# New
# 20th-Century
# Encyclopedia
# of Religious
# Knowledge

**Baker Reference Library**

*Evangelical Dictionary of Theology*
Edited by Walter A. Elwell

*Baker Encyclopedia of Psychology*
Edited by David G. Benner

*Evangelical Commentary on the Bible*
Edited by Walter A. Elwell

*Topical Analysis of the Bible*
Edited by Walter A. Elwell

*New Twentieth-Century Encyclopedia
of Religious Knowledge*
Edited by J. D. Douglas

# New 20th-Century Encyclopedia of Religious Knowledge

## Second Edition

Edited by

## J. D. Douglas

### Consulting Editors

| | |
|---|---|
| Robert G. Clouse | Leon Morris |
| Walter A. Elwell | Richard V. Pierard |
| Irving Hexham | Peter Toon |

**BAKER BOOK HOUSE**
Grand Rapids, Michigan 49516

**Library of Congress Cataloging-in-Publication Data**

New twentieth-century encyclopedia of religious
    knowledge / edited by J. D. Douglas ; consulting
    editors, Robert G. Clouse . . . [et al.]. — 2nd ed.
        p.    cm.
    Rev. ed. of : Twentieth century encyclopedia of
religious knowledge. 1955.
    ISBN 0-8010-3002-1
    1. Theology—20th century—Encyclopedias. 2.
Theology—Encyclopedias.  I. Douglas, J. D. (James
Dixon) II. Clouse, Robert G., 1931–   .
III. Twentieth century encyclopedia of religious
knowledge.
BR95.N395    1991
230'.03—dc20                           90-29129
                                            CIP

Printed in the United States of America

# Preface

The *New Twentieth-Century Encyclopedia of Religious Knowledge* (*NTCERK*) maintains the venerable tradition that was established by the *Realencyklopädie für protestantische Theologie und Kirche* (1853–68) in Germany, brought to the English-speaking world by the *Schaff-Herzog Encyclopedia of Religious Knowledge* (1886), and continued by the *Twentieth Century Encyclopedia of Religious Knowledge* (1955).

The 1955 work was designed to supplement the *Schaff-Herzog* and to parallel it in scope, dealing with "all the principal areas of theological scholarship," according to editor Lefferts A. Loetscher. "Biblical archeology, texts and versions, languages, criticism, history, exegesis, and theology are treated in the light of most recent scholarship." Church history received considerable emphasis, "and careful coverage has been given to the religious history not only of the English-speaking world but also of the European Continent . . . and of other areas of world Christianity. Articles on individual nations summarize leading religious developments within those nations during the twentieth century. . . . Considerable attention has been given to biographies of contemporaries, some of whom are not elsewhere listed. . . . While the chief concern . . . continues to be with the Christian religion, . . . [this work does] provide important material on Judaism, Islam, and other non-Christian religions. Numerous entries deal with theology and ethics as well as with broader cultural and social backgrounds that are of interest for religion."

The subject matter of the present edition, "religious knowledge," generally follows the scope of the *Schaff-Herzog* and the *Twentieth Century Encyclopedia of Religious Knowledge*. *NTCERK* contains about 2,100 articles. For the sake of continuity and comprehensiveness, some of the 1955 entries, especially the biographical sketches, have been repeated. A number of previous entries have been revised and bibliographies updated, reflecting the theological, social, and political ferment of a truly remarkable era. There are many new articles on contemporary issues. *NTCERK* is strong in theology, biblical studies, church history, and comparative religion. It features articles on major fields of study and attempts to integrate those fields with Christian belief. *NTCERK*'s defined scope is limited to the twentieth century. It covers pre-twentieth-century developments only where necessary to explain twentieth-century events and movements. The dynamic nature of those events has demanded review and updating even of new articles to reflect the implications for religious life lying just behind the news headlines.

*NTCERK* is more a new work than a revision. While the present edition follows the tradition of its predecessors, it does not do so slavishly. It differs from the *Twentieth Century Encyclopedia of Religious Knowledge* in several important ways. It is not a supplement to the *Schaff-Herzog*. The reader need not have access to the thirteen-volume work in order to use *NTCERK* to full advantage. It is more consistently and intentionally evangelical in viewpoint and interests than was the 1955 edition, although the word "evangelical" is here used in a broad sense, and not all the contributors consider themselves evangelical. The contributors are less American in orientation; there are more authors from Commonwealth and other nations, including third world countries.

Through the pages of this volume we hope to present a retrospective view of one period in church and world history that we have been privileged to share. It is not too early to begin to contemplate how people, events, and ideas have shaped our present and even now are shaping life as we enter the twenty-first century.

—THE PUBLISHER

# Abbreviations

## General

| | |
|---|---|
| c. | circa, about |
| cent., cents. | century, centuries |
| ed., eds. | editor, edition, editors, editions |
| ET | English translation |
| et al. | and others |
| f., ff. | following |
| Fr. | Father |
| ft. | foot, feet |
| Ger. | German |
| Gk. | Greek |
| Heb. | Hebrew |
| km. | kilometer(s) |
| Lat. | Latin |
| LXX | Septuagint |
| m. | meter(s) |
| mi. | mile(s) |
| mm. | millimeter(s) |
| MS, MSS | manuscript(s) |
| MT | Masoretic Text |
| NT | New Testament |
| OT | Old Testament |
| pl. | plural |
| repr. | reprint edition |
| rev. ed. | revised edition |
| sq. | square |
| St. | Saint |
| suppl. | supplement |
| v., vv. | verse(s) |
| v. | versus |
| vol., vols. | volume(s) |

## Publications

| | |
|---|---|
| AAS | Acta apostolicae sedis |
| AFER | AFER: African Ecclesial Review |
| AmJThPh | American Journal of Theology and Philosophy |
| ATR | Anglican Theological Review |
| Biblica | Biblica Sacra |
| BJEP | British Journal of Educational Psychology |
| BJRL | Bulletin of the John Rylands Library of Manchester |
| BT | The Bible Translator |
| CBQ | Catholic Biblical Quarterly |
| CIL | Corpus inscriptionum latinarum |
| EKL | Evangelisches Kirchenlexikon |
| ET | Expository Times |
| ETS | Erfurter theologische Studien |
| EvQ | Evangelical Quarterly |
| HJP | History of the Jewish People |
| HTKNT | Herders theologischer Kommentar zum Neuen Testament |
| HTR | Harvard Theological Review |
| IBMR | International Bulletin of Missionary Research |
| IBS | Irish Biblical Studies |
| IEJ | Israel Exploration Journal |
| IJGPP | International Journal of Group Psychotherapy and Psychopathology |
| IJMES | International Journal of Middle East Studies |
| IndChHR | Indian Church History Review |
| ISBE | International Standard Bible Encyclopedia |
| JAAR | Journal of the American Academy of Religion |
| JAOS | Journal of the American Oriental Society |
| JBL | Journal of Biblical Literature |
| JChSt | Journal of Church and State |
| JPT | Journal of Psychology and Theology |
| JRTheol | Journal of Religious Theology |
| JRAS | Journal of the Royal Asiatic Society |
| JSJ | Journal for the Study of Judaism in the Persian, Hellenistic and Roman Period |
| JSSR | Journal for the Scientific Study of Religion |
| JTS | Journal of Theological Studies |
| LThK | Lexikon für Theologie und Kirche |
| LuthThJ | Lutheran Theological Journal |
| MQR | Mennonite Quarterly Review |
| NCE | New Catholic Encyclopedia |
| NIDNTT | New International Dictionary of New Testament Theology |
| NovT | Novum Testamentum |
| NovTSup | Novum Testamentum (Supplements) |
| NTS | New Testament Studies |
| OBO | Orbis biblicus et orientalis |
| RGG | Religion in Geschichte und Gegenwart |
| RHPR | Revue d'histoire et de philosophie religieuses |
| SJT | Scottish Journal of Theology |
| SNTS | Society for New Testament Studies |
| SWJTh | Southwestern Journal of Theology |
| TBT | The Bible Today |
| TDNT | Theological Dictionary of the New Testament |
| TGl | Theologie und Glaube |
| TLZ | Theologische Literaturzeitung |
| TU | Texte und Untersuchungen zur Geschichte der altchristlichen Literatur |
| TZ | Theologische Zeitschrift |
| VT | Vetus Testamentum |
| ZAW | Zeitschrift für die alttestamentliche Wissenschaft |
| ZNW | Zeitschrift für die neutestamentliche Wissenschaft |

# Contributors

**Aikins, Gregory,** The Greater Europe Mission, Reykjavík, Iceland

**Albright, Raymond W.,** late professor of church history, Episcopal Theological School, Cambridge, Massachusetts

**Albright, William F.,** late professor of Semitic languages, Johns Hopkins University, Baltimore, Maryland

**Allbeck, Willard D.,** late professor of historical theology, Hamma Divinity School

**Allwardt, Paul,** late professor of music, Gustavus Adolphus College, St. Peter, Minnesota

**Ammundsen, Peter,** late manager, the Danish Parole and Probation Service

**Amstutz, Mark R.,** professor of political science, Wheaton College, Wheaton, Illinois

**Andrén, Carl-Gustaf,** late clergyman, Lund, Sweden

**Angel, Gervais,** theological consultant, South American Missionary Society

**Archer, John Clark,** late professor of comparative religion, Yale University, New Haven, Connecticut

**Armerding, Carl E.,** professor of Old Testament, Regent College, Vancouver, British Columbia, Canada

**Askew, Thomas A.,** professor of history, Gordon College, Wenham, Massachusetts

**Athyal, Saphir,** former principal, Union Biblical Seminary, Pune, India

**Aubrey, Edwin E.,** late professor of religious thought, University of Pennsylvania, Philadelphia, Pennsylvania

**Bachmann, E. Theodore,** late professor of church history and missions, Pacific Lutheran Theological Seminary, Berkeley, California

**Barclay, Oliver R.,** editor, *Science and Christian Belief*

**Barrois, Georges A.,** late professor of biblical literature and theology, Princeton University, Princeton, New Jersey

**Bates, Miner Searle,** late professor of missions, Union Theological Seminary, New York, New York

**Baxter, Edna M.,** late professor of religious education, Hartford Seminary Foundation

**Baynes, Norman H.,** late professor of Byzantine history, University of London, England

**Bebawi, George,** lecturer, St. John's College, Nottingham, England

**Beck, James R.,** associate professor of counseling, Denver Conservative Baptist Seminary, Denver, Colorado

**Benner, David G.,** professor of psychology, Redeemer College, Ancaster, Ontario, Canada

**Bergendoff, Conrad,** late resident, Augustana College, Rock Island, Illinois

**Berger, William H.,** co-pastor, Tippah Presbyterian Parish, Ripley, Mississippi

**Birdsall, J. Neville,** professor emeritus of New Testament studies and textual criticism, University of Birmingham, England

**Bixler, Julius Seelye,** late president, Colby College, Waterville, Maine

**Blackwood, Andrew W.,** late professor of homiletics, Yale University, New Haven, Connecticut

**Braden, Charles S.,** late professor of history and literature of religion, Northwestern University, Chicago, Illinois

**Bray, Gerald,** tutor, Oak Hill College, London, England

**Brenner, Scott F.,** late pastor, United Presbyterian Church, Carnegie, Pennsylvania

**Brewster, David,** vicar, Brockenhurst, Hants, England

**Bright, John,** late professor of Hebrew and Old Testament, Union Theological Seminary, Richmond, Virginia

**Brilioth, Yngve,** late archbishop, Stockholm, Sweden

**Brock, Sebastian P.,** reader in Syriac studies, Oxford University, Oxford, England

**Brown, Arthur S.,** pastor, Wilmore Free Methodist Church, Wilmore, Kentucky

**Bruce, F. F.,** late professor of biblical criticism and exegesis, University of Manchester, England

**Bryan, Rita,** Indiana State University, Terre Haute, Indiana

**Buckwalter, H. Douglas,** doctoral candidate, University of Aberdeen, Scotland

**Buehring, Paul,** late professor of historical theology, Lutheran Seminary, Columbus, Ohio

**Burkman, Thomas W.,** associate professor of history, Old Dominion University, Norfolk, Virginia

**Burrows, Millar,** late professor of biblical theology, Yale University, New Haven, Connecticut

**Burrows, Robert,** Spiritual Counterfeits Project

**Cadbury, Henry J.,** professor emeritus of divinity, Harvard University, Cambridge, Massachusetts

**Cairns, Earle E.,** professor emeritus of church history, Wheaton College, Wheaton, Illinois

**Calverley, Edwin E.,** late professor of Arabic and Islamics, Hartford Seminary Foundation

**Cameron, Charles M.,** minister, St. Ninian's Parish Church, Dunfermline, Scotland

**Carmony, Marvin,** professor of English and linguistics, Indiana State University, Terre Haute, Indiana

**Carpenter, Joel A.,** director of religious programs, The Pew Charitable Trusts

**Cashman, Robert,** Springfield, Missouri

**Chadwick, Anthony S.,** late professor, Oxford University, Oxford, England

**Chakmakjian, Hagop Apraham,** lecturer on Islamic culture and faith, Armenian affairs, and Arab-Israeli conflict

**Chamberlain, W. D.,** late professor of New Testament, Louisville Presbyterian Theological Seminary, Louisville, Kentucky

**Chao, Jonathan,** director, Chinese Church Research Center, Hong Kong.

**Christian, William A., Jr.,** late professor of religion, Yale University, New Haven, Connecticut

**Clark, Elmer T.,** former executive secretary, Association of Methodist Historical Societies

**Claxton, Robert H.,** professor of history, West Georgia College, Carollton, Georgia

**Clouse, Bonnidell,** professor of educational and school psychology, Indiana State University, Terre Haute, Indiana

**Clouse, Robert G.,** professor of history, Indiana State University, Terre Haute, Indiana

**Cobain, Robert,** information and publications officer, Church House, Belfast, Northern Ireland

**Cochrane, A. C.,** Dubuque Theological Seminary, Dubuque, Iowa

**Collins, Gary R.,** professor of psychology, Liberty University, Lynchburg, Virginia

**Come, Arnold B.,** professor emeritus of systematic theology, San Francisco Theological Seminary, San Francisco, California

**Cornett, Norman F.,** researcher and doctoral candidate, McGill University, Montreal, Quebec, Canada

**Count, Earl W.,** late professor of anthropology, Hamilton College, Clinton, New York

**Coward, Harold,** director, Calgary Institute for the Humanities, University of Calgary, Alberta, Canada

**Cressey, Earl H.,** late professor of Chinese studies, Hartford Seminary Foundation

**Cross, Frank Moore, Jr.,** professor of Hebrew and other oriental languages, Harvard University, Cambridge, Massachusetts

**Cruz, Virgil,** senior professor of New Testament, Louisville Presbyterian Seminary, Louisville, Kentucky

**Daniel, J. T. K.,** principal, Serampore College, West Bengal, India

**da Silva, António Barbosa,** assistant professor of philosophy of religion, University of Uppsala, Sweden

**Davidson, Robert,** professor of Old Testament, Glasgow University, Scotland

**Davis, Davina,** doctoral candidate, McGill University, Montreal, Quebec, Canada

**Dawes, Peter S.,** bishop of Derby, England

**De Jong, James A.,** president, Calvin Theological Seminary, Grand Rapids, Michigan

**Detzler, Wayne,** senior pastor, Castleview Baptist Church, Indianapolis, Indiana

**Dibelius, M. M.,** wife of Martin F. Dibelius, late professor of New Testament exegesis and criticism, University of Heidelberg, Germany

**Dickie, E. P.,** late professor of divinity, St. Andrews University, Scotland

**Dicks, Russell L.,** late professor of pastoral care, Duke Divinity School, Durham, North Carolina

**Dieter, Melvin E.,** professor of church history and historical theology, Asbury Theological Seminary, Wilmore, Kentucky

**Dillistone, F. W.,** late chancellor, Liverpool Cathedral, England

**Douglas, J. D.,** editor-at-large, *Christianity Today*

**Drennan, Ollin J.,** professor of physics and natural science, Northeast Missouri State University, Kirksville, Missouri

**Drummond, Alistair J.,** minister, Kelty Church, Fife, Scotland

**Dunnett, Walter McGregor,** professor of Bible and Greek, Northwestern College, St. Paul, Minnesota

**Eller, David B.,** editorial director, Brethren Press, Elgin, Illinois

**Eller, Paul H.,** late president, Evangelical Theological Seminary, Naperville, Illinois

**Ellingworth, Paul,** translation consultant, United Bible Societies, Aberdeen, Scotland

**Elliott, J. K.,** senior lecturer in New Testament, language, and literature, Leeds University, England

**Ellis, John Tracy,** late professor of church history, Catholic University of America, Washington, D.C.

**Elwell, Walter A.,** professor of Bible and theology, Wheaton College, Wheaton, Illinois

**Enroth, Ronald,** professor of sociology, Westmont College, Santa Barbara, California

**Estep, W. R.,** professor of church history, Southwestern Baptist Theological Seminary, Fort Worth, Texas

**Evans, Robert P.,** historian, Billy Graham Evangelistic Association

**Fairbanks, Rollin J.,** late professor of pastoral theology, Episcopal Theological Seminary, Cambridge, Massachusetts

**Faupel, D. William,** professor of bibliography and research, Asbury Theological Seminary, Wilmore, Kentucky

**Fear, John L.,** broadcaster, FEBC, Seychelles

**Ferguson, Ronald,** former leader of the Iona Community, Scotland

**Ferm, Vergilius,** late professor of philosophy, College of Wooster

**Fernando, Ajith,** national director, Youth for Christ, Colombo, Sri Lanka

**Filson, Floyd V.,** late professor of New Testament, McCormick Theological Seminary, Chicago, Illinois

**Finegan, Jack,** professor emeritus of New Testament history and archeology, Pacific School of Religion and Graduate Theological Union, Berkeley, California

**Finkelstein, Louis,** late chancellor and president of the faculties, Jewish Theological Seminary of America, New York, New York

**Fisch, Max H.,** late professor of philosophy, University of Illinois, Champaign-Urbana

**Flack, Elmer E.,** late professor of exegetical theology, Hamma Divinity School

**Fletcher, Joseph,** late professor of social ethics, Episcopal Theological Seminary, Cambridge, Massachusetts

**Florovsky, Georges,** late dean and professor of divinity, St. Vladimir's Theological Seminary, New York

**Foord, Dudley,** presiding bishop, Church of England in South Africa, Cape Town, South Africa

**Forell, George W.,** professor of religion, University of Iowa, Iowa City, Iowa

**Foreman, Kenneth J.,** late professor of doctrinal theology, Louisville Presbyterian Theological Seminary, Louisville, Kentucky

**Forest, James H.,** staff member, Fellowship of Reconciliation, The Netherlands

**Forrester, Duncan B.,** professor of Christian ethics and practical theology, Edinburgh University, Scotland

**Forrester, W. R.,** late professor of practical theology and Christian education, St. Andrews University, Scotland

**Fraenkel, Peter,** late pastor, Evangelical Lutheran Church of France

**France, Richard T.,** principal, Wycliffe Hall, Oxford, England

**Franklin, Stephen T.,** pastor, Evangelical Covenant Church, Big Falls, Minnesota

**Friend, J. Alan,** honorary assistant registrar, Australian College of Theology

**Fry, C. George,** Protestant chaplain, St. Francis College, Fort Wayne, Indiana

**Furcha, E. J.,** professor of church history, McGill University, Montreal, Quebec, Canada

**Gaer, Joseph,** late author

**Garrett, James Leo, Jr.,** professor of theology, Southwestern Baptist Theological Seminary, Fort Worth, Texas

**Gay, Arthur Evans, Jr.,** senior minister, South Park Church, Park Ridge, Illinois

**Gehman, Henry S.,** late professor of Old Testament literature, Princeton Theological Seminary, Princeton, New Jersey

**Gezork, Herbert,** former president, Andover-Newton Theological School, Newton Centre, Massachusetts

**Gibson, George M.,** late professor of preaching, McCormick Theological Seminary, Chicago, Illinois

**Gill, David W.,** author, lecturer, and co-founder, New College for Advanced Christian Studies, Berkeley, California

## Contributors

**Gillman, Ian,** senior lecturer, department of religious studies, University of Queensland, Australia

**Ginsberg, H. Louis,** professor emeritus of Bible, Jewish Theological Seminary of America, New York, New York

**Goodykoontz, Harry G.,** late professor of Christian education, Louisville Presbyterian Seminary, Kentucky

**Grant, Frederick C.,** late professor of biblical theology, Union Theological Seminary, New York, New York

**Grant, Robert M.,** professor emeritus of New Testament, University of Chicago, Chicago, Illinois

**Grimley, Liam K.,** professor of educational and school psychology, Indiana State University, Terre Haute, Indiana

**Grogan, Geoffrey W.,** principal emeritus, Bible Training Institute, Glasgow, Scotland

**Guelzo, Allen C.,** academic dean, Reformed Episcopal Seminary, Philadelphia, Pennsylvania

**Hall, Joseph H.,** associate professor of church history and librarian, Knox Theological Seminary, Fort Lauderdale, Florida

**Hamilton, Ian,** minister, Loudoun Church, Newmilns, Ayrshire, Scotland

**Handy, Robert T.,** professor emeritus of church history, Union Theological Seminary, New York, New York

**Hardy, Edward R.,** late professor of church history, Berkeley Divinity School, Berkeley, California

**Hartman, Grover L.,** former executive secretary, Council of Churches of St. Joseph County, South Bend, Indiana

**Hayes, Stephen,** lecturer in missiology, University of South Africa, Pretoria, Republic of South Africa

**Heinecken, Martin J.,** late professor of systematic theology, Lutheran Theological Seminary, Philadelphia, Pennsylvania

**Heino, Harri,** director, Research Institute of the Lutheran Church of Finland

**Heinze, Rudolph W.,** senior tutor, Oak Hill College, Southgate, London, England

**Hendry, George S.,** late professor of systematic theology, Princeton Theological Seminary, Princeton, New Jersey

**Henry, Carl F. H.,** visiting professor of systematic theology and biblical studies, Trinity Evangelical Divinity School, Deerfield, Illinois

**Hesselgrave, David J.,** professor of mission, Trinity Evangelical Divinity School, Deerfield, Illinois

**Hetle, Erik,** late professor, St. Olaf College, Northfield, Minnesota

**Hexham, Irving,** professor of religious studies, University of Calgary, Alberta, Canada

**Hicks, Peter,** minister, Bushey Baptist Church, Herts, England

**Hillyer, Philip,** freelance editor and researcher

**Holmes, David L.,** professor of religion, College of William and Mary, Williamsburg, Virginia

**Homrighausen, E. G.,** late dean and professor of pastoral theology, Princeton Theological Seminary, Princeton, New Jersey

**Hooper, Robert E.,** chair, department of history and political science, David Lipscomb University, Nashville, Tennessee

**Hope, Norman V.,** late professor of church history, Princeton Theological Seminary, Princeton, New Jersey

**Horton, Walter M.,** late professor of theology, Oberlin College, Oberlin, Ohio

**Hough, Lynn Harold,** late dean, Drew Theological Seminary, Madison, New Jersey

**Houghton, Graham,** principal, South Asia Institute of Advanced Christian Studies, Bangalore, India

**Hudson, Winthrop S.,** late professor of the history of Christianity, Colgate-Rochester Theological Seminary, Rochester, New York

**Hume, Wilson M.,** late associate general secretary, National Council of YMCAs in Egypt

**Hunt, Keith** and **Gladys,** authors, Inter-Varsity Christian Fellowship staff

**Hunter, Harold D.,** executive director, Sunday school department, Church of God of Prophecy, Cleveland, Tennessee

**Hutchinson, Paul,** late editor, *Christian Century*

**Hyma, Albert,** late professor of history, University of Michigan, Ann Arbor, Michigan

**Iglehart, Charles,** professor emeritus of missions, Union Theological Seminary, Richmond, Virginia

**Jackson, John A., Jr.,** Latin American analyst, Department of the Army

**James, Edwin O.,** late professor of history and philosophy of religion, London University

**Jeffrey, Arthur,** late professor of Semitic languages, Columbia University, Columbia, South Carolina

**Jennings, George J.,** missions consultant, Middle East Mission Research, Le Mars, Iowa

**Johnson, D. L.,** professor of humanities, Indiana State University, Terre Haute, Indiana

**Johnson, Sherman E.,** dean emeritus, Church Divinity School of the Pacific, Berkeley, California

**Kassis, Hanna,** professor of religious studies, University of British Columbia, Canada

**Kerr, Hugh Thomson, Jr.,** late professor of systematic theology, Princeton Theological Seminary, Princeton, New Jersey

**Kerstan, Reinhold J.,** director of promotion and development, Baptist World Alliance

**Kirk, J. Andrew,** dean, Selly Oak Colleges, Birmingham, England

**Klein, H. M. J.,** late professor of history, Franklin and Marshall College, Lancaster, Pennsylvania

**Knox, D. Broughton,** principal emeritus, Moore College, Sydney, Australia

**Knudsen, Johannes,** late professor of church history, Chicago Lutheran Seminary, Chicago, Illinois

**Krahn, Cornelius,** late professor of church history, Bethel College

**Kuecklich, Reinhold,** late president, Evangelical Theological School, Reutlingen, Germany

**Kuhn, Harold Barnes,** professor emeritus of the philosophy of religion, Asbury Theological Seminary, Wilmore, Kentucky

**Kuyper, E.,** late friar, OFM, The Netherlands

**Labrentz, H. L.,** clinical psychologist, LaBrentz Associates, Terre Haute, Indiana

**Langley, Myrtle S.,** director, Carlisle Diocesan Training Institute, Carlisle, Cambria, England

**Layman, Fred D.,** professor of biblical theology, Asbury Theological Seminary, Wilmore, Kentucky

**Lazell, David,** author and editor

**Lee, Martha F.,** doctoral candidate, University of Calgary, Alberta, Canada

**Lehmann, Paul L.,** late professor of applied Christianity, Princeton Theological Seminary

**Lenton, Tim,** chief subeditor, *Eastern Daily Press,* Norwich, England

**Lewis, Michael,** associate professor of history, Michigan State University, East Lansing, Michigan

**Liggitt, Eugene,** late professor of Bible and social philosophy, Grove City College, Grove City, Pennsylvania

**Linder, Robert D.,** professor of history, Kansas State University, Manhattan, Kansas

**Lints, Richard,** associate professor of systematic and philosophical theology, Gordon-Conwell Theological Seminary, South Hamilton, Massachusetts

**Livingston, G. Herbert,** professor emeritus of Old Testament, Asbury Theological Seminary, Wilmore, Kentucky

**Lockerbie, D. Bruce,** scholar-in-residence, Stony Brook School, Stony Brook, Long Island, New York

**Lodwick, Kathleen L.,** associate professor of history, Southwest Missouri State University, Springfield, Missouri

**Loetscher, F. W.,** late professor of church history, Princeton Theological Seminary

**Loetscher, Lefferts A.,** professor of American church history, Princeton Theological Seminary, Princeton, New Jersey

**Louden, R. Stuart,** late minister, Kirk of the Greyfriars, Edinburgh, Scotland

**Love, Julian P.,** late professor of biblical theology, Louisville Presbyterian Theological Seminary, Louisville, Kentucky

**Lundin, Roger W.,** professor of English, Wheaton College, Wheaton, Illinois

**Lyman, Mary Ely,** late professor of English Bible, Union Theological Seminary, New York, New York

**Lynch, John E.,** professor of canon law and medieval history, Catholic University of America, Washington, D.C.

**McCarthy, John W.,** late professor of philosophy, University of Louisville, Kentucky

**McCarthy, Thomas J.,** National Catholic Welfare Conference

**Macaulay, Ronald,** director, L'Abri Fellowship, Switzerland

**McClanahan, James,** assistant minister, Southaven Presbyterian Church, Mississippi

**MacDonald, Fergus,** general secretary, National Bible Society of Scotland

**MacDonald, Leslie J.,** Department of Religious Studies, University of Ottawa, Ontario, Canada

**McGregor, Marjorie,** deacon, All Saints' Anglican Church, Victoria, Australia

**Mackay, John A.,** late president, Princeton Theological Seminary, Princeton, New Jersey

**McKelvey, R. J.,** principal, Northern College, Manchester, England

**Mackie, Alexander,** late president, Presbyterian Ministers' Fund

## Contributors

**McKim, Donald,** interim pastor, Trinity Presbyterian Church, Berwyn, Pennsylvania

**MacLeod, Murdo A.,** director, Christian Witness to Israel, Kent, England

**McRay, John,** professor of New Testament and archeology, Wheaton College Graduate School, Wheaton, Illinois

**Magnuson, Norris A.,** professor of history, Bethel Theological Seminary, St. Paul, Minnesota

**Malony, H. Newton,** professor of psychology, Graduate School of Psychology, Fuller Theological Seminary, Pasadena, California

**Manross, W. W.,** late librarian, Church Historical Society, Philadelphia, Pennsylvania

**Marsden, George M.,** professor of the history of Christianity in America, Duke University, Durham, North Carolina

**Martin, Dennis D.,** Institute for Research and Humanities, University of Wisconsin, Madison, Wisconsin

**Matsunami, S.,** Tokyo University, Tokyo, Japan

**Mattsson-Bozé, M. Howard,** professor of history and sociology, Geneva College, Beaver Falls, Pennsylvania

**Mayer, Frederick E.,** late professor of systematic theology, Concordia Seminary, St. Louis, Missouri

**Metzger, Bruce M.,** professor emeritus of New Testament language and literature, Princeton Theological Seminary, Princeton, New Jersey

**Meynell, Hugo A.,** professor of religious studies, University of Calgary, Alberta, Canada

**Michalson, Carl,** late professor of systematic theology and the philosophy of religion, Drew University, Madison, New Jersey

**Middlebrook, Charles W.,** faculty member, Life Bible College at Los Angeles, Los Angeles, California

**Mills, David R.,** lecturer in physics, Monash University, Clayton, Australia

**Mitchell, Jack,** teaching elder, Sunset Presbyterian Church, Portland, Oregon

**Moffett, Samuel Hugh,** professor of ecumenics and mission, Princeton Theological Seminary, Princeton, University, Princeton, New Jersey

**Morris, Leon,** principal emeritus, Ridley College, Melbourne, Australia

**Morrison, Robert L.,** doctoral candidate, Boston University, Boston, Massachusetts

**Muck, Terry C.,** associate professor of comparative religion, Austin Presbyterian Theological Seminary, Austin, Texas

**Muller, William A.,** late professor of philosophy of religion, Southwestern Baptist Theological Seminary, Fort Worth, Texas

**Murray, John,** late professor of systematic theology, Westminster Theological Seminary, Philadelphia, Pennsylvania

**Murray, S. W.,** retired government official, Belfast, Northern Ireland

**Muyumba, Patrice,** associate professor of Afro-American Studies, Indiana State University, Terre Haute, Indiana

**Nash, Ronald H.,** professor of philosophy, Western Kentucky University, Bowling Green, Kentucky

**Needham, Nick,** Rutherford House, Edinburgh, Scotland

**Nelson, John Ogden,** professor of philosophy, University of Colorado, Boulder, Colorado

**Nichols, Alan,** archdeacon, Melbourne, Australia

**Oates, Wayne E.,** professor of psychiatry, University of Louisville School of Medicine, Louisville, Kentucky

**Oddo, Gilbert L.,** late professor, St. Mary's College, Emmitsburg, Maryland

**O'Malley, J. Steven,** professor of church history and historical theology, Asbury Theological Seminary, Wilmore, Kentucky

**Orr, Robbie,** former missionary in Pakistan

**Ostling, Joan,** author

**Parker, Francis H.,** professor emeritus of philosophy, Colby College, Waterville, Maine

**Parker, George F.,** late professor, Berea College, Berea, Kentucky

**Parsons, Martin,** Church Pastor Aid Society, London, England

**Parsons, Michael,** lecturer in theological ethics, London Bible College

**Payne, P. B.,** president, Linguist's Software, Edmonds, Washington

**Pelikan, Jaroslav,** professor of history, Yale University

**Penelhum, Terry,** associate professor of religious studies, University of Calgary, Alberta, Canada

**Perlman, Susan,** associate executive director, Jews for Jesus, San Francisco, California

**Perry, Eleanor H.,** doctoral candidate, Indiana State University, Terre Haute, Indiana

**Perry, Glenn E.,** professor of political science, Indiana State University, Terre Haute, Indiana

**Petersen, Rodney L.,** adjunct professor, Webster University-in-Geneva, Geneva, Switzerland

**Pfeiffer, Robert H.,** late professor of Hebrew and Oriental languages, Harvard University, Cambridge, Massachusetts

**Pickens, Claude L., Jr.,** late secretary, Overseas Department, National Council of the Protestant Episcopal Church

**Pierard, Richard V.,** professor of history, Indiana State University, Terre Haute, Indiana

**Pierce, Richard D.,** late professor of history, Emerson College

**Pinomaa, Lennart,** late professor of systematic theology, Helsinki University, Helsinki, Finland

**Piper, Otto A.,** late professor of New Testament, Princeton Theological Seminary, Princeton, New Jersey

**Poewe, Karla,** assistant professor of anthropology, University of Lethbridge, Alberta, Canada

**Pollard, Noel S.,** vice-principal, Ridley Hall, Cambridge, England

**Poloma, Margaret M.,** professor of sociology, University of Akron, Akron, Ohio

**Rasmussen, Carl Christian,** late professor of systematic theology, Lutheran Theological Seminary, Gettysburg, Pennsylvania

**Rausch, David A.,** professor of history and Jewish studies, Ashland University, Ashland, Ohio

**Reed, Gerard A.,** professor of history, philosophy, and religion, Point Loma Nazarene College, San Diego, California

**Reid, J. K. S.,** professor emeritus of Christian dogmatics, Aberdeen University, Scotland

**Rennie, Ian S.,** vice-president and academic dean, Ontario Theological Seminary, Willowdale, Ontario, Canada

**Rhodes, Arnold B.,** late professor of Old Testament, Louisville Presbyterian Theological Seminary, Louisville, Kentucky

**Rightmyer, Nelson,** late rector, St. John's Church, Worthington Valley, Maryland

**Rissler, Herbert J.,** professor of history, Indiana State University, Terre Haute, Indiana

**Ritter, Gerhard,** late professor of modern history, University of Freiburg i. Breisgau, Germany

**Robeck, Cecil M., Jr.,** associate dean and associate professor of church history, Fuller Theological Seminary, Pasadena, California

**Robert, Dana L.,** associate professor of international mission, Boston University, Boston, Massachusetts

**Rockwell, W. W.,** late librarian, Union Theological Seminary, New York, New York

**Rolston, Holmes,** late editor-in-chief, Board of Christian Education, PCUS

**Rowdon, Harold H.,** senior lecturer in church history, London Bible College, London, England

**Rowley, Harold H.,** late professor of Hebrew, University of Manchester, England

**Rule, Andrew K.,** late professor of apologetics and church history, Louisville Presbyterian Theological Seminary, Louisville, Kentucky

**Sand, Faith Annette,** publisher, Hope Publishing House, Pasadena, California

**Saulpaugh, Ivane,** late secretary of information, Church World Service

**Schilson, Elizabeth A.,** professor of counseling psychology, Indiana State University, Terre Haute, Indiana

**Schiotz, Fredrik A.,** late president, Evangelical Lutheran Church

**Schneider, Carl E.,** late professor of church history, Eden Theological Seminary, St. Louis, Missouri

**Schnucker, Robert V.,** professor of history and religion, Northeast Missouri State University, Kirksville, Missouri

**Schwiebert, Ernest G.,** late professor of history, Air/Research/Development Command, Baltimore, Maryland

**Scorgie, Glen G.,** associate professor of theology, Canadian Bible College, Regina, Saskatchewan, Canada

**Scott, J. Julius, Jr.,** professor of biblical and historical studies, Wheaton College Graduate School, Wheaton, Illinois

**Segal, Eliezer,** associate professor of religious studies, University of Calgary, Alberta, Canada

**Seltzer, George R.,** late professor of liturgics and church art, Lutheran Theological Seminary, Philadelphia, Pennsylvania

**Sharkey, Michael,** Sacra Congregazione per l'Educatione Cattolica, Vatican City

**Shaw, Duncan,** minister, Craigentinny St. Christopher's Church, Edinburgh, Scotland

**Shaw, Mark R.,** professor of church history, Westminster Theological Seminary, Philadelphia, Pennsylvania

**Shelley, Bruce L.,** professor of church history, Denver Seminary, Denver, Colorado

**Shepherd, Massey H., Jr.,** late professor of liturgics, Church Divinity School of the Pacific, Berkeley, California

**Sherlock, Charles,** senior lecturer, Ridley College, Melbourne, Australia

## Contributors

**Singer, C. Gregg,** professor of church history and historical theology, Greenville Presbyterian Theological Seminary, Greenville, South Carolina

**Siromoney, Gift,** vice-principal, Madras Christian College, Madras, India

**Smith, Clyde Curry,** professor of ancient history and religion, University of Wisconsin-River Falls, River Falls, Wisconsin

**Smits, Karel,** late librarian, Catholic University, Nijmegen, The Netherlands

**Smyth, W. Martin,** member of parliament, Belfast South, Northern Ireland

**Sng, E. K. Bobby,** secretary, Graduates' Christian Fellowship, Singapore

**Spinka, Matthew,** late professor of church history, Hartford Theological Seminary, Hartford, Connecticut

**Steere, Douglas V.,** late professor of philosophy, Haverford College, Haverford, Pennsylvania

**Steeves, Paul D.,** professor of history, Stetson University, DeLand, Florida

**Stone, Anthony P.,** administrator, Interserve, London, England

**Stupperich, Robert,** late professor of church history, University of Munster, Germany

**Sweet, W. W.,** late professor of the history of American Christianity, University of Chicago, Chicago, Illinois

**Tappert, Theodore,** late professor of church history, Lutheran Theological Seminary, Philadelphia, Pennsylvania

**Tarr, Leslie K.,** senior editor, *Faith Today*

**Taylor, Charles L.,** late dean, Episcopal Theological Seminary, Cambridge, Massachusetts

**Taylor, James,** pastor, Stirling Baptist Church, Stirling, Scotland

**Theron, Daniel J.,** late professor of New Testament, Princeton Theological Seminary, Princeton, New Jersey

**Thiede, Carsten Peter,** member of the board, German Institute of Education and Knowledge

**Thomas, Edith Lovell,** former consultant, teacher, and writer on music and children in the church

**Thomas, John N.,** late professor of systematic theology, Union Theological Seminary, Richmond, Virginia

**Thomson, William,** professor emeritus of Arabic, Harvard University, Cambridge, Massachusetts

**Toon, Peter,** William Adams Chair of Systematic Theology, Nashotah House, Nashotah, Wisconsin

**Torbet, Robert G.,** late editor, Board of Education and Publication, American Baptist Convention

**Towns, Elmer L.,** dean of the School of Religion and vice-president, Liberty Baptist Seminary, Lynchburg, Virginia

**Traylor, Jack W.,** professor of history, Bryan College, Dayton, Tennessee

**Trueblood, D. Elton,** late chief of religious information, U.S. Information Agency

**Tucker, Ruth A.,** visiting professor, Trinity Evangelical Divinity School, Deerfield, Illinois

**Turner, Max,** lecturer in New Testament, University of Aberdeen, Scotland

**Urwin, Evelyn, C.,** late honorary secretary, Department of Christian Citizenship, Methodist Church of Great Britain

**Vande Kemp, Hendrika,** associate professor of psychology, Graduate School of Psychology, Fuller Theological Seminary, Pasadena, California

**Van Der Bent, A. J.,** librarian, World Council of Churches, Geneva, Switzerland

**Van Til, Cornelius,** late professor of apologetics, Westminster Theological Seminary, Philadelphia, Pennsylvania

**Waine, Ronald J.,** missionary emeritus, North Africa Mission, England

**Walters, Philip,** research director, Keston College, Kent, England

**Warfield, Benjamin Breckinridge,** late professor of didactic and polemic theology, Theological Seminary of the Presbyterian Church in the U.S.A., Princeton, New Jersey

**Watson, Philip,** late lecturer in church history, Garrett Evangelical

**Weaver, Glenn D.,** professor of psychology, Calvin College, Grand Rapids, Michigan

**Webber, Robert,** professor of theology, Wheaton College, Wheaton, Illinois

**Weber, Charles W.,** professor of history, Wheaton College, Wheaton, Illinois

**Welch, Claude,** late professor of theology, Yale University, New Haven, Connecticut

**West, W. M. S.,** principal, Bristol Baptist College, England

**Westmarland, Colin A.,** minister, St. Andrews Church, Valletta, Malta

**Wilder, Amos N.,** late professor of New Testament interpretation, Harvard Divinity School, Cambridge, Massachusetts

**Will, Robert,** late honorary professor, Strasbourg University, Strasbourg, France

**Willaert, Leopold,** late professor in the Faculty of Notre-Dame de la Paix, Namur, Belgium

**Williams, C. Peter,** vice-principal, Trinity College, Bristol, England

**Williams, D. Newell,** associate professor of church history, Christian Theological Seminary, Indianapolis, Indiana

**Williams, David John,** vice-principal, Ridley College, Melbourne, Australia

**Williams, George H.,** late professor of church history, Harvard University, Cambridge, Massachusetts

**Williams, Philip J.,** assistant professor of political science, University of Florida, Gainesville, Florida

**Wilson, J. Christy, Sr.,** late professor of ecumenics, Princeton Theological Seminary, Princeton, New Jersey

**Wilson, J. Christy, Jr.,** professor of world evangelization, Gordon-Conwell Theological Seminary, South Hamilton, Massachusetts

**Wilson, R. McL.,** professor emeritus of biblical criticism, University of St. Andrews, Scotland

**Winquist, Alan H.,** professor of history, Taylor University, Upland, Indiana

**Winter, R. Milton,** pastor, First Presbyterian Church, Holly Springs, Mississippi

**Winter, Ralph D.,** general director, U.S. Center for World Mission

**Wirt, Sherwood E.,** editor emeritus, *Decision*

**Wolseley, Roland E.,** late professor of journalism, Syracuse University, Syracuse, New York

**Woodberry, J. Dudley,** associate professor of Islamic studies, Fuller Theological Seminary, Pasadena, California

**Woolley, Paul,** late professor of church history, Westminster Theological Seminary, Philadelphia, Pennsylvania

**Wright, David F.,** dean of the faculty of divinity, New College, University of Edinburgh, Scotland

**Wright, G. Ernest,** late professor of Old Testament, McCormick Theological Seminary, Chicago, Illinois

**Yarbrough, Robert W.,** associate professor of New Testament studies, Wheaton College, Wheaton, Illinois

**Zabriskie, Alexander C.,** late professor of church history, Protestant Episcopal Seminary, Richmond, Virginia

**Zeps, Michael,** professor of history, Marquette University, Milwaukee, Wisconsin

**Zockler, Otto,** late professor of church history, University of Greifswald, Germany

**Zuck, Lowell H.,** professor of church history, Eden Theological Seminary, St. Louis, Missouri

# Aa

**Abbott, Lyman** (1835–1922). American Congregational pastor and editor. Born in Roxbury, Mass., he was educated at New York University. After practicing law for several years, he was ordained and served pastorates in Terre Haute, Ind. (1860–65), and New York City (1865–69). He then resigned to devote himself to literary work. In 1888 he succeeded Henry Ward Beecher as pastor of Plymouth Church, Brooklyn, serving there until his resignation in 1898. He supported numerous social, charitable, and religious organizations. His many published books include *Jesus of Nazareth* (1869), *How to Study the Bible* (1877), *In Aid of Faith* (1886), *Evolution of Christianity* (1896), *The Theology of an Evolutionist* (1897), *Christianity and Social Problems* (1897), *Life and Letters of Paul* (1898), *Henry Ward Beecher* (1903), *Industrial Problems* (1905), *The Spirit of Democracy* (1910), *America in the Making* (1911), *Reminiscences* (1915), *The Twentieth Century Crusade* (1918), and *What Christianity Means to Me* (1921). He edited the *Illustrated Christian Weekly* (1871–76), the *Christian Union* (1876–81, with Henry Ward Beecher), and the *Outlook* (1881–93).

**Abel, Charles William** (1863–1930). Pioneer missionary in Papua New Guinea. Born in London, he became a Christian during D. L. Moody's first visit to England. As a young man he spent several years in New Zealand, becoming a rugged individual. He returned to England, where he studied at Chestnut College. In 1889 Abel was accepted for service in New Guinea under the auspices of the London Missionary Society (LMS). Initially associated with the pioneer James Chalmers, in 1891 he helped establish the mission station at Kwato with which he was associated for the rest of his life. He was diligent in his efforts to overcome local opposition and indifference, largely through his capacity for friendship and his promotion of justice. Abel was a fervent evangelist intent on building up the Papuan church, but he realized that the gospel created a vacuum in the lives of converts from paganism. Abel encouraged the people to become disciplined and reliable. Always a keen sportsman, he introduced the young people of Kwato to the game of cricket. He established schools, a saw mill, a printing press, a boat yard, and cocoa plantations. He believed that the introduction of industries would give those converted from barbaric and primitive ways "a new, healthy, useful, progressive life." He believed that the policies adopted at Kwato would result in a strong and independent Papuan Christian community and would also save the race from ultimate extinction. His methods did not prove popular with some in Britain and he resigned from LMS in 1917. He became an honorary missionary of the society and formed the Kwato Extension Association. In the USA Abel's work was supported by the New Guinea Evangelisation Society. He died following a car accident during a visit to Britain. Biographies of him have been written by A. G. Hall (1921), R. W. Abel (1934), and M. K. Abel (1954).

JAMES TAYLOR

**Aberhart, William** (1878–1943). Canadian political leader and Baptist lay preacher. Born in Ontario, he trained as a teacher at Hamilton Normal College and Queen's University. He was a teacher (1906–14) and high school principal (1915–35) in Calgary. Aberhart's Bible class at Westbourne Baptist Church evolved into the Calgary Prophetic Institute (1918). Meanwhile, the modernist-fundamentalist controversy raged, and Aberhart's preaching and strong premillennial emphasis drew large crowds and propelled him into a popular radio evangelistic ministry (1925). Concurrently, the worldwide depression settled on the Canadian prairies along with a 10-year drought. Enamored with the theories of English social economist C. H. Douglas, Aberhart began to weave a "social credit" theory into his radio broadcasts as a proposal to solve economic problems and to build a new society. Running on this platform, the Social Credit party won a landslide

1

victory in 1935, and Aberhart became premier of Alberta and minister of education; he was reelected in 1940. Aberhart was succeeded by his ablest pupil, Ernest C. Manning.

JACK MITCHELL

**Abhishiktananda, Swami** (1910–1973). Pioneer of Hindu-Christian dialog. A Benedictine monk from Brittany, Henri Le Saux came to India in 1947 to live a life of *sannyasa* (detachment). With Fr. Jules Monchanin (1895–1957), he founded the Saccidananda Ashram of Santivanam in 1950 on the banks of the sacred river Kaveri in South India. They adopted Indian dress, customs, and names, Le Saux taking the name "Abhishiktananda" (joy of Christ). During this period, described in *Guru and Disciple* (1974) and *The Secret of Arunachala* (1979), Abhishiktananda took instruction from Ramana Maharshi (1879–1950) and Guru Gnanananda, and made several retreats in the caves of the holy mountain Arunachala. There he received the spiritual enlightenment that underlies his theology of Hindu-Christian dialog and fulfillment in experience or "the cave of the heart," later worked out in *Saccidananda* (1974). After Monchanin's death in 1957, Abhishiktananda moved north to the Himalayas and built a hermitage beside the Ganges at Gyansu, inviting Bede Griffiths to take over Santivanam. At Gyansu Abhishiktananda combined a contemplative life with intense literary activity; he took pilgrimages and journeys throughout India and conducted conferences on Hindu and Christian spirituality. His approach to mission and dialog, summarized in *The Church in India* (1969) and *Hindu-Christian Meeting Point* (1976), stands in the tradition of Brahmabandhav Upadhyaya (1861–1907) and the Vatican II call to indigenization, but in sharp contrast to the approach of those like M. M. Thomas (1916– ) who advocate a theology related to the secular world of modern India. Abhishiktananda's other works available in English include *Prayer* (1967) and *The Further Shore* (1975), the latter containing an essay on *sannyasa*.

**Bibliography.** Robin Boyd, *An Introduction to Indian Christian Theology* (2d ed., 1975); Emmanuel Vattakuzhy, *Indian Christian Sannyasa and Swami Abhishiktananda* (1981).

PHILIP HILLYER

**Abortion.** Expulsion or removal of a fetus from its mother's womb. Spontaneous abortions (or miscarriages) occur naturally, often in the case of a nonviable fetus. The term, however, is generally used for the induced abortion of a fetus at the request of its mother. The father may or may not have given his permission; if the woman is young, her parents' permission may not have been sought. Surgical abortions are generally legal in the West, and often are rebatable on health insurance. A therapeutic abortion is legally permitted under most state and federal laws after two medical practitioners testify that the mother's mental or physical life is threatened by the fetus's presence in the womb.

Abortion is available on demand in most states of Australia, some states of the USA, Canada, New Zealand, and Great Britain. Illegal but condoned abortions are available through the public health care systems of many other countries.

The reaction of Christians to the present situation varies greatly. Some fundamentalists and conservative evangelicals and virtually all Roman Catholics oppose the practice, and in some places are pledged to resist its legality by nonviolent means. The Right to Life movement has become internationally active in this cause. The basis of such opposition is that human life is the ongoing process of our creation by God. As it is sinful to take a human life, the abortion of a human fetus is sinful.

Some Christians advocate a theology of relative right to life, based to some extent on the self-preservation aspect of the "just war" theory of ethics. They permit the abortion of a fetus if the mother's life is seriously threatened. Most Christians would permit abortion in the case of rape, incest, or the likelihood of extreme handicap. These are difficult issues for strict Roman Catholics, who hold an absolute right-to-life position.

One reason so many Christians have attenuated their stance against abortion may be the use of contraceptives. The "pill" has been accepted by most Christian churches (not the Roman Catholic Church) on the basis that it prevents unwanted pregnancies and overpopulation. The ethical basis for such approval is the same as for any scientific or technological discovery. Many see only a marginal difference between preventing conception before intercourse and removing the consequences thereafter.

**Bibliography.** D. Callahan, *Abortion: Law, Choice and Morality* (1970); J. Noonan, ed., *The Morality of Abortion* (1971); R. F. R. Gardner, *Abortion: The Personal Dilemma* (1972); O. O'Donovan, *The Christian and the Unborn Child* (1973); F. Colquhoun, *Moral Question* (1977); P. E. Hughes, *Christian Ethics in Secular Society* (1983); J. K. Hoffmeier, ed., *Abortion: A Christian Understanding and Response* (1987).

ALAN NICHOLS

**Abramsky, Yehezkiel** (1886–1976). Jewish rabbi and scholar. Born in Grodno, Russia, he served as rabbi at Smolevitch and then at Slutzk, but fell into disfavor with Soviet authorities when he discussed the lack of religious freedom with a visiting group from America in 1930. He served one year in prison before being expelled, and thereafter was rabbi in London. He retired to Israel in 1951. Abramsky is best known for his

28-volume commentary on oral traditions concerning Jewish law (the Tosefta).

J. D. DOUGLAS

**L'Abri Fellowship.** Christian organization founded in Huémoz, Switzerland, by Francis and Edith Schaeffer to be a "demonstration of the existence and the character of God." The work of the Schaeffers began when they opened their home to friends of their oldest daughter, who was a student at the University of Lausanne. Many of these students became Christians, and the Schaeffers recognized that God was calling them to this work. They formally incorporated L'Abri Fellowship in 1955. There are presently seven branches in Switzerland, England, Holland, Sweden, and the USA. The organization is, however, small, with only about 50 workers. It is open to visitors and students. L'Abri conferences have been held in Europe, Australia, the USA, and South Africa. The principal conviction of the fellowship is that God exists. This means that Christianity is *objectively* true (able to provide "honest answers to honest questions") and *experimentally* true (able to provide answers not merely for the mind but for life).

RONALD MACAULAY

**Absoluteness of Christianity.** Affirmation of the Christian faith that God has given the full and final revelation of himself in Jesus Christ. This is implicit in the doctrine of the deity of Christ. "In the past God spoke to our forefathers through the prophets at many times and in various ways, but in these last days he has spoken to us by his Son" (Heb. 1:1–2a). The eternal Son, the second Person of the Trinity, has become man and is the revealer of God in the context of our earthly life. If Christ is fully God, it follows that there cannot be a revelation which goes beyond him. Paul writes to the Galatian converts that the gospel which he had received was not man-made but God-given and that its terms cannot be altered (Gal. 1:1–12).

The belief in the absoluteness of Christianity does not mean, however, that Christians attribute finality to any of the human systems in which people have sought to express for themselves the meaning of the light of the knowledge of the glory of God which they have seen in Jesus Christ. These systems partake of the frailty and the error which are characteristic of all things human. And the full meaning of Christian truth is seen only as that truth is related to the contemporary questions which agitate the church and the world. Christian thinkers must constantly seek to understand more perfectly the revelation which they have received and to state in each generation the relevance of divine truth for the actual human situation which people confront in their time.

Acceptance of the absoluteness of Christianity inevitably affects the attitudes of Christians toward non-Christian faiths. We do not need to brand as false all that is taught by other religions because we believe that Christianity gives us the full and final revelation of the character of God and of his will for us. Christianity may come as the fulfillment of truth that has already been disclosed in part in other religions. But at the same time Christian thinkers cannot be content with the statement that Jesus Christ is one of many roads that lead to God. They cannot agree that the various ways of approaching God are all equally valid. Christians must continue to hold that "there is one God and one mediator between God and men, the man Christ Jesus, who gave himself as a ransom for all men" (1 Tim. 2:5–6). For this reason there must be at the heart of Christianity a certain intolerance of other religions as these faiths seek to prevent people from coming to the knowledge of God in Christ.

*Bibliography.* E. Brunner, *The Mediator* (1927); R. E. Speer, *The Finality of Jesus Christ* (1933).

HOLMES ROLSTON

**Academies, Evangelical.** Learned societies which bring together theologians and Christian laypeople to address contemporary issues in the light of the gospel. The first evangelical academy was founded in 1945 in Bad Holl, Germany, by Eberhard Müller, general secretary of the German Christian Student Association (1935–38) and student chaplain in Tübingen. Other academies soon followed. Among these are Berlin, Erfurt, Hamburg, Iserlohn, Magdeburg, Mühlheim (Ruhr), and Tutzing. The movement has also spread to Austria, Japan, and South Africa. Study sessions are arranged during vacation periods and on weekends to allow professionals from all walks of life to participate. Clergy and university professors often serve as resource persons. A typical session includes Bible study, theme addresses, and wide-ranging discussion on how to relate one's faith to the workplace. Some 15,000 persons annually have become involved in academy-sponsored sessions since the inception of the movement.

*Bibliography.* E. Müller, *Lutheran World Review* 11 (1949): 27; A. Kunstad and S. Grundmann, eds., *Evangelisches Staatslexikon* (1966); P. Erkelenz, *Der Akademiegedanke im Wandel der Zeiten* (1968); *World of Learning* (1970).

**Access.** Privilege of admittance to, and of conversation with, one of higher station. If the seeker must stand silent in the presence of another, then, even though freely admitted, there is no real access. In Eastern courts it was the custom to appoint an officer who would vouch for suppliants to the throne. This custom is reflected in several situations in the Bible, such as the introduction of David by one of the servants at the court of Saul (1 Sam. 16:14–21) and of Paul to the Jerusalem church by Barnabas (Acts 9:26–29).

Paul uses the word "access" (Gk. *prosagogē*) three times. He applies the figure to the right of Christians to approach God and enjoy fellowship with him because Christ has "introduced" them (Rom. 5:2; Eph. 2:18; 3:12). In the first passage, the access is to the grace that follows justification. In the second, there is assurance that the same access to the Father has been provided for both Jew and Greek through Christ in the Spirit. In the third, the stress is on the bold confidence in which we may make use of our access to God, since Christ has opened the way. Here the note of fellowship with him in prayer is in the writer's thought. Thus access is distinguished from any merely formal judicial right obtained through great effort; the believer is warmly welcomed before the throne of grace. This may have been what moved Tyndale to translate *prosagogē* as "an open way in."

In the background of Paul's thought is the temple and the priest's entrance into the presence of God. The elaborate ritual of atonement that is developed in the Book of Leviticus culminates in the high priest being admitted to the Holy Place only once a year (Lev. 16). It is this restriction that fires the imagination of the author of Hebrews to contrast the free access to God in Christ (Heb. 10:19–23). Because Jesus has entered, not a temple made with hands, but heaven itself; because he comes, not with the blood of animals, but with his own blood, he is able to bring with him all those whom he has redeemed, not into a mere symbol of God's existence, but into his living presence. Here again the high notes of joy and fellowship are sounded. Similarly, the author of 1 Peter writes of Christ's purpose, "to bring you to God" (1 Pet. 3:18), and the Fourth Gospel recalls that Jesus had admonished his inner circle, "I am the way. . . . No one comes to the Father except through me" (John 14:6). The NT makes it clear that we can never enter God's presence in our own right, but that we need Christ to present us.

In the Roman Catholic and Anglican Churches the term has attained a technical meaning. "Prayers of access" are offered in connection with the serving of the Eucharist, the Anglican custom being to make these prayers just before the prayer of consecration of the elements.

*See also* SALVATION.

JULIAN P. LOVE

**Acolyte.** *See* ORDERS, MINOR.

**Acquired Immune Deficiency Syndrome.** *See* AIDS.

**Acts of the Apostles.** This NT book is of tremendous importance in that it is our only independent account of the history of the early church. It is the second part of a two-volume work (the Gospel of Luke is the first part) dedicated to a certain Theophilus (see Luke 1:1–4; Acts 1:1).

***Author and Date.*** From the 2d century on it has been held that the author was Luke, one of Paul's companions on some of his missionary journeys. No other name is attached to the writing in the tradition. In modern times some have doubted whether the book could have been written by a companion of the great apostle, partly because it shows no signs of acquaintance with the Pauline epistles, and partly because there are difficulties in reconciling some of the statements of Acts with some in the Pauline letters. The first point scarcely proves more than that Acts was written at an early date when Paul's letters would not yet have attained a wide circulation (even those who journeyed with the apostle would not have been likely to have had access to copies of what he had written to the churches). As for the second, it certainly shows that the two wrote independently, but it scarcely shows more than that. It cannot be proved beyond all doubt that Luke was the author of Acts, but he is the most likely candidate.

Acts concludes with Paul in Rome awaiting trial, so it cannot have been written before about A.D. 60. The book makes no mention of such events as the deaths of James (A.D. 62) and Paul or of the fall of Jerusalem (A.D. 70). This leads some scholars to favor a date in the early 60s. Others argue that Luke's use of the Gospel of Mark puts him later than this, and urge that there is no reason why his Gospel should be put at a date far from that of Matthew. So they opt for a date in the 80s with Acts, of course, correspondingly later. On the whole there seems to be said for the earlier date.

***Historical Value.*** Luke's account is regarded by some scholars as unreliable because of the difficulty they see in reconciling what he says with what Paul says in his epistles. They point, for example, to problems in reconciling Luke's narrative of the Council of Jerusalem (Acts 15) with what Paul says in Gal. 2. It is not certain, however, that Acts 15 refers to the same events as Gal. 2; it may be that Acts 11:30 is Luke's account of the visit mentioned in Gal. 2. The differences between the two seem to be rather the result of the way two different people viewed the same events than a reflection of irreconcilable discrepancies. Similar comments may be made at other points. To some it seems that Luke contradicts Paul, to others that these are simply independent accounts. It is to be borne in mind that Luke is remarkably accurate. For example, he has the correct names for a bewildering variety of governing authorities like the city officials (politarchs) at Thessalonica (17:6, 8), the provincial officials (asiarchs) at Ephesus (19:31), and the chief official of Malta (28:7). He sets his story in the framework of contemporary history, and it rings true.

Part of Luke's placing of the early church in contemporary history is his consistent demonstration that the Christian way is no threat to good government. He shows that believers obeyed the laws, and he records numerous occasions when just rulers gave their verdicts in favor of Christians. It is true that Christians feature in riots on quite a few occasions, but Luke shows that this was due to the way their opponents (mostly the Jews) stirred up opposition. The Christians did not instigate such tumults.

Luke records a considerable number of speeches; they take up more than a quarter of his book. They start early, for we have an account of what Peter said on the day of Pentecost, and they continue right through to Paul's address to the Jews in Rome. They are obviously summaries; not all those who gave addresses spoke as briefly as these accounts. But there is no reason for thinking that Luke has not given a fair account of what was said, and this allows us to see something of what the preaching of the early church was like. It differed from the way Jesus preached and from the way Christians like Paul wrote.

Luke has given us an account of the way the Christian movement spread in its early days. Interestingly he begins in Jerusalem, not Galilee as we might have anticipated from the Gospels. He has not tried to give a complete account, but centers his early narratives around Peter and the later ones around Paul. There is not much about what the other apostles did. But it is Luke who enables us to see something of the process whereby a movement that was at first exclusively Jewish became largely Gentile. He also shows us how it came about that a religion that originated in Asia began to turn westward, and thus in time would become associated with Europe. Without Luke our knowledge of what went on in the early days of the church would be very much poorer.

***The Spirit of God.*** Luke puts a great deal of emphasis on the importance of the Holy Spirit. The coming of the Spirit is foreshadowed in Acts 1, and Acts 2 contains a vivid account of the Pentecostal outpouring of the Spirit. From then on the book is, as has been rightly said, the "Acts of the Holy Spirit." The Spirit is present in the church, guiding and enabling believers so that God's purpose may be realized. The Spirit guides Peter (10:19), Philip (8:29, 39), and Paul and his companions (16:6–7), and it is interesting to see the way he features in the letter from the Jerusalem Council (15:28).

**Bibliography.** F. J. Foakes Jackson and K. Lake, *The Beginnings of Christianity*, 5 vols. (1920–33); F. F. Bruce, *The Acts of the Apostles* (1951); H. J. Cadbury, *The Making of Luke–Acts* (1958); E. Haenchen, *The Acts of the Apostles* (1971); W. Neil,

*The Acts of the Apostles* (1973); W. W. Gasque, *A History of the Criticism of the Acts of the Apostles* (1975); I. H. Marshall, *The Acts of the Apostles* (1980).

LEON MORRIS

**Adam, Karl** (1876–1966). Roman Catholic theologian. Born in Pursruck, Bavaria, Adam studied at the Philosophical and Theological Seminary in Regensburg and at the University of Munich, where he received his doctoral degree in 1904. He was ordained as a priest in 1900. From 1908 until 1915 Adam was a privatdocent. In 1915 he became a professor at the University of Munich. In 1917 he took the chair of moral theology at the University of Strasbourg. Adam lectured at the University of Tübingen from 1919 until 1950. In January 1934 he had difficulties with the Nazis because of his opposition to the so-called German religion. In 1947 he gave three lectures on the problem of a union between Catholics and Protestants (*One and Holy*, 1951). His writings include *Tertullian's Conception of the Church* (1907), *The Eucharistic Teaching of St. Augustine* (1908), *Christ Our Brother* (1931), *The Son of God* (1934), and *The Spirit of Catholicism* (1954).

**Adams, Theodore Floyd** (1898–1980). Baptist minister, educator, and author. Born in Palmyra, N.Y., he was educated at Denison College in Granville, Ohio, and Colgate Rochester Divinity School. Ordained in 1925, he served as pastor of the First Baptist Church of Richmond, Va. (1936–68), vice-president (1947–51) and president (1955–60) of the Baptist World Alliance (BWA), and visiting professor of preaching at Southeastern Baptist Theological Seminary (1969–78) in Wake Forest, N.C. As president of BWA, he visited the Soviet Union and became the first American Protestant clergyman to administer communion to Soviet churchgoers after the communist takeover in 1917. He was founder and member of the board of CARE, an international relief organization. His books include *Making Your Marriage Succeed* (1953), *Making the Most of What Life Brings* (1954), *Tell Me How* (1964), and *Baptists around the World* (1967).

JACK MITCHELL

**Addams, Jane** (1860–1935). Social worker and peace advocate. Born in Cedarville, Ill., she studied at Rockford (Ill.) College before spending two years in Europe. She and Ellen Gates Starr opened the social settlement of Hull House in Chicago in 1889. Addams later became head resident and is best remembered for her unselfish social work in that neighborhood. She was president of both the national Conference on Charities and Corrections and the Women's International League for Peace. In 1931 she won the Bryn Mawr Achievement Award and the Noble

Peace Prize (which she shared with Nicholas Murray Butler). Her writings include *Democracy and Social Ethics* (1902), *Newer Ideals of Peace* (1907), *The Spirit of Youth and the City Streets* (1909), *Twenty Years at Hull House* (1910), *A New Conscience and an Ancient Evil* (1911), *The Long Road of Women's Memory* (1916), *Peace and Bread in Time of War* (1922), *The Second Twenty Years at Hull House* (1930), and *The Excellent Becomes the Permanent* (1932).

**Bibliography.** J. W. Linn, *Jane Addams* (1935); W. E. Wise, *Jane Addams of Hull House* (1935); L. H. de Bowen, *Open Windows* (1946).

RAYMOND W. ALBRIGHT

**Addison, James Thayer** (1887–1953). Episcopalian priest and educator. Born in Fitchburg, Mass., he studied at Groton, Harvard, and the Episcopal Theological School. Ordained in 1913, he served the parishes of St. Mark's, Nowata, and St. Paul's, Claremore, Okla. (1913–15). He taught history of religion and missions in the Episcopal Theological School, Cambridge, Mass. (1915–40), and was acting master at Kirkland House, Harvard (1932/33). He taught at St. John's University, Shanghai, China (1909/10). During his incumbency at the Episcopal Theological School he taught at intervals in Japan, China, Egypt, and Lebanon. He was a chaplain in World War I. He was vice-president of the National Council of the Protestant Episcopal Church and director of the Overseas Department (1940–47). He was a trustee of the American University in Cairo, Egypt. His writings include *The Story of the First Gas Regiment* (1919), *Chinese Ancestor Worship* (1925), *Our Father's Business* (1927), *Francis Xavier* (1929), *François Coillard* (1929), *Our Expanding Church* (1930; repr. 1951), *Religion in India* (1930), *Life beyond Death in the Beliefs of Mankind* (1932), *The Way of Christ* (1934; repr. 1949), *The Medieval Missionary* (1936), *The Lord's Prayer* (1938), *World of Islam* (1938), *Variety in the Devotional Life* (1939), *Parables of Our Lord* (1940), *Why Missions* (1940), *The Christian Approach to the Moslem* (1940), *The Episcopal Church in the United States* (1951), and *War, Peace and the Christian Mind* (1953). He also contributed to *The Church's Teaching* (vol. 6).

RAYMOND W. ALBRIGHT

**Adler, Alfred** (1870–1937). Austrian psychiatrist and founder of the school of individual psychology. Adler was born in Vienna, Austria. His fascination with human disease led him to the study of medicine at Vienna University. Specializing first in internal medicine, he later turned to neurology and psychiatry. His study of children with congenital somatic difficulties, *Study of Organ Inferiority and Its Psychical Compensation* (1907), indicated that inferiority feelings are compensated for by achieving superiority at some point. Adult personality, therefore, is to be explained in terms of early inferiority. In 1907 he joined Sigmund Freud and adopted, disseminated, and contributed to the latter's views. Adler was a loyal and ardent admirer of Freud, defending him vigorously. Whereas Jung finally broke with Freud in 1911, it was another year before Adler and Freud separated because of disagreement over Freud's theory that the libido is the force behind neurosis. Adler held instead that a sort of will to power or "guiding fiction," when excessive and unreal, precipitates neurosis. He rejected Freud's theory that infantile wishes affect behavior. Whereas Freud emphasized the influence of the past, Adler stressed that an individual's future (i.e., potentialities and expectations) was the determining factor. He believed that people are restrained by organic inferiorities, but compensations are encountered in community life. Personality is the product of our relationship to society, work, and love. By cooperating, the ego can meet basic needs (id) within communal activity. The meaning given to experiences is self-determined. Behavior patterns are acquired through identification and not by inheritance. Prestige and superiority are purely compensatory and do not solve real problems. Serving the community is the healthy and mature way out.

Adler's views on religion are not well known. Born a Jew, he converted to Christianity at the age of 34. Although his conversion may have been genuine, Adler was probably trying to rid himself of all traces of Judaism, a religion he strongly criticized.

After World War I, Adler's views spread rapidly to England and the USA. His concept of the inferiority complex was widely, if not always accurately, known and used. He founded the International Society for Individual Psychology, was made an honorary citizen of Vienna (1930), lectured at Vienna University and at Columbia University, and became a professor at Long Island College of Medicine (1934). Like Freud he was a prolific writer. His writings include *The Neurotic Constitution* (1926), *The Practice and Theory of Individual Psychology* (1927), *Understanding Human Nature* (1927), *The Case of Miss R.* (1929), *The Science of Living* (1929), *The Education of Children* (1930), *The Pattern of Life* (1930), and *What Life Should Mean to You* (1931).

ROLLIN J. FAIRBANKS

**Adler, Felix** (1851–1933). Educator and ethical reformer. Born in Germany, he came to America in 1857 when his father became rabbi of Temple Emanu-El in New York City. He graduated from Columbia College in 1870, and pursued studies in Berlin and Heidelberg (Ph.D., 1873). He was professor of Hebrew and Oriental literature at

Cornell (1874–76), then returned to New York City and established the Society for Ethical Culture, a nonreligious association for the ethical improvement of its members. He was active in various philanthropic enterprises and in popular education. He was professor of political and social ethics at Columbia University (1902–21) and served on the editorial board of the *International Journal of Ethics*. His books include *Creed and Deed* (1877), *The Moral Instruction of Children* (1898), *Life and Destiny* (1903), *Marriage and Divorce* (1905), *Essentials of Spirituality* (1905), *The World Crisis and Its Meaning* (1915), *An Ethical Philosophy of Life* (1918), and *The Reconstruction of the Spiritual Ideal* (1923).

**Adventism.** American millennial movement tracing its beginnings to the preaching of William Miller (1782–1849), a veteran of the War of 1812 who settled in New York State and after a period of intensive Bible study became convinced that Christ's return was imminent. Miller began to preach about 1831, and a revival broke out under his labors. For several years he received invitations from churches of many denominations; after a time many of the established denominations closed their doors to the "Millerite" preachers. Miller was convinced that the symbolic "day" of Bible prophecy was really a year. He also concluded that the 2300 days of Dan. 8:14 were concurrent with the "seventy weeks of years" of Dan. 9. These having begun in 457 B.C. by his calculation, Miller asserted that the longer of the two periods would end about the year 1843. Christ would return and fulfill the prophecy that the sanctuary of the temple would be cleansed. Miller thought the sanctuary mentioned in Dan. 8:14 was the earth (or the church), which would be cleansed by fire at Christ's second advent. He set forth his views in *Evidences from Scripture and History of the Second Coming of Christ about the Year 1843* (1836).

The movement gained many followers, some of them members of existing churches, many others adherents of no church at all. Until 1843 Miller was vague about the time of the second coming ("about the year 1843"), but on January 1, 1843, he committed himself to a definite stance, saying, "I am fully convinced that somewhere between March 21st, 1843 and March 21st, 1844, according to the Jewish mode of computation of time, Christ will come." Tension ran high among Miller's followers and was heightened when an unexpected comet appeared in late February 1843. Many were convinced to leave their churches and join the Millerite movement. However, as March 1844 came and went, Miller was forced to revise his views. A new date of October 22, 1844, was set; but this date, too, resulted in disappointment. The "Great Disappointment," as Adventists termed the reaction to

the failure of Christ to return in this period, caused many to leave the movement. Some returned to their former churches while others gave up their Christian profession entirely. But forces already in operation formed the remaining believers into several denominational bodies, the largest of which is now the Seventh-day Adventist Church.

Since Miller was a Baptist, the doctrinal position of Adventist groups closely resembles Baptist theology at many points. At first Adventists agreed that Christ's return would be premillennial—that it would precede the thousand-year period foretold in Rev. 20. Today, many in the Advent Christian Church maintain an amillennial position. Many Adventists also are known for their advocacy of the idea that the dead await the resurrection in an unconscious state. Adventists generally emphasize the importance of the OT Law. Some worship on Saturday in order to be faithful to the literal import of the fourth commandment, "Remember the Sabbath day by keeping it holy" (Exod. 20:8). Some groups celebrate Jewish holidays and dietary laws. Adventists term baptism and the Lord's supper "ordinances" rather than "sacraments," and often practice foot-washing as a preparation for the Lord's supper. Pacifism is a common Adventist position.

R. MILTON WINTER

**Advocate.** One who assists, and often pleads, the cause of another; an intercessor. A judicial term, its only occurrence in the English Bible is in 1 John 2:1, where it is the translation of *paraklētos*. Christ is here called our "paraclete," our advocate. Since the believer is accused of having sinned, Christ pleads for him before the Father. His pleading is acceptable, both because he is righteous and because he has made expiation for sins. It is at this point that John's soteriology comes closest to that of Paul (cf. Rom. 3:25).

The Greek word *paraklētos* in the Gospel of John (14:16, 26; 15:26; 16:7) obviously refers to the Holy Spirit. In these passages the legal term "advocate" hardly does justice to the richness of the thought. In most English versions the term "comforter" is used, but in the Revised Standard Version the more general word "counselor" appears; the Spirit not only consoles, but encourages to action. In addition to any pleading that may be necessary for disciples, he gives them needed guidance (14:16); he testifies in their hearts to the truth (14:26); he brings Jesus back to their memories (15:26); and he convinces the world that it is sinful, that the righteousness of God is possible, and that judgment is real (16:7–11).

Although the use of this term is limited, the idea of the timely advocate is common in the

Bible. The synoptic Gospels recall Jesus' promise that when his disciples are brought before councils for his sake, they are not to worry, since they will be directed in what they ought to say (Mark 13:11 and pars.). Throughout the Bible the intercessor is a frequent figure. Jonathan intercedes for David before his father Saul (1 Sam. 19:1–7); David intercedes with God for his child (2 Sam. 12:15–17). The psalms are full of intercessory prayers. Paul urges intercession (1 Thess. 5:25; 1 Tim. 2:1). Christ is said to be our intercessor, the one who "happens in on our behalf" (Rom. 8:27, 34; 11:2; Heb. 7:25). And the Holy Spirit is said to intercede with God in prayer for believers who do not know how to pray (Rom. 8:26).

In the Latin church the term "advocate" became associated with ecclesiastical rights. The 11th Council of Carthage (A.D. 407) appointed certain officers as *advocati ecclesiae*, one of their duties being to defend the rights of the church before the state. During the Middle Ages, the office tended to become hereditary, although always the nomination of the church had to be approved by the civil power. It is easy to understand how the office readily lent itself to abuse and even to extortion. In the Roman Catholic Church, whenever there is a move to canonize a new saint, there is always an appointed *advocatus diaboli*, a devil's advocate, who is to list all possible objections to the proposed beatification. He is answered in turn by an *advocatus dei*.

JULIAN P. LOVE

## Aesthetic, Religion and the.

The arts delight us and to that extent anticipate the vision of God by extending our capacity to use our senses, to feel, to judge, and to grasp intelligible order or structure. Good art as such works directly against self-deception and "false consciousness," and so indirectly against the devil who is the "father of lies." "There is life and there alone is life worth living for man, while he contemplates Beauty itself" (Plato, *Symposium* 211C). No theist could possibly doubt that the supremely beautiful which is Beauty itself could be none other than God. This is not so obvious, however, from a reading of the works of the majority of theologians, who by no means exemplify Karl Barth's dictum that theology is the most beautiful of the sciences. Since medieval times, theologians have been prone to envisage the divine from the point of view of the true and the good rather than of the beautiful. An important corrective has been offered in our own time by Hans Urs von Balthasar. As he says, the ancient world refused to understand itself without beauty; but the modern world has largely abandoned her, and so is inevitably left to its own avarice and sadness. Since we no longer believe in beauty, we make a mere appearance of her in order the more easily to dispose of her. However, "we can

be sure that whoever sneers at her name as if she were the ornament of a bourgeois past—whether he admits it or not—can no longer pray and soon will no longer be able to love." Short of beauty, the good loses its attraction, and the true no longer fascinates anyone but becomes submerged in a dry clutter of evidence and argument. This applies to the life of the mind and of the heart in general, but more especially to religion and theology; it is at their peril that biblical theologians forget that it is from the beautiful form constituted by OT and NT together that there shines out the glory of God. As Christian masters of a "theological aesthetics," von Balthasar singles out Irenaeus, Augustine, Denys, Anselm, Bonaventure, Dante, John of the Cross, Pascal, Hamann, Soloviev, Hopkins, and Péguy. The work of these masters of theological aesthetics has nothing to do with that superficial aestheticism which seeks to supply a sort of cosmetics by way of commending religious doctrines and practices. On the role of aesthetics in worship, opinions among Christians vary in a striking way; yet the question posed by the judicious Richard Hooker is always pertinent: "Touching God Himself, has He anywhere revealed that it is His delight to dwell beggarly?"

*See also* ART AND THE CHURCH.

**Bibliography.** H. U. von Balthasar, *The Glory of the Lord: A Theological Aesthetics* (1982); H. A. Meynell, *The Nature of Aesthetic Value* (1986).

HUGO A. MEYNELL

## Afghanistan.

Land-locked nation known as the "crossroads of Central Asia." It borders with the USSR on the north; it has a short contiguous mountainous area at the end of the Wakhan Corridor with China to the east; it possesses a long boundary with Pakistan to the east and south; and it shares a common border with Iran to the west. The area of the country is 647,500 sq. km. (250,000 sq. mi.). It consists of a high arid plateau with mountain ranges across the center of the country and deserts to the north and south. Although no official census has ever been taken, the population is estimated at 16 million, of whom 5 million became refugees because of the Soviet invasion and occupation of this nation. The capital city is Kabul, which is 6000 feet in elevation and has a population of nearly 2 million.

Over 50 languages are spoken in the country, with the two main ones being Dari (Afghan Persian, the lingua franca) and Pashto. The varied linguistic and ethnic mixture in this nation has resulted from invasions down through history. These include the incursions of Alexander the Great, Arab Muslim conquerors in the 7th and 8th centuries A.D., Genghis Khan, Tamerlane, the British, and the USSR.

Most Afghans practice Sunnite Islam, although many adhere to Shiite Islam. There is also a group of Ismailis. Giant statues carved out of the cliffs in the Bamian Valley of the central part of the country bear testimony to the country's Buddhist past. One of these statues is higher than Niagara Falls. The Assyrian or Ancient Church of the East used to have bishoprics in Kabul and Herat. Today Nestorian crosses are woven into Afghan carpets as art forms and are a silent witness to the former Christian presence even though most of the craftspeople who weave these are unaware of the significance of these designs.

A small Armenian church was built in Kabul in the 1800s but was destroyed at the end of the 19th century in the fighting between the British and the Afghans. A Roman Catholic priest was allowed to come to the Italian embassy in Kabul in 1932 and establish a chapel on this expatriate property.

Following the partitioning of India in 1947 and the withdrawal of the British Empire from the subcontinent, Afghanistan was free to follow its own foreign policy, and invited teachers and engineers from other countries to help with their development. This enabled Christian "tentmakers" to enter the country from 1948 on. In 1966, the Afghanistan government allowed missionaries to come in to help with medical projects. An eye hospital in Kabul continues to offer services to the people.

In the 1960s, the Afghanistan government gave permission for a Protestant church to be built. This was dedicated on May 17, 1970. However, since the Muslim law of apostasy states that anyone leaving that religion should die and since some Afghan nationals were becoming Christians, the Kabul Community Christian Church building was destroyed in 1973 and some expatriate Christian workers were expelled.

On July 17, 1973, a coup took place and the monarchy was abolished. The country became a republic under Muhammed Daoud until his government was taken over by a communist revolt in 1978. Russian armies invaded on December 25, 1979, to prop up the faltering regime. Thus there has been a clash in Afghanistan between the two great "Christian heresies" of Islam and communism.

During Russian occupation in the 1980s, Afghan refugees scattered around the world, providing new evangelization opportunities. Radio broadcasts in Pashto and Dari were beamed into the country. By the time of the withdrawal of Russian forces many new connections with the West had been made, although religious resistance to outside, non-Islamic influence remained strong.

*Bibliography.* R. E. Hedlund, *World Christianity, South Asia* (1980); D. B. Barrett, *World Christian Encyclopedia* (1982); J. C. Wilson, Jr., *Today's Tentmakers* (1984); P. Johnstone, *Operation World* (1986).

J. CHRISTY WILSON, JR.

**African Methodist Episcopal Church.** *See* METHODISTS.

**African Methodist Episcopal Zion Church.** *See* METHODISTS.

**Aggrey, James Emman Kwegyir** (1875–1927). African missionary and educator. A Fanti tribesman born in Anamabu, Ghana, West Africa, he converted to Christianity at age eight, was baptized at 14, and taught school (1890–98) while faithfully preaching the gospel in West Africa. After attending the Methodist Missionary School in Cape Coast, he trained as a missionary at Livingstone College, N.C. For the next 20 years he taught English literature at Livingstone, held two small pastorates, and labored for the material benefit of rural blacks. As one of its most useful members, he was the only black on the Phelps Stokes Commission (1920), which studied educational affairs in Africa. He returned to Africa in 1924 to help establish Prince of Wales College on the Gold Coast. Slated to be assistant vice-principal, he died suddenly of meningitis while completing his Ph.D. in America. Intensely proud of his race, he consistently advocated cooperation between blacks and whites.

JACK MITCHELL

**AIDS (Acquired Immune Deficiency Syndrome).** Disease that impairs the immune system's ability to fight disease, leaving an infected person vulnerable to pathologies which a healthy body normally counters. The condition is "acquired," that is, contracted, not inherited. It destroys the body's defense against disease, the immune system. "Deficiency" indicates that the system does not function in the normal manner, while "syndrome" refers to a group of specific diseases accompanying the disorder. AIDS is a fatal illness; there is no cure.

AIDS is contracted through sexual intercourse, contaminated needles or syringes, and, less frequently, through infected blood or blood products used in transfusions. It has also been transmitted by infected mothers to babies during the birth process. The common form of transmission is through exposure of mucus membranes or the blood system to infected blood or semen. The virus causing AIDS, however, is fragile. Outside the body it is easily killed with soap, alcohol, hydrogen peroxide, or a chlorine bleach solution. Touching, shaking hands, or hugging an infected person does not transmit the disease.

AIDS is thought to be caused by the human immunodeficiency virus (HIV). Yet, a specific viral cause for all cases of AIDS has not been isolated; mutant forms complicate research.

AIDS itself does not kill. Rather, the disease is the endpoint of a spectrum of HIV-related infections. Because the immune system is severely damaged and rendered inoperative, opportunistic infections wreak havoc on the human body. AIDS is, therefore, a group of HIV-related diseases, often including Kaposi's sarcoma (cancerous skin lesions), persistent swelling of the lymph nodes, pneumonia, and asymptomatic infections.

Ethical issues associated with AIDS are complicated by a widespread assumption that modern medicine is winning the fight against disease. Medicine has advanced from a profession providing care and comfort to one which offers cures. AIDS challenges this view and turns medical attention toward questions of an earlier era: What obligations are there to treat contagious but incurable diseases? How is personal risk to be weighed against the needs of the sick? A further complication is the fact that the majority of those affected are homosexual men. Antipathy toward both homosexuality and sexual promiscuity distorts much social, religious, and medical thought about AIDS.

Ethical issues fall into three general categories: obligations of health professionals, obligations of researchers, and obligations of society. Obligations of health professionals are conditioned by the history of health care itself: the practice of medicine is a dangerous profession (until the discovery of antibiotics, to care for the sick was to risk sickness and death). The American College of Physicians and the Infectious Disease Society of America both assert that a professional commitment to medicine means little if it applies only under safe conditions. In a joint statement concerning AIDS released in 1986 they stated: "Denying appropriate care to sick and dying patients for any reason is unethical." A 1988 statement by the American Medical Association noted that "a physician may not ethically refuse to treat a patient whose condition is within the physician's current realm of competence."

Related to the professional obligations concerning treatment are the obligations of researchers. In both care and research the issue of confidentiality is critical. Physicians and researchers gather information of a sensitive and potentially damaging sort. Patients and research subjects are asked to reveal intimate details about personal sexual history, practices, and partners. Doubts concerning confidentiality inhibit cooperation by those from whom information is necessary and for whom information might finally be of greatest benefit. On the other hand, disclosure of some information could lead to criminal prosecution, since sodomy remains a crime in many places and use of dangerous drugs is a crime everywhere. Moreover, loss of income, loss of insurance coverage, and loss of status within a community might follow breaches of confidentiality.

Balancing obligations to protect privacy (and civil rights) on the one hand with obligations to safeguard public health on the other is a major ethical dilemma facing researchers and health care workers. Questions to guide research and health care professionals include the following: For whose benefit is information being requested? What is to be done with information obtained? Who will have access to such information? And might there be less intrusive means to obtain necessary information?

Moral obligations of a society faced with an AIDS epidemic have to do initially with the issue of resource allocation. How much public money should be allocated for AIDS treatment and research? Do all members of a society have rights to medical resources sufficient to assure protection from disease and avoidable death? Or do some personal choices eliminate rights to public health assistance? Are there moral criteria that exclude assistance for illnesses that result from homosexual behavior?

Other social considerations include issues of whether surveillance of suspected carriers of the AIDS virus is appropriate and whether compulsory testing and quarantine (compulsory deprivation of liberty) are justifiable responses to an AIDS epidemic. In the USA, section 504 of the Federal Rehabilitation Act of 1973 prohibiting discrimination against the handicapped has been used to protect AIDS sufferers on the grounds that the disease is a handicap limiting major life functions. Court rulings thus generate public policies aimed at education and persuasion rather than coercion. Reasoning reflects a consequentialist ethic: coercive measures are likely to discourage those who most need it from being tested.

*Bibliography.* A. G. Fettner and W. A. Check, *The Truth about AIDS: Evolution of an Epidemic* (1984); R. Steinbrook, et al., *Annals of Internal Medicine* 103 (1985): 787–90; D. Altman, *AIDS in the Mind of America* (1987); V. Gong and N. Rudnick, eds., *AIDS: Facts and Issues* (rev. ed., 1987); A. Zuger, *Hastings Center Report* (June 1987).

D. L. JOHNSON

**Ainslie, Peter** (1867–1934). Disciples of Christ pastor and editor. Born in Dunnsville, Va., he attended Transylvania College. After two years as temporary supply pastor in Newport News, Va., he became pastor of the Disciples of Christ congregation in Baltimore (1891–1934), where he erected the Christian Temple and also developed nine branch churches. He was greatly interested in the world peace movement and in Christian unity, founding and editing the *Christian Union Quarterly* (1911–34). In addition to his successful pastoral work he attended most of the major world conferences on peace and Christian unity. His writings include *Religion in Daily Doings* (1903), *Studies in the OT* (1907), *Among the Gospels and the Acts* (1908), *God and Me* (1908), *The Unfinished Task of the Reformation* (1910), *Introduction to the Study of the Bible* (1910), *Brother and I* (1911), *The Message of the Disciples for the Union of the Church* (1913), *Christ or Napoleon—Which?* (1915), *Working with God* (1917), *If Not a United Church—What?* (1920), *The Way of Prayer* (1924), *The Scandal of Christianity* (1929), and *Some Experiments in Living* (1933). He also coauthored *Christian War* with H. C. Armstrong.

RAYMOND W. ALBRIGHT

**Aland, Kurt** (1915– ). German biblical scholar and NT textual critic. Born in Berlin, he studied there, and has since taught in the theological faculties at Berlin, Halle, and (from 1958) Münster. A versatile scholar whose interests range widely in church history and Old and New Testaments, he has been editor-in-chief of the Commission on the Church Fathers of the Berlin Academy, and has also edited several theological journals. His writings include *Kirchengeschichtlichen Entwürfe* (1960), *Hilfsbuch zum Lutherstudium* (1970), *Neutestamentlichen Entwürfe* (1979), *Geschichte der Christenheit*, 2 vols. (1980–82), and *The Text of the NT* (ET, 1987). He has brought out new editions of F. Loofs's *Dogmengeschichte* (1951) and P. Feine's *Theologie des Neuen Testaments* (1951).

**Albania.** The People's Socialist Republic of Albania, the smallest country in the Balkan peninsula. Albania is a mountainous and underdeveloped region. It has an area of 28,748 sq. km. (11,100 sq. mi.) and a population of almost 3 million. During the Middle Ages the territory of Albania moved back and forth between the ecclesiastical jurisdictions of Rome and Constantinople. At the time of the Turkish conquest in the 15th century northern Albania was predominantly Catholic while the rest of the country was Greek Orthodox. Albania was part of the Ottoman Empire for almost 450 years, during which time there was widespread conversion of the population to Islam. When Turkish rule came to an end in 1912, Albania had become the only European country with a Muslim majority. In the period between the two World Wars independent Albania was continually under threat of foreign domination. The 1937 census showed that nearly 70 percent of the population was Muslim, just over 20 percent Greek Orthodox, and just over 10 percent Roman Catholic.

Albania was invaded by Italy in 1939, and the country remained under foreign occupation until the national resistance movement set up a communist-dominated government under Enver Hoxha in 1941. Religious persecution began immediately, on the grounds that each major religion had been promoted by various invaders at different times and that religion was therefore a divisive factor in the national life. Catholicism, whose links with the West were feared, was especially suspect. Legislation set firm limits to religious freedom.

A totally new state of affairs was inaugurated in 1967. All decrees on religion were abolished, all places of worship were shut down, and Albania declared itself the first atheist state in the world. Albania remains to this day the only country in the world in which it is illegal to practice a faith. There is only patchy evidence of what has happened to believers. In 1971 there were said to be only 14 Catholic priests still alive, 12 in concentration camps and two in hiding. The Catholic bishop Coba was murdered in a concentration camp in 1979 for having celebrated Mass there. Nevertheless, the Albanian media constantly call for an increase in atheist vigilance and there is evidence that faith is still secretly alive. In 1975, for example, an atheist specialist wrote that religious ideas were "still strong and influential" in the family circle.

Events since November 1989 had the least impact on Albania of any Eastern bloc nation. In late 1990 reports of unrest and reforms were surfacing, but no substantive change in Albania's atheistic stance had occurred.

**Bibliography.** G. Sinishta, *The Fulfilled Promise: A Documentary Account of Religious Persecution in Albania* (1976); T. Beeson, *Discretion and Valour: Religious Conditions in Russia and Eastern Europe* (1982).

PHILIP WALTERS

**Albright, Raymond Wolf** (1901–1965). Educator and author. Born in Akron, Pa., he attended Albright College, Franklin and Marshall College, Reformed Theological Seminary (Lancaster), and Divinity School of the Protestant Episcopal Church (Th.D., 1933). His pastoral ministry included three churches in Pennsylvania (1922–27) before he became professor of church history at the Evangelical School of Theology, Reading, Pa. (1926–52). He was also professor of church history at Temple University (1935–45), and in 1952 he took the same position at the Episcopal Theological School in Cambridge, Mass., a position that he held until his death. His career included visiting professorships at the University of Marburg (1956) and Boston University (1906), and a lectureship at the Radcliffe Seminars (1957–65). Albright was a member of numerous societies. His writings include *History of Religious Education in the Evangelical Church* (1932), *History of the Peace Movement* (1935), *History of the Evangelical Church* (1942), and *Focus on Infinity: A Life of Phillips Brooks* (1961). He was department editor of the *New Schaff-Her-*

*zog Encyclopedia,* and a contributor to numerous other encyclopedias.

JACK MITCHELL

**Albright, William Foxwell** (1891–1971). Biblical scholar and archeologist. Born of missionary parents in Coquimbo, Chile, he cultivated an early interest in linguistics and archeology. He received a doctorate in Semitic languages from Johns Hopkins University in Baltimore. Albright served as director of the American Schools of Oriental Research in Jerusalem (1920–29), having been appointed fellow in 1919. Beginning in 1933, he later served as its director, and the institute now bears his name (W. F. Albright Institute of Archaeological Research). He directed excavations at many sites, including Gibeah and Tell Beit Mirsim, making significant advances in W. M. F. Petrie's technique of dating ancient stratigraphy through ceramic typology. He also worked in Jordan and Arabia. In 1929 Albright was appointed professor of Semitic languages at Johns Hopkins, a position he held until his retirement in 1958. His publication record is astonishing. The bibliography in his 1961 festschrift, *The Bible and the Ancient Near East,* has 887 entries. His most influential books are *The Archaeology of Palestine and the Bible* (1932), *The Archaeology of Palestine* (1949), *Archaeology and the Religion of Israel* (4th ed., 1956), *From the Stone Age to Christianity* (2d ed., 1957), and *Yahweh and the Gods of Canaan* (1965).

JOHN McRAY

**Alcuin Club.** Association of Anglicans, chiefly English, founded in 1897 with the aim of promoting the study and use of the Book of Common Prayer and encouraging the practical study of English liturgical traditions. The aim was modified in 1966 to include the publication of manuscripts concerned with current liturgical developments. Representative members include Percy Dearmer, Athelstan Riley, Christopher Wordsworth, Charles Gore, and Walter Howard Frere.

TIM LENTON

**Alexander, Samuel** (1859–1938). Jewish philosopher. Alexander's reconciliation of science and values was reminiscent of Spinoza's mechanical interpretation of nature. He modernized Spinoza's thought by making time central. In Alexander's thought, Nisus was the creativeness of time that evolved successive levels of existence from space-time, which was pervasive to deity. God was conceived both immanently and transcendentally, that is, as both process and as process directed toward deity. Alexander's principal works are *Moral Order and Progress* (1906), *Space-Time and Deity* (1920), and *Beauty and Other Forms of Value* (1933).

JOHN W. McCARTHY

**Algeria.** *See* NORTH AFRICA.

**Alleman, Herbert Christian** (1868–1953). Lutheran theologian. Born in Bloomsburg, Pa., he studied at Pennsylvania College, Lutheran Theological Seminary, and the University of Pennsylvania. Ordained in 1891, he served as pastor of Trinity Church, Chambersburg, Pa. (1891–96), College Church, Gettysburg, Pa. (1896–1900), and Messiah Church, Philadelphia (1900–1911). He became professor of OT literature and theology at Lutheran Theological Seminary in 1911. His works include *The Gist of the Sermon* (1905), *The Book—A Brief Introduction to the Bible* (1908), *Prayers for Boys* (1925), *The OT—A Study* (1934), *The NT—A Study* (1934), and *NT Commentary* (1936). He coedited *OT Commentary* (1948) with E. E. Flack.

**Allen, Alexander Viets Griswold** (1841–1908). American church historian. Born in Massachusetts, he was educated at Kenyon College, Gambier, and Andover Theological Seminary, and in 1865 was ordained in the Protestant Episcopal Church. He was the founder and first rector of St. John's Church, Lawrence, Mass. (1865–67), and then was professor of church history at the Episcopal Theological School, Cambridge, Mass., until his death. His principal works are *Continuity of Christian Thought* (1884), *Life of Jonathan Edwards* (1889), *Religious Progress* (1893), *Christian Institutions* (1897), *Life and Letters of Phillips Brooks* (1900), *Phillips Brooks* (1907), and *Freedom in the Church* (1907).

**Allis, Oswald Thompson** (1880–1973). OT scholar. Born in Wallingford, Pa., into a family having deep roots in colonial America and an unusually deep loyalty to historic Presbyterianism, he entered the University of Pennsylvania intending to major in scientific studies. He came under the influence of Edgar Fahs Smith, president of that institution, who was a devoted Christian. Allis entered Princeton Theological Seminary in 1902, where he studied under Benjamin B. Warfield, William Benton Green, Jr., Robert Dick Wilson, and Geerhardus Vos. Upon his graduation from Princeton, he studied archeology under Friedrich Delitzsch at the University of Berlin (Ph.D., 1913). In the meantime he had joined the faculty at Princeton Seminary and became a colleague of Robert Dick Wilson in the department of OT studies. In 1922 he was made professor of Semitic studies at Princeton. When conflict broke out between liberals and conservatives over the propriety of Harry Emerson Fosdick's call to fill the pulpit of the First Presbyterian Church in New York City, Allis took his stand with Clarence Edward McCartney, his Princeton classmate and friend, against Fosdick's liberalism. In 1929, along with Robert Dick Wilson and J. Gresham Machen, he left Princeton Seminary to become a member of the faculty of the newly formed Westminster Seminary. Allis was the author of nine outstanding books, the most important of which are *The Five Books of Moses* (1943), *Prophecy and the Church* (1945), and *The Unity of Isaiah* (1950).

C. GREGG SINGER

**All Souls' Day.** Annual Roman Catholic Church commemoration of the faithful departed. It occurs on November 2, the day after All Saints' Day. While the latter has been kept since the 9th century, the former became common only two centuries later. This was due to the influence of Odilo, abbot of Cluny, who required its celebration in 998 in the religious houses of his Benedictine congregation. From these monasteries it entered into the whole Western Church.

It was immensely popular for it provided the faithful on earth an opportunity to pray for Christ's merit to be transferred to their family and friends, who, it was held, were in a process of purification on their way through purgatory to heaven. In fact All Souls' Day was widely observed before the church officially had a doctrine of purgatory (which only came in 1254 in a pontifical definition from Pope Innocent IV). The day has kept its popularity into modern times in Catholic countries.

PETER TOON

**Alt, Albrecht** (1883–1956). OT scholar. Born in Stuebach, Bavaria, he studied at the universities of Erlangen and Leipzig, where he concentrated on OT and Oriental research. He was a privatdocent (1909–12) at the University of Greifswald, and professor at the universities of Greifswald (1912–14), Basel (1914–21), Halle (1921/22), and Leipzig (1923–56). He occasionally worked at the German Evangelical Institute for the Antiquities of the Holy Land in Jerusalem, editing the yearbooks of this institution (1927–41), and was president of the German Palestine Exploration Society (1926–49). His writings include *Israel und Aegypten* (1909), *Die griechischen Inschriften der Palaestina Tertia* (1921), *Die Landnahme der Israeliten in Palaestina* (1925), *Der Gott der Väter* (1929), *Die Staatenbildung der Israeliten in Palaestina* (1930), and *Die Ursprünge des israelitischen Rechts* (1934). He coedited the *Biblia Hebraica* (1905–7) with Rudolf Kittel and others.

**Althaus, A. W. H. Paul** (1888–1966). Lutheran theologian. Born in Obershagen, Hanover, he studied at Göttingen, Tübingen, and the theological seminary at Erichsburg, Hanover. He was a privatdocent at Göttingen (1914) before serving as a chaplain in the German army (1915–18). Althaus taught at Rostock (1920–25), and was professor of systematic theology and NT at

Erlangen from 1925. A specialist in dogmatics and ethics, he stood in opposition to the dialectical theology of Karl Barth. His works include *Die letzten Dinge* (1922), *Communio Sanctorum* (1929), *Grundriss der Dogmatik*, 2 vols. (1929, 1932), *Grundriss der Ethik* (1931), *Der Römerbrief* (1932), *Paulus und Luther über den Menschen* (1938), *Die Christliche Wahrheit* (1948), *Die Theologie M. Luthers* (1962), and *Das sogennante Kerygma und der historische Jesus* (1963).

**American Baptist Churches in the USA (ABC).** Successor to the Northern Baptist Convention (NBC). During the post-Civil War era in the USA, Baptists in the North and South went their separate ways. Although they held firmly to congregational autonomy, they formed local associations and state conventions and utilized societies to carry out larger ministries; the Southerners even had their own convention. In the North there was no overarching denomination as such, but in 1908 representatives of the foreign missions, home missions, and publications societies who had long seen the need for cooperative effort took the lead in organizing the Northern Baptist Convention. These and the other societies (education and women's) which hitherto had been independent agencies now became boards, and a central administrative body (board of managers) was created and a unified budget adopted, although the denominational machinery was actually rather loose. The fundamentalist controversy of the 1920s with its attacks on the missionary, educational, and publications program of NBC greatly weakened the denomination. One group separated from NBC in the early 1930s while others remained and promoted a conservative reform program. Frustrated in their efforts, several of these pulled out in 1947 to form the Conservative Baptist Association.

Meanwhile, the leaders of NBC grew dissatisfied with its loose organization and regionalism. In 1950 it was significantly restructured and renamed the American Baptist Convention (ABC). This included the creation of a stronger central board and the office of general secretary and the promotion of closer cooperation among the program agencies. The body was further unified by the establishment of a new headquarters at Valley Forge, Pa., in 1960, which brought foreign missions, home missions, education, and publications work under one roof. At the same time, ABC worked diligently to effect closer relationships with black and ethnic Baptists. It also faced the challenge of the Southern Baptists, who were now aggressively planting congregations in the North and West.

A potentially far-reaching change occurred in 1972 when the report of the Study Commission on Denominational Structure was accepted. This discarded the term "convention" and renamed the denomination "American Baptist Churches in the USA," thus emphasizing that it was an association of churches, not just a "meeting" as such. Extensive power was given to a general board of about 200 members (composed of equal numbers of clergy, laity, and women) which made most of the policy decisions, while the biennial general meeting concentrated mostly on inspiration and fellowship. A new system of representation was introduced to enable more churches to send delegates to the national convention.

ABC emphasizes that it is ecumenical, evangelical, interracial, and international. It participates fully in the National Council of Churches and various ecumenical organizations, and associates with other churches of like faith in the Baptist World Alliance. It is not a credal or liturgical church, and the Bible plays a central role in its worship and life, as does the rite of believer's baptism. Stress is placed on preaching, personal commitment to Jesus Christ, the priesthood of all believers, and religious freedom. Missionary and evangelistic work have also been hallmarks of the denomination.

Sociologically, ABC is characterized by smaller congregations (almost two-thirds of them have fewer than 200 members), ethnicity (over one-third of the membership is black, Native American, Hispanic, or Asian), and its middle-class character. The latter has proven to be an impediment to church growth because upwardly mobile people perceive ABC as being lower on the social scale and gravitate to other churches, while ethnics and inner city residents regard it as being higher than it really is and show limited interest in its programs. The membership has remained steady at about 1.6 million for some years; ABC is the only "mainline" Protestant denomination in the USA that has not suffered a serious decline. Much of this must be attributed to the influence of the evangelical wing of the church which has been steadily increasing in numbers and strength in recent years.

ABC conducts its foreign outreach under the auspices of the Board of International Ministries, which besides sending out missionaries, has channeled much of its resources into national leadership and turned many of its institutions over to local control. The Board of National Ministries engages in home mission work and church planting, especially among immigrants and ethnics. The Board of Educational Ministries is responsible for Sunday school literature, book publication, the promotion of higher education, men's and women's ministries, the American Baptist Historical Society, and the conference center at Green Lake, Wis. ABC supports a half-dozen theological seminaries in various parts of the country.

RICHARD V. PIERARD

## American Council of Christian Churches.

Council formed by Carl McIntire in 1941 to provide organized evangelical opposition to the liberal policies of the Federal Council of Churches (which became the National Council of Churches of Christ in 1950). It was, and remains, a conservative body committed to the defense of historic Christianity and conservatism in national affairs. In 1967 it became an affiliate of the International Council of Christian Churches which had been organized by Carl McIntire in 1947. At its 1967 convention in Seattle, Wash., the American Council declared that "it is the only council of churches in the United States today giving a truly biblical assessment of Christianity today." It also asserted its opposition to membership in the United Nations and to abortion on demand (1971). It has called for the reinstatement of Bible reading and voluntary prayers in public schools. In recent years its influence in evangelical circles and national affairs has greatly diminished.

C. GREGG SINGER

## American Friends Service Committee. See FRIENDS SERVICE COMMITTEE, AMERICAN.

## American Jewish Congress. See JEWISH CONGRESS, AMERICAN.

## American Schools of Oriental Research (ASOR).

Consortium of educational institutions, libraries, and museums concentrating on archeology in the Middle East founded in 1900. In addition to its focus on the material remains of ancient cultures, the organization promotes the study of the history, language, art, architecture, literature, religion, and social world of early cultures in the Middle East. In order to do this it maintains institutes of research in four overseas locations. The W. F. Albright Institute of Archaeological Research in Jerusalem was founded in 1920 and is the oldest American institution of archeology in the Middle East. It was known as the American School until 1970 when it was renamed for its renowned early director. The American Center of Archaeological Research was established in Amman, Jordan, in 1968 to serve as liaison between the Jordanian Department of Antiquities and field archeologists working in Arab countries. The Cyprus American Archaeological Research Institute was established in Nicosia in 1978 to serve both Near Eastern and classical scholars. The fourth institute, the Baghdad School, was founded in 1923 in modern Iraq to serve the needs of those interested in the archeology of ancient Mesopotamia. However, due to the political situation in that area since 1967, the school has been virtually inoperative. Efforts to establish a fifth program were initiated in the summer of 1984 with the establishment of the Damascus Advisory Committee within the structure of ASOR.

Standards in excavation, research, and publication are maintained through ASOR's Committee on Archaeological Policy, which oversees approximately 35 projects in Israel, Jordan, Syria, Cyprus, Tunisia, Egypt, and Yemen. In addition to almost nine decades of commitment to research, the American Schools have also dedicated themselves to providing training for American graduate and undergraduate students working on Middle Eastern culture. Grants and scholarships are given to both students and visiting professors each year for study in these institutes.

The American Schools generate a number of important publications which include the following: the *Biblical Archeologist,* an illustrated quarterly on the semipopular level; the *ASOR Newsletter,* also published quarterly; the *Bulletin of ASOR,* a quarterly for those with advanced interests in the fully documented results of excavations; the *Journal of Cuneiform Studies,* published semiannually for those interested in the archeology of Mesopotamia, Syria, Anatolia, and Iran; the *Annual of ASOR,* a monograph series on projects of the Schools; *ASOR Dissertations,* a series of recent doctoral dissertations relating to the Middle East; and the *ASOR/SOT* series of monographs published in conjunction with the *Journal for the Study of the OT.*

JOHN MCRAY

## Americans United for Separation of Church and State (AU).

Advocacy group that strives to defend, maintain, and promote religious liberty and the constitutional separation of church and state. Known originally as Protestants and Other Americans United, it was formed in 1947 to combat Roman Catholic efforts to secure public assistance for their parochial schools. (The group popularized the term "parochiaid" for this.) It is a nonsectarian organization with broad-based support among mainline and evangelical denominations, Baptists, Seventh-day Adventists, Unitarians, and Jews. Although in its early years AU was perceived by critics as anti-Catholic, the focus of its attention broadened in the 1960s to encompass a wide variety of new threats to the First Amendment's guarantee of state noninvolvement in religious matters. These included mandatory prayer and religious activities in public schools, government intrusion into the internal affairs of churches, meddling in partisan politics by religious groups, and the establishment of formal diplomatic relations with the Holy See.

The 50,000-member organization is administered by a national advisory council comprised of 125 religious, educational, and civic leaders which in turn elects a board of trustees and an executive director to carry out its wishes. This position was held for three decades by Glenn L. Archer, a Free Methodist layman and former dean of the Washburn University law school, who was the leading light in the organization. After a brief interim, Robert L. Maddox, a Southern Baptist minister, was named to the post in 1984. AU publishes a monthly magazine, *Church and State,* and issues papers, reference materials, books, and curricular materials for use in schools. Its staff lobbies Congress and state legislatures, appears on national news broadcasts and discussion programs, and informs the public about religious liberty questions. It also initiates litigation to counter breaches in the separation of church and state, provides legal counsel and support in other cases, and serves as a partner in joint lawsuits.

**Bibliography.** R. L. Maddox, *Separation of Church and State* (1987); A. J. Menendez, *The Best of Church and State* (1975).

RICHARD V. PIERARD

## Ames, Edward Scribner

(1870–1958). Disciples of Christ professor and pastor. Born in Eau Claire, Wis., he studied at Drake University, Yale, and the University of Chicago (Ph.D., 1895). He taught philosophy and pedagogy at Butler (1897–1900), and then taught philosophy at the University of Chicago until his retirement (1900–1935). He was also dean of the Disciples Divinity House in Chicago (1927–45) and pastor of the University Church of the Disciples of Christ (1900–1940). His writings include *Psychology of Religious Experience* (1910), *Divinity of Christ* (1911), *The Higher Individualism* (1915), *The New Orthodoxy* (1918), *Religion* (1929), and *Letters to God and the Devil* (1933). He coauthored *Varieties of American Religion* (1936) and *American Philosophies of Religion* (1936). He contributed to *Contemporary American Theology* (1933) and *The Church at Work in the Modern World* (1935).

RAYMOND W. ALBRIGHT

## Amillennialism. *See* MILLENNIUM.

## Amish.

Conservative Protestant group that originated in Europe as a sect of the Mennonite Church. The group emerged around 1693 when the Bernese Anabaptist Jacob Ammann caused a division in Mennonite ranks of Switzerland, the Palatinate, and Alsace on three or four issues: shunning (*Meidung*), whether persons who speak falsehoods should be banned, whether the so-called true-hearted (sympathetic non-Anabaptist Christians) would or could be saved, and footwashing. Ammann attracted a substantial following in his efforts to consolidate Anabaptists into a reactionary, ultraconservative group. Efforts at reconciliation within Mennonite circles over the next two decades failed. Ammann "excommunicated" anyone who opposed his views. He introduced harsh regulations in dress and customs, insisted on untrimmed beards among the male members of the Amish, retained a certain style of hat, shoe, and stocking, and forbade members to attend worship services in state churches.

Major migrations to the USA, as early as 1720 and largely in the 1820s, led to the establishment of larger Amish communities in Central Illinois, Ohio, Ontario, and Pennsylvania. Later splits brought to the fore controversies between progressives and adherents to the Old Order, resulting in the formation of such groups as the Evangelical Mennonite Church, the Beachy Amish, and the Conservative Amish Mennonites. Only the Old Order Amish have retained the strict discipline and practices introduced by the founder. Since the Amish for much of their history have tended to ignore the preservation in writing of their history and teachings, accurate information about them is hard to obtain. However, in 1912, the Amish Mennonite Publishing Association was established. It publishes, among other Amish literature, the *Herold der Wahrheit*. The production of an Amish Mennonite yearbook and directory in 1938 was not repeated. Amish congregations and conferences are generally governed by periodically updated constitutions or rules and discipline statements.

Like other Mennonites the Amish are pacifists. While they render obligation to their respective governments, such as the payment of taxes, they refuse civil obedience when, in their view, political authority appears to be contrary to the "teaching of Christ." They adhere to the conviction that all of Scripture is inspired and the only true and infallible guide for life. Water baptism, administered to true believers, is by pouring. Members do not take out life insurance, are not allowed to join secret societies, and refuse to swear oaths.

*Bibliography.* M. Gascho, *MQR* 11 (Oct. 1937): 235–66; J. B. Mast, ed. and trans., *The Letters of the Amish Division of 1693–1711* (1950); J. A. Hostetler, *Annotated Bibliography on the Amish* (1951) and *Amish Society* (1963); O. Gingerich, *The Amish of Canada* (1972).

E. J. FURCHA

## Ammundsen, Ove Valdemar (1875–1936).

Lutheran professor and bishop. Born in Denmark, he graduated with a divinity degree before studying in Germany. He was professor of church history in Copenhagen (1901–23) and bishop of Haderslev (1923–36). At the time of his death he was president of the World Alliance for International Friendship through the Churches and joint president of the Universal Christian Council for Life and Work. His works include *The Young Luther* (1907), *English Labour Leaders on Christianity* (1911), *The Youth of S. Kierkegaard* (1912), *The Christian Church of XIX Century* (1925), *The Age of Enlightenment* (1930), and *Social Christianity* (1932).

*Bibliography.* H. L. Henroid and W. H. Drummond, *In Memoriam Bishop Valdemar Ammundsen* (1937).

PETER AMMUNDSEN

## Amsterdam Assembly. First assembly of the

World Council of Churches (WCC) held in 1948. Its theme, "Man's Disorder and God's Design," was discussed under four heads: the universal church in God's design; the church's witness to God's design; the church and the disorder of society; and the church and international disorder.

At this inaugural assembly, 146 churches officially constituted WCC. Only 30 churches came from Asia, Africa, and Latin America. Among the oldest churches represented were the Church of Ethiopia and the Orthodox Syrian Church of Malabar. Some of the youngest were also present, such as the Old Catholic Church and the Salvation Army. The strength of this new beginning was in the realization, already tested in experience, that churches separated by history and tradition were being brought together by the one Lord.

The theological groundwork expressed the indissoluble connection between unity and inner renewal: "We pray for the churches' renewal as we pray for their unity. As Christ purifies us by His Spirit we shall find that we are drawn together and that there is no gain in unity unless it is unity in truth and holiness." It was also strongly realized for the first time that evangelism is the common task of all the churches, and that "the present day is the beginning of a new epoch of missionary enterprise." No distinction was drawn any longer between missions and evangelism, because it was recognized that the traditional distinction between "Christian" and "non-Christian" countries no longer existed. Recognition of the importance of the laity in the church was also one of the outstanding features.

The ecumenical concept of the "responsible society" emerged as an alternative to laissez-faire capitalism on the one hand and totalitarian communism on the other. In order "to prevent an undue centralization of power in modern technically organized communities" it was suggested that society should have "a rich variety of smaller forms of community," which would insure scope for personal responsibility. On the other hand, it was also agreed that "no civilization, however 'Christian,' can escape the radical judgment of the Word of God, and none is therefore to be accepted uncritically." Two other points had significance for the assembly as a whole and for the future of the council: (1) the rejection of war in principle ("war is contrary to the will of God") but also the inability to accept this attitude unanimously as Christians; (2) the political statement that "Christianity cannot be equated with any political system." Every kind of tyranny and imperialism is a call for struggle and for efforts to secure human rights and basic liberties, especially religious liberty.

This first assembly adopted the constitution of WCC, laid down conditions for membership, issued a statement on the nature of the council, outlined the programs of its departments and secretariats, described relationships with other ecumenical bodies, and addressed a message to the churches—a practice repeated by following assemblies.

*See also* WORLD COUNCIL OF CHURCHES (WCC).

A. J. VAN DER BENT

**Amsterdam Itinerant Evangelist Conference.** *See* INTERNATIONAL CONFERENCE OF ITINERANT EVANGELISTS.

**Anderson, Charles Albert** (1889–1962). Presbyterian churchman and college president. Born in Orange, N.J., he was educated at Williams College, Auburn (N.Y.) Theological Seminary, the University of Pennsylvania, Tusculum College (D.D., 1931), and Williams College (D.D., 1934). He began his long career as an assistant minister of the First Presbyterian Church of Watertown, N.Y. (1916/17). He then served as pastor of the Prospect Presbyterian Church in Mapleweed, N.J. (1917–21). Following a 10-year term as university pastor at the University of Pennsylvania (1921–31), Anderson served successive presidencies at Tusculum College in Greenville, Tenn. (1931–42), and Coe College in Cedar Rapids, Iowa (1942–44). He then became director of the Presbyterian Historical Society (UPC) and editor of its journal (1944–60). He wrote *Young People's Topics* (1929) and *The Presbyterian Enterprise* (1956).

JACK MITCHELL

**Anderson, (Sir) James Norman Dalrymple** (1908– ). English lawyer, writer, and churchman. After a brilliant law career at Cambridge, he became a missionary with the Egypt General Mission (1932) and studied Arabic in Cairo. During World War II he joined the Intelligence Corps (not without misgivings), rising to the rank of colonel and Chief Secretary for Arab Affairs. The same swift progress marked his postwar career when he taught Islamic law at London University. By 1954 he was professor of Oriental laws; in 1958 he became director of the Institute of Advanced Legal Studies. When the General Synod of the Church of England was inaugurated in 1970, he became the first chairman of its House of Laity. He was knighted in 1974. A regular supporter of evangelical causes, Anderson wrote many religious works, including *The Need and Limits of Christian Involvement* (1968), *Christianity and Comparative Religion* (1970), *A*

*Lawyer among the Theologians* (1973), *God's Word for God's World* (1981), *Christianity and World Religions* (1984), and the autobiographical *An Adopted Son* (1986).

J. D. DOUGLAS

**Anderson, (Sir) Robert** (1841–1918). Presbyterian layman and dispensational Bible teacher. Born in Dublin, he was educated at Trinity College, Dublin. From 1868 to 1888, he was adviser to the Home Office in London on political crime, and in 1888 was appointed head of the Criminal Investigation Department. He received an LL.D. from Trinity College in 1875. He is best known as a popular exponent of dispensational theology, and wrote prolifically on the subject. His works include *The Silence of God* (1897), *The Bible and Modern Criticism* (1902), *The Bible or the Church?* (1908), *The Lord from Heaven* (1910), *The Hebrews Epistle* (1911), and *Misunderstood Texts of the NT* (1916).

IAN HAMILTON

**Andrae, Tor Julius Efraim** (1885–1947). Swedish bishop. He became professor of the history of comparative religion in Stockholm in 1927 and Uppsala in 1929, minister of ecclesiastical affairs and public instruction in 1936, and bishop of Linköping in 1936. He did research on comparative religion, especially Islam, and on the psychology of religion. Andrae was a low churchman with literary interests. In 1932 he was elected a member of the Swedish Academy.

*Bibliography.* *Tor Andrae in Memoriam* (1947).

CARL-GUSTAF ANDRÉN

**Andrew, Agnellus Matthew** (1908–1987). Roman Catholic bishop and religious broadcaster. Born in Glasgow, Scotland, he was educated there and at London University. Having entered the Franciscan order in 1925, he was ordained in 1932. Until 1954 he worked in Manchester as missionary, retreat director, assistant university chaplain, and Roman Catholic adviser to the British Broadcasting Corporation. He joined the BBC's London headquarters staff thereafter, and was the first Catholic priest to appear on British television. He proved to be an effective and enterprising broadcaster. He was one of the instigators of the Catholic Radio and Television Centre, which trained clergy, nuns, and other church people in television and radio skills. In 1980 he was summoned to Rome and made director of the Vatican's press and broadcasting organization and titular bishop of Numana. He returned to England in 1983, and until his death was chairman of the communications committee of the Episcopal Conference of England and Wales.

J. D. DOUGLAS

**Andrews, Charles Freer** (1871–1940). British publicist. Born in Newcastle-on-Tyne, he was educated at King Edward VII School (Birmingham) and Pembroke College (Cambridge). He was head of Pembroke College Mission (1896), fellow of Pembroke College (1900), and vice-principal of Westcott House (1900). He joined Cambridge Brotherhood, Delhi (1904). After being a fellow of Punjab University (1908), he joined Rabindranath Tagore's settlement at Santiniketan in 1913. He supported Gandhi's advocacy of the claims of Indian laborers in South Africa and assisted in the Smuts–Gandhi agreement (1913–15). Afterward he represented the Indians of Fiji, Kenya, and British Guiana. His writings include *Renaissance in India, Christ and Labour, Mahatma Gandhi's India, Sadhu Sundar Singh, The Challenge of the North-West Frontier,* and *Rise and Fall of the Congress in India.*

EDWIN O. JAMES

**Andrews, Elisha Benjamin** (1844–1917). American Baptist scholar and administrator. Born in Hinsdale, N.H., he was educated at Brown University, Newton Theological Institution, and the Massachusetts Institute of Technology; thereafter he spent a year in German universities. He was president of Denison University (1875–79), professor of homiletics and practical theology at Newton Theological Institution (1879–82), professor of history and political economy at Brown University (1882–88), and professor of political economy and finance at Cornell University (1889–98). Briefly superintendent of Chicago schools, he was finally made chancellor of the University of Nebraska (1900–1908). He was a member of the U.S. delegation to the Brussels International Monetary Commission in 1892. His works include *Institutes of Economics* (1889), *The Problem of Cosmology* (1891), *Eternal Words* (1893), *Wealth and Moral Law* (1894), *History of the United States in Our Own Times* (1904), and *The Call of the Land* (1913).

**Anglican Communion, The.** Worldwide fellowship of Christian churches in communion with the see of Canterbury in England. Each of the present 28 provinces has an independent history. To maintain some cohesion and unity of purpose in faith, order, thought, and action between these various provinces, some central consultation was needed. In 1867 the archbishop of Canterbury invited Anglican bishops from all parts of the world to consult with each other. This led to Lambeth Conferences, held approximately every 10 years in London for the purpose of consultation rather than legislation. Lambeth Conference resolutions act as guides for legislation in the self-governing provinces and do not necessarily reflect views held in the Church of England. For example, in 1968 the Doctrine Commission of the Church of England suggested that the normal test of orthodoxy among Anglican clergy, the Thirty-Nine Articles framed in the 16th century, should not be removed from copies of the Prayer Book, and that clergy should still be required to assent to them in some form or another as a condition of ordination. Resolution 43 of the 1968 Lambeth Conference suggested that each province should decide for itself whether to print the articles with their Prayer Book and not require assent to them from their ordinands.

In addition to these gatherings of bishops, three Anglican congresses (London, 1908; Minneapolis, 1954; Toronto, 1963) have been held, attended by bishops, clergy, and laity from each Anglican diocese in the world.

Since several dioceses and provinces were formed in the 20th century (e.g., the diocese of Europe, 1980; the provinces of West Africa, 1951; Central Africa, 1955; Kenya, 1960; Uganda, 1961; the Southern Cone of South America, 1983), Lambeth Conferences became too large and infrequent to enable the communion to react quickly to current affairs. Consequently the 1958 Lambeth Conference requested a liaison officer to coordinate thought and action within the communion. Bishop Stephen Bayne was the first such executive officer. Support for him was given by the Anglican Consultative Council, set up by the 1968 Lambeth Conference. Its Resolution 69 set up the council to share information, to advise on inter-Anglican collaboration with other churches, to guide Anglican participation in the ecumenical movement, and to review needs. The council met first in Limuru, Kenya, in 1971, when the executive officer was appointed as the first secretary-general of the council. In addition to council meetings the 1978 Lambeth Conference set up occasional meetings of the primates (archbishops) of the provinces.

Out of a division of the world into 209 countries, the 68 million Anglicans live in 147, the majority in Europe, Africa, and North America. Since former Anglican provinces have become part of united regional churches, normally the right of full communion is shared with members of these churches (the Church of South India, North India, Pakistan, Sri Lanka, Bangladesh) and with members of some other churches (Mar Thoma Syrian Orthodox, Old Catholics, Scandinavian Lutherans, Philippine Independent Catholics). Besides these formal arrangements for communion, several local parish churches within the Church of England offer an open invitation to the communion table to communicant members of other churches.

The culture of Anglican churches can vary widely between dioceses or even parish churches due to both social and religious factors. A common bond is the use of Prayer Books (compendia of services and selected prayers and Scripture readings), based either on the 1549 or 1662 editions of the Book of Common Prayer in the Church of England. The *Lambeth Quadrilateral* (1888) as a contribution to church unity affirms belief in Holy Scripture "as the record of God's revelation of himself to man, as being the rule and ultimate standard of faith"; the Nicene and Apostles' Creeds as baptismal confessions of belief; the sacraments of baptism and communion; and the historic episcopate. In plans for union with other denominations these four propositions have been treated by Anglicans as essential conditions.

**Bibliography.** J. W. C. Wand, *The Anglican Communion* (1948); A. M. G. Stephenson, *The First Lambeth Conference* (1967); S. C. Neill, *Anglicanism* (1977); J. Howe, *The Report of the Lambeth Conference 1978* (1978); A. M. G. Stephenson, *Anglicanism and the Lambeth Conferences* (1978); J. I. Packer, *A Kind of Noah's Ark: The Anglican Commitment to Comprehensiveness* (1981); D. R. Barrett, *World Christian Encyclopedia* (1982); J. I. Packer and R. T. Beckwith, *The 39 Articles: Their Place and Use Today* (1984); Anglican Consultative Council, *Bonds of Affection* (1985); *Church of England Year Book 1986* (1986).

GERVAIS ANGEL

**Anglo-Catholicism.** Movement within the Church of England and the Anglican Communion emphasizing the religious teachings and practices of High Churchmen in 17th- and 18th-century England, the pre-Reformation Western Church, and Roman Catholicism. It can be characterized as: a conservative reaction against radical reform by the government which widened political privilege beyond membership in the Church of England and rationalized the distribution of church funds and deployment of clergy; an esthetic longing for pre-Renaissance medievalism; a High Church affirmation that the church was founded by the apostles without dependence on the state and that their authority continues in the Church of England via an unbroken chain of successive bishops; and an inculcation of doctrines and practices of other churches which trace their origins by unbroken episcopal succession to the apostles. In theory this included the Russian and Greek Orthodox Churches, the Lutheran (Episcopal) Church in Sweden, and the Old Catholic Church in Holland. In practice the movement tended to borrow from the culture of post-Tridentine Roman Catholicism.

John Henry Newman used the term "Anglo-Catholic" in 1837 to describe 17th-century High Church English divines such as William Laud. Newman and Hurrell Froude were inspired to unite the Churches of England and Rome in conversation with Nicholas Wiseman, head of the English College, at Rome in April 1833. On July 14 John Keble, their colleague at Oriel College Oxford (hence the term "Oxford movement"),

preached against reform of the church by radicals and non-Anglicans and in favor of tracing the authority of the church to the apostles. Within 11 days Froude helped form a group committed to maintain the doctrine, services, and discipline of the Church of England along High Church lines. From September 1833 to January 1841, Newman, Keble, Edward Pusey, and others published 90 *Tracts for the Times* (hence the term "Tractarian") promoting their views and basing them on 17th- and 18th-century High Church writings. *Tract XC* presented the Protestant Thirty-Nine Articles, the test of Anglican ministerial orthodoxy, as a critique not of Roman Catholic doctrine but of popular abuse. Protest against this interpretation ended publication of the tracts, but from 1841 to 1863 the Library of Anglo-Catholic Theology published works of post-Reformation High Church divines in 88 volumes.

Visible expression of these ideals covered several areas of church life. Anglo-Catholic missionary work was headed by bishops, thus insuring apostolic succession in the new churches. New church buildings were Gothic-style, even overseas, their architects influenced by the promedieval Cambridge Camden Society (founded 1839), to which belonged John Mason Neale, the translator of pre-Reformation hymns. High Church principles were taught at new theological colleges from 1839 (Chichester) and Anglican monastic communities were set up from 1848 (Wantage). Changes were most obvious within local parish churches, where in the 1840s services were intoned, candles were lit, and preachers wore surplices, not the traditional black gown. By the 1860s the priest stood with his back to the congregation at communion services, wore vestments on the Roman model, mixed water with wine, used unleavened bread for communion, lit candles, and spread incense. This style marked Anglo-Catholicism in the early 20th century until the influence of the liturgical movement and reform of some Roman Catholic practices fostered simplicity and greater congregational participation. In England, Anglo-Catholicism was affirmed by a public statement of Catholic principles in 1977 followed by a conference attended by 3000 in 1978 and local Catholic renewal groups nationwide. Their opposition to the ordination of women is balanced by increasing support for union with the Church of Rome fostered by the Anglican-Roman Catholic International Commission.

**Bibliography.** R. W. Church, *The Oxford Movement* (1891; repr. 1970); W. Walsh, *Secret History of the Oxford Movement* (1897); W. O. Chadwick, *The Victorian Church*, 2 vols. (1966–70); I. Mackenzie, ed., *Loughborough Conference Report* (1979); G. Rowell, *The Vision Glorious* (1983); G. Rowell and P. Cobb, eds., *Revolution by Tradition: The Catholic Revival in Nineteenth Century Anglicanism* (1983); D. N. Samuel, *National*

*Apostasy: 150 years of the Oxford Movement* (1983); N. Yates, *The Oxford Movement and Ritualism* (1983).

GERVAIS ANGEL

**Anglo-Israel.** *See* BRITISH ISRAELITISM.

**Angola.** The People's Republic of Angola on the western coast of Africa covers 1,246,700 sq. km. (481,350 sq. mi.) and has a population of approximately 9 million. About two-thirds of the people are nominally Roman Catholic, one-fifth are Protestant, and most of the others adhere to some form of tribal religion. Angola was a Portuguese possession until 1975. Although Baptists, Methodists, and other missionary bodies had a long-established work in various areas under a comity agreement, their rights were never confirmed by the colonial authorities and their status was ambivalent. In 1940 Roman Catholics comprised only 22 percent of the population. A substantial number of Christians left the country for Zaire in 1961 when the revolution started (strengthening the church in the latter country), at which time also many missionaries left Angola. The 1976 constitution allowed freedom of religious belief irrespective of denomination. Strong measures have nonetheless at times been taken against the Roman Catholic Church and groups such as Jehovah's Witnesses. Religious holidays were abolished in 1978, and the government has pursued an antireligious policy, resulting in a growing number of nonreligionists and atheists. Missionary activity is restricted to a greater or lesser extent according to area, but a substantial ministry continues in medical and educational work and the distribution of Bibles. The Evangelical Alliance of Angola, founded in 1922, includes the main Protestant bodies except for the Adventists, but its operations are limited. Here as elsewhere Christians differ in how they come to terms with an authoritarian regime.

J. D. DOUGLAS

**Anthony (Khrapovitzky)** (1864–1936). Russian Eastern Orthodox theologian. Born in the Novgorod district, he studied at St. Petersburg Theological Academy and lectured there on the OT. He was rector of the Moscow Theological Academy, rector of the Kazan Academy, bishop of Kazan, Oufa, Volynia, and Kharkov, and metropolitan of Kiev. He left Russia after the Revolution and settled in Yugoslavia, where he became president of the Synod of the Russian Church. Conservative and even reactionary, he was widely known for his political ideas and activities. In theology he insisted on an ethical interpretation of dogmas. His programmatic essay, "Concerning the Dogma of Redemption," was published in English in the *Constructive Quarterly* (June 1919).

GEORGES FLOROVSKY

**Anthony (Vadkovksy)** (1864–1912). Russian Eastern Orthodox theologian. Born in the Tambov district, he studied at the Theological Academy of Kazan. He was professor of homiletics there before becoming rector of the Academy of St. Petersburg, bishop of Vyborg, archbishop of Finland, and metropolitan of St. Petersburg and the presiding member of the Holy Synod. He vigorously promoted the freedom and independence of the church in Russia. He was chairman of the commission to discuss these matters prior to the council slated for 1906/7 but which was never convened. His scholarly work was confined to the history of preaching in the Slavic East during the early Middle Ages.

GEORGES FLOROVSKY

**Anthropology of Religion.** The study of human behavior in relation to religious belief. The study of religion by anthropologists remains wedded to the method of participant-observation and to grass-roots events. It has nevertheless become highly diversified, not only because the reality we study has changed, but because the analytical or theoretical approaches have multiplied.

The classic study is E. E. Evans-Pritchard's *Witchcraft, Oracles and Magic among the Azande* (1937) in which he details the internal logic of Azande belief. It became the model for later works by John Middleton, Mary Douglas, Max Marwick, and S. F. Nadel as they sharpened the contrasts among witchcraft, sorcery, and divination and attempted to correlate these with forms of social organization and kinship ties.

Having laid solid foundations, the British school of thought with its heyday in the late 1950s and early 1960s was superseded by new approaches developed in North America and France. In America, anthropologists like Victor Turner, Clifford Geertz, and Marshall Sahlins developed what may be called symbolic approaches to religion. Turner elaborated the analysis of the semantic structure of dominant symbols with their emotive and cognitive poles. Geertz concentrated on the conceptual aspects of religion, on its ability to provide a framework of general ideas which make sense of a wide range of experiences, whether intellectual, emotional, or moral. Finally, Sahlins treated religion as part of a cultural design that gives order to practical experience, customary practices, and the relationship between the two.

The idea that religion provides order and meaning was continued, almost to the point of obsession, by French structuralists like Claude Levi-Strauss, and returned to the English world by Edmund Leach. Leach's analysis of the properties of metaphor and, especially, metonymy takes religion out of its cognitive quagmire back into the world of ecstatic and charismatic religions as they occur in the third world as well as the highly industrialized societies of Europe, America, and Japan.

As societies of the third world changed, so did the study of religion. Processual analyses became important. The works of greatest impact were those of Kenelm Burridge and Harold Turner on millenarian or nativistic movements, and Anthony F. C. Wallace on revitalization movements. Wallace's study of religion and the Seneca Indians provides us with a detailed picture of the forces that threaten to destroy a society and the stages of the subsequent revitalization process. More important, Wallace understands the fragile boundaries among religion, politics, and the military and, indeed, their interpenetration or alternation depending on conditions.

In recent times, less dynamic conceptions of religion as, for example, R. N. Bellah's concern with evolution or Bryan Wilson's concern with secularization have been challenged by studies that show the reverse process. Modernization does not produce, as is so often assumed, "rational" individuals whose behavior loses symbolic dimensions. Quite the opposite is the case. Emiko Ohnuki-Tierney, Winston Davis, Irving Hexham, and Karla Poewe, among others, argue that industrialization furthers the growth of new religions, magical religions, charismatic religions, and urban magic.

Among charismatic religions must be included the thousands of independent black churches which started in the late 1800s in southern Africa and have grown phenomenally since. F. B. Welbourn, Bengt Sundkler, Martin West, G. C. Oosthuizen, and M. L. Daneel have produced classic case studies of these independent black churches, while I. M. Lewis and Sudhir Kakar have produced remarkable comparative studies of mystical or ecstatic religions in other areas of the world.

Following the counterculture of the 1960s and the highly controversial work of Carlos Castaneda, anthropological findings have become so popularized as to be considered a major factor in the development, not only of new religions, but especially of the new mystical movement. The latter is a thoroughly cross-cultural and exotic phenomenon consisting of East Indian gurus, North American neoshamans, trance channelers, and other ethnic practitioners who have revived old practices and ancient wisdom to suit the Western religious market.

In the new mystical movement a long occult tradition, peripheral and despised, has come into its own. That it has done so has to do with our increased knowledge of non-Western cultures, with the easy importation of non-Western religious fragments and practitioners, and with the sophisticated use of high technology. Above all, the public, far from being thoroughly modern,

secular, and disenchanted, is, in fact, hungry and pays large sums of money for reenchantment, a magical view of the world, phenomena, and charismatic gifts.

Finally, it must be mentioned that the highly urbanized middle classes—whether of Europe, Japan, North America, or white South Africa—have actively contributed to the growth of neopentecostalism and its concomitant independent churches. Current research points to a curious link between mystical and practical attitudes of the middle class and charismatic or neopentecostal behavior. This attitude combination is noticeable, for example, in the emphasis on the fivefold ministry, intercessory prayer, and healing. Works in progress have Walter Hollenweger's classic *Pentecostals* (1972) to build on.

***Bibliography.*** R. N. Bellah, *Tokuqawa Religion: The Values of Pre-Industrial Japan* (1957); K. Burridge, *New Heaven, New Earth* (1971); M. L. Daneel, *Old and New in Southern Shona Independent Churches* (1971) and *The God of the Matopo Hills* (1970); W. Davis, *Dojo: Magic and Exorcism in Modern Japan* (1980); M. Douglas, *Purity and Danger* (1966); E. Evans-Pritchard, *Witchcraft, Oracles and Magic among the Azande* (1937); C. Geertz, *The Interpretation of Cultures* (1973); I. Hexham and K. Poewe, *Understanding Cults and New Religions* (1986); W. Hollenweger, *The Pentecostals: The Charismatic Movement in the Churches* (1972); S. Kakar, *Shamans, Mystics and Doctors* (1982); E. Leach, *Culture and Communication: The Logic by Which Symbols Are Connected* (1976); C. Levi-Strauss, *Structural Anthropology* (1963); I. M. Lewis, *Ecstatic Religion* (1971); M. Marwick, *Africa* 22, 2/3 (1952); J. Middleton and E. H. Winter, *Witchcraft and Sorcery in East Africa* (1963); S. F. Nadel, *Nupe Religion* (1954); E. Ohnuki-Tierney, *Illness and Culture in Contemporary Japan* (1984); G. C. Oosthuizen, *Post-Christianity in Africa* (1968) and *Pentecostal Penetration* (1975); K. Poewe, *The Namibian Herero: A History of Their Psychosocial Disintegration and Survival* (1985); M. Sahlins, *Culture and Practical Reason* (1976); B. Sundkler, *Bantu Prophets in South Africa* (1961); H. Turner, *Journal of Religion in Africa*, 2:43–63; V. Turner, *The Forest of Symbols* (1967); A. F. C. Wallace, *Religion: An Anthropological View* (1966); F. Welbourn, *East African Rebels* (1961); M. West, *Bishops and Prophets in a Black City* (1975); B. Wilson, *Contemporary Transformations of Religion* (1974).

KARLA POEWE

**Anthroposophy.** A pseudo-Christian form of theosophy in which Jesus Christ is held to be the one avatar and fully initiated person in human history. Jesus' life, death, and resurrection are interpreted as master symbols far more powerful than those of Eastern religious origin. Anthroposophy was founded in 1912 by Rudolf Steiner (1861–1925). Steiner was an occultist who was said to have had great clairvoyant psychic powers. Prior to World War I he was famous as a healer among the German elite. Anthroposophy teaches that people originally shared the spiritual consciousness of the cosmos, and that our present knowledge is only a vestige of our original endowment. However, we possess the capacity for limitless knowledge through the practice of spiritual disciplines and our eventual cosmic evolution. Today anthroposophy is perhaps best known through the Rudolf Steiner Schools and writers like Owen Barfield. It remains, however, a small group with a distinctly European ethos reminiscent of the decadent intellectualism of the Weimar Republic with its mixture of esthetic sensitivity and mystical idealism.

KARLA POEWE

## Anti-Defamation League. *See* B'NAI B'RITH.

## Antigua. *See* WEST INDIES.

## Antimodernist Oath.
Profession of faith instituted by Pope Pius X, *motu proprio "Sacrorum Antistitum,"* September 1, 1910, in connection with the condemnation of modernism. The antimodernist oath is to be taken by clerics prior to their ordination to the subdeaconate; by priests admitted to the ministry of confession and preaching; by rectors and diocesan or papal dignitaries before entering office; by superiors of religious orders; and by doctors and teachers in ecclesiastical institutions of learning.

It supplements the profession of Catholic faith prescribed by canon law, which is based on the Nicene Creed, on articles from the Council of Trent (profession of Pius IV), and Vatican I.

The first part of the oath affirms the following: The existence of God can be proved rationally. The divine nature of Christianity is manifested most certainly by external facts, namely by miracles and the fulfillment of prophecies. Christ personally founded the Roman Catholic Church, the papal system being an essential feature thereof. The traditional doctrine of the church was handed down unchanged from the time of the apostles and is not subject to evolution. Christian faith is a true and objective assent of the human intellect to revealed truth.

The second part of the oath bears on modernist principles condemned in the decree *Lamentabili sane exitu* and the encyclical *Pascendi dominici gregis*. It specifically repudiates any distinction between historical and dogmatic truth, and the interpretation of Scripture at variance with tradition, as well as the modernists' denial of supernatural elements in history and their pantheistic view of the universe.

*Bibliography.* *Acta Apostolicae Sedis* (1910), 2: 669ff.; H. Denzinger, *Enchiridion Symbolorum* (1937), nos. 2145–47.

## Anti-Semitism.
Expression of dislike, distaste, hostility, enmity, or revulsion for Jews or Jewish culture and life. Anti-Semitism bases its tenets on the belief that Jews are different and alien, not only in religious faith but also in physical appearance and character; they are power-hungry, materialistic, aggressive, clannish, and dishonest. In a behavioral sense, anti-Semitism is demonstrated by the tendency to shun Jews, speak disparagingly of them, subject them to social discrimination, or deny them the social and legal rights that non-Jews possess, all because they are allegedly an alien or malevolent people. The term itself lacks technical precision in that the word "Semite" is derived from biblical scholarship (the descendants of Noah's son, Shem) and linguistic studies (a subfamily of Afro-Asiatic languages) and thus refers to certain peoples who originated in southwestern Asia, including Jews and Arabs. The term was first used in the 1870s by German ideologues who dissociated themselves from traditional religious bigots by ascribing a scientific basis that stressed race to their hatred of Jews. Because of the term's unsavory origin and imprecise character, some commentators now prefer to use "anti-Jewish" or "Judeophobia" to designate the phenomenon.

The first manifestations of anti-Semitism were in the Hellenistic (persecution by Antiochus IV Epiphanes) and early Roman imperial (anti-Jewish riots in Alexandria and the crushing of the Palestinian revolt) eras. Upper-class Greek and Roman intellectuals contemptuously viewed the Diaspora Jews as a contaminated rabble who rejected the civic gods. Much more serious was the contest of Judaism with Christianity. Both faiths gained converts from paganism. Judaism continued as a viable alternative to the offspring which claimed to have superseded it, and this evoked bitter condemnation from the church fathers. After the political triumph of Christianity, the old pagan image of the Jews as a God-forsaken people was revived, and they were gradually deprived of all political and civil rights.

During the Crusades their position rapidly deteriorated. Crusaders on their way to recover the holy places took time out to brutally massacre the "enemies" of Jesus. Jews were accused of deicide and criminal conspiracies against Christianity—desecrating the host on the altar and using the blood of Christian children in their rites. Although they provided capital for the commercial expansion of the Middle Ages, Jewish "moneylenders" were objects of envy. As the strictures against usury fell away and their services were no longer seen as needed, they were expelled from England, France, and various German towns. The "reconquest" of Spain resulted in forced conversions to Christianity ("Marranos") and finally expulsion. Judeophobia declined to some degree during the Reformation, especially in those territories where Calvinism prevailed, but in his later writings Luther displayed remarkable hostility toward Jews.

The Enlightenment, with its deemphasis on revealed religion, opened the way for Jewish emancipation, even though most philosophes had little regard for Jewish religion and culture. In the USA and France, Jews for the first time gained equal status before the law, but their troubles did not cease. By now it was becoming clear that anti-Semitism was really a form of xenophobia, and it shifted from a religious to a racial basis. Further, with the rapid industrialization of Europe in the 19th century, Jews were an easily identifiable and highly vulnerable element in capitalist society, and so the victims of the new order, the lower middle classes, found their scapegoat in the Jews. Radicals on both the left and right blamed them for the evils of capitalism, while traditionalists like the German historian Heinrich Treitschke portrayed the legally emancipated and acculturated Jews as aliens who corrupted society. Such propagandists as Count Gobineau, Houston S. Chamberlain, Adolf Stoecker, and Edouard Drumont spread the idea of Jewish racial and moral inferiority, while anti-Semitic political parties sprang up in Germany and Austria. Starting in the 1880s, Jews endured intense persecution in Russia and Romania; the Dreyfus affair convulsed French society in the 1890s. The deteriorating position of the European Jews sparked both a massive immigration to the USA and the birth of Zionism.

After World War I anti-Semitism reached even greater heights, as exemplified by the reactionary identification of Judaism with Bolshevism, the wide dissemination of the notorious tract, *The Protocols of the Learned Elders of Zion*, quota systems and anti-Jewish propaganda in the USA, and anti-Semitic political campaigns in Hungary and Poland. The most devastating of all was the conscious endeavor of the National Socialist regime in Germany to destroy the entire Jewish population of Europe. Although undercurrents of anti-Semitism persist to the present, the Holocaust effectively discredited it in the Western world. Most Christian communities have firmly repudiated their anti-Semitic past, as seen in the pronouncements of the Second Vatican Council, the numerous dialogs between various Christian bodies and Jews, and the strong backing Christians give to Israel.

The establishment of a homeland is the direct result of anti-Semitism and the Holocaust, and it provides Jews with a renewed sense of confidence and ability to combat anti-Semitism. Unfortunately, the very existence of the Jewish state has itself become the focal point of a new and highly virulent anti-Semitism emanating from the Arab states, their third world allies, and leftist sympathizers in the West who regard Israel as the last vestige of Western imperialism, facilely equate Zionism with racism, and spread a message of hatred throughout the world. Also, Soviet "anti-Zionist" policies scarcely cloak what really is a reemergence of traditional Russian anti-Semitism, and in fact an element of Stalin's cold war strategy.

*See also* HOLOCAUST, THE; JEWS, MISSIONS TO.

**Bibliography.** J. W. Parkes, *Conflict of the Church and Synagogue* (1931); S. W. Baron, *The Russian Jew under Tsars and Soviets* (1964); J. Isaac, *Teaching of Contempt: Christian Roots of Anti-Semitism* (1964); *Encyclopaedia Judaica* (1972), 3:87–159; L. Poliakov, *The Aryan Myth* (1974); L. E. Quinley and C. Y. Glock, *Anti-Semitism in America* (1979); P. E. Grosser and E. G. Halperin, *Anti-Semitism, Causes and Effects* (1983); J. Katz, *From Prejudice to Destruction* (1984); D. A. Gerber, *Anti-Semitism in American History* (1986); B. Lewis, *Semites and Anti-Semites* (1986); D. A. Rausch, *A Legacy of Hatred* (1990).

**Apartheid.** Legal policy of racial segregation in South Africa which attempts to impose ethnic pluralism on the country. The term comes from the Afrikaans word meaning "apartness" or "separation." Proponents call it "separate development," "parallel development," or "cooperative coexistence" and claim that the country's complex racial make-up requires such a solution to guarantee peace, freedom, and prosperity for all. Opponents insist that it is merely a device to uphold white political and economic power at the expense of the majority.

Racial segregation goes back to the beginnings of white settlement in the 17th century, but the apartheid doctrine itself rose out of the conflict between the Dutch-speaking Boers (Afrikaners) and the British settlers who entered the territory after the Napoleonic era. The Boers resented the British policy of allowing limited rights to non-whites at the Cape and moved to the interior where they maintained strict white supremacy. Large numbers of Indians entered Natal after 1860 and they too were subjected to discrimination. Friction between the English and Afrikaners became more intense after the discovery of diamonds and gold, and the British effort to dominate South Africa culminated in the Boer War (1899–1902). The British then endeavored to appease the defeated Afrikaners, even to the point of granting virtual independence to the new country.

With the creation of the Union of South Africa in 1910, the Afrikaners regained political strength. The first three prime ministers—Louis Botha, J. B. M. Hertzog, and J. C. Smuts—had been Boer War generals. The more militant Afrikaners created the National party to represent their interests, while the British went along with the diminution of black rights. The Nationalists were primarily interested in improving the socioeconomic status of the Afrikaners vis-à-vis the more prosperous British and at the expense of the blacks.

The Act of Union recognized the unequal voting practices of the various colonies, and in 1913 the Native Land Act set aside reserves for blacks which resulted in a nationwide system of segregation. This was much worse than the pass laws which had been introduced in the previous century to restrict black freedom of movement. In the next few years, the legal reservation of jobs for certain races, banning of strikes, and the color bar in employment were firmly established. In 1934 Hertzog and Smuts formed the United South African Nationalist party, a coalition between British and Afrikaners which was intended to help revive the country's flagging economy, but the hard-liners saw this as a defection. They created the semifascist *Broederbond* to strengthen Afrikanerdom and formed a "purified" National party.

The latter was led by Daniel F. Malan, a former Dutch Reformed clergyman. His goal was to regain for the Afrikaner "children of Israel" the land that had been stolen from them by the British. His group promoted Afrikaner supremacy and South African withdrawal from the British Commonwealth. Smuts, on the other hand, sought to weld the Afrikaners and British into one nation. Either way, blacks were to be relegated to a secondary role. By the 1930s an Afrikaner civil religion had emerged that portrayed them as a covenant people who were doing battle with the British who still possessed their land.

The British Empire was likened to Assyria, the incarnation of evil and the object of God's wrath. Blacks, meanwhile, were a lowly people who could be kept in their place. Whereas Smuts and Hertzog maintained that the white race and civilization had to be protected by policies of racial segregation, Malan went further to argue that God had chosen the Afrikaner people to preserve the white race.

During World War II the power of Afrikaner extremism weakened somewhat, as many of them were pro-German and vast numbers of black workers served in the burgeoning war industries. After the war, however, Malan and his supporters renewed the struggle against the British. They utilized the term "apartheid" as a slogan to win votes. It was the one issue which could arouse poor whites and farmers alike and unite Afrikanerdom behind Malan's party. At the same time, Smuts's deputy and minister of finance Jan Hofmeyr argued in vain for a more liberal racial policy, and foreign criticism of South African race relations increased rapidly. In the 1948 election Malan campaigned on a platform of white supremacy (*baaskap*) and the eventual goal of total apartheid between whites and natives, even though these contradicted the economic and social realities of the country. The Nationalists' narrow victory over the United party and its more liberal position of gradually "uplifting" the blacks opened the way for the imposition of radical apartheid policies. To fulfill its primary objective of uniting the poorer Afrikaners against the more wealthy and socially advanced English-speaking citizens, the National party trampled on the rights of nonwhites. As a result, relations with the British Commonwealth steadily deteriorated and South Africa finally withdrew in 1961 to become a republic.

Numerous pieces of apartheid legislation were enacted, mainly under the aegis of Hendrik Verwoerd who later became prime minister. The Population Registration Act (1950) classified people into various racial groups—white, Coloured, Indian, and Native—on the basis of appearance, general acceptance, and repute, and racial identification cards had to be carried. The Prohibition of Mixed Marriages Act (1949) made marriages between whites and those of other racial groups illegal. The Immorality Amendment Act (1957) strengthened a 1927 law forbidding sexual relations between whites and people of other races. The Group Areas Act (1950) specified places where the various races might live. The Reservation of Separate Amenities Act (1953) decreed segregation in public buildings, hospitals, sports facilities, parks, beaches, hotels, and restaurants, while other laws segregated public transportation and schools. The Promotion of Bantu Self-Government Act (1959) provided for the establishment of 10 "homelands," territories which would be "national units" where Africans could exercise their political rights and have the option of "sovereign independence." These were in fact poor, overcrowded areas located far from the industrial and mining centers where employment was available. A large army and police force was given enormous powers under such legislation as the Suppression of Communism Act (1950), and they acted arbitrarily and brutally to enforce the laws and smother any semblance of resistance.

In the 1960s and 1970s apartheid came under increasing attack from both without and within the country. South Africa was ousted from most international organizations and subjected to various boycotts. Opposition grew at home, although both moderate critics and illegal resistance groups like the African National Congress (ANC) and the Pan-Africanist Congress (PAC) were ruthlessly dealt with by the security police. From a religious standpoint, the various Dutch Reformed churches were essentially pro-apartheid, but in recent years many of them have turned against it. Such individuals as Anglican archbishop Desmond Tutu, Beyers Naudé of the Christian Institute, and Reformed minister Allan Boesak, groups like the South African Council of Churches and Africa Enterprise, and the burgeoning charismatic churches are all forces working within South Africa to break down the apartheid system. Because of the growing pressure on the regime, by the late 1980s the more odious legislation was gradually being dismantled. Concomitant with this welcome change, however, has been an escalating cycle of violence that has left the country in turmoil and uncertainty.

*See also* RACE RELATIONS; SOUTH AFRICA.

*Bibliography.* T. Dunbar Moodie, *The Rise of Afrikanerdom* (1975); P. Walshe, *Church versus State in South Africa* (1983); L. Thompson, *The Political Mythology of Apartheid* (1985); J. Lelyveld, *Move Your Shadow* (1986); B. Lapping, *Apartheid: A History* (1987); R. Omond, *The Apartheid Handbook* (1987); M. de Villiers, *White Tribe Dreaming* (1988).

RICHARD V. PIERARD

## Apocalyptic Literature. *See* PSEUDEPIGRAPHA, OT.

## Apocrypha, OT.

"Apocrypha" is a Greek word in the plural meaning "hidden (things)," applied first to works considered not suitable for circulation, but coming to mean "spurious, non-canonical (books)." For Roman Catholics the term indicates the books which Protestants call Pseudepigrapha, while Protestants understand by the term the books outside of the Hebrew Bible included in the Septuagint and in the Vulgate. Consideration of the Apocrypha brings to the fore the whole question of canon and what criteria determined and still determine what is Scripture. When the canon of the Hebrew Bible was fixed at the Council of Jamnia (c. A.D. 90) the books of the Apocrypha were excluded for one of the following reasons: some books survived only in Greek after the Hebrew or Aramaic original was lost (Tobit, Judith); others were patently written later than Ezra, after whom prophecy, and consequently inspired writings, were believed to have ceased (1 Maccabees, Ecclesiasticus); others had been written in Greek (Wisdom of Solomon, 2 Maccabees). But in Alexandria this chronological limitation was unknown: all writings translated from Hebrew or Aramaic were included in the canonical Scriptures in Greek, and even some Jewish books written in Greek were regarded as inspired. The Jewish LXX probably did not differ materially from the Christian copies, which include the Apocrypha. Allusions to the Apocrypha are quoted as Scripture by Tertullian, Clement of Alexandria, Origen, Cyprian, and later fathers. Cyril of Jerusalem and Jerome denied the canonicity of the Apocrypha, but the Roman Catholic Church at the Council of Trent (1546) and at the Vatican I Council (1870) declared these books "sacred and canonical," except 1 and 2 (3 and 4) Esdras and the Prayer of Manasses, printed after the NT in the Vulgate. Protestants limit the OT to the Hebrew Bible, although the Apocrypha has often been and sometimes still is printed as an appendix. However they may be regarded in terms of their canonicity, the books of the Apocrypha provide an invaluable background to the theology and hermeneutics of the NT writers. No study of the origins of Christianity can afford to overlook them.

*See also* CANON OF SCRIPTURE; PSEUDEPIGRAPHA.

*Bibliography.* R. H. Charles, *The Apocrypha and Pseudepigrapha of the OT, in English* (1913); W. O. E. Oesterley, *An Introduction to the Books of the Apocrypha* (1935); L. H. Brockington, *A Critical Introduction to the Apocrypha* (1961); B. M. Metzger, *The Apocrypha* (1977); N. De Lange, *Apocryphal Jewish Literature of the Hellenistic Age* (1978); Sheppard Guald, *Wisdom as a Hermeneutical Construct* (1980).

*Special Studies.* A. B. Kolenkow, *JSJ* 6 (1975): 57–71; D. J. Harrington, *CBQ* 42 (1980): 147–49; M. Stone, *EBA* 46 (1983): 235–43; T. D. J. Lea, *ETS* 27 (1984): 5–75.

ROBERT H. PFEIFFER AND DAVID JOHN WILLIAMS

## Apocrypha, NT.

Documents from the early Christian milieu which purport to reflect the ministry of Jesus and the apostles but are not in the NT. Clement of Alexandria (late 2d cent.) talks of "apocryphal books" used by gnostic heretics, and both Irenaeus and Tertullian (2d–3d cents.) refer to unacceptable "apocryphal" and "false" books. Origen (3d cent.) applies the term "apocrypha" to Jewish documents rejected in synagogues; the term came to mean by A.D. 400 writings which should not be read in the churches. This process paralleled the selection of the documents which now form the NT (*see* CANON). Up until the time of the Easter letter of Athanasius (A.D. 367) no list of acceptable Christian documents was entirely consistent with the NT, and some earlier lists approved documents which were later not accepted in the church. For example, the Muratorian fragment (c. A.D. 200) accepts the Apocalypse of Peter but rejects Paul's letter to the Alexandrians. Rejected documents were withdrawn, and the term "apocrypha" was reserved within the church for certain Jewish books which were included in the Greek OT canon (LXX) but not in the Hebrew canon. There is one group of apocryphal documents not admitted to the NT canon but whose reading by Christians was permitted. These are now part of the group called the apostolic fathers (1 and 2 Clement, the Didache, the letters of Ignatius, and the Shepherd of Hermas).

Since noncanonical documents illustrate the behavior of people interested in Christianity, form critics use them as evidence of the history of the early church. From this perspective W. Schneemelcher offers a definition: "the NT Apocrypha are writings which have not been received into the canon, but which by title and other statements lay claim to be in the same class with the writings of the canon, and which from the point of view of Form Criticism further develop and mould the kinds of style created and received in the NT, whilst foreign elements certainly intrude" (*NT Apocrypha,* 1: 27). Following the apostolic fathers, acceptable noncanonical Christian literature continues with the apologists and Greek and Latin fathers.

The NT apocrypha includes a vast and increasing body of literature. The writings imitate Gospel material (sayings and experiences of Jesus; Gospels attributed to Jesus, or an apostle, to the Twelve, holy women and arch-heretics; to relatives of Jesus or others such as Gamaliel; Gospels with general titles such as the "Gospel of Truth"; conversations between Jesus and his disciples). They offer sermons by Peter and letters from Paul or Titus, acts of individual apostles (John, Peter, Paul, Andrew, Thomas, Philip, Matthew, Bartholomew, Thaddaeus, Barnabas, Simon, and Jude) and later (c. 5th–6th cents.) acts continuing the earlier ones. They contain the apocalypses of Peter, Paul, and Thomas and other apocalyptic material. Most of this material is commonly dated from the 1st to 3d centuries A.D. In 1946 several new apocryphal documents were discovered at Nag Hammadi, Egypt, and as these are published they are classified among NT apocrypha if they conform with Schneemelcher's definition.

Since these apocryphal gospels, acts, and apocalypses are similar to the canonical material some theorists suggest that they influenced the formation of the latter and that they represent a genuine and independent tradition concerning the ministry of Jesus and the apostles. However, close comparison of canonical with apocryphal material tends to confirm that the latter draws either on the traditions underlying canonical or on heretical imagination (J. Dunn, *The Evidence for Jesus*, 1985, p. 101, on the Gospel of Thomas).

**Bibliography.** M. R. James, *The Apocryphal NT* (1924); W. C. van Unnik, *Newly Discovered Egyptian Writings* (1960); E. Hennecke, W. Schneelmelcher, and R. M. Wilson, *NT Apocrypha*, 2 vols. (1963, 1965); A. Bolis and F. Weiser, *Gospel of the Egyptians* (1975); J. M. Robinson, ed., *The Coptic Gnostic Library* (1975); *Nag Hammadi Library in English* (1975).

GERVAIS ANGEL

## Apologetics.

Branch of theology concerned with providing a defense of belief in God. The Christian apologist attempts to provide a reasoned defense of Christian theism. It should be obvious that apologetics is not limited to the Christian tradition, although that will be the focus here.

Apologetics may be positive in nature, providing grounds for the belief in Christian theism, or negative in nature, providing answers to the criticisms leveled against Christian theism. The former task examines the nature of evidence, the weight of evidence, the relationship between belief and proof, and the concept of revelation and its role in apologetics. The negative task attempts to provide answers to attacks against Christianity such as the problem of evil, the conflict between science and religion, the alleged meaninglessness of theistic beliefs, and the problem of pluralism. The task of apologetics concerns not only the actual defense of Christian theism but also the question of what method is most appropriate to that defense. The categories here are not nearly as neat as one might hope, but broadly speaking there have been two main

camps of apologetic methodologies. One is revelation-based and the other is reason-based.

The central conviction of revelation-based methodologies is that a defense of Christian theism must begin with the revelation of God in Scripture. The mind has been so affected by sin that it cannot effectively reason without the aid of Scripture. The claim is often made that Christian truth cannot be subjected to alien standards of judgment. If this happens then it comes under the control of a particular secular philosophy and its uniqueness is lost. There is no common ground between Christian theism and non-Christian thought from which the apologist may build a case in defense of Christianity. The apologist's only recourse is to divine revelation which supposedly creates its own conditions of reasonableness. In this sense it is said to be self-authenticating.

Modern proponents of this type of method include figures as diverse as Karl Barth and Cornelius Van Til. Traces of this method also appear in classic European Reformed theology—especially in the thought of Abraham Kuyper and Herman Bavinck. In the early church Tertullian stands out as the clearest representative. He asked the rhetorical questions: What has Athens to do with Jerusalem? What has the academy to do with the church? What has Plato to do with Christ?

The main conviction of reason-based methodologies is that the mind is capable of finding evidences in nature for the truth of Christianity. Creation contains abundant evidences of the Creator to which the mind has access and can forcefully bring before the unbelieving world. There is in this sense common ground between the believer and the unbeliever. The apologist attempts to find a shared criterion of rationality or morality and from there construct a case which effectively answers the critic's questions or the problems posed by the philosophy and culture of the age. It is hard to see how any real defense of Christian theism could occur otherwise.

Contemporary proponents of this method again include figures who are very diverse in theological conviction. Names which might be mentioned include C. S. Lewis, Emil Brunner, and Wolfhart Pannenberg. B. B. Warfield and Charles Hodge, Princeton theologians of the 19th century, were also well known for their advocacy of this type of apologetics. The most famous proponent is undoubtedly the medieval theologian, Thomas Aquinas, whose work has been most unfortunately neglected by contemporary mainstream Protestants.

Contemporary apologetics has tended to be divided between popular approaches and more technical scholarly defense. Popular apologists such as Francis Schaeffer, C. S. Lewis, Josh

McDowell, and Paul Little have had a tremendous influence upon the resurgence of conservative Christian theism in the West. On a more technical level the work of Alvin Plantinga stands out. One important feature of his work (and that of others such as William Alston, George Mavrodes, Nicholas Wolterstorff, and C. S. Evans) is that the traditional categories of evidentialism and presuppositionalism (similar to the categories mentioned above) have begun to be broken down. There remains much creative work to be done in the field of apologetics in the last part of the 20th century.

Bibliography. F. F. Bruce, *The Apostolic Defense of the Gospel* (1959); J. K. S. Reid, *Christian Apologetics* (1969); A. Dulles, *A History of Apologetics* (1971); R. Swinburne, *The Coherence of Theism, The Existence of God*, and *Faith and Reason* (1979–83); A. Plantinga and N. Wolterstorff, eds., *Faith and Rationality* (1983).

RICHARD LINTS

**Apostasy.** Total abandonment of one's faith, principles, profession, or political affiliation. The Greek word *apostasia* ("rebellion") bears a political sense in classical Greek writers like Plutarch, as well as in 1 Esdras and Josephus. It is used of religious desertion in the Septuagint of Josh. 22:22; 2 Chron. 29:19; 33:19; Jer. 2:19; and 1 Macc. 2:15. Apostasy from the true God is the subject of description or warning in many OT passages, including Deut. 27–28; Josh. 23–24; Judg. 2; 2 Kings 17; and Jer. 2. Apostasy or faithfulness was the issue that caused the Maccabean revolt against the pagan Seleucids of Syria.

In the NT the actual Greek word *apostasia* occurs in Acts 21:21 in Jewish accusations against Paul and in 2 Thess. 2:3, where Paul gives warning of a great apostasy before Christ's return. Apostasy is a frequent NT theme (Matt. 22:9–12; Luke 8:13; Acts 20:29–30; 2 Thess. 2:3–12; 1 Tim. 4:1–3; Heb. 3:12; 6:4–8; 10:26–31; 2 Pet. 2; 3:17; 1 John 2:18–19; Jude).

Apostasy is largely the result either of false teaching or of persecution, which produces "voluntary" and "involuntary" apostasy, respectively. So-called involuntary apostasy became a feature of church history during the Roman persecutions, especially those under Decius and Diocletian. The church then had to face the problem of the lapsi, defectors who wished to return to the faith and to the fold. Julian the Apostate is really misnamed, as he seems simply to have emerged from concealed to avowed paganism after being declared emperor.

Medieval Catholicism used civil power against apostates, and during the Reformation Protestants followed this practice. The Roman Catholic Code of Canon Law distinguishes between apostasy from religion (unlawful renunciation of the religious life) and apostasy from the faith, which is complete renunciation of the Catholic faith.

Apostasy raises theological issues. Augustine held doctrines of temporary faith and of election to perseverance. Calvinists deny the possible apostasy of a true believer, while Arminians (after initial hesitation by the Remonstrants) held it to be possible.

GEOFFREY W. GROGAN

**Apostles' Creed in Worship.** Both liturgical and nonliturgical bodies use this creed in public worship more often than any other "form of sound words." In length and in clarity it is a suitable expression of common faith. Many nonliturgical churches omit the obscure clause "He descended into hades." Some say "Holy Spirit," not "Holy Ghost." Lutherans and others employ the word "Christian" instead of the "Holy Catholic Church."

Customs vary concerning the place of this creed in the service. Some have it early in the worship service, others before the sermon. Some use the creed after a hymn, and then have the *Gloria in Excelsis*. Others prefer recital of the creed after the main lesson from Scripture, thus letting the people voice their response to God's revelation of himself. The creed throughout stresses objective facts about the Triune God. Toward the end it might also voice Christian beliefs about other aspects of revealed truth, such as the kingdom of God, interracial brotherhood, and world missions. Lovers of the creed all agree that worshipers should stand during the recital and few would object to the custom of bowing the head at each naming of a Person in the Trinity.

ANDREW W. BLACKWOOD

**Apostolicity.** See MARKS OF THE CHURCH.

**Appasamy, Aiyadurai Jesudasen** (1891–1975). Indian bishop, theologian, writer, and speaker. Appasamy believed that many aspects of Hindu culture could enrich the Christian church. He stressed the Hindu tradition of *bhakti* (devotion to a personal god), used ideas from the modified nondualism of Ramanuja, and interpreted union with Christ in terms of fellowship rather than identity. He also strove to make known the life and thought of Sadhu Sundar Singh, who was a personal acquaintance. Appasamy was ordained in 1930 and was involved in the negotiations leading to the establishment of the Church of South India (1947). He was the first bishop of the Church of South India (1950–57). On his consecration, he felt guided by God to call for a year of prayer in his diocese in preparation for outreach. The result was spiritual awakening and church growth. His books include *Christianity as Bhakti Marga* (1928), *Temple Bells* (1930), *What Is Moksa?* (1931), *The Gospel and India's Heritage*

27

(1942), *Sundar Singh: A Biography* (1958), and *A Bishop's Story* (1969).

*Bibliography.* R. H. S. Botd, *An Introduction to Indian Christian Theology* (1969).

ANTHONY P. STONE

## Archeology, Biblical (to 1950).

Since the early years of the 20th century this subject has been completely revolutionized by the tremendous progress of field archeology. The use of the stratigraphic method, chiefly responsible for this change, was initiated by Schliemann at Troy (1870) and inaugurated on a more scientific basis by Flinders Petrie at Tell el-Hesi in Palestine (1890). Two Americans, G. A. Reisner and his disciple, C. S. Fisher, brought the technique to its present level. Today, careful study of the successive strata or layers of human occupation at an ancient site is considered the first duty of an archeologist. Hand in hand with stratigraphy goes typology, the study of types of man-made objects divided into classes, types, and varieties roughly parallel to biological families, genera, species, and varieties. In the case of archeological objects the uniformity produced by imitation and standardization corresponds to biological (genetic) uniformity. While the methods of stratigraphers correspond to those of geologists, the methods of typologists parallel those of biologists. Excavators date archeological deposits by their vertical relationship to one another; comparative archeologists date them by comparing human artifacts from them with typologically identical artifacts found elsewhere under controlled observation. Archeology has thus become scientific in its principles and techniques.

At the same time that biblical archeology has been transformed by these new methods, the study of written materials has also been revolutionized. The progress achieved by philologians in interpreting ancient writing has been accelerated in recent decades by the use of more scientific methods of decipherment, constructing grammars and dictionaries, and developing philological research in ways unimagined by early decipherers and interpreters of hieroglyphic and cuneiform. Since the Bible is a collection of ancient books, written in the midst of this archeological world, it is obvious that the interpreter of ancient written documents from Bible lands will often have more material bearing directly on the Bible than the excavator of ancient mounds. Both must work together in order to obtain the fullest return from the investment in archeology.

*Excavations in Bible Lands. Palestine.* Passing over the first excavations undertaken after 1890 by Bliss and Macalister, we come to R. A. S. Macalister's work at Gezer (1902–9), published in 1912. While representing almost incredible industry his results were very unsatisfactory from the standpoint of chronology and were inadequately recorded, with poor photographs or none at all and with sketchy plans and rough drawings. The early Austrian and German work at Taanach and Megiddo under Sellin and Schumacher (1901–5) was better in some ways (e.g., plans and photographs) than Macalister's, but paid much less attention to pottery and so did not provide enough material for future scholars to work with. It was not until the work of Sellin and Watzinger at Jericho (1907–9) and of Reisner and Fisher at Samaria (1908–10) that any Palestinian excavations were properly staffed and that modern archeological technique was fully introduced. An unhappy blunder in dating at Jericho, influenced by Macalister's errors, threw the chronology of this excavation entirely off, and the otherwise excellent publication of the results in 1913 misled biblical scholars for a decade. The exceedingly well-executed work of Reisner at Samaria, with its generally reliable chronology, was not published until 1924, although Fisher was able to employ the methods he had learned from Reisner in organizing the work at Bethshan (1921–33) and Megiddo (1925–39), as well as in teaching younger men, who carried his principles to many other sites. Directly influenced by Fisher's methods were the American excavations at Tell Beit Mirsim (Kyle and Albright, 1926–33), Tell en-Nasbeh (Badè, 1926–35), Beth-shemesh (Grant, 1928–33), Beth-zur (Sellers and Albright, 1931), and Bethel (Kelso and Albright, 1934). Among major excavations of this period the German excavation of Shechem (1913, 1926–34) should be mentioned, although its poor organization greatly reduced the significance of its results. In 1927 Petrie returned to Palestine, where he dug until 1934 at Tell Jemmeh (Gerar), Tell el-Far'ah (Sharuhen), and Tell el-Ajjul, all in the extreme south. Although he had introduced both stratigraphy and sequence dating into archeology, he had by now sacrificed his leadership to a 40-year-old habit of disregarding the work of other scholars. As a result his methods were out of date and his chronology was almost invariably far out of line with the actual state of knowledge. However, first-class excavations were launched soon afterwards under British auspices at Samaria (Crowfoot, Sukenik, and others, 1931–35) and Lachish (Starkey, Harding, Inge, 1932–38). Major work under Jewish auspices was undertaken at Ai near Bethel (Marquet-Krause, 1933/34), as well as at many synagogues and smaller sites. For lack of space we must pass over many other meritorious excavations carried out between the two World Wars.

Excavation was slowed down by the outbreak of the Arab rebellion in 1936 and was almost entirely halted by World War II in 1939. Fortunately, Nelson Glueck was able to continue his archeological survey of Trans-Jordan (1933–43) and to dig at Tell el-Kheleifeh (Ezion-geber) in 1937–40. Even during the war some Jewish work continued, and in 1944 Maisler and Stekelis began digging at the great Canaanite site of Khirbet Kerak (Beth-yerah); in 1947 Maisler commenced the excavation of Tell Qasileh at the mouth of the 'Auja. Meanwhile R. de Vaux began excavating at Tell el-Far'ah northeast of Shechem (1946). In 1950 and 1951 work at Herodian Jericho was undertaken by Kelso and Pritchard, while work was also started by Winnett at the old Moabite capital of Dibon. Future progress in Palestinian archeology will probably come largely through the intense activity of the well-staffed Israeli Department of Antiquities, headed by Yeivin and Ben Dor, together with that of the archeologists of the Hebrew University in Jerusalem, under Sukenik and Maisler. The chief curator of antiquities in Jordan, G. L. Harding, is a first-class man, but more people and money are needed.

*Syria.* Before World War I little had been done in Syrian archeology. Ernest Renan's expedition to Phoenicia (1860/61) was mainly a surface reconnaissance. In 1887 the Germans dug at Zincirli (ancient Sham'al) in the extreme north, in 1908–11 Garstang dug at another Hittite site in the neighborhood (Sakcegözü), and in 1911–14 (also briefly in 1920) Woolley and Lawrence excavated at Carchemish on the Euphrates. When the French occupied Syria after the war and set up their mandate, excavation began at a number of important sites, especially at Byblos (Montet and Dunand, 1921), Dura on the Euphrates (Cumont, Pillet, Hopkins, 1923), Ugarit (Schaeffer, 1929), at Hamath on the Orontes (Ingholt, 1931–38), at several mounds in the Plain of Antioch (McEwan and Braidwood, 1932–37), at Mari on the Euphrates (Parrot, 1933), and at Alalakh (Woolley, 1936). While much of the early work in Syria (before the late 1920s) was inferior in scientific standards to the better work of the time in Palestine, much of the more recent work has been extremely good. In keeping with the far greater natural wealth of ancient Syria as compared to Palestine, the excavations there have been much more rewarding, especially in the discovery of written records and objects of art.

Because of the present political divisions we shall also include excavations in northwestern Mesopotamia, from the Upper Tigris westward to the Euphrates, under the head of "Syria." Baron Oppenheim carried on important excavations at Tell Halaf, biblical Gozan at the source of the Khabur, before World War I. We may also mention Thureau-Dangin's dig at Khadatu, modern Arslan Tash (1928), and Mallowan's work at Harran (1951). This region is rich in important ancient sites, whose contents are certain to throw much light on the Bible.

*Babylonia and Assyria.* Excavations were begun by Botta in Assyria in 1842 and by Layard in the same region in 1845. These intrepid explorers, followed by others, exhumed the lost civilization of the great kings of Assyria between 900 and 612 B.C. The finding of great numbers of cuneiform inscriptions at Nineveh led speedily to the completion of the task of deciphering cuneiform, which had begun a half-century earlier but had made little progress. Work then shifted to Babylonia, where de Sarzec began digging at Lagash (Telloh) in 1877 and the University of Pennsylvania commenced work at Nippur in 1889. These excavations recovered the lost Sumerian civilization of the 3d millennium, and expanded the horizon of the Assyriologist enormously.

The next great step forward was taken by the Germans, who introduced scientific archeology into the Mesopotamian field at Babylon in 1899 and at Assur, the earliest capital of Assyria, in 1903. Long-continued excavations at these cities unfolded the splendors of Chaldaean civilization under Nebuchadnezzar and the culture of Assyria in the 2d millennium. It was not, however, until after World War I that scientific methods (including the use of pottery chronology, which the Germans had neglected) were extended to cover all the work in the field. Since 1919 prehistoric Mesopotamia has been recovered, from the first traces of early settlers through the successive stages of progress toward literate civilization. In 1922–34 Sir Leonard Woolley undertook a series of brilliant campaigns at Ur of the Chaldees; in 1928 the Germans began work at Erech (Warka), where they uncovered a remarkable civilization of the first literate ages. American excavations at Nuzi (Nuzu) in 1925 and following years disclosed a Horite civilization of the late patriarchal age which has thrown important light on the traditions of the Book of Genesis.

The high-water mark of scientific excavation in Mesopotamia is represented by the University of Chicago excavations in the Diyalah district east of Baghdad (1931) under Frankfort's direction. The methods employed here have been copied elsewhere and are being applied at such sites as Nippur (where excavation was resumed after more than 45 years of neglect) and Eridu (Abu Shahrein). Work was also resumed in Assyria where Frankfort dug at Khorsabad and Mallowan at Calah (Nimrud).

*Egypt.* The discovery of the famous trilingual inscription of Ptolemy V (the Rosetta Stone) in 1798 led to the decipherment of Egyptian in 1802–22. This great achievement was followed by several major expeditions to explore and record Egyptian monuments, notably the Prussian mission headed by Richard Lepsius (1842–45). In 1850 Mariette's 30-year monopoly of Egyptian excavation began, and although many important discoveries were made during this period there was no scientific recording whatever and valuable data were irretrievably lost. The monopoly was broken by Mariette's death in 1881, and three years later Petrie began his remarkable career as an excavator. Since he was easily the most original archeologist of modern times, it is scarcely surprising that he was able to revolutionize the science of archeology by introducing stratigraphic excavation and sequence dating of pottery, two principles that are now generally taken for granted.

An important step forward was taken in 1901, when the Germans began digging at Abusir in Middle Egypt, under the direction of Ludwig Borchardt. From then on scientific methods were applied to the excavation and analysis of Egyptian architectural monuments. Moreover, the methods of Borchardt were combined with those of Petrie by an American archeologist, G. A. Reisner (see above), who continued to work in Egypt until shortly before his death in 1942. Reisner contributed systematic recording and photography to the basic insights of his predecessors, and his methods have become standard in all well-organized excavations. Another first-class American excavator, Herbert Winlock, worked for many years at Medinet Habu in Upper Egypt.

Egypt is quite different from Mesopotamia in one outstanding respect: its monuments are largely accessible without excavation, and accurate recording of their reliefs and inscriptions is often more important than new excavation. The early expeditions were devoted largely to the recording of such monuments, but the introduction of photographic methods has made much of their work unsatisfactory in comparison with present possibilities. This was recognized long ago, and German Egyptologists performed a very valuable service by photographing reliefs of historical importance. No one saw the need as clearly as J. H. Breasted, who organized several expeditions for the purpose of recording the reliefs of temples and tombs, especially at Medinet Habu and Karnak (1924). The method here developed for making reproductions of such material is the most accurate ever devised.

Among the most striking series of discoveries made in Egypt since the introduction of more scientific methods of excavation has been the recovery of the Egyptian historic and prehistoric past before the Great Pyramids of the 4th Dynasty (1895), the discovery and study of the contents of the fabulous tomb of Pharaoh Tutankhamun (1922), and the discovery of the royal and noble tombs of the 21st and 22nd Dynasties (10th–9th cents. B.C.). Many other individual finds are mentioned below in connection with our survey of the contributions of archeology to biblical studies.

*Arabia.* The rediscovery of ancient Arabia began in the early 19th century and was spurred by the decipherment of the Sabaean inscriptions by Gesenius and Roediger in 1841. The explorations in Yemen of Arnaud, Halévy, and especially Eduard Glaser (between 1882 and 1894) yielded thousands of copies and squeezes of Sabaean, Minaean, and Qatabanian inscriptions. These documents were studied by Rhodokanakis, Hoefner, and Ryckmans, among others, and valuable results were obtained. Excavation was, however, essential to any reconstruction of the history and civilization of ancient Arabia. Aside from a few small digs, there were no excavations in Arabia until the campaigns of 1950/51 in ancient Qataban (modern Beihan at the southeastern corner of Yemen), under the auspices of the American Foundation for the Study of Man. These two seasons were exceedingly successful, establishing the evolution of ancient South Arabian culture and the chronology of its inscriptions on a solid basis. They were followed in 1951 by the beginning of systematic excavation in Maryab (modern Marib), the ancient capital of Saba (Sheba).

Meanwhile the work of collecting the accessible inscriptions of ancient North Arabia, mostly on the walls of rock scarps, has continued and it has become possible to correlate the development of the north with that of the south. The contribution to our knowledge of the background of Israelite history and religion is greater than one might think, since Arabia played an important part in OT history. Moreover, its thousands of inscriptions from about 1000 B.C. to A.D. 600 often reflect early Hebrew times, since the direction of migration as well as of cultural diffusion tended to be from north to south, and South Arabia may thus preserve early elements of Israelite culture.

*Persia.* The archeology of Iran has seldom been of direct significance for biblical archeology. However, the excavation of Susa (biblical Shushan) has yielded the Code of Hammurabi and other important monuments, and the work of the University of Chicago at Persepolis has resulted in the discovery of thousands of documents from the late 6th and 5th centuries B.C., illustrating the period from the rebuilding of the temple under Darius Hystaspes to the time of Nehemiah. The great Behistun Inscription of Darius is of the greatest value for our understanding of the Books of Haggai and Zechariah.

*Asia Minor and the Aegean.* Here, too, archeology abounds with material useful to the Bible student. Asia Minor has revealed the secrets of Hittite civilization, especially at the ancient capital of Khattusas (Boghazköy), excavated since 1907. Cyprus was so closely related in culture to Phoenicia that it has yielded many objects of interest to the student of Canaanite and Phoenician civilizations, and hence instructive for our reconstruction of the material culture of Israel. For NT times we have in Asia Minor and Greece sites and individual finds which shed light on the travels and adventures of Paul. Particularly interesting has been the excavation of such sites as Ephesus, Sardis, Corinth, and above all, Athens. The American excavation of the Agora (marketplace and civic center) of Athens has yielded buildings and inscriptions of interest to the student of Acts.

**Archeology and the Bible.** *Prepatriarchal Traditions.* The discoveries of the 19th century were too isolated to throw much light on the first 11 chapters of Genesis. Only in the 1920s did information really begin to become coherent, and it was not until the 1940s that it became possible to see the picture of human beginnings and of the early traditions of the ancient East as a whole. We now know, thanks to the work of Dorothy Garrod and others, that the development of prehistoric man in the East followed the same general lines as in the West. The latest work of physical anthropologists, on the basis of finds in western Europe, eastern Asia, South Africa, and especially in the Near and Middle East, confirms previous results in large part, but also shows that the number of extinct races of man was much greater than used to be thought and that there is no real basis for assuming the existence of different human species. Just as Neanderthal man is now known to have interbred with *Homo sapiens* in the Mousterian Age of Palestine, so we may safely suppose that this was true of other so-called fossil types, which were races and varieties, not true species at all. Radiocarbon dating of archeological material of organic origin by Carbon-14 content proves that the end of the Old Stone Age (Palaeolithic) must be brought down to not over 10,000 years ago, but the chronology of the latter remains uncertain and extreme dates for the earliest flint tools (artifacts) of human manufacture vary from 500,000 to less than 200,000 years ago. It has frequently been thought by scientists that there was a catastrophic break in the continuity of Stone Age culture between the Old Stone and the Middle Stone (Mesolithic) Ages which might be identified with the deluge of Genesis. Certainly there was a relatively fast retreat of the icecaps which probably caused tremendous floods about 10,000 years ago, and their memory may be preserved in the traditions of a great flood which are diffused among primitive peoples over most of the world.

The stories of Gen. 1–11 are very ancient, and can in large part be traced eastward to the valleys of the Euphrates and Tigris. This is particularly true of the account of creation in Gen. 2:4ff., of the story of Eden, of the lists of antediluvian patriarchs, of the story of the flood and the tower of Babel. Since these stories have nothing in common with Egyptian and Canaanite accounts of beginnings and since the Hebrew patriarchs came from Mesopotamia, there seems to be no escape from the conclusion that they belong to the oldest traditions of the Hebrew people. Where we have close contacts, as in the account of the flood, it is clear that the biblical tradition does not depend upon the Babylonian, but that both go back to a common older source. Not all these narratives are of equal age: for instance, the tower of Babel must reflect the temple tower of Babylon (Babel in Hebrew), built originally perhaps in the 24th century B.C. (under Sargon I of Accad). Here and there, scattered throughout the first chapters of Genesis, are details which come from early non-Babylonian sources, probably from the Northwestern Semites of patriarchal times. The table of nations (Gen. 10) seems to reflect the 10th century B.C., since the Arabs and other peoples who emerged after that date do not appear in it at all, and famous peoples of earlier centuries are also missing.

*The Patriarchal and Mosaic Ages.* Archeological research has not disclosed any specific reference to individuals named in the Pentateuch, but it has completely transformed our knowledge of the background of these periods. We now know the archeological and cultural history of Palestine and Syria through the entire 2d millennium. Egyptian political, cultural, and literary history is well known with the exception of a gap in the Hyksos period (late 18th to early 16th cents.). Until recently there was no definitive chronology of Mesopotamian history before the 14th century. But the discovery of the Khorsabad List of the Assyrian kings and especially the finding of nearly 20,000 cuneiform tablets at Mari on the Middle Euphrates has made it possible to fix Mesopotamian dates within a century, and most scholars now date Hammurabi of Babylon about 1728–1686 B.C. Cross-datings are established between Egypt, Syria-Palestine, and Mesopotamia, so a fairly accurate history of the 2d millennium B.C. can be written.

It is almost certain that the Hebrew patriarchs lived in the Middle Bronze Age (2000–1500 B.C.), since historical background, personal and place-names in Genesis, and many other details fit perfectly with this dating, whereas the only other possible date in the Late Bronze Age does not suit the picture in Genesis nearly so well. Personal names like "Abraham" and "Jacob," tribal names like "Benjamin" and "Zebulun," and place-names like "Nahor" (Gen. 24:10) are common in documents of the Middle Bronze Age. The patriarchal customs are strikingly like those of northern Mesopotamia, as reflected in the Nuzi tablets of the 15th century B.C., which reflect practices from earlier centuries. Unfortunately, the one most likely source of historical information, Gen. 14, has hitherto proved refractory, although individual names and various details have turned up in inscriptions from the early centuries of the 2d millennium.

The Late Bronze Age, during which the exodus and the wilderness wanderings occurred, is best known in Egypt. It was ushered in by the Egyptian conquest of Palestine immediately after the expulsion of the Hyksos from Egypt. The Egyptians ruled Palestine, Phoenicia, and southern Syria about 300 years. Monuments of Egyptian domination are scattered throughout this region. Among the most important finds from this period are several hundred cuneiform tablets discovered chiefly at Tell el-Amarna in Egypt; they throw much light on the language and culture of the Canaanites during the three centuries preceding the conquest. Among the most interesting of these tablets are the letters of 'Abdu-Kheba, prince of Jerusalem about 1370 B.C. Two basalt stelae, covered with Egyptian hieroglyphs and dated in the reign of Sethos I (c. 1309–1290), give us details about local civil wars between settled and nomadic groups just before the probable date of the exodus.

Since the Israelites were a very insignificant seminomadic tribe in Egyptian eyes, there are no direct references to them. The exploration of Serbit el-Khadim northwest of Mount Sinai by Petrie and others since 1905 has yielded about 25 short inscriptions in the Canaanite alphabetic script dating from the 15th century B.C. Partly deciphered by Alan Gardiner and the present writer, these inscriptions and the accompanying drawings and sculptures reflect the life of partly Egyptianized Semitic laborers more than a century before the time of Moses; there are strong arguments in favor of including them among the Hebrews of the period "which knew not Joseph." Other interesting traces of the Hebrews in Egypt during this age have been found, and the names of Moses and other members of his family can be identified with Egyptian names popular at that time. There are also many indications of indirect Egyptian influence on Mosaic thought and life, especially in connection with the abortive religious revolution of the Amarna Age, which introduced a number of concepts later to become characteristic of the Mosaic movement, in spite of vital differences between the two forms of monotheism. For instance, the Egyptian solar disk was the "god beside whom there is none other" (cf. Exod. 20:3), the god "who creates what comes into existence," like Israelite Yahweh; his followers also emphasized the importance of the "teaching" (Heb. *torah*).

Of steadily increasing significance for our understanding of the biblical background is the discovery of three Babylonian collections of laws from the 19th to the 17th centuries B.C.: the Code of Hammurabi (1901), the fragmentary Sumerian Code of Lipit-Ishtar (published in 1948), and the shorter Code of Eshnunna (also published in 1948). Together with the remains of an Assyrian law code from about 1100 B.C. and of the Hittite code of the 13th century B.C., these documents furnish extraordinary insight into the background of the Book of the Covenant (Exod. 21–23) and other Mosaic jurisprudence.

*Period of the Judges and the United Monarchy.* While we have comparatively little direct light on this period from inscriptions, there is a rapidly increasing fund of indirect written illustration, while our knowledge of the material background is already very considerable. Direct information on the Israelite occupation of Canaan comes from the Israel Stele of Pharaoh Marniptah (c. 1223–16), where the Israelites appear as nomads who threaten Egyptian control of Palestine and are duly punished. Indirect evidence comes, for example, from the ruins of such important Canaanite towns as Lachish, Bethel, and Tell Beit Mirsim (Debir?), all destroyed by fire in the 13th century B.C. and reoccupied by bearers of a different and much cruder material culture. From the results of excavations we see that most of these destroyed towns were rebuilt almost immediately, but that towns such as Jericho were not rebuilt for centuries (cf. Josh. 6:26). Many new towns and villages sprang up in Israelite territory; their existence was made possible by the rapid spread of the then recent art of lining cisterns with water-tight plaster made with baked lime.

Thanks to the monuments of Rameses III at Medinet Habu in Upper Egypt, we know the date of the Philistine invasion of Palestine, several decades after the principal phase of the Israelite conquest, and we know something about their customs, dress, and the like. The report of the Egyptian envoy Wen-Amun on his mission to Byblos for the purpose of procuring cedar beams from Lebanon (c. 1060 B.C.) gives us extremely interesting information about the Philistines and allied sea-peoples on the coast of Palestine not long before their conquest of Israel after the defeat of the latter at Ebenezer (1 Sam. 4). The Danish soundings at Shiloh prove that the town never recovered from its destruction at the hands of the Philistines shortly after the middle of the 11th century. The excavations at Bethel and Beth-shemesh, in particular, illustrate the life of typical Israelite patriarchal families during this age. The ivories of Megiddo from the first half of the 12th century B.C. show how Canaanites and Israelites lived and dressed.

While no inscriptions throwing direct light on internal affairs in Israel under the united monarchy have yet been discovered, much has been learned of their material culture. Saul's citadel at Gibeah (Tell el-Ful) was very simple, although solidly constructed. There was nothing simple, however, about the constructions of Solomon, known especially from Megiddo. The stables of this period at Megiddo held at least 450 chariot horses, and indications of similar stables have been found at several contemporary sites. Glueck's excavation of the Solomonic seaport at Ezion-geber has brought to light copper refineries of a degree of development not hitherto considered possible in such an early period. Although no remains of the temple of Solomon have been found, its traditional plan appears in a Syrian temple from the 9th century B.C. excavated by the University of Chicago at Tainat in the Plain of Antioch. Moreover, many close parallels to its decorative elements and furnishings have been found in Palestine, Syria, and Cyprus, especially in contexts dated to the 11th–9th centuries B.C. It is now clear that Greek Doric temples of the 6th century B.C., which resemble the temple of Solomon in a number of respects, also owe their architecture largely to Phoenician models.

Until the discovery at Ugarit and decipherment of the long-lost Canaanite religious literature in the 1930s, it was impossible to present an objective argument for dating much Hebrew poetry before the 9th century B.C., in accord with biblical tradition. Now the situation has changed drastically. A great many Hebrew poems employ poetic forms and stylistic devices characteristic of Canaanite poems composed before the 14th century B.C. Among such common elements are climactic or repetitive parallelism, usually consisting of patterns of repeated words arranged in clusters of two or three poetic units (bicola or tricola); parallelism of pairs of given words which recur scores of times without variation in Canaanite and Hebrew literature; and use of stock appellations and phrases, often coinciding exactly in the two literatures. We also have the common use of many archaic grammatical phenomena, unrecognized in the Bible until found in the Ugaritic tablets, and of many ancient words whose meaning had often been completely forgotten. That the Song of Deborah (Judg. 5) swarms with stylistic peculiarities also found in earlier Canaanite literature might be expected, since it is almost universally held to be an authentic document from the 12th century B.C.; it is more surprising to find the same peculiarities in the Song of Miriam (Exod. 15) and elsewhere in poems attributed by tradition to the earliest history of Israel. Moreover, the Psalter includes many archaic psalms (29, 68, etc.) which contain much phraseology of Canaanite origin and which must therefore go back to before the 9th century B.C. In particular we have many psalms which date back to about the 10th century and may easily reflect David's love for music and poetry, as recorded by tradition.

*The Divided Monarchy.* The period from the death of Solomon to the destruction of Jerusalem by the Chaldaeans, covering over three centuries, is now very well illustrated by archeology. Until systematic excavations began in Palestine in 1890, pertinent finds almost all came from outside the borders of Israel. Among them is the list of towns in Judah (including Edom) and North Israel taken by Shishak, king of Egypt (1 Kings 14:25), inscribed on the walls of Karnak in Upper Egypt. Another very important find is the Mesha Stone, which describes the victories of Mesha, king of Moab (2 Kings 3), over the Israelites in the late 9th century B.C. During the excavations at Dibon in Moab in 1951 a fragment of a still earlier Moabite stele was discovered. The excavations carried out in the ancient capitals of Assyria yielded references to Ahab, Jehu, Menahem, Pekah, and Hoshea of Israel; to Azaraiah (Uzziah), Ahaz, Hezekiah, and Manasseh of Judah; to events which preceded and accompanied the fall of Samaria; and especially to the campaign of Sennacherib against Judah (2 Kings 18–19). In 1923 a portion of the Babylonian Chronicle was published, giving a detailed account of the events preceding and following the fall of Nineveh in 612 B.C.; it greatly increased our understanding of the course of Jewish history in the last decades before the fall of Jerusalem in 587 B.C. This was followed in 1939 by the publication of ration lists from the time of Nebuchadnezzar, mentioning Joniachin, king of Judah, and five of his sons, as well as many other captives from Palestine and Phoenicia.

The systematic excavation of ancient Israelite towns since 1890 has given us detailed information about the development of material civilization. The excavations at Samaria and Megiddo, Beth-shemesh and Tell en-Nasbeh, have thrown much light on life in Israel during the period between 900 and 750 B.C., while the following period (750–587 B.C.) has been illuminated by the results of excavations at Tell Beit Mirsim and Lachish (Tell ed-Duweir), to mention only the most important sites. We know how the art of building houses and fortifications developed, how pottery changed, how the crafts expanded, what amulets the women employed, how writing evolved. Among written documents we may cite in particular the ostraca of Samaria from the early 8th century B.C, the Siloam inscription from the end of the 8th century, and the ostraca of Lachish from the last months before the Chaldaean invasion. A great many seal inscriptions have been recovered, and some of them mention the name of the reigning king: Jeroboam II, Uzziah, Jotham, Ahaz, Joniachin. Names of high officials mentioned in the Bible also occur. These documents are significant not only for the direct information they contain, but much more for the light they shed on the evolution of Hebrew spelling and language, as well as on dialectal differences between the speech of Judah and northern Israel.

*Exile and Restoration.* Our knowledge of the period from the fall of Jerusalem to the Macedonian conquest in 330 B.C. owes even more than that of the preceding period to archeology. Excavation and surface examination of scores of sites of preexilic towns of Judah have proved conclusively that the Chaldaean conquest was accompanied by a thoroughgoing devastation of the country, whose towns were not rebuilt for generations, if at all. There is no archeological basis for the frequently expressed view that life continued in Judah during the exile much as it had before—that there was no real break in Jewish life at this time. The traditional view is correct, although it must naturally be modified at points, where new information fills previous gaps in our knowledge.

The most valuable source of new evidence for the age of the restoration comes from finds of Aramaic papyri of the 5th century B.C. in Egypt. The principal finds were made at Elephantine in Upper Egypt in 1904–7, but some papyri and ostraca had already been discovered previously and more have come to light in other sites since then. They are all in biblical Aramaic and provide a wealth of detail with regard to the life and culture of a Jewish colony at the southern boundary of Egypt in the age of Nehemiah and Ezra. Together with other data from contemporary Babylonian and Elamite tablets, they enable us to reconstruct the official life of the Persian Empire and to demonstrate the authenticity of the Aramaic documents in Ezra. It is no longer possible seriously to reject the historicity of the memoirs of Nehemiah and Ezra or to date them after the 5th century B.C.

Strata of this age excavated in Palestine have not yielded much material, but we gain some idea about the reoccupation of the country after the exile, the extent of Persian control, and the spread of Greek civilization generations before Alexander the Great. Coins of the 4th century B.C. bearing the name "Judah" (*Yehud*) show that the little country had been granted a measure of autonomy, like several contemporary Phoenician and Syrian districts.

*The Intertestamental Period.* The three centuries of Macedonian control before the birth of Christ are much better known than they were at the beginning of this century, thanks to discoveries of papyri like the Zeno archives at Philadelphia (Gerza) in Egypt and of the leather scrolls from the Dead Sea cave (since 1947). The Zeno archives throw light on conditions in Palestine under Ptolemy Philadelphus (285–246 B.C.). The leather scrolls from the last two centuries B.C. have revolutionized our knowledge of the history of the Hebrew text of the OT and of Jewish religion and literature in the period immediately before the rise of Christianity.

Excavations in Palestine have uncovered the Hellenistic town of Marisa in Idumaea (Maresha of preexilic Judah), together with two extremely interesting painted tombs from the 3d and 2d centuries B.C. A campaign at Beth-zur north of Hebron (1931) disclosed remains of successive occupations and destructions in the Maccabaean age, when it was one of the most contested fortresses in Judah. Nearly 125 coins of Antiochus Epiphanes alone show the importance of the town at that time. The history of the Tobiad house of Ammon is illuminated by the discovery of a mausoleum and a neighboring tomb, inscribed with the name "Tobiah." Discovery of coins portraying Hasmonaean princes has shed much light on this time; many of their constructions have been uncovered in Jerusalem, Gezer, Samaria, and elsewhere. Such Hasmonaean fortresses as Alexandrium, although identified, have not yet been dug.

*The NT Age.* The last century of the second temple, from the accession of Herod the Great (37 B.C.) to the capture of Jerusalem by Titus (A.D. 70), is now far better known than it was in the middle of the 19th century. Our knowledge of the background of the NT is immeasurably richer. Taking up different classes of material which have contributed to this state of affairs in their order of significance, we come first to one of the most recent discoveries, the Dead Sea Scrolls. These documents belonged in large part to an Essene sect which flourished in the last two centuries B.C.; they bridge the gap between such apocryphal and pseudepigraphic literature as Ecclesiasticus (Ben Sira), the Book of Jubilees, and the Testaments of the Twelve Patriarchs, on the one hand, and the NT on the other. John the Baptist was certainly influenced by them, and we find their language and style strikingly similar to corresponding features of the Gospel of John, with echoes in the synoptic Gospels and the Pauline epistles. It is no longer possible to attribute the Gospel of John to a gnostic writer; we have in these scrolls part of the pregnostic background of thought and language in which Jesus grew up.

After scattered earlier finds of Greek papyri in Egypt, discovery of such material began in earnest in 1897 and has continued ever since. A great mass of private documents in the vernacular Greek (*koinē*) of the Hellenistic-Roman period has made it certain that the authors of the Greek translations and original Greek books which we possess in the NT were writing the actual spoken language of their time, influenced only slightly by literary Attic Greek. Many details of life and speech have been clarified and illustrated by these extraordinary documents. Since 1930 there have also been remarkable discoveries of NT papyri from the 2d century A.D., far earlier than anything previously known, and a whole library of lost early gnostic literature from the 3d and 4th centuries A.D. has come to light since 1947 at Schoenoboskion in Upper Egypt. The importance of this last discovery lies particularly in the fact that the new picture of gnostic beliefs in their formative period confirms and greatly expands the reports of Hippolytus, Irenaeus, and Epiphanius. The gnostics of the subapostolic age held even stranger and more pernicious doctrines than have been credited to them by modern scholars, and it becomes dangerous nonsense to fuse their ideas with those of Jesus and the apostles, as has been popular in certain circles since the early 20th century.

Turning to Palestinian archeology in the narrow sense, many buildings of this age have been excavated. The excavations in Jerusalem have brought to light extensive remains of Herodian and early Roman times in the temple area, especially the exterior of the retaining wall of the Herodian temple enclosure and the substructure and pavement of the praetorium at the tower of Antonia. The line of the first and second walls of Herod has been traced in large part, and the long-lost line of Agrippa's wall is now known. Early Roman remains have been cleared in the southern part of the Western Hill (the traditional Mount Zion) and north of Herod's palace near the present Jaffa Gate. A great many mausolea and tombs of the last century of the second temple have been cleared, with very important results. Two excavations in NT Jericho have brought to light building remains from the time of Herod and his son, Archelaus, who was reigning in Jesus' boyhood. Herodian masonry and building plans have been uncovered elsewhere in the country, especially at Samaria, while Herodian buildings at Hebron and elsewhere have been carefully studied.

Clearance of the tombs of the NT period in and around Jerusalem has brought to light hundreds of short inscriptions in Aramaic, Hebrew, and Greek. For the first time these Aramaic inscriptions yield living evidence of the Aramaic used by Jesus, since all Aramaic literature from this age had perished. The names of the deceased often appear on bone caskets (ossuaries); we find Miriam (Mary), Martha, Elizabeth, Salome, and Sapphira. Common male names include Joseph and Jeshua (Jesus); we also find Simon, John, Matthew, Ananias, Silas, and even such rare names as Alphaeus. A man is called "master, teacher" (*didaskalos*), like Jesus in the Gospel of John, although this appellation has been cited as a supposed indication of a 2d-century date. The most interesting of these inscriptions tells us of the removal and reburial of the bones of Uzziah, who had died nearly eight centuries before.

One unexpected gap in our information about Palestine in the time of Christ is our failure to locate a single synagogue of this period in Pales-tine. Pre-Christian synagogues have been found outside of Palestine, and a Greek inscription found by Weill in Jerusalem probably refers to the synagogue of the libertines (freedmen) mentioned in Acts 6:9, but all the synagogue remains found in considerable numbers throughout the land, especially in Galilee, belong to the late 2d century A.D. and subsequent centuries. Earlier synagogues will undoubtedly be discovered, either in hitherto untouched sites or under the remains of Roman and Byzantine synagogues. There was unquestionably a wholesale destruction of synagogues at the time of the First Revolt (A.D. 66–70), in keeping with other archeological evidence for an almost complete break in the continuity of Jewish and early Christian life in Palestine. Without archeology it thus becomes impossible to understand NT history.

**Bibliography.** R. W. Rogers, *History of Babylonia and Assyria* (5th ed., 1915); A. Deissmann, *Licht vom Osten* (4th ed., 1923); H. Gressmann, *Altorientalische Texte und Bilder zum Alten Testament* (2d ed., 1926/27); L. Speleers, *Les fouilles en Asie Antérieure à partir de 1843* (1928); C. Watzinger, *Denkmaeler Palaestinas* (1933–35); W. F. Albright, *The Archaeology of Palestine and the Bible* (3d ed., 1935); A. G. Barrois, *Manuel d'archéologie biblique* (1939); M. Burrows, *What Mean These Stones?* (1941); C. C. McCown, *The Ladder of Progress in Palestine* (1943); W. F. Albright, *Archaeology and the Religion of Israel* (2d ed., 1946); *From the Stone Age to Christianity* (2d ed., 1946); R. Engelbach, *Introduction to Egyptian Archaeology* (1946); J. Finegan, *Light from the Ancient Past* (1946); A. Parrot, *Archéologie mésopotamienne* (1946); S. Lloyd, *Foundations in the Dust* (1947); W. F. Albright, *OT Commentary* (1948); J. B. Pritchard, ed., *Ancient Near Eastern Texts Relating to the OT* (1950); W. F. Albright, *Archaeology of Palestine* (2d ed., 1951); idem, in H. H. Rowley, ed., *The OT and Modern Study* (1951).

WILLIAM F. ALBRIGHT

## Archeology, Biblical.

**Archeology, Biblical.** The systematic and scientific study of material evidence from biblical times. Activity in biblical archeology has been lively over the past 35 years, although plagued by the instability and repeated warfare among nations clustered in the Middle East. During the 1940s, the British and French mandates, which governed much of the area taken from the defeated Ottoman Empire, rapidly fell apart. The British withdrew their troops from Egypt in 1947, although that land had been technically independent since 1923. Iran became a nation in 1943; Israel and Jordan in 1948; Iraq in 1958. Lebanon became fully independent in 1944 and French troops left in 1946; Syria elected its first parliament in 1947.

Under the guidance of British, French, and American archeologists, each of these nations soon established government agencies to regulate excavations led by experts from the Western countries, and developed staffs that led their own excavations. Excellent museums were built and staffed by native scholars. By the mid-1950s major digs were in progress in all of these countries.

A series of short but intense wars between Israel and her Arab neighbors interrupted archeological activity repeatedly over a period of 20 years. One result of these disruptions has been to confine biblical archeological endeavors largely to Israel and Jordan. Elsewhere, archeological goals and interpretations have been primarily secular. There have been those who have sought to displace biblical archeology with a discipline called Syro-Palestinian archeology. Yet so long as there is a concern to relate the references in the Bible to geography, to historical sites, and to events narrated as occurring at certain places and between inhabitants of known cities or villages, there will be activity in biblical archeology.

Since the British were the dominant influence in Jordan, archeologists from England initiated major excavations in that nation. The most prominent was Kathleen Kenyon, who supervised the excavation at Jericho and started work on the Hill of Ophel south of the present walled city of Jerusalem. She introduced and brilliantly demonstrated the worth of the Wheeler–Kenyon method of digging and analyzing the debris left behind by early inhabitants of a site. She trained a number of younger archeologists and thus made a lasting impact on the discipline.

In Israel archeology became almost a way of life for many in the land, and a number of native-born scholars soon became famous. Prominent among them were Johanan Aharoni and Yigael Yadin, both now deceased. The methods and concepts of W. F. Albright were widely accepted and followed.

The interaction of these methodologies has brought about a synthesis of procedures in both work on the site and analysis of structures and artifacts. The interactions of scholars from a number of countries with archeologists belonging to universities in Jordan and Israel have been productive in developing new techniques.

Yigael Yadin, who excavated Hazor in the 1950s, was the first to use volunteer workers on a dig. The practice soon became standard at most excavation sites. During the 1960s, it became acceptable to combine academic study with field work. Thus students and young professors were given academic training as they participated in a dig. Earned credits were transferred to degree programs pursued at recognized colleges and universities. This procedure has become characteristic of most excavations, with tuition charged and scholarships made available.

Of particular importance for archeological work have been extensive and more accurate survey maps of all the lands in the Middle East. Detailed surveys of regions within nations have brought to light ruins of many small villages of all periods of occupation. Laws regulating construction require that unearthing ancient ruins brings work to a stop until archeologists can examine the ruins and report to the government. These surveys have sparked a study of environmental and geographic factors that doubtless played important roles in the life and practices of the people who lived in key cities and neighboring villages in each region. Archeologists can no longer ignore the network of villages surrounding a city or the overall geography or history of the region in which a site is located.

A number of cities partially excavated in earlier decades have been revisited and, in new areas of the mounds, dug again. The reevaluation of debris and buildings has added greatly to knowledge about each city. This procedure has taken place at Gerash, Amman, and Petra in Jordan; and Jericho, Megiddo, Ai, Gezer, Shechem, Lachish, Tell el Hesi, Tell Qasile, Jerusalem, and others in Israel. In almost every instance, corrections of dating and identification of structures have been made.

Archeologists are now careful to leave areas of a site untouched, so future excavations can apply new technologies with the aim of gaining knowledge beyond the reach of those engaged in current field work.

Significant new discoveries have come to light at new excavations. These places include Hazor, Dan, Joppa, Gibeon, Arad, Beer-sheba, Masada, and Ashdod in Israel; and Bab-ed-Dhra, Heshbon, Dibon, Pella, Zarethan, and Succoth in Jordan.

Although Iraq and Syria have strongly denied any ties to the Bible, work has continued at Nippur, Uruk, Babylon, and other locations in Iraq. The discovery of a hitherto unknown 3d-millennium B.C. civilization at Ebla in northwestern Syria has amazed historians. The discovery has also created much excitement among biblical scholars due to the closeness of Ebla to the patriarchal homeland around Harran. Also the similarity of the language of the people of Ebla to Ugaritic, Aramaic, and Hebrew has been difficult to ignore.

There has been a noticeable increase of specialists on the staffs of many excavations. Professionals such as geologists, geographers, physical and cultural anthropologists, paleoethnobotanists, architects, epigraphers, and many others have made significant contributions to accurate interpretations of artifacts and their relationship to ancient practices and achievements.

Along with the specialists have come new types of tools, including magnetometers, resistivity instruments, laser-guided transits, geological saws, and drafting machines. The photographer has long been with the archeologist, but now offers new techniques, such as ground photogrammetry, aerial photogrammetry, and the use of satellite photographs. Pottery has been scrutinized after kiln refiring, and by neutron activation analysis or microscopic thin-section analysis.

One of the most exciting new trends has been the installation of computer systems, with appropriate software, at a number of archeological laboratories. Portable computers have been taken to the field to record a multitude of facts and to rapidly classify and analyze important data. These machines have the capacity to eliminate many long hours of drudgery and, it is hoped, speed up publication of field reports.

Not only has the discipline of biblical archeology been hampered by inadequate or delayed in-depth reports of important digs, but many archeologists who gave leadership during the past four or five decades have died. Giants such as William F. Albright, Nelson Glueck, G. Ernest Wright, Kathleen Kenyon, Roland de Vaux, Johanan Aharoni, and Yigael Yadin are not easily replaced.

As yet new leaders of the same quality have not moved to the front. Encyclopedias, atlases, and commentaries have not been kept up-to-date; adequate textbooks have not been published.

Yet biblical archeology is neither dead nor dying. Much needs to be done on the field and in the laboratories, and excited, well-trained professionals are available to do the job. The future should provide a knowledge explosion that will greatly facilitate the task of studying the written Word and applying its truths to everyday life.

**Bibliography.** D. Lance, *Biblical Archeologist* 45 (1982): 97–101; J. Maxwell Miller, *Biblical Archeology* 45 (1982): 211–16; A. E. Rainey, *Biblical Archeology* 45 (1982); E. E. Rosen, *Biblical Archaeology Review* 8 (1982): 46–48; J. A. Saur, *Biblical Archeologist* 45 (1982): 73–84; L. E. Toombs, *Biblical Archeology* 45 (1982): 89–91; H. Shanks, ed., *Recent Archaeology in the Land of Israel* (1985); J. F. Strange, *Biblical Archaeology Review* 11 (1985): 66–68.

G. HERBERT LIVINGSTON

# Archeology, Christian.

Systematic and scientific study of material evidence from the time of Christ to the 3d or 4th century A.D. As with biblical archeology, the objective of Christian archeology is essentially to authenticate Scripture, at least in the broad terms of its cultural setting, but, where possible, in the specific terms of its actual narrative. The recent trend in archeology has been away from the narrower pursuits of biblical and Christian archeology to a broader concern with the whole history of a region (such as Near Eastern or Syro-Palestinian archeology).

Specific objects connected with the life of Jesus have not been found, although the Turin shroud has had many advocates for its authenticity. The early presence of Jesus' followers in Palestine, however, has been clearly established. The first discoveries of Palestinian Jewish Christian material, the ossuaries of Bat'n el-Hawa, were made more than a century ago. More recent discoveries include the Jewish Christian burial

ground of Dominus Flevit on the slopes of the Mount of Olives, dating from the 1st century; the excavations at Nazareth, which have revealed early Christian inscriptions and symbols, the latter closely resembling those of Dominus Flevit; the possibly Christian funerary symbols of Khirbet Kilkish (near Hebron) and of the ossuaries of Bethphage; the lamella (metal foil inscription) of the Oil of Faith, again possibly Christian and of the 1st century A.D.; and the evidence of 1st-century (and later) Christian worship at Capernaum. Such evidences of an early Christian presence in Palestine are complemented by other discoveries of coins, artifacts, inscriptions, and buildings which either throw direct light on the text of the NT or, in a more general way, help to establish its milieu.

The story of Paul in the Book of Acts and a number of references in his own epistles have been corroborated and complemented by archeological discoveries. For example, an inscription found at Soloi on the north coast of Cyprus may refer to the Sergius Paulus of Acts 13:7. Another found at Antioch of Pisidia confirms the accuracy of the reference in Acts 13:49 to the region of which Antioch was the center. Discoveries at Philippi have made an important contribution to the story of Paul's visit to that town (Acts 16:12–40) and similarly the archeology of Athens bears out the accuracy of Paul's description of the Athenians as "very religious" and of his reference to an altar inscribed "To the Unknown God." At Corinth, an inscription uses the Latin word for "market" which corresponds to the Greek of 1 Cor. 10:25; another inscription reads "Synagogue of the Hebrews" (cf. Acts 18:4); and yet another mentions an aedile Erastus who may perhaps be identified with the city treasurer of that name in Rom. 16:23. An inscription found at Delphi referring to the proconsul Gallio (Acts 18:12) provides an invaluable clue to the dating of Paul's visit to Corinth. At Ephesus, the temple of Artemis (Acts 19:27) and the theater (Acts 19:29) have been found and inscriptions both there and elsewhere bear out the accuracy of Luke's account of Paul's time in Ephesus. At Herculaneum, destroyed by Vesuvius in 79, there is the impression of a Latin cross on the wall of a small upper room. This room may have been a private Christian chapel; its decoration is indicative of the preaching of the cross by Paul, who stopped at nearby Puteoli on his way to Rome (Acts 28:13; cf. 1 Cor. 1:23). In Rome, much of the city seen by Paul has now been revealed, including the forum, aqueducts, temples, theaters, and basilicas.

To the extent that the scope of Christian archeology is extended beyond the 1st century, so the evidence for the presence and the practice of the church multiplies (e.g., the employment of catacombs as burial places in Italy, North Africa,

Egypt, and elsewhere). The catacombs at Rome are the best known and most extensive. The oldest Roman catacombs probably date from the middle of the 2d century, although some scholars put them as early as the 1st century. The Crypts of Lucina contain the oldest paintings. The Catacomb of Domitilla is probably named after the Domitilla who was banished by the emperor Domitian. The Catacomb of Priscilla contains in the Cappella Greca the greatest series of early Christian paintings preserved in any single room of the catacombs. In a painting of the resurrection of Lazarus is the earliest known picture of Jesus, dating from about the middle of the 2d century. At the Catacomb of Sebastian is a room where numerous graffiti contain appeals to Paul and Peter, whose remains appear to have been temporarily interred there in the middle of the 3d century.

Sculptured sarcophagi (stone tombs) were employed occasionally in the catacombs and frequently in and around the churches which were built above ground after the conversion of Constantine. The oldest Christian sarcophagi are dated in the middle of the 3d century.

The first Christians met in homes (e.g., 1 Cor. 16:19) and this continued to be the case throughout the early centuries of the church. A house church has been excavated at Dura-Europos on the Euphrates, a city which was abandoned after 256. The Christian chapel in this house was adorned with wall paintings showing both OT and NT subjects. The figure of Jesus in a picture of the healing of the paralytic is the second oldest known painting of Christ. In Palestine the most famous churches were the Church of the Holy Sepulchre, erected by Constantine over the traditional site of the tomb of Christ, and the Church of the Nativity, built by Helena at Bethlehem over the grotto in which Christ was supposed to have been born. In Rome the churches of St. Peter and St. Paul outside the walls, founded by Constantine, commemorate the traditional last resting places of the two apostles. It is highly unlikely, however, that these are actual graves, as has sometimes been claimed. Excavations under St. Peter's Church have revealed what was probably an early memorial to the apostle.

The oldest known MSS of the NT were written on papyrus. A tiny papyrus fragment of the Gospel of St. John probably dates from the first half of the 2d century. An extensive codex of the Pauline epistles comes from around A.D. 200. From the middle of the 4th century on, we have MSS on parchment and vellum. Among the oldest and most important are Codex Vaticanus, preserved in the Vatican Library at Rome; Codex Sinaiticus, found in the monastery of St. Catherine at Mount Sinai and now in the British Museum; Codex Alexandrinus, also in the British Museum; Codex Ephraemi rescriptus, in the Bib-

liotheque Nationale in Paris; and the Freer Gospels in Washington.

**Bibliography.** E. F. Campbell and D. N. Freedman, *The Biblical Archaeologist Reader*, 3 vols. (1959); I. Mancini, *Archaeological Discoveries Relative to the Judaeo-Christians* (1970); H. T. Frank, *An Archaeological Companion to the Bible* (1972); G. Cornfield, *Archaeology of the Bible Book by Book* (1976); K. M. Kenyon, *The Bible and Recent Archaeology* (1978); W. Keller, *The Bible as History* (1980); E. M. Meyers and J. F. Strange, *Archaeology, the Rabbis and Early Christianity* (1981); J. A. Thompson, *The Bible and Archaeology* (1982); R. E. Brown, *Recent Discoveries and the Biblical World* (1983).

JACK FINEGAN AND DAVID JOHN WILLIAMS

**Archer, John Clark** (1881–1957). Disciples of Christ pastor, professor, and theologian. Born in Wilna, Md., he studied at Hiram College, Yale University (Ph.D., 1922), and Harvard Divinity School. He was minister at Christian Church, Newton Falls, Ohio (1905–07), minister at Congregational Church, Avon, Conn. (1912–14), assistant minister at South Congregational Church, Brockton, Mass. (1914/15), and interim minister, First Baptist Church, New Haven, Conn. (1918/19). He lectured at Christian College, Jabalpur, India (1907–11), Khalsa College, Amritsar, India (1937, 1946), and Hartford Institute (1926). He served as an officer of the American Oriental Society (1923–26). He was professor of comparative religion at Yale (1915–50) and held the Hoober Chair from 1932 to 1950. His works include *A New Approach in Missionary Education* (1926), *Youth in a Believing World* (1931), *Mystical Elements in Muhammed* (1940), *The Sikhs* (1946), and *Faiths Men Live By* (7th ed., 1948).

**Argentina.** Large South American republic occupying most of the southern half of the continent. One-third of Argentina's population, estimated to reach nearly 33 million by 1990, lives in the capital city and environs of Buenos Aires, a cultured and cosmopolitan city rocked by years of repressive military rule. In a recent and startling act similar to that of their Brazilian neighbors to the north, the liberal senate voted to relocate the capital to a still-to-be-determined site in the southern Patagonia region. Although purportedly the shift would spread the populace across the country's area of 2,776,889 sq. km. (1,072,163 sq. mi.), it has not gone without notice that this remote region faces the Falkland/Malvinas Islands, the scene of the short-lived 1982 skirmish with the British over their possession. Most observers are skeptical about the actuality of this move, but it reflects the strident nationalistic tone being set by those who replaced the military and were willing to arrest the junta leaders on charges of killing 5000 "disappeared" persons and torturing thousands of prisoners. On December 9, 1985, after a trial which involved 5000 witnesses and lasted five months, the five former junta members were found guilty of murder and widespread human rights violations.

Historically Argentina has been a sophisticated and prosperous society whose people, 98 percent European by descent, have mixed little with the indigenous tribes. During the colonial era the Spaniards, threatened by their Portuguese neighbors and wanting to monopolize the country's commerce, prohibited any dealings with the Portuguese who controlled the slave trade. By 1890 the remnant of indigenous people and the few blacks who entered the country had virtually disappeared—not only because they were discriminated against and killed outright, but also because they were conscripted to the front lines in the border wars that erupted in the 19th century where they suffered enormous casualties.

Independence from the Spaniards was achieved in 1816, but as in most of Latin America the European colonial system was replaced with a homegrown variety under the jurisdiction of local nobility. The locus of power, however, was affected by large-scale European immigration which spurred modernization and facilitated the exploitation of the country's vast natural resources and the fertile land, 13 percent of which is arable.

A group of army officers was able to overthrow the conservative government in June 1943. One of their number, the charismatic Colonel (later General) Juan B. Peron, soon asserted leadership and in 1946 was elected president, chiefly through the support of the laboring classes, the Roman Catholic Church, and the army. He was elected for a second term in November 1951—the first time an Argentine president had succeeded himself.

Peron promised his followers great social reforms and a redistribution of power and wealth. Although he affected some land reform and enacted some policies to create a welfare state, he not only ran the country into debt, but began to crush his opposition, suppressing the freedom of the press and of speech. When he closed religious schools and turned on the Catholic Church, the religious leaders returned the favor. Deposed in 1955, Peron went into exile.

Peron's ardent followers clamored for his return, which occurred in 1973 when he was elected to the presidency. He died 10 months later and was succeeded by his wife, Isabel, who became the first woman head of state in the Western hemisphere. In 1976 Isabel was ousted by a military junta amid charges of untoward corruption, and placed under house arrest.

With all its potential, the country is hopelessly in debt, underemployment is rampant, and inflation is out of control. Observers felt that the Argentine invasion of the Falkland/Malvinas Islands in April 1982 was a diversionary tactic meant to distract the nation from its incredible ills. After 12 days of fighting—and hundreds of casualties on both sides—the Argentines surrendered. Three days later the president resigned and civilian rule was established within the year.

Even though there is a 94 percent literacy rate, only 21.5 percent of school-age children finish secondary school. Yet Argentina has traditionally been a center of learning and culture. Life expectancy here is highest in all of Latin America and infant mortality is 34.1 per 1000 births. Per-capita income is $2390 a year, yet 70 percent of the workforce earns less than $1115 annually (1987). Together with Brazil and Mexico, Argentina is responsible for 78 percent of the industrial output of Latin America.

There is no state religion but 91.9 percent of the population are on the Roman Catholic Church rolls, and constitutionally the president and vice-president must be Roman Catholics. All other faiths are tolerated and there is freedom of conscience. The president also exercises the right of patronage in the appointment of bishops and grants or withholds the publication of papal communications. Likewise the government claims the right to appoint parish priests.

Argentina has three cardinals, 14 archbishops, 69 bishops, 5496 ordained priests, 12,709 nuns, 1159 brothers, 1940 seminarians, and a pontifical university serving the church which is divided into 2234 parishes in 13 archdioceses and 45 dioceses (1983). The Church has been discredited in the past few years because of its silence during the years when thousands of people were disappearing. Church officials refused to condemn the evident abuses and instead maintained close ties to those in power. When the infamous military regime was toppled in 1983 the Catholic hierarchy published a white paper citing ways they had privately called the military to task, but their credibility had been damaged and they were judged as compromisers with the evil forces which had been in power.

During the 1977 Latin American conference of bishops (CELAM III) held in Puebla, Mexico, to which the mothers of the disappeared ones had traveled to petition for help in finding their lost children, the Argentine bishops turned a deaf ear—much to the chagrin of their confreres. These same Argentine bishops condemned the purveyors of liberation theology and joined the conservative wing of the Church in an effort to stop identification with the problems of the poor and the marginalized.

Massive emigration from Europe meant the emergence of significant Protestant groups in the country which in 1987 constituted 4.7 percent of the population with 1.5 million members. In Buenos Aires alone there are 25 different seminaries and 58 Protestant denominations. Some 590 foreign missionaries serve in the country and Argentina in turn has sent an estimated 50 missionaries to other countries. Among evangelicals there is a strong presence of the pre-Protestant Waldensian church as well as a significant group from the conservative Plymouth Brethren. In a strange union during the 1970s this latter group joined forces with some pentecostal churches working among the slum dwellers ringing Buenos Aires. A nascent revival movement begun among these disparate groups was cut short by internal disputes. Two brothers-in-law emerged from this movement, Juan Carlos Ortiz and Luis Palau, who migrated north, becoming world-renowned evangelists.

The pressures of World War II brought many Jews to the country. Most of these settled in Buenos Aires so the community there today, 500,000 strong, has one of the highest concentrations of Jews in the world (1987).

*Bibliography.* E. Dussel, *Los últimos 50 Años (1930–1985) en la Historia de la Iglesia en América Latina* (1986); F. A. Foy, ed., *1986 Catholic Almanac* (1986); Comissão Missionária Ibero Americana, *Atlas de Comibarn, Edição Comemorativa Comibam 87* (1987).

FAITH ANNETTE SAND

## Argue, Andrew Harvey

**Argue, Andrew Harvey** (1886–1959). Canadian pentecostal evangelist. Born in Ontario as one of a line of Methodist lay preachers dating back to George Argue, who immigrated from Ireland in 1821, he became a successful and prosperous realtor in Winnipeg. Argue came under the influence of a number of holiness preachers. When news of the Azusa Street revival in Los Angeles (1906) and the revival in Chicago (1907) reached him, he went to Chicago to investigate. While attending services held by William Durham, he had an ecstatic religious experience and spoke in tongues. Through his preaching, his leadership, and his publication of *The Apostolic Messenger,* a pentecostal revival began which saw his Winnipeg assembly grow to be one of the largest pentecostal churches in Canada. Argue toured extensively in Canada and the USA, conducting large revival meetings, establishing churches, and evangelizing Indians until his death.

JACK MITCHELL

## Armageddon

**Armageddon.** The site of the final battle between the forces of good and the forces of evil (Rev. 16:16). The word "Armageddon" probably comes from the two Hebrew words *har* and *megiddow,* meaning "Mount Megiddo." This mountain was located at the upper end of the Plain of Esdraelon, from which entrance was made onto the great battlefield where Israel's fortune was so often decided. In this region Deborah and Barak defeated the Canaanites in spite of almost insuperable odds (Judg. 5:19); Saul and Jonathan met their death at the hand of the Philistines (1 Sam. 31:1); and the fate of Judah was sealed when Josiah fell before the Egyptians (2 Kings 23:29). Wars with Damascus and later with Assyria tortured the valley time and again. Even after Israel ceased to rule the land, Mount Megiddo still presided over this scene of decisive contests. Alexander the Great entered by way of Esdraelon when he brought Hellenistic culture to Palestine and the east. By the time of the later prophets Megiddo had become the symbol of mourning over ruin (Zech. 12:11). Literalists interpret the passage in Revelation to mean that God and the devil will engage in mortal combat at Armageddon. Apocalyptists take it as symbolic of the finality of the struggle between good and evil by which the victory of God in the broadest spiritual sense is assured.

JULIAN P. LOVE

## Armenia

**Armenia.** Region including Soviet Armenia (Armenian Soviet Socialist Republic) and Turkish Armenia. Armenia is located in the center of Soviet Transcaucasia and covers 29,800 sq. km. (11,510 sq. mi.). Over half of the 3 million Armenians live in urban areas.

Over its three-millennium history, Armenia has been subject to many foreign powers. Ancient Uratu fell to the Armens in the 7th century B.C., who in turn fell to the Persian Empire in the 6th century B.C. Alexander the Great conquered the region in 331 B.C., and it was divided between Greece and Persia. Armenia regained its independence in 190 B.C., and Tigranes the Great (94–56 B.C.) extended his kingdom to Palestine and Ecbatana. Caught between Persia and Rome, Armenia was divided between the two powers in the late 4th century A.D. Muslim Arabs occupied Armenia from the 7th century until successive waves of Turkish and Mongol forces overran the country (11th cent.). The Ottoman Turks subjugated Armenia from 1450 to 1915. Armenian nationalists gained sympathy from Russia in the 19th century. At the Congress of Berlin (1878), Great Britain opposed Russia's proposal to annex Armenia. Continued nationalism provoked a series of massacres (1893–95, 1909), culminating in the Armenian Genocide (1915–18). In 1920, a Soviet republic was established. Armenia presently ranks third among the 16 Soviet states.

The Armenians are Christians. The Armenian Apostolic Church claims that the apostles Thaddaeus and Bartholomew were the first missionaries to Armenia. St. Gregory the Illuminator converted Tiridates III to Christianity in A.D. 301. The king declared Christianity the official state religion and cultural ties with Persia were broken. Pagan temples were demolished and churches were built on their sites. The church was organized as a hierarchy with Gregory as the Supreme Patriarch (Catholicos), residing in Echmiadzin near Yerevan. St. Mesrob translated the Bible into Armenian in the 5th century. The Armenian church condemned the decrees of the

Council of Chalcedon (451) and took the path of monophysitic self-isolation (551). Many attempts by the Roman and Greek Churches to reunite the Armenian church have failed.

The Armenian Evangelical movement, a 1930s reform venture in Istanbul, has made an impact on the Armenian church by introducing a Western Armenian translation of the Bible and an erstwhile chain of evangelical churches, high schools, and colleges all over the country.

Syria, Lebanon, France, and the USA have large enclaves of Armenians, while there are smaller numbers in Egypt, Italy, Latin America, Canada, and Australia.

The evangelical and Catholic Armenian communions have provided incentive for change within the Armenian Apostolic Church. The evangelicals represent barely 10 percent of the total Armenian population, yet their spiritual, social, and cultural impact has been altogether out of proportion to their numerical strength, mainly because their sole aim is the spiritual revitalization of their church rather than proselytization.

HAGOP APRAHAM CHAKMAKJIAN

**Armstrong, William Park** (1874–1944). Presbyterian NT scholar. Born in Selma, Ala., he studied at Princeton University, Princeton Theological Seminary, and the universities of Marburg, Berlin, and Erlangen. He was instructor in NT literature (1899–1903), professor of NT literature and exegesis (1903–40), and graduate professor of NT exegesis (1940–44) at Princeton Theological Seminary.

F. W. LOETSCHER

**Armstrongism.** Movement founded in 1933 by Herbert W. Armstrong (1909– ) which represents an Americanized form of British Israelism. Otherwise known as the Worldwide Church of God, this group has been made famous by its free magazine *Plain Truth* and its radio and television broadcasts. Its headquarters are located at Ambassador College, a lavish complex in Pasadena, Calif. Armstrong's son, Garner Ted Armstrong (1930– ), headed the group for many years until accusations of sexual immorality and corruption forced him to resign in 1974. Armstrongism draws upon ideas derived from the Adventist tradition and the Jehovah's Witnesses. It teaches a form of premillennialism with an Arian Christology. Various nations are seen as threats to the future of America; the Germans, however, seem singled out for special attention and are often seen as the cause of Armageddon.

IRVING HEXHAM

**Arndt, Elmer Jacob Frederick** (1908–1969). Educator and clergyman. Born in New Orleans, he received degrees from Eden Theological Seminary, Washington University (St. Louis), Union Theological Seminary, and Yale University (Ph.D., 1944). He was professor of historical theology and Christian ethics at Eden Theological Seminary (1931–69), and chairman and general manager of Church Worldwide Service Center, St. Louis (1946–64). As chairman of the commission on Christian Social Action of the Evangelical and Reformed Church, he participated in negotiations with the Congregational Christian Church, which resulted in a merger (1957) to form the United Church of Christ. He was chairman of a commission to prepare a statement of faith for the United Church of Christ (1958–62), and in 1963 he was an official observer at the Vatican II Council held in Rome. An editor and essayist, he died in St. Louis.

JACK MITCHELL

**Arndt, William Frederick** (1880–1957). Lutheran theologian, educator, and NT scholar. Born in Mayville, Wis., he was educated at Concordia College (St. Paul), Concordia College (Milwaukee), Concordia Seminary (St. Louis), the University of Chicago, Concordia College (Adelaide, Australia, D.D., 1930), and Washington University (St. Louis; Ph.D., 1935). After Lutheran ordination in 1903, he pastored for nine years. He then taught Latin, Greek, and Hebrew at St. Paul's College, Concordia, Mo., until 1921, when he became professor of NT and classical philology at Concordia Seminary. Holding that position until his death, he was editor of many periodicals and author of numerous books, including a joint translation and adaption of W. Bauer's *Lexicon of the Greek NT* with F. W. Gingrich. A devoted churchman, he was chairman of the Missouri Synod Committee on Doctrinal Unity that reached agreement on doctrine with the American Lutheran Church. He died in Cambridge, England, where he was helping the Evangelical Lutheran Church establish a seminary in conjunction with Cambridge University.

JACK MITCHELL

**Arnold, Eberhard** (1883–1935). Founder of the Bruderhof movement in Nazi Germany. Son of a Breslau church history professor, he early linked spiritual authenticity with a concern for economic justice. He studied theology at Halle, disqualified himself for the degree through his insistence on being baptized upon profession of faith, and subsequently obtained a doctorate in philosophy with a dissertation on Nietzsche (1909). Arnold became associated with the Student Christian Movement and edited its periodical from 1915. He also became a convinced pacifist, and began to write extensively and to republish Christian classics on spiritual renewal. In 1930/31 he visited Bruderhof colonies in North America; one of the Alberta congregations commissioned him as its missionary to Europe. Inevitably he incurred the hostility of the Gestapo, which saw danger in a peace-loving religion that did not regard allegiance to the state as its highest priority. "The most sinister powers of our civilization," said Arnold in 1934, "are the State, the military and the capitalist structure. . . . The tremendous edifice built up by a fallen creation is incredible. But it will end in death." A selection of Arnold's writings and addresses, *God's Revolution*, was edited in 1984 by the Hutterian Society of Brothers and J. H. Yoder.

J. D. DOUGLAS

**Arnot, Frederick Stanley** (1858–1914). Pioneer missionary in Central Africa. He was influenced as a boy by David Livingstone and resolved to go to Africa. Although reared in the Free Church of Scotland he became associated with the Christian Brethren. He first left for Africa in 1881, supported by a group of friends. He worked initially among the Barotse who lived between the Zambesi and Chobe rivers. He believed that the higher ground would prove healthier for the missionaries he hoped to introduce. Although he faced many obstacles, including the opposition of Jesuits, he was favorably received by the king of the Barotse and taught his children. Arnot believed that his simple existence delivered him from the attention of those who wished only to rob a white man. He made nine journeys to the center of Africa, establishing good relations with the chiefs of the tribes he contacted, preaching the gospel, and exploring. He was made a fellow of the Royal Geographical Society chiefly as a result of discovering the source of the Zambesi. He inspired many other Christian Brethren missionaries to go to Africa. By the time of his death 61 missionaries were working in 16 mission stations in five areas of Central Africa.

JAMES TAYLOR

**Art and the Church.** Does art enhance worship or does it distract the worshiper from the proper Object of worship? On the one hand religion, engaging as it does the whole human personality and not merely the intellect, is more naturally expressed through the medium of art than by doctrinal formulations. And, for better or worse, much of the greatest art has been based upon religious themes. Furthermore, in places and at times when only a minority has been literate, art has been a chief means of edifying the faithful, and has been so employed by Buddhists, Hindus, Sikhs, and Christians alike. On the other hand, the terms of the OT ban on idolatry (Exod. 20:4–5; Deut. 5:8–9) may well be taken to imply that all religious art, at least of a representational sort, should be forbidden. It is of interest in this connection that within Islamic civilization a similar ban against representation has led to nonrepresentative art, which makes its impact entirely by means of composition, color, rhythm, and abstract design.

In spite of the biblical prohibition, Jewish colonists in the eastern regions of the early Roman Empire decorated the walls of their synagogues with depictions of events and persons from sacred history; and the early Christian artists whose work survives in the catacombs adopted the same practice, although they did not at first depict Christ. After official recognition of Christianity by the Roman State under Constantine early in the 4th century, the decoration of churches presented a problem. While all devout Christians at the time objected to statues, they differed in their attitude toward paintings. Some regarded the latter as useful in reminding the faithful about aspects of the church's teaching, a stance later adopted by Pope Gregory the Great at the end of the 6th century; but others were much less permissive.

From A.D. 725 to 842, the Eastern Church was torn by the iconoclastic (image-smashing) controversy. The iconoclasts argued that images of Christ presupposed either the monophysite or Nestorian heresy; since it is, as would universally be conceded, impossible to represent the divinity of Christ, one must either confound or divorce his divine and human natures in order to represent him at all (in the one case, confusing his divinity with his humanity; in the other, presuming that the human nature can be represented independently of the divine). As to images of the saints, it would be blasphemous to purport to represent in dead wood or stone those who live with God. On the other side, it was urged (by the so-called iconodules) that the iconoclasts themselves were implicitly involved in christological heresy, as they were overlooking an essential element of Christ's human nature; if this cannot be represented graphically, its reality and material quality are impugned. The monasteries were centers of resistance to iconoclasm; John of Damascus, the most distinguished theologian of the iconodule party, was safe from persecution because he lived under Islamic rule. After the iconoclastic controversy ended, Byzantine art at its best may be said to have achieved, from the 10th to the 14th centuries, the highest artistic expression of Christian dogma ever realized.

Western art, by contrast, tended to be an expression, crude in its initial stirrings after the barbarian invasions, of ecstatic piety. As greater skill at representation and sophistication in composition were gradually achieved, there was a tendency for these elements to be cultivated at the expense of one another and of the religious subject matter; but in the great masterpieces of the Renaissance, such as Leonardo da Vinci's

*Last Supper* and Michelangelo's paintings for the ceiling of the Sistine Chapel, there is a consummate mutual enhancement of composition, accurate representation, and dramatic suggestiveness with regard to the scenes of sacred history. The Protestant Reformation saw a revival of iconoclastic attitudes, at least in some of its manifestations; however, Rembrandt, one of the greatest Christian artists of all time, was a Protestant.

In spite of the strong drift of modern art toward the secular, religious art of great power and subtlety was still produced (e.g., Rouault, Matisse). In recent times, religious devotion has been lamentably productive of kitsch. However, one should not infer too readily, from the annoyance and even scandal that this causes to the artistically educated or refined, that it lacks genuine religious value.

**Bibliography.** C. T. Morey, *Christian Art* (1958); E. H. Gombrich, *The Story of Art* (1967).

HUGO A. MEYNELL

## Artificial Insemination.

Process of introducing semen into a woman's reproductive tract by means other than coitus. This is a widespread legal medical practice in most Western countries, despite the opposition of the Roman Catholic Church and others.

It is now estimated that as many as 10 percent of couples are infertile in many countries. The major reasons are: damage to the woman's genital tract from abortion; the extended use of oral contraceptives; damage from communicable diseases; and genetic malformation such as blocked fallopian tubes. The latter case has evoked the greatest sympathy from the churches in terms of ethical response. Most Protestant churches, and certainly the Anglican Church in Great Britain and Australia (where biomedical procedures have been initiated), have given ethical approval to artificial insemination by the husband's sperm in the case of blocked fallopian tubes or genetic problems. One facet of the Catholic Church's objection is that sperm are obtained through masturbation. Official Roman Catholic spokespersons cannot grant this concession, although infertile Catholics take as little notice of the official disapproval as they do of disapproval of the oral contraceptive.

There has been consistent Christian objection to freezing sperm for a later conception, to laboratory experiments on frozen or live sperm or ova, and to allowing single women to undergo artificial insemination by donor (AID) in order to become pregnant. All these issues are complicated by technological advances in bioethics such as in vitro fertilization, embryo freezing, and embryo transfer.

Artificial insemination using the husband's sperm is regarded by most as ethically permissible on the ground that it creates the possibility of children, as a gift from God, for otherwise childless couples. Artificial insemination by donor is regarded as acceptable provided certain safeguards about security of the donor records and telling the child are maintained, parallel with adoption practice.

*See also* BIOETHICS.

**Bibliography.** A. Nichols and T. Hogan, eds., *Making Babies: The Test Tube and Christian Ethics* (1984).

ALAN NICHOLS

## Artificial Intelligence (AI).

Branch of computer science concerned with the intelligence levels of computer programs. Interest in AI began in the 1950s after the advent of digital computers, and has connections with logic, physics, mathematics, linguistics, physiology, and philosophy. Today AI has achieved the status of a new discipline in and of itself, as demonstrated by the recent appearance of substantial literature on the subject.

For purposes of analysis, there are at least two forms of approach to the study of AI: the inferential-psychological and the cognitional.

The inferential or analogical approach to AI has for its most obvious source the conception and development of the computer culture. The video game, for example, confronts the ordinary individual with a larger culture simulation. Video games encourage people to believe that they can create and conquer new mysteries. In this light, some are striving to transcend the gap between "computer chess" and real human intelligence.

Psychoanalysis proclaims a new way of seeing and interpreting both the self and human culture as a whole. In terms of AI, this has produced a new way of thinking, often in computer categories, with the parallel discovery of computational language. The use of the computer in language translation and speech production would lend some support to new and sensational linkages between the computer and human psychology.

Many AI researchers are themselves ambivalent about machines, being on the one hand impressed by their promise while at the same time depressed by the fact that computers do not seem to think, but merely simulate thought. These researchers also note that computers tend to turn their users from thinking to feeling, leaving them vulnerable to the progress of technology.

Many proponents of AI have a romantic inclination to draw definitive conclusions from the reaction of children to advances in computer science, particularly in their tendency to see the self in mechanical terms. To say the least, this inferential approach to electronic technology gives impetus to the belief that programming offers the best clue to man's self-awareness and self-structure.

43

The cognitional approach to the quest for AI is complex, and the related literature is prolific. Knowledge engineering quite normally involves analysis of the power of the mind for storage and recall of data, since the computer is visibly at its best in this area.

Maria Nowakowska sees the goal of AI research to be the discovery of the means of programming to enable computer technology to perform certain acts currently limited to people. This involves as a corollary acceptance of the computer as a companion which makes no emotional demands and whose deliverances represent pure thought.

In her analysis of cognition, Nowakowska leaves very few areas untouched. Not all of these bear directly upon the question of the quest for AI, but many do. Among the more significant are the following:

1. the mind-set which motivates the quest for a bona fide form of technologically crafted intelligence
2. the psychological components which afford encouragement, however great or small, that such discovery or discoveries may prove to be of abiding worth
3. the elements which emerge from the study of cognition which offer to knowledge engineers promise for the ultimate production of AI

With regard to the first of these, Nowakowska sees in the contemporary AI quest the extension of the search for the "second self" of the mid-1960s. This mind-set, which loved the machine for itself, resulted in the establishment about 1965 of the Artificial Intelligence Laboratory at MIT.

Concerning the second of these, Nowakowska notes that the quest for AI reflects a mentality which seeks to simulate its own perceptions and processes. This serves to encourage technological research which offers the greatest potential for successful achievement of AI, whether by intent or serendipity.

The third element, itself a derivative of the in-depth analysis of cognitive processes, is characterized by special exploratory techniques. These emerge in three forms or modes which expand the possibilities of cognition: the heuristic, the stochastic, and the anisotrophic. These have as a common denominator the use of data for exploratory purposes with no concern for their validity or nonvalidity, their truth or falsity, their possibility or impossibility. Research on these modes is free to proceed with pure variables.

Thus the quest for AI is for a super machine, whose invention may come by what may be likened to the quantum leap in science, which would lead from the living to that which simulates accurately the nonliving. It would seem to require the discovery or crafting of a totally new language, suited only to the articulation of high-technological constructs. Whether this quest proves to be a possible one or merely represents an expression of human hubris remains to be seen. Quite probably AI research may carry investigation to the very boundary between life and nonlife. Whether it succeeds in penetrating and surmounting this frontier remains an unanswered question.

*Bibliography.* C. R. Poss, ed., *Handbook of Research Methods in Human Memory and Cognition* (1982); S. Turkle, *The Second Self: Computers and the Human Spirit* (1983); M. Nowakowska, *Cognition Sciences: Basic Problems, New Perspectives and Implications for Artificial Intelligence* (1986).

HAROLD BARNES KUHN

## Asch, Sholem

**Asch, Sholem** (1880–1957). Jewish novelist and playwright. Born into a large and poor Jewish family in Kutno, Poland, he soon displayed talent as a writer of stories and plays in Yiddish, notably *Our Town* (1907) and *The God of Vengeance* (1910). He settled in America in 1914 and was naturalized six years later. Asch became best known for his biblical novels: *The Nazarene* (1939), *The Apostle* (1943), and *Mary* (1949). He traveled often to Europe and Israel, and constantly sought to portray Christianity as the logical continuation of Judaism. His other works, all of which were translated into English, include *Mottke the Thief* (1935), *The War Goes On* (1936), and *The Prophet* (1955).

J. D. DOUGLAS

## Ashram

**Ashram.** Indian religious community. In origin the term was applied chiefly to the forest-retreat of those engaged in the third of the four stages (*āsrama* or *ashrama*) of the ideal Hindu life, and more popularly to the hermitage of a sage (*rishi*). The term was revived in the 20th century to describe the pursuit of religious and secular ideals in a community headed by a charismatic leader. Rabindranath Tagore founded Shantineketan to encourage education and creativity; Sevagram grew up around Gandhi's training of political leaders. Sivananda Ashram near Rishikesh, which has steadily expanded as the world headquarters of the Divine Life Society, founded in 1936 by Swami Sivananda (1887–1963), promotes ayurvedic medicine as well as its founder's religious message. The almost inevitable process of expansion and institutionalization is well illustrated in the development of the much older Ramakrishna Mission, founded in 1897 by Swami Vivekananda (1863–1902), and in the history of Aurobindo Ghose's ashram at Pondicherry.

Claims have been made that India has hundreds if not thousands of ashrams, but if one excludes the 80 or so Ramakrishna Mission ashrams or *maths* (monasteries), there are perhaps 30 relatively permanent Hindu ashrams and 20 or so Christian foundations. Paradoxically perhaps, as with the pursuit of indigenous theology in general, most Christian ashrams in India were set up by foreign missionaries. The first Protestant foundations—the Christu-Kula Ashram (1921) and the Christa Prema Seva Ashram (1922, refounded 1928, reopened in 1972 as an ecumenical ashram run by Catholics and the Church of North India)—were inspired by Gandhian ideals. Later, Catholic ashrams like Santivanam (1950) and Kurisumala (1958), associated with Abhishiktananda and Bede Griffiths, have sought an Indian expression of the monastic life. Although (in Western monastic terms) Christian ashrams of Protestant origin have tended to be active in outlook, and Catholic ones until very recently, when they have been influenced by political or liberation theology, generally contemplative, the "style" of an ashram is strictly secondary to its primary aim. For, in the understanding of the Ashram Aikiva (the Fellowship of Catholic Ashrams, formed in 1978), an ashram is a place of *shram* (hard work) involving a group of people intent on seeking God under the guidance of a person of deep spiritual experience. Members follow a simple lifestyle and devote themselves to *sādhanā* (spiritual exercises) which follow one or more of the classic *mārgas* (ways) of *jnāna* (knowledge), *bhakti* (devotion), and *karma* (action) toward achieving union with God.

*Bibliography.* P. Chenchiah, et al., *Ashrams: Past and Present* (1941); Sr. Vandana, *Gurus, Ashrams and Christians* (1978) and *Social Justice and Ashrams* (1982).

PHILIP HILLYER

## Asmussen, Hans Christian (1898–1968).

German pastor and biblical scholar. Born in Flensburg, he served in the German army (1917/18), and then studied at the universities of Kiel and Tübingen. He was assistant to the rector of the deaconess home in Flensburg (1922–25), and pastor in Albersdorf, Dithmarschen (1925–32), and Altona, suburb of Hamburg (1932–34), when he was dismissed by "German Christians." He served as adviser of the Confessing Church at Oyenhausen (1934–36) and was on the faculty of the clandestine theological seminary in Berlin (1936–43). After World War II he was head of the chancellery of the Evangelical Church in Germany, and from 1949 he was dean of Kiel in the church of Schleswig-Holstein. His works include *Offenbarung und Amt* (1932), *Seelsorge* (1934), *Politik und Christentum* (1934), *Galaterbrief* (1934), *Gottesdienstlehre* (1936), *I. Samuelisbuch* (1938), *Johannesbriefe* (1939), *Rechtglaubigkeit und Frömmigkeit* (1938), *Bergpredigt* (1939), *Epheserbrief* (1949), *Warum noch Lutherische Kirche* (1950), *Maria, die Mütter*

*Gottes* (1951), *Geheimnis der Liebe* (1952), and *Römerbrief* (1952).

## Assemblies of God, General Council of the.

One of the largest pentecostal denominations in the USA. Currently the denomination boasts a membership in excess of 2 million who worship in some 10,800 churches. In addition to having congregations in every state of the Union, the denomination has also been instrumental in establishing national churches in 115 countries.

Doctrinally, the denomination stands within the evangelical wing of Protestant Christianity. It teaches a modified form of John Nelson Darby's dispensationalism, holding to a premillennial, pretribulation rapture of the church. With other pentecostal bodies, it teaches that the baptism of the Holy Spirit is a second normative experiential work in the life of the Christian believer which comes subsequent to regeneration. Speaking in unknown tongues is viewed as a necessary initial physical evidence which accompanies this experience. The purpose of this baptism is to empower the believer for Christian service. The church practices believer's baptism by immersion and holds to a Zwinglian "memorial" view of the Lord's supper.

Founded in Hot Springs, Ark., in April 1914, the Assemblies of God is part of a revival movement that began in a black holiness mission at Azusa Street in Los Angeles, Calif., some eight years before. Within three years the pentecostal revival had circled the world, making beachheads in over 100 countries.

The central teaching of this revival was "Jesus Is Coming Soon." Early adherents believed that they had been given a twofold commission: to proclaim the imminent return of Christ to the nations as a witness, and to urge the church to put on her bridal garments in preparation for the coming Bridegroom. Speaking in tongues, the unique feature of the pentecostal message, likewise had a twofold function. First, adherents believed this gift would enable them to proclaim the message to the nations in the language of the people. Second, they believed this gift was the seal of the Holy Spirit necessary to assure membership in the bride of Christ.

Missionary field experience soon showed that the tongues received were not actual languages. Missionary effort continued to be an emphasis but was conducted through more conventional means. Nonpentecostal churches quickly rejected the teaching that tongues was a necessary prerequisite to becoming part of Christ's bride. Most adherents also dropped this teaching. By the time the Assemblies of God was founded, speaking in tongues was seen as the necessary evidence of Spirit-baptism. This teaching has come to be regarded as "the pentecostal distinctive."

While the established churches rejected the early pentecostal message, large numbers of church members were swept into the movement. Many of these new adherents were drawn from the Wesleyan/holiness tradition. Indeed several small holiness denominations accepted the teaching as a whole. Other holiness converts joined these denominations.

Several new pentecostal converts, however, were drawn from those Reformed Christians who had accepted the Keswick doctrine of the higher Christian life. These new adherents tended to cluster into independent pentecostal congregations. The call to organize the General Council of the Assemblies of God was directed to these bodies. The effort had a fivefold purpose: (1) to try to achieve better understanding and teach a common message; (2) to conserve the movement's work at home and abroad; (3) to provide a mechanism to raise and protect funds for the mission field; (4) to charter local churches under a legal name; and (5) to establish a Bible school to train ministers for the growing movement.

After a shaky beginning, which included great protest from independent groups who refused to join "a man-made organization" on theological grounds and a doctrinal controversy over the nature of the Trinity which resulted in a loss of membership in 1916, the Assemblies of God nonetheless established itself as the leading pentecostal body.

In 1943, the Assemblies of God emerged from several decades of isolation to accept an invitation to join the National Association of Evangelicals. The denomination also sought closer ties with other pentecostal bodies. Following World War II it helped establish the World Pentecostal Fellowship. The denomination's leadership was instrumental in creating the Pentecostal Fellowship of North America in 1948. Following the widespread appearance of glossolalia in more traditional churches in the 1960s the Assemblies of God has also engaged in cautious informal dialog with churches holding membership in the National Council of Churches and the World Council of Churches. They have also had conversations with the Vatican.

Based on its history and present rate of growth it is clear that the Assemblies of God will face the 21st century with the full confidence that it has established itself as a peer among its older Protestant siblings.

*Bibliography.* W. W. Menzies, *Appointed to Serve: The Story of the Assemblies of God* (1971); W. J. Hollenweger, *The Pentecostals: The Charismatic Movement in the Churches* (1972); R. W. Anderson, *Vision of the Disinherited: The Making of American Pentecostalism* (1979).

D. WILLIAM FAUPEL

## Assumption, Dogma of the.

Roman Catholic doctrine defined as an article of faith by Pope Pius XII on November 1, 1950, which holds that Mary was taken, body and soul, to heaven.

The earliest account of the death and assumption of Mary is found in an apocryphal writing commonly known as the *Liber transitus* (Book of the Passing [of Mary]), falsely attributed to Meliton of Sardes. Various recensions of this writing were circulated during the 5th century.

The *Liber transitus* states that Mary died in Jerusalem, and not, as another tradition has it, in Ephesus, where she was believed to have followed the apostle John. The Ephesus tradition is endorsed by the synodical letter of the bishops who met in this city for the Council of 431.

The Jerusalem story, as it was told to the pilgrims, may be summarized as follows. Mary had a premonition of her death. The apostles, miraculously summoned by angels, were with her during the last moments of life. During the funeral procession, a Jew was stricken with the palsy for having laid his hands on the bier. The body of Mary, placed in a new sepulcher, was carried to heaven by angels. The apostles witnessed the miracle; the virgin dropped her sash in order to convince Thomas, who had come late and was skeptical.

Before the close of the 5th century, a feast of the assumption was observed in Palestine, probably in August. The Egyptians, however, celebrated it in January, and the Gallican liturgy followed the Egyptian usage until the adoption of the Roman rite. In the Greek church, a decision of Emperor Maurice (d. 702) prescribed the celebration of the feast on August 15, and this date prevailed also in Rome.

No extensive reference to the assumption is found in patristic literature prior to the 7th century. In the West, the sermons of Jerome and Augustine for the feast are spurious. Gregory of Tours (d. 594) simply reproduces the testimony of the Apocrypha.

In the East, the earliest doctrinal developments occur in the writings of Modestus (d. 634), Andrew of Crete (d. 740), and John Damascene (d. 749). The speculations of the Eastern doctors are also based on the testimony of Juvenal and the Apocrypha.

Most medieval theologians regarded the assumption as a historical fact, rather than an object of doctrinal speculation. That is particularly noticeable in Aquinas, who takes the assumption for granted, and studies in its light the sanctification of Mary and other such mysteries.

It is chiefly the post-Tridentine theology which endeavors dogmatically to establish the belief in the assumption on grounds of convenience, stating that Mary, because of her sinlessness and the fact that she was the mother of Jesus, was fittingly spared the horrors of the grave.

Prior to its official definition, the doctrine of the assumption was regarded as probable. Denial of it was considered impious and blasphemous. During Vatican I (1869–70), a petition signed by 197 bishops was presented to Pope Pius IX to the effect that the doctrine of the assumption be declared an article of faith. However, no action was taken. Later, various petitions addressed to Rome resulted in the appointment of experts to study the whole matter, and in a poll of the members of the Catholic hierarchy as to the possibility and desirability of a dogmatic definition.

The bull *Munificentissimus Deus,* issued on November 1, 1950, points to the unanimous faith and desire of the hierarchy and the faithful as the primary ground for the definition of the dogma. The bull does not consider the testimony of the Apocrypha, but reviews such evidence as may establish that the tradition of the assumption of Mary was consistently held in the church throughout the ages. It insists on the harmony which exists between the dogma of the immaculate conception and the doctrine of the assumption.

The dogmatic definition reads as follows:

We declare and define this to be a revealed dogma, namely that the Virgin Mary, the Immaculate Mother of God, when the course of her life was finished, was taken up, body and soul, into the glory of heaven.

GEORGES A. BARROIS

**Astrology.** Study of the movements of the sun, moon, and planets in the belief that they influence the movement of life on earth. Early astrologers predicted strictly by observation of celestial and atmospheric events. Developments in mathematical astronomy led to predictions from calculated positions of the heavenly bodies.

Astrology developed differently in different regions. East Asian astrology uses a cycle of 12 animals, while Western astrologers start the signs of the zodiac from the vernal equinox and Indian astrologers from various fixed points. Indian astrology has connections with Tantric religion, which contributed to more than 40 methods of dividing a person's life into periods under different rulerships. Tantric methods are usually simpler than those of mainstream Indian astrology, although the rationale is often more obscure. Western astrologers concentrate on delineating character and personality; others predict events and auspicious times.

Astrology developed in a completely different way than science: rules found to be inadequate were not rejected; additional nonphysical planets were introduced. Astrology is properly described as divination because of its use of chance, symbolic connections, inconsistent rules, lack of explanation of rules, and toleration of failed predictions. Divination has been classified as *inductive* (applying fixed rules to external signs), *intuitive* (using insight or inspiration), and *interpretive* (a combination of the previous types where the rules are not rigidly fixed). Astrology is interpretive divination, consisting of many alternative or inconsistent rules and systems that call for the judgment of the astrologer in each particular case. Hence only the pronouncements of astrologers can be tested, not astrology per se.

The scope of astrology is divination involving the heavenly bodies in any way. Proposals as to how astrology works have included the following: actions of deities, inspiration of spirits (good or evil), karma, universal sympathy, synchronicity, physical influence, gullibility, universal validity, and self-fulfilling predictions. Such theories have little effect on the actual procedures of astrologies. Physical influence, when established, is science, not astrology.

Most forms of Hinduism are congenial to astrology. Islam, officially at least, is opposed to its use. The Bible condemns both divination (e.g., Deut. 18:9–14, where the spiritual danger is stressed) and explicit astrology (Jer. 10:2 forbids taking notice of astrological predictions or getting involved in its study).

*Bibliography.* R. C. Thompson, *The Reports of the Magicians and Astrologers of Nineveh and Babylon in the British Museum* (1900); K. E. Koch, *Christian Counseling and Occultism* (1965) and *Between Christ and Satan* (1968); K. Thomas, *Religion and the Decline of Magic* (1971); M. Gauquelin, *Astrology and Science* (1972) and *The Cosmic Clocks* (1973); G. Dean, *Recent Advances in Natal Astrology* (1977); A. P. Stone, *Light on Astrology* (1979) and *Hindu Astrology: Myth, Symbols and Realities* (1981); M. Gauquelin, *The Truth about Astrology* (1983).

ANTHONY P. STONE

**Athearn, Walter Scott** (1874–1934). Disciples of Christ educator. Born in Marengo, Iowa, he studied at Drake, Iowa, and Chicago. After five years as principal of schools in Delta, Iowa (1894–99), he taught pedagogy at Drake (1900–1904), was dean at Highland Park Normal College (1906–9), was professor of religious education at Drake (1909–16), and was professor of religious education at Boston University (1916–29), where he was also dean of the School of Religious Education and Social Service (1918–29). He also served as president of Butler University (1931–34). In addition to active participation in the religious education movement, he wrote *The Church School* (1914), *The City Institute for Religious Teachers* (1915), *The Organization and Administration of the Church School* (1917), *Religious Education and American Democracy* (1917), *The Malden Leaflets* (1917), *A National System of Education* (1920), *An Introduction to the Study of the Mind* (1921), *Character Building in a Democracy* (1924), *An Adventure* *in Religious Education* (1930), and *The Minister and the Teacher* (1932).

RAYMOND W. ALBRIGHT

**Atheism, Christian.** *See* DEATH OF GOD THEOLOGY.

**Athenagoras I** (1886–1972). Archbishop of Constantinople, New Rome, and ecumenical patriarch of the Eastern Orthodox Church. Born in Vasilikon in present-day Greece, he received his early education at Vasilikon where, encouraged by his devout mother, he decided to enter the Orthodox priesthood. He studied at the Holy Trinity Theological Seminary on the island of Halki, Istanbul (1903–10), after which he discarded his baptismal name (Aristokles Spirou) in favor of Athenagoras, was ordained a deacon, and, a year later, a priest. He subsequently served as archdeacon to the metropolitan of Pelegonia (1910–19), archdeacon and secretary to the archbishop of Athens (1919–22), and metropolitan of Corfu (1922–30). In 1930 he was chosen as archbishop of the Greek Orthodox Church of North and South America. During his American pontificate (1930–48), Athenagoras added to his growing reputation for tact and diplomacy by bringing an end to factionalism in his archdiocese and serving as spokesperson for the Greek community in the USA. He also established an Orthodox seminary in New York—the first in the Western hemisphere—for the training of American-born priests. In 1948, he was elected ecumenical patriarch, a position which he held for nearly 24 years. After establishing his supremacy vis-à-vis the patriarch of Moscow, Athenagoras spent most of the remainder of his patriarchate trying to bring unity to the sometimes unruly world of Eastern Orthodoxy and attempting to reach a new understanding with Rome. In the case of the former, he initiated the Panorthodox Conferences held at Rhodes beginning in 1961. In terms of the latter, he suggested that the first step toward unity between East and West should be in the area of practical cooperation with a union of dogma left to some unspecified future date. His ecclesiastical *westpolitik* resulted in three dramatic meetings with Pope Paul VI: in 1964 on the Mount of Olives in Jerusalem; in July 1967 in Istanbul; and in October 1967 in Rome. Practical results of these meetings included the 1965 mutual revocation of the 11th-century anathemas of one another by Rome and Constantinople; an accord on the protection of the holy places in and around Jerusalem; and an agreement on the part of the two communions to explore new pathways of common endeavor.

*Bibliography.* Athenagoras, Oikoumenikos Patriarches, *o epeirotes* (1975); Aristeides Panotes, *Les pacificateurs: Jean XXIII, Athenagoras, Paul VI, Dimitrios* (1974); G. Papaioannou, *From Mars Hill to Manhattan: The Greek Orthodox in America under Patriarch Athenagoras I* (1976); D. Tsakonas, *A Man Sent by God: The Life of Patriarch Athenagoras of Constantinople* (1977).

ROBERT D. LINDER

**Atkins, Gaius Glenn** (1868–1956). Congregationalist pastor and seminary professor. Born in Mount Carmel, Ind., he studied at Ohio State University, Cincinnati Law School, and Yale Divinity School. He was head of the department of history at Mount Hermon Fitting School (1892–95). He served pastorates at Greenfield, Mass. (1895–1900), Burlington, Vt. (1900–1906), First Church, Detroit (1906–10), Central Church, Providence, R.I. (1910–17), and First Church, Detroit (1917–27). He was professor of homiletics and sociology at Auburn Theological Seminary (1927–39). His writings include *Pilgrims of the Lonely Road, Modern Religious Cults and Movements, Reinspecting Victorian Religion, The Making of the Christian Mind, The Procession of the Gods, Life of Cardinal Newman, Religion in Our Times, Preaching and the Mind of Today, From the Cross—a Study of the Seven Last Words, Resources for Living,* and *From the Hillside.* He contributed to the *Interpreter's Bible* and was editor of the *Minister's Quarterly.*

**Atkinson, Henry Avery** (1877–1960). Congregationalist minister. Born in Merced, Calif., he studied at Pacific Methodist College and Garrett Biblical Institute. Ordained to the Congregational ministry in 1902, he served as pastor of First Church, Albion, Ill. (1902–4), First Church, Springfield, Ohio (1904–8), and Central Church, Atlanta, Ga. (1908–11). After seven years as the secretary of the Special Services Commission of the Congregational Churches in the United States (1911–18), he became general secretary of the Church Peace Union and the World Alliance for International Friendship Through the Churches. His writings include *The Church and Industrial Welfare* (1914), *The Church and People's Play* (1915), *Men and Things* (1918), *Causes of War* (1932), and *Prelude to Peace* (1937).

RAYMOND W. ALBRIGHT

**Atom Bomb.** *See* NUCLEAR QUESTION.

**Atonement.** *See* SALVATION.

**Atonement Friars.** Branch of the Franciscan order founded in 1898 by Lewis Thomas Wattson (1863–1940), an Episcopalian clergyman. Originally an order of the Protestant Episcopal Church when Wattson and Laurana Mary White (1870–1935) jointly established monastic orders for men and women at Graymoor, Garrison, N.Y., the orders were by the unprecedented action of Pope Pius X received into the Roman Catholic Church in 1909. The initial intent was to establish a preaching order like the Paulists based on the ideas of St. Francis. After reception into the Roman Catholic Church, the Society of the Atonement devoted its energy to prayer for Christian unity as well as mission work in the USA, Canada, Japan, Great Britain, Brazil, and Rome. The order has houses of study at Graymoor and Montour Falls, N.Y., and at Washington, D.C.

**Bibliography.** D. Gannon, *Father Paul of Graymoor* (1951); T. F. Cranny, *Father Paul: Apostle of Unity* (1955).

R. MILTON WINTER

**Attwater, Donald** (1892–1977). Roman Catholic author and editor. After serving as a soldier in the Near East during World War I, he developed a keen interest in the Eastern Church and the lives of the saints. Educated in legal studies, he turned to writing and was a regular contributor to Roman Catholic reference books and encyclopedias. In World War II, he was a civilian lecturer on history and current affairs. His writings include *Christian Churches of the East* (1935–37), *St. John Chrysostom* (1939), *Martyrs* (1957), *Saints of the East* (1963), and *A Cell of Good Living* (1970). He edited the *Catholic Herald, A Catholic Dictionary* (1931), and the *Penguin Dictionary of Saints* (1965). With Jesuit scholar Herbert Thurston he updated Butler's *Lives of the Saints* (rev. ed., 1956). He also translated Hippolyte Delehaye's classic *Legends of the Saints* (1962).

TIM LENTON

**Aubrey, Edwin Ewart** (1896–1956). Baptist professor and theologian. Born in Glasgow, Scotland, he studied at Bucknell University and the University of Chicago (Ph.D., 1926). He taught at Carleton College, Miami University, and Vassar College before returning to the University of Chicago as professor of Christian theology and ethics (1929–44). After five years as president of Crozer Theological Seminary (1944–49), he went to the University of Pennsylvania where he established the department of religious thought. His writings include *Religion and the Next Generation* (1931), *Present Theological Tendencies* (1936), *Living the Christian Faith* (1939), and *Man's Search for Himself* (1940).

**Auburn Affirmation.** Document published in January 1924, with 150, and republished in May 1924, with 1274 signatures of Presbyterian ministers. The General Assembly of the Presbyterian Church in the USA in 1923, following similar action by the assemblies of 1910 and 1916, had declared each of five designated doctrines to be "essential." The affirmation stated that each of these five Christian truths might, in accordance with historic Presbyterian liberties, be legitimately stated in other ways as well. The affirmation also declared the General Assembly's action to be unconstitutional because it in effect amended the church's constitution without the required concurrent action by the church's presbyteries; and the General Assembly of 1927 later affirmed this principle.

**Bibliography.** L. A. Loetscher, *The Broadening Church: A Study of Theological Issues in the Presbyterian Church since 1869* (1954); R. H. Nichols, *J RTheol* 5 (1925): 14–36.

L. A. LOETSCHER

**Augustinian Canons.** Religious order originating in northern Italy and southern France in the middle decades of the 11th century. The Augustinian canons (also known as canons regular, regular clerics, religious clerics, or black canons) lived in communities leading the life of religious and reciting the Divine Office daily. They were also prepared, at the bidding of their superiors, to preach, teach, administer the sacraments, tend the sick, and offer hospitality to pilgrims and wayfarers. Erasmus, himself a regular canon, remarked that they constituted a sort of mean between the monks and the secular clergy. A 12th-century authority says that the canons were spared the stern discipline, sharp reproofs, long chanting of the office, and spartan diet and vesture, to which monks were subjected. Their watchword was moderation, in imitation of their reputed lawgiver, St. Augustine. The Augustinian rule had the reputation of being at once simple and profound: "an elephant can swim in it and a lamb can walk in it safely." Their essential and characteristic habit was the rochet; the remainder of their dress conformed with that of the other clergy. The Augustinian hermits or friars were a religious order formed from a number of Italian congregations of hermits and combined for administrative convenience by the pope under the rule of St. Augustine in 1256. Originally located in remote places, they soon moved to the towns. In the later Middle Ages there arose a number of local reformed congregations; Martin Luther belonged to one of these.

HUGO A. MEYNELL

**Aulen, Gustaf Emanuel Hildebrand** (1879–1978). Swedish theologian and bishop. Born in Ljungby, county of Kalmar, he studied at the University of Uppsala, was professor of systematic theology at the University of Lund (1913–33), and bishop of Strangnas (1933–52). He was a prominent voice in the World Council of Churches whose first assembly was held in 1948. Among his published works are *Christus Victor* (1931), *The Faith of the Christian Church* (1948), *Church, Law and Society* (1948), *Reformation and Catholicity* (1959), and *Jesus in Contemporary Historical Research* (1973).

**Australia.** Continent and independent nation in the Southern hemisphere lying between the Indian and Pacific oceans. It is the smallest continent, with an area of 7,682,300 sq. km. (2,966,155 sq. mi.). In the mid-1980s it had a population of just over 15 million, which is expected to rise to 20 million by the year 2000. This population is spread over six states and two territories, with the greatest contribution in the southeast segment bounded by Adelaide and Brisbane, and with 70 percent of it in 12 major cities.

While its constitution forbids favoring any particular religion and from imposing religious tests, Australia is not as rigorous as is the USA in separating church and state. Religious freedom is guaranteed, and in recent years a society which once knew only Anglican worship and sermons now knows the full range of world religions.

European settlement began in January 1788, but the aboriginal population had already been in Australia for at least 40,000 years, possibly more than 100,000 years according to recent archeological evidence. Grouped in what could rightly be called "sacred societies," they filled both their everyday world and the transcendental world with religious significance, expressed through totem and ritual. Each aborigine is thought to have two souls, one from natural parents and the other from a totemic ancestor. The latter, together with the social group, is the controlling forces in a person's life.

In sharp contrast to European attitudes toward individual and community ownership and exploitation of land, the aborigines believed that they were owned by and intimately dependent on the land. As a consequence, their culture and religion were ignored and discounted as "stone age" and unworthy of attention, let alone respect, until some 60 years ago. Belatedly the complexities of both are now recognized and admired by those who have studied them carefully.

Earliest missionary endeavors came to naught, as aborigines showed little inclination to adopt the white man's culture-cum-religion package. Harried and decimated, they were expected to die out by the beginning of the 20th century, but in 1976 their numbers had reached 161,000. It is projected that by the year 2000 they will number 300,000, which is at least the aboriginal population of 1788, the first year of European settlement.

Missionary efforts—notably by Catholics, Moravians, Lutherans, Anglicans, Methodists, and Presbyterians—were made from the late 19th century. As a result some 72 percent of aborigines claim membership in Christian churches (1976), with 28 percent regarding themselves as Anglicans, 21 percent as Catholics, 7 percent as Methodists and Presbyterians (Uniting Church), 3 percent as Lutherans, 2.5 percent as Baptists, and other Christian groups making up 11 percent.

Elements of ancient culture remain among aboriginal Christians today, and indigenous expressions of Christianity are encouraged. All major Christian denominations have ordained aboriginal priests and pastors, and by 1986 both an aboriginal and a Torres Strait Islander had been consecrated as assistant Anglican bishops in North Queensland. In addition, in 1985 an aborigine was installed as moderator of the Northern Synod of the Uniting Church in Australia. Special provision has also been made for autonomous development among aboriginal church members. A distinct theological education college for aboriginal people is conducted jointly in Darwin (Nungalinyah College) by the Anglican and Uniting Churches.

Christianity was introduced in Australia in 1788 in the penal colony in New South Wales. A single Anglican chaplain, Richard Johnson (1753–1827), served there. As a result, an Anglican religious monopoly existed for some three decades in New South Wales and off-shoot settlements at Hobart and Norfolk Island. Seen as a possible aid to maintaining the social status quo and to assist in securing and improving morality, the chaplains, sworn to uphold the Anglican "establishment," were subject to the directions of naval and army governors.

It was not that other Christians, particularly Catholics, and non-Christians (e.g., Jews) were not to be found among convicts and guards. Rather, no provision for other than Anglican clergy was made until 1803, when a Catholic convict-priest was allowed to say Mass until an unsuccessful Irish-dominated convict uprising early in 1804. London Missionary Society agents, a few of whom were ordained, were permitted to minister to some inhabitants from 1798, but the quasi-establishment of Anglicanism was strictly enforced. In part this was due to the belief that the religious situation which prevailed in England under the remnants of the Clarendon Code also applied in Australia. It was also due to the suspicion that non-Anglican forms would foster instability if not division and rebellion in the predominantly penal colonies.

While Congregationalists, led by London Missionary Society missionaries, were clearly in existence from 1810 onwards, although not formally and permanently organized, the Anglican monopoly was broken by the arrival in 1815 of the Methodist clergyman Samuel Leigh (1785–1852). He came in response to the appeal of Methodists already in the colony and received support from the senior Anglican chaplain, Samuel Marsden (1765–1838), who, like Johnson whom he succeeded, had evangelical sympathies.

After another false start in 1817 by an unauthorized priest, the first fully accredited Catholic priests, John Joseph Therry (1790–1864) and Philip Connolly (1786–1839), arrived in 1820.

Readily welcomed by some 5000 Catholics, they laid the foundations for future growth.

The first Presbyterian ministers to work among the predominantly free settler Scots were Archibald Macarthur (d. 1841) and John Dunmore Lang (1799–1878). Lang, as a minister of the "established" Church of Scotland, demanded assistance from the government on the same basis as that given to the other "established" denomination in Great Britain, the Church of England.

Such assistance on a general scale was limited to Anglicans until 1832. By then other denominations had emerged, along with the reform era in British politics and the repealing of most discriminatory religious legislation by the end of the previous decade. Congregationalists were in Tasmania in 1827 and in Sydney in 1830. The year 1832 saw the appearance of Baptist, Quaker, and Jewish congregations. To these were added Lutherans in 1838, Christian Israelites in 1843, the Swedenborgians in 1844, and the Churches of Christ in the late 1840s. Unitarians organized in 1850, Mormons in 1851/52, and Christadelphians in 1866. "Plymouth" Brethren followed in the 1870s and the Salvation Army in 1880, with Seventh-day Adventists in 1885. Greek Orthodox and Christian Scientists were both established in 1898, and Jehovah's Witnesses by 1904. A pentecostal group was in existence by 1909, with the Reformed Churches and the Nazarenes appearing after World War II. Along the way small groups of Sikhs were in Australia by 1840, along with Muslims, Confucians, Buddhists, and Taoists from the 1850s.

The challenge to favored treatment for Anglicans came not only from Presbyterians but also from Catholic leaders like John Bede Polding (1794–1877), the first bishop. Anglican claims were defended by William Broughton (1788–1853), the first and only bishop of Australia. (In 1847, other dioceses were formed, and Broughton became bishop of Sydney and metropolitan of Australia and New Zealand.)

A great deal of energy in religious circles was absorbed in campaigns for and against state aid to churches, which continued until 1860–70 in most states and until the close of the century in western Australia. Along with the traditional and new dogmatic claims of the Catholic Church this issue kept sectarian antipathy alive. Such antipathy was strengthened by the Protestant majority's suspicions of Irishism, its association with the Labor party, and its Catholic loyalty.

With the granting of state aid to church schools and the upsurge of ecumenical thought and practice since the establishment of the World Council of Churches in 1948 and Vatican Council II, the sectarian spirit has diminished greatly. It is still found among elderly people and highly conservative Protestant denominations

and the Low Church Anglican archdiocese of Sydney.

Once founded, the various Christian denominations faced great challenges in serving a relatively small population scattered over tremendous distances. Twentieth-century advances in transportation helped Presbyterian minister John Flynn (1880–1951) pioneer both the pedal radio network and flying doctor services in the 1930s.

The churches also faced changes in Australian society, which came in the 1850s with the cessation of the transportation of convicts to the eastern states and the discovery of gold in New South Wales and Victoria. The predominantly free nature of society was confirmed, and the discovery of gold saw rapid increases in wealth and in population (from 265,500 in 1850 to 1.2 million in 1860). The foci of political power and social prestige shifted, while the appearance of Chinese gold seekers led to increasing anti-Asian racism. This in turn led to a restrictive "White Australia" immigration policy, which prevailed until the 1960s.

The Protestant churches set out on their own versions of the USA's "Benevolent Empire" crusades, but without the impetus of the Great or Second Awakenings. Campaigns of moral enlightenment, focused particularly on temperance, gambling, and Sabbath day observance, were sparked by occasional evangelistic crusades.

The Catholic Church had most of its energies absorbed with its school policy but shared some concern for temperance. It also grappled more successfully with the issues which arose out of industrial union unrest in the late 1880s and 1890s. Increasingly the Catholic Church became associated with the working-class aspirations of most of its members, while Protestant churches identified more readily with the middle-class concerns of most of their members. This division along denominational lines was lessened only by Catholic socioeconomic upward mobility by World War II, and by the association of the mildly socialistic Labor party with "communism" in the minds of not a few Catholics during the cold war period.

While the churches in Australia involved themselves in missionary work among aborigines, they also undertook work in New Zealand and the other islands of the South Pacific, Papua New Guinea, Indonesia, Malaysia, Korea, Japan, China, India, East Africa, and South America.

The racial background of most Australians until 1945 was predominantly Anglo-Celtic. Even with 20 to 25 percent of the population having an Irish background there was ready identification with the fortunes of the British Empire. This identification extended to the dependence of churches in Australia on Great Britain and Ireland to supply bishops, clergy, teaching orders, theological educators, and hymn and service books until after World War II.

World War II led Australians to look less toward Great Britain, and more toward the USA, not only for military protection but also for more relevant theology. The emergence of the European Economic Community further shifted Australian interests from Europe to Asia and the Pacific. Postwar immigration from southern Europe and the Middle East weakened British hegemony.

Australian Catholicism became less predominantly Irish because of the influx of Italians, Spaniards, Poles, Croatians, and Lebanese. Orthodox churches grew in number and membership, as Greeks were strengthened and joined by Russians, Ukrainians, Serbs, Bulgarians, Romanians, and Syrians. Coptic Christians arrived from Egypt and Muslims from Turkey, Lebanon, and the Middle Eastern countries. Following the conflict in Indo-China considerable numbers of Buddhists arrived, mainly from Vietnam. Consequently, the proportions of the population which claimed to be related to the founding churches of the late 18th and 19th centuries in Australia decreased markedly.

The significance of religious belief and practice for Australians at large has varied over the years, but at no stage has more than 33 percent of the population been in a church on any given Sunday. The latest figures (1981) indicate that this now stands at about 20 percent—about twice the figure in Great Britain but less than half that in the USA.

Secularism has been a pronounced feature of Australian life throughout its history. Nowhere is this more evident than in the fact that the most "sacred" day in the Australian calendar is April 25, "Anzac Day," commemorating the landing of Australian and New Zealand troops in Gallipoli in 1915. The day is celebrated in a tribal festive spirit.

Statistics, of course, give no indication of the actual religious commitment of the respondents, least of all among Anglicans. Indeed they may indicate for the majority of respondents only the particular denomination which they choose to avoid out of all those available to them.

Given the new multicultural nature of Australian society there will be necessary adjustments in religious attitudes. Mosques and Hindu, Baha'i, and Sikh temples have made their appearance on the religious landscape. Their very presence demands a new awareness of the one world within which religious loyalties are to be expressed and tolerance exercised—and these within a social and legal framework redolent with the Judeo-Christian heritage.

If the Christian churches have never commanded the commitment of more than a distinct minority of Australians there is no evidence that the churches themselves are disappearing. In fact there is some recent evidence that they may be making modest advances in some quarters. There has been a new self-conscious awareness of Australian identity, related only in part to the autonomy gained by the Anglican Church of Australia in 1962 and the revocation of the missionary status of the Catholic Church in the 1970s. It will go on expressing itself in more than Australian hymnals, bishops, and theological educators. Against a past which is religiously inspiring only in infrequent patches, and a present which shows some signs of hope, the future is by no means daunting, if not a religiously exhilarating one.

**Bibliography.** J. D. Bollen, *Religion in Australian Society* (1972); P. O'Farrell, *The Catholic Church and Community in Australia* (1972); F. Crowley, ed., *A New History of Australia* (1974); D. Harris, et al., *The Shape of Belief, Christianity in Australia Today* (1982); *The Australian Encyclopedia* (4th ed., 1983); M. C. Charlesworth, ed., *Religion in Aboriginal Australia* (1984); D. Hynd, ed., *Australian Christianity in Outline* (1984); J. J. Mol, *The Faith of Australians* (1985); *Year Book Australia* (1985); R. Humphrey and R. Ward, *Religious Bodies in Australia* (1986); I. Gillman, *Many Faiths—One Nation* (1987).

IAN GILLMAN

**Austria.** Independent Central European country with an area of 83,855 sq. km. (32,377 sq. mi.). This republic has a population of 7.6 million (1985), of which 96.6 percent are Roman Catholics, 6.1 percent are Protestants, and 0.1 percent are Jews. The first half of the 20th century has seen an increase in the Protestant minority. At the close of World War I there were about 600,000 Protestants in the Austro-Hungarian Empire; about 177,178 of these remained in Austria. The downfall of the Hapsburgs adversely affected the dominance of the Roman Catholic Church. Furthermore, there developed an anticlerical movement in Austria analogous to movements in France and Germany.

When the fascists aligned with the Roman Catholic Church in 1934, about 25,000 Catholics turned to Protestantism. Hitler's annexation of Austria increased this exodus to Protestantism. On the eve of World War II there were about 342,000 Protestants in Austria, with 40,000 evangelicals ensconced in a relatively closed community in Burgenland.

During World War II, Nazi persecution of Protestants reduced their number to 317,331. When the wave of refugees from Eastern Europe came after the war, Protestantism enjoyed something of a renaissance. The number of congregations swelled to 140 and the number of communicants rose to 411,872. Under the Constitution of 1949 both Lutheran and Reformed Confessions were granted toleration. In general, Austrian Protestantism is more evangelical than its German and Swiss counterparts.

In addition to the Helvetic and Augsburg Confessions, there are several smaller Protestant groups in Austria. Among these are the Moravians and Methodists, as well as Baptists, Christian Brethren, Friends, and pentecostals.

The Jewish population has declined over the past century. In 1900 there were 166,000 Jews in Austria. By 1945 that number had shrunk to 4000. Since the fall of nazism the Jewish population in Austria has climbed to 10,000 (1975), and it is holding steady at about 9500 (1985). Of these 80 percent are liberal and 20 percent are orthodox. The main reason for this decline in Austrian Jewry is emigration to Israel.

Since Vatican Council II (1963–65) the face of Austrian Catholicism has changed. Basic beliefs have lost adherents. By 1985 only 69 percent believed in life after death and 50 percent in a bodily resurrection, while attendance at Mass had declined substantially. In 1971, 31 percent of all Austrians attended Mass weekly, but that figure had fallen off to 20 percent by 1985.

A similar decline has been noted in religious vocations. In 1949 there were 4443 secular priests and 1129 religious priests in Austria. By 1971 there remained 3987 secular priests and 1106 religious priests. The number of nuns in Austria had fallen from 16,356 (1950) to 13,574 (1972).

With the influx of foreign workers, the number of practitioners of non-Christian religions has arisen. In 1900 there were neither Muslims, Baha'is, nor Buddhists. By 1985 there were 45,000 Muslims, 2120 Baha'is, and 1020 Buddhists.

Recently, Protestant missionary organizations from Great Britain and the USA have sent workers into Austria. Among these organizations are TEAM, the Conservative Baptist Foreign Missionary Society, the Southern Baptist Convention, Greater Europe Mission, and European Christian Mission. Student ministries are being carried on by OSB (IFES), Campus Crusade for Christ, and the Navigators.

*Bibliography.* E. Bodzenta, *Die Katholiken in Österreich: ein Religionssoziologischer überblick* (1962); F. Klostermann, et al., *Kirche in Österreich 1918–1965* (1966); D. B. Barrett, *World Christian Encyclopedia* (1982).

WAYNE DETZLER

## Autocephalous Church.

The word "autocephalous" is roughly synonymous with "autonomous." In the time of the Byzantine Empire, it designated those Eastern churches whose heads were exempt from the jurisdiction of the metropolitan and depended immediately on the patriarch. Such privileges were granted by decree from a council, or, for political reasons, by the basileus. The word "autocephalous" also applies to Eastern churches whose historical ties with a patriarchate were entirely dissolved, as, for instance, the Church of Cyprus in the 12th century. The situation resulting from the Turkish conquest multiplied autocephalous churches on a national or territorial basis. Their heads are called either patriarchs, exarchs, or archbishops and metropolitans. This diversity of titles does not imply any subordination of their bearers with regard to each other, the relationship between autocephalous bodies being conceived as a communion of federated churches, not as an administrative unity.

GEORGES A. BARROIS

## Ayer, Joseph Cullen, Jr.

(1866–1944). American church historian. Born in Newtonville, Mass., he was educated at Harvard, Berlin, Halle, and Leipzig universities, and at the Episcopal Theological School, Cambridge, Mass. After serving various Episcopalian churches in New England he was appointed in 1901 as lecturer on canon law at the Cambridge Theological School, and thereafter was professor of ecclesiastical history at the Divinity School of the Protestant Episcopal Church in Philadelphia (1905–36), combining this with a lectureship on the history of Christian thought at the University of Pennsylvania (1927–36). He wrote *Die Ethik Joseph Butlers* (1893), *The Rise and Development of Christian Architecture* (1902), and *A Source Book for Ancient Church History* (1913). He made substantial contributions to the multivolume *World's Orators* (1900).

## Aylward, Gladys

(1902–1970). English missionary to China. Born near London, she spent her early working life as a nanny and parlormaid. In 1929 she was accepted provisionally by the China Inland Mission for missionary training, but was soon rejected for poor academics. This depressed her greatly at first, but she soon resolved to press on with her hope of being a missionary to the Chinese. Through great determination she paid her own way to China, where she engaged in evangelism. In 1936 she became a Chinese citizen. During the war with Japan in 1940, she led 100 children to safety after a long, arduous, and dangerous trek. After a serious illness, she continued her evangelistic work among lepers. In 1949 she returned to England. A popular biography was written of her life and adventures in 1957, and a film (part of which she strongly disapproved of) was made of her life and work in 1959 entitled *The Inn of the Sixth Happiness*, starring Ingrid Bergman. Two popular biographies have been written of her life: Allan Burgess' *Small Woman* (1957) and Phyllis Thompson's *London Sparrow* (1971).

IAN HAMILTON

## Azariah, Vedanayakam Samuel

(1874–1945). Bishop, evangelist, teacher, and writer. While YMCA Secretary for South India, Azariah responded to God's guidance and initiated the

Indian Missionary Society of Tirunelveli (1903). Hearing a call from God, Azariah himself went as a missionary to Dornakal in the Telugu area and was ordained (1909). In 1910 he moved the Edinburgh Missionary Conference by his plea for friendship between foreign and national workers—something he himself had enjoyed.

In 1912 Azariah became bishop of the small diocese of Dornakal (later extended) and assistant bishop in the diocese of Madras. Azariah stressed discipline, witness, Christian education, proper instruction of converts from the mass movements, and more Indian clergy. He pro-moted Indian cultural forms in church services, teaching, evangelism, and architecture, while repudiating syncretism. He was also concerned for women's work, Christian marriage, and Christian giving. Azariah was prominent in national and international Christian forums and worked incessantly for church union. He was one of two conveners of the Tranquebar Conference (1919), which eventually led to the formation of the Church of South India (1947).

*Bibliography.* V. S. Azariah, *Christian Giving* (1954); B. G. M. Sundkler, *Church of South India* (rev. ed., 1965); C. Graham, *Azariah of Dornakal* (2d ed., 1972); *IBMR* (Jan. 1985): 16–18.

**Baab, Otto Justice** (1896–1958). Methodist minister and educator. Born in Chicago, he was educated at Hamline University, Garrett Biblical Institute, Northwestern University, and the University of Chicago (Ph.D., 1928). He served as a Methodist pastor in Nashwauk, Minn. (1921–24), Mount Greenwood, Ill. (1925/26), and Hegewisch, Ill. (1926/27), and was ordained to the Methodist ministry in 1927. He served as an instructor in Oriental languages at the University of Chicago (1929/30), as professor of religion, Illinois Wesleyan University (1930–34), and as professor of OT at Garrett Biblical Institute (1934–58). He also was acting president of Garrett Biblical Institute (1953–55). During World War II he served as a member of the national War Labor Board (1942–45), and continued to be active in labor mediation and negotiations in the years following the war until his death, including a stint as executive secretary of the Citizens Committee on Industrial Relations (1948/49). A man of broad social interests and liberal theological views, he participated widely in community life and belonged to a variety of scholarly religious societies and professional labor arbitration organizations. His writings include *Jesus Christ Our Lord* (1937), *The Theology of the OT* (1949), and *Prophetic Preaching: A New Approach* (1958). He was a contributor to the *Schaff-Herzog Encyclopedia of Religious Knowledge* (1956).

ROBERT D. LINDER

**Back to God Hour (BGH).** Begun in 1939 as "the radio voice of the Christian Reformed Church," BGH now broadcasts in nine languages (English, Arabic, Spanish, French, Chinese Mandarin and Cantonese, Japanese, Indonesian, Portuguese, and Russian). Peter Eldersveld, BGH's first full-time radio minister (1946–65), designed a format with a clear biblical message, a discussion of contemporary issues, an evangelistic appeal to believe, and dignified music. Listeners are offered printed materials to inform and deepen their faith, counsel by telephone or letter, and sometimes church-planting assistance. BGH publishes *Today*, a booklet of daily devotional readings. "Faith 20" (English) and "Reflexion" (Spanish) are BGH television broadcast series. BGH offices are in Palos Heights, Ill.

JAMES A. DE JONG

**Bacon, Benjamin Wisner** (1860–1932). American biblical scholar. Born in Litchfield, Conn., he graduated from Yale and the Yale Divinity School, and held Congregationalist pastorates at Old Lyme, Conn. (1884–89), and Oswego, N.Y. (1889–96). He returned to Yale in 1896 as instructor in NT Greek, and was appointed to the chair of NT criticism and interpretation (1897–1932). Among his works are *The Genesis of Genesis* (1891), *Triple Tradition of the Exodus* (1894), *Introduction to the NT* (1900), *The Story of St. Paul* (1905), *Beginnings of the Gospel Story* (1909), *Commentary on Galatians* (1909), *The Fourth Gospel in Research and Debate* (1909), *Jesus the Son of God* (1911), *Christianity Old and New* (1913), *Is Mark a Roman Gospel?* (1919), *Jesus and Paul* (1920), *The Teaching Ministry for Tomorrow* (1923), *The Apostolic Message* (1925), *The Story of Jesus* (1927), and *Studies in Matthew* (1930).

**Baha'ism.** A syncretistic world religion founded in 1863 by Mirzá Husayn 'Alí Núrí (1817–92), known as Bahá'u'lláh (Glory of God). In origin an Islamic sect derived from Babism, Baha'ism made converts in the West from 1894 onwards and consciously presented itself as a new religion under the leadership of Bahá'u'lláh's successors, his eldest son 'Abdu'l-Bahá 'Abbás (1844–1921) and 'Abdu'l-Bahá's eldest grandson, Shoghi Effendi Rabbání (1897–1957). Baha'ism has undertaken a plan of worldwide expansion since 1937, and missionary success outside the West since the 1950s has distributed about three-fourths of the faith's adherents in Africa, Asia, and South America. A strong base of 150,000 to 300,000 is maintained in Iran despite discrimination and persecution. The total formal or active membership of Baha'ism is difficult to establish; most estimates vary from 1.3 to 2 million.

Baha'i doctrines and practices are not universally known or followed outside Islamic countries, but most reflect their Islamic and Shi'ite inspiration. Nevertheless, the revelation in Islam is seen only as the culmination of a 6000-year "prophetic cycle" which gave way to the "Baha'i cycle" of about 500,000 years. This was inaugurated by Sayyid 'Alí Muhammad Shírází (1819–50), the *Bab* or "gate" to the truth, announcing himself on May 22, 1844, to be the forerunner of the twelfth Imam, who was expected to reappear that year after a thousand-year absence. The Bab is thus seen by Baha'is as the precursor of Bahá'u'lláh whose thousand-year dispensation will, it is believed, see the world united under Baha'i teaching. Baha'is treat the writings of the Bab, Bahá'u'lláh (who quoted the NT and the Sufis) and 'Abd al-Baha' as scripture, and regard the interpretative writings of Shoghi Effendi as infallible. The latest leader, the first and only Guardian of the Cause of God, had no personal successor, so the unity of Baha'ism has come to be focused on the internationally elected Universal House of Justice (founded 1963) and the Baha'i World Centre in Haifa, Israel, near the tombs of Bahá'u'lláh and the Bab. Baha'is have their own calendar, reckoning the Badi era from the New Year (March 21) before the Bab's 1844 announcement, and dividing the year into 19 months of 19 days each, with four (or in a leap year, five) extra days to harmonize it with the solar year. Baha'is come together for the Nineteen-Day Feast on the first day of each month and fast throughout the 19th month. They also observe nine holy days on which work is suspended. They pray daily and abstain from alcohol.

**Bibliography.** W. M. Miller, *The Baha'i Faith: Its History and Teachings* (1974); M. Momen, ed., *The Babi and Baha'i Religions, 1844–1944: Some Contemporary Western Accounts* (1981), and *Studies in Babi and Baha'i History* (1982); M. Momen and J. R. Cole, eds., *From Iran East and West* (1984); D. MacEoin, "Baha'ism" in J. R. Hinnells, ed., *A Handbook of Living Religions* (1985); A. Bausani, "Baha'ism" in *The Encyclopaedia of Religion* (1987).

PHILIP HILLYER

**Bahamas.** *See* WEST INDIES.

**Bahrain.** *See* GULF STATES.

**Baillie, Donald Macpherson** (1887–1954). Scottish theologian. Born in Gairloch, Ross-shire, Scotland, he studied at Edinburgh, Marburg, and Heidelberg. He was minister at Bervie (1918–23), St. John's, Cupar (1923–30), St. Columba's, Kilmacolm (1930–34), and was professor of systematic theology at St. Andrews University from 1935. In theology he occupied a mediating position between old liberalism and neo-orthodoxy.

He was active in ecumenical work, especially in the Faith and Order movement. His writings include *Faith in God* (1927) and *God Was in Christ* (1948).

**Baillie, John** (1886–1960). Scottish theologian. Born in Ross-shire, Scotland, he studied at the universities of Edinburgh, Jena, and Marburg, and served with the YMCA in France (1915–19). He taught theology at Auburn Theological Seminary (1919), Emmanuel College, Toronto (1927), and Union Theological Seminary, N.Y. (1930), before he became professor of divinity at Edinburgh in 1934, with which post he combined the principalship of New College from 1950 until his retirement in 1956. He was moderator of the Church of Scotland General Assembly in 1943, and made a Companion of Honour by Queen Elizabeth in 1957—a rare distinction for a churchman. As a theologian he is said to have combined traditional liberalism and Barthianism with a pronounced mystical tendency. He was an early supporter of the World Council of Churches, and became one of its presidents. He was also prominent in an unsuccessful move in 1957 to further the cause of union with the Church of England. Baillie's many published works include *The Roots of Religion in the Human Soul* (1926), *The Place of Jesus Christ in Modern Christianity* (1929), *And the Life Everlasting* (1934), *A Diary of Private Prayer* (1936), *Our Knowledge of God* (1939), *Invitation to Pilgrimage* (1942), *What Is Christian Civilization?* (1945), *Belief in Progress* (1950), *The Human Situation* (1950), and *Natural Science and the Spiritual Life* (1951). His Gifford Lectures, *The Sense of the Presence of God*, were published just after his death.

J. D. DOUGLAS

**Bainton, Roland.** (1894–1984). Congregational minister and Reformation scholar. Born in Ikeston, Derbyshire, England, Bainton was brought to Canada in 1898 and to the state of Washington in 1902 by his father. He was educated at Whitman College and Yale University, and from 1920 until his retirement taught at Yale as professor of ecclesiastical history in the divinity school. During his long tenure, Bainton was the best known scholar of the Protestant Reformation in America. His books were translated into 12 languages. A Christian pacifist, Bainton did intensive research into issues of religious persecution and toleration in the 16th century. He was a prolific writer. Some of his most important books are *Sebastian Castellio Concerning Heretics* (1935), *David Joris* (1937), *Bernardino Ochino* (1940), *The Church of Our Fathers* (1950), *Here I Stand: A Life of Martin Luther* (1950), *The Travail of Religious Liberty* (1951), *The Reformation of the Sixteenth Century* (1952), *Hunted Heretic: The Life and Death of Michael Servetus, 1511–1553* (1953), *The Age of* the *Reformation* (1956), *Yale and the Ministry* (1957), *Christian Attitudes Toward War and Peace* (1960), *Early and Medieval Christianity* (1962), *Erasmus of Christendom* (1969), *Women of the Reformation in Germany and Italy* (1971), and *Women of the Reformation in France and England* (1973). He coauthored *Bibliography of the Continental Reformation: Materials Available in English* (2d ed., 1972) with Eric W. Gritsch.

R. MILTON WINTER

**Balfour, Arthur James** (1848–1930). Philosopher and statesman. Born in Whittinghame, Scotland, he was educated at Trinity College, Cambridge. He entered Parliament as a Conservative in 1874, and was prime minister from 1902–5. He served in other prominent capacities in public life, and became earl of Balfour in 1922. His philosophic aim was the defense of Christian theism. His writings include *The Foundations of Belief* (1895), *The Defence of Philosophic Doubt* (1899), *Theism and Thought* (1922/23), and *Theism and Humanism* (1923).

ANDREW K. RULE

**Ballard, Guy.** *See* I AM MOVEMENT.

**Bangladesh.** An Islamic democracy with a population of about 105 million, of which 80 percent are Muslims, 14 percent Hindus, and 0.3 percent Christians. For centuries Bangladesh was part of a larger political entity centered around the port city of Calcutta. Then, in 1947, when Britain was withdrawing from the subcontinent, India and Pakistan were constituted as separate nations, more or less according to religious majorities of Hindus and Muslims. By this procedure the state of Bengal was further divided. By reason of their Hindu majority, the western districts opted for union with India, while the predominantly Muslim eastern sector became East Pakistan. Even so, the relationship between East and West Pakistan was never very satisfactory. The differences between the Bengalis of the east and their Urdu-speaking compatriots in the west, and the fact that they were separated by 1000 miles and by the modern state of India, proved to be too great to sustain.

East Pakistan complained it was being exploited by West Pakistan. In 1966 an East Pakistan People's League, under the leadership of Sheikh Mijibur Rahman, emerged and quickly gained widespread support for autonomy. In 1971 full-scale war broke out between government troops and the People's League. India then invaded East Pakistan in December 1971 and quickly forced the Pakistani army to surrender. The government of Bangladesh was established under Mijibur Rahman in January 1972. Since then there have been at least two military coups and Mijibur Rahman has been assassinated. In 1986 civilian rule was once again introduced under the presidency of Mohammed Ershad, the former military ruler.

Nearly 97 percent of the population is of Bengali extraction, while the remaining 3 percent are made up of several tribal groups, who for the most part occupy the nation's hilly eastern boundary area. Bangladesh is perhaps the world's most densely populated nation. This partially explains its extreme poverty. The per capita income may be as low as US$150 per annum. More than 80 percent of the population is Muslim, mostly of the Sunni sect. At one time the Hindus were in the majority. Reasons for the increase of Islam are several. First, the missionary activity of Muslim preachers and mystics produced converts among the lower caste Hindus. Second, over the years an influx of Muslims from other parts of North India has increased Islam; and third, the Muslims have had a higher birth rate than the Hindus.

Despite the witness to the gospel by numerous missionaries and local evangelists over the years, most Bangladeshis remain resistant to the gospel of Christ. There is, however, little overt opposition to Christianity.

The earliest missionary effort was launched by William Carey and his colleagues from Serampore about 1800. This work of the Baptist Missionary Society continues to the present, in association with the Bangladesh Baptist Union. About the same time, two Anglican agencies, the Church Missionary Society and the Society for the Propagation of the Gospel, also began work in the country. Subsequently the Australian Baptists, the New Zealand Baptists, the Southern Baptists, the Baptists for World Evangelization, the Lutherans, the International Christian Fellowship, and the Assemblies of God have also established work in Bangladesh. These groups are engaged in evangelistic medical and educational ministries.

In more recent years a major factor of Christian work has been the activity of development agencies that have acted generously in response to the constant food shortages and natural disasters that have repeatedly assailed the country. These include the Church World Service, Lutheran World Relief, Mennonite Central Committee, World Relief Commission, World Vision, and a number of smaller programs.

The total Christian community in the country is estimated to be only 300,000. Of this number, Roman Catholics are in the majority. The Muslim community has not been very responsive to Christ but many from among the low caste Hindus and the more animistic tribals have been responsive. In fact, there are not enough missionaries and evangelists to adequately service all requests received. It is observed that the ratio of missionaries to population is a mere 1:300,000.

Literacy work has been an important aspect of Christian outreach over the years. Also, a number of churches conduct their own Bible correspondence courses. These have perhaps been more effective and influential than statistics reveal, because they provide a rather clandestine opportunity for people to inquire about the Christian faith.

Several missions and churches have conducted Bible schools to provide theological education for the training of pastors and evangelists. Recently the College of Christian Theology of Bangladesh was established on a cooperative basis to provide degree level biblical studies. Even in the face of many difficulties, the Christians of Bangladesh are trusting God for the day to come when thousands of their people will turn to Christ.

*Bibliography.* R. E. Hedlund, ed., *World Christianity: South Asia* (1980); H. J. Kane, *A Global View of Christian Missions from Pentecost to the Present* (1975).

GRAHAM HOUGHTON

**Banks, Louis Albert** (1855–1933). Methodist Episcopalian pastor, writer, and supporter of the Temperance movement. Born in Cornwallis, Oreg., he studied at Philomath College and Boston University, and held pastorates in Oregon, Washington, Idaho, Ohio, New York City, Massachusetts, and Colorado. He was Prohibition candidate for governor of Massachusetts in 1893. He became an evangelist for the American Antisaloon League and also for the World Prohibition Movement (1913–33). He was the author of numerous books, including *The People's Christ* (1891), *Common Folks' Religion* (1894), *The Great Sinners of the Bible* (1899), *Fresh Bait for Fishers of Men* (1900), *Ammunition for the Final Drive on Booze* (1917), *The New Ten Commandments* (1922), *Christ's Soul-Searching Parables* (1925), and *Sermons for Reviving* (1928).

**Baptismal Service.** Older controversies about the mode of baptism have largely died away. Believers in immersion as biblical hold their ground, and keep winning adherents, the majority of whom do not look on this mode as essential to salvation. Some Baptist churches admit to membership persons baptized in other ways. Instead of infant baptism, such churches in growing numbers have public services for the dedication of infants to God. On the other hand, many churches that practice sprinkling for infants and adults do so because they believe in the guidance of the church through the Holy Spirit, and not because of a clear warrant from the NT. On the mission field these matters have assumed new prominence, practically, rather than controversially. Among newer churches, baptism means a complete break with the past and the beginning of a new life in Christ. As these newer churches have grown stronger, they have begun to share with older bodies a sense of baptism as close to the heart of Christianity. On the Continent, also, theologians have in a sense rediscovered Christian baptism. For example, Karl Barth and Oscar Cullmann called on the church to make more out of what in some quarters had become largely a matter of form. About many aspects of baptism theologians have differed widely, but the majority have agreed that it symbolizes cleansing from sin, uniting with the church, and beginning a new life in Christ. They have also insisted that pastors and local churches take measures to put baptism in a place of prominence almost equal to that of the Lord's supper. Why call the latter "The Sacrament," as though there were only one? Details of practice will necessarily differ according to the history and traditions of the local church, but everywhere the ideal calls for sermons about baptism, not in its controversial aspects, but in its central meaning and glory; more careful instruction of boys and girls in "communicants' classes"; more faithful preparation of adults about to be baptized and parents about to present their children; and solemnity in performing this holy rite so that it will become a memorable part of Christian experience, both for those being baptized and for all who share in the service. These ideals call for a new kind of training in practical liturgics by every school of theology.

ANDREW W. BLACKWOOD

**Baptists.** A worldwide movement voluntarily linked in the Baptist World Alliance with a membership of 136 member denominations or unions in 143 countries. Within these unions are about 126,000 local churches having a total membership of around 5 million and an estimated congregational strength of 65 million.

Originating in Europe in the 17th century, the predominant Baptist strength now lies in North America. Seventy-one percent of all local congregations are in North America, 11 percent in Asia, and 8 percent in Europe. Membership distribution is about 82 percent in North America, 5 percent in Asia, and 4 percent each in Africa and Europe.

*Origins.* The modern Baptist movement arose in Europe early in the 17th century as a later result of the Reformation. In 1609 a Separatist group of English exiles in Holland organized along congregational lines to practice baptism only of confessing believers. The leader, John Smyth (1570–1612), argued that the true church was constituted by believers who entered by baptism after repentance and confession of faith. Smyth contended that churches practicing infant baptism were of false constitution and that to institute the practice of believer's baptism is to create a church of a true constitution. Smyth's group met in a bakehouse belonging to Mennonites who represented a remnant of the Anabaptist movement of the 16th century. Smyth discussed union with the Mennonites, but many of his congregations would not follow his lead, and in 1612 Thomas Helwys (d. 1616), a layman, led part of the Smyth group back to England where they founded the first known Baptist church at Spitalfields in London. Theologically they were Arminian, and as their congregations increased in number, they showed a strong sense of interdependence. They became known as the General Baptists.

Another strand of English Baptist life began in 1633 when a group connected with a Calvinist separatist church in London broke away to adopt believer's baptism. They remained Calvinistic in theology, but their church order was more independent.

The resulting churches slowly spread through the British Isles. The first Baptist church in Wales was founded in 1649 at Ilston, Gower, Swansea. Baptists in Scotland appeared in 1765. There is some evidence that when Cromwellians came to Dublin in 1650 they found a Baptist community already in existence, but the continuing Irish Baptist Church dates from 1813, when two ministers arrived for the Baptist Missionary Society.

**Baptist Emphases.** The independence of the various Baptist communions has led to diversity in spirit, but the *Declaration of Principles of the Baptist Union of Great Britain and Ireland* provides the historical principles for most: (1) "That our Lord and Saviour Jesus Christ, God manifest in the flesh, is the sole and absolute authority in all matters pertaining to faith and practice, as revealed in the Holy Scriptures, and that each Church has liberty, under the guidance of the Holy Spirit, to interpret and administer his laws"; (2) "That Christian Baptism is the immersion in water into the Name of the Father, the Son, and the Holy Ghost, of those who have professed repentance towards God and faith in our Lord Jesus Christ who 'died for our sins according to the Scriptures; was buried, and rose again the third day'"; (3) "That it is the duty of every disciple to bear personal witness to the Gospel of Jesus Christ, and to take part in the evangelization of the world."

As a body Baptists generally stress: (1) the acceptance of the authority of the Scriptures as revelation of the will and purpose of God in Christ; (2) the understanding of the church as theocratic assembly, visibly manifested in the local community of believers which is competent, under Christ, to administer God's purpose in the control of its own affairs; (3) entry into the gathered community through baptism on profession of repentance and faith reflected in daily life; (4) the conviction that each believer must work out his or her faith in the world as an individual and as part of the local church gathered in church meeting.

Baptists also have been in the forefront of the claim for religious toleration. An Anabaptist, Balthasar Hubmaier, in 1525 issued the first call in the Protestant Reformation for religious toleration in his writing *Concerning Heretics*. Whether the 16th-century English Baptists can claim a direct lineage from the Anabaptists is debated, but Helwys wrote the first English printed book to plead for full religious freedom when he published *A Short Declaration of the Mistery of Iniquity* in 1612.

***The Development and Spread of the Baptists.*** During the 18th century Calvinistic or Particular Baptists in England grew in strength while the General Baptists declined, a number of churches becoming Unitarian. In 1770, under the influence of the Methodist revival, a "New Connexion" of the more evangelical General Baptists brought new life. At the same time the Particular Baptists, largely as a result of the work of Andrew Fuller (1754–1815), became less rigid with the development of what has become known as evangelical Calvinism. This allowed renewed evangelistic zeal, particularly in such people as William Carey (1741–1834) who was instrumental in the formation of the Baptist Missionary Society in 1792 and who became the society's pioneer missionary in India. In 1812/13 the Baptist Union of Great Britain and Ireland was formed among Particular Baptists. During the 19th century the General Baptists drew closer to the Particular Baptists, and in 1891 the General Baptists of the New Connexion united with the Baptist Union.

Not all Particular Baptists were willing to be associated with the Baptist Union. These churches have remained more strictly Calvinistic and in general refuse to have fellowship or take communion with any who have not been baptized as believers and who do not belong to the same local church. These are known as Strict Baptist churches and have a union of their own, the Strict Baptist Assembly.

During the 20th century, the Baptist Union of Great Britain and Ireland has strengthened its denominational leadership. The Baptist Union as a voluntary fellowship coordinates the work of 29 Baptist associations, representing nearly 1900 churches, through the Baptist Union Council and the annual Baptist Union Assembly. Since World War I, the Baptist Union has been divided into 12 geographical areas, each with a general superintendent generally responsible for leadership and oversight. These developments suggest centralization and a movement toward a conception of England's Baptist Union as a churchly body. In fact, however, the conviction of the local church as properly responsible for its own life under God remains strong. Nevertheless, there is a continuing, conscious attempt by Baptists in England to ensure that their practice reflects clearly their theology and their doctrine of the church.

***In Continental Europe.*** Baptist Churches are to be found in very nearly every European country. The Baptist thrust into Europe occurred early in the 19th century, primarily through the efforts of Johann Gerhard Oncken. The vast majority of Baptist church membership today in Europe outside the British Isles is to be found in communities established by Oncken and his coworkers or by those who were influenced by them. Oncken was born in 1800 in Varel, Germany, in Oldenburg, but as a young man came to England where he became a committed Christian. In 1823 he returned to Germany as a missionary for the Continental Society, attracting large crowds with his preaching. His study of the Bible led him first to challenge infant baptism, and then to desire believer's baptism. He was baptized in the Elbe near Hamburg on April 22, 1834, and the following day in Hamburg a small community of believers was constituted a church with Oncken as pastor. Effectively this marks the beginning of the modern Baptist movement on mainland Europe.

Oncken was joined by Julius Köbner, a Jew and native of Denmark, and by Gottfried Lehmann, a native of Hamburg. This triumvirate became an effective evangelical force in developing Baptist witness. Their enthusiasm for evangelism became a distinctive characteristic of European Baptist churches. The motto "Every Baptist a missionary" is attributed to Oncken. From Germany the Baptist movement spread through Köbner to Denmark in 1839 and to Holland in 1845, through Oncken to Switzerland in 1847. In 1849 Oncken encouraged six Hungarian workers whom he had baptized in Hamburg to return to Budapest to commence Baptist work there. In 1862 when members in Oncken's church decided to develop their trade in Romania, he encouraged them to act as Baptist missionaries as well, initiating Baptist work in Bucharest. Another Baptist movement in Transylvania was initiated from Hungary. The founder of Baptist work in Sweden, F. O. Nilsson, was baptized in Hamburg in 1847 and organized the first Baptist church in Sweden in 1848. The Swedish movement spread to Norway and Finland.

In France, Belgium, Italy, Spain, and Portugal there are relatively small numbers of Baptists. In France there was an indigenous church in the early 19th century which spread to Belgium. In Italy the church was stimulated in 1863/64 by two English ministers, James Wall and Edward Clark, while Spanish Baptists trace their origins in 1869 to the pioneer work of an American, William Knapp. Portugal owes its Baptist witness to Brazilian Baptists who began work in Oporto in 1907.

Perhaps most remarkable has been the story of the Baptists in the Soviet Union. The All Union Council of Evangelical Christians and Baptists traces its origins to at least three incidents. In 1867 Nikita Voronin was baptized by Martin Kalweit, leader of a small group of German Baptists in the Georgia city of Tbilisi. In 1869 the indefatigable Oncken was active in the Ukraine and in contact with Mennonites. Oncken seems to have been instrumental in forming a Baptist church which transmitted its influence into Estonia and Latvia. Then in the 1870s, an English peer, Lord Radstock, who had served in the Crimea and was greatly attracted to the Russian people, began evangelical preaching among the aristocracy in St. Petersburg (now Leningrad). He had considerable success and an evangelical Christian movement began under the leadership of Colonel Pashkoff. This developed into the Evangelical Christian Union.

During the Czarist period, life was difficult for these evangelical Christians and the slowly growing Baptists. The situation worsened after the 1917 October Revolution. From 1929 on all Christians suffered greatly. When in 1935 the Russian Baptist Union was forced to close its church in Moscow, the congregation was welcomed by the evangelical Christians. During the critical years of World War II from 1943 on, the state relaxed its pressure on the church, resulting in a revival among Orthodox and Baptist evangelicals. In October 1944 evangelical Christians and Baptists formally united. Since 1945 the Baptist and evangelical cause has continued and developed, although state pressure has at times been severe.

From 1959–64 under N. Khruschev a seven-year plan was launched to rid the state of religion. This resulted in a split in Baptist ranks in 1960 when the influential Baptist body, the AUCECB (the All Union Council), sent out to member churches new rules and a letter advising careful observance of existing laws, suggesting that children should not be brought to worship services and that no one under age 18 should be baptized. In addition, a curtailment of evangelical activities was recommended with a concentration upon consolidation rather than expansion. The "New Statutes" resulted in strong opposition from within Baptist ranks and an "Action Group" (*Initsiativnya gruppa*) was formed. Upon this latter group state persecution fell and imprisonment resulted.

In 1964 Khruschev was overthrown and the situation eased, but the Baptist split had gone too far for easy reconciliation and the Reform Baptists, although a small minority, formed the Council of Churches of Evangelical Christians—Baptists (CCECB). The original Union modified considerably its statutes as state pressure relaxed. Since 1964 the two Baptist groups have been drawing somewhat closer to each other, although the difference in policy as to how to respond to state decrees remains.

***Outside Europe.*** American Baptists largely trace their origins to the English. As early as 1631

Roger Williams left England to escape the persecution of Archbishop Charles Laud. He led the church at Salem, Mass., and then was banished because of his demand for the separation of church from state. In 1636 he founded the colony of Rhode Island from which stems the much prized guarantee of religious liberty. Williams was quickly followed by other Baptist exiles from England, Scotland, Wales, and Ireland.

Baptist work in Asia and Africa, in its earliest days, developed from British and American missionary initiative with William Carey from England going to India in 1792 and the Virginian David George arriving in Sierra Leone in the same year. Further development has been shared among British and American missionaries and more recently by Baptist missionaries from Australasia. Movement toward indigenous leadership of Baptist work in Asia and Africa has advanced rapidly in recent years. From the earliest beginnings of Baptist witness, there has been a consistent witness to the necessity of the separation between church and state. At the same time Baptists have maintained the responsibility of Christian citizens to be involved in all sectors of society. There have been Baptists, for example, in high public office, in the judiciary, and in the universities. Baptists have been involved in social reforms, from the abolition of slavery in the 19th century to the opposition to all forms of racism in the late 20th century. Mainline Baptists have become deeply involved in various forms of ecumenism, with several Baptist groups, including the English Baptist Union, the American Baptist Convention, some Soviet Baptists, and some unions from Africa and Asia, being active members of the World Council of Churches.

*Bibliography.* E. A. Payne, *The Free Church Tradition in the Life of England* (3d ed., 1951), and *The Baptist Union: A Short History* (1959); W. L. Lumpkin, *Baptist Confession of Faith* (1959); R. Torbet, *A History of the Baptists* (rev. ed., 1966); B. R. White, *The English Baptists of the 17th Century* (1983); H. O. Russell, *The Baptist Witness: A Concise Baptist History* (1983).

## Baptist World Alliance.

A voluntary world fellowship of 136 conventions and unions serving more than 35 million Baptists in 143 countries. It was founded in London in 1905 "to promote the spirit of fellowship, service and cooperation, while recognizing the independence of each particular church and not assuming the functions of any existing organization." Member denominations have historically maintained that through the alliance, as a recognized international body, they are able to carry on ministries with greater depth and impact than any could accomplish on their own.

Four divisions deal with the ministries of relief and development, communications, evangelism and education, and study and research. The latter division has six commissions, where international scholars discuss Baptist doctrine and interchurch cooperation, Baptist heritage, Christian ethics, human rights, ministry of the laity, and pastoral leadership. Three departments serve men, women, and youth.

Every five years Baptists from around the world gather at a Baptist World Congress, at which strong emphasis is placed on fellowship and unity in Christ. World Congresses have met in London (1905), Philadelphia (1911), Stockholm (1923), Toronto (1928), Berlin (1934), Atlanta (1939), Copenhagen (1947), Cleveland, Ohio (1950), London (1955), Rio de Janeiro (1960), Miami Beach (1965), Tokyo (1970), Stockholm (1975), Toronto (1980), and Los Angeles (1985).

The alliance is divided into six regional fellowships which coordinate the world ministry on a more expedient regional level: All Africa Baptist Fellowship, with headquarters in Ibadan, Nigeria; Asian Baptist Fellowship, Quezon City, Philippines; Caribbean Baptist Fellowship, Kingston, Jamaica; European Baptist Federation, Copenhagen, Denmark; North American Baptist Fellowship, Washington, D.C.; and the Baptist Union of South America, Asunción, Paraguay. Each is directed by a regional secretary.

*See also* BAPTISTS.

REINHOLD J. KERSTAN

## Barbados. *See* WEST INDIES.

## Barclay, William

(1907–78). Scottish biblical scholar. Son of a banker and lay preacher in Wick, he studied at Glasgow and Marburg universities, and after ordination in 1933 became a parish minister in Renfrew. From 1947 he lectured in NT at Glasgow University, where he was belatedly made a professor in 1964. Meanwhile he had become known worldwide for his *Daily Study Bible*, the NT lay commentary series which sold 1.5 million copies in two decades and was translated into many languages, including Estonian and Burmese. Barclay disclaimed originality, explaining his success to be a result of a good memory, hard work, an ability to work to order, a facility with words, and a capacity for thinking in pictures rather than theological abstractions. Some found his theological position elusive: he had doubts about the virgin birth and the inspiration of Scripture, but claimed to be the only member of his divinity faculty who believed that Matthew, Luke, and John wrote the Gospels attributed to them. Although brought up in an evangelical home, he rejected the concept of substitutionary atonement and regarded miracles as symbols of what God can still do. Barclay's ability to speak to the condition of ordinary people was confirmed in a long-running and very successful religious television series that reached millions. Nonetheless it was the ministry of print, he insisted, that reached places inaccessible to the ministry of the voice and manifested "the true ecumenical movement." Of his many books his autobiography *A Testament of Faith* (1975) gave him the greatest satisfaction. After retirement in 1974 Barclay became visiting professor of biology at Strathclyde University; the title was an administrative expedient to enable him to lecture on professional ethics.

J. D. DOUGLAS

**Barfield, Arthur Owen** (1898– ). English lawyer and writer. Born in London, he attended Highgate School and served in the Royal Engineers (1917–19). After the war he read English at Wadham College, Oxford, and then spent seven years as a freelance journalist and author. Marriage and financial considerations, however, forced him to enter his family's legal firm in London, where he remained until his retirement in 1965. In his first term at Oxford he began a lifelong friendship with C. S. Lewis. They shared literary interests and an appreciation for George Macdonald. Barfield acted as Lewis's legal adviser and counseled Lewis in financial matters after the unexpected success of his *Screwtape Letters*. Soon after he graduated Barfield became a disciple of Rudolf Steiner and a member of the Anthroposophical Society. His later writings were largely on the subject of anthroposophy, a movement growing out of theosophy. Lewis found Barfield's position impossible to accept and they ceased discussions on his religious views. Barfield received numerous invitations to lecture in American universities as well as a number of honorary degrees.

NOEL S. POLLARD

**Baring-Gould, Sabine** (1834–1924). Anglican cleric, hymn writer, and author. Born in Exeter and educated at Cambridge, he was a schoolmaster at Hurstpierpoint College until his ordination in 1864. A high churchman, he served various parishes. In 1911 he became vicar of the parish of Lew Trenchard, Devon, where he remained until his death. He was a prolific author of 159 separate publications. His income and independence gave him leisure to travel and write. His writings included novels, travel books, studies of folklore, biographies, and contributions to specialist journals. His material was not historically accurate, but his lively style and fresh observations made his work popular. His major works were *Origin and Development of Religious Belief* (1871) and his various studies on the lives of the saints, which were placed on the Roman Catholic index of forbidden books. He also wrote the hymns, "Onward, Christian Soldiers" and "Now the Day Is Over."

NOEL S. POLLARD

**Barmen Declaration.** A confession of Christian principles in the face of totalitarianism adopted unanimously by the 139 delegates to the First Confessing Synod of the German Evangelical (Protestant) Church which met in Wuppertal-Barmen on May 29–31, 1934. The synod was convened to counter the growing nazification of the church administration and the influence of pro-Nazi "German Christians," and it was a pivotal event in the unfolding church struggle. The original draft was penned by Karl Barth, and it was modified somewhat during the debate at Barmen. The brief document consists of six theses, each introduced by a biblical text and followed by an affirmation based on this text and identification of a false doctrine which is rejected. Doctrines condemned include teachings that there are other sources of revelation besides Scripture, that some areas of life are not under the lordship of Christ, that the church's message and order may be modified in response to political conditions, that special leaders may be established with ruling authority, that the German state was the single, totalitarian order of human life, and that the Lord's word and work could properly serve human powers. After World War II the statement had a profound impact on the emerging ecumenical movement and the shaping of newer confessions of faith, especially in Reformed circles.

*See also* CONFESSING CHURCH.

RICHARD V. PIERARD

**Barnardo, Thomas John** (1845–1905). Evangelist and philanthropist. Converted in 1862, he was for a time associated with the Plymouth Brethren. As a medical student at the London Hospital he was introduced to the spiritual and material needs of the East End. When he was turned down by the China Inland Mission he discontinued medical studies and plunged into evangelistic and social activities. The founder of the East End Juvenile Mission (1868), he became involved in a free school for destitute English children and other social work. In the winter of 1869/70, his encounter with Jim Jarvis, a destitute child, launched him on the activity for which he was to become famous; his first home for destitute boys was opened in 1870. The first of his "cottage homes" (for girls) followed in 1876 at Ilford. In 1882 he began to arrange for children to emigrate to Canada, and in 1886 boarding arrangements for children commenced. In 1872 he acquired the Edinburgh Castle, a notorious gin palace and music hall, which he turned into a coffee palace with library, reading, smoking, and club rooms, and a mission church. Abandoning his earlier refusal to appeal for funds (in the manner of George Müller) he used his journalistic talent to raise money and his organizational skills to develop a thriving network of activities. Small in stature, he was both energetic and autocratic. By the time of his death he had admitted almost 60,000 children to his homes, helped 20,000 to emigrate, and assisted 200,000 others in various ways.

HAROLD H. ROWDON

**Barnes, Ernest William** (1874–1953). Bishop of Birmingham. Born into a Baptist family in suburban Birmingham, he distinguished himself as a mathematician at Cambridge. Ordained in 1902 in the Church of England, he continued to lecture in mathematics until his appointment in 1915 as master of the Temple (incumbent of the Temple Church), London. In 1918 he was appointed canon of Westminster before going to Birmingham (1924–53). A prominent modernist, he instigated numerous controversies. When his book *The Rise of Christianity* (1947) raised doubts about historic Christian doctrine, he was denounced by the archbishop of Canterbury. Barnes profoundly distrusted the Roman Catholic Church's political activity. In 1933 he publicly protested against the Nazi treatment of the Jews. He championed the cause of women's ordination and the need for women judges in divorce courts. He also supported missionary work in China, upheld sexual purity, wanted the Anglican Communion service open to all Christians, and would not have a Sunday newspaper in his house. He called for greater Christian education in England and saw a natural alliance between Christianity and the Kingsley–Maurice type of socialism. His other major writings were *Should Such a Faith Offend?* (1927) and *Scientific Theory and Religion* (1933).

J. D. DOUGLAS

**Barnett, Samuel Augustus** (1844–1913). Church of England clergyman. Born in Bristol and educated at Wadham College, Oxford, he was incumbent of St. Jude's, Whitechapel (1872–93). Here he used his social reforming ideas in an effort to win the working class back to the church—often by unorthodox means. In the tradition of the Christian socialists he worked to provide better housing and education. He was a creative pioneer in the settlement movement, inviting university students to live in English city slums. The first settlement he founded was Toynbee Hall in London's East End. He was its first warden (1884–1906). Such was the growing influence of social reforming ideas in the Church of England at the turn of the century that he was made canon of Bristol Cathedral in 1893 and later canon of Westminster Abbey, which freed him to pursue social reform. He helped send many East End children on country holidays.

NOEL S. POLLARD

**Barnhouse, Donald Grey** (1895–1960). American Presbyterian clergyman, radio preacher, editor, and author. Born in Watsonville, Calif., he earned a Th.D. from Aix-en-Provence, France, after attending Biola, Princeton Seminary, the University of Chicago, and the University of Pennsylvania. During World War I he served in the Army Signal Corps, and afterward under the Belgian Gospel Mission (1919–21) was director of a Bible school in Brussels and pastor of two French Reformed churches in southern France. Called to the Tenth Presbyterian Church in Philadelphia (1927), he began a 33-year pastorate and radio ministry that brought him international recognition. He conducted weekly Monday night Bible classes in New York's theater district. So great was his influence that after 1940 he was absent from his pulpit six months each year preaching and teaching at Bible conferences. He authored numerous books as well as founded and edited two monthly magazines: *Revelation* (1931–49) and *Eternity* (1950–60).

JACK MITCHELL

**Baron, Salo Wittmayer** (1895– ). Jewish scholar. Born in Tarnow, Austria, he obtained three doctorates at the University of Vienna, and was ordained rabbi after studies at the Jewish Theological Seminary there. He was a history professor at the Jüdisches Paedagogium in Vienna (1919–25), professor of history at the Jewish Institute of Religion, New York City (1926–30), professor of Jewish history, literature, and institutions at Columbia University (1930–63), director of the Columbia Center of Israel and Jewish studies (1950–68), and visiting professor at Jewish Theological Seminary (1954–72). He chaired the Commission on Survey, National Jewish Welfare Board (1946–48), and presided over the Conference of Jewish Social Studies (1941–55; 1959–68), the American Academy for Jewish Research (1940–43, 1958–63, 1965–67, 1969–79), the American Jewish Historical Society (1953–55), and the Jewish Cultural Reconstruction (1947–80). His principal publications include *A Social and Religious History of the Jews*, 15 vols. (2d ed., 1952–73), *The Jewish Community: Its History and Structure to the American Revolution*, 3 vols. (1942, repr. 1972), *Modern Nationalism and Religion* (1947, repr. 1971), *World Dimensions of Jewish History* (1962), *Ancient and Medieval Jewish History: Essays* (1972), and *The Contemporary Relevance of History* (1986). He coauthored *Economic History of the Jews* (1975) with Arcadius Kahan. He also served as editor of *Bibliography of Jewish Social Studies* (1938/39, 1941) and *Essays on Maimonides* (repr. 1966). He coedited *Judaism: Postbiblical and Talmudic Period* (1954) with Joseph L. Blau and *Violence and Defense in the Jewish Experience* (1977) with George S. Wise. He edited memorial volumes in honor of George A. Kohut (1935) and Morris R. Cohen (1951).

H. DOUGLAS BUCKWALTER

**Barrois, Georges Augustin** (1898– ). Biblical scholar and church historian. Born in Hautes Rivières, France, he entered the Dominican order and studied at the *Stadium Generale*, Tournai, Belgium. Following duty in the armed forces, he was ordained (1923), and graduated from the Dominican College of Theology (S.T.D., 1924). He taught archeology and OT at the *École Biblique* in Jerusalem (1924–34), was active in several excavations in the Middle East, and was the professor of OT at the *Stadium Generale*, Étoilles, France (1935–39). After World War II began, he was called as visiting professor to the Catholic University in Washington, D.C. He left the Roman Catholic Church and joined the Presbyterian Church in the USA. Upon receiving the Th.D. degree (1945) from Princeton Seminary, he became professor of history and theology of the medieval church until his retirement in 1968; he then joined the Orthodox Church in America. He has written extensively on archeology and other subjects; his works include *The Face of Christ in the OT* (1974) and *The Fathers Speak* (1986).

JACK MITCHELL

**Barth, Karl** (1886–1968). Swiss Reformed theologian. Born in Basel, he studied theology at Bern, Berlin, Tübingen, and Marburg universities, then ministered in the church at Safenwil, Switzerland. He later became professor of theology at Göttingen (1921–25), Münster (1925–30), and Bonn (1930–35) universities. With the rise of Hitler he became prominent in the Confessing Church and was the principal author of the Barmen Declaration (1934). Barth was dismissed by Hitler (1935) and returned to Basel, where he remained professor of theology until his retirement in 1962.

He early battled with Emil Brunner over natural revelation, and with Friedrich Gogarten over the theology of the state. Barth's theology is influential, his work massive. He published over 550 books, sermons, tracts, addresses, and letters. His major work, *Church Dogmatics*, comprises 13 large volumes and more than 6 million words. During his long life his theology developed remarkably. Influenced by J. G. W. Herrmann, Barth began holding a liberal position; he later held a dialectical one (crisis theology) in which he proclaimed God as the "Wholly Other." In this, impressed by the Religious Socialist movement, Christoph and Johann Blumhardt, and Søren Kierkegaard, he wished to stress the "Godness of God" as the starting point of his theology. Later, responding to L. A. Feuerbach, Barth adopted a dogmatic stance seeking to show that God was not made in man's image. In this he moved from the positions of Friedrich Schleiermacher, Rudolf Bultmann, and the liberal tradition. Barth concluded his life's work emphasizing "the humanity of God": God with and for man. Such growth and development were consistent with Barth's view of theology. It was not an examination of truth, but "a conversation, a process, an active struggle, an act of guidance."

For Barth the person of Christ is the sole key to understanding God, the universe, and man. Theology is christologically determined; Barth works from Christ outward. Barth sought to escape traditional, static concepts of dogmatics. God's "word," for instance, comes in three interrelated forms: Christ, the Scriptures, and the proclamation of the church. It confronts, indicates, warns, and instructs. The church is an event—it exists as Christ exists; it has a dynamic of its own. The parousia has three successive stages, essentially the same in substance, scope, and content: Christ's resurrection, the Spirit's coming at Pentecost, and the *telos* of history. The believer lives in "the time between the times."

More than any other theologian Barth attempted methodologically to bring ethics totally into theology. "Theology is ethics" was Barth's premise, since knowing God entails doing his will. Barth taught that a separation of ethics and theology would be harmful to both, for theology would become intellectualistic, while ethics would adopt the wrong approach to conduct. Barth regarded ethics as the doctrine of God's commands as Creator, Reconciler, and Redeemer. This structure permeates much of Barth's thinking. Man has, inherently, the character of responsibility before God; he is a being in encounter, free only when he conforms his decisions to the divine decision.

Barth's most important works include *Romans* (1919), *Word of God and Word of Man* (1928), *The Resurrection of the Dead* (1933), *Credo* (1936), *God in Action* (1936), *Church Dogmatics* (1936–77), *The Holy Ghost and the Christian Life* (1938), *The Knowledge of God and the Service of God* (1938), *Church and State* (1939), *No!* [in *Natural Theology*] (1946), *Against the Stream* (1946–52), *Teaching of the Church Regarding Baptism* (1948), *The Faith of the Church* (1958), *God, Grace and Gospel* (1959), *Letters* (1960–68), *Humanity of God* (1961), *Philippians* (1962), *Theology and Church* (1962), *Prayer and Preaching* (1964), *Revolutionary Theology in the Making: Barth–Thurneysen Correspondence* (1964), *Evangelical Theology* (1968), *On Marriage* (1968), *Ethics* (1981), *Theology of Schleiermacher* (1982), and *Witness to the Word* (1986).

**Bibliography.** G. C. Berkouwer, *The Triumph of Grace in the Theology of Karl Barth* (1956); T. F. Torrance, *Karl Barth: An Introduction to His Early Theology* (1962); G. H. Clark, *Karl Barth's Theological Method* (1963); H. Hartwell, *The Theology of Karl Barth: An Introduction* (1964); C. Brown, *Karl Barth and the Christian Message* (1967); R. Willis, *The Ethics of Karl Barth* (1971); J. Thompson, *Christ in Perspective: Christological Perspectives in the Theology of Karl Barth* (1978); S. W. Sykes, *Karl Barth: Studies of His Theological Method* (1979); S. D. McLean,

Humanity in the Thought of Karl Barth (1981); P. J. Rosato, The Spirit as Lord (1981).

MICHAEL PARSONS

**Barton, George Aaron** (1859–1942). Biblical and Semitics scholar. Born in East Farnham, Canada, he was educated at Haverford College and at Harvard University (Ph.D., 1891). He was teacher of mathematics and classics at the Friends' School, Providence, R.I. (1884–89), and lecturer on biblical languages at Haverford College (1891–95). Meanwhile he had become also professor of biblical literature and Semitic languages at Bryn Mawr College (1891–1922), and subsequently was professor of Semitic languages and history of religions at the University of Pennsylvania (1922–32), and professor of NT literature and language in the divinity school of the Protestant Episcopal Church in Philadelphia (1921–37). An acknowledged minister of the Society of Friends (Orthodox) (1879–1918), he was ordained in the Protestant Episcopal Church in 1918. Member of several international societies and institutes, he was director of the American School of Oriental Research in Baghdad (1921–34). His many books include *The Religious Use of the Bible* (1900), *A Sketch of Semitic Origins, Social and Religious* (1902), *The Haverford Library Collection of Cuneiform Tablets or Documents from the Temple Archives of Telloh* (1905, 1909, 1914), *Ecclesiastes* (1908), *The Heart of the Christian Message* (1910), *Commentary on Job* (1911), *The Origin and Development of Babylonian Writing* (1913), *Archeology and the Bible* (1916), *Religions of the World* (1917), *The Religion of Israel* (1918), *Jesus of Nazareth, a Biography* (1922), *Studies in NT Christianity* (1928), *A History of the Hebrew People* (1930), *Christ and Evolution* (1934), and *The Apostolic Age and the NT* (1936).

**Barton, William Eleazar** (1861–1930). Congregational pastor and writer. Born in Sublette, Ill., he was educated at Berea College and Oberlin Theological Seminary, and after ordination in 1885 held pastorates in Tennessee, Ohio, and Massachusetts before going to First Congregational Church, Oak Park, Ill. (1899–1924). At Chicago Theological Seminary he lectured on applied practical theology (1905–9) and on ecclesiastical law (1911–24), and later taught biographical leadership and practical theology at Vanderbilt University (1928–30). He was a delegate to 14 triennial national councils of the Congregational Church, the secretary of its commission on polity, and principal author of its Kansas City Creed (1913). He was also a delegate to the International Council (1899–1930) and the author of its constitution (1920). His writings, in addition to numerous sermons and works of fiction, include *The Psalms and Their Story* (1898), *Old Plantation Hymns* (1899), *Faith as Related to*

*Health* (1901), *Jesus of Nazareth* (1904), *Four Weeks of Family Worship* (1906), *Congregational Creeds and Covenants* (1917), *The Parables of Safed the Sage* (1917), *More Parables of Safed the Sage* (1923), and *My Faith in Immortality* (1926).

**Bashford, James Whitford** (1849–1919). Methodist Episcopal bishop. Born in Fayette, Wis., he was educated at the University of Wisconsin and Boston University (Ph.D., 1881). He was tutor in Greek at the University of Wisconsin, and held pastorates in Massachusetts, Maine, and New York. He was president of Ohio Wesleyan University (1889–1904), then was chosen bishop, and in this capacity went to Shanghai, China. He believed that Christianity could be better interpreted from the point of view of evolution rather than creation, and he was confident that higher criticism, if used with sound scholarship, would not endanger the fundamentals of Christianity. He remained in China for 14 active years. Among his books are *Science of Religion* (1893), *Wesley and Goethe* (1903), and *Methodism in China* (1906).

**Bates, Miner Searle** (1897–1978). Educator and missionary to China. Born in Newark, Ohio, he received degrees from Hiram College, Oxford, as a Rhodes scholar, and Yale University (Ph.D., 1935). During 1917/18 he served the YMCA in India and Mesopotamia, and from 1920–50 was professor of history at the University of Nanking, China, under the United Christian Missionary Society. Returning to the United States, he was professor of missions at Union Theological Seminary (1950–65). His books include *Religious Liberty: An Inquiry* (1945), *Missions in Far Eastern Cultural Relations*, and *The History of the Christian Church in China, 1900–1950* (1984). With Wilhelm Pauck he edited *The Prospects of Christianity Throughout the World* (1964).

JACK MITCHELL

**Battles, Ford Lewis** (1915–1979). American church historian. Born in Erie, Pa., he was educated at West Virginia University, Tufts University, Oxford University, and Hartford Seminary Foundation (Ph.D., 1950). During World War II he had a distinguished career as an intelligence officer. Thereafter he was associate professor of English at West Virginia University (1945–48), professor of church history at Hartford Theological Seminary (1950–68), and professor of church history and historical doctrine at Pittsburgh Theological Seminary (1968–79). During the last year of his life he taught at Calvin Seminary, Grand Rapids, Mich. Among his many accomplishments are the definitive translation of Calvin's 1559 *Institutes* in the Library of Christian Classics series; the first-ever translation into English of the 1536 *Institutes;* numerous translations of patristic texts; a translation of John Eck's *Enchiridion;* and an unfinished translation of Peter Lombard's *Four Books of Sentences.* Battles served on the Commission on Hymnody of the United Church of Christ (1966–73), and translated many hymns from classic texts of Christian tradition, inspiring his students to do likewise. He also applied the computer to concordance and humanistic studies.

*Bibliography.* B. A. Gerrish and R. Benedetto, *Reformatio Perennis: Essays on Calvin and the Reformation in Honor of Ford Lewis Battles* (1981).

E. J. FURCHA AND JACK MITCHELL

**Bauer, Walter** (1877–1960). Lutheran NT scholar. Born in Königsberg, he studied at Marburg, Berlin, and Strasbourg. He taught NT at Marburg (1903–13), Breslau (1913–16), and Göttingen. His chief works include *Mündige und Unmündige bei Ap. Paulus* (1902), *Der Apostolos der Syrer* (1903), *Das Leben Jesu im Zeitalter der neuentestamentlichen Apokryphen* (1909), *Ein Handbuch zum N.T.: Johannes evangelium* (3d ed., 1933), *Die Briefe des Ignatius und der Polykarpbrief* (1920), *Der Wortgottesdienst der Ältesten Christen* (1930), *Die Oden Solomans* (1933), *Rechtgläubigkeit und Ketzerei im ältesten Christentum* (1934), and *Griechisch-deutsches Wörterbuch zu den Schriften des Neuen Testaments und der übrigen urchristlichen Literatur* (4th ed., 1952).

RAYMOND W. ALBRIGHT

**Baumgärtel, Friedrich** (1888–1981). German OT scholar. Born in Plauen, he began his career at Leipzig (1916–22), and was professor of OT at Rostock (1922–28), Greifswald (1928–37), Göttingen (1937–41), and Erlangen (1941–56). He belonged to the school of Rudolf Kittel. A conservative theologian, he strove to connect the results of modern science of the OT with its value as God's revelation. He wrote *Elohim ausserhalb des Pentateuchs* (1914), *Die Bedeutung des Alten Testaments für den Christen* (1925), *Ist die Kritik am Alten Testament berechtigt?* (1927), *Die Eigenart der alttestamentlichen Frömmigkeit* (1932), *Der Hiobdialog* (1933), and *Zur Frage der theologischen Deutung des Alten Testaments* (1938).

**Baumgartner, Walter** (1887–1970). German OT scholar. Born in Winterhur, Switzerland, he studied at the Universities of Zurich (D.Phil., 1913), Marburg, and Giessen. He was professor of OT at Marburg (1920–28), Giessen (1928/29), and Basel (1929–47) before finally lecturing in Semitic languages at Zurich (1947–58). Regarded as a liberal evangelical, he wrote *Kennen Amos und Hosea eine Heilseschatologie* (1913), *Die Klagegedichte des Jeremia* (1916), *Das Buch Daniel* (1926), and *Israelitische und altorientalische Weisheit* (1933).

**Baumstark, Anton** (1872–1948). Roman Catholic Orientalist. Born in Konstanz, Germany, he studied Oriental languages at Heidelberg, Leipzig, Rome, and Jerusalem. After various teaching assignments he became professor of Oriental languages at the University of Münster (1930) and simultaneously at Utrecht, Holland. His books include *Aristoteles bei den Syrern vom 5.–8. Jahrhundert* (1900), *Die Messe im Morgenland* (1906), *Die konstantinopolitanische Messliturgie vor dem 9. Jahrhundert* (1909), *Die christliche Literatur des Orients* (1911), *Nichtevangelische syrische Perikopenordnungen des ersten Jahrtausends* (1921), *Geschichte der syrischen Literatur mit Ausschluss der christlich-palästinensichen Texte* (1922), *Vom geschichtlichen Werden der Liturgie* (1923), *Sacramenta anni circuli* (1927), and *Missale Romanum. Seine Entwicklung, ihre wichtigsten Urkunden und Probleme* (1930). He founded and edited *Oriens Christianus.* He also edited *Die Ostkirche betet. Hymnen aus den Tageszeitender byzantinischen Kirche,* 4 vols. (1934–37).

OTTO A. PIPER

**Bausman, Benjamin** (1824–1909). German Reformed pastor and editor. Born in Lancaster, Pa., he was educated at Marshall College and the Theological Seminary, Mercersburg, Pa., and held successive pastorates within that state at Lewisburg (1853–61), Chambersburg (1861–63), First Reformed Church, Reading (1863–73), and St. Paul's Reformed Church, Reading (1873–1909), which he founded. He wrote *Sinai and Zion* (1860), *Wayside Gleanings in Europe* (1878), *Bible Characters* (1893), and *Precept and Practice* (1901). He was editor of the *Guardian* (1867–82) and founder and editor of *Der reformierte Hausfreund* (1867–1909).

**Bavinck, Herman** (1854–1921). Dutch theologian. Born in Hogeveen, he studied at the gymnasium in Zwolle, the Theological School of the Christian Reformed Church in Kampen, and the University of Leiden (Ph.D., 1880). From 1881 to 1882 he ministered in the church at Franeker. He was professor of systematic theology at Kampen (1882–1902), and then succeeded Abraham Kuyper in the chair of systematic theology at the Free University in Amsterdam from 1902 until his death. In the Dutch Reformed Church, Bavinck was instrumental in reconciling theologically opposed groups, in enhancing the educational system, and in voicing social concerns. His magnum opus was his four-volume *Reformed Dogmatics* (*Gereformeerde Dogmatiek,* 1911, 2d ed.; only vol. 2, *The Doctrine of God,* is translated into English). Other works translated into English include *Our Reasonable Faith* (1956), *The Cer-*

*tainty of Faith*, and *Philosophy of Revelation* (1953).

H. Douglas Buckwalter

**Bavinck, Johan Herman** (1895–1965). Dutch missionary, educator, and author. Born in Rotterdam, he served as missionary to the Dutch East Indies from 1919 to 1939 and occupied the chair of missions at the Free University in Amsterdam from 1939 until his death. His tenure was interrupted by Nazi occupation of the Netherlands, during which Bavinck worked in the Dutch underground. His writings include *The Impact of Christianity on the Non-Christian World* (1948), *The Riddle of Life* (1958), *Faith and Its Difficulties* (1959), *An Introduction to the Science of Missions* (1960), and *The Church Between Temple and Mosque: A Study of the Relationship Between the Christian Faith and Other Religions* (1966).

H. Douglas Buckwalter

**Bayne, Stephen Fielding** (1908–1974). Anglican bishop and educator. Born in New York City, he earned degrees at Amherst College and General Theological Seminary, and was ordained priest in 1933. He served parishes in St. Louis (1934–39), and Northampton, Mass. (1939–42), then was Episcopal chaplain and chairman of the department of religion at Columbia University (1942–47, broken by a two-year stint as a U.S. Navy chaplain). In 1946 he was elected bishop of Olympia, Wash., the membership of which doubled by 1958. He became executive officer of the 40-million-member Anglican communion in 1960, and exercised worldwide influence second only to that of the archbishop of Canterbury. After resigning in the mid-1970s, he returned to General Seminary as professor of Christian mission and ascetical theology, and later served as dean of the seminary until he retired in 1973.

Jack Mitchell

**Baynes, Norman Hepburn** (1877–1961). Historian. Born in London, he studied at Eastbourne College and New College, Oxford. He was professor of Byzantine history at the University of London. His works include *The Byzantine Empire* (1925), *Israel Amongst the Nations* (1927, 1928), *Constantine the Great and the Christian Church* (1929), and *A Bibliography of the Works of J. B. Bury* (1929). He coedited *Byzantium, An Introduction to East Roman Civilization* (1948) with St. L. B. Moss and *Three Byzantine Saints* (1948) with Elizabeth Dawes. He was also coeditor of volume 12 of the *Cambridge Ancient History* (1939).

**Bea, Augustin** (1881–1968). Roman Catholic cardinal and ecumenist. Born in Baden, Germany, he entered the Jesuit order in 1902. From 1924 he worked in Rome, chiefly as professor at the Biblical Institute, where he was rector for 19 years. From 1945 to 1958 he was confessor to Pope Pius XII. In 1959 he was made a cardinal by Pope John XXIII. In 1960 he was appointed to the influential post of president of the Secretariat for Promoting Christian Unity. During Vatican Council II he played a prominent role. Most of his publications focus on the theme of Christian unity. His works include *The Unity of Christians* (1963), *Unity in Freedom* (1964), *The Study of the Synoptic Gospels* (1965), *Ecumenism in Focus* (1969), and *We Who Serve* (1969).

Ian Hamilton

**Beach, Harlan Page** (1854–1933). Missiologist. Born in South Orange, N.J., he was educated at Yale College and Andover Theological Seminary and was ordained as a Congregational minister in 1883. He was a missionary in China for seven years, and from 1892 to 1895 was instructor and later superintendent of the School for Christian Workers, Springfield, Mass. He was educational secretary of the Student Volunteer Movement for Foreign Missions (1895–1906), professor of theory and practice of missions at Yale Divinity School (1906–21), and lecturer on missions at Drew Theological Seminary (1921–28). His publications include *The Cross in the Land of the Trident* (1895), *NT Studies in Missions* (1898), *Protestant Missions in South America* (1900), *Geography and Atlas of Protestant Missions*, 2 vols. (1901–3), *India and Christian Opportunity* (1904), and *Missions as a Cultural Factor in the Pacific* (1927). He was also coauthor of *World Atlas of Christian Missions* (1911), *World Statistics of Christian Missions* (1916), and *World Missionary Atlas* (1925).

**Beatitudes.** *See* Sermon on the Mount.

**Beaven, Albert W.** (1882–1942). Baptist clergyman and ecumenical leader. Born in Moscow, Idaho, he studied at Shurtleff College and Colgate-Rochester Divinity School. He was minister of Lake Avenue Baptist Church, Rochester, N.Y. (1909–29) and president of the Colgate-Rochester Divinity School (1929–43). He was president of the Northern Baptist Convention (1930/31), president of the Federal Council of Churches (1932–34), vice-president of the Baptist World Alliance (1934–39), and president of the American Association of Theological Schools (1940–42). He wrote *The Fine Art of Living Together* (1927), *Putting the Church on a Full Time Basis* (1928), *Fireside Talks for the Family Circle* (1928), *Sermons for Everyday Living* (1933), *The Lift of a Far View* (1936), *The Local Church* (1937), and *Remaking Life* (1940).

*Bibliography.* O. H. Baker, ed., *Albert W. Beaven: Pastor, Educator, World Christian* (1944).

Winthrop S. Hudson

**Beaver, Robert Pierce** (1906– ). Educator, missionary, and author. Born in Hamilton, Ohio, he was educated chiefly at Oberlin College and Cornell University (Ph.D., 1933). A pastor in Cincinnati (1932–36) and Baltimore (1936–38), he was then a missionary teacher in China (1938–42). Returning to the USA, he was professor of missions at the Theological Seminary of the Evangelical and Reformed Church (1944–48), and director of missions research and the Missionary Research Library in New York City for the National Council of Churches (1948–55). From 1955 to 1971 he was professor of missions at the University of Chicago, and prior to retiring he was director of Overseas Ministries Study Center, N.J. (1972–76). He has published a number of articles and authored many books, including *Ecumenical Beginnings in Protestant World Mission* (1962) and *Native American Christian Community* (1979).

JACK MITCHELL

**Beckmann, Joachim** (1901– ). German theologian. Born in Wanne-Eickel (Ruhr Area), he studied at the universities of Marburg, Tübingen, Münster (Dr. Phil.), and Göttingen. He was pastor of the Innere Mission at Berlin, Wiesbaden, and Soest (1926–33), and then became pastor of the Evangelical parish at Düsseldorf. He was cofounder of the Bekennende Kirche and member of the Reichsbruderrat of the German Evangelical Church. From 1945 he was lecturer (from 1951 professor) on dogmatics and liturgics at the Kirchliche Hochschule at Wuppertal, and from 1958 to 1971 president of the Evangelical Church in the Rheinland. He published numerous pamphlets against the Nazi Weltanschauung and the so-called German-Christians. His publications include *Vom Sakrament bei Calvin* (1925), *Ruf zum Gehorsam* (1941), *Die Kirchliche Ordnung der Taufe* (1950), *Quellen zur Geschichte des Christl. Gottesdienstes* (1956), and *Im Kampf für die Kirche des Evangeliums* (1961).

**Beckwith, Charles Minnigerode** (1849–1931). Protestant Episcopal bishop of Alabama. Born in Prince George County, Va., he studied at the University of Georgia, was master of the Sewanee Grammar School, University of the South (1873–79), and graduated from Berkeley Divinity School, Middletown, Conn., in 1881. Ordained that year, he was rector in Atlanta, Ga. (1881–86), Houston, Tex. (1886–92), and Galveston, Tex. (1892–1902) before consecration as the fourth bishop of Alabama (1902–28). He wrote *The Trinity Course of Church Instruction* (1898), *The Teacher's Companion to the Trinity Course* (1901), and *Rightly Instructed in God's Holy Word* (1902).

**Bedikian, Antriganik Arakel** (1885–1980). Scholar of Armenian language and literature. Born in Constantinople, he graduated from Robert College and the University of Chicago. He served for many years as a minister, notably in the Armenian Evangelical Church of New York, and taught at the University of Chicago and at Columbia University in the department of Indo-Iranian languages. His works include *Sketches of the Village of Bardizag* (1950) and *The Golden Age: An Introduction to Armenian Literature in Perspective* (1963). He was coeditor of the oldest Armenian weekly, *Gotchnag*.

R. MILTON WINTER

**Beets, Henry** (1869–1947). Christian Reformed pastor, writer, and editor. Born near Alkmaar, Netherlands, he came to the United States at an early age and studied at Calvin College and Theological Seminary in Grand Rapids, Mich. He was pastor in Sioux Center, Iowa (1895–99), at LaGrave Avenue Christian Reformed Church, Grand Rapids (1899–1915), and at Burton Heights Christian Reformed Church, Grand Rapids (1915–20), and secretary and director of missions for his denomination (1920–39). He was also stated clerk (1902–42). He served on the joint American and Canadian church committee to revise the metrical version of the psalms (1902–9), was associate editor of *Gereformeerde Amerikaan* (1898–1916), editor-in-chief of the *Banner* (1904–29), and editor and publisher of the *Reformed Review* and *Heidenwerld* (1915–40). A firm Calvinist who adhered strictly to the Canons of Dort and the Westminster Standards, he wrote many books, including *Compendium of the Christian Religion* (1903), *The Christian Reformed Church, Its History, Work and Principles* (1923), *The Reformed Confession Explained* (1929), *Bible History, Book by Book* (1934), *The Man of Sorrows* (1935), and *Toiling and Trusting, for Indians and Chinese, Fifty Years of Christian Reformed Mission Work* (1940).

**Begbie, Harold** (1871–1929). English journalist and author. Born in Farnham, St. Martin, Suffolk, he was educated at Merchant Taylors' School. He began to farm, but then turned to journalism. He wrote children's stories, novels, and biographies. Eventually he focused on movements directed toward religious and social reform. He visited the USA and the USSR during World War I. His works include *Broken Earthware* (1909), *Other Sheep* (1911), *The Life of General William Booth*, 2 vols. (1920), and *Life Changers* (1927).

F. W. DILLISTONE

**Belgium.** A North European country of about 10 million, of whom 91 percent are Roman Catholic. There are about 90,600 Protestants, 60,000 evangelicals, 115,000 Muslims, and 42,000 Jews. Belgium has an area of 11,783 sq. km. (30,518 sq. mi.).

Belgium gained its independence in 1830 from William I of Holland, and was a country in which Roman Catholicism flourished and grew. Most notable in Belgium's modern development was the restoration of religious orders, the virility of parish ministries, and the multiplication of charitable institutions. A Catholic bias remains in such secular organizations as trade unions, hospitals, schools, and universities. More recently, however, the Catholic Church has experienced reverses analogous to those seen in other European countries. Regular attendance at Mass fell from 45 percent in 1964 to 34 percent in 1972. Priestly vocations have dropped from 156 in 1964 to 57 in 1973. Some Belgian theological seminaries have closed.

Fidelity to the Catholic faith also is dependent upon the cultural and linguistic heritage of the region. In 1968 two-thirds of all who attended Mass were found in the Flemish regions. Sixty percent of rural residents attended Mass weekly, and 40 percent of urban residents. By way of contrast, in the Walloon or Francophone region of Belgium, only 25 percent attended Mass each Sunday. This same figure held for Brussels.

Belgian Protestantism can be traced back to the Reformer Guy de Brès, who brought the Reformation message to that country in 1561. However, when Belgium gained its independence in 1830, only a few Protestant churches remained. Although there are now about 90,000 Protestants in Belgium, many of these are foreigners who work in this center of European government and commerce. In fact, approximately 20,000 of the Belgian Protestants are not Belgian but foreign. Most of these are Africans, Germans, and Scandinavians.

The oldest Protestant church is the Union des Eglises Evangélique or Belgische Nationaal Protestantse Kerk. Founded in 1830 it merged with Methodists in 1969 and still dominates the Protestant community. However, in 1849 the British and Foreign Bible Society gave birth to the Société Evangélique des Eglises Chrétiennes Missionaires or the Belgische Christelijke Zendingskerk.

Since 1920 the Gereformeerde Kerken in Holland have had several congregations in Belgium. Additionally, the Methodists have a denominational headquarters in Brussels. The Salvation Army and the Baptists likewise have several centers in Belgium.

One of the more spectacular phenomena in Belgium and many other European countries is the presence of large populations of foreign workers who have come from less privileged countries to gain employment in northern Europe. As early as 1970 there were 40,000 Muslims working in Belgium, mainly from Morocco (25,000), Turkey (10,000), Algeria (2000), and Tunisia (3000). By 1974 there were nearly 100,000 Muslims in Belgium, and they were served by three imams and 20 mosques. In 1985 the number of Muslims had escalated to 110,000, surpassing traditional Protestantism.

Because of its accessibility to Britain and the Atlantic seaports, Belgium has been the scene of much foreign missionary work since the early 19th century. The British and Foreign Bible Society blazed the trail, and others followed. Today there are approximately 225 foreign workers in Belgium. Greater Europe Mission operates a large educational institution in Louvain, and they have 27 foreign workers in Belgium. The Belgian Evangelical Mission has about 103 workers, many of whom are part-time or summer members. Operation Mobilization has 47 workers and administrators at its headquarters in Zaventem. The Assemblies of God have a center.

**Bibliography.** E. de Moreau, *Histoire de l'Eglise en Belgique,* 2 vols. (1949); D. B. Barrett, ed., *World Christian Encyclopedia* (1982).

WAYNE DETZLER

**Belize.** A constitutional monarchy of Central America within the British Commonwealth with an area of 22,963 sq. km. (8866 sq. mi.) and a population of 176,000 (1987 est.).

Early attempts by the Spanish to establish missions among native Mayans were largely unsuccessful. The Anglicans founded the first church in the early 19th century, followed by the Baptists and Methodists. An influx of refugees from Yucatán led to the establishment of the first Roman Catholic church (1848–51). The Catholic Church has grown to include approximately 62 percent of the total population. The Anglican Church claims 12 percent of the population. In recent years, the pentecostals and Adventists have been most successful in gaining new adherents. Belize gained its independence from Britain in 1981.

**Bell, Bernard Iddings** (1886–1958). Episcopalian clergyman, professor, and educator. Born in Dayton, Ohio, he studied at the University of Chicago and Western Theological Seminary. After he was ordained in 1910, he became vicar at St. Christopher's Church, Oak Park, Ill. (1910–13), dean of St. Paul's Cathedral, Fond du Lac, Wis. (1913–18), warden of St. Stephen's College (1919–33), professor of religion at Columbia University (1930–33), preaching canon at St. John's Cathedral, Providence, R.I., and educational consultant to the bishop of Chicago. He was a radical independent in politics and a progressive leader for a religious base for modern education. His books include *The Good News* (1921), *Post-Modernism and Other Essays* (1925), *Common Sense in Education* (1928), *Beyond Agnosticism* (1929), *Unfashionable Convictions* (1931), *The Holy Week* (1933), *Preface to Religion* (1935), *O Men of God*

(1936), *In the City of Confusion* (1938), *The Priestly Way* (1938), *Religion for Living* (1939), *Christian Virtues* (1940), *Understanding Religion* (1941), *Still Shine the Stars* (1941), *The Church in Disrepute* (1943), *The Altar and the World* (1944), and *God Is Not Dead* (1945).

RAYMOND W. ALBRIGHT

**Bell, George Kennedy Allen** (1883–1958). Church of England clergyman and exponent of the ecumenical movement. Born in Hayling Island, England, he was educated at Westminster and Christ Church, Oxford, where he was subsequently tutor and student (1910–14). Ordained to the ministry of the Church of England in 1907, he served three years as assistant curate at Leeds Parish Church. From 1914 to 1924 he was resident chaplain to Randall Thomas Davidson, archbishop of Canterbury, and served as assistant secretary to the Lambeth Conference of 1920. As dean of Canterbury (1924–29) he founded the Friends of Canterbury Cathedral. In 1929 he was consecrated bishop of Chichester. He was very active in his contacts with the Lutheran churches of Germany and Scandinavia. He was first chairman of the central committee of the World Council of Churches. He was also a patron of ecclesiastical arts, especially mural painting and religious drama. His works include *The Life of Randall Davidson* (1935), *The Church and Humanity* (1946), and *Christian Unity: The Anglican Position* (1948).

**Bell, Lemuel Nelson** (1894–1973). Missionary surgeon and editor. Born in Waynesboro, Va., he studied at Washington and Lee University and the Medical College of Virginia. He served 25 years as chief surgeon at Tsing-kiangpu General Hospital, under the Presbyterian Mission in China. Following private practice in Asheville, N.C. (1941–56), he and his son-in-law, evangelist Billy Graham, were prime movers in founding *Christianity Today*, of which he was executive editor (1955–73). He also cofounded and was associate editor of the *Presbyterian Journal* (1941–73), moderator of the Presbyterian Church in the USA (1972/73), and a member of its Board of World Missions (1948–66). A recipient of numerous editorial awards, Bell authored two books, contributed regularly to *Christianity Today*, the *Presbyterian Journal*, and medical journals, and wrote thousands of articles in religious magazines. He spoke Chinese fluently and was consulted by President Richard Nixon before his historic trip to China. He died a few hours after addressing a mission conference.

JACK MITCHELL

**Bell, Richard** (1876–1952). Presbyterian clergyman and Islamics scholar. Born in Cummertrees, Dumfriesshire, he studied at the University of Edinburgh and in Germany. He was assistant professor of Hebrew at Edinburgh University (1901–4), assistant minister at Burntisland (1904–6) and at Greenside, Edinburgh (1906), minister at Wamphray (1907–21), and lecturer in Arabic at Edinburgh University (1921–47). His works include *The Origin of Islam* (1926), *The Qur'an Translated* (1937, 1939), and *Introduction to the Qur'an* (1952).

**Bell, William Melvin** (1860–1933). Bishop in the Church of the United Brethren in Christ. Born in Whitley County, Ind., he studied at Roanoake Classical Seminary, was ordained in 1882, and served several pastorates in Indiana before becoming general secretary of home and foreign missions for his denomination (1893–1905). He was elevated to the episcopate in 1905 and was bishop of the eastern district (1917–29). He wrote *The Love of God* (1902), *The Social Message of Our Lord* (1909), *Torches Aloft* (1913), and *Biography of Bishop Nicholas Castle* (1923).

**Bender, Carl Jacob** (1869–1935). Missionary and evangelist. Born in Germany, he emigrated to America with his family at age 12. He attended German Baptist Seminary in Rochester, N.Y., and, supported by American churches, was appointed to Kamerun (now the nation of Cameroon) in 1899 under the Berlin-based German Baptist Missionary Society. After initial service in Douala, he took charge of the Soppo station on Mount Cameroon in 1909. He established a school and a missionary rest center, and while engaged in evangelistic work, he founded more than two dozen outstations by 1919. During World War I he was the only German missionary allowed to remain in the former German protectorate by virtue of his U.S. citizenship. He left Soppo in 1919 with the work entirely in indigenous hands, and returned in 1929 to supervise reconstruction until his death.

JACK MITCHELL

**Bender, Harold Stauffer** (1897–1962). Mennonite churchman, theologian, historian, and educator. Born in Elkhart, Ind., he earned degrees from Goshen College, Garrett Biblical Institute, Princeton Theological Seminary, Princeton University, and Heidelberg University (D.Theol., 1935). He became dean of Goshen College in 1933, and served as dean of Goshen College Biblical Seminary from 1944 until his death. Within the Mennonite Church he was active in many organizations and committees, most notably as chairman of the Historical and Research Committee and the Peace Problems Committee. He also served as president of the Mennonite World Conference (1952–62). He contributed regularly to scholarly journals and wrote numerous books, including *Two Centuries of American Mennonite*

*Literature* (1929), *Conrad Grebel, First Leader of the Swiss Brethren* (1950), and *Menno Simons (1496–1561)* (1936). His literary endeavors also include the founding and editing of the *Mennonite Quarterly Review* (1927–62), and editing the monumental four-volume *Mennonite Encyclopedia*.

JACK MITCHELL

## Benedict XV—Giacomo della Chiesa

(1854–1922). Pope (1914–22). Born in Genoa, he was a member of the titled aristocracy of feudal Italy. He completed his academic preparation for a church career as a student of the Capranica College, Rome, and as a member of the Pontifical Academy of Noble Ecclesiastics, obtaining the degree of Doctor of Theology in 1882. Ordained a priest in 1878, he quickly rose from private secretary to the papal nunciature in Spain to the Section of Ordinary Ecclesiastical Affairs of the Secretariat of State (1887). Pope Pius X made him archbishop of Bologna (1907) and cardinal in 1914.

After the death of Pius X on August 20, 1914, Cardinal della Chiesa was elected pope on September 3, 1914, and took the name Benedict XV, nearly one month after the outbreak of World War I. Benedict's early appeals for peace were ignored by the belligerents, and the entry of Italy into the war on the side of the entente powers (1915) made it plain that the pope would have to limit his efforts to counteracting the most disastrous effects of the war. The Vatican successfully negotiated the exchange of disabled war prisoners and the repatriation of interned civilians unfit for service in the armed forces, in cooperation with neutral Switzerland and the International Red Cross. Information about missing persons was also collected to reunite scattered families, and the pope initiated and promoted relief organizations in occupied or war-torn countries.

In the fall of 1917 Benedict XV made public a specific plan for a negotiated peace in which he stressed the moral force of right over against the brutal force of arms. The plan recommended the restitution of occupied territories, and suggested that the legitimate aspirations of people be given due weight in view of the difficult problems of countries culturally tied to one country but politically under another, such as Poland, Alsace-Lorraine, and the territory of Trieste. The pope's plan was presented to Emperor Wilhelm II on June 29, 1917, by Msgr. Pacelli, then nuncio in Bavaria and later Pope Pius XII. It was turned down by the powers of the entente. The diplomatic activity of Benedict XV at the war's conclusion aimed at normalizing relations between the secular powers and the Holy See. A modus vivendi was established with the French government. In Germany, Msgr. Pacelli negotiated the preparations for a series of concordats which, however, were not concluded until the pontificate of Pius XI.

Benedict XV promulgated the *Codex Juris Canonici*, the compilation of which had been ordered by Pius X on May 27, 1917, and decreed that the new canon law would take effect on the day of Pentecost, May 19, 1918. A new impulse was given to Scripture studies in the encyclical *Spiritus Paraclitus* (1920).

*Bibliography.* H. le Flock, *La politique de Benoît XV* (1920); F. Vistalli, *Benedetto XV* (1928); M. C. Carlen, *A Guide to the Encyclicals of the Roman Pontiffs from Leo XIII to the Present Day, 1878–1937* (1939); F. Hayward, *Un Pape méconnu: Benoît XV* (1955); W. H. Peters, *The Life of Benedict XV* (1959).

GEORGES A. BARROIS

## Benedictines.

Monastic order founded by Benedict of Nursia, the "Patriarch of Western Monasticism," and organized under his *Rule for Monks*. About 529, Benedict founded the order's mother monastery at Monte Cassino, Italy. The order spread slowly, but by the time of Charlemagne it had permeated Western Christendom.

Benedict's *Rule*, largely based on the rules of John Cassian and Basil of Caesarea, greatly influenced the order but also allowed for diversity among the monasteries. Although it urged monks to renounce self-will so that they might live in obedience to Christ, it was more flexible and lenient than the instructions of many earlier ascetics. The *Rule* tempered synergism and individualism with a recognition of human failure and of the importance of community.

The center of Benedictine life was the Divine Office, which Benedict called the *opus Dei* ("work of God"). The Divine Office consisted of prayers and praises to God at seven intervals during the day. Benedictine monks also worked to support themselves and shared their goods in common. Since they were not under rules of strict poverty, the monks were able to assist the needy, who were to be treated as Christ. Benedictine vows required the monks to reside permanently in the locale of their monastery and to obey their monastery's abbot. Abbots, elected for a lifetime tenure, were given much authority, but were expected to consult the entire community in important matters. Apart from the pope, the order lacked an official leader. The Benedictines did much to preserve learning in the Middle Ages and to set an example for later Western monasticism.

Together with his sister Scholastica, Benedict also founded an order for nuns based on his *Rule*. Throughout the Middle Ages, Benedictine nuns remained enclosed in their convents; in modern times, however, many sisters have taken on the tasks of charity, education, and missions.

ROBERT L. MORRISON

## Benediction.

In most evangelical churches the benediction comes at the close of public worship, to crown it with the blessing of God. The minister pronounces the words while standing with arms uplifted and palms toward the people, as a symbol of mercies coming down. In some places the people also stand, but custom favors having them kneel or bow down, and then remain in silent prayer. Not magically but by faith they receive the blessing God bestows and conveys through his ministering servant. Occasionally, the minister can preach on one of the benedictions, such as the apostolic benediction (2 Cor. 13:14). In keeping with the tone of various services he can use other benedictions, such as the priestly (Num. 6:24–26), the covenant (Heb. 13:20–21), or the peace benediction (derived from Phil. 4:6–7). Custom typically calls for a benediction at the end of public worship.

ANDREW W. BLACKWOOD

**Benin.** See WEST AFRICA.

**Bennett, John Coleman** (1902– ). Theologian, educator, and clergyman. Born in Kingston, Ont., Canada, he graduated from Williams College, Oxford University, and Union Theological Seminary. He taught theology at Union Theological Seminary (1927–29), Auburn Theological Seminary (1930–38), and the Pacific School of Religion (1938–43) before returning to Union. He was professor of Christian theology and ethics (1943–57), professor of applied Christianity (1957–60), professor of social ethics (1960–70), and president of the seminary (1963–70). Subsequently he was visiting professor of Christian ethics at the Pacific School of Religion (1970–75), and from 1975 adjunct professor of theology at Claremont. The author of many books, he was from 1943 an officer and participant in numerous national and international conferences on social and ethical concerns.

JACK MITCHELL

**Benson, Clarence Herbert** (1879–1954). Christian educator, author, and minister. A fourth-generation minister following Moravian missionary grandparents, he studied at the University of Minnesota, Macalester College, and Princeton Seminary. After serving five pastorates in New York and Pennsylvania from 1908 to 1919, he was called to pastor the Union Church in Kobe, Japan. Upon returning to the USA, he was invited to teach at Moody Bible Institute, and in 1924 was made director of the Christian education department. In the following years, he wrote a number of textbooks on Christian education, produced the *All-Bible Graded Series* of Sunday school lessons and cofounded Scripture Press to publish them (1934), helped to found both the Evangelical Teacher Training Association (1931) and the National Sunday School Association, and

served as associate editor of *Moody Monthly* (1926–41).

JACK MITCHELL

**Benson, Louis Fitzgerald** (1855–1930). Presbyterian lawyer, pastor, and editor. Born in Philadelphia, Pa., he studied at the University of Pennsylvania and Princeton Theological Seminary. He practiced law (1877–84) prior to his ordination in 1888. He was pastor of the Church of the Redeemer, Germantown, Pa. (1888–94), after which he became an editor. He was also a member of the committee which prepared the Presbyterian *Book of Common Worship*. His personal library contained 9000 works on hymnology. His writings include *Hymns and Verses* (1897), *The Best Church Hymns* (1898), *Best Hymns—A Handbook* (1899), *Studies of Familiar Hymns* (1903, 1923), *The English Hymn—Its Development and Use in Worship* (1915), *Hymns Original and Translated* (1925), and *The Hymnody of the Christian Church* (1927). He edited the Presbyterian (1895) and Congregational (1896) hymnals and the *Journal of the Presbyterian Historical Society* (1903–11).

RAYMOND W. ALBRIGHT

**Berdiaev (or Berdyaev), Nicolas** (1874–1948). Eastern Orthodox philosopher and author. Born in Kiev, Russia, he studied science at the University of Kiev and philosophy at Heidelberg. He was an author all his life except for a brief period after the Russian revolution, when he lectured on philosophy at Moscow University. Because of his strong spiritual resistance to the new regime, in 1923 he was exiled from the Soviet Union. He spent the rest of his life in Berlin and finally Paris. He organized free courses in philosophy and religion, and from 1925 to 1940 was editor of the Russian magazine, *Put (The Way)*, collaborating with a wide group of Russian scholars and thinkers in the emigration. He was a prolific writer. He began as a Marxist, but soon abandoned this position under the strong influence of Kant and German idealistic philosophy. Later, another German influence was added—the mysticism of Jacob Boehme. Berdiaev was widely read in various fields and usually wrote in response to some external challenge. Polemical dialectics is a distinctive feature of his thought. His main problem was always the problem of man, and his main emphasis on man's freedom. He strongly insisted on the prophetic character of his thinking and did not pretend to be an accurate exponent of any confessional tradition. He was very much concerned with the problem of Russian destiny and insisted on the critical meaning of the present historical age. He wrote in Russian, but most of his books (especially those written abroad) are available in various translations.

**Bibliography.** M. Spinka, *Nicolas Berdyaev: Captive of Freedom* (1950); O. F. Clarke, *Introduction to Berdyaev* (1950); G. Seaver, *Nicolas Berdyaev: An Introduction to His Thought* (1950).

GEORGES FLOROVSKY

## Bergendoff, Conrad John Immanuel

(1895– ). Lutheran educator and churchman. Born in Shickley, Nebr., he was educated at Augustana College, Rock Island, Ill., the University of Pennsylvania, Columbia University, and the universities of Chicago (Ph.D., 1928), Uppsala, and Berlin. After pastoring the Salem Lutheran Church of Chicago (1921–31), he became professor of systematic theology and dean of the theological seminary at Augustana College (1931–35). From 1935 to 1962 he was president both of Augustana College and of the Augustana Swedish Institute (1940–67). Bergendoff served on several commissions of the World Council of Churches and the Lutheran World Federation. His books include *Olavus Petri and the Ecclesiastical Transformation in Sweden* (1928), *I Believe in the Church* (1937), *Christ as Authority* (1947), and *The Church of the Lutheran Reformation* (1967). He edited the *Augustana Quarterly* (1929–48) and the *Lutheran Quarterly* (1949–52).

JACK MITCHELL

## Berger, Daniel

(1832–1920). United Brethren in Christ pastor and editor. Born near Reading, Pa., he taught school for a time before graduating from Ohio State University in 1856. For six years he was a pastor before becoming editor in the publishing house of the United Brethren in Christ in Dayton, Ohio (1869–93). His *History of the United Brethren in Christ* (1897) was for a generation the definitive work in its field.

## Berggrav, Eivind

(1884–1959). Lutheran clergyman and editor. Born in Stavanger, Norway, he studied at the universities of Oslo, Copenhagen, and Marburg, and was a graduate student at Oxford, Cambridge, and Oslo. He was headmaster of a *Volksschule* (1909–19), minister at Hurdal (1919–25), chaplain at the Oslo prison (1925–28), bishop of northern Norway (1929–37), and bishop of Oslo and primate of the Church of Norway (1937–50). He was imprisoned from 1942 to 1945. He was president of the United Bible Societies and president of the World Council of Churches. His major interests were in ecumenical movements and the psychology of religion. He led the resistance against Nazi occupation of Norway, and promoted spiritual freedom in the Church of Norway. His works include *The Prisoner's Soul and Our Own* (1932), *The Land of Suspense* (1943), and *Man and State* (1951). He also edited the monthly journal *Kirke und Kultur*.

**Bibliography.** O. Godal, *Eivind Berggrav, Leader of the Christian Resistance* (1949); S. Stolpe, *Eivind Berggrav, Norwegens Bischof* (1951).

RAYMOND W. ALBRIGHT

## Bergson, Henri Louis

(1859–1941). French philosopher. Born of Jewish parents, he became a "Catholic of intent" although never baptized. At the École Normale Superieure, his alma mater, and at the Collège de France he became famous as a brilliant lecturer (1900–1914) and exerted powerful influence on the artists, writers, and philosophers of his time. His books were scientific and philosophic studies of successive problems: psychology, biological evolution, and sociology of religion. He opposed the positivism of his day, declaring that scientific knowledge is the refinement of a broader intuitive faculty, without whose imaginative flexibility it is incapable of learning the truth about spirit, change, and God. Bergson's interest in psychology and religious mysticism led to friendship with William James and to the presidency of the Society for Psychical Research (1913). He lectured in Great Britain and America, starting a series of Gifford Lectures which were interrupted by World War I. His most influential book, *Creative Evolution* (1907), appeared at the time of the Roman Catholic "modernist" controversy, with which many of his friends and students were associated. His major books were placed on the index of forbidden books in 1914. Honored by his admission to the French Academy in 1914, he won the Nobel Prize for literature in 1927. In his last book, *The Two Sources of Morality and Religion* (1932), Bergson maintained that as man is the freest, most creative product in nature, so the Christian saint is the highest development within humanity.

GEORGE F. PARKER

## Berkhof, Louis

(1873–1957). Christian Reformed theologian. Born in Emmen, the Netherlands, he studied at Calvin College and Seminary, Princeton Theological Seminary, and the Divinity School of the University of Chicago. He was pastor at Allendale, Mich. (1900–1902) and Oakdale Park Church, Grand Rapids, Mich. (1904–6). He was professor of exegetical theology (1906–14), NT exegesis (1914–26), and dogmatic theology (1926–44) and president (1931–44) of Calvin Seminary, Grand Rapids, Mich. His writings include *Het Christelijk Onderwijs en Onze Kerkelijke Toekomst* (1905), *Beknopte Bijbelsche Hermeneutiek* (1911), *Christendom en Leven* (1912), *The Church and Social Problems* (1913), *Life under the Law in a Pure Theocracy* (1914), *Biblical Archaeology* (1915; 3d ed., 1928), *NT Introduction* (1915), *Paul the Missionary* (1915), *The Christian Laborer in the Industrial Struggle* (1916), *Subjects and Outlines* (1918), *Pre-millennialisme* (1918), *De Drie Punten in Alle Deelen Gere-*

*formeerd* (1925), *The Assurance of Faith* (1928; 2d ed., 1939), *Reformed Dogmatics*, 4 vols. (1932–37; 3d ed. of Dogmatics proper, 2 vols., 1946), *Manual of Reformed Doctrine* (1933), *Vicarious Atonement Through Christ* (1936), *Summary of Christian Doctrine* (1938), *Principles of Biblical Interpretation* (1950), *The Kingdom of God* (1951), *Aspects of Liberalism* (1951), and *The Second Coming of Christ* (1953).

**Berkouwer, Gerrit Cornelis** (1903– ). Dutch theologian. He studied at the Christian Gymnasium and at the Free University of Amsterdam, obtaining a doctorate there in 1932. As pastor in the Gereformeerde Kerken (1927–45), he served in Oudehorne and Amsterdam. Also lecturer in modern theology at the Free University of Amsterdam (1940–45), he became professor of systematic theology there in 1945 and continued until his retirement in 1973. He was an observer at Vatican Council II (1962) and a member of the Royal Academy of the Sciences. His *Studies in Dogmatics* (14 vols., 1952–76) have earned high praise. "The importance of Berkouwer lies in his refusal to accept simplistic either-or's . . . in which the fulness of truth is torn apart" (*A Half Century of Theology*, 208) and his "conviction that theology, if it is to be meaningful . . . had to be a theology directed to the pulpit" (L. B. Smedes). Other significant works include *The Triumph of Grace in the Theology of Karl Barth* (1956), *The Second Vatican Council and the New Catholicism* (1965), and *A Half Century of Theology* (1977).

**Bernard, John Henry** (1860–1927). Irish clergyman and educator. Born in India, he was a brilliant student at Trinity College, Dublin, where he became fellow and tutor in 1884 and professor in 1906. In 1911 he became bishop of Ossory, Ferns, and Leighlin, and in 1915 archbishop of Dublin, a position he relinquished in 1919 to become provost of Trinity College, where he played a key role following the Treaty of 1922. His statesmanship had already been in evidence after the Easter Rising of 1916 when he spoke for the Southern Unionists in an unsuccessful attempt to frame a new constitution. Always eager to establish links with the Church of England, he preached often at Westminster Abbey and was several times select preacher at Oxford and Cambridge. He was president of the Royal Irish Academy (1916–21). He received honorary doctorates from Oxford, Durham, and Aberdeen. His writings include *The Pastoral Epistles of St. Paul* (1899), *The Second Epistle to the Corinthians* (1903), *The Prayer of the Kingdom* (1904), *The Psalter in Latin and English* (1911), *In War Time* (1917), and *Critical and Exegetical Commentary on the Gospel According to St. John*, 2 vols. (1929). He published the first English translation of Kant's *Critique of Judgment* (1892).

TIM LENTON

**Bertholet, Alfred** (1868–1951). Swiss OT scholar. Born in Basel, he was educated at the universities of Basel, Strasbourg, and Berlin, and was Protestant pastor at the Franco-German church at Leghorn (1892/93). He was privatdocent for OT exegesis at the University of Basel (1896–99), associate professor (1899), and professor (1905–13). He was then professor of OT at Tübingen (1913/14), Göttingen (1914–28), and Berlin (1928–43). He was general secretary of the Second International Congress for the History of Religion at Basel in 1904. His writings include *Der Verfassungsgesetzentwurf des Hesekiel in seiner religionsgeschichtlichen Bedeutung* (1896), *Die Stellung der Israeliten und der Juden zu den Fremden* (1896), *Zu Jesaja 53* (1899), *Buddhismus und Christentum* (1902), *Die Gefilde der Seligen* (1903), *Kulturgeschichte Israels* (1919), *Kultur und Religion* (1924), and *Die Religion des Alten Testaments* (1932). He also wrote commentaries on Leviticus, Deuteronomy, Ruth, Ezra, Nehemiah, and Ezekiel in K. Marti's *Kurzer Handkommentar zum Alten Testament* (5 vols., 1897–1902), and the section on the Apocrypha and Pseudepigrapha in K. Budde's *Geschichte der althebräischen Literatur* (1906).

**Bertocci, Peter Anthony** (1910– ). Philosopher and educator. Born in Elena, Italy, he was brought to the USA when less than a year old. He studied at Boston, Harvard, and Cambridge universities, and taught philosophy and psychology (1935–44) at Bates College, Lewiston, Maine, before becoming professor of philosophy at Boston University (1944–75). A specialist in the philosophy of religion, metaphysics, and psychology, his works include *Empirical Argument for God in Late British Thought* (1938), *Introduction to the Philosophy of Religion* (1951), *Sex, Love, and the Reason* (1967), *Is God for Real?* (1971), and *The Goodness of God* (1981). Following retirement, he taught at Boston University, contributed to *An Encyclopedia of Religion* (1976), and continued work on *The Person and His Primary Emotions*.

JACK MITCHELL

**Bethune-Baker, James Franklin** (1861–1951). Anglican clergyman and professor. Born in Birmingham, England, he studied at Pembroke College, Cambridge. Ordained in 1888, he was dean of Pembroke College, Cambridge (1889–1906), and professor of divinity, Cambridge University (1911–35). His writings include *The Influence of Christianity on War* (1888), *The Sternness of Christ's Teaching* (1889), *The Meaning of Homoousious in the Constantinopolitan Creed* (1901), *Christian Doctrines and Their Ethical Significance* (1905), *An Introduction to the Early History of Christian Doctrine* (1908), *The Faith of the Apostles' Creed* (1918), *The Way of Modernism*

(1927), *Early Traditions about Jesus* (1929), and *The New View of Christianity* (1930).

F. W. DILLISTONE

**Betts, George Herbert** (1868–1934). Methodist educator. Born in Clarksville, Iowa, he was educated at Cornell, Iowa, Chicago, and Columbia (Ph.D., 1909). He taught psychology at Cornell, Iowa (1901–18), and was professor of religious education at Boston University (1918/19), the University of California (1921–22), and Northwestern University (1919–21; 1922–26). He was also professor of education and director of research at Northwestern University (1926–34). His writings include *The Mind and Its Education* (1906), *Function and Distribution of Mental Imagery* (1909), *Social Principles of Education* (1912), *How to Teach Religion* (1919), *The New Program of Religious Education* (1921), *The Curriculum of Religious Education* (1921), *The Beliefs of 700 Ministers* (1929), and *Character-Outcome of Present Day Religion* (1931). He coauthored *Laboratory Studies in Educational Psychology* (1924) with E. M. Turner and *Method in Teaching Religion* (1925) with M. O. Hawthorne.

RAYMOND W. ALBRIGHT

**Bewer, Julius August** (1877–1953). Congregational theologian. Born in Ratingen, Germany, he studied at Union Seminary, Columbia University (Ph.D., 1900), and the universities of Basel, Halle, and Berlin. He was professor of OT at Oberlin Theological Seminary (1902–4) and Union Theological Seminary (1904–45), lecturer in biblical literature, Teachers College (1912–28), and a member of the faculty of philosophy, Columbia University (1913–45). He was also a member of the revision committee of the American Standard Version (1937–53). In theology he was a liberal evangelical of the critical school in biblical interpretation. He was the author of a critical and exegetical commentary on Obadiah and Joel (1911), *Jonah* (1912), *Der Text des Buches Ezra* (1921), *The Literature of the OT* (1922), *Ezechiel* (in R. Kittel, *Biblia Hebraica*) (1932), *The Book of the Twelve Prophets* I, II (1949), *Isaiah* I, II (1950), and *Jeremiah* I, II (1951/52).

**Bhutan.** Himalayan kingdom of 46,600 sq. km. (18,147 sq. mi.) and a population estimated at more than one million. Most are either Buddhists or Hindus, with a Muslim minority. The country has three main languages and about 20 dialects. In the northwest, people of Tibetan ancestry speak the related Dzongkha language. In the northeast, descendants of original inhabitants speak Shashap. In the south, a large, mainly Hindu Nepali, population speak Nepali. Only those who entered before 1959 qualify for Bhutanese citizenship.

Since 1907 the country has been ruled by a hereditary monarchy. Earlier there was both a temporal and a spiritual ruler. The office of spiritual ruler, who was identified as a reincarnation of the Buddha, survived until 1950.

Buddhism first reached Bhutan in the 7th century. The official state religion is the Drukpa Kargyupa sect of Tantric Buddhism; Kargyupa is a sect founded in Tibet in the 11th century, and Drukpa is a variation of it founded in the 13th century. These sects include elements from the pre-Buddhist Shamanist Bon religion. Bon involves worship of natural objects, good and evil spirits, magic, and divination.

Drukpa is a form of Tantric Mahayana Buddhism plus some contributions from the Bon religion. Worship is given to the Buddha; Guru Padmasambhava; Bodhisattvas; other gods, goddesses, and demons; and female consorts of gods. Monks engage in meditation, tantric yoga, regular rituals, the use of *mantras* (formulae uttered in order to deal with evil spirits and diseases or to obtain other desired results), divination, astrology (for auspicious times such as the coronation of a king), and the development of occult powers. They have a rule of celibacy. The scriptures of Tibetan Buddhism (the *Tanjur* and the *Kanjur*) are studied, as well as some other texts. *Karma* and rebirth, with the ultimate aim of attaining *nirvana*, are fundamental doctrines.

Religious art, which has a distinct Bhutanese style, includes representations of Padmasambhava and other deities, elaborate *mandalas*, which are believed to bless any who look at or pass under them, and pictures of the Buddhist cycle of existence. Ritual dances are performed at all religious festivals. Many of them represent, and are intended to effect, the destruction of evil spirits, establishment of the Buddhist religion, and peace. Lamas guide the religious life of the people. Every Buddhist home performs daily worship. Each valley has its guardian deity.

At least 70 percent of the Bhutanese are Buddhist, about 25 percent are Hindu, and 5 percent are Muslim. There are fewer than 1000 Christians, and most of them are Indian nationals working in Bhutan. Christian evangelism is strictly forbidden.

***Bibliography.*** L. A. Waddell, *The Buddhism of Tibet or Lamaism* (1895); N. Singh, *Bhutan: A Kingdom in the Himalayas* (1978); *Bhutan: Himalayan Kingdom* (Royal Government of the Kingdom of Bhutan) (1979); M. Aris, *Bhutan, the Early History of a Himalayan Kingdom* (1979); B. J. Hasrat, *History of Bhutan* (1980).

ANTHONY P. STONE

**Bible Belt.** An area, reputed to be devoutly religious, in the southern USA. The Bible Belt is found on either side of a line extending from Greenville, S.C., through Atlanta, Ga., Birmingham, Ala., and Jackson, Miss., and westward to Dallas, Tex. This predominantly rural area is traditionally considered the center of strongly conservative, often anti-intellectual, religious belief in America. The religious fervor among the common people in this region had its origin in revivals of religion during and after the Civil War.

R. Milton Winter

## Bible in Christian Education.

Before Christ the OT was used to teach truth and duty, and in apostolic days the NT began to be added as writings were disseminated. In medieval times Bible teaching went into eclipse, but such pre-Reformation sects and mystical groups as the followers of John Wycliffe, John Hus, and Peter Waldo recovered the Bible. Through preaching and teaching they insisted on lay knowledge of Scripture. The Reformation restored the Bible to the laity through translations into the vernacular and constant biblical preaching and teaching. The great catechisms (e.g., Lutheran, Heidelberg, and Westminster) formulated the faith for laypersons and supported it with biblical references. In the state schools of Europe (except in France and Russia, since their revolutions) the Bible became the chief text in religion courses. The publicly supported schools of England used an "agreed syllabus," prepared by the various Protestant bodies and containing basic materials from the Bible. In the American colonies the first educational materials were the *Horn Book* and the *New England Primer,* both full of Bible content. Later, during the rise of the Sunday school movement, the Bible was the fountain of all curricula. Its preeminence continued until changes caused by the new interpretations, the use of extrabiblical materials, and pupil-centered educational philosophy.

After 1900 liberalizing forces shifted emphasis from objective content to personal and social experience, and the struggle to mediate between the two continues. Four positions regarding the study of the Bible seem to obtain: the conservative, the liberal, the neo-orthodox, and the neoliberal. Under the World Council and the National Council a more ecumenical approach was attempted, with varying degrees of success. Curricula devoted to a study of the Bible, but assuming and drawing on historical and literary studies, came to be regarded as ideal since it made of the Bible less a static volume of proof texts and more a record of God's redemptive acts in history, centering in the person and work of Christ. Carrying out that ideal in practice, however, has often added to strife among the four positions. The Bible remains for Christian education, however, the source of all knowledge of God's unique work for the salvation of humankind, and the guidebook for Christian faith and practice.

E. G. Homrighausen

## Bible Societies.

Organizations whose basic purpose is to promote the translation of the Bible into all spoken languages, and then to publish and distribute these as widely as possible at a price ordinary readers can afford. The earliest body bearing the name "Bible Society" was founded in 1710 in Halle, Germany, 100 miles southwest of Berlin, by Baron Karl Hildebrand von Canstein who printed Bibles and offered them to the poor at cost. However, the Bible Society movement is normally traced to the founding of the British and Foreign Bible Society (BFBS) in 1804 under the stimulus of Thomas Charles, a Welsh minister with the stated aim "to encourage a wider circulation of the Holy Scriptures without note or comment." From its inception BFBS supplied Scriptures at subsidized prices. And, as well as providing Bibles and Testaments in English and Welsh, it set out to publish Scriptures in foreign languages for missionary use.

Small local Bible societies quickly sprang up throughout the British Isles with the aim of supporting BFBS as well as distributing Scriptures cheaply in their own areas. Some, however, like the Edinburgh Bible Society (founded 1809) and the Glasgow Bible Society (founded 1812)—which joined forces in 1861 to form the National Bible Society of Scotland (NBSS)—directly supported the translation and distribution of the Scriptures on mission fields as well as contributing to the work of BFBS.

With financial help and through its agents BFBS inspired Christians in other countries to found national Bible societies in Germany (1804), Ireland (1806), Finland (1812), Holland (1814), Russia (1814), Denmark (1814), Sweden (1815), Iceland (1815), Norway (1816), and the USA (1816). In German-speaking Europe regional Bible societies were founded in Württemberg (1812), Zurich and Basel (1812), and Prussia (1814). By 1820 "Auxiliaries" of BFBS had been formed by local initiative in Canada, India, Australia, and South Africa.

Throughout the 19th and early 20th centuries the bulk of Bible production and distribution worldwide was carried out by BFBS and the American Bible Society (ABS). Scotland's NBSS and the Netherlands Bible Society (NBS) also worked overseas, but on a much more limited scale. Together these four societies provided a vital back-up service to the expanding Protestant missionary movement.

In some cases more than one Bible society was at work in the same country, and in 1910 BFBS and ABS agreed to adopt a mutual consultation procedure. But a proposal by ABS in 1919 to form a world federation of national Bible societies was resisted by BFBS on the grounds that it considered itself already to be "a World Society." However, in 1932 a series of conferences convened in London by ABS, BFBS, and NBSS resulted in integration by the two large societies of work in specific countries. The work was carried on under one or the other society and in some cases by joint supervision. By 1946 Bible work in most of South America, in the Near East from Bulgaria and Greece to Iraq, and in the Sudan had been integrated. NBSS also cooperated with BFBS and ABS in China and Japan, while in Singapore it integrated its work with BFBS. In Indonesia the work of BFBS and NBSS was united with that of NBS under Dutch supervision.

The advisory councils established by BFBS and ABS for joint agencies developed in time into new national Bible societies. The China Bible House (or Society) was founded in 1937, the Japan Bible Society in 1939, and the Bible Society of Brazil in 1948. In 1940 the Korean Bible Society was formed to continue the work of BFBS there. In 1944 the auxiliaries of BFBS in India were combined to form the Bible Society of India and Ceylon (later to become four Bible societies—of India, Ceylon, Pakistan, and Bangladesh).

In 1932 ABS and BFBS agreed in principle to the "ultimate creation of a world federation of Bible Societies" and in 1939 a conference of six Bible societies in Woudschoten, Holland, resolved to form a "Council of Bible Societies." The intervention of World War II, however, meant that it was not until 1946 that this vision became a reality. In that year the United Bible Societies (UBS) was formed at Elfinsward, England, as a world fellowship of national Bible societies by delegates from 13 countries (Czechoslovakia, Denmark, Finland, France, Germany, Great Britain, Netherlands, Norway, Poland, Scotland, Sweden, Switzerland, and the USA) who were "moved by the need of the world for the Word of God and by the deep Christian fellowship of those who work together for its spread." By 1950 there were 24 member societies, and that number grew steadily as responsibility for Bible work in the newly independent countries passed from expatriots to nationals.

By its 40th anniversary in 1986 UBS was comprised of 70 member societies and 31 Bible society offices. Its global program of translation, production, and distribution—sustained by a budget of $30 million—had extended into 180 countries and territories. UBS consultants were assisting local translation teams in more than 550 languages, and annual distribution exceeded 12 million Bibles, 12 million Testaments, and hundreds of millions of Scripture portions and selections. Other significant developments of these four decades include simplified new reader Scriptures for use in literacy programs, global coordination of Scripture production, growing cooperation with the Roman Catholic and Orthodox Churches, and research into the use of the non-print media and of nondoctrinal helps for readers.

*Bibliography.* E. A. Nida, ed., *The Book of a Thousand Tongues* (1972); United Bible Societies, *The UBS at 40* (1986).

FERGUS MACDONALD

## Bible Text (OT).

At the end of the 19th century virtually the only witnesses available for the text of the Hebrew Bible were medieval manuscripts. All printed editions were derived from late examples of these. These manuscripts were based on the work of the scholars of Tiberias known as Masoretes (from Masorah, "tradition"—the term "Masoretic Text"). There is remarkably little variation among Masoretic MSS, in sharp contrast to the situation in the Greek NT.

Two new groups of earlier (although fragmentary) witnesses have subsequently become available. Vast numbers of fragments of biblical manuscripts have come from the Geniza, or store room, of the Old Synagogue in Cairo, Egypt, the earliest dating from the 7th or 8th century. These reached Western libraries around the turn of the 20th century and even now have only partly been exploited. Fragments of biblical MSS have come from Qumran (the "Dead Sea Scrolls") and elsewhere in the Judean desert, dating from as early as the 3d century B.C. to the 2d century A.D. Although the first discovery of texts from Qumran was made in 1947, several small but important biblical fragments still await publication.

*The Hebrew Text.* These two groups of finds throw new light on two important stages in the history of the transmission of the Hebrew text. Through the Cairo Geniza fragments scholars have learned much about the way in which the original text, comprised only of consonants, came to have vowel signs added. Three primary systems of marking these vowel signs are now known: the Palestinian, the Babylonian, and the Tiberian. The first is known only from a limited number of MSS; the second (where all vowels are written supralineally) was widely current in Babylonia and the Yemen; the third became the norm and is found in printed Hebrew Bibles today. The consonantal text of the Geniza fragments, like that of later medieval MSS, is very stable.

Some indication of how this fixed consonantal text came into being is now provided by the second group of finds, those from the Judean desert. The latest of these texts (2d cent. A.D.) have a consonantal text almost identical with that found in MSS written a thousand or more years later (and thus with the text of modern printed editions). If one turns to the earlier fragments, however, some have a text close to the later standard text, while others show remarkable variations, some of which were the basis for the Greek translation known as the Septuagint (3d–2d cents. B.C.).

Since the 19th century scholars had deduced that in some books the LXX must have been translated from a Hebrew text which at times differed considerably from the one with which we are familiar. The Qumran finds have now provided evidence (often very fragmentary) of such variant Hebrew texts. A particularly dramatic case is provided in Jeremiah, where the original form of the LXX was translated from a Hebrew edition of the book which was both shorter and arranged quite differently from the form familiar today. Fragments of a Hebrew text similar to the one which must lie behind the LXX have now been identified from Cave 4 at Qumran.

Thanks to the new evidence now available from the Dead Sea manuscripts it is clear that in the course of the 1st century A.D., perhaps with the emergence of rabbinic Judaism after the destruction of the second temple in A.D. 70, a conscious effort was made by religious authorities to standardize the text of the Hebrew Bible. How one particular text type came to be chosen is not clear, but the choices made by scribes and scholars in the 1st century A.D. are hardly likely always to be the ones which modern scholars would make, hence the importance of textual scholarship in biblical studies today. This standardized consonantal text must have emerged in about A.D. 100, and apart from a few minor details it was probably very close to the consonantal text of modern printed editions. Hebrew texts very similar to this standardized text also underlie the other ancient versions of the Hebrew Bible in Aramaic (the Targums), Syriac (the Peshitta), and Latin (Jerome's Vulgate). All of these versions, however, occasionally imply a different reading (or vocalization) from the tradition which eventually was fixed by the Masoretes. Early revisions of the LXX (of which fragments have also been found in the Judean desert) provide further witness to the process of standardizing the Hebrew text in the 1st century A.D.

The biblical texts from Qumran are important since they take scholars directly back to a period immediately prior to the standardization of the text, offering tantalizing glimpses of the variety of text forms which were circulating from the 3d century B.C. to the 1st century A.D. They corroborate the indirect evidence already provided by some books of the LXX.

For the period even earlier, between the earliest Qumran fragments and the originals of the various OT books, no direct evidence is available. During this long period two significant things are known to have happened. First, at the time of the return from the exile the Paleo-Hebrew script was replaced by the Aramaic script (the ancestor of the "square Hebrew" script of today). At Qumran a few MSS were still written in the old script, but its use was confined to the Pentateuch and Job (the latter evidently because Job was identified as Jobab). Only in the Samaritan community has the Paleo-Hebrew script been preserved to this

day. Second, around the time of the exile spelling conventions were changing, so in the process of transition some ambiguities in the older system would have led to the possibility of misinterpretation, especially in archaic poetic texts (e.g., as in the suffixes denoting his and hers).

***Important Manuscripts and Editions.*** Among the biblical texts, all fragmentary, from Qumran and the Judean desert the most important are two scrolls of Isaiah, of which the more extensive is of considerable textual and linguistic interest (Qumran, Cave 1); a scroll containing Psalms, but not in the traditional order and with some non-biblical psalms included (Qumran, Cave 11); small fragments of Exodus, Samuel, and Jeremiah with a variant text that has affinities to the Hebrew text presupposed by the LXX of these books (Qumran, Cave 4); and a scroll with the Minor Prophets, an early witness to the standardized consonantal text (Murabba'at, Judean Desert). Prior to the Qumran finds the earliest Hebrew biblical fragment was the Nash papyrus, dating to the 2d to 1st century B.C., containing the Decalogue.

Of the Cairo Geniza fragments the most important are those with non-Tiberian vocalization (*see* DEAD SEA SCROLLS).

The oldest complete Hebrew Bible is the Leningrad Codex, dated A.D. 1008–9; other important early medieval MSS are the Cairo Codex, dated A.D. 895 (historical and prophetic books), and the Aleppo Codex, about A.D. 930 (parts of a complete Hebrew Bible). Some 6000 medieval Hebrew MSS survive. The oldest Samaritan MSS (Pentateuch only) date from the 10th or 11th century (fragments) and the 12th century onwards (complete).

The earliest printed edition of part of the Hebrew Bible was a Psalter (1477). Until 1937 practically all printed editions of the Hebrew Bible went back directly or indirectly to the Second Rabbinic Bible, published by David Bomberg in Venice in 1524/25. In 1937 the third edition of R. Kittel's *Biblia Hebraica* adopted the text of a single MS, the Leningrad Codex, and this practice is continued in its successor, the *Biblia Hebraica Stuttgartensis* (1967–77). Other modern editions based on single MSS include the British and Foreign Bible Society edition (ed. N. H. Snaith, 1958), using a MS of 1482, and the Hebrew University edition (Jerusalem, in progress), using the Aleppo Codex.

The current chapter divisions were introduced into the Hebrew Bible from the Vulgate in 1518, while the verse divisions are the work of the Masoretes. The oldest form of division, already found in some Qumran MSS, is into sections (*parashoth*). The codex or book form was introduced for the Greek NT in the 2d or 3d century and was only much later used for the Hebrew Bible; thus all the Qumran fragments belong to scrolls, while the Cairo Geniza fragments and the medieval MSS may be either in scroll or in book form (those for liturgical use are scrolls).

*See also* DEAD SEA SCROLLS.

**Bibliography.** B. J. Roberts, *The OT Text and Versions* (1951); P. Kahle, *The Cairo Geniza* (2d ed., 1959); J. D. Purvis, *The Samaritan Pentateuch and the Origin of the Samaritan Sect* (1968); S. Talmon, "The OT Text," in P. R. Ackroyd and C. F. Evans, eds., *The Cambridge History of the Bible*, vol. 1, *From the Beginnings to Jerome* (1970), reprinted in F. M. Cross and S. Talmon, *Qumran and the History of the Biblical Text* (1975); R. W. Klein, *Textual Criticism of the OT* (1974); D. Barthelemy, *The Interpreter's Dictionary of the Bible, Supplementary Volume* (1976), pp. 878–84; OBO 21 (1978); I. Yeivin, *Introduction to the Tiberian Masorah* (1980); E. Würthwein, *The Text of the OT* (4th ed., 1980); G. Vermes, *The Dead Sea Scrolls: Qumran in Perspective* (2d ed., 1982).

SEBASTIAN P. BROCK

# Bible Text (NT).

**Sources.** The books in the NT were originally written in Greek, and, although the originals are not extant, many MSS descended from the autographs have survived and are, in general, available in various collections throughout the world. The largest numbers of MSS are housed in libraries in Athens, Paris, Rome, London, and Leningrad and in monasteries on Mount Sinai and Mount Athos. More than 5000 MSS containing all or part of the NT in Greek are now cataloged, and most have been microfilmed. The films are on deposit at the Institut für neutestamentliche Textforschung in Münster, Westphalia. About 60 MSS contain the whole NT; most contain only one section of the canon. About 2000 are Gospel MSS, and about 220 contain only the Book of Revelation. Most of these are complete, but many early MSS are fragmentary, containing in some cases only a few verses.

The earliest MS is dated about A.D. 125 and is the fragment known in the official Gregory-von Dobschütz-Aland list as $\mathfrak{P}^{52}$. The bulk of surviving MSS are dated in the 11th to 15th centuries. Catalogs usually separate the MSS by function (continuous text MSS are separated from lectionaries); by writing material (continuous text MSS are divided into those written on papyrus and those written on parchment or paper); and by script (the parchment MSS are separated into uncials, written in capital letters throughout, and minuscules, written in a cursive hand). Most uncials date from before the 9th century; most minuscules date from the 10th century to and even beyond the invention of printing.

In addition to the Greek MSS sources used in the recovery of the original text include the early versions and patristic citations. The NT was translated at an early date into Western languages such as Latin and Eastern languages such as Coptic, Syriac, and Armenian. These and other versions (e.g., Ethiopic, Georgian, and Gothic) can often aid an investigation into the identification and understanding of the underlying Greek text as well as being of significance for the language,

culture, and history of the communities which used them. In some cases the number of extant MSS is very high: the Latin Vulgate survives in over 10,000 MSS; there are also large numbers of Coptic MSS. Quotations of the NT in the writings of the early church fathers can also be instructive for determining the nature of the biblical text known to them. Both these additional sources have to be handled with care.

**Textual Criticism.** Inevitably with any long document copied by hand, accidental errors arise. In the case of the NT MSS, no two of which agree in all particulars, deliberate alterations can also be detected: some scribes made grammatical or linguistic changes, others theological or exegetical alterations. It has been estimated that most deliberate changes can be dated as originating before A.D. 200: scribes in orthodox circles would have been disinclined to tamper with the text once it had achieved canonical status. The bulk of medieval Greek MSS is fairly uniform, and in general often conforms to the text of the Byzantine lectionaries, but there are important exceptions. Many of the earlier MSS betray significant variation when compared not only with these medieval MSS but with each other.

Each monastery, church, and individual would have considered its own MS of the Scriptures as the one and only form of Holy Writ. Only when two or more copies were compared and differences between them noted was it necessary to reach a decision as to which had the more reliable text, and which had a secondary form of it. Such comparative study was rare in early centuries, although both Jerome and Origen were alert to variants in MSS. Early printed editions of the Greek NT text tended to reproduce a text approximating the majority text of the medieval MSS (the so-called Textus Receptus). It was only when increasing numbers of newly discovered MSS were systematically collected, collated, and compared with one another that a scientific approach to the editing of a critical text became necessary. From the middle of the 19th century on various critical editions appeared, many of which print different forms of the text, reflecting the way in which their editors have reacted to variants in the MSS. A list of 19th- and 20th-century editions is to be found in Amphoux's revision of Vaganay's *Initiation* (see bibliography below).

Most modern editions are eclectic texts and do not represent throughout the readings in one particular MS or one group of MSS. They are texts created by the editors from the fund of variant readings available to them. Nestle-Aland's *Novum Testamentum Graece* (26th ed.) and the United Bible Society's Greek NT (3d ed.) use the same editor-prepared text. Scholarly debate about the principles adopted by editors and their choice of readings may be seen in reviews of these editions. There is thus no consensus as to which edition, if any, is superior to others on the market. A scientifically established critical edition that enables its readers to consult the text in conjunction with the marginal apparatus of variants is required before readers can study the NT text with a fair degree of confidence.

The critical apparatuses in printed editions currently available contain a small fraction of the many thousand Greek and versional MSS listed in catalogs. Attempts are being made to increase the number of manuscripts accessible to the scholarly world for evaluation. Samples are being taken from the microfilmed medieval MSS at Münster to simplify the task of identifying and reading in full the MSS deemed significant. Others are attempting to group or classify types of MSS. As more of this information becomes available, the apparatus notes of editions in print will need to be updated; eventually the principles on which the printed text itself is established will be improved.

***Bibliography.*** *Textual Criticism.* B. M. Metzger, *The Text of the NT: Its Transmission, Corruption, and Restoration* (1968); K. Aland, and B. Aland, *Der Text des Neuen Testaments: Einführung in die Wissenschaftlichen Ausgaben und in Theorie wie Praxis der modernen Textkritik* (1982); L. Vaganay, *Initiation à la Critique Textuelle du Nouveau Testament* (2d ed., 1986).

*Greek Manuscripts.* K. Aland, ed., *Kurzgefasste Liste der griechischen Handschriften des Neuen Testaments* (1963), with supplements and corrections in "Die griechischen Handschriften des Neuen Testaments. Ergänzungen zur 'Kurzgefassten Liste'" in K. Aland, ed., *Materialen zur neutestamentlichen Handschriftenkunde* (1969); see also in *Bericht der Stiftung zur Forderung der Neutestamentlichen Textforschung* (1972, 1974, 1977); J. Finegan, *Encountering NT Manuscripts: A Working Introduction to Textual Criticism* (1974).

*Versions.* B. M. Metzger, *The Early Versions of the NT: Their Origin, Transmission and Limitations* (1977).

*Critical Printed Texts.* C. Tischendorf, *Novum Testamentum Graece* (1869–72); H. von Soden, *Die Schriften des Neuen Testaments* (1902–13); Nestle-Aland, *Novum Testamentum Graece* (26th ed., 1983); K. Aland, et al., *The Greek NT* (3d ed., 1983).

*Analyses of Critical Apparatuses.* J. K. Elliot, *A Survey of Manuscripts Used in Editions of the Greek NT, Supplements to Novum Testamentum* 25 (1983): 97–132; *Biblica* 92 (1985): 539–56.

J. K. ELLIOTT

# Bible Translations (Modern Versions).

***Introduction.*** The history of Scripture translation is continuous from pre-Christian times to the present day. The two major turning points in modern history are the invention of printing from movable type (c. 1438) and the foundation of the British and Foreign Bible Society (1804).

The first Bible to be printed in a modern European language was the German Bible of 1466, followed by translations in Italian (1471), Low German, and Catalan (both 1478). By 1500 significant parts of the Bible had been printed in 11 languages, all European except Hebrew; the OT had also been printed in Aramaic. By 1600 at least one book of the Bible had been printed in 38 languages: 30 European (including the first English Bible, 1535), five Asian (Arabic, ancient Armenian, Persian, ancient Syriac, and Yiddish), and one African (Ethiopic). By 1700 the number had increased only to 50, including four more Asian languages: Formosan, Malay, Nogai, and Samaritan. The first whole Bible in a modern Asian language, Arabic, was published in 1671, followed by Tamil in 1727 and Malay in 1733. By 1800 another 15 languages had been added; the total of 66 then comprised 47 European, 16 Asian, two American, and one African languages.

Within the next 25 years, the number of languages almost doubled, to 125. This total included 45 new Asian languages, especially Indian; two African languages, Bullom and Amharic; and the first Oceanic language, Tahitian. The total of Asian languages, 61 by 1825, had overtaken the total of European languages, now 56.

By 1850 the total number of languages in which some Scripture had been printed had almost doubled again, reaching 204. By this time their geographical spread was more balanced, including for the first time significant numbers of African languages (20, including Malagasy, Xhosa, Zulu, Efik, and Yoruba) and Oceanic languages (5: Hawaiian, Cook Island Maori [Rarotonga], Samoan, Fijian, and Tongan). The first whole Bible for the African region was printed in Malagasy in 1835, followed by the first continental African Bible, Amharic, in 1840. The first Bible in an Oceanic language, Tahitian, was published in 1838, followed by Hawaiian in 1837–39.

Progress since 1850 has been increasingly rapid. The total number of languages having some Scripture rose to 345 by 1875, 527 by 1900, 781 by 1925, 1060 by 1950, and 1829 by 1985. By 1985 the complete Bible had been translated into 293 languages and the NT into 618; 544 translation projects were in progress.

The foundation of the first Bible societies, and the consequent expansion in Bible translation, coincided with the beginning of "the great century of missions" (Latourette). The great majority of non-European translations were made by missionaries, although even in the 19th century the contribution of national "informants" was often underestimated. As new churches have been established and theological education has developed in non-Western countries, it has become normal for Bible translations to be made by native speakers of the receptor language. The United Bible Societies (UBS), founded in 1946 as an association of national Bible societies, has set up a network of specialized translation consultants to advise local translation teams. Similar work is carried on by the Wycliffe Bible Translators/Summer Institute of Linguistics (WBT/SIL), founded in 1934, exclusively in languages that do not yet have the Bible. Translation work is also carried on by other organizations such as the Lutheran Bible Translators; the International

Bible Society (formerly the New York Bible Society), publishers of the (English) New International Version (NIV); Living Bibles International, publishers of Kenneth Taylor's Living Bible (1971); and the Institute for Bible Translation (formerly the East Bible Institute), founded in 1973 in Stockholm. In addition to specialized agencies such as those just mentioned, individual churches often make Bible translations (e.g., the English Authorized Version, by scholars of the Church of England), although a more normal pattern is now that of interdenominational cooperation, as in the New English Bible (by Protestants and Anglicans), or interconfessional translations (e.g., the French Traduction Oecuménique de la Bible). In Scandinavian countries Bible translations for use in the national (Lutheran) churches sometimes receive some form of state sponsorship and financial support.

The specialized agencies engaged in Bible translation clearly have much in common. There are frequent examples of cooperation, especially between Bible societies and the WBT/SIL; yet each organization maintains its distinctive scope and identity. Most member societies of the United Bible Societies are engaged in translation, publication, distribution, and the encouragement of effective use of the Scriptures. They are not, however, involved directly in catechesis, as is the World Catholic Federation for the Biblical Apostolate, based in Stuttgart, which conversely does not undertake translation. In some countries WBT/SIL (headquarters in Dallas) prepares the way for the use of Scripture by undertaking literacy programs. It does not, however, publish Scripture under its own imprint; many of its translations are published by the International Bible Society (see below) and the World Home Bible League. The work of WBT/SIL is confined to languages in which a translation of the Bible does not yet exist. The Lutheran Bible Translators seeks to achieve generally similar aims within the Lutheran communion. The International Bible Society, based in New York, sponsors translations on the same general principles as the (English) New International Version, which are thus described as International translations. Living Bibles International (International Office in Naperville, Ill.) undertakes translations from, or based on, the English Living Bible. The Institute for Bible Translation is concerned with translations into non-Slavic languages of the USSR; it publishes Bibles but does not directly distribute them.

Historically, most Bible translation during the period 1800–1950 was done by Protestants, since Roman Catholics traditionally stressed the authority of the Vulgate, the Greek Orthodox Church used the Septuagint and the traditional Greek NT text, and the Orthodox Church in most other countries used older translations that had acquired ecclesiastical authority. In the period of the Reformation and Counter-Reformation, it was common practice for annotated Bibles to be prepared by both sides for use as weapons in confessional polemic. This practice was avoided by the Authorized (King James) Version of 1611. It remains common, however, especially in developed countries, for different translations in the same languages to be commissioned and used by different Christian (and Jewish) traditions. The first charter of the British and Foreign Bible Society stated that its publications were to be "without note or comment." UBS member societies now publish Bibles "without doctrinal note or comment" to allow for the inclusion of readers' helps that are not denominationally controversial.

In 1968 a growing tendency toward interconfessional cooperation was officially recognized in a joint publication of UBS and the Vatican's Secretariat for Christian Unity, entitled "Guiding Principles for Interconfessional Co-operation in Translating the Bible," upon which 172 translation projects were based by 1985.

Since the 1960s it has become increasingly recognized that even within a single-language community different groups of readers require different types of Scripture translations. General distinctions are made between: (1) translations in literary or liturgical language, which may in principle use the entire resources of the target or receptor language (e.g., the New English Bible); (2) common language translations, which use only those language resources that will be understood by the great majority of native speakers (e.g., the Good News Bible [Today's English Version]); (3) simplified translations, especially for new readers (e.g., the UBS new reader selections in various languages). Common language translations are to be distinguished from translations, such as the NT in Basic English, which use an artificially restricted vocabulary. "Language resources," in this context, refers not only to vocabulary but to grammatical constructions and other aspects of written language.

Assessments of Bible translation work still to be done depend partly upon the goal to be reached: Is it that every individual should be able to read the whole Bible in his or her mother tongue, or that everyone should have access to part of the Bible in a language that he or she can understand? Assessments also depend on how a language is distinguished from a dialect, a matter upon which linguists disagree.

The effect of Bible translation on the life of the church is difficult to quantify. In Western Europe there was a coincidence in the 16th century between Renaissance, Reformation, and the development of national languages; the translation of the Scriptures by Martin Luther and Lefèvre d'Etaples was related to all three developments. Since Vatican II the replacement in the

Roman Catholic Church of Latin by the vernacular in public worship has stimulated the production of official Catholic translations such as that commissioned by the Italian Bishops' Conference; it has also indirectly stimulated the making of interconfessional translations. Since Cyril and Methodius in the 9th century A.D., the Orthodox Church has favored the use of the vernacular in worship, and thus translation of the Scriptures. Yet the high value placed on ancient tradition has often led to the virtual canonization of classic translations such as the Septuagint in Greece and the Church Slavonic Bible in Russia; however, in Greece modern translations are widely used outside the liturgy. In Africa the translation of Scripture has been found to be a significant factor in the formation of independent churches.

The following notes on individual languages illustrate the Western bias of the Bible translation enterprise. Western languages have a much longer history of Bible translation and a much wider variety of current versions than others. Also, until rather recent times, most translators were Western missionaries. Apparent Western predominance in the second sense also illustrates the earlier understanding of the translator's task, which gave priority to expert knowledge of the original languages over native-speaker competence in the receptor language. The following list includes, in alphabetical order, languages spoken by at least 10 million people; numbers refer to paragraphs below:

| | | | |
|---|---|---|---|
| Amharic | 48 | Nepali | 54 |
| Arabic | 5 | Oriya | 33 |
| Assamese | 51 | Oromo | 55 |
| Azerbaijani | 49 | Panjabi | 11 |
| Bengali | 6 | Pashto | 37 |
| Bihari | 14 | Persian | 27 |
| Burmese | 29 | Polish | 24 |
| Chinese | 1 | Portuguese | 8 |
| Czech | 59 | Quechua | 56 |
| Dutch | 35 | Rajasthani | 39 |
| English | 2 | Romanian | 34 |
| French | 12 | Russian | 7 |
| Fulfulde | 43 | (Ki)Rwanda- | |
| German | 10 | (Ki)Rundi | 42 |
| Greek | 52 | Serbo-Croatian | 40 |
| Gujarati | 25 | Sindhi | 57 |
| Hausa | 32 | Sinhala | 50 |
| Hindi | 4 | Spanish | 3 |
| Hungarian | 47 | Sundanese | 36 |
| Indonesian | 28 | Swahili | 38 |
| Igbo | 45 | Tagalog | 46 |
| Italian | 16 | Tamil | 18 |
| Japanese | 9 | Telugu | 17 |
| Javanese | 13 | Thai | 26 |
| Kannada | 30 | Turkish | 22 |
| Korean | 15 | Ukrainian | 21 |
| Kurdish | 58 | Urdu | 23 |
| Malay | 53 | Uzbek | 44 |
| Malayalam | 31 | Vietnamese | 20 |
| Marathi | 19 | Yoruba | 41 |

Except where otherwise indicated, population figures refer to those who regularly speak the language at home, and are estimates given by Gunnemark and Kenrick in 1985. Unless otherwise stated, it is assumed that Roman Catholic translations of the Bible include the Apocrypha, and Protestant translations do not. Bibliography, except for Scripture, covers the period 1955–1986, and is selective.

*1. Chinese Translations.* There are 1050 million Chinese speakers, and over 1000 million of these live in the People's Republic of China. Numerous early translations have disappeared, beginning with the Gospels prepared for the Emperor Ta'i-Tsung in A.D. 640 by a group of Nestorian missionaries under Alopen. The earliest extant translation is that by Emanuel Diaz; it consisted of liturgical selections and was printed in 1636 in Beijing (Peking). Around 1700 the French Protestant missionary Jean Basset translated Matthew–Philemon; his translation, although apparently not published in its original form, influenced Morrison (see below), and through him later translators. Several lost and probably unpublished translations were made in the 18th century, the most extensive being one of the NT and most of the OT by Louis de Poirot (1735–1814).

Throughout the 19th century, Bible translations were made and distributed against the intense opposition of the Chinese government, which decreed the death penalty for those engaged in this work.

Two separate translations of the Bible were begun in 1810 and completed respectively in 1822 and 1823: the first by Johannes Lassar and Joshua Marshman, published in Serampore; the second by Robert Morrison, with the help of William Milne for the OT, published in Malacca. Other versions were made by Walter H. Medhurst, Karl F. A. Gutzlaff, and Elijah C. Bridgman (Singapore, 1838); Medhurst and others (Shanghai, 1853; known as the Delegates' Version, and widely retranslated into other languages); Gutzlaff alone (Hong Kong, 1855); E. C. Bridgman and Michael S. Culbertson, who withdrew from the Delegates Committee in 1853 (Shanghai, 1863); members of the Russian Ecclesiastical Mission in Beijing (Peking) (NT, 1864; rev. ed., 1884); William Dean (Hong Kong, 1870); and John Chalmers and Martin Schaub (tentative NT, 1897; published at their own expense by two members of the Union Bible Committee, on which see below).

All the translations mentioned above were in the Wenli style of Chinese, sometimes known as High Wenli. In the Putonghua style, also known as Kuoyü and formerly called Mandarin by foreigners, a group appointed in 1861 and known as the Peking Committee produced the Gospels and Acts in 1866, Romans–Revelation in 1870, and a revised NT in 1872. This group comprised Protestant and Anglican missionaries from the United States (William A. P. Martin, Samuel I. J. Schereschewsky, and Henry Blodget) and the United Kingdom (Joseph Edkins and John Shaw Burdon); publication was shared by BFBS and ABS. Schereschewsky also translated the OT (1874; rev. ed., 1899), which was published with the Peking Committee NT in 1878; this publication became the standard Putonghua Bible until the appearance of the Union version of 1919 (see below).

In addition Schereschewsky translated the Bible into Easy Wenli (Psalms, 1880; NT, 1898; Bible, 1902). His NT was preceded by that of Griffith John, published by the National Bible Society of Scotland in 1885 (John also translated much of the OT), and that of J. S. Burden and H. Blodget, published in Fuzhou (Foochow) in 1889.

The General Conference of Protestant missionaries held at Shanghai in 1890 felt the need for a translation of the Scriptures that would be generally accepted. As a result of this conference, plans were made for new "union" (i.e., interdenominational) versions in three styles of Chinese: Wenli (otherwise known as High Wenli), Mandarin (now known as Kuoyü or Putonghua), and Easy Wenli. Joseph Edkins, John Wherry, D. Z. Sheffield, and others produced a translation of the Bible into High Wenli. Work in Putonghua was begun in 1898 by a committee including C. W. Mateer, C. Goodrich, and F. W. Baller. Both these Bibles were published by BFBS in Shanghai in 1919. Translations in Easy Wenli appeared in 1897, leading to a NT in 1903 (rev. ed., 1904), but the project was abandoned in 1907 in favor of a single Union Wenli version.

Versions in Wenli were begun in 1945 by G. Allegra and others under the auspices of the Franciscan Studium Biblicum, resulting in a Bible (Hong Hong, 1968), and by Lü Chen-chung (Hong Kong, 1970).

A translation in simplified characters sponsored by Asian Outreach was published in Hong Kong (NT, 1974; OT, 1979); a Living Bible appeared in Hong Kong in 1979. Today's Chinese Version, a common language translation by Moses Hsü, Evelyn Chiao, Martin Wang, Lien Hua Chow, and I-Jin Loh, was published in Hong Kong in 1980, revised in 1985, and printed in simplified script in 1982.

**2. English.** This language has over 320 million home speakers and is the official language for over 1450 million. The first Old English (or Anglo-Saxon) Scripture may have been the 7th-century Psalms said to have been translated by Bishop Aldhelm, but now lost. Six Old English versions of the Gospels from before or shortly after the Norman Conquest (1066) are extant. A Middle English poetical version of the Gospels

and Acts, called Ormulum, was written about 1215 by an Augustinian monk called Orm or Ormin, and the whole Bible is said to have been translated by John of Trevisa (1326–1412). Versions by followers of John Wycliffe (d. 1384) circulated in manuscript.

The first complete printed English NT was published by William Tyndale in Worms in 1526; the first Bible, by Myles Coverdale in Marburg, or possibly Cologne, in 1535. The Tyndale and Coverdale versions were united into Matthew's Bible in 1537 ("Matthew" is probably a pseudonym). This began a continuous tradition of translations or revisions that may be called the mainstream of the English Bible, which includes the "Great Bible" (London, 1539); the Bishops' Bible (London, 1568); the "Authorized Version" or "King James Version" (London, 1611); the Revised Version (Oxford and Cambridge, 1881–85), and its American counterpart, the American Standard Version (New York, 1901); the Revised Standard Version (New York, 1952); the New American Standard Version (La Habra, Calif., 1963 [NT]; 1971 [OT]); and the New King James Version (NT, 1979; OT, 1982).

Among other versions too numerous to list, the "Geneva Bible" (Geneva, 1560), otherwise known as the "Breeches Bible" from its translation of Gen. 3:7, was the first to include verse divisions; it was especially popular among the Puritans. The first English Roman Catholic Bible, known as the Rheims-Douay or Douai Version (Rheims, 1582 [NT]; Douai, 1609/10 [OT]), was translated from the Vulgate; it was frequently revised, notably by Richard Challoner (1749/50), and remained standard for Roman Catholics until the 20th century. More recent Roman Catholic versions, based on the original texts, include the New American Bible (Paterson, N.J., 1970); the Jerusalem Bible (London, 1966), and its successor, the New Jerusalem Bible (London, 1985). Jewish versions of the Hebrew Bible (= OT) include those by Isaac Lee (London, 1845–54), Abraham Benisch (London, 1851–61), the Jewish Publication Society of America (Philadelphia, 1917; new translation, 1962–82). The Jehovah's Witnesses' New World translation of the Bible first appeared in New York in 1961. The Anchor Bible, translated with commentary by Roman Catholic, Protestant, and Jewish scholars, has been in progress since 1964.

Versions by a single translator do not often extend to the whole Bible; exceptions are those by J. M. Ray (London, 1798–99); Charles Thomson (Philadelphia, 1808, from the LXX); Robert Young (Edinburgh, 1863); J. N. Darby, leader of the so-called Plymouth Brethren (London, 1871 [NT]; 1885 [OT]); Ferrar Fenton (London, 1903); James Moffatt (London, 1913 [NT]; 1924 [OT]); Edgar J. Goodspeed (Chicago, 1923 [NT]; 1927 [OT]; 1938 [Apocrypha]); Ronald A. Knox (London and New York, 1956 [Roman Catholic]); and William F. Beck (St. Louis, 1963 [NT]; New Haven, Mo., 1976 [OT]). Edgar J. Goodspeed translated the NT (1923) and Apocrypha (1938); the corresponding OT translation (1927) was made by four other scholars.

In addition to the more recent publications mentioned above, currently used versions include the Good News Bible (= Today's English Version) (New York, 1966 [NT]; New York and London, 1976 [Bible]), a dynamic equivalence ("meaning for meaning") translation; the New International Version, produced by a committee of evangelical scholars (Grand Rapids, 1973 [NT]; 1978 [Bible]); and the Living Bible, a paraphrase by Kenneth N. Taylor assisted by a committee (Wheaton, Ill., 1967 [NT]; 1971 [Bible]).

**Bibliography.** J. R. Harris, *TBT* 9 (1958): 70–73; E. H. Robertson, *The New Translations of the Bible* (1959); R. G. Bratcher, *TBT* 12 (1961): 97–106; M. T. Hills, *The English Bible in America* (1961); J. Reumann, *Four Centuries of the English Bible* (1961); S. L. Greenslade, *Cambridge History of the Bible* (1963), 3:141–74; R. G. Bratcher, *TBT* 17 (1966): 159–72; M. Deansley, *The Lollard Bible* (2d ed., 1966); A. S. Herbert, *A Historical Catalogue of Printed Editions of the English Bible, 1525–1961* (1968); R. W. F. Wootton, *TBT* 19 (1968): 42–45; R. G. Bratcher, *TBT* 20 (1969): 36–39; G. Shepherd, *Cambridge History of the Bible* (1969), 2:362–87; K. R. Crim, *TBT* 21 (1970): 149–54; R. G. Bratcher, *TBT* 22 (1971): 97–107; R. Steiner, *Jahrbuch des Evangelischen Bibelwerkes* 13 (1971): 155–69; C. H. Dodd, *TBT* 27 (1976): 301–11; 28 (1977): 101–16; O. E. Evans, *On Translating the Bible* (1976); J. van Bruggen, *The Future of the Bible* (1978); R. G. Bratcher, *Review and Expositor* 76 (1979): 299–314; F. F. Bruce, *History of the Bible in English* (3d ed., 1979); D. A. Carson, *The King James Version Debate* (1979); P. J. Sjölander, *Some Aspects of Style in Twentieth-century English Bible Translation. One-man Versions of Mark and the Psalms* (1979); B. M. Newman, *TBT* 31 (1980): 325–36; J. P. Lewis, *The English Bible from KJV to NIV* (1981); L. R. Bailey, ed., *The Word of God* (1982); S. Kubo and W. F. Specht, *So Many Versions? Twentieth-century English Versions of the Bible* (1983); R. G. Bratcher, *Harper's Bible Encyclopedia* (1985), 263–67; F. F. Bruce, *The English Bible* (4th ed., 1985); B. F. Chilton, *Beginning NT Study* (1986): 95–119.

**3. Spanish.** This language has over 260 million home speakers in Spain and Latin America; in addition, about 100,000 Sephardic Jews use a variety of Spanish in Hebrew characters. The Castilian dialect is the basis of modern literary Spanish.

A vernacular Bible tradition was slow to develop in Spain, largely because of the opposition of the Inquisition. Translations of parts of the Vulgate were made about 1250–60, but King James I of Aragon, who reigned from 1213 to 1276, forbade both clergy and laity to own a copy of the OT in the vernacular. A translation of the OT known as the Alphonsian was incorporated by King Alfonso X of Castile (reigned 1262–84) in his *Grande e General Estoria*. This was based partly on two earlier versions by Christian scholars, partly from the Vulgate and partly from the Hebrew; the translator of one of these versions of the Psalms was Hermann el Alemán. Spanish Jews worked on various OT translations from the Hebrew, the most notable of which was made

from 1422 to 1431 by Rabbi Moses Arragel of Maqueda (or Guadalajara), under the supervision of the Franciscan Arias of Enzinas (Enciena). The Complutensian Polyglot published in Alcalá in 1514–17 and the Antwerp Polyglot of 1569–73 included Spanish texts, but were not intended for widespread distribution. In about 1561 the poet, theologian, and mystic Luis de León made a translation of the Song of Songs, but this was not printed until 1798. In 1572 he was imprisoned by the Inquisition for making this translation and for introducing doctrinal errors; however, in 1576 he was exonerated and released.

Further Jewish versions of the OT include the Ferrara Bible (1533), made by Tobias Athias and Abraham Usque for Spanish refugees in Italy, and published in two editions, a word-for-word translation for Jews, and a modified version for Christians; also included among these Jewish versions is the Constantinople Pentateuch of 1547.

Juan de Valdés, exiled to Naples by the Inquisition, translated the NT and Psalms between 1531 and 1541; only Mark, Luke, and the Pauline Epistles survive. A translation of the NT was made in Wittenberg by Francisco de Enzinas (Dryander), a student of Melanchthon, and printed in Antwerp in 1543. It was suppressed by order of the Emperor Charles V, and few copies survive. A fresh translation of the NT from the Greek was made by Juan Pérez de Pineda and published in 1556 (officially in Venice, but actually in Geneva). Most copies smuggled into Spain were destroyed.

Meanwhile, translations of Job by Alonso Alvarez of Toledo had appeared in 1514, probably at Toledo; of the Psalms by Juan Roffense in 1550 in Lyons; of the OT by Abraham Usque (otherwise known as Eduardo Pinhel or Duarte Pinel), a Jew from Portugal, published in 1553 in Ferrara under the patronage of the duke of Ferrara; and of the NT at Valencia in 1556.

The first Spanish Bible, known as the "Bear Bible" from the picture on its title page, appeared in 1569, probably in Basel. It was translated by the Catholic reformer Casiodoro de Reina, and included the Apocrypha. A revised NT was published in London in 1596 by Ricardo del Campo (Richard Field), and the whole Bible in Amsterdam in 1602, again revised by Cipriano de Valera. This Reina–Valera translation is still considered the classic translation by Spanish-speaking Protestants. Revised versions without the Apocrypha were published by the British and Foreign Bible Society (BFBS) (London, 1861); by the Society for Propagating Christian Knowledge (SPCK) (London, rev. ed., 1862); and by Angel de Mora and H. B. Pratt of the American Presbyterian Mission for ABS (New York, rev. ed., 1865). Pratt was also responsible for the Versión Moderna Bible (1893), corrected versions of which appeared in 1929 and 1939. The most recent revision of Reina–Valera was published in 1960 by the Bible Societies in Latin America.

William (Guillermo) Rule, the first Protestant missionary to Spain, translated the Gospels (Gibraltar, 1841), Acts (London, 1877), and Revelation (London, 1880). A translation of Isaiah from the Hebrew was made by Luis de Usoz y Río and was published in Madrid in 1863. Federico Fliedner's translation of Matthew–Philemon was published in 1885; the translation of the NT was completed by his grandson and published in 1933 with "polemical and apologetic notes" by F. Faivre.

The earliest Roman Catholic translations, based upon and often printed with the Vulgate, were costly. The first, by Felipe Scío de San Miguel, appeared in Valencia in 1790–93 in 10 volumes; a corrected edition in 19 volumes appeared in 1794–97. In a nine-volume translation (Madrid, 1823–29), Félix Torres Amat, bishop of Astorga, took sufficient account of the original texts for the NT to be revised and reprinted in London by SPCK in 1837 and 1847, and the Bible without the Apocrypha, revised by Juan Calderón, in 1853. William (Guillermo) Norton and Calderón made a very literal translation of the NT (Edinburgh, 1858). In 1850 ABS published a Bible revised by J. C. Brigham and Alberto Tornos, based upon a combination of the Scío and Reina–Valera versions.

The first Spanish Bible printed in Latin America was a Roman Catholic translation commissioned by Mario Galván, based on the 1743 French Vence version; it appeared in Mexico in 1831–33.

New translations of the Gospels were published by ABS in 1910, based on the Greek text of Westcott and Hort; in the same year, BFBS published in Madrid a new translation of Matthew based on the Nestle text. The two projects combined, and the Hispano-American version of the NT, based on Nestle, was published jointly by ABS and BFBS (Madrid, 1916). This was revised in 1953 and published in a diglot with the English RSV. Meanwhile, in 1919 Pablo Berson, a Baptist pastor in Argentina, published a translation of the NT based upon Westcott and Hort.

Rival versions of the NT based on a variety of texts continued to appear. Whole Bibles included a revision of the Torres Amat version by Severiano del Páramo (1928); an interconfessional version by Serafín de Ausejo and others, including, for the NT, the Protestants Gonzalo Béz-Camargo and Ignacio Mendoza (1965); the first Roman Catholic version based on the original texts, made by Eloíno Nácar Fuster and Alberto Colunga (1944; rev. ed., 1947, 1966); Roman Catholic translations by José María Bover and Francisco Cantera Burgos (1947; rev. ed., 1966); Evaristo Martín Nieto and others (1964); the Nueva Biblia Española in modern literary language, by L. A.

Schökel and L. Mateos (NT, 1966; Bible, 1976), widely used in the liturgy throughout the Spanish-speaking world; Bibles by Pedro Franquesa and José M. Solé with others (1966); the Spanish Jerusalem Bible in 1967 (based on the Ausejo version of 1965) by José Angel Ubieta with others; Ramón Ricciardi with others (1971; rev. ed., 1972); and José M. Valverde, José R. Díaz and others (NT, 1966; OT, 1975). Of special importance for Latin America was the Catholic NT by Juan Straubinger (Buenos Aires, 1944). Notable individual translations include those by Felipe de Fuenterrabía (NT, 1964; rev. ed., 1973), Carlos de Villapadierna (NT, 1967), and the Catholic M. Miguens, whose NT was privately printed in 1971.

The Versión Popular was prepared by a Bible Society committee, including W. L. Wonderly, J. D. Galindo, G. Báez-Camargo, A. Lloreda, Elizabeth P. Marroquín, and others, and, in its later stages, some Roman Catholics. The pilot edition of Luke (1954; NT, 1966) was the first consistently dynamic equivalent Scripture in common language; a European version appeared in 1971, and the whole Bible with the Apocrypha, Dios habla hoy, in 1979. The NT of Armando J. Levoratti, Mateo Perdia, and Alfredo B. Trusso (Buenos Aires, 1967) was the first Catholic version to conform to common language, notably in its use of personal pronouns. Also significant for Latin America was the Catholic Biblia Latinoamérica (or Latinoamericana) of Ramón Ricciardi and Bernardo Hurault, later reprinted and revised.

Non-Roman Catholic translations also include the Watchtower NT (1973); the paraphrastic Living Bible (NT, 1973; Bible, 1979); the Biblia de las Américas (NT, 1973), translated for the Lockman Foundation and based on the English NASV; and the Spanish counterpart of the English NIV (NT, 1980).

An ecumenical version by Serafín de Ausejo, F. de Fuenterrabía, and others was reviewed by the French Jerusalem Bible translators (NT, 1968; OT, 1975); the NT of an Interconfessional Bible, based on the UBS Greek Text, also appeared (Madrid, 1978).

*Bibliography.* S. Rypins, *The Library* 5 (1955): 244–67; G. Marin, *Versiones española de la Biblia* (1958); H. T. Marroquín, *Versiones Castellanas de la Biblia* (1959); M. Morreale, *Sefer* 20 (1960): 66–109; E. A. Nida, *TBT* 12 (1961): 107–19; W. L. Wonderly, *TBT* 12 (1961): 107–19, 169–77; G. Marin, *Jahrbuch des Evangelischen Bibelwerkes* 12 (1969): 86–99; L. A. Schökel, *TBT* 22 (1971): 38–44; *TBT* 24 (1973): 118–29.

**4. Hindi.** There are over 750 million speakers of languages in the Hindi group, including over 220 million as home speakers in Hindi proper.

The first Hindi Scriptures were published by the Serampore missionaries under William Carey (NT, 1811). (The statement that the Gospels were published in 1806 has been disproved.) The Pentateuch followed (1812), and the rest of the OT, together with a revision of the NT (1818). In 1826 the BFBS Calcutta Auxiliary published a NT and in 1834 an OT based on the AV, except for the Psalms, which were from Bishop Lowth's English translation. In 1848 a new version was published, begun by W. Yates and a group of nationals and completed by A. Leslie. In 1849 the North India Auxiliary of BFBS published a NT at Allahabad (rev. ed., 1860), and in 1850–55 an OT (rev. ed., 1866–69), edited by committees under Joseph Owen of the American Presbyterian Mission and F. E. Schneider of the Church Missionary Society. In 1914 the BFBS North India Auxiliary published a whole Bible based partly upon translations of portions published from 1878 onwards, but also including new work in which for the first time Indians, Prem Chand and Vishweshwar Dutt, are named as joint translators.

The first published Roman Catholic Scripture was a translation of Matthew (Calcutta, 1917). It was followed by Mark (1937), the Gospels and Acts (1940), the entire NT (1958), and the OT (1965). The translations of the OT and NT were edited by S. N. Wald, who was also the main OT translator. The Apocrypha was revised from the 1965 Wald version and published in 1980. An individual translation of the NT by Camille Bulcke was published in 1980.

Samuel Dutt drafted a common language translation of the NT in 1976; in unofficial cooperation with two Roman Catholics, J. H. Anand translated the corresponding OT. In 1978 the Bible Society of India published a Bible known as the Revised Version, a reedited version of the Tiwari translation of 1967. The Lockman Foundation commissioned a translation of the NT published in Lucknow in 1978. A Living NT also appeared in 1978, as well as a new translation of the NT published by India Bible Publishers in New Delhi.

*Bibliography.* T. G. Bailey, *JRAS* (1936).

*5. Arabic.* This is the official language for over 175 million people and the home language for over 150 million, with considerable variations in colloquial speech from the standard literary Arabic, known as Fasih.

There were Christians in Arabia from the 4th century A.D., but no Arabic translation of the Bible is known to have existed until after Mohammed, although John of Seville is said to have produced an Arabic Bible about 737, and a minority of scholars argue in favor of a pre-Islamic date for the earliest Arabic versions. The chronicle of Michael Syrus mentions an Arabic translation of the Gospels made under the direction of John, patriarch of Antioch, at the command of Emir Amru. Extant biblical MSS in Arabic, from the 9th century onwards, are translated from Coptic, Syriac, Latin, and even Samaritan, in addition to Hebrew and Greek. Ninth-century MSS of Acts, the Pauline Epistles, and the Catholic Epistles from the Monastery of St. Catherine at Mount Sinai were edited by Margaret D. Gibson and published in *Studia Sinaitica* in 1894 and 1899.

The most important early translation of the Hebrew Bible was by Saadia ben Joseph (d. 942), also known as Saadia Gaon; his translation of the Pentateuch was printed in 1546 in Hebrew letters with the Hebrew text, Targum, and a Persian translation. Isaak, son of Velasquez, a Spanish Christian, translated the Gospels in the 10th century. The 11th-century Aleppo Psalter was published in 1706. The Alexandrian Vulgate was translated from Coptic in the 13th century.

There is an especially strong tradition of translating the Psalms into Arabic. The Psalms in Arabic were first published together with Hebrew, Latin, Greek, and Aramaic in an edition prepared by Augustino Giustiniani and Baptista Cigala (Genoa, 1516); in 1610 on Mount Lebanon in Carshuni characters, with Syriac, translated by Maronite monks; in Rome in 1614 with Latin, translated by Gabriel Sionita and Victorio Seialac; and most notably the Aleppo Psalter, published initially as a Melchite liturgical work and subsequently often republished.

Galatians, edited by Rutgherus Spey, appeared in Heidelberg (with Latin) in 1583, and the Gospels, edited by G. B. Raimondi from the Alexandrian Vulgate, in Rome in 1590/91. The same text, complemented by MSS in the Leiden Library, underlay the 1616 Leiden NT edited by T. Erpenius and F. Raphelengius; the Pentateuch followed in 1622.

The Paris Polyglot (1645), edited by Gabriel Sionita, Joannes Hesronita, and others, contained a complete Bible (except for Esther) in Hebrew, Aramaic, Greek, Latin, Samaritan, and Arabic. The Arabic Pentateuch is the translation by Saadia; the prophets are an Alexandrian text by Al 'Alam. The London Polyglot (1657) generally followed the Paris text with slight modifications by E. Castell and E. Pococke; it was reprinted in Newcastle in 1811 with further editing by Joseph D. Carlyle and Henry Ford.

A separate Arabic Bible was prepared by the Sacra Congregatio de Propaganda Fide (Rome, 1647–59), but withdrawn. It was replaced in 1671 by a diglot with Latin edited by Sergius Risius and others; the Arabic text was based on the Vulgate. The NT in this version was reprinted by BFBS in 1820, and the OT in 1722; OT portions and the NT were reprinted by ABS about 1842. A distinct edition of the NT by Salomon Negri was published by SPCK in 1727.

Editions of ancient versions continue to be published; a text of the Pentateuch based on Saadia, adapted to the Samaritan Pentateuch by Abu 'l-Hassan in the 11th century, and edited by Ahmad Hegazi el-Sakka, was published in 1978 in Cairo; and a transcription by Harvey Stool of a Sinai manuscript of Romans–Jude dated 867 was published in Louvain.

In the 19th century, however, there was a general development toward the preparation of new translations. The NT was translated by Nathaniel Sabat and Thomas Thomason and published by BFBS (Calcutta, 1816); a revision by Samuel Lee and J. D. Macbride was published in 1825. In 1851 SPCK published a NT translated by Faris Al-Shidyak, S. Lee, and Thomas Jarrett; in 1857 an OT was planned, but never published. In 1860 the ABS in Beirut published a NT, and in 1865 an OT, begun by the Baptist Eli Smith, and completed by his colleague Cornelius Van Dyck; both were assisted by native speakers of Arabic. Known as the Van Dyck translation, this version remains standard for Protestants. A partial revision by Butrus Abd al-Malik, John A. Thompson, and others was published by the Bible Society in the Near East (Proverbs, 1960; NT, 1967–72); a fresh revision is in progress (1986).

A Dominican translation of the Bible under the direction of Joseph David was published in Mosul in 1875–78, and a Jesuit version, edited by Augustin Rodet, appeared from 1876 to 1880 (repr. 1929–32; NT revised by Subhi Hamawi and Yusuf Kushakji with Butrus Bustani, 1967–69). A translation of the NT was made by the Greek Catholic George Fakhoury and published at Harissa in 1953. A translation of Romans by Abdel Atif was published in 1957; it is described as the first translation since the Middle Ages made solely by a native speaker. A Coptic Orthodox committee published the synoptic Gospels from 1972 to 1978. A Maronite NT translated by Jusif 'Awn appeared in Beirut in 1978.

The UBS in Beirut has published Arabic common-language translations by Yusuf el-Khal and Antoine Naguib of the NT (1978; rev. ed., 1980) and Psalms (1980); work on the OT continues. A NT based on the English Living NT was published in 1982.

Between 1885 and 1906 a number of Arabic Scriptures appeared in Hebrew script. Some were transliterations of Van Dyck. Perhaps the most important among the new translations was that of the Pentateuch by Hezekiel Shemtob David (Bombay, 1891).

**Bibliography.** J. A. Thompson, *TBT* 6 (1955): 2–12, 49–55, 98–110, 146–50; *The Major Arabic Bibles* (1956); K. E. Bailey, *Near East School of Theology Theological Review* 5 (1982): 155–43.

**6. Bengali.** This language has over 150 million home speakers and is the official language for 95 million in Bangladesh and West Bengal (India).

The first Bengali Scriptures were translated by William Carey of the Serampore mission (Matthew, 1800; NT, 1801; OT, 1801–7; rev. ed. Bible, 1832). A NT translated by John Ellerton, an indigo planter at Malda, was revised by a committee of the BFBS Calcutta Auxiliary, and published by the auxiliary in 1819. The BFBS Calcutta Auxiliary began a fresh project with Genesis

in 1832, but no further books were published. William Yates, assisted by John Wenger, produced a series of translations and revisions, including the Psalms (1826; rev. ed., 1838), Gospels (1831), NT (1834; rev. ed., 1841), OT (1844), and revised Bible (1845). Most of these were published by various agencies in Calcutta, but the BFBS in London published a NT in Roman script in 1839. The Yates–Wenger version was repeatedly revised, notably the OT by Wenger (1861), the NT by Krishna Mohun Banerji (1853), and the Bible (1897, 1902, 1909). In Calcutta CMS missionary C. Bomwetsch, assisted by David Rajanee Kanta Biswas, translated the NT in 1885, which was revised in 1905. K. M. Banerji continued his translation work from 1885 as joint director, with Kali Charan Banerji, of a colloquial NT translation published by the BFBS Calcutta Auxiliary; the work was continued by S. C. Mukerji and W. H. G. Holmes. Publication continued until 1916, with various revisions of the Gospels and Acts, but nothing beyond Romans was published.

The first Roman Catholic Scriptures were the Gospels and Acts translated from the Vulgate by S. Taveggia (Calcutta, 1906).

Various private and experimental translations of individual books were made from time to time, including a version of Matthew translated by members of the Aryan Historical Society (1895), Luke in colloquial Chalti Bhasha (1910), a verse translation of the Psalms by E. T. Sandys with Medan Mohan Biswas (1916), and Luke translated into colloquial Bengali by W. McCullough and others, and printed in a simplified phonetic script (1921).

An interdenominational revision of the NT, begun by A. G. MacLeod and Priyar Kumar Barui, was published in 1963 by the Bible Society of India and Ceylon. In 1977 the Bangladesh Bible Society published a common language NT by Basanti Dass and Lynn Silvernale, assisted by Polycarp Dores from 1976. In 1980 the Bible Society of India published another common language NT translated by Deepali Roy, S. B. Dutt, and Arindam Nath. A NT by Arabinda Dey, founder of Christ's Disciples' Fellowship, was also published (Calcutta, 1980; rev. ed. 1983).

**7. Russian.** There are over 150 million home speakers of Russian, the official language for over 275 million people.

Despite the long history of Christianity in Russia, the first publication of a book of the Bible in Russian (Romans, translated by Mikhail Alekseyevich Smirnov [Archbishop Mefodiy]) was published only in 1794 (by the Moscow Synodal Press, in a diglot with Slavonic; rev. ed., 1815). The reason for this late development was the predominance of Slavonic as the liturgical language, long after it had ceased to be used as the vernacular.

The first NT appeared in 1821, and was generally available from 1822. It was published by the Russian Bible Society, in a diglot with the Slavonic text. The Russian translation had been made by a committee appointed by the Holy Synod at the request of Tsar Alexander I. The Russian text was reprinted alone by the Russian Bible Society in 1823, and republished in 1838 in Leipzig, with covert BFBS support.

In 1822, under the direction of Gerasim P. Pavsky, professor of Hebrew at St. Petersburg (Leningrad) Theological Academy, the Russian Bible Society published a translation of the Psalms based primarily on the Hebrew text. A commission was delegated by the Holy Synod to oversee the translation. Genesis–Ruth was printed in 1825, but the project was discontinued when the Russian Bible Society was closed in 1826. Copies circulated unofficially in the early 1830s. An edition lightly revised by E. Stallybrass was published by BFBS in London in 1861. Pavsky later translated other OT books for his students, who from 1838 to 1842 published them without official authority until halted by synodal investigations; they were republished 20 years later in a review.

A new translation of the OT, except Ruth and Psalms, was made by M. Y. Glukharev (Archimandrite Makariy). Makariy died in 1847, but his translation was not published until 1860–67, and then only in a review. L. I. Mandelstam published a rival OT translation in 1862–65 for Russian Jews; a revised edition of the Pentateuch appeared in 1871 with the Hebrew text. The Jewish tradition was maintained by the Society for the Enlightenment of Jews in Russia by the publication of J. Gerstein and J. L. Gordon's translation of the Pentateuch together with the Hebrew (Vilna, 1875), and by David Yosippon's OT (Jerusalem, 1975–78).

The first one-volume Russian Bible became available in 1877. It was published by BFBS in Vienna, and is known as the 1876 edition. It consisted of the 1860–62 NT, and a translation of the OT by V. A. Levinson and D. A. Khvolson, which had been originally published in parts between 1866 and 1875.

The only standard translation for Russian Orthodox is the Synodal Version. Official publications of the Gospels (1860), Acts–Revelation (1862), and the complete NT (1863) were followed by the Pentateuch (1868), Joshua–Esther (1869), and Job–Ecclesiasticus (1872); the complete OT appeared in 1875, and the whole Bible in 1876. It was made by a committee including D. A. Khvolson, E. I. Lovyagin, and M. A. Golubev, who was succeeded by P. I. Savvaitov. BFBS published an edition of this in Vienna in 1877.

A translation of the NT by V. A. Zhukovsky (d. 1852) was belatedly published in Berlin in 1895. A NT by K. P. Pobedonostsev, procurator of the Holy Synod, appeared in St. Petersburg in 1906. The Synodal Bible was reprinted by Protestants (Leningrad, 1926; Kiev, 1927 [both in the new Soviet orthography]); a light revision was published in 1956 by the Moscow Patriarchate. Then the Russian Baptist Union reprinted this revision without the Apocrypha (Moscow, 1957).

Since 1956 the Moscow Patriarchate has sponsored several reprints of the Synodal text, using the new Soviet orthography. Other Scripture publications have taken place outside the USSR. They include a NT by J. Schweigl of the Russian Pontifical College (Rome, 1944–46); a NT based on a critical text, prepared by Orthodox and Protestant scholars in Paris, and published by BFBS in 1958–70; a pilot translation of the Gospel of John by K. I. Logachev, published by UBS in 1978; and a Children's Bible published by the Institute for Bible Translation in Stockholm in 1983.

**Bibliography.** R. A. Klostermann, *Probleme der Ostkirche* (1955): 361–416; A. Osipoff, *TBT* 7 (1956): 56–65; A. Osipoff, *TBT* 7 (1956): 98–101; K. I. Logachev, *Journal of the Moscow Patriarchate* 11 (1969): 61–68; *TBT* 25 (1974): 313–18; *TBT* 25 (1974): 318–31; *TBT* 25 (1975): 138–43; *TBT* 29 (1978): 312–16; M. I. Rizhsky, *Istoriya Perevodov Biblii v Rossii* [The History of Bible Translations in Russia] (1978); S. K. Batalden, *The Study of Russian History from British Archival Sources* (1986), 147–71.

**8. Portuguese.** This language has over 140 million home speakers, mainly in Brazil and Portugal, and is the official language for over 160 million.

A Gospel harmony and liturgical selections were both published in 1495. In 1505 a volume appeared that included an expanded version of Acts and a relatively restrained paraphrase of the Catholic Epistles, together with some nonbiblical material. It had been prepared earlier by Bernardo de Brivega and was printed by order of Queen Leonora. The first Portuguese Scripture in the strict sense was a NT published in Amsterdam in 1681, and in revised form in Batavia (Djakarta, 1693), and often subsequently. It remains the standard version for Protestants. The translator was João Ferreira d'Almeida, who also made an unpublished translation of Genesis–Ezekiel. His MS, except for the Pentateuch, formed the basis of the OT prepared by Danish missionaries at Tranquebar, and published from 1719 to 1751. The Almeida version was independently revised and completed in the East Indies, and published in Batavia in 1753 (OT) and 1773 (NT). It was also revised by T. Boys of the Trinitarian Bible Society (1842–47), by G. Bush of ABS (New York, 1847), by M. Soares for BFBS (Lisbon, 1875), and others.

The standard Roman Catholic version was made by Antonio Pereira de Figueiredo from the Vulgate, with reference to the original texts. The NT was first published in 1778–81 and the OT in 1782–90, and later revised by the translator. BFBS published a revision of this version in 1886. A further revision, begun in 1886, was intended for use in both Portugal and Brazil, but only the European (mainly British) translators continued their work, publishing portions until 1901.

The first Brazilian NT was prepared by Franciscans with the approval of the bishops of the First Brazilian Catholic Congress. The translation was modeled after the Italian San Girolamo version of 1902. The NT appeared in Ratisbon in 1923. A corrected version was published in Bahia in 1955.

ABS and BFBS jointly commissioned a translation, known as the Brazilian version, by a committee most of whose members were native speakers. The NT was issued in sections from 1904 to 1908, and the entire OT in 1917. A generation later, the Bible Society of Brazil undertook the Revised Authorized (or Revised Modernized) version, based jointly on Almeida and the Brazilian version. The NT appeared in 1951 and the Bible in 1958. The 26 translators included Antonio de Campos Gonÿalves and Robert G. Bratcher. Gonÿalves also participated in a NT based on a critical text, and published by the Brazilian Bible Press (Rio de Janeiro, 1949). The Roman Catholic Liga de Estudos Bíblicos published a translation of the NT (1955–61; rev. ed., 1970) and parts of the OT and Apocrypha. Luis G. de Fonseca and others published a Roman Catholic NT (Lisbon, 1957–60). A whole Bible based on the original texts and modeled after the French Maredsous Bible was translated at the Catholic Biblical Center of Sao Paulo and published in 1959.

For linguistic reasons it was necessary to prepare separate common language translations for Brazil and Portugal. The Brazilian NT was published in 1973, and the Portuguese NT in 1978. The Portuguese committee included both Roman Catholics and Protestants. Work on the OT continues in both projects.

Numerous individual and denominational versions have appeared, notably a Bible by Matos Soares (NT, 1930; OT, 1934; Bible, rev. ed., 1956). Several Roman Catholics have also translated the NT, namely, Huberto Rohden (1934; rev. ed., 1938), Alvaro Negromonte (1948), and Lincoln Ramos (1956–58). A Portuguese Watchtower Bible was published in 1967.

**Bibliography.** J. L. Swellengrebel, *TBT* 23 (1972): 126–34; H. Wendt, *Die Portuguesischen Bibelübersetzüngen*, diss. (1964).

**9. Japanese.** This language has nearly 120 million home speakers, but is the official language for over 120 million.

The first Scriptures arrived in Japan with Christianity in 1549 when Francis Xavier brought with him a MS of Matthew, translated in Goa by a Japanese convert called Yajiro or Anjiro. Juan Fernandez and Manoel Barreto later translated much of the NT, but neither of these versions was ever printed. In 1587 a decree mandated expulsion from Japan as punishment for any foreigner engaged in Christian missionary activities. Christianity was then suppressed.

In 1837 the American Board of Commissioners for Foreign Missions made a fresh start in Singapore with the publication of John's Gospel and Epistles, translated by Karl F. A. Gutzlaff of the Netherlands Missionary Society. Later, B. J. Bettelheim made a translation of Luke, John, Acts, and Romans into the Luchu dialect (Hong Kong, 1955), which BFBS later revised (Vienna, 1873/74). Nothing more was published until the American Baptist Missionary Union published the first complete Japanese NT, a work translated by John Goble and Nathan Brown and edited with interlinear references and critical notes by Tetsuya Kawakatsu (Yokohama, 1871–79; rev. ed., 1900 by F. G. Harrington). J. C. Hepburn, of the American Presbyterian Mission, produced an independent translation of Mark, John (1872), and Matthew (1873) in Yokohama. Under the guidance of C. Carrothers, Japanese Christians produced translations of Matthew and Mark (Tokyo, 1875, 1876).

From 1876 to 1880 ABS, BFBS, and NBSS published a NT that was revised by BFBS in 1884. This revised NT, together with an OT published by the same three societies in 1882–87, became known as the Standard Version or Motoyaku ("first version"). Its various parts were all published in Yokohama. The translators of OT and NT worked separately until 1878, when a permanent translation committee was formed that included J. C. Hepburn, S. R. Brown, and D. Crosby Greene, assisted from 1884 by Takayoshi Matsuyama, Masahisa Uemura, and Kajinosuke Ibuka. The NT was revised in 1917, and thus became known as the Kaiyaku or Revised Version. It was published with the Standard Version OT. A revision of the OT was undertaken with Job (1950) and Psalms (1951), but was then abandoned in favor of a new translation.

The Orthodox Ivan D. Kasatkin, chaplain to the Russian Consulate and later Archbishop Nicolai, translated the Psalms (1885) and the NT (1901), with the help of Paul Zukumaro Nakai.

The Roman Catholic Press in Tokyo produced Bible selections and stories (1879), followed by Matthew and Mark (1895), and the other Gospels (1897). The Gospels were translated by Goro Takahashi with the assistance of Michael Steichen and Noel Peri. In 1910 a NT appeared that was translated by Emile Raguet, who was assisted by Yoshikazu Kako and others. Although Raguet was a Protestant missionary of the Paris Missionary Society, his version was often reprinted. It became the standard Roman Catholic version. A colloquial revision of the Gospels appeared in 1963/64, in a diglot with English. Eusebius Breitung and Shigeo Kawanami translated from the Vulgate an OT in moderately literary Japanese and published it from 1954 to 1959. Under the direction of Bernardin Schneider from 1958, Franciscans in Tokyo translated the NT and most of the OT.

Various efforts were made to translate the Scriptures into simple or colloquial Japanese. These efforts culminated in 1955 with the Japan Bible Society's publication of a colloquial Bible, translated by Senji Tsuru (OT), T. Matsumoto (NT), and other native speakers. In 1964 Federico Barbaro and others translated another Bible in colloquial language. The Lockman Foundation sponsored a New Japanese Bible (NT, 1965; OT, 1970). A Living Bible appeared in 1978, and a Watchtower Bible in 1982. The Japan Bible Society published a common language NT in 1978, and three OT books appeared in 1984. In 1983 the Modern Japanese Bible Publishers published a Bible in modern speech, translated by Reiji Oyama. An annotated Franciscan translation is in progress.

Scriptures have also been printed in adapted Chinese *(kunten)* and Roman scripts.

*Bibliography.* J. van Hecken, *Neue Zeitschrift für Missionswissenschaft,* XVI (1960): 81–94; E. F. Rhodes, *BT* 18 (1967): 61–70.

***10. German.*** Home and official language for nearly 100 million people in Germany, Austria, and Switzerland.

Ancestors of German Scriptures include the (Visi) Gothic translation of the Bible (except Kings) by Ulfilas or Wulfila (d. 383), a Frankish translation of Matthew made in 738 at the Abbey of Mondsee in Bavaria, and an East Frankish Gospel harmony, made about 830 at Fulda. Notker Labeo of St. Gallen (d. 1022) made translations of Job (now lost) and of the Psalms (largely reconstructed from his commentary on them). William, abbot of Ebersberg in Bavaria after 1048, made a translation of the Song of Songs that was widely copied. Several translations of the Psalms were made, some interlinear with Latin, and some based, not on the Vulgate, but on Jerome's translation from the Hebrew.

Among the earliest German texts are biblical glosses from the 8th century onward. There are translations of the Lord's Prayer from before 800, and Psalm translations from the 9th century. The Mondsee–Vienna fragments, probably from the 8th century, include a translation of Matthew. A Gospel harmony from about 830 was influential for over 400 years. Also, a verse life of Jesus called "Heliand" appeared about 830, followed by a translation of Genesis, both works in the Old Saxon dialect. In the early 11th century, Notker Labeo wrote an annotated commentary on the Psalms, and this model was applied by others to other biblical books.

In the Middle Ages verse translations of lections from Genesis appeared in Vienna (1100–50) and elsewhere. Some translations, such as Psalters, Gospel harmonies, and lectionaries, were produced to meet liturgical needs, while others, such as the "Worms Prophets," an Anabaptist publication of 1527, stemmed from groups critical of the church.

The first Bible printed in a modern language was published not later than 1466 by J. Mentelin of Strassburg; it was based on an anonymous 14th-century translation from the Vulgate. Between 1466 and 1521 at least 14 editions of High German Bibles were printed, some in language already antiquated. They were rapidly superseded by the translations of Martin Luther (penitential Psalms, 1517; NT, 1522; Pentateuch, 1523; historical books and Job–Song of Songs, 1524; Isaiah–Malachi, 1532; Bible with Apocrypha, 1534 [all published in Wittenberg]). It is estimated that by 1533, one German household in 10 had a Luther NT. The 8th edition of the Luther Bible (1545) is the last for which Luther himself was entirely responsible. Based on the original texts, Luther's translation had a major influence on the development of a unified German language, and remains the standard Bible for Protestants. His *Sendbrief vom Dolmetschen* (1530) remains a classic for Bible translation theory. The influence of Luther's translation extended to the Danish (1524), Swedish (1526), Dutch (1526), and Icelandic (1540) translations, and through Tyndale had some influence on the English Authorized Version (1611). Revisions by Luther himself were published in 1541 ("Melanchthon's Bible"), 1545 (the "standard Luther text"), and 1568 (the first with verse divisions).

Light Roman Catholic adaptations of Luther's NT were made, notably by Hieronymus Emser (1527), reprinted until the 18th century. Emser's NT and Luther's OT were the main sources of a Bible translation by the Dominican Johann Dietenberger, published in 1534; this was revised in 1630 and 1662, and came to be known as the "Catholic Bible of Mainz." This was followed in 1537 by the Roman Catholic Bible of Johann Eck.

Luther's translation was least easily understood in the southern part of the German-speaking area, and adaptations of his NT were published in 1522 and 1523 by Adam Petri and Thomas Wolf. The Zurich Bible of 1524–29 consisted of Luther's translation of Genesis–Song of Songs and NT, the rest of the Hebrew OT (not yet available in Luther's translation) by a committee of Zurich ministers, including Huldrich Zwingli who translated the Psalms, and a version of the Apocrypha by Leo Jud (Juda), adapted to Swiss German usage. This translation was reprinted in 1531 with 200 illustrations, many by Holbein. It was revised in 1540 by Jud with the help of the Jewish scholar Michael Adam for the OT. Some editions of the Zurich Bible included expansions, marked by square brackets, and alternative translations in the margin. It was further revised in 1559 (the "Baptist Bible"), 1772, 1817, 1882, and more extensively in 1931 (the "Zwingli Bible"). A Bible translated by Johannes Piscator was published in Herborn in 1602–6, and was adopted in 1684 as the official translation for the canton of Bern (Berne); a revision appeared in Bern in 1823. The Berleburger Bible, a sectarian version showing mystical tendencies, appeared in 1726–42.

Further revisions of Luther's work appeared in 1870 (NT), 1892 (Bible), 1912, 1956 (NT), 1964 (OT), 1971 (Apocrypha), and 1984 (NT). Several revisions were also made by individual scholars.

An outstanding feature of the German biblical tradition is the number of translations produced by leading scholars in the course of their academic work. New translations by individuals include those by T. Crell and I. Stegmann (NT, 1630); C. Möller (NT, 1700); Thomas A. Erhard (Bible, 1722); J. A. Bengel (NT, 1753); J. D. Michaelis (Bible, 1769–90); J. H. D. Moldenhaur (Bible, 1774–90); Moses Mendelssohn (Pentateuch, 1780–83, in Hebrew characters; Joshua and Judges, 1805); G. M. Wittmann (NT, 1808, called the "Regensburg Version"); W. M. L. de Wette with J. C. W. Augusti (Bible, 1809–14; rev. ed., 1831/32); Johann Gossner (NT, 1815); J. H. Kistemaker (NT, 1825; rev. ed., 1834, often reprinted by BFBS); Asher ben Joseph (Joseph Johlson) (OT in Hebrew script, 1827–36); Moses Landau (OT in Hebrew script, 1833–37); L. Zunz (OT, 1837); V. Loch and W. K. Reischl (Bible, 1851–66); Carl Brockhaus (NT, 1855; Bible, 1871); C. Weizsäcker (NT, 1875, from Tischendorf's 8th ed. of the Greek text); H. L. Strack and O. Zöckler (Bible with Apocrypha, 1886–94); F. E. Schlachter (NT, 1903; Bible, 1905); J. Weiss (NT, 1906/7); E. Dimmler (NT, 1911–17; OT, 1920–22); V. Schweitzer (commissioned by the Roman Catholic Bishop Keppler and thus known as the Keppler Bible [NT, 1915; rev. ed., 1948, 1964; Psalms, 1937]); N. Schlögl (NT, 1921; OT, 1922); H. Menge (NT, 1923; OT, 1926; Apocrypha, 1928; Bible, rev. ed., 1949); P. Riessler (OT, 1924) and R. Storr (NT, 1926), issued together since 1934; M. Buber and F. Rosenzweig (OT, 1925–29 [a very literal Jewish translation]; reissued 1930–48, 1956–58); F. Tillmann (NT, 1927; rev. ed., 1947, based on the Vogels Greek text); A. Schlatter (NT, 1931); A. E. Knoch (NT, 1939, following the English Concordant NT of 1921); N. H. Tur-Sinai (Harry Torczyner) and others (OT, 1937); L. Thimme (NT, 1946); O. Karrer (NT, 1950; rev. ed., 1954); H. Bruns (NT, 1959; rev. ed., 1965; OT, 1962; rev. ed., 1965); A. Zwettler (NT, 1960); J. Zink (NT, 1965); U. Wilckens and others (NT, 1970).

An important strand in the Roman Catholic biblical tradition was a translation with commentary begun by Heinrich Braun, published in 1789–1807; the third edition was done by J. F. Allioli (1830–37), and was thereafter known as the Allioli Bible (rev. ed. by B. Weinhart [1865];

by A. Arndt [1899–1902]; by K. Thieme [1949]). The NT was revised by J. Kürzinger in 1953, and from the Greek in 1957, and combined with an OT by V. Hamp and M. Stenzel (1955; rev. ed., 1962). The Allioli NT was again revised in 1965 by Eleonore Beck and Gabriele Miller. Two cousins, Leander and Carl van Ess, produced a NT in 1807 that was the first Roman Catholic translation from the Greek; the 1816 edition brought the text into line with the Vulgate, but Greek variants were noted. The same translators published an OT (Genesis–Esther, 1822; Job–2 Maccabees, 1836); the complete Bible appeared in 1840. K. Rösch and E. Henne produced a NT in 1914–21 (rev. ed., 1924, 1936, 1967) and a Bible in 1934; the NT followed the Nestle Greek text until 1936, thereafter the Merk text. In 1934 the Klosterneuburg Bible, edited by Pius Parsch from other Roman Catholic translations, appeared in Austria. The Herder Bible Commentary included a new translation edited by R. Pesch and U. Schütz, and was later revised with reference to the French Jerusalem Bible (NT, 1958; Bible, 1966; rev. ed., 1968). The "Einheitsübersetzung" (NT, 1972; rev. ed., 1975; OT, 1974; Bible with Apocrypha, rev. ed., 1980) owes its name to the fact that it was intended for use in all German-speaking Roman Catholic dioceses; however, there was some Protestant cooperation. A light revision of the text was issued with Jerusalem Bible notes in 1986.

A first attempt at a common-language translation of the NT was published in 1967 under the title *Gute Nachricht für Sie;* it was based on the English *Good News for Modern Man* (1966). A fresh start was made with *Die Gute Nachricht* (1971); the complete Bible with Apocrypha appeared in 1982. The translation was jointly commissioned by the Bible societies and Catholic Bible work agencies in the four German-speaking countries.

A Watchtower Bible appeared in 1971 (NT, 1963), and was revised in 1986.

**Bibliography.** W. Walther, *Die deutsche Bibelübersetzungen des Mittelalters* (repr. 1966); K. E. Schöndorf, *Die Tradition der deutschen Psalmenübersetzung* (1967); E. Fascher, *Luthers Bibelübersetzung im Wandel der Zeiten* (1968); E. Arndt, *Weltwirkung der Reformation* (1969), 2:416–22; BGDS(T) 92 (1970): 1–20; S. Hahn, *Luthers übersetzungsweise im Septembertestament von 1522* (1972); W. Kolb, *Die Bibelübersetzung Luthers* (1972); E. Mühlhaupt, *Luthers Testament* (1972); K. Weber, *Bibelübersetzungen unter der Lupe* (2d ed., 1973); R. Steiner, *Neue Bibelübersetzungen vorgestellt, verglichen und gewertet* (1975); S. Meurer, ed., *Verrat an Luther?* (1977); K.-H. zur Mühlen, *Jahrbuch des Evangelischen Bibelwerkes* 18 (1978): 90–97; K. A. Strand, *Catholic German Bibles of the Reformation Era* (1982); H. Reinitzer, *Biblia deutsch. Luthers Bibelübersetzung und ihre Tradition* (1983); S. Meurer, ed., *Die neue Lutherbibel. Beiträge zum revidierten Text 1984* (1985).

***11. Panjabi (Punjabi).*** This language includes 70 million speakers in Pakistan and India.

The Serampore missionaries supervised a translation of the NT (dated 1811 but not issued until 1815) and parts of the OT (Pentateuch,

1818; Joshua–Esther, 1819; Job–Song of Songs, 1821; Isaiah–Ezekiel 26, 1826). Between 1840 and 1902 ABS and BFBS alternated in publishing a translation by American Presbyterian missionaries J. Newton, L. Janvier, and J. Harvey of the NT (1868) and large parts of the OT (1874–1902). A revision of the NT was published by BFBS between 1895 and 1900; Proverbs followed in 1913. A new translation of Isaiah (1902) and Psalms (1913) was made by H. E. Perkins and revised by E. Guilford of CMS.

The Bible Society of India and Ceylon commissioned from 1950 a translation by Sundar Singh, C. H. Loehlin, Harbans Singh, and Sachha Singh Taj (NT, 1955; OT, 1959; Bible repr., 1981). The Bible Society of India also published a translation by James Massey (NT, 1976; Bible, 1984).

**12. French.** With nearly 70 million home speakers, French is the official language for 220 million in France, Belgium, Switzerland, Canada, and elsewhere.

Not later than the early 12th century, the Psalms were translated by Eadwin (c. 1120) into Norman French in two forms: one based on Jerome's translation from the Hebrew, and the other on the Gallican Psalter, revised by Jerome from the LXX. Norman translations of Revelation and Samuel–Kings followed about 50 years later, and translations of Scripture multiplied in the 12th and 13th centuries. About 1170 the Waldensians were active in this area, but their translations were suppressed under Popes Lucius III and Innocent III.

In 1180 a work appeared that was entitled *Historia scholastica*. Completed in 1170 by Peter Comestor, the work contained a digest of Bible history. From 1291 this was translated into French and expanded, with the addition of more biblical text, by Guyart des Moulins, whose work appeared in 1295. Successive editions progressively increased the amount of Scripture, and the work became known as the *Bible historiale*, often reproduced with additional material. The first printed Scripture was an abridgement of the *Bible historiale*, published at Lyon in 1496, probably by the Augustinian monks Julien Macho and Pierre Farget. The same translators published at Lyon about 1477 a NT based on Guyart's work. The Psalms were printed at Lyon about 1483. The *Bible historiale* also formed the basis of a Bible edited by the king's confessor, Jean de Rely. This Bible was issued in Paris by order of Charles VIII, probably about 1495–96, and reprinted 12 times by 1545.

The first printed Bible was translated from the Vulgate by the humanist Jacques Lefèvre d'Étaples (Faber Stapulensis) (NT, 1523; Psalms, 1525; OT, 1528; Bible, 1530). The NT was published anonymously in Paris, but the rest of the Bible in Antwerp, since those who published Scriptures in French were suspected of reforming tendencies.

The NT was revised by Lefèvre in 1534 and 1541. Eliminating reforming prefaces and notes, Catholic versions followed by Nicolas de Leuze, François van Larben, and others in 1550, and Michel de Bay (Baïus) in 1573. A Catholic adaptation of the Geneva Bible (see below) by R. Benoist, the confessor of Henri IV, appeared in Paris in 1566. The Benoist NT was improved by Jacques de Bay, the nephew of Michel de Bay, and formed part of his *Bible de Louvain*, published in Anvers in 1578 and reprinted several times in Paris.

The Reformer Pierre Robert, also known as Olivetan, a cousin of Calvin, translated the OT from Hebrew, and revised Lefèvre's Apocrypha and NT, in the Neuchâtel Bible of 1535, with a preface by Calvin. Olivetan died in 1538, but his translation continued to be printed and revised. The 1553 edition was the first whole Bible to contain the system of chapter and verse division devised by the publisher, Robert Estienne (Stephanus), the system still generally in use. The 1588 revision, edited by B. C. Bertram with the help of Calvin's successor Théodore de Bèze (Beza) and others, became known as the (French) Geneva Bible; it was further revised by G. Diodati (Geneva, 1644), Samuel des Marets (Amsterdam, 1669), David Martin (Utrecht, 1696 [NT], 1707 [Bible]), David Durand (London, 1740 [NT]), Pierre Roques (1744), Louis Gaussen and others (NT, 1839), W. H. Kirkpatrick and L. Durand for BFBS (Brussels, 1869; Oxford, 1872), C. L. Frossard (NT, 1869) and others. A revision of the Geneva Bible was published by J. F. Ostervald in 1724, itself revised in 1744, and became the basis of the Synodal version (NT trial ed., 1894; NT, 1903; Bible, 1910).

The Roman Catholic Jacques Corbin translated the Bible from the Vulgate (1641–42). A French-Latin diglot NT, the French translated by M. de Marolles from Erasmus's Greek text, appeared in 1649. In 1667 the Jansenists of Port-Royal published a NT, called the Mons NT, prepared by a group of translators under the leadership of Le Maître de Sacy, who took the Vulgate as their base text, but corrected it from the Greek. The Vulgate, corrected from the Hebrew, formed the basis of the corresponding OT (1672–96). The whole work became known as the Port-Royal or de Sacy Bible; its excellent style made it popular among Catholics and Protestants alike. It was revised by L. de Carrières (1701–16); H. François (1743); and N. le Gros (1753). L. de Carrières adapted it for Canada with a paraphrase (1846). The Port-Royal version strongly influenced a NT by Denis Amelote (1666–70), which was revised by Genevan Protestants in 1835.

Under the direction of the Protestant ministers of Geneva, Hugues Oltramare published a fresh translation of the NT in 1872. The OT counterpart by Louis Segond appeared in 1874 and became in time the standard Bible for French Protestants. Segond's NT appeared in 1880; his translation was successively revised by J. H. Alexander and others (Bible, 1975), and by J.-M. Nicole and others (Bible, 1978).

Other committee translations include the Jewish OT (1899–1906); the "Centenary Bible" (1916–47) published to celebrate the centenary of the Protestant Bible Society of Paris; a NT under the direction of M. Goguel and H. Monnier (1929); a Bible by members of the Society of St. Paul (1932); the Maredsous Bible (NT, 1948; Bible, 1950; rev. ed., 1968), by P. G. Passelecq and other monks of Maredsous; the Jerusalem Bible (1948–54; rev. ed., 1973), later adapted into other languages; a Bible by A. Liénart and other scholars of the Ligue Catholique de l'Evangile (1951); the "ACEBAC Version" by Canadian Roman Catholics (Gospels, 1951; NT, 1953); the Pléïade translation by E. Dhorme and others (OT and Apocrypha, 1956–59; NT, 1971); the Watchtower NT (1963); an ecumenical edition of Luke and Acts (1966), the forerunner of the TOB (Ecumenical Translation of the Bible, prepared jointly by Catholics and Protestants, with some Orthodox participation; NT, 1972; OT, 1975); and the common language translation (NT, 1971; Bible with Apocrypha, 1986).

Numerous individual translations include a Bible in popular language by Sébastien Châteillon (1555); a NT mainly by D. Bouhours (1697–1703); a NT by the early biblical critic, R. Simon (1702); a NT by I. de Beausobre and J. Lenfant (1718); a Bible by Eugène Genoude, a Roman Catholic layman (1819–24 [?]; rev. ed., 1841; rev. ed. by A. Gaume, 1863); a NT by A. Rilliet from the Codex Sinaiticus (1858); a NT and Bible by J. N. Darby, founder of the so-called Plymouth Brethren (1859; 1885); a NT and Bible by J. B. Glaire, from the Vulgate with papal authorization (1861; 1877); OT books with notes by E. Renan (Job, 1859; Song of Songs, 1860; Ecclesiastes, 1882); a Pentateuch by L. Wogue, a rabbi (1869); a Bible by A. Arnaud (1880–81); a Bible by A. Crampon (1885, 1894–1904); a Bible by E. Ledrain (1886–99); a NT by A. Loisy (1922); a NT from the Greek by B. Botte, a Roman Catholic (1944); a NT and a Bible by E. Osty with J. Trinquet (1949; 1974); a NT by P. de Beaumont in simplified French (1973; rev. ed., 1976); a Bible by A. Chouraqui (1975–77); a NT (1976) and OT books (from 1982) by A. Kuen, based on a comparison of 80 modern versions; a Bible by P. de Beaumont in consultation with S. Lyonnet (1981); Living Bible paraphrase of NT books (from 1973); translations of NT books in "basic French" by L. Rivière and others (from 1982).

**Bibliography.** R. A. Sayce, *Cambridge History of the Bible* (1963), 3:113–22; C. A. Robson, *Cambridge History of the Bible* (1969), 2:436–52; M. Carrez, *RHPR* 57 (1977): 335–41; J. Ellington, *TBT* 31 (1980): 135–40; H. Blocher, *TBT* 32 (1981): 145–48.

**13. Javanese.** This language has nearly 70 million home speakers, mainly in Indonesia.

The NT was first translated into a dialect of northern Java by the Baptist missionary Gottlob Brückner, and published at Serampore by the BFBS Java Auxiliary. A fresh translation was commissioned by the Netherlands Bible Society (NT, 1848; rev. ed., 1860; OT, 1854). BFBS published a translation by the Dutch Baptist (Mennonite) P. Jansz (NT, 1889; rev. ed., 1895–97; OT, 1890–95; Bible, 1906). All these publications were in Javanese script.

The first Scriptures in roman script were transliterations of Jansz's work (NT, 1909–11). A revision of Jansz in roman script was begun by D. Bakker and P. A. Jansz, the son of the translator, and completed by F. L. Bakker, son of D. Bakker (NT, 1929–40; rev. ed., 1956, 1978; OT, 1948–50; rev. ed., 1961). The OT MS, completed in 1941, survived a long stay in a concentration camp. A committee including Sularso Sopater, R. Prawiraatmadja, and Budi Mardono prepared a NT for the Reformed churches in 1972. An interconfessional common language NT prepared by a committee was published in 1980.

The first Scriptures in Arabic script were the Gospels and Acts, lightly revised by P. Penninga and published in 1893–1900. Matthew (1935) and Genesis and John (1939) in the Jansz–Bakker text were transliterated into Arabic script.

**14. Bihari.** Related to Hindi (see 4 above), this language has 65 million speakers in India and Nepal. Bihari has five dialects: (1) Bhojpuri (John, 1911; rev. ed., 1934); (2) Kortha (Mark, 1895); (3) Magahi (NT, 1818, but apparently not issued until 1826; Mark, rev. ed., 1890, retranslated, 1903); (4) Nagpuria (Matthew–1 Corinthians, 1907–14; Gospels, 1962–65, rev. ed., 1971); and (5) Maithili.

**15. Korean.** This language has over 60 million speakers.

Luke and John were printed privately in 1882; the NT in 1887 by BFBS, both at Mukden; the translators were John Ross and John Macintyre of the Church of Scotland Mission, assisted by Saw Sang Yun. A NT by the Baptist M. C. Fenwick appeared in 1919. A combined project of ABS, BFBS, and NBSS in Seoul produced a NT in 1900 (rev. ed., 1904, 1906) and a complete Bible in 1911. A rather free translation of the Bible by J. S. Gale with Korean assistants was issued in 1925. Translations by the Roman Catholics Laurence Syen (OT) and Paul Han (NT) were published, first privately, then by the Korean Catholic Federation (Gospels, 1910; Acts, 1922; Romans–Revelation, 1941; Genesis–1 Kings and Isaiah, 1958–61). A complete Bible was published by BFBS and the Korean Bible Society (KBS) in 1938, and a revision by KBS in 1952. An interconfessional translation by native speakers was published by KBS (NT, 1971; Bible with Apocrypha, 1977). A Living NT appeared in 1977.

*Bibliography.* Nosoon Kwak, *TBT* 27 (1976): 121–27.

**16. Italian.** With nearly 60 million home speakers, Italian is the official language for 65 million.

The earliest extant Scriptures are 14th–century MSS of Venetian and Tuscan Gospel harmonies, but probably by 1260 most of the Bible had been translated into Italian, and was circulating with additional material in the form of a *Bibbia Historiale.* The Franciscans, Dominicans, and Waldensians made wide use of translated biblical passages, sometimes translated not from the Vulgate but from French or Provençal. Two separate editions of the Bible appeared in Venice in 1471. The first, based on the Vulgate, was translated by Niccolò Malermi and often reprinted until 1567. The second was based partly on a 13th–century MS of Psalms 17–150, and followed Malermi from 2 Macc. 2:22 to the end of the NT. The translation of Antonio Brucioli, a lay humanist exiled from Florence, was also published in Venice (NT, 1530; Bible, 1532), and often revised and reprinted (1536, 1538, 1567). Its text, prefaces, and notes were influenced by Erasmus; it was placed on the index in 1559, the year in which it was decreed that vernacular translations must be authorized by the Inquisition. In Venice two Dominicans, Zacheria and Marinochino, published a Bible based closely on the Vulgate (1538). Massimo Teofilo, a former Benedictine converted to Protestantism, published in Lyon a NT based upon the Greek (1551). An idiomatic revision of Brucioli's Bible, intended primarily for Italian Protestant exiles, appeared in Geneva in 1562.

The standard Bible for Protestants was for long the translation by Giovanni Diodati (1607; rev. ed., 1641, 1711, 1744, 1819, 1850, 1854, 1855, 1885), now superseded by the Riveduta (revised) version, prepared under the leadership of Giovanni Luzzi (1916–24; NT, rev. ed., 1982).

The Pontifical Biblical Institute in Rome published the first volumes of a translation by A. Vaccari and others (Pentateuch, 1922; OT, 1943–58), and also sponsored a revised edition (1965). In 1929 the Cardinal Ferrari Society in Florence published a Bible translated by G. Ricciotti and others. The Marietti publishing house in Turin published a NT (1960) and an OT (1961), translated under the direction of S. Garofalo, and a separate translation of Genesis–2 Kings in diglot with Hebrew (1960–62). In 1964 there appeared an annotated Bible translated by E. Galbiati and others. In 1967 the pope commissioned a special translation of Acts by C. M. Martini (later, one of the editors of the UBS Greek text, and archbishop of Milan) and N. Venturini for presentation to distinguished guests. An ecumenical translation, known as the "Bibbia Concordata," translated by Catholic, Protestant, Orthodox, and Jewish schol-ars, was published in 1968. A Bible authorized by the Italian Episcopal Conference, and translated under the direction of E. Florit, was published in the Vatican in 1971.

An interconfessional common language translation of the NT appeared in 1976; the complete Bible followed in 1985.

Among individual and denominational translations are the NT translated from the Greek by M. Teofilo (1551); the Bible of A. Martini (NT, 1769–71; OT, 1776–81) translated at the suggestion of Pope Benedict XIV; the NT by the Waldensian A. Revel, arranged in chronological order (1881); the NT of E. L. Bevir (1891); the Bibles of M. Sales and E. Tintori (1931); the Bible of F. Nardoni (1960); the Watchtower NT (1963); the NT by F. Montixi (1972), based on the German Riethmüller version; and the Living NT (1981).

*Bibliography.* K. Foster, *Cambridge History of the Bible* (1969), 2:110–13; 3:452–65.

**17. Telugu.** With over 55 million speakers, this language is found mainly in India.

Early in the 18th century the Lutheran Benjamin Schultze translated the whole Bible into Telugu, and about 1795 James Dodds, a Scottish layman, translated the NT. The first published Scriptures were the synoptic Gospels translated by Augustus Desgranges of the London Missionary Society (1812). The Serampore missionaries translated and published the NT in 1818 and the Pentateuch in 1821. The BFBS in Madras published a NT in 1818 and Genesis in 1831, both translated from the English Authorized Version by E. Pritchett and J. Gordon assisted by A. Rayar. Pritchett's MSS were revised by a committee that published the OT (1851–54; rev. ed., 1857) and Matthew–Acts (1840–48). A separate version of the NT was prepared by J. S. Wardlaw and J. Hay (NT, 1856; rev. ed., 1860). Hay then started his own revision and was later joined by others (NT, 1878; Bible, 1881–1904; rev. ed., 1912, 1953); this long remained the standard version. In 1913–16 the non-Christian translator Bhujanga Rao published a poetical version of the NT.

D. Thomas, a Roman Catholic, translated the NT from the Vulgate (Gospels–Acts, 1914; Romans–Revelation, 1924). An annotated edition was published in 1966. A translation of various OT and NT books (Psalms, 1966; Acts–James, Revelation, 1974), based on the English Confraternity version, was made under the direction of Bishop I. Mummadi. Other translations include a separate Catholic translation by J. Wijngaards and K. V. Kavi of the Gospels (1973), a Living NT (1976), an interdenominational Protestant version of Ruth (1976), a Bible sponsored by India Bible Literature (Madras) and Grace Ministries (1984), and a Gospel harmony (1974), Luke (1979), and John (1980) in common language.

**18. Tamil.** This language has 55 million speakers in Sri Lanka, India, and Singapore.

In 1578 Roman Catholic missionaries published the first book ever printed in an Indian language; it contained Scripture selections. The Danish Lutheran Bartholomäus Ziegenbalg translated the NT with the help of Johann Ernst Gründler (Gospels–Acts, 1714; Romans–Revelation, 1715; rev. ed., 1722 [by Benjamin Schultze]). Between 1723 and 1728 Ziegenbalg and Schultze translated the OT with the Apocrypha. The whole Bible was revised by J. P. Fabricius in 1772–96, and the NT by C. T. E. Rhenius in 1833. The Fabricius OT and Rhenius NT were published in one volume in 1840, tentatively revised in 1850 (the "Jaffna Version"), and more thoroughly in 1871 by H. Bower (NT, 1864; OT, 1868); this edition became known as the "Union Version."

A MS version by P. Baldeus and A. de Mey was revised by others and published in 1759. A translation of the Gospels and Acts by French Catholic missionaries appeared in 1857. The NT was translated from the Vulgate by J. B. Trincal in 1891 and revised in 1906. A Catholic translation of the OT by H. M. Bottero and others appeared in 1904, and was revised in 1972. A further Catholic NT was published in 1953, and a new translation of the whole Bible, under the direction of Archbishop R. Arulappa of Madras, in 1970–72 (NT, rev. ed., 1974).

A new translation by L. P. Larsen and others was published by BFBS in Madras and later revised (NT, 1929; rev. ed., 1941–42, 1954; OT, 1936; rev. ed., 1949, 1954); the revision committee included C. E. Monahan, V. S. Azariah, S. C. Neill, and H. K. Moulton. The Bible Society of India published a common language NT in 1977; an interconfessional translation of the OT is in progress. A Living NT appeared in 1977, and an edition for Sri Lanka in 1981.

**Bibliography.** S. Kulandran, *A History of the Tamil Bible* (1967); *Missionsinsamlning och den nya Tamilbibeln* (1956).

**19. Marathi.** With over 50 million speakers in India, this language was formerly known as Mahratta.

The Serampore missionaries translated the whole Bible between 1807 and 1821 (NT, 1811; rev. ed., 1824), but unfortunately into the local dialect of Nagpur. American Board missionaries retranslated the NT (1826; rev. ed., 1830); revisions of the whole Bible were published in 1837–48; of the NT in 1851 and the whole Bible in 1855 and 1857; of the NT in 1907 and the Bible in 1924; of the NT in 1964 and Psalms in 1971.

Among individual translations, perhaps the most noteworthy is that by Ramabai Dongre Medhavi, known as Pandita Ramabai, in simple Marathi (NT, 1912; Bible, 1924). A NT by the Roman Catholic Yesu Das (a pseudonym for Maximillian Zinzer, S.J.) also appeared (Gospels–Acts, 1963; Romans–Revelation, 1967).

B. S. Jadhav and an interconfessional committee published a common language NT (1981) and

Bible (1987). A Living NT appeared (1978) as well as a Living Bible (1982).

**20. Vietnamese.** With over 50 million speakers, this language was formerly known as Annamese. In 1872 the Catholic liturgical Gospels and Epistles were published in Bangkok. Luke was translated in 1890 by M. Bonet from the French Ostervald version and published by BFBS in Paris. Mark (1899), John (1900), and Acts (1903) were translated by Walter James of BFBS. Mark was retranslated by P. M. Hosler (1913).

A. Schlicklin published a translation with Latin from the Vulgate (1913–16). W. C. and Mrs. Cadman and John D. Olsen, with other Christian and Missionary Alliance missionaries, translated a Bible (1925; NT, 1923; Genesis, rev. ed., 1922; NT, rev. ed., 1954) that was published by BFBS. Tran Duc Huan (NT, 1961; Bible, 1971), the Roman Catholics G. Gagnon (NT, 1962; OT, 1962–63), and Nguyên thẽ Thuân (NT [from the Greek], 1969; Bible, 1976) also made translations. The NT of Nguyên thẽ Thuân was lightly revised in 1970 in the direction of common language. Meanwhile, NT books were published between 1969 and 1973 in a common language translation by Nguyên van Nha and others. A Living NT appeared in 1976.

**21. Ukrainian.** This language has over 45 million speakers in the USSR. Translations include the Pentateuch by P. A. Kulisch (1869); NT (1880) and Bible (1900) by P. A. Kulisch and D. I. Puluj; NT (1939; rev. ed., 1971) and Bible (1962) by I. Ohienko.

**22. Turkish.** Nearly 45 million speakers. In Arabic script: a NT (1819), and an OT (1827), revised from Ali Bey's text by H. F. Diez and J. D. Kieffer (rev. ed., 1885). (Ali Bey was the name adopted by Albertus Bobovius, a Pole, taken to Turkey as a child, who translated the Bible from French in the mid-17th century.) In Armenian script: a liturgical Psalter with Armenian (1800); Khojentz NT (1819); an OT by W. Goodell with P. Constantinides (1839–42); revised Bible (1887/88). In Greek script: Psalms, translated by Seraphim, metropolitan of Caramania (1782); his NT (1826) and Bible (1866; rev. ed., 1835–38, 1905). In Roman script: the Bible (1941; corrected 1949) and the NT by T. Cosmades (1986).

**Bibliography.** P. H. Nilson, *TBT* 17 (1966): 133–38.

**23. Urdu.** Over 40 million speakers in Pakistan and India. In Devanagari script: Gospels by William Hunter and Mirza Fitrat (1805); NT by Henry Martyn with M. Fitrat (1817); OT books by W. Bowley (1828–40); Luke (1934). In Arabic script: NT by Henry Martyn with M. Fitrat (1814); much of OT by M. Fitrat (1821–29); Bible by W. Yates (1837–49); NT by A. Hartmann (rev. ed., 1930); Catholic Bible (1958). In roman script: Matthew (1834); NT (1841); Bible (1843); new NT (1984).

**24. Polish.** Nearly 37 million speakers. Translations include a Psalter (13th cent.); much of OT (mid-15th cent.); beginning of John (1516); Ecclesiastes (1522); NT by Jan Sieklucki, a friend of Luther (1553); Krakow Bible (1561), superseded as standard for Catholics by Jakub Wujek's translation (NT, 1593; Bible, 1599); Brest Bible (1563), superseded as standard for Protestants by Danzig Bible (NT, 1606; Bible, 1632); translation by members of the Polish Academy of Science (NT, 1966; Bible, 1975); official Catholic "Millennial Bible" (1965); Catholic Bible by M. Peter, M. Wolniewicz, and others (1973–75); common language Gospels (1979).

**Bibliography.** F. Manthey, *TGl* 52 (1962): 462–67; B. Enholc-Narzyánska, *TBT* 14 (1963): 133–38; J. Narzyánski and B. Enholc-Narzyánska, *The Activity of the British and Foreign Bible Society in Poland 1816–1966* (1966); J. Narzyánski, *Jahrbuch des Evangelischen Bibelwerkes* 10 (1967); M. Wolniewicz, *Les Sciences bibliques en Pologne après a guerre (1945–1970)* (1974), 19–41.

**25. Gujarati.** Over 35 million speakers in India. Translations include Matthew (1809) and the NT (1820), under the supervision of the Serampore missionaries; NT (1821; rev. ed., 1832); OT (1823), by James Skinner and others; common language NT (1976), by N. Oliver and others; Living NT (1985).

**26. Thai.** Over 35 million speakers. Translations include Luke, by K. F. A. Gutzlaff (1834); NT (1835–43; rev. ed., 1843–50); OT (1860–83); NT (1880–83); Bible, by American Presbyterian missionaries (1896); Roman Catholic Bible, by G. Phimphisan and others (1960–68 [?]); interconfessional popular language NT (1977, corrected 1984; OT, 1981); Living NT (1977).

**27. Persian (Farsi).** Over 30 million speakers in Iran and Afghanistan. Translations include Jewish OT translations from at least the early 14th century; Pentateuch in Hebrew script (1546); Gospels (1657); Matthew, by Muhammed Fitrat, under the supervision of R. H. Colebrook (1805); Gospels, by the Roman Catholic Leopoldo Sebastiani (1813); NT (1815) and Psalms (1816) by Henry Martyn, assisted by Saiyad Ali Khan; OT, by T. Robinson (1828–38); revised Bible (1895); common language NT, by Shams-e-Eshaq, E. H. Jaeger, and others (1976).

**28. Indonesian.** Over 17.5 million home speakers; official language for 89 million. Although Indonesian has been the national language of Indonesia since 1945, Klinkert's Malay OT (1879) and Bode's NT (1938) continue to be used. Other translations include individual Bible books, mostly in pilot translations, from 1955; pilot NT (1971); Bible (1975), in new orthography with Apocrypha (1975); directed by J. L. Swellengrebel until 1959, and J. L. Ch. Abineno from 1962. Common language interconfessional NT (1977), revised 1978, Ruth and Song of Songs (1980), Bible (1985), Apocrypha in preparation; Living NT (1976).

**Bibliography.** J. L. Swellengrebel, *TBT* 6 (1955): 110–19.

**29. Burmese.** 27 million speakers. Translations include Matthew by Felix Carey (1815); NT (1831); OT by Adoniram Judson (1834–35); NT by Tun Nyein (1903); Living NT (1985); common language NT by Sein Pe and others (1986).

**30. Kannada.** Over 25 million speakers in India. In Telugu script: Gospels–Acts (1820); OT (1827–31); Romans–Galatians, Colossians–Revelation, by John Hands with other missionaries of the London Missionary Society (1830). A new translation of the NT appeared in 1906, and of the Bible in 1928. In Kannada script: Mark (1852); NT (1854); pilot OT (1860); Bible (1865); Living NT (1980); interconfessional common language NT by Vasanthkumar and others (1982).

**31. Malayalam.** Over 25 million speakers in India. The first Scriptures were prepared for the ancient Syrian Church in Travancore. The Gospels were translated by Timapah Pillay and Philippos (1811); NT (1829); OT by Benjamin Bailey of the Church Missionary Society (1839–41; rev. ed., 1859); NT (1854); Job–Song of Songs (1859; rev. ed., 1881); Isaiah–Malachi by Hermann Gundert of the Basel Evangelical Mission (1886); interdenominational "Union version" (NT, 1873–80; OT, 1910); NT, published by the San Jose Book Stall (1978); Living NT (1980); common language NT by T. Chandy and P. K. Nainan (1980); NT by F. Muliyil and others (1981); NT (1977) and Bible (1981) by the Kerala Catholic Bishops' Council's Bible Commission; interconfessional Bible with Apocrypha, directed by J. Pulikunnel (1983).

**Bibliography.** R. Wagner, *Ind Ch H R* (1968).

**32. Hausa.** Nearly 25 million speakers, mainly in Nigeria and Niger. Translations include Matthew, John, and Acts (1857); Genesis (1858); Exodus (1859); NT (1880); Isaiah by James Frederick Schön (1881); NT by W. R. S. Miller and others (1912); Bible by Miller and others (1932; NT, rev. ed., 1972); interconfessional Bible with Apocrypha by Daniel Wambutda and others (1980).

**33. Oriya.** Nearly 25 million speakers in India. Translations include NT (1807); Job–Malachi (1809); Joshua–Esther under the supervision of the Serampore missionaries (1811); OT by Amos Sutton (1842–44); Gospels–Acts (1918); "Union" Bible (1953); Living NT (1978); common language NT by C. Mohi Mohan and others (1986).

**34. Romanian.** Over 20 million speakers. Translations include MSS of Psalms, Acts, and some Epistles from the late 13th century; Scripture selections in the Sibiu Catechism (1541); Gospels by Coresi, a Walachian deacon (1560/61); NT by a monk named Silvestru and others (1648); Bible by Nicolae Milescu and others, the standard Orthodox Bible, often reprinted (1688); Bible by Ion Eliade Rădulescu (1858); Bible by P. D. Cornilescu, adopted as the Bible Society text, and much used by Protestants (1921; rev. ed., 1924);

Orthodox NT (1927), Psalms (1929), Bible (1936) by V. G. Galaction (Gregorie Pisculescu); Bible, including light revision of Galaction Psalms and NT (1968); Catholic NT, with notes by Emil Pascal (1975).

**35. Dutch.** 20 million speakers. Dutch is similar to Flemish and indistinguishable from it until at least 1600. About 1200 a "life of Jesus," known as the Liège Diatessaron, appeared and was widely used. About 1390 Johan Schutken translated the NT with Psalms and some other OT portions; this was printed in 1477. The OT without Psalms (the so-called Delft Bible, based on a 14th-century MS) was also printed in 1477, as was a translation of the liturgical Gospels and Epistles. Schutken's Psalms were reprinted in 1480. The Psalms based on Luther's version appeared in 1520; it was later attacked by the Inquisition, and only one copy of the original edition has survived. In 1522 the Franciscan friar Johan Pelt translated Matthew from Erasmus's Latin; this was condemned for its reforming tendencies. Other translations include a NT based on the Vulgate (1522); a NT based on Luther's translation (1522); the first complete OT (1525), with Genesis–Psalms influenced by Luther, and Proverbs–Malachi by the Delft Bible. Based upon Luther and upon the Vulgate where Luther was not available, the first complete Bible was published in Antwerp by Jacob van Liesveldt. An unofficial Catholic revision appeared in 1528. The first Catholic Bible, by Nicolaas van Winghe and others, was published in 1548 and was widely used. A Bible edited by Jan Cheylliaert in 1556 and popular in the Reformed Church was partly influenced by the German Zurich version and the 1526 Dutch Bible; it was not widely used. Jan Utenhove's NT (1556), the first translation from the Greek, was never reprinted. The 1558 "Biestkins Bible" (NT, 1554) was used by Mennonites and Dutch Lutherans until 1648. It was followed by the Bible by Govaert van Wingen (1561/62), used by the Reformed Church until 1637, and the 1599 revision of the Louvain Bible, often reprinted and revised as the standard Catholic Bible. In 1618 the decision was taken to make a new translation from the original languages; the result was the 1637 States-General Bible, the standard text of the Dutch Reformed Church (rev. ed., 1977). Later translations include the Old Catholic Bible (1732); the NT based on the Greek text underlying J. N. Darby's translation (1877); the Synodal NT (1897); the Leiden translation, based on the results of modern biblical studies, and popular in liberal circles (1901); the Utrecht NT, with conservative notes by A. M. Brouwer (1927); the interdenominational translation by the Netherlands Bible Society (NT, 1939; Bible, 1951; Apocrypha, 1975); the Katholieke Bijbelstichting translation (NT, 1961; corrected, 1966; OT, 1968–73); the Watchtower translation (NT, 1963; Bible, 1969);

interconfessional common language translation (NT, 1972; Bible, 1982); Living NT (1976); numerous other translations by individual and groups of scholars, including books in contemporary Dutch published by the Netherlands Bible Society (1961–75), and a translation of the Psalms in which Catholics, Protestants, Jews, and Muslims participated (1965).

*Bibliography.* C. C. de Bruin, *De Statenbijbel en zijn voorgangers* (1937); B. M. F. van Iersel, et al., eds., *Van taal tot taal. Opstellen over het vertalen van de Schriften* (1977); C. C. de Bruin, ed.; *Corpus sacrae scripturae neerlandicae medii aevi: series maior* (1978–); C. Houtman, *Nederlands Vertalingen van het Oude Testament* (1980); H. W. Hollander and E. W. Tuinstra, eds., *Bijbel Vertalen, Liefhebberij of wetenschap?* (1985).

**36. Sundanese.** Over 22 million speakers in Indonesia. Translations include Matthew by an assistant of Isaac Esser (1854); Luke by G. J. Grashuis (1866); NT (1877) and Bible with revised NT (1891) by S. Coolsma; and a common language NT by Kasim Aniroen, Odeli Suardi, and Eddy Sastradinata (1977).

**37. Pashto.** Over 19 million speakers in Pakistan and in Afghanistan where the language is called Pakhto. Translations include the NT (1818) and Pentateuch, under the supervision of the Serampore missionaries (1824); Bible, by T. J. Lee Mayer with T. P. Hughes, T. Valpy French, and others (1890–95); NT (1945; rev. ed., 1968); portions of a new translation based on the NEB, published by the Pakistan Bible Society (1981) and NT by M.-L. Pajari and others (1986).

**38. Swahili (KiSwahili).** Over 4 million home speakers; everyday language for about 15 million more; lingua franca for about 30 million more, in Tanzania, Kenya, and elsewhere. In Southern KiSwahili (traditionally taken as the basis of literary or standard KiSwahili): Ruth, Jonah (1868); NT, by Edward Steere and others (1869–79; rev. ed., 1883, 1892, 1893, 1921); Psalms, by Steere (1871); Psalms, by F. R. Hodgson (1891); OT, by Hodgson with Jessie Hodgson (1895); Gospels–Acts, by E. Brutel (1913); Union NT (1950); OT, by A. M. Hellier and others (1952); interconfessional NT, by P. Renju, D. Mhina, and D. Waruta (1977). In Zaire KiSwahili: NT (1955; rev. ed., 1972); OT (1960; rev. ed., 1975); NT, by M. A. Ipuma and others (1981).

*Bibliography.* H. van't Veld, *TBT* 17 (1966): 74–80.

**39. Rajasthani (Marwari).** 18 million speakers, mainly in India. Translations include a NT, by the Serampore missionaries (1821); John (1969) and Mark (1974) by P. Domji and others. The Serampore missionaries published a NT in the Bikaneri dialect (1820); Matthew in the Mewari (Oodyapoora) dialect (1815); the NT in Malvi (southeastern Rajasthani) (1826); the NT in Harauti (1821); Matthew in Jaipuri (1815).

**40. Serbo-Croatian.** Over 17 million speakers in Yugoslavia; Serbian occurs in Cyrillic script, Croatian in Latin script. Liturgical Gospels and Epistles were translated by Bernardin of Spalato

(1495). Antun Dalmatin and Stipan Konzul Istrianin, Protestant refugees in Germany, translated the NT in Glagolitic script (1562/63) and Cyrillic (1563). Other Scriptures in Cyrillic, as used in Serbia, include: Bible (1804); NT, by Vuk S. Karadžić, an influential and often reprinted work, but not approved by the Serbian Orthodox Church (1847); lightly revised NT with new OT by G. Daničić (1868); NT, by E. M. Čarnić and others (1973). In roman script, as used in Croatia: Isaiah–Malachi by Dalmatin and Istrianin (see above), with others (1564); annotated Bible, literally translated from the Vulgate by M. P. Katančić (1831); transliteration of Vuk's NT (1864); transliteration of Vuk-Daničić (see above), often revised (1868); Bible with notes, translated from the original texts by I. E. Šarić, Roman Catholic Bishop of Sarajevo (1941–42); interconfessional revision of NT (1969); NT by L. Rupčić (1961; rev. ed., 1967), and embodied in the Croatian counterpart of the Jerusalem Bible (1968); Gospels by B. Duda and J. Fućak (1973); Living NT (1981).

*Bibliography.* A. Bierwisch and P. Ellingworth, *TBT* 24 (1973): 234–40.

**41. Yoruba.** Over 17 million speakers, mainly in Nigeria. The first Yoruba Bible is the only first Bible translation in a major African language made by local Christians. The work was supervised by Samuel Adjai Crowther, the first (Anglican) bishop on the Niger. Until 1856 he worked alone (Romans, 1850), then until 1862 he worked with Thomas King, a Yoruba, who had drafted Matthew (1853). The NT was revised by Charles A. Gollmer (1862), who worked with Crowther on the OT (1867–84). After 1880 Adolphus Mann became chief translator, assisted by D. O. Williams. The Yoruba Bible has been repeatedly revised, most recently in 1980.

**42. Rwanda-Rundi.** A group of languages including Kinyarwanda, spoken in Rwanda, and Kirundi, spoken in Burundi; over 15 million speakers in total. In Kinyarwanda: Catholic School Bible (1910); Gospels, by the Protestant Karl Roehl (1914); NT (1931; rev. ed., 1957), Psalms (1933), OT (1954), by H. E. Guillebaud and others; Catholic NT, by Alexis Kagame (1966; rev. ed., 1979); interconfessional translation of Mark (1981). In Kirundi: liturgical Gospels (1909); Luke, by Catholic missionary P. Bonneau (1920); Matthew and John, by N. P. Andersen, H. P. Jensen, and others (1935); NT, by H. E. and Rosemary Guillebaud with others (1951); Bible, by Rosemary Guillebaud and others (1967); Catholic translations of Matthew (1956), Mark (1957), and Gospels–Acts (1960).

**43. Fulfulde (Ful, Fulbe, Fula, Fulani, Peul, Peulh).** This language is spoken in different forms by 15 million people in Nigeria, Guinea, Senegal, and other West African countries. Translations include John (1919) and Mark (1922), by A. W. Olsen of the Sudan United Mission; Genesis, by F. W. Taylor (1927); NT, by E. M. and Violet Roulet and Ruth Christiansen (1956–63; rev. ed., 1964); common language translation, by R. Kassühlke (Mark, 1971; NT, 1982; Bible, 1983).

*Bibliography.* E. Roulet, *TBT* 7 (1956): 30–33.

**44. Uzbek.** Over 14 million speakers in the USSR and Afghanistan. Translations include the Gospels, by M. Ostroumoff (1891); Mark (1981); Genesis, Jonah, and John, under the auspices of the Institute for Bible Translation in Stockholm (1983).

**45. Igbo (Ibo).** Over 14 million speakers in Nigeria. Scriptures have been published in four dialects and a Union version. This includes Matthew (1860), NT (1860–66), by John C. Taylor with John F. Schön; Gospels (1893), Psalms and Acts–Colossians (1896), by H. H. Dobinson with T. D. Anyaegbunam and others; NT (1900), OT (1901–6), by T. J. Dennis, T. D. Anyaegbunam, and others, revised for Union Igbo (NT, 1908; Bible, 1913; corrected, 1952); Living NT (1980); interconfessional common language NT (1981; rev. ed., 1985).

**46. Tagalog (Pilipino).** Over 14 million speakers in the Philippines. Translations include the synoptic Gospels–Acts, by Pascual H. Poblete with R. O. Walker (1898); NT (1902; rev. ed., 1911, 1930; OT, 1905; rev. ed., 1915, 1930); Roman Catholic NT, by J. Trinidad and others (1952); OT and Apocrypha, by J. C. Abriol and based on the original texts (1962); interconfessional popular language (NT, 1973; Bible with Apocrypha, 1980); Living NT (1977).

Tagalog is closely related to Hiligaynon, with 4 million speakers, and translations of Mark (1900), NT (1903), OT (1912), interconfessional common language (NT, 1974; OT with Apocrypha, 1982); Cebuano, with 13 million speakers, and translations of Matthew (1902), NT (1908), OT (1917), and interconfessional popular language (NT, 1973; Bible with Apocrypha, 1981); and Samarenyo, with 3 million speakers, and translations of Mark–Acts (1908), NT (1928), OT (1937), and common language NT (1979).

**47. Hungarian.** Nearly 14 million speakers. Pauline Epistles, by Benedek Komjáthy from the Vulgate (1533); NT, by János Erdösi (Sylvester) (1541); standard Protestant Bible with Apocrypha, by Gaspar Károli (1590; rev. ed., 1908, 1938, 1975); Roman Catholic Bible, by György Káldi (1626; rev. ed., 1865); Jewish OT (1898–1907); NT, by G. Budai (1967); Bible (1971; rev. ed., 1975); Bible with Apocrypha, by F. Gál and others (1976); Pentateuch, with Hebrew and commentary by J. B. Hertz and others (5 vols., 1984).

*Bibliography.* I. Czegle, *Jahrbuch des Evangelischen Bibelwerkes* 11 (1968): 51–78; K. Pröhle, *TBT* 22 (1971): 133–41; J. Bottyán, *A magyar Bibliaévszázadai* [The History of Hungarian Bible translation] (1982); G. Radó, *TBT* 37 (1986): 144f.

**48. Amharic.** 13 million speakers; official language of Ethiopia. Translations include the Gospels (1824); NT (1829); Bible (1840), which was corrected in 1844 by Abu Rumi (Abba Abraham), edited by Thomas Pell Platt and others, and later revised (1864–73, 1886); the Imperial Authorized revision (1961); the interconfessional common language NT (1980); and the Living NT (1985).

*Bibliography.* A. F. Matthew, *TBT* 7 (1956): 72–76; E. Ullendorff, *Ethiopia and the Bible* (1968); J. Fellman, *TBT* 28 (1977): 154f.

**49. Azerbaijani.** 12 million speakers in the USSR and Iran. The following translations occur in Arabic script unless otherwise noted: Matthew, by Mirza Ferukh and Felix Zaremba (1842); NT, by M. Ferukh and K. G. Pfander (1878); OT, by A. Amirchanianz (1891); NT in Cyrillic script, by Mirza Mikailov for the Institute for Bible Translation (1982).

**50. Sinhala (Sinhalese).** Over 11 million speakers in Sri Lanka. Translations include the Gospels, by Willem Konijn (1739); NT, by Simon Cat, J. J. Fybrands, and H. Philipsz (1771–76); NT (1817; rev. ed., 1827) and OT (1823; rev. ed., 1830), by W. Tolfrey, A. Armour, and others; Cotta version in simple Sinhala (NT, 1832; OT, 1834); Union version (1855; rev. ed., 1938; NT, 1862, rev. ed., 1881, 1899; OT, 1876, rev. ed., 1905), by C. Carter and a committee; NT from the Vulgate by C. Chounavel (1897); Bible, by S. Colfes, C. W. de Silva, and others (1910); interconfessional common language NT (1973) and Bible (1983), by A. P. Fernando and others; Living NT (1980).

**51. Assamese.** Nearly 11 million speakers in northeast India. Translations include the NT (1813), Pentateuch (1822), by the Serampore missionaries; OT, by Akmassam Harmma (Atma-ram Sharma) under the supervision of William Carey (1833); NT, by Nathan Brown (1848; rev. ed., 1849, 1898); OT translated and revised (1903); Bible (1934; rev. ed., 1954, 1984); common language Jonah (1975).

**52. Modern Greek.** Over 10 million speakers. Translations include the Pentateuch, by E. Soncino (1547); NT, by Maximus, a monk of Gallipoli (1638; rev. ed., 1703, 1710, 1824, 1827, 1830); NT and Psalms, by Hilarion, later bishop of Tirnova (1827–28); OT (1840), NT (1844), and revised Bible (1851), by N. Bambas and others (the standard text, especially for Protestants); Matthew (1901), and Gospels (1902), by A. Pallis from Codex Vaticanus (following the publication of Matthew, all modern translations were prohibited by the Greek constitution); NT, by P. N. Trembelas (1937–53); Bible, by A. Chastoupis and N. Louvaris (1954–55); free translation, by J. T. Kolitsaras (NT, 1963–64; OT, 1971–73); NT, by B. Vellas and others (1967); Living OT (portions, 1971; NT, 1981); and the interconfessional common language NT, by S. Agourides and others (1985).

*Bibliography.* E. Oikonomos, *TBT* 21 (1970): 114–25; S. N. Sakkos, *Peri tes metafraseos tes Kaines Diahekes* (1970).

**53. Malay.** This language, which is related to Indonesian, has over 10 million speakers in Malaysia. Translations include the Gospel of Matthew (1629), Gospels–Acts (1651), and Psalms (1652), by Albert C. Ruyl, Jan van Hasel, and Justus Heurnius; NT, by Daniel Brouwerius (1668); NT (1731), OT (1733), and Bible in Arabic script (1758), begun by Melchior Leidekker (d. 1731), and completed by Pieter van der Vorm; Bible (rev. ed., 1821), NT (1820, 1831, 1853, 1866, 1910), OT (1826, 1856); NT (1870) and OT (1879), by H. C. Klinkert; NT (1910), OT (1912 [in Arabic script]), and NT (1927 [in Latin script]), by W. G. Shellabear and others; NT (1938), by W. A. Bode, Inche Mashohor, and others (published with the Klinkert OT, and used also in Indonesia); common language NT (1976) and Bible (1986), by E. T. Suwito.

**54. Nepali.** Over 10 million speakers. Translations include the NT (1821), by the Serampore missionaries; Luke (1850) and Acts (1851), by W. Start; OT (1877, 1883) and NT (1902), by E. MacFarlane, A. Turnbull, and G. P. Prodhan; Roman Catholic NT (1975), by H. B. Chhetri and F. J. Farrell; common language NT in progress.

**55. Oromo.** Over 10 million speakers in central Ethiopia and Kenya. Translations occur in several dialects, including the western (or northern) dialect translations of Luke (1870), John (1871), Genesis and Psalms (1872), Acts–Revelation (1874), Matthew and Mark (1875), NT (1876), Exodus (1877), all by L. Krapf with Debtera Saneb and Roofo (from 1875 with other nationals); common language NT (1979; rev. ed., 1986) and Psalms (1981), by T. Qanaa, G. Bonga, and M. Zach; eastern Oromo (or eastern Shoa) translations of Matthew (1886), by Hajlu; northern dialect translations of the NT (1893) and Bible (1899), by Onesimus Nesib and based on Krapf's translations; southern dialect (now identified with Boran; see below) translations of Jonah (1878) and John (1889), by Thomas Wakefield, and Matthew (1904), by R. M. Ormerod; southern Shoa (or central Oromo) translations of John 1–5 (1839) and Matthew (1841), by Krapf; and Boran dialect translations of Luke (1934), John (1945), and Acts (1954), by E. J. Webster and others; and John–1 Corinthians, James, and 1 John (1966), and NT (1978), by S. M. Houghton and others.

**56. Quechua.** Over 10 million speakers of various distinct dialects. The most widely spoken dialects that have Scripture translations are Chimburazo in Ecuador (Luke [1917]; NT [1954, 1973]; Genesis [1983]), Cuzco in Peru (John [1880]; NT [1947, 1969]; Genesis [1979]; Ruth, Amos, and Proverbs [1982]), Ayachucho in Peru (Luke and John [1954]; NT [1958]; Genesis and Ruth [1974]; NT and Amos [1981]; Bible [1986]), and Bolivian Quechua (John [1907]; NT [1922,

1952]; OT books [1957, 1968]; Bible [1986]; international NT [1976]; interconfessional NT [1977]).

**57. Sindhi.** Over 10 million speakers in Pakistan and India. Translations include the Gospel of Matthew (1825), under the auspices of the Serampore missionaries; Gospels–Acts and Genesis by A. Burn with A. Matchett; NT (1890), by G. Shirt and C. W. Isenberg; OT (1954) and NT (1961), by C. Ray and others; NT books for Hindu readers (1966–82), and for Muslim readers (1978–84).

**58. Kurdish.** Probably about 30 million speakers in Turkey, Iran, Iraq, Syria, and Lebanon. The most widely spoken dialect is Kurmanji, which has Scripture translations of Matthew (1856), the Gospels (1857), the NT (1872), Proverbs (1947), Luke (1953; repr. 1984). Other dialects having translations are Kermanshahi (John [1894]; Gospels [1900]), Mukri (Mark [1909]; Gospels [1919]), and Sorani (Living John [1972]).

**59. Czech.** 10 million speakers; closely related to Slovak. The whole Bible had been translated into Czech by 1370 by an unknown Hussite translator, possibly Tomáš Štítný. Printings include the NT (1475), Psalms (1487), and the Bible (1488, 1506). Other translations include a NT (1533) from Erasmus's Latin; the standard Kralice Bible (OT, 1579–87; Apocrypha, 1588; NT, 1594; one-volume Bible, 1596; rev. ed., 1613, 1722, 1766, 1808, 1887, 1915); Wenceslaus Bible (NT, 1677; OT 1712–15); Bible translated from Vulgate with notes (1917–25; NT, rev. ed., 1946, 1947, 1961, 1970); NT, by F. Zilka (1933; rev. ed., 1970); OT translated from the Hebrew by J. Heger (1955–58); interconfessional Bible (1979; Apocrypha, 1985), directed by M. Bič and J. B. Souček.

*Bibliography.* J. Merell, *Bible v ceskych zemich od estarick dob do soucasnosti* (1956); J. B. Souček, *Jahrbuch des Evangelischen Bibelwerkes* 6 (1963): 90–109; J. Manek, *Tschechischer Ökumenismus* (1977); *Czech Ecumenical Fellowship* (1981); K. Gabris, *TBT* 11 (1960): 145–52.

Details of all printed Scriptures are contained in UBS's biennial *Scriptures of the World* (see below).

*General Bibliography* (from 1955). W. Schwarz, *Principles and Problems of Biblical Translation* (1955); *EKL* (1956), 1:480–89; *RGG* (1957), 1:1201–24; J. Schmid, et al., *LThK* (1957), 2:401–11; J. Wicki, *Neue Zeitschrift für Missionswissenschaft* 16 (1960): 95–109; F. C. Grant, *Translating the Bible* (1961); J. W. F. Bessem, *AFER* 4 (1962): 201–11; D. G. Dance, *Oceanic Scriptures* (1963); J. S. M. Hooper, *Bible Translation in India, Pakistan and Ceylon* (2d ed., 1963); J. Metzler, *Neue Zeitschrift für Missionswissenschaft* 20 (1964): 195–202; E. A. Nida, *Toward a Science of Translating* (1964); D. J. Fant, *The Bible at Work in New York* (1965); *The Gospel in Many Tongues* (9th ed., 1965); J. M. Roe, *A History of the BFBS 1905–1954* (1965); G. E. Coldham, *A Bibliography of Scriptures in African Languages* (1966); J. Beckmann, ed., *Die Heilige Schrift in den katholischen Missionen* (1966), 271–78; *New Catholic Encyclopedia* (1967); D. B. Barrett, *Schism and Renewal in Africa* (1968); *Nyöversattning av Nya testamentet* (1968); A. P. Smit, *God Made It Grow: The History of the Bible Society Movement in Southern Africa* (1970); *Encyclopedia Judaica*, 4:864–89; E. A. Nida, ed., *The Book of a Thousand Tongues* (2d ed., 1972); *Att översätta Gamla testamentet* (1974); C. Buzzetti, *La Parola tradotta* (1973); J. Beekman and J. Callow, *Translating the Word of God* (1974);

M. Black and W. A. Smalley, eds., *On Language, Culture, and Religion: In Honor of Eugene A. Nida* (1974); R. G. Bratcher, et al., *Understanding and Translating the Bible: Papers in Honor of Eugene A. Nida* (1974); K. Callow, *Discourse Considerations in Translating the Word of God* (1974); E. A. Nida and C. R. Taber, *The Theory and Practice of Translation* (2d ed., 1974); H. M. Orlinsky, *Essays in Biblical Culture and Bible Translation* (1974); J. L. Swellengrebel, *In Leijdeckers Voetspoor. Anderhalve eeuw bibelvertaling en taalkunde in de Indonesische talen*, 2 vols. (1974, 1978); G. E. Coldham, *Supplement to the Bibliography of African Scriptures, 1964–74* (1975); E. Dammann, *Die übersetzungen der Bibel in afrikanischen Sprachen* (1975); M. Larsen, *A Manual for Problem Solving in Bible Translation* (1975); E. A. Nida, *Language Structure and Translation* (1975); H. W. Spillett, *A Catalogue of Scriptures in the Languages of China and the Republic of China* (1975); [G. E. Coldham], *Historical Catalogue of Printed Christian Scriptures in the Languages of India and of the Indian Sub-Continent* (1977); C. Lacy, *The Word Carrying Giant: The Growth of the American Bible Society* (1977); S. Meurer, ed., *Eine Bibel—viele* (1978); R. W. F. Wootton, *The Lion Encyclopedia of the Bible* (1978), 72–84; *British Library General Catalogue of Printed Books to 1975*, vols. 28–31 (1979); G. M. Cowan, *The Word That Kindles* (1979); J.-C. Margot, *Traduire sans trahir. La théorie de la traduction et son application aux texts bibliques* (1979); *TRE* (1980), 6:228–331; *The Bible, Texts and Translations . . . from the National Union Catalog, Pre-1956 Imprints*, 5 vols. (1980); E. H. Glassman, *The Translation Debate: What Makes a Bible Translation Good?* (1981); E. A. Nida and W. D. Reyburn, *Meaning Across Cultures* (1981); *UBS Bulletin*, no. 124/125 (1981); S. Meurer, ed., *Mittelpunkt Bibel. Ulrich Fick zum 60. Geburtstag* (1983); R. Kassühlke, in *Sprechend nach Worten suchen*, ed. K. Mönig (1984); E. A. Nida, et al., *Style and Discourse* (1983); C. Buzzetti, *La Bibbia e le sue trasformazioni* (1984); B. F. Grimes, *Ethnologue* (10th ed., 1984); E. A. Nida, *Signs, Sense, Translation* (1984); S. Strohm, et al., *Die Bibelsammlung der Württemburgischen Landesbibliothek Stuttgart* (1984); A. S. Duthie, *Bible Translations and How to Choose Between Them* (1985); T. W. Dye, *Bible Translation Strategy* (rev. ed., 1985); J. Gnilka and H. P. Rüger, eds., *Die übersetzung der Bibel—Aufgabe der Theologie Stuttgarter Symposion 1984* (1985); E. Gunnemark and D. Kenrick, *A Geolinguistic Handbook* (2d ed., 1985); K. Barnwell, *Bible Translation* (3d ed., 1986); J. de Waard and E. A. Nida, *From One Language to Another* (1986); J. S. Mbiti, *Bible and Theology in African Christianity* (1986), chap. 2; *UBS Bulletin*, no. 140/141 (1985); *Meta* 32 (1987).

*Serials. Scriptures of the World* (biennial); *TBT* (1950– ); *Die Bibel in der Welt. Jahrbuch des Evangelischen Bibelwerkes* (1961– ); *Notes on Translation* (1962– ).

PAUL ELLINGWORTH

**Biblical Introduction. OT.** Fifty years ago, as the methods and results of literary criticism made their impact on OT studies, the task of introduction was conceived largely as one of presenting the problems of composition, date, and authorship that attach to the various books, and to show how those books reached their present form. To a large degree this viewpoint still obtains. Although chapters are given to text and canon and brief sections devoted to the message of each book, the bulk of the space is concerned with matters of literary criticism. Other treatments approach the subject chronologically, rather than book by book, but here, too, literary criticism is given paramount importance. These two approaches reflect the fact that the OT may be viewed either as a body of canonical writings or as a developing literature, so that an introduction to it may proceed from either viewpoint, or both.

But a tendency has developed to broaden the scope of the subject. As other ancient literature has been made available, and as the value of form-critical studies and the importance of oral tradition have become apparent, more attention has been given in recent works to the history of the literary types and the traditions which underlie the finished documents. Introductions of the conventional type give this feature little or no attention, but it finds increasing place in recent treatments. In another direction, since the line between the two is sharp, more OT introductions have come to include a discussion of noncanonical Jewish writings. At the same time, perhaps because the field has grown so large, special introductions to various subjects, such as the prophets, the Apocrypha, or the text appear in great number.

Increasingly, introductory matter discusses the formation of the OT literature itself. An introduction is needed to the world of the OT and its history and culture so the biblical record is more understandable. This feeling has produced collections of ancient texts relevant to the Bible, introductions to biblical archeology, works synthesizing the thought world of the ancient Orient and Israel, and numerous efforts to set forth the distinctive features of OT faith. Some of these efforts seem to derive from dissatisfaction with a discipline which covers critical problems but gives scant attention to the validity of the OT message.

*Bibliography.* J. A. Bewer, *The Literature of the OT* (2d ed., 1933); W. O. E. Oesterley and T. H. Robinson, *Introduction to the Books of the Bible* (1934); W. F. Albright, *Archaeology and the Religion of Israel* (1942); G. E. Wright, *The OT Against Its Environment* (1950); F. G. Kenyon, *Our Bible and the Ancient Manuscripts* (1958); H. H. Rowley, ed., *A Companion to the Bible* (2d ed., 1963); M. Noth, *The OT World* (1966); G. Fohrer, *Introduction to the OT* (1968); P. R. Ackroyd, et al., eds., *The Cambridge History of the Bible*, 3 vols. (1975); J. H. Hayes, *An Introduction to OT Study* (1979); L. Ryken, *Words of Delight: A Literary Introduction to the Bible* (1987).

JOHN BRIGHT

## Biblical Theology (OT). *Introduction.* The

concept of "biblical" theology developed in reaction to theology based on church tradition and scholasticism in the late Reformation era, but in recent years its meaning has come to depend somewhat on the outlook of the group using the term.

Originally biblical theology referred to ideas consistent with the Bible. Development of systematic theology, however, made such a broad definition obsolete. Systematic theology proposed to unify or organize theology, allowing creative speculation and philosophical input. John Calvin's *Institutes of the Christian Religion* pioneered this approach, which was biblical but did not follow the Bible's organization of doctrine. Friedrich Schleiermacher unveiled classic liberalism around a systematic, rather than a biblical, theology. Already in 1787 Johann Gabler had called for

care in defining biblical theology. Dogmatic theology, he said, builds around ideas. True biblical theology is more descriptive in relating what is found in Scripture. Biblical theology bore the brunt of higher criticism which made the thought and actions of biblical writers moot, but it was revived by 20th-century German theology in the "biblical theology movement." Various strains of theology sought to reinsert the unity of the Bible and the distinctiveness of Hebrew and Greek thought into modernist formulations.

Most theologians, conservative and modernist, would agree that, in general, biblical theology is not propositional, nor dogmatic, although it builds their foundation. True biblical theology avoids abstraction and accentuates history. It describes God by recounting what God has done. It must be defined as the confessional recital of the acts of God in history, together with what must be inferred from those acts.

The Bible is primarily a literature in which history and historical traditions are taken seriously because they are interpreted as the handiwork of God, or as man in revolt against God. While this story began with creation, its particular focus is in the story of Israel as the chosen people and of the new people of God established in Jesus Christ, who was and is the climactic event in the series of divine acts for the redemption of the world.

***The Redemptive Acts of God.*** The central confession of the people of Israel was that God, who created the world and man upon it as its ruler, chose the fathers (patriarchs) and promised to make of their progeny a nation in possession of a land and of a blessing in which all peoples of the world would find their own blessing (Genesis). In fulfillment of these promises he delivered Israel from Egyptian slavery with remarkable proofs of his power, made the people into a nation in covenant with himself at Mt. Sinai (Exodus–Deuteronomy), and gave them a land in which to dwell (Joshua).

The central event in Israelite history was the exodus, or deliverance from slavery. What the people learned of God from this event was that: (1) The Power which had saved them was the same as the God of the fathers. (2) This God was the greatest of all powers in the world because he was able to make both the greatest monarch on earth (Pharaoh), as well as the forces of nature, serve him. His mighty acts in Egypt were a testimony to the world of his identity, power, and sovereignty (e.g., Exod. 7:1–5; 15:11–18). (3) As remarkable as his power was the completely unmerited demonstration of his grace toward a weak and outcast people. His righteousness had within it a special concern for the weak who had no other savior, and even his severity had redemption within it. (4) The object of this unmerited love, Israel, could only infer that she was God's chosen people. Since God had shown himself to be the Lord of events, the purpose of his choice was to be made clear in history. His seeming favoritism did not contravene his righteousness because his chosen people were given a vocation. Israel was to play a role in his establishment of the world as his kingdom. Hence the conception that God had a purpose in history was understood to involve his choice of human agents, of whom the central and special "servant" was Israel. Historical choice involved historical vocation and a grave responsibility.

The conception of the conquest of Canaan as God's gift of the land further acknowledged his lordship over history and his direction of events for his own ends. In this case Israel as his agent was rewarded in conquest (Deut. 9:1–6), although in subsequent centuries others were called to be God's agents against Israel, and the tables were turned (e.g., Judges; Isa. 10:5–11). The land as God's gift meant that there could be no idea of the natural right of private property. All that one owned was given as a conditional loan and was to be used faithfully as though one were a steward (e.g., Lev. 25:33). Since the righteousness of God was especially concerned not only with evil, but with justice for the needy, one's administration of God's property must have the same ends in view.

The conceptual language describing the relation of God and people was drawn from common law; the religious vocabulary thus abounded with legal terms. God's compact with Israel was most frequently called a "covenant" (although Hosea likened it to a marriage pact). This covenant rested upon a political anthropomorphism which furnished the basic religious vocabulary. In it God appeared as the actual Ruler or Lord of the people, who ruled by means of leaders whom he provided (judges, kings, priests), through his revealed law, and by royal heralds or messengers whom he sent (prophets). The people, on their part, freely accepted his leadership and acknowledged themselves to be his subjects or servants whose task was to hearken to him and to obey him. Righteousness was thus covenant keeping while sin was more than infraction of law; it was disobedience, rebellion, and betrayal of commitment to the Ruler. The attempt was constantly made, however, to transcend the legalism of the relationship by the appeal to the unmerited grace of God in the exodus and conquest, a grace which should bind the people to him with an attachment stronger than legal bonds could portray. In the deepest reaches of Israelite faith gospel preceded law without negating the latter's necessity, even as was the case in the early church.

***The Creative Acts of God.*** God was affirmed as the Creator because he was known to be the Lord of history and of nature. As such he was believed to stand in a completely free, unconfined, and unlimited relationship to all that exists as his creation. His will is the basis of the world's unity and of the inner relationship between nature and history. This meant that no dualism of opposing forces was needed to explain the world, and it excluded every form of pantheism in which deity and world are in any measure identified or in which the divine is believed to be immanent in the evolving process.

The center and climax of God's creative work was seen to be man. He alone of the creatures of earth had a special relationship with God. It was a relationship which acknowledged man's dependence, his capacity to hear and obey (his free nature), and his responsibility to assume a God-given vocation. In Gen. 1 this was stated as a similitude between God and man which could be expressed by the metaphor "image" (man "in the image of God"). Yet this likeness was not such as to permit confusion between the two. God remained Lord, and man his servant. The latter, however, was no automaton; his freedom and power were given to enable him to work out his vocation, but he could also misuse them by trying to make himself "like God."

God as Creator and Lord thus preserved a gulf between himself and his world which could be bridged only as he himself chose. The means by which he chose to reveal himself were many. The "signs and wonders" of nature and of history were always viewed as his handiwork and to be interpreted for their meaning. Nature, however, was no focus of concern in itself, as in polytheism. God used it as the handmaiden of his historical work. The latter was the chief means by which and in which he revealed his will and purpose; and at every juncture of history he was believed to provide for his people spokesmen, or prophets, to whom he revealed his interpretative Word. These men were raised up and empowered by his Spirit, whom he sent into the world as an extension of his presence. Similarly, in describing past events, the writers employed the category of heavenly messengers (angels) as a means whereby God actively governed the world and revealed himself to men. So direct was God's control over the world he created and so manifold his manner of exercising that control that the problem of immanence and transcendence was not acute. Only in the skepticism which was peculiarly biblical was the divine transcendence so emphasized that God's control over history could be doubted. This, however, was considered the skepticism of sinners who wished to remain in their sins (as in Jer. 5:12; Zeph. 1:12).

***The Wrath and Salvation of God.*** Inasmuch as God is primarily known by what he does, it was understood in Israel that God's righteousness encompassed crisis and tragedy, wrath and judgment. The compromises of history were seen as sins against the Lord which were visited by his judgment. This interpreted the history of Israel among the nations, especially in Judges, 1–2 Kings, and 1–2 Chronicles. Historical crisis was searched for meaning in the context of sin and judgment, and the imperialism of the nations was used by God to effect his judgment. This involved a view of sin as both an act of will on the part of man and a state in which he lived. It was something man did which was accompanied or followed by a disruption of well-being ("peace") in social and material life (God's judgment). It was occasioned by a "stiffnecked," "hardhearted," or "uncircumcised" spirit which not only violated one's dependent relationship to God, on which life was based, but also the covenant relationship with the neighbor. Every sin was both willful and a burden to be borne. Consequently, the search for release and security was often desperate and always intense. The pathways chosen were many. One was idolatry, a compromise with neighboring religions which made fewer demands upon the will. Others were faith in king, state, and political alliances, in the exterior observances of cultus and temple, and even in a prudential wisdom which sought the golden mean between extremes (Proverbs). The last was acclimated to the faith, although not without theological controversy as illustrated by Job and Ecclesiastes.

Yet the prophets proclaimed true security to exist in God alone and not in any substitute for him and his law. He alone could relieve men from the burden of evil, and it was confidently asserted that, inasmuch as he was the righteous Lord of history, he had not promised in vain but would do what he had promised. Consequently, to the prophets the Assyrian and Babylonian crises were the day of the Lord, the beginning of his fulfillment of history in which the present orders of the world would be destroyed and, beyond that, restoration in his kingdom. Beyond the suffering of the present with its purging of evil there would be the new covenant (Jer. 31:31–40), the gift of a new heart and a new spirit (Ezek. 36:26), the new heavens and earth (Isa. 65:17–25), and the new Jerusalem as the capital of the world (Isa. 2:2–4; 60). The promises of God to the Davidic king as preserved in the theology of kingship were recalled by certain of the prophets and seen fulfilled in this goal of history. God would raise up his true Anointed (Messiah), and so empower him with his Spirit that the government of the world-kingdom would be upon his shoulders to the end that justice and peace would finally be achieved (Isa. 9, 11). God the Lord could not be defeated by sin, but would accomplish what he purposed (Isa. 43:11–13; 45:23). It was thus characteristic of his nature to instill hope, not in man's capacity to save himself, but in his own righteous power. He alone controlled and interpreted the history which proved the death of the nation's gods (Isa. 41:21–29).

***The Worship and Service of God.*** Because God's first requirement in the covenant was an unreserved and undivided loyalty to himself as Lord, he demanded a worship based upon: (1) a holy fear or reverence which acknowledged complete dependence; (2) faith in his complete control of all things so that the faithful could obey and wait upon him in confidence and without anxiety; and (3) a love which his own grace called forth and which made all obedience a matter of response in gratitude rather than simply a matter of duty. This deep, inner basis of worship meant rejection of the overt practices of magic which dominated pagan worship, and a far different interpretation of the sacrificial cultus which Israel shared with her neighbors. This cultus with its variety of practice and ritual had no automatic efficacy, although of course it was often interpreted in a pagan way. But in theology it was God's gift whereby he could be formally worshiped by gifts from the worshiper's substance, by prayers, by confession, and by praise. It was valid, however, only for faithful members of the covenant community who possessed true reverence and true faith. Their unwitting sins could find atonement (as in Lev. 4–7:10). But the cultus had no efficacy for flagrant covenant breakers who believed they could live as they chose and find security in splendid worship. When the means of worship were used in this manner, the prophets proclaimed that they became practices which God hated and would destroy.

As for daily life in God's service, it may be observed that, in the covenant, common law became religious law and religious law became common law; that is, there was no separation of sacred and secular. The society as ruled by God was a religious, chosen society of divine formation. Hence all law was covenant law, given to the nation as its guide to life, much of it as in the Decalogue addressed to individuals in whom and by whom decisions were made ("thou shalt"). All life was responsible, obedient life, and God's claim upon both individual and society was unconditional. Individual life, therefore, possessed a dignity and meaning unknown elsewhere because in God's "Thou shalt" each person was singled out as the recipient of God's personal address. At the same time, man's life and law must reflect the righteousness of God. This meant that his institutions must function without regard for the community status of individuals and that justice was distributive according to need rather than according to class, power, ability, or possessions. For this reason, the most surprising thing about Israelite law in its ancient setting was its conception of the function of economic life. That function was not profit but the fulfilling of need, based upon the principle of neighborly love (Lev. 19). It thus exhibited a deep concern for the victims of exploitation and a violent distrust of the rich and the powerful who turned the weakness of the weak into an occasion for profit.

Hence, Israel's worship and service of God were the response to the divine nature as it had been revealed in redemptive history. This response took its form in overt practices, many of which had their counterpart in paganism. Yet behind them was a faith and spirit which transformed their inner meaning.

**Bibliography.** M. Burrows, *An Outline of Biblical Theology* (1946); E. J. Young, *The Study of OT Theology Today* (1958); T. C. Vriezen, *An Outline of OT Theology* (1960); G. S. Glanzman and J. A. Fitzmyer, *An Introductory Bibliography for the Study of Scripture* (1961); G. von Rad, *OT Theology*, 2 vols. (1962, 1965); W. Eichrodt, *The Theology of the OT*, 2 vols. (1962, 1967); R. C. Dentan, *Preface to OT Theology* (rev. ed., 1963); H. L. Ellison, *The Message of the OT* (1969); G. Hasel, *OT Theology: Basic Issues in the Current Debate* (1972); S. B. Ferguson and D. F. Wright, *New Dictionary of Theology* (1988): 96–99.

G. ERNEST WRIGHT

# Biblical Theology (NT). *The Point of View.*

Fruitful study of NT biblical theology rests on certain basic convictions: (1) The unity of the Bible. Without denying or minimizing the Bible's diversity of literary form and thought, we may hold that a central theme binds the whole together. It is this unity of theme that justifies the formation of the canon. The books of the NT especially are united in explicit statement of the one basic gospel. (2) God is the axiomatic fact for every NT writer and speaker. The NT is a book about God, and specifically about what he has done through Christ and the Spirit. (3) Hence Christ is central. The gospel story and teaching focus on him and on the effects of his work. (4) This reminds us that history is essential in the NT gospel, which does not present timeless truths but reports and interprets the working of God in a series of purposeful events. (5) Since history is involved, diligent critical study of that history is necessary. The study of NT theology includes honest historical investigation. (6) But the eye of faith is equally necessary. This group of writings gives a unified witness to the working of God, which only the believer can discern and understand. Pure objectivity, in the sense of neutrality, is impossible in God's world, and particularly in dealing with the story of God's redemptive working. (7) The gospel is God's answer to man's sin rather than to his intellectual curiosity.

*Christ the Risen Lord.* No book of the NT is satisfied to present Jesus merely as a great teacher, noble example, or powerful personality. Every book represents him as the risen Christ who is the living Lord of his church. The resurrection is the key fact of the story, the interpreting center.

The resurrection interprets the cross. Only in the light of the Easter story did the Christians understand the cross as God's way to effect his redemptive purpose. The ministry also, with its patient friendship, its authoritative teaching, its healing power, and its faithfulness under opposition, is rightly understood only when seen as part of the total working of God through a living Christ who carries God's purpose to victory. The resurrection results in the active lordship of Christ over his church. It does not speak to believers merely of his personal survival. Christ risen is exalted to the right hand of God; so say 11 NT books by seven writers. As Lord, he rules actively now in this time of conflict with evil, and his followers are assured that he will "reign until he has put all his enemies under his feet" (1 Cor. 15:25). Thus the resurrection interprets the earlier career of Christ and opens the way to his further victorious working.

*Christ and the Father.* While every NT writer, and every book except the epistles of John, call Jesus Lord, he is not regarded as a rival of God the Father. Rather, it is always taken for granted that God the Father was involved in and behind whatever Christ did. "All this is from God" (2 Cor. 5:18). God is known most fully through the works of Christ. Christ is sent by God in the divine redemptive work. He is called by many significant titles: prophet, Messiah, Son of Man, King, Lord; his unique relation to the Father comes to expression in the frequent reference to him as Son or Son of God. The NT clearly recognizes Christ's (preexistent) activity in creating and sustaining the world (John 1:1–18; 1 Cor. 8:6; Col. 1:15–20; Heb. 1:1–3). But no great emphasis is placed on this fact. It prefers to stress the redemptive work which Christ in his historical career began and as Lord is now carrying to completion.

*Christ and Israel.* The history in which Jesus of Nazareth was central was not unprepared. It was the climax of God's work with Israel: he chose Israel, freed her, bound her to himself in covenant, and persisted in his faithfulness to her even when she proved stubborn and rebellious. The OT leaves Israel at a crossroads: either she will draw back within herself and seek in isolation the fulfillment of God's promises, or she will open her eyes and heart to the world vision that challenges her in such writings as Isaiah and Jonah. Christ makes that choice as he fulfills the promises made to Israel and calls out a people to become God's instrument in effecting his full purpose. Thus the work of Christ and the mission of the church continue, fulfill, and expand the work of God with Israel. The biblical story is one story, entirely centered in Christ and united in God's ongoing purpose for world mission.

This unity explains why Jesus and the church inevitably accepted and used the Scriptures of Israel. From the outset the OT was their possession. The NT holds that it is the Christians who rightly see the meaning and connection of the OT. It is the church's book, a witness to Christ. Even though some NT interpretations of OT passages are strained, yet the truth remains that the work of Christ and the apostles carries forward the OT as Christian Scripture.

***Christ and the Church.*** The NT church is not an entirely new creation. It continues and enlarges the OT people of God. It finds the basis of its fellowship in faith in Christ, who fulfilled the OT promises. The church is not a voluntary human association, for it is built by God. The historical work of Jesus Christ gathered together a nucleus. God exalted the risen Christ to lordship and made him head of the church. The gift of the Holy Spirit, sent by the Father, or by Christ for the Father (John 14:16, 26; 15:26; 16:7; Acts 2:33), brings God's active presence, guidance, and power to the church. Thus the church looks back to God's work in Israel and especially in Christ, but Christ's present lordship and the Holy Spirit's active work direct its life.

The fellowship of the church is called by many names, including the disciples, those of the Way, the Israel of God, the body of Christ, and the temple of the Spirit. Because the church has one Lord, it is one. It belies its true nature when it splits into parties. The church's task is to worship in gratitude, to maintain unity in brotherly fellowship, to witness to the gospel in the world, to foster growth in faith and good living in its members, and to live in confident hope of the full, final triumph of the cause of God.

***Christ and the Christian.*** Behind all the redemptive working of God is the sin and need of humanity. Jesus referred to this sinful condition, and it is explicitly discussed in Rom. 1–3. This universal need for redemption is common NT teaching, and the gospel is God's answer to that need. The God who created man and cares for him in daily providence also redeems man through the life, death, resurrection, and living power of Christ, who continues his work through the Spirit. Man must accept what he can never earn or deserve. He must turn in repentance from his sin, accept in faith the freely offered salvation, and live in grateful worship and loyal obedience. He lives in the fellowship of the church, but he is personally responsible for maintaining loyalty to his Lord. In the church he hears God's word in Scripture and the preaching of the gospel, shares in the sacraments of baptism and the Lord's supper, and accepts his share of the church's task. In daily life he walks by the Spirit, with love for his neighbor. God's grace in Christ is not a substitute for moral fruitfulness; its creative working makes possible good living. The fruit of the Spirit working in the believer is love and all its expressions.

***Christ and the World.*** The basic task of church and Christian is evangelistic, to witness to the gospel as widely as possible. The world is the scene of this witness, but the world is not a neutral stage. Forces of evil are active, and the church is in conflict with agencies that openly or subtly resist its witness. The NT church is a perse-cuted church, and these writings treat opposition as inevitable. Christ is Lord; he has won the essential victory over evil; his final triumph is certain and will be complete. But not all are aware of the lordship of Christ, and faithful witness to God's grace in Christ is the church's constant task. Christians give active witness in personal and social situations, but they do not expect that social plans without spiritual conversion can effect radical and permanent improvement in society. The early Christians were a small minority, living in a totalitarian system. They succeeded as they fixed on the necessity of faith, renewal, obedience, and love as the basis of a durable and wholesome fellowship.

***Christ and the Final Goal.*** The NT breathes confidence that full victory will rest with Christ's cause. This hope rests on what God has already done. In the work of Jesus Christ he has defeated sin and evil and determined the outcome of the struggle. The risen Christ carries forward this work, and God's full purpose will be realized. Most NT writers expected this victory rather soon, but they never attempted to fix the exact time, nor did they describe in specific detail the conditions of the time to come. It would be a blessed life with God and Christ. It would be the permanent joy of all who have been faithful to God and looked for his kingdom. This new order began with the coming and work of Jesus Christ, and the life of faith, under the guidance of the Spirit, is the foretaste of what is to come. The final defeat of evil, the final judgment, and the establishment of the eternal kingdom will thus not be a totally new order. It will complete and free from conflict that life which the people of Christ know even now.

*Bibliography.* A. M. Hunter, *Introducing NT Theology* (1958); A. Richardson, *An Introduction to the Theology of the NT* (1958); R. Schnackenburg, *NT Theology Today* (1963); J. Jeremias, *NT Theology* (1971); W. G. Kümmel, *The Theology of the NT According to Its Major Witnesses* (1973); G. E. Ladd, *A Theology of the NT* (1974).

FLOYD V. FILSON

# Biblicism.

**Biblicism.** Originally, a term used to describe the practice of medieval scholastics who depended on a strictly literal interpretation of the Bible for their line of argument. The biblicists were among the formal rationalists who employed Aristotle's system and method in dealing with biblical thought. In 20th-century theology biblicism has also been used as a negative epithet against all theologies holding to inspiration and inerrancy of Scripture. Its essence lies in adhering to the letter of the Scripture and often ignoring the context or historical situation. Thus, a true biblicist abjures oath swearing and turns the other cheek when smitten, as commanded in Matt. 5:34, 39. The tendency toward biblicism is seen most markedly in some strains of millennialism and fundamentalism. Millennialists tend to emphasize a literal application of biblical references to eschatological events. In some instances they are considered biblicists for not taking into account the use of poetic expression or literary device. Fundamentalists are often charged with biblicism for defending certain basic beliefs largely on a literal interpretation of statements of Scripture. As with millennialists, what comes under this description varies. Those who oppose biblicism point to Paul's dictum that the letter kills while the Spirit gives life (2 Cor. 3:6) and to his principle of testing and holding fast that which is good (1 Thess. 5:21).

**Bigamy.** A polygamous marriage limited to two wives (bigyny) or two husbands (biandry). It was practiced among the ancient Hebrews, associated with concubinage, and the law did not condemn it. It began to disappear after the exile but continued into the Christian era. The rare cases of bigamy among early Christians probably were entered into prior to conversion. Polygamy among primitive peoples is rarely concupiscent; it reflects the need for domestic labor and for progeny. Christian asceticism rejects both bigamy and digamy (remarriage of a widowed spouse). This prohibition was later applied only to clergy, and then became a policy of clerical celibacy in a double-standard morality as between clergy and laity. Some post-Reformation Catholic moralists have argued that monogamy is a part of the "natural law," but this is disputed by most Protestant scholars. Jesus' ethical sayings do not touch on the issue of polygamy versus monogamy. Neither do St. Paul's but 1 Cor. 7 seems to assume monogamy. Modern legal codes enforce monogamy.

*Bibliography.* G. E. Howard, *A History of Matrimonial Institutions*, 3 vols. (1904); E. Westermarck, *A History of Human Marriage*, 3 vols. (1921), and *Christian Morals* (1939); M. Cronin, *The Science of Ethics*, 2 vols. (1939).

JOSEPH FLETCHER

**Billing, Einar Magnus** (1871–1939). Swedish theologian. Born in Lund, he studied at the University of Uppsala, and became professor of systematic theology there (1908–20). He was bishop of the diocese of Västerås (1920–39). Billing inaugurated a revival of the Luther investigation in Sweden. His analysis of the idea of the church was pioneering. Most important, however, was his view of revelation. Through his remarkable theological work Billing helped to create a new, vigorous Swedish theology. He wrote *Luthers lära om staten* (1900), *De etiska tankarna i urkristendomen* (1907, 1936), *Försoningen* (1908), *Vår kallelse* (1909), *Herdabrev* (1920), *Den svenska folkkyrkan* (1930), and *Kyrka och stat* (1942).

*Bibliography.* *Einar Billing in Memoriam* (1940); E. Montan, *Einar Billing* (1943); A. Ihrmark, *Från Einar Billings ungdomstid* (1945).

RAYMOND W. ALBRIGHT

**Bingham, Rowland Victor** (1872–1942). Founder of SIM International (formerly Sudan Interior Mission). Born in East Grinstead, England, he moved in 1889 to Canada where he was challenged by the spiritual needs of the Sudan region of Africa. Going in 1893 to Africa with two other young men, they were afflicted with malaria, and his companions died before reaching the field. In 1898 he organized a mission council to recruit candidates for central interior Africa. Although his health never permitted him to stay long in Africa, he was the driving force behind SIM which has become one of the world's largest independent mission agencies. He also founded Evangelical Publishers, *Evangelical Christian* magazine, and Canadian Keswick Conference.

LESLIE K. TARR

**Bioethics.** An umbrella term which seeks to recognize God's sovereignty in a vast range of medical and technological procedures connected with sanctity of life and artificial conception medical technologies. Science has accumulated ethical questions rapidly over the past 20 years because of its work to solve increasing infertility problems, especially among women, caused by such factors as blockage of the fallopian tubes, damage from abortion and communicable disease, and extended use of the oral contraceptive. Major areas of Christian concern include, but are not limited to, the following bioethics issues:

*Abortion* is a spontaneous or induced termination of pregnancy before the embryo or fetus is capable of sustaining life on its own. Abortion falls within bioethics because it is legal in many countries and is used as a form of contraceptive or family planning. Almost all Christian traditions oppose using abortion in this way. Many give ethical permission in the cases of rape, incest, or likelihood of abnormality. The "just war" argument is often applied when there is a real threat to the life of the mother. It is in those cases regarded as the lesser of two evils. Other Christians regard abortion as a rebellion against God's sovereignty even under these conditions.

*Amniocentesis* is the technique of withdrawing fluid around the fetus prior to birth to enable diagnosis of abnormalities. Although there is some risk in this procedure, most Christian ethicists approve it where abnormality is suspected. This is only morally possible when a therapeutic abortion is regarded as defensible.

*Artificial insemination* is the injection of semen donated by the patient's husband or an anonymous donor into the vagina by artificial means. Roman Catholics are opposed to this, but many other Christian traditions permit it.

*Ectogenesis* is growth of a fetus outside the human body. All Christian traditions condemn this practice, because it denies the future child the mother-child bonding in the womb which is essential for the development of humanity, security, and affection.

*Embryo freezing*, once it became possible, was adopted by *in vitro* fertilization (IVF) programs in Australia and England of keeping on hand embryos from a couple, to increase the chances of successful pregnancy. Roman Catholics oppose the practice, but most Protestants regard it as ethically permissible, for the reasons that it increases the chance of pregnancy and reduces the number of surgical operations the woman has to undergo. However, most commentators are opposed to "spare" embryos being put aside for the birth of a twin years later, or for donation to another couple. Frozen embryos are technically property, subject to inheritance and divorce property settlement. Their full legal status may introduce yet other legal and ethical dilemmas.

*Embryo transfer* is the transfer of an early embryo, after fertilization of the egg *in vitro* ("in glass") in the laboratory, to the womb. This is an essential part of *in vitro* fertilization, and ethical approval is linked with that.

*Eugenics* is the study of possible influences as a means of improving hereditary characteristics of a race. As a sociological interest eugenics has been debated by ethicists for many years. Scientific experimentation to this end is now possible as an offshoot of *in vitro* fertilization, but it is strongly opposed by all Christian thinkers. The marginal question is the propriety of experimentation on "spare" sperm, eggs, or embryos to determine the cause of genetic disease such as multiple sclerosis. Christians are divided on this.

*In vitro fertilization* is a process of fertilizing egg with sperm in a laboratory, and then inserting the embryo in a womb. Roman Catholic official spokespersons are opposed to each element in this process (masturbation to produce semen, fertilization outside the womb, taking more than one egg, reimplanting in a womb, the use of donated egg or sperm, and the freezing of spare embryos). But most Protestants and many individual Catholics approve the basic process on the basis that it increases the chances of conception, thus conforming to God's will for married couples to have children. But many aspects of the IVF program are questioned, particularly the use made of spare embryos, the very high failure rate of the program, and the fact that many couples need IVF because of irreversible sterilization during or at the end of a previous marriage.

*A surrogate mother* is a substitute mother who bears a child for a woman who cannot bear children herself. Sometimes this is a relative; sometimes she is paid. Illegal in most countries, it is possible in California. It has produced court cases in which the surrogate mother, having carried the child in the womb for nine months, wants to keep it, and the "customer" couple sue for breach of contract. Because of this complication, and because natural law demands that the mother who carries the child is the mother, regardless of where the genetic material came from, Christian ethicists usually oppose this practice and many have spoken against bills to make it legal.

ALAN NICHOLS

**Birth Control.** *See* SEX, ETHICS OF.

**Bishop.** A church leader, normally one who has oversight of churches within a defined area (*see* DIOCESE). The title is applied to some church leaders with specialist tasks and to those who assist diocesan bishops to perform duties reserved for bishops (*see* BISHOP, SUFFRAGAN). Although Roman Catholic theory teaches that their authority derives from the apostle Peter through the pope or from the apostles as a group, there is no evidence that bishops referred to in the NT had apostolic status. The NT *episcopos* was a church leader (1 Tim. 3:1–7; Titus 1:5–9), probably coextensive with the *presbyteros*.

Today a group of bishops with dioceses may be presided over by an archbishop or metropolitan, whose group of dioceses is called a province. In the Roman Catholic Church bishops are answerable to the pope, whom they are to visit in person or through a deputy every five years. In other churches bishops have a constitutional authority, in the Church of England derived from the Crown.

The title is used in several churches which do not subscribe to the theory of the historic episcopate in succession from the apostles (*see* EPISCOPACY). It is used also by individuals who appeal to the theory but are not recognized as bishops by the historic churches. On the latter see H. R. T. Brandreth, *Episcopi Vagantes and the Anglican Communion* (1961). Several are listed in a private publication by Alan Bain (*Bishops Irregular* [1985]).

*See also* BISHOP, SUFFRAGAN; DIOCESE; EPISCOPACY.

GERVAIS ANGEL

**Bishop, Auxiliary.** In the Roman Church, any bishop appointed to help a residential bishop on account of his incapacity to meet the duties of his charge, because of age, ill health, or an excessive working load. Canon law distinguishes the auxiliary bishop from the coadjutor, who has the right of succession to the bishop he assists. Auxiliaries and coadjutors are consecrated with a title to a church not having a residential bishop.

GEORGES A. BARROIS

**Bishop, Suffragan.** Assistants to the bishop of a diocese. Suffragan bishops were used in the Western Church (from at least 1240 to 1592 in England), especially as deputies for absentee diocesans. From 1870 suffragans were appointed to assist with episcopal duties in the busy diocese of Canterbury and the vast diocese of Lincoln. Suffragans now outnumber diocesan bishops in the Church of England, but because they do not have sees of their own, their responsibilities are delegated by the diocesan and not defined uniformly, and they have no independent leadership role within a diocese.

*See also* EPISCOPACY.

GERVAIS ANGEL

**Bixler, Julius Seelye** (1894–1985). American theologian, philosopher, and educator. Born in New London, Conn., he graduated from Amherst College, and then pursued additional studies at Harvard University, Union Theological College, New York, and Yale University (Ph.D., 1924). After a period overseas as student and instructor, he taught religion and biblical literature at Smith College (1924–33) before appointment as professor of theology at Harvard (1933–42). In 1942 he became president of Colby College, Waterville, Maine, which rapidly expanded and gained increased recognition under his leadership. He was the recipient of numerous honors, and for 20 years after retirement was much in demand as visiting professor at home and abroad, during which time he also continued to write prolifically. His interests were wide: he was a friend of Albert Schweitzer whom he visited several times in Lambarene, a linguist, an accomplished cellist, and while himself liberal in theology an encourager even of those whose position was more conservative. His publications include *Religion in the Philosophy of William James* (1926), *Immortality and the Present Mood* (1931), *Religion for Free Minds* (1939), *Conversations with an Unrepentant Liberal* (1946), *A Faith that Fulfills* (1951), and *Education for Adversity* (1952).

HAROLD BARNES KUHN

**Black, Hugh** (1868–1953). Scottish preacher and professor. Born in Rothesay, he graduated from Glasgow University, studied theology at the Free Church College, Glasgow, and upon ordination became minister of Sherwood Church, Paisley (1891–96). He served as Alexander Whyte's associate minister at Free St. George's, Edinburgh, for nearly a decade before accepting an invitation to Union Theological Seminary, New York, where he became professor of practical theology (1906–38). He was recognized as having great gifts as a preacher, and he exercised them widely during his teaching years. Among his publications are *The Dream of Youth* (1894), *Culture and Restraint* (1901), *Work* (1903), *The Practice of Self-Culture* (1904), *Edinburgh Sermons* (1906), *Happiness* (1911), *According to My Gospel* (1913), *The New World* (1916), *The Adventure of Being Man* (1929), and *Christ or Caesar* (1938).

**Black, James Macdougall** (1879–1949). Presbyterian clergyman. Born in Rothesay, Isle of Bute, he was educated at Glasgow University, Marburg, and United Free Church College, Glasgow. Ordained in 1903, he was minister of Broughton Place Church, Edinburgh (1907–21), and St. George's West, Edinburgh (1921–49). He was also moderator of the General Assembly (1938–39). He wrote *The Mystery of Preaching* (1935), *The Dilemmas of Jesus* (1925), *New Forms of the Old Faith*, and *His Glorious Shame*.

F. W. DILLISTONE

**Black, Matthew** (1908– ). Scottish biblical scholar. Born in Kilmarnock and educated at the universities of Glasgow and Bonn, he taught Hebrew in Glasgow, Manchester, and Aberdeen (1935–42). He was Church of Scotland minister at Dunbarney (1942–47), but returned to academic life as lecturer in NT at Leeds (1952–54) before he became professor of biblical criticism at Edinburgh (1952–54), then professor of divinity and biblical criticism and principal of St. Mary's College, St. Andrews (1954–78). His publications include *The Scrolls and Christian Origins* (1961), *An Aramaic Approach to the Gospels and Acts* (3d ed., 1967), *Commentary on Romans* (1973), and *The Book of Enoch or I Enoch* (1985). He was editor of *NT Studies* (1954–78).

J. D. DOUGLAS

**Black Muslims ("The Nation of Islam").** A religious/political group originating in Detroit, Mich., in 1931. Its founder, Wallace Farad, combined Islam and black nationalism into a potent doctrine that rapidly gained followers. Elijah Muhammad, Farad's successor as leader, consolidated the movement and moved its headquarters to Chicago, Ill., in 1934. Elijah interpreted himself as the last messenger of Farad, said to be Allah incarnate.

The Muslims' original doctrine was millenarian, prophesying an imminent fall of America. The corrupt world of the "white devils" would eventually destroy itself; black Americans, the chosen people, would then assume their rightful place as world leaders. Until that time, the Muslims demanded a separate state for black Americans.

Members of the Nation followed a strict moral code, including observance of dress and dietary regulations. Education and the family unit were the focus of Muslim life. Their doctrine emphasized "knowledge of self," thus promoting an awareness of black history and a collective identity for blacks. Symbolizing the unknown and infinite power of the black nation, members often assumed the surname "X." The most controversial element of their doctrine was a belief that all Caucasians were intrinsically evil.

This belief system led the Muslims to prepare for the fall of America in ways that improved members' socioeconomic standing and insured the group's survival after the "failure" of Elijah's prophecy. The Nation developed its own school system and amassed large property holdings. At the peak of its success the Nation of Islam owned mosques, office buildings, restaurants, supermarkets, bakeries, factories, and farms. Its newspaper, *Muhammad Speaks*, had the highest circulation of any black publication in the United States.

Malcolm X, the Nation's best-known convert, came to believe in a more orthodox form of Islam after making his pilgrimage to Mecca in 1964. The first major disruption in the movement's history came with his expulsion in 1965 and his subsequent assassination.

Elijah Muhammad's apocalyptic rhetoric diminished gradually as the 1970s approached, and after his death in 1975 the movement moved swiftly toward orthodox Islam. Elijah's son Wallace permitted all races to join the Muslims, disbanded the Nation's secret police, and relegated previous leaders to the status of mere men, albeit divinely inspired. Marking its move toward orthodoxy, the Nation underwent three changes in name: in 1976 they became the World Community of Al-Islam in the West, the Bilalians; in 1980 the American Muslim Mission; and in late 1985 simply a Muslim community.

Although most Muslims accepted this doctrinal moderation, some were dissatisfied. In 1977, Minister Louis Farrakhan left, and, returning to Elijah Muhammad's original doctrine of racial separation and millenarianism, created a devout religious group, also called the Nation of Islam. The "new" Nation became politically notorious through Farrakhan's controversial statements in support of Jesse Jackson in the U.S. presidential primaries of 1984.

Today both groups are well established. Although no exact membership figures have ever been published, a generous estimate of Wallace Muhammad's Muslim community would be 80,000 adherents, and Farrakhan's Nation of Islam has perhaps 20,000. Both organizations have their headquarters in Chicago and regularly publish newspapers. Muhammad's group distributes the *Muslim Journal*, and Farrakhan's group publishes the *Final Call*.

**Bibliography.** E. U. Essien-Udom, *Black Nationalism: A Search for Identity in America* (1962); Malcolm X and A. Haley, *The Autobiography of Malcolm X* (1964); E. Muhammad, *The Message to the Blackman in America* (1965); C. E. Lincoln, *The Black Muslims in America* (rev. ed., 1973); L. Mamiya, *JSSR* 21 (1982): 138–52; C. Marsh, *From Black Muslims to Muslims* (1984).

MARTHA F. LEE

**Black Religion in America.** Black religion is a vibrant and dramatically varied reality in America with potential for even greater service to the black community. During the last two decades scholarship has focused on its origins, denominational configurations, worship characteristics, and important leaders. Far more black scholars are involved, and their research has significantly advanced understanding and brought to light bias which in the past has skewed the conclusions of some white scholars.

*Roots of Black Religion in America.* The main issue is the degree to which the African past has influenced the religion of the slave in America. E. F. Frazier contends that the treatment of captured individuals in Africa and the disruptive nature of the institution of slavery itself practically insured that traditions and practices would be stripped away. He found no evidence of "syncretism or fusion of Christian beliefs and practices with African ideas and rituals."

Recently several scholars are firmly espousing the opposite side in this debate. Henry Mitchell's thesis is that during slavery profound integration followed confrontation between the African corpus of belief and Christianity. G. Wilmore holds essentially the same position, speaking of an "aboriginal Black Religion" which, while deeply influenced by the belief system of the missionaries, retained sufficient substance from African traditions that it was—and continues to be—"something less and something more than what is generally regarded as the Christian religion."

Several black scholars have reasoned that syncretism was likely since at numerous points compatibility existed between African beliefs and doctrines of Christianity. For example, in the "high theology" which existed in Africa before the days of slavery, God was represented as a God of mercy, Creator, and Arbiter of justice much as in Judeo-Christian thought. It is likely that the earliest black preachers were drawn in part from the ranks of slaves who already possessed the mantle of leadership in the African religions, thus almost guaranteeing the integration of the two belief systems. Assimilation could have been initiated in Africa through encounter with missionaries during the period of slave trading.

Recent research recognizes early and continuing evidence of the African presence. African concepts and practices are easily identified in certain contemporary black cults. Voodooism in its less lurid and sensational forms addresses worship to an all-powerful supernatural being, petitioning him for deliverance from evil. Containing vestigial remains of African religions, it flourishes not only in Caribbean lands but also in many sections of the USA.

With respect to more orthodox contexts, Mitchell lists "strong component beliefs" alive in black religion, such as the providence of God, the grace of God, and the work of the Holy Spirit, which represent traditional African beliefs continued and strengthened by encounter with the relevant Christian affirmations. In the persistent refusal to "surrender(ed) their humanity under the most exasperating circumstances of their enslavement," black religionists "relied upon the most elemental presuppositions of a primitive religious consciousness to give consolation and meaning to their existence" (*Black Religion and Black Radicalism*, p. 14), additional indication of appropriation of the African mindset.

***Denominational Configurations.*** Systematic missionary activity among the slaves was begun by the English in 1701 through the Society for the Propagation of the Gospel in Foreign Parts. In the earliest periods, blacks customarily worshiped with their masters, albeit in segregated seating. However, from the beginning, black believers also managed private quasi-religious opportunities which made possible explicit consideration of the situation of oppression. Following numerous slave uprisings—especially the insurrection led by preacher Nat Turner—it became illegal in several states for slaves to meet in worship without white supervision.

The transition to independent black churches was not smooth and natural. Absalom Jones and Richard Allen were among those who resolved to reject segregation and discriminatory treatment. After they were forcibly removed from a Philadelphia white Methodist church while kneeling in prayer they organized black churches in that city during the 1790s. These black congregations were not merely replicas of their white counterparts; rather, they almost always gave vital support to freedom movements, encouraged by white abolitionists.

By denomination, 85 percent of all black Christians in the USA are either Baptist or Methodist; of that number, 65 percent are Baptist (1965). Blacks have also formed pentecostal congregations, and they were instrumental in the early development of American pentecostalism. In 1990 the major black denominations were the African Methodist Episcopal Church, the African Methodist Episcopal Zion Church, the Christian Methodist Church, the National Baptist Convention of America, and the National Baptist Convention, USA, Inc.

***Worship Characteristics.*** The long-held opinion of many whites has been that "the uniqueness of black religion lies in 'barbaric' spontaneity, expressiveness, excitement, rhythm, interest in the dramatic, love of magic, fascination with power and the absence of morality of the ethical sense" (Joseph Washington, *Black Sects and Cults*, p. 89). Researchers explain that many such features are drawn from the evangelistic religion of the white Baptists, Methodists, pentecostals, and others in the revivalist tradition.

Beyond such manifestations, it is possible to isolate particularly black emphases which reveal that black religion was more than an offshoot of southern Methodists and Baptists. Since survival itself was assumed to be possible only through God's providence, worship was a joyful and grateful praise of his presence, protection, and ultimate vindication. Hence, the worship service was not a time of propounding doctrinal teaching but rather an occasion for restorative rehearsal of God's goodness and concern for his servants' existential plight and renewal of faith in a theodicy which delivers justice.

Black preaching and black music similarly reflected these premises. Intensely biblical, both sought by means of the worship experience to direct hope and healing upon the day-to-day struggles of the masses of black Christians. Again, such concerns reveal ties to stresses in African religions.

***Leading Spokespersons for Black Religion.*** Among those who have contributed to the message of black religion are many unnamed early religionists. Inspired by insights produced in the meeting between African and Christian traditions, they bequeathed to black religion strong faith in God's mercy, providence, and justice. Turner, leader of a slave rebellion in 1831, deserves mention not for his bloody uprising but for his perception of God as Liberator. Turner's mission resembled that of the religious mystics who led peasant revolts in medieval Europe. Richard Allen worked to establish black churches that would combine relevance with deep spirituality in simple, informal faith. David Walker set the agenda for black militancy. As an early 19th-century abolitionist he issued a passionate call to arms, for, "They want us for their slaves, and think nothing of murdering us in order to subject us to that wretched condition—therefore, if there is an attempt made by us, kill or be killed" (*Black Religion and Black Radicalism*, p. 58). His call for reconciliation was just as passionate: "Throw away your fears and prejudices then, and enlighten us and treat us like men, and we will like you more than we do now hate you" (p. 60). Other leaders brought high scholarship and deep spirituality to black religion and to the black movement for liberation, among them W. E. B. DuBois, Benjamin Mays, Howard Thurman, and John Hope Franklin. Dr. Martin Luther King, Jr., initiated far-reaching changes in destructive attitudes entrenched for centuries, and his impact as a charismatic leader and innovative theologian was such that his death occasioned an act of national mourning. Scholars working with black theology, including James Cone, G. Wilmore, Henry Mitchell, and James Deotis Roberts, have led one of the few authentically indigenous North American theological movements, reapplying the message of liberation known in black religion from its earliest days in America.

*Summary.* In its most authentic expressions black religion is anything but escapist. The recent developments of black theology are committed to the continuing battle with white racism and the amelioration of the condition of black people. Black religion has largely been a radical movement. "Deradicalization" of the black community is properly associated with the ascendancy of Booker T. Washington, a nonradical leader whose strategy was pietism and accommodation. The result was that the liberation movement was carried forward by entities outside the church, particularly the Black Muslims. The efforts of Cone, Wilmore, and others are directed to calling the church back to its traditional role of striving for righteousness and justice under a liberation theology conception of God.

The potential for benefit to the mainline Christian church through dialog with black religion is enormous, and even conservative Christians have been challenged by the movement to address the continuing dichotomy between the spiritual and the social. Black religion, with long experience in joining a deeply spiritual religious experience with a worldly social action, could be an able tutor.

*See also* BLACK THEOLOGY; CIVIL RIGHTS MOVEMENT.

**Bibliography.** E. F. Frazier, *The Negro Church in America* (1963); J. O. Buswell, III, *Slavery, Segregation, and Scripture* (1964); J. H. Cone, *Black Theology and Black Power* (1969); M. Marty and D. G. Peerman, eds., *New Theology 6* (1969): 178–84; L. Lucas, *Black Priest/White Church: Catholics and Racism* (1970); H. H. Mitchell, *Black Preaching* (1970); G. S. Wilmore, *Black Religion and Black Radicalism: An Interpretation of the Religious History of the Afro-American People* (1972); *Christian Century* (March 28, 1973): 369–72; J. R. Washington, Jr., *Black Sects and Cults* (1973); H. H. Mitchell, *Black Belief: Folk Beliefs of Blacks in America and West Africa* (1975); G. S. Wilmore, *Black and Presbyterian: The Heritage and the Hope* (1983); W. A. Elwell, ed., *Evangelical Dictionary of Theology* (1984), 158–61; H. H. Mitchell and N. C. Cooper-Lewter, *Soul Theology: The Heart of American Black Culture* (1986).

VIRGIL CRUZ

**Black Theology.** A North American theological movement brought into existence in the late 1960s almost entirely as a result of the work of James H. Cone. Black theology has four main roots: traditional black Christianity; the civil rights movement of the 1950s and 1960s; the publication of Joseph Washington's *Black Religion;* and the rise of the Black Power concept and the Black Muslims.

Traditional black religion is a largely unexplored source of black theology. Yet, beyond doubt, traditional spirituals, black preaching, and an experiential religion which drew upon biblical examples such as the exodus theme played a significant role in shaping what eventually became black theology.

The civil rights movement, which was initially ignored and even rejected by mainline churches, forced black members of the Southern Christian Leadership Conference (SCLC) and similar groups to reflect on their situation and develop a theological rationale for their struggle. The resulting search brought a renewed awareness of the work of leaders such as Richard Allen, the founder of the African Methodist Episcopal Church; Henry Highland Garnet, a Presbyterian preacher who urged fellow blacks to resist slavery; Nat Turner, a Baptist preacher who led a slave revolt; and Henry McNeal Turner, an AME bishop who claimed that God was a black.

The publication in 1964 of Joseph Washington's *Black Religion,* which argued that "Negro congregations are not churches but religious societies" and suggested that blacks had only folk religion and folk theology rather than a genuine Christianity, stung black Christians. Black theologians sought a positive and clearly black response.

The Black Muslims, in particular Malcolm X, challenged black Christians to abandon the ideal of integration and seek a true black cultural identity.

Things came to a head in 1966 when white church leaders urged black Christian leaders to denounce the Black Power movement as racist. Instead of obeying they published the statement "Black Power" in the *New York Times* on July 31, 1966, affirming their solidarity with the black cause. This statement was the first step in the self-conscious development of black theology.

The first full-scale study of black theology was James Cone's *Black Theology and Black Power* (1969), which argued that the liberating elements in black power were identifiable with the Christian gospel. His sequel, *A Black Theology of Liberation* (1970), made liberation the central theme of his theology.

J. Deotis Roberts took up Cone's challenge to produce a black theology in *Liberation and Reconciliation: A Black Theology* (1971). Roberts claimed that, while Cone's direction of thought was essentially correct, he had overlooked the great importance of reconciliation. Major Jones also reacted to Cone's arguments in his book *Black Awareness: A Theology of Hope* (1971), asserting that Cone was too dependent on the white theological tradition. Various other contributions were made by able black writers who developed Cone's arguments and gradually introduced themes from African and other third world theologies.

In 1970 the white Methodist secretary of the South African University Christian Movement (UCM) imported black theology to South Africa with a paper *Towards a Black Theology* (1970) and organized a conference at Roodepoort in March 1971 which Cone addressed. The black theology movement in South Africa quickly stimulated interest in traditional African religion, the theologies of independent African Christian churches, and various theologies of liberation. On the political front it greatly strengthened the growth and self-confidence of groups such as the South African Students Organization (SASO) and various other black consciousness movements. Today black theology continues to play an important and highly political role in the South African situation and has helped raise the consciousness of black leaders. Yet, although they have contributed to its growth, neither Alan Boesak nor Desmond Tutu can be seen as purely "black" theologians. Rather they have contributed from a perspective rooted in the Reformed and Anglican traditions informed by insights from black theology.

In North America black theology continues to develop but is now dividing over the role of organizations such as CAUSA, the Unification Church's anticommunist political front which is attracting the support of a significant number of former SCLC leaders. Thus a split is developing between left- and right-wing blacks, all of whom are seeking to develop a black consciousness appropriate to a changed and changing situation.

*Bibliography.* T. Skinner, *How Black Is the Gospel?* (1970); G. S. Wilmore, *Black Religion and Black Radicalism: An Interpretation of the Religious History of the Afro-American People* (1972); B. Moore, *Black Theology: The South African Voice* (1973); G. S. Wilmore and J. H. Cone, eds., *Black Theology: A Documentary History, 1966–1979* (1979).

IRVING HEXHAM

## Blackwood, Andrew Watterson (1882–1966).
Homiletics professor. Born in Kansas, he graduated from Harvard University in 1905 and after training at United Presbyterian seminaries he was ordained (1908) and engaged in home mission work until 1911. He served pastorates in Pittsburgh, Columbia, S.C., and Columbus, Ohio (1908–25), before becoming professor of English and Bible at the Louisville Presbyterian Seminary in 1925. In 1930 he was called as professor of homiletics at Princeton Theological Seminary and remained there until his retirement in 1950. For eight years thereafter he served as professor of homiletics at Temple University School of Theology. His works include *The Fine Art of Public Worship* (1939), *Evangelism in the Home Church* (1942), *Pastoral Work: A Source Book for Ministers* (1945), and *The Growing Minister, His Opportunities and Obstacles* (1960).

C. GREGG SINGER

## Blaiklock, Edward Musgrave (1903–1983).
Baptist lay leader and classics professor. Born in Birmingham, he emigrated with his family to Auckland, New Zealand, in 1909 and was educated at Auckland Grammar School and the University of Auckland (Litt.D.). He taught classics and biblical and ancient history at Auckland University for 42 years and was professor of classics for 20 years until his retirement in 1968. He dedicated much of his life to the academic and administrative work of the university and had the

distinction of serving as its first public orator. While his teaching and writing were strictly on the classics of the ancient world, his main interest was the Bible. He frequently led tours to important archeological sites in Bible lands and lectured on the Bible in many parts of the world. Blaiklock was a leading layman of the Baptist Union of New Zealand and was its president in 1970. He supported and offered leadership to many evangelical and interdenominational organizations in New Zealand. He was an apologist for the Christian faith both in newspapers and on radio. His works include *The Acts of the Apostles: An Historical Commentary* (1959) and *The Archaeology of the NT* (1970). He was also coeditor of *The New International Dictionary of Biblical Archaeology* (1983) and editor of the *Zondervan Pictorial Bible Atlas* (1969).

NOEL S. POLLARD

## Blake, Eugene Carson (1906–1985).
American Presbyterian ecumenist. Born in St. Louis, he graduated from Princeton University in 1928. Deterred by the fundamentalist controversies at Princeton Seminary, Blake took his first year of theological studies at New College, Edinburgh, returning to Princeton to complete his divinity degree in 1932. He was a pastor for 20 years, including service at the First Presbyterian Church of Albany, N.Y. (1935–40), and at the Pasadena, Calif., Presbyterian Church (1940–51). He became stated clerk of the Presbyterian Church, USA (later, the United Presbyterian Church in the USA) in 1951, serving until 1966. Blake made the office of stated clerk a powerful and publicly visible position through his advocacy of racial justice, support for the ordination of women, work in behalf of the National and World Councils of Churches, and opposition to the Vietnam War. With John A. Mackay of Princeton Seminary, Blake issued in 1954 "A Letter to Presbyterians" opposing the slanderous anticommunist rhetoric of U.S. Senator Joseph McCarthy. This letter, which stirred much comment, was the first public stand taken by any major Protestant group against possible loss of individual freedoms and constitutional rights in the name of patriotism and opposition to communism. Strongly influenced by the writings of Reinhold Niebuhr, Blake espoused what he called an "ecumenical consensus theology," which aimed to enrich every church's appreciation of the truth, not to reduce or relativize that truth. In 1960, he gave a famous sermon at Grace Cathedral (Episcopal) in San Francisco, where he called for the formation of a church that would be "truly reformed, truly catholic, and truly evangelical." This sermon led to the formation of the Consultation on Church Union (COCU). Blake served as general secretary of the World Council of Churches from 1967 to 1972. During his tenure Pope Paul VI paid an

unprecedented visit to the WCC headquarters in Geneva, Switzerland.

R. Milton Winter

**Blake, Robert Pierpont** (1886–1950). Born in San Francisco, Calif., he studied at the University of California and at Harvard University (Ph.D., 1916). He studied and taught for a number of years in Russia and the Georgian Soviet Socialist Republic. He taught at Harvard for 30 years on the economic development of the ancient and medieval Mediterranean world and on the Byzantine and Ottoman empires. He also taught Armenian and Georgian. His most notable works are his editions of various Armenian and Georgian texts, including the OT Prophets and the Gospels. He took part in the search for MSS and archeological remains in expeditions to Athos, Sinai, Samaria, and Van. He served as director of the Harvard University library from 1928 to 1937. In 1938 he was an exchange professor at the University of Sorbonne.

*Bibliography.* Harvard University Gazette 46/6 (1950/51): 34f.

Henry J. Cadbury

**Blanch, Baron Stuart Yarworth** (1918– ). Archbishop of York. After war service as an air force navigator, he graduated from Oxford, was ordained, and served a number of Church of England parishes (1849–57). He was vice-principal of Wycliffe Hall, Oxford (1957–60), warden of Rochester Theological College (1960–66), bishop of Liverpool (1966–75), and archbishop of York (1975–83). After this he became a life peer. His works include *The World Our Orphanage* (1972), *For All Mankind* (1976), *The Christian Militant* (1978), *The Burning Bush* (1978), *The Trumpet in the Morning* (1979), *The Ten Commandments* (1981), *Living by Faith* (1983), and *Way of Blessedness* (1985).

Tim Lenton

**Blanke, Fritz** (1900–1967). German church historian and theologian. Born in Kreuzlingen, son of a publisher and bookseller, he was early influenced by a pietistic group on the fringe of the Reformed state church which he later joined. After primary school he attended the gymnasium in Constance and the universities of Tübingen, Heidelberg, and Berlin. He obtained his doctorate under Karl Holl. Although he passed the required examinations for ordination in the Evangelical Church of Baden in 1923 and 1924, he decided to pursue an academic career and accepted a position as private lecturer at the University of Königsberg (1926–29). In 1929 he became professor of church history and the history of dogma at the University of Zurich. During a distinguished career as professor, spiritual counselor, devoted churchman, and politically and socially engaged citizen, Blanke published nearly 400 articles, books, sermons, reviews, and analyses. Among his students were pastors and prospective scholars from Europe, Asia, and North America. In addition to being coeditor of the modern critical edition of Zwingli's works in the *Corpus Reformatorum,* he coedited a popular edition, *Zwingli Hauptschriften* (1940) with Rudolf Pfister and Oskar Farner. The *Mennonite Quarterly Review* devoted its January 1969 issue to Blanke. The Zwingli Verlag in 1960 published a bibliography of his works from 1926 to 1959, and *Zwingliana* 12/9 (1968) contains his publications from 1960 to 1967. Tributes to him can be found in *Corpus Reformatorum,* vol. 93, in *Zwingliana* 12/7 (1967), and in the *Neue Zürcher Zeitung* (March 9, 1967), no. 1010.

E. J. Furcha

**B'nai B'rith.** Originally established in 1843 as a fraternal order for Americanizing German-Jewish immigrants to the USA, cultivating esoteric rituals and regalia, and offering mutual aid to members, in a Jewish equivalent of the exotic fraternal societies common at the time. B'nai Brith ("sons of the covenant") avoids specific religious or dogmatic affiliation, striving for harmony among all segments of the Jewish community.

By the end of the 19th century the organization had evolved away from ritualism and fraternal functions to emphasize philanthropy and public service. By the 1940s leadership moved to Eastern-European Jews, and under the presidency of Henry Monsky it became one of the foremost American Jewish organizations. Its important arms include the Anti-Defamation League (to fight anti-Semitism), and the Hillel Society, a Jewish framework for college students.

It has about 500,000 members, mostly in America, but including affiliates in 48 countries.

*See also* Anti-Semitism.

*Bibliography.* E. E. Grusd, *B'nai Brith: The Story of a Covenant* (1966); D. D. Moore, *B'nai Brith and the Challenge of Ethnic Leadership* (1981).

Eliezer Segal

**Boe, Lars Wilhelm** (1875–1942). Lutheran clergyman, politician, and educator. Born in Calumet, Mich., he studied at St. Olaf College, Northfield, Minn., and Luther Theological Seminary, St. Paul, Minn. He was pastor in Lawler, Iowa (1901–4), president of Waldorf College, Forest City, Iowa (1904–15), a member of the Iowa legislature (1909–11), a state senator (1913–15), executive secretary, board of trustees and board of education, United Norwegian Lutheran Church (1915–17), general secretary, Norwegian Lutheran Church of America (1917/18), and president of St. Olaf College (1918–42).

Erik Hetle

**Boehmer, Heinrich** (1869–1927). Lutheran church historian. Born in Zwickau, Saxony, he studied theology and history. He then served on the editorial board of *Monumenta Germaniae Historica*. He taught church history in Leipzig (1898–1903), Bonn (1903–12), Marburg (1912–15), and again in Leipzig (1915–27). He wrote *Kirche und Staat in England und der Normandie im 11. und 12. Jahrhundert* (1899), *Die Fälschungen des Erzbischofs Lanfrank von Canterbury* (1902), *Die Bekenntnisse des Ignatius von Loyola* (trans. 1902), *Analekten zur Geschichte des Franziskus von Assisi* (1904), *Luthers Romfahrt* (1914), *Studien zur Geschichte der Gesellschaft Jesu* (1914; later published under the title *Ignatius von Loyola*, 1941); *Luther im Lichte der neuern Forschung* (1918), *Die Jesuiten* (1921), *Urkunden zur Geschichte des Bauernkrieges und der Wiedertaufer* (1921), *Loyola und die deutsche Mystik* (1921), *Luthers erste Vorlesungen* (1924), *Der junge Luther* (1925, 1951), *Gesammelte Aufsätze* (1927), and *Thomas Munzers Briefwechsel* (1931). He also brought out volume 5 of Albert Hauck's *Kirchengeschichte* (1920).

RAYMOND W. ALBRIGHT

**Bohlin, Torsten Bernhard** (1889–1950). Swedish bishop. He became professor of systematics at Åbo in 1925 and at Uppsala in 1929, and bishop of Härnösand in 1934. Bohlin's dogmatic and ethical writings are distinguished by a liberal-theological and Christian-humanistic attitude. He is best known as one of the foremost apologists of Christianity in Sweden. Bohlin was a zealous and inspiring supporter of youth work, popular education, and the Christian Temperance movement.

*Bibliography.* Torsten Bohlin. *En minnes—och vänbok* (1950).

CARL-GUSTAF ANDRÉN

**Boisen, Anton T.** (1876–1965). Congregationalist clergyman. Born in Bloomington, Ind., he studied at Indiana University, Union Theological Seminary, and Harvard. He was instructor in Romance languages, Indiana University (1899–1903), field investigator, Presbyterian Department of Country Church Work (1911–12), pastor, Congregational Church, Wabaunsee, Kans. (1913–15), and North Anson, Maine (1915–17), supervisor of the Interchurch World Movement (1919–20), chaplain at the Worcester (Mass.) State Hospital (1924–32), and the Elgin (Ill.) State Hospital, research associate and lecturer at Chicago Theological Seminary (1925–42), lecturer at Boston University School of Theology (1929–31), and research consultant of the Council for Clinical Training of Theological Students. His writings include *Exploration of the Inner World* (1936) and *Problems in Religion and Life* (1946). He also edited *Hymns of Hope and Courage* (4th ed., 1950).

**Bolivia.** A land-locked Andean republic of some 1,098,590 sq. km. (424,165 sq. mi.). The least densely populated country in Latin America, its population is estimated at 7,314,000 (1990). Spanish is the official language. Thirty percent of the people are Quechua, 25 percent Aymara, 31 percent are mestizo, and 14 percent European by descent. Europeans have long controlled Bolivia with a contentiousness that has provoked 189 coups d'état from the time independence was won from Spain in 1825 through 1980. Bolivia has had one of the world's highest inflation rates and was the first Latin American country to unilaterally suspend payments on its foreign debt; incoming factions have had little desire to pay off nefarious debts incurred by predecessors who had pocketed much of the proceeds.

Human rights violations have frequently been cited by international observers against the fascist military who harbored Nazi criminals after World War II. In three costly wars between 1879 and 1935 Bolivia lost its Pacific coast to Chile, its oil-laden Chaco to Paraguay, and its rubber-growing areas to Brazil. As a result it is the poorest country in South America with 55 percent of the population rural and a per capita income (1985) of $536, a life expectancy of 48.6 years (male) and 53.0 years (female), and an infant mortality rate of 123 per 1000 births. A 75 percent literacy rate is claimed and compulsory education is mandated for those seven to 14 years of age.

Most of Bolivia's agricultural products come from farms cleared out of the semitropical forests of the Amazon headwaters in the northeast which fall off to the sparsely inhabited Chaco lowlands of the southeast. The Andes range runs down the middle of the country with three of the highest peaks in South America, making it costly to transport commodities to the west where most of the populace lives on the great altiplano plateau. Few cash crops, aside from potatoes and barley, grow at such altitudes and in this unfortunate void cocaine traffic has reached uncontrollable dimensions.

Roman Catholicism, Bolivia's official religion, claims 94.6 percent of the population (1983). About 44 percent mix Catholicism with pagan holdovers. Due to a 1951 Concordat with the Holy See the state nominates candidates for bishoprics. One cardinal, seven archbishops, 20 bishops, 828 priests, 1732 nuns, and 176 brothers serve the church which is divided into 443 parishes in four archdioceses and four dioceses (1983).

As of 1987 Protestants claimed 422,500 members and 6.5 percent of the population. Their fast-growing churches are served by 650 foreign missionaries mainly working among the indigenous populations, and 35 recognized denominations.

Recent proselytizing of the Baha'i faith has resulted in 3000 baptisms annually (1987).

FAITH ANNETTE SAND

**Bonhoeffer, Dietrich** (1906–1945). Lutheran pastor and theologian. Born in Breslau, he was the son of a professor of psychiatry. During theological studies at Tübingen and Berlin he was influenced by Karl Barth. After a brief period pastoring a Lutheran congregation in Barcelona, he spent one year at Union Theological Seminary in New York. In 1931 he returned to Berlin to lecture at the university. From the outset he was a vocal opponent of nazism, wholeheartedly supporting the Confessing Church and signing the Barmen Declaration in 1934. For one year thereafter he served as pastor to a Lutheran congregation in London, after which he returned to Germany to become head of a small seminary for the Confessing Church. Forbidden by the Nazis to teach, he was banned from Berlin and dismissed from the seminary in 1936. In 1939 he rejected the offer of a job in America in order to stay and face the difficulties ahead with his fellow Christians in Germany. He was active in German opposition to Hitler, and became deeply involved in a plot to kill Hitler and overthrow the Nazi state. He was arrested in 1943 for helping to smuggle a number of Jews into Switzerland. On April 8, 1945, he was hanged along with Admiral Canaris and others who had plotted against Hitler. His life and published writings have had a considerable influence upon postwar theology. His major works include *The Cost of Discipleship* (1937), *Ethics* (1949), *Letters and Papers from Prison* (1953), and *Christology* (1960).

IAN HAMILTON

**Booth, Ballington** (1857[?]–1940). Founder in 1896 of the Volunteers of America. Born in Yorkshire, England, he was trained by his father, William Booth, to lead the Salvation Army, and was commissioner in Australia (1884–87) and in the USA (1887–96). He left the Salvation Army because he perceived it as too authoritarian, and with his wife organized the more democratic Volunteers of America, retaining the use of uniforms and ranks. He led the organization until his death. He was ordained as presbyter in the Evangelical Church in Chicago in 1896.

EARLE E. CAIRNS

**Booth, Evangeline Cory** (1865–1950). Daughter of General William Booth, founder of the Salvation Army. She was educated in London and soon took a leading place in the army. She was field commissioner in London for five years, principal of the International Training Colleges, commander of the army in Canada for nine years,

and commander-in-chief in the USA (1904–34). She then served as general of the world army and resided in London (1934–39). Upon retiring, she returned to the USA. She wrote many songs of the army and published *Songs of the Evangel* (1927). Among her other books are *Love Is All* (1925), *Towards a Better World* (1928), and *Woman* (1930). With Christian romance novelist Grace Livingstone Hill she wrote *The War Romance of the Salvation Army* (1919).

RAYMOND W. ALBRIGHT

**Booth, William** (1829–1912). Founder of the Salvation Army. Born in Nottingham, he grew up amid poverty and became a pawnbroker's assistant. He was converted in 1844, and later became a minister of the Methodist New Connexion. Even when preaching to a full congregation on Tyneside, however, he was uneasy about his limited outreach. For Booth, the Lord's requirements involved loosing the chains of injustice, freeing the captive and oppressed, sharing food and home, clothing the naked, and carrying out family responsibilities. To speak of godly poverty in no sense indicated that God approved of destitution. In 1865 he began "The Christian Mission" in London's East End which became the Salvation Army in 1878. By 1884 some 600 Salvationists had been jailed for insisting on preaching in the open air. Booth fought on; his men and women soldiers waged war against such evils as sweated labor and girls sold into prostitution. Accused of embezzling funds, he was totally exonerated. His army spread throughout the world, with a whole network of social and regenerative agencies. He was freeman of London, honorary doctor of Oxford, and guest at King Edward's coronation and of the U.S. Senate, which he opened with prayer. His book *In Darkest England and the Way Out* (1890) tells of his motivation and philosophy. When he died—the official notice said that "the General has laid down his sword"—150,000 people from all classes filed past his coffin.

J. D. DOUGLAS

**Boreham, Frank William** (1871–1959). Baptist preacher and writer. Born in Tunbridge Wells, England, he left school early and suffered an injury at work that made him lame for the rest of his life. Although born an Anglican, at age 20 he was baptized in a London Baptist Church. He immediately began preaching as a layman and wrote his first book. In 1892 he entered Spurgeon's College, London, and in 1894 was called to a Scots community near Dunedin, New Zealand, as minister. He was elected president of the New Zealand Baptist Union in 1902. In 1906 he was called to the Baptist tabernacle in Hobart, Tasmania, and 10 years later to the Baptist church in Armadale, Victoria. The rest of his ministry was based in Australia. In four decades he published

80 books and wrote a stream of articles for daily papers and the Baptist religious press. His fame led to invitations to preach overseas and in the churches of other denominations in Australia. His writings include *A Bunch of Everlastings* (1920), *The Heavenly Octave: A Study of the Beatitudes* (1936), *My Christmas Book* (1953), and *The Last Milestone* (1971).

NOEL S. POLLARD

**Bornkamm, Heinrich** (1901–1977). German church historian. Born in Wuitz, Saxony, he studied at the universities of Jena, Tübingen, and Berlin (D.Theol.), taught church history at Tübingen, and was professor of church history at Giessen (1927–35), Leipzig (1935–48), and Heidelberg from 1948 until his retirement. His major interests were Luther, the Reformation, mysticism, 18th-century church history, and modern Catholicism. In 1935 he became president of the Evangelischer Bund, holding this position for many years; from 1948 he was also head of the Verein für Reformationsgeschichte, and from 1938 a coeditor of *Archiv für Reformationsgeschichte*. His numerous books include *Luther und Boehme* (1925), *Mystik, Spiritualismus und die Anfänge des Pietismus im Luthertum* (1926), *Der protestantische Mensch nach dem Augsburgischen Bekenntnis* (2d ed., 1936), *Eckhart und Luther* (1936), *Luthers geistige Welt* (1947), *Luther und das Alte Testament* (1948), *Die Staatsidee im* (1950), *Die authentischen lateinischen Texte der Confessio Augustana* (1958), *Luther als Schriftsteller* (1965), *The Heart of Reformation Faith* (1965), *Thesen und Anschlag Luthers* (1967), and *Luther im Spiegel der deutschen Geistesgeschichte* (2d ed., 1970).

**Bosanquet, Bernard** (1848–1923). Anglican philosopher. Born in Alnwich, England, he studied at Balliol College and became a fellow and tutor at University College, Oxford (1871–81). He then lived in London (1881–1903) where he worked with his wife in behalf of the Charity Organization Society and finally served as professor of moral philosophy at St. Andrews University (1903–8). He delivered the Gifford Lectures in 1911 and 1912. Although he wrote several works on logic, ethics, and esthetics, his main contribution to religious thought was his attempt to develop from the Christian doctrine of the Holy Spirit a philosophical conception of the dynamic unity of the world. He is best known for his insistence that the Absolute is impersonal. His principal works are *The Civilization of Christendom* (1893), *The Principle of Individuality and Value* (1912), *The Value and Destiny of the Individual* (1913), *What Religion Is* (1920), and *The Meeting of Extremes in Contemporary Philosophy* (1920).

*Bibliography.* H. Bosanquet, *Bernard Bosanquet: An Account of His Life* (1924); J. H. Muirhead, *Bernard Bosanquet and His Friends* (1935).

EDWIN E. AUBREY

**Bosley, Harold Augustus** (1907–1975). Methodist clergyman and author. Born in Burchard, Nebr., he was educated at Nebraska Wesleyan University and the University of Chicago (Ph.D., 1933). Ordained by the United Methodist Church in 1933, he became director of religious activities at Iowa State Teachers College in Cedar Falls, Iowa (1934–38), and then successively pastor of Mount Vernon Place Church in Baltimore (1938–47), dean of the divinity school, Duke University (1947–50), pastor of First Methodist Church of Evanston, Ill. (1950–62), and senior minister of Christ Church Methodist in New York, N.Y. (1962–74). As the founder of the interreligious Appeal of Conscience Foundation, he tried unsuccessfully in 1966 to ship 10,000 Jewish prayer books to the Soviet Union. He wrote a dozen books, among which are *The Quest for Religious Certainty* (1939), *On Final Ground* (1946), *The Church Militant* (1952), *The Mind of Christ* (1966), and *Men Who Build Churches* (1972).

JACK MITCHELL

**Bosworth, Edward Increase** (1861–1926). Congregationalist clergyman. Born in Dundee, Ill., he studied at Oberlin, Yale, Leipzig, and Athens. After a pastorate in Mount Vernon, Ohio (1886–87), he taught NT at Oberlin (1887–1926), serving as dean of the school of theology (1921–23) and acting president of Oberlin College (1918–19). Among his books are *Studies in the Acts and Epistles* (1898), *Studies in the Teaching of Jesus and His Apostles* (1901), *Studies in the Life of Jesus Christ* (1904), *New Studies in Acts* (1908), *Christ in Everyday Life* (1910), *Thirty Studies about Jesus* (1917), *Commentary on Romans* (1919), *What It Means to be a Christian* (1922), and *Life and Teaching of Jesus According to the First Three Gospels* (1924).

RAYMOND W. ALBRIGHT

**Bousset, Johann Franz Wilhelm** (1865–1920). German NT and patristics scholar. Born in Lübeck, he was educated at Erlangen, Leipzig, and Göttingen, and taught NT at Göttingen before transferring to a similar post at Giessen, where he remained until his death. One of the founders of the History of Religion School of biblical study, he was the author of *Evangeliencitate Justins des Märtyrers* (1891), *Jesu Predigt im Gegensatz zum Judentum* (1892), *Textkritische Studien* (1894), *Antichrist* (1895), *Kommentar zur Offenbarung des Johannes* (1896), *Religion des Judentums im neutestamentlichen Zeitalter* (2d ed., 1906), *Kyrios Christos. Geschichte des Chris-*

*tenglaubens von den Anfängen des Christentums bis auf Irenaeus* (1913), *Das Wesen der Religion* (4th ed., 1920), and *Jesus* (4th ed., 1927).

**Bower, William Clayton** (1878–1954). Disciples of Christ educator. Born in Wolcottville, Ind., he was educated at Tri-State, Butler, and Columbia. He specialized in the functional nature of religion, experience curriculum, creative method, and the value content of public education. He served pastorates in Indiana, New York, and California. He was professor of religious education at Transylvania and the College of Bible (1912–26) and the University of Chicago (1926–43). He was advisor to the Kentucky Department of Education on Moral and Spiritual Values. His publications include *Survey of Religious Education in the Local Church* (1919), *Educational Task of the Local Church* (1921), *Curriculum of Religious Education* (1925), *Religious Education in the Modern Church* (1929), *Character Through Creative Experience* (1931), and *Religion and the Good Life* (1933). He was editor of and contributor to *The Church at Work in the Modern World* (1935), *The Living Bible* (1936), *Christ and Christian Education* (1943), *Church and State in Education* (1944), and *Moral and Spiritual Values in Education* (1951). He coedited *The Disciples and Religious Education* (1936) with Roy G. Ross and *Protestantism Faces Its Educational Task Together* (1949) with P. R. Haywood.

**Bowie, Walter Russell** (1882–1969). Episcopalian clergyman and professor. Born in Richmond, Va., he studied at Harvard University, Union Theological Seminary, and Virginia Theological Seminary. He was ordained in the Protestant Episcopal Church (1908), and served parishes in Virginia (1908–23) and New York City (1923–39). He was professor of practical theology, Union Theological Seminary, N.Y. (1939–50), dean of students (1945–50), professor of homiletics, Virginia Theological Seminary (1950–55), visiting lecturer at Yale, and lecturer at Seabury Divinity School (1955–69). He was chaplain in France during World War I (1918–19). He wrote *The Inescapable Christ* (1925), *On Being Alive* (1931), *The Light Shineth in Darkness* (1933), *Remembering Christ* (1940), *Jesus and the Trinity* (1960), *The Living Story of the OT* (1964), *What Is Protestantism?* (1965), and *Learning to Live* (1969), as well as numerous children's books and several pageants. He was associate editor of *The Interpreter's Bible* and a member of the committee that produced the RSV NT.

H. Douglas Buckwalter

**Bowman, John Wick** (1916– ). American Presbyterian NT scholar. Born in Brownsville, Pa., he studied at the College of Wooster (Ohio) and Princeton University. Bowman taught at the United Theological College, Saharanpur, India, Western Theological Seminary, and San Francisco Theological Seminary. The first theologian to receive a Fullbright Scholarship (1949–50), Bowman served on the advisory committee for the RSV. His most important books are *The Intention of Jesus* (1943), *The Religion of Maturity* (1948), *Prophetic Realism and the Gospel: A Preface to Biblical Theology* (1955), *Jesus' Teaching in Its Environment* (1963), *The Fourth Gospel and the Jews* (1975), and *The Samaritan Problem* (1975).

R. Milton Winter

**Bowman, Thomas** (1836–1923). Bishop of the Evangelical Association. Born in Lehigh township, Northampton County, Pa., he studied at the Vandermeers Seminary and entered the ministry of the Evangelical Association. He was pastor in the eastern Pennsylvania conference (1859–75) and presiding elder (1870–75). He was made bishop in 1875. He also served at the Union Biblical Institute (now Evangelical Theological Seminary) at Naperville, Ill. (1891–1911). He frequently represented his denomination at national and world gatherings. Among his publications are *Historical Review of the Disturbances in the Evangelical Association* (1894), *A Reply to a Pack of Lies* (1894), *The Revised Catechism of the Evangelical Association* (1905), *The Great Salvation* (1909), and *Der Kleine Katechismus* (1909).

Raymond W. Albright

**Boys Brigade, The.** A Christian boys' organization founded in Glasgow, Scotland, in 1883 by William A. Smith. The first of its kind, it rapidly became international, starting in the USA in 1887, in Australia in 1891, and in the Caribbean in 1892. The object is to help boys toward true Christian manliness through Christian education and a range of activities to develop obedience, discipline, and self-respect. Its motto is "Sure and Steadfast." In 1984 there were 422,000 members and leaders in over 7000 companies in 44 countries. The largest national memberships are in Britain, Finland, Nigeria, and Denmark. The World Conference Committee, comprising representatives from eight regions of the world, was established in 1976 and meets every three years to hear reports, discuss development plans, and decide on priorities. In 1983 the centenary in Britain was marked by celebrations throughout the year, honored by the presence on one occasion of Queen Elizabeth II, the organization's patron in Britain.

Alistair J. Drummond

**Braden, Charles Samuel** (1887–1970). Methodist missionary, editor, author, and educator. Born in Chanute, Kans., he studied at Baker University, Union Theological Seminary, and the Uni-

117

versity of Chicago (Ph.D., 1926). Following ordination (1914), he was a missionary in South America (1912–22), and assistant secretary, Methodist Board of Foreign Missions (1923–25). From 1926 he taught religious history and literature at Northwestern University until his retirement in 1954. He continued teaching as visiting professor at Scripps College, Claremont, Calif. (1954–56), Facultad Evangelica de Teologica, Buenos Aires (1957), Perkins School of Theology (1954, 1959), and until his death was resident scholar at Perkins School of Theology. He served as editor of *El Heraldo Christiano*, Santiago, Chile (1916–22), founder and editor of *World Christianity* (1936–39), and editorial adviser to the *Journal of Bible and Religion* (1943–49). He contributed over 150 articles to encyclopedias, periodicals, and journals, and authored a dozen books concerned with world religions.

JACK MITCHELL

## Bradley, Francis Herbert (1846–1924).

Philosopher. Educated at Cheltenham and Marlborough, Bradley spent most of his life as a fellow of Merton College, Oxford, where his activity was limited by ill health. Opposed to utilitarianism and naturalism he sought, as an objective idealist and in a somewhat neo-Hegelian way, to reconcile the heroic and worshipful God demanded by religion with an absolute and infinite deity. His published works include *The Presuppositions of Critical History* (1874), *Ethical Studies* (1876), *The Principles of Logic* (1883), *Appearance and Reality* (1893, 1914), *Essays on Truth and Reality* (1914), and *The Principles of Logic* (1922).

*Bibliography.* H. Rashdall, *The Metaphysic of F. H. Bradley* (1912); C. A. Campbell, *Scepticism and Construction, Bradley's Sceptical Principle as the Basis of Constructive Philosophy* (1931); T. K. Segerstedt, *Value and Reality in Bradley's Philosophy* (1934); R. G. Ross, *Scepticism and Dogma: A Study in the Philosophy of F. H. Bradley* (1940).

RAYMOND W. ALBRIGHT

## Brahmanism. *See* HINDUISM; INDIA.

## Brahmo Samaj, The. A pioneer Hindu reform movement founded by "the prophet of Indian nationalism," Ram Mohan Roy (c. 1772–1833). A Bengali Brahman attracted by the monotheism of Islam and the ethical teaching of Jesus, Ram Mohan Roy sought to promote a rationalistic and unitarian religion based on the *Upanishads* (Hindu philosophical writings). The Atmiya Sabha (Spiritual Association) of 1815 was followed by a "Unitarian Mission" (1821) and the Brahma Sabha (1828), later called the Brahmo Samaj (One God Society). Ram Mohan's unitarianism, expressed in *The Precepts of Jesus* (1820) and other writings, was opposed by the Serampore missionary Joshua Marshman (1768–1837) and later by Indian Christians such as Lal Behari Day (1824–94) and Nehemiah Goreh (1825–95),

although both the latter supported the Brahmo Samaj concern for Indian-ness in religion.

Services in the first Brahmo Samaj "church," opened in 1830, included readings from the *Upanishads*, a sermon, and the singing of theistic Sanskrit and Bengali hymns composed by Ram Mohan and his friends. Prayer was added by one of Ram Mohan's successors as leader, Debendranath Tagore (1817–1905), father of the poet Rabindranath, who joined the Brahmo Samaj in 1842. Debendranath also compiled *Brahma Dharma*, a selection of passages chiefly drawn from the *Upanishads* which supported the sect's outlook and became its main sacred text. The next important leader, Keshab Chandra Sen (1838–84) joined the Brahmo Samaj in 1857 and was instrumental in replacing Hindu rites with its own. He parted company, however, with Debendranath in 1865 on the question of repudiating caste, and took the more radical members of the sect with him to form the Brahmo Samaj of India in 1866, leaving Debendranath with what became known as the Adi Samaj (Original Samaj).

Sen followed in the social reform tradition of Roy, who had successfully campaigned to get *sati*, the self-immolation of widows on their husband's funeral pyre, declared illegal in 1829, by working to improve the position of Hindu women and girls. Largely due to pressure from the Brahmo Samaj the government passed laws to abolish child marriages, permit intercaste marriages and the remarriage of widows, and recognize Brahmo Samaj marriages. On the religious front Sen became interested in non-Hindu and especially Christian scriptures, and at the next schism in the Brahmo Samaj took his followers into the eclectic "Church of the New Dispensation," holding that theirs was the third dispensation after the OT and NT. The Church of the New Dispensation did not long survive Sen's death in 1884, but its theological ideas were to continue in the thought of Sen's biographer and successor, P. C. Mozoomdar (1840–1905), and bear new Christian fruit in the theology of one of its members who became a Roman Catholic, Brahmobandhav Upadhyaya (1861–1907). Sen's opponents founded the rival Sadharan Brahma Samaj in 1878, which still exists, with about 1500 members in India altogether.

Although torn by schism and limited in its influence to the intellectual elite of Indian society, the Brahmo Samaj promoted a social conscience in Hinduism and inspired other groups like the Prarthana Samaj in Bombay, led by Mahadev Govind Ranade (1842–1901), to work for social reforms. It thus has a permanent place in the development of 20th-century Hinduism.

*Bibliography.* R. Boyd, *An Introduction to Indian Christian Theology* (1975); M. M. Thomas, *The Acknowledged Christ of the Indian Renaissance* (2d ed., 1976); D. Kopf, *The Brahmo Samaj and the Shaping of the Modern Indian Mind* (1978); A. Kolencherry, *The Universality of Modern Hinduism* (1984).

PHILIP HILLYER

**Branscomb, (Bennett) Harvie** (1894– ). Methodist philosopher and theologian. Born in Huntsville, Ala., he studied at Birmingham-Southern College, Oxford University, and Columbia University (Ph.D., 1924). During World War I he served on the commission for relief in Belgium (1914–15). He taught philosophy at Southern Methodist University (1919/20), and NT at Duke University divinity school (1921–45; dean, 1945/46). He was chancellor of Vanderbilt University. He was chairman of the Commission of the American Library Association to Brazil (1945) as well as of the United States Advisory Committee for Educational Exchange (1947–51). His writings include *The Message of Jesus* (1925), *Jesus and the Law of Moses* (1930), *The Teaching of Jesus* (1931), *The Gospel of Mark* (1937), and *Teaching with Books* (1940). He was also editor of the *American Oxonian* (1943–46).

BRUCE M. METZGER

**Brazil.** The largest country of South America, sixth in population and fifth in land area among the nations of the world. With a south Atlantic coastline of 4500 miles, its western and southern borders touch all the South American countries except Ecuador and Chile. The land area is 8,511,965 sq. km. (3,286,473 sq. mi.) and the population is 141.5 million (1987 est.).

Brazil is a rapidly developing nation with abundant resources and voluminous trade. The foreign debt, which in 1987 was over $100 billion, largely resulted from borrowing for development. The large foreign debt necessitates a yearly trade surplus of exports over imports of about $8 billion. Agriculture, enhanced by immense areas of arable land and a year-round temperate climate, contributes to Brazilian trade with crops of coffee, soybeans, cocoa, citrus fruits, and bananas. Brazil exports iron ore, bauxite, uranium, gold, diamonds, and semiprecious stones. Discovery of large reserves of petroleum off the Atlantic coast has moved Brazil toward energy self-sufficiency. Industrialization proceeds at a rapid pace and Brazilian cars, trucks, steel piping, and shoes account for billions of dollars yearly in exports.

Ethnically, Brazil is highly varied. The original population, Amerindian, was scattered sparsely over the land. About 150,000 Amerindians remain in the jungles. Portuguese settlement, beginning in 1500, brought the white man. Later influxes of European settlers have resulted in a white majority. Negroes, brought as slaves from Africa, were emancipated in 1893 and comprise 11 percent of the population. An immigration of more than one million Japanese since 1900 produced another significant segment.

Classes for adults and compulsory elementary education for children have drastically reduced the level of illiteracy from one-half in the 1950s to less than one-third in the early 1970s. The Brazilian system offers four years of compulsory elementary education, four years of *ginasio* (gymnasium), then three years of *segundo grau* (second degree), which corresponds to the American high school. College and university study may begin after the passing of entrance examinations. Full educational programs are available in the populated and more developed areas.

Brazil's most serious social problem is urban crime. For unskilled labor the current minimum salary is 2640 cruzados, the equivalent of $40 per month. Millions of Brazilians live in *favelas*, slums scattered through the metropolitan areas, without basic comfort and sanitation. The result is the proliferation of disease and crime. The need for a significant rise in the real wages of the working class and better-trained police was acute by the late 1980s. An estimated 300,000 Brazilian homeless street-children survived in groups on their own by begging and theft.

After a military dictatorship (1964–86) Brazil returned to representative republican government with an elected national president, bicameral legislature, and elected governors in 23 states.

Although at different periods of Brazil's history Roman Catholicism has been the official religion, freedom of worship for non-Catholics has been the norm. At the birth of the republic in 1889, church and state were separated. The official census of 1980 showed 106 million Roman Catholics, 4 million Protestants, 3.8 pentecostals, 860,000 spiritualists *(Kardecistas)*, 678,000 Afro-Brazilian spiritists, 257,000 oriental religionists, 91,795 Jews, and 2 million professed atheists.

Roman Catholic missionaries arrived among the first settlers and catechized the native Indians. The Roman Catholic Church of the late 1980s had 31 archdioceses, 118 dioceses, and 4947 parishes, according to available statistics. Cardinals preside over the archdioceses in Sao Paulo, Rio de Janeiro, and Fortaleza. There are 70 seminaries. The total number of priests was 12,589—7263 Brazilians, 1409 Italians, 990 Germans, 967 Dutch, and 562 Spanish. The 178 bishops, five of whom were cardinals, formed the National Council of Brazilian Bishops (CNBB) which was divided ideologically between conservatives and liberals endorsing liberation theology. A movement for lay and grass-roots Catholic involvement in social struggles, promoted by the liberal clergy, gained momentum, particularly in the northeast drought area, with the formation of hundreds of neo-Marxist cells called *Comunidades Eclesiais de Base* (Church Base Communities). The conservative bishops and priests support the status quo.

The Protestants have grown significantly since 1850, and the pentecostals, since 1900. Although much smaller numerically than the Catholics, according to official figures, the church attendance is about equivalent. On a given Sunday there will be about 10 million Catholics and about the same number of non-Catholic Christians in church services. There are 2400 evangelical foreign missionaries in Brazil, serving under 127 different agencies. The largest evangelical mission agencies include the Southern Baptists with 276; New Tribes Mission, 180; Wycliffe Bible Translators, 175; Unevangelized Fields Mission, 122; Baptist Mid-Missions, 188; Association of Baptists for World Evangelism, 67; Christian Missions in Many Lands, 63; Presbyterian Church, 58; Bethany Fellowship, 48; Baptist Bible Fellowship, 42. The ministries of the evangelical missions are directed to the general Brazilian population in evangelism, Bible teaching, literature publication, and Bible translation. Specific group efforts are made toward the Amerindians in the jungle, Jews, orientals, children, youth, athletes, professionals, the incarcerated, and addicts.

Among active sects are the Jehovah's Witnesses, Mormons, Rosicrucians, Baha'i, Unification Church, Perfect Liberty, and other oriental groups. Spiritualism and spiritism attract Brazilian people from all social levels. Spiritualism, of European origin, more refined and philosophical, is the religion of many in the middle and upper classes. Its main doctrines are reincarnation and communicating with the dead. Spiritism is essentially African animism brought to Brazil by slaves from Nigeria and other western African lands and syncretized with Roman Catholic beliefs. It emphasizes potions, curses, incantations, dances, drum beating, and animal (and sometimes human) sacrifices. The popularity of spiritualism and spiritism in Brazil derives from the healing of sicknesses, removal of tumors, and other surgical operations by untrained mediums using primitive means, ostensibly under the spiritual control of deceased doctors. Public revolt is aroused from time to time by the discovery of the practice of human sacrifice, usually of children, in the ritual.

LEONARD MEZNAR

**Breasted, James Henry** (1865–1935). Historian and orientalist. Born in Rockford, Ill., he studied at North Central College, Chicago Theological Seminary, Yale, and Berlin (Ph.D., 1894). Thereafter he was associated with the University of Chicago, teaching Egyptology, Semitic languages, and oriental history (1894–1933). From 1895 he was associated with the Haskell Oriental Museum, of which he was director (1901–31). He led many research projects in the Near East and in the museums of Europe. He was relieved of all responsibility for teaching after August 1925 in order to make it possible for him to take charge

of the Oriental Institute, of which he was the director (1919–35). Among his many publications, those of greatest interest to students of religion are *Egypt Through the Stereoscope* (1905), *A History of Egypt* (1905, 1909), *Ancient Records of Egypt, Historical Documents* (5 vols., 1906), *The Temples of Lower Nubia* (1906), *A History of the Ancient Egyptians* (1908), *Development of Religion and Thought in Ancient Egypt* (1912), *Survey of the Ancient World* (1919), *Conquest of Civilization* (1926), and *The Dawn of Conscience* (1923).

RAYMOND W. ALBRIGHT

**Breen, Quirinus** (1896–1975). Presbyterian scholar. Born in Orange City, Iowa, he studied at Calvin College and Theological Seminary and the University of Chicago (Ph.D., 1931). He served two pastorates and taught history at Hillsdale College (1931–33), Albany (Oreg.) College (1933–38), and the University of Oregon (1938–64). Following his retirement he was resident scholar in Princeton's Institute for Advanced Study, later teaching at Grand Valley State University in Michigan. His special scholarly interest was in Renaissance humanism and its influence on the Protestant Reformers. He is the author of *John Calvin: A Study in French Humanism* (1931) and *Christianity and Humanism: Studies in the History of Ideas* (1968).

R. MILTON WINTER

**Brenner, Scott Francis** (1903– ). Reformed and Presbyterian pastor and scholar. Born in Harmony, Pa., he was educated at Ursinus College, the Theological Seminary of the Reformed Church in the United States, Lancaster, Pa., and the Divinity School of the Protestant Episcopal Church (Th.D., 1938). He served pastorates in the Evangelical and Reformed Church and later in the Presbyterian Church, USA. He served on denominational boards and committees concerned with Christian worship and authored several books on worship. Among the most important are *A Handbook on Worship* (1941), *The Way of Worship* (1944), *The Book of Worship of the Evangelical and Reformed Church* (1945), *The Art of Worship* (1961), and *Ways of Worship: New Forms of Mission* (1968).

R. MILTON WINTER

**Brent, Charles Henry** (1862–1929). Protestant Episcopal missionary bishop. Born in Newcastle, Ont., he graduated from Trinity College, Toronto, in 1884, and after ordination was curate of St. Paul's Cathedral, Buffalo, N.Y. (1887–88), and St. John the Evangelist, Boston (1889–91), and associate rector of St. Stephen's, Boston (1897–1901). In 1901 he was consecrated first bishop of the missionary district of the Philippines, and transferred in 1908 to the diocese of Washington and in 1919 to the diocese of Western New York, with which he combined latterly the charge of the Protestant Episcopal churches in Europe (1926–28). He was largely responsible for promoting and conducting world church conferences, beginning with the first conferences in Stockholm and Lausanne. His idea of Christian unity was analogous to the unity in the British Empire, where personal loyalty to the monarch rather than organic, constitutional, or legislative ties bind vastly different groups into one whole. He felt that every Christian group could contribute something to all others in a great church which would become the heir of all the spiritual, moral, and intellectual wealth of the Christian centuries. He was the author of many publications, including *With God in the World* (1899), *The Consolations of the Cross* (1902), *With God in Prayer* (1907), *The Mind of Christ in the Church of the Living God* (1908), *The Conquest of Trouble and the Peace of God* (1916), *Understanding* (1925), *The Commonwealth: Its Foundation and Pillars* (1930), and *Adventures in Prayer* (1932).

**Brethren, Church of the.** *See* DUNKERS.

**Brethren in Christ, United.** *See* UNITED BRETHREN IN CHRIST.

**Brethren of Christ.** *See* CHRISTADELPHIANS.

**Breviary.** Official prayerbook of the Roman Catholic Church. Obligatory for the clergy and monastic and other religious communities, and recommended for laity, the breviary was originally a compilation or abridgement of the psalter, the antiphonal, and the hymnal. For centuries referred to as *The Divine Office*, it is today properly known as *The Liturgy of the Hours*. Its purpose is to sanctify the day and the work of the Christian. In accordance with the injunction of Christ to "pray always" (Luke 18:1; 21:36) and in imitation of the early church (Acts 2:42; 3:1; 10:9; 16:25), the day is divided into the office of readings, morning prayer (lauds), the daytime hours (terce, sext, none), evening prayer (vespers), and night prayer (compline). For each there is an opening hymn, psalms, a Scripture reading, and prayers. In a four-week cycle almost all psalms are read or sung. The breviary is usually printed in four volumes, one each for Advent and Christmas season; the Lenten and Easter seasons; "ordinary time," weeks 1–17; and "ordinary time," weeks 18–34. Before the Second Vatican Council the entire office was said in Latin, but now the vernacular language may be used. The liturgy is designed as a communal prayer, and bishops, priests, and deacons are required by canon law "to fulfill the liturgy daily."

**Bibliography.** *The Divine Office* (1974); C. Jones, G. Wainwright, and E. Yarnolds, eds., *The Study of the Liturgy* (1978).

JOHN E. LYNCH

**Bridges, Robert Seymour** (1844–1930). English poet and essayist. Educated at Eton and Oxford, he studied medicine at St. Bartholomew's, London, and became consulting physician at Great Ormond Street Children's Hospital. He gave up medicine in 1882 and settled in Yattendon, Berkshire, devoting himself to literature. He became precentor in the village choir, and in 1899 published the *Yattendon Hymnal*, which revived 16th- and 17th-century melodies and emphasized a close relationship between text and tune. It was drawn on for the *English Hymnal* (1906) and the *Oxford Hymn Book* (1908). He published volumes of *Shorter Poems* in 1873 and 1890 and was appointed poet laureate in 1913. Eight plays published between 1885 and 1894 were applauded by classical scholars. In 1904 he moved to Oxfordshire, and in 1918 performed a literary service by publishing a collection of the poems of his friend, Gerard Manley Hopkins, which he had rescued from obscurity. An intellectual innovator, avoiding emotion, Bridges would not "write to order" as poet laureate. In his most widely known work, *Testament of Beauty* (1929), he attempted to reconcile scientific knowledge with faith. He was founder of the Society for Pure English.

TIM LENTON

**Briggs, Charles Augustus** (1841–1913). American biblical scholar. Born in New York City, he was educated at the University of Virginia, Union Theological Seminary, and the University of Berlin. He was ordained to the Presbyterian ministry and was pastor at Roselle, N.J., from 1870 to 1874, when he was appointed professor of Hebrew at Union Theological Seminary, New York City. In 1891 he was transferred to the chair of biblical theology, and then from 1904 he was professor of theological encyclopedia and symbolics. In 1892 he was tried for heresy by the Presbytery of New York, but was acquitted, although in the following year he was suspended by the General Assembly. In 1899 he was ordained in the Protestant Episcopal Church. In addition to numerous studies in various theological periodicals, he wrote many books, including *Biblical Study* (1883), *American Presbyterianism* (1885), *Messianic Prophecy* (1886), *The Authority of Holy Scripture* (1891), *The Bible, the Church and Reason* (1892), *The Higher Criticism of the Hexateuch* (1893), *The Messiah of the Gospels* (1894), *General Introduction to the Study of Holy Scripture* (1899), *The Incarnation of the Lord* (1902), *Ethical Teachings of Jesus* (1904), and *Critical Commentary on the Psalms* (1906). He was editor of the *Presbyterian Review* (1880–90), and collaborated with S. D. F. Salmond in editing the *International Theological Library* from 1891, with S. R. Driver and A. Plummer in editing the *International Critical*

*Commentary* series from 1895, and with F. Brown and S. R. Driver in preparing the *Hebrew and English Lexicon of the OT* (1891–1906).

**Bright, John** (1908– ). American Presbyterian OT scholar. Born in Chattanooga, Tenn., and educated at Union Theological Seminary in Virginia and Johns Hopkins University, Bright continued the tradition of OT scholarship established by W. F. Albright at Johns Hopkins, which emphasized restoration of confidence in the antiquity and basic reliability of the OT historical accounts. He served for many years as professor of OT interpretation at Union Seminary in Richmond, Va. Bright's scholarship blended careful use of literary criticism of the OT text with copious citation of archeological evidence. Bright maintained that "Israel's history is a subject inseparable from the history of Israel's religion." Among his most significant books are *The Kingdom of God* (1953), *The Authority of the OT* (1967), *Covenant and Promise: The Prophetic Understanding of the Future in Pre-Exilic Israel* (1976), and *A History of Israel* (3d ed., 1981).

R. MILTON WINTER

**Brightman, Edgar Sheffield** (1884–1953). Philosopher. Born in Holbrook, Mass., he studied at Brown University, Boston University (Ph.D., 1912), and in Germany. He taught philosophy and Greek at Brown (1906–8), philosophy and Bible at Nebraska Wesleyan University (1912–15), ethics and religion at Wesleyan University (1915–19), and philosophy at Boston University (1919–53). He was an ordained minister of the Methodist Church; fellow of the American Academy of Arts and Sciences and of the Conference on Science, Philosophy, and Religion; and president of the American Philosophical Association, American Theological Society, and National Association of Biblical Instructors. His chief interests were epistemology, metaphysics, axiology, philosophy of religion, Hegelianism, and Latin-American and Indian philosophy. His chief contribution was to an empirical personalism, resulting in the idea of a temporalistic, finite God within whose eternal, unified personality will is limited by eternal experiences called the rational and the nonrational "Given." God is then Controller of the Given. His chief works are *Sources of the Hexateuch* (1918), *Introduction to Philosophy* (1925, 1951), *Religious Values* (1925), *Philosophy of Ideals* (1928), *Moral Laws* (1933), *Philosophy of Religion* (1940), and *Nature and Values* (1945). He edited *Personalism in Theology* (1943). He contributed to the *Encyclopedia of Religion* (1945), *History of Philosophical Systems* (1950), and *Radhakrishnan* (1951).

**Brilioth, Yngvo Torgny** (1891–1959). Lutheran professor and clergyman. Born in Sweden, he studied at the University of Uppsala (Ph.D., 1916). Ordained in Uppsala in 1918, he became lecturer in church history in Uppsala (1919), professor of church history at Åbo University (1925), professor of practical theology at the University of Lund, and dean of Lund (1928). He was bishop of Växjö (1937–50), and archbishop of Uppsala. He was a member of the central committee and executive committee of the World Council of Churches and chairman of the Commission on Faith and Order of the World Council of Churches. His publications are *The Anglican Revival* (1925), *Eucharistic Faith and Practice* (1930), *Three Lectures on Evangelicalism and the Oxford Movement* (1934), and *Landmarks in the History of Preaching* (1950).

**Brinton, Howard Haines** (1884–1973). Quaker author and educator. Born in West Chester, Pa., he was educated at Haverford, Harvard, and the University of California. He taught at Guilford, Earlham, and Mills colleges. From 1936 he was director of Pendle Hill Graduate School, Wallingford, Pa. Among Brinton's works were *Mystic Will* (1930), *Critique by Eternity and Other Essays* (1943), *The Quaker Doctrine of Inward Peace* (1948), *Quaker Education in Theory and Practice* (1948), *Quakerism and Other Religions* (1957), *Ethical Mysticism in the Society of Friends* (1957), *Ethical Mysticism in the Society of Friends* (1967), and *Quaker Journals: Varieties of Religious Experience among Friends* (1972). He was also editor and contributor to *Children of Light* (1938) and *Byways in Quaker History* (1944).

**British Council of Churches (BCC).** An ecumenical council for the churches of Great Britain and Ireland. Constituted in September 1942, its formation climaxed increased cooperation among the non-Roman Catholic churches involving conferences on "Life and Work" (Oxford, 1937) and "Faith and Order" (Edinburgh, 1937). William Temple's influence in its formation and his involvement in its early years were crucial. Sixteen denominational bodies and several interdenominational organizations (including the YMCA, YWCA, and SCM) were among the initial members. By a special doctrinal arrangement the Society of Friends, the Unitarian Church, and Free Christian Churches were able to associate with the council. The council has gradually widened its membership. In 1964 representatives of the Lutheran Council of Great Britain and the Greek Orthodox Church were added, and in 1972 a number of black-led churches joined. Despite long negotiations the Roman Catholic Church, although working closely with the council, has retained the observer status granted in 1965.

Reports have been issued on a variety of subjects reflecting concern on a range of religious, social, political, moral, and interdenominational issues. Although the council cannot directly take part in church union negotiations it has been responsible, through group study schemes, conferences, and various initiatives, for a growing understanding among member churches. Departments of the council include Christian Aid, the Divisions of Ecumenical Affairs, International Affairs, Community Affairs, and the Conference for World Mission which was formed in 1978 when BCC incorporated the Conference of Missionary Societies of Great Britain and Ireland.

**Bibliography.** E. A. Payne, *Thirty Years of the British Council of Churches, 1942–1972* (1972).

JAMES TAYLOR

## British Israelitism.

A nationalistic eschatological theory rather than a separate sect and movement. Its adherents, mainly Protestant, prefer to remain members of their churches. The publication of *Our Israelitish Origin* by John Wilson in 1840 probably marked the popular emergence of its teachings. Three convictions are central. First, the OT prophecies must be literally fulfilled or God is a liar and unfaithful to his word. Second, British Israelitism believes that the prophecies require for their fulfillment the persistence, as a nation, of the 10 tribes of the northern kingdom of Israel under a king of David's dynasty. The tribes were taken into captivity in Assyria in the 8th century B.C. Third, they believe that the people of Britain and the USA are the descendants of the 10 tribes and are, therefore, the inheritors of God's promises. The lost tribes are to be identified with the Scythians, Cimmerians, and Goths who eventually, as the Angles, Saxons, Jutes, and Normans, reached England after being "sifted through many nations" (Amos 9:9). As a result, it is claimed, the English language contains many words similar to Hebrew: "Scot" derives from "Scythian," "Saxon" is from "Isaac's son," and "Britain" derives from "b'rith," the Hebrew for "covenant." British Israelitism is characterized by a literalist interpretation of the Bible. For example, the promise in Gen. 22:17, "Thy seed shall possess the gate of his enemies," is taken to refer to the British possession of Gibraltar and Malta. It has also been charged with encouraging a false sense of racial security and pride. Few historians support its theories, and it can be dismissed on ethnological and philological grounds. Its method of interpreting Scripture allows serious distortion of truth to conform to modern-day events.

JAMES TAYLOR

## Brotherhood Movement.

A philosophical men's organization developed from a Sunday afternoon Bible class for young men inspired in 1875 by an English midlands draper, John Blackham. Especially popular with Congregationalists, it became an interdenominational movement. At its zenith it attracted attendance at its Sunday afternoon meetings of up to 300,000. It was organized into local societies, county and area federations, and a national council and conference with various social service departments. Combining a somewhat vague belief in the fatherhood of God, the saviorhood of Jesus Christ, and the sacredness of man, it has been described as "a religious equivalent of pre-war Progressivism" (McLeod). By World War II it had begun to lose its appeal, but it still continues, although in an attenuated form. A parallel Sisterhood was organized in 1891.

HAROLD H. ROWDON

## Brotherhood of Man.

The conception of a fundamental kinship among humanity has origins in both Greek and biblical thought. Greeks of the classical period divided the human race into Greeks and non-Greeks, described the latter as barbarians, and regarded them as an inferior stock. Plato said that all barbarians were enemies by nature, and Aristotle believed that they lacked the qualities of freemen, being destined by nature to serve as slaves. Although this view was occasionally challenged and a more cosmopolitan outlook expressed, especially by the Cynics, it is to the Stoics that we owe the first expressions of human brotherhood as an ideal of conduct. In Zeno's *Republic* all distinctions of earthly rank and race have been abolished, and there is neither Greek nor barbarian in his world-city, from which only the unworthy are excluded. In the writings of the later Stoics, Epictetus and Marcus Aurelius, Zeus is regarded as the father of all mankind, and men are therefore brothers, possessing a common reason, and alike subject to the universal law of nature which prescribes their mutual obligations and establishes their freedom and equality. Epictetus demands that a master should refrain from anger with a neglectful slave on the grounds of their common kinship: "Slave, will you not bear with your own brother, who has Zeus for his forefather, and is born as a son of the same seed as you and of the same heavenly descent? . . . Will you not remember what you are and whom you are ruling? That they are kinsmen, born your brothers, children of Zeus?" (*Discourses* 1.15).

In the OT there is much emphasis on the ties of kinship that bind together the Israelites, and on the unique bond that unites them as the chosen people of Yahweh. There is, however, an incipient universalism in the Book of Amos, where neighboring nations stand equally under the judgment of Yahweh; in Isaiah, where Israel is to be the instrument for the conversion of the Gentiles; and in the short books of Ruth and Jonah, where national exclusiveness is transcended. The accounts of the creation and the flood in Genesis clearly indicate that all men are descended from a common stock, and the sons of Noah are regarded as the progenitors of the various races of mankind. Yet the symbol of brotherhood is never extended explicitly beyond the limits of Israel, and, although Yahweh is occasionally referred to as a Father, it is always in relationship to the nation. At the same time, mercy and kindness are to be shown, not only to the poor and needy of Israel, but especially to slaves and foreigners within her borders, and the messianic kingdom is to initiate universal peace for all mankind.

In the NT, the prevailing sense of the word "brother" (*adelphos*) is "fellow-Christian," and the community of believers is called the "brotherhood" (*adelphotēs*, 1 Pet. 2:17; 5:9). "Brotherly love" (*philadelphia*) is the duty of Christians toward each other (1 Thess. 4:9–10; 1 John 2:9–11; 3:10, 14). Beyond this more intimate circle of discipleship, however, there is also a universal bond uniting all men in a natural brotherhood, which is generally assumed rather than asserted. Jesus refers to God as "Father" without any restrictions upon the term's sphere of reference, and also uses "brother" in the general sense of "fellow-man" (Matt. 5:22, 23; 7:3; 18:15, 35; 23:8). It is probably to the Stoic Cleanthes that Paul refers when he uses at the city of Athens the quotation "For we are also his offspring" (Acts 17:28).

The reason for this ambivalence in the NT is that sin has alienated people from God and from others, so that the relationship is more potential than real. So Jesus has come to establish a *new* brotherhood of those who are obedient to God's will (Mark 3:32–35); Paul speaks of being *adopted* into sonship through God's grace (Rom. 8:15); and the Fourth Gospel says that those who receive Christ are given "the right to *become* children of God" (John 1:12). This brotherhood is, among believers, quite universal in its scope: "For ye are all sons of God, through faith, in Christ Jesus. . . . There can be neither Jew nor Greek, there can be neither bond nor free, there can be no male and female: for ye are all one man in Christ Jesus" (Gal. 3:26, 28). The Christian's relation to all people, whether in Christ or unbeliever, is also marked by an outgoing love which is given unconditionally to every "neighbor" and is not withheld even from his enemies, because it has its origin in the love of God himself; "for he maketh his sun to rise on the evil and the good, and sendeth rain on the just and the unjust." It is in this way that the disciples show that they are sons of their Father in heaven (Matt. 5:43–48).

The concept of human brotherhood has exercised a potent influence on Western thought and action which is difficult to accurately assess. It has been an ideal of personal ethics, stimulating acts of charity and attitudes of brotherly love. It has at times served as an ideal to challenge social

inequalities and injustices. Examples include the Christian response to the institution of slavery and other forms of racism, national exclusivity, and warfare. In the 18th-century Enlightenment the universalism of Stoicism blended with Christian idealism in contributing to the concept of a natural right to freedom and equality. This proclamation of inherent human rights powerfully influenced the American and French revolutions, and the slogan of the latter included "fraternity" as one of its objectives.

In the liberal theology of the latter half of the 19th century the "kingdom of God" in the Gospels was interpreted to imply the brotherhood of man and the Fatherhood of God, and these were the ideals that inspired the social gospel at the beginning of the present century. A vigorous protest was made against social inequalities and the injustices of laissez-faire capitalism, and pacifism became widely accepted as the only Christian attitude toward international tensions. The neo-Reformation reaction to liberalism has often been less concerned with man's natural brotherhood than with his innate selfishness and his need of redemption. The kingdom of God will never be fulfilled within history, and the Christian must therefore pursue the more modest social aim of achieving a tolerable justice between men's competing interests.

*See also* PEACE MOVEMENTS.

ANTHONY S. CHADWICK

## Brown, Arlo Ayres

**Brown, Arlo Ayres** (1883–1961). Methodist clergyman and educator. Born in Sunbeam, Ill., he received his education at Northwestern University, Drew Seminary, and Union Theological Seminary. After serving as an associate at the Madison Avenue Church in New York City (1907–9) and pastor of the Mount Hope Church, N.Y. (1909–12), he became the agent for the Board of Foreign Missions of the Methodist Church in Jerusalem (1912/13), an executive of the Newark district of his church (1913/14), superintendent of teacher training of the Board of Sunday Schools of the Methodist Church (1914–21), president of the University of Chattanooga (1921–29), and president of Drew University (1929–47). His writings include *Studies in Christian Living* (1914), *Primer of Teacher Training* (1916), *Life in the Making* (1917), *A History of Religious Education in Recent Times* (1923), and *Youth and Christian Living* (1929).

RAYMOND W. ALBRIGHT

## Brown, Charles Reynolds

**Brown, Charles Reynolds** (1862–1950). Congregationalist clergyman and lecturer. Born in Bethany, W.Va., he studied at the University of Iowa and the School of Theology of Boston University. He was pastor of Wesley Chapel Methodist Episcopal Church, Cincinnati, Ohio (1889–92), Winthrop Congregational Church,

Boston (1892–96), and First Congregational Church, Oakland, Calif. (1896–1911). He was dean of the Yale Divinity School (1911–28), where he had a distinguished career as teacher, preacher, and administrator. He wrote *The Strange Ways of God* (1908), *The Young Man's Affairs* (1909), *Faith and Health* (1910), *The Modern Man's Religion* (1911), *The Latent Energies in Life* (1912), *The Quest of Life* (1913), *Yale Talks* (1919), *The Master's Way* (1919), *Living Again* (1920), *The Religion of a Layman* (1921), *The Greatest Man of the Nineteenth Century* (1921), *The Art of Preaching* (1922), *Why I Believe in Religion* (1923), *What Is Your Name?* (1924), *Where Do You Live?* (1925), *Ten Short Stories from the Bible* (1925), *These Twelve* (1926), *The Making of a Minister* (1927), *The Gospel for Main Street* (1929), *My Own Yesterdays* (1931), *Have We Outgrown Religion?* (1932), *They Were Giants* (1934), *Finding Ourselves* (1935), *The Master's Influence* (1936), *Being Made Over* (1939), and *Dreams Come True* (1944).

RAYMOND W. ALBRIGHT

**Brown, William Adams** (1865–1943). American theologian. Born in New York City, he was educated at Yale University, Union Theological Seminary, and the University of Berlin. From 1892 he taught at Union Theological Seminary, notably as professor of systematic theology (1898–1930) and as research professor in applied theology (1930–36). He gave much time to the work of the Federal Council of Churches, home missions, and the ecumenical movement. He was a member of the Society of Biblical Literature and Exegesis, and contributed to Hastings' *Dictionary of the Bible*. His works include *Musical Instruments and Their Homes* (1888), *The Essence of Christianity* (1892), *Christ the Vitalizing Principle of Christian Theology* (1898), *Modern Theology and the Preaching of the Gospel* (1914), *Is Christianity Practicable?* (1916), *Modern Missions in the Far East* (1917), *The Church in America* (1922), *The Life of Prayer in a World of Science* (1926), *God at Work* (1933), *The Church, Catholic and Protestant* (1935), *Church and State in Contemporary America* (1936), *The Minister—His World and His Work* (1937), *The Case for Theology in the University* (1938), *A Creed for Free Men* (1941), and *The New Order in the Church* (1943).

**Browne, Laurence Edward** (1887–1986). British OT scholar and professor of comparative religion. Born in Northampton, he graduated from Cambridge, was ordained in 1911, and served the Church of England at home for 10 years. An OT specialist, he developed his interest in Islam while lecturing in India. Another period of parish work in England followed, during which time he became professor of comparative religion at Manchester University (1941–46). In 1946 he was appointed to the chair of theology at Leeds University, retiring in 1952. He served further parishes in Yorkshire and Sussex until 1964. His publications include *Early Judaism* (1920), *From Babylon to Bethlehem* (1926), *The Eclipse of Christianity in Asia . . . to the Fourteenth Century* (1933), *Prospects of Islam* (1944), *Where Science and Religion Meet* (1950), *Ezekiel and Alexander* (1952), and *The Quickening Word* (1955).

TIM LENTON

**Browne, Lewis** (1897–1949). Jewish author. Born in London, England, he was educated at the University of Cincinnati, Hebrew Union College, Rabbinical Seminary, and Yale. He served as rabbi of Temple Israel, Waterbury, Conn. (1920–23), and Free Synagogue of Newark, N.J., where he was associated with Stephen S. Wise (1924–26). He resigned his rabbinate to devote his time to lecturing and writing. Among his noteworthy books are *Stranger Than Fiction* (1925), *This Believing World* (1926), *The Graphic Bible* (1928), *Why Are Jews Like That?* (1929), *Since Calvary* (1931), *Blessed Spinoza* (1932), *How Odd of God* (1934), *All Things Are Possible* (1935), *The Wisdom of Israel* (1945), and *The World's Great Scriptures* (1946).

RAYMOND W. ALBRIGHT

**Bruce, Frederick Fyvie** (1910–1990). Scottish biblical scholar. Born in Elgin and educated at the universities of Aberdeen, Cambridge, and Vienna, he taught Greek at the universities of Edinburgh (1935–38) and Leeds (1938–47). He was professor of biblical history and literature at Sheffield (1947–59) before moving to the historic Rylands chair of biblical criticism and exegesis at Manchester (1959–78). He was also well known as speaker and lecturer in evangelical, especially Plymouth Brethren, circles. Among his numerous publications are *The NT Documents* (1943), *The Books and the Parchments* (1950), *Second Thoughts on the Dead Sea Scrolls* (1956), *The Spreading Flame* (1958), *Paul and His Converts* (1962), *Israel and the Nations* (1963), *NT History* (1969), *Paul and Jesus* (1974), *Paul: Apostle of the Free Spirit* (1977), *History of the Bible in English* (1979), *The Pauline Circle* (1985), *The Real Jesus* (1985), and commentaries on Acts (Greek text and commentary, 1951; English, 1954), Ephesians (1961), Romans (1963), Hebrews (1964), First and Second Corinthians (1971), Galatians (1982), First and Second Thessalonians (1982), Philippians (1983), Gospel of John (1983), and Colossians, Philemon and Ephesians (1984). His biographical *In Retrospect* was published in 1980. He also edited the *Evangelical Quarterly* (1949–80) and *Palestine Exploration Quarterly* (1957–71).

J. D. DOUGLAS

**Brunei.** *See* SOUTHEAST ASIA.

**Brunner, (Heinrich) Emil** (1889–1966). Swiss Reformed theologian. Born in Zurich, he studied at the universities of Zurich and Berlin, and at Union Theological Seminary, N.Y. He taught languages in England (1913–14), was pastor of the mountain parish of Obstalden (1916–24), and professor of theology at Zurich (1924–53) and at Christian University, Mitaka, Tokyo, Japan (1953–55). Known as one of the founders of the so-called dialectical school of theology and a collaborator of Karl Barth, he disagreed with Barth in allowing a place for natural theology. He lectured widely at universities in Europe and the USA, and participated in the preparation of theological materials for the ecumenical assemblies at Oxford and Amsterdam. Among his most important books are *The Mediator* (1926), *The Divine Imperative* (1932), *Man in Revolt* (1936), *The Divine-Human Encounter* (1937), *Revelation and Reason* (1942), *Justice and the Social Order* (1944), *Dogmatics* (3 vols., 1946–60), and *Christianity and Civilization* (1948, 1949).

*Bibliography.* *Das Menschenbild im Licthe des Evangeliums* (1949); C. W. Kegley, ed., *The Theology of Emil Brunner* (1962).

**Bryennios, Philotheos** (1833–1914). Greek metropolitan of Nicomedia. He was educated at the "Theological School in Chalce of the great Church of Christ" (1856), and the universities of Leipzig, Berlin, and Munich. In 1861 he became professor of ecclesiastical history, exegesis, and other studies at Chalce, of which he was appointed master and director in 1863, although he soon resigned the latter positions. In 1867 he was called to Constantinople to be the head of the "Great School of the Nation" in the Phanar, or Greek quarter of Constantinople, and remained there until, in 1875, he was sent by the synod of metropolitans and patriarchs to the Old Catholic conference at Bonn, where he was appointed metropolitan of Serrae in Macedonia. In 1877 he was transferred to the metropolitan see of Nicomedia, and three years later went to Bucharest as commissioner of the Eastern Orthodox Patriarchal and other independent churches, to investigate and report on monasteries which had been plundered in Moldavia and Wallachia. He wrote a reply to the encyclical letter of Pope Leo XIII concerning the Slavic apostles Cyrillus and Methodius, which was published at Constantinople in 1882. His fame rests upon his discovery in 1873 in the Jerusalem Monastery of the Most Holy Sepulcher in the Greek quarter of Constantinople of a manuscript containing a synopsis of the OT and NT in the order given by St. Chrysostom; the Epistle of Barnabas; the First and Second Epistles of Clement of Rome to the Corinthians; the Teaching of the Twelve Apostles; the spurious letter of Mary of Cassoboli, and 12 pseudo-Ignatian Epistles. He edited the Epistles to the Corinthians with prolegomena and notes at Constantinople in 1875, and published the "Teaching of the Twelve Apostles" (1883).

*Bibliography.* P. Schaff, *Teaching of the Twelve Apostles* (1890), 8–9, 289–95.

**Buber, Martin** (1878–1965). Jewish philosopher. Born in Vienna, he received his early education from his grandfather, the noted scholar Solomon Buber. He studied philosophy and history of art at the universities of Vienna, Leipzig, Berlin, and Zurich, was Zionist political writer and editor of the Vienna *Welt* in 1901, and studied philosophy of religion in Berlin. From 1916 until 1924 he was the editor of *Der Jude*, a periodical for German-speaking Jews which he had founded. He held the first chair of Jewish philosophy of religion and ethics in Germany at Frankfort-Main from 1923 to 1933. After his exile from Germany in 1938 he emigrated to Israel and became professor of social philosophy at Hebrew University. He was a leader of the German religious socialist movement and is noted for his reinterpretation of Hasidism, a philosophy which has had a profound influence on Western thought. His early Zionist activities were partly responsible for transforming Zionism from a purely political to a cultural movement. His writings contain some of the most profound, original studies in Judaism and the philosophy of religion. With Franz Rosenzweig and later alone he made a revolutionary translation of the Bible into German. His influence has been widely felt throughout the world. Among his most significant works are *I and Thou* (1937), *Moses* (1944), *For the Sake of Heaven* (1945), *Tales of the Hasidim* (2 vols., 1947), *Between Man and Man* (1947), *Israel and the World* (1948), *Prophetic Faith* (1949), and *Two Types of Faith* (1951).

LOUIS FINKELSTEIN

**Buchman, Frank Nathan Daniel** (1876–1961). Founder of Moral Re-Armament. Ordained as a Lutheran clergyman in 1902, Buchman soon made social work a prominent part of his ministry. Following a radical spiritual awakening at Keswick, England, in 1908, he gradually developed the principles and procedures that convinced him that his calling was to raise a force of persons dedicated to the task of building a "hate-free, fear-free, greed-free world." His movement first took firm shape at Oxford University in 1921, a connection that eventually gave the First Century Christian Fellowship, as it was at first known, the name "Oxford Group," by which the movement subsequently became widely identified. Working at first largely among undergraduates on college and university campuses, Buchman gradually came to focus primarily on wealthy and influential persons. His retreatlike "house parties," as well as rallies that by the

1930s drew crowds purportedly as large as 100,000, gained him increasing publicity and growing influence. His principles included the belief that men and women were sinners who could be radically changed through conversion and "guidance" by God and fellow believers. Conversion and guidance focused on four "absolutes" which Buchman considered essential to personal and societal reconstruction: purity, honesty, unselfishness, and love. The growing threat of war brought an intensification of evangelistic efforts and the beginning of a shift of focus when, in 1938, Buchman appealed for moral and spiritual rearming to save Europe and the world. From that appeal came the name "Moral Re-Armament" by which the movement has since generally been known. Following World War II Buchman increasingly emphasized social and political aims, with a strongly anticommunist stance as well as a broadened appeal to persons of all faiths. The first World Assembly of Moral Re-Armament was held at Caux, Switzerland, in 1946. During ensuing years a center there, as well as centers in Michigan and Japan, trained thousands of persons in the movement's principles. Buchman's message, while shifting from its original base of Christian personal evangelism, continued to focus on renewal of moral and spiritual resources for a world in crisis. The worldwide impact of Buchman and his movement is evident not only in his being decorated by eight governments, but also in the fact that at his death, numerous eminent government officials sent messages. Moral Re-Armament, which claimed some 4000 full-time workers in the 1960s, including about 1000 in the USA, has lost much of its strength since Buchman's death.

*Bibliography.* F. Buchman, *Remaking the World* (1949); W. H. Clark, *The Oxford Group* (1951); A. Lunn, *Enigma: A Study of Moral Re-Armament* (1957); G. Marcel, *Fresh Hope for the World* (1960); P. Howard, *Frank Buchman's Secret* (1962); J. P. Thornton-Duesbery, *The Open Secret of MRA* (1964); T. Driberg, *The Mystery of Moral Re-Armament* (1965); G. Ekman, *Experiment with God* (1972); T. Spoerri, *Dynamic out of Silence* (1976); G. Lean, *Frank Buchman, A Life* (1985).

NORRIS A. MAGNUSON

**Buddhism.** An Eastern religion, founded in India by Siddhartha Gautama (c. 566–486 B.C.). Buddhism teaches that suffering and existence are inseparable; salvation, or more properly liberation from suffering, comes only from realizing that each person is part of this inseparable connection. That knowledge leads to an inward extinction of self and the senses until it culminates in a state of illumination that is beyond suffering and existence. This final state of illumination is called nirvana.

Siddhartha Gautama realized the truth of nirvana without the help of any supernatural gods. He did it through observation of the suffering around him. He was the son of a feudal king, one of many in fragmented northeastern India. As a child, the prince was sheltered from the world's suffering. His father never let him see the ravages of illness, old age, or death. Not until he was a young man, married with an infant son himself, did he venture out of the protection of the palace and see firsthand the realities of the world. The truth of suffering was such a shock that he renounced his princely prerogatives, left his wife and son, and took the life of a wandering ascetic. After trying and discarding all the religious options of the day (largely the varieties of Hindu philosophy and ascetic technique common in India), he finally became fully enlightened to the truth of suffering while under a tree in modern-day Bodh Gaya. He became "the Buddha," the enlightened one.

Although Gautama was only one of many "Buddhas" throughout history, he was unique because he developed a teaching that became the model for others seeking final illumination. One cannot achieve nirvana by believing in Gautama Buddha; one must fully understand Gautama Buddha's teaching or *dhamma*. The essence of that teaching is summarized in four statements known as the Four Noble Truths:

1. Everything is suffering.
2. Suffering comes from the desire for existence.
3. Suffering is eliminated when desire for existence is eliminated.
4. Desire for existence is eliminated by following the eightfold path.

The eightfold path is the ethical driving force of the Buddhist life. A good Buddhist is expected to have correct views, good intentions, restrained speech, and to act ethically. A good Buddhist is also expected to engage in a reputable livelihood, live energetically, be sensitive to the consequences of actions, and singlemindedly pursue the religious life.

For 40 years the Buddha traveled around northern India teaching this simple doctrine. It proved an attractive alternative to the bewildering variety of Hindu gods that had previously been the religion of choice. The Buddha's simple, deity-free path to freedom provided an egalitarian way to escape the sufferings of poverty, slavery, and caste, and the capriciousness of the Hindu pantheon. Although the Buddha never promised the eradication of any of these economic, social, and religious roadblocks, he did claim to offer a transcendent end-run around them.

Indicative of the popularity of his message was the eagerness with which his followers saved his homilies. They were collected in an immense catalog of teachings called the *Tripitaka*, the Buddhist equivalent of sacred scripture. Originally written in Pali, a simplified dialect of Sanskrit, they have been embellished over the years with an elaborate monastic code and a scholastic distillation of the Buddha's parable-like sermons. Many of the original Pali scriptures, which have been kept with an inerrant mindset by the Theravada tradition of Buddhism, were translated into Sanskrit, Tibetan, Chinese, and Japanese. Those cultures added their own Buddhist scriptures and variants of the faith, which make up the other major division of Buddhism called Mahayana. In addition, Tibetan Buddhists developed Tantric Buddhism and a meditative variety called Zen arose in Japan.

Indeed, an astounding variety of religious forms has grown out of the Buddha's teachings. Since the original teachings had little ritual and downplayed the importance of deities, later followers satisfied their need for worship-related activities in different ways. Legends surrounding the Buddha's life quickly turned into miracle stories, and after the Buddha died (from eating a poisoned meal) his bones and teeth were spread far and wide as holy relics. In that way the original teachings quickly spread to Ceylon, where the early texts were kept pure. Yet even there, where today the purest form of Buddhism endures, Buddhism is no longer simply a way to enlightenment for the individual but a religion for an entire nation with all the institutional and denominational accoutrements that requires.

In its homeland, India, Buddhism took more diverse forms. While not rejecting the original teachings, proponents argued that those teachings were incomplete, and they set about to complete them, similar to the way the Christian NT completes the OT. Buddhist knowledge, they claimed, needed to be perfected. At issue in most of these developments was the nature of the absolute. Since Buddhists do not believe in a god or gods, the primary distinctive of their religious tradition is how they view and describe to others the nature of transcendence. These additional teachings, which were various attempts to deal with this knotty problem, were laid down in their present form probably between the 1st and 5th centuries A.D.

In India, two primary schools, Shunyavada and Yogacara, set the agenda for the discussion as it later developed in Tibet, China, and Japan. Shunyavada, or the doctrine of the void, tried to solve the question of the existence of the liberated in nirvana by denying both that the self existed in nirvana and that the self did not exist. The answer lies in the "emptiness" (sunyata) in between those two alternatives. It is a state that cannot be described, because description would make it either relative or absolute, both unacceptable alternatives. Thus, the question of the absolute is in the end a false one.

Although such descriptions of emptiness are satisfying to philosophers, they leave the common man floundering. The Yogacara school added more concrete meaning to the concept. Without denying that emptiness means rising above the mundane/supernatural dichotomy, Yogacara teachers began to describe it in terms of a "Buddha nature," which they described as inexpressible and without multiplicity, but an identifiable nature all the same. This teaching, which eventually fused with the teaching of Shunyavada, became the accepted version of Buddhism in 5th-century India, and set the stage for the spread of Buddhism throughout East Asia.

The most extreme development took place in Tibet, where Tantric Buddhism (vajranaya) and its belief in the magic effect of rituals and ceremonies held sway. Buddhism arrived in China as early as the 1st century, but solved the need for ritual and transcendence without resorting to the extremes of Tibet. In China, Amida Buddhism developed, named after a Buddha called Amitabha, who was capable of leading believers to liberation through their trust in him. Both Tantric Buddhism and Amida Buddhism took Gautama Buddha's early teachings of self-salvation and turned them upside down, one stressing the value of ritual and ceremony, the other the importance of trust or faith in an outside agent, a Buddha especially concerned with helping others to salvation.

Amida Buddhism spread to Japan and has had strong influence there. However, another form of Buddhism became very important in Japan. Called Zen, it made the practice of meditation its central feature. Meditation on the difficult concept of emptiness (shunyata) can consume a lifetime, but is the only way to ultimately understand that which is neither part of the conditioned or the unconditioned. Short poems of free verse, called *koans*, are used by Zen masters to focus on freeing their minds and thinking from conditioned existence.

Buddhism remains today a strong force in most countries of Southeast and East Asia, with the exception of India, where the Muslim invasions of the 11th and 12th centuries largely wiped it out. Since the beginning of the 20th century, Buddhism has begun to find followers in Europe and North America. In England, for example, the publication in 1879 of Sir Edwin Arnold's long poem, *The Light of Asia*, opened the way for the acceptance of Buddhism. In the USA, the participation of two Buddhists at the "World Parliament of Religions" in 1893 marked the beginning of a Buddhist movement there. The two main forms of Japanese Buddhism, Zen and Amida (or Jodo Shinshu after Shinran-Shonin, a 13th-century teacher who stressed the grace of believing in Amitabha), have proved to be the most popular to the American religious consumer.

In both Europe and America there has been a marked increase in scholarly study of Buddhism on the university level. In recent years, the wave of Southeast Asian refugees to the USA has resulted in the formation of many ethnic Buddhist churches.

*Bibliography.* C. N. E. Eliot, *Japanese Buddhism* (1935); G. C. Pande, *Studies in the Origins of Buddhism* (1957); P. V. Bapat, ed., *2500 Years of Buddhism* (1959); D. T. Suzuki, *Outlines of Mahayana Buddhism* (1963); H. Nakamura, *Ways of Thinking of Eastern People: India, China, Tibet, Japan* (rev. ed., 1964); E. B. Cowell, *Buddhist Mahayana Texts* (1965); W. T. DeBary, *The Buddhist Tradition in India, China, and Japan* (1969); E. Thomas, *The Life of Buddha* (1969); M. Winternitz, *A History of Indian Literature,* S. Ketar, trans. (1971); W. Rahula, *What the Buddha Taught* (1974); E. M. Layman, *Buddhism in America* (1976); *The Pali Canon and Its Commentaries* (n.d.).

TERRY C. MUCK

## Buehring, Paul Henry (1880–1958).
Lutheran theologian. Born in Elkhorn, Wis., he studied at Wartburg College, Capital University Seminary, Columbus, Ohio, the divinity school of the University of Chicago, and Augustana Seminary. Ordained in 1905, he was pastor at St. Mary's, Ohio (1905–11), president of Hebron (Nebr.) Academy (1911–19), and professor of historical theology and dean at Columbus Seminary. He served as chairman of the Board of Foreign Missions of the American Lutheran Church. He wrote *The Spirit of the American Lutheran Church* (1940) and co-authored *Christian Ethics* (1935) with J. Michael Reu.

## Bulgakov, Sergius (1870–1944).
Eastern Orthodox professor and author. Born in Livny, Russia, he studied at the University of Moscow, where he received a doctorate (1912). After a two-year research trip to Western Europe he became professor of national economy in the Polytechnical Institute, Kiev (1901), and in 1906 at the Moscow Institute of Commercial Science; in 1917 he was elected to the same chair at Moscow University. He began as a Marxist, but soon abandoned this position and gradually came back to the faith of the Eastern Orthodox Church. Religious and theological interests became dominant in his studies and writing. In 1906 he was a member of the Governmental Duma (representing Moscow). In 1917 he was a member of the All-Russian Church Council, and was elected to the Supreme Church Board. In 1918 he took holy orders. For political reasons he left Moscow in the same year and settled in Sympheropol, Crimea, where he was for some time professor at the university. In 1923 he was expelled from Russia by the government and went to Prague, Czechoslovakia, to become professor of political economy at the Russian Graduate School of Law. In 1925 he went to Paris and became professor of divinity at the newly founded Orthodox Theological Institute; later he was appointed its dean. He actively participated in the ecumenical movement as well as in the Anglo-Russian Fellowship of St. Sergius and St. Alban (in England). His most important books were written in his last years. His ambition was to give an inclusive and comprehensive interpretation of all main traditional Christian doctrines in light of "Sophia," or Holy Wisdom. His ideas met with strong opposition in certain quarters and his orthodoxy was challenged, yet no close examination of his views was ever made. Books translated into English were *The Orthodox Church* (1935) and *The Wisdom of God, A Brief Summary of Sophiology* (1937). Two volumes of his theological trilogy were made available in French—*Du Verbe Incarne* (1943) and *Le Paraclet* (1946)—and one work was published only in German: *Die Tragödie der Philosophie* (1927).

*Bibliography.* P. B. Anderson, *The Living Church* (1935); L. A. Zander, *God and the World—The System of Father Sergius Bulgakov,* 2 vols. (1948).

GEORGES FLOROVSKY

## Bulgaria.
An Eastern bloc nation on the Balkan Peninsula. The People's Republic of Bulgaria covers 110,912 sq. km. (42,823 sq. mi.). The Bulgarian Orthodox Church was by far the largest Christian denomination in Bulgaria in 1990. It had some 3720 churches administered by 1500 priests, and over half the population probably retained at least some sentimental attachment to it. The percentage of practicing Orthodox was about 2.3 million or 25 percent of the 9.2 million people (1982). The Latin- and Eastern-rite Catholics numbered about 60,000 and 10,000, respectively. The mainstream pentecostals included some 7000 members, the Congregationalists 4000, the Adventists 3000, the Methodists 1500, and the Baptists 800. Officially unrecognized groups include unregistered pentecostals, Tinchevists, Jehovah's Witnesses, and Brethren. Other branches of the Orthodox communion were represented, as was the Armenian Apostolic Church.

Most Muslims in Bulgaria were of the one million Turkish minority, although the gypsies (possibly 400,000) also tended toward Islam. The Pomaks (Muslims of Bulgarian extraction) were estimated at about 200,000. Only about 5500 remained of the 50,000 Jews who lived in Bulgaria at the end of World War II. Some 3200 of these lived in Sofia, but only about 50 attended the synagogue.

The Bulgarian Constitution states that "citizens shall be guaranteed freedom of conscience and religion." It permitted the performance of "religious rites" and provided for the conduct of "antireligious propaganda." In practice, permitted religious activity was mainly confined to approved forms of worship within the walls of registered churches and mosques, conducted by clergy acceptable to the authorities. A committee chaired by a deputy minister for foreign affairs regulated religious affairs, and the government had the power to suspend or remove clergy and exercises ultimate control over practically every aspect of organized religious activity. There was one seminary and one theological academy, both under the Bulgarian Orthodox Church. Formal religious instruction to minors by clergy was forbidden.

After the period of severe religious persecutions during the postwar Stalinist period, the Orthodox Church reached an accommodation with the government, but at the sacrifice of principles and independence. The Catholics of both rites, working together, showed great integrity and faithfulness despite hardships and privations. Protestants, both registered and unregistered, experienced intermittent pressure from the state, but reported cases of violent persecution of Christians generally were rare. Nevertheless, cases of harassment and the arrest, suspension, and exile of pastors occurred through the 1980s.

The mainly Islamic Turkish minority was the object of a vigorous campaign of "assimilation" from late 1984. Authorities denied reports of killings, imprisonments, and discrimination against Muslims during this campaign to "Bulgarise" this ethnic minority and destroy its identity in the interests of a one-nation state. Evidence of such persecution was overwhelming, however. Jews were also affected less violently by the process of assimilation. Mixed marriages became the rule rather than the exception, and the tiny Jewish community, without a single rabbi (1985), faced the complete loss of its identity. Bulgaria seemed less affected in 1989 and 1990 by the openness of Eastern Europe. As this publication went to press little was known about Bulgaria's potential for new freedom.

In the wake of the anticommunist revolutions of late 1989 small inroads by both Christians and Muslims were almost immediate. December 1989 saw a public demonstration by 7000 Orthodox, Protestants, and Roman Catholics in Sofia. Pentecostals quickly convened a national congress and elected Viktor Virchev as their leader, and the patriarch gave a Christmas address on television, the first Christian program ever broadcast over government media. In late 1990 Bulgaria remained materialistic communist officially but religious interest seemed on the rise.

**Bibliography.** T. Beeson, *Discretion and Valour* (rev. ed., 1982).

PHILIP WALTERS

**Bultmann, Rudolph Karl** (1884–1976). Protestant theologian and NT scholar. Born in Wiefelstede, Oldenburg, Germany, he studied theology at the universities of Tübingen, Berlin, and Marburg. He lectured at Marburg (1912–16), Breslau (1916–20), and Giessen (1920/21), returning to Marburg as professor of NT (1921) until his retirement (1951). Together with Martin Dibelius and Karl L. Schmidt, Bultmann pioneered the development of form-critical methods for examining the Gospels. The influences on his work were numerous including his theology teachers, from whom he inherited the liberal belief in the priority of experience over against doctrine, philosophy, and dialectical theology. However, Bultmann's methodological starting point was rooted in existentialism. Perhaps the early Heidegger, particularly his *Being and Time* (*Sein und Zeit*), was most influential. From Heidegger Bultmann gained the concept of human nature as something that is created only in moments of decision, not as something static. Theology is anthropologically based. Bultmann held that the worldview of the prescientific age of the NT writers was now untenable and no longer viable for modern man. It had become theologically insupportable and culturally obsolete. In Bultmann's early work he came to skeptical conclusions about the historical reliability of the Gospels; and, later, from 1941 onward (i.e., the essay "NT and Mythology"), he began his program of demythologizing (*Entmythologisierung*). The mythological statements of the NT need to be interpreted—and this he attempted to do existentially. Bultmann's major publications are largely translated and include *Jesus and the Word* (1935), *Jesus Christ and Mythology* (1946), *Gnosis* (1952), *Essays: Philosophical and Theological* (1955), *Theology of the NT* (2 vols., 1951, 1955), *Primitive Christianity in Its Contemporary Setting* (1956), *History and Eschatology* (1957), *Existence and Faith* (1961), *The History of the Synoptic Gospels* (1963), *Faith and Understanding* (1969), *The Gospel of John: A Commentary* (1971), *A Commentary on the Johannine Epistles* (1973), and *The Second Letter to the Corinthians* (1985).

**Bibliography.** H. P. Owen, *Revelation and Existence* (1957); C. E. Braaten and R. A. Harrisville, *Kerygma and History* (1962); I. Henderson, *Rudolph Bultmann* (1965); C. W. Kegley, *The Theology of Rudolph Bultmann* (1966); W. Schmithals, *Introduction to the Theology of Rudolph Bultmann* (1967); R. C. Roberts, *Rudolph Bultmann's Theology: A Critical Interpretation* (1976); N. Perrin, *The Promise of Rudolph Bultmann* (1979).

MICHAEL PARSONS

**Bund, Evangelischer (Evangelical Union).** W. Beyschlag contributed significantly to the formation in 1886 of an association of Protestant (evangelical) churches in Germany "to preserve German Protestant interests and to strengthen evangelical consciousness." One of the primary contributions of the Bund at the turn of the last century was the support—financially and through literature—of the "Los-von-Rom" movement.

In its current focus, the Bund keeps alive the message and significance of the 16th-century Reformation in social, confessional, and ideological responses to the issues of today. Among the activities of the Bund is the maintenance since 1947 of an institute for confessional studies and the publication since 1949 of the journal *Materialdienst* which provides subscribers with theological and historical information for use in keeping alive a vibrant Reformed Protestant tradition and witness. H. Bornkamm and Martin Schmidt have been among leading theologians of the Bund. The former headquarters in Berlin were destroyed during World War II. Current head offices are in Bensheim, Hesse, Germany.

E. J. FURCHA

**Bund der evangelischen Kirchen in der deutschen Demokratischen Republik.** Evangelical churches in the German Democratic Republic established a structural link to foster mutual support and make effective Christian witness to the nation easier. As a result there is mutual recognition of ministries and communion fellowship. The federation involves seven Protestant territorial churches: Evangelische Landeskirche Anhalt, Evangelische Kirche Berlin-Brandenburg, Evangelische Landeskirche Greifswald, Evangelisch Lutherische Landeskirche Mecklenburg, Evangelisch Lutherische Landeskirche Sachsen, Evangelische Kirche der Kirchenprovinz Sachsen, Evangelisch Lutherische Kirche in Thüringen. There is no longer a structural link with similar Protestant churches in the Federal Republic of Germany, although an intimate relationship is maintained.

*Bibliography.* R. Henkys, ed., *Bund Der Evangelischen Kirchen in der D.D.R., Dokumente* (1971).

E. J. FURCHA

**Bund Evangelisch-Freikirchlicher Gemeinden (Freikirchen).** An association of three disparate groups of "free churches" formed in Germany in 1941. The Baptists, the oldest of the three, date to 1849. The Elim Movement, a pentecostal group, and the Bund freikirchlicher Christen (1947) are of recent origin. Current membership is 150,000. The Bund maintains a seminary for training its clergy and a youth seminary, both in Hamburg. Its publishing house (Oncken Verlag) is in Kassel and the headquarters of the denomination is in Bad Homburg.

Among the most significant contributions of the Bund to spiritual life in the Federal Republic of Germany are its four deaconess houses, several youth centers, an extensive Sunday school movement, and the active pursuit of evangelism through "tent missions." The official monthly publication, *Die Gemeinde*, has a wide readership.

Formation of the Bund was made possible when the Baptists gave up their practice of closed communion, the Elim Christians ceased the practice of simultaneous prayer during public worship in favor of ordered participatory prayer, and the free church movement accepted public believer's baptism in place of "secret" baptism.

The polity of the Bund is congregationalist, coordinated through an executive. Membership

in congregations of the Bund is by public profession of faith and baptism by immersion. Activities of the denomination are reflected in the annual publication of the *Jahrbuch des Bundes Evangelisch-freikirchlicher Gemeinden in Deutschland*.

E. J. FURCHA

**Burkina Faso.** *See* WEST AFRICA.

**Burkitt, Francis Crawford** (1864–1935). English biblical and patristics scholar. A brilliant student at Cambridge, he spent nearly all of his life there. After a year as lecturer in paleography he was appointed in 1905 professor of divinity, a post he retained until his death. An eminent Syriac scholar, he contributed many articles to journals and symposia. His books include *Early Christianity Outside the Roman Empire* (1899), *Early Eastern Christianity* (1904), *The Gospel History and Its Transmission* (1906), *Earliest Sources of the Life of Jesus* (1910), *The Failure of Liberal Christianity* (1910), *Jewish and Christian Apocalypses* (1914), *Eucharist and Sacrifice* (1921), *Christian Beginnings* (1924), *Christian Worship* (1930), and *Church and Gnosis* (1932).

**Burleigh, John Henderson Seaforth** (1894–1985). Church historian and Church of Scotland minister. Born in Kelso, he was educated at the universities of Edinburgh, Paris, Strasbourg, and Oxford and received the D.D. from Aberdeen University in 1937. He ministered in the charges of Fyvie (1924–28) and St. Enoch's, Dundee (1928–31), before appointment to Edinburgh University where he was professor of ecclesiastical history for 33 years until his retirement in 1964. He convened the influential Church and Nation Committee (1949–54), was principal of New College, Edinburgh (1956–64), and was moderator of the General Assembly in 1960, presiding over the additional meeting of the assembly that year, attended by Queen Elizabeth II, to mark the 4th centenary of the Reformation in Scotland. His writings include *The City of God: A Study of St. Augustine's Philosophy* (1944) and *A Church History of Scotland* (1960). He edited the *Evangelical Quarterly* (1943–49) and *Augustine's Earlier Writings* (1953).

ALISTAIR J. DRUMMOND

**Burma.** A "socialist democracy," of whose 40 million population 80 percent are Buddhists and 4 percent Christians. Modern Burma was incorporated, piecemeal, into British India in the 19th century. In April 1937, Burma became a separate state within the British Commonwealth as a result of its opposition to British rule on the one hand, and the India connection on the other. After the 1942–45 Japanese occupation Britain returned, but resistance to colonial rule was mounting. A group, led by Aung San, pressed for independence, which was granted on January 4, 1948. In 1962 the elected government of Prime Minister U Nu was overthrown by the army, whose commander, Ne Win, intent on creating a socialist Burma, seized power. The new regime allowed greater religious tolerance and revoked an earlier ruling that had established Buddhism as the state religion. At the same time, political opposition was outlawed and between 1963 and 1966, most private sector services were nationalized, including those sponsored by mission agencies, such as church schools and hospitals.

The most significant cultural divisions among the peoples of Burma are between Buddhists and the non-Buddhists, and between those who live in the lowlands and practice settled, wet-rice agriculture and those who live in the more hilly areas in the west, north, and east of the country, and practice dry-rice agriculture. Meanwhile, the popular Buddhism of the majority of the population is blended in a rather accommodative fashion with folk and local religion. Still, Christianity has not made a significant impact among the Buddhist population. The church, for the most part, is made up of believers from among the country's various tribal groups.

The Roman Catholics were the first to enter Burma, along with the Portuguese in the mid-16th century. Tentative Protestant attempts were launched by William Carey from Serampore, India, in the early 1800s. The first sustained missionary effort was begun by the Baptist Adoniram Judson, who, along with his wife Ann, arrived in Rangoon in 1813 after authorities refused to allow him to work in Calcutta. Judson immediately gave himself to learning the language and translating the Bible into Burmese. During the 1824 Anglo-Burma war, Judson was thrown into prison in Mandalay on suspicion of spying for the British. For nearly two years he was treated inhumanely and suffered from the most extreme deprivation.

The Baptists expanded their endeavors to the Karens in 1827, the Chins in 1845, and the Kachins in 1876. This work has continued to grow up to the present, making the Burma Baptist Convention the largest Christian denomination in the country, with about 3500 congregations and a community of about 600,000. The Anglican Society for the Propagation of the Gospel entered Burma in 1859, followed by the Lutherans and the American Methodists, but their work has remained small. British Methodists arrived in 1896 and concentrated in the northern regions of the country. Also beginning work in Burma were the Salvation Army (1915), the Seventh-day Adventists (1919), the Bible Churchman's Missionary Society (1920s), the Assemblies of God (1930), and the Church of Christ (1949). In 1954 the Presbyterian Church was introduced by immigrant

Lushais from northeast India who brought their faith with them.

In 1966, all foreigners were summarily asked to leave the country; overnight, the church in Burma was without missionary assistance. Even though some difficulties have been experienced and some programs and projects have had to be abandoned, the church has risen to the occasion, developed remarkably and, by the 1980s was expanding ministry. Given certain government limitations, Christians are permitted to continue their activities openly. These even include witnessing, the baptizing of new believers, and the opening of church buildings.

Nationalization has not interfered with the operation of the more than 20 Bible schools, institutes, and seminaries in the country. Classes were meeting and most had full enrollment. In the late 1980s Burmese Christians were optimistic and their church growing. Some tribal groups were more than 50 percent Christian and their leaders were planning further evangelism.

*Bibliography.* C. Anderson, *To the Golden Shore: The Life of Adoniram Judson* (1956); R. E. Hedlund, ed., *World Christianity: South Asia, Eastern Asia* (1980).

GRAHAM HOUGHTON

**Burney, Charles Fox** (1868–1925). Anglican Semiticist. He studied at St. John's College, Oxford, gaining many university distinctions. He was Fellow of St. John's College until 1914, then professor of biblical interpretation at Oxford (1914–25). He was a noted authority on Semitic languages. His writings include *Outlines of OT Theology* (1899), *Israel's Settlement in Canaan* (1918), *The Book of Judges* (1918), and *The Aramaic Origin of the Fourth Gospel* (1922).

F. W. DILLISTONE

**Burrows, Millar** (1889–1980). Presbyterian OT scholar. Born in Wyoming, Ohio, Burrows graduated from Cornell University, Union Theological Seminary, N.Y., and Yale University (Ph.D., 1925). He served on the faculties of Tusculum College in Tennessee (1920–23), Brown University (1925–34), and Yale Divinity School (1934–58). He was also visiting professor at the American University of Beirut and director of the American School of Oriental Research in Jerusalem (1931/32; 1947/48). An authority on the Dead Sea Scrolls, his major works include *Founders of Great Religions* (1931), *The Basis of Israelite Marriage* (1938), *Outline of Biblical Theology* (1946), *The Dead Sea Scrolls* (1955), *More Light on the Dead Sea Scrolls* (1958), and *Jesus in the First Three Gospels* (1977).

R. MILTON WINTER

**Burton, Ernest De Witt** (1856–1925). American NT scholar. Born in Granville, Ohio, he was educated at Denison University and at Rochester

Theological Seminary, and pursued further studies at the universities of Leipzig and Berlin. He was associate professor (1883) and professor (1886) of NT interpretation at Newton Theological Institution, then in 1892 went to the University of Chicago where he was professor of NT literature and interpretation, and then head of the department of biblical and patristic Greek. In 1923 he became president of the University of Chicago, a post he held until his death. Among his publications were *Syntax of the Moods and Tenses in NT Greek* (1893), *Records and Letters of the Apostolic Age* (1895), *Handbook of the Life of Paul* (1899), *Studies in the Gospel of Mark* (1904), *Commentary on Paul's Epistle to the Galatians* (1920), and *Sourcebook for the Study of the Teaching of Jesus* (1923). He coauthored *Harmony of the Synoptic Gospels in English* (1917) and *Harmony of the Synoptic Gospels in Greek* (1920) with E. J. Goodspeed.

**Burundi.** A central African nation of 27,834 sq. km. (10,747 sq. mi.) and a population of over 5 million (1988), the country attained independence from Belgium on July 1, 1962. Since then, Burundi's religious history has been characterized by the growing conflict between state and religious authorities. Traditional religious beliefs refer to Imana, the great God who is normally invisible but sometimes visits his people in the form of a white lamb. The people who worship Imana are known as "initiates," or the children of Imana or also *Abana* or *Mbana.* These initiates make up about one-fifth of the Burundi population. In the traditional religious story good conquers evil and death and promotes the good from within. A constant demand is made for initiates to respect God, the greater supreme Being. Rearing good children is not only very important for Burundi, but it also fulfils the will of the greater Imana.

In recent years the importance of the Roman Catholic Church is reflected by the fact that about 74.5 percent of the population consider themselves Roman Catholics. The White Fathers Order established missions in Burundi in 1879 during German occupation of East Africa. Resistance to Christianity at that time was strong and two priests and a lay helper were killed in 1881 and were not replaced until 1899. By 1916, the Belgian army forced the Germans out of East Africa as Burundi and Rwanda became a Belgian-mandated territory. The Belgians used religion as part of their socialization activities, allowing Catholicism to flourish by 1922.

Since independence, the relationship between the political authorities and the Catholic Church has not always been smooth. In the 1980s the government accused the church of conducting a smear campaign against the country. The government rejected claims made by Pope John Paul II in 1986, who condemned the repression of the church and deplored the restriction of religious activities, the expulsion of Belgian missionaries, the imprisonment of several priests, the nationalization of secondary schools and seminaries, the closure of catechist training centers, and the suppression of the Action Catholique movement.

The Lutherans arrived in Burundi in 1907 and established the first Protestant station. By 1914, they had stations at Ibanga, Cogabami, Rubura, and Muyabe. After World War I, the Seventh-day Adventists, Danish Baptists, and others took over stations previously established by the Lutherans. Overall the Protestant community in Burundi remains small and voiceless.

The most indigenous Christian church in Burundi is the Church of God (Eglise de Dieu), which grew out of Anglican missions in southern Burundi.

The growing fear among religious leaders in the late 1980s was that the government might establish monopolistic control over the religious as well as secular educational institutions. Churches are responsible for much of Burundi's educational program. This neutralization of schools would provide the state with unique control over the training and allocation of leadership positions. Political developments in Burundi reflect an ongoing conflict of interests among the religious and political leaders which, if not carefully watched, might lead to crises in the socioeconomical, political, and national culture of the country.

*Bibliography.* L. Brenneman, et al., *Area Handbook for Burundi* (1969); W. Weinstein, *Historical Dictionary of Burundi* (1976); P. Falk, *The Growth of the Church in Africa* (1979); R. F. Manyeto, *The ABC of Modern Africa* (1979); C. Legum, *African Contemporary Record* (1984/85); *New African* 23 (Nov. 1986): 28; *African Confidential* 28 (Jan. 1987); E. P. Dostert, *Africa* (1987).

PATRICE MUYUMBA

**Bury, John Bagnell** (1861–1927). Irish historian. Born in the County of Monaghan, Ireland, he studied at Trinity College, Dublin, became fellow of Trinity College (1885), professor of modern history in Dublin (1893), and professor of modern history at the University of Cambridge (1902). He is best known for his work on the history of the Byzantine Empire. His works also include *A History of Freedom of Thought* (1914), *The Life of St. Patrick* (1905), and *The Idea of Progress* (1924).

*Bibliography.* N. H. Baynes, *A Bibliography of the works of J. B. Bury* (1929); H. Temperley, ed., *Selected Essays of J. B. Bury* (1930).

NORMAN H. BAYNES

**Buswell, James Oliver, Jr.** (1895–1975). Clergyman, theologian, and college president. Born in Wisconsin, he graduated from the University of Minnesota and McCormick Theological Seminary, and subsequently earned the Ph.D. from New York University. He was army chaplain

(1917/18), pastor in Minnesota, Wisconsin, and Brooklyn, N.Y. (1919–26), and president of Wheaton College (1926–40). A strong conservative, he served from 1941 to 1955 at what became Shelton College, and helped found the American Council of Christian Churches and the International Council of Christian Churches. From 1956 to 1969 he taught at Covenant Theological Seminary in St. Louis, Mo. He was a founder of the Bible Presbyterian Church. He wrote *A Systematic Theology of the Christian Religion* (2 vols., 1962/63).

EARLE E. CAIRNS

**Butterfield, Herbert** (1900–1979). British historian and Methodist layman. Born in Yorkshire, he graduated from Cambridge where he was to spend nearly all of his working life—first as lecturer (1930–44), then as professor (1944–63) of modern history. He was also master of Peterhouse, the university's oldest college (1955–68). Butterfield was concerned with the relationship between the historian and Christianity, science and political morality. He edited the *Cambridge Historical Journal* (1938–52), was a fellow of the British Academy (1965), and was knighted by Queen Elizabeth (1968). His many publications include *Christianity and History* (1949), *Christianity in European History* (1951), *Liberty in the Modern World* (1952), and *International Conflict in the Twentieth Century* (1960).

TIM LENTON

**Buttrick, George Arthur** (1892–1980). Presbyterian pastor and professor. Born and educated in England, Buttrick was ordained in the Congregational Church in the United States in 1915 and served pastorates in that denomination before becoming pastor of the First Presbyterian Church of Buffalo, N.Y., in 1927. He was later chosen to succeed Henry Sloane Coffin at the prestigious Madison Avenue Presbyterian Church of New York City, where he served with distinction (1927–54). In addition he also taught preaching at Union Theological Seminary in New York City. In 1954 Buttrick became professor of Christian morals and chairman of the board of preachers at Harvard University where he also taught preaching in the divinity school. He served as editor-in-chief of *The Interpreter's Bible*, a 12-volume commentary on the OT and NT. He was also editor of *The Interpreter's Dictionary of the Bible* (4 vols., 1962; supp. vol., 1976). He published many books

of sermons as well as books on prayer and spiritual life.

R. MILTON WINTER

**Byzantine Rite.** The system of prayers and ceremonies developed at first in the Patriarchate of Byzantium (Constantinople) for public worship and the administration of the sacraments. The rite is used today throughout the four patriarchates of Constantinople, Alexandria, Antioch, and Jerusalem, as well as in the Church of Cyprus, and such national bodies as the Russian, Greek, Bulgarian, Serbian, Romanian, Georgian, and Polish Orthodox Churches. The Byzantine rite should be distinguished from such other Eastern rites as the Coptic, Syrian, or Armenian rites, although there is some analogy of form.

The churches of the Byzantine rite use the so-called liturgies of Saint John Chrysostom and Saint Basil for the celebration of the Eucharist. The liturgy of the Presanctified, also known as the liturgy of Saint Gregory, is substituted during Lent for weekday services. The original language is Greek, but national or missionary churches outside the Greek-speaking area have the liturgy in their own tongue.

The architecture and decoration of church buildings of the Byzantine rite have individual characteristics. The nave is preceded by a narthex or vestibule. The sanctuary, with the altar in the middle and the *prothesis* and *diakonikon* on either side, is divided from the nave by the *ikonostasis*, which is a screen or wall decorated with images of Christ, the virgin, and the saints. These decorated panels separate three doors through which the officiating ministers gain entrance into the sanctuary. Statues are prohibited, as well as the use of musical instruments. The laity partakes of both elements in the eucharistic communion.

Some groups within the Byzantine rite seceded from their parent church and acknowledged the authority of the pope. Although they passed to the Roman communion, they generally were allowed to retain their original language and ceremonial.

*See also* EASTERN ORTHODOX CHURCHES.

**Bibliography.** C. E. Hammond, comp., *Liturgies, Eastern and Western*, vol. 1 (1896, 1965); B. J. Kidd, *The Churches of Eastern Christendom from A.D. 451 to the Present Time* (1927, 1974); S. Salaville, *An Introduction to the Study of the Eastern Liturgies* (1938).

GEORGES A. BARROIS

**Cabala (Kabbala).** System of esoteric wisdom primarily associated with Judaism but having affinities with forms of mysticism in other religions, including Christianity and Buddhism. The term undoubtedly derives from the Hebrew verb, *qābal,* meaning "to receive," and thus refers to a tradition that has been orally passed down from generation to generation. Cabala has a long history, demonstrable from about the 11th century A.D. climaxing in its period of greatest prestige in the 16th and 17th centuries. At this time Isaac Luria (1534–72) of Safed, Palestine, promulgated the idea that one could explain by cosmic events both the Jewish exile (diaspora) and the future redemption, which gave fresh expression to the hope of Israel. The mystic could find reunification with God apart from the world of material things, a hope that was especially meaningful to Jews dispersed in Africa, Asia, and Europe; the system was prominent in France and Spain during the Middle Ages.

The *Zohar* (Book of Splendor), the primary text of Cabalism, offered the possibility of expanding those religious and philosophical horizons for Jews exiled from Spain and Portugal in 1492. Written in Hebrew it is largely untranslated. The French edition, the only complete one yet attempted, contains 1,250,000 words filling six substantial volumes. Cabala concerns itself with philosophical questions such as the Godhead, creation, good and evil, the communication of God to man, the nature and preexistence of the soul, its union with matter and the question of metempsychosis, the Messiah and his kingdom, the state of the soul after death, and the resurrection of the dead. The Cabala is, therefore, the "hidden thought of Israel" about teachings of the Jewish religion that often parallel both Greek philosophical thought and Christian doctrine.

To Cabalists the means of deriving this hidden meaning from the Scripture is esoteric. Since the Scripture contains many names and symbols which have only figurative representation, the Cabalists developed a figurative language to deal with them. The highly mystical and symbolic nature of the Cabalistic writings makes it impossible for the "outsider" to understand much of what is written. Cabalism commonly employs such esoteric systems of thought as: (1) Gematria, which assigns numerical values to letters and words, whose arithmetical values are then used to explain their hidden meanings; (2) Notarikon, a system of shorthand in which each letter of a word is taken as the initial of another word, or conversely, in which the initial letters of an entire sentence are combined to form a word which is held to throw light on the sentence; and (3) Themurah, the transposition of letters in a word or sentence.

JOHN McRAY

**Cable, Alice Mildred** (1877–1952). British pioneer missionary, writer, and traveler. Qualified as a chemist with additional training in anatomy, surgery, and midwifery, she sailed to China in 1892 with the China Inland Mission and began a lifelong partnership with Evangeline French and then her sister Francesca. She first settled in Hwochow in Shansi Province following the Boxer uprising, and concentrated on educational work among women and girls with some itinerant evangelism in the area. With her two companions she set out in 1923 "to visit every city of the Kansu Province situated beyond the Great wall," so beginning a series of intrepid missionary journeys to areas hitherto unreached by the Christian gospel and where no Western single women had ever traveled. Several times they covered the northwest area from Inner Mongolia to Tibet and from the Kansu Province to Sinkiang. Her travels are described in several books that she wrote with her friends, including *The Fulfilment of a Dream, Something Happened, Through Jade Gate and Central Asia, A Desert Journal,* and *The Gobi Desert.* Following her retirement, she visited Australia, New Zealand, India, and South America.

*Bibliography.* W. C. Northcott, *Star over Gobi: The Story of Mildred Cable* (1957); E. M. Sawyer, *Mildred Cable* (1962); W. J. Platt, *Three Women* (1964).

JAMES TAYLOR

**Cabot, Richard Clarke** (1868–1939). Unitarian physician and theologian. After graduating from Harvard, he taught clinical medicine at Harvard Medical School (1899–1929), social ethics at Harvard College (1920–34), and natural theology at Andover Newton Theological School, Newton Centre, Mass. (1935–39). He initiated medical social work at Massachusetts General Hospital, Boston, in 1905. A pioneer in religion and health, he urged physicians to tell their patients their true condition. He wrote "A Plea for a Clinical Year for Theological Students" (*Survey-Graphic*, Dec. 1925). In 1925 he founded the Council for Clinical Training under leadership of Anton T. Boisen, Protestant chaplain at Worcester State Hospital, Worcester, Mass. He was noted in the field of medicine as a teacher and diagnostician, and he originated the now internationally accepted method for teaching diagnosis, known as clinicopathological conference. He wrote *Physical Diagnosis* (1901), *Social Service and the Art of Healing* (1909), *Differential Diagnosis* (1911), *What Men Live By* (1914), *Laymen's Handbook of Medicine* (1916), *Social Work* (1919), *Facts on the Heart* (1926), *Adventures on the Borderlands of Ethics* (1926), *The Meaning of Right and Wrong* (1933), and *Christianity and Sex* (1937). He wrote *The Art of Ministering to the Sick* (1936) with Russell L. Dicks.

ROLLIN J. FAIRBANKS

**Cabrini, Frances Xavier** (1850–1917). America's first canonized saint. Born in St. Angelo, Italy, Cabrini immigrated to the USA in 1889. Originally she had wanted to go to the Far East to do missionary work, but at the request of Pope Leo XIII she came instead to the USA to work among her fellow Italian immigrants. In America she founded many hospitals, schools, nurseries, and other welfare institutions. In 1952 her order of Catholic sisters, Missionaries of the Sacred Heart, had 4000 members who oversaw 97 welfare institutions worldwide. Cabrini was canonized in 1946.

*Bibliography.* T. Maynard, *Too Small a World* (1945).

GILBERT L. ODDO

**Cabrol, Fernand** (1855–1937). Roman Catholic scholar. Born in Marseille, he was a Benedictine monk from 1878. He served as prior of the celebrated Abbey of Solesme and abbot of Farnborough from 1909. An eminent liturgist, he edited the *Monumenta ecclesiae liturgica* and *Dictionnaire d'Archéologie chrétienne et de Liturgie* with fellow-scholar Henri Leclercq. His works include *Histoire du Cardinal Pitra* (1893), *Études sur la Peregrinatio Silviae* (1895), *Les livres de la Liturgie latine* (1903), *Les origines liturgiques* (1906), *Introduction aux études liturgiques* (1907), *L'Angleterre avant les Normands* (1909), *Le livre de la Prière antique* (1910, 1921), *La prière pour la France* (1916), *La prière des anciens chrétiens* (1929), and *La Messe en Occident* (1932).

ROBERT WILL

**Cadbury, Henry Joel** (1883–1974). American educator. Born in Philadelphia, he was educated in classics and biblical studies at Haverford College and Harvard (Ph.D., 1914). He taught Bible at Haverford College (1910–19) and at Bryn Mawr College (1926–34); at Harvard he taught NT (1919–26) and subsequently held a chair in divinity (1934–54). A member of the Religious Society of Friends (Quakers), he was active particularly in the work of the American Friends Service Committee, serving as chairman between 1928 and 1934, and again for a time after 1944. A member of many learned societies, he was also director of Andover-Harvard Theological Library (1938–54). His many publications include *Style and Literary Method of Luke* (1920), *National Ideals in the OT* (1920), *The Making of Luke–Acts* (1927), *The Peril of Modernizing Jesus* (1937), *George Fox's Book of Miracles* (1948), *The Book of Acts in History* (1955), *John Woolman in England* (1971), *Friendly Heritage* (1972), and *Narrative Papers of George Fox* (1972).

**Cadoux, Cecil John** (1883–1947). Congregational professor of NT and church history. Educated at King's College, London, and Mansfield College, Oxford, he became professor of NT criticism and theology at Yorkshire United Independent College (1919–33) and professor of church history at Mansfield College (1933–47). His works include *The Early Christian Attitude to War* (1919), *The Early Church and the World* (1925), *Catholicism and Christianity* (1928), *The Case for Evangelical Modernism* (1938), and *The Life of Jesus* (1947).

F. W. DILLISTONE

**Cailliet, Emile** (1894–1981). Presbyterian professor of Christian philosophy. Born and educated in France, Cailliet studied at the universities of Montpellier (Ph.D., 1926) and Strasbourg (Th.D., 1936). Cailliet's early education was nonreligious; he saw his first Bible at age 23. He became an enthusiastic scholar of Christian philosophy. In his teaching he sought to relate religious philosophy to the insights derived from the physical sciences. An authority on Pascal, Cailliet also contributed to the literature of symbolism and mysticism. He served for many years as professor of Christian philosophy at Princeton Theological Seminary. During his later years Cailliet assisted Young Life, a nondenominational evangelistic ministry to American high school students. His most important books include *The Life of the Mind* (1942), *The Clue to Pascal* (1943), *Pascal, Genius in the Light of Scripture* (1945), *The Beginning of Wisdom* (1947), *Great Shorter Works of*

*Pascal* (1948), *The Dawn of Personality* (1955), *The Recovery of Purpose* (1959), and *Young Life* (1963).

R. MILTON WINTER

**Cairns, David Smith** (1862–1946). Scottish theologian and minister. Educated at the universities of Edinburgh and Marburg, he trained in theology at the United Presbyterian College, Edinburgh. He ministered at Ayton (1895–1907) before appointment as professor of apologetics and dogmatics in Aberdeen College (1907–1929). After the union of his church with the Church of Scotland he continued as professor of systematic theology and master of Christ's College, Aberdeen, until retirement in 1937. He took a prominent part in the 1910 Edinburgh World Missionary Conference. King George V bestowed on him a rare honor for a minister, making Cairns an Officer of the British Empire (O.B.E.). His writings include *Christianity in the Modern World* (1906), *The Reasonableness of the Christian Faith* (1918), *Life and Times of A. R. Macewen, D.D.* (1925), and *The Faith That Rebels* (1928).

ALISTAIR J. DRUMMOND

**Calendar, Christian.** Index of the year arranged according to months and weeks, giving a list of feasts, fasts, and saints' days, to which data of a more miscellaneous character may be added.

***Origin of the Christian Calendar.*** In its most general character as an annual list of days and feasts, the Christian calendar dates from the primitive church, which found its model in classical antiquity, particularly the Romans. Numerous Roman calendars of the imperial period have been preserved either in whole or in part. They were designed for public use for areas ranging from a town to an entire country. These calendars contained astronomical information as well as lists of religious feasts and civic celebrations, some of which were connected with the cult, such as many of the public games, while others commemorated historic events. The transition from pagan to Christian usage may be seen in two calendars from the middle of the 4th and 5th centuries. One of these was drawn up at Rome in the reign of Constantine II and is evidently a revision of a pagan calendar, omitting all feasts of a distinctively religious character, both heathen and Christian, but retaining the purely civic feasts. Christian influence is visible, however, in the recognition of the Christian weeks beside the Roman system, since the year, which here begins with January 1, falls in two regular divisions, one of eight days each (the *nundinae*) represented by the letters A–H, and the other of seven days, indicated by A–G. The second calendar was prepared in 448 during the reign of Valentinian III, and although pagan in basis, contains for the first time a small number of Christian feasts—five festivals of Christ and six saints' days. The oldest exclusively Christian calendar is a Gothic fragment, apparently prepared in Thrace in the 4th century, containing the last eight days of October and the entire month of November. Seven days have the names of saints attached to them, two from the NT, three from the general church, and two from the Goths.

***The Calendar in the Early Church.*** Even before the inclusion of Christian feasts in the Roman calendar, however, the church had lists of saints' days arranged according to the date of their celebration, although not yet incorporated in a formal calendar. Allusions to such lists of memorial days are found in Tertullian and Cyprian, but the earliest one extant was prepared at Rome in the middle of the 4th century. It consists of an enumeration of 12 Roman bishops and a list of martyrs for 24 days, including feasts in commemoration of the birth of Christ and of Peter (Feb. 22), the remainder being festivals of martyrs, generally of local origin. The next oldest calendar is a list of the festivals of the Church of Carthage, which apparently dates from the end of the 5th or the beginning of the 6th century, and contains the names of bishops and martyrs, most of whom were natives of Carthage. From such beginnings a wealth of calendars soon developed throughout the Latin world, and the lists of the days of the month received an increasing proportion of martyrological, hagiological, and heortological material. The interaction of the churches, especially of Rome with Africa, Gaul, Spain, and England, resulted in the addition of so many foreign saints that those who received honor throughout the church exceeded the saints of local fame; finally there was no day of the year which did not honor a saint.

***Complications in Dating.*** Since martyrs were commemorated in the early church (especially in the place where they had suffered), each community originally had its own list of feasts and its own calendar. This practice was of long duration, despite the frequent interchange of names and despite the increasing prestige of the Roman calendar and list of feasts. The diversity of calendars was augmented, moreover, by the reverence paid to the local saints of individual countries and dioceses, while a still more important factor was the discrepancy in the dating of the beginning of the year. The first of the year was reckoned from no less than six days: (1) the Feast of the Circumcision (Jan. 1; used in conformity to the Julian calendar); (2) March 1 (Merovingian France, the Lombards, Venice, and, for a time, Russia); (3) the Feast of the Annunciation (Mar. 25; first in Florence and Pisa, whence it extended to France, Germany, England, and Ireland, being retained in the latter two countries until the 18th cent.); (4) Easter (especially in France); (5) September 1

(Byzantine Empire, and, until modern times, Russia); and (6) Christmas (Carolingian France, the Anglo-Saxons, Scandinavia, Prussia, Hungary, and portions of Holland, Switzerland, etc.). The problem was further complicated by the various methods of indicating the day of the month, of which at least five systems were used contemporaneously: (1) the ancient Roman method of calends, ides, and nones; (2) the Greco-Christian consecutive numbering of the days of the month, now generally used; (3) the *consuetudo Bononiensis*, which divided the month into two halves, in one of which (*mensis intrans*) the days were numbered forward from 1, while in the other (*mensis exiens*) they were reckoned backward from 30 or 31; (4) the method of Cisiojanus or Cisianus, which designated the days of the month by the syllables of arbitrary mnemonic verses (long popular in Poland and North Germany); and (5) the designation of the day by the feast celebrated on it. This confusion was confounded by the various reckonings of Easter, while the movable feasts based upon it and running side by side with the fixed festivals, or even crossing them, added to the confusion.

***Early Medieval Calendars.*** In the Middle Ages calendars were multiplied, partly in consequence of the chronological intricacies already noted and partly because of the universal need for ecclesiastical data of this character. It is true that there are few calendars still extant which were prepared previous to the 8th century, but this deficiency is compensated for, especially by the sacramentaries which give the list of feasts, while liturgical books, particularly manuscripts of the Psalter, frequently have a calendar prefixed to them. Such calendars are generally perpetual, that is, available for any year, but are usually provided with methods for the determination of the movable feasts of any particular year. Not only are the letters A–G repeated in them from January 1 to designate the days of the week, but they also contain the numbers 1–19 to denote all new moons which fall, in the course of a cycle of 19 years, on the day of the month designated by one of these numbers.

***Greek and Slavic Calendars.*** All calendars of the Greek and Slavic churches begin their ecclesiastical year, as already noted, with September 1. The great majority of their immovable feasts are consecrated to the saints and Mary, while a number of movable feasts are consecrated to Christ. The latter, like the Sundays of the year, are divided into three periods: *Trioidion* (beginning with the 10th Sunday before Easter), *Pentēkostarion* (from Easter to the close of the second week after Whitsuntide), and *Oktoēchos* (extending from the second Sunday after Whitsuntide to the Western Epiphany). The calendar of the Greek Church is characterized by numerous fasts, partly of single days and partly of several weeks. To the latter belong the four "great fasts." In a number of the more important feasts the Greek calendar harmonizes with the Western, but it deviates in numerous instances from the latter in its dating of the feasts of saints and martyrs.

***Later Medieval Calendars.*** In the Western Church the majority of calendars were written in Latin until the end of the Crusades. Among them special mention may be made of the ancient list of feasts prepared at Rome during the reign of Gregory II or Gregory III and noteworthy as giving the Roman stations in which the feasts were celebrated and the lessons from the Gospels.

The invention of printing in the 15th century brought about important changes in the calendar, although the first printed specimens resemble those in manuscript and, like them, are perpetual. The first calendar for a definite year was printed at Nuremberg in 1475 in German and Latin. It was designed for the years 1475, 1494, and 1513 as the first of a triple cycle of 19 years each, and was so constructed that the dates for other years might be derived from these three, so that it really extended from 1475 to 1531. The ecclesiastical portions, however, were in perpetual form, since the calendar contained, in addition to the letters A–G for the days of the week, only the names of the saints for a limited number of days without division into weeks and without movable feasts. It was not until the middle of the 16th century that calendars arranged according to the weeks and feasts of a definite year came into general use.

***Easter.*** The reckoning of Easter hitherto employed had long been recognized as inadequate, and the elimination of the errors which this system had caused was an urgent task. Since the second half of the 3d century the rule had been adopted by the Alexandrian Church, and confirmed by the Council of Nicea, that Easter should fall on the Sunday after the spring full moon, that is, on the first Sunday after the full moon on or following the vernal equinox. The date of this equinox was to be March 21, while the full moon was to be reckoned according to a cycle of 19 years. This system of reckoning was introduced into the Roman Church in 525 by Dionysius Exiguus, spread throughout Italy, Gaul, and Spain, and was given to the Anglo-Saxon churches by Bede in 729. This method, however, had two faults. In the first place, by its assumption that the vernal equinox falls on March 21 it adopted the entire Julian system which makes the year 365¼ days in length and intercalates a day every four years. In reality this year is 11 minutes too long, so that an extra day is intercalated every 128 years. In the second place, by its reckoning of the spring full moon according to a 19-year cycle of 235 months or 6939¾ days, it made the cycle an hour too long, thus making a discrepancy of a day between the real and the theoretical new moon every 210 years. It was not until the 13th century that this error attracted attention, the first works to note it being the *Computus* of Master Conrad in 1200 and a similar work by an anonymous author in 1223. The problem was likewise taken up by Johannes de Sacro-Busto about 1250 in his *De anni ratione* and by Roger Bacon in a treatise addressed to Clement IV (*De reformatione calendarii*), while among the Greeks the monk Isaac Argyros wrote on the problem in 1272. In the 15th century the reformation of the calendar was discussed in the great councils of the Roman Catholic Church, especially by Pierre d'Ailly at Kostnitz in 1414 and by Nicholas of Cusa at Basel in 1436, the latter proposing to begin the correction of the calendar in 1439.

*The Gregorian Calendar.* The actual reform of the calendar was first carried out by Gregory XIII (1572–85) in conformity with a resolution of the Council of Trent. In 1577 the pope appointed a committee which held sessions at Rome to carry out the plan proposed by the Calabrian astronomer Aloigi Ligli, and confirmed this reformed calendar, which was called the Gregorian in his honor, by a bull of February 24, 1582. The reform was designed, on the one hand, to regulate Easter with reference to the solar and lunar revolutions, thus restoring the year of the lunar cycle according to the date and intention of the Nicene Council, and, on the other, to avoid any future shifting of the vernal equinox and the spring full moon. To restore the vernal equinox to March 21, the 10 days between October 4 and 15 were dropped, while for the correction of the spring full moon the new moons were set back three days from January 3 to December 31. These corrections were assured by retaining the Julian system of intercalation and the 19-year lunar cycle for a century. The intercalary day was to be omitted thrice in four centuries, and the new moon was to be retarded one day eight times in 25 centuries (seven times after each 300 years and the eighth time after 400). For the correction of the lunar cycle the reckoning of epacts, or the age of the moon on January 1, was introduced according to the cycle proposed by Ligli.

The Gregorian calendar was adopted in Roman Catholic countries either immediately or in the course of a few years. The Protestant districts, on the other hand, opposed it, partly on account of their hostility to Rome and partly on account of its chronological discrepancies. Its inaccuracies were recognized by William IV of Hesse-Cassel, and Joseph Justus Scaliger issued repeated warnings against it. At the end of the 16th century the Julian calendar existed in Germany side by side with the Gregorian, the two being designated as old and new style, respectively. The movable feasts of the two faiths accordingly differed, and the advocates of the new style dated the days of the month 10 days in advance of the old until the end of the 17th century. In view of the discrepancies between the two systems the German Protestants devised a third calendar, which was to agree neither with the Gregorian nor the Julian and was to take effect in 1700. In its reckoning of time it agreed with the Gregorian, but its feasts were calculated astronomically according to the meridian of Uraniborg and the Rudolphinian Tables of Kepler. The result was increased confusion and embitterment between Roman Catholics and Protestants, particularly in 1724, 1744, and 1788, when there was a divergency of a week between the Gregorian and the astronomical Easter. This Protestant calendar was finally suppressed by Frederick the Great in 1775, and the Gregorian calendar became supreme throughout Germany.

*Reforms of the Calendar.* The evangelical reforms of the calendar thus far considered were concerned only with chronology, without regard to the traditional Christian lists of saints and martyrs. There is, however, a tendency among Lutherans to revise the hagiology of the church, in view of the Protestant skepticism regarding the existence of many of the saints of tradition and the Christianity ascribed to others. They are offended, furthermore, by the names of such heroes of the Counter-Reformation as St. Ignatius Loyola and other opponents of their sect, while prominent Protestants, it is felt, should be recognized in an ecclesiastical calendar designed for Lutheran use. Such an attempt was made by Ferdinand Piper in his *Evangelischer Kalender* (1850–70), in which he sought to transform the hagiology of the Western Church according to evangelical ideas. To increase the interest of the laity in this new list of names, 399 brief biographies were added and were later published separately under the title *Zeugen der Wahrheit* (4 vols., 1874). Piper's calendar, however, failed to secure official recognition in any German church, although in various revisions it has been included in a number of popular calendars in Germany. It is self-evident that only partial success can be attained by any Protestant hagiological calendar in view of the diversity of Protestant conditions and requirements. Apparently, the most that can be done is to add new dates and names, whether these be supplementary or corrective, to the traditional hagiology of the church, so that, according to the requirements of time or place, a choice may be made from the names associated with any particular day.

*Bibliography.* W. S. B. Woolhouse, *Analysis of the Christian, Hebrew and Mahometan Calendars* (1881); J. C. Macdonald, *Chronologies and Calendars* (1897); A. A. MacArthur, *The Evolution of the Christian Year* (1953); E. Achelis, *The Calendar for the Modern Age* (1959); W. M. O'Neil, *Time and the Calendars* (1975); A. Adam, *The Liturgical Year* (1981).

OTTO ZÖCKLER

# Calendar, Muslim.

**Calendar, Muslim.** Year with 12 lunar months, in accordance with Koran 6.96 and 9.36–37, and reaffirmed in the traditional report of Muhammad's Farewell Address. The Muslim era was established by the second caliph, 'Umar, in A.D. 639 (A.H. 17) to begin with the new moon of the first month (*Muharram*) of the year in which the migration (*hijrah*) of Muhammad from Mecca to Yathrib, later called "the City (*al-Madīnah*) of the Prophet," took place. That first day was June 16, 622, of the Julian calendar and July 16, 933, of the Persian Seleucid era. The Persian Yezdegird era began just 10 years later, on June 16, 632, the reckoning of which was corrected by Malik Shah's Jalali calendar in A.D. 1074/75. Egypt and India kept using the Julian calendar for agricultural purposes. On January 1, 1926, the Republic of Turkey definitely abandoned the old Hijrah (Hegira) calendar, after trying the combination of lunar and solar calendars begun by the Ottomans. On May 28, 1935, Turkey adopted Sunday instead of Friday as the weekly day for closing commercial establishments.

*Bibliography.* S. B. Burnaby, *The Jewish and Muhammadan Calendars* (1901).

EDWIN E. CALVERLEY

## Calhoun, Robert Lowry (1896–1983).

Congregational theologian, historian, educator, and author. Born in St. Cloud, Minn., he studied at Carleton College and at Yale (Ph.D., 1923). After teaching philosophy and education at Carleton (1921–23), he taught historical theology at Yale for 43 years before retiring in 1965. As chairman of the Commission of Christian Scholars, he protested America's use of atomic weapons against Japan during World War II, and later opposed a commission position statement justifying the theoretical retaliatory use of nuclear force by the USA. He held important committee positions with the World Council of Churches and the Federal Council of Churches that recommended church polity on contemporary moral and theological issues. Additionally, he helped the Protestant churches find a unity of ancestry with the Orthodox and Roman Catholic churches. His books include *God and the Common Life* (1935) and *The Place of Religion in Higher Education* (1942).

JACK MITCHELL

## Calverley, Edwin Elliott (1882–1971).

Presbyterian missionary, teacher, and editor. Born in Philadelphia, Pa., he studied at Princeton University, Princeton Theological Seminary, and Hartford Seminary Foundation (Ph.D., 1923). Ordained by the Philadelphia Presbytery in 1908, he joined the Arabian Mission of the Reformed Church in America, arriving in Bahrain on December 31, 1909. He also served at Basrah and Amarah in Iraq but mostly at Kuwait, Arabia, until 1930, when he became a teacher of Arabic and Islamics in the Kennedy School of Missions

of the Hartford Seminary Foundation. He became professor emeritus in 1951. He was visiting professor in the School of Advanced International Studies, Johns Hopkins University, Washington, D.C. (1953/54). He published *The Arabian Readers* (1920), *Worship in Islam* (1925), and articles on missionary and Islamic subjects in the *Royal Central Asian Society Journal* and *The Moslem (Muslim) World*. He was coeditor with Samuel M. Zwemer (1938), editor (1947–52), and coeditor with A. Kenneth Cragg (1952–54) of *The Moslem World*.

## Calvinism. *Meaning and Uses of the Term.*

Calvinism is an ambiguous term insofar as it is currently employed in two or three closely related senses. Sometimes the term designates the teaching of John Calvin. Sometimes it designates, more broadly, the doctrinal system confessed by Protestant churches known historically, in distinction from Lutheran churches, as Reformed or Calvinistic churches. Sometimes it designates, more broadly still, the entire body of conceptions—theological, ethical, philosophical, social, and political—which, under the influence of Calvin, raised itself to dominance in the Protestant lands of the post-Reformation age, and has left a permanent mark not only upon the thought of mankind, but upon the life-history of men, the social order of civilized peoples, and even the political organization of states. In the present article, the term will be taken, for obvious reasons, in the second of these senses. Fortunately this is also its central sense; and there is little danger that its other connotations will fall out of mind while attention is concentrated upon this.

On the one hand, Calvin, although always looked upon by the Reformed churches as an exponent rather than as the creator of their doctrinal system, has nevertheless been both reverenced as one of their founders and deferred to as the one to whom their doctrinal system has perhaps owed most. In any exposition of Reformed theology, therefore, the teaching of Calvin must always take a high, and, indeed, determinative place. On the other hand, although Calvinism has dug a channel through which not merely flows a stream of theological thought, but also surges a great wave of human life, its fountain-head actually lies in its theological system—or rather, to be perfectly exact, one step behind even that, in its religious consciousness. For the roots of Calvinism are planted in a specific religious attitude, out of which is unfolded first a particular theology, from which springs on the one hand a special church organization, and on the other a social order, involving a given political arrangement. The whole outworking of Calvinism in life is thus but the efflorescence of its fundamental religious consciousness, which finds its scientific statement in its theological system.

*The Fundamental Principle of Calvinism.* The exact formulation of the fundamental principle of Calvinism has challenged a long series of thinkers. Perhaps the simplest statement of it is the best: that it lies in a profound apprehension of God in his majesty, with the inevitably accompanying poignant realization of the exact nature of the relation sustained to him by the creature as such, and particularly by the sinful creature. He who believes in God without reserve, and is determined that God shall be God to him in all his thinking, feeling, and willing and in the entire compass of his life-activities is a Calvinist. In Calvinism, then, objectively speaking, theism comes to its rights; subjectively speaking, the religious relation attains its purity; soteriologically speaking, evangelical religion finds its full expression and its security. Theism comes to its right only in a teleological conception of the universe, which perceives in the entire course of events the orderly outworking of the plan of God, who is the Author, Preserver, and Governor of all things, whose will is consequently the ultimate cause of all. The religious relation attains its purity only when an attitude of absolute dependence on God is not merely temporarily assumed in the act, say, of prayer, but is sustained through all the activities of life. And evangelical religion reaches stability only when the sinful soul rests in humble, self-emptying trust purely on the God of grace as the immediate and sole source of all the efficiency which enters into salvation.

*Relation to Other Systems.* The difference between Calvinism and other forms of theistic thought is a difference not of kind but of degree. Calvinism is not a specific variety of theism, religion, or evangelicalism set over against other specific varieties. It differs from them not as one species differs from other species, but as a perfectly developed representative differs from an imperfectly developed representative of the same species. There are not many kinds of theism/religion/evangelicalism, among which men are at liberty to choose to suit their individual taste or meet their special need, all of which may be presumed to serve each its own specific uses equally worthily. There is but one kind of theism/religion/evangelicalism; and the several constructions laying claim to these names differ from each other not as correlative species of a broader class, but as more or less perfect, or more or less defective, exemplifications of a single species. Calvinism conceives of itself as simply the more pure theism/religion/evangelicalism, superseding as such the less pure. It has no difficulty, therefore, in recognizing the theistic character of all truly theistic thought, the religious note in all actual religious activity, the evangelical quality of all really evangelical faith. It refuses to be set antagonistically over against any of these things, wherever or in whatever degree of imperfection they

may be manifested; it claims them in every instance of their emergence as its own, and strives only to point out the way in which they may be given their just place in thought and life. Whoever believes in God; whoever recognizes in the recesses of the soul an utter dependence on God; whoever in all thought of salvation hears the echo of the *soli Deo gloria* of the evangelical profession Calvinism recognizes as implicitly a Calvinist, and as only requiring to permit these fundamental principles—which underlie and give its body to all true religion—to work themselves freely and fully out in thought and feeling and action, to become explicitly a Calvinist.

*Calvinism and Lutheranism.* It is unfortunate that a great body of the scientific discussion which, since Max Göbel (*Die religiöse Eigenthümlichkeit der lutherischen und reformirten Kirchen* [1837]) first clearly posited the problem, has been carried on somewhat vigorously with a view to determining the fundamental principle of Calvinism, has sought particularly to bring out its contrast with some other theological tendency, commonly with the sister Protestant tendency of Lutheranism. Undoubtedly somewhat different spirits inform Calvinism and Lutheranism. And undoubtedly the distinguishing spirit of Calvinism is rooted not in some extraneous circumstance of its antecedents or origin—as, for example, Zwingli's tendency to intellectualism, or the superior humanistic culture and predilections of Zwingli and Calvin, or the democratic instincts of the Swiss, or the radical rationalism of the Reformed leaders as distinguished from the merely modified traditionalism of the Lutherans—but in its formative principle. But it is misleading to find the formative principle of either type of Protestantism in its difference from the other; they have infinitely more in common than in distinction. And certainly nothing could be more misleading than to represent them (as is often done) as owing their differences to their more pure embodiment respectively of the principle of predestination and that of justification by faith. The doctrine of predestination is not the formative principle of Calvinism, but one of its logical consequences, one of the branches which it has inevitably thrown out. It has been firmly embraced and consistently proclaimed by Calvinists because it is an implicate of theism, is directly given in the religious consciousness, and is an absolutely essential element in evangelical religion, without which its central truth of complete dependence upon the free mercy of a saving God cannot be maintained. And so little is it a peculiarity of the Reformed theology, that it underlay and gave its form and power to the whole Reformation movement; which was, as from the spiritual point of view, a great revival of religion, so, from the doctrinal point of view, a great revival of Augustinianism. There was accordingly no difference among the Reformers on this point: Luther and Melanchthon and the compromising Butzer were no less jealous for absolute predestination than Zwingli and Calvin. Even Zwingli could not surpass Luther in sharp and unqualified assertion of it: and it was not Calvin but Melanchthon who gave it a formal place in his primary scientific statement of the elements of the Protestant faith.

Just as little can the doctrine of justification by faith be represented as specifically Lutheran. Not merely has it from the beginning been a substantial element in the Reformed faith, but it is only among the Reformed that it has retained or can retain its purity, free from the tendency to become a doctrine of justification on account of faith. Here, too, the difference between the two types of Protestantism is one of degree, not of kind. Lutheranism, the product of a poignant sense of sin, born from the throes of a guilt-burdened soul which cannot be stilled until it finds peace in God's decree of justification, is apt to rest in this peace; while Calvinism, the product of an overwhelming vision of God, born from the reflection in the heart of man of the majesty of a God who will not give his glory to another, cannot pause until it places the scheme of salvation itself in relation to a complete worldview, in which it becomes subsidiary to the glory of the Lord God Almighty. Calvinism asks with Lutheranism, indeed, that most poignant of all questions, What shall I do to be saved? and answers it as Lutheranism answers it. But the great question which presses upon it is, How shall God be glorified? It is the contemplation of God and zeal for his honor which in it draws out the emotions and absorbs endeavor; and the end of human as of all other existence, of salvation as of all other attainment, is the glory of the Lord of all. Full justice is done in it to the scheme of redemption and the experience of salvation, because full justice is done in it to religion itself which underlies these elements of it. It begins, it centers, it ends with the vision of God in his glory; and it sets itself before all things to render to God his rights in every sphere of life-activity.

*Soteriology.* One of the consequences flowing from this fundamental attitude of Calvinistic feeling and thought is the high supernaturalism which informs both its religious consciousness and its doctrinal construction. Calvinism would not be badly defined, indeed, as the tendency to do justice to the immediately supernatural. The strength and purity of its belief in the supernatural Fact (God) saves it from all embarrassment in the face of the supernatural act (miracle). In everything which enters into the process of redemption it is impelled by the force of its first principle to place the initiative in God. A supernatural revelation, in which God makes known to man his will and his purposes of grace; a super-

natural record of this revelation in a supernaturally given book, in which God gives his revelation permanency and extension—such things are to the Calvinist almost matters of course. And, above all, the Calvinist can but insist with the utmost strenuousness on the immediate supernaturalness of the actual work of redemption itself, and that no less in its application than in its impetration. Thus it comes about that the doctrine of monergistic regeneration—or as it was phrased by the older theologians, of "irresistible grace" or "effectual calling"—is the hinge of the Calvinistic soteriology, and lies much more deeply embedded in the system than the doctrine of predestination which is popularly looked upon as its hallmark. Indeed, the soteriological significance of predestination to the Calvinist consists in the safeguard it affords to monergistic regeneration—to purely supernatural salvation. What lies at the heart of soteriology is the absolute exclusion of the creaturely element in the initiation of the saving process, that so the pure grace of God may be magnified. Only so could the Calvinist express man's complete dependence as a sinner on the free mercy of a saving God; or extrude the evil leaven of synergism by which God is robbed of his glory and man is encouraged to think that some power, some act of choice, some personal initiative contributes to that salvation which is in reality all of grace. There is accordingly nothing against which Calvinism sets its face with more firmness than every form and degree of autosoterism. Above everything else, it is determined that God, in his Son Jesus Christ, acting through the Holy Spirit whom he has sent, is our Savior. To it sinful man stands in need not of inducements or assistance, but of actual saving; and Jesus Christ has come not to advise, or urge, or induce, or aid man but to save man. This is the root of Calvinistic soteriology; and it is because this deep sense of human helplessness and this profound consciousness of indebtedness for all that enters into salvation to the free grace of God is the root of its soteriology that to it the doctrine of election becomes the *cor cordis* of the gospel.

*Historic Development.* Historically Reformed theology finds its origin in the reforming movement begun in Switzerland under the leadership of Zwingli (1516). Its fundamental principles are already present in Zwingli's teaching, although it was not until Calvin's profound and penetrating genius was called to their exposition that they took their ultimate form or received systematic development. From Switzerland Calvinism spread outward to France, and along the Rhine through Germany to Holland, eastward to Bohemia and Hungary, and westward, across the Channel, to Great Britain. In this broad expansion through so many lands its voice was raised in a multitude of confessions; and in the course of the centuries which have elapsed since its first formulation, it has been expounded in a vast body of dogmatic treatises. Its development has naturally been much richer and far more many-sided than that of the sister system of Lutheranism in its more confined and homogeneous environment; and yet it has retained its distinctive character and preserved its fundamental features with marvelous consistency throughout its entire history. It may be possible to distinguish between those Reformed confessions which bear more and those which bear less strongly the stamp of Calvin's personal influence; and they fall into two broad classes. Those formulated after the Arminian defection (c. 1618) demanded sharper definitions on the points of controversy raised by that movement. A few German confessions also bear traces of the influence of Luther. And, of course, no more among the Reformed than elsewhere have all the professed expounders of the system of doctrine been true to the faith they professed to expound. Nevertheless, it is precisely the same system of truth which is embodied in all the great historic Reformed confessions; it matters not whether the document emanates from Zurich or Bern or Basel or Geneva, whether it sums up the Swiss development as in the Second Helvetic Confession, or publishes the faith of the national Reformed Churches of France, or Scotland, or Holland, or the Palatinate, or Hungary, Poland, Bohemia, or England; or republishes the established Reformed doctrine in opposition to new contradictions, as in the Canons of Dort (in which the entire Reformed world concurred), or the Westminster Confession (to which the whole of Puritan Britain gave its assent), or the Swiss Form of Consent (which represents the mature judgment of Switzerland upon the recently proposed novelties of doctrine). And despite the inevitable variety of individual points of view of the many writers who have sought to expound the Reformed faith through these four centuries—and the grave departures from that faith made here and there among them—the great stream of Reformed dogmatics has flowed essentially unsullied, straight from its origin in Zwingli and Calvin to its debouchure, say, in Chalmers, Cunningham, Crawford, Hodge, Thornwell, and Shedd.

*Varieties.* It is true an attempt has been made to distinguish two types of Reformed teaching from the beginning: a more radical type developed under the influence of the peculiar teachings of Calvin, and a more moderate type, chiefly propagating itself in Germany, which exhibits rather the influence, as was at first said (Hofstede de Groot, Ebrard, Heppe), of Melanchthon, or, in its more recent statement (Gooszen), of Bullinger. In all that concerns the essence of Calvinism, however, there was no difference between Bullinger and Calvin, German and Swiss: the Heidelberg Catechism is no doubt a catechism and

not a confession, but in its presuppositions and inculcations it is as purely Calvinistic as the Genevan Catechism or the catechisms of the Westminster Assembly. Nor was the substance of doctrine touched by the peculiarities of method which marked such schools as the so-called scholastics (showing themselves already in Zanchius [d. 1590] and culminating in theologians like Alsted [d. 1638] and Voetius [d. 1676]); or by the special modes of statement which were developed by such schools as the so-called federalists (e.g., Cocceius [d. 1669], Burman [d. 1679], Wittsius [d. 1708]; cf. Diestel, *Studien zur Federaltheologie,* in *Jahrbücher für deutsche Theologie,* vol. 2 [1862]; G. Vos, *De Verbondsleer in de Gereformeerde Theologie* [1891]; W. Hastie, *The Theology of the Reformed Church* [1904], pp. 189–210). The first serious defection from the fundamental conceptions of the Reformed system came with the rise of Arminianism in the early years of the 17th century (Arminius, Uytenbogaert, Episcopius, Limborch, Curcellæus); and the Arminian party was quickly condemned by the whole Reformed world. The five points of its "Remonstrance" against the Calvinistic system were met by the reassertion of the fundamental doctrines of absolute predestination, particular redemption, total depravity, irresistible grace, and the perseverance of the saints (Canons of the Synod of Dort). The first important modification of the Calvinistic system which has retained a position within its limits was made in the middle of the 17th century by the professors of the French school at Saumur, and is hence called Salmurianism, or Amyraldism, or hypothetical universalism (Cameron [d. 1625], Amyraut [d. 1664], Placæus [d. 1655], Testardus [d. ca. 1650]). This modification also received the condemnation of the contemporary Reformed world, which reasserted the importance of the doctrine that Christ actually saves by his Spirit all for whom he offers the sacrifice of his blood (e.g., Westminster Confession, Swiss Form of Consent).

Three "varieties of Calvinism" can be identified: supralapsarianism, infralapsarianism, and postredemptionism, all of which (as indeed their very names suggest) take their point of departure from a fundamental agreement in the principles which govern the system. The difference between these various tendencies of thought within the limits of the system turns on the place given by each to the decree of election, in the logical ordering of the "decrees of God." The supralapsarians suppose that election underlies the decree of the fall itself, and conceive the decree of the fall as a means for carrying out the decree of election. The infralapsarians, on the other hand, consider that election presupposes the decree of the fall, and hold, therefore, that in electing some to life God has mankind as a *massa perditionis* in mind. The extent of the difference between these parties is often, indeed usually, grossly exaggerated: and even historians of repute are found representing infralapsarianism as involving, or at least permitting, denial that the fall has a place in the decree of God at all: as if election could be postposited in the *ordo decretorum* to the decree of the fall, while it was doubted whether there were any decree of the fall; or as if indeed God could be held to conceive men, in his electing decree, as fallen, without by that very act fixing the presupposed fall in his eternal decree. In point of fact there is and can be no difference among Calvinists as to the inclusion of the fall in the decree of God. To doubt this inclusion is to place oneself at once at variance with the fundamental Calvinistic principle which conceives all that comes to pass teleologically and ascribes everything that actually occurs ultimately to the will of God. Accordingly even the postredemptionists (Salmurians or Amyraldians) have no difficulty with this point. Their peculiarity consists in insisting that election succeeds, in the order of thought, not merely the decree of the fall but that of redemption as well, taking the term "redemption" here in the narrower sense of the impetration of redemption by Christ. They thus suppose that in his electing decree God conceived man not merely as fallen but as already redeemed. This involves a modified doctrine of the atonement from which the party has received the name of hypothetical universalism, holding as it does that Christ died to make satisfaction for the sins of all men without exception if, that is, they believe, but that, foreseeing that none would believe, God elected some to be granted faith through the effectual operation of the Holy Spirit. The indifferent standing of the postredemptionists in historical Calvinism is indicated by the treatment accorded it in the historical confessions. It alone of the "varieties of Calvinism" here mentioned has been made the object of formal confessional condemnation; and it received condemnation in every important Reformed confession written after its development. There are, it is true, no supralapsarian confessions; many, however, leave the questions which divide supralapsarian and infralapsarian wholly to one side and thus avoid opting for either position; and none is polemically directed against supralapsarianism. On the other hand, not only does no confession close the door to infralapsarianism, but a considerable number explicitly teach infralapsarianism which thus emerges as the typical form of Calvinism. That, despite its confessional condemnation, postredemptionism has remained a recognized form of Calvinism and has made a place for itself in the Calvinistic churches (especially in America) may be taken as evidence that its advocates, while departing in some important particulars from typical Calvinism, have nevertheless remained, in the main, true to the fundamental postulates of the system. There is another variety of postredemptionism, however, of which this can scarcely be said. This variety, which became dominant among the New England Congregationalist Churches about the second third of the 19th century attempted, like the "congruists" of the Church of Rome, to unite a Pelagian doctrine of the will with the Calvinistic doctrine of absolute predestination. The result was, of course, to destroy the Calvinistic doctrine of irresistible grace, and as the Calvinistic doctrine of the "satisfaction of Christ" was also set aside in favor of the Grotian or governmental theory of atonement, little was left of Calvinism except the bare doctrine of predestination. Perhaps it is not strange, therefore, that this "improved Calvinism" has crumbled away and given place to newer and explicitly anti-Calvinistic constructions of doctrine.

***Epistemology.*** Calvinism maintains without qualification the Protestant conception of Scripture as self-authenticating. The God of the Bible cannot appeal to anything beyond himself to corroborate the truth of his Word. Even in paradise man, made in the image of God, surrounded by the universe, itself a revelation of God, needed the self-authenticating, supernatural revelation of God. As all men see the revelation around and within them, so all men, through Adam (Rom. 5:12), have heard the voice of God. All men, therefore, know the true God, their Creator (Rom. 1:19–20; 2:14–15). Men cannot escape knowing their responsibility to God.

Yet, having sinned in Adam, all men seek to suppress this knowledge, devising systems by which it becomes dependent upon the autonomous human will and the movements of time. Only if God in sovereign grace and providence brings men into contact with the gospel and, through the regenerating power of the Spirit, enables them to receive this gospel will men accept the truth.

In apologetics, therefore, Calvinism does not, like Romanism and varying forms of evangelical Protestantism, begin with "natural theology," to lead on to the "mysteries" of the faith. Such a procedure presupposes the autonomy of man. On the contrary, Calvinism asks men to presuppose God as the one through whose revelation, natural plus supernatural, any human knowledge has significance.

***Ontology.*** Calvinism maintains without qualification the Protestant conception of God as self-independent and of the creature as God-dependent. Man's knowledge is inherently analogical of God's knowledge because man's being is analogical of God's being.

Calvinism stands opposed, therefore, to the Romanist conception of the "analogy of being," according to which God and his creatures are subject to a common species of being; to the dialectical notion of the "analogy of faith," according to which God and man exist as aspects of the one Event called Christ; and to varying forms of evangelical Protestantism which, by virtue of a measure of ultimacy or autonomy attributed to human being, make concessions to the Romanist or to the dialectical idea, or to both.

*Ethics.* Calvinism maintains without qualification the Protestant doctrine of self-conscious submission to the revealed will of God. Man's ethical reaction is inherently analogical. But, as a sinner in Adam, the "natural man" seeks to suppress the originally proper reaction of the will. Only on the basis of the substitutionary work of Christ and by the regenerating power of the Holy Spirit can the sinner do the will of God.

Calvinism is therefore opposed to the Romanist scheme of ethics, based upon the "analogy of being"; to the ethics of dialectical theology whereby the will of God and the will of man are reduced to unity in the Event of Christ; and to the varying schemes of evangelicalism to the extent that they, because of their views of the autonomy of the human will, make concessions to Romanism and dialecticism.

*Bibliography.* R. H. Tawney, *Religion and the Rise of Capitalism* (1926); M. Weber, *The Protestant Ethic and the Spirit of Capitalism* (1926); A. Kuyper, *Lectures on Calvinism* (1931); A. Hyma, *Christianity, Capitalism and Communism* (1937); A. Dakin, *Calvinism* (1940); E. A. Dowey, *The Knowledge of God in Calvin's Theology* (1952); J. T. McNeill, *The History and Character of Calvinism* (1954); J. T. McNeill, ed., *Institutes of the Christian Religion* (1960); E. S. Morgan, *Visible Saints: The History of a Puritan Idea* (1963); C. Van Til, *The Case for Calvinism* (1964); A. S. Kistemaker, *Calvinism, Its History, Principles and Perspectives* (1966); R. Stauffer, *Dieu, la creation et la providence dans la predication de Calvin* (1978).

B. B. WARFIELD AND CORNELIUS VAN TIL

**Cambodia (Kampuchea).** *See* SOUTHEAST ASIA.

**Cameroon.** *See* WEST AFRICA.

**Campaign for Nuclear Disarmament (CND).** Campaign launched in 1958 to oppose Great Britain's nuclear weapons policy and calling for unilateral nuclear disarmament by organizing marches between the Atomic Weapons Research Establishment at Aldermaston and London. Membership declined after 1962, partly due to the Cuban missile crisis and the Vietnam war. The movement began to revive in the 1970s and was relaunched in 1980, expressing particular opposition to the siting of American Cruise and Trident missiles in Great Britain. Membership grew tenfold in five years.

CND strategy depends largely on public meetings, leaflets, lobbying, and demonstrations; official policy includes the advocacy of a certain degree of civil disobedience. CND is linked with peace movements worldwide, particularly in Europe and the USA. CND supporters have secured resolutions in favor of Great Britain's unilateral nuclear disarmament at Labour party conferences in 1960 and the early 1980s.

Christian CND is a specialist section of CND founded in the mid-1960s and relaunched in 1978. It seeks to present CND's message in the light of the gospel and to build interest in unilateral nuclear disarmament in churches of all denominations.

PETER HICKS

**Campbell, Reginald John** (1867–1956). English clergyman. Born in London he studied at University College, Nottingham, and Christ Church, Oxford. He entered the Congregational ministry in 1895 and served at the Union Church, Brighton, until 1903, when he went to the City Temple, London. His *New Theology* (1907) aroused controversy because of liberal elements in its evangelicalism, and he withdrew it from circulation. He was ordained in the Church of England and served the parishes of Christ Church, Westminster (1917–24) and Holy Trinity, Brighton (1924–30), thereafter becoming residentiary canon in the diocese of Chichester (1930) and subsequently its chancellor (1936–46). His publications also include *The Restored Innocence* (1898), *A Faith for Today* (1900), *The Ladder of Christ* (1912), *Life of Christ* (1921), *Christian Faith in Modern Light* (1932), *The Peace of God* (1936), and *The Life of the World to Come* (1948).

TIM LENTON

**Campenhausen, Hans Erich Freiherr Von** (1903– ). Lutheran church historian. Born in Rosenbeck (Livland, Russia), he studied theology in Marburg and Heidelberg (D.Theol., 1926) and in Göttingen, and taught church history in Heidelberg, where he later transferred to NT studies. His major interest has been in early church history. His works include *Ambrosius von Mailand als Kirchenpolitiker* (1928), *Die Passionssarkophage* (1930), *Die Idee des Martyriums in der alten Kirche* (1936), *Polykarp v. Smyrna und die Pastoralbriefe* (1951), *Der Ablauf der Osterereignisse und das leere Grab* (1952), *Kirchliches Amt und geistliche Vollmacht in den ersten drei Jahrhunderten* (1953), *Die griechische Kirchenväter* (1955), *Die lateinische Kirchenväter* (1960), *Tradition und Leben: Aufsätze und Vorträge* (1960), *Die Jungfrauengeburt in der Theologie der Alten Kirche* (1962), and *Aus der Frühzeit des Christentums* (1963).

**Campus Crusade for Christ.** *See* STUDENT ORGANIZATIONS, RELIGIOUS (NORTH AMERICA); STUDENT ORGANIZATIONS, RELIGIOUS (WORLDWIDE).

**Canada.** The world's second largest country with an area of 9,976,140 sq. km. (3,851,809 sq. mi.). Canada has one of the world's lowest population densities (6.10 per sq. mi.). The majority of its population of 25.7 million are located in a narrow southern fringe bordering on the USA. The distribution of its population and its proximity to the more populous United States, with whom it shares the same language, culture, and open border, have shaped Canadian development.

Although English is the first language for the majority of the population, French is also one of two official languages of Canada and is the first language of 26 percent of the population. The majority of Francophones, whose rights are entrenched in law, are to be found in the province of Quebec, northern New Brunswick, eastern and northern Ontario, and southeastern Manitoba.

Immigration has brought cultural diversity to Canada. Immigrants from Eastern and Western Europe came in large numbers to western Canada in the final decade of the 19th century and the beginning of this century. Post-World War II immigration brought immigrants from Europe, the Caribbean, and Southeast Asia. The cultural diversity is especially evident in major urban centers.

Canada's native population consists of three groups—Indian, Inuit (or Eskimo), and Metis. Status Indians (those registered under the Indian Act) number about 330,000. The Inuit population is about 28,000, and the vast majority live in the northern territories, northern Quebec, and Labrador. The Metis (mixed native Indian and non-Indian ancestry) and nonregistered Indians number about one million. Since 1973 considerable progress has been made in settling aboriginal land claims with the country's native peoples.

An autonomous member of the British Commonwealth of Nations, Canada is a constitutional monarchy with a parliamentary form of government. The British monarch is the official head of state, represented by a resident governor-general. The Constitution Act of 1982 severed the last formal legislative link with Britain and included a formula whereby the federal parliament can make constitutional changes with the support of seven provinces representing 50 percent of the population. In practice the government is under the direction of the prime minister, the leader of the political party that is able to command the support of a majority in the 282-member House of Commons. An appointed Senate, composed of 104 members and selected on the basis of regional representation, exercises limited review powers.

Canada is a federal state, composed of 10 provinces and two large northern territories (Yukon and Northwest Territories). Federal and provincial spheres of responsibility are delineated in the British North America Act of 1867.

Since the coming of the first European settlers from France in the 16th century, the Roman Catholic Church has figured prominently in the nation's history, especially in Quebec where the overwhelming majority are French-speaking and Roman Catholic. That church is the largest single religious body in seven of Canada's 10 provinces and in the two territories. The Roman Catholic share of the population has grown steadily over the past century. In 1931, it was 39.5 percent. The 1981 census revealed that 47.3 percent of Canadians claimed to be Roman Catholic. The strength and vitality of the national church is reflected in the number of Canadians who are members of the College of Cardinals (five in 1986).

The overall Protestant share of the population has steadily declined from about 53.3 percent in 1931 to about 40 percent in 1981. That decrease was most evident in the mainline Protestant denominations (United, Anglican, Presbyterian, and Lutheran).

The United Church of Canada, the nation's largest Protestant denomination, had 15.6 percent of the population in 1981, compared to 19.5 percent in 1931. That church is the product of a merger in 1925 of the Methodists, Congregationalists, and a majority of the Presbyterians. Since then it has absorbed the eastern conference of the Evangelical United Brethren Church (1968); merger discussions with the Anglican Church of Canada, launched in 1944, broke down in 1975.

The Anglican Church of Canada is the second largest Protestant body. Its share of the population has steadily declined from 15.8 percent in 1931 to 10 percent in 1981.

A minority of Presbyterians voted against the church union proposal of 1925 and constituted the continuing Presbyterian Church in Canada. Their share of the population in 1981 was 3.4 percent, compared to 6.4 percent in 1931. Mergers have resulted in consolidation of Canada's Lutherans into fewer church bodies. The two major groups are the Evangelical Lutheran Church of Canada and the Lutheran Church—Canada (affiliated with the Lutheran Church—Missouri Synod in the USA).

In 1981 Canadian Baptists had 2.9 percent of the population, compared to 4.3 percent in 1931. The two largest Baptist groupings are the Canadian Baptist Federation (1200 congregations in three regional conventions and a Francophone convention) and the Fellowship of Evangelical Baptist Churches in Canada (475 congregations). Other major Baptist groups are the Baptist General Conference of Canada, North American Baptist General Conference, and the Southern Baptist Churches of Canada.

Pentecostal churches have increased in numbers since the denomination made its debut in the first decade of the century. In the decade of 1971 to 1981, they grew by 54 percent. The pentecostal share of the population in 1981 was 1.3 percent. The largest pentecostal entity is the Pentecostal Assemblies of Canada, with its sister body, the Pentecostal Assemblies of Newfoundland.

The newer evangelical bodies, such as the Christian and Missionary Alliance and the Free Methodist Church, have registered steady growth.

Immigration has increased the size of the country's Buddhist and Muslim populations, and the Jewish proportion has declined only slightly.

In common with the rest of the industrialized world, Canada has witnessed an increase in the number of unchurched people. The number of those claiming no religious affiliation increased from 930,000 in 1971 to 1,790,000 in 1981, which placed this group in fourth position—behind the Roman Catholic Church, the United Church, and the Anglican Church.

Fourteen Canadian denominations, including the mainline Protestant churches (except for the Lutheran Church—Canada) and Orthodox denominations, are members of the Canadian Council of Churches. Twenty-two smaller Protestant bodies belong to the Evangelical Fellowship of Canada.

LESLIE K. TARR

## Canadian Baptist Federation (CBF).

Religious body composed of three regional conventions and a union of Canadian Francophone churches—the United Baptist Convention of the Atlantic Provinces, the Baptist Convention of Ontario and Quebec, the Baptist Union of Western Canada, and the Union d'églises baptistes françaises au Canada. Founded in 1944, CBF serves as a liaison between member bodies and coordinates national Baptist initiatives in Christian education, overseas missions, relief and development programs, army and prison chaplaincies, communications, and youth ministry. Member bodies include about 1200 congregations. CBF is a member of the North American Baptist Fellowship and the Baptist World Alliance.

LESLIE K. TARR

## Canadian Council of Churches (CCC).

National ecumenical organization that fosters consultation, planning, and common action for member churches. Founded in 1944, it now includes in its membership 14 Protestant and Orthodox denominations (in addition, the Canadian Conference of Catholic Bishops is an associate member). The council holds a triennial assembly which formulates policy. Representation at the assembly and membership on the general board reflect the size of the council's member bodies. Three commissions (Faith and Order, Justice and Peace, Ecumenical Foundation and Communication), the general secretary, and council staff oversee operations. The council works closely with many Canadian interchurch coalitions which address national and international issues. CCC cooperates with other national ecumenical councils and with the World Council of Churches.

LESLIE K. TARR

## Canon Law.

The legislation of the church as distinguished from that of the civil government. While all Christian denominations have established regulations in some form or other, the term is most often used by the Anglican, the Orthodox, and especially by the Roman Catholic Church which has the most elaborate system today. Of Greek derivation, "canon" meant a rule used by masons or carpenters. In ecclesiastical terminology it became the standard by which something was measured. Thus one could speak of the canon of Scripture, the recognized list of sacred books; the canons or approved clergy; the canon or unvarying part of the Mass; or, later, the canonization of saints. In its most widespread usage, however, it referred to the enactment of councils, the norms regulating the behavior of Christians.

While there was undoubtedly previous legislation dealing with such concerns as the nonreiteration of baptism or the reconciliation of apostates, the earliest series of canons that have come down to us date from the beginning of the 4th century. The first are possibly from the Councils of Elvira (c. 309) and Arles (314). The main development, however, took place in Asia Minor and Syria. There five regional councils were held just before and after the Council of Nicea in 325. The canons of these councils—Ancyra, Neocaesarea, Gangra, Antioch, and Laodicea—when joined with those of Nicea became the nucleus of all future collections. The legislation dealt mainly with the hierarchical structure of the church, the dignity of the clergy, the punishment of heinous sin, the readmission of schismatics, and certain liturgical practices.

John the Scholastic, patriarch of Constantinople (c. 565), edited a remarkable collection of the canons of councils and a number of letters from St. Basil treating disciplinary questions. His anthology was particularly useful because the canons were arranged according to subject matter instead of chronologically. He also collected laws of the emperors which regulated affairs of the church. The combination of ecclesiastical and imperial legislation, peculiar to the East, became known as nomocanons. The Council of Trullo in 692 defined the sources of Eastern law and added about 100 enactments of its own. The Council of Trullo is still normative for the Orthodox Church.

In the West, Dionysius Exiguus (c. 500) at Rome made a new Latin translation of the canons of the nuclear and ecumenical councils. He also collected 39 decretals of the popes. (Decretals are authoritative papal decisions on questions of discipline posed by various bishops.) Thus the notion of canon law in the West, as well as in the East, began to embrace more than conciliar legislation.

As a result of the barbarian invasions and the subsequent introduction of the penitentials a body of Franco-Germanic law developed that was not wholly consistent with the classical tradition. Remarriage after divorce, for example, was tolerated under certain circumstances. The Gregorian reformers in the last half of the 11th century sought to purify the church and to liberate it from secular domination. The movement led to renewed interest and research in the field of law. About the year 1140 Gratian, known as the father of the science of canon law, compiled his *Decretum* in which he sought to bring together in one volume all existing law and to reconcile or harmonize conflicting texts. This work became almost immediately the basic textbook in the schools of canon law which were beginning to spring up in Western Europe. The close study of the law stimulated a flood of questions on substance and procedure for the papacy to resolve. The lawyer popes of the Middle Ages were delighted to oblige, so that soon there were thousands of decretals eagerly copied and circulated. It finally became necessary for Pope Gregory IX to commission Raymond of Penafort to organize these decretals in some systematic way. When published in 1234 the collection was known as the *Extravagantes* because the decretals had been "wandering outside" the *Decretum* of Gratian. The continued profusion of decretals led to other collections: the *Liber Sextus* of Boniface VIII (1298; because there were five books in the *Extravagantes*); the *Clementinae* (1317); the *Extravagantes* of John XXII (1325); and the *Extravagantes communes* (1503). The *Decretum* plus the five collections of decretals became known as the *Corpus Iuris Canonici*. The *Corpus* remained the basic law of the Roman Catholic Church until the second decade of the 20th century. The canon law of the Church of England "presupposes . . . the general pre-Reformation Canon Law of the Western Church except where that Canon Law has been affected by contrary statute or custom in England" (*Canons of the Church of England*, xii).

Since the *Corpus* did not extend beyond the 15th century, it had to be supplemented with later legislation. For Catholics the most important additions were made by the Counter-Reformation Council of Trent (1545–63) and occasional decrees of the popes and Roman congregations (offices). Because this mass of material lacked organization and included prolix as well as outdated legislation, Pope Benedict XV in 1917 promulgated the first Code of Canon Law. Unlike the medieval collections which retained narrative sections, expository material, and the motivations of the legislator, the code sought expression in abstract principles. Cardinal Gasparri, the chief architect, took as a model the civil codes which many European countries had adopted during the 19th century. The Code of Canon Law contained 2414 canons arranged in five books. The general principle of organization was borrowed from Roman law: persons, places, and things.

When Pope John XXIII summoned the Second Vatican Council (1959), he also called for the renewal of canon law. The revision could not get underway until the council had finished its work (1965). The consultative process took so long that the new code was not ready for promulgation until 1983. With 1752 canons it is considerably shorter than the first code. The new code has seven books, partially based on the threefold *munera* (offices) of Christ: the kingly or ruling office, the priestly or sanctifying office, and the prophetic or teaching office.

Book 1, General Norms (203 canons), includes: the nature of ecclesiastical laws; custom; general decrees and instructions; individual administrative acts; physical and juridic persons; juridic acts; the power of governance; ecclesiastical offices; prescription; and the computation of time. Book 2, The People of God (503 canons), is divided into three parts. After listing the obligations and rights of all the Christian faithful, it treats clerics and associations of the faith. Part 2 is concerned with the hierarchical constitution of the Church: the Roman pontiff and the college of bishops; the synod of bishops; the cardinals; the Roman curia; particular churches (diocese); bishops; provinces; conferences of bishops; and the internal ordering of particular churches. Part 3 deals with institutes of consecrated life and societies of apostolic life (popularly known as religious orders). Book 3, The Teaching Office of the Church (87 canons), includes: preaching of the Word of God; catechetical instruction; missionary action; Catholic education; books and the media; and the profession of faith. Book 4, The Office of Sanctifying in the Church (420 canons), regulates baptism, confirmation, the Eucharist, penance, the anointing of the sick, marriage, the liturgy of the hours, funeral rites, the veneration of saints, sacred places, and sacred times. Book 5, The Temporal Goods of the Church (57 canons), governs the acquisition and administration of property, contracts, and wills. Book 6, Sanctions in the Church (89 canons), deals with ecclesiastical penalties such as excommunication. Book 7, Processes (353 canons), is concerned with trials, matrimonial procedures (annulments), recourse against administrative decrees, and the removal and transfer of pastors.

A special pontifical commission has been established to make authentic interpretations of the canons when it seems advisable.

***Bibliography.*** R. C. Mortimer, *Western Canon Law* (1953); *The Canons of the Church of England* (1969); *The Code of Canon Law in English Translation* (1983).

JOHN E. LYNCH

**Canon of Scripture.** Those books in the Jewish and Christian Bible considered to be Scripture and therefore authoritative in matters of faith and doctrine. In the course of its history the term "canon" (Gk. *kanōn*, "rod"; Heb. *qāneh*, "reed") has acquired a variety of meanings. Originally referring to a straight rod, it came to signify anything straight—a rule, standard, model, measure, criterion, or norm. It eventually came to be applied to a rule of faith. While the Hebrews regarded their Scriptures as inspired, they did not refer to them as "canonical." Church fathers in the 4th century A.D. first applied the term to the sacred Scriptures to distinguish them as the authoritative writings recognized by the church.

*OT Canon.* The crystallization of what is now the OT was a long and complicated process, marked by several stages.

Cultic interests in Israel contributed much toward the recognition of sacred writings. The religious community gradually collected and preserved early songs, narratives, laws, annals, psalms, prophecies, and other literary remains (see Exod. 40:20; Deut. 31:24–26). Godly men spoke and what they said was immediately recognized as inspired. Consequently there was no early demand for formal canonization. The first public acknowledgment of a sacred document seems to have taken place in 621 B.C. when "the book of the law" which Hilkiah found in the temple was formally recognized by King Josiah (2 Kings 23). This marked the beginning of the subtle process which in time brought public recognition of the tripartite canon.

Scholars are not agreed as to the time each of the three parts received formal approval. Pfeiffer, for example, suggests that the canonization of the Law took place c. 400 B.C.; the Prophets, c. 200 B.C.; and the Hagiographa, c. A.D. 90. Oesterley and Robinson, following Hoelscher, recognize no canon of the OT before the Council of Jamnia (A.D. 90). G. R. Driver questions the theory that the issue was settled at Jamnia. Rowley and many others feel that the fixation of the canon was by general consent and not by formal decision.

Doubtless, the Torah acquired earliest recognition as authoritative. Long after the crystallization of the Prophets and the Writings the primacy of the Pentateuch prevailed. The fixation of the literary strata and eventually the books of the Pentateuch was an involved process. Apparently it was complete by the time of Nehemiah (432 B.C.), for when the Samaritans withdrew from the Jews they adopted the Pentateuch as their sole canon. At least by c. 250 B.C., when the Torah was translated into Greek (LXX), it had become the Bible of Judaism. In all the synagogues the Law was read and regarded as authoritative.

The historical narrative begun in the Pentateuch is continued in the Former Prophets. Within this framework numerous documents sprang up only to be lost in the process of selection, evaluation, assimilation, and preservation (1 Kings 11:41; 14:19, 29; 1 Chron. 29:29). These materials were organized, adapted, and edited during the exile (c. 550 B.C.), preserving the prophetic record of the history and faith of Israel, which had become vitiated by the fall of Jerusalem in 587 B.C. Later editors made additional alterations to the text.

The Latter Prophets had a somewhat different development. Projected for the most part independently and limited in use by reason of the primacy of the Law, the writings of the prophets acquired public recognition slowly. During the exile, under the influence of Ezekiel and Isaiah, who projected great hopes for Israel's future, there sprang up a revival of interest in prophecy, particularly predictive passages envisioning the coming of a deliverer and the overthrow of Israel's enemies. As reverence for the written Law increased, appreciation for the word of the prophet also grew. But in spite of this, countless interpolations were made in the text to bring books up to date and to enhance their value for current religion and morality. The presence of late sections in some prophecies and the absence of the Book of Daniel from the collection place the fixation of the prophetic canon late, c. 200 B.C. Writing c. 180 B.C. Ben Sira recognizes the "Law and the Prophets" (Ecclus. 44–49). In 132 B.C. the grandson of Ben Sira refers repeatedly to these two divisions, both of which by that time had been translated into Greek.

The process by which the Writings attained canonical status was much more subtle. This was due to their independent character, varied contents, and loose connection. About all that they had in common was the claim to inspiration. Yet wide appeal and circulation ensured their ultimate preservation. Some of the books, such as Psalms and Proverbs, include separate collections. By 132 B.C. there existed a fluid grouping, for Ben Sira's grandson refers to "the Law and the Prophets and the rest of the books." But while the third division in general had become crystallized before the beginning of the Christian era (see Luke 24:44), some of the books, such as Esther, Ecclesiastes, and the Song of Solomon, long remained under dispute. The destruction of Jerusalem in A.D. 70, the disorganized state of Judaism, controversies over the status of certain books, and the influence of Christianity led to the fixation of the canon of 24 books (22, with Ruth combined with Judges and Lamentations with Jeremiah). The formal recognition of the complete OT is usually regarded as having taken place at the Council of Jamnia, although the general pattern appeared much earlier and some books came into question later.

Besides the 24 canonical books (39 in the English Bible), there are numerous documents from the last centuries B.C. and the first century A.D. known as the Apocrypha and Pseudepigrapha. Jews in Alexandria treated Scripture more casually than Palestinian Jews. The latter held that prophecy ended in the time of Ezra, thus precluding admission to canonical standing of any document recognized as later; the former, on the other hand, held to the continuity of inspiration and the sanctity of books translated from Hebrew or Aramaic into Greek. Hence they included in their collection not only the books of the Hebrew canon but also the Apocrypha, which they interspersed among the canonical writings; they also made other alterations to the text. They did not, however, set up a special Alexandrian canon. The witness of the LXX is to the effect that the OT canon had not become fixed when the Greek version was projected. Bentzen, following Kahle, suggests that the Greek Bible was the creation of the Christian church.

The NT bears testimony to the free use of Scripture on the part of early Christians. It includes, besides numerous quotations from each of the three parts of the OT, adduced largely, though not exclusively, from the LXX, several references to or reminiscences of writings outside the Hebrew canon (see Heb. 11:35–37; James 1:19; Jude 5, 14–16). This practice of employing a larger collection obtains also in the writings of the apostolic and early church fathers. While the LXX was long used by the church, the acceptance of the Apocrypha was by no means universal. There was, in fact, considerable variation in usage in both East and West. Jerome, for example, protested vigorously against the inclusion of these books, but Augustine and the Roman Church, following him, accepted them. At the time of the Reformation the Protestant churches returned to the original Palestinian canon as the basis for doctrine, but retained the arrangement of books as handed down by the LXX and the Vulgate, which make no distinction between the second and third divisions of the tripartite canon. In his German Bible of 1534 Luther placed the Apocrypha at the end of the OT, noting that these books were inferior but "good and useful for reading."

**Bibliography.** M. L. Margolis, *The Hebrew Scriptures in the Making* (1922); H. E. Ryle, *The Canon of the OT* (2d ed., 1925); S. Zeitlin, *An Historical Study of the Canonization of the Hebrew Scriptures* (1933); O. Eissfeldt, *Einleitung in das Alte Testament* (1934); W. O. E. Oesterley and T. H. Robinson, *An Introduction to the Books of the OT* (1934); R. H. Pfeiffer, *Introduction to the OT* (1941); A. Bentzen, *Introduction to the OT* (1948), 1:20–41; Artur Weiser, *Einleitung in das Alte Testament* (1949); H. H. Rowley, *The Growth of the OT* (1950); G. Ostborn, *Cult and Canon: A Study in the Canonization of the OT* (1951); A. Jeffrey, *Interpreter's Bible* (1952), 1:32–45.

ELMER E. FLACK

**NT Canon.** Although recognition of the canon of the NT was one of the most important developments in the early church, there is a surprising absence of contemporary references to the order in which the various parts of the NT achieved general currency and the reasons which led the church to make the selection that ultimately prevailed. There are a number of theories on both of these matters.

Harnack held that the Gospels were the nucleus of the canon, and that the Pauline Epistles followed. The Acts of the Apostles was added chiefly to vindicate the authority of Paul and to join his writings to the Gospels.

According to E. J. Goodspeed the first collection of NT books was made by a Christian, perhaps at Ephesus, whose interest in Paul had been roused by reading the recently published Acts of the Apostles (shortly after A.D. 90). This admirer composed a prefatory encyclical (Ephesians) and published the corpus of 10 letters (i.e., all but the Pastorals), which in turn stimulated the composition of other letters, namely Rev. 1–3, Hebrews, 1 Peter, and 1 Clement. John Knox conjectured that the collector and publisher of the preliminary Pauline corpus was Onesimus.

Hans Windisch thought that the Book of Revelation, because it contained words of Jesus Christ, history of the kingdom, and letters, supplied the pattern for the canonization of documents in each of these three areas.

The question whether the church's canon preceded or followed Marcion's canon continues to be debated, but in view of the consistent representation in the fathers that Marcion *rejected* certain books, the great probability is that the church's canon was previous to Marcion's rival canon.

John Knox proposed the elaborate hypothesis that Marcion had a kind of proto-Luke which the church later enlarged in the interest of anti-Marcionite polemic, producing our present Luke sometime after A.D. 150. He fails, however, to show that after A.D. 150 conditions prevailed in the church to render possible the immediate general acceptance of a newly redacted Gospel.

J. H. Ropes hazarded the theory that the formation of the basic canon took place early in the 2d century, perhaps at Antioch. The Western text (found today in such manuscripts as Codex Bezae, the Old Latin manuscripts, and other witnesses) was the text of the primitive canon, expressly created for that purpose.

Various answers have been given to the question of why the church approved certain books and rejected others. According to Harnack, the canon constituted one of the three barriers (the other two being the creed and the bishops) which the church erected in its struggle with heresy, particularly gnosticism. The process involved essentially the competition of many and the survival of the fittest. Juelicher, on the other hand, stressed the importance of *anagnōsis* (public reading) of NT documents along with OT documents, already regarded as canonical, with the consequent impartation of the authority of the latter to the former. Conflict, so far from decreasing the canonical material by selection, actually worked to increase the amount subsequently canonized by expanding the church's acquaintance with acceptable literature. According to Westcott, the formation of the canon was among the first instinctive acts of Christian society, resting upon the general confession of the churches and not upon the independent opinions of its members. The canon was not the result of a series of contests; rather, canonical books were separated from the others by the intuitive insight of the church.

***Theology of the Canon.*** Discussion of the canon must distinguish between the ground of canonicity and the grounds of the conviction of canonicity. The latter were variously apprehended by different elements in the early church. In some areas such as Alexandria the process of canonization proceeded by way of selection, moving from many to few; in other areas like Syria the church was content with a canon of 22 books. The ground of canonicity, on the other hand, rests ultimately upon what God has accomplished through Christ and the Spirit. Luther recognized as canonical those writings which preach Christ. Calvin defined the authority of the Scriptures in terms of the activity of God's Spirit (*testimonium Spiritus Sancti internum*). In this sense, the church did not create the canon, but came to recognize and acknowledge the self-authenticating quality of the canonical documents which imposed themselves as such upon the church.

***Bibliography.*** A. Souter, *The Text and Canon of the NT* (1913); M. L. Margolis, *The Hebrew Scriptures in the Making* (1922); A. von Harnack, *The Origin of the NT and the Most Important Consequences* (1925); N. B. Stonehouse, *The Apocalypse in the Ancient Church* (1929); M. J. Lagrange, *Histoire ancienne du canon Nouveau Testament* (1933); R. P. C. Hanson, *Tradition in the Early Church* (1962); Hans von Campenhausen, *The Formation of the Christian Bible* (1972); M. G. Kline, *The Structure of Biblical Authority* (1972); J. A. Sanders, *Torah and Canon* (1972); S. Z. Leiman, *The Canonization of Hebrew Scripture* (1976).

BRUCE M. METZGER

**Capitalism.** Economic system characterized by private or corporate ownership of goods, private investment decisions, and a competitive free market. Usually the term "capitalist" is reserved for an individual whose major economic activity is the ownership and use of capital in large amounts. Strictly regarded, the borders of such a definition are flexible and unclear, but the usage works well enough in practice.

Commonly, also, an economy such as the "American" is distinguished, as capitalism, from a socialist or communist economy, which is not capitalist. But capital is employed in the latter economies also. Thus, if capitalism were defined as suggested above, a socialist and a communist economy would also be capitalistic, and the dis-

tinction drawn between them and the American economy would be invalid. Sometimes, the distinction is described as one between "private" capitalism, on the one hand, and "state" or "public" capitalism, on the other. This comes nearer to the truth; but it also requires qualification because, on the one hand, private capitalists are not absent either from recognized socialist theory and practice or from the present "socialist" stage of the Soviet economy, and, on the other hand, capital is both privately and publicly owned and controlled in America. The real difference, then, is one of proportion and of specific programs— what proportion of the economy and what specific economic programs and institutions should be privately controlled and what publicly, and how each kind of ownership and control might be exercised so as to bring about the highest level of productivity, the right amount and kind of personal freedom and prosperity, and the greatest personal and social security and attainment of culture.

Criticisms of capitalism have been theoretical and practical, superficial and profound; the proposed remedies have ranged, and still range, all the way from comparatively minor readjustments and "improvements" of capitalism to sweeping, utopian, or more sober and practical demands for its abolition. Practically all of the more sweeping criticisms and programs of improvement have rested upon an estimate of man's rational and moral stature which is probably too high—apart, at least, from man's regeneration; and upon an estimate of the cause of man's predicament which does not recognize the true location of the trouble or its profound seriousness. Most of them have been intellectually unclear and practically unworkable, due in part probably to the white heat of emotion in which they were generated.

The claim that the most thorough of these proposals, both theoretically and practically, is that of the communists is probably just. Marx saw clearly enough certain real dangers in modern capitalism, especially perhaps its inherent tendency to concentrate, in the hands of the few, power which would inevitably be or become socially irresponsible in several ways—such as exploiting women and children and destroying the home; competing for raw materials and markets, eventually on a world scale, leading to war; and generating cycle of "boom and bust." What he did not allow for, because there was little to suggest it in the society of his time, was the inevitable development of controls, such as the spreading of ownership through the establishment of joint-stock, limited liability companies; the strengthening of the middle classes; the more or less successful expedients of democratic governments; and the various movements looking to the establishment and preservation of world peace, and possibly leading in the future to some form of world government.

In religious circles, the liberal movement, with its Christian socialism and its social gospel was perhaps the most earnest indictment of the profit motive and of other evils in capitalistic society. It was also the most widespread effort to think out and to apply remedies. That movement is, for the present, in eclipse. But Christianity, with its doctrine of brotherhood in Christ and its essential sympathy for all who are oppressed, can never surrender its function of criticism of all systems erected by finite and sin-perverted man; and it is to be hoped that the objectives of the social gospel will presently be revived, on more realistic theological and sociological foundations and with more practical programs.

Along with this religiously motivated criticism of capitalism, there has been a persistent effort to lay the blame for capitalism, or for its evils, upon Protestantism, and more specifically upon John Calvin and his followers. Its first expression was an essay of Max Weber's (1904/5), later translated into English by T. Parsons and published as *The Protestant Ethic and the Spirit of Capitalism* (1930). But the theory, along with criticisms and modifications of Weber's formulation and exposition of it, had already been made familiar to English readers through R. H. Tawney's *Religion and the Rise of Capitalism* (1926). It has been widely discussed in America, Great Britain, and Europe; but the student who is not a specialist may find a brief and adequate consideration of it in *John Calvin: The Man and His Ethics* (1931). It is true that Protestantism did contribute to the rise of modern capitalism by justifying the relief of industry from ecclesiastical, especially monastic, control; by announcing and defending the legitimacy of interest and credit; and by emphasizing individualism and the so-called economic virtues. As a result, "there is a historical correlation, which cannot be explained by an accidental conjunction, between the growth of Calvinism and the growth of capitalism" (*John Calvin*, p. 190). But, on the other hand, "before Calvin was born, forces were at work which were calculated inevitably to bring about a transition to a new economic order" (p. 191); "capitalism existed, both in form and spirit, before Calvin's day" (p. 187); and Calvin labored to instil a religiously sanctioned ethic which, had it been followed, would largely have obviated the formation of that soulless, godless, greedy system which critics see, apparently, in capitalism.

Some, in their effort to rebut Weber's charge, appear to agree that capitalism is an evil thing, but deny that Protestantism had any significant part in its development. Perhaps more commonly, Protestants regard capitalism, with all its acknowledged faults, as the best economic system available. They hope for and confidently expect a progressive remedying of its more obvious defects; they point out that, human nature being what it is, competition is useful and necessary, and may be carried out under conditions which at least greatly minimize its potentially destructive character; and they expect no substitution of the very different spirit of Christian *agapē* for it, in the economic order, until the kingdom of God has come, or at least until a much closer approximation of it has been achieved than seems likely in the near future.

***Bibliography.*** M. Weber, *The Protestant Ethic and the Spirit of Capitalism* (1930); R. H. Tawney, *Religion and the Rise of Capitalism* (1947); W. A. Orton, *The Economic Role of the State* (1950); F. M. Stern, *Capitalism in America* (1951); G. Spiro, *Marxism and the Bolshevik State* (1951); F. Sternberg, *Capitalism and Socialism on Trial* (1952); V. A. Demant, *Religion and the Decline of Capitalism* (1952); W. W. Rostov, *The Stages of Economic Growth* (1960); J. K. Galbraith, *The Affluent Society* (1961); Ayn Rand, *Capitalism: The Unknown Ideal* (1966).

ANDREW K. RULE

# Capital Punishment.

Penalty of death imposed upon those found guilty of certain specified crimes by a recognized public authority. The primary debate within the Christian tradition concerns the severity of such punishment in the light of biblical ethics. The parties to the debate have largely agreed that punishment of some kind is necessary but have disagreed over the type of punishment demanded.

Most ancient Middle Eastern societies (Israel being no exception) held to a version of the lex talionis: punishment was meted out according to the seriousness of the crime (a life for a life, an eye for an eye, etc.). In its original intent this type of legal code attempted to safeguard against excessive punishment as well as insure "just" penalty where due. The extension of this code to the death penalty seemed obvious enough and there were few objections in these early societies.

Several passages in the NT raised the issue anew for the early Christian church. Jesus' teaching in the Sermon on the Mount contains cautions about exacting vengeance, and the Pauline corpus contains several warnings about usurping the role of God as Avenger (cf., e.g., Rom. 12:19). As a result there began a movement within Christendom to abolish the death penalty.

This is not to say, however, that the NT does not contain passages which might be taken to support the imposition of the death penalty. The powers given to the state include the power of the sword (Rom. 13:1–5). It is also imperative to understand the relationship between social ethics (the principles governing social structures) and personal ethics (the principles governing the behavior of individuals) as it relates to the issue of punishment. Do the Scriptures forbid private vengeance (cf. the episode of the woman caught in adultery in John 8:1–11) and thereby also legal sanctions imposed by the state, or merely the first of these? Also to be considered is the relationship between the clear commands of the OT regarding capital punishment and the teaching of the NT.

There is no developed criminal law in the Koran, but the crime of homicide is treated with meticulous detail and is instructive in regard to the Islamic view of capital punishment. The actual punishment in the case of a homicide is to be carried out by the relatives of the slain victim. Just retaliation means either demanding the murderer's life, accepting compensation, or pardoning the offense altogether. Capital punishment is not mandatory although it nonetheless retains its status as just. This surely stems from the Islamic conviction about the value of life (especially if that life is a Muslim's). It is interesting to note that the individual rather than the state has the authority to punish in this instance.

The modern debate about capital punishment centers far less on ethical principles than on political expediency. The death penalty is now largely prohibited in the European West (with notable exceptions); this has come about for primarily two reasons. The judicial system in most countries has been deemed not safe enough to guard against the possible condemnation of innocent people. Furthermore, ethnic minorities have constituted the majority of those found guilty of capital crimes. On the other side of the debate, the calls for the continuation (or reinstatement) of the death penalty have focused on the rising crime rate in society and the need for stricter and swifter methods of punishment to deal with these trends. The debate itself is not likely to conclude until sin in all its manifold forms has been abolished.

*Bibliography.* C. S. Lewis, Report of the Royal Commission on Capital Punishment (1953); W. Moberly, *The Ethics of Punishment* (1968); J. N. D. Anderson, *Issues of Life and Death* (1976); O. O'Donovan, *Measure for Measure: Justice in Punishment and the Sentence of Death* (1977).

RICHARD LINTS

## Capuchins.

Franciscan reform group founded by Matteo di Bascio of Urbino in 1525. As part of an effort to reestablish the original ideals of St. Francis, the Capuchins adopted his unique style of clothing and grooming, including sandals, a beard, and a pointed hood or *capuche*, from which the Capuchins take their name. The group began to care for plague victims at Camerino, where it was established with the approval of Pope Clement VIII in 1528. Its rule, adopted in 1529, emphasized austerity, charity, and poverty. The early Capuchins faced many difficulties: their founder returned to the Observants; their second vicar-general, Louis of Fossombrone, was deposed; and their fourth vicar-general, Bernardino Ochino, became a Protestant. These crises served to kindle the disapproval of other Franciscans. Eventually, however, the group gained recognition for its preaching and missionary work. Despite the Capuchins' sectarian beginnings, they fought ardently to advance the Counter-Reformation. In 1619 the Capuchins became a fully independent branch of the Franciscan order by decree of Pope Paul V. They have retained this status, alongside the Coventuals and the Observants, until the present day.

ROBERT L. MORRISON

## Cardinals, College of.

Group of cardinals in the Roman Catholic Church with the exclusive right of electing the pope in conclave. The Sacred College also assists the pope collegially by its counsel on questions of major importance. The pope personally chooses those cardinals who are to be promoted to the college. Up until the time of Pope John XXIII (1959) the upper limit of cardinals, rarely reached, was set at 70. Pope Paul VI in 1970 decreed that a cardinal who had reached the age of 80 was no longer eligible to participate in a papal election. In 1973 he created 30 new cardinals, increasing the membership of the college to 145. Although the college is divided into three ranks (episcopal, presbyteral, and diaconal), all cardinals enjoy episcopal consecration. Up until the 1917 Code of Canon Law it was possible for a layman to be named cardinal. Giacomo Antonelli, secretary of state for Pope Pius IX and promoted to the cardinalate in 1847, remained in deacon's orders throughout his life. All cardinals (except Eastern patriarchs) are assimilated to the clergy of Rome, symbolized by their assignment of a title to one of the ancient churches of that city. In the 1983 Code of Canon Law cardinals are treated in canons 349–59.

Historians disagree about the origin of the cardinalate, basing their arguments partly on the etymology of the term. Some maintain that it derives from the Latin noun *cardo* (hinge). Figuratively the Latin adjective *cardinalis* would indicate something central or fundamental, as in cardinal numbers or cardinal virtues. A cardinal, then, was a chief official upon whom the administration of a major church revolved. Other scholars prefer a liturgical derivation from the ecclesiastical concept *incardinare* as used especially in the letters of Gregory the Great (590–604). Thus a cardinal was a minister serving in a church for which he was not ordained. Somewhat later the canonical status of incardination evolved into a position of dignity.

The modern history of cardinals begins with Pope Leo IX (1049–54), who employed them as his principal assistants and invited foreigners into their ranks. To end the turmoil frequently accompanying the succession of a new bishop of Rome, Pope Nicholas II at a Lateran synod (1059) decreed that henceforth the election would be entrusted to the cardinals. Because the decree had failed to prevent a schism in 1130 due, in part, to an ambiguity about the dominating role of the cardinal bishops, the Third Lateran Council in 1179 declared that all cardinals were to be considered equal and that a two-thirds majority of votes was necessary for a valid election. To speed up the deliberations Pope Gregory X in 1274 inaugurated the conclave system whereby the cardinals were to be strictly isolated. Pope Pius IV in 1562 issued detailed regulations for voting during the conclave. A final step was taken by Pope Pius X in 1904. He formally abolished the veto power (*jus eclusivae*) which Spain, Austria, and France claimed to be able to exercise once in a conclave. The current law regulating the government of the Church after the death of a pope and the subsequent election procedures was promulgated by Pope Paul VI in 1975.

**Bibliography.** C. G. Fürst, *Cardinalis: Prolegomena zu einer Rechtsgeschichte* (1967); S. Kuttner, *The History of Ideas and Doctrine in the Middle Ages* (1980).

JOHN E. LYNCH

**Caritas.** International Roman Catholic organization that aims to "help its members to promote the practice of charity and social justice, not only among Christians, but also among all persons of good will." It is a confederation that participates fully in the larger social mission of the Roman Catholic Church, expressed most visibly on the parish, diocesan, and national levels. Representatives of the worldwide confederation meet every four years to "build solidarity among each other and to seek mutual inspiration and support." Caritas works closely with Protestant, Jewish, and nondenominational agencies in international relief activity. Caritas became well known in the late 1960s because of its concern and aid for the Nigeria/Biafra war victims.

**Carlile, Wilson** (1847–1942). Founder of the Church Army. Born in London, he was in business until 1878, when he entered the London College of Divinity to study for the ministry of the Church of England. Ordained in 1880, he founded the Church Army to work in the Westminster slums two years later. He was rector of St. Mary-at-Hill, London (1892–1926), and on his retirement King George V made him a Companion of Honour, a rare award for a clergyman. He wrote *The Church and Conversion* (1882), *Spiritual Difficulties* (1885), *Continental Outcast* (1906), and *Baptism of Fire* (1907).

J. D. DOUGLAS

**Carmelites.** Roman Catholic religious order founded by St. Berthold on Mount Carmel in 1154. The order originally claimed continuity with Elijah and the "sons of the prophets" (2 Kings 2), but now regards this claim as spurious. The order's primitive rule, composed by Albert of Jerusalem in 1209, called for poverty,

solitude, and abstinence from meat. It was approved by Pope Honorius III in 1226.

After the fall of the Crusader states in 1187, many Carmelites returned to Europe; they reorganized under the leadership of St. Simon Stock in 1247, becoming one of the mendicant orders. The Carmelite sisters were founded in 1452 and the order soon spread through Europe. In 1562, St. Teresa of Avila launched a reform movement in which she urged Carmelite nuns to return to the order's original austerity. She also inspired St. John of the Cross to follow suit among the friars. The movement's followers became known as the "discalced" (barefoot) Carmelites because of their austerity. The reform spread throughout much of the Carmelite order, despite the persecution of John by his superiors. The discalced Carmelites received their own general in 1593 and thus became independent of the calced or mitigate Carmelites. In 1634, a small group of discalced Carmelites returned to Palestine.

Between 1770 and 1870 Carmelites in France, Italy, Spain, Germany, and Belgium were severely oppressed by absolutist governments. Only four general assemblies were held during this time; usually they are held every six years. With the end of the oppression, the order was able to rebuild and resume the missionary activity that had begun following the Council of Trent. In 1964 there were about 3000 mitigated Carmelites and over 4000 discalced Carmelites.

ROBERT L. MORRISON

**Carmichael, Amy Wilson** (1867–1951). *See* DOHNAVUR FELLOWSHIP.

**Carnell, Edward John** (1919–1967). American scholar of apologetics. Born in Antigo, Wis., Carnell was trained at Wheaton College, Westminster Theological Seminary, Harvard Divinity School (Th.D.), and Boston University (Ph.D.). He served on the faculties of Gordon College and Gordon Divinity School and later taught for many years at Fuller Theological Seminary. Carnell was a leading thinker in the neoevangelical movement of the 1940s and 1950s. His apologetic approach has been termed "verificational apologetics." Carnell's major works include *An Introduction to Christian Apologetics* (1948), *A Philosophy of the Christian Religion* (1952), *Christian Commitment: An Apologetic* (1957), *The Case for Orthodox Theology* (1959), *The Kingdom of Love and the Pride of Life* (1960), *The Theology of Reinhold Niebuhr* (1960), *The Burden of Soren Kierkegaard* (1965), and *The Case for Biblical Christianity* (1969).

R. MILTON WINTER

**Carpenter, Joseph Estlin** (1844–1927). English Unitarian scholar. Born in Ripley, Surrey, he was educated at University College, London, and Manchester New College, and was successively minister of Oakfield Road Church, Clifton, Gloucestershire (1866–69), and Mill Hill Chapel, Leeds (1869–75). From 1875 to 1906, he lectured on Hebrew, OT literature, and comparative religion at Manchester New College, first in London, then at Oxford, where he was appointed principal in 1906. His works include *Life and Work of Mary Carpenter* (1879), *Life in Palestine When Jesus Lived* (1889), *The First Three Gospels, Their Origin and Relations* (1890), *Composition of the Hexateuch* (1902), *The Bible in the Nineteenth Century* (1903), *The Place of Christianity among the Religions of the World* (1904), and *James Martineau, Theologian and Teacher* (1905). He wrote *Studies in Theology* (1903) with P. H. Wicksteed. He edited volumes 3–5 of Ewald's *History of Israel* (1871–74), a portion of the *Sumaāngala Vilāsinī* (1886), the *Dīgha Nikāya* (2 vols., 1890–1903; both in collaboration with Rhys Davids), and *The Hexateuch According to the Revised Version* (2 vols., 1900; in collaboration with G. Harford-Battersby). He translated C. P. Tiele's *Geschiedenis van den Godsdienst tot aan de heerschappij der Wereldgodsdiensten* (1876) under the title *Outlines of the History of Religion* (1878).

## Carthusians.

Roman Catholic monastic order founded by St. Bruno of Cologne in 1084 at the Grand Chartreuse near Grenoble, France. Since their beginning, the Carthusians have focused on living a contemplative, solitary, and semieremitical life. The order prohibits frequent conversation among the brothers, fasts often, and eats no meat. Material needs are met by lay brothers; the monks devote their time to private prayer as well as the daily office, Mass, and conventual.

In 1127 the Dom Guigues compiled the order's rule (*Consuetudines*). It was approved by Pope Innocent II in 1133; although it has been subsequently modified, the rule remains essentially the same in its austere requirements. In its latest revision (1924), the rule was aligned with the Code of Canon Law.

From 1378 to 1409, the order underwent the "Great Schism." During this period, the houses of Italy and Germany followed the Roman pope, Urban VI, while the houses of France and Spain followed the pope of Avignon, Clement VII. The opposing Carthusian groups also had separate generals. The schism was resolved when the two separate generals resigned and were replaced by a single general. During the Reformation, the order was persecuted in Austria, England, France, Holland, and Yugoslavia; it was also later persecuted during the French Revolution in its home country. The order flourished after it was allowed to return to the Grand Chartreuse in 1816, but in the early 20th century it was once again forced to vacate the monastery as a result of France's anticlerical legislation of 1901. The monks returned to the monastery in 1940.

Since the 12th century, a few convents have been associated with the order. The nuns live a similar, although less solitary, lifestyle. Like their brothers, Carthusian nuns devote their efforts to the pursuit of contemplative union with God. Carthusian spiritual writers include Hugh of Balma, Denis the Carthusian, and Lanspergius. The Carthusians have also edited and published the works of many non-Carthusian mystics such as St. Gertrude, Tauler, Suso, and Ruysbroeck.

Robert L. Morrison

## Carus, Paul

**Carus, Paul** (1852–1919). Philosopher of comparative religion. Born in Ilsenburg, Germany, he was educated at the universities of Tübingen, Greifswald, and Strasburg (Ph.D., Tübingen, 1876), and after teaching in two realgymnasia in Dresden and in the Royal Saxon Cadet Corps, he came to America in 1883. From 1887 he was editor of *The Open Court* (Chicago) and from 1890 edited *The Monist* (Chicago). He was secretary of the Religious Parliament Extension from its inception, and had an active interest in ethnic religion. He was a member of the Leopoldina, the Press Club, the American Oriental Society, and the American Association for the Advancement of Science. In theology he held that religion is to be purified by scientific criticism and ultimately to be based upon the facts of experience. His works include *Helgi und Sigrun, ein episches Gedicht der nordischen Sage* (1880), *Metaphysik in Wissenschaft, Ethik und Religion* (1881), *Algenor, eine epischlyrische Dichtung* (1882), *Gedichte* (1882), *Lieder eines Buddhisten* (1882), *Ursache, Grund und Zweck* (1883), *Aus dem Exil* (1884), *Monism and Meliorism* (1885), *Fundamental Problems* (1889), *The Ethical Problem* (1890), *The Soul of Man* (1891), *Homilies of Science* (1892), *Primer of Philosophy* (1893), *The Religion of Science* (1893), *Truth in Fiction* (1893), *The Gospel of Buddha, According to Old Records* (1894), *De rerum natura, philosophisches Gedicht* (1895), *Religion of Enlightenment* (1896), *Buddhism and Its Christian Critics* (1897), *Chinese Philosophy* (1898), *Kant and Spencer: A Study of the Fallacies of Agnosticism* (1899), *Sacred Tunes for the Consecration of Life* (1899), *The Dawn of a New Era, and Other Essays on Religion* (1899), *Whence and Whither: An Inquiry into the Nature of the Soul, Its Origin and Its Destiny* (1900), *The History of the Devil and the Idea of Evil* (1900), *The Surà of Metaphysics* (1903), *Friedrich Schiller* (1905), *Magic Squares* (1906), and *The Rise of Man* (1906). His works of fiction include *Karma: A Story of Early Buddhism* (1895), *Nirvana: A Story of Buddhist Psychology* (1897), *The Chief's Daughter: A Legend of Niagara* (1901), *The Crown of Thorns: A Story of the Time of Christ* (1901), and *Amitabha* (1906). He also translated from Latin the *Eros and Psyche* of Apuleius (1900), and from German the *Xenions* of Goethe and Schiller (1896) and Kant's

*Prolegomena to Any Future Metaphysics* (1902). He also edited and translated the Chinese texts of Lâo-tse's *Tao-Teh-King* (1898), *Kan Ying P'ien* (1906), and *Yin Chih Wen* (1906).

RAYMOND W. ALBRIGHT

**Carver, William Owen** (1868–1954). Baptist theologian. Born in Wilson County, Tenn., he studied at Boyle College, Tenn., Richmond College, Va., Southern Baptist Theological Seminary (Th.D., 1896), and in Europe. He was ordained to the Baptist ministry (1891) and served as a pastor (1889–1907). He was professor of philosophy and ancient languages at Boscobel College, Nashville, Tenn. (1893–95). He taught NT interpretation at Southern Baptist Theological Seminary (1896–1923) and was also professor of comparative religion and missions (1899–1943; retired 1943), acting professor (1947–48), and Norton Lecturer (1933–34, 1945–46). His works include *History of New Salem Church* (1903), *Baptist Opportunity* (1908), *Missions in the Plan of the Ages* (1909), *Missions and Modern Thought* (1910), *Acts Commentary* (1916), *All the World in All the Word* (1918), *The Bible a Missionary Message* (1921), *The Self-Interpretation of Jesus* (1926), *Thou, When Thou Prayest* (1928), *The Course of Christian Missions* (1932), *How the NT Came to Be Written* (1933), *The Rediscovery of the Spirit* (1934), *The Furtherance of the Gospel* (1935), *Sabbath Observance* (1940), *Christian Missions in Today's World* (1942), *If Two Agree* (1942), *Why They Wrote the NT* (1946), and *The Glory of God in the Christian Calling* (1949). He was managing editor of the *Review and Expositor* (1919–42), and contributing editor of *The Commission*.

WILLIAM A. MUELLER

**Case, Adelaide Teague** (1887–1948). Episcopalian educator. Born in St. Louis, Mo., she studied at Bryn Mawr and at Teachers College, Columbia (Ph.D., 1924), where she taught (1919–41). She was professor of Christian education at the Episcopal Theological School (1941–48). She wrote *Liberal Christianity and Religious Education* (1924), *As Modern Writers See Jesus* (1927), *Seven Psalms* (1935), and *The Servant of the Lord* (1940). She contributed to *Religion: The Dynamic of Education* (1929), *Our Children* (1932), *Liberal Catholicism and the Modern World* (1934), and *The Church Through Half a Century* (1936).

CHARLES L. TAYLOR

**Case, Shirley Jackson** (1872–1947). Baptist scholar. Born in Hatfield Point, New Brunswick, Canada, he was educated at Acadia University, Yale (Ph.D., 1906; D.D., 1917), and Marburg. He taught at academies in New Brunswick and New Hampshire (1893–97); was instructor in NT Greek at Yale (1905/6); was professor of the his-

tory and philosophy of religion at Bates College (1906–8); taught NT interpretation at the University of Chicago (1908–17); taught the history of early Christianity at the University of Chicago (1917–38); and was dean of the University of Chicago Divinity School (1933–38). After retirement from the University of Chicago he became professor of religion and dean of the School of Religion at Florida Southern College. A theological liberal, he made distinguished contributions in the field of the historical study of the NT and the history of the early church, particularly stressing environmental influences. Among his numerous books the most notable are *The Historicity of Jesus* (1912), *Evolution of Early Christianity* (1914), *The Millennial Hope* (1918), *The Revelation of John* (1919), *Social Origins of Christianity* (1923), *Jesus, A New Biography* (1927), *Experience of the Supernatural in Early Christian Times* (1929), *Jesus Through the Centuries* (1931), and *The Social Triumph of the Early Church* (1933). He edited the *American Journal of Theology* (1912–20) and the *Journal of Religion* (1927–39).

W. W. SWEET

**Cassells, William Wharton** (1858–1925). Missionary bishop. One of the "Cambridge Seven" who created something of a sensation when they volunteered for missionary service overseas in 1884, he was posted to Shansi by the China Inland Mission (CIM). Cassells subsequently settled in Szechwan, a western province of China with a population of 68 million which Hudson Taylor, a leader of the mission, decided to make a Church of England district. Cassells was consecrated first bishop of Szechwan by Archbishop Benson of Canterbury, with responsibility to give episcopal supervision both to the Church of England section of CIM and to the Church Missionary Society mission. The society guaranteed his stipend and he came on to their roll of missionaries, while fully retaining his position in CIM.

HAROLD H. ROWDON

**Castro, Emilio E.** (1927– ). Pastor, educator, and ecumenical leader. Born in Montevideo, Uruguay, he received his theological education at Union Theological Seminary in Buenos Aires and engaged in postgraduate studies at Basel, Switzerland (1953/54). He was a pastor of the Methodist Church in Uruguay and Bolivia, and taught theology at the Mennonite Seminary in Montevideo (1959–64). He was the coordinator of Commission Pro Evangelical Unity in Latin America (UNELAM) from 1965 to 1972. From 1973 to 1983 he served as director of the Commission on World Mission and Evangelism of WCC. In 1984 he obtained a doctorate from the University of Lausanne Theological School. He assumed the leadership of WCC in January 1985. His latest book is *Sent Free—Mission and Unity in* *the Perspective of the Kingdom* (1985). His main concern is that every program and service of WCC keep in mind the holistic nature of the gospel Christians preach and of the vocation they have. Liberation theology and evangelism must be kept together.

A. J. VAN DER BENT

## Catechisms, Roman Catholic.

The best-known catechisms in the Roman Catholic Church are the *Summa of Christian Doctrine* by Peter Canisius (1555) and the *Catechism of the Council of Trent* (1566). Numerous catechisms have been published since then authorized by the Roman Catholic hierarchy in each country (e.g., the *Penny Catechism* in Britain and the series of Baltimore Catechisms in the USA). Since the Second Vatican Council there have been further modern catechisms produced in Roman Catholic countries, but each has had to be approved by the Vatican. Now (1989) the Roman Catholic Church is waiting for an authoritative catechism being produced by the Vatican and to be authorized by the pope. This will then assume the position which the Catechism of the Council of Trent held for centuries.

PETER TOON

## Catholic.

Transliteration of the Greek term *katholikos*, meaning "general" or "throughout the whole." The phrase *hē katholikē ekklēsia* ("the catholic church") was first used by Christian writers to distinguish the entire body of believers from individual bodies. It then came naturally to designate the orthodox in distinction from heretics and schismatics. Later it was applied to faith, tradition, and doctrine; it was understood to express the universality of the church ("in Greek that is called 'catholic' which is spread through all the world" [Augustine, *Epist.* 52.1]); it distinguished a cathedral from parish churches, or the latter from oratories or monastic chapels. After the separation of the Greek and Latin churches, the epithet "catholic" was assumed by the latter, as "orthodox" was by the former. At the Reformation the term was claimed by the Church of Rome in opposition to the Protestant or Reformed churches; in England the national church was said to be the true catholic church of the land, and the expression "Roman Catholic" came into use for the sake of distinction. "Anglo-Catholic" was coined by analogy with this at the time of the Tractarian movement. On the Continent the single word "catholic" is the common designation for that branch of the church in affiliation with Rome. Protestants have generally interpreted the term to mean the entire communion of the saved at all times and in all places. The word "catholic" in the phrase "the holy catholic church" of the Apostles' Creed is explained by Pearson (*Exposition of the Creed*, art.

9) as indicating that the church is to be disseminated through all nations, extended to all places, and propagated to all ages; that it contains in it all necessary truths, exacts absolute obedience from all men to the commands of Christ, and furnishes us with all graces necessary to make us acceptable and our actions well-pleasing to God. The word was not in the earliest form of the creed.

## Catholic Action.

Any act conforming to the principles of the Roman Catholic Church. In a letter to Cardinal Betram of Breslau (Nov. 12, 1928), Pope Pius XI wrote:

> Catholic Action is a true apostolate in which Catholics of every social class participate, and thus come to group themselves, in thought and in work, around centers of sound doctrine and manifold social activity, legitimately constituted, and assisted and sustained accordingly by the authority of the bishops.

Catholic action can be understood in a wide or narrow sense. Catholic action in the wider sense involves an association or specific work of Catholics which is apostolic in scope and is approved by the proper ecclesiastical authority. For example, Catholics working on behalf of educational causes, for the stimulation of the fine arts, for a society on behalf of the Catholic press, or in an organization striving to improve public morals—these are all examples of Catholic action by the apostolate for the application of Catholic teaching to a wide scope of social endeavor.

Catholic action, in the more narrow sense, involves laypeople directly assisting the ecclesiastical hierarchy. Not only is this form of Catholic action carried out by the laity at the prompting of the hierarchy, but also under the direct supervision of the clergy. When endowed with these requisites Catholic action can call itself official in the sense that it is officially willed and recognized by the church.

Both in the wide and narrow senses, however, Catholic action constitutes apostolic activity of laypeople in conformity with the principles of the Catholic faith.

***Bibliography.*** L. Civardi, *A Manual of Catholic Action* (1943).

GILBERT L. ODDO

## Catholic Apostolic Church.

Religious movement which began in Scotland in 1830. It grew out of the conviction of a group of clergy and laypeople of the Church of England that the Lord could not return until spiritual preparation had been made in the church. They maintained that this could be effected only through the Spirit. The group also believed that God wanted to restore the ministry of the apostles; 12 men were designated as such through prophecy. Since the last "divinely called apostle" died in 1901, there have been no ordinations in this religious body which is popularly called Irvingite. On this account, as well as on account of the absence of missionary activity, there has been no growth. The U.S. religious census of 1936 reported seven congregations with 2577 members. The New Apostolic Church of North America, which claims to uphold the original teachings of the movement, is more vigorous.

*Bibliography.* P. E. Shaw, *The Catholic Apostolic Church, Sometimes Called Irvingite* (1946).

THEODORE TAPPERT

## Cavert, Samuel McCrea (1888–1976).

Presbyterian ecumenical leader. Born in Charlton, N.Y., and educated at Union College, Columbia University, and Union Theological Seminary in New York, Cavert joined the staff of the Federal Council of Churches and was elected general secretary in 1921. He served until 1950, when the Federal Council joined with other agencies to form the National Council of the Churches of Christ in the USA, of which he became the first general secretary. Cavert chaired the committee on arrangements for the first assembly of the World Council of Churches (WCC), held in Amsterdam in 1948. He served as executive secretary for the United States of WCC (1953–57). Cavert's more important books include *The Adventure of the Church* (1927) and *The American Churches in the Ecumenical Movement: 1900–1968* (1968).

R. MILTON WINTER

## Celibacy. *See* CHASTITY; CONTINENCE.

## Censorship.

Provision that no publication will be issued without examination and permission of ecclesiastical authorities. According to the actual discipline of the Roman Catholic Church, the following categories of books and periodicals are to be submitted to the judgment of ecclesiastical authorities before being printed: Bible texts and studies; devotional and theological books; books whose subject matter is formally related to religion and morals; devotional pictures; documents concerning procedures of beatification or canonization not yet terminated; lists of current indulgences; collections of decrees from the Roman Congregations; liturgical books; and versions and new editions of books already approved.

The responsibility of presenting such writings for examination rests with the author and publisher, not with the printer. The ordinary of the author or the bishop in whose diocese the publishing house or the printing shop is located, is generally competent in granting the imprimatur, by which permission is given to print the book submitted for approval.

Writings printed in violation of the above rules, as well as any books which are blasphemous,

obscene, or foster heresy, may not be read by unauthorized Roman Catholics, even though such books are not actually inscribed in the *Index Librorum Prohibitorum*, the catalog of books listed by the Congregation of the Holy Office as subversive of Christian faith and morals.

GEORGES A. BARROIS

## Censures.

Penalties inflicted on baptized Christians for sinful acts committed deliberately and with obstinacy against public order in the Roman Catholic Church. The purpose of such penalties is to vindicate the inviolability of Church laws and to induce delinquents to amend their ways. In order to achieve this goal, the transgressor is deprived of some spiritual privileges otherwise enjoyed by the faithful until he recants. These privileges include reception of the sacraments, participation in or attendance at the ceremonies of the church, any public ecclesiastical office or dignity, the reception of income from benefices, and the exercise of functions proper to ordained clerics. It is to be noted that censures and their absolution belong to the external order of the church, and are distinct from the administration of the sacrament of penance, which belongs to the *forum internum* or order of conscience.

Canon law recognizes two kinds of censures according to the manner in which they are inflicted. Some are individually notified following a judicial sentence, when a previous admonition has failed to elicit a favorable response from the guilty party (censures *ferendae sententiae*). Others are prescribed once and for all as prospective sanctions of specific infractions described by the Code of Canon Law, no admonition or sentence being necessary (censures *latae sententiae*).

Censures fall into three categories: (1) excommunication, by which individual transgressors are withdrawn from the communion of the faithful; (2) interdict, a collective penalty by which an entire group, while remaining in the communion of the church and still enjoying its essential ministrations, is deprived of the external pomp and solemnity with which the liturgical ceremonies are normally conducted; and (3) suspension, which deprives a cleric of his office or benefice, or both.

Although absolution from censures is an act of jurisdiction *in foro externo*, that is, of administrative concern, priests empowered to receive confessions may absolve penitents from ordinary censures. However, the authority competent *in foro externo* may demand proof that absolution was actually granted.

Special faculties are required to absolve from censures inflicted by decision of an ecclesiastical superior, also known as censures *ab homine*, and of censures "reserved" by law. The absolution from the former belongs to the one who inflicted the penalty, his delegate, or successor. Absolution from the latter is reserved to the ordinary or, in proportion to the offense, to the Holy See, "commonly," "specially," or "most specially."

A penitent in danger of death may be absolved by any priest. Should he recover, however, he is under strict obligation to notify within a month the authority which pronounced the sentence in the case of a censure *ab homine,* or, in the case of a censure *latae sententiae* reserved "most specially" to the Holy See, the Roman tribunal of the *Sacra Poenitentiaria.*

**Bibliography.** *Codex juris canonici,* canons 2241–85; F. M. Cappello, *Tractatus canonico-moralis de censuris* (1933); "Censura," *Enciclopedia Cattolica,* vol. 3 (1949).

GEORGES A. BARROIS

**Census.** Count of the population (especially males) and a property evaluation. It is generally admitted that a census, as described in Luke 2:1–3, may have taken place during Herod's reign; may have involved the return of everyone to his original home; and may have formed part of an empirewide enrollment.

Josephus states that toward the end of Herod's reign Augustus treated him as a subject rather than as a friend, and that all Judea took an oath of allegiance to Augustus and Herod (*Antiquities* 16.290; 17.42; cf. the census imposed in A.D. 36 on the client kingdom of Antiochus [Tacitus, *Annals* 6.41]).

A papyrus from A.D. 104 describes how the prefect of Egypt ordered Egyptians to return home so that the customary census by household might be carried out. Luke, then, "seems to have been recording a custom familiar in Judaea when he says that everyone was ordered to go to his own city" (F. G. Kenyon and H. I. Bell, *Greek Papyri in the British Museum* [1907], 3: 131).

There is scattered evidence of census activity in various parts of the empire between 11 and 8 B.C., the evidence for a census in Egypt in 10/9 B.C. being practically conclusive. Such a census by households may have been the first of a 14-year census cycle certainly attested from A.D. 33/34 on.

When Quirinius was legate of Syria (A.D. 6), he conducted a census in that province and also organized the census in Judea necessitated by its reduction to provincial status after the deposition of Archelaus (Josephus, *Antiquities* 17.355; 18.2). This latter census is referred to by Gamaliel in Acts 5:37. If the *titulus Tiburtinus* (*CIL* 14.3613) refers to Quirinius, then his legateship of Syria in A.D. 6 was his second tenure in office; whether his earlier legateship was in Syria or elsewhere is uncertain. But the identity of the official whose career is outlined in the *titulus Tiburtinus* is doubtful. Quirinius may have commanded the campaign against the Homanadensians (an unruly tribe in the Taurus region) as extraordinary legate of Syria between 12 and 6 B.C. But he more probably commanded the Homanadensian

campaign as legate of Galatia. Certainty must await further evidence. Any solutions which require alteration of basic texts are suspect. Some render Luke 2:2, "This census took place before that held when Quirinius was governor of Syria."

**Bibliography.** F. Bleekmann, *Klio* 17 (1921): 102–12; E. Groag, *Realencyclopaedia* 2/7 (1931): 822–43; A. G. Roos, *Mnemosyne* 3 (1941): 306–18; H. Braunert, *Historia* 6 (1957): 192–214; E. Stauffer, TU 77 (1961): 9–34; A. N. Sherwin-White, *Roman Society and Roman Law in the NT* (1963); A. Dupraz, *De l'association de Tibère au Principat à la naissance du Christ* (1966); G. Ogg, *ET* 79 (1967–68): 231–36; A. Schalit, *Koenig Herodes* (1969): 265–78; H. R. Moehring, *NovTSup* 33 (1972): 144–60; E. Schürer, *HJP* 1 (1973): 399–427; C. F. Evans, *JTS* n.s. 24 (1973): 24–39; I. H. Marshall, *Commentary on Luke* (1978).

F. F. BRUCE

**Center Party (Zentrumspartei).** The political voice of German Catholicism organized in 1871. The party's name came from the location of its deputes in the parliamentary seating plan. Its efforts were largely defensive in nature, because it saw its task to be that of safeguarding Catholic rights in a Protestant-dominated Reich, especially in the realms of education and public finance. All attempts to broaden its appeal to include non-Catholics were blocked by the party's leadership. Although adherents spanned the socioeconomic spectrum from industrial workers to landed gentry, it attracted the ballots of mainly middle- and upper-class voters and those in rural areas. After 1918, the Center accepted the new democracy of the Weimar Republic, showed increased concern for the working classes and social welfare issues, and entered into government coalitions, while at the same time it continued to uphold Catholic interests. It failed to resist Hitler's rise to power, and under Nazi pressures was dissolved in 1933. After World War II, old Center elements joined with some anti-Nazi Protestant conservatives to form the new Christian Democratic Union, an important political party in West Germany.

RICHARD V. PIERARD

**Certainty.** Quality or state of being certain. The Christian doctrine of religious certainty has its scriptural basis chiefly in Rom. 8:15–16 and Gal. 4:6, where it is said that the divine Spirit bears witness within the spirit of man. The NT often speaks of full assurance (see Col. 2:2; 1 Thess. 1:5; Heb. 6:11; 10:22). What is presented to us is not a rational certainty, but the certainty of encounter. It is more than knowing *what* we believe; we know *whom* we have believed (2 Tim. 1:12; 1 John 4:16). It is impossible for us by any observation or any thinking of our own to reach what God is and wills. We are thrown back on his own revelation. There are differences in the mode of conceiving the impact of this revelation.

Certainty is based on inner experience. This does not demand minimizing the value of Scripture or the church. Frank of Erlangen pointed to the convincingness of one particular inner experience, that of regeneration, which is beyond all questioning and free from all doubt (*System of Christian Certainty*). He did not, however, rest in that subjective experience, for the consciousness of being reborn leads to other certainties.

Certainty is based on some form of authority. Augustine (*Commentary on St. John's Gospel* 29.6) makes use of the principle contained in the Septuagint version of Isa. 7:9: "Unless you believe, you will not understand." At one point (*Contra epistolam Manichaei quam vocant fundamenti* 6) he even declares, "I would not believe the gospel unless the authority of the Catholic Church compelled me thereto." It should be noted, however, that Augustine was speaking in the heat of controversy and nowhere repeats this assertion; that "authority" here means "testimony"; and that, even if the sentence were taken at face value, it would still be necessary to inquire what the Catholic Church is. The truth in this doctrine of authority lies in the contention of Aquinas that God seldom makes use of direct assurance. There are some individuals who have passed beyond all doubt in their religious life; but it is also true that it is unusual, in many cases impossible, to have certainty in isolation from the fellowship of believers.

Certainty is based on Scripture and the Holy Spirit. Luther put the testimony of the Holy Spirit in the forefront of his teaching as guarantor of Scripture and guarantor of personal certainty. He thus challenged the church for seeking certainty in doctrine declared on authority to be infallible. No authority can do that; certainty can come only through a more than human source. Calvin developed the doctrine of the *testimonium Spiritus Sancti internum* in book 3 of the *Institutes*, anchoring the doctrine in election and God's hidden decree. Many Calvinists realize that there is the suggestion of a circular movement in the argument at this stage. Man cannot have assurance until he has assurance; there is in fact as much room for doubt and despair as in certain aspects of the Roman system. In both, men may rest in doubt rather than in assurance, in one case because there is ambiguity in our interpretation of the eternal divine decree, in the other because the final decision seems to lie in the power of the church.

The divine speech can become historically clear only in the existential situation; the voice of God can be heard only in sublime moments. But existential situations do arise; sublime moments do occur; and God does indicate when he is "making a special announcement." He may do so through special clarity in the soul, and we speak of vision; or through his prophets, and we look on them as inspired; or by the testimony of his church; or by his Word in Scripture speaking with inescapable force. The witness of the luminous moment will be found to coincide with the evidence received from sound authority and tradition, from the Bible, the church, and the Christian fellowship, and that coincidence will provide the highest form of religious conviction.

*Bibliography.* K. Heim, *Das Gewissheitsproblem* (1911); *Glaubensgewissheit* (1920); God Transcendent (1935); F. R. Tennant, *Philosophical Theology*, 2 vols. (1928–30); J. Dewey, *The Quest for Certainty* (1929); W. A. Brown, *Pathways to Certainty* (1930); E. P. Dickie, *Revelation and Response* (1938); E. Brunner, *Revelation and Reason* (1947); *Westminster Confession of Faith*, chap. 18.

E. P. DICKIE

## Chad. See WEST AFRICA.

## Chafer, Lewis Sperry (1871–1952).

Presbyterian evangelist and teacher. Born in Rock Creek, Ohio, he studied at New Lyme (Ohio) Academy and at Oberlin College. He also studied under Frank E. Fitch in Buffalo, N.Y. He was a traveling evangelist (1900–1914); an internationally known Bible teacher and lecturer (1914–24); founder, president, and professor of systematic theology at Dallas Theological Seminary from 1924; and editor of *Bibliotheca Sacra* from 1940. He wrote *Satan* (1909), *True Evangelism* (1911), *The Kingdom in History and Prophecy* (1915), *Salvation* (1916), *He That Is Spiritual* (1918), *Grace* (1922), *Major Bible Themes* (1926), *The Ephesian Letter* (1935), and *Systematic Theology* (8 vols., 1948).

## Chalmers, James (1841–1901).

London Missionary Society (LMS) missionary. Born in Ardrishaig, Argyleshire, Scotland, he was converted at the age of 14. After studying at Cheshunt College and Highgate, an LMS institution, he was sent by LMS to Raratonga, one of the Cook Islands in the southern Pacific (1867). The island had been partially Christianized, but he furthered the work of education and evangelization. In 1877 he went to New Guinea. He was later killed by natives.

*Bibliography.* J. Chalmers, *Pioneer Life and Work in New Guinea, 1877–1894* (1895); R. Lovett, *Autobiography and Letters* (1902).

## Chamberlain, Jacob (1835–1908).

Dutch Reformed missionary. Born in Sharon, Conn., he was educated at Western Reserve College, Reformed Theological Seminary, New Brunswick, N.J., and the College of Physicians and Surgeons, N.Y. In 1859 he went as a medical missionary to the Arcot Mission, Madras, and was stationed successively at Palmaner, Madras (1860–63), and Madanapalli, Madras (1863–1901). From 1891 he was lector in biblical languages and prophecy and acting principal of the Theological Seminary in the Arcot Mission, Palmaner. He was chairman of a committee for the translation of the Bible into Telugu (1873–94); member of the Telugu Revision Committee of the Madras Tract Society (1873–80); and in 1878 was elected vice-president of the American Tract Society for India. In 1901 he was first moderator of the South India United Church Synod. He was also engaged in literary work in Tamil and Telugu. He translated the liturgy of the Dutch Reformed Church into Telugu (1873), and also prepared a Telugu version of the *Hymns for Public and Social Worship* (1884), as well as other devotional works in the same language. His English works include *The Bible Tested* (1878), *Native Churches and Foreign Missionary Societies* (1879), *The Religions of the Orient* (1896), *In the Tiger Jungle* (1896), *The Cobra's Den, and Other Stories of Missionary Work among the Telugus of India* (1900), and *The Kingdom in India* (1908).

**Chambers, Oswald** (1874–1917). British Bible teacher. Born the son of a Baptist pastor in Aberdeen, Scotland, he became a Christian following a service conducted by C. H. Spurgeon, who earlier had greatly influenced his parents. While his early interests and studies were in art leading to distinction in fine art and archeology at Edinburgh University, he eventually entered the Dunoon Training College in 1897 to study for the ministry. While there he revealed outstanding gifts of faith, self-sacrifice, concern for the spiritual welfare of others, and prayer. Following visits to America and Japan he became a traveling missionary for the Pentecostal League of Prayer in 1909 before becoming principal (1911–15) of the Bible Training College founded at Clapham Common, London. In 1915 he became superintendent of the YMCA huts in Egypt, beginning an effective and lasting ministry among military personnel. His many books are largely notes of his Bible studies and talks, including the devotional classic *My Utmost for His Highest*.

JAMES TAYLOR

**Chancel.** In a church edifice the area beyond the nave and transepts reserved for the altar or communion table, the minister, and the choir. In Roman churches, it is often known as the sanctuary. The altar stands against the wall farthest from the congregation, and serves as the focal point of interest. A communion table, if in use, stands away from this wall, so that the minister can stand behind it and face the people. Except when ministering at the lectern or in the pulpit he sits near one of the side walls, so as not to turn his back toward the altar or table. For the same reason members of the choir sit in two sets of parallel pews facing each other, rather than the people. This arrangement emphasizes the worship of God, not the entertainment of an audience. Even in nonliturgical bodies the chancel arrangement is becoming common. In time it may practically supplant the central pulpit.

ANDREW W. BLACKWOOD

**Chantepie de la Saussaye, Pierre Daniel** (1848–1920). Dutch Protestant scholar. Born in Leeuwarden, the Netherlands, he studied at the University of Utrecht (D.D., 1878). After serving as a pastor of the Reformed Church (1872–78), he taught at the universities of Amsterdam and Leiden (1878–1916). He was a member of the Royal Academy of Sciences at Amsterdam. He wrote *Zekerheid en Twijfel* (1893) and *Religion of the Ancient Teutons* (1901). He is known chiefly for his *Lehrbuch der Religionsgeschichte*, published first in 1887–89. (The final edition was completely revised under the direction of A. Bertholet and E. Lehmann.)

GEORGES A. BARROIS

**Chaplain.** A minister who provides spiritual care in a secular setting. The most visible chaplains are those in the military services. Chaplains have become key members of hospital, hospice, and nursing care teams. Police departments rely on chaplains to deal with work stresses. Jail and prison chaplains counsel both inmates and staff. Industrial chaplaincies have been instituted at large plants. College campus ministries are chaplain-style works. Legislative chaplains serve in a largely ceremonial capacity.

Modern chaplains have tended to be ordained with specialized counseling training, commissioned by their denominations and the secular organization to which they are attached. This is the ideal, however, and chaplains may be unpaid volunteers, part-time employees, or lay counselors. The chaplain exists in an uncertain territory, caught between church and state. Military chaplains, for example, are commissioned staff officers, lacking command. By law they must provide for Christian and other religious worship; conduct marriages, baptisms, and funerals; hold prayer breakfasts; plan cultural activities; teach religious education and leadership development classes; and maintain a pastoral relationship to both active and retired military personnel. They also report on the state of morale to commanding officers. The work has unusual problems. A total of 134 USA chaplains died in combat in World War I and World War II, and another 16 in the Vietnam conflict. Particularly in Vietnam, chaplains complained of ministering to men who lived in hopeless and subhuman circumstances. Interpersonal conflicts with field commanders who did not understand their function were frequent. When they returned to their annual denominational meetings in the midst of the anti-Vietnam sentiment, many were booed and hissed for "prostituting their ordination" in the military.

Other types of chaplains experience similarly unusual conflicts. Prison chaplaincy is normally a primarily administrative position involving reports and arrangements for all sorts of activities and meetings. These staff often arrange psychological, spiritual, and vocational testing and treatment programs, leaving little time for personal pastoral contact. Administrations, however, found stable pastoral relationships important to avoiding difficulties among inmates, guards, and other staff in a highly stressful environment. From the 1930s, prison chaplains were no longer political appointees, and the quality of care increased radically. Still, finding qualified pastors willing and able to cope with the frustrations and low pay remained a serious problem. The perception of the ministerial work was also an issue. Prison staffs crave information often most available through counselors and chaplains, yet pastoral trust is particularly fragile there.

Industrial chaplains may be seen as management by workers and as labor pacification servants by management. Hospital chaplains often find themselves as liaisons between distraught patients and families and doctors who consider their efforts interference.

The most serious conflict remained between the military and federal prison chaplain and the U.S. Constitution. James Madison complained that a military chaplaincy was too close to establishing one faith over another to be acceptable. Legal challenges have been frequent since the 1840s over the establishment issue. In the 1870s a coalition of groups, the Liberal League, was formed expressly to end the military chaplaincy and other public religious symbols. The American Civil Liberties Union actively opposes the concept.

The programs have survived so many challenges because of a long-standing judicial doctrine that the government must hold in balance the establishment clause with the rights to free exercise of religious belief. In Elliott v. White (1928) it was explained that without chaplains free exercise would not be available to servicemen or to convicts. Judicial opinion was divided, though; in Engle v. Vitale (1962) Justice William O. Douglas wrote that in his opinion public chaplaincy was clearly as unconstitutional as the inscription, "In God we trust," on American coinage. In the school prayer decision, Abington v. Schempp (1963), the view was reaffirmed that there are individuals whose lives are so regulated by government that they could not voluntarily worship without government help. Theriault v. Silber (1977) and Katcoff and Wieder v. the Army (1979) reconsidered the issue for prisons and the military, respectively.

Some denominations do not participate in public chaplaincies for church-state reasons, and others are prepared to pay chaplains from church sources if required. Chaplaincies of all types reached both higher levels of competence and greater challenges in the late 1900s.

**Bibliography.** C. P. Lutz, *Christian Century* (Feb. 28, 1973); D. K. Pace, *A Christian's Guide to Effective Jail and Prison Min-* istries (1976); C. L. Greenwood and P. J. Weber, *Chaplaincy,* 4: 1/2 (1981); E. I. Swanson, *Chaplaincy,* 4: 4 (1981); J. S. Boozer, *Edge of Ministry . . . The Chaplain Story* (1984).

**Chapman, James Wilbur** (1859–1918). Presbyterian pastor and evangelist. Born in Richmond, Ind., he was educated at Lake Forest University and Lane Theological Seminary. He was pastor of the First Reformed Church, Albany, N.Y. (1883–88); pastor of Bethany Presbyterian Church, Philadelphia (1888–93); evangelist (1893–99); and pastor of the Fourth Presbyterian Church, New York City (1899–1903). He spent the last 15 years of his life as a representative-at-large for the Evangelistic Commission of the Presbyterian Church. His works include *Ivory Palaces of the King* (1893), *Received Ye the Holy Ghost?* (1894), *"And Peter"* (1895), *The Spiritual Life of the Sunday School* (1899), *Present-Day Parables* (1900), *Revivals and Missions* (1900), *Present-Day Evangelism* (1903), *Fishing for Men* (1904), *Samuel Hopkins Hadley of Water Street* (1906), *Another Mile* (1908), *The Lost Crown, The Secret of a Happy Day, The Surrendered Life, Chapman's Pocket Sermons* (1911), *Revival Sermons* (1911), and *When Home Is Heaven* (1917).

RAYMOND W. ALBRIGHT

**Charismatic Movement.** A Christian worldwide phenomenon whose distinctive stress on experience, action, and behavior contrasts with the traditional Western Protestant and Catholic emphases on teaching Scripture and administering the sacraments. Its common characteristics of baptism in the Spirit, speaking in tongues, direct revelations from God, and divine intervention in response to prayer for well-being (conversion, physical and emotional healing, exorcism, and deliverance from evil) have formed a distinctive common culture. This character is normally labeled "charismatic," although its leading exponents deplore the suggestion that the phenomenon is other than biblical and Christian.

The culture of the charismatic movement is enjoyed not only by charismatics who maintain or have had some link with historic churches, but also by millions of Christians whose charismatic churches have arisen in the 20th century on all continents. The precise expressions of charismatic convictions and ideals vary from country to country, denomination to denomination, and local church to local church.

***The Christian Charismatic Movement.*** From one standpoint, speaking in tongues sounds like gibberish; expecting divine intervention for healing or exorcism is magic; and "resting in the Spirit" (a swoon following prayer for divine intervention), "singing in the Spirit" (a musical sound in gatherings for worship reminiscent of medieval chant), and exuberant emotional cries of joy or wailing are typical of religious ecstasy. Such comparison has reinforced a widely held theory that no place has remained in Christian practice since the apostolic age for "signs and wonders" (Acts 14:3) such as healing or exorcism by direct (i.e., without clinical and medical procedure) divine intervention.

Several considerations counter such an assessment of charismatic behavior. First, the motive is Christ- or Jesus-centered. Charismatic worship is directed to the Trinity, not to God alone. Focus on the glory of God makes praise central to worship. The fatherhood of God justifies much of the concentration on human welfare in the exercise of gifts such as healing. The roles of Jesus as Savior, Lord, Baptizer in the Spirit, and coming King dominate the renewed evangelism, the heightened enthusiasm for and obedience to the biblical teaching of Jesus, the insistence that communication with Jesus is the object of baptism in the Spirit, and the world-denying expectation of the alternative Christian society with its stress on personal holiness and authoritarian community discipline.

Second, the movement has originated in historical Christian settings. In the USA and Europe contact between Christians in pentecostal churches and Christians from other churches accounts for the beginning of several charismatic ministries. For example, Cecil Cousen and Harold Horton from Great Britain, and David du Plessis with his contacts at the World Council of Churches and the Vatican, David Wilkerson via his book *The Cross and the Switchblade,* and Demos Shakarian, founder of the Full Gospel Businessmen's Fellowship International, all of the USA, came originally from pentecostal churches. In Latin America progress among pentecostal churches stimulated interest among Roman Catholics. Where people have received baptism in the Spirit from an informal source such as private prayer or Bible study, their identity as charismatics has been established by communion with like-minded people from neopentecostal groups. The common identity of charismatic with pentecostal means that the orthodoxy of the latter is regarded as a measure of the orthodoxy of the former.

Third, the theory that "signs and wonders" are no longer a legitimate expression of authentic Christianity is designed to protect the supreme authority of Scripture from claims to right doctrine emanating from other sources, such as direct revelation (claimed, e.g., by Muhammed or the Mormon Joseph Smith) or religious experience (claimed, e.g., by Spiritualists). By contrast, charismatics regard "miracles" as a ministry exercised on the authority of Scripture (1 Cor. 12:28), not as a ground for establishing the truth of the text. Finally, parallels between pagan and Christian behavior or teaching are not confined to charismatic practice.

***The Worldwide Charismatic Movement.*** The charismatic movement is not an institution. It has no formal gathering of official delegates as the pentecostal churches do. It has no general secretary or representative council. It is a popular culture more than a structured movement. But within countries, within church denominations, and within local church groups, charismatics gather for worship, teaching, and ministry. Some local churches are uniformly charismatic in culture, while others of mixed culture have charismatic elements. Because of the informal and eclectic adherence of Christians to charismatic culture it is impossible to offer an accurate numerical figure. For example, two independent sources estimated Roman Catholic charismatics worldwide in 1985 at 7.5 million and 20 million. One calculation in 1980 of charismatics worldwide in Catholic, Protestant, Orthodox, Anglican, and black churches was 11 million, 4.5 million of them in the USA. Independent indigenous churches whose culture contains charismatic elements were calculated at 82 million, the majority being in Africa and the USA (24.5 million and 21.4 million, respectively). Both groups are spread in Africa, North and South America, East and South Asia, Europe, Oceania, and the Soviet Union (Orthodox). Worldwide pentecostal denominations were calculated at 22 million.

The 11 million charismatics in the denominational churches sprang up within 20 years (c. 1960–80). North American and British Protestant charismatics appeared around 1960, and North American Catholic "pentecostals" in 1967, although pentecostal influence on Roman Catholics in South America occurred earlier. By Western standards this religious growth is rapid, but it does not compare with the speed of indigenous church development in Africa, North America, and South Asia.

***Common Characteristics.*** The central reality in the movement is baptism in the Spirit. Theoretically this baptism is independent of baptism by water and conversion/justification by faith and of the regeneration by the Spirit associated with them by Catholics and Protestants. Baptism in the Spirit is an experience received from God, often after prayer, the laying on of hands, and a period of waiting on God. Pentecostals teach that speaking in tongues is normal evidence of reception of this baptism. Some charismatics insist on this evidence, and various effects of reception are recognized:

1. Heightened sense of the presence of the risen and indwelling Christ, God the Father, and the Holy Spirit.
2. A more avid desire to spend time in prayer, to learn from Scripture, and to "hear God" in novel ways (receiving direct words, impressions, and pictures from God) in

order to build up personal Christian lifestyle, to develop community life, or even to address contemporary political and social issues.

3. Greater flexibility in relating to others, with fewer social inhibitions and often with more care for others and with greater participation in communal worship.
4. Praise of God in private and public worship, exercising the gift of tongues, singing in the Spirit, and expressing devotion with greater physical freedom in dance, colorful dress, novel church decor, and raising hands.
5. Keener personal evangelism and more trust in God's readiness to work in ministry to people at all levels (spiritual, physical, mental, emotional, social).

Charismatics committed to the priority of evangelism and ministry to people stress the need for the power which accompanies baptism in the Spirit.

The expected visible behavior of people baptized in the Spirit varies from group to group and even person to person. Insisting on particular expressions of authentic baptism in the Spirit centers on the interpretation and application of biblical texts on spiritual things/men (1 Cor. 12:1). Charismatics claim that baptism in the Spirit restores to the church or to the individual all the gifts listed by Paul and Peter (Rom. 12; 1 Cor. 12; Eph. 4; 1 Pet. 4) as well as others. Furthermore, the exercise of the listed gifts is regarded as distinctively supernatural, although a natural potential to exercise a particular gift might underlie the possession. Others, especially within the Catholic tradition, stress that gifts are given to the community and to individuals serving the community rather than to individuals per se. Some charismatic communities exist for the primary exercise of particular gifts, such as healing.

Critics of charismatic practice and teaching on baptism in the Spirit and on spiritual gifts point to several problematic areas. Does a Christian who has been baptized in the Spirit automatically reject Christians unfamiliar with this new experience or regard them as lacking an essential component of biblical Christianity? Does the effective exercise of spiritual gifts make redundant or demote to second-best the exercise of natural, trained talents? Since charlatans and magicians can deceive people into believing that they observe a change where there is either delusion or illusion, what assurance can charismatics give that their claims to new spiritual dimensions or to physical and other changes are not subject to self-deception and the unwitting deception of others?

No serious reply to such radical questions will convince an inquirer committed to debunking the movement. But certain considerations can tem-

per their force. First, Christian discipleship is necessarily progressive. Holiness teachers who insist on instant and complete personal change are proved false by the Pauline stress on gradual maturity, imperfection, and partial ignorance prior to the return of Christ (1 Cor. 13:10–12; Phil. 3:12). Christians may expect to differ on what they believe is essential to discipleship. Second, polarizing the effects of supernatural gifts and natural trained talents arises from an inadequate appropriation of the power of the Trinity. Creation undergirds natural talent; regeneration is the mainspring of supernatural gifts. Regeneration happens to created people, and the right exercise of every God-given element in life is a basic Pauline rule (1 Cor. 10:31). Paul is more concerned with the use to which gifts are put than with their origin (1 Cor. 14). Third, there is no guarantee against deception in any area of life where the human senses are at work. However, responsible charismatics are concerned to "test everything" (1 Thess. 5:21 RSV), to seek in ministers a concern for conversion to Christ, and to subject claims of healing to clinical medical examination. Sadly, irresponsible charismatics have sought to inflate the evidence of the senses or to attribute the absence of an observable response to lack of faith.

*Ecumenism.* In 1971 the Roman Catholic Secretariat for Promoting Christian Unity planned a series of dialogs on charismatic renewal with representatives of pentecostal churches and charismatics in Protestant, Orthodox, and Anglican churches. The first dialog was co-chaired by David du Plessis and Kilian McDonnell. In the 1970s several charismatics saw their movement as a means of healing denominational divisions. Underlying their hopes was the ease with which Protestant and Catholic charismatics worshiped and ministered together, especially in war-torn Ireland. The overtures of David du Plessis led to a mutual understanding between the World Council of Churches (WCC) and several pentecostal churches, and to "charismatic events" at WCC meetings. However, as the movement has progressed, charismatics have tended to strengthen their ties with their denominations. Others have left their churches to join new "restorationist" churches which hold that the recovery of spiritual life requires the foundation of new institutions, not the reform of existing ones.

*Bibliography.* D. J. du Plessis, *The Spirit Bade Me Go* (1970); W. J. Hollenweger, *The Pentecostals* (1972); K. McDonnell, *Charismatic Renewal and the Churches* (1976); R. Quebedeaux, *The New Charismatics: The Origin, Development and Significance of Neo-Pentecostalism* (1976); M. Harper, *Let My People Grow* (1977); R. Davis, *Locusts and Wild Honey* (1978); C. E. Hummel, *Fire in the Fireplace* (1978); E. Sullivan, *Baptized into Hope* (1980); K. McDonnell, *Presence, Power, Praise: Documents on the Charismatic Renewal*, 3 vols. (1980); D. Barrett, *World Christian Encyclopedia* (1982); A. Walker, *Restoring the Kingdom* (1982); D. Martin and P. Mullen, eds., *Strange Gifts: A Guide to Charismatic Renewal* (1984); P. Hocken, *Streams of Renewal* (1986).
GERVAIS ANGEL

**Charity, Christian.** Love of one's fellowman. While love comprehends the whole of the Christian's moral obligations (Rom. 13:9–10), charity is its manifestation toward one's neighbors. The Good Samaritan is both the model and source of real charity, and Christians show their fellowship with him by it (Matt. 9:13).

With the rise of Protestantism, the concept of Christian charity was subjected to reformulation and redirection. The Reformers sharply criticized the selfish motives which prompted much of the almsgiving in the medieval church (merit for penance, the gaining of heaven). They called for a recapture of the impulse of godly love which had prompted the early church to care not only for its own poor but for all broken and destitute people. Such teaching, combined with the unsettled state of affairs in the 16th century, led to a temporary disruption of charitable activities among Protestants. But in the next three centuries the Protestant ethic gradually created a fervent concern for physical and spiritual needs.

Protestantism, especially the Reformed tradition, influenced Christian charity in yet another way. It stimulated the ideal of Christianizing social, economic, and political institutions. It condemned any otherworldly attitude which encouraged complacent acceptance of non-Christian social practices and institutions. Everyone was encouraged to be self-supporting and thrifty, thus eliminating in large measure those people in society who previously had been the object of so much Christian charity.

As nations took shape, however, and as religious toleration grew and the line between the Christian church and secular society was sharpened, the conditions of Christian charity changed radically. Masses of physically and spiritually impoverished people mushroomed in the new industrial societies. The first reaction of Christians was to fall back on direct benevolence and charitable institutions, the latter updated to meet new problems. But the Protestant ideal gradually reasserted itself.

In the 19th and 20th centuries this ideal attempted to meet the needs of the industrial world in two ways. Some Christians attacked the non-Christian moral principles and social attitudes of the upper classes. The practical effect of this effort was to inspire the large-scale paternalistic philanthropy of industrial magnates. Other Christians, in terms of the so-called social gospel, attempted to transform the socioeconomic structure of society. With its optimistic faith in the possibility of a thoroughly Christian culture, this movement contributed to the gradual removal of charitable activities from the direct promotion and supervision of the church and the assumption of them by secular social organizations or governmental bureaus. This led in time to the cutting away of the peculiarly Christian foundations of charity and to their replacement by an empirical ethic guided by detached scientific objectivity.

As the optimism of liberal Christianity was shattered by war, the Great Depression, and ideological conflict with fascism and communism, a reborn Christian orthodoxy brought to bear on the needs of people a more complex and critical dialectical approach. Dialectical theology stressed the need of both an individual-spiritual and a sociostructural resolution of the evils which beset mankind, insisting at the same time that all resolutions will be relative and imperfect until God brings his kingdom in its fullness.

***Since 1955.*** After World War II the extent of social needs and privation around the world became a greater issue for Christians than it had been, yet the church had been replaced by government in Western Europe and North America as the dominant institution of response to suffering. Through ecumenical and parachurch organizations, Christians began, haltingly, to recover the thrust of relief work at home and abroad.

This effort was fragmented by differing social agendas which reflected Christianity's theological chasms. The attempts at charity can be divided into three sectors: (1) efforts growing out of world ecumenical dialog, which tended to be based on dialectical theology and had a Marxist philosophical bent; (2) evangelical parachurch and denominational organizations that followed the Salvation Army's model into widening areas of endeavor from the 1960s to 1980s; and (3) local, diaconal ministries, which enjoyed something of a resurgence as government backed off from its "war on poverty" in the late 1970s and 1980s.

In the third world those with needs were utterly dependent on government, community, or outside intervention. The African church, though, began to assume a social consciousness and maturity. In China, particularly during the persecution of the Cultural Revolution, the growing underground church was forced to meet its own needs and did so with great courage and sacrifice.

***Government Relief.*** Throughout the West the dramatic shift in benevolent care from church, community, and family to government was made necessary by the Great Depression in the USA and by the rise of totalitarianism in Europe. The social gospel movement, however, may be credited with riveting national attention on poverty in many countries, particularly industrial England and the USA. A 1903 census report found that one-third of all benevolent institutions in the USA were church-related. A 1940 study of urban life reported that 96 percent of all poor relief funds and 90 percent of health and welfare money came from government. New Deal legislation in the USA introduced minimum wage laws, Social Security, Aid to Families with Dependent Children (AFDC), workman's compensation, and unemployment insurance. In the private sector the United Fund intertwined Christian and secular efforts. Christians pressured at work to give to these community benevolent agencies lost control of what agencies and social causes would receive funds.

In 1964 U.S. President Lyndon Johnson made charity a government preoccupation in his declared "unconditional war on poverty." The Department of Health, Education and Welfare (HEW) began this crusade with a $2-billion budget. Eventually 100 programs were begun or expanded, including Medicare, Medicaid, Supplemental Security Income, and food stamps. By 1969 the budgeted HEW programs consumed 25 percent of the American GNP and employed one percent of the population.

Government impetus continued to the 1990s, but began to lose ground for various reasons. Public disenchantment with the incredible costs and resulting inflation was not helped by reports that both unemployment and the percent of dependent persons in poverty had drastically grown. A severe recession from 1978 to 1984 closed thousands of businesses, and put millions of Americans under public assistance. England was suffering from similar problems and a nearly bankrupt national economy.

*Christian Responses.* Roman Catholics and mainline Protestants were among, those most interested in social action and most supportive of government efforts. Church agencies working with government grants sprang up and tried desperately to fill social needs. In the USA black churchmen began to take leading roles made possible through their growing civil rights political power. Evangelicals continued to channel their efforts into Salvation Army and similar programs, which were far less visible. As a result the impression continued that conservative Christians were disinterested. This was more true after the fundamentalist-modernist controversy which publicized the liberal social agenda and distanced conservatives from the social ideas so identified with modernism.

Dialectical theology expressed itself through that modernist social agenda, as well as in the national and international councils of churches, ecumenical movements which participated heavily in charitable endeavors. Its ideas became more controversial when augmented by Marxist dialectics by liberation theologians who sought social and economic justice in Central and South America. The movement remained widely influential in the church, but its identification with communism, with revolution in Africa and the Americas, and with Mideast terrorism caused growing opposition.

The late 1900s' most striking developments, however, may have come from within the evangelical community, which developed a vocal social justice agenda of its own and organized a variety of local, parachurch, denominational, and interdenominational actions. Much of the impetus for this social consciousness started in the National Association of Evangelicals (NAE) and *Christianity Today* Magazine. Housing and urban renewal were pioneered by such groups as Habitat for Humanity and Voice of Calvary Ministries. Prison Fellowship made a national Christian issue of helping and evangelizing exploding inmate populations and criminal justice reform. The right-to-life movement spawned a multitude of organizations which not only fought abortion but aided impoverished families. Disaster and world hunger relief became major endeavors. Local churches developed word-deed ministries and diaconal need-response teams on an unprecedented scale.

Development of a biblical theology for dealing with poverty was a difficult challenge for Christians of various viewpoints. Liberation theologians J. B. Metz, Jürgen Moltmann, and Gustavo Gutiérrez worked through an intense "critical reflection on praxis" based in a sociological interpretation of biblical concepts. This model influenced black theology, feminists, and other social justice movements. Among a number of key influences on conservative thought were the books of Jacques Ellul and Francis and Franky Schaeffer. Specifically geared to framing an unabashedly biblical and practical response to poverty, George Grant's *Bringing in the Sheaves: Transforming Poverty into Productivity* (1985) set the stage for more study applying traditional concepts of Christian charity to new situations in a biblical way.

*Bibliography.* K. S. Latourette, *Three Centuries of Advance,* and *The Great Century* (1939); C. H. Hopkins, *The Rise of the Social Gospel in American Protestantism* (1940); J. C. Bennett, *Christian Ethics and Social Policy* (1946); C. F. H. Henry, *The Uneasy Conscience of Modern Fundamentalism* (1947), and *Aspects of Christian Social Ethics* (1964); D. O. Moberg, *The Church as a Social Institution* (2d ed., 1984); G. Grant, *Bringing in the Sheaves: Transforming Poverty into Productivity* (1985).

ARNOLD B. COME

## Charles, Robert Henry

**Charles, Robert Henry** (1855–1931). Irish biblical scholar and archdeacon of Westminster. Born in County Tyrone, he was educated at Queen's University, Belfast, and Trinity College, Dublin, and after ordination served curacies in London (1883–89). He then lectured in Dublin, London, and Oxford before appointment as canon of Westminster in 1913, later adding to this the post of archdeacon (1919–31). A master of biblical and cognate languages, he is probably best remembered as general editor of and substantial contributor to *The Apocrypha and Pseudepigrapha of the OT in English* (1913). In addition to work done for major encyclopedias and dictionaries he was editor or translator of texts in many languages. His own books include *Forgiveness and Other Sermons* (1886), *Critical History of the Doctrine of a Future Life in Israel, in Judaism, in Christianity* (1899), *Immortality* (1912), *Studies in the Apocalypse* (1913), *Religious Development Between the Old and the New Testaments* (1914), *A Critical and Exegetical Commentary on the Revelation of St. John* (1920), *The Teaching of the NT on Divorce* (1921), *The Decalogue* (1923), and *A Critical and Exegetical Commentary on the Book of Daniel* (1929).

**Charteris, Archibald Hamilton** (1835–1908). Church of Scotland minister and professor. Born in Wamphray, Dumfriesshire, he studied at Edinburgh, Tübingen, and Bonn. He was minister of St. Quivox, Ayrshire (1858–59), New Abbey, Dumfriesshire (1859–63), and The Park Parish, Edinburgh (1863–68). From 1868 to 1898 he was professor of biblical criticism at Edinburgh University. He was chairman of the general assembly's committee on Christian life and work (1869–94), and was instrumental in establishing the Young Men's Guild, the Women's Guild, and the Deaconesses' Hospital. He also revived the order of deaconesses as a part of the organization of the Church of Scotland. He was appointed a chaplain to the queen in 1869, and was moderator of the general assembly of the Church of Scotland in 1892. From 1901 to 1908 he was chaplain in ordinary to the king of Scotland. In theology he was a conservative. He wrote *Life of Professor James Robertson* (1863), *Canonicity: A Collection of Early Testimonies to the Canonical Books of the NT* (1880), *The NT Scriptures* (1888), and *The Church of Christ* (1905).

**Chastity.** Self-imposed regulation of the thoughts and actions of human sexual expression. Within Christian ethics chastity might be more exactly defined as refraining from sexual behavior and thoughts forbidden by Scripture and affirming the sexual relationship and attitudes acceptable to God.

In Roman Catholic usage chastity is a synonym for continence—complete abstinence form sexual intercourse. The "vow of chastity" negatively renounces marriage and sexual intercourse and positively sets the person apart for single-minded service to Christ. Under John Paul II considerable pressure was exerted to drop chastity as a clerical vow in order to increase the number of men and women choosing vocations, to stem the trend of priests and nuns leaving their vows for marriage, and to conform church practice to post-Vatican II openness. In the 1980s widowed persons were for the first time in modern history accepted for ordination, but the vow of chastity was deemed inviolable by John Paul and other conservatives.

In its more general ethical sense both the term and concept of chastity seemed in danger of extinction. Christians have often been pulled between the philosophies of hedonism of surrounding culture and desires for godly discipline or inner asceticism. Ascetic celibacy is usually based on two NT warrants, Jesus' saying that some "renounced marriage because of the kingdom of heaven" (Matt. 19:12), and Paul's saying that "it is good for a man not to marry" (1 Cor. 7:1). Philosophically the idea of continence conveys a dualistic view of the spiritual as holy and physical life as base. This dualism has been attributed to Paul, yet his constant interchange of the words *sarx* (flesh) and *sōma* (the whole person) suggest that he maintained that the flesh is not inherently evil but only subject to temptation (see Rom. 7:22). Ascetic chastity also emphasizes Jesus' demand for self-denial, forsaking life in the interest of shouldering the cross (as in Matt. 16:24–26).

Martin Luther set out a dramatic reinterpretation of Scripture and Christian ethics by doing away with the double morality between the "religious" and the laity. He exhorted all Christians to observe chastity while leaving continence to an individual's sense of vocation. Various Protestant ascetic groups (e.g., the 19th-century Rappites and Shakers) practiced continence, but without children growth had to come from conversion, and the groups faded as founders died.

The historical Christian ideal of chastity is continence outside marriage and fidelity within a heterosexual marriage covenant. The Christian is to keep self-control in deed (1 Cor. 6:15), word (Eph. 5:3, 12), and thought (Matt. 5:28). Christian ethical chastity also sets apart the body as a dwelling place for God's Holy Spirit destined for God's presence (1 Cor. 6:12–20). Chastity observes a sanctity of God's creation purpose for male and female (Gen. 2:20–25). It respects other persons as fellow image-bearers instead of as objects useful to gratify desires (Eph. 5:1–2). It lifts humanity above the meaninglessness of assuaging the appetite (Gal. 5:16–26). Ultimately a chaste life recognizes the right of a Creator to set standards of conduct for those created and redeemed (Eph. 2:10).

Twentieth-century Christians struggled to apply such principles. The signal collapse of standards in Western sexual ethics followed World War I. Outward Victorian and liberal Christian morality gave way to rootless search for freedom in the 1920s. In this generation's children of the 1960s the attempt was made to sweep away all moral codes. The most significant Christian trend away from code ethics was engineered by Joseph P. Fletcher in a 1959 address at Harvard Divinity School. Fletcher's "situation ethics" tied ethical decision making to the subjective, relative standard of love rather than to fixed referents of codes, applying John Dewey's philosophy of pragmatism to Christian morality. The act which is thought to best bring love to a particular situation or context is the absolute morality. The Christian church through the early 1990s debated whether a true sexual standard could any longer be applied. Tolerance of adultery, homosexuality, and other behaviors not traditionally accepted as Christian was a serious issue in the lives of clergy as well as laity. Those groups that sought to apply relativism found themselves swept along with a society of no rules, unable to proclaim an objective ground for chastity. Chastity and monogamy regained some popularity as a utilitarian response to the AIDS crisis, but no moral code based on Scripture was widely accepted, except by those who maintained the integrity of the Bible.

*See also* CONTINENCE.

**Bibliography.** O. Hardman, *The Ideal of Asceticism* (1924); W. E. H. Lecky, *The History of European Morals*, 2 vols. (1927); C. F. H. Henry, *Christian Personal Ethics* (1957); J. P. Fletcher, *Situation Ethics: The New Morality* (1966); C. F. H. Henry, ed., *Baker's Dictionary of Christian Ethics* (1973); P. E. Hughes, *Christian Ethics in Secular Society* (1983).

JOSEPH FLETCHER

**Chautauqua Movement.** Movement which originated at the summer camp meeting grounds at Lake Chautauqua, N.Y., in 1874, and developed into a summer educational institution.

The Chautauqua idea was actually an adaptation of the camp meetings of the American frontier. Its purpose was to combine religious education for adults with outdoor recreation. The plan was devised by Lewis Miller of Akron, Ohio, and John H. Vincent of New York, a Methodist minister. Chautauqua soon became an established institution. As early as 1875 the study of Hebrew was introduced, and this augured the development of a fairly complete offering of liberal arts and biblical subjects. However, the immediate result was the establishment of a school of biblical languages under the leadership of William Rainey Harper.

In 1902 the charter of the institution was changed to allow it "to promote the intellectual, social, physical, moral and religious welfare of the people." As a result, the original evangelical character of the institution was replaced by a more openly cultural and secular tone. The movement proved to be very popular and by 1900 had spread to nearly every section of the country.

C. GREGG SINGER

**Cheney, Charles Edward** (1836–1916). Reformed Episcopal bishop. Born in Canandaigua, N.Y., he was educated at Hobart College and at the Protestant Episcopal Theological Seminary, Alexandria, Va., from which he graduated in 1859. He was ordered deacon in 1856 and ordained priest two years later. After serving as curate of St. Luke's, Rochester, N.Y. (1858/59), and of St. Paul's, Havana, N.Y. (1859/60), he became rector of Christ Church, Chicago, in 1860. His pronounced evangelicalism, however, caused him to be tried by Bishop Whitehouse, although the verdict was overruled by the civil courts. His church, nevertheless, seceded from the Protestant Episcopal communion, and in 1873, upon the organization of the Reformed Episcopal Church, he was elected first bishop, still retaining his rectorate. His jurisdiction was changed in 1878 from the Northwest to the Synod of Chicago, and in 1905 he served as president of the Synod of Reformed Episcopal Churches of the Central States. While in the Protestant Episcopal Church he was, naturally, an adherent of the pronounced Low-church party, and described himself as "believing heartily in the great fundamental principles held by all *evangelical* Christians," and as "totally opposed to all that leans toward any compromise with Romanism, and equally opposed to the radicalism involved in the destructive criticism of God's Word." He wrote *Twenty-Eight Sermons* (1880), *A Word to Old-Fashioned Episcopalians* (1884), *What Is the Reformed Episcopal Church?* (1885), *What Do Reformed Episcopalians Believe?* (1888), *The Enlistment of the Christian Soldier* (1893), *A King of France Unnamed in History* (1903), and *The Second Norman Conquest of England* (1907).

**Chesterton, Gilbert Keith** (1874–1936). Born in London, he studied at Saint Paul's School and audited university courses in journalism. He was converted to Roman Catholicism in 1922. He maintained that the church (i.e., the Roman Catholic Church) is the only institution in which true humanism can develop. He wrote *Orthodoxy* (1908), *Tremendous Trifles* (1909), *Fancies versus Fads* (1923), *The Thing: Why I Am a Catholic* (1929), *Resurrection of Rome* (1930), and *The Well and the Shallows* (1935). He also wrote monographs: *Robert Browning* (1903), *Charles Dickens* (1905), *George Bernard Shaw* (1909), *Saint Francis of Assisi* (1923), *Chaucer* (1932), and *Saint Thomas Aquinas* (1933). His autobiography was published in 1936.

**Bibliography.** H. Belloc, *The Place of Chesterton in English Literature* (1937); M. Ward, *Gilbert Keith Chesterton* (1944); D. Attwater, *Modern Christian Revolutionaries* (1947); D. Barker, *G. K. Chesterton* (1973).

GEORGES A. BARROIS

**Cheyne, Thomas Kelly** (1841–1915). Church of England theologian. Born in London, he studied at Worcester College, Oxford, and at the University of Göttingen. He was ordered deacon in 1864, and ordained priest in the following year. From 1868 to 1882 he was fellow of Balliol College, Oxford, in addition to being a college lecturer on Hebrew and divinity in the same college from 1870 to 1871. He became rector of Tendring, Essex (1880–85), was Oriel professor of the interpretation of Scripture, Oxford (1885–1908), and became canon of Rochester (1885). He was a member of the OT Revision Company (1884), Bampton Lecturer (1889), and American Lecturer on the History of Religions (1897/98). He was one of the leaders of the higher criticism of the Bible in the English-speaking world. His independent works include, in addition to numerous contributions to standard works of reference and to theological periodicals, *Notes and Criticisms on the Hebrew Text of Isaiah* (1868), *The Prophecies of Isaiah* (2 vols., 1880/81), *Micah* (1882) and *Hosea* (1884) in *The Cambridge Bible, Jeremiah* in *The Pulpit Commentary* (1883/84), *The Book of Psalms, A New Translation* (1884), *Job and Solomon* (1887), *Jeremiah, His Life and Times* (1888), *The Origin and Religious Contents of the Psalter* (1891, the Bampton Lectures for 1889), *Aids to the Devout Study of Criticism* (1892), *Founders of OT Criticism* (1893), *Introduction to the Book of Isaiah* (1895), *Book of Isaiah* (critical text and translation) in the Polychrome Bible (2 vols., 1898/99), *Jewish Religious Life after the Exile* (1898, American Lectures on the History of Religions for 1897/98), *The Christian Use of the Psalms* (1899), *Critica Biblica* (1904), *Bible Problems and the New Materials for Their Solution* (1904), and *Traditions and Beliefs of Ancient Israel* (1907). He also wrote *The Book of Isaiah Chronologically Arranged* (1870) in collaboration with S. R. Driver. He coedited the *Encyclopaedia Biblica* with J. S. Black (4 vols., 1899–1903).

## Chicago School of Theology.

Dominant set of theological perspectives at the divinity school of the University of Chicago from the turn of the century to the mid-1960s. While showing considerable diversity, the theologians of the Chicago School shared some common commitments. First, they were committed to modernism. Modernism was the view that the values of modern democratic culture were consonant with Christianity and had cosmic sanction. The members of the Chicago School, usually but not always, called this cosmic support "God." An exception was George Burman Foster who, at the turn of the century, struggled with the meaning of the "death of God" for Christianity. Second, the Chicago School accepted the historical-critical method of studying the Bible, the origins of Christianity, and the development of Christian doctrine. Shirley Jackson Case and Shailer Mathews represented this emphasis. Third, most members of the Chicago School used some type of empirical philosophy as a tool for stating the Christian faith. In the earlier decades, they typically appealed to pragmatism. In 1927 Henry Nelson Wieman joined the faculty and championed the use of process philosophy as developed by Alfred North Whitehead. While Wieman's own orientation later shifted away from Whitehead, the use of process philosophy became common at Chicago.

The very course of history in the 20th century deeply challenged the modernist basis of the Chicago School. The two World Wars and the Great Depression made it difficult to believe that the progressive values of Western culture were somehow divinely—or at least cosmically—sanctioned. Theologically this skepticism was represented by the neo-orthodox movement. In the 1960s, new faculty, with a wider range of theological methods, were appointed to the University of Chicago Divinity School. This may be taken as the end of the Chicago School. Its influence is still widely felt, however, particularly in the contemporary movement of process theology.

*Bibliography.* C. H. Arnold, *Near the Edge of Battle* (1966); B. E. Meland, ed., *The Future of Empirical Theology* (1969); W. Hynes, *Shirley Jackson Case and the Chicago School* (1981).

STEPHEN T. FRANKLIN

## Children at Worship.

Since worship is largely a matter of habit, church leaders have devised three ways of promoting the church attendance of boys and girls. A separate children's church seldom proves satisfactory. A children's sermon is good, especially when children remain for the entire service. Family worship offers something for children during each part of the service. The last suggestion is the best; adults gain much from public worship when it appeals to children.

The character of a child's worship depends largely on the adults with whom he lives and the children with whom he mingles. Both at home and in church school adults should teach children to follow the forms of the church to which their parents belong. Early in life children should be taught to revere the church and its ways of worship. Inner character should be nurtured so that children will express themselves in song and prayer, in contemplation of things holy, and in silence. Under skillful leadership and in the presence of others, children can learn by participating actively in the public worship of God. Such an approach assumes that both the individual and the group can best grow in the Christian life as they are led to express their thoughts and feelings in acts of worship. While the ecclesiastical approach has its place, the main reliance must be on experience, as children respond to the leadings of the Holy Spirit.

Teachers, parents, pastors, and other leaders find that as children advance into the teen-age years this experiential approach helps them to become more firmly rooted. Instead of withering, their personal and corporate devotional lives tend to flourish. But the beginnings must come early in life. At home small children should learn to worship as members of the family, with appropriate songs, readings, prayers, and confessions of faith. The end result will depend on whether the growing child has become a Christian. Has he learned to know God in Christ for himself, or merely learned to follow forms of worship? Like Samuel, every child needs to discover God. Then forms will begin to have meaning.

*See also* CHILDREN'S WORK.

EDITH LOVELL THOMAS

**Children's Work.** Ever since biblical times the chief factor in Christian education has been the home. At the time of the Reformation the Bible became the chief authority. This emphasis continued in colonial America. Between 1787 and 1847, however, there was a gradual withdrawal of religious materials from public school curricula, so that the teaching of religion became increasingly the responsibility of the church. Between 1790 and 1815, teaching in the Sunday school centered in the catechism; many contemporary churches still stress this. By the second decade of the 19th century emphasis had shifted to Bible study. Children memorized large portions of Scripture, which were recited each Sunday with little supervision; prizes were the chief incentive. Selections of biblical passages were made with little regard to the capabilities of the children. By the third quarter of the 19th century some attention was given to their capacities, but unfortunately the same passages were used for all ages. Such uniform lessons continued until 1910, when closely graded lessons were introduced. Later, group-graded lessons were used. Many children are still being taught uniform lessons.

Many graded lesson materials are biblical. They tend toward moralizing and the "trait theory" of teaching. Weekday religious classes are generally biblical. Yet Bible stories have often been used with little sensitivity to children's limited knowledge, and verbalization has often been confused with education. More recent pioneers have stressed building proper foundations for later religious education in early childhood. Young children are guided to think religiously in terms of their own world and experiences. Meanings and motives are regarded as more important than verbalization of adult ideas. Christian conceptions of God are fostered in connection with the child's actual experiences with persons, the church, and the world. More direct Bible study can begin some time after the third grade, when children are becoming conversant with geography, time, and foreign affairs. Such courses usually begin with the NT and are taught in long units, to provide an understanding of Jesus as a real person in his own world. Vivid experiences are provided and questions are encouraged so that children gain more knowledge and better understanding. In teaching older children, attention is given to different cultural and racial groups, the local church and other churches in the community, and creation, the universe, life

and death, and the practice of prayer and worship. The practice of Christian living precedes the theoretical teaching of a faith. Thus prepared, adolescents seem more ready to progress through courses in Bible, church history, worship, Christian vocation, and other practical subjects involving Christian service.

*See also* CHILDREN AT WORSHIP.

EDNA M. BAXTER

**Chile.** Officially called the Republic of Chile, it is a country on the southwestern coast of South America with an area of 756,945 sq. km. (292,258 sq. mi.) and a population of 12.5 million (1987 est.).

Roman Catholicism was the official state religion until 1925, when a new constitution provided for the separation of church and state. Before that time, the church had allied itself with a series of conservative governments to protect its privileged position. Despite the formal separation of church and state in 1925, succeeding governments did not attempt to restrict the church's activities.

Since the 1960s the Chilean church has been at the forefront of the renewal within the Latin American church as a whole. As early as 1961 the hierarchy drafted a national pastoral plan calling for greater lay participation. In 1962 the bishops published two important pastoral letters discussing socioeconomic problems in the country. The hierarchy's reformist position during the 1960s coincided with the growing ascendancy of the Christian Democratic party which gained power in 1964. During the leftist Popular Unity government of Salvador Allende (1970–73) progressive clergy and religious leaders became increasingly influential within the church. In 1971 they launched the Christians for Socialism movement which spread to many other Latin American countries. The Allende period was marked by a highly fruitful dialog between Marxists and Christians and the willingness of a substantial number of priests to collaborate with the government. By 1973, however, the increasing political polarization had spilled over into the church, leaving the clergy sharply divided over the military coup that year.

As the repressive nature of the Pinochet dictatorship became apparent, the church assumed an increasingly critical attitude toward the government. Cardinal Raul Silva, the archbishop of Santiago, was particularly outspoken in his criticisms of the regime. He founded the Vicariate of Solidarity in 1976, which provided legal and humanitarian assistance to victims of repression and their families. In 1985 Cardinal Fresno, Silva's successor, was instrumental in bringing together the various opposition parties to sign a National Accord, calling for the restoration of democracy.

Like the Catholics, Protestants are divided regarding the Pinochet dictatorship. While some conservative pentecostal churches have provided the government with a degree of religious legitimacy, a number of Protestant churches have been highly critical of government repression. Since the arrival of the first Protestant missionary in 1821, the number of Protestants has grown rapidly. While Roman Catholicism still claims some 80 percent of the population, by 1984 pentecostals accounted for 16.5 percent, as compared to nonpentecostal Protestants who constituted 2 percent of the population.

*Bibliography.* B. Smith, *The Church and Politics in Chile* (1982); T. Beeson and J. Pearce, *A Vision of Hope* (1984).

PHILIP J. WILLIAMS

**China.** China has a population of 1.1 billion and a land mass of 9,560,940 sq. km. (3,691,500 sq. mi.). China's recorded history dates back to about 1700 B.C. Since 1949 the People's Republic of China has been ruled by the Chinese Communist party.

***Christianity in Chinese History.*** Christianity first came to China through Nestorian missionaries from the Middle East in A.D. 635. After 210 years of propagation, Nestorian Christianity was practically wiped out during the anti-Buddhist persecution of 845 in the Tang Dynasty (618–905). The Nestorian Tablet, erected in A.D. 781 and now on display at the Forest of Tablets in Xian, bears testimony to their missionary efforts.

Nestorian Christians returned to China as scribes and teachers during the Yuan Dynasty (1279–1368), when China was under Mongol rule. During that time Catholic missionaries were sent to the Mongol capital Cambaluc (today's Beijing). Franciscan missionary John of Montecorvino (1247–1328) spent 30 years ministering in the Yuan capital. He tried to establish a native clergy by training orphan children, but without much success.

The third attempt to evangelize China came during the late Ming Dynasty (1368–1644), beginning with the Jesuit Francis Xavier. Forbidden to set foot on Chinese soil, Xavier could only visit Portuguese trading posts like Macau. Faced with a wall of resistance, Xavier died on Shangchuan Island near Macau in 1552.

Xavier's noble example was not forgotten. The Jesuits continued to send missionaries to China. The most successful was Father Matteo Ricci (1552–1610), who first reached China in 1582 and, with much patience and prudence after 18 years of intensive labor and bridge building, was able to find a warm reception in Peking in the year 1601. Before his death in 1610, Ricci had established a good basis for subsequent mission work. Ricci won the respect of the Chinese officials through his friendship and his contribution of Western scientific learning to the Chinese court.

Ricci was followed by a succession of able Jesuit scientists and philosophers, the most distinguished being Father Jean Adam Schall von Bell (1591–1666) of Germany. The Kangxi emperor, of the Qing Dynasty (1644–1912), was tutored by Jesuit fathers and almost became a second Constantine.

However, the Jesuits were not able to continue their missionary approach to the Chinese people by way of accommodation. The arrival of the Franciscans and of the Dominicans brought about an internal conflict over the issue of ancestor worship, known as the "Rites Controversy." It developed into a conflict of authority between the Chinese emperor and the pope. This conflict was exacerbated to the point where an imperial edict was issued in 1724 expelling all Catholic missionaries, Dominicans and Franciscans as well as Jesuits, from China, leaving only a few Jesuit scientists in the court of Peking serving as astronomers. What followed was a century of sporadic state persecution against Catholic Christianity, continuing until 1860. Believers were pressured to recant, and propagators of the faith were punishable by strangulation.

The arrival of Robert Morrison of the London Missionary Society (LMS) in 1807 marked the beginning of the fourth missionary attempt. Morrison worked with great dedication as a student of the Chinese language, Bible translator, and scholar of Chinese culture. By the time he died in 1834, he had produced a dictionary of the Chinese language and a full translation of the Bible. Other missionaries from LMS followed in Morrison's footsteps and engaged in language study and literature distribution prior to China's opening to the outside world.

Western colonial pressure forced China to open her doors to the West and hence to the gospel. Between 1839 and 1842 the British fought against China when the latter refused to allow the import of opium. In 1842 China was forced to sign the Treaty of Nanking by which Hong Kong was ceded to Britain, and China opened five ports to foreign trade. They were Shanghai, Ningbo, Fuzhou, Xiamen, and Guangzhou.

With the opening of these five ports to foreign residence, missionaries such as William Lockhart of LMS, Elijah C. Bridgman of the American Board of Missionaries for Foreign Missions, William Martin of the Presbyterians in North America, William C. Burns (Scottish) of the English Presbyterian Mission, and, of course, Hudson Taylor began to establish themselves there. Missionaries began to evangelize the Chinese people and build churches. Although Chinese law forbade missionaries to leave the treaty ports, nevertheless during those years they made frequent itinerant trips to the inland villages as scouts for the gospel.

When China lost the Second Opium War in 1858, she was forced to sign the Treaty of Tianjin which was ratified in 1860. In this treaty there was a "toleration clause" that granted foreign missionaries the right to propagate the Christian faith in China and the right for the Chinese people to believe in the Christian religion. Foreigners were also granted the right to travel in China with a passport. Thus missionaries began to move into China's interior.

***Development of Protestant Missions in Modern China.*** During the early years of penetration (1860–70), there were numerous antimissionary riots as missionaries sought to establish themselves in the interior. In 1865 Hudson Taylor, who had first gone to China in 1854, founded the China Inland Mission and began to appeal for a thousand missionaries to go into the Chinese interior. From 1865 to 1895 China witnessed the first wave of frontier missionary advance. Missions that had bases in the five ports had a head start, establishing themselves in the major cities of north, central, and southeast China.

The method of evangelism established by missionaries in the treaty ports was applied to work expanded into the interior of China and followed by missions that came to China subsequently. Basically, they developed a threefold approach to mission work: medical, educational, and evangelistic. Nearly every mission established clinics that grew into hospitals as a means of evangelistic contact. They established primary schools for children of converts, and these schools later developed into high schools and eventually into 13 Christian universities. Their evangelistic work concentrated on street preaching and the establishment of gospel halls that grew into churches in the villages as well as in the cities. This form of mission work continued right up until 1949.

The period of 1895–1912 was a period of political and cultural disintegration for China. The disintegration stemmed from China's humiliation when she lost a war with Japan in 1895. This triggered a reform movement in 1898, an attempt at political institutional reform that lasted 100 days. The disintegration also stemmed from the pressure of foreign powers to partition China by increased demands for more foreign concessions in the major cities. The anti-Manchu and antiforeign Boxer uprising, which resulted in the deaths of nearly 200 missionaries and over 2000 Chinese Christians in North China, and the abolition of the traditional examination system in 1905 all contributed to disintegration.

***The Rise of the Church in the Republic of China.*** In 1911 the Qing Dynasty was toppled by Sun Yat-sen's democratic revolution. A republic was officially founded the following year, bringing to an end two millennia of monarchal rule. How-ever, the new republic was not strong enough at first to deal with the anarchy in the country. Various warlords competed for power in China during 1916–28.

Nevertheless, the spirit of independence contributed to the rise of a Chinese independent church movement in north, east, and southern China, the beginning of a later Chinese indigenous church movement. After the civil service examination system was abolished young students began studying abroad, and when they returned to China they started a new thought movement.

On May 4, 1919, Chinese students staged a huge anti-Japanese demonstration in Beijing against the international injustice meted out to China in the Treaty of Versailles in France. This demonstration has since come to be known as the beginning of the Chinese intellectual revolution in modern China. Continued interest in political and cultural reform extended the initial intellectuals' and the students' patriotic movement into a New Culture movement during the period of 1920–22. They believed that only science and democracy could save China.

In their acclaim of science, the young intellectuals denounced traditional Chinese culture and beliefs, rejecting also all religions, including Christianity, as superstitious. An anti-Christian movement broke out in March 1922 when delegates to Lenin's Moscow conference for Far Eastern Toilers (Jan. 1922) returned to China and began to attack the World Student Christian Federation's international conference, which was to meet in Qinhua University in April 1922. This anti-Christian movement was later revived and spread throughout China with great intensity and directness of attack during the years of collaboration between the Kuomintang and Chinese Communist party (1924–27). Christianity was attacked as the cultural arm of Western imperialism. The church also came under severe attack. In response, many churches separated themselves from foreign missions, and began to establish independent churches. Chinese church leaders engaged themselves in a long debate on how to create Chinese indigenous churches.

During the Northern Expedition (1926/27) led by Chiang Kai-shek, the revolutionary army was preceded by anti-Christian propaganda spread by the Communists. They attacked churches and forced some pastors to parade through the streets. In March 1927 nearly all of the 6000 Protestant missionaries had to evacuate from the interior to find refuge in the treaty ports or flee to the Philippines and Japan. Christians became timid and confused. Anti-Christian propaganda did not cease until after the split between the Kuomintang and the Communists in April 1927 when the latter were driven underground.

After the pacification of China in June 1928, Chiang Kai-shek imposed a military peace on the country, establishing his capital in Nanjing, and for 10 years he worked to reconstruct the economy. During this decade the church enjoyed a breathing space as the Nanjing government adopted a friendlier attitude toward Christianity. The National Christian Council launched a five-year plan (1929–34) to stimulate evangelism and to revive the spirit of shaken believers. The 1930s also witnessed the rise of Chinese indigenous evangelists such as Wang Mingdao, John Sung, and Watchman Nee, who all contributed significantly to the revival movement of that decade.

When the Japanese invaded China in 1937, the life of the nation and of the church was once again thrown into turmoil. Missionaries had to evacuate, Christian institutions had to relocate, and believers suffered much. However, in spite of the suffering during the war years, the number of believers did not decrease. In fact it had grown from 560,000 in 1936 to nearly 700,000 in 1945.

In less than a year following the Japanese surrender, civil war between the Kuomintang and the Communists broke out into full-scale conflict and it continued until the defeat of the Nationalists in 1949. Chiang Kai-shek fled to Taiwan, and Mao Zedong (Mao Tse-tung) established the People's Republic on October 1, 1949.

At that time there were 840,000 Protestant believers, 20,000 churches, 5600 missionaries, 8500 Chinese evangelists, 3500 Bible women, and about 2100 Chinese ordained pastors. (In 1948 the Catholics reported 3,274,000 believers, 3090 foreign priests, and 2698 Chinese priests.)

The history of the suffering church in socialist China since 1949 may be divided into seven periods, each determined by China's major political developments.

*The Church under Trial (1949–58).* During the first nine years after the Chinese communist takeover, the Protestant church was brought under the full control of the state through the formation and work of the Three-Self Patriotic Movement (TSPM), a "religious patriotic organization" created under the directives of the party to implement the party's religious policy among the Protestants. For the Catholics a similar organization called the China Catholic Patriotic Association was created (1957).

The party's policy then was to cut off the churches in China from their Western mother churches on the grounds that Christianity had been used by the capitalist imperialists to conduct cultural aggression. To do this the party used a few Protestant liberal leaders, headed by Wu Yaozong, to establish a Three-Self (self-supporting, self-governing, and self-propagating) Reform Movement, the earlier name of TSPM, to do its bidding.

Under Wu's leadership and assisted by party officials, a "Christian Manifesto" was published on July 28, 1950, together with the signature of 40 well-known church leaders. Thereafter, all Chinese pastors and parachurch leaders were required to demonstrate their patriotism by signing this document, which declared Christians' separation from Western imperialism and their support for the new China. In 1951 TSPM launched an accusation campaign, urging pastors to accuse those colleagues who were unfriendly to the CCP. In 1954 TSPM was formally organized, and churches were told to join it as a declaration of their support for the party's leadership. Those who refused to join were condemned as antirevolutionaries, and most of them were imprisoned during 1955 and again in 1958. Under such pressures the majority of Protestant church leaders submitted themselves to the leadership of the party as implemented by TSPM.

By 1958 practically all churches had been brought under the control of the state through TSPM. As the shepherds were attacked, the flock scattered. Country churches were closed down under the "great leap forward" movement. Even the pastors who declared their support for TSPM were forced to do political studies for six months. When they realized that they belonged to the class of exploiters, they "volunteered" to work in the factories or on the farms. A church union movement was launched to close down half-empty churches. The 200 plus churches in Shanghai were reduced to eight; the 66 churches in Peking were reduced to four.

*The Church Suppressed (1958–66).* After 1958 Christianity in China existed on two levels: a few TSPM churches open for public worship and closely supervised by the state through the Religious Affairs Bureau and TSPM, and small underground house groups meeting clandestinely. The open TSPM churches could not do things according to the demands of Scripture, and the underground house churches could not do things openly according to their conscience. House church activities were considered illegal, and violators were prosecuted, often resulting in long years of imprisonment, or were forced to do hard labor. Forbidden to have visitors, deprived of the privilege of Bible reading, and isolated from their friends and relatives, they suffered 10 to 20 years of internment. But most learned to witness of Christ to their fellow prisoners, and as a result secret prison fellowships emerged.

Deprived of their menfolk and without income, wives and children of the imprisoned found themselves destitute. Often they were driven out of their parish houses when their churches were taken over by the state. In addition to financial and physical hardships, their friends and relatives would avoid contact with them because they were labeled as "antirevolutionary families." Their children were also deprived of opportunities for higher education. Without pastors, believers began to meet secretly in their homes to comfort each other and to uphold each other in the faith. That was the beginning of the house church movement.

*The Church in Suffering (1966–76).* In August 1966 the Great Proletarian Cultural Revolution broke out at Mao's instigation. Young radical Red Guards sprang up and went on a rampage all over China. Armed with the "little red book" and encouraged by Chairman Mao, they set out to destroy old ideologies, customs, ideas, and habits. They stormed city halls, broke into party and police headquarters, took over university administration buildings, and publicly humiliated and beat up party officials, intellectuals, and anyone whom they considered not totally "proletarian." In the sphere of religion, they destroyed temples, monasteries, and stormed the few churches that remained. They searched the believers' homes, looking for Bibles, hymnals, and Christian literature to confiscate or to burn. In Xiamen, southeast China, the Red Guards gathered all the Bibles that they could find, piled them into a great heap in the public square, and set fire to them. Believers were rounded up and forced to kneel in front of that pillar of fire. In those days practically all Christians, including TSPM leaders, were attacked and forced to parade the streets. Some of the believers were literally beaten to death. Others suffered permanent paralysis. Not a few house church leaders who propagated the gospel were arrested and sent to labor camps.

After the first wave of attack, all traces of visible Christian activity were removed from the face of Chinese society. All Christians had to go through the baptism of suffering and humiliation. For a while even clandestine house church activities were suspended. The church in China appeared to be dead and buried.

But God did not depart from his people in China. Instead, a great spiritual army began to rise up. It was a slow process that began after the initial waves of attack during 1966–69. A few young men lamented over the situation of spiritual desolation that characterized the church and began to pray for a revival. They went about the villages in search of remnant believers and urged them to rise up from their fears and to start calling upon the name of the Lord again. Small groups began to meet secretly to pray and to encourage each other by recalling God's Word and by sharing God's grace in their lives. Gradually these small groups grew into house churches of 50 to 200 members. Deprived of ministerial leadership, lay leaders rose up to lead prayer meetings and to minister to a growing number of God's people. God was at work all over China, and house churches began to spring up in cities, towns, and in countless numbers of villages. Out

of suffering and death a new Chinese church was born. This new church believed that God had called them not only to believe in Christ, but also to suffer for his sake (Phil. 1:29).

*The Risen Church (1976–80).* After the death of Mao Tse-tung and the arrest of the "gang of four" in 1976, China began to change. Politically China moved away from Mao's radical leftist line of continuous revolution to a new program of socialist modernization, which implied a more open attitude toward the West. The period of 1976–80 was an era of transition from the rule of Hua Guofeng, Mao's designated heir, to that of Deng Xiaoping, China's strong man and reformer. During the first two years of the transition (1976–78), Chinese society began to thaw, and underground house churches began to surface in semiclandestine activities. In March 1979 the Chinese Communist party began to restore its religious policy of limited toleration under the united front policy, namely, a policy of friendly cooperation with ideological enemies in order to enlist the support of the religious masses for the Four Modernizations program. This was followed by the restoration of the Three-Self Patriotic Movement in August 1979 and the reopening of churches under TSPM in the large cities. TSPM was not fully reconstituted on the national level until October 1980, when it held its third national conference in Nanjing.

During 1979/80 the house church movement enjoyed a short period of unprecedented freedom, especially in the countryside. Politically, Chinese Communist cadres adopted a laissez-faire attitude, and administratively, TSPM had not yet been fully organized to implement religious control. It was during this period of transition before the control apparatus was restored that house churches grew in size and number. The church that had suffered so long was able to enjoy a temporary season of peace, and the people of God took advantage of it to preach the gospel. Even atheistic Communist party and Youth League members believed in Christ. It was a time of unprecedented revival.

*The Church in Spiritual Conflict (1980–82).* In December 1980 the Chinese Communist party held a work conference to evaluate the progress of the Four Modernizations program and to set new agendas after the dismissal of Hua Guofeng. Economically, the government sought to restore centralized planning and control. Politically, Deng Xiaoping restored political studies in schools and work units, which had been suspended since 1977. The party's new leadership was determined to eliminate leftist officials and to reshape the party with old ideals represented by the "four insistences": (1) on the ideology of Marxism, Leninism, and the thought of Mao Tse-tung; (2) on the dictatorship of the proletariat; (3) on the leadership of the Chinese Communist party; and

(4) on walking the path of socialism. The spirit of the four insistences dominated the constitutional revision of 1982, the 12th Party Congress (Sept. 1–12, 1982), and the ensuing religious policy.

This political tightening since early 1981 resulted in increased control by the Religious Affairs Bureau and TSPM over house church activities. As TSPM became more organized, establishing branches at the provincial and county levels, house church activities in the cities and in the villages came under pressure. On March 31, 1982, the Central Committee of the Chinese Communist party issued a document, known as Document No. 19, on religious policy, which is summarized as the "three designates" policy: (1) Christians may worship only in churches designated by TSPM; (2) only designated pastors are allowed to preach; and (3) they can do so only within their own designated districts. Under this new policy house church leaders were forbidden to do itinerant preaching and churches not approved and controlled by TSPM were told to close down.

The renewed restrictions came at a time when house churches were enjoying a season of great revival at the grass-roots level. A system of itinerant evangelism was developing in many parts of China, especially in Zhejiang and Henan. Preachers became more bold, preaching even in their neighboring provinces. As a result many became Christians, and the number of Christians in China grew from less than one million in 1949 to over 35 million, if not 50 million, in 1982. Desiring to see the whole nation turn to Christ, many house churches organized evangelistic teams to do cross-county and cross-provincial missions. These evangelistic outreaches ran into direct conflict with the government's religious policy of containing Christian activities within the four walls of TSPM churches. As a result, many incidents of conflict developed between TSPM officials and house churches, the more publicized ones occurring in Dongyang and Yiwu counties in Zhejiang province. Many itinerant preachers were arrested by the local public security bureaus. Others became fugitives. House churches in the cities also came under pressure. Park meetings stopped, and the Bible delivery ministry slowed down.

*The Church under Persecution (1983–84).* The implementation of the three designates became more vigorous in 1983, especially during the latter part of the year, when the Religious Affairs Bureau declared Witness Lee's group to be counterrevolutionaries in May, and when the government launched an "anticrime campaign" in September and an "antispiritual pollution campaign" in October. In conducting these campaigns, independent house church meetings were disbanded, itinerant preachers became targets of arrest and many were imprisoned, some being detained for one to two years without trial, others being sentenced to five years "for disturbing social order," or to 15 years as "counter-revolutionaries." Those who recanted their faith would be released. Such believers and preachers were subjected to severe physical punishment.

The renewed persecution forced many house churches to go underground. The itinerant evangelists in Henan province had to flee to the neighboring provinces of Shaanxi, Shanxi, Hebei, Anhui, Sichuan, Shandong, and Inner Mongolia. In their flight they developed new horizons of missions.

In the heat of this persecution house church leaders searched the Scriptures in an effort to find spiritual strength to endure suffering. They concluded that suffering for Christ is an integral part of discipleship. With this thought they equipped themselves for renewed expansion. As a result, they developed a "seven-point mission strategy": (1) preach the Word of God so that hearers can be born again; (2) walk the pathway of the cross; (3) know TSPM as a secular power; (4) establish churches as the goal of evangelism; (5) nurture the young churches with Scripture and spiritual life training; (6) develop and organize spiritual fellowship among established churches; and (7) engage in pioneer evangelism and reach out to hitherto unreached areas.

With this new breakthrough one central China group began to link up the churches they had founded with other isolated house churches and thus formed an organizational structure similar to presbyteries (pastoral districts) and synods (councils). A pastoral district is comprised of 30–50 meeting points, and 10 districts constitute a council. As of 1987 they organized eight councils, stretching over 22 provinces, and shepherding some 400,000 believers. During this period many house churches joined TSPM under pressure, and the number of TSPM churches began to grow from 600 in 1982 to 2000 in 1984. TSPM organizations by then had reached down to the township level.

*The Missionary Church (1985–87).* In October 1984 the Chinese Communist party passed a resolution on economic structural reform—a significant milestone in Deng Xiaoping's reform movement designed to stimulate greater and faster economic growth. China became even more open to the outside world in order to attract foreign capital, expertise, and scientific knowledge. For the church it meant less persecution, fewer arrests, and greater opportunity for church growth.

During this period TSPM continued to put pressure on independent house churches, and TSPM churches increased from less than 2000 in 1984 to over 5000 in 1987. Bishop K. H. Ting, head of TSPM and of the China Christian Council, declared in 1987 that there were now 4 million Christians in China, although house church leaders estimate that there are at least 50 million believers, if not more, meeting in at least 200,000 or more meeting points.

Early in 1985 TSPM established an Amity Foundation to receive donations from foreign churches. The United Bible Societies donated a modern press to this foundation, which promised to use it to print Bibles along with other things. By 1986 TSPM had opened 10 regional theological seminaries, each having a two-year program. The Nanjing Seminary runs a four-year program. It also printed on the average 250,000 Bibles per year plus a similar number of hymnals. *Tian Feng*, TSPM's official magazine, reported numerous ordination events taking place during 1985/86. Local authorities were also more willing to return former church buildings to local believers.

In 1985 house churches in Central China started to establish underground seminaries of three months duration to train full-time itinerant evangelists. Between 1986 and 1987 they established 11 such "seminaries of the field," each having graduated several classes. Their graduates were sent out to outlying provinces to do pioneering mission work.

After Hu Yaobang, the secretary general of the Chinese Community party, was removed from power in January 1987 due to his liberal reform views and his sympathies with the students' democratic movement, a stream of leftist propaganda followed, and consequently another wave of persecution against independent house meetings set in after April 1987. The pressure from TSPM, the Religious Affairs Bureau, and the Public Security Bureau on house churches is similar to that exerted on them during 1982–84, namely, to stop all private religious activities outside of government control. However, in spite of the severity of the current persecution, most house church leaders remain committed, although not a few are joining TSPM.

Christian-state relations seemed especially promising early in 1990, when the government instituted some reform measures in reaction to events in Eastern Europe. Caught up in the democracy ferment, university students demanded more immediate reforms during the momentous days of June 1990, including a large number of Christians. Christians were also among those killed in the bloody crackdown on the student protest, and the conservative backlash affected hopes for quick reform of religious controls. Anti-student propaganda included reference to religious agitation against the government. Chinese officials in the province of Fujian, which had been one of the most relaxed governments in its relations with Christians, officially "abolished" unregistered religious meetings in a crackdown late in 1990, declaring Bibles and Christian litera-

ture to be "tools of subversion." Arrests of house-church leaders increased. Still, contacts between Chinese and churches outside China remained. Bibles were printed with government permission. In late 1990 the status of house churches and China's religious policy remained in a state of flux.

The future of the church in China looks promising. The government is committed to the reform policy, as shown by the trend set at the 13th Party Congress. This trend will usher in even greater openness in the future. For economic structural reform is demanding political structural reform, and in due time political reform will necessarily require ideological structural reform. In another 10 to 15 years it is most likely that China will evolve into a pluralistic society, including ideological pluralism, and in that process the propagation of the gospel might be legalized. Presently Chinese people are free to believe or not to believe in a religion, but they are not free to propagate their faith outside of government control. Legalized or not, the Christian church has been firmly established in China, and Chinese Christians are giving themselves to the evangelization of China as their primary task.

**Bibliography.** K. S. Latourette, *A History of Christian Missions in China* (1929); P. M. D'Elia, *The Catholic Missions in China* (1941); P. A. Varg, *Missionaries, Chinese and Diplomats* (1958); S. M. Bates, *Frontiers of the Christian World Mission since 1938* (1962), 1–22; F. P. Jones, *The Church in Communist China* (1962); G. Patterson, *Christianity in Communist China* (1969); R. Bush, *Religion in Communist China* (1970); P. E. Kauffman, *China, the Emerging Challenge* (1982); G. T. Brown, *Christianity in the People's Republic of China* (1985); L. Ladany, *The Catholic Church in China* (1987); J. Chao, *China's Religious Policy Toward Christianity* (ET, 1987).

JONATHAN CHAO

## Chorley, Edward Clowes

**Chorley, Edward Clowes** (1865–1945). Episcopalian historiographer. Born in Manchester, England, he studied at Richmond College and the Philadelphia Divinity School. In 1915 he was appointed historiographer of the diocese of New York, and in 1919 he was made historiographer of the Episcopal Church. He was the founder and editor of *The Historical Magazine of the Protestant Episcopal Church* from its inception in 1932 until his death. His writings include *The New American Prayer Book, Its History and Contents* (1929) and *Men and Movements in the American Episcopal Church* (1946).

**Bibliography.** *Historical Magazine of the P. E. Church* (Dec. 1949); *The Living Church* (Nov. 9, 1949).

MASSEY H. SHEPHERD, JR.

## Christadelphians

**Christadelphians.** Sect founded in 1848 in America by an English physician, John Thomas. The name of the sect comes from the Greek words meaning "brothers of Christ." They accept the Bible as God's infallible revelation but reject the Christian doctrine of the Trinity and the deity of Christ. Highly millenarian, they expect the imminent return of Christ to establish a thousand-year theocracy at Jerusalem. They teach baptism by immersion and the annihilation of the wicked. Christ's death was not expiatory but rather an example of God's love. Salvation is through good works and the acceptance of "true" beliefs. They have no ministers but follow a Brethren-type church order. Although they probably number no more than 40,000 members worldwide, it is likely that Christadelphian beliefs influenced the development of Adventism and the Jehovah's Witnesses as well as several other similar Arian-type movements in the 19th and early 20th centuries.

IRVING HEXHAM

**Christengemeinschaft.** Protestant group founded in 1922 by Friedrich Rittelmeyer and Emil Bock. Its headquarters are located in Stuttgart, Germany, where the group maintains a seminary for the training of its leaders. Members are found mainly in Germany and North America. Chief characteristics include an act of consecration by which members become partakers in the death and resurrection of Christ, seven sacraments, and a strong emphasis on a personal religious experience that seems to replace almost completely the traditional Protestant teaching of justification by faith. Christendom is viewed as the fellowship of all those who have had a personal religious experience and have been consecrated into the sacrificial death and resurrection of Christ. Jesus is viewed as a spiritual being at the head of "cosmic hierarchies." Those who enter into this spiritual world receive "gnosis" as a form of liberation from spiritual bonds. Death is viewed as a step toward reincarnation. Rittelmeyer, Bock, and R. Steiner, whose anthroposophic ideas greatly influenced the founders, have left an extensive literary legacy detailing the polity and theology of the group. The liturgy was allegedly "revealed" to Steiner; it resembles the Roman Catholic Mass. Since 1950 the rites of the church are no longer accepted as valid by other German churches.

E. J. FURCHA

**Christian.** Term designating a follower of Christ which arose in the Greek-speaking world. The use of the ending *-ianos* (of Latin origin) on the stem of the Greek *Christos* (often confused by pagans with *chr*, "good," "serviceable") could not occur in an Aramaic-speaking situation. Origin of the designation at Antioch in Syria (Acts 11:26) was fitting. There, for the first time, a considerable number of Gentiles followed Christ; the group could no longer be regarded as a Jewish sect. A new name was needed, and since the disciples baptized "in the name of Christ," the name "Christian" was apt. We need not seek its origin at Rome; Roman influence was prominent at Antioch, where the first noncanonical Christian writer to use the title (Ignatius) lived. The name was not originated by the disciples themselves, nor did it arise in the offices of the provincial administration to describe the group as revolutionary. It probably arose among the people of Antioch who heard the new group confess Christ as Lord and so coined the title. Nothing proves that its original intent was abusive, but as the Christian group grew and people and rulers saw clearly its threat to pagan faith and ways, the term inevitably acquired a note of reproach. The Christians at first preferred other names, but in the 2d century they gradually adopted and defended it.

FLOYD V. FILSON

*In the 20th Century.* Mirroring the early clash with the Roman world, the name "Christian" was again used as a reproach and a signal for persecution. It seems certain that more Christians have been persecuted and martyred for their faith during the course of the 20th century than in all previous periods of church history combined. Christianity as a social system was deemed a threat particularly within the communist world, to native religionists in general and Islamic fundamentalists in particular, to the national socialist movement of the 1930s and 1940s, and to Western secular humanists.

As a holdover from the medieval concept of "Christendom," many Western nations had accepted and even relished their status as "Christian" countries. The U.S. Supreme Court recognized the fundamental basis of law in English jurisprudence and the Judeo-Christian ethic. As secularism came to dominate Western thought, however, reinterpretation of those roots was used to sanitize society from identification with Christianity.

Within the church the term came to have changing definitions. Modernist movements made the term "Judaism" more a cultural heritage than a religion; the same process occurred within Christianity. That fact was seen by conservative Christian leader J. Gresham Machen, whose *Christianity and Liberalism* (1923) warned that there must be limits to the range of beliefs which can be called "Christian" if the word is to retain any meaning at all. Conservatives came to be called "fundamentalists" and eventually came to grudgingly accept that name as distinguishing them from what they found to be non-Christian elements who refused to give up their rights to the name. Other groups preferred to call themselves "orthodox" Christians by way of distinction; followers of Karl Barth were quickly identified as "neo-orthodox" Christians and mainly accepted that description. Finally in the 1940s conservative Christians sensed the need for unity and gathered under the banner of "evangelical Christianity" or "evangelicalism." Those who saw the members of the National Association of Evangelicals as still too inclusive retained the name "fundamentalist." With some variations and taking into account the strong preference of some groups to be known as pentecostals, that state of affairs prevailed through the 1980s.

Despite wide disagreements about what the term meant, opinion polls over the USA and other Western countries found that most people still generally identified themselves as Christians. How vast the inclusiveness of that identity had become might be indicated by Shailer Matthews, dean of Chicago Divinity School (1908–33), one of the few leaders who relished being called a modernist. In *The Faith of Modernism* (1924) Matthews wrote that modernism was nothing more or less than Christianity without a confession—each person endeavoring to reach beliefs by empirical methods to apply inherited values to the needs of a modern world. In 1966 William Hamilton, one developer of the death of God theology, was asked whether radical theologies might still be considered Christian, despite taking an atheistic position. He said that he and his colleagues remained Christians, defining Christianity as a "choice of comrades" and an affirmation of relation to Jesus Christ.

*Bibliography.* A. Gercke, *Festschrift zur Jahrhundertfeier der koenigl. Universitaet zu Breslau* (1911): 360–73; R. Paribeni, *Nuovo Bullettino di Archeologia Christiana*, 19 (1913): 37–41; P. de Labriolie, *Bulletin du Cange 5* (1929–30): 69–88; E. Peterson, *Miscellanea Giovanni Mercati* 1 (1946): 355–72; E. J. Bickerman, *HTR* 42 (1949): 109–24; E. S. Gaustad, ed., *A Documentary History of Religion in America*, 2 vols. (1983); W. A. Elwell, ed., *Evangelical Dictionary of Theology* (1984); S. Neill, *Christian Faith and Other Faiths* (1984).

**Christian Aid.** British Council of Churches (BCC) agency which raises and distributes relief and development funds. The roots of Christian Aid extend back to the immediate postwar period when the U. K. Committee for Christian Reconstruction in Europe was formed in 1945. In 1950 this committee was absorbed into the British Council of Churches as its Department of Inter-Church Aid and Refugee Service. It has remained a part of BCC ever since, although physically separate and financially independent. In 1957, as the Inter-Church Aid and Refugee Service, it initiated what was to become an annual campaign in which member churches of BCC cooperated at the local level to inform the general public about acute human need around the world and invited donations.

In 1964 the name of the organization was changed to Christian Aid, a term associated with the week-long campaign each May observed in parts of England, Scotland, Wales, and Ireland. Approximately half of Christian Aid's regular income (i.e., excluding what is raised by appeals for emergencies such as drought or flood relief or the rehabilitation of earthquake victims) is raised during Christian Aid Week.

As a division of BCC, Christian Aid is answerable to that body (to which its constituent churches appoint delegates). In its grant making it gives priority to overseas development programs in the fields of agriculture, health, trade and technical training, and nonformal education. Christian Aid employs no overseas staff, but works through indigenous organizations, such as national councils of churches and other church groups or agencies.

Christian Aid bases its convictions concerning aid on an evolving theology and the requirements of the gospel. It is particularly sensitive to the experiences and views of the churches and Christian partners overseas. These are consciously sought as a contribution to Christian Aid's policies, philosophy, and Christian insight.

**Christian and Missionary Alliance (C&MA).** Conservative evangelical group with origins in a movement begun in New York City in 1881 by A. B. Simpson (1843–1919). The Christian Alliance, formed in 1887 to promote Simpson's distinctive views on sanctification and divine healing, and the Evangelical Missionary Alliance, formed in 1887 to promote pioneer foreign missions, merged in 1897 as the Christian and Missionary Alliance. Having survived early secessions to pentecostalism, C&MA has grown to embrace approximately 250,000 members and adherents in the USA, another 60,000 in Canada, and about 2.3 million worldwide. It operates five colleges and two seminaries in North America, and supports some 1200 missionaries in 52 countries. Initially intended as a parachurch society, it has evolved into a self-conscious denomination. Its executive powers rest in a president, board of governors, and district superintendents; its legislative powers reside in a representative general council. Autonomous Alliance national churches cooperate in a fraternal World Alliance Fellowship. The international headquarters is in Nyack, N.Y. C&MA attained its goal of doubling in size between 1978 and 1987, which has increased the challenge of maintaining its original emphases on sanctification as a crisis subsequent to conversion, on physical healing as a provision in the atonement, and on world evangelization as a means of hastening the premillennial return of Christ.

GLEN G. SCORGIE

**Christian Atheism.** *See* DEATH OF GOD THEOLOGY.

**Christian Blind Mission International (CBMI).** Largest independent mission agency serving blind and handicapped individuals in more than 90 countries on all six continents. A division of Christoffel Blinden Mission, whose international headquarters are in Bensheim, West Germany, CBMI has national branches in the USA (1975), Canada (1978), and Australia (1983). The mission, organized in 1908, grew out of the ministry of a Lutheran missionary, Ernest Christoffel, who sought to reach Muslims through schools for the blind and homes for the handicapped and orphans in Turkey and Iran. Through its "love in action" emphasis, the agency seeks to meet the physical and spiritual needs of the world's blind, visually handicapped, and other physically and mentally handicapped people. It is especially active in outreach to the more than 40 million of the world's blind, most of whom live in third world nations. Emphasizing Christian unity, CBMI cooperates with a broad cross-section of denominations and mission agencies, thereby avoiding needless duplication. It supports, for instance, eye doctors, mobile eye clinics and camps, and other handicapped-related services of existing Christian hospitals and national churches throughout the third world. CBMI-sponsored mobile eye clinics and eye camps annually treat more than 100,000 cataract sufferers in remote places. Its doctors perform simple 10-minute operations on location, which restore sight to those otherwise resigned to a life of blindness. Included in 861 projects supported by CBMI are 101 boarding schools for the blind, 26 training farms for the blind, 33 homes for the multiple handicapped, 186 eye hospitals, and numerous other institutions. It supports more than 2500 workers, including doctors, nurses, national evangelists, and paramedical workers.

LESLIE K. TARR

## Christian Brethren. See PLYMOUTH BRETHREN.

## Christian Church. See DISCIPLES OF CHRIST.

## Christian Endeavor Society.

An interdenominational, interracial organization founded by Francis E. Clark in 1881 for the purpose of training young people in the duties of church membership and Christian activities. Its principles included open confession of Christ, active service for him, loyalty to his church, and fellowship with his people. At its peak, thousands of societies were to be found in numerous denominations and in nearly every country. Many of the denominations involved substituted their own societies for young people, yet even in the mid-1950s the active membership of Christian Endeavor was still estimated at about 3 million, since which time numbers have shown a marked decrease.

## Christian Peace Conference (CPC).

Conference founded in 1958 at the instigation of the Comenius Faculty of the University of Prague, Czechoslovakia, to bring together Christian churches in Eastern Europe in their search for peace. CPC has played a significant role in the East-West dialog of Christian churches and peace groups.

Its initial objective addressed at congresses in 1959 and 1960 was to speak against the build-up of atomic weapons and to work toward demilitarizing the world's superpowers. The first All Christian Peace Assembly sponsored by CPC met in Prague in 1961. In its 30-year history six such assemblies have been held at irregular intervals; the most recent took place in Prague in the summer of 1985 with some 800 delegates and observers from 90 countries. The president and general secretary along with an advisory committee of about 100 members function on behalf of CPC in the intervening years.

J. L. Hromádka, former member of the World Council of Churches and a winner of the Lenin Peace Prize, resigned his position as the first president of CPC in 1969 over alleged curtailment of the freedom and sovereignty of "a body of devout Christians" who act "in the perspective and under the guidance of the Gospel." In recent years the leadership of the Russian Orthodox Church has had a distinct impact on the working of CPC. All pertinent statements issued by CPC are reported in the official monthly *Journal of the Moscow Patriarchate.*

CPC has championed Christian-Marxist dialog, sought to be an "apostle of the pilgrim church moving through a revolutionary age," and issued the challenge that Christians must abandon the notion of just war and advance just peace. Foremost on the agenda of CPC in the 1980s are three issues: imperialism, anticommunism, and the nuclear question. At least one-third of its current membership comes from the so-called two-thirds world.

## Christian Reformed Church in North America (CRCNA).

A confessional church in the Continental Reformed tradition. Its three standards of unity, to which all office bearers (pastors, elders, deacons, professors) subscribe, are the Belgic Confession (1561), the Heidelberg Catechism (1563), and the Canons of Dort (1619). Weekly sermons and several years of church education for youth follow the catechism. In 1986 CRCNA approved a contemporary testimony on ethical issues of the day; entitled "Our World Belongs to God," it does not share equal status with the three confessions.

CRCNA is organized into 860 congregations, 41 classes or districts, and an annual synod. Each officially constituted congregation is governed by a consistory of office bearers, which delegates two of its members to two or three classis meetings a year. Each classis delegates four elders and pastors to the synod, which considers proposals from the denomination's committees and agencies, makes major appointments, adjudicates differences, takes doctrinal positions, and determines general policy affecting all the congregations. The 306,000 members (73,000 families) reside throughout Canada (30%) and the USA (70%).

CRCNA dates from 1857, when a small group of recent Dutch immigrants in western Michigan broke a tenuous, seven-year union with the Reformed Church in America. Issues were RCA toleration of lodge membership, use of hymns, lack of regular catechism preaching, and lax church discipline. CRCNA increased through both internal growth and Dutch immigration, especially to the USA before World War I and to Canada after World War II. It also gained membership from the RCA in the 1880s as a result of the lodge issue. Most immigrants originally settled in Dutch communities, where CRCNA still has its greatest numerical strength. Since World War II CRCNA has become more ethnically diverse because of its vigorous home missions and church-planting program and through its relief and relocation work among Cuban and Southeast Asian refugees and Korean immigrants.

The character of CRCNA includes strains of confessional pietism from the 1834 Secession in the Netherlands; of cultural transformation from turn-of-the-century Dutch neo-Calvinism; and of Americanizing influences from the dominant culture and from healthy associations with American Presbyterianism. A theological emphasis on the covenant is expressed in the baptism of infants, strong and spiritually nurturing family ties, and the establishment of parentally controlled Christian elementary and high schools. Regarding all areas of life as belonging to Christ, members have often undertaken nonecclesiastical Christian endeavors in labor, politics, journalism, social services, recreation, business, and education. Unfortunately, these group efforts have often isolated CRCNA members from other Christians.

The oldest church agency is Calvin Theological Seminary (1876), which offers five degree programs. Calvin College developed out of the seminary and offers an undergraduate liberal arts program. Missions began with outreach to Native Americans in the 1880s. The world mission board presently sponsors work in 21 countries, while the home mission board supports efforts in some 175 locations. The Back to God Hour broadcasts the gospel in eight languages around the world. The Christian Reformed World Relief Committee (CRWRC) undertakes disaster relief and has development projects on four continents. A chaplains committee and a committee on race relations are also active. The Christian Reformed Board of Publications produces a weekly denominational paper, the *Banner*, and markets church education materials for churches in several denominations. CRCNA offices and most agencies are located in Grand Rapids, Michigan.

CRCNA maintains contact with confessionally compatible denominations through the Reformed Ecumenical Synod and the National Association of Presbyterian and Reformed Churches. It cooperates in certain activities with the World Alliance of Reformed Churches, although as a nonmember. For doctrinal reasons it does not belong to the World Council of Churches, the National Council of Churches, or the National Association of Evangelicals.

While it has openly faced many recent issues (hermeneutics, new forms of worship, the role of women, neopentecostalism, modern warfare, divorce and remarriage, homosexuality), it has also lately reaffirmed historic positions (the infallibility of Scripture, reprobation, Christ's atonement, the historicity of Genesis) and remains a strong confessional church.

**Bibliography.** H. Zwaanstra, *Reformed Thought and Experience in a New World* (1973); P. De Klerk and R. De Ridder, eds., *Perspectives on the Christian Reformed Church* (1983), J. D. Bratt, *Dutch Calvinism in Modern America* (1984); H. W. Van Brummelen, *Telling the Next Generation* (1986).

JAMES A. DE JONG

## Christian Science.

Religious system founded by Mary Baker Eddy (1821–1910) in 1879 on the basis of her book *Science and Health with Key to the Scriptures* (1875). Baker Eddy believed that she had been divinely healed of a severe injury in 1866 and that as a result she had discovered the secret of healing and life which she described as "Christian Science." From the time of her recovery she dedicated her life to an emphasis on healing through Christianity which she interpreted in terms of Eastern religious ideas derived from Hinduism and Buddhism.

The doctrines of Christian Science are often confusing. The basic premise is that God is the "divine Principle of all that really is." Mind and spirit are eternal realities while matter is an illusion subject to dissolution and decay. Since evil is connected with matter it is therefore unreal. Therefore, the only reality of sin, sickness, and death is in the awful fact that these unrealities seem "real" to humans through their erroneous beliefs. But God can strip away the unreality; "healing" becomes not something "miraculous" but rather the "divinely natural." Heaven is harmony and spirituality while hell is the reign of mortal and carnal belief.

Always a predominately middle-class group dominated by women, Christian Science is today in severe decline. However, the newspaper it publishes, the *Christian Science Monitor*, is probably the best in the world and is remarkable testimony to the ideals of Baker Eddy and the movement she founded.

**Bibliography.** W. R Martin and N. H. Klann, *The Christian Science Myth* (1954); C. S. Braden, *Christian Science Today*

(1958); R. Peel, *Christian Science: Its Encounter with American Culture* (1958).

IRVING HEXHAM

## Christian Socialism.

The Christian theory or practice of those who support a social system in which the producers possess political power and the means for producing and distributing goods. The term does not denote a clearly delineated or readily definable group or movement, although the beginnings of modern Christian socialism can be traced to the 19th century. Its diverse exponents include Adolf Stoecker, Philip Jacob Spener, A. H. Francke, Wilhelm von Ketteler, F. D. Maurice, and W. Rauschenbusch. Some of these individuals sought better conditions for laborers and for the poor and dispossessed by changing social conditions, while others undertook measures to improve the lot of the poor through acts of charity. Christian socialist thought often displayed an uncritical application of NT concepts to contemporary social situations—at times assimilating secular socialism, occasionally being diametrically opposed to movements that address material change at the expense of the transcendent dimensions of human life.

In the Roman Catholic tradition, Wilhelm von Ketteler, bishop of Mainz, Germany, was one of the foremost exponents of Christian socialist action, addressing social problems in his sermons as early as 1848 and later calling for cooperative Christian labor movements. These ideas were more fully developed in Catholic associations that combined the social demands of the gospel with notions of solidarity for greater social equality. Pope Leo XIII firmly established the Roman Catholic Church's commitment to Christian socialist tenets in his encyclical *Rerum novarum* (1891).

Three principles are at the heart of Christian social movements of the last two centuries: (1) the incarnation calls Christians to be actively involved in all aspects of the human situation (Pius XII); (2) obstacles to building up the Christian life must be overcome; and (3) the church has its own principles for social change, contained in natural law and in divine revelation; it must not depend on secular forces to inform its involvement in the world. Christian social teaching is all-encompassing enough to adapt to changing human situations.

Within Protestantism, Christian social awareness found expression on several fronts. Foremost among these was the *Hallesche Stiftung* of A. H. Francke and the *Rauhe Haus* of J. H. Wichern. In England, prominent leaders of organized Christian socialism were Charles Kingsley (1819–75), J. M. Ludlow (1821–1911), and F. D. Maurice (1805–72). They carried on a multifaceted attack on social inequities by calling for cooperative workshops and better education for the working class (adult education was born in principle), and by demanding social legislation. In the latter part of the 19th century the Guild of St. Matthew (1877) and the Christian Social Union (1889) were concrete expressions of the concerns these visionaries had espoused earlier in the century.

In North America, Christian socialist thought gained widespread acceptance through the work of Washington Gladden (1836–1918) and W. D. P. Bliss who organized the Society of Christian Socialists in 1889. The Baptist pastor Walter Rauschenbusch (1861–1918), son of a German immigrant, formulated the theology of the social gospel in several important publications. His ideas have had far-reaching effects well into the 20th century, shaping Christian social thought and placing it firmly as a legitimate heir of the gospel in its application of "eternal principles" to every facet of human life.

**Bibliography.** A. Cunningham, *Slant Manifesto: Catholics and the Left* (1968); W. R. Coats, *God in Public: Political Theology beyond Niebuhr* (1974); J.-B. Metz and J.-P. Jossua, eds., *Christianity and Socialism* (1977); W. R. Ward, *Theology, Sociology and Politics: The German Protestant Social Conscience, 1890–1933* (1979); R. J. Ederer, *The Social Teachings of Wilhelm Emmanuel von Ketteler: Bishop of Mainz (1811–1877)* (1982); W. S. Hudson, ed., *Walter Rauschenbusch: Selected Writings* (1984).

E. J. FURCHA

## Christmas.

Christian holiday commemorating the anniversary of Christ's birth, celebrated on December 25. The exact date of the birth of Jesus is unknown, although modern scholarship favors a date a year or two before 4 B.C., when Herod the Great died. Luke's reference to shepherds out in the fields (Luke 2:8) does not support a winter date.

Mid-winter was a time of celebration in the Greco-Roman world, as the winter solstice marked the turn of the year. Saturnalia extended from December 17 to 24 and in A.D. 274 the emperor Aurelian made December 25 a feast of the invincible sun. January 6 was sacred to Dionysus. With the toleration of Christianity under Constantine, both December 25 and January 6 became Christianized feasts (Christmas and Epiphany, respectively). It is known that Christmas was celebrated in Rome before A.D. 336.

Eastern (Greek-speaking) Christians celebrated both the birth and the baptism of Christ at Epiphany, but Christmas was the Western celebration of both. Late in the 4th century, Gregory of Nazianzus and Chrysostom promoted a dual celebration in the East. Jerusalem favored Epiphany, resisting Christmas until the 6th century. Later, in the West, Epiphany became separated from Christmas and was linked to the visit of the magi.

Symbols, originating largely from classical or Teutonic-Celtic paganism, such as lights, greenery, and special foods, gradually became associated with Christmas, as did St. Nicholas, whose feast on December 6 had been a time for giving gifts, especially to children.

The Puritans rejected Christmas because of its pagan origin, and this affected the beginnings of American Christianity. Scotland, traditionally the country least enthusiastic about Christmas except for Armenia, which never accepted it, has lowered its resistance to it somewhat in recent decades.

*See also* CHURCH YEAR.

GEOFFREY W. GROGAN

**Christology.** The study of the person and work of Christ. On the historical level, numerous attempts have been made to reconstruct the "real" Jesus of Nazareth in the context of 1st-century Jewish society, on the assumption that the portrait offered in the Gospels is that of the "Christ of faith" rather than the "Jesus of history"; thus Jesus has been seen as an orthodox Pharisee, an eschatological prophet, a failed Zealot leader, a magician and practictioner of secret necromantic rites, and in many other guises which make him unrecognizable as the divine Savior of traditional Christian belief.

On the theological level, the issue has been primarily how a divine figure, as traditional orthodoxy has assumed Jesus to be, can also be a genuine human being. This question has led to widespread dissatisfaction with the classical statement of the Council of Chalcedon (A.D. 451), which many feel has protected belief in Christ's full divinity at the expense of cutting him off completely from the actual human figure. From this dissatisfaction two main questions have arisen: How (and when) did belief in a divine Jesus actually originate? Where should we begin in constructing our own understanding of Jesus?

*The Origin of Christology.* C. F. D. Moule (1977) made an important distinction between two essentially different ways of understanding the origin of Christology, which he labels "evolution" and "development." On the evolutionary view, an original simple recognition of Jesus as a purely human Jewish figure was increasingly overlaid with mythological ideas of a divine savior descending from heaven which were derived from other religious systems; the result was a Christology which was quite alien to the historical Jesus and his teaching. On the developmental view the presentation of Jesus in the NT as a preexistent, divine Savior, while more explicit and theologically sophisticated than the direct teaching of Jesus himself before Easter, was merely the drawing out of what was already present in the historical life and teaching of Jesus.

On the evolutionary view, then, Jesus was a man, and nothing more. He was, of course, a supremely good and godly man, one who lived so close to God that in a sense others could see God in him. But the idea of the incarnation of a preexistent being in the human life of Jesus of Nazareth is a product of mythology, unrelated to what Jesus actually was. (This approach was summed up in the title of a volume of essays published in 1977, *The Myth of God Incarnate*.) Suggestions for the real origin of this myth have been varied, some looking to Jewish speculation about the personal existence of God's Wisdom as an "independent" being, some to pagan ideas of the gods coming to live among men, or to the dying-and-rising gods of some mystery religions. For those who hold this sort of view, clearly the Christology of Chalcedon has no root in historical reality.

J. D. G. Dunn (1980) has argued that the idea of Jesus' preexistence (and with it a true doctrine of incarnation) is not found in most of the NT. He finds, rather, two unrelated strands of thought: first, the tradition that Jesus spoke of himself as the Son of God (which need not in itself imply his preexistence); and second, the tendency to see the creative wisdom of God (an idea, not a person) supremely revealed in Jesus. It was the author of the Fourth Gospel who first brought these strands together to create the new doctrine of the incarnation of a personally preexistent divine being; and it was from John's insight that later Christian orthodoxy developed. Dunn sees John's "innovation," however, as the proper conclusion to be drawn from earlier Christian thought, not as an illegitimate "evolution."

Against both these positions, authors such as Moule and Martin Hengel (1975) trace the idea (if not necessarily the explicit language) of incarnation back to (and behind) the earliest NT statements. While there was necessarily a growth in perception and articulation of the truth about Jesus, the impact he made on his first disciples was itself the basis of this doctrinal development; they came to see him as the one in whom they met God, and so they began to worship him even before they had worked out the revolutionary theological implications of such an attitude. And in this developing NT response to the earthly Jesus as divine are to be found all the raw materials from which Chalcedonian orthodoxy was constructed. While Moule argues for this "development" only within the NT, E. L. Mascall (1985) sees it as continuing legitimately in the increasingly sophisticated Christology of the postapostolic church, of which Chalcedon is the high point.

*The Starting-Point of Christology.* Much debate has focused recently on whether Christology should begin "from above" or "from below." Those who question the value of the Chalcedonian definition often do so on the grounds that it begins from above, that is, that it starts with an a priori concept of Jesus as a divine being, the second Person of the Trinity, and then tries to fit the facts of the earthly life of Jesus in with this prior concept, with the result that the human Jesus is never taken seriously.

These terms (originally used by Luther) have become prominent in modern debate, particularly through the work of Wolfhart Pannenberg (1964). In opposition to those who see history as irrelevant to faith (e.g., Rudolf Bultmann), Pannenberg insists that Christology must begin from below, with the facts of the historical Jesus. For Pannenberg the resurrection in particular is the key to Christology, for here history points unambiguously to the divine dimension in Jesus. Belief in the incarnation of a preexistent divine being, while not a legitimate starting-point for Christology, is its appropriate conclusion. For Pannenberg, beginning from below does not mean that the divinity of Jesus is automatically excluded from the resultant Christology. Indeed, in the sense that they take the historical record seriously as their starting-point, virtually all modern Christologies begin from below.

The term has been pressed further, however, by J. A. T. Robinson (1973), whose Christology from below focuses so completely on the reality of Jesus' humanity, which must be just like ours, that he is unable to give any substantial meaning to Jesus' divinity. Jesus is the man in whom we see God, the man who is so open to God that he is effectively "God for us." But this is not to speak of a distinct divine "nature." Rather the divine and human "stories" are two different ways of speaking about the same fully human person.

Robinson's work is one of the most lucid examples of what has become a dominant trend in modern Christology: to make the humanity of Jesus the starting-point (in conscious opposition to the method of Chalcedon), and to allow only so much meaning to talk of "divinity" as can be fitted into a real humanity. The result is that "incarnation" has become for many an empty theological term, a "myth."

The work of A. T. Hanson (1975) is typical. He claims that Chalcedon followed the "Johannine" route, whereas Scripture offers other, more suitable models for understanding Jesus. Jesus is the one in whom "grace and truth," the essential characteristics of God in the OT, are most fully revealed. Hanson offers a Christology of revelation rather than incarnation.

A related point is made by those who see christological language as "functional" rather than "ontological." Oscar Cullmann (1957) insisted that the only Christology known to the NT is a functional one; it speaks of what Jesus does rather than of his eternal being. More recently, however, it has increasingly been recognized that a functional route to the understanding of Jesus does not rule out an ontological conclusion (nor, indeed, did Cullmann wish to do so). Through

Christ's work we have (and the NT writers had) access to an understanding of him, but this does not mean that statements about his essential nature are either impossible or even logically subordinate to statements about his work. Through what he *does* we can see who he must *be* in order to fulfill this function. In this connection a helpful distinction is sometimes drawn between the "order of being" and the "order of knowing."

A new dimension has been brought into Christology by the attempt to relate it to politics. The leading figures here have been Jurgen Moltmann (1972) and the Latin American liberation theologians, particularly Jon Sobrino (1976). Moltmann, together with most modern theologians, did not accept the patristic belief in the impassibility of God. He was, therefore, able to portray Jesus as "the crucified God," who in his suffering shares in the realities of suffering and oppression experienced by millions in the world today. Sobrino also stressed the involvement of Jesus in the realities of earthly life; for him Jesus is supremely a man of faith, in whose relationship with God the Father God the Son is revealed, and who in his teaching on the kingdom of God brought God's perspective to bear on the realities of his world. In following him and in sharing his perspective we find God at work for the liberation of oppressed humanity today.

All these trends in modern Christology bear witness to a desire to escape from merely abstract philosophical speculation about Christ's divine and human natures and how they might be combined in one person, to a more direct engagement both with the historical record of Jesus as he actually was on earth and with the realities of the world in which he must be preached today. The old christological questions which centered around Greek philosophical terms (*hypostasis, physis, ousia,* etc.) are less prominent, and attention has focused on the more fundamental issue of whether there is any real sense in which Jesus may be described as "divine" at all, and how such language may be given meaning in the context of modern secular thought. To ask such questions is not, of course, necessarily to abandon the essentials of Chalcedonian orthodoxy; such scholars as Cullmann, Pannenberg, and Moltmann remain "Chalcedonian" (in that they affirm Jesus as truly God and truly man), despite their untraditional ways of approaching the issue.

The question then arises as to how the more recent expressions of Christology should be addressed in relation to the older formulations. This issue has been particularly acute in the Roman Catholic Church, and has focused on the massive works of Edward C. F. A. Schillebeeckx (1974, 1977), in which traditional terminology is used, but often in contexts which suggest a different perspective from that of the "orthodox" Christology of Chalcedon. Investigations of the orthodoxy of Schillebeeckx and of Hans Küng by the church authorities have been a marked feature of recent Catholic theology. In Protestant circles there is perhaps a greater willingness on the part of some modern theologians to declare an explicit break with Chalcedonian orthodoxy, so that the lines are more clearly drawn between a traditional doctrine of incarnation and the various forms of "reductionist," nonincarnational Christology.

Among those who still wish to speak of the divinity of Jesus as an ontological truth, the problem of how a preexistent divine being could meaningfully share in real human experience remains a serious one. It is widely recognized that popular Christian devotion, based on Chalcedonian orthodoxy, has almost inevitably tended toward a sort of docetism which refuses to take Jesus' humanity seriously. In the attempt to curb this tendency, kenotic theories continue to be advanced in order to explain how Jesus could genuinely have shared in such human limitations as temptation and ignorance, although the nature of the kenosis proposed varies considerably.

**Bibliography.** V. Taylor, *The Person of Christ in NT Teaching* (1958); O. Cullmann, *The Christology of the NT* (1959); R. H. Fuller, *The Foundations of NT Christology* (1965); W. Pannenberg, *Jesus—God and Man* (1968); J. A. T. Robinson, *The Human Face of God* (1973); J. Moltmann, *The Crucified God* (1974); A. T. Hanson, *Grace and Truth: A Study in the Doctrine of the Incarnation* (1975); M. Hengel, *The Son of God* (1976); I. H. Marshall, *The Origins of NT Christology* (1976); J. Hick, ed., *The Myth of God Incarnate* (1977); G. W. H. Lampe, *God as Spirit* (1977); C. F. D. Moule, *The Origin of Christology* (1977); J. Sobrino, *Christology at the Crossroads* (1978); M. D. Goulder, ed., *Incarnation and Myth: The Debate Continued* (1979); E. Schillebeeckx, *Jesus: An Experiment in Christology* (1979); L. Boff, *Jesus Christ Liberator: A Critical Christology of Our Time* (1980); J. D. G. Dunn, *Christology in the Making* (1980); E. Schillebeeckx, *Christ: The Christian Experience in the Modern World* (1980); A. T. Hanson, *The Image of the Invisible God* (1982); H. H. Rowdon, ed., *Christ the Lord: Studies in Christology Presented to Donald Guthrie* (1982); C. E. Gunton, *Yesterday and Today: A Study of Continuities in Christology* (1983); K. Runia, *The Present-Day Christological Debate* (1984); E. L. Mascall, *Jesus: Who He Is—And How We Know Him* (1985).

RICHARD T. FRANCE

# Church and State.
The complex relationship between church and state has been a significant part of human history from the 1st century to the present day. The Christian faith has been from the beginning a missionary and, hence, a world-transforming movement. Because of its proclamation of a coming new order, it has been essentially a dynamic force in society and, consequently, has never been at peace with the world around it. This has led to continuous tension and conflict, usually dealt with by historians under the general heading of "church and state." This phrase includes a wide variety of historical relationships between the spiritual and temporal authority structures. These two authority structures have long attempted to define and give form to the lives of human beings—the state being primarily concerned with temporal life

as an end in itself and the church being concerned with temporal life as a means to spiritual ends. Tension and conflict have resulted when at certain points in history their interests have intersected and/or overlapped.

***Historical Background.*** Christian leaders made no attempt to formulate a theory of church-state relations until Christianity became a state religion in the 4th century. Before that time, even though they had no legal standing, believers generally followed Paul's admonition to "be subject to the governing authorities" (Rom. 13:1) except when that subjection conflicted with explicitly understood commands of God or the proclamation of the gospel (Acts 5:29). Moreover, the duty of obedience to civil rulers was always qualified by the condition that these authorities were doing their appointed work of restraining evil and seeking peace and safety (cf. Rom. 13:1–7; Rev. 13).

Widespread persecution of the early Christians was frequent, with the final official Roman effort to eradicate them from the empire taking place under Diocletian in 303. It failed, and with the Edict of Milan in 313 Christianity became an officially recognized religion in the Roman Empire. By the end of that century the Roman rulers had decreed that Christianity was the sole official religion of the state.

This new arrangement created a need for closer definition of the relationship between the church and the state, especially since the church had become an institution in the modern sense during this period. From the 4th century through the Middle Ages, the accepted idea was that church and state, while in principle distinct societies, were united in one commonwealth, namely, the *Corpus Christianum.* The distinction between them was manifested mainly in their separate hierarchies (pope and emperor) with their different functions and in the systems of law which they administered. After the Great Schism (1054) between the Eastern and Western churches, there were two commonwealths of this kind—otherwise the main idea was not affected, except that in the Byzantine East the emperor became the dominant partner. In the West there was ever-recurring tension or rivalry between the ecclesiastical and civil authorities, culminating in the Investiture Controversy in the 11th century, after which a rejuvenated and powerful papacy increasingly began to assert its prerogatives over those of the secular rulers. This trend continued until the creation of "the papal monarchy" of the 13th century when the church was clearly in ascendancy over the state. This arrangement began to crumble in the 14th century, mostly because of internal ecclesiastical problems and monarchical restiveness but also because of growing numbers of groups designated by the church as "heretical" which questioned papal power and called for a return to NT norms.

The coming of the Protestant Reformation in 1517 disrupted the unity of the Western Church and led to the formation of a variety of national churches. Some continued to be in communion with Rome while claiming a considerable degree of independence (e.g., Gallicanism in France) while others rejected papal authority altogether (e.g., the Lutheran, Reformed and/or Presbyterian, and Anglican churches). The Lutherans and Anglicans were much more willing than the Reformed churches (Calvinists) to allow the civil power ("the godly prince") to manage the affairs of the church. Still, the accepted idea was that in each country church and state were one commonwealth.

However, the Reformation spawned other movements with a different concept of church-state relations. These groups, especially the Anabaptists, criticized the various Reformation church establishments and, in a manner reminiscent of the medieval sects, pleaded for the creation of a "true church" which consisted only of those who were called out of the world into separate communities of genuine believers. In short, they preached against nominal Christianity encouraged by the national churches and instead called for "gathered churches" and separation of church and state. They argued that churches should not be established or depend on civil governments for support because this not only violated NT teachings but also inevitably led to worldliness, compromise, and sacrilege.

Nevertheless, until the French Revolution and the gradual disintegration of the old order elsewhere, the alliance of church and state was generally maintained in Europe, with a more or less precarious toleration of dissenting minorities in most countries. It was not until the founding of the USA in 1789, especially with the adoption of its Bill of Rights in 1791, that full blown religious liberty and separation of church and state became accepted political principles. In America, a combination of religious leaders (mostly Baptists, Quakers, Mennonites, and assorted Calvinists) and intellectual leaders (mostly in the Enlightenment tradition) supported separation of church and state as the best way to guarantee religious freedom—by keeping the state out of church affairs and the church out of state affairs.

In Europe in the 19th century, most civil governments ceased to be professed upholders of the church or even recognizably Christian. At the same time, many perceptive church leaders began to question the validity of the concept of establishment (e.g., the Oxford movement in England and the Disruption in Scotland). During the course of the century, the idea of the union of church and state gave way to a commitment to religious pluralism in a liberal state. The new ideal was one in which the state was religiously neutral as it maintained law and order and preserved the freedom of citizens to profess and practice any religion or none. In this arrangement, churches would be voluntary societies left to their own devices while separation of church and state became axiomatic.

However, the rise of totalitarian states (Marxist and fascist) and various kinds of dictatorships in Europe and elsewhere in the 20th century challenged traditional liberal assumptions and led to new church-state conflict and tensions. Pluralism and liberalism, and the religious liberty these were supposed to secure, have been shaken by the appearance of these new states which have attempted to impose a secular faith on all their citizens and to tolerate churches only if they are content not to challenge or criticize the political order. In this arrangement, churches are expected to confine themselves to the private sphere of personal religion, and nothing else.

Historically speaking, then, there have been many different expressions of the church (papal, episcopalian, presbyterian, congregational, independent) and of the state (monarchical, republican, democratic, dictatorships, fascist, Marxist) which have affected the character and extent of church-state relations. In addition, the problem has been posed differently according to whether the membership of a church was coterminous with that of a state, or a church was a small minority within a state, or there were several churches or only one church in a state. This makes any simple description of the history of church-state relations impossible and any simple prescription for church-state relations difficult.

Nevertheless, there seem to have been three broad categories of church-state relations in the past. First, there have been and continue to be those states in which there is no separation of church and state. Second, there have been and continue to be those states in which there is a friendly separation—that is, where the entities of church and state are separate but primarily in order to protect the interests of the church from government intrusion and to enhance religious freedom, as in the USA. In this arrangement, church and state are separate but religion and politics are not. Third, there have been and continue to be those states in which there is an unfriendly separation—that is, where the entities of church and state are separate but mainly in order to free the state from religious intrusions into its interests. In this arrangement, both the church in particular and religion in general are relegated to the private sphere. Once mostly the purview of radical republicanism, this approach is now more commonly found in Marxist regimes, as in the Soviet Union.

***Recent Developments.*** Church-state relations during the past century have been characterized by volatility and change. The main theme in church-state relations in the USA in the 20th century has been increasing tension. This has been generated from two sources. First, there has been a rift in the ranks of American evangelicals with the Anabaptist/Baptist wing calling for continuance of the Jeffersonian "wall of separation" between church and state and an emerging fundamentalist/Calvinist coalition arguing that the First Amendment has been inverted during the past few decades to mean protection *against* religion rather than freedom *for* religion. In other words, the latter group (neoconservative evangelicals) has claimed that the USA has moved from friendly to unfriendly separation. A second source of tension has been the growing religious pluralism in the country at large brought about by the penetration of the American religious mind by Eastern thought and by the dramatic increase in immigration from the Orient and Middle East since World War II.

Volatility and change also have been the hallmarks of church-state relations worldwide in this century. First, there has been an increasing constitutional separation of church and state in most modern nations, for a variety of reasons. Second, contrary to optimistic expectations around the turn of the last century, many modern governments have turned on the church with increasing hostility. This has been true in many areas of the world which have experienced revolution in the 20th century. Third, the "Declaration on Religious Freedom" adopted by Vatican Council II (1962–65) has opened up new possibilities for church-state relations, especially in the heavily Roman Catholic countries of southern Europe and Latin America. Even though this declaration was aimed primarily at governments which suppressed religious liberty, especially the freedom and independence of the Catholic Church, it has led to separation of church and state in a number of predominately Catholic countries since 1965.

***Church and State in the USA since 1950.*** In the USA since 1950, there has been an erosion of the traditional view, which has supported a wall of separation between the institutions of church and state, on the one hand, and the preservation of the principle of a friendly separation which permitted a generous interplay of religion and politics, on the other. This, in turn, has led to growing disagreements among the religious, political, and intellectual leadership of the nation concerning whether the independence of church and state should be one of segregation, neutrality, or mutual support.

Further, in this same period, the meaning of the term "pluralism" has been expanded to include other, very diverse groups. Recent decades have been marked by a willingness on the part of many American institutions to give recognition to claims for equal treatment made by a variety of ethnic, racial, religious, and other minority bodies. But not all Americans have welcomed this new religious and cultural pluralism, which extends well beyond the traditional Judeo-Christian mainstream. As a result, a great struggle has ensued over the appropriate place of religion in society. The essential question in post-World War II America has become: Should the government disregard or take formal account of those Judeo-Christian values which many believe to be the foundation of the national culture? Broadly speaking, the main church-state issue of the last half of the 20th century separates those who think that government should accommodate and encourage the sort of religion which they see as foundational to American culture, and those who believe that the government should not extend aid or support to religion in any way.

The focus of this new tension has been varied. In the political realm, it often has centered on the place of the Roman Catholic Church in American life. For example, in 1960, the U.S. public elected John F. Kennedy as the nation's first Catholic president. During that campaign, Kennedy confronted "the religious issue" both directly and often. Because he was willing to discuss it and because he assured his critics that he was an American first and a Catholic second, he was elected, but the issue remained in the campaign to the end. Nevertheless, Kennedy's election was a milestone in church-state relations for it was a precedent-setting event which demonstrated that Catholics were, at last, a fully accepted part of the Judeo-Christian tradition upon which the country allegedly was founded. Another breakthrough (some would say breakdown) in church-state relations occurred in 1984 when President Ronald Reagan established full diplomatic relations with the Vatican for the first time in 117 years. Meanwhile, in the 1980s, the issue of the church's activity in the political arena returned with a vengeance as groups as diverse as the Moral Majority and the National Conference of Catholic Bishops lobbied in God's name for a variety of political programs.

Even more important, the new tensions have involved the U.S. Supreme Court with increasing frequency and intensity since 1950. Court decisions concerning church and state fell into four categories in that period: foundational ideology, upholding the wall, breaching the wall, and sitting on the wall of separation. In the case of *Zorach* v. *Clauson* (1952), Justice William O. Douglas delivered the court's majority opinion which upheld the right of the public schools to allow children who requested it to be released during regular classroom time to receive religious instruction in church buildings. Foundational to the court's decision and foundational to church-state relations in the USA was Douglas's dictum: "We are a religious people whose institutions presuppose a Supreme Being." This seemed to authorize certain actions concerning religion in the public schools based on the nation's civil religion, which at the time rested on the Judeo-Christian tradition.

Several decisions upholding the wall of separation between church and state followed in the next decade. The most important of these were the Regent's Prayer Case (*Engel* v. *Vitale*) in 1962, which outlawed the recitation of state-sponsored prayers in the public schools; the decision which in 1963 made illegal daily Bible readings as a part of opening school exercises (*Abington School District* v. *Schimpp*); a 1968 ruling (*Epperson* v. *Arkansas*) which struck down an Arkansas law forbidding the teaching of the theory of evolution in any state-supported school or university; and another decision the same year (*Flast* v. *Cohen*) which gave taxpayers standing in federal courts to challenge public expenditures relating to religion on First Amendment grounds.

During this same period, the court made decisions which appeared to breach the wall. For instance, in 1961 (*McGowan* v. *Maryland*) the high tribunal upheld state-imposed Sunday closing laws in Maryland on the basis that they were not primarily religious in nature, thus secularizing the Christian Sabbath. In 1981 (*Widmar* v. *Vincent*), the court upheld an approach to religion in the public schools often referred to as "equal access." Under equal access, public schools having extracurricular activities must provide equal opportunity for both religious and secular organizations. Moreover, the court upheld the practice of having a chaplain paid with tax dollars deliver an invocation prior to each session of a state or federal legislature in 1983 (*Marsh* v. *Chambers*) in a case involving the Nebraska lawmaking body. In 1984 (*Lynch* v. *Donnelly*), the High Court ruled that a Pawtucket, R.I., tradition of providing a city-sponsored "Seasons Greetings" display which included a nativity scene along with secular symbols of the holiday was constitutional. This last decision, while implying that Jesus was in some way a secular figure, argued that these symbols posed no real danger of the establishment of a state church and suggested that the tribunal had moved from a position of "segregation" manifested during the 1960s in the school prayer and Bible-reading cases to an approach of "benevolent neutrality" in this case in the 1980s.

In addition, since the 1950s the court has handed down decisions which can be interpreted as wall-straddling, or as sometimes belonging on one side of the wall and sometimes on the other. A number of these have related to state aid to religious schools. For instance, in 1971 in *Lemon* v. *Kurtzman*, the court ruled that states could not provide financial support to nonpublic elementary and secondary schools by way of reimbursement for the cost of teachers' salaries, textbooks, and instructional materials in specified secular subjects or provide supplements to the annual salaries of nonpublic school teachers. In the same case, it formally introduced the concept that "political divisiveness" may be a part of the "entanglement test" (the doctrine that church and state each can best work to achieve their aims if each is left free from the other within its respective sphere and that there be no excessive entanglement which leads to a dangerous or compromising relationship between the two entities). However, in 1983 in *Mueller* v. *Allen*, the high tribunal permitted unprecedented support for parochial schools by upholding a Minnesota statute which allowed taxpayers, in computing their state income tax, to deduct certain expenses incurred in providing for the education of their children in religious schools. This decision reflected the continuous campaign for parochial aid (any form of direct or indirect tax aid for sectarian private schools from any level of government) that has been carried on in America since World War II as well as the favorable climate for such aid created in the 1980s by the Reagan presidency. Other major examples of the High Court's church-state schizophrenia included the *Roe* v. *Wade* case in 1973, unusual because it took control of abortion from states and authorized abortion on demand in certain circumstances while at the same time denying that abortion was a moral issue. On the other hand, a 1988 court decision (*Kendrick* v. *Bowen*) allowed religious groups which receive federal funds to continue to counsel teenagers to seek alternatives to abortion.

All of these post-1950 developments in church-state relations at the political and legal levels have been complicated by a resurgent American civil religion in the same period. Civil religion, which experienced a revival under President Dwight D. Eisenhower (1953–61), is that generalized common public faith which binds most Americans together, upon which the operative common values of the society are based, and which permits Americans to mix their religion and politics. Presidents John F. Kennedy (1961–63), Lyndon B. Johnson (1963–69), Richard M. Nixon (1969–74), Gerald R. Ford (1974–77), Jimmy Carter (1977–81), and Ronald Reagan (1981–89) continued to support this revival with Nixon and Reagan giving it major formative impetus in terms of public piety and priestly leadership. This, in turn, created a certain amount of confusion in the public mind concerning the separation of church and state, on the one hand, and the mixture of politics and religion, on the other—leading some to consider them one and the same thing and others to try to conflate them.

### Church and State in the Other Western Democracies since 1950.
In the 20th century, most Western governments have adopted policies and laws that insulate the state against undue ecclesiastical influence and protect a pluralism of religious groups and beliefs. Vestiges of establish-

ment policies still remain in Great Britain, Scandinavia, Spain, and parts of Germany, largely in the form of financial support and special protection of certain churches and religious institutions, and minor regulation of church property, doctrine, and liturgy. All of this is most true of Great Britain, where the Anglican Church still enjoys some of the privileges and burdens of being the established religion of England, and where various schemes are used to grant state aid to parochial schools, especially in Northern Ireland. Constitutional battles between church and state continue to be waged in some countries over such matters as government taxation of the churches, government support of religious education, and the giving of religious instruction in state-supported schools. This has been more true of Italy and Spain than elsewhere. Also, papal concordats with most of the predominately Roman Catholic countries of Europe affect the way in which church-state relations are spelled out, especially in the case of education. Within the churches themselves, a growing academic movement, particularly among neo-Thomists and neo-Calvinists, has brought the issue of church-state relations to the forefront of theological debate in many countries.

With the exception of Great Britain and the Republic of Ireland, there are no established churches in the English-speaking community of nations, although church-state relations everywhere for the most part have been friendly. The British Parliament, where certain bishops are members of the House of Lords, maintains in many ways the right to determine the doctrine and liturgy of the Church of England. The special status of the Church of England does not preclude the fact that religious freedom is guaranteed and all citizens enjoy full equality before the law; still, both the Sovereign and the Lord Chancellor must be members of the Anglican communion. The Sovereign is also the Supreme Governor of the Church of England (Anglican) while in England and head of the Church of Scotland (Presbyterian) when in Scotland, and consequently is an Anglican while in England and a Presbyterian when in Scotland. In Ireland, the Roman Catholic Church is not officially established but historically and constitutionally has enjoyed a special position of favor tantamount to establishment as the guardian of national morality. In Canada, Australia, and New Zealand, separation of church and state is not as sharp as in the USA. In all three countries church schools receive financial assistance from public sources in various forms, and in Australia the Anglican Church still enjoys a position of preeminence among the various religious communities.

Religious freedom is guaranteed in all of the other Western democracies but church-state relations vary from country to country. For example,

Lutheranism is still the official faith of Sweden, Norway, Denmark, Finland, and Iceland, while the established religion of Greece is the Orthodox Church. In Norway and Sweden, the sovereign is also head of the established church while the Danish national church really has no head. In Finland, the president nominates bishops of both the Lutheran and the Orthodox Churches, and both churches are financially supported by the state and their synodal decrees confirmed by parliament. Switzerland is a special case in a number of respects. Some cantons (e.g., Zürich, Waadt) have a Reformed (Calvinist) established church or, having separated church and state, recognize only the Reformed Church as existing in law (e.g., Basel, Appenzell-Ausserrhoden). Some cantons treat only the Roman Catholic Church in the same way (e.g., Ticino, Valais). Most cantons recognize both the Reformed and the Catholic Churches, either as the established churches of the canton or, where church and state have been separated (e.g., Neuchâtel, Geneva), as the only churches with a legal existence.

Church and state are sharply separated in France but relations between the government and the various churches have been increasingly cordial since World War I. Diplomatic relations were resumed with the Vatican in 1921, and it was agreed to hold consultations before bishops were appointed—but so far there has been no concordat. Church and state are separate but friendly in West Germany, and the Evangelical Church (Lutheran and Reformed) and the Roman Catholic Church enjoy special privileges in the various constituent states of the German Federal Republic on the basis of the fundamental law of 1949 and various concordats which several states have made with the Vatican since 1945. Special federal legislation allows the churches to engage in public activities, especially social and relief work, and provides them with substantial funds to do so. Austria provides for separation of church and state with the Roman Catholic Church enjoying certain privileges, especially in education, based on a concordat with the Vatican. In Belgium and Luxembourg, all churches are guaranteed freedom from state control but the government in each state pays the salaries of all clergy—Catholic, Protestant, and Jewish. Church and state are completely separate in the Netherlands although the monarch is required to be of the Reformed faith. Portugal has separation of church and state with special ties to the Vatican by means of a concordat. The Roman Catholic Church was the official religion of Spain until 1976, when it was disestablished following the death in 1975 of Francisco Franco, the Spanish dictator. Previous to this, a law of 1967 removed the most severe disabilities on non-Catholics and granted them a measure of religious liberty. With the establishment of a constitutional monarchy similar to that of Great Britain in 1975, church and state became separate with the Catholic Church retaining a number of privileges, particularly in education and in the armed forces chaplaincy. The Lateran Treaty of 1929, which established the Roman Catholic Church in Italy, was confirmed by the republican constitution of 1946 following World War II. However, the 1946 constitution also guaranteed freedom of religion and organization for non-Catholics, providing for their exact relationship with the state to be established by special agreements. Later, a concordat with the Vatican in 1984 abrogated the treaty of 1929, disestablished the Catholic Church, desacralized the city of Rome, and sharply separated church and state in Italy.

**Church and State in the Soviet Union and Other Marxist Countries since 1950.** The Soviet Union, as the most powerful communist country in the world, has set the pattern for church-state relations in most of the other Marxist states. In 1918, immediately following the 1917 Bolshevik Revolution, V. I. Lenin, the Soviet leader, issued a declaration concerning the place of religion in the new regime. The Russian Orthodox Church was disestablished, church and state were strictly separated, the oversight of education was taken from the church and the church itself deprived of juridical personhood, thus making it impossible to hold property or manage a church budget. As the Soviet state developed, it became apparent that this was definitely an unfriendly separation.

However, the configuration of church-state relations in the Soviet Union was determined more by Josef Stalin than by Lenin. During his years as the Soviet dictator (1927–53), Stalin defined church-state relations—always officially separated—usually in terms of harsh repression; sometimes, depending upon the political needs of the regime, in terms of toleration; but never in terms of religious freedom. The principal religious code of the Stalinist era was the Legislation on Religion of 1929 which caused the virtual destruction of the churches as vital organizations. It reiterated Lenin's prohibition against property holding and budgetary activity and added new restrictions: all congregations had to be registered with the state, no religious activity could take place outside the walls of the buildings provided for worship by the state, public religious instruction of the young was prohibited, participation in a religious group disqualified one for membership in the Communist party, and all baptisms had to be registered and receive prior approval from the state. A Minister of Cults was appointed to oversee the activities of the officially registered churches. During the first years of the Stalinist regime, the Russian Orthodox Church, which experienced something of a revival, and the evangelical Christian churches emerged as the strongest Christian bodies in the Soviet Union.

Because they strongly supported the Soviet effort during World War II, Stalin permitted the reopening of many churches at the end of the conflict, the establishment of a central church administration under the Russian Orthodox patriarch, and the formation of a church organization of evangelicals called the All-Union Council of Evangelical Christians and Baptists. This thaw lasted only a few years and repression was reinstituted under the leadership of Nikita Khrushchev (1959–64). During these years, there was a campaign to eliminate religion, deregister churches, and arrest resisting clergy, climaxed in 1962 by a secret revision of the 1929 legislation on religion which was designed to rid the USSR of all religion (including Judaism and Islam) within a few years.

The Brezhnev dictatorship (first secretary of the Communist party, 1964–82) were years of uncertainty for church-state relations as policy fluctuated between harsh repression to mild toleration, often depending upon Soviet relations with the USA. Repression lessened with the establishment of detente early in the 1970s. In 1975, the law of 1929 was revised extensively, making it more moderate than in 1962 but still more restrictive than in 1929. Some relief from repression and harassment began with the Brezhnev Constitution of 1977 after which churches experienced a slow but steady gain in concessions. These included permission to import limited quantities of Bibles, to renovate and construct new church buildings, to increase opportunities for theological education, and to enlarge the circulation of certain religious publications. However, harassment increased once again beginning in 1979–81, with the Soviet invasion of Afghanistan, the end of detente, and the election of Reagan as president. Many religious and political dissidents were put in prison or psychiatric hospitals and churches once again had difficulties meeting the demands of local Soviet administrators. Uncertainty continued from 1982 to 1985 under Brezhnev's successors. Repression continued but some improvements were noted beginning in 1983 with the return of the Danilov monastery to the Russian Orthodox Church by the Soviet government.

A new era of cautious optimism for improved church-state relations was inaugurated in 1985 with the coming to power of Mikhail Gorbachev (first secretary, beginning in 1985; president beginning in 1988). Gorbachev's policies of glasnost (openness) and perestroika (restructuring) unleased new forces in Soviet society that will not be easily reversed. In church-state terms, Gorbachev has condemned past antireligious repression, called for a more tolerant attitude toward religion in the interest of national unity, and initiated legislation to modify previous laws regulating religion and to guarantee "freedom of conscience." He also has authorized the publication and importation of tens of thousands of once prohibited Bibles, reduced the number of Christian prisoners in the Soviet gulags, and joined the churches in promoting the celebration of the millennium of Christianity in Russia in 1988. On the other hand, at the end of the 1980s, a Council on Religious Affairs still closely supervised the activities of the churches—albeit more benignly than at any time since World War II—according to the rules laid down by Lenin in 1918 and the KGB (the security police) continued to be the most troublesome institutional restraint on believers. Moreover, the study of atheism was still compulsory in universities and a consciously atheistic approach still permeated all of education; there were still Christian prisoners in the gulags; the Uniate Church, an autonomous Ukrainian Orthodox Church, and various autonomous branches of the Baptists, pentecostals, and Seventh-day Adventists were still illegal; and Christian believers were still subject to myriads of informal civil, economic, and educational disabilities.

In terms of church-state relations, the constitutions and practices of the Soviet Bloc countries of Eastern Europe are closely patterned on those of the USSR. In each country, church and state are strictly separated in an unfriendly manner, and in each atheism is given official state support. However, concrete practice varies from country to country and from time to time, depending upon a given country's historic and/or current relationship with the Soviet Union, the ability of its indigenous leadership to manage domestic politics and economics, and its geographic proximity to the West. Immediately following World War II, all of the Soviet Bloc countries tried to eradicate religion and destroy the influence of the churches. However, as regimes changed and Soviet military and economic influence fluctuated, historic religious patterns reasserted themselves and a religious revival of significant proportions occurred in some parts of Eastern Europe. Thus, in general, the churches of Poland, Hungary, and Yugoslavia have retained their vitality and influence and, in the long run, benefited from separation more than those in the other Soviet Bloc states. In Poland, the Roman Catholic Church has remained powerful and dominant and served as a rallying point for national resistance to Soviet/Marxist domination in the 1980s. In Hungary, after an abortive attempt to gain independence from Soviet control in 1956, the nation as a whole has gradually restored a measure of freedom, and the churches have benefited from this development. The Roman Catholic, Reformed, and Lutheran Churches experienced renewal in Hungary in the 1970s and 1980s. Although the churches of Yugoslavia have not demonstrated as much vitality as those in Poland and Hungary since World War II, they have enjoyed the fruits of President Tito's independent

brand of national communism which he established after breaking with Moscow in 1948. Thus, not only are church and state separate in Yugoslavia but that separation is the "least unfriendly" and allows the greatest amount of religious freedom of any Soviet Bloc country. At midpoint in terms of continuous repression is the German Democratic Republic (East Germany). The churches of the GDR have diminished in official membership since 1945 but often have more people in attendance than they did before the war. Although the churches are subject to all of the restrictions common to Marxist governments everywhere, they enjoy more peripheral freedoms, such as the publication of Bibles in sufficient numbers and the maintenance of theological faculties at universities and of independent theological schools.

The most repressive and unfriendly regimes in terms of church-state relations have been those in Czechoslovakia, Romania, and Bulgaria. Religious believers in Czechoslovakia enjoy considerable formal rights. Freedom of conscience and worship is constitutionally guaranteed, children are allowed to receive religious instruction, religious higher education is allowed, and the overwhelming majority of Czechoslovaks remain Catholic or Protestant. However, the authorities frequently have violated these rights and often severely restrict church activities. Partly because of the unsuccessful 1968 attempt to establish an independent Czech socialist "Action Program" and partly because of a major religious revival in 1968/69, the 1970s and 1980s has been a time of a sustained campaign on the part of the government to combat church influence. Despite political and economic pressures and years of intense antireligious propaganda, only one in five Czechoslovaks professes atheism, and there is evidence that a growing number of young people see in religion one of the most satisfying outlets for dissent. Romania perhaps has been the most consistently religiously repressive regime in Eastern Europe. Even so, more than 80 percent of the Romanian people continue to be religiously affiliated with either the Romanian Orthodox Church or Lutheran Church or the growing numbers of Baptist and pentecostal churches in the country. Religious restrictions generally follow the Soviet pattern and persecution of Christians was especially severe during the 1980s, mostly in response to the Ceauşescu regime's need for a scapegoat in light of the nation's faltering economy. Bulgarians have looked with genuine affection upon the Russians ever since the 19th century when they helped the Bulgarians gain their independence from the Turks. Consequently, the post-World War II Bulgarian Marxist government has consistently followed the Soviet lead in most matters, including religion. Church and state are separate, Soviet style. Constitutionally, citizens have the right to religious beliefs as long as there is no political basis to any religious organization they join. However, there are many restrictions and disabilities connected with identification with a church, all churches are registered and subject to state supervision, and religious instruction is forbidden in the schools. The 1970s and 1980s were times of considerable repression, but the Soviet example of glasnost began to make some impact late in the latter decade.

One other Marxist state in Europe is worth mentioning because of its extreme attitude toward religion, and that is Albania. This country became Marxist immediately following World War II as a result of Soviet military might. Its constitutions of 1946 and 1950 guaranteed freedom of conscience and religion, separated church and state, and sharply curtailed religious activities. All religious organs and spokespersons were heavily censored and a Stalinist type of religious supervision was established. Then, in a speech in 1967, Albanian dictator Enver Hoxha declared that Albania was now the first atheist state in the world and announced that all religion in the country had been abolished, all places of worship had been confiscated by the government, and all religious feasts and other customs related to religion had been replaced by new festivities and customs which were socialist in content. Since 1967, the entire population has been officially atheist and the regime has declared that the only religion of the state is now "Albanism."

In contrast to tiny Albania, the People's Republic of China, the most populous Marxist state in the world, has had a turbulent political, social, and cultural history since the Communist Revolution of 1949. The original constitution of the People's Republic of China said simply that "all citizens are free to believe in religion." Since the Chinese as a people have never been fanatically religious and since Christianity was only a small minority of the population at the time, there was no attempt to formalize the separation of church and state, even though it was a practical fact in an unfriendly vein. Like all new Marxist regimes, that in China was militantly atheist and did what it could to spread atheism and hinder religion. The leaders of the Cultural Revolution (1966–68) promulgated a new constitution which declared that "citizens have the freedom to believe in religion and the freedom not to believe in religion and to propagate atheism." They also initiated a vigorous campaign to eradicate all religion in China, and temples and churches virtually disappeared from the land. In the years following the Cultural Revolution, religion experienced a resurgence in Chinese life during a period of quest for stability. The new constitution of 1982 reaffirmed that the state was officially atheist. Once again, it made no reference to an established religion or to separation of church and state but it did reaffirm

religious freedom, outlaw discrimination on religious grounds, and stipulate that religions in China had to be administered by Chinese adherents and not by foreigners. During the 1970s and 1980s, many churches were rebuilt (Protestants built or restored an average of one per day from 1979–89), theological training schools reopened, religious publishing houses were established, millions of believers were added to the churches—and the general attitude of the government concerning religion during the period was "live and let live."

Church and state are separated in all other Marxist countries, with the degree of hostility or cordiality largely dependent upon the religious history of the nation and the current domestic economy. In countries like Vietnam, where the vast majority of people have never believed in a single road to truth, the Communist party is unlikely to monopolize people's minds in the way it has succeeded in monopolizing the country's institutions. Therefore, in Vietnam most church-state tension centers on institutions. For example, since the mid-1950s, the Communist party of Vietnam has required that religious hospitals, clinics, schools, and orphanages be turned over to the state and that church property be limited to specific meeting places. Church and state are constitutionally separate and freedom of conscience officially guaranteed. This arrangement is, of course, designed to keep religion out of politics and the church out of the affairs of the state. Other than that, since only about 10 percent of the population is Christian (the overwhelming majority of whom are Roman Catholic) and since Hanoi's relations with the Vatican improved following the American departure in 1975, the Vietnamese communists do not see any pressing need to convert Vietnamese Christians to atheism. Nevertheless, no Catholic or Protestant can be a member of the Communist party and all Christians suffer limited opportunities for education and career advancement. Similar situations exist in most third world Marxist nations such as Angola, Benin, the Congo, Ethiopia, Mongolia, Mozambique, Somali, and South Yemen.

In Latin America, Marxist regimes, such as those which came to power in Cuba in 1959 and in Nicaragua in 1979, constitutionally separate church and state and grant religious freedom. However, in the 1980s there was a growing trend toward benevolent neutrality between church and state in Cuba whereas in Nicaragua there was an increasing threat of open warfare between the Sandinista government and the Roman Catholic Church. The Catholic hierarchy in Nicaragua has often expressed its hostility toward Sandinista policies in general and toward Marxism in particular, a sure formula for confrontation between church and state in a Latin American Marxist nation.

***Church and State in the Latin American Countries since 1950.*** Mexico is unique among the nations of Latin America and perhaps the entire world in its approach to church and state. The constitution of 1917 (now in effect) went beyond separation of church and state and denied all churches legal existence and tried to eliminate all church influence. This measure was, of course, aimed at the Roman Catholic Church which in the eyes of the revolutionaries of 1917 was a part of an oppressive land-owning establishment which they had overthrown. The constitution made the government officially anticlerical and outlawed all religious associations known as churches. Therefore, churches in Mexico cannot own property, the government has the power to determine the number of priests in each state, foreign clergy are prohibited from working in the country, and public displays of religion are forbidden. In short, the goal of the constitution of 1917 was to annihilate the influence of the Catholic Church in Mexico.

Yet that nation has continued to be the most heavily Catholic country in the Western Hemisphere throughout the 20th century and the church there has not faded. Each year, millions of people take part in illegal public religious processions and forbidden Catholic schools teach millions of students, including the children of most of the leaders of government. This internal contradiction raised increasing concern among political leaders in the late 1980s and led some to call for the nation to come to terms with the reality of the situation by restoring the Roman Catholic Church to normal status and creating a more friendly separation of church and state. The issue divided the country in the latter part of the 20th century.

In other Latin American countries, the decisions of Vatican II led to a major reassessment of church-state relations everywhere. Before 1965, the Roman Catholic Church, the established religion in most Latin American countries, had generally supported the status quo, which usually meant repressive and exploitive regimes. As the Church began to identify less and less with the political elites and more and more with the poor and oppressed, increasing tension developed between the Catholic Church and the governments of the Latin American dictatorships, and there was a shift from friendly separation to a more hostile variety. Nevertheless, most of the Latin American nations (with a few exceptions, such as Colombia where the Catholic Church is officially established and Protestants still suffer some disabilities) constitutionally guarantee religious liberty, even if they still maintain an established church. This is the case in Argentina, Bolivia, Costa Rica, the Dominican Republic, Haiti, and Paraguay. Costa Rica and Bolivia still retain the right to nominate bishops, once the prerogative of the Spanish crown, while Venezuela and Argentina surrendered that right in 1964 and 1966, respectively.

***Church and State in the Muslim Countries since 1950.*** Islam has not produced a doctrine of separation of church and state comparable to that championed by evangelical Protestants and Enlightenment rationalists in America and eventually implemented throughout most of the Western world. By strong tradition based on the *Sharia* or religious law, which is also the law of society and of the state, Islam controls the entire life of its members. Religion, state, and community are one, and their authority is absolute. Orthodox Islam knows nothing of religious liberty in the Western sense, in principle forbids apostasy under dire penalty, and provides for change of faith only toward Islam. In those Muslim nations where there is a procedure for the recognition of conversion from Islam to another religion—such as Syria, Iraq, Pakistan, and Indonesia—all of them have been subject to strong influences from without the Islamic culture to bring about such an innovation.

Among modern Muslim nations, Turkey and Indonesia are among the most advanced in terms of religious liberty and separation of church and state. Although both are heavily Muslim countries (Indonesians constitute the world's largest single Muslim group, but, interestingly enough, the country also contains a growing Christian population which currently makes up 10 percent of the population), both are also republics which provide for separation of church and state. Islam is favored in the sense that it is the dominant religion of both states and Islamic strictures are incorporated into the sociopolitical life of the nation. Egypt is generally considered a moderate Muslim state and this is illustrated in its 1971 constitution which reflects both Islamic and Western influences. It provides for religious toleration but recognizes Islam as the official religion and, by a 1980 amendment, the *Sharia* as "the principal source of law" in the land.

Iran and Saudi Arabia are the most conservative of the modern Muslim countries. Iran became an Islamic Republic on April 1, 1979, following the overthrow of the former sovereign, the Shah (Muhammad Reza), on January 16, 1979. The constitution adopted on December 2–3, 1979, established Shi'ite Islam as the official state religion, placed supreme power in the hands of the Muslim clergy, and named Ayatollah Ruhollah Khomeini as the nation's religious leader (*velayat faghi*) for life, with powers superior to those of the president of the republic. An Assembly of Experts, composed of 83 mullahs (a Muslim religious teacher or leader), was elected in December 1982, to choose a successor to the *velayat faghi.* Limited toleration is extended to Christians and other religious groups but there is no religious freedom and no "separation of church and state" in Iran. Saudi Arabia is equally conservative in these matters. It is a traditional absolute monarchy with all power ultimately vested in the king, who is also the country's supreme religious leader. The judicial system is largely based on the *Sharia* but tribal and customary law is also applied. The government is guided by Islamic principles and Islam is the only officially recognized religion. Non-Muslim foreign workers are allowed to practice their religion only in the privacy of their own quarters. As in Iran, there is no religious liberty nor any concept of "separation of church and state" in Saudi Arabia.

***Church and State in Other Important Nations since 1950.*** India was established as a secular republic in 1947 when it gained its independence from Great Britain. With a population of more than 770 million (1986), it is the world's largest republic. The constitution provides for religious liberty and separation of religion and state. However, the country's overwhelmingly Hindu population (around 83 percent in 1986) has often asserted its political muscle through state governments which have passed legislation of a specifically Hindu character. On the other hand, the national government has introduced laws offensive to traditional Hindu teachings, the foremost example being the forbidding of all forms of discrimination against "untouchables," although it has been impossible to enforce this statute in every case.

Japan was established as a constitutional monarchy in May 1947, following its defeat in World War II. The secular constitution adopted that same year contains an extensive enumeration of civil rights including freedom of thought, conscience, and religion, and provides for complete separation of religion and state. However, there stands alongside of secular society in Japan the indigenous religion of the country, Shinto ("the way of the gods"), marked by the veneration of nature and of ancestors. Shinto, "the religion of Japaneseness," historically has served as the civil faith of the nation and provided a bridge between the state and the religious needs of the Japanese people. In the 1970s and 1980s, there was a revival of Shintoism in Japan which reemphasized traditional values and national identity.

***Conclusion.*** Worldwide trends in church-state relations continue to be toward separation of the two historic authority structures. As in the past, this has been for a variety of reasons, but predominately in order to keep the church out of the affairs of state. In this respect, the trend has been increasingly toward unfriendly separation. However, although there is some division in the ranks, most Christians still support separation as the best way to preserve religious liberty.

As this article demonstrates, the flashpoint of much modern church-state tension is education.

For example, as soon as education, in which both church and state have an essential interest, becomes universal and compulsory, either collaboration or conflict appears inescapable. This is a particularly thorny problem even in the USA where there traditionally has been a wall of separation between church and state. This raises the concomitant problem of the demarcation of the provinces of church and state which liberalism in the past has presupposed. On the one hand, how can secular politicians be convinced that churches have an inherent authority directly derived from God, that is, rights which the state does not confer but may be required to acknowledge? Conversely, on what basis can a church, whose freedom is being restricted by a state, persuasively and effectively construct its resistance?

**Bibliography.** C. Dawson, *Religion and the Modern State* (1935); A. P. Stokes, *Church and State in the United States*, 3 vols. (1950); C. Dawson, *Understanding Europe* (1952); F. H. Littell, *From State Church to Pluralism* (1962); R. F. Drinan, *Religion, the Courts, and Public Policy* (1963); S. Mead, *The Lively Experiment: The Shaping of Christianity in America* (1963); D. Oaks, ed., *The Wall Between Church and State* (1963); D. E. Boles, *The Bible, Religion and the Public Schools* (1964); A. G. Huegli, ed., *Church and State under God* (1964); K. F. Morrison, *The Two Kingdoms* (1964); M. A. C. Warren, *The Functions of a National Church* (1964); M. D. Howe, *The Garden and the Wilderness: Religion and Government in American Constitutional History* (1965); W. M. Abbott, ed., *The Documents of Vatican II* (1966); L. Pfeffer, *Church, State and Freedom* (1967); J. Tonkin, *The Church and the Secular Order in Reformation Thought* (1971); R. E. Morgan, *The Supreme Court and Religion* (1972); R. N. Bellah, *The Broken Covenant: American Civil Religion in Time of Trial* (1975); L. Pfeffer, *God, Caesar and the Constitution* (1975); A. J. Menendez, *Church-State Relations: An Annotated Bibliography* (1976); R. T. Handy, *A History of the Churches in the United States and Canada* (1977); E. Helmreich, ed., *Church and State in Europe* (1979); S. Picken, *Shinto: Japan's Spiritual Roots* (1980); J. H. Whyte, *Church and State in Modern Ireland, 1923–1979* (1980); B. Szajkowski, ed., *Marxist Governments: A World Survey*, 3 vols. (1981); H. B. Clark, II, ed., *Freedom of Religion in America: Historical Roots, Philosophical Concepts, Contemporary Problems* (1982); R. J. Neuhaus, *The Naked Public Square: Religion and Democracy in America* (1984); J. E. Wood, Jr., ed., *Religion, the State and Education* (1984); L. Pfeffer, *Religion, State and the Burger Court* (1985); A. J. Reichley, *Religion in American Public Life* (1985); J. E. Wood, Jr., ed., *Religion and the State: Essays in Honor of Leo Pfeffer* (1985); J. F. Wilson, ed., *Church and State in America: A Bibliographical Guide (The Colonial and Early National Periods)* (1986); R. T. Miller and R. B. Flowers, *Toward Benevolent Neutrality: Church, State and the Supreme Court* (1987); P. Mojzes, *Church and State in Postwar Eastern Europe: A Bibliographical Survey* (1987); J. F. Wilson and D. L. Drakeman, eds., *Church and State in American History* (1987); R. V. Pierard and R. D. Linder, *Civil Religion and the Presidency* (1988); R. S. Alley, ed., *The Supreme Court on Church and State* (1988).

ROBERT D. LINDER

**Church Army.** Group of trained evangelists founded in England in 1882 by Prebendary Wilson Carlile. The group works in the dioceses and parishes of the Anglican Church and in many ecumenical settings. The social work of the Church Army is coordinated with local authorities and other voluntary organizations providing residential establishments for unemployed young people, the single homeless, and the elderly. The society is also concerned with the rehabilitation of addicts. The Church Army runs youth centers and works closely with the chaplains' department in the armed forces and in prisons.

Church Army captains and sisters are to be found in areas of great need, including inner cities. There is constant seeking of new ways to bring the Good News of Jesus to people. Teams of evangelists can be found on the Norfolk Broads, at the seaside, and in many parishes. A roadshow bus uses theater, music, and drama to bring the message alive. The organization always strives to provide Christian service in areas of need. It has the active support of Queen Elizabeth and the archbishop of Canterbury.

Overseas daughter societies have been set up in Australia, New Zealand, Canada, the USA, the Caribbean, and East Africa.

**Churches of God.** The list of churches with some variant of the name "Church of God" is substantial. The churches selected for inclusion here are those which have distinguished themselves by their influence in the USA and abroad. The gravitation around this name is a result of a restorationist impulse.

The first denomination to use the name "Church of God" was the Holiness group led by Daniel S. Warner (1881). All the churches have had small segments of their constituency secede and form other denominations. Among the most notable was the 1919 withdrawal from the Church of God (Cleveland) of a group opposed to tithes, led by J. L. Scott, that incorporated in 1922 as the Original Church of God. Headquartered in Chattanooga, Tenn., a representative body meets annually for the 3000 members. In 1943, Homer A. Tomlinson failed to succeed his father as general overseer of the Church of God of Prophecy and pontificated over his Church of God (World Headquarters) out of his residence in Queens, N.Y. Tomlinson was legendary because of his coronation in 101 capitals of the world; he declared himself "King of All Nations of Men" and proclaimed prosperity as a result of the act. He also obtained considerable notoriety by his 1952, 1960, 1964, and 1968 campaigns as the Theocratic party candidate for president of the USA. At his death in 1968 his responsibilities were assumed by Voy M. Bullen, who runs the almost nonexistent denomination from his home in Huntsville, Ala. The Church of God (Jerusalem Acres) was started in 1957 when Grady R. Kent left the Church of God of Prophecy because of his preoccupation with apocalypticism. He expanded this emphasis beyond the restoration of the offices of 12 apostles and seven spirits of God and added what he called "New Testament Judaism"—observance of the Sabbath, various Jewish festivals, and dietary laws. The church

survived his death in 1964, but the small membership base continues to erode.

***Church of God (Anderson, Ind).*** The earliest significant breach among Holiness believers occurred within a group of German Baptists in Indiana and Ohio known as the Church of God of North America General Eldership. In 1878, several members of this group led by Daniel Sidney Warner, editor of the *Gospel Trumpet,* seceded and established a new organization (Northern Indiana Eldership). By 1881, Warner and his associates withdrew and created another religious fellowship, the Church of God Reformation. One of Warner's noted characteristics was his desire to unite all Christians, a by-product of which is that the church to this day does not keep a membership roll. Their report system does, however, allow them to reckon 250,000 adherents, with racially inclusive congregations in the USA, with the majority of communicants outside the USA since 1983. An international convention drawing 20,000 attendees is convened each June in Anderson. They officially disallow a formal creed, while publishing "teachings." Their theological nuances are from the Holiness movement and include immersion of recognized believers, resistance to Protestant charismatic distinctives, apocalypticism, and a foot-washing service as part of the Easter celebration. However, they deny a connection of Christ's second coming with the millennium, they have worked with the National Council of Churches (NCC) while observing National Association of Evangelicals (NAE) functions, and the Anderson college and seminary have been accused of being liberal by their majority conservative constituency. They have been self-described as combining Wesleyan soteriology, radical reformation ecclesiology, and experiential epistemology. The Winebrenneran connection is maintained to this day as well as direct fellowship with restorationist groups like Disciples, Brethren, and Friends.

***Church of God in Christ.*** This church, predominantly but not exclusively black, projected in 1982 a worldwide membership of 3,709,661. This would make it second only to the affiliated membership of the Assemblies of God. The church owes its earliest moorings to the Holiness movement.

Charles H. Mason was born in 1866 on the Prior Farm near Memphis, Tenn. Both his parents had been slaves and both became members of the local Missionary Baptist Church. Converted in 1878, Mason recorded a personal healing in 1880, and by 1893 he had preached his first sermon. The Mount Gale Missionary Baptist Church issued him a local license and his thoughts turned toward a domestic ministry. By 1894, however, he left the Arkansas Baptist College and began an evangelistic ministry which emphasized divine healing and sought to reach people of "all colors."

During 1885/86, Elder Mason and other Missionary Baptist Church ministers from Mississippi, including Elder C. P. Jones, openly propagated the Holiness teaching of entire sanctification. They were soon ejected from their Baptist Association and in 1897 held a revival that became the organizational meeting for a burgeoning denomination that would be called "The Church of God in Christ" (cf. 1 Thess. 2:14) to distinguish itself from other Churches of God. Later that year the group was incorporated in Memphis, Tenn. Since they were the first Holiness denomination to incorporate, a variety of ministers, including whites, were ordained by Mason; this practice continued after the group became pentecostal.

When news of the Azusa Street Revival came to Mason and Jones in 1907, they reacted differently. Jones was uninterested, but Mason traveled to Los Angeles and returned with the pentecostal experience and doctrine. There was a division at the 1907 annual assembly which resulted in Presiding Elder Jones withdrawing the right hand of fellowship from Mason who assumed the leadership of the church. Mason retained this position until his death in 1961 at the age of 95.

The leader since 1968 has been its first elected presiding bishop, James O. Patterson, Sr., who has served several consecutive four-year terms. His unique leadership skills not only pulled the church through an ominous transition period (1961–68), but have creatively moved the church to new heights (e.g., education, doctrine, polity, social responsibility, finances, publishing, etc.). Patterson presides over the annual convocation in Memphis that is said to attract 40,000. The church has kept many of the early Holiness pentecostal tenets and has taken part in social and political matters such as those connected with Martin Luther King, Jr., and Malcolm X. Mason Theological Seminary was established in Atlanta, Ga., in 1970, making it the first pentecostal seminary, and it was the first such seminary to receive accreditation.

***Church of God (Cleveland, Tenn.).*** The third largest pentecostal church in the world is the Church of God (Cleveland). Less than one-third of its 1,703,678 members (1986) reside in the USA and, among the 114 countries, there are affiliations in South Africa, Indonesia, and Romania. The roots of the church reach back to the short-lived Christian Union (1886) in Tennessee, formed by Richard G. Spurling, and an 1896 revival in Cherokee County, N.C., in which, reportedly, 100 people experienced tongues-speech. In 1902, W. F. Bryant and R. G. Spurling, Jr., organized a small band as the Holiness Church at Camp Creek. A. J. Tomlinson joined the group in 1903 and was chosen as pastor.

During January 1906, four affiliated congregations convened their first annual gathering and evidenced their biblicist orientation by first resolving that they were not "legislative or executive" but "judicial only." In 1907 the name "Church of God" was adopted, and in 1909 Tomlinson was chosen as the head of the fledgling denomination. In early 1910, R. M. Evans arrived in the Bahamas to establish the Church of God, and later that year the newly created "[The Evening Light and] Church of God Evangel" published 25 teachings. These teachings, adopted by the assembly of 1911, were grounded in the Holiness movement and evidenced the 1908 move of the church into the emerging pentecostal movement. Important polity decisions were made, first in 1910 with the adoption of state overseers, and then in 1917 with the formation of the Council of Elders. The Bible Training School was opened in 1918 and an orphanage was begun in 1920. By the end of 1923, a new general overseer, F. J. Lee, was chosen.

A significant occurrence was the role of the Church of God at the 1942 constitutional meeting of NAE. The extent of the evangelical influence was evident in the 1948 formation of the Pentecostal Fellowship of North America (PFNA), which took the NAE statement of faith and added an affirmation of Spirit-baptism with initial evidence. The Church of God was also integral to the formation of the World Pentecostal Fellowship (1947), which has never produced a doctrinal statement.

The biennial assemblies (since 1946), governed by ordained male ministers, convene in various cities in the USA. The body supports, in the USA, Lee College, three Bible colleges, a seminary, and the Pentecostal Resource Center. The assembly of 1986 enlarged the executive council to 18 members; the six new members were not from the USA. The Church of God is a multifaceted body whose ministries also focus on modern media, youth, military personnel, lay responsibility, stewardship, and cross-cultural concerns.

***The Church of God of Prophecy.*** The Church of God of Prophecy (the name since 1952) officially claims to own the early years of the Church of God (Cleveland). As a result of numerous sociological, theological, historical, and personal factors, the Church of God of Prophecy came into existence in 1923/24. A. J. Tomlinson served as general overseer of the church until his death (1943), at which time his youngest son, Milton A. Tomlinson, was chosen for the position. Tomlinson remains the head of the 237,142-member (1986) international church (89 countries). In addition to Tomlinson College, there are international departments which direct prayer groups, organize missions, work with young people, utilize modern media, seek out military personnel, and encourage Bible study and evangelism. One department maintains and operates the multimillion-dollar, 216-acre biblical theme park in western North Carolina known as the Fields of the Wood. Displayed there, and at each church facility, is the distinctive church flag (1933).

The term "theocracy" is employed to describe a government that proclaims the annual general assembly to be the highest tribunal, while the entire ecclesiastical structure collapses on the office of the general overseer. All of the general assembly resolutions, which are projected to be unanimous decisions of all male members of the 20,000 attendees, have been predicated on Holiness pentecostal thought, like the prohibition of multiple marriages of adulterous persons and affirming immanence-oriented eschatologies. The Holiness influence has been keenly felt in matters of clothes and recreation, while the restorationist impulse was manifested in an exclusive body ecclesiology. The latter has accounted for the church's lack of membership in organizations like PFNA and WPF. At the same time, it has influenced the fact that the Church of God of Prophecy has a high percentage of female pastors and may be the church most racially inclusive at all levels in the USA.

**Church of God (Apostolic).** The classical pentecostal movement has three main segments. There are Keswickian pentecostals, like Assemblies of God and International Church of the Foursquare Gospel, and Holiness pentecostals, like the Pentecostal Churches of God in this article along with the Pentecostal Holiness Church. The third segment is determined by a unitarian doctrine centered in Jesus Christ; thus devotees have been labeled "Jesus Only," and may be called Oneness Pentecostals.

One of the oldest churches in this stream was organized in Danville, Ky., as the Christian Faith Band by Elder Thomas J. Cox in 1897, who served as general overseer until his death in 1943. It was a 1915 move toward a "more scriptural" name that led the group into the Oneness stream. Along with traditional Oneness Pentecostal doctrines, the church has not opposed medicine, has opposed war, and has ordained female ministers. The total membership may be no more than 1000.

*Bibliography.* E. L. Simmons, *History of the Church of God* (1938); J. O. Patterson, et al., *History and Formative Years of the Church of God in Christ* (1969); *Official Manual with the Doctrines and Discipline of the Church of God in Christ* (1973); C. T. Davidson, *Upon This Rock*, 3 vols. (1973–76); C. W. Conn, *Like a Mighty Army* (1977); J. Stone, *The Church of God of Prophecy: History and Polity* (1977); A. C. Peipkorn, *Holiness and Pentecostal* (1979); J. R. W. Smith, *The Quest for Holiness in Unity* (1980); J. R. W. Smith, *I Will Build My Church* (1985).

HAROLD D. HUNTER

**Church Discipline.** *See* DISCIPLINE, CHURCH.

**Churches of Christ.** Independent, autonomous churches emphasizing a return to the pattern of the NT church. Even though indigenous congregations in many countries around the world share basically the same views, the vast majority of Churches of Christ are located in the USA; as of 1987 there were approximately 12,000 congregations with some 1.2 million members. A number of minor theological differences separate the fellowship, but all are united on such things as a cappella music, limited public roles for women, and opposition to organized societies outside the local church that would do the work of the local congregation.

Churches of Christ were recognized as a separate religious movement in the U.S. religious census of 1906. Until this century, Churches of Christ did not have a separate existence from the larger body often referred to as Disciples of Christ. Thus the history of Churches of Christ includes such men as Thomas and Alexander Campbell who brought their ideas of religious change to America from Northern Ireland. Alexander Campbell's views, first enunciated in his *Christian Baptist*, have had a tremendous impact upon many leaders of Churches of Christ. His series of articles entitled "Ancient Order of Things" posited a strong inductive method of formulating the pattern of the 1st-century church. This method continues to dominate the thought of many in the fellowship.

Second-generation leaders emphasized different aspects of the early restorers. Tolbert Fanning and David Lipscomb, editors of the *Gospel Advocate*, emphasized a conservative interpretation of the Bible, often recalling Campbell's ideas from the *Christian Baptist*. When higher criticism emerged late in the 19th century, David Lipscomb gave direction to conservative Disciples. Parallel to much of American religion during the era, the segment of the Disciples that came to be known as Churches of Christ rejected the conclusions of liberal theology. These positions were enunciated in an article by Lipscomb in 1907 when he recognized two religious bodies—Disciples of Christ and Churches of Christ.

Although Churches of Christ are located in all states of the USA, the vast majority of the membership remains in the South and Southwest, with Tennessee and Texas having the largest numbers. Members of the fellowship support nine senior colleges and six junior colleges in the USA and Canada. Numerous elementary and secondary schools are supported within Churches of Christ. The oldest school among Churches of Christ is David Lipscomb College in Nashville, Tenn., founded in 1891 by David Lipscomb and James A. Harding as the Nashville Bible School.

The American Restoration movement historically has placed a strong emphasis on journalism. This has especially been true among Churches of Christ. Because of the autonomous nature of individual congregations, new ideas found their way into the fellowship through the printed page.

The oldest journal continuing to publish among Churches of Christ and the Restoration movement is the *Gospel Advocate*, begun by Tolbert Fanning in 1855.

The greatest growth of Churches of Christ took place from the late 1940s to the 1960s. The fellowship has often been included in the lists of the fastest-growing religious bodies in the USA. In recent years, growth has been minimal, with the largest growth being in the Northeast. On the other hand, the largest numbers of new converts can be counted in countries of the third world, especially in Africa and Central America. The most successful effort in Europe has been through an indigenous movement in Spain.

*Bibliography.* Earl West, *Search for the Ancient Order*, 3 vols. (1949, 1950, 1979); James De Forest Murch, *Christians Only* (1962); Bill Humble, *The Story of the Restoration* (1969); Leroy Garrett, *The Stone–Campbell Movement* (1981).

ROBERT E. HOOPER

## Churches of Christ, World Convention of.
A periodic, inspirational global fellowship composed of churches and individuals from 60 countries associated with the Campbell–Stone movement. Founded in 1930, it meets in assembly every four years for proclamation of the gospel, Christian education, evangelistic emphasis, inspiration, ecumenical concerns, and fellowship.

## Church Growth.
Term coined by Donald A. McGavran to describe the dynamic Christian mission of spiritual outreach to the non-Christian populations of the world. Its meaning in his usage is illuminated by three facts:

1. He was a third-generation missionary in India where the ancient system of caste divides the population into thousands of social pockets. He and others observed the tendency of whole groups to make decisions such that people movements resulted—in contrast to the evangelical/pietist expectation of purely individual decisions.
2. He came from the Campbellite/Disciples of Christ tradition which emphasized the primacy of the local congregation as the essential existence of the church of Jesus Christ, a fact which again made him uneasy with any evangelism which did not result in new Christians becoming incorporated into congregational life.
3. After many years of mission administration he became displeased with the static character of much of the work in India.

Thus, McGavran chose the term "church growth" in conscious reaction to the trend in conciliar circles to redefine missions and evangelism so as to allow churches to occupy themselves with all kinds of things other than outreach, and in protest against the evangelical employment of mass evangelistic techniques (radio, literature, large meetings) which often had no verifiable results in congregational life.

The polemic impact of the concept significantly increased when McGavran was allowed by the Northwest Christian College of Eugene, Oreg., to found there the Institute of Church Growth. It was there he completed his classical work *The Bridges of God*. This book was printed by the National Council of Churches, and almost overnight became both widely read and controversial. His passion for true church growth, even in the form of people movements involving group conversion, raised many eyebrows. Some denied the possibility of whole groups being converted, while others recoiled at the thought of ethnically homogeneous units becoming the locus of church life and perhaps even perpetuating racism.

By 1965 the term "church growth" had gained additional backing as McGavran was invited to move his Institute of Church Growth to Fuller Theological Seminary in Pasadena, Calif., where he was heard more extensively than ever, especially in nonconciliar circles. Alan Tippett accompanied him; J. Edwin Orr, Ralph Winter, Charles Kraft, Arthur Glasser, and Peter Wagner soon joined him.

The church growth perspective was embraced by the Evangelical Foreign Missions Association, which for some years sponsored annual church growth seminars for missionaries on furlough, highlighting McGavran and his faculty members. Equally influential in the church growth movement was the decision of Overseas Crusades, Inc., to publish the *Church Growth Bulletin*. Articles like "Will Uppsala Betray the 3 Billion?" disturbed the thinking at World Council of Churches meetings.

Thus, despite his move to an interdenominational evangelical seminary McGavran retained his influence in the conciliar world, and in 1968 was asked to write an article for the *International Review of Missions* which touched off a global debate. A whole issue of the journal was later employed to sum up the backwash of response, much of it negative, coming from people with backgrounds in European church situations where the growth of the church (unlike in India and the mission field in general) is in one sense meaningless since most of the population is involved only minimally in the church. At the same time the emphasis on the growth of the church along the lines of homogeneous population units antagonized both conciliar and evangelical thinkers alike, in an age when racial integration was high on the agenda of Christian thought.

Nevertheless a church growth school gradually emerged with mounting influence and a growing literature. Even the World Council's Iberville statement conceded a great deal to this school of thought.

Meanwhile Fuller Seminary's School of World Mission and Institute of Church Growth grew steadily so that by 1987 enrollment was over 700, with at least 300 overseas national leaders; the largest group was comprised of experienced missionaries on furlough. Unquestionably, no other school in modern times has affected as many missionaries and thus promoted church growth thinking. The higher degrees offered there have been the basis for a large number of professorships in dozens of other schools, both in North America and in non-Western countries.

On the other hand, the term "church growth" has attained a great deal of acceptance outside the world of the missionary. Peter Wagner in particular, but McGavran himself also attempted to adapt the concept for the use of churches in North America. Wyn Arn founded the Institute for American Church Growth to foster this dimension of the movement. Eventually the Fuller Evangelistic Association opened the Fuller Institute for Evangelism and Church Growth, with Carl George as its director. A whole flurry of books appeared in North America. Eddie Gibbs adapted some of the concepts in a book that challenged England along the same lines.

In one way or another dozens of North American denominations have launched multimilliondollar efforts to expand their membership in a secular world increasingly hostile in some ways and increasingly open in others.

A characteristic of the original church growth concern was the determination both to plant more churches where conditions seemed favorable and to penetrate groups which seemed resistant. The latter emphasis unfortunately has been lost in many popular interpretations of church growth thinking, which have simply stressed the possibilities of the growth of existing churches, not the venturesome penetration of unreached peoples.

RALPH D. WINTER

**Church History Studies.** Since 1900, and especially since 1950, there has been an explosion of scholarship in the study of church history. In terms of the loci of this scholarship, the dominant trend has been out of the seminaries and into theological faculties related to private universities and the history departments of the state universities. A roll call of the dominant historians of Christianity during the century illustrates this: Sweet, Latourette, Bainton, Mead, Ahlstrom, and Marty. The main methodological trend has been away from the von Rankian scientific school of the 19th century and the old liberal school of the early 20th century to an age of methodological conservatism and considerable uncertainty. Although there has been some inclination toward

the new social history, most church historians have relied little on psychohistory, cliometrics, the French *Annales* school, and the like. Finally, there has been a shift in the foci of subject matter, deemphasizing church union and the development of a common theology and emphasizing spiritual legacies and the study of how Christianity has affected culture and vice versa. The following works are representative of the increasingly high quality of scholarship in church history studies during this century.

*Encyclopedias and Dictionaries.* The New *Catholic Encyclopedia* (16 vols., 1967) is an outstanding multivolume work. The best single-volume dictionaries dealing with church history are J. C. Brauer (ed.), *The Westminster Dictionary of Church History* (1971); F. L. Cross (ed.), *The Oxford Dictionary of the Christian Church* (1974); J. D. Douglas (ed.), *The New International Dictionary of the Christian Church* (rev. ed., 1978); and W. A. Elwell (ed.), *Evangelical Dictionary of Theology* (1984).

*General Works.* Kenneth Scott Latourette's work dominates the general histories: *A History of Christianity* (1953); *History of the Expansion of Christianity* (7 vols., 1937–45); and *Christianity in a Revolutionary Age* (5 vols., 1958–62). Also important are Williston Walker's *History of the Christian Church,* rev. by R. A. Norris, D. W. Lotz, and R. T. Handy (4th ed., 1985); and Kurt Aland's *History of Christianity* (2 vols., 1985/86). Jaroslav Pelikan's monumental *Christian Tradition: A History of the Development of Doctrine* (5 vols., 1971–85) covers this topic admirably, but Paul Tillich's *History of Christian Thought* (2d rev. ed., 1968) also should be mentioned because of its original insights. The best layperson's general history of the Christian faith is Timothy Dowley (ed.), *Eerdmans' Handbook to the History of Christianity* (1977), while Jacques Ellul, *The Subversion of Christianity* (1986), offers a challenging new interpretation.

*The Ancient Period.* No student of this era can ignore W. H. C. Frend's magisterial *Rise of Christianity* (1984). Central to the study of NT history are Rudolf Bultmann, *Primitive Christianity in Its Historical Setting* (1956); Bruce Metzger, *The NT: Its Background, Growth and Content* (1965); and F. F. Bruce, *NT History* (1970). Also important are C. H. Dodd, *The Founder of Christianity* (1970); Henry Chadwick, *The Early Church* (1968); J. N. D. Kelly, *Early Christian Doctrines* (rev. ed., 1978); C. J. Cadoux, *The Early Church and the World* (1925); R. M. Grant, *Early Christianity and Society* (1977); and Peter Brown, *Augustine of Hippo* (1967).

*The Medieval and Renaissance Periods.* Classic interpretations include Christopher Dawson, *Religion and the Rise of Western Culture* (1950), and R. W. Southern, *Western Society and the Church in the Middle Ages* (1970). Other important studies worthy of note are H. C. Lea, *History of the Inquisition in the Middle Ages* (3 vols., 1922); Gerd Tellenbach, *Church, State and Christian Society at the Time of the Investiture Controversy* (1940); Matthew Spinka, *John Huss and the Czech Reform* (1941); Steven Runciman, *A History of the Crusades* (3 vols., 1951–54); Brian Tierney, *Foundations of the Conciliar Theory* (1955); Walter Ullmann, *The Growth of Papal Government* (1955); and G. B. Russell, *Witchcraft in the Middle Ages* (1972). Since mid-century, attention has focused on the late medieval and Renaissance periods as the key to understanding the coming of the Protestant Reformation. In this category are the following first-rate studies: L. W. Spitz, *The Religious Renaissance of the German Humanists* (1963); H. A. Oberman, *Forerunners of the Reformation: The Shape of Late Medieval Thought* (1966); Charles Trinkaus, *In Our Image and Likeness: Humanity and Divinity in Italian Humanist Thought* (2 vols., 1970); Charles Trinkaus and H. A. Oberman (eds.), *The Pursuit of Holiness in Late Medieval and Renaissance Religion* (1974); Francis Oakley, *The Western Church in the Late Middle Ages* (1979); and Steven Ozment, *The Age of Reform, 1250–1550* (1980).

***The Reformation Era.*** Reformation historians have been among the most prolific of 20th-century students of Christian history. Commanding the heights of Reformation historiography is A. G. Dickens and John Tonkin, *The Reformation in Historical Thought* (1985). The dominant surveys include G. R. Elton, *Reformation Europe, 1517–1559* (1963); H. J. Grimm, *The Reformation Era* (rev. ed., 1973); and P. J. Klassen, *Europe in the Reformation* (1979); while L. W. Spitz, *The Protestant Reformation, 1517–1559* (1985), covers a more limited segment of the period. Lutheran Reformation studies have been well served by hundreds of competent scholars, including E. G. Rupp, *The Righteousness of God: Luther Studies* (1953), and Joseph Lortz, *The Reformation in Germany* (2 vols., 1968). Luther himself has been the focus of scores of biographies and special monographs. Among the best are the classic biography by R. H. Bainton, *Here I Stand: A Life of Martin Luther* (1950); as well as the work of E. G. Schwiebert, *Luther and His Times* (1950); Erik Erikson, *Young Man Luther: A Study in Psychoanalysis* (1958); and James Atkinson, *The Trial of Martin Luther* (1971). Calvin studies have featured the work of J. T. McNeill, *The History and Character of Calvinism* (rev. ed., 1967); R. M. Kingdon, *Geneva and the Coming of the Wars of Religion in France, 1555–1563* (1956) and *Geneva and the Consolidation of the French Protestant Movement, 1564–1572* (1967); and E. W. Monter, *Calvin's Geneva* (1967). First-rate Calvin biographies include T. H. L. Parker, *John Calvin* (1975), and W. J. Bouwsma, *John Calvin* (1987). A. G. Dickens, *The English Reformation* (rev. ed., 1988),

dominates that area of Reformation studies while the Puritan movement has received quality attention from William Haller, *The Rise of Puritanism* (1938); Christopher Hill, *Society and Puritanism in Pre-Revolutionary England* (1964); and Patrick Collinson, *The Elizabethan Puritan Movement* (1967). Alan Simpson straddled the Atlantic with his *Puritanism in Old and New England* (1955); while Cromwell received insightful treatment from R. S. Paul, *The Lord Protector: Religion and Politics in the Life of Oliver Cromwell* (1955). Two excellent biographies which provide understanding of Knox and the Scottish Reformation are those of Jasper Ridley, *John Knox* (1968), and W. S. Reid, *Trumpeter of God: A Biography of John Knox* (1974). Studies in the Radical Reformation in general and Anabaptism in particular experienced a giant leap forward with the publication of G. H. Williams, *The Radical Reformation* (1962); supported by John Wenger (ed.), *The Complete Writings of Menno Simons* (1956); F. H. Littell, *The Anabaptist View of the Church* (1957); H. J. Hillerbrand, *A Bibliography of Anabaptism, 1528–1630* (1962); Claus Peter Clasen, *Anabaptism: A Social History* (1972); and W. R. Estep, *The Anabaptist Story* (rev. ed., 1975). Outstanding surveys of the Catholic Reformation include Pierre Janelle, *The Catholic Reformation* (1949), and M. R. O'Connell, *The Counter Reformation* (1974), while Hubert Jedin, *The History of the Council of Trent* (2 vols., 1957–61), and Jean Delumeau, *Catholicism Between Luther and Voltaire* (1977), have added new dimensions of understanding to this corner of the Reformation era. In addition, E. Harris Harbison's classic *Christian Scholar in the Age of the Reformation* (1956) and Keith Thomas's groundbreaking *Religion and the Decline of Magic* (1971) deserve special mention.

***Wesley and the Wesleyan Tradition.*** Much work needs to be done in this area of church history, and the definitive biography of John Wesley remains elusive. However, certain aspects of Wesley's life and ministry have been illuminated by G. E. Harrison, *Son to Susanna* (1937); W. R. Cannon, *The Theology of John Wesley* (1946); V. H. H. Green, *The Young Mr. Wesley* (1961); Martin Schmidt, *John Wesley: A Theological Biography* (2 vols., 1962–73); A. C. Outler (ed.), *John Wesley* (1964); A. S. Wood, *The Burning Heart: John Wesley, Evangelist* (1967); and R. G. Tuttle, *John Wesley, His Life and Theology* (1980). Valuable studies of various facets of Wesleyan history include E. P. Thompson, *The Making of the English Working Class* (1963); Bernard Semmel, *The Methodist Revolution* (1973); and David Hempton, *Methodism and Politics in British Society, 1750–1850* (1984).

***Modern Western Church History.*** G. R. Cragg, *The Church and the Age of Reason, 1648–1789* (rev. ed., 1966), and Alex Vidler, *The Church in the*

*Age of Revolution: 1789 to the Present Day* (rev. ed., 1971), are useful surveys of this period of Christian history. Other scholarly studies cover sundry important subtopics such as W. K. Jordan, *The Development of Toleration in England* (4 vols., 1932–40); J. H. Nichols, *Democracy in the Churches* (1951); Karl Barth, *Protestant Theology in the Nineteenth Century* (1959); and Owen Chadwick, *The Victorian Church* (2 vols., 1966–70).

**Eastern Church History.** The pioneering work of Matthew Spinka is still foundational for the study of the history of Christianity in Eastern Europe: *The Church and the Russian Revolution* (1927) and *History of Christianity in the Balkans* (1933). More recent works of note include Nicholas Zernov, *Eastern Christendom* (1961); G. P. Fedotov, *The Russian Religious Mind* (2 vols., 1966); Michael Bourdeaux, *Faith on Trial in Russia* (1971); and Jane Ellis, *The Russian Orthodox Church: A Contemporary History* (1986).

**History of Ecumenism and Missions.** The dominant tome in this field is Ruth Rouse and S. C. Neill (eds.), *A History of the Ecumenical Movement, 1517–1948* (2d ed., 1967). Also important are J. T. McNeill, *Unitive Protestantism* (1935), and H. E. Fey (ed.), *The Ecumenical Advance, 1948–1968* (1970). A significant work on the history of missions is Stephen Neill, *A History of Christian Missions* (1964).

*American Church History.* The lively nature of Christianity in America has captured the interest of an increasingly large number of dedicated scholars. W. W. Sweet dominated the historiography of American Christian history in the first half of the century with such landmark works as *Religion on the American Frontier, 1783–1850* (4 vols., 1931–46). Most influential in the last half of the century have been Sidney Mead, *The Lively Experiment: The Shaping of Christianity in America* (1963); Sydney Ahlstrom, *A Religious History of the American People* (1972); and M. E. Marty, *Pilgrims in Their Own Land: 500 Years of Religion in America* (1984). Above all, Ahlstrom's magisterial volume with its insistence on the Puritan theme, in the broadest sense of that term, has been the protagonist in the study of the history of American Christianity since its publication. Two other general surveys of the history of religion in America deserve mention, not because of their interpretive hegemony, but for other reasons. These are W. S. Hudson's synthesizing *Religion in America* (4th ed., 1987); and C. L. Albanese's attempt to subvert official establishment history, *America: Religions and Religion* (1981). After falling on evil days in the first decades of the century, Puritan studies have made a comeback with a vengeance, thanks mostly to the yeoman work of Perry Miller: *Orthodoxy in Massachusetts* (1933); *The New England Mind: The Seventeenth Century* (1939); *The New England Mind: From Colony to Province* (1953); and *Errand into the Wilderness* (1956), to cite a few. Other important contributions to Puritan history are E. D. Morgan, *Visible Saints: The History of a Puritan Idea* (1963), and Sacvan Bercovitch, *The Puritan Origins of the American Self* (1978). Echoes of Puritan intellectual influence can be found in the important studies of Alan Heimert, *Religion and the American Mind from the Great Awakening to the Revolution* (1966), and Norman Fiering, *Jonathan Edwards' Moral Thought and Its British Context* (1981). Henry May, *The Enlightenment in America* (1976), and W. G. McLoughlin, *Revivals, Awakenings and Reform* (1978), provide insights into two seemingly antithetical yet often complementary aspects of America's religious heritage. Protestant history has been covered thematically in M. E. Marty, *Righteous Empire: The Protestant Experience in America* (1970, rev. ed., with the title *Protestantism in the United States: Righteous Empire* [1985]); while Catholic history has been handled synoptically in J. P. Dolan, *The American Catholic Experience: A History from Colonial Times to the Present* (1985). Similarly, G. M. Marsden, *Fundamentalism and American Culture: The Shaping of Twentieth-Century Evangelicalism, 1870–1925* (1980), and W. R. Hutchison, *The Modernist Impulse in American Protestantism* (1976), treat two sides of the modern American religious coin. Two landmark books have contributed greater understanding to the history of Christianity in the South: Donald Mathews, *Religion in the Old South* (1977), and Albert Raboteau, *Slave Religion: The "Invisible Institution" in the Antebellum South* (1977). Exemplary denominational histories include R. A. Baker, *The Southern Baptist Convention and Its People, 1607–1972* (1974), and F. A. Norwood, *The Story of American Methodism* (1974). Important themes in the history of revivalism have been highlighted in the pioneering works of W. R. Cross, *The Burned Over District: The Social and Intellectual History of Enthusiastic Religion in Western New York, 1800–1850* (1950); T. L. Smith, *Revivalism and Social Reform in Mid-Nineteenth-Century America* (rev. ed., 1980); and D. L. Weddle, *The Law as Gospel: Revival and Reform in the Theology of Charles G. Finney* (1985). Two important works on Catholic development in America are R. D. Cross, *The Emergence of Liberal Catholicism in America* (1968), and D. J. O'Brien, *American Catholics and Social Reform: The New Deal Years* (1968). The pioneer work of J. W. James (ed.), *Women in American Religion* (1980), deserves mention, as do the enduring classics: H. R. Niebuhr, *The Kingdom of God in America* (1937); C. H. Hopkins, *The Rise of the Social Gospel in American Protestantism* (1940); and A. P. Stokes, *Church and State in the United States* (3 vols., 1950).

**Journals.** The leading journals devoted to the scholarly study of the history of Christianity in its various expressions are the *Catholic Historical Review* (founded 1915); *Church History* (founded 1932); *Journal of Ecclesiastical History* (founded 1953); *Journal of Religious History* (founded 1960); and *Fides et Historia* (founded 1968).

ROBERT D. LINDER

**Church of Christ, Scientist.** *See* CHRISTIAN SCIENCE.

**Church of England in South Africa.** The oldest of the republic's English-speaking churches. Although the first service on record was held in 1749, it was only in 1848 that Robert Gray was appointed as first bishop. A strong Tractarian, Gray, seeking to be free from what he called the "bonds and fetters of the Reformation," leaned strongly toward the doctrines of the Church of Rome, and founded the Church of the Province of South Africa in 1870. With the exception of the bishop of Natal, the rest of the bishops of the Church of England in South Africa followed Gray, and the Church of the Province was recognized as a member of the Anglican Communion whereas, illogically, the original Church of England in South Africa came to be ignored by that body. However, both the Supreme Court in South Africa and the Privy Council in England on appeal, held the Church of the Province to be separate from the Church of England on the grounds of no "identity in standards of faith and doctrine."

From 1870 until 1932 Bishop Gray's successors accepted a dual status. Consecrated in England, they were bishops of the Church of England and as such ministered to the congregations of the Church of England in South Africa. Elected as bishops by the Church of the Province, they ministered as such to that church. But the dual status was brought to an end by the election in 1932 of the first archbishop of Cape Town who had not been consecrated in England.

Successive pleas to the archbishop of Canterbury that he should appoint a bishop for the Church of England in South Africa were rejected and it struggled for survival until in 1955 G. F. B. Morris, who had been bishop in North Africa, accepted election as bishop of the Church of England in South Africa. Although sharply criticized for this by the archbishop of Canterbury and ignored by the Lambeth Conference, the Church of England in South Africa then consolidated and rapidly expanded.

In 1983 Canon Dudley Foord of Sydney, Australia, was elected presiding bishop and was consecrated by the archbishop of Sydney, with the primate of Australia, 12 other Australian bishops, and the bishop of Kimberley (a bishop of the Church of the Province), participating in a gesture of goodwill. But no acceptable formula for coexistence between the two "Anglican" churches has as yet been found, and the presence of two separate Anglican churches in the same country is unique to South Africa. The position is hardly known outside of that country, more especially because the Church of England in South Africa tends to keep a low profile, concentrating on preaching and teaching the historic Christian faith, planting churches, and strengthening the life of each congregation, whereas the Church of the Province of South Africa maintains a very high profile on political matters under the leadership of Archbishop Desmond Tutu.

Currently the Church of England in South Africa has churches in Namibia and all four provinces of South Africa, where the gospel of Jesus Christ is faithfully proclaimed. The church has six bishops and over 100 ordained clergy, and is growing rapidly.

DUDLEY T. FOORD

**Church of the Brethren.** *See* DUNKERS.

**Church of the Nazarene.** *See* NAZARENE, CHURCH OF THE.

**Church of the New Jerusalem.** *See* NEW JERUSALEM, CHURCH OF THE.

**Church Peace Union.** *See* PEACE MOVEMENTS.

**Church Socialist League.** League established by members of the Church of England in 1906 to pioneer in social theory and action in directions in which the great bulk of their fellow-churchmen were not willing to follow. An off-shoot of the same name was organized by Episcopalians in the USA in 1911. Leading British figures were Lewis Donaldson (who summed up the league's position: "Christianity is the religion of which socialism is the practice"), P. E. T. Widdington, and James Adderley; American leaders included B. I. Bell, Lyford Edwards, and Bishop Spaulding, who called himself a Christian Marxist. The league never exerted influence in the Protestant Episcopal Church, partly because the term "socialist" was equated in most minds with anti-American tenets, partly because some of its leaders were pacifists. It was absorbed by the Church League for Industrial Democracy in 1919.

ALEXANDER C. ZABRISKIE

**Church Society.** Senior evangelical body of the Church of England committed to upholding the 39 Articles of Religion. It seeks to do this through meetings, conferences, publications, and education. The Church Society was formed in 1950 from two previously existing bodies: the Church Association founded in 1865, which supported most of the prosecutions against ritualism; and the National Church League, organized in 1906 from several groups devoted to more positive methods of spreading Reformation principles and teachings. The Church Society currently publishes two quarterlies: a theological journal, *Churchman*, and the magazine *Cross+Way*. The society has a council of 20, roughly half lay and half clergy, which meets each month. Through the Church Society Trust it appoints clergy to over 100 parishes.

## Church Union, The.

English organization founded in 1859 as an offshoot of the Oxford movement to help misunderstood and abused priests and parishes; to restore to the church the fullness of Catholic faith, life, and practice; and to work for the conversion of England to Christ. The union is active today in the areas of church defense, prayer, social and youth work, and publishes the *Church Observer*.

## Church Universal and Triumphant, The (CUT).

Cult founded in 1958 which holds to an eclectic blend of Eastern mysticism, unorthodox Christianity, and patriotic Americanism. The cult's founder, Mark Prophet, claimed to receive spiritist revelations from the "ascended masters," deceased persons of spiritual significance who had joined the ranks of the "Great White Brotherhood." He later met and married Elizabeth Clare Wulf, 21 years his junior. Mark and Elizabeth considered themselves to be specially anointed "messengers" of the ascended masters. Their role was to disseminate the teachings of the spirit beings (including Jesus) which they received in the form of dictations. In 1973 Prophet died and his wife assumed sole leadership of the group. Prophet is believed to maintain communication with the movement as the ascended master Lanello.

CUT has been influenced by both theosophy and the I AM movement of Guy and Edna Ballard. It views itself as the true church of Jesus Christ and Gautama Buddha. It venerates Mary and teaches the deification of humanity, reincarnation, and the evolution of all life toward the Godhead. Special spiritual significance is attached to colors, auras, jewels, and vibrational frequencies. Religious practices include prayer, affirmations, and "decreeing," a form of rapid chanting. A special subgroup known as the Keepers of the Flame Fraternity remains at the core of the movement.

In recent years controversy has swirled around the group because of allegations by ex-members and other critics of financial irregularities, racism, and control-oriented leadership. In the early 1980s the church purchased 33,000 acres of land near Yellowstone National Park in Montana and has relocated its headquarters there.

*Bibliography.* *Spiritual Counterfeits Project Journal* (1984); J. G. Melton, *Encyclopedic Handbook of Cults in America* (1986); R. Enroth, *The Lure of the Cults and New Religions* (1987).

RONALD ENROTH

## Church World Service.

Organization founded in May 1946 to integrate and carry forward the work of three emergency relief organizations established by the Protestant churches of the USA: (1) the Church Committee for Relief in Asia, an expansion of the Church Committee for China Relief, begun in 1938; (2) the Church Committee on Overseas Relief and Reconstruction, succeeding the Committee on Foreign Relief Appeals in the Churches, organized in 1938, developing a program of contributed relief supplies; and (3) the Commission for World Council Service, organized in 1945 to carry on relief and reconstruction services in Europe in connection with the World Council of Churches, then in process of formation. Later, Church World Service absorbed the American Committee for Christian Refugees.

During its separate existence, Church World Service, Inc., received cash contributions of $19,202,304 directly and through Protestant and Orthodox denominations, and contributions of relief supplies valued at $36,504,998. It disbursed these in relief activities in Europe and Asia, and also in its program for the resettlement of 51,000 Protestant and Eastern Orthodox displaced persons in the USA.

On January 1, 1951, it became a department of the newly established National Council of the Churches of Christ, USA.

IVANE SAULPAUGH

## Church Year.

Christian year which has as its basis the first day of every seven-day week, together with the annual festivals of Christmas and Easter. Its primary purpose is kerygmatic although it also has a pedagogical role.

The beginning of the church year is fixed with respect to Christmas: a four-Sunday period of preparation is called Advent and the first of these is the first day of the church year. Thus it begins either in late November or early December of the "secular" year. Although Christmas is on a fixed date, Easter is a movable festival, occurring sometime between late March and late April. This is because it is fixed with reference to the Jewish Passover and the new moon. Forty days after Easter Sunday is Ascension Day (thus always on a Thursday) and 10 days later (50 days after Easter) is the Festival of the Holy Spirit (Pentecost/Whitsuntide). Therefore each year the church lays hold by faith of the mystery of the birth, death, resurrection, and ascension/exaltation of Jesus and of the sending in his name of the Holy Spirit to his followers. And each Sunday is, as it were, the whole church year compressed into one day. In keeping this year the church is acting in much the same way as did ancient Israel, with its weekly Sabbath and annual festivals of Passover, Unleavened Bread, Booths, and Pentecost.

Into this annual cycle of weekly remembrance and major festivals, some churches/denominations have inserted memorial days to point to various aspects of the life of Jesus, to Mary his mother, to the apostles, and to martyrs and saints. In the Roman Catholic calendar, for example, there is the remembrance of someone on every day of the year but this (since 1969) is not allowed to detract from the unique character of each Sunday as a weekly festival of the resurrection of Jesus. The Roman Catholic Church claims that by celebrating the anniversaries of saints and martyrs, it is acknowledging that the saints who have suffered and been glorified with Christ have achieved the paschal mystery and are thereby examples to the faithful.

The church year as we now experience it is the result of gradual development from the time of the apostles to the end of the patristic period. The weekly festival of the Lord's Day was fixed in apostolic teaching and was always a day of joy. Easter, being intimately related to the Passover, also originated at a very early period and was at first a simple, unitive festival before Christ's death was commemorated on Friday and his resurrection on Sunday. The 50 days of Easter are the oldest part of the church year and correspond to the period in the Jewish calendar between the Feast of Unleavened Bread and the Feast of Firstfruits (Equals Weeks or Pentecost); they were regarded as "the great Sunday," the time between the resurrection and the descent of the Holy Spirit (Acts 2). Only later was the 40th day made especially the Day of Ascension and the 50th that of the Holy Spirit.

The fixing of the date of Christmas came later. December 25 was the *natalis solis invieti* from A.D. 274 and the church took over this date to make it the festival of the nativity. Earlier the important date had been January 6, the feast of the Epiphany, which was celebrated as a commemoration of both the nativity and the baptism of Jesus. The nativity being transferred to December 25, the Epiphany on January 6 was kept as a celebration of the baptism of Jesus in the East, but in the West it also took on the commemoration of the visit of the magi.

Thus the Christian year was fixed by the 5th century, with some differences between East and West. With very few exceptions Christians have accepted its minimum—the weekly celebration of the Lord's Day. And the 20th century has seen a growing interest in holding to the year from denominations which traditionally have paid minimal attention to it.

PETER TOON

# Civil Rights Movement.

The modern civil rights movement in the USA was initiated in 1954 with the historic Supreme Court decision of *Brown* v. *Board of Education of Topeka* (Kansas),

which abolished segregation in public schools, and ended with the assassination of Martin Luther King, Jr., in 1968. Civil rights, meaning those rights which a citizen possesses over against the state or other citizens as contained in a constitution or statutory law, has had a long history of progressive development in the Western world. This development has centered around the attempt to reconcile the concept of freedom with the idea of equality.

In the West, freedom, having been promoted through a variety of means but primarily by popular revolutions, has been established gradually at the expense of arbitrary power formerly exercised by monarchs, dictators, and privileged groups. The most important of these have been the liberal revolutions, in Great Britain in 1688, America in 1776, and France in 1789, which set the tone for all those which followed. In America the acceptance of democratic principles has led to the broadening of the concept of freedom to include more and more people. At the same time, the expansion of freedom ran headlong into the increasing demand for equality by both older and newer minority groups within the American population. These increasing demands were based on the theoretical pronouncement in the Declaration of Independence that God had created all men equal and that every man had certain inalienable rights, among which were life, liberty, and the pursuit of happiness.

The sticking point revolved around the fact that both freedom and equality involved human relationships. If every person attempts to be free, every freedom-seeking individual becomes in some way an obstacle in the path of someone else's freedom. Historically, freedom has depended on power. But as political power in America became more broadly based, freedom became more widely distributed. However, with this democratization of power, there arose a new problem in the determination of freedom. Over time, democracy in America resulted in the unequal division of freedom, thus allowing for a superior freedom to the majority while often denying freedom to minority groups, especially blacks. In this context, the measure of equality has increasingly become the standard for settling disputes over freedom. In America, historically speaking, equality has not meant that all people are in fact equal, but that people should treat one another in religious, racial, and legal affairs as if they were equal. This attempt to balance freedom with freedom and freedom with equality was present in the beginning of the nation's history with the adoption of the Bill of Rights, the first 10 amendments to the U.S. Constitution. However, the list of civil rights enumerated and protected by the Bill of Rights was not definitive, and these rights were not applied evenhandedly to the entire population, especially to blacks who were given special noncitizen status by the original Constitution.

Nor has it been clear what rights a citizen may expect to claim. Some have argued that these should be limited to the more procedural questions such as due process under the law. Others have asserted that they must include equal access to the material resources by which one's social well-being is guaranteed. The debate over what constitutes an individual's civil rights has been the focal point of the modern civil rights movement in America and underlies much of the civil strife in the modern world.

The modern civil rights movement has roots reaching far back into the ancient world. Natural law is one cornerstone of civil rights theory. Greek, Roman, Hebrew, and Christian writers have affirmed that certain laws are eternal and that every human being is capable of recognizing them. Natural law theory reached its political zenith in the 18th-century Enlightenment, concluding that all people are in some sense equal. Of equal importance in the development of Western concepts of civil rights has been the Judeo-Christian faith. The Hebrew OT laws surpassed other contemporary codes in affirming the equal treatment of all citizens regardless of social standing. The Israelites' deep sense of social justice was based largely on their belief in Yahweh's creative activity. Since all humans have been created in the very image of God, to mistreat them is an inherent violation of their dignity and rouses both the compassion and wrath of God. Likewise, teachings concerning human rights were within the prophetic tradition of the OT, which was highly critical of unjust treatment of disenfranchised groups. Moreover, the entire burden of the NT account of the incarnation and of the way of salvation through the finished work of Christ on the cross stresses that a human being is of the greatest value. The writings of Paul and the communal practices of the early church also reflect much of the same moral and theological grounding for civil rights as is found in the OT and the teachings of Jesus.

This theory, based on natural law and the Judeo-Christian tradition, ran up against the facts of race relations in the USA, which is a story of sin and retribution, of prolonged transgression and embittered expiation. The institution of chattel slavery was a crime against the most fundamental principles of the American experiment. Civil rights movements and violent repression alternated in the South in a 100-year rhythm: before the Revolution, at the time of the Civil War, and again in the modern civil rights movement of the 1950s and 1960s. The ferocity of these struggles for human dignity and rights has been intensified by America's all-pervasive messianic eschatology, disseminated through the churches and often expressed through political ideology in public acts. This messiaism, based on a future hope which is combined with faith in its realizability on earth, fermented in the First and Second Great Awakenings, Jacksonian democracy, the social gospel movement, and the civil rights movement.

The immediate background of the modern civil rights movement in America was a dramatic shift of viewpoint by leaders of the white community and a considerable shift in public opinion. In the wake of World War II (1939–45), as complacency began to yield to guilt and concern, the basically racist character of many American institutions came to be recognized to an unprecedented degree, and grave doubts began to corrode the old assumption that the American ideals of freedom and equality of opportunity had been achieved. Blacks had served loyally and in substantial numbers in the military during the war, yet had to return home to a still largely segregated society. Nazi anti-Semitism and atrocities in the name of Aryan supremacy caused a revulsion against racist theory. Furthermore, the movement of large numbers of blacks from the South brought them into political significance in the North and awakened whites there to the existence of a problem that many hitherto had regarded as being peculiar to the South. President Harry S. Truman responded in part to this growing feeling of unfulfilled citizenship for black Americans by establishing by executive order in 1946 the President's Committee on Civil Rights. The committee recommended antilynching and anti-poll tax laws, a permanent Fair Employment Practices Committee, a strengthening of the civil rights section of the Justice Department, and the use of the Federal Bureau of Investigation in cases involving violations of civil rights. Although Truman asked Congress every year thereafter to enact such laws, nothing happened, mostly because of Southern opposition. However, in 1948, Truman by executive order ended segregation in the armed forces and began the practice of having the Justice Department aid private parties in civil rights cases.

There were other federal initiatives against the illegal abridgement of civil rights during the decade immediately following World War II, but the real beginning of the modern civil rights movement came with the historic Supreme Court case of *Brown* v. *Board of Education of Topeka* in 1954. In 1896, the Court had decided in the case of *Plessy* v. *Ferguson* that even in places of public accommodation such as railroads and, by implication, schools, segregation was legal so long as "separate but equal" facilities were provided. The 1954 Court invalidated the "separate but equal" doctrine by asserting that "separate educational facilities are inherently unequal" and that "segregation in public education" denied blacks "equal protection of the law." This largely unanticipated event galvanized opposition to further denial of civil rights to blacks, transformed a hopeless passive minority into a self-conscious force, and touched off more than a decade of domestic upheaval that led the nation to the brink of racial civil war.

The Rev. Dr. Martin Luther King, Jr., soon became the central figure in the civil rights movement. King led American blacks from indirect to direct action and gave them a new sense of racial identity and purpose. He was able to do this because of his place of leadership in the black community based on his authority as a black Baptist minister, his superior educational credentials which commanded the attention of the white religious community, and his Christ-centered nonviolent theology. His theology, based in part on his reading of Paul Tillich and his study of Mohandas Gandhi but mostly on the teachings of Jesus Christ, shaped the modern American civil rights movement. King's emphasis that Christian love must always be at the heart of the struggle and his insistence on the nonviolent way placed him between two competing ideological extremes: a single-minded pious concern for the development of a church which preached only a message of otherworldly salvation on the one hand and a secularist outlook which regarded the institutional church as no more than an assembly-point for community action on the other. Instead King developed from his rich evangelical Baptist resources his view of black suffering and the meaning of historical travail, and a faith in God's ultimate victory. In short, he combined conservative theology with liberal politics and shaped the cause of modern civil rights into what historian Stephen B. Oates has called "a movement that was designed to save the soul of a nation."

But King and his theology were many times tested in action. The shift from legal struggles in the courts to black protest in the streets began on December 1, 1955, in Montgomery, Ala., when Rosa Parks—a black seamstress who had been active in the local chapter of the National Association for the Advancement of Colored People—violated a city ordinance by refusing to give up her seat to a white person on a local bus. After her arrest, blacks gathered to protest and found an eloquent leader in King, who only the year before had begun his first pastorate at the city's Dexter Avenue Baptist Church. He organized a massive boycott of the city's bus system, which depended heavily on black patronage, and eventually won a stunning victory when a year later the Supreme Court ruled the Alabama segregated-seating law unconstitutional. In so doing, King had won far more than a limited dent in the wall of segregation. He had provided blacks with a new weapon with which to fight racial oppression.

Highlights of the civil rights movement included King's founding of the influential Southern Christian Leadership Conference in 1957—which in many ways became the real locus of black civil rights leadership during the next decade, largely replacing the NAACP. This was followed by almost unceasing activity on behalf of civil rights, in conjunction with both his own organization, of which he was president, and other new civil rights organizations like the Congress of Racial Equality and the Student Nonviolent Coordinating Committee. Together they participated in the unfolding of events, including the beginning of passive resistance in 1960, voter registration drives beginning in 1962, and the march on Washington of over 250,000 people under King's leadership in 1963. Beyond the pale of King's control were the massive urban race riots in New York, New Jersey, and the Watts district of Los Angeles in 1964/65.

The culminating event and high water mark of the civil rights movement occurred in Selma, Ala., in 1965, when 25,000 people from all over the country converged on that city. The event took on almost pentecostal significance for many who were there and caused President Lyndon Johnson to declare along with the participants that "we shall overcome." On the other hand, it also marked the beginning of the end of joint interracial protest. In the following summer, on June 9, the murder of James Meredith during a march from Memphis, Tenn., to Jackson, Miss., led to a coalescing of the other black leaders on that march, and from that time on a new sense of black responsibility apart from white participation became more manifest. Moreover, beginning in 1966, King began to turn his attention increasingly to the injustices of the Vietnam War, radicals like Black Muslim leader Malcolm X began to challenge King's nonviolent strategy, and Black Power advocates began to call for more rapid and far-reaching change. Tension and frustration mounted, culminating in the rage and violence of the riots in Newark, N.J., and Detroit, Mich., in the "long hot summer" of 1967. On April 4, 1968, King was assassinated in Memphis by a gunman firing from ambush while he stood on a balcony of the Lorraine Hotel talking with friends and aides. There was one last convulsive round of rioting in the big cities of America, and the modern civil rights movement came to an end. At his death, most Americans, both black and white, still believed that King's way was the best road to amity and justice. The more militant and separatist spirit of the later 1960s had no single theologian or ideological leader with anything like King's steady sustaining power.

Although the movement ended with the murder of its most important leader, the gains during 1954–68 were impressive. The Civil Rights Act of 1957, the first such federal legislation since 1875, created a temporary Federal Civil Rights Commission to investigate denials of civil rights and make recommendations for further legislation, and it authorized federal district courts to issue injunctions against interference with the right to vote. President Dwight D. Eisenhower put new teeth into this renewed federal interest in civil rights when he sent 1000 U.S. Army paratroopers into Little Rock, Ark., in 1957 to insure the racial integration of the city's Central High School. Also under Eisenhower, the Civil Rights Act of 1960 authorized the federal courts to appoint referees to enroll qualified voters in districts where local officials were found to be systematically excluding blacks. During the Johnson administration, the landmark Civil Rights Acts of 1964 and 1968 outlawed discrimination in education, housing, employment, voting, and public accommodations.

The relative success of the civil rights movement inspired other groups to press for their full rights as citizens. Since the 1960s, these have included Native Americans, women, prisoners, mental patients, homosexuals, tenants, the handicapped, the aged, children, aliens, refugees, the poor, the unborn, consumers, and employees. Moreover, the civil rights movement sparked debates which continued into the 1970s and 1980s concerning the extent to which federal, state, and local authorities should go in obtaining racial and gender balance in the classroom and in the job market.

Christians have a clear duty to support continuing efforts toward full implementation of a broad scale of civil rights in the areas of education, employment, and participation in the political process. The Bible teaches believers that all people are of one blood (Acts 17:26), and clearly indicates that all individuals are equal in God's sight in terms of eligibility for his grace offered to them in his Son, Jesus Christ. Moreover, the teachings of the NT are clearly on the side of freedom, equality of opportunity, and social justice. It is to their credit that although many white evangelical Christians were slow in coming to the side of their black counterparts in the struggle for civil rights when it began in the 1950s, since the 1960s they have joined with many church groups and organizations of nearly all theological persuasions in active support of those Americans who are still in the process of procuring their civil rights.

See also KING, MARTIN LUTHER, JR.; PEACE MOVEMENTS; RACE RELATIONS.

**Bibliography.** M. L. King, Jr., *Why We Can't Wait* (1964); F. R. Dulles, *The Civil Rights Commission, 1957–1965* (1968); P. E. Kraemer, *Awakening from the American Dream: The Human Rights Movement in the U.S. Assessed During a Crucial Decade, 1960–1970* (1973); A. Meier and E. Rudwick, *CORE: A Study in the Civil Rights Movement* (1975); W. Laqueur and B. Rubin, eds., *The Human Rights Reader* (1979); W. Harrelson, *The Ten Commandments and Human Rights* (1980); S. B. Oates, *Let the Trumpet Sound: The Life of Martin Luther King, Jr.* (1982); A. Swidler, ed., *Human Rights in Religious Traditions* (1982); C. S. Bullock, III, and C. M. Lamb, *Implementation of Civil Rights Policy* (1983); J. Moltmann, *On Human Dignity: Political Theology and Ethics* (1984); A. R. White, *Rights* (1984); C. Fager, *Selma, Nineteen Sixty-Five: The March That Changed the South* (1985); J. Farmer, *Lay Bare the Heart: An Autobiography of the Civil Rights Movement* (1985); R. Farley, *Blacks and Whites* (1986); R. K. Fullinwider and C. Mills, eds., *The Moral Foundations of Civil Rights* (1986); G. H. Hill, *Civil Rights Organizations and Leaders: An Annotated Bibliography* (1986); J. W. Montgomery, *Human Rights and Human Dignity* (1986); R. F. Drinan, *Cry of the Oppressed: The History and Hope of the Human Rights Revolution* (1987); J. Williams, *Eyes on the Prize: The Civil Rights Movement in America, 1954–1965* (1987).

ROBERT D. LINDER

**Clark, Elmer Talmage** (1886–1966). Methodist clergyman, editor, and author. Born in Randolph County, Ark., he was educated at Hendrix College, Southern College, Vanderbilt, Temple (S.T.D., 1925), and George Peabody College. Ordained by the Methodist Episcopal Church, South (1911), he pastored churches in Missouri (1908–17) and then worked as a foreign correspondent during World War I for the *New York Tribune* and *St. Louis Republic*. He subsequently became a missionary secretary of the Methodist Church in charge of literature, and was for 35 years (1927–52) editor of *World Outlook*, a Methodist missionary magazine. From 1952 to 1961 he was secretary of the World Methodist Council, and until his death was editorial secretary. A historian, he served as executive secretary of the Association of Methodist Historical Societies, and wrote missions-promoting works which include *The Small Sects in America* (1937), *The Chiangs of China* (1943), and *The Warm Heart of Wesley* (1950), and edited three volumes of journals and letters of Francis Asbury (1958).

JACK MITCHELL

**Clark, Francis Edward** (1851–1927). Congregational minister and founder of the Christian Endeavor movement. Born in Aylmer, Quebec, he graduated from Dartmouth and Andover Theological Seminary, and was thereafter pastor of Williston Church, Portland, Maine (1876–83), and Phillips Church, South Boston (1883–87). In 1881 he founded the Society of Christian Endeavor (SCE), and in 1887 resigned his pastorate to devote his whole time to its promotion. During the next 40 years he traveled around the world five times representing SCE. He was editor of *The Christian Endeavor World*, and also served as president of the World's Society of Christian Endeavor. His publications include *Young People's Prayer Meetings* (1887), *World-Wide Endeavor* (1897), *A New Way Around an Old World* (1900), *Training the Church for the Future* (1902), and *The Christian Endeavor Manual* (1903).

See also CHRISTIAN ENDEAVOR.

**Clark, Gordon Haddon** (1902–1985). Born in Philadelphia, the son of a Presbyterian minister, he took both his undergraduate and graduate work at the University of Pennsylvania where he received the Ph.D., and continued his graduate studies at the Sorbonne in Paris. Returning to Philadelphia he taught philosophy at the University of Pennsylvania (1924–36) and then at Wheaton College in Illinois (1936–44). Leaving Wheaton, he taught philosophy at Butler University (1945–73) and became the chairman of the department of philosophy at that institution in 1946. In his later years he taught philosophy at Covenant College (1974–84) in Lookout Mountain, Tenn. He was a prolific writer in the fields of theology and philosophy, producing many scholarly articles for numerous journals, and wrote many books, including *A Christian Philosophy of Education* (1946), *A Christian View of Men and Things* (1952); *What Presbyterians Believe* (1956), *Biblical Predestination* (1969), *Historiography: Secular and Religious* (1971), *Three Types of Religious Philosophy* (1973), *Language and Theology* (1980), and *The Biblical Doctrine of Man* (1984).

C. GREGG SINGER

**Clarke, Charles Philip Stewart** (1871–1947). Anglican clergyman. Born in Whiteshill, Gloucestershire, he was educated at Clifton College and Christ Church, Oxford. Ordained in 1895, he served Eastleigh, Hants; he pastored Christ Church Mission, Poplar (1898–1901); he was vicar of High Wycombe (1910–16); he was donhead of St. Andrew's and examining chaplain to the bishop of Salisbury, subsequently becoming a prebendary in Salisbury Cathedral. In 1934 he became archdeacon of Chichester. His publications include *A Short History of the Christian Church*, *The Oxford Movement and After*, *Everyman's Book of Saints*, *Church History from Nero to Constantine*, and *Via Media*.

EDWIN O. JAMES

**Clarke, William Newton** (1841–1912). Baptist theologian. Born in Cazenovia, N.Y., he studied at Madison (now Colgate) University and Hamilton Theological Seminary, Hamilton, N.Y. He held Baptist pastorates at Keene, N.H. (1863–69), Newton Centre, Mass. (1869–80), and Montreal, Canada (1880–83). He was professor of NT interpretation at the Toronto Baptist College (1883–87) and pastor in Hamilton, N.Y. (1887–90). From 1890 he was professor of Christian theology at Colgate University. His theological position was "intended to present the substance of the Scriptural teaching, interpreted by Christian thought, in the light of modern knowledge." He wrote a *Commentary on the Gospel of Mark* (1882), *Outline of Christian Theology* (1898), *What Shall We Think of Christianity?* (1899), *Can I Believe in God the Father?* (1899), *A Study of Christian Missions* (1900), and *The Use of the Scriptures in Theology* (1905).

**Clay, Albert Tobias** (1866–1925). Orientalist. Born in Hanover, Pa., he studied at Franklin and Marshall College, Mount Airy Seminary, and the University of Pennsylvania (Ph.D., 1894). He taught Semitics at the University of Pennsylvania (1893–95; 1899–1910), Chicago Lutheran Seminary (1895–99), and Yale University (1910–25). His works include *Amurru, the Home of the Northern Semites* (1910), *The Empire of the Amorites* (1919), and *The Origin of the Biblical Traditions* (1923).

ELMER E. FLACK

**Clayton, Philip Thomas Byard** (1885–1972). Founder of Toc H. While a chaplain with the British Army, Clayton, with Neville Talbot, a fellow chaplain, rented a house in Poperinghe in 1915 and turned it into a club for soldiers, with a chapel in the loft. Named after Talbot's younger brother, recently killed, Talbot House in signaler's shorthand is Toc H. Clayton started Toc H in 1919 to provide fellowship for veterans and to attract younger men to its principles (summarized in the four points of the Toc H compass: fellowship, service, fairmindedness, the kingdom of God). Houses were set up in London and elsewhere.

In 1922 Clayton became vicar of All Hallows by the Tower in London, which soon became the spiritual center of the movement. The lamp of maintenance was adopted as symbol (incorporating the double cross from the arms of Ypres) and every meeting commenced in a darkened room with a ceremony of light. The original house in Poperinghe was purchased in 1922 and became the center of pilgrimage. Toc H currently functions as an ecumenical voluntary movement.

HAROLD H. ROWDON

**Clinical Training of Ministers.** Practical training afforded Christian theological students or ordained clergy in general and mental hospitals, prisons, social service agencies, and counseling centers. Such training has typically involved the supervision of a full-time chaplain, coupled with intensive self- and theological reflection. Clinical training was initiated by Anton Boisen in 1925 when, as the chaplain of Worcester State Hospital in Massachusetts, he invited several theological students to become hospital attendants and reflect with him on the theological meaning of mental illness resulting from their contact with "living human documents." Boisen began this training program in collaboration with Richard Cabot, a professor in the Harvard Medical School, who had challenged seminary professors to develop a "clinical theology" which ministers could use in contact with those of their congregants under stress. He had issued a plea for a "clinical year" in theological education.

In 1930 Cabot, Boisen, and interested others formed the Council for Clinical Training of Theological Students. Two centers, in New York and Boston, were soon formed. Somewhat different traditions emerged from these groups. The Boston group, which eventually became the Institute of Pastoral Care, was more concerned with training ministers for parish work. Thus, their training centered in general hospitals. The New York group, which retained the title "Council for Clinical Training," was more concerned with training pastors for specialized ministries. Thus, their training centered in mental hospitals.

Boisen was more interested in helping ministers engage in theological reflection on persons undergoing the stress of mental illness than on either informing ministers about psychiatric or psychological insights or training them in ministry to the sick. However, in the ensuing years, his influence was felt more in the New York group with its emphasis on depth psychology and assisting persons in becoming free from the constraints of social and moral expectations. These themes remain integral to clinical training. Self-understanding in both the trainee and the client is still emphasized.

The Boston tradition became epitomized in *The Art of Ministering to the Sick* (1936), coauthored by Cabot and Russell Dicks, then chaplain of Massachusetts General Hospital. They were concerned with normal spiritual and moral growth enhanced through "pastoral conversation." The analysis of verbatim reports of these contacts became the prime focus of training. This emphasis on directed listening still characterizes clinical training. In addition, the theological reflection recommended by Boisen has become standard. This type of reflection has come to be defined not only as character development, which Cabot recommended, but also as the probing of assumptions about cosmology, anthropology, theodicy, and soteriology.

The Association for Clinical Pastoral Education, Inc. (ACPE), defines standards for clinical training, certifies supervisors, establishes liaisons with seminaries, and accredits centers to offer programs in parishes as well as correctional institutions, community mental health centers, counseling agencies, children's homes, rehabilitation centers, and general or mental hospitals.

Although by the mid-1940s over 2000 seminary students had received clinical training, over 30 training centers had been established, and more than 75 seminaries required at least three months of CPE (clinical pastoral education) for graduation, by 1975 Hiltner estimated that less than 10 percent of American clergy had had such training. Nevertheless, clinical pastoral training has spread to many other nations through supervisors trained in the USA. Programs in Holland, the Philippines, Bolivia, Singapore, England, Switzerland, and Germany are but a few examples.

The most highly developed tradition of clinical training outside the USA is found in Great Britain. In 1962, Frank Lake founded the Clinical Theology Association which offered a 12-week residential course which could be followed by two years of short-term seminars at over 90 centers. In addition, a degree program in pastoral studies was established in 1965 at Birmingham University under the leadership of R. A. Lambourne. It included a number of placements in medical, psychological, and social work settings. In 1958 Ellie Jansen founded the Richmond Fellowship which treated emotional disturbance in hostel settings. She established courses for clergy in these hostels in 1966. Finally, W. Kyle opened the Westminster Pastoral Foundation in 1970 and offered training for ministers. Collaborating with the British Council of Churches and the Roman Catholic Church, an Association for the Advancement for Pastoral Care and Counseling was founded in 1972. This organization paralleled ACPE in America.

At least two statements have been made as to the expected outcomes of clinical training for ministers. Anderson (1980) expressed the desires of seminaries while Rowatt (1982) reported a survey of what supervisors expected to happen in CPE. Anderson suggested that seminaries expected CPE to result in increased pastoral role identity but that the clinical setting had not been as effective in relating clergy to their parish church roles. Next, he affirmed that CPE should result in greater self-understanding. Again, although he concluded that CPE was peculiarly effective in self-reflection, this self-understanding had been insufficiently linked to students' pastoral identities. Further, he suggested that where CPE was an ordination requirement, the seminary expected evaluation of students' fitness for ministry but that CPE centers had been less than helpful in this task—largely because they considered student personal growth a private issue. Finally, seminaries have expected CPE to result in greater proficiency in theological reflection, but this has not occurred to the desired degree. While Anderson concluded that seminaries do not expect students to have answers after CPE, they have expected an increased awareness of the relationship between theology and practice as well as some appreciation for how experiential theology relates to the classical traditions of the Christian gospel.

Rowatt reported a survey of ACPE supervisors and educators as to what they expected of ministry in comparison to the categories reported in the Readiness for Ministry Project of the Association of Theological Schools. They agreed with the ratings given by a national sample of laypersons but, in general, emphasized the importance of ministry to individuals and the importance of acknowledging, accepting, and relating to the life experience of persons. They evidenced less concern for church organizations and community systems than the laypersons. The ACPE sample placed strong emphasis on the minister as reflective theologian and the importance of relating faith to life. Finally, they showed less concern for daily piety and traditional morality. They emphasized human limitations and the importance of self-insight and personal ethical decisions.

In general, it seems that clinical training has been a personally transformative yet liberating experience for clergy who have had to look to other settings for fostering their traditional parish roles and lifestyle.

**Bibliography.** E. Thornton, *Professional Education for Ministry: A History of Clinical Pastoral Education* (1970); R. C. Powell, *50 Years of Learning Through Supervised Encounter with Living Human Documents* (1975); J. C. Carr, J. E. Hinkle, and D. M. Moss, III, *The Organization and Administration of Pastoral Counseling Centers* (1981); E. B. Holifield, *A History of Pastoral Care in America* (1983); R. J. Wicks, R. D. Parsons, and D. E. Capps, *Clinical Handbook of Pastoral Counseling* (1985).

H. NEWTON MALONY

**Coadjutor.** *See* BISHOP, AUXILIARY.

**Cockburn, James Hutchison** (1882–1973). Church of Scotland minister. Born in Paisley, he graduated from Glasgow University and was ordained in 1908. He ministered at Mearns (1908–14), Battlefield (1914–18), and Dunblane Cathedral (1918–45), then went to Geneva as director of the World Council of Churches department of reconstruction and interchurch aid. During his ministry in Scotland he was convenor of several influential church committees. His publications include *Religious Freedom in Eastern Europe* (1951), *The Celtic Church in Dunblane* (1954), and *The Medieval Bishops of Dunblane and Their Church* (1959).

**Codex Juris Canonici (Code of Canon Law).** *See* CANON LAW.

**Coffin, Henry Sloane** (1877–1954). Presbyterian minister and educator. He was educated at Yale, Edinburgh, and Union Theological Seminary, N.Y. He was pastor at Bedford Park, New York City (1900–1905), and Madison Avenue, New York City (1905–26). He also taught practical theology at Union Theological Seminary (1904–26), and became professor of homiletics and pastoral theology (1926–45). He also was a fellow of the corporation of Yale University (1921–45). He wrote *The Creed of Jesus* (1907), *Social Aspects of the Cross* (1911), *University Sermons* (1914), *The Ten Commandments* (1915), *Some Christian Convictions* (1915), *In a Day of Social Rebuilding* (1918), *A More Christian Indus-*

*trial Order* (1920), *What Is There in Religion?* (1922), *Portraits of Jesus Christ* (1926), *What to Preach* (1926), *The Meaning of the Cross* (1931), *What Men Are Asking* (1933), *God's Turn* (1934), *Religion Yesterday and Today* (1940), *The Public Worship of God* (1946), *God Confronts Man in History* (1947), *Communion Through Preaching* (1952), and *2 Isaiah* in *The Interpreter's Bible.*

**Coggan, F. D.** (1909– ). Archbishop of Canterbury. After a brilliant career at Cambridge he taught Semitic studies and literature at Manchester University from 1931. He was very much involved with the Inter-Varsity Fellowship, editing its magazine and its then definitive history—*Christianity and the Colleges* (1934). After studying at Wycliffe Hall, Oxford, he was ordained and became a curate at St. Mary's, Islington. For the next 20 years he was a teacher in theological colleges, first as professor of NT at Wycliffe College, Toronto (1937–44), and then as principal of London College of Divinity (1944–56). During this period he established himself as a sound biblical scholar with particularly strong convictions about the importance of preaching, seen in the books *A People's Heritage* (1944), *The Ministry of the Word* (1946), *The Glory of God* (1950), and *Stewards of Grace* (1958). His abilities as a theologian and a communicator and his energetic and inspirational leadership marked him out. In 1956 he was consecrated as bishop of Bradford, and was appointed to be archbishop of York in 1961 and of Canterbury in 1974. His literary output continued: *Five Makers of the NT* (1962), *Christian Priorities* (1963), *The Prayers of the NT* (1967), *Sinews of the Faith* (1969), *Word and World* (1971), *Convictions* (1975), *On Preaching* (1978), *Sure Foundation* (1981), and *Mission to the World* (1982); his scholarship was given further outlet through his chairmanship of the commission that produced *The Revised Psalter* (1963) and, in its later stages, of the Joint Committee on the New Translation of the Bible, which was responsible for the New English Bible (1970). His concern for preaching was a major factor in the foundation of the College of Preachers (1960).

His time at Canterbury has been variously assessed. He has been called the layperson's archbishop, and certainly he had an ability to communicate with ordinary people. He continued the impetus that Archbishop Ramsey had given to improved relationships with the Roman Catholic Church. His obvious impatience with the obstacles to intercommunion indicated perhaps a more uncertain touch than that of either his predecessor or his successor when dealing with the nuances of ecumenical theology. It has been said that he "disappointed the clergy," and it is probably true that he was "a little too liberal to retain the full confidence of Evangelicals but too Evangelical to be quite on the wavelength of either

Liberals or Anglo-Catholics" (A. Hastings, *A History of English Christianity* [1986], p. 556). His essential evangelical instincts were seen in an ecumenical evangelistic drive while he was at York ("Call to the North," 1973). This was followed in 1975 by "The Call to the Nation." The call was much criticized for lack of organization and simplicity of analysis, particularly because of its emphasis on individual rather than corporate responsibility. He also gave the strongest support to the ecumenical "Nationwide Initiative in Evangelism" (1976–81) but this again was, at best, only half successful. History may judge that his impatience for action amidst the uncertainty, disillusionment, and division of the 1960s and 1970s was a proper call to faith in a sea of unfaith. Certainly his appeal for more ordinands (1978), in a climate where many church leaders apparently accepted, and even seemed gratified by, the prophecies of retrenchment and decline, was significant in retaining a vision of hope within the church.

*Bibliography.* A. Arnott, *Wife to the Archbishop: The Lifestory of Jean Coggan* (1976); P. A. Welsby, *A History of the Church of England, 1945–1980* (1984); R. Manwaring, *From Controversy to Co-Existence: Evangelicals in the Church of England, 1914–1980* (1985); A. Hastings, *A History of English Christianity, 1920–1985* (1986).

C. PETER WILLIAMS

## Collins, Lewis John (1905–1982).

Anglican social activist. Educated at Cambridge, in 1931 he became a minor canon at St. Paul's Cathedral and deputy priest-in-ordinary to King George V. Promoted to priest-in-ordinary in 1934, he was made vice-principal at Westcott House, Cambridge, but moved to Oriel College, Oxford, in 1937 as fellow, lecturer in theology, and chaplain. He became dean in 1938 and stayed with the college until 1948, but from 1940 to 1945 was chaplain of the RAF voluntary reserve. He was founder-chairman of Christian Action, formed following a public meeting in Oxford in 1946. At first promoting a united Europe, it switched in 1953 to passive opposition to apartheid. He resigned as chairman in 1973, but was president from 1959 until his death. Founder of the Campaign for Nuclear Disarmament in 1958, he opposed the formation of the civil disobedience "Committee of 100" in 1960, and resigned as chairman in 1964 because of leftist domination. He was chancellor of St. Paul's Cathedral (1948–53), precentor (1953–70), and treasurer (1970–81). He was nominated three times for the Nobel Peace Prize, was awarded a gold medal in 1978 by the UN Special Committee Against Apartheid, and was chairman of the Martin Luther King Foundation (1969–73). Publications include *The NT Problem* (1937), *A Theology of Christian Action* (1949), and his autobiography, *Faith under Fire* (1966).

TIM LENTON

## Colombia.

With an area of 1,141,748 sq. km. (440,831 sq. mi.), Colombia's population is estimated to reach 31,820,000 by 1990. The diverse ethnic groups—68 percent mestizo, 5 percent black, and 7 percent indigenous—are dominated by the 20 percent European-descent who have held power since the Spanish colonial system was overthrown in 1819. Spanish is the official language, and the dialect spoken here is most similar to the Castilian spoken in Spain.

Three cordilleras of the Andes separate the country, whose population is concentrated along the coast and in two highland valleys—Cauca and Magdalena where the capital Bogotá sits at 2624 m. (8659 ft.). The eastern half of the country, the Amazon headwaters beyond the Andes, is thinly inhabited, mostly by the tribal populations.

Life expectancy in the country is 61.4 years for males and 66 years for females with an infant mortality rate of 62 per 1000 births. Although 80 percent of the populace is literate, only 28 percent finish primary school.

Even though Colombia is the continent's fourth largest country, only 5 percent of the land is arable and the per capita income is $1112 (1981). The economy is bolstered by the legal exportation of coffee and the illegal exportation of cocaine.

Two powerful political parties, the Conservatives and the Liberals, have been factiously engaged during much of this century and "La Violencia" of 1948 to 1958 claimed 200,000 lives. The Conservative party is ardently supported by the Roman Catholic Church, which claims 94.6 percent of the population and has a privileged and established position guaranteed by a Concordat signed with the Vatican in 1973. One of the country's two cardinals, López Trujillo of Medellín, has led a continent-wide campaign to halt liberation theology's efforts at consciousness-raising.

The Colombian church is organized into 2367 parishes in 11 archdioceses and 32 dioceses ministered to by 15 archbishops, 57 bishops, 5355 priests, 18,171 nuns, and 889 brothers. There are two pontifical universities and 2443 seminarians in the country (1983).

In spite of its conservative Catholic power, Colombia possesses the fastest-growing Protestant church in Spanish South America. Its 717,000 members (1987) constitute only 2.4 percent of the populace but they are served by 51 Protestant denominations and 1150 foreign missionaries who work mainly among the many ethnic groups in Colombia.

FAITH ANNETTE SAND

## Colored Methodist Episcopal Church. *See* METHODISTS.

## Colors, Liturgical.

Western liturgical usage prescribes certain standard colors for the vestments worn during altar functions by officiating ministers. In the Roman rite, white is the festive color, which may be replaced by gold or silver brocade on solemn occasions; red is worn at Pentecost and on the feasts of martyrs; green is employed on ordinary Sundays and nonfestive days throughout the year; violet is reserved for Sundays and nonfestive days in Advent and Lent; rose color may be substituted for violet on the third Sunday in Advent and the fourth Sunday in Lent. Black is used for the office of the dead and on Good Friday. The draperies of the altar generally match the color of the vestments.

GEORGES A. BARROIS

## Colossians, Epistle to the. *See* PAUL, THE APOSTLE.

## Colwell, Ernest Cadman (1910–1974). NT scholar, educator, and author. Born in Hallstead, Pa., he held degrees from Emory University and the University of Chicago (Ph.D., 1930). He served successively as instructor in English literature and Bible at Emory (1924–28), professor of NT at Emory (1951–57), president of South California School of Theology, Claremont (1957–68), then distinguished professor of the NT (1968–71), and until his death, as visiting professor of Greek at Stetson University, Deland, Fla. While at Chicago, he formed the Federated Theological Faculty, uniting four theological schools into the country's largest Protestant faculty. Known as a leading NT scholar and authority on NT MSS, he was a prolific writer, producing more than 12 books and over 70 journal articles, as well as co-authoring the Goodspeed translation of the Bible (1948).

JACK MITCHELL

## Comfort, William Wistar (1874–1955). Society of Friends scholar. Born in Philadelphia, he studied at Haverford College, Harvard University, and in Europe. He taught at Cornell University and Haverford College; later he became president emeritus of Haverford College. He wrote *Just among Friends* (1941), *Stephen Grellet* (1942), *William Penn: A Tercentenary Estimate* (1944), and *Quakers in the Modern World* (1949).

## Common Grace. *Nature of the Concept.* The concept of common grace has its historical origin in the theology of Calvin. Charles Hodge, Herman Bavinck, and especially Abraham Kuyper sought to develop the idea of common grace as a part of the Calvinist philosophy of history and culture.

Common grace, like special or saving grace, according to Kuyper, presupposes the idea of total depravity. But whereas special grace regenerates the hearts of men, common grace restrains the process of sin in mankind and enables mankind positively to develop the latent forces of the universe and to do works of "civic righteous-

ness." Without common grace there would be no field of operation for special grace. Yet the purpose of common grace is not exhausted by serving as the historical basis for special grace. According to the principle of *Heteregonie der Zwecke*, common grace has as its *Nebenzweck* the general development of human culture.

***Recent History.*** During the second decade of the present century opposition arose among Reformed theologians to the idea of common grace. It was said to tone down the doctrine of total depravity and to be, of necessity, a steppingstone toward the Arminian idea of grace as God's desire to save all men. This opposition has been expressed with vigor in a number of publications on the part of Herman Hoeksema and others.

In 1924 the Synod of the Christian Reformed Church affirmed the idea of common grace under three heads pertaining to: (1) a favorable attitude of God toward mankind in general; (2) the restraint of sin in the life of the individual and in society; and (3) the performance of civic righteousness by the unregenerate.

***Relation to Natural Theology.*** In the Netherlands Valentine Hepp developed the views of Kuyper and Bavinck in the direction of a natural theology similar to that of scholasticism. He sought for an area of knowledge and ethical response where there is commonness without difference between the believer and the unbeliever (*Het Testimonium Spiritus Sancti*). Accordingly, he developed a method of apologetics in which appeal is made to an area of knowledge (general truths about God, man, and the world) that unbelievers have in common with believers. The great stress that Calvin lays on the fact that by their systems of philosophy unbelievers seek to suppress their own inescapable knowledge of God as their Creator and Judge is not denied but largely ignored by Hepp (*Gereformeerde Apologetick*, 1920).

***Integration with Other Doctrines.*** Thus the pendulum is swinging back and forth between the two extremes of a total denial of common grace (difference without sameness) and a scholastic affirmation of common grace (sameness without difference). On either position it is impossible to integrate the idea of common grace with the genius of Calvinism. According to Calvinism, the self-sufficient God of Scripture works out his purpose for mankind covenantally, that is, by way of challenge and response. At the beginning of history God gave mankind life and favor. He offered mankind still higher life and favor on condition of obedience (covenant of works). Thus sameness is basic to the idea of the conditional as the conditional is constitutive of the covenantal, and the covenantal is the means by which God accomplishes the differentiation between the "vessels of mercy" and the "vessels of wrath."

After mankind fell into sin, God continued his conditional dealings with mankind. He continued to give life and favor, and he restrained man in his path "unto death," so that man could give some measure of externally favorable response to the striving of God's Spirit with him. Thus, in spite of his hatred of God, the sinner is bound to respond with some measure of respect for the laws and favors of God. Every fact about and within him speaks to man of the goodness of God. Every fact is to the sinner a call to repentance for sinning against the goodness of God. Every fact says to him, "Do this and you will live; do that and you will die." Only thus is civilization to be accounted for. And thus the stage is set daily for the "vessels of mercy" and for the "vessels of wrath," each to react significantly in his own way, in faith or in disobedience, toward his own ultimate destiny.

Thus the idea of common grace is integrally related to the idea of God as the sovereign determiner of the ultimate destinies of men, of the genuine meaning of history, and of the conditional in relation to human choice. Only thus can Calvinism be distinguished as a life- and worldview from all systems based on the "autonomy" of man. Thus Calvinism is shown to be theism and Christianity come to its own, a life- and worldview on the basis of which human history has genuine significance. For thus it is possible to prevent falling into the idea of absolute identity (univocism) or into the idea of absolute difference (equivocism) between God and man. Progress on the idea of common grace is likely to come with progress on the idea of analogy, based on the idea of God as sovereign, over against the Romanist-evangelical idea of analogy of being and the dialectical idea of analogy of faith.

Cornelius Van Til

**Common Prayer, Book of.** Book containing prescribed worship forms of both the Church of England and the churches of the Anglican Communion. This volume was used without change until the mid-19th century. The Oxford movement brought about a return to careful observation of the rubrics of the Book of Common Prayer, the frequency and standard of public worship increasing accordingly.

Pressure for change arose during the second phase of the Oxford movement, when some clergy believed the eucharistic theology of the 1662 book was deficient. Controversy arose concerning the growth of ceremonies (such as signing with the cross, elevation of the consecrated bread and wine, the use of incense) and ornaments (e.g., candles, vestments) accompanying the actual rites (text) of the book. Such practices spread rapidly among Anglican churches in mission areas, both in England and overseas.

Legal battles saw these practices rejected by the courts. But such rulings were not accepted by Anglo-Catholics, on the grounds that the courts were judicial, not spiritual, in their power. Some ritualist clergy were jailed, which gained them public sympathy. A key ruling was the "Lincoln Judgement," following prosecution of Bishop King of Lincoln. The archbishops of Canterbury and Ireland sought to calm matters by issuing the "Lambeth Opinions," but little resolution was obtained.

A Royal Commission was called in 1906, as a result of which deliberations within the church continued until a report recommending revision was issued in 1920. Various parties then produced draft books (e.g., the "Green Book" of the Anglo-Catholics) and a book agreed upon by Convocation and the (newly set up) Church Assembly was deposited with Parliament in 1927. It was passed in the House of Lords, but was narrowly rejected in the Commons. After further small changes it was re-presented, but again failed, by a narrower margin.

The English bishops then indicated that they would not regard as disloyal clergy who stayed within the limits of the Deposited Book. It thus became the de facto standard of ceremonies, ornaments, and ritual. (New rules were eventually adopted in the 1960s.) However, apart from the marriage service (in which the preface removed explicit references to sexual union, and the word "obey" from the woman's vow), the book did not win widespread acceptance. It went too far for evangelicals, not far enough for Anglo-Catholics. The variations allowed in the holy communion were used in many parishes, but usually piecemeal: many Anglo-Catholic churches produced liturgies of their own, to which most bishops raised little objection. Evangelicals continued to use the 1662 version without change.

The toleration of various liturgies in the Anglican Communion saw the end of the principle of uniformity and the growth of local uses. In Scotland, the USA, Canada, and South Africa local prayer books came into being in 1928–30, representing a wide range of churchmanship. In East Africa, Australia, and New Zealand the use of the 1662 book continued, but the English practice of bishops allowing local variation grew (despite several court cases).

The "Parish and People" movement in the 1930s and 1940s brought a growth of parish eucharists followed by meals. The frequency of communion, use of services, candles, and other innovations so controversial in the 1880s came to be accepted as normal in many places. The standard of traditional church music improved (under the impetus of the Royal School of Church Music). But little liturgical change took place until well into the 1960s.

Decolonization saw formal ties with the Church of England severed in the 1960s, as indigenous churches and leaders began to emerge. The Liturgical movement came to influence Anglican liturgical practice and research. The impact of the modern media—especially television—and the spread of the charismatic movement brought further pressure for change. In these cases, however, the issues were less doctrinal than cultural. Experimental liturgies were developed in many branches of the Anglican Communion, with considerable involvement of local parishes (a feature absent from the 1920–28 processes).

The late 1970s saw a growing consensus between the various parties in the Church of England, based on modern liturgical research (e.g., the "fourfold shape" theory of eucharistic liturgy, the Holy Spirit's role in baptism). Rapid development of lay involvement, and the use of contemporary music, visual arts, and drama has brought about a new atmosphere in public liturgy.

As a consequence, revised Prayer Books have emerged in Australia (1978), the USA (1979), England (the Alternative Service Book, 1980), and New Zealand (1984). The 1662 book (or its derivatives) continues to be the official standard in some churches. Its actual use is declining, but it is expected that it will continue for some time yet, supported in particular by the Prayer Book Society.

*Bibliography.* A. G. Hebert, *Liturgy and Society* (1935); G. Dix, *The Shape of the Liturgy* (1945); M. J. Hatchett, *Commentary on the American Prayer Book* (1980).

CHARLES SHERLOCK

# Communism, Marxist.

Social theories which may properly be characterized as communist, and efforts to translate them into practice have appeared in Western history, with impressive frequency, at least since the time of Plato. Those responsible for such efforts have not been uniformly simpleminded or wicked people. They have indeed included men of outstanding character and intellect, such as Plato and Thomas More. R. N. Carew Hunt explains this phenomenon by saying, "For nearly two thousand years European civilization has rested upon a contradiction—between a philosophy and a religion which teach that all men are brothers, and an economic system which organizes them as masters and servants," thus involving "inequalities of human life" which "are seen largely to derive from private property" (*The Theory and Practice of Communism*, [1950], p. 3). In general it may be said that the several theories have not won serious allegiance on a large scale or for long. The experiments have been local and short-lived; and the attitude of others toward both theories and experiments has commonly been easy tolerance and good-humored rejection.

But when communism is mentioned in America today, it is not these theories and experiments of the past but the Marx–Engels—Lenin–Stalin succession that is referred to; and the attitude expressed, if it is not a devotion which approaches religious veneration, is one of intense hostility and fear or of bewilderment and frustration. Apart from a "hard core" of devoted communists which has persisted in every Western nation (comparatively large in some, almost insignificant in others), the West has passed through a "honeymoon period" with communism into one of growing disillusionment and hardening opposition. Apparently, also, the relatively stable numerical strength of the Party and its "fellow-travelers" in America has been maintained only by the constant flowing into it and out again of numerous inarticulate people who must therefore also have shared the experience of attraction and subsequent disillusionment. It is claimed that many more would like to leave the Party but are prevented from doing so, partly by a realization of the intense spiritual suffering which almost all the former communists have found to be involved in making such a break, and partly by the combination of persecution pressures from their former comrades and the lack of an intelligent, understanding inducement on the part of noncommunist society. On the other hand, communism has been able to win, and to retain to the point of imprisonment, ruin, and even death, the allegiance of many whose education, social, and financial status, and future prospects in noncommunist society, were above average.

Marxist communism is thus a very challenging phenomenon—challenging in several senses of the word. In its first formulation, and in the adherence to it of much of its subsequent leadership, it appears as a missionary movement of certain intellectuals on behalf of the oppressed proletariat, a movement in which a genuine social sympathy and the pangs of conscience accusing the person for his undeserved privileges both seem to play a part in varying proportions. But certainly also adherence to it may be due to the lust for self-vindication on the part of people who feel themselves to be failures, the lust for power over others, an intense desire to "belong" to a devoted group, a liking for a "cloak and dagger" life, a hatred for organized society, or to any of a number of similar questionable motivations; as membership in it may also issue in such motivations.

The theory was hammered out by Karl Marx (1818–1883) in association with Friedrich Engels (1820–1895), and in an environment of constant, intense cooperation with and dissention from, other revolutionaries on the basis of the philosophy of such left-wing Hegelians as Ludwig Feuerbach (1804–1872), the writings of the classical, mainly English, economists, and some acquaintance with English social conditions in that comparatively early stage of the Industrial Revolution when its socially disruptive effects were much in evidence and remedial measures had not yet begun to take effect. Engels, who had operated mills in England, was much more aware of the latter than was Marx, whose mind remained largely Continental to the last. The "catechism" of Marxist communism is *The Communist Manifesto*, the work of Marx and Engels, first published in German in February 1848. Its "bible" is Marx's *Capital*, the first volume of which was published in German in 1867, the second, by Engels, in 1885 after Marx's death.

The history of this movement has been characterized throughout by internal controversy, as a result of which numerous people who thought of themselves as true and loyal communists have been constantly expelled from the Party, often, although not always, for theoretical divergencies, and often also through party manipulation rather than through the winning of theoretical arguments. The agreement within the triumphant faction has often been achieved without those who participated knowing what it was that they were agreeing on. It is therefore very difficult for the dispassionate student to decide whether the officially orthodox developments at the hands of Lenin and Stalin are a true expression of the spirit of the original or not. This has been a hotly debated, and a bloodily contested, question, especially in the case of Stalin. It is not difficult to agree with Spolansky's assertion that Marx, if he were alive today, would totally fail to understand the discussions in contemporary communist groups (*The Communist Trail in America* [1951]). However that may be, within the Party the works of Lenin and Stalin (unless, as is suspected by some, the latter is now in a slow process of repudiation) are regarded also as authoritative.

Communist theory was little more than a ferment, and their activity only a "nuisance," within the labor movement until, in 1917, Lenin was transported in a closed railway car across Germany by the German High Command, from his exile in Switzerland to Petrograd, in the hope that his activity there might hasten that disintegration of Russia which had already begun, and thus take Russia out of World War I. Under his inspiration and guidance, the Kerensky government, which had taken over at the time of the czar's abdication in March, was overthrown. There followed a long and bitter struggle to reclaim Russia from domestic and foreign military opposition, to hammer out a consistent Soviet policy, and to clamp its hold upon the country as a whole (see E. H. Carr, *The Bolshevik Revolution, 1917–1923* [1951]). Events connected with World War II severely tested the stability of the Soviet regime; but the test was met and ultimately Soviet power was vastly extended, so that now it controls a large portion of the human race.

Marxist communism is essentially a program based on, and guided by, a philosophy of violent revolution in which, so it is confidently believed, the proletariat will ultimately seize power on a worldwide basis. After this revolution there will be an intermediate "socialist" period in which, under the "dictatorship of the proletariat," all remnants of "bourgeois" thinking and practice, and those who entertain them, will be ruthlessly exterminated. When this has been accomplished the communist stage of history will have been achieved, the classless society will be finally ushered in, all exploitation of man by man will disappear, each will voluntarily contribute according to his ability and receive according to his needs in a situation of plenty for all, and the state, which is essentially coercive power in the hands of a few, will wither away.

The inevitability of this outcome is guaranteed by the dialectical character of historical evolution, through class conflict. This theory of "historical materialism" rests on the belief that the principle which ultimately conditions all human relationships is the production of the material means to support life. It is believed that a primitive communism, on a low social level, was disrupted by the institution of private property. Although a disruption, it was also an advance. But a society so organized has within it the seeds of its own destruction and of the creation of a higher social stage because it divides mankind into two warring classes: the owners and exploiters, on the one hand, and the larger and growing class of the dispossessed, on the other. Thus the class struggle is inevitably generated. The dominating class develops, by conscious and unconscious processes, a superstructure of culture, including political institutions and theories, ethics, religion and philosophy, the real purpose of which is self-justification, and which is therefore relative purely to the interests of the class. The exploited class presently begins to do the same. Since the dominant class will never willingly yield up its privileges, and since it controls for the time being the means of power, the transition from one stage of historical evolution to another will always involve violence. It is believed that history has thus passed from the primitive communism to a slave economy; from that to feudalism; and from that to capitalism (*see* CAPITALISM). The latter is the present stage of history. It must develop all of its potentialities for good before the inner contradictions will destroy it and usher in the final victory of the proletariat. It was this latter belief which caused considerable confusion in communist minds when power came to them, not as was anticipated in the most advanced industrial societies, but in the mainly peasant economy of Russia. The problem was whether they should first develop an advanced, capitalist society in Russia before their communism could really take hold there; or perhaps mark time in Russia until the expected revolution should take place in Germany; or proceed to communize Russia at once, and, if so, how that could be done.

But this "historical materialism" itself rests, in communist theory at least, upon a more ultimate philosophy of "dialectical materialism" which, so it is maintained, is the only real alternative to idealism. The latter is the philosophy of the bourgeois society, and all the current philosophies of bourgeois society which seem to be opposed to idealism are really disguised forms of it. Such a philosophy the communists strenuously reject and combat. Their philosophy must be "scientific" which means, for them, that it must be materialistic, and its laws must be those of, or similar to, classical physics. At the same time, it must be able to guarantee that development is in the direction of the desired revolution and to provide a guide to revolutionary action. This seemed to mean that its laws must be dialectic in character. There must be opposites, which are yet interconnected, so that they will conflict and result in revolutionary change. Whether any philosophy could satisfy such requirements may well be doubted, but Marx was sure that his dialectical materialism could. "With me," he wrote in the introduction to the first volume of *Capital*, "the ideal is nothing else than the material world reflected by the human mind and translated into terms of thought." But, it may be asked, if matter is ultimate, and if matter is conceived, as Marx thought that he conceived it in the manner of 19th-century physics, what is the character of his "human mind," where did it come from, how can it translate the material world into "terms of thought," and how can we be sure that thereby objective truth may be known? Marx himself, apparently, became impatient with such questions. They are, he says, not questions of theory at all, but practical questions. We may agree that practical life does answer them; but that a theoretical answer is desirable also in a philosophy of any kind would seem to be obvious, and also that the answer must be in harmony both with the practical answers and with the philosophical theory. It cannot be admitted that Marxism meets this test.

Furthermore, as a revolutionist Marx had to find a justification in his philosophy for his conviction that human free choice influences events, and a guide to such choice. He and Engels, like their successors, are forever urging the proletariat to exercise their free choice and to unite for revolution, and assuring them that the resultant action will influence the course of history; and the former bitterly condemned the proletariat for their lethargy and refusal. But if matter is pri-

mary and if it is the matter of classical physics, how could beings having freedom of choice have come into existence and, if they did, how could their free actions influence an evolution which is determined by iron laws? The compromise often suggested is that human free action can hasten, or delay, but that it cannot otherwise change the inexorable outcome. But that is an evasion, not a solution, of the problem.

Some characteristic and essential features of this theory and program call for further emphasis. First, worldwide revolution by violence belongs to its essence. Marx came repeatedly into contact with those who advocated revolution by means of gradualism and constitutional procedures. He always and emphatically repudiated such ideas. Only violent and bloody revolution would work. Every responsible organ of communist expression has reiterated this judgment, openly and many times. Any retreat from this view, such as the suggestions of Stalin and Malenkov that communism and capitalism can have a peaceful coexistence, are purely strategic and intended for outside consumption to aid the world revolution by disarming opposition. The communists entertain, and openly express, nothing but contempt for those well-meaning individuals who think that they can be persuaded to compromise this issue, or to abandon this program. The "subversive" activities in other countries are intended only to soften them up and thus prepare the way for the inevitable bloody revolution there. Stalin's "socialism in one country" is also simply a strategic and temporary retreat.

Second, communist theory acknowledges, and its procedures admit, none of our ethical and religious restraints upon either their subversive activities, their international diplomacy, their domestic administration, or the violent revolution. Our ethics belongs to the bourgeois superstructure and is purely relative to it; their ethics belongs to their superstructure and consists, at present, of anything which actually aids their cause. Thus deceit and untruth, when practiced by them and not against them, is a virtue so long as it is successful. Religion not only belongs to our superstructure and is in the interest simply of bourgeois dominance, as an "opiate of the people"; it is also repudiated by their materialism, which is aggressively atheistic. In the last year of his life, Engels did recognize that Christianity had once proved to be, not an opiate, but a marvelously successful revolutionary force. Presumably, if it played that role once, it could do so again, as of course it has repeatedly. But this acknowledgment and its implications have played no part in communist theory or practice. They will tolerate the church, as a temporary strategy, if and insofar as they think it to be necessary and can use it for their own purposes; but they have not abandoned, and will not abandon, their essential atheism, and their goal is the destruction of the church.

Third, communist theory, and much of communist practice, involves no respect for present individuals. The outlook is so futuristic that present standards of living and present individuals are cheerfully sacrificed in the supposed interest of the future; and the individual is merged in, and readily sacrificed to, the group. Thus, although the communists commonly describe themselves as democratic, the term as they use it means something very different from our understanding of the word. They have toyed with the idea that the classless society will be a pure democracy, without any coercion and even without any delegated authority. Lenin seems to have thought, when he wrote his pamphlet "How to Organize Competition" in January 1918, that something approaching this would work in the Russia of that time; but by April of that year, when his "Immediate Tasks of the Soviet Government" appeared, he had begun to change his mind. Stalin seems to have completely repudiated the whole idea.

*See also* COMMUNISM, RECENT TRENDS IN.

**Bibliography.** J. C. Bennett, *Christianity and Communism* (1951); I. Deutscher, *Stalin: A Political Biography* (1949); A. Koestler, *The Yogi and the Commissar* (1946); M. Lovell, *The Soviet Way of Life* (1948); G. V. Plekhanov, *Fundamental Problems of Marxism; In Defence of Materialism;* D. Runes, *The Soviet Impact on Society* (1953); R. Schlesinger, *Marx: His Time and Ours;* L. Schwarzschild, *The Red Prussian* (1947); V. Venable, *Human Nature, The Marxian View* (1946).

ANDREW K. RULE

## Communism, Recent Trends in.

Communism is any economic scheme that advocates common ownership of property to the exclusion of private property. The term usually refers to Marxism. Less than 70 years after the death of Karl Marx (1818–83), one-third of the world lived under political systems claiming direct inspiration from his ideas. In fact, Marx's ideas now influence almost all aspects of human thought and affairs, including politics, economics, sociology, psychology, history, and religion. Recent trends in Marxism have centered around three intractable problems: the nonoccurrence of a proletarian revolution in the West; the phenomenon of Stalinism in the USSR and most Soviet Bloc countries; and the continuing vitality of religion, especially Christianity, in the various Marxist countries of the world.

First, the various Marxist parties of Western Europe and the USA have spent a great deal of time in the last half of the 20th century trying to explain why communist revolutions have not occurred in any of the most industrialized countries of the world where Marx believed they were historically inevitable and where they should erupt first. For example, the Italian Communist party, building upon the work of Antonio Gramsci (d. 1937), probably the most original Marxist thinker of the 20th century, during the past 50 years has strongly modified the ideas of both Marx and Lenin. Gramsci saw Marx as having greatly underestimated the resilience of capitalist society. One of the main reasons why revolution had failed in the West, according to Gramsci, was that the mass of the people was not convinced of the value of socialism and still clung to capitalist versions of liberty, equality, and nationalism. He argued that not until the power of bourgeois ideology had been broken could Marxism become attractive to large numbers of people. Thus, one of the major tasks of communists in the West was to establish a kind of socialist counterculture, an alternative vision of the world to the current prevailing attitudes of capitalism. Only then could the proletariat gain hegemony over all the forces in society that opposed capitalism.

Nor had Lenin provided a satisfactory revolutionary program for the West, according to Gramsci. The strategy of frontal assault may have been successful in Russia where the state was a tottering autocratic structure imposed on a society with no solid middle-class institutions, but it would not do for Western Europe where political authority was much more firmly supported by society. In other words, one of the major tasks confronting contemporary Marxists was to undermine the political concepts of capitalist society as a necessary preliminary to any revolution.

Building upon the ideas of Gramsci and under the leadership of Palmiro Togliatti, the Italian Communist party after World War II developed a middle course between the mid reforms of the social democrats and the uncompromisingly revolutionary stance of Lenin. Thus, the Italian Communists took issue with Moscow over Poland, where they strongly supported Solidarity, and over Afghanistan, where they claimed the Soviets had endangered world peace by invading that country in 1980. Moreover, they have joined with other communist parties in Western Europe to form "Eurocommunism," dedicated to holding Moscow at arm's length and traveling the parliamentary road to socialism. Beginning in the 1970s, Italian, Spanish, and French Communists openly affirmed that the construction of socialism was possible in a multiparty state and that the worldwide communist movement had become a polycentral system in which Moscow no longer held the unique place. Thus, the Italian Marxists have touted their "third way," the French have insisted on a socialism "in French colors," and the Spanish Communists have gone so far as to abandon any specific reference to Leninism in its self-definition. All of the communist parties of Western Europe now officially see the gaining of an electoral mandate as an essential step in the struggle to transform capitalism and bring about "the revolution." However, none has any coherent strategy for working out long-term policies and most still feel trapped between the legacy of Lenin and the temptations of bourgeois democracy.

Moreover, even though Marxist ideology has long been influential among intellectuals in the USA, the American Communist party continues to be almost nonexistent. As long ago as 1906, sociologist Werner Sombart noted that in the USA socialism had "foundered upon shoals of roast beef and apple pie." It is also important to remember that, unlike Europe, the USA has no feudal past and that the American struggle for democracy has not been conducted against the background of entrenched social privilege. Thus, the very openness of the American political system has made it responsive to the demands of organized workers in a way unheard of in the Old World. Consequently, there has never been a real threat of Marxist revolution in the USA, except perhaps in the imagination of certain politicians and religious leaders.

However, for a brief period, an ephemeral and mutated form of Marxism was successful in America, Great Britain, and Western Europe. In fact, it has been the only Marxist movement to have made any impact on the Anglo-Saxon world. Beginning in the USA in the 1960s, the New Left spread quickly throughout the universities of America and Europe. Basing its ideology largely upon German Marxist philosopher Herbert Marcuse's *One-Dimensional Man* (1964), the New Left was defined more by what it rejected than by what it affirmed—it opposed both the shallow materialist capitalism of the West and the authoritarian Leninist tradition of the East and instead looked to the third world for its heroes. The product of affluence more than poverty, the New Left was a revolt against the kind of society produced by the long postwar capitalist boom, and it disappeared with the end of that boom in the early 1970s. Its apogee was reached in the events of 1968, such as the huge anti-Vietnam War demonstrations in the USA and the student revolt in Paris.

The New Left was by nature and inclination amorphous. Nevertheless, three main themes can be discerned. First, New Leftists rejected wholesale the existing order of things. They rejected reform because of the total corruption of contemporary society and called for a revolution that was worldwide and total. Second, they distrusted the workers of the Western industrial countries because they had been irredeemably infected by the system. Third, as a consequence, liberation had to come from those supposedly outside the system, whether students and other minority groups in the West, or from the third world where New Leftists found their chief exemplars. In sum, the New Left was often more a state of mind than

a theory of society. It had more in common with anarchism and extreme versions of Maoism than it did with mainstream Marxism. The only area where some New Left thinkers lined up with the main socialist tradition was in their advocacy of workers' control of production. Nevertheless, most New Leftists insisted that they were the "true heirs" of Karl Marx.

The second main theme of Marxist history in the last half of the 20th century has been the progressive repudiation of Stalinism. Joseph Stalin's death in 1953 unleashed long pent-up resentment against Stalinism, a Russian version of Marxist-Leninism which included the heresy of "socialism in one country." Soviet Marxists denounced Stalin's long record of failed economic politics while Communists in other countries decried his geopolitical foreign policy which was little more than a naked expression of power that long predated Marxism. Moreover, many Marxists in and out of the USSR criticized the "cult of personality" upon which he had built his brutal regime and the terror which sustained it.

Then, in 1956, Nikita Khrushchev (1894–1971), who succeeded Stalin as first secretary of the Communist party in the USSR, startled the delegates to the Twentieth Party Congress when he declared that Stalin had "sanctioned in the name of the Central Committee of the All-Union Communist Party the most brutal violation of socialist legality, torture and oppression which led to the slander and self-accusation of innocent people." The speech had a profound impact on the communist world, especially among party intellectuals and theoreticians. In practical terms, it signaled the diminution of terror in Soviet society, a new openness in Soviet society, the reduction in the number of political prisoners held in camps, and the possibility of criticizing certain aspects of the regime without risking persecution. Although Khrushchev attenuated Stalinist terror, he did not abolish it altogether and continued to use ruthless measures to rule the USSR and to keep Soviet Bloc countries in line. Anti-Stalinist demonstrations were allowed throughout the Marxist world (especially Eastern Europe) but when the Hungarians went too far in their quest for freedom in 1956, Khrushchev did not hesitate to send Soviet tanks into Budapest.

Still, on the whole, Khrushchev's de-Stalinization program marked a new phase in Marxist development. The Soviets adopted a policy of peaceful coexistence with the capitalist West while Khruschchev's speech gave the Italian Communist leader Togliatti the opportunity to broaden his position by declaring that the mere criticism of Stalin as a person was too superficial and that the entire system which he had constructed needed to be examined. In China, Mao, already embarked on an independent course, now combined a version of Marxism with nationalism which allowed Chinese communism to function as an ideology for mass participation in the modernization process. In other Marxist countries, reaction to de-Stalinization ranged from destroying statues of the former Soviet dictator to calls from intellectuals for renewed study of Marx's ideas in order to provide foundations for reform.

Khrushchev's successor as first secretary of the Soviet Communist party, Leonid Brezhnev (1906–82), continued to move away from Stalinism by joining with U.S. leaders in establishing a policy of détente in East-West relations. Even though these relations could sometimes be rough and tense, overall the 1970s was a period of expanding contact between the Marxist East and the democratic West. These broadening contacts, in turn, affected life in all of the Marxist world, including intellectual and religious currents.

After the short-lived regimes of Yuri Andropov (1982–84) and Konstantin Chernenko (1984/85), Mikhail Gorbachev resumed the de-Stalinization of Soviet Marxism in 1985. Following his announced policy of *glasnost* (openness) and methodology of *perestroika* (restructuring), Gorbachev during the 1980s embarked on an aggressive new policy of arms control with the USA and a program of limited private enterprise and economic freedom at home. Most important, his regime has granted new freedom of thought to Soviet intellectuals and freedom of expression to political dissidents. Many Marxist countries which traditionally have been heavily influenced by Moscow have followed suit.

Third, the continuing vitality of religion in all Marxist countries (with the possible exception of Albania) has perplexed and concerned many Marxist thinkers. For example, observers of European religion have noted that there has been more regular manifest religious devotion in Marxist countries in Eastern European nations in the post-World War II period than there has been in Western Europe. In fact, religion illustrates better than anything else the changing world of Marxism in the last half of the 20th century. Early in 1918, Lenin personally drafted a document which separated the church from the state and the schools from the churches. Among other things, Lenin's decree forbade the churches to hold property and to manage a church budget. The Russian Orthodox Church, as the established state religion, understood this decree as an unfriendly gesture while the other confessions generally regarded it as a hopeful sign of more tolerance than they had enjoyed in the past under Tsarist-controlled Orthodoxy.

Stalin promulgated the Legislation on Religion of 1929 which virtually destroyed the freedom of the churches as ecclesiastical organizations and brought them under direct state supervision. This law made it illegal for churches to own property or enter into contracts and specified that buildings could be used for religious services only upon application to government authorities and by a petition with 20 or more signatures. (Processing of these applications was at the whim of local authorities as was the tenure in assigned buildings.) Religious activities outside of the church building itself were prohibited, all auxiliary services (such as libraries, women's societies, and youth organizations) were forbidden, and the religious instruction of children was disallowed. In addition, participation in a religious group disqualified an individual for membership in the Communist party and usually kept him or her out of the professions. Concomitant with this, antireligious propaganda by the Knowledge Society (formerly the League of the Militant Godless) was financed by the government, medical personnel were trained to warn patients of the harm ensuing from religious faith, and baptisms, church marriages, and religious funerals were discouraged by the authorities.

The level of enforcement of this law varied, according to external pressures and domestic crises, from routine harassment to active persecution, up to the Nazi attack on the Soviet Union in 1941. However, in appreciation of the strong support by both the Orthodox Church and evangelical Christians during World War II, Stalin permitted the reopening of many churches at the end of the war, the establishment of a central church administration under the Russian Orthodox patriarch, and the formation of a church union of evangelicals. But the situation took a turn for the worse under Khrushchev when in 1962 he initiated a secret revision of the special Legislation on Religion calculated to deregister churches, arrest resisting clergy, and speed up the elimination of religion, the presence of which he considered a continuing embarrassment to the Soviet regime. Behind the scenes, both the Orthodox Church and the Baptist Union were required to adopt new constitutions, further weakening their legal status and making them more amenable to the goals of the state. When the Baptist Union agreed to these more restrictive rules, it precipitated a major split in its ranks, resulting in the establishment of an alternative and illegal "underground" union. After some initial resistance, the Orthodox Church also agreed to a new constitution which severely restricted the role of the clergy in local church affairs and precipitated a dissident movement.

The 1970s marked another period of greater tolerance of the churches by the authorities, mostly due to the pressure of world opinion and the mellow Soviet-U.S. relations during détente. In 1975, the 1929 law was amended, making it more moderate than in 1962 but still more restrictive than in 1929. Overall, there was less harassment under Brezhnev than under Khrushchev, and permission was given for the first time to import limited quantities of Bibles and to build a few new church buildings.

Détente ended in 1980 and harassment of believers increased once again. During the Andropov—Chernenko years, ambivalent policies, negative and positive, haunted church-state relations in the Soviet Union. On the one hand, there was a crack-down on evangelical groups, while on the other, the Soviet authorities in 1983 gave the Danilov Monastery back to the Orthodox Church to be renovated in anticipation of the celebration of the millennium of Christianity in Russia in 1988.

The Gorbachev era, beginning in 1985, has been characterized by a marked decrease in official pressure on the churches. Moreover, the government made the millennium a national event, openly acknowledging the long-term impact of Christianity on Russian culture, and for the first time allowing the publication of large numbers of Bibles and the importation of substantial amounts of religious literature from the West. In addition, during the 1980s there was a dramatic drop in the number of religious prisoners in the Soviet Gulag; the head of the Council of Religious Affairs (which supervises all religious activities in the USSR) adopted a more positive attitude toward the churches and appointed new staff committed to perestroika in church-state relations; and Gorbachev himself called for a more tolerant attitude toward religion in the interest of national unity. In his many speeches about perestroika in this period, the first secretary repeatedly insisted on a return to the spirit of Leninism (meaning the Leninism of 1918) in order to overcome Stalinism—in the realm of religion as well as politics and economics. At the same time, Stalin's 1929 legislation remained in effect.

Soviet Bloc countries in Eastern Europe have tended to follow Moscow's leadership in their religious policies during the post-World War II period. In the 1980s, Gorbachev's religious glasnost was readily adopted by Poland, the German Democratic Republic, Hungary, and Bulgaria; and Yugoslavia already had it. Only Czechoslovakia and Romania have been reluctant to reduce official pressure on their respective religious communities. Outside the Soviet Bloc, Marxist countries like China also adopted a more relaxed attitude toward religion, but for reasons different from Moscow's. China's revised policies came mostly in response to internal upheaval and economic problems and renewed contacts with the USA. Thus, churches were allowed to reopen and the importation of Bibles was allowed to resume, but Western missionaries were not allowed to return. On the other hand, Albania has not abandoned its policies; religion there remains outlawed and all vestiges thereof severely persecuted in that Balkan Marxist state.

Because of de-Stalinization there also has been a movement among Marxist intellectuals to reassess the relationship of modern communism to Christianity. In this regard, the French Marxist thinker Louis Althusser has been extremely influential on many Christian proponents of Marxism, especially during the 1960s and 1970s. Using structuralist linguistics, psychology, and anthropology, Althusser attempted to "rehabilitate" Marx as a structuralist before his time. (Structuralism is the view that the key to the understanding of a social system is the structural relationship of its parts—the way these parts are related by the regulative principle of the system.) In his work, Althusser emphasized Marxism as a scientific method distinct from Marxism as an ideology. Since a major obstacle to Christian acceptance of Marxism has been its adherence to an atheistic ideology and its reduction of religion to a reflection of societal sickness, Althusser's criticism of reductionist uses of Marxism and his separation of scientific method from ideology made Marxism more acceptable to some Christians.

On the other hand, his interpretation of Marxism has made it more difficult to reconcile it with Christianity. Althusser has been criticized for eliminating the role of free human creativity by his stress on the scientific study of structures alone as determinants of society. Thus, he holds to a rigorous, monistic materialism which treats free will as an ideological illusion and which sees Christianity as an ideology using this illusion of free will to justify itself. Nevertheless, his interpretation of Marx has been used as a crack through which a number of so-called Christian Marxists have attempted to squeeze their liberation theology.

Critical Marxism, another attempt to relate Marxist thought to the conditions of the second half of the 20th century, also grew up in the 1960s and 1970s. The term "critical Marxism" underscores a common epistemological note which characterized those who can be included in this intellectual movement—the criticism of at least some aspects of the dominant Marxist tradition with a greater awareness of the subjective factors that influence society and Marxism itself. Further, this movement commonly desired to dissociate Marxist socialism from existing communist nations and their ideology while maintaining "Marxist analysis." In Eastern Europe, it often expressed dissatisfaction with statism, party-rule, and dogmatism, in an effort to create a "truer" Marxist socialism. Most important, in Latin America it enabled several important Christian thinkers to distinguish between Marxist analysis and Marxist atheism-materialism. Among those who have been included in this school of thought have been Gramsci, Marcuse, George Lukacs,

Jurgen Habermas, Ernst Bloch, Roger Garaudy, Jean-Paul Sartre, and even Althusser.

Another major movement on the religious front was the development of a Marxist-Christian dialog in Eastern Europe beginning in the 1960s. This dialog has continued, with serious disruption caused by the Soviet crushing of the Czech bid for independence from Moscow in 1968, throughout the last decades of the 20th century. Moreover, the dialog spread to West Germany, France, and even the USA during the 1960s and 1970s. In Czechoslovakia, for example, Protestant theologians carried on lengthy and serious exchanges with Marxist theoreticians, contributing to the effort of the Dubcek regime to create "socialism with a human face" before it was crushed by Soviet military might. At other meetings, motifs from the writings of "the young Marx" were rediscovered, especially his idea of alienation, and their common ancestry in Christianity stressed. These dialogs brought some Christians face-to-face with a number of apparently forgotten social demands of faith, and some communist participants found authentic Marxist tools with which to criticize their dogmatic and repressive regimes. Unfortunately, several Marxist participants, like the French Marxist Garaudy, were expelled from the party for bending too far in the direction of Christianity.

A final meeting place of Marxism and Christianity in the period since World War II has been liberation theology, especially in the 1970s and 1980s. In considering liberation theology, the focus shifts from a critique of Christianity offered by Marxists to a reformulation of Christianity by Christians who are either Marxists themselves or are strongly influenced by some aspect of the Marxist tradition. Although in reality a diffuse movement with a growing number of adherents all over the world, liberation theology historically has centered in Latin America and has been largely Roman Catholic in orientation. It differs from previous systematic expressions of Christianity in that it seeks to interpret the faith from the perspective of the poor and oppressed. Because the problems of the third world are different, liberationists struggle with issues of faith and postcolonial deprivation as they search for hope in a world of poverty. Their concern is to locate the God of righteousness in a world of injustice.

The most basic source of liberation theology is the experience of poverty, destitution, and repression in a region which Christendom has dominated for centuries. Liberation theologians believe that this suffering is against the will of God. Some of the theological roots of the movement can be traced to Europe's political theology and to Jurgen Moltmann's theology of hope. The deepest theological roots, however, stem from the growing interest of the Roman Catholic Church in dialog with the world, a dialog initiated by Vatican II (1962–65). To a Latin American priesthood increasingly involved with the poor, this signaled the opportunity for a new examination of past answers (such as Marxism and other brands of socialism) formerly prohibited by the Church. These possibilities were explored and amplified at the Medellín Conference of Latin American bishops held in Colombia in 1968.

A final source of liberation theology is not Christian in origin at all, but Marxist. In fact, the continuing use of Marxism has caused considerable conflict between the more conservative Vatican and the more radical liberationists. However, it is not Marxism as a philosophy or as a holistic plan of political action that they adapted for use, but Marxism as an instrument of social analysis. The focus has been on the economic system as a key factor in oppression and the class struggle as the battleground for that oppression. Finally, also borrowed from Marxism is the concept of praxis—that is, theology must be done and not just learned. This praxis describes the interaction that is always going on between reflection and action, a dialectical engagement with the world which results in transforming action. Like Marx, liberationists argue that it is the precondition of knowledge, in which people seek not merely to understand the world but to change it. Through praxis, individuals enter into their sociohistorical destiny. Among those who have been active in the formulation and espousal of various forms of liberation theology are Catholics Gustavo Gutierrez, Leonardo and Clodovis Boffo, Juan Luis Segundo, and Protestants Jose Miguez Bonino and Samuel Escobar.

Recent trends in Marxist communism have not altered the fact that the movement is still based on Marx's materialistic conception of history and its ultimate goal is still the destruction of capitalism and the establishment of a classless society. On the other hand, Marxism in the second half of the 20th century has been a volatile movement because it has had to try to explain the vagaries of its history—including why the revolution has not occurred in the most industrialized areas of the West where Marx predicted it would happen— and because of the progressive de-Stalinization of the movement since 1956. Moreover, Marxism has had to deal with the fact that religion has not begun to wither away in Marxist countries, as Marx said it would *after* the revolution. Numerous Marxist thinkers have spent a great deal of time grappling with these issues in the closing decades of the 20th century.

Implicit in each of these issues is the fact that many of Marx's expectations have remained unfulfilled. In the first place, for example, there is the lack of revolutionary drive among the working class in the West. Second, Marx underestimated the persistence and growth of nationalism in the world. Third, Marx did not foresee the resurgence of Christianity with a social conscience. Finally, many Marxists are beginning to realize that Marx often indulged in a shallow optimism about the possibilities open to human nature, which they fear he may have misread. Christian thinkers no doubt will continue to find the Marxist critique of capitalism helpful in their own attempts to relate the teachings of Jesus to the social issues of the day, and many will continue to find Marxism fascinating as a vehicle of protest. However, Christians also will continue to find Marxism inadequate to answer the fundamental questions of meaning because it still maintains that these questions can be solved by a reorganization of the relations of production. If socialism is to have a future, it will have to go beyond any society describable in Marxist terms—and at that point biblical theology seizes the initiative.

Drastic economic reforms and political restructuring throughout Eastern Europe occurred in 1990, resulting in the reunification of East and West Germany. The full impact of this realignment, politically, economically, or religiously, has not yet been realized.

*See also* COMMUNISM, MARXIST.

**Bibliography.** L. Kolakowski, *Main Currents of Marxism* (1978); K. Bockmuehl, *The Challenge of Marxism* (1979); J. A. Kirk, *Liberation Theology: An Evangelical View from the Third World* (1979); D. Lyon, *Karl Marx* (1979); R. Heilbroner, *Marxism: For and Against* (1980); J. A. Kirk, *Theology Encounters Revolution* (1980); A. F. McGovern, *Marxism: An American Christian Perspective* (1980); D. McLellan, *Marxism after Marx* (1980); P. Mojzes, *Christian-Marxist Dialogue in Eastern Europe* (1981); B. Szajkowski, ed., *Marxist Governments: A World Survey*, 3 vols. (1981); A. Westoby, *Communism after World War Two* (1982); D. McLellan, *Marx: The First 100 Years* (1983); N. Piediscalzi and R. G. Thobaben, eds., *Three Worlds of Christian-Marxist Encounters* (1985); S. N. Gundry and A. F. Johnson, eds., *Tensions in Contemporary Theology* (1986); D. McLellan, *Marxism and Religion* (1987); J. Ellul, *Jesus and Marx: From Gospel to Ideology* (1988).

ROBERT D. LINDER

**Community Churches.** In many smaller American towns and villages one Protestant church serves most of the inhabitants. While there are a number of reasons for this, the urban movement, failure of economy, impatience with denominational structures, and the desire to make the church reflect the community are among the chief causes for the single community church phenomenon.

There are two basic types of community churches: the single denominational church and the nondenominational Protestant church. First, in a highly unified religious or ethnic community the church will frequently reflect a particular denomination. Historically, in some cases for one or more of the above reasons, where several community churches existed their members voted to become a single body, such as the Presbyterian community church. In other cases—particularly

during the early community church movement—federations were made whereby members of previously existing denominational churches would meet together in a nondenominational structure but keep separate rolls and affiliation for the constituent denominational interests.

More frequently a community church took on nondenominational status either from a union among previous denominational churches or from the desire of community members to establish a new nonaffiliated church. In either case there existed a preference for local control and reflection of broad community religious ideals. Such a church normally took on the following characteristics: it was community-centered, democratic, nonsectarian, and non- or transdenominational.

Since the 1920s a self-conscious community church movement has taken place, encouraged in part by various social and religious surveys as well as ecumenical interests. The first orderly survey of community churches published in 1922 revealed the existence of 713 clearly defined community churches. Five years later the number had increased to 1296. Twenty-five years later, in 1952, community churches numbered well over 3000.

Concomitant with this growth was the formation of a nationally organized community church service agency which culminated in the formation of the International Council of Community Churches (1950). This international organization resulted from the merger of the Biennial Council of Negro Churches, the National Council, a predominantly white organization, and more than 65 churches located outside the USA.

The International Council, in its ecumenically minded documents, sought both the development of the local community church and its cooperation toward a united church. Since its inception the council has been a member of the National Council of Churches of Christ and the World Council of Churches. Nevertheless, the International Council is remarkably free from coercive governmental structures, and allows local community church members to vote themselves in or out of the council.

Since its purpose is to include rather than to divide, one discovers that the community church council represents both a blend of traditional Christian concepts and an openness to change. Great stress is laid upon love which includes, rather than upon creeds which, it believes, divide.

The openness of the council is especially revealed in its broad position on divine revelation. While conceding that inviolate truths are contained in the Bible, declared to be written in language subject to debate, the council also values truths found in the writings of Buddhism, Hinduism, and Islam.

After weathering a difficult decade during the 1970s the International Council of Community

Churches regained composure and now serves approximately 1300 community churches in 50 states and several other nations. In addition to encouraging its member churches to serve human social and economic needs, the council provides services such as ecclesiastical endorsement, personnel placement, insurance, and continuing education. The council also publishes a monthly newspaper (*Christian Community*) and a quarterly (*Pastor's Journal*).

In recent years the multiplicity of new denominational and independent churches has caused a considerable setback to the community church movement with its pluriform ideals and structures.

**Bibliography.** D. R. Piper, *Community Churches* (1928); F. D. Wentzel, *Once There Were Two Churches* (1950); J. R. Shotwell, *Unity Without Uniformity: A History of the Postdenominational Community Church Movement* (1984).

JOSEPH H. HALL

**Community of the Resurrection.** Founded in 1892 by Church of England priest Charles Gore (consecrated bishop of Worcester, 1902) the Community of the Resurrection is a male religious order with community houses in Mirfield, London, and Huntingdon, England, and in Rosettenville, South Africa. Their culture is Anglo-Catholic, liberal in spirit, and related to modern trends. Their work is scholarship, preparing Anglican candidates for the ordained ministry (at Mirfield), supervising retreats and giving spiritual direction, leading parish missions and helping in running local parish churches. Some were chaplains in World War I. Their work among the Bantu poor in Johannesburg, publicized by the community member Trevor Huddleston (later bishop) in *Naught for Your Comfort* (1956), alerted Anglicans outside South Africa to social aspects of apartheid. Their central emphasis is on living happily together under community rule, but their best-known work is markedly related to others. A need to train men called to ministry and who did not have the means to enter the universities of Oxford and Cambridge in the early 20th century led to the conversion of the house stables into quarters, setting up a bursary fund, staffing a pre- and postgraduate training program, and establishing a hostel at Leeds for trainees prepared by the community to study at the university.

GERVAIS ANGEL

**Comparative Religion.** The study of comparative religion began with the Greek historian Xenophanes in the 6th century B.C. when he observed that Thracians and Ethiopians both depicted their gods after their own image. However, although writers like Saint Augustine made some acute observations on the differences between religions it was not until the theory of evolution gained popularity in the late 19th century that the serious study of comparative religion began.

Under the influence of Darwin various scholars discovered what they believed to be evolutionary links between different religions. F. Max Muller, E. B. Taylor, and Sir James Frazer were among the founders of the "new" science. The discipline rapidly gained respectability through the immense linguistic abilities of people like Muller, and soon chairs were established in various institutions, particularly the new universities of North America.

In Britain the study of non-Christian religions tended to be linked to the needs of empire and had a more anthropological bias than had the theologically orientated Americans. The study of Asian languages and the history of various subject peoples were also part of the British contribution. In Germany it was the history of religions in an essentially evolutionary and Hegelian framework which predominated, while in the United States, under the influence of the newly formed University of Chicago, comparative religion became an important element in the cultural pluralism of the prevailing liberal consensus.

During the 1960s comparative religion, renamed "Religious Studies," became a popular course in many American universities and was introduced to Britain by professor Ninian Smart at the new University of Lancaster in 1967. A practical side to religious studies appeared in Britain due to the great increase in Asian immigration during the 1960s. As a result, through the efforts of semigovernment bodies like the Schools Council, the teaching of comparative religion quickly replaced more traditional biblical studies in British schools where religious instruction is a compulsory subject.

At its crudest, comparative religion teaches that all religions are essentially equal and originate from one underlying reality. Thus the Ten Commandments of Judaism, Jesus' Sermon on the Mount, the four noble truths of Buddhism, and Hindu teachings derived from the Bhagavad Gita are placed alongside each other to show that all religions teach "the same" moral code. Often this ethical element is reduced to "love thy neighbor as thyself." In a similar way the worship of God or gods and the attempt by Buddhists to gain nirvana is reduced to the statement that "all religions worship a supreme being."

Some modern religious movements, such as Baha'i and the Unification Church, make the unity or rather commonality of religion a central aspect of their teachings. In a sense these and similar movements are truly comparative religions. At the same time certain streams in liberal Protestantism and more recently Roman Catholicism lead in a similar direction even though they would violently reject the pietistic dogmatism of groups like the Unification Church.

One fundamental problem for the more popular forms of comparative religion is the simple observation that all religions are not equal and that in fact upon closer study the teachings of the major world religions are at least as different as they are similar. To argue that Ugandan women regularly use umbrellas and that British housewives do also tells us very little about the realities of female society in Uganda and Britain. In Uganda the umbrella is used as protection against the sun while in Britain it protects against the rain. Similarly prayer in Christianity is very different from meditation in Buddhism, and the Christian belief in the individual person cannot be equated with Buddhist claims that no person exists.

Religions such as Theravaden Buddhism present a strong argument against the crudest forms of comparative religion because of their rejection of the importance of belief in God or the gods and denial of the existence of an individual self. Similarly African religions which do not possess a sacred/secular distinction and often lack a European form of the idea of god also present serious problems for the development of a comparative theology which might perhaps lead to a world religion.

Equally important as purely intellectual considerations are sociological realities. It is easy to talk about pluralism in an essentially secular country. But as soon as any form of classical or traditional Islam is considered, the problem of religious toleration and the American assumption of the separation of church and state becomes acute. Many religions simply do not separate religion and politics and indeed it is often impossible to make such a separation without doing serious violence to the integrity of the religion concerned.

Despite problems like those stated above, some scholars persist in seeking a basic unity between all religions. Their efforts are well meaning and are often explicitly motivated by a deep commitment to political and social liberalism. But their approach in turn often creates the problem of the illiberal liberal who can tolerate strong religious beliefs among all people except his or her own.

The study of comparative religion is in many ways the last frontier of modern theology. To date most scholars who have approached the topic have been theological liberals or agnostics. Few traditional Roman Catholics or conservative evangelicals have ventured into the area. Exceptions to this rule are the Catholic theologian Karl Rahner and the Reformed theologian J. H. Bavinck. The Anglican theologian Stephen Neill has also made significant contributions to the field from a relatively conservative perspective.

Originally, in the work of writers like Max Muller the study of African and other "primitive" religions played a key role in developing theories of comparative religion. Thus missionary writers like Bishop Henry Callaway were considered to have made an important contribution to the field through studies like Callaway's *Religious System of the Ama-Zulu* (1870). But during the 20th century the religions of India have taken central place in the development of religious studies. Thus while literally hundreds of North American universities offer thousands of courses on "Hinduism" and "Buddhism" only half a dozen colleges in North America offer a dozen or so courses on African religions. The neglect of African and other religious traditions lacking written scriptures is a serious gap in the current state of religious studies.

The rise of new religious movements in Western society which are often called "cults" emphasizes the interconnectedness of the world and the need for Christians to take seriously the challenge of non-Christian world religions and newer forms of Christianity which often incorporate elements from other religious traditions. Today for the first time since the late Roman Empire Western Christians live in a religiously plural world which they are only beginning to recognize and respond to. At the same time many non-Western societies, such as Japan, are having to cope with the impact of the West and various aspects of Christianity. Thus the serious study of the similarities and differences between various religions becomes an important theoretical and existential challenge.

**Bibliography.** N. Smart, *Reasons and Faith* (1968); H. Kraemer, *World Cultures and World Religions* (1960); S. G. F. Brandon, ed., *A Dictionary of Comparative Religion* (1970); E. J. Sharpe, *Fifty Key Words: Comparative Religion* (1971); R. S. Ellwood Jr., *Religious and Spiritual Groups in Modern America* (1973); H. G. Coward, *Pluralism: Challenge to World Religions* (1985).

IRVING HEXHAM

**Computer-Aided Biblical Research.** The advent of enormous data bases of Greek and Hebrew literature and search tools permits the analysis of material in minutes that formerly could take a lifetime. The largest body of computerized ancient Hebrew literature, including the entire Talmud, has been amassed in the Global Jewish Database of Bar Ilan University. The Thesaurus Linguae Graecae (TLG) project of the University of California, Irvine, includes 58.5 million words of Greek literature written prior to A.D. 600, including all of the Greek classics, Philo, Josephus, medical texts, and the Greek church fathers.

Many educational centers are working on specialized data bases, including Brown, Duke, Harvard (Perseus Project, coordinated by Gregory Crane and the Photogrammetry and Archaeological Data Base Projects, coordinated by R. Saley), Hebrew University (Armenian inscriptions, coordinated by M. Stone), Hebrew Union College

(Comprehensive Aramaic Lexicon, coordinated by S. Kaufman), Maredsous Centre for Informatique et Bible, Oxford, Packard Humanities Institute, Pennsylvania (CCAT project), Stellenbosch (Syriac Peshitta and Qumran Text Projects, coordinated by J. Cook), Toronto, and Westminster Seminary (Hebrew Bible Morphological Analysis, coordinated by A. Groves).

The TLG project began in the early years of computers, when most computer entry was limited to capital letters. Unfortunately, its encoding system has not been brought into conformity with any of the international standards organizations (ANSI, NISO, ISO). The advent of graphics-oriented computers has permitted screen display and printing of fully pointed and accented Greek and Hebrew. Linguists' Software pioneered Greek and Hebrew display with automatic nondeleting backspacing accents, unlimited overstrike capability, and PostScript laser fonts for typeset quality publishing. They provide the full texts of the BHS OT, UBS NT, and LXX.

Tools for sophisticated analysis of the texts are now widely available, including GRAMCORD (coordinated by Paul Miller of Trinity Evangelical Divinity School) for grammatical analysis of the NT, and Hypertext Biblical Data Project (coordinated by R. Cover of Dallas Seminary). Star Software's program can do complex searches of the entire Bible in as little as one second. Linguists' Software's programs convert any TLG data into properly accented Greek and convert any portion of the BHS into a wide variety of formats for specialized searches.

The 1986 release of the CD ROM disk containing the TLG corpus for analysis on the IBYCUS microcomputer marks the beginning of a new age of widespread immediate access and analysis of vast amounts of data. The subsequent use of other micros to access this data and the forthcoming CCAT CD ROM disk with its focus on biblical texts confirm the importance of these developments. Computer tools are already providing new insights into the meanings of words and use of grammatical and syntactical structures in the Bible.

P. B. Payne

**Concordats.** The period of 1955–84 witnessed the addition of 37 new corcordats to the list of 148 church-state agreements identified in the *Raccolta di concordati su materie ecclesiastiche tra la Santa Sede e le autoritá civili* (rev. ed., 1954), or about 20 percent of the concordats in papal history. Before 1955 the matters most often dealt with in concordats were the rights and privileges of the Roman Catholic Church; the establishment, suppression, and division of dioceses and ecclesiastical provinces; the appointment of bishops; the establishment of military chaplaincies and their manner of support; Catholic schools

and religious education; and questions pertaining to marriage. After 1955 these matters continued to occupy the attention of papal treaty makers but after 1965 were overshadowed by attempts to implement the decrees and declarations enacted by Vatican Council II (1962–65), especially the Declaration of Religious Freedom.

Pope Pius XII (1939–58) added two concordats to the list during the last years of his pontificate: (1) with North Rhineland-Westphalia, December 19, 1956 (text in *Acta Apostolicae Sedis* 49 [1957]: 201–5); and (2) with Bolivia, February 1, 1958 (*AAS* 50 1958: 68–81). The former was a minor "housekeeping" treaty, the latter a concordat regulating Church missionary activities.

John XXIII (1958–63) concluded five concordats: (1) with Austria, May 13, 1960, modifying the concordat of 1933, concerning patrimonies (*AAS* 52 [1960]: 933–41); (2) with Austria, June 3, 1960, concerning the Apostolic administration of Burgenland (*AAS* 52 [1960]: 941–45); (3) with Bolivia, March 15, 1961, concerning the military vicariate (*AAS* 53 [1961]: 299–303); (4) with Paraguay, December 20, 1961, concerning the military vicariate (*AAS* 54 [1962]: 22–27); and (5) with Austria, July 9, 1962, concerning education (*AAS* 54 [1962]: 641–52).

Paul VI (1963–78) produced 20 concordats, many of them stemming from Vatican Council II. Others addressed strained relations with some traditionally Catholic areas such as the Iberian Peninsula and Latin America. These concordats included: (1) with Lower Saxony, February 26, 1965 (*AAS* 57 [1967]: 834–56); (2) with the Saarland, April 19, 1968, establishing a chair of Catholic theology at the University of Saarland (*AAS* 60 [1968]: 780–81); (3) with El Salvador, July 11, 1968, concerning the military vicariate (*AAS* 60 [1968]: 382–84); (4) with Switzerland, July 24, 1968, concerning the creation of the diocese of Tessin (*AAS* 63 [1971]: 212–13); (5) with Austria, October 7, 1968, concerning the establishment of the diocese of Feldkirch (*AAS* 60 [1968]: 782–85); (6) with Bavaria, October 7, 1968, revising the concordat of 1924 (*AAS* 61 [1969]: 163–68); (7) with the Rhine Palatinate, April 29, 1969 (*AAS* 62 [1970]: 157–62; (8) with the Saarland, November 12, 1969, concerning the formation of a Catholic teachers' union (*AAS* 62 [1970]: 499–505); (9) with Bavaria, September 17, 1970, concerning church relationships with the department of theology at the University of Augsburg (*AAS* 62 [1970]: 821–25); (10) with Austria, March 8, 1971, concerning Catholic schools (*AAS* 64 [1972]: 478–81); (11) with the Rhine Palatinate, May 15, 1973, concerning Catholic schools (*AAS* 65 [1973]: 631–42); (12) with Lower Saxony, May 21, 1973, revising the concordat of 1965 (*AAS* 65 [1973]: 643–46); (13) with Bavaria, September 4, 1974, revising and adding to the concordat of 1924 (*AAS* 66 [1974]: 601–19); (14)

with Portugal, February 15, 1975, modifying the concordat of 1940, mostly by reducing the privileges of the church (*AAS* 67 [1975]: 435–36); (15) with the Saarland, February 21, 1975, concerning Catholic schools (*AAS* 67 [1975]: 248–54); (16) with Colombia, July 2, 1975, concerning the church and religious liberty (*AAS* 67 [1975]: 421–34); (17) with Austria, January 9, 1976, modifying the concordat of June 1960 (*AAS* 68 [1976]: 422–24); (18) with Bavaria, July 7, 1978, modifying the concordat of 1924 (*AAS* 70 [1978]: 770–75); (19) with Switzerland, July 19, 1978, concerning changes in the diocese of Basel (*AAS* 70 [1978]: 468–70); and (20) with Spain, July 28, 1976, modifying the concordat of 1953, and disestablishing the Catholic Church in Spain (*AAS* 68 [1976]: 509–12).

John Paul II (1978– ) also has been an active papal diplomat, concluding 10 post-Vatican II concordats with six different nations: (1) with Spain, January 3, 1979, addressing unresolved juridical issues between the church and Spain resulting from the concordat of 1976 (*AAS* 72 [1980]: 29–36); (2) with Spain, January 3, 1979, concerning teaching and cultural issues (*AAS* 72 [1980]: 37–46); (3) with Spain, January 3, 1979, concerning the military chaplaincy and military service by ecclesiastics and religious (*AAS* 72 [1980]: 47–55); (4) with Spain, January 3, 1979, concerning church property and other economic issues (*AAS* 72 [1980]: 56–62); (5) with Peru, July 26, 1980, modifying church privileges and rescinding the right of the state to participate in the selection of bishops (*AAS* 72 [1980]: 807–12); (6) with Austria, July 24, 1981, clarifying several previous concordats concerning financial arrangements between church and state (*AAS* 74 [1982]: 272–74); (7) with Monaco, July 25, 1981, updating the papal bull of 1886 (*AAS* 73 [1981]: 651–53); (8) with Ecuador, March 26, 1983, concerning religious assistance to the armed forces and the national police (*AAS* 75 [1983]: 481–84); (9) with Italy, February 18, 1984, abrogating the concordat of 1929 concluded by Mussolini and Pius XI, disestablishing the Roman Catholic Church, and desacralizing the city of Rome (*AAS* 77 [1985]: 1055–59); and (10) with Haiti, August 8, 1984, revising the concordat of 1860, reducing church privileges, and excluding the state from the selection of bishops (*AAS* 76 [1984]: 953–55).

The most important of these recent concordats was the historic 1984 treaty with Italy that ended Roman Catholicism's status as the established religion of that country. Also, under the new pact, Rome ceased to be a "sacred city," but Italy continued to recognize the Vatican City State as an independent and sovereign enclave in the middle of Rome. Other important aspects of the new treaty included the stipulation that henceforth parents who desire Catholic religious instruction in the state schools for their children will have to request it (whereas before they had to ask for an exemption from such instruction), and that the state will exercise primary responsibility for marriage, marriage annulment, and divorce. In summary, the church lost its official standing and most of its prerogatives in Italy; yet, as Cardinal Agostino Casaroli, the papal secretary of state, observed, the concordat was a fulfillment of the promises of Vatican II and "a document of mutual agreement, not one of privilege."

Historically, concordats have tried to resolve conflicts between the ecclesiastical and civil powers through a variety of means, especially through a mutual recognition of interests. Among other things they also have made provision for state support for Catholic schools, the teaching of Catholic religion courses within state-supported schools, theological faculties in state universities, the support of the clergy, maintenance of church buildings (especially in countries where church real estate has been nationalized), and various aspects of the apostolate. In previous concordats, the state has been given certain rights in the naming of bishops for the area, but since Vatican II the church has been attempting to rescind such secular privileges so that the selection of bishops is entirely in the hands of the church. Moreover, post-Vatican II concordats have accepted the disestablishment of the church in many traditionally Catholic countries as well as the principle of religious freedom for all peoples. In the meanwhile, as the newly revised Code of Canon Law of 1985 affirms, concordats existing before the present Code took effect remain intact, even if they contain provisions contrary to the new Code.

**Bibliography.** W. M. Abbott, ed., *The Documents of Vatican II* (1966); A. de Jong, *Concilium* 8 (1970): 104–12; H. E. Cardinale, *The Holy See and the International Order* (1976); A. Vallini, *Apollinaris* 49 (1976): 235–50; V. C. Orti, *Apollinaris* 53 (1980): 83–130; P. Tocanel, *Apollinaris* 54 (1981): 183–96; and J. A. Coriden, T. J. Green, and D. E. Heintschel, eds., *The Code of Canon Law* (1985).

ROBERT D. LINDER

## Concupiscence.

The simple and natural act of desiring a thing for the satisfaction to be derived from it. In this sense of the term, Pelagians maintain that concupiscence is perfectly natural, normal, and therefore good. Concupiscence becomes evil only when excessive because any excess violates the principle of moderation dictated by reason.

The Pauline-Augustinian tradition has held that the Pelagian view is too simple and too Hellenistic. According to it, the satisfaction of physical desire in man is indeed not evil in itself since it is inherent in the constitution of man as created by God. But the Pelagians fail to recognize that the nature of man as created by God is corrupted by sin. Although sin is primarily spiritual, it manifests itself also in the corruption of all phases of man's physical nature. So thirst becomes an excuse for drunkenness; hunger, for gluttony; sex, for lust. Because these forms of sin are more obvious, they have sometimes been thought of as independent kind of sin or even as the essence of sin itself. The Pauline contrast between spirit and flesh is taken to mean that physical desire and its satisfaction is evil in itself and is the source of sin. This latter view has found expression especially in some of the statements on sex in the Augustinian-Catholic tradition. But even this tradition at its heart recognizes that sin is essentially spiritual and that physical sins are derivative and secondary in nature.

The exact relation, however, between spiritual and physical sin is obscure and not easy to analyze. It can be said with Paul (Rom. 1:26–30) that, because men refused to worship God, he "gave them over to shameful lusts," and so the spirit became subservient to the flesh, became *kata sarka* instead of *en sarki* (2 Cor. 10:3). Or it may be said that because man in self-love sinned against God with a consequent disintegration in their relationship, so man in sensuality now sins against himself with a consequent disintegration in his own nature. However, the apparent independence and initiative of sensuality as a principle of sin in man's life requires a definition of it as something more than an extension of self-love. R. Niebuhr indicates that sometimes sensuality actually deifies or idolizes something or someone outside the self in a vain attempt to escape the self; and further, as a last resort, it sometimes is an attempt at resignation of both self and world to a common dissolution in the depths of the impersonal ocean of subconsciousness. But it must be stressed that concupiscence, whatever its motive, has a great variety of forms and consists of "any inordinate devotion to a mutable good," of which sexual license is only the most striking example.

*Bibliography.* R. Niebuhr, *The Nature and Destiny of Man* (1941); A. Harnack, *History of Dogma* (1900); R. Seeberg, *History of Doctrine* (1905); O. Piper, *The Christian Interpretation of Sex* (1941); N. P. Williams, *The Ideas of the Fall and Original Sin* (1927); T. Aquinas, *Summa Theologica*, vol. 2.

ARNOLD B. COME

## Conditional Immortality.

Doctrine which maintains that people are naturally and entirely mortal, but that those who enter into living communion with God are granted immortality. Theories which either imply or directly teach annihilationism, or conditional immortality, have continued to appear in the current century. A form of this doctrine, based on evolutionary points of view, was enunciated by McConnell in his *Evolution of Immortality* and a similar view, that man is not immortal but "immortable," was independently reached by J. Y. Simpson, and elaborated in his *Man and the Attainment of Immortality*. The theory is, in brief, that when the evolutionary process, operating under the kind of

law made familiar by Darwin, had produced man, a stage was reached when further evolution was dependent only or mainly on moral and spiritual laws; and that immortality was achieved only when a certain stage in moral and spiritual evolution had been attained.

Since this view was presented in support of the Christian system, it was natural and inevitable that critics should raise the question of the immortality of those dying in infancy. Since they have had no opportunity to achieve such spiritual development through their own efforts, it would seem to follow that they must perish. Simpson noted that those dying in infancy could not have willed themselves out of relationship with God. The reply, however, is not conclusive. It assumes that human individuals are in that relationship with God which guarantees their immortality until they will themselves out of it; but the theory is that human individuals are not in that relationship until they have reached a stage of spiritual development at which they may will themselves into it—and that presumably infants have not done.

The theory also, by its insistence on human achievement as a condition of immortality, seems at least to obscure the distinction between immortality and eternal life and to do less than justice to the doctrine of regeneration as a creative act of God alone.

ANDREW K. RULE

## Conference on Christian Politics, Economics, and Citizenship (COPEC).

Conference of 1400 delegates, which met at Birmingham for a week in April 1924, and began a new stage in Christian social thinking in Great Britain and contributed to the ecumenical movement, especially to the formation of the British Council of Churches. Among its significant leaders were William Temple, Charles E. Raven, Lucy Gardiner, and Malcolm Spencer.

ALEXANDER C. ZABRISKIE

## Conference on Science, Philosophy, and Religion.

Conference founded in 1940 through the efforts of Louis Finkelstein, president of the Jewish Theological Seminary of America, with the aid of about 100 leaders in American academic and intellectual life, headed particularly by Lyman Bryson and Harlow Shapley. Annual meetings of the conference have taken place—generally in September—since 1940. Its constitution has changed gradually, and there are now a body of fellows, selected from among the convoking members and participants of earlier years, and a board of directors. Many different religious groups—Protestant, Catholic, and Jewish—and all shades of philosophical approach are represented in the papers which are read and published annually. Finkelstein was president of the conference from 1940 to 1951.

**Bibliography.** Proceedings of each annual conference, 1941ff.

WILLIAM F. ALBRIGHT

**Confessing Church.** *See* BARMEN DECLARATION; GERMANY, FEDERAL REPUBLIC OF.

**Confessional, Secrecy of the.** Roman canon law states the absolute inviolability of the "seal," or secrecy, of the confession. It must be kept by the priest, by persons acting as interpreters, and by anyone who might have overheard a confession. The penalty for direct violation by the priest is excommunication, the absolution from which is reserved to the Holy See in the most exclusive manner, *specialissimo modo.* A priest guilty of indirect violation may be barred from sacred functions, charges, and privileges. The following rules tend to protect the secrecy of the confession and to prevent abuses: (1) a priest may not bear witness in ecclesiastical courts as far as his penitents are concerned; (2) confessors are forbidden to use what they have learned in the confessional, in a manner detrimental to their penitents; (3) superiors of institutions or masters of novices in religious orders may not hear the confessions of their charges, except upon the formal request of the latter.

GEORGES A. BARROIS

**Confession of 1967.** A statement of faith composed as part of the 1958 merger of the United Presbyterian Church of North America and the Presbyterian Church in the USA; its expressed purpose was to "call the church to that unity in confession and mission which is required of disciples today." The confession was first published in 1965 along with eight traditional creeds; it was approved in 1967. The document was written by a committee chaired by Edward A. Downey, Jr., of Princeton Seminary.

The confession claims at its outset that the reconciling work of God the Father, Son, and Holy Spirit is the foundation of all confessions concerning God, man, and the world. It then proceeds to set forth several doctrines related to God's work of reconciliation. These doctrines are grouped under five umbrella categories: (1) the grace of our Lord Jesus Christ, (2) the love of God, (3) the communion of the Holy Spirit, (4) the mission of the church, (5) and the equipment of the church. The doctrines presented include those of the person and work of Jesus Christ, human sinfulness, the new life, the Bible, revelation and religion, reconciliation in society, baptism, and the Lord's Supper. The confession identifies racial injustice, international discord, poverty, and moral confusion in sexual relationships as specific matters that the church's mes-

sage addresses, and it urges the faithful to seek and discern the will of God and to act accordingly.

ROBERT L. MORRISON

**Confucianism.** A system of social, political, and ethical thought and action that for centuries molded the life of Chinese, Korean, and Japanese societies. Some argue that Confucianism is a philosophy and not a religion, but close examination reveals unmistakable religious elements centering on the veneration of ancestors and practical assistance in daily living through what can only be termed magical means. In essence Confucianism represents a primal religion with a rich ethical, social, and political tradition.

The term "Confucianism" is a Western one. In Chinese the tradition is called the "School of the Literati." These literati are the scholars and teachers of the ancient literature, especially the Five Classics, which according to tradition were edited by Confucius (551–479 B.C.). The Five Classics consist of *The Book of Poems, The Book of Rites, The Book of History, The Spring and Autumn Annals,* and *The Book of Changes.*

Classical Confucianism emerged in the centuries following Confucius's death. This system embraced the belief of two individuals and two other main doctrines: Mencius, who held that human nature is inherently good and should strive for harmony with heaven; "The Great Learning," which formulated a means for attaining world peace and stressed the need for exhaustive effort in learning; "The Doctrine of the Mean," which emphasized the metaphysical nature of human potentiality; and Hsun Tzu (298–238 B.C.), who questioned Mencius' faith in human goodness and proposed that human nature was neither good nor bad but required restraint and training.

From 206 B.C.–A.D. 220 Confucianism was the official state creed of the Han Dynasty and a Confucian canon was established. During this period Confucian scholars were used exclusively in government service and a cult of Confucius was encouraged. This form of Confucianism remained essentially dominant in China until the early years of the 20th century.

Beginning about A.D. 960 a new form of Confucian orthodoxy known as Neo-Confucianism developed which divided into two schools: the School of Principle and the Ch'eng-Chu School. Neo-Confucianism was characterized by its willingness to incorporate aspects of Buddhism and Taoism into its beliefs and practices as well as a strong reformist tradition that sought to recreate a pure, undefiled form of Confucianism.

Neo-Confucianism differed from Buddhism in its unabashed humanism and emphasis on this life. Neo-Confucianism strongly asserted the importance of man, not simply people, and his place in the universe. Countering Buddhism, Neo-Confucianism stressed rationality and the rational investigation of principle. A sense of history and the necessity of studying history was also part of the Neo-Confucian tradition, because history was seen as a guide to right action and an understanding of ethical decisions. Later, during the Ming and Ch'ing dynasties, Neo-Confucianism gave rise to various mystical movements and an emphasis on the inner self.

For Confucianism the state, family, and individual are a unified whole. Rites of propriety cement society and reflect a formal humanism in which the relationship between father and son is the primary social relationship. Worship in this context takes the form of filial piety where the true gentleman shows respect for his ancestors through acts of virtue. For the common people this veneration of the ancestors often degenerates into crude magical acts and lavish feasts. Sacrifice both to one's own ancestors and the civic sacrifices to Confucius take the form of elaborate rituals and solemn banquets.

In 1905 the imperial system of examinations was abolished in China and in 1928 official sacrifices to Confucius ended, thus abolishing the formal association of Confucianism and the Chinese state. Within the People's Republic of China there have been periodic persecutions of Confucianism and a general burning of Confucian literature. Yet to many observers China remains a profoundly Confucian state. Although Confucian beliefs and practices can be found in most Chinese societies outside China as well as in Japan, South Korea self-consciously keeps alive a Confucian tradition and is the site of the world's remaining Confucian university. In North Korea Kim III Sung has founded a highly successful communist state with many Confucian features including an "ancestor's day" and the veneration of political leaders, especially Sung himself.

Confucian influences in Europe and North America can be seen in the theology and practices of groups like the Korean-based Unification Church, the more orthodox Christian Korean Universities Bible Students, the works of Watchman Nee, and in the group known as "The Local Church," which has its origins in Chinese culture. These often creative adaptations of Confucian social norms to biblical teachings demonstrate the continuing vitality of Confucian classics and their ability to appeal to people living in technological societies outside of the Orient. Formal Confucianism, however, seems in general decline, although some observers speculate that it could reemerge in mainland China in harmony with Marxism.

*Bibliography.* H. G. Creel, *Confucius, the Man and the Myth* (1949); Wu-chi Liu, *Confucius: His Life and Time* (1955); D. S. Nivison, ed., *Confucianism in Action* (1966).

**Congo, People's Republic of the.** This country has an area of 342,000 sq. km. (132,00 sq. mi.) and a population of 1.8 million people (1985), concentrated mostly around Brazzaville and Pointe Noire. After a long period of French influence (1785–1885), French colonization followed. In 1910 the Congo became a French colony. The Congo attained its independence from France in 1960. Since 1970 the Congo has adopted a socialist political system that has guided its development plans.

The Congo's religious history presents a mixture of traditional Christianity and modern indigenous beliefs and practices that reflect the diversified Congolese religious movements.

*Traditional Religions.* The Congo's non-Christian religions are still followed by a large segment of the Congolese population. In late 1960 about 11 percent of the population belonged to the traditional religions. Some traditional beliefs are closely related to certain Christian concepts so that in the present day Congolese Christianity has begun to accept some of the fundamental ideas that were originally rejected by the Christian missionaries. Most Congolese share a common name for God: Nzambi (among Kongo-Sundi, Dondo, Ndasa), Nzama (Teke), and Nziame (Kuta). Nzambi is the all-powerful, self-created being by whom the earth and sky, man, and everything were created. Nzambi is also omnipresent in heaven as well as on earth. He is "Nzambi Watanda" when he reflects love, goodness, grace, and holiness to us. He can easily become "Zambi Wamutsele" as he exposes his anger to us. This double-sidedness reflects the divine binary nature of Nzambi. "Nzambi," or God the creator, in most African beliefs cannot be approached except through the intermediary of the spirits of one's ancestors, because dead ancestors have some degree of binary features allowing them to intercede on behalf of the living by asking favors and pray-talking to the divine.

Islam is developing slowly in the Congo—Muslims number 0.4 percent of the population. Many of these are expatriates from northern African countries. Since 1966 the Tenrikyo religion, whose origins date back to Japan (1838), has also been present in the Congo. Since 1971 a Tenrikyo Center in Brazzaville has attracted some 250 followers. There are three mission stations and a dispensary staffed by a doctor and some nurses. Tenrikyo theology promotes good health care and healing as a precondition for salvation.

*Christianity.* Christianity in the Congo can be divided into three major systems: Catholicism, Protestantism, and indigenous churches.

*Catholicism.* A Portuguese explorer's visit to the Congo in 1482 opened doors to this vast kingdom and caused Christianity to flourish in the 16th century under the leadership of Alfonso I and his son Henrique. Although devastated and disintegrated by slavery and slave trading in the 17th and 18th centuries, the Congolese Catholic Church maintained several underground institutions. The first Congolese priests of modern times were then ordained in 1895.

After World War II some progress was made in the structural organizations of the Congolese Catholic Church. The archdiocese of Brazzaville with two subdioceses was established in 1955, and a Congolese bishop consecrated in 1961. The estimated number of Congolese Catholics in 1970 was 376,000. The importance of the Congolese Christianity is reflected by the fact that the first president of the Congo, Filbert Youlou, was himself a Catholic priest. In the late 1980s there were almost one million Congolese Catholics.

*Protestantism.* Congolese Protestants constitute one of the most complex religious communities in Africa. The work started in the Congo in 1909 and was the direct result of the expanding Swedish Evangelical Mission (Svenska Mission) established first in Zaire (then Belgian Congo). In the late 1970s the Congolese Protestant Church grew to some 350,000 and by the mid-1980s there were some 650,000 adherents.

Religious freedom is symbolic of Protestantism and is reflected by the development of several indigenous Christian movements (sometimes prophetic, sometimes spiritualistic) which added several levels of difficulties to the early work of the Swedish missionaries, but is now credited with early efforts to Africanize the gospel. As early as 1961 the Congolese Evangelical Church became one of the few African Protestant churches to acquire autonomy. Today it is by all measures one of the country's most reliable socializing agents. The Protestant Church, together with the Catholic and Kimbanguist churches, participates in broadcasting the gospel, in running schools, and in the dissemination of information about health care and healing. The Protestant Churches in the Congo have also grown in numbers and now include the Salvation Army, the Swedish Pentecostal Church, and others.

*Indigenous Churches.* The people of the Congo have also been known for their religious inventiveness and creativity. There are numerous indigenous initiatives, which have qualitatively and quantitatively changed Congolese religious life. Because of limited space, only two major indigenous initiatives will be discussed here.

*Kimbanguism.* The church begun by Simon Kimbangu is the largest independent church in Africa. It has a large following in Zaire where it started, and it exists now in the Congo because of the numerous Kongo people who live there. After a long history of persecution (especially during the Colonial era), Kimbanguism flourished in the 1960s as it acquired a recognizable political status and became almost identical with the nation-

alist interests of the Kongo and people on both banks of the Congo River. Today, Kimbanguists are well respected and belong to the World Council of Churches, to the all-African Council of Churches, and to the newly established Federation of Christian Churches in the Congo.

*Croix-Koma.* A more recent religious movement of indigenous creation is the Croix-Koma founded by Ta Molanda (or Father Molanda), a Catholic of Lari origins. In 1964 Molanda organized the Catholics against witchcraft, magic, sorcery, and other diabolical beliefs and practices. This charismatic movement attracted some 30,000 persons a year to attend its seven-day period of structured, step-by-step teaching intended to lead them to Christ from paganism, irreligion, and immoral behaviors. The followers came from Catholic and Protestant churches, and from traditional religions. The movement attained its peak in 1966/67, when President Massamba Debat proposed it as the official Congolese state religion. Molanda rejected this, and by 1970 Croix-Koma was attracting about 200,000 pilgrims to Kankata, their headquarters. It is estimated that by 1988 about 20 to 35 percent of the Congolese people visited Kankata for the seven-day teaching program.

The relationship between the religious authorities and the state is defined more clearly by the 1969 constitution that established the Congo as a People's Republic—one, indivisible, and secular. This constitution also promotes the ideas that citizens should enjoy freedom of speech, press, association, procession, and demonstration under conditions specified by the law. Freedom of conscience and religion are also guaranteed to all citizens. While religious communities are free in all questions relating to their beliefs and their external practices, the state forbids the misuse of religious institutions and religion itself for political ends.

**Bibliography.** J. F. Vincent, *Cahiers d'Études Africaines* 24 (1966): 527–63; Paradi's *Sarea Handbook for People's Republic of the Congo* (1970), 83–84; P. Falk, *The Growth of the Church in Africa* (1979); R. F. Manyeto, *Yhr SBC of Modern Africa* (1979); C. Legum, *African Contemporary Record* (1984/85); P. Goetz, *Encyclopedia Britannica* (1986); A. Rake, *New African Year Book* (1985–86).

PATRICE MUYUMBA

# Congregationalists.

Congregationalism was officially born when in 1582 the English Parliament considered it treason to worship apart from the Church of England. "Separatists," "Non-conformists," and "Puritans" were names for congregationalists. Robert Browne, the 16th-century Separatist leader, described the qualities of the new congregationalists: (1) they are a company of true believers who confess Christ alone as Savior and Lord; (2) authority in the church rests solely in Christ as the head; (3) teachings from the Bible as the Scriptures are perspicuous; (4) the church shall be self-disciplining with pastor, elders, deacons, and members keeping watch over the conduct of the church; (5) all congregational churches are interdependent and should fellowship for mutual benefit. Robert Browne's church at Norwich, England, in 1580 was to serve as the model from which future congregational churches developed. Browne's contemporary, Henry Barrowe, fostered a plan with a stronger eldership. This concept was debated for many generations because of what was feared to be excessive authority of a few over the congregation. This more presbyterian form became part of the system of the United Reformed Church in England and the United Church of Christ in America in the 20th century. Congregationalists in England and America agreed that these independent congregations should be free from the authority of the state. In its heritage, the word "evangelical" was descriptive of these churches. In submission to the sole authority of Scripture and dependence on the grace of God, they determined to preach the gospel to a world in need of salvation.

With the writing of the Westminster Confession of 1647, Congregationalism had a confession of faith around which to rally. In 1658 the Savoy Declaration of Faith and Order was written as the Confession of Faith of the Congregational-Independents. It was the Westminster Confession without its presbyterian form of government and with Congregationalism's separation from civil authority.

Even as Congregationalism seemed to be established on solid credal ground and agreed on polity from its heritage, movement away from these basics happened quickly. In Massachusetts the Congregational Church became identified with the state with all the celebrated difficulties of that commonwealth during colonial days. The blight of the Half-way Covenant saw the early demise of Congregationalism. When a baptized person grew up and married but did not join the church, the church extended baptism to his or her children. In a few short generations of such compromise and laxity the church had practically abandoned the orthodoxy of Westminster and Savoy. The struggles with deism and unitarianism have been documented as theological debates within Congregationalism that, in some sense, have never been resolved.

The diversity in Congregationalism is seen in the proliferation of groups. In 1957 after 15 years of negotiations, the United Church of Christ was formed from the General Council of Congregational Christian Churches and the Evangelical and Reformed Church. The Constitution of 1961 commissioned the new church as presbyterian in polity but congregational in much of its style. The United Church of Christ in its ecumenical relations is a member denomination of the National

Council of Churches of Christ and the World Council of Churches headquartered in Geneva, Switzerland.

In a centrist position is the National Association of Congregational Christian Churches (NACCC), formed in 1955 in Detroit, Michigan. With strong emphasis on the "Congregational Way," the National Association formed a fellowship of churches without ecclesiastical authority and binding creeds. Although sympathetic to conciliar movements, NACCC has not joined any ecumenical group.

The Conservative Congregational Christian Conference was incorporated as a denomination in 1949. Concerned to be a consistently evangelical expression of Congregational heritage, the conference adopted a Statement of Faith and Polity that all ministers and churches support. Early in its history, the conference joined the National Association of Evangelicals (NAE) to identify with American evangelicalism. Through its membership in NAE, the Conservative Congregational Christian Conference is affiliated with the World Evangelical Fellowship headquartered in Singapore.

There have been some attempts over the years to bring Congregationalists worldwide together. The International Christian Congregational Fellowship has brought delegates from many nations in an international forum to discuss heritage and program. The International Christian Congregational Fellowship has most often met in England. The World Evangelical Congregational Fellowship (WECF) began in 1986 with the originating convocation held at Westminster Chapel in London, England. Founding members from Brazil, Portugal, Great Britain, Ireland, Australia, the United States, Canada, Truk, and South Africa affirmed the traditional Congregational value of worship and fellowship. WECF has as its purpose: cooperative endeavor in the faith, preservation of the historical Congregational commitment to the lordship of Christ and the infallibility of his Word, and to present to the world a witness of oneness in Christ as evangelical Congregationalists.

Congregationalism maintains its lively heritage and historical diversity—from independent churches and interdependent fellowship to a more presbyterian form with denominational authority, from no creeds to Westminster and Savoy, from fellowshiping in conciliar movements to no ecumenical attachments. Congregationalism continues as a pluralistic movement, sometimes proud and sometimes frustrated by that fact. In 1984 the United Church of Christ listed 6419 churches, 1,694,107 members, and 10,157 ministries. The National Association of Congregational Christian Churches listed 462 churches, 108,150 members, and 826 ministries. The Conservative Congregational Christian Conference listed 157 churches, 28,383 members, and 386 ministries.

**Bibliography.** M. W. Kohl, *Congregationalism in America* (1977); G. T. Booth, *Evangelical and Congregational* (1981); *Yearbook of American and Canadian Churches* (1986).

ARTHUR EVANS GAY, JR.

**Congregations, Roman.** The various departments or agencies of the Roman Curia that exercise administrative powers. Since the overhaul of the Curia in 1908, they have undergone numerous changes, most notably through the apostolic constitution *Regimini Ecclesiae Universae*, promulgated by Pope Paul VI on August 15, 1967, which put into effect the recommendations of a papal commission headed by Cardinal Francesco Roberti. Through this, the secretariat of state was assigned the coordinating role among these bodies, and placed under the secretariat's immediate jurisdiction was the former Congregation for Extraordinary Ecclesiastical Affairs. Renamed the Council for the Public Affairs of the Church, it is a sort of "foreign ministry" which cares for relations between the church and civil governments.

The number of the "Sacred Congregations" was reduced through various reorganizations from 11 in the early part of the century to 10 currently. They are composed of cardinals and some diocesan bishops and each is presided over by a cardinal prefect (except the Doctrine of the Faith, Bishops, and Oriental Churches, which the pope reserves the prefecture to himself). The prefect is assisted by a secretary and subsecretary, also selected by the pontiff, and a number of minor officials, lay and clerical. Most important matters are resolved at plenary meetings of a congregation, which all member cardinals attend, while the presiding cardinal may meet with the major officials of the congregation to deal with minor concerns.

The Congregation for the Doctrine of the Faith (originally the Roman Inquisition, and from 1908 to 1965 known as the Holy Office) is responsible for safeguarding Catholic faith and morals. It scrutinizes all matters relating to new doctrines and opinions, critiques books sent for its examination (the Index of Prohibited Books was abolished in 1966), and deals with marriage laws and laicization of priests. It is assisted by an International Theological Commission (formed in 1969), which is comprised of no more than 30 members named by the prefect in consultation with episcopal conferences, and by the Pontifical Biblical Commission, reorganized in 1971.

The Congregation for Oriental Churches (formerly Congregation for the Eastern Church) deals with all questions involving persons, things, or rites of the Eastern churches. Provision is made for membership from all the Eastern rite churches in communion with Rome, and it includes cardinals, patriarchs of the Eastern churches, and major archbishops who are equivalent to patriarchs. The congregation includes the Pontifical Mission for Palestine and maintains a special relationship with the Secretariats for Promoting Christian Unity and for Non-Christians.

The Congregation for Bishops was formerly the Consistorial Congregation. It creates and modifies dioceses, ecclesiastical provinces, and regions, and is charged with nominating bishops, apostolic administrators, and military vicars.

The Congregation for the Sacraments and Divine Worship was created in 1975 and replaced agencies that dealt with a variety of worship and sacramental themes, but in 1984 Pope John Paul II divided it into two bodies. The Congregation for the Sacraments is responsible for questions relating to the discipline of the seven sacraments that are not handled by the Congregation for the Doctrine of the Faith (especially marriage and holy orders). The Congregation for Divine Worship has competence over all worship and liturgical matters.

The Congregation for the Causes of Saints also resulted from the 1975 reorganization. Its predecessor was the Congregation of Rites. It deals with the beatification of servants of God, the canonization of saints, and the preservation of relics.

The Congregation for the Clergy, earlier called the Congregation of the Council, fosters the spiritual, intellectual, and pastoral growth of the diocesan clergy. It monitors cathedral chapters, pastoral councils, and priests' senates, promotes the adequate distribution of clergy throughout the world, furthers catechetical work, and is concerned with the administration of the church's temporal properties.

The Congregation for Religious and Secular Institutes oversees the life and work of men and women living in spiritual (religious) communities and the progress of renewal in these bodies.

The Congregation for Catholic Education was previously the Congregation for Seminaries and Universities, and it supervises the training of priests and the education of clerics and laypeople in the faith. It exercises control over theological seminaries (except those specifically under the jurisdiction of the Congregation for the Evangelization of Peoples), superintends universities, faculties, and colleges that are dependent on church authority, and cares for diocesan and parochial schools.

The Congregation for the Evangelization of Peoples directs the missionary activity of the church. Formerly known as the Congregation for the Propagation of the Faith (Propaganda), its competence extends to all missions established for the preaching of the gospel throughout the world. Along with the assigned cardinals, the presiding officers of the Secretariats for Promoting Christian Unity, for Non-Christians, and for Nonbelievers serve as consultants. It is assisted by various commissions which foster the spiritual vitality of missions, oversee the educational institutions under the congregation's jurisdiction, administer mission enterprises, and promote missiological research.

RICHARD V. PIERARD

**Congruism.** Hypothesis devised to reconcile the predetermination of God with the freedom of man, especially with regard to saving grace. Congruism is associated with Francisco Suarez, a Jesuit scholastic (1548–1617), who, in swinging back toward Augustinianism from Molina's doctrine of relative free will, developed this theory. According to congruism, the nature or essence of grace that saves (efficacious grace) is not specifically different from that which does not save (sufficient grace, to use the Thomist word). Efficacious grace is thus *ex eventu* (from its effect). According to Molinism, the effectiveness of grace comes in the last analysis from the free choice of any individual who avails himself of it. According to congruism (which, according to Garrigou-Lagrange, is "white-washed Molinism"), its effectiveness comes from the foreseen congruity or precise suitability of the grace, the person involved, and the circumstances. As a congruist sees it, God knows in the case of every man infallibly what combination of circumstances and motives will induce him to turn to God and be saved; and therefore, for the elect, God predetermines those circumstances which are "congruent" with his choosing the highest good, and bestows his grace under those precise circumstances.

Congruism is not accepted by Reformed theologians, who teach that saving grace is not only essentially different from any other kind of grace, but is irresistible. It is rejected also by strict Thomists in the Roman Catholic Church, but is current as a minority view and has never been specifically condemned, although it seems to be in conflict with, for example, canon 9 of the Council of Orange: "Whatever good we do, God operates in us and with us that we may operate."

*Bibliography.* R. Garrigou-Lagrange, *Grace* (1952).

KENNETH J. FOREMAN

**Connell, Francis J.** (1888–1967). Roman Catholic theologian, educator, and author. Born in Boston, he graduated from Mount St. Alphonsus Seminary, N.Y., and the University of Angelico, Rome, Italy (S.T.D., 1923). He entered the Redemptionist Order in 1907, and was ordained a priest in 1913. From Mount St. Alphonsus Seminary, where he was professor of dogmatic theology (1915–21; 1924–40), he moved to the Catholic University (Washington, D.C.), as associate and then professor of moral theology (1940–58), and dean of the School of Sacred Theology (1949–57). He served as a theological expert and a member of the American Bishops' press panel at Vatican Council II from 1962–65. As a leading Catholic moral theologian, he spoke widely and was heard frequently on Catholic radio. His works include *Our Lady of Perpetual Help* (1940), *Baltimore Catechism No. 3* (1954), and *The Seven Sacraments: What They Are, What They Do* (1965).

JACK MITCHELL

**Conscience.** Internal monitor of thought and behavior by which one evaluates the self in accordance with a fixed standard or belief. Psychologists view conscience from different theoretical frameworks. Psychoanalysts believe conscience is part of the *superego*, one of three components of the personality, along with the *id* and the *ego*. Sigmund Freud saw the superego as composed of two subsystems, one called the *ego ideal*, which is the self-image of what the person feels he or she should be, and the other called the *conscience*, which is a self-criticizing agent that produces feelings of guilt when societal demands are not met. The ego ideal is positive, creating feelings of esteem and pride; the conscience is negative, bringing punishment for infractions from within the person. The optimal time for the formation of the conscience is the first few years of life when children identify with their parents who represent the mores and normative demands of the culture. By internalizing the superego, the child incorporates the expectations of the society and as an adult passes them on to the next generation.

Social-learning psychologists find the principal components of a conscience to be the emotion of guilt, the need to confess, and a resistance to temptation. The investigations of Robert Sears show that conscience is more apt to occur if parents are accepting of the dependency needs of the child, if they take the time to reason with the child regarding the consequences of behavior, and if they use love-oriented techniques of discipline. Justin Aronfreed held that conscience develops when the aversive states of fear, guilt, and shame following transgression are tied to cognitions that precede the intent to engage in wrong doing.

An alternative to psychoanalytic and social-learning psychologies is behavioristic psychology that views conscience as being classically conditioned. When a child links self-punitive behavior, such as confession, to a reduction of external punishment, he or she may continue as an adult to engage in self-criticism even though external punishers no longer are present. Some people acquire a conscience more readily than others. Hans Eysenck found psychopaths who are deficient in conscience development harder to condition than neurotics who have "a conscience much more tender than the average person."

Theologians believe that the conscience, rather than being a product of human development, is given to all humankind by God and as such is natural, uncreated, and absolute. Father Grancis Chiaramonte wrote, "Where Freud insists that man creates and controls his own conscience, theologians see conscience as an innate driving force towards objective good and truth" (p. 132). Clark Pinnock affirmed that the conscience is the natural property of all men putting them in touch with the moral code of the universe rather than its being a phenomenon occurring from cultural mores.

The word "conscience" is not found in the OT nor was it used by Jesus or his disciples. In the NT it was mentioned first by the apostle Paul who wrote that the conscience was to the Gentiles what the law was to the Jews (Rom. 2:14–15), a moral law written in their hearts. A conscience can be good or bad, "good" when coupled with a pure heart and a sincere faith (1 Tim. 1:5), making for healthy relationships with others (Rom. 14:1–23) and contributing to one's spiritual well-being; and "bad" when restricting behavior that is not truly detrimental (1 Cor. 8:4, 7–8), thereby inhibiting believers from enjoying the freedom that is rightfully theirs in Christ. The conscience may be adversely affected by the way one lives (1 Tim. 4:2; Titus 1:15), yet reparation is possible (Heb. 10:22). One is not to violate the conscience given by God; nevertheless, because it is subject to evil influences, it cannot be relied on as the sole guide to a moral life.

**Bibliography.** H. Eysenck, *BJEP* 30 (1960): 11–12; R. Sears, *Personality Development in Children* (1960), 92–111; S. Freud, *Standard Edition of the Complete Works of Sigmund Freud* (1961); *Civilization and Its Discontents* (1961); J. Aronfreed, *Conduct and Conscience: The Socialization of Internalized Control over Behavior* (1968); F. Chiaramonte, *Children, Psychology, and the Schools* (1969), 128–32; C. Pinnock, *Baker's Dictionary of Christian Ethics* (1973), 126–27.

BONNIDELL CLOUSE

**Conscientious Objectors.** *See* PACIFISM; PEACE MOVEMENTS.

**Contemplation.** As a religious experience, the simple, undivided attention of the soul upon God, intent on knowing and loving him. As a philosophical exercise, the concentrated, intellectual thinking on absolute Good or absolute Truth. It usually involves the blending of the cognitive and affective powers and brings profound delight.

The pursuit of contemplation entered Christian experience and vocabulary primarily from Neo-Platonic philosophy; however, it was given direction by its fusion with the injunction to draw near to God found in both the OT and NT.

For Plato the act of contemplation was the consummation of a fruitful life: "Let those who have distinguished themselves in every action of their lives and in every branch of knowledge come at last to their consummation: the time has now arrived at which they must raise the eye of the soul to the universal light which lightens all things, and behold the Absolute Good" (*Republic* vii). Aristotle saw the contemplative life as the height of happiness: for him there was no virtuous activity so pleasant as that of philosophical reflection and speculation (*Ethics* x).

In both the OT and NT to know, love, and "see" God is presented as the highest privilege of believers and as the gift of eternal life. In God's own light they see light (Ps. 36:9), and as the deer pants for streams of water so the soul of the believer is to thirst for the living God (Ps. 42:1–2), longing for communion with the Lord (Ps. 73:26). According to Jesus the gift of eternal life consists in knowing (i.e., having communion with) God the Father; and Paul prayed that the interior, spiritual eyes of his converts would be fully opened in order that they might see the riches of the grace and glory of God (Eph. 1:15ff.; Col. 1:3ff.).

For Augustine of Hippo, who had such a profound influence upon the church in the West from the 5th century onwards, contemplation was both an intellectual and a spiritual (religious) experience. It was far more than the joy felt by the philosopher in his speculations. For the bishop of Hippo, intellectual perception of truth was religious, and his religious experience was intellectual. Into this approach flowed both Platonic philosophy and biblical theology.

Augustine was convinced that the eternal happiness of the saints in heaven consists in their contemplation of God. Further, he held that some beginnings of this contemplation are possible (even if merely passing glimpses and intuitions of deity) in this life. Various references to the joy of contemplation occur in his *Confessions* (see vii, 10, 17; ix, 10, 23, 24, 25), while the second part of *De Trinitate* provides an exposition of the soul's ascent to God. For Augustine knowledge of God and love of him join here so that one without the other is inconceivable.

But how is contemplation to be fitted into a busy life? Building on Augustine's insights in *City of God* (xix), Gregory the Great offered this statement:

> The active life consists in giving bread to the hungry, in teaching wisdom to him who knows it not, in bringing the wanderer back to the right way, in recalling one's neighbour to the path of humility from that of pride, in giving to each what he needs, in providing for those who are committed to our care.
>
> In the contemplative life, however, while maintaining with his whole heart the love of God and his neighbor, a man is at rest [*quiescere*] from exterior works, clinging by desire to his Maker alone, so that, having no wish for action and treading underfoot all preoccupations his soul is on fire with longing to see the face of his Creator (*Homilies on Ezekiel* ii, 2, 8).

In the East, however, the active life was seen more in terms of the personal activity to overcome, mortify, and repudiate sin in the human heart, mind, and will. And, accompanying this approach, contemplation was related specifically to an apophatic doctrine of God.

Since God is a mystery beyond words and understanding, Evagrius Ponticus (the most influential spiritual writer in the Greek East) taught that the human mind has to rise above concepts, words, and images and above discursive thinking in order to apprehend and gaze upon God intuitively. Thus abstract concepts about God are replaced by a deep sense of the immediacy of the presence of God. This noniconic, nondiscursive consciousness of God's presence is often called *hesychia* (tranquility and inner stillness).

This Greek approach entered into Western spirituality through the influence of the writings of Dionysius the Pseudo-Areopagite. His teachings on mystical theology and the threefold pattern of union with God (purgative, illuminative, and unitive) became available when John Scotus Erigena translated them into Latin in the 9th century A.D. One important effect of this mystical theology was to help to cause the general abandonment of the Platonic-Augustinian synthesis of knowledge and love in contemplation.

Though only indirectly influenced by the Greek tradition, St. Teresa of Avila and St. John of the Cross set forth in the 16th century a doctrine of contemplation that was similar to that of Evagrius. And this teaching has been widely received within the Roman Catholic Church. In contrast, Protestants have been suspicious of it, believing that its emphasis on mystical union with God does not take account of the doctrine of justification by faith.

The Spanish mystics (Teresa and John) made a distinction between acquired and infused contemplation. Acquired contemplation, also known as the prayer of simplicity, is the simple, loving gaze of the believer upon God: the intellect, heart, and will are quiet and still, attracted and (to some extent) overwhelmed by the presence and glory of God in Jesus Christ. Such contemplation is open to all who have proceeded through the purgative and illuminative ways towards God.

Infused or supernatural contemplation is only possible and can only begin when the Holy Spirit gives the believing soul an experimental knowledge of God through the operation of the spiritual gifts of wisdom and understanding. When this happens the Spirit testifies to the believer that he or she is truly a child of God. St. Teresa distinguished five grades to this unitive path to God: (1) infused contemplation, (2) the prayer of quiet, (3) prayer of union, (4) prayer of conforming union, and (5) prayer of transforming union. She believed that few people were given grace to enter into this deepening mystical experience of God.

Protestant attacks upon this mystical approach to contemplation have often been based on mis-understanding. This is certainly true of F. Heiler in (1937) and A. Nygren in his *Agape and Eros* (ET, 1953). In contrast, there is greater appreciation of Hans Urs von Balthasar's work on prayer because it has an Augustinian and Barthian ring to it. In fact, Protestants have tended to see meditation and contemplation as pointing to the same activity, the prayer arising from sincere consideration of God's Word.

*Bibliography.* V. Lossky, *The Mystical Theology of the Eastern Church* (1957); C. Butler, *Western Mysticism* (3d ed., 1967); H. Urs von Balthasar, *On Prayer* (1973); J. Aumann, *Spiritual Theology* (1980); A. Louth, *The Origins of the Christians Mystical Tradition: From Plato to Denys* (1981).

PETER TOON

**Continence.** Abstinence from sexual intercourse, not to be confused with chastity or celibacy (the unmarried state, in which there may be neither continence nor chastity). This confusion is to be seen in the Roman Catholic vow of "chastity" taken by "religious," which really means continence. From primitive times it has often been a policy of cults to require continence of the charismatic figures (priests, priestesses, shamai, fakirs, etc.), because of the psychosexual tendency to find an opposition between "holiness" and sexuality. The Hebrew priests were an exception. For all others, continence has ordinarily been regarded as unnatural and antisocial, except in the prenuptial state. Deviation from this norm has been found only in extreme ascetical movements demanding continence of their followers. Jesus says in Matt. 19:12 that some made themselves eunuchs for the kingdom of heaven. This statement is often taken as a scriptural basis for continence. But only the most absolute literalism would take this to mean emasculation; "eunuch" is most obviously a metaphor meaning a self-denying son of God who is prepared to forego even good things, if need be, out of loyalty to God's will. Paul in 1 Cor. 7 seems to recommend (but not to require) continence but this is to be seen as uttered in an apocalyptic context.

**Conversion.** The idea of conversion so differs in its nuances among various cultures and is so differently perceived by those who study it that an agreed-upon definition is unrealistic. In a religious context, however, some elements are incontrovertible. First, conversion is an inward, personal, affective experience. Second, while personal views are sometimes rethought, what is meant by conversion is centered in a god or ultimate reality. Third, this god-centered process of change begins in dissatisfaction, involves a conscious crisis of self-identity, and culminates in a conscious turning from one way of looking at life to another. Fourth, the results of true religious conversion pervade the individual's outlook on life and approach to living. This result is variously called a new worldview, an altered perceptual grid, a changed "universe of discourse," or a rebirth. It is a mental, social, and spiritual metamorphosis.

***Biblical Conversion.*** Nowhere is the concept of conversion so dramatically or comprehensively systematized as in biblical Christianity. Fallen humanity is morally and spiritually dead, at total enmity with its Creator, and condemned to an eternal existence of meaninglessness and misery (Gen. 3; Eph. 2:1–3). This hopeless condition is described as idolatry, lawlessness, and perversion (Jer. 2:5; Rom. 1:18–32). To humanity wallowing in this grotesque state God reaches down with a way of escape (Rom. 5; 2 Pet. 1:3–4). The penalty for sins is paid by God in Christ, and man's inability to see and respond to God is overcome as the Holy Spirit deals with the inner person (John 1:12–13; 3:16; Rom. 8:14; 28–39). All the while God the Father is pictured as waiting, calling, and loving. Jesus' profound picture of the effect of conversion is that of the prodigal son (Luke 15:11–24).

The experience of Christian conversion may be explosively sudden and radical, as was Paul's, or quiet and subtle. Whatever the extent of catharsis, the hallmark of the Christian concept of conversion is that it is accompanied by personal conviction of sin, remorse for that sin, a belief in and acceptance of Jesus Christ's death as the answer to that sin, and a thankful love for Christ and commitment to do God's will (Acts 26:18; 1 Thess. 1:9–10).

***Sociological and Psychological Dynamics.*** Sociological and psychological disciplines during the 1900s were extremely interested in applying scientific methodology to such a uniquely personal phenomenon. This interest has occasionally been stimulated by religious movements, such as the modern version of the "born again" phenomenon and the rise of a plethora of new religious expressions involving various forms of conversion. One model for how people may react in conversion remains that of Augustine. In his *Confessions* he depicts his conversion drama as follows. First, he described his inner state in terms of increased inner tension, a sense of special encounters, a preoccupation with themes of searching, dying, madness, and sickness. Second, he described divine intervention or what is commonly known as self-surrender accompanied by voices, lights, and visions. Third, he described his new inner state in terms of a surge in confidence, a sense of liberation, a sense of mission. In the process, Augustine relocated himself within a new symbolic universe in terms of which he reconstructed his biography. The latter is an activity engaged in by all converts, be they secular, occult, or religious. Its aim seems to be the disclosure, not only of God's ways, but of a divine plan for one's life.

In short, conversion consists both of a radical shift from one private master symbol (e.g., lust) to another (e.g., continence), and of a simultaneous shift from one conventional symbolic framework (e.g., Manichaeism) to another (e.g., Christianity).

Social science studies are moving away from William James' psychological emphasis on conversion as characterized by the ecstasy of happiness. Likewise, there is a loss of interest in distinguishing Christian evangelical conversion from other conversions by way of permanence, surrender, and sense of sin. Instead, recent studies see conversion as a radical change in one's "universe of discourse." In other words, one recognizes a convert by studying his rhetoric and reasoning.

"Universe of discourse" starts with the assumption that human beings orient themselves to the world from the perspective of symbolic frameworks that provide a language for giving meaning to human existence. By looking at this symbolic language, we shall discover several rhetorical indicators, among them the following: (1) biographical reconstruction, which refers to the fact that converts reconstruct and reinterpret their past lives from the perspective of the present, as did Augustine; (2) adoption of a master attribution that explains all causes and effects; (3) abandonment of analogical reasoning, which allows converts to insulate and protect their new beliefs and state of being from others; (4) assumption of a master role or master relationship, which informs and directs all other activities.

Because the last three rhetorical indices are also found among committed nonconverts, other indices may be suggested. For example, converts commonly "burn the bridges" to their pasts. They claim to have made conscious and explicit decisions to commit themselves to a "new master" or new faith. They voice a strong urge to share, testify, or proselytize on behalf of the new faith.

Sociological analyses, however, suffer from a major shortcoming. They cannot show how an individual's discovery of God unifies his cognitive, affective, moral, and faith dimensions into a thoroughgoing reorientation of life. Such a reorientation is only weakly seen in the person's rhetoric. If Lonergan is right when he says that in a "religious" conversion one falls-in-love with God and so is grasped, possessed, and owned through a total, otherworldly love, then we are left without sociological tools for objectification.

Finally, we turn to converts of new religions. One adds only the refreshing fact that such converts usually experience a shift in causal locus from external to internal sources. Indeed, one might go so far as to say that without looking at one's own failings, no conversion is possible. Finally, when Christians and others do not experience multiple conversions within their own faith, they rely on other ritual milestones (e.g., Spirit baptism, tongues, consecration, etc.) to mark their spiritual development.

*Bibliography.* W. Conn, *Christian Conversion* (1986); I. Hexham and K. Poewe, *Understanding Cults and New Religions* (1986); C. L. Staples and A. L. Mauss, *JSSR* 26 (1987).

KARLA POEWE

## Conviction of Sin.

The state of moral certainty or persuasion that one is a sinner. It is not itself an experience of conversion but is a path leading in that direction. It may come quietly as the result of deep contemplation, or it may burst upon the soul suddenly in anguish of fear or remorse. It is often induced by a weariness with sin which has long been practiced, and by a growing hatred of its power. In its more terrifying forms it is typical of those who have come through experiences of stubborn resistance, as Paul, or of gross wrongdoing, as Augustine. Conviction may soon find relief in an assurance of the regenerating work of God, or it may continue for some time before the sense of forgiveness assuages its grief. Especially during revival meetings of high emotional appeal, it may be attended by prolonged physical and mental sufferings.

Scripture teaches that conviction of sin is essentially the work of the Holy Spirit (John 16:8–10), and must be followed by conviction of righteousness and of judgment before that work is finished. God uses various means to bring the individual to a conviction of sin. Thus the Bible can speak of it as the work of the Lord (Jude 1:5) and especially of the law (Titus 1:9). So also a spiritually minded church or preacher can be said to bring conviction of sin, the sense of moral blame being awakened by public refutation (Acts 18:28; 1 Cor. 14:24). The need for conviction of sin is universal, the unique exception being Jesus who challenged anyone to convict him (John 8:46).

JULIAN P. LOVE

## Conwell, Russell Herman

(1842–1925). Baptist minister and educator. Born in Worthington, Mass., he entered the law school at Yale in 1860, but interrupted his studies at the outbreak of the Civil War, and rose to the rank of lieutenant colonel in the Union Army. He resumed his studies at Albany University, and practiced law in Minneapolis and Boston. During this period he had a two-year stint as foreign correspondent of the *New York Tribune* and the *Boston Traveler*. Ordained to the Baptist ministry in 1879, he pastored Grace Baptist Church, Philadelphia (1881–91), and the Baptist Temple in the same city (1891–1925). In 1888 he founded Temple College (later Temple University), and served as its president (1888–1925). In 1890 he established Samaritan Hospital. His famous lecture on *Acres of Diamonds* (1888) provided funds that he gave entirely to Temple, especially in the form of aid

for needy students. He wrote biographies of presidents Hayes (1876) and Garfield (1881), and of C. H. Spurgeon (1892). Among his other publications are *Observation* (1916), *What You Can Do with Your Will Power* (1917), *Effective Prayer (1920)*, *Sermons for Occasions* (1921), *Why Lincoln Laughed* (1922), and *Borrowed Axes* (1923).

## Conybeare, Frederick Cornwallis

(1856–1924). Scholar in Armenian studies. Born in Kew, England, he was educated at Oxford where in 1880 he was elected fellow of University College. In 1887 he resigned in order to give his whole time to research work in the Armenian field, which earned him international recognition and a fellowship of the British Academy in 1903. The range of his interests gradually extended and covered other areas such as church history and political issues. Among his numerous publications are *The Apology and Acts of Apollonius and Other Monuments of Early Christianity* (1894), *The Key of Truth, A Manual of the Paulician Church of Armenia, the Armenian Text edited and translated* (1898), *The Story of Ahikar, from the Syriac, Arabic, Armenian, Ethiopic, Greek and Slavonic Versions* (1898), *The Dialogues of Athanasius and Zachaeus and of Timothy and Aquila* (1898), *The Dreyfus Case* (1898), *Roman Catholicism as a Factor in European Politics* (1901), *Old Armenian Texts of Revelation* (1906), *Myth, Magic and Morals: A Study of Christian Origins* (1909), *History of NT Criticism* (1910), *The Historical Christ* (1914), and *Russian Dissenters* (1921). In 1922 he prepared the section on Old Armenian liturgies for *Patrologia Orientalis*. From 1913 until his death he catalogued Armenian MSS, first in the British Museum, then in the Bodleian Library at Oxford, and finally at the Vatican.

## Cook, Stanley Arthur

(1873–1949). Born in Kings Lynn, he studied at Cambridge, where he became a fellow of Gonville and Caius College (1904–49). He taught Hebrew (1904–32) and comparative religion (1912–20), and was Regius Professor of Hebrew (1932–38). He was a pupil of W. Robertson Smith, with whom he collaborated in working on the *Encyclopaedia Biblica*. His range of interest was extraordinarily wide, and his power to stimulate and encourage younger scholars exceptional. His publications include *A Glossary of the Aramaic Inscriptions* (1898), *The Laws of Moses and the Code of Hammurabi* (1903), *Critical Notes on OT History* (1907), *The Religion of Ancient Palestine in the Second Millennium B.C. in the Light of Archaeology and the Inscriptions* (1908), *The Study of Religions* (1914), *The OT: A Reinterpretation* (1936), *The "Truth" of the Bible* (1938), *The Rebirth of Christianity* (1942), and *An Introduction to the Bible* (1945). In addition he completed W. Wright's *A Catalogue of the Syriac Manuscripts Preserved in the Library of* the University of Cambridge (1901), and edited W. R. Smith's *Religion of the Semites* and a posthumous volume of essays by R. H. Kennett. He was joint editor of the *Cambridge Ancient History,* for which he wrote a number of chapters. His work for the *Encyclopaedia Britannica* (11th ed.) received far less notice than it deserved. A volume of essays was prepared in his honor, but was not published until after his death, under the title *Essays and Studies* presented to Stanley Arthur Cook by members of the Faculty of Divinity and Oriental Languages in the University of Cambridge.

HAROLD H. ROWLEY

**Cooke, Terence James** (1921–1983). Roman Catholic cardinal, educator, and editor. Born in a slum tenement in New York City, he studied for the priesthood at Cathedral College and St. Joseph's Seminary, was ordained in 1945, and served as a parish priest for two years in the South Bronx. Following graduation from Catholic University (1949), he taught at Fordham University. In 1957 he became personal secretary to Cardinal Francis Spellman of the archdiocese of New York, and upon Spellman's death (1968), he was installed as archbishop, and later cardinal (1969). As head of the richest see in Roman Catholicism and most important outside of Rome he was conservative in matters of theology and liturgy, but more progressive on social and political questions, where he campaigned tirelessly for charitable causes related to health care, social service, and education. He was vicar, overseeing all Roman Catholic chaplains in the armed forces, and until his death retained the simplicity and soul of a village priest.

JACK MITCHELL

**Cooneyites.** A sect founded about 1885 in Northern Ireland by William Irvine and George Walker but later dominated by Edward Cooney. Also called Go-Preachers (Mark 16:15), its traveling exhorters attacked churches and clergymen, education and luxury, smoking and drinking. It spread to other parts of Great Britain and to North America but gradually declined.

THEODORE TAPPERT

**Cope, Henry Frederick** (1870–1923). Baptist educator. Born in London, he was educated privately in England and after arrival in the USA studied at Ripon College and the Southern Baptist Theological Seminary. After ordination to the Baptist ministry in 1893 he served pastorates in Rochester, N.Y. (1894/95), Plano, Ill. (1895–98), and Dillon, Mont. (1898–1903). For two years he taught and lectured in Chicago and thereafter was associated with the Religious Education Association (assistant secretary, 1905–7; general secretary, 1907–23). He wrote *The Modern Sun-*

day School in Principle and Practice (1907), *Levels of Living* (1908), *The Friendly Life* (1909), *The Efficient Layman* (1910), *Efficiency in the Sunday School* (1912), *Religious Education in the Family* (1915), *The Modern Sunday School and Its Present-Day Task* (1916), *Religious Education in the Church* (1917), *The School in the Modern Church* (1919), *Parent and Child* (1921), *The Week-Day Church School* (1921), and *Principles of Christian Service* (1921). He edited *Religious Education* from 1906 to 1923.

RAYMOND W. ALBRIGHT

**Coptic Church.** The largest Christian church body in Egypt.

*History.* According to tradition, Christianity was established in Egypt in A.D. 42 as a direct result of the preaching of St. Mark. Derived from the Greek *Aigyptios* which, after the Muslim (Persian and Arab) conquest of A.D. 640, evolved into the Arabic *Qibto,* the word "Copt" was first used in Europe in the 16th century to describe the Christian inhabitants of Egypt.

The social, economic, and political fortunes of the once powerful church have waned in inverse proportion to the growth and often ruthless domination of the Muslim community. At present the majority of its members—representing less than 20 percent of Egypt's population—are poverty-stricken peasants. They are fearful of absorption by Islam, and obliged to subsist in Christian ghettos, which are largely isolated from and (unofficially) discriminated against by the Muslim-Egyptian mainstream populace.

Despite strict laws prohibiting Christians from proselytizing among Muslims, the Coptic Orthodox Church, with a membership of perhaps 7 million, continues to be the numerically most significant Christian community in the Arab world. In recent years it has shown signs of revitalization, with a concomitant increase in church schools, monastic vocations, and religious literature.

*Teaching and Practice.* Egyptian church leaders—both native and Greek (along with those of Syria, Malabar, and Armenia)—took issue with the Council of Chalcedon's condemnation of monophysitism in A.D. 451 and united under one leadership to establish a patriarchate independent of the rest of Christendom.

The Cairo-based Coptic patriarchate oversees dioceses which in turn are presided over by bishops (until 1971 called metropolitans and metropolitanates, respectively). Some of the older dioceses trace origins back to the time of Athanasius (A.D. 293–373).

During its 4th century apex the Coptic Church comprised 100 dioceses or bishoprics, with this number reduced to 12 during the 10th and 17th centuries. At the time of the accession of Shenouda III in 1971, the church was organized into 24 dioceses, a number subsequently modified due to the division of several of the larger dioceses, and the merging of some of the smaller ones. As of 1977 the Holy Synod comprised 40 bishops, five abbots, and the vicars of Alexandria and Cairo. Also, bishops have been assigned jurisdiction over each of four special functions within the church: (1) public, ecumenical, and social relations; (2) theological and educational institutions; (3) higher studies and Coptic culture; and (4) African affairs, specializing in liaison with African indigenous churches.

Rites of worship are derived from the original Greek liturgy of Alexandria and are celebrated in the now-dead Coptic language, along with a large amount of Arabic. A recent development within the church has resulted in the enrollment of more than one million children in church Sunday schools.

Monasticism continues to be a significant feature of the Coptic Church, with the majority of its bishops being former monks. Whatever credence is given to the tradition that monasticism originated in Egypt, it is a fact that significant numbers of Christians in Egypt early came to grips with radical biblical teaching on money and possessions, and shunning material goods, devoted themselves to extensive periods of solitary meditation and prayer.

*Bibliography.* E. R. Hardy, *Christian Egypt: Church and People* (1952); C. Kopp, *Glaube und Sakramente der Koptischen Kirche* (repr. 1963); E. Wakin, *A Lonely Minority: The Modern Story of Egypt's Copts* (1963); W. F. Adeney, *The Greek and Eastern Churches* (repr. 1965); M. Roncaglia, *Histoire de l'Eglise Copte,* 6 vols. (1966– ); A. S. Ativa, *History of Eastern Christianity* (1967); A. J. Butler, *Ancient Coptic Churches of Egypt,* 2 vols. (repr. 1970); O. F. A. Meinardus, *Christian Egypt, Ancient and Modern* (2d ed., 1976); I. Habib el-Masry, *The Story of the Coptic Church of Egypt, Established by St. Mark* (1978); D. B. Barrett, ed., *Encyclopedia of World Christianity* (1983); D. Bundy, *ATLA Proceedings* 39 (1985): 102–29; B. C. Carter, *The Copts in Egyptian Politics* (1986); B. A. Pearson and J. A. Goehring, eds., *The Roots of Egyptian Christianity* (1986).

JON BONK

## Corinthians, Epistles to the. *See* PAUL, THE APOSTLE.

## Corruption. Both a manifestation and a result of sin. God made man perfect and placed him in a perfect environment. But by sinning against God, man became guilty (subject to condemnation) and corrupt. The idea of guilt and corruption are supplemental. Because of sin man is loathsome in his guilt and guilty in his vile estate. Moreover, the idea of ethical corruption in man and physical corruption in his environment are supplemental.

In nonbiblical thought there was no perfect creation of man or the world. Thus the corruption of man does not involve guilt. Nor is the corruption of the universe directly dependent upon human sin. Corruption is an inherent aspect of reality.

In biblical thought, the Son of God has come to remove corruption from the heart of man and, eventually, in the regeneration of all things, from the cosmos. He does so by dying for his own, removing their guilt, and meriting eternal life for them. Thus, the corruption of their hearts is, in principle, removed. And, in the new heavens and on the new earth, all corruption in man and in the cosmos will have disappeared.

CORNELIUS VAN TIL

## Corson, Fred Pierce (1896–1985). Methodist clergyman, educator, and author. Born in Millville, N.J., he graduated from Dickinson College and Drew University, was ordained in 1920, ministered in Connecticut and New York (1920–29), and was then appointed superintendent of the Brooklyn South District of N.Y. East Conference (1930–34). He was president of Dickinson College (1934–44) before being named bishop of the Methodist Church in 1944, a position he held until his retirement in 1968. He was president of the World Methodist Council (1961–66), and delegate observer at the Vatican Council II (1962–65). He founded the "Bishops' Crusaders," a worldwide youth movement, and after retirement was titular pastor of historic St. George's United Methodist Church in Philadelphia. Besides contributing to religious journals, he wrote *The Pattern of a Church* (1946), *Your Church and You* (1951), *Pattern for Successful Living* (1953), and *Steps to Christian Unity* (1964).

JACK MITCHELL

## Costa Rica. A republic of Central America with an area of 52,100 sq. km. (19,730 sq. mi.) and a population of 2.7 million (1987 est.).

Roman Catholicism is the official state religion. The Catholic diocese of Costa Rica was not established until 1850, before which the church came under the diocese of Nicaragua. In 1852 a concordat was signed with the Holy See defining church-state relations. The Costa Rican church was largely unaffected by the liberal-spearheaded anticlerical campaign that swept through most of Central America during the late 19th century. From 1901 to 1930 the church maintained harmonious relations with a series of liberal governments. During the 1940s, under the leadership of Archbishop Víctor Sanabria, the church actively collaborated with the social reforms of President Calderón Guardia and even developed warm relations with the Communist party leader, Manuel Mora.

Since Sanabria's death in 1952, the church hierarchy has been comparatively inactive in social issues, assuming a position of passive collaboration with a series of moderate reformist governments. Progressive currents, such as liberation theology, have had much less impact in Costa Rica than elsewhere in Central America. A small group of progressive clergy is dedicated to playing a more active role in promoting social change, however, but since the late 1960s it has continually come into conflict with conservative bishops. In 1982 there were 454 priests (295 secular and 159 religious) spread over 178 parishes.

The number of Protestant churches has been steadily increasing since World War II. In 1980 Protestants constituted 6.6 percent of the total population. Since 1978 the growth of pentecostal sects has been remarkable; pentecostals now account for approximately half of all Protestants in the country.

PHILIP J. WILLIAMS

**Counseling, Pastoral.** Pastoral care is a part of the ministry of the church that involves acts of helping, done by Christians (especially pastors), with the goal of bringing encouragement and practical assistance to people who are physically or spiritually needy, in conflict with others, experiencing crises, or needing help in decision making. Throughout the Christian era, pastors and other religious leaders have been engaged in four functions of pastoral care: (1) healing (restoring individuals to wholeness and helping them move beyond their previous levels of functioning); (2) sustaining (encouraging people, helping them to endure and rise above difficult circumstances); (3) guiding (assisting people as they face difficult decisions); and (4) reconciling (helping individuals build relationships with other people and with God). Pastoral care is a broad form of people-helping that includes counseling, but is not limited to it.

Pastoral counseling is a modern and psychologically sophisticated form of pastoral care. Usually offered by a minister, priest, rabbi, or chaplain, pastoral counseling seeks to combine skilled counseling methods with the moral guidelines and spiritual values that come from religion. The evangelical pastoral counselor seeks to counsel in ways that will honor Christ, help troubled individuals, and bring changes in thinking and behavior that are consistent with scriptural truths.

The Bible is filled with examples of dedicated men and women who encouraged, guided, supported, confronted, comforted, advised and in other ways counseled people in need. Jesus is described in Scripture as the "Wonderful Counselor" (Isa. 9:6), the early church is pictured as a caring community of believers, the writers of the epistles frequently dealt with the personal and congregational problems of their readers, and the NT instructs all believers to be burden bearers who care for, encourage, edify, and help one another.

The modern pastoral counseling movement began in the 1920s, largely as a reaction both against traditional theological education, with its lack of emphasis on practical and pastoral caring, and against early psychiatric treatment which had little place or respect for the healing power of religion. From these beginnings, Clinical Pastoral Education (CPE) was born and soon developed into a highly organized movement, ecumenical in emphasis and generally liberal in theology. Much of its work has been to provide standards and guidelines for the training of pastoral counselors; to show both theological educators and professional counselors that pastoral involvement is relevant and effective in treating psychological and physical illness; to investigate ways by which theology and the psychological sciences can be related; to produce books and journals that show how counseling can be done as part of the pastoral ministry; and to demonstrate that the personal and spiritual development of seminarians and pastors is at least as important as intellectual training for the ministry.

Theologically conservative Christians have tended to avoid close contact with the mainstream pastoral counseling movement, primarily because of its liberal emphasis and its close affiliation with secular psychology. Even so, almost all seminaries and Bible colleges, regardless of theological persuasion, now offer courses in pastoral counseling. Some have degree programs with an emphasis on counseling, and many give training in related areas such as crisis intervention, the psychology of religion, or pastoral psychology.

Within recent years several journals and a number of books on Christian counseling have appeared. Many are helpful although some propose counseling approaches that claim to be "biblical" but that contradict and sometimes condemn the approaches of other writers. Regrettably, this has led to mutual criticism among a few leaders in the field and confusion among pastors who are seeking more effective ways to counsel.

Pastoral counselors seek to help people with religious issues, including doubts and theological questions. However, most pastoral counseling deals with personal, social, marital, and family problems. The emphasis in pastoral counseling is on coping with present problems, helping those who suffer, and giving spiritual guidance. Rarely does the pastoral counselor attempt to deal with the unconscious, uncover repressed experiences, remold the personality, or engage in other long-term, in-depth forms of counseling.

Few pastors have the privilege of deciding whether to do counseling. Counseling is widely perceived to be a part of the pastor's responsibilities and church members bring their problems. As pastoral counseling has become more popular and its effectiveness more widely recognized, increasing numbers of pastors are finding themselves swamped with requests for counseling. Some pastors, especially those who have training in this area, are capable, effective counselors. Others feel inadequate and find the counseling experience to be frustrating, unproductive, and a distraction from other ministerial duties.

Pastoral counseling takes place not only in pastors' offices and other church settings, but also in hospital rooms, prison cells, parishioners' homes, restaurants, military settings, and funeral homes. Hospital and military chaplains usually identify themselves as pastoral counselors, as do college chaplains, prison pastors, and chaplains who are associated with major league sports teams.

Within recent years several new trends have appeared within the pastoral counseling field. These include the training and use of lay counselors within local congregations; increased communication and cooperation among pastors and professionals in the helping fields; the establishment of the church-sponsored pastoral counseling centers; the involvement of pastors in new and established counseling clinics or community centers; the consideration of ways by which problem prevention can be stimulated by and through the congregation; the increased use of sermons and small study groups as ways of stimulating mental and spiritual health; the development of films, seminars, and training programs that can supplement, replace, and sometimes prevent the need for counseling; the application of pastoral counseling to missions, along with the adaptation of pastoral counseling methods for use in other cultures; the development of self-help and mutual aid groups, including Bible study groups, as adjuncts to pastoral counseling; and an emphasis on ways in which pastors, burdened with the demands of the ministry, can get pastoral counseling for themselves.

When they leave their training programs and enter the pastoral ministry, many Christian leaders are surprised to discover the existence of so many needs and personal problems that do not respond to traditional pastoral care. Pastoral counseling is a part of the ministry that appears to be increasing in its influence, impact, and importance.

**Bibliography.** H. Clinebell, *Basic Types of Pastoral Care and Counseling* (rev. ed., 1984); G. R. Collins, *Innovative Approaches to Counseling* (1986); R. Hurding, *Roots and Shoots: A Guide to Counseling and Psychotherapy* (1987); G. R. Collins, *Christian Counseling: A Comprehensive Guide* (rev. ed., 1988).

GARY R. COLLINS

**Courts, Ecclesiastical.** The Roman Catholic Church claims full judicial power over its members. The bishop delegates his jurisdiction to a judge-official, assisted eventually by vice-officials, and who is competent in matrimonial causes, in causes involving the validity of ordination, and in matters of discipline and ecclesiastical privileges. The court of appeal is that of the metropolitan.

In addition anyone may appeal to the tribunals of the Roman Curia, namely, the *Rota*, which

among other functions, judges matrimonial causes appealed from diocesan or metropolitan courts; the *Poenitentiaria*, which grants absolution from censures and dispensations; and the *Signatura*, which acts as Supreme Court (see *Codex Iuris Canonici*, can. 1569–1607).

GEORGES A. BARROIS

**Covenant Theology.** *Meaning of the Term.* Covenant theology sprang up naturally as the most consistent expression of Calvinism, in which the idea of the self-sufficient, ontological Trinity is the final reference point in all predication. It is this idea that lies at the center of covenant theology. The three Persons of the Trinity have an exhaustively personal relationship with one another. And the idea of exhaustive personal relationship is the idea of the covenant.

*Covenant of Works.* Since the internal relationships of the triune God are covenantal, God's relation to mankind is also covenantal. God dealt covenantally with mankind through its representative head, Adam (Rom. 5:12). Made in the image of God, Adam received supernatural, positive communication from God (G. Vos, *Biblical Theology* [1948]). God promised to reward fully self-conscious obedience and threatened to punish disobedience. Thus man was called upon to think God's thoughts after him and to obey God's will. Man was, in short, expected to think and act analogically.

Man's task was as wide as the universe. He was asked to subdue the powers of the created world. He was to do all to the glory of God. As philosopher, scientist, artist, in short, with all the gifts God had bestowed, man was to act analogically or covenantally.

*The Sinner as Covenant Breaker.* When Adam disobeyed God he broke the covenant. In him mankind broke the covenant. Men are therefore covenant breakers, under God's wrath and corrupt in nature.

As covenant breakers men assume that they are not created by God. The covenant breaker makes himself the final reference point in all predication. In theology he reduces God to a projection of himself. In philosophy he holds that ultimate coherence lies in Reality, enveloping God and man. In science, he assumes that reality is nonstructural in nature (irrationalism) and that God is subject to the structure of reality (rationalism).

*Covenant of Grace.* The sinner as covenant breaker cannot succeed. His program is inherently destructive. But the sovereign God rules. Covenant theology holds that whatever comes to pass does so by virtue of the ultimate plan of God.

Accordingly, even the "wrath of man" must praise God. God sees to it that mankind fulfills its task. He sent his Son, through whom the world was made, into the world as Savior. He died for his own and merited life for them. Thus he maintains the covenant of works, fulfills its obligations, and thereby assures the accomplishment of the covenantal task of mankind. Through Christ man knows God truly and knows the universe truly. Thus not only theology, but also philosophy and science are saved. Those in Christ are covenant keepers.

***The Covenant of Common Grace.*** But not all men are covenant keepers. Many have never heard of Christ. Others, having heard of him through the general offer of the gospel of grace, have rejected him. Still others, born within the fold of the church and given in a special sense the promises of the covenant of grace, with Esau break the covenant and crucify the Son of God afresh. They are "covenant breakers" in the narrower sense of the term.

Even so, God, through Christ, restrains the wrath of men as covenant breakers. Through his Holy Spirit, God strives with men, preventing them from fully expressing their hostile, self-frustrating policy as covenant breakers. God keeps the consciousness of himself as Creator and Judge alive in men's minds, however much they, as covenant breakers, seek to suppress it (Rom. 1). As a result, although in principle covenant breakers, they yet can make great contributions to the work and program of Christ, through whom mankind fulfills its covenant responsibilities and reaps its covenant rewards.

***History.*** The idea of covenant theology has only in modern times been thus broadly conceived. As the term indicates, the idea of the covenant has usually been limited to theology. And among covenant theologians there has been a difference of opinion on the nature and extent of the covenant. Some hold that God made his covenant of grace with the elect only, while others hold that God made his covenant with "believers and their seed." The former stress the "unconditional" or sovereign character of the promises of God. The latter stress the "conditional" character of the promise given to "children of believers" as a class. But such differences do not in the least undermine the common presuppositions of Calvinism, especially that of the counsel of God as controlling whatsoever comes to pass. Even those who stress the conditional character of the covenant maintain that back of the will of man is the ultimate, all-determinative will of God.

**Bibliography.** G. Vos, *De Verbondsleer in de Gereformeerde Theologie* (1891); H. H. Kuyper, *Hamabdil* (1907); W. Hendriksen, *The Covenant of Grace* (1932); G. Ch. Aalders, *Het Verbond Gods* (1939); P. Y. De Jong, *The Covenant Idea in New England Theology* (1945).

CORNELIUS VAN TIL

**Cox, Harvey Gallagher** (1929– ). Baptist theologian, educator, and author. Born in Phoenixville, Pa., he studied at the University of Pennsylvania, Yale Divinity School, and Harvard University (Ph.D., 1963). Ordained as a minister of the American Baptist Church in 1956, he served as director of religious activities at Oberlin College (1955–58), program associate for the American Baptist Home Mission Society (1958–63), and fraternal worker with Gossner Mission in East Berlin, Germany (1962/63). In 1962 he acted as consultant to the Harvard Divinity School department of church and society at the Third Assembly of the World Council of Churches in New Delhi, India, and chaired the boards of Blue Hill Christian Center (1963–66) and the Boston Industrial Mission. He taught as assistant professor of theology and culture at Andover Newton Theological School (1963–65), associate professor of church and society at Harvard (1965–70), and since 1970 has been professor of divinity at Harvard. He is also a research associate of the Harvard University program on technology and society (1967– ).

His many publications include *God's Revolution and Man's Responsibility* (1965), *The Secular City: Secularization and Urbanization in Theological Perspective* (1965), *On Not Leaving It to the Snake* (1967), (with members of the seminar on technology and culture at Massachusetts Institute of Technology) *Technology and Culture in Perspective* (1967), (with Mary Corita Kent and Samuel A. Eisenstein) *Sister Corita* (1968), *Feast of Fools: A Theological Essay on Festivity and Fantasy* (1969), *The Seduction of the Spirit: The Use and Misuse of People's Religion* (1973), *Turning East: The Promise and Peril of the New Orientalism* (1977), and *Religion in the Secular City* (1984). He edited *The Church Amid Revolution* (1967), *The Situation Ethics Debate* (1968), *Military Chaplains: From Religious Military to a Military Religion* (1973), and is presently a member of the editorial board of *Christianity and Crisis*.

H. DOUGLAS BUCKWALTER

**Cragg, Albert Kenneth** (1913– ). Islamics scholar and Anglican bishop. After graduating from Oxford he was ordained in the Church of England and served as curate in Birkenhead (1936–39) and as chaplain of All Saints', Beirut (1939–47), where he also taught philosophy at the American University. In 1947 he returned to England as rector of Longworth (1947–51) before going to America as professor of Arabic and Islamics at Hartford Theological Seminary (1951–56). He was canon of St. George's Church, Jerusalem (1956–61), and warden of St. Augustine's College, Canterbury (1961–67), then was consecrated assistant bishop to the Anglican archbishop in Jerusalem (1970–74). Since returning to England he has served as reader in religious studies at Sussex University and assistant bishop of Chichester (1974–78), after which he served in the diocese of Wakefield (1978–81). In semiretirement he became assistant bishop in the

Oxford diocese in 1982. His publications include *The Call of the Minaret* (1956), *Sandals at the Mosque* (1959), *The Dome and the Rock* (1964), *Counsels in Contemporary Islam* (1965), *Christianity in World Perspective* (1968), *The History of Islam* (1969), *Alive to God* (1970), *The Mind of the Qur'ān* (1973), *The Christian and Other Religions* (1977), *Islam from Within* (1979), *This Year in Jerusalem* (1982), and *Jesus and the Muslim* (1985).

J. D. DOUGLAS

## Craig, Archibald Campbell (1888–1985).

Scottish Presbyterian minister. Born in Kelso, he was educated in the University of Edinburgh and at New College, Edinburgh. During World War I he won the Military Cross (1918), but later he became a convinced pacifist. He was minister of Galston Erskine (1921–26), then of Hillhead U. F. Church, Glasgow, through the reunion of the churches in 1929. During 1930–39 he was the first chaplain to Glasgow University. In 1939 he was appointed a secretary with the BBC. He served the church as secretary to the Churches Commission on International Friendship and Social Responsibility (1939–42), as secretary of the newly formed British Council of Churches (1942–46), as a lecturer in biblical studies at Glasgow University (1947–57), as convener of the Inter-Church Relations Committee at the time of the Bishops Report (1957), and as moderator of the General Assembly (1961). As moderator he visited the Vatican and met Pope John XXIII, which aroused controversy in Scotland but aptly expressed his lifelong commitment to ecumenics. In 1970 he was admitted to the Order of St. Mark of Alexandria. His published writings include *University Sermons* (1937), *Preaching in a Scientific Age* (1954), *God Comes Four Times* (1956), *The Church in the World* (1961), and *Jesus* (1968).

ALISTAIR J. DRUMMOND

## Craig, Clarence Tucker (1895–1953). Methodist theologian. Born in Benton Harbor, Mich., he studied at Morningside College, Boston University (Ph.D., 1924), Harvard, Basel, and Berlin universities. After serving Methodist pastorates in Cincinnati and Brooklyn, he was NT professor at the Oberlin Graduate School of Theology (1928–46) and Yale Divinity School (1946–49), and became dean of Drew Theological Seminary in Madison, N.J. After serving on the American Standard Bible Translation Committee, he spent six months as its educational representative in 1946. He participated extensively in work of the World Council of Churches. In addition to editing and contributing to five volumes, he wrote *The Christian's Personal Religion* (1925), *Jesus in Our Teaching* (1931), *We Have an Altar* (1934), *The Study of the NT* (1939), *The Beginning of Christi-*

*anity* (1943), *One God, One World* (1943), and *The One Church* (1951).

**Bibliography.** L. A. Weigle, *Religion in Life* 23 (1954): 451–57.

## Cram, Ralph Adams (1863–1942). Author and architect. Born in Hampton Falls, N.H., he was supervising architect at Princeton (1907–29) and construction architect at Bryn Mawr and Wellesley colleges. Among his many books on art are *The Decadent, Black Spirits and White, Church Building* (1901), *The Ruined Abbeys of Great Britain* (1906), *The Gothic Quest* (1907), *Excalibur* (1908), *The Ministry of Art* (1914), *Heart of Europe* (1915), *The Substance of Gothic* (1917), *The Nemesis of Mediocrity* (1918), *The Great Thousand* (1918), *The Catholic Church and Art* (1929), *The Cathedral of Palma de Mallorca* (1933), *Convictions and Controversies* (1935), and *My Life in Architecture* (1936).

RAYMOND W. ALBRIGHT

## Crawford, Daniel (1870–1926). Brethren missionary to Central Africa. One of a large party who accompanied F. S. Arnot, a fellow Scot, on his second visit to Central Africa in 1889, he settled in Katanga. After the murder of Chief Msiri in 1891 he spent some time doing itinerate work before settling in 1895 at Luanza on Lake Mweru. A rugged pioneer and individualist, he preached and taught the Bible, setting up local churches wherever possible. He translated the Bible into Luba (NT, 1904; OT, 1926). His book, *Thinking Black*, reveals his insight into African ways of thinking at the time, but seems paternalistic and patronizing today.

HAROLD H. ROWDON

## Cremation. The disposal of the dead by reducing the body to ashes. Cremation's extent among primitive societies is a matter of debate, but it was common in the ancient world, except in Egypt, Judea, and China. Cremation was practiced along with burial in Greece and Rome, but gave way to burial in the Roman Empire from the 2d century A.D. and, under Christian influence, disappeared by the 5th century. It was revived in Europe and North America in the late 19th century, often for practical and hygienic reasons connected with the rapid growth of cities, but also by freethinkers wishing to ridicule Christian belief in the resurrection of the body. Hence the Roman Catholic Church prohibited cremation for its members from 1886 to 1963. The relaxation of the Catholic ban was accompanied, if not caused, by a desire to see death given a simple, realistic, and final context, in contrast to the expensive and euphemistic trends that had developed in North American funeral parlors.

Cremation has been usual in Hinduism since the mid-Vedic period (except for infants, yogis, and sadhus), where it forms part of extensive rites lasting several days. It is normal in Buddhist culture, although not predominant in Tibet. It is practiced by Jains and some Zoroastrians, but thought undesirable by Baha'is. The Egyptians, for example, believed that the preservation of the body was essential for the next life. Hindus, however, hold that the corpse must be completely consumed to allow the spirit to depart to a new body.

Cremation and burial practices may not always be directly related to beliefs about the afterlife. Orthodox Jews have always buried their dead, although belief in the resurrection of the body emerged late in Judaism. The early Christians were as much influenced by the burial of Jesus as by any considered concept of general resurrection, and the later entry of the Greek idea of the immortality of the soul into Christian thought had little if any practical effect. On the other hand, more recent reevaluation of the "resurrection of the body" as a unitary concept combining "body" and "soul" similar to our modern concept of "person," offers no philosophical or theological obstacles to preferring cremation to burial. The choice between them would seem to involve only pragmatic considerations, or possibly pastoral concern for the one that has the most psychological effectiveness for the mourners.

*Bibliography.* R. W. Habenstein and W. M. Lamers, *Funeral Customs the World Over* (1963); *NCE* (1967) 4:439–41; 16:108–9; B. Walker, *Hindu World* (1968): 146–49; J. S. Curl, *A Celebration of Death* (1980).

PHILIP HILLYER

## Cremer, August Hermann (1834–1903).

German theologian. Born in Unna, he studied at Halle and Tübingen, and in 1859 was appointed pastor at Ostönnen, near Soest, Westphalia. Eleven years later he became professor of systematic theology at Greifswald and pastor of St. Mary's. His principal works were *Die eschatologische Rede Jesu Christi, Matthäi 24. 25* (1860), *Über den biblischen Begriff der Erbauung* (1863), *Über die Wunder im Zusammenhang der göttlichen Offenbarung* (1865), *Biblisch-theologisches Wörterbuch der neutestamentlichen Gräcität* (1866–67), *Vernunft, Gewissen und Offenbarung* (1869), *Die Auferstehung der Todten* (1870), *Der Gott des Alten Bundes* (1872), *Über die Befähigung zum geistlichen Amte* (1878), *Die Bibel im Pfarrhaus und in der Gemeinde* (1878), *Über den Zustand nach dem Tode, nebst einigen Andeutungen über das Kindersterben und über den Spiritismus* (1883), *Zum Kampf um das Apostolikum* (1893), *Glaube, Schrift und heilige Geschichte* (1896), *Die christliche Lehre von den Eigenschaften Gottes* (1899), *Die paulinische Rechtfertigungslehre im Zusammenhang ihrer geschichtlichen Voraussetzungen* (1900), *Taufe, Wiedergeburt und Kindertaufe* (1900), *Weissagung und Wunder* (1900), *Bedeutung des Artikels von*

*der Gottheit Christi für die Ethik* (1901), *Das Wesen des Christenthums* (1901), and *Grundwahrheiten der christlichen Religion nach D. Seeberg* (1903).

*Bibliography.* August Hermann Cremer, *Gedenkblätter* (1904).

## Crisis, Theology of.

Early 20th-century theology which combined certain ideas about God's self-revelation in Jesus Christ and a certain method of theological analysis. The term "theology of crisis" is often used interchangeably with two others: dialectical theology and neo-orthodoxy.

*Dialectical theology* denotes the method of analysis characteristic of the theology of crisis. Dialectical thinking in the Western intellectual tradition goes back to the time of Socrates. Such thinking tries to arrive at truth by setting opposites over against each other. The opposites with which the theologians of crisis are concerned are not statements (as in the case of Socrates and the Sophists); not the antithetical rhythm of thought regarded as the ultimately real (Hegel); but the contradictions of human existence (Kierkegaard) as these contradictions are sharpened when they are considered in the context of God's self-revelation in Jesus Christ.

*Neo-orthodoxy* denotes the historical position of the theology of crisis in the course of theology since the Protestant Reformation. The theologians of crisis are *orthodox* in the sense that they accept the central conceptions and doctrinal formularies of the 16th-century Reformation as reliable guides to the understanding of what the Bible says about God's action in Jesus Christ for man's salvation and the world's redemption. But they are also *neo*-orthodox because the theologians of crisis regard it as a primary responsibility of theology to give to the doctrinal conceptions and creeds of the past a contemporary formulation and significance. They consider it the business of theology not to restate truths as they have once been stated, but to make room by fresh thinking and statements for the living Truth to which all authentic theological thinking points. The theology of crisis, strictly considered, denotes the theological movement which seeks—by dialectical thinking and in the light of the central theological insights and concerns of the Reformation—to give contemporary meaning and relevance to the interpretations of the relations between God and man and the world, established and illuminated by God's self-revelation in Jesus Christ.

It is not yet possible to accurately assess the permanent contribution of the theology of crisis to Christian theology in the 20th century. Nevertheless, it is possible to distinguish the narrower from the broader boundaries of the movement. The pivotal date is the year 1919, when Karl Barth published the first edition of his commentary on the letter of Paul to the Romans (*Der Römerbrief*). The broader boundaries would then include those antecedent tendencies and movements in post-Reformation theology which tried with varying degrees of authenticity and effectiveness to interpret the central insights of the Reformation and those ways in which, since 1919, the thought of Barth and his more intimate associates has affected the theological thinking of their contemporaries. The narrower boundaries may be drawn around the original collaborative work of Barth and his more intimate associates, that is, between the publication of the *Römerbrief* in 1919 and the cessation of the publication of the initial periodical series, *Zwischen den Zeiten* (*Between the Times*) in 1933. Since 1933, the apparently inevitable parting of the ways which overtakes creative cultural movements set in upon the theology of crisis and its continuing story is the story of divergent accents from the unfolding thoughts of those who first set the movement going or of those chiefly influenced by them.

The theology of crisis is a theology of the parish rather than of the schools. It was inspired by the predicament of the Christian minister under the weekly obligation of preaching a sermon. Karl Barth, the creative genius of the movement, was a pastor in the village of Safenwil, in the canton of Aargau, in Switzerland. Eduard Thurneysen, Barth's intimate friend and associate, was a pastor in the neighboring village of Leutwil. The *Römerbrief* grew out of the searching conversations of these two friends as they tried to take seriously their responsibilities as Christian ministers toward the Bible from which they spoke each Sunday in their pulpits, and for the people assembled with them as a congregation of believers in Jesus Christ. It was not long until they were joined by Emil Brunner, a Swiss pastor, and by two Germans, Friedrich Gogarten, a professor of theology at Breslau, and Rudolf Bultmann, a professor of NT at Marburg on the Lahn. Barth, Thurneysen, and Brunner were members of the Reformed Church of Switzerland; Gogarten and Bultmann of the Evangelical Lutheran Church of Germany. Owing to the vitality and substance of their writings, Barth and Brunner moved from the parish ministry to theological professorships, while Thurneysen added a professorship in practical theology in Basel (1935) to his preaching and pastoral duties at Muenster. Brunner began at Zurich in 1924, where he remained until his retirement in 1953, when he joined the faculty of the newly formed International Christian University at Tokyo. Barth was called in 1921 to the professorship of Reformed theology at Göttingen; in 1925, to the chair of theology at Muenster in Westphalia; and in 1929 to the Protestant faculty at Bonn. Owing to the totalitarian government of Adolf Hitler, Barth was compelled to leave Bonn, and assumed the chair of theology at Basel.

The controversy among the theologians of crisis is the outgrowth of the characteristic doctrines of the movement. Among these doctrines the following may be mentioned.

*The Sovereign Freedom of God.* God is free and sovereign in and over the world which he has created and redeemed. In particular, he is free to reveal himself or to withhold himself, according to the mystery of his being and activity.

*God's Self-Revelation.* God's revelation is always both a dynamic act of self-disclosure and a free gift of grace.

*The Word of God.* The knowledge of God and of his self-revealing activity comes through Jesus Christ in a threefold form characteristic of the life of the church in the world. According to the order of God's self-revelation, there is first of all the historical life of Jesus Christ: his birth, ministry, death, and resurrection, which point to his ascension and exaltation, his preexistence and his second advent. Jesus Christ is the Word of God in the sense that he is God's personal giving and communicating of himself in personal involvement and encounter with men in the world. In short, Jesus Christ is the "Word made flesh." Then, there is the Bible. The Bible is the Word of God because it is the report of Jesus Christ, the Word. As in the theology of the Reformers, so in the theology of crisis, the maxim of *sola scriptura* is pragmatically, and in principle, the point of departure for and the norm of theological thinking and interpretation. And third, there is the proclamation of the church in the sermon. The sermon is God speaking in and to the fellowship of believers through human words. What distinguishes the Word of God from the word of man in the sermon is the faithfulness of what is said in the pulpit to the biblical report of Jesus Christ, and the degree to which human words become the vehicle of God's Holy Spirit, that is, God's contemporary self-communication.

*The Crisis of Human Existence.* Crisis means both turning-point and decision. According to the theology of crisis, when man is confronted through the preaching of the gospel by the self-revealing God, the actual character of human existence is exposed. The actual character of human existence is its alienation from God and consequent internal disorder and disintegration. A radical turnabout is the only way to wholeness and to health. It is God in his dynamic activity of self-revelation in his Word who requires the decision to turn about and who gives the power to make the decision. Thus, crisis is the central characteristic of the relations between God and man.

*The Paradox.* The relations between man and God can be described appropriately only in paradoxical terms. This is the case, first of all, because the Bible describes God's activity paradoxically. God is holy love. Man is the forgiven sinner. Jesus Christ is the God-man. And then, human existence is paradoxical. Man is both believer and unbeliever, obedient and disobedient, child of death and of eternal life.

Sooner or later the question of how these paradoxical facets of God's relations with men are to be interpreted was bound to arise. And over this question the theology of crisis fell apart. How are these paradoxes to be referred to God's self-revealing activity as Redeemer or as Creator? How is man prepared to respond to, or to apprehend the meaning of Jesus Christ? Barth, and Thurneysen with him, remained adamantly christocentric. Gogarten, however, found it necessary to stress creation, according to an elaborate doctrine of the "orders of creation." Brunner and Bultmann emphasized the problems involved in the knowledge of God. The debate between Brunner and Barth centered on the problem of the "point of contact" (*Anknüpfungspunkt*); between Bultmann and Barth on the problem of the preparatory knowledge of God, that is, preparatory to the revelation in Christ (*Vorverständnis*).

Whatever the ultimate significance of the theology of crisis may be, certain impressive contributions have already become plain. The theology of crisis has given fresh and contemporary understanding to the initiative and sovereignty of God, so that once again it is possible to think about the world and about human life in the world in the context of clearly formulated apprehensions of the divine activity. The theology of crisis, while taking full account of the higher criticism of Scripture, has restored the sense of the unity of the Bible, and opened the way for the instruction and guidance of religious faith through the inner logic of biblical events and ideas. The theology of crisis has given significant emphasis to the Christian church as the fellowship of believers in which a continuing creative conversation is going on in two directions. On the one hand, the church is engaged in a living conversation with itself, that is, with the faith and thoughts of those who in all the times and places of the church's history have given faithful and creative witness to God's self-revelation in Jesus Christ. Perhaps the most striking fact about the Christian church in the 20th century is its movement toward ecumenical unity. Such a unity requires a common mind, which transcends the particular formulations of the separate confessional traditions. And no single theological influence has been more operative in the emergence of an ecumenical theology that of the theology of crisis. On the other hand, the church is engaged in a living conversation with those outside the church, whose creative labors of mind and spirit determine the making and the remaking of culture. There are those who believe that it is largely owing to what the theology of crisis has contributed to the restoration of theology as an independent science, that Christian thought in the 20th century can participate constructively

and critically in the cultural enterprise as it has not been able to do since the Middle Ages.

But these contributions have also raised certain problems which point beyond the theology of crisis, and for the solution of which the insights and the method of the theology of crisis are inadequate. How shall the unity of biblical faith and thought, and the diversity of biblical experience and development be meaningfully related and understood? What is the relation between revelation as act and revelation as knowledge? Some answer to this question must be worked out along lines which transcend the hitherto fruitless correlation or juxtaposition of natural and revealed theology. Can theology discharge its cultural responsibility without an ontology? And if not, what are the nature and terms of a theological ontology? It is with these problems that the next chapter of Protestant theology in the 20th century must be concerned. And the theologians who are dealing with these problems most constructively are the theologians who have been at once the severest critics of the theology of crisis, and the most deeply influenced by it.

**Bibliography.** K. Barth, *Epistle to the Romans* (1933); *The Doctrine of the Word of God* (1936); *Church Dogmatics* (1936–81); E. Brunner, *Revelation and Reason* (1946); *The Divine Imperative* (1947); *Man in Revolt* (1947); *The Mediator* (1947); *The Christian Doctrine of God* (1950); *The Christian Doctrine of Creation and Redemption* (1952); C. Kegley, ed., *The Theology of Emil Brunner* (1962); C. Van Til, *Christianity and Barthianism* (1962); C. Brown, *Karl Barth and the Christian Message* (1967); J. Macquarrie, *Twentieth Century Religious Thought* (1973); S. Sykes, ed., *Karl Barth—Studies of His Theological Methods* (1979); P. Avis, *The Methods of Modern Theology* (1986).

# Croce, Benedetto

**Croce, Benedetto** (1866–1952). Italian philosopher, historian, and critic. Born in Pescasseroli (Aquila), he studied briefly at the University of Rome and in later life received honorary degrees from Oxford, Freiburg, and Marburg universities but was largely self-educated. He developed a "philosophy of the spirit" in which philosophy was identified with history and history eventually with liberty, and in which four grades or realms of spirit are distinguished: the esthetic, logical, economic, and ethical. He founded and edited the influential journal *La Critica* (1903–44) and its continuation *Quaderni della Critica* (1945– ). In politics he long remained independent but joined the Liberal party in 1924 and was its president for a time after World War II. He was a senator from 1910, minister of education in Giolitti's cabinet (1920/21), and minister without portfolio in the cabinets of Badoglio and Bonomi (1944). In 1946 he founded the Italian Institute of Historical Studies, a postgraduate school adjoining his library in Naples. Critical of both Catholicism and Protestantism, he thought of himself as having continued the work of philosophers like Vico, Kant, Fichte, and Hegel. Some of his more important philosophical works in English translation are *Philosophy of the Spirit*,

*Aesthetic* (1909), *Philosophy of the Practical* (1913), *Logic* (1917), *Theory and History of Historiography* (1921), *The Philosophy of Giambattista Vico* (1913), *Historical Materialism and the Economics of Karl Marx* (1914), *What Is Living and What Is Dead of the Philosophy of Hegel* (1915), and *History as the Story of Liberty* (1941).

**Bibliography.** H. Wildon Carr, *The Philosophy of Benedetto Croce* (1917); R. Piccoli, *Benedetto Croce, An Introduction to His Philosophy* (1922); B. Croce, *An Autobiography* (1927); D. Mack Smith, *The Cambridge Journal*, vols. 1–2 (1947–49).

MAX H. FISCH

**Cronin, John Francis** (1908– ). Roman Catholic priest, educator, and social activist. Born in Glens Falls, N.Y., he studied at Holy Cross College, Worcester, Mass., and Catholic University of America, Washington, D.C. (Ph.D., 1935). In 1932 he was ordained a priest. He taught as professor of philosophy and economics, St. Mary's Seminary, Baltimore, Md. (1932–45), was associate director, Department of Social Action, U.S. Catholic Conference, Washington, D.C. (1946–67), professor of Christian ethics, St. Mary's Seminary (1967–78), and retired in 1978. From 1968 to 1972 he was president of the Maryland Project for Equality (interreligious civil rights program for fair employment). In the economic field he has stressed labor-management cooperation and has often served as arbitrator and conciliator in labor disputes. His literary works include *Cardinal Newman: His Theory of Knowledge* (1935), *Economics and Society* (1939), *Economic Analysis and Problems* (1945), *Catholic Social Action* (1948), *Catholic Social Principles* (1950), *The Catholic as Citizen* (1963), *Government in Freedom* (1965), *Christianity and Social Progress* (1965), and *Social Principles and Economic Life* (1966).

H. DOUGLAS BUCKWALTER

**Cross, Frank Leslie** (1900–1968). Anglican scholar. After studies at the universities of Oxford, Marburg, and Freiburg, he was ordained in 1925. He was tutor at Ripon Hall, Oxford (1924–27), librarian of Pusey House, Oxford (1927–44), and lecturer in natural and comparative religion, Oxford (1935–38), where he became professor of divinity from 1944. His publications include *Religion and the Reign of Science* (1930), *John Henry Newman* (1933), *The Tractarians and Roman Catholicism* (1933), *1 Peter* (1934), *Anglicanism* (with P. E. More, 1935), *St. Athanasius: De Incarnatione* (1939), and *The Early Christian Fathers* (1960). He is probably best known, however, for his editorship of the monumental *Oxford Dictionary of the Christian Church* (1957; 2d ed., 1974).

J. D. DOUGLAS

**Cuba.** See WEST INDIES.

**Cullmann, Oscar** (1902– ). Lutheran theologian. Born in Strasbourg, France, he was a member of the Lutheran Church of Alsace, although never ordained. He took three degrees at the University of Strasbourg, including a doctorate in theology in 1930. He did further studies at the Sorbonne, University of Paris. He taught both at Strasbourg (1927–38) and Basel (1938–72), the latter paralleled by teaching at the Sorbonne (1951–72). He was cofounder of the Ecumenical Institute at Jerusalem and was an active participant in the furtherance of Protestant-Roman Catholic dialogs. For nearly 40 years he was the leading advocate of the salvation-historical interpretation of the NT and a major opponent of the reigning existentialist school led by Rudolf Bultmann. His various writings insist on an inductive approach to the study of Scripture whereby the reader sets aside improper presuppositions and methodologies—especially 19th-century historicism and 20th-century existentialism—and simply listens to what the authors have to say. Cullmann made free but qualified use of form-critical methodology to arrive at an understanding of the faith of the early church, the forms within which it expressed that faith, and the development of those forms in its life and worship. He contended that the foundation and unifying theme of the NT—and, indeed, the entire Bible—is *Heilsgeschichte*, that is, the history of the self-disclosure and saving action of God in the events which lead up to and follow from the Christ event. The life, death, and resurrection of Christ thus constitute the midpoint and consummation of this saving history and determine its meaning all along the line. From that perspective, *Heilsgeschichte* is also always Christ-history. It is for that reason that Christology and *Heilsgeschichte* are interwoven in the NT. The time before the Christ event was the period of Israel. The time since the Christ event is the period of the church. But the latter is characterized as eschatological time because the Christ event inaugurated the eschatological age and is thus qualitatively different from the time that preceded Christ. In its life, worship, and service, the church therefore lives in eschatological tension between the "now" and the "then," the "already," and the "not yet." The end of history will disclose nothing new but will be the universal manifestation of that decisive battle against the principalities and powers that was already won in the Christ event. Cullmann insisted that every attempt to isolate the biblical message from its salvation-historical moorings inevitably ends in a distorted docetism.

**Bibliography.** O. Cullmann, *The State in the NT* (1963); *The Christology of the NT* (1963); *Christ and Time: The Primitive Christian Conception of Time and History* (1964); *Salvation in History* (1967); *Early Christian Worship* (1978).

FRED D. LAYMAN

**Cult.** See SECTS AND CULTS.

**Cunningham, John Rood** (1891–1980). Presbyterian minister, college president, and educator. Born in Wiliamsburg, Mo., he studied at Westminster College (Fulton, Mo.) and Louisville Presbyterian Seminary. Ordained in 1917 by the Presbyterian Church in the USA, he then served with the War Work Council, Presbyterian Church (1918/19), and afterwards ministered successively at Presbyterian Church, Grenada, Miss. (1919–23), First Presbyterian Church, Bristol, Tenn. (1928–30), and First Presbyterian Church, Winston-Salem, N.C. (1936–41). From 1930 to 1936 he was president of Louisville Presbyterian Theological Seminary. He was also president of Davidson College (1941–57), and executive director of the Southern Presbyterian Foundation (1957–64). A leader in national and international church organizations, he was active in groups dedicated to world peace and to solving social, religious, and racial problems.

JACK MITCHELL

**Curia.** *See* CONGREGATIONS, ROMAN.

**Cutts, Edward Lewes** (1824–1901). Anglican scholar. Born in Sheffield, England, he studied at Queen's College, Cambridge. He was ordained in 1848, became vicar of Haverstock Hill (1871), and remained there until his death. He was appointed to visit the Syrian and Chaldean Churches in 1876 and described his travels in *Christian under the Crescent in Asia* (1877). His books include *A History of Early Christian Art* (1893), *St. Augustine of Canterbury* (1895), *Parish Priests and Their People in the Middle Ages in England* (1908), and *Turning-Points of General Church History* (rev. ed., 1928).

F. W. DILLISTONE

**Cyprus.** An Eastern Mediterranean island republic with an area of 9251 sq. km. (3572 sq. mi.) and a population of just under 700,000. The population is 75.5 percent of Greek origin (all but a fraction linked with the Greek Orthodox Church); 18.5 percent are Turkish Muslims. Armenian, Maronite, British; and other minorities comprise the remaining 6 percent. Under British administration from 1878, Cyprus was a crown colony from 1925 to 1960, when it became independent. Protestant work has always been difficult in a land where Orthodox bishops have traditionally been national leaders. The limited freedom evangelical workers had exercised before independence was much more severely restricted when the Greek majority under Archbishop/President Makarios effectively renounced the arrangement by which the Turkish minority's rights were safeguarded. Violence ensued between the two races. Despite the efforts of a resident United Nations peacekeeping force, the situation erupted in 1974 when what was seen as a mainland Greece threat was countered by an invasion of Turkish forces that occupied some 37 percent of the northern section of the island. In 1988 there was no prospect of that partition's being removed. In addition to Armenian, Maronite, and Anglican congregations, there is a community church in Nicosia, chiefly for British and American expatriates, and some 15 congregations with 4000 members of the Catholic church of Cyprus. The Reformed Presbyterian Church (USA) operates two schools, and a number of other missionary workers are involved in literature work and in a broadcasting ministry to Cyprus. With the exception of a very few longtime non-Greek residents, the Turkish part of the republic is entirely Muslim.

J. D. DOUGLAS

**Czechoslovakia.** A central European country whose population is 15.7 million (1988) and whose area is 127,896 sq. km. (49,381 sq. mi.). The country came into existence in 1918 at the end of World War I and the dissolution of the Austro-Hungarian Empire. It consisted of the Czech lands (Bohemia and Moravia), Slovakia, and Carpatho-Ukraine. The country was divided during World War II, and reunited afterwards, apart from Caphartho-Ukraine, which was claimed by the Soviet Union. Historically and culturally, Slovakia is Catholic, while the Czech lands have a strong Protestant tradition.

A census taken soon after the communist takeover in 1948 recorded that 94.6 percent of the population of Czechoslovakia described themselves as religious believers. From the outset the communist government was hostile to Christianity and especially to the Roman Catholic Church. In the 1950s the religious orders were outlawed, and many priests and religious people were imprisoned. The authorities hoped to destroy the Church from within by installing proregime clergy who would head a schism from Rome. Ultimately, this plan failed, largely because of the firm resistance of the head of the church in Czechoslovakia, Cardinal Beran. The 1960s saw a great relaxation of government interference in Church affairs until the invasion of Czechoslovakia by the Soviet army in 1968. Liberals in the government were replaced by hardliners under Gustav Husák.

Czechoslovakia in 1990 was experiencing political and societal uncertainties with other Eastern European nations. Churches were gradually enjoying more freedoms. The government continued to exercise a large measure of control over the churches. One of its most effective methods of control was the legal requirement that a priest or minister of any denomination should have a state license to carry out his pastoral duties. If he was too zealous in performing his ministry, he risked losing his license. The government also controlled the number of men training for the priesthood and blocked Vatican nominations for new bishops. Eight of the country's dioceses were without a bishop until 1989, when five bishops and one archbishop were installed without government opposition. Previously the Roman Catholic hierarchy was dominated by members of the government-sponsored priests' organization, "Pacem in Terris," which had the support of approximately 10 percent of the country's Catholic clergy, although Pope John Paul II forbade priests to belong to it. The country's primate, Cardinal Frantissek Tomásek, the 87-year-old archbishop of Prague, had nothing to do with the movement and frequently voiced his opposition to it. *Pacem in terris* voluntarily disbanded in 1989, signaling the restoration of much autonomy to the church.

The non-Catholic denominations had not suffered as much opposition under the regime as had the Roman Church. By and large, they accepted the restrictions imposed on them by the government. Those ministers and laypersons who did stand against the authorities only rarely received any support from their churches. Pentecostal churches for many years were recognized only in Slovakia. In 1989, however, pentecostals were allowed to surface freely in Bohemia and Moravia.

Despite the severe restrictions imposed on Christianity in Czechoslovakia, the country saw a considerable religious revival in recent years. Only one-third of the population attended church in the mid-1980s, with Catholics outnumbering Protestants by two to one, but an increasingly large number, especially young people, were turning to religion. Unofficial religious activity was on the increase with suspended priests performing their duties secretly. A considerable amount of religious *samizdat* (unofficially produced literature) appeared in order to provide believers with spiritual material that would not otherwise have been available to them. Literature was allowed to circulate more widely under the new, more open society of 1980, and hundreds of radio programs were beamed into the region each month. Nearly 40 years of communist rule had taken their toll on Czechoslovakia's believers, but Christianity had survived and continued to grow. Its greatest new challenge in the 1990s seemed to be how to minister to the new social problems, especially drug addiction and alcoholism, that were emerging in their changing social structure.

**Bibliography.** T. Beeson, *Discretion and Valour* (rev. ed., 1982); A. D. Moore, *Christianity Today* (April 23, 1990): 19–23.

PHILIP WALTERS

# Dd

**Daane, James** (1914–1983). Born in Grand Haven, Mich., he graduated from Calvin College and Calvin Theological Seminary, and was ordained in 1942. He served three Christian Reformed congregations until he joined the editorial staff of *Christianity Today* in 1961. From 1966 through 1981 he was professor of pastoral theology at Fuller Theological Seminary. Under Josef Hromadka he earned a Princeton Seminary Th.D. in 1945. A founder of the *Reformed Journal* in 1951, he served as an editor until his death. In *A Theology of Grace* (1954) Daane keenly argued that Cornelius Van Til's critique of Herman Hoeksema's rejection of common grace was as enmeshed in non-Christian philosophical rationalism as Hoeksema's theology; he found that both theologies threaten the church's effectiveness in society. Divine election as appealing and gracious is further developed in *The Freedom of God: A Study of Election and Pulpit* (1973) and in *Preaching with Confidence* (1982).

JAMES A. DE JONG

**Dahl, George** (1881–1962). Congregational Christian. He studied at Yale University (Ph.D., 1913), and in Germany. He taught OT in the Yale Divinity School (1912–49). He edited the *Journal of Biblical Literature* (1921–41) and was a member of the OT committee of the RSV from 1940. He wrote *Materials for the History of Dor* (1915), and *Heroes of Israel's Golden Age* (1923).

**Dalman, Gustaf Herman** (1855–1941). German Lutheran. Born in Niesky, Silesia, he studied at the Moravian theological seminary in Gnadenfeld, where he was professor of OT exegesis and practical theology (1881–87). In 1887 he became a Lutheran, studied at Leipzig (Ph.D., 1887), and until 1902 was professor and later director of the Institutum Delitzschianum at Leipzig. He was privatdocent (1891–96) and after 1896 was associate professor of OT exegesis. In 1902 he was named president of the German Evangelical Archeological Institute, and was appointed honorary Swedish consul for Palestine and Damascus in 1903. In theology he avoided disputes and tried to unite Evangelical Christian faith with scientific thought. Among his publications were *Studien zur biblischen Theologie* (2 vols., 1889, 1897), *Jesaja 53, das Prophetenwort vom Sühnleiden des Heilsmittlers* (1890), *Kurzgefasstes Handbuch der Mission unter Israel* (1893), *Grammatik des jüdisch-palästinischen Aramäisch* (1894), *Eben Ezer, Gedenkbuch der Familie Julius Marx* (1897), *Aramäisch-neuhebräisches Wörterbuch zu Targum, Talmud und Midrasch* (2 vols., 1897, 1901), *Christentum und Judentum* (1898, trans., *Christianity and Judaism*, by G. H. Box, 1901), *Die Worte Jesu mit besonderer Berücksichtigung des nachkanonischen jüdischen Schrifttums und der aramäischen Sprache*, i. (1898; trans., *The Words of Jesus Considered in Light of Post-Biblical Jewish Writings and the Aramaic Language*, by D. M. Kay, 1902), and *Palästinischer Diwan* (1901). He edited the monthly *Berith Am* from 1893 to 1902 and the annual report of the *Deutsches Evangelisches Institut für Altertumswissenschaft des heiligen Landes* after 1905.

**D'arcy, Martin** (1888–1976). Roman Catholic. Born in Bath, Somerset, he studied at Stonyhurst College and Oxford University. Ordained a priest of the Society of Jesus (1921), he became master of Campion Hall, Oxford (1932–45), and lectured on philosophy. He was appointed graduate dean of philosophy, Fordham University (1939/40), lecturer at Institute of Advanced Study, Princeton (1941/42), and English provincial of the Society of Jesus (1945–50). His writings include *The Mass and the Redemption* (1925), *Catholicism* (1928), *The Spirit of Charity* (1929), *Mirage and Truth* (1930), *The Nature of Belief* (1931), *Christ as Priest and Redeemer* (1933), *Thomas Aquinas* (1935), *Christian Morals* (1937), *The Problem of Pain* (1938), *Death and Life* (1942), *Belief and Reason* (1943), and *The Mind and Heart of Love* (1945).

**Dargan, Edwin Charles** (1852–1930). Southern Baptist pastor, educator, and writer. Born in Darlington County, S.C., he studied at Furman University and Southern Baptist Theological Seminary. He pastored Baptist churches in Roanoke County, Va. (1877–81), Petersburg, Va. (1881–87), Dixon, Calif. (1887/88), and Charleston, S.C. (1888–92). After a period as professor of homiletics at the Southern Baptist Theological Seminary (1892–1907), he returned to the pastorate at First Baptist Church, Macon, Ga. (1907–17), and finally was editor of the Sunday School Lesson Helps of the Southern Baptist Convention, Nashville, Tenn. (1917–27). Described as Calvinistic in theological views, he was a prolific writer. Among his works were *Ecclesiology* (1897), *A History of Preaching, from* A.D. *70 to 1572* (2 vols., 1905, 1912), *The Doctrines of Our Faith* (1905), *Society, Kingdom, and Church* (1907), *The Art of Preaching in the Light of History* (1922), and *The Bible Our Heritage* (1924). He also wrote commentaries on Colossians (1890) and Romans (1914).

**Darlington, James Henry** (1956–1930). Protestant Episcopal bishop. Born in Brooklyn, he studied at the University of the City of New York and at Princeton Theological Seminary, and was licensed by the presbytery of Newark in 1879. Thereafter, however, he was made deacon and ordained priest in the Protestant Episcopal Church, and became rector of Christ Church, Brooklyn (1883–1905), serving briefly in the diocese also as archdeacon. In 1905 he was consecrated bishop of Harrisburg, Pa. He wrote *Pastor and People* (1902) and *In Memoriam . . . Verses by the Way* (1923) and edited *The Hymnal of the Church* (1900). He composed hymn tunes, songs, instrumental music, and a symphony, *The Sea and the Sea Gulls* (1929). A prominent ecumenist, he was chairman of his denomination's committee that conferred with the Eastern Orthodox Churches and the Old Catholic Church (1910–25).

**Davidson, Randall Thomas** (1848–1930). Archbishop of Canterbury. Born in Scotland and educated at Oxford, he was successively curate of Dartford (1874–77), chaplain to Archbishop Tait (1877–82) and Archbishop Benson (1882/83), dean of Windsor and domestic chaplain to Queen Victoria (1883–91). In 1891 he was consecrated bishop of Rochester, transferring to Winchester in 1895, before becoming archbishop of Canterbury in 1903. On retirement in 1928 he was made first Baron Davidson. His publications include *Life of Archbishop Tait* (2 vols., rev. ed., 1891), *The Christian Opportunity* (1904), *Captains and Comrades in the Faith* (1911), *The Testing of a Nation* (1919), and *Occasions* (1925).

**Dawson, Christopher** (1889–1970). Roman Catholic. Born in Hay Castle, Breconshire, he was educated at Winchester and Trinity College, Oxford. He joined the Roman Catholic Church in 1913. He lectured on the history of culture, University College, Exeter (1925–33). In 1940 he took part with Cardinal Hinsley in the foundation of the Sword of the Spirit Movement. His publications include *The Age of the Gods* (1928), *Progress and Religion* (1929), *Christianity and the New Age* (1931), *The Modern Dilemma* (1932), *The Making of Europe* (1932), *The Spirit of the Oxford Movement* (1933), *Enquiries into Religion and Culture* (1934), *Mediaeval Religion* (1935), *Religion and the Modern State* (1935), *Beyond Politics* (1939), *The Judgment of the Nations* (1943), *Religion and Culture* (1948), *Religion and the Rise of Western Culture* (1950), and *Understanding Europe* (1952).

**Day, Albert Edward** (1884–1973). Methodist. Born in Euphemia, Ohio, he studied at Taylor University (D.D., 1918) and the University of Cincinnati. Ordained to the ministry of the Methodist Episcopal Church (1904), he served as pastor in Ohio, Pennsylvania, Maryland, and California. He was director of the New Life Movement of the Methodist Church (1945–47) and founded the Disciplined Order of Christ (1945). He was the author of *Present Perils in Religion* (1928), *Revitalizing Religion* (1930), *Jesus and Human Personality* (1934), *God in Us—We in God* (1938), *The Evangel of a New World* (1939), *The Faith We Live* (1940), *Discipline and Discovery* (1946), and *An Autobiography of Prayer* (1952). He was coauthor of *Whither Christianity* (1929) and *Contemporary Preaching* (1931).

**Deaconess.** Since the middle of the 19th century women have exercised a ministry in many churches as deaconesses. This has not been seen as something new, but as having its origins in the early days of Christianity. Evidence in both the NT and the early church indicates that women exercised officially recognized diaconal-style mercy ministry alongside male deacons. It is, however, more accurate regarding the early church to speak of women deacons as there is no certainly attested use of the word "deaconess" (*diakonissa*) before A.D. 325. Modern usage reflects these different expressions.

The 19th-century revival of this type of ministry began in Kaiserswerth, Germany, within the Motherhouse communities, and with some modifications it has continued to be the dominant model in Europe, especially Germany and Switzerland. Deaconesses are traditionally linked to one another through their allegiance to the Motherhouse. There is an emphasis on community and practical diaconal work, particularly in institutions such as hospitals and homes for the elderly. A common characteristic is their independence of official church structures. Overseas missions, particularly from Germany, have established the pattern of work in some African and Asian-Pacific countries. A different development emerged in the United Kingdom, Sweden, USA, and countries influenced by them. The chief characteristic in these countries was that deaconesses or women deacons have been integrated into church structures, and authority for their work has rested with church organizations. Deaconesses now work in parishes, in chaplaincy positions, or in specialist church agencies. There are variations within this broad group. Some churches see diaconal ministry as an ordained ministry alongside the presbyterate, while others emphasize its lay status. Another difference lies in the liturgical functions of the deaconess; Anglicans in particular have preserved the diaconal role in worship, but others minimize this aspect.

One organization promoting this role has been Diakonia, the World Federation of Sisterhoods and Diaconal Associations, which manages to contain within it the enormous differences in the interpretation of diaconal ministry. Since the formation of Diakonia in 1946, it has grown from a largely European organization to a worldwide ecumenical fellowship. Its membership of more than 10,000 represents more than 50 associations from 30 countries. Diakonia maintains links with the World Council of Churches and since 1979 has included both men and women in its fellowship, although in practice it mainly represents the female diaconate. Its purpose is to provide for the sharing of ideas, for reflecting on the meaning of diaconal ministry, and for mutual practical assistance.

Two recent developments have radically affected the deaconess movement, particularly in English-speaking countries. The first is the recent renewed emphasis on the diaconate in the life of the church. The Brotherhoods of Deacons in European Protestant churches, the renewal of the permanent diaconate in the Roman Catholic Church since Vatican Council II, research interest within the World Council of Churches, and renewed emphasis on diaconal ministry, have contributed to this new impetus. The second is the opening of the presbyterate of mainline denominations to women. A shortage of presbyters in local churches has increased the demand for women to serve as presbyters rather than in diaconal ministry. Often, once the presbyterate has been opened to women, no more women have become deaconesses. Some churches, and deaconesses in particular, are more closely studying the distinctive nature of the diaconate and how it relates to other ministries.

In the 1980s the ministry and status of deaconesses radically changed. It is still too early to predict what the prevailing nature and style of the future diaconate will be, but women deacons may be at the center of these changes.

*Bibliography.* R. Felgentriff, *Diakonia from Utrecht to Bethel 1946–1975* (1975); J. Grierson, *The Deaconess* (1981); J. Barnett, *The Diaconate: A Full and Equal Order* (1981); *Contemporary Understandings of Diakonia*, World Council of Churches (1982); J. E. Booty, *The Servant Church: Diaconal Ministry and the Episcopal Church* (1982); G. Swensson, ed., *The Churches and the Diaconate, a Festschrift for Inga Bengtzen* (1985).

MARJORIE McGREGOR

## Dead Sea Scrolls. *Discovery.*

The first discovery of MSS popularly known as the Dead Sea Scrolls was made by an Arab goatherd in 1947 in a cave near the northwest corner of the Dead Sea, in the area called Qumran. Some of these MSS were purchased by the Syrian Orthodox Monastery of St. Mark in Jerusalem, others by the Hebrew University. Those acquired by the Syrian Monastery were later purchased in 1955 on behalf of the government of Israel.

Between 1950 and 1956 10 other caves in the same area proved to contain further MSS, almost all in a fragmentary condition. For scholarly reference the caves containing MSS are numbered serially by order of discovery. The greatest abundance of material was found in Cave 4. When the tens of thousands of fragments from Cave 4 were pieced together, they amounted to nearly 400 separate books, about 100 of these being books of the Hebrew Bible.

The scrolls in Cave 1 were better preserved than those in the other caves because they had been placed in earthenware jars. They included two copies of the Book of Isaiah in Hebrew, one practically complete, the other less so; a commentary on the Book of Habakkuk, relating its prophecies to persons and events of the commentator's day; the "rule" of a Jewish religious order; a collection of hymns of thanksgiving; directions for the waging of the last great war by the "children of light" against the "children of darkness"; and a work called the "Genesis Apocryphon," an imaginative expansion of the stories of the Hebrew patriarchs.

Many of the documents from the caves describe the beliefs and practices of a religious community, presumably the community to whose library the MSS originally belonged. Some account of the origins of this community is given in the *Book of the Covenant of Damascus* (CD), also called the *Zadokite Work*. This work has been known since early in the 20th century, when two mediaeval copies, both imperfect, were identified among MSS from the Cairo genizah. The Qumran texts had not long been discovered when it was realized that they came from the same milieu as the *Zadokite Work*, and in fact fragments of the *Zadokite Work* dating from the 1st century B.C. were subsequently found at Qumran.

One of the last scrolls from Qumran to be acquired by Israeli authorities in 1967 is called the *Temple Scroll,* a revised edition of Deuteronomy, its provisions adapted to life in Israel during the last century or two of the temple's existence.

**Date.** The date of the MSS was disputed at first, but it is now generally agreed on paleographical grounds that most of them belong to the period between the 2d century B.C. and the 1st century A.D. A few are older. The paleographical dating agrees reasonably well with the dating of the jars in which the scrolls were placed in Cave 1, and even with the date of the linen in which some of them were wrapped before being placed in the jars (as determined by radiocarbon dating).

An ancient building complex in the vicinity of the caves was excavated between 1953 and 1956. Its ruins had been known to the local Arabs as Khirbet Qumran. It now proved to have been the headquarters of a religious community, almost certainly the community to which the scrolls belonged; moreover, it is the only site that can be identified with an Essene settlement mentioned by the Roman writer Pliny the Elder (d. A.D. 79) in that neighborhood.

One of the principal criteria for dating the phases of occupation of Khirbet Qumran was the evidence of coins found in the course of excavation. There were two main phases of community occupation: the first began before 100 B.C. and continued until about 31 B.C., when an extensive and destructive earthquake is known to have taken place in that region; the second lasted from about 4 B.C. until about A.D. 68, when the place was destroyed by fire, after some fighting. The site was occupied by a Roman garrison between A.D. 68 and 90 and again by insurgents in the second Jewish war against Rome (A.D. 132–135). One of the most impressive features of the two phases of community occupation is the elaborate organization of a plentiful water supply (there is ample evidence of the damage caused to it by the earthquake of 31 B.C.).

**Significance.** The documents reflect the conditions of more than two centuries following the attempt of Antiochus IV (175–164 B.C.) to suppress the practice of the Jewish religion. That attempt provoked a revolt which resulted in the triumph of the Hasmonean family (Judas Maccabeus and his brothers and their descendants), who established a dynasty of priest-kings which endured until the Roman occupation of Judea in 63 B.C. The founders of the community rejected the Hasmoneans' claim to be high priests; in their eyes the high priesthood in Israel belonged exclusively to the family of Zadok, who had been chief priest under Solomon. In Qumran terminology each Hasmonean high priest, from Jonathan (152 B.C.) onwards, is called the "wicked priest," the illegitimate high priest. Their tenure of the sacred office conveyed defilement to all public life in Israel, so the community, led by their chief organizer and instructor, the Teacher of Righteousness, withdrew to the wilderness of Judea. Their objectives were to preserve the laws of purity and to make ready for God's imminent intervention in judgment, when they would be prepared instruments in his hand. After the extermination of the Kittim (that is, the Romans) and the punishment of their own unworthy leaders (the wicked priesthood and its associates), a new age of righteousness and peace would be established under a great priest of the house of Zakok and a military and civil ruler of the house of David.

The Qumran community was probably one branch of the Essene order. Its members were sharply critical of the Pharisees, whom they described as "seekers after smooth things" or "givers of smooth interpretations," because they considered them to be deplorably lax in their pursuit of holiness and purity. They would have been much more critical of Jesus for freely consorting with all types of men and women—especially disreputable types. Their literature provides valuable background material for NT studies and early Christianity as well as for our knowledge of Judaism in the age preceding A.D. 70.

As for the OT, the Qumran documents throw much light on the history of the Hebrew text of that period. They include MSS of Hebrew Scripture 1000 years older than anything of the kind known before 1947. They bear witness to at least three types of Hebrew text current before A.D. 70—first, the type which, in due course, formed the basis of the Masoretic Text; second, the type which underlay the earliest Greek version of the Hebrew Bible (the Septuagint); and third, a type (for the Pentateuch) closely related to the Samaritan Bible.

**Bibliography.** *Texts.* M. Burrows, J. C. Trever, and W. H. Brownlee, *The Dead Sea Scrolls of St. Mark's Monastery* (1, 1950; 2.2, 1951); E. L. Sukenik, *The Dead Sea Scrolls of the Hebrew University* (1955); D. Barthélemy, et al., *Discoveries in the Judaean Desert* (1955ff.); N. Avigad and Y. Yadin, *A Genesis Apocryphon* (1956); Y. Yadin, *The Scroll of the War of the Sons of Light against the Sons of Darkness* (1962); Y. Yadin, *The Temple Scroll* (1983).

*Translations.* A. Dupont-Sommer, *The Essene Writings from Qumran* (1961); G. Vermes, *The Dead Sea Scrolls in English* (2d ed., 1975); T. H. Gaster, *The Dead Sea Scriptures* (2d ed., 1976).

*Studies.* M. Burrows, *The Dead Sea Scrolls* (1955); M. Burrows, *More Light on the Dead Sea Scrolls* (1958); J. T. Milik, *Ten Years of Discovery in the Wilderness of Judaea* (1959); M. Black, *The Scrolls and Christian Origins* (1961); G. R. Driver, *The Judaean Scrolls* (1965); A. R. C. Leaney, *The Rule of Qumran and Its Meaning* (1966); R. de Vaux, *Archaeology and the Dead Sea Scrolls* (1973); F. M. Cross, Jr., *The Ancient Library of Qumran and Modern Biblical Studies* (3d ed., 1967; repr. 1980); G. Vermes, *The Dead Sea Scrolls: Qumran in Perspective* (2d ed., 1982).

MILLAR BURROWS AND F. F. BRUCE

**Dearmer, Percy** (1867–1936). Anglican. Born in London, he was educated at Christ Church College, Oxford. He was rector of St. Anne's, South Lambeth (1891–94); St. John the Baptist, Great Marlborough (1894–97); Berkeley Chapel,

Mayfair (1897); St. Mark's Marylebone Road (1898–1901); and Vicar of St. Mary the Virgin, Hampstead (1901–15). From 1914 to 1918 he was a chaplain to the British Red Cross and from 1919 to 1931 was lecturer in art and professor of ecclesiastical art in King's College, London. He became canon of Westminster (1931–36) and also served there as librarian (1933–36). A leading liturgiologist, he was a major authority in this field and his books are still widely used in these studies. He tried to recall the church to the native English traditions in liturgy and to improve church music. He wrote *Religious Pamphlets* (1898), *The Parson's Handbook* (1899), *Highways and Byways in Normandy* (1900), *The English Liturgy* (1903), *The Server's Handbook* (1904), *The Sanctuary* (1905), *Body and Soul* (1909), *Everyman's History of the English Church* (1909), *Reunion and Rome* (1910), *Fifty Pictures of Gothic Altars* (1910), *The Dragon of Wessex* (1911), *The Ornaments of Ministers* (1911), *Illustrations of the Liturgy* (1911), *Everyman's History of the Prayerbook* (1912, rev. as *The Story of the Prayerbook*, 1933), *The English Carol Book* (1913), *The Art of Public Worship* (1919), *Linen Ornaments of the Church* (1919), *Power of the Spirit* (1920), *Lessons on the Way* (5 vols., 1921–25), *The Church at Prayer* (1923), *Eight Preparations for Communion* (1923), *Sanctuary* (1923), *Art and Religion* (1924), *The Truth about Fasting* (1928), *The Sin Obsession* (1929), *The Legend of Hell* (1929), *A Short Handbook of Public Worship* (1931), *Our National Church* (1934), and *The New Reformation, The Church of England and the Fellowship of Churches* (1934). He edited *The English Hymnal* (1906), *The Necessity of Art* (1924), *Songs of Praise* (1925; enlarged ed., 1931), *Affirmations: God in the Modern World* (1928), *Oxford Book of Carols* (1928), *Songs of Praise for Boys and Girls* (1929), *Songs of Praise Discussed* (1933), and *Christianity and the Crisis* (1933).

*Bibliography.* N. Dearmer, *Percy Dearmer* (1940).

RAYMOND W. ALBRIGHT

**Death of God Theology.** "God is dead" is a slogan used by several different theologians and critics of orthodox Christianity. In the 2d century A.D. Praxeas taught that God (the Father) and the One who died on the cross were so completely unified that God died there (patripassianism). Jean Paul Richter fascinated romantics and promoted atheism with his "Speech by the Dead Christ . . . that there is no God" (1796/97). In 1802 G. W. F. Hegel spoke of the death of God on Good Friday as the key to contemporary religious awareness. More dramatic was the despair experienced by Friedrich Nietzsche at the historical, social, and political manifestation of the church and its desire for power and influence over Western man and contemporary civilization. Of the God of the Western church he wrote in 1882,

"Where is God gone? I will tell you—we have killed him, you and I—we all are his murderers. . . . God is dead. God will remain dead."

Three young American theologians and a sociologist in the 1960s used "God is dead" as the central theme of their published teaching. In 1963 Thomas J. J. Altizer taught the death of God is a historical event: God has died in *our* time, in *our* history, in *our* existence . . . we can know neither a trace of God's presence nor an image of his reality." In 1966 he affirmed that "the first duty of the Christian theologian must be seen as not loyalty to the Church but loyalty to Christ as he is met in the totality of human experience" (*The Gospel of Christian Atheism*, p. 130). Altizer rejected historic expressions of doctrine, community organization, and lifestyle of Western Christian faith to the 20th century and saw contemporary secular culture as the place where God operates. In 1966 his associate, William Hamilton, asserted that technology, not a transcendent object of worship, is the answer to human problems, and that Christian discipleship is to altruistically follow the model of Jesus as a "man for others." Whereas Altizer and Hamilton rejected the worldviews of traditional Christianity on the ground that they are culturally out of date, Paul van Buren criticized the language of Christian theism for being incompatible with empirical standards of what is to count as true or false. His *Secular Meaning of the Gospel* (1965) culled and collated the conclusions of logical empiricists and philosophers of religion, together with Karl Barth's original rejection of natural theology. Van Buren offered a dramatic but naive verdict that religious language is meaningless. Like Hamilton he affirmed the agapeistic moral example of "the historical Jesus." These "God is dead" theologians were extreme propagandists within a wider circle of world-affirming teachers (e.g., Paul Tillich and J. A. T. Robinson) who accepted the split between God and man asserted by Barth and Rudolf Bultmann but who sought to "locate" him not in otherworldly transcendence, but in human society. In 1961 the sociologist Gabriel Vahanian observed that mass church membership in America from 1945 was a human religiosity based on an unconscious idea that the transcendent God is dead.

*Bibliography.* T. J. Altizer, *Mircea Eliade and the Dialectic of the Sacred* (1961); with W. Hamilton, *Radical Theology and the Death of God* (1966); *The Gospel of Christian Atheism* (1967); G. Vahanian, *The Death of God* (1961); P. van Buren, *The Secular Meaning of the Gospel: An Original Inquiry* (1965); W. Hamilton, *The New Essence of Christianity* (1966); K. Hamilton, *God Is Dead: The Anatomy of a Slogan* (1966); J. C. Cooper, *The Roots of the Radical Theology* (1967).

GERVAIS ANGEL

**De Blois, Austen Kennedy** (1866–1945). Baptist. Born in Wolfville, Nova Scotia, he studied at Acadia College; in Europe; at Brown (Ph.D., 1889); and at the Newton Theological Institute.

He was principal, Union Baptist Seminary, St. Martins, New Brunswick (1892–94); president, Shurtleff College, Alton, Ill., (1894–99); pastor of First Baptist Church, Elgin, Ill. (1899–1902); First Baptist Church, Chicago, Ill. (1902–11); First Baptist Church, Boston, Mass. (1911–26); editor, *The Watchman-Examiner* (1926–28); and president of the Eastern Baptist Theological Seminary, Philadelphia, Pa. (1926–36). He wrote *Bible Study in American Colleges* (1899), *The Pioneer School* (1900), *Imperialism and Democracy* (1901), *History of the First Baptist Church in Boston, 1665–1915* (1916), *Life of John Mason Peck, Prophet of the Prairies* (1917), *The Message of Wisdom, Studies in the Book of Proverbs* (1920), *Some Problems of the Modern Minister* (1928), *John Bunyan, The Man* (1928), *Fighters of Freedom* (1929), *Evangelism in the New Age* (1933), *The Church of Today—and Tomorrow* (1934), *The Making of Ministers* (1936), and *Christian Religious Education: Principles and Practice* (1939). He also edited and translated Borelius's *Grundriss der jetzigen Lage in der deutschen Philosophie.*

RAYMOND W. ALBRIGHT

**Declaratory Act.** An enactment by the highest legislative court of a Presbyterian denomination, stating that church's attitude to its confessional standards. The first such act was passed by the Synod of the United Presbyterian Church in Scotland in 1879, and it decreed that ministers and elders of that church would no longer be required to subscribe literally to the Westminster Confession but would enjoy liberty in interpretation in such matters as did not enter into the substance of the faith. The Free Church of Scotland passed a similar act in 1892, and the established Church of Scotland in 1910. In America the Presbyterian Church in the USA adopted a similar measure in 1903.

*Bibliography.* J. R. Fleming, *The Church in Scotland, 1875–1929* (1933).

NORMAN V. HOPE

**Deems, Mervin Monroe** (1899– ). Congregational minister, educator, and author. Born in Baltimore, he studied at Johns Hopkins University, Southern Baptist Theological Seminary, and the University of Chicago (Ph.D., 1928). He was assistant professor of history at William Jewell College (1924–26), assistant professor of history and religion at Carleton College (1928–31), pastor of the Second Congregational Church, Norway, Maine (1932–36), professor of ecclesiastical history and missions at Bangor Theological Seminary (1936–43), professor of the history of early Christianity and missions while a member of the Federated Theological Faculty at the University of Chicago (1953–54), dean and professor of sacred rhetoric at Bangor Theological Seminary (1954–68), and then pastor and interim pastor of several churches in Maine (1968–82). He had served as assistant secretary of the American Society of Church History, and editor of the Chicago Theological Seminary *Register* (1947–54). He remained active in local church ministries in his late 80s, and wrote two books and a number of articles for encyclopedias and journals.

JACK MITCHELL

**Deferrari, Roy Joseph** (1890–1969). Roman Catholic educator and author. Born in Stoneham, Mass., he studied at Dartmouth College and Princeton University (Ph.D., 1915). He was instructor in classics at Princeton (1915–17), head of the department of Greek and Latin at Catholic University of America (1918–49), professor of Greek and Latin (1922–60), dean of the graduate school (1930–37), secretary-general (1937–67), member of the U.S. Educational Mission to Japan (1946), and on the managing committee of American Schools for Classical Studies in Athens.

Among his works are *Some Problems of Catholic Higher Education in the United States* (1963), *A Layman in Catholic Higher Education: His Life and Times* (1966), and *A Handbook for Catholic Higher Education* (1966). He was author or editor of *Selections from Roman Historians* (1916), *Essays on Catholic Education in the United States* (1942), *A Lexicon of St. Thomas Aquinas* (1948–53), *St. Augustine: Treatises on Marriage and Other Subjects* (1955), *A Complete Index of the Summa Theologica of St. Thomas Aquinas* (1956), and *A Latin-English Dictionary of St. Thomas Aquinas* (1960). He translated *Saint Basil* (1926–34); Eusebius Pamphili, *Ecclesiastical History* (1953); St. Cyprianus, *Treatises* (1958), and *Saint Ambrose: Theological and Dogmatic Works* (1963).

H. DOUGLAS BUCKWALTER

**De Foucauld, Charles Eugene** (1858–1916). French soldier, explorer, missionary-monk, and mystic. Cashiered from the army in 1881 for conduct unbecoming an officer, the young aristocrat began his moral regeneration by returning to lead his men in the Sud-Oran campaign and completed it by exploring the closed land of Morocco in 1883/84. His spiritual regeneration was marked by a return to Roman Catholicism in 1886 and subsequent periods as a Trappist monk in France and Syria (1890–97); a hermit in Nazareth (1897–1900); a priest at Beni-Abbès, an Algerian garrison on the edge of the Sahara (1901–5); and finally as a nomadic hermit among the Tuareq, based at Tamanrasset and Asekrem from 1905 until his murder in December 1916.

Advised by his spiritual director, the famed Abbé Huvelin (1838–1910), who pointed him toward the spirituality of Chrysostom, Teresa of Avila, and John of the Cross, Charles saw himself as a "little brother" of Jesus called to live in imitation of Christ, following the Gospels and the French 17th-century focus on the hidden life of Jesus with Mary and Joseph at Nazareth. This vocation seemed to require a life of real rather than merely institutional poverty, and Charles wrote a number of Rules for small contemplative communities that would exist alongside the poor, supporting themselves by manual labor and living rather than preaching the gospel.

Although Charles failed to find followers during his lifetime, his ideas germinated later with the foundation of the Little Brothers of Jesus by René Voilaume in 1933 and the Little Sisters of Jesus by Sister Magdeleine in 1939. Both now exist in small groups worldwide, as do a number of other organizations directly drawing on Charles' spirituality, besides those like the Taizé communities and some Indian ashrams that have developed similar approaches to Christian presence in society, independently.

PHILIP HILLYER

**Deism.** Belief in God as creator, and perhaps as a moral guide and judge, which rejects the claim that God intervenes in the world. Deists deny miracles and special acts of revelation, although they may acknowledge God's immanence in nature or conscience. Deism was widespread in Britain, Europe, and North America in the 17th and 18th centuries, in part because it seemed to many to avoid the sectarian divisions and intolerance that followed the Reformation. It is commonly said to be extinct, but this is far from clear, even though few would be happy with the title, which has become somewhat pejorative.

Historically, deism occupied a precarious middle ground between Christian orthodoxy and atheism or agnosticism. It had something in common with those Christian thinkers who accepted the distinction between natural religion (religion that could be supported by unaided human reason) and revealed religion (religion based on divine revelation). It accepted the former, rejected the latter, and agreed with atheistic freethinkers that institutionalized religion was primitive and destructive at its worst, and at its best did no more than provide moral guidance that the enlightened individual could obtain by reason and conscience without it. Some deists were openly or disguisedly anti-Christian, whereas others said they were Christians who were merely seeking to rid their faith of undesirable traditional accretions.

In Britain, the best-known deists were probably John Toland (1670–1722) and Matthew Tindal (1657–1733). The titles of their best-known works, Toland's *Christianity Not Mysterious* (1696) and Tindal's *Christianity as Old as the Creation* (1730), indicate that they saw themselves as rationalizing the Christian religion rather than as undermining it. The deists' most famous opponent, Joseph Butler (1692–1752), argued in *The Analogy of Religion* (1736) that anyone prepared to accept the reality of God on the basis of reason should nevertheless acknowledge that some of his purposes are likely to be beyond comprehension. He said deists should not pretend to know that God would never intervene in nature or reveal his intentions through miracle or revelation.

In Europe, where orthodoxy was more intolerant, deism was more overtly anti-Christian. Its most illustrious representative was Voltaire (1694–1778). He is famous for the remark that if God did not exist, it would be necessary to invent him; but his thought is fiercely anticlerical and he crusaded for religious tolerance. Jean-Jacques Rousseau (1712–78) wrote a deistic confession in the "Profession of Faith of a Savoyard Vicar," which is part of *Emile*. Rousseau argued against institutionalized religion and saw God as immanent in the individual human conscience. In America, deism had varying but often great influence among the major formative figures of the Revolution, such as Washington, Jefferson, and Franklin. The most famous literary embodiment of it is in Thomas Paine's *Age of Reason* (1794). This book, still widely read, argues for the claims of natural religion, and attacks the OT and NT as full of stories and teachings that cannot reasonably be ascribed to the inspiration of a benevolent God.

The supposed death of deism has been due to the attacks on natural religion in the works of David Hume (1711–76) and Immanuel Kant (1724–1804), and the negative impact of Darwinism on the belief in God's design in nature. In addition, advances in toleration for which the deists fought have made atheism no longer unthinkable.

But its obituaries have been premature. Deism was the source of many attempts to adapt Christian theology to a scientific and secular culture, and positions markedly similar to it are to be found among many liberal theologians. It stirred interest in comparative religion. Some Christians who have been influenced by the study of other faiths have been inclined to follow the classical deists in identifying the core of religion with commitments that do not of necessity include the specifically Christian doctrines of incarnation and Trinity. Deism was also an impetus for higher textual criticism, and it is hard to deny long-term deistic influence on those scholars who see no alternative but to set aside any belief in divine intervention or miracle when assessing the origin or reliability of biblical texts. A substantial discussion of neodeistic Christian thought from an orthodox perspective has recently been written by David Brown, who revives arguments similar to Butler's. A movement with such controversial descendants is hardly dead.

**Bibliography.** E. Cassirer, *The Philosophy of the Enlightenment* (1951); L. Stephen, *English Thought in the Eighteenth Century*, 2 vols. (1876; repr. 1963); P. Gay, *The Enlightenment*, 2 vols. (1966); E. C. Mossner, *Encyclopedia of Philosophy*, 8 vols. (1967), 2:326–36; J. H. Hick *God and the Universe of Faiths* (1974); ed., *The Myth of God Incarnate* (1977); M. F. Wiles, *The Remaking of Christian Doctrine* (1974); D. E. Nineham, *The Use and Abuse of the Bible* (1976); D. Brown, *The Divine Trinity* (1985); T. Penelhum, *Butler* (1985).

TERRY PENELHUM

**De Jong, Johannes** (1885–1955). Ecclesiastical historian, church administrator, and cardinal. Born on the isle of Ameland, Netherlands, he was educated in seminaries at Culemborg and Rijsenburg and ordained in 1908. He continued his studies in history and theology in Rome at the Academy of St. Thomas Aquinas (Ph.D., 1910) and the papal Gregorian University (S.T.D., 1911). He served as vicar at Amersfoort (1911/12), conrector of the mother institution of the Sisters of Our Holy Lady at Amersfoort (1912–14), professor of ecclesiastical history in the seminary in Rijsenburg (1914–31), seminary president (1931– 35), titular archbishop of Rusio and coadjutor to the archbishop of Utrecht (1935/36), archbishop of Utrecht (1936–51), and was elevated to the cardinalate in 1946 with San Clemente at Rome as his titular church. During the Nazi occupation of the Netherlands (1940–45), Archbishop de Jong was the main Roman Catholic proponent of ecclesiastical-religious resistance. For example, the Dutch Catholic episcopate, under de Jong's leadership, forbade its communicants to take part in manhunts organized by the Nazis: for Jews, for labor draftees, and for Dutch veterans threatened with reinternment. De Jong urged noncooperation with the Nazis and Catholics who lost jobs because of civil disobedience were financially supported by the church. He retired in 1951 because of poor health incurred during the strenuous years of the Nazi occupation. De Jong published (with W. Knuif) *Philippus Rovenius en zijn bestuur der Hollande Missie* (1925), and *Handboek voor de Kerkgeschiedenis* (2 vols., 1929–31; 5th ed., in 5 vols., 1962).

**Bibliography.** H. W. F. Aukes, *Kardinaal de Jong* (1956); Werner Warmbrunn, *The Dutch under German Occupation, 1940–1945* (1963); Walter B. Maass, *The Netherlands at War: 1940–1945* (1970).

ROBERT D. LINDER

**De La Bedoyère, Michael** (1900–1973). Roman Catholic writer and editor. After graduating from Oxford he lectured for a year at the University of Minnesota, then became assistant editor of the *Dublin Review* (1931–34), editor of the *Catholic Herald* (1934–62), and *Search Newsletter* (1962–68). His publications include *Christianity in the Market Place* (1943), *No Dreamers Weak* (1944), *Living Christianity* (1954), and biographies of Catherine of Siena (1946), Friedrich von Hügel (1951), Cardinal Griffin (1955), Francis de Sales (1959), and Francis of Assisi (1962). He also edited *Objections to Roman Catholicism* (1964) and *The Future of Catholic Christianity* (1966).

**Delegate, Apostolic.** The title of some representatives of the pope. The nature of their office is described summarily in the *Codex Juris Canonici*, can. 267, par. 2. Apostolic delegates are usually titular archbishops assigned permanently to represent the papal government in its relations with the ecclesial hierarchy of a given country. It should be emphasized that their functions are not of a diplomatic character since they are not accredited to the sovereign of a nation, as nuncios and internuncios are. However, they may have to deal occasionally with political matters, and they are often granted quasi-diplomatic privileges by civil governments. The ordinary duties of apostolic delegates are to ascertain that the laws of the church are observed correctly, to inform the Holy See of the state and progress of the church in their circumscription, to communicate special instructions of the pope to ordinaries and to grant papal dispensations, absolutions, and similar privileges within the limits of their faculties, or to transmit petitions and appeals to the proper Roman agencies. There are actually 23 apostolic delegations, of which five depend on the Congregation of the Consistory, eight on the Congregation for the Eastern Church, and 11 on the Congregation of the Propaganda.

GEORGES A. BARROIS

**Demant, Vigo Auguste** (1893–1983). Anglican theologian. Born in Newcastle upon Tyne, he studied at the universities of Durham and Oxford, and at Ely Theological College before ordination in the Church of England. He served curacies in Oxford and London, and was then successively director of research for the Christian Social Council (1929–33), vicar in Richmond (1933–42), canon residentiary of St. Paul's Cathedral (1942–49), and professor of moral and pastoral theology at Oxford (1949–71). His published works include *God, Man and Society* (1933), *Christian Polity* (1936), *The Religious Prospect* (1939), *Theology of Society* (1949), *Religion and the Decline of Capitalism* (1952), *A Two-Way Religion* (1957), and *Christian Sex Ethics* (1963).

**Democracy.** Literally "rule (Gk. *kratos* ) by the people (Gk. *demos*)." In Abraham Lincoln's words, democracy is government "of the people, by the people, and for the people." Such a definition, however, is not universally accepted. Since many communist leaders regard their governments as democratic, they would likely reject the phrase "by the people" and consider a democratic government to be one that is "for the people." The government of the USA has occasionally been declared not to be democratic on the ground that it is "for Wall Street." Stalin openly acknowledged that his rule was not by the people. Under a move toward a more open society in the 1980s some communist countries moved toward the holding of elections with a choice among candidates and other Western-style democratic reforms. These moves varied with current political and economic realities. In China tentative work toward a more representative government was crushed in a bloody government-student confrontation in June 1989.

The term "democracy" is thus by no means easy to define, and it is commonly employed more as a term of emotional approval than as a description. Democracy might be defined as "a form of government in which sovereignty resides in the people as a whole and is exercised either directly by them or by officers elected by, and responsible to, them," but some reply that such a democracy only exists when sovereignty is directly exercised by the people as a whole. When authority is delegated to elected officials, it is maintained, a republic, not a democracy, exists. Both forms are generally considered democratic, while government without delegation of authority is characterized as "pure democracy."

The relationship between democracy and equality also is debated. It is occasionally denied that Great Britain, for example, is a democracy, although it has representative government based on universal adult suffrage. The democratic principle of "equality before the law" does not extend to the person of the sovereign, and Britain retains some feudal forms and privileges. The French revolutionists emphasized equality (without defining it), and experimented with it in practice, but their experience, and the subsequent instability of French society, showed that they did not succeed in solving the equality problem. Marxist leaders have tended to reject equalitarianism. Democracy requires a large measure of individual liberty; liberty, in turn, requires a degree of equality. The problem governments which want to be identified as democratic face is how to deal with equality. Unrestricted individual liberty is impossible in a social situation, and each governing style must define what parameters it will allow without unleashing anarchy. It cannot be justly admitted that any precise solution of this problem in theory or in practice, is available.

It is generally agreed that an undue restriction of the franchise is undemocratic, but a commonly accepted definition of "undue restriction" has not been achieved. People who regard the protection of property rights as the main or sole function of government have seen no challenge to democracy in restricting the voting privilege to those owning property. Others have proposed restrictions based on education or intelligence. A "racial" restriction is still practiced in some countries. Democracies

have seen no contradiction in restricting the franchise to adult males. Age restrictions have been debated. Assuming that democracy calls for as little restriction as possible, the exercise of the franchise calls for responsibility, and defining who is responsible is often a perilous judgment.

As states become larger, democratic processes also tend to be slow, blundering, and quite wasteful in their proximate operation. It has been judged by some that for this reason alone no true democracy could long survive. Others have felt that democracy can function securely only if power is delegated to a strong central government. Such powers risk the rights of individuals or lesser governmental units and call into question whether such a state may be called democratic. Others have contended that a strong central government is necessary in times of internal or external stress, but that in less pressing circumstances the "emergency powers" should be surrendered.

Democracy attributes to the individual a comparatively high level of mental capacity and moral judgment. At the same time, it is usually recognized that men commonly lack knowledge, wisdom, or moral reliability. In order to succeed, stable democratic governments must provide certain safeguards, negative and positive. Typical of the negative safeguards are the American constitutional system of checks and balances, relatively frequent elections, and, in some instances, provision for referendum and recall. Typical of positive safeguards is the strong emphasis, characteristic of democracies, on free, universal education, freedom of speech and the press, and freedom of assembly.

Such a high evaluation of the individual requires a supporting philosophy. Democracy is not simply a form of government; it is a way of life which makes assumptions about the purpose and worth of an individual. A religious faith must underlie such assumptions. Historically, in ancient Athens and in the modern West, that religious philosophy has prevailingly been a naturalistic humanism. Such a philosophy is itself not stable. The ruin of democracy in Athens is attributed to the abandonment of religious sanctions. Challenges to the stability of the West in the 20th century, including the Nazi and fascist movements, are attributed to the progressive secularization of European and American culture. James Hastings Nichols in *Democracy and the Churches* (1951) sought to show historically that modern democracy has been really at home only where the Reformed branch of Protestant Christianity has been strong. Nichols acknowledged only the Scandinavian countries, prevailingly Lutheran, as exceptions to this generalization, and there he found exceptional circumstances at work. More recently evangelicals such as Peter Marshall and Francis Schaeffer have made similar theses regarding Europe and the USA. There does seem to be a profound affinity between democracy and Christianity. This affinity must not be pressed too far, as some do who, in incautious enthusiasm, appear to teach that the establishment of democracy was the sole or central purpose of Christ's incarnation. Not all forms of Christianity are organized democratically and Christianity can and does work effectively in any form of social organization.

*Bibliography.* Aristotle, *Politics;* Plato, *Laws;* P. Blanshard, *Communism, Democracy and Catholic Power* (1951); L. Smith, *American Democracy and Military Power* (1951); A. Brady, *Democracy in the Dominions* (2d ed., 1952); R. M. MacIver, *Democracy and the Economic Challenge* (1952); A. Ross, *Why Democracy?* (1952); F. Somary, *Democracy at Bay* (1952); M. Einaudi and F. Goguel, *Christian Democracy in Italy and France* (1953); W. H. Riker, *Democracy in the United States* (1953); A. T. Vanderbilt, *The Doctrine of the Separation of Powers and Its Present-Day Significance* (1953); W. Lippmann, *The Public Philosophy* (1955); R. A. Dahl, *A Preface to Democratic Theory* (1956); S. Hook, *The Paradoxes of Freedom* (1962); C. B. Macpherson, *The Life and Times of Liberal Democracy* (1977); P. Marshall and D. Manuel, *The Light and the Glory* (1977), and *From Sea to Shining Sea* (1985); F. Schaeffer, *Is Capitalism Christian?* (1985); J. Eidsmoe, *Christianity and the Constitution: The Faith of Our Founding Fathers* (1987).

ANDREW K. RULE

**Demythologization.** See MYTH IN THE NT.

**Denmark.** A North European monarchy of 43,080 sq. km. (16,633 sq. mi.) surrounded on three sides by water. It has a population of 5.1 million which is comprised of about 4,850,000 Protestants, 20,000 Roman Catholics, 12,500 Muslims, and 7100 Jews (1985). Denmark is essentially a Lutheran country, as is its sole colony on the Faeroe Islands, which enjoy autonomy. Both the universities of Copenhagen and Aarhus have theological faculties.

One of the most influential movements within Danish Christianity is the Inner Mission of the Lutheran Church which led the way in drawing urban people of Copenhagen into the church; its Magdalene Home cares for homeless girls in the capital city. The Church Army carries on active missionary work in the underprivileged areas of the city and country. Since 1878 the YMCA and YWCA have also shared in the social involvement of the Danish Church. A concerted social activity established in 1902 operates under the title of Co-operative Congregational Relief Work (*De samvirkende Menighedsplejer*). It coordinates church provision for the needy. The Copenhagen Church Fund (*Kobenhavns Kirkefond*) was established to build churches in about 1900. As the city grew, some parishes had expanded to 50,000 to 80,000 persons. The church fund provided for the construction of churches, so that no parish should have more than 10,000 and no pastor should be responsible for more than 5000. Within 50 years the Copenhagen Church Fund provided for the construction of 39 churches.

Six major movements distinguish the Danish church from other European Lutheran confessions: (1) the Inner Mission, which combines social action and parish-based evangelism; (2) the books and songs of N. F. S. Grundtvig (1783–1872), which continue to be read and sung, so his higher critical scholarship and sacramentalism continue to influence his Danish church; (3) the Church Center, which was influenced by the philosophical synthesis of J. P. Mynster (1775–1854) and H. L. Martensen (1808–1884); (4) a return to Sören Kierkegaard's teachings and an antihumanistic philosophy fed on the teachings of Karl Barth; (5) the Oxford Group, which arose between the wars and drew into its circle many clergy and laypersons; (6) the liturgical movement called the Oratorians.

Despite the religious affiliation of most Danes, religious practice is minimal. Weekly church attendance in most parishes has fallen to 2 to 4 percent of membership. Among Denmark's small Roman Catholic population about 40 percent go to Mass each week. Only 5 to 7 percent of the Danish people can be classified as evangelical, although on the Faeroe Islands 27 percent of the population claim to be evangelical Christians.

In addition to the Lutheran Church there are several nonestablished free churches. Baptists claim about 6828 adult members, Elim Churches have 5000 members, and there are 4000 pentecostals and 3900 salvationists. Neopentecostal groups grew from 5000 in 1975 to 12,000 in 1985. Several peripheral movements have grown. There are 13,620 Jehovah's Witnesses, 2700 Mormons (1985), and 10,000 practitioners of transcendental meditation (1975). In 1900 there were no Muslims in Denmark. Now there are about 13,000, mainly foreign workers from Pakistan, Turkey, and Yugoslavia.

Although the religious activity of foreigners was largely made illegal in the 1970s, several major evangelistic events have occurred. In 1965 Billy Graham conducted a campaign in Copenhagen which drew total attendances of 67,000 and 681 enquirers. His EURO-70 television relay crusade was also broadcast into Denmark. In 1979 Campus Crusade for Christ conducted "Here's Life Roskilde" mission.

*Bibliography.* E. P. Hartling, *The Danish Church* (1964); D. B. Barrett, ed., *World Christian Encyclopedia* (1982), pp. 262–65.

WAYNE DETZLER

**Denney, James** (1856–1917). Scottish theologian. Born in Paisley, he graduated from Glasgow University, studied theology at the Free Church College, and in 1886 was ordained and inducted to his denomination's East Church in Broughty Ferry. From 1897 he was professor of systematic theology in his former college, but after three years transferred to the chair of NT, a post he held until his death, along with being the college principal for the last two years. He was a warm supporter of his church's merger with the United Presbyterians in 1900 to form the United Free Church, and helped lay the foundations for the more significant union with the national Church of Scotland in 1929. He wrote commentaries on Thessalonians (1892), 2 Corinthians (1894), and Romans (1900). His other works include *The Death of Christ* (1903), *Jesus and the Gospel* (1908), *The Way Everlasting* (1911), and the posthumous *Christian Doctrine of Reconciliation.*

J. D. DOUGLAS

**Depravity.** The witness of Scripture to the depravity of fallen mankind is consistent and pervasive. No more incisive and comprehensive indictment is found than in Gen. 6:5: "The Lord saw how great man's wickedness on the earth had become, and that every inclination of the thoughts of his heart was only evil all the time." The implications respecting the intensity, inwardness, inclusiveness, exclusiveness, and continuousness of the evil are to be distinctly noted. The witness of the Scripture throughout, particularly of our Lord and the apostle Paul (see Mark 7:15–23; John 3:6; Rom. 3:9–15, 8:6–8), is to the same effect. To try to evade the conclusion that depravity is total would be futile. Man as depraved is destitute of all that is well-pleasing to God—"those controlled by the sinful nature cannot please God" (Rom. 8:8); "there is no one who does good, not even one" (Rom. 3:12). And, more positively, man as depraved is in a condition of active enmity toward God and his law—"the sinful mind is hostile to God. It does not submit to God's law, nor can it do so" (Rom. 8:7). This condition is universal (Rom. 3:9–18), a fact no one indicates more plainly than our Lord himself when he says, "Flesh gives birth to flesh" (John 3:6). That which is propagated by human nature is human nature controlled and dominated by sin. It is not proper to speak of degrees of total depravity. But it is necessary to recognize that there are degrees of development and manifestation of this depravity with which all are equally afflicted. It is this fact of depravity that establishes the necessity of regeneration as the only way of appreciating the things of the Spirit of God and of entrance into the kingdom of God (see 1 Cor. 2:14, 15; John 3:3, 5).

*See also* MAN, DOCTRINE OF.

JOHN MURRAY

**Depression, The Churches and the Economic.** The history of economic depressions in the USA shows that, previous to the Great Depression of the 1930s, the general effect of widespread distress has been a contributing cause of an increased interest in religion. Thus the great revival of the late 1850s had a definite tie with the great financial panic of 1857, and the revival reaped its largest results where the depression hit the hardest. The depression of the early 1890s also had a definite effect on the revivals of Dwight L. Moody, J. Wilbur Chapman, and B. Fay Mills. However, contrary to predictions of religious leaders, the depression of the 1930s, the most disastrous depression of modern times, did not drive men to God. That this was true of the larger denominations is demonstrated by a study of membership statistics during and immediately following the depression years.

One of the direct consequences of the Depression was the rapid growth of holiness, pentecostal, and millennial sects throughout the nation. Preaching of premillennialism was stimulated. It has been explained that premillennialism is always a particularly effective doctrine among poor people disastrously affected by depressions. Such doctrines are sometimes called "poor men's doctrines." Seeing little chance for better things in this life, poor people look forward longingly to the second coming of Christ which will put an end to poverty and injustice. Such church bodies held that the sufferings, privations, and catastrophes which accompany depressions are but signs of the last days and indications that the second coming of the Lord is imminent. The rapid growth of these bodies during the Depression years is illustrated by the increase in membership of the Assemblies of God and the Church of the Nazarene. Assemblies membership grew from 48,000 in 1926 to 175,000 in 1937, and Nazarene membership doubled during the same period. Numerous pentecostal and premillennial sects arose during the Depression years, as A. T. Boisen showed in a study of the effect of the Depression on the above sects made in three areas of Indiana.

The Depression had a disastrous economic effect upon all churches. The easy money of the prosperous 1920s stimulated great building programs. Congregations all over the country, especially in the cities, built costly buildings which they were unable to carry financially in the 1930s; there were many foreclosures. Church budgets sharply declined, reducing ministers' salaries and cutting benevolent giving. The episcopal fund of the Methodist Church, for instance, was so depleted that bishops' salaries were cut in half. The enrollment in denominational colleges sharply declined, as did income from gifts and endowments, causing the sweeping dismissal of instructors. The Depression also created new duties for ministers, especially in the area of counseling, due to personal crises created by the Depression. Large churches were compelled to reduce their staffs of paid workers, which increased burdens on the ministers and volunteer workers. Ministers' attitudes toward economic and social questions became more liberal as a result of what they had seen and experienced. This led to the formation of unofficial social agencies in larger Protestant and Roman Catholic bodies.

**Bibliography.** S. C. Kincheloe, *Research Memorandum on Religion in the Depression* (1937).

W. W. SWEET

**Devotional Literature.** Personal writings of inner worship and praise; this rich field of religious writing has become less known in the 20th century. Many religious leaders are acquainted with famous works of doctrine, such as Calvin's *Institutes of the Christian Religion* and Butler's *Analogy of Religion,* but not with the *Prayers and Devotions* of Lancelot Andrewes or the *Pensées* of Blaise Pascal. Those who know the secular writings of Samuel Johnson are unaware that this great lexicographer left at least 100 prayers of profound and enduring devotional appeal.

A striking feature of devotional classics is the degree to which they are independent of time and changing social conditions. Old books about science seem quaint, works about theology are easily dated, but writings that reveal the depths of religious experience are remarkably the same through the generations.

There are four major classifications within the devotional writing genre. First, perhaps the largest group, are the strictly biographical writings. Eminent examples include *The Confessions of St. Augustine, The Autobiography of Richard Baxter,* Cardinal Newman's *Apologia pro Vita Sua,* and various Quaker *Journals,* notably those of George Fox and John Woolman. Such authors bare their soul, showing how God has dealt with them. This is preeminently the literature of witness.

Second are admonitions and spiritual counsels. Men who have lived wisely and well share their wisdom, sincerely and humbly, with all who listen. Examples are such writings as Thomas à Kempis's *Imitation of Christ,* Jeremy Taylor's *Holy Living* and *Holy Dying,* and William Law's *Serious Call to a Devout and Holy Life.*

Third are scattered thoughts, with the work of Pascal as the best-known and loved example. On pieces of paper of all sizes Pascal wrote down ideas just as they came, leaving to others after his early death the task of organization. This is powerful writing, chiefly because it is unadorned and never toned down for publication. Some of S. T. Coleridge's writing is similar.

Fourth are actual prayers, devotional literature at its most intense level. The prayers of Bishop Andrewes, who helped translate the Authorized Version of the Bible, have long been loved by those fortunate enough to own copies. At most other points Christian literature is *about* religion; the best devotional literature is comprised of books *of* religion.

D. ELTON TRUEBLOOD

**Dewey, John** (1859–1952). Philosopher and educator. Born in Burlington, Vt., he studied at the University of Vermont and Johns Hopkins (Ph.D., 1884). He taught philosophy at Michigan (1884–88; 1889–94); Minnesota (1888/89); Chicago (1894–1904; director of the school of education, 1902–4); and at Columbia from 1904. A Hegelian who applied Darwinian science to sociology and education, his philosophy of "progressive education" continues to influence teachers and schools in methodology and philosophy. In both areas he stressed the human need to think experimentally, manipulating and experiencing environment. In education this developed into the theory of learning by doing. His teaching methods, which permitted students to select subjects appealing to them, first were put into practice at the University of Chicago High School. Soon "new" schools and "progressive" methods were announced, tried, and sometimes grossly distorted. In his later years Dewey said that progressive education had been distorted into a belief that he sanctioned unlimited freedom from discipline. His major contributions to education include such ideas as that the child is more important than the subject matter, that learning must be related to its time, that schools should be democratic and not authoritarian in spirit, that discipline comes from within and not from without, that learning can be taught by experience, that education must aim at developing character, and that an adequate philosophy of education must underlie the teaching process. In his system the teacher is a social servant maintaining proper social order and securing right social growth. Many religious leaders and educators feel that his materialistic and humanistic approach to the individual has been inimical to religion and that because he failed to take religion seriously into his purview his educational philosophy is inadequate. Like his educational methods, his deterministic philosophy has been taken to extremes in modern humanism. Among his books are *Psychology* (1886), *Leibnitz* (1888), *Critical Theory of Ethics* (1894), *Study* (1894), *School and Society* (1899), *Studies in Logical Theory* (1903), *How We Think* (1909), *How We Think* (1910), *Influence of Darwin on Philosophy and Other Essays* (1910), *German Philosophy and Politics* (1915; rev. ed., 1942), *Democracy and Education* (1916), *Reconstruction in Philosophy* (1920), *Human Nature and Conduct* (1922), *Experience and Nature* (1925), *The Public and Its Problems* (1927), *The Quest for Certainty* (1929), *Art as Experience* (1934), *A Common Faith* (1934), *Liberalism and Social Action* (1935), *Logic: The Theory of Inquiry* (1938), *Culture and Freedom* (1939), and *Problems of Man* (1946).

*See also* INSTRUMENTALISM.

RAYMOND W. ALBRIGHT

**De Witt, John** (1842–1923). Presbyterian educator. He studied at Princeton University, studied law for a year, and then theology at Princeton and Union seminaries. He held pastorates at Irvington-on-Hudson, N.Y. (1865–69), Central Congregational Church, Boston (1869–76), and Tenth Presbyterian Church, Philadelphia (1876–82). He was professor of church history at Lane Theological Seminary (1882–88); professor of Christian apologetics at McCormick Theological Seminary (1888–92); and professor of church history at Princeton Theological Seminary (1892–1912) and a member of the Presbyterian Church, USA, General Assembly committees that drafted the revisions to the Westminster Confession of Faith (1901–2) and the Book of Common Worship (1903–6). While modestly maintaining anonymity, he was editor-in-chief of the *Princeton Theological Review* (1903–8), and was a trustee of Princeton University (1904–19).

*Bibliography.* F. W. Loetscher, *Princeton Theological Review* 22 (1924): 177–234.

L. A. LOETSCHER

**Dewolf, L. Harold** (1905–1986). Methodist minister, educator, and author. Born in Columbus, Nebr., he graduated from Nebraska Wesleyan and Boston University (Ph.D., 1935). After ordination (1926), he pastored in Nebraska and Massachusetts (1922–36). He began as fellow and then professor of philosophy (1933–44) at Boston University, and then professor of systematic theology at Boston University School of Theology (1944–65). From 1965 to 1972 he was dean and professor of systematic theology at Wesley Theological Seminary (Washington, D.C.). Moving to Florida Southern College (Lakeland), he was distinguished visiting professor until his death. A contributor to religious, philosophical, educational, and psychological journals, his books include *A Theology of the Living Church* (1953), *The Enduring Message of the Bible* (1960), *Galatians: A Letter for Today* (1971), and *Eternal Life: Why We Believe* (1980).

JACK MITCHELL

**Dialectical Theology.** The methodological approach of neo-orthodox theology, which seeks insights in the apparent paradoxes of faith, rather than in propositional statements. Dialectic is as old as philosophy, for philosophy does not exist, except as assertion, until the possibility of another point of view is acknowledged. In his friendly discussions in the marketplace Socrates carried it to a high level, being convinced that truth could be found—in contrast to the Sophists who generally argued merely for the sake of argument. Socrates fought not for victory but for the truth. Among his last words (*Phaedo* 91) were, "Pay little attention to Socrates, but much more to the truth." For Aristotle, dialectic is contrasted with metaphysic, because of its tentativeness, and with sophistic, which is the pretense of knowledge without the reality (*Meta.* 2, 1004. b.); and whereas disciplines like mathematics can give certainty, there is much in human experience which allows only discussion. Abelard, who "preferred the strife of disputation to the trophies of war," by his *Sic et Non* won a permanent place for reverent but thorough inquiry into matters of faith, on the ground that "by doubting we are led to inquire, by inquiry we perceive the truth." Every question can be argued for or against. He thus anticipated the "modern dialectic" in which Aquinas followed the practice of Aristotle, whose works had been newly translated into Latin. The dialectic of Immanuel Kant was chiefly concerned with the problem of knowledge and its limitations. He was the "old pedant guarding the frontier against the trespassing of reason." For Georg Hegel the very nature of reason is the thinking out of contradiction; and to think out contradiction is to abolish it. The higher truth contains and fulfils the contradictions out of which it emerges; the conclusion is a "both . . . and."

At this point Søren Kierkegaard joins issue. Like Karl Marx with dialectical materialism, he reverses Hegel's system. For "both . . . and" he substitutes "either . . . or." The "yes" is not derived by thinking out the implications of the "no." That must be given as something new. The positive is not discovered by reason, but is received through revelation. Truth is subjective. There is no clear-cut argument in the human intellectual treasury that will lead to God. There is urgent need of God, because every instant is wasted when the person has him not. Dialectical contradiction brings the individual's passion to despair and helps the sufferer, by means of "the category of despair" which is faith, to embrace God, taking a leap of passionate faith into the face of objective reason.

Thus the dialectical theology, notably connected with the name of Karl Barth, denies the existence of an analogy of being (*analogia entis*) and the doctrine that creation is a similitude of God's being. Fr. Przywara, in *Polarity*, a reply to Barth, indicates the limits of the application of the idea as given in the Fourth Lateran Council, 1215, cap. 2, *Inter creatorem et creaturam non potest tanta similitudo notari, quin inter eos major sit dissimilitudo notanda*. Barth made use of the phrase *finitum non capax infiniti*, indicating that since we are still *in via* and not *in patria*, we can make no theological pronouncement that can claim finality, but must proceed by statement and counterstatement. In Augustine's words, our life on earth is a watchnight between dusk and dawn; between our Lord's ascension and his return. (The organ of the theological group, which included Emil Brunner, Friedrich Gogarten,

Edward Thurneysen, and others, was called *Between the Ages*.) Indeed the situation is much worse than that. We are not only finite; we are sinners. And Barth soon replaced *finitum non capax infiniti* with *homo peccator non capax Verbi Divini*. Every human thought concerning what we are contains its opposite in the thought of what we are not. We know the image of God only because we see its degradation in our sinfulness; and the glory of nature is evident because of its opaqueness. This is the negative standpoint taken by Barth in *Das Wort Gottes und die Theologie* (1925). The thought, however, can be applied in a positive direction to indicate that we would not know our unredeemed condition if we were not within the redemption; and we should not, as Pascal said, be seeking for God at all, if we had not already found him.

Dialectical theology thus takes paradox and makes it the pattern of theological thinking. The dialectic theologian speaks of "the timeless entering time," or "the beyond that is within," or "eternity as a present possession." But in his *Dogmatics* (ET, by G. T. Thomson, 1955: xii) Barth explicitly rejects the claim to present the case for "dialectical theology." He wishes to be indebted to no human philosophy and to form no "school"; so that a better name for the movement is the "theology of crisis" or, perhaps best, "theology of the Word." Like all Calvinism, it seeks to build a system of theology under the dominating idea of the absolute sovereignty of God. God is "wholly other" from creation. Therefore we can learn about him, not by interpreting our experience, but by turning away from it to revelation. Our human values do not reveal God; but we are driven to him by ignorance, vanity, poverty, infirmity, depravity, and corruption.

It is natural, therefore, that the Calvinistic heritage of the dialectical theology should be strongest in the account it gives of natural theology. Calvin directs attention to the self-revelation of God in nature, in history, and in human experience, but he makes the qualification, "if Adam had remained innocent" (*Inst.* 1.2.1.). To an innocent mind, the works of God in nature and in providence would speak of God's essential attributes; but to perverted humanity no such message is conveyed. True, the image of God was not altogether blotted out (1.15.4), yet what remained was wretched and insufficient. The faculty for perceiving God in creation and in history is not just weakened; it is lost. Must we not go, for insight into the nature of God, to the revelation through which God undertook the work of restoring the fallen world and redeeming sinful man? Must we not go, in fact, to the history of Israel, the Scriptures, and the life and death and resurrection of Jesus? In our subjective response to this revelation God's grace becomes a "yes" which affirms instead of the world's "no," which

has taken away our authentic humanity. The confrontation of the Word's "yes" and the world's "no" is the crisis every person must face.

The controversy between Karl Barth and Emil Brunner on natural revelation can be followed in its earlier stages in *Natural Theology* (ET by P. Fraenkel, 1944, 1962). Its later stages are to be seen in Barth's *Die Kirchliche Dogmatik* II.1 and Brunner's *Revelation and Reason* (ET by O. Wyon, 1946). Barth seeks to draw a distinction between "natural theology" and "Christian natural theology"; between a doctrine of revelation through creation which can be gathered from mere observation of the created world and one which can be gathered only from the Scriptures. Brunner believes this introduces a confusion. Created things bear the divine stamp upon them; they do not first have to acquire it through the historical revelation given in Christ. We simply cannot see the truth of these analogies without the historical revelation in Christ and the faith which it creates. In this debate Barth is defending an important element in Reformed theology. The analogy of being does not give a sound basis for the construction of a natural theology; for when man is left alone with these analogies he will certainly interpret them in a pantheistic sense. But it is foolish, Brunner considers, to go further and say that the analogies only exist because of faith. It would be better to say that they become visible only to faith. (See further C. C. J. Webb, *Religious Experience*; H. Kraemer, *The Christian Message in a Non-Christian World*; N. Macnicol, *Is Christianity Unique?*)

According to the dialectical theology, God is always Subject. When the person presumes to treat of him as Object—as we necessarily do both in preaching and in theology—we are looking on him as the other member of an "I-object" relation and not, as we ought, as the one who addresses us. Therefore we are bound to fall into paradox and contradiction. Necessarily, the Word of God as objective revelation is not a real issue in the subjective values of dialectical theology. For this reason the primary battleground of the modernist controversy from the 1930s on has involved the implications of dialectical analysis. Brunner most clearly explained the problem from a dialectic viewpoint. While Barth always tried to retain a *sola Scriptura* stance, Brunner observed dryly that "The Devil would pass the most rigorous examination in dogmatic and Biblical theology with distinction." His point is that, under a dialectical theology, the Christian faith can take root only in the heart which recognizes its need as so desperate that an experience regarding Christ can conquer reason and make it free to serve. Revelation only has meaning if it serves that existential purpose.

*See also* CRISIS, THEOLOGY OF.

*Bibliography.* K. Barth, *Epistle to the Romans* (1933); *The Doctrine of the Word of God* (1936); and *Church Dogmatics* (1936–81); E. Brunner, *Revelation and Reason* (1946); *The Divine Imperative* (1947); *Man in Revolt* (1947); *The Mediator* (1947); *The Christian Doctrine of God* (1950); *The Christian Doctrine of Creation and Redemption* (1952); C. Kegley, ed., *The Theology of Emil Brunner* (1962); C. Van Til, *Christianity and Barthianism* (1962); C. Brown, *Karl Barth and the Christian Message* (1967); J. Macquarrie, *Twentieth Century Religious Thought* (1973); S. Sykes, ed., *Karl Barth—Studies of His Theological Methods* (1979); P. Avis, *The Methods of Modern Theology* (1986).

E. P. DICKIE

## Dibelius, Friedrich Karl Otto (1880–1967).

Lutheran bishop of Berlin and Brandenburg following World War II. Born in Berlin, he studied at the University of Berlin (Ph.D., 1901) where he was greatly influenced by Adolf von Harnack. Dibelius was ordained to the Lutheran Church in 1906 and served pastorates at Crossen-on-the-Oder, Danzig, Lauenburg, and Berlin. In 1925 he was appointed general superintendent in East Prussia and then bishop in 1945. He became a member of the council of churches in 1921 and served on the central committee of the World Council of Churches (WCC) beginning in 1948. During the 1930s and 1940s, he was one of the foremost opponents of the Nazi state in Germany, which resulted in his suspension from office and incarceration on several occasions. He was a major leader in the reconstitution of the Lutheran Church in Germany following the war. Most of the members of his diocese lived behind the Iron Curtain during that period and he remained a consistent and outspoken critic of communist totalitarianism, particularly from 1949 onward. He functioned not only through the German church, but he also expressed his concerns through his extensive opportunities as a speaker in various international forums of WCC. He insisted that genuine faith and piety depend on human freedom and that the state must observe proper limitations. His ministry was characterized by intellectual integrity and great personal courage. Dibelius authored numerous books and articles on church history, social ethics, and Christian devotional practices.

FRED D. LAYMAN

## Dibelius, Martin Franz (1883–1947).

Lutheran. Born in Dresden, Saxony, he studied at the universities of Neuchatel, Leipzig, Berlin, and Tübingen (Ph.D., 1905). He taught at Berlin (1908–15) and was professor of NT in Heidelberg (1915–47). He was a pupil of Adolf von Harnack and Hermann Gunkel; he was founder of the *formgeschichtliche Schule* of biblical criticism, the form-critical method which calls for the treatment of Gospel accounts as separate units, theorizing that the present composition of the NT was made at a time subsequent to the writing of the accounts themselves. Among his many pupils, the best known was Ernst Lohmeyer. He wrote *Die*

*Geisterwelt im Glauben des Paulus* (1909), *Die urchristliche überlieferung von Johannes dem Täufer* (1911), *Die Formgeschichte des Evangeliums* (1919), *Geschichte der christlichen Literatur* (1926), commentaries on the small epistles of St. Paul, *Evangelium und Welt* (1929), *Paulus* (1951), and *Aufsätze zur Apostelgeschichte* (1951).

*See also* FORM CRITICISM.

MRS. M. DIBELIUS

## Dickie, Edgar Primrose (1897– ).

Scottish theologian. Born in Dumfries, he graduated from Edinburgh and Oxford. After ordination in the Church of Scotland he ministered in Lockerbie (1927–33) and Edinburgh (1933–35) before appointment as professor of divinity in the University of St. Andrews, a post he held until 1967. A decorated officer in World War I, he took charge of his church's work in France in World War II, and was later appointed chaplain to the queen. His gift of humor was reflected in various children's books and in contributions to *Punch*. His theological publications include *Spirit and Truth* (1935), *Revelation and Response* (1938), *The Obedience of a Christian Man* (1944), *The Fellowship of Youth* (1947), *God Is Light* (1953), *Thou Art the Christ* (1954), *A Safe Stronghold* (1955), *The Unchanging Gospel* (1960), and *The Father Everlasting* (1965).

J. D. DOUGLAS

## Dickinson, Clarence (1873–1969).

Presbyterian church musician and professor of church music. Born in Lafayette, Ind., Dickinson studied at Miami (Ohio) University Preparatory School and Northwestern University (Mus. Doc.). A founder of the American Guild of Organists (1896), Dickinson was organist and director of music at the Church of the Messiah (1892–98), St. James Episcopal Church (1902–9), the Sunday Evening Club, Orchestra Hall (1906–9), all in Chicago, and later for many years at the Brick Presbyterian Church of New York City. He was the founder and conductor of numerous choral societies in the Chicago and New York areas. He was also a lecturer in church music and director of sacred music at Union Theological Seminary in New York (1928–45). Dickinson edited hymnals for the Presbyterian Church, USA in 1933 and for the Evangelical and Reformed Church in 1941. Dickinson's published works include Storm King Symphony for Organ (1919), The Coming of the Prince of Peace, a Nativity Play in Ancient Christmas Carols (1919), Book of Antiphons (1920), Historical Organ Recital Series (vol 1, 1920; vol. 2, 1939), Sacred Solos for Voice (1930), *German Masters of Art* (1914), *Excursions in Musical History* (1917), *The Troubadours and Their Music* (1920), *The Technique and Art of Organ Playing* (1921), *Choirmasters Guide* (1924), *A Treasury of Worship* (1927), *Choir Loft and Pul-*

*pit* (1943), and *Sacred Choruses Ancient and Modern.*

R. Milton Winter

**Dicks, Russel L.** (1906–1965). Methodist chaplain, lecturer, and author. Born in Stillwater, Okla., he graduated from the University of Oklahoma and Union Theological Seminary. Following ordination in 1933, he served as Protestant chaplain at the Massachusetts General Hospital, Boston (1933–38), chaplain at the Presbyterian Hospital, Chicago (1938–41), and the Wesley Memorial Hospital, Chicago (1944–48), associate professor of pastoral care, Duke University Divinity School (1948–58), and until his death as director of the Central Florida Counseling Center in Orlando. He was cited by the National Council of Churches of Christ in America for outstanding work for the welfare of the people. He served as the general editor of the Westminster Pastoral Aid books; was on the editorial board of *Pastoral Psychology,* and was the founder and editor of *Religion and Health.* He authored numerous books and manuals concerned with pastoral ministry to the sick, including *Meditations for the Sick* (1938), *When You Call On the Sick* (1940), *Thy Health Shall Spring Forth* (1943), *Pastoral Work and Personal Counseling* (1944), *Comfort Ye My People* (1946), and *My Faith Looks Up* (1950).

Jack Mitchell

**Diem, Hermann** (1900– ). Lutheran theologian. After studies at Tübingen and Marburg (1910–23), he was a pastor in the state church of Württemberg, a part-time lecturer at Tübingen, and a leading member of the Confessional Church. He was a well-known writer on Kierkegaard, and theologically stood close to Karl Barth. That stance changed significantly in 1957 when, at his inaugural lecture as professor of systematic theology at Tübingen, he sought to build a bridge between Barth and Bultmann—and did so with what Barth called "marked originality of character." In the 1959 foreword to his *Dogmatics,* Diem stated that he had "cut through all sorts of fixed positions" in order to help "those who will not or cannot simply adhere to one of the major schools of theological thought and . . . subscribe like disciples to the teaching of one master and read nothing else." His earlier writings, which reflect his interest also in practical theology and church organization, include *Warum Textpredigt?* (1939), *Restauration oder Neuanfang in der evangelischen Kirche?* (1946), *Der Abfall der Kirche Christi in die Christlichkeit* (1947), *Amerika-Eindrücke und Fragen* (1949), *Grundfragen der biblischen Hermeneutik* (1950), and *Theologie als kirchliche Wissenschaft* (1951).

Charles M. Cameron

**Dietrich, Christian** (1844–1919). Leader in the Evangelical National Church of Germany. He was rector of the Evangelical Daughter-Institute at Stuttgart. As president of the old pietistic associations of Württemberg, he worked for their close unification. Open to the influences of the younger Free Church movements of evangelicals, nevertheless he worked to preserve the same heritage of the Swabish pietism and to make it influential within the groups of evangelicals inside the National Church of the larger Germany. He was editor of *Philadelphia,* a periodical of the national church evangelicals.

Reinhold Kuecklich

**Dillenberger, John** (1918– ). Minister, educator, and college president. Born in St. Louis, he graduated from Elmhurst College, Union Theological Seminary, and Columbia University (Ph.D., 1948). After ordination in the United Church of Christ (1943), he served as a chaplain in the U.S. Navy (1943–46). He began teaching as a tutor at Union Theological Seminary (1947/48), and continued as an instructor at Princeton University (1948/49), assistant and associate professor at Columbia University (1949–54), professor of theology at Harvard Divinity School (1954–58), professor of systematic and historical theology at Drew University (1958–62), professor of historical theology and dean of graduate studies at San Francisco Theological Seminary (1962–64), professor, dean, and president at Graduate Theological Union, Berkeley, Calif. (1964–78), and professor and president of Hartford Seminary (1978–83). His written works include *God Hidden and Revealed* (1953), *Perceptions of the Spirit in Twentieth Century American Art* (1977), *The Visual Arts and Christianity in America* (1984), *A Theology of Artistic Sensibilities* (1986), as well as edited selections of Luther's (1961) and Calvin's (1971) works.

Jack Mitchell

**Dillistone, Frederick William** (1903– ). English theologian. Born in Sussex, he graduated from Oxford, trained for the ministry at Wycliffe Hall, Oxford, and was ordained to a curacy in the diocese of Portsmouth in 1928. He lectured at various theological colleges: Wycliffe Hall, Oxford (1924–31) and the theological college at Saharampur in India (1931/32). He was professor of systematic theology, Wycliffe College, Toronto (1938–45), vice-principal of the revived London College of Divinity (1945–47), and professor at the Episcopal Theological School, Cambridge, Mass. (1947–52).

Thereafter he served the Anglican cathedral in Liverpool, England, as canon and chancellor (1952–56) and dean (1956–63). He was appointed fellow and chaplain of Oriel College, Oxford (1964–70). His books as a theologian and biographer are his most important contribution to the Church of England. Publications include *The Significance of the Cross* (1944), *The Holy Spirit in the Life of Today* (1946), *The Structure of the Divine Society* (1951), *Jesus Christ and His Cross* (1953), *Christianity and Symbolism* (1955), *The Christian Faith* (1964), and *C. H. Dodd: Interpreter of the NT* (1977). He was joint editor of the *Westminster Study Bible*.

NOEL S. POLLARD

**Diocese.** The geographical area within which an ecclesiastical leader exercises episcopate authority over churches (*see* EPISCOPACY). The word originates from the ancient Greek for the process of administering a home, a city-state, or finance. The 1st-century B.C. Roman politician Cicero applied it to smaller territorial areas than provinces, the standard Roman units of government. The 5th-century Christian writer Apollinaris Sidonius used it of a bishop's area of control. The earliest bishops had sees which might be coextensive with cities. But with Diocletian's secular division of the Roman Empire into 12 dioceses (c. 293) and the later involvement of bishops in state affairs, the word "diocese" replaced "parish" to denote a bishop's territory in the Western Church. In the 20th century the changes in boundaries for units of local government have confused traditional diocesan boundaries so that the custom of maintaining bishops with sole pastoral responsibility for a geographical area has often been impractical.

GERVAIS ANGEL

**Disciples of Christ.** Variously known as the Disciples and the Christian Church, this denomination adopted "Christian Church (Disciples of Christ)" as its official name in 1968. All of these names and variants are used to identify institutions and publications, such as *The Disciple*, the monthly magazine of the denomination, Texas Christian University, the largest institution of higher education related to the group, and the Division of Overseas Ministries of the Christian Church (Disciples of Christ). Members of the denomination most often refer to themselves as Disciples or members of the Christian Church.

A mainline Protestant denomination numbering one million members in the USA and Canada, the Disciples have an inclusive membership policy and participate in the ecumenical movement. Persons join the Disciples by a simple confession that Jesus is the Christ, the Son of the living God, linked with the declaration that they accept him as Lord and Savior, followed by baptism or transfer of membership from another denomination. Disciples have historically practiced believer's immersion as baptism. Some congregations do not recognize any other form as baptism and require persons transferring from other denominations who have not been immersed as believers to be baptized as a condition of membership. The decided trend among Disciples congregations is to recognize the baptism of other denominations, regardless of form.

The Disciples is a member of the National Council of Churches (NCC), the World Council of Churches, and the Consultation on Church Union (COCU). They have contributed numerous leaders to the ecumenical movement, including Jesse Bader, who was head of evangelism in NCC, and Paul Crow, who served as general secretary of the Consultation on Church Union. In recent years Disciples have entered bilateral conversations with the Roman Catholic and Russian Orthodox churches and the World Alliance of Reformed Churches. Disciples are also involved in local and regional ecumenical organizations.

The Disciples as a movement first identified itself as "Reformation of the Nineteenth Century." This movement resulted from the 1830s union of two frontier American groups: the Christians and the Reformers. The Christians, led by Barton W. Stone, separated from the Presbyterians over what they perceived to be the use of the Westminster Confession rather than the Bible as the test of fellowship. Desiring to proclaim that the unity of Christ through the Holy Spirit is manifested in the visible church, they chose to be known only as Christians and to accept no standard for faith and practice but the Bible. The Reformers, led by former Presbyterian Alexander Campbell (1788–1866), separated from the Baptists in a similar controversy involving the use of confessions. This call for church union by rejecting extrabiblical standards was an attempt toward unity through restoration of what Campbell believed to be the divinely authorized "ancient order" of the church revealed in the Scriptures. While continuing to work for Christian unity 20th-century Disciples have largely abandoned the restoration principle on the grounds that it is based on a faulty understanding of the character of the biblical witness and that it has failed to produce church union. Disciples share their 19th-century heritage with two other groups, the Churches of Christ and the Christian Churches, which continue to seek Christian union according to the restoration principle.

Disciples practice a covenantal polity that is neither congregational, presbyterian, nor episcopal. Rather, the church is understood as "expressing itself" in congregational, regional, and general manifestations. Since each manifestation is a gathering of believers in the name of Jesus Christ, each is "the church" and contributes in its own way to the ministry of the whole.

Polity is characterized, under the lordship of Christ, by self-government and by rights and responsibilities appropriate to its tasks. Congregations have the task of ordering their life and witness. Each selects its own ministers and determines the basis of membership. Regions, comprised of members in a geographic area (usually a state or group of states), have the tasks of extending the Christian mission in their region, nurturing ministers and congregations, and relating to the worldwide mission of the denomination. Regions typically work through committees and employ one or more regional ministers. They authorize ordination to the ministry in accord with policies developed by the general manifestation.

The general manifestation, comprised of all Disciples in the USA and Canada, represents the whole denomination and maintains national and world ministries. Governed by a general assembly made up of all ordained ministers and representatives selected by the congregations and regions, the general manifestation works through administrative units responsible for publishing, ecumenical relationships, assistance to institutions of higher education related to the denomination, benevolent agencies, assistance in the construction of church facilities, financial support of regional and general ministries, a historical society, pension and health care programs for employees of the denomination, and home and overseas missions. The general assembly authorizes church union negotiations with other denominations.

Disciples are distinguished among mainline Protestants by the weekly observance of the Lord's supper and the practice of electing nonprofessionally educated elders from the congregation to share with the minister in administering the supper.

*Bibliography.* W. E. Tucker and L. G. McAllister, *Journey in Faith* (1975); J. O. Duke, *What Sort of Church Are We?* (1981); W. Baird, *What Is Our Authority?* (1983); D. N. Williams, *Ministry among Disciples* (1985); C. M. Williamson, *Baptism: Embodiment of the Gospel* (1987).

D. NEWELL WILLIAMS

## Discipline, Church.

This term is used in two senses, one relating to the nurturing regulation of church members, the other to correction aimed at restoration of fellowship and the guarding of body purity. In earlier times almost every branch of the church had its Book of Discipline, or some other means of regulating beliefs, conduct, and worship. Today most of this lies in abeyance, although conservative evangelical bodies have become more active in its exercise. Churches have had corrective measures for admonition, punishment, or expulsion of members who broke the laws of God and the church, based mainly on Matt. 18 and Paul's counsel to the Corinthians. Seldom today does any local body discipline a member, even for gross iniquity. In the late 20th century secular courts have ruled that churches may be actionable for public rebuke, even in cases of gross immorality. There was a growing opinion that private conduct was not church business. Occasionally the church at large rebukes or silences a clergy in cases where the person is deemed to disturb church unity or teach doctrines not in keeping with the church's position. While church discipline is warranted and commanded in both OT and NT, the best discipline is nurture, in which each congregation takes loving measures to "discipline" her members, especially the young, in training them for Christian life and service.

ANDREW W. BLACKWOOD

## Dispensationalism.

A method of biblical interpretation first systematically formulated in the 19th century by John Nelson Darby (1800–1882), dynamic leader of the Plymouth Brethren. Darby's ideas captured the imagination of large numbers of evangelicals, pervaded late 19th-century millenarianism in Britain and the USA, and became a prominent element in 20th-century American fundamentalism. Dispensationalism was spread and institutionalized through the popular Scofield Reference Bible (1909; rev. ed. 1917, 1967), the numerous lectures and writings of James M. Gray and Lewis Sperry Chafer, and the influential Dallas Theological Seminary in Texas (founded by Chafer), which requires all faculty and graduates to subscribe to dispensational theology.

Disillusioned with the contemporary church and convinced of its apostasy, Darby developed an elaborate philosophy of history based on biblical prophecy. He divided all history into separate eras or dispensations (from Lat. *dispenso*, "to weigh out, to administer as a steward," which translates Gk. *oikonomía*, "rule or management of the household"), each of which contained a different order by which God worked out his redemptive plan. The sixth age, in which he believed himself to be living, the age of the church, would, like all preceding periods, end in failure because of humanity's sinfulness. Darby departed from previous millenarian teaching by asserting that Christ's second coming would occur in two stages: (1) an invisible "secret rapture" of true believers could happen at any moment, ending the great "parenthesis," or church age, which began when the Jews rejected Christ; (2) followed by the literal fulfillment of OT prophecies concerning Israel and of NT prophecy regarding the great tribulation. Christ's return would be completed when he established a literal 1000-year kingdom of God on earth, manifest in a restored Israel.

Dispensationalism is built on the concept of divine stewardship (Eph. 1:10; 3:2, 9; Col. 1:25), the teachings of human depravity and God's sovereign grace, a premillennial understanding of Scripture, the principle of progressive revelation

(God unveiled truth over time in stages of revelation), and the hermeneutical principle of the literal interpretation of the Bible, including the belief that every biblical figure of speech should, if practical, be interpreted literally. With these theological presuppositions and this hermeneutical principle, the dispensationalists distinguish between God's program for Israel and his program for the church. The church is seen as beginning on the day of Pentecost, and promises made to Israel in the OT have not yet been fulfilled.

According to Darby's American disciple, C. I. Scofield (1843–1921), a dispensation is "a period of time during which man is tested in respect of obedience to some great revelation of the will of God." Christian teaching traditionally has identified two biblical economies or dispensations (law and grace), but Scofield and other dispensationalists have identified as many as seven: (1) innocence—continuing to the expulsion from Eden (Gen. 1:28–3:13); (2) conscience or moral responsibility—which continued to the flood (Gen. 3:22–7:23); (3) human government (in which God delegates his authority to human agencies)—which lasted until the call of Abraham (Gen. 8:20–11:9); (4) promise (the test of Israel's stewardship of divine truth)—which extended to the giving of the Law (Gen. 12:1–Exod. 19:8); (5) the Law (disciplinary correction)—lasting until the death of Christ (Exod. 19:8–Matt. 27:35); (6) the church (the dispensation of the Holy Spirit)—which will continue until Christ's return (John 1:17; Acts 2:1); and (7) the millennial kingdom (the thousand-year reign of Christ)—continuing until to the eternal state (Eph. 1:10; Rev. 21:4).

Nondispensationalists have pointed out that dispensationalism is of recent origin and appears to represent a departure from historic evangelical eschatological interpretation. They also criticize dispensationalists for selectively relegating some NT Scriptures, such as the Sermon on the Mount, to the next age. In addition, critics claim that the dispensationalists rest their basic beliefs on a few scriptural passages taken out of context and, therefore, their theology is arbitrary and unbiblical. Many biblical scholars question the dispensationalist conclusion that the kingdom will be a racial, nationalistic Jewish one.

*Bibliography.* O. T. Allis, *Prophecy and the Church* (1945); G. E. Ladd, *The Blessed Hope* (1956); C. N. Kraus, *Dispensationalism in America: Its Rise and Development* (1958); C. B. Bass, *Backgrounds to Dispensationalism* (1960); E. R. Sandeen, *The Roots of Fundamentalism: British and American Millenarianism, 1800–1939* (1970); C. C. Ryrie, *Dispensationalism Today* (1973); G. M. Marsden, *Fundamentalism and American Culture: The Shaping of Twentieth-Century Evangelicalism, 1870–1925* (1982).
ROBERT D. LINDER

**Divination.** The discovery and foretelling of the will and operation of the supernatural. It assumes a realm of spirit: for example, the *mana* of some religions—not an entity, but a dynamism which permeates the universe; the *ch'i*, perhaps, of the Chinese, an item in their classical tradition; and, to some degree, the *pneuma* of Western thought and the *anima* of Hinduism. It assumes spirits and gods also, in great numbers, whose will and works are subject to interpretation by signs and acts of theirs and whose meanings may be "read" by diviners.

On man's part, charms are much in use as guarantees of divine behavior favorable to the wearers. New Age "channeling" and horoscopes are tools for the examination of wisdom and fortune with reference to marriage, agriculture, travel, and appropriate times for ceremonies in some cultures. "Mediums" gained popularity in the 19th-century Western spiritualist movement. In the New Age movement Eastern forms of mystic divination enjoyed popularity.

Divination is of low or high degree, but places emphasis on man's own responsibility for the avoidance of evil and adherence to the good.

*Bibliography.* C. H. Troy, *Introduction to the History of Religions* (1913); R. H. Lowie, *Primitive Religion* (1924), H. L. Friess and H. W. Schneider, *Religion in Various Cultures* (1932); D. K. Clark and N. L. Geisler, *Apologetics in the New Age* (1990).
JOHN CLARK ARCHER

**Divine Decrees.** The decrees of God have reference to that which God willed to be and therefore to all that is comprised in the works of creation and providence. They do not denote, however, the actions of God in creation and providence but only the eternal counsel of God respecting all that comes to pass in these spheres. Decrees are distinct from their execution—they are eternal, the execution is temporal. Eternity as predicated of the decrees is to be distinguished from eternity as it applies to God himself. The decrees arise from God's sovereign will, but God did not will himself to be. Decrees are not to be identified with the commandments of God—decrees refer to what God has determined to come to pass, commandments to what he has revealed to be the rule of thought and action for rational and responsible creatures. Events in contravention of divine command are nevertheless embraced in the divine decree (Acts 2:23).

JOHN MURRAY

**Divine, Father.** See FATHER DIVINE'S PEACE MISSION.

**Divine Healing.** The supernatural cure of disease through faith in God. Faith healing may be similarly defined but commonly is associated more directly with the work of faith healers who claim the personal gift of healing. Numerous examples of healing through divine intervention appear in both the OT and NT and in the history of the church (e.g., 2 Kings 5:14; 20:5–7; Mark 1:30–34, 40–42; Luke 7:2–10; 8:43–48; John

9:1–7; Acts 3:1–10; 9:32–41; 14:8–10). Healing is one of the gifts which the Holy Spirit gave to the church (Mark 16:17–18; 1 Cor. 12:28–30). Believers are urged to seek healing (James 5:14–15).

Many of the most influential early church fathers indicate that the practice of healing continued in the postapostolic church (Irenaeus, Justin Martyr, Tertullian, Augustine). During the course of the development of the medieval Roman Catholic tradition, the rite of prayer for the sick was shaped by its sacramental theology into the ritual of extreme unction, and was reserved mainly for the moment of death. Smaller, more evangelical groups, such as the Waldensians and some of the monastic orders, continued to incorporate a more active use of healing in their group practices.

The Reformers' study of the practices of the early church in their reaction to medieval Catholicism led to a revival of divine healing. Both Lutherans and Anglicans took up its use again in the established Protestant churches. However, the expansion of the doctrine within the Reformed traditions was retarded by the common belief that the operation of the charismatic gifts within the church had ceased with the death of the apostles and the establishment of the canon of Scripture. John Wesley, the Anglican founder of Methodism, showed interest in divine healing. Although he too believed that the operation of the charismatic gifts had ceased generally, he did allow for their contemporary extraordinary demonstration. The main renewal of the teaching, however, arose within revivalistic Protestantism in the 19th century during the same period in which the medical community was locked in a battle between homeopathic healing and invasive therapy. It was also the time in which new psychosomatic theories were being developed, and the rise of Christian Science provided an alternate interpretation to the contemporary preachments of either medicine or religion.

The healing revival in America was directly rooted in a new healing impulse among pietistic cells within the Reformed churches in southern Germany and Switzerland. The faith cure work of Dorothea Trudel in Mannedorf, Switzerland, and the teachings of Swiss pastor Otto Stockmayer and German pastor Johann Blumhardt (1805–80) were among the more influential European models for the movement in America. The work of Trudel especially influenced physician Charles Cullis, an Episcopal convert of the American holiness revival. He made divine healing a prominent feature of the faith cure home he founded in Boston in the mid-19th century. He maintained the institutions on the faith principles of his contemporary George Müller (1805–98) and of August Francke (1663–1727), the prominent 17th-century leader of the German pietist institutions at Halle.

Cullis's work quickly became the center of a rising interest in divine healing within the American holiness revival. The Willard Tract Repository, the publishing arm of Cullis's faith cure home, printed holiness and healing literature. John Inskip, a Methodist minister and most prominent leader of the holiness camp meeting movement, testified to being healed through Cullis's prayers. Cullis also strongly influenced William E. Boardman, the Presbyterian higher-life advocate, to give himself to pioneering healing ministries in England and Europe. In 1881 Cullis's faith conventions inspired Albert B. Simpson to incorporate divine healing within the basic doctrinal commitments of the emerging Christian and Missionary Alliance movement. A. J. Gordon (1836–95), the prominent Baptist pastor and revivalist of the higher-life movement, promoted faith healing. J. Alexander Dowie (1847–1907) established his famous religious societal experiment at Zion, Ill., at the end of the century within this context.

Three main doctrinal positions developed out of the extensive debate over the teachings that such movements promoted within the churches. Most of the ecclesiastical establishment of the time maintained the traditional Reformed stance that declared that the completion of the biblical canon marked the end of the need for miracles and gifts. A second and more aggressive position was taken by most leaders of the Methodist holiness revival. They allowed and even expected divine interventions such as miracles of healing by the prayer of faith; but at the same time they maintained that how and when God responded to such prayers for divine healing was a part of his providential working. Illness was not caused by God but allowed and used by God for the formation of the spiritual life. Prayer for divine healing by such advocates was always closed with the petition, "Nevertheless, Thy will be done." The mid-20th-century revival of healing in some Episcopal circles also represents such a mediating stance. The third and most radical healing theology, however, maintained that in the atonement Christ not only assured believers of present forgiveness of sins, but freedom from all physical illnesses; therefore, to append "Thy will be done" to a prayer for physical or mental healing is as much in error as it would be to add such a petition to a prayer for salvation from sin. Pentecostal and charismatic groups generally have accepted this position. Most contemporary faith healers espouse some variation of this view. They maintain that if one is not healed, the primary problem is a lack of faith, because the work of Christ has already assured us of God's will and purpose in relation to illness.

***Bibliography.*** E. Front, *Christian Healing* (1954); M. Kelsey, *Healing and Christianity in Ancient Thought and Modern Times*

(1973); D. Harrell, Jr., *All Things Are Possible: The Healing and Charismatic Revivals in Modern America* (1975).

MELVIN E. DIETER

**Divine Science.** *See* NEW THOUGHT.

**Divini Redemptoris.** Encyclical of March 19, 1937, in which Pope Pius XI condemns Bolshevist communism for its materialism, it conceptions of man and society, and its atheism and terrorism. The Catholic Church has a better plan for reconstructing the social order. "There would be neither Socialism nor Communism today if the rulers of the nations had not scorned the teachings and material warnings of the Church." Spiritual renewal and Catholic Action are recommended as countermeasures.

**Bibliography.** Latin text in *Acta Apostolicae Sedis*, vol. 29: 65–106; ET in J. Husslein, *Social Wellsprings* (1942), 2:341–74.

THEODORE TAPPERT

**Divino Afflante Spiritu.** Encyclical of Pope Pius XII, issued on September 30, 1943, on the best means of promoting the study and diffusion of Scripture. It outlines a complete program of scientific investigation of the Bible, starting from the necessity for the exegete to be thoroughly acquainted with the principles of modern linguistics and the methods of textual criticism. It stresses the importance of patristic, ecclesiastical, and profane literatures for a theological interpretation of the sacred text. While acknowledging the necessity of taking into account the literary patterns and formulas used by the inspired writers, it recommends some caution in appraising the bearing of the same upon the substance of the biblical message.

**Bibliography.** Original text in *Acta Apostolicae Sedis*, vol. 35: 297–325. ET in J. E. Steinmueller, *A Companion to Scripture Studies* (1946), 1:460–83.

GEORGES A. BARROIS

**Divorce.** The loosening or dissolution of the marital bond. The term has had a number of meanings. In ecclesiastical law the decision that there had never been a marriage, now called a *decree of nullity*, was known as divorce *a vinculo matrimonii*, and what is now called *judicial separation* (in which the marriage continues to exist) was known as divorce *a mensa et thoro* (from bed and board). The third and now universal meaning of the word (and the one used in this article) is the dissolution of a valid marriage with freedom to contract another marriage.

All marriage (as distinguished from concubinage) is intended to be lifelong. This does not mean that it is indissoluble, but it is not entered into with the intention of dissolving it. Differing societies have varied divorce customs and rules which span the spectrum between complete freedom, where either husband or wife can leave at will, and strict indissolubility of the marriage.

The great majority of societal customs fall between the two. However, among most peoples divorce is far less frequent than the laws allow.

In ancient Israel liberty of divorce was allowed only to the husband. It was to be based on the ground of "something indecent" in the wife and involved a written document (Deut. 24:1). In ancient Athens divorce was free to the husband and almost as free to the wife, but the latter was protected by her dowry, which had to be returned on her divorce. The marriage laws of Rome in the 1st century A.D. allowed full freedom to the husband or to the wife to withdraw consent to the marriage. Divorce and remarriage were frequent in ancient Rome. Pompey was married six times, Caesar four, and Jerome relates that he had seen in Rome a man living with his 21st wife, who herself had had 22 husbands.

From the beginning the Christian community disapproved of divorce, but its rules have varied in strictness. The Eastern Church has allowed divorce, but not more than once. In the early days of the church in England the *Penitential* of Theodore of Canterbury allowed considerable liberty for divorce and remarriage. In the Roman Empire the law allowing divorce by mutual consent on numerous grounds remained till the time of Justinian. Thus the strict indissolubility of marriage cannot be regarded as Catholic tradition. However, it became the rule for Christians in the Western Church throughout the Middle Ages and is still the canon law of the Roman Catholic Church. The Reformers taught that marriage was not a sacrament but "a worldly thing" (Luther). Since divorce and remarriage were permitted in Scripture for something unseemly, divorce was believed to be permitted to Christians. John Milton stressed that, since God had permitted divorce in Deuteronomy, it could not be sinful in itself. The Church of England, however, continued the indissolubility of marriage in all circumstances and also swept away many of the grounds of nullity of the medieval church which had provided relief from the strictness of indissolubility (an Act of the Reformation Parliament denounced the evils which arose from the ease of establishing nullity of a marriage). A large number of members of the Church of England from the Reformation on (including Archbishop Cranmer and the Caroline divines J. Cosin and H. Hammond) approved of permitting divorce on the grounds of adultery and malicious desertion (and some also for cruelty and other serious causes). However, the Canon of 1604 was not altered but fell into desuetude. Divorce was obtainable by act of Parliament after matrimonial offense had been proved in the ecclesiastical court. From the time of the Reformation to 1857, 317 marriages in England and 146 in Scotland were dissolved by act of Parliament. In 1857 a divorce court was established by the Parliament of the United Kingdom to provide availability of divorce to the populace who were not able to afford the promotion of a private act of Parliament. In 1969 Parliament enacted provision for divorce for the irretrievable breakdown of the marriage.

Absolute indissolubility of marriage has tended to lead to infidelity and a lowering of the community's standards. However, divorce is condemned by Jesus and Christian ethics in general. The ideal is that it not be even thought of by married people, for love and the enjoyment of the marriage relationship normally deepen as time goes on. But the ideal is different from a strict law. Divorce is not the cause of the breakdown of the marriage but its result. Yet easy divorce may prevent a troubled marriage from being retrieved.

***Bible Teaching on Divorce.*** Gen. 2 tells how in marriage a man is to leave his father and his mother to be united to his wife so that they become one. The implication is clear; marriage is a lifelong, monogamous, exclusive basis of the family. Experience confirms that the mutual tender emotions evoked by being in one another's company in marriage bonds the marriage into a permanent relationship. The breaking of this unity is painful emotionally, and the Scripture makes clear that it is against the ethical standard of the Creator (Mal. 2:14–16). Yet the Lord permitted divorce if the husband found something indecent in his wife. If he divorced her he must give her a written document to that effect (Deut. 24:1). He could never remarry her (Deut. 24:4). When Jesus was questioned as to what might be included as grounds for divorce, he replied with the principle that if a man or a woman divorced their spouse and married again they committed adultery (Mark 10:2–12). Luke 16:18 reports that Jesus extended this description of adultery to include a man who married a divorced woman. Jesus explained that God's permission for divorce was the result of humankind's sinfulness; the godly person ought not to divorce and remarry if he (or she) has been given the nature that can take this path (Matt. 19:8–12). The one ground for divorce given by Jesus is unchastity (Gk. *porneia*), although he does not fully explain what this might entail.

Paul, instructing the Corinthians, repeated Jesus' prohibition of husband and wife separating but made the interesting addition that if a wife left her husband she ought not to remarry but be reconciled to her husband. He added a second comment, that if an unbelieving partner leaves the marriage, the other is not "bound"—is presumably free from the command of the Lord which Paul had just quoted. By implication this would allow the abandoned partner to enter a new marriage.

From the biblical account it would appear that Christian ethics may allow divorce at least for the grounds of adultery and desertion. There may well be more grounds in practice under the Deut. 24:1 principle of indecency, which may correspond to Jesus' ground of *porneia*. Underlying these permissions is the human hardness of heart. Men and women are created as they are physically and emotionally in order that their relationship in marriage should last as long as life. It would seem that the construction of Jesus' absolute prohibition of divorce in Mark and Luke has the character of his absolute statement, "Ask and you shall receive," which is true and yet the rest of Scripture makes clear that there are conditions (as in 2 Cor. 12:8–9; James 4:3). Jesus was not contradicting or correcting the OT Scripture, but protecting it from the abuse of interpretation which made the lawful permission for divorce the means for lustfully taking a new wife. Such divorce counted for nothing in God's eyes.

D. BROUGHTON KNOX

## Dix, George Eglinton Alston (1901–1952).

Anglican Benedictine monk known as Dom Gregory. He was educated at Merton College, Oxford, and Wells Theological College. Ordained in 1924, he was history lecturer at Keble College, Oxford, before joining the Nashdom community in 1926. His special interest was the development of Christian thought and its manifestation in liturgical uses. He was sharply critical of certain Anglican movements toward reunion. He wrote *The Apostolic Tradition of Hippolytus* (1937), *A Detection of Aumbries* (1942), *The Shape of the Liturgy* (1944), and contributed to *The Apostolic Ministry*.

F. W. DILLISTONE

## Dobschütz, Ernst (Adolf Alfred Oskar Adalbert) Von (1870–1934). NT scholar. He

was professor of NT at Halle (1913 until his death in 1934; rector, 1922/23) and exchange professor at Harvard (1913/14). His work assumed an international character when he succeeded C. R. Gregory in the task of assigning official numbers to newly found MSS of the NT (published in *ZNW*) and when he became director of a projected *Corpus Hellenisticum zum NT* (see *ZNW*, 34 [1925]: 43ff.).

Representative publications include *The Eschatology of the Gospels* (1909), *Die Thessalonischerbriefe, Meyers Kommentar* (7th ed., 1909), *The Apostolic Age* (1910), *The Influence of the Bible on Civilization* (1914), *Nestle's Einführung in das griechische Neue Testament* (4th ed., 1923), *Der Apostel Paulus*, 2 vols. (1926–28), *Das Neue Testament* (1927), *Das Apostolicum in biblisch-theologischen Beleuchtung* (1932), *Die Bibel im Leben der Völker* (1934). He edited (with O. von Gebhardt) *Die Akten der Edessenischer Bekenner, Gujas, Samonas, und Abibos* (*TU*, 37, 2, 1911).

**Bibliography.** E. Stange, ed., *Die Religionswissenschaft der Gegenwart in Selbstdarstellungen* (1928), 4: 31–32 (with picture and full list of publications); obituary notice, *JBL* 54 (1935): vi.

BRUCE M. METZGER

**Doctrinal Preaching.** The pulpit interpretation of Christian truth for practical ends. Preaching may be doctrinal directly or indirectly. At its core every message ought to have such a truth as God's providence. Doctrinal "preaching" began with the prophets. "Jesus came preaching the kingdom." The apostles preached doctrine, as did many of the early fathers. The Reformation brought a return to the practice. Such preaching calls for mastery of the truth, clarity of thought, sturdiness of structure, simplicity of style, and ability to meet human needs. Instead of confining a sermon to abstractions about God's omniscience, omnipresence, omnipotence, and transcendence, the effective preacher normally deals with one such truth in thought-forms of today. He may teach about God as Light, Life, Love, Spirit (Person), or Father. Literature about doctrinal preaching was for a time scant and disappointing, but in the 1970s and 1980s there was a resurgence of evangelical interest on the subject. Reprints of great sermons and better homiletic instruction in many seminaries was aimed at revitalizing the pulpit's biblical and doctrinal fidelity. Because of present doctrinal concern in seminaries, the church should continue to witness a revival of such preaching, to alleviate "religious illiteracy."

ANDREW W. BLACKWOOD

**Dodd, Charles Harold** (1884–1973). British biblical scholar. Born in Wrexham, North Wales, he graduated from Oxford in 1906. In the following years he spent a semester at Berlin, pursued research in ancient history and archeology there and at Magdalen College, Oxford, and, turning to theology, became a student at Mansfield College, Oxford. Ordained in 1912, he served as minister of the Independent or Congregational Church at Warwick (1912–15, 1918/19). Recalled to Mansfield College, he taught NT there until 1930, when he became professor of biblical criticism and exegesis at Manchester University. In 1935 he was elected Norris-Hulse professor of divinity at Cambridge. He retired in 1949 and was active during the following years as director of the New English Bible (1970). He was made a Companion of Honour by Queen Elizabeth in 1963 in recognition of his achievements. His published works include *The Authority of the Bible* (1928), *The Bible and the Greeks* (1935), *Parables of the Kingdom* (1935), *The Apostolic Preaching and Its Developments* (1936), *History and the Gospel* (1938), *Gospel and Law* (1951), *According to the Scriptures* (1952), *The Interpretation of the Fourth Gospel* (1953), *Historical Tradition in the Fourth Gospel* (1963),

*The Founder of Christianity* (1970), and commentaries on Romans (1932) and the Johannine Epistles (1946).

**Bibliography.** G. B. Caird, *Proceedings of the British Academy* 60 (1974): 497–510; F. W. Dillistone, *C. H. Dodd: Interpreter of the NT* (1977).

F. F. BRUCE

**Dohnavur Fellowship.** An evangelical and interdenominational faith mission in South India. Founded in 1901 by Amy Carmichael (1867–1951), it was the first mission supported by the Keswick Convention. After brief service in Matsuye, Japan (1893/94), Amy Carmichael went to India in 1895 and remained there until her death. She was initially engaged in itinerant village evangelism, but from 1901 onwards became increasingly concerned about the fate of young girls who had been dedicated to temple prostitution, and others who had become homeless. By 1904 Amy—known as Amma (mother)—and her Indian colleagues were caring for 17 children; by the 1940s the fellowship at Dohnavur, a village in the Tirunelveli (Tinnevelly) district of Tamil Nadu, numbered more than 900. The story of the fellowship's growth is told in the prose, verse, and photographs of Amy Carmichael's many books, especially *Gold Cord* (1932) and *Gold by Moonlight* (1935), and by Frank Houghton's biography, *Amy Carmichael of Dohnavur* (1953). The community numbers 500 girls and women of all ages today. It looks after 200 girls in danger of exploitation or abuse, provides schools for its own members and for the children of Indian missionaries, has its own farms, workshops, and a cottage industry project for mentally and physically handicapped women and girls, operates a hospital, and maintains its founder's concern for village evangelism.

PHILIP HILLYER

**Dominican Republic.** *See* WEST INDIES.

**Dominicans.** An Order of Preachers (*Ordo fratrum Praedicatorum*), often described also as Black Friars or Jacobins. It was founded by Dominic (1170–1221), an Augustinian canon secular who saw the need for a body of well-educated preaching friars. Legalized in 1216, it adopted Augustinian rules, and added some features Dominic adapted from the Norbertines, a German preaching community. Its constitution, adopted in 1220, included the obligation to renounce the ownership of property, but the emphasis upon evangelical poverty was less pronounced than among the Franciscans. The order was not permitted to own land, although it might acquire monasteries and churches. By the 14th century it had 21 provinces and 562 houses. The second order, for women, originated in the convents of La Prouille and of St. Sixtus in Rome and received from Dominic the Augustinian rule in

1217, again with additions. At its peak this order counted some 350 houses. The third order, founded during the career of Dominic, was open to men and women, and was given a rule in 1285 by the general Munio de Zamora. Its members are not restricted to the cloisters.

The greatest of the scholastics, Thomas Aquinas (1224–74), and his versatile teacher, Albertus Magnus, are but two of many distinguished theologians among Dominicans of the later Middle Ages. While their involvement in staffing the Inquisition brought unpopularity, Dominicans have made notable contributions in other fields, not least as missionaries. Their services in art and the advance of learning have been considerable. The Reformation greatly reduced the number of their houses, and many were confiscated under the secularizing policy of Joseph II (1780–90), which was emulated in Germany, and the Revolution suppressed the order in France for many years.

In the early years of the 20th century there were about 300 houses with some 3000 members. Under Pope Leo XIII, a great admirer of Thomas Aquinas, the order once more assumed importance by its influence on theological learning. There have been four Dominican popes: Innocent V, Benedict XI, Pius V, and Benedict XIII.

Missionary work is still a significant feature of Dominican activity. In the late 1980s they were working in about 60 countries or territories with a missionary force numbering 7275.

J. D. Douglas

## Dooyeweerd, Herman (1894–1977).

Dutch theologian. Born in Amsterdam, he graduated from the Free University there, and was assistant director of the Kuyper Institute, The Hague (1922–26), before appointment as professor of the philosophy of law in the Free University (1926–65). His major work, *A New Critique of Theoretical Thought* (4 vols., 1953–58), challenged the "pretended autonomy" by which philosophical thought asserts self-sufficient independence from divine revelation. He attacked speculative metaphysics, insisting that true knowledge of God and self-knowledge come from the working of God's Word and Spirit in the heart. Accepting the concepts of general revelation and common grace, he held that neither provides any foundation for natural theology based on man's unaided reason. Moreover, orthodox theology was no guarantee of true spiritual understanding; the latter comes through submission of the whole person to the message of Holy Scripture concerning "redemption by Jesus Christ." Acceptance or rejection of this was "a matter of life and death to us, and not a question of theoretical reflection." In 1935 Dooyeweerd cofounded the journal *Philosophia Reformata*, and was prominent in the establishment of the Association for Calvinistic Philosophy (later called Christian Philosophy). From 1948 he was a member of the Royal Dutch Academy of the Sciences.

Charles M. Cameron

**Doubt.** A state of uncertainty as to the truth or reality of something, or as to the reliability of a person. It may involve a factual and disinterested recognition that sufficient evidence is lacking, but there may also be a more positive element resulting in either a wavering of opinion or a tendency to accept or reject without strong conviction. Especially if the object is a person, the tendency to rejection may take the form of suspicion, mistrust, or fear.

The term is sometimes employed in a purely descriptive sense, expressing or implying no evaluation of the attitude of the doubter. An example is the statement (Acts 2:12) that some of those who witnessed the outpouring of the Holy Spirit were "amazed and perplexed." More commonly, however, some evaluation of the attitude of doubt is indicated or implied.

In the Scriptures, and in the Christian tradition, the evaluation of doubt is usually unfavorable. "The Lord will give you an anxious mind . . ." (Deut. 28:65) is one of the disabilities which is predicted for failure to observe the Law of God. Jesus censured Peter for doubting (Matt. 14:31). To deal with the doubts of Thomas, the evidence which he demanded is presented, but he is commanded "Stop doubting and believe" and others are commended who shall believe without such evidence (John 20:24–29). In Christian ethics, doubt has historically been classified as doublemindedness—a sin—for which the cure is prayer of confession and petition (James 1:5–8). The reason is that the Christian life is one of humble reliance on God through Christ. All the fruits of a God-controlled life flow from trust in him (Gal. 5:22). Doubt, lack of such trust, frustrates such a life. Christianity also maintains that man was made by God for such a life of trust, that refusal to trust was an element of the first sin, and that our failure to trust is the fruit of sin.

But doubt has also been highly commended, especially when it involves a refusal to accept anything on the basis of untested authority and is a first, negative, step in the quest for truth. This sort of positive, epistemological doubt was characteristic of Socrates and much of Greek philosophy, and the search for a reliable authority for discerning truth empowered the Bereans (Acts 17:11), John Wyclif, Jan Hus, and the later Reformers to doubt of ecclesiastical authority and turn to Scripture as God's objective revelation. In a corollary movement doubt of any belief not founded on precise observation and sound reasoning founded modern science. Descartes became the "father of modern philosophy" through his methodological determination to doubt everything that could be doubted, always convinced, however, that thus he would reach an indubitable foundation for his system.

As an epistemological method, therefore, doubt has value so long as it honestly seeks an infallible source of truth. The Christian ethical system finds that foundation only in Scripture.

ANDREW K. RULE

**Dougherty, Dennis Joseph** (1865–1951). Cardinal. Born in Honesville, Pa., he studied at Saint Mary's College, Montreal; at Saint Charles Borromeo Seminary, Overbrook, Pa., and at the North American College, Rome. Ordained to the priesthood in 1890, he served on the faculty of Saint Charles Borromeo Seminary (1890–1903). He was appointed successively bishop of Nueva Segovia (1903), and of Jaro (1908), in the Philippine Islands. He was called back to the USA as bishop of Buffalo, N.Y. (1915), and he became archbishop of Philadelphia (1918). He was created cardinal on March 7, 1921, under the pontificate of Benedict XV.

GEORGES A. BARROIS

**Douglas, Lloyd Cassel** (1877–1951). Minister and novelist. Born in Columbia City, Ind., he studied at Wittenberg College and the Hamma Divinity School, Springfield, Ohio. He served in various pastorates from 1903 to 1933, including the Luther Place Memorial Church, Washington, D.C. (1908–11); the First Congregational Church, Ann Arbor, Mich. (1915–21); the First Congregational Church, Akron, Ohio (1921–26); the First Congregational Church, Los Angeles, Calif. (1926–29); and St. James United Church, Montreal (1929–33).

In 1929 he published *Magnificent Obsession*, the first of a number of novels with religious themes, many of which found a very large audience. These include *Forgive Us Our Trespasses* (1932), *Green Light* (1935), *The Robe* (1942), and *The Big Fisherman* (1948). He spent his later years in Los Angeles and Las Vegas.

Douglas attributed his narrative ability to his childhood experience of riding out with his father, Alexander Jackson, on pastoral calls and hearing him tell stories of his rural parishioners.

AMOS N. WILDER

**Douglass, Harlan Paul** (1871–1953). Congregational pastor and leader. Born in Osage, Iowa, he studied at Grinnell College. Following Congregational pastorates in the Midwest, he was for 11 years executive secretary of the American Missionary Association. He was editor of *Christendom* (1938–48). He was part-time consultant in the newly organized Department of Research and Survey of the National Council of the Protestant Episcopal Church from 1951.

**Doukhobors.** A sectarian, spiritualistic group that emerged in Russia during the 18th century. Their name means "spirit wrestlers." They were severely persecuted by the state at the instigation of the Russian Orthodox Church. In 1898 many Doukhobors emigrated to Canada where they were promised land and the freedom to practice their religion according to their traditions.

In Canada they established themselves across the prairie provinces and are particularly strong in central British Columbia where they have their headquarters. Today there are several Canadian Doukhobor groups as well as smaller groups in Russia and parts of South America. The Canadian groups are generally peaceful and respected citizens. However, a radical breakaway sect called "The Sons of Freedom" has given Canadian Doukhobors an extremist image through their arson and their public nudity when arrested or taken to court.

They interpret Christian doctrines in terms of manifestations of human nature. Thus the Trinity is seen as light, life, and peace, to which may be linked by human memory, understanding, and will. Orthodox critics intended their name to suggest that they resisted, or fought with, the workings of the Holy Spirit. The Doukhobors accepted the name but argued that indeed they wrestled by means of the Holy Spirit, striving to serve God. Doukhobor teachings about the Holy Spirit probably derive from Shamanistic beliefs found in Russian folk culture.

In many ways the Doukhobors are similar to Quakers and historically they both influenced and were guided by Leo Tolstoy (1828–1910) who helped them emigrate to Canada. Doctrinally they believe in continuing revelation, and argue that the life of Jesus is a model for human spiritual development so that all people may become sons of God. They tend to be pacifists who are inclined to communal living and an agricultural way of life which stresses a simple lifestyle. The group is, however, changing and many Doukhobors are gradually integrating into Canadian society as a rather odd form of charismatic Christianity.

*Bibliography.* The Book of Discipline; F. C. Conybeare, *Russian Dissenters* (1921); G. Woodcock and I. Avakumovic, *The Doukhobors* (1968).

IRVING HEXHAM

**Drama, Religious.** Virtually all traditions of drama have origins in religious rite or celebration. Some of the earliest Egyptian texts for funerals and occasions of state are plays. Ancient Hindu drama still celebrated in Kerala, India, and the earliest examples of Japanese or Chinese theater, are religious, as is the so-called *Passion Play of Abydos*, which covers the death, burial, and resurrection of the god Osiris, as a directive for community religious observance. The shamanistic masked performances of native American,

Siberian, and Inuit peoples reenact primary myth. The earliest actors were priests, and the "action" essentially liturgical.

Early Greek drama reflected liturgical forms, including the statutory 50-member chorus, an altar of Dionysus at center stage, preference for mythic plots over innovative stories, and the use of masks. In Greece the move from ritual to theater was associated with Thespis, an innovative choral leader who gave a separate voice and impersonation to the god or hero and scripted dialog between this figure and the chorus. Thespian productions in Greece could be tragic (from *tragos*, a sacrificial goat) and expiatory—the idea behind Aristotle's notion of catharsis as an experience of release enjoyed by the audience. They could also be comic (*comos*, a revel) and anesthetic, as typically associated with extravagant festivals. Even in later Greek secular drama the fact that female roles were played by male actors hinted at ancient religious taboo.

The earliest record of religious drama in Christendom is the *Christos Paschon*, written in Greek sometime after the 5th century. It is a pastiche, in that it brings the styles of Euripides and others to a telling of the biblical story. It seems to be designed as a type of dramatic sermon which was later to emerge in the West. It falls far short of the oldest Greek passion play, which survives in a 13th-century Vatican MS. Roman Christians were enjoined by Augustine, Jerome, and others to eschew the degenerate Roman theater of the 4th century, and the professions of *historio* (actor), *pantomimus* (male dancer, mime), or *mimus* (mimic actor) were explicitly forbidden to Christians in the 5th and 6th centuries. It is unsurprising, then, that later religious drama was not inspired by Roman theater.

In European Christendom, the most dramatic spectacle sanctioned was the celebration of the Mass itself. Pageantry accompanied the Eucharist celebration for a high feast day and the doctrine of the real presence of Christ's body intensified the emotion within the worship experience. The Mass had always an evident narrative structure, retelling the story of salvation in precis and in more depth through the liturgical cycle of the year. Allegorical interpretation of the Mass, reflected in vestments and sacred objects as well as action, began with the liturgical writer Amalarius of Metz (c. 780–c. 850). *Liber officialis* became widely popular. An even more explicit connection between the Mass and the theater is in the *Gemma animae* of Honorius of Autun (1090–1156). In this liturgy the Eucharist enacts a conflict between Christ the hero and his antagonist. Action intensifies through the passion and burial, followed by the dramatic reversal of the resurrection. Identification by the worshiper is achieved in the communion and catharsis in the *gaudium* as worship culminates in rejoicing.

Liturgical tropes developed after the 9th century, notably the *quem quaeritis* trope of the Easter liturgy. Such verbal amplifications of a passage in the liturgy highlighted its emotional appeal. Some of these simply elaborated antiphonal responses in the choir, but the suggestion of dialog could be more explicit. An increasing number of examples with dramatic impersonation and individualized speaking parts occur from the 10th century Easter trope of St. Gall and various French and Italian examples of the next two centuries. Elaborate examples such as the *Visitatio sepulchri* trope were written by the 14th and 15th centuries. All of these continued to employ Latin.

The old evolutionary hypothesis for medieval drama imagined that vernacular cycles, saints, and morality plays gradually progressed toward secularization. Such a view has been largely discarded. Rather, parallel lines of development—with a high degree of shared purpose and certain crossover of influence—are suggested by the evidence. There was an ongoing tradition of Latin religious plays. In France two examples are the Beauvais *Daniel* (12th cent.) and Philippe de Mezières *Presentation of the Virgin Mary in the Temple* (c. 1385). Later plays are similarly influenced by scriptural history. Meanwhile there also appeared the popular morality and miracle plays of Hrosvit or Hrosthwitha, a 10th-century Benedictine nun of Gandersheim in Saxony, whose work most directly imitates that of the Roman comedian Terence. The German-authored *Play of Antichrist* (c. 1160) combines the legend of the "Last Roman Emperor" with the theme of the "end times" drawn from Daniel, but it is an isolated example of Latin religious drama rather than part of a distinct tradition.

Vernacular material tended to have more consistently biblical plots. The Anglo-Norman *Jeu d'Adam*, one of the earliest surviving examples of its type, is a vigorous yet reflective treatment of the Eden narrative. Influenced by Cistercian spirituality and its well-developed theology of play, this work was a harbinger of lively later enlargements of biblical story in the *Corpus Christi* plays of England and suggests ways in which western European vernacular poetry joined the liturgical organization of biblical material.

The Franciscans also had an influence on these developments. The first record of a nativity play is a request for permission to perform made by St. Francis in 1220. Italian Franciscans employed vernacular scriptural plays in their evangelistic program. Lay confraternities such as the *Companie del Gonfalone* in 1260 were founded to give annual dramatic performances of the passion events in the Roman Colosseum. As the Franciscans spread into Europe they emphasized the use of vernacular song, theater, and pantomime as communications media. Their stress on affective personal response to the atonement and emotional identification with the passion is shown in their extensive use of the *sermone semidrammatico*, a homily accompanied by impersonation and sometimes extensive theatrical development. Staging directions accompany texts of "dialogue" poems such as Jacopone's *Donna del Paradiso* and versions of the *stabat mater;* English examples include a dramatic sermon preached at Wells Cathedral on Palm Sunday 1300 in which the friar-homilist impersonated Caiaphas, "bysschop of ye lawe," to highlight his appeal to the "new law in Christ."

The *Corpus Christi* cycles in England may constitute the high-water mark of vernacular biblical drama in the West. Four major complete texts survive (York, Wakefield, Chester, and a traveling cycle, "N-Town") and there are records of many others, now lost. Best known of these is the York cycle, which still is frequently performed in England and North America. Most accomplished of the many dramatists whose work makes up the generational accretions of these cycles is the "Wakefield Master," whose *Second Shepherds' Play*, with its localization of the nativity among Yorkshire shepherd villages and pastures, is typical of the incarnational ambition of the English cycle plays. Performed on or about the Feast of *Corpus Christi*, itself a recapitulation of the liturgical year, these multipageant representations of the events of salvation history from creation to last judgment were performed in the open air on elevated stations, sometimes wagons, to whole communities over two or three days.

Some 15th- and 16th-century French passions, including the *Passion d'Arras* and Arnoul Greban's *Mystère de la Passion*, took four days. Confraternities of the Virgin in the Lowlands, in one of which the painter Hieronymus Bosch took an active part, also produced biblical drama and morality plays. One of these, the Dutch *Elckerlye* (1495), shows Franciscan influence and parallels or is the source for the 16th-century English *Everyman*.

Other morality plays, including the Middle English plays *Wisdom* and *Castle of Perseverance*, emphasized faculty psychology in the tradition of Prudentius (4th cent.) and, in the latter case, established traditions of theological allegory. The largest category of late medieval religious drama was probably the saints' play, of which the *Jeu de St. Nicholas* of Jean Bodel (c. 1200) and *Le Miracle de Theophile* of Rutebeuf (1261) are examples. The saints' play abounded throughout Europe, although in Reformation countries most texts have perished. In England, for example, where Wycliffian opposition began early in the 15th century, only two plays from the early 16th century survive, and these concern biblical saints, Paul and Mary Magdalene.

The older type of play survived on into the 17th and early 18th centuries in Roman Catholic Europe. The two surviving MSS of medieval shepherds' plays from Hungary and the only surviving Czechoslovakian cycle play from this period are Franciscan, and the style remains in the Jesuit-inspired and Benedictine-edited Oberammergau Passion play or in the Spanish-American Passion Play of Albuquerque, N. Mex. Nevertheless, the Reformation marked a decisive change in the character and development of religious drama. Theodore Beza, John Calvin's notable disciple, is typical in his *Abraham Sacrifeant* (1550) in using the genre as a vehicle for Reformed apologetics. Less skillful and more polemical is the large body of Tudor biblical drama in England, exemplified by Bishop John Bale's *King Johan* and *God's Promises* (1577). Perhaps the last great English witness to the once-vigorous medieval tradition is Christopher Marlowe's *Dr. Faustus* (1604). Its theologian's devil's pact, sin against the Holy Spirit, and borrowing of allegorical devices from the morality plays created a kind of inversion of the saints' play—a "deconversion" begun in satanic invocation and concluded with a rapture into hell.

With the Puritan opposition to theater of any kind and the general secularization of drama, there was nothing in Renaissance England that compared to the spectacles of the Valenciennes Passion Play (1547). As in the Lowlands, so also in Elizabethan England, biblical subjects, such as Nicholas Udall's *Jacob and Esau* (1557), quickly gave way to dramatic farce; Thomas Garter's *Commody of the most vertuosu and Godlye Susanne* (1564) teeters on the brink of parody.

In the 17th century there appeared, as in Milton's *Samson Agonistes* (1671), a kind of biblical closet drama such as reemerged in the 19th century in E. B. Browning's *Drama of Exile* (1844). But religious drama no longer had center stage. The Restoration featured a few polemical farces. *Rome's Follies, or the Amorous Fryars* (1681) and Arrowsmith's *Reformation* (1673) were more political than religious, while John Dryden's *State of Innocence and Fall of Man* (1677) was a hybrid. Edward Ecclestones' *Noah's Flood* (1679), like Roger Boyle's *Tragedy of King Saul* (1763) and Aaron Hill's *Saul* (1769), anticipated the fate of biblically based works in the 18th century, such as Oliver Goldsmith's oratorio, *The Captivity* (1764), and Hannah More's *Sacred Dramas* (not published until 1835).

In the early 19th century Lord Byron's *Cain* (1821) illustrates a romantic vogue for recasting biblical figures: Cain becomes a Manfred-like hero. The play was swiftly answered by William Battine's *Another Cain* (1822), yet found a later appreciative echo in Howard Nemerov's *Cain* (1959), in which God is made to order Cain to murder Abel. The fascination with biblical antiheroes seen in Henry Milman's *Belshazzar* (1822) became a major theme in 20th-century biblical drama, including Oscar Wilde's *Salome* (1893), Barnard's *Jezebel* (1904), Gwen Lally's *Jezebel* (1912), Clemence Dane's *Naboth's Vineyard* (1925), A. P. Herbert's *Book of Jonah (as almost any Irishman would have Written it)* (1921), and Lionel Abel's *Absalam* (1956). Central biblical heroes are subjected to demotion or parody: Arnold Bennet's *Judith* (1919), George Bernard Shaw's *Back to Methuselah* (1922), James Barrie's *Boy David* (1938), Paddy Chayefsky's *Gideon* (1962), Archibald MacLeish's *J. B.* (1956), and Wofl Mankowitz's *It Should Happen to a Dog* (1956) are luminous examples. More sober treatments of biblical story, such as John Masefield's *Esther* (1922) and *The Trial of Jesus* (1925), the plays of Charles Williams, or even Christopher Fry's *Firstborn* (1948) have sustained less interest than dramatizations of heroes from the apocrypha such as T. S. More's *Judith* (1911), Jean Giradoux's play of the same name (1956), and James Bridie's *Susannah and the Elders* (1937). Marc Connelly's rollickingly reverent adaptation of hexaemeral narrative to black American culture, *Green Pastures* (1930), was a striking exception to the trend, both in its success and in its sympathetic comic mode. A decade later in England, Dorothy L. Sayers' confessional dramas, *He That Should Come* (1939) and *The Man Born to Be King* (1943), were also successful, the latter especially as a radio play.

Biblical drama in the 20th century has often taken up religious questions ranging outward from the biblical sources employed. Michel de Ghelderodes, the Belgian dramatist, offered a brilliant and religiously serious look at the events of Christ's passion from an oblique angle in *Barabbas* (1928). But perhaps the most influential practitioners of religious drama in this period were those who broke away from purely biblical subjects to focus on spiritual struggle and questions of religious identity in historical contexts while maintaining contemporary idiom. Jean Anouilh's *Beckett, or the Honour of God* (1960), like T. S. Eliot's *Murder in the Cathedral* (1935) and *The Cocktail Party* (1950), or Rolf Hochhuth's *Deputy* (1964), is a probing of national as well as individual religious conscience. If Samuel Beckett's *Waiting for Godot* (1955) can be seen as an ironic treatment of the quest for religious meaning, these plays, like Ghelderodes's *Barabbas*, can be seen as attempts to articulate that possibility of meaning in secular society. Within the modern churches themselves where foot-washing ceremonies and liturgies of baptism are still often self-consciously representational and dramatic in character, interest in religious drama has produced a tradition of traveling theater companies which are, in some respects, a throwback to the medieval period.

*Bibliography.* S. W. Cheney, *The Theatre: Three Thousand Years of Drama, Acting, and Stagecraft* (1929); K. Young, *The Drama of the Medieval Church*, 2 vols. (1933); O. B. Hardison, Jr., *Christian Rite and Christian Drama in the Middle Ages: Essays in the Origin and Early History of Modern Drama* (1965); M. Rosten, *Biblical Drama in England: From the Middle Ages to the Present Day* (1968); E. D. Coleman, *The Bible in English Drama* (1968); D. L. Jeffrey, *Mosaic* 8 (1975): 17–46.

DAVID L. JEFFREY

**Driver, (Sir) Godfrey Rolles** (1892–1975). English biblical scholar. Born in Oxford as the son of a distinguished Hebraist, he was decorated for valor in World War I, graduated from Oxford, and spent nearly all of his life there, notably as professor of Semitic philology (1938–62). In 1965 he was appointed joint director with C. H. Dodd of the New English Bible project (himself heading the distinguished group of OT scholars). His own publications include *Letters of the First Babylonian Dynasty* (1925), *Problems of the Hebrew Verbal System* (1936), *Semitic Writing* (1948), ed., *Aramaic Documents of the Fifth Century B.C.* (1954), *Canaanite Myths and Legends* (1956), and *The Judaean Scrolls* (1965).

**Driver, Samuel Rolles** (1846–1914). OT scholar. Born in Southampton, he studied at Oxford, and was fellow (1870–82) and tutor (1875–82) there before his appointment as professor of Hebrew (1882–1914). He was a member of the OT Revision Company (1876–84). His many writings include *Isaiah: Life, Times, and Writings* (1888), *Notes on the Hebrew Text of the Books of Samuel* (1890), *Introduction to the Literature of the OT* (1891), *Deuteronomy* (1895), *Leviticus* (in *The Polychrome Bible*, 2 vols., 1894–97), *The Parallel Psalter* (1898), *Daniel, Joel, and Amos* (in *The Cambridge Bible for Schools*, 1900–1901), *Genesis* (in *The Westminster Commentaries*, 1904), *Deuteronomy* and *Joshua* (in R. Kittel's *Biblia Hebraica*, 1905), *The Minor Prophets* (in *The Century Bible*, 1906), *The Book of Job* (1906), and *The Book of the Prophet Jeremiah* (1906). He collaborated with F. Brown and C. A. Briggs in *A Hebrew and English Lexicon of the OT* (1892–1905).

**Drugs.** See SUBSTANCE ABUSE.

**Drummond, James** (1835–1918). Irish Unitarian scholar. Born in Dublin, he studied there at Trinity College and at Manchester New College in London, and was thereafter assistant minister at Cross Street Chapel, Manchester (1859–69). He was then appointed professor of NT divinity in Manchester New College, which was removed to Oxford in 1889 and called Manchester College in 1893. He was also principal of the college from 1885. After retiring in 1906 he continued his literary work, which included *The Jewish Messiah* (1877), *Introduction to the Study of Theology* (1884), *Philo Judaeus, or the Jewish-Alexandrian Philosophy in Its Development and Completion* (2 vols., 1888), *The Character and Authorship of the*

*Fourth Gospel* (1904), *Studies in Christian Doctrine* (1908), *The Transmission of the Text of the NT* (1909), *Lectures on the Composition and Delivery of Sermons* (1910), and *Paul: His Life and Teaching* (1911). He also wrote commentaries on most of Paul's Epistles, and published his Hibbert Lectures under the title *Via, Veritas, Vita* (1894).

**Drury, Augustus Waldo** (1851–1935). United Brethren scholar and pastor. Born in Pendleton, Ind., he studied at Western College, Toledo, Iowa, Union Biblical Seminary, Dayton, Ohio, and the University of Berlin. He was professor of classics of Western College (1872/73), held various pastorates in his denomination (1873–80), was professor of church history at Union Biblical Seminary (1880–92), and professor of systematic theology there (1892–1935) in what was later called Bonebrake Theological Seminary. In addition to biographies of P. W. Otterbein (1884) and J. J. Glossbrenner (1889), his published works include *Disciplines of the United Brethren in Christ* (1895), *Baptism* (1902), *History of the Church of the United Brethren in Christ* (1924), and *Outlines of Doctrinal Theology* (rev. ed., 1926).

**Drury, Clifford Merrill** (1897–1984). Presbyterian minister, educator, and author. Born in Early, Iowa, he graduated from Buena Vista College, San Francisco Theological Seminary, and Edinburgh University (Ph.D., 1932). After ordination in 1922, he pastored the Community (American) Church, Shanghai, China (1923–27), and the First Presbyterian Church, Moscow, Idaho (1928–38). From 1938 to 1963 he was professor of church history at San Francisco Theological Seminary. In 1933 he was commissioned as a chaplain in the U.S. Naval Reserve, a position he held until 1958. He was the official historian of the U.S. Navy Chaplain Corps (1944–56), and received the Secretary of the Navy Commendation medal. He authored numerous historical books concerning the early settlement of Oregon, Washington, and California. He also compiled *The History of the Chaplain Corps, United States Navy* (5 vols., 1948–57), contributed over 40 articles to historical journals, and wrote an autobiography entitled *My Road from Yesterday* (1984).

JACK MITCHELL

**Drury, Marion Richardson** (1849–1939). United Brethren minister. Born in Pendleton, Ind., he studied at Western College, Toledo, Iowa, and Union Biblical Seminary, Dayton, Ohio, and held pastorates in Toledo (1875–87) and Cedar Rapids, Iowa (1878–81). For 16 years thereafter he was associate editor of the *Religious Telescope*, then resumed the pastorate at Toledo (1898–1907), Oakland, Calif. (1907–10), and Cedar Rapids, Iowa (1917–19), interspersed with brief stints as president of Philomath College, Oreg.

(1910–13) and of Leander Clark College, Toledo (1913–16). After being student secretary for Coe College (1919–22), he spent his latter years as a missionary for his denomination at Ponce, Puerto Rico (1922–39). His publications include *Pastor's Pocket Record* (1883), *Handbook for Workers* (1888), *Our Catechism* (1897), *Life and Career of Bishop James W. Hott, D.D.* (1902), *After Eighty Years* (1930), *Reminiscences of Early Days in Iowa* (1931), and *Life of Augustus Waldo Drury* (1936).

**Druze, The.** A religious group that branched off from the Ismāʿīlīya sect of Shīʿa Islam. Because of their beliefs the Druze can no longer be considered Muslims. Today they are concentrated mainly in the mountains of Syria (Jabal Ḥawrān and the Jawlān), Lebanon (the Shūf), and upper Galilee.

The movement developed in the 11th century when al-Ḥākim, the Fāṭimid Ismāʿīlī caliph in Cairo (A.D. 996–1021), was perceived to be a manifestation of God. Although their name is derived from that of al-Darazī, one of the initiators of the movement, their doctrines in large measure were formulated by Ḥamza, who argued that al-Ḥākim was more than a mere imām in the prevailing Shīʿa Ismāʿīlī sense but was rather the incarnation of divinity and its embodiment, while Ḥamza was the imām—the intellect (al-ʿaql)—who perceived and communicated this reality. According to these doctrines, cosmic intelligence was initially made incarnate in the creation of Adam and was revived in ʿAlī (the cousin of the prophet and the primary imām, according to the Shīʿa) and his descendants, of whom al-Ḥākim was the seal. Contrary to Shīʿa doctrine, ʿAlī and al-Ḥākim were placed in a position superior to that of Muhammad. Al-Ḥākim was thus perceived as the embodiment of divine unity and therefore was beyond categorization in terms of good or evil. His actions, though they may have appeared at times to be cruel, were beyond comprehension and their creative symbolism was known only to Ḥamza as imām.

Opposition to these doctrines by the Sunnī majority and by most Ismmāʿīlīs was seen as part of the cosmic plan of the confrontation of good and evil, to be resolved in the eschatological battle that would take place upon the return of al-Ḥākim, whose disappearance was interpreted as an occultation (ghayba).

Al-Ḥākim, as the manifestation of the divine unity (al-waḥda), and Ḥamza, as imām, were followed hierarchically by human representatives of five cosmic principles (ḥudūd): cosmic intelligence (al-ʿaql), cosmic self (al-nafs), cosmic utterance (al-kalima), cosmic precedent (al-sābiq) and cosmic imminence (al-tālī). Under these five were missionaries or proselytizers (dāʿīs), preachers (maʾdhūns), persuaders (mukāsirs), and the bulk of the believers.

The doctrines of the Druze were put in writing primarily in the many epistles written by the tālī al-Muqtaná. Together with the epistles by Ḥamza, al-Ḥākim, and others these form the scriptures of the Druze, *Rasahl al-Ḥikma* ("Epistles of Wisdom").

Initially a proselytizing movement, the missionary activity of the Druze ceased after the withdrawal of the tālī al-Muqtaná, who had acted as intermediary between Ḥamza (who had also gone into occultation, thus becoming the hidden imām) and the believers. From that time the Druze became a closed community, strictly adhering to its code of conduct and closed to intermarriage. The code of conduct includes the following principles: (1) to recognize the oneness of the One Lord (mawlānā al-Ḥākim); (2) to submit to the orders of the One or, until his return, his agents; (3) to tell the truth, to believers by necessity and to nonbelievers unless the interests of the community are otherwise affected; (4) to aid and protect one another; and (5) to dissociate from the nonbelievers.

After the 15th century, the Druze were divided into two groups; the select few who were endowed with the knowledge of the religious mysteries ('uqqāl), and the majority of believers who were not (juhhāl).

The Druze Calendar begins in A.D. 1017 (A.H. 408), the date of Ḥamza's declaration of the divinity of al-Ḥākim.

**Bibliography.** S. de Sacy, *Exposé de la religion des Druzes*, 2 vols. (1838); P. K. Hitti, *Origins of the Druze People and Religion* (1928); J. N. D. Anderson, *The World of Islam* (1952): 1ff., 83ff.; M. G. S. Hodgson, *JAOS* 82 (1962): 5–20.

HANNA KASSIS

## Du Bose, William Porcher (1836–1918).

Philosophical and biblical theologian. Born in South Carolina, he taught at the University of the South from 1871 until his death. Profoundly affected by religious experiences, the Civil War (in which he was wounded and captured), the death or maiming of many close friends, and the South's plight in the Reconstruction era, he rejected traditional answers to the problem of evil and sought to address the questions raised for Christian faith by science. The material for his answers came from the NT and human experience, his method from Aristotle.

Du Bose's books include *The Soteriology of the NT* (1892), *The Ecumenical Councils* (1896), *The Gospel in the Gospels* (1906), *The Gospel According to St. Paul* (1908), *High Priesthood and Sacrifice* (1908), *The Reason of Life* (1911), and *Turning Points in My Life* (1911).

**Bibliography.** J. O. Murray, *Du Bose as a Prophet of Unity* (1924); T. D. Bratton, *Apostle of Reality: The Life and Thought of the Rev. William Porcher Du Bose* (1936).

ALEXANDER C. ZABRISKIE

## Dubs, Homer Hasenpflug (1892–1969).

Philosopher, theologian, and sinologist. Born in Deerfield, Ill., he studied at Yale University, Columbia University, Union Theological Seminary, the University of Chicago (Ph.D., 1925), and Oxford University. He was an ordained minister of the Evangelical Church (1917), and served as a missionary in the China Mission of the Evangelical Church in Hunan, China (1918–24). He also was instructor of philosophy, University of Minnesota (1925–27), professor of philosophy, Marshall College (1927–34), director of Translation of Chinese Histories Project of the American Council of Learned Societies (1934–37), acting professor of philosophy, Duke University and Duke Divinity School (1937–43), visiting professor of Chinese, Columbia University (1944/45), professor of Chinese studies, Kennedy School of Missions, Hartford Seminary Foundation (1945–47), professor of Chinese, Oxford University (1947–59), and professor emeritus (1959–69). His writings include *Hsuntze: The Molder of Ancient Confucianism* (1927), *Rational Induction: An Analysis of the Method of Philosophy and Science* (1930), and *China, the Land of Humanistic Scholarship* (1949). Along with B. H. Niebel, he wrote *Evangelical Missions* (1919), and he edited and translated from Chinese *Hsuntze: The Works* (1928).

H. DOUGLAS BUCKWALTER

## Duchesne, Louis Marie Olivier (1843–1922).

French Roman Catholic. Born in St. Servan, he studied in Paris and in Rome from 1873 to 1876, visiting Epirus, Thessaly, Macedonia, and Mt. Athos in 1874 and touring Asia Minor in 1876. From 1877 to 1895 he was professor of church history in the Institut Catholique de Paris, and thereafter was director of the French school at Rome. He was also maître de conférences and later directeur d'études at the École des Hautes Études, Paris (1885–95), and in 1888 was elected a member of the Académie des Inscriptions et Belles-Lettres. He wrote *De Macario Magnete et scriptis ejus* (1877), *Étude sur le Liber Pontificalis* (1877), *Mémoire sur une mission au Mont Athos* (with C. Bayet, 1877), *Vita Sancti Polycarpi auctore Pionio* (1881), *Le Liber Pontificalis: Texte, introduction et commentaire* (2 vols., 1886–92), *Origines du culte chrétien* (1889; ET by M. L. McClure under the title *Christian Worship: Its Origin and Evolution* [1902]), *Les Anciens Catalogues épiscopaux de la province de Tours* (1890), *Fastes épiscopaux de l'ancienne Gaule* (2 vols., 1894–99), *Autonomies ecclésiastiques* (1896), *Les Premiers Temps de l'état pontifical* (1898), *Le Forum chrétien* (1899), *Autonomies ecclésiastiques; églises séparées* (1904; ET, *Churches Separated from Rome* [1908]).

**Dugmore, Clifford William** (1909– ). Anglican church historian. Born in Birmingham, he graduated from Cambridge and Oxford, and after ordination served in various posts in the Church of England (1935–47). Thereafter he lectured in ecclesiastical history at the University of Manchester before appointment in 1958 as professor of ecclesiastical history in King's College, London, from which post he retired in 1976. His publications include *Eucharistic Doctrine in England from Hooker to Waterland* (1942), *The Influence of the Synagogue upon the Divine Office* (1944), *The Mass and the English Reformers* (1958), and *Ecclesiastical History No Soft Option* (1959). In 1944 he edited *The Interpretation of the Bible*, and from 1950 was editor of the *Journal of Ecclesiastical History*.

J. D. DOUGLAS

**Duhm, Bernhard** (1847–1928). German OT theologian. Born in East Frisia, Holland, he obtained a Ph.D. degree at Göttingen, where he taught OT (1871–89). He then became professor of OT at Basel, a post he held until his death. He specialized in the internal criticism and understanding of the prophetic literature. In addition to highly regarded commentaries on Isaiah, Jeremiah, Job, and the Psalms, his works included *Über Ziel und Methode der theologischen Wissenschaft* (1889), *Kosmologie und Religion* (1892), *Das Geheimnis in der Religion* (1896), *Die Entstehung des alten Testaments* (1897), and *Israels Propheten* (1916).

**Dukhobors.** *See* DOUKHOBORS.

**Dun, Angus** (1892–1971). Episcopalian bishop, educator, and author. Born in New York City, he studied at Yale University, the Episcopal Theological School, Cambridge, Mass., and the universities of Oxford and Edinburgh (1919/20). Ordained in 1917, he was an instructor and professor of theology at the Episcopal Theological School (1920–40) and dean (1940–44). He served as bishop of Washington, D.C. (1944–62), during which he officiated at Franklin D. Roosevelt's funeral. He was an energetic advocate of ecumenism and peace, serving as chairman both of the Federal Council of Churches and the Commission on Ecumenical Relations of the Protestant Episcopal Church, in addition to 10 years as a member of the central committee of the World Council of Churches. Afflicted with crippling prenatal injuries, many corrective surgeries, paralysis due to polio, and a leg amputation, he overcame them and as a result was a man of compassion and humor. His books include *The King's Cross* (1926), *We Believe* (1934), and *Prospecting for a United Church* (1948).

JACK MITCHELL

**Dunbar, Helen Flanders** (1902–1959). Psychiatrist. Born in Chicago, she was a graduate of Bryn Mawr College, Columbia (Ph.D., and Med. Sc.D.), Union Theological Seminary, N.Y., and Yale. She received clinical training at the Worcester (Mass.) State Hospital and the hospitals of the universities of Vienna and Zurich. She was associated with the College of Physicians and Surgeons (Columbia University), Presbyterian Hospital and Vanderbilt Clinic, Bellevue Hospital (N.Y.), and the Greenwich (Conn.) Hospital. She helped found the Council for Clinical Training of Theological Students and was its first director. As a practicing psychiatrist and psychoanalyst she pioneered particularly in psychosomatic medicine. She inaugurated and was editor-in-chief of *Psychosomatic Medicine* (1938–47). Her publications include *Symbolism in Medieval Thought; Emotions and Bodily Changes*, and *Psychosomatic Diagnosis*.

ROLLIN J. FAIRBANKS

**Duncan, George Simpson** (1884–1965). Scottish NT scholar. Born in Forfar and educated at the universities of Edinburgh and Cambridge, he was chaplain to Earl Haig during World War I (1915–19), and thereafter taught NT (1919–54) and was principal (1940–54) at St. Mary's College, St. Andrews. He was moderator of the General Assembly of the Church of Scotland in 1949, and one of the translators of the NT in the New English Bible. His own publications include *St. Paul's Ephesian Ministry* (1929), *St. Paul's Epistle to the Galatians* (1934), and *Jesus, Son of Man* (1948).

J. D. DOUGLAS

**Dunkers.** Also called Dunkards, Tunkers, and Dompelaars; the name "Dunkers" can be traced to a group of "baptists"—possibly Anabaptists with pietistic leanings—who originated in Schwarzenau near Wittgenstein, Ruhr, Germany, in 1708. Under the leadership of Alexander Mack, eight persons covenanted with one another to be governed by NT principles. They seem to have been influenced by the 17th-century historian of Christianity, Gottfried Arnold, whose pietist tenets they modified to suit their unregulated religious individualism. One of their subgroups emerged in Krefeld in 1715, but emigrated to Pennsylvania in 1719 to escape severe persecution. Adherents of the original group also left for Pennsylvania in 1729, settling near Germantown. While two small splinter groups are still known by the names Old Order Dunkards and Dunkard Brethren, the majority have been known since 1770 as the Church of the Brethren. A major break occurred in about 1882 when the Progressive Dunkers, known as the Brethren Church, left the main body because it was not progressive enough. The Old Order Dunkards, on the other

$$\mathbb{E}e$$

**East Africa.** *Introduction.* The area comprising today's nations of Kenya, Uganda, and Tanzania. In 1498 there appeared off the coast of eastern Africa, at the important trading center of Malindi, three large sailing ships. On their sails they bore a large red cross, symbolic of Christianity. Aboard one was the Portuguese explorer Vasco da Gama, accompanied by Roman Catholic priests who made some contact with the local people. It was East Africa's first introduction to both Christianity and Europeans; by the end of the 16th century there were missionary priests at Lamu and Augustinian friars in Mombasa with 600 African converts.

Long before, however, supporters of the Prophet Muhammad's grandson established themselves on the East African coast in the 8th century, while from at least the 13th century permanent Muslim settlements had grown up along the coast and on the offshore islands. In 1631 the first Christian king of Mombasa, installed only the previous year, expelled his Portuguese masters and had all Christian converts forcibly reconverted to Islam, deported as slaves to Mecca, or killed.

Subsequently Christian work lapsed until the arrival in Zanzibar of the Church Missionary Society (Anglican) and the Holy Ghost Fathers (French Roman Catholic) in 1844 and 1863, respectively, and in Mombasa of British Methodists in 1862. Much of their early work involved freed slaves. Both Christianity and Islam are missionary faiths, and each set about converting the local Bantu, Nilotic, and Paranilotic peoples. The cultures of these peoples were deeply religious but their religious belief systems varied along a continuum, from the Bantu and settled Baganda recognition of a pantheon of gods and spirits to the Paranilotic and pastoral Masai's firm belief in one God. Neither Islam nor Christianity was able to penetrate much into traditional African religions until the late 19th and well into the 20th centuries, but after World War I much ground was won, and both religions became powerful forces. Since independence from colonial rule one of the features of Christianity has been the development of African leadership and the handing over of denominational authority from the missions to the churches.

Other world faiths represented in East Africa today include Baha'ism, Hinduism, Jainism, Sikhism, Judaism, and Zoroastrianism. All but Baha'i are the faiths of original settlers, mainly from the Indian subcontinent, who continued to make their way to Africa from colonial times until well after independence.

Kenya, Uganda, and Tanzania are separate republics, Tanzania uniting the former states of Tanganyika and Zanzibar. The area was under colonial rule from the 1870s when the king of Buganda accepted help from Britain to maintain his position against other foreigners. In 1884 there was the beginnings of a German empire in Tanganyika. Colonialism gathered momentum with the establishment of British protectorates in Zanzibar (1890), Uganda (1894), and British East Africa (Kenya; 1896), and culminated after World War I when Germany's East African territory was placed under British administration as Tanganyika Territory. Tanganyika obtained independence from Britain in 1961, followed by Uganda in 1962 and Kenya and Zanzibar in 1963.

The three states have long attempted to act as a single economic trade unit through the East African High Commission from 1948 and the East African Common Services Organization and East African Community from the 1960s. This cooperative arrangement has suffered many setbacks in a series of major political and social upheavals. For different reasons the religious organizations of the three countries have developed separate identities and grown apart.

*Kenya.* Kenya won independence from Britain in 1963 and was constituted as a parliamentary democracy in 1964 and as a one-party republic in 1969. Its population in the mid-1980s was 16 million with a growth rate of 3.38 percent a year, while in 1975–80 life expectancy was 52.5 years and the household size 5.6 persons. Its area is 582,645 sq. km. (224,961 sq. mi.), with 9.5 percent of the land devoted to agriculture.

An area of relatively low land runs along the coast and spreads out to cover a wide area in the northeast. To the southwest are high plateaus and mountains. Mount Kenya sits astride the equator, its top covered by ice and snow all year round. At 5195 m. (17,058 ft.), it is the country's highest point and a much-loved landmark. The northern climate is hot and dry; that of the southwestern highlands is wetter and somewhat cooler, and the coastal lowland is hotter and in parts wetter than the highlands. The two major cities, the capital of Nairobi and Mombasa, are situated in the highlands and on the coast, respectively.

The population comprises many ethnolinguistic groups, the largest four being the Kikuyu (20.1 percent), Luo (13.9 percent), Luhya (11 percent), and Kamba (9.7 percent). The Kikuyu occupy in the main the highlands area between Mount Kenya and Nairobi, the Luo and Luhya the southwestern country bordering on Lake Victoria, and the Kamba the plains to the east and southeast of Nairobi. Although all peoples communicate in their vernacular, English is the official and Swahili (a trade language originating with the coastal Swahili peoples of mixed Arab and African descent) the national language.

Following on the success of the initial Christian missions in the late 19th century a variety of others, including the Society of Friends, the Salvation Army, Presbyterians, and Baptists, made Kenya their mission field. And because of the laws of comity which most missions upheld as well as for various other reasons the different denominations are inclined to predominate in certain areas of the country and among particular ethnic groups. Moreover, African Christians were quick to want "a place to feel at home" and the first of Kenya's many African Independent Churches was founded in the west of the country as early as 1914. In the mid-1980s, 11.4 million or 73 percent of Kenya's population were professing Christians and of these 4.1 million or 26.4 percent were Roman Catholic, 3 million or 19.3 percent were Protestant, 2.8 million or 17.6 percent were African Independent, 1.1 million or 7.2 percent were Anglican, and 392,000 or 2.5 percent were Orthodox.

The remaining 27 percent comprised about 3 million or 18.9 percent African traditionalists, 941,300 or 6 percent Muslims (strongest at the coast and in the northeastern area where the Somalis are 100 percent Muslim), 3000 Ahmadis, 180,000 Baha'is, 80,000 Hindus, 40,000 Jains, 17,000 Sikhs, 4000 nonreligious, 980 Jews, and 370 Parsis.

*Uganda.* Since independence from Britain in 1962 the Republic of Uganda has had a checkered political history. Sir Edward Mutesa, last *kabaka*

(king) of Buganda, was president until he was deposed in 1966 by Milton Obote who set up a one-party republic. A military coup brought General Idi Amin to power in 1971. Under his military dictatorship Uganda became increasingly friendly with the Muslim countries of North Africa, resulting in growing Muslim aggressiveness. Christian missionaries were expelled and widespread persecution of Christians culminated in the banning of 28 Christian denominations as subversive organizations in 1973. Janani Luwum, the Anglican archbishop, was murdered in 1977. By then Amin's government was recognized internationally as a lawless regime, and in 1979 with the help of Tanzania it was replaced by a parliamentary democracy, followed by a succession of short-lived regimes including another government under Obote, another military takeover, and a reconciliation government with its National Resistance Council under President Yoweri Museveni.

Uganda's population in 1988 was 17 million, while in 1975–80 the growth rate per year was 3.05 percent and the average household size 4.9 persons. Its geographical area is 241,139 sq. km. (93,104 sq. mi.) with 42.95 percent of the land devoted to agriculture.

The southeastern regions around Lake Victoria are about 1200 m. high; to the north the land falls to a slightly lower level; in the west the Ruwenzori Mountains rise above 4550 m. (15,000 ft.) and in the east Mount Elgon rises to 4321 m. (14,178 ft.). Lakes cover one-sixth of the total area. Uganda enjoys a cool season in July and August; the hot season lasts from December to March. The average annual rainfall varies between about 1500 mm. (60 in.) in the highlands and 500 mm. (20 in.) in the northeast near the Kenyan border.

The population comprises a number of ethnolinguistic groups, the largest group being 16.3 percent Ganda; several others range between 5 and 8 percent: 8.1 percent Nkole, 8.1 percent Teso, 7.8 percent Soga, 7.1 percent Kiga, 5.9 percent Ruanda, 5.6 percent Lango, and 5.1 percent Gisu. Traditionally many of these were organized into centralized kingdoms, a factor which contributed greatly to the rapid spread of Christianity in the late 19th century. A wide variety of vernacular languages is spoken, with some Swahili but the official language is English. Kampala, situated near the northern shores of Lake Victoria in the former kingdom of Buganda, is the capital.

Traditional religionists in Uganda are a rapidly decreasing minority, as are Hindus since the exodus of the Asian community under Idi Amin. Islam was brought to Uganda in the mid-19th century by Arab traders from the coast and by Sudanese troops from the north and has a significant following. Uganda is a major mission field of the Baha'i faith, Kampala having one of its seven temples worldwide.

Uganda's Christians, mainly Anglican and Roman Catholic, are among the most vigorous in Africa. Anglicans pioneered the Christian missionary expansion with a visit to the king of Buganda in 1875. They were quickly followed by the French Roman Catholic White Fathers in 1878. The early history of modern Uganda involves a complex interaction of political and religious forces, with Anglicans, Roman Catholics, and Muslims all playing a role. Among the outcomes was the early expulsion of Christian missionaries and the martyrdom of 200 to 300 African Christians, Anglican and Roman Catholic, at Namugongo in 1885–86. Both could be said to have encouraged the growth and spread of the Christian faith. In the mid-1980s Uganda's professing Christians numbered 10.4 million or 78.3 percent of the population; of these 6.6 million or 49.6 percent were Roman Catholic, 3.5 million or 26.2 percent were Anglican, 251,000 or 1.9 percent were Protestant, 66,000 or 0.5 percent were African Independent, and 15,000 or 0.1 percent were Orthodox. The remaining 21.7 percent comprised 1.7 million or 12.6 percent African traditionalists, 872,700 or 6.6 percent Muslims, 4400 Ahmadis, 330,000 Baha'is, 4000 nonreligious, and 700 Jews.

*Tanzania.* The United Republic of Tanzania is made up of the country formerly called Tanganyika and the islands of Pemba and Zanzibar. Since gaining independence from Britain in 1961 it has been a one-party socialist republic. Its first and long-time president, Julius K. Nyerere, has been one of Africa's most visionary, outspoken, and stable leaders.

Tanzania's geographical area covers 945,087 sq. km. (364,900 sq. mi.) with 54.7 percent of the land devoted to agriculture. Its population in the mid-1980s was 18 million, while in 1975–80 the growth rate per year was 3.13 percent and the average household size 4.4. persons.

From a coastal plain of Tanzania about 200 m. above sea level the country rises to a high plateau 200 to 1000 m. in places. In the south mountains rise to over 2000 m. (7000 ft.) and in the north looms Kilimanjaro, Africa's highest mountain at 5896 m. (19,340 ft.) high and one of several old volcanoes found in the region of the Eastern Rift Valley. The coastal plain is hot and wet, with average temperatures ranging from about 23°C to 27°C (73°F to 81°F), and an average rainfall of more than 1000 mm. (40 in.) each year. The highlands are cooler and in the north, near the equator, rain falls at all seasons, but in the south there is a dry season between June and September. The chief cities are Dar es Salaam (the former capital), Zanzibar, and Dodoma (the new capital from 1982).

Tanzania comprises a great number of ethno-linguistic groups, the largest being the Sukuma (13 percent), the Rufiji cluster (9 percent), the Rukwa cluster (5 percent), the Makonde (3.7 percent), the Chagga (3.5 percent), and the Haya (3.5 percent); Zanzibari (with Swahili, Arab) make up 2.3 percent, while the number of British Asians has declined from 50,000 in 1968 to 8000 by 1977. Many vernacular languages are spoken but the speaking of Swahili, the primary official language (with English), is widespread.

African traditional religions were followed by 32 percent of the population in 1970, mainly among the Sukuma, but have declined since then by about one percent per year. Islam is strongest on the coast, while along the traditional caravan routes Baha'i and Hinduism have sizable followings.

After the disintegration of the church in the 17th century Christianity made new beginnings in Tanzania when Roman Catholic missionaries moved from the island of Reunion to Zanzibar in 1860 and missionaries of the (Lutheran) Berlin Mission arrived in Zanzibar in 1886, moving to the mainland the following year. Since then the church has experienced steady growth, missions from many other denominations gradually joining the Roman Catholics and Lutherans. Growth in the Anglican Church (as in Kenya and Uganda) was greatly aided by African teachers and evangelists belonging to the East African Revival. This renewal movement originated in Uganda and Rwanda around 1928 and began to spread throughout East Africa in the 1930s–40s, reaching Buhaya, Tanzania, as early as 1935 through a visit of one of its European founders and leaders, Dr. Joe Church. In the mid-1980s 8 million or 44 percent of Tanzania's population professed to be Christian; of these 5 million or 28.2 percent were Roman Catholic, 2 million or 11.2 percent were Protestant, 722,100 or 4 percent were Anglican, 90,300 or 0.5 percent were African Independent, and 794,400 or 4.4 percent were Orthodox.

The other 56 percent of the population comprised 4.1 million or 22.8 percent African traditionalists, 5.9 million or 32.5 percent Muslims, 8000 or 0.1 percent Ahmadis, 60,000 or 0.3 percent Baha'is, 19,000 Hindus, 40,000 nonreligious, 5000 atheists, 2000 Sikhs, 600 Jains, 120 Jews, and 100 Parsis.

*Bibliography.* R. A. Oliver, *The Missionary Factor in East Africa* (1952); J. V. Taylor, *The Growth of the Church in Buganda: An Attempt at Understanding* (1958); F. B. Welbourn, *East Africa Rebels: A Study of Some Independent Churches*; J. V. Taylor, *The Primal Vision: Christian Presence amid African Religion* (1963); J. S. Trimingham, *Islam in East Africa* (1964); F. B. Welbourn, *East African Christian* (1965); C. J. Hellberg, *Missions on a Colonial Frontier West of Lake Victoria* (1965); F. B. Welbourn and B. A. Ogot, *A Place to Feel At Home: A Study of Two Independent Churches in Western Kenya* (1966); D. B. Barrett, *Schism and Renewal in Africa: An Analysis of Six Thousand Contemporary Religious Movements* (1968); P. M. Miller, *Equipping for Ministry in East Africa* (1969); P. M. Holt, A. K. S. Lambton, and

B. Lewis, eds., *The Cambridge History of Islam* (1970); N. Q. King, *Religions of Africa: A Pilgrimage into Traditional Religions* (1970); R. Macpherson, *The Presbyterian Church in Kenya* (1970); J. S. Mbiti, *Concepts of God in Africa* (1970); S. von Sicard, *The Lutheran Church on the Coast of Tanzania, 1887–1914* (1970); J. S. Mbiti, *NT Eschatology in an African Background* (1971); P. St. John, *Breath of Life: The Story of the Rwanda Mission* (1971); A. J. Temu, *British Protestant Missions (East Africa)* (1972); A. Shorter, *African Culture and the Christian Church: An Introduction to Social and Pastoral Anthropology* (1973); M. S. Langley and T. Kiggins, *A Serving People: A Textbook on the Church in East Africa* (1974); W. B. Anderson, *The Church in East Africa, 1840–1974* (1977); A. Wipper, *Rural Rebels: A Study of Two Protest Movements in Kenya* (1977); V. J. Donovan, *Christianity Rediscovered: An Epistle from the Masai* (1978); R. W. Strayer, *The Making of Mission Communities in East Africa: Anglicans and Africans in Colonial Kenya, 1875–1935* (1978); M. Louise Pirouet, *Black Evangelists: The Spread of Christianity in Uganda, 1891–1914* (1978); T. Tuma and P. Mutibwa, eds., *A Century of Christianity in Uganda, 1877–1977* (1978); A. Shorter, *Priest in the Village: Experiences of African Community* (1979); J. E. Church, *Quest for the Highest: An Autobiographical Account of the East African Revival* (1981); D. B. Barrett, ed., *World Christian Encyclopedia: A Comparative Survey of Churches and Religions in the Modern World, A.D. 1900–2000* (1982); H. Okullu, *Church and Politics in East Africa* (n.d.).

MYRTLE S. LANGLEY

**Easter.** The most important of the Christian festivals, celebrating the resurrection of Jesus Christ. It was instituted at an early date in the history of the church and probably was observed by A.D. 110 in Antioch as a Christian parallel to the Jewish Passover (14 Nisan) on the following Sunday. Controversy raged in the 2d and 3d centuries over whether it should be observed on 14 Nisan or the following Sunday. An added controversy arose between those who used astronomical means to determine the date and those who fixed the date in relation to the Jewish Passover. The Council of Nicea decided in 325 that the date should be established astronomically on the first Sunday after the first full moon following the spring equinox. The continuing debate over the date between the Eastern Orthodox and the Western churches arises from discrepancies between the Julian and Gregorian calendars. No resolution is yet apparent to the problem of a fixed (favored by secular authorities) or an agreed date (favored by the churches).

*See also* CHURCH YEAR.

JAMES TAYLOR

**Eastman, Fred** (1886–1963). Congregationalist professor and dramatist. Born in Lima, Ohio, he studied at the College of Wooster, Ohio, Columbia University, and Union Theological Seminary. He was pastor, Reformed Church, Locust Valley, N.Y., (1912–17); business manager, *Red Cross Magazine* (1917–19); director of educational work, Board of Home Missions of the Presbyterian Church, USA (1919–23); managing editor, *Christian Work* (1924–26); contributing editor, *Christian Century* (1926–36); professor of biography and drama, Chicago Theological Seminary, from 1926, and Federated Theological Faculty, University of Chicago, from 1943. In addition to many plays he wrote *Books That Have Shaped the World* (1937), *Men of Power* (5 vols., 1938–40), *Christ in the Drama* (1947), and *Writing the One-Act Religious Drama* (1948). He coauthored with L. Wilson, *Drama in the Church* (1933; rev. ed., 1942), with E. Oullette, *Better Motion Pictures* (1936), and with Bailey, Conant, and Smith, *The Arts and Religion* (1944).

**Easton, Burton Scott** (1877–1950). Anglican NT scholar. Born in Hartford, Conn., he was educated at the universities of Pennsylvania (Ph.D., 1901) and Göttingen, and Philadelphia Divinity School (1906). Ordained in 1905, he taught NT first at Nashotah House, then at Western Theological Seminary, Chicago (1911–19), and at General Theological Seminary, New York (1919–48), where he was also subdean and librarian. He was most eminent as an exegete; his commentaries on Luke (1926) and the pastoral epistles (1947) and his translation and interpretation of *The Apostolic Tradition* of Hippolytus (1934) are noted works of scholarship.

*Bibliography.* F. C. Grant, ed., *Memorial Volume of NT Essays* (1954).

FREDERICK C. GRANT

**Eberhardt, Paul** (1876–1923). A mystic and philosopher of the Evangelical National Church of Germany. Born in Strausberg, Mark Brandenburg, he was a philosopher of religion. As a mystically thinking free author (Romance: *Wohin der Weg? Das Jahr einer Seele*, 1920) he penetrated the depths of non-Christian, especially Eastern, religions. Their most sublime products he tried to make available for home-devotion through *Das Buch der Stunde* (1916 and 1920). With his series of publications, *Der Aufbau, Blätter für Suchende* (1914), he influenced his contemporaries ethically and religiously. In the same way he worked after 1919 through pamphlets and the journal, *Der deutsche Pfeiler* (1921ff.). His writings and thought gained new popularity in the 1970s and 1980s in New Age and Eastern mystical movements in the West.

REINHOLD KUECKLICH

**Ecuador.** One of the smallest Latin American countries, Ecuador's 283,560 sq. km. (109,483 sq. mi.) stretch from sweltering tropical coastal areas to cool mountain valleys that lie directly beneath the equator and down the Andes again to the rainy, tropical Amazon jungle in the east. South America's most densely populated country, Ecuador has a population estimated at about 10.8 million (1990). Of these, 25 percent are indigenous, mainly living in the Amazon jungles; 10 percent are blacks, concentrated along the coast with one-half the country's population; 55 percent are mestizo, spread throughout the country; and 10 percent of European-descent control most land and resources.

Quito, at 2838 m. (9320 ft.), has been the capital since independence from Spain in 1822. Although Quechuan is widely spoken, Spanish is the official language. There is a 90 percent literacy rate, and attendance through the sixth grade is required. The law has a 76 percent compliance record in urban areas and a 33 percent compliance record in rural areas.

The discovery of oil in the 1960s revolutionized this primarily agricultural country. Although Ecuador has been the world's largest exporter of bananas, oil and gas exports came to represent 72 percent of the country's total export revenue in the early 1980s. A democratic form of government put in place in 1979 ended 16 years of a repressive military regime. The oil recession of the 1980s added to a huge foreign debt (much of it resulting from corruption in the military). Per-capita income is $1299 (1985), and life expectancy is 59.8 years (male) and 63.6 years (female), while infant mortality is 63 per 1000 births.

The Catholic Church has had strong leaders in the liberation theology movement, including Bishop Leonidas Proaño of Riobamba who in 1969 divested the church of 3000 hectares in a private land reform movement and called on others to follow this lead with "voluntary acts of impoverishment." The military regime took umbrage at what they called his "subversive acts," and to embarrass him they arrested and deported 17 bishops and 20 priests from all over South America who had gathered in August 1976 in Riobamba for a church conference.

Relations between the Holy See are regulated by a 1937 agreement. Divorce is permitted. There are 820 parishes in three archdioceses and 10 dioceses ministering to 92 percent of the population with one cardinal, three archbishops, 24 bishops, 1537 priests, 4112 nuns, and 329 brothers. A pontifical university serves the church community.

In spite of a large Protestant foreign missionary population (702 in 1985) Ecuador has one of the smallest percentages of evangelicals in South America (3.2 percent in 1987). Many of the overseas personnel work in Quito with the powerful radio station *Hoy Cristo Jesus Bendice* (HCJB) or in rural tribal work. The country's 320,000 Protestants are distributed among 36 denominations. Among Andean peoples a mixture of Roman Catholicism and ancestral pagan beliefs is widely practiced.

FAITH ANNETTE SAND

**Ecumenical Movement.** The word "ecumenical" comes from the Greek *oikoumenē*, which has among its meanings the inhabited world and humanity. The first meaning stressed cultural unity, as in the integrated culture of the Roman Empire (Luke 2:1); the second emphasized universality, embracing the human race (Matt. 24:14). In Christian usage these meanings persisted. The ecumenical councils purposed to safeguard the religious unity of the empire and claimed to have universal validity. In contemporary theological thinking the adjective is used to describe both organized and general concerns among Christians for the cultural unity of the church and the unity of all things in Christ.

***Origins and Developments.*** By the beginning of the 20th century, Christianity was a genuinely international religion. The 19th-century missionary expansion, notably in Africa and Asia, gave birth to the ecumenical movement, which generally is reckoned to have begun at the World Missionary Conference at Edinburgh, Scotland, in 1910. Various transdenominational bodies had been formed during the 19th century, such as the Evangelical Alliance (1846), and international youth movements such as the YMCA (1844), the YWCA (1858), and the World Student Christian Federation (1895). Two principal architects of the Edinburgh Conference were John R. Mott and J. H. Oldham. Together with William Temple, later archbishop of Canterbury, they played a leading role in the formation of the World Council of Churches (WCC) in 1948. The Edinburgh Conference led to creation of the International Missionary Council (IMC) in 1921 "to help coordinate the activities of the national missionary organizations of the different countries and to unite Christian forces of the world in seeking justice in international and inter-racial relations." In 1961 IMC became the Division of World Mission and Evangelism of WCC.

Bishop Charles Brent, who attended the Edinburgh Conference, proposed a conference on faith and order to include representatives of "all Christian communions throughout the world which confess the Lord Jesus Christ as God and Saviour." The first fully constituted World Conference on Faith and Order took place at Lausanne, Switzerland, in 1927. Other world meetings followed at Edinburgh (1937), Lund, Sweden (1952), and Montreal, Canada (1963). The Faith and Order gatherings were concerned not only with organic church union but also with seeking a common position on theology, tradition, and renewal. Those within the Faith and Order movement discussed founding a federation of independent churches and even more innovative and far-reaching possibilities.

Ecumenism developed a service aspect known as the Life and Work movement. Archbishop Nathan Söderblom of Sweden in 1925 convened the Universal Christian Conference on Life and Work at Stockholm to study how to apply Christian principles to international relations and to social, industrial, and economic life. The movement in its early stages avoided discussions of a doctrinal nature. The report of the Oxford Life and Work Conference (1937) remains the most comprehensive ecumenical statement on problems of church and society and Christian social responsibility. The Third World Conference on Church and Society, held in Geneva in 1966, confronted the technological expertise of the Western industrialized world with the revolutionary politics of the third world, particularly in Latin America.

From 1948 ecumenical concerns and actions have been promoted by numerous other national and regional ecumenical bodies. Among the older Christian councils are the British Council of Churches (1942), the National Christian Council of India (1947), the National Council of Churches of Christ in the United States of America (1950), and the Christian Council of Asia (formerly the East Asia Christian Conference, 1959). The Roman Catholic Church has become a member of 24 national councils of churches and also of the Caribbean and Pacific regional councils. Twelve international confessional organs—now called Christian world communions—also exist. Their programs continue to emphasize the theological contributions Christian world communions can make to the entire ecumenical movement. Another 200 ecumenical institutes around the world offer a variety of programs. European ecumenical institutes have made scholarly contributions to ecumenical theology, social ethics, and spirituality, while Asian and African study centers have deepened the understanding of the Christian faith in a multireligious environment.

On the local level the ecumenical movement fostered changes in ecclesiastical and social structure. The Week of Prayer for Christian Unity has been celebrated for several decades. Joint catechetical classes are conducted by Roman Catholic priests and Protestant ministers. Mixed-marriage groups are active, and ecumenical baptisms and marriages are more commonly administered. New building designs have experimented with housing different denominations under one roof. Ecumenical groups share everything from Bible study to sponsorship of third world projects.

Evangelical academies and lay training centers, formed around ministry to contemporary disorder of life in society, have provided another challenge to established ecumenism. These academies and centers were born in Germany as a result of the ruin caused by World War II. Lay institutes have been organized outside Europe in Japan, Korea, Zambia, Australia, Canada, the United States, and other countries to bring Christianity to grips with the secular world. In West Germany, for example, the *Kirchentag* meets every two years, bringing together tens of thousands of church leaders for several days of intensive education and argument. These rallies provide a meeting point for German Christians from the East and the West with international visitors. The charitable and liturgical community of Taizé in France has joined Protestants of various communions and Roman Catholics in monastic vows. The growth of pentecostalism has added to the ecumenical impetus over recent decades. Attaching great value to simplicity and fervor pentecostal communities in Europe and North and South America tend to be ecumenical in their belief that the baptism of the Holy Spirit is available to believers in all ages. A number of pentecostal churches have joined the World Council of Churches, although many pentecostal groups remain suspicious of the official ecumenical movement. Conservative evangelicals also avoid affiliation and support for WCC, accusing it of a lack of true missionary concern and activity and in many cases of departing from biblical Christianity.

***Roman Catholic Church.*** Roman Catholicism has radically changed its attitude toward the ecumenical movement since Vatican Council II and the influence of Pope John XXIII. Before Vatican II (1962–65) Roman Catholic doctrine was negative toward rapprochement with other churches. In 1961, Rome agreed to send official observers to the third assembly of WCC at New Delhi, India, and a number of delegated observers from various denominations were invited to attend the Vatican Council. The Council's Decree on Ecumenism praised "the ecumenical sincerity and energy of the separated brethren." Pope John XXIII created in 1960 a Secretariat for the Promotion of Christian Unity which coordinates all ecumenical relations with non-Roman Catholic churches. Since 1965 a Joint Working Group—its members appointed by the Vatican Secretariat for Christian Unity and the World Council of Churches—has met annually to discuss common concerns. The Week of Prayer for Christian Unity has been annually prepared by a group of World Council and Roman Catholic members. Since 1980, when the Committee on Society, Development and Peace (SODEPAX) concluded its 12-year mandate, cooperation in social questions has continued informally, and the WCC Faith and Order Commission now includes Roman Catholic members. For more than 15 years any important World Council conference or consultation has been attended by several official and fully participating Roman Catholic delegates. Pope Paul VI, visiting the World Council at Geneva in 1969, called the occasion "a prophetic moment and truly blessed encounter." Pope John Paul II visited the council headquarters in 1984 and referred to the Bishop of Rome as the symbol of unity. The Roman Catholic Church continues to be engaged in bilateral dialogs with Anglican, Reformed, Lutheran, Methodist, and other churches.

In spite of growing collaboration between the Roman Catholic and the WCC constituencies serious obstacles remain to doctrinal agreement and visibly restored unity. Because of its hierarchical structure and its sheer numerical weight, the Roman Catholic Church would create administrative and psychological problems, not to mention theological tensions, if it entered the World Council as a full member. Its membership would require a change in the council's constitution and alter the council's character.

***Orthodox Churches.*** In 1920 the Ecumenical Patriarchate of Constantinople issued an encyclical pleading that "above all, love should be rekindled and strengthened among the churches, so that they should no more consider one another as strangers and foreigners, but as relatives, and as being part of the household of Christ and 'fellow heirs, members of the same body and partakers of the promise of God in Christ' (Eph. 3:5)." Since the Stockholm Conference on Life and Work in 1925, the Eastern Orthodox churches have participated actively in the ecumenical movement. They helped to face the issues of proselytism and religious liberty in the 1950s, and Orthodox churches in East Europe joined WCC in 1961. They have made many contributions to the work of the Faith and Order Commission.

***Bibliography.*** R. Rouse and S. Neill, eds., *A History of the Ecumenical Movement, 1517–1948* (1954); *Journal of Ecumenical Studies* (1964–present); H. E. Fey, ed., *The Ecumenical Advance: A History of the Ecumenical Movement*, vol. 2, 1948–1968 (1970); *Classified Catalog of the Ecumenical Movement*, 2 vols. (1972); W. A. Visser 't Hooft, *Has the Ecumenical Movement a Future?*, in C. G. Patelos, ed., *The Orthodox Church in the Ecumenical Movement: Documents and Statements, 1902–1975* (1978); A. J. Van der Bent, ed., *Major Studies and Themes in the Ecumenical Movement* (1981); *Classified Catalog of the Ecumenical Movement* (1982); T. S. Derr, *Barriers to Ecumenism: The Holy See and the World Council of Churches on Social Questions* (1983).

A. J. VAN DER BENT

**Eddy, Mary Baker** (1821–1910). Founder of the Church of Christ, Scientist. Since her death Christian Science has grown from its Boston "Mother Church" to approximately 8000 branches worldwide (1982). Membership is uncertain, since leaders are loathe to disclose such statistics. Eddy's latter years were filled with bickerings with the board of directors of her movement; yet, despite this internal difficulty and the fact that no single person was ever to assume her position of leader, the impetus of her earlier leadership kept the movement going during the crucial years immediately following her death. Her publications include *Historical Sketch of Christian Science Mind Healing* (1888, 3d ed., 1890), *Christian Science Series* (vol. 1, 1889; vol. 2, 1890—treatises by Mrs. Eddy and her students), *Retrospection and Introspection* (1891), *No and Yes* (1891), *Rudimental Divine Science* (1891), *Personal Contagion* (1909), and *The First Church of Christ, Scientist, and Miscellany* (1913).

*See also* CHRISTIAN SCIENCE.

***Bibliography.*** S. Wilbur, *The Life of Mary Baker Eddy* (1907); A. Brisbane, *Mary Baker G. Eddy* (1908); G. Milmine, *Life of Mary Baker G. Eddy* (1909); H. A. Studdert Kennedy, *Mrs. Eddy* (1910, 1947); H. W. Dresser, *The Quimby Manuscripts* (1921); E. M. Ramsay, *Christian Science and Its Discoverer* (1923); A. Dickey, *Memoirs of Mary Baker Eddy* (1927); E. F. Dakin, *Mrs. Eddy, The Biography of a Virginal Mind* (1929).

RAYMOND W. ALBRIGHT

**Eddy, Sherwood** (1871–1963). Born in Leavenworth, Kans., he studied at Yale and Union Seminary. In 1896 he went to India for 15 years in student work, then spent 15 years as secretary for Asia of the YMCA. For 20 years he conducted seminars on European leadership. His books include *India Awakening* (1911), *The New Era in Asia* (1913), *The New World of Labor* (1923), *New Challenges to Faith* (1926), *Religion and Social Justice* (1928), *The Challenge of Russia* (1930), *The Challenge of the East* (1931), *The Challenge of Europe* (1933), *Russia Today* (1934), *A Pilgrimage of Ideas* (1935), *Europe Today* (1938), *Revolutionary Christianity* (1939), *The Kingdom of God and the American Dream* (1934), *Man Discovers God* (1934), *A Portrait of Jesus: A Twentieth Century Life of Christ* (1943), *Pathfinders of the World Missionary Crusade* (1945), *God in History* (1947), and *You Will Survive after Death* (1950).

***Editae Saepe Dei.*** Encyclical of Pope Pius X issued on May 26, 1910, on the centenary of the canonization of Cardinal Borromeo who had been active in fighting the Reformation. The pope refers derogatively to the Reformers as rebels, full of arrogance and immorality, "enemies of the cross of Christ." The evangelical princes of the Reformation era and their subjects are equally charged with moral corruption. Energetic protests from evangelical church circles in Germany, as well as from the royal government of Prussia, prevented the encyclical from being promulgated in the dioceses of the *Reich*. The Vatican declared unofficially that the pope's intentions were misunderstood, no offense being meant to German Protestantism as such.

***Bibliography.*** Original text in *Acta Apostolicae Sedis* (1910), 2: 357–80. ET in *American Catholic Quarterly Review* 35 (1910): 394–412.

GEORGES A. BARROIS

**Edman, Victor Raymond** (1900–1967). Educator and author. Born in Chicago, he was educated at the University of Illinois, Columbia University, Boston University, and Clark University (Ph.D., 1933). During World War I he served in Europe with the U.S. Army infantry. He was an instructor at the Missionary Institute, Nyack, N.Y. (1921–22), and continued successively as director of the Christian and Missionary Alliance's El

Institute Biblico del Ecuador (1923–28), pastor of the Gospel Tabernacle, Worcester, Mass. (1929–35), and associate professor of political science (1936–39), professor (1939–42), acting president (1940–41), and president at Wheaton College (1941–65). He was editor of *The Alliance Witness*, an international missionary magazine, and wrote 19 books on religion and philosophy before his death from a heart attack while speaking at a chapel service at Wheaton College.

JACK MITCHELL

## Education, Christian. *Biblical Warrants.*

The mandate for Christian education (CE) derives from the Abrahamic covenant and the Mosaic command for parents to instruct their children in the *shemah* (Deut. 6:4–5); Wisdom literature's many references to reciprocal responsibilities within families for teaching and heeding knowledge and understanding that lead to godly behavior; Jesus' reiterations of the Great Commandment, to love the Lord with one's whole being, including the mind (Matt. 22:37–40); various Pauline exhortations to parents and others regarding the nurture and discipline of children (Eph. 6; Col. 3); and Paul's specific references to Timothy's training in righteousness (2 Tim. 1, 3).

Paul uses two terms familiar to Greek education, *paideia* and *nouthesia*. *Paideia* refers to the total education of the young—intellectual, physical, moral, cultural, and social. *Nouthesia* specifies the rigorous and admonishing nature of such education, which for the Greek schoolboy literally meant the probability of a whipping administered by a family slave or *paidagōgos*, to punish any lapse in learning. Transferred to the figurative, Paul refers to the Law as this "schoolmaster" (KJV) or "custodian" (RSV) or "tutor" (NEB), responsible for our moral instruction until faith in Christ replaces adherence to the Law (Gal. 3:24–25).

*In the Home.* Throughout the Christian era, CE has always been regarded as a primary parental obligation. "Christian nurture" was Horace Bushnell's mid-19th century term for instruction by example and precept. For most of the 20th century, however, CE took the Christian family for granted, dealing pleasantly with stable families and ignoring most others. Nearing the end of the 20th century, CE has revived this emphasis upon parent-generated nurture for all households, largely through the popularity of extramural, interdenominational agencies and their publications, films, seminars, radio and television broadcasts. Such groups offer counseling to intact as well as divided families, to single-parent households, families disrupted by abuse or addiction, and others once ignored by CE's focus on ideal relationships.

Christian publishing houses have begun to compete favorably in the marketplace with children's books and Bible-study guides; some have also entered successfully the burgeoning videotape industry, offering a biblical alternative to secular television.

*In the Church.* Historically, within the community of faith, candidates for baptism (catechumens) received formal instruction in doctrinal orthodoxy from the church's preceptors—elders, pastors, bishops. The Apostles' Creed may have developed as a compact expression of Christian doctrine for just such indoctrination. Also useful in CE were elements of the Latin Mass intoned, processions and vestments, pageants, and mystery plays; even statuary and stained glass windows told the story of the gospel and its heroes to those incapable of or otherwise prevented from reading the Scriptures.

The Protestant Reformation ended the Latin barrier to CE, bringing the Scriptures to the vernacular languages. Congregational singing of hymns and chorales also contributed to learning, especially among the still largely illiterate populace. Not until the late 18th and early 19th centuries, when the Sunday school movement began in Great Britain and America, did the church find a means—other than its own formal education—to help alleviate gross ignorance until a common or public school system could take root. Following the spread of Sunday schools, summer conferences to train teachers sprang up, such as the Chautauqua movement, founded in 1874 in western New York, which in time gave its name to a circuit of traveling exhibitions of culture and entertainment. These ventures developed into the summer adult Bible conference and camps for youth. Some of these have since declined into resorts with little or no reminder of their roots.

The success of the Sunday school movement gave rise to other types of youth work, now frequently referred to as youth ministries. These include both church-based efforts, such as the nondenominational Christian Endeavor societies, as well as so-called parachurch organizations, working outside the church, such as the Young Men's Christian Association. Established in London in 1844 and seven years later in Boston, the YMCA sought "the improvement of the spiritual condition of young men," offering tradesmen instruction for body, mind, and spirit. Both Dwight L. Moody and William A. "Billy" Sunday were YMCA workers. In 1988, the YMCA was sued to remove the word "Christian" from its name; in defense, officials acknowledged that the official name and all charter references to Christ are mere "institutional rhetoric."

In spite of such decline in purpose, the growth of CE through modern church-based organizations (among them, Christian Service Brigade, Pioneer Clubs, AWANA, and denominational entities such as the Baptist Young People's Union), as well as through parachurch groups primarily working with school and college students (such as Inter-Varsity Christian Fellowship, Campus Crusade for Christ, Young Life, the Navigators, Fellowship of Christian Athletes, Fellowship of Christians in Universities and Schools, Youth for Christ, and Campus Life) dramatizes the continuing need for Christian educators professionally trained and vocationally committed to work both in and beyond the local church.

Nor is CE, whether under church sponsorship or not, restricted to youth ministries. Adult education opportunities, including Bible studies, experimentation with liturgy and other worship patterns, participation in home and foreign mission ventures, as well as seasonal emphases during Advent or Lent, must also be regarded as ongoing elements of CE.

***Schools, Colleges, and Seminaries.*** The history of CE is also the history of general education. Prior to the Edict of Milan in 313, Christian scholarship had been practiced in schools founded by Clement of Rome and Justin Martyr. During the 3d century, Christians hid from persecution in desert monasteries such as those in Egypt, the Sinai, or Syria, there preserving, copying, and teaching young men to copy the precious manuscripts and documents of the church. Following Constantine, these schools were free to send missionaries (such as Columba, Patrick, Boniface, and Alopen) to convert and instruct the lost.

By the middle of the 8th century, bishops' schools had been founded. Charlemagne invited Alcuin of York to teach his son Pepin at Aachen; before his death in 899, the godly King Alfred the Great had established schools in England, spending one-eighth of his income on education. In the 10th century cathedrals began sponsoring grammar schools, which eventually grew into universities.

With the invention of Johann Gutenberg's movable type in the mid-15th century and the arrival in Europe of scholars capable of reading ancient Hebrew and Greek MSS, Christian humanism brought new dimensions to CE, including advocacy of popular literacy by Erasmus to make the Bible more accessible. In 1423, Vittorino da Feltre founded the first boarding school, the House of Joy, in Mantua, Italy. There he hoped to bring his pupils under the daily tutelage of faithful teachers, whose example his students might emulate. The 17th-century Moravian pastor Jan Amos Comenius offered radical ideas about compulsory schooling for all children, which in time were implemented throughout Europe; he is rightly regarded as the "father of modern education." All across Africa, Latin America, and Asia, Christian mission schools have long been the starting point for eventual leaders in developing countries.

All these instances foreshadow today's Christian day school movement, as well as Christian colleges and universities, in which students are taught by faculty committed in faith to Jesus Christ. To such Christians, all education is CE because, in the words of Frank E. Gaebelein, "All truth is God's truth." Christian educators, particularly in evangelical schools, colleges, and seminaries, strive to achieve an "integration of faith and learning." Recently these institutions tend to consider CE as "Christian formation and discipleship," the designation preferred at Fuller Theological Seminary, for instance.

Beyond religious instruction, however, attitudes within the Christian community toward general education have swung like a pendulum. Basil the Great (c. 329–379), Gregory of Nazianzus (330–389), and Augustine of Hippo (359–430) all advocated the broadest possible acquisition of knowledge, which Gregory called "the first of our advantages as Christians." On the other hand, Tertullian (c. 160–215) seemed to disparage learning, setting up a dichotomy between "Athens and Jerusalem," as representatives of pagan knowledge and Christian faith.

Since then, the church or parties within the church have approved positions opposed to the growth of human knowledge, particularly in areas of scientific inquiry. In 1632 the Roman Church punished Galileo as a heretic; in America, the 1925 Scopes trial set a negative perception of fundamentalism toward education. Generations later several state laws mandating the teaching of "scientific creationism" in public schools have been ruled unconstitutional and many laws forbid or discourage any creationist instruction. Some Christians have taken an anti-intellectual view, disdaining formal education because of its supposed power to corrupt. To these believers, CE remains a narrow field related to salvific knowledge and nurture in it. Suspicion of public and even parochial education, however, has grown rapidly among evangelicals. In America, where in 1647, the Commonwealth of Massachusetts enacted legislation requiring schooling to combat "ye olde deluder Satan," many parents now instruct their children at home rather than expose them to the perceived spiritual antipathy of a public school or the possible heterodoxy of a Christian school.

***The Future of Christian Education.*** In Great Britain and North America, increasingly secularistic modes of thought have all but stripped religious content from the formal public education curricula, as well as from daily life, leaving their citizenry lacking in religious aspects of "cultural literacy." Even the remaining pluralistic civil religion can no longer rely on common knowledge of religious terms and references once taken for granted.

For CE, conditions are not much more sanguine. Even among evangelicals, biblical literacy may no longer be assumed. In many Christian families, the custom of daily Bible reading has disappeared with the traditional family dinner. In many evangelical churches, topical preaching has largely replaced biblical exposition; many churches have abandoned the hymnal for current songs projected on a screen. Christian schools have slowed in growth; economic pressures compel contraction, merger, or dissolution. Only those with strong programs survive; the same is true of Bible and liberal arts colleges and seminaries.

If CE is to succeed in spite of hostile secular attitudes external to the church, it must first overcome the handicaps it faces within the church. Characteristically, CE is a low-budget item in most churches and in many denominational headquarters. To succeed CE will need to be given the highest priority, and without the *paideia* and nurture necessary for growth, there will be no evangelism, no mission effort, no Christian publishing and broadcasting, no Christian endeavor worthy of the name. Christians also may no longer assume that secular public institutions can be redeemed by petitions or constitutional amendments. Instead, the future of CE will reflect how Christians answer Joshua's summons to make a decision, choosing either to serve secularism or the Lord (Josh. 24:14–15) in covenantal and discipling tasks.

*Bibliography.* F. E. Gaebelein, *Christian Education in a Democracy: The Report of the NAE Committee* (1951); *The Pattern of God's Truth: Problems of Integration in Christian Education* (1954); E. H. Harbison, *The Christian Scholar in the Age of the Reformation* (1956); K. B. Cully, *The Search for a Christian Education since 1940* (1965); J. Cogley, *Religion in a Secular Age: The Search for Final Meaning* (1968); K. G. Howkins, *The Challenge of Religious Studies* (1972); K. O. Gangel, W. E. Benson, *Education: Its History and Philosophy* (1982); P. F. Parsons, *Inside America's Christian Schools* (1987); D. B. Lockerbie, *Renewed and Transformed: Thinking and Acting Like a Christian* (1989).

D. BRUCE LOCKERBIE

**Eekhof, Albert** (1884–1933). Reformed church historian. Born in Steenwijk, the Netherlands, at an early age he accompanied his father to the USA, but later returned to study theology at the University of Leiden. After completing his work there he did thorough research work in the USA, investigating church history. In 1910 he became Reformed pastor at Diemen, and in 1924 professor of church history at Leiden. He was deeply interested in the first Protestants who emigrated to America, and worked as a leading editor of the *Nederlandsche archief voor kerkgeschiedenis*. He wrote *Bastiän Jansz. Krol* (1910), *De Hervormde Kerk in Noord-Amerika* (1913), *De Avondmaalsbrief van Cornelius Hoen* (1917), and *De Theologische Faculteit te Leiden in de 17e eeuw* (1921).

ALBERT HYMA

**Ego and Egoism.** The "I" that is an experiencing or acting agent. The ego is variously defined, and the attitude of psychology toward the problems of metaphysics and ethics depends on how this inner self is conceived. The ego is usually related to the individual's self-identification within the limits of the body. The ego is "first and foremost a body-ego," according to Freud. But this overlooks the fact that only self-conscious beings can be said to have an ego, and self-consciousness refuses to identify itself absolutely with the bodily organism.

Psychologically, the self-reference involved in thinking, feeling, and acting helps a self-conscious person learn from his or her environment. Many elements of experience are not conscious yet they help to build the structure of the world as it is perceived, and the structure of an individual's personality. The different levels of self-reference, conscious and subconscious, are distinguished by Sigmund Freud and Friedrich Nietzsche in the ego, id, and superego phraseology. Martin Buber expressed similar concepts in a different sense in his "I-thou-it" distinction. To Freud, the ego is concerned with perception and therefore has direct relations with reality ("the ego is the representative of the outer world to the id"), while the id is concerned with instinct, and therefore is "subjective." But instinct influences the ego also. The ego is "subject to the influence of the instincts, too, like the id, of which it is in fact only a specially modified part." The id is a kind of storehouse of the experiences of the ego, and is the "great storehouse of libido," for the pleasure-principle "reigns supreme in the id." The ego represents what we call reason and sanity, in contrast to the id which contains the passions. So "the ego's position is like that of a constitutional monarch," striving to be moral, while the id is nonmoral, and the superego may be hypermoral, although Freud is not very clear as to the relations of the ego and the id to the superego.

Buber picks up on Søren Kierkegaard in this as Freud draws from Nietzsche. He starts from the way an individual relates to things on the one hand, and to other persons on the other. The ego can never learn from itself. Humans are not equipped with that degree of self-discernment. Rather the ego acquires personality by recognizing the "thouness" of other individuals, treating them with respect as persons, instead of as things. "As I say thou, I become I. All real life is meeting." Buber tries to find an antidote for isolationism in psychology, as well as the cure for "egoism" in ethics. This has been the recurring danger of all modern philosophy, since René Descartes's *cogito ergo sum* apparently gave the primacy to thinking as the constitutive principle of reality. If that be so, the ego acquires a magisterial authority; for, as George Berkeley showed, even the external world could only be established as an inference from the primal reality of the thinking subject. To Buber, the source of all social sin is to treat the thou as it. The source of neighborliness is to rejoice in the otherness of the thou, not to desire to possess or dominate, but to enrich the soul by respect for the personality of others.

One of the main problems of ethics is to escape from the egocentric predicament caused by psychological presuppositions and necessities. Egoism tends ethically to be identified with systematic selfishness. It believes and behaves as if nothing counts except personal good, the satisfaction of self-interest. Although modern psychology has disposed of the theory at the basis of hedonism—that the only effective human motives are the pursuit of pleasure and the avoidance of pain—hedonism in some form will probably persist. As feeling is always the most individualistic of our experiences, the hedonist is invariably confronted with the difficulty of reconciling individual self-interest with the "common good." In the process it becomes apparent that the "greatest happiness of the greatest number" is a psychological monstrosity.

In economics, the same theory of human nature led to the development of "enlightened self-interest" as the only possible motive in industry and commerce, on the assumption that "economic man" must be led to see that unenlightened self-interest means defeat in a war of all against all. If unrestrained egoism is man's natural way of life, all government, all rules, and even all scruples are artificial restraints upon his "natural" activities. Thus an overly pessimistic view of human nature leads to an impossible view of social structures, in which nature, "red in tooth and claw," is disciplined into "moral" behavior through artificial restrictions imposed on man's true self. Bishop Joseph Butler has a sounder psychology and the ground for a better ethic when he says the indications are just as real "that we were made for society and to do good to our fellow-creatures; as that we were intended to take care of our own life and health and private good." Butler's view of human nature offers a balance between self-love and benevolence under the sway of conscience. It allows for the effects of the fall, yet gives a truer and less cynical reading of the facts of human nature than did Thomas Hobbes and his followers. It preserves us against the opposite, idealist extreme which refuses any legitimate place to self-interest, attempts to banish the profit motive from industry and commerce, and builds "castles in Spain" that contribute nothing to the housing of humanity.

The Freudian analysis of human nature, which begins and ends in crass materialism, gives little help in the integration of character or in devising patterns for social institutions. Buber's distinctions are of more value in showing how, from the religious point of view, the otherwise irreconcilable conflict between egoism and altruism need not arise. True personality, in the religious sense, is not a development of the libido—the lust for pleasure, power, wealth, or any "thing." Its essence is the capacity for fellowship; and in true religion the relation of faith as a fellowship-experience determines the character of all our relations to other persons and to things. This is a byproduct of conversion, in which human nature is redeemed from self-striving toward enlightenment and the impossible task of restraining a primitive selfishness. The liberated individual becomes in very truth, although not in immediate perfection, the child of God.

*Bibliography.* M. Buber, *I and Thou* (1937), and *Between Man and Man* (1947); S. Freud, *The Ego and the Id* (1940).

W. R. FORRESTER

**Egypt.** Officially the Arab Republic of Egypt, an arid country of 1,001,449 sq. km. (386,662 sq. mi.), and about 42 million people (1985 est.). In 1882, Britain occupied Egypt after a short war, initiating a chain of events that drew Egypt into European life, systems, and political life. The first organized revolt against the British in 1919 is a landmark in the modern political life of Egypt. It led to the emergence of the first Egyptian political party (the Wafd), which was followed by others. The link between Egypt and Europe in 1923 inspired the newly elected democratic government to promulgate the first Egyptian constitution.

The interaction between the European model of a state and the long inherited ideas of an Islamic society and state was never a quiet subject and, in fact, never was forgotten. Ali Abdel-Parzek, a sheikh and leading Muslim theologian writer at Al-Azhar University, challenged the old concept of the Islamic state in his book *'Al-Islam wa usul Al-Hukm* (*Islam and the Principles of Government*), published in 1925. As a result he was stripped of his degree and dismissed from Al-Azhar, and the book was banned. Al-Azhar is not only a university for Islamic studies but also one of the most influential religious organizations in Egypt. Abdel-Parzek advocated a separation of the religious from the worldly (secular) life and insisted that Islam has no revealed model of a state or even of government.

This book came two years after the first constitution of Egypt, and three years after its publication Hasan Al-Banna founded the Society of the Muslim Brethren or the Muslim Brotherhood. This was the society essentially responsible for the Islamicization of Egypt. The Brotherhood gained most support from the working class and some land owners who were not attracted by the secular political Egyptian leadership. World War II created stronger dreams of freedom since Egypt, after supporting the Allies, thought to gain independence but that dream was shattered. More important was the creation of a Jewish state in Palestine in May 1948, which sparked many of the subsequent events.

The "free officers" led by Gamal Abd al-Nasser and the Brotherhood volunteers were among those who fought the Israelis in Palestine. Whether the Arab-Israeli war in 1948 caused the formation of the secret paramilitary society of the Brotherhood or whether it began earlier is not clear. In January 1948 the Egyptian secret police uncovered various caches of arms belonging to the Brotherhood. The paramilitary secret society was involved in the assassination of Al-Nokrashy (Dec. 1948), the minister of the interior and high court judge, and also dynamited a company that supported the political left wing. The political police assassinated Al-Banna. The struggle for political parties led to the great Cairo fire in January 1952 which was aimed at Western interests. The government declared martial law, leading to a decisive confrontation and near civil war. The army, led by General Muhammad Nagib, took over, declared Egypt a republic, and dissolved all political parties except the Brotherhood. The struggle for political power between the Brotherhood and Nasser, who became the sole leader of the free officers in 1954 after deposing General Nagib, culminated in an attempt to assassinate Nasser in Alexandria in July 1954. The Brotherhood was outlawed and six defendants were hanged. Nasser announced his plans to develop the army, the economy, and agriculture under a one-party system.

From 1954 to 1967 the Brotherhood was not a popular subject and many members suffered in concentration camps. Nasser improved the lot of the average Egyptian through the nationalization of all foreign interests and more money for education, health, and industrialization. Egypt's involvement in the Arab world led to the formation of the union of Egypt and Syria (1958–62); Egypt mobilized to lead the Arab world and Nasser dealt with internal political forces. That plan came to an end in 1967 when Israel defeated Egypt in six days. Nasser's regime was collapsing, giving the Brotherhood another chance.

The first generation of Al-Banna and Al-Hudaybi, who were social and religious reformers, was more moderate than the second generation who had reorganized the movement in the detention camps. They saw what had happened to their leaders and decided to declare "Takfir" or excommunication of the whole society. The earliest systematic vision of "Takfir" was spelled out in a book that became one of the main documents of the new movement—Signposts by Sayyid Qutb, who was a prisoner and was hanged by Nasser in 1966. The death of Sayyid Qutb marked the end of all possible dialog between the movement and the Egyptian government. The third generation which appeared after 1967 was more determined to fight to the death. Among these were the four Muslims who murdered Anwar al-Sadat in 1981.

Today the Islamic movement in Egypt is divided. The old program of the 1940s is no longer attractive to the third generation who are university graduates who face unemployment, a housing shortage, and both social and political decay. They see Islam as both the Koran and the sword, and believe that salvation will be secured only when an Islamic state is founded. Answers still vary as to the character of an Islamic state and whether it should have a constitution, a parliament, banks, and other modern institutions. The movement is divided between those who accept the Saudi and Pakistani model, and those who want to return to the golden dream of early Islam and the Islamic state as it was founded by the Prophet Muhammed and the four enlightened caliphs.

This issue remains, among others such as human and civil rights of non-Muslims, one of the most difficult to be faced. Social custom makes employment and marriage so restrictive that 7000 Coptic Christians each year convert to Islam for practical reasons. The answers to the problems vary according to the education and political vision of those engaged in the debate.

*Bibliography.* R. P. Mitchell, *The Society of the Muslim Brothers* (1969); M. Berger, *Islam in Egypt Today: Social and Political Aspects of Popular Religion* (1970); R. H. Dekmejian, *Egypt under Nasser* (1972); S. E. Ibrahim, *IJMES* 12 (1980): 423–53; B. Kepel, *The Prophet and the Pharaoh: Muslim Extremism in Egypt* (1984).

GEORGE BEBAWI

## Eichrodt, Walther

**Eichrodt, Walther** (1890–1978). German OT scholar. Born in Gernsbach, Baden, he studied theology first at the seminary in Bethel, and later at the universities of Griefswald and Heidelberg. He taught at the University of Erlangen (1918–21), then from 1921 at the University of Basel where he became professor of OT and the history of religion in 1934. He was a pioneer of the Biblical Theology movement. He continued to teach at the University of Basel until 1961, and was rector of the theological faculty from 1953. As a churchman he was active in both the synod of the Reformed Church in Basel and the Basel Mission. His published works include *Die Quellen der Genesis* (1916), *Die Hoffnung des ewigen Friedens* (1920), *Theology of the OT*, 3 vols. (1933–39; ET, 1961), *Man in the OT* (1944; ET, 1951), *Israel in der Weissagung des Alten Testaments* (1951), *Gottes Ruf im Alten Testament* (1951), and *The Book of the Prophet Ezekiel* (1965/66).

**Eire.** *See* IRELAND, NORTHERN; IRELAND, REPUBLIC OF.

**Eiselen, Frederick Carl** (1872–1937). Methodist biblical scholar. Born in Mundelsheim, Germany, he received his preparatory education in Germany and later studied at New York University, Drew Theological Seminary, the University of Pennsylvania, Columbia University (Ph.D., 1907), and Berlin. He was professor of Semitic languages at Garrett Biblical Institute (1902–32), dean (1919–24), and president (1924–32). He also served as professor of biblical literature at Northwestern University (1918–24). He wrote *Sidon—A Study in Oriental History* (1907), *A Commentary on the Minor Prophets* (1907), *Prophecy and the Prophets* (1909), *The Christian View of the OT* (1912), *Books of the Pentateuch* (1916), *The Psalms and Other Sacred Writings* (1918), and *The Prophetic Books of the OT* (2 vols., 1923). He was also coeditor of *The Abingdon Bible Commentary* and coauthored with W. C. Barclay, *The Worker and His Bible* (1909).

RAYMOND W. ALBRIGHT

**Election.** The decree of God whereby from eternity he chose unto everlasting life a certain number of angels (1 Tim. 5:21) and men (Rom. 8:28, 29; Eph. 1:4; 2 Tim. 1:9; 1 Pet. 1:1, 2). It is with the election of men that the revelation in Scripture is mainly concerned. The discrimination which election implies appears in the OT most conspicuously in the choice of Jacob over Esau (Gen. 25:23; Mal. 1:2, 3; compare with Rom. 9:11–13). The choice of the children of Israel as God's peculiar people is the typical example which sets the points for our understanding of what election involves—sovereign election in love unto redemption and the adoption of sons (Deut. 4:37; 7:7, 8; 10:15; 14:2; 33:3). Election guarantees all the means and provisions necessary for the achievement of its purpose. The choice in Christ before the foundation of the world is the source from which all saving grace proceeds as it is bestowed and exercised in the believer (Eph. 1:4–14). Foreknowledge (Rom. 8:29; 1 Pet. 1:2) cannot be construed as the mere foresight of believing and persevering grace but must be understood in the pregnant sense of distinguishing and purposive love (see Amos 3:2 and Rom. 11:2). The reason for God's election lies hidden in the unsearchable riches of his own sovereign good pleasure. It is not ours to comprehend but to bow in holy amazement.

JOHN MURRAY

**Eliot, Thomas Stearns** (1888–1965). Anglo-Catholic English-American poet, literary critic, essayist, and lecturer. Born in St. Louis, he studied at Harvard University where he was influenced by the anti-Romanticism of Irving Babbitt, George Santayana, and Bertrand Russell. He studied in France for a year and was at the University of Marburg, Germany, in 1914 when World War I broke out. At Merton College, Oxford, he completed his dissertation on the philosophy of F. H. Bradley. Harvard accepted the dissertation but Eliot never returned to complete the degree. In 1929 he was baptized and confirmed in the Anglican Church; a few months later he renounced his American citizenship to become British. He once announced himself as a "classicist in literature, royalist in politics, and anglo-catholic in religion."

Eliot's public literary life began in 1915 when Chicago's *Poetry* magazine published *The Love Song of J. Alfred Prufrock*. He supported himself briefly as a teacher, then in a position with Lloyd's Bank until 1926, and finally as an editor for Faber & Faber, the London publisher. His literary reputation was established in 1922 with publication of *The Waste Land*. For the next two decades Eliot dominated poetry and literary criticism in English-speaking countries on both sides of the Atlantic.

Eliot's early poems renounced soft Georgian Romanticism; he wrote of the decay of Western culture, expressing the disillusionment of the post-World War I age. Blending verbal wit into flexible blank verse with colloquialism, irony, precise imagery, and allusiveness, he startled early readers by eliminating transitions, juxtaposing images into kaleidoscopic patterns. After Eliot's conversion to Christianity, poems such as *Ash Wednesday* (1930) and the *Four Quartets* (1935–43) express a search for spiritual peace, a concern over the relationship between time and eternity. In addition to his literary criticism he wrote two long essays on Christian political theory, reflecting a conservative cast of mind: *The Idea of a Christian Society* (1940) and *Notes Towards the Definition of a Culture* (1949). He also wrote five successful plays in poetic idiom, dealing with religious themes: *Murder in the Cathedral* (1935), *The Family Reunion* (1939), *The Cocktail Party* (1950), *The Confidential Clerk* (1954), and *The Elder Statesman* (1958). In 1958 Eliot was awarded the Nobel Prize for Literature and was also named by Queen Elizabeth to the prestigious Order of Merit.

JOAN OSTLING

**Elicott, Charles John** (1819–1905). Anglican scholar and bishop. Born in Lincolnshire, he was educated at Cambridge and was rector of Pilton (1842–58). Briefly professor at King's College, London, and at Cambridge, he was appointed dean of Exeter in 1861, and bishop of Gloucester and Bristol in 1863. He retained the Gloucester section when the see was divided in 1897. For 11 years he was chairman of the NT Revision Committee. He published commentaries on most of the Pauline Epistles (1856), on the NT (3 vols., 1878–79), on the OT (5 vols., 1882–84), and on the complete Bible (7 vols., 1897).

**Elliott, Grace Loucks (Mrs. Harrison S.)** (1891–1979). Methodist. Born in Alverton, Pa., she studied at Findley College, Teachers College and Union Theological Seminary, and Columbia University (Ph.D., 1936). She was on the staff of the National Board of the YWCA, visiting colleges and universities (1917–25); lectured in colleges, conferences, and social and religious agencies on religious education and family relations (1925–43); and was general secretary of the YWCA (1943–53). She contributed to education, social, and religious journals. She wrote (with H. Bone) *The Sex Life of Youth* (1929), *Understanding the Adolescent Girl* (1930), (with H. S. Elliott) *Solving Personal Problems* (1936), and *Women after Forty* (1936).

**Elliott, Harrison S.** (1882–1951). Methodist. Born in St. Clairsville, Ohio, he studied at Antioch College, Valparaiso University, Ohio Wesleyan University, Drew Theological Seminary, Teachers College, Columbia University, and Yale University (Ph.D., 1940). He was secretary to Bishop James W. Bashford of the Methodist Church in China (1905–8); assistant secretary of the African Diamond Jubilee of the Methodist Church (1909/10); secretary of the International Committee, YMCA (1910–22); instructor in religious psychology, Drew Theological Seminary (1921–23); and professor of practical theology and head of the department of religious education and psychology, Union Theological Seminary (1925–50). He was ordained to the ministry of the Methodist Church (1944); chairman of the National Boys Work Committee of the YMCA (1927–46); president of the Religious Education Association (1939–42), and general secretary of the Religious Education Association (1950/51). He was one of the outstanding leaders in the field of religious education and in the field of group dynamics. He directed the first large-scale use of group discussion in conferences at the international conference of the YMCA, in Poertschach, Austria (1923); at the Student Volunteer conference of the United States in Indianapolis, Ind. (1924); and at the world conference of the World Alliance of the YMCA in Helsingfors, Finland (1926). He was greatly interested in mental hygiene and helped to introduce courses in mental hygiene into the curriculum of theological seminaries. He wrote *How Jesus Met Life Questions* (1920), *The Bearing of Psychology upon Religion* (1927), *The Process of Group Thinking* (1928), *Group Discussion in Religious Education* (1930), and *Can Religious Education Be Christian?* (1940). He coauthored with E. Cutler, *Student Standards of Action* (1914), and with G. L. Elliott, *Solving Personal Problems* (1936).

**Ellis, John Tracy** (1905– ). Roman Catholic educator, editor, historian, and author. Born in Seneca, Ill., he holds degrees from St. Viator College and the Catholic University of America (Ph.D., 1930). He taught history at St. Viator College (1930–32), College of St. Teresa (1932–34), and while studying for the priesthood at Sulpician Seminary (1934–38) was director of the Southern Branch Summer Session, the Catholic University of America, San Antonio, Tex. (1935–37). Later he taught history at the Catholic University of America (1938–41), was professor of American church history (1947–64), professor of church history at the University of San Francisco (1964–76), and professorial lecturer in church history at the Catholic University of America (1977– ). He served as managing editor of the *Catholic Historical Review* (1941–63), secretary of the American Catholic Historical Association, and censor of books, archdiocese of Washington. He has written many articles and books, including *The Formative Years of the Catholic University of America* (1946), *A Select Bibliography of the History of the Catholic Church in the United States* (1947), and *The Life of James Cardinal Gibbons* (2 vols., 1952).

JACK MITCHELL

**Ellul, Jacques** (1912– ). French sociologist, historian, and Christian ethicist. Born in Bordeaux, he was educated at the University of Bordeaux (Doctor of Law, 1936). In 1940 he was dismissed from his university teaching post at Strasbourg for his opposition to Marshal Pétain and the Vichy government. An active participant in the Resistance movement during the occupation of France by Germany, he was afterward appointed deputy major of Bordeaux in charge of public works (1944–46). From 1944 to his retirement in 1980 he served as professor of the history and sociology of institutions in the Faculty of Law and Economic Sciences at Bordeaux, and also held a chair in the Institute of Political Studies (1947–80). An active lay leader in the Reformed Church of France, Ellul served on its National Council (1951–70) and also served on World Council of Churches commissions (1947–51).

As a historian and sociologist owing much to (but going beyond and often against) Marx and Weber, Ellul is best known for his broad-ranging studies of *la technique* as the 20th century's definitive mode of thought and action and its driving spiritual force, subordinating all of life to rationalistic, quantitative analyses. Technique progressively eliminates tradition and spiritual and human values and installs the rule of measurable effectiveness in politics, the media, economics, education, religion, art, and the popular culture. Against this faceless, global, totalitarian force which creates the true infrastructure of modern life Ellul calls for the rediscovery and renewal of true individuality.

As a theologian and ethicist (with deep roots in Scripture and influenced greatly by Kierkegaard and Barth), Ellul is best known for his criticism of all conformism to the world and its philosophical or social systems. He proposes a radical, biblical, Christian ethics of freedom, holiness, and love over against the tyranny of the principalities and powers inhabiting the institutions and collective realities of the world.

Ellul has written more than 600 published articles and nearly 50 books, the best known of which are *The Presence of the Kingdom* (ET, 1951), *Histoire des Institutions* (5 vols., 1951–80), *The Technological Society* (ET, 1964), *The Political Illusion* (ET, 1967), *The Meaning of the City* (1970), *The Ethics of Freedom* (French, 3 vols., 1976–84; ET, 1976), *The Humiliation of the Word* (ET, 1985), *The Subversion of Christianity* (ET, 1986), and *Le Bluff Technologique* (1987).

*Bibliography.* J. Ellul, *In Season, Out of Season* (ET, 1982); (1988); D. W. Gill, *The Word of God in the Ethics of Jacques Ellul* (1984); J. M. Hanks, *Jacques Ellul: A Comprehensive Bibliography* (1984).

DAVID W. GILL

**El Salvador.** A Central American republic with an area of 21,331 sq. km. (8236 sq. mi.), a population of 4.86 million (1985), and an annual per capita income of $710 (1985). Most live on as little as $10 a month. Roman Catholicism is the dominant religion in El Salvador, although it is often mixed with traditional Mayan tribal beliefs. The influence of the church was substantially weakened but not neutralized by the liberal reforms of 1871–88. Marriage, education, and cemeteries were secularized; monastic orders were abolished; and the concordat with the Vatican was annulled. Nevertheless, because of the church's relative poverty, the measures were not as severe as those in Guatemala. A demonstration of the church's resilience was its success in regaining much of its lost influence during a series of liberal governments (1890–1931). A military coup precipitated the massacre of 4 percent of the population in 1932 and destabilized both society and church.

The dominant figure in the Catholic Church throughout most of the 20th century was Archbishop Luis Chávez y González. During the 1950s and 1960s he promoted priesthood vocations and the formation of agricultural cooperatives. His close ties to the Christian Democratic party and enthusiastic adoption of Vatican II reforms led the church away from its traditional support for the military dictatorship. Because of Chávez's relatively tolerant attitude, liberation theology had a profound impact on the Salvadorean church. During the 1970s significant sectors of the church were active in the formation of Christian base communities and peasant organizations, and in advocating radical socioeconomic change. The military responded to these activities with a ruthless attack on the church. During 1977–81, 10 priests and hundreds of church workers were assassinated. On March 24, 1980, Chávez's successor, Archbishop Oscar Arnulfo Romero, was murdered while saying Mass. Since Romero's death the church hierarchy has actively sought a negotiated settlement to the country's civil war.

Among 46 Protestant denominations (15–20 percent of the total population), pentecostals dominate. Traditional denominations account for only a small percentage of the recent growth in Protestant converts. By the early 1970s the annual rate of conversion to Protestantism had already reached 11 percent. By the late 1980s the figure was considerably higher.

**Emerton, Ephraim** (1851–1935). American church historian. Born in Salem, Mass., he studied at Harvard, Berlin, and Leipzig universities. Thereafter he taught history and German before appointment as professor of ecclesiastical history (1882–1918). A Unitarian by affiliation, he wrote *Introduction to the Study of the Middle Ages* (1888), *Mediaeval Europe, 814–1300* (1894), *Desiderius Erasmus* (1899), *Unitarian Thought* (1911), *Beginnings of Modern Europe* (1917), *The Defensor Pacis of Marsiglio of Padua* (1920), *Learning and Living* (1921), and *Humanism and Tyranny—Studies in the Italian Trecento* (1925). He also translated *Correspondence of Pope Gregory* (1931) and *Correspondence of St. Boniface* (1934).

**Empirical Theology.** The philosophy that internal and external experience is the sole foundation for knowledge. An empirical or pragmatic element has characterized Christian thought since the time of Christ (Acts 4:20). The Christian experience of salvation has affected what are apparently its most metaphysical affirmations, as in Athanasius's battle on soteriological grounds for the deity of Christ. In modern times the pioneer of empirical theology as such was Friedrich Schleiermacher who, instead of beginning with general principles or "revealed truths," proposed to "elucidate the contents of the Christianly pious soul." Since then there have been many exponents of this point of view, beginning with the data of experience, proceeding chiefly by the inductive method to validate doctrine. The examples below illustrate various forms of empiricism. Albrecht Ritschl, while repudiating Schleiermacher's subjectivism, laid the foundations of his system empirically in the historical Jesus, and found religion's validity in the support it offers to empirically observed values. Ernst Troeltsch found Christianity not absolute, but best (for us)—not because it is more true but only because it is more fitting. *Varieties of Religious Experience* by W. James (1902) is a classic of sympathetic case studies, for the most part waiving ontological questions. F. R. Tennant's *Philosophical Theology* (1928–30), excluding specifically religious experience, builds strictly on sensory experience. D. C. Macintosh in *Theology an Empirical Science* (1919) and *The Reasonableness of Christianity* (1926) takes a critical realist stance. Macintosh builds on the admittedly optimistic standpoint that the "highest Christian ideals are practicable, progressively realizable, and the values thus produced will be ultimately conserved."

The claims of empirical theology are summarized in the statement by Macintosh that "genuine knowledge of a divine Reality has been gained through religious experience at its best"; also that "this knowledge may be formulated and further developed by means of inductive procedure." Empirical theology is a protest against theology exclusively based on or concerned with metaphysical assumptions; on general "truths of reason"; or on the bare authority of church, religious literature, or individual. That theology is focally concerned with experience is widely admitted. Empirical theology insists that theological propositions contrary to observable fact must be rejected.

Some criticisms of empirical theology are beside the mark. It is not purely individualistic and subjective; it has always tended to stress the universal rather than the particular. It is not pure psychologism or positivism, although sometimes it tends in that direction. It constantly asks to what objective reality the observed data point.

The following summarizes the criticism of the weaknesses or dangers inherent in empirical theology. Empiricists may claim too much, as when H. N. Wieman asserts that the evidence for God is of the same order and cogency as for any physical fact. Again, empirical theologies have by no means reached identical conclusions; pure and indisputable fact can never be the sole basis for construction. Further, empiricists themselves do not agree as to what can be called basic data. Are sense perceptions alone admissible (Tennant), or is personal religious experience a primary datum as well (Schleiermacher, Macintosh, and most others)? Is faith founded on history empirical (Ritschl) or are historical events irrecoverable so that succeeding generations can only infer their existence? Even assuming that all religious experience were uniform, might not the inferences drawn therefrom be colored by the wishes or the training of the observer? Further, in the Christian religion, the most decisive elements go beyond direct experience and observation and are not susceptible to empirical demonstration. If it were otherwise there would be no true walk by faith. The theology of revelation and the theology of experience are not mutually exclusive. Trustworthy revelation is supported by experience; on the other hand the most poignant questions of man cannot be answered from within but require answers from outside the perceptual system.

KENNETH J. FOREMAN

**Encounter Groups.** A variety of planned, intensive group experiences designed to help individuals deal with emotional and personal problems. Participants are encouraged to strip away the facades that mask their true natures and reveal their innermost thoughts, feelings, and aspirations. The encounter's purpose is to fill a void created by a societal emphasis on social adjustment rather than personal adjustment, on duty rather than pleasure, on intellect rather than emotions. The theory is that growth occurs as the person develops an understanding and appreciation of self and others.

Based on humanistic principles, encounter groups are geared to meet the needs of people who do not suffer severe psychopathology. Each of the eight to 20 members of the group, together with a leader or "facilitator," share their concerns, reveal their fears, and express their hopes. It is important to know that others care, that others will listen and understand, and that others want to help. Games may be used to enable group members to become more aware of their own bodies and to act out feelings of aggression, dependency, and affection. Emphasis is placed on the "here and now" and on the potential within each person, seeking to go beyond past failings and feelings of guilt. Encounter groups meet in homes, churches, industries, hospitals, correctional institutions, and universities. Some meetings may last for hours, continue all night, or over a nonstop three-day weekend. The more elaborate sessions may meet at resorts with beautiful accommodations, elaborate meals, and possibilities for yoga, dancing, and nude swimming.

The encounter movement began with Kurt Lewin's group dynamics studies in 1946 at the Massachusetts Institute of Technology. He designed training sessions to help managers and executives better understand the importance of the affective component of workers' lives. Known as T-groups, these training sessions soon expanded to include educators and those wishing to ease international tensions and improve race relationships. The emphasis of the T-group was more on group interaction and less on the intrapersonal adjustment of individual members. But as the movement grew in the 1950s and escalated in the 1960s and 1970s, the term "encounter" became associated with meeting the affective needs of the participants. A large variety of strategies—including Gestalt therapy, synanon (developed for the treatment of drug addiction), creativity workshops, transactional analysis, psychodrama, Esalen eclectic, sensitivity training, and various self-help groups—became associated with the encounter label.

Popularity for such groups waned during the 1980s. This was due partly to incorporation of its methods into other forms of therapy not associated with humanistic psychology and partly because of mounting criticism of both methodology and consequences of the encounter session.

Some facilitators are trained, experienced mental health professionals. Others are charlatans and hucksters who often do not function effectively as leaders and would not know how to handle an emergency should one occur. Although nearly 90 percent of encounter-group leaders and 60 percent of encounter-group members say the sessions are beneficial, research does not support this. In one study of 200 encounter-group participants, only about one-third appeared to receive any lasting benefits. In another study, the experience was damaging to 8 percent of group members.

**Bibliography.** H. E. Klingberg, Jr., *JPT* 1 (1970): 31–39; M. Lundberg, *Potomac Magazine, The Washington Post* (July 5, 1970); C. R. Rogers, *Carl Rogers on Encounter Groups* (1970); R. S. Smith, *IJGPP* 20 (1970): 192–209; E. E. Mintz, *Marathon Groups: Reality and Symbol* (1971); A. Kadis, et al., *Practicum of Group Psychotherapy* (2d ed., 1974); R. D. James, *The Wall Street Journal* 59 (April 16, 1979): 1, 18.

BONNIDELL CLOUSE

**Encyclical.** In current usage, a formal pastoral letter sent by a pope or Anglican bishops on doctrinal, moral, or disciplinary matters. Originally an encyclical was a circular letter from a Christian leader of recognized authority to the churches of a given area. The first recorded modern papal encyclical was *Ubi primum*, discussing episcopal duties, issued by Benedict XIV (1740–58) on December 3, 1740. Like other pontifical documents, papal encyclicals are indexed by their opening words. Since 1867, the term "encyclical" also has been used for the letters issued by the Anglican bishops at the end of their Lambeth conferences once each decade.

Encyclicals are circulated by the pope as an activity proper to his offices of shepherd of the Church and head of the episcopal college, and thus are a part of his *ordinary magisterium* as opposed to his *extraordinary infallible magisterium*, exercised in such solemn functions as the definition of dogma or the official approbation of the decrees of an ecumenical council. While these pastoral letters are not of themselves infallible pronouncements and although their teachings are subject to change, nevertheless Catholics are obligated to assent to their doctrinal and moral content. The following list includes more significant encyclicals of the popes since Pius XII.

**Encyclicals of Pius XII (1939–58).** *Summi pontificatus*, 1939 (Christian idea of the state); *Mystici corporis*, 1943 (the church as the body of Christ); *Divino afflante Spiritu*, 1943 (biblical studies); *Mediator Dei*, 1947 (liturgy); *Humani generis*, 1950 (subversive doctrines); *Evangeli praecones*, 1950 (missions); *Ad caeli reginam*, 1954 (queenship of Mary); *Musicae sacrae*, 1955 (sacred music); *Haurietis aquas*, 1956 (devotion to the sacred heart); *Luctuosissimi eventus*, 1956 (urging prayers for peace and freedom for the people of Hungary); *Laetamur admodum*, 1956 (exhortation for prayers for peace in Poland, Hungary, and the Middle East); *Datis nuperrime*, 1956 (lamenting Hungary's sorrows and condemning the ruthless use of force there); *Fidei donum*, 1957 (present condition of Catholic missions, especially in Africa); *Invicti athletae*, 1957 (honoring St. Andrew Bobola, martyred in 1657, Polish Jesuit missionary); *Le pelerinage de Lourdes*, 1957 (warning against materialism on the centenary of the visions at Lourdes); *Miranda prorsus*, 1957 (morality and motion pictures, radio, TV); *Ad apostolorum principis*, 1958 (communism and the Church in China); *Meminisse iuvat*, 1958 (prayers for the persecuted Church).

**Encyclicals of John XXIII (1958–63).** *Ad Petri cathedram*, 1959 (truth, unity and peace in a spirit of charity); *Sacerdotii nostri primordia*, 1959 (honoring St. John Vianney, died, 1859, French saint); *Princeps pastorum*, 1959 (missions, native clergy, and lay participation); *Mater et magistra*, 1961 (Christianity and social progress, reaffirming the fundamental social teachings of Leo XIII); *Aeterna Dei Sapientia*, 1961 (commemorating the 15th centennial of the death of St. Leo I, and affirming the See of Peter as the center of Christian unity); *Paenitentiam agere*, 1962 (need for interior and exterior penance); *Pacem in terris*, 1963 (concerning the establishment of universal peace in truth, justice, charity, and liberty).

**Encyclicals of Paul VI (1963–78).** *Ecclesiam suam*, 1964 (the Church's duty to other Christians and to nonbelievers, and its future development); *Mense maio*, 1965 (prayers for the preservation of peace); *Mysterium fidei*, 1965 (Holy Eucharist); *Christi Matri*, 1966 (prayers for peace); *Popularum progressio*, 1967 (the development of peoples); *Sacerdotalis caelibatus*, 1967 (the necessity of priestly celibacy); *Humanae vitae*, 1968 (the regulation of birth).

**Encyclicals of John Paul II (1978– ).** *Redemptor hominis*, 1979 (redemption and the dignity of the human race); *Dives in misericordia*, 1980 (the need to demonstrate the mercy of God in an increasingly threatened world); *Laborem exercens*, 1981 (the dignity of labor and the rights of workers); *Slavorum apostoli*, 1985 (commemorating the 11th centennial of the death of St. Methodius, died in 885, who with his brother St. Cyril, died in 869, evangelized the Slavs in the 9th cent.); *Dominum et vivificantem*, 1986 (the role of the Holy Spirit in the life of the Church); *Redemptoris Mater*, 1987 (announcing a holy year of the Virgin Mary).

The most important of John XXIII's encyclicals were *Mater et magistra*, 1961, and *Pacem in terris*,

1963. The former commented on modern social questions in the light of Christian doctrine, evinced a decided bias in favor of the "lowly and oppressed," and called on Catholics to cooperate with other people in the task of humanizing and christianizing modern civilization. The latter, uniquely addressed to "all men of good will," discussed the quest for international peace and identified it with that unity of order which is based on respect for the Law of God. Paul VI's most discussed encyclicals included his radical *Populorum progressio*, 1967, and his controversial *Sacerdotalis caelibatus*, 1967, and *Humanae vitae*, 1968. The first of these documents condemned war, injustice, violence, and economic exploitation as well as governments which supported economic systems which kept a majority of their people in degradation. The *Sacerdotalis caelibatus* reaffirmed clerical celibacy in the Western Church and *Humanae vitae* outlawed for Catholics all artificial means of birth control. John Paul II's most influential encyclical has been his *Laborem exercens*, 1981, in which he insisted on the primacy of humanity over "things," and called for a new economic order, neither capitalist nor Marxist, based on the rights of workers and the dignity of labor. He also, on several occasions, has pointedly endorsed Paul VI's *Humanae vitae*.

**Bibliography.** A. Fremantle, ed., *The Papal Encyclicals in Their Historical Context* (1956); J. N. Moody and J. G. Lawlor, eds., *The Challenge of Mater et Magistra* (1963); P. Riga, *Peace on Earth* (1964); Paul VI, *The Teachings of Pope Paul VI*, 9 vols. (1968–75); M. C. Carlen, ed., *The Papal Encyclicals*, 5 vols. (1981); P. Hebblethwaite, *Introducing John Paul II* (1982); J. W. Houck and O. F. Williams, eds., *Co-Creation and Capitalism: John Paul II's Laborem Exercens* (1983); *The Pope Speaks* (1954– ).

ROBERT D. LINDER

**Enelow, Herman Gerson** (1877–1934). Rabbi. Born in Russia, he studied at the University of Chicago, Cincinnati, and Hebrew Union College (doctorates, 1900 and 1925). He served as rabbi of Temple Israel, Paducah, Ky. (1898–1901); Temple Adath Israel, Louisville, Ky. (1901–12); and Temple Emanu-El, New York (1912–34). He was president of the Central Conference of American Rabbis (1927–29). His books include *Aspects of the Bible* (1911), *The Effects of Religion* (1917), *The Varied Beauty of the Psalms* (1917), *The Faith of Israel* (1917), *The Allied Countries and the Jews* (1918), *A Jewish View of Jesus* (1920), *The Adequacy of Judaism* (1920), *The Jew and the World* (1921), *The Diverse Elements of Religion* (1924). He edited *Yahwism* (1903), *Origins of Synagogue and Church* (1929), and Al-Nakawa's *Menorat Ha-Maor* (1929–31).

RAYMOND W. ALBRIGHT

**England.** The country of England comprises the southern two-thirds of the island of Britain. England and Wales were politically joined in 1536, but Wales maintains a separate social and ecclesiastical identity. Including Wales, England covers 151,126 sq. km. (58,350 sq. mi.) with a population of about 50 million (1985). Although England is a constitutional monarchy, the role of the monarch has devolved into a ceremonial position, including nominal leadership of the Church of England. Political leadership rests in the prime minister and a bicameral parliament. Parliament retains final authority over the Church of England, which was established by Henry VIII through a series of antipapal acts in the 1530s. There are an estimated 4.6 million Christians in England itself and 5 million in Wales, about 19 percent of the total population (1985).

Anglican communions still hold some dominance over the religious life of England and Wales. Like other Western European countries, however, the prevailing religious mood of the English people has become firmly secularist. Two-thirds of England's people have been baptized, but only one-third undergo confirmation. Some 38 percent of church members in England and Wales identify themselves as Anglican, about 33 percent as Roman Catholic, and 29 percent with other denominations. A total of 77 percent of the people of Wales and 87 percent of those in the rest of England do not consider themselves to be members of any church. A continuing migration to England from former colonies and world trading partners has introduced an array of world faiths to the English urban scene. By 1985 estimate there were: nontrinitarians, 348,000; Muslims, 900,000; Sikhs, 175,000; Hindus, 140,000; Jews, 111,000; Krishnas, 50,000; and Buddhists, 20,000.

From a height of undisputed leadership within the world church in the 19th century, England's Christian presence reached such an ebb that by the late 20th century some churches received aid and missionaries from nations whose churches their countrymen founded. Several factors have been suggested for England's drastic spiritual decline. Nearly 80 percent of all English now live in densely populated urban areas where social disintegration has been a byproduct of industrialization. The social problems attending the Industrial Revolution hit England hard and early. Human needs within the urban slums bred such pioneering Christian efforts as the Sunday school movement, the Salvation Army, and the YMCA and YWCA. Classical liberalism drawn from Romantic philosophy and European theologies after Friedrich Schleiermacher fit this social activist need, as did the Christian Socialist movement. The social gospel gave Christians tools with which to reconstruct their degraded society but distracted them from missions, evangelistic outreach, and biblical studies. England was far slower than continental Europeans to embrace the neo-orthodox constructs of Karl Barth.

Barthian theology arose as England was struggling to cope with the devastating human losses suffered in World War I. In many ways more debilitating than the material devastation of World War II, the nation lost such a percentage of its young adult men that religious answers seemed unavailing, and the national consciousness retreated into skepticism.

Politically, as England lost its role as a colonial power it also lost a world missions vision such as dominated English Christianity in the 19th century. One notable exception to this 20th-century decline was the Welsh revival of 1903–5. Wales was the scene of several dramatic evangelical awakenings during the 19th century. The early 20th-century revival in the coal fields, however, stirred such a profound outpouring of zeal for home and world evangelism that Welsh missionaries spread throughout the world. An outgrowth of this revival was the request for disestablishment of Welsh Anglicans from the Church of England. The Church in Wales was split off from the archbishopric of Canterbury by act of Parliament in 1915. Final separation was accomplished after the war in 1920. By the later 1900s, although still nominally established, the Church of England lacked its once-powerful leading of social and political life in a metropolitan and sophisticated pluralistic society. Most active in leading the Church of England toward a stronger position through ecumenism was archbishop of York and later of Canterbury, William Temple (1881–1944). Founder of the British Council of Churches, Archbishop Temple added social mission and world focus to the moribund church in the 1930s and early 1940s.

By the 1980s signs of renewal were emerging within individual English churches, while overall denominations continued to slide. Estimates for 1985, which included Scotland and Ireland as well as England and Wales, showed a 10 percent loss in membership among Roman Catholics since 1970 and about a 25 percent loss among Methodists and Presbyterians. On the other hand, Lutheran membership had increased slightly, some conservative Presbyterians affiliated with the Free Church of Scotland were planting congregations, and pentecostal and Holiness and Orthodox churches were growing. A house church movement of small study groups independent of denominations, had also drawn nearly 200,000 since 1970.

If health had not returned to the English church it did show some signs of recovery from what may have been the nadir of its influence.

*See also* ENGLAND, CHURCH OF.

**Bibliography.** K. S. Latourette, *A History of Christianity* (1953); A. D. Gilbert, *Religion and Society in Industrial England: Church, Chapel, and Social Change* (1976); D. Barrett, *World Christian Encyclopedia* (1982); J. L. Gonzalez, *The Story of Christianity*, vol. 2, *The Reformation to the Present Day* (1984).

PETER TOON

**England, Church of.** By 1900 the Church of England, although retaining the trappings of establishment, had lost most privileges associated with it. In no real sense could Parliament be regarded as its lay synod. Thus the movement already begun in the Victorian period to give the church a greater control of its own structures was a marked feature of the 20th century.

Clerical assemblies or convocations had been revived (Canterbury 1852, York 1861), but had no formal ecclesiastical power. Inspired by the dynamic energy of William Temple, later archbishop of Canterbury, what became known as the "Life and Liberty movement" sought a greater degree of self-government. This was achieved by the Enabling Act (1919) which created a new body called church assembly. Made up of clergy and laity, including women, it had the right to legislate, subject to parliamentary veto. It was not a synod. The influence of the laity was limited, since many doctrinal and other matters were still reserved for the purely clerical convocations. Parliament did, in fact, exercise its right of veto in 1928 when it rejected the Revised Prayer Book which, although it had failed to commend itself to many evangelicals and Anglo-Catholics, had the support of a clear majority in church assembly and convocations. In the face of this rejection the bishops maintained the right of the church to decide its own patterns of worship by allowing the use of the 1928 book.

The limitations of the power of the laity in church assembly became increasingly frustrating, particularly when it was realized that they had no right to be consulted about canon law revision which began in 1947. In 1953 the church assembly appointed a commission "to consider how the clergy and laity can best be joined together in the synodical government of the Church." This eventually led to the replacement of the church assembly by general synod (1970). The new body was linked to diocesan and deanery synodical structures and gave a considerably greater role to the laity, although certain protections were provided for the clergy.

Meanwhile, a number of commissions sat in 1935, 1952, and 1970 to seek resolution of the tensions and anomalies in the relationship between church and state. The key areas were the right of the church to govern itself and to have a greater involvement in the appointment of its higher clergy. These were in measure resolved in the 1970s. The Worship and Doctrine Measure (1974) gave the Church of England freedom to legislate for itself in matters of doctrine and worship, except in liturgical matters where the Book of Common Prayer, or parts of it, were involved. In 1976 Prime Minister James Callaghan, while retaining the formal rights of appointment, allowed the church very substantial influence in the process of selecting diocesan bishops. In these ways real power has devolved to the church, but the continued role of the state remains an object of criticism for many.

In the course of the 19th century three clear theological groups emerged: evangelicals, Anglo-Catholics, and liberals. Although each had its own internal differentiation and many members and clergy of the Church of England resisted such classification, they do represent significant strands. At the beginning of the 20th century the Anglo-Catholics, with their highly sacramental and ritualist emphasis, were extremely influential. Such advanced ritualism allowed a measure of unity to be sustained, but at the cost of much bitterness and large-scale breakdown of effective diocesan discipline in liturgical matters. Gradually some of the liturgical emphases of the Anglo-Catholics became normative in much Church of England worship. However, partly because of its success, partly because of suspicions of authority based on tradition, and partly because of its own internal uncertainties, Anglo-Catholicism as a distinct movement declined significantly by the late 1970s, although there was something of a resurgence in the 1980s.

In the first half of the 20th century the influence of evangelicals was marginal. For much of the period evangelical leadership was weak. The 1920s saw a sharp split between liberal and conservative evangelicals, primarily over different responses to biblical criticism, but also over the degree of "compromise" that could be allowed other views within the church. The conservative success in helping to defeat the 1928 Prayer Book made them the object of much calumny and suspicion. They in turn became extremely defensive and generally retired to the parishes and their own organizational network. The rise of leaders such as John R. W. Stott, J. I. Packer, and Colin Buchanan after World War II brought new commitment to theology, to institutional structures, to liturgical developments, to ecumenical activity, and to social awareness. These objectives were endorsed by the National Evangelical Assembly meetings at Keele (1967) and Nottingham (1977). Still, significant elements within the evangelical constituency remained unhappy with compromises that closer involvement with the wider church brought.

The "broad church" heritage of the 19th century had, particularly through F. D. Maurice, urged an inclusiveness able to hold together apparent polarities. If this was one part of the liberal heritage, another was the diluted doctrinal package of liberal Protestantism. Before World War I there was considerable debate between liberals and conservatives about whether acceptance of the virgin birth and the physical resurrection of Christ should be required for ordination. Bishop Charles Gore urged that they should. Archbishop Randall Davidson was less certain.

Immediately after World War I, a more extreme form of modernism, which questioned not only the miraculous in general, but also the divinity of Christ in particular, became notorious. As a result, Archbishop Davidson was pressured into appointing a doctrine commission (1922). Its work was to describe the opinions of its supposedly representative cross-section of members rather than those of the Church of England as a whole. It met for many years under the chairmanship of Temple. Its report, *Doctrine in the Church of England* (1938), was liberal-Catholic in its ethos—it firmly rejected the modernist position, but remained open on miracles and was largely unaware of neo-orthodoxy.

After World War II liberalism was comparatively weak, but the 1960s brought a new burst of radicalism that was symbolized in the questioning of Bishop J. A. T. Robinson's *Honest to God* (1963). The argument regarding the theological boundaries of the Church of England remained, but the doctrine commission report *Christian Believing* (1976) seemed to reveal that they were very wide indeed. The so-called Durham Controversy over Bishop David Jenkins' views on the virgin birth and the physical resurrection of Christ, however, produced a statement from the bishops, *The Nature of Christian Belief* (1986), which is cautiously orthodox in its approach.

Throughout the period the Church of England had to battle with the task of adjusting to an increasingly secularized society. All church statistics have been downward—the number of ordained parochial clergy: 1901, 23,670; 1971, 15,223; 1980, 11,235; 1984, 10,749; Easter communicants: 1901, 1,902,000; 1971, 1,631,506; 1980, 1,764,000; 1983, 1,668,000; baptism: 1901, 566,221; 1970, 347,161; 1980, 272,000; 1983, 239,000. Its inherited income, although well-managed by church commissioners, has had to be supplemented on an increasing scale. Many new dioceses have been created and suffragan and (more recently) area bishops appointed. The *Alternative Service Book* (1980), although much criticized by the traditionalists, achieved a remarkable degree of acceptance. Many were disappointed that the challenges which came from the report of the Archbishop's Commission on Evangelism, *Towards the Conversion of England* (1945), were not taken more seriously. Certainly the failure to give enough attention to evangelism was a major weakness identified by the Partners in Mission survey of the Church of England, *To a Rebellious House?* (1981). A key question, still unresolved, is whether the Church of England remains the church of all the people of England or is, in ways which affect structures and strategy, the church of its committed members.

While remaining predominantly middle-class in character, significant attempts have been made to understand and resolve social problems. Two archbishops' reports—*Christianity and Industrial Problems* (1918) and *Faith in the City* (1985)—have been notable, although politically controversial.

The Church of England, as an established church with strong Protestant and Catholic traditions and an inclination to be tolerant of most views as long as they do not threaten the functions of the institution, has as wide a spectrum of belief as any major church in Christendom. Its polarized elements are able to coexist more because of their particular traditions and the freedom they enjoy, than because of any agreement.

This has made ecumenical relationships very difficult. Despite occasional agreements and the influence of the charismatic movement in breaking down some barriers, the polarities still tend to dampen unity with others whose views are no different than those already within the Church of England. Thus in the late 1950s proposals for unity with the Church of Scotland (Presbyterian) collapsed, as did those with Methodists (1972), and others which sought a covenant among the Church of England, the United Reformed Church, the Methodists, the Churches of Christ, and the Moravian Church (1982). The ordination of women, accepted by the majority, was in the 1980s, for similar reasons, being vigorously opposed.

**Bibliography.** G. K. A. Bell, *Randall Davidson: Archbishop of Canterbury* (1935); R. B. Lloyd, *The Church of England, 1900–1965* (1972); E. R. Norman, *Church and Society in England, 1770–1970* (1976); A. Wilkinson, *The Church of England and the First World War* (1978); A. D. Gilbert, *The Making of Post Christian Britain: A History of the Secularization of Modern Society* (1980); P. A. Welsby, *A History of the Church of England, 1945–1980* (1984); R. Manwaring, *From Controversy to Co-Existence: Evangelicals in the Church of England, 1914–1980* (1985); A. Hastings, *A History of English Christianity, 1920–1985* (1986).

C. PETER WILLIAMS

**Ephesians, Epistle to the.** *See* PAUL, THE APOSTLE.

**Episcopacy.** A system of church government whereby ultimate local church jurisdiction resides in the office of one person, the bishop. Modern discussion of episcopacy centers on how oversight (Gk. *episcopē*) can be exercised. In the NT responsibility for *episcopē* belongs to Christ (1 Pet. 2:25), the Twelve (Acts 1:20), and presbyters (Acts 20:28; Titus 1:5–7; 1 Pet. 5:2, some MSS). Whether a presbyter exercised oversight as part of a team or on individual initiative is not clear from Titus 1:7, nor is it clear that the overseeing group in a church were always presbyters (Phil. 1:1).

Oversight was exercised in practice, if not specifically described as such, by Paul and his delegates Timothy and Titus. Ignatius of Antioch attributed to the single *episcopos* the ultimate authority in a local church: "Follow the bishop, as Jesus Christ followed the Father; and follow the *presbyterion* as the Apostles . . . reverence the deacons. Let that eucharist be considered valid which is under the bishop or him to whom he commits it. It is not lawful apart from the bishop either to baptise or to hold a love-feast" (Ignatius, *To the Smyrnaeans* 8). The 2d-century bishop was expected to guard the faith, give pastoral care to clergy and people, govern, discipline, and administer the community of his see, and symbolize the unity of the church on behalf of Christ. Each see could only have one symbol of unity, and no bishop could exercise this function without having a see. By the 3d century ultimate jurisdiction by one bishop over a local church (a see) was the rule, and bishops as a group had collegial authority over the church while exercising independent authority within their sees. Oversight of a see or diocese is normally today exercised as the bishop receives Christians into full membership of a local church (confirmation) on the recommendation of ministers who are licensed to exercise the bishop's responsibility to evangelize and pastor (ordination) and instituted to carry out these duties in a particular area/local church (institution and induction).

Overall management of all the local churches within a see was joined in time by political and social expectations secular rulers and society placed on bishops. Some became secular rulers themselves, especially under the feudal system in the West. Today, diocesan bishops have responsibilities within their diocese toward the clergy and laity, to appoint clergy and confirmation, administer services and church property, and to oversee diocesan committees and the cathedral. The bishop also is concerned with the denominational church and with cooperatively relating to other denominational churches where the church has an organic relationship. The bishop speaks for his diocese with government and in society at large. The pressure of the various demands is eased both by the synodical system of corporate responsibility (such as synods, committees, and executive staff) and by sharing responsibility with bishops who have no see.

Several issues have been raised in this century concerning the nature of episcopacy: How does the oversight assumed by a bishop represent Christ's oversight if Christ's oversight is a responsibility of his whole body, all Christians in one place? If oversight is exercised by a person toward persons, can a bishop oversee all Christians in a diocese or should oversight be confined to a certain sector of the community, such as the clergy? Since most bishops can only oversee a limited proportion of the community, is monepiscopacy (one bishop symbolizing the unity of the Church in one see) an impossible system for exercising oversight?

A different approach to episcopacy arises from the modern theory of apostolic succession. The theory is based on the 2d-century plan to protect against heresy by insisting that a physical link from the apostles to the current rule of faith, ministers, sacred writings, and churches authenticate them. The modern theory locates authentic Christianity in the bishops who can trace a physical link (the laying-on-of-hands) to the bishops of the 2d century, who were appointed by the apostles or by Christians in the apostolic age. Such bishops qualify to exercise oversight by virtue of their appointment (consecration) as bishops—not their election and mission to oversee a particular diocese. This approach validates the use of bishops without sees to assist diocesan bishops and the appointment as bishops of members of the Vatican Curia and other church leaders by Pope John XXIII.

While the approach eases episcopal workload by providing more bishops than dioceses, it has created a barrier to schemes of union with episcopal churches and churches who have not included episcopal succession among their traditions.

*Bibliography.* J. B. Lightfoot, *The Christian Ministry* (1868, repr. ed., 1901); R. Whateley, *Apostolic Succession Considered* (1912); H. B. Swete, *Essays on the Early History of the Ministry* (1921); C. Jenkins and K. D. Mackenzie, eds., *Episcopacy Ancient and Modern* (1930); K. E. Kirk, ed., *The Apostolic Ministry: Essays on the History and Doctrine of the Episcopacy* (1946); J. W. C. Wand, *The Church, Its Nature, Function, and Ordering* (1948); A. Ehrhardt, *The Apostolic Succession* (1952); K. Carey, ed., *The Historic Episcopate in the Fulness of the Church: Seven Essays by Priests of the Church of England* (1954); D. T. Jenkins, *The Protestant Ministry* (1958); A. T. Hanson, *The Pioneer Ministry* (1961); W. Telfer, *The Office of Bishop* (1962); *Anglican-Presbyterian Conversations: The Report of the Panels Appointed by the Church of Scotland, the Church of England, and the Episcopal Church in Scotland* (1966); R. C. Moberly, *Ministerial Priesthood* (repr., 2d ed., 1969); P. A. Welsby, *Episcopacy in the Church of England* (1973); P. Moore, ed., *Bishops, But What Kind?* (1982).

GERVAIS ANGEL

**Episcopalians.** *See* ANGLICAN COMMUNION.

**Episcopalians, Protestant.** *See* PROTESTANT EPISCOPALIANS.

**Episcopalians, Reformed.** *See* REFORMED EPISCOPALIANS.

**Epistles.** *See* HEBREWS, EPISTLE TO THE; JAMES, EPISTLE OF; JOHN, EPISTLES OF; JUDE, EPISTLE OF; PAUL, THE APOSTLE; PETER, THE APOSTLE.

**Erdman, Charles Rosenbury** (1866–1960). Presbyterian. Born in Fayetteville, N.Y., he was a graduate of Princeton University and Princeton Theological Seminary. He was pastor of the Overbrook (Pa.) Church (1891–97); First Church, Germantown, Pa. (1897–1906); First Church, Princeton, N.J. (1924–34), and professor of practical theology, Princeton Seminary (1906–36). He was moderator of the General Assembly of the Presbyterian Church, USA (1925); president of its Board of Foreign Missions (1926–41); and the author of more than 20 volumes, mainly expositions of NT books.

F. W. LOETSCHER

**Eschatology, Christian.** Referring to future events which will end present history and inaugurate the age to come as those events are described in the Scriptures. The term "eschatology" is derived from the Greek words *eschatos*, meaning "last," and *logos*, in the sense of "science" or "subject." The traditional definition of eschatology requires some modification, however. Rather than referring exclusively to events which are yet to transpire at the end of present history, the NT proclaims that the *eschaton* has begun in and with the Christ event, giving an eschatological dimension to present existence.

Expectations about the end of the world existed among many ancient peoples. These expectations usually assumed a cyclical view of history drawn from the model of nature. Just as the seasons of the year follow one another in due course, so the corresponding periods of the world will complete their cycle in a "great world-year." One world-year is then succeeded by another in which all of the events of previous cycles occur again with the regularity of natural events.

According to these extrabiblical views, each period of the world-year has its own characteristics, determined by the character of the people who live during that epoch. The overall course of the cycle is in the direction of deterioration, however, like nature which decays and withers away. Among the late Babylonians, for instance, the periods of the historical cycle were designated by metals of successively inferior quality. Thus Nebuchadnezzar had a dream in which he saw a great image with a golden head, a body and arms of silver, hips of brass, legs of iron, and feet which were a mixture of iron and clay. This was interpreted by the prophet Daniel to refer to the succession of Gentile empires which would extend from Babylon until the time of the end (Dan. 2).

The Hebrews appear to have been the first people in the ancient world to break through the cyclical understanding of history and eschatology. Their self-identity was conditioned by the history of God's saving actions which constantly intersected their national history. What emerged in the OT was a linear perception of history with a beginning point and an end point and which consisted of a sequence of redemptive events that supplied the fundamental meaning for national and personal history.

At least by the time of the prophets (8th cent. B.C. and following), history was understood as unfolding in two epochs, the current age and the ideal age of the future. Present history was characterized by human sinfulness, oppression, and exploitation, especially among the Gentiles. The future age was to be characterized by messianic rule, justice, righteousness, peace, and abundance. These two epochs were separated by a cluster of eschatological events which were gathered under the inclusive term "the day of the Lord." The day of the Lord was understood to be a day of judgment upon the enemies of God and his people and a day of salvation for Israel, the covenant nation. It was thus anticipated as the time when the epoch of sinfulness would end and the ideal age would begin.

NT writers announced that the Christ event inaugurated a new era which was qualitatively different from the history that preceded it. Jesus proclaimed that the time of the law and the prophets reached its terminus in John the Baptist and that the eschatological kingdom was present in his person and ministry (Matt. 11:7–15; Luke 17:21). He announced the imminent arrival of the kingdom which had been promised in the OT (Matt. 4:17, 23; 10:7), as John the Baptist had before him (Matt. 3:2). He interpreted his mission in terms of the fulfillment of OT messianic prophecies (Luke 4:16–22; 24:25–27, 44–46; Matt. 11:2–6). The thrust of his ministry was to assemble the messianic community, beginning with Israel (Matt. 10:5–7; 23:37), and to endow the community with the eschatological Spirit (John 7:37–39; Luke 24:49). He granted the blessings of salvation (Luke 19:9–26; John 5:24), healing (Matt. 4:23–24), forgiveness (Mark 2:10), justifying righteousness (Matt. 5:6), and eternal life (John 5:21, 24; 6:40, 47, 51, 54; 17:2), blessings which OT hope anticipated only at the *eschaton*. His death and resurrection established the time of the new covenant which had been prophesied by Jeremiah (Luke 22:20; cf. 2 Cor. 3:6; Heb. 8:8–13; Jer. 31:31–34).

The NT thus affirms that eschatological events have already occurred within history. The present epoch is therefore the end of the ages (1 Cor. 10:11) or the times (1 Pet. 1:20). It is the "last days" (Heb. 1:2), or even the "last hour" (1 John 2:18). Such phrases were not intended to imply a commitment to the belief in a chronological imminency of the final eschatological events; rather, they reflect an awareness of the intrusion of the eschatological into the historical. They testify that there will be no succeeding ages prior to the full manifestation of the *eschaton*. The early church realized that the Christ event was the turning point of the ages and that the threshold had been crossed into eschatological times. The NT writers consistently maintained a suspended judgment as to the nearness or distance of the final events and the end of the present age.

The NT in various ways reflects Jesus' use of history and eschatology. The presence and operation of the eschatological kingdom was foundational to early preaching according to the Book of Acts (8:12; 19:8; 20:25; 28:23, 31). The resurrection of Jesus was perceived to be the beginning of the eschatological resurrection (Acts 4:2; 26:23), by which Jesus was designated both Messiah and Lord of the new creation (Acts 2:30–36). The outpouring of the Holy Spirit on the day of Pentecost was interpreted to be the fulfillment of Joel's eschatological prophecy (Acts 2:16–21; cf. Joel 2:28–32). The early church understood itself to be the messianic community already experiencing the blessings of the age to come (Acts 2:43–47), in accordance with promises made in the OT which were now being fulfilled in their appointed time (Acts 2:23–35; 3:24–26).

Paul shared this perspective with the early church. The death and resurrection of Christ constituted the decisive conquest over the kingdom of evil (Col. 2:15) and was the basis upon which Christians were delivered from the fallen world order (Gal. 1:4) to participate in Christ's kingdom and the new creation (Col. 1:13; 2 Cor. 5:17). Christ abolished death and brought life and immortality into present existence (2 Tim. 1:10). In this way, the glory which belongs to the age to come has been manifested in the world (2 Cor. 4:6). Christ's resurrection is the first fruits of the eschatological resurrection (1 Cor. 15:20), and he is the first born of the new eschatological humanity which has its existence in him (Col. 1:18). Christians participate in his eschatological existence as they are baptized into him (Rom. 6:3–11).

These NT passages, although not exhaustive, illustrate an important aspect of the eschatological outlook and understanding. The early church recognized that the *eschaton* had its inauguration in the Christ event and that eschatological realities have become part of present history and experience. Eschatological realities exist, however, as mystery and are perceived only by faith. The kingdom, although operative, cannot be seen nor entered except by a new birth in the Spirit (John 3:3, 5). It is known exclusively by revelation (Matt. 13:11–17). The blessing of salvation is experienced only by faith (Rom. 1:16–17). Participation in death to the old creation and resurrection to the new eschatological life is a present reality only in the spiritual and sacramental senses (Rom. 6:3–11; Col. 2:11–15).

This brings into focus an eschatological reservation in the NT, the tension between the "already" and the "not yet." It is recognized that the Christ event inaugurated eschatological events and conditions. Christ came to fulfill OT messianic prophecies. The decisive battle with the demonic and evil has been won. The messianic community has been formed and has received the eschatological Spirit. The time of the new covenant has begun and eschatological blessings are being experienced. But it is equally recognized that Satan and the fallen world order continue as historical realities and that they represent a negative moral and spiritual dynamic in the Christian's environment, challenging new existence. The kingdom has not yet had its universal and visible manifestation. The resurrection of the body has not yet occurred. The messianic community has not yet attained the fullness of Christ's perfection (Eph. 4:13–16). The final judgment lies yet in the future.

Nonetheless, the Christian hope for the future is based on events which have already occurred. The final events will be a visible and universal manifestation of the triumph of God that was realized in the Christ event. This triumph now is experienced spiritually and partially—by faith. In the end it will be exhibited for all the world to see.

Like the OT, the NT can refer to these future eschatological events under the broad term "the day of the Lord" (Acts 2:20; 1 Thess. 5:2; 2 Pet. 3:10–12). Sometimes an abbreviated form is used: "the last day" (John 6:39–40, 44, 54), or "that day" (Matt. 7:22; Luke 21:34). The day of the Lord takes on a christological dimension in the NT since Christ has been invested with the role of eschatological judge (John 5:22, 27; Acts 10:42; 17:31). It can thus be referred to as "the day of the Lord Jesus" (2 Cor. 1:14; 1 Cor. 1:8), or "the day of Christ" (Phil. 1:6, 10; 2:16).

The day of the Lord will be initiated by the return of Christ to earth from his throne in heaven. The words chosen by the NT writers to describe the return of Christ emphasize his visibility, his glory, and his unmistakable triumph. In contrast to his first coming as an obscure peasant teacher and humble son of man, his return will be a public "unveiling" (Gk. *apokalupsis*, 1 Cor. 1:7; 2 Thess. 1:7; 1 Pet. 1:7, 13), an "appearance" (Gk. *epiphaneia*, Titus 2:13), a personal "arrival" (Gk. *parousia*, Matt. 24:27; 2 Thess. 2:8) of the victorious Lord on the stage of human history. Every eye will see him when he comes with great power and glory (Rev. 1:7; Mark 13:26).

Throughout the Scriptures, the day of the Lord is both a day of salvation and a day of judgment. When Christ returns, he will resurrect the dead in Christ (1 Cor. 15:23; 1 Thess. 4:13–18) and gather his people to himself (2 Thess. 2:1; Matt. 24:31). The resurrection will bring their salvation to completion, when they are presented in perfection before him and are transformed to receive incorruption, glory, and power (1 Thess. 5:9–10; 1 Cor. 15:42–57). But the return of Christ will also be a day of judgment upon evildoers and the manifestation of divine wrath upon the enemies of God (2 Thess. 1:6–9; Rev. 19:11–16). All human creatures have an appointment with the final judgment, before which they must appear and give an account of their deeds and the stewardship of their lives (Heb. 9:27; Rom. 14:10; 2 Cor. 5:10). The destiny of the faithful is to be with God in the

new heavens and the new earth (1 Thess. 4:17; Rev. 21:1–4). The fate of the disobedient and unbelieving is to be excluded from the presence of God in a place of eternal destruction (Matt. 8:12; 13:4–43, 49–50; 2 Thess. 1:9; Rev. 20:11–15).

The consummation of the eschatological events will be the subjugation of all evil (Phil. 2:10–11; 1 Cor. 15:24–28; Rev. 20:1–3, 7–10), the liberation of the creation from the presence and effects of sin (Rom. 8:19–23), and the transformation of the universe (Rev. 21–22). The new heavens and the new earth will be characterized by righteousness (2 Pet. 3:13) and the exclusion of all sin and suffering (Rev. 21:4, 8, 27; 22:3). God's final triumph will be manifest when he has reconciled all things to himself in Christ (Eph. 1:10; 1 Cor. 15:24, 28) and "the kingdom of the world has become the kingdom of our Lord and of his Christ," over which "he will reign for ever and ever" (Rev. 11:15 NIV).

*See also* MILLENNIUM.

**Bibliography.** R. Bultmann, *History and Eschatology* (1957); O. Cullmann, *Christ and Time* (1964); R. C. Dentan, ed., *The Idea of History in the Ancient Near East* (1955); G. E. Ladd, *Theology of the NT* (1974); J. D. G. Dunn, *Unity and Diversity in the NT* (1977).

FRED D. LAYMAN

## Eschatology, Muslim. *See* ISLAM.

## Esher, John Jacob (1823–1901). Evangelical United Brethren theologian. Born in Baldenheim, Germany, he entered the ministry of the Evangelical Association in the Illinois Conference in 1845. He represented that body in general conference sessions from 1851 to 1863, when he was elected bishop. He organized the first annual conferences in Europe and Asia and was the first bishop of the church to visit the missions in the Orient and travel around the world. He wrote the first comprehensive theology of his denomination. At the time of the division of the Evangelical Association (1891–94) and the formation of the United Evangelical Church he was the senior bishop of the church and leader of the group which continued the original church.

He wrote *Katechismus der Evangelischen Gemeinschaft* (1882; 2d ed., 1901), *Über Länder und Meere* (1886), *Die Evangelische Gemeinschaft und Zwei Predigten* (1894), and *Christliche Theologie* (vol. 1, 1899; vol. 2, 1901).

RAYMOND W. ALBRIGHT

## Essays Catholic and Critical. A 1926 volume of essays written by 13 British Anglican scholars. Among them were A. E. Taylor, Kenneth E. Kirk, and A. E. J. Rawlinson. Often classed as "liberal Catholics," the authors proposed to restate and synthesize the Catholic faith with the methods of modern theological study in the tradition of the *Lux Mundi* essays of 1888. Their emphasis was that the church is the living Body of Christ: "For

the Catholic Christian *'Quid vobis videtur de Ecclesia?'* What think ye of the Church? is not merely as pertinent a question as *Quid vobis videtur de Christo?* What think ye of Christ? it is the same question differently formulated." The volume has had a wide and deep influence within the Anglican communion and has affected the Anglican approach to church unity.

NELSON RIGHTMYER

**Eternal Life.** The origins of this phrase are to be found in the ancient Jewish rabbinical writings which are throughout deeply eschatological in outlook. The primary meaning is "life in the age that is eternal." The rabbis saw eternal life in terms of its quality rather than its quantity. Eternal life signified "life in the eschatological age that is to be realized." Hence, to Jesus' hearers, his use of this phrase would have an eschatological implication.

The key to an understanding of the meaning of eternal life in the Gospels may lie in the fact that in John's Gospel "eternal life" has taken the place of the term "kingdom of God" or "kingdom of heaven" so frequently found in the three synoptic Gospels. "Kingdom of God" is to be understood eschatologically in Jesus' teaching. The kingdom of God is the new age breaking into history in the Person of Jesus Christ, the age and realm in which God the Father reigns as sovereign Lord in majesty. Life in that kingdom, or in the age to come, is free from the limitations of time, decay, evil, and sin. Thus "eternal life" is life in the kingdom of God. Eternal life signifies this basic eschatological idea of life in the inaugurated divine kingdom, where evil is at an end.

The accent is on life. Examples are found in the synoptic Gospels of the use of "life" in exactly the same sense as "eternal life" is used (Matt. 7:14, 19:17; Mark 9:43). Jesus Christ's offer to men is life, not the frustrating, sin-corroded life of this age, but life that is in harmony with man's destiny as the child of God, life that belongs to the coming age. This use of the term "life" is virtually equivalent to the "kingdom of God" in Jesus' thought, for the two expressions seem interchangeable on his lips (Mark 9:43, 45, 47).

The phrase "eternal life" occurs explicitly as well as implicitly in the synoptic Gospels, most notably in the question put to Jesus by the inquiring ruler: "What shall I do to inherit eternal life?" (Matt. 19:16; Mark 10:17; Luke 18:18). The phrase was evidently current in thoughtful Jewish religious circles, and summed up what the coming Messiah would have to offer. Jesus answered the rich young ruler with a call to more perfect obedience to God's rule and Law. The expected kingdom or realm of God offered men eternal life.

Eternal life is the chief topic in the record of Jesus' teaching found in the Fourth Gospel, just as the kingdom of God is the emphasis in the synoptic account of his teaching. The phrase, "eternal life," occurs 17 times in John's Gospel and six times in his first epistle, while the equivalent use of "life" is found many times as well. Here the eschatological idea, still fundamental to the right understanding of the term, has become more inward and spiritualized. There appears to be even less interest in duration in regard to eternal life which is presented as a potential present inward possession. The age to come has already broken into history with the coming of Jesus Christ; and those who believe in him, who are "in Christ," can already enjoy the life of the new age. Christian life is in this sense "realized eschatology."

Jesus teaches that his supreme gift to men is "eternal life" (John 17:2). Everlasting life is the form in which that offer is made in our Lord's great summary of what God's saving visitation means (John 3:16). It might almost be said that we have a precise definition of eternal life in this Fourth Gospel: "Now this is eternal life, that they may know you, the only true God, and Jesus Christ, whom you have sent" (John 17:3). As one of God's own children, to know the Father through saving faith in the Lord Jesus Christ is man's entry into the life of the world to come, and it is an inward possession here and now, as well as the pledge of fully realized "life" hereafter.

A believer then enters upon "eternal life" through the appropriation of the saving benefits offered in Jesus Christ. This emphasis on faith in the sense of personal trust in, and commitment to, Jesus, is underlined in his statement, "Whoever eats my flesh, and drinks my blood, has eternal life" (John 6:54a). Whosoever receives Christ by faith is the possessor of eternal life; the life of the age to come is here and now. Nevertheless a "not yet" still remains: "and I will raise him up at the last day" (John 6:54b).

The synoptic account of the promises made to these who accept Christ tells of blessings here and now, "and in the age to come, eternal life" (Mark 10:30). After the final judgment, the righteous enter into eternal life (Matt. 25:46). Still, in regard to eternal life, the main emphasis of the Gospels remains on a realized spiritual possession rather than on immortality in any detached philosophical sense. The weary burden of hope deferred is not a NT conception, and the Christian hope is closely linked to the life of the kingdom, discoverable within the here and now. Even judgment is withdrawn from futurity: "we know that we have passed from death to life" (1 John 3:14). The new age is present in Jesus: "God has given us eternal life and this life is in his Son" (1 John 5:11).

The present and future aspects of eternal life are drawn together in the Person of Jesus Christ, who can himself claim to be the Resurrection and the Life, both the future realization and the present possession of eternal life in one living Savior

305

(John 11:25–26). The essential eschatology of Jesus' teaching, which has continually to be recognized, is realized eschatology.

The life of the age to come has broken into history with Jesus Christ's coming as Savior. Eternal life is life in contrast to death; it is the full realization of our redemption in Jesus Christ. "The gift of God is eternal life in Jesus Christ our Lord" (Rom. 6:23b).

R. STUART LOUDEN

**Eternity.** Wherever this concept is involved, whether in the foreground or in the background of thought, we need to be peculiarly wary of the fallacy of equivocation of terms. For, although it is used in at least four different senses, it always expresses a certain superiority to the limitedness and relativity of the temporal, and thus it tends to evoke an emotion which, in proportion to its strength, threatens clarity of thought and causes the various senses to be confused.

We speak of "the eternal hills," knowing full well that they are not strictly eternal, but, while the poetic mood prevails, feeling pity or resentment for the philistine soul who would dare to mention that prosaic fact.

We identify eternity with time projected to infinity—either toward the past ("the eternity before time was"), or toward the future ("he now dwells in eternity"), or in both directions but on the same level as experienced time, or as "located" somehow "above" our finite time.

Eternity is regarded as infinite time, somehow "transcended." In this sense, eternity is not "when time shall be no more." Time remains real in eternity. It is infinite in dimension, but it is seen from a higher point of view. It is perhaps impossible for finite minds fully to transform the concept of infinite time into that of eternity; but at least some things can be said about it. Eternity must be a degree and kind of *unity* which is not suggested by the term "infinite time." It must have at least the unity experienced by an Infinite Mind which, although it can move freely through infinite time, can also see it as a single "now." It is suggested, in popular terms, by such scriptural passages as "before Abraham was born, I am" (John 8:58); "For a thousand years in thy sight are like a day that has just gone by, or like a watch in the night" (Ps. 90:4); "With the Lord a day is like a thousand years, and a thousand years are like a day" (2 Pet. 3:8). We find analogies to such experience in our own ability, in memory and in anticipation, to transcend the succession of finite moments. Perhaps a better analogy may be found in the experience of the psychological time concept of a specious present, which can hold both something of the "no longer" and something of the "not yet" in the unity of a single "now." The fact that the length of this intuitive present, as measured by clock time, is vari-

able suggests the possibility that a mind of infinite capacity might be able to treat infinite time as specious present. This would be a first approach to the kind of unity which must distinguish eternity from infinite time; but certainly it must have more of unity in it than that.

In stark opposition to all these senses in which the term eternity is used, we also employ the term to signify that which negates time entirely, either in the sense that, when eternity is present, time has ceased to be, or in the sense that considerations of time are wholly irrelevant to it. In the latter category fall such experiences as logical validity ("once true, always true"), esthetic values (e.g., "a thing of beauty is a joy for ever"), and moral values (e.g., "kind words can never die").

*See also* TIME.

**Bibliography.** A. S. Pringle-Pattison, *The Idea of God* (1920); Karl Heim, *The New Divine Order* (1930)

ANDREW K. RULE

**Ethiopia.** Officially a People's Democratic Republic in northeast Africa. Ethiopia has a population of 46 million (1987) and covers an area of about 1,221,900 sq. km. (471,778 sq. mi.).

The 20th century brought Ethiopia into closer contact with the rest of the world than ever before and showed the continuing importance in its life of the (Orthodox) national church. Addis Ababa became the ecclesiastical center, and some efforts were made to secure independence from the Coptic church which traditionally supplied the *abuna* (patriarch), but not until 1951 was the first native *abuna* installed. Foreign contacts of the Ethiopian church included membership of the World Council of Churches (WCC), and closer relations with other churches of the monophysite communion. In 1959 the Ethiopian church became independent of Egypt.

Among its distinctive features are its acceptance of some apocryphal books in the canon, Sabbath observance, circumcision, and a distinction between clean and unclean meats. Christ is held to have one nature but to be perfectly human as well as perfectly divine. Until the deposition of Emperor Haile Selassie in 1974 the country was open to foreign missionaries, albeit with restrictions. Selassie participated in the 1966 Berlin World Congress on Evangelism and was host to the WCC central committee meeting in Addis Ababa in 1971. He died in 1975. He claimed to have been the 225th descendant of King Solomon and the Queen of Sheba.

Under the socialist regime many bishops (including, in 1976, the *abuna*) have been compulsorily retired and replaced by others not known for strong views against the revolution. The Lutheran World Federation's Radio Voice of the Gospel was suppressed in 1977. The country has been disrupted by a major locust infestation, a series of famines, an ongoing civil war both in

Eritrea and in Tigré, and sporadic recurrence of the age-old rivalry between Orthodox (more than 24 million members in 1986) and Muslims (14.5 million). About 5.25 million adhere to traditionalist beliefs. A further 1.5 million are in other Christian churches, and there are tiny communities of Jews and Baha'is.

GEORGE BEBAWI

**Ethiopian Orthodox Church.** *History.* Tracing its origins back to the early 4th century, the Ethiopian Orthodox Church is among the most venerable in Christendom. While popular tradition links the eunuch of Acts 8 with Ethiopian Christianity, there is no evidence to support such a view, since the term "Ethiopia" in its biblical usage does not refer to any particular nation. Derived from two Greek words meaning "to burn" and "face," Ethiopia meant, literally, "land of burnt faces." It is generally agreed that Candace's converted treasurer came from the Nubian state of Cush, with its capital at Meroë, north of what is now Ethiopia.

Christianity is thought to have been introduced to Ethiopia by two Syrian Christians, Frumentius and Aedesius. Victims of either shipwreck or piracy on the Red Sea, they were transported inland to Aksum, the ancient capital of what is now Ethiopia, where they became wards of the emperor Ezana, whose conversions they accomplished in due course.

Granted their freedom by the now Christian king, Frumentius proceeded to Alexandria where he reported to Athanasius (A.D. 297–373, patriarch of the Alexandrian church). He then returned to that country after being consecrated "Bishop of Ethiopia" in A.D. 340, thus beginning a Coptic jurisdiction which was to last until 1959, when the Ethiopian Orthodox Church achieved complete autonomy, and the right to appoint its own *abuna* (patriarch).

Today, with an estimated 16 million adherents, it is the largest of the five monophysite or Eastern Orthodox churches which parted theological company with the rest of Christendom after the Council of Chalcedon (A.D. 451) over disagreement on the precise relationship between Christ's human and divine natures.

The revolution in 1975 resulted in the loss of its privileged status as state church, and the confiscation of all of its considerable land holdings which for centuries have been the source of most of the church's revenues. Furthermore, the then Abuna Theopholes was arrested, charged with crimes "against the oppressed masses," declared guilty, and deposed. His place, under the watchful eye of the military regime, was filled on August 29, 1976, by the present patriarch, Abuna Tekle Haimonot.

*Teaching and Practice.* The 1000-year ecclesiastical isolation resulting from the successful conquest of northern Africa by Islam in the 7th century is reflected in the present-day church's unique and colorful blend of indigenous, Judaic, and Christian elements.

Theologically, the Ethiopian church closely resembles the Coptic church in its understanding of monophysitism, church order, eschatology, liturgy, monasticism, as well as biblical and hagiographical literature. Of the seven sacraments recognized by the church, four (baptism, communion, confirmation, penance) are required of all members, and three (unction, holy orders, holy matrimony) are optional.

The church is characterized by an elaborate angeology and by its veneration of the virgin Mary as paramount intercessor with Christ on behalf of believers. Numerous sacred fasts (more than 200 per year), holy festivals, and Judaic dietary taboos further distinguish it from Christian practice elsewhere.

Pervasive Judaic elements are especially obvious in the architecture and furnishings of churches, each being patterned after the OT Jewish temple, and each containing a representation of the ark of the covenant, the *tabot*.

While the church is no longer in a position to directly influence the state, it continues to play a significant role in the lives of nearly half of the country's population.

*Bibliography.* J. M. Harden, *Introduction to Ethiopic Christian Literature* (1926); H. M. Hyatt, *The Church of Abyssinia* (1928); J. S. Trimingham, *The Christian Church and Missions in Ethiopia* (1950); E. Isaac, *The Ethiopian Church* (1967); E. Ullendorff, *Ethiopia and the Bible* (1968); S. H. Selassie, ed., *The Church in Ethiopia: A Panorama of History and Spiritual Life* (1970); F. M. Snowden, *Blacks in Antiquity: Ethiopians in the Greco-Roman Experience* (1970); A. Wondmagegnehu and J. Motovu, *The Ethiopian Orthodox Church* (1970); J. Bonk, *An Annotated and Classified Bibliography of English Literature Pertaining to the Ethiopian Orthodox Church.*

JON BONK

**Ethiopian Jews.** See FALASHAS.

**Eucharist.** See SACRAMENTS.

**Eucharistic Theology.** See LITURGICAL WORSHIP, RECENT TRENDS IN.

**Eucken, Christian Rudolph** (1846–1926). Lutheran. Born in Aurich, East Friesland, he studied at Göttingen and Berlin. He taught at the Frankfurt Gymnasium (1869–71), was called to a professorship in philosophy at the University of Basel (1871–74), and finally served as professor of philosophy at Jena (1874–1920). In 1908 he was awarded the Nobel Prize for Literature. In 1912 he visited the USA. Against the naturalistic positivism of his time he developed a neoidealist metaphysics and advocated the concept of spiritual activity as the source of the unity and evolution of the universe. Eucken's principal works of religious significance were *Die Einheit des Geist-*

*eslebens* (1888), *The Problem of Human Life* (ET, 1909), *The Truth of Religion* (ET, 1913), *Life's Basis and Life's Ideal* (ET, 1911), *The Life of the Spirit* (ET, 1909), *Present-Day Ethics and Their Relation to the Spiritual Life* (ET, 1912), and *Can We Still Be Christians?* (ET, 1914).

**Bibliography.** W. R. B. Gibson, *Rudolf Eucken's Philosophy of Life* (1906); W. S. Morgan, *The Religious Philosophy of Rudolf Eucken* (1914); P. Kalweit, *Euckens Religionsphilosophie* (1927).
EDWIN E. AUBREY

**Euthanasia.** Literally, "to die well," the word has become established in common usage with a more precise meaning: the deliberate ending of life to enable, in the given circumstances, the sick person to die in dignity and peace. Further, euthanasia is normally used in a "voluntary" sense in that it has been requested by the patient or is done to fulfill what is believed to be the person's desire. It is not to be confused with the prescribing of drugs for the relief of pain and distress in the knowledge that such treatment will probably shorten life.

At the heart of the modern call for voluntary euthanasia is the concept of human rights—here "the right to die." The argument maintains an individual should be free to determine whether to live or die and, in the event of choosing to die, may be assisted in doing so by the medical profession. This concept is supplemented by arguments based on "quality of life" and compassion—that a person has no capacity for rational existence, an incurable or fatal illness, or no hope for treatments to give long-term help.

With the possible exception of emergency situations Christians have generally opposed any right to voluntary euthanasia. While there is debate on the issue, Christians have traditionally offered arguments based on practical legal and moral considerations. For example, it is difficult to be absolutely sure the patient's full consent has been given; it is impossible to frame laws which contain adequate safeguards to prevent misuse and abuse; and someone (a doctor) has to assist in what is an act of voluntary suicide (thus there is a question of guilt). To these are added theological arguments centering on the fact that God is the Creator and Judge and that, as creatures made in his image, human beings have no right to determine the times of their deaths but ought to be cared for, when sick, by fellow human beings.

Another important part of the Christian response has been to call for, and to be involved in, the improvement of care for those known to be dying. This includes better techniques of nursing care, of alleviating pain and distress, and of counseling to prepare for "dying well." Christians have actively participated in care for the terminally ill through a growing number of "hospices." As Western society responds to mounting health care costs and a growing number of elderly people and in the face of growing efforts for euthanasia-promoting legislation in some countries, the church is being called more and more to work through its response to questions relating to medical ethics and the supposed "right to die."

**Bibliography.** Board for Social Responsibility, Church of England, *On Dying Well: An Anglican Contribution to the Debate on Euthanasia* (1975); J. Rachels, *The End of Life: Euthanasia and Morality* (1986).
PETER TOON

**Evangelical Academies.** *See* ACADEMIES, EVANGELICAL.

**Evangelical Alliance.** A world body founded at an 1846 London conference attended by 800 leaders from 52 branches of the Christian church in Europe and North America. It functioned for more than a century mainly as a number of alliances in various countries but in 1951 formed the World Evangelical Fellowship to strengthen its global dimension, particularly through the work of its theological commission.

The Evangelical Alliance was designed as a confederation of church leaders on the basis of "great evangelical principles" spelled out in some detail in the original basis of faith. These principles included the eternal punishment of the wicked, and the perpetuity of the Christian ministry. In 1912 a less specific basis of faith was introduced and this was revised in 1970. Until the 1960s membership was on an individual basis, but it is now open to local evangelical fellowships, societies, denominations, and individual churches which are in agreement with its doctrinal basis, aims, and objects.

The organizational structures of the alliance have always been minimal, particularly until the 1890s. Its aims also have been somewhat indefinite, going little further than the cultivation of brotherly love and the furthering of common purposes. One of its best-known activities has been the promotion of a united week of prayer throughout the world, traditionally during the first week of January. During the 19th century it convened international conferences which were important because of their size, character, and wide representation of evangelical Christianity (such as London, 1851; New York, 1873). It disseminated a vast amount of information through these conferences—which included thorough surveys of the religious scene worldwide—and through the British organ, *Evangelical Christendom*. It was a powerful advocate of world missions and promoted the first united evangelical missionary conferences in 1854 (New York and London). It also exerted pressure on foreign governments on behalf of persecuted Protestant minorities.

The fortunes of the alliance have reflected those of evangelical Christianity, declining in influence in the 20th century until after World War II. It then sponsored a united evangelistic exhibition in Central Hall, Westminster, at the time of the Festival of Britain (1951); opened the first of several hostels for overseas students in London (1952); and sponsored the Harringay Billy Graham crusade (first in 1954/55). Subsequently it launched a magazine, *Crusade* (later renamed *Today*), and launched a relief fund, the TEAR Fund (1967), which by the mid-1980s raised as much as £11 million annually. In 1958 it formed the Evangelical Missionary Alliance which links nearly 100 evangelical missionary societies and training colleges.

**Bibliography.** J. W. Ewing, *Goodly Fellowship* (1946); J. B. A. Kessler, *A Study of the Evangelical Alliance in Great Britain* (1968); D. Howard, *The Dream That Would Not Die: The Birth and Growth of the World Evangelical Fellowship, 1846–1986* (1986).

HAROLD H. ROWDON

**Evangelical and Reformed Church.** An ecclesiastical union of the Evangelical Synod of North America and the Reformed Church in the United States. Informal conversations preceded discussions between official commissions which in 1932 adopted a basic Plan of Union. This document became the basis on which the union was effected at the first general synod of the united church in June 1934.

The new body had 2648 pastors, 2929 congregations, and 631,271 communicant members. The union also brought into affiliation 30 educational institutions (including those on foreign fields); 9 hospitals; 10 orphanages; 11 homes for the aged; and 2 homes for epileptics and the feeble-minded.

Pending the acceptance of a constitution (1940), the congregations, regional conferences, classes, districts, synods, boards, committees, commissions, and the governmental and administrative bodies of both churches continued to be governed by the plan of union and by their own constitutions and by-laws. The respective boards and agencies effectively merged before 1940. Union was hastened by the redivision, in 1938, of 56 classes (Reformed) and 20 districts (evangelical) into 24 synods.

In 1934 Central Theological Seminary, Dayton, Ohio (Reformed), merged with Eden Theological Seminary, Webster Groves, Mo. (evangelical). Two years later, periodicals of the two bodies merged into *The Messenger* and *Friedensbote*. In 1940 the boards for home and foreign missions were transformed respectively into the Board for National and the Board for International Missions. The church had stations in Africa, China, Honduras, India, Iraq, Japan, and South America. Similar mergers formed the Women's Guild and the Churchmen's Brotherhood.

The new constitution was approved at the 1936 and 1938 general synods and accepted by the respective classes and districts but it did not become effective until the convening of the 1940 general synod.

The doctrinal standards of the Evangelical and Reformed Church are the Heidelberg Catechism, Luther's Catechism, and the Augsburg Confession. The formal position of the church is that they "are accepted as an authoritative interpretation of the essential truth taught in the Holy Scriptures. Wherever these doctrinal standards differ, ministers, members, and congregations, in accordance with the liberty of conscience inherent in the gospel, are allowed to adhere to the interpretation of one of these confessions."

In 1937 union was suggested as possible with the Congregational-Christian Churches. By 1942 union conversations had become public. Legal efforts by Congregational dissenters failed to prevent the union and in 1957 at Cleveland, Ohio, 629,000 members of the Evangelical and Reformed Church joined 1,420,000 Congregational-Christians as a new United Church of Christ (*see* UNITED CHURCH OF CHRIST). By 1959 a *Statement of Faith* for the new denomination had been approved by the second general synod, and a Constitution for the United Church of Christ was adopted in 1961. More than 100,000 Congregationalists chose to enter a Wisconsin-based National Association or the Illinois-based Conservative Congregational Christian Conference rather than adhere to the United Church of Christ. Within the Evangelical and Reformed Church, only the small former Eureka Classis chose to remain independent of UCC in the upper Midwest. Toward the end of the 20th century, a united church consciousness was gradually replacing former loyalties among the 6500 congregations who had combined their separate identities.

**Bibliography.** Minutes of General Conferences and files of the *Messenger* and *Yearbook* (1934– ); J. H. E. Horstmann and H. H. Wernecke, *Through Four Centuries: The Story of the Beginnings of the Evangelical and Reformed Church, in the Old World and the New, from the Sixteenth to the Twentieth Century* (1938); E. J. F. Arndt, *The Faith We Proclaim; The Doctrinal Viewpoint Generally Prevailing in the Evangelical and Reformed Church* (1960); D. Dunn, et al., *A History of the Evangelical and Reformed Church* (1961); L. H. Gunnemann, *The Shaping of the United Church of Christ: An Essay in the History of American Christianity* (1977); E. J. F. Arndt, *History and Program: A History of the United Church of Christ* (1982).

LOWELL H. ZUCK

**Evangelical Association.** See EVANGELICAL CHURCH; UNITED METHODIST CHURCH.

**Evangelical Church.** A merger in 1922 in Detroit, Mich., of the Evangelical Association and the United Evangelical Church. The church no longer exists as an independent body.

*See also* UNITED METHODIST CHURCH.

**Evangelical Church in Germany.** *See* GERMANY, FEDERAL REPUBLIC OF.

**Evangelical Congregational Church.** A denomination formed by 20,000 members of the Evangelical Congregational Church who were dissatisfied with the direction of the Evangelical Church after its 1922 merger. The bulk of congregations is located in the East Pennsylvania Conference, with scattered congregations in Illinois, Pittsburgh, Ohio, and West Virginia conferences. ECC adheres to Methodist polity and an Arminian doctrine. To avoid "usurpation of powers in violation of the discipline," bishops and presiding elders are chosen to an eight-year term of office.

Annual and general conferences are comprised of clergy and lay delegates in equal numbers. An itinerant ministry, appointed yearly by the annual conferences, serves some 38,500 members in 160 congregations. The 1985 *Yearbook of American and Canadian Churches* lists 271 clergy for the denomination. ECC adheres to the inspiration of the Bible but follows an inclusive membership policy in maintaining a "fellowship of all followers of Christ." The board of missions oversees all mission work at home and abroad. Summer gatherings in parks within the boundaries of the conferences imitate traditional "camp meetings." Headquarters of the denomination, a publishing house, and a theological training center are in Myerstown, Pa. The denominational periodical is the *United Evangelical*.

E. J. FURCHA

**Evangelical Covenant Church.** Formerly the Swedish Evangelical Mission Covenant Church, the present name was adopted in 1957. Its historical influences include the 16th-century Reformation, the Swedish Lutheran state church, and the 19th-century spiritual awakenings in Scandinavia. In the 1870–80s various groups in Sweden and North America broke with the main body and formed free churches which eventually coalesced into the new denomination. Doctrinally it is broadly Lutheran, but it emphasizes the sovereignty of the Word of God over all creedal interpretations, a pietistic restatement of justification by faith as basic to evangelism and Christian nurture, and the necessity for personal faith in Jesus Christ as Savior and Lord. Baptism and the Lord's supper are seen as divinely ordained sacraments, and both infant and adult baptism are recognized. Personal freedom is highly valued, but this is distinguished from individualism which disregards the centrality of the Word of God and the mutual responsibilities and discipline of the spiritual community. Because of the theological diversity that characterizes its membership, the church identifies itself as neither liberal nor fundamentalist. It is congregational in polity, but the denomination ordains clergy. The principal institutions of higher education are North Park College and Theological Seminary in Chicago. It publishes the *Covenant Companion* (monthly) and *Covenant Quarterly*, and supports missionaries in seven countries and several schools, hospitals, and retirement facilities. In 1987 the adult membership was 85,150 in 566 churches.

RICHARD V. PIERARD

**Evangelical Fellowship of Canada (EFC).** A national church agency organized in 1964 to foster cooperation among evangelical denominations, parachurch agencies, and individuals. The 22 member denominations have a constituency of about one million. Its membership includes a large number of individual evangelicals who are members of mainline denominations and other churches not affiliated with EFC, and its general council includes members of all Canadian Protestant denominations. Three EFC presidents have been ministers of mainline Protestant churches. EFC seeks to promote renewal in the churches and to serve as a forum for interaction and stimulation; it is also an evangelical voice to media, government, and the general public. A full-time executive director, task forces on evangelism and family, and a social action commission implement its program. Its official publication is *Faith Today*, published bimonthly. EFC is a member of the World Evangelical Fellowship.

LESLIE K. TARR

**Evangelical Foreign Missions Association (EFMA).** Formed in 1945 under the aegis of the National Association of Evangelicals (NAE) to assist theologically conservative denominational and independent mission boards. It helps to obtain travel documents and supply diplomatic information, aid missionaries and executives in their travel arrangements, advise on tax matters and living costs abroad, and provide opportunities for spiritual fellowship and mutual encouragement through workshops, briefings, consultations, and retreats. It encourages cooperative endeavors among evangelical missionary societies, and, in conjunction with the Interdenominational Foreign Mission Association (IFMA), it operates the Evangelical Missions Information Service which publishes the *Evangelical Missions Quarterly* (founded 1964) and a newsletter. The EFMA-IFMA have also jointly sponsored various conventions and cooperative undertakings, the most noteworthy being the Congress on the Church's Worldwide Mission in Wheaton, Ill., in 1966. Some 83 agencies, deploying more than 12,000 missionaries in 130 countries, comprise the EFMA membership.

*See also* NATIONAL ASSOCIATION OF EVANGELICALS (NAE).

RICHARD V. PIERARD

**Evangelical Free Church of America (EFC).** A Reformed body with historical roots imbedded in 19th-century Scandinavian pietism. Its parent churches were the Swedish Evangelical Free Church, organized in the USA in 1884, and the Norwegian and Danish Evangelical Free Church Association, organized in 1909. In June 1950 these churches merged and took the name Evangelical Free Church of America. In June 1950 the groups merged into the Evangelical Free Church of America. The EFC statement of faith proclaims the Bible to be without error in its form as originally written and the imminent premillennial second coming of Jesus. EFC is an association of about 880 independent congregations (1987) with a vigorous publishing arm, a vital foreign missionary outreach, and a keen interest in education at all levels, from day schools through seminaries. The official denominational publication is the *Evangelical Beacon*. In 1987 the church was approaching a membership of 100,000. It maintains a headquarters in Minneapolis, Minn.

ROBERT V. SCHNUCKER

**Evangelicalism.** A modern Christian movement which transcends confessional and denominational boundaries to emphasize conformity to the basic principles of the Christian faith and a missionary outreach of compassion and urgency. An evangelical is one who believes and proclaims the gospel of Jesus Christ, the message that Christ died for human sins, was buried, and rose again on the third day in fulfillment of the prophetic Scriptures, thereby providing the means of redemption for sinful humanity (1 Cor. 15:1–4).

While such a definition is generally true, by the late 20th century it was difficult to say how evangelicals differed from other kinds of Christians, since the term had been used in a variety of ways. The definition commonly used by opinion pollsters—that an evangelical is someone who believes in the inerrancy of Scripture, has had a born-again experience through Jesus Christ, and seeks to share his faith with others—was woefully inadequate. Donald W. Dayton points out that it is impossible to develop a single definition that applies to all the groups it has been used to describe.

The term first came into use during the Reformation to distinguish Protestants from Roman Catholics, and it stressed the centrality of Christ, grace, faith, and Scripture. In Germany it gradually came to be applied collectively to Lutheran, Reformed, and Union communions, and even today evangelical (Ger. *evangelisch*) is synonymous with "Protestant" in much of Europe.

Although much of the spiritual vigor of the Reformation eroded during the ensuing age of orthodoxy, three movements in the late 17th and 18th centuries—German pietism, Methodism, and the Great Awakening—led to the renewal of the Protestant church. These were rooted in Puritanism, which had emphasized biblical authority, divine sovereignty, human responsibility, and the need for personal piety and discipline. The pietism identified with Philipp Spener (1635–1705), August Francke (1663–1727), and Nikolaus von Zinzendorf (1700–1760) was characterized by Bible study, preaching, personal conversion and sanctification, missionary outreach, and concern for the physical needs of others. Their work in turn influenced renewal efforts in Britain and North America and laid the foundations for the later revival in Germany.

In spite of the chilling effect of the Enlightenment, the Methodist revival of John and Charles Wesley and George Whitefield in Britain and the Great Awakening in America transformed the religious experience of many at the grass-roots level. The new fervor spread into the Church of England by the late 18th century, where the evangelical party of Henry Venn, Isaac Milner, Charles Simeon, John Newton, William Wilberforce and the Clapham Sect, and numerous others fought against social ills at home and abroad, and founded Bible and missionary societies. Well into the 1800s similar developments occurred in the Scottish church under Thomas Chalmers and Robert and James Haldane, while the Baptists, Congregationalists, and Methodists in Britain all created foreign mission agencies. In Germany, where the old pietism had waned, a new wave of evangelical enthusiasm spread across the land, known as the *Erweckung*, which cross-fertilized with the British movements. A parallel development, *Le Réveil*, occurred in Holland and France. Both words and the character of the movements may be translated "The Awakening."

Common to these movements were a rather simplistic emphasis on a conversion experience of some kind, the need to live a "holy life," and personal evidence of newly found or renewed faith in good works of evangelism and social concern. The result was that the 19th century became the evangelical age. In Britain the evangelical party was represented in public life by such distinguished personalities as Lord Shaftesbury and William E. Gladstone, while nonconformist groups such as the Baptists and Christian (Plymouth) Brethren reached many with the gospel. Other examples of evangelical vitality included the YMCA founded by George Williams, the Salvation Army of Catherine and William Booth, the social ministries of George Müller and Thomas Barnardo, and the China Inland Mission of Hudson Taylor, and the Keswick Convention.

In the USA the distinguishing feature of evangelical religion was revivalism. The Second Great Awakening in the early 19th century culminated in the urban efforts of Charles Finney and D. L. Moody. Rural and frontier movements continued throughout the 1800s among the Disciples of Christ, Baptists, Methodists, and Presbyterians, as did the growth of holiness perfectionism movements. All served to make Protestantism in the new nation clearly evangelical. The deep, personal evangelical faith struck deep roots among American blacks, both in slavery and freedom, and it sustained their community through the deepest adversities.

Evangelicalism shaped the nation's values and civil religion and helped form the vision of Americans as God's chosen people. Political leaders publicly expressed evangelical convictions and relegated non-Protestant and foreign elements to a second-class status. Revivalism also provided the reforming impetus to create a righteous republic where social evil as well as unbelief would be purged. The antislavery and temperance campaigns, innumerable urban social service agencies, and the nascent women's movement reflected this.

The 19th-century evangelical impulse was spread through the world by the foreign missionary advance which proceeded from the Protestant churches of the North Atlantic region. Before long, the evangelical revivals that had repeatedly swept the Western world began to occur in Africa, Asia, and Latin America as well. The Evangelical Alliance was formed in London in 1846 to unite Christians (but not churches or denominations as such) in common endeavor to promote religious liberty, missions, and evangelism. National alliances came into being in the USA, Germany, and elsewhere. In 1951 the international organization was replaced by the World Evangelical Fellowship.

Another use of the term "evangelicalism" arose in the 20th century in the wake of the struggle of the orthodox Protestants (known in North America as fundamentalists) with theological liberalism and the social gospel. The orthodox were overwhelmed, or so it appeared, by the flood of such new ideas as German higher criticism, Darwinian evolution, Marxist socialism, Nietzschean nihilism, and the naturalism of the new science. In concert with the stress on material prosperity, rugged individualism, and nationalistic jingoism the taproot of Christian social concern was severed. Confidence also was undermined in the infallibility of the Bible, the existence of the supernatural, and the possibility of bringing in the kingdom of God once the Great Commission was fulfilled. Disillusionment produced by the bloodbath of World War I, the rise of totalitarian systems like Soviet communism and German nazism, and the continuing spread of secularism further eroded the position of Christian orthodoxy. Protestantism faced a crisis of monumental proportions as church attendance and interest in Christianity in general declined steadily, and the conservatives seemed unable to do anything about the situation. The fundamentalists withdrew to lick their wounds and build a new set of institutional structures to replace those over which they had lost control, while many of the orthodox elsewhere, both in the mainline churches in the USA and the established churches in other countries, continued to hold and practice their beliefs as before, but they remained in obscurity.

Around the time of World War II, some elements within the conservative or fundamentalist party grew dissatisfied with their isolation and wished to see a more broadly based cultural, theological, and ecclesiastical engagement. Describing themselves as "evangelicals," they set out to build coalitions of cooperation in evangelism, missionary work, and unity against liberalism, especially as it affected the integrity of the Scriptures. Their work bore fruit in a blossoming of foreign missionary endeavors, Bible institutes and colleges, student ministries, and radio and literature works. The evangelistic campaigns of the youthful Billy Graham gave them global significance. Conservative evangelicals emerged in Britain and *Evangelikalen* in Germany, who were joined by such groups as the National Evangelical Anglican Congress and the German Conference of Confessing Fellowships. In the USA the National Association of Evangelicals (NAE) (1942), Fuller Theological Seminary (1947), *Christianity Today Magazine* (1956), and the ministries of Youth for Christ and the Billy Graham Evangelistic Association expressed this "new" evangelicalism, a term which Harold J. Ockenga coined in 1947.

Leaders of new (or "neo") evangelicalism rejected the separatism, anti-intellectualism, legalism, and moralism that had come to be identified with the older fundamentalism. They endeavored to bring about renewal in the church through evangelism, built some ecumenical bridges, and even manifested a renewed interest in the social dimension of the Christian message. By the 1960s they had claimed the mainstream in the conservative church, called themselves simply "evangelicals," and labored to bring together people of like mind from all the various Christian communions, whether or not they had been involved in the earlier struggles for doctrinal purity. The Graham organization was the major catalyst for evangelical ecumenism, since it (in collaboration with *Christianity Today*) called the World Congress on Evangelism (Berlin, 1966) and the International Congress on World Evangelism (Lausanne, 1974). The subsequent meetings sponsored by the Lausanne committee, including a second congress in Singapore in 1989, together with the activities of the World Evangelical Fellowship and the regional organizations formed by evangelicals in Africa, Asia, Latin America, and Europe have fostered closer relations and cooperative efforts in evangelism, relief work, and theological development.

As the movement for evangelical ecumenism proceeded apace, it became increasingly clear that the term now encompassed so complex a sociological reality that it was losing its descriptive power. Included under one label were traditionalists, restorationists, adventists, pentecostals, Holiness people, fundamentalists, and pietists, as well as hierarchical, Episcopal, Presbyterial, and Congregational churches. They could no longer be distinguished from people in "mainline," "liberal," or "ecumenical" churches. In effect it had become a generic term for all kinds of Christian orthodoxy, and with the indigenization of mission society operations, the multinational character of relief and evangelistic organizations, and the sending of missionaries by people in third world countries themselves, this broad evangelicalism was a global phenomenon.

**Bibliography.** J. D. Douglas, ed., *Evangelicals and Unity* (1964); P. Scharpff, *History of Evangelism: Three Hundred Years of Evangelism in Germany, Great Britain, and the United States of America* (1966); B. L. Shelley, *Evangelicalism in America* (1967); J. B. A. Kessler, *A Study of the Evangelical Alliance in Great Britain* (1968); R. V. Pierard, *The Unequal Yoke: Evangelical Christianity and Political Conservatism* (1970); J. R. Orr, *Evangelical Awakenings*, 8 vols. (1973–78); D. W. Dayton, *Discovering an Evangelical Heritage* (1976); C. F. H. Henry, *God, Revelation, and Authority*, 6 vols. (1976–82), and *Evangelicals in Search of Identity* (1976); C. R. Padilla, ed., *The New Face of Evangelicalism: An International Symposium on the Lausanne Covenant* (1976); D. McGavran, *The Conciliar-Evangelical Debate: The Crucial Documents, 1964–1976* (1977); R. Webber and D. Bloesch, *The Orthodox Evangelicals: Who They Are and What They Are Saying* (1978); M. A. Inch, *The Evangelical Challenge* (1978); D. G. Bloesch, *Essentials of Evangelical Theology*, 2 vols. (1979); R. Lovelace, *Dynamics of Spiritual Renewal: An Evangelical Theology of Renewal* (1979); D. F. Wells and J. D. Woodbridge, eds., *The Evangelicals: What They Believe, Who They Are, Where They Are Changing* (1979); J. D. Woodbridge, M. A. Noll, and N. O. Hatch, *The Gospel in America: Themes in the Story of America's Evangelicals* (1979); E. Dobson, E. Hindson, and J. Falwell, eds., *The Fundamentalist Phenomenon* (1981); R. Webber, *The Church in the World* (1986); G. M. Marsden, *Reforming Fundamentalism: Fuller Seminary and the New Evangelicalism* (1986); R. Webber, *The Church in the World* (1986).

RICHARD V. PIERARD

## Evangelical Mission Covenant Church. *See* EVANGELICAL COVENANT CHURCH.

## Evangelischer Bund. *See* BUND, EVANGELISCHER.

## Evangelism.
The strategies and endeavors of Christians to communicate the gospel of Jesus Christ as Lord and Savior and call people to become his disciples. Evangelism derives from the NT term *euangelion*, which means good news or gospel. Thus to engage in evangelism, according to the Lausanne Covenant of 1974, "is to spread the good news that Jesus Christ died for our sins and was raised from the dead according to the Scriptures, and that as the reigning Lord he now offers the forgiveness of sins and the liberating gift of the Spirit to all who repent and believe." Evangelism is basic to the church's mission, in which it joins with works of justice and compassion, and the purposes of worship, fellowship, and spiritual maturity.

Christianity has been an evangelistic religion from its inception, as Jesus Christ commissioned his followers to "go into all the world and preach the good news (Gk. *euangelion*) to all creation" (Mark 16:15 NIV). Since the days of the apostles, Christians have felt called by God to share the good news with their families, their neighbors, their fellow citizens, and people of other cultures and races.

This mandate is a continuing NT theme. The Acts of the Apostles in particular recounts the evangelistic work of Peter, Philip, Paul, and their associates. These examples, along with the instruction of the epistles, became a model for subsequent Christians. References in the NT to the second coming of Christ have added a note of urgency to the evangelistic task, reminding Christians that their time is limited.

Zeal for doing evangelistic work has not been constant in the history of the church, however, and commitment is usually culturally conditioned. The religious plurality in the Mediterranean world of the 2d century A.D. seemed to encourage early Christians to share their faith even in the face of persecution. While the church dominated European society during the Middle Ages, however, great zeal could be mustered for crusades to conquer and "christianize" Muslim lands, but the faith of people within Europe often seemed to be taken for granted. Evangelical movements of the past two centuries have stressed more consistently the need for personal faith in Christ as Savior and the work of evangelism as an ongoing priority of the church, wherever it is situated. These movements have generally welled up from social groups, such as the working poor of John and Charles Wesley's England, or the modernizing middle class of 20th-century Korea, whose religious needs were not being met by the older and more established faiths. Churches of evangelical origin, however, have often lost their zeal for evangelism over time, especially as their members have become more comfortable in their social circumstances and less willing to endure opposition.

From the earliest days Christians have pursued evangelism in a variety of forms. NT believers shared their faith in personal encounters, in homes or on the streets, while preaching in synagogue or in the public square, or even while giving testimony in court. Through the centuries people have come to Christ one at a time, in families, or in some instances, as whole villages or tribes. Modern Christians have thus felt free to use a variety of tools for evangelism, including printed books, Bible portions, tracts, magazines, or advertisements. As they developed, such media as phonograph and audio tapes, radio, film, and television joined the evangelism arsenal. Audiences and settings also varied, from spontaneous witness to friends and strangers, from door-to-door canvass to preaching on street corners, in parks, in churches, and in city-wide crusades at vast arenas.

These methods normally have met with the wide approval of orthodox Christians so long as they were used with honesty, love, and respect for hearers, and so long as they presented the gospel clearly and without the calculated intrusion of other messages. Cases of evangelistic ministries which have failed to meet these standards have been frequent throughout the 20th century, however. Such episodes tend to tarnish the reputation and credibility of all evangelists in popular opinion.

Conscious emphasis upon methodology in evangelism has grown since the Great Awakening in America to the point where evangelism sometimes appears today to demand special expertise. Early Christians and pioneers of evangelical movements seem to have shared the gospel with greater spontaneity than is now common. Many contemporary 20th-century evangelists spent such immense amounts of time and effort to streamline and polish their techniques that the question was often asked whether methodology had become a substitute for compassionate zeal. This raised the more important issues of whether the engineering of religious consent had come to be equated with conversion and whether evangelism was a profession for specialists rather than an integral aspect of the church's common life. In Christian evangelism, as in other spheres of late 20th-century life, technical knowledge had often outstripped clear thinking about the relation among means, ends, and identity.

The end of evangelism is to see people become reconciled to God through the saving work of Jesus Christ, and by the Holy Spirit's power to begin to live as Christians. Scripturally it is one of the ways communities of Spirit-filled people bear fruit. Evangelism, then, needs to be shaped by these ends, obliging its hearers to count the cost of becoming Christ's disciples, showing the redeeming love of Christ at work in the church and inviting them to join this redemptive community. True evangelism is more a vital function in the church's total mission than a device or a profession.

*Bibliography.* E. M. Green, *Evangelism in the Early Church* (1970); A. C. Outler, *Evangelism in the Wesleyan Spirit* (1971); J. D. Douglas, ed., *Let the Earth Hear His Voice: Official Reference Papers and Responses, International Congress on World Evangelization, Lausanne, Switzerland* (1975); D. C. K. Watson, *I Believe in Evangelism* (1977); H. M. Conn, *Evangelism: Doing Justice and Preaching Grace* (1982); M. L. Rudnick, *Speaking the Gospel Through the Ages: A History of Evangelism* (1984); V. Samuel and C. Sugden, eds., *Sharing Jesus in the "Two-Thirds" World* (1984).

JOEL A. CARPENTER

## Evangelization of Peoples, Sacred Congregation for the.

The department of the Roman Curia charged with the supreme direction and administration of the Catholic Church's missionary activity. Founded in 1622, it was known until August 15, 1967, as the *Congregation for the Propagation of the Faith* or simply the *Propaganda* (from its Latin name *Propaganda Fide*). Prior to the 20th century its competence embraced all matters in the lands designated as mission territories, but Pius X's constitution of 1908 transferred its jurisdiction over questions of faith, marriage, discipline of the sacred rites, and the activities of religious orders' missionaries to other Roman congregations. In 1931 its jurisdiction over ecclesiastical institutions of learning was assumed by the Congregation for Seminaries and Universities (now the Congregation for Catholic Education). Thus the Congregation for Evangelization maintains administrative and executive authority over everything connected with missions for the spread of the faith, but judicial matters are left to other bodies. It designates mission territories, appoints bishops or other ordinaries, and oversees the ecclesiastical government there. It has charge of all institutions, schools, home bases, funds, and properties related to the operation and promotion of foreign missions.

Canon law defines the Congregation's status and competence in the territories where the hierarchy is not yet established or is in an initial state of development. These districts may be in non-Catholic but Christian regions or in non-Christian lands. Various dioceses in northern Europe are under its jurisdiction, and only in 1908 were Great Britain, the Netherlands, southern Canada, and the USA removed from its control. Today, scattered and usually remote areas in the Western hemisphere are under the Congregation's authority, as are most of Africa, Asia, and Oceania. In 1938 some regions in North Africa and western Asia were shifted to the jurisdiction of the Congregation for the Eastern Church.

The Congregation for the Evangelization of Peoples is comprised of cardinals chosen by the pope, together with a number of prelates. The cardinal prefect regularly reports to the pontiff, who approves all major decisions. To aid in planning and development, the body maintains an extensive archive and library. The territories under its jurisdiction are divided into dioceses, vicariates, and prefectures, and are ruled over by bishops, vicars apostolic, and prefects apostolic, all of whom are chosen by the congregation. In a few places, independent missions *(missiones sui juris)* existed but these were gradually phased out. Archdioceses and dioceses in former missionary countries often continue for some time under the authority of the congregation, and it communicates with the ordinaries of these territories, either directly or through the regional representatives (apostolic delegates and papal nuncios) of the Holy See.

Traditionally, upon opening a new mission region the congregation entrusted the work to a particular religious order or mission society and appointed an ecclesiastical superior as a member of the group to oversee the work, but current practice is to place indigenous bishops at the head of dioceses as quickly as possible. This enables expatriate missionaries to work unitedly in a given region and at the same time to develop indigenous leadership within the local church. After World War I Benedict XV assigned Propaganda the task of building up an indigenous clergy and hierarchy as quickly as possible, and the first Asian bishop was consecrated in 1923 and the first African apostolic vicars were named in 1939. The creation of an indigenous episcopacy and hierarchy in nearly all mission lands is one of the most important developments in the Roman Catholic Church's recent history. The ongoing world mission testifies to the genuinely universal character of the church.

RICHARD V. PIERARD

**Evanston Assembly (1954).** The second assembly of the World Council of Churches. Its theme, "Christ—The Hope of the World," was discussed under six heads: *faith and order:* our oneness in Christ and our disunity as churches; *evangelism:* the mission of the church to those outside her life; *social questions:* the responsible society in a world perspective; *international affairs:* Christians in the struggle for world community; *intergroup relations:* the churches amid racial and ethnic tensions; and *the laity:* the Christian in his vocation.

The so-called younger churches, except those in China, were strongly represented, and their presence was felt in the form of an impatient urge for concrete action. As the assembly was held in the USA, it gave the powerful churches an opportunity to acquaint themselves directly with WCC. Theologically speaking, Evanston was one of the most carefully prepared assemblies. The theme gave rise to differing opinions. The concept of the Christian hope held by European churches tended to be eschatological, whereas the concept of North American churches was more optimistic and more concerned with the Christian's hope in the world here and now. There was also no agreement that the Jewish people occupy a special place in the history of salvation.

The phrase "the responsible society" was more clearly defined; it was made clear that it did not indicate "an alternative social or political system," but "a criterion by which we judge all existing social orders and at the same time a standard to guide us in the specific choices we have to make." Priority was especially given to the social and economic "problems in the economically underdeveloped regions," a question to which WCC paid increasing attention. The assembly affirmed its responsibility for international peace and justice and issued an appeal to governments urging the prohibition of all weapons of mass destruction, and abstention from aggression. Statements on religious liberty and on "intergroup relations," insisting on racial equality, were issued. In continuation of the Amsterdam Assembly, the missionary task of the laity was strongly stressed since it "constitutes more than 99 percent of the Church," "bridges the gulf between the Church and the world," and "stands at the very outposts of the Kingdom of God."

The Evanston Assembly was careful to identify with the continuation of ecumenical efforts dating back to the Edinburgh Missionary Conference of 1910. One of its convenors, Dr. John R. Mott, continued to be honorary president of WCC until his death in 1955 and another pioneering ecumenicist, Bishop George K. A. Bell, was honored with the same title. WCC presidents elected for the next seven years were: Principal John Baillie (Scotland), Bishop Sante Uberto Barbieri (Argentina), Bishop Otto Dibelius (Germany), Metropolitan Juhanon Mar Thoma (Syrian Church), Archbishop Michael (Greek Orthodox, USA) (succeeded in 1959 by Archbishop Iakovos), and Bishop Henry Knox Sherill (USA). Moderator of the central committee was Bishop Bell.

*See also* WORLD COUNCIL OF CHURCHES (WCC).

A. J. VAN DER BENT

**Everlasting Life.** See ETERNAL LIFE.

**Exaltation of Christ.** The doctrine relating to the state of majesty of Jesus as Christ and Son of God. The word occurs rarely in the NT with reference to Christ, but the idea is prominent. In contrast to his "state of humiliation," his incarnate state as the Jesus of Nazareth who suffered under Pontius Pilate, Christ's state of exaltation begins with the resurrection and continues forever, a state of majesty no longer at the mercy of men or nature. The Apostles' Creed denotes the exaltation by the phrases "rose again . . . ascended . . . sitteth at the right hand . . . shall come to judge." The word can refer to the act of God the Father or to the "state" of Christ. The *locus classicus* is in Phil. 2:9, the verb used here not occurring elsewhere in the NT. Acts 2:33 and 5:31 use a less emphatic word which elsewhere refers to Christians (2 Cor. 11:7) or to men in general (Matt. 23:12). The church doctrine uses Paul's word but with John's meaning. The surface impression a reader would derive from Paul is that of an assumption of glory, whereas the impression gained from John (John 17) is that of a resumption of former glory. Hebrews stands closer to Paul than to John, although in harmony with both. The Father is always represented to be the source and agent of exaltation. Even in the exalted state Christ is still the Son. Concrete definiteness is lent to the concept by such words as "glory," "power," "authority," as well as by "he sat down at the right hand of the Majesty in heaven" (Heb. 1:3). Eph. 1:19–23 unites the cosmic exaltations of Christ with his headship of the church. The title of Christ by which the church most succinctly confesses his exaltation is "Lord." There is both a present and a future aspect of the exaltation, both expressed in Christian hymns and liturgy. Christ's exaltation now is seen with the eyes of faith. Not everywhere is he acknowledged to be Lord. But it is the church's belief that "every eye will see him" (Rev. 1:7) and "every tongue confess that Jesus Christ is Lord" (Phil. 2:11; cf. 1 Cor. 15:24). The difference between present and future is not in the exaltation itself, but in the degree and extent to which it is acknowledged on earth.

KENNETH J. FOREMAN

**Ex Cathedra.** Lat., "from the chair." A term which applied originally to all manner of authoritative pronouncements, but which now is reserved for infallible utterances of the pope. The Vatican Council (1870) proclaimed as an article of faith that the pope, whenever he speaks *ex cathedra*, that is, in his capacity as the pastor and doctor of the Church Universal, by virtue of his supreme apostolic authority, and in order to define a doctrine regarding faith and morals to make it binding for all Christians, is personally infallible. These stipulations were shaped after the terms used in conclusion of the Bull *Ineffabilis Deus*, by which Pope Pius IX had defined the dogma of the Immaculate Conception (1854). Since the proclamation of the papal infallibility in 1870, the only *ex cathedra* definition actually delivered is that of the assumption of Mary by Pope Pius XII (1950).

GEORGES A. BARROIS

**Excommunication.** *See* CENSURES.

**Exegesis.** *See* HERMENEUTICS.

**Existentialism, Christian.** A philosophy which in the Christian context is meant to express a concern for the individual person and personal freedom. It represents an approach to Christian life and existence rather than a prescribed set of doctrines or specific theological content.

Søren Kierkegaard (1813–55) was key to the development of Christian existentialism. Mostly unnoticed in his own time, Kierkegaard was rediscovered in the 20th century by European theologians such as Karl Barth (1886–1968). Others who adopted a Christian existential approach to faith were Karl Jaspers (1883–1969), Gabriel Marcel (1889–1973), and Nikolai Berdyaev (1874–1948). The Jewish theologian Martin Buber (1878–1965) in *I and Thou* (ET, 1937) showed his debt to Kierkegaard. Existentialism as a secular philosophical movement was fostered in the 20th century by Martin Heidegger (1889–1976), Maurice Merleau-Ponty (1908–61), and Jean-Paul Sartre (1905–80).

These writers seek the meaning of human existence and believe such meaning can be found only from within human experience. They reject the Western philosophy which, since René Descartes (1596–1650), has tried to explore objectively "beings-in-general." Their concern is with human subjectivity. Any approach to knowledge or truth-seeking using categories disengaged from human experience ignores both the enigmatic nature of personal existence and the immense differences between human and nonhuman being. Detached, impersonal investigations—as in the natural sciences—cannot deal with issues such as the meaning of life because they sever the human subject from the object of knowledge. Kierkegaard's aphorism, "truth is subjectivity," captured the need for human involvement and personal participation in knowledge and truth.

Kierkegaard rejected Georg Hegel's (1770–1831) absolute idealism that proposed a basic continuity between all things. Hegel tried to assimilate the individual into the universal, the finite into the infinite, and the human into the divine. He believed reason could uncover the developmental process of the universe as truth inevitably emerged through stages of thesis and antithesis toward synthesis. Kierkegaard contended this eliminated the "infinite qualitative difference" between God and humanity and thus was blasphemy. He rejected attempts to unite God's revelation and human reason, faith and human culture, or holiness and human ethics.

For Kierkegaard, Christianity was an absolute paradox. God is transcendent and holy; humans are finite and sinful. Christianity teaches that the chasm between God and humans has been bridged by God's Son, Jesus Christ. God has appeared as the promised Messiah in the human man Jesus; the infinite has become the finite. This conviction is not derived from human reason or rational proofs. It comes from inward faith. The Holy Spirit grants faith that God is revealed in Jesus Christ and that the barrier of sin has been broken down. Reconciliation is actualized by faith. God communicates "indirectly" through Jesus who is the only point of contact between God and humans. This paradox cannot be comprehended rationally or explained intellectually. Reason is finite and unable to grasp what cannot be known or verified by the dialectical processes of history.

Kierkegaard said a person must take a leap of faith to become a Christian. One chooses to accept the Christian gospel with its ethical demands and embraces in a personal way God's claims upon one's life. Humans created in the image of God are responsible for reflecting what God is: love. Since humans have free powers to choose, they may shape themselves either as God wishes or against God's wishes. For Kierkegaard, "the individual existing" is prior to "the individual thinking."

Atheistic existentialists such as Sartre have argued that since there is no God, humans *are* this freedom in themselves. "Existence precedes essence," they said. Humans must make choices within their historical circumstances and the "givenness" of their lives. They are responsible only to themselves and encounter the anguish and despair of craving a completeness for life which because of their freedom—which always leads them to changes—they can never find. Without God, there are no values except those that humans themselves project. Anxiety or dread (Ger. *angst*) is a basic part of the human condition since it describes the dissatisfaction between the self one is and the authentic self one has the possibility to become.

For Christian existentialists the basic insecurities of life are expressed in Kierkegaard's works, *The Concept of Dread* (ET, 1944) and *The Sickness unto Death* (ET, 1941). Angst is caused ultimately by sin and escaped only through one's personal encounter with God in Christ. In the "moment" of this encounter faith finds true peace through the forgiveness of sins and the renewal of life provided by God. The human decision for faith, temporally made, has eternal aspects.

The early writings of Barth echoed Kierkegaard's attacks on the objectivism of theological systems that sought by reason to come to a knowledge of God. Barth spoke of the "Godness of God" and God the "Wholly Other," stressing with Kierkegaard the "infinite qualitative difference" between the transcendent God and sinful humanity. Barth and his colleagues developed a "crisis" or "dialectical" theology in which they viewed the world as under God's judgment in Christ. Humans either receive the gift of God's grace in Christ by faith or experience spiritual death by rejecting Christ. The "grace" and "judgment" of God are the points of the dialectic or word. The response of humanity must be to answer either "yes" or "no" to Christ. By 1921, Barth named his theological ancestry as extending "through *Kierkegaard* to *Luther* and *Calvin*, and so to *Paul* and *Jeremiah*." Later Barth began to emphasize the "humanity of God." Yet he always saw himself as faithful to "Kierkegaard's reville" which led him to reject the liberalism of

19th-century theology that stressed the continuity rather than the discontinuity between humans and God.

Christian existentialism is prominent in the works of the biblical scholar, Rudolf Bultmann (1884–1976). Bultmann was a student of Heidegger's and reinterpreted his philosophical existentialism within a Christian framework. He blended Heidegger's views of "inauthentic existence" with what he regarded as the biblical myth of the fall. He saw humanity as in subjection to the elements of the world, having lost its true freedom and selfhood; this is the essence of sin. In Jesus Christ God delivers from the bondage to the inauthentic self and gives the freedom of authentic existence. This freedom comes from the decision of faith. To believe in the cross of Christ is to appropriate personally the message that one can be reconciled to one's true being and to God by giving up self-sufficiency and living by grace.

Paul Tillich's (1886–1965) theology was heavily influenced by existential themes. He wrote that "existential philosophy asks in a new and radical way the question whose answer is given to faith in theology." For Tillich, God is "Being itself" or "the Ground of being." All that participates in God "stand-out" (Lat. *ex-sistere*) from God. Humans are estranged or separated from their ground of being (God ) in the condition called sin. Biblical symbols, centering in the key symbol of "Jesus as the Christ," are the means of gaining "an existential understanding of revelation, that is, a creative and transforming participation of every believer in the correlation of revelation." In Jesus as the Christ, the power of the "new Being" was uniquely present. "Revelation" and "salvation" are the healing events mediated by the Christ which convey the power of the new being to people of faith.

Christian existentialism in varied forms continues to have immense impact on contemporary theology. Protestants such as John Macquarrie (1919– ) and Roman Catholics such as Karl Rahner (1904–84) have applied existential approaches and themes. As a call for the personal appropriation of faith and the need for free, human decision, existential motifs will have an ongoing role in the development of Christian theology.

*Bibliography.* A. C. Cochrane, *The Existentialists and God* (1956); D. E. Roberts, *Existentialism and Religious Belief* (1957); J. Macquarrie, *An Existentialist Theology: A Comparison of Heidegger and Bultmann* (1960); W. Barrett, *Irrational Man: A Study in Existential Philosophy* (1962); J. Macquarrie, *Existentialism* (1973).

DONALD MCKIM

**Exorcist.** *See* ORDERS, MINOR.

**Expansion of Christianity (Modern).** After World War II it became apparent that Christian missions had been successful to a degree that had not been fully appreciated. Henry P. Van Dusen could write about the existence of the church in the outposts of the world. Kenneth Scott Latourette located the church in almost every country. Stephen Neill noted that for the first time in history there was a universal religion, and identified that religion as Christianity. The gains, however, have been in geographical expansion and an increase in the absolute number of Christians. On a percentage basis the number of Christians in the world has been in a slow decline through the 20th century and by 1990 was the religion held by fewer than one-third of the world's population.

*Background.* After the war Christian expansion confronted unprecedented and accelerated change in the world. Western domination of the non-Western world collapsed almost completely within about 25 years. Newly independent nation-states were born in record numbers. While secularization and the disestablishment of the church characterized the Western world to the extent that it became common to speak of a post-Christian age, religion generally was not necessarily in eclipse. Tribal (primal) religions won new attraction as the newly free nations affirmed their selfhood. Revitalization movements breathed new life into historic faiths, including Christianity. Eastern mystical movements found acceptance in the West. Islam capitalized on oil riches and believer devotion to make significant inroads into Europe and the Americas as well as elsewhere. The division between the communist and free worlds, so apparent immediately after the war, became indelibly impressed on every sphere of life—political, social, economic, ideological, and religious. Eastern Europe and China were sealed off from, and largely antagonistic to, the Western world, and their communist governments persecuted Christian minorities and extended leftist influence in Asia, Latin America, and Africa. The gap between rich and poor nations, and between the rich and the poor within nations, plagued the world and clouded the future as never before. Analysts interpreted the gap differently, but most agreed that rising expectations in the third world especially were largely unattainable and that the gap would be a destabilizing influence for decades to come. The technological revolution resulted in almost instantaneous communication worldwide and in greatly increased traffic among nations. The industrial base of the West began to erode as Japan, South Korea, Taiwan, and other nations stepped up production. Predictions were that information would eventually be the prime commodity of the USA and certain other Western nations. Finally, the eyes of the world became focused on the Middle East where much of the world's oil reserves are centered and where renewed antagonisms between Arabs, Muslims, Jews, and Christians (and factions within these groups) stirred periodic wars and unrelenting terrorism.

*The Churches and Their Missions.* The Christian response to the unchanged commission to disciple the nations (Matt. 28:16–20) on the one hand, and rapidly changing world conditions on the other, has been varied. Due to Soviet domination in Eastern Europe, Muslim power in the Middle East, and internal factors the Orthodox churches have made a very limited contribution to the expansion of Christianity over the past generation, although modest gains increased their membership to slightly over 173 million by 1987. Most of this can be accounted for on the basis of biological growth within the families of members. One Orthodox analyst, Ion Bria, says that most Orthodox churches "find it very difficult to speak of foreign missions. It certainly is not a live option for many national Orthodox churches. Their duty remains primarily within the churches and the nations in which they find themselves. Yet, other Orthodox churches are to be challenged for having both the opportunity and the resources, and not responding to the charge to 'make disciples of all nations.'"

The Sacred Congregation for the Propagation of the Faith of the Roman Catholic Church did not experience as much disruption in its missionary outreach during World War II as did most Protestant missions. The curia adopted a policy of appointing national leaders to places of increased responsibility and of accommodating indigenous religious and cultural preferences, and this mitigated problems associated with nationalism. The movement, however, bit into the monolithic nature of Roman Catholicism and fostered such unwelcome (to Rome) developments as a gradual decline in the number of foreign missionaries and personnel sent out from Europe and North America. Native leaders also contributed to the inroads of liberation theology in Latin America and elsewhere. By 1986, the world total of Roman Catholics had reached approximately 887 million.

Overall, Protestant churches and their missions have experienced significant growth since World War II. Including approximately 100 million non-white indigenous Christians of the world—most of whom have a Protestant orientation—the number of world Protestants reached nearly 379 million by 1986. The growth has not been uniform, however, and the various major divisions of Protestantism responded to world challenges in different ways.

In 1961 in New Delhi the International Missionary Council (IMC) became the Division of World Mission and Evangelism (DWME) of the World Council of Churches (WCC). At meetings of IMC in Willingen and Ghana, of DWME at Mexico City, Bangkok, and Melbourne, and of WCC in Uppsala, Nairobi, and Vancouver discussions revolved around the mission of all the churches on all six continents. Churches connected with WCC tended to shift their emphasis from missions and the sending of missionaries to sociopolitical concerns. More conservative Protestants responded with the Wheaton Declaration (1966), the Frankfurt Declaration (1973), and the Lausanne Covenant (1974).

In Europe, there have been attempts to integrate traditionally independent mission organizations into existing church structures. Beginning in the early 1970s, the Lutheran Church in West Germany developed six regional centers to coordinate the efforts of independent missions within church organizations. This has been motivated in part by the conviction that mission is integral to the overall ministry of the church. Speaking generally, however, both church attendance and mission involvement have declined.

A general decline in membership in the mainline denominations of the United States (with the exception of the Southern Baptists) has been accompanied by a dramatic reduction in the number of foreign missionaries. By 1960 the number of personnel in agencies affiliated with the Division of Overseas Ministries of the National Council of Churches (NCC) in the United States was exceeded by nonconciliar Protestant overseas personnel, a trend which has continued. On the other hand, evangelical churches of various strains have almost uniformly experienced growth through outreach. In North America the missions connected with the Interdenominational Foreign Mission Association (IFMA) and the Evangelical Foreign Missions Association (EFMA) (an affiliate of the National Association of Evangelicals [NAE]) have shown consistent if not dramatic growth. A rapid increase in the number of mission agencies (approximately 100 each decade since 1950) has been accompanied by rapid growth and notable contributions from unaffiliated groups such as the Southern Baptists, Operation Mobilization, and Youth with a Mission and from specialist missions such as Wycliffe Bible Translators, Missionary Aviation Fellowship, and several missions concentrating on radio communication. Evangelical student organizations such as InterVarsity Christian Fellowship, Campus Crusade for Christ, and the Navigators have given significant impetus to world missions.

The most spectacular growth has occurred among pentecostals and charismatics. An almost insignificant phenomenon at the beginning of this century, they had combined to become the largest sector of Protestantism and perhaps the most pervasive force for church growth, church renewal, and world missions by the mid-1980s. There were then as many as 51 million believers in some 1200 pentecostal denominations worldwide. Add charismatics to this number and the figure comes to over 100 million. The latter especially are scattered throughout the ecclesiastical spectrum, including Roman Catholicism. Through their own organizations and through their participation in a variety of denominations and missions, their impact on Christianity around the world has been considerable.

Another significant phenomenon of recent years has been the rise of missions in the younger Protestant churches of the third world. As these churches have gained in leadership, membership, and overall strength they have increasingly become involved in the organization of mission boards and the sending of missionary personnel. By 1986 as many as 380 such agencies were entirely autonomous under which 20,000 cross-cultural national missionaries were serving.

Missiology also developed as a discipline with the emergence of professional organizations such as the Association of Professors of Missions, the Association of Evangelical Professors of Missions, and the American Society of Missiology in North America. Missiological periodicals and textbooks increased drastically.

***Areas of Growth.*** Growth in the evangelical, especially pentecostal, sectors of the church in the USA and various countries of Europe and elsewhere was offset by losses in other communions, resulting in little or no growth overall. Rapid church growth through the 1970s and 1980s took place largely in the third world. Most notable is the growth in Africa where Christians of all types numbered more than 196 million in 1986. Much of this growth is occurring in more than 6000 indigenous or nativistic church groups prone to varying degrees of syncretism. Growth is running somewhat behind earlier predictions that Christians would constitute a majority in Africa by the year 2000, but it is still great.

Some countries of Asia and the Pacific have also witnessed great growth. Most attention has been focused upon China, which was sealed off from missionary activity from the outside world in 1950. Within one generation after Mao's takeover, however, the state-recognized Three-Self Patriotic Movement Church was allowed to open churches in major centers, a major seminary opened, and a limited number of Bibles were printed. Nevertheless, an estimated 80 percent of some 40 million to 50 million Christians in China remained in house churches. South Korea now claims the largest churches in the world, one church in Seoul alone numbering more than 500,000 members. Approximately 25 percent of South Korea was Christian by 1990. Although growth was less spectacular, the church made significant gains in India, Taiwan, Indonesia, and elsewhere.

The vast majority (87 percent) of Latin America was still nominally Roman Catholic but the late 1900s brought profound changes in that church and in the religious situation. Theological and political division and the inroads of animism and spiritism threaten Roman Catholicism. By the mid-1980s the number of Protestants reached at least 22 million (some estimates were as high as 30 million), or 7.5 percent of the population. Some 70 percent of these were pentecostals.

By the mid-1980s one of the most significant developments of the 2000 years of the Christian era had occurred: The center of gravity in the Christian church had shifted from the Western to the non-Western world. Membership for all communions in Europe (including the USSR) and North America reached 695 million, but in Africa, East and South Asia, Latin America, and Oceania the total membership was 753 million.

*Major Concerns.* In the 1980s considerable attention was given to trends, issues, or problems of the task of carrying out the Christian mission and discipling the nations. The nature of the church's mission itself emerged as a major concern. In the conciliar churches mission was often understood horizontally in terms of humanization, effecting justice, eliminating poverty, and aiding organizations and efforts purporting to accomplish these ends. Conservative evangelicals stressed the vertical relationship with God implicit in world evangelization, personal redemption, and discipleship, with appropriate sociopolitical action an outgrowth of new life or a lesser partner in mission. The divisions occasioned by these very different understandings characterized the missionary enterprise at almost every level.

A major concern of evangelicals in the forefront of the effort to evangelize the world was the existence of unreached peoples. Vagueness existed in attempts to define such terms as "unevangelized" and "unreached." Defining the unevangelized as those who have not had the gospel offered to them, the estimated percentage of the world's unevangelized population decreased from 48.7 percent in 1900 to 27.3 percent in 1986 and it was projected that the percentage might be reduced to 16.6 percent in A.D. 2000. Another approach spoke of unreached peoples as homogeneous groupings within which there is no viable, evangelizing church. There were approximately 17,000 such groups in the world. This latter approach linked evangelization with church planting and growth, one of the major evangelical emphases of the postwar era.

Diversity in the church and its missions occasioned considerable debate. Worldwide, an average of five new denominations were born each week in the 1980s. There were over 13 times as many Christian service agencies and six times as many foreign mission agencies in the mid-1980s as in 1900. In North America alone, more than 100 new mission agencies formed during each decade between 1950 and 1990; by far the most rapid growth occurred in unaffiliated agencies and in the number of short-term missionaries (30,000 in 1985). A large but undetermined number of Christians offered themselves as "tentmaking missionaries" and a large percentage of new missions were "specialized missions." Some insist that the overlap and misunderstandings occasioned by such a state of affairs is one of the strongest arguments for mergers of denominations and missionary organizations, and a renewed emphasis on the church itself as the instrument of mission in the world. Others insist that the multiplication of mission agencies and opportunities is a sign of vitality and bodes well for the future of church expansion.

The degree of accommodation to the various cultures and religions of the world was yet another concern. Leaders agreed that the Christian faith could and must be expressed in forms meaningful to the people of a given culture. The term "contextualization" was most often used to refer to this process. The perplexing questions involved how to go about this, the kinds and extent of cultural accommodation, and the potential loss of the essence of the gospel itself inherent in contextualization.

Similarly, it was apparent that Christianity faced a religiously pluralistic world. This led to rethinking such issues as the source of these religions, the extent of truth inherent in other religious faiths, the nature of interreligious dialog, and strategies for Christian witness among adherents of other religions.

Finally, within a generation or so after World War II it became apparent that in the future Christianity must find its way in the world amidst new waves of opposition. Secularism, humanism, and materialism in the free world, religious persecution in Marxist states, increasing restrictions upon missionary activity in non-Christian nations, and the growing number of martyrs worldwide testified to this trend. By 1980 25 countries were closed to foreign missionaries, 24 were partially closed, and 18 severely restricted their entrance and activities. These 67 countries had a combined total of 3.1 billion inhabitants. The number of Christian martyrs grew. In the face of this opposition much encouragement has been drawn from the Scriptures and the history of Christian expansion, particularly the expansion under fire of the church in China.

*Bibliography.* D. B. Barrett, *World Christian Encyclopedia. A Comparative Survey of Churches and Religions in the Modern World, A.D. 1900–2000* (1982); I. Bria, comp., ed., *Go Forth in Peace: Orthodox Perspectives on Mission* (1986); P. Brierley, ed., *UK Christian Handbook, 1985/86 ed.* (1986); P. Johnstone, *Operation World, A Day-to-Day Guide to Praying for the World* (4th ed., 1986); S. Wilson and J. Siewert, eds., *Mission Handbook: North American Protestant Ministries Overseas* (13th ed., 1987).

DAVID J. HESSELGRAVE

# Ff

**Fahs, Sophia Lyon (Mrs. Charles H. Fahs)** (1876–1978). Unitarian. Born in Hangchow, China, she studied at the College of Wooster, Columbia University, and Union Theological Seminary. She was traveling secretary for the Student Volunteer Movement in American Colleges (1899–1901); YWCA student secretary at the University of Chicago (1901/2); lecturer in religious education, Union Seminary (1926–44); and editor of children's materials for the American Unitarian Association (1936–51). She edited the New Beacon Series in Religious Education, including 35 titles. She wrote *Uganda's White Man of Work* (1907), *Red, Yellow and Black* (1918), *Beginnings of Earth and Sky* (1937), *Teacher's Guide to Beginnings of Life and Death* (1939), *Leading Children in Worship* (1943), *Jesus: The Carpenter's Son* (1945; Teacher's Guide, 1945), *From Long Ago and Many Lands* (1948), and *Today's Children and Yesterday's Heritage* (1951). She coauthored *Exploring Religion with Eight-Year-Olds* (1930), *Martin and Judy* (3 vols., 1939–43), and *Consider the Children: How They Grow* (1940, rev. ed., 1950).

**Fairbairn, Andrew Martin** (1838–1912). Scottish Congregational theologian. Born in Fife, he had little formal education, but read avidly as he worked for a living, and eventually was able to study at Edinburgh University. After ordination he was minister in Bathgate and Aberdeen before becoming principal, first of Airedale Theological College (1877–86), then of the newly founded Mansfield College, Oxford (1886–1909). In theology he reflected the views of modern German thinkers. His writings include *Studies in the Philosophy of Religion and History* (1876), *Studies in the Life of Christ* (1880), *Christ in Modern Theology* (1893), and *The Philosophy of the Christian Religion* (1902). Much sought after because of his clear and refreshing style, he paid several visits to the USA. He was also active at home in the field of both secular and religious education, in which causes he did not shrink from political controversy.

J. D. Douglas

**Fairbanks, Rollin Jonathan** (1908–1983). Episcopal educator, clergyman, and editor. Born in Watertown, N.Y., he studied at the University of Michigan, the Episcopal Theological School, Cambridge, Mass., Worcester (Mass.) State Hospital, and the Massachusetts General Hospital, Boston. After ordination in 1936, he became rector of St. John's Church, St. Johns, Mich. (1936–39), and of St. James' Church, Grosse Ile, Mich. (1939–42). He served as Protestant chaplain at the Massachusetts General Hospital (1943–50), lecturer (1943–50), assistant professor (1950–53), and professor of pastoral theology at the Episcopal Theological School, Cambridge, Mass. (1953–74), lecturer at Harvard Divinity School (1941–54), instructor at Boston University School of Theology (1947/48), and professor at the Episcopal Divinity School (1974–77). He founded the Institute of Pastoral Care (1944), and served as its executive director (1944–50), field secretary (1951), and member of the board of governors. He started the *Journal of Pastoral Care* (1947) and was editor-in-chief (1947–50), associate editor (1951–65), and book review editor (1965–70). He was director of the Pastoral Counseling Center, Boston (1949–53).

Jack Mitchell

**Faith and Order.** *See* Ecumenical Movement.

**Faith Missions.** *See* Expansion of Christianity, Modern.

**Falashas.** Ethiopian national-religious group following a distinctive brand of Jewish observances. The group claims descendancy from followers of Menelik I, an alleged son of Solomon and the queen of Sheba. Modern scholarship suggests that they may have come from Jewish settlements in southern Arabia or first-temple Jewish settlements in Upper Egypt. Their sacred texts—

mostly biblical and apocryphal materials—are preserved in Ge'ez, an ancient literary dialect, in essentially the same versions used by their Christian neighbors (close to the LXX). They do not speak Hebrew, nor are they aware of the Maccabees or Hanukkah, indicating that they separated from mainstream Judaism before the Maccabean era. From the late 13th century, their powerful kingdom, centered around the fortress of Simin, conducted military campaigns against hostile Christian neighbors and missionary Ethiopian rulers. After their loss of independence in the 17th century, the Falashas continued to adhere to their religion. A responsum of the Egyptian rabbi David Ibn Zimra generally accepts them as Jews, although he admits that they are misguided in their practices. Since the 19th century they have been in contact with other Jewish communities, especially through travelers such as Joseph Halévy who visited them and then described their customs and literature. In the 1980s many were airlifted to Israel where their absorption has been generally successful.

Distinctive Falasha practices include emphasis on ritual purity regarding corpses and menstruation; differences in festivals (they continue to offer the Paschal sacrifice, have a different date for the Day of Atonement, and do not celebrate New Year's Day); and acceptance of all their members as qualified for the priesthood. They hold traditional Jewish beliefs.

**Bibliography.** A. Z. Aescoly, *Sefer ha-Falashim;* W. Leslau, *Falasha Anthology: The Black Jews of Ethiopia* (1951); S. W. Baron, *A Social and Religious History of the Jews* (1983).

ELIEZER SEGAL

## Falwell, Jerry

**Falwell, Jerry** (1933– ). Fundamentalist and independent Baptist pastor. Born in Lynchburg, Va., he was an alcoholic in early life, but became a Christian in 1952. Graduating from the Baptist Bible College (Mo.) in 1958, he returned to Lynchburg and founded the Thomas Road Baptist Church, which by the 1980s claimed a membership of about 17,000. He soon started a radio and television ministry, known as the Old Fashioned Gospel Hour which by the 1980s was broadcast by nearly 400 television stations and about 500 radio stations. By 1980 contributions to his ministry amounted to nearly $1 million per week. Falwell also founded Liberty Baptist College in 1971, now known as Liberty University.

In the early years of his ministry Falwell had strongly opposed the involvement of ministers in the political life of the nation; however, the increasing corruption in the moral standards of some Americans, marked by the legalization of abortion in *Roe* v. *Wade* in 1972, caused him to radically shift his position. Thus he founded the Moral Majority in an attempt to reform the American people who sponsored this immoral endorsement and to bring them back to biblical standards. Declaring that he was neither a Democrat nor a Republican, Falwell pushed his way into the mainstream of politics and claimed that he had helped Ronald Reagan to win the presidency. He added to this claim that his Moral Majority had also brought about the defeat of several liberal Democratic senators, namely, George McGovern of South Dakota, Frank Church of Idaho, and Birch Bayh of Indiana.

C. GREGG SINGER

**Famine.** Severe shortage of food within a local district or major region. During the late 19th century and for a short period following World War II, it seemed that mankind had the potential to banish famine from the face of the earth. Books like H. G. Wells' *Outline of History* (1920) reflect such an optimistic faith in progress. The success of the Marshall Plan in Europe following the Second World War added vigor to this view, and Western governments and church groups embraced the need for the "development" of "underdeveloped" countries.

The 1960s saw a shift in terminology and worldview. Underdeveloped countries became the third world as optimism about newly independent states formed by the breakup of colonial empires surged. Yet by the mid-1960s new voices warned of impending doom. Books like *Famine 1975* reflected a new mood of pessimism which had become the dominant intellectual trend after the publication of *Limits to Growth* by the Club of Rome in 1972. This vision was given semiofficial status by the publication of President Jimmy Carter's 1980 *Global 2000 Report to the President* which exacerbated secular pessimism about the future of industrial society.

The scientific flaws in such studies have been largely ignored. Few people are aware of *Models of Doom* (1973), which completely demolishes the credibility of *Limits to Growth*. Similarly, *The Resourceful Earth* has received relatively little attention despite its devastating critique of *Global 2000*. Christian writers have generally accepted the vision of doom presented by the secular pessimists as can be seen from Ronald J. Sider's bestselling *Rich Christians in an Age of Hunger* (1977). Although the book has many merits, its essential premise is that we face imminent social and economic collapse. In his first edition Sider relied heavily on the work of the Club of Rome; in his second edition he incorporated *Global 2000*, apparently unaware of the very serious defects of these works.

Today we hear a great deal about famine in Africa and other parts of the globe. But, in fact, famines are far less devastating than at any time in the past. The question we now face is one of marshaling the will to overcome the effects of famine. But how we do this depends on our vision of the future and our assessment of available resources.

Optimists like Herman Kahn, who have a biblical vision of reality, believe that the earth can sustain a far higher population than at present and that population growth is in fact good. Pessimists like the Club of Rome believe that our world's population is already too large and that drastic reductions in the number of people are necessary for the future survival of the human race. Behind the pessimistic vision is a semipagan understanding of nature with an appeal to evolutionary science, that sees the earth as a living organism (sometimes named *gaia* after the Greek god of nature). All of this is in sharp contrast to biblical teachings.

The Bible sometimes treats famine as a simple historical fact (see Gen. 12:10; 26:1; Acts 11:28). On other occasions divine providence is operative (see Amos 4:6; Rev. 6:8). The biblical view of famine contrasts markedly with that of ancient Canaanite religion and other religious systems, which deify nature and treat famine as the result of the anger of the gods or other nonhumans disturbed by human action.

God controls the forces of nature and orders the seasons. As Creator and Sustainer of human life God enters into a covenant with humans. Morality, then, and not some ontological necessity, the whim of the gods, or a fixed "natural" law, becomes the central issue in understanding the reasons for famine and other natural disasters.

God's creation is good and mankind has the duty to nurture it. Yet as a result of the fall, sin has entered creation and a certain natural historical development takes place which allows the outworking of the effects of the fall over millennia. In the history of Israel God used famines to warn the people and to indicate his displeasure (1 Kings 17:1; Hag. 1:9–11; 2:16–17). On the other hand, blessing and prosperity come as a result of obedience (Ps. 1:1–3; Prov. 3:7–10). The key biblical passage for understanding God's providential action in the history of Israel and, by extension, the human race is Deut. 29. The Bible makes it clear that it is the duty of Christians to work together to relieve suffering and to overcome its effects (cf. Acts 11:28–29; 1 Cor. 16:1–4; Gal. 6:9–10).

*Bibliography.* D. H. Meadows, et al., *Limits to Growth* (1972); H. S. D. Cole, et al., eds., *Models of Doom: A Critique of Limits to Growth* (1973); R. J. Sider, *Rich Christians in an Age of Hunger* (1977, 1984); Council on Environmental Quality and the Department of State, *The Global 2000 Report to the President* (1980); P. Laslett, *The World We Have Lost: England Before the Industrial Age* (1984); J. L. Simon and H. Kahn, eds., *The Resourceful Earth* (1984).

IRVING HEXHAM

**Farmer, Herbert Henry** (1892–1981). English Presbyterian minister, educator, and theologian.

Born in London, he studied at Cambridge, was ordained, and was minister of Stafford Presbyterian Church (1919–22) and St. Augustine's Presbyterian Church, New Barnet, London (1922–31). Thereafter he was professor of Christian doctrine, Hartford Seminary Foundation (1931–35), professor of systematic theology at Westminster College, Cambridge (1935–60), and, combined with his appointment at Westminster College, lecturer in the philosophy of religion, Cambridge University (1937–40) and professor of divinity, Cambridge University (1949–60). A distinguished preacher, he delivered numerous prestigious lectures in Britain and the USA. Farmer belonged to the last generation of English theologians influenced by German philosophical idealists like Albrecht Ritschl and Friedrich Schleiermacher, as mediated by John Oman, his teacher at Westminster College. However, he grew to intellectual maturity during the decline of liberal theology, in the years of disillusionment following the holocaust of World War I and under the intellectual influence of Karl Barth. Thus Farmer became a transitional figure in English theology, deeply influenced by his own Reformed background and the existentialism of Martin Buber, but never quite able to embrace the old orthodoxy or the new. Rather, with some success, he tried to pick his way through the theological minefields of his day, stressing a kind of "radical personalism" and struggling to replace the formulas of Christian belief in the orthodox phraseology with a fresh approach and up-to-date language. His published works include *Things Not Seen* (1927), *The Experience of God* (1929), *The World and God* (1935), *The Healing Cross* (1938), *The Servant of the Word* (1941), *Towards Belief in God* (1942), *God and Men* (1948), *Revelation and Religion* (1954), and *The World of Reconciliation* (1966). Ironically, his introductory article, "The Bible: Its Significance and Authority," in the *Interpreter's Bible* (1952) has been more widely influential than any of his books.

ROBERT D. LINDER

**Farrar, Frederic William** (1831–1903). Anglican scholar. Born in India of missionary parents, he studied at King's College, London, where he came under the influence of F. D. Maurice. After some years as a schoolmaster, Farrar (who had earlier been ordained) became first a canon of Westminster, then dean of Canterbury (1895–1903). His *Life of Christ* (1874) and *Life and Works of St. Paul* (1879) were bestsellers, but his *Eternal Hope* (1878) aroused much controversy because it threw doubt on the doctrine of the eternal punishment of the wicked—a view modified in his *Mercy and Judgment* (1881).

J. D. DOUGLAS

**Farrer, Austin Marsden** (1904–1968). Theologian, philosopher, and priest of the Church of England. He was educated at Oxford, was ordained, and in 1931 became chaplain and tutor at St. Edmund Hall, in 1935 fellow and chaplain at Trinity, and in 1960 warden of Keble, all in Oxford. He wrote what is now a classic in theistic metaphysics, *Finite and Infinite* (1943). He delivered the Bampton Lectures for 1948, *The Glass of Vision*, the Edward Cadbury Lectures for 1953/54 on *St Matthew and St Mark*, the Gifford Lectures for 1957 on *The Freedom of the Will*, the Nathaniel Taylor Lectures for 1961, *Love Almighty and Ills Unlimited*, and the Deems Lectures in 1964, later to be incorporated into *Faith and Speculation*. He was a founding member of the Metaphysicals, an informal society of Oxford dons responsible for publishing *Faith and Logic*, to which he was a contributor. From 1962 he was a member of the Church of England's Liturgical Commission. Shortly before his death he was elected a fellow of the British Academy. The depth and integrity of his Christian thought and character shine through in all his writings and published sermons.

ALISTAIR J. DRUMMOND

**Father Divine's Peace Mission.** Eclectic cult combining elements from the Holiness, New Thought, Perfectionist, and Adventist movements with the unique belief that its founder, Father Divine, was not simply a prophet or a messianic figure but God incarnate.

The movement's founder, George Baker, was born into a poor Negro family in rural Georgia about 1878–80. This religiously sensitive boy attracted little attention until he was about 20 years of age. While serving as a part-time Baptist minister in Baltimore, he met Samuel Morris, an itinerant preacher who declared that he himself was the Father Eternal. Baker became Morris's "Messenger" or "God in the sonship degree." After quarrels fragmented that group, Baker gathered a following in Valdosta, Ga., but was arrested as a public nuisance and was forced to leave the state. Initially he moved to Brooklyn, and then to Sayville, N.Y., where as Reverend Major J. Devine, he organized numerous followers into the Peace Mission Movement.

Attracted by the provision of bountiful dinners and clean sleeping quarters, his followers multiplied through the Depression era. In 1930, Baker was reborn as Father Divine, and in 1941, moved his residence and headquarters to Philadelphia. The movement grew to over a million members and had major centers in Philadelphia and New York, with smaller ones in several states and foreign countries. At his death in September 1965, Father Divine's leadership fell to his white widow, Mother Divine.

This success was the result of Father Divine's flamboyant personality and his alleged divinity. These factors also formed the basis for the movement's theology, ethics, and liturgy. Because of his divinity, Father Divine's words were transcribed and published in the magazine *New Day* as sacred scripture. He taught that heaven was now on earth; holy communion was celebrated at banquets with God himself; the church age and water baptism were obsolete; and there was no clergy-laity separation. Sin, sickness, and death were consequences of unbelief, for true victory and holiness were possible in this life.

Such perfectionist doctrines also affected ethics. Vices such as drinking, smoking, gambling, and adultery were condemned. Father Divine affirmed racial equality, public education, mass production to eliminate poverty, and cash-only business transactions.

Logically, the liturgy stressed the Last Supper. The banquet table, loaded with food, was a religious symbol. There were songs and impromptu sermons, but no formal service, no Scripture reading, and no clergy. In theory and practice, then, the movement advocated a mass cooperative or primitive communism.

JACK MITCHELL

**Fatherhood of God.** The name of Father is infrequently applied to God in the OT, and mostly in a figurative sense. God is the Father of Israel because he is the Creator of Israel's existence as a people, not by physical generation (as the relation of God to people was conceived in some heathen religions), but by sovereign divine election (Hos. 11:1). Israel was a foundling child on whom God took pity (Deut. 32:10, 18–22; Ezek. 16:5–7), and God's fatherly love toward Israel as his adopted child constituted a claim upon Israel's obedient service. The Fatherhood of God in the OT has its meaning in the context of the covenant and it relates primarily to Israel as a people. Rarely is it extended to individuals (Ps. 68:5). The invocation of God in prayer by the name of Father, which became current in postcanonical Judaism, is found in the OT only in Jer. 3:4, 19, and there only by inference.

Fatherhood is ascribed to God with such great frequency in the NT, especially in the teaching of Jesus, that it has been regarded as the distinctive mark of the Christian conception of God. Its OT connotation is enriched with the thought of God's fatherly readiness to forgive (Matt. 6:14; Luke 15:11–32). The question has been much debated whether the Fatherhood of God proclaimed by Jesus is to be understood as extending to all men, or only to believers. Since both views can be supported by passages in the Gospels, it is evident that the Fatherhood of God is indeed universal in common grace, extending his providential care to all men indiscriminately (Matt. 5:45), but it is not effectively realized as a personal relationship except where it is correlated with sonship (Matt. 11:27). Jesus' proclamation of the Fatherhood of God is thus at the same time the benediction (Matt. 5:9), the challenge (Matt. 5:48), and the authorization (John 1:12) of divine sonship to men; for Jesus himself is *the* Son who alone can properly speak of God as *my* Father (Matt. 11:27) and who by sharing his sonship with men can direct them to *your* Father (Matt. 6:8) and authorize them to say together *our* Father (Matt. 6:9). The name of Father is applied to God with great frequency in the Fourth Gospel and also in the Pauline Epistles, where it is expressly signified that God is our Father, but primarily the Father of our Lord Jesus Christ (2 Cor. 1:3). We, through Jesus' sonship, are adopted (Gal. 4:5; Eph. 1:5), and by Jesus' indwelling Spirit we are enabled to be the children of God (Rom. 8:14–16; Gal. 4:6).

The Fatherhood of God in no wise precludes his holy wrath against sin and his disciplinary treatment of sinners (Deut. 8:5; Heb. 12:5–8). It was a sentimentalized conception of the Fatherhood of God that was used by some liberals in the Ritschlian tradition in an attempt to turn the flank of the historic doctrine of the atonement.

The gospel of the Fatherhood of God not only brings men into a relation of sonship to him, but unites them together as a family which is animated by brotherly love (1 Thess. 4:9; Rom. 12:10), reconciliation (Matt. 18:21–35), and mutual submission (Eph. 5:21; Phil. 2:3). It is the ground of the catholicity and the ecumenical mission of the church.

*Bibliography.* P. T. Forsyth, *The Holy Father and the Living Christ* (1897); J. S. Lidgett, *The Fatherhood of God* (1902); A. Harnack, *What Is Christianity?* (1904); T. W. Manson, *The Teaching of Jesus* (1931); W. B. Selbie, *The Fatherhood of God* (1936); G. Vos, *Biblical Theology* (1948); H. Bavinck, *The Doctrine of God* (1951); J. I. Packer, *Knowing God* (1973); R. C. Sproul, *The Holiness of God* (1985); J. M. Frame, *The Doctrine of the Knowledge of God* (1987); K. Mains and D. Mains, *Abba: How God Parents Us.*

GEORGE S. HENDRY

**Fatima, Our Lady of.** Popular title given to Mary in honor of apparitions at Cova da Iria, near Fatima, Portugal, in 1917. On May 13, 1917, three shepherd children related that the virgin had appeared to them and recounted how she would reappear to them at that spot on the 13th of every month until October. The children later said that in her July 13 appearance she declared that the Lord desired devotion to her Immaculate Heart to be established throughout the world and that the faithful should offer a communion of reparation on the first Saturday of each month.

Seventy thousand people gathered at the appointed place on October 13 to behold the predicted miracle. The vision was not apparent to the assembled throng, but the three children testified that the Lady appeared and announced that she was the Lady of the Rosary, warned the people that they must not continue to offend God, and urged them to recite the rosary. Suddenly a heavy downpour of rain, which had been drenching the assembled thousands, abruptly ceased and the sun appeared to revolve, throwing out shafts of varicolored light through the clouds.

In October 1930, Roman Catholic ecclesiastical authority declared the apparitions worthy of belief, and devotion to Our Lady of Fatima was authorized under the title of Our Lady of the Rosary. Millions of pilgrims have since visited the site, which is regarded as a religious and national shrine.

*Bibliography.* W. T. Walsh, *Our Lady of Fatima* (1950); C. C. Martindale, *The Meaning of Fatima* (1950); J. M. Alonso, *The Secret of Fatima: Fact and Legend.*

THOMAS J. MCCARTHY

**Faunce, William Herbert Perry** (1859–1930). Ecumenist. He was president of Brown University (1899–1930) and was widely interested in ecumenical and international affairs. He was once president of the World Peace Foundation. His later books include *The Educational Ideal in the Ministry* (1908), *What Does Christianity Mean?* (1912), *Social Aspects of Foreign Missions* (1914), *Religion and War* (1918), and *The New Horizon of State and Church* (1918).

RAYMOND W. ALBRIGHT

**Fausset, Andrew Robert** (1821–1910). Biblical scholar. Born in Ireland, he graduated from Trinity College, Dublin, was ordained in the Church of England, and served parishes in Durham and York (1848–1910). An excellent classicist, he translated Bengel's *Gnomon of the NT* from Latin and published a very good *Bible Cyclopaedia* (1878). His other works included *The Millennium* (1880), *True Science Confirming Genesis* (1884), *Critical and Expository Commentary on the Book of Judges* (1885), and *Spiritualism* (1885). He is perhaps best known for his contribution to the Jamieson, Fausset, and Brown commentary on the Bible.

J. D. DOUGLAS

**Fear.** Human emotion signifying the confrontation or anticipation of danger or power. Fear is a subject of common interest in psychology and religion, one of the points at which the two fields converge. As a motivating factor in religious behavior and a component part of religious experience, it has caused much discussion among psychologists and theologians.

Rudolph Otto explained fear as a religiously significant emotion. In the presence of the numinous, the individual feels a sense of *mysterium tremendum*, which is composed of awe and fascination. Elements of fear are present in religious experience both because humans tend to become religious in the presence of the mysterious and because a sense of guilt causes fear that the true self is about to be revealed.

Psychologists of every variety have paid attention to fear. John B. Watson saw in newborns only two basic and inherited fears–the fears of "a loud sound and the loss of support." These, however, are neurologically complicated experiences which contemporary psychologists regard as arising out of maturation and learning, rather than from heredity. The impulse toward survival quite often is reversed into a fear of death, and one may wisely ask if such experiences as Watson mentions, and countless others, are not derivatives of this parent fear with which each individual has to deal, creatively or destructively, from very early in life.

Among depth psychologists, the difference between *fear* and *anxiety* has occasioned much discussion. Among Freudians, fear is defined as directed toward an externally real object, while anxiety arises from a psychic condition which tends "to ignore the object." Fear, for Sigmund Freud, is a necessary and normal part of the individual's self-preservative impulse as he responds to external, reality-based danger; anxiety is an internally structured and derived psychic reality which is much more serious and which merits medical attention. In one way or another, psychoanalysts make distinctions of this kind.

Otto Rank draws attention to the "fear of life," where the individual is reluctant to enter into responsible living situations because he basically fears responsibility, preferring to be passive, dependent, and irresponsible; but he also makes much of the opposite kind of fear–that of "having to live as an isolated individual." The death fear, then, is the fear of going back into nonbeing, of losing individuality, or never having achieved a sustained place in the human community.

This latter opinion is closely akin to the thought of Søren Kierkegaard, in *The Sickness unto Death*. He relates fear, or "despair," to the experience of becoming a self. The achievement of selfhood, of individuality, of personhood, he regards as the core of intentionality in personality. To do this without at the same time losing the approval of one's community is the dilemma of human existence. In the matrix of this dilemma fear is born.

Clinical psychiatrists call attention to another type of fear–that of the phobic and deluded neurotic and psychotic person. Usually these fears take a persecutory bent; the individual projects his inner fears upon the outer environment and reads them back as persecutions. Such persons are often completely incapacitated for effective family living and vocational pursuits; they are most often candidates for hospital care. They are thought of medically as psychotic.

An individual's fear may be organized into compulsive thoughts and acts which are extremely annoying to him, which he may keep secret, but which do not keep him from a minimum degree of function at home and at work. These compulsive feelings may issue into obsessive thoughts, such as thinking something extremely vulgar and fearing that he will say it. Or they may crystallize into compulsive phobias or manias. The person with a compulsive phobia will fear entering closed places, leaving the house, or handling certain things. It is a procedure of abstinence. The person with a compulsive mania cannot keep from doing certain things. He *must* touch every hand rail; or he *must* go through the elaborate ritual of arranging his shoes, evening his trouser legs, and tying a string across the back door before he can go to bed.

These fears are clearly irrational, compulsive, involuntary, and arise from distorted psychic processes in the individual. They painfully hamper the creative expression of life. Modern medical psychologists have made great progress in treating these disorders, and pastoral psychologists in interpreting their religious significance. The biblical concept of fear as opposed to *agapē* love is the most rewarding interpretation. Paul repeats the theme that God has not given a spirit of fear but of power and love and self-control (2 Tim. 1:7). John insists that perfect love casts out fear (1 John 4:18).

*Bibliography.* R. May, *The Meaning of Anxiety* (1950); B. W. Overstreet, *Understanding Fear in Ourselves and Others* (1951).

WAYNE E. OATES

**Fedorov, Nicolas** (1828–1903). Eastern Orthodox. Probably an illegitimate son of Prince Paul Gagarine, he studied at Odessa Richelieu-Lycaeum, but did not complete the course. In 1854–68 he was a schoolmaster in various small cities of Central Russia. After 1868 he was a library clerk at the Rumjanzev Museum in Moscow, and later in the Moscow Archives of the Foreign Office. He was a close friend of Fyodor Dostoyevski, Vladimir Soloviev, Leo Tolstoy, and other prominent people in Moscow. He was a man of peculiar habits and convictions, a solitary thinker and dreamer. Probably inspired by French positivism and French utopian socialism, Fedorov attempted a striking synthesis of Christianity and a religion of humanity, centered around the idea of resurrection, which he interpreted as a task committed to humanity. Humankind must resurrect dead ancestors, and for that purpose erotic energy must be diverted from the procreation of children to the raising up of the fathers. This strange conception exercised a considerable influence, even on such philosophers as Soloviev, who was himself developing ideas to the same effect. The alleged influence of Fedorov on Dostoyevski is not to be exaggerated. After the Russian Revolution Fedorov's ideas were reinterpreted in a secular manner by a group of followers in the Soviet Union and outside Russia. Fedorov's papers were published (in Russian) in two volumes.

GEORGES FLOROVSKY

**Fedotov, George P.** (1886–1951). Eastern Orthodox. Born in Saratov, Russia, he graduated from the University of Petrograd and studied history at Berlin and Jena. He taught the history of Middle Ages as privatdocent in Petrograd and as professor in Saratov. He left Russia in 1925 for France, where he taught church history at the Paris Orthodox Theological Institute (1925–40). He came to America in 1941 and taught as lay professor of church history at the St. Vladimir Russian Orthodox Seminary in New York (1941–51). He was coeditor in Paris of the review *New City* (1930–39). He has published the following books in English: *The Russian Church since the Revolution* (1927), *Russian Religious Mind* (1947), and *Treasury of Russian Spirituality* (1949, 2d ed., 1950). Some of his Russian books are *Saints of Ancient Russia, St. Philip: Metropolitan of Moscow,* and *Russian Religious Songs.*

**Fellowship of Evangelical Baptist Churches in Canada.** Denomination formed in 1953 by the merger of two evangelical groups which had been established following the modernist-fundamentalist controversy–the Union of Regular Baptist Churches of Ontario and Quebec (1927) and the Fellowship of Independent Baptist Churches of Canada (1933). Through church planting and absorption of two regional groups of Regular Baptist Churches, it has grown from about 200 to 475 congregations with approximately 67,000 members (1986). Ninety of these churches are Francophone, and 15 are ethnic congregations. The denomination has churches in all 10 provinces and the northern territories. Its foreign mission board, which was established in 1962, now supports 76 missionaries in nine countries of Asia, Africa, South America, and Europe. The denomination has remained aloof from the Canadian Council of Churches and the World Council of Churches. Its official publication is the *Evangelical Baptist,* published monthly from the national office in Toronto.

LESLIE K. TARR

**Fellowship of Independent Evangelical Churches (FIEC).** Organization formed in England in 1922 originally as the Fellowship of Undenominational and Unattached Churches and Missions at the instigation of E. J. Poole-Connor, a gifted preacher and Bible expositor, "to advance the evangelical Christian faith." The aim was to bring together for mutual encouragement small, isolated evangelical churches throughout England, Wales, and Scotland, with the subsidiary purpose of compiling a register of ministers. The ideal, then as now, was to combine the oneness of the true church of Christ with the liberty of individual congregations within fundamental doctrinal restrictions, resisting and rejecting the modernism and liberalism which had infiltrated mainstream denominations. Independent and uncompromising, FIEC has held strong views on the position of evangelicals remaining in the denominations; but a more open, though still nonecumenical, approach is now evident. Well over 400 churches are affiliated, and a home missions department aims to plant churches in areas where there is no evangelical witness. A national council of elected members also contains representatives of the 16 regional auxiliaries. A bimonthly magazine, *Fellowship,* has a circulation of about 4000.

TIM LENTON

**Ferm, Vergilius Ture Anselm** (1876–1974). American Lutheran scholar. Born in Sioux City, Iowa, he studied at Augustana College, Augustana Theological Seminary, and Yale University (Ph.D., 1925). He was ordained in 1919 and pastored churches in Iowa and Connecticut (1919–26). He was professor of philosophy at Albright College, Reading, Pa. (1926/27), professor of philosophy at the College of Wooster (1928–38), professor of philosophy and department head (1938–64), and president emeritus (1964–74).

His works include *The Crisis in American Lutheran Theology* (1927), *First Adventures in Philosophy* (1936), *What Can We Believe?* (1948), *A Protestant Dictionary* (1951), *A Concise Dictionary of Religion: A Lexicon of Protestant Interpretation* (rev. ed., 1965), *A Dictionary of Pastoral Psychology* (1955), *Pictorial History of Protestantism* (1957), *Toward an Expansive Christian Theology* (1964), and *Cross-Currents in the Personality of Martin Luther* (1972). He also edited *What is Lutheranism?: A Symposium in Interpretation* (1930), *Contemporary American Theology: Theological Autobiographies* (2 vols., 1932, 1933), *An Encyclopedia of Religion* (1945), *Forgotten Religions, Including Some Living Primitive Religions* (1950), *Ancient Religions* (rev. ed., 1965), *A History of Philosophical Systems* (1950), *The American Church of the Protestant Heritage* (1953), *Puritan Sage: The Collected Writings of Jonathan Edwards* (1953), *An Encyclopedia of Morals* (1956), and *Classics of Protestantism* (1959).

H. DOUGLAS BUCKWALTER

**Ferré, Nels F. S.** (1908–1971). Swedish-American theologian. Born in Lulea, Sweden, he studied at Boston University, Andover Newton Theological School, and Harvard (Ph.D., 1938). Ordained as a Congregational minister in 1934, he was instructor in philosophy at Andover Newton (1937–39), professor of Christian theology there (1939–50), and professor of philosophical theology at Vanderbilt University (1950–57). He then returned to his old post at Andover Newton (1957–65), and later was professor of philosophy at the College of Wooster (1968–71). His books include *Swedish Contributions to Modern Theology* (1939), *The Christian Fellowship* (1940), *The Christian Faith* (1942), *Return to Christianity* (1943), *Faith and Reason* (1945), *Evil and the Christian Faith* (1946), *Pillars of Faith* (1948), *Christianity and Society* (1950), *Strengthening the Spiritual Life* (1951), *The Christian Understanding of God* (1951), *Christian Faith and Higher Education* (1954), and *The Living God of Nowhere and Nothing* (1966).

**Fey, Harold Edward** (1898– ). Disciples of Christ minister, editor, and author. Born in Elwood, Ind., he held degrees from Cotner College, Lincoln, Nebr., and Yale University Divinity School. Ordained in 1923, he served pastorates in Lincoln (1925/26) and Hastings, Nebr. (1927–29). He also was professor at Union Theological Seminary, Manila, Philippines (1929–31), editor of *World Call* (1932–35), editor of *Fellowship*, and secretary of Fellowship of Reconciliation in New York (1935–40). In 1940 he joined *Christian Century* as associate editor (1940–47), and then became managing editor (1947–52), executive editor (1952–55), and editor (1956–64). Until his retirement in 1968 he was professor of social ethics at Christian Theological Seminary, Indianapolis. He was an accredited correspondent to the UN forces in Japan and Korea (1951) and to Vatican Council II (1962). His books include *The Lord's Supper: Seven Meanings* (1948), *The Christian Century Reader* (1962), *With Sovereign Reverence* (1974), and an autobiography entitled *How I Read the Riddle* (1982).

JACK MITCHELL

**Figgis, John Neville** (1866–1919). Anglican historian. After graduating from Cambridge he was ordained and was a curate at Great St. Mary's, Cambridge (1895–98), and lecturer at St. Catharine's College, Cambridge (1895–1901). He was a rector thereafter in Dorset (1901–7), and in 1909 he became a member of the Community of the Resurrection. His reputation as a historian steadily grew, and he was much in demand as lecturer in the USA. His publications include *Divine Right of Kings* (1896), *Christianity and History* (1904), *From Gerson to Grotius* (1907), *The Gospel and Human Needs* (1909), *Religion and English Society* (1910), *Civilization at the Cross Roads* (1912), *Antichrist* (1913), *Churches in the Modern State* (1913), *Fellowship of the Mystery* (1914), *Some Difficulties in English Religion* (1916), and *The Will to Freedom* (1917).

**Fiji.** See SOUTH PACIFIC, ISLANDS OF THE.

**Filson, Floyd Vivian** (1896–1980). American NT scholar. Born in Hamilton, Mo., he studied at Park College, McCormick Theological Seminary, and the University of Basel (Th.D., 1930). He taught NT Greek at McCormick Theological Seminary (1923–30), NT literature and exegesis (1930–34), and NT literature and history (1934–67). He was made dean of the seminary in 1954. He was a member of the Society of Biblical Literature, the National Association of Biblical Instructors, the American Oriental Society, and the translation committee for the Revised Standard Version of the Bible. His works include *St. Paul's Conception of Recompense* (1931), *Origins of the Gospels* (1938), *Pioneers of the Primitive Church* (1940), *One Lord, One Faith* (1943), *The NT Against Its Environment* (1950), *Jesus Christ the Risen Lord* (1956), *Which Books Belong in the Bible?* (1957), *The Gospel According to John* in *The Laymen's Bible Commentary* (1959), *A Commentary on the Gospel According to St. Matthew* (1960), *Three Crucial Decades* (1963), and *A NT History: The Story of the Emerging Church* (1964). He was coauthor with G. Ernest Wright of *The Westminster Historical Atlas to the Bible* (1945; rev. ed. 1956), coeditor of *The Westminster Study Bible* (1948), cotranslator of Rudolph Otto's *Kingdom of God and the Son of Man* (1938), and translator of Oscar Cullmann's *Christ and Time* (1950).

JACK MITCHELL

**Finegan, Jack** (1908– ). American educator and minister. Born in Des Moines, Iowa, he studied at Drake University, Colgate Rochester Divinity School, and the University of Berlin. He was minister, First Christian Church, Ames, Iowa (1934–39), professor of religious education, Iowa State College (1939–46), and professor of NT, Pacific School of Religion and Graduate Theological Union, Berkeley (1946–75). He wrote *Light from the Ancient Past* (1946), *The Archeology of World Religions* (1952), *Handbook of Biblical Chronology* (1964), *The Archeology of the NT* (2 vols., 1969, 1981), *Encountering NT Manuscripts* (1974), *Archaeological History of the Ancient Middle East* (1979), *Tibet–A Dreamt-of Image* (1986), and many more books and articles.

SHERWOOD E. WIRT

**Finkelstein, Louis** (1895– ). Jewish theologian. Born in Cincinnati, Ohio, he studied at the College of the City of New York, Columbia University (Ph.D., 1918), and the Jewish Theological Seminary of America. He was rabbi of Congregation Kehilath Israel, New York City (1919–31). At the Jewish Theological Seminary he was instructor in Talmud (1920–24), lecturer in theology (1924–30), associate professor (1930/31), professor of theology from 1931, assistant to the president (1934–37), provost (1937–40), president (1940–51), chancellor (1951–72), and since 1972, chancellor emeritus. In 1939 he founded the Institute for Religious Studies at the seminary, a graduate school conducted with the cooperation of Jewish, Catholic, and Protestant scholars. He also served as religious adviser to President Roosevelt (1940–45) and ambassador of President Kennedy to the Papal Coronation (1963).

Among his writings are *Jewish Self-Government in the Middle Ages* (1924; 2d ed., 1964), *Akiba—Scholar, Saint, Martyr* (1936), *The Pharisees, The Sociological Background of Their Faith* (1938), *New Light from the Prophets* (1969), *Social Responsibility in the Age of Revolution* (1971), *Pharisaism in the Making* (1972), and *Sifra* (1985). He coauthored *Religions of Democracy* (1941) and *Faith for Today* (1941). He also edited *Kimchi's Commentary on Isaiah* (1926), *Sifre on Deuteronomy* (2 vols., 1936, 1937), *Saadia Gaon Abot of Rabbi Nathan* (1950), *The Jews: Their History, Culture and Religion* (3 vols., 1949), and is coeditor of the *Science, Philosophy and Religion Annual Symposia* (1942– ).

H. DOUGLAS BUCKWALTER

**Finland.** A constitutional republic of Scandinavia with 338,145 sq. km. (130,559 sq. mi.) and 5 million people (1985). The Christian faith reached Finland from the East and the West, beginning in the 10th and 11th centuries. The Orthodox faith took root among the easternmost part of the population, while other sections were evangelized by the Western Church. This also meant a division between the Catholic and Orthodox churches. Karelia, a region along Finland's border with the USSR, remained a battleground between East and West, both politically and with regard to religion. As the national border has been moved several times, there has always been an Orthodox minority in Finland.

Over four centuries, the Catholic Church constructed a system of ecclesiastical order in Finland, which at that time belonged to Sweden. The Lutheran Reformation was carried through in the 16th century relatively peacefully in Finland. In 1809 Finland was annexed to Russia and given inner autonomy. The position of the church did not change, although the head was now the Orthodox ruler of Russia. A remarkable change in the inner autonomy of the church was brought about by the enacting of the Ecclesiastical Law of 1869. The church got its own parliament, the synod. This law was based on the principle of religious freedom, although Protestant dissenters, who began to get a foothold in Finland from the latter half of the 19th century, could not leave the Lutheran Church until a special law had been enacted in 1889.

Finland declared her independence on December 6, 1917. Complete freedom of religion was granted by the Religious Freedom Act of 1922.

***The Lutheran Church.*** The Evangelical Lutheran Church of Finland is the traditional church of the majority of Finns; it still embraces nearly 90 percent of the population. Up to the latter half of the last century it was a typical state church. The church's dependence on the state has gradually diminished. It has become a folk church. It still, however—like the Orthodox Church—fulfills certain functions which in principle might belong to state or municipality.

The legal status of the Evangelical Lutheran Church is guaranteed in the constitution and in a special Ecclesiastical Law in whose legislation the supreme body of the church, the synod, plays a central role. The Evangelical Lutheran Church is mainly responsible for public cemeteries and the official registration of its own members. The state pays the salaries of members of the chapter and of ministers to the armed forces and the prisons. In comparison with sister churches in other Scandinavian countries, however, the Evangelical Lutheran Church in Finland enjoys a very large measure of autonomy.

The Church lives and functions in its 595 independent parishes. Each parish elects its own workers and officials and decides on its own activities and finance. However, certain matters must be submitted to higher authority for ratification. The smallest of the congregations comprise no more than a few hundred members, the largest tens of thousands. The greater part of the activity of the church and its parishes is financed out of tax revenues levied in the local parishes, each of which, either individually or in federation, independently sets the tax rate for its own area.

***Diversified Activity.*** Despite low figures for church attendance (weekly, 4 percent; monthly, 12 percent; annually, 66 percent), few religious communities in the world have developed as diverse a range of activities as the Finnish Evangelical Lutheran Church. Part of its work covers a very considerable proportion of the population in the age-groups concerned.

Most extensively, the congregation embraces its members in the context of church rites. The proportion of baptisms and funerals has constantly been higher than that of church members among the population. On the average every Finn attends some church ceremony once in a year. Also confirmation classes and work among children involve the greater part of the relevant age groups.

***Revival Movements.*** Throughout the whole of the present century Finnish Christianity has been characterized by dozens of religious societies and four national revivalist movements. Revival movements grew up in Finland, principally in the 19th century. Although there were foreign contacts, these movements grew into distinctively Finnish expressions of Lutheranism. Their memberships included both clergy and laity. Each of the four revival movements of the last century was principally restricted to its own geographical area. All these movements spread a personal religious life to the population at large. Meetings were usually held in people's homes, and laymen also preached at them. The movements found a place within the church as free expressions of religious life.

***The Orthodox Church.*** Although Finland has always been considered part of the Western Christian sphere, the Karelians, whose homeland straddles the great cultural divide, have been strongly influenced by the Byzantine tradition for nearly a millennium and many of them belong to the Russian Orthodox Church. Although the membership of the Orthodox Church in Finland is under 58,000, this body is, for historical and cultural reasons, the nation's second folk church. It has been a majority church only among the easternmost population. Its status is similar to that of the Lutheran Church, although its administration falls under the ecumenical patriarchate of Constantinople.

***Other Churches and Religious Communities.*** In Finland's religious life diversification has been notably slow, even though the Evangelical Lutheran and Orthodox churches have in some measure lost followers to other religious communities. Most of those who have relinquished their membership in the church have not joined any other religious group. For example, the Roman Catholic Church in Finland has a membership of only 4000. In addition to the traditional churches there are almost 30 communities; but among them they represent only about one percent of the population.

Pentecostals likewise number about one percent but have not officially formed a separate church or denomination. Some small communities are markedly active in relation to their membership. Among these are Jehovah's Witnesses (11,700); Free (Congregational) (11,200); and Adventist (5100).

HARRI HEINO

**Fisher, Geoffrey Francis** (1887–1972). Archbishop of Canterbury. Educated at Oxford, he taught at Marlborough College (1911–14) and was headmaster of Repton School (1914–32) before his surprise appointment in 1932 as bishop of Chester. He was translated to London in 1939 and to Canterbury in 1945 (on the premature death of William Temple). In London during the war years he once housed in Lambeth Palace 300 people made homeless by enemy bombs. While he concentrated on canon law revision and church administration, he voiced strong views on other topics: he favored capital punishment for

certain offenses, defended the atom bomb as a "lifesaver and deterrent," and was a firm opponent of divorce. He made history in 1960 as the first archbishop of Canterbury to visit the pope (John XXIII) since the Reformation. He also sought to improve relations with Orthodox and Protestant churches. An early president of the World Council of Churches, he was nonetheless against organic unity, and notably raised his voice against a proposed merger between the Church of England and the Methodists. On retirement he was known as Baron Fisher of Lambeth.

J. D. DOUGLAS

**Fjellbu, Arne** (1890–1962). Norwegian bishop. Born in Decorah, Iowa, he studied at Oslo, was ordained in the Lutheran Church, and subsequently became dean of Nidaros. From this post he was ejected by Quisling, a Norwegian put into power by the Nazis, to whom Fjellbu was strongly opposed. After the war he became bishop of the diocese (1945–61). A specialist in pastoral theology and Christian ethics, he wrote several books in Norwegian. One of them was translated into English as *Memoirs from the War Years* (1959).

**Fleming, Daniel J.** (1877–1969). Presbyterian. Born in Xenia, Ohio, he studied at Wooster College and Columbia (Ph.D., 1914). He taught at Forman Christian College, India (1904–12), and was professor of missions, Union Theological Seminary (1915–44). He was a member of the International Commission on Village Education in India (1919/20); member of the India Staff of Laymen's Foreign Missions Inquiry (1930/31), and a consultant on India, Department of State (1945/46). Among his books are *Each with His Own Brush: Contemporary Christian Art in Asia and Africa* (1938), *The World at One in Prayer* (1942), *Bringing Our World Together: A Study in World Community* (1945), and *Living as Comrades: A Study of Factors Making for Community* (1950).

**Flew, Anthony Garrard Newton** (1923– ). English atheistic theologian. From his study of theology, he concluded that there is no God. Flew, who held chairs of philosophy at Keele (1954–71) and Reading (1973–82), is perhaps best known for the argumentative device sometimes called "Flew's fork"; while naive believers appear committed to propositions of science or history that may be shown to be false as conclusively as is possible in the nature of the case, sophisticated believers, by denying these, are apt to subject their faith to "the death of the thousand qualifications." The defining characteristics usually ascribed to God, moreover, seem incompatible with one another and with known facts. Flew has also written with memorable force and wit on politics, education, psychical research, and the philosophy of David Hume, of whom he may be regarded as a disciple.

HUGO A. MEYNELL

**Flew, Robert Newton** (1886–1962). English Methodist scholar. Born in Devon, he was educated at the universities of Oxford, Marburg, and Fribourg. He was an assistant tutor at Handsworth College, Birmingham (1910–13), a Methodist minister in London (1913–18), and a military chaplain (1918–20). After further ministries in London (1921–27) he became first professor of NT in Wesley House, Cambridge (1927–37), where subsequently he was principal and professor of systematic and pastoral theology (1937–55). He was also moderator of the National Free Church Federal Council of England and Wales (1945/46), and president of the Methodist Conference of Great Britain and Ireland (1946/47). Among his publications are *The Teaching of the Apostles* (1915), *The Forgiveness of Sins* (1916), *The Idea of Perfection in Christian Theology* (1934), *Jesus and His Church* (1938), and *The Hymns of Charles Wesley* (1953).

**Fliche, Augustin** (1884–1951). Roman Catholic. Born in Montpellier (France), he studied at the University of Paris (Sorbonne; docteur des lettres, 1912). He lectured at the University of Bordeaux (1913); he was maître de conférences at Montpellier (1919), professeur (1923); dean of the Faculté de Lettres (1934–46). He was vice-president of the National Committee of Historical Sciences; and membre de l'Institut de France (1941). He exerted a very wide and deep influence by his lectures on medieval church history. He is most widely known both for his works on the period of Gregory VII and for the collections which he directed: *Bibliothèque de l'enseignement ecclésiastique* and, in collaboration with V. Martin and E. Jarry, *Histoire de l'Eglise depuis les origines jusqu'à nos jours*, vol. 8, *La Réforme grégorienne et la reconquête chrétienne* (1940), *Du premier concile de Latran à l'avènement d'Innocent III (1123–1198)* (1944–46), and *La chrétienté romaine (1198–1274)* (1950). He also published *La réforme grégorienne* (3 vols., 1925), *La querelle des investitures* (1946), and *L'Europe occidentale de 888 à 1125* (1930).

*Bibliography.* F. L. Ganshof, *Revue belge; de philologie et d'histoire*, 30 (1952): 649.

LEOPOLD WILLAERT

**Flight, John William** (1890–1964). Congregational clergyman and educator. Born in Cleveland, Ohio, he was educated at Hope College, Hartford Theological Seminary (Ph.D., 1921), Strasbourg, Paris, and Yale universities. He was ordained in 1918 and served pastorates in Waterbury, Winsted, and Georgetown, Conn. He was instructor in Hebrew at Yale University (1927–29)

and professor of biblical literature at Haverford College (1929–60). He served as secretary (1934–47) and president (1948) of the Society of Biblical Literature and Exegesis, and associate editor of the *Journal of Bible and Religion*. He wrote *The Nomadic Ideal in the OT* (1923), *The Book of the Bible* (1929), *Moses: Egyptian Prince, Nomad Sheikh, Lawgiver* (1942), and *The Drama of Ancient Israel* (1949).

JACK MITCHELL

**Florensky, Paul** (1881–1949). Eastern Orthodox. Born in Tiflis, he studied at the University of Moscow and the Moscow Theological Academy. He was lecturer and then professor of the history of philosophy at the Moscow Academy (1908–18). He was editor of *Theological Messenger* (*Bogoslovsky Viestnik*), published by the academy faculty. In 1910 he took holy orders, and after the closing of the academy continued for some time his pastoral activities as a chaplain of a convent at Sergievsky Posad (now Zagorsk). Later on he was working for a period as engineer and scientific consultant, and was even chairman of the Technical Commission of the Sovnarkom. He was arrested (probably in 1929 or 1930) and confined first at Solovki, and then exiled to far eastern Siberia. Florensky published a number of articles, but his place in the history of Russian thought and literature was established by *The Pillar and Foundation of Truth: An Essay Towards an Orthodox Theodicy* (1914). It is a sketch of a religio-philosophical system, based on the doctrine of St. Sophia, which Florensky developed much further than had been done by Vladimir Soloviev. The approach to theology is deeply esthetic. Portions of this work, in German, are in Hans Ehrenberg, ed., *Das Oestliches Christenthum*, vol. 2 (1925).

*Bibliography.* D. S. Mirsky, *A History of Russian Literature* (1949), 427–28.

GEORGES FLOROVSKY

**Florovsky, Georges V.** (1893–1979). Greek Orthodox clergyman, educator, and author. Born in Odessa, Russia, he graduated from the universities of Odessa and Prague. He was lecturer in philosophy, Odessa University (1919/20), taught philosophy of law at the Russian Graduate School of Law, Prague (1922–26), was professor of patristics and systematic theology at the Orthodox Theological Institute, Paris (1926–48), professor of divinity (1948–55) and dean (1950–55) at St. Vladimir's Theological Seminary, adjunct professor of Eastern church history at Harvard Divinity School (1956–64), associate professor of dogmatic theology at Holy Cross Greek Orthodox Theological School (1955–59), and visiting professor at Princeton Theological Seminary from 1972 until his death. He was very active in the rapprochement between the Orthodox and Anglican churches, and was the foremost member of the

Orthodox constituency to the World Council of Churches. His *Collected Works of Georges Florovsky* are in four volumes.

JACK MITCHELL

## Foakes-Jackson, Frederick John (1855–1941).

Church historian. He was dean and tutor in Jesus College, Cambridge (1895–1916), after which he served with distinction as Briggs Graduate Professor of Christian Institutions at Union Theological Seminary in New York (1916–34). He also lectured in the Jewish Institute in New York and in the General Theological Seminary. After coming to America he published *St. Luke and a Modern Writer* (1916), *English Society, 1750–1850* (1916), *Introduction to Church History, 590–1314* (1921), *Anglican Church Principles* (1924), *Studies in the Life of the Early Church* (1924), *Life of St. Paul* (1926), *Rise of Gentile Christianity* (1927), *Peter, Prince of Apostles* (1927), *Josephus and the Jews* (1930), *The Church in England* (1931), *Eusebius, Bishop of Caesarea and First Christian Historian* (1933), *The Church in the Middle Ages* (1934), and *History of Church Historians* (1939). He edited *Parting of the Roads* (1911), *Faith and War* (1916), and with K. Lake, *The Beginnings of Christianity* (5 vols., 1919–32).

RAYMOND W. ALBRIGHT

## Foley, George Cadwalader (1851–1935).

Episcopalian. Born in Philadelphia, he studied at Griswold College (1872) and the Philadelphia Divinity School of the Protestant Episcopal Church (D.D., 1899). Ordained to the priesthood in 1875, he served as rector of St. James Church, Pittston, Pa. (1875–79), and Trinity Church, Williamsport, Pa. (1879–1905). In 1905 he became professor of homiletics and pastoral care in the Philadelphia Divinity School and later professor of systematic theology there (1915–35). He edited *The Church Standard* (1907/8) and wrote *Anselm's Theory of the Atonement* (1909).

RAYMOND W. ALBRIGHT

## Folklore.

All the beliefs, traditional customs, tales, songs, sayings, superstitions, and legendary materials created and preserved by a people or a nation. Almost all folklore has its beginning in religion, and is related to it. Religions produced myths, beliefs, concepts, proverbs, customs, songs, superstitions, and precepts to serve basic purposes. Religious lore developed literary forms suited to its purposes, just as each religion developed rituals and rites. These folklore forms comprise: the myth, the fable, the allegory, the legend, the parable, and the proverb. But however different a folklore may be in its *forms* from others, it is very similar to all others in probing toward an understanding of truth and dealing with "good" and "evil."

Folklore, in all its varied forms, came into being because people wanted to know the truth about the origin and meaning of the universe, in general, and human destiny in particular. They were concerned with the problem of how man ought to shun "evil" and attain the "good." Although it is often difficult to see any obvious affinity between these objectives and the extreme manifestations of given superstitions, yet, if carefully traced to their origins, it would be found that their mainspring is to resolve doubt or to ward off some evil.

Folklore concerns itself with every conceivable human experience, from before birth to life after death. Folklore reflects every conceivable human emotion, and every conceivable relationship between man and man, between man and his God, and between man and his own inner self. Since the basic human needs are the same, and the quest for certainty is the same the world over, great similarities or parallels are to be found in practically all folklore customs, beliefs, and superstitions.

Every religion has inspired its own folklore, revolving around, mainly, its sacred scriptures. The lore represents the interpretation of the scriptures as conceived by the folk imagination, which often differs greatly from its conception in the mind of the writers. For example, the OT is held in reverence, although in differing degrees, by three very divergent religions–Judaism, Christianity, and Islam, plus sects within those religions. The Bible has thus been the source of much folk inspiration. Even outside these faiths, the Bible is known and read by more people, and in more languages, and in a greater variation of versions, than any other religious scriptures. And as long as the Bible continues to hold the folk attention, the folk mind will continue to create lore, in all its forms, which will present a great variation of interpretation of the ethics and the precepts contained in the Bible.

Folklore is vast and complex; it ranges from the simple precept and readily acceptable proverb, to the most abstruse symbolism and weird incantation. Lore has developed an almost endless scheme of divination by oracles, the stars, sacrificed animals, the behavior of birds, mirrors and reflections, writing in ashes, walking in circles, dropping molten wax into cold water, and a vast variety of other methods. For each kind of evil, feared and anticipated, lore has produced the proper remedy in the form of a talisman, a magic wand, an amulet, or one of the many other shields conjured up by the magician. Yet even at the lowest level of voodoo and superstition, religious lore reflects the folk concern with truth, and the determined struggle for "good" and against "evil." Folklore, more than any other branch of man's creativity, reflects more completely what the people really know, what they really fear, and to what they really aspire.

**Bibliography.** A. Lang, *Custom and Myth* (1885); A. van Gennep, *The Rites of Passage* (1908, repr. ed., 1960); J. G. Frazer, *Folk-Lore in the OT*, 3 vols. (1918; abr. ed., 1923); H. J. D. Astley, *Biblical Anthropology* (1929); A. H. Krappe, *The Science of Folk-Lore* (1962); E. A. Westermarck, *The History of Human Marriage*, 3 vols. (repr. ed., 1971); M. Edmonson, *Lore: An Introduction to the Science of Folklore and Literature* (1971); R. J. Adams, *Introduction to Folklore* (1973); A. Dundes, *Interpreting Folklore* (1980); E. Oring, ed., *Folk Groups and Folklore Genres* (1986).

JOSEPH GAER

## Footwashing.

A ritual cleansing of the feet preparatory to worship based on the example of Christ (John 13:1–17). The patristic writers also note its practice (Tertullian [*De corona* 8]; Athanasius [*Canon* 66]).

Scholars commonly interpret Christ's act not as the establishment of a sacrament or ordinance, but rather as a rebuke of the disciples for their lack of humility and servanthood. Consequently, the practice has not been followed widely in the church in spite of Christ's injunction that his disciples are to wash one another's feet (John 13:14). The Roman Catholic and Greek churches observed the rite mainly as a ceremonial recognition of servanthood among the higher clergy. Within Protestantism the practice has survived in small primitivist movements. Churches in the Anabaptist tradition (e.g., Church of the Brethren, Amish, Brethren Church [Ashland, Ohio]) commonly accept footwashing as an ordinance along with adult baptism and the Lord's supper; it usually is one of three parts of the ritual of the love feast along with the agape meal and the Eucharist or communion. Many pentecostal churches and some Baptist and Adventist churches also observe it as an ordinance.

MELVIN E. DIETER

## Ford, Leighton Frederick Sandys (1931– ).

North American evangelist and church leader. Born in Toronto, he was educated at Wheaton College, Ill., and Columbia Theological Seminary, Decatur, Ga. In 1955 he was ordained to the ministry of the (southern) Presbyterian Church of the USA, now part of the Presbyterian Church, USA, and joined the Billy Graham team as an associate evangelist. He traveled widely, preaching to millions and conducting evangelistic crusades in 35 countries. Author of six books and popular speaker on radio and television, he was chosen Clergyman of the Year in 1985 by Religious Heritage of America. In 1986 he founded the Leighton Ford Ministries as an independent evangelistic enterprise, while continuing as chairman of the Lausanne Committee for World Evangelization.

SHERWOOD E. WIRT

## Foreign Missions Conference of North America (FMC).

Organization of Protestant missionary agencies from the United States and Canada founded in 1911 to consider questions relating to the administration of foreign missions and other matters of particular interest to the participating boards and societies. In 1917 the Committee of Reference and Counsel was incorporated as FMC's executive committee.

FMC fostered cooperative work in Latin America, created the Missionary Research Library (1914), took part in founding the International Missionary Council (1921), promoted joint efforts by its members in such areas as rural and medical missions, and absorbed the Federation of Women's Boards of North America (1934). Prominent in the early years were John R. Mott, Robert E. Speer, and Arthur J. Brown. FMC participated in the planning work for the National Council of Churches (NCC) and after a temporary delay joined the new group. With 83 agencies as full members and 15 with consultant status, FMC on January 1, 1951, became the Division of Foreign Missions (from 1965 the Division of Overseas Ministries) of NCC. Five American boards withdrew membership, while the Canadian societies affiliated with the Canadian Council of Churches.

RICHARD V. PIERARD

## Foreign Missions Inquiry, Laymen's.

A controversial survey of Christian mission fields in Asia by a commission representing seven USA Protestant churches. The areas studied were India, Burma, China, and Japan. The commission of 15 was chaired by William Ernest Hocking, professor of philosophy at Harvard University. The laymen were of American Baptist, Congregational, Dutch Reformed, Protestant Episcopal, Methodist Episcopal, Presbyterian Church, USA, and United Presbyterian churches.

Impelled by an apparent decline of missionary interest in the churches, the inquiry made an unofficial examination of the principles, aspects, and administration of the missionary enterprise. The Institute of Social and Religious Research assembled a mass of data. The commission studied the data and visited the mission fields. In 1932 it published its findings in a volume, *Rethinking Missions*. In 1933 appeared the *Regional Reports of the Commission of Appraisal* (3 vols.) and the *Fact-finders' Reports* (4 vols.).

Although the findings were partly commendatory, their adverse criticisms received greater publicity and fueled the modernist-conservative debate. The report was sharply criticized, especially for defining the missionary task as one of making common cause with other religions in the search for truth. Hocking defended the work in *Living Religions and a World Faith* (1940).

WILLARD D. ALLBECK

**Forgiveness.** The possibility of the forgiveness of sins is grounded in the nature of God, whose covenant with his people is unchangeable. God's will for men, as expressed in that covenant, includes devotion and obedient living. Where men transgress his will, the covenant God is at once wrathful and gracious. The Bible is the only book of religion that posits faith in the God who completely forgives sin. In the OT sin was often immediately followed by its consequence–death in the case of Achan's lust for gold (Josh. 7) or Saul's disobedience (1 Sam. 15, 31), or Uzzah's irreverence (2 Sam. 6:1–11). Yet David could cry out in penitence for forgiveness of his great transgression (2 Sam. 12:1–23). Leaders often interceded with God for their people's forgiveness, as Moses after the making of the golden calf (Exod. 33), and the priests in postexilic times (Ezra 9; Neh. 9; Dan. 9). The psalms abound with the pleadings and the joyful release of men who have sought forgiveness (Pss. 6, 25, 32, 51, 107, 130.) The prophets proclaim the forgiving nature of the Lord, but insist that the experience of his grace must be attended by a change of heart and life (Isa. 1:18; Jer. 31:31–34; Hos. 14:1–2; Amos 5:24).

In the NT, the thought of forgiveness is not so common as that of salvation and its cognates, although Paul identifies redemption with the forgiveness of sins (Col. 1:14). Of the two most frequently occurring words for forgiveness, *aphesis* denotes the bearing away of sin, as in Zechariah's song (Luke 1:77), John the Baptizer's preaching (Luke 3:3), and Jesus' identification of himself with the Paschal lamb (Matt. 26:28). The other word, *charisesthai*, found more often in Paul (2 Cor. 12:13; Col. 2:13), means "to treat graciously." Thus both terms stress the initiative of God in forgiveness. Hence, forgiveness as viewed in the Bible is more than the remittance of a penalty; it is the establishment of a warm personal relationship with God. This note is sounded often in the Gospels, especially in the parable of the gracious father (Luke 15:11–32), who yearns for the prodigal while he is yet "at a distance" and entreats the cold-hearted elder son who is proud of his uprightness.

Yet, like the prophets, the NT emphasizes also the need of change in men who are forgiven. According to the preaching of both John and Jesus, there must be repentance and faith (Mark 1:4, 14–15). The man forgiven by Christ's act must become "a new creation" (2 Cor. 5:17). Especially strong is the urgency that relations with our fellows test the reality of our own forgiveness. The woman who "loved much" could be forgiven gross sins, while the unloving Pharisee could receive no forgiveness (Luke 7:36–50). We may know that we have passed from death unto life only if we love (1 John 3:14). The debtor who had been forgiven an impossible debt had his forgiveness revoked when he refused remission to one who owed him (Matt. 18:23–35). We are taught to pray for forgiveness only in so far as we are willing to forgive (Matt. 6:12; Mark 11:25). The classic biblical examples of men who forgave those who wronged them, such as Joseph and his brothers (Gen. 45), David and Saul (1 Sam. 24), and Stephen and those who stoned him (Acts 7:54–60), must all be tested in the light of the spirit of Jesus' forgiveness of his enemies on the cross (Luke 23:34).

There are in the Gospels three difficult passages on forgiveness. In one, Jesus declares that he who "blasphemes against the Holy Spirit never has forgiveness" (Mark 3:29). In its setting this seems to mean that the man who fails to sense that all good comes from the Spirit of God is so spiritually dull as to be past forgiveness. A second (Mark 4:12) declares that the parables blind those who are spiritually perverted so they will not be forgiven. The third (Matt. 18:15–18), which represents Jesus as giving to the church the right to "bind" or "loose" from Christian fellowship, is often interpreted to mean that there is vested in the church the right to refuse forgiveness of sin or to grant it. This would signify that to the fellowship of believers there comes the understanding that enables them to know when a sinner is truly repentant and should be forgiven. It is, of course, a misinterpretation and misuse of this scripture for a church to arrogate to itself the right of forgiveness as an ecclesiastical prerogative. This led the medieval church to impose penance as a means for obtaining forgiveness. Later it sold indulgences through which the temporal pains of purgatory were remitted. From the whole tendency of prescribed acts the Protestant Reformation revolted to a more dynamic doctrine of the forgiveness of sin.

JULIAN P. LOVE

**Form Criticism.** Translation of the German *Formgeschichte*, lit., "history of form." Form criticism studies the literary form of documents that preserve earlier tradition. Its basic assumption is that the earlier, oral use of the tradition shaped the material and resulted in the variety of literary forms found in the final written record. Study of these forms, therefore, according to this theory, throws light on the life and thinking of the people who thus preserved tradition.

*Types of Oral Tradition.* Ancient writings reflect many special types of oral tradition. The Homeric poems are regarded as the written record of the work of numerous ancient bards. The Greek diatribe reflects discussion methods of Greek philosophical circles. Surviving missionary discourses, E. Norden argued, show a typical form. The Mishnah and later the Talmud preserve in writing the rabbinic tradition which had been orally shaped and transmitted through many generations.

Particularly influential in biblical study, however, was Olrik's analysis of the 13 laws or principles that govern the form of oral tradition in the folk tales of common people. He laid bare the simple, concrete, vivid, and effective patterns that prevail where many people share through many generations in handing on a tradition.

***OT Record of Oral Tradition.*** H. Gunkel first applied this viewpoint to OT study. Particularly in the third edition of his commentary on Genesis (1917), but also in other writings, he called attention to the various *Gattungen* or literary forms in which ancient oral tradition had taken shape. In narrative he finds fable, myth, saga, legend, brief tale, and historical narrative. Lyric compositions include funeral hymns, love songs, taunt songs, wedding songs, royal songs, hymns for public worship, thanksgiving hymns, and laments of individual or congregation. In prophetic writings he finds visions in narrative form and various forms of prophetic sayings, including threat, promise, and rebuke. Gunkel's concern is to understand the literary forms by reconstructing the life situation in which they arose and developed.

Gunkel's pioneer work has left its mark deeply on OT studies, and the form-critical approach has become pervasive. Many specialist studies have been undertaken, with Alt working on OT law (distinguishing apodictic from casuistic law), G. E. Mendenhall on covenant forms (showing, he maintained, the influence of the Hittite suzerainty treaties), Hempel and Wolff distinguishing the primary prophetic oracles from the development of them by the prophets themselves, and Westermann concentrating on the prophetic "woe" oracles. S. Mowinckel studied under Gunkel but also under the anthropologist Grønwald. His work has had a massive influence, especially in psalm study, for he related many of the psalms to a new year festival which he held was patterned on that observed in Babylon. Some OT scholars have developed his thesis further while others have reacted against it. Other form-critical positions have also come under fire; for instance, D. J. McCarthy's studies have produced a reaction against the Hittite treaty theory.

***Form Criticism of the Synoptic Gospels.*** In NT study, and especially in regard to the synoptic Gospels, form criticism has received vigorous development. It appeared as a clear-cut method in works by K. L. Schmidt (1919), M. Dibelius (1919), and R. Bultmann (1921), the three scholars whose work still dominates this field of study. It built upon many forerunners: Olrik's studies of folktales; Gunkel's identification of oral traditions embedded in the OT; Wellhausen's critical attention to the individual items of the gospel tradition and to the early stages of that tradition; Norden's study of prose style and mission discourses, among others. It built upon the concept that identification of written sources could not fully bridge the gap between Jesus and the written Gospels. A period of oral tradition had intervened and called for study. The prevailing sociological interest encouraged scholars to ask what part the total group of early Christians had in handing down the gospel.

Form criticism follows this sociological interest. It minimizes the role of the individuals who finally wrote down the tradition. It views the synoptic Gospels as a collection of many separate units whose present order in the Gospels is the result of late editorial grouping and so does not reflect the actual sequence of events and teaching in Jesus' ministry. It holds that these units can be classified according to their form, and that the *Sitz im Leben*, the life situation in the early church, determined the form each unit took. Therefore, from the form, these scholars believe that they can deduce the situation in the church that shaped this unit of tradition. The material thus becomes a source of information about the life and interests of the church, and is of little use in determining what Jesus did and said. Form critics differ among themselves as to how clearly the tradition gives a true picture of the historical Jesus, but most of them agree that the Gospels are primarily witnesses to the life and teaching of the early church. They are viewed as preserving this developed tradition as it had been selected and shaped by use in worship, instruction, counseling, and controversy. They see parallels not in the cultured literature of great writers but in the popular writings of ancient times that preserve the traditions of common people.

***Types of Gospel Tradition.*** Attempts to classify the forms have not led to clear agreement. Form critics agree that the passion story took form first; form criticism here sees one exception to its claim that each event or teaching of the gospel account was originally a separate unit. This is essential to their principle of procedure. A connected story of the passion was needed from the first to make clear the innocence of Jesus and the meaning of his death and resurrection. The "pronouncement story," to use V. Taylor's term, is a prominent form of the gospel tradition. Starting with a problem, controversy, or miracle, it comes to a climax in a saying or pronouncement of Jesus. "Parables" and "sayings" take form according to their purpose. "Miracle stories" have a typical form: the great need, the word or action of Jesus, and the amazing result. Various stories about Jesus, including those that give clues to his origin, greatness, and destiny, center attention upon him and his significance for faith. They remind us that the tradition was preserved in constant touch with the worship and teaching of the church, to which Jesus was "Lord and Christ."

***Other Oral Tradition of the Early Church.*** Form criticism deals essentially with the synoptic

Gospels. The Fourth Gospel is too plainly the work of personality to be regarded as the product of popular tradition. Attempts to apply the method in Acts have limited justification. The speeches, for example, present in summary fashion the main points of the basic gospel message, the kerygma. Most of them follow a typical pattern, as C. H. Dodd has shown; the speeches in Acts 7:2–53; 14:15–17; and 17:22–30 diverge most from this common pattern, whose content is well represented in Acts 10:34–43. J. A. T. Robinson led a reaction against Dodd's concept of one basic kerygma, and he stressed kerygmatic diversity and development.

Contemporary religious and philosophical traditions throw light on NT letters. There has been much study of early Christian confessions by scholars like O. Cullmann and Hunter, while possible early Christian hymns have attracted particular attention. Phil. 2:6–11, Col. 1:15–20, 1 Tim. 3:16, and the hymns of the Apocalypse have been the subjects of special studies by R. P. Martin, J. T. Sanders, and others. First Peter has been subjected to full analysis form-critically, and has been described by scholars such as Perdelwitz and Cross as a baptismal worship service, perhaps held at Passover time. Patterns have been discerned in the NT doxologies, and also a standard form of ethical parenesis in Ephesians, Colossians, 1 Peter, and elsewhere. Lists of vices and virtues, and of duties of household members, parallel somewhat similar lists found elsewhere.

**Criticism and Evaluation.** Criticism of form criticism has not been wanting. It includes the following points: Form criticism has not been able to assign all the gospel material to clear forms; it forgets the role of eye witnesses in preserving the original tradition; it does not do justice to the historical sense, intelligence, and integrity of the early Christians; while it rightly recognizes the extensive topical grouping of material in the Gospels, it goes too far in discrediting their basic outline of Jesus' ministry; while it correctly sees the importance of the early oral period, it hardly gives adequate weight to the fact that within some 20 years the writing of written sources began, and so the process of oral tradition was not so long as in folk tales; its tendency to assume radical distortion of the tradition in the Hellenistic church is refuted by the prevailingly Semitic character of the common synoptic tradition, and its results are warped by unexamined assumptions, such as that miracle stories are largely late creations and that explicit Christology arose first in the church rather than in the mind of Jesus.

**Bibliography.** E. Norden, *Agnostos Theos* (1913); H. Gunkel, *Genesis* (1917); K. L. Schmidt, *Der Rahmen der Geschichte Jesu* (1919); M. Dibelius, *From Tradition to Gospel* (1934); R. H. Lightfoot, *History and Interpretation in the Gospels* (1935); V. Taylor, *The Formation of the Gospel Tradition* (1933); S. Mowinckel, *The Psalms in Israel's Worship* (1962); R. Bultmann, *The History of the Synoptic Tradition* (1963); G. Von Rad, *The Problem of the Hexateuch and Other Essays* (1964), 1–78; C. K. Barrett, *Jesus and the Gospel Tradition* (1967); H. Gunkel, *The Psalms: A Form-Critical Introduction* (1967); K. Koch, *The Growth of the Biblical Tradition: The Form-Critical Method* (1967); N. Perrin, *Rediscovering the Teaching of Jesus* (1967); C. Westermann, *Basic Forms of Prophetic Speech* (1967); E. P. Sanders, *The Tendencies of the Synoptic Tradition* (1969); G. Lohfink, *The Bible: Now I Get It: A Form Criticism Handbook* (1979); F. McConnell, ed., *The Bible and the Narrative Tradition* (1986); M. Gerhart and J. G. Williams, *Genre, Narrative, and Theology* (1988)

FLOYD V. FILSON AND GEOFFREY W. GROGAN

**Formosa.** See TAIWAN.

**Forsyth, Peter Taylor** (1848–1921). Scottish Congregationalist theologian. Born in Aberdeen, he studied at Aberdeen and Göttingen. He was principal of Hackney Theological College, Hampstead, London (1901–21) and chairman of the Congregational Union of England and Wales. Coming under the influence of strong teachers such as Albrecht Ritschl and Andrew Fairbairn, he turned his thought and creative energies into applying the unique claims of Christianity to modern, positive, and social outlooks. In addition to earlier books and *Children's Sermons*, his later books are *Positive Preaching and the Modern Mind* (1907), *Missions in State and Church* (1911), *The Cruciality of the Cross* (1911), *The Person and Place of Christ* (1911), *The Work of Christ* (1911), *Christ on Parnassus* (1911), *Faith, Freedom and the Future* (1912), *The Religion and Ethic of Marriage* (1912), *The Principle of Authority* (1913), *Theology in Church and State* (1915), *The Christian Ethic of War* (1916), *The Justification of God* (1916), *The Soul of Prayer* (1916), *The Church and the Sacraments* (1917), and *This Life and the Next* (1918).

RAYMOND W. ALBRIGHT

**Fortescue, Adrian** (1874–1923). English Roman Catholic scholar. He studied at Rome (Ph.D., 1894) and Innsbruck (D.D., 1905), and was parish priest at Letchworth, Herts, from 1907 to 1923. Devout, erudite, and sprightly, he was most widely known for his practical manual, *The Ceremonies of the Roman Rite Described* (1917), and was distinguished for scholarly work in liturgics, such as *The Mass, a Study of the Roman Liturgy* (1912), and Eastern church history. After his death in 1923 *The Uniat Eastern Churches* (1923) was published; edited by J. Maspero, *Histoire des Patriarches d'Alexandria;* and an edition of Boethius, *De Consolatione Philosophiae* (1924).

**Bibliography.** J. G. Vance and J. W. Fortescue, *Adrian Fortescue, A Memoir* (1924).

EDWARD R. HARDY

**Fosdick, Harry Emerson** (1878–1969). American Baptist minister. Born in Buffalo, N.Y., he graduated from Colgate University and Union

Theological Seminary, and became minister of the First Baptist Church, Montclair, N.J. (1904–15). During this period he also began a long association as professor of practical theology at Union Theological Seminary, N.Y. (1908–46). In World War I he served with the YMCA in France, and on his return became guest preacher at the First Presbyterian Church, New York City. Attacked by fundamentalists for his liberal theological views, he resigned this position in 1925 to become minister of Park Avenue Baptist Church. Under his leadership this became the interdenominational Riverside Church, where he was minister until his retirement in 1946. For 20 years his radio ministry was carried by the nationwide National Vespers. One of his major interests was the development of personal counseling in the churches in cooperation with psychiatric help. He wrote 30 books, including *The Manhood of the Master* (1913), *The Meaning of Prayer* (1915), *The Modern Use of the Bible* (1924), *On Being A Real Person* (1943), *On Being Fit to Live With: Sermons on Post-War Christianity* (1946), *Rufus Jones Speaks to Our Times: An Anthology* (1951), his autobiography *The Living of These Days* (1956), and *Dear Mr. Brown: Letters to a Person Perplexed* (1961). He also wrote the hymn "God of Grace and God of Glory."

J. D. DOUGLAS

# Foursquare Gospel, The International Church of the.

Church incorporated under the leadership of Aimee Semple McPherson (1890–1944), a well-known evangelist in the early 20th-century pentecostal movement. McPherson went to serve as a missionary in China in 1910 with her husband, Robert Semple, who died shortly after their arrival. She returned to the United States and remarried. In 1915 McPherson began holding evangelistic campaigns throughout the United States and other countries. In 1923 in Los Angeles, Calif., she built Angelus Temple, a church seating 5300 people. McPherson had a dynamic preaching style that included illustrated sermons and full-length sacred operas. Angelus Temple was often filled to capacity several times each Sunday. McPherson had envisioned the "Foursquare Gospel" in 1921 at a meeting in Oakland, Calif. The Foursquare Gospel stands for Jesus Christ the Savior, Jesus Christ the Healer, Jesus Christ the Baptizer with the Holy Spirit, and Jesus Christ the Coming King. Other aspects of doctrine are stated in a declaration of faith. LIFE Bible College, one of the denomination's ministerial training centers, has published a systematic theology entitled *Foundations of Pentecostal Theology* (1983).

The International Church of the Foursquare Gospel meets in convention at least once every two years for business and planning purposes. Corporate activities are transacted by a board of directors consisting of seven to 12 members. The board appoints district supervisors who name local pastors. A church council oversees the business of the local congregation. Women have been ordained from the church's earliest years. There are 1250 Foursquare churches in nine districts in the United States with 188,757 members and adherents (1986). There are Foursquare missions in 60 countries with 13,762 churches and 912,174 adherents (1986). Throughout its history, the Foursquare Church has shown interest in the material needs as well as the spiritual concerns of persons. Angelus Temple Commissary, for example, opened in 1927. During the Great Depression, it fed and clothed over 1.5 million people. The commissary has continued to offer food and clothing to needy persons in the inner city regardless of race or creed. The International Church is often involved in disaster relief in foreign countries. The International Church of the Foursquare Gospel is a member of the National Association of Evangelicals and the Pentecostal Fellowship of North America.

*Bibliography.* A. Semple McPherson, *The Foursquare Gospel* (1969); Aimee, *Life Story of Aimee Semple McPherson* (1979).

CHARLES W. MIDDLEBROOK

# Fowler, Henry Thatcher

(1867–1949). University professor. Born in Fishkill, N.Y., he studied at Yale (Ph.D., 1896). He taught biblical literature and philosophy at Yale (1895–97) and Knox College (1897–1901) and was professor of biblical literature and history at Brown University (1901–34). His major works of religious interest include *The Prophets as Statesmen and Preachers* (1904), *Studies in the Wisdom Literature of the OT* (1907), *History of the Literature of Ancient Israel* (1912), *The Origin and Growth of the Hebrew Religion* (1916), *Great Leaders of Hebrew History* (1920), and *The History and Literature of the NT* (1925). He coauthored, with M. C. Hazard, *The Books of the Bible with Relation to Their Place in History* (1903), and with F. K. Sanders, *Outlines for Study of Biblical History and Literature* (1906).

RAYMOND W. ALBRIGHT

# Frame, James Everett

(1868–1956). Presbyterian clergyman. Born in Boston, he studied at Harvard, Union Theological Seminary, and Berlin and Göttingen. He taught NT (1897–1905), biblical theology (1905–19), and sacred literature (1919–38) at Union Theological Seminary. He was professor emeritus after 1938. He insisted upon a thorough knowledge of Hebrew and cognate languages as an aid to understanding the deepest thought of the NT authors. Howard Chandler Robbins aptly characterized him theologically as a representative of "liberal Presbyterianism in its scholarly aspect." He wrote articles on the Epistles to the Colossians and to the Thessalonians, *Encyclopaedia Britannica*, 11th ed. (1910–11); *JBL*

49 (1930): 1–12; book reviews for *The Nation;* and *A Critical and Exegetical Commentary on the Epistles of St. Paul to the Thessalonians, International Critical Commentary* (1912).

BRUCE M. METZGER

**France.** The French Republic is the largest European country west of the USSR, covering 547,026 sq. km. (211,208 sq. mi.). It has a population of 55.1 million (1988). There are four main religious groups in France. Most numerous are the Roman Catholics, followed by the Muslims. The Reformed-Lutheran bloc comes third, while the Protestant evangelicals are in fourth place.

The Roman Catholic Church continues to decline. Although approximately 80 percent of the population are baptized Catholics, recent surveys show that only about 11 percent participate regularly in church life. In major cities the observance is even lower; only 7 percent of Parisians practice the faith. Parochial education has sharply decreased. Over half of parishioners say they no longer believe in purgatory or the need of confession. Between 1960 and 1986 the number of priests fell from 41,704 to 28,000. By 2000 the church predicts that perhaps only 12,000 priests will be available to serve the nation's 36,000 municipalities. The average age of priests is 65, while the number of ordained replacements fell from 708 in 1966 to 111 by 1980. This situation has caused many country priests to care for from six to 12 parishes. Half of all the parishes do not have resident priests.

Pope John Paul II, who visited France three times between 1980 and 1986, maintains that materialism, secularism, and humanism are the major causes of dechristianization. The French are not so much antireligious as indifferent, even though France is the "elder daughter of the church." Only 15 percent actually claim to be irreligious or atheistic. In this discouraging Catholic scene some sociologists now note a renewal movement among laity, especially among youth, but along innovative lines that stretch the Church's rules.

Islam is the second largest religion in France, with some 2.7 million adherents. Of these, 1.5 million are foreigners, mostly Arab and Algerian. Another 1.1 million Muslims are French citizens. About 900,000 Muslims live in the greater Paris area; 148,000 are in the south, especially in Marseilles; 110,000 live in the Rhone-Alpes region; and 67,000 live in Languedoc-Roussillon. The economic and educational levels of Muslims vary, but most have menial employment. Since adults often fervently practice their faith in order to preserve their roots, there are hundreds of mosques and prayer halls. Their children tend to repudiate or ignore the Muslim tradition. So far there is no sign of militant fundamentalism. Some French political leaders take an anti-immigrant line. A certain percentage of the public is racist, especially in times of high unemployment. A Christian witness to Muslims exists, but is very limited. Most of the response to the gospel comes from young people who are more open to outside influences.

Before 1980 the older Protestant bodies (Reformed and Lutheran) claimed about 800,000 parishioners (1.6 percent of the population), including pastors and sympathizers. But a poll taken that year showed that 2.4 million people, or 4.5 percent of the population, claimed to be "close to Protestantism." Protestant leaders were elated that their numbers had somehow tripled without their knowledge, since they had done little to account for it. Most of those in question, however, were either lapsed Protestants or nonmembers. Interviews with respondents revealed that only a minority were baptized members. More of these newly discovered "Protestants" considered Jesus Christ as a moral ideal rather than as the Son of God. One-third never read the Bible, and almost half did not believe in the resurrection of Christ. Given such a tenuous relationship, the respondents appeared as admirers or sympathizers of Protestantism. Thus, slightly over a million seems to be a more likely estimate of true Protestant strength. Although the Reformed Church boasts of having the most members, some of the church's own leaders believe it to be in a state of decline. Alsace and Lorraine are the main areas of Lutheran strength.

The theology of French Protestants was heavily Barthian before World War II, and Barth continued to dominate the scene until the early 1960s. Since then no single theological system has prevailed. A small number of Reformed and Lutherans are evangelical. In the 1960s and 1970s France's new prosperity produced a "society of consummation," which drew much attention from the Protestants. The most newsworthy event for mainline Protestants since World War II was the Reformed Church's publication of the *Eglise et Pouvoirs* report in 1971, which strongly attacked the role and misuse of money. Other central interests during the 1970s and 1980s included pacifism, ecumenism, socioeconomic justice, abortion, the east-west confrontation, and the death penalty. Only a small number of leaders and laypersons were concerned with evangelism and church expansion. Relations with the World Council of Churches and the Roman Catholic Church grew closer.

A phenomenon of the 1980s is the rising strength of evangelical Protestants. Pentecostal denominations make up the largest element, followed by Christian Brethren, Baptists, Free Churches, Mennonites, the independent Reformed, missionary-founded denominations, and others. The impact of their growing number, estimated by some at 200,000 in 1986, was reflected earlier in the Plett report on evangelicals, published in 1981 by the Reformed Church. That document called the evangelicals an "important reality" and attempted to identify and locate them in French society. André Benoit of the Protestant faculty of theology at Strasbourg University notes that "today we meet more and more Christians who claim the name evangelical." The enlarged evangelical ranks are the result of evangelism, which is in turn their primary concern. A second dominant interest is the planting of new churches. In 1983 a study by Michel Evan of Operation Mobilization claimed that over 400 new evangelical churches had emerged in the previous decade, many of them founded by some of the 600 foreign missionaries in France. Evangelicals had discovered each other in evangelism conferences sponsored by evangelist Billy Graham in Berlin (1966), Amsterdam (1971), Lausanne (1974), and Amsterdam (1983, 1986). The French Evangelical Alliance (1846), the Federation of French Evangelicals (1969), and the Association of Confessing *(Professants)* Churches (1957) form important links between churches and believers. A growing number of books, periodicals, camps, musical groups, theological seminaries, Bible institutes, and parachurch evangelistic movements have been supportive of the evangelical cause. An event which both symbolized and strengthened the new evangelical unity was Mission France, the third Billy Graham crusade, held in 1986. This eight-day mission attracted 100,500 people in Paris and 182,204 more by live satellite and video transmission in 31 other French cities, as well as in Switzerland and Belgium. A grand total of 282,704 attended, and 13,840 responded to the evangelist's invitation to give themselves to Jesus Christ.

**Bibliography.** G. Matagrin, *Préparer Aujourd'hui l'église de Demain* (1976); A. Woodrow, *L'Eglise Déchirée* (1978); J.-P. Richardot, *Le Peuple Protestant Aujourd'hui* (1980); G. Plett, *Les Courants Evangéliques dans et hors de l'Eglise Réformée de France* (1981); R. Mehl, *Le Protestantisme Francais dans la Société Actuelle* (1982); A. Encrevé, *Les Protestants en France de 1800 à Nos Jours* (1985); M. Arkoun, *Le Nouvel Observateur* (Feb. 7–13, 1986); G. Dagon, *Annuaire Evangélique, 1986* (1986).

ROBERT P. EVANS

**Franciscans.** Various religious groups who profess to follow some form of the rule of Saint Francis of Assisi (1181–1226). Although reared in an atmosphere of luxury, following his conversion Francis devoted himself to a life of poverty and humility as exemplified by Christ. He attracted many followers but they soon divided into three autonomous groups: the Friars Minor, the Poor Clares, and the Third Order (or Order of Penance). Despite their shared tradition these groups have been bitterly divided over exactly how they should imitate the poverty and simplicity of Christ.

The Friars Minor were approved by the papacy in 1210. At first they were itinerant preachers and social workers who supported themselves by whatever means they could. However, their rapid growth led to a need for financing and organization. All such businesslike activities were discouraged by Francis who asked that the vow of poverty not be violated. Shortly after his death the pope declared that the order could hold property. A conflict arose between the Spirituals, who insisted on keeping the founder's request, and the Conventuals, who accepted the new approach. Eventually, the papacy condemned the belief that Christ and his apostles lived in absolute poverty (1323). This led to persecution of the Spirituals and they became associated with several heretical movements.

The Franciscan Order declined during the 14th and 15th centuries but a reform movement, the Observants, developed in its ranks. In 1517 Leo X officially separated the order into two independent branches: the Friars Minor of the Regular Observance and the Friars Minor Conventual. Further discord among the Observants led to several factions, including the Capuchins, the Discalced (Shoeless), and the Recollects. Increasing division caused Leo XIII (1897) to unite all the Observants except the Capuchins.

The Poor Clares were founded by a noblewoman of Assisi who followed Francis. Her order of nuns, organized in 1219, was devoted to a life of prayer and penance. Despite the contemplative character of the group they also faced the same struggles over the practice of poverty found among the friars.

The Third Order consisted largely of laypeople. An important force in late medieval society, this group grew rapidly among women in the 19th century. They presently devote themselves to teaching, nursing, and other charitable acts.

Franciscans have contributed in important ways to the Christian tradition. During medieval and Reformation times they led the way in evangelism. Five of their members have served as pope and many popular practices of the Roman Catholic Church such as the devotion to the Sacred Heart, the Precious Blood, and the Stations of the Cross have been encouraged by the Franciscans. The order continues to demonstrate vitality through a wide variety of attempts to help the poor. These vary from the approach of liberation theology to advocacy of the teachings of leading medieval scholars such as Bonaventura.

**Bibliography.** M. D. Lambert, *Franciscan Poverty: The Doctrine of the Absolute Poverty of Christ and the Apostles in the Franciscan Order, 1210–1323* (1961); J. R. H. Moorman, *History of the Franciscan Order: From Its Origins to the Year 1517* (1968); R. Brown, *St. Francis of Assisi: Omnibus of Sources* (1983); I. de Aspurz, *Franciscan History: The Three Orders of St. Francis of Assisi* (1983).

ROBERT G. CLOUSE

## Frazer, James George (1854–1941). Anthropologist. Born in Glasgow, he was educated at Larchfield Academy, Helensburgh, Glasgow University, and Trinity College, Cambridge, where he was a classical scholar and subsequently a fellow. From 1907 until 1919 he was professor of social anthropology at the University of Liverpool. He was instrumental in founding *The Cambridge Review* (1879), and in 1911 he delivered the first of his Gifford Lectures at St. Andrews on "Belief in Immortality and the Worship of the Dead." He was an original fellow of the British Academy and a fellow of the Royal Society of Edinburgh. Between 1890 and 1912 he produced his monumental work, *The Golden Bough*, in 12 volumes and three editions. He also published *Pausanias and Other Greek Sketches* (1900), *Lectures on the Early History of Kingship* (1905), *Totemism and Exogamy* (1910), *Folk-Lore in the OT* (3 vols., 1918), *Sir Roger de Coverley and Other Literary Pieces* (1920), *The Worship of Nature* (1926), *The Gorgon's Head* (1927), *The Fasti of Ovid* (5 vols., 1929), *Myths of the Origin of Fire* (1930), *The Fear of the Dead in Primitive Religion* (1933/34), and *Totemica* (1939). *The Golden Bough* and *Folk-Lore in the OT* were issued in abridged form in 1922 and 1923, respectively.

EDWIN O. JAMES

## Fredericq, Paul (1850–1920). Born in Ghent, Belgium, he became professor at the University of Liège in 1882 and at the University of Ghent in 1883. He taught principally history and Flemish literature. In 1876 he became a Protestant. He played an important role in the Flemish movement. His works are *Geschiedenis der Inquisitie in de Nederlanden* (2 vols., 1892, 1897), *Religieuze twisten in de Nederlanden* (1894), and *Corpus documentorum inquisitiones haereticae Nederlandicae* (3 vols., 1900–1906).

ALBERT HYMA

## Free Christianity, German Alliance for. Organization of liberal groups within German Protestant territorial churches founded in 1948 by E. Meyer. Among the groups that joined were the *Protestantenverein*, the Friends of Evangelical Freedom, and the *Volkskirchliche Vereinigung*. Its first congress was held in Frankfurt am Main in 1948. The stated objectives of the alliance were to apply theological insights and the best findings of the humanities and the sciences to the process of clarifying Christian faith and to make apparent the relevance of faith to contemporary social and ethical norms of behavior. In addition, the alliance has sought to counteract the "confining" impact of post–World War I neo-orthodox trends and to stem the tides of clericalism in the church.

Its monthly publication, *Freies Christentum*, promotes piety without the shackles of dogmatism, uncensored theological inquiry, and individual liberty of conscience. It has worked, in addition, toward the goal of establishing territorial churches free of state control.

Since its inception, the alliance has been a member of the International Association for Liberal Christianity and Religious Freedom (IARF).

E. J. FURCHA

## Free Church Federal Council of England and Wales. A body constituted in 1940 by the fusion of the National Free Church Council and the Federal Council of the Evangelical Free Churches. The National Free Church Council was established in 1896 on a basis of personal membership and includes representatives of local councils of Free churches throughout the country. The Federal Council was set up in 1919 on a more official basis to represent the Free churches.

The council now consists of representatives of 15 denominations, prominent among which are the Baptist Union of Great Britain and Ireland, the Methodist Church, the Presbyterian Church of Wales, the Salvation Army, and the United Reformed Church.

The council has special responsibility for: (1) *legislation:* representing to the government the principles and judgments of the Free churches on legislative matters which directly or indirectly affect them; (2) *representation:* providing means whereby the Free churches may be represented at official functions and on national committees; (3) *social issues:* sponsoring projects to arouse Christian responsibility in industrial and civic life and safeguarding public and social righteousness; (4) *faith and order:* imparting knowledge of Free Church history and principles, and promoting mutual understanding among Christians of different communions; (5) *education:* securing the due rights of the Free Churches in educational legislation and administration; (6) *hospital chaplaincy service:* the "appropriate church authority" for consultation regarding the appointment of chaplains; (7) *evangelism:* encouraging and advising local councils in the planning and conducting of campaigns and other methods of united witness.

The constituent churches claim more than one million committed members, with nearly 10,000 ministers. The total adult community within their influence is probably well over double the committed membership, and at least one half million children and young people are also associated with their local churches.

## Free Church of America. *See* EVANGELICAL FREE CHURCH OF AMERICA.

## Free Church of Scotland. Church formed at the Disruption of 1843 when, under the leadership of Thomas Chalmers, about one-third of the ministers and members seceded from the Church of Scotland in protest against state control of the

church. In 1900 the majority of the then Free Church of Scotland entered into union with the United Presbyterian Church to form the United Free Church of Scotland. The present Free Church of Scotland took shape from the minority who refused to enter the union of 1900. Their refusal to unite was based on the fact that the United Presbyterian Church in its constitution of 1847 had accepted the principle of voluntaryism, which seemed to them to compromise the goal of a national church or national recognition of the Christian religion.

After 1900 the now divided Free Church was involved in a battle in the civil courts over claims to church property. The dissenting minority claimed rights to all the property formerly held by the Free Church. They lost in the Scottish courts but then won a House of Lords appeal in 1904. The outcome was a distribution of the property proportionate to the strengths of the two groups.

The present Free Church of Scotland holds to the Westminster Confession of Faith as its doctrinal standard without qualification or reservation. In worship it maintains a simplicity of form with the singing of metrical psalms unaccompanied by musical instruments. The church is served by about 100 ministers and engages in overseas work in India, South Africa, and Peru. It maintains its own theological college for the training of its ministers, which is also attended by extradenominational students. In common with most other Scottish bodies, numbers have declined in recent years. No precise statistics are readily available, but it is unlikely that the Free Church now has more than about 18,000 members and adherents.

ALISTAIR J. DRUMMOND

**Freemasonry.** World's largest fraternal organization. Emphasizing morality, charity, and brotherhood, Masonry is veiled in allegory and symbolism. Although Masons must profess faith in a Supreme Being, the order's moral principles are concerned with man's duties to his fellowmen and not to the Creator. While numerous Christian denominations have criticized Freemasonry for being a secret society and a false religion, neither charge is probably justified. Masonry is an organization with secrets but not a secret society in the traditional meaning of the term. Moreover, its acknowledgment of the Great Architect of the Universe and the immortality of the soul is not tantamount to the doctrines of a new religion.

Freemasonry has adopted an extensive legendary history replete with the rites and trappings of antiquity. Much of its intricate symbolism is associated with the order's supposed Egyptian origins and with the building of Solomon's temple. However, there is no authentic evidence for the latter.

In actuality, Freemasonry evolved from medieval stonemaking guilds. When the era of cathedral building ended after the Reformation, these declining guilds began admitting nonworking, honorary members. In the 17th and 18th centuries, these guilds evolved into "speculative" bodies which maintained the symbolic tools of "operative" Masonry. In 1717 four London lodges formed the first Grand Lodge. Thereafter, the order abandoned its strictly Christian tone to adopt the general tenets of deism. Members were free to belong only to that "Religion in which all men agree . . . to be Good Men and True."

Masonry was transplanted from Great Britain to the United States in 1733. There is some evidence that the American Revolution was inspired by Freemasons, or, at least, that colonial lodges served as a vital communications link between Revolutionary leaders. Although officially divorced from partisan politics in the United States, Masonic membership became an almost essential prerequisite for political success in the Midwest and South during the 19th and early 20th centuries.

From Great Britain, speculative Masonry moved to the Continent where it was often revolutionary and opposed to ecclesiastical and political authority. In France, Belgium, Spain, and Portugal, it was stridently anti-Catholic. In Latin America, lodges served as cells for revolutionary, anticlerical activity. Almost from its inception, Freemasonry encountered opposition from organized religion. Until recently, the Roman Catholic Church viewed it as a cover for conspiracy against government and religion, and several papal bulls expressly forbade Catholic membership in the organization. Protestant churches which condemn membership include the Lutheran, Quaker, Brethren, Mennonite, Mormon, Christian Reformed, Nazarene, and Seventh-day Adventist. The order has also been banned in the Soviet Union, Poland, Hungary, Spain, Portugal, China, Indonesia, and the United Arab Republic.

In most Masonic lodges worldwide, three basic degrees–entered apprentice, fellowcraft, and master mason–comprise the central core of the order's symbolic work. Superimposed on these Blue Lodge degrees are many higher degrees offered by two rites–the Scottish and the York–which lead ultimately to the 32nd degree.

In the United States, only white males are eligible for Masonic membership. However, Negro Prince Hall Lodges, still considered "clandestine" by regular U.S. lodges, were first chartered in 1775 by England's Grand Lodge. Several social organizations, although they have no official standing in the order, are affiliated with Freemasonry in the United States. The Shrine, the Grotto, and the Tall Cedars of Lebanon are well known for their charitable and benevolent civic and educational endeavors. Female relatives of Master Masons may join the order of the Eastern Star; boys, the order of DeMolay; and girls, the order of Job's Daughters.

It is estimated that there are about 6 million Freemasons worldwide, 4 million of whom reside in the United States and one million in Great Britain. A steadily declining membership in recent years seems to threaten the vitality and continuing existence of the order. But the ties to tradition and antiquity, which are the very essence of Masonry, will probably make change and adaptation difficult.

*Bibliography.* A. G. Mackey, *An Encyclopedia of Freemasonry* (1887); H. W. Coil, *A Comprehensive View of Freemasonry* (1954); L. Dumenil, *Freemasonry and American Culture, 1880–1930* (1954); B. Ray, *Revolution and Freemasonry, 1680–1880* (1981); M. C. Jacob, *The Radical Enlightenment: Pantheists, Freemasons and Republics* (1981).

HERBERT J. RISSLER

**Free Methodist Church.** American denomination organized in 1860 in Pekin, N.Y., as part of mid-19th–century revivalism. It presently serves in 26 countries with a membership of 220,808. Benjamin Titus Roberts, John Wesley Redfield, and I. M. Chesbrough were among its principal founders. Early emphases were freedom in worship, the doctrine of entire sanctification, ministry to the poor, and abolition of slavery. Laypeople were instrumental in the church's formation and even today have equal representation with clergy at all levels of church government. The Holiness Movement Church of Canada merged with the Free Methodist Church in 1959.

The church functions with a modified episcopal form of government. Local churches are represented at an annual conference by their pastor(s) and at least one lay delegate. Each annual conference has both lay and clerical delegates to the general conference. Bishops are elected by the general conference and stand for reelection. Pastors are appointed by the ministerial appointment committee of their annual conference.

The church sponsors six institutions of higher education in North America: Aldersgate College, Central College, Greenville College, Roberts Wesleyan College, Seattle Pacific University, and Spring Arbor College. Bible schools, colleges, and seminaries serve the church in other countries. Social ministries include retirement centers, nursing homes, primary schools, hospitals, and a rescue mission.

The Free Methodist Church has adopted the following statement of mission: "The Mission of the Free Methodist Church is to make known to all people everywhere God's call to wholeness through forgiveness and holiness in Jesus Christ, and to invite into membership and to equip for ministry all who respond in faith." The Free Methodist Church is a member of the Christian Holiness Association and the National Associa-

tion of Evangelicals. Its headquarters is located in Winona Lake, Ind.

*See also* HOLINESS CHURCHES.

*Bibliography.* B. T. Roberts, *Fishers of Men* (1904); W. T. Hogue, *History of the Free Methodist Church* (1915); L. R. Marston, *From Age to Age a Living Witness* (1960); D. E. Demaray, *Snapshots, The People Called Free Methodist* (1985).

**Free Presbyterian Church of Scotland.** Ecclesiastical body which emerged from the Free Church of Scotland in response to its adoption of the Declaratory Act of 1892 concerning adherence to the Westminster Confession of Faith. The act stated that the Free Church disclaimed intolerant or persecuting principles; and that in pledging adherence to the Confession of Faith her office-bearers were not inconsistent with liberty of conscience and the right of private judgment. After the birth of the Free Presbyterian Church, the post–1900 Free Church, being the conservative minority of the original Free Church, repealed the act. However, the Free Presbyterians have felt constrained to continue a separate witness alongside the Free Church. Although they have many similarities, the origin of the present Free Church remains a stumbling block to union between the two churches. Their numerical strength in 1987 was probably about 10,000 members and adherents.

ALISTAIR J. DRUMMOND

**Freud, Sigmund** (1856–1939). Father of psychoanalysis. Born in Freiberg, Moravia, he studied both medicine and psychology at Allgemeines Krankenhaus under Ernst Bruecke, receiving an M.D. (1881) from Vienna University where he became a lecturer (1885), extraordinary professor (1902), and ordinary professor (1919). He was the first to discover the anesthetic properties of cocaine (1884). He studied under Charcot at Salpetriere Hospital, Paris (1885/86), and in Vienna with Joseph Breuer with whom he wrote *Studies in Hysteria* (1893), which explained that physical symptoms of hysteria are rooted in highly emotional experiences in early life, which have been "forgotten," that is, repressed into the unconscious part of the mind and therefore normally inaccessible to the conscious mind.

Freud developed a therapeutic process called *catharsis* which was produced through hypnosis; later he substituted free association for hypnosis and, adding the interpretation of dreams, he produced the psychological therapy called psychoanalysis which is based upon an original theory of personality. This theory, now widely accepted, states that there are three parts to the mind: the *id*, the amoral, primeval, instinctive self composed of needs, desires, and passions; the *ego*, that part of the mind which implements the *id* in reality, and the *superego*, which roughly is the conscience, the standards and conventions inherited from and imposed by society. The ego is caught in the crossfire between the incessant demands of the id and the stern voice of the superego. Emotional maturity is achieved only when a healthy and harmonious compromise is achieved by the ego between the impossible demands of the id and the superego. Until there is honest recognition of the demands of the id, self-deception and rationalization dominate. Variations of this theory were developed by two students of Freud, Alfred Adler and Carl Gustave Jung.

Freud's insistence that the *libido* or sex drive constituted the primary factor in all emotional life set off an avalanche of criticism and misunderstanding. His theory of "infantile sexuality" (theorizing that the sex instinct begins with birth, subsides at about the age of five, and reappears at puberty) proved equally unacceptable at the time.

Further hostility was engendered by his attack on religion as an illusion concocted by man to explain the unknown. As the frontiers of ignorance shrank, man would become emancipated from his dependence upon the supernatural (*The Future of an Illusion*, 1927). Many of his most ardent disciples deplore this book as "regrettable" and "unscientific." In *Moses and Monotheism* (1939) he examined the nature of religion, argued that monotheism was a distinctly Jewish contribution, offered a theory on recurring anti-Semitism, and maintained that Moses was an Egyptian. Despite all attacks and criticism, Freud is gratefully acknowledged today as the father of "depth psychology" or dynamic psychiatry and a monumental contributor to contemporary culture. His studies continue to shed new light on sociology, anthropology, biography, literature, history, ethics, and religion.

Included among his many publications are *The Interpretation of Dreams* (1900), *The Psychopathology of Everyday Life* (1905), *Three Contributions to the Theory of Sex* (1905), *Wit and Its Relation to the Unconscious* (1905), *Leonardo Da Vinci* (1910), *Totem and Tabu* (1913), *The Ego and the Id* (1923), *Repression, Symptoms and Anxiety* (1926), and *The Discontents of Civilization* (1930).

ROLLIN J. FAIRBANKS

## Fridrichsen, Anton Johnson (1888–1953).

Lutheran. Born in Meråker, Norway, he studied at the University of Oslo. He served in the pastoral office (1913/14). He was assistant professor at the University of Oslo (1915–28); and was professor of NT at the University of Uppsala, Sweden, from 1928. He founded several scientific societies (such as the Uppsala exegetiska sällskap) and publications (such as *Svensk exegetisk årsbok*, Acta seminarii neotestamentici upsaliensis, Coniectanea neotestamentica, and Symbolae biblicae upsalienses) for the furtherance of biblical studies. He especially worked in the fields of NT

philology and biblical theology. He wrote *Hagios-Qados. Ein Beitrag zu den Voruntersuchungen zur christlichen Begriffsgeschichte* (1916), *Le problème du miracle dans le christianisme primitif* (1925), and *The Apostle and His Message* (1947). He coauthored with I. Heikel, *Grekisk-svensk ordbok till Nya Testamentet och de apostoliska fäderna* (Greek-Swedish Dictionary to the NT and the Apostolic Fathers, 1934), and with others, *Svenskt-Bibliskt Uppslagsverk* (Swedish Biblical Encyclopaedia, 1948–52).

*Bibliography.* ZNW, 45 (1954): 123–29.

## Friedrich, Johannes (1836–1917). German

church historian. Born in Upper Franconia, Germany, and educated at Bamberg and Munich, he taught at the University of Munich from 1862. His ability brought him to the attention of J. A. Hohenlohe, archbishop of Ephesus *(in partibus)*, and he was appointed his secretary. In 1870 he went with the archbishop to the Vatican Council, where he, along with J. J. I. von Döllinger, opposed the proposed definition of papal infallibility. In 1871 he was excommunicated by the Roman Catholic Church for refusing to accept the decrees of the council. In 1872 he was appointed to the chair of church history at Munich. His more important writings include *Johann Wessel* (1862), *Die Kirchengeschichte Deutschlands* (2 vols., 1867–69), *Geschichte des Vatikanischen Konzils* (3 vols., 1877–87), *Beiträge zur Geschichte des Jesuitenordens* (1881), *Johann Adam Mohler* (1894), and *Ignaz von Döllinger* (3 vols., 1899–1901).

IAN HAMILTON

## Friends, Society of. Religious movement

founded in the 17th century by George Fox (1624–1691). Fox was regarded by his contemporaries as a crazed revolutionary and was jailed eight times for disturbing the peace. After members of the sect emigrated to America several of them were hanged and others imprisoned for creating public disorder.

Initially the Quakers experienced considerable opposition because of their mystical theology and rejection of orthodox teachings such as the Trinity and the importance of celebrating the sacraments. Their emphasis on the illumination of human minds by God's "inner light" led to a belief in continuing revelation and further deviation from traditional Christian teachings. But, in the 19th century, the teachings of Joseph John Gurney (1788–1847) led many Quakers to accept an orthodox form of evangelical theology.

From the beginning Quakers were known for their radical social programs, which included the emancipation of women, opposition to slavery, prison reform, and the extension of education to all classes in society. They were also known for their simple lifestyle, plain worship, and modest dress. Pacifism is an important element in Quaker belief, and throughout their history they have actively worked for world peace and conflict resolution. Probably the best-known Quaker after Fox is William Penn (1644–1718), who established Pennsylvania as a "holy experiment" based on toleration and Christian charity.

The simple Quaker meeting and use of an unpaid, unordained ministry clearly influenced the early Brethren movement while Quaker social concerns have affected most mainline churches. Today there are about 21,000 Quakers worldwide but their influence far exceeds their numbers.

*Bibliography.* H. R. Brinton, *Friends for 300 Years* (1952); A. N. Brayshaw, *The Quakers, Their Story and Message* (1953); D. E. Trueblood, *The People Called Quakers* (1966).

IRVING HEXHAM

## Friends Service Committee, American (AFSC).

Committee established in 1917 by American and Canadian Friends to relieve human suffering and explore new approaches of service for conscientious objectors. Both efforts were successful, providing alternative means of service for those opposed to war and helping rehabilitate devastated areas of France, Russia, Germany, Austria, and Poland. Between World War I and World War II, AFSC was very active in the Peace movement and continued to work to improve the lives of conscientious objectors, to give aid and assistance to the unemployed and refugees, and to provide medical services and food to those suffering from famine, tumult, or the devastation of war anywhere in the world. The creative and ingenious use of the media has done much to spread their ideas of peace and nonviolent action. AFSC uses radio, television, speakers, pamphlets, an office in the United Nations building, seminars, campus organizations, and printed materials to make their viewpoint public. Their fivefold program includes international service, community relations, peace education, international affairs, and youth affairs. AFSC's Voluntary International Service Assignments (VISA) apparently served as the model for the Peace Corps, which was established by the Kennedy administration. In 1947 AFSC and its British counterpart won the Nobel Peace Prize. AFSC headquarters is in Philadelphia, Pa.

ROBERT V. SCHNUCKER

## Fritsch, Charles Theodore (1912– ). OT

scholar, educator, and author. Born in Allentown, Pa., he studied at Muhlenberg College, Princeton Theological Seminary, and Princeton University (Ph.D., 1940). He was ordained a Presbyterian minister in 1940. He was instructor (1937–40), assistant professor (1940–50), associate professor (1950–57), and professor (1957–77) of Hebrew and OT literature, and professor of OT (1977–79) at Princeton Theological Seminary, and adjunct professor at Dropsie College (1968–78). An expert on the LXX, he cofounded the International Organization for Septuagint and Cognate Studies. While he continued to contribute to journals up to 1985, his major works include *The Qumran Community: Its History and Scrolls* (1956), "Proverbs" in the *Interpreter's Bible* (1955), "Genesis" in the *Layman's Bible Commentary* (1959), "1 & 2 Chronicles," "Ezra," and "Nehemiah" in the one-volume *Interpreter's Bible Commentary* (1972), and *A Classified Bibliography of the Septuagint* (1973).

JACK MITCHELL

## Froom, Leroy Edwin (1890–1974). Seventh-

day Adventist editor. Born in Belvedere, Ill., he studied at Walla Walla and Pacific Union colleges, Washington Seminary, and the University of Nanking. He was a pastor in Baltimore and Wilmington, Del. (1913–15), editor of *Signs of the Times Magazine* (1915–18), the Chinese *Signs of the Times* (1918–21), *Watchman Magazine* (1922–26), and *The Ministry* (1928–50). In 1939 he became professor of history of prophetic interpretation at his church's theological seminary in Washington, D.C. His most widely known writing is *The Prophetic Faith of Our Fathers* (4 vols., 1946–54).

H. DOUGLAS BUCKWALTER

## Fry, Franklin Clark (1900–1968). American

Lutheran pastor and leader. Born in Bethlehem, Pa., he graduated from Hamilton College (1921), and was ordained as a Lutheran minister (1925), pastoring churches in Yonkers, N.Y. (1925–29), and Akron, Ohio (1929–44). He served as second president of the United Lutheran Church in America (1945–62), vice-chairman of American Relief for Korea (1950–54), chairman of the policy and strategy committee, National Council of Churches of Christ in USA (1954–60), president of the Lutheran World Federation (1957–63), chairman of the central and executive committees, World Council of Churches, and president of Lutheran World Relief, Inc.

## Fürbringer, Ludwig E. (1864–1947). Born in

Frankenmuth, Mich., he graduated from Concordia Seminary, St. Louis, Mo. (1885), and pastored a Lutheran church at Frankenmuth (1885–93). He was professor of biblical interpretation and liturgies at Concordia Seminary (1893–1947) and president (1931–43). He was president of the Evangelical Lutheran Synodical Conference (1920–47). For more than 45 years he was editor of the German biweekly religious periodical *Der Lutheraner*. His publications include *Letters of C. F. W. Walther* (2 vols., 1915, 1916), *The Book of Job* (1927), *The Eternal Why* (1947), and *Persons and Events* (1947). He was editor of M. Guenther's *Populaere Symbolik* (3d ed., 1898; 4th ed.,

1913), *Men and Missions Series* (1924–33), *Concordia Cyclopedia* (1927), *Die evangelischen Perikopen des Kirchenjahrs in Predigtstudien ausgelegt* (1932), *Thomasius Gospel Selections* (1937), and the autobiographical *Eighty Eventful Years* (1944).

FREDERICK E. MAYER

**Fuller, Charles E.** (1887–1968). California orange grower and Baptist pastor. Fuller was perhaps the most popular grass-roots evangelist in North America during the 1940s. Converted under the preaching of Paul Rader after graduating from Pomona College, Fuller later studied at the Bible Institute of Los Angeles. After some radio pioneering, in 1937 he persuaded the Mutual Broadcasting System to air his Old Fashioned Revival Hour, which quickly became a favorite Sunday afternoon radio program for millions of Americans. The live broadcasts from the Long Beach, Calif., Municipal Auditorium were heard over 625 stations during the 1940s. Fuller's programs were light, featuring letters and gospel music, while his messages were folksy, fatherly, and biblical, accenting the return of Christ. In 1947 Fuller provided the funds to launch the Fuller Theological Seminary in Pasadena, named for his father, now one of the largest theological schools in America with a strong evangelical commitment.

SHERWOOD E. WIRT

**Fundamental Churches of America.** *See* INDEPENDENT FUNDAMENTAL CHURCHES OF AMERICA.

**Fundamentalism.** Movement which first took shape primarily in the United States as a protest of conservative Protestants against theological modernism in the early 20th century. In reaction to more naturalistic theologies, fundamentalists emphasized certain fundamental doctrines such as the inerrancy of Scripture, the virgin birth of Christ, substitutionary atonement, the resurrection of Christ, and the second coming. (The exact list of these "fundamentals" has varied.) The term "fundamentalist" might be used to refer to any Christian who subscribes to such fundamentals, and in the British Isles the term often has that broad meaning.

In America, the principal center of fundamentalism, the movement has developed through a number of historical stages; accordingly the word has taken on more specific (though changing) meanings. In this primary context, "fundamentalism" refers to a movement among evangelical Protestants. The one definition that applies in almost all such cases is that fundamentalism is militant antimodernism. Since the 1970s, "fundamentalism," which initially had an almost exclusively evangelical Protestant reference, has been applied to other militantly antimodernist religious movements, especially Islamic fundamentalism.

The term "fundamentalism" was coined in 1920 by Curtis Lee Laws, a theologically conservative editor in the Northern Baptist Convention. He referred to the antimodernist party in his denomination. He also implicitly alluded to *The Fundamentals*, a 12-volume set of popular defenses of conservative evangelical Christianity, published from 1910 to 1915. William B. Riley, a Minnesota Baptist pastor, had also founded the World Christian Fundamentals Association (WCFA) in 1919.

The leadership behind *The Fundamentals* and WCFA was dispensationalist premillennial and represented the most important party shaping the new antimodernist coalition. Dispensationalists held that the Bible divided history into seven dispensations of differing administrations of God's rule, ending with the coming millennial reign of Christ in Jerusalem. They saw the return of the Jews to Palestine as an important part of the fulfillment of biblical prophecies. The most important vehicle for spreading dispensationalism was the *Scofield Reference Bible*, first published in 1909. Dispensationalists also stressed the inerrancy of Scripture and the prophesied apostasy of the major churches. Accordingly, they were especially militant antimodernists. They also preserved 19th-century revivalism's enthusiasm for aggressive evangelism and missions.

Another major component of the fundamentalist coalition that was emerging by 1920 was the Princeton theological tradition. The Princetonians were strict Presbyterian confessionalists. Their antimodernism and emphasis on the inerrancy of Scripture brought them into alliance with dispensationalists.

These early fundamentalist traditions may be distinguished from the separatist Holiness movements and from pentecostalism, with whom most fundamentalists disagreed doctrinally, despite many common traits and mutual influences. Many American fundamentalists did hold to the more moderate Holiness doctrines of the English Keswick Convention, a connection that illustrates the transatlantic dimension present in the movement.

During the 1920s denominationalist conservatives and dispensationalists led attacks on theological modernism in major American (and some Canadian) denominations, especially the Northern Baptist Convention and the (northern) Presbyterian Church in the USA. The fundamentalism of the 1920s took on a political dimension as well, as some fundamentalists emphasized preserving the United States as a Christian nation. Opposition to teaching biological evolution in public schools became their leading concern and led to antievolution legislation in a number of Southern states. William Jennings Bryan led this crusade, which reached a sensational focal point with the 1925 trial of John T. Scopes in Dayton, Tenn.

Although fundamentalism as organized antimodernism began in the Northern United States, it had counterparts in the heavily conservative Protestant South, from which it continued to draw strength in later decades.

After the controversies of the 1920s, many fundamentalists withdrew from major American denominations and formed their own networks of organizations. While most of America's major denominations declined, fundamentalism grew.

During the 1940s and 1950s the American fundamentalist coalition divided. Stricter fundamentalists remained militant, began to demand ecclesiastical separatism, and were usually dispensationalists. Other fundamentalists practiced or tolerated nonseparatism and stressed their broader Christian heritage. The latter, associated most notably with Billy Graham, became known as "neoevangelicals" or as simply "evangelicals."

In the South, fundamentalism continued to grow, not only in separate organizations but also in the Southern Baptist Convention. Southern Baptist fundamentalists were not separatists, since by the 1970s and 1980s they had prospects for controlling the convention and purging it of its moderates. The inerrancy of Scripture became the central symbol of their defense of the faith.

Beginning in the 1970s American fundamentalism became perceptibly more political. The most prominent manifestation of this activism was the Moral Majority, organized by Jerry Falwell in 1979. Political fundamentalists emphasized a return to traditional American Protestant values, antiabortion, antievolution, anticommunism, and support for Israel. Many pentecostals and charismatics took on similar political militancy.

Though Protestant fundamentalism has been primarily an American phenomenon, it has always had counterparts, especially in Canada and the British Isles. As a result of missionary efforts, it also has many international manifestations.

*Bibliography.* G. W. Dollar, *A History of Fundamentalism in America* (1973); G. M. Marsden, *Fundamentalism and American Culture: The Shaping of Twentieth-Century Evangelicalism* (1980); R. V. Pierard, *Evangelicalism and Modern America* (1984), 161–74, 206–12; E. R. Sandeen, *The Roots of Fundamentalism: British and American Millenarianism: 1800–1930* (1970); F. M. Szasz, *The Divided Mind of Protestant America, 1880–1930* (1982); T. P. Weber, *Living in the Shadow of the Second Coming: American Premillennialism, 1875–1982* (1982).

GEORGE M. MARSDEN

## Fundamentals Association, World Christian.

An organization originating in large interdenominational conventions held by evangelicals in the USA during and immediately after World War I. The World Conference on Christian Fundamentals, which convened in Philadelphia in May 1919, was the immediate stimulus. The association requires its members to subscribe to a nine-point doctrinal statement affirming belief in the inspiration and inerrancy of the Scriptures; the Trinity; the deity and virgin birth of Christ; the creation and fall of man; the substitutionary atonement; the bodily resurrection and ascension of Christ; the personal, premillennial, and imminent return of Christ; the regeneration of believers; and the bodily resurrection of men to everlasting blessedness or everlasting conscious punishment.

The president of the association from its founding until 1930 was William B. Riley. Under his leadership mass meetings were held throughout the USA to promote conservative Christian principles, premillennial eschatology, and opposition to the teaching of organic evolution. Interest lessened after the first decade. From 1930 to 1952 Paul W. Rood was president, with headquarters in Glendale, Calif., where the quarterly organ, *The Christian Fundamentalist*, was issued. A merger with the Slavic Gospel Association in 1952 brought an end to the separate existence of the organization.

*See also* FUNDAMENTALISM.

*Bibliography.* Conference Report, *God Hath Spoken* (1919); S. G. Cole, *The History of Fundamentalism* (1931).

PAUL WOOLLEY

**Gaebelein, Arno Clemens** (1861–1945). Evangelical scholar. Born in Thuringia, Germany, he emigrated to America at age 18 and was ordained in the Methodist Episcopal Church. During his 20s he held pastorates in Maryland and New Jersey before moving to New York City and beginning a ministry to Jews. In 1894 Gaebelein founded *Our Hope* magazine, devoting it to exposition, prophecy, and Jewish evangelism. It soon acquired worldwide circulation and continued until 1958. Gaebelein also lectured widely in the Bible conference movement. His 50 books, mostly on prophecy, contain a wealth of biblical detail and a strong sense of Zionist orthodoxy. Several of his works are *Commentary on Matthew* (2 vols., 1908), *Studies in Prophecy* (1917), *The Jewish Question* (1917), *His First and Second Coming* (1941), and the autobiographical *Half a Century* (1930).

SHERWOOD E. WIRT

**Gaebelein, Frank Ely** (1899–1983). American educator and biblical scholar. After graduating from New York and Harvard universities, he organized Stony Brook School on Long Island in 1921, and was its headmaster until 1963. He then became coeditor of *Christianity Today* magazine, during which time he participated in the 1965 civil rights march at Selma. A frequent speaker at educational and religious institutions and conferences, he also played a key part in preparing the New International Version of the Bible, bringing to the task a great concern for literary and stylistic excellence. Another major project was *The Expositor's Bible Commentary* series, of which he was general editor from its beginning in 1972 until his death. His many publications include *Down Through the Ages* (1924), *Exploring the Bible* (1929), *Philemon: The Gospel of Emancipation* (1939), *Christian Education in a Democracy* (1951), and *A Varied Harvest* (1967).

J. D. DOUGLAS

**Gairdner, William Henry Temple** (1873–1928). Scottish missionary to Egypt. Born in Ayr-shire, the son of a medical professor, he graduated from Oxford, was ordained in the Church of England in 1899, and at once went to Egypt where he was a missionary for the rest of his life. He became proficient in Arabic and Islamic studies, was cofounder with Douglas Thornton of the magazine *Orient and Occident*, and by the sanctity of his life made a profound impression for Christianity in an area not normally susceptible to the gospel.

J. D. DOUGLAS

**Galatians, Epistle to the.** *See* PAUL, THE APOSTLE.

**Gallagher, Buell Gordon** (1904–1978). Congregational minister and educator. Born in Rankin, Ill., he studied at Carleton College, Northfield, Minn., Union Theological Seminary, London School of Economics and Political Science, and Columbia University (Ph.D., 1939). He was instructor of economics, Doane College, Crete, Nebr. (1925–26), ordained as a Congregational minister (1929), national secretary of the National Interseminary Movement (1930–31), minister of the First Congregational Church at Passaic, N.J. (1931–33), president of Talladega (Ala.) College (1933–43), professor of Christian ethics, Pacific School of Religion (1944–49), consultant to the U.S. Office of Education (1950/51), assistant commissioner (1951/52), president of College of the City of New York (1952–61, 1962–69), chancellor of California State Colleges (1961/62), and president emeritus (1970–78). He chaired the U.S. general committee of World University Service (1953–66) and international assembly (1962–66), and was the democratic nominee for U.S. Congress from California in 1948. He wrote *American Caste and the Negro College* (1938), *Portrait of a Pilgrim: A Search for the Christian Way in Race Relations* (1946), *Color and Conscience: The Irrepressible Conflict* (1946), *A Preface to the Study of Utopias* (1960), and *Campus in Crisis* (1974). He also edited *College and the Black Student: National Association for the*

*Advancement of Colored People Tract for the Times* (1971).

H. DOUGLAS BUCKWALTER

**Galloway, George** (1861–1933). Presbyterian. Born in Stenton, Fifeshire, he studied at the universities of St. Andrews, Edinburgh, Göttingen, and Berlin. He was minister of Kelton Parish Church (1891–1915), when he became principal and primarius professor of theology, St. Mary's College, St. Andrews. He wrote *Studies in the Philosophy of Religion* (1904), *The Principles of Religious Development* (2 vols., 1909), *The Philosophy of Religion* (1914, 1935), *The Idea of Immortality* (1919), *Religion and Modern Thought* (1922), *Faith and Reason in Religion* (1929), and *Religion and the Transcendent* (1930).

ANDREW K. RULE

**Gambia.** *See* WEST AFRICA.

**Gambling**. Risk taking in games or sports involving chance. Risk associated with skill increases interest and excitement in life. It becomes an ethical problem when exploited to redistribute wealth without relation either to merit or to responsibility. Some forms of sport have existed mainly as a basis for gambling, and the temptation to "rig" results tends both to destroy sport and to corrupt society.

Christians historically have condemned gambling as akin to intemperance and sexual vices. It is an escapist device which preys on human weakness and greed, trading prudent use of personal resources for an infinitesimal chance of success. Even psychology treats gambling as an addiction, and support groups for compulsive gamblers have become common. From a religious standpoint, a consistent belief in chance renders belief in a sovereign, life-controlling God inconsistent.

Several phenomena made gambling more of an issue to 20th-century Christians. Gambling became accepted as a legitimate money-raising device for local churches. Raffles, bingo, and even casino-type games have been used; occasionally states have had to restrict more flagrant abuses by churches. State governments themselves began to sponsor lotteries and to license parimutuel racetracks and casino gambling to fund education and replace federal grants no longer available. In the 1830s poorly planned lotteries conceived to fund canal and road projects led several states into bankruptcy or recession. Many feared this new dependence on institutionalized gambling to be, at best, another secularizing and self-destructive influence on society.

**Gamertsfelder, Solomon J.** (1851–1925). Evangelical Association pastor and educator. Born near Warsaw, Ohio, he received his education at North Central College, Evangelical Theological Seminary, Wooster College (Ph.D., 1893), and Harvard University and the University of Chicago. After serving five pastorates of his denomination in Ohio, he became assistant editor of the denominational weekly, *The Evangelical Messenger* (1887–95). He was professor of systematic theology at Evangelical Theological Seminary (1895) and its president (1908–20). He wrote *Systematic Theology* (1921), and edited *The Baccalaureate Sermons and Addresses of President A. A. Smith* (1895).

PAUL H. ELLER

**Gandhi, Mohandas Karamchand (Mahatma)** (1869–1948). Vaishnavite Hindu. Born in Porbander, India, a true *karmayogin* (devotee of pathway of selfless action) in the tradition of the *Bhagavadgita*. Profoundly influenced by Henry Thoreau, Leo Tolstoy, and the Sermon on the Mount, he was a London matriculate, studied law at Inner Temple, and was called to the bar in 1891. In 1893 he went to Durban, Natal, took leadership of the 20-year nonviolent struggle for civil rights of Indians in South Africa, and in 1915 returned to India. He was engaged until 1947 in a nonviolent *Satyagraha* campaign of civil resistance to attain Indian independence. He spent 249 days in South African prisons, 2089 days in Indian jails, and fasted 12 times as vicarious penance. He was the architect of India's freedom through nonviolence and an unusual combination of saint, lawyer, and politician. He sought to apply the principles of *Satyagraha* (truth-force), *Ahimsa* (nonviolence), *Brahmacharya* (chastity), nonattachment to possessions, and renunciation, all for the attainment of complete self-rule for India through *Swadeshi* (indigenous self-sufficiency), the removal of untouchability for *Harijans* (God's children, his name for outcastes), Hindu-Muslim unity, and village uplift. He aimed to free India through the moral emancipation of her people and the awakening of the soul. Regarding religion he wrote: "All faiths constitute a revelation of Truth; but all are imperfect and liable to error. . . . We would think it our duty to blend into our faith every acceptable feature of other faiths." He was assassinated in New Delhi by a Hindu zealot in 1948.

*Bibliography.* R. Rolland, *Mahatma Gandhi* (1924); M. K. Gandhi, *An Autobiography; or the Story of My Experiments with Truth* (1927, 1929, 1945); M. K. Gandhi, *Satyagraha in South Africa* (1928); M. K. Gandhi, *Speeches and Writings of Mahatma Gandhi* (1933); S. Radhakrishnan, ed., *Mahatma Gandhi: Essays and Reflections on His Life and Work* (1939); E. S. Jones, *Mahatma Gandhi: An Interpretation* (1948); H. S. L. Polak, H. N. Brailsford, and Lord Pethick-Lawrence, *Mahatma Gandhi* (1949); V. Sheean, *Lead Kindly Light* (1949); L. Fischer, *The Life of Mahatma Gandhi* (1950); G. Ashe, *Gandhi* (1969); M. Chatterjee, *Gandhi's Religious Thought* (1983); and M. Juergensmeyer, *Fighting with Gandhi* (1984).

WILSON M. HUME

**Gandz, Solomon** (1884–1954). Jewish educator. Born in Tarnoberzeg, Austria, he studied at the University of Vienna (Ph.D., 1911) and at the Jewish Theological Seminary, Vienna. He taught Jewish history and religion at the Junior Colleges of Vienna (1915–19). From 1923 he lived in New York City, becoming a naturalized citizen in 1929. He was librarian and research professor at Yeshiva College (1924–34), research professor in the history of Semitic civilization, Dropsie College, Philadelphia (1942–54), Guggenheim Fellow (1936/37), and an associate editor of *Isis*. He wrote about 50 articles on the history of mathematics and civilization of the Semitic peoples and *Die Muallaqa des Imrulgais* (1913), *Monumenta Talmudica II* (1913/14), and *The Dawn of Literature, Prolegomena to a History of Unwritten Literature* (1939).

**Garbett, Cyril Forster** (1875–1955). Archbishop of York. He studied at Keble College, Oxford. Ordained a deacon in 1899 and a priest in 1901, he served at Portsea (1899–1919), Portsmouth (1915–19), and as dean of Southwark (1919–32). He was consecrated bishop of Southwark in 1919, where he served until translated to Winchester in 1932. Ten years later he became archbishop of York. He wrote *The Church and Modern Problems* (1911), *The Challenge of the King* (1915), *The Work of a Great Parish* (1919), *After the War* (1924), *Authority, Obedience and Reservation* (1925), *Secularism and Christian Unity* (1929), *In the Heart of South London* (1931), *The Challenge of the Slums* (1933), *A Call to Christians* (1935), *The Church and Social Problems in Peace and War* (1940), *We Would See Jesus* (1941), *Physician, Heal Thyself* (1945), *The Christian Churches and International Peace* (1945), *The Claims of the Church of England* (1947), *Watchman, What of the Night?* (1948), and *Church and State in England* (1950).

RAYMOND W. ALBRIGHT

**Garrard, Lancelot Austin** (1904– ). Unitarian scholar. Born in Yorkshire, he studied at the universities of Oxford and Marburg, and served Unitarian congregations in Dover, Bristol, and Liverpool (1932–52), during which time he was also tutor in the Unitarian colleges in Oxford and Manchester. In 1952 he returned to Oxford as tutor at Manchester College, and later served as principal (1956–65). He has been president of the college since 1980. He wrote *Duty and the Will of God* (1938), *The Interpreted Bible* (1948), *The Gospels To-day* (1953), *The Historical Jesus: Schweitzer's Quest and Ours* (1956), and *Athens or Jerusalem?* (1965). He was also editor of the *Hibbert Journal* (1951–62).

J. D. DOUGLAS

**Garrison, Winfred Ernest** (1874–1969). Disciples of Christ educator. Born in St. Louis, he studied at Eureka College, Yale, and Chicago (Ph.D., 1897). He was associate in history, Chicago (1897/98); professor of church history and Hebrew, Butler College (1898–1900; president 1904–6); president, New Mexico Normal University, Las Vegas (1907/8); president, New Mexico State College, Las Cruces (1908–13); headmaster and proprietor, Claremont School for Boys, Claremont, Calif. (1913–21); associate professor, then professor of church history, University of Chicago and Disciples Divinity House (1921–43); and literary editor of *The Christian Century* from 1923. He was president of the New Mexico Educational Association (1909/10) and of church history organizations. He also was associate at the Life and Work Conference, Oxford, 1937; a delegate to the Faith and Order Conference, Edinburgh, 1937; a consultant at the World Council of Churches Assembly, Amsterdam, 1948; a member of the Faith and Order Commission, Theological Commission on the Church, and American Theological Committee, as well as the New Mexico Constitutional Convention, 1910. He is the author of *Wheeling Through Europe* (1900), *Alexander Campbell's Theology* (1900), *Catholicism and the American Mind* (1928), *Affirmative Religion* (1928), *Religion Follows the Frontier* (1931), *The March of Faith: Religion in America since 1865* (1933), *Intolerance* (1934), *Faith of the Free* (1940), *An American Religious Movement* (1945), *Religion and Civil Liberty* (1946), and *Disciples of Christ: Whence and Whither* (1948). He wrote with A. T. DeGroot, *Disciples of Christ, A History* (1948), and edited with T. C. Clark, *100 Poems of Peace* (1934), and *100 Poems of Immortality* (1935).

**Garstang, John** (1876–1956). Archeologist. A mathematical scholar at Jesus College, Oxford, he served as an honorary reader in Egyptian archeology at Liverpool (1902) and taught the methods and practice of archeology (1907–41). From 1897 he conducted excavations on Roman sites in Britain, Egypt, Nubia, Asia Minor, and North Syria (1900–8); in the Sudan at Meroë (1909–14); and in Palestine at Ashkelon (1920/21) and Jericho (1930–36). He served as the director of the British School of Archeology in Jerusalem (1919–26) and directed the department of antiquities for the government of Palestine (1920–26). His publications include *El Arâbah: A Cemetery of the Middle Kingdom* (1901), *Tombs of the Third Egyptian Dynasty* (1904), *The Burial Customs of Ancient Egypt* (1907); *The Land of the Hittites* (1910), *Meroë: The City of the Ethiopians* (1911), *The Hittite Empire* (1930), *The Foundations of Bible History: Joshua, Judges* (1931), *The Heritage of Solomon* (1934), and *Reports on the Excavations* *of Abydos, Meroë, Jericho and Mersin* in *Annals of Archeology* (1908–40).

RAYMOND W. ALBRIGHT

**Gasparri, Pietro** (1852–1934). Cardinal. Born in Capovallazza, Italy, he studied at the *Seminario Romano,* and was ordained in 1877. He taught canon law in Rome and Paris, and held various charges in the Vatican diplomacy. A cardinal from 1907 he headed the Commission for the Codification of Canon Law. Secretary of state under Benedict XV and Pius XI, he prepared the accords of the Lateran between the Vatican and Italy (1929). In 1930, he published the *Catechismus Romanus,* as a model for the reduction of diocesan catechisms.

**Bibliography.** F. M. Taliani, *Vita del cardinale Gasparri, segretario di Stato e povero prete* (1938).

GEORGES A. BARROIS

**Gavin, Frank Stanton Burns** (1890–1938). Episcopalian educator and author. Born in Cincinnati, Ohio, he studied at the University of Cincinnati, Hebrew Union College, General Theological Seminary, Columbia University (Ph.D., 1923), and Harvard University (Th.D., 1919). Gavin was a novice in the Society of St. John the Evangelist (1916–21), taught NT at Nashotah House, Wis. (1921–23), and church history at General Seminary (1923–38). After living a year in Athens, he wrote *Some Aspects of Contemporary Greek Orthodox Thought* (1923). He also wrote *Aphraates and the Jews* (1923), *Jewish Antecedents of the Christian Sacraments* (1928), *Seven Centuries of the Problem of Church and State* (1938), and edited *Liberal Catholicism and the Modern World* (1934).

EDWARD R. HARDY

**Gehman, Henry Snyder** (1888–1981). OT scholar. Born on a farm near Ephrata, Pa., he studied at Franklin and Marshall College and later at the University of Pennsylvania (Ph.D., 1913). He taught Semitics for several decades, first at Princeton University and later at Princeton Seminary. He was instrumental in changing the seminary's climate from traditional orthodoxy to an atmosphere hospitable to higher criticism. He earned a doctorate in 1927 at the Philadelphia Divinity School of the Protestant Episcopal Church, and joined the Presbyterian Church. His grasp of Semitic languages, and his insistence on the union of piety and learning (in opposition to fundamentalism) profoundly affected the direction of theological education at Princeton. His published works included *The Interpreters of Foreign Languages among the Ancients* (1914), *The Sahidic and the Bohairic Versions of the Book of Daniel* (1927), and *Some Present-Day Values of OT Studies* (1934). He edited the OT section of the *Westminster Study Bible* (1948), and revised an earlier Bible dictionary which was published as the *Westminster Dictionary of the Bible*.

**Gemeinschaftsbewegung.** A pietist movement of German Christians dating back to 1848. Efforts to combine the aims and objectives of pietist circles in the Rhineland led to the formation of an evangelical fellowship in Germany which combined influences from a Holiness movement emanating from Oxford, England, and the stress on evangelizing all levels of society through socially aware evangelical piety, promoted by A. Stoecker and J. H. Wichern. Branch organizations evolved in the 1880s, supported by leading Christian laypersons and theologians. Some groups within the "fellowship" movement, such as the Gnadauer Verband, saw themselves as *ecclesiolae in ecclesia.* The Blankenburger Allianz (1888), on the other hand, sought to distance itself from ecclesial structures.

One century later the movement stresses evangelization, sanctification of its members, intensive spiritual nurture of members of the territorial churches through regular study of the Bible and Christian tradition and by maintaining active prayer cells. Members are encouraged to turn away from the world and to focus on the "inner life." The loosely organized groups stress personal Christian commitment, pastoral care, and mutual spiritual nurture. The celebration of agape-like communion is frequent. There is a common disregard of "nonessentials" in corporate worship and in the daily conduct of the members.

The movement's positive impact on Protestant church life has been to stimulate large-scale missionary activity at home and abroad and charitable work in the core of large cities. Negative factors are a rather conservative approach to Christian teaching, perfectionist tendencies, and a narrow view of the world.

*See also* GNADAUER VERBAND.

E. J. FURCHA

**General Synod.** The central legislative body of the Church of England, part of the system of synodical government introduced in 1970. Some parts of the new system, such as parish church councils, were already in existence. The deanery and diocesan conferences were modified to become deanery and diocesan synods. Reform simplified church governance. In the general synod one body replaced five, the upper and lower houses of the convocations of York and Canterbury and the Church Assembly. The governing bodies at most levels were also smaller and efficiently organized. There were, however, more lay electors from the deanery level instead of, as before, from the diocese, involved in electing the general synod. Another purpose for reorganization might be described as "linking." Matters could be referred in a systematic way, either down from the general synod to lower levels, including the parish, or from the parish, through the various levels, up to the general synod.

The general synod consists of three houses: bishops, clergy, and laity. The house of bishops includes 43 diocesan bishops plus nine suffragan bishops. The house of clergy consists of 15 representatives from deans and provosts, one archdeacon from each diocese, a small number from specialized areas of work, and the rest, known as proctors, are elected by clergy in each diocese. The house of laity consists of representatives from each diocese, elected by the lay members of the deanery synod. Elections take place once every five years.

The primary purpose of the general synod is to prepare legislation, since the nature of the relationship with the state requires Parliament to approve some changes. The general synod is the only body in England which has the right to present measures to Parliament, which can be rejected but not amended. However, such legislation is less frequent since 1974 when the church was given permission by Parliament to order its own worship and doctrine. One consequence of this was the production in 1970 of an alternative to the 1662 Prayer Book, known as the Alternative Services Book. Much of the general synod's business is channeled through its four main boards: mission and unity, ministry, social responsibility, and education. While many of its deliberations concern the life of the Church of England directly, there are also debates on matters of national and international importance. Decisions are usually made by simple majority votes, though more serious matters need a two-thirds majority. The general synod is also responsible for central church finances, especially the cost of training for ordination.

Since 1977 there has been a new method in the Church of England for appointing bishops. The general synod elects six of its members, three clergy and three laity, to sit with the two archbishops and four members elected from a vacant diocese, to send two names forward to the crown for consideration to fill the bishopric.

PETER S. DAWES

## Gerhardt, Martin (1894–1952).

Lutheran educator. Born in Berlin, Germany, he studied at the universities of Berlin, Tübingen, and Erlangen (Ph.D., 1924). He was lecturer at Erlangen University (1922), archivist of the Rauhes Haus at Hamburg (1923–31), established the Wichern archives and edited the youth diaries of Wichern (*Der junge Wichern*) and The Inner Mission (*Die Innere Mission*), a memorandum to the German Evangelical Church by J. Hinrich Wichern. From 1931 to 1937 he was archivist of the Kaiserswerth Deaconess-Institution and established the Fliedner archives and the special library on deaconess

service. In 1937 he was appointed professor of church history at Göttingen University with an interruption (1940–45) for army service in Norway. He wrote *Johann Hinrich Wichern* (3 vols., 1926–31), *Theodor Fliedner* (2 vols., 1933–37), *Norwegische Geschichte* (1942), *Ein Jahrhundert Innere Mission* (1948), *Friedrich von Bodelschwingh* (2 vols., 1950, 1952), and coauthored *Deutschland und Skandinavien im Wandel der Jahrhunderte* (1950).

## German Evangelical Synod of North America. See EVANGELICAL AND REFORMED CHURCH.

## German Democratic Republic (GDR).

Popularly known as East Germany, a nation of 108,333 sq. km. (41,828 sq. mi.) and approximately 17 million population (1988). When Germany was partitioned following World War II East Germany joined the Warsaw Pact alliance and became a strongly Marxist and militantly atheistic East bloc satellite, despite historic ties to the Protestant Reformation and a large population who retained Christian identification. A revolution on Nov. 9, 1989, left the country's political status uncertain and world superpowers immediately began discussions aimed at developing a much more open and democratic society and possibly political reunification with West Germany.

Even before the revolution, the DGR was almost exclusively Christian and overwhelmingly Protestant in its religious life, apart from tiny communities of Jews who continued to experience some anti-Semitic pressure. Most Protestants belong to the eight regional churches which, with the Moravian church, make up the GDR's Federation of Evangelical Churches. Owing to the one-time established position of Lutheranism in German society, over three-quarters of the population were reckoned Protestant when the GDR was established in 1949. At reunification estimates of practicing Protestants ranged from 3 million to 5 million. Nevertheless, despite difficulties, the parish system continued as the churches tried to adapt themselves to new conditions. For instance, *Kirchentage*, congresses which include services, meetings, exhibitions, and discussions extending over several days, might attract more than 100,000 people.

An estimated total of 1.25 million Roman Catholics in 1949 did not decline markedly. As a minority in a largely atheist state whose religious life is dominated by Protestantism, the Catholic Church often tended toward a defensive mentality, with the faith carefully taught, good attendance at Mass, and parish life excellently organized. Pilgrimages and processions displayed the gospel to the outside world.

Other confessions include Orthodox, Old Catholics, Old Lutherans, Methodists, Mennonites, and various Free Evangelical congregations. Among other recognized groups and sects the New Apostolic Church is notable. The GDR's third strongest confession, with at least 100,000 members, the group survived the Nazi era without being banned and afterward grew. The Jehovah's Witnesses have been the only proscribed sect.

Churches play an active social role in the area of the former GDR. Both Protestants and Catholics run hospitals, nursing and convalescent homes, homes for the elderly, and children's care centers. There are Protestant and Catholic publishing houses. Church music flourish, and a Christian presence was even felt in broadcasting and television under the communist government.

With the 1989 revolution a radically new role opened for the church in the new political affairs. Before 1990 there existed in theory, and to a considerable extent in practice, a strict division between church and state. The churches appointed their own officers and own buildings and land. A policy of avoiding involvement with the state as far as possible and concentrating on religious activities was followed by the Roman Catholic Church, the New Apostolic Church, and the smaller confessions. The majority Protestants (members of the Federation), with their watchword "the Church within socialism," sometimes insisted on voicing the claims of the gospel in social and political affairs. On important questions church and state disagreed: the treatment of conscientious objectors; different understandings of the terms "peace" and "justice"; the state's assumed right to train the young in Marxism; and the imprisonment of individual believers who campaigned publicly for what they believe to be Christian causes. High-status occupations contained only a tiny handful of believers. State spokesmen claimed that Christian candidates were never rejected on religious grounds, but because they did not have a positive attitude toward Marxist society, an indispensable qualification for influential positions. This assessment turned out to understate Christian disaffection with Marxism. Lutheran churches in particular were critical to sparking the peaceful overthrow of Marxism. Weekly prayer meetings in churches became rallying points for Germans who supported democratization. Whether that influence would continue to pervade a new government and the secular society that would eventually emerge remained to be seen.

PHILIP WALTERS

## Germany, Federal Republic of (FRG).
Until reunification with East Germany in 1990, known popularly as West Germany. With 60.5 million (1988) West Germany was the most populated nation of Europe. Southern West Germany and the Rhineland are heavily Roman Catholic while the rest of the country is nominally Protestant, augmented by Protestant refugees from Eastern Europe since World War II.

Roman and other non-Germanic enclaves of Christians in German lands are reported as early as the late 2d century A.D. Germanic nations themselves adopted Christianity somewhat later–first an Arian faith and, by the end of the 5th century, the "catholic" form. Among the Franks in Gaul structures emerged which integrated territorial interests and a certain political autonomy, vested in the emperor, with the spiritual authority which was centered in Rome. At the height of this development, the "holy Roman Empire of the German Nation" incorporated the emperor and pope as two poles within which various ethnic and political forces were held in unified tension. This fundamental structure remained until the Reformation of the 16th century.

During the Reformation religious, economic, and social forces contributed to the emergence of new political constellations. The Peace of Westphalia (1648) helped settle religious conflicts by recognizing the Reformed, Lutheran, and Roman Catholic expressions of the Christian faith as legitimate religious entities within territorial boundaries. The operative principle was that the religious confession of the regent of a territory determined the religious affiliation of the subjects in that area. Dissenters were free to leave one territory for another germane to their persuasion. These stringent rules were relaxed in the wake of the Enlightenment. Not until the 19th century, however, did religious minorities gain legal status as "free churches."

Clearly, the geographic and political shape of Germany underwent significant changes after the days of the Holy Roman Empire, none more traumatic than those which succeeded the unconditional surrender in May 1945 of the Nazi regime. In the partition of Germany after the war were born the German Democratic Republic (GDR) and the Federal Republic of Germany (FRG) in 1949. Independent monetary reforms during the summer of 1948 and the cold war between the former allies contributed to the growing separation between the GDR and the FRG. The Federal Republic came into being when the 11 western territories (*Länder*)—which were under a form of trusteeship of the French, British, and USA governments—adopted a new constitution (*Grundgesetz*) on August 23, 1949. Because of the continuing special status and the location of the former capital, Berlin (it was surrounded by territories under control of the USSR), Bonn was chosen as the capital of the FRG. After Germany reunited, Berlin was again named as the capital.

Church life in the FRG has undergone similarly far-reaching changes since 1945. Under the Nazis, the Protestant churches in Germany were shaken by severe theological and administrative conflicts. These were caused, in part, by the emergence of the government collaborating "German-Christians" and by far-reaching interference through organs of the state in spiritual life and ecclesiastical affairs. The Confessing Church movement, developed by signers of the Barmen Declaration, was intended to counteract these pressures; its influence, however, was limited. After 1945 German Protestantism (and to a lesser extent the Roman Catholic Church) had to find new structures and appropriate ways of proclamation and outreach to survive the crisis.

The rebuilding process began with a church conference at Treysa in 1945, which laid the foundation for the Evangelical Church of Germany (EKD). Another helpful event was the adoption of a declaration of guilt (*Stuttgarter Schuldbekenntnis*) by the council of the EKD in October 1945. The EKD worked to establish new constitutions which would order church life in the Lutheran, Reformed, and United territorial churches and safeguard against future interference in church affairs by external forces. To preserve the confessional nature of the Lutheran tradition the United Evangelical Lutheran Church of Germany (VELKD) was created. At the same time, the ecumenical nature of German Protestantism was underlined in the reshaping of the Evangelical Church of the Union (EKU). Both bodies belong to the EKD and take an active part in the World Council of Churches (WCC) and in the Lutheran World Federation. Through these bodies a vital spiritual link between Protestant Christians in the two German states is maintained.

Largely because of major population movements after 1945, changes in the regional distribution of the major Christian confessions have taken place. Many formerly predominantly Roman Catholic or Protestant areas tended toward a balance or showed marked increases in the erstwhile minority, particularly in Bavaria and Nordrhein-Westphalia. The impact of secularizing trends eventually reduced the Christian population until it was a minority in the GDR.

According to the 1950 census 51.7 percent of the population was nominally Protestant, 45.2 percent Roman Catholic, 3.5 percent listed no religious affiliation, and 0.2 percent were estimated to belong to other religious communities. These figures have since changed to show a higher percentage of people with no religious affiliation and of those who belong to non-Christian religious communities.

In the 1980s congregational life in Protestant churches had not changed significantly from what it was prior to 1945. The clergy was accorded high social standing and assumed major responsibility in administration and spiritual leadership. In addition to traditional Sunday worship pastors handled most religious instruc-

tion of young people prior to confirmation and performed the rituals related to birth, marriage, and death. Congregations and higher church courts suffered from the resulting lack of active lay involvement and occasionally even from a shortage of clergy. Ordination of women clergy eased this gap. Ecumenical cooperation among Protestants, Roman Catholics, and Free Churches was more prominent than before 1945. Most major universities continued to have theological faculties for Protestants and Catholics.

The Roman Catholic Church in Germany involved itself in parochial and the socioreligious concerns of many of its church-related organizations. Despite a shortage of priests and less interest among young people in religious orders, the Roman church remained a significant force in the spiritual life of its people.

In late 1990 the effect of reunification on the church remained uncertain. Commentators generally were afraid that the East Germans would bring into the church organizations far more impetus toward materialism than spirituality.

One early indication of the lack of enthusiasm for religion came even before October 1990 reunification. Since West Germany has long collected a tax from Christians to support churches, East Germans were given an opportunity in advance to sign up for the exemption from religious taxes. They did so in enormous numbers. One respected polling organization estimated the number of Protestants in what was East Germany at 3 million, instead of the 5 million which had been estimated.

Reunification also was expected to make united Germany a slightly more Protestant than Roman Catholic nation. West Germany had 26.5 million Catholics and 25 million Protestants in late 1990. The merger made the figures about 27.2 million Catholics and 28 million Protestants. Virtually all additions were to state churches. Baptist, Methodist, and Episcopal churches (the free church bodies) were few but more spiritually healthy. A drastic increase in those bodies was anticipated by some analysts.

*See also* BARMEN DECLARATION; GERMAN DEMOCRATIC REPUBLIC.

**Bibliography.** RGG (3d ed., 1958) (see esp. "Deutschland"); R. Kunze, *Kooperativer Föderalismus in der Bundesrepublik* (1968); U. Scheuner, *Kooperation und Konflikt* (1972); *Evangelisches Staatslexikon* (1975) (see esp. "Bundestaat" and "Deutsches Reich").

E. J. FURCHA

**Gerstenmaier, Eugen** (1906–1986). Born in Kirchheim unter Teck, he studied in Tübingen, Rostock, and Zurich, and was ordained in the Lutheran Church. He was a parish minister before entering political life in 1936. Until 1944 he worked in external affairs within the German Evangelical Church. For his activities in the Confessing Church and in the resistance movement against Adolf Hitler (the Kreisauer Circle) he was arrested and held in a concentration camp until the end of World War II. In 1945 he founded the Evangelische Hilfswerk and served as its director until 1951. He joined the Christian Democratic Union (CDU), and became a member of the Bundestag (1948) and later became its president (1954–59). In 1950 he became a delegate to the Council of Europe. As a member of the CDU caucus and its vice-chairman (1956–69), he played a leading role in representing the Protestant interests within CDU. Many of his writings reflect the interaction of ecclesiastical and political power in international relations. Notable publications include *Kirche, Volk, und Staat* (1937), *Die Kirche und die Schöpfung* (1938), *Hilfe für Deutschland* (1946), *Reden und Aufsätze* (2 vols., 1956–62), and *Neuer Nationalismus? Von der Wandlung der Deutschen* (1965). H. Kunst published a festschrift in 1966, *Für Freiheit und Recht: Eugen Gerstenmaier zum 60. Geburtstag.* F. von Schlabrendorff assessed his career during the Hitler years in *Eugen Gerstenmaier im Dritten Reich* (1965).

E. J. FURCHA

**Gezork, Herbert** (1900– ). Baptist minister, educator, and leader. Born in Insterburg, Germany, he studied at the University of Berlin, the Divinity School in Hamburg, and Southern Baptist Theological Seminary, Louisville (Ph.D., 1930). He was associate minister, First Baptist Church, Berlin (1925–28); general secretary, German Baptist Youth Movement (1930–34); professor of religion, Furman University, Greenville, S.C. (1937/38); professor of social ethics, Andover Newton Theological School (1939–50); lecturer, Wellesley College (1939–50); Chief of Evangelical Affairs, U.S. Military Government in Germany (1946–48); president, Andover Newton Theological School (1950–65); visiting professor, Harvard Divinity School (1965–68); and director, department of religion, Chautauqua Institution (1968–72). He was president of the American Baptist Convention (1959–60). He wrote *Die Gottlosenbewegung* (1932), and *So Sah Ich die Welt* (in German, Dutch, Finnish, 1933).

**Ghana.** *See* WEST AFRICA.

**Ghéon, Henri** (1875–1944). Pseudonym of Leon Vangeon, a Roman Catholic dramatist. Born in Bray-sur-Marne, France, he promoted a revival of the Christian theater in the spirit of the medieval scenic plays, through *Nos directions* (1911), *L'homme né de la guerre* (1919), and *Parti pris* (1924). His religious dramas usually borrowed their theme from the legends of the saints, as, for instance, *Le comédien et la grâce*, *Les trois miracles de Sainte Cécile*, and *Saint Maurice ou*

*l'obéissance*. He also wrote hagiographic fragments and a few poems of mystical inspiration.

GEORGES A. BARROIS

**Gibbons, James** (1834–1921). Roman Catholic cardinal. Born in Baltimore, he received his early education in Ireland, but returned to the USA in 1851, and lived for several years in New Orleans. He studied at St. Charles' College, Ellicott City, Md. (1855–57), and at St. Mary's Seminary, Baltimore (1857–61), and after ordination served in Baltimore until 1868 when he was consecrated titular bishop of Adramytum and appointed vicar apostolic of North Carolina. In 1872 he became bishop of Richmond, Va., and in 1877 he returned to Baltimore as archbishop coadjutor for five months before succeeding to the see, thus becoming primate of the Roman Catholic Church in the USA. He presided over the Third Plenary Council at Baltimore in 1884, and was made cardinal by Leo XIII in 1886. He was the first chancellor of the Catholic University of America (1889), and contributed impressively against strong opposition to the acceptance of his church in America. He was author of *The Faith of Our Fathers* (1871), *Our Christian Heritage* (1889), *The Ambassador of Christ* (1896), and *A Retrospect of Fifty Years* (1917).

**Gibraltar.** Since 1713, a British fortress colony on the Spanish side of the Straits of Gibraltar in the eastern Mediterranean. Gibraltar has a unique ecclesiastical as well as political status. The local population of about 28,000 is largely of Italian origin, and about 78 percent are Roman Catholic. In 1806 Gibraltar was made a Vicariate Apostolic, and in 1910 a diocese directly subject to the Holy See. The Church of the Holy Trinity, built in Moorish style in 1825, is the cathedral of the Anglican diocese of Gibraltar, established in 1842, with jurisdiction over the English churches and chaplaincies in southern Europe. The first bishop, George Tomlinson, was active in reopening communications between the Church of England and the Eastern churches, and several other distinguished scholars and missionaries have occupied the see. One of the few British Crown Colonies left, Gibraltar has a substantial garrison force which, with British civilian residents, has consolidated the presence also of Presbyterian and Methodist congregations.

**Gideons International, The.** An association of Christian business and professional people founded in 1899 in Boscobel, Wis. In 1908 the group began what became its primary evangelistic focus, to distribute free Bibles and New Testaments. There are now more than 88,000 members of the Gideons in more than 130 countries. These laypersons speak at churches to raise funds for Bible printing and place Scriptures in public places such as hotels, motels, and hospitals. Where allowed Gideons personally distribute Scriptures at schools, colleges, and prisons and to military personnel and nursing staffs, among others. As of July 1986 more than 385 million Scriptures in 55 languages have been placed worldwide.

**Gifford, William Alva** (1877–1960). Canadian church historian and theologian. Born in Ottawa, he graduated from the University of Toronto and Victoria College, Toronto. His first pastorate after ordination (1908) was in British Columbia. From 1910 to 1912 he taught classics at Columbian College, Vancouver, before pursuing graduate studies at Harvard (D.Th., 1915). For a time after World War I he taught at the Kakhi University, Ripon, England. His outstanding contribution to theological education spanned 34 years as professor of church history and historical theology at Wesleyan College, Montreal, and after joining the United Church in the 1925 union of churches at its United Theological College in Montreal. During this time he served both at the college and as professor of religion in the faculty of divinity, McGill University, until his retirement in 1949.

His writings reflect what might be called a liberal evangelicalism, proffering challenge and encouragement to Christians whom he believed to be living at the end of the era of triumphalist Christendom. His best known books were *The Christian and War* (1926), *The Eternal Quest* (1939), *The Story of the Faith* (1946), and *The Seekers* (1954). In addition, he delivered numerous speeches and wrote articles on topics of historical and current interest.

E. J. FURCHA

**Gilkey, Charles W(hitney)** (1882–1968). Baptist. Born in Watertown, Mass., he was educated at Harvard, Union Theological Seminary, Berlin, Marburg, and at United Free Church College, Glasgow, New College, Edinburgh, and Oxford. He was the student secretary of the International Committee of the YMCA (1903–5). After ordination to the Baptist ministry in 1910 he became pastor of the Hyde Park Church, Chicago (1910–28). After teaching homiletics at the divinity school of the University of Chicago (1926–47), he became the dean of the chapel at that university (1928–47), and associate dean of the divinity school (1938–47). After 1948 he became lecturer on homiletics at Andover-Newton Theological School. In 1924/25 he was Barrows Lecturer to university centers in India. He wrote *Jesus and Our Generation* (1925), *New Frontiers for Faith* (1926), *Present Day Dilemmas in Religion* (1927), and *Perspectives* (1933).

RAYMOND W. ALBRIGHT

**Gilmore, George William** (1857–1933). American Congregational scholar. Born in London, he studied at Princeton University and Union Theological Seminary, N.Y. In 1886 the U.S. Commissioner of Education, at the request of the king of Korea, appointed Gilmore to found the Royal Korean College at Seoul. He returned to America in 1889, and after various teaching appointments went to Bangor Theological Seminary, Maine, where he taught Bible and comparative religion (1893–99), after which he was professor of OT language and literature and the history of religion at Meadville Theological School (1899–1906). From 1905 he was a member of the editorial staff of the *New Schaff-Herzog Encyclopedia of Religious Knowledge,* to which he contributed the main part of its bibliography and numerous articles, especially on comparative religion. In addition to many studies in scientific and theological periodicals and book reviews on OT subjects and comparative religion, he was the author of *Korea from Its Capital* (1892), *The Johannean Problem* (1895), *Animism—Thought Currents of Primitive Peoples* (1919), *Tax Talks* (1925), and was editor of *Selections from the Classics of Devotion* (1916) and *Cobern's Archaeological Discoveries* (1922, 1924, 1929). He also translated several German theological works into English.

**Gilson, Etienne Henry** (1884–1978). French scholar. Born in Paris, he studied at the university there and at the Collège de France. After teaching philosophy in various colleges (1908–12) he taught briefly at the University of Lille before becoming a decorated army officer during World War I (1914–18). Thereafter he was professor at the universities of Strasbourg (1919–21) and Paris (1921–32), and at the Collège de France (1932–50). Having played a major role in the founding of the Pontifical Institute of Medieval Studies at the University of Toronto in 1929, he made this the center for his academic activity in latter years. A Thomist and an authority on the history of philosophy, he published many highly acclaimed works, including *The Spirit of Mediaeval Philosophy* (1936), *Reason and Revelation in the Middle Ages* (1939), *God and Philosophy* (1941), *History of Christian Philosophy in the Middle Ages* (1955), and, along with Thomas Langan, *Modern Philosophy: Descartes to Kant* (1963).

J. D. DOUGLAS

**Gingerich, Melvin** (1902–1975). Mennonite writer and educator. Born in Kalona, Iowa, into a distinguished family of Amish Mennonites, he graduated from Goshen College and the University of Iowa (Ph.D., 1938). Between 1927 and 1941 he taught at junior schools; from 1941 to 1947 he lectured at Bethel College before being called to Goshen College in 1949. In 1947 he became the first director of the Mennonite

Research Foundation, serving concurrently as archivist of the Mennonite Church until 1970. His major contribution to Mennonite life came through his editorial work with the *Mennonite Quarterly Review,* the *Mennonite Encyclopedia,* the *Mennonite Historical Bulletin,* and *Studies in Anabaptist and Mennonite History.* Among his own publications are *Mennonites in Iowa* (1939), *Service for Peace* (1949), *Youth and Christian Citizenship* (1949), and *Mennonite Attire through 4 Centuries* (1970). His private papers and unfinished manuscripts further attest to his work in the cause of Mennonite history. An autobiography, "The Making of a Mennonite Historian," was published in *Mennonite Life* 26 (1971). The *Mennonite Quarterly Review* dedicated its April 1978 issue to Gingerich.

E. J. FURCHA

**Ginsberg, Harold Louis** (1903– ). Leading scholar of Hebrew Bible and related fields. Born in Montreal, Ginsberg studied in London and began publishing in 1928. From 1941 he taught Bible at the Jewish Theological Seminary of America, New York. His approach was philological, interpreting the biblical text in the light of Near Eastern languages and cultures. He has devoted special studies to Ecclesiastes and Daniel. In *The Israelian Heritage of Judaism* (1982), he argued for an Israelite provenance for the Book of Deuteronomy, and traced its influence on biblical writings. He served as vice-president of the American Academy for Jewish Research (1969/70), honorary president of the American Society of Biblical Literature (1969), and was an editor of the American Jewish Publication Society translation of the Prophets.

ELIEZER SEGAL

**Girgensohn, Karl** (1875–1925). Lutheran theologian and educator. Born in Oesel, Latvia, he taught theology at Dorpat, Estonia (1903–18), Greifswald, Germany (1919–22), and Leipzig (1922–25). He was a conservative theologian, and a leader in experimental psychology of religion. His principal works are *Die Religion, ihre psychischen Formen und ihre Zentralidee* (1903), and *Der seelische Aufbau des religiösen Erlebens* (1921).

*Bibliography.* Autobiography in *Die Religionswissenschaft in Selbstdarstellungen,* Vol. 2 (1926).

OTTO A. PIPER

**Gladden, Washington** (1836–1918). Congregationalist pastor and writer. Born in Pottsgrove, Pa., he graduated from Williams College, and held pastorates in Brooklyn and Morrisania, N.Y., and North Adams and Springfield, Mass., before beginning in 1882 a 32-year ministry at the First Congregational Church, Columbus, Ohio. During the early part of his career he had served on the editorial staff of the New York *Independent,* and

while at Springfield he also edited the *Sunday Afternoon* for two years. Among his many books are *Plain Thoughts on the Art of Living* (1868), *Workingmen and Their Employers* (1876), *Being a Christian* (1876), *The Lord's Prayer* (1880), *The Young Men and the Churches* (1885), *Applied Christianity* (1887), *Who Wrote the Bible?* (1891), *The Church and the Kingdom* (1894), *Social Facts and Forces* (1897), *Art and Morality* (1897), *The Christian Pastor* (1898), *Straight Shots at Young Men* (1900), *The Practise of Immorality* (1901), *Christianity and Socialism* (1905), *The Church and Modern Life* (1908), *Recollections* (1909), *Present Day Theology* (1913), and *Live and Learn* (1914).

**Glegg, Alexander Lindsay** (1882–1975). British lay evangelist. Born in London of Scottish parents, he trained at London University as an electrical engineer and was in business for much of his life. After conversion at the Keswick Convention in 1905, however, his great love was evangelism. For nearly five decades he maintained a ministry in a deprived area of London. As a Free Churchman he surprisingly won acceptance in Anglican circles and once preached (and made an evangelistic appeal) in Westminster Abbey. His meetings during the dark days of World War II crowded out London's Albert Hall. He was a spiritual encourager and financial supporter of many young evangelists and of missionary societies, and founded an annual holiday camp that brought thousands of families to North Yorkshire. Fellow evangelist Billy Graham acknowledged a great debt to Glegg. His popularly styled evangelical writings, which went all over the world, include *Life with a Capital "L"* and *Four Score and More.*

J. D. DOUGLAS

**Glossolalia.** A phenomenon related to human speech dating back to the earliest periods of recorded history. It has been defined by W. J. Samarian as "a meaningless but phonologically structured human utterance believed by the speaker to be a real language, but bearing no systematic resemblance to any natural language, living or dead." It appears to have played a part in the experience of folk religion in ancient Mesopotamia, Egypt, and even Greece. As a general rule, however, such ecstatic utterances were considered to be outside the generally accepted boundaries of the upper classes of these societies.

While there is some evidence to suggest that the phenomenon occurred in the context of prophecy in ancient Israel, there is no explicit mention of it in the OT. Reference to glossolalia in the NT is found in Acts and the epistles of Paul, most explicitly in 1 Cor. 12–14. The author of the Acts clearly understood the utterances on the day of Pentecost to be of known languages which were understood. The early church accepted the occurrence of this phenomenon as evidence that God was extending his mission to the Gentile world (Acts 11:15–18).

Paul assumes that normally the tongues phenomenon should be actual language, although he allowed for ecstatic utterances as (facetiously?) "the language of angels" (1 Cor. 13:1). It is clear that the utterances were not understood by the Corinthian church. Thus Paul instructed that while such languages might be a gift of the Holy Spirit, they must be interpreted when uttered in a public meeting.

Data on glossolalia following the NT era are scarce and often ambiguous. Often it is not clearly differentiated from the gift of prophecy. Although evidence suggests that the phenomenon was experienced in almost every century of the Christian era, most manifestations appeared among groups who were labeled heretical by the mainstream of the church. Little is known about the significance or meaning these groups placed upon the presence of this phenomenon.

A major origin of the modern expression of glossolalia in the church is eschatological in nature and can be traced to the events which led to the establishment of the Catholic Apostolic Church in 1835. The phenomenon began to occur throughout Scotland earlier in the decade. Interpretations of these "messages" suggested that Christ was returning soon. The phenomenon and interpretation supported the expectations of several prominent churchmen in England, who, in a study of biblical prophecy, came to believe that the world was entering a final tribulation period before the "biblically predicted" end of history. Believing themselves to be the restored Apostolate, they established the new church in the conviction that through it would come a worldwide "end-time" revival, which would, among other things, restore the gifts of the Spirit to the church.

In this mission, the new church failed, and indeed became cultic in nature. However, many of its themes were shared by emerging groups of the 19th century. The Plymouth Brethren, the Adventists, such Restoration movements as the Church of Christ and Church of God, the Prophecy Conference Movement, the Wesleyan/Holiness Movement and Keswick Higher Life Movement were some of the groups which emerged during the century that looked for the imminent close of the church age. Most, if not all, felt that the charismatic gifts would be restored during a final worldwide outpouring of the Holy Spirit upon the church. Glossolalia, in particular, was anticipated as the means to carry the end-time message to the nations of the world.

Sporadic expressions of glossolalia did occur in many of these groups during the late 19th century. It was the emergence of the pentecostal movement, however, at the turn of the 20th century that brought the phenomenon into the church on a sustained basis. Following on the heels of the 1904 Welsh revival, pentecostal adherents concurred that the anticipated end-time worldwide revival had begun. Glossolalia, they said, distinguished it from all other revivals in church history, and as such signified a second Pentecost. The phenomenon served three functions: (1) it was the eschatological sign marking the end of the church age; (2) it was the means by which the end-time message would be proclaimed to the nations as a warning; and (3) it was the seal of the Spirit designating those who would be the bride of Christ.

Rejection by mainstream Christendom, disconfirmation that glossolalia was actual language spoken at will, and the delay of the parousia led pentecostals to gradually drop the eschatological significance to the phenomenon. They continued to insist, however, that it was a necessary evidence for the "baptism of the Holy Spirit," which they believed was an experience subsequent to regeneration which empowered the Christian believer for Christian service.

By the 1960s the phenomenon began to transcend the pentecostal boundaries and was experienced in all major Christian communions. It is also commonplace in almost all indigenous third world churches. Conservative estimates have been made that by the year 2000 over 100 million living Christians will have spoken in tongues at least once.

***Bibliography.*** C. Brumback, *"What Meaneth This?" A Pentecostal Answer to a Pentecostal Question* (1947); W. J. Samarian, *Tongues of Men and Angels: The Religious Language of Pentecostalism* (1970); C. G. Williams, *Tongues of the Spirit: A Study of Pentecostal Glossolalia and Related Phenomena* (1981); H. N. Malony and A. A. Lovekin, *Glossolalia: Behavioral Science Perspectives on Speaking in Tongues* (1985).

D. WILLIAM FAUPEL

## Gloubokovsky, Nicholas (1863–1937).

Russian Orthodox NT scholar. Born in Kitchmensky Gorodok, Vologda district, he studied at the Theological Seminary of Vologda and the Theological Academy of Moscow. He was lecturer and professor of NT at St. Petersburg Theological Academy (1893–1918), at the University of Belgrade (1923/24), and Sofia (from 1924). The main field of his research was Pauline theology. In 1918 he delivered the Olaus Petri lectures at the University of Uppsala. He took interest in the ecumenical movement and was present at the Lausanne Conference (1927). In Russia he was an active member of the commission revising the Slavonic text and translation of the NT. His major works are in Russian, including especially *St. Theodoret of Cyrus: His Life and His Writings* (2 vols., 1890) and *The Gospel of St. Paul* (3 vols., 1905, 1910, 1912). His Olaus Petri lectures are published in Swedish and Bulgarian: *Den ortodoksa kyrkan och frogan on sammanslutning mellan den kristna kyrkorna* (1921). He was editor of the *Orthodox Theological Encyclopaedia* (14 vols.).

GEORGES FLOROVSKY

**Glover, Terrot Reaveley** (1869–1943). Baptist. Born in Bristol, England, and educated at St. John's College, Cambridge, he was professor of Latin, Queen's University, Kingston, Canada (1896–1901); classical lecturer, St. John's College, Cambridge (1901–39); and public orator, University of Cambridge (1920–39). He also served as Sather Professor, University of California. He was president of the Baptist Union of Great Britain and Ireland in 1924. He wrote *Studies in Vergil* (1904), *The Conflict of Religions in the Early Roman Empire* (1909), *The Jesus of History* (1917), *Jesus in the Experience of Men* (1921), *The Pilgrim* (1921), *Paul of Tarsus* (1925), *The Influence of Christ in the Ancient World* (1929), *The World of the NT* (1931), *Greek Byways* (1932), *Horace* (1932), *The Disciple* (1941), *The Challenge of the Greek* (1942), and *Cambridge Retrospect* (1943).

**Bibliography.** H. G. Wood, *Terrot Reaveley Glover; A Biography* (1953).

F. W. DILLISTONE

**Glueck, Nelson** (1900–1971). American biblical archeologist. Born in Cincinnati, Glueck studied Bible with Julian Morgenstern and was ordained at Hebrew Union College in 1923, and received his doctorate at Jena (Ph.D., 1927). From 1929 he taught Bible at Hebrew Union College. During much of the period between 1932 and 1947 he was also director of the Jerusalem School of the American School of Oriental Research. He directed excavations at Jebel el-Tannur (1937), Ezion-Geber (1938), and the Negev (from 1952). He made important contributions to our knowledge of Edomite, Moabite, Ammonite, and especially Nabatean cultures. In 1941 he was appointed director of the Union of American Hebrew Congregations (the central organization of American Reform Judaism), and in 1947 he was elected president of the Hebrew Union College. In 1949 Glueck assumed the leadership of the other main Reform seminary, the New York Jewish Institute of Religion. Later he was responsible for the amalgamation of the two schools, and for the opening of branches in Los Angeles and Jerusalem. He was a strong representative of Zionist ideology, which was often viewed with disfavor by the Reform movement.

ELIEZER SEGAL

**Gnadauer Verband (GV).** This organization of "awakened Christians" has a prominent place within the general movement of lay organizations. It originated in Gnadau, near Magdeburg (now in the German Democratic Republic, GDR), on Pentecost Sunday, 1888, out of concern to evangelize nominal Reformed Christians. Its name may be translated as the "Association of Gnadau."

Conferences were held every other year until 1903 and annually thereafter. In 1897 the association was registered as a corporation under the initial presidency of the Christian layman, Count von Pückler.

Among the many activities of GV are the dissemination of tracts and Bibles, the training of lay preachers, youth workers, deaconesses, and colporteurs, and the maintenance of an active temperance movement known as *Blaukreuz.*

Persons who have experienced a "conversion" are admitted into membership. Regular prayer groups are maintained and Bible reading and study is encouraged, as is volunteer service in hospitals, orphanages, and other institutions. Although occasional outbursts of enthusiasm occurred in the history of GV, its distinctive marks are loyalty to the established church, rejection of perfectionist tendencies, and the promotion of Christian literature and music. After the division of Germany GV maintained separate organizational structures in the Federal Republic of Germany and in the GDR.

E. J. FURCHA

**Gnosticism (Gnosis).** A religious and philosophical movement roughly contemporary with early Christianity. For centuries gnosticism was considered as only a Christian heresy, the result of a fusion of Christianity with Greek philosophy. Some scholars, though, have stressed an oriental element in gnostic belief. With the rise of the history of religions school (Richard Reitzenstein, Hans Jonas) and investigation of other Greco-Roman religions this view gained credibility. Some traced the origins of gnosticism to Egypt, Mesopotamia, and particularly Persia. M. Friedlander argued for a pre-Christian Jewish gnosticism.

One common methodological error was to identify the origin of gnostic concepts and motifs with the system itself. A term was traced back to its first occurrence in history, and that first use was labeled "gnostic." It is now recognized that gnostic writers borrowed and adapted ideas for their own purposes without regard to the original intent of those ideas. The concepts and terms became gnostic only when used in the context of a gnostic system.

A related problem was that of definition. Some scholars, particularly British, argued the traditional view of gnosticism as a Christian heresy. Others, particularly in Germany, broadened the terms used to cover a movement that influenced Christianity but was independent of it. They have preferred to speak of *gnosis.* When a German study of gnosis is translated into English the dif-

358

ferences in meaning inevitably cause confusion. It is, therefore, important to recognize whether the terms are used in a wider or a narrower sense. In general we may think of a movement developing alongside, and interacting with Christianity, and which finally culminated in the "classic" systems of the 2d century A.D. The precise details of the development are still obscure, especially for the early stages.

In recent years there has been a strong emphasis on the Jewish element, although the suggestion of a Jewish *origin* has been opposed, among others, by Hans Jonas, author of one of the most influential works in this field in the 20th century, *The Gnostic Religion* (1958). A modified English presentation was published. Certainly a large place is given in gnostic texts to reinterpretation of the OT, but this was also done by Christians and affords no proof that the originators of the movement were necessarily Jews.

Until 1955 all information about the gnostics came from the writings of early heresiologists, whose work was suspect since it was propaganda of the opposition. The only actual gnostic documents extant, apart from extracts and quotations in the works of the early fathers, were from a late period when the movement had gone into decline. Publication in 1955 of the Berlin Gnostic Codex (actually known to exist as far back as 1896) yielded three original gnostic documents, the Gospel of Mary, the Apocryphon of John (Ap. John), and the Sophia Jesu Christi, one of which (Ap. John) was for a time thought to be the source of a similar passage in *Adversus Haereses* by Irenaeus. Gnostic studies were revolutionized through the discovery in 1946 of a gnostic library in Nag Hammadi, Egypt. A complete facsimile edition was finally published, and while editing and evaluating its contents progressed, the library was effectively used to survey the gnostic movement by Kurt Rudolph. Early on the research confirmed the general reliability of the patristic reports and shed light on the ways in which gnostics modified and adapted their literature (there were at least four versions of the Apocryphon of John and two of the Sophia of Jesus Christ, and also a document on which Sophia may have been based). The texts raised questions about alleged gnostic libertinism since the dominant tone was rather ascetic. Perhaps most important, the new resources gave insight into what gnosticism meant to a gnostic. Gnosticism has often been considered bizarre and grotesque, but in fact it was an attempt to deal with the human predicament and to resolve the problem of evil–not a counsel of despair but a religion of hope.

The NT uses terms and concepts later incorporated into developed gnostic systems, but they were not necessarily gnostic at the NT stage or derived from gnosticism; in fact, echoes and allusions and sometimes direct quotations demonstrate Christian influence on gnosticism. Interaction with the ideas which became gnosis, in the wider sense, is another matter. There are indications in the later strata of the NT of a growing resistance to mystical patterns of philosophy within churches.

The main characteristics of gnosticism in its classic form were: (1) a radical cosmic dualism which rejected this world and all that belonged to it; (2) a distinction between the Creator of this world, often identified with the God of the OT, and the unknown transcendent supreme God; (3) the belief that the human soul essentially belongs to the realm of the supreme God, a spark of divine light imprisoned in a material body; (4) a myth, often incorporating a precreation fall, to explain the origin of the world and the problems of human existence; and (5) the saving *gnosis*, which is not a rational knowledge but secret knowledge conveyed by revelation. Classic forms of gnosticism, such as the Valentinian system, show clear Christian influence, but there are indications that the movement was of wider scope and did not necessarily originate within Christianity. Hermetic literature of the 2d and 3d centuries shows little if any Christian influence, and Hermetic texts appear in the Nag Hammadi library. In some documents of that library the Christian element *could* have been imposed on an originally non-Christian text; but no older text is available; indeed no gnostic text in its present form is older than the NT.

A later off-shoot of the gnostic movement, Manicheism, was widely spread and reached the status of a world religion. There are at least affinities with gnosticism in the medieval Bogomils in the Eastern Church and Cathari, who arose in southern France. Modern splinter groups occasionally use similar forms of doctrine and sometimes seem to borrow directly from gnostic concepts.

**Bibliography.** *Theologische Realenzyklopädie* (1970– ), 13:519–50; D. M. Scholer, *Nag Hammadi Bibliography 1948–1969* (1971) (supplemented annually, except 1976, in *Nov. Test.*); J. M. Robinson, ed., *The Nag Hammadi Library in English* (1977); K. Rudolph, *Gnosis: The Nature and History of an Ancient Religion* (ET, 1983).

R. McL. WILSON

**God.** At the close of the 19th century the emphasis in the doctrine of God was upon the divine immanence. The emphasis of classic liberalism harmonized with the prevailing interest in evolution as the key to the understanding of human life. The kingdom of God was interpreted as being progressively realized in history by men working with God to the building of a better society. The doctrine of the universal Fatherhood of God was generally accepted, sometimes in terms that obscured the divine wrath and the necessity for the new birth.

World War I and the difficult situation in postwar Europe gave a severe shock to this easy idealism with which the 20th century had opened. The Great Depression, World War II, and the world conflict with communism have deepened the sense of tension and the understanding of the seriousness of the human dilemma. The history of the concept of God in this period reflects and interprets these tensions.

About the middle of the 19th century Søren Kierkegaard had pointed out the chasm between the Christianity of the NT and the Christianity of Europe in general and of Denmark in particular. The translation of his works into German prepared the way for his influence on the men who were to found the theology of crisis. The latter first attracted world attention with the publication of a commentary on Romans in 1918 by Karl Barth. Barth developed the doctrine of the unknown God, particularly against the teaching of Friedrich Schleiermacher that the task of theology is the explication of the religious consciousness. Barth asserts that there is no way to God from man, but there is a way from God to man. God is known as he makes himself known to human hearts in his "word." On a subjective level he recovered the concept of the word of God as the starting point of knowledge of God. The Scripture is accepted as the written witness to the word of God. But the word of God is conceived in dynamic rather than in static terms. The word of God is God's manifestation of himself in history, given to a chosen people and culminating in the life, death, and resurrection of Jesus Christ. The word of the Lord, given in history and witnessed to in the Scripture, becomes the word of God as the Holy Spirit brings the message of Scripture home to those who are willing to hear it. This doctrine of the word of the Lord is directed against the idea of a knowledge of God that is general, timeless, and nonhistorical, and against mysticism in the sense that the great mystics claim a direct and unmediated knowledge of God.

The theology of crisis has also been called the theology of paradox. At times, knowledge of truth must be stated in seemingly contradictory statements. This view affirms both that God is sovereign and that man, as a responsible being, is given a limited amount of freedom. He has the freedom to hear or not to hear the word of the Lord. In Jesus, God was manifest in the flesh, but also in Jesus God was veiled in the flesh.

Barth insists that the image of God in man has been completely destroyed by sin and must be recreated by a gracious act of God before man can hear the word of God. Emil Brunner, however, who, as against the teaching of Schleiermacher and Albrecht Ritschl, has much in common with Barth, holds that the image of God in man has been marred, but not utterly destroyed. Barth proclaims a knowledge of God based on revelation alone. With Brunner there is an effort to build a bridge between the message received in the word of the Lord and the truth that has come from other sources.

Theologians of this school insist that people receive their knowledge of God as God confronts them in his word. This prepares the way for the note of crisis or decision. When God speaks the person must hear or refuse to hear the word that comes. This means that obedience to the word of God is the road to spiritual knowledge.

The impact of the theology of crisis has profoundly influenced the concept of God in contemporary America. At the far left of the spectrum there are those in the radical or neoliberal groups, who hold to some sort of doctrine of divine immanence of classic liberalism or the strains of pantheistically-oriented thought drawn from Alfred North Whitehead and Martin Buber. Neo-orthodox theology dominates the mainstream church and accepts many of the ideas which were emphasized in the theology of crisis. Neo-orthodox Christians have sought to identify themselves as conservative, orthodox, and even evangelical. All within historic Christianity have come to be labeled as "fundamentalist." As a result it has become increasingly difficult to categorize groups according to their conceptions of God and revelation.

The general movement of theological thinking in the 20th century has been to call Christian thought back from vague generalities to a faith that takes into account the Bible as the only valid source of knowledge of God. God has revealed himself in Jesus Christ. In him is the light of the knowledge of the glory of God. The written witness to this revelation has been preserved in the Bible in either a subjective or an objective historical sense. The Spirit who spoke through prophet and apostle bears witness to the truth of the word of God. This word of the Lord is the only basis upon which man can build an abiding civilization.

HOLMES ROLSTON

**Goebel, Louis William** (1884–1973). Evangelical and Reformed. Born in Carlinville, Ill., he was educated at Elmhurst College and Eden Seminary, and ordained in 1907. He was chairman of the committee on union of the Evangelical Synod of North America during negotiations which led to union with the Reformed Church in the United States in 1934, vice-president of the Evangelical and Reformed Church (1934–38) and president (1938), and delegate to world conferences in Oxford, Edinburgh, and Amsterdam. He was a member of the Central Committee of the World Council of Churches.

**Göhre, Paul** (1864–1928). German Lutheran and socialist. He established personal contact with the labor movement by working in a factory. He was pastor in Frankfurt-Oder (1894–1907), particularly active in social work and cooperatives. Attacked by ecclesiastical circles, he left the church in 1901. He joined the Social Democratic party and represented it in Reichstag (1903–18), and was a member of the Prussian Cabinet (1918–23). He advocated close cooperation of socialism and undogmatic Christianity. His books include *Drei Monate Fabrikarbeiter* (1891) and *Der Unbekannte Gott* (1919).

OTTO A. PIPER

**Goforth, Jonathan** (1859–1936). Canadian Presbyterian missionary to China. Born in Western Ontario, Goforth graduated from Knox College, Toronto. In 1887 he and his wife went to Honan province in China to open a station in Changte. Goforth determined to teach Chinese scholars the gospel and did, in fact, successfully evangelize that highly esteemed class. Committed to indigenous church development, he saw 50 of his converts proceed to full-time service in the national church. In 1907 he visited Korea, the scene of an extensive revival. Returning to Manchuria, he led in the revival there, and then returned to Changte where revival also broke out. Those revivals are described in his *By My Spirit*. When the majority of Canadian Presbyterians entered the new United Church of Canada in 1925, Goforth remained with the continuing Presbyterian Church. Because the Honan field was taken over by the United Church, Goforth went to Manchuria and opened a new field where he ministered for his remaining days in China. Afflicted with blindness in 1933, he remained in China until 1934, when he returned to Canada, actively preaching and promoting missions to the end. His wife Rosalind wrote *Goforth of China*, a popular missionary biography.

LESLIE K. TARR

**Gogarten, Friedrich** (1887–1967). Born in Dortmund, Germany, he studied under Ernst Troeltsch and at the age of 40 became privatdocent at Jena. Three years later he was called to become professor of systematic theology at Breslau (1930–35) and taught theology at Göttingen from 1935. His theological positions shifted radically. Even at the beginning, and in contrast to Troeltsch, he sought idealistically for a faith to support reason. Although enamored of Martin Luther and Søren Kierkegaard, and even after he had supported Karl Barth enthusiastically, he turned against their supernaturalism. He eventually reached a position similar to that of Martin Buber. During the Nazi period he gave his theological support to the "German Christians," in contrast to the "Confessional Church." His major works include *Die religiöse Entscheidung* (1921; 2d ed., 1924), *Von Glauben und Offenbarung*

(1923), *Ich glaube an den dreieinigen Gott* (1926), *Politische Ethik* (1932), *Gericht oder Skepsis: eine Streitschrift gegen Karl Barth* (1937), *Weltanschauung und Glaube* (1937), and *Das Bekenntnis der Kirche* (1939).

RAYMOND W. ALBRIGHT

**Goguel, (Henry) Maurice** (1880–1955). Born in Paris, he received his education at the University of Paris (Th.D., 1905) and l'Ecole des Hautes Etudes. He was on the faculty of Protestant theology at Paris from 1906, director of studies at l'Ecole des Hautes Etudes from 1927, and also dean of the faculty of letters at Paris from 1937. He wrote *L'apôtre Paul et Jésus Christ* (1904), *Wilhelm Hermann et le problème religieux actuel* (1905), *L'Evangile de Marc* (1910), *L'Eucharistie des origines jusqu'à Justin Martyr* (1910), *Introduction au Nouveau Testament* (1922–26), *Jésus de Nazareth, mythe ou histoire* (1925), *Jean-Baptiste* (1928), *Vie de Jésus* (1932), *La naissance du christianisme* (1946), and *L'Eglise primitive* (1947).

RAYMOND W. ALBRIGHT

**Golden Rule.** The saying of Jesus in Matt. 7:12 and Luke 6:31 has been called "the golden rule" at least since the 18th century. In Matthew's Sermon on the Mount it is a summary and climax which comes just before the final series of warnings. In Luke's Sermon it fits gracefully between commands of nonresistance and generosity. Matthew adds the clause, "for this is the law and the prophets," thus making it a summary of the whole will of God, similar to Mark 12:29–31. The saying, in negative form, is frequently found in Jewish literature, its earliest appearance being in Tobit 4:15, where it occurs with counsels of prudence and generosity. The most famous Jewish form is that of Hillel, "What is hateful to you, do not do to your neighbor; this is the whole Torah, all the rest is interpretation" (Shabbôt 31a). Other forms are found in a quotation from Philo (Eusebius, *Preparation for the Gospel*, 8, 7.6); in Testament of Naphtali, 1 (Heb. text); and in Letter of Aristeas, 207, which connects the principle with the example of God, "who draws all men by forbearance." From Jewish tradition the negative form comes into Christian literature in a later "Western" variant of Acts 15:29 (which adds the negative command after the warning not to partake in sexual immorality). Didache 1:2 couples the rule with the commandments to love God and neighbor. The positive form appears in the church fathers only as a quotation from the Gospels. Sayings similar to the golden rule, usually in negative form, are found in the sayings of Confucius and in Hindu scriptures, in both forms in Greek philosophy from Thales (c. 640–546 B.C.) on, and in Muslim tradition. Jesus' positive statement of the principle accords with his presentation of righteousness as the active doing of good rather than the avoidance of evil. Christians generally prefer the positive form, while Jewish teachers have contended that the negative is more realistic and profound. Taken out of its context, the golden rule need be no more than a prudential maxim which often proves practically advantageous. Jesus' teaching is, however, set against the background of God's goodness and constant activity. The good that his followers do to others, and that they wish may be done to them, is the outgoing love which exists among children of a heavenly Father.

*Bibliography.* I. Abrahams, *Studies in Pharisaism and the Gospels,* Series 1 (1917): 21–25; L. J. Philippidis, *Die "Goldene Regel" religionsgeschichtlich untersucht* (1929); R. H. Pfeiffer, *History of NT Times* (1949), 384.

SHERMAN E. JOHNSON

**Goldin, Judah** (1914– ). Noted American scholar of Jewish literature and history. Born in New York City, Goldin was ordained by the Jewish Theological Seminary of America in 1939. From 1959 he taught classical Judaica at Yale University. His many studies in the area of rabbinic Judaism are notable for the way in which he integrated Jewish subjects into a broad cultural context. He also produced English translations of important Talmudic texts (*Living Talmud* [1957]; *The Fathers According to Rabbi Nathan* [1955]). He also served in several scholarly organizations, such as the American Academy for Jewish Research and the Yale Judaica Research Committee.

ELIEZER SEGAL

**Goldman, Solomon** (1893–1953). Jewish rabbi and author. Born in Kozin, Russia, he studied at New York University, Columbia University, University of Chicago, Yeshiva Rabbi Isaac Elchanan, and Jewish Theological Seminary of America. He served Congregation B'nai Israel, Brooklyn (1917–19), Cleveland Jewish Center (1921–29), and Chicago, Anshe Emet from 1929. He associated with the Reconstructionists in American Judaism. He is the author of *A Rabbi Takes Stock* (1931), *The Jew and the Universe* (1936), *The Golden Chain* (1937), *Crisis and Decision* (1938), *Undefeated* (1940), *The Book of Books* (1948), and *In the Beginning* (1949).

**Gollwitzer, Helmut** (1908– ). German theologian. Born in Pappenheim, the son of a Lutheran pastor, he studied philosophy and theology at the universities of Munich, Erlangen, Jena, and Bonn, and succeeded Martin Niemoller as pastor in Berlin-Dahlem (1938–40). A prisoner-of-war in Russia for some years after World War II, Gollwitzer became professor at Bonn (a post once held by Karl Barth) before transferring to the Free University of West Berlin in 1957. He acknowledged his debt to Martin Luther and Karl Barth, and has been described as the latter's "most controversial living disciple." He was prevented from succeeding Barth at Basel by "political difficulties." Gollwitzer's *Introduction to Protestant Theology* (ET, 1982) is "in the tradition of Barth and Bonhoeffer" and was said to have been "a theology of freedom and solidarity." His other writings include *Unwilling Journey: A Diary from Russia* (1953), *The Demands of Freedom: Papers by a Christian in West Germany* (1965), *The Existence of God as Confessed by Faith* (1965), and *The Christian Faith and the Marxist Criticism of Religion* (1965).

CHARLES M. CAMERON

**Good, James Isaac** (1850–1924). German Reformed church historian. Born in York, Pa., he graduated from Lafayette College and Union Theological Seminary, N.Y., and pastored Reformed churches in Pennsylvania (1875–95). For the latter part of that period he taught church history at Ursinus College, Philadelphia, before becoming its professor of dogmatics and pastoral theology, and later its dean (1893–97). He was then professor of Reformed church history and liturgics at Central Theological Seminary (1907–24). He was president of the general synod of the Reformed Church in the United States (1911–14). His many published works include *Origin of the Reformed Church of Germany* (1887), *History of the Reformed Church of Germany* (1894), *History of the Reformed Church in the United States* (1899), *Famous Women of the Reformed Church* (1902), *Famous Missionaries of the Reformed Church* (1903), *Famous Places of the Reformed Churches* (1910), *History of the Swiss Reformed Church since the Reformation* (1913), *The Heidelberg Catechism in Its Newest Light* (1914), *Famous Reformers of the Reformed and Presbyterian Churches* (1916), and *The Reformed Reformation* (1917).

**Goodall, Norman** (1896–1985). English Congregational scholar and ecumenist. Educated at Oxford, he served Congregational churches in Walthamstow (1922–28) and New Barnet (1928–36) before appointment as foreign secretary of the London Missionary Society (1936–44). He then became secretary of the International Missionary Council (1944–61), and subsequently assistant general secretary of the World Council of Churches (1961–63). He wrote *With All Thy Mind* (1933), *Pacific Pilgrimage* (1941), *One Man's Testimony* (1949), *History of the London Missionary Society, 1895–1945* (1954), *The Ecumenical Movement* (1961), *Christian Missions and Social Ferment* (1964), *Ecclesiastical Progress* (1972), and *Second Fiddle* (1979).

J. D. DOUGLAS

**Goodspeed, Edgar J.** (1871–1962). Baptist. Born in Quincy, Ill., he studied at Denison University, the University of Chicago (Ph.D., 1898), Berlin, and Oxford. He was associate in biblical and patristic Greek, University of Chicago (1900–1902); instructor (1902–5); assistant professor (1905–10); associate professor (1910–15); professor (1915–37); secretary to the president (1920–24); and chairman of the NT department (1923–37). He lectured widely in the USA in defense of modern-speech translation of the NT. He was active in beginning to collate the NT Greek manuscripts in America (1898–1907), and in introducing the study of Greek papyri to America, collaborating in the Tebtunis Papyri, vol. 2 (1907).

He is best known for his American translation of the *NT* (1923). It was republished in 1931 as part of *The Bible, an American Translation*, and again with his *The Apocrypha, an American Translation* (the first such translation made throughout from the Greek) as part of *The Complete Bible, an American Translation* (1939). He collaborated with Prof. Ernest D. Burton in a *Harmony of the Synoptic Gospels* (1915) and *A Greek Harmony of the Synoptic Gospels* (1920). He wrote *The Story of the NT* (1916), *The Story of the OT* (1934), *The Story of the Bible* (1936), and *The Story of the Apocrypha* (1939). A fuller *Introduction to the NT* appeared in 1937. He lectured in history at Scripps College (1938) and at U.C.L.A. (1938–51).

Other books include *Index Patristicus* (1907), *Index Apologeticus* (1912), *Die ältesten Apologeten* (1914), *Making of the English NT* (1925), *Formation of the NT* (1926), *Strange New Gospels* (1931), *Ethiopic Martyrdom* (1931), *New Chapters in NT Study* (1937), *Christianity Goes to Press* (1940), *The Curse in the Colophon* (1935), *The Junior Bible* (1936), *The Four Pillars of Democracy* (1940), *How Came the Bible* (1940), *History of Early Christian Literature* (1942), *Goodspeed Parallel NT* (1943), *Problems of NT Translation* (1945), *How to Read the Bible* (1946), *Paul* (1947), *The Apostolic Fathers, an American Translation* (1950), and *A Life of Jesus* (1950). He coauthored with J. M. P. Smith, *The Short Bible* (1933), and with D. W. Riddle and H. R. Willoughby, *The Rockefeller McCormick NT* (3 vols., 1932). He published a number of essays, chiefly in the *Atlantic Monthly*, two volumes of which were collected in *Things Seen and Heard* (1925), and *Buying Happiness* (1932). He was a member of the Revised Standard Bible Committee from its organization in 1930.

**Gordis, Robert** (1908– ). Distinguished rabbi, biblical scholar, and theologian. Born in New York City, he studied and received ordination at the Jewish Theological Seminary of America (JTS) there in 1932. From 1931 to 1968 he held a pulpit at the Conservative congregation Beth El, Rockaway Park, N.Y. From 1940 to 1981 he was professor of Bible at the JTS. He also taught briefly at Columbia University, Union Theological Seminary in New York, and Temple University. Since 1951 he has been editor of *Judaism*, one of the most prestigious of American Jewish journals.

Gordis's biblical scholarship has been directed primarily toward wisdom literature, including major studies of Job, Ecclesiastes, and Esther. His theological writings have been concerned with the confrontation between Judaism and modern culture. He is considered one of the foremost spokesmen for the ideology of the conservative movement in American Judaism.

ELIEZER SEGAL

**Gordon, Alexander Reid** (1872–1930). Presbyterian. Born in Inverurie, Aberdeenshire, he studied at Aberdeen, Edinburgh, Freiburg, Göttingen, and Berlin universities. Ordained in 1898, he was minister at Monikie, Forfarshire (1898–1907), professor of OT at Presbyterian (now United Theological) College, Montreal (1907–30), and McGill University (1914–30). His works include *The Poets of the OT* (1912), *The Prophets of the OT* (1917), *The Faith of Isaiah* (1919), and *The Prophetical Literature of the OT* (1919).

ELMER E. FLACK

**Gordon, Cyrus Herzl** (1908– ). Jewish scholar. Born in Philadelphia, he was educated at the University of Pennsylvania (Ph.D., 1930) where he taught Hebrew (1930/31) before becoming field archeologist in Bible lands with the American Schools of Oriental Research (1931–35). Thereafter he was teaching scholar in Semitics at Johns Hopkins University (1936–38), variously lecturer in Bible and Religion at Smith College and member of the Institute for Advanced Study at Princeton (1938–42), professor of Assyriology and Egyptology at Dropsie College, Philadelphia (1946–56), and professor of Near Eastern studies at Brandeis University (1956–73). Among his many books are *The Living Past* (1941), *Ugaritic Handbook* (1947), *Ugaritic Manual* (1955), *Adventures in the Near East* (1957), *The Ancient Near East* (1965), *The Common Background of Greek and Hebrew Civilization* (rev. ed., 1965), *Ugaritic Textbook* (rev. ed., 1967), and *Forgotten Scripts* (rev. ed., 1982).

**Gordon George Angier** (1853–1929). Congregationalist pastor and author. Born in Aberdeenshire, Scotland, he studied at Bangor Theological Seminary and Harvard University. He pastored a church in Greenwich, Conn. (1881–84), and the Old South Church in Boston (1884–1927). He was lecturer in the Lowell Institute in 1900 and Lyman Beecher Lecturer at Yale in 1901, in addition to being university preacher at Harvard (1886–90) and Yale (1888–1901). Also, he was an overseer at Harvard (1897–1916). His published works include *The Witness to Immortality* (1893), *The Christ of To-Day* (1895), *Immortality and the New Theodicy* (1897), *The New Epoch for Faith* (1901), *Through Man to God* (1906), *Ultimate Conceptions of Faith* (1903), *Religion and Miracle* (rev. ed., 1910), *Revelation and the Ideal* (1913), *Aspects of the Infinite Mystery* (1916), *Humanism in New England Theology* (1920), and *My Education and Religion* (1925).

RAYMOND W. ALBRIGHT

**Gore, Charles** (1853–1932). Anglican bishop. Born in Wimbledon, Surrey, he graduated at Oxford and was ordained in 1878, serving later as vice-principal of Cuddesdon College (1880–83) and librarian of Pusey House, Oxford (1884–93). His advanced theological views led to his resignation, however. From 1894 to 1902 he was canon of Westminster and became also a royal chaplain. He was consecrated bishop of Worcester in 1902 and two years later became the first bishop of Birmingham. He was the editor of *Lux Mundi* (1890), to which he also contributed chapters on "The Holy Spirit" and "Inspiration." His own books included *Leo the Great* (1880), *The Church and the Ministry* (1889), *The Incarnation of the Son of God* (1891), *The Creed of the Christian* (1896), *The Sermon on the Mount* (1897), *Prayer and the Lord's Prayer* (1898), *The Body of Christ* (1901), *The New Theology and the Old Religion* (1907), *Orders and Unity* (1909), *Son of Man* (1913), *A Prayer Book Revised* (1913), *The Basis of Anglican Fellowship* (1914), *Christianity Applied to the Life of Man and Nations* (1920), *The Proposed Scheme of Union in South India* (1921), *Belief in Christ* (1922), *Catholicism and Roman Catholicism* (1923), *Holy Spirit and the Church* (1924), *The Anglo-Catholic Movement Today* (1925), *Can We Then Believe?* (1926), *Strikes and Lock-Outs* (1926), *The Prevention of Conception* (1927), *Christ and Society* (1928), *Jesus of Nazareth* (1929), and *Reflections on The Litany* (1932). He also wrote commentaries on Ephesians (1898), Romans (1899), and the Johannine Epistles (1921), and edited G. Romanes' *Thoughts on Religion* (1894), *Essays in Aid of the Reform of the Church* (1898), and *The New Commentary on the Holy Scripture* (1928).

**Gospel and Gospels.** *Introduction.* In the early church the word "gospel" was used in the singular, for it was important to the Christian witness that there was only one gospel (Gal. 1:8–12). But accounts were drawn up of the saving events, and in time it became customary to attach the name "gospel" to each of these (see the opening reference to the beginning of "the gospel of Jesus Christ" in Mark 1:1). From the time of Justin in the 2d century the word was used of the four canonical Gospels. These Gospels form a unique type of literature. The ancient world knew of biographies of famous people, but the Gospels are not biographies. They record what God has done in Jesus, and thus are "good news." They all came to have the names of authors attached to them, but were anonymous in the autographs.

*Dates of the Gospels.* Dating the Gospels is difficult, and agreement has not been reached. At first the Christian message, including all the information about Jesus, seems to have been transmitted orally, but in time some of it was written down. Fuller narratives were probably seen to be required when the eyewitnesses of the saving events began to die off. There is considerable agreement that all four Gospels should be dated within the period A.D. 60–100, but little evidence provides precise dates. Most scholars would date Matthew in the 80s, Mark somewhere from 65 to 75, Luke in the 70s or 80s, and John near the end of the 1st century A.D. Conservative scholars consider earlier dates more probable, although how much earlier is not easy to determine. In any case, whatever the dates of writing, it is clear that early tradition attests the existence of all four.

*The Synoptic Gospels.* Form critics have made much of the fact that the Christian message was transmitted orally for some time, and they have given a good deal of attention to the way oral tradition was handed on. They draw attention to the use of small units and to the tendency for classes of units to emerge, such as miracle stories or stories that end in a significant saying. In the latter the details of the story are not important; it is the saying to which everything leads. Some form critics insist so strongly on the handing on of nothing more than the individual units that they disregard the possibility of anything in the way of a connected narrative. They also can be so single-minded in discovering a life setting for Gospel stories in the early church that they give little attention to the possibility that individual accounts may also reflect a life setting in the ministry of Jesus. In any case those who wrote our Gospels were not simply compilers of anthologies. They were serious authors, and attention must be given to their editorial activity, as redaction critics maintain. Each shaped his material to bring out what he saw to be important.

The relation between the three synoptists is much debated. There are passages which correspond almost word-for-word in Matthew, Mark, and Luke, and other passages are shared by two of them. The resemblances extend to unimportant particles and are found in accounts of events as well as in reports of Jesus' teaching. Sometimes Matthew and Mark agree in their wording where Luke differs, sometimes Mark and Luke agree, and more rarely Matthew and Luke agree. The first and third Gospels also have passages that are absent from the corresponding parts of

Mark. Of course each Gospel has material that is absent from the others. Oral tradition can explain some of these facts, but not nearly all of them.

Most critics hold that Mark was written first and that Matthew and Luke made use of it. Almost all of Mark is contained in the other two; about 90 percent is in Matthew and about half in Luke; only four paragraphs of Mark are not found in one of the others. The Markan order of events is mostly followed in both Matthew and Luke, and where one of them differs the other generally follows it. Interestingly, although Matthew is so much longer than Mark, where the two have a common narrative, Mark's version tends to be longer and more lifelike. This sort of evidence has convinced most critics that Mark is the earliest of the three and that the two others have made considerable use of his work. The view put forward in the early church that Mark is an abbreviation of Matthew is still held in some form by a few scholars, but Markan priority seems to be more probable.

Scholars also consider it likely that another source, usually designated Q, was involved. Sometimes Matthew and Luke share matter which Mark lacks, and when reporting what is in Mark they may agree in including something Mark does not have. The resemblances in the common matter may be close, but the differences are so great that most believe it unlikely that Matthew made use of Luke or that Luke made use of Matthew. To explain the similarities scholars posit Q or perhaps a number of sources. That there were such sources we know from the reference to the "many" who have written (Luke 1:1). Q material seems to be in sayings rather than narratives.

Since some material occurs only in Matthew or Luke, scholars agree that these evangelists themselves contributed as well as borrowed from other sources. Clearly the relationship between the three synoptists is complex. The most likely solution is that Matthew and Luke used Mark, some common sources such as Q, and matter peculiar to themselves. Little more can be certain.

*Matthew.* Although most Christians would probably affirm that Luke or John is their "favorite Gospel," in practice Matthew seems to be used most of all. It has many of Jesus' teachings, and it has always lent itself to liturgical use. Its first place in all the lists of Gospels that have come down from the early church points to its popularity.

It appears to have originated in a Greek-speaking, Jewish-Christian community, and its author was likely a Jewish Christian himself. Many quotations from the OT are a feature of this writing. But despite its "Jewishness" this Gospel emphasizes the universality of the gospel. Early in Matthew is the story of the Gentile magi who came to the Christ child, and the Gospel ends

with a command of the risen Christ to take the gospel message into all the world. It is an "ecclesiastical" Gospel not only because it is the only one of the four to refer explicitly to the church, but also because much of what it says would aid church leaders (the use of the Sabbath, the errors of the scribal tradition, the response to persecution, and the like). The tradition of the ancient church unanimously ascribes this Gospel to the apostle Matthew, and while this view is mostly rejected by modern scholarship, R. T. France argues that it fits the facts.

Matthew offers a good deal of teaching, and there are five great discourses which are often compared to the five books of Moses. But the conclusion sometimes drawn that Matthew sees Christianity as the "new law" is to be rejected firmly. As much as any of the NT writers he sees gospel, not law, as the essence of the Christian way. Matthew finds the teaching of Jesus of utmost importance for those who want to live the Christian life. The Sermon on the Mount in particular has had immense influence on Christians of all persuasions, and indeed it has affected the thinking of many who would not call themselves Christians.

*Mark.* If, as seems probable, this is the oldest written Gospel, then Mark is the originator of the Gospel form, which is no mean achievement. Traditionally it has been held that John Mark wrote this book and embodied in it reminiscences of the apostle Peter. This cannot be proved, and scholars differ, but there is no doubting the freshness and vitality of this book, even if the Greek is more rugged than that of the other Evangelists. Mark wastes no time in telling us what he is about; his opening words are "the beginning of the gospel about Jesus Christ, the Son of God" (1:1). Mark uses the word "gospel" seven times, more often than anyone else in the NT except Paul. He is telling his readers of "good news" and speaks of Jesus proclaiming "the good news of God" (1:14). Mark is concerned with what God has done in Christ. There is not much teaching in Mark. The author tells what Jesus did rather than what he said. He shows Jesus the man, but he also shows Jesus the Son of God and connects the importance of both natures to explain what God is doing. He puts emphasis on the cross, both in the space he allots to it, and in teaching that brings out its meaning (e.g., Mark 10:45). Modern scholars have given increasing attention to the *kerygma*, the message the early Christian preachers proclaimed. Interestingly, the outline of Mark is much the same as the outline of the *kerygma*. Mark gives us the basic message that the early preachers proclaimed when they went out with the gospel.

*Luke.* There is considerable agreement that the third Gospel is part of a two-volume work with Acts as the second volume. In earlier days there was considerable discussion as to the author's merits as a historian, but today interest tends to focus on his status as a theologian; he is sometimes thought to have been one of the greatest theologians of the early church. With his second volume giving something of the history of the early church, he shows interest in the continuing activity of God after the death and resurrection of Christ. Despite the emphasis on the work of the Holy Spirit in Acts, Luke is said by many to have little interest in the "charismatic" aspects of early church life and to be one of the authors of "early catholicism." He is interested in the church as an institution, and this is said to have replaced the typical early Christian conviction that Christ would come back in the immediate future. Luke is thought to have lost a good deal of an early eschatological enthusiasm. This, however, is scarcely fair. He says much about eschatology, including quite a few things the other writers do not mention. His explicitly stated interest is to produce a reliable record of what God had done in Christ and of what he was continuing to do in the life of the church.

Luke has a deep interest in salvation. He makes more use of the salvation terminology than do the other evangelists and his interests range far beyond Israel. He refers to Samaritans on a number of occasions, including the grateful leper whom Jesus healed and the parable of the Good Samaritan. His universalism does not mean that all will be saved, for he distinguishes between "the sons of this world" and "the sons of light" (16:8). Luke is concerned to bring out the truth that God has a purpose that he is working out, first in the life, death, resurrection, and ascension of Christ, then in what is happening in the church. No NT writer has a greater interest than Luke in people who were disadvantaged in 1st-century society. He has a lot to say about women, children, the poor, and the disreputable. Though society at large relegated all such people to a very minor place, Luke was concerned to show that God's purpose was wide enough to include them all. As all the Evangelists, Luke gives evidence of a deep interest in the passion, and he is the only one to tell us of Jesus' ascension. He tells us a good deal about the Holy Spirit, more so than the other Evangelists (and, of course, he has much more to say when he comes to Acts). He puts emphasis on the importance of prayer and records seven prayers of Jesus that nobody else includes. This also is a singing Gospel. Luke records great Christian hymns such as the *Magnificat* (1:46–55) and the *Nunc Dimittis* (2:29–32), and he strikes the note of joy, for example, when he tells of the joy in heaven over one sinner who repents (15:7, 10, 11–31).

*John.* This Gospel has been regarded by many critics as composed toward the end of the 1st century or early in the 2d. Some have thought the author was John the apostle, but others believe an unknown disciple has reflected long and deeply about the life and teaching of Jesus and about the Christian life, and has put down some of his thoughts in this Gospel. Whatever the date of composition, its author had access to an early, reliable tradition independent of that behind the synoptic Gospels. Many scholars hold that the author is more interested in theology than in history, and accordingly they hesitate to accept as history what is attested by John alone. There is a theory of "the Johannine circle," a community out of which this Gospel arose and in which it was originally intended to be read. Some scholars have apparently gone beyond the evidence in this area of Johannine criticism, but John does exhibit a unique expression of Christianity.

That the author was a theologian is clear from his use of the *Logos* concept from the opening line to the very end. Among the discourses he records are teachings of priceless value, unlike anything in the other Gospels. John includes the seven "I am" sayings, and such concepts as the *Logos* and the preexistence of Christ ("Before Abraham was I am" [8:58]). The writer tells us that he has written so that his readers may believe that Jesus is the Christ and believing might have life (20:31). The theological purpose is very plain. But we should not therefore conclude that the writer was not interested in history. On the contrary, he has recorded things about Jesus found nowhere else.

Attempts have been made to find sources behind this Gospel (e.g., some theorize a "signs" source and a "discourse" source), but such attempts do not appear to have been successful. They fail to carry conviction in the light of the uniformity of the style and the theology throughout the whole book. It may be that the writer did have sources, but if so he has rewritten them so completely that there is no way to separate them from his own contribution.

***Bibliography.*** *General.* B. H. Streeter, *The Four Gospels: A Study of Origins, Treating of the Manuscript Tradition, Sources, Authorship, and Dates* (4th ed., 1930); C. F. D. Moule, *The Birth of the NT* (1962); D. Guthrie, *NT Introduction: The Gospels and Acts* (1965); R. H. Fuller, *A Critical Introduction to the NT* (1966); W. G. Kummel, *Introduction to the NT* (rev. ed., 1975); R. P. Martin, *NT Foundations: A Guide for Christian Students*, vol. 1, *The Four Gospels* (1975); B. S. Childs, *The NT as Canon: An Introduction* (1985).

*Matthew.* W. C. Allen, *A Critical and Exegetical Commentary on the Gospel According to St. Matthew* (1907); A. W. Argyle, *The Gospel According to Matthew* (1963); J. C. Fenton, *Saint Matthew* (1963); W. F. Albright and C. S. Mann, *Matthew* (1971); D. Hill, *The Gospel of Matthew* (1972); E. Schweizer, *The Good News According to Matthew* (1975); F. W. Beare, *The Gospel According to Matthew* (1981); R. H. Gundry, *Matthew: A Commentary on His Literary and Theological Art* (1982); D. A. Carson, "Matthew," in *Expositor's Bible Commentary* (1984); R. T. France, *The Gospel According to Matthew* (1985).

*Mark.* C. E. B. Cranfield, *The Gospel According to Saint Mark: An Introduction and Commentary* (1959); V. Taylor, *The Gospel According to St. Mark* (1959); D. E. Nineham, *The Gospel of St. Mark* (1963); W. Marxsen, *Mark the Evangelist: Studies on the*

*Redaction History of the Gospel* (1969); R. P. Martin, *Mark: Evangelist and Theologian* (1973); W. L. Lane, *The Gospel According to Mark* (1974); E. Trocmé, *The Formation of the Gospel According to Mark* (1975); H. Anderson, *The Gospel of Mark* (1976); M. Hengel, *Studies in the Gospel of Mark* (1985).

*Luke.* W. Manson, *The Gospel of Luke* (1930); J. M. Creed, *The Gospel According to St. Luke* (1950); H. J. Cadbury, *The Making of Luke–Acts* (2d ed., 1958); H. Conzelmann, *The Theology of Saint Luke* (1960); G. B. Caird, *The Gospel of St. Luke* (1963); E. E. Ellis, *The Gospel of Luke* (1966); L. E. Keck and J. L. Martyn, eds., *Studies in Luke–Acts: Essays Presented in Honor of Paul Schubert* (1966); H. Flender, *St. Luke: Theologian of Redemptive History* (1967); I. H. Marshall, *Luke: Historian and Theologian* (1971); *The Gospel of Luke: A Commentary on the Greek* (1978); J. A. Fitzmyer, *The Gospel According to Luke* (2 vols., 1981, 1985); D. Juel, *Luke–Acts: The Promise of History* (1983).

*John.* P. Gardner-Smith, *Saint John and the Synoptic Gospels* (1938); W. F. Howard, *Christianity According to St. John* (1943); E. Hoskyns and F. N. Davey, *The Fourth Gospel* (2d ed., 1947); C. H. Dodd, *The Interpretation of the Fourth Gospel* (1953); W. F. Howard, *The Fourth Gospel in Recent Criticism and Interpretation* (4th ed., 1955); R. Bultmann, *Das Evangelium des Johannes* (1956); C. H. Dodd, *Historical Tradition in the Fourth Gospel* (1963); R. E. Brown, *The Gospel According to John* (2 vols., 1966, 1970); J. Marsh, *The Gospel of St. John* (1968); R. Schnackenburg, *The Gospel According to John* (3 vols., 1968, 1982); L. Morris, *The Gospel According to John* (1971); R. Kysar, *The Fourth Evangelist and His Gospel: An Examination of Contemporary Scholarship* (1975); C. K. Barrett, *The Gospel According to St. John* (2d ed., 1978); J. L. Martyn, *History and Theology in the Fourth Gospel* (2d ed., 1979); E. Haenchen, *John* (2 vols., 1984); J. A. T. Robinson, *The Priority of John* (1985).

LEON MORRIS

**Gospel Songs.** A distinct, American Christian music arising in the late 19th century to dominate nonliturgical worship, popular performance, and revivals. It technically differs from the "hymn," although in worship services during the 1900s hymns and gospel songs often came to be used interchangeably. A hymn is a lyric poem designed to express a worshiper's attitude toward God and God's purposes in human life. It is objective in content, usually lacking a refrain. Hymn tunes are normally stately and dignified with strict, even time values given to notes. Gospel music is more informal, both in content and musicality. Its purpose is to set Bible teachings to music for a mass audience, usually with an evangelistic or subjective worship intent. A chorus or refrain is standard. The gospel song became an important part of Christian music from its birth in the 1870s urban revival. It was also a means of contextualizing the gospel for divergent cultures within American society. Its fluidity has made it a vital evangelistic tool for third world countries.

Modern gospel music is unique in blending African and European artistic traditions into a single genre or set of genres. From Africa the rhythmical forms of drum-beat accompaniment and antiphonal tribal singing both influenced the American spiritual and through it, gospel forms. The spiritual as a folk music form used hand clapping and drums and vocal rhythms from its beginning. Instrumentation thus was a vital part of singing a spiritual; the spiritual was ready-made for tambourine, horn, organ, and piano. The content drew on the Bible story, but the lyrics could be changed at will to pass messages secretly among slaves. The mood expressed the emotions of everyday life and the future hope for freedom on earth and in heaven. The songs were communal. Songs such as "Swing Low, Sweet Chariot" and "Steal Away" were meant to be antiphonal; a leader's call is followed by a congregational response.

European contributions to gospel owe much to German pietism, particularly the Moravians, and through Moravian influence on John and Charles Wesley, the Methodist Church. The strain was first popularized by Isaac Watts (1674–1748). Within the nonconformist church Watts introduced an alternative to the staid Anglican psalter. English Calvinism added to the mix the hymns of August Toplady (1740–78).

These musical traditions began to meld in the fire of the Second Awakening, especially at its peak in the southern camp meetings of 1798–1804. Other melting pots were the revival and world missions movements which grew from the awakening and sought music with evangelistic fervor. The Sunday school movement, which began in England but took on a distinctly American hue by mid-century, looked for a musical catechism. William J. Kirkpatrick (1838–1921) set the tone for the Sunday school chorus with his book *Devotional Melodies* and such songs as "Jesus Saves," "He Hideth My Soul," and "Redeemed." Mrs. Alexander van Alstyne (1820–1915), using her maiden name of Fanny Crosby, produced 8000 songs for the Sunday school and later urban revivals, including "Blessed Assurance," "Rescue the Perishing," and "Jesus, Keep Me Near the Cross." The subjects of the new type of song were those of 20th-century gospel music: the love of Jesus, the joys of heaven, the call of the gospel, and the last days.

The crusades of Dwight L. Moody (1837–99) and song-leader Ira D. Sankey (1840–1908) made the gospel song the property of the revival movement and the churches which grew through it. The tradition continued through the 1900s with Billy Sunday (1862–1935) assisted by Homer A. Rodeheaver (1880–1955) and then Billy Graham and Cliff Barrows.

Meanwhile the spiritual had been refined and was ready for a second infusion into the white churches. That infusion was primarily the result of the success of black gospel singer Mahalia Jackson (1911–72) in the 1940s. The southern impact added what was known as "soul" styling, with an intense personal feeling which dated back to slavery days. Through the 1950s and 1960s Christian (and even secular) rock-and-roll became a revolutionary force in American life through the blend of jazz, blues, and gospel. Rhythm-and-blues style brought a solitary and introspective, rather than a community, aura to much of the new Christian "pop" market. Records and mass media caused new movements to run through and intermingle music with amazing rapidity.

As the 20th century neared its conclusion many groups who had continued to hold steadfastly to psalters and hymns were switching to new hymnals which dropped older pieces in favor of hymns and songs with a gospel flavor. On the negative side few pieces of objective-worship music were written, and the American understanding of a biblical theology of worship had suffered a decline as songs about the individual's emotional response to Jesus were stressed. In the pop market, songs which emphasized musicianship and electronically produced innovative sounds drawn from rock and jazz often muscled out lyrics with solid teaching. Christian music in general was still in the midst of change by the 1990s, and few knew what directions the gospel song would finally take.

**Bibliography.** A. Heilbut, *The Gospel Sound: Good News and Bad Times* (1975); J. Sallee, *A History of Evangelistic Hymnody* (1978); R. Anderson and G. North, *Gospel Music Encyclopedia* (1979); V. Broughton, *Black Gospel: An Illustrated History of the Gospel Sound* (1985).

## Gottheil, Richard James Horatio (1862–1936). Jewish orientalist. Born in Manchester, England, he was educated at Columbia College, and the universities of Berlin, Tübingen, and Leipzig (Ph.D., 1886). From 1887 he was professor of rabbinic literature and Semitic languages at Columbia University, and served also for a period as president of the Federation of American Zionists (1898–1904). He was founder and president of the Jewish Religious School Union, and head of the Oriental department of the New York Public Library.

His own works include *Zionism* (1914), *The Belmont-Belmonte Family* (1917), and *The Life of Gustav Gottheil: Memoir of a Priest in Israel* (1936). Among other works he edited *A Treatise on Syriac Grammar by Mar Eliâ of Sôbhâ* (1887), *Selections from the Syriac Julian Romance* (1906), *The Syriac-Arabic Glosses of Isha bar Ali* (1910–27), and *Fragments from the Cairo Genizah in the Freer Collection* (1927). He was editor of the *Columbia University Oriental Series* and (with Morris Jastrow) of the *Semitic Study Series*. In addition he was a department editor of the *Jewish Encyclopedia* (12 vols., 1901–6). He also made numerous contributions to Oriental and popular periodicals and to standard reference works.

## Gräbner, Theodore (1876–1950). Lutheran pastor, educator, and author. Born in Watertown, Wis., he was a graduate of Concordia Seminary, St. Louis, Mo. (1897), taught in Lutheran secondary schools (1897–1906), and was pastor of Lutheran parishes in Chicago (1906–13). He taught homiletics and also NT interpretation, dogmatics, and philosophy at Concordia Seminary (1913–49). He championed such causes as Christian elementary education, youth programs, Lutheran unity, and problems related to separation of church and state. His many writings include *Dark Ages* (1917), *Spiritism* (1920), *Bible Student Quarterly* (1921–47), *Essays on Evolution* (1925), *God and the Cosmos* (1932), *Borderland of Right and Wrong* (1938), *Toward Lutheran Union* (1943), and *A Handbook of Organizations* (1948). He edited *Lehre und Wehre* and *The Lutheran Witness* (1914–49).

FREDERICK E. MAYER

## Graham, William Franklin (1918– ). American evangelist. The son of a North Carolina dairy farmer and grandson of a Confederate soldier wounded at Gettysburg, Graham was converted when barely 16 years old at an evangelistic meeting in Charlotte. He was educated at Bob Jones College, Florida Bible Institute, and Wheaton College, Ill., where his leadership qualities became apparent early. After a brief pastorate, Graham became vice-president of Youth for Christ and began his lifelong traveling evangelistic ministry. Between trips he served four years as president of Northwestern College, Minneapolis. In 1949 his first major crusade in Los Angeles attracted nationwide attention, and the following year he founded the Billy Graham Evangelistic Association with headquarters in Minneapolis. His earnest delivery and striking physical appearance made a powerful impression on England during his 1954 London Crusade; over 50 Anglican clergymen traced their conversion to those meetings. The new queen, Elizabeth II, invited him to Windsor Castle. For the next 33 years he and his team traveled the world, preaching to crowds as large as one million (in South Korea) as well as to remote African villagers. Heads of state sought his counsel; academic honors came. He sponsored world evangelistic congresses in Berlin (1966), Lausanne (1974), and Amsterdam (1983, 1986), which spawned similar gatherings on every continent. His books, beginning with *Peace with God* in 1952, became best-sellers. His magazine *Decision* reached a total circulation of 5 million in six languages; he also conceived the magazine *Christianity Today*. His films, radio outreach, weekly newspaper column, and telecasts have made his message known worldwide, while his personal charm, humble bearing, and model family life have made him one of the world's most-admired men.

SHERWOOD E. WIRT

## Grant, Frederick Clifton (1891–1974). Anglican biblical scholar and theologian. Born in Beliot, Wis., he studied at Lawrence College, Nashotah House, General Theological Seminary,

N.Y., and Western Theological Seminary, Chicago (Th.D., 1922). After five parish ministries he became dean of Bexley Hall, Gambier, Ohio (1924–26), president of Western Theological Seminary during its relocation to Evanston, Ill., and merger with Seabury Divinity School (1927–38), and then professor of biblical theology, Union Theological Seminary, N.Y., from 1938 onward. He was editor of the *Anglican Theological Review* (1924–55). He expressed his liberal Anglicanism in such works as *New Horizons of the Christian Faith* (1928), and his ecumenical spirit and first-hand observations of Vatican II in *Rome and Reunion* (1965). He contributed greatly to the historical understanding of early Christianity through such works as *The Economic Background of the Gospels* (1926), *The Growth of the Gospels* (1933), *An Introduction to NT Thought* (1950), *Hellenistic Religions* (1953), *Ancient Roman Religion* (1957), *Ancient Judaism and the NT* (1959), and *Roman Hellenism and the NT* (1962).

GLEN G. SCORGIE

**Grant, Robert McQueen** (1917– ). NT and patristics scholar. Born in Evanston, Ill., he studied at Northwestern University, Union Theological Seminary, N.Y., and Harvard (Th.D., 1944). Following ordination by the Protestant Episcopal Church, and parish ministry (1942–44), he taught NT at the University of the South (1944–53) and, from 1952, at the University of Chicago Divinity School where he was professor of humanities from 1973. He was president of the Society of Biblical Literature, the American Society of Church History, and the North American Patristic Society. His many works include *Second-Century Christianity* (1946), *The Bible in the Church* (1948), *Miracle and Natural Law* (1952), *The Sword and the Cross* (1955), *The Letter and the Spirit* (1957), *Gnosticism and Early Christianity* (1959), *A Historical Introduction to the NT* (1963), *The Formation of the NT* (1965), *The Early Christian Doctrine of God* (1966), *After the NT* (1967), *Augustus to Constantine* (1971), *Eusebius as Church Historian* (1980), *Christian Beginnings* (1983), and *Gods and the One God* (1986).

GLEN G. SCORGIE

**Gray, George Buchanan** (1865–1922). English Congregationalist. Born in Blandford, Dorsetshire, he was educated at New College and University College, London, and Mansfield College, Oxford. He entered the Independent ministry in 1893 and was fellow and tutor at Mansfield College (1891–1900). From 1900 he was professor of Hebrew and OT exegesis at Mansfield and lecturer on the OT at the Friends' Summer School (1897–99). He was a member of the Board of the Faculty of Oriental languages at Oxford University from 1896, and of the general and executive committees of the Palestine Exploration Fund from 1905. In theology he was a liberal evangelical. He wrote *Studies in Hebrew Proper Names* (1896), *The Divine Discipline of Israel* (1900), *Numbers* in *The Temple Bible* (1902), *A Critical and Exegetical Commentary on Numbers* (1903), *A Critical and Exegetical Commentary on the Book of Isaiah*, vol. 1 (1912), *A Critical Introduction to the OT* (1913), *Forms of Hebrew Poetry* (1915), and *Sacrifice in the OT: Its Theory and Practice* (1925).

**Gray, James Martin.** (1851–1935). A New York City native, Gray was rector of First Reformed Episcopal Church, Boston (1879–94), as well as lecturer, Reformed Episcopal Seminary and Gordon College. Gray joined the faculty of Moody Bible Institute, Chicago, Ill. in 1893 and became dean in 1904. He was president of Moody from 1925 to shortly before his death. Gray helped guide the development of the 20th-century Bible college form and curriculum, and he influenced American dispensationalist thought as an editor of the Scofield Reference Bible (1909). He wrote *Synthetic Bible Studies* (1900), *How to Master the English Bible* (1904), *Primers of the Faith* (1906), *The Antidote to Christian Science* (1907), *Great Epochs of Sacred History* (1910), *Progress in Life to Come* (1910), *Bible Problems Explained* (1913), *Christian Workers' Commentary on the Old and New Testaments* (1915), *Picture of the Resurrection* (1917), *Prophecy and the Lord's Return* (1917), *A Text-book on Prophecy* (1918), *Spiritism and the Fallen Angels* (1920), *My Faith in Jesus Christ* (1927), and *Steps on the Ladder of Faith* (1931).

RAYMOND W. ALBRIGHT

**Greece.** Of the republic's 9.08 million population, 8.86 million are Orthodox, 38,200 are Roman Catholic, and 11,400 are Protestant. The country has an area of 131,944 sq. km. (50,944 sq. mi.).

Christianity came to the Greek peninsula through the apostle Paul. He touched such centers as Athens, Corinth, Thessalonica, and Berea, and the first Christian church in Europe was founded at Philippi. After 330, when Constantine built a new capital at Byzantium, which he called Constantinople, the church in Greece gravitated toward the East, and in 1054 the Great Schism divided the Eastern from the Western Church. The main issue in the division was the inclusion in the Nicene Creed of the *"filioque* clause," which said that the Holy Spirit was given by the Father and the Son.

The Orthodox Church still differs fundamentally from the Roman Catholic and Protestant churches. Heavy emphasis is placed on the transcendence of God. Man is not totally depraved and is capable of striving for salvation. Icons (religious engravings) are used as aids to worship. The archbishops are chosen by and responsible to the government of Greece; the country is one of the last bastions of "caesaropapism" in which the church works in close concert with the state.

Secularism is affecting Greece as it is other European countries. In 1961 the newspaper *Nea* surveyed the Greek population, and it was discovered that 30 percent attended church every Sunday. In the rural areas attendance was only 5 to 10 percent. By 1971 the number of weekly worshipers had fallen to 20 percent. It remains the established religion, and strict laws forbid proselytizing by other faiths.

Several religious societies strive to keep alive the Orthodox faith. *Zoe* (life) was formed in 1911, and it emphasizes Bible study and communion. *Soter* (savior) split from *Zoe* in 1960 and opposes any attempt at ecumenism with the Roman Catholic Church. A third movement, *Apostolike Diakonia* (apostolic service), propagates traditional Orthodox doctrine by the circulation of literature.

There is a small Roman Catholic community in Greece divided into three rites: Latin, Byzantine, and Armenian. These were restored as the Greeks won independence from Turkey during the 19th century.

There are several small and struggling Protestant communions in Greece. In 1858 Michael Kalopothakes founded the Greek Evangelical Church. As a graduate of Union Theological Seminary he returned to his native Greece and founded a church in Athens and a Sunday school. The first building of the Greek Evangelical Church was built in 1871. Kalopothakes was underwritten by the British and Foreign Bible Society. By the 1980s there were 32 congregations with 3000 members.

A second Protestant church is the Free Evangelical Church, which began in 1908 and eventually had 40 congregations and 1000 members. It is congregational in polity in contrast to the more Presbyterian approach of the Greek Evangelical Church.

The Jehovah's Witnesses entered Greece in 1900, although this movement was officially banned until 1974. They came to have 409 worship centers and 15,753 members.

Inasmuch as Greece was occupied by Turkey for nearly 400 years (1453–1827), there was a large Muslim population. In 1923 400,000 Muslims remained and were repatriated to Turkey in exchange for 1.5 million Greeks from Turkey. Now there are about 131,000 Turkish-speaking Muslims in Turkey. Many Turkish people have converted to the Orthodox Church.

Approximately 25 American missionary sending agencies work in Greece. Greater Europe Mission has a Bible training center near Athens. The Assemblies of God conduct church-planting work, as does the Oriental Missionary Society. Trans World Radio broadcasts regularly into the country.

Greece has exported many workers to Europe and America. Today there are approximately 2.2 million Greeks in the USA, Germany has 294,000, Australia has 250,000, and South Africa has 60,000.

*Bibliography.* E. Benz, *The Eastern Orthodox Church: Its Thought and Life* (1963); M. Rinvolucri, *Anatomy of a Church: Greek Orthodoxy Today* (1966); D. B. Barrett, ed., *World Christian Encyclopedia: A Comparative Survey of Churches and Religions in the Modern World*, A.D. *1900–2000* (1982), 328–33.

WAYNE DETZLER

**Greek Rite.** *See* BYZANTINE RITE.

**Greenberg, Simon** (1901– ). American Jewish rabbi, educator, and theologian. Born in Russia, he lived in the USA from 1905. Educated at the Teachers Institute of the Jewish Theological Seminary (JTS) in New York and other institutions, he received rabbinical ordination from JTS in 1925. From 1925 he served as rabbi at the important Conservative synagogue Har Zion in Philadelphia. From 1946 he filled major administrative posts in the conservative movement of American Judaism, and in 1957 was appointed vice-chancellor of JTS, where he had been professor of homiletics and education since 1948. Considered one of the leading spokesmen for the conservative movement, he wrote widely on Jewish education (emphasizing the centrality of Zionism and Hebrew), and the relationships between Judaism and American civilization.

ELIEZER SEGAL

**Greene, Theodore Meyer** (1897–1969). Philosopher and educator. Born to missionary parents in Constantinople, he studied at Amherst College and Edinburgh University (Ph.D., 1924). After serving as a YMCA secretary in Mesopotamia, he taught at Forman Christian College, Lahore, India (1919–21), Princeton (1923–45; professor of philosophy, 1941–45), Yale (1946–55), and Scripps College, Claremont, Calif. (1955–61). He was an outstanding teacher and popular advocate of the humanities. He was principally a philosopher of education, art, and religion. In addition to scholarly editions of selected writings of Kant, his chief works include *The Meaning of the Humanities* (1938), *The Arts and the Art of Criticism* (1940), *Our Cultural Heritage* (1956), *Liberalism* (1957), and *Moral, Aesthetic and Religious Insight* (1958).

GLEN G. SCORGIE

**Greenland.** A self-governing overseas territory of Denmark, Greenland has an area of 2,175,600 sq. km. (840,000 sq. mi.) and a population of about 54,000 (1985). Christianity arrived in about A.D. 990 with the first Scandinavian colonists. Missionary and trade stations were founded by the Danes and Moravians in the 1720s and 1730s. Missionaries, who had worked only on the western coast, founded their first station on the eastern coast at Angmagssalik in 1894. In 1906 the "Greenland Church Cause" (*Den gronlandske Kirkesag*) was founded in Copenhagen. In cooperation with the Danish Society for Foreign Missions, this Lutheran foundation sent out missionaries among the Greenlanders on the northeastern coast of the island. In 1937 the missionary work was brought to an end with the evangelization of all Eskimo groups.

Virtually all indigenous Christians on the world's largest island are Lutherans. By 1951 Greenland had one dean, one vice-dean, and 23 pastors; seven of the pastors were Danes, the rest were Greenlanders. The parishes tend to be extensive–40 to 90 miles in each direction from a church center. Travel in the summer is by motorboat and in the winter by dogsled; wind and ice often impede pastoral work. The 18 clerical districts in the late 1980s had the assistance of about 180 lay catechists who play a significant part in the Lutheran Church of Greenland. The Lutheran bishop of Copenhagen has supervision over Greenland. There is a seminary in Godthaab, the capital. From 1970 the population has been augmented by some 3000 U.S. troops who have expanded considerably the meager numbers of non-Lutheran Christians.

In 1960 the Roman Catholic diocese of Copenhagen founded the largest geographic parish in the world on Greenland, but it contains only a few hundred members.

J. D. DOUGLAS

## Grenfell, Wilfred Thomaston (1865–1940).
Labrador missionary doctor. Born in Parkgate, near Chester, England, he studied at Marlborough College, Oxford University, and London Hospital. In 1889 he joined the Royal National Mission to Fishermen and in 1892 went to Labrador. During 40 years he established hospitals, nursing stations, orphanages, schools, and other enterprises, and operated medical ships. He wrote 24 books, of which *A Labrador Doctor* (1922) and *Forty Years for Labrador* (1932) are autobiographies.

EDWIN E. CALVERLEY

## Grensted, Laurence William (1884–1964).
Anglican. Born in Blundellsands, near Liverpool, he studied at Oxford and Manchester. He was principal of Egerton Hall Theological College, Manchester (1919–24); fellow and chaplain of University College, Oxford (1924–30); and professor of philosophy of the Christian religion, Oxford (1930–50). He is known for work in the psychology of religion, writings on doctrine, and as an entomologist. Among his books are *Psychology and God* (1930), *The Person of Christ* (1933), *This Business of Living* (1939), and *The Psychology of Religion* (1952).

## Griffiths, Bede (1906– ).
Promoter of intrareligious dialogue. As Griffiths recounts in *The Golden String* (1954), he was converted to Catholicism in 1931 by the argument of Newman's *Development of Christian Doctrine*. Griffiths then became a Benedictine monk at Prinknash Abbey and was later prior of Farnborough Abbey. Attracted by Gandhi's life and spirituality, Griffiths went to India in 1955 and helped Francis Mahieu, a Belgian Cistercian, found Kurisumala Ashram, a monastery of the Syrian rite, in Kerala.

In 1968 Griffiths took over the Saccidananda Ashram at Santivanam which had been started by Jules Monchanin (1895–1957) and Henry Le Saux (1910–1973). Here residents and visitors met for prayer three times a day, using the scriptures of different religions in order to grow together toward the truth that they all sought. As Griffiths explained in *Return to the Centre* (1976), "I have to be a Hindu, a Buddhist, a Jain, a Parsee, a Sikh, a Muslim, and a Jew, as well as a Christian, if I am to know the Truth and to find the point of reconciliation in all religion" (p. 71). And for Christianity to be a truly world religion, a union must take place, so that Christianity "abandons its Western culture with its rational masculine bias and learns again the feminine intuitive understanding of the East" (*The Marriage of East and West* [1982], pp. 198f.).

PHILIP HILLYER

## Grimm, Harold John (1901–1983).
Historian of the German Reformation. Born in Saginaw, Mich., he studied at Capital University, Evangelical Lutheran Theological Seminary in Columbus, Ohio, the universities of Leipzig and Hamburg, and Ohio State University (Ph.D., 1932). He taught history at Capital University (1925–37), Ohio State University (1937–54; 1958–72), and Indiana University (1954–58). His work was characterized by regard for both the social and religious dynamics of the Reformation. He was a founder of the American Society for Reformation Research, and an editor of the *Archive for Reformation History* (1949–63). Among his many honors from students and peers were professor of the year award at Ohio State (1950), the presidency of the American Society of Church History (1961), and a festschrift entitled *The Social History of the Reformation* (1972). He wrote *Martin Luther as a Preacher* (1929), *The Reformation Era* (1954), *Luther and Culture* (1960), *The Reformation in Recent Historical Thought* (1964), and *Lazarus Spengler* (1978). Along with Tschau and Squires, Grimm wrote *Western Civilization* (2 vols., 1942).

GLEN G. SCORGIE

**Gros, Erwin** (1865–1927). German Evangelical National Church pastor and author. A teacher's son, he was pastor of Hartenrod, Hoechstenbach, Esch and Gonzenheim, parishes of the Hessian National Church. He was a popular author. He published his sermons in eight small volumes, *Auf der Dorfkanzel,* and in two books of sermons, *Im Frieden Gottes* and *Mit Gott zu Gott.* He wrote many rural romances, the most famous being *Der Bauernpfarrer.* Also, he was the author of thrilling historical stories, the most famous being *Die letzte Nonne von Walsdorf, Elsbeth von Helkhoven,* and *Es geht eine dunkle Wolke herein.*

REINHOLD KUECKLICH

**Groulx, Lionel** (1878–1967). French-Canadian historian and nationalist. Abbé Groulx was professor of Canadian history at the Université de Montréal from 1915 to 1949. His influence as a historian was supplemented by his use of the novel to popularize his historical thesis of the clerical-agrarian basis of French-Canadian nationality. His two best-known novels, *Chez nos gens* (1920) and *L'Appel de la race* (1922), sold widely. Groulx's work was important in setting the *nationaliste* trend of French-Canadian fiction in the 1920s. Moreover, through *l'Association catholique de la jeunesse canadienne française,* which he helped establish in 1904, and as director of the Montréal periodical *l'Action française* from 1920 to 1928, as well as his some 20 books and innumerable articles, Groulx was the leader of French-Canadians between the World Wars. An ultramontanist-nationalist, historically characteristic of French-Canadian nationalism, Groulx nationalized social catholicism, which significantly influenced him through the work of J. B. H. Lacordaire, C. Montalembert, J. de Maistre, F. Ozanam, and L. Veuillot. Groulx's social catholic understanding of the incarnation was the core of his practical theology and consequent religious rationale for French-Canadian nationalism. Further, Groulx was influenced by French romanticism through his extensive study of French literature as well as philosophy and theology at the University de la Minerve, Rome, University of Fribourg (Ph.D., 1907), and at Montreal (docteur ès lettres, 1932). Much of his work can be interpreted as the development and promotion of the individuality of the French-Canadian community over the Canadian Confederation. Likewise his case for French-Canadian nationalism can be seen as collective individualism and cult of self. Groulx's ideology rejected the religiopolitical French-Canadian nationalism of the early 20th century for a secular *quebeçois* militancy. It prepared the "Quiet Revolution" of French-Canada in the 1960s, although Groulx, because of his intellectual and ecclesiastical intransigence, vigorously repudiated its secular character. The *Institut d'histoire de l'amérique française* in Montreal he founded in 1946 houses all documents pertinent to Groulx.

*Bibliography.* M. Wade, *The French Canadians* (1968); J. P. Gaboury, *Le Nationalisme de Lionel Groulx* (1970); L. Groulx, *Mes Mémoires* (1970); S. Trofiemenkoff, ed., *Abbé Groulx: Variations on a Nationalist Theme* (1973); M. Filion, ed., *Hommage à Lionel Groulx* (1978); G. Fregault, *Lionel Groulx Tel Qu'en Lui-Même* (1978); R. Bergeron and G. Huot, eds., *Journal 1895–1911 Lionel Groulx* (1984).

NORMAN F. CORNETT

**Grubb, Sir Kenneth George** (1900–1980). Missionary and ecclesiastical statesman. As a missionary associated with the Heart of Amazonia Mission, he was commissioned to conduct a linguistic survey of the lowland Indians of Amazonia. The results were published in 1927, the first of a series of surveys produced during the next decade. These included volumes on Bolivia (1932), the northern republics of South America (1931), Brazil (1932), Spain (1933), Mexico (1935), and Central America (1937). Meanwhile he had joined the staff of the World Dominion Press as survey editor and become managing trustee of the Survey Application Trust. Between 1949 and 1968 he was joint editor of the *World Christian Handbook.* Before and during World War II he worked for the Ministry of Information, becoming a controller (1941–46) and being made Companion of St. Michael and St. George in recognition of his services.

He became deeply involved in the World Council of Churches, serving as director and then chairman of the Commission of the Churches on International Affairs (1946–68). He was president of the Church Missionary Society (1944–69) and was the first evangelical to serve as chairman of the House of Laity of Church Assembly of the Church of England (1959–70) and the first to be elected to three successive terms of office. He was knighted in 1953.

HAROLD H. ROWDON

**Grundemann, Reinhold** (1836–1924). German Evangelical National Church pastor and author. Born in Baerwalde, Neumark, he pastored churches in Bitterfeld (1861), Frankfurt/Oder (1862–64), and Moerz near Belzig (1869–1912). From 1865 to 1869 he was a cartographer at Perthes in Gotha. He was author of mission books and was well known as the coeditor of *Allgemeine Missionszeitschrift,* and through the pioneer drawing of a large and a small mission atlas: *Allgemeiner Missions-Atlas* (1868–71), *Neuer Missions-Atlas* (1895–1903), and *Kleiner Missions-Atlas* (1883, 1905). He was the founder of the Brandenburgische Missions-Konferenz and its president for 25 years.

REINHOLD KUECKLICH

**Guatemala.** A republic of Central America with an area of 108,889 sq. km. (42,042 sq. mi.) and a population of 8.9 million.

Most Guatemalans are Roman Catholic or Christo pagan, mixing Catholicism and Mayan deities. The liberal repression against the Catholic Church during the 1870s and 1880s in Guatemala was probably the most severe of any country in Latin America. Church property was confiscated and religious orders were dissolved. By the time it was over only about 100 priests remained. Significantly weakened institutionally, the church was never able to develop a strong native clergy. The Catholic hierarchy accommodated itself to a series of dictatorships lasting until 1944. In 1954, Archbishop Mariano Rossell was a key figure in the successful overthrow of the democratically elected Jacobo Arbenz Guzmân government. Succeeding military regimes rewarded the church by lifting previously imposed restrictions.

One important consequence of the improving church-state relations was the influx of foreign missionaries after 1954. The number of priests increased from 132 in 1950 to 483 in 1965. Many of the foreign priests who arrived during the 1960s were greatly influenced by Second Vatican Council reforms, and became active in the formation of agricultural cooperatives and in community development. These activities brought many church people into conflict with the government. Beginning in 1976, at least 16 priests and religious and thousands of Catholic lay leaders were murdered or disappeared. In 1980 the bishop of Quiché was forced into exile. Despite the government's measures of repression against the church, the hierarchy maintained a very cautious attitude during this period, largely neutralized by conservative Cardinal Mario Casariego, who opposed any church involvement in "political" issues. In contrast a number of independent Christian groups, such as the Commission for Justice and Peace, actively monitored human rights abuses. After Casariego's death in 1983 the hierarchy became more openly critical of government abuses.

Protestant churches have been increasingly influential since their arrival in 1882. The liberal reforms created many opportunities for Protestant missionaries, allowing them to construct numerous schools and the first full-service hospital. By the late 1970s 67 different denominations operated in the country. In 1984 it was estimated that 22 percent of the population belonged to Protestant churches. Most of the inroads have been made by fundamentalist and pentecostal sects.

PHILIP J. WILLIAMS

**Guiana, British.** *See* GUYANA.

**Guiana, French.** A former French colony on the northern coast of South America, bounded by Brazil and Surinam. French Guiana was founded in 1604 and became a department of Metropolitan France in 1946, having a local governor and general council of 15 elected officials, with representation in Paris by a senator and deputy. The land area is 91,000 sq. km. (35,100 sq. mi.). The economy is based on lumber, silver, cocoa, coffee, and fishing. Substantial aid is given by France, which uses French Guiana as the launching pad for her spacial program.

The total population was about 70,000 in 1981, with 36,000 in the capital, Cayenne. Of these, the majority were Creole (35,000) with 7000 French. Other Caucasians, blacks, Amerindians, and Orientals (Laotians and Vietnamese since 1979) made up the total. Approximately 65,000 were Roman Catholic (mid-1980s).

Religious work was first begun by the Jesuits and Capuchins in 1643. The Carib tribe (1400) is nominally Roman Catholic. Traditional Protestantism is represented by a French Reformed and a Presbyterian congregation. Evangelical witness, including church planting, has been most actively carried out by Assemblies of God, Southern Baptists (since 1982), Salvation Army, Brethren (with two congregations of Laotians by the late 1980s), and smaller ethnic groups like Chinese evangelicals from Surinam.

LEONARD MEZNAR

**Guignebert, Charles** (1867–1939). Born in Villeneuve Saint Georges near Paris and baptized a Roman Catholic, he studied at the Lycée de Versailles and at the Sorbonne, Paris. His teaching career began in the Lycées of Evreux, Pau, Toulouse, and Paris. In 1906 he was appointed by the minister of national education to a newly created chair of history of Christianity at the Sorbonne, which he occupied until retirement. A theological liberal, he was primarily a historian, but his presentation of Christianity was so profound that many regarded him a specialist in NT. His main works are *Tertullien. Étude sur ses sentiments à l'égard de l'empire et de la société civile* (1901), *Manuel d'histoire ancienne du Christianisme* (1906), *Modernisme et tradition catholique en France* (1908), *Le primauté de Pierre et la venue de Pierre à Rome* (1909), *Le problème de Jésus* (1914), *Le Christianisme antique* (1921), *La vie cachée de Jésus* (1921), *Le Christianisme médiéval et moderne* (1922), *Le problème religieux dans la France d'aujourd'hui* (1922), *Christianity: Past and Present* (1927), *L'evolution des dogmes* (2d ed., 1929), *Jésus* (1933, ET, 1935), *Le monde juif vers le temps de Jésus* (1935, ET, 1939), and *Le Christ* (1944). He translated *A Short History of the French People* (1930).

***Bibliography.*** M. Brunot, *Les Annales de l'Université de Paris* 4/5 (1939); A. Loisy and M. Simon, *Revue Historique* 188 (1940).

DANIEL J. THERON

**Guilday, Peter** (1884–1947). Catholic historian. Born in Chester, he studied at St. Charles Borromeo Seminary, Philadelphia, and the Catholic University of Louvain (D.Sc.Hist., 1914); taught American church history in the Catholic University of America, Washington (1914–47); was ordained to the priesthood in 1909; founded the *Catholic Historical Review* (April 1915), of which he remained editor to his death; and founded the American Catholic Historical Association (1919). He was noted as an orator, a stimulating teacher, and a historical researcher. He wrote *The English Colleges and Convents in the Low Countries, 1558–1795* (1914), *An Introduction to Church History* (1925), *The Life and Times of John Carroll, First Archbishop of Baltimore, 1735–1815* (2 vols., 1922), *The Life and Times of John England, First Bishop of Charleston, 1786–1842* (2 vols., 1927), and *A History of the Councils of Baltimore, 1791–1884* (1932).

*Bibliography.* J. J. Kortendick, *Catholic Library World* (May 1941); J. T. Ellis, *Catholic Historical Review* 33 (Oct. 1947): 257–68.

JOHN TRACY ELLIS

**Guinea.** *See* WEST AFRICA.

**Guinea-Bissau.** *See* WEST AFRICA.

## Gulf States (Kuwait, Bahrain, Qatar, the United Arab Emirates [UAE], and Oman).

A cluster of small, oil-rich Arab states in the area of the Persian Gulf and the Gulf of Oman. Because of their rich resources these tiny countries have been significant in the ongoing struggles of the Middle East. In 1990 Kuwait was invaded and its government overthrown by neighboring Iraq after a lengthy land dispute over islands in the Persian Gulf. Religious tensions also helped precipitate what began as a bitter and bloody occupation which divided the Islamic world. Their religious makeup is complicated by large minorities (in the UAE about 80 percent of the population) who are temporary workers with foreign nationality. Most of these people share the Muslim faith of the indigenous population, but there are also large numbers of Christians (notably from the Philippines), Hindus, and others. While such expatriates, Muslims included, generally cannot hope to become citizens of the countries where they live and suffer serious disabilities as aliens, they do enjoy freedom of religion. The shifting nature of this sector of the population, which shrank considerably during the mid-1980s due to the downturn in oil revenues, dictates concentration on these countries' more permanent inhabitants.

The indigenous population of the Gulf states is Muslim, virtually without exception. Aside from Oman, all are ruled by Sunni dynasties, and Sunni members dominate their societies, although substantial portions of the population in each case are Shi'ites (Twelvers). In Bahrain in particular a Shi'ite majority of perhaps 70 percent or more has deeper roots in the archipelago, since the Sunnis are relatively recent conquerors. Shi'ites make up about one-fourth of Kuwait's population and between 15 and 20 percent of Qatar's and the UAE's. The Shi'ites are victims of much discrimination in such matters as governmental employment and tend to cluster in the lower economic rungs, although the merchant class includes some wealthy Shi'ites. When Kuwait had an elected parliament before 1986, districts were gerrymandered to minimize Shi'ite representation.

Often reflecting tribal divisions, at least three of the four Sunni schools of Muslim jurisprudence have a substantial following in these states. Kuwait's Sunnis are mainly Malikis, as is the ruling family of Bahrain. Shafa'is form much of the population of Bahrain and of the UAE. The rulers and much of the people of Qatar and four of the smaller member states of the UAE (Ash Shariqah, Ra's al-Khayma, Ujman, and Umm al Qawain), as well as some of the people in the al-'Ain (Buraimi) Oasis) region of Abu Dhabi (the largest member of the UAE), are Hanbalis (that is, Wahhabis) but appear generally to lack the strictness of the followers of the same movement in Saudi Arabia.

Oman is unique in that it is the one Muslim country in which both Sunnis and Shi'ites exist as relatively small minorities among its nationals. Instead, both the ruling dynasty and the majority of the people belong to the Ibadi sect, which is the only surviving–and the moderate–branch of the militant, puritanical Kharijites (Seceders). The Kharijites, who form small minorities in other Gulf countries (particularly the UAE), Zanzibar, Algeria, and Libya, date back to the beginning of the caliphate, A.D. 660, when they seceded from Muhammed's son-in-law, Ali, in protest because he agreed to submit the conflict over who should be successor to the Prophet to arbitration. The Kharijites, who declared themselves the only true Muslims, rejected the need for a caliph or imam. Should one prove necessary, they insisted, he must be elected by the whole community, and any Muslim, regardless of tribe, is qualified to rule. If such a ruler deviates from justice he should be overthrown. These strongly democratic ideas have no effect on Omani politics today. The Ibadis differ from now-extinct branches of Kharijism in not calling for war against other Muslims, advocating instead their peaceful conversion. In fact, the ruling dynasty (sultanate) of the 1980s had no particular religious sanction. A theocratic imam representing the "fundamentalist" side of Ibadism ruled the interior of the country largely independently of the sultan until the latter defeated him during the 1950s and forced him into exile in Saudi Arabia.

Islam is the official religion of all of these states. Like other traditional Arab monarchies, the Gulf regimes have always based their legitimacy heavily on their devotion to Islam. The Iranian Revolution in 1979, pressures from Saudi Arabia in some cases, and the resurgence of religious sentiment among their own populations evoked renewed efforts by governments to bolster their Islamic credentials during the 1980s. Government money was lavished on building mosques and for other religious purposes. Although a variety of decrees and codes of law were adopted, the Shari'a is defined everywhere as a main source of jurisprudence. The Shari'a applies particularly in the area of personal status (marriage, divorce, inheritance, and related matters). Even modern codes draw on the Shari'a, and Kuwait and Jordan still use the Ottoman civil code (the Majalla) that was issued in the 1870s. The Majalla is a mere systematization of Islamic rules of the Hanafi school. Regimes were lax in their enforcement of some Islamic prohibitions in the 1980s. Everywhere except in Kuwait liquor was served to foreigners in hotels and scantily attired Western women could be seen in lobbies and swimming pools. The availability of alcohol and other religiously forbidden things in Bahrain made it a major attraction for less strict Saudis.

Confronting this "official" (or "establishment") Islam was the new momentum of "popular Islam"—movements demanding fuller implementation of the Shari'a, condemning corruption, emphasizing social justice, calling for solidarity with fellow Muslims (as in Palestine and Afghanistan), and rejecting monarchical regimes and dependence on Western powers. Among Shi'ites movements also asserted demands for ending discrimination against themselves. Such movements varied in their agenda from country to country. Sunni fervor ranged from the revolutionary Salafi movement to reformists and organizations of Muslim Brethren able to work with spokesmen for official Islam.

As the self-proclaimed champion of the dispossessed everywhere and enemy of superpower domination, the Iranian Revolution provided both a fillip and a complication for popular Islam in the Gulf states. It inspired and apparently supported local groups but also induced the regimes to try to co-opt the moderate ones. Particularly at first, in keeping with the Ayatollah Ruhollah Khomeini's deemphasis on sectarian differences, the Iranian Revolution's appeal extended to Sunnis, particularly to the poor, as well as to Shi'ites. Some Sunni preachers called for support of Khomeini. But, as Iran experienced turmoil and as local regimes cultivated an image of the Shi'ite character of the movement centered in Tehran, support for it seemingly came to be more restricted to Shi'ites, and sectarian conflict showed signs of renewal. Revolutionary Shi'ite groups, allegedly supported by Iran, engaged in guerrilla activity in Kuwait, whose ruler gave financial and other support to Iraq's war against Iran through the 1980s. A truck-bombing was directed at the United States and French embassies in 1983, an attempt failed to assassinate the emir in 1985, and a group plotted to blow up oil installations in 1987. In Bahrain, a coup involving Shi'ite nationals of several Gulf states was aborted by security forces in 1981.

**Bibliography.** R. G. Landen, *Oman since 1856: Disruptive Modernization in a Traditional Arab Society* (1967); J. D. Anthony, *Arab States of the Lower Gulf: People, Politics, Petroleum* (1975); T. E. Farah, *Islamic Resurgence in the Arab World* (1982), 170–77; J. A. Bill, *Foreign Affairs* 63 (Fall 1984): 108–47; R. H. Dekmejian, *Islam in Revolution: Fundamentalism in the Arab World* (1985); M. C. Peck, *The United Arab Emirates: A Venture in Unity* (1986); R. K. Ramazani, *Shi'ism and Social Protest* (1986), 30–54; R. M. Wright, *Sacred Rage: The Wrath of Militant Islam* (1986).

GLENN E. PERRY

### Gummey, Henry Riley, Jr. (1870–1941).

Protestant Episcopal educator. Born in Philadelphia, Pa., he studied at the University of Pennsylvania, and the divinity school of the Protestant Episcopal Church, where he was professor of liturgics and canon law (1929–41). His chief literary contribution is *The Consecration of the Eucharist—A Study of the Prayer of Consecration in the Communion Office from the Point of View of the Alterations and Amendments Established Therein by the Revisers of 1789* (1908).

SCOTT F. BRENNER

### Gunkel, Johann Friedrich Hermann

(1862–1932). German biblical scholar. Born in Springe, near Hanover, he was educated at the universities of Göttingen, Giessen, and Leipzig, and thereafter taught OT at Halle, Giessen, and Berlin before returning to Halle. In collaboration with W. Bousset from 1903 he edited the *Forschungen zur Religion und Literatur des Alten und Neuen Testaments,* and developed the religious-historical approach to biblical literature— the forerunner of form criticism. His *Die Wirkung des Heiligen Geistes nach den populären Anschauungen der apostolsichen Zeit und nach der Lehre des Paulus* (1888) was reissued in a third edition in 1909. He also wrote *Schöpfung und Chaos in Urzeit und Endzeit* (1895), *Der Prophet Esra* (1900), *Genesis übersetzt und erklärt* (1900), *The Legends of Genesis* (1901), *Israel and Babylon* (1903), *Zum religionsgeschichtlichen Verständnis des Neuen Testaments* (1903), *Ausgewählte Psalmen* (1904), *Literaturgeschichte Israels und des alten Judentums* (1906), *Die Propheten* (1917), *Das Märchen im Alten Testament* (1917), and *Einleitung in die Psalmen* (1928–33).

### Gunsaulus, Frank Wakeley (1856–1921).

Congregationalist pastor and scholar. Born in Chesterville, Ohio, he graduated from Ohio Wesleyan University, and after four years as a Methodist Episcopal minister he became a Congregationalist. He held pastorates in Columbus, Ohio (1879–81), Newtonville, Mass. (1881–85), Baltimore (1885–87), and Plymouth Church, Chicago (1887–89). Shortly after transferring to the Central Church in Chicago (1889–1919) he also became president of the Armour Institute of Technology, a post he held until 1921. He also lectured regularly at the University of Chicago. He wrote *Metamorphoses of a Creed* (1879), *Transfiguration of Christ* (1886), *The Man of Galilee* (1889), *Life of William Ewart Gladstone* (1898), *Paths to Power* (1905), *Higher Ministries of Recent English Poetry* (1907), *Paths to the City of God* (1907), and *The Minister and the Spiritual Life* (1911).

**Guru.** Historically the teacher of the Hindu *Vedas*. Since the *Upanishads* were written (c. 600s–500s B.C.) when Hinduism turned its orientation from the seen to the unseen, from dualism to monism, and from liberation as intuition and ecstasy to liberation as *bhakti* or devotion, the guru has become the center of Hindu tradition. To his disciple he is mentor, judge, and symbol of the Absolute—indeed, a god. He has his own ashram or establishment of instruction and is no longer the lonely ascetic or divine madman drawn to live in filthy places.

The guru serves as guide on the "paths" to liberation. Although these paths are called devotion, knowledge, work, or mind, they have nothing to do with the outer world but refer entirely to subjective states. The more altered the states of consciousness experienced, the closer one is to liberation. One advances from the trance state of devotion to that of pure awareness until body-consciousness is lost and the mind has died, guaranteeing no further rebirth.

The essence of the guru phenomenon is the guru-disciple relationship, which is dependent upon the all-pervasive domination of the guru and the absolute surrender of the disciple. The relationship has its source in Indian society and so demands emotional suppression; thus it is ascetic and repressive. "Detachment" from the world of duty and "attachment" to the god within by merging with the guru has special significance.

With the decrease in the value of an individual, a lower priority given to rational knowledge since the 1960s and 1970s, and the popularity of transpersonal ties and altered states of consciousness, the guru-disciple relationship has become popular in the West. The guru was, of course, known to Westerners and was cultivated for his "ancient wisdom" since at least the beginning of theosophism under Helena Blavatsky (1831–91) and Annie Besant (1847–1933). The latter started an organization to sponsor the mystic Jidder

Krishnamurti as a messiah-like guru. Although Krishnamurti left the theosophist fold, its sponsorship of gurus remained a central purpose.

The import of the Indian guru became big business in America with the rise of interest in experiential religions. The promise of self-realization appealed to American notions of success and dovetailed with the human potential movement and experimentation with alternate lifestyles and medicine. Indeed psychotherapists and psychotherapies have played an important role in Bhagwan Shree Rajneesh's organization.

Today, the degenerate side of the guru phenomenon is clearly visible in the inability of many of its fans to tolerate criticism and doubt, their demand to remain childlike and totally dependent, and their demand to relate to the guru as divine lover or loving father. The idea is cultivated through guru-based mysticism that solutions to life's problems are purely relational in nature. Above all, it is now recognized that "guru-salvation," based as it is on simple rescue themes, subjective states, impressionistic ways of experiencing the world, and dramatic behavior, is one expression of hysteria and hysterics. It is not surprising, therefore, that outside Hindu circles the guru is being replaced by trance channelers whose "how to" formulas are more direct ways of helping wealthy clients discover the god within.

**Bibliography.** W. Donkin, *The Wayfarers* (1948); P. Brent, *Godmen of India* (1972); S. Kakar, *Shamans, Mystics and Doctors: A Psychological Inquiry into India and Its Healing Traditions* (1982); I. Hexham and K. Poewe, *Understanding Cults and New Religions* (1986).

KARLA POEWE

**Gustav-Adolf-Verein (Gustavus Adolphus Association).** Established in 1832 as the Gustav-Adolf-Stiftung, it was renamed in 1842 the Evangelischer Verein der Gustav-Adolf-Stiftung when it joined forces with the Verein für Unterstützung hilfsbedürftiger Protestantischer Gemeinden. Its efforts were focused on areas where Protestants constituted a denominational and linguistic minority. It offered material support and spiritual aid through lecture series, literature, the building of schools and churches, and the training of catechetical instructors and preachers. Finances were secured through annual collections in churches of the Evangelische Kirche Deutschland (EKD).

After World War II in Germany the association was particularly a boon to Protestant refugees who had been resettled in largely Roman Catholic areas. The 1980s headquarters for the Western churches was Kassel (FRG), while the head office for the Eastern churches continued to be Leipzig in East Germany. The work is done through subgroups and women's groups within the various territorial churches of EKD. It publishes *Die evangelische Diaspora* (1919–41, 1953– ).

E. J. FURCHA

**Guyana.** Founded in 1831 as a crown colony and formerly British Guiana. Guyana became an independent member of the British Commonwealth in 1966. In 1987 the country became officially the Cooperative Republic of Guyana. The nation of 214,969 sq. km. (83,000 sq. mi.) is a military and Marxist regime with close diplomatic and personal ties to East Europe. Bounded by Brazil, Venezuela, and Surinam on the Caribbean Sea, Guyana is largely tropical forest land. Its total estimated population was 884,000 (mid-1980s), the majority of which was East Indian; about 40 percent was black, and 5 percent was Amerindian.

Although the government was officially atheist at the end of the 1980s, religious activity was tolerated and involved most citizens. About 300,000 East Indian Hindus, brought to Guyana by the British as farm laborers in the 1800s, formed the largest religious group. The largest Christian groups were Roman Catholic and Anglican, with a little more than 140,000 in each communion. Protestants were found among 51 denominations, and there had been marked growth in the number of pentecostals. The largest pentecostal group, the Elim Pentecostal Church, had 8500 members. There were 16 evangelical missionary agencies in the country in the 1980s with 50 missionaries. The largest was World Team, working among Wyano Indians and planting churches among blacks in the bush and Hindustani sugar cane workers. Unevangelized Fields Mission maintained a Bible institute in Georgetown, the capital. The people of Guyana tend to be strongly nationalistic, and indigenous church movements have been popular. In 1976 foreign missions in Guyana were affected by the government's nationalization of all schools.

In November 1976, Guyana was thrust into both religious and secular spotlights as the site of Jonestown and the People's Temple Movement. More than 900 members of the sect who had moved to Guyana from the USA died in a mass suicide.

LEONARD MEZNAR

**Gwatkin, Henry Melvill** (1844–1916). English church historian. Born in Barrow-on-Soar, Leicestershire, he graduated from Cambridge University, and remained there all his life, notably as professor of ecclesiastical history (1891–1916). Highly regarded as teacher and scholar, he wrote *Studies of Arianism* (1882), *The Arian Controversy* (1889), *Selections from Early Christian Writers* (1893), *The Eye for Spiritual Things* (1906), *The Knowledge of God* (1906), and *Early Church History to A.D. 313* (2 vols., 1909). He also served as joint editor of the *Cambridge Medieval History* after 1911.

# Hh

**Haas, John Augustus William** (1862–1937). Lutheran pastor and educator. Born in Philadelphia, he was educated at the University of Pennsylvania, the Lutheran Seminary at Mt. Airy, Philadelphia, and the University of Leipzig. He held pastorates at Grace Lutheran Church, New York City (1888–96) and St. Paul's Lutheran Church in the same city (1896–1904) before appointment as president of Muhlenberg College, Allentown, Pa. (1904–37), during the earlier part of which period he also taught religion and philosophy. While generally conservative in theology, he respected other positions, particularly in the field of biblical research. His major books were *Commentary on the Gospel of Mark* (1895), *Bible Literature* (1903), *In the Light of Faith* (1922), *Freedom and Christian Conduct* (1923), *The Unity of Faith and Knowledge* (1926), *The Truth of Faith* (1927), *What Ought I to Believe?* (1929), *The Christian Way of Liberty* (1930), and *Christianity and Its Contrasts* (1932).

**Habgood, John Stapylton** (1927– ). Archbishop of York. After graduating from Cambridge he pursued theological studies at Cuddesdon College, Oxford. He returned to his scientific interests as demonstrator in pharmacology at Cambridge (1950–53), but was ordained in 1954 and was successively curate of St. Mary Abbots, Kensington (1954–56), vice-principal of Westcott House, Cambridge (1956–62), rector of St. John's, Jedburgh (1962–67), principal of Queen's College, Birmingham (1967–73), bishop of Durham (1973–83), and archbishop of York (from 1983). He has written *Religion and Science* (1964), *A Working Faith* (1980), and *Church and Nation in a Secular Age* (1983).

**Häring, Theodor** (1848–1928). German theologian. Born in Stuttgart, he studied at the universities of Tübingen and Berlin. He lectured in the evangelical theological seminary at Tübingen (1873–76) and was pastor in Calw (1876–81) and in Stuttgart (1881–86). After three years as profes-

sor at Zurich (1886–89), he was chosen to succeed Albrecht Ritschl at Göttingen. From 1895 he was professor of NT exegesis, dogmatics, and ethics at Tübingen. He was influenced much by Württemberg's pietism and the teaching of Ritschl. He developed, nevertheless, an individual theological system and influenced an entire generation of pastors. Häring was associate editor of *Theologische Studien aus Württemberg* (1880–89), and he wrote *Über das Bleibende im Glauben an Christus* (1880), *Die Theologie und der Vorwurf der doppelten Wahrheit* (1886), *Zu Ritschls Versöhnungslehre* (1888), *Zur Versöhnungslehre* (1893), *Unsere persönliche Stellung zum geistlichen Beruf* (1893), *Die Lebensfrage der systematischen Theologie* (1895), *Das Christliche Leben* (1902), and *Der Christliche Glaube* (1906). His chief later works were commentaries on Romans, Hebrews, and the Pastoral Epistles, collections of sermons, and *Von Ewigen Dingen* (1922).

RAYMOND W. ALBRIGHT

**Häring, Theodor Lorenz** (1884–1964). Philosophy educator. Born in Stuttgart, Germany, he studied theology and philosophy at Tübingen, Halle, Berlin, and Bonn. He taught at Tübingen (1912–51), and devoted himself primarily to the history of philosophy and related fields. His chief works are *Der Duisburgische Kantnachlass um 1775* (1910), *Untersuchungen zur Psychologie der Wertung* (1913), *Die Materialisierung des Geistes* (1919), *Die Struktur der Weltgeschichte* (1921), *Philosophie der Naturwissenschaft* (1923), *Hegel, sein Wollen und sein Werk* (2 vols., 1928, 1938), *Individualität in Naturund Geisteswelt* (1925), *Grundprobleme der Geschichtsphilosophie* (1924), and *Schwabenspiegel* (1950).

RAYMOND W. ALBRIGHT

**Haiti.** *See* WEST INDIES.

**Haldane, John Burdon Sanderson** (1892–1964). Educator. He was educated at Eton and New College, Oxford. He taught biochemistry at Cambridge (1922–32), genetics at London University (1933–37), and thereafter was professor of biometry at University College, London. His religious books include *Science and Ethics* (1928), *The Inequality of Man* (1932), *The Causes of Evolution* (1933), *Fact and Faith* (1934), *The Marxist Philosophy and the Sciences* (1938), and *Science Advances* (1947).

RAYMOND W. ALBRIGHT

**Hall, Granville Stanley** (1846–1924). Protestant psychologist and educator. Born in Ashfield, Mass., he studied at Williams College, Union Theological Seminary, and the universities of Berlin, Bonn, Heidelberg, and Harvard (Ph.D., 1878). He taught psychology at Antioch College (1872–76), English at Harvard (1876/77), psychology at Harvard and Williams (1880/81), and psychology at Johns Hopkins (1881–88), where he founded one of the first psychology laboratories in the country and included among his students John Dewey and Joseph Jastrow. When Clark University was opened in 1889 in Worcester, Mass., he was appointed president and professor of psychology. During his administration considerable educational research was carried out. He resigned in 1920, but continued to write until his death. While his methods often lacked the precision of other social scientists in his day, he precipitated active interest and research in psychology and education. He was best known as an advocate of the culture-epoch theory which was set forth in his most influential book, *Adolescence* (1904).

His publications include *Aspects of German Culture* (1881), *Contents of Children's Minds on Entering School* (1884), *Hints Towards a Select and Descriptive Bibliography of Education* (1886), *Youth—Its Education, Regimen and Hygiene* (1907), *Educational Problems* (1911), *Founders of Modern Psychology* (1912), *Jesus Christ in the Light of Psychology* (1917), *Morale: The Supreme Standard of Life and Conduct* (1920), *Senescence* (1922), and *Life and Confessions of a Psychologist* (1923).

He was the founder and editor of the *American Journal of Psychology* (1887–1921), *American Journal of Religious Psychology and Education* (1904–15), and the *Journal of Applied Psychology*.

ROLLIN J. FAIRBANKS

**Haller, William** (1885–1974). Born in New York, N.Y., he studied at Amherst College and Columbia University (Ph.D., 1916). He was instructor and professor of English at Barnard College and on the faculty of philosophy, Columbia University (1909–50). He was coeditor of the Columbia edition, *Works of John Milton*, edited *Tracts on Liberty in the Puritan Revolution* (1944), and wrote *The Rise of Puritanism* (1938). His studies in the history of Puritanism and related topics were the outgrowth of his studies in

English literature and English and American history.

**Hallesby, Ole Kristian** (1879–1961). Norwegian Lutheran theologian and writer. Theologically liberal as an undergraduate, Hallesby experienced a conversion in 1902 that returned him to the Haugean tradition of piety and orthodoxy of his heritage. Ordained in 1903 and an itinerant preacher for several years, he studied at Erlangen and other centers in Germany before being appointed professor of systematic theology in the recently founded Free Faculty of Theology in Oslo in 1909. Hallesby taught there until 1951. Increasingly prominent and widely traveled abroad, he became the central figure in the conservative opposition to theological liberalism. He was also a leader of the religious resistance during the German occupation of Norway (1940–45). In addition to his leadership within the Norwegian Church, he became the first president of the International Fellowship of Evangelical Students in 1947. A prolific and influential author of more than 40 widely translated volumes, his book *Prayer* (ET, 1948) has gone through more than 50 printings.

NORRIS A. MAGNUSON

**Hallucination.** Sensory experience—usually of sight or hearing, but also occasionally involving smell, taste, or touch—which has no objectively real, external stimulus. Hallucination can force the body to perceive a whole complex of sense experiences. Sleep perceptions and illusion, in which the body misperceives for an external reason, are not regarded as hallucination, nor are experiences shared by a group.

Scripture does not specifically deal with hallucination. Some examples of demon possession may have been related to mental disorders. The epistles warn Christians to test with skepticism or to disregard personal revelation, presumably including mystical visions which might arise from hallucination. The vision of the ascetic, from whatever source, has alternately been condemned and credulously affirmed. Comparing the mystical visions of hermits, monks, and other ascetics with hallucination he has encountered in his practice, counselor Jay E. Adams suggests that at least some revelations were caused by sins against the body rather than holiness. Loss of sleep, perceptual deprivation, and poor eating habits are regarded by Adams as common causes of perceptual disturbances not related to organic dysfunction. He believes a related type arises from personal problems, a taxing lifestyle, and feelings of guilt. The individual under pressure does not take care of the body and cannot sleep. Misperceptions, whether mystically revelatory or nightmarish, may result.

Whatever their form and cause, human perceptions are notoriously undependable at interpreting reality. The study of how the brain perceives and the factors which may alter perception is ongoing. Western society historically has normally regarded bizarre perceptions as evidence of mental illness, and some forms do require hospitalization and medication. Abnormal perceptions may have clearly organic causes, such as alcohol- and drug-induced episodes. Hallucinations are expected in some drug withdrawal. Medical science has also become more knowledgeable about perceptual problems related to brain tumors and chemical imbalances.

Counselors confronted with persons who experience hallucination, are taught to first look for lifestyle and environmental causes. Psychologists also tend to regard the content of the visions as an indication of their seriousness. A pioneer pastoral counselor, Anton T. Boisen, long ago called counselors to take seriously what goes on in a hallucination. The fact that a person hears voices, he said, is not so important as what the voices say. It is the task of the professional to try to make sense, with the individual, out of nonsense.

*Bibliography.* A. H. Maslow and B. Mittleman, *Principles of Abnormal Psychology* (rev. ed., 1951); A. T. Boisen, *The Exploration of the Inner World* (1951); J. E. Adams, *The Christian Counselor's Manual* (1973); J. E. Adams, *Lectures on Counseling* (1978); T. G. Esau, *Baker Encyclopedia of Psychology* (1985), 490–91.

## Hamilton, John Taylor (1859–1951).

Moravian bishop. Born in Antigua, West Indies, he was educated at Moravian College, Bethlehem, Pa., and the Moravian Theological Seminary in the same town. He was a teacher at Nazareth Hall Military Academy (1877–81), pastor of the Second Moravian Church, Philadelphia (1881–86), and professor of Greek, church history, and practical theology in the Moravian Theological Seminary (1886–1903). Thereafter he was the American member of the Mission Board of the Moravian Church, Herrnhut, Saxony, and in 1905 was made bishop. He retired in 1928. Among his published works are *History of the Moravian Church in America* (1895), *History of the Moravian Church during the Eighteenth and Nineteenth Centuries* (1900), *History of the Missions of the Moravian Church during the Eighteenth and Nineteenth Centuries* (1901), and *Twenty Years of Pioneer Missions in Nyasaland* (1912).

## Hamilton, Kenneth Gardiner (1893–1975).

Moravian bishop, scholar, and missionary. Born in Bethlehem, Pa., he was educated in Moravian schools in America and Germany (including Herrnhut, Saxony), the Moravian College and Seminary in Bethlehem, Pa., and Columbia University (Ph.D., 1941). He served successively as a pastor (1914/15), YMCA secretary among prisoners of war in Europe (1915–18), missionary in

Nicaragua (1919–37), professor and subsequent dean at Moravian Theological Seminary (1937–46), denominational archivist (1937–63), member and subsequent president of the executive board of the Northern Province of the Moravian Church in America (1946–61), and executive officer of his church's board of foreign missions (1949–56). He was consecrated a bishop in 1947. He wrote *Meet Nicaragua* (1939) and *John Ettwein and the Moravian Church during the Revolutionary Period* (1941), and revised and expanded his father's *History of the Moravian Church* (rev. ed., 1967) and edited various Moravian archival materials.

GLEN G. SCORGIE

## Handy, Robert Theodore (1918– ).

American church historian. Born in Connecticut and educated at Brown University, Colgate Rochester Divinity School, and the University of Chicago (Ph.D., 1949), he was an American Baptist pastor, an army chaplain, and a teacher at Shimer College until he became an instructor and professor of church history at Union Theological Seminary, N.Y. (1950–86). He was president of the American Society of Church History (1959) and was for 20 years a member of the Faith and Order Commission of the World Council of Churches. He is the author of *A Christian America: Protestant Hopes and Historical Realities* (1971, 1984), *A History of the Churches in the United States and Canada* (1977), and *A History of Union Theological Seminary in New York* (1987). He also edited *The Social Gospel in America* (1966) and *The Holy Land in American Protestant Life, 1800–1948* (1981), and was coauthor of *American Christianity* (2 vols., 1960–63) and of *A History of the Christian Church* (4th ed., 1985).

## Harkness, Georgia Elma (1891–1974).

American Methodist scholar and writer. Born in Harkness, N.Y., she was educated at Cornell University, Boston University (Ph.D., 1923), and at Harvard, Yale, and Union Theological Seminary, N.Y. After teaching at Elmira College (1922–37), Mount Holyoke College (1937–39), and Garrett Biblical Institute (1939–50), she became professor of applied theology at the Pacific School of Religion, Berkeley, Calif. (1950–61). Her major interests were world peace, the devotional life, and the interpretation of theology to the laity. She was a prolific writer; her books include *The Church and the Immigrant* (1921), *John Calvin: the Man and His Ethics* (1931), *Holy Flame* (1935), *The Faith by Which the Church Lives* (1940), *Prayer and the Common Life* (1948), *The Gospel and Our World* (1949), *The Sources of Western Morality* (1954), *Christian Ethics* (1955), *The Providence of God* (1960), *The Church and Its Laity* (1962), *Stability amid Change* (1969), *Women in Church and Soci-*

*ety* (1972), and *Biblical Backgrounds to the Middle East Conflict* (1976).

**Harnack, (Karl Gustav) Adolf von** (1851–1930). German theologian and church historian. Born in Dorpat, Livonia, he was educated there, and in 1874 became privatdocent at Leipzig, where he was appointed associate professor in 1876. He was full professor of church history at Giessen (1879–86), Marburg (1886–89), and Berlin (1889–1921). At Berlin he was also librarian of the Prussian State Library. One of the leaders of the critical school of theology and an authority on the history of the antenicene period, he was also from 1881 one of the editors of the *Theologische Literaturzeitung*, and from 1882 of *Texte und Untersuchungen zur Geschichte der altchristlichen Litteratur*, to which series he contributed many monographs. His numerous works in English translation include *History of Dogma* (7 vols., 1895–1900), *Monasticism: Its Ideals and Its History* (1895), *Christianity and History* (1900), *What Is Christianity?* (1901), *The Apostles' Creed* (1901), *The Mission and Expansion of Christianity in the First Three Centuries* (2 vols., 1904/5), *Luke the Physician* (1907), *The Sayings of Jesus* (1908), *The Acts of the Apostles* (1909), *The Constitution and Law of the Church in the First Two Centuries* (1910), *The Date of the Acts and of the Synoptic Gospels* (1911), *Bible Reading in the Early Church* (1912), and *Essays on the Social Gospel* (1917).

**Harner, Nevin Cowger** (1901–1951). Evangelical and Reformed educator. Born near Berlin, Pa., he studied at Franklin and Marshall College, Theological Seminary of the Reformed Church in the USA, Union Theological Seminary, and Columbia University. He was professor of Christian education at the Theological Seminary of the Evangelical and Reformed Church (1929–45, 1947–51). He was the president of Heidelberg College (1945–47), visiting professor at Union Theological Seminary, Princeton Theological Seminary, and Garrett Biblical Institute, vice-chairman of the division of Christian education, National Council of the Churches of Christ in the USA, and executive secretary, American Association of Theological Schools. Among his publications were *The Educational Work of the Church* (1939), *Youth Work in the Church* (1942), with D. Baker, *Missionary Education in Your Church* (1942), *Religion's Place in General Education* (1949), and *I Believe: A Christian Faith for Youth* (1950).

**Harper, William Rainey** (1856–1906). Baptist educator. Born in New Concord, Ohio, he was educated at Muskingum College, New Concord, and Yale (Ph.D., 1875). After being principal of Masonic College, Macon, Tenn. (1875/76), he was tutor (1876–79) and principal (1879/80) of the preparatory department of Denison University and professor of Hebrew and OT exegesis at Baptist Union Theological Seminary (1880–86). He then went to Yale as professor of Hebrew, where he remained until 1891, when he became president and head professor of Semitic languages and literatures in the newly established University of Chicago. He was also principal of the Chautauqua College of Liberal Arts (1885–91), Woolsey professor of biblical literature at Yale University, and instructor in Semitics at Yale Divinity School (1889–91), a member of the Chicago board of education from 1896 to 1898, and director of the Haskell Oriental Museum at the University of Chicago. In 1881 he began to teach Hebrew by correspondence, inaugurating what became the American Institute of Sacred Literature, and three years later (1884) he founded the American Institute of Hebrew. His remarkable ability as an organizer was strikingly exemplified by his development of the University of Chicago into a leading American institution. Harper was an editor of *The Biblical World*, the *American Journal of Theology*, and the *American Journal of Semitic Languages and Literatures*. Among his numerous publications were *Elements of Hebrew* (1881), *Elements of Hebrew Syntax by an Inductive Method* (1883), *Constructive Studies in the Priestly Element in the OT* (1902), *Religion and the Higher Life* (1904), *The Structure of the Text of the Book of Amos* (1904), *The Prophetic Element in the OT* (1905), *The Structure of the Text of the Book of Hosea* (1905), *The Trend in Higher Education* (1905), and *A Critical and Exegetical Commentary on Amos and Hosea* (1905). With R. F. Weidner he wrote *Introductory NT Greek Method* (1888).

*Bibliography.* R. F. Harper, F. Brown, and G. F. Moore, eds., *OT and Semitic Studies. In Memory of William Rainey Harper*, 2 vols. (1907).

**Harris, George Kaufelt** (1887–1962). Baptist missionary. Born in Winona, Minn., he studied at the Moody Bible Institute, Chicago. He went to China as a missionary of the China Inland Mission in November 1916. His main evangelistic efforts were among the Chinese Muslims, mostly in Sining, Tsinghai, the political capital of Chinese Islam. He translated a series of seven booklets, *The Sevenfold Secrets*, by Lilias Trotter. He wrote *How to Lead Moslems to Christ* (1946) and articles on Chinese Islam for *Muslim World*.

CLAUDE L. PICKENS, JR.

**Harris, James Rendel** (1852–1941). English Quaker scholar. Born in Plymouth, he graduated from Cambridge, was a fellow of Clare College there for various periods, then professor of NT Greek at Johns Hopkins University (1882–85) and at Haverford College (1886–92). From 1892 he was university lecturer in paleography at Cambridge, and after less than a year's tenure of the chair of theology at the University of Leyden, he was appointed director of studies at the Friends' Settlement for Social and Religious Study at Woodbrooke, near Birmingham, in 1904 (he had forsaken Congregationalism in 1880 and joined the Society of Friends). In 1918 he became curator of MSS at the John Rylands Library at Manchester, whence he traveled extensively in the East. Among other works he wrote or edited *NT Autographs* (1882), *The Teaching of the Apostles and the Sibylline Books* (1885), *Biblical Fragments from Mount Sinai* (1890), *A Study of Codex Bezae* (1890), *The Apology of Aristides* (1891), *Popular Account of the Newly Recovered Gospel of St. Peter* (1892), *Lectures on the Western Text of the NT* (1894), *Union with God* (1895), *The Guiding Hand of God* (1905), *Cult of the Heavenly Twins* (1906), *Side-Lights on NT Research* (1909), *An Early Christian Psalter* (1909), *Boanerges* (1913), *The Suffering and the Glory* (1916), *The Origin of the Prologue to St. John's Gospel* (1917), *The Origin of the Doctrine of the Trinity* (1919), *Leyden Documents Relating to the Pilgrim Fathers* (1920), *The Mayflower Song Book* (1920), *Eucharistic Origins* (1927), *The Twelve Apostles* (1927), and *The Migration of Culture* (1936). Along with his wife, Helen B. Harris, he wrote *Letters from Armenia* (1897). From 1914 to 1929 he contributed regularly to the *Bulletin* of the John Rylands Library. A wide range of interests, biblical, literary, and archeological, is revealed by five series of essays written between 1927 and 1935, and given successively the titles, *Woodbrooke, Caravan, Sunset, Evergreen,* and *After-Glow.*

**Hart, Hornell Norris** (1888–1967). American Quaker scholar. Born in St. Paul, Minn., he was educated at Oberlin College, University of Wisconsin, and State University of Iowa (Ph.D., 1921). He was professor of social economy, Bryn Mawr College (1924–33), professor of social ethics, Hartford Theological Seminary (1933–38), and spent the rest of his teaching life at Duke University as professor of sociology. He wrote *Living Religion* (1937), *Sceptic's Quest* (1938), *New Gateways to Creative Living* (1941), edited *Toward Consensus for World Law and Order* (1950), and made various contributions to symposia.

**Hartshorne, Hugh** (1885–1967). Congregationalist. Born in Lawrence, Mass., he attended Amherst College, Yale University, Teachers College, Columbia University (Ph.D., 1913), and Union Theological Seminary. He was ordained in 1913. From 1912 to 1922 he was principal of the Union School of Religion, and instructor and assistant professor of religious education at Union Seminary from 1912 to 1922. In 1922 he went to the University of Southern California as professor of religious education and in 1924 to

Teachers College, Columbia University, as codirector with Mark A. May of the Character Education Inquiry. In 1929 he became research associate in religion at Yale and from 1950 was professor of the psychology of religion there. For many years he was connected with various national youth organizations. He wrote *Worship in the Sunday School* (1913), *Childhood and Character* (1919), *Character in Human Relations* (1932), and *Friendship Triumphant* (1937). He coauthored several books including, with M. A. May, *Studies in Deceit* (1928), *Studies in Service and Self-Control* (1929), and *Studies in the Organization of Character* (1930).

**Hastings, James** (1852–1922). Scottish editor and scholar. Born in Huntly, he was educated at Aberdeen University, and after ordination ministered in the Free Church (1884–1901) and the United Free Church (1901–11). After this he returned to Aberdeen to give his whole time to a literary career. He had previously edited the *Dictionary of the Bible* (5 vols., 1898–1904), *Dictionary of Christ and the Gospels* (2 vols., 1906/7), and had begun work in 1908 on his *Encyclopaedia of Religion and Ethics* (12 vols., 1908–22). He also edited *The Dictionary of the Apostolic Church* (2 vols., 1915, 1918), *Great Texts of the Bible* (1910ff.), *Greater Men and Women of the Bible* (1913ff.), and another series on *Great Christian Doctrines* (3 vols., 1915–21). He also edited *The Expository Times* (1890–1921).

**Hatch, William Henry Paine** (1875–1972). Episcopal educator. Born in Camden, N.J., he studied at Harvard (Ph.D., 1904), the Episcopal Theological School, Union Theological Seminary (D.D., 1915), and the University of Strasbourg (D. Theol., 1925). He taught NT at General Theological Seminary (1908–17) and at Episcopal Theological School (1917–46). In theology he was a liberal. He wrote *The Pauline Idea of Faith* (1917), *The Idea of Faith in Christian Literature from the Death of St. Paul to the Close of the Second Century* (1925), *Greek and Syrian Miniatures in Jerusalem* (1931), *The Greek Manuscripts of the NT at Mount Sinai* (1932), *The Greek Manuscripts of the NT in Jerusalem* (1934), *The "Western" Text of the Gospels* (1937), *The Principal Uncial Manuscripts of the NT* (1939), *An Album of Dated Syriac Manuscripts* (1946), and *Facsimiles and Descriptions of Minuscule Manuscripts of the NT* (1951). With C. C. Edmonds he wrote *The Gospel Manuscripts of the General Theological Seminary* (1918).

BRUCE M. METZGER

**Hazelton, Roger** (1909– ). American theologian. Born in River Forest, Ill., he was educated at Amherst College, Chicago Theological Seminary, the University of Chicago, and Yale University (Ph.D., 1937). He served as a Congregational pastor in Oak Park, Ill., and in Chester, Conn., was tutor in religion at Olivet College, Mich. (1936–39), dean of chapel at Colorado College (1939–45), professor of philosophy of religion and Christian ethics (1945–51) and of Christian theology (1951–57) at Andover Newton Theological School, professor of theology and dean of the Graduate School of Theology, Oberlin College (1960–65), and professor of Christian theology at Andover Newton (1965–78). He has served on the Consultation on Church Union, and was secretary (1961–71) and president (1971/72) of the American Theological Association. His works include *The Root and Flower of Prayer* (1943), *The God We Worship* (1946), *Renewing the Mind* (1949), *On Proving God* (1952), *God's Way with Man* (1956), *New Accents in Contemporary Theology* (1960), *Christ and Ourselves* (1965), *A Theological Approach to Art* (1967), *Knowing the Living God* (1968), *Blaise Pascal: The Genius of His Thought* (1974), *Ascending Flame, Descending Dove* (1975), and *Graceful Courage: A Venture in Christian Courage* (1985).

WILLIAM H. BERGER

**Headlam, Arthur Cayley** (1862–1945). Anglican bishop and theologian. Born in Whorlton, County Durham, he was educated at Oxford, and was ordained in the Church of England in 1889. He held various posts at Oxford University (1885–1896), then was rector of Welwyn (1896–1903) before appointment as principal of King's College, London (1903–12), during which period he was also professor of dogmatic theology (1903–17). He then returned to Oxford as professor of divinity (1918–23), and finally was consecrated bishop of Gloucester (1923–45). His many published works include *Teaching of the Russian Church* (1897), *The Dates of the NT Books* (1902), *Sources and Authority of Dogmatic Theology* (1903), *History, Authority and Theology* (1911), *Christian Miracles* (1911), *St. Paul and Christianity* (1913), *The Study of Theology* (1918), *The Doctrine of the Church and Christian Reunion* (2d ed., 1923), *Life and Teaching of Jesus Christ* (1923), *The Church of England* (1924), *Economics and Christianity* (1926), *The New Prayer Book* (1927), *What It Means to Be a Christian* (1933), *Christian Theology* (1934), *The Doctrine of God* (1934), *The Task of the Christian Church* (1942), *The Holy Catholic Church* (1945), and *The Fourth Gospel as History* (1948), and a commentary on Romans (1895) in collaboration with W. Sanday.

**Hebrew University of Jerusalem.** A leading academic center of Israel and world Jewish studies. Founded in 1918 and opened in 1925, the university was designed by the Zionist movement to play a role in the Jewish national revival. In addition to pursuing academic excellence, it was to serve the Jewish communities of "Eretz Israel" (and later the state of Israel) and of the world. When the Mount Scopus campus (near Jerusalem at the edge of the Mount of Olives) was rendered inaccessible in the 1947 War of Independence, a new campus was inaugurated at Givat Ram in 1955. After the Six-Day War of 1967, the regained Mount Scopus facilities were rebuilt and expanded. In addition to its internationally known work in sciences and humanities, the university has always been prominent in religious studies. It houses top schools of Jewish studies, archeology, and Islamic studies, as well as the extensive collections of the Jewish National and University Library. Hebrew University also publishes several distinguished journals and maintains an active foreign student program. In 1986 it had an estimated 16,000 students.

ELIEZER SEGAL

**Hebrews, Epistle to the.** This writing does not begin like a letter, but it ends like one. References to the recipients (such as 5:12; 6:9; 13:18–24) show that a definite group is in mind, so the work may fittingly be called an epistle. It is intended for a small group whose members "ought to be teachers" (5:12). The writer calls his work "my word of exhortation" (13:22), which may mean that he has included the substance of a sermon (as in Acts 13:15).

Traditionally the recipients have been understood to be Christian Jews tempted to relapse into Judaism. The constant appeal to the OT and frequent references to Jewish liturgy support this, as does the fact that the title "To the Hebrews" is found in the oldest extant MSS. The elegant Greek in which the letter is written is no argument against this, for many Jews of the Dispersion were fluent in Greek. Nor is it convincing to say that Gentile Christians would use the OT as much as Jews, for Scripture would be authoritative for Gentiles only as long as they were Christians; it would have no validity if they were apostasizing. The fundamental teachings in 6:1–2 are held by some to be what would be taught in the Gentile mission. This may be so, but it would have been equally necessary to teach Jewish converts that Jesus is the Christ; the basics followed from that. Complete certainty is unattainable, but the balance of evidence favors the view that the work was initially addressed to a small group of Jewish Christians who were in danger of returning to Judaism.

The epistle is anonymous, and a variety of possible authors has been suggested. The writing and organizational style and subject matter argue strongly against the supposition that Paul wrote it, and other suggestions (such as Barnabas, Apollos, or Priscilla) are no more than guesses. There is no evidence, and we must leave the question of authorship open. The date is also unknown, but perhaps the absence of any reference to the destruction of Jerusalem (which would have strengthened the argument that Judaism is superseded) favors a date prior to A.D. 70 (although many favor the 80s).

The writer makes a strong case for Christianity as the final religion. He argues that the thrust of OT teaching points to the coming of Jesus, in whom the climax of God's purpose is to be seen. Judaism is not seen as erroneous but as preparatory: the Sabbath rest for which the OT worthies looked is found in Christ (4:1–11), Melchizedek teaches important lessons about Christ (5:6–10; 6:20–7:28), the new covenant of Jer. 31 becomes a reality in Christ and is a far better covenant than the one it superseded (8:8–13), while the death of Christ perfectly fulfills all that the old sacrifices pointed to (chaps. 9–10). It is Jesus' offering of himself once and for all that is central to salvation. And the portrait gallery of faith in chap. 11 is a Christian classic.

*Bibliography.* B. F. Westcott, *The Epistle to the Hebrews* (1892); W. P. DuBose, *High Priesthood and Sacrifice* (1908); J. Moffatt, *A Critical and Exegetical Commentary on the Epistle to the Hebrews* (1924); A. Nairne, *The Epistle to the Hebrews* (1933); T. H. Robinson, *The Epistle to the Hebrews* (1933); W. Manson, *The Epistle to the Hebrews* (1951); A. Snell, *New and Living Way* (1959); H. W. Montefiore, *A Commentary on the Epistle to the Hebrews* (1964); J. Hering, *The Epistle to the Hebrews* (1970); G. W. Buchanan, *To the Hebrews* (1972); D. Hagner, *Hebrews* (1983); F. F. Bruce, *The Epistle to the Hebrews* (rev. ed., 1990).

LEON MORRIS

**Heenan, John Carmel** (1905–1975). Roman Catholic cardinal. Born in Ilford, Essex, he was educated at the English College, Rome, and ordained in 1930. For 16 years thereafter he worked in London's East End before becoming successively bishop of Leeds (1951–57), archbishop of Liverpool (1957–63), and archbishop of Westminster (1963–75). He was made cardinal in 1965. While not an enthusiastic ecumenist even after Vatican II, he was personally on good terms with many leaders of other denominations. His publications include *Priest and Penitent* (1936), *Cardinal Hinsley* (1945), *The People's Priest* (1951), *Our Faith* (1957), *My Lord and My God* (1958), and the two autobiographical volumes *Not the Whole Truth* (1971) and *A Crown of Thorns* (1974).

J. D. DOUGLAS

**Heidegger, Martin** (1889–1976). German philosopher. Born in Messkirch, Baden, he taught at Freiburg University before becoming professor of philosophy at Marburg (1923–28). He then returned to Marburg and was appointed rector there in 1928, in which post his support for Hitler caused considerable dismay and damaged his reputation. In an idiosyncratic style Heidegger attempted to revitalize the problem of "being," which had been neglected in Western philosophy (he contended) since pre-Socratic times. Though his objective was a comprehensive ontology, his fragmentary major work, *Sein und Zeit* (1927; ET, *Being and Time* [1962]), and his later essays are largely existential in execution. Starting with the Kierkegaardian antithesis of the authentic versus the unauthentic life, he analyzes standard existential themes—care, dread, nothingness, estrangement, being-in-the-world, being-toward-death—with a view to providing ontological insights. Although Heidegger denied that he was an existentialist, he exercised a marked influence on those of that viewpoint, and also on some theologians, notably Rudolf Bultmann. Among his books in English translation are *Kant and the Problem of Metaphysics* (1929), *What Is Philosophy?* (1956), *The Question of Being* (1958), and *On the Way to Language* (1971).

**Heiler, Friedrich** (1892–1967). German scholar and ecumenist. Born in Munich, he studied and obtained a doctorate there, and then taught history of religions first at Munich (1918–20), then from 1920 at Marburg. He was a Roman Catholic, became a Lutheran in 1919, and was consecrated by a Gallican bishop in 1930. Influenced by Nathan Söderblom he established himself as a champion of Christian unity, and helped evolve a sort of Protestant catholicity, his views reflected in his best-known work *Das Gebet* (1918; ET, *On Prayer* [1923]). Other notable works include *Die buddhistische Versenkung* (1918), *Die Mystik in den Upanishaden* (1925), *Christlicher Glaube und indisches Geistesleben* (1926), *Evangelische Katholizität* (1926), *Urkirche und Ostkirche* (rev. ed., 1971), *Altkirchliche Autonomie und päpstlicher Zentralismus* (1941), and *Form and Essence of Religion* (1961). A collection of his sermons appeared in 1949 as *Mysterium caritatis*. G. Lanczkowski prepared a tribute to Heiler in *Zeitschrift der deutschen morgenländischen Gesellschaft* 119 (1969).

E. J. FURCHA

**Heim, Karl** (1874–1957). Lutheran. Born in Kreis Heilbronn, Württemberg, he studied at Tübingen (Dr. Phil., 1899). He became general secretary of the German Christian Student Association (1900–1903). He taught theology at Halle (1903–14), at Münster (1914–20), and at Tübingen (1920–39), where he was also morning preacher (1920–48). In the German church crisis of Nazi rule his sympathies were with the Confessional Church. His life's ambition was to build a bridge between theology and the natural sciences. He wrote *Psychologismus oder Antipsychologismus?* (1902), *Das Weltbild der Zukunft* (1904), *Das Wesen der Gnade bei Alexander Halesius* (1907), *Das Gewissheitsproblem in der Systematischen Theologie bis zu Schleiermacher* (1911), *Leitfaden der Dogmatik zum Gebrauch bei akademischen*

*Vorlesungen* (1912), *Glaubensgewissheit* (1916), *Glaube und Leben* (1926), *Der evangelische und Glaube und das Denken der Gegenwart* (5 vols., 1931–51).

RAYMOND W. ALBRIGHT

**Henderson, George David** (1888–1957). Scottish church historian. Born in Airdrie, he was educated at the universities of Glasgow, Berlin, and Jena, and after ordination was minister of Greenock East (1916–22) and St. Mary's, Patrick, before his appointment as professor of divinity and church history at Aberdeen University (1924–57). He was moderator of the Church of Scotland general assembly in 1955. His publications include *Mystics of the North-East* (1933), *The Scottish Ruling Elder* (1935), *Religious Life in 17th Century Scotland* (1937), *The Church of Scotland: A Short History* (1939), *Heritage: A Study of the Disruption* (1943), *The Claims of the Church of Scotland* (1951), *Why We Are Presbyterians* (1953), and *Presbyterianism* (1954).

J. D. DOUGLAS

**Henderson, Ian** (1910–1969). Born in Edinburgh, he was educated at the universities of Edinburgh, Zurich, and Basel, was ordained in the Church of Scotland, and served the parishes of Fraserburgh South (1938–42) and Kilmany (1942–48) before appointment as professor of systematic theology at Glasgow University (1948–69). A scholar who acknowledged a great debt to Rudolf Bultmann, he was nonetheless enough of an individualist to launch a savage and satirical attack on the World Council of Churches in his *Power Without Glory* (1967). His other publications include *Can Two Walk Together?* (1948), *Myth in the NT* (1952), *Rudolf Bultmann* (1965), and *Lüthi, In Time of Earthquake* (1969).

J. D. DOUGLAS

**Hendry, George Stuart** (1904– ). Presbyterian theologian. Born in Scotland, he studied at the universities of Aberdeen and Edinburgh, followed by brief periods at Tübingen and Berlin, and was then ordained in the Church of Scotland. He ministered at Bridge of Allan (1930–49) before going to Princeton Theological Seminary as professor of systematic theology (1949–72). His major works are *The Holy Spirit in Christian Theology* (1956), *The Gospel of the Incarnation* (1958), and *The Westminster Confession for Today* (1960).

J. D. DOUGLAS

**Henry, Carl Ferdinand Howard** (1913– ). American theologian. Born in New York City, he forsook professional journalism after conversion, and after graduating from Wheaton College and Northern Baptist Theological Seminary (Th.D., 1942) he was ordained to the ministry. He taught theology at Northern Baptist Seminary (1942–47)

before joining the founding faculty of Fuller Theological Seminary, Pasadena, Calif. (1947–56), during which time he earned the Ph.D. degree from Boston University. In 1956 he became the first editor of *Christianity Today* (1956–68; editor-at-large, 1968–77), which quickly established itself as the voice of mainline evangelicalism. Its incisive editorials were complemented by a proficient and informed news section. Henry was chairman of the 1966 World Congress on Evangelism in Berlin, lecturer-at-large for World Vision International (1974–87), has been visiting professor at numerous North American institutions, and has lectured in different parts of the world, notably in Southeast Asia. His many publications include *The Uneasy Conscience of Modern Fundamentalism* (1948), *Fifty Years of Protestant Theology* (1950), *Christian Personal Ethics* (1957), *Aspects of Christian Social Ethics* (1964), *Frontiers in Modern Theology* (1966), *Evangelicals in Search of Identity* (1976), *God, Revelation and Authority* (6 vols., 1976–83), and *Christian Countermoves in a Decadent Culture* (1986). Among works he has edited are *Contemporary Evangelical Thought* (1957), *Revelation and the Bible* (1959), *The Biblical Expositor* (1960), *Basic Christian Doctrines* (1962), and *The Christian Mindset in a Secular Society* (1984). He was also editor-in-chief of *Baker's Dictionary of Christian Ethics*, and in 1986 he wrote the autobiographical *Confessions of a Theologian*.

J. D. DOUGLAS

**Henson, Herbert Hensley** (1863–1947). Church of England bishop. Educated at Oxford, he was ordained and ministered in Barking (1888–95) and in an Ilford hospital (1895–1900) before becoming canon of Westminster Abbey and rector of St. Margaret's, Westminster (1900–1912). He became dean of Durham in 1912, was consecrated bishop of Hereford in 1918 (an appointment that caused much misgiving because of his liberal views), and returned to Durham as bishop in 1920, retiring in 1939. Among his numerous publications are *Apostolic Christianity* (1898), *Preaching to the Times* (1903), *Moral Discipline in the Christian Church* (1905), *Christian Marriage* (1907), *The Liberty of Prophesying* (1909), *Christian Liberty* (1918), *Anglicanism* (1921), *Notes on Spiritual Healing* (1925), *Disestablishment* (1929), *The Oxford Groups* (1933), *The Church of England* (1939), *Retrospect of an Unimportant Life* (3 vols., 1942–50), and *Bishoprick Papers* (1946).

J. D. DOUGLAS

**Hepburn, James Curtis** (1815–1911). Presbyterian missionary. Born in Milton, Pa., he was educated at Princeton and the University of Pennsylvania (M.D., 1836), and in 1840 went to China as a medical missionary. He served in Singapore from 1841 to 1843, and in Amoy from 1843 to 1846. He resided in New York until 1859, when he went to Japan, in Yokohama until 1892. In 1905 he received the decoration of the Order of the Rising Sun, third class, from the emperor of Japan. He wrote *Japanese and English Dictionary* (1867; abr. ed., 1873) and a Bible dictionary in Japanese (1889). He prepared Japanese translations of the Westminster Confession, the Westminster Shorter Catechism, the Decalogue, the Lord's Prayer, and the Apostles' Creed. He contributed to the translation of the Bible into Japanese.

**Herbergen der Christenheit.** A yearbook devoted to German ecclesiastical history, first published with the 1957/58 edition by Franz Lau. Since its 1973/74 volume it has been under the general editorship of Karl-Heinz Blaschke of Leipzig. The editor works with an editorial committee of church historians. The journal is published by the Evangelische Verlagsanstalt, Berlin, GDR. Its primary focus is on church history in the territories of the GDR within the Evangelische Kirche Deutschland. Special attention is given to research on the church's place in its sociopolitical context and to discussion of relevant issues of culture, society, and religion.

E. J. FURCHA

**Herbergen zur Heimat.** German lodging houses or hospices. In 1854 Clemens Theodor Perthes established a Christian hospice to provide home-like living quarters for young journeymen artisans. In 1882 Friedrich von Bodelschwingh expanded the concept to include shelters for jobless itinerants. During the two World Wars of the 20th century most of the hospices were transformed into homes for the aged. After 1945 hospices were reopened to provide temporary shelter and food for economically and socially uprooted persons. Hospices are associated with the "evangelical professional association for aid to non-resident people."

E. J. FURCHA

**Hermann, Johann Georg Wilhelm** (1846–1922). German Protestant theologian. Born in Melkow, he studied at the University of Halle, and four years later, after serving in the Franco-Prussian war, became privatdocent at Halle in 1875, and professor ordinarius at Marburg in 1879. He followed Albrecht Ritschl's attempts to divorce theology from philosophical systems by concentrating on practical ethics and the historical Jesus. Regarding the NT records as historically unreliable, he sought to discover the "inner life of Jesus" in its ethicoreligious significance, assuring men that, as they unite their imperfect moral lives with the universal ethical ideal revealed in the inner Jesus, they might be able to do good.

The effect of Christ's work thus terminates, for Hermann, on men, and need not produce any change in God's attitude toward sinners. Like Ritschl he would not attribute metaphysical deity to Jesus, but he was intensely devoted ethically to the person of Jesus.

His best known book, first published in 1886, was translated into English as *The Communion of the Christian with God.* His lectures on dogmatics were published in 1925 by M. Rade, and were translated into English in 1927 as *Systematic Theology.*

ANDREW K. RULE

**Hermann, Rudolf** (1887–1962). German Lutheran theologian. Born in Barmen, he studied at Marburg, Halle, and Greifswald, and taught systematic theology at Göttingen (1916–19) and Wroclaw (1919–26) before appointment as full professor of theology at Greifswald from 1926. He contributed extensively to *Beiträge zur Förderung Christlicher Theologie,* to *Zeitschrift für systematische Theologie,* and to *Deutsche Theologie.* His own most notable publications are *Christentum und Geschichte bei Wilhelm Hermann* (1914), *Zur Frage des religionspsychologischen Experiments* (1922), *Das Verhältnis von Rechtfertigung und Gebet* (1926), *Luthers These: Gerecht und Sünder zugleich* (1930), and *Die Bedeutung der Bibel in Goethes Briefen an Zelter* (1948).

E. J. FURCHA

**Hermansson, Oskar Herman** (1889–1951). Swedish State Church and Svenska missionary. Born in Östergötland, Sweden, he studied at Missionsförbundets Training College (1914–18), and, after ordination, ancient languages and Arabic. He served in Sinkiang, East Turkestan (1920–38) and in India (1939–45). In 1933 Muslim rebel rulers at Yarkand condemned to death Hermansson and four other leading Christians, one Turki being martyred, the others reprieved. During 1934–46 he translated the Bible into Turki, mostly alone. Elected an honorary member of the British and Foreign Bible Society, he saw the Turki translation to publication (1946–51).

EDWIN E. CALVERLEY

**Hermeneutics, Biblical.** The study of the interpretation of the biblical text, both what it meant to its original readers and what it means for modern readers.

***The Importance of Hermeneutics.*** The inspiration of Scripture establishes the importance of hermeneutics and of understanding rightly. This is emphasized in the Bible itself (through such passages as Neh. 8:7–8; Matt. 13:51; 15:16, 17; Luke 24:27, 32, 44, 45; Acts 8:30–35; 2 Tim. 2:14–19; 3:15–17; and 2 Pet. 3:15–17). Acceptance of Scripture as the Word of God is merely theoretical unless its interpretation is guided by objective ways to be sure of what God is saying through it.

***The History of Hermeneutics.*** The process of hermeneutics can be seen at work within the Bible itself. Its writers give an inspired interpretation of historical events in terms of the punitive and redemptive acts of God. Any record of events is interpretation, because judgments must be made as to their relative importance. Many OT passages (such as Deuteronomy and the historical psalms) recite the mighty deeds of God and link them to a theological theme, as Pss. 105 and 106 give complementary accounts of earlier history. The prophets apply the Law and the lessons of the history to their contemporaries. NT interpretation of the OT is of special importance, establishing norms for the interpreter who accepts biblical inspiration.

Jewish hermeneutics of the intertestamental and early Christian periods has been the subject of much scholarly work. An element of interpretation is inevitable in translation; thus the Targums, the Midrash, and the Talmud reflect rabbinic understanding and application of the OT. Qumranic exegesis, as seen for instance in the Habakkuk Commentary, is controlled by the community's belief in itself as the people of a new covenant. *Midrash Pesher*, in which commentary is incorporated within the body of the text, is also a characteristic of Qumran. The LXX reveals its origin in Alexandrian Judaism, and it shows the reservations of late pre-Christian Judaism about anthropomorphisms and other features of the biblical text which seemed unfitting. Philo, a scholar within Alexandrian Judaism, in his many commentaries showed his nurture in Greek as well as biblical thought by adopting an allegorical hermeneutic, enabling him to find philosophical concepts in the Hebrew literature as Greek philosophers were finding Platonism in Homer. This type of approach was carried to its ultimate pole early in the Christian era in some of the gnostics such as Valentinus, in whose thought the OT foundations of the gospel are completely overshadowed by Hellenistic and Oriental concepts, so that NT words carry an alien burden of meaning.

Origen (c. 185–254) had a tendency to allegorize, but this represents only one side, the more speculative, of his thought; there is also much literal exegesis in his many works. Allegorizing seems, however, to have been endemic in much Alexandrian theology. The School of Alexandria, with its Platonic background, clashed with the School of Antioch, with its much more literal exegesis. Theologically the clash focused on Christology during the Nestorian debate, but the literal and practical Antiochene exegesis is to be found at its best in the homiletical commentaries of John Chrysostom (c. 344–407).

Augustine (354–430) had a Neo-Platonic background but avoided the worst aspects of allegorizing. He recognized that both the OT and NT needed to be approached with a sense of their relationship. To Augustine the exegetical principle was that all Scripture contributed to the practical purpose of expressing love to God and neighbor. Medieval hermeneutics recognized a fourfold sense in Scripture: the literal or surface meaning, the allegorical or doctrinal application, the anagogical which looked for spiritualized interpretation, and the tropological or morally edifying sense. Thomas Aquinas drew attention to the importance of analogy in the Bible.

In the Middle Ages biblical interpretation was somewhat stagnant, as biblical study was largely governed by patristic traditions of interpretation. The Reformation broke this strait-jacket. The Reformers emphasized the right of private judgment, but rejected idiosyncratic interpretation, teaching that the one Spirit gives believers unanimity on the great doctrines of the faith. Martin Luther and John Calvin stressed literal interpretation according to the ordinary rules of grammar, and Ulrich Zwingli emphasized the perspicuity of the Bible. The Counter-Reformation reasserted the sole right of the Catholic Church to interpret Scripture and to do so according to "the unanimous consent of the Fathers."

In the 18th century, rationalistic presuppositions increasingly affected biblical scholarship and inevitably influenced the understanding of the text. Biblical cosmology, history, theology, and even ethics were subjected to criticism on the basis of the so-called canons of rational thought, and the supernatural was set aside. Friedrich Schleiermacher was very interested in hermeneutics, and emphasized the role of the interpreter's preunderstanding. His own theology shows strong evidence of influence by the philosophy of Romanticism; although he uses classic theological terms, they tend to describe subjective states rather than doctrines grounded in the objective acts of God. This virtual control of theology by anthropology set a pattern for the 19th century. The Hegelian idealist school moved away from Schleiermacher's stress on feeling to emphasize the mind, and the Neo-Kantian school of Albrecht Ritschl highlighted the will in its ethical emphasis. Under the influence of Immanuel Kant, not only was much in the history of Christian doctrine dismissed as metaphysical, but the same was held to be true of much biblical thought. Such a question as, "Is Jesus God incarnate?" was held to be invalid, so the interpreter was largely limited to asking ethical questions of the text. Every change in the prevailing philosophy heralded a different approach to hermeneutics. Under the influence of philosophical evolutionism the stress on development, already fostered by Hegelianism, was strengthened, and documentary analysis produced a revised conception of biblical literary chronology. At the same time the "quest for the historical Jesus" was being pursued, to ultimately skeptical conclusions.

At the turn of the 20th century a number of new factors began to influence the general intellectual climate. Inevitably they affected the preconceptions of biblical interpreters. Freudian psychoanalysis (and later two World Wars) began to shatter 19th-century utopian optimism. W. Dilthey's philosophy of history directed attention from the objective data to the historian's presuppositions, and he seemed to put historical certainty in doubt. Kant's rejection of metaphysics continued to exercise a powerful influence, and rationalism was still evident in widespread reluctance to accept biblical supernaturalism.

After World War I existentialism came into its own as a major philosophical influence on hermeneutics. Søren Kierkegaard's dictum, "subjectivity is truth," and Martin Heidegger's teaching that the individual faces the challenge to authentic existence through personal decision, caused Rudolf Bultmann to ask questions about human existence when he came to the Scriptures. His subsequent program of demythologizing was a product both of his rationalism and of his preoccupation with the existential challenge of Jesus rather than "objective" questions about His person and work. Later, Ernst Käsemann and other pupils of Bultmann reacted against his failure to provide a firmer objective basis for faith's existential response.

Meanwhile, Karl Barth called for greater attention to those elements in Scripture which challenged modern thought, and commentaries produced under his influence became distinctly more theological. That Barth was a "modern," however, was revealed in his desire not to tie the biblical message too strongly to history and in his insistence that the Bible is not in itself objectively the Word of God, but that it becomes so in the context of human experience. Revelation for Barth and other neo-orthodox theologians is an encounter rather than a propositional statement.

Existentialism deeply influenced Paul Tillich and the "death of God" theologians, while process philosophy lies behind the approach of Charles Hartshorne, John Cobb, and Norman Pittenger to the Bible. A kind of technological philosophy pressed its attention on Dietrich Bonhoeffer and Harvey Cox. On the other hand, Near Eastern studies led Scandinavian and other OT form critics to stress the hermeneutical value of comparing Christian Scripture with ancient Near Eastern texts.

While Christian linguistic philosophers, particularly of the Neo-Thomist school, were seeking to answer the claim of the logical positivists that all metaphysical statements (including, in their judgment, theological statements) are nonsense because they are not verifiable, Jürgen Moltmann was responding to the Marxist criticisms of religion in his "theology of hope." Ernst Bloch's "philosophy of hope" had developed Karl Marx's call to be less concerned to understand history than to change it. The interpreter, Moltmann maintained, should go to the Bible for a plan of social action, asking questions therefore about the future rather than the past or present. He was followed by the liberation theologians, who maintained that only the socially concerned have the right to interpret the Bible, because they alone share the Bible's own concern for social justice. Under such views the interpreter, as well as the interpretation, is under scrutiny. Recent structuralism focuses attention on the Bible as literature, subject to literature's laws of structure.

***Hermeneutics as "Given" with the Biblical Revelation.*** Classic Christian hermeneutics accepts the principle that the Bible contains the main principles of its own interpretation and that these principles are as authoritative and reliable as is the whole of biblical revelation. The interpreter's main task therefore is to discover and apply them. The way the NT interprets the OT becomes the model. There has been much recent interest in this. Barth followed the principle that the Bible is self-interpreting when he endeavored to purge his theology of existentialism. In every age of the church's life the effects can be seen of getting one's hermeneutical bearings from the prevailing philosophy of the day rather than from the Bible itself. This does not mean that Scripture is to be treated in isolation from either the currents of thought or the world of its modern interpreters. But it does mean that the biblical concepts themselves are to furnish the interpreter with hermeneutical guidelines.

***What the Biblical Text Meant.*** Grammatico-historical interpretations must always be the first stage. The historical circumstances of writer and first readers, and the straightforward grammatical sense of the literature must be considered. Technical and nontechnical word usage, the use of analogy and symbolism, the way the book's message is conveyed (by narrative, visions, meditation, or dialog, for example), the literary genre, the place of the book within the literary output of the human author, the organization of particular passages within a book as a whole—these and many other matters occupy the exegete and are featured in exegetical commentaries. The Antiochenes and later the Reformers contended for the importance of such painstaking work. The purpose is to ascertain, as far as is possible, the meaning of the text for its original readers. In this way, the modern interpreter seeks to hear and feel the power of the Word of God from within its original setting.

***What the Biblical Text Means.*** If we follow the Reformers' dictum that each thought unit of the Word of God has only one propositional meaning, perhaps *means* should be amended, as has been suggested, to *signifies,* although many use the two words as synonyms. Theological interpretation follows grammaticohistorical methods, for inspiration means the Bible has a divine author—the Holy Spirit—as well as human authors. The passage in view must be understood not only in its literary and historical contexts, but in that of the divine revelation as a whole. The exegete seeks the theological interpretation in the context of the whole Bible and in relation to the interpreter's own day. Perhaps the major clues to such theological interpretation are the consistency of God and the Christocentric nature of Scripture, both of which are taught within the Bible itself. Promise and fulfillment relate to both principles. Differences of emphasis exist, for example, between interpreters who hold to a dispensational scheme (stressing the difference in God's dealing with his people in different periods) and those who stress the covenant motif as binding together revelatory history. The laws and limits of typology and the principles of prophetic interpretation are also points of debate. Theological commentaries major in relating particular books to the Bible as a whole and to Christian historical debate, and the best homiletical commentaries take the work both of the exegete and the biblical theologian as their basis.

**Bibliography.** R. T. Chafer, *The Science of Biblical Hermeneutics* (1940); L. Berkhof, *Principles of Biblical Interpretation* (1950); B. Ramm, *Protestant Biblical Interpretation* (1950); C. H. Dodd, *According to the Scriptures* (1952), and *Interpretation of the Fourth Gospel* (1953); R. Bultmann, *Essays Philosophical and Theological* (1955); D. Daube, *The NT and Rabbinic Judaism* (1956); E. C. Blackman, *Biblical Interpretation* (1957); E. E. Ellis, *Paul's Use of the OT* (1957); F. F. Bruce, *Biblical Exegesis in the Qumran Scrolls* (1960); R. Bultmann, *Jesus Christ and Mythology* (1960); J. Macquarrie, *The Scope of Demythologising: Bultmann and His Critics* (1960); J. Barr, *The Semantics of Biblical Language* (1961); J. D. Smart, *The Interpretation of Scripture* (1961); C. Westermann, ed., *Essays in OT Interpretation* (1963); J. Barr, *Old and New in Interpretation* (1964); C. E. Braaten, *History and Hermeneutics* (1968); D. L. Baker, *Two Testaments, One Bible* (1976); I. H. Marshall, *NT Interpretation* (1977); E. Ellis, *Prophecy and Hermeneutic in Early Christianity* (1978); G. W. Anderson, ed., *Tradition and Interpretation* (1979); A. C. Thiselton, *The Two Horizons* (1980); D. A. Carson, ed., *Biblical Interpretation and the Church* (1982).

GEOFFREY W. GROGAN

## Herron, George David (1862–1925).

Congregational social reformer. He sprang into national prominence as a social prophet in the early 1890s. A midwestern Congregational minister, he lectured and wrote extensively on social Christian themes. Called in 1893 to be professor of applied Christianity at Iowa (now Grinnell) College, he became the central figure in the influential "Kingdom movement." As he moved in a radical direction, both socially and theologically, he was rejected by the churches and found his support in certain religiosocial reform movements of the late 1890s. He resigned his chair in 1900 and became a leading figure in the organization of the American Socialist party in 1901. That same year he was divorced by his wife, speedily remarried, and was deposed from the ministry. Living abroad, he was conspicuous as a socialist leader until 1914; through the Woodrow Wilson administration he served as a diplomatic agent in Europe.

**Bibliography.** M. P. Briggs, *George D. Herron and the European Settlement* (1932); R. T. Handy, *George D. Herron and the Social Gospel in American Protestantism, 1890–1901* (1949).

ROBERT T. HANDY

## Hershberger, Guy Franklin (1896– ).

Mennonite scholar. Born in Kalona, Iowa, he studied at Heston College and the universities of Chicago, Michigan, and Iowa (Ph.D., 1935). He taught history and sociology at Goshen College (1925–65). A leading scholar in the field of Christian nonresistance, he served for 20 years as the executive secretary of the Mennonite Church's Committee on Economic and Social Relations. His published works include *Can Christians Fight?* (1940), *Christian Relationships to State and Community* (1942), *War, Peace, and Nonresistance* (rev. ed., 1953), and *The Mennonite Church in the Second World War* (1951). He edited *The Recovery of the Anabaptist Vision* (1957). A festschrift in his honor, *Kingdom, Cross, and Community* (1976), discusses major questions of ethics, social concerns, and the form and mission of the church from the Anabaptist-Mennonite ethos.

JAMES MCCLANAHAN

## Heschel, Abraham Joshua (1907–1972).

American Jewish philosopher and scholar. Born in Warsaw, Poland, of Hasidic lineage, he had a traditional Jewish religious education, later studying at the University of Berlin and the Hochschule für die Wissenschaft des Judentums, where he taught Talmud. In 1937 he succeeded Martin Buber at the Jüdisches Lehrhaus. In 1938 he was transported by the Nazis to Warsaw, then he fled to London. From 1940 to 1945 he taught at Hebrew Union College in Cincinnati, and afterwards moved to the Conservative Jewish Theological Seminary of America, where he taught Jewish ethics and mysticism until his death. He achieved eminence as both a scholar of Jewish philosophical and mystical thought, and as an influential philosopher in his own right. He published scholarly studies on the thought of the biblical prophets, the Talmudic rabbis, medieval rationalists, and Hasidic teachers. His theological writings focus on the existential situation of man's relationship to God and the world. He emphasized God's concerned call to mankind, and man's response to this call in the realms of faith, deeds, and prayer. In *The Sabbath: Its Meaning for Modern Man* (1952) Heschel described Judaism as a hallowing of time. In *Israel: An Echo of Eternity* (1969) he offered a theological exposition on the place of Zionism in

Judaism. Heschel was prominent in his support of social causes, notably the civil rights movement and opposition to the Vietnam War, and was active in Jewish-Christian dialog.

ELIEZER SEGAL

**Higger, Michael** (1898–1952). Jewish Talmudic scholar. Born in Rogovo, Lithuania, he studied at New York University, at Columbia University (Ph.D., 1926), and at the Jewish Theological Seminary of America, becoming a rabbi in 1926. Higger published critical editions and English translations of the minor tractates of the Talmud (1929–37), and wrote *Intention in Talmudic Law* (1927) and *The Jewish Utopia* (1932), a reconstruction of the rabbinic concept of the ideal social life on earth. He also published the 10–volume *Ozar Ha-Beraitot* (1938–48), classifying and listing the Baraitot, statutes not found in the Mishnah but cited in the discussions of the Amoraim, and found scattered through the Babylonian and Palestinian Talmuds.

**Higginbottom, Sam** (1874–1958). Presbyterian missionary. Born in Manchester, England, he studied at Mt. Hermon School, Amherst College, Princeton University, and Ohio State University. He served in India from 1903 to his retirement. He organized an Agricultural Institute to improve crop production in India. He also worked to raise the status of lepers and the blind. He was president of Allahabad Christian College and was moderator of the General Assembly of the Presbyterian Church, USA, in 1939. After his retirement he founded and directed the Christian Service Training Center, Inc., at Babson Park, Fla., to prepare foreign missionaries for customs and conditions of their assignments. He wrote *The Gospel and the Plow* (1921), *What Does Jesus Expect of His Church?* (1940), and *Sam Higginbottom, Farmer* (1949).

RAYMOND W. ALBRIGHT

**Hilfswerk, Evangelisches.** Shortly after the end of World War II, the Evangelical Church in Germany (EKD) created a relief agency, largely supported by laypersons. Its objectives were to assist refugees and displaced persons, returning prisoners of war, and those who had lost their possessions in air raids. Eugen Gerstenmaier, theologian and later active member of the Christian Democratic Union (CDU) and president of the Bundestag, became its first director from 1945 to 1951. With headquarters in Stuttgart, Gerstenmaier engaged parish clergy as coordinators and established branch offices in each territorial church which saw to the distribution of food, clothing, Bibles, and Christian literature.

To accommodate the many needs of some 12 million refugees and countless impoverished German citizens, the Hilfswerk expanded to include the three mainline Protestant churches (Lutheran, Reformed, and Church of the Union) as well as the Free churches. This united Protestant agency complemented the Roman Catholic Caritas. Churches outside Germany and, since 1948, denominations within the World Council of Churches (WCC) channeled much of their support for Germany during the postwar rehabilitation years through the Hilfswerk.

Another focus of this well-structured diaconate in action has been the erection of temporary structures for churches and schools, of homes for apprentices and for the aged, and of housing cooperatives to help in the permanent relocation of displaced persons. In 1957 the Hilfswerk joined its network and resources with the "Innere Mission der Evangelischen Kirche Deutschland."

*Bibliography.* *Jahrbuch des Hilfswerks der E.K.D.* (1950); G. Noske, *Heutige Diakonie der Evangelischen Kirche* (1956).

E. J. FURCHA

**Hillis, Newell Dwight** (1858–1929). American pastor and writer. Born in Magnolia, Iowa, he graduated from Lake Forest University and McCormick Theological Seminary, entered the Presbyterian ministry, and held pastorates at Peoria, Ill. (1887–90), Evanston, Ill. (1890–94), and Central Church, Chicago, an independent church (1894–99). He then began a 25-year ministry at Plymouth Congregational Church, Brooklyn, becoming well known as a preacher at home and in Britain, and serving also as president of Plymouth Institute (1914–29). His numerous books include *A Man's Value to Society* (1896), *William Ewart Gladstone* (1898), *Right Living as a Fine Art* (1899), *Influence of Christ in Modern Life* (1900), *David the Poet and King* (1901), *Building a Working Faith* (1903), *Contagion of Character* (1911), *Anti-Slavery Epoch* (1911), *Studies of the Great War* (1915), *German Atrocities* (1918), *Rebuilding the Ruined Lands of Europe* (1919), and *The Better American Lectures* (1921). He also compiled *Lectures of Henry Ward Beecher* (1913).

**Hilprecht, Hermann Vollrath** (1859–1925). Assyriologist. Born in Hohenerxleben, Germany, he studied theology, philology, and law at Leipzig (Ph.D., 1883). He taught OT theology in Erlangen (1885/86), and was professor of Assyrian and comparative Semitic philology at the University of Pennsylvania (1886–1911). He was also curator of the Semitic section of the university museum (1887–1911), containing more than 50,000 original Babylonian antiquities largely presented by him. From 1895 he was the scientific director of the University of Pennsylvania's four expeditions to Nippur, Babylonia, and editor-in-chief of *The Babylonian Expedition of the University of Pennsylvania* (1893–1911). He reorganized the Babylonian section of the Imperial Ottoman Museum in Constantinople (1893–1909) and made frequent scientific researches in Asia Minor and Syria as well as in India, China, Ceylon, Korea, and Japan. He was a leading authority on cuneiform research. His works include *Mathematical, Metrological and Chronological Tablets from the Temple Library of Nippur* (1906), and *Assyriaca, Eine Nachlese auf dem Gebiete der Assyriologie* (1894). He and A. T. Clay edited *Business Documents of Murashû Sons of Nippur, Dated in the Reign of Artaxerxes I* (1898).

RAYMOND W. ALBRIGHT

**Hiltner, Seward** (1909–1984). American Presbyterian theologian. Born in Tyrone, Pa., he studied at Lafayette College, the Divinity School of the University of Chicago (1931–35), and the University of Chicago (Ph.D., 1952). He was secretary of the Westminster Foundation, University of Chicago (1933–35), executive secretary, Council for Clinical Training (1935–38), executive secretary in the department of pastoral services, Federal Council of Churches of Christ in America (1938–50), professor of pastoral theology at the University of Chicago (1950–61), and professor of theology and personality at Princeton Theological Seminary (1961–80). His writings include *Religion and Health* (1943), *Pastoral Counseling* (1949), *Self-Understanding Through Psychology and Religion* (1951), *The Counselor in Counseling* (1952), *Sex and the Christian Life* (1957), *Preface to Pastoral Theology* (1958), *The Christian Shepherd* (1959), *Ferment in the University* (1969), and *Theological Dynamics* (1972).

**Hinduism.** *Introduction.* A family of religions which has evolved over 4000 years on the Indian subcontinent. In the late 20th century it was estimated to be the world's third largest religious grouping. All but 36 million of an estimated 583 million Hindus lived in India where they made up 79 percent of the population (1980). Indeed, it is easier to define Hinduism as the religion and way of life of all Indians who belong to no other faith than to define the precise beliefs and practices which bind Hindus as coreligionists. No religious leader or organization can speak on behalf of all Hindus, though many political parties claim to do so. Hindu beliefs are so diverse it has been suggested that a "Hindu religion" does not exist, that it is "nothing but an orchid cultivated by European scholarship"—a term which conveniently but misleadingly unites a whole collection of Indian religions that have interacted during their long development. There are, however, some strands or emphases that are shared among Hindus and which have impressed themselves on 20th-century observers.

*Life and Society.* Scholarship on Hinduism is often focused on the study of philosophical Hinduism on the one hand and of popular Hinduism on the other. There are literary sources, ancient and medieval, which form the basis of the study of philosophical Hinduism. Popular or folk Hinduism is studied by observing the different practices over India.

In Hindu society people are divided into castes (*varnas*) on the basis of their birth. The Brahmans (also Brahmins), who are scholars and priests, form the highest stratum, which itself is divided into castes. For instance, among the Brahmans, the worshipers of *Vishnu* form a separate caste and so do the worshipers of *Siva*. The warriors (*Kshatriyas*), the traders (*Vaisiyas*), and the agriculturists (*Sudras*) form three more strata in which the agriculturists are given a rank lower than the traders who, in turn, are of a rank lower than the warriors. The rest of the population forms the fifth and the lowest stratum. Those of this section are outcastes—outside the four main *varnas* of traditional Hindu society. For many ritual purposes women are treated on a par with the fourth *varna*, the *Sudras*. The highest *varna* is that of the fairskinned Brahman, whereas to the lowest *varna* (which literally means color) belong Sudras who are darkskinned. The Brahmans refrain from consuming meat and liquor, whereas the outcastes partake of them. The outcastes have historically been regarded as "untouchables," although that distinction is now illegal under Indian law.

Rules of pollution and purity have a strong influence among the Hindus, especially in rural India. Some objects such as gold and silk cannot be polluted. Objects such as a dead body pollute other objects that come into contact with it. Fire and running water can remove pollution. A person touching a polluted object becomes polluted, and can pollute another person by touch. The cow is treated with veneration, and products of the cow, including dung, are used to cleanse. Since a carcass is polluted, those whose work is to remove dead animals remain polluted and are treated as outcastes. There are detailed rules about the degrees of pollution and the remedies for removing each.

In modern India special efforts are being made to improve the position of the outcastes, renamed the *Harijans* (people of god) under reforms designed by Mahatma Gandhi (1869–1948). There are reservations in government jobs, and special scholarships for their children, and they are listed as "scheduled" castes or tribes. The *Harijans* who become Christian or Muslim converts are not eligible for such scholarships. Many state governments also give scholarships and provide reservations in educational institutions to people classified as "backward classes," and Christians and Muslims are eligible for these. There is also official encouragement for intercaste marriages.

***Religious Beliefs.*** Among the Hindu scriptures the four parts of the *Veda*—*Rig, Yajur, Sama,* and *Atharva*—are the most important. They were composed in Sanskrit over 3000 years ago and are passed on from generation to generation by oral tradition. Among the important gods of the Vedic religion of the Indo-Aryans are *Agni* (fire), *Vayu* (wind), *Varuna* (sea), and *Indra* (mountain, thunder, and rain). The practice of fire worship has continued over the centuries, and has a place in the marriage rituals of the higher castes even today. Hinduism gives highest importance to the worship of three deities—*Siva, Vishnu,* and *Sakti.*

The adherents of *Siva* are called *Saivaites,* and there have been many sects within *Saivism.* The sect called the *Vira Saivas* worships *Siva* alone. But this still is a broad classification which includes the worshipers of *Shanmuga* and *Ganesha,* who are treated as sons of *Siva. Parvati,* the daughter of the mountains, is treated as a consort of *Siva.* Thus different faiths are absorbed into *Saivism* as sects through the mechanism of family relationship among deities.

The adherents of *Vishnu* are the *Vaishnavites. Sri Devi* (also called *Lakshmi,* the goddess of wealth) and *Bhu Devi* (earth) were once independent deities but now are worshiped as consorts of *Vishnu. Vishnu* is believed to have had 10 major *avatars* or incarnations, including different animal forms, such as the fish, the boar, and the tortoise. His human forms include epic heroes such as *Rama,* the hero of *Ramayana; Krishna* of the story of *Mahabharata,* and one historic person, Siddhartha Gautama or the Buddha. By this mechanism of *avatar,* Buddhism could be partly absorbed into *Vaishnavism.*

*Sakti* (lit. "power") is a general name for female deities. *Parvati,* the consort of *Siva,* is worshiped in different forms. In South Indian villages, the worship of the Seven Virgins, who are also consorts of various male deities, is fairly common. Worship of *Kali* is practiced throughout India, and animal sacrifices are associated with *Kali* worship. During the medieval times warriors would immolate themselves before an image of *Kali* for the prosperity of their nation.

In rural areas there are many non-Brahman priests. Recent studies in the villages of the state of Tamil Nadu (Madras) have identified several thousand gods and goddesses who are worshiped as part of the folk tradition. Some deities are worshiped by individual families, some by certain castes, and some by a whole village. Village deities may be worshiped in certain regions during an epidemic, drought, or famine. Guardian deities are worshiped as protectors of individual villages, often with annual festivals of singing and dancing. Village deities, in general, have their place outside Brahmanism. Animal sacrifices were once common in village festivals, but over the years the practice has slowly diminished.

Among the different schools of philosophical Hinduism, *Vedanta* is widely known. Sankara, a *Saivite* reformer of the 9th century, propounded

his philosophy of *advaita* or nonduality. Brahman is the principle of reality coexisting with *maya* or unreality. Ramanuja, a *Vaishnavite* reformer of the 12th century, taught a philosophy of *vishistadvait* (modified nonduality) in opposition to *advaita.* During the 14th century, Madva preached the philosophy of *dvaita* or pure duality. He held that the Supreme Being and the soul are different from matter which is real and eternal. To the *Saivite* the Supreme Being is *Siva* but to the *Vaishnavite* it is *Vishnu.*

Both *Saivism* and *Vaishnavism* also have strong traditions of devotion or *bhakti.* As part of the *bhakti* movement, their saints went from place to place singing devotional songs at every major shrine. Their songs in the Tamil language have been collected and are still used for devotion and worship. The classical music and dance of India are highly devotional.

Painters and sculptors have left a rich variety of themes. The bronze sculptures of South India made by the lost wax process are known for their exquisite craftsmanship. Sculptor craftsmen could choose from specific forms set out in literary works on iconography. Each deity was distinguished by its special emblems. For example, *Siva* is shown holding a trident and an ax, and *Vishnu* is shown with a shell and a discus. The discus was used on the battlefield as a weapon and the conch shell as a trumpet. *Rama* is shown with a bow and arrow, *Durga* with the same emblems as *Vishnu,* and *Kali* with the emblems of *Siva.*

The devotees of *Vishnu* at the time of rituals wear a special "V"-shaped mark chalked in white with a vertical red (or yellow) stroke in the middle on their forehead and sometimes on their forearms. There are subtle variations in the mark to distinguish northern from southern sects of *Vaishnavites.* Two white vertical bars represent the feet of *Vishnu* planted on the forehead of the devotee, indicating complete submission. The devotees of *Siva* display three horizontal lines across the forehead. Priests and artisans and others who claim high status in society wear the sacred thread across their chest.

GIFT SIROMONEY

***20th-Century Developments.*** Hinduism was first presented as an integrated universal faith as recently as 1893, when Swami Vivekananda (1863–1902), chief disciple of Ramakrishna Paramahamsa (1836–86), expounded his interpretation of *Advaita Vedanta* at the World Parliament of Religions in Chicago. This "Neo-Vedanta" might be said to bear the sort of relationship to Hinduism that Neo-Thomism bears to European Christianity, but Vivekananda's espousal of a combination of advaitic spirituality and social service in the Ramakrishna Mission institutionalized on a much larger scale the reforming outlook of the

Brahmo Samaj. The redefinition of *Advaita Vedanta* for the intellectuals of modern India and for Western readers was taken further in *The Hindu View of Life* (1927), *Eastern Religions and Western Thought* (1939), and later writings of the philosopher-statesman Sarvepalli Radhakrishnan (1888–1975).

On the practical level, the principles of *swadeshi* (service), *ahimsa* (nonviolence), and *satyagraha* (commitment to truth) inspired the political activity of Gandhi for Indian independence and the rights of the outcastes. His disciple Vinoba Bhave (1895–1982) later started the *Sarvodaya* (uplift of all) movement and the *Bhoodan* (land-gift) campaign to persuade village landlords to donate land to landless laborers.

Other Hindu figures who have had influence beyond India include Aurobindo Ghose (1872–1950), Ramana Maharshi (1879–1950), and Jiddu Krishnamurti (1895–1986). Aurobindo attracted large numbers of Westerners to his Auroville ashram at Pondicherry, while Krishnamurti, once supreme world teacher of the Theosophical Society (which was founded in the USA in 1875), dissolved the organizations that had grown up around him in 1929 and settled in California, from which base he wrote numerous books and lectured worldwide on the principles of self-knowledge.

The 1960s and 1970s saw publicity given to the spread in the West of movements such as the Divine Light Mission, the International Society for Krishna Consciousness (ISKCON) or Hare Krishna movement, and transcendental meditation (TM), which is presented as a scientific philosophy rather than a religion. Numerical gains among these Neo-Hindu movements were modest, though sufficient to provide bases for future growth.

Reform movements among the educated Brahman elite must be seen in their social context. The overwhelming majority (98 percent) of India's 547 million Hindus are neither Brahman nor followers of *Advaita Vedanta*. Instead they worship individual gods within the Hindu pantheon. *Vaishnavites* claim 70 percent of the people, *Saivites*, 25 percent, and the other 5 percent *Shaktas* and followers of various *avataras* or incarnations of the gods. With such a syncretistic base Hinduism has easily been molded by such modern reformers as Vivekananda and Gandhi. These men and other leaders have tried to unify and reinterpret Hinduism as one of a variety of paths (none of them exclusive) which lead to God. Christians and Christian principles borrowed by Gandhi have had a social impact. Christians helped end such practices as *sati*, the immolation of widows on their husbands' funeral pyres. Modern Hinduism also interacted with the secularizing influences of nationalism, humanism, communism, and the Western scientific outlook on religion.

It would be rash to generalize from particular studies how all Hindus, urban and rural, have reacted to 20th-century changes. Serious attempts are being made to bring the outcastes into the mainstream of Hinduism. Untouchability is prohibited, and temples have been thrown open to the Harijans. Harijans have started asserting their rights. The influence of astrology over the lives of people is also slowly diminishing, notwithstanding computer-produced horoscopes used by families for arranging marriages. Still there are grounds for expecting that the 80 percent of the population in India's half million villages remained in the 1980s more conservative religiously and that city dwellers were more open to secularization. On the other hand, the same rural conservatism has resulted in instances of mass conversion, particularly among low castes, to Christianity in the 1930s, Buddhism in the 1950s, and Islam in the 1980s. There have also been reconversion movements to Hinduism through the influence of the *Arya Samaj*, a mission organization founded by Dayananda Sarasvati (1824–83) in 1875.

*See also* INDIA.

**Bibliography.** *Religion and Society* (journal of the Christian Institute for the Study of Religion and Society); F. Kingsbury and G. E. Phillips, *Hymns of the Tamil Saivite Saints* (1921); C. G. Diehl, *Instrument and Purpose* (1956); R. C. Zaehner, *Hinduism* (1962); A. L. Basham, *The Wonder That Was India* (3d ed., 1967); T. A. Gopinatha Rao, *Hindu Iconography*, 2 vols. (repr., 1971); D. L. Gosling, *Science and Religion in India* (1976); H. Whitehead, *The Village Gods of South India* (rev. ed., 1976); K. M. Sen, *Hinduism* (1982); C. Srinivasa Rao, *Vedanta: Some Modern Trends* (1982); A. M. Abraham Ayrookuzhiel, *The Sacred in Popular Hinduism* (1983); S. Weightman, *A Handbook of Living Religions* (1984).

PHILIP HILLYER

## Hinke, William John

**Hinke, William John** (1871–1947). Reformed educator and author. Born in Giershofen, Rhein Province, Germany, after early training in Germany he studied at Calvin College, Ursinus School of Theology, Princeton Seminary, and the University of Pennsylvania (Ph.D., 1906). He taught Latin and Greek at Calvin College (1890–92), German and Hebrew at Ursinus College (1892–1907), and OT in the School of Theology at Ursinus (1907–9). He was professor of Semitic languages and religions at Auburn Theological Seminary (1909–39), and librarian (1923–39). He wrote *Bibliography of the Reformed Church in the United States* (1901), *A New Boundary Stone of Nebuchadnezzar I, from Nippur* (1907), *Selected Babylonian Kudurru Inscriptions* (1911), *Life and Letters of the Rev. John Philip Boehm* (1916), *History of Goshenhoppen Reformed Charge, 1727–1833* (1920), and *History of the Tohickon Union Church, 1745–1854* (1925). He also edited and translated *The Minutes and Letters of the Coetus of Pennsylvania 1747–1792*

(1903), *General Biographical Catalog of Auburn Theological Seminary, 1818–1918* (1918), *The Latin Works of Huldreich Zwingli* (vol. 2, 1922), and *Pennsylvania German Pioneers* (3 vols., 1934).

RAYMOND W. ALBRIGHT

**Hinsley, Arthur** (1865–1943). Roman Catholic educator and cardinal. Born in Carlton, Yorkshire, he was educated at Ushaw, the English College, Rome, and the Gregorian University. He was professor at Ushaw (1893–97), and headmaster of St. Bede's Grammar School, Bradford (1899–1904). He also served in several pastorates (1904–17), as rector of English College, Rome (1917–28), visitor apostolic to the Catholic missions in Africa (1927), titular archbishop of Sardis (1930), apostolic delegate to Africa (1930–34), archbishop of Westminster (1935–43), and cardinal (1937–43).

F. W. DILLISTONE

**Hirsch, Emanuel** (1888–1972). Lutheran writer. Born in Bentwisch, Brandenburg, he studied at the University of Berlin, was assistant at Göttingen, docent at Bonn (D.Theol., 1921), and professor at Göttingen (1921–45). His literary work may be divided into four sections: (1) Studies of the history of modern philosophy and theology: *Fichte's Religionsphilosophie* (1914), *Luthers Gottesanschauung* (1918), *Die Theologie des Andreas Osiander* (1919), *Christentum und Geschichte in Fichte's Philosophie* (1920), *Die idealistische Philosophie und das Christentum* (1926), *Kierkegaard-Studien* (2 vols., 1930–33), *Geschichte der neuern evangelischen Theologie im Zusammenhang mit den allgemeinen Bewegungen des europäischen Denkens* (5 vols., from 1949). (2) Biblical research: *Jesus Christus der Herr* (1926), *Das vierte Evangelium verdeutscht und erklärt* (1936), *Studien zum vierten Evangelium* (1936), *Die Auferstehungsgeschichten und der christliche Glaube* (1940), *Frühgeschichte des Evangeliums* (2 vols., 1941). (3) Problems of Christian doctrine: *Deutschlands Schicksal* (1920), *Der Sinn des Gebets* (1921, 1928), *Staat und Kirche im 19. und 20. Jahrhundert* (1929), *Schöpfung und Sünde* (1931), *Die gegenwärtige geistige Lage* (1934), *Das Alte Testament und die Predigt des Evangeliums* (1936), *Zweifel und Glaube* (1937), *Der Weg der Theologie* (1937), *Leitfaden zur christlichen Lehre* (1938), *Das Wesen des Christentums* (1939). (4) Practical books: *Luthers deutsche Bibel* (1928), *Der Wille des Herrn* (1925), *Das Evangelium* (1929), *Hilfsbuch zum Studium der Dogmatik* (1937), *Die Umformung des christlichen Denkens* (1938). He was editor of *Theologische Literaturzeitung* (1921–30).

**Hirsch, Emil Gustav** (1852–1923). Jewish rabbi. Born in Luxemburg, then part of Germany, he was educated at the universities of Pennsylvania, Berlin, and Leipzig (Ph.D., 1876), and the Hochschule für die Wissenschaft des Judentums, Berlin (1872–76). Returning to the United States, he was rabbi of Har Sinai Congregation, Baltimore (1877/78), Adas Israel Congregation, Louisville, Ky. (1878–80), and Sinai Congregation, Chicago (1880–1923). He was also professor of rabbinical literature and philosophy at the University of Chicago (1892–1923). He was one of the founders of the Jewish Manual Training School, Chicago, the Associated Jewish Charities, the Civic Federation, and other similar movements. He was well known as an orator, and in theology belonged to the advanced wing of reformed Judaism. He edited *Der Zeitgeist* (1880–83), *Hebraica* (in collaboration with W. R. and R. F. Harper and I. M. Price) (1892–95), *The Reformer* (1886–92), *The Reform Advocate* (1886–92), and was editor of the biblical department of *The Jewish Encyclopedia*.

**History, The Christian Interpretation of.** If history studies human actions and decisions, its interpretation relates the past to a philosophy of truth, God, and human purpose. History may be viewed through several philosophical grids.

*Philosophies of Interpretation.* Life may be uncontrolled and meaningless, as the natural man of the Book of Ecclesiastes complains, "a chasing after the wind" (Eccles. 1:14). This theme of Greek philosophy has sometimes infected Christianity with pessimism. Some cultures see the past as the only source of meaning for the present. The life-force of today is drawn from the spiritual power of ancestors. Augustine in *The City of God* confronted this idea in Roman thought. A similar conception might be seen in the medieval church's adoration of saints as mediators for the Christian before God, their works of supererogation available as indulgences to forgive sin. The dominating Eastern philosophy of history is the cyclical view. World events and epochs arise from a mystical source, transverse a pattern, and submerge again into the void, only to rise again. There are many variations of this interpretative philosophy, and it empowers the concept of reincarnation and much of modern occult and New Age mysticism. A similar view is a base for Marxist dialectic history.

Biblical Christianity takes its interpretative theme from a linear, progressive model: (1) God is Lord over history, the ground for an absolute historical perspective. All reality has its source in sovereign design. (2) History flows as a stream from its origin toward its goal. There is a cyclical quality of life, but new material is continually introduced. All the seemingly meaningless vanities arise from human abuse of the exalted position of "image-bearer of God," yet even this failure is given timeless significance in Jesus Christ's victory over sin and death. (3) Thus, history is the study of human destiny within a kingdom. It had a definite beginning and two major axial points, God's first personal intervention in history in Jesus Christ, and his future intervention in the eschaton. (4) History is time surrounded by eternity, finitude in the midst of infinity. Therefore, a human understanding is necessarily proximate and subjective. The historian cannot be detached from the flow of events being studied. (5) The course of history is God's reaching out in love to all of humanity, and the place of the church in history is to join in that work of grace. (6) Within history the transformation of humanity is far from complete. By faith Christians know the certainty that all things will be brought under Christ.

*Influences on Christian Interpretation.* Linear history is the firm Judeo-Christian interpretative framework which guided Western civilization well into the Enlightenment. Its goal-centered view of time and events, however, has been questioned. A few of the major influences within the church must be noted. In 18th-century idealism, history was perceived as being moved by good forces which some originating force worked into its fabric. No ongoing Mover was required, the basic goodness of humanity being sufficient. An evolutionary developmental progress logically followed. Radical postmillennialism, social activism, and the 19th-century awakenings in Europe and the USA were touched. German idealists, beginning with Johann Herder and progressing through Georg Hegel, spread this conception through theology. A variety of opinions of history spread from Germany through Europe to the USA. The French philosopher Auguste Comte argued that history is deterministically, even pantheistically moved by social laws which differ only in degree from natural laws. A progressive and meaningful history was rejected. Such ideas were explored by Horace Bushnell in American theology, Darwinian evolutionists, John Dewey-influenced educators, and Marxian dialectic history. Friedrich Nietzsche took these positivistic views to their ultimate conclusion in a chaotic history with no ethical standards beyond the exercise of power. Nietzsche's conception influenced German national socialism.

Aghast at where positivism had taken the world, German theology led by Karl Barth, Rudolf Bultmann, and Reinhold Niebuhr fought to return the Christian view of history, as well as the Bible, to a firm foundation. Their view of revelation was subjective, so they could not posit an objective history which could be studied. They saw history as "God's mighty acts," salvific themes which gain reality and meaning as applied by the Holy Spirit in the heart. Bultmann saw the historical event of the resurrection as irrelevant. Its significance lies in the faith event. This view has gained a strong following within mainline Christianity, but it has been fiercely reacted to by defenders of objective history; Jürgen Moltmann and liberation theology have demanded that Christianity not be divorced from human realities, and some later 20th-century theologies regard the philosophy of Alfred North Whitehead, conceiving of God as lord of history in the form of a chess player struggling to counter impersonal laws and world forces of which he himself is part. The interplay of Christianity and history is far from over.

*Bibliography.* G. H. Clark, *A Christian View of Men and Things: An Introduction to Philosophy* (1952); H. Berkhof, *Christ the Meaning of History* (1966); R. Nash, ed., *Ideas of History,* vol. 1 (1969); W. Corduan, *Handmaid to Theology: An Essay in Philosophical Prolegomena* (1981).

## Hocedez, Edgar (1877–1948).

Jesuit. Born in Ghent, Belgium, he studied at the Philosophical and Theological College of the Society of Jesus at Louvain. He taught theology at Kurseong, India (1908–12), at Louvain (1912–14); at Hastings (1914–19), at Louvain (1919–28); and at the Gregorian University, Rome (1928–40). He was editor of the *Nouvelle Revue Théologique* from 1920 to 1926. He is most widely known for his studies in the history of philosophy and theology in the Middle Ages, published mainly in *Gregorianum.* He wrote *Richard de Middleton* (1925), *Aegidii Romani Theoremata de esse et essentia* (1925), and *Histoire de la théologie au XIXe siècle* (3 vols., 1947–52).

*Bibliography.* J. Levie, *Nouvelle Revue Théologique* 70 (1948): 786–93.

## Hocking, William Ernest (1873–1966).

Born in Cleveland, he was educated in physical sciences at Ames, Iowa, and in philosophy at Harvard (Ph.D., 1904) and Germany. He taught in California, Yale, and Harvard (1914–43), and lectured in England, Scotland, Holland, Germany, Syria, India, China, and other places. He visited the Near East in 1928, to study the working of the mandates, and in the Far East in 1931/32, to study the working of certain Protestant missions. The result of the former journey is embodied in *Spirit of World Politics* (1932); of the second in *Re-Thinking Missions* (1932). His major works bearing directly on religion are *The Meaning of God in Human Experience* (1912), *Human Nature and Its Remaking* (1918), and *Living Religions and a World Faith* (1940). The first of these contained two theses which have influenced religious and metaphysical thinking, especially in France and Germany: that in experience the "I" and the "Thou" are inseparable—a fundamental revision of Descartes; and that God is to be experienced not alone in the universal, but also in the particular, in sensation. Both of these concepts have played a part in the existentialist movements. Hocking has written 18 books and some 200 articles.

**Hodges, George** (1856–1919). Protestant Episcopalian scholar. Born in Rome, N.Y., he was educated at Hamilton College, and ordained to the priesthood in 1882. After being curate (1881–89) and rector (1889–94) of Calvary Church, Pittsburgh, he became dean of the Episcopal Theological School at Cambridge, Mass. (1894–1919), where he was actively involved also in community interests. He published many books, among them *The Episcopal Church* (1889), *This Present World* (1896), *Faith and Social Service* (1896), *William Penn* (1900), *The Human Nature of the Saints* (1904), *When the King Came* (1904), *Three Hundred Years of the Episcopal Church in America* (1906), *Everyman's Religion* (1911), *A Child's Guide to the Bible* (1911), *Class Book of OT History* (1914), *The Early Church* (1914), and *Religion in a World at War* (1917).

**Hodgson, Leonard** (1889–1969). Anglican theologian. Born in London, he was educated at Oxford and at St. Michael's College, Llandaff. After a curacy in Portsmouth (1913/14) he was vice-principal of St. Edmund's Hall, Oxford (1914–19), fellow and dean of divinity at Magdalen College, Oxford (1919–25), professor of Christian apologetics, General Theological Seminary, New York City (1925–31), residentiary canon of Winchester Cathedral (1931–38), professor of moral and pastoral theology at Oxford (1938–44), and professor of divinity at Oxford (1944–58). His numerous publications include *The Place of Reason in Christian Apologetic* (1925), *And Was Made Man* (1928), *Eugenics* (1933), *The Lord's Prayer* (1934), *Democracy and Dictatorship in the Light of Christian Faith* (1935), *The Grace of God in Faith and Philosophy* (1936), *This War and the Christian* (1939), *The Christian Idea of Liberty* (1941), *The Doctrine of the Trinity* (1943), *Theology in an Age of Science* (1944), *Biblical Theology and the Sovereignty of God* (1946), *The Doctrine of the Atonement* (1951), *The Ecumenical Movement* (1951), *For Faith and Freedom* (1956), and *Sex and Christian Freedom* (1967).

J. D. DOUGLAS

**Hoeffding, Harald** (1843–1931). Danish philosopher. Born in Copenhagen, he was educated at the university there (Ph.D., 1870), and after teaching in schools for several years became in 1880 privatdocent for philosophy at his alma mater, where he was full professor of philosophy from 1883. Under the influence of Kierkegaard he showed interest in ethical and religious values, and with his "conservation of values" concept he himself influenced the Chicago School of Theology. Among his works available in English are *Outlines of Psychology* (1891), *History of Modern Philosophy* (2 vols., 1900), *Problems of Philosophy* (1906), and *Philosophy of Religion* (1906).

**Hoffman, Conrad** (1884–1958). American Presbyterian administrator. Born in Chicago, he studied at the universities of Wisconsin, Halle, and Göttingen. He served as a student YMCA secretary at the University of Kansas (1913–15), senior secretary for prisoner of war work in Germany (1915–19), director of European student relief under the World Student Christian Federation (1921–27), and director of the Committee on the Christian Approach to the Jews, International Missionary Council (IMC) (1930–36). He was then appointed secretary of the Christian Approach to the Jews of the Board of National Missions, Presbyterian Church, USA, and became secretary of evangelism for the same board in 1943. He returned as director of IMC's Committee on the Christian Approach to the Jews (1945–51). He wrote *In the Prison Camps of Germany* (1920), *The Jews Today, A Call to Christian Action* (1941), and *What Now for the Jews?* (1948).

**Hoh, Paul Jacob** (1893–1952). Lutheran pastor, educator, and author. Born in Reading, Pa., he studied at the University of Pennsylvania, and at the Lutheran Theological Seminary in Philadelphia. He was pastor at St. Mark's Church, Bethlehem, Pa. (1918–20), Holy Trinity Church, Wildwood, N.J. (1920/21), and Ascension Church, Philadelphia, Pa. (1921–30). He also was editor of the Parish and Church School Board of the United Lutheran Church in America (1930–37), professor of practical theology at Lutheran Seminary in Philadelphia (1937–52), and president of the seminary (1945–52). He wrote *Little Children Come unto Me* (1927), *The Gospel according to St. Luke, A Study* (1936), *Studies in First Corinthians* (1937), and *Parish Practice* (1944).

**Holiness Churches.** A family of American churches which grew out of the 19th-century Holiness revival. The common point of identity is commitment to the Wesleyan doctrine of entire sanctification as a second work of grace subsequent to regeneration. This group of churches is to be distinguished from pentecostal churches, which may also espouse Holiness theology but whose common identity is commitment to glossolalia as evidence of the fullness of the Spirit.

Except for their common adherence to the doctrine of entire sanctification, Holiness churches represent one of the most diverse groups of churches in the religious world. Many of the groups are strongly influenced by Methodist polity and practice as well as by its central doctrine of Christian perfection; but others accommodate disparate Mennonite, Quaker, Baptist, Presbyterian, or Congregational traditions to Wesleyan teachings on Christian holiness.

The largest Holiness church is the Salvation Army, with approximately 2.5 million members (mid-1980s). Among the others are the Church of the Nazarene, about 800,000 members; the Church of God (Anderson, Ind.), 350,000 members; the Wesleyan Church (which resulted from the merger of the Pilgrim Holiness and Wesleyan Methodist churches), about 200,000 members; and the Free Methodist Church, about 200,000 members. Scores of smaller bodies make up the remainder of the more than 7 million members of the movement around the world. The churches of the movement maintain more than 50 accredited colleges, universities, and seminaries in the United States, in addition to educational institutions they support in international fields. Several interdenominational schools and mission agencies serve Holiness adherents in mainline Methodism as well as the smaller Holiness denominations.

All of these churches are rooted in revivals which began in frontier churches in the early 19th century and continued through the end of the century. By the 1830s many Methodist bishops, ministers, and laypeople became concerned because of the relaxation of spiritual discipline and the decline of the preaching of entire sanctification within the church. The Holiness revival which arose in response to such concerns had a focal point in a weekly meeting for the promotion of holiness at the New York City home of Walter and Phoebe Palmer, two Methodist laypersons. The general success of the revival in reaching beyond Methodism was abetted by revivalists Charles G. Finney and Asa Mahan of Oberlin College who, with some other New School Presbyterians, encouraged believers on to a second crisis of faith which would bring cleansing from inbred sin and the fullness of the Spirit.

The Holiness revival came to full bloom in American evangelicalism after the Civil War. It was chiefly promoted by the National Campmeeting Association for the Promotion of Holiness, established in 1867 (later the National Holiness Association [NHA] and now the Christian Holiness Association). The success of NHA, its state and local affiliates, its publishing agencies, and the hundreds of independent Holiness associations which informally identified themselves with the Holiness revival, led to increasing tension between the movement and the churches to which its associates belonged. In one sense the movement was conservative. It grew out of a motive to preserve piety and discipline common to the Christian Holiness traditions. In other ways it was both radical and progressive. It fostered ecumenical concerns when sectarianism was rampant. It received women into the ordained ministry and the legislative councils of the church. It accepted and encouraged lay ministries as essential to accomplishing the Christian mission. It became the seedbed for a more holistic view of persons and life; the modern faith healing movement developed mainly under its auspices.

It provided significant impetus to the inner-city missions movements in the USA and Europe.

By the closing decades of the 20th century Holiness movement adherents began to form new churches either from choice or because of ecclesiastical pressure from their home communions. Out of this confrontation with the religious establishment more new churches were formed than had ever been established before in American history in so short a period. However, not all of the Holiness advocates left the larger churches to join the new Holiness churches. Holiness and deeper life elements continued to influence Methodism from within, often in close cooperation with the Holiness churches. The Keswick Convention movement, which has a similar theology and also was born out of the 19th-century American Holiness revival, constitutes the most significant contemporary influence of the Holiness revival in the evangelical Reformed churches and the Church of England.

The work of the Salvation Army represents the strongest continuing expression of the Wesleyan emphasis upon social as well as personal holiness. The social conscience of other bodies, once expressed in the ardent abolitionism of the early Wesleyans and Free Methodists, tended to be blunted over the years (with that of other conservative evangelical churches) in reaction to the theological liberalism which ruled the social programs of the larger Protestant churches in the first half of the 20th century. In recent years, however, the Holiness churches have shown revived concern for social witness reinforced by the consciousness of the past commitments of the movements.

*Bibliography.* T. Smith, *Revivalism and Social Reform: American Protestantism on the Eve of the Civil War* (1957); V. Synan, *The Holiness-Pentecostal Movement in the United States* (1971); C. Jones, *Perfectionist Persuasion* (1974); D. W. Dayton, *Discovering an Evangelical Heritage* (1976); M. E. Dieter, *The Holiness Revival of the Nineteenth Century* (1980).

MELVIN E. DIETER

**Holl, Karl** (1866–1926). German Protestant church historian. Born in Tübingen, he studied at the university there (Ph.D., 1889). After having been an assistant for two years in the preparation of the edition of the church fathers by the Berlin Academy of Science, he became privatdocent at the University of Berlin in 1896. In 1898 he was made titular professor at the same university, but resigned in 1900 to accept the position of associate professor of church history at Tübingen, returning to Berlin as full professor in the same subject (1906–26). He wrote *Die Sacra Parallela des Johannes Damaszenus* (1896), *Enthusiasmus und Bussgewalt beim griechischen Mönchtum* (1898), *Fragmente vornicänischer Kirchenväter aus den Sacra Parallela* (1899), and *Modernismus* (1908). Holl taught and wrote most extensively on the early and Reformation periods of Christianity.

In addition to his earlier works he produced in the former area the critical edition of *Epiphanius* in the Berlin edition of the Greek Fathers (2 vols., 1915, 1922); and in the latter area his great late achievement was *Gesammelte Aufsätze zur Kirchengeschichte* (1922–28), of which the first volume deals with *Luther;* the second with *Der Osten;* the third with *Der Westen.* In many ways Holl was responsible for the renewed interest in Luther studies.

**Holland.** *See* NETHERLANDS.

**Holman, Charles T.** (1882–1968). Baptist. Born in Cheltenham, England, he studied at McMaster University, University of Chicago, and Indiana University. He was pastor of Baptist churches in Canada; Bloomington, Ind.; and Chicago, Ill. (1907–23). He taught pastoral duties, Federated Theological Faculties, University of Chicago (1923–47), and was dean of Baptist Divinity House, University of Chicago (1942–47). He was pastor of Union Church of Guatemala (1947–52). He was a pioneer in relating psychological and social sciences to pastoral counseling. He is the author of *The Cure of Souls: A Sociopsychological Approach* (1932), *The Religion of a Healthy Mind* (1939), *Getting Down to Cases* (1942), and *Psychology and Religion for Everyday Living* (1949).

**Holmes, John Haynes** (1879–1964). Clergyman, social activist, and author. Born in Philadelphia, he studied at Harvard College and Harvard Divinity School. He received the annual Gottheil Medal for outstanding service of Jews (1933). He was ordained and installed as minister of the Third Religious Society (Unitarian), Dorchester, Mass., in 1904. Holmes was minister of the Church of the Messiah (now Community Church), New York (1907–49). He was vice-president of the National Association for the Advancement of Colored People from 1909 and director of the American Civil Liberties Union from 1917 and chairman, 1939 to 1949. He is the author of *The Revolutionary Function of the Modern Church* (1912), *Marriage and Divorce* (1913), *Is Death the End?* (1915), *New Wars for Old* (1916), *Religion for Today* (1917), *Life and Letters of Robert Collyer* (1917), *Readings from Great Authors* (1918), *The Grail of Life* (1919), *Is Violence the Way Out?* (1920), *New Churches for Old* (1922), *Patriotism Is Not Enough* (1925), *Palestine Today and Tomorrow* (1929), *The Heart of Scott's Poetry* (1932), *The Sensible Man's View of Religion* (1933), *Through Gentile Eyes* (1938), *Rethinking Religion* (1938), *Out of Darkness* (1942), *The Second Christmas* (1943), and *The Affirmation of Immortality* (1947). With R. Lawrence he wrote the play, *If This Be Treason* (1935).

**Holocaust.** A term derived from the Septuagint *holokautoma* (complete burning), used as a reference to the extermination of Jews in Europe between 1939 and 1945. In the OT the word and its derivatives refer to total sacrifice by fire to Yahweh, normally of an unblemished male animal. In the original "sacrifice by fire" rigid rules determined the time and manner of the sacrifice and the conduct of the priests presiding at it (see Lev. 1:3–17, 6:8–13). The notion of "holocaust" occurs infrequently in Christian or Jewish literature until after World War II, when it is given a radically new interpretation in attempts to describe the systematic efforts by Adolf Hitler and the Nazi regime to eradicate the European Jewish people in the so-called solution to the Jewish question. Since about the late 1950s the term has gained currency in literature, historical accounts, and theology with almost exclusive reference to the indiscriminate mass murder in Germany and in territories under its control of up to 6 million men, women, and children who were defined by the Nazi regime as "belonging to the Jewish race." This figure represents some 90 percent of East European Jewry or 30 percent of the entire Jewish people in 1939. Political enemies, gypsies, the mentally ill, and other groups were included.

To give the appearance of decency and civilized action Nazis justified their actions as protecting the world from the alleged threat to the purity of the Aryan race and maintaining German national unity and security. Legislation initially singled out persons of the Jewish race (anyone with one or more "Jewish" grandparents). Everyone with such ancestry had to register from 1940/41; businesses maintained or financed by Jews also had to be registered. Failure to do so might lead to deportation or execution. In a second stage Jews were moved into urban ghettos and dismissed from prominent work positions. This stage was rapidly followed by confiscation of valuable or essential property and transportation to "work camps" and/or concentration camps which became extermination centers. From September 1941 on, every racial Jew (regardless of religious affiliation or citizenship) had to wear a yellow star prominently displayed on the left chest (in Poland such a "badge" was introduced two years earlier). Different colored "J"s were stamped on identity papers, indicating "grades of Jewishness" or preferred treatment for political or other reasons. By 1943/44 most intended victims were also tattooed on their arms.

The department of "Jewish Affairs for the Third Reich" under Adolf Eichmann coordinated all matters pertaining to this obsession with "purity of the Aryan race." By the end of World War II, 395 camps for men and 17 camps for women had been set up to gather, quickly and efficiently, all who were deemed undesirable. As soon as a person had become useless or was deemed a threat or a nuisance, extermination through gassing, shooting, or incineration was carried out. Freight trains (often open cattle cars) transported these prisoners, generally under the command of SS officers and soldiers. Most notorious among the camps were Bergen-Belsen, Auschwitz-Birkenau, Buchenwald, Dachau, Treblinka, Mauthausen, Sobibor, Gross-Rosen, and Vught. The relatively few survivors told of atrocities committed on hapless victims. Meticulous records of confiscated Jewish treasures and possessions kept by local and camp authorities corroborate these stories.

The Jewish holocaust combines the forces of historical fact and literary truth. Some have compared the Nazi extermination of Jews to the death of Jesus, suggesting that radically new ways of thinking, speaking, and living are the only acceptable response to the phenomenon, to the extent that some writers would redate future history, beginning with the holocaust as point zero.

Among the most prominent characteristics of postholocaust literature are the demand for silence, on the one hand, and the challenge to bear unrelenting witness to its tragic dimensions, on the other. In response to the latter challenge, an ever-growing literary legacy contains documentation, narrative, poetry, drama, and theological reflection. The goal is that out of the fragmentation and madness of attempted genocide may come discovery of truth and out of the *"l'univers concentrationnaire,"* true liberation for all humankind.

**Bibliography**. E. Wiechert, *Der Totenwald (The Forest of the Dead)* (1947); H. Arendt, *Eichmann in Jerusalem: A Report on the Banality of Evil* (1963; rev. ed., 1965); T. Borowski, *This Way to the Gas, Ladies and Gentlemen* (1967); J. Presser, *The Destruction of the Dutch Jews* (1969); E. L. Fackenheim, *God's Presence in History: Jewish Affirmations and Philosophical Reflections* (1970); L. L. Langer, *The Holocaust and the Literary Imagination* (1975); E. Fleischner, ed., *Auschwitz: Beginning of a New Era?* (1977); A. H. Rosenfeld and I. Greenberg, eds., *Confronting the Holocaust: The Impact of Elie Wiesel* (1978); A. L. Sachar, *The Redemption of the Unwanted, From the Liberation of the Death Camps to the Founding of Israel* (1983).

E. J. FURCHA

## Holtzmann, Heinrich Julius (1832–1910).
German Protestant. Born in Carlsruhe he was educated at the universities of Heidelberg and Berlin and, after being a pastor in Baden from 1854 to 1857, became privatdocent at Heidelberg in 1858. Three years later he was appointed associate professor and was advanced to a full professorship in 1865. In 1874 he accepted a call to Strasbourg as professor of NT exegesis, a position which he retained until 1904, when he became professor emeritus. In theology he is one of the leading representatives of historical-critical analysis. His writings include *Kanon und Tradition* (1859), *Die synoptischen Evangelien, ihr Ursprung und geschichtlicher Charakter* (1863), *Kritik der Epheser- und Kolosserbriefe auf Grund einer Analyse ihrer Verwandschaftsverhältnisse* (1872), *Die*

*Pastoralbriefe, kritisch und exegetisch behandelt* (1880), *Lehrbuch der historischkritischen Einleitung in das Neue Testament* (1885), *Lehrbuch der neutestamentlichen Theologie* (2 vols., 1896–97), *R. Rothes speculatives System* (1899), *Gesammelte Predigten* (1901), *Die Entstehung des Neuen Testaments* (1905), and *Das messianische Bewusstsein Jesu* (1907). He contributed material on the Apocrypha and the NT to C. C. J. Bunsen's *Bibelwerk* (2 vols., 1866, 1869), on John, the Synoptic Gospels, Acts, the Johannine Epistles, and Revelation to the *Hand-Kommentar zum Neuen Testament*, which he edited in collaboration with R. A. Lipsius, P. W. Schmiedel, and H. von Soden (1889–91), and edited with K. Budde *Eduard Reuss' Briefwechsel mit seinem Schüler und Freunde Karl Heinrich Graf* (1904). He coauthored with G. Weber, *Geschichte des Volkes Israel und die Entstehung des Christentums* (2 vols., 1863), and with R. Zöpffel, *Lexikon für Theologie und Kirchenwesen* (1882).

## Holy Land.
Name commonly given to the land of Israel because of the veneration of sacred sites by adherents of Christianity, Islam, and Judaism. Judaism's traditional emphasis has been on the entire land (*Eretz Yisrael*) rather than venerating the holy places upon which Christianity came to focus. With the fall of Jerusalem to the Romans in A.D. 70 and the accompanying expulsion of many Jewish inhabitants from the land, pilgrimage to the Mount of Olives and the graves of biblical and rabbinical figures became increasingly popular. The most venerated place of Jewish prayer in the 20th century has been the Western Wall (often referred to as the "Wailing Wall"), a relic of the temple of Herod. Under the control of Jordan from 1948, the wall was forbidden ground to Jews under Arab occupation, but the reunification of the city of Jerusalem under Israeli control after the 1967 Six-Day War opened this sacred site to pilgrims of all faiths. Jewish prayer services are held there during the day, and individual meditation occurs well into the night.

Almost every Christian holy site in Israel is connected with the life of Jesus, although the authenticity of the holy places is open to dispute. When church and state were linked in the early 4th century, Emperor Constantine's mother, Helena, visited the Holy Land and established the places of Jesus' birth, death, and resurrection. Magnificent churches were built upon these sites, as well as upon the sites where miracles were performed and where saints ministered. Although the present sanctuaries date from various periods and religious rights are shared by both Roman Catholic and Eastern Orthodox communions, the Church of the Nativity stands upon the traditional site of Jesus' birth in Bethlehem, while the Church of the Holy Sepulcher (and Calvary) is found in Jerusalem. The garden of Gethsemane and the stations of the cross on the Via Dolorossa in Jerusalem are points of Christian prayer and pilgrimage, as is the Hall of the Last Supper. Around the Sea of Galilee, the site of Jesus' baptism in the Jordan River, the site of the Sermon on the Mount (the Mount of Beatitudes), and the sites of Jesus' miracles in Capernaum are points of pilgrimage.

Jerusalem is the third holiest city in Islam (Mecca and Medina being the first and second), and most Muslim holy places in the Holy Land are connected with the lives of the biblical heroes of Judaism and Christianity whom Islam has adopted as its own. The main Muslim holy site is *Haram al-Sharif*, a complex of buildings built in A.D. 691 which are dominated by the beautiful Dome of the Rock. It is from the rock at the center of this mosque that Muhammad is said to have ascended to heaven.

After the Arab-Israeli cease-fire agreement in June 1967, all of these holy sites were situated in the territory of the State of Israel. On June 27, 1967, Prime Minister Levi Eshkol affirmed to invited Christian, Jewish, and Muslim officials that Israel was committed to protecting the holy places of all religious traditions in the Holy Land. The Knesset (the Israeli Parliament) passed a strongly worded Law for the Protection of the Holy Places on the same day. In spite of periodic clashes between a variety of religious traditions, the holy places are more accessible today than at any other time in the history of the Holy Land.

*Bibliography.* F. M. Field, *Where Jesus Walked: Through the Holy Land with the Master* (1977); M. Davis, ed., *With Eyes Toward Zion: Scholar's Colloquium on America-Holy Land Studies*, vols. 1–2 (1977, 1986); S. Doyle, *The Pilgrim's New Guide to the Holy Land* (1985); D. Rossoff, *Land of Our Heritage: An Overview for the Jewish Traveller in Israel* (1987).

DAVID A. RAUSCH

## Holy Name, Society of the.
A Roman Catholic society of laymen whose object is to promote reverence for the holy name of God and Jesus Christ, and to suppress blasphemy, profanity, and the taking of unlawful oaths. It originated in Dominican circles following the Council of Lyons in 1274, and it was repeatedly approved by the popes. Local branches of the society in various American churches have been organized into diocesan unions since 1882, under the authority of a director general appointed by the hierarchy. The society has its headquarters in New York.

## Holy Spirit, The. *In the OT.*
The OT offers us a variety of perspectives on the Spirit of God (referred to as the Holy Spirit only in Ps. 51:11; Isa. 63:10–14), but the Spirit is primarily portrayed through the activity of God in power and his presence in revelation. The Spirit is thus possibly related to God's act in creation, as in Gen. 1:2 and Pss. 33:6; 104:30, although such assertions are rare and not unambiguous. *Rûaḥ* in

Gen. 1:2 may be interpreted "a mighty wind from God"; in Ps. 33:6 "the breath (*rûaḥ*) of his mouth" may refer to God's word of command; and in Ps. 104:30 God's *rûaḥ* might indicate the vitality he gives living organisms (note Ps. 104:29; Job 27:3; 33:4; 34:14–15), rather than what might properly be called "the Spirit of God." God's Spirit more typically is related to God's covenantal activities in and on behalf of Israel, so the locus of the Spirit's work is restricted almost exclusively to the holy nation.

The Spirit is thus said to be "on," "with," or "in" (the terms are used interchangeably) Israel's *leaders*, enabling them to act with God's power or to reveal his will. Accordingly God's *rûaḥ* is portrayed as a charismatic endowment on the judges, such as Othniel (Judg. 3:10), Gideon (Judg. 6:34), and Jephthah (Judg. 11:29), flaring into action on behalf of the covenant people in times of crisis. Indeed, even the at-first-sight bizarre eruptions of the Spirit through Samson (Judg. 13:25; 14:6, 19; 15:14) act as divine protection of Samson and the routing of Israel's enemies. More personally the Spirit of the Lord is an endowment on Moses (Num. 11:17, 29) through which he liberates and leads Israel at God's direction. Joshua has a similar endowment noted in Num. 27:18 and elsewhere. Subsequently, with the 70 elders (Judg. 11:25–29), Moses is enabled to adjudicate her disputes (as in Neh. 9:20, a retrospective view). God's wisdom and enabling are also portrayed as given by God's Spirit to the craftsmen who make the cultic furniture (Exod. 28:3; 31:3; 35:31). Later, God's Spirit acts in power on behalf of Israel, the unseen scepter of his righteous rule through her kings, such as Saul in 1 Sam. 10:1–11 and notably through David in 1 Sam. 16:13 and elsewhere (see Zech. 4:6).

The Spirit of God acted as the channel of communication between God and man. This was the Spirit of prophecy as Judaism came to understand it. The Spirit made God's will and wisdom known to the charismatic leader, to the king, and even to the cult carpenter, characteristically through the phenomenon of oracular speech termed "prophecy," in which a message of the Lord was granted by the Spirit in a dream vision or word. Thus God's revelation is directly or indirectly traced in early prophecy to the Spirit (as in Num. 11:25–29; 24:2; 1 Sam. 10:10; 19:20), and in classical prophecy. Mic. 3:8 and Hos. 9:7 equate *prophet* with man of the Spirit. A similar message is expressed in Ezek. 11:5–25 and elsewhere (Isa. 48:16; 61:1–3; Zech. 7:12). The character of prophecy in the history of Israel was probably more varied than many scholars admit. The usual simplified schemas identify, for example, an "early ecstatic" type in 1 Sam. 19:20; 10:1–13; Num. 11:25; but then what of the "late ecstatic" Ezekiel and Zechariah? Such theories fit no more than a small part of the evidence and tell us more about the critical proclivities of the analyst than about the primary material.

In the OT the personal ministry of the Spirit seems limited to the leaders and prophets; theirs is the responsibility to bring Yahweh's direction to his people. By contrast a future is anticipated in which *all* Israelites will share in the Spirit of prophecy (Joel 2:28; Num. 11:29); indeed, such immediate knowledge of God lies at the heart of the hoped-for new covenant. In the new covenant each would "know the Lord" for himself (Jer. 31:34). The future is thus expected to be an epoch characterized by the lavish outpouring of God's Spirit (as in Isa. 32:15; 44:3; Ezek. 39:29) and the revelation of his glory and power (Hab. 2:14). This would be accomplished in a righteous, prophetic liberator (Deut. 18:15; Isa. 61) and king endowed with the Spirit of wisdom and power (Isa. 11:1–9), and by the consequent deep existential renewal that recreates the very heart of man in obedience (Jer. 31:31–40; Ezek. 36:24–29). This recreation is in view in Ps. 51:10–14.

Despite some degree of personification of the Spirit (notably at Isa. 63:10–14; Neh. 9:20; Ps. 143:10; but also in the Spirit "speaking" in 2 Sam. 23:2; Ezek. 2:2; 3:24; 11:5), this seems a literary device. The Spirit in the OT is rather a mode of God's presence (as in Pss. 51:11; 139:7). The OT reference to his "arm" or "hand" means *God's Spirit* rather than *God the Spirit*.

**In the NT.** By the time of the NT it was a commonplace of Jewish belief (albeit not universal) that God had withdrawn the Spirit from Israel, but that the Spirit would return in overflowing measure at the end. At the heart of the NT proclamation lies the conviction that, in and through Jesus, these promises of Ezek. 36:24–29 (the recreative Spirit in men's hearts) and Joel 2:28–32 (the pouring out of the Spirit of prophecy) had already begun to be fulfilled. The three chief theological witnesses are Luke–Acts, John, and Paul.

*Luke–Acts.* In his writings Luke builds the conception of John the Baptist and Jesus on the framework of the return of the Spirit to pious Israel who is awaiting her Messiah (Luke 1:15–17, 41, 67; 2:25–32, 36–38). John is to be filled with the Spirit from his birth (1:15), and the Spirit, the power of the Most High, overshadows Mary (1:35) so that the very existence of the one conceived by the Spirit, the Son of the Most High, is also stamped by the Spirit (1:32). As the one so conceived, he, from youth, lives in intimate relationship with the Father (2:40, 52) and knows his calling uniquely to be "about my Father's business" (2:49). Jesus' reception of the Spirit at his baptism (3:21–22) has nothing to do with deepening his own relationship to God or with entry into new covenant or new age existence. Rather, as 4:16–21 vividly quotes from Isa. 61:1–2, it is his empowering as the messianic Servant and King (note also the reference to Ps. 2:7 at Luke 3:22)

and Mosaic prophet in 4:18–21 (compare with Acts 3:22–26; 7:37). The messianic purpose is to bring release (as in the *aphesis* of Luke 4:18), and the joy of the kingdom of God, to Satan's captives (compare especially 11QMelch use of Isa. 61:1–3). Luke 7:21–23; 11:20–22, and 13:16, and Acts 10:38 point out that this had occurred. In salvation the Spirit at work through Jesus is a power that molds an individual's life and beliefs. In this people begin to experience the promised recreation and to taste the life of the kingdom of God.

With his death, resurrection, and ascension, Jesus, according to Acts 2:33, receives the gift of the Spirit a second time in the sense that he becomes Lord of the gift of the Spirit promised by Joel 2:14–39. The Spirit of prophecy which had been the channel of communication between Yahweh and the leaders now ties the risen Lord to the disciples. The Spirit of the Lord, operating as the Spirit of prophecy, has become the Spirit of Jesus (Acts 16:7), and *he* distributes its charismata, as in Acts 2:33. Commensurate with the Spirit of prophecy in Judaism, in Acts the risen Lord gives visions and dreams (2:17–28), crucial theological visions (10:10–20), personal direction (9:10–16), or comfort (7:55; 18:9–10). Joel's promised gift is also traced to the charismata of tongues which punctuate Acts, a form of inspired speech which Judaism would immediately recognize as belonging in the category of prophetism and issuing from the Spirit of prophecy. By the same gift the risen Lord gives direction in words in 10:19 and 13:2. Charismatic wisdom and discernment are also given through the Spirit of prophecy, as when Luke 21:15 is fulfilled in Acts 5:3; 6:9–10, and 16:18. This gift also is related to power in preaching—a major emphasis in Acts not to be confused with the essence of the Pentecost gift. Power in preaching is merely an activity of the Spirit as the Spirit of prophecy. Through this gift Jesus directs and empowers the church's mission to outsiders (Acts 2:4, 33; 4:8, 31; 8:29; 11:12–15; 13:2–9). He gives charismatic wisdom and revelation where it is needed for the defense and propagation of the gospel (5:1–11; 6:3, 5, 10) or for the direction, sanctification, and upbuilding of the church (9:10–16, 31; 11:28; 13:52; 15:28).

The Pentecostal gift of the Spirit is thus no *donum superadditum* but the link between Jesus in heaven and his disciples on earth by which he continues to announce his messianic liberation; it is the very life of the church. For this reason the gift is promised to all who believe (Acts 2:38–39). Although the Spirit has been active through Jesus in the lives of the disciples before Pentecost—and perhaps through Philip in the lives of the Samaritans before they receive the Spirit in Acts 8:17—Jesus' removal from earth in death, resurrection, and ascension makes the Pentecost gift the authentication of Christian existence. Without it there can be no continuing communion and communication between the disciple and his Lord, which is the mark of Christian life.

*John.* John presents a similar picture in different form. Because Jesus is richly empowered by the Spirit (1:33; 3:34) the disciples can experience his words as "Spirit" and "life" (6:63) and be told they are "clean" "through the word I have spoken to you" (15:3; compare with 13:10). A Samaritan woman can be told that through Jesus she might be given "living water" (4:10), and that worship could be performed in Spirit and in truth (4:23). Finally, in 20:22, Jesus "breathed the Spirit into the disciples" (the same rare word, *enephusēsen* as is used in the LXX version of Gen. 2:7 to relate how God breathed life into Adam). The process of birth by "water" and "Spirit" in 3:5 refers to the fulfillment of Ezek. 36:24–27). The echo of Gen. 2:7 in 20:22 indicates a climax in the process.

But, as with Luke–Acts, Jesus' ascension out of the world poses a problem. How will the disciples continue to experience him? This question is answered by John in the farewell discourse. Jesus is going to the Father, but he will not leave the disciples as defenseless orphans (14:18); he will send them an advocate (*paraclētos*). The first two Paraclete promises are sandwiched with sayings about Jesus' "leaving" and yet "returning" (with the Father) to dwell with the obedient disciple. If Jesus and the Father are going to make their abode with the Christian (14:23), if Jesus is to appear to the disciples but not to the world (14:17, 19, 22–24), and if he is not going to abandon them it is because the coming Paraclete will mediate the presence of the Father and the Son just as the Son has represented the Father in his earthly life (14:7–11). As R. E. Brown puts it, "John represents the paraclete as the Holy Spirit in a special role, namely as the personal presence of Jesus in the Christian while Jesus is with the Father."

The Paraclete comes as Jesus' *replacement* at Jesus' permanent removal to be with the Father (7:38–39), and the fulfillment of the promises of the Paraclete (and of 7:37) takes place beyond the chronological framework of the Fourth Gospel. The nature of the gift promised, restoring communion between the disciple and the risen Lord, leading the church into all truth (15:26–27; 16:14), and convicting the outsider of the gospel (16:8–11), invites comparison with Luke's description of the Pentecostal gift. John's more personal presentation of the Spirit, however, especially in respective roles of Jesus and the Spirit in relation to the disciple, to the Father, and to the world, provides one basis for the doctrine of the Trinity.

Luke–Acts and John tell how the disciples of Jesus received the Spirit in a twofold experience: within the ministry of Jesus, and beyond the salvation-historical turning point of his death, resurrection, and exultation. For neither can this second gift be a continuing pattern, except, perhaps, in the most abnormal of circumstances, such as at Samaria in Acts 8. There is no authentic Christian existence for one who does not have what Luke would call Joel's promised gift, and John "the Paraclete."

*Paul.* The apostle expresses certainty that the Galatians will remember that they "received the Spirit" not by circumcision and commitment to Torah, but by believing what they heard preached: the gospel of Christ crucified (3:1–5). He assumes the Galatians will freely admit that they received the Spirit as they started their Christian lives. The whole argument of Gal. 3:1–5, 15, in its context, shows that Paul considered reception of the Spirit as a necessary and sufficient condition of authentic Christian existence. The same assumption is made in Rom. 8:9–11. The following points show how Paul describes the character of the gift of the Spirit.

a. For Paul the Spirit is the Spirit of the new covenant. The promises of a new heart, new knowledge of God, and new obedience of Jer. 31:31–34 and Ezek. 36:24–27, given by the indwelling Spirit, are regarded as fulfilled. The Christ-event inaugurates a new covenant of freedom and life through transformation by the Spirit into ever-increasing glory (2 Cor. 3:3–18).

b. The Spirit received is the eschatological Spirit, the matrix of the new creation. When Paul speaks of each convert as a new creation (*kainē ktisis*) in 2 Cor. 5:17, he not only has in mind that the indwelling Spirit has made them new in heart, spirit, and relationship. He also means that this new state of affairs is the beginning of something much bigger—cosmic renewal. This is made clear in 2 Pet. 3:13 and Rev. 21:1–3. Each conversion is an installment of the new creation, and the Spirit received is the downpayment (*arrabōn* in 2 Cor. 1:22; 5:5; Eph. 1:14) of the eschatological order, its firstfruits (Rom. 8:23). Similarly the Spirit can be called God's seal on his people (2 Cor. 1:22)—the mark of God's ownership and of his intent to redeem. For Paul the Spirit is the power of the age to come—a power anticipated in us through the Christ-event, but a power, nevertheless. It orientates our existence toward the end, for which, with creation, we groan (Rom. 8:22–27).

c. The Spirit received is the Spirit of Christ. The new heart and spirit promised by Ezekiel turn out, for Paul, to be nothing other than Christ in us (Rom. 13:14; Gal. 3:27; Eph. 4:24; Col. 3:4, 10). If this new creation made "in Christ" by the indwelling Spirit is none other than the image of Christ it is hardly surprising that Paul refers to the Spirit (as in Rom. 8:9–11) as the "Spirit of Christ." It also becomes obvious how in Rom. 8 Paul can move directly from speaking of the Spirit of God to asserting that those without the Spirit of Christ do not belong to Christ, and how he can then start the next sentence, "if then Christ is in you." Paul is not referring to different entities nor failing to distinguish Christ and the Spirit. Rather since the resurrection the primary focus of the Spirit's function has been to impress Christ on the life of the convert; the Spirit of God is experienced as the Spirit of Christ.

d. The Spirit received is the Spirit of God's Son and the matrix of our sonship (Gal. 4:6; Rom. 8:15). The Spirit who recreates us in the image of God's Son reproduces in us the beginnings of Jesus' full filial relationship to the Father and so, for example, brings us to pray, "Abba," with him. The Spirit is thus appropriately characterized as the Spirit of adoption in Rom. 8:15.

e. The Spirit we receive will one day fully conform us to the Son's glorious resurrection existence as a "spiritual body." Our new existence will manifest the Christ-centered focus of the new creation by the Spirit (1 Cor. 15:45–49; Phil. 3:21).

f. In the meantime the Spirit is the author of the eschatological tension we experience between the "already" and the "not yet" of conformity to Christ's image. Paul may speak at times as though the battle is over, as in Rom. 6:6, 1 Cor. 5:17, Gal. 2:20, and Col. 3:9, or that we are involved passively in transformation (2 Cor. 3:18), but Paul also emphasizes that the "flesh"—sinful human nature—remains a potential threat (Gal. 5:13; 6:8). The difference between the Christian and the man outside Christ is not that the former has sloughed off the sinful caterpillar nature and emerged a beautiful butterfly. Rather the man outside Christ is totally determined by his rebellious nature while the Christian has the Spirit, so that in God's grace he can manfully resist the flesh (Gal. 5:17). However much Paul's term "the fruit of the Spirit" might suggest passive growth, Paul stresses that the Christian must fight the flesh to the death in Rom. 8:13 (see 1 Cor. 9:24–27; Gal. 5:13–26; Phil. 2:12–13; 3:13–14.)

Clearly the gift of the Spirit as Paul understands it is the ground of Christian life; it could not possibly be postponed to a "second blessing," although equally clearly Paul expects this gift of the Spirit to be experienced in the variety of charismata spoken of in Rom. 12, 1 Cor. 12–14, and Eph. 4, and there is no scrap of credible evidence he expected such gifts as tongues or prophecy to cease before the parousia (see 1 Cor. 13:10). The charismata are not a distinct set of workings of the Spirit that can be set over against and added to our experience of new covenant relationship, sonship and resurrection "life"; they are themselves specific aspects and experiences of those privileges.

***Doctrinal Developments.*** Since the biblical period reflection and controversy have focused on many different major areas of the doctrine of the Spirit. A few of the primary issues are:

*The Spirit as a Member of the Trinity.* The NT leaves the status of the Spirit somewhat unclear.

Triple references to God, Christ, and Spirit in Matt. 28:19; 1 Cor. 12:4; 2 Cor. 13:13; Eph. 4:2–6; and 2 Thess. 2:13–14 fall somewhat short of proving a belief in the Spirit as a divine Person, coeternal with Father and Son, and some triads such as 1 Tim. 5:21 omit the Spirit. Passages describing the *role* of the Spirit are not much help, though arguably from the Paraclete passages something approaching a trinitarian view might be inferred.

So it is not surprising to find a measure of confusion in the apostolic fathers and the apologists. In the 3d and early 4th centuries (to the Council of Nicea, A.D. 325) controversy raged rather on the question of the divinity of the Son, debates on the Spirit playing second fiddle. Only from the mid-4th century does the deity of the Spirit emerge as an issue. Cyril of Alexandria and Athanasius, followed more definitely by Basil the Great and Gregory of Nazianzus, affirmed the Spirit's pretemporal divinity against semi-Arians. Hard on the heels of this discussion came the more recondite controversy regarding whether the Spirit proceeds from the Father *and* the Son, the position argued by most Western theology and which prevailed with the addition of the *filioque* clause at the Council of Toledo in 589, or from the Father *through* the Son. This issue, which in 1054 split the Western from the Eastern churches, did not concern the affirmation of Christ's lordship in sending the Spirit at Pentecost but how the divine Persons relate in eternity, and in what senses they are coequal.

Unitarianism attempted to cut the Gordian knot, questioning whether the Spirit is truly a third divine person, rather than a referring expression for God himself, especially in relation to his power at work in the world. As "Spirit" has come to be stressed as God's mode of immanence in creation in idealism and classic liberalism, theological studies in pneumatology have tended to go in pantheistic directions and lost sight of the biblical focus on the Spirit as the redeeming presence of God in the people of God (for counterblasts, see Karl Barth and Jürgen Moltmann).

*Spirit and Word.* The NT regards the OT Scripture as the product of the Spirit, and with the notable exception of Marcion, the church has extended the claim to the NT too, albeit with varying theories on the method of inspiration. With the Reformation confirmation that the Word is God's is itself attributed to the inner witness of the Spirit, rather than to church authority or to features of the Bible itself. To the Spirit too is traced the effectual call of a person through the gospel and saving faith. The Spirit also is credited with illumination to read the Word with understanding. The conservative church's understanding in these areas was worked through in the Reformation by John Calvin. A modern defender of the work of the Spirit in Scripture is Helmut Thielicke.

*Reception of the Spirit and Baptism.* The early church appears to have hovered between assigning the receiving of the Spirit to baptism and dividing the gift between baptism and confirmation (see L. S. Thornton and G. W. H. Lampe for different assessments), and similar positions are held today. The NT identifies the gift of the Spirit primarily and intrinsically with conversion–regeneration and secondarily to baptism. Baptist circles tend to identify the receiving of the Spirit as a much later witness to prior conversion. Sacramentalism tends to reverse the theological order to accord priority to baptism (J. D. G. Dunn v. Lampe). Confirmationists such as Thornton see the more significant reception of the Spirit attaching to postbaptismal confirmation. It is unclear how their position establishes which graces are afforded by the Spirit in baptism and which pertain only to the second rite. Insofar as they place theological emphasis on a *second* gift of the Spirit, they appear to differ from the NT. The same danger attaches to pentecostalism and the related charismatic and neo-pentecostal theologies. Their emphasis on immediate and charismatic experience of the Spirit accords with the NT, but when they require a second-blessing reception of the Spirit their views differ from Luke–Acts where the Pentecost gift is a sine qua non of authentic Christian existence—experienced initially with charismata, not at a secondary "empowering."

*Bibliography.* L. S. Thornton, *Confirmation: Its Place in the Baptismal Mystery* (1950); N. Q. Hamilton, *The Holy Spirit and Eschatology in Paul* (1957); D. E. Holwerda, *The Holy Spirit and Eschatology in the Gospel of John* (1959); G. R. Beasley-Murray, *Baptism in the NT* (1962); G. W. H. Lampe, *The Seal of the Spirit* (2d ed., 1967); J. D. G. Dunn, *Baptism in the Holy Spirit* (1970); R. E. Brown, *The Gospel According to John* (1971), 1135ff.; L. Neve, *The Spirit of God in the OT* (1972); J. D. G. Dunn, *Jesus and the Spirit* (1975); E. Schweizer, *The Holy Spirit* (1980); Y. M. J. Congar, *I Believe in the Holy Spirit*, vols. 1–3 (1983); A. Heron, *The Holy Spirit* (1983); T. Smail, *The Giving Gift* (1988).

MAX TURNER

**Holy Week.** The week from Palm Sunday to Holy Saturday, originally called the "great week." Celebration of the week had arisen in Palestine by the 4th century, as a fast period lasting from two days to a week. Prisoners and slaves were released and alms were given to the poor. Public offices were closed, and a liturgical celebration was practiced. In the 5th century a festival of palms spread through Palestinian churches. Through the medieval period it was a time of mourning. Holy Week is the Christian church's most pervasive celebration. In the Greek and Roman churches and in the majority of Protestant communions the days have similar themes. Christians observe the week as the high drama of faith, reliving the events of the final days before

triumph on Easter. The designations are: Palm Sunday, the "triumphal entry" into Jerusalem; Monday, Jesus' cleansing of the temple; Tuesday, conflicts between Jesus and the religious authorities; Wednesday, the day of silence, with Jesus and the Twelve; Maundy Thursday (Lat. *mandatum*, "command," referring to John 13:34), a time of special communion (using the Lord's supper or footwashing); Good Friday, the crucifixion, now often celebrated with ecumenical community services (three-hour services, signifying the hours of darkness, are a disappearing custom); and Holy Saturday or Easter Saturday, the day in the tomb, in the Greek Church a day of strict fasting, in the Roman liturgy a Mass day of both mourning and joyful anticipation. In the USA Good Friday has traditionally been a legal holiday. Concern over church-state issues in the late 20th century, however, caused the creation of a "spring holiday" weekend generally coinciding with neither Holy Week nor Passover.

*See also* CHURCH YEAR; EASTER.

**Holy Year.** *See* JUBILEE, YEAR OF.

**Homiletics, Teaching of.** The training of future pastors to communicate through preaching. There are three ways to study the mastery of homiletics, all in use: (1) Many come to homiletics as a science, applying rules of rhetoric, which go back to Greece and Rome. (2) Others have dealt with preaching as an art or craft. This approach has led to increased appreciation of master preachers, and more study of history. (3) Another group stresses the study of master sermons, past and present. Each approach has merits and limitations. Some seminary curricula allow the student to integrate the three methods. Most probably learn how to preach after ordination. Many have become master preachers out on the field: H. W. Beecher, Phillips Brooks, J. H. Jowett, and Alexander Maclaren. A graduate may serve an apprenticeship under a mature pastor, or enter a field that affords time to master this art. Some denominations have come to require an internship before ordination, a period of licensure; work as an assistant pastor also encourages homiletic training.

Many observers feel the need for changes in the teaching of homiletics. The professor should know the history of preaching, beginning with the prophets. He should have had pastoral experience, to understand human needs. Then he should coach each student. Such a plan calls for small classes; in a large seminary it requires a large staff. "Practice preaching" before students has an air of unreality. Video and recording technology allows a student to reproduce an actual service and then go over it with the instructor, perhaps in the presence of other students. Gradually a student should develop the art of self-criticism, so that he will never rest content with second-rate delivery. Fortunately, most professors of homiletics have also developed the art of self-criticism. Hence the teaching of tomorrow ought to be less wooden and more rewarding.

*Bibliography.* J. H. Jowett, *The Preacher—His Life and Work* (1912); A. W. Blackwood, *The Fine Art of Preaching* (1937); G. Campbell Morgan, *Preaching* (1937); R. E. Sleeth, *Persuasive Preaching* (1956); P. T. Forsyth, *Positive Preaching and the Modern Mind* (1957); R. R. Caemmerer, *Preaching for the Church* (1959); E. Clowney, *Preaching and Biblical Theology* (1961); C. H. Spurgeon, *Lectures to My Students* (repr. ed., 1965); P. Brooks, *Lectures on Preaching* (repr. ed., 1969); D. M. Lloyd-Jones, *Preaching and Preachers* (1971); J. D. Baumann, *An Introduction to Contemporary Preaching* (1972); D. Demaray, *An Introduction to Homiletics* (1974); J. A. Broadus, *On the Preparation and Delivery of Sermons* (1979); W. C. Kaiser, Jr., *Toward an Exegetical Theology* (1981); F. Craddock, *Preaching* (1985); S. T. Logan, Jr., ed., *The Preacher and Preaching: Reviving the Art in the Twentieth Century* (1986); G. Spring, *The Power of the Pulpit* (repr. ed., 1986); D. G. Buttrick, *Homiletic: Moves and Structures* (1987).

ANDREW W. BLACKWOOD

**Homosexuality.** Sexual attraction to members of one's own sex; homosexual practice refers to sexual activity with someone of the same sex. Female homosexuality is also called lesbianism. There continues to be great debate among psychologists and theologians about whether there is an inherited predisposition toward homosexuality or whether it is a learned response to certain conditions, particularly poor parent-child relationships. It does not seem possible, on the evidence so far available, to entirely rule out genetic or hormonal influences. However, the more objective studies suggest that it is primarily a learned behavior.

All sexual acts outside marriage, and homosexual lifestyles by name, are condemned in the Bible. In ancient Israel homosexuality was a capital crime (Lev. 18:22; 20:13). Paul is particularly direct in regard to homosexuality in Rom. 1:26, 27; 1 Cor. 6:9, 10, and 1 Tim. 1:9, 10. On the other hand, Scripture allows and encourages strong friendships between members of the same sex, such as that between David and Jonathan. Men and women are also encouraged to display and develop characteristics often regarded by society as belonging to the opposite sex. The Bible, for example, encourages men to be gentle and forgiving (Eph. 4:1–3). Strong condemnation of homosexuality in early Christian history was influenced both by the OT and by Roman law, where it also was punishable by death. Greek society was more open to such practices. Later, Thomas Aquinas developed the concept that the sexual organs must not be used for any acts which preclude generation; this institutionalized the ascetic view that sex was not for pleasure but only for conception—a view which continues to influence Roman Catholic attitudes to contraception and biomedical procedures such as artificial insemination and in vitro fertilization. Other ethical considerations are raised in regard to biomedical issues, however.

Traditional Christian morality, based on biblical precepts, has declared homosexual practices to be sinful, but (like other sins) capable of forgiveness. Homosexual lifestyle is contrary to the biblical ethic and should be neither practiced nor taught. The church biblically stands especially strongly against any sexual actions which exploit others. Christian attitudes toward the criminality of homosexual acts between consenting adults are far more ambivalent. Sin and crime are quite different categories, and where government does not declare adultery a crime it is difficult to justify declaring consenting adult homosexual acts in private to be a crime. By the 1980s many states had decriminalized all or most homosexual activity, with the support of civil libertarians and many Protestant churches. Such groups were taking principial stands that homosexuals should not be targets for discrimination or exploitation, whether by law or social ostracism.

The spread of AIDS-related diseases complicated the ethical issues since homosexual practices contributed significantly to its incidence. The AIDS problem was greeted by various responses from the church. Some called it "the wrath of God" and called for severe penalties for spreading it by giving blood, sharing needles, or homosexual acts. Other sections of the church were more permissive, calling on the "gay" community to restrict its behavior and be more responsible for other people's well-being. Most groups, whatever their views on drug abuse and homosexuality, sought ways to offer sympathy and pastoral care, through chaplaincies, education programs, and hospices.

ALAN NICHOLS

**Homrighausen, Elmer George** (1900–1982). Presbyterian (formerly Reformed Church in the United States) scholar. Born in Wheatland, Iowa, he studied at Mission House College, Princeton Theological Seminary, and the University of Dubuque (Th.D., 1931). He was pastor of the English Reformed Church at Freeport, Ill. (1924–29), and the Carrollton Avenue Evangelical and Reformed Church, Indianapolis (1929–37). He was professor of Christian education at Princeton Theological Seminary (1938–54), professor of pastoral theology there (1954–70), and dean from 1955. His works include *Christianity in America—A Crisis* (1937), *Current Theological Trends* (1938), *Let the Church Be the Church* (1940), and *I Believe in the Church* (1951). He also helped to translate sermons by Barth and Thurneysen.

**Honduras.** A republic of Central America, with an area of 112,088 sq. km. (43,277 sq. mi.) and a population of 4.66 million (1987). The Roman

Catholic Church is the dominant faith (about 94 percent of the people in 1982). The fate of Catholicism in Honduras was closely linked to that of Guatemala during the 19th century. The terms of the Concordat of 1861 between Honduras and the Vatican were almost identical to those negotiated by Guatemala in 1852. Similarly, during the 1880s the Honduran government implemented a series of anticlerical measures fashioned after President Justo Rufino Barrios' Liberal Reforms in Guatemala. These measures, combined with the country's relative impoverishment, have made the Honduran church one of the weakest in Central America.

Church-state relations improved during the 1950s, culminating in the 1957 constitution which reversed most of the previous restrictions on the church. Since then, the influx of foreign missionaries has partially mitigated the shortage of native clergy. As a response to the shortage of priests, especially in the countryside, in 1966 missionaries introduced a program called Delegates of the Word. Peasants received training in the gospel teachings and were authorized to give Celebrations of the Word. In this way, delegates could celebrate services in between the pastoral visits of the local priest (sometimes only twice a year). In rural areas the church also became active in promoting peasant organizations and cooperatives. Because of these activities, the military government blamed the church for a wave of peasant agitation in 1975. The murder of two priests during the same year resulted in the hierarchy's curtailing of some of these activities.

It was not until the 1950s that the Protestant community, about 94,000 in 1982, began to show a dramatic increase. Between 1936 and 1950 the average annual Protestant growth rate was 1.6 percent. From 1965 to 1978, however, the annual growth rate was 12.4 percent. Although the Methodist and Episcopal churches are dominant among the English-speaking population, fundamentalists and pentecostals account for much of the recent growth.

**Honesty.** Qualities of inward and outward integrity, candor, and social justice. Honesty is closely related to honor, which has been described as a system of reciprocal rights and obligation belonging to a social relationship, and also the individual's recognition of these. Each social system develops its own code of "honor," which may be almost identical with proper ethical standards, but may also be supplementary, indifferent, or even hostile to them; every craft and profession develops its own honor, but "honor among thieves" bears little relation to honesty, commonly understood. Honor here means fidelity to those associated with us and observance of their accepted code. In Christian ethics the conception of "honor" is governed by

the belief in a moral Judge who is also Redeemer, in what is due to him as such, and in consequence is due to another person—who is regarded as made in the image of God, standing under his judgment, and claiming his forgiveness.

That a wide variety of meanings attach to "honesty" is due to the fact that it is the characteristic excellence of the just man in different surroundings. Honesty can mean conformity to codes. At its best it involves integrity in thought, word, and deed. Honest motives rise above mere respect for a properly constituted social order or desire for esteem to devotion to an ideal of righteousness and truth. This explains what the English logician Richard Whately meant when he said, "Honesty is the best policy, but he who acts on that principle is not an honest man." Honesty in its highest sense is not refined and enlightened self-interest, but a sincere devotion to principle.

As civilized society has become more commercialized, honesty has tended to become identified less with respect for moral rights in general, and more with the rights and laws of property in particular. The honest person is trustworthy and conscientious in work and business relationships, refraining from lying, cheating, or stealing. Honesty, so regarded, becomes the supreme virtue of a commercialized society. But even here professional and other standards may claim a relative autonomy. What is perfectly justifiable and even meritorious in business may be unprofessional conduct in a lawyer. The general principle of honesty must be articulated in each sphere. It is probable that only a strict sense of individual and corporate responsibility to God can enable adjustments to be made. The honest person retains integrity and fidelity to principle amid the compromises of policies, programs, and practical necessities; with a strong sense of duty, the individual of honor cannot but be honest before God.

W. R. FORRESTER

**Hong Kong.** A British crown colony with an area of 1068 sq. km. (412 sq. mi.) and 5.84 million population (1988). The vast majority of the inhabitants (98 percent) are Chinese. Christianity was introduced to Hong Kong by Protestant missionaries from both Europe and America who moved to the colony shortly after Great Britain took possession of it in 1842 following the Opium War. The first Roman Catholic missionaries, from Italy, arrived in 1858. Many of the early converts to Christianity and their descendants were prominent in the political and economic development of the colony, despite racial tensions. Since they had been educated in English by missionaries, they were familiar with Western ways and the English language. The philanthropic contributions of these converts aided many church-related institutions, particularly educational institutions and hospitals, many of which continue their work. (Other educational institutions moved from China to Hong Kong in 1949.) The Christian population of the colony increased dramatically in 1883 to 1885 as a result of persecution in neighboring Kwangtung province.

Hong Kong has been a center of Christian publishing since a number of presses were established in the 19th century. The 1960s and 1970s saw a rapid increase in Christian publishing houses in the colony, most of them run by Chinese. By the 1980s there were approximately 90 Christian publishing houses and presses in Hong Kong. Of these about 50 are Protestant, 30 are Roman Catholic, and the others identify with specific Protestant denominations. Most are small, employing fewer than 20 people, but several employ 50 or more staff members. Radio and television programs are a widely used source of spreading Christianity, and Roman Catholic and Protestant groups have studios.

Pentecostal groups first located in Hong Kong in 1910, and, along with evangelical churches, are presently experiencing rapid growth. The Christian population of Hong Kong is approximately 600,000, nearly evenly divided between Protestants and Roman Catholics.

KATHLEEN L. LODWICK

**Hoover, Harvey Daniel** (1880–1958). Lutheran. Born in New Oxford, Pa., he was educated at Gettysburg College, Susquehanna University, and at Illinois Wesleyan University (Ph.D., 1907). He also studied at Union Theological Seminary. He was pastor of churches in Friedens, Pa. (1902–4), and East Pittsburgh, Pa. (1904–7). He was professor of theology and sociology at Susquehanna University (1907–9) and president of Carthage College (1909–26). He then became professor of practical theology in the Lutheran Theological Seminary, Gettysburg, Pa. He was editor of *Light for Today* (1935–47), associate editor of *The Lutheran Church Quarterly* (1938–48), editor of five volumes of the annual publication of the National Lutheran Education Association (1920–25), and editor of *The Bible Reading Fellowship* from 1930.

**Hope.** In the Christian context the believer's response in trust to the relationship he has with God. In the OT God is recognized as the hope of Israel; hope springs from God's covenant promises. The OT emphasizes trust, dependence, expectation, and patience. Hope is to be accompanied by the fear of God. The believer expects God to help in the present and ultimately to put an end to distress. Hope becomes increasingly eschatological, related to messianic expectation.

The NT concept of hope is determined by the OT. The chief characteristic of hope is that it is a gift of God (2 Thess. 2:16–17; 1 Pet. 1:3); it is a concomitant part of the gospel (Col. 1:23). Without God, a person is without hope (Eph. 2:12). Hope includes expectation (1 Cor. 1:7), trust (Rom. 15:13), and patience (Rom. 8:25; 1 Thess. 1:3). It is inseparable from faith. On the one hand, faith is the foundation upon which hope rests (2 Cor. 5:7; Rom. 8:24); on the other hand, hope enlivens faith (Gal. 5:5; Col. 1:5).

Hope is inherent in the believer's relationship with Christ—looking to his death, resurrection, and parousia as its basis and stimulus. The object of hope is clearly defined with its foundation in God's acts in Christ (Eph. 1:12; Col. 1:27; 1 Pet. 1:21). Hope has certainty because of its connection with the historical Christ and the promises of God (Col. 1:23). Hope is also eschatological. It is grounded in the work of the Holy Spirit (Rom. 8:23–25) and focuses on the future realities of Christ's return.

Christian hope directs present life. It is a stimulus to godliness (1 John 3:3). It is essentially related to love (1 Cor. 13:13; Col. 1:4–5). It matures in suffering (Rom. 5:1–5). It results in steadfastness (1 Thess. 1:3; Heb. 6:11), in confidence (2 Cor. 3:12), and in joy (Rom. 5:1–2; Heb. 3:6). Hope is the basis upon which the believer labors for the Lord (1 Cor. 15:58).

*Bibliography.* A. Pott, *Das Hoffen im NT* (1915); E. Brunner, *Eternal Hope* (1954); J. E. Fison, *The Christian Hope: The Presence and the Parousia* (1954); P. S. Minear, *Christian Hope and the Second Coming* (1954); C. F. D. Moule, *The Meaning of Hope* (1963); J. Moltmann, *A Theology of Hope: The Ground and the Implications of a Christian Eschatology* (1964); *NIDNTT* (1976): 2:238–46; *TDNT* (1978) 2:517–35.

MARTIN PARSONS

**Hope, Norman Victor** (1908–1983). Presbyterian scholar. Born in Edinburgh, Scotland, he studied at the University of Edinburgh (Ph.D., 1944). He was minister of Busby West Church in Glasgow (1935–38), taught theology at New Brunswick Theological Seminary, New Brunswick, N.J. (1938–46), and was professor of church history at Princeton Theological Seminary (1946–78). He is the author of *One Christ, One World, One Church: A Short Introduction to the Ecumenical Movement* (1953). He translated Karl Holl's *Urchristentum und Religionsgeschichte*, under the title, *The Distinctive Elements in Christianity* (1937). He also contributed to the 1955 edition of the *Twentieth Century Encyclopedia of Religious Knowledge* and to Baker's *Dictionary of Practical Theology* (1967).

JAMES McCLANAHAN

**Horn, William** (1839–1917). Evangelical Association bishop. Born in Oberfischbach, Prussia, he was self-educated. After a number of pastorates in his denomination (1861–71), he became editor of the German Sunday school literature of the Evangelical Association in 1872, a post he held until 1879. He was then editor of the *Christlicher Botschafter* (1879–91) before becoming a bishop of his denomination. In theology Horn laid special stress on the love of God and on the redeeming work of Christ. His published works include *Präsident James A. Garfields Lebens- und Leidensgeschichte* (1881), *Life of Bishop John Seybert* (1894), *Illustrationen oder Bilder und Beispiele zum Gebrauch für Prediger, Eltern und Lehrer* (1900), *Life of Bishop John J. Escher* (1907), *Wegeblüthen* (1907), and *Erfüllte Prophezeiungen* (1907).

**Horton, Walter Marshall** (1895–1966). Congregational Christian theologian. Born in Somerville, Mass., he studied at Harvard, Columbia (Ph.D.), Union Theological Seminary, N.Y., Paris, Strasbourg, and Marburg. He was instructor at Union Theological Seminary (1922–25), and thereafter taught theology at the Oberlin Graduate School of Theology. Described as a "realist" in theology, he tried to purge liberal theology of idealistic illusions while retaining its sound elements. His principal writings were *Theism and the Modern Mood* (1930), *A Psychological Approach to Theology* (1931), *Theism and the Scientific Spirit* (1933), *Contemporary English Theology* (1936), *Contemporary Continental Theology* (1938), *Can Christianity Save Civilization?* (1940), *Our Eternal Contemporary* (1942), *Our Christian Faith* (1945), *Toward a Reborn Church* (1949), *Christian Theology: An Ecumenical Approach* (rev. ed., 1958), and *The God We Trust* (1960).

**Hoskier, Herman Charles** (1864–1939). Episcopalian NT textual critic. Born in London, he studied at Eton College, in France and Germany, and at Amsterdam (Th.D.). He served in the French army (1914–19). He entered banking and brokerage in New York and retired to devote himself to NT textual criticism. He was particularly interested in interrelationships among the Syriac, Coptic, Ethiopic, Latin, and Greek texts of the NT. His main writings include *Account and Collation of the Greek Codex Evangelium 604* (1890), *The Golden Latin Gospels JP in the Library of J. Pierpont Morgan* (1910), *Concerning the Genesis of the Versions of the NT* (2 vols., 1910–11), *Concerning the Date of the Bohairic Version* (1911), *Codex B and its Allies* (2 vols., 1913/14), *Immortality* (1925), *Concerning the Text of the Apocalypse* (2 vols., 1929), *The Complete Commentary of Oecumenius on the Apocalypse* (1928), *Bernard of Cluny's De contemptu mundi* (1929), *In Tune with the Universe* (1931), and *The Back of Beyond* (1934).

DANIEL J. THERON

**Hoskyns, Edwin** (1851–1925). Anglican leader. Born in Aston-Tirrold, Berkshire, he studied at Jesus College, Cambridge, where he became a fellow. Later he was ordained a deacon (1874) and a priest (1875). He then became curate, Welwyn,

Herts, and Quebec Chapel, London (1879–81), vicar, St. Clements, North Kensington (1881–86), rector, St. Dunstan, Stepney (1886–95), vicar of Balton (1895–1901), honorary canon of Manchester from 1899, rector of Burnley (1901–4), bishop of Burnley (1901–5), and bishop of Southwell (1905–25). He devoted himself to the improvement of the workers' conditions.

*Bibliography.* Alumni Cantabrigienses, vol. 2, 1752–1900; *The New International Year Book* (1925).

DANIEL J. THERON

**Hospice.** As early as the reign of Constantine hospices appeared as shelters for the sick, the poor, orphans, the old, and travelers. Through the centuries, as hospitals, orphanages, and other specialized agencies arose to meet the needs of specific groups, the term "hospice" came to apply only to shelters for travelers. Established in uninhabited areas, at difficult mountain passes, and in other places of extreme need, hospices served thousands of the faithful who in the Middle Ages undertook pilgrimages.

In modern times the hospice of the Great St. Bernard Pass in the Swiss Alps has been the best known. It was founded by St. Bernard of Menthon in 962 and has sheltered as many as 25,000 travelers a year. From the hospice and small huts on adjacent mountains the monks of St. Bernard with their famous dogs have gone out to search for travelers lost in the snow. Once hospitality was free to all. Because of abuse by tourists the Great St. Bernard Hospice today receives, between July and September, only pedestrians and travelers definitely in need. Others are referred to a standard hotel on the grounds.

Among Protestants the name "hospice" has been applied to guest houses in which people are offered a substitute for the atmosphere of a Christian home while traveling or during temporary residence in a town. Since 1860 more than 125 such hospices were established in Germany, Austria, Switzerland, and Sweden to supplement the *Herbergen zur Heimat*, and in 1904 they formed an Association of Christian Hospices.

In Great Britain and the USA the YMCA and YWCA performed a similar function. However, some church bodies and the Salvation Army also established what were variously called hospices, hostels, shelters, residence houses, and residence clubs to provide accommodation and a Christian environment for students, young men or women employed in business or industry, and others who were temporarily away from home.

In about the 1970s the "Hospice movement" arose in the USA to give a new dimension to hospices. With medical costs rising and new concerns being expressed about the quality of life in a hospital environment, some large medical institutions began to provide monitored but lower-cost and more homelike accommodations for the terminally ill. While these were normally secular agencies they provided ministry opportunities for urban churches. By the later 1980s social and Christian groups had set up some hospice care centers specifically for persons with terminal AIDS-related illnesses.

GROVER L. HARTMAN

**Hough, Lynn Harold** (1877–1971). Protestant educator and writer. He studied at Scio College and Drew Theological Seminary (Th.D., 1919). He was pastor, among other churches, of Central Methodist, Detroit, and American Presbyterian Church, Montreal. He was professor of historical theology at Garrett Biblical Institute (1914–19), and dean of Drew Theological Seminary (1934–47). Among his books are *Athanasius the Hero* (1906), *The Theology of a Preacher* (1912), *The Man of Power* (1916), *A Living Book in a Living Age* (1918), *The Significance of the Protestant Reformation* (1918), *The Productive Beliefs* (1919), *The Opinions of John Clearfield* (1921), *Life and History* (1922), *The Strategy of the Devotional Life* (1922), *The Inevitable Book* (1922), *Synthetic Christianity* (1923), *Evangelical Humanism* (1925), *Adventures in the Minds of Men* (1927), *Imperishable Dreams* (1929), *The Artist and the Critic* (1930), *Personality and Science* (1930), *The University of Experience* (1932), *Vital Control* (1934), *The Church and Civilization* (1934), *The Great Evangel* (1935), *The Civilized Mind* (1937), *Free Men* (1939), *The Christian Criticism of Life* (1941), *Adventures in Understanding* (1941), *Patterns of the Mind* (1942), *Living Democracy* (1943), *The Meaning of Human Experience* (1945), *Christian Humanism and the Modern World* (1947), and *The Dignity of Man* (1950).

**Houtin, Albert** (1867–1926). Roman Catholic modernist, priest, and historian. His *Question biblique*, written at modernist leader Alfred Loisy's suggestion, was placed on the index of banned books (1903). He left the church in 1912, shortly before publishing his *Histoire du modernisme catholique*.

WALTER M. HORTON

**Howard, Peter** (1908–1965). Oxford Group (Moral Rearmament) movement leader. Born in Maidenhead, England, and educated at Oxford, he was an international rugby player and also became known as a political columnist (1933–41). He relinquished this line of work after conversion to the so-called Oxford Group, and divided his time between the movement and his farm in East Anglia. After Frank Buchman's death in 1961 he became the movement's leading spokesman. Among his publications were *Innocent Men* (1941), *Ideas Have Legs* (1945), *That Man Frank Buchman* (1946), *The World Rebuilt* (1951), *Remaking Men* (1954), *Frank Buchman's Secret* (1961), and *Design for Dedication* (1964). He was also the writer of numerous plays.

**Howard, Wilbert Francis** (1880–1952). Methodist pastor, NT scholar, and author. Born in Gloucester, England, he studied at Manchester and London. After several pastorates (1905–19), he became professor of NT language and literature at Handsworth College, Birmingham (1919–51), and later its principal (1943–51). He was editor and joint author of J. H. Moulton's *Grammar of NT Greek*, vol. 2 (1929), sections on 1 and 2 Corinthians in *The Abingdon Bible Commentary* (1929), John in the *Interpreter's Bible* (1952), *The Fourth Gospel in Recent Criticism and Interpretation* (1931), *Christianity according to St. John* (1943), and *The Romance of NT Scholarship* (1949).

**Howison, George Holmes** (1834–1916). Educator and author. Born in Montgomery County, Md., he studied at Marietta College, Lane Theological Seminary, and Berlin. He taught mathematics and political economy at Washington University, St. Louis, Mo. (1864–69), was professor of logic and philosophy of science at Massachusetts Institute of Technology (1871–79), lectured on ethics at Harvard (1879/80), on philosophy at Michigan (1883/84), and was professor of philosophy at the University of California (1884–1909). An inspiring and successful teacher of philosophy, Howison stressed a theistic personalism in which he defined God as perfect person, final cause, and center of the republic of persons, with emphasis on the freedom and dignity of the soul. Among his books are *Limits of Evolution, and Other Essays in Philosophy* (2d ed., 1904) and *Philosophy—Its Fundamental Conceptions and Methods* (1904). He contributed to *The Conception of God* (1897).

*Bibliography.* J. W. Buckham, *Harvard Theological Review* 9 (1916); J. W. Buckham and G. M. Stratton, *George Holmes Howison, Philosopher and Teacher* (1933); C. M. Bakewell, *Philosophical Review* 49 (1940).

RAYMOND W. ALBRIGHT

**Hromadka, Josef Luki** (1889–1969). Czech Reformed theologian. Born in Hodslavice, Moravia, he studied at Basel, Heidelberg, Vienna, Prague (Ph.D., 1920), and the United Free Church College, Aberdeen. He was professor of systematic theology at Prague (1920–39) and at Princeton (1939–47). He returned to Prague in 1947 and became dean of the Comenius Faculty in 1950. From its inception he was active on the executive of the World Council of Churches, sharply criticizing Western culture at the Amsterdam Assembly in 1948. He was a vice-president of the World Alliance of Reformed Churches, and helped establish the Christian Peace Conference and served as its president (1959–68). In helping to reorient the

Christian church to promoting the reconciliation of nations, he contributed significantly to Christian-Marxist dialog and to an easing of East-West tensions. His major writings include *Principles of the Evangelical Church of Czech Brethren* (1927), *Masaryk* (1930), *Christianity in Thought and Life* (1931), *Luther* (1935), *Calvin* (1936), *Theologie und Kirche zwischen gestern und morgen* (1957), *Doom and Resurrection* (1945), *The Gospel for Atheists* (1958), and *My Life between East and West* (1969). J. Smolik published a festschrift, *Von Amsterdam nach Prague. J. L. Hromadka* (1969).

E. J. FURCHA

**Hubbard, Lafayette Ronald** (1911–1986). A highly successful science fiction writer and adventurer, he developed his own unique and highly unorthodox form of therapy known as "dianetics." In 1951 he published *Dianetics: The Modern Science of Mental Health,* which provoked a strong and somewhat violent reaction from psychiatrists, psychologists, and other mental health professionals. Hubbard founded the Church of Scientology in 1955. For the remainder of his life he developed the teachings of scientology, which consist of a blend of primal experiences such as "soul travel" and "the remembrance of past lives," Hindu and Buddhist metaphysics, and a rich pseudoscientific mythology, the essence of which he outlined in novels like his best-selling *Battlefield Earth: A Saga of the Year 3000* (1982). Hubbard's teachings created one of the most original and influential new religious movements of the 20th century and have given rise to many similar groups such as EST, Lifespring, and Eckenkar.

IRVING HEXHAM

**Hudson, Winthrop Still** (1911– ). American Baptist church historian. Born in Schoolcraft, Mich., he studied at Kalamazoo College, Colgate-Rochester Divinity School, and the University of Chicago (Ph.D., 1940). He was minister of the Normal Park Baptist Church, Chicago (1937–42), instructor at the Colgate-Rochester Divinity School (1942–44), assistant professor at the University of Chicago (1944–47), and professor of the history of Christianity at the Colgate-Rochester Divinity School (1948–77). He was president of the American Society of Church History (1948), and editor of *Church History* (1950). His writings include *John Ponet: Advocate of Limited Monarchy* (1942), *The Great Tradition of the American Churches* (1953), *The Story of the Christian Church* (1958), *Understanding Roman Catholicism* (1959), *American Protestantism* (1961), *Nationalism and Religion in America* (1970), and *Religion in America* (rev. ed., 1973). He also edited Henry Scougal's *Life of God in the Soul of Man* (1948) and Roger Williams' *Experiments of Spiritual Life and Health* (1951).

**Hügel, Friedrich Von** (1852–1925). Roman Catholic philosopher. Of Austrian and Scottish parents, he inherited a barony and had some wealth. As an interpreter of religion he warned against the impoverishment that inevitably came to any form of the Christian religion that neglected to hold the three principal elements of the mystical, the institutional, and the intellectual together in a dynamic tension. A leader of the Roman Catholic modernist movement, he sought to join elements of religion, science, and philosophy. His influence on Protestant thought in England, where he resided from 1867, was immense. His *Mystical Element of Religion* (2 vols., 1908; 2d ed., 1923) is a classic study of the phenomena of the mystical life and of their psychological and philosophical interpretation. His emphasis on the givenness of God and upon the transcendent quality of the reality of God antedated by a decade the Barthian accent in this direction and prevented Barthianism from sweeping England with its novelty. This interpretation of the essential religious experience in a realist frame appears with increasing clarity in his writings: *Eternal Life* (1912), *Essays and Addresses in the Philosophy of Religion* (1921, 1926), *Selected Letters* (1927), and *The Reality of God* (1931).

DOUGLAS V. STEERE

**Hughes, Edwin Holt** (1866–1950). American Methodist bishop. Born in Moundsville, W.Va., he studied at Ohio Wesleyan University and Boston. He pastored churches in Massachusetts (1892–1903) and was president of De Pauw University from 1903 to 1908. A distinguished scholar, educator, and preacher, he served as a bishop (1908–40), and was the senior bishop from 1936. He began his episcopal service in California and after his retirement served again in the Washington, D.C., area (1943–47), and in Wisconsin (1947/48). He was the acting president of Boston University (1923) and acting chancellor of American University (1933). He was the chairman of the joint commission on the union of the American Methodist churches. In theology he described himself as a moderate progressive. His later books are *Thanksgiving Sermons* (1909), *The Teaching of Citizenship* (1909), *A Boy's Religion* (1914), *The Bible and Life* (1914), *God's Family* (1926), *Christianity and Success* (1928), *Are You an Evangelist?* (1937), *Evangelism and Change* (1938), and *I Was Made a Minister* (autobiography, 1943). He was coauthor of *Worship in Music* (1929).

RAYMOND W. ALBRIGHT

**Hughes, Philip** (1895–1967). Roman Catholic historian. Born in Manchester, England, he graduated from the seminary at Leeds (1920). After his ordination he went to the University of Louvain, became a member of the Seminar Historique, and did research in Rome (1921–23). He worked in the parishes of Manchester, England (1924–31), and was archivist of Westminster (1934–39). Later he became a professor in the College of St. Thomas at St. Paul, Minn. His works include *A History of the Church* (3 vols., 1934–49), *Pope Pius the Eleventh* (1937), *The Faith in Practice: Catholic Doctrine and Life* (1938), *Pope's New Order* (1943), *A Popular History of the Catholic Church* (1947), and *The Reformation in England* (1963).

**Humani Generis.** An encyclical issued by Pope Pius XII on August 12, 1950. It denounces "historicism," which tends to reinterpret Christian doctrines on the basis of an evolutionistic philosophy, and "existentialism," a system which, according to the pope, "neglects the immutable nature of things, while being concerned exclusively with the 'existence' of individual realities." Both ideologies are held responsible for introducing elements of relativity into dogmatics, and for tying essential Christian beliefs to the passing conditions of history, thus threatening faith itself. A strict adherence to the philosophy of Aquinas is considered the best way to secure a foundation for theology. Catholics are urged to observe extreme caution in meeting non-Roman scholars, lest they may be tempted to harmonize their differences of belief at the expense of the official teaching of the church. The encyclical concludes by urging Roman Catholic exegetes to follow scrupulously the decree of the Pontifical Biblical Commission (June 30, 1909), on the interpretation of the first 11 chapters of Genesis as history, not myth.

GEORGES A. BARROIS

**Human Rights.** Prerogatives of persons or communities which are granted by God or the state on the basis of citizenship, membership, or humanity. Paradoxically, by the late 1900s advocacy of human rights was almost universal, yet they have existed in only a minority of countries, and there only imperfectly. Moreover, as the vocabulary of human rights has become universalized, it has also become politicized. Governments and organizations have been unable to arrive at a universally accepted definition. In general, the term "human rights" is a 20th-century rendition of such concepts as "natural rights" and "the rights of man" which became commonplace in Western language in the 18th century. Thus, human rights are those rights enjoyed equally by all human beings simply because they are human beings.

There is no worldwide consensus concerning the concretization of these rights. The classical list of human rights includes equality before the law and security of person. Freedoms usually thought to be covered are religion, conscience,

expression of opinion, press, association, and disposal of property. But in the 20th century there is some warrant, by virtue of usage at the UN and elsewhere, to distinguish among civil and political rights, economic and social rights, and perhaps even collective rights. Civil and political rights include the rights to life, liberty, security of person, privacy, and property; the right to marry and establish a family; the right to a fair trial; freedom from slavery, torture, and arbitrary arrest; freedom of movement and the right to seek asylum; the right to a nationality; freedom of thought, conscience, and religion; freedom of opinion and expression; freedom of assembly and association, and the right to free elections, universal suffrage and participation in public affairs. Economic and social rights include the right to work and to earn a just reward for labor; the right to form and join trade unions; the right to rest, leisure, and periodic holidays with pay; the right to a standard of living adequate to health and well-being; the right to social security; the right to education, and the right to participation in the cultural life of a community. Collective rights include those of nations to self-determination, of races to freedom from discrimination, and of classes to freedom from neocolonialism.

Several historical streams converge into the modern river of human rights. Major sources have been the Judeo-Christian tradition, Renaissance humanism, and Enlightenment liberalism. Although modern human rights terminology is not especially biblical, the notion is found in both the OT and NT.

First, the Bible contains a doctrine of divinely inspired duties (including, e.g., the Ten Commandments) which, taken to their ultimate conclusion, form the basis of what moderns call human rights. The commandment, "You shall not murder," teaches that human life is sacred and implies that there is a right to life. Thus, although Yahweh's commandments are formulated as human obligations to God and not as explicitly conferring tangible rights or benefits upon humanity, they do, in fact, provide a philosophical basis for highly valuing and properly treating humans. Moreover, in Christian thought, all human duties to God are ultimately reduced to two: love God with one's whole being, and love others as oneself (Matt. 22:34–40). Therefore, although some modern scholars argue for human rights only on metaphysical or sociological grounds and deny that there is a biblical foundation, human rights are inherent in a correct understanding of Scripture, and biblical theology can be used to promote the human rights agenda. The notion of human rights derived from divinely imposed duties is reinforced by portions of the Mosaic law which guard the dignity of strangers, widows, and neighbors. Further, both Moses and the prophets emphasized justice and love, not only in the treatment of individual people, but also in the social solidarity and integrity of corporate life.

Second, human rights are also grounded in the Hebrew-Christian idea of God and share the belief that all humans are created in the *imago Dei*. The concept of human dignity, as well as the ideas of justice, righteousness, and human freedom (esp. freedom from oppression), flows from this doctrine. Moreover, the moral imperative of human rights is based solidly on the biblical vision of *shalom*. This vision entails peace in its largest sense; it includes God's intended state of well-being, wholeness, justice, completion, and harmony for all God's creatures.

Third, the NT doctrine of the incarnation demonstrates the ultimate worth of human beings: "For God so loved the world that he gave his one and only Son, that whoever believes in him shall not perish but have eternal life" (John 3:16). Through Jesus, the NT shows God's interest in people from all segments of society. Jesus demonstrated the respect due Samaritans, tax collectors, and harlots, even in their sin and alienation. Salvation dramatically redirects people into a fellowship which overcomes barriers of nationality, class, sex, and race. According to the NT, the ultimate realization of the kingdom of God proclaimed by Jesus will be a universal society of justice and the full realization of humanity.

While the human rights tradition that emerged in the West was deeply rooted in the Bible, it was also nurtured and shaped by Athenian democracy and Roman jurisprudence. Greek and Roman sages spoke of natural law and held that deity was immediately accessible to human reason. Medieval scholasticism built on these foundations and "Christianized" natural law theory, resting its case on the assumption that human reason, apart from divine disclosure, could identify a normative objective moral order. Medieval natural law advocates insisted that a universally shared body of law and ethics survived the fall as a present possession of humankind. A practical outcome of this development was the Magna Carta in 1215. Heavily influenced by University of Paris-trained theologian and archbishop of Canterbury Stephen Langton, this document embodied in rudimentary form many basic civil and political rights, which were later more fully developed in the modern era.

The scholastic tendency to marginalize revelation led to a secularizing of natural law theory, beginning around the time of the Renaissance. Combined with the idea of the fundamentally free, autonomous, and self-determining human person, natural law became, in the hands of Renaissance humanists, an important impetus to champion elementary human rights. This development found support among many Protestant thinkers as well, such as Martin Luther (1483–1546) and John Calvin (1509–64). Although Luther and Calvin did not accept a natural law independent of Scripture or recognize a natural law founded on a metaphysical natural order, they nevertheless accepted the concept as a reflection of the original endowment of human nature which, despite perversion by sin, survives by common grace. Thus, echoes of human dignity and liberty can be found in their writings. Even more important in the early modern period in the development of a natural law theory that would sustain a modern human rights movement was the Dutch Protestant jurist Hugo Grotius (1583–1645). Heavily influenced by his Calvinist background, Grotius was a transitional figure who linked medieval scholasticism to the Enlightenment. He argued that there was a universal law of nature which derived from God's will and was known by human reason. He also held that this natural law was self-evident and so unalterable that not even God could change it. Thus, even though he did not mean to be, Grotius became the founder of the humanistic natural law theory that dominated Western legal and political thought for nearly 200 years when the historical school of law emerged.

The Enlightenment thinkers built upon the work of the Renaissance humanists and Grotius, whose work in turn rested on Judeo-Christian and classical foundations. These thinkers first joined the idea that all individuals everywhere are entitled to life, liberty, and the pursuit of happiness on this earth to the concept of natural law. They also championed the notion that natural rights have an immediate, concrete and universal application. John Locke (1632–1704), father of modern liberalism and a fountainhead of the Enlightenment, illustrates the fusion of the biblical, classical, scholastic, and humanistic tributaries of Western thought at this point. In turn, Locke's contract theory, philosophy of limited government, and affirmation of inalienable human rights were the immediate ideological influences on the founding documents of American constitutionalism.

However, the heirs of the Enlightenment concept of human rights soon split into two main camps. The liberal democrats emphasized political rights, such as those found in the modern liberal state (e.g., life, liberty, and freedom of religion, press, and assembly). The classical economists stressed economic rights, such as those found in the modern capitalist state (freedom from state interference in the economy and in society in general). Those who emphasized economic rights divided further in the 19th century with the emergence of modern socialism, especially Marxism, which stressed socioeconomic rights for workers (such as the right to form trade unions, the right to work for fair wages, the right to decent housing, and, ultimately, economic equality).

In the 20th century, Christians have once again become active in the struggle to establish human rights throughout the world. Among many and varied roles have been World Council of Churches social programs, Martin Luther King, Jr.'s (1929–68) leadership of the Southern Christian Leadership Conference in the civil rights movement of the 1950s and 1960s in the United States, the work of the Evangelicals for Social Action (formed in 1974) in North America, the presidential leadership of Jimmy Carter (1977–81), the activities of JustLife (established in 1986 as a broadly ecumenical, Catholic-Protestant coalition to work through the American political process for a consistent prolife ethic), and the impact of liberation theology, especially in Latin America.

Aside from the problems of definition and realization, the key question in the modern human rights movement has been, "Who will guarantee these rights?" The Enlightenment answer has been that the state has the primary responsibility. Thus, the various historical ideological streams eventually flowed into three constitutional gulfs: (1) the bill of rights enacted by the British Parliament in 1689; (2) the Declaration of the Rights of Man and the Citizen promulgated by French revolutionalists in 1789; and (3) the first 10 amendments to the Constitution of the United States adopted in 1791. All of these documents emphasized political rights and were framed to protect individuals against political oppression and to limit governments. Moreover, they became the forerunners of rights language now found in the fundamental documents of virtually every state around the world.

The individualistic concepts of human freedom and political rights were implemented in most Western countries in the 19th century. However, they failed to produce the predicted social harmony. Further, the social question erupted in the 19th century to complicate the picture as rights began to include claims to a just share of wealth and economic opportunity. In the 20th century third world theorists have added survival needs and rights and cultural authenticity to the ideological mix.

The current human rights movement emerged from the ashes of World War II and has been embodied in a growing number of international agreements. The most important of these have been the United Nations' Universal Declaration of Human Rights (1948), the European Convention on Human Rights (1953), and the Helsinki Conference Accords (1973–75). Of these the European Convention is the most sophisticated of modern international human rights treaties and the most consistent with biblical norms. In addition to problems of enforcement, these new documents raise questions concerning the nature of the state and society they will produce or reinforce and in what kind of state and society they can flourish. There also are questions of limitations. The UN declaration says there is a right to marriage and to raise a family—but at what age, and how large?

Three main streams of rights language dominate the human rights scene in the world today. Western nations tend to view rights in individualistic and political terms. Eastern bloc countries perceive rights mostly in a corporate sense. The third world is more inclined to see survival and liberation as rights of necessity that precede rights of preference. All converge at the historic point of emphasis on human dignity and social justice.

This returns the rights movement to its need for a firm ideological base upon which to build the future. What kind of foundation is needed for a contemporary philosophy of rights which can, with logical consistency, uphold human dignity and social justice? The Christian faith can provide this base if it keeps four facts in mind. First, Christians must remember that biblical authority is the source of the Christian's concern for human rights. Thus, God's concern for human dignity and social justice becomes the Christian's concern for human dignity and social justice, and these concerns coincide to produce human good and happiness. Second, the Christian also needs to remember that in a sin-ridden world, human rights will never be a popular cause. In this regard, the Christian's commitment is to human dignity and human personality. As believers work with others of good will in the pursuit of human rights it is well to keep in mind that the temptations to compromise and the pressure of other interests mean most human initiatives in the public order are motivated by pragmatic political concerns. Third, Christians must maintain an independent prophetic voice. If believers are serious about human rights, they will have to be scrupulous in seeing the totality of the picture and be constantly on guard lest they become unwitting partisans in a less than righteous cause. Fourth, Christians need to realize that they possess several unique resources in their witness for human dignity and well-being. Foremost of these resources is a worldwide network of support and correction, providing the Church can transcend boundaries of nationality and class. Thus, when one part of the body suffers, there will be resonating voices of encouragement from other parts; and when another part of the body becomes too comfortable with status and power, a word of admonition will be forthcoming.

**Bibliography.** C. J. Friedrich, *Transcendent Justice: The Religious Dimensions of Constitutionalism* (1964); M. Cranston, *What Are Human Rights?* (1973); J. N. D. Anderson, *Liberty, Law and Justice* (1978); G. W. Forell and W. H. Lazareth, eds., *Human Rights: Rhetoric or Reality* (1978); W. Laquer and B. Rubin, eds., *The Human Rights Reader* (1979); A. O. Miller, ed., *A Christian Declaration on Human Rights* (1979); C. J. H. Wright, *Human Rights: A Study in Biblical Themes* (1979); D. F. Wright, ed., *Essays in Evangelical Social Ethics* (1979); J. Finnis, *Natural Law and Natural Rights* (1980); W. Harrelson, *The Ten Commandments and Human Rights* (1980); A. Swidler, ed., *Human Rights in Religious Traditions* (1982); R. A. Evans and A. F. Evans, eds., *Human Rights: A Dialogue Between the First and Third Worlds* (1983); D. P. Forsythe, *Human Rights and World Politics* (1983); P. Marshall, *Human Rights Theories in Christian Perspective* (1983); J. Moltmann, *On Human Dignity: Political Theology and Ethics* (1984); M. F. Plattner, ed., *Human Rights in Our Time: History, Theory, Policy* (1984); A. R. White, *Rights* (1984); J. R. W. Stott, *Issues Facing Christians Today* (1985); C. H. Esbeck, ed., *Religious Beliefs, Human Rights, and the Moral Foundation of Western Democracy* (1986); N. S. S. Iwe, *The History and Contents of Human Rights: A Study of the History and Interpretation of Human Rights* (1986); J. W. Montgomery, *Human Rights and Human Dignity: An Apologetic for the Transcendent Perspective* (1986); M. Novak, *Human Rights and the New Realism: Strategic Thinking in a New Age* (1986); M. L. Stackhouse, *Creeds, Society, and Human Rights: A Study in Three Cultures* (1986); R. J. Vincent, *Human Rights and International Relations* (1986); R. F. Drinan, *Cry of the Oppressed: The History and Hope of the Human Rights Revolution* (1987).

ROBERT D. LINDER

## Hume, Basil George

**Hume, Basil George** (1923– ). Roman Catholic cardinal. After studying at the universities of Oxford and Fribourg, he was ordained in 1950. He was appointed to the teaching staff at Ampleforth College, and was professor of dogmatic theology there (1955–63). He was elected abbot of Ampleforth in 1963, and only reluctantly relinquished that post to become archbishop of Westminster and cardinal in 1976. Contrary to the expectations of some, the promotion of a godly recluse to be Roman Catholic leader in England and Wales proved to be a great success. His publications include *Searching for God* (1977), *In Praise of Benedict* (1981), and *To Be a Pilgrim* (1984).

J. D. DOUGLAS

## Hungary

**Hungary.** A socialist republic of 93,033 sq. km. (35,920 sq. mi.) and a population of about 10.6 million (1985). The largest church in Hungary was the Roman Catholic Church with over 6.3 million nominal adherents (59.2 percent of the population). The Reformed Church had 1.8 million members (16.8 percent), and the Lutheran Church 350,000 (3.3 percent). Over a dozen other Protestant denominations, some called collectively the "free churches," tallied a total membership of some 50,000. There were 231,000 Eastern-rite Catholics (Uniates) and 13,000 Orthodox. Jehovah's Witnesses totaled 4800, and there were 80,000 Jews. Sociological surveys conducted in the early 1980s indicate that only about 38 percent of the population regarded itself as religious. Among this religious minority only 20 percent believed their religious convictions to be in accordance with the teachings of the church. Less than 10 percent of the population attended church regularly.

The communist transformation of Hungary after World War II brought about profound changes in the relationship of the churches to the state. The constitution grants freedom of religion and stipulates the separation of church and state; the policy of the state, however, restricted the role of religion to private life and sought the active political support of church leaders. Most Roman Catholic associations were dissolved and church schools, which formed the majority of the country's educational institutions, were nationalized. Compulsory religious education in schools was abolished, and obstacles discouraged children from registering for optional instruction. Evangelical organizations were disbanded. Nearly all Catholic monasteries were dissolved in 1950. Believers often faced discrimination in housing, education, and employment. Because believers were barred from membership in the Communist party, they could play no more than a secondary role in political life. This changed somewhat in July 1989, when the government lifted its bans against believers.

Repressive measures were resisted by the leaders of the Catholic, Reformed, and Lutheran churches. Cardinal Jozsef Mindszenty was arrested in December 1948. In the same year the Reformed and Lutheran churches entered into agreements with the state which set legal limits on church activity and regulated state subsidies. Progovernment leaders were appointed. The Catholic Church yielded two years later after thousands of priests and religious had been arrested and a state-sponsored "peace priest movement" had been established. The 1950 Agreement was more onerous than those signed by the two major Protestant churches; and Archbishop Jozsef Grosz, who signed it, was imprisoned in the following year. In 1956 uprising brought about the temporary return of Cardinal Mindszenty; but when Soviet troops occupied Budapest he sought refuge in the American embassy and stayed there until 1971. During this period the free churches tended to be much more cooperative with the authorities and thereby avoided arrests and enforced resignations.

From 1956 the state concentrated on consolidating its political control of the churches. Until July 1989, when the State Office of Church Affairs was abolished in the reform movement that swept Eastern Europe, government approval was required for most senior church appointments. State-approved church leaders had broad powers to discipline politically unacceptable clergy. Long before the reforms, however, repression characteristic of the Stalinist era was eased. In 1964 an agreement with the Vatican led to the completion of the hierarchy. Laszlo Lekai was appointed archbishop of Esztergom in 1976.

Since the mid-1970s the churches have been allowed greater opportunities for worship, witness, and education. Several Western evangelists have been able to hold large public meetings. On

July 29, 1989, Billy Graham spoke to 90,000 in Budapest's Nep Stadium, an event advertised and broadcast to the nation over state-run television. Missions to alcoholics and wayward youth have been established. Before the reforms of 1989 this seemed a pragmatic government effort to solve the country's pressing social problems, rather than an abandonment of the state's ideological position. Political support from the churches was still mandatory. This situation changed drastically, however, in 1989. Within the span of a summer all conscientious objectors were released from prison, religious orders were legalized, and believers were accepted into the Socialist Workers' party. Symbol of the Hungarian mood came on August 20, when hundreds of thousands of Hungarians paraded through the streets of Budapest, marking for the first time in many years Saint Stephen's Day.

*Bibliography.* T. Beeson, *Discretion and Valor: Religious Conditions in Russia and Eastern Europe* (rev. ed., 1982); E. Andras and J. Morel, eds., *Church in Transition: Hungary's Catholic Church from 1945 to 1982* (1983).

PHILIP WALTERS

**Hunt, William Holman** (1827–1910). English artist. Born in London, he was educated in private schools and entered the Royal Academy Schools in 1843. At the academy his great friendship with Sir John Everett Millais (1829–96) began. In 1840, with the eminent artists, Millais and Dante Gabriel Rossetti (1828–82), Hunt laid the foundation of the Pre-Raphaelite Brotherhood. His painting, "The Light of the World," was exhibited in 1854. Hunt benefited much from the support of the writer John Ruskin, traveled in Europe, and made several visits to Palestine. He developed a profound religious passion, desiring to illuminate the scenes of Scripture in his work. He liked to think of himself as an artistic priest, interpreting the beauty of the work of God. His great paintings were all the products of long work. He received the Order of Merit in 1905, and at death he was buried in Saint Paul's Cathedral. He wrote *Pre-Raphaelitism and the Pre-Raphaelite Brotherhood* (2 vols., 1905).

LYNN HAROLD HOUGH

**Hunzinger, August Wilhelm** (1871–1920). After teaching theology at Leipzig and Erlangen he became the chief pastor in Hamburg yet continued his major theological interest, seeking especially a possible resolution of the differences between the liberal and conservative theologies which were agitating the church. His major works include *Lutherstudien* (1906), *Der Glaube und das religionsgeschichtliche Christentum der Gegenwart* (1907), *Zur apologetischen Aufgabe der evangelischen Kirche in der Gegenwart* (1907), *Probleme und Aufgaben der gegenwärtigen systematischen Theologie* (1909), *Theologie und Kirche* (1912), *Das Wunder* (1912), *Hauptfragen der Lebensgestaltung* (1916), and *Das Christentum im Weltanschauungskampf der Gegenwart* (3d ed., 1919).

RAYMOND W. ALBRIGHT

**Hurlbut, Jesse Lyman** (1843–1930). Methodist Episcopalian minister, editor, and author. Born in New York City, he studied at Wesleyan University. After teaching in Pennington Seminary (1864/65), he held pastorates from 1865 to 1879 and then was appointed an agent of the Methodist Episcopalian Sunday School Union. He was assistant editor (1884–88) and then editor (1888–1900) of Sunday school literature for the Sunday School Union and Tract Society. In 1900 he returned to the ministry, taking a pulpit at Morristown, N.J. He later served Methodist churches at South Orange (1904–5) and Bloomfield (1906–9), and was named district superintendent of the Newark district (1909–14). In his later years he became a counselor for the Chautauqua Literary and Scientific Circle. His many books include *Life of Christ* (1882), *Studies in the Four Gospels* (1889), *Studies in OT History* (1890), *Story of the Bible told for Young and Old* (1904), *Stories from the Old and New Testaments* (1905), *Handy Bible Encyclopedia* (1906), *Teacher Training Lessons* (1908), *Organizing and Building Up the Sunday School* (1909), *Story of Jesus* (1915), *Story of the Christian Church* (1918), and *The Story of Chautauqua* (1921). He also prepared many volumes of Sunday school lessons, many in collaboration with J. H. Vincent.

RAYMOND W. ALBRIGHT

**Hutchinson, Paul** (1890–1956). Methodist editor. Born in Madison, N.J., he graduated from Lafayette College and Garrett Biblical Institute. He began his career as a church journalist on the *Epworth Herald*, Methodist youth weekly published in Chicago, and in 1916 went to China, where he edited the *China Christian Advocate* and *Tsing Hua Pao*, and had general supervision of Methodist publications. In 1942, after returning to the USA, he became managing editor of *The Christian Century*. In 1947 he became editor. He wrote for many magazines and newspapers, and was the author of *The Next Step* (1921), *The Spread of Christianity* (1922), *China's Real Revolution* (1924), *What and Why in China* (1927), *The United States of Europe* (1929), *Men Who Made the Churches* (1930), *World Revolution and Religion* (1931), *Storm over Asia* (1932), *The Ordeal of Western Religion* (1933), *From Victory to Peace* (1943), *The New Leviathan* (1946), and *The New Ordeal of Christianity* (1957). With H. E. Luccock he wrote *The Story of Methodism* (1926, rev. ed., 1951).

**Hutten, Kurt** (1901– ). German Lutheran scholar. Born in Langenburg, he studied at the universities of Berlin, Marburg, and Tübingen (1919–23). He was assistant minister in Lutheran congregations in Württemberg (1923–27) and he taught at the seminary at Urach (1927–29). After earning his doctorate (1928) he worked as a teaching assistant before becoming director of the Evangelical Press Service in Stuttgart. On account of his involvement with the Confessing Church he was temporarily removed from his office and forbidden to do press work. After conscription in 1943 and being wounded in Russia he was taken prisoner of war by the Americans. Discharged in 1945, he returned to press work on behalf of the territorial church of Württemberg. His publications include *Die Bhakti-Religion in Indien und der christliche Glaube im Neuen Testament* (1928), *Kulturbolschewismus* (1932), *Um Blut und Glauben—Evangelium und völkische Religion* (1934), *Ein neues Evangelium?* (1936), *Christus oder Deutschglaube?* (1936), *Seher, Grübler, Enthusiasten- Sekten und religiöse Gemeinschaften der Gegenwart* (1950), *Die Glaubenswelt der Sektierers* (1957), and *Iron Curtain Christians in Communist Countries Today* (1967). Hutten was awarded an honorary doctorate from the University of Tübingen. In active retirement, he continues to write and maintain an interest in current affairs.

E. J. FURCHA

**Hutterian Brethren.** *See* MENNONITES.

**Hutton, John Alexander** (1868–1947). Presbyterian minister, editor, and author. Born in Coatbridge, Scotland, he studied at Glasgow University and was ordained in Alyth, Perthshire (1892). He served as minister in Newcastle-on-Tyne (1900–1906), Glasgow (1906–23), and Westminster Chapel, London (1923–25). From 1925 to 1946 he was editor of *The British Weekly*. He often preached and lectured in the USA. He published many volumes of sermons and essays, including *Pilgrims in the Region of Faith* (1906), *Loyalty: The Approach to Faith* (1917), *The Proposal of Jesus* (1920), and *Finally* (1935).

F. W. DILLISTONE

**Hyatt, James Philip** (1909–1972). Disciples of Christ scholar. Born in Monticello, Ark., he was educated at Baylor, Brown, and Yale universities (Ph.D., 1938), and at the American School of Oriental Research in Jerusalem. He taught biblical history at Wellesley College (1935–41), then from 1941 he was professor of OT and head of the department of religion at Vanderbilt University. He was also a member of the Revised Standard Bible Committee from 1945, and wrote *Treatment of Final Vowels in Early Neo-Babylonian* (1941), *Prophetic Religion* (1947), *Jeremiah: Prophet of Courage and Hope* (1958), *The Heritage of Biblical Faith* (1977), and a commentary on Exodus (2d ed., 1980).

**Hyde, William DeWitt** (1858–1917). American Congregationalist educator. Born in Winchendon, Mass., he studied at Harvard, Union Theological Seminary, and Andover Theological Seminary. After pastoring in Paterson, N.J., he became president of Bowdoin College and also taught mental and moral philosophy (1885–1917). Among his books were *Practical Ethics* (1892), *Social Theology* (1895), *Practical Idealism* (1897), *The Evolution of a College Student* (1898), *God's Education of Man* (1899), *The Art of Optimism* (1900), *The Cardinal Virtues* (1901), *Jesus' Way* (1902), *The New Ethics* (1903), *From Epicurus to Christ* (1904), *Abba Father: or the Religion of Everyday Life* (1908), *Self-Measurement* (1908), *The Teacher's Philosophy in and out of School* (1910), and his most popular work, *The Great Philosophies of Life* (1911).

RAYMOND W. ALBRIGHT

**Hyma, Albert** (1893–1978). Renaissance-Reformation historian. Born in the Netherlands, he immigrated to America with his parents when he was 17. Hyma attended Calvin College and the University of Michigan (Ph.D., 1922). From 1922 to 1924 he taught history at the University of North Dakota. Returning to the University of Michigan in 1924, he held continuous history department appointments until his retirement in 1962. Throughout his life he lectured at many North American universities and colleges and received numerous awards, including election to the Royal Historical Society (1926), a Guggenheim Fellowship (1928/29), and appointment to the Maatschappij der Nederlandsche Letterkunde (1957). In 1936 he was knighted by Queen Wilhelmina of the Netherlands for his work in the area of Dutch history. Hyma was a founding editor of the *Journal of Modern History* and medieval and Reformation period editor of the *Twentieth Century Encyclopedia of Religious Knowledge*. His reputation was built on a superb study entitled *The Christian Renaissance: A History of the 'Devotio Moderna'* (1924). Hyma's publications include textbooks, biographies (Erasmus, Luther, Calvin), and studies of Dutch colonialism, Dutch immigrants, and Michigan topics. His Christian sensitivities are seen in over 40 books and 200 articles and reviews.

*Bibliography.* The American Historical Review 85 (1980): 279–81.

JAMES A. DE JONG

**"I AM" Movement.** Organization founded in 1930 by Guy and Edna Ballard which assigns primary importance to interaction with the "Ascended Masters" of the Great White Brotherhood. These "Ascended Masters" are spiritual teachers who have completed their earthly pilgrimage, ascended into a higher state of being, and assumed responsibility for the destiny of humanity. Contact with this group of beings was initiated through their Authorized Messengers, the Ballards, and is a central goal of each member's life. The communications (dictations) from the Ascended Masters are transmitted via a monthly periodical, *The Voice of the "I AM,"* and through textbooks published by the Saint Germain Press.

The teachings of the "I AM" movement are directed toward the individual and collective well-being of the human race through realization of a threefold Truth: (1) knowledge of the "Mighty I AM Presence"; (2) use of the Violet Consuming Flame of Divine Love; and (3) use of God's Creative Name, "I AM." The divine spark exists within each individual as the Christ Self. Happiness, health, and prosperity are available to seekers who attune themselves to their "I AM Presence" through contemplation and the repetition of affirmations and decrees. Abuse of the divine energy by humankind results in discord, hatred, imperfection, and death.

The movement began when Guy Ballard, already familiar with theosophical/occult literature, had a series of mystical experiences at Mount Shasta in northern California. The Ascended Master, Saint Germain, appeared to him and designated Ballard, his wife Edna, and their son Donald as the only official messengers of the cosmic hierarchy. Shortly before Ballard's death in 1939, disgruntled former members initiated lawsuits against the movement's corporate expression, the Saint Germain Foundation. The organization suffered legal difficulties until the 1950s. After Edna Ballard's death in 1971, leadership was transferred to a board of directors. The foundation's international headquarters moved to Schaumburg, Ill., in 1978.

*Bibliography.* G. R. King (pen name of Guy W. Ballard), *Unveiled Mysteries* (1934); C. S. Braden, *These Also Believe* (1949); J. G. Melton, *Encyclopedic Handbook of Cults in America* (1986).

RONALD ENROTH

**Iceland.** An independent republic since 1944, Iceland has an estimated population (1986) of 246,000 and a land area of 103,000 sq. km. (39,800 sq. mi.).

Settled by Norsemen between A.D. 870 and 930, Iceland adopted Christianity in the year 1000. The "folk-church" that resulted from this act subsequently became a national institution. Iceland's conversion to Lutheranism became complete in 1550 with the beheading of its last Roman Catholic bishop. Following the Reformation, Gudbrandur Thorláksson translated the Bible into Icelandic—an event of immense significance, since it helped preserve the Icelandic tongue from foreign linguistic influence. A stream of liturgical and devotional literature did much to foster a unity of Christian tradition and practice among the far-flung settlements of that medieval agrarian society. An outstanding example is Hallgrimur Pétursson's (1616-74) *Hymns of the Passion*.

Urbanization and industrialism in the 19th and 20th centuries undermined the strong religious traditions of the old society. Continental theologies influenced the thinking of church leadership and brought, each in its turn, rationalism, spiritism, theosophy, and liberal theology. Highwater marks in Christian work during the modern era were: mass distribution of the Icelandic Bible and the formation of the Icelandic Bible Society (1815); the establishment of the YMCA by Fridrick Fridricksson (1899); the beginnings of the Salvation Army's work in Reykjavik and the Plymouth Brethren mission in Akureyri around the turn of the century; and the initiation of the Sunday school by Arthur Gook from England in 1906. A charismatic awakening, which began as a result of a student movement in 1975, has been important and continues to grow.

The Church of Iceland is the Evangelical-Lutheran Church, claiming 92.6 percent of the population as adherents. Some 7 percent of the population are comprised of the Evangelical-Lutheran Free churches, Roman Catholics, pentecostals, Adventists, Plymouth-Brethren, and others. The results of a survey in 1984 indicate that the majority of Icelanders (85 percent) are more or less in conformity with their religion. However, those that would classify themselves as definitely "Christian" would represent only about 8.5 percent of the population.

**Bibliography.** R. F. Tomasson, *Iceland: The First New Society* (1980); T. K. Thórdarson, *Iceland, 1966* (1967); J. Hood, *Icelandic Church Saga* (1946).

GREGORY AIKINS

**Ihmels, Ludwig Heinrich** (1858–1933). German theologian and Lutheran bishop. Born in Middels, East Frisia, he was educated at the universities of Leipzig, Erlangen, Göttingen, and Berlin, and was a pastor thereafter in East Frisia (1881–94). He was then director of studies at the monastery of Loccum (1894–98) and professor of systematic theology at Erlangen (1898–1903) and at Leipzig (1903–22) before becoming bishop of Saxony in 1922. He presided over the first Lutheran World Congress at Eisenach in 1923. His books include *Rechtfertigung des Sünders vor Gott* (1888), *Wie werden wir der christlichen Wahrheit geweiss?* (1900), *Die Selbststandigkeit der Dogmatik gegenüber der Religionsphilosophie* (1900), *Theonomie und Autonomie im Licht der christlichen Ethik* (1902), *Wer war Jesus, was wollte Jesus?* (1905), *Die Auferstehung Jesu Christi* (1906), *Centralfragen der Dogmatik in der Gegenwart* (1911), and *Das Christentum Luthers in seiner Eigenart* (1917).

**Immanence and Transcendence.** Divine attributes of being and providential activity (Lat. *in manere*, "dwell in"; *trans scandare*, "climb across"). The generic meaning of "immanence" is "being within"; of "transcendence," "being apart or independent." The problem of divine immanence and transcendence is posed by the very existence of both philosophical theology and religion, for they are based on the thesis that God causes (philosophical) or cares for (religious) the world. Since this implies that God must be distinct from, yet at work in, the world, extreme immanence and extreme transcendence set limits logically and chronologically for a scale of relative immanence and transcendence. Along this scale or continuum God may be regarded as almost completely transcendent, and related to the world solely by an original creative act (deism). God may also be conceived as a being whose *substance* is apart from the world but whose *activity*

or handiwork the world is ("effective" immanence, or theism in a narrow sense). A position of extreme immanence may see God as a being whose substance and activity are almost identical with the world ("substantial" immanence), either wholly (pantheism) or partially (panentheism: the world is in God). Such substantial immanence may so identify the world with God that it deifies the world (as in Neo-Platonism and medieval mysticism), or it may so identify God with the world that it naturalizes God (as in Renaissance mysticism and modern romanticism). Thus each of the extreme positions tends to be incompatible with its own philosophical and religious framework. Extreme transcendence tends to destroy God's efficacy and hence man's religiosity, while extreme immanence tends to destroy either man's humanity—his individual freedom and ethical categories—or God's divinity—his perfection and power.

The history of the problem of divine immanence and transcendence consists largely in a constant swinging of the theological pendulum from one extreme to the other, seeking for a "vital center." The swing of the pendulum started with the hylozoism of the pre-Socratic Greeks (c. 600–450 B.C.), when the divine was conceived immanently either as reality itself (e.g., Anaximander and the Eleatics) or as the governing law of reality (Heraclitus). From Socrates through Plato to Aristotle (450–322 B.C.) the transcendence of God was increasingly stressed to the point that in Aristotle, God, as "self-thinking thought," is unaware of the world. This was followed by a rapid return toward substantial immanence in Stoicism (c. 322 B.C.–A.D. 200), in which God was conceived as the indwelling semipersonal logos of nature.

The swing from Aristotelian transcendence to Stoic immanence set the pattern for the theologians of the Christian era. Stoic pantheism was transformed into a panentheism where God's being and activity were understood as being identical with the world, though transcending it. The divine "one" of Neo-Platonism "emanates" the world, which yearns through *epistrophē* for reunion with it; and for the Christian Scotus Eriugena (c. 800–877), God as Father "unfolds" the Son and through him the world, which then returns again to its source. Since, however, a more moderate position of substantial transcendence and effective immanence had already been maintained, in the midst of Neo-Platonism, by Augustine and some of the early church fathers, the swing was increasingly away from immanence toward the extreme transcendence of 13th- and 14th-century nominalism (William of Occam and Nicholas of Autrecourt). In nominalism God was above knowledge, although he could be seen through the study of creation. But there arose, almost simultaneously, a return to substantial immanence in the pantheism and panentheism of the 13th- and 14th-century Christian mystics (Meister Eckhart) and the modern, more rationalistic, mysticism of Giordano Bruno (1548–1600) and Benedict Spinoza (1632–77). For them God is the sole substance and *natura naturans* in contradistinction to *natura naturata* which is the world.

With the development of the physical sciences in the 17th and 18th centuries and the consequent picture of the world as a machine, there was again a swing toward transcendence, beginning with René Descartes (1596–1650) and Thomas Hobbes (1588–1679) and culminating in 18th-century deism, where God was needed only to start a world machine whose internal laws of motion were adequate for its continuance. Meanwhile, however, German pietism and English evangelicalism stressed God's role in the human heart, and with the rise of the biological sciences in the 19th century and the description of the world as an organism, there was a return toward substantial immanence. God was conceived as the inner meaning and life of the world—a position whose emotional expression in romanticism and rational expression in Hegelianism Friedrich Schleiermacher (1768–1834) attempted to synthesize. Beginning in the last half of the 19th century, finally, and continuing to the late 20th century, the swing has been back toward substantial transcendence with effective immanence, in both Protestantism and Catholicism, on the basis, this time, of ethical and religious, rather than scientific, considerations. The two most active agents in this movement have been the existentialism of Søren Kierkegaard and his followers (such as K. Barth and P. Tillich in Protestantism and G. Marcel and J. Maritain in Catholicism), the Protestant "neo-orthodoxy" exemplified by Barth and E. Brunner in Europe and Reinhold Niebuhr in America, and in Catholicism the papal condemnation of the "modernists" in 1907 and the development from 1879 of Neo-Thomism (as in E. Gilson).

*Bibliography.* J. Orr, *Christian View of God and the World* (1908); A. S. Pringle-Pattison, *The Idea of God* (1917); W. Temple, *Nature, Man and God* (1934); K. Barth, *The Doctrine of the Word of God* (1936); H. R. Mackintosh, *Types of Modern Theology* (1939); G. Vos, *Biblical Theology* (1948); P. Tillich, *Systematic Theology* (1951); H. Bavinck, *The Doctrine of God* (1951); J. Parkes, *The Foundations of Judaism and Christianity* (1960); J. I. Packer, *Knowing God* (1973).

FRANCIS HOWARD PARKER

**Implicit Faith.** In Roman Catholic theology, faith which gives whole-hearted assent to a doctrine, even when all the particulars or consequences of the doctrine are not understood. Such particulars or consequences are believed implicitly, inasmuch as they are assumed to be implied in a given article of faith. For instance, the Roman Catholic Church teaches that the early church implicitly believed in the immaculate conception and in the assumption of Mary, which are deemed to be organically related to her election as the mother of Christ, although the former two articles of faith were not defined respectively until 1854 and 1950.

The notion of implicit faith has a direct bearing on the problem of the salvation of Christians and eventually of unbaptized persons who, through no fault of their own, are unable to give specific assent to all the revealed truths explicitly defined by the church. Thus the minimum faith requirements for salvation, as held by most Roman Catholic theologians, are belief and trust in God as Lord and Judge of all men, and in Jesus Christ as Savior, or in such provisions as were made by God for the salvation of men from sin and death.

It may be assumed that the faith of many church members remains, to a certain extent, implicit, inasmuch as they give their assent to "all truths that are taught by the church" generally, even though they are not always in a position to give a satisfactory account of the specific objects of their belief. The term "implicit faith" is often used by Protestant polemicists with reference to these blanket endorsements of ecclesiastical tenets by uninformed Roman Catholics.

*Bibliography.* H. Davis, *Moral and Pastoral Theology*, vol. 1 (1938); F. Tillmann, *Die Katholische Sittenlehre* 4/1 (1935).

GEORGES A. BARROIS

**Incarnation.** *See* CHRISTOLOGY; SALVATION.

**Independent Fundamental Churches of America.** Organization founded in June 1930, at Cicero, Ill., to succeed the American Conference of Undenominational Churches. It is a fellowship of churches which have no denominational affiliation. Its individual membership includes ministers, Bible teachers, evangelists, missionaries, editors of Christian periodicals, and those training for full-time Christian service.

Membership is conditioned upon assurance of desire to cooperate with the fellowship's purpose and to oppose and counteract apostasy from biblical truth. Members are required to maintain the fellowship's standard of Christian ethics, morals, and conduct. A chief requirement is written assurance of belief, without reservation, in the doctrinal platform, which is ultraorthodox in its adherence to every foundational phase of the historic Christian faith. Annual renewal of membership is required.

Each congregation and individual member is assured full liberty of conscience regarding methods of operation and service. The constitution forbids organization as a denomination. The fellowship does not own property. It cannot own or administer any church, mission, missionary society, or school. Ordination is conducted and controlled by local churches.

In the early 1980s there were some 900 churches with about 100,000 adult members. The fellowship functions through trustees elected on a rotary system by an annual national convention. Auxiliary regional organizations function in portions of certain states; in greater areas, in an entire state. The national executive secretary and office headquarters are in Chicago. An annual directory and an official monthly magazine, *The Voice*, are published.

**India.** Large Asian subcontinent with an area of 3,287,593 sq. km. (1,269,346 sq. mi.) and a population of 725 million (1983). As an independent nation committed to democracy since 1947, the vast country of India continues to enjoy a rich diversity of religious traditions and practices. From the mid-20th century remarkable development has taken place, not only in the multireligious milieu, but also in the social, economic, cultural, and political spheres of life.

Although India is a secular state, its secularism is not simply the absence of religion, as it is normally understood in the West. Sarvepalli Rādhakrishnan, for example, explains that "to be secular is not to be religiously illiterate; it is to be deeply spiritual and not narrowly religious." The background of this view is motivated by the philosophy of *Sarva Dharma Sanabhava*, which implies equality of all religions, castes, and persuasions. According to the 1981 census, 83 percent of India's population are Hindu, 11 percent Muslim, 2.4 percent Christian, 2 percent Sikh, 0.7 percent Buddhist, 0.5 percent Jain, and the remaining 0.4 percent followers of other persuasions. Many years before the separation of Pakistan, anyone who lived in the land of the Indus who had not become a Muslim was called a "Hindu"—a word of Persian etymology, mainly used to distinguish the Islamic faith from that of the other people of India.

***Indian Religion.*** Extensive excavations carried out at the two principal sites of Mohenjo-Daro and Harappa in the Indus Valley in 1920 provided archeological evidence of pre-Aryan civilization, resembling that of Dravidian Saivism of South India. These finds further confirmed that this ancient civilization was quite advanced. There is evidence of well-constructed streets, elaborate drainage systems, and international commerce and shipping activities; these finds also confirm that the beginning of Indian civilization can be dated to the pre-Vedic period. When the Aryans arrived in India in the middle of the 2d millennium B.C., they were nomads. Their religious experience and social order were conditioned by nature and its rhythms. *Indra* (sky); *Vayu* (wind); *Agni* (fire); and *Surya* (sun) were some of the early Aryan deities. The *rita* or order in nature which the people observed caused them to believe that the undergirding values of the whole cosmos upheld both the social order and ethical systems. This belief became the basis of the doctrines of *karma* and *dharma*. The doctrine of *karma* holds that present life can be traced back to previous life ad infinitum and that each act produces automatically the "fruit" for which it was intended. Man can liberate himself from this continuous bondage through the redemptive grace of God which helps him to perform *karma* (deed), practice *bhakti* (devotion), and pursue *jman* (knowledge). According to a survey conducted in Tamil Nadu in 1981 on the extent of belief in *karma* theory, 70 percent of the young in the universities reject it, whereas 60 percent of illiterates above 60 years of age uphold it.

The Hindu scriptures represent a considerable library. The ancient liturgical chants of the *Rig Veda*, the sacrificial forms of *Yajur Veda*, the chants of *Sama Veda*, and the incantations of *Atharva Veda* are considered divinely inspired. The six *darsanas* are *Nyaaya, Vaiseshika, Saankhya, Yoga, Meemaamsa*, and *Vedanta*, and their many schools have an abundance of literature in Sanskrit and other Indian languages. The word *Upanishad* ("sitting down near") probably refers to the method a guru uses to communicate spiritual truth to the people fathered around him. The climax of spiritual quest by ancient philosophers in the *Upanishads* may be brought under a significant formula, *tat tvam asi* ("that art thou"), claiming *Brahman* as the ultimate reality beyond all vicissitudes and change. There are also important *Upanishads* in which the whole idea of impersonal *Brahman* is rejected and the Ultimate Reality is understood in personal terms. While the *Advaitic Vedaanta* of Sankara, *Visistavaita* of Ramanuja, and *Saiva Siddhanta* continue to dominate Hindu thought and philosophy, the *bhakti* movements have been inspired by both *Vaishnavism* and *Shaivism*. Appar, Sambandhar, Manickavasagar, and Tayumanevar have contributed poems in the *bhakti* tradition within *Shaivism* whereas Kabir, Tulsidas, Tukuram Chaitanya, and Alvars belong to *Vaishnavism*. The sacred literature of Hinduism falls into either the category of *Shruti*, (knowledge directly heard by and revealed to the sages) or the category known as *Smriti* (knowledge remembered and traditionally passed on by the sages). The *Vedas* belong to the first category, whereas the epics, such as Ramayana and Mahabharata (which contains the *Bhagavad Gita*), belong to the second category. The tranquility in the midst of change attained by discharge of one's duty with disinterest for reward, or the doctrine of *nishkama karma*, is an admirable teaching of the *Gita*.

A religion needs theological and doctrinal foundations. Nevertheless, the many festivals, ceremonies, and meticulous details of temple worship in diverse traditions throughout rural India form the religious life and practice of the people, many of whom have little knowledge of the different schools of thought within Hinduism.

*Religious Leaders.* Among the social reformers of the Indian renaissance, Ram Mohan Roy (1772–1833), the founder of *Brahma Samaj,* was the foremost. He was undoubtedly influenced by the ethical message of the gospel of Jesus Christ and by the monotheistic teaching of the Koran. He campaigned unflinchingly for the abolition of child marriage and *sati.* While Roy took an eclectic approach to religion, Dayanand Sarasvati (1824–1883), the founder of *Arya Samaj,* firmly believed that the *Vedas* were the books of true knowledge and rejected the institution of castes.

Ramakrishna Paramahamsa (1834–1886), after whom the Ramakrishna Mission Centres were established, was an ascetic known for his religious experience of God. Although he had little formal education, he taught Hindu tenets through parables. For him, all religions—including Islam and Christianity—were different paths to the same goal. His sayings have been extensively preserved and propagated by his disciples, chief of whom was Vivekananda (1863–1902), a graduate of the Scottish Church College, Calcutta. Vivekananda argued eloquently in favor of Hinduism at the Parliament of Religions held in Chicago in 1893, and established the Vedānta Society in the USA. He worked diligently to promote social consciousness among Hindus and expressed the dire need for religious people to wake up from their spiritual complacency and serve the poor and needy. The Ramakrishna Mission continues to carry out an extensive program of cultural, educational, and religious activities.

Following Vivekananda's teaching, the Theosophical Society was founded in 1875 in New York by Madame Helena Blavatsky. It became popular mainly because the followers of any religious faith were eligible for membership. Its headquarters was established in Adayar, Madras, in 1882. A well-known convert from England, Annie Besant, was zealously involved in the social and educational enterprises of this society. The library maintained at Adayar by this society contains a commendable number of manuscripts on religious literature, which are of immense value for research and study.

Aurobinda Ghose (1872–1950) was a man of great intellect, a reformer, and an outstanding graduate of Cambridge University. There are some parallels between his thought and that of Teilhard de Chardin. According to Ghose, a nucleus of new humanity can be formed by those who discipline their body, mind, and spirit with the help of integral yoga. After a period of imprisonment by the British for his political involvement, he repudiated politics altogether and established an ashram for his disciples at Pondicherry, a French colony, where he spent the rest of his life as a voluntary exile.

Many charismatic leaders have been responsible for the emergence of a number of popular cults both in India and abroad. Miracle-working gurus arouse a great deal of excitement among people and invariably have a huge following. In many instances, guruism is an alternative to traditional religion. The movement associated with Sai Baba is *bhakti* in character, and claims to be a spiritual path which any religionist might follow. Four gurus of this tradition—Sai Baba of Shirdi, Govind Upsasani, Godavari Metaji, and Sheherarji Irani—hail from Maharashtra, but the fifth one, Satyanarayana Sai Baba, is from Andhra Pradesh. They perform many miracles and help people to achieve a knowledge of "self" and its identity with *Brahman.* Swami Sivananda Saraswati, born in 1887, founded the ashram at Rishikesh and the Divine Life Society in 1937, which has at least 300 branches around the world. This society has a preaching, publishing, and medical program.

Chinmayananda, a disciple of Swami Sivananda, established Chinmaya Mission in 1953 in Madras which has about 100 centers around the world. With his brilliant oratory, Chinmayananda attempts to relate advaitic philosophy to national life and interprets the same to be rational and scientific. Jiddu Krishnamurthy (1895–1986) of Andhra Pradesh pleads for a radical transformation in the deepest recesses of human consciousness, as any society is the outcome of the outward projection of people's psychological states. For him, truth is only isness, and is neither absolute nor relative. Six international schools founded by Krishnamurthy aim to help children grow up without identifying themselves with any particular religion, nation, or ideology but with a great deal of feeling for man and nature. The Hare Krishna movement propagates the chanting of the holy names of God. Followers believe that the chanting of *mantras* makes one attain a transcendental ecstasy with the energy of God himself (*Hare* refers to the energy of God). This spiritual exercise is said to remove one's consciousness from material desires and anxieties. Transcendental meditation, inaugurated by Maharishi Mahesh Yogi (b. 1918) of Madhya Pradesh, claims to reduce hypertension and is considered to be a scientific technique for peace and happiness. Although the goal of transcendental meditation appears to be secular, it has as its foundation advaitic philosophy.

A popular movement among people of all walks of life in South India is focused on the god Aiyappa, born of Siva and Vishnu and enshrined in Sabarimala, a forested pilgrim center. The devotees wear black clothing and take a vow to follow a 41-day discipline of abstinence from pleasure before they start their trek to the hills. They believe that their annual pilgrimage will have the blessing of the Almighty for the whole year. Ayyappa Seva Sangam, the reconstructed Sabarimala temple, and the mass media have increased the flow of pilgrims from many communities, especially from Tamil Nadu and Kerala.

The Rashtriya Swayamsevak Sangh (RSS), founded in 1925 by Hedgewar at a camp in Amaravati, claims to be a cultural organization. A large number of Swayamsevaks attend daily drills and meetings and get involved in social action programs. After Gandhi's assassination by Godse, RSS was declared unlawful. RSS is accused of operating like an Indian version of nazism or a gang of fascists out to destroy the minorities. Although it is supposed to be only a cultural organization, its clearly defined political goal is to attain Hindu Rashtra or Hindustan. It has also introduced the *Shuddhi* ceremony to bring converted Muslims and Christians into the Hindu fold. RSS works with the misgiving that the Muslims, Christians, and communists in India have extraterritorial loyalties. Despite the admirable social work done by RSS, it is extremely fanatical, breeding cultural hatred toward people of other faiths. The *Sarvodaya* (welfare for all) and *Boodan* (land gift) movements founded by Gandhi (1862–1948) and Vinoba Bhave (1895–1982), respectively, recognize all religions and want every man to follow the Truth according to his light. These movements serve the poor and needy with disinterest in any personal reward. Through transformation of all aspects of life, including that of socioeconomic and political orders, they want to establish *Ram Raj* (kingdom of God).

A secular movement called *Dravida Kazhagam*—whose chief exponent is E. V. Ramasamy, a rationalist—has far-reaching effects in South India. The movement has challenged the anachronistic code of Manu on the stratification of Indian society based on castes and has helped depressed people attain social emancipation.

***Neo-Buddhism.*** Buddhism probably arose in the 6th century B.C. as a lay movement in protest against Brahminism and the sacrificial systems of ancient *Vedas*. The low castes and outcastes found their dignity in Buddhism. Nevertheless, after the glorious period of the Emperor Ashoka, Buddhism declined in India, although it had become strong in some of the neighboring countries in Asia. This century witnessed a revival of Buddhism after Ambedkar embraced it on October 14, 1956, at Nagpur. There was a mass conversion of about 400,000 untouchables. This Neo-Buddhism takes into consideration a religious protest movement of the untouchables against Hindu society based on three fundamental principles: *prajna* (understanding against superstition), *karuna* (love), and *samata* (equality). Further, the converts to Neo-Buddhism gained considerable socioeconomic status. It should be noted that religion, status, and property play an important role in Indian society and should be taken into account in any interpretation of the liberation of people.

***Christianity.*** India is as old as Christianity itself; there is archeological, topographical, and literary evidence besides the continued existence of Christian communities in Kerala and Madras from the 1st century A.D. Further, there is documentary evidence of affirmation made to the Nicene Creed (A.D. 325) on behalf of the churches "in the whole of Persia and in the great India" by a representative bishop called John. After the Portuguese discovery of the Cape route to India by Vasco da Gama in 1498, many Christian missions were established. Francis Xavier, who arrived in India in 1542, worked indefatigably among the pearl fishers and won many to the Christian faith. Robert de Nobli (1577–1656), an Italian Jesuit, followed cultural adaptation and called the NT which he translated into Sanskrit, the Fifth *Veda*. The Protestant mission began with the arrival of Ziegenbalg and Pluetschau, German Lutherans sent by Frederick IV of Denmark in 1706. Ziegenbalg translated the Bible into Tamil in 1725. The Serampore Trio—William Carey, Joshua Marshall, and William Ward—translated the Bible into many Indian and Asian languages. The Christian missionaries of the West have done pioneering work in education from primary village schools to colleges, literary development, medical work, industrial enterprises, and a variety of philanthropic programs.

There have been many direct and indirect influences on the life and thought of the people for the Christian faith. The reform movements of worship, such as *Brahma Samaj* and *Prarthana Samaj*, the rise of theism, and the work of service agencies such as Ramakrishna Mission have all been undoubtedly due to the Christian influence. The impact of Christian morality can be discerned in the extension of educational facilities without any bias of castes, the cessation of *sati* and temple prostitution and emancipation of women, and the transformation of anachronistic worldviews and superstitious beliefs. The Indian government awarded Mother Teresa the *Bharat Ratna* in 1984 for her work among the poor in Calcutta. Since a large section of the Indian population is illiterate and economically poor, there is ample opportunity to establish Christian service and development programs. The opportunity to serve the poor and needy is also undertaken rightly by Christian groups in collaboration with people of other faiths wherever possible.

A large number of tribal peoples, especially those in northeast India, have responded to the Christian gospel, not only because of the liberating power of the gospel from the evil spirits of their traditional animism, but also for the sake of the transformation of their lifestyle with new values of self-reliance and dignity. A number of indigenous missionary societies continue to send dedicated young people to serve in places where Christian witness is almost nonexistent. Response to mass communication programs of the gospel, especially through film and radio, is on the increase. According to a survey made in Madras in 1980, a growing percentage of people of other faiths are becoming believers in Christ and worship him only, although they may not join the church through baptism. These people are usually called Non-Baptised Believers in Christ (NBBC). Christian schools and colleges continue to provide lay and pastoral leadership for church and society, although many of them have the tendency to lose the cutting edge of Christian witness due to secularism.

The Union of the Church of South India, uniting four branches of the Christian church in South India in 1947, and the Union of the Church of North India, uniting six branches in 1970, are indeed great new facts of modern ecumenism. They have a strong basis for a more meaningful mission to a pluralistic and multireligious society. All those committed to confess their faith in Christ today have to take the social, political, economic, and religious contexts in which people live seriously. Sporadic attempts of inculturation in church music, liturgy, architecture, and theology are being made in order to avoid loss of Indian identity. The articulation of the Christian faith in indigenous expression has tremendous value for the Christian community of the world. Both the living experience of people of many faiths and formal interfaith dialog have challenging relevance. In spite of many challenges such as theological liberalism, secular humanism, and religious apathy, there are signs of hope, as more and more people are making a sincere commitment to Christ.

*Islam.* Approximately 11 percent of the Indian population are Muslims, the second largest religious community in India. The faith and practice of the Muslims have exerted a strong monotheistic flavor to Indian thought. The Hindu temples with gods and goddesses became victims of Muslim iconoclasm. In the northwest, conversions to Islam were substantial. Among the Mughal emperors, Akbar the Great (1542–1605) was unique in his eclectic approach to religion.

The Muslim League was born partly out of a keen desire to revive Muslim culture throughout India and partly out of the fear of Hindus. In the 1940s the league established a distinct identity by moving out of the Indian National Congress under the leadership of Jinnah and working for a separate state which resulted in the formation of Pakistan. The Indian Union Muslim League (IUML) was formed in 1947 mainly to safeguard the interests of all Muslims in India. In 1975 there was a split to form the All India Muslim League (AIML). Both IUML and AIML are political and communal. Jamaat-E-Islami Hind, established in 1941, is determined to reconstruct Indian society on the basis of Islamic principles, and to convert everyone to Islam. Because of its narrow communal outlook, it is considered to be the Islamic version of RSS and was banned during the Emergency. It is no wonder that the conservative element of Islam won the day even on the recent divorce bill for Muslim women.

*Sikhism.* Guru Nanak, the founder of Sikhism, was born in A.D. 1469. The final version of the *Adi Granth*, the holy book of the Sikhs, was compiled by Guru Gobind Singh, the last of the 10 original gurus. The minority community of 14 million Sikhs who remain concentrated in and around the state of Punjab suffer from an identity crisis and attempt to strengthen their commitment to the tenets of Sikhism. The Sikh Nirankari movement founded by Baba Dayal attempts to preserve Sikh purity in the face of all brahminical influences, especially casteism and idolatry. The Nirankaris have their center at Chandigarh. They greet one another with the words, "Dhan Nirankar" ("all glory to the Formless"). They stress prayer and listening to the reading of the *Granth*. They believe in the divine trusteeship of all wealth and assets. Sikhs are generally patriotic and have fought with distinction in all wars to preserve India's territorial integrity. Nevertheless, a concept of a separate state was debated in 1981 and is supported by a small percentage of Sikhs both in India and abroad.

Under the direction of militant Sikh leader Sant Jarnail Singh Bhindrenwale, the shrine of the Golden Temple was used as a storehouse for illegal arms and as a sanctuary for terrorists. The government used the army to flush out the terrorists from the Golden Temple complex in 1984. This action resulted in the disapproval of a large section of Sikhs and has led to many acts of violence and terrorism, including the assassination of former prime minister Indira Gandhi. Although the Longowal–Rajiv accord brought some understanding in the political leadership given by the ruling party of *Akali Dal* in the state of Punjab, there is little rapprochement between Sikh religious leaders and the government. Religion and politics are not kept apart, and this has created at times an ugly conflict among the people of different communities.

All well-meaning citizens of India, whatever their religion, are expected to promote the ideals of a secular state with no established state religion as such, although all persons are equally entitled to freedom of conscience and the right to freely profess, practice, and propagate religion subject to public order, morality, and health, even as the founding fathers of the Indian constitution dreamed of a multireligious, but peace-promoting nation.

*Bibliography.* M. Hiriyanna, *Essentials of Indian Philosophy* (1951); N. Smart, *Doctrine and Argument in Indian Philosophy* (1951); R. Ranikkar, *The Unknown Christ of Hinduism* (1964); R. C. Zachner, *The Hindu Scriptures* (1966); B. and R. Allchin, *The Birth of Indian Civilization* (1968); S. Nikhilananda, *Hinduism: Its Meaning of the Liberation of the Spirit* (1968); D. A. Thangasamy, *The Theology of Chanchiah* (1968); P. T. Thomas, *The Theology of Chakkarai* (1968); R. H. S. Boyd, *An Introduction to Indian Christian Theology* (1969); K. Klostermaier, *Hindu and Christian in Vrindaban* (1970); E. G. Parrinder, *Avatar and Incarnation* (1970); R. D. Ranade, *Vedanta: The Culmination of Indian Thought* (1970); M. M. Thomas, *The Acknowledged Christ of the Indian Renaissance* (1970); J. R. Hinnels and E. J. Sharpe, eds., *Hinduism* (1972); N. V. Banerjee, *The Spirit of Indian Philosophy* (1974); V. A. Devasenapathy, *Saiva Siddhanta* (1974); F. W. Clothey, ed., *Images of Man: Religion and Historical Process in South India* (1982); G. S. S. Rao, *Vedanta: Some Modern Trends* (1982); F. W. Clothey and J. B. Long, eds., *Experiencing Siva* (1983); J. T. K. Daniel and R. Gopalan, eds., *A Vision for India Tomorrow* (1984); S. Doraisamy, *Christianity in India* (1986); T. M. Philip, *The Encounter Between Theology and Ideology* (1986); E. O. Shaw, *Rural Hinduism* (1986); R. Sunder, *The Confusion Called Conversion* (1986).

J. T. K. DANIEL

## Indians of North America, Missions to the.

Missions to North America's Indians began with the European conquest and colonization of the continent. Consequently, 20th-century missions to Native Americans bears the imprint and lengthening shadows of the colonialism of earlier centuries.

Overtly successful, if coercive, Spanish missions penetrated the American Southwest; thus today some 20,000 Pueblo belong to parishes which are more pastoral than missionary. French missionaries established extensive work among the tribes of the St. Lawrence and Great Lakes areas, traces of which yet remain. Russian Orthodox missionaries planted churches in Alaska, and 22,000 natives today consider themselves Orthodox.

Apart from their work among the Southern Indians (mainly the "Five Civilized Tribes"), Protestant missionaries had minimal success while the American frontier expanded westward. Tribes suffering annihilation and removal rarely responded favorably to the Christianity of their foes. Following the American Civil War, however, under President Ulysses S. Grant's "Quaker Peace Policy," various denominations received exclusive access to newly defined reservations in the trans-Mississippi West. Christian missionaries endeavored both to convert "pagans" to Christianity and "civilize" them in accord with the American model. The federal government suppressed traditional religious expressions such as the sun dance and forced Indians into the mainstream of American culture.

By establishing schools and hospitals as well as churches, some denominations enjoyed apparent, if limited success from 1870 to 1910. In 1908, however, 14 Protestant denominations joined the Home Missions Council under the guidance of the Federal Council of Churches, consequently fusing their missions' structures (and ultimately defusing their energies).

By the 1920s, many "humanitarian" reformers openly questioned and criticized the missions' approach to Native Americans. Under Franklin D. Roosevelt's New Deal, the federal government, through its Bureau of Indian Affairs headed by Commissioner of Indian Affairs John Collier, implemented sweeping changes which largely eliminated federally sustained denominational programs and encouraged Indians to recover their traditions, most of which remain rooted in tribal ceremonies and religion. In many ways, the 20th century has witnessed some turning away from Christianity by alienated Indians—exemplified by Vine Deloria, Jr., the son of an Episcopal priest, who expressed his disillusionment in such books as *Custer Died for Your Sins* and *God Is Red.*

Despite certain obstacles, however, Christian work has endured throughout this century. Once called the "vanishing Americans," numbering only 250,000 in the 1890 census, Indians today may number as many as 2 million. It is difficult to estimate the Indian population, for data may reflect either tribal roles, bureaucratic surveys, or individual testimony. Of those claiming Indian ancestry, most are mixed-bloods; only tribes such as the Sioux and Navajo, which have been preserved from extensive exposure to Anglo-Americans, maintain sizable full-blood populations. Most tribes, particularly in Oklahoma where some 100 were removed during the 19th century, include numbers of thoroughly assimilated mixed-bloods. Some play prominent roles in their tribes. Such mixed-bloods, while defining themselves as "Indian," frequently join non-Indian churches, especially in urban areas.

While recognizing the incompleteness of data concerning christianized Indians, it is still possible to indicate a 20th-century pattern by statistical study. In 1921 a survey of 26 Protestant denominations revealed 32,000 active adherents with an additional 80,000 communicants; in 1950, 36 denominations claimed 39,000 members, with 140,000 communicants; by 1970, 42 denominations, with over 2000 local churches, had 90,000 members, with a total of 120,000 identifying with them. The two largest Protestant denominations were Southern Baptist (36,000) and Episcopal (20,000).

In 1921, Catholic missions reported 61,000 members; in 1970, 177,000. Thus the Catholic Church claims the largest number of Indians on its rolls. Catholic statistics, however, reflect baptized, not active believers, and indicate growing congregations rather than successful missionary outreach. Combining data for both Catholic and Protestant work among Native Americans enables one to estimate that at least 250,000 of them claim they are Christian.

During this century, denominational missions have shifted from "foreign missions" to "home missions" to "indigenous" ministries (although few denominations have recruited and educated native ministers). Indigenous work has often been done by concerned bivocational persons (often of Indian descent) who establish purely congregational churches. Rapid church growth has occurred in the Navajo Nation under Navajo-speaking workers.

The success of indigenous work illustrates perhaps the most significant shift in the history of missions to the Indians: colonialism has ended. Non-Indian missionaries no longer preside over subjugated natives. Indians have increasingly assumed responsibility for preaching the gospel and planting churches. The drive for self-determination, which has marked Indian affairs in general since World War II, is slowly transforming the churches.

**Bibliography.** E. E. Lindquist, *Indians in Transition: A Study of Protestant Missions in the United States* (1951); C. F. Starkloff, *The People of the Center: American Indian Religion and Christianity* (1974); K. R. Philip, *John Collier's Crusade for Indian Reform, 1920–1954* (1977); H. W. Bowden, *American Indians and Christian Missions: Studies in Cultural Conflict* (1981).

GERARD A. REED

# Individualism.

A state of mind or attitude produced by a social milieu which pays little respect to tradition or authority. Tribal custom and convention have little control, there exists no overpowering social unity, and individual initiative is unconfined. An individualistic society is one where people "think for themselves." Persons are not simply absorbed into the social organism as nonentities who comprise a larger entity. There are evidences of such a spirit among the philosophers of Greek society. The ideal of self-sufficiency is an element in the Socratic character, and the political theory of individualism is proposed by Plato in the *Republic.*

Modern individualism rests upon two concepts: the idea of the worth of the individual from a religious view and the commercial practice of free exchange. Individual worth was strong during the early Christian period and was revived in the time of the Reformation. Individualism in economics has asserted that if the processes of free exchange were allowed to operate without check, then the greatest good to the greatest number would automatically result. The Western concept of a "free-enterprise system" is rooted in the individual ideal. It became a particularly strong tradition in the English Puritan and Scotch Presbyterian society of frontier North America.

Religious individualism did not originate in the Christian religion nor is it characteristic of earlier Judaism. The main strain of Hebrew literature makes Israel, the people or nation, the primary concern of God, although OT Law is greatly concerned with personal value and holiness. But with the collapse of national hopes there emerges through the prophets a new sense of God's dealings directly with the individual. The Gospels take for granted the direct relation of the individual with God, which is a particular implication of the Christian emphasis on the Fatherhood of God. The supreme value of the individual and the idea of human equality are complementary concerns of the NT. A central doctrine of the Reformation was the universal priesthood of believers—in its didactic expression individualistic and democratic.

The rise of individualism in commercial enterprise appears in the spirited mercantile cities of the Renaissance. The broad horizons opened by discovery and the stimulation of trade with the East called for resourcefulness and activity. While medieval man had been organized and unified, this new European was incited to inventiveness, diversity, and enterprise. The theory of economics devolved that exchanging parties in commercial dealings have a common interest; free exchange and the division of labor lead to an increase in human satisfactions and happiness. Indeed the good of the community is served when man may trade without restraint. Under the philosophical school named utilitarianism, the view sought the simplification of antiquated laws. The proposed theory was that law was not to make people do what was right but that law simply maintained a system of equal rights and provided men with the liberty essential to living the good life. A magnificent presentation of the principle of individualism was made by the last great utilitarian, John Stuart Mill (*On Liberty* [1859]).

In the absolute sense, consistent individualism is not reasonable in a society. There is an interdependence and interaction between the individual and the group. Even the most pronounced individualists must recognize the role played by institutions and society at large in the development of individuality. When individualism is considered a tradition or "modus operandi" which must be defended to the bitter end, then it loses its force and dwindles to mere egoism or hedonism.

**Bibliography.** J. Mill, *On Liberty* (1859); R. H. Tawney, *Religion and the Rise of Capitalism* (1926); J. Dewey, *Individualism, Old and New* (1930); M. Weber, *The Protestant Ethic and the Spirit of Capitalism* (1930); R. W. Lane, *The Discovery of Freedom: Man's Struggle Against Authority* (1943); E. Laszlo, *Individualism, Collectivism, and Political Power* (1963); C. Derber, *The Pursuit of Attention: Power and Individualism in Everyday Life* (1979); F. R. Dallmayr, *Twilight of Subjectivity; Contributions to a Post-Individualist Theory of Politics* (1981); J. Harland, *Word Controlled Humans: A Brief History* (1981); G. C. Lodge and E. F. Vogel, *Ideology and National Competitiveness: An Analysis of Nine Countries* (1987).

EUGENE LIGGITT

# Indonesia.

Large republic occupying thousands of islands from the northern tip of the Malay Peninsula to the northern tip of Australia. It has an area of 1,919,270 sq. km. (741,034 sq. mi.).

Religion permeates all of life in Indonesia. Almost everyone holds some form of religious belief and participates in religious ceremonies at home or in community gatherings as well as in formal worship. Sacred sites can be found in the jungle, in fields, or on mountaintops where food, cigarettes, and flowers are offered to the spirits. Elaborate mosques, temples, and churches in the cities demonstrate the religious plurality of the nation. Religion is a compulsory subject at all schools, with weekly classes even for tertiary students. Public transport vehicles bear stickers and slogans invoking God's protection. People talk about religion.

In the world's fifth most populous nation (170 million in 1987) the majority are Muslims, yet Indonesia is not an Islamic state. Its laws specifically recognize Islam, Christianity, Hinduism, and Buddhism, and all citizens are expected to belong to a recognized religion. Monotheism is part of the state ideology adopted in the 1945 Constitution, which states as the first of the *Pancasila* (Five Principles) "Belief in One Supreme God." A policy of religious tolerance in the framework of communal harmony is promoted by the government. The Department of Religion provides grants for buildings and scriptures for each of the faiths, and teachers of religion for each of the faiths are on an equal basis with other teachers.

Indonesia is characterized by diversity. Its 3000 islands are inhabited by over 300 ethnic groups, with another 250 small tribes in Irian Jaya. Distinctive regional differences are found in culture, history, and economic development, and religion is no exception. The people of Sunda in the province of western Java, the Acehnese north of Sumatra, and the Minang-kabau of western Sumatra are strongly Muslim; the island of Bali is predominantly Hindu; in Irian Jaya and the eastern Lesser Sunda Isles, a high percentage of the population are Christians. This diversity reflects the radically different orientation of each ethnic group.

Hinduism and Buddhism came to Java from India 20 centuries ago and quietly penetrated the whole of society in central and western Java, climaxing in two great Hindu dynasties in southern Sumatra and Java between the 8th and 15th centuries. This Hindu influence still pervades Javanese culture, evidenced by its social system, ceremonies, and epic poems. Undoubtedly, Hinduism's tendency to syncretism has contributed to the various strands of religion in Java, a melding of earlier animism, Hinduism, and later Islam, with one or other predominant depending on the strata of society and the local tradition. In modern Indonesia, Buddhism and other Chinese religions are followed by the majority of Chinese (approximately 4 percent of the population), and Hinduism is strong among the Indian immigrants.

Islam took root in Indonesia late in the 13th century, brought for the most part by traders from India. Islam originated in the seaports of Sumatra, western Java, and Macassar, and spread extensively into the interior. In the western islands, Malay people in the coastal regions are solidly Muslim, but in the eastern islands on the whole, Islam has not achieved the same penetration among the interior tribal peoples. In the rural inland of central and eastern Java, Islam is another veneer over layers of Hindu-Buddhism and animism, where worship of a multitude of spirits is common.

Census results in 1971 identified 87.5 percent of the population as Muslim. These figures reflect a large number of "statistical Muslims," including those who have been married by a Muslim official and in so doing have recited the Islamic confession but may not otherwise be practicing Muslims. A large number of Javanese belong to the mystic sects, and they account for a significant fraction of those listed as Muslims. Details from the 1982 census have not been released. The number of practicing Muslims has been estimated at slightly under half the population, and growing.

There has been a widespread missionary effort to consolidate the faith among nominal Muslims, as well as to reach animist tribes people. Islamic village schools provide approximately one-third of all primary education, and there is a vigorous building program for mosques, Islamic hospitals, and universities with both government and overseas aid. Each year about 60,000 Indonesians make a government-organized pilgrimage to Mecca. A Koran-chanting competition attracts much attention on local, regional, and national levels.

Christianity was planted by Roman Catholic missions in the eastern islands commencing in 1522 with Portugese Franciscans in the Moluccas. When the Dutch East India Company took control in 1605, the congregations became Protestant. It appears, however, that evangelism took second place to the commercial interests of the company. In the early 19th century, separate work by the lay settlers Emde and Coolen led to the birth of an indigenous Javanese church. Growing missionary concern in Germany, the Netherlands, and America brought many missionaries. Work in some sensitive Muslim areas was restricted by the Dutch government, but several tribes which had not previously been influenced by Islam and which still followed their primitive tribal religions responded to the gospel. One of the notable people movements was among the fierce Toba Bataks of northern Sumatra, who were reached by Nommensen in 1862. Batak Christians presently number over 2 million. Roman Catholic missions were recommenced, resulting in strong churches in the Moluccas, Flores, and Timur islands, and significant work also took place in northern Sumatra and central Java.

These early movements have grown into separate denominations mainly along ethnic lines, such as the Batak Christian Protestant Church, the Moluccan Protestant Church, the Java Christian Church, and the Timor Evangelical Christian Church. Several achieved autonomy in the 1930s and the remaining control by Western churches was severed by the Japanese occupation and independence after World War II. Most of these older churches have an ongoing partnership with Western Lutheran or Dutch Reformed churches and mission agencies. Various denominational missions have established churches during this century, including Methodist, CMA, Baptist, Assemblies of God, and other pentecostal churches. Outreach among unreached people has continued to bear fruit, notably among the Dayaks of Kalimantan, the Karo Bataks of northern Sumatra, the many tribes of Irian Jaya, and in the Lesser Sundas and interior Sulawesi. Both Indonesian and foreign missionaries have taken initiatives in this work. However, several Muslim groups remain resistant to the gospel. Education has been influential alongside evangelism, and today Christian schools are to be found throughout the archipelago.

In the wake of the abortive communist coup on September 30, 1965, those who had no religious affiliation were afraid of being suspected as communist sympathizers. Multitudes came to Christianity for refuge if not salvation, in particular in Java and parts of Sumatra. Some estimates place the numbers as high as 2 million. In many instances the churches were unable to provide adequate nurture for the new converts, which, combined with the manifold motives for adopting Christianity, has undoubtedly added to the number of nominal Christians. Many Chinese, perhaps 20 percent, have become Christian both prior to 1965 and since.

Since the early 1970s, church growth has steadied in most older denominations, although still double the natural population growth rate, and some pentecostal and evangelical churches have reported substantial increases. It is difficult to obtain reliable data since the 1971 census, which recorded 7.4 percent of the population as Christians, but conservative estimates for 1986 placed the number at 11 percent, which included nominal Christians. There are now over 50 member denominations of the Indonesian Communion of Churches (ICC, formerly the Indonesian Council of Churches). The Roman Catholic Church represents about 25 percent of Christians in Indonesia, and the proportion of pentecostal and non-ICC Protestant churches (11 percent in 1975) is growing.

Increasing urbanization is bringing both problems and opportunities to Christians in Indonesia. Churches have mostly had beginnings in rural districts, where 80 percent of the population still lives. Cities and large towns allow greater freedom for witness than a close village community. Social visiting on religious holidays is reciprocal, and there is no hesitation to include prayer and testimony when guests of another religion are present. House churches and cell-groups are expanding in the larger cities, and are more effective in reaching non-Christians. Christian programs are broadcast on radio and government television stations.

One of the difficulties facing the churches in Indonesia is the lack of trained personnel. Only 30 percent of ministers serving in ICC churches in the late 1970s had tertiary theological qualifications. Most ordained clergy serve between six and 15 congregations, and many congregations are led by laypersons with no special training. Two major concerns are universalism and syncretism. The suggestion that all religions are ultimately the same (all use the word *Tuhan* [Lord]) and the timidity associated with being a small minority in a Muslim majority combine to hinder many Christians from witnessing. Laws which prohibit the offer of enticements and proselytization directed toward adherents of another faith were introduced in 1978, ostensibly to minimize friction between the faiths. More recently, all community organizations in Indonesia have been required to adopt the *Pancasila* as their founding principle, which has posed a serious dilemma for churches which hold to the Bible as their sole point of reference. Similarly, custom law (*adat*) is a powerful force in Indonesian culture, and Christians who lack clear teaching face difficulties in knowing which practices are acceptable and which stem from beliefs contrary to the gospel. Worship of ancestor spirits and the work of traditional healers pose continual problems. There is, in each of these challenges, a need for both individual Christians and churches alike to be willing, irrespective of the cost, to live out their faith in Christ.

**Bibliography.** D. Bentley-Taylor, *The Weater-Cock's Reward: Christian Progress in Muslim Java* (1967); F. Cooley, *Indonesia, Church and Society* (1968); A. T. Willis, *Indonesian Revival: Why 2 Million Came to Christ* (1977); D. C. E. Liao, *East Asia* (1979); F. Cooley, *The Growing Seed: The Christian Church in Indonesia* (1981); D. B. Barrett, *World Christian Encyclopaedia* (1982); F. Cooley, *Indonesia 1986—An Official Handbook* (1986); P. Johnstone, *Operation World* (1986).

DAVID R. MILLS

**Infinite, Infinity** (Lat. *infinitus*, "not limited"). Indeterminate, either extrinsically endless (the number series) or intrinsically indefinite (space or time continua); complete or perfect (not necessarily all-inclusive). While science deals in extreme immensity, the conception of utter limitlessness is untestable, incomprehensible, and inimical. Much of current theology is related to science, so issues relating to God's infinity have become a battlefield.

The only direct OT reference to the infinitude of God's being is Ps. 147:5, which uses the Hebrew *'ên mispār* ("no number") to refer to God's understanding. The conception of limitless being is assumed, however, by the prophets and in the psalms. One of its clearest statements is Solomon's dedicatory prayer for the temple (1 Kings 8:23, 27; 2 Chron. 6:14, 18) in which God's infinity is contrasted with the finitude of a place of worship. A vivid OT picture is the unconsumed yet all-consuming fire of the burning bush in Exod. 3 and the revelation of God's name, "I AM." It was from that form of the Hebrew verb "to be" that the Hebrews took the tetragrammaton "YHWH." The reverence with which they regarded this attributive name was intense. Before writing it a scribe purified himself. When Torah was read in the synagogue, the Hebrew *'Adonai* ("Lord") was verbalized for YHWH. In the context of limitlessness Jesus subscribed to himself deity (John 8:58). It is assumed by NT writers that infinity of being belongs to YHWH. A key proclamation was that God's infinity belongs to the Christ (e.g., in John 1, Heb. 1, and Revelation). Until modern times the infinity of the being and attributes of God has seldom been an issue. Those who ascribed limits to the divine nature of Jesus Christ normally were regarded as suborthodox. The ultimate Christian statement to the point was attempted by the Westminster Assembly (1643–49). After a complex definition of God's infinite being in the Westminster Confession, a more succinct version set it as a simple faith tenet of the Shorter Catechism: "God is a Spirit, infinite, eternal, and unchangeable, in his being, wisdom, power, holiness, justice, goodness, and truth" (Q. 4).

In modern theology infinity as an attribute of God is often related to his transcendency of being. The definition preferred is that of Greek philosophy, a negative sense of indeterminancy, which for the Greeks was rooted in polytheism. For Aristotle matter (potentiality) is the only infinite, although Aristotle's "unmoved mover" was a being of pure actuality which anticipated modern thought. The theologies of transcendence do not speak to the issue of infinity in themselves. In some form all regard God as "Wholly Other" (Søren Kierkegaard's term), which limits God's ability to be immanent and so his power to protect his infinite being. Theologies of immanence (from 19th-century classical liberalism on) must necessarily limit God, so they either redefine infinitude as completeness or else reject the concept entirely. Man-transcendent theologies which seek to lift man deterministically or ascribe an evolutionary infinity to human potential are atheistic in base, and their view of infinity refers to its quality of expanding indefiniteness.

Of the major world views current in the late 1900s, atheism ascribes no infinity; pantheism defines nature as infinite (complete but impersonal); panentheism allows the potentiality of an infinite being (though logically never without limits); and finite godism and polytheism deny the possibility of infinite being. Only deism and theism attribute to God a boundless nature. Only in theism is God truly infinite in power.

*Bibliography.* S. Alexander, *Space, Time, and Deity*, vol. 2 (1920); A. N. Whitehead, *Process and Reality* (1929); F. J. Tennant, *Philosophical Theology*, vol. 2 (1930); E. Brunner, *The Christian Doctrine of God* (1950); P. Tillich, *Systematic Theology* (1951); L. Berkhof, *Systematic Theology* (1953); J. A. T. Robinson, *Honest to God* (1963); T. J. J. Altizer, *The Gospel of Christian Atheism* (1966); J. Moltmann, *The Theology of Hope* (1967); S. Charnock, *Discourses upon the Existence and Attributes of God* (repr. 1979); N. Geisler and W. Corduan, *Philosophy of Religion* (1988).

## Inge, William Ralph

**Inge, William Ralph** (1860–1954). Anglican scholar. Born in Crayke, Yorkshire, he graduated from Cambridge, was ordained in the Church of England, and was fellow and tutor of Hertford College, Oxford (1889–1904) and vicar of All Saints', Knightsbridge (1905–7). He then returned to Cambridge as professor of divinity (1907–11) before becoming dean of St. Paul's, London (1934). Known widely as the "gloomy dean," he realistically faced the problems of the church and his times, was a progressive leader in the Church of England, occupied major theological lectureships in Britain and America, and especially championed the cause of Christian devotion. His prolific writings reflected his many interests. His writings include *Society in Rome under the Caesars* (1886), *Christian Mysticism* (1899), *Truth and Falsehood in Religion* (1906), *Faith* (1909), *The Church and the Age* (1912), *Outspoken Essays* (2 vols., 1919, 1922), *The Idea of Progress* (1920), *Lay Thoughts of a Dean* (1926), *Christian Ethics and Modern Problems* (1930), *God and the Astronomers* (1933), *Vale* (1934), *Freedom, Love and Truth* (1936), *A Pacifist in Trouble* (1939), *Talks in a Free Country* (1943), and *Diary of a Dean* (1949).

RAYMOND W. ALBRIGHT

## Inner Light.

**Inner Light.** A doctrine that the gospel is known in the hearts of all humanity, characteristic of the Quakers. It is perhaps most fully developed by Robert Barclay in his *Apology for the True Christian Divinity*, although he uses the term "saving light" instead. As he expounds the doctrine, this light is in all as a supernatural gift. Thus, it is not to be identified with the natural conscience, nor is it a relic of the light remaining in Adam after the fall. It is not an accident but a real, spiritual substance. If it were an accident, when a man has it he would be holy since "no accident can be in a subject without it give the subject its own denomination"; but this light "subsists in the hearts of wicked men," since it is universal.

Barclay describes this light as "the gospel which the apostle saith expressly is preached "in every creature under heaven." He distinguishes it from the "outward gospel" which apparently he identifies with the declaration of the history of Jesus as the Christ. He strenuously maintains that man can be and is saved apart from the outward knowledge of Jesus, but none can be saved apart from the saving light. "For to speak properly, the gospel is this inward power and life which preacheth glad tidings in the hearts of all men, offering salvation unto them, and seeking to redeem them from their iniquities, and therefore it is said to be preached 'in every creature under heaven': whereas there are many thousands of men and women to whom the outward gospel was never preached." This saving light is sufficient for salvation, but it can be resisted. Therefore, although none of those to whom the outward gospel is preached are saved, except by the inward operation of this light, not all men are saved through this light.

ANDREW K. RULE

**Innere Mission.** Freely translated into English as "Home Mission." The term gained currency in the territorial Protestant churches of Germany during the early 19th century through the work of Johann Hinrich Wichern. He used it to describe the specific mission activities that needed to be done within Christendom (because of moral decline and growing alienation from NT values) in all aspects of life. Activities within the scope of Innere Mission were to express Christian love in deeds that would demonstrate "Christ's saving love" to renew those masses of people who had come under the dominion of sin.

Wichern established his *Rauhes Haus* in 1833. Its initial focus was to save children from being exploited. Similar institutionalized "attacks" on an inadequate social system for the disenfranchized sprang up elsewhere in major industrial centers, often combining care, protection, and Christian education. The work eventually extended to prison reforms and to the active dissemination of evangelical notions through tracts known as *Fliegende Blätter*.

Much of the impetus for such evangelical socialist activity came out of Lutheran pietism and the Awakening, which was particularly effective and long-lasting in Württemberg. Most notable precursors were the *Franckeschen Stiftungen*, Halle, the *Lutherhof* in Weimar, and several Bible Societies.

The movement gained some popularity after the first *Kirchentag*, held in 1848 in Wittenberg. Wichern's challenge on that occasion led to the formation of a central committee within the German Evangelical Church. Two offices were set up in Berlin and Hamburg respectively to coordinate activities and promote the expansion of interior mission. A yearly congress assured continuing momentum. Associations for young men and women, Sunday school work, alcoholics, wayward youth, and to serve other needs were established. During war years the work of interior mission extended to soldiers in the field, the wounded, prisoners of war, and refugees.

Among the leading personalities within the movement was Friedrich von Bodelschwingh, who in the 1870s founded the Bethel institutions for people afflicted by leprosy, depression, and related illnesses. By 1900 land reform, innovative agricultural practices, and "make-work" programs were instituted within the purview of internal mission.

Adolf Stoecker, biblically conservative but socially radical, gave the movement a high profile in the last two decades of the 19th century, relating ecclesiastical activities inspired by the motive of love of neighbor to emerging sociopolitical interests. Stoecker's work contributed significantly to the formation of the Christian-Socialist party in 1878.

Since World War II *Innere Mission* has built and supported homes for senior citizens, worked extensively in train depots in aid of homeless persons, and worked among displaced persons, especially those of German descent from Eastern countries and the Balkan States. More than 100 "sister houses," with a membership of more than 40,000, maintain or service hospitals, orphanages, and institutions for health care, education, and social welfare. The services of *Innere Mission* are extended to everyone in Germany and continue to address spiritual, ethical, social, and political issues.

*Innere Mission* work in Scandinavian countries tended to retain its strong evangelical focus and, more than in the German developments, integrated work aimed at the renewal of the individual with activities that addressed social problems. Societies founded in Sweden and Norway in particular combined home and foreign missions, working among seafarers and sending lay preachers to China and elsewhere. In the USA, Lutherans tended to promote institutions for children, immigrants, and seafarers, and hospitals. Since 1920 several of the smaller societies are united as the Hauge Lutheran Mission Federation, whose activities are focused in the Midwest.

The work covered by *Innere Mission* falls within the category of the Christian diaconate, and is related not only to NT practices but to the historic practice of the church to care for widows, orphans, the homeless, and the destitute. Although *Innere Mission* is often understood to refer to specific institutions, Wichern and others in the history of the movement tended to use the notion as applying to all works of love by concerned Christians.

**Bibliography.** J. F. Ohl, *The Inner Mission* (1911); M. Hennig, *Quellenbuch zur Geschichte der Inneren Mission* (1912); S. S. Gjerde and P. Ljostveit, *The Haugean Movement in America* (1941); H. H. Ulrich, *Die Kirche und ihre missionarische Aufgabe* (1955); C. Bourbeck and H. D. Wendland, *Diakonie zwischen Kirche und Welt* (1958); *Das missionarische Wort* (from 1947).

E. J. FURCHA

**Innitzer, Theodore** (1875–1955). Cardinal. Born in Neugeschrei, Erzgebirge, and educated at the University of Vienna and its theological school, he was ordained there in 1902 and served in the parish at Pressbaum, Niederösterreich. After serving several years as Studienpräfekt and Subregens at the theological seminary in Vienna, he taught NT in the theological faculty at the University of Vienna and served three terms as dean of the theological faculty. During 1928 and 1929 he was minister of social administration. In 1932 Pope Pius XI named him archbishop of Vienna. He was named cardinal, with the titular church San Crisogono, on March 13, 1933.

RAYMOND W. ALBRIGHT

**Inquisition.** Originally the *Inquisitio haereticoe pravitatis* or "Holy Office," established by the Roman Catholic Church to detect and punish those whose opinions differed from church doctrines. Efforts at doctrinal discipline which extended into the 20th century were primarily through the "Holy Roman and Universal Inquisition," organized as a congregation by Paul III in 1542 as a measure of the Counter-Reformation. It is officially designated since 1908 as the "Congregation of the Holy Office." It has exclusive jurisdiction in matters concerning the Catholic faith and the validity of the sacraments. It has charge of the index of forbidden books and several other matters previously under the "Congregation of Indulgences," which was suppressed.

GEORGES A. BARROIS

**Institutional Churches.** An outreach-oriented structure popular in the late 19th and early 20th centuries in urban churches. The accelerated industrialization of the USA after the Civil War resulted in crowded living conditions for workers who were predominantly non-Nordic, non-Protestant immigrants. Even many Protestants of this impoverished labor class became alienated from the churches. The then widely discussed problem was how to reach the masses. City evangelism and the institutional church were the two most frequently attempted solutions.

The institutional program was experimental and fluid—recreation for children, adult education, clubs, forums, even financial assistance. A well-rounded institutional program of such Christian friendliness often involved a special building, social and medical workers, overseeing ministers, and a large budget. Neighborhood and settlement houses were closely akin while denominational and nondenominational "missions" and church extension societies often supported "institutional" features. Such institutional work grew mainly from the social gospel ideology.

Institutional churches were not notably successful in bringing non-Protestants into Protestant church membership, but they fostered good will and understanding and helped many needy people. They gave the churches new realization of social needs and thus indirectly strengthened many reform movements such as those for free pews, temperance, better housing, suppression of vice, industrial justice, and adult education. In a somewhat less patronizing and more democratic form, social and "institutional" features have remained characteristic of many urban ministries.

**Bibliography.** T. Abel, *Protestant Home Missions to Catholic Immigrants* (1933); A. I. Abell, *The Urban Impact on American Protestantism 1865–1900* (1943).

L. A. LOETSCHER

**Instrumentalism.** A form of pragmatism sponsored by functionalists in psychology and philosophy associated with the thought of John Dewey (1859–1952). Under this deterministic view the mind is the instrument or tool of the organism; it cannot be separated philosophically from the body. What is called the mind is a complex set of habits formed in evolutionary response to the environment. In order to survive organisms must adapt to their environment. Ideas are a means of getting on in the world, true if successful and wrong if unsuccessful. Instrumentalism rejects the view of the mind as a spectator looking out at the world, a soul-like substance having its origin in special creation or in a world of spirit. It is, instead, an evolving tool in nature, useful biologically and fundamentally functional.

The first manifesto of the theory of instrumentalism appeared in *Studies in Logical Theory* (1903), although William James in *Principles of Psychology* (1890) had already toyed with the view. In 1899 Dewey's address "Psychology and Philosophic Method" banished the assumption of the soul or ego from psychological language and substituted the concept of behavior—experience in which mind has its setting and function. Behaviorism in psychology is an applied form of instrumentalism. Thus mind is simply living tissue capable of responding. In psychological literature this is referred to as an *SR* (stimulus-response) or, as more conservative functionalists now say, *SOR* (stimulus-organism-response). The mind thus is part and parcel of nature (not something supernatural), and so there is no innate worth in the individual as a reasoning creature, let alone as an image-bearer of God.

Instrumentalism has had a successful vogue in recent psychology and philosophy largely because of the importance given to the evolutionary viewpoint; it also has enjoyed acclaim in the hope that by its basic conception of mind more progress may be made in understanding behavior through scientific procedures. If mind is something unique, something supernaturally grounded, it is supposed that no scientific psychology can be constructed since a scientific method presupposes cause and effect. Further, the old view of mind rested upon philosophical premises (such as Plato's theory of the soul) and to a theology in which the soul issued from God and returned to God. Such views make impossible the extension of scientific method and hinder full and proper investigation of behavior. Moreover, animal psychology has prepared the way.

Instrumental logic (functional logic) looks upon thought as a means by which the stimulus of experience is deliberately organized. Its challenge is to reconstruct experience effectively, facing facts and issues and solving problems. Ideas are tools, platforms of response, tentative and uncertain until tested by their results. Knowledge is functional and instrumental—both a science and an art. Logic is a practical discipline which has nothing to do with absolute truth. Truth is forged on the anvil of experience and is truth in that it is found useful in framing an adequate response.

VERGILIUS FERM

## Interchurch World Movement of North America.
Movement which grew out of a meeting of representatives of various Protestant home and foreign missionary boards meeting in New York City on December 17, 1918. The national organization consisted of a General Committee of more than 100 persons nominated by the cooperating boards, and an Executive Committee of which Dr. John R. Mott was chairman, and a Canadian Council to consider matters peculiar to Canada. There was a staff headed by a general secretary, S. Earl Taylor, and associate general secretaries. A full organization of interdenominational forces was also contemplated for each state and local community.

The Interchurch World Movement was not an effort to achieve organic unity among churches, nor was it intended to be like the Federal Council of Churches—a federation of church bodies limited in its powers and authority by the constituting churches. It was patterned more after the cooperative financial "drives" of World War I, and was an effort of numerous interdenominational and denominational agencies to coordinate various home and foreign missions, Christian education, and social services in the interests of greater efficiency.

The movement contemplated two types of activity: (1) There was to be extensive fact finding through national and community surveys around the world which would examine modern society,

analyzing the church's efficiency in these areas. The social horizons were to be broad, and the viewpoint superdenominational. (2) The movement also planned to deal with the raising of funds and greater coordination of all services rendered. The movement was not to dictate to the denominations and was to have actual control only over its own administrative budget.

The movement collapsed in less than two years. It had presupposed a greater unity of ideas and objectives than yet existed among the American churches. It had counted on large financial support from unchurched friends which did not materialize. Its sociological emphasis far overshadowed its theological emphasis. Its bold stand on the steel strike alienated some potential supporters, and it suffered from postwar weariness and disillusionment.

Part of the research program of the Interchurch Movement was later carried out in distinguished surveys by the Institute of Social and Religious Research. Most notable perhaps of its achievements was a courageous report on the steel strike of 1919 which informed and powerfully influenced public opinion, and produced direct effects on industrial conditions.

*Bibliography.* Interchurch World Movement, *The Handbook* (1919); *Report on the Steel Strike of 1919* (1920), and other writings.

L. A. LOETSCHER

## Intercommunion.
The practice of interchurch participation in eucharistic celebration. The problem of intercommunion is a byproduct of the denominational development of Protestantism, in which differences regarding the theology of the Lord's supper have been prominent since the Reformation. In the period of the Reformation the issue of intercommunion arose in areas of Germany and Switzerland where Reformed and Lutheran groups were in close contact. Generally speaking, the Reformed were inclined to favor the practice, while the Lutherans were opposed to it; but there were many exceptions on both sides.

In the USA the issue assumed major proportions. During the intense denominational rivalries of the 19th century, a number of Protestant groups observed what came to be termed "close communion." With the decline of those rivalries in the 20th century the ecumenical movement raised the question of intercommunion as a demonstration of the unity of the church. The European churches participating in ecumenical activity were also compelled to reexamine their positions on the matter. Out of this discussion several answers to the problem have arisen.

Those who favor the practice of intercommunion maintain that the Lord's supper was instituted as a means for unity rather than division. Unity of a doctrinal or confessional nature, therefore, logically follows joint communion, instead of preceding it. The ultimate responsibility for worthy participation lies with the conscience of the communicant rather than with that of the officiant. This viewpoint has been instrumental in the arrangement of community communion services, in which congregations of various denominations have participated.

At the other extreme are those who hold that joint participation in the sacrament is a confession of a common faith; therefore only those who share a common doctrinal faith ought to commune together. They regard it as the duty of the church to deny the privilege of the Lord's table to those who are not thus qualified, and many require registration prior to communion as a means for carrying out this duty. Between these two viewpoints lie many varieties and combinations, for only rarely has either of these positions been maintained with complete consistency.

A special problem has been posed by the contention of Roman Catholic, Eastern Orthodox, and some Anglican theologians, that only legitimate ordination in the apostolic succession can validate the administration of the Eucharist, and that therefore communion at the hands of a priest lacking such ordination is a mutilated sacrament or none at all. They have consequently discouraged or prohibited their members from communing with others.

Particular instances of the problem have included the communion services at ecumenical conferences, where churches of several different denominations celebrated simultaneously, each at its own altar or table. The administration of the sacrament to the armed forces has been complicated when chaplains of the various denominations might not be available, as was the situation of German Protestantism during and since the era of National Socialism, when circumstances seemed to make intercommunion expedient.

In recent years, practical intercommunion has become commonplace among different Protestant denominations (including the Anglican Communion) as a result of wider ecumenical convergence. Formal steps have seldom been taken, however, and most actual instances of intercommunion have emerged as exceptions to the general rules of a particular church order. Thus it may happen that in a local ecumenical project the normal rules of each participating denomination are suspended and complete interchange of ministries and sacraments encouraged. Individuals are also widely expected to participate fully in the activities of other denominations when opportunities occur and this can now be said to have become the norm in the mainline Protestant world.

In the Roman Catholic Church matters are more complicated, but since Vatican Council II (1962–65) individuals from Orthodox and Anglican churches have been allowed, and in many cases encouraged, to receive communion in Roman Catholic churches, particularly in countries where the ministrations of their own church are not readily available. Many parish priests in Europe and Latin America seem prepared to go further and recognize Orthodox or Anglican eucharistic celebrations as valid, but this has not received official approval.

It would appear that cooperation will continue to develop along these lines, with as little recourse to formal agreements as is necessary. Laypeople in particular are already much more advanced along these lines than most of the clergy, who are in danger of being left behind in a general movement toward greater convergence. Liturgical revision, which has now made many Roman Catholic and Protestant services virtually indistinguishable from each other, has undoubtedly furthered this trend, and it seems likely that intercommunion will soon be accepted most places, at least in practice.

JAROSLAV PELIKAN

**Bibliography.** H. Asmussen, ed., *Abendmahlsgemeinschaft?* (1937); J. T. Christian, *Close Communion;* E. S. Freeman, *The Lord's Supper in Protestantism* (1945); D. Baillie and J. Marsh, eds., *Intercommunion* (1952); World Council of Churches, *Baptism, Eucharist and Ministry* (1982); J. E. Griffiss, *Church, Ministry and Unity* (1983); Y. Congar, *Diversity and Communion* (1984); H. Meyer and L. Vischer, eds., *Growth in Agreement* (1984); J. Matthews, *The Unity Scene* (1986).

GERALD BRAY

## Interdenominational Foreign Missions Association (IFMA).

Organization founded in 1917 which is comprised solely of "faith missions," that is, groups which rely on God through faith and prayer for the provision of their needs and are not formally affiliated with any denomination. Its purpose is to strengthen the effectiveness and outreach of its constituents by means of spiritual fellowship and prayer, sponsoring consultations and conferences on missionary principles and practices, and providing a united testimony to the need for a speedy and complete evangelization of the world. Approximately 100 agencies deploying 11,000 missionaries belong to IFMA. All members must subscribe to a conservative doctrinal statement which essentially excludes pentecostals. Its organ is the *IFMA News*. Several societies are affiliated with the Evangelical Foreign Missions Association as well, and the two agencies cosponsor the Evangelical Missions Information Service and periodic joint consultations.

RICHARD V. PIERARD

**Interdict.** *See* CENSURES.

**Interfaith Relations.** Although relations among religions have been ongoing down through the centuries, interfaith relations have become very important in this century. In the last two decades theologians of all religions have devoted themselves to relating the truth claim of their own religion to the truth claims of other religions largely because the breaking of cultural, racial, linguistic, and geographical boundaries is on a scale that the world has not previously seen. For the first time in recorded history there would seem to be a true world community. The West can no longer regard itself as the historical and cultural center of the world and as possessing the only valid way of worship. The same is true for the East. Today everyone is the next-door neighbor and spiritual neighbor of everyone else. Today every religion, like every culture, is an existential possibility offered to every person. Alien religions have become part of everyday life, and we experience them as a challenge to the claims of truth of our own faith.

Judaism is an appropriate religion with which to begin. From the destruction of the second temple in Jerusalem (A.D. 70), and especially since the failure of the Bar-Kokhbah revolt (A.D. 135), Judaism has lived as a diaspora—as widely scattered communities of believers living as minority groups within other societies. The experience of being a minority group in other cultures, which is now becoming commonplace for all world religions, has been the norm for Judaism for countless generations. From the biblical period to the present, Judaism has had to formulate its beliefs and practices in the face of challenges from other cultures and religions. The events of the 20th century, and the Holocaust in particular, have given fresh intensity and sharpness to the old question "How does one sing the Lord's song in an alien land?" Of the three Western monotheistic religions of biblical origin (Judaism, Christianity, and Islam), Judaism provided the context out of which Christianity and Islam arose. This integral relationship (somewhat like that of Hinduism and Buddhism in the East) has caused Jewish thinkers to examine their stance in relation to the viewpoints of the other religions with which they are so closely connected.

Jews trace their beginnings to Abraham, who left Mesopotamia and migrated to Canaan. The religious significance of Abraham's journey is that in leaving Mesopotamia he also left the worldly gods and nature deities in order to serve the Lord who created heaven and earth. The early experience of the Jewish people with the God of Abraham took the form of a covenant relationship. The Book of Deuteronomy understands the Jews to be in bondage to God through the covenant entered into by Moses on Mount Sinai. Instead of being held in worldly vassaldom as they were in Egypt, the Jews are committed to a relationship of service and obedience to God. It is this notion of being committed to God that is fundamental to the Jewish understanding of itself and of other religions. Just as God has entered into a special covenant relationship with the Jews, there is no reason why God could not enter into covenant relationships with other peoples. Thus, from the Jewish perspective, the various religions may be seen as the expressions of the relationships obtained between other peoples and God. While for Jews it is the Mosaic covenant that is true and authoritative, for other peoples (e.g., the Christians or Muslims) it will be their particular relationship with God that will be true and authoritative. Indeed, in the most ancient covenant relationship, described in Gen. 9:8–17, God enters into a covenant with Noah, his family, and with every living person and animal.

This approach has led Jews to see themselves as a special people set apart by God. Conversion of others to Judaism has not been judged appropriate; rather, it is the role of Jews to help other peoples to better fulfill their own covenant relationship with God. Contemporary American thinkers such as Abraham Heschel emphasize an ecumenical perspective in which the Jew's task is to be deeply religious *Jewishly* and thus to deepen the spiritual content of America communally—to reawaken other religions to their different covenant commitments to God. While this approach works reasonably well relative to Christianity or Islam, it works less well in Hinduism (where some denominations are monistic rather than theistic) and not at all with Buddhism where there is no God with which to enter into a covenant relationship.

The relationship between Christianity and other religions is one of the key issues in Christian self-understanding, perhaps because of the exclusivist missionary approaches adopted by Christianity over the past several hundred years. Today Christians recognize that, far from disappearing, the religions of Judaism, Islam, Hinduism, and Buddhism are alive and well—in spite of Christian missionary efforts. This fact is causing Christians to reassess their understanding of scriptural teachings and the doctrines of Christology and evangelism. Can Christianity accept other religions as ways to salvation without giving up its fundamental conviction in the absoluteness and uniqueness of Jesus Christ?

The NT contains both narrow christocentric lines of thought and more open theocentric points of focus; both inclusive and exclusive interpretations can be found in it. These two poles created problems for NT Christians in their relations with persons of other religions. Early Christianity had to establish itself in relation to Judaism, since Jesus was born a Jew. If Christianity were simply a variant of Judaism, Gentile converts would have to submit to circumcision, dietary injunctions, and other aspects of Jewish law. While the Jerusalem Christians were in favor of such requirements, Paul argued that for Christians to insist on Jewish law was to fail to understand the essence of the gospel. Paul's view helped Christianity to separate itself from Judaism.

Next Christianity was challenged by Greek dualism, especially in the form of gnosticism. Gnosticism minimized the historical element in Christianity and attempted to divorce the teachings of Jesus from his life, death, and resurrection. The claims of the Gnostics and others such as Marcion compelled Christians to systematize the gospel. This response took three forms; (1) identifying authoritative lines of succession among the bishops; (2) determining the writings to be included in the canon of Christian Scripture; and (3) formulating clear, brief statements of Christian doctrine (e.g., the Apostles' Creed and the doctrine of the Trinity).

From A.D. 622 Christianity was challenged by the younger and more vigorous religion of Islam. Muhammad knew of Christianity and honored Jesus as a prophet but denied the incarnation. This remains a fundamental point of difference between Islam and Christianity. During the medieval period missionaries were sent to Europe and Asia. Missions were established in India and China, bringing Christianity into contact with Hinduism, Buddhism, Confucianism, and Taoism.

Early modern Christian thinkers made a variety of moves which resulted in a more open Christology. Kant, through reason, and Schleiermacher, through the subjective feeling of absolute dependence, grounded Christianity in human universals that opened the door to a more positive view of other religions. Biblical scholars like David Friedrich Strauss called the historical reliability of the Gospels into question. In the 20th century the idea of evolutionary progress was introduced by Ernst Troeltsch, who understood the various religions as evolving toward a common universal perfection. Jesus Christ is not to be identified with God but is placed alongside the founders of the other great religions which are seen as forging alternate pathways to God—impelled by the Spirit to evolve to a final ultimate unity. Karl Barth, however, reacted by presenting an uncompromising and exclusivist view of God's self-revelation in Jesus Christ. Barth restricts God's saving grace to Jesus Christ who judges not only the other religions but Christianity as well.

In the past few decades Christian theologians have taken various positions along the spectrum between the religious pluralism of Troeltsch and the exclusivism of Barth. More open theocentric approaches which shift the focus from Christ to God and open the way for dialog with Jews, Muslims, and many Hindus have been proposed by thinkers such as Paul Tillich, John Hick, Wilfred Cantwell Smith, Paul Knitter, and Kristen Stendahl. Christocentric approaches to other religions ground themselves in Jesus Christ as the unique incarnation of God. Older views of this kind often consigned other religions to spiritual darkness and damnation. Such views have become unacceptable in the light of increasing contacts with other religions. Christocentric theologians have been laboring to avoid the unacceptable implications of the older views without having to implicitly renounce them.

The Roman Catholic theologian Karl Rahner has presented the most sophisticated and influential proposal of this kind. Rahner suggests that God's saving grace revealed to us in Jesus Christ can be seen to be at work in other religions where the devotees have not heard of Jesus. God's grace can, in such circumstances, lead to salvation. Christians should regard such persons as "anonymous Christians." Rahner accommodates both the universal saving grace of God and the exclusiveness of Christ. Christ remains the explicit criterion for God's grace wherever it is found. In Rahner's view allowing for the reality of God's grace in other religions gives the Christian a basis to be tolerant, humble, and yet firm toward all believers of other religions.

A third approach is that of dialog. Dialog theologians such as Raimundo Panikkar and Stanley Samartha reinterpret Christian theology so as to make room for dialog with other religions on the grounds of full commitment and mutual respect. They attempt to express Christianity not just in terms of its own heritage but also in relation to the spiritual heritage of others. The approach of dialog is exemplified in the way in which Jesus deals with Nicodemus, the Samaritan woman, and the Roman centurion. Free and open exchange of various experiences of commitment are seen to result in a deepening of each religion without loss of distinctiveness. Christ is seen as both the exemplar of how to dialog and the universally present Holy Spirit that makes dialog possible.

An unresolved problem for all of these approaches is the Buddhist and Advaita Vedanta Hindu rejection of God as ultimate reality. Christian theologians have yet to come to grips with this problem.

Islam was born within the context of Judaism and Christianity. Indeed Muhammad understood his revelation to be a continuation and fulfilment of the Jewish and Christian biblical tradition. This initial openness hardened because of the basic Islamic requirements of the absolute allegiance to one God, Allah, and rejection of all other gods as false idols. The unforgivable sin of idolatry was called *shirk*. *Jihād*, the holy war, develops in part as a response to idolatry. Allah is understood as the creator of all and is thus the God to be accepted and worshiped by all. After having had time to learn of Allah (a four-month grace period), an idolator is subject to attack as a threat to Islam and a performer of *shirk*. In Islamic countries minority group members of other "religions of the book" were allowed to retain their faith if they submitted to the Muslim government and paid a special tax. This was quite fair, however, since all Muslims had to pay a tithe to the state.

One effect of the *jihād* was to rapidly expand Islam during the period A.D. 634–732 into Spain, France, Syria, Iraq, and Iran. In later years expansion continued into Africa, India, and further eastward. During the modern period Islam spread to North America where it is learning to live as a minority religious group—causing a reassessment of the traditional notions of *shirk* and *jihād* as guides for response to other religions. The Koran itself offers a helpful lead. In it the messages spoken by the prophets of the various religions all emanate from a single source called "the Mother of the Book" (43:4; 13:39). Thus all scriptures are but earthly copies of a single source book in heaven and so ought to agree. The reason they do not is not due to any fault of the founding prophets but because the followers of Moses, Jesus, Buddha, and the *Vedas* have corrupted the original texts revealed to them. Only the Koran has been handed down uncorrupted. Given this situation it is not surprising that when the Koran (5:48) calls all religions "to compete with one another in goodness"—a kind of spiritual olympics—it is confidently expected that Islam will win.

In India and the Far East, the Sufi influence has produced an essentially mystical response to the encounter with other religions. For example, the Sufi master Jalal al-Din Rumi provides Islam with a way of recognizing truth within other religions—they are divergent paths to the *kaaba*, the experience of unity with the one God. Because Islam has the full uncorrupted revelation and experience of the *kaaba*, its role is to be the guide for others on their upward journey.

Unlike the other religions, Hinduism does not have an identifiable founder or beginning. Hinduism provided the context out of which Buddhism arose and both religions share the presuppositions that *karma* (the mental trace or seed left behind by each thought or action that predisposes one to a similar thought or action in the future), *samsāra* (rebirth), and *jiva* (the empirical self which is reborn) are *anādi* (beginningless) and that by following a particular spiritual path (*marga*) release can be realized. In Hinduism it is only by the revelation of the Hindu scriptures that release or salvation can be obtained. Hindu theology, however, does make room in its scheme for other religions. The one God, or Brahman, revealed through the scriptures is also given secondary revelation in the form of *avatars* or incarnations of the divine. Hindu *avatars* such as Kishna or Rama are seen to be paralleled by *avatars* in other religions: Moses, Jesus, Muhammad, and the Buddha—all of whom are understood to be incarnations of Brahman. Thus Jews, Christians, Hindus, and Buddhists are seen by Hindus as following spiritual paths. If they advance far enough in this life then they will be reborn as Hindus in the next life and will be able to reach full release through the Hindu scriptures. This is the basis of the Hindu claim for tolerance of all religions, and the Hindu metaphor that the various religions are but different paths up the mountain. In the Hindu view all other paths merge into the Hindu path before the top is reached—and at the top is Brahman.

As is the case with the other religions, Hindus do not take the Buddhist negation of God seriously. Instead Hindus simply superimpose their own theology on Buddhism and the other religions as a way of embracing them.

The Buddhist attitude toward other religions may be described as critical tolerance combined with a missionary goal. Buddhism has spread widely from Hindu India—where it began as a new religion at the time of Gautama Buddha about 500 B.C.—south to Sri Lanka and Southeast Asia, north to Tibet, east to China and Japan, and recently west to Europe and North America. Although Buddhism encountered established religions in all of these regions, there is little evidence of war or persecution. Buddhism has demonstrated a remarkable degree of tolerance and flexibility throughout the course of its expansion. In addition to its attitude of critical tolerance Buddhism's stress on compassion provides a natural point of contact with other religions. Buddhism rejects the worship of God or gods and the performance of religious rituals as a means of release. It also rejects speculations about ultimate beginnings, especially about whether the self and the world are eternal, and speculations about the ultimate state of the self in the future as being unhelpful.

The missionary motivation originated with Buddha's directive that the *dharma* (the truth or the way) is to be preached to all persons so as to encourage those who are spiritually minded to test it for themselves (*Aṅguttara Nikāya* 1.20.1). All this allows for spiritual growth in other religions. Some Buddhist thinkers divide other religions into two categories: (1) false religions, those which deny moral responsibility and free will (e.g., materialism, deterministic Calvinism); and (2) unsatisfactory but not necessarily false religions, those which posit a God with supernatural grace or maintain the omniscience of a founder or revelation. Religions of the second sort, so long as they maintain moral responsibility and free choice, may provide useful "psychological crutches" (e.g., the belief in a God who gives grace) to help one advance through the beginning stages of spiritual growth. Eventually, however, one will outgrow such childish beliefs and experience reality directly without the superimposition of fictions such as a transcendent God. Then the way is open for the full realization of the Buddhist *dharma*. In contemporary circles the Dalai Lama diplomatically manifests this approach when he suggests that the various religions are suited to persons of different dispositions and mental outlooks. We should therefore value the techniques for spiritual improvement developed by the various religions as useful in progressing toward the common goal. But for the Buddhist there is no doubt that the common goal involves the transcending of helpful fictions such as belief in God and the direct realization of the *dharma* which the Buddha experienced.

With increasing travel and mixing of cultures, along with the availability of better knowledge of the world religions, there is bound to be increasing interaction among religions in the future. Such interaction is not to be feared, but, as the past experience of the religions shows, provides the creative challenge for new growth and insight within each religion. The prospect is not that all religions will become one, but that through interaction they will deepen, vitalize, and renew one another in their differences.

*Bibliography.* S. Radhakrishnan, *Recovery of Faith* (1967); K. Klostermaier, *Hindu and Christian in Vrindalan* (1968); W. C. Smith, *The Faith of Other Men* (1972); J. Neusner, *The Way of the Torah* (1974); W. Rahula, *What the Buddha Taught* (1974); K. Cragg, *The House of Islam* (1977); D. Swearer, *Dialogue: The Key to Understanding Other Religions* (1977); R. Panikkar, *The Intra-Religious Dialogue* (1978); J. Hick and B. Hebblethwaite, eds., *Christianity and Other Religions* (1980); R. Panikkar, *The Unknown Christ of Hinduism* (1981); S. J. Samartha, *Courage for Dialogue* (1981); W. C. Smith, *Towards a World Theology* (1981); J. Newman, *Foundations of Religious Tolerance* (1982); W. Ariarajah, *The Bible and People of Other Faiths* (1985); H. Coward, *Pluralism: Challenge to World Religions* (1985); P. F. Knitter, *No Other Name?* (1985); H. Coward, *Word and Text: Scripture in World Religions* (1988).

HAROLD COWARD

## International Conferences for Itinerant Evangelists.
Conferences sponsored by the Billy Graham Evangelistic Association in Amsterdam which had as their purpose the stimulation of evangelism and the encouragement of evangelists from all over the world. The 1983 conference brought almost 4000 itinerant evangelists from more than 130 countries for an intense 10-day schedule of meetings, workshops, informal discussions, and outreach. There was a comprehensive examination of itinerant evangelism, including the personal and spiritual life of the evangelist. The latter's code and conduct were the subject of 15 one-sentence "Affirmations." The 1986 conference had more than 8000 participants from some 173 countries and territories, and was more representative than any other Christian meeting in recorded history. Billy Graham was honorary chairman and a major speaker at both conferences, which were presided over by Walter H. Smyth. The addresses and much of the workshop material were incorporated into official conference volumes entitled *The Work of an Evangelist* (1984) and *The Calling of an Evangelist* (1987).

## International Congregational Council (ICC).
Council first convened in London in 1891 composed of representatives from Congregational churches throughout the world. A constitution was adopted which fixed the size of the council at 450 members—150 from Great Britain, 150 from the USA, and 150 from other countries. Subsequent meetings (1899, 1908, 1920, 1930, 1949) took place on an alternating but irregular basis on opposite sides of the Atlantic. At these meetings the delegates discussed a broad range of theological, ecclesiastical, critical, and social issues relating to Congregationalism and promoted international understanding and good will among the various communities. After World War II the council met every four or five years. It adopted a more formal organizational structure, appointed permanent leadership, and created a special service fund to finance interchurch visits, scholarships for foreign seminars, and research projects. It also became increasingly involved in ecumenical ventures and engaged in social action linked with evangelism. At its 1966 conclave ICC voted to undertake discussions with the World Presbyterian Alliance regarding possible union, and the merger was carried out at a joint assembly in Nairobi, Kenya, on August 20, 1970. The new organization was called the World Alliance of Reformed Churches (Presbyterian and Reformed).

RICHARD V. PIERARD

## International Council of Christian Churches.
Council founded in 1948 under the leadership of Carl McIntire, president of the American Council of Christian Churches, for the purpose of offsetting the liberalism of the World Council of Churches (WCC) which held its first postwar conference in the same year. The council has consistently followed the basic policy and principles of the American Council of Christian Churches and has denounced WCC for its tolerance of the USSR and its communistic regime. It has also opposed the policies of the United Nations and American involvement in that international organization for the same reasons. In recent years its influence has greatly declined.

C. GREGG SINGER

## International Missionary Council (IMC).
Organization founded in 1921 in Mohonk Lake, N.Y., which brought together about 30 regional and national Christian groups in the interest of bringing the gospel to the non-Christian world. From this meeting came increased coordination of missionary activity, the development of common study programs, the use of consultations,

and united action. The movement enjoyed the stellar leadership of J. H. Oldham, John R. Mott, and William Paton. A number of important conferences were held to facilitate the work of IMC. In 1928 IMC met in Jerusalem; in 1938 in Madras; in Whitby, Ontario, in 1947; in Willingen, West Germany, in 1952; and in Ghana in 1958. In 1961 in New Delhi, IMC joined with the World Council of Churches and is now the Division of World Missions and Evangelism.

Throughout its history of promoting Christianity in the non-Christian world, IMC has acknowledged the variety and complexity of beliefs of its constituent members. It has not insisted upon a single doctrinal statement but has emphasized the need for Christian fellowship and united action. Thus it became a key element in the development of the ecumenical spirit among the main branches of the non-Roman Catholic churches. Among its many publications which advocated fellowship and cooperation in missions, the most important is the quarterly journal, *International Review of Missions*.

ROBERT V. SCHNUCKER

**Inter-Varsity Fellowship.** *See* STUDENT ORGANIZATIONS, RELIGIOUS (NORTH AMERICAN); STUDENT ORGANIZATIONS, RELIGIOUS (WORLDWIDE).

**Intuitionism.** The position that there is a mystical kind of knowledge that comes to the mind itself. It is to be distinguished from mediated knowledge or discursive reasoning. Mediate knowledge is acquired by sense experience through ideas or by the process of thinking through to conclusions. Intuitionists affirm that under certain conditions there comes a flash of insight, or they concur with Henri Bergson that certain areas of experience (such as motion or life itself) are not amenable to rational processes since reason distorts the very fluidity of the subject. Reason chops up experience into static and frozen items or entities; life is a process like motion which by its nature cannot thus be abstracted. A bird on the wing can only be intuited since intuition takes in the whole flash of motion; reason moves dialectically from position to position, noting only a series of rests, points, or positions.

Intuitionists generally believe that this form of knowing is altogether unlike sense experience and reason and is higher and more profound. The critic may suggest that the flash-form of knowledge itself is rooted in reason and sense experience and that an intuition is only the rearrangement of items already acquired in the ordinary way by accumulated experience and thought.

Intuitionism is most generally associated with the emotional life rather than with any a priori category of the mind. Feelings, it is said, furnish cognitive experience unlike any other. Such

knowledge that is rooted in deep feeling goes under the name of mysticism. It is an insight that comes with power of conviction of its reality, its own authenticity which needs no other corroboration. It is personally and passively appropriated, and passively as though the subject had no hand in the matter.

Both in ethics and in religion intuitionists challenge the claims of rationalists and empiricists. Religious history is full of testimonies and defenses of religious experience as the ground of belief in God, special information regarding religious ideas or action, and supernatural clues or a "call" of God. Intuition and imagination are closely related; both imply a fertility of mind which does not resist impressions. Some philosophers have regarded intuitive insight as the highest achievement of wisdom, including Plato and Benedict Spinoza in Western thought and the Upanishads in the East.

*Bibliography.* H. Bergson, *Creative Evolution* (1913); W. P. Montague, *The Ways of Knowing* (1925); H. Bergson, *The Two Sources of Morality and Religion* (1935); D. C. Macintosh, *The Problem of Religious Knowledge* (1940).

VERGILIUS FERM

**Iona Community, The.** Ecumenical community seeking new and radical ways of living the gospel in today's world. Although the historic island of Iona is its spiritual home, the community's main work is in the world, particularly in notoriously difficult urban areas.

The community was founded in 1938 by George F. MacLeod. Appalled by the church's lack of impact in working-class communities at a time of high unemployment, MacLeod initiated an experiment on Iona, the Scottish Hebridean island from which Columba had launched a great missionary movement in A.D. 563. The Iona Community, consisting of ministers and craftspeople, began to rebuild the ruins of the medieval Benedictine abbey which had replaced the Celtic Columban foundation. MacLeod's intention was to train young ministers for work in the industrial parishes of inner-city and housing scheme areas of Scotland. He believed that clergy should work alongside industrial men, living together in Christian community. By 1967, when the rebuilding was completed, the Iona Community had trained many young ministers for work in urban areas.

The Iona Community today consists of 185 members, 800 associates, and 2500 "friends." Its members—ordained and lay, Protestant and Roman Catholic, men and women, married and celibate—share a fivefold rule of prayer, economic sharing, planning of time, meeting together, and work for justice and peace. They live in many parts of the world.

On Iona, the community welcomes many people from all over the world every year. The pilgrims come as day visitors, or to live in the restored abbey to share in the community's weekly program of worship, work, recreation, healing, and study. Young people come to the MacLeod Centre, a new international youth center completed during the Iona Community's 50th anniversary celebrations in 1988. On the mainland of Great Britain, the community has several Columban houses—experimental communities living out the concerns of the Iona Community—and has staff members engaged in peace and justice work, urban mission, and renewal of worship.

**Bibliography.** G. F. MacLeod, *We Shall Rebuild* (1944); R. Morton, *The Iona Community: Personal Impressions of the Early Years* (1977); R. Ferguson, *Chasing the Wild Goose: The Story of the Iona Community* (1988).

RONALD FERGUSON

**Iran.** Large western Asian country occupying 1,648,000 sq. km. (636,300 sq. mi.) with a population of 47.8 million (1987). To the north it borders on the USSR at the Caucasus, the Caspian Sea, and Russian Central Asia. To the east it shares a common border with Afghanistan and Pakistan. To its south are the Gulf of Oman, the Straits of Hormuz, and the Persian Gulf. To the west it borders on Iraq and Turkey. The population is divided into over 45 groups speaking 31 languages. Approximately three-fourths of the people speak Persian or Farsi while another one-fifth are Turkish speakers. This latter group is located mainly in the northwestern province of Azerbaijan. The major cities are Tehran (7 million population), Isfahan, Mashad, and Tabriz. Urbanization has reached 50 percent.

Iran is the major center of Shiah Islam with over 90 percent of the people belonging to that division of the Muslim religion. With the overthrow of the Shah in 1979, the theocratic Islamic Republic was formed under Khomeini. Shiah Islam continues to be the official state religion. This division of Islam recognizes 12 Imams who were descended from Mohammed through his daughter Fatima and son-in-law Ali, whom they count as the first legitimate caliph, although he was actually the fourth to hold that office. In Iran, Muslim saints are widely venerated and their shrines are often heavily endowed. Qum and Mashad are centers of pilgrimage.

The Kurds, who are a minority in the western part of the country, are Sunnis. The Baha'i Islamic sect originated in Iran in 1844 and was severely persecuted by the Khomeini regime. Some of the sect who have left Iran have become missionaries of the Baha'i World Faith. There has been a small group of Jews in Iran since the Babylonian captivity as well as Zoroastrian remnants of the official pre-Islamic religion.

Christians constitute less than one-half of one percent of the population. The largest group comes from the Armenian Apostolic Church, followed by the Assyrian or Ancient Church of the East (traditionally termed Nestorian Christians), Roman Catholics, and Protestants.

Henry Martyn translated the NT into Persian in less than a year, doing most of his work in Shiraz in the southern part of the country. Anglican missionaries from the Church Missionary Society worked for many years in southern Iran until they were forced out by Khomeini. Presbyterians were the main Protestant mission in the northern part of the nation. These along with workers in the International Missionary Fellowship and the Seventh-day Adventists were also expelled by the Islamic Republic, but small churches they planted continue to grow. The Khomeini regime persecuted Muslim converts to Christianity, killing an Anglican priest, trying to shoot the bishop, and murdering his only son.

Freedom to sell and distribute Bibles has continued and more copies of the Scriptures have been sold in the last few years than in the history of the country. Daily Christian radio broadcasts are beamed into Iran. There is also more openness to the gospel by Iranians who are scattered around the world, since many are disillusioned with Islam and the war with Iraq.

In late 1990 the war between Iran and Iraq was largely forgotten in the aftermath of Iraq's invasion of Kuwait and the resulting international turmoil. Iran seemed ready to stand in solidarity with their Arab neighbor, an event which could have widespread ramifications for the long-standing conflicts between the nations' Muslims. There also were indications of new policies affecting Christians. The Iranian Bible Society, which operated openly in Teheran after the Islamic revolution, was subjected to increasing harassment in the late 1980s, and its offices were closed and files confiscated in 1990. Importation of Persian Bibles and other religious literature was forbidden. Christian activities were increasingly restricted by the Office of Religious Minorities of the Ministry of Islamic Guidance.

**Bibliography.** D. N. Wilber, *Iran, Past and Present* (1967); R. E. Waterfield, *Christians in Persia* (1973); D. M. McCurry, *World Christianity, Middle East* (1979); H. B. Dehquani-Tafti, *The Hard Awakening* (1981); D. B. Barrett, *World Christian Encyclopedia* (1982).

**Iraq.** Independent Arab republic in southwest Asia covering 438,317 sq. km. (169,235 sq. mi.) and with a population of 15.5 million. Islam has dominated Iraq's religious scene since the 7th century. Over 95 percent of the population are Muslims; 62 percent of these are Shias (Shi'ites). Despite this, Sunnis of both Hanafite and Shafiit rites are a minority with preponderant influence in the nation, especially as an urban middle class in government. The 2 million Kurds in Iraq follow basically the Shafiite (Sunni) rite, although some are either Christians or Yazadis.

Yazidi religion (0.9 percent of the population) is a syncretism of Manichean, Zoroastrian, Jewish, Nestorian, and Muslim elements, the last of these dominating in belief and practice. Yazadis are devil worshipers who revere the fallen angel Malak Ta'us who manifested himself in Shaikh Adi, the 12th-century founder. Their two sacred books are the Black Book and the Book of Revelation. Mandeanism (0.2 percent of the population) originated in 2d-century gnosticism. Its syncretistic tenets include ancient Mesopotamian, Iranian, Jewish, and Christian beliefs. Today the followers call themselves Mandaiia, but others refer to them as Christians of John the Baptist, Dippers, or Sabeans. Their faith centers on a fertility cult and they have sacred books to support their rites.

Judaism has all but disappeared in Iraq. Before World War II about 250,000 Jews lived in Iraq, but since then they have emigrated in large numbers to Israel. The continuing Arab-Israeli hostilities make the 100 or so in Baghdad live in difficult circumstances. The Baha'i faith came to Iraq 150 years ago. Followers have experienced severe repression. A 1970 decree banned their rites; only about 700 live in Baghdad (1986).

Today, Christians number less than 500,000 (3.5 percent of the population) and follow a Syriac liturgy. There are Chaldeans, Nestorians (Assyrian Church of the East), Syrian Catholics, and Syrian Orthodox (the last known also as Jacobites). Syriac continues to be the language in some rural areas for the liturgies. After 1917 Armenian Orthodox (Gregorians) and Armenian Catholics fled Turkey to escape persecution. Greek Orthodox and Greek Catholics form small communities made up of those from Syria, Lebanon, and Palestine. The few Latin Catholics are mostly expatriates. Their clergy head schools and medical and seminary programs, as well as oversee parish and interrite efforts. Latin Catholics represent about 1.8 percent of the total population—about a quarter of million in 1985. Since 1970 over half of Syria's 463,500 Christians (1985) reside in Baghdad. Reasons include: (1) Kurdish revolts and repression in the north; (2) greater opportunity for education and employment, especially for youth; (3) urban amenities; and (4) urban anonymity. Emigrés to Australia, Canada, and the USA have numbered thousands in the last 25 years.

Catholics represent the largest number of Iraqi Christians (74 percent of Christians); they are largely Chaldeans, in 10 dioceses served by as many bishops. The patriarch is in Baghdad. In 1970 innovative Chadean priests founded the Chaldean Sacerdotal Alliance intended to renew missionary zeal and to implement Vatican II decisions. Syrian Catholics (30,000) are in two dioceses under 32 priests and two bishops. Three thousand Armenian Catholics are ministered to by four priests and an archdiocese in Baghdad. Three hundred fifty Greek Catholics are under one priest's care in that city, while 3500 Latin Catholics are present as expatriates there as well. Religious instruction is permitted in communities when a Christian community actually represents a majority; outside of major cities, there is no religious instruction other than sporadic sessions by churches during holidays or as they prepare for first communion. Nearly one-half of all Christian children receive no religious training. Missionary activities have stimulated the formation of evangelical congregations mostly from converts out of Eastern churches. Some of these numerous but small Protestant groups continued under nationals after American missionaries were evicted in 1969.

In church and state relations, a provisional constitution in 1970 declared Islam to be the state religion but "all citizens are equal before the the law without distinction of religion." Of course observance of this enactment finds a hiatus in general and varies from place to place. Religious judges (*qadi*) regulate the individual affairs and rights of Muslims. For non-Muslims there is no governmental bureau of religious affairs; everything pertaining to the administration of church property or individual rights is regulated by civil courts. In civil court, one judge is particularly charged with non-Muslim affairs; usually his verdict takes into consideration the customs of each community in consultation with its leader.

Iraq achieved international centerstage in August 1990 when a long-standing territorial dispute with Kuwait escalated into Iraq's invasion of Kuwait and overthrow of its government. Atrocities were reported against Kuwaiti nationals and foreigners. A mass of refugees fled to Jordan. In late 1990 Iraq was isolated literally by an economic blockade and figuratively by international condemnation of its actions. A United Nations force made up largely of U.S. troops was standing in Saudi Arabia.

**Bibliography.** A. S. Atiya, *A History of Eastern Christianity* (1968); R. F. Nyrop, *Iraq: A Country Study* (1979); T. Y. Ismael, *Iraq and Iran: Roots of Conflict* (1982); G. J. Jennings, *Welcome into the Middle East* (1986).

GEORGE J. JENNINGS

**Ireland, Northern.** Northeast section of the island of Ireland which is an integral part of Great Britain. It covers only 14,121 sq. km. (5452 sq. mi.) and is often called Ulster because it includes part of the old province of that name. From 1801 to 1921 Ireland as a whole formed part of the United Kingdom and as such was governed by laws made by Parliament (which included Irish members). In 1921 the partitioning of Ireland took place based on the principle of self-determination. The newiy formed Irish Free State in the course of time deepened the economic, political, and cultural differences between it and the six northern counties of Ulster which were left to shape their own political future. In 1925 six of the counties of the northern province of Ulster retained their links with Great Britain and formed what is now known as Northern Ireland with its capital in Belfast. Eventually the Republic of Ireland was established in 1949.

The census figures of 1981 showed the population of Northern Ireland dropping from 1,536,065 to 1,507,065. However, the satellite towns ringing Belfast, the capital, showed an increase of around 50,000—a sign of redevelopment.

In Northern Ireland there are scores of religious sects, but the 1981 census figures provide less information about the religious breakdown than the 1971 census. On that occasion just under 10 percent of the population did not disclose their religion, but the 1981 figures for Belfast showed over 20 percent of people in the city refusing to answer the question and 18 percent for the whole of Northern Ireland.

The 1981 figures for Northern Ireland showed that there were 414,532 Roman Catholics, 339,818 Presbyterians, 281,472 Church of Ireland, and 58,731 Methodists. Other denominations totaled 112,822. Population experts reckoned that the Roman Catholic percentage had risen from just over 31 percent to around 39 percent.

The long drawn-out conflict in Northern Ireland which began in 1969 has been a source of contention within Great Britain. The conflict has not been merely a church-state problem or even a Protestant-Catholic issue, since there are many political, social, and economic factors involved. Nevertheless, this is clearly an area where religion has become the focus of unrest within the body politic.

ROBERT COBAIN

**Ireland, Republic of.** State occupying approximately 83 percent of the island of Ireland. It has an area of 70,283 sq. km. (27,136 sq. mi.). The republic was formed in 1949 when a unanimous vote of the Irish Parliament (Dail Eireann) agreed to break completely with Great Britain and with the British Commonwealth. Great Britain acknowledged Ireland's right to take that step, and the nation changed its name from Eire to the Republic of Ireland.

The first step toward the independence of that part of the country came in 1921 when the Irish Free State was established with its own parliament but still owing allegiance to the British crown and still a member of the British Commonwealth. Six of the northern counties resisted this change and remained in the United Kingdom.

Those of more Republican views in Ireland believed that a complete break with Great Britain should have been made at that time. The Irish Republican Army (IRA), an illegal organization, started a campaign of violence against the Irish government and all who supported the Irish Free State as constituted. The government introduced a law under which anyone found to be unlawfully in possession of firearms could be executed. Some Republicans were in fact put to death for this offense.

In 1925 the border between the Free State and Northern Ireland was finally fixed and customs posts were put into operation. This was opposed by Nationalists who saw it as giving recognition to Northern Ireland instead of trying to unite the whole country as an independent state. In 1932 a general election brought Eamonn de Valera, leader of the Republicans, into power in the Dublin government. One of his first steps was to abolish the oath of allegiance to the British crown. In 1937 a new constitution was put into effect and the name of the country was changed from the Irish Free State to Eire. A president was appointed in place of the British governor-general. The first president was Douglas Hyde, a Protestant Gaelic scholar.

According to the 1981 census, the population of the Republic was 3.4 million, of which 3.2 million were Roman Catholics. The largest Protestant denomination was the Church of Ireland (part of the Anglican Communion, but separate from the state), with a membership of 95,366. There were 14,255 Presbyterians, 5790 Methodists, 2127 Jews, and 10,843 in other religious bodies. Those who professed no religion numbered 39,572, and no information was forthcoming on 70,976 others.

All the main denominations, including Roman Catholics, disregard the border and administer their respective churches as a single unit, whether they are in the Republic or in the British province of Northern Ireland. The House Church movement has grown considerably since the 1960s. There has also been a fourfold increase in people who classify themselves as professing no religion.

Since the 1960s many of the barriers between Catholics and Protestants have been broken down in the republic. Ecumenical meetings are held regularly, including hundreds of small prayer groups where Catholics and Protestants pray and study the Bible together.

J. ERIC MAYER

**Ironside, Henry Allen** (1876–1951). Home missionary, evangelist, and Bible teacher. Born in Toronto, he organized and became president of the Western Book and Tract Company in 1914. He later taught at the Evangelical Theological College in Dallas, Tex. (1924–30). Although never ordained, he was pastor of the Moody Memorial Church in Chicago (1930–48). As a young man he had joined the Plymouth Brethren, but his interdenominational tendencies were reflected as he lectured extensively throughout the United States, speaking at the Mt. Hermon Bible conferences, at Winona Lake, Stony Brook, and addressing Keswick gatherings, among others. He died while on a preaching tour of New Zealand, and was buried there. His writings include *Notes on Daniel* (1911), *Lectures on Romans* (1928), *In the Heavenlies* (1937), *The Unchanging Christ* (1938), *The Lamp of Prophecy* (1940), *A Historical Sketch of the Brethren Movement* (1942), *The Great Parenthesis* (1943), *Expository Notes on the Epistles of James and Peter* (1947), and *Expository Notes on Ezekiel, the Prophet* (1949).

**Irrationalism.** Divergent constructs which share the basic theory that reality cannot be captured within, or reduced to, intellectual concepts. Truth must arise from within the individual's free choice (existentialism); it is the interplay of cause-and-effect relationships on the individual (instrumentalism, behaviorism); it is personal revelatory experience (mysticism); it is knowledge built on faith perceptions (romanticism). Many philosophies have drawn deliberately or by implication on irrationalism, although the label has been tainted since the beginning of the Enlightenment, and it has often been used as an epithet categorizing a group as being antirational or illogical. Few today use the term self-descriptively.

Two types of irrationalism have historically influenced Christianity. The form most prevalent in the past was "experiential." While it is still common, a second type has been more crucial to theological inquiry since Søren Kierkegaard and Karl Barth. What might be called "revelational" came to dominate much of 20th-century mainline Christianity.

***Experiential.*** The knowledge of God is considered to be appropriated in a personal religious experience that transcends man's rational capacity.

*Mysticism.* In reaction to Platonic Stoics in Greek philosophy, Plotinus (205–70) argued that the "Divine Mind" is above all sensation and knowledge. To reach it the pilgrim must seek unconscious absorption in which the soul no longer knows it has a body. Description of such experience is meaningless; it may be known only to the one who undergoes it, and truth gained is incommunicable. This thinking induced hermits to spend decades sitting on pedestals or in caves. When Anselm of Canterbury (1033–1109) drew on the Stoics to define God as an object for human reason in medieval theology and Peter Lombard and other scholastics reduced his will to ecclesiastical manuals of morality and law, the mystics became a counterpoint. Such monks as Bernard of Clairvaux (1090–1153) and Hugh of St. Victor (1096–1141) believed it possible to experience God through disciplined affection

instead of reflection. Pauline theology has a surface mysticism and Paul and John speak of mysti-clike trances. The difference is that the NT writers took away and applied knowledge from these experiences. A true mystic would not admit this to be possible.

*Pietism, Moralism, Romanticism.* A similar clash of method came in the reaction of German pietists to 17th-century Protestant scholasticism and Immanuel Kant's rejection of rationalism. Such evangelicals as Charles Wesley and Jonathan Edwards and such nonevangelical romanticists as Friedrich Schleiermacher similarly fought the deist and other natural religion forces they saw at work in the church. The pietist pioneers Philipp Spener and August Francke taught that God is not known in the theological formulas but in meditation and prayer. Kant placed moral experience above natural science and rational metaphysics, believing that only by obeying an inner imperative can any conception of the infinite be framed. Puritan pietists and later evangelical revivalists such as Timothy Dwight and Asahel Nettleton struggled to redefine theology to give primacy to affection. Romanticists rejected theological truth altogether and looked to inner truth that elicited social action. Albrecht Ritschl and Wilhelm Hermann modified theological irrationalism, but Rudolf Otto's *Idea of the Holy* (*Das Heilige,* 1917) is the most competent of the modern efforts to perpetuate this line. Otto associated the relation to God (whom he described as knowable objective reality, in contradistinction to Schleiermacher) as something which can only be awakened inside the self and only described through analogy and metaphor.

*Philosophy.* In the warfare of irrationalism with rationalism, philosophy has often honored the irrational. Socrates relied on an inner voice, and Plato's "idea of the good" transcended rational penetration. The most notorious philosophical rationalists (such as the Stoics, Benedict Spinoza, Georg Hegel, and F. H. Bradley) did not identify truth with rational exactitude. They found aesthetic and supracognitive functions for love, art, and religion. Process and existential philosophies affirm an open and incremental universe, and have to that extent committed themselves to irrationalism.

***Revelational.*** The second form of irrationalism developed to apply theological convictions which secular philosophies had not taken into account. Revelational irrationalism attacks the supposition that truth about God can be discerned through sensory experience. God manifests himself as he wills; when God reveals himself he does so freely, by grace. Human reason is not involved nor autonomy in any form—be it rational processes or works righteousness.

*In History.* Early Christian apologists assumed a certifiable intellectual content to reside in truth.

Tertullian, however, said Christian truth was involved in the paradox of a God-man, and the paradox could only be resolved in an act of faith. To the Averroists of the Middle Ages, man's reason had independent access to the divine mysteries. Thomism regarded the most rational human act as a dependence on God's truth as revealed to the church. Thomas Aquinas, however, defined a large body of "natural theology" which could be seen through reason. In the face of this autonomy the voluntarists and nominalists, such as Duns Scotus and William of Occam, reduced man's ability almost to nothing, paving the way for Martin Luther, in whom the knowledge of God is *sola gratia, sola fide*. Nicholas of Cusa and Jacob Boehme saw such depth and contradiction to God's nature that every human effort to know him is frustrated.

At the beginning of modern Western thought René Descartes equated truth with clear rationality, but Blaise Pascal more mystically affirmed a mysterious Christ in whom faith from a rational standpoint is hazardous. Hegel equated truth with the universals, but Kierkegaard identified it with the particular reality of Christ. For these irrationalists truth was incarnated by a gracious act of God in the person of Jesus Christ, and faith to appropriate Christ is a subjective experience without a firm epistemology in the senses.

*In 20th-Century Theology.* This form of irrationalism is suggested by neo-orthodox theology. There is an irrationality in God's free decision, in his gracious love in Christ, in the Godless nature of man, and in the cosmos itself as the battlefield between God and demonic powers. Its meanings cannot be translated into the language of natural science (logical positivism). Nor are they humanly communicable (Karl Jaspers' existentialism). Theologians outside neo-orthodoxy charge that this system amounts to epistemological agnosticism, although the neo-orthodox reject that label, preferring to say that there is an epistemological silence which the human can overcome as the Holy Spirit reveals truth through revelation and its proclamation. There is, they admit, no revelation which has objective truth-bearing content. Scripture only becomes God's revelation subjectively, and its factual historicity is irrelevant. The action of God, according to the revelatory irrationalist, restores and orients the reason instead of destroying it.

**Bibliography.** E. Brunner, *Erlebnis, Erkenntnis, und Glaube* (1921); K. Jaspers, *Vernunft und Existenz* (1935); E. Brunner, *The Philosophy of Religion* (1937); E. Lewis, *A Philosophy of the Christian Revelation* (1940); D. C. Macintosh, *The Problem of Religious Knowledge* (1940); R. Niebuhr, *The Meaning of Revelation* (1941); S. Kierkegaard, *Philosophical Fragments* (1942); P. Tillich, *Systematic Theology*, vol. 1 (1951); G. Clark, *Thales to Dewey: A History of Philosophy* (1957).

**Irvingites.** *See* Catholic Apostolic Church.

**Irwin, William Andrew** (1884–1967). Methodist. Born in Ontario, he was educated at Toronto, Victoria, and Chicago universities. He taught in the department of Semitics, Toronto (1919–30); in OT at Oriental Institute and Divinity School, Chicago (1930–50); and at Southern Methodist from 1950. He was a member of the 1934 Oriental Institute Megiddo Expedition and the Standard Bible Committee. He was editor of J. M. P. Smith, *The Prophets and Their Times* (2d ed., 1941), (with A. P. Wikgren) I. M. Price, *The Ancestry of our English Bible* (2d ed., 1949), and the revised edition of the OT in *The Bible, an American Translation* (1954). He is the author of *The Problem of Ezekiel* (1943), (with Frankfort, Jacobsen, and Wilson) *The Intellectual Adventure of Ancient Man* (1947), and (with H. R. Willoughby et al.) *The Study of the Bible Today and Tomorrow* (1947).

**Islam.** Term referring to both the religion of about 800 million persons in Asia, Africa, and parts of Europe and the entire body of believers and the countries they live in.

***Muhammad's Life and Work.*** Muhammad (A.D. 570–632) is the founder of Islam. His early life is shrouded in mystery and legend. Born in Mecca, he grew up as an orphan and was probably reared by a grandfather and an uncle. As a young man, he was a successful caravan conductor. His meditations on the issues of life and death finally crystallized with the approach of his 40th birthday. An angel appeared to Muhammad and summoned him to preach. Muhammad began his ministry as the prophet of God's wrath and the preacher of righteousness.

Muhammad did not regard his religion as a new creation, but as a restoration of the religion of Abraham. He proclaimed himself to be the last and true prophet of God. His message caused his native city to despise and persecute him. His flight from Mecca to Medina, the *Hijra* (Sept. 22, 622), under threat of death, opened up a new era for Islam and the world.

In Medina Muhammad set about to establish a new community organized on the revolutionary principle of obedience to God and to himself as God's apostle. This eventually led to war with Mecca; Muhammad was eventually victorious. Although Muhammad remained a prophet, he became a militant ruler over an aggressive political state. At his death he left a powerful religiopolitical heritage to his followers.

***The Muslim World.*** Islam is second only to Christianity as a world religion, having approximately 800 million adherents as against Christianity's one billion. The Muslim population is concentrated in a broad belt running deep into North Africa from the Atlantic to the Red Sea and into Somalia; the Balkans, Turkey, and the Arabian peninsula; Iraq, Iran, and Afghanistan; southern

USSR and western China; the Indian subcontinent, Malaysia, and Indonesia. About 12 percent of the population of China is Muslim, compared with 10 percent in India. Islam sees itself as universal; its aim is Islamization of the world.

Although Islam is thought of as a religion, it is important to remember that it is a total way of life, governing the social relationships of man with man, as well as offering religious guidance. (In contrast with the Christian view, guidance is considered the paramount need of man, since man, being essentially good, will walk straight if only he is shown the right path.) The *'Umma* (the community of believers) is the bearer of the *Sharī'ah* (the Law, expressing the will of God for man), which can be fully implemented only under an Islamic government. The separation of religion and politics is an alien concept to Islam. Indeed Pan-Islamism envisages a worldwide political framework for the implementation of its religious, social, and cultural values—"a living family of Muslim republics," to quote Iqbal (1876–1938), its greatest modern visionary. Yet although the creation of Pakistan (1947) is the supreme result of Iqbal's concept, the ideal has been seriously set back by a great deal of ideological and sectarian infighting.

### Islam Defined and Demonstrated.

The abstract noun "Islam," and its active participle "Muslim," are derivatives of the Arabic root *s-l-m* (familiar in one of its variants as the greeting of peace, *Salaam*), bearing the idea of submission to God. The basic idea of Islam is expressed in its creed: "There is no god but Allah, and Muhammad is the Apostle of Allah." The Quranic doctrine of God is emphatically and rigorously monotheistic; the sin of all sins is *shirk*, the attribution of partners to Allah. For the Koran, the Christian doctrine of the Trinity is *shirk*. Allah, the Eternal Alone, is creator and judge of all; he is all-knowing and compassionate, granting guidance to those who call on him.

The Five Pillars of Islam are: (1) recitation of the creed, in Arabic, with understanding and sincerity; (2) the five daily prayers in Arabic, directed toward Mecca, with the prescribed postures; (3) the payment of *zakāt*, a charitable tax on grain, cattle, and one's bank balance; (4) rigorous fasting during daylight hours in the month of Ramadan; and (5) the *hajj*, or pilgrimage to Mecca, made at least once in one's lifetime, if means permit.

The conventional Muslim is religiously observant, disciplined and sober, careful of the food laws (distinguishing *halāl* [lawful] from *harām* [forbidden]). Notably *harām* are meat not ritually slaughtered, pork, and intoxicants, but in practice tobacco, tea, and coffee are allowed. The family structure is patriarchal and closely knit, and the marriages of children are arranged by parents. Polygamy is officially discouraged on the ground

that it is practically impossible for a mere man to render the equal justice inculcated by the Koran to a plurality of wives. The Muslim temperament is characteristically serious and resigned, corresponding to a view of God's dealings with man as severe and arbitrary. But having spoken of the "conventional Muslim" we must add that so many ethnic groups and cultures are included in the Muslim family of nations that it can be misleading to speak in general terms.

### The Muslim View of Christianity.

On the one hand, Christians are respected (along with Jews) as people of Scripture, and it is permitted to eat with them and to take their daughters in marriage; on the other hand, their polytheism, their reprehensible choice of food and drink, and their permissive lifestyle are held in abhorrence. In doctrine there is so much superficial similarity—in the understanding of the nature of God; of heaven, hell, and angels; of the prophets and scriptures; of the virginal conception and sinless character of Jesus and his expected second coming—that Muslims frequently tell Christians, "We all believe the same thing; it's just that you call Jesus the Son of God, while we call him a Prophet." But beneath these similar labels there is radical disparity of content. The two distinctives of the Christian faith—the incarnation and the atonement—are most emphatically denied. Jesus did not die, but was taken up alive into heaven, while a substitute (usually believed to be Judas) was mistakenly crucified.

### Islam and the Bible.

From the Muslim point of view, Islam is coeval with the human race. Adam was the first Muslim, indeed the first prophet of Islam. Noah in turn was a great prophet, followed in due course by Abraham the friend of God, and his honored elder son and fellow prophet Ishmael, progenitor of the Arabs, from whom Muhammad was born in or around the year 570 of the Christian era. But from the non-Muslim point of view, Islam is seen as commencing with Muhammad, and firmly centered in his great master work, the Koran—regarded by Muslims as of eternal, quasi-divine status. (Here a basic difference from Christianity may be observed: the focus of the gospel is on its divine Founder, the NT having the secondary status of witness to him. With Islam it is the book which is divine, the Prophet being only the human instrument.) In keeping with the character of a scripture-based religion, Islam claims to be the heir of all authentic religious tradition, specifically of the biblical prophets and their books (including the NT), of which the Koran is the definitive repository. Discrepancies between the earlier scriptures and the Koran are explained as deliberate falsifications made by Jews and Christians in their own interests.

### The Roots of the Law.

The literary authorities are two books which can readily be purchased and studied by the ordinary Muslim or interested inquirer: they are the Koran and the Hadith. The Koran, hailed by Muslims as Muhammad's only miracle, is the primary and unquestioned source of authority. The Hadith is a vast assemblage of over half a million sayings attributed to the Prophet, of varying degrees of credibility, put together in writing in the 3d century A.H. (9th cent. A.D.). The Hadith is the literary embodiment of the Sunnah, the tradition of the manner of life of Muhammad. Its actual effect on belief and practice is enormous, and the critical evaluation of Hadith and the consequent refashioning of theology is perhaps the most daunting challenge which Muslim theologians face.

The concepts and processes by which orthodox Islam developed are complex. Four roots of the law are recognized. Basic to the whole structure is the Koran, which dealt in an ad hoc manner with the religious, moral, and political issues which arose during Muhammad's lifetime. But how were the sentences of the Koran to be applied by succeeding generations to new situations? In the early days, social and theological problems were tackled by individual scholars with "utmost exertion of the faculties" (*ijtihād*). The consensus (deemed unanimous) of the *salaf*—the contemporaries of Muhammad and the two succeeding generations—is termed *ijmā'*. The subjects of *ijmā'* are considered as having been settled once for all. But after the *salaf* had passed on and *ijmā'* was consolidated, *ijtihād* tended to give way to the more formal process of *qiyās* (deduction of a solution by analogy with the text of the Koran and the emergent Hadith). The "gate of *ijtihād*" was then deemed to be closed; but throughout the history of Islam various eminent scholars have claimed the right to exercise *ijtihād*. This remains at the present time as a possible instrument of reform. *Ijmā'* regulated not only the interpretation of the Koran, but gave form to the Hadith.

***Islamic Chronology.*** The decisive date for the establishment of Islam is that of the Hijra, the flight from Mecca to Yathrib (later known as Medina) in A.D. 622. The Islamic era commences from the setting up of the community in that year. The issue is complicated, however, by the fact that a lunar calendar is followed, each month commencing at the sighting of the new moon, with 12 months in the year. It follows that each year is about 11 days shorter than the solar year, and so each festival occurs that much earlier each successive year. Similarly the century is shorter; we are now in the early years of the 15th century A.H. As among Jews, the yearly festivals are the great landmarks of the year. The most important are *'īd-al-fitr* (after the Fast), *'īd-al-adḥā* (commemorating Abraham's sacrifice of his son), and *'īd-Milād-al-Nabī*, celebrating the birth of the Prophet. For the Shī'ah, the 10th of Muḥarram is

observed with tremendous zeal, with beating of breasts and self-flogging with chains, in mourning and protest at the death of Husain, in A.D. 680 at the hands of the ruling Muslim majority.

***Islamic Eschatology.*** The fifth article in the orthodox Muslim creed discusses the last day, and all credal statements ('aqā'll) from the time of Abū Ḥanifah (d. 767) on contain some elaboration of this doctrine. Muhammad himself had been greatly concerned about judgment and life after death; as a result the doctrine of last things occupies a large portion of the Koran. Topics covered include the coming day, the resurrection, the torment of the tomb, the balance, the bridge, the grand assizes, and paradise and hell. For the most part Islamic theologians have been uncomfortable about these doctrines, stating that they are to be believed simply because they are mentioned in the Koran and the traditions. Rationalistic Mu'tazilites denied their literal reality; philosophic theologians attempted to spiritualize or allegorize them; the orthodox labored to systematize the material in the sources. In the devotional literature, however, eschatology lent itself to elaborate development for purposes of edification. The favorite topics of this treatment are death and the grave, the intermediate state, the signs of the hour, resurrection, assembling for judgment, the search for an intercessor, the weighing at the balances, the bridge crossing, and the life of the blessed in paradise and of the damned in hell. A number of early tractates dealt with individual matters of eschatology, but the treatment of this subject largely formed part of larger works of edification. From the 10th century on, however, there has been a growing number of independent treatises devoted solely to these matters, such as the pseudo-Ghazalian *al-Durra al-Fākhira*, the *Tadhkira* of al-Qurtubī, Ibn Makhlūf's *al-'Ulūm Al-Fākhira*, 'Abd al-Raḥmān's *Daqā'iq al-Akhbār*, and the many little eschatological treatises of al-Suyūṭī.

***Outline of History and Division.*** The meteoric spread of Islam in the 1st century of its history was due to the enthusiasm and mental vigor of Arabs united in one faith, the weakness of the mutually hostile Byzantine and Persian empires, and the general decay of the church. Before Muhammad's death in A.D. 632, not only was the whole Arabian peninsula brought under Islam, but in its onward course all Semitic peoples except the Jews embraced Islam. Under the 'Umayyad caliphs in Damascus (from A.D. 660) and then the Abbasid caliphs in Baghdad (from A.D. 750) Islam advanced toward its climax in the splendor and intellectual brilliance of the Arab Muslim Empire in the 8th and 9th centuries, covering a great band of territory from Spain in the west over to India and Central Asia, and south into sub-Saharan Africa. In the 10th century it disintegrated, although the fiction of splendor was maintained until the Mongols sacked Baghdad in 1258 and killed the last Abbasid caliph.

The second great renaissance and expansion of Islam in the 14th century (8th cent. A.H.) occurred chiefly through the activities of Sufi traders and preachers in Turkey, Central Asia, India, China, and central Africa. Toward the close of this movement Islam was also brought to Indonesia, but had hardly begun to take root before the European colonizers took over. It is not therefore surprising that Islam in that region—although numerically very strong—has weak roots. Not to speak of the great movements in Iran, Egypt, and Syria, in the 16th century two great Muslim empires were established—the Mogul (Mongol) in Delhi and the Ottoman in Istanbul, both with pervasive Sufi influence. Neither of these survived the rise of European colonial power and ultimate domination. Yet by the middle of this century every Muslim state was once more free of foreign control.

Muslims are not impressed by claims of Christian unity. It is Islam which is one over all the earth. Yet the divisions in Islam are hard to deny, when Iran (backed by Syria and Libya) has been locked in mortal combat with Iraq (backed by Saudia Arabia, Jordan, and Egypt)—all Muslim states—since 1980. The main Muslim body is that of the Sunnis—about 90 percent of the whole. They claim to follow the *sunnah* (the orthodox traditions of the Prophet) and also to revere equally the first four caliphs. The principal minority is that of the Shi'ah, whose separatism has historical roots in the struggle for succession after the death of Muhammad.

The Sufis are the mystics of Islam. The Ahmadi sect is quite small, but has an influence out of all proportion to its numbers. They are the followers of Ghulam Ahmad Mirza (1839–1908) of Qadian in North India (hence one of their names, the Qadiani). They are strong anti-Christian polemicists, but they themselves fell on hard times in their own homeland of Pakistan, when, in 1974, the National Assembly declared them non-Muslim. This was on account of their breach of the doctrine of the finality of the prophethood of Muhammad by their ascribing prophethood—and that of an exalted nature—to Ghulam Ahmad Mirza.

Discernment should be exercised in assessing the claims of various groups to speak for Islam. For example, the Islamic Foundation in Leicester, England, is an arm of the Jama'ati-Islami—the reformist party led by Sayyid A. A. Mawdudi (d. 1979) which led the campaign to reestablish strict Islamic orthodoxy in Pakistan, and which in the past 10 years (in parallel with a movement of similar character in Iran) has been in the vanguard of the general resurgence of Islamic conservatism. Again, the influential commentary on

the Koran by Muhammad Ali represents Ahmadiyya teaching.

*Bibliography.* F. Rehman, *Islam* (1966); M. Geibels, *An Introduction to Islam*, 5 vols. (1975–77); K. Ahmad, ed., *Islam: Its Meaning and Message* (1976); A. A. Mawdudi, *Women in Islam* (1978); *Towards Understanding Islam* (1980); *The Islamic Movement* (1984); A. Cooper, *Ishmael My Brother* (1985).

ROBBIE ORR

**Israel.** The name *Eretz Yisrael* (the land of Israel) is the biblical Hebrew designation that took on the connotation of the promised land during the Second Temple period. Prior to this, there was no one name in general use that denoted the land that God had promised to give Abraham and his descendants through Isaac and Jacob. By the time of Jesus, the term *Eretz Yisrael* was widely used among the Jewish people. The Romans recognized this important link between the Jewish people and their land, the Jewish people and their God. They determined to use the Greek term *Palestine* (derived from ancient Philistia) to replace the province of Judea and the concept of Eretz Yisrael. Emperor Hadrian, after the Second Jewish Revolt (A.D. 132–135), hoped to eradicate both Jewish tradition and Jewish culture (as well as the Jewish God) by calling the area Palestine. This designation was commonly used until 1948 and the founding of the modern State of Israel. Ironically, the Jewish people in the later 19th and early 20th centuries in the Holy Land were referred to as "Palestinians."

Although banned by Roman law from even gazing upon Jerusalem after their Second Revolt, some Jews tenaciously remained in Eretz Yisrael throughout the Roman occupation. By the time the Muslims conquered Eretz Yisrael from the Christian Byzantines during a seven-year siege (A.D. 633–640), Jewish communities dotted the landscape. Most Jews, however, remained outside of Eretz Yisrael, and the desire to return to the promised land permeated the religious thought and daily prayers of traditional Judaism.

The 19th century found nearly all of the Jewish communities in Eretz Yisrael located in Jerusalem, Hebron, Safed, and Tiberias, suffering under heavy Muslim taxation by a corrupt and declining Ottoman Turkish administration. Jewish immigration in the latter 19th and early 20th centuries was stimulated by a religious zeal to settle in the promised land as well as by widespread anti-Semitism and persecution in the Western world. The rise of political Zionism gave added impetus with the belief that Jewish people would never be free as long as they lacked a legal homeland in Eretz Yisrael. Acreage was purchased in the Holy Land and reclaimed.

When the Ottoman Empire became the ally of the Germans in World War I, the British sought and gained the support of both Arabs and Jews. As the war progressed, the British promised to support the founding of an Arab state in the Middle

East. This state was to include areas of present-day Syria (east of Damascus), Iraq, and Saudi Arabia. The British also promised the Jews (in the Balfour Declaration of 1917) a national home in Palestine. Neither the Arabs nor the Jews had a state in this area, and both groups appeared to be in good rapport when the Ottoman Turks were defeated with Germany in World War I. The French and British moved into the area and carved out "mandates": the French were to control the Syria-Lebanon area; the British the Palestine and Iraq area. When the French ousted Emir Faisal (moderate leader of the Arab movement who had declared himself king of Syria), the British quickly moved to make him king of Iraq. They also created Trans-Jordan out of the Palestine mandate area west of the Jordan River and made Faisal's brother, Abdullah, king of that territory. The League of Nations approved these actions in 1922.

Radical Arabs grew alarmed at Jewish settlement and the possibility of a Jewish state. Anti-Jewish riots broke out in Jerusalem in April 1920, and to appease the nationalist Arabs, the British appointed the right-wing Palestinian Arab leader, Hajj Amin al-Husseini, to be Mufti (official expounder of Muslim law) of Jerusalem in 1921 and chairman of the Supreme Muslim Council in 1922. Anti-Jewish and anti-British, this Grand Mufti of Jerusalem was directly responsible for the horrendous anti-Jewish riots in 1929 and 1936, and for leading a full-scale rebellion against the British from 1936 to 1939. Finally, the Mufti strengthened ties with Adolf Hitler, accepted $500,000 from the Nazi leader, and used his forces to fight for the Nazis during World War II. Unfortunately, most Arabs in the Middle East declared on the side of the Nazis, because Hitler's forces were seen as liberators from the British and French Mandates.

Ultimately, the horror of the Nazi Holocaust, in which 6 million Jews were exterminated, united Jewish Zionist and non-Zionist factions with a considerable number of worldwide sympathizers to support a Jewish commonwealth in Palestine. In 1947, the United Nations Special Committee on Palestine recommended the partition of the remaining Palestine mandate to solve the Arab-Jewish conflict. During the resolution debate in the United Nations, the newly formed Arab League of Nations threatened war. Nevertheless, the United Nations on November 29, 1947, voted in favor of the partition plan, which it believed fairly divided the remaining area of the Palestine mandate along Jewish owned-Arab owned territorial lines. Both the USA and the Soviet Union endorsed the plan, while Great Britain abstained during the vote.

The Arabs firmly rejected the partition plan, as well as any future proposal for a Jewish state in Palestine, and within a week over 100 Jews were killed by Arab guerilla attacks and terrorist explosions in Palestine. In January 1948 the first detachments of the Arab Liberation Army entered Palestine from Syria and Trans-Jordan. In fear, the United Nations Security Council did not put the partition resolution into effect, but at the same time did not rescind the order. The State of Israel was formally recognized on May 14, 1948, when British rule ended.

Five Arab armies (Egypt, Syria, Trans-Jordan, Lebanon, and Iraq) with help from Arab allies such as Saudi Arabia immediately invaded Israel, claiming that they would exterminate the Jews and push them into the sea. At great personal cost, Israel won this War of Independence. The Egyptians agreed to a United Nations armistice only after Israeli fighting units were expanding territorially and moving into the Sinai. The Arab nations appear to have regarded the armistice (which required Israel to pull back to her original partition territory) as only an intermission in war. Hundreds of thousands of Jewish refugees from Arab lands and from the Holocaust poured into the new Jewish State. Hundreds of thousands of Palestinian Arabs had left Israel. The complicated Arab-Israeli conflict was not settled. This would lead to the 1956 conflict over the Suez Canal, the 1967 Six-Day War (when Israel would capture the Sinai, Gaza, West Bank, and East Jerusalem), and the 1973 Yom Kippur War.

Although nothing in history could be compared to an ancient people returning to their land after 19 centuries of enforced exile, the Jews of Israel have spent the past four decades in an atmosphere of hostility, war and siege with their Arab neighbors. Even the return of the Sinai to the Egyptians for recognition by Anwar Sadat and a peace treaty resulted in Sadat's assassination and unbelievable pressures on his successor, Hosni Mubarak, to scrap the treaty.

Internally the pressures mount as well. Before the Six-Day War there were approximately 220,000 Arabs in Israel. When East Jerusalem was captured during the Jordanian attack, 55,000 Muslim Arabs and 12,000 Christian Arabs were added to Israel proper. By the 1973 Yom Kippur War, Arabs were 15 percent of the population; in 1986, they were 17 percent of the population; and by the year 2000 projections are that they will be 22 percent of the population (Israeli Jews growing to 4.1 million; Israeli Arabs growing to 1.2 million). One-half of these Arabs are youths under age 14, generally dedicated to Palestinian nationalism and the elimination of the Jewish state of Israel. Added to this are the explosive situations in the Gaza strip and the West Bank, where an additional 1.2 million Arabs live. The Palestinian Arab "intifada" of the latter 1980s is testimony to the volatile nature of the tensions in Eretz Yisrael.

In spite of this, Israel is the only democracy in the Middle East. Israel's parliament, or Knesset (Hebrew for "assembly"), is the supreme authority in the Jewish State for a four-year period. It can only dissolve itself and call new elections before the four-year term is up if the majority of its members "lose confidence" in the way the government is being run. The 120 representatives to the Knesset (MK's—Members of the Knesset) are elected for four-year terms and must be 21 years of age. Judges, civil servants, rabbis paid by the state, active army officers, and other officials are not permitted to run for office.

Every citizen over the age of 18 is eligible to vote, and the country is treated as one district. Any political party, group, or individual may submit a list of candidates for the Knesset, provided the group or individual obtains the signatures of 750 citizens. This includes Arab citizens, and there are Arab representatives in the Knesset. Nevertheless, one of the problems Israeli Arabs have is that if they accept citizenship, they are looked upon as traitors to the Arab cause. Israeli voters choose from the many submitted national lists of political candidates (each list containing 120 names). The 120 Knesset seats are distributed according to the percentage of votes each list obtains. For example, if the Likud party receives 40 percent of the national vote for its list of candidates, the first 48 names (40 percent of 120) on its list become members of the Knesset. If one of those members resigns or dies, the next person on the list automatically takes his or her place. Because this system encourages a large number of parties (it is not uncommon to vote on 20 lists), coalitions are needed to gain a majority of seats in the Knesset. In Israel, a president is elected by the Knesset, but he is mainly a ceremonial figure. The key leader is the prime minister, who is the leader able to form a majority coalition.

Because Israel is a Jewish state, most Israeli Jews believe Judaism is entirely relevant to public order and to Israel's political system. Judaism is not separated from the state, and Jewish religious tradition provides Israel's political symbols for official state ceremonies. The close relationship stems from the inability to separate the Jewish state from Jewish nationality, rather than from legal favoritism of individual Jews over non-Jews. This certainly does not mean that most Israelis favor the imposition of *halakhah* (the collected legal rulings of the scribes) by the Orthodox religious establishment. On the contrary, Israeli definitions of Jews, Judaism, and Jewish law are hotly debated.

For most Israeli Jews, Jewish identity transcends a religious identity. It is a peoplehood. Non-Jewish religions, however, are accorded full rights. Muslim and Christian religious courts are recognized by Israel and are given exclusive judicial authority in matters of their members' "personal status"—marriage and divorce. This extends to the Temple Mount, where Jerusalem police have standing orders not to let Jews pray on the Temple Mount because of the offense it would give to Muslims.

Creativity has flourished in the State of Israel. The country is blessed with some of the finest musicians, scholars, scientists, archeologists, and doctors in the world. Kibbutzim and development towns have turned the desert into productive fields and gardens. It has been a haven for refugees around the world and, currently, the people of Israel are sacrificing to provide homes for hundreds of thousands of Russian Jews who are allowed finally to leave the Soviet Union because of the glasnost reforms of the 1980s. A kaleidoscope of opinions, Israel is mindful of her special 4000-year heritage. The mind-set, rugged individualism, and pride of the Israeli can never be severed from the events and lessons of four millennia of historical experience, including the sobering losses and hopeful gains of four decades of modern statehood.

*Bibliography.* W. Laqueur and B. Rubin, eds., *The Israel-Arab Reader*(4th rev. ed., 1984); H. M. Sachar, *A History of Israel: From the Rise of Zionism to Our Time* (1986); C. H. Voss and D. A. Rausch, *American Jewish Archives* 40 (1988): 41–81.

DAVID A. RAUSCH

**Italy.** Independent republic in southern Europe covering 301,225 sq. km. (116,304 sq. mi.). Its population in 1985 was 56.3 million of which 47.1 million (83.6 percent) were Roman Catholic, 225,000 were Protestants, and 45,000 (0.1 percent) were Muslims.

Christianity came to Italy during the apostolic age. Italians were present at the birth of the church at Pentecost. The Book of Romans was written to an existing church in that city about A.D. 56/57. In about A.D. 60 Paul arrived in Rome (Acts 28:15). He suffered martyrdom there, and many believe that Peter also met his death in Rome.

In 324 Constantine officially recognized Christianity as the state religion, and the emperor moved his capital to Constantinople. This left a power vacuum in Rome, which was filled by the Lombards and Goths from the North. In 476 the city was sacked and the emperor deposed. This is sometimes regarded as the fall of the Roman Empire; the process had, however, been going on for several centuries.

As the political power of Rome waned, the religious power escalated. As bishop of Rome, Damasus (366–384) asserted that Peter had been buried in Rome. Leo the Great (440–461) claimed Petrien power over the church in general, and traced this power backward through Peter to Christ on the basis of Matt. 16:18. Gregory the Great (590–604) undertook to christianize the barbarians of northern Europe, and sent the missionary Augustine to England. Sylvester (314–335) received the "Donation of Constantine," which granted the bishops of Rome territorial sovereignty over much of the Italian peninsula. (This so-called Donation of Constantine was, however, proven to be a forgery by Lorenzo Valla in the 15th century.) This "donation" was discovered, and probably written, in the 8th century.

In 1054 Constantinople and Rome were separated from each other. The Orthodox and Catholic churches went their own way. Two Italian reformers were at the forefront. Peter Waldo's followers became the Waldensians of southern France and northern Italy, and there are still 29,413 members of that community (1985). Another Italian voice of the Reformation was Girolamo Savonarola (1452–1498), whose reforms in Florence were cruelly crushed.

In the 19th century the face of Italian Catholicism changed dramatically. The period between the Congress of Vienna (1815) and the Liberation of Rome (1870) is called "Risorgimento." At the dawn of the 19th century, the vast majority of the Italian peninsula was under the control of the Vatican. When the revolutions of 1848 swept Europe, the pope resisted this democratic movement. However, by 1870 the geographical control of the Vatican had been successfully limited to the small plot of land called the Vatican and Castel Gandelfo, the summer residence of the popes.

In the face of this loss of temporal power, the popes tried to bolster their spiritual power. Gregory XVI (1831–46) restored the Inquisition to crush non-Catholic ideas and movements. Pius IX (1846–78) promulgated the Immaculate Conception of Mary (1854), issued the Syllabus of Errors (1864), and summoned the First Vatican Council (1869–70), which gave official approval to the dogma of papal infallibility. Nevertheless, these doctrinal bulwarks could not withstand the wind of change in the modern world.

The decline in the spiritual power of the Vatican was initiated by the Second Vatican Council (1962–65). Attendance at Mass has declined to 20 to 25 percent, depending on what part of Italy one considers. The Roman Catholic Church could claim 99.6 percent of all Italians in the year 1900; now that percentage has fallen to 83.6 percent. The gains have not come to Protestantism, but rather to irreligion and apathy. In 1900, 50,000 claimed they were irreligious and 10,000 said they were atheists. Now 5,820,400 (10.6 percent) say they are irreligious and 1,265,500 profess to be atheists.

Although the Roman Catholic Church still dominates the religious life of Italy, Protestantism has gained a respectable foothold since the mid-19th century. In 1848 religious liberty was a popular principle in Europe, and the revolution of 1848 issued in tolerance for the Waldensian Church. In 1953 there were 26,297 Waldensians in Italy, and that number has grown only marginally to the present figure of 29,413. The emigration of Waldensians to Uruguay in 1856 and 1860, and to North Carolina in 1893, has kept the movement small. Furthermore, there appears to be little evangelism to draw in new members. The major cause of growth is biological.

In 1861 the Wesleyan type of Methodism was established in Italy. This was followed by the episcopal form of Methodism from America in 1873. By 1946 these two branches merged to form the Evangelical Methodist Church in Italy. In all the church numbered 7000 in 1953. By 1985 that religious community had shrunk to 6000.

Baptist missionaries came from England in 1866, and were joined by American Baptist missionaries in 1870. However, the Southern Baptist Convention took over the entire movement in 1923. Altogether there were 9000 Baptists in 1953. The community had grown to 10,000 by 1985.

Other Protestant movements in Italy are the International Evangelical Church (15,000), New Apostolic Church (20,000), Greek Orthodox Church (25,000), and Churches of Christ (6000). The Jehovah's Witnesses in Italy claim a total membership of 80,000.

Several third world movements have also opened headquarters in Italy. From Korea has come the Holy Spirit Association for the Unification of World Christianity and from Nigeria the Christ Apostolic Church.

Citywide evangelistic activities have traditionally been carried on by North American missionaries. Among the most well-known thrusts have been Billy Graham's brief Turin Crusade in 1967, the Conservative Baptist Foreign Mission Society campaign in Naples in 1968, and the Southern Baptist Crusade in all of Italy in 1968.

As immigrants have come to Italy, non-Christian religions have also appeared. For instance, in 1900 there were 1000 Muslims in Italy, but by 1985 there were 45,000 (0.1 percent). There were no Buddhists in Italy in 1900; now, however, there are 2050. There were no Baha'is in 1900, but now 4400 live in Italy.

The Jewish population has remained comparatively stable over the past century. In 1900 the Jewish community numbered 35,000. Even with the emigration from the Soviet Union into Italy, there are still only 38,900 Jews. Many Soviet Jews use Italy as a waystation on their way to Israel.

Many North American missionaries are at work in Italy. Greater Europe Mission has 21, Conservative Baptists have 19, Bible Christian Union has 19, Campus Crusade for Christ has 18, European Christian Mission has 11, and European Missionary Fellowship has three. Because of the freedom to broadcast by radio in Italy, several major radio missions have entered that country. Among them are HCJB, European Christian Mission, and Gospel Missionary Union. By 1986 there were 80 religious broadcasting stations in Italy.

**Bibliography.** A. C. Jemelo, *Church and State in Italy* (1960); *Dati Statici Dela Diocesi Italione* (1967); E. R. Hedlund, *The Protestant Movement in Italy* (1970).

WAYNE DETZLER

**Ivory Coast.** *See* WEST AFRICA.

**Jacks, Laurence Pearsall** (1860–1955). Unitarian. Born in Nottingham and educated at the University of London, Manchester College, Nottingham, and Harvard, he entered the ministry as assistant to Stopford Brooke in 1887. He ministered in Liverpool and Birmingham. He became professor of philosophy, Manchester College (1903), and principal of Manchester College (1915–31). He was the editor of the *Hibbert Journal* from its foundation in 1902 to his retirement in 1947. He wrote *Life and Letters of Stopford Brooke, The Legends of Smokeover, Constructive Citizenship* (1927), *The Education of the Whole Man* (1931), *Elemental Religion* (1934), *The Confessions of an Octogenarian* (1942), *A Living Universe, The Challenge of Life, Religious Perplexities*, and numerous other books, including translation of works by A. Loisy.

F. W. DILLISTONE

**Jackson, Frederick John Foakes.** *See* FOAKES-JACKSON, FREDERICK JOHN.

**Jackson, Samuel Macauley** (1851–1912). Presbyterian. Born in New York City, he studied at the College of the City of New York, Princeton Theological Seminary, Union Theological Seminary, and abroad. Ordained in 1876 he served as pastor of the Presbyterian Church, Norwood, N.J., and was professor of church history at New York University (1895–1912). He was president of the board of trustees of the Canton Christian College in China and an honorary fellow of the Huguenot Society of London, having edited the Papers and Proceedings of the Huguenot Society of America (*Tercentenary of the Edict of Nantes*, 1899, and additional volumes in 1902 and 1904). Much of his life was devoted to literary work. He was a member of the publication committee of the Ecumenical Missionary Conference held in New York (1900) and edited a *Missionary Bibliography* and the *Report of the Centenary Conference on the Protestant Missions of the World* (1888). His major publications include *The Latin Works and the Correspondence of Huldreich Zwingli, together with Selections from his German Works, in English Translation* (vol. 1, 1912), *Zwingli's Selections* (1901), *Huldreich Zwingli* (Heroes of the Reformation Series) (1901), and *The Source of Jerusalem the Golden and other pieces attributed to Bernard of Cluny* (1910). He was editor-in-chief of the *New Schaff-Herzog Encyclopedia of Religious Knowledge* (12 vols., 1907–11); associate editor of the 1884 edition; assistant editor of *Schaff's Bible Dictionary* (1880); editor for religious literature in *Johnson's Universal Cyclopaedia* (1893–95, 1900); editor of the department of religion in *New International Encyclopaedia* (1902–4), and joint editor of *Cyclopaedia of Living Divines* (1887). He also edited the *Concise Dictionary of Religious Knowledge* (1891), *Heroes of the Reformation* (1898–1906), church terms in *Standard Dictionary* (1895), and the *New International Dictionary* (1900).

RAYMOND W. ALBRIGHT

**Jacobs, Charles Michael** (1875–1938). Lutheran. Born in Gettysburg, Pa., he studied at the University of Pennsylvania, the Lutheran Theological Seminary at Mt. Airy and Philadelphia, and did graduate study at Pennsylvania and Leipzig. Ordained to the Lutheran ministry in 1899, he served pastorates at St. Peter's Church, North Wales, Pa. (1899–1904), and Christ Church, Allentown, Pa. (1904–13). He became professor of church history and director of the graduate school at the Lutheran Seminary, Philadelphia (1913–38; president, 1927–38). He was coeditor of *Luther's Works in English* (6 vols., 1915–32), and (with Preserved Smith) *Luther's Correspondence*, vol. 2 (1916). He also wrote *The Way—A Little Book of Christian Truth* (1922) and *The Story of the Church—An Outline of Its History* (1925), and translated W. Elert, *An Outline of Christian Doctrine* (1926).

RAYMOND W. ALBRIGHT

**Jacobs, Henry Eyster** (1844–1932). American Lutheran scholar. Born in Gettysburg, Pa., he

449

graduated from Pennsylvania College, Gettysburg, and Gettysburg Theological Seminary, and was a tutor at Pennsylvania College (1864–67). He was then pastor and principal of Thiel Hall, Phillipsburg, Pa. (now Thiel College, Greenville) (1868–70); professor of Latin and history (1870–80), classics (1880–81), and Greek (1881–83) at Pennsylvania College; and professor of systematic theology at Lutheran Theological Seminary, Philadelphia (1883–1932), of which he became dean (1894–1920) and president (1920–27). His own books include *The Lutheran Movement in England during the Reigns of Henry VIII and Edward VI, and Its Literary Monuments* (1891), *A History of the Evangelical Lutheran Church in the United States* (1893), *Elements of Religion* (1894), *Martin Luther, the Hero of the Reformation, 1483-1546* (1898; repr., 1973), *German Emigration to America, 1709-1740* (1899), *Summary of the Christian Faith* (1905), and *Lincoln's Gettysburg World Message* (1920). He edited *The Lutheran Review* (1882–1896) and, among other volumes, *The Lutheran Commentary* (13 vols., 1895–99), to which he contributed the sections on Romans and 1 Corinthians, and *The Lutheran Cyclopaedia* (1899).

**Jacquier, Eugene** (1847–1932). French Roman Catholic scholar. Born in Vienne, he was ordained in 1871 and studied at Lyons (Th. D., 1891). He was professor of biblical studies, Catholic faculties, Lyons (1894–1927). His works include *Histoire des livres du Nouveau Testament* (4 vols., 2d ed., 1903; ET, *History of the Books of the NT*, vol. 1, 1907), *Le Nouveau Testament dans l'Eglise chrétienne* (2 vols., 1911–13), *Etudes de critique et de philologie du Nouveau Testament* (1920), and *Les Actes des Apôtres* (Etudes Bibliques) (1926).

OTTO A. PIPER

**Jainism.** Ancient Indian religion with 3.2 million adherents (1981) living mostly in the states of Gujarat, Rajasthan, and Karnataka. Jainism recognizes 24 Tirthankaras or leaders; the 24th Tirthankara, Mahavira, was an older contemporary of Gautama Buddha. Even though Jainism existed before the time of Mahavira, he was the one who made it a strong religious movement during the 6th century B.C.

The Jainist concept of *ahimsa* (noninjury) opposes any killing of animals—even insects. It began as a protest movement against the mass sacrifice of animals practiced by the ancient Hindus. Contemporary Vedic Hindus no longer follow the custom of sacrificing birds and animals, and even in popular Hinduism the incidence of animal sacrifice has declined; it is in fact prohibited by law in India. Since *ahimsa* is a fundamental precept of Jainism, Jains do not consume meat and laypersons prefer professions where they can practice *ahimsa*. Money lending and trading are preferred professions.

There are many features that distinguish Jainism from Vedic Hinduism. Jainism rejects the authority of the *Vedas*, disapproves of bloody sacrifices, prescribes asceticism, allows women to become nuns, and allows nudity of monks. Jains do worship Hindu gods, mostly on festive occasions. Jainism is classified along with Buddhism as a heterodox religion, as opposed to Hinduism which is an orthodox religion. Jainism does not maintain that death is the end of life and that nothing exists after death. It believes in the doctrine of *karma* and in the transmigration of souls as does orthodox Hinduism.

The Jain community is divided into two main sects—the Svetambaras and the Digambaras—and each is divided in turn into many subsects. The Digambara monks have practiced nudity from the days of Mahavira, and the images of Jain saints are shown in the nude, either standing or seated.

Jain monks once lived in caverns around Madurai, the capital of the ancient Pandya kingdom, and they have left the earliest known inscriptions in the Tamil-Brahmi script. The Jains made valuable literary contributions to Tamil and Telugu. Ethical works such as Naladiyar, poetic works such as Jivakacintamani, and grammatical works such as Nannul and Neminatham represent some of their contributions to Tamil literature. Cave painting, illustrated manuscripts, and carvings of Tirthankaras and Gomateswara are examples of their contribution to Indian art.

In South India, the Jains suffered religious persecution during the 8th and 9th centuries and again during the 12th century, which led to a great reduction in their numbers. Discarded statues of seated Tirthankaras are now worshiped as Muniswara or holy men by simple village folk.

Even though the Jains form less than half a percent of the Indian population, they play an important role as financiers, educators, and entrepreneurs.

**Bibliography.** S. Stevenson, *The Heart of Jainism* (1915); M. S. Ramaswami Ayyangar and B. Seshagiri Rao, *Studies in South Indian Jainism* (1922); K. K. Dixit, *Jaina Ontology* (1971); N. R. Gusev, *Jainism* (1971); R. S. Gupte, *Iconography of the Hindus, Buddhists and Jains* (1972); S. Gopalan, *Outlines of Jainism* (1975).

GIFT SIROMONEY

**Jamaica.** *See* WEST INDIES.

**James, Edwin Oliver** (1888–1972). Anglican cleric and professor. Born in London and educated at the universities of Oxford and London, he was ordained in the Church of England in 1911 and served various parishes, mainly in London and Oxford. The last of these he combined with a lectureship in anthropology at Cambridge (1928–33). He was professor of the history and philosophy of religion at Leeds University (1933–45), at King's College, London (1945–48), and at London (1948–55). He was president of the Folk-Lore Society (1930–32) and edited its journal. His publications include *Primitive Ritual and Belief* (1917), *Introduction to Anthropology* (1920), *Origins of Sacrifice* (1933), *Christian Myth* (1933), *The Social Function of Religion* (1940), *The Concept of Deity* (1950), *Marriage and Society* (1952), *The Nature and Function of Priesthood* (1955), *The History of Religions* (1956), *Myth and Ritual in the Ancient Near East* (1958), *Sacrifice and Sacrament* (1962), *Christianity and Other Religions* (1967), and *Creation and Cosmology* (1969). He was a contributor to encyclopedias and dictionaries.

## James, Epistle of. *Authorship and Date.*

These two matters together constitute one of the most vexing questions of NT scholarship. Tradition ascribes the epistle to James, the Lord's brother, known also as James the Just; but many dispute this ascription. One difficulty is that not until Origen (c. 185–254) is there a clear reference to the book having been written by James and regarded as Scripture. The Western Church did not completely accept the epistle until the Synod of Hippo (A.D. 393) and the Third Council of Carthage (A.D. 397).

An examination of the internal evidence for date and authorship must begin with the claim to authorship in 1:1. The very simplicity of this greeting lends support (against theories of pseudonymity or that another James was the author) to the traditional authorship. It finds further support in the "Jewishness" of the epistle as a whole. Indeed, so Jewish is the epistle that some claim that it is not essentially Christian at all, although it may have had a Christian redactor. But such suggestions must be rejected in the light of the epistle's affinities with other NT literature and its probable allusions to the (preliterary) words of Jesus (e.g., 1:2 compared with Matt. 5:10–12; 1:4 with Matt. 5:48; 1:5, 17 with Matt. 7:7–11; 1:6 with Matt. 8:23–26; 1:22 with Matt. 7:21–27; 2:10 with Matt. 5:19; 3:18 with Matt. 5:9; 4:4 with Matt. 6:24; 4:12 with Matt. 7:1 and 10:28; 5:10 with Matt. 5:12, and 5:12 with Matt. 5:34–37).

For all its Jewishness the epistle represents some of the best Greek in the NT, and it is possible that the author read the OT in the LXX rather than in the Hebrew. Yet the Hellenism of the epistle does not go beyond what could be expected of a Palestinian Jew and a Galilean in particular, and it certainly does not rule out James as the author. He may have used an amanuensis. Other considerations bearing on the date and the authorship are the epistle's lack of an explicit Christology, its primitive ecclesiology (Jewish-sounding references to the church), and its lack of a missionary concern. These are best accounted for by an early date and the apparent situation of its readers. The discussion of faith and works in James 2:14–26 is not inconsistent with such a date. In short, there is more reason to retain than to reject the traditional authorship of the epistle by James, the Lord's brother, and, on this basis, it may well be the earliest book in the NT, composed c. A.D. 45, not long after Paul had begun preaching at Antioch. James may have wished to clarify Paul's teaching on faith and works, which was still largely misunderstood and misrepresented.

***Destination and Purpose.*** The epistle was probably written from Jerusalem to the church in Judea. Evidently those addressed were passing through a time of severe trial (James 1:1–18). They were being persecuted and dragged before the courts (2:6). The name of Jesus was blasphemed by their enemies (2:7). It may well be that the persecution in question was that instigated by Herod Agrippa I (Acts 12). In view of their trials, the readers are encouraged to patience (5:7–11), being reminded that there is a divine purpose behind what was happening (1:1–4, 12). But, at the same time they are rebuked for their love of money (4:13–5:6), their profession without practice (1:22–27; 2:14–26), their partiality (2:1–13), and their argumentativeness (3:1–18). The epistle is practical rather than doctrinal, concerned to teach its readers how to bear their troubles bravely and to live worthily.

***Bibliography.*** *Commentaries.* C. L. Mitton, *The Epistle of James* (1966); J. B. Adamson, *The Epistle of James* in NICNT (1976); B. Reicke, *The Epistles of James, Peter, and Jude* (1982); S. Laws, *A Commentary on the Epistle of James* (1986).

*Studies.* K. L. Carroll, *BJRL* 44 (1961); K. G. Eckart, *TLZ* 89 (1964); C. E. B. Cranfield, *SJT* 18 (1965); J. A. Brooks, *SWJTh* 12 (1969); P. B. R. Forbes, *EvQ* 44 (1972); A. W. Argyle, *NTS* 20 (1973); H. P. Hamann, *LuthThJ* 9 (1975); P. H. Davids, *Scripture, Tradition, and Interpretation* (1978).

DAVID JOHN WILLIAMS

## James, Fleming (1877–1959). Episcopalian OT

scholar. Born in Gambier, Ohio, he studied at the University of Pennsylvania (Ph.D., 1899) and at the Philadelphia Divinity School. He was deacon at a small church in Philadelphia (1901/2); priest at the Church of Our Saviour in Shangahai, China (1902–6), and St. Anna's Mission in Philadelphia (1906–12); and rector of St. Paul's, Englewood, N.J. (1912–21). He was professor of OT literature and interpretation at Berkeley Divinity School (1921–40), and taught OT at Yale Divinity School. He was dean of the School of Theology, University of the South, Sewanee, Tenn. (1940–47). Thereafter he served as executive director of the OT section of the Revised Standard Bible Committee until its publication in 1952. He was coauthor of *The Beginnings of Our*

*Religion* (1935) and author of *Thirty Psalmists* (1938) and *Personalities of the OT* (1939).

JOSEPH FLETCHER

**James, William** (1842–1910). American psychologist and philosopher. Born in New York, he studied in private schools, then at the Lawrence Scientific School and the Harvard Medical School (M.D., 1869). After having suffered mental illness, he recovered in 1872 and began a teaching career at Harvard. He held various posts in philosophy, anatomy, and physiology at Harvard where he also became professor of philosophy (1885–89), psychology (1889–97), and philosophy again from 1897. He held a position in the front rank of modern psychologists, and in this field exercised a potent influence both in Europe and America. In philosophy he represented what may be called empirical idealism, as opposed to absolute idealism. In his radical empiricism he accepted religious phenomena as real experience, making extensive use of analytical psychology. In his famous *The Will to Believe* (1897) he propounded the thesis that when we are faced with two undemonstrable alternatives, the course of wisdom is to choose tentatively the one that reflects our hopes rather than our fears, and to act as if it were true. His works have been widely translated, and are characterized by keen analysis, apt illustration, lucid exposition, and a charm of style rarely encountered in works on philosophy. Among his other works were *The Principles of Psychology* (2 vols., 1890), *Human Immortality: Two Supposed Objections to the Doctrine* (1898), *Talks to Students on Psychology, and to Teachers on Some of Life's Ideals* (1899), *Varieties of Religious Experience: A Study in Human Nature* (1902), *Pragmatism: A New Name for Some Old Ways of Thinking* (1907), and *Pluralistic Universe* (1909). In 1908 a volume of *Essays Philosophical and Psychological* was published in his honor in New York.

**Japan.** Northern Pacific island nation occupying 372,197 sq. km. (143,706 sq. mi.). The 120 million Japanese who inhabit four major islands off the coast of East Asia and who operate the world's second largest economy are a profoundly religious people possessing a rich and varied religious tradition. Despite the outward trappings of secularism, particularly among the young, the lives of nearly all Japanese involve socially mandatory rituals of an essentially religious nature. Society requires that families contribute financial support to local religious institutions and festivals, and the major stages of life—birth, puberty, marriage, death, and remembrance—are marked by ceremonies rooted in the Shinto and Buddhist faiths. Moreover, the rules for social intercourse are based on the precepts of Confucianism.

While Western faiths posit a singular supreme deity and a unique, authoritative holy book, in Japanese religion there are multiple deities and many scriptures. Ritual impurity and consciousness of human imperfection replace the preoccupation with sin as disobedience against the will of a supreme god. The Japanese have a clear sense of the separation from fellow human beings and from the *kami* (deities) which is caused by such impurities as sickness and death, and religious rituals are offered to remedy these defects. Worship takes place in conjunction with seasonal festivals and celebration of significant points in the lifecycle rather than on a weekly holy day. The lengthy New Year celebration brings crowds to Shinto shrines and Buddhist temples, and most homes mark the summer Bon festival of the dead. While religious exclusivity is positively appraised in the West, the Japanese value the complementarity of religious traditions. Hence it is common for a person to be married in a Shinto ceremony, conduct mundane affairs in accordance with Confucian rules of behavior, and be buried with Buddhist rites—all with a sense of wholeness rather than contradiction.

***Shinto.*** Shinto ("the way of the gods") is an animistic faith, the only such cult to maintain mainstream status in one of the world's technological societies. It is the indigenous religion of Japan, although its systematization through the accretion of ritual, a priesthood, icons, and buildings for worship in the 6th and 7th centuries A.D. involved the ingesting of a great deal of continental and Buddhist influence. Shinto is practiced only in Japan; 20th-century efforts to export it to Taiwan, Korea, Manchuria, and the Pacific islands came to naught with the collapse of the empire in 1945. Rooted in the cycles of agriculture, Shinto is closely associated with the imperial family and the ethos of Japanese-ness, and hence has served as a tool for nativist and nationalistic movements from ancient times to the present day.

Early Shinto involved the veneration of *kami* thought to inhabit such imposing phenomena as mountains, rivers, waterfalls, aged trees, and wind. Related to this was the concept of sacred space; shrine ground was usually fenced or roped off and located close to special natural objects. Later, the *torii* gateway formed the entrance to such precincts. In such purified places divinities were called upon and their powers invoked to safeguard the essentials of life—fertility, health, and favorable weather. Suppliants ritually purified themselves by rinsing their mouth and hands with water. Ceremonies marked sacred time, and rites and prayers were gradually codified over the course of history. Food offerings formed the center of each ceremony; products of the sea, rivers, plains, and mountains were presented to the spirits.

As Shinto absorbed many of the concepts and practices of the more sophisticated Buddhism, the two faiths became, at times, almost indistinguishable. Shinto *kami* were regarded as Japanese manifestations of Buddhist saints, and rites to the gods and the Buddha were practiced in the same edifices. In the early Meiji period (1868–1912), there was a forced separation of the religions as part of the nativist movement to elevate the imperial family as an ethereal focus of national loyalty. Formally shorn of governmental subsidy and regulation as a consequence of postwar reforms, Shinto today supplies the rituals for the felicitous, productive aspects of life. Marriages, harvest festivals, and dedications of new buildings typically incorporate Shinto ceremonies.

**Buddhism.** Nearly a millennium after the followers of the original Buddha in India founded the religion, Buddhism flowed into Japan in its Mahayana form from China. The new faith, rich in literary, philosophical, artistic, and architectural achievement, rode the tide of the expansive culture of China's Tang Dynasty. A Korean king is said to have sent sutras and images to the Yamato court in A.D. 552, although a slightly earlier date is likely. Buddhism flourished under the sponsorship of Empress Suiko and her devout regent Prince Shotoku (574–622) who lectured on the sutras and established many monasteries, including the notable Horyuji in Nara. During the Nara period (710–794), Buddhism became the state religion and imposing new temples reflected the prestige of the imperial court. Also from China came the sectarian proclivities of Buddhism, and by the 13th century all the major sects of contemporary Japanese Buddhism were established in Japan: the Tendai sect, the Shingon sect, Zen, the Pure Land sects, and the Nichiren sect. The Pure Land sects (Jodo), which emphasize salvation in an afterlife attained through faith in the vow of the Amida Buddha, has the greatest number of adherents today.

Japanese Buddhism has a number of unique features. While Indian and Chinese Buddhism tends to be reclusive, the Japanese variety has emphasized human relations and institutions. Worship of the founders of the various sects is widespread. Japanese Buddhism tends to be non-rationalistic, intuitively reciting invocations without developing grand doctrinal systems—even though Japan for most of the 20th century has been the world center for Buddhist scholarship. Japanese Buddhism also tends to equate the real world with the absolute Buddha, thus lacking an ideological, reformist impulse. Hence, among the Japanese—the majority of whom formally identify themselves as Buddhists—the sutras and scriptures are treated as empty formulas and the teachings of the faith are not morally compelling. Buddhist-based new religion such as Soka Gakkai

are seeking to restore vitality to the faith and apply its precepts to such issues as world order, local and national politics, and human suffering.

**Christianity.** The 16th century brought Jesuit Christianity and Spanish missionary Francis Xavier to Japan along with European firearms and recent scientific discoveries. The Catholic faith spread rapidly in an interregnum period dominated by warring local lords. Aided by mass conversions decreed by sympathetic *daimyo*, a church of perhaps 300,000 baptized adherents and a growing native priesthood was established by 1600. After the Tokugawa shoguns consolidated national political hegemony, however, the foreign faith was viewed as potentially subversive, and was brutally suppressed and virtually wiped out by the state. The prevention of Christian evangelization was one motive behind the Tokugawa policy of national isolation which prevailed until the mid-19th century.

When Japan's doors were forced open to the West in the 1850s, French priests and American and British Protestant missionaries reintroduced Christianity to Japan. After anti-Christian edicts were dismantled in 1873, new churches spread and a number of Christian schools—some of which evolved into influential private universities—were founded. As in the case of Buddhism's introduction in the 6th century, Christianity in the 1870s and 1880s rode the tide of an advanced foreign civilization. Progressive Japanese regarded the Christian faith as an essential energizer of Western science and industrialization. In the early 20th century, Japanese social and political activists were attracted to Christianity as a basis for the democratic spirit. Many prominent Japanese intellectuals and socialists in the 1920s began their careers as Christians.

Despite another surge of popularity in the unsettled post-World War II years, Christianity has never grown beyond a tiny minority in modern Japan. Statistics from 1980 showed 973,340 Christians—a little under one percent of the population—roughly one-third Roman Catholic and two-thirds Protestant. The Christian movement remains on the periphery of Japanese society, particularly in the world of business where few Christian leaders are found. Christianity's failure to become mainstream is attributable both to the unwillingness of Japanese culture to admit the alien system (particularly with its Euro-American additives) and to the sectarian tendency of Japanese Christians to segregate themselves, even from other Christians, within their own churches and denominations.

**Bibliography.** J. M. Kitagawa, *Religion in Japanese History* (1966); R. H. Drummond, *A History of Christianity in Japan* (1971); S. D. B. Picken, *Shinto: Japan's Spiritual Roots* (1980); J. M. Phillips, *From the Rising of the Son: Christians and Society in Contemporary Japan* (1981); S. D. B. Picken, *Buddhism: Japan's Cultural Identity* (1982); *Christianity and Japan: Meeting,*

*Conflict, Hope* (1983); J. M. Kitagawa, *On Understanding Japanese Religion* (1987).

THOMAS W. BURKMAN

**Jaspers, Karl Theodor** (1883–1969). German existentialist philosopher. Born in Oldenburg, he early forsook law for medicine, which he studied at the universities of Berlin, Göttingen, and Heidelberg. He was a research assistant at the psychiatric clinic in Heidelberg, a voluntary post filled for six years without salary. Concerned by the imbalance created because of the current concentration on diagnosis, he labored to articulate principles of psychopathology, and in 1913 broke new ground in psychiatric studies by the publication of his *Allgemeine Psychopathologie*. Hailed as a remarkable work for a young man, its significance was underlined in an English translation more than half a century later (*General Psychopathology* [1965]). In 1916 he was appointed professor of psychology at Heidelberg, but his increasing interest in philosophy was reflected in his *Psychologies der Weltanschauungen* (1919), and he transferred to the chair of philosophy in 1921. Further works followed as he expanded his existentialist views, notably the three-volume *Philosophie* (1932). With Hitler's rise to power, Jaspers' opposition to National Socialism, and the fact that his wife was Jewish, greatly inhibited his university position, leading to his removal from it and a ban that prevented further publication of his work. In the postwar years he gave himself to the rebuilding of the universities and to the moral transformation of society. That the German people had a collective culpability for the Nazi years was a deeply held view expressed in *Die Schuldfrage* (1946), rendered into English the following year as *The Question of German Guilt*. An ambivalent reception to this led Jaspers to accept a chair of philosophy at Basel in 1948. When further criticism of Germany met with resentment he became a Swiss national in 1967. Among his many books were some on theological topics, showing his dislike for dogmatic Christianity. They included *Nietzsche and Christianity* (1946), *The Perennial Scope of Theology* (1948), and *Myth and Christianity* (1954).

CARSTEN PETER THIEDE

**Jefferson, Charles Edward** (1860–1937). Congregational pastor and writer. Born in Cambridge, Ohio, he was educated at Ohio Wesleyan University. He later was superintendent of public schools in Worthington, Ohio (1882–84), and then studied at the School of Theology at Boston University (1884–87). He was then pastor of the Central Congregational Church, Chelsea, Mass. (1887–98), before beginning his long ministry at the Broadway Tabernacle, New York City (1898–1937). He also served widely beyond his denomination, and was known as one of the great preachers of his day. His books include *Quiet Talks with Earnest People in My Study* (1898), *Things Fundamental* (1903), *Faith and Life* (1905), *The Minister as Prophet* (1905), *Character of Jesus* (1908), *The Building of the Church* (1910), *Why We May Believe in Life after Death* (1911), *The Minister as Shepherd* (1912), *Old Truths and New Facts* (1918), *The Character of Paul* (1923), *Cardinal Ideas of Isaiah* (1925), *Cardinal Ideas of Jeremiah* (1928), *Christianizing a Nation* (1929), and *Like a Trumpet* (1934).

RAYMOND W. ALBRIGHT

**Jehovah's Witnesses.** Religious movement begun by Charles Taze Russell (b. 1852) in Pittsburg, Pa. Its earliest roots stem from a Bible class he organized in 1868. At first commonly known as Russellites, the group adopted their present name in 1931. Under Adventist influence, Russell came to believe that Christ would return in 1914. The formation of the Bible class eventually led to the publication of a magazine, *Zion's Watch Tower and Herald of Christ's Presence* in 1879 and the organization of the Zion's Watch Tower Tract Society in 1884. The society's avid distribution of literature and aggressive witnessing set up an active antagonism between it and the established churches which continues unabated to the present. Nevertheless, the movement grew steadily throughout the rest of the century. Russell died in 1916, having lived two years beyond the 1914 date in which he had declared Christ would return to earth to establish his millennial kingdom.

Joseph Franklin Rutherford (b. 1869) assumed leadership of the movement after Russell's death. Schism sparked by the posthumous publication of Russell's last volume of *Studies in the Scriptures* led to the formation of the rival Dawn Bible Student's Association. In 1918 Rutherford and other members of the headquarters staff were imprisoned for suspected pro-German activities; the sentence was later reversed, but the incident reinforced the persecution complex the societies were already experiencing. They stepped up their antireligious establishment rhetoric; the significance of Russell and his writings was diminished. The loose autonomous local societies were reorganized into a strong hierarchical organization which portrayed itself as a theocracy. The society utilized the latest media technology both to witness door to door with the newly developed portable phonograph and to produce millions of copies of the *Watchtower* and other printed materials which poured from the Brooklyn, N.Y., headquarters which it occupied in 1909.

Rutherford died in 1942. Nathan H. Knoor (b. 1905) succeeded him as president. Knorr strengthened the educational programs of the movement. The Watchtower Bible School of Gilead, N.Y., was begun in 1943 and *The New*

*World Translation of the Christian Greek Scriptures* and *The New World Translation of the Hebrew Scriptures* were published in 1950. Knorr died in 1977. Fredrick Franz presently serves as the fourth president of the society. Within recent years his presidency has been racked by dissension and defection within the Bethel headquarters community in Brooklyn.

In many ways the Jehovah's Witnesses are a contemporary expression of the Arian movement of the 4th century. They deny the doctrine of the Trinity, attributing its origins to satanic deception. Christ is a "mighty God," the highest creation, and first witness to the authority of the almighty God whose only true name is Jehovah. Evil forces, led by Satan, seek to besmirch the honor of Jehovah's name. Humankind is part of the conspiracy of evil through the fall, but may be freed from their participation in this by accepting the redemption which Christ won for them when he paid the ransom for their sin to Jehovah on the cross. Those who now witness in Jehovah's name and proclaim his final vindication at the last great battle between good and evil at Armageddon will continue to live on the redeemed earth; a smaller number (144,000) of select saints will be resurrected to a heavenly spiritual kingdom and will rule over the restored earth. All other souls will be annihilated either at their death or at subsequent judgment if they finally fail to give witness to Jehovah. The movement denies the doctrine of eternal punishment.

The Witnesses' understanding of salvation lacks any dominant sense of grace. Personal and corporate witness in vindication of Jehovah's honor gives assurance that they are on the path to final salvation from death. Biblical literalism and rationalism have led not only to their Arianism, but to their refusal to receive blood transfusions and to a severe separation from all other social groups, especially governments and churches. To participate in any way in such systems is to give allegiance to the satanic order. Thus, they are pacifists and will not salute the flag, although they do pay taxes in obedience to Christ's command to render unto Caesar the things which are his. They celebrate no holidays, not even their own birthdays. Christmas and Easter are considered pagan. Their strict separation is enforced by the absolute prohibition of any communication between Witnesses and those (even spouses) who deny the faith.

Jehovah's Witnesses number 3 million in more than 200 countries. They publish more than 50 million books and pamphlets annually in addition to the almost 500 million copies of their *Watchtower* and *Advance* magazines. Although their growth has slowed somewhat in recent years to about 6 percent per annum, they still rank at the forefront of religious organizations in annual membership gains. Their aggressive witnessing

tactics have frequently brought them into conflict with the laws of the countries in which they work; they have been banned in some African nations. In countries like the USA where minority rights are protected, legal defense of their beliefs has forced clearer definitions of civil rights statutes by the nation's highest courts.

*Bibliography.* R. Franz, *Crisis of Conscience* (1983); H. and G. Botting, *The Orwellian World of Jehovah's Witnesses* (1984); *Yearbook of Jehovah's Witnesses* (1986).

MELVIN E. DIETER

**Jenkins, Claude** (1877–1959). Anglican church historian. Born in Staffordshire, he was educated at Oxford, ordained in the Church of England in 1903, and was lecturer and then professor of ecclesiastical history at King's College, London (1905–34), and professor of ecclesiastical history at Oxford (1934–59). Among his publications were *An Unpublished Visitation of Archbishop Parker* (1911), *The Monastic Chronicler* (1922), *Sir Thomas More* (1935), and *F. D. Maurice and the New Reformation* (1938).

**Jenkins, David Edward** (1925– ). Anglican bishop and theologian. After school, he went into the army and served in India in World War II. He returned to England to study at Queen's College, Oxford. After ordination he became a fellow and chaplain at Queen's (1954–69), then served the World Council of Churches in Geneva as director of Humanum Studies. This experience and the travel entailed developed his interest in church and society, Marxism, liberation theology, and health services. In 1973 he returned to England to be director of the William Temple Foundation in Manchester, and in 1979 he was appointed professor of theology at the University of Leeds.

In 1984 he became the bishop of Durham. Before his actual consecration he made public some of his doubts about the vocabulary and concepts of traditional theology. In particular, his comments on the traditional doctrines of the virginal conception and bodily resurrection of Jesus were interpreted by many as being heretical. Despite protests he was consecrated and entered upon his episcopate. His way of presenting Christian faith is more in terms of "living with questions" than "living with certain truths."

His books include *Guide to the Debate about God* (1966), *The Glory of Man* (1984), *Living with Questions* (1969), *What Is Man?* (1970), and *The Contradiction of Christianity* (1976).

PETER TOON

**Jeremias, Joachim** (1900–1979). German NT scholar. Born in Dresden, he studied at the theological seminary of the Brüdergemeinde in Herrnhut and at the University of Leipzig (Dr. Phil.). He taught in the University of Berlin and was director of the Institutum Judaicum (1928), was professor of NT at the University of Greifswald (1929–35), and at Göttingen (1935–79). His writings touched almost every field of NT studies, including theology, linguistics, archeology, criticism, hermeneutics, and history. Having spent part of his childhood in the vicinity of Jerusalem, he was fluent in Hebrew and Arabic. He was noted especially for his insistence that the life of Jesus must be understood against the background of contemporary Judaism, a field in which he was an acknowledged authority. This is seen most clearly in such works as *Jesus' Promise to the Nations* (1958), *The Parables of Jesus* (rev. ed., 1963), *The Sermon on the Mount* (1963), *The Central Message of the NT* (1965), *The Eucharistic Words of Jesus* (1966), *Jerusalem in the Time of Jesus* (1969), and in his important contributions to Kittel's *Theological Dictionary of the NT.*

JOHN McRAY

## Jerusalem Conference (1928).

A meeting of the International Missionary Council (IMC), as well as laypersons and a large number of representatives from third world churches. The two-week conference's most influential paper was "Christianity and the Growth of Industrialism in Asia and Africa," which attracted the attention of the international labor movement. However, the emphasis on social concerns led many delegates to question whether the gospel of individual salvation was not being lost. Only the careful diplomacy of John R. Mott, who had chaired the Edinburgh Conference in 1910, prevented open division.

William Paton, founder of the National Christian Council of India, argued that social questions were of great importance to third world Christians, many of whom would be disappointed at the more lukewarm attitude of Western Europeans and Americans. The conference eventually produced a statement which said that "the Gospel of Christ contains a message, not only for the individual soul, but also for the world of social organization and economic relations in which individuals live." Missionaries in the field were encouraged to report on local industrial conditions to IMC for further, concerted action. The probability that IMC would change its character, and the dominance at committee and administrative levels of conservative Westerners ensured that the recommendations of the conference were never really put into effect. Nevertheless, they helped to persuade conservative evangelicals that IMC was becoming a liberal organization, and dissuaded them from taking an active part in its affairs.

*Bibliography.* S. Neill, *A History of Christian Missions* (1964); D. Hudson, *The Ecumenical Movement in World Affairs* (1969).

GERALD BRAY

**Jesuits.** Members of the largest Roman Catholic male religious order. Founded in Paris in 1534 by Ignatius Loyola, a Basque nobleman, the order was officially approved by Pope Paul III in 1540. Ignatius used his *Spiritual Exercises* to mold and guide his earliest followers at the University of Paris. This book continues to have an important influence on the training and formation of contemporary members of the order.

Although the Society of Jesus was not founded by Ignatius for the specific purpose of initiating a Catholic Counter-Reformation, Jesuits assumed a leadership role in the 16th-century revival of Catholic theology. In particular, at the Council of Trent (1545–63) Jesuit theologians had an important impact on the many reforms that were initiated. Among the earliest well-known Jesuit theologians were two Doctors of the Church, Peter Canisius and Robert Bellarmine.

In the 16th century Jesuits showed remarkable zeal for work among the poor and the plague-stricken. Ignatius demanded that even the greatest scholars of his order should regularly teach catechism to young children and minister to the poor. At the same time, all the French kings for two centuries, from Henry III to Louis XV, requested Jesuits as their confessors. All dukes of Bavaria after 1579 and all German emperors after the early 17th century had Jesuit confessors. Not surprisingly, the order attracted much jealousy and hostility. Eventually in 1773, under pressure from the Bourbon monarchs and other rulers in Europe, the Jesuits were suppressed by Pope Clement XIV. After the suppression its members continued to maintain contact with one another and some lived together in small communities as secular priests. Following the downfall of Napoleon and the release of Pope Pius VII from captivity in France, the order was officially restored in 1814. From a membership of about 600 in that year the order rapidly grew to more than 15,000 members by the end of the 19th century.

Among the various apostolates undertaken by the Jesuits, missionary work has always held an important place. Within months of the founding of the order, Ignatius sent his closest confidant, Francis Xavier, on a missionary journey to the East. In 12 years of traveling from India to Japan, Xavier became one of the greatest missionaries since Paul. He was designated by Pope Pius XI as patron of all missions of the Catholic Church. Although Francis Xavier died on Sancian Island in 1552 without accomplishing his dream of reaching China, other Jesuits later labored in that vast country. Among the most notable was Matteo Ricci who, through his knowledge of mathematics and astronomy, gained a welcome place at the imperial court. As missionaries the Jesuits introduced many cultural adaptations, such as use of the vernacular in liturgical worship. The resultant

Chinese rites controversy lasted more than a century. There was also controversy regarding the missionary work of the Jesuits in South America, notably in Paraguay. Early in the 17th century Jesuits had initiated idyllic Christian village communities, known as Reductions, to protect the native Catholic Indians in Paraguay from exploitation by white colonists. The reductions among the Guaranis, with a population that exceeded 140,000, were the most notable before the Jesuits were expelled from Spanish America in 1767. In North America the best-known Jesuit missionary work was that of the North American Martyrs, including Isaac Jogues and John de Brébeuf, who labored among the Iroquois Indians in Canada in the 17th century. From Canada the work of the Jesuits spread eastward into New York and northern New England and southward to the Gulf of Mexico. Jesuits also won renown as explorers, including Jacques Marquette who accompanied Joliet in the exploration of the Mississippi River in 1673.

As part of their missionary endeavor Jesuits generally established schools and universities wherever they settled. Indeed education at all levels has been a principal work of the order almost from the time it was founded. By the time Ignatius died in 1556 about three-fourths of the members of his order were engaged in educational work. Almost the same proportion of the order's members have been consistently involved in education over the past four centuries. Students in Jesuit schools have been drawn from all social classes. Norms for the organization, curriculum, and methods used in Jesuit schools were first set forth in the document *Ratio Studiorum* in 1599. Some of the most famous Jesuit universities in the USA include Boston College, Fordham, Geogetown, Gonzaga, Loyola, Marquette, and Xavier.

The Society of Jesus has a constitution which deals with governance, ministries, and manner of life but, contrary to the belief of some of the order's enemies, it does not have any secret rules or regulations. At the head of the order is a superior general who is elected for life by a general congregation of the order. But in 1981 Pope John Paul II intervened in the affairs of the order in an unprecedented manner. In that year, Fr. Pedro Arrupe, superior general of the Jesuits, was disabled by a severe stroke. Although the constitutions of the Society of Jesus specify how a superior general should be replaced, the pope intervened directly to appoint 80-year-old Paolo Dezza as his personal delegate and Giuseppe Pittau as coadjutor. Never before had a pope taken action independently of the Jesuits' constitutions. Pedro Arrupe became the first Jesuit superior general who did not die in office. In September 1983 the Jesuits held a general congregation at which they elected on the first ballot a Dutch Jesuit, Peter Hans Kolvenbach, as their 29th superior general. Some of the most famous Jesuits of the 20th century include theologians Karl Rahner, Jean Daniélou, and Henri de Lubac; the noted ecumenist Augustin Cardinal Bea; the philosopher Bernard Lonergan; poet and peace activist Daniel Berrigan; and French paleontologist Teilhard de Chardin.

**Bibliography.** M. Moerner, ed., *The Expulsion of the Jesuits from Latin America* (1965); J. de Guilbert, *The Jesuits: Their Spiritual Doctrine and Practice* (1970); Ignatius of Loyola, *The Constitutions of the Society of Jesus* (1970); J. Brodrick, *The Origin of the Jesuits* (1971); W. V. Bangert, *A History of the Society of Jesus* (1972); D. Mitchell, *The Jesuits, A History* (1981); H. Aveling, *The Jesuits* (1982); G. J. Garraghan, *The Jesuits of the Middle United States* (1984).

LIAM K. GRIMLEY

**Jesus as a Preacher.** An aspect of Jesus' ministry which is prominent in the Gospels. He did not deliver sermons, in the modern sense, but in a fashion all his own he served as the supreme Interpreter of God's truth for sinful men. The Gospels show: (1) Usually he preached from the Bible. (See Luke 4:14–27, which A. B. Bruce calls the "frontispiece" of the gospel.) (2) He preached about the kingdom of God and called for repentance. (3) He preached much about divine mercy and redeeming grace. (4) He spoke much about the "last days," an aspect of his preaching and teaching that has caused much debate and confusion. (5) He set an example of how to gain a hearing even for an unwelcome message. Frequently he began with a question of interest to everyone; often also with a problem, or a "life situation." He showed how to start with the hearers "where they are," mentally. (6) He constantly appealed to the imagination. According to Horace Bushnell, his gospel is "the gift of God to the imagination." (7) He employed the language of the common people, who heard him gladly, as one of themselves. Even in English, the reports of his spoken words impress us with what A. E. Wendt calls "pregnant simplicity." (8) He preached with authority, like no other. In various ways as preachers, the prophets and apostles resembled him, but he towered above them as much in the spoken word as in character. (9) While he preached by word of mouth, he taught more by what he did. Often he employed miracles as "signs" of truths he wished the hearers to see as well as hear. Thus he employed the "case method," which is now considered a modern invention. (10) As the divine Truth through the divine personality he taught and preached by being what he was as the sinless Son of God, Savior of the world, and Lord of glory. This aspect of his work is stressed in the Book of Acts. The Lord's supper might also be seen as a sermon in action. In 1 Cor. 11:26 the word translated "proclaim," or "show," is the term often rendered, correctly, as "preach." Herein lies much truth, but it is also full of the mystery of how the two natures of Christ interrelate. Perhaps for this reason few writers have dealt with Christ's preaching.

*See also* JESUS AS A TEACHER; JESUS CHRIST.

ANDREW W. BLACKWOOD

## Jesus as a Teacher.

**Jesus as a Teacher.** The Gospels contain about 200 references to Jesus as teacher, or rabbi. He taught "with authority," and not as the scribes, that is, with an inherent sense of firsthand knowledge. He was a preacher-teacher, always striving to bring about a decision in the lives of the hearers. They were amazed at what he taught and how he taught. At the age of 12 he was in the temple among the doctors (teachers), "hearing them and asking them questions." During his ministry he encountered persons and groups as a teacher, asking and answering questions, telling parables, performing signs and wonders. Through these he revealed his character and power and confronted the people with vital truths. By his various acts (such as washing the disciples' feet and instituting the Lord's supper), he taught truths unforgettably. His crucifixion was not only an atoning sacrifice but also a supreme lesson. Through it he has taught men with finality his obedience to the Father's will and the nature, extent, and power of divine love for sinful men.

Jesus as teacher used effective methods. Often he introduced a subject by raising a question or posing a problem. "Whose superscription is this?" "Whosoever shall humble himself as this little child." He took advantage of every opportunity to help others learn. He used the principle of apperception, always approaching persons with an appreciation of what they already knew or had experienced. He used illustrations from ordinary life and made his teaching vivid by putting truths in recognizable forms. Although the Son of God incarnate, Christ's teaching used humor. By winsome grace he awakened latent possibilities and encouraged men to express that potential. Recognizing individual differences, he treated each one uniquely.

Master teachers work with a clear purpose in view. Jesus as teacher had a profound sense of mission to save lost humanity. His divine consciousness gave him a unique love for persons, a passionate desire to help them know God and themselves, and a sacrificial spirit. He taught abstract truth, communicating effectively to those who received and followed him. Although he is still our supreme example, as teacher Christ is uniquely the living, personal truth that he taught. As the teacher come from God he used methods to teach the truth that in his own person he exemplified. Today, through the Holy Spirit Christ still serves as our supreme teacher.

*See also* JESUS AS A PREACHER; JESUS CHRIST.

*Bibliography.* H. H. Horne, *Jesus the Master Teacher* (1920); C. F. McKay, *The Art of Jesus as a Teacher* (1930); N. E. Richard-son, *The Christ of the Class Room* (1932); H. R. Sharman, *Jesus as Teacher* (1934); L. A. Weigle, *Jesus and the Educational Method* (1939); W. A. Curtis, *Jesus Christ the Teacher* (1943); D. Guthrie, *A History of Religious Educators* (1975); L. L. Benni-son, *Jesus the Master Teacher* (1980).

E. G. HOMRIGHAUSEN

## Jesus Christ.

**Jesus Christ.** *General Survey.* In *Quest of the Historical Jesus* (1910), Albert Schweitzer contended that the writing of a "Life of Jesus" would be impossible in the future. His prediction rightly expressed the mood of Continental Protestant theology, for the number of "Lives" published after World War I in that part of the world is negligible. The reason for that dearth, however, probably lies in theological outlook rather than in methodological difficulties. In the Anglo-Saxon world a few hundred works were published in that period, Roman Catholics produced a number of outstanding critical and devotional works, Jews struggled with questions of how to interpret and evaluate the gospel story, theosophical and mystical groups claimed Jesus for themselves, and a host of writers composed more or less fictional biographies.

The modern Christian "Lives" can be divided into three groups: harmonies of the Gospels, critical studies, and devotional-interpretative works. The second group was what Schweitzer had in mind. The principal reason modern scholars are reluctant to compose a critical "Life of Jesus" is that the Gospels were never intended to present a purely historical view. Rather, they proclaim Jesus of Nazareth as the Lord and Savior of mankind, combining the record of facts with the Christian valuation. Those scholars who consider this combination a distortion of the records must confine themselves to a discussion of the historical circumstances of Jesus' life, and to parallels and antecedents of his teaching. They may not furnish a total picture of his personality or of his life work. This is unfortunate, however, because apart from the personality of Jesus the gospel proclamation makes no sense historically or theologically.

*Harmonies.* Compiling an annotated harmony of the Gospels is the simplest way to write a life of Jesus, but also the least satisfactory. Unless the life of Jesus is reinterpreted the narratives of the single Gospels are preferable to a harmony, in which their individual viewpoints are lost. Nor are matters improved by adding apocryphal material, as did H. Daniel-Rops and A. Séché. The majority of harmonies differ only by the quantity and the nature of the explanatory material added. Most of them follow tradition (such as S. J. Andrews, A. I. Dushaw, W. Lowrie, W. S. Morris, A. W. Ross, J. J. Scott, B. S. Whitman, and Beaufays and F. Klein among the Roman Catholics). Critical elements are introduced by P. Gardiner-Smith, G. R. Lees, J. Moffatt, A. R. Whitman, and the Roman Catholics A. Fahling and Lagrange.

***Critical Works.*** The few works that in a strict sense continue the critical tradition (M. Goguel, C. A. Guignebert, W. Heitmueller, J. Mackinnon, C. W. Quimby, P. Wernle) all bear witness to the almost insurmountable methodological problem. Even when dealing primarily with the historical "background" they have to integrate their material to show that it refers to the Jesus of history. Thus they try to give either a psychological portrait of Jesus or a systematized presentation of his teaching. The majority of the "critical" works, however, are hardly more than continuations of the older liberal "Lives." Emphasis is placed upon Jesus the teacher or on his exemplary life and personality.

Even so, the positivistic scholar cannot deny that the portrayal of the personality of Jesus as given in the Gospels is a perplexing contrast between his claims and the actual circumstances of his life. According to some, Jesus was mistaken in considering himself as the Messiah (C. J. Cadoux, S. J. Case, Schweitzer, H. Warschauer). This interpretation was taken by others to indicate that Jesus was eccentric (V. P. Gronbech) or motivated by ecstatic experiences (Oscar Holtzmann). No wonder that some psychologists contended that Jesus belonged to the neurotic (Baumann, Van Delius, Rasmussen) or even paranoiac type (Binet-Sanglé, William Hirsch, de Loosten). These views were refuted, however, by Schweitzer and W. E. Bundy.

The attempt to prove the nonhistoricity of Jesus and to explain the Gospels as myths was continued (for example, by A. Niemojewski, J. M. Robertson, G. T. Sadler, W. B. Smith, P. Thielscher). This view was modified by P. L. Couchoud and, in a different way, by form criticism, especially in R. Bultmann and M. Dibelius. The latter school holds that the original historical nucleus of the Gospels became so overgrown by legend and myth that the historian must be content with the portrait of Jesus as seen by the primitive church. Others abandon the idea of a biography and simply present Jesus as teacher. Opinions concerning his message are divided, however. Some consider him as the prophet of a new type of ethics (W. H. Cadman, C. W. Gilkey, Shailer Mathews, C. C. McCown, C. C. Morrison, E. M. Poteat, K. S. Ross, F. K. Stamm, Bouck White) or of a deepened religion (D. E. Adams, Bundy, O. Cone, F. Paradise, H. R. Purinton-S. B. Costello, R. W. Stewart). Others, following W. Herrmann, focus upon the inner life or character of Jesus (e.g., F. D. Adams, F. L. Anderson, W. R. Bowie, M. E. Lyman, A. W. Martin).

A number of Roman Catholic scholars defended the historical reliability of the Gospels (e.g., J. Lebreton, L. C. Fillion, L. de Grandmaison, Lagrange, M. Lepin, F. Prat, G. Ricciotti). They tried with remarkable success to beat the critics with their own weapons by showing that the "critical" approach was never as unbiased as it pretended to be. Less convincing are the Protestant apologetic works, in which a "Life of Christ" is established upon a "critically defendable residue" of Gospel material (e.g., F. C. Burkitt, H. Carpenter, G. W. Fiske, T. R. Glover, A. W. Hall, W. B. Hill, A. C. Headlam, L. Lemme, R. Nordsten, H. Rimmer, E. H. Sawyer). These lack the firm position from which their Roman Catholic colleagues are able to set definite limits to critical research.

***Interpretations.*** Most 20th-century writers have realized that to be relevant, any historical presentation of the Gospel material requires an interpretation of the life of Jesus. An attempt is often made to weld the traditionally interpreted Gospel materials into a consecutive story (e.g., D. A. Edwards, A. C. Garrett, C. Gore, K. F. B. Mackay, D. A. Poling, R. E. Speer, T. Zahn). Purely pragmatic narrative does not do justice to the Gospels, however, because it fails to bring the personality of Jesus to life.

Various approaches to that goal are possible—there is, for example, a tendency among certain writers to point out the naturalness of Jesus and the significance of his out-of-door life (B. Barton, W. A. Grist, T. Kagawa, W. F. Kirkland, J. E. McIntyre, J. Skinner, W. A. Quayle). Schweitzer advocated "consistent eschatology," according to which Jesus acted in his ministry as a fanatical believer in an apocalyptic program. That view was modified by Cadoux, H. G. Hatch, R. L. Hartt, Hooke, A. G. Paisley, Peck, and Warschauer. Others (such as W. R. Bowie, C. R. Brown, B. W. Robinson, D. M. Ross, M. H. Shepherd) describe Jesus as a person whose whole life was motivated by goodness and sympathy. Strength of character and spiritual power form the characteristics of Jesus according to such scholars as E. Hodgkin, E. Russell, David Smith, and A. P. Terhune. Such approaches tend, however, to bring Jesus down to the level of the average man, and in some Unitarian "Lives" this tendency assumes pathological features (e.g., J. G. F. Raupert, A. M. Rihbany). Yet it is obvious that the Gospels would never have been written unless Jesus had been an eminent personality. Hence, in order to do him full justice, writers will emphasize the uniqueness of his personality (F. V. Filson, Ray O. Miller, W. E. Leonard, Purinton, W. B. Riley), his character (J. M. Murry, Martin J. Scott), his spiritual insight (F. W. Lewis, G. T. Tolson) or his spiritual life (Frame, A. F. Irvine, F. Rittelmeyer, Sledd, D. Van Steere). These presentations assume that Jesus differed only by degree from other people.

No less violence is done to the Gospels, however, when their material is used merely as a collection of evidences for the truth of the christological dogma (e.g., L. Boettner, G. R. Negley, W. C. Robinson, Schaller, F. J. Sibley, R. A. Torrey,

W. E. Vine). Such procedure neglects considerable portions of the Gospels and treats their arrangement as irrelevant. On the whole, Roman Catholic scholars better blended the Gospel story with the dogma (e.g., Beaufays, W. Dawson, Fahling, Fernessole, Lagrange, C. Morino, A. Reatz).

***The Transcendence of Jesus.*** The real problem of the life of Jesus consists in fully utilizing the Gospels in presenting Jesus so that the divine purpose and power of his life become manifest to the people of our generation. A number of remarkable solutions to this problem have been offered. Like the critics they take the human life of Jesus seriously, but they show how in his very human life Jesus transcended all other people (Berger, Paisley). Some describe this element of transcendence as the irresistible challenge that emanates from the Gospel portrait (C. and M. Carnson, P. C. Simpson, F. Gogarten). Others consider his perfection as a revelation of God that overawes the reader (J. Bos, Douglas Edwards, John Knox, Macaulay, F. Mauriac, G. Campbell Morgan, A. W. Robinson, David Ross, C. A. Johnston Ross, Charles A. Anderson Scott). Witness is borne by others to the strange paradox that in all he is and does, Jesus shocks people, and yet they feel attracted to him (G. L. Borchert, G. Fiske, R. Mackintosh, Richard Roberts, K. Schilder, A. Schlatter, W. Spens). Finally there are those who confess that it was the picture of Jesus' life that changed their lives completely, thereby disclosing his divine dignity and power (T. H. Davies, Otto Dibelius, George S. Duncann, E. L. Pell, P. Whitwell Wilson).

OTTO A. PIPER

***The Last Half of the 20th Century.*** In recent critical investigation about Jesus skepticism of the supernatural continues, but existentialism replaced rationalism, idealism, and Hegelianism as its philosophical setting. Bultmann and his followers assumed the historical Jesus to be of little consequence and the Gospels to be mythological expressions of the experience and preaching of the church (*kerygma*). They became primarily concerned with the achieving of one's own existential being.

In 1953 E. Kasemann asserted that the preaching (*kerygma*) of the early church did, in fact, point to the Jesus of history and called for a "new quest for the historical Jesus," thus inaugurating a post-Bultmannian era. E. Fuchs, G. Bornkamm, and J. M. Robinson joined the effort to discover what could be learned about the man, Jesus, who stands behind the *kerygma*. They recognized the futility of attempting biographies and sought in Jesus the basis of the church's existential message. Authentic elements in the Gospels, they believe, attest Jesus' belief in his own divinity and inspiration, his gracious attitude toward social outcasts, his ability to forgive, and especially his authority and lordship in the church.

Critical tools such as form, source, and redaction criticism became indispensable in the effort to distinguish the authentic Jesus material from that created by the early church. The "minimalist" view accepted as authentic only those words and actions for which no question could be raised. Any statement ascribed to Jesus with a parallel in the Greco-Roman or Jewish world of his day, which assumed supernatural intervention, or which fit into certain literary types was rejected as an invention. J. M. Rohde, following in Schweitzer's footsteps, worked to summarize the findings of 20th-century works on Jesus. He also helped define for redaction criticism an increasingly significant role of identifying the contribution of each final Gospel editor. W. Marxsen, E. Schweizer, and N. Perrin are examples of nonconservatives committed to the discipline. The latter, in a reductio ad absurdum, affirmed that only two, or at the most four, sayings of Jesus in the Gospels are authentic. In the 1980s the "Jesus Seminar" of the Society of Biblical Literature attracted widespread attention by conducting a vote among scholars to determine which sayings of Jesus were then considered to be authentic. The effort actually attempted to popularize the methodology and assumptions of liberal scholarship.

E. Stauffer and J. Jeremias stood in marked contrast to the position influenced by Bultmann. Both employed critical methodology but grounded their interpretations of Jesus in his historical setting and life. O. Cullmann did not write extensively on the life of Jesus, but his interpretation of the NT insists that the historical Jesus is central in the history of salvation, in opposition to Bultmann's thought.

The use of redaction criticism by conservatives was controversial. Some rejected it totally, some used it to identify the distinctiveness of each Gospel, and still others employed it to uncover the creativity of the writers and editors. R. Meye, W. L. Lane, and I. H. Marshall exemplify conservatives who made cautious use of redaction criticism, while R. H. Gundry suggested that much of Matthew is "midrash," that is, stories created as commentary and illustration.

Such conservatives as D. Guthrie and E. F. Harrison produced "harmonies" and "devotional-interpretative" works which embody a sophistication and awareness of historical-cultural and literary matters often missing from earlier works of this type.

Investigation of literary forms in the Gospels (form criticism) came to include considerations of the form of the works as a whole. Some studied the Gospels to determine the cause of their writing (etiology), while for others the Gospels were classed as ancient literature created to praise or aggrandize notables of the past (pane-gyric). Finally "Gospel" came to be identified as a separate genre.

Jewish writings attempted primarily to show Jesus' affinity with his nation and to include him among its famous men. Noteworthy Jewish writers on Jesus include S. Sandmel, G. Vermes, D. Flusser, A. G. Fruchtenbaum, and J. Jocz.

Contemporary liberal studies of Jesus seemed in disarray. Conservatives either continued the harmonization and the devotional-interpretative approaches, or struggled with the relevance of critical methodologies shorn of naturalistic presuppositions. Contributions from the study of Jesus' environment (intertestamental Judaism) and the findings of archeology offered the hope of combining with textual, linguistic, and other approaches to produce better understanding of the historical Jesus and his significance.

*See also* CHRISTOLOGY; SON OF MAN.

J. JULIUS SCOTT, JR.

**Bibliography.** *Survey Works to 1950.* A. Schweitzer, *The Quest of the Historical Jesus* (1910); S. J. Case, *The Historicity of Jesus* (1912); S. J. Case, *Jesus Through the Centuries* (1932); C. C. McCown, *The Search for the Real Jesus* (1940); A. Schweitzer, *The Psychiatric Study of Jesus* (1948); A. M. Hunter, *Interpreting the NT, 1900–1950* (1952).

*Critical Works to 1950.* W. Heitmueller, *Jesus* (1913); P. Wernle, *Jesus* (1916); E. Meyer, *Ursprung und Anfänge des Christentums*, 3 vols. (1921–23); J. Mackinnan, *The Historic Jesus* (1931); M. Goguel, *Life of Christ* (1933); R. Bultmann, *Jesus and the Word* (1934); C. Guignebert, *Jesus* (1935); P. Gardner-Smith, *The Christ of the Gospels* (1938); C. Guignebert, *Le Christ* (1948); M. Dibelius, *Jesus* (1949); M. Goguel, *Jesus* (1950); C. W. Quimby, *Jesus as They Remembered Him* (1951).

*Aspects of the Life of Jesus to 1950.* G. S. Hall, *Jesus the Christ in the Light of Psychology*, 2 vols. (1917); P. Gardner-Smith, *Narratives of the Resurrection* (1926); W. B. Hill, *The Resurrection of Jesus Christ* (1930); J. G. Machen, *The Virgin Birth of Christ* (1930); W. E. Bundy, *Psychic Health of Jesus* (1932); H. G. Hatch, *Messianic Consciousness of Jesus* (1939); E. Hirsch, *Auferstehungsgeschichten und der Christliche Glaube* (1940); J. W. Bowman, *The Intention of Jesus* (1943); D. Edwards, *Virgin Birth in History and Faith* (1943).

*Mythical Views to 1950.* A. Niemojewski, *Gott Jesus im Lichte fremder und eigener Forschungen* (1910); W. B. Smith, *Ecce Deus* (1912); G. T. Sadler, *Has Jesus Lived on Earth?* (1914); J. M. Robertson, *The Historical Jesus* (1916); G. T. Sadler, *Behind the NT* (1921); P. L. Couchoud, *Le Mystère de Jésus* (1924); P. Thielscher, *Unser Wissen um Jesus* (1930); P. L. Couchoud, *Creation of Christ* (1939).

*Conservative, Apologetic "Lives" to 1950.* W. B. Hill, *Life of Christ* (1917); A. C. Headlam, *Jesus Christ in History and Fact* (1925); T. Zahn, *Grundriss der Geschichte des Lebens Jesu* (1928); C. Gore, *Jesus of Nazareth* (1929); F. C. Burkitt, *Jesus Christ, an Historical Outline* (1932); A. C. Garrett, *The Man from Heaven* (1939); D. A. Edwards, *Jesus, the Gospel Portrait* (1947).

*Liberal Interpretations to 1950.* W. F. Cooley, *Aim of Jesus Christ* (1925); S. J. Case, *Jesus* (1927); W. R. Bowie, *The Master* (1928); W. E. Bundy, *Our Recovery of Jesus* (1929); R. Norwood, *The Man Who Dared to be God* (1929); K. Page, *The Personality of Jesus* (1932); S. Eddy, *A Portrait of Jesus* (1943); H. J. Cadbury, *Jesus, What Manner of Man?* (1947).

*Naturalistic Interpretations to 1950.* B. Barton, *The Man Nobody Knows* (1924); W. A. Quayle, *Out-of-Doors with Jesus* (1924); J. E. McIntyre, *Idealism of Jesus* (1928); W. F. Kirkland, *Portrait of a Carpenter* (1931); T. Kagawa, *Jesus Through Japanese Eyes* (1934).

*Philosophical Interpretations to 1950.* P. E. Moore, *Christ of the NT* (1924); J. M. Murry, *Life of Jesus* (1926); R. Rojas, *The Invisible Christ* (1931); J. Erskine, *Human Life of Jesus* (1945); G. Santayana, *The Idea of Christ in the Gospels* (1946).

*Transcendental Interpretations to 1950.* P. W. Wilson, *The Christ We Forget* (1917); A. Schlatter, *Geschichte des Christus* (1923); T. H. Davies, *Gospel of the Living Jesus* (1928); C. Carnson and M. Carnson, *The Christ of the Twentieth Century* (1930); J. Bos, *The Unique Aloofness of Jesus* (1931); A. G. Paisley, *Emotional Life of Jesus* (1931); O. Borchert, *The Original Jesus* (1933); G. Campbell Morgan, *The Great Physician* (1937); M. Spens, *Concerning Himself* (1937); J. Knox, *The Man Christ Jesus* (1942); G. S. Duncan, *Jesus, Son of Man* (1947); F. Gogarten, *Die Verkuendigung Jesu Christi* (1948).

*Roman Catholic Works to 1950.* G. Papini, *Life of Christ* (1923); G. K. Chesterton, *The Everlasting Man* (1925); L. de Grandmaison, *Jesus Christ* (1928); A. Reatz, *Jesus Christ* (1933); J. Lebreton, *Life and Teaching of Jesus Christ Our Lord* (1934); F. J. Sheen, *The Eternal Galilean* (1934); F. Mauriac, *Life of Jesus* (1937); G. Ricciotti, *Life of Christ* (1947).

*Jewish Works to 1950.* S. Krauss, *Das Leben Jesu nach juedischen Quellen* (1912); B. Pick, *Jesus in the Talmud* (1913); A. L. Williams, *The Hebrew Christian Messiah* (1916); J. Klausner, *Jesus of Nazareth* (1925); E. F. Trattner, *As a Jew Sees Jesus* (1931); H. J. Schonfield, *According to the Hebrews* (1937); M. Goldstein, *Jesus in the Jewish Tradition* (1950).

*Since 1950.* G. Ogg, *Chronology of the Public Ministry of Jesus* (1940); J. Jocz, *The Jewish People and Jesus Christ* (1949); J. M. Robinson, *The Problem of History in Mark* (1957), and *The New Quest for the Historical Jesus* (1958); O. Cullmann, *The Christology of the NT* (1959); G. Bornkamm, *Jesus of Nazareth* (ET, 1960); E. Stauffer, *Jesus and His Story* (1960); J. Jeremias, *The Parables of Jesus* (ET, 1963); N. Perrin, *The Kingdom of God in the Teachings of Jesus* (1963); H. Anderson, *Jesus and Christian Origins* (1964); O. Cullman, *Christ and Time* (2d ed., 1964); J. Jeremias, *The Problem of the Historical Jesus* (ET, 1964); E. Kasemann, *Essays on NT Themes* (ET, 1964); J. Jeremias, *The Eucharistic Words of Jesus* (1966); O. Cullmann, *Salvation in History* (ET, 1967); N. Perrin, *Rediscovering the Teachings of Jesus* (1967); D. Flusser, *Jesus* (1968); R. Meye, *Jesus and the Twelve* (1968); J. M. Rohde, *Rediscovering the Teaching of the Evangelists* (ET, 1968); C. C. Anderson, *Critical Quests of Jesus* (1969); E. F. Harrison, *A Short Life of Christ* (1969); H. K. McArthur, *In Search of the Historical Jesus* (1969); I. H. Marshall, *The Work of Christ* (1969); W. Marxsen, *Mark the Evangelist* (1969); J. W. Bowman, *Which Jesus?* (1970); D. Guthrie, *A Shorter Life of Christ* (1970); I. H. Marshall, *Luke the Historian and Theologian* (1970); J. Jeremias, *The Proclamation of Jesus* (ET, 1971); E. Schweizer, *Jesus* (ET, 1971); C. C. Anderson, *The Historical Jesus: A Continuing Quest* (1972); D. Guthrie, *Jesus the Messiah* (1972); H. W. Hoehner, *Chronological Aspects of the Life of Christ* (1973); S. Sandmel, *We Jews and Jesus* (1973); F. F. Bruce, *Jesus and Christian Origins Outside the NT* (1974); A. Fruchtenbaum, *Jesus Was a Jew* (1974); W. L. Lane, *Commentary on the Gospel of Mark* (1974); G. Vermes, *Jesus the Jew: A Historian's Reading of the Gospels* (1974); G. Aulen, *Jesus in Contemporary Historical Research* (ET, 1976); M. Grant, *Jesus: An Historian's View of the Gospels* (1977); H. C. Kee, *Jesus in History* (2d ed., 1977); I. H. Marshall, *I Believe in the Historical Jesus* (1977); R. H. Stein, *The Method and Message of Jesus' Teaching* (1978); R. H. Gundry, *Matthew: A Commentary on His Literary and Theological Art* (1982); G. R. Habermas, *Ancient Evidence for the Life of Jesus* (1984); J. D. G. Dunn, *The Evidence for Jesus* (1985); G. Vermes, *Jesus and the World of Judaism* (1985); F. F. Bruce, *Jesus: Savior and Lord* (1986).

**Jewish Congress, American (AJC).** The leading community-relations organization of the American Jewish community. The beginnings of AJC date to a temporary assembly of Jewish organizations convened in Philadelphia in 1918 to formulate a postwar program for the Jewish people and to send a delegate to the Versailles Peace

Conference. Although disbanded in 1920, a number of representatives, led by Stephen S. Wise, immediately began plans to reestablish the congress, and a permanent organization was established in 1928. Since 1930 membership has been on an individual rather than organizational basis. Originally designed primarily to fight anti-Semitism in America and abroad (esp. during the Nazi era), the congress since 1945 has identified with and supported liberal programs in a general American context, combating all forms of racism and supporting human rights, separation of church and state, as well as defending the state of Israel. A governing council of 150 members and an administrative committee of 50 govern AJC. It publishes *Congress Bi-Weekly* as well as the distinguished intellectual quarterly *Judaism*.

ELIEZER SEGAL

## Jewish Congress, World.

International assembly of Jewish organizations. It first met in Geneva in 1936, although it had a number of forerunners and preparatory conferences. It includes delegates from Jewish communities, national organizations, and other autonomous and democratically constituted bodies. It is headed by a plenary assembly, its highest decision-making organ, as well as an executive committee and governing council. Its purposes are to further the interests of Jews and Jewish communities in all countries, to serve as a spokesorgan for the Jews in international and governmental contexts (without interfering in any country's domestic political affairs), to actively promote Jewish cultural and social welfare, and to coordinate the interests of constituent organizations. The activities of the congress were heavily influenced by the powerful personality of its president, Nahum Goldmann, from its establishment until his retirement in 1978 (when he was succeeded by Edgar Bronfman). It played an important role in negotiations for the rescue of Jews from Nazi Europe, as well as the post-World War II relief and rehabilitation efforts, and the prosecution of war criminals. It represented Jewish positions in the arrangements for indemnification of Jewish Holocaust victims. In general, the organization has defended the interests of persecuted Jewish communities, especially in communist and Arab states, and has represented Jewish positions before international organizations (e.g., United Nations agencies) and in interreligious forums. Although supportive of the state of Israel, the congress's internationalist stands have sometimes created friction with Israeli positions.

ELIEZER SEGAL

## Jews, Missions to the.

Jesus proclaimed the gospel exclusively to the Jews and initially instructed his disciples to do the same; but after the resurrection he commanded that the gospel be preached in all the world.

The early church was almost exclusively Jewish. The response on the day of Pentecost came from the Jews in Jerusalem, and a large number of the priests also became followers of Jesus (Acts 6–7). One of the earliest problems confronting the church was not "the Jewish question" but "the Gentile question"—should the gospel be preached to them? The Council of Jerusalem affirmed that the gospel was for all men, Jews and Gentiles alike (Acts 15). A later disagreement between Peter and Paul insured a continuing particular approach to the Jewish people alongside the worldwide mission of the church (Gal. 2). Christianity was at first regarded as a sect of the Jews by the Roman and Jewish authorities. The final breach between church and synagogue took place only after the Bar Kochba revolt (A.D. 132–135). It was not occasioned primarily by theological but by political differences, because the Jewish believers did not take part in the revolt but withdrew to the wilderness. Throughout subapostolic times the church continued to present Christ to the Jews even though in its own midst serious errors began to arise from the Judaizing party. The controversy with Judaism is witnessed by Justin Martyr's *Dialogue with Trypho* and Tertullian's *Adversus Judaeos*. Endeavors to turn the Jews to Christ continued throughout the Middle Ages, sometimes in ways that respected the integrity of the Jews, but often by compulsion. In England during the 12th century such large numbers of Jews turned to Christianity that King William II endeavored (unsuccessfully) to have them return to Judaism because of the complaints of their fellow Jews.

The need for the Jews to hear the gospel was not questioned by Calvin or Luther. The latter was at first favorably inclined toward them and expected their mass conversion to Christ. When this did not transpire he became a bitter enemy. In the Calvinist churches perhaps the most eminent Jewish believer was Tremellius, one of the compilers of the Heidelberg Catechism. Contrary to popular belief Calvin expected the future restoration of Israel although he took seriously the present rejection. He adopted no systematic stance with regard to their future but a tension in his thought later resulted in misunderstandings. His successors also looked for the ingathering of Israel. This was particularly true among the English Puritans and the Dutch Calvinists in the years following the Reformation. The Westminster Directory of Public Worship required that prayer for the conversion of the Jews be made each Lord's Day.

Subsequently in England Jewish evangelism was neglected until a growing interest in eschatology stirred the London Missionary Society to appoint Joseph Frey, a young Hebrew Christian, to minister to his fellow Jews in London. The response was such that a specific society became an evident necessity. In 1809 together with some other eminent evangelicals he founded the London Society for Promoting Christianity among the Jews (now the Church's Ministry among the Jews, CMJ). It was modeled on the British and Foreign Bible Society as an interdenominational foundation. Of the four ministerial vice-presidents two were Episcopalian and two were Nonconformist. It continued as such until 1815, when the dominance of episcopal forms made it impossible for the Nonconformists to remain within it. In the meantime a commission was sent out from Scotland to determine the condition of Jewry in Palestine and Europe. The report brought back by Andrew Bonar and Robert M. McCheyne from Palestine resulted in the commencement of a Jewish mission under the direction of the Church of Scotland. The report was also the stimulus to the Nonconformist churches in England to begin a similar work. In 1842 the British Society for the Propagation of the Gospel among the Jews, now Christian Witness to Israel (CWI), was inaugurated and presently has branches in many parts of the world. The Presbyterian churches in the United Kingdom have maintained their interest in Jewish missions while also engaging in dialog with representatives of Judaism.

A similar concern developed on the Continent. There were numerous conversions to Christianity in Germany during the early part of the 19th century. Several organizations were established in the German states, and in 1871 the *Evangelisch-lutherischer Centralvarein für Mission unter Israel* was formed in an attempt to unite the various missions to the Jews. In 1972 the *Evangeliumsdienst für Israel Sudwest* was founded in Stuttgart to continue the interest in that part of Germany previously organized from Switzerland by the *Schweizer Evangelisch Judenmission* (1830) but which renounced any missionary intent (later called *Stiftung für Kirche und Judentum*). Jewish missionary activity has been organized in several other European countries including Norway, Denmark, and Finland. The Norwegian mission, *Den Norske Israelsmisjon* (DNI), carried out an extensive ministry in Romania.

World War II and the ensuing Holocaust in which 6 million Jews perished almost totally destroyed the Jewish community in Europe and radically altered the operations of most of these missions. The establishment of the State of Israel in 1948 was a further reason for the transfer of a considerable emphasis in Jewish mission to Israel. The post-Holocaust situation also caused the approach of many Jewish missions to change. In 1948 the First Assembly of the World Council of Churches meeting in Amsterdam could say of the missionary commission of Jesus, "The fulfillment of this commission requires that we include the Jewish people in our evangelistic task." Very shortly afterwards, however, the situation altered radically for most of the larger denominational churches. The rise of covenant theology saw mission no longer as legitimate in the case of Israel—only dialog in which each party spoke from positions of equal validity.

The main societies in Israel today are DNI, the Finnish Evangelical Lutheran Mission (FELM), CMJ, and CWI. The two main centers of the Norwegian mission are Haifa and Jerusalem. In Jerusalem they run the Caspari study center in conjunction with FELM and provide a theological extension course for local believers as well as a research center. CMJ operates in Tel-Aviv and Jerusalem. In the former a study center, Immanuel House, provides short-term study courses mainly for Israeli Christians. The main thrust of CWI is in Rishon LeZion where Hagefen Press translates evangelical literature into Hebrew and produces indigenous writing by way of two regular magazines in Hebrew. The Baptists, mainly from the USA, are also prominent in various capacities. The United Council of Christian Churches in Israel acts as a common platform for many of these and other organizations working in the same sphere. It also publishes *Mishkan*, a theological journal for the study of the concerns of Jewish evangelism.

The State of Israel (excluding occupied territories) has a population of 3.7 million, of which 3.2 million are Jewish, 475,000 are Muslim, and some 80,000 are Christians. Of these, no more than 2500 are known to be Protestant (of whom 2000 belong to the Arab Episcopalian Church), 500 are dispersed through various expatriate denominations. In addition there are some 3000 Jewish Christians who are not registered as such in any public registry. These belong to about 28 independent Hebrew-speaking congregations of Israeli citizens. These have recently begun a vigorous evangelistic program in Israel.

In the USA during the 19th century many of the larger denominational churches maintained a mission to the Jews but these no longer have a specific missionary emphasis, many having largely adopted covenant theology. The Lutheran Church—Missouri Synod still has an active missionary involvement with the Jewish people. Several independent Jewish mission boards have continued a missionary emphasis although some of them have been more concerned with the promotion of dispensational theology centering on Israel. The larger and more active are Jews for Jesus, the American Board of Missions to the Jews (1894), and the Friends of Israel (1938). A recent development which may prove an effective missionary method is the growth of messianic fellowships and congregations, although the latter is still a matter of some controversy. Most Jewish missions now meet and consult regularly under the auspices of the Lausanne Consultation on Jewish Evangelism.

*See also* HOLOCAUST, THE.

**Bibliography.** A. A. Bonar, *Narrative of a Mission of Enquiry to the Jews from the Church of Scotland* (1854); J. Dunlop, *Memories of Gospel Triumphs among the Jews during the Victorian Era* (1894); W. T. Gidney, *The Jews and Their Evangelisation* (1898); F. J. Exley, *Our Hearts' Desire* (1942); G. Hedenquist, *The Church and the Jewish People* (1954); J. Jocz, *Jesus Christ and the Jewish People* (1954); R. N. Longenecker, *The Christology of Early Jewish Christianity* (1970); P. Osterbye, *The Church in Israel* (1970); B. Bagatti, *The Church from the Circumcision* (1971); P. van Buren, *Discerning the Way* (1980); *A Christian Theology of the People of Israel* (1983); O. Kvarme, *Let Jews and Arabs Hear His Voice* (1981); David W. Torrance, ed., *The Witness of the Jews to God* (1982).

MURDO A. MACLEOD

**Jews for Jesus.** Jewish missionary organization founded in 1973 by Moishe Rosen in San Francisco. It is one of the youngest Jewish missionary organizations in America, but the largest in the world. Moishe Rosen was a veteran missionary to Jews with the American Board of Missions (ABMJ) to the Jews. Rosen learned communications from the antiwar protesters and the "turn-on, tune-in, drop-out" movement. By 1972 Rosen had gathered a highly creative, activistic group of Jewish believers in Jesus.

Jews for Jesus was not an appellation, but one of several slogans by which the group was identified. In September 1973, Jews for Jesus became an independent organization and called itself "Hineni Ministries," although everyone called the group "Jews for Jesus." The generic slogan became synonymous with the organization. Within three years it had over 120 full-time Christian workers.

Some of the distinctives of their outreach are "broadside" gospel tracts. These are done in cartoon-style calligraphy. Over 25 million have been distributed, making Jews for Jesus the largest producer and distributor of gospel tracts in the USA. A branch in Toronto has its own council and budget, and there is a cooperative agreement with Christian Witness to Israel, a Jewish missionary society with ministries in Israel, Great Britain, India, South Africa, and Australasia.

Other evangelistic distinctives include Jewish gospel music, traveling evangelistic music teams such as "The Liberated Wailing Wall," and the Jewish gospel drama ("parabolic preaching"). Full-page advertisements offering free evangelistic books are placed in secular newspapers and magazines throughout North America, Europe, and Israel.

Jews for Jesus engages in traditional missionary endeavors such as door-to-door work, personal Bible instruction, telephone evangelism, hospital work, and fellowship meetings. Other aspects of the work include messianic Jewish worship celebrations and family events such as weddings, funerals, and Jewish-Christian Passover feasts.

All the front-line missionaries of Jews for Jesus are Jewish or are married to Jews. They are the best trained, best disciplined, best paid force of missionaries to the Jews worldwide. Continual training is required for all staff, and in 1988 a new degree program was introduced, the Master of Arts in Jewish Missions, which all staff must complete. The program is under the auspices of the School of World Missions at Fuller Theological Seminary, Pasadena, Calif.

SUSAN PERLMAN

**Joad, Cyril Edwin Mitchinson** (1891–1953). Anglican. Born in England, he was educated at Blundell's, Tiverton, and Balliol College, Oxford. He served in the civil service, board of trade (1914–30), and in his later years taught philosophy at the University of London (1930–53) and achieved fame for his participation in broadcasts. An agnostic until his later years, he was converted to Christianity and became a strong Anglican. His books on ethics and philosophy have achieved enduring acclaim among both Christian and non-Christian academicians. Some which have been reprinted include *God and Evil* (repr. ed., 1972), *The Present and Future of Religion* (repr., 1974), and *The Recovery of Faith: A Restatement of Christian Philosophy* (repr., 1976).

RAYMOND W. ALBRIGHT

**Johansson, Gustaf** (1844–1930). Archbishop of Finland. He became professor of systematics at Helsinki (1877), bishop of Kuopio (1885) and Nyslott (1896), and archbishop of Åbo (1899). Johansson was early influenced by the pietistic revival in Finland and was a disciple of J. T. Beck at Tübingen. He repudiated the new currents in theology and the ecumenical movement. Through his powerful religious personality he exercised a great influence. He was maligned for his passivity during Russian attempts to exert political and social control over Finland from 1904 until Finland's independence and civil war (1917–19).

CARL-GUSTAF ANDRÉN

**John, Epistles of.** *Authorship*. The similarity between the epistles and the Gospel binds the question of the authorship of the epistles with that of the Gospel. Critical scholars tend to assert that the apostle John was not directly responsible for any of the Johannine literature, although he may have influenced those who were—a "school," perhaps, of Christian thinkers gathered about John. The suggestion is favored by many that "John the elder," who is referred to by Papias, was the author. But it is not certain whether Papias intended to distinguish between John the Elder and John the apostle. In the same context he refers to the apostles as "elders." The traditional view, therefore, that "the elder" who wrote 2 and 3 John, was the apostle is logical, and the same author appears also to have written 1 John and the Gospel. The authoritative tone of the epistle and the claim of the author in 1 John to have been an eye witness of the historical events of the Gospel, are consistent with the view that they were written by an apostle.

***Purpose.*** It is clear that 1 John was written to counter those who denied that Jesus was the Christ and the Son of God (2:22), that is, who denied the reality of the divine incarnation (4:2, 3) and, consequently, the significance of Jesus' death (5:6–8). In 3 John there is no mention of such teaching, but in 2 John there is reference again to those who deny the reality of an incarnation of Christ (vv. 7, 9). From this it would seem that the Johannine church was faced with an incipient docetic gnosticism. On the practical side gnosticism often showed itself in neglect of Christian morality. It is not certain whether this was the case here, but the author stresses the importance of holiness and of love outworking in life (1 John 2:4–11; chap. 3; 4:7–21). It is difficult to identify John's opponents. Links can be found with Paul's opponents in Corinth, with Cerinthus at Ephesus, and with Ignatius's opponents at Antioch, but in no case is the identification complete. It may be best to regard them simply as a group who had broken away under docetic influence from the Johannine church, claiming to be "spiritual." Some scholars suggest that their docetism stemmed from a misinterpretation of the Gospel of John and that 1 John was an attempt to present a more orthodox interpretation. The problem with Diotrephes (3 John 9–10) seems distinct from the main concern of the epistles. He appears simply to have disagreed with John over the latter's policy on hospitality.

***Destination and Date.*** We have no means of identifying the Gaius to whom 3 John was addressed. The "elect lady" of 2 John has been variously understood, but most likely was a church rather than an individual. No indication is given of the recipients of 1 John. External evidence, however, links the apostle John with Ephesus, so the church addressed is probably the church in Ephesus or, more broadly, in the province of Asia. The nature of the false teaching suggests a date near the end of the 1st century. The date of the epistles relative to the Gospel is the subject of much disagreement, especially among scholars who see the Gospel as having passed through several redactions.

***Literary Form and Structure.*** The second and third epistles are clearly real letters. First John, on the other hand, lacking as it does an address and final greeting, might be a tract, a pamphlet, or a sermon. The structure of 1 John is determined by the author's purpose to counter false teaching by promoting faith in Jesus as the Christ

and love among Christians (3:23). However, it is difficult to find any clear development of thought in 1 John other than that the author proceeded around a central idea.

***Bibliography.*** *Commentaries.* C. H. Dodd, *The Johannine Epistles* (1946); R. Schnackenburg, *Die Johannesbriefe* in *HTKNT* 13³ (3d ed., 1965; sup., 5th ed., 1975); R. Bultmann, *The Johannine Epistles* (1973); J. Painter, *John: Witness and Theologian* (1975); I. H. Marshall, *The Epistles of John* (1978); S. S. Smalley, *1, 2, 3 John* (1984).

*Special Studies.* W. F. Howard, *The Fourth Gospel in Recent Criticism and Interpretation* (rev. ed., 1955); J. A. T. Robinson, *Twelve NT Studies* (1962); U. B. Müller, *Die Geschichte der Christologie in der johanneischen Gemeinde* (1975); R. E. Brown, *The Community of the Beloved Disciple* (1979); M. de Jonge, *Text and Interpretation* (1979); J. Painter, *NTS* 32 (1986).

DAVID JOHN WILLIAMS

**John, Gospel of.** *See* GOSPEL AND GOSPELS.

**John, Griffith** (1831–1912). Welsh Congregational missionary. Born in Swansea, Wales, at the age of 14 he began to preach in Welsh, and studied at Brecon College and the Missionary College at Bedford, England. In 1855 he was assigned by the London Missionary Society to China. Until 1861 he lived in or near Shanghai. Then he went to Hankow, where he became the first Protestant missionary in Central China, and made that city his headquarters until 1906. He made numerous journeys into the surrounding country and established many churches and missions in neighboring provinces. He lived in the USA after 1906, when he retired from missionary life. He wrote tracts in Chinese and also translated the NT and a portion of the OT into both easy Wen-li and Mandarin colloquial.

***Bibliography.*** R. W. Thompson, *Griffith John, the Story of Fifty Years in China* (1908).

**John XXIII** (1881–1963). Pope from 1958 to 1963. Born Angelo Giuseppe Roncalli in Sotto il Monte, near Bergamo, Italy, he was ordained to the priesthood in 1904. Having obtained a theology doctorate in Rome, he served as secretary to the bishop of Bergamo until 1915. After the war, he entered the Vatican's diplomatic service, and in 1925 was appointed apostolic visitor to Bulgaria; in 1934, he became apostolic delegate to Turkey and Greece. In both posts he had to protect the interests of a Roman Catholic minority in unfriendly Eastern Orthodox and Muslim environments. In 1944, he became papal nuncio in newly liberated France, where his task was to heal divisions caused by the experience of occupation. In 1953 he was created a cardinal and became patriarch of Venice.

After Pius XII's death, Roncalli was elected on the 12th ballot, taking the name John, after John the Baptist. John XXIII was not expected to live long (he was 77 when elected), and it was thought he would continue the conservative policies of his predecessor. The reverse proved true when in January 1959, under what he claimed was divine inspiration, he announced the convening of an ecumenical council mandated to regenerate the spiritual life of Catholics, update teaching, organization, and image, and promote Christian unity. He named it Vatican Council II, declaring that he hoped it would inaugurate a new Pentecost. Conservative members of the Curia resisted his plans, but Roncalli stood firm, and the council officially opened on October 11, 1962. Pope John invited Eastern Orthodox and Protestant churches to send observers to the council; 39 delegates attended, as well as 86 missions from governments and international bodies. He himself followed the council's discussions on closed-circuit television. He made only one serious intervention, when he instructed that the schema on revelation (which the council had rejected) be discussed no further, but instead be revised by a special commission. The original schema had anathematized those who denied the literal truth of Christ's words and deeds as narrated in the Gospels. The pope's decision encouraged liberal council members, and the final Constitution on Divine Revelation affirmed simply that Scripture inerrantly taught "that truth which God wanted put into the sacred writings for the sake of our salvation."

As pope Roncalli maintained a high international and ecumenical profile. A variety of representatives of other religious traditions was warmly received, including Archbishop Fisher of Canterbury, and such political figures as Harold Macmillan of Britain and the son-in-law of Soviet Premier Nikita Khrushchev. In East-West relations Pope John worked for reconciliation, and received the Balzan Peace Prize in 1963 in recognition of his services to world peace.

Roncalli was ill for some time with gastric cancer before his death. His posthumously published *Journal of a Soul* (1965) provides valuable insights into the inner life of one called the most revolutionary of modern pontiffs. He released eight encyclicals, including *Mater et magistra* (1961), dealing with labor and colonialism, and *Pacem in terris* (1963), a plea for world peace and cooperation.

NICK NEEDHAM

**John Paul** (1912–1978). Pope from August 26–September 28, 1978. Born Albino Luciani in Forno di Canale, Italy, he was ordained to the priesthood in 1935 and obtained a theology doctorate in Rome in 1937. After teaching and administrative posts at Belluno Seminary, in 1958 Luciani became bishop of Vittorio-Veneto. He took part in Vatican Council II as a supporter of its forward-looking attitudes. He disagreed, for instance, with the Church's official prohibition of contraception, although loyally submitting to the encyclical *Humanae vitae* of 1968, which reiterated the ban. His loyalty was rewarded in 1969 when Pope Paul VI appointed him archbishop and patriarch of Vienna; in 1973 he received a cardinal's hat.

Luciani's unexpected election to the pontificate after Paul VI's death brought to the papal throne a man of warmth, simplicity, and integrity who was committed to taking his church farther along the reforming path mapped out by the Vatican Council II. His sudden death under puzzling circumstances only a month after his election has occasioned some controversy. He wrote *Catechesi in bricole* (*Catechism in Crumbs*) and *Illustrissimi* (*The Most Illustrious Ones* [1976]).

NICK NEEDHAM

**John Paul** (1920– ). Pope since 1978. Karol Wojtyla is the first non-Italian to hold the papal office since Adrian V (1522–23) and the first Polish pope. Born in Wadowice, Poland, Wojtyla studied at Jagellonian University until the German occupation of Poland in World War II. He spent the war years doing manual labor and studied at a secret seminary at Kraków for the priesthood. He was ordained in 1946 and obtained doctorates from the Pontifical Angelicum University in Rome and Catholic University, Lublin. He served as a parish priest, lectured on social ethics at Kraków Seminary, and was professor of ethics at Lublin before he was appointed bishop of Omri in 1958, archbishop of Kraców in 1964, and cardinal in 1967. He also gained an international reputation as a member of the preparatory commission for Vatican Council II and through service on various postconciliar commissions after playing a prominent role at the council from 1962 to 1965. In 1971 he became a permanent member of the council of the Roman Synod of Bishops. He became widely known through his lectures and publications and led the struggle of the Polish church against the communist government.

He was elected pope in October 1978 when the conclave could not agree on an Italian candidate. A simple ceremony of inauguration set the tone for his pontificate, which has been characterized by his visibility to ordinary Christians throughout the world. Beginning with a trip to Mexico in 1979, he traveled extensively in third world countries. His travels were interrupted when he was shot in an assassination attempt in May 1981 in St. Peter's Square. After major surgery and a long period of recuperation he resumed his busy schedule, becoming the first pope to visit England in 1982.

His encyclicals had a strong emphasis on human freedom and dignity, but he opposed liberation theology and was conservative in theology and ethics, affirming the church's traditional teaching on clerical celibacy, contraception, abortion, and homosexuality. During his pontificate action was taken against Roman Catholic theologians whose teachings were considered unorthodox. Despite his sincere concern for human rights and his warm likeable personality, these actions led some to assess his pontificate negatively, while others stressed his importance in preserving the Christian heritage and emphasizing the international nature of the Roman Catholic Church. His encyclical, *The Social Concerns of the Church* (1988), spoke out against abuses of power under both capitalistic and communistic systems.

*Bibliography.* P. Hebblethwaite, *Introducing John Paul II* (1982); P. Johnson, *Pope John Paul II* (1982); Lord Longford, *Pope John Paul II: An Authorized Biography* (1982).

RUDOLPH W. HEINZE

**Johnson, Amandus** (1874–1974). Swedish educator and historian. He studied at Gustavus Adolphus College, Colorado, Berlin, and Pennsylvania (Ph.D., 1908). He taught in Pennsylvania (1910–22) and directed the West African Educational Exposition (1922–25). He was founder and director of the American Swedish Historical Museum (1926–40). He wrote *The Swedish Settlements on the Delaware* (2 vols., 1911), *Religious and Educational Contributions of the Swedes to American Culture* (1922), *In the Land of the Marimba* (1929), *Mbundu English-Portuguese Grammar and Dictionary* (1930), and *The Journal and Biography of Nicholas Collin (1746–1831)* (1936). He also wrote a multivolume work on Swedish contributions to American life (1953–57). He translated and edited *The Records of the Swedish Lutheran Churches of Raccoon and Penns Neck, New Jersey* (1938).

**Johnson, Elmer Ellsworth Schultz** (1872–1959). Schwenkfelder. He studied at Princeton University and the Hartford Theological Seminary (Ph.D., 1911). He was pastor of the First Schwenkfelder Church, Philadelphia (1902–4). From 1904 to 1919 he lived in Wolfenbüttel, Germany, as a member of the editorial staff of *Corpus Schwenkfeldianorum* (letters and treatises of Casper von Schwenkfeld [1490–1561]). He later served as editor in chief. He was Waldo professor of medieval and modern church history at Hartford Theological Seminary (1923–43) and pastor of Hereford Mennonite Church, Bally, Pa. (1921–47). He also was a member of the editorial staff of *The Schwenkfeldian* (1903–53).

RAYMOND W. ALBRIGHT

**Johnson, Frederick Ernest** (1884–1959). Methodist. Born in Ontario, he was educated at Albion College, Union Theological Seminary, and Columbia University. He was executive secretary, Department of Research and Education, Federal Council of Churches (1924–50), and executive director, Central Department of Research and Survey, National Council of Churches, and editor for the *Information Service*. He held a professor-

ship in Teachers College, Columbia University (1931–50). He directed an international survey of YMCA and YWCA facilities (1929–31). He was the author of *The New Spirit in Industry* (1919), *Economics and the Good Life* (1934), *The Church and Society* (1935), and *The Social Gospel Re-examined* (1940). He coauthored with Arthur E. Holt, *Christian Ideals in Industry* (1924), and with H. S. Warner, *Prohibition in Outline* (1927). He edited *Social Work of the Churches* (1930), *Religion and the World Order* (1944), *World Order: Its Intellectual and Cultural Foundations* (1945), *Foundation of Democracy* (1947), and *Wellsprings of the American Spirit* (1949).

**Johnson, Hewlett** (1876–1986). Dean of Canterbury. Born in England and educated at Manchester and Oxford universities, he was ordained in 1905 and was vicar of St. Margaret's, Altrincham (1908–24), dean of Manchester (1924–31), and dean of Canterbury (1931–63). He worked in the Manchester slums, and although he had wealthy parents, he made no secret of his socialist tendencies. He visited Russia in 1938 and thereafter published *The Socialist Sixth of the World*, which went through some two dozen editions and was translated into at least as many languages. Although never a member of the Communist party, he was awarded the Stalin Peace Prize in 1951, and caused uproar by charging the Americans with using germ warfare in Korea. His other publications include *Soviet Success* (1947), *China's New Creative Age* (1953), *Eastern Europe in the Socialist World* (1954), *Christians and Communism* (1956), and *The Upsurge of China* (1961).

J. D. DOUGLAS

**Johnson, Paul Emanuel** (1898–1974). American psychologist, philosopher, and pioneer in clinical pastoral education. Born in Niantic, Conn., he studied at Cornell College, Mount Vernon, Iowa, the University of Chicago, and Boston University (Ph.D., 1928). He was ordained a Methodist minister, served as a missionary in China (1925–27), then was successively associate professor of philosophy at Hamline University (1928–36), dean and professor of philosophy and religion at Morningside College, Sioux City, Iowa (1936–41), and professor of psychology of religion (1941–57) and of psychology and pastoral counseling (1957–63) at Boston University. With others he founded the Institute of Pastoral Care (1943), the *Journal of Pastoral Care* (1950), and the Danielson Pastoral Counseling Center in Boston. His work on pastoral care was rooted in his personalist philosophy of life, and stressed the dynamic potential of interpersonal relations. His writings include *Psychology of Religion* (rev. ed., 1959), *Christian Live* (1951), *Psychology of Pastoral Care* (1953), *Personality and Religion* (1957), *Person and Counselor* (1967), (with L. Colston)

*Personality and Christian Faith* (1972), and *Dynamic Interpersonalism for Ministry* (1973).

GLEN SCORGIE

**Jones, Eli Stanley** (1894–1973). Missionary to India. Born in Clarksville, Md., he studied at Asbury College, and went to India as a missionary of the Methodist Episcopal Church. After serving at the Lal Bagh Methodist Church at Lucknow (1907–10), he was appointed to Sitapur. He conducted religious retreats in India and America, and was an evangelist to the educated classes of India. After his retirement in 1954 he continued evangelistic work in the Far East six months each year. He was the recipient of the Gandhi Peace Prize in 1961. His writings include *The Christ of the Indian Road* (1925), which was translated into 20 languages and sold more than 700,000 copies, *Christ at the Round Table* (1928), *The Christ of Every Road* (1939), *The Christ on the Mount* (1931), *Christ and Human Suffering* (1933), *Christ's Alternative to Communism* (1934), *Victorious Living* (1936), *Along the Indian Road* (1939), *Abundant Living* (1942), *The Christ of the American Road* (1944), *How to Be a Transformed Person* (1951), *Christian Maturity* (1957), *Victory Through Surrender* (1966), *A Song of Accents—A Spiritual Autobiography* (1968), *The Reconstruction of the Church—On What Pattern?* (1970), and *The Unshakable Kingdom and the Unchanging Person* (1972).

**Jones, Rufus Matthew** (1863–1948). American Quaker. He studied at Haverford College and Harvard. He helped interpret Quaker mystical religion and taught philosophy in Haverford College for 40 years. He was the founder and lifetime chairman of the American Friends Service Committee. He was the acknowledged leader of Quaker thought and was largely responsible for renewing its outreach to the world. He wrote *Studies in Mystical Religion* (1908), *Spiritual Reformers in the 16th and 17th Centuries* (repr. 1959), *The Later Periods of Quakerism* (repr. 1970), *Fundamental Ends of Life* (1924), *Pathways to the Reality of God* (1931), *New Eyes for Invisibles* (1943), *The Luminous Trail* (1947), and *A Call to What Is Vital* (1948), in which he sought to make the appeal of spiritual religion reach out to those of all faiths. His autobiography is carried through his middle life in *Finding the Trail of Life* (1926), *The Trail of Life in the Middle Years* (1934), and *A Small-Town Boy* (1941).

DOUGLAS V. STEERE

**Jordan.** Middle East Kingdom located on the northwest corner of the Arabian peninsula. It has an area of 97,740 sq. km. (37,738 sq. mi.). Of Jordan's 2 million people (1985), 93 percent are Muslims (mostly Sunnis of the Shafiite rite). The Chechens, a small group of Caucasian extraction, are Shias. Most well-established families living in urban and village communities observe orthodox Muslim customs, but the nomadic Bedouin follow pre-Islamic tribal law (*urf*). Baha'i is represented by a very small community in the northern Jordan Valley. A few hundred Druze live along the Syrian border. The sect's leading tenet is that Hakim (the divine sixth Fatimid caliph) is alive and in hiding. There are also about 3000 Alawites living in Jordan.

An interesting statistic indicating Islam's strength in Jordan is the increase of Hajj pilgrims to Mecca. In 1969 about 6376 visited Mecca while in 1976 the number of visitors had increased to 23,427.

Christians in Jordan represent 4.9 percent of the population, but the percentage is declining annually at a rate of 0.1 percent. The survival of Christianity in the Muslim world can be explained by the extraordinary zeal of the orthodox clergy and existing tribal structures which have conditioned and stabilized the various religious alliances. Christianity tends to be best preserved in rural areas. However, Christians are present in all social strata, except among the nomads (5 percent of total population) and, with rare exceptions, among the Palestinians in refugee camps. Christians tend to be involved more and more in rapid urbanization as they become middle-class merchants and office workers. Limited economic opportunities, however, have led to emigration of many Jordanian Christians.

The Greek Orthodox Church with 36,000 members is the largest Christian group. Parish priests and laity are for the most part Palestinian Arabs whereas the patriarch, bishops, and monks are Greeks. The patriarchate sponsors schools, an orphanage, and a home for the aged. The Armenian Apostolic Church (1500 members) has suffered most from emigration. There are about 27 Christian denominations in all, with membership numbering only in the hundreds. Interestingly, one identification of a group with 4100 members is "Isolated Radio Churches" which suggests groups united by radio broadcasts and perhaps correspondence.

In church and state relations, the Constitution of 1952 (subsequently amended several times) establishes Islam as the state religion, prohibits all religious discrimination, and guarantees the free exercise of religion and belief. There is no government ministry or department dealing with religious affairs. To be recognized and to receive state protection, minority religious groups must register with the Ministry of the Interior. The state has refused to recognize some religious groups (e.g., Jehovah's Witnesses) because of alleged subversive activities. Eviction of individuals who aggressively engage in "evangelism" by expatriates has occurred.

No school, Christian or otherwise, can be opened without approval of the Ministry of Education. From a practical standpoint, the Ministry of Education, somewhat under the influence of the Muslim Brotherhood, tends to frustrate more than to facilitate the functioning of Christian schools. In official schools, Muslim religious instruction is obligatory for Muslim students and constitutes a subject for examination.

With some reservations in view of social pressure, one can say that Christians enjoy a number of advantages in Jordan. They are well represented in the government, and in cases of conflict between Christians and Muslims, the Hashemite monarchy has often conciliated. Paradoxically, the monarchy has had to conciliate on occasion between rival Christian groups.

*Bibliography.* A. J. Arberry, ed., *Religion in the Middle East*, 2 vols. (1969); W. Lancaster, *The Rwala Bedouin Today* (1981); P. Gubser, *Jordan: Crossroads of Middle Eastern Events* (1983); K. Cragg, *The Call of the Minaret* (1985); G. J. Jennings, *Welcome into the Middle East* (1986).

GEORGE J. JENNINGS

**Jourdan, George Viviliers** (1867–1955). Church of Ireland church historian. Born in Dublin, he was educated at Trinity College and the University of Dublin. He held curacies in Cavan, Westmeath, and Cork; became incumbent of Rathbarry, Ross (1906); St. Mary Shandon, Cork (1915); and Dunboyne, Meath (1940); was elected canon of St. Patrick's Cathedral, Dublin (1931); and was appointed professor of ecclesiastical history at the University of Dublin (1933). His publications include *The Movement Towards Catholic Reform in the Early Sixteenth Century* (1914), *The Stress of Change* (1931), and seven chapters in W. A. Phillips, ed., *The History of the Church of Ireland* (1933/34).

**Jowett, John Henry** (1864–1923). English Congregational preacher and writer. Born in Halifax, Yorkshire, he was educated at the universities of Edinburgh and Oxford, and ministered at St. James' Congregational Church, Newcastle-on-Tyne (1889–95), Carr's Lane Congregational Church, Birmingham (1895–1911), Fifth Avenue Presbyterian Church, N.Y. (1911–18), and Westminster Chapel, London (1918–23). He was a prominent speaker in the Northfield Conference in 1909. His publications include *From Strength to Strength* (1898), *Thirsting for Souls* (1902), *The Epistles of Peter* (1905), *The High Calling: Meditations on St. Paul's Letter to the Philippines* (1909), and various other devotional works.

**Jubilee, Year of.** Roman Catholic institution which began with medieval pilgrimages to the tombs of the apostles in Rome. The essential ceremony of the jubilee consists in the solemn opening of the *Porta Sancta*, the walled "Holy Door" in the Roman basilicas of St. Peter, St. John Lateran, St. Mary Major, and St. Paul. After the conclusion of the jubilee, the Holy Door is walled again. Considerable indulgences are granted to the pilgrims who visit the aforesaid basilicas and fulfill certain conditions, which usually are the reception of the sacrament of penance, holy communion, and the offering of prayers. Persons physically unable to travel to Rome may earn similar indulgences in their home country, according to the provisions specified in the bull proclaiming the jubilee or in a similar document.

Extraordinary jubilees with special indulgences were proclaimed by Pius X on the 50th anniversary of the definition of the Immaculate Conception (1904); and on the 16th centennial of the Edict of Constantine (1913); by Pius XI on the 50th anniversary of his ordination (1929); and on the 19th centennial of "the redemption of mankind" (1923), in which instance the *Porta Sancta* was solemnly opened. Paul VI proclaimed a jubilee indulgence for most of 1966 to celebrate the end of the Second Vatican Council.

**Judaism, Recent.** The word *Judaism* was derived from the Greek *'Ioudaismos* and came to signify among the Greek-speaking Jews of the Roman Empire their religion, philosophy, and way of life. The term was used to distinguish Jewish culture from the Greek or Hellenistic culture that permeated the ancient Western world. The apostle Paul used the word twice in his letter to the Galatians (1:13–14) to describe his firm adherence to the Jewish way of life and traditions of his ancestors before his conversion experience. The term has no other parallels either in the Hebrew or Greek Scriptures or in rabbinic literature (although it is popularly used today). Torah is the term generally used in ancient Hebrew sources for the whole gamut of Jewish teaching.

Although Judaism and Jewish people have historically emphasized particular aspects of their belief, they have always put more stress on the actual living of one's faith rather than on a particular creed or doctrinal formula. The cornerstone of Judaism is *deed*, not *dogma*. Nevertheless, there are basic concepts in traditional Judaism that have not only held during the ancient period, but also have permeated the 20th century.

***Basic Concepts.*** In every Jewish worship service today, the Shema is recited. It literally means "Hear!" (or "Understand!") and is the first word of Deut. 6:4, which the congregation sings in unison: "*Shema Yisrael Adonai Eloheinu Adonai Echad*" ("Hear, O Israel: The Lord our God, the Lord is One"). Judaism has traditionally held to the unity and eternal spirit of the one true God. God created everything and actively governs the universe. Monotheism is never questioned and, historically, God's existence can never be proved. It is taken for granted. Whereas the essence of God is hidden and unfathomable, the attributes of God (such as justice, mercy, and wisdom) are visibly active in the universe.

For the Jew, the weekly Sabbath observance symbolizes the truth of God's personal activity in the affairs of humankind. On the seventh day of the week God culminated his work of creation and declared the day blessed and holy. The Sabbath also celebrates God as the Redeemer of his people in world history. The day commemorates the exodus from Egypt, in which God liberated the Hebrew slaves, presented the Torah, and led his people into the promised land.

In Judaism, the relationship between God and man is one of grace and faith. Grace is the divine side of the connection, and *hesed* is the word used for the undeserved love that God has for his creation and in his covenant with the Jewish people. Faith that leads to devotion is the human side, and the Jewish concept of faith is one of being faithful or holding firm in the faith. Faith is an ongoing process and must mirror God's faithfulness. It links the soul of the human being to God, creating an awareness of and an attachment to the divine that produces deeds of kindness. In this way, the "faithful ones" (*emunim*) mirror the grace of God in acts of human grace.

Judaism teaches that God has shown men and women the way of truth. One learns the will of the Father through Torah (a word that is related to the root "to teach" or "teachings," rather than "law"). In the most narrow sense, it specifically refers to the first five books of the Bible (Genesis–Deuteronomy), the foundation stones of Jewish tradition. In the broader sense, Torah encompasses the total revelation of God—interpretation as well as revelation. In this expanded view, far from being a narrow law code, Torah is a "way of life"—God's way of life.

Broadly conceived, Torah presents the Jewish people with the opportunity for individual salvation as well as national redemption. The famed 20th-century scholar and philosopher, Rabbi Abraham Joshua Heschel (1907–72) declared: "A Jew must strive to be Torah incarnate." In Judaism, *mitzvot* ("good deeds" or "commandments," both ritual and ethical) are not what one does above and beyond, but rather are the expected thing to do—the way of the faithful's life. The Hebrew admonition is *zedek zedek tirdof* ("Justice, Justice pursue"). Through such a way of life and drawing close to God's gracious deliverance, a Jewish person becomes a *ben Olam Haba*, a son of the world to come. Non-Jews are also provided the opportunity for salvation by following God's way as he instructed in the seven commandments given to Noah (Gen. 9). In Judaism, the "righteous" from all nations who follow God's way inherit the "world to come."

Judaism is a liturgical religion. It has a prayer book and a fixed liturgy for worship. Although spontaneous prayer and private expression toward God are never discouraged, the prayer book (known as the *Siddur*, "order") is used in both the synagogue and the home. While individual prayer is important, communal prayer in Judaism has greater worth and effect. The local community reflects in miniature the entire covenanted congregation standing before God. Each Jewish person derives strength and purpose from uniting with the congregation under God in prayer. The yearly cycle of fasts, festivals, and holy days in Judaism internalizes this Jewish experience and dictates an understanding of life itself. Birth, circumcision, bar/bat mitzvah, marriage, and death are milestones that are marked with religious significance and ritual.

In Judaism the preservation of life supersedes the fulfillment of all commandments (except prohibitions against murder, unchastity, and idolatry). For the Jewish people, this means that they are not only responsible for their lives before God, but are responsible for the well-being of all men, women, and children. In Judaism, one should be concerned as much with the preservation of others' lives as with one's own life. Such righteousness is not without its rewards, both in this world and in the "world to come." God will reunite body and soul in *tehiyyat hametim* ("the revival of the dead") at the end of world history.

***Groups and Experience***. Historical circumstances have molded and transformed the face of Judaism in the 20th century, and yet the basic concepts of modern Judaism have shaped the character and actions of Jews around the world. Building upon the concept of the sanctity of human life, for example, Jewish men and women have been in the vanguard of social reform movements throughout the 20th century and, as a people, in the area of charitable giving they are second to none (the Hebrew word for charity, *tzedakah*, literally means "righteousness"). From helping the boat people of Cambodia to the starving masses of Africa, from providing homes for orphans to local charity campaigns, the Jewish people are often at the forefront of leadership and the backbone of support. Jewish Nobel Prize winners have been so prevalent in the 20th century that their number is approximately 25 times their percentage in the world population. In the last few decades 30 to 40 percent of the American Nobel laureates in science have been Jewish, rising to prominence at the very same time that science began to explode within the cutting edge of human knowledge.

Adaptation to this modern world and bitter tragedy have altered Judaism and its traditions. Nowhere are these factors more visible than in the USA. The American Jewish community was destined to become the largest Jewish community in the world in the 20th century and the home of the three large traditions of Judaism.

Reform Judaism was the first of the contemporary reinterpretations of Judaism to emerge in response to the modern technological world and newly won freedoms. Early reformers were German laypeople who had no intention of breaking with Jewish tradition. They sought only to adapt and modify the traditional synagogue service to modern culture, such as shortening the liturgy by avoiding repetition and using German as well as Hebrew, introducing the sermon, adding mixed choral singing, and so on. A new generation of university-educated rabbis, familiar with modern biblical criticism, added theological impetus to the lay reform movement.

Quite independently, Jewish laypeople in the USA incorporated such changes in their synagogues. German Reform rabbis immigrating to America in the 19th century solidified the Reform movement in the USA. In a pioneer atmosphere with no traditional or organizational restraints, Reform Judaism in America went far beyond the more traditional Reform movement in Europe. In some cases, Reform synagogues became almost indistinguishable from liberal Protestant churches. The Union of American Hebrew Congregations (UAHC) was founded in 1873 by Reform rabbi Isaac Mayer Wise (1819–1900). To Wise's delight, Reform Judaism's Hebrew Union College (HUC) followed in Cincinnati, Ohio, in 1875, the first extant institution of Jewish higher learning in America. Currently, Hebrew Union College-Jewish Institute of Religion has centers in Cincinnati, New York, Los Angeles, and Jerusalem. In 1889, the third arm of the Reform movement was created—the Central Conference of American Rabbis (CCAR). This national association of Reform rabbis today has a membership of approximately 1500.

At the founding of the Union of Orthodox Jewish Congregations of America (UOJCA) in 1898, the Orthodox rabbis present made it clear that they were "anti-Reform" and that Reform views were totally unacceptable. Orthodox Judaism considers itself the authentic bearer of the religious Jewish tradition. The term "orthodoxy" first appeared within Judaism at the end of the 1700s in response to the reform impulse and the attempt of some Jews to adapt Judaism to Western culture. The word "orthodox" means "right belief," and yet most of the early disputes were over "right practice." The Orthodox movement stresses the importance of *halakhah*, the legal part of Torah and Talmudic tradition.

Through its organization for rabbis, the Rabbinical Council of America (founded in 1923), UOJCA supervises the *kashrut* (Jewish dietary laws that assure food is *kosher*, "religiously proper" in both slaughter and preparation). They are responsible for the "U" symbol that appears on some kosher products (signifying Orthodox Union). The "K" found on other products certifies

that the food has been processed as kosher under rabbinic supervision. Observant Jews maintain the Jewish dietary laws faithfully, and Orthodoxy in America, Israel, and other nations is painstakingly involved in monitoring the process.

Although the 1890 census gave Reform Judaism more than half of the congregational memberships and synagogue buildings in the USA, a new surge of 2 million Jewish immigrants from the Russian Empire, Austria, Poland, Hungary, Romania, and other areas of Eastern Europe would infuse an Old World spirit into Jewish religion and culture. Many of these Jews had suffered from anti-Semitic attack and were escaping the horror of pogroms, especially in Russia. In stark contrast to most new immigrants (27 million would travel to America's shores between 1880 and 1930), the Jewish immigration was a movement of families. They had little incentive to return to their former countries and were determined to make the USA their home.

Among new arrivals to America between 1880 and 1910, Jews were second in number only to the Italians. Most of them were committed to traditional Judaism, and Yeshiva University in New York became Orthodox Judaism's largest educational institution. By 1919, the American Jewish community was the largest Jewish community in the world. By 1930 Jews constituted 3 percent of the total population of the USA. Today, more than 11 percent of the Jewish families in the USA describe themselves as "Orthodox." A complex movement, an Orthodox synagogue may belong to one of three councils (UOJCA, the National Council of Young Israel, or the Yeshiva University Synagogue Council). Hardly monolithic, Orthodox rabbis may be members of one of six rabbinical organizations, or they may be privately ordained and not part of any such organization. The largest centers of Hasidic Jews, the rigorously observant East European charismatic pietists of Judaism who follow a *tzaddik* (or *rebbe*), have been replanted in the USA and Israel. Progressively during the 20th century, they have been guardedly accepted as the right-wing of the Orthodox movement.

The question that faced these Jewish immigrants was how they could maintain traditional Judaism in an industrial and urbanizing nation such as the United States of America. For many, the answer was Conservative Judaism, the third major grouping of Judaism. Like Reform Judaism, Conservative Judaism has roots firmly planted in the soil of Western Europe. Its leaders insisted that only moderate reforms that were not in conflict with the spirit of historical Judaism should be permitted in traditional ritual. The Conservatives believe that modern culture necessitates some adaptation and change. They believe that the entire history of Judaism was a succession of changes, and that change is valid in light of biblical and rabbinic precedents. Conservative Judaism's educational institution, Jewish Theological Seminary of America (JTS), was founded in 1887 in New York City as an alternative to Reform Judaism's Hebrew Union College, and under the leadership of its president Solomon Schechter (1847–1915) the United Synagogue of America was founded in 1913. Today, this association consists of approximately 850 Conservative synagogues in the USA and Canada. The Rabbinical Assembly (RA) is Conservative Judaism's international association of rabbis.

To Conservatives, the Jewish peoplehood is a living organism that historically responded with creativity to new challenges. And yet, such change is to be made with only the greatest reluctance, because Conservative Judaism maintains the validity of the traditional forms and precepts of Judaism. There is an essential commitment of Conservative Judaism to the observance of kashrut, the Sabbath, the yearly and life cycles, the importance of the State of Israel, and devotion to the Hebrew language. For many immigrants, Conservative Judaism was the in-between group. It provided a way to adapt to modern culture without compromising the essence of traditional Judaism. By the 1950s, every study of religious preference among Jews showed that approximately half of all Jews in the USA considered themselves Conservative Jews.

***The Holocaust and Israel***. In 1951 the Israeli Knesset set aside the 27th day of Nisan as a "perpetual remembrance" of the 6 million Jewish men, women, and children exterminated by the Nazi regime and its collaborators. *Yom Ha-Shoah* (Holocaust Remembrance Day) became a part of the religious calendar of the Jewish people, a time of reflection that more Jews were killed in the period from 1939 to 1945 than in all the previous persecutions and massacres in Jewish history. During the Holocaust, one-third of world Jewry and two-thirds of European Jewry were killed. The 3.3 million Polish Jewish community was decimated to less than 10,000. The Holocaust is an atrocity in Judaism's history that has burned itself on the Jewish community's psyche and soul.

Eight days after *Yom Ha-Shoah*, *Yom Ha-Atzmaut* (the Israeli "Fourth of July") is observed on the fifth day of Iyyar. Religious services around the world include prayers for Israel and thankfulness to God for a homeland. After 19 centuries of enforced exile, the Jewish people once again have a homeland in the Holy Land, the State of Israel being formally recognized on May 14, 1948. Although Jewish people consider their country of residence their home and Jewish tradition teaches that one must be a good citizen of the country in which one lives, the importance of the State of Israel to the survival of the Jewish people is incalculable. During the Holocaust, there was no place for most Jewish people to go—no country that would take them in. The State of Israel promises citizenship to Jewish people from any nation and pledges to be a haven in time of trouble.

Both the Holocaust and the modern State of Israel have become an intrinsic part of 20th-century Judaism. They have had an important effect on Jewish groups everywhere. During the Holocaust, Zionist and non-Zionist Jews came together to support a Jewish State. Although some Orthodox rabbis at first opposed political Zionism because of its secular base, and others today oppose the State of Israel because the Messiah did not establish it, most Orthodox rabbis, leaders, and laypersons view the State of Israel as "the beginning of the redemption," God's guiding of human beings to prepare for the Messiah. Orthodox Jews believe in a personal Messiah, an individual who will be a charismatically endowed descendant of David who will reign in Jerusalem, will rebuild the temple, and will reinstitute the sacrificial system.

The horror of the Holocaust has moved Reform Judaism from a position of opposition to the reestablishment of a Jewish state in the latter 19th century and early 20th century to a wholehearted support of the necessity for Israel. Conservative Judaism has been a firm supporter of the State of Israel, but along with Reform Judaism it has been contending with Orthodox Judaism in Israel for the right of equal recognition and the right to found synagogues, camps, and schools in the Jewish state. Reform Judaism believes in a coming messianic age, rather than in a personal Messiah. Most Conservative Jews concur with this assessment.

Reform Judaism's Columbus Platform of 1937 was a watershed for a change of direction toward less radical and more traditional respect for Torah and the uniqueness of Judaism. Reform Judaism continues to believe, however, that halakhah is created by human beings, not God. Because Judaism is a changing, evolving, and growing religious tradition, human beings have the option to change or modify Jewish practices. Today, Reform Judaism and Conservative Judaism are much closer than at any other time in history, and Reform Judaism often shares its abundance of rabbis with the Conservative movement. Reform Judaism ordained its first female rabbi in 1972 and, after much debate, Conservative Judaism finally permitted female ordination in the early 1980s. Both movements contend with a high rate of intermarriage and low synagogue attendance that portend to decimate the Jewish population. Reconstructionism, a movement that originated with Conservative Judaism's Mordecai Kaplan (1881–1983) and emphasized Judaism as a civilization, is a very small movement today, as is purely secular Judaism. Only a small percentage of Jews question the existence of God, and more than 80 percent of American Jews define themselves in religious terms or as part of a religious movement.

Today, the largest Jewish community in the world is in the USA, with approximately 5.9 million. The second largest is in Israel, with approximately 3.6 million. These Jewish communities are currently consumed with the task of helping the 2 million Jews of Russia to escape the bonds of communist anti-Semitism in the respite of glasnost.

**Bibliography.** *Encyclopedia Judaica*, 16 vols. (1972, plus update supplements); *Gates of Prayer: The New Union Prayerbook* (1975); B. Greenberg, *How to Run a Traditional Jewish Household* (1983); Y. Eckstein, *What Christians Should Know About Jews and Judaism* (1984); J. D. Sarna, *The American Jewish Experience* (1986); L. Fein, *Where Are We?: The Inner Life of America's Jews* (1988); D. A. Rausch, *Building Bridges: Understanding Jews and Judaism* (1988); A. Lerman, *The Jewish Communities of the World: A Contemporary Guide* (4th ed., 1989); E. Friesel, *Atlas of Modern Jewish History* (1990).

DAVID A. RAUSCH

## Jude, Epistle of. *Authorship and Date.* There

is no reason to doubt that the Jude of the opening verse is the brother of James "the Just" and, indeed, of Jesus himself. Modern scholars do disagree about whether Jude was the actual author of the epistle or a pseudonym used by another. The latter opinion is held largely on the grounds of the language of the epistle; it is doubted that a Palestinian Jew would have had the command of Greek of this author. But there is no a priori reason why a brother of Jesus, a Galilean, should not have known Greek from his childhood and refined his knowledge as a Christian missionary. The author was undoubtedly familiar with the Hebrew scriptures, he probably read the book of Enoch in Aramaic, and he owed much to Jewish haggadic traditions. From this it seems likely that the epistle belongs to the milieu of 1st-century Jewish Christianity. Certainly nothing in the matter it deals with is without parallel elsewhere in the NT (for example, the antinomianism of the Corinthians). A date in the 50s is not out of the question and there are possible (but not proven) references to the epistle in Clement of Rome, Polycarp, Barnabas, and the Didache. An early date would add weight to the argument that Jude was the author. It should be noted, however, that some hesitation was felt in the later church in accepting the epistle as authentic.

*Destination and Purpose.* We can only guess at the location of the church(es) addressed, taking into account the probability that they were a predominantly Jewish Christian community (if the writer's "Jewishness" is any guide to that of his readers') and that they were being threatened with an antinomianism which is more easily associated with a Gentile rather than a Jewish environment. A location in Asia Minor, with its large Jewish communities, its links with Paul, and its antinomian movements attested in Rev.

2:14, 20 is a possibility. Others have suggested Syria and Egypt.

The purpose of the epistle is clearly set out at the beginning. The author states that he had intended writing about "our common salvation," but instead felt it necessary to urge his readers "to contend for the faith that was once for all entrusted to the saints" (v. 36, NIV). The reason for this was the appearance among these Christians of teachers who claimed to be Christian but who rejected the moral authority both of Christ (vv. 4, 8) and the Scriptures (vv. 8–10) and turned the (Pauline) doctrine of salvation by grace to their own antinomian ends (v. 4)—a problem with which Paul himself constantly contended. These teachers claimed the authority of a direct inspiration (v. 8). They cannot be called gnostics, but they represent a form of incipient gnosticism.

**Bibliography.** B. Reicke, *The Epistle of James, Peter, and Jude* (1964); A. R. C. Leaney, *The Letters of Peter and Jude* (1967); E. M. Sidebottom, *James, Jude and 2 Peter* (1967); M. Green, *The Second Epistle General of Peter and the General Epistle of Jude* (1968); J. N. D. Kelley, *A Commentary on the Epistles of Peter and Jude* (1969); J. Cantinat, *Les Epitres de Saint Jacques et de Saint Jude* (1973); R. J. Bauckham, *Jude, 2 Peter* (1983).

DAVID JOHN WILLIAMS

## Jung, Carl Gustav (1875–1961). Protestant

psychotherapist. He was born in Basel, Switzerland, the son of a clergyman. He studied at Basel University (M. D., 1902). He was a disciple of Sigmund Freud until 1911, when he founded a new school at Zürich. Preferring the term "analytical psychology" to "psychoanalysis," Jung believed that everyone is both an introvert and an extrovert, and that how a person individualizes the self from others is determined by which predominates. The primary functions of the mind are thinking, feeling, sensation, and intuition. He acknowledged the conscious and the unconscious, but he differed from the Freudians in teaching that the unconscious is made up of undeveloped, rather than repressed, material. The unconscious also includes both personal and collective factors, the collective factors inherited from ancestors. He stressed "individuation" which is similar to religious conversion. Less of a scientist than a philosopher, Jung gave a religious emphasis to many of his ideas. His use of religious symbols attracted religious people, but he often gave such symbols different meanings. His works include *Psychology of the Unconscious* (1916), *Studies in Word Association* (1918), *Psychological Types* (1923), and *Modern Man in Search of a Soul* (1934).

ROLLIN J. FAIRBANKS

## Justification. The act of declaring, or the pro-

cess of becoming just or righteous. The theme of the divine righteousness/justice in human salvation is prominent in the Book of Romans, where

Paul explains how God can forgive sinners, be they Jewish or Gentile.

Because of the great influence of Augustine of Hippo, Paul's teaching was misunderstood for centuries. Because Augustine did not know Greek he judged that *dikaioun* (Lat. *justificari*) meant "to make righteous"; he rejected the possibility that it meant "to pronounce righteous." So he thought of the principle of righteousness being infused into the soul at baptism and of the Christian life being a process of being made righteous just in order that, after death, God (for Christ's sake) could pronounce the Christian justified. This approach became standard doctrine in the Middle Ages and was confirmed by the Roman Catholic Church at the Council of Trent (1545–63).

Martin Luther was the first to clearly see that *dikaioun* was to be interpreted as the declaration by God with respect to a sinner who believes the gospel. That is, for Christ's sake, God the Father declares a believing sinner to be forgiven and to be perfectly righteous as viewed "in Christ": further, because God's word does not return unto him void this declaration also is the origin of the regeneration and conversion of the believing sinner. This insight was a liberating force for Luther and he became the leader of the Protestant Reformation. All the Protestant churches have followed Luther in insisting that the primary meaning of justification is the declaration of God who accounts a sinner to be righteous in his sight for the sake of Jesus Christ, the Righteous One. Not surprisingly, there have been many bitter and erudite controversies between Catholic and Protestant theologians over this doctrine.

As a result of the ecumenical movement of the 20th century, it has been possible for theologians from the Roman and Protestant churches to meet in order to discuss amicably different doctrines. Although this has not led to any agreement, it has helped to sort out where there are differences and where there have been, and remain, misunderstandings. Most important of the reports from this dialog is *Justification by Faith: U.S. Lutheran-Roman Catholic Dialogue* (1983). This sets out the issues with great clarity and integrity. Less important, but a significant sign of mutual understanding, is *Salvation and the Church: An Agreed Statement by the Second Anglican-Roman Catholic International Commission* (1987). It appears to be the case that while theologians can agree as to what Paul taught in the context of his mission as apostle to the Gentiles, they cannot as yet agree how this ought to be stated in the context of the modern world as doctrine/dogma for today. The Roman Catholics have the further problem that their received dogma is viewed as without essential error and that dogma commits them to a doctrine which is apparently at odds with what Paul actually taught. Interestingly, justification never seems to have a major issue for the Orthodox and Eastern churches and so they have little or nothing to contribute to this continuing debate.

**Bibliography.** P. Toon, *Justification and Sanctification* (1983); A. E. McGrath, *A History of the Doctrine of Justification* (1986).

PETER TOON

# Kk

**Kaftan, Julius Wilhelm Martin** (1848–1926). German Lutheran theologian. Born near Apenrade in Schleswig-Holstein, he was educated at the universities of Erlangen, Berlin, and Kiel, and in 1873 was appointed associate professor of systematic theology at Basel, and was full professor from 1881. In 1883 he became professor of apologetics and the philosophy of religion at Berlin, a post he held until his death. A member of the religiohistorical school, he wrote extensively on Kant and his influences on Protestant thought. Among his works were *Sollen und Sein in ihrem Verhältnis zu einander* (1872), *Die Predigt des Evangeliums des Apostels Paulus in Predigten der Gemeinde dargelegt* (1879), *Das Wesen der christlichen Religion* (1881), *Die Wehrheit der christlichen Religion* (1888), *Dogmatik* (1897), and *The Philosophy of Protestantism* (1917).

**Kaftan, Theodor** (1847–1932). Lutheran church administrator and theologian. He spent many years as the general superintendent of the church in Schleswig. Theologically he was opposed to Ernst Troeltsch and tried to develop a new support for the traditional faith by a use of modern developments in science and thought. His publications include *Moderne Theologie des alten Glaubens* (1905), *Zur Verständigung über moderne Theologie des alten Glaubens* (1909), and *Ernst Troeltsch* (1912).

RAYMOND W. ALBRIGHT

**Kagawa, Toyohiko** (1888–1960). Japanese Christian leader. Born in Kobe, he was disinherited when at 15 he became a Christian, having been greatly influenced by American missionaries C. A. Logan and H. W. Myers. He studied at Meiji Christian College in Tokyo and at Kobe Seminary. He entered the slums of Kobe on Christmas Eve 1909, to devote himself to Christian service among the poor, helpless, and fallen. Later he studied at Princeton Theological Seminary (1914–16). He became an outstanding evangelist and Christian leader, distinguished social worker,

and leader of labor movements and cooperatives of various kinds. He was a Christian poet and author of 180 books on religious, social, scientific, and other subjects. He was chairman of many organizations, among them the Mission to Lepers, the International Peace Association (he was imprisoned as a pacifist during World War II), the Moral New Life Society, and the Tree Crop Agricultural Research Institute. He was president of the All Japan Farmers' Association, the Japan Co-operative Association, and the Christian News Weekly.

He established churches, missions, kindergartens, nurseries, and gospel schools in cities and in rural mining and fishing districts. He received 225,000 decision cards from Japanese audiences who wanted to follow Christ. He traveled widely abroad on evangelistic tours, being heard on four continents. Among his books in English translation are *Before the Dawn* (1925), *Love, the Law of Life* (1930), *Christ and Japan* (1934), *Song from the Slums* (1935), *Brotherhood Economics* (1937), and *Behold the Man* (1941).

**Kähler, Carl Martin August** (1835–1912). German Protestant. Born in Neuhausen, he studied law at Königsberg and theology at Heidelberg, Halle, and Tübingen. He became privatdocent at Halle in 1867, and was professor of systematic theology and NT exegesis in Halle from 1879. His writings include *August Tholuck, ein Lebensabriss* (1877), *Julius Müller, der hallische Dogmatiker* (1878), *Neutestamentliche Schriften in genauer Wiedergabe ihres Gedankenganges dargestellt* (3 vols., comprising Hebrews, Galatians, and Ephesians, 1880–94), *Die Wissenschaft der christlichen Lehre* (3 vols., 1883–87), *Der sogenannte historische Jesus und der geschichtliche Christus* (1896), *Jesus und das Alte Testament* (1896), *Dogmatische Streitfragen* (2 vols., 1898), *Wiedergeboren durch die Auferstehung Jesu Christi* (1901), and *Die Sakramente als Gnadenmittel* (1903).

**Kahle, Paul Ernst** (1875–1964). German orientalist. Born in Hohenstein, East Prussia, he studied at Marburg, Halle (Ph.D., 1898), and Berlin, and was German pastor in Cairo, Egypt (1903–8). He taught Oriental languages at Halle (1909–14), Giessen (1914–23), and Bonn (1923–38). He lived in England, mainly at Oxford, from 1939 until 1963. His major works were *Masoreten des Ostens* (1913), *Masoreten des Westens* (1927, 1930), *Biblia Hebraica, ed. Kittel: Textum masoreticum curavit* (1927), *The Cairo Geniza* (1947), *Die Hebräischen Handschriften aus der Höhle* (1951), *Piri Re'is, Bahrije* (das türkische Segelhandbuch für das Mittelmeer) (1926), *Leuchtturm von Alexandria* (1930), *Die verschollene Columbuskarte von 1498* (1933), *Chronik des Ibn Ijas* (1931, 1932, 1935), and *Der Hebräische Bibeltext seit Franz Delitzsch* (1960).

RAYMOND W. ALBRIGHT

**Kampuchea (Cambodia).** *See* SOUTHEAST ASIA.

**Kattenbusch, Friedrich Wilhelm Ferdinand** (1851–1936). German Lutheran theologian. Born in Kettwig, near Essen, he studied at Bonn, Berlin, Halle and Göttingen, and was professor of systematic theology at Giessen (1878–1904), Göttingen (1904–6), and Halle (1906–23). He was made a privy ecclesiastical councillor in 1897 and from 1903 was a member of the Norwegian *Videnskabsselskabet*. In theology a follower of Albrecht Ritschl, he was particularly interested in historical theology and doctrine, and especially comparative symbolics. His published works include *Lehrbuch der vergleichenden Confessionskunde* (1892), *Das apostolische Symbol, seine Entstehung, sein geschichtlicher Sinn und seine ursprüngliche Stellung im Kultus und in der Theologie der Kirche* (2 vols., 1894, 1900), *Das sittliche Recht des Krieges* (1906), *Deus absconditus bei Luther* (1920), *Der Quellort der Kirchenidee* (1921), *Die Doppelschichtigkeit in Luthers Kirchenbegriff* (1928), and *Die deutsche evangelische Theologie seit Schleiermacher* (6th ed., 1934).

**Keller, Adolphe** (1872–1963). Swiss Protestant ecumenist. Born in Rüdlingen, Switzerland, he studied theology at the universities of Basel, Berlin, and Geneva. He was pastor in Cairo, Egypt; Stein am Rhein, Switzerland; Geneva; and Zurich. He served as general secretary of the International Christian Social Institute founded by the Ecumenical Conference at Stockholm; secretary of the Swiss Church Federation; assistant professor of ecumenism and descriptive ecclesiology at the universities of Zurich and Geneva (1929); director of the European Central Office for Inter-Church Aid, Geneva (1922); and founder and director of the Ecumenical Seminar, Geneva. His books include *Eine Sinai-Fahrt* (1901), *A Phi-* *losophy of Life* (1914), *Dynamis: Forms and Forces of American Protestantism* (1922), *Die Kirchen und der Friede* (1927), *Der Schweizerische Evangelische Kirchenbund* (1928), *Auf der Schwelle* (1929), *Der Weg der dialektischen Theologie durch die christliche Welt* (1932), *Karl Barth and Christian Unity* (ET, 1933), *Vom unbekannten Gott* (1933), *Von Geist und Liebe* (1934), *Religion and the European Mind* (1934), *Church and State on the European Continent* (1936), *Five Minutes to Twelve* (1938), *Am Fusse des Leuchtturms* (1940), *Christian Europe Today* (1942), *Amerikanisches Christentum Heute* (1943), *Unbekanntes Amerika* (1944), *Wiederaufbau der Welt* (1944), and *Zeit-Wende* (1946). With G. Stewart he wrote *Protestant Europe* (1927).

**Kelso, James Anderson** (1873–1951). Presbyterian educator. Born in Rawal Pindi, India, he studied at Washington and Jefferson, Western Theological Seminary, Berlin, and Leipzig (Ph.D., 1900). He was professor of Hebrew and OT (from 1901) and president of Western Theological Seminary (1909–43). He wrote *Die Klagelieder, Der Massoretische Text und die Versionen* (1901), *Hebrew-English Vocabulary to the Book of Genesis* (1917), *A History of the Hebrews in Outline* (1921), and *The Hebrew Prophet and His Message* (1922).

ALEXANDER MACKIE

**Kelso, James Leon** (1892–1978). American archeologist and biblical scholar. He served as professor of OT history and biblical archeology at Pittsburgh Theological Seminary, and briefly as director of the American Schools of Oriental Research in Jerusalem (1949/50). He worked on 10 different archeological expeditions to Israel from 1926 to 1964. At Tell Beit Mirsim he served as assistant director to W. F. Albright in 1926, 1930, and 1932. The two worked together again on the Bethel expedition in 1934, when he served as president of the staff and later became director of Bethel excavations in 1954, 1957, and 1960. In 1950 he was director of the excavations at Hasmonean Jericho and Nitla, Jordan.

JOHN MCRAY

**Kennedy, Geoffrey Anketell Studdert** (1883–1929). Anglican clergyman. Irish in origin, he was educated at Trinity College, Dublin, and Ripon College. After ordination in 1908 he was curate in Rugby and Leeds before becoming vicar of St. Paul's, Worcester (1914–21), but for part of this time he was a military chaplain in World War I. He was awarded the military cross for bravery, and became affectionately known among the troops as "Woodbine Willie." Later he was rector of St. Edmund, Lombard Street, London (1922–29), and a royal chaplain, and was closely associated with the work of the Industrial Christian Fellowship. He wrote books in a popular style, including *Rough Rhymes* (1918), *The Hardest Part* (1918), *The Wicket Gate* (1923), and *The Word and the Work* (1925).

**Kennett, Robert Hatch** (1864–1932). Church of England OT scholar. Born in Nether Court, St. Lawrence-in-Thanet, he studied at Cambridge, became lecturer in Hebrew, Syriac, and Aramaic (1887–1903), and then regius professor of Hebrew and canon of Ely (1903–32). His works include *The Composition of Isaiah* (1910), *The Servant of the Lord* (1911), *Deuteronomy and the Decalogue* (1920), *Sacrifice* (1924), *OT Essays* (1928), and *Ancient Hebrew Social Life and Custom* (1931).

ELMER E. FLACK

**Kent, Charles Foster** (1867–1925). American biblical scholar. Born in Palmyra, New York, he was educated at Yale (Ph.D., 1891), Yale Divinity School, and the University of Berlin. He was an instructor at the University of Chicago (1893–95), professor of biblical literature and history at Brown University (1895–1901), and professor of biblical literature at Yale University (1901–25). He founded the National Council on Religion in Higher Education to train candidates for positions in colleges in the field of religion. Besides his work as editor of *The Historical Series for Bible Students* and his six-volume *Historical Bible* and two-volume *Shorter Bible*, he published many books, including *Outlines of Hebrew History* (1895), *The Wise Men of Ancient Israel and Their Proverbs* (1895), *A History of the Hebrew People* (2 vols., 1896, 1897), *A History of the Jewish People: The Babylonian, Persian, and Greek Periods* (1899), *The Messages of the Later Prophets* (1900), *Israel's Historical and Biographical Narratives* (1905), *Origin and Permanent Value of the OT* (1906), *Israel's Laws and Legal Precedents* (1907), *Heroes and Crises of Early Hebrew History* (1908), and *Kings and Prophets of Israel and Judah* (1909).

**Kenya.** *See* EAST AFRICA.

**Kenyon, Frederic George** (1863–1952). English classical scholar and textual critic. Born in London, he was educated at Winchester and New College, Oxford, and at Halle (Ph.D.). He was director and principal librarian, British Museum (1909–30) and professor of ancient history at the Royal Academy (1918). He wrote *Aristotle on the Constitution of Athens* (1891, 1904, 1920), *Classical Texts from Papyri in the British Museum* (1891), *Catalogue of Greek Papyri in the British Museum* (3 vols., 1893–1907), *Our Bible and the Ancient Manuscripts* (1895, 1939), *Palaeography of the Greek Papyri* (1899), *Facsimiles of Biblical Mss. in the British Museum* (1900), *Handbook of Textual Criticism of the NT* (1901, 1912), *Recent Developments in the Textual Criticism of the Greek Bible* (1933), *The Chester Beatty Biblical Papyri*, (8 vols., 1933–41), *The Text of the Greek Bible* (1937, 1949), *The Story of the Bible* (1937), *The Bible and Archaeology* (1940), *Reading the Bible as History* (1944), and *The Bible and Modern Scholarship* (1948).

DANIEL J. THERON

**Kepler, Thomas Samuel** (1897–1963). Methodist professor, author, and journalist. Born in Mount Vernon, Iowa, he studied at Cornell College, Boston University (Ph.D., 1931), Marburg, and Cambridge. He was professor of Bible and philosophy at Mount Union College, Alliance, Ohio (1930–34), professor of Bible and religion at Lawrence College, Appleton, Wis. (1934–46), and professor of NT at Oberlin College Graduate School of Theology (1946–63). His many biblical, devotional, and inspirational writings include *Why Was Jesus Crucified?* (1937), *Credo: Fundamental Christian Beliefs* (1945), *A New Look at Old Doctrines* (1949), *The Fellowship of the Saints* (1948), *Jesus' Spiritual Journey–And Ours* (1952), *Religion for Vital Living* (1953), *Finding God with the Saints* (1955), *The Book of Revelation* (1957), *The Meaning and Mystery of the Resurrection* (1963) and *The Oxford NT Introduction* (1963). He also edited *World Devotional Classics* (12 vols., 1952–56), helped to edit *The Interpreter's Dictionary of the Bible* (4 vols., 1962), and wrote a religious column for a major newspaper syndicate.

GLEN G. SCORGIE

**Kerr, Hugh Thomson** (1871–1950). Presbyterian. Born in Elora, Ontario, he was educated at the University of Toronto and Western Theological Seminary. He held several pastorates, the last at Shadyside Presbyterian, Pittsburgh (1913–45). He was moderator of the General Assembly (1930); president of the board of Christian education (1923–40); and secretary of the Pitcairn-Crabbe Foundation (1941–50). He was one of the first radio preachers in America (1922–42) and the author of more than 20 books, including *Children's Story Sermons* (1911), *The Gospel in Modern Poetry* (1926), *A God-Centered Faith* (1935), and *The Christian Sacraments* (1944).

HUGH THOMSON KERR, JR.

**Kerr, Hugh Thomson, Jr.** (1909– ). American Presbyterian theology professor. Born in Chicago and educated at Princeton University, Western Theological Seminary, and the universities of Pittsburgh and Edinburgh, Kerr taught doctrinal theology at Louisville Presbyterian Seminary (1936–40) and Princeton Seminary (1940–72). At Princeton he edited the quarterly *Theology Today*. Among his most important works are *A Compend of Calvin's Institutes* (1939), *A Compend of Luther's Theology* (1943), *Positive Protestantism* (1950), *Sons of the Prophets: Leaders in Protes-*

*tantism from Princeton Seminary* (1963), *Protestantism: A Concise Survey of Protestantism and Its Influence on American Religious and Social Traditions* (1979), and, with John M. Mulder, *Conversion: The Christian Experience* (1983).

R. MILTON WINTER

**Keswick Convention.** An annual gathering in England formerly for one week and now for two, for "the promotion of personal, practical and Scriptural holiness," held in July at Keswick in Cumbria since 1875. It is the spiritual child of the 1859 revival and the campaigns of D. L. Moody and Ira Sankey. It was preceded by gatherings at Brooklands, Oxford, and Brighton (1874/75). Canon Hartford-Basttersby, vicar of Keswick, and Robert Wilson, his Quaker friend, established the convention at Keswick. It was to be for "Christians of every section of the Church of God" and its motto became "All one in Christ Jesus."

It grew rapidly, and now uses two large tents and has well over 5000 people attending it each week, many from overseas. The Keswick movement inspired local conventions in cities and towns and many overseas national "Keswicks," including the great one at Maramon in South India, regularly assembling over 100,000 people.

Keswick produced several hymn books, the latest being *Keswick Praise*, and regular publications like *The Life of Faith* and *Keswick Week*. There are now over fifty Keswick tape libraries in many parts of the world. Bible exposition is given a place of priority. A week's ministry normally follows a pattern, from the call to penitence through victory to world mission. Keswick teaches that victory in Christ comes by the Holy Spirit's counteraction of sin rather than its eradication. Many missionary leaders first responded to God's call to missionary service at Keswick.

**Bibliography.** J. C. Pollock, *The Keswick Story* (1964).

GEOFFREY W. GROGAN

**Kevan, Ernest Frederick** (1903–1965). English Baptist minister and college principal. After serving as minister of Baptist churches at Walthamstow (1924–34), New Cross (1934–44), and Upper Tooting (1944–46), he became first principal of London Bible College (1946–65), an interdenominational, evangelical theological institution. His insistence on high academic standards, a deep devotional tone, "guided self-discipline," and close relationships with the churches gained widespread respect for the college, which drew students from many parts of the world and grew to a student body of more than 200.

A convinced Calvinist, although scrupulously fair in his presentation of other points of view, his doctoral thesis, published in 1964 under the title, *The Grace of Law*, was a careful examination of Puritan theology on the role of the Law of God. Other influential, though shorter, works were

*Keep His Commandments: The Place of Law in the Christian Life* and *The Moral Law* (1963). He was an editor and commentator of *The New Bible Commentary* (1963), and both his series of Bible readings given at the Keswick Convention were published, as well as brief treatments of *Salvation* (1963) and *Going on in the Christian Faith* (1964).

Outwardly somewhat reserved and even austere, he was an impressive preacher; his talks to children were masterly. He played an important part in the postwar evangelical resurgence.

HAROLD H. ROWDON

**Kidd, Beresford James** (1864–1948). Anglican church historian. Born in Birmingham, he was educated at Keble College, Oxford. Ordained in 1887, he was assistant curate of Saints Philip and James, Oxford (1887–1900), vicar of St. Paul's, Oxford (1904–20), chaplain and lecturer in theology at Pembroke College, Oxford, warden of Keble College, Oxford (1920–39), prolocutor of the Convocation of Canterbury (1932–36), and honorary canon of Christ Church (1915). He taught in the School of Theology, Oxford, and wrote *The Thirty-Nine Articles* (1899), *The Continental Reformation* (1902), *Documents Illustrative of the Continental Reformation* (1911), *Documents Illustrative of the History of the Church to A.D. 461*, *A History of the Church to A.D. 461* (3 vols., 1922), *The Churches of Eastern Christendom from A.D. 451* (1927), *The Counter-Reformation* (1933), and *The Primacy of the Roman See* (1936).

F. W. DILLISTONE

**King, Henry Churchill** (1858–1934). American educator, philosopher, and theologian. Born in Hillsdale, Mich., he studied at Oberlin College, Oberlin Theological Seminary, Harvard, and Berlin. While a seminary student he was a tutor in Latin (1879–81) and mathematics (1881/82) in the preparatory department of his college. He returned to Oberlin in 1884 and was successively associate professor of mathematics (1884–90) and professor of philosophy (1890–97), professor of theology (1897–1925), and president (1912–27). He was a member of the committee of 10 appointed in 1893 by the National Education Association to report on studies in secondary schools. He lectured widely, and from 1919 to 1921 was moderator of the National Council of Congregational Churches. His works include *Outline of Erdmann's History of Philosophy* (1892), *Appeal of the Child* (1900), *Reconstruction in Theology* (1901), *Theology and the Social Consciousness* (1902), *Personal and Ideal Elements in Education* (1904), *Seeming Unreality of the Spiritual Life* (1908), *Laws of Friendship–Human and Divine* (1909), *The Ethics of Jesus* (1910), *Religion as Life* (1913), *Fundamental Questions* (1917), *For a New America in a New World* (1919), *A New*

478

*Mind for the New Age* (1920), and *Seeing Life Whole* (1923).

**King, Martin Luther, Jr.** (1929–1968). Baptist minister and American civil rights leader. He studied at Morehouse College, Atlanta, Crozer Theological Seminary, and Boston University (Ph.D., 1955). He was pastor of the Dexter Avenue Baptist Church, Montgomery, Ala. (1954–59), and copastor with his father, Martin Luther King, Sr., of Ebenezer Baptist Church, Atlanta (1960–68). He also served as president of the Montgomery Improvement Association (1955–59) and helped found the Southern Christian Leadership Conference (SCLC) in Atlanta in January 1957 and was its president (1957–68). The former spearheaded the drive to desegregrate Montgomery and inaugurated the national quest for full civil rights for blacks in 20th-century America; SCLC became the organization through which King channeled most of his civil rights activities after 1957. A dynamic preacher, he became the youngest person ever to receive the Nobel Peace Prize in 1964.

Beginning in 1955, King became the dominant leader in a moral crusade against racial segregation in the American South, a movement which eventually became known nationally as "the civil rights revolution" of 1960 to 1968. Heavily influenced by Walter Rauschenbusch and Reinhold Niebuhr but taking his fundamental ideas from the teachings of Jesus and his operational techniques from Mohandas K. Gandhi, King preached nonviolence as the most effective weapon in the quest of black Americans for civil rights and social justice. Arrested more than 15 times, often assaulted, continually threatened, he came to symbolize the courage, sacrifice, and suffering of struggling blacks. The peak of his influence came on August 28, 1963, when he led the largest civil rights demonstration in American history. Nearly 250,000 people took part in the historic "March on Washington," mainly to support the civil rights bill then pending in Congress. The highlight of the march was King's memorable "I Have a Dream" speech, delivered from the steps of the Lincoln Memorial. Almost a year later, Congress passed the landmark Civil Rights Act of 1964. King continued to lead massive voter-registration drives and to press for more jobs for the poor. Early in 1967 he began to include opposition to the Vietnam War in his litany of concerns—a shift which cost him much grass-roots support and the loss of a great deal of sympathy in the administration of President Lyndon B. Johnson.

During the last year of his life his interests were divided and his influence somewhat diminished, but he continued his nonviolent quest for rights and jobs. King's influence and leadership during the troubled 1960s may have saved America from a bloody racial civil war, and he did more than any other individual of the 20th century to make black emancipation a political and social fact in modern America. He was assassinated in early April 1968, in Memphis, a crime which sparked riots among blacks across the USA. In 1985 Congress enacted legislation which, beginning in 1986, established King's birthday as a federal holiday. He wrote *Stride Toward Freedom* (1958), *Strength to Love* (1963), *Why We Can't Wait* (1964), and *Where Do We Go From Here: Chaos or Community?* (1967).

**Bibliography.** C. S. King, *My Life with Martin Luther King, Jr.* (1969); H. Walton, Jr., *The Political Philosophy of Martin Luther, Jr.* (1971); L. Bennett, *What Manner of Man: A Biography of Martin Luther King, Jr.* (4th rev. ed., 1976); S. B. Oates, *Let the Trumpet Sound: The Life of Martin Luther King, Jr.* (1982); D. J. Garrow, *Bearing the Cross: Martin Luther King, Jr. and the Southern Christian Leadership Conference* (1986).

ROBERT D. LINDER

**Kingdom Movement.** *See* HERRON, GEORGE DAVID.

**Kingdom of God.** *See* MILLENNIUM; SOCIAL GOSPEL.

**Kingdom of God, League of the.** English social reform organization. Founded in 1906 by P. T. R. Widdrington, priest of the Church of England prominently identified with the existing Christian Social Union of the same communion, the league carried on the Christian socialist tradition of Frederick Denison Maurice (1805–72). Widdrington's concern was to find a theological basis for a Christian sociology. The league contributed powerfully to the growth of a school of Catholic sociology in the Church of England, based on the doctrines of the incarnation, the atonement, and the Trinity. It cooperated in the holding of the Anglo-Catholic Summer School of Sociology in 1925, out of which grew the Christendom movement, in which the league is now merged.

**Bibliography.** M. B. Reckitt, *Maurice to Temple: A Century of the Social Movement in the Church of England* (1947).

EVELYN C. URWIN

*Kirchenaustritt.* The decision by persons 14 years or older to leave the church into which they were baptized, thus freeing themselves from its spiritual tutelage and from the obligation to pay "church taxes" collected by the state on behalf of the officially recognized and incorporated territorial or state churches. Before changes in legislation governing church membership in 1873, as a result of the *Kulturkampf*, such exodus from one church was followed normally by transfer of membership to another mainline church, sect, or free church. Since that date, members may exit or transfer without having to justify their decision to an official of the church, although formal notification of an appropriate ecclesial or state agency is still required. In some political jurisdictions in Germany a specified waiting period is established before a decision to leave the church is final. Reentry into a church of one's choice is not regulated by law.

In the Roman Catholic tradition leaving the church is considered apostasy. Protestant church law and practice is less stringent, although state and territorial churches tend to look upon baptized members as "merely estranged and not wholly severed from the body of the church."

Discontinued membership in large numbers has been statistically recorded since 1884. Inordinately large numbers of "departing" members in some years have been offset by high numbers of readmissions in other years. Church officials are concerned that alienation from the church in recent years indicates rejection of the church's teaching as no longer significantly contributing to the spiritual well-being of individuals in contemporary society.

E. J. FURCHA

**Kirk, Harris Elliott** (1872–1953). Presbyterian. Born in Pulaski, Tenn., he studied at Southwestern College and Divinity School, Clarksville, Tenn. He was minister of Cottage Church, Nashville, Tenn. (1897–99), First Church, Florence, Ala. (1899–1901), and Franklin Street Church, Baltimore, Md. (1901–53). He was special lecturer at Hartford Theological Seminary on homiletics and psychology of religion (1919–24); annual lecturer at Princeton University on historical Christianity (1924–30); and professor of biblical literature, Goucher College (1928–40). In theology Kirk was a liberal. He wrote *The Religion of Power* (1916), *The Consuming Fire* (1919), *One Generation to Another* (1924), *The Spirit of Protestantism* (1930), *The Glory of Common Things* (1930), *Stars, Atoms and God* (1932), *A Man of Property* (1935), and *A Design for Living* (1939).

**Kirkridge.** Retreat-and-study center in the Pennsylvania Appalachian Mountains. Begun in 1942, the movement has its center at Bangor, Pa., in a 350-acre mountain tract with buildings for religious retreats. Original inspiration came from the Iona Community in Scotland, work-camps, and other semimonastic retreat systems. Since 1942 a group of as many as 150 has participated in the Kirkridge Discipline, devotional and ethical rules and intentions for daily life. The object of the program is to sharpen the devotional and vocational relevance of Christianity by retreats (silence, manual work, worship, and instruction), by colloquies on the arts and other areas of expression, and by maintaining fellowship among a widely scattered membership of ministers and laypersons, men and women. Originally Presbyterian, Kirkridge is widely inclusive and has inspired similar programs elsewhere.

JOHN OGDEN NELSON

**Kittel, Gerhard** (1888–1948). German NT scholar. Born in Breslau, Germany, he was privatdocent at Kiel and Leipzig, and professor of NT at Greifswald (1921–26) and Tübingen (1926–45). Kittel's work was mainly devoted to the study of the Jewish background of the NT. In his opinion the Jewish element prevailed over the Hellenistic element in the making of the NT books. Kittel edited the voluminous *Theologisches Wörterbuch zum Neuen Testament* (1933). He insisted that a NT lexicon must fully trace the history of each word, noting its secular usage in classical Greek and *koine* and the religious connotations derived from the LXX and its Hebrew background. His pamphlet *Die Judenfrage* (1934) aroused a bitter controversy and his propagandistic writings during World War II landed him in prison when the Allies occupied Germany in 1945. Other works included *Jesus und die Rabbinen* (1914), *Der Midrasch Sifre zum Deuteronomium* (1922), *Das Problem des spätpalästinensischen Judentums und des Urchristentums* (1926), *Urchristentum, Spätjudentum, Hellenismus* (1926), and *Die Religionsgeschichte und das Urchristentum* (1932).

OTTO A. PIPER

**Kittel, Rudolf** (1853–1929). German OT scholar. Born in Ehningen, Württemberg, he studied at Tübingen (Ph.D., 1879). After pastoring from 1876 to 1879 he was a lecturer at Tübingen (1879–81), professor in a gymnasium at Stuttgart (1881–88), and professor of OT exegesis at the University of Breslau (1888–97), where he was rector from 1896 to 1897. He was professor of OT exegesis at the University of Leipzig from 1898 to 1924. He is best known for his critical Hebrew OT text, *Biblia Hebraica* (3d ed., 1929–37). He translated OT and pseudoepigraphical works for several German publications, and edited many works, including C. F. A. Dillmann's *Handbuch der alttestamentlichen Theologie* (1895). His later works include *The Scientific Study of the OT* (1910), *Die Religion des Volkes Israel* (1921), *Geschichte des Volkes Israel* (3 vols., 1929), and *Great Men and Movements in Israel* (1929).

ELMER E. FLACK

**Klett, Guy Soulliard** (1897–1984). Presbyterian educator and historian. Born in Rexmont, Pa., he studied at Lafayette College, Gettysburg College, Penn. State University, the University of Pennsylvania, and the University of Michigan. He was instructor of English and history at Gettysburg College, and taught briefly also at other institutions, including Heidelberg College (1925–29), before taking up his main life's work as research historian for the department of history of the Presbyterian Church, USA (1936–62). He wrote *Presbyterians in Colonial Pennsylvania* (1937), *Scotch-Irish in Pennsylvania* (1948), and he edited *Presbyterian Church and Our National*

*Foundations: Minutes of the Presbyterian Church in America, 1706–1788* and *Journals of Charles Beatty, 1762–69.*

**Knights of Columbus.** A fraternal benefit society of Roman Catholic men established in the USA in March 1882. By 1940 its membership stood at about 785,000, but 40 years later this figure was doubled, with representatives in every American state, Canada, Mexico, Puerto Rico, the Canal Zone, and the Philippines. Its charter defines the society's purposes as: to render pecuniary aid to its members and the beneficiaries of its members; to render assistance to sick and disabled members; to promote social and intellectual intercourse among its members; and to promote and conduct educational, charitable, religious, social, and relief work. The society is devoted to the guiding ideals of charity, unity, fraternity, and patriotism. Contributions and endowments by the local and national bodies of the Knights have been registered at many colleges and academies. Scholarship funds are distributed by the Catholic University of America, where the Knights of Columbus have endowed a chair of American history. After World War II an educational trust fund insured the college education of sons and daughters of members killed in active service. The society has an extensive youth program, and through advertising in secular periodicals and through literature distribution it seeks to explain Roman Catholic doctrine and practice.

**Knowles, Michael Clive** (1896–1974). Roman Catholic historian. Born in Studley, Warwickshire, England, he studied at Christ's College, Cambridge, and Collegio Saint Anselmo, Rome, and was ordained priest in 1922. He was fellow of Peterhouse (1944–63), university lecturer in history (1946/47), professor of medieval history (1947–54), and professor of modern history (1954–63). He wrote *The Monastic Order in England* (1940), *The Religious Houses of Mediaeval England* (1940), *The Religious Orders in England* (1948, 1955, 1959), *The Monastic Constitutions of Lanfranc* (1951), *The English Mystical Tradition* (1961), *Saints and Scholars* (1962), *The Evolution of Medieval Thought* (1962), *The Historian and Character* (1963), *Great Historical Enterprises* (1963), *From Pachomius to Ignatius* (1966), *What Is Mysticism?* (1969), *The Christian Centuries* (1969), and *Thomas Becket* (1970).

**Knox, Edmund Arbuthnott** (1847–1937). Bishop of Manchester. Born in Bangalore, India, he graduated from Oxford, and was fellow and dean of Merton College (1869–84). He was a rector in Leicester (1884–91) and in Birmingham (1891–94) before his consecration as suffragan bishop of Coventry (1894–1903). He was transferred to Manchester as diocesan in 1903, holding that post until his retirement in 1921. Even then he was still active as an evangelical and successfully mustered support against the revised Prayer Book (1927/28). Among his writings were *Sacrifice or Sacrament* (1914), *Glad Tidings of Reconciliation* (1916), *On What Authority?* (1922), *John Bunyan in Relation to His Time* (1928), *Robert Leighton, Archbishop of Glasgow* (1930), *The Tractarian Movement, 1833–1845* (1933), and *Reminiscences of an Octogenarian, 1847–1934* (1935).

**Knox, John** (1900– ). American NT theologian. Born in Frankfort, Ky., he studied at Randolph-Macon College, Emory University, and the University of Chicago (Ph.D., 1935). He served as minister in the Methodist Episcopal Church, South, in West Virginia and Baltimore (1919–24), was assistant professor of Bible at Emory University (1924–27), minister of Fisk University (1929–36), and taught briefly at Hartford Theological Seminary and the University of Chicago before becoming professor of sacred literature at Union Theological Seminary, N.Y. (1943–66). In 1962 he was ordained to the ministry of the Protestant Episcopal Church. From 1966 to 1972 he was professor of NT at the Episcopal Theological Seminary of the Southwest in Austin, Tex. His works include *He Whom a Dream Hath Possessed* (1932), *Philemon among the Letters of Paul* (1935), *The Man Christ Jesus* (1941), *Christ the Lord: The Meaning of Jesus in the Early Church* (1945), *The Fourth Gospel and the Later Epistles* (1945), *On the Meaning of Christ* (1947), *Chapters in a Life of Paul* (1950), *Criticism and Faith* (1952), *The Early Church and the Coming Great Church* (1955), *The Death of Christ* (1958), *The Ethic of Jesus in the Teaching of the Church* (1961), *Life in Christ Jesus* (1961), *The Church and the Reality of Christ* (1962), and *The Humanity and Divinity of Christ* (1967).

**Knox, Ronald Arbuthnot** (1888–1957). Roman Catholic. Educated at Eton and Balliol College, Oxford, he was a fellow and lecturer of Trinity College, Oxford (1910–17). Originally ordained into the Church of England, he was received into the Church of Rome in 1917. He was Roman Catholic chaplain to the University of Oxford (1926–39), and a protonotary apostolic from 1951. His literary work included a translation of the Bible (NT, 1945; OT, 1949). A notable historical study is *Enthusiasm, A Chapter in the History of Religion* (1950). In addition his apologetic, satire, instruction, and mystery works include *Some Loose Stones* (1913), *Reunion All Round* (1914); *A Spiritual Aeneid* (1918), *The Belief of Catholics* (1927), *Let Dons Delight* (1939), *God and the Atom* (1945), *A Retreat for Priests* (1946), *The Mass in Slow Motion* (1948), *The Creed in Slow Motion* (1949), and *On Englishing the Bible* (1949).

F. W. DILLISTONE

**Knudson, Albert Cornelius** (1873–1953). Methodist theologian. Born in Grandmeadow, Minn., he was educated at the University of Minnesota, Boston University (Ph.D., 1900), and the universities of Jena and Berlin. After brief terms of service as professor in Denver and Baker universities and Allegheny College, he became professor at Boston University School of Theology (1906–43), where he also served as dean (1926–38) and dean emeritus (1938-53). Early in his career he wrote books on OT subjects, among them *The Beacon Lights of Prophecy (1914), The Religious Teaching of the OT* (1918), and *The Prophetic Movement in Israel* (1921). But under the inspiration of Borden Parker Bowne, the founder of American personalism, he gradually transferred his literary activities to philosophical theology. Three books have a more or less apologetic purpose: *Present Tendencies in Religious Thought* (1924), *The Philosophy of Personalism* (1927), and *The Validity of Religious Experience* (1937). Three others are strictly theological, two of them systematic theology: *The Doctrine of God* (1930), *The Doctrine of Redemption* (1933), and *Basic Issues in Christian Thought* (1950). He also wrote *The Principles of Christian Ethics* and *The Philosophy of War and Peace.* Knudson's sustained effort to rethink Christian theology as a whole resulted in a personalistic system that belongs to the Arminian tradition but has its own distinctive character.

**Köberle, Adolf** (1898– ). Lutheran theologian. Born in Bad Berneck, he began his career in a parish in Bavaria in 1922, after studies at the universities of Erlangen, Munich, and Tübingen. In 1926 he became lecturer at and director of the seminary for missionaries at Leipzig. From 1930 to 1939 he was professor at Basel, and from 1939 until his retirement, at Tübingen. Since 1950 he has sought to apply depth psychology and theology to pastoral care. His life has been dedicated to drawing the evangelical church of Germany out of its isolationist mentality. Köberle lives in active retirement in the Federal Republic of Germany. For many years he edited the *Zeitschrift für Systematische Theologie* and worked on the editorial committees of *Deutsche Theologie, Evangelisches Missionsmagazin* (1932–39), *Evangelische Weihnacht* (1946–49), and *Wege zum Menschen* (1957– ). Some of his many writings have been translated into French and English. Most notable are his *Rechtfertigung und Heiligung* (1928, 1938), *Evangelium und Zeitgeist* (1934), *Das Glaubensvermächtnis der schwäbischen Väter* (1959), *Rechtfertigung, Glaube und neues Leben* (1965), *Besuch am Krankenbett* (2 vols., 1970–72), and *Heilung und Hilfe* (1968). One of his most recent contributions is the biographical sketch, "Professor D. Justus Köberle, 1871–1908. Ein Lebensbild in Briefen," in *Zeitschrift für bayerische Kirch-engeschichte,* 55 (1968). The festschrift *Die Leibhaftigkeit des Wortes* (1958) was published in his honor.

E. J. FURCHA

**Koehler, Ludwig Hugo** (1880– ). Reformed pastor, OT scholar, and lexicographer. Born in Neuwied am Rhein, Germany, during military service at Freiburg im Breisgau he studied Heinrich Rickert's *Logik und Erkenntnistheorie.* After becoming a Swiss citizen (1903), he studied theology and Oriental languages at Zurich (Th.D., 1909) under Paul Wilhelm Schmiedel. He was ordained in the Reformed Church of Zurich (1904) and served as the pastor in a rural community. In 1908 he was named assistant professor of OT and biblical geography at Zurich, and then ordinary professor (1923–47). He was dean of the theology faculty (1916–18; 1926–28) and rector of the university (1930–32). His books include *Amos* (1917), *Religion und Menschheit* (2d ed., 1923), *Deuterojesaja stilkritisch untersucht* (1923), *Die Offenbarung des Johannes und ihre heutige Deutung* (1924), *Das formgeschichtliche Problem des Neuen Testaments* (1927), *Theologie des Alten Testaments* (2d ed., 1948), *Kleine Lichter* (1945), and *Lexicon in Veteris Testamenti Libros* (1951–53).

RAYMOND W. ALBRIGHT

**Koehler, Walther** (1870–1946). Lutheran church historian. Born in Elberfeld, Germany, he studied at the universities of Halle, Heidelberg, and Tübingen. He taught church history in Giessen (1900–1909), Zurich (1909–29), and Heidelberg (1929–46). He was a specialist in German and Swiss Reformation history and an important contributor to the Weimar edition of Luther's works and the critical edition of Zwingli's works. His most important publications include *Luthers Schrift an den christlichen Adel deutscher Nation im Spiegel der Kultur- und Zeitgeschichte* (1895), *Luther und die Kirchengeschichte,* vol. 1 (1900), *Reformation und Ketzerprozess* (1901), *Dokumente zum Ablassstreit von 1517* (1902), *Luthers 95 Thesen und Gegenschriften* (1903), *Bibliographia Brentiana* (1904), *Konrad Ferdinand Meyer als religiöser Charakter* (1911), *Luther und die Lüge* (1912), *Luther und die deutsche Reformation* (2d ed., 1917), *U. Zwingli und die Reformation in der Schweiz* (1919), *Die Geisteswelt U. Zwinglis* (1920), *Zwingli und Luther, ihr Streit um das Abendmahl* (2 vols., 1924, 1952), *Das Marburger Religionsgespräch 1529* (2 vols., 1929), *Historie und Metahistorie in der Kirchengeschichte* (1930), *Zürcher Ehegericht und Genfer Konsistorium* (2 vols., 1932, 1942), *Luther und das Luthertum in ihrer weltgeschichtlichen Auswirkung* (1933), *Dogmensgeschichte als Geschichte des christl. Selbstbewusstseins* (2 vols., 1938, 1951), *Omnis ecclesia Petri propinqua* (1938), *Ernst Troeltsch* (1941),

*Huldrych Zwingli* (1943), and *Der verborgene Gott* (1946).

RAYMOND W. ALBRIGHT

## Koestler Arthur (1905–1983).

Writer on politics and science. Born in Budapest and educated in Vienna, Koestler's early career as a journalist, political novelist, essayist, and activist took him to Palestine, the Soviet Union, and the Spanish Civil War. He was interned in Paris in 1940 and escaped to England, where he was to campaign for the abolition of capital punishment.

Koestler's life up to this point is chronicled in *Dialogue with Death* (1937), *Scum of the Earth* (1941), *Arrow in the Blue* (1952), *The Invisible Writing* (1954), and the unfinished *Stranger on the Square* (1984). These autobiographical writings, like Koestler's occasional essays and the novels *The Gladiators* (1931), *Darkness at Noon* (1940), *Arrival and Departure* (1943), *Thieves in the Night* (1946) and *The Age of Longing* (1951), reveal preoccupations similar to those of his friend George Orwell (1903–50). But after the abolitionist *Reflections on Hanging* (1956) Koestler exchanged politics for the history and philosophy of science, taking a special interest in the thought of the astronomer Johannes Kepler (1571–1630). A trilogy on the place of creativity in scientific advancement, *The Sleepwalkers* (1959), *The Act of Creation* (1964), and *The Ghost in the Machine* (1967), was followed by *The Roots of Coincidence* (1972) which brought to public notice Koestler's long-held interest in extrasensory perception (ESP) and the paranormal.

In later years a sufferer from Parkinson's disease and leukemia, Koestler became vice-president of the Voluntary Euthanasia Society. He and his wife took drug overdoses and were found dead in their London flat. The endowment Koestler left for a professorial chair in parapsychology was taken up by Edinburgh University.

PHILIP HILLYER

## Koran, The.

The holy book of Islam, believed by Muslims to be the uncreated Word of God (Allāh), revealed for the guidance of mankind through the intermediacy of the Prophet Muhammad. According to hagiographic sources, the first revelation descended on Muhammad on the 27th night of Ramadān (the Muslim month of fasting) about A.D. 610 in the cave of Ḥarrā', outside Mecca, to which he had withdrawn to contemplate. Not surprisingly, the illiterate and simple merchant was astounded when an unknown voice commanded him *"iqra'"* ("Read!" or "Proclaim!"), the first revealed word, to which the term "Koran" is generally related.

Muslim belief in revelation differs from the Judeo-Christian conception. Their actual Scripture exists only in heaven. Muhammad wrote down, as Allāh's scribe, a replica of the eternal original. Muhammad had no choice in deciding the time, location, content, or vocabulary of these revelations, which continued to descend on him until his death in A.D. 632. The Koran constitutes the collection of these revelations initially in the memory of individuals and subsequently in a written form. It contains 114 chapters, each of which is known as a *sūra* and which, with the exception of the first, are arranged according to length rather than chronologically (not unlike the arrangement of the prophetic books in the Bible). Each *sūra* has a title (in some cases more than one), which usually is a word taken from the *sūra* without any indication of its subject. Each chapter may contain more than one subject, giving the casual reader a sense of discontinuity. To the believer, however, the unity and continuity of the text are powerfully evident and arises from the majesty of its divine source. With the exception of chap. 9, each *sūra* begins with the invocation of "the Name of God, the Merciful, the Compassionate." This invocation, known as the *"basmalah,"* is said, on the authority of the Prophet, to contain the essence of all the teachings of the Koran. It is employed as the opening phrase of all that is written, said, or done by Muslims.

The chapters are divided into verses, each of which is known as an *"āya,"* a term which has two primary meanings. The first refers to a literary unit, a grouping of words, in the same sense as the terms *stanza, couplet,* or *pentad.* The verses of the Koran are defined by a rhyming ending rather than by a completed thought. Consequently, one verse may end and another begin in the middle of a sentence. The second meaning of *āya* refers to a sign or manifestation of divine power (as in biblical usage). Thus when it is said that the *āyāt* (pl. of *āyā*) of the Koran were well-devised (by God), both senses of the term *āyā* are employed.

Unlike the Bible, the Koran owes its text and canon to one man, Muhammad. Early textual variations are minimal and were corrected by the corporate recollection of the community of faith. The revelations descended mainly in two locations: Mecca, the birthplace of the Prophet and the stage of his early preaching, and Medina, the city that became the center of a growing Muslim state, guided by the teachings of the Koran. The change was brought about by the forced migration (*hijra,* Lat. *hegira*) of Muhammad and the believers in A.D. 622 (the beginning of the Muslim calendar).

While all chapters of the Koran focus on one central theme, namely, the proclamation of God's uniqueness and all-embracing sovereignty, there is a marked difference between the earlier and later *sūras.* In the earlier chapters—short and rhapsodic—one senses jubilation at the recognition of God's creative and merciful omnipotence. Clearly articulated are the rewards of paradise for those who believe and the horrors of punishment for those who, having been given the guidance, reject it insolently. While the later chapters (especially those revealed at Medina) retain the same theme throughout, new revelations pertaining to the juridical issues arising from the social and economic needs of the nascent community of faith, now living as a political entity, are predominant. In addition to religious matters (such as prayer, fasting, alms-giving, pilgrimage, sin, rewards, punishments, and forgiveness), more mundane issues are covered. Ordinances treat such details as marriage, divorce, inheritance, debts, food and drink, and slavery.

A sizeable portion of the Koran deals with biblical topics; reference is made to events surrounding some of the major figures of the OT and NT to demonstrate God's continued concern for humanity and their persistent rebellion against him. One finds here the main theological divergences between Islam and Christianity: the affirmation of Christ's prophethood while denying as blasphemous the Christian claim to his divinity, the affirmation of God's oneness while rejecting the concept of the Trinity, and the affirmation of God's victory over man's design to kill Jesus who, accordingly, was not crucified.

The Koran was revealed in Arabic and may only be written and recited in that language. The sanctity of the revealed Word is in the language of revelation itself. A translation cannot truly be the Koran. In the Muslim world only a small minority possess command of Arabic grammar and lexicography so a Muslim would ecstatically hear the Koran recited without necessarily understanding that which is said. The hearer is satisfied by the fact that it is the word of God and subsequently seeks its interpretation.

The style of the Koran is different from that of the collected sayings of Muhammad (*Hadith*), and Muhammad himself challenged his detractors to produce one verse similar in style or content to that of the Koran. The style is prosodic but not prose in that it rhymes as does poetry; neither is it poetry. While there are hints at narrative, it is not narrative in style. One exception is chap. 12 which deals in narrative style with one theme: the story of Joseph. Thus, the Koran cannot be retold in simplified form, as would the Bible, nor can it be used as source material for the reconstruction of the life of the Prophet or the history of the early Muslim community. At the same time, it is not a collection of precepts or instructions as is the case of some other scriptures. It is not a book by Muhammad or about him or about Muslims; it is—so the Muslims believe—the divine word in a perceivable or legible form.

**Bibliography.** A. J. Arberry, *The Koran Interpreted* (1963); J. Jomier, *The Bible and the Koran* (ET, 1964); W. M. Watt, *Bell's Introduction to the Qur'ān* (1970); K. Cragg, *The Event of the Qur'ān* (1971); "Studies in Qur'ān and Tafsīr" in supp. to *JAAR* (1979); H. E. Kassis, *A Concordance of the Qur'ān* (1982).

HANNA KASSIS

**Korea.** *Introduction* The divided nation of Korea is one of the world's oldest, occupying a peninsula that extends southeast from Manchuria near Japan. A mountainous region with fertile river valleys and deltas, its population in 1980 was estimated at 55.9 million, including nearly 18 million in North Korea and 38 million in South Korea. North Korea has an area of 120,538 sq. km. (46,540 sq. mi.); South Korea has an area of 98,477 sq. km. (38,022 sq. mi.).

Occupied after World War II by the Soviet Union north of the 38th parallel and by Western allied forces below, the de facto creation of North and South Korea was to be temporary expedient, which was entrenched by both sides, especially after the Korean War. Reunification was discussed in the 1970s, without success, and military incursions near the border were continual from the 1950s into the 1980s. Some thaw in relations was accomplished in moves toward cooperation between the two Koreas.

*Before World War II.* The Protestant churches in Korea in the first half of the 20th century were characterized as evangelistic—especially after widespread revivals of 1908, with personal witnessing the rule for all members; Bible-centered—with all members in Sunday schools, and as many as 3000 Bible training institutes annually; self-reliant—with lay leadership and general emphasis on self-support; a worshiping community—almost the entire membership attending church services; and disciplined—with high standards of individual conduct.

Until the war in 1950 it was largely a rural church. Presbyterians predominated, outnumbering the older Roman Catholic community, and Methodists were third in number of adherents, followed by Pentecostals, Evangelicals (Holiness), Baptists, and the Salvation Army. By the 1930s these churches were all under National leadership: in the Presbyterian churches from 1907, the Methodists from 1930, and Roman Catholics gradually after 1931. Christian schools began as training institutions for the children of members, but became centers of general education, culminating in the Yonsei University and the Ehwa Women's University (Seoul), the Presbyterian Theological Seminary (originally in Pyongyang, now in Seoul), and the Union Methodist Seminary (Seoul).

Medical work was maintained in 50 hospitals and clinics, capped by the Severance Medical College, Seoul. The Bible Society (Korean Bible Society, 1940), Christian Literature Society, YMCA, rural reconstruction, and city settlement projects served the wider public. Between 1910 and 1940 the Protestant churches grew from 120,000 to about 220,000. Roman Catholic growth was steady, from about 40,000 in 1908 to just over 130,000 in 1940. Much work has been done for women, with a staff of foreign and Korean sisters. More than 500 grade schools were reported, together with homes for orphans, lepers, and the aged.

With annexation by Japan (1910) churches underwent constant trials. These were first intermittent, as in the "Conspiracy Case" (1912), the Independence movement (1919), and during the 1930s. After 1937, Japanese wartime pressures were continuous until the surrender (1945). The problem of compulsory attendance at Shinto shrines rent the Christian educational world, and led to the loss of several institutions to the Christian movement.

The year 1941 has been called the year of pro-Japanese renovation of the churches; 1942 the year of resistance; 1943 the year of persecution, with many arrests and the dissolution of Holiness and Seventh-day Adventist churches; 1944 the year of church ruin; and 1945 the year of emancipation.

CHARLES IGLEHART

*Since World War II.* At the close of World War II in 1945 which ended Japanese occupation, the total number of Christian adherents was estimated at about 750,000, of whom 600,000 were Protestant and 150,000 Catholic. Two-thirds of all Protestants were in the north. The tragic division of the country and the ensuing Korean War in 1950 changed everything. In the communist north, fierce persecution wiped out almost all visible signs of Christianity, and no organized church is left, although there are some small signs that a token reappearance may be allowed.

In South Korea, however, the growth of the church has been explosive. By 1986 a conservative estimate reports a total of about 10 million Christian adherents, or 25 percent of the population. Of these, 8.15 million are Protestant and 1.85 million Roman Catholic. This does not include some 650,000 in new semi-Christian cults such as the Unification Church. The older religions have sharply declined. Buddhist estimates range from 5 to 12 million adherents, while Confucianism as a religion has virtually disappeared. Shamanism is still a pervasive but unpublicized influence.

Among reasons advanced for the growth of Christianity, the more significant are: the evangelistic zeal of lay Korean leadership, emphasis on Bible study, and wise mission policies, notably the "Nevius Plan" of self-support, self-government, and self-propagation. To these theological and strategic factors must be added the social and political changes in Korea since the fall of the Yi Dynasty in 1910, which destroyed confidence in Korea's traditional religions and led to colonization by Japan (1905–45), and the restoration

of independence in the south after World War II. Christian leadership in the struggles for independence during this period, and for social welfare and human rights, won the favorable attention of the whole nation.

Protestant Christianity brought modern medical practice to Korea. Western education, introduced by the missionaries and linked to an insistence on providing education for women, challenged Confucian control of the nation's intellectual community. Three of the five most prestigious universities in the country are mission-founded: Ewha by Mary Scranton, a Methodist; Yorsei by Horace G. Underwood, a Presbyterian; and Sogang by the Jesuits. The Presbyterian Seminary of Korea, founded by Samuel A. Moffett, is the largest Presbyterian seminary in the world.

But in many ways the most radical factor for change in Korean Christianity has been the revival movement which unexpectedly broke upon the church in 1907 and introduced into Korean Protestant orthodoxy waves of purification and renewal which still continue. The Christian community in South Korea expands at four times the rate of population growth, and, despite omens of a possible dampening effect due to economic affluence, secularism, and ecclesiastical schisms, Christianity in Korea nearly doubles in membership every 10 years.

**Bibliography.** J. C. M. Kim and J. J. S. Chung, *Catholic Korea* (1964); A. D. Clark, *A History of the Church in Korea* (1971); G. L. G. Paik, *The History of Protestant Missions in Korea* (rev. ed., 1975); M. Huntley, *To Start a Work: The Foundations of Protestant Mission in Korea 1884–1919* (1987).

SAMUEL HUGH MOFFETT

## Kraeling, Carl Hermann

**Kraeling, Carl Hermann** (1897–1966). American archeologist. Born in Brooklyn, N.Y., he studied at the University of Heidelberg (Dr. Theol., 1935), Columbia University, and Union Theological Seminary (Ph.D., 1928), and at the University of Pennsylvania and the Lutheran Theological Seminary, Philadelphia. He taught at the latter (1920–29) and at Yale Divinity School (1929–41) before becoming professor of NT criticism and interpretation (1941–50) and chairman of the department of Near Eastern languages and literatures (1947–50) at Yale University. He was the professor of Hellenistic oriental archeology and director of the Oriental Institute of the University of Chicago (1950–62). A former president of the American Schools of Oriental Research at Jerusalem and Baghdad, he was known especially for his work in the Hellenistic and Roman phases of Near Eastern cultural history developed in the course of his association with the excavations of Yale University and the American Schools of Oriental Research at Gerasa, and in connection with the excavations of Yale University and the French Academy at Dura-Europos on the Euphrates. Among his published works were *Anthropos and the Son of Man* (1937), *A Greek Fragment of*

*Tatian's Diatessaron* (1935), *Excavations at Dura-Europos* (1936), *John the Baptist* (1951), and *The Christian Building* (1967). He was editor of the *Journal of Biblical Literature* (1931–33), and editor and contributor to *Gerasa, City of the Decapolis* (1938).

**Kraeling, Emil Gottlieb** (1892– ). Lutheran. Born in Brooklyn, he studied at New York University, the Lutheran Theological Seminary in Philadelphia, Leipzig, Pennsylvania, and Columbia (Ph.D., 1918). He was associate pastor in Brooklyn (1914–40) and taught OT at Union Theological Seminary (1919–43) and at Columbia University (1919–26, 1945/46). He wrote *Aram and Israel* (1918), and *The Book of the Ways of God* (1939).

**Kraemer, Hendrik** (1888–1965). Dutch missionary, translator, historian of religions, and ecumenist. Having been commissioned to "study the spiritual life of the Javanese people," Kraemer served the Dutch Bible Society in Indonesia from 1921 to 1935. While there he developed a theology of missions that showed particular concern for the indigenous Christian church in a culture shaped by Islam and Dutch colonialism. In 1937 he became professor of the history and phenomenology of religions at the University of Leiden in Holland. He prepared a memorable study guide entitled *The Christian Message in a Non-Christian World* (3d ed., 1956) for the 1938 World Missionary Conference at Tambaram, India. In it he argued that all religions are unique realities rather than continuous levels or varying appearances of a single, underlying reality as the evolutionary and unity of religions theories had suggested. He also emphasized the primacy of Christianity's "biblical realism." These views served to restore the importance of conversion as a missionary goal distinct from dialog and social ministry. Kraemer held his teaching position at Leiden until 1947 with the exception of a term of imprisonment by the Nazis during World War II. Following the Leiden years, he became the first director of the World Council of Churches' Ecumenical Institute at Château de Bossey, Switzerland. He taught at Union Seminary, N.Y., from 1955 until 1957, and then returned to Holland. In the last decade of his life, Kraemer wrote several books, including *The Communication of the Christian Faith* (1956), *Religion and the Christian Faith* (1957), *World Cultures and World Religions* (1960), and *Why Christianity of All Religions?* (1962). In these latter works, he softened his earlier dichotomy between Christianity and other religions as a result of his struggle with Rom. 2:1–16. As in his earlier work, however, he sharply criticized relativism and upheld Christianity.

ROBERT L. MORRISON

**Krahn, Cornelius** (1902– ). Mennonite historian. Born in Rosenthal, Russia, into a Mennonite family of Dutch-Prussian origin, he studied at the universities of Amsterdam, Berlin, Bonn, Heidelberg, and Wisconsin, becoming one of the leading Mennonite historians of the early 20th century. He taught at Tabor College (1939–44) and at Bethel College of the General Conference Mennonite Church, North Newton, Kans., until his retirement, and was editor of *Mennonite Life* and coeditor of the *Mennonite Encyclopedia*. His books include *Menno Simons (1496–1561), Ein Beitrag zur Geschichte der Taufgesinnten* (1936), and *Adventure in Conviction* (1952). He also edited C. Henry Smith's *Story of the Mennonites* (3d ed., 1950).

E. J. FURCHA

**Kroner, Richard** (1884–1974). German philosopher of religion. Born in Wraclaw (Breslau), Silesia, he studied at the universities of Berlin, Wraclaw, Heidelberg, and Freiburg/Breisgau, then served as assistant and professor of philosophy at Freiburg (1912–24), taught at the Technological Institute, Dresden (1924–28), and at the University of Kiel (1928–34). Because of pressures from the Hitler regime, he left for England in 1938 and for the USA (Yale and Union Seminary, New York) in 1941. An appointment to McGill University in 1940 as professor of metaphysics was never realized.

In 1910 he cofounded *Logos*, an international journal for the philosophy of culture, serving as its editor until 1934. Along with Dutch scholars he established the International Hegel Society in 1930, acting as its president until 1935.

He was influenced by southwest German Neo-Kantianism and contributed significantly to Neo-Hegelianism through his two-volume publication *Von Kant bis Hegel* (1921–24; 2d ed., 1961). Other works include *Die Selbstverwirklichung des Geistes* (1928), *Kulturphilosophische Grundlegung der Politik* (1931), *The Religious Function of Imagination* (1941), *The Primacy of Faith* (1943), *Speculation and Revelation in the History of Philosophy* (3 vols., 1957–61), *Between Faith and Thought* (1966), and *Freiheit und Gnade* (1969).

E. J. FURCHA

**Ku Klux Klan.** Following the defeat of the Confederate armies in the American Civil War, the Union forces devastated the South, burning and plundering in an act of unrestrained vengeance. Even medical schools and university libraries were burnt to punish the "rebels." For a short while a Union army of occupation controlled the South, and blacks were elected to the legislatures and other civic offices. Although the blacks played an important role in Reconstruction and showed themselves responsible citizens, Southern whites sought their own vengeance and, at times, self-defense by forming various secret organizations. The Ku Klux Klan was formed in Tennessee in 1866 as a support group for Civil War veterans. But in 1867 it became the "Invisible Empire of the South" with an extensive hierarchy controlled by the "Grand Wizard." Klansmen terrorized freed blacks and their supporters, lynching and torturing all who opposed them. With the end of the Reconstruction Era and the Compromise of 1877, white vigilante actions increased and blacks were deprived of political power and the franchise. Lynchings reached their peak in 1896 when 161 blacks died at the hands of white fanatics. In 1915 the Klan, which had ceased to operate, was revived in Georgia and became a vigorous political force that spread across the USA, gaining members in both North and South. The target of Klan activities now extended to radical whites, Roman Catholics, and Jews, as well as anyone deemed "undesirable." By 1928 the Klan was once more in decline and was officially dissolved for financial reasons in 1944. Once again, however, the Klan was revived in 1949 in Alabama, where they organized bitter opposition to desegregation. During the 1960s, especially after the brutal murder of three civil rights workers, the Klan came under increasing federal scrutiny. Today the Klan appears to be more in decline again although it seems to have given birth to, or at least encouraged, the growth of a number of white supremacist organizations such as the "Aryan Nations." What is significant about the present era is the extensive use of computer networks by Klan-related groups and their dissemination of antiblack and anti-Semitic propaganda through the computer.

*Bibliography.* C. C. Alexander, *The Ku Klux Klan in the Southwest* (1966); M. Chalmers, *Hooded Americanism* (1965); W. P. Randel, *The Ku Klux Klan* (1965).

IRVING HEXHAM

**Küng, Hans** (1928– ). Swiss-German theologian. Born in Sursee, Lucerne, Switzerland, he spent eight years in studies at the Pontifical Gregorian University in Rome (1948–55), residing in the German College, where he received licentiates in philosophy and theology and was ordained to the priesthood in 1954. Then he studied in Paris at the Catholic Institute and the Sorbonne and received a Th.D. in 1957 for a dissertation on Karl Barth's doctrine of justification. After a brief pastorate in his native country, he assumed a chair in theology at Tübingen in 1960. He worked on preparations for the Second Vatican Council and served as an official theological adviser to it. Paul VI did not renew the appointment and Küng returned to Tübingen in 1963 as professor of dogmatic and ecumenical theology and director of the Institute for Ecumenical Research. An extraordinarily prolific scholar who authored or edited dozens of books and hundreds of articles

and possessed a worldwide following, he was increasingly drawn into controversy with church hard-liners. On December 18, 1979, Rome formally relieved him of professorial responsibilities in the Catholic faculty at Tübingen, but the university retained him with a secular contract.

Küng's primary interest lay in ecumenism. He wanted to bring together the Catholic emphasis on the community of faith in space and time with the Protestant emphasis on constant recourse to Scripture and practical reform in accordance with the norms of the gospel. For him reform was not in doctrine but in spiritual renewal, to be expressed in reconciliation between Christians both in and outside the church. The universal church does not prove itself by authoritarian power or absolute formulations of dogma but by extending witness through its presence and action in the world. Remaining in the truth is more a matter of orthopraxy than orthodoxy. Thus, his views about the nature of the priesthood, papal authority, centralization in the church, justification, and reunion with Protestantism were the source of unending controversy with Rome. Although he stayed in the church, Küng's "Evangelical Catholicity" or "Neo-Catholicity," expressed in such best-selling books as *On Being a Christian* (1974), *Does God Exist?* (1976), *Eternal Life after Death* (1984), and *Why I Am Still a Christian* (1987), made him enormously popular, even in non-Catholic circles.

*Bibliography.* H. Haring and K.-J. Kuschel, eds., *Hans Küng: His Work and His Way* (1980); J. Kiewit, *Hans Küng* (1985).

RICHARD V. PIERARD

**Künneth, Walter** (1901– ). Lutheran theologian and churchman. Born in Etzelwang, Bavaria, he studied theology and philosophy at the universities of Erlangen and Tübingen (D. Phil., 1924). He taught at the Berlin-Spandau Apologetics Centre and at the University of Berlin. He emerged as a leader of Kirchenkampf resistance to National Socialism. He conducted a literary fight from 1935 to 1937 against Adolf Hitler's chief ideologist, A. Rosenberg. His efforts led to persecution by the Gestapo, loss of his offices, and enforced silence for the remaining period of the Third Reich. Erlangen University awarded him an honorary doctorate (1945) and appointed him to a chair (1946; professor of dogmatics and ethics, 1953–69). He served on the Church Council of the Evangelical Lutheran State-Church of Bavaria. His many awards include the Distinguished Service Cross of the West German Republic. His writings include *Antwort auf den Mythus* (1935), *Der grosse Abfall* (1947), *Theologie der Auferstehung* (1933; 6th ed., 1981), *Glaube an Jesus?* (2d ed., 1961), *Politik zwischen Dämon und Gott* (1954), *Fundamente des Glaubens* (4th ed., 1980), and *Der Christ als Staatsbürger* (1984). With Peter Beyerhaus he coedited *Reich Gottes oder Weltgemeinschaft* (1975), a critique of the World Council of Churches. He has also written an autobiography, *Lebensführungen* (1979).

GLEN G. SCORGIE

**Kutter, Hermann** (1863–1931). Swiss Protestant. Until his retirement in 1926, Kutter served parishes in Vinelz, Bielersee, and Zurich. He was an early influence on Karl Barth. He provided the chief impetus for the formation of the Christian Socialist movement in Switzerland, and his influence extended far beyond his native country, especially through his writings *Sie müssen* (1903), *Gerechtigkeit* (1905), *Die Revolution des Christentums* (1908), and *Not und Gewissheit* (1926).

THEODORE TAPPERT

**Kuwait.** *See* GULF STATES.

**Kuyper, Abraham** (1837–1920). Dutch Protestant theologian and statesman. Born in Maassluis, near Rotterdam, he studied in Leiden and was pastor at Beest (1863–68), Utrecht (1868–70), and Amsterdam (1870–74). Thereafter he became a figure in the political life of Holland, being a member of the States-General for Gouda from 1874 to 1877. In 1894 he again returned to the same body for Sleidrecht, and in 1901 he became prime minister until 1905. In 1880 he founded at Amsterdam the Free University, where he taught for many years, lecturing on various topics as the need arose. In theology a strict orthodox Calvinist, he founded the Reformed Free Church in 1886. He lectured extensively in the USA. He made a lasting impact on primary and secondary education, politics, and literature in the Netherlands. Besides editing the daily *Standaard* for nearly 50 years, he also edited the weekly *Herout*, and published many works. Among these were *Calvinism* (1899), *The Work of the Holy Spirit* (ET, 1900), *His Decease* (ET, 1928), *Asleep in Jesus* (ET, 1929), and *The Revelation of John* (ET, 1935). In addition, portions of his *Encyclopaedie der heilige Godgeleerdheid* (3 vols., 1894) have been translated into English under the title, *Encyclopaedia of Sacred Theology: Its Principles* (1898).

**Kyle, Melvin Grove** (1858–1933). United Presbyterian archeologist. Born near Cadiz, Ohio, he was educated at Muskingum College and Allegheny Theological Seminary. He taught biblical theology and archeology at Xenia Theological Seminary (now Pittsburgh-Xenia) (1908–30; president, 1922–30; later research lecturer). He was editor of *Bibliotheca Sacra* (1921) and lecturer in the American School of Oriental Research, Jerusalem (1921). He made exploration at Sodom and Gomorrah (1924) and at Kirjath-sepher (1926–28). He wrote *The Deciding Voice of the Monuments in Biblical Criticism* (1912), *Moses and Monuments* (1920), *The Problem of the Pentateuch* (1933), and *Excavating Kirjath-Sepher's Ten Cities* (1934).

RAYMOND W. ALBRIGHT

# Ll

**Labor and the Church.** Initially, many religious bodies opposed the labor movement. In many cases opposition stemmed from religious beliefs. Some religious teachings viewed the "sweat of thy face" (Gen. 3:19) as ordained by God for the descendants of the disobedient Adam and Eve. Others justified toil for its redemptive value toward salvation. Because the writings of Marx championed atheism as well as the plight of the laboring masses, the labor movement became inextricably linked with Marxism in the eyes of many. Churches condemned the bargaining tactics of using strikes, pickets and any resulting violence as a violation of natural economic law. Manual labor was vindicated and encouraged by religious leaders who, like those in management, were usually spared physical drudgery. Thus, the clergy with its influence identified itself with management early in the struggle between labor and management.

During the 19th century in both Europe and the United States the trend began to change in the relationship between churches and labor. Religious bodies moved away from a position of opposition to labor. Some groups went further than others in supporting the union movement. By 1824 Great Britain had repealed laws which repressed labor unions. The enactment of the Reform Act of 1867 further strengthened British workers in political power. Labor had already gained the rights to organize and bargain collectively when the Church of England proclaimed its support of labor in pronouncements of the Lambeth Conference in 1920. In America the Knights of Labor was a fraternal society dedicated to Christian piety and temperance as strongly as it was committed to advancing the cause of the worker. In founding the Federal Council of the Churches of Christ, the group asserted the rights of labor in principle and action. Even though the ecumenical movement favored shorter working hours in 1908, they did not press for the eight hour day until the 1930s.

The Roman Catholic Church began taking action on behalf of organized labor in 1891 when Pope Leo XIII issued the encyclical, *Rerem novarum*. Pope Pius XI expanded its doctrine with the 1931 encyclical, *Quadragesimo anno*. Thirty years later under John XXIII, a third encyclical, *Mater et magistra*, reiterated the stance of both previous papal documents in recognizing the rights of workers.

The relationship between religion and labor has progressed from antagonism to support. Among religious scholars and theologians of international note who have lauded the efforts of labor and, thus, furthered its cause were Taylor, Rauschenbusch, Tillich, Lehmann, Temple, Cardijn, and Barth. Christian involvement in the union movement remains active. Current noteworthy examples of Christian effectiveness in the labor movement stand out in Europe and Africa. During its inception in 1980, the Solidarity movement found much of its power based in its alliance with the Roman Catholic Church to confront the communist regime in Poland. Similarly, the National Union of Mineworkers has been aided in the quest for black equality by the Anglican Church in South Africa. Through the efforts of Christian supporters, both organizations have championed the rights and dignity of individuals in all levels of society.

While communism in Poland isolated the people from the regime, the Roman Catholic Church provided a sense of unity for the dominated society which lacked an access to the centers of power. Preceding the strikes in August of 1980 the Church had already widened its reach to the public through periodicals and the Clubs of Catholic Intellectuals. When Polish Cardinal Wojtyla, who associated closely with the workers movement, was elected Pontiff in 1978, Poland gained international attention. John Paul II's 1979 visit to his homeland inspired Polish workers to bridge the gap between society and unapproachable government leaders.

The Solidarity movement resulted from a series of strikes in August 1980. Lech Walesa, an electrician, led his coworkers in a series of work stoppages at the Gdansk shipyard which abruptly grew into a national struggle. When the shipyard management conceded to wage demands on August 15, 1980, a turning point occurred. The shipyard workers refused to end the strike out of solidarity for other laborers who still lacked wage concessions. The formation of a strike committee to draw up a list of demands immediately followed this action. The Inter-Factory Strike Committee called for a free trade union, free elections, and the dissolution of censorship.

During the August strikes, the role of the Roman Catholic Church intertwined with the labor movement as masses were celebrated in the shipyard and within the factories. Leaders of the movement recognized the importance of the Church in gaining support among dissatisfied elements in the society. In a meeting with Father Jankowski, a parish priest in the Gdansk shipyard district, strike leaders urged him to secure approval from the church hierarchy for the strikers. On August 22, Cardinal Wyszynski proclaimed his sympathy with the movement in a letter which was censored in an address broadcast to pilgrims at Czestochowa. The Church followed with an expression of its unqualified support for Solidarity. In negotiations at the shipyard, government representatives sat beneath a statue of Lenin while their labor counterparts chose seats beneath a cross. By August 31, 1980 the government reached a twenty-one point agreement with Solidarity. Solidarity retained legal status for sixteen months until marshal law was declared outlawing the organization in December, 1981. Although Solidarity had been legally abolished, the movement endured under conditions of duress, harassment and imprisonment until the Polish reestablished its legality in 1989.

South Africa is another area where the union movement has been supported by the church in a struggle for social justice. The Apartheid system is not only a means of social and racial control but it also involves economic injustice and the maintenance of dangerous working conditions for blacks. For example, a black miner in 1986 was paid about one-fifth of what a white miner earned for the same job. Also a clear illustration of the need for safer mining practices was the death of 67 workers in a disaster at the Hlobane mine in 1983. Because of an inquiry supported by black union leaders, the mining company was found to be criminally liable for the deaths and a white miner was proven to be responsible for the blast.

In reaction to the inequality of wages and working conditions in the mines, there were a series of violent demonstration beginning in 1982 when several of the largest mines in South Africa were closed by rioting. The riots stopped gold production and resulted in the destruction of millions of dollars worth of property. After these job actions were suppressed, the government realized that the problem had arisen because of an absence of a structure for bargaining and communication between the 456,000 black miners and company management. Although the miners had been dissatisfied before, they had lacked a leader capable of galvanizing them into action. In 1982 this changed, however, when a consensus began to form around a black lawyer named Cyril Ramaphosa who was able to represent the cause of the workers in an effective way to the mines.

In June 1983 Ramaphosa's union group, the National Union of Mineworkers (NUM) was able to secure recognition from the government and to negotiate for a rational nonracial wage for all miners. In addition, he exposed dangerous working conditions in the mines, sought paid vacations, accident insurance, and other fringe benefits for workers. Perhaps, more important than any of these accomplishments was his insistence that racial discrimination in the mines should be ended by opening up the better job positions, which were reserved for whites only, to black workers. By 1986 the NUM conducted one of the largest strikes in South African mining history when about 300,000 black miners in 44 mines stopped working. This resulted in increased pay and benefits for miners.

Ramaphosa also organized the Congress of South African Trade Unions (COSATU) in December 1985 which brought together 32 unions under his leadership. He attempted to work with political and religious groups to achieve greater equality and a more democratic economy in South Africa. His movement, supported by individuals such as Desmond Tutu and Allen Boesak as well as certain elements of the Roman Catholic Church in South Africa, has brought greater dignity to labor in that nation.

These events involving church support in Europe and Africa for the union movement provide a microcosm of the progression in the relationship between labor and religion since the Industrial Revolution. The success of church involvement with labor in Poland has taken hold in eastern Europe where the pattern of church support for the union movement in its call for social justice and greater freedom has been repeated behind the disintegrating Iron Curtain. From antagonistic disapproval during the 19th century, the attitude of religious leaders has changed to one of active support as the 21st century approaches.

RITA G. BRYAN AND ROBERT G. CLOUSE

## Ladd, George Eldon

**Ladd, George Eldon** (1911–82). Canadian NT scholar. Born in Alberta, he graduated from Gordon College and Gordon Divinity School, served several Northern Baptist churches as minister, and studied at Boston University and Harvard (Ph.D., 1949). He taught at Gordon College and Divinity School, and from 1950 until his death, NT theology at Fuller Theological Seminary. Ladd was a major American scholar who sought consciously to make evangelical scholarship credible following the fundamentalism-modernism controversies of the 1930s, and he was an effective bridge between evangelical and modern scholarship. Ladd's primary contributions were in NT theology, particularly concerning the kingdom of God and biblical eschatology. His considerable success is evidenced by the reception of his works in the academic world, his inspiration to many of his students to pursue scholarship, and the particular honor of being one of a handful of contributors to the 25th anniversary issue of the journal of biblical scholarship, *Interpretation* (January 1971). Ladd's works include *Crucial Questions about the Kingdom of God* (1952), *The Blessed Hope* (1956), *Jesus and the Kingdom* (rev. ed., 1964), *The Presence of the Future* (1974), *The NT and Criticism* (1967), and *Theology of the NT* (1974). A feschrift in his honor is entitled *Unity and Diversity in NT Theology* (1978).

JAMES MCCLANAHAN

## Lagrange, Albert (Marie Joseph) (1855–1938).

Roman Catholic. Born in Bourg-en-Bresse, France, he received a doctorate in civil law in Paris. Turning to theology, he entered the Seminary of Saint Sulpice (1878), and became a Dominican in 1879. After his ordination (1883), he studied at Salamanca and attended courses in Semitic languages at the University of Vienna. In 1890 he founded the *Pratique d'Bibliques* in Jerusalem, where he resided until his retirement at Saint Maximin (1935). He played an important part in the revival of biblical studies in the Roman Church, advocating the use of historical criticism. Among his principal works are his commentaries on the four Gospels, (1911–25) followed by a volume of synthesis, *l'Évangile de Jésus-Christ* (1928). He also wrote *Études sur les Religious Sémitiques* (1903), *Le Messianisme chez les Juifs* (1909), *Épître aux Romains* (1915), *Épître aux Galates* (1918), *Le Judaïsme avant Jésus-Christ* (1931), and *Introduction à l'étude du Nouveau Testament* (vol. 1, *Canon du N.T.*, 1933; vol. 2, *Critique textuelle*, 1935, and vol. 3, *Critique historique*, 1937).

**Bibliography.** F. M. Braun, *L'oeuvre du Père Lagrange* (1943); R. T. Murphy, *Père Lagrange and the Scriptures* (1946).

GEORGES A. BARROIS

## Lake, Kirsopp (1872–1946).

Anglican church historian and archeologist. He was educated at Lincoln College, Oxford, and served curacies at Lumley, Durham (1895–97), and St. Mary the Virgin, Oxford (1897–1904). He taught at the University of Leyden, Holland (1904–13). At Harvard University he taught Christian literature (1914–19), was Winn Professor of Ecclesiastical History (1919–32), and professor of history (1932–38). He visited Mt. Athos and other libraries to investigate Greek manuscripts, and directed archeological expeditions to Serabit (1930, 1935), Samaria (1932–34), and Lake Van (1938/39). His books include *Text of the NT* (1898), *Codex 1 of the Gospels* (1900), *Texts from Mt. Athos* (1901), *The Athos Leaves of Codex H—Paul* (1904), *The Historical Evidence for the Resurrection of Jesus Christ* (1905), *The Athos Leaves of the Shepherd of Hermas* (1908), *Professor von Soden's Treatment of the Text of the Gospels* (1909), *The Earlier Epistles of St. Paul* (1910), *The Codex Sinaiticus,* (2 vols., 1911, 1921), *The Stewardship of Faith* (1914), *The Beginnings of Christianity* (5 vols., 1920–33), *Landmarks in the History of Early Christianity* (1921), *Immortality and the Modern Mind* (1922), *Religion Yesterday and Tomorrow* (1925), *Paul, His Heritage and Legacy* (1934), and *An Introduction to the NT* (1937). He translated *The Apostolic Fathers* (1912), *Eusebius* (1927), and *The Serabit Inscriptions* (1927). He edited *The Caesarean Text of Mark* (1928), *Six Collations of NT Manuscripts* (1–9, 1934–41), and *Studies and Documents* (9 vols., 1934–37).

RAYMOND W. ALBRIGHT

## Lamaism.

Tibetan form of Buddhism. Buddhism appears to have entered Tibet in the 7th century A.D., where the indigenous religion consisted of a set of shamanistic practices called Bon. Bon emphasized magic, both good and evil, and the many spirits, also both good and evil. Buddhism's earliest Tibetan patrons appear to have been royalty who found it a helpful political support.

Tibetan Buddhism drew upon the Tantric form of Indian Buddhism, alternatively called Tantrayana, Vajrayana, or Mantrayana. Vajrayana claims to be a superior form of Buddhism, with its own esoteric tradition of a higher wisdom. Tibetan Tantric Buddhism emphasizes the role of dualities (such as male and female, good and evil, wisdom and method) and their resolution into unity, or at least harmony, through meditation, chanting, painting, statuary, liturgy, and other highly symbolic forms. The symbols and deities may be interpreted as objective realities, as psychological truths, as meditational correlates, or as cosmic forces. Tantric Buddhism thus allowed the Tibetans to incorporate many magical, shamanistic, and spiritualist motifs and practices from the Bon religion. It has also encouraged certain practices originating in Indian Buddhism, such as the cult of Tara, a protective female deity who has been worshiped by people from every level of society. Tantric Buddhism also asserts the possibility of becoming a Buddha in this life and in this body.

The possibility of becoming a Buddha or Bodhisattva has resulted in one of Tibetan Buddhism's more striking characteristics. Many of the more prestigious monks, either because of achievement or rank, are considered to be living Buddhas and Bodhisattvas, stimulating respect, awe, and occasionally worship. The term *lama*, associated with the Indian term *guru*, means "superior one" and is applied to the Tibetan monks and Buddhist leaders.

Buddhism has gone through several cycles of decay and revival in Tibetan history. One of the most significant of the reform movements is known as the Yellow Hat party (in distinction to groups with red hats and black hats). It has stressed monastic discipline and the study of traditional Mahayana texts as well as the esoteric texts of Tantric Buddhism.

Buddhists from Tibet converted the Mongolians at two different times and through them reached into the imperial court of China. The first major convert was Kublai Khan (1215–94) who conquered China and established the Mongol dynasty (c. 1280–1368). Most ordinary Mongolians, however, did not become Buddhist until the second round of conversions. In the 16th century one of the recently converted Mongol chieftains bestowed the title of Dalai Lama upon a Yellow Hat leader. This title was retained by his successors (as well as applied retroactively to his two immediate predecessors).

The Dalai Lamas are considered to be the incarnation of Avalokitsvara. Each Dalai Lama is also believed to be the reincarnation of the previous Dalai Lama. Because of their connections with the Mongols, the Dalai Lamas have held political as well as spiritual authority. This contrasts with another office, known as the Panchen Lama. The Panchen Lama, considered to be the incarnation of Amitabha, holds spiritual authority only. The political value of the Mongolian support for the Dalai Lamas increased when the Mongolians conquered China, establishing the Manchu (Qing or Ching) Dynasty (1644–1911). Tibetan religion received high status in the Manchu Court in Beijing. This patronage, however, cost the Tibetans dearly, because it meant the inclusion of Tibet in the traditional zone of Chinese sovereignty.

In 1951, the Chinese communists invaded Tibet. During an uprising in 1959, the Dalai Lama fled the country. The communists snapped the Buddhist tradition of Tibet, which, while showing some signs of revival in the 1980s in Tibet itself, survived mostly in the ceremonies of a handful of refugees.

*Bibliography.* G. Tucci, *Tibetan Painted Scrolls*, 3 vols. (1949); S. V. Beyer, *The Cult of Tara* (1973); E. M. Dargyey, *The Rise of*

*Esoteric Buddhism in Tibet* (1977); G. Tucci, *The Religions of Tibet* (1980); M. H. Franz, *Rule by Incarnation: Tibetan Buddhism and Its Role in Society and State* (1982).

STEPHEN T. FRANKLIN

**Lambeth Conference.** Gathering of bishops of the Anglican Communion held every 10 years. The first Lambeth Conference was called by Archbishop Longley in 1867. Moderate High Church men in the Church of England, such as Bishop Samuel Wilberforce, had become increasingly conscious of the need for the church to make its own decisions, and were critical of what they regarded as an inappropriate dependence on the state. At the same time Anglicanism in many British colonies quite rapidly discarded its establishment trappings and set up an independent government akin to that which had characterized the Episcopal Church in the USA and Scotland. Consequently a synodical form of government emerged as the norm and, from about 1860, important colonial church leaders such as Bishop Gray of Capetown began to call for a higher synod "to crown the edifice" of the provincial and diocesan synods. Most evangelicals and many liberals opposed such synodical developments, believing that they were likely to enhance authoritarian clerical and episcopal claims by decreasing the lay voice in the church. Bishop Gray, however, pressed the case particularly strongly when he found, in his efforts to deal with the heretical Bishop Colenso, his authority frustrated by the residual rights of the establishment. Archbishop Longley, as a High Church man, was very sympathetic to such appeals. He agreed to hold a meeting of bishops, although, significantly, it was not given synodical status and therefore had no formal authority to settle matters of canon law and doctrine.

One hundred and fifty-one bishops were invited to the first conference and 76 attended. Many, including those from York Province, were intensely suspicious and absented themselves. Momentum had, however, been achieved and Archbishop Tait, although he shared none of his predecessor's High Church liking for synods, considered it advisable to call another conference in 1878. This was much more representative and established the precedent for conferences every 10 years or so which has been the subsequent pattern (1888, 1897, 1908, 1920, 1930, 1948, 1958, 1968, 1978, 1988).

Lambeth Conferences have been important in developing the mind of the Anglican Communion on many issues, particularly in the area of ecumenism. The Lambeth Quadrilateral (1888) and the Lambeth "Appeal to all Christian People" for reunion (1920) were particularly important in defining Anglican ecumenical attitudes.

The 1958 conference had as its theme "The Holy Bible: Its Authority and Message." An emphasis upon the supernatural activity of God was struck against the background of growing theological pessimism. But the public statement which gained considerable interest was a strong, positive declaration of the importance of sexual relationships in marriage. This included support for birth control as a means of family planning.

The exclusively episcopal character of Lambeth was balanced by the first international Anglican gathering held outside Great Britain, in Minneapolis, Minn. (1954). A similar congress was held in Toronto in 1963, from which the Mutual Responsibility and Interdependence (MRI) program emerged. This encouraged less dependence upon the older churches, as Anglicanism developed outside Great Britain, the USA, Canada, and Australasia. MRI has played a large part in the growing independence and diversity of churches within Anglicanism. The influence of the Second Vatican Council furthered the sense of mutual collegiality among Anglican dioceses. In particular, the years between the conferences of 1978 saw the rapid emergence of revised liturgies of considerable diversity.

The 1968 conference was a more collegiate gathering, the English bishops being in a minority. The Lambeth Quadrilateral was further modified; explicit reference to the episcopate in the fourth point was replaced by a general reference to "ministry which is a channel of grace." This was due in part to the strong support given to the proposed union between the Church of England and the Methodist Church in Great Britain. Considerable attention was given to contemporary issues—revolution, racism, and poverty—as well as current church concerns—the place of the 39 Articles and the diaconate, for example. The ordination of women was discussed but without any particular conclusion.

The conference set up a permanent body, eventually called the Anglican Consultative Council (ACC) including lay and clerical as well as episcopal representatives from each church. ACC has met approximately every three years since, and is growing in importance as a forum for Anglicans, as the older ties of common liturgy and history diminish.

The 1978 conference continued to move away from any appearance of being an international governing body for Anglicanism. Bishops worked in small groups on a wide range of issues. The emphasis fell upon equipping them for their ministries and enabling them to share mutual concerns. The conference passed comparatively few resolutions. These included firm statements on justice and human rights, and the upsurge of interest in the work of the Holy Spirit in the 1970s.

The ordination of women had been an issue since Lambeth 68. Resolution 21 acknowledged this and called for churches to remain in full communion despite differences on this issue. The Partners in Mission program was initiated; this has led to critical review and planning of each church's mission, with help and interaction from other member churches. A further development was the beginning of an association of French-speaking dioceses.

Progress was made in reaching agreement with the Roman Catholic Church on intermarriage, and the reports of the Anglican-Roman Catholic International Commission (ARCIC) were endorsed. Relations with the Orthodox churches were furthered by a joint Anglican-Orthodox Commission in the 1970s; its work was supported by Lambeth, though the differences over the ordination of women, among other matters, was substantial. The relationship of Anglicanism to non-Christian religions and ideologies was given careful consideration.

Since 1978 the growth of Anglicanism in developing countries has continued, especially in Africa and South America. In Great Britain and elsewhere there has been sharp debate about the limits of theological pluralism, due partly to the growing diversity of liturgical practice, partly to disagreement over the ordination of women, but more especially because some bishops have failed to adhere firmly to the Catholic faith in their public ministry. An interchurch theological commission was set up to further theological discussion among Anglicans, and so far has published one report on the church and the kingdom of God in the contemporary world.

The Lambeth Conference is attended by most bishops in the Anglican Communion (407 in 1978), and since 1968 has benefited from non-Episcopal consultants and non-Anglican observers. Its resolutions are a useful, if very general, yardstick of Anglican attitudes on theological, ecclesiological, and moral questions.

*Bibliography.* D. Morgan, *The Bishops Come to Lambeth* (1958, 1968, 1978); A. M. G. Stephenson, *Anglicans and the Lambeth Conferences* (1978).

PHILIP J. WILLIAMS AND CHARLES SHERLOCK

***Lamentabili Sane Exitu.*** Decree issued by the Roman Congregation of the Holy Office and signed by Pope Pius X in 1907. It lists 65 propositions taken from the writings of modernist scholars, particularly A. Loisy, but also G. Tyrrell and E. Le Roy. It condemns as errors the claim that scientific research, even in theological matters, ought to be free from ecclesiastical control; the rejection of scriptural inerrancy; a subjective notion of revelation; religious pragmatism and an evolutionistic conception of the dogmas and institutions of the church, whose objective character and absolute value was denied by modernism. The decree was followed after an interval of two months by the encyclical *Pascendi diminici gregis.*

The original Latin text is in *Acts Sanctae Sedis*, vol. 40 (1907), while the English translation is in J. E. Steinmueller, *A Companion to Scripture Studies*, vol. 1 (1946).

GEORGES A. BARROIS

**Lampe, Geoffrey William Hugo** (1912–1980). Anglican clergyman, theologian, and educator. Born in Bournemouth, England, he was educated at Oxford University and Queen's College, Birmingham University. He was ordained in 1937, and served as curate of Okehampton (1937/38), assistant master, King's School, Canterbury (1938–41), chaplain in the British army (1941–45), fellow and chaplain of St. John's College, Oxford (1943–53), professor of theology, Birmingham University (1953–59), and, combined with this appointment, dean of the faculty of arts (1955–59) and vice-principal, Birmingham University (1957–59), professor of divinity, Cambridge University (1959–71), and Regius professor of divinity, Cambridge University (1971–79). A recipient of the Military Cross for bravery during World War II, he was elected a fellow of the British Academy (FBA) in 1963, and, for his promotion of ecumenical relations between the Church of England and the Scandinavian churches, was made a Commander of the Northern Star by the king of Sweden in 1978. Lampe was in many ways a typical liberal mid-20th-century Anglican theologian, grounding his theology on the critical-historical study of the NT and the Christian fathers but with virtually no philosophical dimension. In other ways he was a radical thinker, especially in later life, about such matters as total openness and freedom in thinking about the central issues of Christian doctrine. Thus he sought a fresh interpretation of the patristic understanding of the deification of Christ and of the doctrine of the Trinity. In *God as Spirit* (1977), he repeatedly returned to the theme of the Spirit of God as the Spirit of Christlikeness as an existential reality in society. Moreover, in his reflections on death—both his own, which he knew would occur a few days later, and that of Christian believers in general—he tiptoed to the edge of agnosticism before reaffirming the biblical promise that death will not separate the believer from "the love of God, which is in Christ Jesus our Lord." As an active member of the National Synod of the Church of England, he worked tirelessly for ecumenism, liturgical reform, and the ordination of women. Lampe's scholarly reputation rests largely on his editorship of the massive *Patristic Greek Lexicon* (5 vols., 1961–69) and the second volume of *The Cambridge History of the Bible: The West from the Fathers to the Reformation* (1969). In addition to *God as Spirit*, his other important works include *Aspects of the NT Ministry* (1948), *Reconciliation in Christ* (1956), *I Believe* (1960), *The Seal of the Spirit* (rev. ed., 1967), *St. Luke and the Church of Jerusalem* (1969), and *Explorations in Theology 8* (posthumously, 1981).

ROBERT D. LINDER

**Lampe, William Edward** (1875–1950). Evangelical and Reformed. Born in Frederick, Md., he studied at Princeton University, Princeton Theological Seminary, and the Theological Seminary of the Reformed Church. A missionary to Japan (1900–1907), he organized the Layman's Missionary Movement in the Reformed Church (1908). He served as president of the United Stewardship Council of the Churches of Christ in America, and was a member of the Federal Council of Churches and of its executive committee. He was secretary of the general synod and general council of the Evangelical and Reformed Church.

H. M. J. KLEIN

**Lang, Cosmo Gordon** (1864–1944). Archbishop of Canterbury. Born of Presbyterian parents in Aberdeen, he was educated at the universities of Glasgow and Oxford, and was studying law when he changed course and studied theology at Cuddesdon. After ordination he was fellow of All Souls', Oxford (1888–93), curate of Leeds (1890–93), fellow of Magdalen College and dean of divinity (1893–96), vicar of St. Mary the Virgin, Oxford (1894–96), and vicar of Portsea and prison chaplain (1896–1901). In 1901 he was consecrated suffragan bishop of Stepney, and in 1908 became archbishop of York, and in 1928 archbishop of Canterbury. He retired in 1942, at which time he was created baron. During his early ministry he wrote *Miracles of Jesus as Marks of the Way of Life* (1900), *Thoughts on Some of the Parables of Jesus* (1905), *Opportunity of the Church of England* (1905), and *Principles of Religious Education* (1906). He was deeply interested in ecumenical relations, but is remembered most widely for his part in events that led to the abdication of King Edward VIII in 1936.

**Laos.** *See* SOUTHEAST ASIA.

**Larsen, Peter Laurentius** (1833–1915). Pioneer Norwegian Lutheran pastor and educator. Larsen emigrated to America in 1857. After home mission work in Minnesota, he served the Norwegian Synod's students at Concordia Seminary, St. Louis, Mo. (1859–61). Civil War tensions took him and his students to Decorah, Iowa. There, as president of Luther College, Larsen committed his synod to the advancement of higher education. Involved periodically in controversies over slavery, absolution, and predestination, he held the respect of friend and foe by his integrity and wisdom. College president until 1913, he was also vice-president of the Norwegian Synod

(1876–93), and editor of *Evangelisk Luthersk Kirketidende*.

**Bibliography**. K. Larsen, *Laurentius Larsen, Pioneer College President* (1936).

E. Theodore Bachmann

**Latourette, Kenneth Scott** (1884–1968). American church historian. Born in Oregon, he studied at Yale University (1904–9), where he became involved in the work of the Yale Mission. After graduation he was an active participant in the Student Volunteer Movement. He also taught in China but illness forced him to return home in 1912. Latourette then turned his attention to historical scholarship, centering his attention on the history of Christian missions, the expansion of Christianity, and the history of the Far East. In 1921 he returned to Yale University as a member of the faculty and remained there until his retirement in 1953.

Academic life and its demands did not prevent him from taking an active part in the life of the church, particularly in the affairs of the American Baptist Convention in which he served a term as president. He also assumed an active role in historical activities and was elected president of the American Historical Association.

Latourette was a prolific writer. His best-known works include *The History of Christian Missions in China* (1929), *History of the Expansion of Christianity* (7 vols., 1937–1945), and *Christianity in a Revolutionary Age* (5 vols., 1958–1962).

C. Gregg Singer

**Laubach, Frank Charles** (1884–1970). Congregationalist missionary, linguist, and philosopher on prayer. Born in Benton, Pa., he was educated at Princeton and Columbia (Ph. D., 1915) and Union Theological Seminary. In 1915 he began his long career as a missionary, first to the Philippines and later with an increasingly worldwide ministry. Dissatisfied with what he termed the "pettiness and futility" of his life, he began an experiment in prayer—a "practice of the presence" of God—that became one of the two major emphases of his life. In 1929 he undertook the second project that was to dominate his energies—literacy work among the poor and illiterate people of the world. In that year he received government permission to work among the Morotribe on the island of Mindanao. In the course of his efforts to teach the Moros to read, he began developing the charts that were to characterize his literacy work, and adopted the motto, "Each One Teach One," that came to be known as the "Laubach Method." The program soon expanded to other provinces and then, beginning in 1935, to other countries. He visited Malaya, India, Egypt, Ceylon, Palestine, and Turkey, and initiated work on charts for each nation. Laubach was eventually responsible for the development of literacy primers for about 300 languages and dialects in more than 100 countries. The Committee on World Literacy and Christian Literature of the Foreign Missions Conference of North America, as well as Laubach Literacy International, resulted from those efforts. He wrote more than 30 books on such wide-ranging subjects as Philippine history, literacy, prayer, the Bible, and world needs. Among his books were *Letters by a Modern Mystic* (1937), *Prayer, the Mightiest Force in the World* (1951), *The World Is Learning Compassion* (1958), *Thirty Years with the Silent Billion* (1960), and *Toward World Literacy* (1960).

**Bibliography**. D. Mason, *Frank C. Laubach* (1967).

Norris A. Magnuson

**Lausanne Committee for World Evangelization.** A body formed after the 1974 Congress on World Evangelization, held in Lausanne, Switzerland, involving 2750 participants from 150 nations. One of the widest-ranging meetings of Christians ever held, the congress adopted the Lausanne Covenant, a 3000-word 15-point document which enunciated a contemporary expression of historical evangelical commitments on a broad range of essential doctrinal tenets and practical implications of those commitments. The covenant, which has been translated into many languages, has been widely accepted. Congress participants indicated a desire for a continuing committee to spread the "Lausanne spirit" and vision. Linked by the Lausanne Covenant and a shared vision, the 75-member committee, through congresses, conferences, publications, and networking, seeks to be a catalyst and facilitator for world evangelization. Its members are from a broad regional and denominational cross-section, with the majority from the third world. The international office is now located in Singapore.

Leslie K. Tarr

**Lawrence, William** (1850–1941). Protestant Episcopal bishop. Born in Boston, he studied at Harvard and at the Episcopal Theological School, Cambridge, Mass., and after ordination was rector of Grace Church, Lawrence, Mass. (1876–84), professor of homiletics and pastoral theology in the Episcopal Theological School (1884–93), and bishop of Massachusetts (1893–1926). He was largely responsible for the enlargement of the pension fund of the Episcopal Church. His published works include *Visions and Service* (1896), *Study of Phillips Brooks* (1903), *The American Cathedral* (1921), *Fifty Years* (1923), *Memories of a Happy Life* (1926), *The New American* (1929), and *Life of Phillips Brooks* (1930).

**Laws, Robert** (1851–1934). Scottish medical missionary. Born in Aberdeen, he worked his way through university and college in Glasgow, and having qualified as doctor and minister, went in 1875 to Central Africa under the auspices of the United Presbyterian Church. Due to his pioneering activities, stations were established, agricultural work was begun, the slave trade was countered in Livingstonia, and eight languages were written down for the first time. By 1901 the Livingstonia Mission had six main and 112 preaching stations, five African congregations with 1576 members, 142 schools with 11,000 students, and 531 native teachers and preachers. By 1914 the work begun by Laws had 49 missionaries, over 9000 communicants, and 57,479 students. In 1924 the Synod of the Church of Central Africa was formed, with Laws as moderator. After 52 years on the field, he retired in 1927. His labors had been acknowledged at home when in 1908 he was elected moderator of the general assembly of the United Free Church of Scotland.

**Lay Preaching.** One mark of growth in religious consciousness in the 20th century has been the increasing currency of the term, "the ministry of the laity," which once would have seemed to many a self-contradictory expression. The notion that preaching and other ministries should be limited to those ordained by churches is now widely looked upon as being invalid. Beginning in the 1950s one evidence of this trend appeared in many conferences in the USA.

The church has a tradition of powerful lay preaching. Most early Christians were what today would be called laity. Aquila and Priscilla were tent makers, yet their appearance in three NT books is evidence of their powerful ministry in the early church. The contention is that Christianity won largely because of its adoption of a universal ministry, and because early lay Christians were also ministers.

Lay preaching has sometimes been more effective than that of professionals. St. Francis of Assisi and George Fox were effective lay preachers. Work to enable lay workers is fostered by several national and international organizations, by denominations, and local congregations. Videotape and audiotape courses offered by some seminaries are designed to better prepare lay workers for an amazing variety of tasks once regarded as clergy responsibilities.

D. ELTON TRUEBLOOD

**Leach, William Herman** (1888–1962). Presbyterian. Born in Shingle House, Pa., he studied at Alfred University, Syracuse University, Auburn Theological Seminary, and Union Theological Seminary. He was pastor of First Congregational, Port Leyden, N.Y.; Cochran Memorial Presbyterian Church, Oneida, N.Y.; First Presbyterian Church, Alden, N.Y., and Walden Presbyterian Church, Buffalo, N.Y. He was editor of religious literature, George H. Doran Company (1925–28),

and founder and editor of *Church Management* (from 1924). Among his guides and manuals were *How to Make the Church Go* (1922), *Church Finance* (1928), *Church Publicity* (1930), *Cokesbury Funeral Manual* (1932), *Sermon Hearts from the Gospels* (1934), *Sermon Hearts from the Psalms* (1936), *The Making of the Minister* (1938), *Cokesbury Marriage Manual* (rev. ed., 1939), *Sermon Hearts* (1931), *The Improved Funeral Manual* (1946), *Toward a More Efficient Church* (1948), and *Protestant Church Building* (1948). He coauthored with J. W. G. Ward, *The Tragedy and Triumph of Easter* (1933), and *Special Day Sermons with Worship Outlines* (1935), and, with Marcus L. Bach, he wrote *Vesper Dramas* (1938).

**League of Nations, The Churches and the.** The league (1919–45), which aimed at cooperation for peace, was originated and organized under conspicuously Christian leaders, including Woodrow Wilson, Jan C. Smuts, and Robert Cecil. Many Christians welcomed it with enthusiasm, notably in Scandinavia, Great Britain, and the USA, and established or joined supporting associations. Resolutions of approval were adopted by church bodies, and some declarations of church leaders were as enthusiastic as Archbishop Nathan Söderblom of Sweden who in 1926 asserted: "The fundamental idea of the League of Nations . . . constitutes in my judgment a continuation of the divine work of creation."

In Germany, France, Italy, and the USA there were various objections to the entire settlement of World War I, with which the league was identified, and political leaders tended to oppose or to distrust the concept. The USA, despite a herculean campaign by President Wilson, stood outside, cooperating occasionally. The Roman Catholic hierarchy generally maintained a cautious reserve.

Moreover there developed an increasing disappointment that international relations still were mostly motivated by national reasons of state, and the presence in the league covenant of economic sanctions and potential military sanctions against aggressors created some nervousness. To this the Briand–Kellogg Pact (1928), renouncing war as an instrument of national policy, afforded an emotional outlet. Church opinion was increasingly confused by the rise of Adolf Hitler, the Spanish Civil War, and the nominal sanctions against Italy for its conquest of Ethiopia.

Church members generally approved—only a few with knowledge—the social and humanitarian activities of the league and its efforts to protect minorities and mandated populations from abuses. The churches did not put forth sufficiently strong or persistent effort, in the USA or elsewhere, to persuade governments to act in accord with the political program of the league, which provided means for peaceful adjustment.

*Bibliography.* A. Keller, *Die Kirchen und der Friede, mit besonderer Berücksichtigung ihrer Stellung zum Völkerbund* (1927).

MINER SEARLE BATES

**Lebanon.** Arab republic on the eastern coast of the Mediterranean with an area of 10,300 sq. km. (4015 sq. mi.).

A unique feature of Lebanon is its variety of religious communities. The state recognizes 15 such groups. The constitution identifies these religious communities as juridical bodies with specific prerogatives, notably in the field of law. Religious courts enact legislation concerning marriage, separation, divorce, and inheritance. Each citizen has an official identification card which also indicates state-registered religious affiliation. As of yet there is no civil marriage. Religious chanceries issue official certificates of baptism and death. In the Muslim community judicial officers are civil servants of the state. Before the civil war (pre-1975) all religious communities received subsidies for social work, courts, and schools. The constitution allows involvement of the various religious groups in education. Political parties in Lebanon are usually associated with religious communities. This fact lies behind much of the unrest in the country.

Statistics are of doubtful accuracy; the last official census was in 1932 and that figure still appears in recent publications. Although Muslims probably constitute the majority of the population, this is impossible to verify because of the horrendous number of casualties, displaced people, and emigration since the advent of the civil war in 1975. An unofficial estimate of the total population is 2.7 million (1986), which is divided into Shia Muslims (35 percent), Maronite Christians (25 percent), Sunni Muslims (25 percent), Greek Orthodox (7.5 percent), and Druze (7.5 percent).

Smaller Orthodox churches include the Russian Orthodox Church, the Russian Orthodox Church Outside of Russia, the Coptic and Syrian Orthodox Churches, and the Ancient Church of the Near East (Nestorians). Protestants include those of the National Evangelical Synod of Syria and Lebanon with the largest Protestant constituency being that of the American United Presbyterians (10,000). Church union discussions with the third largest Protestant body, the National Evangelical Church of Beirut, failed. The Anglican Community has also been approached. There are two Armenian Protestant churches, the Union of Armenian Evangelical Churches and the Armenian Evangelical Spiritual Brethren. This Union is the second strongest Protestant community in the country with an extensive primary and secondary school program. Other religious groups include the Lebanese Baptist Convention, Seventh-day Adventists, Church of God, the Pentecostal Church of God, the Assemblies of God, the Christian and Missionary Alliance, and other smaller bodies.

Community councils and school associations, hospitals, dispensaries, and clubs contributed to the nation's vitality and unity prior to the war. The Near East regional bureau of the World Muslim Congress is located in Beirut; a national Islamic Congress met in 1974 for the first time in Lebanon.

In late 1990 developments in the Lebanese civil conflict gave some hope for resolution. However, the political situation within the war-ravaged country was still unsettled.

*Bibliography.* J. Gulick, *The Middle East: An Anthropological Perspective* (1976); H. Barakat, *Lebanon in Strife: Student Preludes to the Civil War* (1977); D. C. Gordon, *The Republic of Lebanon: Nation in Jeopardy* (1983); G. J. Jennings, *Hadith: Composite Middle Eastern Village* (1983).

GEORGE J. JENNINGS

**Lectern.** A reading stand or desk used to support a large copy of the Bible, lying open during worship. It is used in sanctuaries which have a divided chancery and in High-Church, liturgical forms of worship. From the lectern the minister reads the lesson or sermon pericope, and he may direct other parts of the service from the lectern. Whether and how a lectern is used depends on a church's theology of worship. The focus of attention in worship may be centered around the Bible (the lectern), the preaching from the Word (pulpit), the continuing sacrifice of Christ (altar), or the sacraments (communion table). In High-Church traditions where Scripture is read at a lectern and preaching done from a separate pulpit the lectern is covered with a rich cloth and the Bible decked with one or two colored ribbons. Cloth and ribbons may be adorned with symbolic figures, and their colors will shift with the five seasons of the liturgical year.

**Lectionary.** A list of Bible readings for use in public worship through the year, usually at morning worship. In liturgical bodies, the lectionary is prescribed; in some other communions it is optional; and many groups do not use a lectionary at all. Denominational books of worship have such lists, which many pastors ignore. A good lectionary singles out passages suitable for worship ranging over the Bible. Such a program tends to follow the Christian year, emphasizes the NT but also uses the OT, and encourages the minister to preach from the Bible, with the paragraph as the unit. Lectionaries suffer from a lack of continuity, ignoring the way the Bible was written. In a church which is not liturgical a pastor may prepare a lectionary for the congregation in keeping with the plan for preaching. This leads the people in personal study through the Bible.

ANDREW W. BLACKWOOD

**Lee, Robert Greene** (1886– ). Baptist. Born in Fort Mill, S.C., he was educated at Furman University and Chicago Law School (Ph.D.). After four years as a student pastor in South Carolina, he became pastor of First Baptist Church, Edgefield, S.C. (1919–21); First Baptist Church, Chester, S.C. (1921/22); First Baptist Church, New Orleans, La. (1922–25); Citadel Square Baptist Church, Charles, S.C. (1925–27); and Bellevue Baptist Church, Memphis, Tenn. (1927). He was president of the Southern Baptist Convention for three terms. Among his books are *Glory Today for Conquest Tomorrow* (1941), *This Critical Hour, and Other Heart-Searching Sermons* (1942), *For the Time of Tears* (1949), *The Bible and Prayer* (1950), *Great Is the Lord* (1955), *Bought by the Blood* (1957), *A Charge to Keep, and Other Messages* (1959), *Christ Above All, and Other Messages* (1963), *From Death to Life Through Christ* (1966), and *If I Were a Jew* (1977).

**Lee, Umphrey** (1893–1958). Methodist scholar and educator. Born in Oakland City, Ind., he studied at Trinity University, Southern Methodist University, Columbia University (Ph.D., 1931), and in Germany and England. He was a pastor in Texas, notably at Highland Park Methodist Church (1923–36), taught homiletics in the Southern Methodist University School of Theology (1927–32), was dean of the School of Religion at Vanderbilt University (1936–39), and was president of the Southern Methodist University (1939–54). Among his books are *Jesus, the Pioneer* (1926), *Short Sketch of the Life of Christ* (1927), *The Bible and Business* (1930), *Historical Backgrounds of Early Methodist Enthusiasm* (1931), *The Historic Church and Modern Pacifism* (1943), *Render unto the People* (1947), and *Our Fathers and Us* (1958). He and W. W. Sweet also wrote *A Short History of Methodism* (1956).

**Legates and Nuncios.** Special representatives of the pope. A papal legate (Lat. *legatus*, "one provided with a contract")—technically legate *a lectere* (lit. "from the side," meaning the pope's side)—is always a cardinal who is sent as an alter ego of the Roman pontiff to deal in the pope's name with church affairs or to preside over some major church gathering or liturgical celebration. The nature and extent of the legate's powers are determined by the pope and are of a temporary character. A papal nuncio (Lat. *nuntius*, "a messenger") is a prelate, usually a titular archbishop, who, on a permanent basis, represents the pope before a national government and the Roman Catholic Church in a prescribed geographical area, usually a certain country. Nuncios are normally accorded ambassadorial status and have a twofold mission: (1) to maintain good relations between the Holy See and the civil government to which they are accredited: and (2) to observe and inspect church conditions in the region and to report all relevant matters of concern to the Vatican.

The history of papal legation has been long and varied. As early as the 5th century the bishops of Rome claimed the right of internal legation, that is, legation concerned with the jurisdictional relations of the See of Rome with local churches and other Christian ecclesiastical authorities. For example, special representatives from Rome were present at both the Council of Nicea (325) and Constantinople (381). From the 5th through the 8th centuries, the Roman bishop sent legates in what might be considered the exercises of external legation, that is, legation concerned with the church's international activities and its relations with civil governments. Leo I (440–461) sent the first of these legates to a civil power when he dispatched a personal representative to the imperial court in Constantinople in order to keep Rome informed about the activities of the court there and in eastern Christendom in general as well as to convey to the emperor his instructions concerning doctrinal and disciplinary matters.

Special papal diplomats, officially designated as "sent legates" (Lat. *legati missi*), appeared in the 9th century. Their prestige and importance were enhanced during the pontificate of Gregory VII (1073–85) when their legations, both internal and external, began to be entrusted only to cardinals who in turn were given greater power and the higher title of *legati a latere*. Also in the Middle Ages, the office of "native legate" (Lat. *legati nati*) was created—so-called because they were not "sent" from Rome but received their role, mainly a jurisdictional one in strictly ecclesiastical matters, as incumbents of some important ecclesiastical see, such as Canterbury, Rheims, Cologne, or Toledo. There, and in surrounding territories, these powerful residential archbishops represented the pope and acted in his name. Since the Reformation, this authority has largely been redelegated to papal nuncios with only the empty title still claimed by some of these archbishops.

The modern configurations of the offices of legate and nuncio took place during the Renaissance, the period of the birth of modern diplomacy itself. Beginning in 1436 with Bernard du Rosier's *Short Treatise about Ambassadors*, the first textbook of diplomatic practice in Western Europe, a distinction was made between legates and ambassadors. Formerly all diplomatic agents were called *legati*, but now the term was to be applied only to the cardinal legates of the Holy See while diplomats representing the new secular states would be called ambassadors. Minor papal diplomatic agents, once also called *legati*, would henceforth be designated as "nuncios" and "procurators," according to their functions. During the Middle Ages, the nuncio had been a fiscal officer, charged with the collection of the papal tithe and other monetary contributions to the papacy by the faithful. During the Renaissance, du Rosier and other diplomatic theorists attempted to redefine the medieval office of nuncio and the old Roman office of procurator. The nuncio was to be the "messenger" who spoke with the voice of his principal, empowered to deliver a message or to grace a ceremony, but not to negotiate. The procurator, on the other hand, had no symbolic representative function, but armed with specific legal powers to represent the interest of his principal or to arrange on more or less fixed terms a particular piece of business, could negotiate.

During the course of the 15th century, both terms became confused. The papacy, for reasons of its own, customarily began to restrict legate status to special missions while regarding papal nuncios as having rank and function corresponding to secular ambassadors. The office of procurator was gradually absorbed into that of papal legate in the ecclesiastical world and that of ambassador in the secular world—with most secular ambassadors down to the 17th century being styled as "ambassadors" and "procurators" until the more resounding term "plenipotentiary" finally drove "procurator" out of use.

Meanwhile, Pope Alexander VI (1492–1503) began to adopt the diplomatic institutions of his secular neighbors and established in 1495 a permanent nuncio at the court of the Holy Roman Empire. Also, during most of his reign, Alexander kept a diplomatic representative, Francisco de Prats, in Spain. In 1500, he sent a nuncio to the French court and another to Venice, and kept them at their posts for three years. Julius II (1503–13) followed the general practice established by Alexander and maintained more or less permanent nuncios in most of the city-states of Italy and in several key transalpine courts. However, it was Leo X (1513–21) and Clement VII (1521–34) who made these practices a permanent feature of papal diplomacy. By 1534, papal nuncios were present in nearly all of the capitals of Europe, serving as resident papal diplomatic representatives there, keeping a watchful eye on the political activities in the courts of the various European powers.

The Council of Trent (1545–63), among other things, dealt with complaints concerning the abuse of power by papal legates. It decreed that henceforth the powers of legates were restricted to duties specified by the pope and that bishops were no longer subject to legatine interference except in cases clearly authorized by the papacy. Later in the century, Pope Gregory XIII (1572–85) strengthened the system of papal diplomacy by giving it organic structure and a body of well-defined regulations. The distinctive role, attributions, and economic treatment of various kinds of papal diplomatic agents were clearly set forth. This institutionalization and regularization of papal diplomatic offices and practices ushered in the "golden age of Roman Catholic diplomacy" (1585–1648). Soon after the Treaty of Westphalia (1648) came a decline that lasted until World War I (1914–18). Since 1918, nunciatures and apostolic delegations have grown steadily in number and prestige, especially under the vigorous leadership of Popes John XXIII (1958–63), Paul VI (1963–78), and John Paul II (1978– ). Moreover, the modern papal diplomatic corps is widely known as one of the most well-informed and efficient in the world.

At the Congress of Vienna (1814/15), the powers gathered there agreed that henceforth secular governments would regard papal legates and nuncios as having the rank of ambassadors. This secular recognition of the pope's right to send diplomatic representatives rested partly on his historic position as a temporal sovereign. Since 1870, however, it has been based not so much on his still-asserted claims to that status as on his social and religious importance as spiritual leader of millions of Roman Catholic Christians scattered across the face of the earth. But this recognition extends only to matters spelled out in a nuncio's accreditation to a specific government. In some cases, concordats specify the extent of the legates' and/or nuncios' rights of internal and external legation in a country. In most instances, however, modern non-Catholic governments accept papal legates and nuncios on the same basis as they do ambassadors from any secular state.

*Bibliography.* G. Paro, *The Right of Papal Legation* (1947); W. Gurian and M. A. Fitzsimons, eds., *The Catholic Church in World Affairs* (1954); G. Mattingly, *Renaissance Diplomacy* (1955); R. A. Graham, *Vatican Diplomacy* (1959); H. E. Cardinale, *The Holy See and the International Order* (1976); M. Oliveri, *The Representatives: The Real Nature and Function of Papal Legates* (1980); P. Blet, *Histoire de la representation diplomatique du Saint Siège* (1982).

ROBERT D. LINDER

## Leger, Paul Emile

**Leger, Paul Emile** (1904– ). Canadian Roman Catholic cardinal. Born in Valleyfield, Quebec, he was educated in Canada and France and ordained as a priest (Sulpician Order) in 1929. He founded the Sulpician Seminary in Fukuoka, Japan, and taught philosophy there (1933–39). During World War II he held ecclesiastical posts in Quebec and was rector of the Pontifical Canadian College in Rome (1947–50). Named archbishop of Montreal in 1950, he was appointed a cardinal in 1953. Regarded as a liberal and a progressive, he played a key role in Vatican II (1962–65). He resigned in 1967 as archbishop to undertake missionary work among African lepers and handicapped children in Cameroon. Although he retired in 1979, he has been a tireless advocate and supporter of third world interests.

LESLIE K. TARR

**Lehmann, Johannes Edvard** (1862–1930). Church historian. Born in Copenhagen, he studied in Denmark, Germany, Holland, England, France, and Italy, receiving his Ph.D. from Copenhagen in 1896. He lectured in Copenhagen (1900–1910), and was professor in Berlin (1910–13) and Lund, Sweden (1913–27). His main works were *Zarathustra* (1899–1902), *Mysticism* (1904), *Buddha* (1907), *The Science of Religion* (1914), *The Place and the Way* (1917), and *Grundtvig* (1929). He was coeditor of *Lehrbuch der Religionsgeschichte* (1897) and *Textbuch zur Religionsgeschichte* (1912).

PETER AMMUNDSEN

**Lehmann, Paul Louis** (1906– ). Presbyterian theologian. Born in Baltimore, he was educated at Ohio State University, Union Theological Seminary, N.Y., and at the universities of Zurich and Bonn (1932/33). He was professor of religion and philosophy at Elmhurst College (1933–40), professor of biblical and systematic theology, Eden Theological Seminary (1940/41), professor of biblical history and literature, Wellesley College (1941–46), associate religious editor, Westminster Press, Philadelphia (1946/47), professor of applied Christianity, Princeton Theological Seminary (1947–56), professor at Harvard University (1956–63), and professor of systematic theology, Union Theological Seminary, N.Y. (1963–74). He served as president of the American Theological Society (1969/70). His works include *Forgiveness: Decisive Issue in Protestant Thought* (1940), *Ethics in a Christian Context* (1963), *The Transfiguration of Politics* (1975), "The Anti-Pelagian Writings" in *Companion to the Study of St. Augustine* (1955), and "The Christology of Reinhold Niebuhr" in *Reinhold Niebuhr* (1956).

WILLIAM H. BERGER

**Leiper, Henry Smith** (1891–1975). American missionary, ecumenist, and administrator. Born in Belmar, N.J., he graduated from Amherst College, Union Seminary, and Columbia University, and was a missionary in China under the American Board (Congregational-Christian) from 1918 to 1922. During that period he served in Siberia with the Army YMCA. After holding executive positions in national boards of the Congregational-Christian Churches, he became executive secretary of the American Section of the Universal Christian Council for Life and Work (1930–38), associate general secretary of the World Council of Churches, and general secretary of its Conference of USA member churches (1938–52). He was then executive secretary of the Congregational Missions Council (1952–59), and director of the department of religion, Chautauqua Institution (1959–75).

**Leisure.** Relief from the occupations necessary for physical existence to gain time and energy for the higher interests of life. The concept has positive and negative meanings. The individual at leisure negatively refrains from compulsory occupation and positively uses the opportunity such freedom gives for concerns other than the earning of daily bread.

The possession and use of leisure are important factors in creating culture, and the value set on leisure is an important index to the nature of a culture. Certain elements of culture (for example, the arts) require leisure for proper development; and the more any civilization becomes commercialized, the more important it is to provide spare time to enjoy the "higher interests of life," which seldom have immediate utilitarian value. The games and amusements of a person or nation are important, since what is done in spare time is an indication of character and helps in forming it.

The Jewish Sabbath, and such parallels to it as are known to history, are of the utmost importance in the history of culture. In turning aside to worship, we recognize claims more fundamental and far-reaching than the struggle for existence. In the case of the Jews and Christians this recognition has transformed the human struggle into a daily walk with God. Play is not an exclusively human activity, but worship is; and the provision of opportunities for worship is probably the only way to counteract the stultifying spiritual effects of materialism.

Modern education often concentrates on preparation for life work to the neglect of preparation for the wise use of leisure. Classical education, with its comparative indifference to immediate utilitarian demands, may have been a better preparation for life. Conditions of modern life make "education for leisure" more imperative than in any previous age, not only because modern techniques have reduced back-breaking toil, but also because economic realities often create spells of enforced unemployment. If the person who has no interest in work tends in leisure to fall back on vicarious amusements, the one who has no interest in anything but work tends to go to pieces when this means of fulfillment is denied. Those whose work has some quality of artistic satisfaction are most likely to be able to integrate their work and their recreation into a satisfying unity.

Leisure is customarily contrasted both with haste and with compulsory work, the inference being that what we do on our own initiative we do with deliberation and with a sense of responsibility different from that felt in employments that involve time-pressure. Although neither moral goodness nor worship are spare-time activities, neither can attain its potential expression without leisure; and the pressure of work upon an age preoccupied with money values adds point to the poet's prayer, "Leave us leisure to be good" (Gray).

W. R. FORRESTER

**Lenski, Richard Charles Henry** (1864–1936). Born in Greifenberg, Prussia, he studied at Capital University, Columbus, Ohio and the Lutheran Seminary in Columbus. After ordination (1887) he served pastorates at Baltimore, Md., Trenton, Springfield, and Anna, Ohio. He taught chiefly in the fields of exegesis, dogmatics, and homiletics at the Lutheran Seminary (1911–36; dean, 1919–35). For 20 years he was editor of the *Lutherische Kirchenzeitung.* His greatest literary effort was a commentary on the Greek NT (11 vols., 1931–38). In addition he wrote *Biblische Frauenbilder* (1895), *His Footsteps* (1898), *Eisenach Gospel Selections* (1910), *Eisenach Epistle Selections* (1914), *St. Paul* (1916), *New Gospel Selections* (1919), *The Active Church Member* (1922), *The Eisenach OT Selections* (1925), *Kings and Priests* (1927), *The Sermon, Its Homiletical Construction* (1927), *St. John* (1929), *The Ancient Epistle Selections* (1935), and *The Gospel Selections of the Ancient Church* (1936).

PAUL BUEHRING

**Lent.** Season of preparation for Easter. Possibly a Christian adaptation of pagan springtime awakenings and a recognition of Jesus' 40 days in the wilderness, a Lenten-type period has been observed since at least the Council of Nicea (325). Lent begins on Ash Wednesday and includes the 40 days before Easter, excluding Sundays. While the more rigorous aspects of fasting and self-denial have declined in the 20th century, Protestant and Roman Catholic sermons and readings tend to relate to self-examination, discipline, penitence, and renewal. The mood is introspective, centering on the gifts and means of grace, the events of Christ's life, and his teachings. Ash Wednesday inaugurates the season with a prayerful mood among Protestants and one of suppliant penitence among Catholics. The World Day of Prayer was established for the first Friday in Lent by the National Council of Church Women. Protestantism omits the Ember days, which are observed on the Wednesday following Ash Wednesday and the Friday and Saturday thereafter, as days of welcome to the spring.

The first three Sundays of Lent carry forward the mood of penitence, looking toward the passion and resurrection. The fourth Sunday breaks in as a day of gratitude and rejoicing for forgiveness. This once was the traditional Mothers' Day, or Mothering Sunday, observed as a home-coming time. Passiontide includes the last two weeks in Lent, the fifth Sunday being Passion Sunday. The theme is the redemptive suffering of Christ and the final events of his life on earth. Passiontide is divided into Passion Week and Holy Week.

Holy Week and Lent proper close on Saturday at noon, when Christ lay in the grave. Easter does not belong in Lent but begins Eastertide, the season of resurrection which continues until Pentecost.

*See also* EASTER; HOLY WEEK.

GEORGE M. GIBSON

**Leonard, Graham Douglas** (1921– ). Bishop of London and consistent defender of the orthodox doctrine and traditions of the Church of England. Educated at Balliol College, Oxford, and Westcott House, Cambridge, he was ordained in 1947 after service as an officer in World War II.

In 1964 he was consecrated as bishop of Willesden (1964–73), since when he has been diocesan at and has been successively bishop of Truro (1973–81) and London (1981– ). In 1977 he became a member of the House of Lords. Although a High Churchman, he has always worked with evangelicals to oppose error and commend the gospel. He is acknowledged as the leader of those who oppose the ordination of women to the priesthood. His books include *The Gospel Is for Everyone* (1971), *God Alive: Priorities in Pastoral Theology* (1981), *Firmly I Believe and Truly . . .* (1985), and *Life in Christ* (1986).

PETER TOON

**Leube, Hans** (1896–1947). Church historian. Born in Leipzig, he studied at Leipzig (Ph.D., 1921), lecturing there (1923), and he was professor at Breslau (1931–45). Ejected from there he became professor at Rostock (1946). Leube was stimulated by his teacher Heinrich Boehmer. His early works deal mainly with German church history of the 17th century, and he later wrote on French and English church history. His works included *Reformideen der deutschen lutherischen Kirche* (1924), *Calvinismus und Luthertum 1* (1928), *Reformation und Humanismus in England* (1928), *Der Jesuitenorden . . . in Frankreich* (1935), *Deutschlandbild und Lutherauffassung in Frankreich* (1941), and *Kirche und Glaube in England* (1942).

**Bibliography.** TLZ (1948).

ROBERT STUPPERICH

**Levonian, Loutfy** (1881–1961). OT and Islamics scholar. Born in Turkey, he was the dean and a pillar of the Near East School of Religion, Athens, Greece, and the Near East School of Theology, Beirut. He graduated from the Central Turkey College in Aintab. Following two years of public school teaching he took graduate study at Woodbrooke College in Selly Oak, England (1910–12). Returning to Turkey, he was miraculously delivered from imprisonment and murder. In 1919 he attended Woodbrooke College again and thereafter served as dean and professor of OT and Islamics at the School of Religion Athens

(1922–32) and the Near East School of Theology, Beirut (1932–50). At retirement, Union Theological Seminary, N.Y., called him as visiting professor (1950/51); the Pacific School of Religion in Berkeley, Calif., was his last assignment (1951/52).

Loutfy Levonian was a true teacher and scholar, a member of the Royal Asiatic Society and fellow of Selly Oak colleges. OT and Islamics were his specialities. He was a lucid author, having published *Moslem Mentality* (1928), *Islam and Christianity* (1940), *Turkish Press* (2 vols., 1932, 1936), and 30 *Woodbrooke Tracts* on religious-philosophical subjects, translated into nine languages.

Levonian was an ecumenist; he was a speaker at the International Missionary Council meetings in Madras (1937) and Toronto (1947), and a man of peace and reconciliation.

The Armenian Evangelical churches owe him a boundless debt of gratitude. If they were revived, strengthened, and flourished after the horrendous persecutions and decimation by the 1915 genocide, they owe it first to the mercy of God and then to the spiritual vision, ecclesiastical loyalty, and intellectual integrity infused by Loutfy Levonian to his students who are presently serving Evangelical Armenian churches in many countries.

HAGOP APRAHAM CHAKMAKJIAN

## Lewis, Clive Staples (1898–1963).

British literary scholar and critic, lay theologian and apologist, and Christian mythopoetic novelist. Born in Belfast, he was educated first at home by his mother who died when he was nine, then in various preparatory schools in England and Belfast. Lewis's most important intellectual influence in his pre-Oxford years was the atheist W. T. Kirkpatrick, who tutored him as a private boarder at his home in Great Bookham, Surrey, (1914–17). In 1917 he went to University College, Oxford, with a classics scholarship, but a few months later accepted a commission as second lieutenant to serve in the Somerset Light Infantry. In April 1918, he was wounded in the Battle of Arras near Lillers, France. He returned to Oxford in 1919, the same year his first book, *Spirits in Bondage: A Cycle of Lyrics*, was published, receiving little notice. He received a First Class degree in Classical Moderations in 1920, a First in "Greats" in 1922, then read in the English School, taking a First there in 1923. After one year as a tutor in philosophy at University College, he was elected fellow and tutor in English literature at Magdalen College, Oxford, a position he held from 1925 to 1954 when he was named professor of medieval and renaissance literature at Magdalene College, Cambridge. He was a popular tutor and lecturer, and many of his learned works reflect his urbane wit and magisterial depth of scholarship in medieval and Renaissance literature. Several have become standards in the field, most notably *The Allegory of Love* (1936), a study of the medieval courtly love tradition from Ovid to Spenser, which won the Hawthornden prize; *A Preface to Paradise Lost* (1942), an excellent introduction to Milton's epic; and his contribution to the Oxford History of English Literature series, *English Literature in the Sixteenth Century, excluding Drama* (1954).

Lewis was most widely known, however, for his Christian writings. An atheist from his schoolboy days whose reading was deeply influenced by a taste for myth and medieval romance, Lewis passed from "paganism" into theism in 1929 and into orthodox Christianity shortly thereafter, an intellectual journey he recounted in an allegorical fiction, *The Pilgrim's Regress* (1933), and his spiritual autobiography, *Surprised by Joy* (1955). He had been led, he wrote, by a longing for joy, or *Sehnsucht*, a mystical yearning with the conviction that this material world is a shadow of a deeper reality. A member of the Church of England, he wrote with a unique blend of romanticism and erudite rationalism, and his Christian writings were noted for their wit and clarity. His first popular work was the satirical *Screwtape Letters* (1945), correspondence of a senior devil to a junior devil on how to bring a new Christian convert back into the fold of "our Father Below." It was a best-seller. Other major works included two pieces of apologetic writing, *The Problem of Pain* (1940) and *Miracles* (1947). Other nonfiction Christian writing included *Mere Christianity* (1952), which originated as a series of highly popular radio talks over BBC during World War II, *Reflections on the Psalms* (1958), *The Four Loves* (1960), *Letters to Malcolm: Chiefly on Prayer* (1964), and various collections of essays and occasional pieces. He wrote four adult novels of mythopoetic adult fiction: *Out of the Silent Planet* (1938), *Perelandra* (1943), and *That Hideous Strength* (1945), a space fantasy trilogy, and *Till We Have Faces* (1956), a reworking of the Cupid–Psyche myth, and which Lewis personally regarded as his best work. He also wrote seven volumes of fairy tales for children, the *Chronicles of Narnia* (1950–1956), in which Aslan, a lion, is the Christ symbol. They came to be regarded as classics of children's literature; the concluding volume, *The Last Battle* (1956), was awarded the Carnegie Medal.

JOAN OSTLING

## Lewis, Edwin (1881–1959).

Methodist. Born in Newbury, England, he went to Newfoundland in 1900 to do mission work, and transferred to American Methodism in 1904. He studied at Mt. Allison University, New Brunswick; Middlebury (Vt.) College; United Free Church College, Glasgow; New York State Teachers' College; and Drew

Theological Seminary (Th.D., 1918). He was instructor in English at New York State College (1915/16) and taught theology at Drew (1916–51). He was visiting professor of theology at Temple University from 1951. During 1936 and 1937 he was special lecturer in the seminaries at Tokyo, Seoul, Peking, Nanking, and Jubbulpore, India. His publications include *Jesus Christ and the Human Quest* (1924), *A Manual of Christian Beliefs* (1927), *God and Ourselves* (1931), *Great Christian Teachings* (1933), *A Christian Manifesto* (1934), *The Faith We Declare* (1939), *A Philosophy of the Christian Revelation* (1940), *A New Heaven and a New Earth* (1941), *Christian Truth for Christian Living* (1942), *The Practice of the Christian Life* (1942), *The Ministry of the Holy Spirit* (1944), *The Creator and the Adversary* (1948), *Theology and Evangelism* (1951), and *The Biblical Faith and Christian Freedom* (1953). He was joint editor of *The Abingdon Bible Commentary* (1929) and contributed to *Harper's Bible Dictionary* (1952).

## Liberalism. *Introduction.*

The terms "liberal" and "liberalism" are difficult to define because they have been employed both to describe and also to evaluate in a long, heated discussion. In religious circles, liberalism commonly signifies a more or less coherent body of historicocritical views concerning the Scriptures and a body of philosophicotheological doctrines concerning the content of the Christian faith. Liberals sometimes insist, however, that theirs is not a body of doctrine but a spirit and method. The spirit claimed is that of open-minded investigation of facts, without prior assumptions or commitments. The method is defined as the inductive method of empirical science, in contrast with the alleged dogmatic, deductive method of conservative theology.

Theological liberalism is a comparatively late result of a wider liberal trend to identify with the classical liberalism of Greece and Rome. It first emerged as the Italian Renaissance in the latter half of the 15th century, and ever since has been seeking, with varying success, to express itself in all aspects of culture. The common feature is the modern form of materialistic or naturalistic humanism. Its theological or ecclesiastical tendency is atheistic; liberalism perceives itself as enlightenment in opposition to ignorance, and its political expression in opposition to human tyranny becomes either constitutional democracy or revolutionary Marxism.

*The Influence of Naturalism.* Theological liberalism cannot be completely naturalistic or fully humanistic, but what distinguishes it from a conservative theology is the large measure of control exercised by naturalistic humanism over its spirit, method, and conclusions. Thus the doctrine of God is a vital consideration to liberal theology because of its conception of humankind's inher-

ent rights and need. The key affirmation is the infinite value and dignity, the consequent rights and capacity, of the individual human. Since human value is the foremost assumption, other parts of the system have been deduced from it or introduced in the light of it. Therefore, faith is necessarily naturalistic. Conservatism can maintain that human beings, though weak, fallible, and sinful, are nevertheless very noble creatures because of their high destiny in the purpose of God. Liberalism logically has no God until it has established and elaborated humankind as the "first article" of its "creed."

Negatively, any apparent facts or any doctrines which seem to reduce humankind's value and dignity must be ignored, explained away, or minimized. Our finiteness is countered by emphasizing our power to transcend our limitations and by insisting on a doctrine of divine immanence which makes us akin to the infinite. Sin may not be wholly ignored, since liberalism is a theology of "salvation," but dwelling on it is deprecated as morbid; the Augustinian view of sin must be execrated or emasculated. Evolution's "sin" is merely residual and temporary; absolute idealism insists that the experience of sin vanishes when all things are seen in their proper relationship to the perfect whole, or that the apparent evil is really good as a condition essential to "soul making."

Positively, liberalism has emphasized humankind's high intellectual and moral capacity and achievements. The specific manner of doing so is the characteristic popularly known as "modernism." Modernism is identified with this kind of liberalism, but strictly a modernist is one who uses as the criterion of truth and error what is regarded as the best insights of the culture. Thus the doctrines of the modernism of one era can be (and are) radically different from those of a different era. A 19th-century modernist was bound to point to the achievements of the natural sciences as evidence of humankind's great intellectual capacity. Both the limitless optimism of 19th-century science and the apologetic enthusiasm of the liberal appeal to it were certain to impart to the liberal attitude toward scientific achievement a spirit which can only be regarded as immoderate. Likewise modernism caused its adherents to find their evidence for humankind's high moral capacity in current efforts toward social amelioration. In considering it they too often mistook the will for the deed.

But the science which at that time seemed best to illustrate and demonstrate humankind's great intellectual value was "classical physics"; and this science was confidently claimed to require a mechanistic cosmology. Such a worldview excluded the distinctively human from its picture of reality and thus was directly antagonistic to the humanism of liberalism.

***New Directions.*** How to deal with this difficulty divided American liberalism into two antagonistic camps. On the one hand, a group of thinkers at the University of Chicago dubbed themselves "social theologians." They turned to the social sciences, claiming that these relatively immature disciplines afforded a more authentic picture of reality than did the natural sciences. This device was in harmony with the general liberal claim to be scientific and with the general liberal interest in social reform, and its results were not without value. But it was not a very plausible solution. It was even less plausible when its control by an instrumentalist philosophy was too obvious to be ignored. It was rejected by the majority of the liberal thinkers.

Most American liberals now acknowledged, in spite of their previous claims to be strictly scientific, that their purpose from the first had been evaluation instead of description, so their method was philosophical. Calling themselves "new theists," they turned explicitly to the philosophical system of idealism of the British and American Neo-Hegelians. This system was directly opposed to the mechanism which seemed to be implied in the classical physics. If not a philosophical restatement of Christian truth, it was widely regarded as at least an overt apologetic for the Christian view. It was the most powerful philosophical system at the time and seemed to demonstrate the full liberal claim regarding humankind's great intellectual capacity. What its theological disciples failed at first to observe was that the absolutism of this system granted doubtful status within reality to those finite spirits whose infinite value liberalism guarded. Also, its strong tendency was toward pantheism.

In support of the moral grandeur which liberalism claimed for humankind, it: (1) advocated a romantically light view of sinfulness; (2) represented humankind as the highest evolutionary achievement of an immanent divine principle; (3) enthusiastically pictured humankind as on the verge of realizing, by their own efforts, an idealistic social program which was identified with the kingdom of God; and (4) insisted that humankind had only recently evolved by natural processes from a purely animal stage. That so short a time could have brought about such a glorious achievement seemed to raise humankind's moral greatness, potentially if not yet in actuality, to infinity. All of this was in harmony with the unbridled optimism which then pervaded Western culture.

***In the Reformation.*** The literary humanism of the Renaissance made some contributions to the Reformation so that there was a certain penetration of Christian thought by the humanism of that time. But the claim sometimes made that the Reformation was essentially an abortive, premature expression of liberalism cannot be allowed.

The humanism of the Reformation period either became pagan or secular or remained outside, or was excluded from, the Reformation movement because the two were based on fundamentally different principles. The Reformation did involve a high doctrine of the value of humankind, but it was God-centered, while humanism was man-centered. Luther's cautious, independent attitude toward the humanists, his break with Erasmus, and even his refusal to compromise his differences with Zwingli were not errors in principle, even if their tactical wisdom is debatable. Calvin described his transfer from the camp of the humanists as "a sudden conversion."

***From Schleiermacher.*** It was not until the 19th century that humanism truly penetrated Christian thought. Then it began without any clear awareness of its radical character. The successes of humanism in science and philosophy, in literature and art, and in culture generally had caused humanism to become the prevailing atmosphere, especially in the German universities. The professors in the theological faculties of these universities absorbed this atmosphere during their undergraduate days, lived in it throughout their lives, and carried it over as a matter of course into their theological work. They began to apply, in their historicocritical study of the Scriptures, the methods and principles of secular history and an attitude which was in fact that of naturalistic humanism. At first the naturalism was more in evidence than the humanism; but even then naturalism was not at first, as Albert Schweitzer has shown, a consistent, self-conscious principle. Friedrich Schleiermacher in his apologetic sought to meet the non-Christian world on its own ground, which was naturalistic humanism. Although he remained throughout, as he himself said, "a pietist of a higher type," and to some extent transcended naturalism, he never fully outgrew it. The descent from Schleiermacher, best observed in the field of Christology, makes naturalism increasingly manifest. Schweitzer's comment regarding Schleiermacher was that "no one has shown the same skill in concealing how much in the way of miracle he ultimately retains and how much he rejects." Schleiermacher did posit one genuine miracle as necessary to account for the entrance of Jesus into history. That event is for him, however, less than a true incarnation of God, and he hastens to add that everything else in the life and work of Jesus was within the limits of natural law. If Schweitzer is correct in his statements about Schleiermacher's subtlety, Albrecht Ritschl is certainly subtle enough. It seems impossible to decide with any assurance just what Ritschl did think of Christ. Indeed, his pragmatic epistemology of value judgments appears to make the question of Christ totally irrelevant for theology. When one turns to Harnack and to Schweitzer and their successors, the situation becomes perfectly plain. By the time Harnack's devices of higher and textual criticism have done their work, the "gospel in the gospel" has become a simple, unitarian formula. Jesus has been relegated to the dimension of a human genius and martyr, the sphere of his genius being religion and morality. Harnack was the true father of the movement which, particularly in America, reduced the doctrine of the kingdom of God to the movement known as the "social gospel." Miracles are explained by Harnack as the misconceived and the unexplained. In the writings of Schweitzer, Jesus appears as a man who deserves the loyalty of all who possess a proper "reverence for life." But Schweitzer's "Jesus" entertained a completely mistaken eschatological expectation of the kingdom of God. His delusions of grandeur with respect to his own status in that kingdom raise, in the minds of others if not in that of Schweitzer himself, a serious question as to his sanity. This attitude of respect for Jesus merely as a human teacher and leader, widely held among liberals since Harnack's day, has sometimes been characterized as Jesusism. There followed a rash of books purporting to identify the specific mental disease from which Jesus suffered. The final stage, logically at least, was to say, with Arthur Drews and others, that we have no reason to believe that Jesus ever existed at all. The conservative scholar agrees that no such person as the "liberal" Jesus ever did exist; but he will add that the existence of the real Jesus is historically unquestionable.

***Irreconcilable Worldviews.*** Surveying the long history of liberal christological speculation, from the rationalists to Drews, the pattern and its explanation become obvious. The rationalists began it by employing, without careful scrutiny or even systematic fidelity, a criterion of truth borrowed from secular culture. In this they were preceded by the OT higher critics, and followed by the liberal theologians. They were so aware of the inadequacies of 18th-century conservative apologetics and so enthusiastic about appealing to 19th-century rationalism that they did not pause to discover that their naturalistic criterion of truth could only be an alien intruder into the Christian system. Nor did they anticipate the only possible outcome of their procedure.

Christianity can borrow from secular culture only by first baptizing what it borrows into its own spirit and filling it with an essentially Christian meaning. When, as in the case of liberalism, it fails to do that, the alien element will spread, reducing Christianity to its own dimensions. And so the alien epistemology borrowed by liberalism progressively excluded the authentic Christian point of view. An insane Jesus and the Jesus who never existed at all are characteristic of all that remained.

ANDREW K. RULE

***Contributions of Liberalism.*** From a positive standpoint liberalism made some valuable contributions to theology. God was understood in terms of the divine nearness rather than remoteness, more as Father than as King. He both reached out and was reachable in the life and ministry of Jesus as well as in our own history. He was seen at work in natural and social processes, and his self-revelation was ongoing. Liberalism's antidogmatic and anticreedal temper encouraged a continuing reformulation of Christian theology in response to God's revelation. It placed high esteem on the mutual importance of human experience and biblical witness. By stressing the human element in the formation and transmission of Scripture it distinguished between the spiritual truths that comprise its permanent revelatory significance and the historically conditioned worldview which is limited, transitory, and not normative for our times. Its centering in the life of Jesus rather than his primordial existence enabled appreciation of his human character and single-minded commitment to the will of God. Liberalism portrayed the Christian life as discipleship, that is, the living out of the affirmation that "Jesus is Lord." Obedience to his moral teaching was the basic element in following him; this implied the transformation of both the individual's character and social structures into a clearer image of the kingdom of God. An essential interrelationship was found between the internal and external realms. This resulted in a Christian social agenda that has included environmental protection, economic justice, human rights advocacy, and opposition to war. The emphasis on the oneness of all Christians through faith in a common redeemer and the essential unity of humankind through the fatherhood of God fostered a commitment to ecumenism and interreligious dialog. The result was an optimism rooted in the awareness of a God actively at work in all aspects of creation and the world-redeeming power of his love as revealed in Jesus.

***The Reconsideration.*** After 1870 liberalism seemed to be triumphing, especially in America. The cluster of views that constituted the "new theology" or "modernism," had become widely accepted in the Protestant pulpits and theological schools and publications. In reality, however, it was opposed at every step. Modernism in Roman Catholic circles, both in Europe and America, was essentially checked by Pius X in 1907 in the decree, *Lamentabili sane exitu.* In the Protestant-dominated countries pietist and confessionalist groups offered strong resistance. Most important was the "fundamentalist" movement, named after a 12-volume series of articles authored by distinguished scholars in Britain and North America, which affirmed the central doctrines of Protestant Christianity. Liberalism was aggressively challenged, but the acrimonious controversies in the first quarter of the 20th century led some to doubt whether an irenic, scholarly, broad-minded Protestantism that was in harmony with historic Christian thought could exist any longer.

Other developments also forced a radical reconsideration of liberalism. The catastrophe that engulfed Europe in World War I and the worldwide social upheaval which followed made the dark side of human nature painfully obvious and rendered romantic optimism increasingly implausible. The rise of neo-orthodoxy, with its stress on the absolute transcendence of God, the sinfulness of humankind, the bridging of the chasm between the sovereign God and fallen creation and humanity through Christ, and Jesus as the Word made flesh (rather than the historical Jesus) undercut the premises of liberalism. Advances in scholarship, particularly biblical archeology, textual analysis, and ancient philosophy, destroyed basic assumptions of liberal criticism and strengthened confidence in the accuracy and integrity of Scripture. A vastly different alternative to the liberal understanding of the worldview and teaching of Jesus was available. On the other hand, the history of religions school portrayed Christianity merely as a syncretistic Near East religion, rejecting its significance and denying its claim to finality. The growth of secular humanism as a religious movement confronted liberals with the fact that they had yielded to the same naturalistic philosophy so they had no defense against it. Some humanists repudiated the existence of God, immortality, and the supernatural in general and substituted faith in man and human powers. Others identified with an empirical philosophy of religion grounded on scientific methodology and experience. What, therefore, distinguished the latter? The precipitous decline in church attendance and evangelistic zeal in Europe and North America and the flagging missionary vision revealed the spiritual poverty of liberalism after World War I. By the 1940s a "new evangelicalism" offered the spiritual vision lacking in liberalism. Evangelical scholars challenged the inadequate assumptions of liberalism and wrestled with the necessity for a social vision. Evangelists and missionaries carried the gospel around the world. As a result, Christianity became increasingly a global faith.

In response, some "evangelical liberals" or "neoliberals" in the USA backed away somewhat from modernism and its emphasis upon the "spirit of the age." They began to preach a God who was both immanent and transcendent. Jesus, the Bible, and Christianity were proclaimed to be unique, and the call was made that Jesus should be accepted as Lord of one's life. They were not prepared to accept the premise of alienation and discontinuity between the divine and the human, but they downplayed human progress as the means of God's revelation. While retaining a cordial outlook toward culture and secularity, most liberals stressed the importance of moral attacks upon sin in the world. By the 1960s most of them had abandoned humanistic optimism and the dream of an earthly kingdom, but they retained their views on biblical interpretation and preached the need for social change. The "radical" or "secular" theologians still spoke of the "death" of God in this secular age and were optimistic about the creative possibilities open to humankind. But even as they held up love as the sufficient norm of ethical behavior they reaffirmed some form of lordship of Christ and his call to discipleship. Nevertheless, by the 1980s it had become questionable whether Western liberalism could any longer hold its own in competition with neo-orthodoxy, revitalized evangelicalism, and the influx of new theologies from the third world.

*See also* THEOLOGY, 20TH-CENTURY TRENDS IN.

**Bibliography.** A. Harnack, *What Is Christianity?* (1901); W. Rauschenbusch, *Theology for the Social Gospel* (1917); J. G Machen, *Christianity and Liberalism* (1923); S. Mathews, *The Faith of Modernism* (1924); D. S. Robinson, *The God of the Liberal Christian* (1926); A. Schweitzer, *The Quest of the Historical Jesus* (1926); R. Niebuhr, *The Nature and Destiny of Man*, 2 vols. (1942/43); C. VanTil, *The New Modernism* (1946); P. Tillich, *The Protestant Era* (1948); W. Pauck, *The Heritage of the Reformation* (1950); J. Dillenberger and C. Welch, *Protestant Christianity Interpreted Through Its Development* (1958); L. H. DeWolf, *The Case for Theology in Liberal Perspective* (1959); K. Cauthen, *The Impact of American Religious Liberalism* (1962); J. Dorn, *Washington Gladden: Prophet of the Social Gospel* (1966); L. J. Averill, *American Theology in the Liberal Tradition* (1967); W. R. Hutchison, *American Protestant Thought: The Liberal Era* (1968); L. Gilkey, *Naming the Whirlwind: The Renewal of God-Language* (1969); M. E. Marty and D. G. Peerman, *New Theology No. 6* (1969); M. Ranchetti, *The Catholic Modernists* (1969); W. R. Hutchison, *The Modernist Impulse in American Protestantism* (1976); R. J. Coleman, *Issues of Theological Conflict: Evangelicals and Liberals* (1980); D. E. Miller, *The Case for Liberal Christianity* (1981); R. M. Moats, *Harry Emerson Fosdick: Preacher, Pastor, Prophet* (1985).

RICHARD V. PIERARD

## Liberation Theology.

**Liberation Theology.** Theological movement that emerged in the mid-1960s in response to the poverty and lack of genuine democratic processes in Latin America. Its primary concern has been to reflect upon the meaning for Christian commitment of political and economic systems that have caused a glaringly unequal distribution of wealth among people.

***Historical Development.*** At the end of Vatican Council II (1965), Helder Cámara, Roman Catholic bishop of Orlando and Recife, Brazil, joined other third world bishops in writing a passionate pastoral letter concerning the plight of the poor. They called on the church to involve itself in exposing the extreme poverty of the third world and seeking solutions to the root causes of that poverty. In 1967 Paul VI lent his support in the encyclical, *Populorum progressio*, which, among other things, described the underlying principles of capitalism as immoral.

The Roman Church had long been identified with the systems of the governments under which they ministered in the Americas, although the church-government relationship had often been far from friendly. But in 1968 the church endorsed a major policy shift. The second general conference of the Latin American episcopate, meeting in Medellín, Colombia (CELAM II), took a radical stance on social justice issues against the political and economic oppression they saw manifest throughout the continent. With official church sanction the Latin American bishops defined the situation of their countries, and the 85 percent of the population living in squalid poverty, as an abject dependence upon the decisions of outsiders who controlled technological knowledge and the means of production. The mood was anti-authoritarian, pro-Marxist, and revolutionary. The leaders spoke of the need of their countries to "liberate" themselves from subjugation to the policies of others.

While arising from Central American Roman Catholicism, liberation theology drew from German theology, particularly Jürgen Moltmann and Johann Baptist Metz. Metz challenged theologians to relate their faith to society in a "political theology" which applies or contextualizes the eschatological proclamation of the kingdom of God to the conditions of modern society. In *A Theology of Hope* Moltmann wrote that Christian eschatology must give a living hope in the future. The purpose of the church, Moltmann said, is to participate in the liberating sending of Jesus, becoming creative disciples who anticipate God's coming kingdom by criticizing and changing society.

The movement born at the Medellín conference lacked identity or precepts until 1973 when a Peruvian priest, Gustavo Gutiérrez, published *A Theology of Liberation*. Soon proponents from across the theological spectrum were expanding on his concepts, including Rubem Alves, Hugo Assman, Leonardo Boff, Cámara, Emilio Castro, Samuel Escobar, Paulo Feire, José Porfirio Miranda, Rene Padilla, and Juan Luís Segundo. Gutiérrez and José Míguez-Bonino have remained the most influential liberation theologians.

***Principles and Theology.*** One principle of this method is that theology can only contribute to the task of solving humanity's outstanding conflicts when it allows relevant sociological and economic sciences to guide its thinking. Of these social sciences the most relevant in dealing with poverty is the Marxist analysis of the patterns of capitalist ownership and production. Denying that they were Marxist, the theologians supported the class struggle of Marxist revolutionaries toward some kind of socialist system as the only viable solution to the gap between rich and poor and to political systems controlled by foreign

interests. This identification with both reform and revolution has had historic, often bloody, implications. Positively it gave new relevance and a new role to the church as defender of and liaison for the common person. Negatively, the movement alienated church leaders, especially from 1978 under John Paul II. In the tense Latin America milieu it set laypersons, priests, and nuns at odds with desperate authoritarian systems, leading to arrests, torture, and murder. Where socialist governments achieved power the church found itself in an uncertain situation of continuing tension, given the militantly atheistic beliefs of many leaders.

Despite its negative elements and extraordinary history, the themes of liberation theology have stimulated even evangelicals who cannot accept the theological and economic ideology endemic to the movement. The liberation theologian takes Scripture seriously, but systematically reads into it a self-reflective system of personal mission and God's desire to deliver humanity from everything that destroys and disfigures. Such deliverance is depicted most graphically in a contextualized exegesis of Israel's exodus from Egypt and the prophetic demand for justice for the poor (e.g., Jer. 22:16). Justice brings nearer the kingdom in which all of life will be transformed.

Liberation theology redefines a number of key theological concepts. (1) Jesus is the God of justice, born poor. In the prophetic tradition he attacks the alliance between religion and political life and denounces oppressive legal restrictions which maintain the common people in subservience to the elite. Nevertheless he died as a subversive of public order. Jesus was crucified in order to free ordinary people from the shackles of religious and political domination. (2) The resurrection is God's conquest of sin, the Law, and principalities and powers. Because death has been defeated the world's system of death (social forces which withhold life from the majority) is rendered innocuous. Jesus has entered into a new life so individuals and societies may share in his victory. (3) The church is a base community of God's people, a new model of church for the future. Pregnant with resurrection life, the people do not need God's Word to be mediated through teachers. Their position of material deprivation articulates God's truth to them, and professional theologians should listen to the way the people apply Scripture to their situation so they may reflect on and modify their own theology, attitudes, and structures. (4) Redemption and salvation are by faith, but faith is seen as critical self-reflection and practicing social justice.

This system also has its own eschatological schema. Coupled with stern warnings of impending doom comes the message of restoration and the coming age of reconciled humanity and harmonious nature. This "utopian" motif inspires and motivates social change. Liberation theology also stresses Jesus' solidarity with the outcasts of the present world order, and the base ecclesial communities as a new way of being the church. Liberation theology seeks to make of theology a liberating instrument.

*See also* THEOLOGY, 20TH CENTURY TRENDS IN.

**Bibliography.** J. Moltmann, *A Theology of Hope* (1967); G. Gutiérrez, *A Theology of Liberation* (ET, 1973); J. Míguez-Bonino, *Doing Theology in a Revolutionary Situation* (1975), and *Christians and Marxists: The Mutual Challenge to Revolution* (1976); J. Moltmann, *Politische Theologie–Politische Ethik* (1984); D. J. Hesselgrave and E. Rommen, *Contextualization: Meanings, Methods, and Models* (1989).

J. ANDREW KIRK

**Liberia.** *See* WEST AFRICA.

**Liber Pontificalis.** A manuscript discovered by J. M. March in the library of the Chapter of Tortosa, Spain and published in Barcelona in 1925. It contains the biographies of the popes from John VIII (872–82) to Honorius II (1216–27). The text appears to be more ancient and more correct than that of the basic *codex Vat. lat.* 3764.

GEORGES A. BARROIS

**Liberty, Religious.** According to A. H. Newman, "unrestricted freedom to believe, practise, and propagate any religion whatever or none." During the 20th century religious liberty has gained its widest acceptance among human individuals and groups of any century since its initial advocacy during the 17th century, yet paradoxically the 20th century is said to have witnessed more martyrdoms for the Christian faith than all other centuries in the history of Christianity combined.

*Declarations.* In 1948, 48 members of the United Nations signed the Universal Declaration of Human Rights, article 18, which declares: "Everyone has the right to freedom of thought, conscience and religion; this right includes freedom to change his religion or belief, and freedom, either alone or in community with others and in public or private, to manifest his religion or belief in teaching, practice, worship and observance." Freedom of religion is an important component in a network of associated human rights or freedoms. The World Council of Churches adopted declarations on religious liberty in 1948 and 1961.

*Roman Catholic Church.* This, the largest body of Christians, reversed Pius IX's condemnation of religious liberty in his *Syllabus of Errors* (1864, numbers 15, 79) and a centuries-long tradition inimical to the theory and practice of freedom for non-Catholics. Vatican Council II adopted in 1965 a *Declaration on Religious Freedom (Dignitatis humanae personae).* Preparation for such a declaration had been made by theologians, notably the American Jesuit, John Courtney Murray. Its argument for universal religious freedom was based both on reason and on revelation and was applicable whether Roman Catholics were the majority or a minority religion.

*Marxist-Leninist Regimes in Europe.* Marxist-Leninist principles of a totalitarian state, advantage for atheism, and severe constriction of theistic religions were applied in the USSR beginning with the Bolshevik Revolution (1917) and in the nations of Eastern Europe after World War II. The Russian Orthodox Church and the government were separated, as were schools and the church. Severe persecution occurred during the 1920s. The Soviet constitution, amended in 1929 to guarantee freedom to both "religious worship" and "antireligious propaganda," was altered later in Joseph Stalin's regime (1924–53) to make religious propaganda illegal.

During World War II conditions for believers were less severe, whereas under Premier Nikita Khrushchev (1958–64) the criminal code was stiffened against believers, and churches were forced to decide whether to seek registered status. The emigration of Jews from the USSR was severely limited until the 1970s. Albania, a self-proclaimed atheistic state, absolutely prohibited (from 1968) any function of churches or mosques. In Bulgaria, Hungary, East Germany, Czechoslovakia, Romania, and Yugoslavia, religious bodies and the state lived with an uneasy coexistence, until the easing of church relations under perestroika reforms in the late 1980s. In Poland the predominant Roman Catholicism was able to an extent to challenge the government throughout the communist rule.

*Western Europe.* After the death of General Francisco Franco in 1975 and the restoration of a constitutional monarchy under Juan Carlos, Spain adopted in 1978 a new constitution that guarantees freedom of worship and expression and provides for no established church. Italy disestablished the Roman Catholic Church (1984), guaranteeing freedom of religion to non-Catholics. France increasingly subsidized Roman Catholic schools. In Germany under National Socialism (1933–45) the regime repressed the churches and fostered the Holocaust. After World War II West Germany by concordats and church treaties restored some privileges to Roman Catholic and Lutheran churches. Sweden studied (1958–72) but did not implement independent status for the Church of Sweden. Norway adopted (1964) a constitutional amendment protecting religious freedom for all, and Denmark declined disestablishment (1971). In Northern Ireland serious Roman Catholic-Protestant violence, involving political and economic as well as religious factors, has occurred since 1968.

*North America.* In the USA the Supreme Court on a case-by-case basis made more explicit the meaning of the "free exercise" and "no . . . establishment" clauses of the First Amendment to the Constitution. The court applied "free exercise" to unpopular religious movements, limited religious observances in public schools, prohibited the appropriation of public funds to religious elementary and secondary schools, expanded allowable conscientious objection to war, upheld the rights of sabbatarians, upheld tax exemption of churches, curtailed government intervention in church controversies, and liberalized the legal practice of abortion. In 1960, John F. Kennedy was the first Roman Catholic to be elected as president. Without formal constitutional guarantees Canada similarly guaranteed the free exercise of religion, although with differences as to education.

***South and Central America and Mexico.*** A wave of violence against Evangelicals (Protestants) occurred in Colombia during the early 1950s. Evangelical missionaries were allowed to reenter the regions, but the new concordat (1974) heavily favored the Roman Catholic Church. The effect of Vatican Council II in Latin America was generally to enhance the recognized religious freedom of non-Catholics. Religious liberty was indeed operative in Brazil. Tensions grew, nevertheless, during the latter 1960s and the 1970s between allegedly pro-Marxist Roman Catholic clergy and the Brazilian government and conservative clergy. Divorce was legalized (1977). The Brazilian government (1977) compelled 150 missionaries to leave their work with Indian tribes. Peru had previously terminated (1976) the Bible translation work of the Wycliffe Bible Translators. Religious freedom suffered in Argentina under the military regime that succeeded the government of Juan and Eva Peron. In 1978 and 1979 all religions except the Roman Catholic were forced to register or be banned, and reports of anti-Semitism were frequent. In Chile reports of violation of civil rights under the Augusto Pinochet Ugarte government also abounded.

Following Fidel Castro's Marxist revolution in Cuba (1959) Christian missionaries were jailed and expelled, and severe restrictions were placed on all practice of Christianity. In Nicaragua under the Sandinista government (from 1979) tensions increased between the Roman Catholic Church and the government, and in El Salvador Catholics accused (1982) the government of murder and torture of peasants. Costa Rica, Guatemala, and Mexico afforded greater religious freedom, although Mexico retained its prohibition against church ownership of property.

***Muslim Nations and Israel.*** The enforcement of Islamic law (*Shari*) has varied somewhat in predominantly Muslim nations during the 20th century. In Turkey, where one million Armenian Christians were massacred during World War I for reasons more political than religious, the most

thoroughgoing secularization occurred under President Mustafa Kemal (Atatürk) (1923–38), with the disestablishment of all religions, but since then Islamic religious instruction in public schools has become available (1960) and compulsory (1982). Since 1978 conflicts between Sunnis and Shi'ites increased. According to Indonesia's Constitution of 1945 Islam was no longer the state religion and law was not based on the *Shari;* a modus vivendi prevails among Muslims, Hindus, Buddhists, Catholics, and Protestants. Syria's Constitution of 1973 made Islam only the religion of the head of state and sanctions religious freedom; its government during the 1980s vigorously suppressed the right-wing Muslim Brotherhood. Pakistan's government after a period of moderate secularization was re-Islamicized during the 1970s and 1980s. Egypt under President Anwar Sadat established peace with Israel (1979), and Sadat imprisoned more than 1500 religious leaders, chiefly of the Muslim Brotherhood but also of the Coptic Christians, prior to his assassination (1981). On the other hand, Saudi Arabia fiercely applied the *Shari*, Libya undertook Islamic socialism, and Iran under the revolutionary regime of the Ayatollah Khomeini witnessed a Shi'ite revival that caused Christians to flee, Baha'is to be persecuted, and its emissaries to agitate in other, chiefly Sunni nations. Some nations (e.g., Algeria, Iraq, Jordan) retained Islam as the state religion but guaranteed religious freedom. Lebanon's tragic civil war (from 1975) involved conflict among Sunni Muslims, Maronite Christians, and the influx of Shi'ites.

In Israel there was a continuing struggle between orthodox Jews, who desired a government based on rabbinic law, and non-Orthodox Jews, who preferred a secular government.

***China.*** Religious freedom for adherents of numerous religions was available in China during the first half of the 20th century. After the Marxist forces of Mao Tse-tung assumed control in 1949, Christian missionaries were forced to depart, the practice of Christianity, Buddhism, or Islam by Chinese was severely curtailed, and the Three-Self Patriotic movement was established by the government as the officially sanctioned church. Christians in an underground house-church movement were severely persecuted. During the Cultural Revolution (1966–69) a drastic religious purge was carried out. With the death of Mao (1976) copies of the Chinese Bible and of the Koran were allowed to be printed (1979), a law protecting religious belief was enacted (1979), the Constitution of 1982 deleted the freedom to propagate atheism and pledged state neutrality respecting religion, and during the 1980s nondenominational Protestant and Chinese Catholic worship services were conducted in the major cities, although the Chinese Catholic Church was not recognized by the Vatican.

***South, Southeast, and East Asia.*** India enjoyed considerable religious liberty after its national independence (1948) despite laws enacted by various states to regulate religious conversions, the government's policies (1976) concerning birth control and sterilization, and the increased violence between Sikhs and Muslims during the 1980s. In Burma Buddhism was disestablished as the state religion in 1962, and all foreign Christian missionaries were expelled (1966). From 1983 Sri Lanka had violent conflict between the majority Buddhist Sinhalese and the minority Hindu Tamils, although this was primarily an ethnic, rather than a religious, struggle.

The revolutionary government of Kampuchea (Cambodia) expelled Roman Catholic bishops and priests (1975) and severely restricted Buddhism (1978) but then allowed increasing toleration of Buddhism during the 1980s. Laos deposed Buddhism's leader and forced him to flee the country (1979).

Shintoism was at the pinnacle of its influence in Japan between 1930 and 1945 and was then disestablished after the defeat of Japan by the USA at the end of World War II. With religious liberty sanctioned by its new constitution, Japan became the focus of Christian missionary undertakings by numerous boards and societies. The Soka Gakkai party, allied with the Buddhist sect, Nichiren Shoshu, exerted influence in the parliament. South Korea afforded freedom of worship and witness, but numerous Christians were not supportive of government policies which they reckoned as too restrictive. In the Philippines during the 1970s Muslim insurgents, with the announced goal of secession, fought government forces.

***Non-Muslim Africa.*** The free exercise of religion in South Africa was intertwined with the struggle against and the defense of apartheid (racial segregation), some of whose strongest opponents were church leaders. During the dictatorial rule (1971–79) of Idi Amin, a Muslim, Uganda's government expelled 27 religious groups and reportedly was responsible for the killing of 400,000 Christians. Following the overthrow of Haile Selassie's Christian monarchy in 1974 the Muslim revolutionary government of Ethiopia imposed restrictions upon Christians, and landowners harassed Falashas (black Jews), many of whom were then repatriated in Israel. Malawi outlawed Jehovah's Witnesses in 1967 as "dangerous to the good government of the state" and in 1975 detained 30,000 of them in detention camps, others having fled to Zambia. Jehovah's Witnesses were similarly detained in Mozambique (1976) and were outlawed in Cameroon, Kenya, and Zaire. Burundi expelled large numbers of foreign missionaries (1979, 1985), and Zaire's Christians (1970s) had to cope with the messianic implications and restrictions of the regime of President Mobutu Sese Seko.

***Bibliography.*** F. Ruffini, *La libertà religiosa* (ET, 1912); J. L. Mecham, *Church and State in Latin America* (1934; 1966); M. S. Bates, *Religious Liberty: An Inquiry* (1945); C. Northcott, *Religious Liberty* (1948); A. F. Carrillo de Albornoz, *Roman Catholicism and Religious Liberty* (1959); M. Asad, *The Principles of State and Government in Islam* (1961); A. C. Cochrane, *The Church's Confession under Hitler* (1962); W. Kolarz, *Religion in the Soviet Union* (1962); A. F. Carillo de Albornoz, *The Basis of Religious Liberty* (1963); A. P. Stokes and L. Pfeffer, *Church and State in the United States* (1964); E. I. J. Rosenthal, *Islam in the Modern National State* (1965); J. C. Murray, ed., *Religious Liberty: An End and a Beginning* (1966); A. F. Carillo de Albornoz, *Religious Liberty* (1967); R. C. Bush, Jr., *Religion in Communist China* (1970); H. Welch, *Buddhism under Mao* (1972); T. Beeson, *Discretion and Valour: Religious Conditions in Russia and Eastern Europe* (1974); A. V. Thomas, *Christians in Secular India* (1974); R. T. Miller and R. B. Flowers, *Toward Benevolent Neutrality: Church, State and the Supreme Court* (1987).

JAMES LEO GARRETT, JR.

**Libya.** *See* NORTH AFRICA.

**Licentiate.** One who holds the academic degree of license which, in Roman Catholic institutions of learning and in some secular universities, is intermediate between the bachelor's degree and the doctorate. In some Protestant denominations "licentiate" is the title given to laypersons who are permitted to preach the gospel while preparing for the ordained ministry.

GEORGES A. BARROIS

**Liddell, Eric** (1902–1945). Athlete and missionary. Born in Tientsin, China, he was educated at Edinburgh University. He played rugby for Scotland in seven internationals between 1922 and 1923. In 1924 he won the quarter-mile at the British AAA Championships in London, before taking the bronze medal in the 200 meters and the gold medal in the 400 meters at the Olympic Games in Paris, in which he set a new world record of 47.6 secs. In 1925 he left Scotland for China to begin his missionary work at the Anglo-Chinese Christian College at Tientsin alongside his parents. During his first furlough in 1931 he was ordained to the ministry of the Congregational Church. From the college at Tientsin he was posted to country work in Siaochang in 1937. In 1941 his wife and family were evacuated to Canada. In January 1942, together with other missionaries, he was evacuated in the French Concession in Tientsin but in March 1943 they were sent by the Japanese to Weihsien Interment Camp where in weakening conditions he died of a sustained attack of influenza. Memorial services were held in Glasgow, Edinburgh, and Toronto, followed by many tributes and dedications in his honor. His athletic achievement and spiritual resolve were celebrated in the award-winning film, "Chariots of Fire."

ALISTAIR J. DRUMMOND

**Lie.** It is debatable whether people of Western society have told more lies in personal relations, business transactions, political campaigns, and international dealings, in the 20th century than any other people at any other time. Lies may be disseminated more widely and over far more diverse media than ever before. The use of the lie in public relations has had unique features, and perhaps society has become more cynical.

On the one hand, a sharpened awareness of the moral and social evil of misrepresentation has produced definite efforts to suppress it (such as laws to ensure truth in lending, advertising or labeling), and has occasioned reactions of intense moral indignation in cases where deliberate misrepresentation has been suspected or established.

On the other hand, while the use of deliberate misrepresentation, especially in international dealings, is by no means new, but open manipulation of masses of people through "the big lie," oft repeated, caused unprecedented death and destruction in the practice of the Nazi government. Whole communist societies have proudly subscribed to a philosophical doctrine that all morality, including truth speaking, is purely relative to the interests of the class struggle or state government. The philosophies of naturalism and instrumentalism in the 20th century presented no rational moral logic for telling the truth when a lie serves better, and situation ethics brought that relativity into the 1960s and 1970s church. Such problems have given the question of truth and falsehood a decisive prominence.

ANDREW K. RULE

**Lieberman, Saul** (1898–1983). Jewish scholar of rabbinics. Born in Motol, Poland, he studied at the Theological Seminary of Slobodca, Lithuania (rabbi, 1916), and at the universities of Kiev and Jerusalem. He taught at the Hebrew University of Jerusalem (1931–36) and the Harry Fischel Institute (postgraduate rabbinical school) in Jerusalem (1935–40). In 1940 he emigrated to the USA (naturalized citizen, 1953) to teach at the Jewish Theological Seminary of America in New York (dean of the graduate department from 1949). He served as president of the American Academy for Jewish research and received a number of high honors from Israel. He was one of few to combine "old style" rabbinic knowledge with modern critical methodology. He also revolutionized Jewish studies through his advocacy of the importance of Tosefta, a body of Jewish literature from the first three centuries of the present era. His magnum opus was *Tosefta Kifshutah,* a 10-volume critical edition with commentary (1955–73). His many other scholarly works include *The Talmud of Caesarea* (1931), *Commentary on the Palestinian Talmud* (1934), *Tosefet Rishonim* (4 vols., 1938/39), *Greek in Jewish Palestine*

(1942), *Hellenism in Jewish Palestine* (1950), and *Siphre Zutta: The Midrash of Lydda* (1968).

GLEN G. SCORGIE

**Liebman, Joshua Loth** (1907–1948). Rabbi. Born in Hamilton, Ohio, he studied at the University of Cincinnati, Hebrew Union College (rabbi, 1930), Hebrew University in Palestine, Harvard, and Columbia. He taught at the University of Cincinnati (German tutor, 1925/26; lecturer in Greek philosophy, 1926–29). He held the Leo W. Simon Traveling Fellowship in Philosophy (1930–34). He was a preacher of wide reputation in leading colleges and over national radio chains. Liebman worked tirelessly for racial and religious understanding and regularly interpreted Jewish philosophy and religion in such Protestant theological seminaries as Bangor, Andover-Newton, and Boston University. He wrote *The Religious Philosophy of Aaron Ben Elijah* (1939), *God and the World Crisis—Can We Still Believe in Providence* (1941), *Teleology and Attributes in the Philosophy of Maimonides* (ET, 1943), and *Peace of Mind* (1946).

RAYMOND W. ALBRIGHT

**Liechtenstein.** An independent state since 1719 located between Austria and Switzerland. With a territory of 159 sq. km. (62 sq. mi.), it had in 1986 an estimated population of 27,000. German is the language of its inhabitants, some 23,000 of whom are Roman Catholics, attached to the diocese of Chur.

**Lietzmann, Hans** (1875–1942). Protestant church historian, successor of Adolf Harnack in Berlin. Born in Düsseldorf, Germany, he was instructor (1900) in Bonn and then assistant professor (1905) and professor (1908) in Jena and professor (1924–42) in Berlin. A recognized authority on ancient church history, Lietzmann was the author, among other works, of *Apollinaris von Laodicea* (1904), *Symeon Stylites* (1908), *Petrus und Paulus in Rome* (1915), *Messe und Herrenmahl* (1926), and *The Beginnings of the Christian Church* (4 vols., ET, 1937–52). He edited the *Zeitschrift für neutestamentliche Wissenschaft* (from 1920), and the series, *Kleine Texte für Vorlesungen und Übungen*.

THEODORE TAPPERT

**Life and Work.** *See* ECUMENICAL MOVEMENT.

**Lightfoot, Robert Henry** (1883–1953). English NT scholar. Born in Wellingborough, Northamptonshire, he was ordained in the Church of England and was curate of Haslemere (1909–12). He was then successively bursar (1912/13), vice principal (1913–16), and principal (1916–19) of Wells Theological College, fellow and chaplain of Lincoln College, Oxford (1919–21), and fellow of

New College, Oxford (1921–50), for part of which time he was also professor of exegesis (1935–49). A scholar with a deep respect for German form criticism, he wrote *History and Interpretation in the Gospels* (1935), *Locality and Doctrine in the Gospels* (1938), *The Gospel Message of St. Mark* (1950), and *St. John's Gospel* (1956). He also edited the *Journal of Theological Studies* (1941–53). In 1955 D. E. Nineham edited a collection of essays in Lightfoot's memory, entitled *Studies in the Gospels*.

J. D. DOUGLAS

**Ligon, Ernest Mayfield** (1897–1984). Psychologist. Born in Iowa Park, Tex., he studied at Texas Christian University and Yale (Ph.D., 1927). He was assistant professor of psychology at Connecticut College (1927–29) and professor and chairman of the psychology department at Union College, Schenectady, N.Y. (1929–62). In 1935 he founded the Character Research Project at Union College, a project which endeavored to apply insights of developmental psychology to the task of Christian character formation. Its experimental programs were used in many American churches and YMCAs. Ligon widely publicized the project through his *Psychology of Christian Personality* (1935; repr. 1960). He also wrote *Their Future Is Now* (1939), *A Greater Generation* (1948), *Dimensions of Character* (1956), *Parent Roles* (1959), and (with L. Smith) *The Marriage Climate* (1963).

GLEN G. SCORGIE

**Lilje, Hanns** (1899–1977). German bishop, scholar, and teacher. Born in Hannover, he studied at the evangelical academy at Kloster Loccum and at the universities of Göttingen, Leipzig, and Zurich (Dr. Theol.). He was student chaplain in Hannover (1925) and general secretary of the German Christian Youth Movement (DCSV) and vice-president of the world SCM (1927–34). From 1934 to 1944 he was general secretary of the Lutheran World Convention and in 1947, cofounder of the Lutheran World Federation and its president (1952–57). He was cofounder of the "Jugendpeformatorische Bewegung" from which emerged the Confessing Church. In 1944 he was imprisoned for his activities with the "Confessing Church." In 1945 he was cosigner of the "Stuttgart Declaration," an acknowledgment of the guilt of German Christians in the crimes on humanity perpetrated by the Third Reich. He was a member of the Council of the Evangelical Church of Germany (EKD) (1947–71); he became bishop of the Evangelical Lutheran Church of Hannover in 1949, acting chair of the council, and from 1955 to 1969 was the presiding bishop of the United Evangelical Lutheran Church of Germany (VELKD). In 1950 he became abbot of Cloister Loccum, dedicating himself to revitalizing the evangelical academy there. He was a

widely acclaimed preacher. His publications include *Das technische Zeitalter* (1928), *The Last Book of the Bible* (1940), *Im finstern Tal* (ET, 1966), *Luther: Anbruch und Krise der Neuzeit* (1946), *Atheism, Humanism and Christianity* (1965), *Martin Luther* (1972), and *Memorabilia: Schwerpunkte eines Lebens* (1973). He edited *Junge Kirche* (1933–36), *Die Furche* (1934–41), and *Das Sonntagsblatt* (from 1947), through which he sought to challenge evangelical Christians with contemporary issues.

E. J. FURCHA

**Lindsay, Thomas Martin** (1843–1914). Scottish church historian. Born into a Presbyterian manse in Lanarkshire, he was educated at Edinburgh University, and served there as assistant to the professor of logic and metaphysics. In 1896 he was ordained in the Free Church of Scotland, in whose Glasgow college he became professor of church history in 1872 and principal in 1902 of what was by then the United Free Church College. A defender of Roberson Simth in the heresy trial (1877–81), Lindsay was a staunch supporter of missions. Among his many publications were handbooks on Acts (1884–85), Mark (1884), Luke (1887), and the Reformation (1882), and other works including *Luther and the German Reformation* (1900), *The Church and the Ministry in the Early Centuries* (1902), and *A History of the Reformation* (2 vols., 1906/7). He also contributed to major projects such as the *Cambridge Modern History* and the *Encyclopaedia Britannica*.

**Litany.** In liturgical churches a highly standardized form of prayer. In less liturgical worship the litany assumes various forms, such as prayers of confession, thanksgiving, or supplication. The minister leads in a number of brief petitions or supplications, after each of which the people unite in an appropriate response. Psychologically the effect depends partly on prose rhythm, which tends to draw everyone into the atmosphere of devotion. The value depends on the skill and care of the minister in selecting or preparing a suitable litany and in leading the people clearly but inconspicuously.

ANDREW W. BLACKWOOD

**Literature and Religion.** In the modern world, the relationship of religion and literature involves a paradox. The rise of "English studies" has coincided with the decline of orthodox Christianity in the West. For the first 18 centuries of Christian history there was no such thing as "literature," at least not as it is now known. The discipline called "English" did not exist, nor did the conception of works of the imagination set off from all other forms of writing.

Only with the waning of Christian cultural influence during and after the 18th century, did the modern idea of "literature" arise. In fact, the decline of Christianity is considered one of the important reasons for the rapid development of the fine arts, including literature, in the Enlightenment. As the embodiment of the human imagination and moral sense, the arts were to fill the spiritual void created by the breakdown of a Christian consensus. Figures as diverse as the English Romantic poet William Blake, the American essayist Ralph Waldo Emerson, and the English poet and critic Matthew Arnold developed this view of literature in the 19th century.

To many, poetry and fiction seemed capable of carrying on the Christian tradition by sustaining its vital esthetic and moral heritage without requiring its outmoded theological framework. The human imagination would do the work that at one time had belonged to the transcendent God of Judeo-Christian theism. Grounded in the self rather than in God, spiritual and moral values appeared secure from the type of attacks that had undermined historical Christianity.

This view of literature *as* religion has meant that for 200 years Western literature has been replete with Christian themes and images but increasingly devoid of the substance of Christian belief. Examples might include William Wordsworth's *Prelude* (1805), Herman Melville's *Moby Dick* (1851), Henry David Thoreau's *Walden* (1854), the poetry of Emily Dickinson (1850s and 1860s), George Eliot's *Middlemarch* (1872), James Joyce's *Portrait of the Artist as a Young Man* (1916), T. S. Eliot's *Waste Land* (1922), and William Faulkner's *Absalom, Absalom!* (1936). In each of these works one might hear the cadences of King James prose, find an abundance of Christian images, or discover a telling analysis of the decline of faith. But one is not likely to find an orthodox apprehension of the Christian faith in these modern classics.

Like the literature it discusses, the modern study of religion and literature has often focused upon the spiritual ethos of literary works rather than upon questions of theological commitment or consistency. Among other things, the psychology of Carl Jung, the analysis of comparative religion, and broad studies of cultural criticism have been used to explore the "religious dimensions" of human experience. This brand of criticism emphasizes literature as a unique expression of human spirituality.

At the same time, other schools of literary criticism have emphasized the ability of literature to cultivate and preserve specific Christian values. In particular, the new criticism and archetypal criticism, both of which arose in the mid-20th century, proclaimed the power of imaginative works to maintain a Christian view of reality in a post-Christian world. For the new critic, this task is accomplished when the work of fiction or poetry creatively embodies the ironies of life within its perfected form; for the archetypal critic Northrop Frye, all of literature represents the human attempt to realize the kingdom of God through the creation of imaginative literature. These two schools have been the critical approaches most widely embraced by scholars in recent decades.

During those same decades, however, other visions of literature have displaced new criticism and archetypal criticism in the larger academic community. Although different from one another in a number of ways, these critical perspectives—structuralism and poststructuralism, Freudianism, Marxism, and feminism—share a distrust of authority and a skepticism about claims of purity and power for the imagination. They question whether the self can control the meaning of language and express sharp doubts about religious claims to truth and transcendence. In hindsight, we may see antecedents of these contemporary beliefs in the literature produced after World War I—in the fiction of James Joyce, Ernest Hemingway, Virginia Woolf, Franz Kafka, and William Faulkner and in the poetry of Wallace Stevens and T. S. Eliot.

Christians have yet to thoroughly assess the implications of these developments for the study of religion and literature. Indications are that Christian thinking shaped by these contemporary schools will emphasize the economic, psychological, and social nature of religion. In doing so, such criticism will raise important questions of justice and will provide further corroboration of the doctrine of original sin. Whether this criticism will engage fully questions of truth and spirituality is another matter. After an extended period of peaceful coexistence with the literary academy, Christians studying literature in coming years may find themselves forced into a more combative position than that to which they have been accustomed.

**Bibliography.** W. H. Auden, *The Dyer's Hand* (1962); N. Scott, *The Broken Center* (1966); P. Ricoeur, *The Symbolism of Evil* (1967); M. H. Abrams, *Natural Supernaturalism: Tradition and Revolution in Romantic Literature* (1971); G. Steiner, *In Bluebeard's Castle: Some Note Towards the Redefinition of Culture* (1971); N. Frye, *The Great Code: The Bible and Literature* (1982); H. G. Gadamer, *Truth and Method* (1982).

ROGER W. LUNDIN

**Little Sisters of the Poor.** A religious community of Roman Catholic nuns. Dedicated to work among the aged poor, the community was founded in France in 1839 by Jeanne Jugan (Sr. Mary of the Cross) who was beatified in 1982 by Pope John Paul II. They came to the USA in 1868. Their number has grown rapidly on both sides of the Atlantic. By 1950 there were over 900 professed sisters doing charitable work in 13 large metropolitan cities throughout the USA. Presently the Little Sisters number over 4100 and serve in 28 countries on six continents.

**Liturgical Movement.** One of the significant movements of the 20th-century church has been in liturgical studies, which emerged as a new discipline in theological education. The impact has been felt in the worship of the local church and on a worldwide basis. Specifically, liturgical studies reach into biblical origins, historical developments, theological nuances, the role of the arts in worship including music, art, liturgical dance and drama, studies in the church year, as well as architecture, both interior and exterior.

The origins of the 20th-century liturgical movement extend back to its 19th-century precursors in the Roman Catholic Church. In France, Prosper Gueranger refounded the Benedictine Abbey of Solesmes in 1832 as a monastery dedicated to the recovery of the church's liturgical heritage, especially the Gregorian chant. In 1841 Solesmes published *L'Année Liturgique*, a publication which had a wide influence on the beginnings of liturgical reform. This publication succeeded in awakening the Benedictines, who soon became the pioneers of the liturgical movement. Scholars such as Ferdinand Cabrol and Pierre Batiffol began to investigate the origins and history of the liturgy. Primarily, the interest of scholarship in the 19th century was in the medieval era as this age of history was being rediscovered by scholarship in general and was seen by Catholics as the golden era of the church.

The movement began to get underway in the first two decades of the 20th century. In 1903 Pope Pius X issued an instructional decree on church music. His concern was to restore more active participation on the part of the layperson. Several years later he called for a more frequent reception of holy communion. In 1909, a Catholic conference held in Mannes, Belgium, became the real source for the inauguration of the liturgical movement on a widescale basis. This conference saw the liturgy as a primary means to instruct people in the true meaning of faith and life, and the best source for the nourishment of the faith. It also called for the translation of the Roman liturgy into the vernacular, a centering of the church's life in the liturgy, a restoration of Gregorian chant as a way of increasing participation, and the establishment of retreat centers to foster liturgical renewal. The outstanding leader of this conference was Lambert Beauduin of Mont Cesar in Louvain. His book *La Piété de L'Église*, published in 1914, established the platform for Roman Catholic liturgical renewal, calling for an active participation of the community in worship.

While the work of the first decades of the 20th century was largely pastoral, the next phase of the movement, which occurred between the two World Wars (1918–40), shifted the emphasis toward the search for a theology of worship. In this phase of the movement German scholarship prevailed through the Rhineland Abbey of Maria Laach. In 1918 the publication *Ecclesia Orans* began and the work of Abbot Ildefons Herwegen and Odo Casel became widely known. Soon other theologians and church historians began to study the liturgy. The work of Josef Jungmann, Jean Daniélou, Louis Bouyer, and many others opened up liturgical scholarship as an important field of a major center for the liturgical movement. Their publication, *Orate Fratres* (later named *Worship*), became a major organ for the spread of the movement.

By the end of World War II the liturgical movement had spread widely in Europe and America. In Asia and Africa the church began to search for expressions of local worship drawn from the cultures and to probe the missionary implications of liturgical renewal. Although the movement had not penetrated into South America or Southeast Asia, the nearly worldwide influence of the movement created a growing ferment which eventually resulted in the summoning of Vatican Council II.

Certain promulgations of the Catholic Church paved the way for the liturgical constitution of Vatican II. In 1947 Pius XII issued the encyclical *Mediator Dei et hominum* which some regard as the charter of the liturgical movement. In this document the pope praised the liturgical reforms of the past and advocated them as signs of renewal in the church. Positive steps toward the implementation of the encyclical were taken by reviving Holy Week and reinstituting the Paschal Vigil as the central event of the entire Christian year. This resulted in a reexamination of the church year as ordered by the paschal mystery. In 1955 Pius XII issued another encyclical, *De musica sacra*, which set forth rules for increased participation of the layperson in worship.

When Vatican II convened in 1963, the first order of business was the liturgical constitution which had already been in the making for a considerable time. The constitution, *De sacra liturgia*, was passed by an overwhelming majority and promulgated by Paul VI in 1963. This document is the most important liturgical document of the 20th century, not only because it reflects more than a century of change, but because it is ecumenical in scope, providing principles of worship and objectives for renewal applicable to all the churches.

In the final third of the 20th century the liturgical movement spread to nearly every denomination. The movement has found strong adherents and leaders in the Anglican Church—liturgical scholars such as Dan Gregory Dix, E. C. Ratcliff, Massey E. Shephard, H. B. Porter, J. G. Davies, and others—who have done in the Anglican Church what Catholic leaders have accomplished in the Roman Church. In America the result has been a new Book of Common Prayer, as well as changes in the arts and the church year similar to those in the Catholic Church.

The most pronounced change in Protestant churches can be seen in the liturgy of the Church of South India, a liturgy which is in keeping with the liturgical movement and profoundly relevant to the Christians of South India. Also, the Taizé community in France has had a profound impact on Protestant worship through their common liturgical life, music, and widespread ecumenical influence. Other Protestant bodies, notably mainline Lutherans, Presbyterians, Methodists, and Disciples of Christ, all issued new liturgical books for congregational life in the 1970s and 1980s. The influence of the liturgical movement also shows signs of growth and development among evangelical and charismatic churches.

*See also* LITURGICAL WORSHIP, RECENT TRENDS IN.

**Bibliography.** L. Beauduin, *Liturgy: The Life of the Church* (1926); L. Bouyer, *Liturgical Piety* (1950); J. A. Jungmann, *The Mass of the Roman Rite: Its Origins and Development*, 2 vols. (1951–55); O. Rousseau, *The Progress of the Liturgy* (1951); J. A. T. Robinson, *Liturgy Coming to Life* (1960); W. Bardin, *Studies in Pastoral Liturgy*, 2 (1961); I. H. Dalmais, *Introduction to the Liturgy* (ET, 1961); O. Casel, *The Mystery of Christian Worship, and Other Writings* (1962); J. A. Jungmann, *Pastoral Liturgy* (1962); L. Bouyer, *Rite and Man* (1963); B. Wicker, *Culture and Liturgy* (1963); J. D. Crichton, *The Church's Worship: Consideration on the Liturgical Constitution of the Second Vatican Council* (1964); Y. T. Brilioth, *Eucharistic Faith and Practice* (1965); J. D. Crichton, *Changes in the Liturgy* (1965); A. R. Shands, *The Liturgical Movement and the Local Church* (rev. ed., 1965); M. H. Shepherd, *Liturgy and Education* (1965); E. B. Koenker, *The Liturgical Renaissance in the Roman Catholic Church* (rev. ed., 1966); J. G. Davies, *Worship and Mission* (1967); A. G. Martimort, ed., *The Church at Prayer* (1968); H. Winstone, ed., *Pastoral Liturgy* (1975); J. Ainslie, J. D. Crichton, and H. Winstone, eds., *English Catholic Worship* (1979); B. Morris, ed., *Ritual Murder* (1980); G. Dix, *The Shape of the Liturgy* (repr. 1982); K. Stevenson, ed., *Liturgy Reshaped* (1982); E. Underhill, *Worship* (repr. 1982); J. Wilkinson, *Egeria's Travels to the Holy Land* (rev. ed., 1982).

ROBERT WEBBER

## Liturgical Worship, Recent Trends in.

Worship renewal in the late 1900s focused on a return to the worship principles of the early church. The new interest in patristics among Orthodox, Roman Catholic, and Protestant Christians is tending toward common forms of worship—restoring the importance of both Word and sacraments, simplifying the church year, renewing interest in art and architecture, and recovering the entire treasury of music, especially the singing of psalms and the chant. New prayer books and other revised liturgical materials are becoming available.

*Patristic Sources.* Information on worship in the NT church is scanty, but the pattern of worship seems to have centered around Word and table. The liturgy of the Word was shaped by synagogue worship of Scripture, sermon, and prayer while the Lord's supper was shaped by the institution of the Last Supper which included taking, blessing, breaking, and giving. A comparison of Acts 2:42 with other early writings indicates that the sacrament took place in the context of a full meal known as the *agapē* feast. Some time after Paul's instruction to the Corinthians to separate the meal from worship (1 Cor. 11:17–22), the meal disappeared, and bread and wine were retained in the rite as the elements of the meal. Forms of prayers for the service appear in the *Didache*. Scholars disagree whether these forms are for the *agapē* meal or the Eucharist. The tendency is to see them as *agapē* prayers.

The first writer to give a full account of Christian worship is Justin (A.D. 150), 60th in his *Second Apology for Christians to (the Emperor) Antonius Pius* and in his *Dialogue with Trypho the Jew*. The service consisted of Word and Eucharist. The liturgy of the Word contained Scripture reading, a sermon, and prayers of intercession. Then bread and wine and water were brought to the president, who said a prayer of thanksgiving over them with the congregation saying an amen. After the communion a collection was taken for the needy, and the deacons took the sacrament to those absent.

The first known Eucharistic text is found in the *Apostolic Tradition*, written by Hippolytus, a presbyter in Rome around A.D. 215. The original text has never been found. Consequently, scholars must rely on an early 5th-century Latin version, together with Coptic, Arabic, and Ethiopian translations. Many scholars argue that the text has suffered in transmission. Nevertheless, the text has played a significant role in liturgical renewal of the 20th century. The prayer offers thanksgiving for creation and redemption and the bread and cup in memory of Christ's death and resurrection. It also contains a primitive form of the epiclesis, a prayer for the Holy Spirit to come upon the communicants.

In the 4th century, two influential centers developed in Egypt and Antioch. The most influential prayer book from Egypt was that of Bishop Serapion of Thumis (c. A.D. 350), a collection containing all the elements of the Eucharist as it was celebrated in Egypt. The prayer did not contain the words, "This do in remembrance of me," and there were two invocations, one before and one after the institution narrative. The second, which invoked the Logos, prayed for the consecrated elements. It ended with the intercessions. Serapion influenced the Alexandrine Greek liturgy of St. Mark, which in turn influenced the Coptic liturgy of St. Mark or St. Cyril. In the late 4th century, Antioch's Clementine liturgy in the eighth book of the *Apostolic Constitutions* was most influential. Textually it appears similar to Hippolytus. The preface was very long, the anamnesis included the consummation of all things, and the epiclesis and institution narrative were typically Eastern. This rite influenced the liturgy of St. James, the rites of West Syria, and the orthodox liturgies of St. Basil and St. John Chrysostom.

The development of the liturgy in the West is not as clear as in the East. Almost nothing is known of the liturgy between Hippolytus and Ambrose of Milan who wrote at the end of the 4th century. In his work *De sacramentis*, lectures to the newly baptized, he made numerous references to a Eucharistic text which later appeared in the *Gelasian Sacramentary*. He also wrote of the eucharist in *De mysteriis*, giving insight into the characteristically Roman rite used in Milan. In this liturgy the intercessions came before the institution narrative, consecration was effected by the words of institution (not an epiclesis), and the Lord's Prayer found a place in the rite after the canon.

It appears that a great deal of flexibility regarding worship characterized the first four centuries of the Christian church. While the framework of Word and sacrament remained constant, the place of the prayers, as well as their length and use, were subject to local customs and understanding. In later centuries the tradition became more fixed.

**Orthodox.** In Byzantine churches three liturgies are approved and used throughout the year. These are the liturgies of St. James (used on the Feast of St. James), and the Liturgy of St. Basil the Great (used on Christmas Eve, Eve of Epiphany, Feast of St. Basil, Sundays of Lent except Palm Sunday, and Thursday and Saturday of Holy Week); the Liturgy of St. John Chrysostom is celebrated at all other times.

The liturgies of St. Basil and St. Chrysostom consist of four parts. First, the prothesis concerns the preparing of the bread and wine. Second is the enarxis, which consists of prayers such as the opening blessing of the Trinity, the first litany, anthems, and other litanies. Third, the synaxis includes an entrance rite, readings from Scripture, and the common prayers of the church. Fourth comes the Eucharist or what is called the liturgy of the faithful.

The Byzantine liturgy has not changed substantially. Some orthodox liturgists, such as Alexander Schmemann, have called for new life to be breathed into the liturgy, not through change but through the rediscovery of the original gospel meaning of the liturgy.

**Roman Catholic.** Very little is known about the origin and development of medieval liturgies. From the 5th century ceremonial aspects of worship became more elaborate, compensating perhaps for the fact that the liturgy was fixed in the Latin language. The liturgy also became clericalized, putting the worshipers in the position of observers. The cup was withdrawn from the laity, the doctrine of transubstantiation was affirmed, and proliferation of masses became common. There was little liturgical uniformity.

Liturgical reform was instituted by the Council of Trent and made possible by the printing press.

The introduction of rubrics brought uniformity to worship. By the 19th century Catholic worship became devotional and in need of reform.

The reform of the liturgy was introduced by the *Constitution on the Liturgy* of 1963. This reform returns to sacramentality, wherein the liturgy is seen as the action of Christ through the signs of Word and table mediating to the worshiping people and beyond them to the world, the benefit of Christ's saving death and resurrection. The communal-celebration sharing among worshipers is restored through singing, praying, hearing the Word, passing the peace, and receiving the bread and wine. The centrality of the Word proclaimed also is reintroduced.

These new emphases have changed the celebration of the Eucharist. The priest faces the people, and the church year is reorganized around the paschal mystery. Preaching has returned, as have the arts and new forms of architecture that create more space for the celebration. Because participation is key, the Mass is now said in the vernacular. The prepatory rites are simplified to an entrance song, a greeting, a penitential act, the *Gloria,* and a prayer. The liturgy of the Word calls for three Scripture readings, interspersed by psalms and anthems, a sermon followed by the creed, and the prayers of the people. In the liturgy of the Eucharist the offertory prayers have been shortened, new Eucharistic prayers have been written, the list of saints has been shortened, an acclamation has been introduced after the words "mystery of faith," the central canon may be sung, and the sign of peace is given before the communion. In addition, the new calendar drops many feasts of the saints and makes others optional. The people become participants in a worship that is more in line with the early church, but in keeping with modern times.

**Anglican.** The Anglican liturgy went through significant change due to the work of Thomas Cranmer during the reign of Edward VI (1547–53). Cranmer created a liturgy in the vernacular and eliminated transubstantiation and the Mass as sacrifice. By 1662 a prayer book order was established that still remains in use in many parts of the Anglican community. In the 1960s this prayer book and others formed since (notably the 1928 American version), began to undergo change.

Consequently, emphasis was placed on increased congregational participation, the corporate significance of worship, and an increased note of joy. New features of the liturgy included a rite of penitence and the *Gloria in excelsis Deo* at the beginning, increased use of Scriptures, a creed following the sermon with responsive forms of the intercession, and a restoration of the peace. The Eucharistic prayer was expanded. The whole Eucharistic prayer is now seen as the prayer of consecration rather than the words of institution alone. New rites appeared in the New Book of Common Prayer in America (1979) as well as in Australia (1978), England (1980), Ireland (1984), and Canada (1984). The order of worship, along with the prayers, the singing of psalms, the use of antiphons, and the revised texts of the Eucharistic prayers, have great similarity to the Catholic texts.

*Other Protestant Bodies.* Similar changes occurred among other Protestants. Lutherans began to change their liturgies after Vatican II in keeping with the general ecumenical norms of worship. In America the Lutheran Book of Worship (1978), was published following a 10-year trial use. Similar changes are being made in the Lutheran churches of Hungary, France, Africa, Asia, and Latin America. These changes go beyond the Reformation tradition to reintroduce weekly Eucharist and a structure of worship similar to the ecumenical pattern. Similar developments are discernible in the Reformed community, among Methodists and some Baptists. What is clear is that the pattern of worship set forth in the *Liturgical Constitution* of 1963 has gained general acceptance. While some Western churches have arrived at a fairly fixed order and texts (notably Catholic, Anglican and Lutheran), other Reformed, Methodist, Baptist and Free churches remain more experimental. Nevertheless the main lines of liturgical reform are now present to some degree in almost all Christian churches.

*See also* LITURGICAL MOVEMENT.

**Bibliography.** *Liturgies and Documents. Documents on the Liturgy* (1962); *The Rites of the Catholic Church*, 2 vols. (1976, 1980); *Lutheran Book of Worship* (1978); *Book of Common Prayer* (1979); *Baptism and Eucharist: Ecumenical Convergence in Celebration* (1983); *The Service for the Lord's Day* (Presbyterian, 1984); *The Sacramentary* (1985); *Thankful Praise* (Disciples of Christ, 1987).

*Studies.* E. Schling, ed., *Die Evangelischen Kirchenordnungen des 16 Jahrhunderts* (vol. 1–5, 1902–13; vol. 6, 1955; vol. 11, 1961); P. Graff, *Geschichte des Auflosung der alten gottesdienstlichen Formen in der Evangelischen Kirche Deutschlands*, 2 vols. (1921); H. Holloway, *A Study of the Byzantine Liturgy* (1933); S. Salaville, *Introduction to the Study of Eastern Liturgies* (1938); J. H. Strawley, *The Early History of the Liturgy* (repr. 1947); J. Jungmann, *The Mass of the Roman Rite: Its Origins and Development*, 2 vols. (1951, 1955); A. Baumstark, *Comparative Liturgy* (1958); L. D. Reed, *The Lutheran Liturgy* (rev. ed., 1959); E. A. Payne and S. F. Winward, *Orders and Prayers for Church Worship* (1960); L. C. Sheppard, ed., *True Worship* (1963); J. D. Crichton, *The Church's Worship: Considerations on the Liturgical Constitution of the Second Vatican Council* (1964); F. E. Brightman, ed., *Liturgies Eastern and Western* (repr. 1965); Y. T. Brilioth, *Eucharistic Faith and Practice* (1965); U. Kury, *Die altkatholische Kirche in Kirchen der Welt*, vol. 3 (1966); K. Amon, *Liturgisches Jahrbuch* 18 (1968); C. O. Buchanan, *Modern Anglican Liturgies: 1958–68* (1968); J. E. Skoglund, *A Manual of Worship* (1968); T. Klauser, *A Short History of the Western Liturgy: An Account and Some Reflections* (2d ed., 1969); C. Kucharek, *The Byzantine-Slav Liturgy of St. John Chrysostom: Its Origin and Evolution* (1971); C. O. Buchanan, *Further Anglican Liturgies: 1968–75* (1975); C. G. W. Jones and E. Yarnold, eds., *The Study of Liturgy* (1978); C. O. Buchanan, ed., *The Development of the New Eucharistic Prayers of the Church of England* (1979); M. J. Hatchett, *Commentary on the American Prayer Book* (1980); R. C. D. Jasper and G. J. Cuming, *Prayers of the Eucharist: Early and Reformed Texts* (2d ed., 1980); G. J. Cuming, *He Gave Thanks: An Introduction to the Eucharistic Prayer* (1981), and *A History of Anglican Liturgy* (1982); G. Dix, *The Shape of the Liturgy* (repr. 1982); C. O. Buchanan, *Eucharistic Liturgies of Edward* (1983); C. F. D. Moule, *Worship in the NT* (repr. 1983); J. F. White, *Sacraments as God's Self Giving* (1983); G. J. Cuming, *Hippolytus: A Text for Students* (1984); C. O. Buchanan, *Latest Anglican Liturgies: 1975–1984* (1985).

ROBERT WEBBER

## Lloyd-Jones, David Martyn (1899-1981).

English preacher. Born in Welsh-speaking Wales he moved to London as a child, and spent most of his life there. After highly successful medical studies he was about to embark on a career as a physician when he heard the call of God and decided to become a preacher instead. He maintained that preaching was the highest calling a man could be given, and his sermons were noted for their depth of personal counsel. He entered the ministry at a time when evangelicalism was at a low ebb, and much of his life was spent in controversy with those who would water down the gospel by turning conversion into a purely psychological experience. His medical training gave his voice added weight, and he was able to influence an entire generation of younger preachers, turning them away from dry academic theology and giving them a vision of what could be accomplished by a truly pastoral pulpit ministry.

From 1938 to 1968, Lloyd-Jones was minister of Westminster Chapel in London, and it is from this time that his major published work dates. He wrote an excellent study of *Spiritual Depression* which continues to be a classic in its field, and a number of shorter pieces uphold various points of evangelical teaching. At the same time he developed a regular ministry of expository preaching which eventually led to a complete series of sermons on *Ephesians* and another series covering the major part of *Romans*. His forthright manner and firm convictions made him an object of frequent controversy, especially over the question of mixed denominations. He himself believed firmly in the need to pray for revival as the only answer to the nation's spiritual needs, and he frequently spoke on that subject. However, although his teaching was greatly appreciated by many, on issues such as these he was seldom heeded and was sometimes regarded as eccentric. The earlier part of his career is covered in *Martyn Lloyd-Jones: The First Forty Years* by Iain Murray (1982).

GERALD BRAY

## Loane, Marcus Lawrence (1911– ). Anglican

archbishop and author. Born in Tasmania, he graduated from Sydney University and trained for the ministry at Moore Theological College. After ordination in 1935 he joined the Moore College staff, first as tutor, then vice-principal (1939), and finally as principal (1954–58). During his long period as an academic, he began to write and publish on his two academic themes, the NT and the history of the Reformation and the Evangelical Revival.

During World War II he served with the Australian army as a chaplain in New Guinea. He left Moore College when he became assistant bishop of the diocese of Sydney (1958–66). He was elected as archbishop of Sydney (1966–82) and gained an Australia-wide role in 1978 when he was elected as the first Australian-born primate of the Church of England in Australia; he served until his retirement in 1981. He was knighted by Queen Elizabeth in 1976. Among his works are *Oxford and the Evangelical Succession* (1950), *Makers of Religious Freedom in the Seventeenth Century: Henderson, Rutherford, Bunyan, Baxter* (1961), *The Voice of the Cross* (1963), *Our Risen Lord* (1965), *Life Through the Cross* (1966), *The Hope of Glory: An Exposition of the Eighth Chapter in the Epistle to the Romans* (1969), and *Three Letters from Prison: Studies in Ephesians, Colossians and Philemon* (1972).

NOEL S. POLLARD

**Lods, Adolphe** (1867–1948). French biblical scholar. Born in Courbevoie, he studied at the Sorbonne and the universities of Paris, Berlin, and Marburg. Ordained in 1892, he served as professor of Hebrew, University of Paris (1893–1906) and professor of Hebrew language, and literature, Sorbonne (1906–37). His works include *La Palestine dans l'histoire ancienne* (1921), *Les prophètes d'Israël et les débuts du judaisme* (1935), and *La Religion d'Israël* (1939).

ELMER E. FLACK

**Loetscher, Frederick William** (1875–1966). Presbyterian. Born in Dubuque, Iowa, he studied at Princeton University (Ph.D., 1906), Princeton Theological Seminary, and the universities of Berlin and Strassburg. He was pastor of the Oxford Presbyterian Church, Philadelphia (1907–10), instructor in church history (1903–7), professor of homiletics (1910–13) and of church history (1913–45), Princeton Seminary, and professor of church history, Temple University (1945–51). He was editor of the *Journal of the Presbyterian Historical Society* (1912–42), secretary of the American Society of Church History, editor of its *Papers* (1918–33), and its president (1934), and a departmental editor of *Collier's Encyclopedia* (1950). His writings include a monograph on Schwenckfeld, sermons, addresses, and articles in historical and theological publications.

**Loetscher, Lefferts Augustine** (1904–1981). Presbyterian historian. Born in Dubuque, Iowa, he was educated at Princeton University, Princeton Theological Seminary, and the University of

Pennsylvania (Ph.D., 1943). He became an instructor of church history at Princeton Theological Seminary in 1941 and was appointed professor of American church history there in 1954, retiring in 1974. He served as a member of the board of directors of the Presbyterian Historical Society (1947–72) and as president of the American Society of Church Historians (1962). His works include *A Brief History of the Presbyterians* (3d ed., 1978), *The Broadening Church* (1954), and *Facing the Enlightenment and Pietism: Archibald Alexander and the Founding of Princeton Theological Seminary* (1983). With M. W. Armstrong and C. A. Anderson he wrote *The Presbyterian Enterprise—Sources of American Presbyterian History* (1956), and with H. S. Smith and R. T. Handy, *American Christianity: An Historical Interpretation with Representative Documents* (2 vols., 1960, 1963). He was editor-in-chief of the first edition of the *Twentieth Century Encyclopedia of Religious Knowledge* (1955).

WILL BERGER

**Loewenich, Walter von** (1903– ). German church historian. Born in Nuremberg, he studied at Erlangen, Göttingen, Münster, and Tübingen. He taught church history at Erlangen from 1931. Among his teachers Paul Althaus, Emmanuel Hirsch, and Karl Barth were most influential. Loewenich has combined NT studies with his interest in Catholicism, Luther studies, and the relation of Christian faith and humanist thought. His publications include *Luthers theologia crucis* (1929), *Das Johannesverständnis in zweiten Jahrhundert* (1932), *Luther und das johanneische Christentum* (1935), *Die Geschichte der Kirche* (1938), *Menschsein und Christsein bei Augustin* (1947), *Die Aufgabe des Protestantismus in der geistigen Situation der Gegenwart* (1952), *Modern Catholicism* (1959), *Paul, His Life and Work* (1960), *Luther und Lessing* (1960), *Wahrheit und Bekenntnis im Glauben Luthers* (1974), and *Probleme der Lutherforschung und der Lutherinterpretation* (1984).

E. J. FURCHA

**Lofthouse, William Frederick** (1871–1965). Methodist. Born in South Norwood, Surrey, and educated at Trinity College, Oxford, he taught in Methodist colleges (1896–1901), was minister in Bradford (1901–4), tutor in OT, Handworth College, Birmingham (1904–25), and principal (1925–40). He was president of the Wesleyan Methodist Conference (1929/30). He has written *Ethics and Atonement* (1906), *Altar, Cross and Community* (1921), *The Father and the Son* (1934), *Christianity in the Social State* (1936), and numerous OT studies.

F. W. DILLISTONE

**Loisy, Alfred** (1857–1940). Born in Ambrières, France, he studied at the seminary of Châlons and at the Institut Catholique, Paris, and was ordained to the priesthood in 1879. He taught exegesis and Hebrew at the Institut Catholique, from which his modernist inclinations caused him to resign (1894). After his excommunication from Rome (1908), he was appointed to a professorship at the Collège de France (1909). His most characteristic writings are *L'Evangile et l'Eglise* (1903), *Le quatrième Evangile* (1903), *Les Evangiles Synoptiques* (1907/8), *Les mystères païens et le mystère chrétien* (1919), *Religion et humanité* (1926), and *Les origines du Nouveau Testament* (1936). His autobiographical writings, *Choses passées* (1913), and *Mémoires pour servir à l'histoire religieuse de notre temps* (1930/31), detail the story of modernism in France.

*Bibliography.* F. Heiler, *Der Vater des katholischen Modernismus: Alfred Loisy* (1947).

GEORGES A. BARROIS

**Lonergan, Bernard Joseph Francis** (1904––1984). Canadian Roman Catholic theologian and philosopher. Born in Buckingham, Quebec, he joined the Jesuits in 1922, and taught subsequently in their seminaries in Montreal and Toronto. He was also a consultant to the Second Vatican Council, acknowledged particularly for the way in which he continually stressed the emphasis of Thomas Aquinas on intellectual inquiry. Later he served at Boston College (1975–83) as visiting distinguished professor of theology. His works include *Insight: A Study of Human Understanding* (1957) and *Method in Theology* (1972).

**Long, Ralph Herman** (1882–1948). Lutheran. Born in Loudonville, Ohio, he studied at Capital University, Evangelical Lutheran Seminary in Columbus, Ohio, and the University of Pittsburgh (1925). Ordained in 1909, he served parishes in Newton Falls-Warren, Ohio (1909–13), Coraopolis, Pa. (1913–21), and St. Paul's, Pittsburgh (1921–27). He was the stewardship secretary of the Evangelical Lutheran Joint Synod of Ohio (1927–30), and the executive director of the National Lutheran Council (1930–48).

RAYMOND W. ALBRIGHT

**Lord's Day Alliance of the United States.** Movement organized as the American Sabbath Union in Foundry Methodist Church, Washington, D.C., in 1888, by delegates chosen from six religious bodies: Baptist (Northern), Methodist Episcopal, Presbyterian, USA and US, Reformed Church in America, and United Presbyterian. The alliance subsequently became the agency of many other denominations, including Southern Baptist, United Brethren in Christ, Congregational-Christian, Disciples of Christ, Christian Reformed, Evangelical and Reformed, and Protestant Episcopal. Its headquarters are in New York City.

**Lord's Day Observance Society.** An interdenominational evangelical society founded in London in 1831 to encourage "due observance of the Lord's Day," "to diffuse information as widely as possible on the subject," and "to promote . . . the enactment of such laws as may be necessary for repressing the open violation of the Lord's Day." In the 19th century the society stressed Sabbath observance as Britain's duty as a Christian nation; but it also holds that each of the Ten Commandments is part of the moral law of God and is thus binding on all men, whether professing Christians or not. The society has been particularly active in publishing (sometimes over one million leaflets in a year), and in opposing proposed legislation that might detract from Sunday as a day of worship and rest from unnecessary work; this has involved it in frequent opposition to Sunday trading, sports, and entertainment. It has also engaged in evangelism, particularly among children.

PETER HICKS

**Lord's Prayer, The.** *Use in Worship.* Also called "The Disciple's Prayer," given by Jesus as a model (Matt. 6:9). Jesus evidently used the prayer at least twice, in slightly varying forms to make different points with his followers (compare in context, Matt. 6:9–13; Luke 11:2–4). It has been argued that the prayer was intended as a guide or outline for personal devotion, not as a form of set words. Such forms, however, were then in use in synagogue worship, and Bruce Metzger observes that Jesus likely followed a corporate worship form in the Aramaic.

Whatever Jesus's intent, this prayer has become a part of public worship in almost every branch of the church. The prayer may come early in the service, but more fitly later on, perhaps at the close of the pastoral prayer, if the order calls for that exercise. In the fifth petition most follow the KJV and the NIV and say "debts"; others, following an earlier English version, use "trespasses." As with other forms the danger with repeating this prayer is that it become meaningless ritual. Beginning with family worship the same persons may join in the Lord's Prayer several times over a Sunday, and sometimes it is repeated at almost incredible speed. Probably we use these words too often, and carelessly, so that untaught people attach to them magic power, apart from their meaning. To guard against "vain repetitions" the leader may call for this prayer less frequently, and school people to repeat it deliberately, stressing the important words. Children may also be trained in the meaning and use of this prayer as a vital part of worship. Ministers also guide their congregations into renewed appreciation by preaching sermons about the prayer as a whole, each petition, and the doxology.

ANDREW W. BLACKWOOD

***Text of the Prayer.*** As was undoubtedly the case with most of Jesus' teaching the Lord's Prayer seems to have been given to the disciples originally in Aramaic. Both Matthew's and Luke's forms, when put into Aramaic, exhibit end-rhyme—a circumstance not likely to occur accidentally. Many early synagogal prayers exhibit this characteristic, including the Shemone 'Erse, or "Eighteen" prayers, in their earliest form (the so-called Palestinian recension discovered in the Cairo Geniza) dating from the end of the first Christian century, as well as the piyyutim (synagogal hymns) of the early Middle Ages.

Perhaps the most interesting variant reading in the text of the Lucan form of the Lord's Prayer is in the second petition (Luke 11:2). "Thy Holy Spirit come upon us and cleanse us" or something very similar is found in two minuscule Greek MSS (162, 700) and was quoted by Gregory of Nyssa (A.D. 395) and Maximus of Turin (c. 450). According to Tertullian, in the middle of the 2d century Marcion apparently replaced the first petition by this one. It is likely that the variant form is a liturgical adaptation of the original form of the Lord's Prayer, perhaps used when celebrating the rite of baptism or the laying on of hands. Furthermore, the cleansing descent of the Holy Spirit is so definitely a Christian ecclesiastical concept that, if it were original in the prayer, it should have been supplanted in the overwhelming majority of texts by a concept originally much more Jewish in its piety ("thy kingdom come").

In 1903, it was decided that in future printings of the Anglican Prayer Book the position of the comma be changed (using the Matthean form) from "Thy will be done on earth, as it is in heaven," to "Thy will be done, on earth as it is heaven." According to this punctuation, which follows Westcott and Hort's strophic arrangement of the Greek text and was adopted by the RSV in its rendering of Matt. 6:10, the qualifying phrase, "on earth as it is in heaven," is to be taken with each of the three preceding petitions. The NIV leaves out the comma entirely, in effect suggesting the same interpretation.

The meaning of the word *epiousion* (the only adjective in the entire prayer) in the fourth petition is difficult to ascertain. Part of the difficulty arises from the fact that it has never been found, with one exception, in any context other than those pertaining to the Lord's Prayer. The exception, a fragmentary Greek papyrus of a householder's account book listing the purchase of provisions (published by A. H. Sayce in W. M. Flinders Petrie, *Hawara, Biahmu, and Arsinoe,* 1889), throws little light on its precise meaning. Depending partly on the presumed derivation of the word, the phrase has been taken to mean,

"our daily bread," "our bread for the morrow," "the bread which we need," or simply "our next bread."

Is the verb in the fifth petition (Matt. 6:12) "as we forgive" (KJV) or "as we have forgiven" (RSV)? The latter translates the aorist form of the Greek verb found in the two earliest vellum Greek MSS (Codex Vaticanus and the original scribe of Codex Sinaiticus). On the other hand, many early versions support the present tense of the verb, which is found in later Greek MSS and was followed by the KJV translators from the Old Latin, Jerome's Vulgate, the Sahidic and Bohairic forms of the Coptic, the Gothic, the Armenian, the oldest manuscript of the Old Georgian, and the Ethiopic. The Curetonian Syriac MS, which is thought to preserve a very old form of the text, perhaps 2d century, reads, "And forgive us our debts, so that we also may forgive our debtors" (F. C. Burkitt trans.). Although most scholars believe that codices Vaticanus and Sinaiticus preserve, on the whole, the purest form of the NT text (the Alexandrian), it may be that in this instance the past tense, "as we have forgiven," represents a learned and sophisticated refinement introduced into the Lord's Prayer at Alexandria.

The evidence of the manuscripts shows clearly that the original form of the Lord's Prayer closed with the petition for deliverance. At a very early date, however, the concluding doxology, patterned apparently upon 1 Chron. 29:11–13, was added as an appropriate liturgical close. Thus the prayer as used in most churches begins and ends on the thought of the sovereignty and glory of God.

***Bibliography.*** C. F. Aked, *The Lord's Prayer; Its Meaning and Message for Today* (1910); C. C. Torrey, *Zeitschrift für Assyriologie* 28 (1913); E. von Dobschuetz, *HTR* 7 (1914); G. Walther, *Untersuchungen zur Geschichte der griechischen Vaterunser-Exegese,* in *TU,* 3 (1914); J. W. Thirtle, *The Lord's Prayer, An Exposition, Critical and Expository* (1915); G. Dalman, *Die Worte Jesu,* vol. 1 (2d ed., 1930); F. Rittlemeyer, *The Lord's Prayer* (1931); B. F. Simpson, *The Prayer of Sonship* (1932); J. I. Vance, *Thus Pray Ye* (1935); S. C. Hughson, *The Approach to God, A Study of the Covenant of Prayer* (1937); A. von Schlatter, *Das Unser Vater; eine Auslegung des Herrengebets* (1938); G. Heard, *The Creed of Christ: An Interpretation of the Lord's Prayer* (1940); E. Underhill, *Abba: Meditations Based on the Lord's Prayer* (1940); E. F. Tittle, *The Lord's Prayer* (1942); H. G. Moss, *The Lord's Prayer in the Bible* (1948); P. Schempp, *Der Anruf Gottes; eine Erklaerung der ersten Bitte des Vaterunsers* (1949); M. Boegner, *La prière de l'église universelle* (1951); G. A. Buttrick, *So We Believe, So We Pray* (1951); H. Martin, *The Lord's Prayer* (1951); E. F. Scott, *The Lord's Prayer, Its Character, Purpose, and Interpretation* (1951); K. Barth, *Prayer According to the Catechisms of the Reformation* (1952); J. C. Jeffries, *The Law in the Prayer: The Ten Commandments in the Lord's Prayer* (1952); E. Lohmeyer, *Our Father* (ET, 1965); F. H. Chase, *The Lord's Prayer in the Early Church* (repr. 1967); J. Jeremias, *The Prayers of Jesus* (1967); A. W. Pink, *The Beatitudes and the Lord's Prayer* (1979); B. M. Metzger, *Manuscripts of the Greek Bible* (1981).

BRUCE M. METZGER

## Losskey, Nicholas O. (1870–1965). Eastern

Orthodox. Born in Kreslavka, Russia, he studied in the Imperial University of St. Petersburg, where subsequently he was a professor of philosophy until 1921. In 1922 he was exiled from Russia by the Soviet government and lived in Prague until 1942; from 1942 to 1945 he was a professor of philosophy at Bratislava University, Slovakia. He then became professor of philosophy at the Russian Theological Seminary in New York. His main works (mostly translated from Russian) are *Die Grundlehren der Psychologie vom Standpunkte des Voluntarismus* (1905), *The Intuitive Basis of Knowledge* (ET, 1919), *Handbuch der Logik* (1927), *The World as an Organic Whole* (1928), *Freedom of Will* (1932), *Value and Existence—God and the Kingdom of God as the Basis of Values* (1935), *Sensory, Intellectual and Mystical Intuition* (ET, in five booklets, 1934–38), *God and World Evil* (in Russian, 1940), *Dostoevsky and His Christian World Conception* (in Slovak, 1945), *Les conditions de la morale absolue* (1948), and *History of Russian Philosophy* (1951).

*Bibliography.* Festschrift N. O. Losskij zum 60. Geburtstage (1932).

**Los Von Rom.** A slogan meaning "free from Rome," first coined in a speech made in Vienna in 1897 during a major crisis in the Danube Democracy. It became the motto of the "Los-von-Rom" movement which combined nationalistic sentiments, a marked anticlericalism, Protestant evangelical zeal, and animosity toward Rome. The movement extended to Czechoslovakia, but was strongest in Austrian territories to the end of World War II. Its primary objective was to convince "Germans" that to be Roman Catholic was "un-German." By some estimates there were 100,000 "conversions" to Protestantism by the end of World War I. The *Evanglische Bund* contributed resources and a "back-to-the-gospel" ideology, thus strengthening the movement. Many "converts" joined the Old Catholic Church instead, since it combined Catholic teaching with a rejection of the juridical primacy of the papacy over Christendom. As a result of the impact of this movement, the annexation of Burgenland in 1921 and an influx of Protestant refugees during and after World War II, Protestantism in Austria grew from 107,471 members in 1900 to almost 412,000 in 1950. In 1986 Austrian Protestants numbered about 420,000.

E. J. FURCHA

**Lourdes.** A town in the department of Hautes Pyrénées, France, where between February 11 and July 1858, the virgin Mary reportedly appeared on 18 separate occasions to a peasant girl, Bernadette Soubirous, known since her canonization on December 8, 1933, as St. Bernadette. Some 2 million pilgrims each year, of all nationalities, ages, and classes, visit the place as a shrine to Mary. Thousands of cures have been reported, for example, 5000 of them in 1959, of which 58 were officially declared miraculous. As a result of all this, universal devotion to Mary under the title of Our Lady of Lourdes has been accorded her by Roman Catholics throughout the world.

J. D. DOUGLAS

**Love.** There are two words in the NT which are translated love: *agapan* and *philein*. The love of desire, self-seeking, *eran*, does not occur. The characteristic NT word is *agapan; philein* is much less frequent. *Agapan* is the love that gives itself without counting the cost (1 Cor. 13). The cognate noun, *philia*, friendship, occurs in the NT only once (James 4:4), while *philos*, friend, occurs 28 times, 15 of which are in the Gospel of Luke. It is a love between equals. The love described by *philein* is more emotional than *agapan;* it depends upon the mutual congeniality of the lovers, while *agapan* does not depend on the merits of the one loved. Something like this difference may be involved in the dialog between Peter and Jesus (John 21:15–19). To be sure, Augustine said there was no difference between the two words, but he was confused on the whole doctrine of Christian love, making it more like *eros* than *agapē.*

*Bibliography.* R. G. Moulton and A. S. Geden, *Concordance to Greek Testament* (1897); R. Young, *Analytical Concordance to the Bible* (1919); J. Moffatt, *Love in the NT* (1930); A. Nygren, *Agape and Eros: A Study of the Christian Idea of Love* (1932); G. Kittel, ed., *Theological Dictionary of the NT* (1964).

W. D. CHAMBERLAIN

**Lowrie, Walter** (1868–1959). Episcopalian. Born in Philadelphia, he studied at Lawrenceville School, Princeton University, the University of Greifswald, Germany, and at the American School of Classical Studies in Rome. He was rector of Trinity Church, Southwark, Philadelphia, Trinity, Newport, R.I., and St. Paul's American Church in Rome. He was the author of *Doctrine of St. John* (1899), *Monuments of the Early Church* (1901), *The Church and Its Organization* (1904), *Gaudium Crucis* (1908), *Problems of Church Unity* (1924), *Birth of the Divine Child* (1926), *Jesus According to St. Mark* (1929), *Religion or Faith* (1930), *Our Concern with the Theology of Crisis* (1932), *Kierkegaard* (1937), *SS. Peter and Paul in Rome* (1940), *A Short Life of Kierkegaard* (1942), *The Short Story of Jesus* (1943), *The Lord's Supper and the Liturgy* (1943), *Religion of a Scientist* (1945), *Essential Action in the Liturgy* (1945), *Art in the Early Church* (1947), and a translation of the works of Kierkegaard.

**Low Sunday.** The English name for the Sunday after Easter, also called *Quasimodo* Sunday, from the opening words of the Mass.

**Loyalty.** *Introduction.* Faithful adherence to a person or thing regarded as worthy of, or as having a right to, such commitment. The object of fidelity may be to one's word; husband, wife, or child; business associate; sovereign or other constituted authority, country, moral values, or God. The word derives from the Latin *lex*, meaning "a law," and it is similar in meaning to the term "fealty," which was restricted to certain relations in feudal society, and comes from the Latin *fides*, meaning "faith."

**As Ethical Issue.** Since social life depends on confidence, trust, and trustworthiness, this ethical "law" or "keeping faith" is highly regarded by thoughtful people. Probably the most dangerous result of corruption among public officials, in business dealings, and among prominent athletes is the damage done thereby to the confidence of those who trusted them, which breeds cynicism and destroys social cohesion.

Insofar as a stable social order is good in itself and the basis of the stability of other values, political loyalty may be regarded as good. Grave ethical challenges have arisen in 20th-century life, as at other times, when the conduct of those who wield political authority conflicts with personal and Christian loyalties. When there is no immediate method to peacefully change the authorities, a painful practical moral problem results. Absolutists, of course, such as Thomas Hobbes and the modern "statists," for whom all rights and duties derive from, or have been reposed in, the state, sovereign, or economic class, have denied that any such conflict can properly arise. But it is normally recognized that there are circumstances in which loyalty to other values may require repudiation—by armed violence if necessary—of loyalty to political authority as constituted. The authors of the American Declaration of Independence felt obligated to repudiate the authority of the British government at the cost of bloodshed, but they wrote the declaration to explain their reasons for discovering their loyalty out of "a decent respect for the opinions of mankind."

In the history of ethical thought, loyalty has been emphasized by those who find the essence of moral good not in the consequences of action, but in the attitude of the agent. For Kant, virtue is the attitude of loyalty to the dictates of the categorical imperative, which is laid upon the will by the practical reason (see his *Metaphysics of Morals*). Josiah Royce, however, explicitly worked out ethics of loyalty. "Loyalty to loyalty" was, for him, the supreme good (see his *World and the Individual*, and *Philosophy of Loyalty*). In his *Problem of Christianity*, he sought to interpret Christianity as "the most highly developed religion of loyalty."

Loyalty to God, loyalty of individuals and of God to the covenants, loyalty to the "program of Christ" and to one's fellow Christians, does play a large part in Christianity. Humanity was created to live in loyal, filial dependence upon God, and a repudiation of this relationship constituted the first sin, the consequences of which have brought dire results to the human race. God is repre-

sented as being unswervingly loyal to his covenants and as requiring a depth of loyalty humanity could not provide. Christ was loyal in all things, to the will of God in his redemptive vocation; upon that loyalty human hope absolutely depends. As a fruit of justification and adoption, Christians are required to be loyal to Christ, to his commandments and purposes, to his church, and to fellow Christians, in love.

ANDREW K. RULE

***In Christian Thought.*** The ethics of loyalty have created thorny issues for Christians in the area of relations with the state and with cultural or community groups, particularly in this century. Where missions have reached into closed tribal, Muslim, and eastern cultures, accepting the Christian God is still a treasonous rejection of family, culture, and nation. It has sometimes been deemed so disloyal as to be worthy of the death penalty. In no modern culture is the disciple immune from conflicting loyalties, so scriptural mandates have particular relevance.

In the Bible honor, obedience, and submission are used to define the concept of loyalty. Paul emphasizes submission in human relationships (Rom. 13:1–7; Eph. 5:21–6:9; cf. 1 Pet. 2:13) so long as submission does not mean conformity to the world system (Rom. 12:2; Acts 4:18–20). This suggests that there are ranks of loyalty in biblical Christianity—in family life (Gen. 2:4; Eph. 5:31), among the Christian community (Rom. 12:10; 1 Pet. 2:9, 17), and to God utterly (Deut. 6:4–5; Matt. 22:36–37). Jesus stressed the inevitability of violent conflicts in loyalty (Matt. 10:34–39); yet he equally demanded that the Christian show loving honor to all (as in Luke 10:30–37).

The Christian thus walks a tightrope of proper obedience and loyalty, in which each issue must be evaluated in the light of Scripture and in which Christians may legitimately disagree. Writing in the wake of World War II's violence, C. S. Lewis wrote ("Christian Behavior" in *Mere Christianity* [1952]) that Christian behavior demanded that both English and German believers take up arms when called upon by their governments. Christians might fire on one another, even kill one another, he said, without compromising their mutual unity and love. Those in Quaker or other pacifistic groups put a far different construction on loyalty to authorities. The same principle extends to relationships with non-Christian spouses, parents, or business partners. Christians are ordered not to form loyalties to non-Christians; where loyalty exists, however, submission is to be the rule. Where the actions of authority directly demand an either-or stand, the first loyalty is properly with God. To some Christians this has meant dying rather than cooperating in attempts to kill Jews during the Holocaust. It is used likewise to justify going to prison in the civil rights or the antiabortion struggles. It also has, for some, meant quitting a job rather than violating Christian standards. Such priorities in loyalty continue to create dilemmas in discipleship.

**Luccock, Halford Edward** (1885–1960). Methodist. Born in Pittsburgh, Pa., he was educated at Northwestern University, Union Theological Seminary, and Columbia University. Ordained to the Methodist ministry in 1910, he served appointments at Windsor, Conn. (1910–12), and St. Andrew's Church, New Haven, Conn. (1914–16). He was an instructor at the Hartford Theological Seminary (1912–14), registrar and instructor in NT at Drew Theological Seminary, Madison, N.J. (1916–18), editorial secretary of the Methodist Board of Foreign Missions (1918–24), and an editor of *The Christian Advocate* (1924–28). From 1928 to 1953 he was professor of homiletics at Yale Divinity School. His books include *Fares, Please* (1916), *The Mid-Week Service* (1916), *Five Minute Shop-Talks* (1916), *Studies in the Parables of Jesus* (1917), *The Christian Crusade for World Democracy* (1918), *The New Map of the World* (1919), *Skylines, the Haunted House and Other Sermons* (1923), (with Paul Hutchinson), *The Story of Methodism* (1926; rev. ed., 1950), *Preaching Values in New Translations of the NT* (1928), *Jesus and the American Mind* (1930), *Preaching Values in the OT in Modern Translations* (1933), *Contemporary American Literature and Religion* (1934), *Christian Faith and Economic Change* (1936), *Christianity and the Individual* (1937), *The Acts of the Apostles in Present Day Preaching* (1938), *Social, Ethical and Religious Aspects of American Literature 1930–1940* (1940), *American Mirror* (1941), and *In the Minister's Workshop* (1944).

RAYMOND W. ALBRIGHT

**Luke, Gospel of.** *See* GOSPEL AND GOSPELS.

**Lund Conference** (1952). The Third World Conference of Faith and Order (now attached to the World Council of Churches) in Lund, Sweden. It was largely preoccupied with the subject of intercommunion among different Christian churches. Based on work begun at the Edinburgh Conference of Faith and Order (1937), a preparatory series of papers was drawn up by the Theological Commission on Intercommunion for the conference. These papers dealt with both historical and contemporary issues and have remained a standard reference work on the subject. They are notable for the contributions made by the Russian Orthodox theologian Georges Florovsky at a time when neither the Orthodox nor the Roman Catholic churches were officially involved in ecumenical dialog.

The 225 delegates from 114 church bodies concluded that it was useless to work toward Christian unity from the standpoint of existing divisions within the church, because these tended only to reinforce prejudices already deeply held. Instead, unity could only advance by adopting new methods of cooperation which would penetrate behind existing divisions and reconsider the deeper meaning of the church as a God-given reality.

The conference produced a strong statement reaffirming the saving power of Christ and his lordship over the church, and it also attempted, less successfully, to reaffirm Christian belief in the Trinity. It ended by recommending that in the future ecumenists consider the doctrine of the church in close connection with the doctrine of Christ and the doctrine of the Holy Spirit. On the more specific issue of intercommunion, the conference was unable to advance very far, but it did produce a useful summary of what intercommunion involved and how different degrees of intercommunion actually existed within the Protestant world.

*See also* INTERCOMMUNION.

**Bibliography.** D. Baillie and J. Marsh, eds., *Intercommunion* (1952); O. Tomkins, ed., *The Transactions of the Third World Conference of Faith and Order* (1953).

GERALD BRAY

**Lundensian Theology.** *The Lundensian Theologians.* The work done by a number of 20th-century theologians who have centered about the University of Lund, Sweden. Within the movement have been Nathan Söderblom, a former primate of the Church of Sweden; Einar Billing, considered by some the ablest theologian in Swedish history; Gustaf Aulén and Anders Nygren, bishops in the Church of Sweden, but formerly professors at Lund; and two professors there, Ragnar Bring and Gustaf Wingren. Wingren, who is still an eminent theologian, the successor and one of the critics of Nygren, gave the Lundensian theology a new direction by replacing Nygren's abstract and Neo-Kantian methodology (the a priori concept) by an experiential one ("a phenomenological analysis of human existence"). By such an analysis Wingren attempts to show that morality is inherent in the basic conditions of human existence, giving it a natural foundation which is coherent with the doctrine of natural law found in classical theology and moral philosophy. Wingren connects natural theology (creation theology) to the Law as described in the Bible, and he seems to conceive of a dialectic relationship between the Law and the gospel. To identify the gospel in the Bible is, for him, to discern and account for the biblical message that liberates or releases man from sin. Wingren has been influenced by, among others, the philosopher and theologian K. E. Lögstrup.

The Lundensian theology is often contrasted with the Uppsala school where traditional theology (i.e., normative theology as an academic discipline) has been very seriously called into question. Uppsala has developed an argumentative way of doing systematic theology and theological ethics in opposition to the traditional, intuitional approach. The argumentative method is taken by Uppsala as the proper way of formulating a system since, according to this school, it is in line with the methods of *Religionswissenschaft* which, it affirms, must be sharply distinguished from academic theology. Uppsala prefers *Religionswissenschaft* since they believe it is more practical in serving the specific ideals of the church. The Methods of *Religionswissenschaft* are closer to ordinary means of scientific research and one of its goals is to study the ultimate truth-questions of religion.

*Theological Method.* The historical background of this movement was the Kantian undermining of the ontological-metaphysical presuppositions of Christian theology, and Friedrich Schleiermacher's consequent interpretation of religion in terms of man's feeling of dependence on God. Recognizing the problem addressed by Schleiermacher, the Lundensians affirm the validity of religious experience as God's revelation of himself and his immediate confrontation of man. The Word of God is its own authority. It must be taken seriously, and theology must interpret it in the sense in which God intends, not according to preconceived ideas. The task and method of theology are not apologetic or speculative but scientific—to set forth descriptively what a religion holds to be the way in which God and man come into fellowship with each other. The Lundensians, notably Nygren, hold that religions fall into categories, according to their fundamental answers to this question. The study of these basic answers is called motif research. The pervasive motif of Hellenism was *eros*, man's quest for his *summum bonum*. That of Judaism was *nomos*, man's effort to find favor in the sight of God by faithful obedience to the Law. For Christianity it is God who comes to sinful man, in divine *agapē*. He makes to sinful man the free and unconditioned proffer of restoration to fellowship with God. Motif research says that the specific affirmations of a religion can be understood only in the light of its basic attitude on this point. It is in theological method, rather than in novel theological content, that the Lund theologians have made their most distinctive contribution.

*Theology.* The Lundensians themselves disavow the term "Lundensian theology," declaring that their theology is in no sense distinctive. It is rather a fresh insistence on the evangelical view of Christianity recovered in the thought of Martin Luther. By *agapē* these theologians say they mean nothing different from the historic evangelical affirmation of God's free and utter self-giving grace, and they identify with Philip Melanchthon's statement (*Apology*) that "it is of especial service

for the clear, correct understanding of the entire Holy Scriptures, and alone shows the way to . . . right knowledge of Christ."

In keeping with the fundamental *agapē* motif, the theology dissents from quantitative or penal theories of the atonement. Justification is conceived as free forgiveness and restoration to fellowship with God, rather than in juridical concepts. Pietistic pretensions on the part of the Christian are condemned as an attempt at works-righteousness. And Christian ethics is fulfilled, not in a quest for moralistic excellence, but in self-giving participation in the body of believers and the world. The combination of theology based on the Word of God, and a methodology which sets it in contrast with other views of religion, has marked Christian theology, and the sense of responsibility for sharing its insights has made the adherents eminent in ecumenical activities.

*Bibliography.* English Works by Lundensian Theologians. G. Aulén, *Christus Victor* (1931), *Church, Law and Society* (1948), and *The Faith of the Christian Church* (1948); A. Nygren, *Agape and Eros*, 2 vols. (1932, 1939); *Commentary on Romans* (1949); A. Nygren, ed., *This Is the Church* (1952).

*Swedish Works by Lundensian Theologians.* A. Nygren, *Dogmatikens vetenskapliga grundläggning med hänsyn till den Kant-Schleiermacherska problemställning* (1922); *Filosofisk och kristen etik* (1923); A. Nygren, ed., *En bok om bibeln* (1947); G. Aulén, *Den kristna gudsbilden* (1927); R. Bring, *Dualismen hos Luther* (1929), and *Förhållandet mellan tro och gärningar inom luthersk teologi* (1934); G. Wingren, *Luthers lara om kallelsen* (1948); *Människan och inkarnationen enligt Ireneus* (1947); *Predikan* (1949); N. F. S. Ferré, *Swedish Contributions to Modern Theology* (1939); *Teologins metodfråga* (1954); *Filosofi och teologi hos biskop Nygren* (1956); *Skapelsen och lagen* (1958); *Luthers lära om kallelsen* (1960); *Från ordningsteologi till revolutionsteologi* (1969); *The Flight from Creation* (1971); *Växling och kontinuitet* (1972); *Was geschah eigentlich in Lund in den dreissiger Jahren?* (1972); *Credo. Den kristna tros- och livsåskådningen* (1974); *En kristen människosyn i Årsbok för kristen humanism* (1976); *Värderingar inom den systematiska teologin* (1972); *Token som tiger: vad teologin är och vad den borde vara* (1981); *Människan och kristen. En bok om Irenaeus* (1983); *Tro i en tid av tvivel* (1985); *Gamla vägar framåt: kyrkans uppgift i Sverige* (1986).

*Other Works in English.* N. F. S. Ferré, *Swedish Contributions to Modern Theology* (1939); E. M. Carlson, *The Reinterpretation of Luther* (1948); P. S. Watson, *Let God Be God* (1948).

CARL CHRISTIAN RASMUSSEN AND ANTONIO BARBOSA DA SILVA

## Lunn, (Sir) Arnold Henry Moore (1888–1974).

English Roman Catholic writer. Born in Madras, India, he studied at Oxford and during World War II was press correspondent in the Balkans, Chile, and Peru. He was a ski expert, and wrote many books on the subject, as well as on Switzerland. The son of a Methodist missionary, he turned to Roman Catholicism in midlife, and wrote about his conversion in *Now I See* (1933). He was knighted in 1952. Among his religious works are *Roman Converts* (1924), *Things That Have Puzzled Me* (1927), *John Wesley* (1929), *The Flight from Reason* (1930), *Public School Religion* (1933), *A Saint in the Slave Trade* (1934), *Within That City* (1936), *Communism and Socialism* (1938), *Whither Europe?* (1940), *Come What*

May: An Autobiography (1941), And the Floods Came (1942), The Third Day (1945), and The Revolt Against Reason (1950). He coauthored with R. A. Knox, Difficulties (1932), with C. E. M. Joad, Is Christianity True? (1933), with J. B. S. Haldane, Science and the Supernatural (1935), and with G. G. Coulton, Is the Catholic Church Anti-Social? (1946).

## Lutheran Church in Germany, United Evangelical.

The "Vereinigte Evangelisch-Lutherische Kirche in Deutschland" (VELKD), formed at a general synod at Eisenach on July 8, 1948. The Evangelical-Lutheran territorial churches of Bavaria, Braunschweig, Hamburg, Hannover, Mecklenburg, Saxony, Schaumburg-Lippe, Schleswig-Holstein, and Thuringia formed the union by adopting a constitution which was ratified by the nine participating churches by the end of 1948. The territorial churches of Lübeck and Eutin joined in 1949 and 1967, respectively. VELKD is united by confession and considers itself called to "united confessing and action." Since all churches in VELKD continue membership in the Evangelical Church of Germany (EKD), which unites Lutheran, Reformed, and United churches, the chief focus of VELKD is on internal renewal of faith, witness, and liturgy in keeping with their specifically Lutheran tradition.

At the General Synod, November 1968, the three churches within the geographic boundaries of the German Democratic Republic (GDR) established a separate administrative body which retained the essential constitution of 1948 but set up its own administration (VELKD in the GDR). The Lutheran territorial churches of Württemberg and Oldenburg are not members of VELKD although they maintain fraternal ties.

The constitutions of both branches of VELKD consist of a preamble, a basis, confessional statements which include the Confessio Augustana of 1530 and Luther's Small Catechism, and bylaws which govern the life and work of member churches. Several significant changes of the constitutions have taken place over the years. Member churches recognize one another's ministry and practice open communion. All churches are members of the Lutheran World Federation.

VELKD has three levels of government. The chief legislative body is the general synod which normally convenes once a year to debate and determine policy. Its more than 60 members are appointed to a six-year term. Ten are chosen by the presiding bishop; the remaining members are appointed by the territorial churches in VELKD.

The conference of bishops constitutes the second governing body. It consists of eight bishops and two church leaders each from the churches of Bavaria and Hannover. The bishops of Württemberg and Oldenburg participate as "guests" without vote. The presiding bishop, chosen from among the group, moderates meetings and represents the conference of bishops.

The administration of VELKD is the responsibility of an executivelike group, chaired by the presiding bishop. He is assisted by a vice-bishop. The president of the general synod and seven additional members of synod, five of whom must be laypersons, complete the administrative body. The maximum term of office of the executive is six years.

Headquarters are in Hannover and Berlin. VELKD has published Amtsblatt since 1954, occasional bylaws and announcements, and the minutes of the general synod meetings.

*Bibliography.* P. Fleisch, *Das Werden der VELKD* (1951); RGG, 3d ed.; *Evangelisches Staatslexikon* (1975).

E. J. Furcha

## Lutherans.

*Introduction.* The oldest and largest Christian communion (c. 67 million members) resulting from the 16th-century Reformation in Western Christendom. At first "Lutheran" was a pejorative name applied to the followers of the Augustinian monk and Wittenberg university professor Martin Luther by enemies. Luther had been excommunicated by the pope and banned by the Holy Roman Empire but managed to survive because of the protection of the local Saxon rulers who agreed with Luther and were proud of the fame of their new university. While Luther deplored the name, writing "You should never say I am a Lutheran," his adherents soon called themselves Lutherans and the name became part of the official titles of many of the churches who adopted Luther's reforms. The large national Lutheran churches of Europe, however, call themselves simply Church of Sweden and Norway or Denmark, respectively. The various German Lutheran churches are called Evangelical Lutheran, Evangelical, or Evangelical Church of the Augsburg Confession. Only in North America is Lutheran always in the official title of such churches (as in the Evangelical Lutheran Church in America, the Lutheran Church-Missouri Synod, and the Evangelical Lutheran Church in Canada).

At first largely confined to central and northern Europe, Lutherans spread to all continents as a result of emigration and a missionary movement which began in the 18th century. By the latter 20th century Lutherans could be found in practically every country. In Namibia, as in Denmark, Finland, Iceland, Norway, and Sweden, Lutherans constituted a majority of the population. While there was considerable growth in membership in Africa and Asia, their numbers in the traditionally Lutheran countries in Europe steadily decreased.

*Statistics.* In the late 1960s the largest Lutheran churches were still found in Europe and North America. In the late 1980s their estimated relative sizes were: Federal Republic of

Germany, 19 million; USA, 8 million; Sweden, 7 million; the German Democratic Republic, 6 million; Denmark, 4.5 million; Finland, 4.5 million; and Norway, 3.8 million.

Others with more than 500,000 communicants were: Indonesia, 2.7 million; India, Brazil, and Tanzania, one million; the Republic of South Africa, 710,000; Ethiopia, 660,000; Papua New Guinea, 640,000; Madagascar, 600,000; Namibia, 550,000; and the USSR, 520,000.

***Lutheran Doctrines.*** People considered themselves "Lutherans" for a variety of reasons. Originally all shared a particular understanding of the Christian faith. They emphasized the power and pervasiveness of human sin, the bondage of all men and women to the powers of evil, and their inability to save themselves or even to contribute to their own salvation through good works. They asserted salvation by faith alone (*sola fide*), faith being understood not merely as holding certain teachings to be true but primarily as trust in God's steadfast love. They followed Luther's assertion that faith is divine grace (*fides autem est gratia*). They claimed that the church is the "assembly of all believers among whom the Gospel is preached in its purity and the holy sacraments are administered according to the Gospel." They emphasized the Word of God as the highest authority for their life and teaching, insisting that it should be read in the light of its center, Jesus Christ.

This also meant a distinction between the two ways in which God deals with human beings: (1) the Law which is his demand on everybody and accessible to everybody, since it is written in their hearts; it promotes their earthly welfare, undergirds their communal life, and restrains the power of evil—but it does not save. (2) The gospel is God's gift of his Son, who died for the sins of all so that all might be saved and inherit eternal life, but it is a gift accessible only through faith in Jesus Christ. Lutherans retained only two of the seven sacraments of the medieval church. They affirmed that infant baptism as an outreach of God to humankind rather than an act of public confession on the part of men and women. In their understanding of the Lord's supper they insisted on the real presence of the body and blood of Christ "in, with and under" the elements of bread and wine, in contrast to the Roman Catholic teaching of transubstantiation and other groups' view of the sacrament as a memorial service. The description of the Lutheran view as "consubstantiation" is incorrect since most Lutherans have historically rejected the notions of "substance" and "accident" in reference to the Eucharist as assumed in the doctrine of transubstantiation.

These beliefs were authoritatively formulated in the Lutheran confessions, also known as *The Book of Concord.* It contains besides the three ecumenical creeds (Nicene, Apostles', and Athanasian) *The Augsburg Confession* (1530), *The Apology of the Augsburg Confession* (1531), *The Smalcald Articles* (1537), *Treatise on the Power and Primacy of the Pope* (1537), *The Small Catechism* (1529), *The Large Catechism* (1529), and the *Formula of Concord* (1577).

In their worship Lutherans maintained the basic pattern of the Roman Mass but translated the Latin text into the vernacular and insisted that the entire service be conducted in the language of the people. Congregational singing of hymns was stressed (Luther himself contributed to this development by writing many hymns, including "A Mighty Fortress Is Our God") and the preaching of sermons based on the exposition of Scripture was placed in the center of worship. Because of the centrality of preaching as the proclamation of God's Law and gospel, the education of Lutheran pastors stressed the importance of the original languages of the Bible. Theological students were required to learn Hebrew and Greek.

***Lutheran Ecclesiology.*** Lutherans did not develop a consistent pattern of ecclesiastical organization. For example, they kept the episcopal form of church government in Sweden (where the so-called apostolic succession was maintained since some of the bishops of the old church joined the Lutheran movement), Denmark, Finland, and Norway. In Germany they adopted a presbyterian type of church government very similar to that of the churches of the Calvinistic tradition, reintroducing the title "bishop" only in the 20th century. In America and many non-European countries where Lutheran churches were voluntary religious organizations without any support or special treatment from the state, they adopted a congregational form of government. In the latter part of the 20th century some called their leaders bishops in these countries, but without changing the basic congregationalist structure since these bishops are elected for a term and not for life and their powers are severely limited.

Because so much of their history was determined by events beyond their control Lutherans have been profoundly affected by the social and political situation of the time. Politics contributed to their initial survival. The German emperor was unable to enforce his Edict of Worms which would have destroyed the Lutheran movement because of the threat to his empire from the Turks who had reached central Europe and encircled Vienna in 1529, shortly before the Diet of Augsburg.

The Peace of Augsburg (1555) established the principle in large parts of central Europe that the religion of the ruler was to determine the religion of the citizens (*cuius regio eius religio*); thus one became a Lutheran or had to abandon Lutheran convictions according to the vagaries of governmental succession. Politics saved the Lutherans again in the 17th century when Gustavus Adolphus of Sweden defeated the imperial forces of Roman Catholicism at the battle of Breitenfeld (1631). Later the fact that the Hohenzollern rulers of Prussia were Calvinists compelled German Lutherans in the 19th century to abandon Lutheranism and become members of the so-called Prussian Union, forcing a small but dedicated minority to leave their homes in Prussia and look for the right to be unambiguously Lutheran in Missouri, USA (the ancestors of the Lutheran Church-Missouri Synod).

*The Lutheran Tradition.* Against this complicated historical background being a Lutheran could have at least four different meanings. First, it could signify adherence to a theological system developed by Luther and Melanchthon in the 16th century and Anders Nygren, Werner Elert, Paul Tillich, and others in the 20th. It is a system which indirectly produced the ideas of Georg Hegel, Søren Kierkegaard, and Friedrich Nietzsche, whose thought was formed in sometimes acrimonious debate with their Lutheran heritage.

Second, it represented a moral perspective, characterized by the distinction between Law and gospel which made Lutherans antiutopian and often politically quietistic, doubtful of their ability or anybody else's to bring in the kingdom of God. Even in largely Lutheran countries leaders who attempted to produce a political utopia were not Lutherans (Kaiser Wilhelm II and Adolf Hitler). While Lutherans generally were not found at the center of the political debate, they contributed to the support of welfare institutions in the Scandinavian countries and the diaconal work (schools, homes for the handicapped, hospitals, and other institutions) of Lutheran churches all over the world.

Third, Lutheran faith connoted a kind of religious feeling associated with pietism and expressed eloquently in the writings and hymns of Ludwig, Count Von Zinzendorf, who always asserted that he was a Lutheran in spite of severe criticism from the more orthodox. He exerted profound influence not only on his followers in the *Brüdergemeinde* but also on others who were raised on Zinzendorf's hymns and prayers. This emphasis on religious feeling was particularly strong in North America. These settlers were guided in their initial development by pietist pastors from Germany and the Scandinavian countries, and their churches grew with the aid of the European missionary societies who recruited from among the pietists.

Fourth, Lutheranism also has meant a cultural attachment related to language, literature, and music. There are cultural Lutherans who identify with an ethnic/religious tradition, although they might not accept any traditional Lutheran doctrines or even believe in a personal God. Many were deeply attached to the music of J. S. Bach or even the rituals of baptism and confirmation as important rites of passage, as well as the church services on Christmas, Good Friday, and Easter. While this type of Lutheranism was more common in the former state churches of Europe, it was also found in North America.

*Late 20th-Century Lutheranism.* All these meanings entered into Lutheran identity, and an individual might move from one emphasis to the other, or combine them in a somewhat idiosyncratic fashion. But by the late 20th century dramatic changes were taking place in the self-understanding of many Lutherans. In Europe and North America the ordination of women was widely adopted and generally accepted in mainline churches, slowly changing the customary patriarchal attitudes of Lutherans. Even in non-Western countries women assumed leadership positions. The growth of the Lutheran movement in non-Western countries helped Lutherans to pursue racial inclusiveness and become aware of what they can learn in the understanding of their faith from fellow believers in other cultures. Lutherans became increasingly interested in the results their faith ought to produce in the life of the Christian.

Mainline Lutherans were active in the 20th-century ecumenical movement and engaged in dialogs with Roman Catholics, Anglicans, Reformed churches, and Eastern Orthodox with the hope of better understanding and in some instances eventual union. Conservative Lutherans, especially within the Missouri Synod, insisted that such efforts threatened the preservation of the truth achieved in the Lutheran Reformation.

The future of Lutheranism may depend on the ability of some Lutherans to continue their emphasis on the primacy of faith as trust in the triune God. If they are enamored of the pan-ethical theologies whose agenda arise not from the faith of the Christian church but the fashionable demands of the moment, Lutherans may disappear with most other Protestants into an amalgam of civil religion. On the other hand, the resources in the prophetic gospel of the OT and NT mobilized by Luther in the 16th century—the grace of God made available through faith alone to all in Word and sacrament—may help Lutherans to avoid subservience to him whom Luther called "the prince of this world."

*Bibliography.* M. Luther, *Luther's Works* (1955–86); T. Tappert, *The Book of Concord* (1959); W. Elert, *The Structure of Lutheranism* (1962); J. Bodensieck, ed., *The Encyclopedia of the Lutheran Church*, 3 vols. (1965); C. Bergendoff, *The Church of the Lutheran Reformation* (1967); G. W. Forell and J. F. McCue, eds., *Confessing One Faith, a Joint Commentary on the Augsburg Confession by Lutheran and Catholic Theologians* (1982).

GEORGE W. FORELL

**Lutheran World Federation.** An organization founded in 1947 in Lund, Sweden, by 47 churches from six continents to coordinate relief efforts of Lutherans in war-ravaged Europe and to support the mission churches in Africa, Asia, and Latin America, which had been cut off from their bases of support by World War II. A previous effort to organize Lutherans on an international level after World War I, the Lutheran World Convention, was too loosely organized to be effective. Today LWF consists of more than 100 member churches and LWF-recognized congregations, representing more than 50 million members.

Its constitution defines its doctrinal basis as "The Holy Scriptures of the Old and New Testament as the only source and infallible norm of all church doctrine and practice," and it "sees in the three Ecumenical Creeds and in the Confessions of the Lutheran church, especially in the Unaltered Augsburg Confession and Luther's Small Catechism, a pure exposition of the Word of God." LWF is defined as a free association or agency of Lutheran churches. It does not exercise ecclesiastical functions or have power to legislate for member churches. In spite of this disclaimer, LWF added to its constitution at Budapest (1984) that its affiliated changes "understand themselves to be in pulpit and altar fellowship with each other." Since this amendment was not unanimously adopted it raises questions about the federation's reluctance to legislate for member churches.

LWF is governed by general assemblies consisting of delegates chosen by the member churches, who meet at intervals of five to seven years. Assemblies have met in 1947, Lund, Sweden; 1952; Hannover, Germany; 1957, Minneapolis, USA; 1963, Helsinki, Finland; 1970, Evian, France; 1977, Dar es Salaam, Tanzania; and 1984, Budapest, Hungary. Between assemblies it is led by a president and an executive committee of 29 members, elected by the assembly. The executive committee elects a general secretary whose office and staff are located in Geneva, Switzerland. LWF works through commissions of church cooperation, communication, studies, and world service. An Institute for Ecumenical Research in Strasbourg, France, is closely related to the general secretariat and the department of studies.

Through these commissions LWF functions to: (1) further a united witness before the world to the gospel of Christ as the power of God for salvation; (2) cultivate unity of faith and confession among the Lutheran churches of the world; (3) develop community and cooperation in study among Lutherans; (4) foster Lutheran interest in, concern for, and participation in the ecumenical movement; (5) support Lutheran churches and groups as they endeavor to extend the gospel and carry out the mission given to the church; and (6) help Lutheran churches and groups, as a sharing community, to serve human need and to promote social and economic justice and human rights. In recent years the emphasis has been increasingly concentrated on the 6th function.

*See also* LUTHERANS.

*Bibliography.* J. Bodensieck, ed., *The Encyclopedia of the Lutheran Church* (3 vols., 1965); C. Bergendoff, *The Church of the Lutheran Reformation* (1967); *LWF Report*, 19, 20 (Feb. 1985); *LWF Information* 20–22 (May and June 1987).

GEORGE W. FORELL

**Luwum, Janani** (1922–1977). Archbishop of Uganda and martyr. Born in East Acholi toward the Sudanese border, he was the son of poor Christians who could not afford to send him to school before he was 10 years old. He was a good student and finally went to high school 80 miles away (he walked the distance at the beginning and end of each term). After a missionary-run teacher-training course he took a teaching post near his home. In 1948, however, he was converted, became such a fervent evangelist that he disturbed the somewhat quiescent missionaries, and decided to forsake teaching for a ministry in the Anglican Church. Subsequently he became principal of a theological college and, in 1969, bishop of Northern Uganda. In 1974 he was elected archbishop in a land where in 1971 Idi Amin had established a reign of terror. During the three years remaining to him the archbishop spoke out fearlessly on behalf of the victims and the oppressed. The outcome was inevitable—some say at the hand of the dictator himself—and his body identified by his mother and brother before burial in his Acholi homeland. Anglicans in Kampala were not allowed to hold a memorial service for him. "This," said one of them, "has just put us fifty times forward."

J. D. DOUGLAS

**Luxembourg, Grand Duchy of.** A constitutional monarchy bordering Belgium, France, and Germany, with an area of 2587 sq. km. (999 sq. mi.) and a population 367,000, of which 341,000 are Roman Catholics. Luxembourg fell under the control of Germany during the two World Wars, but has cultural and commercial affinities with the Netherlands and Belgium.

The Roman Catholic Church in Luxembourg traces its roots to the work of the Anglo-Saxon missionary Willibrord (658–739), who built the monastery of Echternach in 698. From 1908 the diocese of Luxembourg was directly under the Holy See. The Catholic religion was practiced more faithfully than in other European countries in the late 1900s; approximately 43 percent attended Mass weekly, according to one modern estimate, and another 30 percent attended from time to time. Tens of thousands thronged to the shrine of the Virgin each year.

The Protestant Church of Luxembourg traces its roots to Prussian occupation after 1813. The Protestant church combines both Lutheran and Reformed traditions, but claimed only about 4000 practicing members in the 1980s. The Protestant community embraced approximately 7000 (2.1 percent of the people). Since 1951 American Mennonite missionaries have worked in Luxembourg. Their main centers of ministry are in Esch-sur-Alzette and Dudelange. The four Mennonite congregations had 65 adults and a circle of 200 adherents in the 1980s. The Jehovah's Witnesses had 591 adult members and 1000 adherents. The New Apostolic Church claimed 350 members and 400 adherents. At the same time the grand duchy had 3800 registered atheists, many of them members of the Communist party which had a draw of 10 percent or higher.

Radio Luxembourg was the world's most powerful radio station. Since 1946 it has carried religious broadcasts in English, German, Slovak languages, and French.

***Bibliography.*** D. B. Barrett, ed., *Annuaire Diocesain de Luxembourg* (1971); *World Christian Encyclopedia* (1982).

WAYNE DETZLER

**Luxury.** From the Latin *luxus,* meaning "abundance." Abundance, of course, is relative to need, or to one's estimate of need; so luxury might, in full harmony with its etymology, have meant simply a sufficiency for actual need. But in the midst of 20th-century Western materialistic culture the term has come to indicate a superabundant condition which conduces to enjoyment over and above what is simply necessary.

The judgment that luxury exists is relative to the condition in which others live, or are thought to live. A man may judge his lot to be luxurious in comparison with that of the poverty-stricken, but he may at the same time feel deprived when he compares it with that of the more wealthy. A possession, such as a particular kind or condition of automobile, may be judged to be a luxury, a bare necessity, or a deprivation, according to the use that a person has for it, and the kind and condition possessed by his neighbor.

The judgment that an abundance or a superabundance exists and is being enjoyed, in itself, does not have explicit moral implications. It is when the personal relations involved are considered that the enjoyment of luxury becomes a moral and spiritual question. Alexis Carrel (*Man, the Unknown*) is one of many who maintain that luxurious living, especially of modern city life, is to be condemned because of its effect on health. It may be replied, though, that it is the abuse of luxury which is inimical to health, so that it is something morally reprehensible which vitiates the luxury and not vice versa. It is commonly and more explicitly on the basis of a person's relations to fellows that luxury is either commended or condemned.

Self-centered persons will commend luxury if they judge that they, and perhaps a relatively small circle of those with whom they feel in sympathy, enjoy it; but will condemn it, or envy those whom they judge to possess it, if they lack it. Altruistic persons, on the other hand, may commend luxury, earnestly desire it for all men, and even advocate and practice a temporary self-deprivation in order that ultimately all may enjoy it. This spirit characterized many of the American theological and social liberals, and it is the appeal of Marxism and some other utopian philosophies. A person who is keenly aware of lack on the part of others, may feel self-condemned. This is regarded as one reason certain privileged people embraced the communist program, particularly in the Depression years in the USA. This Western interest abated by the end of Joseph Stalin's regime in the USSR in 1953 when it became known that the spread of privileges was not being actually narrowed in Russia and that the Russian economic system failed to provide for its people.

However one may morally evaluate luxury as such, 20th-century history demonstrates that the enjoyment of it by the few entails a subtle danger of estrangement from others, a narrowing of their range of interests, a perversion of their values, and a consequent moral and spiritual impoverishment. The individual or nation of wealth and luxury is apt to be the object of open or latent hostility. As a response, the wealthy seek to protect themselves and become suspicious, remote, and self-sufficient in relation both to God and others. Seeking a security which is never fully possible, they become hard, grasping, and perpetually dissatisfied.

Such outcomes are not inevitable, but it is because the danger is so insistent and such outcomes are so common that Scripture issues such solemn warnings and bitter condemnations. The luxurious Ahab is condemned by Elijah for dispossessing (and killing) the poor Naboth (1 Kings 21:20–25), and the prophets thunder against the oppressions and the prideful ostentations of the rich. Thus the writer of Prov. 30:8–9 petitions God to "give me neither poverty nor riches, but give me only my daily bread," for he recognizes that, while the danger of poverty is theft and dishonor to God, the danger of riches is self-satisfaction and the denial of God. In Luke 16:19–31, the rich man enjoys his luxury in a spirit of complete indifference to the needs of Lazarus and suffers in torment as a result; the rich fool of Luke 12:15–21 plans to enjoy material wealth with no thought of others, God, the brevity of life, or other values, and earns God's censure, "You fool!"; the rich young ruler (Matt. 19:16–25) has his scale of values so perverted that, though he yearns to enjoy other values, the primacy of his wealth shuts him out from them. "The deceitfulness of wealth" so chokes out God's Word, Jesus said in Matt. 13:22, and Jesus once exclaimed: "How hard it is for the rich to enter the kingdom of God!" (Mark 10:23).

ANDREW K. RULE

**Lyman, Eugene William** (1872–1948). Congregationalist. Born in Cummington, Mass., he studied at Amherst College, Yale University Divinity School, and was Hooker Fellow at the universities of Halle, Berlin, and Marburg. He was professor of philosophy, Carleton College, Northfield, Minn. (1901–4), professor of theology at Congregational College, Montreal (1904–5), Bangor Theological Seminary (1905–13) and Oberlin Graduate School of Theology (1913–18), and professor of the philosophy of religion, Union Theological Seminary (1918–40). He wrote *Theology and Human Problems* (1910), *Experience of God in Modern Life* (1918), *The Meaning of Selfhood and Faith in Immortality* (1928), *Meaning and Truth of Religion* (1933), and *Religion and the Issues of Life* (1943).

MARY ELY LYMAN

**Lyman, Mary Ely** (1887–1975). Theologian and educator. Born in St. Johnsbury, Vt., she was one of the first women to hold a full professorship in an American theological school. She studied at Mt. Holyoke College, Union Theological Seminary, N.Y., Cambridge University, and the University of Chicago (Ph.D., 1924). She was professor of religion, Vassar College (1921–26), lecturer in English Bible, Union Theological Seminary (1928–40), lecturer in religion, Barnard College, Columbia University (1928–40), dean and professor of religions, Sweet Briar College, Sweet Briar, Va. (1940–50), and dean of women, professor of English Bible, and professor emeritus, again at Union (1950–55; emeritus, 1955–75). Ordained to the Congregational ministry in 1949, she served as honorary vice-president of the International Association of Women Ministers. Her writings include *Paul the Conqueror* (1919), *Knowledge of God in Johannine Thought* (1924), *The Fourth Gospel and the Life of Today* (1931), *The Christian Epic* (1936), *Jesus* (Hazen Series, 1937), *Into All the World* (1956) and *Death and the Christian Answer* (1960).

GLEN G. SCORGIE

**Lyttle Charles Harold** (1884–1980). American Unitarian historian and apologist. Born in Cleveland, Ohio, he graduated from Western Reserve University and Meadville Theological School, then pursued further studies at the universities of Berlin and Marburg. After returning to the USA, he earned a Harvard S.T.M., and in 1914 was ordained to the Unitarian ministry. In 1923 he gained the Th.D. from the Meadville Theological Seminary. The remainder of his life was divided between pastorates in Brooklyn, N.Y. (1914–24), and Geneva, Ill. (1927–77), teaching at Meadville Theological School and the University of Chicago (1924–49), holding numerous positions within his denomination, and writing on behalf of his faith. Two of his most important books are *Freedom Moves West* (1952) and *The Liberal Gospel* (1925), an anthology of the sermons of William Ellery Channing.

ROBERT V. SCHNUCKER

# Mm

**Macao.** Portuguese territory at the mouth of the Pearl River in southern China with an area of 17 sq. km. (6.5 sq. mi.) and a population of 408,500 (1985 est.). Macao (also spelled Macau) has long been the site of Christian activity. The Jesuits entered the colony in 1570. Matteo Ricci, the first missionary to China, arrived a few years later. Protestant missionaries served briefly in Macao in the early 19th century, but the authorities refused to allow them to establish a permanent mission, perhaps at the request of the Portuguese priests who were unwilling to have their non-Portuguese co-religionists live in the colony. Some Protestants translated the Bible and printed tracts for distribution within China without hindrance from civil authorities, but they made few local converts.

Presently, the Christian population of Macao is about 260,000, nearly all of whom are Roman Catholics. Protestants tend to be refugees or recent converts. There are 13 Roman Catholic presses in Macao, one of which dates from 1902 and 8 of which were started in the 1960s and 1970s. They produce printed materials, videocassettes, and films for distribution to Portugal, Brazil, and Canada, in addition to meeting local needs.

KATHLEEN L. LODWICK

**Macartney, Clarence Edward Noble** (1879–1957). Presbyterian scholar. Born in Northwood, Ohio, he graduated from the University of Wisconsin, Princeton University, and Princeton Theological Seminary. He was pastor of the First Church, Paterson, N.J. (1905–14), Arch Street Church, Philadelphia (1914–27), and First Church, Pittsburgh (1927–53). In 1924 he was moderator of the General Assembly of the Presbyterian Church in the USA. He lectured at many conferences, colleges, and seminaries; wrote numerous journal articles; and published over 40 books, mainly sermons and Bible studies, but also substantial volumes on Lincoln and other historical subjects.

F. W. LOETSCHER

**McClure, James Gore King** (1848–1932). Presbyterian minister and educator. Born in Albany, N.Y., he was educated at Yale and Princeton Theological Seminaries, and after ordination was minister at New Scotland, N.Y. (1874–79). After traveling in Europe for two years he was minister at Lake Forest, Ill. (1881–1905), during part of which time he was also president of Lake Forest University (1897–1901). He was then president of McCormick Theological Seminary (1905–28). Among his publications are *Possibilities* (1896), *The Great Appeal* (1898), *Environment* (1899), *For Hearts That Hope* (1900), *Living for the Best* (1903), *The Growing Pastor* (1904), *Loyalty the Soul of Religion* (1905), *Grandfather's Stories* (2 vols., 1926, 1928), *The Story of England's First Library* (1929), and *The History of the Presbyterian Theological Seminary, Chicago* (1929).

**McConnell, Francis John** (1871–1953). Methodist scholar. Born in Trinway, Ohio, he studied at Ohio Wesleyan and Boston University (Ph.D., 1899). Ordained to the Methodist ministry in 1894, he was pastor at W. Chelmsford, Mass. (1894–97), Newton Upper Falls, Mass. (1897–99), Ipswich, Mass. (1899–1902), Harvard St., Cambridge, Mass. (1902–3), and New York Ave., Brooklyn (1903–9). He was president of De Paul University (1909–12). He was elected a bishop in May 1912, and served in the episcopacy until retirement in 1934, being the senior bishop during the latter years. He also taught at Columbia, Drew, Garrett, and Yale; was president of the Federal Council of Churches (1929); and served widely beyond his denomination. A Christian liberal, he won distinction as chairman of the Interchurch World Movement's commission which reported on the Pittsburgh steel strike. In theological outlook and spirit he was a personalist and disciple of Borden Parker Bowne. His books include *The Divine Immanence* (1906), *Religious Certainty* (1910), *Christian Focus* (1911), *The Increase of Faith* (1912), *Personal Christianity*

(1914), *Understanding the Scriptures* (1917), *Democratic Christianity* (1919), *Public Opinion and Theology* (1920), *The Preacher and the People* (1922), *Is God Limited?* (1924), *The Christlike God* (1927), *Humanism and Christianity* (1928), *Borden Parker Bowne* (1929), *Human Needs and World Christianity* (1929), *The Prophetic Ministry* (1930), *The Christian Ideal and Social Control, Christianity and Coercion* (1933), *Christian Materialism* (1936), *John Wesley* (1939), and *Evangelicals, Revolutionists and Idealists* (1942).

**Bibliography.** H. F. Rall, ed., *Religion in Public Affairs* (1937).
RAYMOND W. ALBRIGHT

## McCracken, Robert J. (1904–1973). Baptist preacher and theologian. Born in Motherwell, Scotland, he studied at the universities of Glasgow and Cambridge and was ordained in 1928. He served two Scottish Baptist churches (1928–37) and taught theology at the Baptist Theological College of Scotland (1932–37). Emigrating to Canada, he taught theology and philosophy of religion at McMaster University (1938–46) before succeeding Harry Emerson Fosdick as minister of the Riverside Church in New York City (1946–67). There he consciously abandoned the expository method for "life situation" preaching. Through his Riverside pulpit, practical theology lectures at Union Theological Seminary in New York (1949–67), civic activities, broadcasting, and writing, he became a prominent representative of liberal Protestantism in America. He wrote *Questions People Ask* (1951), *The Making of a Sermon* (1956), *Putting Faith to Work* (1960), and *What Is Sin? What Is Virtue?*

**Bibliography.** P. Sherry, ed., *The Riverside Preachers* (1978).
GLEN G. SCORGIE

## Macdonald, Duncan Black (1863–1943). Semitics and comparative religion scholar. Born in Glasgow, Scotland, he was educated there and at the University of Berlin. He taught Semitics at Hartford Theological Seminary (1892–1931) and Mohammadanism at the Kennedy School of Missions on the same campus (1911–25). He also lectured on comparative religion at the University of Chicago (1905–06). His works include *Development of Muslim Theology, Jurisprudence, and Constitutional Theory* (1903), *Religious Attitude and Life in Islam* (1909), *Aspects of Islam* (1911), *The Hebrew Literary Genius* (1933), and *The Hebrew Philosophical Genius* (1936). He wrote many articles for the *Encyclopaedia Britannica* and the *Encyclopaedia of Islam*. He was editor of the Mohammedan section of Hastings' *Encyclopaedia of Religion and Ethics*, and edited a concordance of the Peshitta. In 1933 his former students and colleagues published the *Macdonald Presentation Volume* in his honor; it contains biographical

sketches, Semitic and oriental articles, and his bibliography to that date.
EDWIN E. CALVERLEY

## Macdonald, George (1824–1905). Scottish minister, poet, and novelist. Born in Huntly, Aberdeenshire, he was educated at King's College, Aberdeen, and the theological college of Highbury. In 1850 Macdonald was ordained minister in a Congregational chapel at Arundel. He left under pressure three years later, his theology suspected of having a heretical German Romantic tinge. He never held a regular pulpit again. Macdonald's writing, influenced by 19th-century English and German Romantics, develops the use of imagination and mystical journeys into life through an acceptance of death and renunciation of the intellect. The dark aspect of his outlook was probably influenced by his personal experience with tuberculosis; it took the life of his mother, his father, four siblings, four children, and finally his own. Twentieth-century critic C. S. Lewis called him a genius at myth making, a writer whose vision of holiness was astringent yet paradoxically radiant. His first literary work, the verse drama *Within and Without*, was published in 1855. Altogether he wrote 52 volumes, including 25 novels, three adult prose fantasies, eight books for children, five collections of sermons, three of essays, two of short stories, and five of poems. With the publication of the dream romance *Phantastes* in 1857, his popularity was assured, and for the rest of his life he remained a best-selling author. His best works are generally considered to be two adult fantasies, *Phantastes* and *Lilith* (1895), and several children's books, *At the Back of the North Wind* (1871), *The Princess and the Goblin* (1872), *The Princess and Curdie* (1873), and *Sir Gibbie* (1879).
JOAN OSTLING

## McDowell, William Frazer (1858–1937). Methodist Episcopal bishop. Born in Millersburg, Ohio, he was educated at Ohio Wesleyan University and Boston University, and after ordination held various pastorates in Ohio (1882–90). He was then chancellor of the University of Denver (1890–99), corresponding secretary of the board of education of the Methodist Episcopal Church (1899–1904), bishop, resident in Chicago (1904–16), and head of the Washington, D.C., area of his denomination (1916–34). He traveled and lectured widely, and wrote *In the School of Christ* (1910), *A Man's Religion* (1913), *Good Ministers of Jesus Christ* (1917), *This Mind* (1922), *Making a Personal Faith* (1924), *That I May Save Some* (1927), *Them He Also Called* (1929), and *Lectures on Christian Biography* (1933).

## Macfarland, Charles Stedman (1866–1956). Clergyman and author. Born in Boston, he stud-

ied at Yale (Ph.D., 1899). He held pastorates in Malden, Mass. (1900–1906), and South Norwalk, Conn. (1906–11). From 1912 to 1931 he was general secretary of the Federal Council of the Churches of Christ in America. For over 50 years he served the churches in America and Europe as teacher, pastor, creative administrator, and author. His works include *The Spirit Christlike* (1904), *International Christian Movements* (1924), *Across the Years* (1936), and *Christian Unity in the Making, The First Twenty-five Years of the Federal Council of the Churches* (1948).

## McGiffert, Arthur Cushman (1861–1933).
Congregationalist church historian. Born in Sauquoit, N.Y., he studied at Western Reserve College, Union Theological Seminary, and in France, Italy, and Germany (Ph.D., Marburg, 1888). He was instructor (1888–90) and professor of church history (1890–93) at Lane Theological Seminary and professor of church history (1893–1927) and president (1917–26) at Union Theological Seminary. His major works include *Protestant Thought before Kant* (1911), *Martin Luther, The Man and His Work* (1911), *The Rise of Modern Religious Ideas* (1915), *The God of the Early Christians* (1924), and *A History of Christian Thought* (vol. 1, 1931; vol. 2, 1932).

RAYMOND W. ALBRIGHT

## McGiffert, Arthur Cushman, Jr. (1892– ).
Congregationalist theologian. Born in Cincinnati, Ohio, he was educated at Harvard, the American School of Archaeology, Athens, Union Theological Seminary, Harvard Divinity School, and the University of Zurich. He was pastor of All Souls Church, Lowell, Mass. (1920–26), professor of Christian theology at the Chicago Theological Seminary (1926–39), and president of the Pacific School of Religion, Berkeley, Calif. (1939–46). He returned to the Chicago Theological Seminary as president and professor of American religious thought in 1946. His works include *Jonathan Edwards* (1932) and *Young Emerson Speaks* (1938). He edited *Christianity as History and Faith* (1934).

## Macgregor, John Geddes (1909– ). Presbyterian minister and philosopher. Born in Glasgow, Scotland, he graduated from the universities of Edinburgh and Oxford, and from the Sorbonne. After ordination in the Church of Scotland, he served as assistant minister of St. Giles', Edinburgh (1939–41), and then as minister of Trinity-Pollokshields, Glasgow (1941–49). He became the first incumbent of a chair of philosophy and religion at Bryn Mawr College (1949–60) before appointment as professor of philosophy at the University of Southern California. Theologian and church historian as well as philosopher, he wrote *Aesthetic Experience in Religion* (1947),

*Christian Doubt* (1951), *Les frontières de la morale et de la religion* (1952), *The Thundering Scot* (1957), *The Coming Reformation* (1960), *The Rhythm of God* (1974), and *Reincarnation in Christianity* (1978).

## McGuigan, James Charles (1894–1974).
Canadian cardinal. Born in Hunter River, Prince Edward Island, he attended several colleges and universities and was ordained priest in 1918. He served as secretary to bishops, professor of theology, and parish priest. After postgraduate studies at the Catholic University of America, he was appointed rector of St. Joseph's in the archdiocese of Edmonton. He was consecrated archbishop of Regina in 1930, and went to the see of Toronto in 1934 where he was cardinal-archbishop until 1971. He was named cardinal in 1945, the first Anglo-Canadian named to the Sacred College. In 1947 he was papal legate *a latere* at the Marion Congress in Ottawa. His only known publication is a collection of sermons.

E. J. FURCHA

## Machen, John Gresham (1881–1937). Presbyterian scholar. Born in Baltimore, he studied at Johns Hopkins, Princeton University, Princeton Theological Seminary, and the universities of Marburg and Göttingen. He taught NT literature and exegesis at Princeton Theological Seminary (1926–29) and Westminster Theological Seminary (1929–37). An outstanding conservative apologist and theologian with a gift for clarity of exposition, he led in the founding of Westminster Theological Seminary (1929) and of the Presbyterian Church of America (1936), later renamed the Orthodox Presbyterian Church. He wrote *The Origin of Paul's Religion* (1921), *Christianity and Liberalism* (1923), *NT Greek for Beginners* (1923), *What Is Faith?* (1925), *The Virgin Birth of Christ* (1930; 2d ed., 1932), *Modernism and the Board of Foreign Missions of the Presbyterian Church in the USA* (1933), *The Christian Faith in the Modern World* (1936), *The Christian View of Man* (1937), *God Transcendent and Other Selected Sermons* (1949), and *What Is Christianity? Sermons and Addresses* (1950). With James D. Boyd, he wrote *A Brief Bible History*.

**Bibliography.** V. Form, ed., *Contemporary American Theology* (1932); *Presbyterian Guardian* 3 (Jan. 23, 1937): 153–72; W. Masselink, *Prof. J. Gresham Machen: His Life and Defense of the Bible* (1938); N. B. Stonehouse, *J. Gresham Machen, A Biographical Memoir* (1954).

BRUCE M. METZGER

## McIntire, Carl (1906– ). American fundamentalist leader. He entered Princeton Theological Seminary in 1928, but left in 1929 to attend the recently established Westminster Theological Seminary in Philadelphia. He was ordained in the Presbyterian Church USA in 1931, and became minister of Chelsea Presbyterian Church, Atlantic

City, N.J. Two years later he was called by Collingswood Presbyterian Church, N.J. In 1936 he and other conservatives were removed from their pastorates when a dispute arose over supporting the Presbyterian Board of Foreign Missions. He joined the Presbyterian Church of America (later called the Orthodox Presbyterian Church) but soon left because he felt that the church lacked an emphasis on a premillennial eschatology and had an erroneous view of Christian liberty. He helped to found the Bible Presbyterian Church in 1937, but in 1955 this church split and a rival ecclesiastical body was started by those who disagreed with his leadership policies. In 1941 he founded the American Council of Christian Churches to oppose the liberalism of the Federal Council of Churches, and in 1948 in Amsterdam he was instrumental in activating a new body, the International Council of Christian Churches, to oppose the World Council of Churches. His views became more widely known through his demonstrations, his broadcasts, and his publication, the *Christian Beacon*.

C. GREGG SINGER

**Macintosh, Douglas Clyde** (1877–1948). Baptist theologian. Born in Breadalbane, Ont., he was educated at McMaster University, Toronto, Chicago (Ph.D., 1909), and Yale. He served as minister of the Baptist church at Marthaville, Ont. (1897–99). He taught philosophy at McMaster (1903–4), and biblical and systematic theology at Brandon (Manitoba) College (1907–9). He began his long service at Yale Divinity School as assistant professor of systematic theology (1909–16), Dwight Professor of Theology (1916–32), and professor of theology and philosophy of religion (1933–42; emeritus, 1942–48). He was also chairman of the department of religion in the Yale Graduate School (1920–38). He served with the YMCA and also as a chaplain in the Canadian Expeditionary Force in England and France in 1916. He lectured in many universities and on many foundations. His application for U.S. citizenship became world news when it was denied by the U.S. District Court for Conn. (1929), granted by the U.S. Circuit Court of Appeals (1930), and reversed by the U.S. Supreme Court (1931). His books include *The Reaction Against Metaphysics in Theology* (1911), *The Problem of Knowledge* (1915), *God in a World at War* (1918), *Theology as an Empirical Science* (1919), *The Reasonableness of Christianity* (1924), *The Pilgrimage of Faith in the World of Modern Thought* (1931), *Social Religion* (1939), *The Problem of Religious Knowledge* (1940), *Personal Religion* (1942), *Thinking about God* (1942), and *Plain Man's Soliloquy*. He contributed to *Humanism, Another Battle Line* (1931), *Is There a God?* (1932), *Contemporary American Theology* (1932), *The Process of Religion* (1933), *Luther, Kant, Schleierma-*

*cher* (1939), *Science, Philosophy and Religion* (1941), *Liberal Theology, An Appraisal* (1942), and *Twentieth Century Philosophers* (1943). He edited G. B. Foster, *Christianity in Its Modern Expression* (1921) and *Religious Realism* (1931). He was associate editor of *Webster's New International Dictionary* (2d ed., 1934).

RAYMOND W. ALBRIGHT

**McIntyre, James Francis** (1886–1979). American cardinal. Born in New York, he studied at City College, N.Y. He held positions in several exchange and banking firms (1899–1915), but then changed course and prepared for the priesthood at Cathedral College and Saint Joseph's Seminary, N.Y. After ordination in 1921 he engaged in pastoral and administrative duties in the archdiocese before appointment as auxiliary bishop of New York (1941), coadjutor (1946), and archbishop of Los Angeles (1948–70; cardinal in 1953). During his incumbency Roman Catholic parishioners in Los Angeles increased from 625,000 to about 1,620,000, and parishes increased from 211 to 313. A strong conservative, he came under fire for not speaking out on racial problems and for disciplining those of his clergy who took a public stand on civil rights.

**MacKay, Donald** (1922–1987). Scientist and Christian apologist. Born in Wick, Scotland, he graduated with a degree in science from St. Andrews University and later obtained a Ph.D. from London University (1951). He began working in radar research at the Admiralty in London (1943–46), then taught physics at King's College, London (1946–60), before becoming professor of communication at the University of Keele (1960–82). A lifelong member of the Plymouth Brethren, he pioneered an approach to the relationship between Christian apologetics and science that encouraged the thinking processes of many generations of students. He stressed that honest doubt, resulting from a love of truth, can itself be a gift from God; to reject doubt is to throw dust in the eyes of the mind. He argued that Christian believers in particular have the best of reasons to seek a scientific understanding of human nature, and that scientists are answerable as God's stewards for the use they make of their talents. In the early 1960s MacKay discussed what he called "mindlike" behavior. Many of his thought-forms have taken shape in informational technology and robotics. A lucid and persuasive speaker and writer, MacKay's influence was deeply felt in the USA, especially among leaders of the American Scientific Affiliation. Among his published works are *Where Science and Faith Meet* (1952), *Freedom of Action in a Mechanistic Universe* (1967), and *Human Science and Human Dignity* (1979).

J. D. DOUGLAS

**Mackay, John Alexander** (1889–1983). Presbyterian scholar and ecumenical leader. Born in Inverness, Scotland, he was educated at the University of Aberdeen and Princeton Seminary. The recipient of a graduate fellowship, Mackay was prevented by World War I from his original intention of studying in Germany, and chose instead to study in Spain. There he worked under Miguel de Unamuno, an existentialist scholar and authority on Søren Kierkegaard. In Spain he developed a lifelong love for the Iberian Peninsula and Hispanic culture. Upon completion of his studies in Spain, Mackay and his wife became educational missionaries to Peru, where in 1917 they founded a Protestant school in Lima now known as the Colegio San Andres. In 1915 he was appointed to the chair of philosophy in Peru's National University of San Marcos, the first Protestant to be named to such a position. From 1925 to 1932, Mackay served as a writer and evangelist for the South American Federation of YMCAs, residing successively in Uruguay and Mexico. He then came to the USA as secretary for Latin America and Africa of the Board of Foreign Missions of the Presbyterian Church of the USA. In 1936 Mackay was elected president and professor of ecumenics at Princeton Theological Seminary, serving until 1959. Just before his arrival Princeton Seminary had been rocked by the withdrawal of J. Gresham Machen and others to found Westminster Theological Seminary in Philadelphia. Mackay brought unity and theological breadth to the beleaguered seminary, inviting world-renowned scholars to lecture and expanding its ecumenical horizons. In 1944 he founded the quarterly, *Theology Today*, successor to the *Princeton Theological Review*. Rejecting the narrowness of his upbringing in a small branch of Scottish Presbyterianism, Mackay became a world leader in the ecumenical movement. He headed the Commission on the Universal Church in Oxford in 1937, where he coined his oft-quoted directive, "Let the Church Be the Church." He was a member of the provisional committee for the World Council of Churches, and later a member of its central committee (1948–54), chairman of the International Missionary Council (1947–58), and president of the World Alliance of Reformed Churches (1954–59). He was moderator of the Presbyterian Church, USA in 1953. In his ecumenical endeavors Mackay argued for a balance of ardor and order of ecclesiastical unity and evangelical mission. In 1954, with E. C. Blake, Mackay published "A Letter to Presbyterians," condemning U.S. Senator Joseph McCarthy's tactic of disparaging and discrediting church leaders and political opponents by labeling them "communists" or "communist sympathizers." Mackay's chief works in English are *The Other Spanish Christ* (1932), *Spain and Latin America: Christianity on the Frontier* (1950), *The Presbyterian Way of Life* (1960), and *Ecumenics: The Science of the Church Universal* (1964).

R. Milton Winter

**Mackie, Alexander** (1885–1966). Presbyterian minister. Born in Philadelphia, he graduated from Princeton University and Princeton Seminary. He was minister of Sherwood Church, Philadelphia (1910/11), and Tully Memorial Church, Sharon Hill, Pa. (1911–36). He became president of the Presbyterian Ministers' Fund (1936). He wrote *The Gift of Tongues: A Study in Pathological Aspects of Christianity* (1921).

**Mackinnon, James** (1880–1945). Presbyterian historian. Born in Turriff, Aberdeenshire, he was educated at the universities of Edinburgh, Bonn, and Heidelberg. He lectured in history at Glasgow and St. Andrews, and was professor of ecclesiastical history at the University of Edinburgh (1908–30). He wrote *A History of Modern Liberty*, *The Social and Industrial History of Scotland*, *Luther and the Reformation* (4 vols., 1925–30), *From Christ to Constantine* (1936), *Calvin and the Reformation* (1936), and *The Origins of the Reformation* (1939).

F. W. Dillistone

**Mackintosh, Hugh Ross** (1870–1936). Church of Scotland theologian. Born in Paisley, he studied at George Watson's College, Edinburgh University (D. Phil.), New College, Edinburgh, and the universities of Freiburg, Halle, and Marburg. He was ordained in the Free Church of Scotland in 1897, and was minister of Queen Street Church, Tayport (1897–1901), and of Beechgrove Church, Aberdeen (1901–4). In 1904 he was appointed professor of systematic theology at New College, Edinburgh, becoming professor of dogmatics at the University of Edinburgh when New College was united with that institution (1935) following the union of the United Free Church of Scotland (1929). In 1932 he was elected moderator of the General Assembly of the Church of Scotland. In theology, he was a conservative liberal, and welcomed, with some qualifications, the theological movement led by Karl Barth. His main emphasis was on the forgiveness of sins as the center of the gospel, but he is better known for kenotic Christology, developed in *The Doctrine of the Person of Jesus Christ* (1912). His other most important works are *Types of Modern Theology* (1937) and *The Christian Experience of Forgiveness* (1927). He co-authored *Selections from the Literature of Theism* (1904), *Life on God's Plan* (1909), *The Person of Jesus Christ* (1912), *Studies in Christian Truth* (1914), *Immortality and the Future* (1915), *The Originality of the Christian Message* (1920), *The Divine Initiative* (1921), *Some Aspects of Christian Belief* (1923), *The Christian Apprehension of God* (1925), and *The Highway of*

*God* (1931). He translated F. Loof's *Haeckel's Riddle of the Universe* (1904) and J. Wendland's *Miracles and Christianity* (1911). He edited and translated volume 3 of A. Ritschl's *Christian Doctrine of Justification and Reconciliation* (1900) and F. Schleiermacher's *Christian Faith* (1928).

**Bibliography.** H. R. Mackintosh, *Sermons, with Memoir* (1938); *Dictionary of National Biography* (suppl., 1931–40).

CLAUDE WELCH

**Maclean, Donald** (1869–1943). Presbyterian church historian. Born in Lochcarron, Ross-shire, he studied at the University of Aberdeen and at New College, Edinburgh. He was licensed in the Free Church of Scotland by the Presbytery of Lochcarron and was inducted to Moy Free Church in 1897 and to Free St. Columbia, Edinburgh, in 1905. In 1900 when the Free Church of Scotland and the United Presbyterian Church of Scotland were united, he was one of the few ministers in the former church who remained outside the Union, and continued in what was still called the Free Church of Scotland. He was appointed professor of church history and church principles in the Free Church College, Edinburgh (1920), and principal (1942). In theology he was an orthodox Calvinist with strong evangelical sympathies. He wrote *Duthil: Past and Present* (1910), *Travels in Sunny Lands* (1911), *The Literature of the Scottish Gael* (1912), *The Law of the Lord's Day in the Celtic Church* (1926), *Aspects of Scottish Church History* (1927), and *The Counter-Reformation in Scotland, 1560–1930* (1931). He edited the *Evangelical Quarterly* (1929–43).

**Bibliography.** G. N. M. Collins, *Donald Maclean, D.D.* (1944).

**MacLeod, George F. (Lord MacLeod of Fuinary)** (1895– ). Presbyterian minister. Born the son of a Conservative member of Parliament, he was educated at Oxford and Edinburgh. He became a pacifist after he served in World War I, and was awarded the Military Cross and the Croix de Guerre. A Church of Scotland minister in St. Cuthbert's, Edinburgh (1926–30), and Govan Old, Glasgow (1930–38), he founded the Iona Community and began the rebuilding of Iona Abbey in 1938. He was the first Presbyterian since the 17th century to be select preacher at Cambridge and to occupy the pulpit of St. Paul's Cathedral in London. In 1954 he became the first Fosdick visiting professor at Union Theological Seminary, New York. In 1956 he was appointed a royal chaplain; in 1957 he was moderator of the general assembly of the Church of Scotland. In 1967 he was elevated to the House of Lords, resigning as leader of the Iona Community, and he became president of the International Fellowship of Reconciliation. While in New York in 1986 he was awarded the Union Medal by Union Theological Seminary. The international youth and reconciliation center on Iona, opened in 1988, was named in his honor. He wrote *We Shall Rebuild* (1944), and *Only One Way Left* (1956).

**Bibliography.** Ron Ferguson, *The Whole Earth Shall Cry Glory: Iona Prayers by Rev. George F. MacLeod* (1986).

RONALD FERGUSON

**Macmurray, John** (1891–1976). Scottish philosopher. Born in Maxwelltown, Dumfriesshire, he studied at the universities of Glasgow and Oxford. He was lecturer in philosophy at Manchester (1919), professor of philosophy at the University of Witwatersrand, South Africa (1921/22), lecturer in philosophy at Balliol College, Oxford (1922–28), professor of philosophy of mind and logic at the University of London (1928–44), and professor of moral philosophy at the University of Edinburgh (1944–58). His works include *Freedom in the Modern World* (1932), *Interpreting the Universe* (1933), *Philosophy of Communism* (1933), *Creative Society* (1935), *Reason and Emotion* (1935), *Structure of Religious Experience* (1936), *The Boundaries of Science* (1939), *Challenge to the Churches* (1941), *Conditions of Freedom* (1949), *Persons in Religion* (1957), *Science, Art and Religion* (1961), and *Search for Reality in Religion* (1965).

J. D. DOUGLAS

**McNeill, John Thomas** (1885–1975). Canadian Presbyterian church historian. Born in Elmsdale, Prince Edward Island, McNeill graduated from McGill University, Westminster Hall (now United Theological College of British Columbia), Vancouver, and the University of Chicago. He served a pastorate and taught in Canada. He was later professor of the history of European Christianity at the University of Chicago (1927–44). From 1944 to 1953 McNeill was professor of church history at Union Theological Seminary in New York City. His principal works are *The Presbyterian Church in Canada, 1875–1925* (1925), *Makers of Christianity* (1935), *Christian Hope for World Society* (1937), *John Calvin on God and Political Duty* (1950), *A History of the Cure of Souls* (1951), *The History and Character of Calvinism* (1954), *Unitive Protestantism: The Ecumenical Spirit and Its Persistent Expression* (1964), and *The Celtic Churches: A History* (1974). With James Hastings Nichols, he wrote *Ecumenical Testimony: The Concern for Christian Unity Within the Reformed and Presbyterian Churches* (1974). McNeill was general editor of *The Library of Christian Classics* and with Ford Lewis Battles produced a definitive new English edition of Calvin's *Institutes of the Christian Religion* (2 vols., 1960).

R. MILTON WINTER

**Macnicol, Nicol** (1870–1952). Missionary and scholar. Born in Catacol, Arran, Scotland, where his father was minister, he studied at Glasgow

536

University and the Glasgow Free Church Theological (now Trinity) College. Ordained as a missionary to India, he served first at Wilson College, Bombay, and from 1901 to 1929 in the United Free Church Mission at Poona, the last three years as secretary of the National Christian Council. In 1930 he returned to India as a member of the Lord Lindsay Educational Commission and was joint editor of its report. From 1932 to 1935 he was Wilde Lecturer on Natural and Comparative Religion at Oxford University. In 1934/35 he was in America as lecturer on the life and religions of India at the Hartford Seminary Foundation. He published two courses of his Wilde lectures as *The Living Religions of the Indian People* (1934); and the third series, given at Hartford and other places in America and at Oxford, as *Is Christianity Unique? A Comparative Study of the Religions* (1936). His other books include *Indian Theism* (1915), *Psalms of the Maratha Saints* (1919), *The Making of Modern India* (1924), *India in the Dark Wood* (1930), and *Hindu Scriptures* (1938).

EDWIN E. CALVERLEY

## McPherson, Aimee Semple. *See* FOURSQUARE GOSPEL, INTERNATIONAL CHURCH OF THE.

## Madagascar.
Independent country made up of the island of Madagascar and a number of smaller islands situated in the Indian Ocean off the southeastern coast of mainland Africa. It has an area of 587,041 sq. km. (226,658 sq. mi.) and a population of 9,490,000 (1983 est.).

Religion in Madagascar is characterized by a Christian majority of historic churches seeking to penetrate a resilient and sizable traditional religion while keeping a wary eye on small but aggressive religious minorities such as Islam, Bahai, and Independent churches.

Traditional religion claims an estimated 47 percent of the population. As with African traditional religion across the continent, Malagasy religion is built around the ancestor cult. Rituals of burial and appeasement of the ancestral spirits (*Razana*) dominate tribal faith. Witchcraft plays a role in the delicate chemistry of appeasement but seems to have declined in significance in recent years.

Christianity made an unsuccessful foray into Madagascar in the 17th century through Jesuit missionaries. None of their work survived into the 19th century when King Radama I (1810–28) opened the country to European and Christian influences. The London Missionary Society (LMS) planted the first Protestant churches in the country and translated the Scriptures into Malagasy by 1830. Persecution became virulent under Radama I's successor. Christianity was encouraged, however, with the ascension of Radama II. Rapid church growth, particularly among the dominant Merinas, enabled Christianity to reach one million adherents by the year 1900. French rule from 1895 provided Catholicism with an opportunity to advance in Madagascar. The Paris Mission Society was able to take over much of the Protestant work of LMS, which had fallen out of favor with the French colonial administration.

The 20th century witnessed disappointing church growth. The rapid expansion of Christianity in the late 19th century came to a halt by World War I. Political independence from France in 1960 began a troubled period for the churches, culminating in the establishment in 1975 of a revolutionary socialist government. The government position began to soften in the early 1980s and new mission efforts such as those of African Inland Mission were permitted by the government.

The current profile of religion in Madagascar includes about 4 million traditionalists, 4.7 million Christians of various denominations, 150,000 Muslims, and a variety of smaller religious minorities supporting the Bahai, Hindu, and Jewish faiths.

*Bibliography.* P. Falk, *The Growth of the Church in Africa* (1979); A. Hastings, *History of African Christianity: 1950–1975* (1979); D. Barrett, ed., *World Christian Encyclopedia* (1982).

MARK R. SHAW

## Magic.
Use of ceremonies, spells, charms, and the like which are believed to have supernatural power to cause a supernatural being to act. Although the term "magic" is probably of Greek origin, the belief and practice of magic are associated more or less with all religions. Magic must be distinguished from religion, although it may be religious even as religion may be magical. Magic is essentially coercive and religion persuasive, but both seek self-preservation.

Magic is most common in primitive religions. Magic can be black (having to do with demons) or white (having to do with friendly powers). The basic principle of imitative magic is that like produces like; contact magic maintains that objects once in contact are always so. In the latter case, possession of a part of another's body which may constitute a "charm" may be used to affect the other's body.

Among Taoists, "magic grannies" have obtained power to cure disease from demons, while geomancers interpret "wind and water." Buddhist monks invoke "dragon-kings." Some Jews have a magical dependence on the Law, while certain Christians expect wonders of the sacraments.

Magic has become increasingly visible in today's technological world. Its growth is closely associated with four major developments.

First, magic is linked with the upsurge of cults and new religions, especially those of the 1960s and 1970s in the USA, Canada, Japan, and Europe. Recent scholarship shows, however, that new religions are neither new nor religious. Their magical aspects involve healing, ritual, language, and *darshan* (sight for the purpose of imbibing the deity's or guru's divine power).

Second, the growth of magic is tenuously linked with the worldwide neopentecostal movement or the charismatic renewal dating back to the late 1950s.

Third, magic plays an important role in the shift from cult groups to individual quests and the associated phenomenon of trance channelers, especially in present-day Sweden and the USA. Eastern and Western myths are manipulated in order to bring about personality and life-style changes. Recalling Helena Blavatsky and mediums, as well as shamans before her, the trance channeler claims to be possessed by an ancient spirit whose behavior and voice are imitated in histrionic fashion. One trance channeler claimed to have infused magical power into her horses which were then sold at exorbitant prices.

Fourth, magic remains closely associated with the occult generally. Horoscopes, tarot card reading, astral travel, and other phenomena, including altered states of consciousness and the power associated with these states, continue their venerable tradition into the present. Now, however, the star occult figure is no longer Helena Blavatsky but Shirley MacLaine.

In the meantime, scholarly opinion about the nature of magic and the difference between magic and religion remains divided. In general, however, later 20th-century anthropologists continue to look to Malinowski when they approach magic from the angle of its social and psychological functions, and to Evans-Pritchard when they approach it from the angle of culture and the symbolic dimension of human behavior.

Given this diversity of views, it is suggested that we refrain from hard and fast definition of magic. Instead, magic is understood in terms of the characteristics imputed to it. Such a list of magic-making characteristics would include the following adjectives: impersonal, mechanical, automatic, compulsive, coercive, manipulative, practical, efficient, palpable, quick, and this-worldly. Thus the magic of different cults may be described in terms of various sets of adjectives. In Japanese cults, such as Mahikari and Soka Gakkai, magic is quick, pragmatic, and this-worldly. "Miracles," the consequences of cult magic, are seen to take place in the form of concrete, visible experiences. These experiences include healing, improved status, or increased wealth which signal the efficacy of magic.

Contrary to Max Weber and Bryan Wilson, the modern world is decidedly not "disenchanted," but is experiencing "reenchantment." The increased use that man makes of his symbolizing capacity and sense of the sacred has given modernization theory an ironic twist, because that with which modern man is "disenchanted" is science, biomedicine, and professional specialization; that with which he is "reenchanted" is supernatural technique, divine healing, and eclectic pluralization, specifically, in the field of medicine. It is people's particularistic conception of salvation that accounts for this thaumaturgical response in the modern world.

Given the definition of magic in terms of magic-making characteristics, we can better understand its association with the concerns of the urban middle class for health, wealth, and self-actualization. The magic of new religions and of some aspects of the neopentecostal movement does not only ritualize optimism and raise self-esteem, but also treats anxiety, depression, social and psychological dislocation, and maladjustment, as well as the more severe conditions of poverty, hysteria, and failure among the traditional poor or upwardly mobile lower middle classes of the third world. To the wealthy it promises eternity, peak experiences, self-actualization, divine identity, the God within, infinite possibilities, and the assurance that the soul lives forever and evermore improves.

Regarding wealth, one either has it, in which case one worries about the accumulation of time as in the Americanized version of reincarnation, or one does not have it in which case one listens to Kenneth Hagin's or Oral Roberts' prosperity gospel. The latter is also known as the "name it, claim it" doctrine. Not only American evangelists of past revivals and the present renewal, but also Japan's Soka Gakkai and India's Rajneeshies, to name but two exported new religions, promise or assume the possession of secular benefits. Josei Toda, head of the Soka Gakkai in the 1950s, likened the sacred tablets (known as *Daigohonzon*) to a machine which produces happiness, large companies, and wealth—all very concrete, this-worldly benefits. It might be noted, although the point is not developed here, that magical results of the prosperity gospel depend on the effectiveness with which "magicians" can hint at covert causalities thus turning metaphors into signs of invisible powers.

Finally, magical characteristics have also found their way into quasi-religious corporations, especially direct sales companies. Like the prosperity gospel of evangelists, these corporations rely on word magic in their testimonies, songs, and prayers. It is a way of infusing the charisma of company leaders into the grass-roots sales forces, just as evangelists or cult leaders infuse their respective charisma into oil clothes, pieces of paper, holy water, and so on which, when touched, heal diseases.

**Bibliography.** B. R. Wilson, *Magic and the Millennium* (1973); W. Davis, *Dojo: Magic and Exorcism in Modern Japan* (1980); E Ohnuki-Tierney, *Illness and Culture in Contemporary Japan* (1984); I. Hexham and K. Poewe, *Understanding Cults and New Religions* (1986).

JOHN CLARK ARCHER AND KARLA POEWE

**Maier, Walter Arthur** (1893–1950). Evangelical scholar and preacher. Born in Boston, he studied at Concordia Collegiate Institute, Bronxville, N.Y., Boston University, Concordia Seminary, St. Louis, Mo., and Harvard (Ph.D., 1929). After two years as executive secretary of the International Walther League (1920–22) he became professor of Semitic languages and OT interpretation at Concordia Seminary (1922–50). He was editor of the *Walther League Messenger* (1920–45); did relief work among German war prisoners (1917–19); was camp pastor at Camp Gordon, Atlanta, Ga. (1918); and served as a technical advisor in the education and religious affairs branch to the military government in Germany (1947). He was best known, however, for his radio preaching which he began as the regular preacher on the Lutheran Hour on the Columbia System (1930/31) and continued on the Mutual Network (1935–50). His messages were christocentric and strongly evangelical. He wrote *The Lutheran Hour* (1931), *For Better, Not for Worse* (1935; 3d ed., 1939), *Christ for Every Crisis* (1935), *Christ for the Nation* (1936), *Winged Words for Christ* (1937), *The Cross from Coast to Coast, The Radio for Christ, Peace Through Christ* (1940), *Courage in Christ* (1941), *For Christ and Country* (1942), *Victory Through Christ* (1943), *America, Turn to Christ* (1944), *Christ, Set the World Aright* (1945), *Jesus Christ, Our Hope* (1946), *Rebuilding with Christ* (1946), *Let Us Return unto the Lord* (1947), *He Will Abundantly Pardon* (1948), *The Airwaves Proclaim Christ* (1948), *1000 Radio Voices for Christ* (1949), and a devotional calendar, *Day by Day with Jesus* (1939–49).

RAYMOND W. ALBRIGHT

**Makarios III** (1913–1977). Archbishop and first president of the Republic of Cyprus. Born Michael Mouskos near Paphos, Cyprus, he entered the monastic life at 13 years of age, graduated from the University of Athens in 1942, and was ordained priest in 1946. He pursued postgraduate studies at Boston University, but was summoned home in 1948 on election as bishop of Kition, and succeeded to the archbishopric of the autocephalous church three years later. Suspected of collaborating with guerrilla forces during the preindependence years, he was exiled to the Seychelles by the British. He later resided in Athens, but returned after participating in a 1959 agreement that gave Cyprus independence, whereupon he became head of state. He had to cope with the island's Turkish Muslim minority, with extremists who wanted union with Greece, and with opposition from clergy and laity within his own church who criticized his dual role. He acted ruthlessly against each group of enemies, and narrowly escaped with his life in 1974 when a short-lived coup removed him briefly from leadership; the invasion of the island by Turkish forces annexed some 37 percent of the area. Makarios was never able thereafter to regain full control of the situation. The Turkish intervention effectively partitioned Cyprus, and through the 1980s there was as yet no prospect of reunion. With the death of the archbishop-president Makarios there closed a chapter of Byzantine history that had somehow lingered into the 20th century.

J. D. DOUGLAS

**Malagasy Republic.** *See* MADAGASCAR.

**Malawi.** *See* SOUTHERN AFRICA.

**Malaysia.** *See* SOUTHEAST ASIA.

**Mali.** *See* WEST AFRICA.

**Malines Conversations.** Historic series of semiofficial discussions between Anglican and Roman Catholic leaders. On the basis of the Appeal to All Christian People of the Lambeth Conference of 1920, the Anglo-Catholic leader Lord Halifax proposed to Cardinal Mercier of Malines (Mechlin) discussions to explore the possibility of Anglican-Roman reunion. With the informal approval of the pope and the archbishop of Canterbury, four conversations were held at Malines in 1921–25; at the first two there were three, at the third and fourth, five on each side. The fourth conversation approached the crucial question of papal supremacy both theologically and canonically; significant contributions were Bishop Gore's paper "On Unity with Diversity," and one presented by the cardinal, written at his request by a Belgian canonist, "L'église anglicane unie, non absorbie." Fundamental differences as well as possible hopes of understanding had been explored when Mercier's death put an end to the series. A fifth conversation was held in 1926 merely to draw up a report. In 1928 the papal encyclical *Mortalium animos* seemed to forbid such discussions, and general Anglican opinion was that no more could be done at present. The conversations record the Anglican determination not to exclude "the great Latin Church of the West" (Lambeth 1908, 1920) from hopes for reunion, and demonstrate the extent to which an irenic approach from the Roman Catholic side was possible.

**Bibliography.** Lord Halifax, *The Conversations at Malines* (1930); J. G. Lockhart, *Charles Lindley, Viscount Halifax* (1936); G. K. A. Bell, *Christian Unity, the Anglican Position* (1948).

EDWARD R. HARDY

**Malta.** A strategic central Mediterranean island south of Sicily, the largest of an archipelago of five, of which only Malta and Gozo are inhabited. The country has a total area of 316 sq. km. (122 sq. mi.) and a population of 20,100 (1983 est.). It was the site of Paul's shipwreck and three-month stay that resulted in the conversion of some of the inhabitants (Acts 27–28). During 1530–1798 the islands were held by the Knights of St. John. Early in their rule they successfully withstood an attempted invasion by the Turkish sultan. From 1814 to 1964 Malta was a British possession, enjoying internal self-government almost continously from 1921. Today it is an independent republic within the British Commonwealth, pursuing a nonaligned foreign policy. Of the estimated 350,000 Maltese, all but about 9000 are Roman Catholic, the official religion according to the constitution, headed by an archbishop of Malta and, since 1864, a bishop of Gozo.

The Methodists opened a church on Malta in 1824; the Anglicans built a cathedral in the capital of Valletta after a royal visit in 1838/39; and the Church of Scotland established a congregation in 1843. The Protestant churches followed a policy of nonproselytization, although in the 19th century Malta was an important center of publication and translation for missionaries working toward the Near East. Today the Anglican Church is part of the diocese of Gibraltar in Europe, and the Church of Scotland and the Methodists worship together in Valletta, meeting the pastoral needs of non-Roman Catholic residents and tourists.

**Bibliography.** *History of the British & Foreign Bible Society,* 3 vols. (1904–10); B. Bluet, *The Story of Malta* (1967).

COLIN A. WESTMARLAND

# Malvern Conference.

Conference held in Malvern, Worcestershire, England, in January 1941, organized by William Temple, archbishop of York, and the Industrial Christian Fellowship. Some 200 English Anglican leaders met to discuss the bearing of faith on social order and post-war reconstruction. The findings of the three-day session were necessarily general; public attention was perhaps unduly attracted by the one disputed resolution which asserted that private ownership of essential resources might be an obstacle to human welfare. The conference "re-published the Christian principles in relation to the world of today" and at a critical moment directed attention to Anglican social concern. Its chief value perhaps was the widespread backing it evidenced for the demand, on Christian principle, that the common life of man be ordered for the common good, and for the expression of this in concrete policies such as Temple vigorously propounded in the speeches and writings of his last years.

**Bibliography.** *The Life of the Church and the Order of Society* (1941); *Malvern* (1941); M. B. Reckitt, *From Maurice to Temple* (1947); F. A. Iremonger, *William Temple* (1948).

EDWARD R. HARDY

# Man, Doctrine of.

While Scripture presents no formal anthropology and Reformed theology has always been reticent in developing formulated doctrines of man, the true knowledge of God will bring us to a true knowledge of ourselves. As Calvin writes, "Again, it is certain that man never achieves a clear knowledge of himself unless he has first looked upon God's face, and then descends from contemplating him to scrutinize himself" (*Institutes* 1.1.2). So it is man from the divine viewpoint, especially as the subject of redemption, who is to be considered. A doctrine of man must move along a line parallel to the movement of divine grace, for man is a being made to know God.

***Imago Dei.*** The important and mysterious words in the Genesis account of man's creation are "image" and "likeness." The *imago Dei* provides intimations of the creatureship of man and the creatorship of God. Man was created with such powers and possibilities and held such a place in the universe that the eternal Son of God could become man and, within the conditions of human life, reveal the glory of the Father. The "image of God" was not lost, although seriously damaged, by man's fall into sin. The image of God is not moral perfection but the possibility of achieving it. It bespeaks the divine purpose and is descriptive of man's nature rather than his character. Man is created in God's image as an intelligent, moral, and free personality. Whatever deadly disorder may come, man remains personal, responsible, and moral. The image of God allows for his redemption and regeneration; by the same token, death and alienation from God are possible.

***Freedom.*** Because man is morally free, he is responsible for his sin. God has infinite mercy for the sinner while condemning his sin. Human sin is not a general calamity which incites divine pity but a crime which deserves divine judgment. The gospel assumes that men have sinned and, although some are worse than others, all need the forgiveness of God. This assumption predicates human responsibility. Man is free in the sphere of all those forces, visible and invisible, which belong to the natural order; indeed, man is free in the presence of God himself. Man can stand in stiff-necked rebellion against the divine intention; he can refuse to submit to God's authority; he can reject God's grace; he can choose to avert the mercy of God; and he can adamantly stand upon his decision against God. For by man's freedom man is man and by this also there are both glory and tragedy in the human destiny.

***Unity.*** Because man belongs to the human race, he is implicated in its achievements and failures. In the OT, this sense of participation in the fortunes of the race became so strong that some lost the sense of individual responsibility. The prophet Ezekiel reminded the people that they must not attribute all their sufferings to the sins of their fathers. But it is also true that we live as members of the human race and share in its sin. Human error and revolt assume a variety of forms, but all have sinned and need redemption.

**Fallen Man.** In the fall man was led to violate the divine will and rebel against God. Each individual human being since has committed acts contrary to the divine Law; each member of the human race possesses a corrupted nature which is the source of actual sin. Fallen man loses his intimacy with God and is heir to depravity, is beset by guilt, and comes under the penalty of death. There is no change in the constitution of man. He still has will and conscience. But his personality is distorted and warped; his knowledge and his will no longer agree; he has lost his delight in God's Law.

Man's fallen state is graphically portrayed in Rom. 5. Our normal sinfulness is connected with Adam's sin; by that connection we inherit condemnation even before we act. For "sin entered the world through one man" (v. 12). For centuries the theologians of the church have discussed this mystery. This mystery cannot be stated in words without contradiction yet is actually experienced. By revelation and conscience we know our responsibility yet we are helpless to carry it out. Thus bereft of self-assurance we turn to the mercy of God and his grace in Jesus Christ.

**The Body.** Man naturally attributes sin to the original constitution of his nature. This makes the body antagonistic to the soul, a prison house in which the ethereal spirit is confined. But according to both Hebrew and Christian thought, both soul and body are necessary and constituent elements of man. God formed man's body and this body is not necessarily and in itself antagonistic to righteousness. The Word—the Son of God— became flesh and dwelt among us; his body was as real as ours and was the instrument by which he demonstrated perfect love for men and perfect obedience to the Father. Moreover, Christ healed sick bodies, mended the broken, and made the incapacitated whole. His church has continued his ministry. The body in the Christian conception is to be a holy sacrifice and a temple of the Holy Spirit. In the life beyond death, after the resurrection, the body will be glorified and redeemed.

**Restoration.** The doctrine of man's restoration falls properly under the work of the Son and Spirit. The individual, from the viewpoint of God, is newly created or regenerated. That individual has in obedience and faith come to Christ. Subjectively, he has undergone a "change of mind" which converts his alienation to faith and love. By the indwelling of the Spirit, man is led to repentance and faith in Christ. By the Spirit, he is united to Christ and receives the blessings of the new covenant.

Man's justification under the divine and perfect Law is through the merits of Christ alone. The theme of the Book of Romans is that believing sinners, by the propitiation of Christ's sacrificial death, fulfill the Law. Man's personal obedience always falls short and man's case, on its own merits, is hopeless. His need is met only and completely by the sacrifice of Christ appropriated by faith. So faith, which is composed of knowledge, commitment, and trust, is the essence of the "good work" which the Spirit begins in man. This faith, which is both God's gift and man's decision, results in obedience and earnest striving after a holy life. This faith is a personal reliance upon Christ as Savior and Lord.

The traditional term for the continuing salutary work of God within man is sanctification. This is the process by which man is transfigured into the fulfillment of God's will and design. The means is still faith. The indwelling of Christ, the indispensable union, is secured by faith; this is not something we achieve through hard work and self-discipline but comes by reverent reliance on God. So man is bound to Christ, the Second Man; so man is personally united to God and from God man derives all grace and virtue. Still the human regenerate will is not passive or absorbed. The will has its work to do, in meditation and prayer, in self-examination and confession, in study of truth and attendance upon conscience.

Thus man restored is man as he should be. He is a child of God, a brother of Christ, the residence of the Spirit of God. His performance is in the sphere of service and duty, in high or humble paths. He no longer lives to himself but whether he lives or dies, it is "to the Lord."

The preaching of the Word is the most critical moment in human life. By it, the Bible speaks, not to interpret human experience or to catalog religious emotions but to give testimony to the eternal Word. As man hears this Word, he is immediately aware of the qualitative difference between this Book and any other. Any other book is the projection of the human mind but this Word of judgment and grace is the projection of God. God's Word descends upon man with crushing, demanding power. It strips him of his imagined worth; it tears away his pretenses to dignity and leaves him in a position where he must assent to the call of God. It rings like God's voice as he called to man in the garden, "Where are you?" The history of humanity is one of a continuous effort to avoid God. Even our religion may be a God-escaping mechanism.

The incarnation, climaxed in the cross and the resurrection, is the act of God by which he entered our perverted order and performed the saving work by which we are reconciled to God. By the Christian *metanoia*, that transformation of the believer by the renewing of his mind, he knows that he has not chosen Christ but that Christ has chosen him. All theological activity must conform to this "descent" of grace; any other protestation is the assertion of self-will. It is by the Word, the lively Image of God, that we may truly know God and it is by this knowledge that we may be what God meant us to be, man in the image of God.

*Bibliography.* J. Laidlaw, *The Bible Doctrine of Man* (1905); H. W. Robinson, *The Christian Doctrine of Man* (1926); J. G. Machen, *The Christian View of Man* (1937); E. Brunner, *Man in Revolt* (1939); R. Niebuhr, *The Nature and Destiny of Man* (1941); J. Orr, *The Christian View of God and the World* (1947); D. M. Baillie, *God Was in Christ* (1948); C. R. Smith, *The Biblical Doctrine of Man* (1951); K. Barth, *Church Dogmatics* (1951); D. Cairns, *The Image of God in Man* (1953); J. Murray, *The Imputation of Adam's Sin* (1959); G. Wingren, *Man and the Incarnation* (1959); G. C. Berkouwer, *The Image of God* (1962); K. Rahner, *Man in the Church* (1963); R. P. Shedd, *Man in Community* (1964); W. Pannenberg, *What Is Man?* (1970); R. Jewett, *Paul's Use of Anthropological Terms* (1971); J. Moltmann, *Man* (1971); P. K. Jewett, *Man as Male and Female* (1975); G. L. Carey, *I Believe in Man* (1977); H. D. McDonald, *The Christian View of Man* (1981).

EUGENE LIGGITT

**Manicheism.** Religion of Manes (or Mani) which arose in Sassanid Babylonia in the early 3d century A.D. as a gnostic sect, and, if one includes the Paulicians, Bogomils, Paparenes, Catharists, and Albigensians as derivatives, not ending before the 17th century. The movement had spread before mid-4th century as far west as Carthage in North Africa, and by the 7th century as far east as Beijing in China. From the beginning it was most successful in Central Asia. It retained a large following in the East until the 13th-century Mongolian invasion of Asia.

*Sources.* Information about Manicheism can be found in fragments of Mani's own writings; writings by Mani's followers (particularly 4th-century papyri found in 1930 in El Faiyum, Egypt, containing a Coptic translation of Mani's writings and those of his early disciples); and writings about Manicheism by others (especially Augustine, who was himself a member of a North African Manichean community [A.D. 376–384], and the Arab author al-Nadim [*Kitab al-Fihrist*, A.D. 988]).

*Mani.* According to al-Nadim, Mani's parents were members of the Mughtasilah cult. "Those who wash themselves" observed ablution as a rite and washed everything they ate. Mani's father had been ordered to join this cult when his wife was pregnant with Mani, and their child was reared in accordance with the cult's teachings.

At the age of 12 the precocious child received revelatory instructions to leave the cult because he was not one of its adherents: "Upon thee are laid purity and refraining from bodily lusts, but it is not yet time for thee to appear openly, because of thy tender years." This message was brought to Mani by the angel Tawm. (Tawm is either a Nabatean word meaning "companion" or more likely a rendering of the Syriac *tuma* ["twin"]. It could also be the Arabic *taw'am*, for the Cologne Greek Codex uses the technical religious term

*syzygy*, with the further metaphorical explanation of *katoptron* ["mirror" or "mirror-image"], to describe not merely the revelatory agent, but the intimate role "she" played in Mani's own self-understanding and development.)

A second revelation, the signal for Mani to begin preaching the gospel of truth, was again brought by Tawm when Mani was 24 years of age. Tawn assured Mani that his time had come and that the Lord had chosen him for this mission. Mani began his ministry on the day of the coronation of Shapur I in A.D. 241.

Mani's missionary efforts, including their geographical dimensions and results, are well chronicled. Al-Nadim claims that Mani traveled 40 years before meeting Shapur, but this cannot be correct because Shapur's reign was not that long. Mani was initially received favorably, but eventually offended the Zoroastrian priests of Belapat and was imprisoned. According to the *Manichaean Homilies*, Mani died in Bahram's prison at the 11th hour on March 2, 276, having designated as his successors 12 "apostle-teachers" and 72 "bishops."

*Teachings.* Manicheism is based on the concept of eternal dualism between two principles, Light (Good) and Darkness (Evil). The powers of Darkness eventually became aware of the desirability of the Light. The demons of Darkness stole parts of the Light from the princes of Light and built the earth and its occupants, both animate and inanimate. While man was thus part of the realm of Darkness, he also had particles of the Light. Man was given a divine message to free the imprisoned Light within him and thus be restored to the realm of Light. Religious teachers such as Buddha, Zoroaster, and Jesus have brought messages of Light, revealing to man his true nature and role in the cosmic process. Mani, however, is the greatest prophet and teacher.

Mani distinguished between the Elect and the Hearers. The Elect were those who could "subdue lust and covetousness, refrain from eating meats, drinking wine, as well as from marriage, and [could] also avoid injury to water, fire, trees, and living things." The Hearers, who were unable to do all these things and yet loved the religion, were called upon to "guard the religion and the Elect," and to offset unworthy actions by devotion "to work and righteousness, nighttime prayer, intercession, and pious humility."

*The Study of Manicheism.* The history of the study of Manicheism began immediately, although the earliest scholars were hardly sympathetic. The movement was immediately perceived as another heresy. Because of the tenor of Christian thought at this time, Manicheism was usually attacked with *ad hominem* denigrations rather than presented with genuine *ad doctrinam* analyses. Nevertheless, actual physical attacks upon Manichees, after those which included the death of Mani and some associates at Sassanian hands, were initiated under the Roman emperors beginning with Diocletian—well before the Christianization of the empire and its legalized opposition to other religions.

Eusebius gives the earliest account of the sect. But it was the *Acta Archelai*, associated with Hegemonios, that became the principal source for all later Greek and Latin works on Manicheism. It presents a dialog between Archelaus, bishop of Qarqar in Mesopotamia, and Mani himself. Early in the 4th century, Alexander of Lykopolis wrote a rather neutral account of Manicheism in Greek.

Another phase in the history of the study of Manicheism is both intended and implied by the developments after the Reformation. Luther, like Augustine before him, had been tagged as a Manichean. Reformed figures like Gottfried Arnold (1699), Isaac de Beausobre (1734), and Johann Lorenz von Mosheim (1739) sought a new view of church history where "true Christianity" originated outside the Catholic Church among the opposition and required an independent, unprejudiced history of heresy. Johann August Wilhelm Neander (1789–1850), Ferdinand Christian Baur (1792–1860), Adolf Hilgenfeld (1823–1907), Richard Adelbart Lipsius (1830–1892), Adolf Harnack (1851–1930), Wilhelm Bousset (1865–1920), Rudolf Bultmann (1884–1976), and our contemporaries Hans Jonas and Kurt Rudolph have continued the pursuit, each reenergized by a new theory or text. As a result, Manicheism has come to be seen within a larger context. Yet all these studies tend to blur the similarities among gnostic grouping and thereby fail to delineate their difference.

*Bibliography.* J. Quasten, *Patrology,* vol. 3 (1960); S. Runciman, *The Medieval Manichee: A Study of the Christian Dualist Heresy* (1960); H. Jonas, *The Gnostic Religion: The Message of the Alien God and the Beginnings of Christianity* (1963); B. Dodge, ed. and trans., *The Fihrist of al-Nadīm* (1970); J. P. Asmussen, *Manichaean Literature* (1975); R. Cameron and A. J. Dewey, trans., *The Cologne Mani Codex* (1979); L. Koenen and C. Römer, eds., *Der Kölner Mani-Kodex* (1985); A. Di Berardino, ed., *Patrology,* vol. 4 (1986); K. Rudolph, *Gnosis: The Nature and History of Gnosticism* (1987); J. Finegan, *Myth and Mystery* (1989).

## Manning, Ernest Charles (1908– ).

Canadian politician, preacher, and broadcaster. Born in Carnduff, Saskatchewan, he was attracted by the preaching and political views of William ("Bible Bill") Aberhart, Baptist preacher and exponent of Social Credit monetary and political views. He was the first student enrolled in Aberhart's Prophetic Bible Institute in Calgary. Following a brief pastoral ministry, he was elected in 1935 to the Alberta legislature where, at the age of 27, he immediately became a member of the cabinet headed by Aberhart. He succeeded Aberhart as premier in 1943 and held that post, without interruption, until he retired in 1968. He resigned from the legislature in 1969 and was appointed to the Senate of Canada in 1970 (retired 1983). Throughout his political life, Manning preached on the "Back to the Bible Broadcast" that was aired weekly on radio across Canada.

LESLIE K. TARR

## Manson, Thomas Walter (1893–1958).

Presbyterian scholar. Born in Tynemouth, Northumberland, he studied at the universities of Glasgow and Cambridge (Westminster College). He was minister at Falstone (1926–32), professor of NT at Mansfield College, Oxford (1932–36), and Rylands professor of biblical criticism and exegesis at the University of Manchester (1936–58). His publications include *The Teaching of Jesus* (1931), *God and the Nations* (1940), *The Church's Ministry* (1948), *The Sayings of Jesus* (1949), *The Beginning of the Gospel* (1950), *The Servant-Messiah* (1953), *Jesus and the Non-Jews* (1955), *Ministry and Priesthood: Christ's and Ours* (1958), *Ethics and the Gospel* (1960), *Studies in the Gospels and the Epistles* (1962), and *On Paul and John* (1963). He edited *A Companion to the Bible* (1939) and *The Bible Today* (1955).

*Bibliography.* M. Black, *Proceedings of the British Academy* 44 (1958): 325–27; H. H. Rowley, *Studies in the Gospels and Epistles* (1962).

F. F. BRUCE

## Marchant, James (1867–1956).

Social worker and writer. Born in London, he was minister of Exeter Street Independent Church and of Trinity Presbyterian Church, London (1895–97), clerical secretary of Dr. Barnado's Homes (1903–6), secretary of the National Birthrate Commission (1913–34), and editor of its reports (1916–20), of the venereal disease report (1921), and of birth control reports (1922–27). He was chairman of Visual Education Ltd., and director of Stoll Picture Productions Ltd. He wrote *Life of Dr. Paton* (1909), *Memoirs of Dr. Barnado* (1907), and *Life and Letters of John Clifford* (1924).

EDWIN O. JAMES

## Marcus, Jacob Rader (1896– ).

American rabbi and historian. Born in Connellsville, Pa., he studied at Lane Theological Seminary, the University of Chicago, the University of Cincinnati, Hebrew Union College, various European academies, and the University of Berlin (Ph.D., 1925). Following U.S. army service overseas, he began his distinguished teaching career as professor of Jewish history at Hebrew Union College in 1920. He established American Jewish history as an academic discipline through his own prolific writings, and by founding (and continuing to direct) the American Jewish Archives (1947) and the American Jewish Periodical Center (1956). He served as president and honorary president of both the Central Conference of American Rabbis and the American Jewish Historical Society. He has received five honorary doctorates and the Frank L. Weil Award for his contribution to American Jewish culture. His many writings include *The Rise and Destiny of the German Jew* (1934), *The Jew in the Medieval World* (1938), *Communal Sick-Care in the German Ghetto* (1947), *Early American Jewry* (2 vols., 1951–53), *Studies in American Jewish History* (1969), *The Colonial American Jew* (3 vols., 1970), *Critical Studies in American Jewish History* (3 vols., 1971), and *The American Jewish Woman, 1654–1980* (2 vols., 1981).

GLEN G. SCORGIE

**Mariavites.** Group founded in 1893 as a result of the visions and revelations received by a Clarissa nun, Felicia Kozlowska (1862–1922). Her clerical followers began a reform movement for which the life of the virgin (*Mariae vita*, hence the name) was to furnish the pattern. The Mariavites were particularly concerned with lay membership. The Curia refused to grant approval to the movement, and in 1906 excommunicated both Kozlowska and the chief clerical leader, Kowalski. In 1909 the Mariavites joined the Old Catholics. Kowalski was consecrated as the first bishop of the group.

MATTHEW SPINKA

**Maritain, Jacques** (1882–1973). French Roman Catholic philosopher and leading figure in Neo-Thomism, the movement which seeks to present the thought of Thomas Aquinas in a form relevant to the 20th century. Born in Paris, he studied at the Sorbonne and Heidelberg. Drawn away from scientism by the lectures of Henri Bergson, he was converted to Roman Catholicism in 1906. He was professor of philosophy and modern history at the Institut Catholique, Paris (1914–39), professor at the Pontifical Institute for Mediaeval Studies, Toronto (1940–44), and professor of philosophy at Princeton University (1948–73). His foundational contribution to philosophy was in the field of epistemology, where he stressed the priority of intuitive reason. He also used Thomistic insights widely in his writings on morals, art, history, and politics. In his retirement years he returned to France. He wrote over 60 books, some co-authored by his wife, Raïssa Oumansoff. His works include *The Philosophy of Art* (1923), *An Introduction to Philosophy* (1930), *The Degrees of Knowledge* (1937), *Redeeming the Time* (1943), and *Moral Philosophy: An Historical and Critical Survey of the Great Systems* (1964). He surveyed his own views in *The Peasant of the Garonne: An Old Layman Questions Himself about the Present Time* (1968).

PETER HICKS

**Mark, Gospel of.** *See* GOSPEL AND GOSPELS.

**Marks of the Church.** External attributes of the Christian church. Roman Catholic theology identifies the marks of the church as unity, holiness, catholicity, and apostolicity. Roman Catholic theologians interpret the unity of the church in the sense that the church is actually one visible society, whose members profess the same belief, partake of the same sacraments, and submit to the one supreme authority of the pope. In contrast, Protestants understand the unity of the church to be the spiritual communion of all who put their trust in Christ, irrespective of denominational allegiance. The Roman Catholic Church claims to be manifestly privileged with the fullness of the means of sanctification by which Christians may achieve holiness. Catholicity, the universality of the church through time and space, is also alleged to belong exclusively to the Roman Communion. While Protestants understand the apostolicity of the church as the fact that Christians strive to live according to the principles and doctrines which the apostles professed, Roman Catholics maintain that apostolicity is the dogmatic and constitutional guarantee found in the apostolic origin and uninterrupted succession of its hierarchy. The pope and the bishops under this authority are, in fact, regarded as the only lawful successors of St. Peter and the apostles.

The Roman Catholic Church distinguishes between the marks of the church and the notes of the church. The notes of the church are: authority (the church has the exclusive right to teach and govern the faith); infallibility (the church cannot err in matters of faith or morals); and indefectability (the church will endure until the end of time).

In contradistinction to Roman Catholic thought, Protestants identify the marks of the church as the preaching of the pure doctrine of the gospel; the rightful administration of the sacraments; and the proper administration of church discipline (*Belgic Confession*, art. 29).

*Bibliography.* H. Dieckmann, *De Ecclesia* (1925); E. S. Berry, *The Church of Christ* (1927); *Psalter Hymnal* (1976).

GEORGES A. BARROIS

**Maronites.** Both a political constituent of Lebanon and an integral part of the Roman Catholic Church. In belief and practice, the Maronite Church frequently follows those of the Eastern rite but accepts the primacy of the pope and basically conforms to Catholic orthodoxy. The Maronites are today most prominent in Lebanon, where they constitute about 30 percent of the population (about 500,000) and have, since independence, traditionally held the presidency. Large groups in Cyprus, Egypt, North America, and Israel bring the total membership of the Maronite Church to approximately 1.4 million.

***Origins and Early History.*** The nucleus of what became the Maronite Church formed around a monastery in northern Syria. Tradition and a biography by the Syrian bishop Theodoret trace the monks' devotion to a hermit named Maron, whose death is placed at A.D. 410. A friend and fellow student of John Chrysostom, Maron undertook a life of prayer and reflection, which led to the founding of the monastery in his memory.

Unlike the so-called monophysite churches (Coptic, Ethiopian, Armenian, and Syrian Orthodox), the Maronites from the 6th century were staunch defenders of the Council of Chalcedon (451) with its doctrine of the dual nature of Christ. Indeed, the monastery became, in the 6th and 7th centuries, the focal point for Chalcedonian missionary activity and religious life. Building on this strength, and in response to a vacuum felt when the Chalcedonian patriarchate of Antioch fell vacant, a Maronite patriarchate was formed—an institution that has remained signally important in church life down to the present. The ongoing relation of the patriarch to Rome has constituted one of the most interesting chapters in Maronite history. Despite ongoing controversy over the subject, some of which can be traced to Western ignorance of the Eastern Church in the years prior to the Crusades, there is evidence that a patriarchate had been established at least by the end of the 7th century (Maronite sources show St. John Maron to have been elected in 685), and that the patriarchate was, from the beginning, at least tacitly approved by Rome. There is no evidence of Rome's disapproval, which surely would have been forthcoming in light of Maronite claims for their bishop with regard to the important see of Antioch.

Even before the rise of Islam in the 8th century, Maronites were coming under increasing pressure from Melchites and Monophysites, from which refuge was eventually sought in the inaccessible mountain fortresses of Lebanon. Such remoteness, by itself, abetted their practical separation from Rome; the spread of Islam throughout the old Christian lands ensured that Maronite isolation would be entrenched until the Crusades.

***Separation from Rome: 8th–12th Centuries.*** The second period in Maronite history was dominated by three conditions: (1) the overwhelming tide of Islam that inundated much of the Levant in the 8th and 9th centuries; (2) the increasing isolation of the Maronites in the mountains of Lebanon, and the growing communal allegiance to their patriarch in all spheres of life; and (3) the formal break between the Eastern and Western churches in the 11th century (which actually only served to legitimize what had already practically taken place). It was but a step, aided by fading memories in Rome and a widespread feeling that everything in the East represented "heresy," to arrive at a point where the Maronites, who had never rejected the primacy of Rome, were linked in popular Western opinion with the various dissident groups that were out of fellowship with the Latin Church.

***Reunion with Rome: 12th Century to Modern Times.*** On their way to Jerusalem, the Crusaders traveled along the coast of the Levant. They were greeted as allies by the Maronites. Exactly what followed has been the subject of considerable faulty reporting over the years, but a formal reunion with Rome was accomplished in Tripoli in 1180/81. Whether remnants of heresy needed to be excised or whether there was simply increasing pressure from Rome to conform to things Latin, the so-called return was not without its problems. Tensions remained at least until the 16th century, when three national synods (1580, 1596, 1598) were held in response to papal initiative. In the meantime, contact between Rome and Lebanon had suffered with the post-Crusade Muslim conquests. But the renewed papal initiatives, while never successful in fully Latinizing the church, did go a long way toward restoring the Maronites as the primary Catholic force in the Levant. In the final analysis, there remain many compromises, such as celebration of the Lord's supper under both kinds, use of the Syriac liturgy, marriage of at least the lower priests, and retention of their own saints and·fast-days.

From the 16th century on the role of the Maronites as the major Catholic presence in the area grew. In 1584 a Maronite College was established in Rome by Pope Gregory XIII; directed or influenced by Jesuits, the college became a center for various attempts in subsequent centuries to bring about a greater conformity to Latin practices. Significant progress was made toward this goal when, in 1736, the Synod of Mt. Lebanon was held from which eventually issued a complete set of Latin decrees that would become the canon for Maronite life and worship for many years. Three editions would be published between 1736 and 1900, all of which are summarized in George Manaš' *Canon Law of the Maronites* (1925).

Under the Ottomans (1516–1914), the "millet" system enabled the Maronites and other non-Muslim groups to administer their own civil and religious laws. It was during this period that Maronite conflict with the Druzes erupted, prompting French military intervention. This event probably led to the French receiving the mandate for Lebanon after 1914 and cemented close Maronite ties with France.

In modern times Lebanon achieved a state of semi-independence and became something of a Catholic stronghold. The Maronite patriarch of Antioch became a rallying point for various dissident Orthodox groups, some of which formally returned to Catholicism. After World War I

Lebanon was ruled by the French until independence was achieved on August 31, 1946. Since that time the president of Lebanon has been a Maronite. The Maronite patriarch remains one of the most influential figures in the country. Maronites continue to be concentrated in the valley and mountain areas of Lebanon, as well as among the professional and upper-middle classes of Beirut society.

***Contemporary Maronite Life.*** With the expulsion of the Palestinians from Israel (1948, 1967) and Jordan and their settlement in Lebanon, the once-fragile but workable compromise has been severely strained. A resurgent Islam, with support from the main body of Palestinian refugees, has called into question Maronite control in Lebanon and has led to increased emigration to the West, particularly to the USA. Large colonies of Maronites are established in cities like New York, Boston, Philadelphia, and Pittsburgh, and throughout the Eastern states. A seminary opened in Washington in 1961 under the auspices of the Roman Catholic archbishop Patrick O'Boyle, and as of 1966 a Maronite was appointed as suffragan to the metropolitan of Detroit. The challenge of the future is thus twofold: Can the old center for Maronite life maintain its position and vitality in the face of increasing pressures in Lebanon? Will the newer centers of Maronite life, particularly in the USA, be able to maintain their rich ethnic and cultural Catholicism in the face of mounting pressures to assimilate?

***Bibliography.*** G. Dandini, *Missione apostolica al patriarca dei Maroniti del Monte Libano* (1656); P. Abraham, *The Maronites of Lebanon* (1931); P. Dib, *Histoire de l'Eglise maronite* (vol. 1, 1962); G. Zananiri, *Catholicism oriental* (1966); E. El-Hayak, *New Catholic Encyclopedia* (vol. 9, 1967); T. Sable, *Encyclopedia of Religion* (vol. 15, 1987).

CARL E. ARMERDING

## Marriage.

Union between a man and woman which is socially recognized and approved and by nature is lifelong and exclusive. Marriage is a fundamental institution in all human societies and the foundation of the family. Sexual activity is the basic expression of marriage, leading to offspring and completion of the full family unit (father, mother, and children). The family provides the fellowship and affection that human nature needs and also the nurture and protection which children require.

All societies have rules regulating who may marry and for the most part celebrate marriage with a public rite or ceremony, frequently at which the guests are witnesses. Marriage law in Western countries is based on Roman law. It is monogamous and the essential requirement is free consent between the parties. In Roman law, divorce was easy, granted by the simple withdrawal of consent by either partner. The church maintained within its own fellowship the Chris-

tian ideal of marriage in which divorce had no place. Clandestine marriage with full consent was recognized by the Western Church as true marriage but was strongly discouraged because of the possibility of abuse. In most Western countries it was eventually declared illegal. Canon law did not regard consummation as essential to constitute marriage but in its absence a marriage could be nullified.

The Bible's teaching on marriage is consistent. In Genesis two principles are clear. First, marriage is for the purpose of fellowship and companionship: "The LORD God said, 'It is not good for the man to be alone. I will make a helper suitable for him'"; "For this reason a man will leave his father and mother and be united to his wife, and they will become one flesh" (Gen. 2:18, 24; cf. Matt. 19:4–6). The implication is that marriage is to be lifelong and monogamous. Second, marriage is for the procreating of children (Gen. 1:28). Parents have the obligation to provide not only for their children's physical sustenance but also for their spiritual growth (Deut. 6:7; Ps. 78:5–6). The NT confirms this OT obligation: children are to be brought up in the training and instruction of the Lord (Eph. 6:4).

Marriage between one man and one woman provides the deepest possible human fellowship. Within the Godhead is fellowship (John 1:18), for "the Father loves the Son and shows him all he does" (John 5:20); the Son loves the Father (John 14:31) and always does what pleases him (John 8:29). Gen. 1:26 suggests that fellowship between men and women is part of being the image of God. In the Bible the relationship between God and his people is described in terms of human marriage and the duties of husband and wife are drawn from the character of God expressed in his relationship with his people.

The basic character of God may be described as absolute "other-person-centeredness." Man, the image of God, is to reflect this basic characteristic of other-person-centeredness. The body is to be used to serve God by serving other people (Rom. 12:1). This basic principle finds its fullest expression in marriage. The body is not to be used selfcenteredly. The wife's body belongs, not to her alone, but also to her husband. "In the same way, the husband's body does not belong to him alone but also to his wife" (1 Cor. 7:4).

In the Bible the sexes are equal in the sight of God and in the community of God's people (1 Cor. 11:11; Gal. 3:28; 1 Pet. 3:7), yet there is an order in the relationship of the sexes corresponding to the order within the Trinity (1 Cor. 11:3). The headship of man in regard to his wife is an image of the headship of God toward his people (1 Cor. 11:3; Eph. 5:22), that of initiating, self-sacrificial, loving service (Eph. 5:25). The response of the wife is like that of the Son to the Father or of the church to the Savior (Eph. 5:24). This relationship of the love of service and the love of response is not appreciated in the world.

Asceticism is never advocated in the Bible. The tendency of human nature to regard sexual activity in marriage as inherently shameful is explicitly contradicted (1 Tim. 4:1–3; Heb. 13:4). Marriage, however, is never an obligation. The unmarried state is honorable (1 Cor. 7:1). Abstinence from marriage may be the right choice, depending on the circumstances and nature of the individual (Matt. 19:11–12; 1 Cor. 7:26). Marriage, or abstinence from marriage, must be for the Lord's sake and for his kingdom (1 Cor. 7:39; 2 Cor. 6:14). Practical considerations in Paul's day suggested that remaining unmarried was advantageous. However, he made it clear that this was his personal advice (1 Cor. 7:25–26), not part of the divine instruction of which his letters to the churches normally consisted (1 Cor. 14:37).

In the OT polygamy was practiced widely among the nations and was often present in Israel. It was neither commanded nor condemned. God is said to have given David the wives of his conquered enemies (2 Sam. 12:8), indicating his complete succession to the throne. In the NT Christian ministers are not to have more than one wife (1 Tim. 3:2).

Remarriage after the death of a spouse is fully permitted in Scripture (Rom. 7:2; 1 Cor. 7:39), and is recommended for young widows (1 Tim. 5:14).

*Bibliography.* J. Milton, *The Doctrine and Discipline of Divorce* (1643); O. D. Watkins, *Holy Matrimony* (1895); S. A. Leathley, *The History of Marriage and Divorce* (1916); E. Westermarck, *The History of Human Marriage* (1921); A. T. Macmillan, *What Is Christian Marriage?* (1944); T. A. Lacey, *Marriage in Church and State* (1947); K. E. Kirk, *Marriage and Divorce* (1948); B. Ward Powers, *Marriage and Divorce—The NT Teaching* (1987).

D. BROUGHTON KNOX

## Marshall, Peter (1902–1949).

Presbyterian minister. Born in Coatbridge, Scotland, he was educated at the technical school and mining college there and then served in the Royal Navy. He believed that he was called to the ministry. Finding entry to a regular theological training college barred because of his inadequate entrance qualifications, he went to the USA in 1927. In 1931 he graduated from Columbia Theological Seminary, Decatur, Ga. Ordained that year, he served pastorates in Covington, Ga., and in Atlanta before his unexpected call in 1937 to the pastorate of New York Avenue Presbyterian Church, Washington, D.C. In 1948 he was named chaplain of the U.S. Senate. While in Washington, Marshall gained a widespread reputation as a master of oratory; listeners found his brief prayers especially memorable. Several of his sermons appear in his book, *Mr. Jones, Meet the Master* (1949), and a biography by his wife Catherine, *A Man*

*Called Peter* (1951), formed the basis for a successful film.

ROBERT L. MORRISON

## Mar Thoma Church.

Syrian church in India which traces its origins to the ministry of the apostle Thomas, who is believed to have landed at Cranganore, north of Cochin in Kerala, in A.D. 52 and was martyred at Mylapore (now part of Madras) around A.D. 72. According to the traveler Cosmas Indicopleustes, there were Christians on the Malabar Coast before A.D. 550. Briefly forced to accept papal jurisdiction at the Synod of Diamper (1599), the "Thomas Christians" declared themselves independent of Rome in 1653. Two-thirds soon recanted, but the rest entered into a relationship with the Syrian Church of Antioch. In the early 19th century, contact between Church Missionary Society missionaries and the Syrian Orthodox Church in India prompted Abraham Malpan (1796–1845) and others to press for reforms, including the use of the Bible and an evangelically modified liturgy in the vernacular, Malayalam, rather than in Syriac. After lengthy disputes and protracted litigation over church property the reforming party formed an autonomous body, the first of its kind in India, the present Mar Thoma Church.

Strongest in its native Kerala, the Mar Thoma Church maintains an ecumenical outlook. It reinforced its 1936 intercommunion agreement—a limited but unique accord between an Eastern and a Western church—with the Anglican Church of India, Burma, and Ceylon in 1957 and established principles of intercommunion with the Church of South India (CSI) in 1958. The Mar Thoma Church, with a present membership of about 400,000, has been linked more formally with CSI and the Church of North India (CNI) since 1978 through a joint council. This has set up theological, peace and justice, and mission commissions and issued the Mar Thoma eucharistic liturgy, the Holy Qurbana, and the CSI and CNI orders of the Lord's supper together in a single booklet to help church members become more familiar with each other's traditions. A 1975 proposal that the three churches commit themselves to union in a "Bharat Christian Church" with a combined membership of over 3 million is still under discussion. There have also been unofficial conversations between the Mar Thoma Church and the Syrian Orthodox Church which resulted in a Common Statement (1971) outlining areas of shared doctrine and practice and acknowledging that many of the issues which caused the 19th-century rupture have since been resolved by reforms in both churches.

*Bibliography.* L. W. Brown, *The Indian Christians of St. Thomas* (1956); C. P. Matthew and M. M. Thomas, *The Indian Churches of St. Thomas* (1967); Church History Association of

India, *History of Christianity in India* (2 vols., 1982– ); S. C. Neill, *A History of Christianity in India,* vol. 1 (1984).

PHILIP HILLYER

**Marty, Martin Emil** (1928– ). Lutheran historian. Born in West Point, Nebr., he studied at Concordia Seminary, St. Louis, Chicago Lutheran Theological Seminary, and the University of Chicago (Ph.D., 1956). He was ordained minister in the Lutheran Church (1952), and pastored churches in Washington, D.C. (1950/51), River Forest, Ill. (1952–56), and Elk Grove Village, Ill. (1956–63). Thereafter he was associate professor of the history of modern Christianity at the University of Chicago. He served as president of the American Society of Church History (1971), president of the American Catholic Historical Association (1981), vice-president of the American Academy of Religion (1986), associate editor (1956–85) and senior editor of the *Christian Century,* and coeditor of *Church History.*

His writings include *A Short History of Christianity* (1959), *The New Shape of American Religion* (1959), *Second Chance for American Protestants* (1963), *Varieties of Unbelief* (1964), *The Modern Schism* (1969), *Righteous Empire* (1970), *Protestantism* (1972), *A Nation of Behavers* (1976), *Religion, Awakening and Revolution* (1978), *By Way of Response* (1981), *A Cry of Absence* (1983), *Pilgrims in Their Own Land* (1984), *Protestantism in the United States* (1985), *Modern American Religion,* vol. 1 (1986), and *An Invitation to American Catholic History* (1986). He edited *New Directions in Biblical Thought* (1960), *The Place of Bonhoeffer* (1962), and *Handbook of Christian Theologians* (1965).

H. DOUGLAS BUCKWALTER

**Marxism.** *See* COMMUNISM, MARXIST.

**Mary, the Virgin Mother.** The role of Mary in salvation history is generally problematic in ecumenical dialog. Such dialog, to be fruitful, must not seek to reduce the various faiths to some lowest common denominator but rather, by making Christians confront the sources of their disunity, must ultimately lead to deeper theological reflection. A theology of Mary must first, of course, be grounded in Scripture.

The Evangelist Mark mentions Mary the mother of Jesus only twice in his Gospel (Mark 3:31–35; 6:3). In the opening chapters of Matthew's Gospel, the focus is on Joseph as the descendant of David (Matt. 1:1–17) and as the one chosen to receive God's messages (1:20; 2:13; 2:20, 22). But in Luke's narrative a clearer picture of Mary emerges. It is Mary who, through the annunciation and visit to her cousin Elizabeth (Luke 1:26–56), first receives the announcement of salvation. And by accepting her role as the

"Lord's servant" (1:38) she makes possible the fulfillment of the plan of salvation.

Outside of the infancy narratives Mary appears on only a few occasions in the synoptic Gospels (Matt. 12:46–50; 13:55; Mark 3:31–35, 6:3; Luke 8:19–21). Where she does appear, the focus is always on her responsiveness to the divine call—even when that entails consternation (Luke 1:29), amazement (1:34), marvel (2:33), and lack of understanding (2:50).

John situated the public life of Jesus between two events that directly involved Mary. At the beginning of the public ministry of Jesus his mother is an intercessor at a wedding feast (2:3–5). At Calvary Jesus assigns a new role of motherhood to her (John 19:25–27).

Throughout the Gospels Mary is presented first and foremost as the mother of Jesus. Motherhood is her role in salvation history, a role which she voluntarily accepts. When the time comes for her son's purification, she presents him to the Lord in the temple. There she receives through Simeon the announcement of his mission (Luke 2:29–32) and of her own share in the work of salvation (Luke 2:35). The Gospels of Luke and John clearly identify two separate stages in this mother-son relationship. The first stage involves the motherly nurturance that was needed while Jesus was "obedient" to his parents (Luke 2:51). At the age of 12 years Jesus tells his mother that he must be in his Father's house (Luke 2:49). Finally at Cana a new relationship emerges as he begins his public ministry (John 2:4). When Jesus addresses Mary at Cana as "woman," Mary's maternal role on his behalf ends. At Calvary he again addresses her as "woman" (John 19:26) and then bestows on her a totally new maternal role.

As the Gospels present Mary as the mother of Jesus, they also affirm, in two separate literary traditions, the virginity of Mary (Matt. 1:18–23; Luke 1:26–38). In Matthew's Gospel the account of the conception of Jesus clearly confirms that Jesus was not conceived of a father but of the Holy Spirit (Matt. 1:18–25). Luke's account of the annunciation also affirms the role of the Holy Spirit in attesting to the virginity of Mary.

It is significant that the title "virgin" or "mother" is never attributed to Mary by the Evangelists in a triumphalist manner. On the contrary, her virginity appears as a unique consecration to the Lord, and her motherhood is presented as an ever-faithful response to the divine call. It is perhaps with focus on these aspects that a theology of Mary can most effectively contribute to ecumenical dialog. She is for all the churches a model of the believer. Protestant traditions, as well as both Eastern and Western Catholic traditions, have recognized the role of Mary in its christological context in their professions of faith in God's salvific work in Christ Jesus. And that role finds its basis in Mary's calling as virgin, mother, and faith-filled model of all Christian believers.

*Bibliography.* D. Flanagan, *Irish Theological Quarterly* 40 (1973): 227–49; D. G. Dawe, *One in Christ* 16/1–2 (1980): 126–36; W. J. Hollenweger, *One in Christ* 16/1–2 (1980): 59–68; A. R. Mackenzie, *One in Christ* 16/1–2 (1980): 68–78; K. Borrensen, *Concilium* 168 (Oct. 1983): 48–56; G. Maron, *Concilium* 168 (Oct. 1983): 40–47; J. Moltmann, *Concilium* 168 (Oct. 1983): xii–xv; N. Missiotis, *Concilium* 168 (Oct. 1983): 25–39; M. Ellingsen, *Journal of Ecumenical Studies* 22 (Summer 1985): 683–84.

LIAM K. GRIMLEY

**Mascall, Eric Lionel** (1905– ). Anglican theologian. Educated at the universities of Cambridge and London, he taught mathematics (1928–31) before his ordination in 1932. He ministered in London (1932–37), was subwarden of Scholae Cancellarii, Lincoln (1937–45), lecturer and tutor at Christ Church, Oxford (1945–62), university lecturer in philosophy of religion, Oxford (1947–62), and professor of historical theology, London University (1962–73). Well known as a churchman of the Anglo-Catholic tradition, his publications include *Death or Dogma* (1937), *The God-Man* (1940), *He Who Is* (1943), *Corpus Christi* (1953), *Christian Theology and Natural Science* (1956), *Words and Images* (1957), *The Recovery of Unity* (1958), *Pi in the High* (1959), *Grace and Glory* (1961), *Theology and History* (1962), *The Secularisation of Christianity* (1965), *Growing into Union* (1970), *Whatever Happened to the Human Mind?* (1980), *Jesus* (1985), and *The Triune God* (1986).

**Mason, C. H.** *See* CHURCHES OF GOD.

**Mather, Kirtley F.** (1888–1978). Professor of geology. Born in Chicago, he studied at Denison University, Granville, Ohio, and the University of Chicago (Ph.D., 1915). He taught at the University of Arkansas (1911–14), Queen's University, Kingston, Ontario (1915–18), Denison University (1918–24), and Harvard (associate professor of geology, 1924–27; professor of geology, 1927–54). He was president of the American Association for the Advancement of Science (1951) and the American Academy of Arts and Sciences (1957–61). He was a wide-ranging scholar, tireless field worker, and outstanding teacher. He was also involved in civil liberties campaigns and YMCA work. He sought to demonstrate the harmony of science and progressive Christianity. He assisted defense lawyer Clarence Darrow in the Scopes evolution trial of 1925, and from that experience wrote *Science in Search of God* (1928). His other writings include *Old Mother Earth* (1927), *Sons of the Earth* (1931), *Enough and to Spare* (1944), *Crusade for Life* (1949), *The World in Which We Live* (1961), *The Earth Beneath Us* (1964; rev. ed., 1975), and *Source Book in Geology, 1900–1950*

(1967). He coauthored *A Source Book in Geology* (1939) with S. Mason.

GLEN G. SCORGIE

**Mathews, Basil Joseph** (1879–1951). Methodist scholar. Born in Oxford, England, he studied at Oxford University. He was a member of the literary staff of *Christian World* (1904–10), editorial secretary for the London Missionary Society (1910–19), chairman of the literature committee of the British Ministry of Information (1917/18), director of the press bureau of the Conference of the British Missionary Society (1920–24), international literature secretary of the World's Committee of the YMCA, Geneva (1924–29), professor of Christian world relations at Andover Newton Theological School and Boston University (1931–44), and professor of world relations at Union College, University of British Columbia, Canada (1944–49). Among his more than 40 books are *Livingstone the Pathfinder* (1913), *Paul the Dauntless* (1916), *The Clash of Color* (1924), *Jesus and Youth* (1929), *A Life of Jesus* (1930), *Shaping the Future* (1936), *The Church Takes Root in India* (1938), *The Jew and World Ferment* (1939), *Supreme Encounter* (1940), *Pattern for Living* (1942), and *Booker T. Washington* (1948).

HERBERT GEZORK

**Mathews, Shailer** (1863–1941). Baptist theologian. Born in Portland, Maine, he was educated at Colby University, Newton Theological Institution, and the University of Berlin. He was associate professor of rhetoric (1887–89) and professor of history and political economy (1889–94) at Colby University. He was then associate professor (1894–97) and professor of NT history and interpretation (1897–1904) at the divinity school of the University of Chicago. He was professor of systematic theology (1904–6) and of historical and comparative theology (1904–33) in the same institution and dean of the school (1908–33). He wrote many books, among them *Select Mediaeval Documents* (1891), *The Social Teaching of Jesus* (1897), *A History of NT Times in Palestine* (1899), *The French Revolution* (1901), *The Messianic Hope in the NT* (1905), *The Church and the Changing Order* (1907), *The Social Gospel* (1909), *The Making of Tomorrow* (1913), *The Spiritual Interpretation of History* (1916), *Patriotism and Religion* (1918), *The Validity of American Ideals* (1922), *The Faith of Modernism* (1924), *The Atonement and the Social Process* (1930), *Creative Christianity* (1935), *New Faith for Old—An Autobiography* (1936), *The Church and the Christian* (1938), and *Is God Emeritus?* (1940). He coauthored the *Dictionary of Religion and Ethics* (1921) with G. B. Smith. He edited *The World Today* and the *NT Handbooks* series.

**Matthew, Gospel of.** *See* GOSPEL AND GOSPELS.

**Matthews, Isaac G.** (1871–1959). Baptist scholar. Born in Middleville, Ont., he studied at McMaster University, McMaster Theological Seminary, and the University of Chicago (Ph.D., 1912). He was pastor at Jackson Avenue Baptist Church, Vancouver, B.C. (1898–1900), pastor at New Westminster Baptist Church, B.C. (1900–1903), professor of OT language and literature, McMaster University (1904–19), pastor at First Baptist Church, New Haven, Conn. (1919/20), professor of OT language and literature at Crozer Theological Seminary (1920–42), and was annual professor in the American School of Oriental Research in Jerusalem (1930/31). He wrote *Jewish Apologetic to the Grecian World in the Apocryphal and Pseudepigraphical Literature* (1914), *How to Interpret OT Prophecy* (1919), *OT Life and Literature* (1923; rev. ed., 1934), *Commentary on 1 and 2 Samuel* (1929), *Commentary on Malachi and Haggai* (1935), *Commentary on Ezekiel* (1937), and *The Religious Pilgrimage of Israel* (1947).

**Matthews, Walter Robert** (1881–1973). Dean of St. Paul's, London. Born in London, he was in business for some years before seeking ordination. Even thereafter he continued his studies as a curate and graduated from King's College, London, in 1912. Six years later he became dean of the college (1918–31), transferring to Exeter as dean (1931–34) before taking up a post at St. Paul's (1934–67). His later books include *The Problem of Christ in the 20th Century* (1951), *Some Christian Words* (1956), *The Search for Perfection* (1957), *The Lord's Prayer* (1958), *The Thirty-Nine Articles* (1961), *Memories and Meanings* (1969), and *The Year Through Christian Eyes* (1970).

J. D. Douglas

**Maundy Thursday.** English name for Thursday in Holy Week. The word "Maunday" is a corruption of the Latin word *mandatum*. It refers to the Roman service of footwashing, during which a choir sings the Latin words of John 13:34.

**Mauriac, Francois** (1885–1970). French Roman Catholic writer. Born in Bordeaux and raised by a well-to-do grandmother and a pious mother with Jansenist leanings, he was educated in a rigorous school operated by the Marist Fathers, and studied at the universities of Bordeaux and Paris. In 1909 he launched his career with a small book of verse and thereafter devoted his time to literature. Rejected for war service in 1914, he volunteered for the medical corps. After 1918 he resumed writing. His first successful novel, *A Kiss for the Leper*, appeared in 1922. By the 1930s he was publishing novels, literary criticism, biographies, plays, and articles on numerous topics. During World War II he joined the resistance and wrote anti-Nazi pieces at great personal risk. In the 1950s he opposed French colonialism in Algeria, supported De Gaulle's return to power, and became a target of right-wing extremists. He received the Nobel Prize for literature in 1952. Religious themes and concepts pervade his novels, and nearly all of them in some way grapple with themes of human sin, greed, lust, hatred, and pride. He was clearly a Christian commentator on human foibles, but at the same time a moralist who illustrated both the best and the worst in God's creatures. In the mid-1920s he experienced a religious crisis and decided to cease writing as a Catholic novelist. Instead he would seek to give an indirect apology for Christianity through an objective rendering of the world which would show the danger posed by an absence of Christian devotion. Some observers believed an actual "conversion" had taken place, while others saw it as a "new profundity" in a man who realized he was approaching the autumn of life. His novel *The Viper's Tangle* (1932) had a particularly evident religious thrust, even though other Catholics were critical of his rather unorthodox expressions of piety. He antagonized many clerics by defending "as a Catholic and because I was a Catholic" the Republican cause in the Spanish Civil War. Mauriac was criticized by some for an alleged obsession with evil. In response, he insisted that his characters differed from others in fiction because they had a soul. As he put it, "Any writer who has maintained in the center of his work the human creature made in the image of the Father, redeemed by the Son, illumined by the Spirit, I cannot see in him a master of despair, however somber his painting may be."

RICHARD V. PIERARD

**Mauritania.** *See* WEST AFRICA.

**Mauritius.** Independent island state in the western Indian Ocean off the coast of East Africa. It has an area of 1865 sq. km. (720 sq. mi.) and a population of 1.1 million (1988). A crown colony until independence in 1968, it remains part of the British Commonwealth. Since its discovery in 1511 by the Portuguese, Mauritius was colonized successively by the Dutch and French before the British took control in 1810. English is the official language, but French is still extensively used in legislative and legal matters. Creole is most widely used by the inhabitants. About 46 percent of the population are Hindus (Sanatanist and Arya Samaj), 34 percent are Christians, and 17 percent are Muslims (mostly Sunnis, with a 10 percent Ahmadi minority). The Christian community is overwhelmingly (about 97 percent) Roman Catholic, but there are some 7000 Anglicans, 3000 Seventh-day Adventists, and 1500 Jehovah's Witnesses. Among the other religious minorities are about 10,000 Baha'is and 5000 Buddhists.

There is no formal state religion. Opportunities in religious broadcasting are minimal nationally, but there is a Scripture distribution ministry. An encouraging ecumenical spirit is reported, and since 1974 Catholics and Anglicans have shared a college.

**Maxwell, Leslie Earl** (1895–1984). Founder of Prairie Bible Institute. Born in Salina, Kans., he served overseas in the U.S. army (1917–19). After graduating from Midland Bible Institute in 1922, he proceeded north to Canada. In the rural community of Three Hills, Alberta, he conducted Bible classes that eventually developed into Prairie Bible Institute. The school stressed Bible instruction, personal spiritual development, and world missions. In Maxwell's lifetime graduates proceeded to overseas missions service, and the school came to be regarded as a major recruiting base for churches and mission agencies. In the wake of the success of Prairie Bible Institute, dozens of similar institutions developed across western Canada. Maxwell also served as pastor of Prairie Tabernacle from its inception in 1922 and, in addition, was a radio broadcaster and in demand as a convention speaker in Canada and the USA. He wrote *Born Crucified, Crowded to Christ, Abandoned to Christ*, and *World Missions—Total War*.

LESLIE K. TARR

**Maxwell, William Delbert** (1901–1971). Church of Scotland minister and scholar. Born in Ripley, Ont., he studied at the University of Toronto, Knox College, Toronto, and the University of Edinburgh (Ph.D., 1929). He was minister at Kensington, London (1928–32), Hillhead, Glasgow (1934–50), and Whitekirk, East Lothian (1950–56). He went to South Africa to serve as professor of ecclesiastical history at Fort Hare University (1956–71). His published works include *John Knox's Genevan Service Book, 1556* (1931), *An Outline of Christian Worship* (1936), *The Book of Common Prayer and the Worship of the Non-Anglican Churches* (1950), *History of Worship in the Church of Scotland* (1955), *The Eucharist in the Light of Our Lord's Resurrection* (1963), and *The Resurrection—Its Significance and Relevance* (1958).

**Mayer, Frederick E.** (1892–1954). Lutheran theologian. Born in New Wells, Mo., he graduated from Concordia Seminary, St. Louis, Mo. He was pastor of Lutheran churches at Sherrard and Kewanee, Ill. (1915–25), professor of systematic theology at Concordia Seminary, Springfield, Ill. (1926–37), and professor of symbolics and dogmatics at Concordia Seminary, St. Louis, Mo., from 1937. He was editor of and contributor to *Concordia Theological Monthly*. He coauthored *Popular Symbolics* (1934), *Jehovah's Witnesses* (1942), *American Churches and Sects* (1946), *The Story of Bad Boll* (1948), and *American Denominations*.

**Meditation.** Private devotional or spiritual exercise consisting of profound reflection on a religious theme. It is essential to distinguish between meditation as practiced in Eastern religions and the classic (Western) Christian approach. The purpose of the former is to achieve a higher consciousness and enjoy psychophysical relaxation; all use of the discursive intellect is rejected. In contrast Christian meditation is centered on the use of the mind, which considers, reflects upon, and thinks about God's revelation in Word and deed in order to prepare the heart for prayer and the will for action. Meditation is sometimes called mental prayer since it is a prayerful, humble consideration of what God has said and done with a view to loving, serving, and trusting him more.

In the Bible, references to meditation are found most often in the Psalter (see, e.g., Pss. 19, 63, 77, 119). Ps. 1, written as an introduction to the whole book, portrays meditation as a key component in the life of the godly person. Since the Psalter was the prayer book of Jesus and the apostolic church, it also became the prayer book of the church throughout the centuries. Meditation was seen as both a preparation for prayer and a form of prayer; it was the connecting link between the written Word of God and the loving of God from the heart. In the monasteries and convents of the Middle Ages it was an important part of the devotions of monks and nuns, who were taught to meditate not only at fixed times but also as they went about their daily duties in the garden or kitchen.

In the 16th century both Protestant and Catholic books containing specific methods of meditation and prayer began to appear. Martin Luther wrote *A Simple Way to Meditate/Pray, for Master Peter, the Barber* (1535); Calvin discussed meditation in his *Institutes of the Christian Religion* (3.9). However, Roman Catholics produced the greatest number of books in the 16th century. Most famous is the *Spiritual Exercises* of Ignatius of Loyola; other influential books were *Introduction to the Devout Life* by Francis de Sales, *Libro de la oración y meditación* by Louis of Granada, and *Tratado de la oración y meditación* by Peter of Alcántara. The Anglican bishop Joseph Hall was guided by these in the writing of his own influential *Art of Divine Meditation* (1606).

Catholic writers made a clear distinction between meditation and contemplation, seeing mental prayer as the first rung of the spiritual ladder and contemplative prayer as a higher form of prayer in which there is a simple, loving gaze upon God in the face of Jesus Christ. In general, Protestant writers saw differing degrees of intensity in meditation and prayer and so often used contemplation and meditation as synonyms. Meditation/contemplation of the glory of Christ in heaven was the highest form.

English Puritans, inspired by the emphasis on meditation in the Bible and learning through Bishop Hall and Catholic writers a variety of methods, produced a great number of books between 1630 and 1690 on both how to meditate and examples of meditation. They saw meditation as a definite means of grace, ordained by God as the normal way for truth received in the mind from the Word to pass into the heart, arouse the affections, and guide the will. God's written Word was to be considered so that it would inflame the heart and energize the will in a Godward direction. The most famous example of a meditation is *Pilgrim's Progress* by John Bunyan and of a method is the second part of Richard Baxter's *Saints' Everlasting Rest.*

Both Catholics and Protestants have insisted on the necessity of meditation as preparation for communion with God in private prayer and corporate worship, especially while receiving holy communion. However, this tradition has been challenged by modern biblical criticism, which has reduced the confidence of Christian pastors/teachers in the authority and inspiration of the Bible. This lack of confidence in the text of Scripture as the basis for meditation has created a kind of vacuum which has been partially filled by the adoption of techniques such as yoga from Eastern religions. Therefore what is often called meditation—especially as practiced on retreats and in meditation groups—is by no means always meditation as it has been understood over the centuries. The Western Church will need to recover confidence in the written Scriptures as God's Word if it is to recapture the practice of meditation as the psalmists, Jesus, apostles, and church fathers knew it.

*Bibliography.* B. Frost, *The Art of Mental Prayer* (1931); J. Leclerq, *The Love of Learning and the Desire for God* (1978); P. Toon, *From Mind to Heart* (1987).

PETER TOON

**Meland, Bernard Eugene** (1899– ). American theologian and educator. Born in Chicago, he studied at Park College, McCormick Theological Seminary, and the universities of Illinois, Chicago (Ph.D., 1929), and Marburg. He taught religion and philosophy at Central College, Fayette, Mo. (1929–36), and at Pomona College, Claremont, Calif. (1936–45), before becoming professor of constructive theology at the University of Chicago (1945–64), to which he returned after retirement as visiting professor of theology (1965–68). He lectured widely in India and Burma on different occasions, and was coeditor of the *Journal of Religion* (1946–64). His publications include *Modern Man's Worship* (1934), *The Church and Adult Education* (1939), *Seeds of Redemption* (1947), *America's Spiritual Culture* (1948), *The Reawakening of Christian Faith* (1949), *Higher Education and the Holy Spirit* (1953), *The Realities of Faith: The Revolution in Cultural Forms* (1962), and *The Secularization of Modern Cultures* (1966). He coauthored *American Philosophies of Religion* (1936) with H. N. Wieman. He edited *The Future of Empirical Theology* (1969) and *Fallible Forms and Symbols* (1976).

**Mennonites.** Protestant denomination founded by Conrad Grebel (1489–1526) in Zürich, Switzerland, in 1525. The first public baptism took place in 1525 at a drinking fountain in Zollikon. Similar groups were soon found in southwest Germany and among the peasants in northern Germany. One of the earliest statements of common purpose and conviction was the Schleitheim Confession (1527).

After the failure to establish a "theocratic" community in Münster (1534), some of the survivors were organized by Obbe and Dirk Philips. Menno Simons (c. 1496–1561), a converted priest, joined the movement through believer's baptism in 1536. Persons of like persuasion were soon widely known as "Menno's followers" or "Mennists." Some of them went to England on the invitation of King Henry VIII.

Since Mennonites opposed "established" churches and sought separation of baptized believers from all temporal matters, they were generally resented by authorities and often persecuted. Mennonites would give up homeland and property rather than accept compromise with the world and the "worldly church" in matters of faith and lifestyle. Many settled in Germantown, Pa., in the late 17th century and spread rapidly into Canada, Illinois, Indiana, Ohio, and Virginia. Others settled in Prussia, Poland, and Russia. Many of these later migrated to Canada and the USA.

The original Mennonites taught a radical NT Christianity. Mennonites today practice nonresistance, refuse to swear oaths, do not join secret societies, and seek to live by a biblical ethic informed by Matt. 5–7. The Lord's supper is celebrated twice a year, in conjunction with footwashing and the exchange of the "kiss of peace." Men and women are separated for the last two acts. Marriage is restricted to members of the Mennonite community.

Although congregations are associated in district or state conferences and maintain a worldwide network through a general assembly and the Mennonite Central Committee (MCC), local churches are autonomous. Rarely are appeals taken to a conference. Church leaders are known as bishops or elders, ministers, and deacons. Since most Mennonite communities are relatively small, their ministers are often self-supporting. Several splits over doctrinal interpretations and conduct have resulted in the formation of subgroups. The earliest of these was the Amish (1693) who, in turn, subdivided into the Conservatives, the Old Order Amish, and the Beachy Amish.

Major subgroups developed as follows:

*The Church of God in Christ (Mennonite)* was founded by John Holdemann in 1859.

*The Conference of the Evangelical Mennonite Church* originated in 1865 with Henry Egly.

*The Conservative Mennonite Conference* (until 1954 known as the Conservative Amish) dates back to 1910. It represents a split over the use of English in worship, the introduction of Sunday schools, and the practice of holding "protracted meetings."

*Evangelical Mennonite Brethren* (Defenseless Mennonites) originated with Russian Mennonite immigrants in 1873/74.

*General Conference Mennonites* date back to 1860. They seek coordination of all Mennonites on principles of church autonomy but insist on freedom from traditional dress and behavior codes. Strong emphasis on education is upheld through a liberal arts curriculum, Bible colleges, and a seminary.

*The Hutterian Brethren* trace their origins to John Hutter, who died a martyr in 1536. They maintain common property and have their own schools. There are currently about 44 colonies in the USA and 74 in Canada.

*The Mennonite Brethren Church* dates back to 1860 in the Ukraine with migration to the USA and Canada in 1876. Merged with the Krimmer Brethren since 1960, the group has a membership of some 30,000 in 160 congregations.

*The Mennonite Church* is the largest single group with some 84,000 members in more than 900 congregations.

*The Old Order (Wisler) Mennonite Church* was founded in 1872 by the first Mennonite bishop, Jacob Wisler, in Indiana. Some 5400 members in 35 congregations maintain German worship services to this day.

*The Reformed Mennonite Church* originated in 1812. John Herr was its first leader. Footwashing and the "kiss of peace" are observed as ordinances of the NT church in addition to baptism and the Lord's supper. Strict codes of belief and behavior are enforced. The group has about 500 members.

*Unaffiliated Mennonites* adhere to a variety of interpretations of Mennonite tenets. About 4500 individuals are loosely attached to the Mennonite communities.

*The Old Order Amish Mennonite Church* dates back to 1720–40. It maintains an exclusive fellowship, has no missionary activity, and refuses to be organized into conferences or to do any work related to the state. Some 21,500 members maintain 280 congregations.

The most recent Mennonite confessional statement of 20 articles dates back to 1963. It summarizes what most Mennonite groups believe. The Mennonites maintain a publishing house which produces a Mennonite year book and directory, numerous journals and periodicals, and a wide selection of devotional, theological, and historical materials. Through their prominence in the peace movement and their willingness to fight poverty and hunger, Mennonites have contributed significantly to the Christian faith and tradition and to the world at large. Schools, colleges, seminaries, libraries, and archives for the preservation of their history are maintained. Worldwide membership (1984) is 730,000 in 57 countries.

*Bibliography.* Mennonite Encyclopedia, 4 vols. (1955); F. Blanke, *Brothers in Christ* (1961); G. H. Williams, *The Radical Reformation* (1962); C. J. Dyck, *An Introduction to Mennonite History* (1966); I. B. Horst, *Anabaptism and the English Reformation to 1558* (1966); Menno Simons, *The Complete Writings* (1978); J. Thieleman van Braght, *Martyrs Mirror* (1982); *Mennonite Yearbook* (1985); *Mennonite Quarterly Review* 60 (1986).

E. J. FURCHA

**Mercati, Giovanni** (1866–1957). Italian cardinal. Born in Villa Gaida, Italy, he studied at Reggio Emilia and the Gregorian University at Rome (Th.D., 1891). Following his ordination to the priesthood, he was doctor of the Ambrosian Library of Milan (1893–98), scriptor of the Vatican Library for the Greek Language (1898–1918), prefect of the Vatican Library (1918–36), and cardinal deacon, librarian, and archivist of the Holy Roman Church after 1936.

**Mercier, Désiré Joseph** (1851–1926). Belgic cardinal. Born in Braine l'Alleud, Belgium, he studied at the Seminary of Malines and at the University of Louvain. He was ordained in 1874. He inaugurated the chair of Thomistic philosophy created at the University of Louvain in 1880, and organized the Institut Supérieur de Philosophie, which received its definitive charter in 1894. He was made archbishop of Malines and cardinal in 1906. His religious leadership and patriotism upheld the morale and spiritual unity of occupied Belgium during World War I. On his own initiative, he met with Lord Halifax and prelates of the Church of England to establish contact between the Roman and Anglican churches (1921–25). These meetings, however, failed to yield positive results. In addition to pastoral addresses and letters, he wrote *Cours de Philosophie* (4 vols., 1892), *Les origines de la psychologie contemporaine* (1897), and *La méditation universelle de la Très Sainte Vierge* (1925).

*See also* MALINES, CONVERSATIONS.

*Bibliography.* G. Goyau, *Cardinal Mercier* (1925); H. J. Dubly, *The Life of Cardinal Mercier* (1928); J. A. Gade, *The Life of Cardinal Mercier* (1934).

GEORGES A. BARROIS

**Merezhkovsky, Dmitry** (1866–1939). Russian Orthodox poet and journalist. Born in St. Petersburg, he studied at the University of St. Petersburg. He began his career as a poet and journalist, but from the beginning was concerned with religious themes. He was very active in the rapprochement of the Russian intelligentsia with the church in the early decades of the 20th century, although his personal religious convictions were unorthodox and syncretistic. He was a prolific novelist, literary critic, and essayist. Most of his books were translated into French, English, and other languages.

*Bibliography.* R. S. Mirsky, *A History of Russian Literature* (1949).

GEORGES FLOROVSKY

**Merk, August** (1869–1945). Roman Catholic biblical and patristics scholar. Born in Achern, Germany, he did graduate study at the universities of Munich and Beyrut. He was a professor at Ignatius College, Valkenburg, Holland (1907–25), professor of NT exegesis at the Pontifical Institute, Rome (1928–45), and editor-in-chief of *Cursus S. Scripturae* (1921–31). His works include *Erloesungsgeheimnis* (1929), and *Novum Testamentum graece et latine* (1933; 5th ed., 1944). He revised the 3d edition of Knabenhauer's *Commentarius in Evangelium sec. Mattaeum* (1922) and Cornely's *Introduction* (9th ed., 1927). He completely rewrote the latter work under the title *Introductionis in S. Scripturae libros compendium* (1940).

OTTO A. PIPER

**Merrill, William Pierson** (1867–1954). Presbyterian scholar. Born in East Orange, N.J., he studied at Rutgers College and Union Seminary. He was pastor of Trinity Presbyterian Church, Chestnut Hill, Philadelphia (1890–95), Sixth Presbyterian Church, Chicago (1895–1911), and Brick Presbyterian Church, New York City (1911–36). He was Lyman Beecher Lecturer at Yale (1922), president of the Church Peace Union (1918–47), member of the executive committee of the World Alliance for International Friendship, member of the Commission on Rethinking Missions in India, China, and Japan (1931–32), and member of the board of directors of Union Seminary (1912–54). He was a liberal in theology and his hymns "Not Alone for Mighty Empire" and "Rise Up, O Men of God" have been widely used. His published books are *Faith Building* (1885), *Faith and Sight* (1900), *Footings for Faith* (1915), *Christian Internationalism* (1919), *Common Creed of Christians* (1920), *Freedom of the Preacher* (1922), *Liberal Christianity* (1925), *Prophets of the Dawn* (1927), *The Way* (1933), and *We See Jesus* (1934).

**Merry del Val, Rafael** (1865–1930). Cardinal. Born in London, he studied in Belgium, England, and at the Gregorian University, Rome. Ordained in 1888, he was appointed private chamberlain to Leo XIII. He was sent to Canada as delegate extraordinary to investigate the Manitoba schools question (1899). A cardinal from 1903, he was secretary of state under Pius X. He drafted the policy of the Vatican in the conflict with the French Republic, which resulted in the denunciation of the Concordat of 1801 and in the separation of church and state (1905). He consistently opposed the claims of the government of Spain to a greater emancipation from church rule.

*Bibliography.* P. Cenci, *Il cardinale R. Merry del Val* (1933).

GEORGES A. BARROIS

**Merton, Thomas** (1915–1968). Roman Catholic monk and priest. Born in Prades, France, he was a convert to Catholicism and was eventually drawn to the monastic life. In 1941 he entered the Trappist community at Our Lady of Gethsemani in Kentucky. Seven years later his autobiography, *The Seven Storey Mountain*, was published. An instant best-seller, it remains in print in English and several other languages; it has been compared with Augustine's *Confessions*. Merton's early books reflect his enthusiasm for the Roman Catholic Church. His later work demonstrates a growing respect for religious life in the wider Christian church and beyond. During the Vietnam War, he associated with the Fellowship of Reconciliation, the Catholic Peace Fellowship, and other peace groups. His opposition to the war resulted in his being silenced for a time. Although living in monastic seclusion, correspondence linked him with writers (among them Boris Pasternak in Russia), religious leaders (including two popes, John XXIII and Paul VI), political figures, scholars, and social activists. His interest in non-Christian religions led him to India and Sri Lanka prior to attending a Christian monastic conference in Thailand, where he died of electrocution. Many of his 60 books are still in print. They include *The Sign of Jonas* (1951), *New Seeds of Contemplation* (1962), *Raids on the Unspeakable* (1964), *Zen and the Birds of Appetite* (1968), *Contemplation in a World of Action* (1971), and *Faith and Violence* (1968). Among works published posthumously are *The Asian Journals* (1973), *The Collected Poems* (1977), *The Literary Essays* (1981), and *The Hidden Ground of Love: Letters of Thomas Merton* (1985).

*Bibliography.* W. Shannon, *Thomas Merton's Dark Path: The Inner Experience of a Contemplative* (1981); M. Shannon, *The Seven Mountains of Thomas Merton* (1984).

JAMES H. FOREST

**Metaxakis, Meletios (Emmanuel)** (1871–1935). Greek Orthodox statesman. Born in Crete, he received his theological education in the School of the Holy Cross at Jerusalem. After serving in various positions at different places, he was consecrated metropolitan of Kitios (Cyprus) in 1910. He was metropolitan of Athens (1918–22), patriarch of Constantinople (1922/23), and, after a short retirement, patriarch of Alexandria (1926). A man of strong will and initiative, he was a leader of the liberal trend in the Greek Church and was in close contact with the West. He was especially interested in the rapprochement between the Greek and Anglican churches and was present at the Lambeth Conference in 1930, on which occasion the problem and ways of a prospective reunion were discussed. It was upon his initiative, and obviously under his influence, that the churches of Constantinople (1922) and Alexandria (1930) recognized the Anglican orders. On his visits to the USA in 1918 and later, Meletios contributed to the establishment of the Greek Archdiocese of the Americas (*see* EASTERN ORTHODOX CHURCHES).

GEORGES FLOROVSKY

## Methodist Council, World.

Organization founded in 1951 to provide forums for fellowship and interaction among member Methodist and United churches. The first Methodist ecumenical conference was held in London in 1881. Similar world conferences were held every 10 years until 1931. World War II delayed the meeting of the next conference until 1947. In the 1951 conference the World Methodist Council was created as a continuing body with provisions for a permanent secretariat and standing committees. Subsequent meetings were scheduled every five years in conjunction with a World Methodist Conference sponsored by the council. There are 500 members representing 64 Methodist and United churches with 25 million members (54 million including United bodies) in 90 countries. The World Methodist Historical Society and the World Federation of Methodist Women are council affiliates.

MELVIN E. DIETER

## Methodists.

Protestant denomination which began as the major expression of the Evangelical Revival movement in the Church of England in the 18th century under the leadership of John Wesley (1703–91).

*The Life and Thought of John Wesley.* As an ordained priest in the Church of England, John Wesley united his sense of churchmanship with an unflagging commitment to preach the gospel in a direct and compelling way throughout the British Isles and to nurture those converts who responded to that message. He was aided in this mission by his effective pastoral and administrative gifts, as well as by capable co-laborers, including his brother Charles, a gifted hymn writer. The status of Methodism was altered from that of a revival movement or society to an independent ecclesial body in the USA in 1784 and in England after the death of John Wesley. The rise of Methodism is also to be viewed within the context of the broader Continental movement of Protestant spirituality that preceded it, as well as in relation to the socioeconomic dislocations that accompanied the Industrial Revolution and the Enlightenment in England.

During Wesley's lifetime, the Church of England was weakened by incursions of natural theology known as deism, which sought to extricate the supernatural from Christian faith in deference to a "Christianity not mysterious." At the same time, the rise of the machine age as a result of the Industrial Revolution was causing massive social and spiritual dislocations as Britons flocked to the growing cities for employment in the new industries. The antiquated parish structure of the Church of England was incapable of responding to these conditions, and its leadership was often perceived as being insensitive to them.

John Wesley was born in Epworth, England. His father, Samuel, was a priest in the Church of England. His early spiritual and educational nurture was provided by his mother, Susannah. After graduating from Christ Church, Oxford, in 1725, he was ordained to the ministry of the Church of England. He also began reading the English spiritual writers, notably William Law. After a period of pastoral service in his father's Epworth parish, Wesley returned to Oxford where he became a tutor at Lincoln College and also became a member of a newly formed "Holy Club" of Oxford students, whose members included his brother Charles and the future evangelist, George Whitefield. They were dubbed "Methodists" because of their fastidious devotion to works of holiness and a plain lifestyle. Wesley thereafter undertook a three-year missionary venture to the new American colony of Georgia. He encountered amid a storm at sea a group of Moravian immigrants whose fearless faith prompted Wesley to seek the assurance of salvation. This assurance was divinely granted to him following his return to London in 1738, when he attended a meeting of Moravians on Aldersgate Street. He thereafter visited the Moravian center, headed by Zinzendorf, at Herrnhut in Germany, where his appreciation of Moravian thought became tempered by theological disagreement with Zinzendorf. As a consequence, while Methodism is indebted to the Moravians for much of its emphasis upon the instantaneous experience of regeneration, the personal assurance of salvation, and the use of small nurturing groups or bands, it was destined to develop its own distinctive theological and organizational identity.

In 1739, the great Evangelical Revival began in Bristol, England, under the preaching of Whitefield, who soon summoned Wesley from Oxford to undertake the work of an itinerant field preacher. Although Wesley responded reluctantly to this novel vocation, his preaching at this industrial center met with spectacular success, as large numbers responded with emotional fervor to his direct invitation to flee the wrath of God and come to salvation in Jesus Christ. He had acted on the grounds of his extraparochial clerical appointment to teach at Oxford. When he was charged by other clergymen with invading their parishes, he responded that, in light of the urgency of the Great Commission, the world was his parish. Wesley soon established the first Methodist class, intended to nurture those won to Christ. Classes met in small groups on a weekly basis under the leadership of lay class leaders, who sought to help students attain the "power of godliness." These classes, graded according to the spiritual level of participants, were grouped into societies. The charge to traveling lay preachers, whose services Wesley began to utilize to assist his mission, was to preach the gospel, to visit the societies, and to increase their strength and numbers. To facilitate this highly mobile structure, Wesley began to hold regular annual conferences in 1744, in order to superintend, instruct, and appoint lay assistants.

The theology of Methodism is Arminian, a term that stems from Wesley's work as editor of the *Arminian Magazine*, a journal that sought to refute the errors of Calvinism. A practical theologian, Wesley's message was based upon the Bible as the inspired Word of God, whose message came to be confirmed and appropriated by the witness of Christian tradition as well as by human experience and reason as these faculties are exercised by the supernatural guidance of the Holy Spirit. Two aspects of Wesley's theology in particular require summarization: his doctrine of salvation and his attitude toward theological controversies.

Wesley distinguished between "essentials" and "opinions" with regard to doctrine. The former included basic biblical doctrines embedded in the Articles of Religion of the Church of England. There were original sin, whereby no one is exempted from the need for grace, and saving grace itself, which Wesley presented in both its objective and subjective aspects. Objectively, saving grace is grounded in the atoning work of Jesus Christ, whose substitutionary, sacrificial death brings to all mankind the possibility of eternal righteousness and life with God as the gift of faith. Subjectively, this grace is appropriated under the inspiration of the Holy Spirit in a threefold manner. Preveniently, the love of God in Christ is available to all and operative in each person before and as that person responds to this offer. Citing John 1:9, Wesley objected to the Calvinist's limitation of saving grace to those elected in an act of divine foreordination, for whom grace was also deemed irresistible. He also objected to the Pelagian appeal to natural human will as the cause of salvation.

Second, saving grace is to be appropriated as God's justification of the sinner. Wesley saw this justification as an instantaneous, full pardon by the imputation and, subsequently, the impartation of Christ's righteousness within the life of the believer as the gift of faith through the Holy Spirit. The Moravians had shown him that the believer may be inwardly assured of this relational change, to which Wesley also referred as the "witness of the Spirit" (Rom. 8:16).

Third, justification is followed by sanctification, that real empowerment of the believer through the Holy Spirit whereby he or she is enabled to attain not merely pardon but victory over all that separates man from God, namely, sin, death, and the devil. Wesley taught that this sanctification is in part gradual, beginning with one's regeneration, but that it is also instantaneously appropriated by the believer in a crisis experience subsequent to regeneration. Wesley pressed all earnest Christians to be cleansed from sin and delivered from its power by faith in Christ, whereby one may attain an unmitigated love for God and neighbor and strive, without spiritual pride, to attain holiness. For Wesley, the principal vocation of Methodism was to spread this message of scriptural holiness over the earth. It was to embody both a personal and a social dimension, as Wesley also found himself combatting such injustices as the West Indian slave trade. In distinction from his pre-Aldersgate stance, Wesley now saw holiness to be the fruit of saving faith, not its condition. In his study of the scriptural basis for this doctrine, he also relied upon insights from the pietists, the English devotional tradition, and certain Greek patristic writers.

Throughout his long ministry, Wesley resisted mounting pressures for the Methodist societies to secede from the Church of England; he forbade his lay preachers to administer the sacraments; and class meetings were held during the week so that Methodists, who remained Anglicans, could participate in regular worship services of the Church of England. He upheld the importance of baptism and the Lord's supper as the "ordinary" channels whereby God's saving grace is communicated to believers. In addition, Wesley inaugurated rituals for his followers that could be administered by laity, such as a New Year's Eve covenant watchnight service and a love feast. Methodist chapels in Britain were not designated as churches, in order that Methodism might avoid the charge of being schismatic as in the case of the Nonconformists in the Puritan tradition. From a legal standpoint, local chapels were held in trust by the congregation for the conference of Methodist preachers and were subject to its authority. This arrangement, which has continued to the present time, incorporates an element of congregational autonomy with an element of centralized authority. Toward the end of Wesley's lifetime, he also acted to ordain ministers for service in the New World. This action occurred only when it became clear to him that the separation of Methodism in America from Anglicanism had, because of the Revolutionary War, become a *fait accompli*, and when it became apparent that these acts of ordination would not be performed by an Anglican bishop. Wesley justified his action on biblical grounds, citing studies by two "latitudinarian" divines (Lords Stillingfleet and King) that had persuasively argued for a twofold order of ministry, that of deacon and elder, thereby indicating that he who functions in an episcopal capacity does so solely as an elder and with no higher spiritual authority.

### The Development of American Methodism.
After Methodists arrived in small numbers as immigrants in the 1760s, Wesley appointed and sent several lay preachers to offer them spiritual leadership and to extend the work in the New World. Methodism reached a low ebb during the Revolutionary War years but one of these early missionaries, Francis Asbury, remained to become the first superintendent, later bishop, of the newly constituted Methodist Episcopal Church in 1784, an office that he shared for a season with Thomas Coke, whom Wesley had commissioned to ordain Asbury at the organizational conference of the new church, the so-called Baltimore Christmas Conference. The Larger Minutes from Wesley's British conference became the basis for the Methodist Book of Discipline, and doctrinal guidelines were provided by the Articles of Religion that Wesley had abridged from the Anglican Thirty-Nine Articles of Religion. Under Asbury's leadership, the new church became mobilized to advance across the American frontier, using with effectiveness lay preachers, who became circuit riders, and being supervised by more experienced preachers known as presiding elders. Entry into the active ministry now involved a twofold process: membership in an annual conference of preachers and episcopal ordination. Laypersons in ministry who were not a part of the itinerant system included local preachers, class leaders, and exhorters.

The rapid growth of Methodism in the early 1800s was hindered by the tensions precipitating the American Civil War. In 1844, Methodism divided into Northern and Southern regional bodies, known as the Methodist Episcopal and the Methodist Episcopal Church, South, respectively. In addition, a smaller group had seceded in 1830 to form the Methodist Protestant Church, due to their opposition to the episcopal polity and their insistence upon lay representation in conferences. The latter demand was met in time by both Northern and Southern Episcopal Methodism.

Smaller schisms included the Wesleyans, who seceded in the 1830s under the leadership of Orange Scott, a New England abolitionist minister who linked a renewed emphasis upon sanctification with his antislavery message. In the 1860s, the Free Methodists seceded, under the leadership of an elder named Benjamin Roberts, in order to maintain the eroding emphasis upon sanctification and disciplined church membership, and also to protest the practice of renting church pews. The message of the gospel was effectively disseminated in the 19th century by the use of camp meetings. Methodists became active in the post-Civil War era in the formation and growth of the interdenominational National Holiness Association.

In the 20th century, Methodism's continued growth was accompanied by an increased involvement in social issues, liberal theological currents, and participation in the ecumenical movement. In 1939, Northern and Southern Methodists joined with Methodist Protestants to form the Methodist Church, which in turn joined with the Evangelical United Brethren in 1968 to form the United Methodist Church, with more than 10 million members.

### The Church of the United Brethren in Christ and the Evangelical Association.
In 1752, Philip William Otterbein (1726–1813) arrived in Pennsylvania as a missionary to the German Reformed immigrants. Educated at the Herborn Academy in Nassau, Germany, where the Heidelberg Catechism was the prized doctrinal standard, he had been deeply influenced at Herborn by Reformed pietism. While initiating pietist conventicles and standards for membership accountability in several pastorates in Pennsylvania, he met an "awakened" Mennonite pastor named Martin Boehm in a barn meeting in 1767, that began an informal brotherhood for the evangelization of German-Americans across confessional lines. He became pastor in the "Evangelical" Reformed congregation in Baltimore, where he became friends with Francis Asbury and where, in 1800, he was elected a superintendent of the rising United Brethren in Christ. Under the leadership of a younger preacher, Christian Newcomer, the United Brethren spread into the Midwestern states, and the majority of their work soon became English-speaking. A modified episcopal polity with more congregational autonomy, a single order of ministry, and a confession of faith reflecting elements of Reformed pietism were developed.

In 1796, a Pennsylvania-born farmer and Revolutionary War soldier named Jacob Albright (1759-1808) was converted and, after a brief time as a member of a Methodist class, responded to a call to minister the gospel among his German neighbors, who became deeply concerned for their godless spiritual condition. He was ordained by his lay associates and, shortly after 1800, the Evangelical Association was formed along lines of Methodist doctrine and polity, although its mission was largely directed to German-speaking Americans for the next century. Following a schism in 1891 that was partially healed in 1922, the newly reunited body became the Evangelical Church, which in 1946 joined the United Brethren to form the Evangelical United Brethren Church (EUB), with almost 750,000 members worldwide.

***The Present Outreach of World Methodism.*** *British Isles and the Americas.* Membership in all branches of Methodism in the British Isles in 1985 was over 465,000—a decline from 969,000 members in 1910. The British Methodist Church is a union of the United Free Churches, the Methodist New Connection and the Bible Christians (united in 1907), and the Primitive Methodists and the Wesleyan Methodists (united in 1932). It now operates theological schools and numerous primary, secondary, and collegiate-level schools, as well as overseas missions. Union with the Church of England was narrowly defeated in the 1970s. There are also some 25,000 Methodists in Ireland.

There are 20 American Methodist denominations, of which the United Methodist Church is largest with 9,519,407 members, although this represents a decline of more than one million members since 1968. Annual conferences are grouped into five regional jurisdictions. Executive leadership is vested in the council of bishops, legislative leadership in the quadrennial general conference, and judicial leadership in the judicial council. Bishops have administrative authority without a superior power jurisdiction. Programs are administered through numerous general agencies; these include mission work in 54 nations, over 100 schools of higher education, and numerous hospitals and homes for the elderly. Below the general conference, there are the annual conferences, district conferences, and charges conferences. An equal number of lay and clerical delegates are elected to conferences. Black Methodists number almost 4 million, including the three largest independent black denominations, the African Methodist Episcopal Church (2,050,000 members, organized in 1816 by a free black, in Philadelphia, Richard Allen), the African Methodist Episcopal Zion Church (1,134,176 members, and organized in New York City in 1821), and the Christian Methodist Church (786,707 members, organized in 1870 among emancipated slaves in Jackson, Tenn.). They share major Methodist emphases in doctrine and polity, and have developed distinctives in hymnody and worship. In 1981, Free Methodists numbered 73,542 members, Wesleyans, who merged with the Pilgrim Holiness Church in 1968, numbered 103,712 members,

and other smaller Methodist-related denominations totaled over 600,000 members.

Methodists and EUBs in Canada have now united with the United Church of Canada, which had 903,302 members in 1981. There were 32,935 members in the Methodist Church of Mexico. Methodist church bodies, numbering 517,847 members, exist with varying degrees of autonomy from parent church bodies in Central, South American, and Caribbean nations, with the largest number being the 72,000-member Methodist Church of Brazil and the 150,000- member Methodist Pentecostal Church of Chile.

*Continental Europe and Africa.* United Methodism in Continental Europe is the result of British Methodist, American Methodist, Evangelical, and United Brethren missionary activity that began in the 19th century. Operating in 15 nations, the work is organized in annual conferences grouped within four central conferences, with more than 148,000 members in 1981. Total membership of all Methodist bodies in Europe, including those in Britain and Ireland, was 749,090, but numbers have since decreased.

All Methodist-related church bodies in Africa, operating in 24 nations, had 2,658,199 members in 1981, and the number is rapidly increasing. The largest bodies include the Methodist Church in Ghana and in Nigeria, with about 300,000 members in each, and the 828,500-member Methodist Church of Southern Africa.

*Asia and the Pacific.* Methodist work in Asia and the Pacific, developed since 1814 with the work of British, North American, and EUB missionaries, has grown to include 19 nations with 4,528,776 members in 1981, including the 600,000-member Methodist Church of India. In several nations, Methodist work has been merged with united indigenous church bodies, as in the United Church of Christ in Japan and the Uniting Church in Australia. Elsewhere autonomous churches have been formed, as the Korean Methodist Church, which has grown dramatically in recent years to 646,840 members in 1981 and today has the largest Methodist congregation. In Asia, as in Europe and the third world, growth has often occurred in spite of oppressive political conditions.

Methodism worldwide is now affiliated in an interdenominational alliance called the World Methodist Council, which represents 25 million church members within a larger community of 54 million persons and 64 member church bodies.

**Bibliography.** W. R. Cannon, *The Theology of John Wesley* (1946); A. Outler, ed., *John Wesley* (1964); R. Davies and G. Rupp, *A History of the Methodist Church in Great Britain,* 2 vols. (1965); A. Outler, *Evangelism in the Wesleyan Spirit* (1971); O. E. Borgen, *John Wesley on the Sacraments* (1972); A. E. Core, *Philip William Otterbein, Pastor Ecumenist* (1972); J. S. O'Malley, *Pilgrimage of Faith: The Legacy of the Otterbeins* (1973); F. Baker, ed., *The Works of John Wesley,* 3 vols. (1975– ); B. Behney and

P. Eller, *A History of the Evangelical United Brethren Church* (1979); T. Langford, *Practical Divinity: Theology in the Wesleyan Tradition* (1983); R. G. Tuttle, Jr., *John Wesley: His Life and Theology* (1978); M. B. Stokes, *The Bible in the Wesleyan Heritage* (1979); K. Steckel and C. E. Sommer, eds., *Geschichte der Evangelisch-Methodistischen Kirche* (1982); J. R. Tyson, *Charles Wesley on Sanctification* (1986); R. Wilke, *And Are We Yet Alive? The Future of the United Methodist Church* (1986); H. A. Snyder, *The Divided Flame: Wesleyans and the Charismatic Renewal* (1986); J. S. O'Malley, *Touched by Godliness: Bishop John Seybert and the Evangelical Heritage* (1986); H. Lindstrom, *Wesley and Sanctification* (n.d.).

J. Steven O'Malley

## Metropolitan Community Church (MCC).

Largest of a number of denominations which arose during the so-called sexual revolution of the 1960s to serve the homosexual community. MCC's first service was held on October 6, 1968, in the home of its founder, Troy Perry. In 1987, the denomination had swelled to 260 churches—200 in the USA and 60 in 10 other countries worldwide, including Australia, Canada, Denmark, England, France, Indonesia, Ireland, Mexico, New Zealand, and Nigeria. In that same year, MCC reported a membership of close to 30,000. MCC trains its ministers at its own Good Samaritan Seminary in Los Angeles, Calif. The denomination is organized along congregational lines, upholding the autonomy of individual churches. The legislative body, comprised of a house of clergy and a house of laity, and the governing body, comprised of a board of elders and district representatives, meets in general conferences biannually.

MCC's founder, Troy Perry, born in 1940 in Tallahassee, Fla., was reared in a rigid pentecostal environment, serving as a pastor in his late teens and early 20s in the Church of God of Prophecy, first in Chicago and then in California. His break with that denomination coincided with his changing views on homosexuality and public acknowledgment of his own homosexual inclinations. He believed that God had called him to establish a church that affirmed the legitimacy of homosexual relationships for Christians. Not surprisingly, homosexuals account for between 75 and 95 percent of MCC's congregations. MCC members come from a range of denominational backgrounds, representing a wide spectrum of theological and liturgical persuasions. This diversity has left its mark on MCC services, which tend to be eclectic, incorporating everything from the spontaneity of pentecostal revivalism to the calculated ritual of Catholicism. Each church is free to determine the form its services take. The church recognizes two sacraments, water baptism and communion, the latter of which is observed each Sunday.

Perry's pentecostal roots point MCC in a theologically conservative direction. MCC's statement of faith is typically evangelical. Where the church departs from the evangelical mainstream is in its teaching on homosexuality. MCC believes that homosexuality, like heterosexuality, is not a matter of individual choice but a natural endowment. Consequently, it is not to be rejected as sin, but actively and responsibly nurtured as a gift from God. Biblical passages dealing with homosexuality are either dismissed as culturally determined and no longer binding or interpreted as prohibitions, not of homosexuality itself but of its wrongful expression. MCC unites homosexual partners in ceremonies it calls "holy unions," which in some ways are analogous to heterosexual marriages. Sexual relationships outside of holy union, however, are not forbidden by the church but are a matter of individual conscience.

In 1982 the denomination applied for membership in the National Council of Churches in the USA. Because of MCC's controversial nature, the council postponed a final decision indefinitely but established a process for ongoing dialog. MCC has, since its inception, been actively involved in the broader gay rights movement. It is in that wider context of cultural change and shifting moral values that the rise and development of MCC is properly understood.

Robert Burrows

## Metzger, Bruce Manning (1914– ).

Presbyterian scholar. Born in Middletown, Pa., he studied at Lebanon Valley College, Princeton Theological Seminary, and Princeton University (Ph.D., 1942). He taught at Princeton Seminary from 1938 to 1985, where he was professor of NT languages and literature. He is a versatile scholar, having done extensive work in paleography, NT manuscripts, textual criticism, philology, early church history, biblical studies, translation, and bibliography. He was chairman of the Committee on Versions, International Greek NT Project; a member of the Revised Standard Bible Committee, Apocrypha section; a member of the American Study Group on Christian Vocation, World Council of Churches; chairman of the American Textual Criticism Seminar; editorial secretary of *Theology Today;* one of four editors of the United Bible Societies' Greek NT; president of the Society of Biblical Literature; president of the Studiorum Novi Testamenti Societas; and corresponding fellow of the British Academy.

Among his more important works are *An Introduction to the Apocrypha* (1957), *The NT: Its Background, Growth, and Content* (1965), *Index to Periodic Literature on Christ and the Gospels* (1966), *The Text of the NT* (1969), *Periodical Literature on the Apostle Paul* (1970), *A Textual Commentary on the Greek NT* (1971), *The Early Versions of the NT* (1977), *NT Studies: Philological, Versional, and Patristic* (1980), *Manuscripts of the Greek Bible* (1981), and *The Canon of the NT* (1987). A festschrift in his honor was published in

1981 entitled *NT Textual Criticism,* edited by E. J. Epp and G. D. Fee.

WALTER A. ELWELL

**Mexico.** Country occupying the northern portion of the isthmus connecting the southern border of the USA with South America. It has an area of 1,972,547 sq. km. (761,605 sq. mi.) and a population of 83 million (1987). Mexico is a predominantly Roman Catholic country. Approximately 95 percent of all Mexicans are baptized Catholics and 77 percent are married in the church. The Mexican church is one of the strongest institutionally in Latin America. In 1979 there were 10,095 priests (7113 secular and 2982 religious) and 26,119 nonordained religious working in Mexico. The church's educational system consists of an extensive network of Catholic primary and secondary schools and the Jesuit-run university. Just under 10 percent of Mexican children are educated in Catholic schools.

With Mexico's independence came the formal unity of church and state, assuring the church a privileged position in society. The first attempt to limit the power of the church in 1833 led to the overthrow of President Gómez Farias and the imposition of a clerical-supported regime. When the liberals gained power in the 1850s they implemented a series of reforms. The 1855 *Ley Juárez* eliminated ecclesiastical jurisdiction over civil court cases and the 1856 *Ley Lerdo* provided for the sale of church properties. The most significant anticlerical measures, the Liberal Reforms, were decreed by President Benito Juárez in 1859. These measures, which significantly curbed the economic privileges and secular power of the church, were eventually incorporated into the constitution of 1873. The church's response to the reforms was to support the French intervention in Mexico during 1861/62.

During the rule of Porfirio Díaz (1876–1910) the church regained some of its prestige and secular influence. As Díaz did not enforce the reform laws with any consistency, the church was able to strengthen and reorganize itself. A reflection of this was the church's involvement in a small-scale union organization and its growing interest in social issues. The Mexican Revolution, however, saw the return of anticlericalism, this time even more radical. A new constitution in 1917 contained a number of articles aimed at weakening the church. The most damaging, article 130, prohibited the church's involvement in politics, banned foreign priests, declared monastic orders illegal, and empowered the government to determine the number of priests in Mexico. Although President Carranza did not enforce the more radical measures, anticlericalism intensified with the expansion of the Mexican state and the continued meddling of the church in secular matters.

The growing church-state tensions burst forth into violent confrontation during the Calles presidency. Calles, an ardent anticlerical, moved to enforce article 130, which the church had publicly disavowed. The ensuing Cristero Rebellion (1926–29) saw the mobilization of thousands of peasants (with church support) against government forces. Although an agreement was worked out in 1929, a second rebellion broke out in response to President Cárdenas's attempt to introduce "socialist" education into the schools. Without church support, however, the movement was doomed from the start.

Since 1940 there has been a modus vivendi between church and state. While no actual settlement was reached, peace has been secured because of the government's nonenforcement of the anticlerical measures. Moreover, the church, recognizing the hopelessness of armed insurrection, has avoided direct confrontation with the government. An important vehicle for Catholic opposition to the government has been the National Action party (PAN). Founded in 1939 to carry the church's struggle into the political arena, PAN has become the largest opposition party in Mexico.

The Catholic Church in Mexico continues to be one of the most conservative churches in Latin America. Nevertheless, it has been inevitably affected by Vatican II. A reflection of this is the fact that Mexico has produced several liberation theologians of international reputation. Moreover, a small sector within the church, influenced by progressive currents of Catholicism, has actively promoted the formation of Christian base communities and struggled for the rights of Mexico's poor and oppressed. The Jesuits have been particularly instrumental in setting up educational programs in some of Mexico's poorest slums.

These activities, however, like elsewhere in Latin America, have drawn progressive clergy and religious into conflict with the government and powerful economic groups. For example, in 1977 two priests were murdered because of their work on behalf of slum dwellers in Chihuahua and Mexico City. To protest the killings, the progressive bishop of Cuernavaca, Sergio Méndez Arceo, led a procession of 70 priests and 5000 faithful to the famous Guadalupe Basilica. As more and more priests come into contact with the harsh realities of poverty in Mexico, they will undoubtedly become more outspoken on behalf of the poor.

Protestants have had a presence in Mexico since the colonial period. However, the first missionaries did not arrive until 1860 when freedom of religious worship was granted by the Mexican government. By 1916 there were 50,000 Protestants in Mexico, Presbyterians and Methodists accounting for three-quarters of them. In 1980 4 million Mexicans identified themselves as Protestants or non-Catholic Christians. The pentecostals have exhibited the most dramatic growth. Whereas pentecostals constituted a tiny fraction of the Protestant community in 1916, in 1980 they accounted for 66 percent of all Protestants. Traditional denominations have slid from 75 percent to 20 percent of Protestants during the same period. While a minority of Protestant churches are active in social issues, most seem to be primarily preoccupied with increasing their membership. Because some churches (particularly the pentecostals) have been accused of serving as instruments of U.S. foreign policy, a lively debate has emerged among Protestants concerning their role in the future of Mexico.

**Bibliography.** R. Quirk, *The Mexican Revolution and the Catholic Church* (1973); J. Meyer, *The Cristero Rebellion* (1976); P. Lernoux, *Cry of the People* (1982); T. Beeson and J. Pearce, *A Vision of Hope* (1984).

PHILIP J. WILLIAMS

## Meyer, Fredrick Brotherton (1847–1929).

English Baptist pastor. Born in London, he studied at Regent's Park Baptist College, graduated from London University, and served as an assistant in Baptist churches in Liverpool and York. At York he helped to make known the American evangelists Moody and Sankey. Meyer ministered in Leicester (1874–88) and London (1888–1921). Three times he left Baptist pastorates for independent churches, and twice he returned to a former charge. A man with profound social concern, he was highly regarded by British statesmen and bishops. It was estimated that he had preached over 15,000 sermons, yet he found time to write devotional and expository books, among them a two-volume commentary on Exodus (reissued in 1951), and these with his tracts had a circulation of some 5 million at the time of his death. He was a welcome visitor to the USA, especially to Moody's Northfield Conferences, and even after his retirement he exercised an itinerant ministry on every continent.

J. D. DOUGLAS

## Michelfelder, Sylvester Clarence (1889–

1951). Lutheran pastor. Born in New Washington, Ohio, he studied at Capital University and Seminary, Columbus, Ohio. He was pastor of Trinity Lutheran Church, Willard, Ohio (1913–21), and of Steward Avenue Lutheran Church (1921–26). He served as superintendent of the Pittsburgh Inner Mission Society (1926–31) and pastor of St. Paul's Lutheran Church, Toledo, Ohio (1931–45). He was representative of the National Lutheran Council to the Reconstruction Department of the World Council of Churches in Geneva. There he founded the Material Aid Division for postwar reconstruction. He became executive secretary of the Lutheran World Convention (1945), which he helped to reorganize as the Lutheran World Fed-

eration (1947). He then served as its executive secretary (1947–51). He wrote *Life Adjustment* and *So You Are Thinking.*

**Bibliography.** P. Fraenkel, *Oekumenische Profile* (1952).

PETER FRAENKEL

## Micklem, Nathaniel (1888–1976). English

Congregationalist scholar. Educated at Oxford and Marburg, he was professor of OT literature and theology, Selly Oak Colleges, Birmingham (1921–27), professor of NT literature and criticism, Queen's Theological College, Kingston, Ontario (1927–31), and principal and professor of dogmatic theology, Mansfield College, Oxford (1932–53). He was the author of *The Theology of Politics* (1941), *Law and the Laws* (1952), *The Box and the Puppets, 1888–1953* (1957), and *Behold the Man* (1969). He was also a regular contributor to the *British Weekly.*

J. D. DOUGLAS

## Millennium.

The earthly reign of the Messiah at the end of history. According to the Book of Revelation, Satan will be bound and thrown into the abyss (20:2–3), there to remain while the saints reign with Christ on earth for 1000 years (20:6). Thereafter Satan is to be released to battle God's people (20:7–9); he will be defeated and thrown into "the lake of burning sulfur" (20:10). This passage is the only clear reference in Scripture to a millennial reign of Christ on earth although several others (e.g., 1 Cor. 15:24–28) may refer to the same period. There are three views of the millennium: (1) premillennialism, (2) postmillennialism, and (3) amillennialism. Their exponents believe that the Lord's second coming will occur, in the first case, before the millennium; in the second case, after the millennium; or in the third case, that the language of Scripture is too highly figurative to suggest in reality any millennium at all.

Although these interpretations have never been without adherents in the history of the church, in certain ages a particular outlook has predominated. During the first three centuries of the Christian era, premillennialism appears to have been the dominant eschatological interpretation. In the 4th century, when the Christian church was given a favored status under the emperor Constantine, the amillennial position was accepted. The millennium was reinterpreted to refer to the church. The famous church father, Augustine, articulated this position, and it became the prevailing interpretation in medieval times.

The Protestant Reformers accepted Augustinian amillennialism. However, they did inaugurate changes in eschatological interpretation that set the stage for a great renewal of premillennial interest during the 17th century. Martin Luther (1483–1546), for example, advocated a more literal approach to the Scriptures, identified the papacy with the Antichrist, and called attention to biblical prophecies. Some later Lutheran scholars redirected this interest to focus on a premillennial interpretation. However, the German Calvinist theologian Johann Heinrich Alsted (1588–1638) revived the teaching of premillennialism in the modern world. Alsted's book, *The Beloved City* (1627), caused the learned Anglican scholar Joseph Mede (1586–1638) to become a premillennialist. The works of both men helped to inspire the desire for God's kingdom on earth which accompanied the outbreak of the Puritan Revolution of the 1640s. But with the restoration of the Stuart rulers, this outlook was discredited.

As premillennialism waned, postmillennialism became the prevailing eschatological interpretation, receiving its most important formulation in the work of Daniel Whitby (1638–1726). According to Whitby, the world was to be converted to Christ, the Jews restored to their land, and the pope and Turks defeated, after which time the earth would enjoy universal peace, happiness, and righteousness for 1000 years. At the close of this period, Christ would return personally for the last judgment. Perhaps because of its agreement with the views of the 18th-century Enlightenment, postmillennialism was adopted by the leading Protestant theologians of the era.

During the 19th century, premillennialism again attracted widespread attention. This interest was fostered by the violent uprooting of European political and social institutions during the French Revolution. One of the more influential leaders at this time was Edward Irving (1792–1834), who published many works on prophecy and helped to organize the Albury Park prophecy conferences. These meetings set the pattern for millennial gatherings throughout the 19th and 20th centuries. The prophetic enthusiasm of Irving spread to other groups and found firm support among the Plymouth Brethren movement.

J. N. Darby (1800–1882), an early Plymouth Brethren leader, articulated the dispensationalist understanding of premillennialism. His teaching, spread by such means as the Scofield Reference Bible, has led to the popularity of dispensational premillennialism in the English-speaking world during the 20th century.

In addition to the premillennial, amillennial, and postmillennial interpretations, some groups such as the Jehovah's Witnesses, the Latter-day Saints, and the Seventh-day Adventists identify their sectarian activities with the millennium. Also, some third world millenarian groups teach the coming of a golden age to earth.

ROBERT G. CLOUSE

## Miller, Perry Gilbert Eddy (1905–1963). Literary scholar. Born in Chicago, he studied at the

university there (Ph.D., 1931) and at Harvard University. He was instructor and professor of American literature at Harvard (1931–63), with a break for army service in World War II (1942–46) and another for a guest professorship at the University of Leiden (1949/50). He wrote *Orthodoxy in Massachusetts* (1933), *The New England Mind* (1939), *Images or Shadows of Divine Things* (1948), *Jonathan Edwards* (1949), *The Transcendentalists* (1950), *The New England Mind: From Colony to Province* (1953), *Roger Williams* (1953), *The Raven and the Whale* (1956), and *Consciousness in Concord* (1958). He coauthored *The Puritans* (1938) with T. H. Johnson. He edited *Major Writers of America* (1960) and *Life of the Mind in America* (1965).

## Milligan, George (1860–1934). Biblical scholar. Born in Kilconquhar, he studied at Aberdeen, Edinburgh, Göttingen, and Bonn. He served at St. Matthew's, Morningside (1883–94) and Caputh (1894–1910), and became regius professor of divinity and biblical criticism at Glasgow University (1910–32). He was convener of the General Assembly's Committee on Religious Instruction for Youth; president of the Oxford Society of Historical Theology (1915/16); moderator of the General Assembly, Church of Scotland (1923); and first chairman of the Scottish Sunday School Union for Christian Education (1926). His main writings are *History of the English Bible* (1895), *The Lord's Prayer* (1895), *The Theology of the Epistle to the Hebrews* (1899), *The Twelve Apostles* (1904), *St. Paul's Epistles to the Thessalonians* (1908), *Selections from Greek Papyri* (1910), *The NT Documents: Their Origin and Early History* (1912), *The Expository Value of the Revised Version* (1917), *The Vocabulary of the Greek Testament* (1919–29), *Here and There among the Papyri* (1922), and *The NT in Its Transmission* (1932).

*Bibliography.* Glasgow Herald (Nov. 26, 1934); Dictionary of National Biography (1931–40).

DANIEL J. THERON

## Mills, Benjamin Fay (1857–1916). Unitarian minister and lecturer. Born in Rahway, N.J., he studied at Phillips Andover Academy, Hamilton College, and Lake Forest University. He was ordained in the Congregational Church, and served churches at Cannon Falls, Minn., Rutland, Vt., and Albany, N.Y. (1878–85). He engaged in evangelistic work (1885–95), withdrew from Orthodox fellowship (1897), and conducted independent work in Boston (1897–99). He was in charge of the First Unitarian Church, Oakland, Calif. (1899–1903), founded the Los Angeles Fellowship (1905) and the Greater Fellowship (1908), and edited the *Fellowship Magazine* from 1905. In 1907/8 he visited China, Japan, and the Philippines. He wrote *Victory Through Surrender* (1892), *God's World and Other Sermons* (1894),

*The Divine Adventure* (1904), and *The New Revelation* (1908). He contributed to *Our Foreign Missionary Enterprise* (1909).

**Mindszenty, Jozsef** (1892–1975). Hungarian cardinal. Born in Csehimindszent in Austria-Hungary, he was imprisoned by the Nazis toward the end of World War II, became primate of Hungary in 1945, and was named cardinal in the following year. In the closing days of 1948, Hungary's communist government charged him with treason and spying, and after a farcical trial he was sentenced to life imprisonment. Released by fellow countrymen during the short-lived insurrection in 1956, he was at once again endangered by invading Soviet forces and was granted asylum in the U.S. embassy in Budapest. His stay there covered the closing years of Pius XII's pontificate, all of John XXIII's, and fully half of Paul VI's. Finally in 1971, having failed to obtain a government declaration of his innocence (his insistence on which had greatly extended his embassy sojourn), he belatedly followed a papal instruction to go to Rome. His voluntary incarceration complicated the position of Hungarian Catholics. Even after he retired to Vienna he continued to embarrass the Vatican by outspoken criticism of any compromise with communism. That implacable opposition was reflected in the dogged way he pursued his principles despite criticism.

J. D. DOUGLAS

**Minear, Paul Sevier** (1906– ). NT biblical scholar. Born in Mount Pleasant, Iowa, he studied at Iowa Wesleyan College, Garrett Biblical Institute, and Yale University (Ph.D., 1932). He taught at the Hawaii School of Religion (1933/34), and was professor of NT at Andover Newton Theological School (1944–56) and Yale University Divinity School (1956–71), during which time he was also professor of biblical theology. Among his books are *An Introduction to Paul* (1936), *And Great Shall Be Your Reward* (1941), *Eyes of Faith* (1946), *The Kingdom and the Power* (1950), *Christian Hope and the Second Coming* (1954), *Jesus and His People* (1956), *Images of the Church in the NT* (1960), *The Gospel of Mark* (1962), *I Saw a New Earth* (1969), *I Pledge Allegiance* (1975), *To Die and to Live* (1977), *NT Apocalyptic* (1981), *Matthew: The Teacher's Gospel* (1982), and *John: The Martyr's Gospel* (1984).

**Minor Orders.** *See* ORDERS, MINOR.

**Mirbt, Carl** (1860–1929). Lutheran church historian. He was a professor at Marburg (1890–1912) and Göttingen (1912–28) and a leading authority on the papacy. His early publications deal with the Hildebrandine controversy of the 11th century. His outstanding source book, *Quellen zur Geschichte des Papsttums und des*

*römischen Katholizismus* (1924), consists of source excerpts or entire documents in Greek, Latin, German, French, and English from nearly every Christian century. He participated as a Konsistorialrat in Lutheran church life. He was a leader in the Evangelischer Bund.

> *Bibliography.* *Die Religion in Geschichte und Gegenwart*, vol. 4 (1930).

W. W. ROCKWELL

**Missionaries of the Sacred Heart.** *See* CABRINI, FRANCIS XAVIER.

**Mission Covenant Church of America, Evangelical.** *See* EVANGELICAL COVENANT CHURCH.

**Missions, Orphaned.** *See* ORPHANED MISSIONS.

**Missions, Promotion of.** When Protestant mission societies were first founded in the 1790s, they were composed of volunteers, frequently members of a particular denomination. For example, the oldest British mission society, the Baptist Missionary Society (1792), was composed of Baptists, the Church Missionary Society (1799) of Anglicans, and the London Missionary Society (1795)—although interdenominational—by mostly Congregationalists. The voluntary nature of Protestant mission activity made promotional work a necessity if a society were to raise money and recruit volunteers for the mission field. Potential missionaries were early promoters of missions because they needed to raise the money to finance their passage overseas. Missionaries and officers of mission societies visited churches, delivered sermons, and encouraged interested church members to found local mission support groups. These ongoing mission circles provided prayer and monetary backing for the missionary and the mission society. Once missionaries arrived in the field, they would write letters home to supporters, mission boards, and denominational periodicals. Because they were the popular romantic and adventure literature of the day, published letters and missionary diaries were a major promotional tool for early 19th-century missions.

The promotion of missions also took place in local churches where there was a mission-minded pastor. Mission sermons, annual local mission conferences, and regular mission study groups all served to keep missionary interest high in local churches. In the late 19th century, women organized women's boards in most American denominations for the support of single women missionaries who worked among women and children around the world. Women in local churches contributed not only to their denominational mission society, but to their women's board. By 1901, nationally coordinated mission texts united

American Protestant women in an annual study of a particular mission field or problem.

Since the early 1800s, student groups have been at the forefront of mission promotion. The first American mission society, the American Board of Commissioners for Foreign Missions (1810), was founded in response to requests by Congregational seminarians. Seminary students began "societies of inquiry," in which they studied and prayed whether to volunteer for mission service. In 1886, student YMCA leaders attended a summer Bible camp hosted by evangelist Dwight L. Moody. While there, 100 college men volunteered to become foreign missionaries, thus creating the nucleus of the Student Volunteer Movement for Foreign Missions, a national student organization designed to promote missions among students. In Great Britain, students created the Student Volunteer Missionary Union. Thousands of European and American student volunteers swelled the ranks of the mission force by World War I, motivated by their promotional motto, "the evangelization of the world in this generation."

In the late 20th century, students have again become a major force in mission promotion. Groups such as the Theological Students for Frontier Missions (1980) organize chapters at seminaries to promote missions. The Inter-Varsity Christian Fellowship (1940) has held triennial Urbana conferences at which American collegians and seminarians dedicate themselves to foreign missions. At the 14th Urbana conference, over 18,000 students participated, more than 85 percent of whom indicated interest in mission service. In 1986, over 10,000 European students gathered in Amsterdam to commit themselves to mission activity. In Africa, Asia, and Latin America, the International Fellowship of Evangelical Students (1946), among other groups, promotes mission commitment among students.

The promotion of missions in the late 20th century varies widely among denominations because of the great differences in their strategies and definitions of missions. Such international groups as the Anglican Communion and the United Methodist Church practice partnership in missions whereby mission assistance is sent at the request of the receiving church. Partnership strategies obviate the need for general mission volunteers, and thus promotion becomes a relatively unimportant part of the denominational mission program. However, denominations, independent churches, and parachurch organizations that see themselves as providing evangelistic missionaries for "people groups" hitherto unreached by the gospel still engage heavily in mission promotion. For example, the Southern Baptists, who boast the largest denominational mission force in America, hold an annual mission fund-raising event in every church. Local mission events and mission education programs occur much as they did a century ago. Most theologically conservative missionaries must raise their own support, and thus travel from congregation to congregation in efforts to raise funds and to promote the cause of evangelistic missions. In general, the church organizations which believe that the world has not yet been adequately evangelized emphasize active promotion of missions, fund raising, and recruitment of missionaries. Groups that emphasize economic development, social liberation, mission partnership, and other nonevangelistic mission strategies tend to deemphasize the promotion of traditional missions.

DANA L. ROBERT

## Modern Churchmen's Union.

Church of England body founded in 1898 as the chief organ of liberal and modernist tendencies in the Church of England, appealing to the Erasmian tradition of Christian humanism. Although never very large (no more than 1200 members in 1948, since which time it has dwindled considerably), the union has included a number of distinguished theologians, such as W. R. Inge and W. R. Matthews, and prominent laypersons. Its influence is exercised largely through an annual conference and a quarterly journal, the circulation of which was 1000 in 1987.

## Moehlman, Conrad Henry (1879–1961).

Church historian. Born in Meriden, Conn., he studied at the University of Rochester, the University of Michigan (Ph.D., 1918), Rochester Theological Seminary, and the University of Chicago. After serving as pastor of the Baptist church in Central City, Nebr. (1905/6), he taught church history at Rochester Theological Seminary (1907/8), Hebrew language and literature (1909–12), NT interpretation (1913), and church history (1919–28). He also lectured on religion at the University of Rochester (1922–28, 1942–46). At the formation of Colgate-Rochester Seminary he became James B. Colgate professor of the history of Christianity (1928–44). He also taught history in schools in Dallas, Tex., and California. He wrote *The Unknown Bible* (1926), *The Story of the Ten Commandments* (1928), *The Catholic-Protestant Mind* (1929), *The Christian-Jewish Tragedy* (1933), *Sayings of Jesus* (1936), *Protestantism's Challenge* (1939), *School and Church* (1944), *The Church as Educator* (1947), *The Wall of Separation between Church and State* (1951), *Ordeal by Concordance* (1955), and *How Jesus Became God* (1960). He edited the *Record of Rochester Theological Seminary* (1913–19; 1921–23) and the *Colgate-Rochester Bulletin* (1930–38).

RAYMOND W. ALBRIGHT

## Möttlingen Movement.

Spiritual revival movement largely inspired by the Blumhardts

564

within the climate of Swabian pietism. Friedrich Stanger (1855–1935), a Protestant pastor who had experienced conversion, started a movement in 1909 in the community of Möttlingen, near Calw, Württemberg, under the motto *Die Rettungsarche* ("Ark of Salvation"). Stanger felt "divine powers flowing through him" through the mediation of the "victorious Christ." Following the principle found in James 5 (the laying on of hands, prayer of faithful believers, anointing with oil, exorcisms), Stanger practiced a ministry of faith healing. The movement attracted followers in southwestern Germany and Switzerland, particularly in Basel and Zurich. Although banned by the Nazis it experienced a brief resurgence after 1945. Since 1924 the group has published the periodical *Jesus ist Sieger*.

E. J. FURCHA

**Moffatt, James** (1870–1944). Scottish biblical scholar. Born in Glasgow, he was educated at the University of Glasgow and the Free Church College. After ordination he was minister at Dundonald (1896–1907) and Broughty Ferry (1907–11). He was subsequently professor of Greek and NT exegesis at Mansfield College, Oxford (1911–15), and professor of church history at the United Free Church College, Glasgow (1915–27), and at Union Theological Seminary, New York (1927–40). He translated a famous work by Adolf Harnack under the English title *Expansion of Christianity in the First Three Centuries* (1904–8), and edited a NT commentary series known by his name. Despite his conservative antecedents he became known for his critical and sometimes idiosyncratic approach to biblical studies, yet his translation of the whole Bible (1913, 1924) was highly acclaimed, widely used, and is still quoted in learned commentaries. Among his other works were *The Historical NT* (1901), *The Golden Book of John Owen* (1904), *Introduction to the Literature of the NT* (1911), *Theology of the Gospels* (1912), *Approach to the NT* (1921), *Hebrews* (in the *ICC* series) (1924), *Everyman's Life of Jesus* (1924), *The Bible in Scots Literature* (1925), *Presbyterianism* (1928), *Love in the NT* (1929), *The Day before Yesterday* (1930), *Grace in the NT* (1931), *The First Five Centuries of the Church* (1938), *First Corinthians* (1938), and *The Books of the Prophets* (1939).

J. D. DOUGLAS

**Moltmann, Jürgen** (1926– ). German theologian. Born in Hamburg, he was a prisoner of war in Belgium and Britain (1945–48). He later studied theology and became a pastor in 1952. He was professor at the church seminary in Wuppertal (1958–67), and since then has been professor of systematic theology in the Protestant faculty of Tübingen University. He is a prolific writer. His main contribution to date is his trilogy *Theology*

*of Hope* (1964), *The Crucified God* (1972), and *The Church in the Power of the Spirit* (1975); each book looks at theology as a whole from a different and specific perspective. This trilogy alone established him as a major theologian of this generation. He is a prominent spokesperson for the theology of hope, affirming the future's ontological priority. Eschatology is not "a loosely attached appendix" to dogmatics; "Christianity *is* Eschatology." History is promise and fulfillment, the basis for Christian hope. God promises; Christ's coming, death, and resurrection confirm and fulfill that promise. God's essential nature is future, yet the cross reveals him in contradiction; he is known in the opposite of himself.

Moltmann argues (following Hegel's analysis of society) that people see the church as socially irrelevant—a church resigned to living in a half-hearted way. The kingdom and righteousness of God demand economic, political, and cultural liberation. His other works include *Religion, Revolution and the Future* (1970), *Hope and Planning* (1971), *Man: Christian Anthropology* (1974), *The Experience of Hope* (1975), *The Future of Creation* (1979), *Experiences of God* (1980), *The Trinity and the Kingdom of God* (1981), *The Power of the Powerless* (1983), *The Open Church* (1983), *On Human Dignity* (1984), and *On Creation* (1985).

MICHAEL PARSONS

**Monaco.** Tiny principality with an area of 1.6 sq. km. (0.6 sq. mi.) on the Mediterranean Sea, surrounded by France and with a population of 29,000 (1986 est.), of which all but 3000 are Roman Catholic. Monaco has had a bishop since 1887. Monaco is governed under a constitution adopted in 1911, and is supported by gambling interests in the town of Monte Carlo.

**Mongolia.** Independent Asian state bounded by both China and the USSR, with an area of 1,565,000 sq. km. (604,250 sq. mi.) and a population of 1,810,000 (1981). During the 20th century, Mongolia has been transformed from a Buddhist theocracy to a Marxist secular state in which organized religion has been virtually eliminated. Before the mid-1920s, Tibetan Lamaism served as both the principal political and belief system. Superficially, Buddhism had centuries earlier replaced native Mongol shamanism. But many of the elements of popular shamanism (such as belief in good and evil spirits inherent in nature, idolatry and blood sacrifices, and reliance upon healers for beneficent intervention between human and spiritual worlds) were actually modified to fit Buddhist beliefs. From the 17th through the 19th centuries, monasteries governed by a "living Buddha" (Yellow Hat sect *Khubilgan* or *Khutukhtu*, if especially distinguished) served as the foci of Mongol religious, political, and economic life. Although a feudal nobility, complete with princely descendants of warrior khan and bound serfs, coexisted with the theocracy into the 20th century, the partnership was by no means equal. From 1911 through 1921, the Khutukhtu of Urga (later, Ulan Bator, the capital) headed an establishment in which 40 percent of the male population served as lamas, the church monopolized at least half the country's land and livestock wealth, and literacy was estimated at about 10 percent of the disease-ridden, impoverished population.

Great power rivalry in and around Mongolia between 1900 and into 1940 hastened the realization that Buddhist rule must end or the Mongols vanish as a people. This view was not only that of Mongolian nationalists and Marxists, but was also widely expressed by Westerners and Christian observers as well. Theocracy blocked secular education with both its beliefs and use of the Tibetan language, obstructed the formation of a state budget, and frustrated all attempts to raise troops for state defense. In 1911, the success of the Chinese Nationalist attempts to overthrow the Ch'ing Dynasty led to a Mongol revolt for independence from the Manchus. Both the church and nationalists appealed to the czarist government for continuing protection from China between 1911 and 1917. After the Bolshevik Revolution, the new Soviet government continued to support Mongol autonomy and treated the region as a nonoccupied buffer zone against possible extension of British, Japanese, and Chinese interests.

Although Soviet protection was initially welcomed by both church and nationalists, it was the latter group that used Marxist solutions to dissolve the theocracy. Relying upon Comintern advice, nationalists such as Sukebator and Choibalsan led an attack upon the nobility and then the church between 1921 and 1940. Initial moves were moderate. Following the establishment of a provisional government in 1921, Jebtsun Damba Khutukhtu was allowed to rule as a politically impotent constitutional figurehead. But upon his death, the Mongolian People's Revolutionary Government forbade both the search for and installation of a new "reincarnation" and Mongolia was officially declared a People's Republic. After 1924, monastic wealth was taxed, lower-ranking lamas driven from monasteries into secular professions, most temples either destroyed or used for nonreligious purposes, and higher lamas forced to flee abroad or face liquidation. Postwar party documents have partially condemned "excesses" and terror aimed at the church, particularly those that occurred during the "Left Deviation" (1929–32) and Choibalsan's creation of a Stalin-like personality cult (1932–39). Nevertheless, treating Buddhists as "class enemies" is more typically explained as having been necessary for creating an autonomous state during a period of external threat, particularly from Japan and China.

By 1940, the use of secret police against lamas and confiscation of church wealth had effectively broken the back of the Buddhist establishment. Where there had been nearly 1000 monasteries and 100,000 lamas in the early 1930s, only two monasteries, manned by a little over 100 lamas, operate today. These institutions have no independence from the state, but serve as government-subsidized centers for the study of church history. Religion has been relegated to the museum where it serves as a reminder of the bad days of poverty, ignorance, and exploitation. The postwar university system curriculum, modeled along Soviet lines, also includes required courses on scientific atheism. Despite this, one still finds new stones piled upon *obo*, ancient cairn at mountain passes where, according to shamanist beliefs, heavenly spirits intersect with those of earth. Also noteworthy are Buddhist religious pictures that can be found on the walls of yurts and apartments of older Mongols alongside larger pictures of family members and political leaders. Party organs still occasionally fulminate against the persistence of shamanism and Buddhist beliefs and authorities sometimes arrest an individual religious leader. But such official concern seems largely misplaced. Owing to demographic changes that have produced a younger Mongol population, educated under a Marxist regime and benefiting from changes that continue to increase their wealth and life expectancies, traditional religions are widely considered to be little more than embarrassing superstitions incompatible with modernism.

**Bibliography.** R. J. Miller, *Monasteries and Cultural Change in Inner Mongolia* (1959); O. Lattimore, *Nomads and Commissars: Mongolia Revisited* (1962); W. Heissig, *A Lost Civilization: The Mongols Rediscovered* (1964); R. Rupen, *Mongols of the Twentieth Century* (1964); C. R. Bawden, *The Modern History of Mongolia* (1968); G. A. Cheney, *The Pre-Revolutionary Culture of Outer Mongolia* (1968); A. Sanders, *The People's Republic of Mongolia: A General Reference Guide* (1968); V. P. Petrov, *Mongolia: A Profile* (1970); R. Rupen, *How Mongolia Is Really Ruled: A Political History of the Mongolian People's Republic, 1900–1978* (1971); A. Sanders, *Asian Survey* 18/1 (Jan. 1978): 29–35; W. Heissig, *The Religion of the Mongols* (1980); T. Haining, *Asian Affairs* (Feb. 1986): 19–32.

MICHAEL LEWIS

## Monod, Wilfred (1867–1943).

Manichean scholar. He taught theology in the Protestant faculty at the University of Paris. He was a liberal dualist with gnostic tendencies, holding that God is of a different order from this world but that ultimately he will win over all the forces at work in this world, even the satanic ones. He wrote *Aux croyants et aux athées* (1906), *Le problème du bien, Somme théologique,* and *Journal d'un pasteur* (3 vols., 1935).

RAYMOND W. ALBRIGHT

**Monotheism.** Belief in one, and only one, God. Monotheism is to be distinguished from polytheism (belief in a plurality of gods), henotheism/monolatry (belief in a supreme god, although not to the exclusion of lesser deities), and atheism (disbelief in the existence of any gods altogether). Monotheism, which commonly refers to OT Israel's belief in one God and adopted by the Christian church, is characteristic of the mainstream of Western religious thought. Some other contemporary religions espouse a form of monotheism (Zoroastrianism, Sikhism), but suggest that God is part of the universe. Only Judeo-Christian religion affirms the one transcendent yet immanent God.

Students of comparative religion have regarded monotheism as the final stage in the development of the religious consciousness of Israel. They posit a number of intermediate stages, beginning with some primitive form of animism (the belief that natural objects are inhabited by supernatural spirits). Gradually the Israelites perceived that some spirits were more powerful than others and were worthy of being recognized as gods. Eventually the people came to believe in and worship the most powerful of these gods.

This hypothesis, however, is suspect. It cannot be categorically concluded that polytheistic religions invariably reduce the number of their gods to one. There are a plethora of Hindu deities (as many as 800 million), for example, and this number is actually increasing. Monotheism did not evolve throughout the course of Israel's history, but was revealed by God to his people.

The entire Bible assumes that there is only one God. Against materialism (which holds that matter is eternal), the creation account teaches that God created nature and the cosmos and is above it (Creator–creature distinction). Against pantheism (which maintains that God is in everything), the Bible shows that God is distinct from his creation. Against dualism (which posits an ongoing struggle between the principles of good and evil), the Bible reveals the good, powerful God.

Contemporary views of God basically fall into three relatively well-defined camps. *Naturalism*, exemplified in the thought of John Dewey (1859–1952), describes nature as self-sufficient; God has no active role. *Finitism*, represented primarily by the thought of Alfred North Whitehead (1861–1947) and his school, distinguishes between God in his primordial nature (as a changeless, actual entity) and God in his consequent nature (as an entity capable of growing in awareness and sympathy). God is an infinite-finite being. There has also been a resurgence of the more traditional *theism*. God is said to participate in the cosmos (as opposed to naturalism) and is infinite (as opposed to finitism).

**Bibliography.** W. Elwell, ed., *Evangelical Dictionary of Theology* (1984); J. Collins, *Collier's Encyclopedia* (1988); S. B. Ferguson, et al., *New Dictionary of Theology* (1988).

**Monsignor.** Title from the Italian meaning "my lord" formerly used when addressing Roman Catholic prelates of all rank. According to modern etiquette, however, the title primarily applies to prelates of the papal household, either honorific or holding office, and of a rank inferior to that of bishop.

**Montgomery, James Alan** (1866–1949). Episcopalian OT scholar. Born in Philadelphia, Pa., he studied at the University of Pennsylvania (Ph.D., 1904), Philadelphia Divinity School, Greifswald, and Berlin. After serving as curate at the Church of the Holy Communion, New York (1892/93), St. Paul's, West Philadelphia (1893–95), and St. Peter's, Philadelphia (1895–99), he became rector of Epiphany, Germantown (1899–1903). He taught OT at the Philadelphia Divinity School (1899–1935) and was professor of Hebrew at the University of Pennsylvania (1909–36). He was the director of the American School of Oriental Research in Jerusalem (1914/15). He wrote *The Samaritans, the Earliest Jewish Sect* (1907), *Aramaic Incantation Texts from Nippur* (1913), *Religions of the Past and Present*, *Commentary on Daniel* (1927), *History of Yaballaha III* (1927), *Arabia and the Bible* (1934), and *Hebraic Mythological Texts from Ras Shamra* (1935).

RAYMOND W. ALBRIGHT

**Moon, Sun Myung.** *See* UNIFICATION CHURCH.

**Mooney, Edward Francis** (1882–1958). Cardinal. Born in Mount Savage, Md., he studied at Saint Charles College, Saint Mary's Seminary, Baltimore, and North American College, Rome. Ordained to the priesthood in 1909, he held several teaching positions and engaged in pastoral work in the archdiocese of Cleveland, Ohio. He served on the faculty of the North American College, Rome (1923–26). He was consecrated archbishop (titular) of Irenopolis and was sent as apostolic delegate to India (1926) and Japan (1931). He was called back to the USA to take over the diocese of Rochester, N.Y. (1933). He became archbishop of Detroit, Mich. (1937), and was created cardinal on February 18, 1946, under the pontificate of Pius XII.

GEORGES A. BARROIS

**Moore, Edward Caldwell** (1857–1943). Presbyterian theologian. Born in West Chester, Pa., he studied at Marietta College and Union Theological Seminary. He also studied at Berlin, Göttingen, Giessen (D.Th., 1926), and Brown (Ph.D., 1891). He served a Presbyterian church in Yonkers, N.Y. (1886–89), and Central Congregational Church, Providence, R.I. (1889–1901). He taught theology and Christian morals at Harvard (1901–29). He wrote *The NT in the Christian Church* (1904), *History of Christian Thought since Kant* (1912), *The Spread of Christianity in the Modern World* (1919), *West and East* (1919), and *The Nature of Religion.* He coedited *The Harvard University Hymn Book* (1925) with A. T. Davison.

RAYMOND W. ALBRIGHT

**Moore, George Foote** (1851–1931). Congregational scholar. Born in West Chester, Pa., he was educated at Yale and Union Theological seminaries. He was a Presbyterian minister in Ohio (1877–83) before becoming professor of Hebrew language and literature at Andover Theological Seminary (1883–1902). Thereafter he was professor of the history of religion at Harvard (1902–4) and professor of the history of religion at Yale (1904–21). Regarded as belonging to the critical school, he was a member of the Deutsche morgenländische Gesellschaft and the Society of Biblical Literature and Exegesis, and recording secretary of the American Oriental Society. A contributor to the *Encyclopaedia Biblica,* he also wrote *Commentary on Judges* (1895), *The Literature of the OT* (1913), *History of Religions* (2 vols., 1913, 1919), *Metempsychosis* (1914), and *Judaism* (2 vols., 1927).

**Moral Development.** Process by which children go from the age of innocence to the age of accountability, from a time when they know neither good nor evil to a time when they understand what is right and what is wrong and choose the right way. The progressive and continuous changes that occur from infancy to maturity to produce this desirable state are generally considered to include the formation of a wholesome character, adjustment to the society in which one lives, and a respect for those in authority.

Psychologists approach the study of moral development from various perspectives. Learning psychology has its roots in the philosophy of British associationist John Locke, who held that the child is born as a tabula rasa or blank slate. It is the experiences a person has that make him whatever he becomes. Behaviorists such as John B. Watson and B. F. Skinner focused on observable behaviors which are shaped by environmental events. Albert Bandura, also a learning psychologist, emphasized the importance of appropriate models. Moral development occurs when the child imitates the actions of responsible adults and is reinforced for socially acceptable behavior and punished for socially unacceptable behavior.

Humanistic psychology stems from the philosophy of Jean-Jacques Rousseau, who saw the child as a noble savage. Children are "noble" in that they are born with the potential for self-development including the propensity to develop morally; they are "savage" in that they seek to go their own ways and make their own decisions. Humanistic psychologists such as Carl Rogers and Abraham Maslow favor the encouragement of the child's natural desire to be moral by letting the child choose his own values and act upon his own decisions. Moral development comes from within the individual rather than being imposed by an outside source.

By contrast, psychoanalytic psychology as proposed by its founder Sigmund Freud views the infant as a depraved creature with irrational passions and instincts. The formation of an ego oriented to a world of reality and a superego embodying societal values and attitudes and oriented to matters of right and wrong is essential in order for the individual to become a moral person.

The bulk of current literature on moral development relates to cognitive psychology with its emphasis on stages of moral reasoning as given by Jean Piaget and developed by Lawrence Kohlberg. Kohlberg adopted the Platonic and Socratic views that virtue is one not many, and justice is its name. Moral development occurs in a series of stages that are invariant, hierarchical, and universal. At each succeeding stage, one advances in an understanding of what is fair or just, incorporating a larger number of persons in a concept of fairness. Kohlberg wrote that at the first stage of moral judgment, a person interprets an action as good or bad according to its physical consequences. Avoidance of punishment and unquestioning deference to power are valued in their own right. At the second stage the individual believes that right action consists of that which satisfies personal needs. Human relations are viewed in terms like those of the marketplace. At stage 3, good behavior is equated with whatever pleases or helps others. Winning the approval of family, friends, and neighbors takes priority. In stage 4 a person is oriented to law and order. Right behavior consists of doing one's duty, showing respect for authority, and maintaining the given social order for its own sake. Those who progress to stage 5 believe that the purpose of the law is to preserve human rights, and they seek to change those laws which do not serve this purpose. In the opinion of those who reach stage 6, morality is grounded not in legality but in abstract principles of justice and respect for every individual. Moral development thus proceeds from a desire to enhance self (stages 1 and 2) to a conformity to social expectations (stages 3 and 4) to a concern for the rights and humanity of every person (stages 5 and 6).

**Bibliography.** S. Freud, *Civilization and Its Discontents* (1930); J. B. Watson, *Behaviorism* (1931); J. Piaget, *The Moral Judgment of the Child* (1932); A. Bandura, *Journal of Personality and Social Psychology* 1 (1965): 589–95; C. Rogers, *Freedom to*

*Learn* (1969); A. H. Maslow, *Dominance, Self-esteem, Self-actualization: Germinal Papers of A. H. Maslow* (1973); B. F. Skinner, *Reflections on Behaviorism and Society* (1978); L. Kohlberg, *Essays on Moral Development: The Psychology of Moral Development* (1984); B. Clouse, *Moral Development: Perspectives in Psychology and Christian Belief* (1985).

BONNIDELL CLOUSE

**Moral Education.** The teaching of morals has long been considered an important part of the educational process. "Listen, my son, to your father's instruction and do not forsake your mother's teaching" (Prov. 1:8), wrote King Solomon thousands of years ago. "Then you will understand what is right and just and fair—every good path" (Prov. 2:9). As these verses imply, moral education was didactic, the wisdom of the ages passed from one generation to the next. Stress was placed on overt behaviors such as obedience, truthfulness, responsibility, and not socializing with those who would deceive or lead one into a life of profligacy. Also emphasized was the knowledge or cognition that accompanies moral behavior. Now known as character education, this method is still commonly used by parents, teachers, and religious leaders. It is based on the universally accepted premise that adults know better than children what is right and what is wrong. Directions and guidelines are essential to the proper development of the young and for the smooth functioning of society. The morally educated person is one whose attitudes and actions correspond to what the culture expects of its members.

Many people feel that the major responsibility for moral education lies with parents or with religious leaders. But some children are not taught in the home and some children do not attend a church or synagogue, making it necessary to provide another avenue of instruction. The school has become the logical choice. A few have argued that the school is even preferable because it introduces the child to a larger, more democratic community. Emile Durkheim maintained that the school frees the child from excessive dependency, from being a slavish copy of the family. Jean Piaget believed that the morality of cooperation (autonomy) encouraged by the school was more mature than the morality of constraint (heteronomy) taught in the home.

Moral education programs have flourished in the past two decades. The trend, however, is away from indoctrination and toward each student developing within the self his or her own understanding of what is good and right. This change has come in part from research that shows that only a minor portion of moral education occurs at the "facts" level. Simply knowing what society expects does not ensure that one will act in accordance with that knowledge. Fluctuations and diversified elements within the social groups that make up the community of the school also complicate the process of moral education.

The two major programs in moral education in the USA are Lawrence Kohlberg's moral reasoning, and Howard Kirschenbaum and Sidney Simon's values clarification. To encourage moral reasoning, stories with a moral dilemma are told; each child is to state a position on the dilemma. The student is naturally drawn to the reasoning of someone at the next higher stage, so that, in time, one's concept of justice includes an ever-expanding circle of humankind. According to this cognitive approach, the morally educated person is one who has advanced in thinking processes from being an egocentric being to a socially responsive and responsible individual.

To enhance the clarification of values, questions are asked about topics such as money, friendship, leisure, religion, or love. The student must be able to choose freely; consider alternatives; choose after thoughtfully considering the consequences of each alternative; be happy with the choice; affirm the choice publicly; act upon it; and incorporate the behavior. According to this humanistic approach, the morally educated person is one who is allowed to choose, affirm, and act upon those values that make him or her a fully functioning individual.

*Bibliography.* H. Hartshorne and M. A. May, *Studies in the Nature of Character*, 3 vols. (1928–30); J. Piaget, *The Moral Judgment of the Child* (1932); E. Durkheim, *Moral Education: A Study in the Theory and Application of the Sociology of Education* (1973); H. Kirschenbaum and S. Simon, eds., *Readings in Values Clarification* (1973); B. Clouse, *Christianity Today* 22 (Dec. 30, 1977): 14–17; L. Kohlberg, *Essays on Moral Development: The Psychology of Moral Development* (1984); H. Blackham, et al., *Journal of Moral Education* 14 (1985): 4–8.

BONNIDELL CLOUSE

**Moral Rearmament.** *See* BUCHMAN, FRANK NATHAN DANIEL.

**Moravian Brethren.** *See* UNITY OF THE CHURCH (MORAVIAN BRETHREN).

**More, Paul Elmer** (1864–1937). Editor and scholar. Born in St. Louis, Mo., he studied at Washington University and Harvard. After teaching Sanskrit at Harvard (1894–95) and Bryn Mawr (1895–97), he became literary editor of the *Independent* (1901–3) and the *New York Evening Post* (1903–9). In addition to his *Shelburne Essays* (11 vols., 1904ff.), he wrote *Life of Benjamin Franklin* (1900), *Platonism* (1917), *The Religion of Plato* (1921), *Hellenistic Philosophies* (1923), *The Christ of the NT* (1924), *Christ the Word* (1927), *The Demon of the Absolute* (1928), *The Catholic Faith* (1931), and *The Sceptical Approach to Religion* (1934). He coedited *Anglicanism* (1935) with F. L. Cross. He edited *The Nation* (1909–14). He

569

translated *Judgment of Socrates, Prometheus Bound,* and *Century of Indian Epigrams.*

RAYMOND W. ALBRIGHT

**Morehead, John Alfred** (1867–1936). Lutheran pastor and theologian. Born in Pulaski County, Va., he studied at Roanoke College, Va., Lutheran Theological Seminary, Mt. Airy, Philadelphia, Berlin, and Leipzig (D.Th., 1922). Ordained in the Lutheran ministry in 1892, he preached at Burke's Garden, Va. (1892–94), and the First English Lutheran Church, Richmond (1894–98). He was president and professor of systematic theology at Southern Lutheran Theological Seminary (1898–1908), president of Roanoke College (1908–19), chairman of the European commission of the National Lutheran Council (1919–23), executive director of the National Lutheran Council (1923–30), chairman of the editorial committee of the *Lutheran World Almanac and Encyclopedia* (1924–30), and gave his full time in his last years as president of the executive committee of the Continuation Work of the Lutheran World Convention (1930–36).

*Bibliography.* S. Trexler, *John A. Morehead* (1938).

RAYMOND W. ALBRIGHT

**Morgan, George Campbell** (1863–1945). British preacher, Bible teacher, and author. After several years as a schoolteacher in Birmingham and after being rejected by the Wesleyan Methodist Church, he entered the Congregational ministry. During his first pastorates in Birmingham and New Court Church, London, he developed the gift of lucid Bible exposition. His abilities earned him recognition in Great Britain and the USA and he was in great demand at D. L. Moody's Northfield Conferences. In 1904 he began the first of two influential ministries at Westminster Chapel, London, which lasted until 1917. His Friday Night Bible School, in which he taught the Bible analytically and systematically, drew large crowds and had a wide influence through the extensive distribution of the *Westminster Bible Record.* He served as president of Cheshunt College, Cambridge (1911–17), and was involved in several missionary societies, particularly the Evangelical Union of South America. From 1919 he spent several years in the USA and Canada in itinerant ministry and serving a number of churches before returning to a second term at Westminster Chapel (1933–45). His colleague in later years and successor was Martyn Lloyd-Jones. He published many books, mainly of expositions and sermons.

JAMES TAYLOR

**Morgenstern, Julian** (1881–1976). Jewish rabbi and scholar. Born in St. Francisville, Ill., he studied at the universities of Cincinnati, Berlin, and Heidelberg (Ph.D., 1904), and the Hebrew Union College. He served as rabbi in Lafayette, Ind. (1904–7), and taught Bible and Semitic languages at Hebrew Union College (1907–47). He was president of Hebrew Union College (1921–47). He delivered the Haskell Lectures at Oberlin Graduate School of Theology (1935), and edited *Young Israel* (1908–11). He was secretary of the Central Conference of American Rabbis (1907–15), trustee of the American Schools of Oriental Research (1921–46), American vice-president of the World Union for Progressive Judaism from 1926, president of the American Oriental Society (1928–29), and president of the Society of Biblical Literature and Exegesis (1941). He wrote *The Doctrine of Sin in the Babylonian Religion* (1905), *A Jewish Interpretation of Genesis* (1919), *Amos Studies,* vol. 1 (1941), *The Ark, the Ephod and the Tent of Meeting* (1945), and *As a Mighty Stream* (1949).

**Mormons.** Name popularly given to members of the Church of Jesus Christ of Latter Day Saints. An orthodox Mormon is one who testifies that the *Book of Mormon* is true, acknowledges that Joseph Smith is a true prophet of God, and agrees to abide by the ordinances of the church. The Mormon Church is one of the fastest-growing in the world. The current president, Ezra Taft Benson, together with the Council of Twelve and the First Council of Seventy, oversees the organization's vast network of missionary activity and considerable financial investments from the group's headquarters in Salt Lake City, Utah. Worldwide membership of the church is more than 5 million.

The church was organized on April 6, 1830, in Fayette, N.Y., by Joseph Smith who claimed to have discovered the "everlasting gospel of Jesus Christ" which had been hidden away for 1400 years on gold and bronze tablets near Palmyra in western New York. Smith's unique claims to apostolicity brought strong opposition from the contemporary religious and political establishment. Smith's and his followers' trek westward took them initially to Kirtland, Ohio, where they built the first temple. From there they migrated to the Missouri Territory, then back to Nauvoo, Ill. There Smith and other leaders were arrested for attacking an opposition newspaper which had revealed the leaders' practice of polygamous marriage. After Smith and his brother Hyrum were lynched by a mob in Carthage, Ill., on June 27, 1844, the main body of Mormons under their new leader, Brigham Young, made their way to the Great Salt Lake in the Utah Territory and settled there. A much smaller group rejected the leadership of Brigham Young and organized themselves under the leadership of Joseph Smith's family as the Reorganized Church of Jesus Christ of Latter Day Saints. Today they maintain their headquarters at Independence,

570

Mo., and report a membership of about 250,000. They are much more traditional in belief.

The teachings and practices of the Mormons can be understood only within the context of the two pillars of their basic confession—the veracity of the *Book of Mormon* and the authority of contemporary revelation entrusted to the first president of the church as the living successor of the founding prophet, Joseph Smith. At crucial points in the church's history the authority of the contemporary prophet has prevailed over the revelations which are fixed in the authoritative books. The living prophet has demonstrated his power to modify or even reverse the past teaching and practices of the church. This has allowed the Mormons to make radical shifts in policy and practice as contemporary issues have challenged them to do so. Two of the most obvious of these instances are the Woodruff Manifesto of 1890 which forbade further practice of polygamy, allowing Utah to achieve statehood, and the pronouncement of President Spencer Kimball in 1978 which permitted nonwhites immediate rights to the full priesthood in contradiction to all previous authoritative teachings and practices of the church. In addition to the *Book of Mormon* the church's other authoritative scriptures are *The Doctrine and Covenants,* the *Pearl of Great Price,* and the Bible, "insofar as it is translated correctly."

Mormon theology may be characterized as polytheistic and anthropological in focus. God the Father was chosen in a council of the gods on the planet Kolab to be the God of the planet earth. God is flesh and bone, has all the attributes of a man, and is married. With his wives he procreated all the spirits which are embodied in men and women on earth. All of these spirits—except the spirit of the man Jesus Christ—fell from God's grace in their prior existence and were in need of redemption. Adam and Eve were placed on the earth to provide bodies for these preexistent spirits so that they might receive God's salvation and prove their faithfulness to him by obedience and good works. The chief consequence of the fall was that men and women discovered their own sexuality; therefore it was a "fall forward," for it made possible the embodiment of the fallen preexistent spirits. Procreation, then, is essential to salvation; this explains the strong emphasis of the Mormons upon marriage and the family and the rationalization for the polygamy they once condoned. The church's fascination with personal genealogies is rooted in these doctrines as well. By identifying one's ancestors and being baptized for them in one of the many regional temples, those who did not hear the "everlasting gospel" as revealed only through Mormonism will be given the opportunity to receive it and be saved.

Exaltation as a god is much more meaningful to a Mormon than salvation from sin. The end of full salvation is one's elevation to a godhood equal to that of God the Father. This exalted state is reserved for males. A woman can share in highest bliss only through her relationship with her husband, who stands in the Melchizedekian priesthood, the highest in the church. Some measure of salvation and entrance into the terrestrial or telestial heaven is open to all persons except the devil and his angels and the most reprobate of humankind. Only those who faithfully follow the mandates of the faith, however, can reach the celestial heaven where they may become gods. Thereafter, they, with their eternal wives, will procreate new spirits and repeat on a planet of their own the cycle of redemption which they experienced on earth and thus eventually redeem the universe.

**Bibliography.** L. C. Scott, *The Mormon Mirage* (1979); J. and S. Tanner, *The Changing World of Mormonism* (1980); K. J. Hansen, *Mormonism and the American Experience* (1981).

MELVIN E. DIETER

**Morocco.** *See* NORTH AFRICA.

**Morris, Leon Lamb** (1914– ). Anglican theologian. Born in Lithgow, New South Wales, Australia, he was educated at Sydney University and Sydney Teachers' College and later took degrees from London and Cambridge (Ph.D.) universities. After three years of teaching, he was made deacon in 1938 and ordained priest in 1939, serving in the diocese of Sydney and then as a Bush Church Aid missioner at Minnipa in the diocese of Willochra, South Australia. From 1945 to 1960 he was vice-principal of Ridley College in Melbourne, Victoria. He left to become warden of Tyndale House in Cambridge (1961–63), but returned to Australia as principal of Ridley College, where he remained until his retirement in 1979. Much of his writing and preaching has focused attention on the atonement. Preaching has always been of paramount importance to Morris, and in the training of others for ministry he has laid particular emphasis on this and on the importance of the minister's pastoral care of his people. A prolific author, perhaps his most significant publications have been *The Apostolic Preaching of the Cross* (1955), *Commentary on the Gospel of John* (1971), *Testaments of Love* (1982), and *Theology of the NT* (1986).

**Bibliography.** R. Banks, ed., *Reconciliation and Hope: NT Essays on Atonement and Eschatology* (1973).

DAVID JOHN WILLIAMS

**Morrison, Charles Clayton** (1874–1966). Disciples of Christ minister. Born in Harrison, Ohio, he graduated from Drake University. He became a fellow in the department of philosophy at the University of Chicago (1902–5). He was a pastor in Clorinda and Perry, Iowa, at Monroe Street Church, Chicago, and at First Church, Springfield, Ill. He is most widely known as editor of the *Christian Century*, which he revamped in 1908 as an undenominational journal of religion and edited until 1947. After 1947, he served as a contributing editor. He was a lecturer on Christianity and public affairs at Chicago Theological Seminary from 1931. He was a delegate at the World Missionary Conference, Edinburgh (1910), the Panama Congress, and regional conferences in South America. He edited the *Proceedings* of the same (1916). He was also a delegate of the Oxford and Edinburgh conferences (1937) and the World Council of Churches, Amsterdam (1948). His books include *The Unfinished Reformation* (1952), *Can Protestantism Win America?* (1948), *The Christian and the War* (1942), *What Is Christianity?* (1940), *The Social Gospel and the Christian Cultus* (1932), *The Outlawry of War* (1926), and *The Meaning of Baptism* (1916). He coauthored *The Daily Altar* (1918) with H. L. Willett. He compiled *Hymns of the United Church* (1916). He founded and edited *Christendom* (1934–39) and the *Pulpit* from 1929.

## Mortalium Animos

**Mortalium Animos.** Encyclical issued by Pope Pius XI on January 6, 1928, on the principles of true religious unity among Christians. It condemns the opinion that all religions are good because they all foster the growth of natural religion in man. It warns against trying to restore Christian unity on the basis of interconfessional encounters. It restates the Roman doctrine of the church as a perfect, visible society gathered under one head, infallible in its teaching and having the divine promises of perpetual duration. It maintains that uniformity of belief and government never existed in the church. The encyclical rejects any attempt to bring about the reunion of the churches in such a way that would place Rome on a par with other denominations.

*Bibliography.* Acta Apostolicae Sedis (1928), 20: 6–16.

GEORGES A. BARROIS

## Mott, John Raleigh

**Mott, John Raleigh** (1865–1955). Ecumenist. Born in Livingstone Manor, N.Y., he was raised in a devout Methodist family. His Christian commitment profoundly intensified during his college years, and he was deeply influenced by D. L. Moody. This remarkable layman was the most prominent person in world missions and ecumenism during the first half of the 20th century. A lifelong officer of the YMCA (general secretary of the American YMCA, 1915–28), Mott was a founder of the Student Volunteer Movement (1888), the World's Student Christian Federation (1895), the Edinburgh Missionary Conference (1910), and the International Missionary Council (1921). Chairperson of SVM and WSCF until 1920, he presided over most of the sessions at Edinburgh in 1910, and chaired its Continuation Committee as well as its successor, the International Missionary Council, for two decades until 1942. Central also in the formation of the World Council of Churches in 1948, he was named an honorary president of that body. In the course of his constant world travels in the interest of missions and ecumenism, Mott was instrumental in organizing Christian youth and student movements around the world, as well as numerous national councils of churches. An exponent and model of social Christianity, Mott labored for reconciliation among the combatants after World War I, and in relief work among Allied troops and prisoners of war during both wars. Among his many honors, he was awarded the Nobel Peace Prize in 1946 for his world service in various causes. His numerous writings include *The Evangelization of the World in This Generation* (1900), *The Decisive Hour of Christian Missions* (1910), *Confronting Young Men with the Living Christ* (1923), *Liberating the Lay Forces of Christianity* (1932), *Five Decades and a Forward View* (1939), and *The Larger Evangelism* (1944).

NORRIS A. MAGNUSON

## Moule, Charles Francis Digby

**Moule, Charles Francis Digby** (1908– ). Anglican clergyman and educator. Born in Hangchow, China, of missionary parents, he was educated at Cambridge University and was ordained a deacon (1933) and a priest (1934) of the Church of England. He served as curate at St. Mark's, Cambridge, and tutor at Ridley Hall (1933/34), curate of St. Andrew's, Rugby (1934–36), vice-principal at Ridley Hall (1936–44), curate of St. Mary the Great, Cambridge (1936–40), dean of Clare College, Cambridge (1944–51), assistant lecturer in divinity at Cambridge University (1944–51), and professor of divinity at Cambridge University (1951–76). He was elected a fellow of Clare College (1944) and a fellow of the British Academy (1966). A distinguished NT scholar, he delivered many prestigious lectures. Critical of systematic theology and all theological systems, of much modern biblical scholarship, and occasionally of even his own theological preferences, Moule could also appreciate other points of view. His magnificent background in classics led him to approach the NT like a classical text, but one with a sacred message. He never established his own school of NT studies but rather showed his students how to use modern critical methods to come to theologically conservative conclusions. His position at Cambridge University made him one of the most influential NT scholars of the mid-20th century. His most notable works include *The Meaning of Hope* (1953), *An Idiom Book of NT Greek* (1953), *The Sacrifice of Christ* (1956), *Commentary on Colossians and Philemon* (1957), *Worship in the NT* (1961), *Commentary on Mark* (1965), *The Phenomenon of the NT* (1967), *The Origin of Christology* (1977), *The Holy Spirit* (1978), *The Birth of the NT* (3d ed., 1981), and

*Essays in NT Interpretation* (1982). He also coedited *Christian History and Interpretation* (1968) and *Jesus and the Politics of His Day* (1984).

ROBERT D. LINDER

**Moule, Handley Carr Glyn** (1841–1920). Anglican bishop and writer. Born in Dorchester, England, he was educated at Cambridge, where after a short period as schoolmaster and curate he returned as dean of Trinity College (1873–77), first principal of Ridley Hall (1881–99), and professor of divinity (1899–1901). He was then consecrated bishop of Durham (1901–20), one of the senior sees of the Church of England. In theology he followed the traditions of the English Reformation, and in later years was greatly influenced by the Keswick movement. Among his numerous writings are *Poems from Subjects Connected with the Acts of the Apostles* (1869), *Justifying Righteousness* (1885), *The Christian's Victory over Sin* (1887), *Secret Prayer* (1889), *Veni Creator* (1890), *At the Holy Communion* (1892), *Charles Simeon* (1895), *Philippian Studies* (1897), *Colossian Studies* (1898), *Ephesian Studies* (1900), *The Evangelical School in the Church of England* (1901), *The School of Suffering* (1905), *Second Epistle to Timothy* (1905), *Faith, Its Nature and Work* (1909), *Messages from the Epistle to the Hebrews* (1909), *Christus Consolator* (1915), *Christ and Sorrow* (1916), *The Call of Lent* (1917), and *Auckland Castle* (1918).

**Moulton, James Hope** (1863–1917). Methodist scholar. Born in Richmond, Surrey, he studied at the Leys School and King's College, Cambridge. He was fellow of King's (1888–94), entered the ministry (1886), assisted his father at the Leys (1886–1902), was classical lecturer at Girton and Newnham Colleges (1887–1901), was tutor at Wesleyan College, Didsbury (1902–17), and was professor of Hellenistic Greek and Indo-European philology at Manchester University (1908–17). He died at sea while returning from India after his ship had been torpedoed. He is noted for his contribution to the study of koine Greek. His main writings are *An Introduction to the Study of NT Greek* (1895), *The Science of Language and the Study of the NT* (1906), *Grammar of NT Greek* (vol. 1, 1906; vol. 2, 1919), *Early Religious Poetry of Persia* (1911), *Early Zoroastrianism* (1912), *Religions and Religion* (1913), *From Egyptian Rubbish Heaps* (1917), *British and German Scholarship* (1915), *The Treasure of the Magi* (1917), *A Neglected Sacrament and Other Studies and Addresses* (1919), and *The Christian Religion in the Study and the Street* (1919).

**Bibliography.** *Dictionary of National Biography* (1912–21), pp. 319f.; *Bulletin of the John Rylands Library* 4 (1917): 10–25; *Times*, Mar. 3, 1941.

DANIEL J. THERON

**Moulton, Richard Green** (1849–1924). Literary critic. Born in Preston, England, he studied at the University of London, Cambridge, and the University of Pennsylvania (Ph.D., 1891). He was Cambridge University extension lecturer in literature (1874–90) and was professor of literature in English at the University of Chicago (1892–1919). In addition to his many books on Shakespeare and literary criticism, those which are of most interest to students of religion are *The Literary Study of the Bible* (1896), *A Short Introduction to the Literature of the Bible* (1901), *World Literature and Its Place in General Education* (1911), *The Modern Study of Literature* (1915), and *The Whole Bible at a Single View* (1918). He edited *The Modern Reader's Bible* (25 vols., 1895–1923), for which he was best known.

RAYMOND W. ALBRIGHT

**Mowinckel, Sigmund** (1884–1965). Lutheran OT theologian. Born in Kjerringy, Norway, he studied at the universities of Oslo, Marburg and Giessen, and Oslo (D.Th., 1916). He was "Adjunktstipendiat" at Oslo (1915; docent, 1917; professor of OT theology, 1922). He also served as dean of the theological faculty for several triennia. He wrote *Zur Komposition des Buches Jeremia* (1914), *Statholderen Nehemia* (1916), *Ezra den skriftlaerde* (1916), *Kongesalmerne* (1916), *Der Knecht Jahwes* (1921), *Psalmenstudien I–VI* (1921–24), *Profeten Jesaja* (1925), *Jesajadisiplene* (1926), *Le Dècologue* (1927), *Die Sternnamen im Alten Testament* (1928), *Die Erkenntnis Gottes bei den alttestamentlichen Propheten* (1941), *Zur Frage nach dokumentarischen Quellen in den Listen in Jos. 13–19* (1946), *Prophecy and Tradition* (1946), *Jesaja* (1949), *Religion og kultus* (1950), *Han som kommer, Messiasforestillingne i Det Gamle Testament og pa Jesu tid* (1951), *Offersang og sangoffer*, and *Salmediktningen i Bibelen* (1951).

**Mowll, Howard West Kilvinton** (1890–1958). Anglican archbishop and evangelical leader. Born in Dover, England, he was educated at Cambridge. He was president of the Cambridge Inter-Collegiate Christian Union and was involved in the first division between conservative evangelicals and the Student Christian Movement. He prepared for ordination at Ridley Hall, Cambridge, and was ordained in England, but immediately served the Anglican Church in Canada. He was on the staff of Wycliffe College, Toronto (1913–22), and was professor of history from 1916. In 1922 Mowll was called from his academic work in Canada to serve as assistant bishop of the missionary diocese in West China. In 1926 he became bishop of the diocese. He served in a war-torn and internally divided China, himself falling into the hands of bandits and being held prisoner for a month in 1924. In 1933 he was elected archbishop of Sydney after a hotly contested election. He accepted and served the oldest Australian diocese until his death 26 years later. His strong conservative evangelical stance at first created some controversy. Mowll supported all the main evangelical causes such as the inter-denominational Scripture Union, of which he was president.

By his sterling work for the church during World War II and his support for the World Council of Churches he gradually gained recognition and support both in his diocese and in the whole Australian church. He became primate of the Church of England in Australia in 1947. He traveled widely after the war and led one of the first Western church delegations to be invited to China in 1955. He was made a Companion of the Order of St. Michael and St. George in 1954.

NOEL S. POLLARD

**Mudge, Lewis Seymour** (1868–1945). Presbyterian pastor. Born in Yonkers, N.Y., he graduated from Princeton University and Princeton Theological Seminary. He was pastor of the First Church, Beverly, N.J.; First Church, Trenton; First Church, Lancaster, Pa.; and Pine Street Church, Harrisburg. He was stated clerk of the general assembly of the Presbyterian Church in the USA (1921–38) and moderator of the assembly of 1931. His writings include sermons, addresses, and pamphlets on ecclesiastical law and procedure.

F. W. LOETSCHER

**Muelder, Walter G.** (1907– ). Methodist educator, personalist ethicist, and Christian ecumenist. Following his graduation from Knox College in 1927, he attended Boston University School of Theology, where he was to teach and serve as dean for much of his career. Following seminary, Muelder studied at the University of Frankfurt before receiving a Ph.D. from Boston University. Muelder's doctoral dissertation, prepared under the direction of E. S. Brightman, dealt with Ernst Troeltsch's philosophy of history. In this study, he attempted to integrate Troeltsch's historicism with the personalism he had learned from Brightman and others. He found that Troeltsch and personalism were compatible in their rejection of positivism. He believed that Brightman's personalism avoided the relativism of Troeltsch's historicism, but that personalism should incorporate Troeltsch's emphasis on the concrete unity of theory and practice. Muelder has also attempted to incorporate a communitarian emphasis in his personalism.

Muelder clung to his youthful pacifist convictions through both wars, although his formal ethical framework, presented in *The Moral Laws*, left the issue open in theory. He has criticized neo-orthodox theologians for separating faith and reason and for their overly pessimistic anthropolo-

gies. Muelder presents instead a qualified Christian perfectionism he calls prophetic meliorism. His emphasis on nonviolence and meliorism strongly influenced his best-known student, Martin Luther King, Jr. Muelder actively participated in several World Council of Church assemblies, including Evanston, New Delhi, and Uppsala. Among his books are *Religion and Economic Responsibility* (1953), *The Church and Social Responsibility* (1953), *American Income and Its Use* (1954), *In Every Place a Voice* (1957), *Foundations of the Responsible Society* (1959), *Methodism and Society in the Twentieth Century* (1961), and *Toward a Discipline of Social Ethics* (1972).

ROBERT L. MORRISON

**Mueller, Wilhelm Max** (1862–1919). Biblical scholar. Born in Gleissenberg, Bavaria, he was educated at the universities of Erlangen, Leipzig (Ph.D., 1893), Berlin, and Munich. In 1888 he left Germany for the USA, and was later appointed professor of OT and NT exegesis at the Reformed Episcopal Seminary, Philadelphia (1890–1919). He wrote *Asien und Europa nach altägyptischen Denkmälern* (1893), *Die Liebespoesie der alten Aegypter* (1899), *Egyptological Researches* (1906), and *Mythology of the Ancient Egyptians* (1918). He was joint editor of *Gesenius' Hebrew Dictionary* (1915).

**Muggeridge, Malcolm** (1903– ). English writer. Born in London and educated at Cambridge, he was lecturer at the Egyptian University, Cairo (1927–30). He followed a career in journalism, interrupted by army service in World War II (1939–45), in which he was a decorated officer. His last full-time post was as editor of *Punch* (1953–57). He was past middle age when he became a Christian, but he still regards himself as a "theological ignoramus" and is critical of the institutional church. He was a speaker at the 1974 Lausanne Congress on World Evangelization, and appeared frequently on television and radio programs. Among his books are *Jesus Rediscovered* (1969), *Something Beautiful for God* (1971), *Chronicles of Wasted Time* (2 vols., 1972/73), *Jesus: The Man Who Lives* (1975), *A Third Testament* (1977), *A Twentieth-Century Testimony* (1979), and *Like It Was* (1981). He wrote *Paul: Envoy Extraordinary* (1972) with A. R. Vidler.

J. D. DOUGLAS

**Muhammad.** *See* ISLAM; KORAN.

**Muilenberg, James** (1896–1974). Congregational scholar. Born in Orange City, Iowa, he studied at Hope College and at the universities of Nebraska, Yale (Ph.D.), and Marburg. He taught at Nebraska (1920–23) and Mount Holyoke (1926–32). He was dean of the College of Arts and

Sciences at the University of Maine (1932–36), professor of OT at the Pacific School of Religion (1936–45), and taught OT at Union Theological Seminary, N.Y. He wrote *Specimens of Biblical Literature* (1923), and *The Literary Relations of the Epistle of Barnabas and the Teaching of the Twelve Apostles* (1929). He was coauthor of *Excavations at Tell en-Nasbeh* (1947).

**Mulert, Herman** (1879–1950). Lutheran theologian. Born in Niederbobritzsch, Saxony, he studied at the universities of Leipzig, Marburg, Berlin, and Kiel under W. Hermann, Adolf von Harnack, and O. Baumgarten. He was lecturer at Kiel (1907), Halle (1909), and Berlin (1912), and professor of systematic theology at Kiel (1917–35) and Leipzig (1948). He advocated Christian tolerance. "Doctrinarianism is unwise, to be imprudent is never Christian" was his motto. He was a disciple of Naumann and an active member of the democratic movement in Germany. He is widely known for his *Schleiermacher* (1918) and his *Konfessionskunde* (1937). He edited the periodical *Christ und Welt* (1932–41), *Leben Schleiermachers* (1922), and *Der vergnügte Theologie*.

MARTIN REDEKER

**Muller, James Arthur** (1884–1945). Episcopalian church historian. Born in Philadelphia, he was educated at Princeton (Ph.D., 1915), Harvard, and the Episcopal Theological School. He taught history at Boone University, Wuchang, China (1917–19), and St. Stephen's College, New York City (1919–23), and was professor of church history at Episcopal Theological School (1923–45). His books are *Stephen Gardiner and the Tudor Reaction* (1926), *The Letters of Stephen Gardiner* (1933), *Apostle of China* (1937), *The Episcopal Theological School, 1867–1943* (1943), and *Who Wrote the New Prayers in the Prayer Book?* (1946).

*Bibliography.* M. H. Shepherd, Jr., *Church History* (Dec. 1945), and *Historical Magazine of the P. E. Church* (Dec. 1945).

MASSEY H. SHEPHERD, JR.

**Mundelein, George William** (1872–1939). Cardinal. Born in New York, he studied at Manhattan College, New York, Saint Vincent's Seminary, Beatty, Pa., and at the College of the Propaganda, Rome. Ordained to the priesthood in 1895, he engaged in pastoral and administrative work in the diocese of Brooklyn, of which he became chancellor in 1897, and auxiliary bishop in 1909. He was appointed archbishop of Chicago in 1915. Anxious to promote the education of the clergy in the Midwest, he founded the Seminary of Saint Mary of the Lake in Mundelein, Ill. (1921). He was created cardinal on March 24, 1924, under the pontificate of Pius XI. He was host to the first International Eucharistic Congress to be held in the USA (Chicago, 1926).

GEORGES A. BARROIS

**Munk, Kaj Harald Leininger Petersen** (1898–1944). Lutheran poet and dramatist. Born in Maribo, Denmark, he studied theology at the University of Copenhagen. He was parish minister at Vedersø (1924–44). Traditionally Lutheran in theology, he was influenced by Grundtvig, the Inner Mission, and especially Søren Kierkegaard. In his fiery preaching he used unique and outspoken methods to relate the gospel to the present day. He was a poet and dramatist. A master of dialog, he chose great persons, good or evil, as his subjects (Herod, David, Henry VIII, Mussolini, Hitler, Brandes, Grundtvig, etc.), always featuring a dualistic struggle between good and evil from a God-centered point of view. "The Word," perhaps his greatest play, is a modern resurrection story. Active in public life, he became a leader in the opposition to the German occupation and was killed by enemy hirelings (Jan. 4, 1944). *Kaj Munk Mindeudgave* (Memorial Edition, 1948–49) contains nine volumes, one of sermons, two of articles, one of poems, one of autobiography, and four of plays.

*Bibliography.* R. P. Keigwin, *Kaj Munk, Playwright, Priest, Patriot* (1944); S. Stolpe, *Kaj Munk* (1945); B. B. Rud, *Kaj Munk* (1938); N. Nøigaard, *Ordets Dyst og Daad* (1946); O. Geismar, *Om Mennesket Kaj Munk* (1946).

JOHANNES KNUDSEN

**Murray, George Gilber Aime** (1866–1957). Professor and scholar. Born in Sydney, New South Wales, he studied at Oxford. He was professor of Greek at Glasgow (1889–99) and Oxford (1908–36). Among his numerous publications, those most directly related to religion are *Five Stages of Greek Religion* (1913, 1925, 1951), *Stoic Philosophy* (1915), *Stoic, Christian and Humanist* (1940), and *Religio Grammatici* (1913f.).

RAYMOND W. ALBRIGHT

**Murray, John** (1898–1975). Presbyterian theologian. Born in Sutherland, Scotland, he served in France during World War I, where he lost the sight of one eye. After graduating from Glasgow University, he studied for the ministry under Free Presbyterian Church auspices, and was then sent by that body for further training at Princeton Theological Seminary, where he graduated with a degree in theology in 1927. After his return to Scotland, differences with his church led to his return to Princeton as assistant to Charles Hodge in the systematic theology department in 1929. Another problem of conscience confronted him there, which was resolved in 1930 when he became an instructor at Westminster Theological Seminary, Philadelphia. He was appointed professor of systematic theology in 1937, in which year he was ordained in the Orthodox Presbyterian

Church; he held the post until his retirement in 1966. He and Paul Woolley were founding editors of the *Westminster Theological Journal*. Among Murray's writings are *Christian Baptism* (1952), *Redemption, Accomplished and Applied* (1955), *Principles of Conduct* (1957), and *Commentary on the Epistle to the Romans* (2 vols., 1959, 1965).

J. D. DOUGLAS

**Murry, John Middleton** (1889–1957). Literary critic and editor. Born in Peckham, London, he was educated at Christ's Hospital and Brasenose College, Oxford. He became a literary critic for the *Westminster Gazette* and then *The Times*. After serving in military intelligence during World War I, he became editor of the *Athenaeum* (1919–21) and founded the *Adelphi* (1923). He wrote a number of books exploring the nature of literary and religious genius: *Dostoevsky* (1917), *Keats & Shakespeare* (1925), *The Life of Jesus* (1926), *God* (1927), *Heaven & Earth* (1938), *The Betrayal of Christ* (1943), and *Adam and Eve* (1945).

**Bibliography.** R. Heppenstall, *John Middleton Murry* (1935).

**Music, Sacred.** Two main lines of development can be traced in sacred music: classical sacred music and popular sacred music. Classical sacred music like Bach's chorales has not been subject to the vicissitudes of time. Consequently, it has not changed over the course of the 20th century. Popular sacred music, on the other hand, has undergone a dramatic transformation. This is particularly true of the church's hymnody. What many term the "hymn explosion" today is a reflection of the fact that the church's music, like its theology, must take its place in an ever-changing world.

The music of the church in the first half of the 20th century was the music of the Moody/Sankey and Sunday/Rodeheaver revival. The gospel song tradition of Ira Sankey, with its warmth and immense popular appeal, was difficult to shake. Little attention was paid to the traditional music of the church, and the church was musically weak. At mid-century, however, the church was faced with a crisis which forced it to reevaluate its music.

The church was struggling by the 1950s to both attract and keep members. This concern led the church to realize that its songs were filled with outdated musical idioms and irrelevant lyrics. The impetus for change came with the performance of Geoffrey Beaumont's *Twentieth Century Folk Mass* (1956). Because he believed that the music of the Church of England was completely foreign to Englishmen, Beaumont turned to the world and wrote his mass in pop style. Beaumont helped usher in the experimentation of the 1960s.

The chaotic 1960s witnessed innovative experimentation in church music and vitriolic debates. The church was confronted with jazz, pop music, aleatoric music, 12-tone music, and rock. Music was no longer associated with organized mass evangelism. The most controversial development of the 1960s was the rock musical. "Jesus Christ, Superstar" and "Godspell" shocked the church. The church's answer was the small, informal youth singing group.

Music styles introduced in the 1960s continued in the 1970s—as did the debate over the place of pop music in the church. There were some new developments. Electronic equipment was brought into the sanctuary. Music publishers and the recording industry capitalized on the popularity of contemporary Christian music. One of the most significant developments in church music was the youth musical.

New hymnals were the hallmark of the 1980s. Many denominations produced supplements to their regular hymnbook, containing guitar chords and new songs. Hymnody's range of subjects was expanded to include topics like the third world, race relations, human rights, and environmental issues. The lyrics of hymns have been changed: there has been an update of archaic language, the use of inclusive language, and a gender-neutral approach to God. Important hymn writers include Albert F. Bayly (1901– ), Fred Pratt Green (1903– ), Fred Kaan (1929– ), and Brian Wren (1936– ).

**Bibliography.** D. P. Ellsworth, *Christian Music in Contemporary Witness* (1979); J. R. Sydnor, *Hymns and Their Uses* (1982); C. Webster, *Our Hymn Tunes* (1983); D. B. Pass, *Music and the Church* (1989).

**Muslim Calendar.** See CALENDAR, MUSLIM.

**Muslim Eschatology.** The fifth article in the orthodox Muslim creed proclaims belief in the Last Day, and all credal statements from the time of Abū Ḥanifah (d. 767) onwards contain some elaboration of this article. Muhammad had shown himself much concerned with matters of judgment and the hereafter, so that the doctrine of "Last Things" bulks largely in the Koran and consequenntly in the traditions. It was details mentioned in the Koranic descriptions of the last things, namely, the coming day, the resurrection, the torment of the tomb, the balance, the bridge, the grand assizes, paradise and hell, which exercised the exegetes and the theologians. For the most part the theologians are uncomfortable about these matters, stating that they are to be believed in because mentioned in the Koran and tradition, but taken without question of why or how. Rationalistic Mu'tazilites denied their literal reality; philosophic theologians attempted to spiritualize or allegorize them, while the orthodox labored to systematize the material in the sources. In the devotional literature, however, this doctrine lent itself to elaborate development for purposes of edification. The favorite topics of this treatment are: (1) death and the grave; (2) the intermediate state; (3) the signs of the hour; (4) resurrection; (5) assembling for judgment; (6) the search for an intercessor; (7) the weighing at the balances; (8) the bridge crossing; (9) the life of the blessed in paradise and of the damned in hell. There are some early tractates dealing with individual matters of eschatology, but for long the treatment of this subject formed part of larger works of edification. From the 10th century onwards, however, there are a growing number of independent treatises devoted solely to these matters, such as the pseudo-Ghazalian *al-Durra al-F,* the *Tadhkira* of al-Qurṭubī, Ibn Makhlūf's *al-al-F,* *'Abd al-Ra's al-Akhb*, and the many little eschatological treatises of al-Suyūṭī.

*See also* ISLAM.

ARTHUR JEFFREY

**Muslim Ethics.** By definition Islam is a system of moral monotheism. As "submission to the will of God," Islam rests on "five pillars" of required conduct (*ibadat*): (1) affirmation of the faith (*shahada*); (2) adoration of God (*salat*); (3) ministration to the needy (*zakah*, obligatory tithe; *sadaqa,* voluntary sharing); (4) repudiation of self, especially by fasting (particularly during Ramadan); and (5) participation in the community, as seen in the pilgrimage (*hajj*) to Mecca. Muslims pray for moral guidance, daily asking God to "show us the straight path, the path of those whom Thou hast favored, not the path of those who earn Thine anger" (Surah 1.5–7).

The sources of Muslim ethics are threefold: a people, a prophet, and a process. A sense of practical morality motivated the behavior of the pre-Islamic Arabs. Desert Arabs (bedouins) had a strict survival ethic that prized patient endurance, self-control, hospitality, loyalty to the group, courage in battle, and honor. Urban Arabs (in the Yemen, the Hijaz, and on the edge of the Fertile Crescent), as a merchant-professional class, esteemed integrity, honesty, shrewdness, managerial skill, wisdom, and the keeping of oaths. Among them the Prophet Muhammad appeared. For Muhammad morality was a divine donation, not a human creation. The eternal Law, however, elicited a temporal and personal response, revealing kindness, equity, compassion, mercy, generosity, self-restraint, sincerity, and ethical solidarity within the community of faith. Muhammad's preaching (between A.D. 610 and 632) initiated Islam, a religion that is an ongoing process of reflection on the Moral Law and its application to all aspects of life. Within that process the Koran (seen as an inerrant, infallible guide) and the Hadith (the traditions of the Prophet) are normative.

The spread of Islam throughout the known world from the Iberian to the Indian peninsula involved Muslims in the complex moral issues posed by life in great commercial cities. Three additional sources of moral insight were added to the Muslim synthesis: (1) the legacy of the Greco-Roman classics, especially Plato's *Republic, Timaeus,* and *Laws* and Aristotle's *Nicomachean Ethics;* (2) the heritage of imperial Iran, with the moral insights of Zoroastrianism and the precedents of the Parthian court; and (3) the Judeo-Christian tradition, from the practices of the desert fathers (asceticism) to the moral preaching of the city pulpits.

As Islam flourished, three ethical styles became evident. Civil ethics, or the morality of palace and market, viewed religion and government as sisters. Islam stressed good character in a ruler, and issued manuals of practical advice for princes and civil servants. This was the case in the Umayyad and Abbasid Caliphates, and later in the Ottoman, Safavid, and Moghul empires. Philosophical ethics, or the morality of the academy, applied rational thought to the theory and practice of consistent behavior. Mystical ethics, or the morality of the Sufis, moved beyond practicality and rationality to stress loving self-surrender as the ultimate ethical act. Rabia, an early Sufi, admitted to God: "I have loved Thee with two loves, a selfish love and a love that is worthy (of Thee)." Denial of self and humility were regarded as the path to perfection.

In the 20th century Muslim moralists have faced unprecedented ethical issues such as organ transplants, nuclear war, ecological pollution, and family planning. Seeking answers to these questions has been difficult. Appeal has been made to secondary sources of authority under the Koran and Hadith. Consensus (*ijma*) is one, although there is debate over which consensus is sought—that of the Muslim people, moral theologians, or legal experts—and by what method such concurrence is to be determined. Analogy (*qiyas*) compares the "known" of the past with the "unknown" of the present. Private opinion (*ra'y*) is another secondary source. The individual confronted with moral choices must follow the dictates of informed conscience, although opponents feel that this is essentially a denial of morality.

Muslim moral theologians since 1945 have been pulled in two opposite directions. Some, like Sir Muhammad Iqbal, spiritual father of Pakistan, have been influenced by Western philosophies as divergent as idealism and existentialism, finding ethical counsel in the common experience of educated men. Others, like the Ayatullah Ruhollah Khomeini, mentor of the Islamic Revolution in Iran, have argued for a return to the basics of the Koran. By the late 1980s the Fundamentalist interpretation proved to be more popular.

Most Muslim moralists envision human conduct as falling into five categories: (1) mandatory acts (*wajib*), that *must* be done (e.g., confession of the faith); (2) meritorious acts (*mustahab*), that *ought* to be done (e.g., extra prayers); (3) permitted acts (*mubah*), that are morally neutral (e.g., eating melon); (4) condoned but reprehensible acts (*makruh*), that *ought not* be done (e.g., divorce); and (5) condemned acts (*haram*), that *must not* be done (e.g., the worship of idols). Some scholars, in the style of Western moralist Joseph Fletcher, can envision the same act as falling into each of the five categories, depending on circumstances.

*See also* ISLAM.

**Bibliography.** D. B. Macdonald, *The Religious Attitude and Life in Islam* (1909); M. Ali, *The Religion of Islam* (1950); D. M. Donaldson, *Studies in Muslim Ethics* (1953); D. Rahbar, *God of Justice: A Study of the Ethical Doctrines of the Qur'an* (1960); J. Schacht, *An Introduction to Islamic Law* (1964); T. Izutsu, *Ethico-Religious Concepts in the Qur'an* (1966).

C. GEORGE FRY

## Muslim Propaganda.

Like Christianity and Buddhism, Islam is one of the great missionary religions of the world. A moral monotheism like Christianity, Islam has claims to universality, finality, and authority. Entrance into the faith requires witnessing (the *shahada*): "There is no god but God and Muhammad is his prophet." That credo, contends the Koran, is intended for all humans.

While an ancient hadith asserts that "disbelief is one religion," from its inception Islam had distinguished between those without revelation (pagans [*kafir*]) and those with a revelation (Jews and Christians, the "people of the book" [*ahl al-kitab*] or "people of the covenant" [*ahl adh-dhimma*]). Pagans are not to be tolerated but are to be converted. "Unbelief," states one hadith, "has no rights." As soon as possible, pagans are to be incorporated into "the house of Islam" (*dar al-Islam*) from "the house of war" (*dar al-harb*). The same invitation is extended to Jews and Christians. "Fight against such of those to whom the Scriptures were given as believe neither in Allah nor the Last Day," teaches the Koran, "who do not forbid what Allah and His apostle have forbidden, and do not embrace the true faith until they pay tribute out of hand and are utterly subdued" (9.29). If Jews and Christians refuse submission to Islam, they are to be "tolerated" as religious subcultures within the community (*umma*) of Islam, as separate "nations" (*millet*). They are permitted to practice their religion, but are forbidden to propagate it, promote it, or proselytize Muslims.

Islam, therefore, is unique among the world religions in that it is the only faith-system from its origins to claim to supersede both Judaism and Christianity. While Jews and Christians regard Islam as something new, the most recent world religion created by Muhammad in the 7th century, Muslims contend that innovation (*bidat*) is the problem of Judaism and Christianity. Islam is "old," indeed, the original faith of humankind. Abraham, affirms the Koran, "was not a Jew nor a Christian but a true Muslim" (3.67). The common plight of Judaism and Christianity is one of apostasy. "When the revelations of the Merciful were recited to them, they fell down on their knees in tears and adoration," teaches the Koran, "but the generations who succeeded them neglected their prayers and succumbed to temptation. These shall surely be lost" (19.58). Now, as a result, "they worship their rabbis and their monks, and the Messiah the son of Mary, as gods besides Allah, though they were ordered to serve one God only. There is no god but Him" (9.31). Jews and Christians have intentionally "corrupted" their books—the *Tawrat* (Torah), the *Zabur* (Psalter), and the *Injil* (Gospel). For Muslims the Koran, received through Muhammad, is not a new revelation, but "it is a transcript of Our eternal book, sublime and full of wisdom" (43.2). Muhammad's message was that of Moses, Jesus, and all the prophets. Jews and Christians share in their rejection of him, the one Muslims assert to be the prophet foretold by Moses (Deut. 18:18) and the comforter promised by Jesus (John 14:16).

According to Muslim teaching both Jews and Christians have unique defects. Judaism errs in its ethnocentricity ("Zionism"), its exclusiveness ("the chosen people"), and its neglect of missionary work (lack of "universalism"). It also suffers from glaring ethical defects (such as usury). Christianity, asserts the Koran, is wrong on a number of points, most of which concern Jesus. Although Muslims believe that Jesus (*Isa*) was sinless, born of the virgin Mary, a prophet powerful in word and deed, who raised the dead, healed the sick, and taught the "gospel," he "was no more than a servant of God" (43.59). Because "Allah is one, the Eternal God," teaches the Koran, ". . . none is equal to him" (112.3). "Those who say, 'The Lord of Mercy has begotten a son,' preach a monstrous falsehood," states the Koran, "at which the very heavens might crack, the earth break asunder, and the mountains crumble to dust. That they should ascribe a son to Merciful, when it does not become him to beget one!" (19.88). Or again, "the Christians call Christ the Son of God . . . but they imitate what the disbelievers of old used to say" (9.30). Not only do Muslims insist "God is one, he has no son," but they also maintain that Jesus did not die on the cross but was taken into heaven and one who resembled him, perhaps Judas or Simon of Cyrene, was killed in his place. Christians also err, confess the Muslims, in teaching the doctrine of the Trinity. "God," reports one hadith, "has no partner." Because of its claims to supersede Christianity, Islam is the only other world religion that has grown greatly at the expense of the church.

The growth of Islam beyond the confines of Arabia has occurred in three great eras. The period of Arab expansion extended from the death of Muhammad (632) to the defeat of Abd ar-Rahman at Tours (732). Military occupation of the Middle East, North Africa, Spain, and Central Asia was followed by indoctrination and the mass conversion of the inhabitants of these areas to Islam. The Muslim renaissance (1300–1699) saw the appearance of the Ottoman, Safavid, and Moghul empires and the evangelization of vast parts of Eurasia as far removed as Albania and Indonesia. In the current period of revival (since 1945) Islam is now represented, through conversion and immigration, in nearly all parts of the earth. By the late 1980s it was estimated that there were one billion Muslims, with an annual growth rate of almost 5 percent. By the start of the 21st century Islam may surpass Christianity as the world's largest religion.

Rarely employing formal missionaries, Islam is spread primarily by individual Muslims living and teaching their faith. With claims to totality (an entire way of life, not simply a religion) and vitality (a source of power, not simply a doctrine), Islam is Christianity's greatest challenge and opportunity.

*See also* ISLAM.

**Bibliography.** L. Levonian, *Studies in the Relationship between Islam and Christianity* (1940); W. C. Smith, *Islam in Modern History* (1957); S. D. Goitein, *Jews and Arabs: Their Contacts Through the Ages* (1964); G. H. Jansen, *Militant Islam* (1979); T. W. Lippman, *Understanding Islam: An Introduction to the Moslem World* (1982); E. Mortimer, *Faith and Power: The Politics of Islam* (1982); D. Pipes, *In the Path of God: Islam and Political Power* (1983).

C. GEORGE FRY

**Muslims, Black.** *See* BLACK MUSLIMS.

**Muslims, Missions to.** Since the rise of Islam early in the 7th century, the conversion of Muslims has been the most difficult of missionary endeavors. Aside from spiritual obstacles, the hindrances are first sociological. Group solidarity commonly leads to family and community ostracism and persecution of the convert. In some cases the Law of Apostasy calls for the death penalty. There are also theological obstacles. Since Islam is the only world religion to rise after Christianity, Muslims believe that all that is of value in Christianity is contained in Islam and commonly hold the Jewish and Christian Scriptures to have been corrupted. They also deny doctrines such as the Trinity and Christ's incarnation, sonship, and crucifixion.

The obstacles are political as well. Since Islam applies to every area of life, including the political, non-Muslims are commonly de facto if not de jure second-class citizens where Muslims are in a majority. Despite the ancient churches in many Muslim lands, many Muslims associate Christianity with the West. This has often raised cultural barriers. Western forms of worship and church structure have been imposed without recognizing that most Muslim forms of worship have been adopted or adapted from Jews and Christians. Finally, the barriers are historical. Much of the contact between Muslims and Christians militarily, politically, and religiously has been hostile.

In the Middle East both Roman Catholic and Protestant missions have addressed themselves to the task of reinvigorating indigenous Christian churches. The Roman Catholic method has been to bring the Eastern churches into communication with Rome, resulting in the Uniate communities of the traditional Oriental rites. Protestants originally strove to revitalize the churches, but most often the groups responding have been driven by conservatives into forming separate evangelical churches. In the political strongholds of Islam the approach to Muslims has been largely a witness through Christian schools, hospitals, and other forms of service.

Denominational groups like the Southern Baptists have initiated work in Lebanon, Jordan, Israel, Egypt, and Cyprus as have a host of interdenominational faith groups like Middle East Christian Outreach, Arab World Ministries, Inter Serv, the Evangelical Alliance Mission, Agape (Campus Crusade for Christ), Frontiers, and Operation Mobilization.

Missions in North Africa have proved more difficult. Following the 1969 revolution in Libya, missionaries have no longer been permitted in the country. Although the constitution of Tunisia guarantees freedom of conscience and the free exercise of religion, the government is not favorable to Christian proselytism. The North African Mission started a Bible correspondence course in 1962 which has since been banned, but Arab World Ministries personnel remain. In Algeria Christian influence has been reduced since independence (1962). The Roman Catholic Church emphasizes service. Proselytism is forbidden, and some violators have been deported. In Morocco there has been growing intimidation of Muslim inquirers since 1968 because of their increase in numbers. All North African countries are reached by Christian radio programs from Liberia and Morocco, and Bible correspondence courses are available.

In sub-Saharan Africa both Islam and Christianity are growing at the expense of animistic tribal groups but not each other. Countries with Muslim majorities include Senegal, Mauritania, Guinea, Mali, Niger, Sudan, Somalia, and Djibouti. Government policies have ranged from religious freedom in Senegal, Mali, and Niger, to the banning of the proselytizing of Muslims in Mauritania, the expulsion of missionaries from Somalia in 1973 and 1974, and the institution of Islamic *shari'a* law in the Sudan in 1983.

Roman Catholics have a small presence in every country but Mauritania, and the Coptic Orthodox are in Sudan and Djibouti. Protestant denominations that have been active in one or more countries are the Anglicans, Methodists, Presbyterians, Finnish Lutherans, Brethren, Mennonites, Christian Reformed, Assemblies of God, the Christian and Missionary Alliance, and various Baptist groups. In addition there are specific ministries such as Bible translation, literature, student work, relief and development, aviation, cassette ministries, and broadcasting. Besides the traditional ministries of church planting, education, and medical aid, missions have responded to the repeated drought with relief to refugees and with development as the desert stretches south and as the political turmoil in countries like Sudan continues. Christian broadcasts are sent from the Seychelles and Kenya, and Somalis and others are evangelized when they are in freer countries like Kenya. The fact that people groups such as Fulani live in more than one country makes it possible for them to carry the gospel across borders.

In a string of countries just to the south, neither the Muslims nor the Christians have a clear majority. In Burkina Faso and Nigeria evangelism among animistic Muslims has been accompanied by reports of miracles. In the former case this has resulted in considerable church growth.

After 1947 Christians entered Afghanistan as tentmakers. Laubach Literacy teachers, also Christians, were invited in 1951. The following year a Protestant expatriate church was organized. Roman Catholic expatriates could meet in the Italian embassy. In 1966 the International Afghan Mission (later the International Assistance Mission) was formed as an umbrella organization for Christian groups to provide social (primarily medical) services for the government, although proselytizing was forbidden. After the Soviet invasion of 1979, IAM continued to work in Afghanistan while other Christian organizations like SERVE aided refugees in Pakistan. Refugees were able to get Persian and Pashtu Bibles and the Dari New Testament. The small groups of national Christians grew inside the country, and Afghans were free to become Christians outside of their homeland.

Today 33 Muslim people groups make up close to 18 percent of the Soviet Union and are in a majority in six republics, nine autonomous republics, and four autonomous regions. Tentmaker organizations in England, Europe, and the USA are developing means of witness, and the Soviet Union is showing greater openness to evangelism. Radio, literature, and cassettes are all being used.

China has 10 national minorities that are Muslim, comprising 2.4 percent of the population. Currently there are Christian teachers in Muslim areas such as Xinjiang Province, where a number of Uighur Muslims are known to have become Christians.

Pakistan, the second largest Muslim country in the world, is more open to the gospel than many other Muslim countries. Missionaries have worked in the area since 1833 and include Roman Catholics, Presbyterians, Anglicans, Methodists, and Conservative Baptists as well faith missions. With most Christians coming historically from Hindu scheduled castes, many have little vision for Muslim evangelism. The Christian Study Centre in Rawalpindi engages in research on local Islam, the training of Christians, and dialog with Muslims. Pakistani Christians are now sending their own evangelists to Azad Kashmir. A Muslim convert runs St. Andrews Fellowship in Lahore for the nurture of new converts. Bible correspondence courses, radio programs, and Christian literature are all being produced locally.

Despite Muslims being a minority in India, it is the third largest Muslim country. The Henry Martyn Institute in Hyderabad teaches Christians about Islam and engages in dialog with Muslims. Although there are severe restrictions on missionary visas, there is freedom for evangelism with greater results than in most Muslim countries.

Bangladesh is the fourth largest Muslim country. Christian missions, particularly Baptist missions, have been in the area for many years with few converts among Muslims. Christians are largely from the lower Hindu castes with little vision for Muslim evangelism. Relief offered by Christian organizations like World Vision, the TEAR Fund, and Global Partners has broken down prejudices. In a few areas church planting among rural Muslims has mushroomed as it has been led by Muslim converts who have retained and adapted Muslim forms of worship.

In Southeast Asia although there are many Muslims in countries like Thailand and Burma, the greatest concentrations are in Indonesia, Malaysia, and the Philippines. Muslims in the Philippines have felt suppressed by the Roman Catholic majority who govern them and have taken over large sections of their ancestral land in the southern region. Of the 14 Muslim peoples the Maranao, Magindanao, and Ilanon live on the major island of Mindanao. SIM (with which International Christian Fellowship merged), the Overseas Missionary Fellowship, RBMU International, and SEND International are jointly ministering to them. International Missions is working in the northern section. All are using contextualized approaches. The Christian and Missionary Alliance has been working among the Tausug, Samal, and Badjao of the Sulu Islands and the city of Zamboanga, and a number of churches have been established. The Summer Institute of Linguistics is engaged in Bible translation among peoples on Palawan Island. A book room is maintained in a Muslim section of Manila.

Although Muslims comprise only 53 percent of the population of Malaysia, Islam is the official and favored religion in Peninsular Malaysia, and there is pressure to do the same in East Malaysia. There has been discriminatory legislation against non-Muslims, the forbidding of proselytizing Muslims, and even attempts to forbid Christians to use religious terms that are now considered Islamic even though historically they were previously used by Jews or Christians. The largest Protestant mission agencies are the Overseas Missionary Fellowship and the Southern Baptist Convention, but many missionary visas are being denied. Nevertheless there is increased interest in evangelism among Malaysian Christians.

Indonesia, the largest Muslim country in the world, has also experienced the largest turning to Christ among Islamized peoples. An abortive communist coup attempt in 1965 led the government to require everyone to belong to one of the recognized religions. Many chose Christianity especially in protest against the subsequent massacre of many communists by Muslim extremists. Many estimate that over 2 million became Christians in the late 1960s. Conversions have been facilitated by the government's ideology of Pancasila, which bases the state on a belief in God rather than just Islam. The Evangelical Theological Seminary in Yogyakarta requires every student to plant a church in the animistic Muslim surroundings before graduation. The Muslim backlash to the church growth in Muslim areas of Sulawesi, Samatra, and Java has led to some violence. In 1989 major ecumenical and evangelical Indonesian church leaders met to discuss how to witness to Muslims most effectively without causing unnecessary alarm.

Islam has spread to every part of the world. It has been in Eastern Europe since the Middle Ages and has also entered Western Europe. North Africans reside in France, Turkish laborers work in Germany, and Pakistanis have moved to England. In the Americas Muslim immigrants have been supplemented by African-American converts. In Europe and England ministries to Muslims have been established like L'Ami in Paris and In Contact Ministries in London. In the Americas the Zwemer Institute has a similar function.

Contemporary missions to Muslims have a number of emphases in common with missions in general. Indigenous churches are increasingly responsible for propagating the faith. These third world churches have sometimes formed their own missions. There is a focus on people groups rather than nations. Tentmaking ministries have received renewed emphasis as countries have closed to traditional missions. Attention has been given to transitional people with the increase in urbanization, refugees from political strife and famine, and migrant workers. As the role of culture has been better understood, there has been increased contextualization—the retention and adaptation of indigenous forms of worship and organization. Finally, increasingly nonpentecostal missionaries are experiencing miraculous signs of God's power. Missionaries to Muslims have also assumed an increasingly informed and cordial perspective toward Muslims as they have come under the influence of scholars like Duncan Black Macdonald (1863–1943) and Kenneth Cragg.

**Bibliography.** J. Richter, *A History of Protestant Missions in the Near East* (1910); L. E. Browne, *The Eclipse of Christianity in Asia* (1933); K. S. Latourette, *A History of the Expansion of Christianity* (7 vols., 1937–45); J. T. Addison, *The Christian Approach to the Moslem* (1942); H. G. Dorman, *Toward Understanding Islam* (1948); N. A. Daniel, *Islam and the West* (1960); *Islam, Europe and Empire* (1966); L. L. Vander Werff, *Christian Mission to Muslims: The Record* (1977); D. C. E. Liao, ed., *Eastern Asia* (1979); D. M. McCurry, ed., *Middle East* (1979); R. E. Hedlund, ed., *South Asia* (1980); D. B. Barrett, ed., *World Christian Encyclopedia* (1982); P. Johnstone, ed., *Operation World* (1986).

J. DUDLEY WOODBERRY

**Mysticism.** *See* CONTEMPLATION.

**Mystic Union.** The vital, dynamic, and spiritual union of the believer with Christ resulting from a personal relationship with the Savior. This union is reflected in such passages as the allegory of the Vine and the branches (John 15:1–8), the frequently repeated Pauline phrase "in Christ," and the NT body of Christ metaphor. The personal identity of the believer is never lost in this union, but at the same time the believer cannot live and bear fruit apart from Christ. As the Christian is in Christ, so also Christ is in the believer. This state is not for the select few who achieve it by contemplation but for all those who believe in Christ as Lord and Savior.

**Myth in the NT.** Since the first known anti-Christian writer, Celsus (2d cent. A.D.), pagans acquainted with Christian teachings have scoffed that stories affirming Jesus' divinity had been invented by the early church. Only with the Enlightenment, however, were theories about a "mythology" of Jesus discussed in Western intellectual circles. In the 19th century the views became known within the church itself via higher critical biblical studies. In the 20th century the thought of Rudolf Bultmann ensconced a form of mythical Christology within mainline Christianity. Bultmann's influence on neo-orthodox theology and the radical neoliberalism of the 1960s were focal points of debate from the 1940s.

While the Greek word *mythos* could include rumor and other meanings, it generally referred to human fabrication. Its five uses in the NT definitely contrast the falsehood of *mythos* with God's revealed truth of *logos*. Myths are contrasted with history (2 Pet. 1:16) and truth (2 Tim.

4:4; Titus 1:14); they are incompatible with God's work accepted by faith (1 Tim. 1:4) and true religion (1 Tim. 4:7). Exactly what "myths" were in view in these passages is argued, since myths of classic paganism had little force in the early Christian centuries. Some have suspected that Paul and Peter were condemning the Jewish *haggada* and its fanciful elaboration of OT stories, the allegorical exegesis of Alexandrian Jews such as Philo, or pregnostic speculation (especially in 2 Pet.). Clearly nothing in the Gospel accounts was labeled false, and when Celsus designated biblical stories as "empty myths," the apologist Origen defended their truth categorically.

***The Modern Concept of Myth.*** The use of mythical language has been explained in two different ways. Myths were considered by the rationalists as erroneous interpretations of nature, due to faulty reasoning (Benedict Spinoza and Thomas Hobbes), to priestly deceit (Lord Herbert of Cherbury), or to exaggerations common to oral communication (David Hume). Insisting on the unrestricted operation of natural causes, the rationalists were forced to attack both pagan mythology and biblical miracle stories.

But a second, quite different, interpretation was developed by the German classical scholar Christian Gottlob Heyne (1729–1812). He explained the myth as language by which primitive man described his inner states, and reacted to his environment. It is the fertile womb out of which eventually historiography, religion, philosophy, poetry, and literature proceed. One theory arising from Heyne's proposed that even language originates in sounds corresponding to a culture's intuitive ideas about its mythical images. Friedrich Schelling (1775–1854), a German idealist philosopher, held that the myth was the first stage in the Absolute's endeavor to attain self-realization. The important idea which was embedded in such a view was that a myth might have a subjective reality or truth, even if lacking in historical fact.

A large number of psychological, sociological, and even political views came from Heyne's and Schelling's basic concepts. One possible reality was that the myths of a people expressed their unique spirit and character, their *Volksgeist*. Modern writers have looked for myths which undergirded totalitarian movements. Voltaire saw such a mythology at work in pre-Revolution France. In ethnology a trend of modern research has been to identify a collective mind of a culture which is affected by life events and forces and personifies those events and forces as myths. Carl Jung was among those who saw this collective mind as a part of humanity in general, and not of social or national groups. Freudian psychology contended that in disguised manner the myth gives expression to the urges and desires of the unconscious, particularly the sexual ones.

***Myth and the Bible.*** For every interpretation of the myth in secular thought a similar application of the term eventually was found in biblical studies. Deists employed the rationalistic theory of myth as a means of discrediting all the biblical stories dealing with miracles and supernatural agents. Adopting Heyne's explanation, Johann G. Eichhorn and his disciple J. P. Gabler sought in the late 18th century to differentiate between the mythical form of the record and the historical fact to which it referred. To the method employed by this "mythical school" Johann Herder and Wilhelm De Wette objected, however. They pointed out that such differentiation was not feasible, since myth infected both form and content of the record. The OT was mythical throughout and had to be enjoyed esthetically as the national epic of the Hebrews. The gospel was myth, whether it had a historical basis or not. Through the mythical symbol of Jesus it allegedly described the right relationship between man and God.

F. C. Bauer, taking up suggestions of Friedrich Schleiermacher, taught that mythology was the language of the natural religion as contrasted with revelation. By applying rationalistic criteria to NT study he radically eliminated all supranatural features as unhistorical. His disciple, David Friedrich Strauss, divided his *Life of Jesus* (1840) into a "Historical Outline" and a "Mythical History of Jesus." Strauss used allegorical interpretation to discern in the mythical history of the Gospels the portrait of the true humanity in whom God dwells.

From an entirely different angle the mythical problem of the Bible was approached by F. Nork. Profiting from the increased knowledge of ancient mythology, he attempted to show that throughout the Bible are the reflexes of Indian, Babylonian, and classical mythology. In them he saw the primordial spiritual wisdom of the race. The mythical features of the Bible, far from detracting from the value of the Bible, enhance it.

Nork's ideas pervaded the growing field of Assyriology. Students were struck by the resemblance of some Babylonian myths to the stories of Genesis. Assuming that the stories were borrowed by the Jews during the exile, H. Winkler and Alfred Jeremias declared the religion of the OT to be a replica of the astral mythology of Mesopotamia. P. Jensen noticed traces of the *Gilgamesh Epic* everywhere he looked in the Bible, and Franz Delitzsch denounced OT religion as a degeneration of Babylonian mythology. Others offered the more positive suggestion that Israel had adopted mythical creation concepts from her neighbors but had strictly controlled, transformed, and adapted them to ethical monotheism.

The standard position of scholars in most seminaries of the late 20th century remained true to these ideas. Myth within the OT arose from its cultural conditioning in the ancient Near East setting. Mythopoeic thought was transformed from polytheism to monotheism and adapted to illustrate Yahwistic religion's concept of God. The OT stories were never intended to be regarded as factual history; therefore they are not myths but symbolic, figurative uses of Near Eastern mythology. Whether any factual history stood behind these symbolic stories was debated. It became the work of modern theology to distinguish the symbols from the facts and use both properly. Ironically, after archeological discoveries and more sophisticated study of the *Gilgamesh Epic* and other Babylonian myths, some scholars doubted their parenthood of Genesis. Conservatives suggested that what the myths do share with Genesis is more adequately explained if the factual history described by Genesis were interpreted by Mesopotamian cultures within mythical history.

**The Mythical Christ.** The interpretation of OT myth soon advanced NT studies far beyond the beginnings of Strauss. Strauss engineered the foundational understanding of myth on which others built. Myth, said Strauss, is the proper mode of expression for all religion. "Religion is by definition imaginative . . . and therefore mythical . . . , for myths are expressions in storylike form of temporally conditioned religious ideas." A host of mythical ideas and images were discovered in the NT canon before the beginning of the 20th century by such interpreters as Hermann Gunkel, Wilhelm Wrede, G. P. Wetter, and Anton J. Fridrichsen. The dominant theme of their work was that Christian religion was an assembly of ideas from many religions and cultures. H. A. A. Kennedy and Carl Clemen cautioned that this did not make Christianity a syncretistic religion, for the NT placed all its emphasis on the work of Jesus—the kerygma. Kerygma was defined as the central message of the gospel which primitive Christians proclaimed and in which God acted to benefit humanity.

It was at this point that Bultmann spoke most forcefully and profoundly changed modern theology in his paper, "NT und Mythologie" (1941). Bultmann proposed that the person and work of the historical Christ is quite properly couched in the language of faith and myth. The mythical imagery used does not form the kerygma but interprets its historical facts and spiritual experiences. As with OT studies, Bultmann and Martin Dibelius contended that it is the task of NT form criticism to separate and interpret kerygma and myth in their proper places. Early Christians, Bultmann said, shared a mythical worldview of a three-level universe. They also shared a gnostic mythical concept of redemption: the "god-man" sent to die and rise again, fighting off demonic forces in a heroic rescue of fallen humanity. Primitive Christianity had formed such myths around its historical facts, and developed cult legends centering in baptism and the Eucharist and the soon return of the heavenly Redeemer. When Bultmann and his disciples thus spoke of "demythologizing" the NT they sought to strip away the fleshly shell to expose the historical kerygma of God's salvific work. That skeletal kerygma as the core of true religion could be shared by all the world. Bultmann was little interested in the historical man named Jesus who was born, lived, and tragically died. Only the kerygmatic Jesus of faith mattered. The mythical forms of belief in miracles, heaven and hell, and a God who tampers with nature had to be discarded in a scientific age.

Karl Barth and Emil Brunner, in applying Bultmann's thought to crisis theology, stressed the difference they saw between Christian myth and pagan myths, for what Bultmann constructed was not far from a pagan conception of mythopoeic reality.

Despite stringent criticisms of the Gospels, Bultmann did not give up Christianity altogether. Rather, by adopting an existentialist interpretation of the Christian faith, for which he was indebted to Søren Kierkegaard, Barth, and Martin Heidegger, he held that Paul and John agreed with him and had already overcome in principle the mythical worldview. Further, the true objective of the gospel message never was to describe supernatural events in space and time but rather, under the mythical garb of the gospel story, to announce God's coming and the radical change thus accomplished in a person's "existence." When the gospel story is proclaimed, the individual thereby becomes aware of the misery of his "existence," that his self is enslaved by the powers of this world, such as worry, sin, and death, and thus unable to live a life truly his own. That change of "existence" is considered as an act of divine grace, and according to Bultmann it is redemption. Yet that result is accomplished by means of the hearing of the gospel story rather than by any activity of the man Jesus.

Bultmann's critics have granted that he emphasized aspects of Christian faith which had been badly neglected, such as the operation of the Holy Spirit in the genesis of faith, the experiential character of faith, the soteriological aspect of biblical history, and the need of something more than belief in the merely "historical Jesus." But there is also wide agreement that his "existentialistic" interpretation of the gospel story is untenable, both for historical and theological reasons. First of all, it is pointed out that in his view of gnosticism, Bultmann reads modern ideas into that movement. Furthermore, Bultmann's contention that the NT message is a myth created by the early church fails to explain how it was possible immediately after Jesus' death for the primitive church to apply such an interpretation to his life, unless in his personality and his work were sufficient evidence for the fact that he was the Messiah and the Son of God.

Moreover, the "demythologization" of the gospel story does violence to the message of the NT. By denying the incarnation and ascribing to Jesus but an incidental role in the formation of the gospel, Bultmann ignores the emphasis all NT writers place upon the necessity of a divine redemption through the agency of an individual man. Nor does Bultmann leave room for the central role which the church is to play in the execution of the saving purpose of God. And his disdain for eschatology not only denies Scripture but robs the believer of hope. Subjective religious experience becomes the only gift available through God.

**Since Bultmann.** Two reactions quickly developed to the demythologizing premise. To Bultmann's theological right Ernst Käsemann delivered the opening salvo in an address on the historical Jesus at Marburg in 1953. The post-Bultmannian movement tried to step back toward a more reasonable treatment of the Gospels as historical sources for the life of Jesus. There also was, moreover, a post-Bultmann movement which complained that he did not go far enough. Neoliberal and radical theologies reached a high point in the 1960s when both Christ incarnate and the very idea of God were seen as ancient myths. The death of God was solemnly intoned by Christian atheists attempting to remove all vestiges of myth from the Christian faith and thus remove every obstacle that hindered thoughtful moderns from accepting Christ. John A. T. Robinson's *Honest to God* (1963) created a whirlwind of controversy, as did Thomas Altizer's *Gospel of Christian Atheism* (1966). The death-of-God theology disappeared rather quickly, owing to its own inherent self-contradiction and the religious revival which began in the West and continued into the 1980s.

In 1977 another attempt was made to discredit the factuality of the gospel message in a book of 10 essays by seven British scholars, *The Myth of God Incarnate.* While these issues quickly took a back seat to other theological interests, the divergence among views of the respective historicity and mythological interference within the gospel colored presuppositions in a variety of issues. The fundamental questions continued as to whether the Christian faith could be found relevant for 21st-century thought if it remained a supernatural religion. Yet could it be regarded as an authentic, historical faith at all if its supernatural, redemptive history was devalued into the category of myth—of whatever definition?

**Bibliography.** *The Concept of Myth.* M. Müller, *Contributions to the Science of Mythology,* 2 vols. (1897); A. Lang, *Myth, Ritual and Religion,* 2 vols. (2d ed., 1906); J. G. Frazer, *The Golden Bough,* 12 vols. (3d ed., 1911–23); B. Malinowski, *Myth in Primitive Psychology* (1926); E. Cassirer, *Language and Myth* (ET, 1946); H. A. Murray, ed., *Myth and Mythmaking* (1960); D. P. Verene, ed., *Symbol, Myth, and Culture: Essays and Lectures of Ernst Cassirer, 1935–1945* (1979).

*Culture and Biblical Studies.* W. M. L. De Wette, *Biblische Dogmatik des Alten und Neuen Testaments* (1813); D. F. Strauss, *The Life of Jesus Critically Examined* (ET, 1840), and *A New Life of Jesus,* 2 vols. (ET, 1879); C. Clemen, *Primitive Christianity and Its Non-Jewish Sources* (1912); H. A. A. Kennedy, *St. Paul and the Mystery Religions* (1913); J. J. Bachofen, *Der Mythos von Orient und Okzident* (1926); H. Gunkel, *Zum religionsgeschichtlichen Verständnis des Neuen Testaments* (3d ed., 1930); H. G. Wood, *Did Christ Really Live?* (1938); A. D. Howell Smith, *Jesus Not a Myth* (1942); G. Ebeling, *The Problem of Historicity in the Church and Its Proclamation* (ET, 1967).

*Bultmannian Theology.* H. W. Bartsch, ed., *Kerygma und Mythos,* 2 vols. (1951/52); M. Eliade, *Myth of the Eternal Return* (ET, 1954); R. Bultmann, *History and Eschatology* (1957), *Jesus Christ and Mythology* (1958), and *Myth and Christianity* (1958); B. S. Childs, *Myth and Reality in the OT* (1958); B. S. Childs, *Myth and Reality in the NT* (1960); C. W. Kegley, *The Theology of Rudolf Bultmann* (1966); N. Perrin, *The Promise of Bultmann* (1969).

*Post-Bultmannian Views.* J. M. Robinson, *A New Quest of the Historical Jesus* (1959); G. Ebeling, *Word and Faith* (ET, 1963); E. Fuchs, *Studies of the Historical Jesus* (ET, 1964); M. Kähler, *The So-Called Historical Jesus and the Historic Biblical Christ* (1964); T. J. J. Altizer, *The Gospel of Christian Atheism* (1966); C. Van Til, *Is God Dead?* (1966); R. A. Kerezty, *God Seekers for a New Age: From Crisis Theology to Christian Atheism* (1970); J. Hick, ed., *The Myth of God Incarnate* (1977); M. Green, *The Truth of God Incarnate* (1977); A. N. Wilder, *Jesus' Parables and the War of Myths* (1982); G. Fackre, *The Christian Story* (1984).

# Nn

**Nairobi Assembly.** Fifth international meeting of the World Council of Churches held in 1975. With the theme "Jesus Christ Frees and Unites," the assembly dealt with six main topics: (1) Confessing Christ Today; (2) What Unity Requires; (3) Seeking Community: The Common Search of People of Various Faiths, Cultures, and Ideologies; (4) Education for Liberation and Community; (5) Structures of Injustice and Struggles for Liberation; and (6) Human Development: Ambiguities of Power, Technologies, and Quality of Life.

The daunting complexity of many world problems was more fully realized at this assembly. The task of evangelism was seen as relating spirituality to involvement. Yet it was also stressed that Christian missions which fails to liberate human beings from crushing poverty, vile working conditions, and evil tyranny is largely irrelevant. The world gathering attempted to raise theological and sociopolitical issues in one breath by stating that faith in the triune God and sociopolitical engagement, the conversion to Jesus Christ, and active participation in changing economic and social structures belong together and condition one another. The search for a "just, participatory and sustainable society" became a major undertaking. Programs on faith, science and technology, disarmament and militarism, ecology and human survival, women in the church and society, and renewal and congregational life received new emphasis.

It was recommended to ask the churches to transmit their responses to the three agreed statements on "Baptism, Eucharist and Ministry," compiled by the Commission on Faith and Order. The document appeared in a final version in 1982. As there were serious objections to the report on dialog with people of other faiths, the report was referred back to the section for reconsideration before it was voted in plenary. A beginning was also made in discussing the "ecumenical sharing of resources."

A. J. Van Der Bent

**Namibia (South West Africa).** Territory in southern Africa with an area of 823,168 sq. km. (317,827 sq. mi.) and a population of 1,146,000 (1985 est.). In the north, Ovambo, Kavango, and Caprivians predominate; the center and south are populated by Herero, Damara, Nama, Coloreds, Bushmen, Basters, Tswana, English, Afrikaners, and Germans.

Namibia has been administered by South Africa since South African forces occupied the territory in 1915 at the request of the Allied Powers in World War I. Before that Namibia had been under German rule dating back to 1884, when it became a German protectorate. Walvis Bay and the Penguin Islands, however, had been annexed by Great Britain and were incorporated into the Cape Colony in 1884. As of June 1985, Namibia has been administered by the Transitional Government of National Unity (TGNU). With petty apartheid laws gone, TGNU is working on a draft constitution for an independent Namibia.

Christian missions have been active in the territory since the early 19th century, especially the Rhenish, London, and Finnish missionary societies. They were followed by others, including the Catholic and Dutch Reformed churches. Often not mentioned is the brief growth spurt of the Marcus Garvey movement during the turbulent 1920s. More important still was the Apostolic movement. It has since mushroomed into hundreds of small African Independent churches with loose ties to Apostolic Faith Healing Mission and Zion Christian Churches in South Africa and Botswana.

Most of the intimate portraits of Namibia's indigenous peoples were provided by missionaries of the *Rheinische Missions-Gesellschaft*. Particularly impressive are the accounts of Dannert (1906), Irle (1906), and Vedder (1922, 1928). These and the *Berichte* of missionaries Kuhlmann and Meier, among others, portray the drastic shifts of black (especially Herero and Nama) church affiliation. Affiliation shifts were in direct response to the Herero and Nama defeats in the

1904–17 colonial war and their efforts to reconstitute themselves as "nations" and later an independent Namibia.

The seed of revitalization was sown as early as 1907, when a group of Herero asked Rhenish missionaries for translations of the OT because they saw in it a blueprint for national revival. From 1909 on Rhenish missionaries were to witness thousands of Herero converting en masse to the Lutheran faith only to witness en masse defections in the 1920s. It was a time when Africans turned to Africanized forms of Christianity, including Oruuano, Orujano, and AFM, and to the rekindling of the holy fires of tribal religions.

While today at least 95 percent of the people formally belong to Christian churches, of which the Evangelical Lutheran Church is the largest, in fact, there is a great deal of church shopping and multichurch attendance. Everyday concerns, especially healing, are brought to African Independent churches (be they Apostolic, pentecostal, or Zionist-based). These churches are growing, especially in the black townships. Their prophets and prophetesses deal primarily with mental and physical ailments, casting out demons and treating multiple personality disorders or possessions, paranoid fears, and catatonic inhibitions.

While these independent churches are as proindependence and antiapartheid as are most mainline churches, their theologies differ. The theology of independent churches is not so much based on abstract Western thought as on encounter, on experiencing the reality of the divine presence. Divine liberation is experienced in ritual, song, and in the midst of historical realities, and is thus the core theological concept. By contrast, mainline churches couch their notions of liberation in the rhetoric of Neo-Marxism and, generally, Western social thought. Historic churches are, therefore, black political organs; they do not have the power, however, to turn the black's life around.

Namibia was affected by Southern Africa's political and intertribal warfare and the struggle against apartheid during the late 1980s. In late 1990 the future of the country and its Christians was unsettled.

**Bibliography.** E. Dannert, *Zum Rechte der Herero* (1906); M. I. Irle, *Die Herero* (1906); M. H. Vedder, *Skizzen aus dem Leben und der Mission in Sudwest* (1922); *The Native Tribes of South West Africa* (1928); K. Poewe, *The Namibian Herero: A History of Their Psychosocial Disintegration and Survival* (1985); J. H. Cone, *The Spirituals and the Blues: An Interpretation* (1972); H. Drechsler, *Let Us Die Fighting* (1980).

KARLA POEWE

**Narcotics.** *See* SUBSTANCE ABUSE.

## National Association of Evangelicals (NAE).

Organization arising out of the revivals of the turn of the 20th century in reaction to the "liberal" Federal Council of Churches. The actual organization of this conservative voluntary association took place in St. Louis in 1942, when 150 evangelical leaders formed the group. NAE does not speak for its members, but keeps them informed about issues of concern to them, such as separation of church and state, violations of the freedom of religion, and various aspects of federal legislation. NAE is active in working with Campus Crusade and Youth for Christ. Today it encompasses 44 denominations, churches from 31 other groups, and nearly 2000 other organizations, associations, and schools. It is estimated to have between 10 and 15 million members. Its headquarters is in Wheaton, Ill.

ROBERT V. SCHNUCKER

## National Church Reform Union.

Organization formed in 1880 by a group of (mainly) Broad Churchmen to avert disestablishment of the Church of England by internal reform and liberalization. Its active existence was brief, but many of its aims have been accomplished since 1919 by the church assembly and parochial church councils.

EDWARD R. HARDY

## National Council of the Churches of Christ in the United States of America (NCCC).

Interdenominational, ecumenical agency of Protestant, Anglican, and Eastern Orthodox denominations. It came into being at a constituting convention held in Cleveland, Ohio, from November 28 to December 2, 1950. It constitutes a merger of 14 interdenominational agencies, including these eight original bodies: the Federal Council of the Churches of Christ in America, the Foreign Missions Conference of North America, the Home Missions Council of North America, the International Council of Religious Education, the Missionary Education Movement of the United States and Canada, the National Protestant Council on Higher Education, the United Council of Church Women, and the United Stewardship Council.

The formation of NCCC brought all phases of interchurch cooperation under the direction of a single agency representing the total life of its 31 member denominations. NCCC includes 135,000 local congregations with more than 40 million members (1987). Its stated purpose is "to serve as a community of its constituent communions in manifesting oneness in Jesus Christ as Divine Lord and Savior, and to do together those things which can better be done united than separated."

NCCC functions through six commissions (communication, faith and order, international affairs, justice and liberation, regional and local ecumenism, and stewardship) and four divisions (church and society, church world service, education and ministry, and overseas ministries). It maintains offices in the areas of finance and services, information, personnel, research, and evaluation and planning.

NCCC produces educational materials; administers disaster and relief funds; supervises refugee placement; advocates the use of the RSV; strengthens family life; promotes world peace; and provides leadership training.

NCCC's activities have received mixed reviews. It is praised for its humanitarian, ecumenical, and family concerns, but criticized for its left-wing social pronouncements, liberal theological bias, and questionable use of funds. Its current headquarters is in New York.

WALTER A. ELWELL

**Nation of Islam.** *See* BLACK MUSLIMS.

**Nazarene, Church of the.** Church taking its name from the Church of the Nazarene established in southern California (Los Angeles) in 1895. An Eastern Holiness group, the Association of Pentecostal Churches of America, formed a year later and then joined with the Nazarenes in 1907 to form the Pentecostal Church of the Nazarene. The southern Holiness Church of Christ joined east and west in Pilot Point, Tex., in 1908, considered to be the year of origin of the denomination. Holiness groups in the South, the upper Midwest, and the British Isles joined with the church over the next several decades. In 1919 the name of the denomination was changed to Church of the Nazarene.

Due partly to its far-flung core areas—eastern (New England and New York), western (Los Angeles and southern California), and southern (Tennessee, Texas, and Oklahoma)—and the early receptivity of Midwesterners to its teachings and practices, the Church of the Nazarene in eight decades has gained standing as a vigorous emerging national church, and an international one also. The church had more than 5000 U.S. congregations in 1987, with its strength concentrated in the Northeast, lower Midwest and Michigan, West, and parts of the Southeast, especially Florida.

Although the Nazarenes take their theological position and most practices from John Wesley and the Methodists, and today are much like the Methodists at large of an earlier time, both the 19th-century Holiness movement out of which the church developed and to some extent the young church itself drew upon other denominations as well, including Baptists, Congregationalists, Episcopalians, Presbyterians, Quakers, and the Salvation Army.

Spreading the doctrine of "scriptural holiness" has occupied such preeminence in the mind of the denomination that its adherence and commitment to mainstream evangelical Christian doctrine, including emphasis upon the new birth and an elevated but nonmechanical view of the bibli-

cal texts, have not always been well recognized, either by observers or its own members. One of the largest and perhaps the most significant of the Holiness churches, the denomination remains resolutely noncharismatic, although fellowship with pentecostals is less distant than in the past. The worship services of the church, today as in the formative years, are marked by a simplicity and warm formality apparent whatever the sophistication of a local congregation.

The church operates in some 75 world areas overall. Membership in 1987 reached 838,000, with the U.S. total 543,762. Other regional totals include Africa with 49,000, Asia Pacific with 53,802, Canada with 10,260, Caribbean with 73,471, Mexico–Central America with 54,229, South America with 41,786, and Eurasia with 11,729. According to 1987 statistics, the greatest growth that year took place in the Caribbean (almost 9 percent) and Mexico–Central America (6.5 percent).

Sunday school enrollment in 1987 was 1,264,876, with some 254,736 enrolled in the Nazarene Youth International auxiliary numbering 6956 societies; and 531,384 enrolled in the Nazarene World Missionary Society, with 7445 societies. With some 8400 congregations worldwide, ordained elders numbered 10,579 and licensed ministers 4086 (1987).

The church today owns and operates a fully accredited theological seminary, 6 liberal arts colleges, 2 universities, and a Bible college in the USA and colleges in Canada, Great Britain, and Japan. It also operates Spanish seminaries in Texas and Costa Rica and Bible colleges in Australia, Switzerland, and South Africa.

The Nazarene Publishing House printed or reprinted some 900,000 books in 1987, with some 62 new titles. Volume of business for the year was $17,000,000.

Radio programs of the church, "Showers of Blessing" and "Master Plan," are carried in 38 languages in 80 countries over some 1000 stations around the world.

Nazarenes in 1987 donated almost $392 million, with a per capita giving of $467.67. Tithing is encouraged but not insisted upon.

Nazarene church government is representative, reflecting a conscious effort to work from a middle position between episcopacy and congregationalism. The quadrennial general assembly is the supreme authority as to doctrine, polity, and practice. Membership is composed of equal numbers of laypeople and clergy, elected by the various district assemblies around the world, and includes missionaries, educators, and the headquarters staff. The general assembly elects six superintendents, who supervise the headquarters staff; and chooses a general board, which carries on between assemblies. District superintendents, elected annually, supervise the work of some 80 districts in the USA and about 120 worldwide. Local churches function under the leadership of pastors selected by local church membership.

The international headquarters, the publishing house, and the graduate theological seminary are located in Kansas City, Mo.

*See also* HOLINESS CHURCHES.

**Bibliography.** T. L. Smith, *Called unto Holiness: The Story of the Nazarenes* (1962); A. C. Outler, ed., *John Wesley* (1964); M. E. Redford, *The Rise of the Church of the Nazarene* (1965); L. Parrott, *Introducing the Nazarenes* (1969); W. M. Greathouse, *Nazarene Theology in Perspective* (1970); *Manual, Church of the Nazarene* (1985); *Statistics, Church of the Nazarene* (1987).

MARVIN CARMONY

## Near East School of Theology (NEST).

Religious institution in Beirut founded in 1932 by the merger of the Near East School of Religion (Athens) and the School of Religious Workers (Beirut). It is supported by the two mission boards, the Episcopal Diocese (Jerusalem), the Lutheran Church (Jordan), the Armenian Evangelical Union, and the Evangelical Synod (Syria–Lebanon). In the 1950s its administration was turned over to indigenous leadership and its property deeded to local evangelical bodies. The faculty and student body are ecumenical. Pursuing an interdenominational policy, it confers B.Th., M.A., M.Th., M.S.Th., and Th.D. degrees.

HAGOP APRAHAM CHAKMAKJIAN

## Nee, Watchman (Henry) (1903–1972).

Chinese Christian leader. Born in Swatow and educated at Trinity College, Foochow, he was active early in preaching the gospel, both indoors and on the streets. He formed an assembly after the Plymouth Brethren manner and other local groups followed, spreading first to Shanghai and then by 1932 farther north. Watchman Nee had been impressed by the writings of J. N. Darby, and through these had written to make contact with believers in the West. A group of Exclusive Brethren were favorably impressed on meeting him in China in 1932. When he visited England and America in 1933, however, he was found to be more "open" than his original contacts approved of. When the Shanghai group persisted in having fellowship with non-Exclusive believers, relations were formally severed. Nee was later successful in business, but turned his successes over to his church (known as Little Flock) in 1948. Because of his opposition to the communist Three-Self movement, he was imprisoned from 1952 until just before he died.

## Negro Churches. *See* BLACK RELIGION IN AMERICA; CIVIL RIGHTS MOVEMENT.

## Negro Spirituals. *See* GOSPEL SONGS.

## Neighbor. OT term similar to "brother," a fellow member of the covenant people (Lev. 25:25; Deut. 15:2–3; Neh. 5:1–13; Jer. 34:8, 17). This link involved moral obligations (Exod. 20; Lev. 19:18) and rights. Relations among neighbors were subject to the Law (Exod. 20:16–17; cf. Lev. 6:2–7; Deut. 19:11–13), because God had established the relationship (Job 16:21). When the rights of neighbors are disregarded, moral disintegration and national catastrophe follow and the divine wrath is incurred (Ps. 12:2; Prov. 11:9)—a situation becoming more common until the judgment (Isa. 3:5; Jer. 9:4–9). Ezekiel regards treatment of neighbor and neighbor's wife as an important factor in distinguishing between the righteous and the sinful man (Ezek. 18:22). In the age of the new covenant the Law will be written on men's hearts and they will live together in peace (Ezek. 31:34). Zechariah envisages a time when "each one of you will invite his neighbor to sit under his vine and under fig-tree" (3:10).

The NT confirms obligations to the neighbor. The theological meaning is presented in the parable of the Good Samaritan (Luke 10:25–37), where it was the man who had compassion who was a neighbor to the man who fell into the hands of robbers. The Christian is exhorted to serve as compassionate neighbor in the world. Both Paul (Rom. 13:9) and James (2:8) regard as the royal law the commandment to "love your neighbor as yourself."

## Neill, Stephan Charles (1900–1984). Missionary and missiologist. After studying classics and theology at Trinity College, Cambridge, he went to South India as a missionary in 1924. In his work as an evangelist, theological teacher, and Anglican bishop of Tinnevely (Tirunelveli), he became deeply concerned with producing Christian literature in Tamil for church workers and in promoting the cause of church unity. He was involved for 10 years in the Joint Council on Church Union working toward the formation of the Church of South India. After returning to Europe in 1944 because of poor health, Neill maintained his ecumenical interests through working with the World Council of Churches. He was professor of missions and ecumenical theology at the University of Hamburg from 1962, and professor of philosophy and religion at University College, Nairobi. He lectured all over the world, and was in demand as a speaker at university missions in Britain.

Neill wrote a large number of books on various topics, including *Anglicanism* (1958), *The Interpretation of the NT 1861–1961* (1962), and *A History of Christian Missions* (1964). *Christian Faith and Other Faiths* (1961) was revised in 1970 and replaced by *Crises of Belief* in 1984, a year which also saw the publication of two other works which symbolized his enduring concerns: *The Supremacy of Jesus* and *A History of Christianity in India* (vol. 1). He edited, with Ruth Rouse, *A*

*History of the Ecumenical Movement 1517–1948* (1954).

PHILIP HILLYER

**Neo-Orthodoxy.** *See* BARTH, KARL; CRISIS, THEOLOGY OF; DIALECTICAL THEOLOGY.

**Neo-Protestantism.** A term intended to distinguish the modern age and its interpretation of Christianity from the Reformation and its interpretation (Old Protestantism). A consciousness of ideological distance from the Reformers was expressed in the period of rationalism, but it was not until the beginning of the 20th century that Ernst Troeltsch formulated the distinction and coined the terms. Others elaborated Troeltsch's theory, pointing out that just as Christianity was Hellenized in the ancient church, so it has been progressively refashioned in modern times by elements of modern culture. In this process historical criticism has modified biblical authority, this-worldliness has supplanted otherworldliness, and every doctrine has somehow been affected by the modern spirit. Some theologians have consciously embraced neo-Protestantism. Others, like Karl Barth and Emil Brunner, although acknowledging the correctness of the analysis, have sharply repudiated neo-Protestant reinterpretations.

THEODORE TAPPERT

**Neo-Thomism.** Revival of interest in the philosophy of St. Thomas Aquinas generally dating from the 1879 encyclical of Pope Leo XIII, *Aeterni patris*, which presented Thomism as the official philosophy of the Roman Catholic Church. The movement bifurcated in the early 20th century. One branch, represented by Joseph Maréchal, Bernard Lonergan, and Karl Rahner, was an adaptation to Kantian thought. It was eager to bring traditional Thomism in line with modern scientific knowledge and postmedieval philosophical thought. While claiming to be loyal to the fundamental principles of Thomism, adherents addressed problems raised by the criteriological and epistemological questions of Descartes and Kant. It is to such thinkers as these that the term "Neo-Thomist" most properly applies, with its suggestion that Thomism needs not only to be resuscitated but also expanded and modified.

The second branch, under the leadership of Étienne Gilson and Jacques Maritain, sought to recover a pure version of Aquinas's teachings. While no less aware of modern questions, they held that Thomism needed only to be restored and applied. Of special interest is the late phase of Gilson's thought, with its insistence that Aquinas alone among philosophers has grasped the true principle of metaphysics. For Gilson, the fundamental doctrine of Thomism is to be found in the distinction between existence (*esse*) and essence. Whereas essence is inherently static and schematic, existence is dynamic and inconceptualizable. Aquinas largely reduced existence to the status of essence. Both Gilson and Maritain assert that the Thomism of Aquinas is radically existential and dynamic.

Since the Second Vatican Council Neo-Thomism has given way to phenomenology and process theology, largely because the movement holds to what is viewed as an outdated Aristotelianism. At the same time, Thomistic philosophical principles have been adopted by some evangelical Protestant thinkers like Norman L. Geisler for apologetic purposes.

*Bibliography.* M. de Wulf, *Scholasticism Old and New* (1907); M. C. D'Arcy, *Thomas Aquinas* (1930); E. Gilson, *The Unity of Philosophical Experience* (1938); J. Maritain, *The Degrees of Knowledge* (1937); E. Gilson, *Being and Some Philosophers* (1949); W. Elwell, ed., *Evangelical Dictionary of Theology* (1984).

**Nepal.** Monarchical Hindu state between India and Tibet, with an area of 145,391 sq. km. (56,136 sq. mi.) and a population of around 17 million (1986 est.). Of these, about 15 million are Hindus, some 900,000 are Buddhists, 465,000 are Muslims, and 115,000 adhere to tribal religions. There are perhaps 80,000 nonreligionists and atheists. Baha'is and Jains total about 7500. The Christian community is tiny and lives under considerable restrictions in a land where baptism and proselytizing are illegal and punishable by imprisonment, and where national believers are not recognized by the state. There are only about 6000 Christians in the country, including resident Europeans and Indians. The largest indigenous church is the Church of Christ in Nepal, formed in 1966.

**Nesmelov, Victor** (1863–1927). Eastern Orthodox philosopher. He studied at the Theological Academy of Kazan, where he was later professor of philosophy. His main work, *The Science of Man* (2 vols., 1893, 1903), was an original reinterpretation of Christian doctrine from an anthropological point of view. Berdiaev very aptly described it as an attempt to "churchify" Feuerbach.

GEORGES FLOROVSKY

**Netherlands, The.** European monarchy covering 40,844 sq. km. (15,770 sq. mi.) with a population of 14,561,000 (1986 est.). Secularization has affected both church and society deeply. An increasing proportion of the population professes to be unaffiliated with any church. The church's encounter with modern society has transformed the face of the ecclesiastical situation. This transformation may be viewed in terms of ecumenical, evangelical, theological, charismatic, and political developments.

Following the formation of the Ecumenical Council of the Netherlands (1946), Amsterdam

589

hosted the first assembly of the World Council of Churches (1948). Ecumenical developments have created tensions within the churches. The issue of WCC membership has become a major focal point of the conflict between progressives who encourage change and conservatives who resist change. Some have left their denominations over this issue. Others remain within their denomination while retaining a personal view rather different from the official position. Many, however, are deeply committed to the determination of Amsterdam (1948)—"that having discovered one another, we intend to stay together." WCC member churches include Nederlandse Hervormde Kerk (Netherlands Reformed Church), Gereformeerde Kerken in Nederland (Reformed Churches in the Netherlands), Algemene Dropsgezinde Societeit (General Mennonite Society), Evangelisch Lutherse Kerk (Evangelical Lutheran Church), Remonstrantse Broederschap (Remonstrant Brotherhood), and the Council of Churches in the Netherlands (Associate Council).

The 1954 visit of Billy Graham was greatly influential. Even more dramatically influential in a pentecostal direction was the 1958 visit of T. L. Osborn. While Baptists number approximately 12,000 (1981), the rise of pentecostalism has been meteoric—379 (1930), 584 (1947), 7590 (1960), 17,480 (1971), 34,190 (1981). While Dutch "evangelicalism" has had a strong American influence, it does have an indigenous Dutch history in the 19th century Reveil (Awakening) movement. Dutch evangelicalism tends to be more Reformed and less premillennialist than American fundamentalism. While there may be a tendency toward otherworldliness in the evangelical movement, its fervor and piety and openness to continuing renewal have much to teach the established churches.

Until the 1960s, the Nederlandse Hervormde Kerk (NHK)—a founding member of WCC and a powerful voice in Dutch public life during the postwar years, although not without significant conservative influence—was quite distinctive in its progressive outlook. Since the 1960s, there have been extraordinary developments in the Roman Catholic Church and the Gereformeerde Kerken in Nederland (GKN). A shaking off of traditional attitudes and ways of life in Dutch Catholic theology has led to the Netherlands being identified with ultraprogressivism. Despite sustained conservative reaction from Rome, this grappling with the issues raised by secularization—particularly evident in A New Catechism, a best-seller since its publication in 1967—is widely regarded as a stimulus toward renewal. GKN, formed in rather conservative isolation following a number of secessions from NHK, has been described as a "thoroughbred horse in blinkers." Since the 1960s, GKN has moved toward a more open stance and was admitted to full membership in WCC in 1971. While the "concerned" within the GKN may disagree with recent trends in their denomination, many beyond the Netherlands see in the theology of GKN theologian G. C. Berkouwer a genuinely evangelical middle way which avoids the extremes of both conservatism and liberalism. Notable Dutch theologians include E. Schillebeeckx (RC), H. Berkhof (NHK), and G. C. Berkouwer (GKN).

While the charismatic movement may be seen in connection with the influence of T. L. Osborn, the rapid rise of pentecostalism and the beginning of charismatic renewal among Roman Catholics in the 1960s, the formation of the task force Charismatische Werkgemeenschap Nederland (CWN) in 1972 is of particular significance. CWN, which includes both Protestants and Roman Catholics, works for the renewal of churches. It does not seek to compete with the churches and takes care to avoid the creation of separate churches. The attempts to be accepted by the churches have been fairly successful without gaining overall uncritical acceptance.

Until 1977, the major political parties in the postwar era were the Catholic People's party (KVP), the Calvinist Anti-Revolutionary party (ARP), the moderate Protestant Christian Historical Union (CHU), Labour (PvdA), and Liberal (WD). Following a federation between KVP, ARP, and CHU in 1976, the three parties, while retaining their separate organizations, contested the 1977 election under a common banner—the Christian Democratic party. This led to a complete merger into the "Christian Democratic Appeal" in 1980. It is this political consolidation which has produced the present Christian Democratic Appeal government. Another aspect of Christian political involvement worthy of note is the call from the Dutch Inter-Church Peace Council for a world free of nuclear weapons, beginning with the Netherlands.

Progressives and conservatives evaluate these changes differently. All are challenged to learn from the past without being locked in the past and to be open to the future without losing direction.

**Bibliography.** N. van der Plas and H. Suer, eds., *Those Dutch Catholics* (1967); M. Schuchart, *The Netherlands* (1972); J. A. Hebly, ed., *Lowland Highlights: Church and Oecumene in the Netherlands* (1972); I. J. Hesselink, *Reformed Review* 26/2 (Winter 1973): 67–89; H. Bakvis, *Catholic Power in the Netherlands* (1981).

CHARLES M. CAMERON

**Neumann, Theresa** (1898–1962). Born in Konnersreuth, Germany, she experienced a normal life until the age of 20. After that, she incurred many injuries and illnesses. As a result of one injury she became totally blind, but suddenly, after four years, she regained her sight. During the period of Lent in 1926 she is said to have received the stigmata of the crucifixion on her side, hands, and feet. Until 1951, each Good Friday, and several other Fridays throughout the year, she bled from the eyes and from the stigmata on her body. Many doctors, theologians, and hundreds of thousands of laypeople witnessed the phenomena, which were much disputed within Roman Catholic circles. Over 100 books, primarily in French and German, were written about the Konnersreuth stigmatic.

**Bibliography.** R. Kraus, *Mystical Phenomena in the Life of Theresa Neumann* (1947); Hilda Graef, *The Case of Theresa Neumann* (1951).

GILBERT L. ODDO

**Neve, Jürgen Ludwig** (1865–1943). Lutheran professor. Born in Schleswig, Germany, he studied at Breklum, Schleswig, and the University of Kiel (Th.D., 1924). He was professor of church history at Chicago Theological Seminary (1887–92) and Western Theological Seminary, Atchinson, Kans. (1898–1909); and professor of symbolics and history of doctrine at Hamma Divinity School (1909–43). Among his books are *Free Church in Comparison with State Church* (1900), *Brief History of the Lutheran Church in America* (1903), *Altered and Unaltered Augsburg Confession* (1910), *The Augsburg Confession, Its History and Interpretation* (1914), *Introduction to the Confessions of the Evangelical Lutheran Church* (1917, 1926), *The Lutherans in the Movements for Church Union* (1921), *Story and Significance of the Augsburg Confession* (1930), *Churches and Sects of Christendom* (1940), and with O. W. Heick, *History of Christian Thought* (vol. 1, 1943; vol. 2, 1946).

RAYMOND W. ALBRIGHT

**New Age Movement.** A general consensus about the sterility of modern society and the need to return to some form of spirituality. New Age thought appeals to many people in all walks of life through talk about reincarnation, the importance of dreams, astrology, psychic or holistic healing, and a host of other popular spiritual exercises and highly romanticized claims about self-fulfillment through a spiritual quest.

The appearance of today's New Age movement was noted as early as 1971 by Irving Hexham in *Some Aspects of the Contemporary Search for an Alternative Society* and *The New Paganism: Yoga and U.F.Os.* Other writers who were committed to New Age beliefs, like Lawrence Blair (*Rhythms of Vision: The Changing Patterns of Belief* [1976]) and Marilyn Ferguson (*The Aquarian Conspiracy: Personal and Social Transformation in the 1980s* [1980]), also heralded the arrival of a New Age. But it was not until the publication of actress Shirley MacLaine's best-selling autobiography *Out on a Limb* (1983) and the subsequent television special based on her book in 1987 that most people became aware of the growth of the so-called New Age movement and Christian groups began to take it seriously.

In North America the publication of various books by Constance Cumby and Dave Hunt brought an awareness of the growth of the New Age movement to the Christian public, especially fundamentalists. Both authors presented useful insights which were marred by a tendency to discover a worldwide conspiracy everywhere. Not until the publication of *Unmasking the New Age* and *Understanding Cults and New Religions* in 1986 did serious critiques of the New Age movement appear from a Christian perspective. Essentially, the New Age movement is neither new nor a movement. Its roots go back to various 19th-century religious movements such as spiritualism and theosophy. In essence it is a modernized magical vision of reality held together by numerous appealing mythologies rather than a coherent worldview. Underlying it is a synthesis between Eastern and Western religious traditions woven together in a pseudoscientific framework which calls discredited ancient traditions "new," "spiritual," and "scientific." These beliefs are given life through the activities of "channelers" or "transchannelers" and similar guru figures who are simply a new, modernized form of spiritualist medium.

Many aspects of the New Age movement have clearly fascist overtones and as a social phenomenon it resembles the romantic movements which flourished in pre-Nazi Germany. G. L. Mosse's *Crisis of German Ideology* and P. F. Drucker's *End of Economic Man* make sober reading in the light of New Age thought. Even so it must be remembered that many similar movements flourished in Great Britain and the USA in the 19th century and prior to World War II and they did not lead to fascism. Therefore while the political implications of the New Age movement bear watching, the likelihood is that it will eventually prove itself to be sterile and like 19th-century spiritualism simply wither away in the face of modern technological society.

**Bibliography.** I. Hexham, *The New Paganism: Yoga and U.F.O.s* (1973); L. Blair, *Rhythms of Vision: The Changing Patterns of Belief* (1976); M. Ferguson, *The Aquarian Conspiracy: Personal and Social Transformation in the 1980s* (1980); C. Cumby, *The Hidden Dangers of the Rainbow* (1983); D. Hunt and T. A. McMahon, *The Seduction of Christianity* (1985); D. J. Groothuis, *Unmasking the New Age* (1986); I. Hexham and K. Poewe, *Understanding Cults and New Religions* (1986); K. Holt, ed., *The New Age Rage* (1988).

IRVING HEXHAM

**New Apostolic Church.** Group formed as the result of a schism in the Catholic Apostolic Church which claims to preserve the original teachings of Edward Irving, Henry Drummond, and other founders of the parent body. The schism originated in Germany where the Catholic Apostolic Church, commonly identified as the

Irvingites, had firmly established itself after 1842. In the late 1850s, some of the German leaders asked that new apostles be named to the ruling council to replace those who had died. The English church refused. In 1860, Heinrich Geyer, a prophet of the German church, felt called to name two new persons as apostles. The schism which this independent action portended was delayed briefly, but in 1862 all compromises on the issues with the English church failed and the parent body excommunicated Geyer and F. W. Schwarz, a Catholic Apostolic pastor who had supported Geyer's actions. In 1865, they formed the General Christian Apostolic Mission, now the New Apostolic Church. Geyer soon fell out with the new church, leaving the leadership of the new body to Schwarz, whom he had previously called to the apostleship.

The church was dramatically reshaped by the influential apostle Fritz Krebs (1832–1905) in the late 19th century. He held that to the apostles alone was assigned the exclusive authority to transmit salvation. The group has modified its patterns of worship, abolishing the use of vestments and simplifying the order of worship. The apostles now number about 50. The current membership, in both German republics, is about 500,000. The international headquarters of the church are at Frankfort-on-Main, West Germany. U.S. headquarters are in Chicago, Ill. The American church, numbering 33,068 members, and the churches in Canada and seven other countries are administered by the president of the Canadian district. Worldwide membership is over 800,000.

**Bibliography.** O. Eggenberger, *Neuapostolische Gemeinde, ihre Geschichte und Lehre* (1953); D. Hesslegrave, *Dynamic Religious Movements* (1978); A. Piepkorn, *Profiles in Belief: The Religious Bodies of the United States and Canada* (1979).

MELVIN E. DIETER

# Newbigin, James Edward Lesslie (1909– ).

Missionary and missiologist. After a time as Student Christian Movement secretary in Glasgow and lecturer at Westminster College, Cambridge, Newbigin went to Madras as a Church of Scotland missionary in 1936. He spent most of the next 38 years in South India. At the inauguration of the Church of South India in 1947, he was appointed bishop of Madurai and Ramnad. He retired in 1959 to become chairman of the International Missionary Council and later was recalled to India to be bishop in Madras (1965–74). Back again in Britain, he lectured at the Selly Oak Colleges (1974–79), was appointed moderator of the United Reformed Church (1978/79), and then in 1980 became a United Reformed Church minister in Birmingham. Not surprisingly, perhaps, his 1985 autobiography is entitled *Unfinished Agenda*. His writings reflect his eclectic career and major concerns, including church theology and Christian defense. They include *Christian Freedom in the Modern World* (1937), *The Reunion of the Church* (1948), *A South India Diary* (1951), *The Household of God* (1953), *A Faith for This One World?* (1961), *Honest Religion for Secular Man* (1966), *The Finality of Christ* (1969), *The Good Shepherd* (rev. ed., 1977), *The Open Secret* (1978), *The Other Side of 1984* (1983), and *Foolishness to the Greeks* (1986).

PHILIP HILLYER

**New Delhi Assembly.** The third international meeting of the World Council of Churches held in 1961. With the theme "Jesus Christ, the Light of the World," the assembly discussed three themes: witness, service, and unity.

Of the 23 new member churches, 11 were in Africa, 5 in Asia, and 2 in South America. Only 5 were in Europe and North America. Two Pentecostal churches from Chile formed a bridge to the evangelical churches, most of which dissociated themselves from WCC, and still do so. The main theme, more regarded as a guiding principle, in comparison to the previous assemblies, was liable to misinterpretation in view of the fact that light is one of the symbols that appear in the Asian religions. Instead of "the ecumenical conscience of the churches" the assembly became visibly the mouthpiece of the member churches. The assembly addressed religious liberty, international crisis, anti-Semitism, and South Africa, and drafted an "Appeal to all Governments and Peoples."

The adhesion of the Orthodox churches in Eastern Europe was rightly regarded as "the opportunity to ensure that a real spiritual dialogue shall take place between the Eastern churches and the churches which take their origin in the West." Out of 400 million Christians today—the total membership of the 310 churches represented in WCC—135 million are Orthodox. With the act of integration, the International Missionary Council ceased to exist as a separate entity and was replaced by the WCC Commission on World Mission and Evangelism. The unity of the church was conceived of as "one fully committed fellowship, holding the one apostolic faith, preaching the one Gospel, breaking the one bread, joining in common prayer, and having a corporate life reaching out in witness and service to all and who at the same time are united with the whole Christian fellowship in all places and all ages."

*See also* WORLD COUNCIL OF CHURCHES (WCC).

A. J. VAN DER BENT

# New Jerusalem, Church of the. Christian

group whose teachings are based on the thought of Emmanuel Swedenborg (1688–1772), a learned Swedish scientist who turned to theology at the age of 55. Swedenborg did not personally organize any group of followers around his theological and philosophical teachings. In 1783

Robert Hindmarsh, a London Methodist, first began to organize those who had been attracted to Swedenborg's writings. The British societies organized the General Conference of New Church Societies in 1815. By 1792 societies began to spring up in Canada and the USA. In 1798 John Hargrove reorganized the Baltimore society, the first in America. This and other American societies organized the General Convention of the New Jerusalem in Philadelphia, Pa., in 1817.

Following the controversy surrounding the founding of the Academy of the New Church at Philadelphia in 1876, the Pennsylvania Association of the General Association was allowed to organize as the General Church of Pennsylvania. The main point of contention was the nature of the authority of Swedenborg's writings. By 1890, the General Church withdrew completely from the General Association; they eventually set up an episcopal form of polity and became known, in 1897, as The General Church of the New Jerusalem. Its headquarters are at Bryn Athyn, Pa. The church has a membership in the USA of 2143 and in Canada of 366. It has a mission in the Republic of South Africa. The General Convention maintains its headquarters at its New Church Theological School, Newton, Mass.; it also has a seminary in London, England. There are affiliated societies in Europe and missions in Korea, Japan, and the Philippines. Inclusive membership in the USA and Canada is 2245. Worldwide membership is estimated to be around 40,000.

Both groups adhere to the fundamental understanding of reality proposed by Swedenborg in his spiritual writings. He believed that all of life and creation (including the Scriptures) are ultimately spiritual and to be spiritually discerned. By the principle of "correspondence" believers are able to discern the spiritual realities lying behind all materiality and to live in the spiritual or true world. Death will free them finally to live in the unencumbered spiritual world. The New Jerusalem represents the new spiritual era which was opened up by Swedenborg's spiritual interpretation of Scripture. Opposing views on the authority of Swedenborg's scriptural interpretations constitute a major point of difference between the General Convention and the General Church. The former accepts the writings as enlightened commentary on Scripture; the latter receives the writings as divinely inspired and equal to or superior to Scripture in their revelation and authority. The General Convention is the more ecumenical of the two bodies, holding membership in the National Council of Churches in the USA. It is congregational in polity and accepts members by baptism and confirmation or by transfer from other Christian churches. The General Church receives members only by its own baptism and holds to an episcopal order of church government.

***Bibliography.*** M. Block, *The New Church in the World* (2d ed., 1968); H. Keller, *My Religion* (1964); H. Odhner, *The General Church of the New Jerusalem* (2d ed., 1965).

MELVIN E. DIETER

## NT Studies, 20-Century Trends in.

This century has seen many developments and innovations in NT studies, some of which have arisen from new discoveries and lines of thought in kindred fields, such as those of the Greco-Roman and Oriental worlds, and some from trends and debates in the fields of philosophy and systematic theology.

Textual criticism lies at the foundation of all other study, concentrating on the text or wording of the component documents. At the beginning of the century the textual theory of Westcott and Hort was paramount: both new discoveries and reconsideration of the data have led either to great modifications or to the total dismissal of that theory. Many documents, previously only known to exist, have now been examined; other documents (particularly on papyrus) have been discovered; many ancient translations have received critical attention and are available in scholarly form; and there have been great advances in the collection and analysis of the quotations from Scripture in the fathers and other writings. The reaction from Westcott and Hort led first to emphasis on the other text which they believed ancient, namely, that of Codex Bezae, the Latin and Syriac versions. This emphasis in its turn gave rise to a theory of "local texts," sponsored by the great sees, any of which might contain acceptable readings. While this stimulating theory might now be looked at once again, textual criticism has not remained content with it but has moved in several divergent directions.

First, especially linked with the name of G. D. Kilpatrick, an eclectic method has been developed, which is willing to accept as original any reading which rational criteria commend. Second, the dominant hand-edition (Nestle-Aland, 26th ed.), produced by Kurt Aland and an editorial board, lays very great stress on the witness of papyrus MSS of the 2d to the 4th centuries. Acknowledging the existence of rescensional forms, it believes these to be the product of the age following the great persecutions. Third, a strong phalanx of American conservative Protestant scholars has sought to establish the originality of the text of the majority of medieval MSS, in spite of the chronological problems involved. Textual criticism then is at the moment a house divided, which is perhaps one reason why it has become so much the preserve of those possessed of specialist skills practiced by few other scholars.

The language of the NT has received much attention, not only from those interested primarily in that collection of 1st-century books alone, for theological reasons, but also from students of the history of the Greek language; these, for their part, have contributed mutually to the study of NT language from their investigations of literary and nonliterary material both of the ancient world and of the period of medieval and modern Greek. Standard grammars are those of Blass-Debrunner (latest ed. by Rehkopf, 1975; latest ET by Funk, 1961) and of Moulton-Howard, Turner (vol. 1, 1908; vol. 2, 1929; vol. 3, 1963; vol. 5, 1976). Among the most important contributions from the side of the history of Greek are Lars Rydbeck, *Fachprosa, vermeintliche Volkssprache und Neues Testament* (1967), B. G. Mandilaras, *The Verb in the Greek Non-Literary Papyri* (1973), and F. T. Gignac, *A Grammar of the Greek Papyri of the Roman and Byzantine Periods* (2 vols., Milan, 1975, 1977). For treatment of syntax by Gignac we must for the present rely on *Yale Classical Studies* 28 (1985): 155–65.

The study of the Aramaic language, the vernacular of Jesus and the first Palestinian Christians, has also advanced. Particularly important have been the writings in Aramaic and Hebrew from Qumran. Valuable summaries of the state of investigation and analysis may be found in Matthew Black, *An Aramaic Approach to the Gospels and Acts* (3d ed., 1966) and various essays of Joseph Fitzmyer, gathered in the collection, *A Wandering Aramean* (1979).

From these advances has continued to flourish the debate over the possibility of Aramaic bases for the traditions of the four Gospels and the Acts of the Apostles. Few, if any, scholars of reputation would today advocate that the Gospels as they stand are translations from Aramaic, but a majority would allow that it is at least probable that the traditions utilized by the Gospel writers and the author of Acts existed in Aramaic, certainly in an oral form. It remains a matter of debate, however, whether in any given case we should see Aramaic behind particular forms of words in the Gospels or elsewhere, if the construction or usage should be paralleled in Greek, contemporary with the NT or in its subsequent history. Here the limits of human mental ability play their part: no scholar can be equally equipped in the Greek language and its history, and in the Aramaic language and its history. Although there are some outstanding scholars, each will be orientated toward the one field of knowledge and expertise rather than to the other. In the case under review, one will interpret in one way, one in another. This author inclines to the view that if a form of words can be paralleled in Greek, its Aramaic origin, however plausible, is not demonstrable; but others will argue otherwise. This is an impasse which cannot be overcome. Aramaic will remain of vast exegetical importance, but absolute certainty about the original form of any saying will not be attainable.

The interrelation of the synoptic Gospels has continued to attract much study. At the beginning of the century, the two-source theory was predominant over other interpretations, which during the earlier half of the century was developed into a four-source theory. More recently, however, the whole structure has come under criticism: minorities of scholars hold either to a view that Luke used both Mark and Matthew, or, reviving the Griesbach hypothesis, that the order and relationship of the Gospels was Matthew, used by Luke, and both by Mark. In all circles the notion of special literary sources for Matthew and Luke has disappeared. Most scholars still hold a two-source theory, however, with Q, the common source of Matthew and Luke, coming back into its own. The emphasis in present work is not upon the historical reliability of the Gospels, but upon the theological emphases and objectives of the Evangelists shown in their editorial work and in their favored terminologies (redaction criticism). This emphasis is also found in work on the Acts of the Apostles.

This change of emphasis is no doubt due to the application and influence of the technique of form criticism. Form criticism arose in the early 1920s in Germany, where it continued to dominate, and found a welcome particularly in American scholarship. The method is derived from anthropological models, which had been fruitfully applied to OT materials. Traditions in the course of transmission within a given society achieve a particular form, which gives the clue to the function played by the unit of tradition in the life of the society, its *Sitz im Leben*. The method is potentially of great exegetical value, and neutral in regard to the historical origins of traditions, but its application has always tended to be weighted by a skeptical view of historical investigation and an overemphasis on the possible creativity of the early Christian society faced with theological and ethical questions unanswered by traditional material. Existentialist philosophy and theology also encouraged form criticism in this direction. Form criticism has been challenged by those with a more confident view of the possibility of historical knowledge by stress upon the reliability of oral tradition when used as a means of instruction, and upon the short length of time elapsed between event and Gospel, too short for creativity to have much scope. But confidence in the outline of the Gospel story has been generally eroded.

Great change has come over the study of the Johannine literature during these years. All would admit development of tradition before the final form of the Gospel. Some have followed Bultmann's hypothesis of a Narrative Source (Book of Signs), although his other, of a Sayings Source, has not survived critical scrutiny. Others pursue a line akin to that of C. H. Dodd, discerning historical material by various methods, including form criticism. Much use has been made of the notion of a school in which "Johannine" material was passed on, reflected upon, and developed. Within such a context, room is often found for the composition of both the Apocalypse and the Epistles. There has not been agreement on which school of theological thought influenced the Evangelist or his sources: Philonic-Platonic thought, pre-Christian or late Jewish gnosticism, and thought akin to that of the Qumran community have all been proposed. Stress has often been laid on the links with the most primitive Christianity, especially in the use of testimonia.

While there has certainly been throughout NT scholarship a tendency to return to positions on authorship closer to traditional ascriptions, there has been more emphasis on continuity and development of thought than upon specific identification of authors as a unifying factor. In the study of the Epistles, both those of the Pauline corpus and those in the Catholic group, much research has attempted to find patterns either of primitive liturgy or of primitive *paraenesis* (ethical instruction).

Doubt has persisted about the authenticity of Ephesians and the Pastoral Epistles in Pauline studies, but attempts to resolve the problem by computerized vocabulary and application of statistical analysis applied to linguistic patterns, while suggestive, have not met with wide approval. Paul has been linked by most scholars closely with the Judaism of his day, which many sources, especially from Qumran, now make better known, but debate persists about the exact nature of this Judaism. There has also been emphasis upon literary links of Paul with the Hellenistic literary forms, and upon the quest for the nature of the communities to which he wrote as a factor in determining the form of his letters.

In this period there has been a move, in regard to the life of Jesus, from historical confidence in many quarters to an emphasis upon the nature of the NT documents as witnesses to the belief of the early church and its religious experience of Jesus as Lord and Savior. Even those convinced that we may discern the "Jesus of Galilee" within or behind the object of devotion stress the limits of this, and the role of interpretation and proclamation in its transmission. An increasing input by post-Christian unbelieving scholars and by Jewish scholars has contributed to this trend, but in general it has been linked with very positive theology and informed by the experience of the church in the 20th century.

In this climate there have flourished recently two further types of approach. First, the attempt to apply to NT interpretation structural analyses which seek to discover how the construction of discourses functions in the reading of it. This discipline seeks to emphasize the impact of the discourses upon the reader, especially those contemporary with their composition, and to understand their structure in the light of this. Second, there has flowered, on the borders of biblical study and philosophical theology, much serious study of hermeneutics, investigating the problems of expounding the content and significance of these documents of the 1st century in the setting of the 20th. These introduce the student of the NT to new fields, in which, if he labors hard, he will find much of vital importance.

**Bibliography.** J. M. Robinson, *A New Quest of the Historical Jesus* (1959); W. G. Kümmel, *The NT: The History of the Investigation of Its Problems* (1973), and *Introduction to the NT* (rev. ed., 1975); P. Vielhauer, *Geschichte der urchristlichen Literatur* (1975); A. C. Thistleton, *The Two Horizons* (1980); R. F. Collins, *Introduction to the NT* (1983); C. M. Tuckett, *The Revival of the Griesbach Hypothesis* (1983); W. Schmithals, *Einleitung in die drei ersten Evangelien* (1985); S. Neill, *The Interpretation of the NT, 1861–1986* (2d ed., 1988).

J. Neville Birdsall

## New Theology, The.

The expression of the implications of the belief that the church in every age has the continuing task of recasting and updating the historic Christian message to suit that generation. It finds its first clear outline in the work of Reginald John Campbell (*The New Theology* [1907]; *New Theology Sermons* [1907]) but more recently in the works of J. A. T. Robinson, D. Nineham, and Maurice Wiles.

No one definite issue comes to the fore as of most significance in the New Theology. Its main thesis, however, has been that man has "come of age" intellectually, psychologically, and religiously. The old images and language of God are both inadequate and unhelpful. The starting point of the New Theology has always been the doctrine of God. The idea of the immanence of God pervades and controls the theology. God is immanent in the universe and in mankind. He is not above or apart from creation; he is the uncaused Cause of all existence (Campbell), the ground of our being (Robinson). Man, therefore, never encounters God directly but always through relationship. In this aspect Robinson followed the lead given by Martin Buber, with his "I-Thou" theology, and the Englishman John Wren Lewis.

Among the secondary concerns are the social implications of the gospel and an attempt to reconcile theology with science. In the former area the New Theology has adopted the idea of the priority of love over law, situational ethics or the new morality. The New Theology almost completely removes the distinction between God and man. "Deity," "divinity," and "humanity" are essentially the same: humanity is divinity viewed from below, divinity is humanity viewed from above. To say "God," according to Robinson, is to say "Love." It is to speak of the creative power between people (termed Ultimate Reality). The whole human race is a unity because God pervades it. The traditional teaching on the person of Christ is incredible to the New Theologians. Christ is both divine and human because he allowed himself to be governed by divine love. The title "Christ," for Campbell, is a quality that any man might attain to in fully realizing his potential as a human being. In this way the New Theology makes the incarnation nothing more than the supreme example of God's indwelling a man. In Robinson's words, Christ is merely "a window into God at work." The New Theology rejects evil, sin, the fall, and the wrath of God.

*Bibliography.* E. L. Mascall, *The Secularization of Christianity* (1965); R. J. Page, *New Directions in Anglican Theology* (1967); K. Hamilton, *What's New in Religion?* (1968); R. J. Blaikie, *"Secular Christianity"and God Who Acts* (1970); J. Bowden, *Voices in the Wilderness* (1977).

MICHAEL PARSONS

**New Thought.** Philosophical perspective which affirms that each individual must be loyal to Truth as he sees it. While New Thought is more a point of view than a definitive movement, it is definitely organized into a number of groups, differing somewhat in their emphases. These groups include Unity, the Institute of Religious Science, and Divine Science. Most of these, excluding Unity, are united in the International New Thought Alliance. In 1917 this body drew up a declaration of principles, affirming the Good as universal and everlasting; health as man's divine inheritance; and the divine supply as abundant and available to those who live with their whole being and thus express fullness. The kingdom of heaven is said to be within us; God is universal love, life, truth, and joy; realizing oneness with him means love, truth, peace, health, and plenty for man. Heaven is here and now. The universe is spiritual, and man is a spiritual being.

The diverse New Thought groups all recognize Phineas P. Quimbly as their founder, although many others, including Warren Felt Evans, Ralph Waldo Emerson, and Julius A. Dresser, have been influential in the development of their thought. The early history of New Thought is closely tied to that of Christian Science since Mary Baker Eddy was once healed by Quimbly and for some time was taught by him. How much the Quimbly influence has affected Christian Science is a moot question.

Some of the groups are closer to orthodox Christian belief than others, notably Unity; some are definitely eclectic, drawing from other faiths and philosophies as well.

*Bibliography.* H. W. Dresser, *History of the New Thought Movement* (1919); E. Holmes, ed., *Mind Remakes Your World* (1944); C. Braden, *These Also Believe* (1949).

CHARLES S. BRADEN

**Newton, Joseph Fort** (1880–1950). Episcopalian minister and writer. Born in Decatur, Tex., he was pastor of the First Baptist Church, Paris, Tex. (1897/98), and associate pastor of a nonsectarian church in St. Louis, Mo. (1898–1900). He founded the People's Church in Dixon, Ill., in 1901. He was pastor of the Liberal Christian Church, Cedar Rapids, Iowa (1908–16); of London City Temple (1916–19); and of the Church of the Divine Paternity, New York (1919–25). Ordained to the ministry of the Protestant Episcopal Church (1926), he served as rector of Christ Church, Overbrook, Philadelphia (1926–30); St. James Church, Philadelphia (1930–35); and of the Church of St. Luke and the Epiphany, Philadelphia (1938–50).

He wrote *David Swing, Poet and Preacher* (1909), *Abraham Lincoln* and *Lincoln and Herndon* (1910), *The Eternal Christ* and *Sermons and Lectures* (1912), *The Builders, a Story and Study of Masonry* and *Wesley and Woolman* and *What Have the Saints to Teach Us?* (1914), *The Ambassador* (1916), *The Mercy of Hell* and *The Sword of the Spirit* (1918), *The Theology of Civilization* (1919), *Some Living Masters of the Pulpit* (1922), *Preaching in London* and *The Men's House* (1923), *Preaching in New York* (1924), *The Truth and Life* (1925), *The Religion of Masonry* (1926), *God and the Golden Rule* (1927), *Altar Stairs* (1928), *The New Preaching* (1929), *Things I Know in Religion* (1930), *The Angel in the Soul* (1931), *The Sermon in the Making* (1932), *Living Every Day* (1937), *We Highly Resolve, the Stuff of Life* (1939), *His Cross and Ours* (1940), *Living Up to Life* (1941), *Live, Love and Learn* (1943), *Where Are We in Religion?* (1944), and an autobiography, *River of Years* (1946).

W. W. MANROSS

**New Zealand.** South Pacific Ocean country southeast of Australia with an area of 268,808 sq. km. (103,787 sq. mi.). In 1985 the population was 3,291,500, 55 percent of which lived in the five principal cities. Under a single parliamentary government, there is guaranteed freedom of religion; the doctrine of separation of church and state is similar to that in Australia.

In 1981 some 10 percent of the population claimed to be Maori, while 3 percent indicated origins in other parts of Polynesia. No one can be sure when the Maoris reached New Zealand, but various groups seem to have arrived between 1000 and 1500 B.C. While to European eyes the Maoris were clearly a more highly developed people than the Australian aborigines, they were equally at odds with Europeans. Their sense of community was high, and this together with their view of the spirit-world, set barriers between them and the "pakehas," or white settlers. Bitter conflicts erupted, particularly from 1844 to 1864;

British troops were hard pressed to subdue the Maori warriors.

The earliest Christian missions were initiated in 1814 under the Anglican Church Missionary Society, with Thomas Kendall (1778–1832) as the local leader. Methodists led by Samuel Leigh (1785–1852) followed in 1822; Catholics arrived in 1838. These, and other labors, led in the 1960s to some 31 percent of Maoris claiming to be Anglicans, 17.2 percent Catholics, 7.5 percent Methodists, 2.4 percent Presbyterians, and 0.9 percent Brethren. Other white Christian-related groups accounted for 1.4 percent of Maoris, but Mormons had the allegiance of 7.3 percent. Of greater indigenous interest are the 13.1 percent who belong to the Ratana Church (established in 1920 by T. W. Ratana) and the 3.2 percent who owe allegiance to the Ringatu Church which dates from 1868 and was founded by Te Kooti Rikivangi. Both the latter combine elements of traditional Maori religion with Christianity; attempts to develop acceptable indigenous expressions of the faith are to be found among most Christian groups.

After some semipermanent contacts by whalers and sealers from late in the 18th century, large-scale permanent British settlement began in the 1840s. It was predated by the work of the missionaries, the Anglicans being inspired by Samuel Marsden (1764–1838) of Sydney. This early missionary work was of considerable value for, while never a penal colony, New Zealand did attract what a contemporary observer described as "the veriest refuse of civilized society." A counterweight to this came through the carefully selected Scots Presbyterian emigrants who came to Dunedin from 1848 and the English Anglicans who came, similarly screened, to Christchurch in 1851. Anglican work continued under supervision from Australia until George Selwyn (1809–1878) was consecrated bishop of New Zealand in 1842. Relative autonomy came with a separate constitution for the province in 1857, with Selwyn as metropolitan from 1858. There are seven dioceses, and 1981 census returns indicated that 25.7 percent of the population claim Anglican allegiance.

New Zealand's Catholics became the sole responsibility of Bishop Jean Pompallier (1801–1871) from 1842, and there are now four dioceses, with some 14.4 percent of the population declaring themselves Catholics in census returns.

Methodists had their first separate conference in 1874, but were linked with Australian Methodists under one general conference until 1913. The various groups came together as the Methodist Church of New Zealand, and in 1981 4.7 percent of the census respondents indicated that they were Methodists.

Presbyterians came to Wellington in 1839, but gathered strength in the southern Otago area, where many emigrated as members of the Free Church of Scotland after 1848. Others came from Nova Scotia in 1851 to Waipu in the north. The Presbyterian Church of New Zealand was united in 1901 and as the second largest Christian denomination accounts for 16.5 percent of census respondents.

Baptists began work in 1851 and in 1981 made up 1.6 percent of the population, being followed in numbers by the Mormons with 1.1 percent. Other groups, including Jews, Buddhists, Hindus, and Muslims, each make up less than one percent of the population, with Brethren at 0.8 percent, the Salvation Army and pentecostals each at 0.6 percent, Jehovah's Witnesses and Seventh-day Adventists at 0.4 percent each, and the Churches of Christ, Lutherans, and Hindus each at 0.2 percent.

While New Zealanders are keen to maintain their distinctiveness from Australians, there are strong parallels between the two countries. Nevertheless, New Zealand retains a stronger British flavor than does Australia, and has far greater contact and involvement with the peoples of the South Pacific. As in Australia, the growth area in the religious profile is that of "no religion," which in the 1981 census stood at 23.6 percent of the population (cf. 14.2 percent in 1971)—25.2 percent if "atheists" and "agnostics" are included.

The spirit of secularism is strong in New Zealand, as in Australia, despite the fact that religion, with a Puritan content, was given a higher priority in certain key areas and periods than in Australia.

*Bibliography.* K. Sinclair, *A History of New Zealand* (1969); B. Colless and P. Donovan, eds., *Religion in New Zealand Society* (1980); J. J. Mol, *The Fixed and the Fickle: Religion and Identity in New Zealand* (1982); J. Irwin, *An Introduction to Maori Religion* (1984); *New Zealand Official Yearbook* (1985).

IAN GILLMAN

# Nicaragua.

**Nicaragua.** Large Central American republic with an area of 130,000 sq. km. (50,200 sq. mi.) and a population of 3,020,000 (1983). Roman Catholicism is the dominant religion in Nicaragua. During the postindependence period, the church allied itself with the Conservatives to protect its privileged position. The most serious attack on the church occurred during the Liberal government of José Santos Zelaya (1893–1909), leading to the confiscation of church property and the annulment of the concordat. During subsequent Conservative governments harmonious church-state relations were restored.

Throughout most of the Somoza dictatorship (1936–79), the church hierarchy served as a strong pillar of support for the regime. This situation began to change after 1970 with the appointment of a new archbishop, Miguel Obando y Bravo. Perhaps even more important were the activities of young progressive clergy influenced by liberation theology. By 1974 most of the bishops were actively collaborating with the moderate opposition to Somoza, while a number of progressive clergy and religious were providing support for the Sandinista insurgency. Since Somoza's fall in 1979, consensus has given way to division within the church, primarily concerning the church's role within the revolutionary process. While progressive clergy and religious have actively collaborated with the Sandinista government, the church hierarchy has become increasingly vocal in its opposition to what it considers a Marxist-dominated government. In 1983 there were 320 priests (128 secular and 192 religious) distributed throughout 178 parishes.

On the Atlantic Coast (which was a British protectorate during much of the 19th century) Protestant groups have been dominant—the Moravians amongst the indigenous Miskito population and the Anglicans amongst the Creole population. In 1982 there were 78 Protestant denominations with 129,727 communicants.

Policies of the Nicaraguan government regarding religious activities remained ambivalent through the late 1980s. In late 1990 both Protestant and Roman Catholic relations with the Sandinistas seemed relatively good, and there were some signs of a religious awakening.

PHILIP J. WILLIAMS

**Nichols, James Hastings** (1915– ). Presbyterian minister and church historian. Born in Auburn, N.Y., he studied at Yale (Ph.D. 1941) and Harvard. He taught at Macalester College (1940–43), the University of Chicago (1943–62), and Princeton Theological Seminary (1962–73). In 1963, he was a Protestant representative to the Second Vatican Council in Rome. He authored *Primer for Protestants* (1947; rev. ed., 1957), *Democracy and the Churches* (1951), and *History of Christianity: 1650–1950* (1956). Nichols' most important contributions have been a major study of the Mercersburg theologians, *Romanticism in American Theology* (1961), and in the area of Presbyterian/Reformed worship and theology, *Corporate Worship in the Reformed Tradition* (1968).

JAMES MCCLANAHAN

**Nichols, Robert Hastings** (1873–1955). Presbyterian. Born in Rochester, N.Y., he graduated from Yale (Ph.D., 1896), and studied theology at Auburn Theological Seminary and Mansfield College, Oxford. After Presbyterian pastorates in Unadilla, N.Y., and South Orange, N.J., he taught church history at Auburn Seminary (1910–44). He was professor of church history at Union Theological Seminary (1939–44; lecturer until 1948). He was active in the American Society of Church History as treasurer (1922–50) and editor of *Church History* (1932–49). He was stated clerk of the Synod of New York of the Presbyterian Church (1922–51). He wrote *The Growth of the Christian Church* (1914; rev. ed., 1941).

**Nicholson, William Patteson** (1876–1959). Irish evangelist. Born into a missionary family in Bangor, County Down, he spent some years at sea, and was converted in 1899. He trained at the Bible Training Institute, Glasgow, and was appointed evangelist of the Lanarkshire Christian Union in 1903. He did evangelistic work in various countries, notably Australia, New Zealand, and North America. He served as evangelist on the team of Wilbur Chapman and Charles M. Alexander in their missions in Australia and America. He was ordained as an evangelist in 1914 in the Presbyterian Church in North America. His most outstanding work was done in Northern Ireland (1921–26) when there was bitter strife and unrest. His uncompromising and ardent preaching found a wide acceptance among the crowds attending. There were thousands of professed conversions, communion rolls greatly increased, and the spiritual life of many churches was revitalized.

S. W. MURRAY

**Nicoll, William Robertson** (1851–1923). Scottish minister, writer, and editor. Son of an Aberdeenshire minister, he graduated from Aberdeen University, then studied theology and was ordained in the Free Church of Scotland. He ministered at Dufftown (1874–77) and Kelso (1877–85), but ill health took him to London, where he embarked on a remarkable literary career. In 1885 he assumed editorship of *The Expositor* and in 1886 of *The British Weekly*, holding both posts until his death. Under his guidance *The British Weekly* made a noteworthy impact on the political scene, especially during World War I. Among many substantial contributions made in the secular literary field was his founding and editing of *The Bookman* (1891–1923). Included in his more religious writings are *Calls to Christ* (1877), *Songs of Rest* (2 vols., 1879, 1885), *The Incarnate Saviour* (1881), *The Lamb of God* (1883), *The Return to the Cross* (1897), *The Church's One Foundation: Christ and Recent Criticism* (1901), *Ian Maclaren: Life of the Rev. John Watson* (1908), *My Father: An Aberdeenshire Minister, 1812–91* (1908), *The Expositor's Dictionary of Texts* (1910), *Reunion in Eternity* (1918), *Letters of Principal Denney* (1920), and *Princes of the Church* (1921). He also edited a number of other works, including *The Theological Educator, The Expositor's Bible,* and *The Expositor's Greek Testament*.

J. D. DOUGLAS

**Niebuhr, Helmut Richard** (1894–1962). Clergyman, philosopher, and educator. He was educated at Elmhurst (Illinois) College, Eden Theological Seminary, Washington University, Yale Divinity School, and Yale University (Ph.D., 1924). Niebuhr was the president of Elmhurst College (1924–27) before returning to Eden Theological Seminary where he wrote his first book, *The Social Sources of Denominationalism* (1929). In 1931 he returned to Yale Divinity School as associate professor of Christian ethics where he stayed until his sudden death. Niebuhr's theological concern throughout his long career was to urge an ongoing reformation of life and thought, seeing the radically transcendent God as the source of all constructive change. He stressed the need for understanding our human life from a Christian point of view. During his Yale years he wrote many significant books, including *The Church Against the World*, co-authored with W. Pauck and F. P. Miller (1935), *The Kingdom of God in America* (1937), *The Meaning of Revelation* (1941), *Christ and Culture* (1951), *The Purpose of the Church and Its Ministry* (1956), *Radical Monotheism and Western Culture* (1960), and posthumously, *The Responsible Self* (1962). Two excellent studies of Niebuhr's thought are John D. Godsey, *The Promise of H. Richard Niebuhr* (1970), and Lonnie D. Kliever, *H. Richard Niebuhr* (1977).

WALTER A. ELWELL

**Niebuhr, Karl Paul Reinhold** (1892–1971). Evangelical and Reformed theologian and churchman. He graduated from Elmhurst (Illinois) College, Eden Theological Seminary (1913), Yale Divinity School, and was ordained in the Evangelical Synod of North America (1915). After serving as minister of the Bethel Church, Detroit (1915–28), he was appointed professor of applied Christianity at Union Theological Seminary, where he served until failing health forced his retirement in 1960. Niebuhr was a central figure in the return of American Protestantism to a more biblical point of view from the naive optimism of early 20th-century liberalism. His belief that although the structures of human existence are fallen, they still demand social involvement brought Niebuhr to propound a radical social gospel for a radically fallen world in the name of the transcendent God. Niebuhr had numerous political involvements, including the Americans for Democratic Action, UNESCO, Committee for Cultural Freedom, the World Council of Churches, the Liberal Party of New York State, the American Association for a Democratic Germany, and the Fellowship of Christian Socialists. He was at one time associate editor of *The Nation* and editor of *Christianity and Crisis* and *Christianity and Society*. His creative brilliance brought him the Presidential Medal of Freedom in 1964, as well as honorary degrees from scores of universities, including Harvard, Yale, and Oxford.

Niebuhr wrote extensively and his magnum opus *The Nature and Destiny of Man* (2 vols., 1941, 1943) is one of the great theological works of the 20th century. Among his other significant works are *Moral Man and Immoral Society* (1932), *Beyond Tragedy* (1937), *The Children of Light and the Children of Darkness* (1944), *The Irony of American History* (1952), *Christian Realism and Political Problems* (1953), *The Godly and the Ungodly* (1958), *The Structure of Nations and Empires* (1959), *Man's Nature and His Communities* (1965), and *Justice and Mercy* (1974) edited by Ursula M. Niebuhr.

Three excellent studies of Niebuhr's life and thought are Gabriel Fakre, *The Promise of Reinhold Niebuhr* (1970); Nathan A. Scott, Jr., ed., *The Legacy of Reinhold Niebuhr* (1975); and Richard Fox, *Reinhold Niebuhr: A Biography* (1985).

WALTER A. ELWELL

**Niemoeller, Martin** (1892–1984). German Lutheran pastor and ecumenical leader. Born into a pastor's family in Lippstadt, Westphalia, he entered the navy after completing high school, and during World War I served as a submarine officer. After the war he married Else Bremer and studied for the ministry. In 1924 he was ordained and took an administrative position with the Westphalian Inner Mission. In 1931 he was called to the Annenkirche in the affluent Berlin suburb of Dahlem. A political conservative, he rejected the Weimar Republic and voted for Hitler but never joined the Nazi party. When Hitler set out to make the Protestant church subservient to his will, Niemoeller became a leader of the clerical opposition. In August 1933 he formed the Pastors' Emergency League which defied the Nazi reorganization scheme for the church and its demand to dismiss clergy of Jewish ancestry. This led to the formation of the Confessing Church which spearheaded the resistance to nazification of the church. As one of the most outspoken critics of the regime—to the extent of confronting Hitler in person—Niemoeller was arrested in 1937 and imprisoned in Moabit. After a mock trial he was incarcerated in the Sachsenhausen concentration camp and in 1941 was transferred to Dachau. Although he had been marked for execution, he survived the camp and participated in the postwar reorganization of the church. He drafted the controversial "Stuttgart Declaration of Guilt" which was signed by several Protestant leaders in October 1945. He was named president of the Evangelical Church of Hesse-Nassau in 1947, serving until 1964. An ardent ecumenist, he was among the founders of the World Council of Churches and was elected one of its presidents in 1961. Niemoeller was also a critic of anticommunism, the division of Germany, the cold war and all wars in general, racism, and anti-Semitism.

He was a popular speaker at church and peace gatherings throughout the world.

*Bibliography.* M. Niemöller, *From U-Boat to Pulpit* (1936), *Here Stand I!* (1937), *God Is My Führer* (1941), *Dachau Sermons* (1946); C. S. Davidson, *God's Man: The Story of Pastor Niemoeller* (1959); D. Schmidt, *Pastor Niemöller* (1959); J. Bentley, *Martin Niemoeller* (1984); H. Locke, ed., *Exile in the Fatherland: Martin Niemöller's Letters from Moabit Prison* (1986).

RICHARD V. PIERARD

**Niger.** *See* WEST AFRICA.

**Nigeria.** *See* WEST AFRICA

**Nikodim (Boris Georgyevich Rotov)** (1929–1978). Metropolitan of Leningrad. Born in Frolovo in the Soviet Union, he entered the Orthodox monastery at Ryazan, and there assumed the name of Nikodim when he was made a deacon in 1947. After ordination as priest two years later he became rector briefly at Davydov, and then at Uglich, combining parochial work with studies at Leningrad Seminary, and afterwards at the Theological Academy. He was subsequently archimandrite in charge of the Russian Orthodox Mission in Jerusalem before consecration in 1960 as bishop of Podolsk and head of foreign relations of the Russian Church. It was he who led the Russian Orthodox Church into the World Council of Churches (WCC) in 1961. In 1963, at only 34, he was appointed metropolitan of Leningrad. He became widely known at ecumenical meetings all over the world, and was elected for a term as one of the WCC's six presidents. He collapsed and died during an audience with Pope John Paul I in the Vatican.

J. D. DOUGLAS

**Niles, Daniel Thambyrajah** (1908–1970). Ecumenical leader and evangelist. A fourth-generation Tamil Christian born near Jaffna, Niles spent a lifetime in the service of the Methodist Church in Ceylon in conjunction with his ever-increasing involvement in the ecumenical movement. The youngest delegate at the International Missionary Council conference held at Tambaram, Madras, in 1938, Niles gave a keynote address at the founding of the World Council of Churches (WCC) in Amsterdam in 1948, and after Uppsala (1968) become one of its six presidents. He was co-chairman of the WCC youth department, chairman of the World Student Christian Federation, secretary of the WCC department of evangelism, and chief founder of the East Asia Christian Conference (EACC). At the time of his death he was chairman of EACC and president of the Methodist Church in Ceylon. His most enduring testament may well be the 45 hymns he wrote for the *EACC Hymnal* (1963), exhibiting as they do Niles' hope that the church would rediscover its faith's "original mood of exhilaration, of challenge and high adventure, of expectant hope and triumphant deed." He wrote nearly a score of books, many based on his sermons or expounding the preacher's vocation. They include *Preaching the Gospel of the Resurrection* (1953), *As Seeing the Invisible* (1961), *Upon the Earth* (1962), *Buddhism and the Claims of Christ* (1967), and *Who Is This Jesus?* (1968). His understanding of the gospel is summarized in the posthumous *Testament of Faith* (1972), compiled by his son Dayalan.

PHILIP HILLYER

**Nock, Arthur Darby** (1902–1963). Theologian and historian. Born in Portsmouth, England, he graduated from Cambridge, taught classics there (1923–30), and then became professor of the history of religion at Harvard, a post he held until his death. A member of many foreign learned academies, he was a specialist in the study of religion between Alexander and Julian. His works include *Sallustius* (1926), *Essays on the Trinity and the Incarnation* (1928), *Conversion* (1933), *St. Paul* (1938), and with A. J. Festugiére, *Hermés Trismégiste* (1946). He edited the *Harvard Theological Review* from 1933, was associate editor of *Vigilae Christianae*, and was one of the editors of the *Oxford Classical Dictionary*.

J. D. DOUGLAS

***Non Abbiamo Bisogno.*** Encyclical issued by Pope Pius XI on June 29, 1931, for the defense of Catholic Action in Italy against fascism. While the purpose of Catholic Action was "to have the laity participate in some measure in the apostolate of the hierarchy," namely, through groups devoted to various social activities, the fascist government endeavored to discredit and eventually to destroy such organizations as being incompatible with the allegiance due to the state. The pope protests against such attacks, denounces the interference of fascist police with the rights of Catholic groups, and reaffirms the spiritual nature and aims of Catholic Action. He expresses concern over the monopoly claimed by the state for the spiritual formation of Italian youth forcibly enrolled in the schools and organizations of the party. The oath exacted from the members of the fascist groups is branded as unlawful, persons who could not avoid taking it being advised to make use of some mental restriction, like "saving the laws of God and of the Church." The document closes with a call to prayer and unity.

*Bibliography.* Original text in *Acta Apostolicae Sedis* (1931), 22: 285–312. English translation of the most significant passages in J. Husslein, *Social Wellsprings* (1942), 2: 235–54.

GEORGES A. BARROIS

**Norelius, Erik** (1833–1916). Lutheran pastor. Born in Hassela, Helsingland, Sweden, he came to America at the age of 17 and prepared himself for the ministry at Capital University, Columbus,

Ohio. For most of his long life he was pastor of the Swedish Lutheran Church, Vasa, Minn. His interests in education, journalism, charity, and church administration made him a leader in the Lutheran Augustana Synod. He was present at its organization in 1860, and subsequently became president (1874–81, 1899–1911). He was editor of various Swedish religious journals, laid the foundations for Gustavus Adolphus College, St. Peter, Minn., and began the Children's Home at Vasa. A careful and observant student, he was interested in the literary documents of Swedish settlements in America, and published an invaluable two-volume work: *De Svenska Lutherska Forsamlingarnas och Svenskarnes Historia i Amerika* (1890, 1916).

CONRAD BERGENDOFF

**Norman, Edward Robert** (1938– ). Anglican scholar. Educated at Cambridge (Ph.D., 1964), he was ordained in the Church of England in 1965, and from 1971 has been chaplain, dean, and fellow of Peterhouse, the oldest Cambridge college. His main area of research has been modern Irish history on which he has published a number of studies, including *A History of Modern Ireland* (1971), which is distinguished for its pro-British line. In 1976 he published a major study entitled *Church and Society in England 1770–1970*, which has established itself as a classic in its field. He became more widely known when he delivered the Reith Lectures in 1978, published subsequently as *Christianity and the World Order* (1979). In these lectures he developed the thesis that the church, and especially the Church of England, had sold out to secularism, and had neglected its chief business, which was the winning of men and women to Christ. The lectures aroused a storm of protest, but little effective opposition, as the justice of his criticism was hard to deny. Since that time, however, he has been less prominent in church and state affairs, and has not followed through on the criticisms he made in the lectures.

GERALD BRAY

**Norregaard, Jens** (1887–1953). Lutheran. Born in Rye, Denmark, he studied at the universities of Copenhagen, Tübingen, Berlin, Edinburgh, Cambridge, and Oxford. He was professor of church history at the University of Copenhagen from 1923, and rector from 1942. He was a member of the Continuation Committee for the Faith and Order movement from 1937. He is the author of *Augustins religioese Gennembrud* (1920), *Augustins Vej til Kristendommen* (1928), *Kirke historie* with Hjalmar Holmquist (3 vols., 1931–40), and *Kristendommens Historie i Romantikens, Liberalismens og Realismens Tidsalder* (2 vols., 1939).

CONRAD BERGENDOFF

**North, Christopher Richard** (1888–1975). British OT scholar. Born into a Methodist manse, he was educated at Didsbury College, Manchester, and at the School of Oriental Studies. After ordination he served various Methodist churches in Wales and England before becoming professor of OT languages and literature at Handsworth College, Birmingham (1925–40). At the end of World War II he became professor of Hebrew at the University College of North Wales, Bangor (1945–53). A member of the New English Bible's OT panel, he wrote *The OT Interpretation of History* (1946), *The Suffering Servant in Deutero–Isaiah* (1948), *The Thought of the OT* (1948), *Isaiah 40–55: Introduction and Commentary* (1952); and *The Second Isaiah* (1964).

J. D. DOUGLAS

**North Africa.** In each of the lands of North Africa today (Morocco, Algeria, Tunisia, and Libya), Islam is the state religion. The large majority are Sunni Muslims. There are small but very active Shia Muslim groups seeking to introduce an Iranian style of Islam. The groups are strongly opposed by the governments, and many of their leaders have been imprisoned. In some areas there are small communities of Sufi Muslims and, in spite of efforts to diminish their influence, Marabouts (local holy men to whom are attributed special powers which can be made to work by the use of charms, amulets, and spells), whose practices still flourish. The Kharidjites, or Ibadis, who separated from the main body (Sunni Muslims) during the period of the third Caliph Othman (A.D. 644–656) and just prior to the major separation of the Shia (the party of Ali, Muhammad's son-in-law), are still in southern Algeria.

The building of mosques has accelerated during the past 25 years while many church buildings have been transformed into libraries, museums, and supermarkets. Some have been "converted" into mosques.

Other religions are permitted to exist in the lands of North Africa when practiced by non-nationals. Any North African thought to be in association with expatriate Christian communities is placed under surveillance. There is no missionary presence, and although the Bible Society is still able to exhibit and sell the Christian Scriptures, the sale of such Scriptures in the languages of North Africa is prohibited.

Small Protestant and Roman Catholic communities meet regularly. These are composed almost exclusively of Europeans, North Americans, and some nationals of other African countries. In the early 1960s the former French Reformed Church and the American Methodist Church formed the Protestant Church in North Africa. The Anglican Church has resident chaplains in each of the North African countries, in which the worship is

601

in English. A Roman Catholic brotherhood of Italian inspiration, the Folkalari, also has a presence in western Algeria.

Recent surveys would suggest that there is in existence a small underground Christian church which is very jealous of its North African heritage, composed of loyal Algerians, Moroccans, and Tunisians. As far as is known no such group exists in Libya. These small groups are self-supporting and are entirely led by North Africans. They are developing a uniquely North African style of worship built on a firm belief in the authenticity and reliability of Scripture.

*Bibliography.* E. F. Gautier, *Le passé de l'Afrique du Nord* (1937); G. M. Wysner, *The Kabyle People* (1945); W. H. C. Frend, *The Donatist Church* (1952); F. R. Steele, *Not in Vain* (1981).

RONALD J. WAINE

## Northcott, William Cecil (1902–1987).

English Congregational pastor, editor, and journalist. Born in Buckfast, Devon, he graduated from Cambridge and then spent three years as a social worker in London's East End. Thereafter he ministered in Congregational churches in Lancashire (1929–35), was home secretary and literary superintendent for the London Missionary Society (1935–50), general secretary and editor of the United Council for Missionary Education (1950–52), and editor with the Lutterworth Press (1952–72). He was also editor of the *Congregational Monthly* (1953–58) and British correspondent for the *Christian Century* (1945–70). Northcott, who earned a London Ph.D. in his 60th year, wrote many books, among them *Time to Spare* (1935), *Who Claims the World?* (1938), *John Williams Sails On* (1939), *Glorious Company* (1945), *Whose Dominion?* (1946), *Religious Liberty* (1948), *Voice out of Africa* (1952), *Robert Moffat: Pioneer in Africa* (1961), *Christianity in Africa* (1963), and *Slavery's Martyr* (1976).

J. D. DOUGLAS

## Northfield Conference.

Conference instituted at Northfield, Mass., by Dwight L. Moody on September 1, 1880. The purpose, according to Moody, was "not so much to study the Bible (though the Scriptures will be searched daily for instruction and promises) as for solemn self-consecration, for pleading God's promises, and waiting upon Him for fresh anointment of power from on high." Over 300 were in attendance at the first meeting in 1880, and during Moody's life the annual conference grew steadily in numbers and popularity. It was Moody's intention that these conferences should avoid sectarian bias and emphasize only broad, inclusive doctrines. Prominent religious leaders of all evangelical Protestant denominations in the USA and abroad were secured to address the conferences from year to year. Missionaries on furlough were constantly in attendance as leaders and participants, and a con-

siderable amount of missionary recruiting resulted from their presence and influence. After Moody's death the conferences continued with large attendance through the years. Various institutes were organized from time to time in connection with the conference, devoting themselves particularly to Bible study and religious education.

*Bibliography.* W. R. Moody, *Life of Dwight L. Moody* (1900); J. Mabie, *Heaven on Earth* (1951).

RICHARD D. PIERCE

## North India, Church of.

Union of six churches inaugurated on November 29, 1970, at All Saints Cathedral, Nagpur. In contrast to the South India scheme which had allowed for an ongoing unification of ministry in which episcopally ordained presbyters would gradually replace those who were not, the Church of North India scheme featured a unification rite with mutual laying on of hands. This combined an affirmation of the reality of each representative minister's existing ordination with a statement of willingness to receive from God whatever "of Christ's grace, commission and authority" he might wish to give.

At its inception CNI had about 650,000 members made up of 280,000 former Anglicans of the church of India, Pakistan, Burma, and Ceylon; 206,000 members of the United Church of Northern India (a 1924 Union of Presbyterians and Congregationalists); 110,000 Baptists of the Council of Baptist Churches in Northern India; 20,000 Methodists (British and Australasian Conferences); 18,000 Brethren; and 16,000 Disciples of Christ. The Union did not include Baptists and Presbyterians who were involved in separate negotiations for a projected Church of North-East India, and also went ahead without the American Methodists. The Methodist Church in Southern Asia, formerly known as the Methodist Episcopal Church, had been party to the long process of unity discussions reaching back to the Lucknow Round Table Conference of 1929, but withdrew at a late stage of the final negotiations. However, unification talks between CNI (recently estimated to have over one million members) and the 900,000-member Methodist Church in India, as MCSA was renamed, reopened in 1985.

CNI has also been involved more closely with CSI and the Mar Thoma Church in a joint council instituted in 1978. The joint council has set up theological, peace and justice, and mission commissions and issued the eucharistic liturgies of the three churches in a single booklet. A 1975 proposal that the three churches commit themselves to union in a single "Bharat Christian Church" is still under discussion. CNI has adopted a flexible approach to liturgy, issuing regular and occasional services in individual booklets generally initially authorized for optional and experimental use pending revision and adoption as definitive. Besides the standard Lord's supper there is an alternative order outlining a "nonliturgical" celebration and also a service derived from the Church of the Brethren in Gujarat that incorporates footwashing and a love-feast. A degree of indigenization in worship is encouraged in the marriage service, which can include garlanding and a number of other traditional ceremonies if desired.

*Bibliography.* Constitution of the Church of North India (1981); *The North India Churchman* (monthly).

PHILIP HILLYER

**Norway.** Constitutional monarchy of northern Europe with an area of 323,895 sq. km. (125,057 sq. mi.). Its population of 4,170,000 (1987) is about 97.5 percent Lutheran. Historically Norway has enjoyed several religious revivals. Perhaps the best known occurred under the influence of Hans Nielsen Hauge early in the 19th century. At the beginning of this century a pentecostal revival introduced this strain of Christian activism into the Norwegian church. As a result of these revivals, Norway has been at the forefront of Lutheran missions. This zeal has also spawned societies for home missions and Christian youth organizations in the schools. Theological and Christian education has produced Christian high schools, folk high schools for further education, and a free faculty of theology.

Norwegians have no tradition of weekly worship. Fewer than 17 percent attend services each week. However, 96 percent of all children are baptized, 80 percent are confirmed in the Lutheran Church, 85 percent are married in the church, and 95 percent are buried by the church. The commitment to the Lutheran Church runs deep in the Norwegian nation. In a survey conducted in 1976, 18 percent of all Norwegians considered themselves to be "born-again" Christians. Among young people 27 percent made the same profession. The Billy Graham Oslo crusade in 1955 drew 77,000, of whom 1000 came forward as enquirers. Billy Graham's EURO-70 crusade was carried by land line to 10 Norwegian cities. Ninety percent of all the homes in Lappland have been reached by the Every Home Crusade with Christian literature.

In addition to the Lutheran Church, the Mission Covenant Church has 120 congregations and 7453 members. Norwegian Methodists have 98 congregations with 17,702 members. Pentecostal churches have 770 congregations and 36,105 members. The Salvation Army has 1200 centers and 44,836 soldiers and officers. The Lutheran Free Church has 64 congregations and 6753 members. The First Roman Catholic Church was organized in 1842. By 1890 there were 1000 Catholics. In 1972 they still numbered only 0.3 percent of the Norwegian population. Most Catholics are immigrants, and 75 percent of the Catholic clergy are also immigrants. About 75 percent of the registered Catholics regularly practice their religion. The Church of Jesus Christ of Latter Day Saints has about 2000 members in Norway. The Jehovah's Witnesses have 158 centers and 5857 members. The Mormon missionaries landed in Norway in 1850, while the Jehovah's Witnesses sent their first missionaries to Norway in 1891.

Conservatism is the hallmark of religious life in Norway. There is no national ecumenical council of churches in Norway. In 1961 the Norwegian Missionary Council voted by one vote not to join the World Council of Churches, when the International Missionary Council was absorbed into the larger body. Non-Christian religious groups are very small in Norway. There are only 4200 Muslims. The Bahais number only 1400, and there are 950 Jews. The immigrant population contains just 100 Buddhists. Religious radio broadcasts are heard by 10 percent of Norway's 3 million adults each morning. The Sunday morning service is heard by 15 to 20 percent, and religious music on Wednesday afternoon is heard by 20 percent of the populace. Norway is the major sending country of missionaries in Continental Europe. Proportionately it leads all of Europe in sending out missionaries. Currently there are 14,000 missionary support groups in Norway. Presently they have 1539 missionaries serving 44 countries worldwide.

*Bibliography.* D. B. Barrett, ed., *World Christian Encyclopedia* (1982); G. Ostenstad, *International Review of Mission* 62/245 (Jan. 1973): 43–50.

WAYNE DETZLER

**Noth, Martin** (1902–1968). German OT scholar. Born in Dresden, he studied at Erlangen, Leipzig, and Rostock. He began his teaching career in 1927 at Greifswald. From 1930 to 1945 he was professor of OT at Königsberg and, from 1945, at Bonn. While on leave from there in 1965, he became director of the German Evangelical Institute for the Study of the Antiquity of the Holy Land, Jerusalem. He helped establish *Vetus Testamentum* in 1950, coediting it for nine years. From 1929 to 1966 he edited *Zeitschrift des Palästinavereins* and from 1932 contributed to *Palästinajahrbuch*. In addition to several commentaries on Exodus, Leviticus, Numbers, and Joshua, and several articles, he published numerous books on the history of Israel and on the transmission of OT literature. Most notable are *Das System der Zwölf Stämme Israels* (1930), *Die Welt des Alten Testaments*, *Die Gesetze im Pentateuch* (1940), *Überlieferungsgeschichte des Pentateuch* (1948), and *Geschichte Israels* (1950).

E. J. FURCHA

**Novice, Novitiate.** In Roman Catholic religious orders or congregations a person undergoing a probation period of at least one year, prior to admittance to profession. According to canon law, the minimum age requirement for entering the novitiate is 15 years (completed). Persons married, unavoidably involved in secular affairs, or supporting close relatives may not be admitted as novices. Novices bear the habit of the order or congregation, share in community observances, and study the rules of the order. They also attend lectures and exercises for the fostering of spiritual life under the direction of a master or mistress of novices. During the novitiate, members occupy secluded quarters in the convent or monastery. They may not renounce their property, and they may freely leave or be dismissed at any time. After completion of the novitiate, novices must either take temporary vows, be dismissed, or have their probation extended for periods up to six months. Male scholastics, professed members engaged in theological studies, are sometimes unofficially referred to as "professed novices."

*Bibliography.* Codex Juris Canonici, can. 553–571.

GEORGES A. BARROIS

**Nuclear Question.** The dropping of atomic bombs on Hiroshima and Nagasaki on August 6 and 9, 1945, raised the nuclear question for the first time. Today's stockpile of nuclear weapons contains the equivalent of one million Hiroshimas with the capacity to kill everyone 12 times. Even before the Soviet Union possessed the atomic bomb the USA relied principally upon the threat of retaliation in pursuit of a policy of containment. Since then the Soviet Union, Great Britain, France, China, and India have become nuclear powers. Pakistan, Brazil, Argentina, South Africa, and Israel have nuclear weapons capabilities.

The nuclear powers argue that nuclear arsenals serve as a deterrent to war; that having preserved peace for several decades they will continue to do so indefinitely. Nuclear deterrence has had an enormous appeal in spite of opposition from scientists, physicians, and social scientists who fear that a disaster might result by accident or by opposing powers being drawn into a conventional war. It is significant that the pastoral letter of American Roman Catholic bishops conceded a "strictly conditioned moral acceptance of nuclear deterrence"; the statement by the Vancouver Assembly of the World Council of Churches (1984) was a compromise between unilateral and multilateral positions.

The nuclear question, then, is whether it is ever morally right to wage war by killing defenseless men, women, and children. Such warfare was accepted by both Hitler and the Allies in World War II. It was pursued by the USA in the Korean and Vietnam wars and then in the bombing of Libya.

In the 1960s many Christian and humanitarian scholars condemned the blasphemy, inhumanity, and insanity of nuclear warfare, including Albert Schweitzer, Karl Barth, Linus Pauling, Norman Cousins, Bertrand Russell, George F. Kennan, Martin Niemoeller, J. L. Hromadka, and Werner Heisenberg. Yet politicians and churches paid little attention to the voices of these scientists, theologians, and humanitarians, both Christian and non-Christian, until recent years.

Talk about nuclear free zones, nuclear freeze, and nuclear disarmament started in Europe, triggered by the announcement that the USA would base missiles in NATO countries. Millions of Europeans realized that there is no defense against nuclear weapons. Protest marches took place in European capitals and the movement spread to the USA and Canada. Churches suddenly found themselves with a new peace agenda.

Although texts like "Christ is our peace" and "Blessed are the peacemakers" are repeated, the emphasis tends to be put on *our* peacemaking work, *our* political action, rather than upon what God has done, is doing, and will do in Jesus Christ. Much of the rhetoric sounds like that of the social gospel and pacifism preached in the 1930s. The kingdom of peace and justice can be realized on earth through education and legislation. The Christian peace movement seems to have been inspired more by fear of the bomb than by a fear of the Lord.

*Bibliography.* R. L. Sivard, *World Military and Social Expenditures* (1986).

A. C. COCHRANE

**Nutting, Wallace** (1861–1941). Congregational minister and antiquarian. Born in Marlboro, Mass., he studied at Harvard, Hartford Theological Seminary, and Union Theological Seminary. Ordained to the Congregational ministry in 1888, he served pastorates in Newark, N.J.; St. Paul, Minn.; Seattle, Wash.; and Providence, R.I. In 1905 he retired from the ministry because of ill health, giving his time thereafter to the publication of books on American life and American and English landscapes. Nutting published a well-known series on landscapes and folklore of Vermont (1922), Massachusetts (1923), Maine (1924), Pennsylvania (1924), Ireland (1925), New York (1927), England (1928), and Virginia (1930). He also published *Old New England Pictures* (1913), *The Windsor Handbook* (1917), *Furniture of the Pilgrim Country* (rev. ed., 1924), *Photographic Art Secrets* (1927), *Furniture Treasury* (vols. 1–2, 1928; vol. 3, 1933), *The Clock Book* (1924), and *Wallace Nutting's Biography* (1936).

RAYMOND W. ALBRIGHT

**Nyasaland (Malawi).** *See* SOUTHERN AFRICA.

**Nygren, Anders Theodor Samuel** (1890–1978). Swedish theologian and philosopher. Born in Göteborg, he studied at the University of Lund and was a minister (1912–1920). He became docent of philosophy of religion (1921) and professor of systematic theology (1924) at Lund. He was president of the Lutheran World Federation (1947–52) and became bishop of Lund (1949), retiring in 1958. He was a delegate to the Ecumenical Councils at Lausanne (1927), Oxford (1937), Amsterdam (1948), and Lund (1952), and was a member of the central committee of the World Council of Churches. His writings address basic issues in systematic theology, philosophy of religion, and ethics. Methodologically speaking, he defended an antimetaphysical standpoint in line with the philosopher Axel Hägerström, his fellow countryman and contemporary. He was also influenced by Kant's conception of a priori, and Schleiermacher's view of religious experience. Nygren became particularly known for his view on the uniqueness of the Christian idea of (God's) love (*agapē*) as opposed to *eros*. Nygren stressed *agapē* as the essential feature of Christianity. Most of his work is available only in Swedish, but among his books available in English are *Agape and Eros* (1932), *Commentary on Romans* (1941), *The Gospel of God* (1951), and *Meaning and Method: Prolegomena to a Scientific Philosophy of Religion and a Scientific Theology* (1972).

**Bibliography.** I. Kegley, ed., *The Philosophy and Theology of Anders Nygren* (1970); *Reply to Interpreters and Critics* (1970).

ANTONIO BARBOSA DA SILVA

**Oblates.** From Lat. *oblatus* ("offered"), a name adopted in modern times by several Roman Catholic institutions. The best known are The Oblates of Mary Immaculate (O.M.I.), founded in France in 1816 by Charles de Mazenod, and The Oblates of St. Francis de Sales, originally founded by St. Francis but refounded in 1871 by Louis Brisson.

In the early Middle Ages an oblate was a child sent to a religious institution to be brought up by a religious order, not all of whom became religious. Later in the Middle Ages an oblate was one who lived a simplified monastic (religious) life outside a religious institution but in association with it. This usage continued in the lay oblate of the 20th century. These modern lay oblates kept certain rules but lived outside the community structure.

**Occultism.** From the Lat. *occultus,* something "hidden" or "concealed," a term which refers to that which is esoteric, mysterious, and beyond the range of ordinary human knowledge. Forms of occultism involve some type of secret technique and secret teaching directed at consciousness alteration and the manipulation of the supernatural. The ultimate objective is to attain psychospiritual power.

Occultism represents an Eastern mystical worldview characterized by monism (the view that "all is one"), the notion that humankind is divine (the "divine within"), the idea that death is an illusion, and a belief that mastery of certain spiritual techniques and knowledge of spiritual laws lead to mystic union with "the One." This union results in an ability to control the forces of the One and thereby to control reality by controlling consciousness.

Occultism claims to be a "spiritual science" rather than a set of beliefs. It offers a system of knowledge focusing on universal energy (the life force). In order to achieve occult knowledge, practitioners stress that one must first concentrate on "bodywork," using various techniques and movements designed to free the body's energy. The second step toward occult proficiency involves knowledge of the *astral body.* Out-of-body experiences and astral projection are within this stage.

In the popular sense of the word, occultism deals with fortune telling, black and white magic, and spiritism (spirit contact). Related occultic practices include: (1) *astrology*—an ancient method of mapping human experience against celestial events by means of a horoscope and the 12 signs of the zodiac; (2) *numerology*—which attaches special occult significance to numbers and relates those numbers to prediction of the future as well as character analysis; (3) *tarot cards*—fortune telling (divination) by the manipulation and placing of cards; (4) *palmistry*—another means of forecasting the future via interpretation of the lines in a person's palms; (5) *meditation*—the repetition of a mantra (a sacred sound, often the name of a god) and the spiritual guidance of a guru; and (6) *automatic writing*—"dictation" or writing done in a trance state without the conscious control of the writer.

Occultists distinguish between "true" magic (white magic) and the practice of sorcery and necromancy (black magic). Sorcery is used for antisocial purposes or for material gain. White or beneficent magic involves the ceremonial evocation and control of spirits, using such ritual tools as the wand, the dagger, the robe, and the belt. White magic is associated with the contemporary practice of witchcraft and the worship of the goddess.

Spiritism is the practice of making contact with discarnate entities or invisible personalities. Typically, this occurs through the practice of mediumship, or trance channeling, a form of voluntary possession.

From the perspective of historic, orthodox Christianity, all forms of occultism are viewed as spiritual counterfeits, demonic in origin, and prohibited by Scripture.

*Bibliography.* F. Leahy, *Satan Cast Out* (1975); H. Berkhof, *Christ and the Powers* (1977); L. Stewart, *Life Forces* (1980);

Studies in Cross-Cultural Psychology Journal (Winter 1980–81); B. Alexander, The Occult (1983).

RONALD ENROTH

**Ockenga, Harold John** (1905–1985). American preacher and educator. Educated at Taylor University, Princeton and Westminster Theological seminaries, and at the University of Pittsburgh (Ph.D., 1939), he was ordained in the Presbyterian Church in 1931 and was minister of Breeze Point Church, Pittsburgh (1931–36), and of Park Street Church, Boston (1936–69). He was a founder of Fuller Theological Seminary, Pasadena, Calif., and of Gordon-Conwell Theological Seminary, South Hamilton, Mass.; he was the first president of the National Association of Evangelicals. He is credited with coining the term "new evangelicals" in reference to a group that repudiated the defensive posture of fundamentalists and called for increased social concern, theological reform, and openness to ecumenical dialog—a group that included Billy Graham, Bernard Ramm, Carl Henry, and E. J. Carnell. Ockenga sought to play down some of the differences between new evangelicals and fundamentalists, claiming that both groups believed in the authority of Scripture and in theological orthodoxy. A gifted and popular preacher, he sought to demonstrate the intellectual respectability of the evangelical movement through his sermons. Among his written works are *These Religious Affections* (1937), *Our Protestant Heritage* (1938), *Everyone That Believes* (1942), *Our Evangelical Faith* (1946), *The Church in God* (1955), *Power Through Pentecost* (1959), *Women Who Made Biblical History* (1961), *Preaching in Thessalonians* (1963), and *Faith in a Troubled World* (1972).

ROBERT L. MORRISON

**Offertory.** That part of the service during which gifts of money are received as well as the music, vocal or instrumental, performed during such reception. While local practices vary widely, most congregations have appointed persons to receive the gifts and to bring them forward for the officiating clergy to place upon the altar or communion table. In some localities the minister offers a prayer of consecration; elsewhere, the choir or congregation sings a more or less suitable text. Ideally the bringing of gifts should have great significance as a token of the dedication of the entire personality to the cause of Christ and his church. In practice it has become a more or less routine gathering in of money for the support of the church, accompanied by music, which only in rare instances has relevance to personal consecration. For the most part music serves merely to minimize the embarrassment most parishioners feel during a silence of some minutes' duration.

PAUL ALLWARDT

**Office.** *See* BREVIARY.

**Old Catholics.** An international group of independent Catholic churches which possess an episcopal polity but do not recognize the primacy of Rome.

***Creation of Old Catholic Churches.*** Old Catholicism was born in the rejection by German Catholic leaders of Vatican Council I's definition of papal infallibility and primacy in 1870. Some, however, trace it back to the Jansenist schism of Utrecht in the Netherlands in 1724 and argue that it also drew ideas from the movements of Josephinism in Austria (1780–90) and Febronianism in Germany and Austria (late 18th cent.), which sought to limit papal power. In 1871 a group of several hundred professors and clerics led by the church historian theologian J. J. I. Döllinger proclaimed in Munich their rejection of Vatican I decrees. They insisted that these and other modern enactments of the Roman Church, such as the Assumption of Mary and the Syllabus of Errors, had in fact created a new church.

Those who persisted in their opposition were excommunicated, but by 1873 they had successfully regrouped and proclaimed themselves "Old Catholics." That year Joseph Reinkens was consecrated the first bishop of the new church by the bishop of Deventer of the Dutch "Little Church of Utrecht." Although excommunicated, Döllinger did not affiliate with the Old Catholics. During the *Kulturkampf* of the 1870s Bismarck backed them as a counterweight to the power of political Catholicism. The movement spread to Switzerland and Austria where its influence was not great, but in Germany it derived sustenance from popular nationalism.

Other Old Catholic bodies emerged during the 1870s in Italy and France, and later in Czechoslovakia, Yugoslavia, and Poland. In 1889 several of these disparate communities joined in the Union of Utrecht under the presidency of a Dutch Old Catholic archbishop, but the independence of each national church was guaranteed. The Declaration of Utrecht remained the official doctrinal standard for the various bodies. Other Old Catholic churches were formed in the USA, England, and the Philippines; some of them did not affiliate with the Utrecht group.

***Doctrinal Basis.*** Old Catholics recognized the doctrines deemed apostolic—those of the seven ecumenical councils prior to 1054—while rejecting many later actions of Rome. The seven sacraments were retained but auricular confession was made voluntary and absolution was regarded as a ceremonial declaration of forgiveness made by the priest as a servant of Jesus Christ. The church was defined as an invisible body headed by Christ, which included all who shared in salvation through faith in him. The church held firmly to apostolic succession with its threefold office of deacons, priests, and bishop; clergy were allowed to marry; and the episcopate was seen as a fraternal community of shepherds. The vernacular was used in all services, and direction over each church was exercised by a board of clerics and laypersons, presided over by the bishop. The synod, as a representative body of all the congregations, had legislative, judicial, disciplinary, and administrative powers. The synod elected the bishop. Priests were chosen by congregations with episcopal approval. The Scriptures possessed primacy in authority, but tradition was still accorded great weight.

*Ecumenical Aspect.* From the outset the Old Catholics had close relations with the Church of England, which was represented at its meetings from the early 1870s. They recognized Anglican ordination in 1925, and in 1931 the Utrecht Union and the Anglican Church concluded the Bonn Agreement (effective 1932) which provided for intercommunion between the two groups. Each recognized the Catholicity and independence of the other and members of each were allowed to participate in the other's sacraments. After World War II the movement diminished in some countries, but it persisted as a viable entity. In the 1970s Old Catholics engaged in conversations with Rome on the issue of primacy in the church, without, however, abandoning their hostility to the 1870 affirmation of papal authority. In 1946 the (Old Catholic) Polish National Church in the United States (founded 1897) entered into intercommunion with the Episcopal Church there. The question of the ordination of women proved to be a barrier to better relations between the Old Catholics and the Anglican and American Episcopal churches. Attempts to establish ties with Orthodox churches were impeded by differences over the Nicene Creed, Eucharist, and holy orders. The Old Catholics have devoted little effort to missionary work and propagation of the faith. The global community in 1980 consisted of 443,600 people in 20 denominations.

*Bibliography.* A. C. Piepkorn, *Profiles in Belief: The Religious Bodies of North America* (vol. 1, 1977); J. G. Melton, *Encyclopedia of American Religions*, 2 vols. (1978); G. Huelin, *Old Catholics and Anglicans* (1983); C. B. Moss, *The Old Catholic Movement, Its Origin and History* (1984).

RICHARD V. PIERARD

## Oldham, George Ashton

**Oldham, George Ashton** (1877–1963). Episcopalian bishop. Born in Sunderland, England, he studied at Cornell and General Theological Seminary, New York City. After two curacies he was chaplain of Columbia University (1905–8). He was rector of St. Luke's Chapel in New York City (1909–17) and then St. Ann's in Brooklyn (1917–22). He was consecrated bishop coadjutor of Albany in 1922 and became bishop in 1929, from which office he retired in 1950. His interest in world order led him into membership in the Committee on World Faith and Order, the Com-

mittee on International Affairs in the World Council of Churches, and similar bodies; as an English-American he was also vice-president of the American branch of the Anglican Society and a member of The Pilgrims. He wrote *A Fighting Church: The Christian Today* and *The Redeemer.*

JOSEPH FLETCHER

**Oldham, Joseph Houldsworth** (1874–1969). Anglican. Educated at Trinity College, Oxford, he was secretary of the Student Christian Movement (1896/97), the Young Men's Christian Association (1897–1900), the World Mission Conference (1908–10), and the International Missionary Council (1921–38). He wrote *Christianity and the Race Problem*, *The Church and Its Function in Society*, and *Real Life Is Meeting*. He edited the *Reports of the Oxford Conference on Life and Work* (1937), the *International Review of Missions* (1912–27), and the *Christian News Letter* (1939–45).

F. W. DILLISTONE

**Old River Brethren.** *See* RIVER BRETHREN.

**OT Studies, 20th-Century Trends in.** Toward the end of the 19th century a consensus in OT studies seemed to be emerging. The first five books of the OT (Genesis to Deuteronomy), traditionally assigned to Moses, were held to be the product of four documentary sources, referred to by the letters JEDP. If the OT had any continuing relevance for Christian faith it would be found in the ethical monotheism of the prophets, the high-water mark of Israel's faith. The 20th century has seen the collapse of this consensus. There are many reasons for this; three major causes deserve explanation.

*New Discoveries.* There was a significant increase in knowledge of the history and cultures of the ancient Near East, the fruits of archeological discoveries at a variety of sites and the publication of texts which provided background to, and comparative material for, an understanding of the OT.

For example, from Syria in the early 1930s came the Ras Shamra/Ugaritic texts, many of them from around 1400 B.C. In addition to historical data, a text called the "Legend of Keret" threw light on social customs and in particular upon kingship of the period. The most interesting texts from the viewpoint of OT studies, however, were religious and mythological texts which introduced the Canaanite pantheon of the day, presided over by a titular head, the god El, but featuring as its most active members the fertility god *Ba'al*, the warrior goddess *Anath*, and adversaries such as *Yam* (Sea) and *Mot* (Death). This gave firsthand documentary evidence of the nature of the religion which the Hebrews encountered when they settled in Canaan. Ugaritic as a language had close affinities with Hebrew, increasing knowledge of the range of meanings of Hebrew words. Ugaritic poetry provided parallels in form and thought to Hebrew poetry. This material was variously and sometimes controversially used to reinterpret the OT, especially the psalms.

At Nuzi, near modern Kirkuk in Iraq, finds included family and legal documents dating to around the middle of the 2d millennium B.C. They dealt, for example, with slavery, adoption, marriage contracts, and wills. Some of the social and legal customs reflected provided links with the patriarchal narratives in Genesis where these narratives differ from later OT law codes. This, together with evidence from sites such as Mari in northern Mesopotamia, has been seen by some as confirmation of the essential historical reliability of the patriarchal narrative. In the enthusiasm to lend support to the biblical material some parallels were overdrawn. Even with such material at hand—possibly reflecting customs which lingered for centuries in parts of the ancient Near East—many scholars remained convinced that the patriarchal narratives in their Genesis form were no earlier than the 6th-century Babylonian exile.

More recently, from Ebla in north Syria thousands of tablets came to light from a hitherto unknown culture which flourished around the middle of the 3d millennium B.C. Startling claims have been made by some and firmly denied by others that in the Ebla texts are to be found, for example, the names of five cities mentioned in Gen. 14:2, parallels to other patriarchal personal names, and the occurrence of a divine name *Ya*, parallel to the Hebrew personal name for God, *Yahweh* (*Yah*). As in the case of earlier discoveries, relationship to the OT was among the least important and most controversial aspects of the Ebla material. It was expected to fill in one further small area of knowledge, which, in spite of discoveries, was still fragmentary.

In Israel itself the most important and spectacular discovery began by accident in 1947 in caves at the northwest end of the Dead Sea. In the caves had been stored the library of a Jewish sect which flourished from around 160 B.C. to A.D. 68. Documents which never became part of the canonical OT and parts of every OT book except Esther were found, as well as commentaries on certain prophetic books. The Dead Sea Scrolls were more informative of sectarian Judaism and NT background than for OT studies, but regarding the history of the OT they were of crucial significance. They provide Hebrew texts a thousand years older than the earliest extant manuscripts of the Hebrew Bible. It was initially claimed that these texts unequivocally supported the reliability of the standard Hebrew texts, but it was not so simple as that. The text of Jeremiah, for instance,

has come down in two forms, Hebrew and Greek, with the Greek text approximately one-eighth shorter than the Hebrew and with some material ordered differently. Some Dead Sea Scrolls fragments of Jeremiah supported the standard Hebrew text, while other Hebrew fragments supported the Greek text. Thus, before Jesus there were two Hebrew versions of the text of Jeremiah known in Palestine, which differed in organization and length. Which more nearly represents the earliest text can only be surmised.

The list of discoveries of the 1900s is almost endless, from Elephantine in southern Egypt to Mari in northern Mesopotamia. Texts include Babylonian historical documents, inscriptions and letters from Palestine, Egyptian love poetry and wisdom documents, and Sumerian, Akkadian, and Babylonian proverbs and wisdom sayings. Despite this wealth archeology neither proves nor disproves the OT; it did help recover something of the world in which ancient Israel lived and enabled more intelligent OT reading. It further helped scholars avoid making superficial and inaccurate claims about the biblical record.

***New Ways of Handling the Literature.*** Much of the approach to the OT which dominated 19th-century studies worked on the assumption that the OT literature consisted of books either written by one author or built up, as in the case of Genesis to Deuteronomy, from written sources. By the end of the 19th century, however, these assumptions were being increasingly questioned by H. Gunkel, who laid the foundations for what became form criticism. This approach stressed the importance of the community as opposed to the individual author and the ways material was handed down orally within the community. It worked to classify material into traditional types (*Gattungen*), common stocks of language, mood, and thought, and a defined *Sitz im Leben* or setting in the life of the community. Thus an attempt was made to get behind the books and isolate, in Genesis for example, family sagas, etiological legends explaining the origin of personal names or distinctive features of the landscape, and cult legends accounting for the worship of the deity at a particular place. Gunkel's work proved particularly helpful in the study of the psalms. He classified such distinctive types as psalms of lament, psalms of individual thanksgiving, hymns, and royal psalms. His theories associated many of them with particular acts of worship in ancient Israel. With modifications this form-critical approach dominated the study of the psalms during the 1900s and was given notable expression in S. Mowinckel's *Psalms in Israel's Worship* (ET, 1962).

In the study of legal material a sharp distinction became drawn between casuistic and apodictic law. The casuistic laws introduce a particular case with "if" or "when"; then an appropriate penalty or consequence is spelled out. Such case law, which apparently was known throughout the ancient Near East, had its natural setting in the administration of justice at the city gate or in the law courts. Exod. 21:1–11 is a good example of such case law. Apodictic law consists of the direct address, "you shall . . . you shall not" or has the participial clause, "whoever does." The setting for such material was worship, with a speaker or priest reminding the people of their unconditional obligations to God. Parallels in Hittite treaty documents from 1500 to 1300 B.C. were used to defend the antiquity and Mosaic authorship of the Decalogue, but those promoting a late date also found close parallels in Assyrian treaty documents of the 7th century B.C.

In the study of the prophets, form criticism theories conceived of the prophets primarily as speakers, not writers. They identified the earliest prophetic material as consisting of the brief, poetic oracle introduced by "Thus says the LORD." The prophet was believed to function as a messenger sent by God, delivering a message in the first person in the name of God (similar to Jacob's use of messengers in Gen. 32:3–5). The prophets made use of many conventional types of speech, such as laments, funeral dirges, and court room speeches.

Form criticism has tended to isolate for study small units within books; it has been the task of tradition history to trace ways in which these units might have been brought together and shaped into larger complexes and handed down. A brief account of one study illustrates the approach. In an essay on the Hexateuch (Genesis–Joshua) G. von Rad argued that the final form of these books was the outgrowth and elaboration of early, short credal statements such as those found in Deut. 26:5b–9 and Josh. 24:2b–13. While such credal statements contain references to the exodus from Egypt and the settlement in the land of Canaan, they say nothing about Mt. Sinai and the giving of the Law. He thus posits that they represent two originally independent traditions: a settlement tradition which developed in the Feast of Weeks celebrated at the sanctuary of Gilgal, and a Sinai tradition from the Feast of Booths celebrated at Shechem. He further argues that it was the author of the "J" strand in the Pentateuch, the "Yahwist," who gathered these traditions and prefaced them with the patriarchal traditions. The thesis is that the Yahwist took traditions originally linked only to separate clan groups and applied them to all Israel to provide a theological rationale for Israel's emergence as a nation. The addition of the primeval stories in Gen. 1 through 11 sought to interpret the story of Israel as the bridge across the gulf which separated God and the entire human race. Inevitably this is speculative, and the separation of the Sinai and settlement traditions especially has been sharply criticized. If form criticism, however, has any validity it must show that in some cases small units with which it deals might have developed to their biblical book form. This study also illustrates how tradition history develops in redaction criticism, interpreting how the final shape of the material might reflect the ideology or theology of a final editor or editors.

Such new attempts to understand much of the literature of the OT opened complex and fascinating directions even for evangelical scholars committed to an inspired Scripture. OT texts are now often regarded as living organisms which continued to grow as people, seeking to understand themselves and their relationship to God, adapted traditions and added new insights.

Nevertheless, books in the OT, even form critics realized, might be a stew of JEDP materials, but it became one story. Irrespective of its historical value, some work was done to ask how to interpret it as a unified story. This kind of question increasingly came to the fore in the later 20th century.

There also was renewed interest in Israel's wisdom literature. This interest was sparked partly by the wealth of comparative material available from other cultures and partly by the recognition that the influence of wisdom thought extended far beyond the wisdom books. The wisdom tradition seems to have contributed, for example, to the Joseph story (Gen. 37–50) and the so-called succession narrative (2 Sam. 9–10; 1 Kings 1–2). This new look for an intermingling and cross-fertilization of what were once regarded as separate traditions—prophecy, wisdom, the Law, and the cult—played a prominent role in OT studies.

There was also a revived interest in apocalyptic literature and an attempt to evaluate its positive theological significance. Interest has shifted from stressing the foreign elements in apocalyptic to tracing its roots in earlier prophetic or wisdom traditions, and in sociological factors and religious tensions in the postexilic Jewish community.

The study of the literature of the OT can never take place in a vacuum. Tools and techniques employed in the study of literature in general have always found their place in OT study. This was noticeably so in the late 20th century with the application of "rhetorical criticism" and "structuralism" in OT study. The results, especially of structuralism, are subject to sharp disagreement.

***The Theological Relevance of the OT.*** The place of the OT in the Christian church has always been argued. Anti-Semitism, particularly in Germany during the 1930s, added sharpness to the debate. An outpouring of books and articles considered the theology of the OT and what is meant by that theology. Was it a purely descriptive discipline, describing various theological views, or a normative discipline, seeking to direct attention to a permanently valid revelation of God? What was the relationship between such a theological approach and a purely historical approach in terms of a history of the religion of Israel? Was one consistent theology at work in the OT or different, perhaps incompatible, theologies? If this theology attempted to present the religion of ancient Israel as a self-contained unity in the face of changing historical conditions, what was the constant in its tendency and character? Any attempt to systematize in terms of "covenant" or "communion with God" presented difficulties. Some categories seemed too precise. The covenant theme was difficult to apply to all of the material in the OT. Others seemed too broad. Saying that the OT was about "the oneness of God" seemed to beg the question, since it is the character of such a God that is central to the discussion. Von Rad broke with the systematic approach by arguing, following his tradition-historical studies, that "an Old Testament theology must have a historical and not a systematic basis." Its true subject was thought to be Israel's own confessions of faith and in particular the concept of *Heilsgeschichte* or salvation history central to such confessions. Since those who followed this view did not believe the OT presented a literal factual history, this sparked a lively debate on how Israel's account of salvation history correlated with fact. What was meant by an act of God? What was the relationship between event and interpretation? Did an approach to OT theology in terms of *Heilsgeschichte* do justice to the wisdom literature, in which appeal to history is conspicuously absent?

Allied to the question of theology was the problem of the relationship between the OT and the NT. If as some claimed, an OT theology must be a Christology, what did this mean in practice for interpretation? To speak of OT promise and NT fulfillment would not do, since these categories operate within the OT itself. If appeal was made to typology, were there any limits to the linking types which might be found?

For a time, notably in the 1950s, there was a confident appeal to a consistent "biblical theology" throughout the Bible. When approached from higher critical perspectives this proved to be built on shaky foundations and to be somewhat disappointing in the practical results it achieved. Out of the ashes of this type of biblical theology came "canonical criticism." Canonical criticism dealt not with what books should or should not be in the canon, but with the shape of the canon as it was passed down. It sought to take seriously the conviction that the canon grew out of and continued to nurture the needs of the believing community. The final form of the canonical text was to be taken seriously since it was this which had spoken, and could still speak, to the commu-

nity of faith. The fruits of this approach, particularly as exemplified in the works of Brevard Childs, left many difficult questions unanswered. It did focus attention on an important issue. To talk about the OT is to use an expression which is specifically Christian, although not one which was used by the first generation of Christians. What Christians call the OT is the Hebrew Bible, the sacred Scriptures of Judaism as a continuing, living faith. Increasingly Jewish scholars contributed to contemporary biblical scholarship, and increasingly Christian scholars recognized the importance of their contribution.

See also APOCRYPHA; ARCHEOLOGY, BIBLICAL; DEAD SEA SCROLLS; RAS SHAMRA.

*Bibliography.* R. De Vaux, *Ancient Israel* (1961); W. Eichrodt, *Theology of the OT*, 2 vols. (ET, 1961, 1964); G. von Rad, *OT Theology*, 2 vols. (ET, 1962, 1965); B. W. Anderson, ed., *The OT and the Christian Faith* (1964); M. Noth, *The OT World* (1966); D. W. Thomas, ed., *Archaeology and OT Study* (1967); K. Koch, *The Growth of the Biblical Tradition: The Form-Critical Method* (1969); J. B. Pritchard, *Ancient Near Eastern Texts Relating to the OT* (1969); J. A. Sanders, *Torah and Canon* (1972); R. E. Clements, *A Century of OT Study* (1976); J. L. Crenshaw, ed., *Studies in Ancient Israelite Wisdom* (1976); W. Zimmerli, *OT Theology in Outline* (ET, 1978); G. W. Anderson, ed., *Tradition and Interpretation: Essays by Members of the Society for OT Study* (1979); B. S. Childs, *Introduction to the OT as Scripture* (1979); P. D. Hanson, *The Dawn of Apocalyptic: The Historical and Sociological Roots of Jewish Apocalyptic Eschatology* (1979); J. H. Hayes, *An Introduction to OT Study* (1979); C. Bermant and M. Weitzman, *Ebla* (1979); J. H. Hayes, *An Introduction to OT Study* (1979); J. Bright, *A History of Israel* (1981); J. Barr, *Holy Scripture, Canon, Authority, Criticism* (1983); N. Frye, *The Great Code, The Bible and Literature* (1983); J. A. Soggin, *A History of Israel* (1984); H. G. Reventlow, *Problems of OT Theology in the Twentieth Century* (1985); W. H. Schmidt, *The Faith of the OT: A History* (1986).

ROBERT DAVIDSON

## Oliver, John Rathbone

**Oliver, John Rathbone** (1872–1943). Episcopalian priest, doctor, and writer. Born in Albany, N.Y., he studied at Harvard, General Theological Seminary, the University of Innsbruck, Austria (M.D., 1910), and Johns Hopkins (Ph.D., 1927). He was master at St. Paul's School, Concord, N.H. (1894–97) and, after ordination as a priest in the Protestant Episcopal Church in 1900, served as curate in St. Mark's Church, Philadelphia (1900–1903). He was a surgeon in the Austrian Army (1914/15); psychiatrist at Johns Hopkins Hospital, Baltimore (1915–17); chief medical officer to the Supreme Bench of Baltimore (1917–30); professor of the history of medicine at the University of Maryland (1927–30); associate professor of the history of medicine at Johns Hopkins (1930–43); warden of Alumni Memorial Hall at Johns Hopkins; a member of the clerical staff at Mount Calvary Church; and also maintained a private practice as a psychiatrist. Among his books are *The Good Shepherd* (1915; rev. ed., 1932), *The Six-Pointed Cross in the Dust* (1917), *Fear* (1927), *Victim and Victor* (1928), *Foursquare* (1929), *Rock and Sand* (1930), *Article Thirty-Two* (1931), *Psychiatry and Mental Health* (1932),

*Tomorrow's Faith* (1932), *Priest or Pagan* (1933), *The Ordinary Difficulties of Everyday People* (1935), *Greater Love* (1936), and *Spontaneous Combustion* (1937).

RAYMOND W. ALBRIGHT

**Oman.** *See* GULF STATES.

**Oman, John Wood** (1860–1939). Professor of theology at Westminster College, Cambridge (1907–35). His major work, *The Natural and the Supernatural* (1931), looks upon man's religious experience as his normal response and adjustment to his environment without explaining away the real essence of religious knowledge and feeling. Among his other books are *The Problem of Faith and Freedom* (1906), *Grace and Personality* (1917), and *Vision and Authority* (1929).

RAYMOND W. ALBRIGHT

**Omnipotence.** A property of God's infinity, affirming an ability, freedom, authority, and power to do whatever is within the divine will. Ultimate power is implicit in the idea of deity and lies below the surface of many religions; a being worthy of worship must be allowed authority and power beyond that of the worshiper. Students of world religion have observed forms of omnipotence even in animism and polytheism, where it may be masked by a plurality of gods who individually are limited in shared authority. Religions which do not subscribe to a personal god acknowledge life or natural forces which have ultimacy. Even some forms of atheism and religious humanism ascribe to humanity an unlimited potential approaching omnipotence.

Christian monotheism is different in its concept of power from Judaism and far beyond Islam in attributing to God an ability that entirely matches will. A qualitative difference is necessary for Christianity if God's freedom and power are believed to have allowed him to both create and govern the universe and be confined in the form of a human infant and die on the cross. Various Hebrew terms are used (from Gen. 17:1 on) to convey the concept of God's utter freedom. The name for God, *El-Shaddai*, refers to omnipotence. In the NT the Gk. *pantokratōr* may be translated "omnipotent" in 2 Cor. 6:18 and several places in Revelation.

Philosophers have struggled with the implications of infinite power and control, using such absurdities as whether God can create a stone too heavy for him to lift to reject the possibility of omnipotence or logically comprehend it. Descartes proposed that a truly infinite God is free from logic and universal law and so is free to create such a stone or a mathematical system where two plus two equals five. Aquinas set the concept of omnipotence, however, within a "law of noncontradiction." Neither God's will nor his power extend to what is self-contradictory, imperfect, or otherwise out of keeping with his holiness.

Scripture affirms such limitations. God cannot deny himself, lie, undo what is done, or do anything out of keeping with his character (see Num. 23:19; 1 Sam. 15:24; 2 Tim. 2:13; Heb. 6:18; James 1:13, 17). Difficulties and issues attending this understanding are numerous. At the root of most problems which occupied the church in the 1900s was some question of human freedom, revelation, and soteriology. Omnipotence was related to all such questions. They can even be considered as a single matter from the perspective of omnipotence.

The question of God's sovereignty over human affairs has long been debated. If God is utterly sovereign, then man seems only an actor on the divine stage. Further, given the evil in the world, if God is good he must not be all-powerful; if he is all-powerful he cannot be good.

Different responses have been taken to this since the 4th century when Augustine first answered these charges. Augustine's philosophy is still followed by the Reformed church. Augustine maintained that God created humanity with freedom within limits to sin or not to sin. Humanity voluntarily surrendered that freedom and became radically depraved. All of life is affected by evil and pain arising from the fall. God allowed this to happen and took it into account in his plan and governance of creation. In his perfection God had limited options. He could either change humanity so he could deal with them or he could destroy them. He omnipotently followed the plan of salvation in Christ's righteousness. Under this he can accept humans without contradiction. In his power he governs so that his ultimate design will be accomplished; he sovereignly mandates even that evil serve his purpose and ultimately be defeated.

Augustine's system seems to many—Christians and unbelievers—to fully protect neither God's goodness nor human responsibility. The Augustinian system, especially as applied in Calvinism, has been accused, further, of introducing in the doctrine of predestination a pessimistic inevitability to life and salvation. For these reasons during the 19th and 20th centuries most conservative Protestants did not follow the Augustinian model. The alternative philosophy, expressed in various forms, asserts that man did not lose all freedom in the fall. God chose to set up the governing of humanity in such a way that he would not control their actions. In Christ the possibility of escape from evil is offered, and God may help to some extent in the individual's decision to come to Christ. God cannot make that decision for the individual, however. Scriptures speaking of predestination refer to omniscience, instead of omnipotence. God knows all possible actions of all possible moments, sees future events and acts accordingly, guiding humans without impeding their freedom.

Two non-Christian philosophies also were reapplied to the Christian setting in modern church movements. One philosophy current in the early Enlightenment was deism, which proposed that God is so utterly removed from the world he has little contact and limited power in the lives of humans. In regard to omnipotence a similar philosophy was developed by Karl Barth and followed by much of the 20th-century church. Barthian theology sets far closer, more personal ties between God and creation, but God remains "wholly other" from reality, in the noumenal or *Geschichte* spiritual sphere and divorced from the phenomenal *Historie* of everyday life. God's power as expressed in salvation and revelation is insubstantial, and human responsibility is needed to apply it to the phenomenal world.

Deism protected God's transcendence at the expense of some power; pantheism does the same with God's immanence, so identifying God with the phenomenal world that the two come to be indistinguishable. Schleiermacher and much of 19th-century German theology followed this view. God lacked personality, although mystically the individual might find union with God. Otherwise God is *all-Welt*, totally immanent and closely identifiable with the world. In the 20th century this conception was maintained by process theology or panentheism. God is independent of the world but interdependent with it. Both need one another and draw meaning from one another. Both are in the process of becoming. God directs, but as an impersonal force. He can in no-wise be responsible for what happens, good or evil.

These overviews hardly do justice to any of the above positions, but they suggest the basic lines of understanding of omnipotence at work in the 20th-century Christian milieu and why these strains contributed to awesome divisions within Christianity.

**Bibliography.** C. Hartshorne, *Reality as Social Process: Studies in Metaphysics and Religion* (1953); A. N. Whitehead, *Process and Reality* (repr. ed., 1960); H. Hartwell, *The Theology of Karl Barth: An Introduction* (1964); E. Jungel, *The Doctrine of the Trinity: God's Being Is in Becoming* (ET, 1976); H. Bavinck, *The Doctrine of God* (repr. ed., 1977); K. S. Kantzer and S. N. Gundry, eds., *Perspectives on Evangelical Theology* (1979); A. Kenny, *The God of the Philosophers* (1979); R. H. Nash, *The Concept of God: An Exploration of Contemporary Difficulties with the Attributes of God* (1983); W. A. Elwell, ed., *Evangelical Dictionary of Theology* (1984).

**Omnipresence.** A property of the immensity and infinity of God, his eternal, inescapable presence. The idea of omnipresence is latent more often than it is explicit. A common definition would be that quality whereby there is no place where its possessor is not. The difference between the Christian and other conceptions is not found in the formal definition but in the kinds of pres-

ence connoted. The traditional terms with which omnipresence is usually contrasted are transcendence and immanence As extremes transcendence is complete separation of God from all else, and immanence is complete absorption of God in and by that which is other. In practice the terms are relative. Immanence in modern theology can convey the idea of the presence of a God who holds himself at the same time aloof, and transcendence the separateness of a God who concedes a presence in some form. Deism and pantheism represent the opposite positions: deism holds that God once discharged the office of creator but now leaves all else severely alone; pantheism in various degrees of strictness, thinks of God as everywhere, to the extent of identifying him with all that is.

The Christian doctrine is particularly rigorous. Perfectly God's divine Being transcends space limitations. At every point of space all of who God is exists. Such omnipresence is different in kind from that found in pantheism. There are in Scripture statements which suggest a sense in which God may be in one place and not in another (1 Sam. 26:19, of Israel, and with Jacob, Gen. 28:16–17). In 1 Kings 20:28 Syria's idea that God could be localized was ridiculed. Prophet and lawgiver protested against idolatry, denying that things could be like God or that God could be localized. The road to the simple pantheistic identification of God and the world is permanently barred by the line dividing creation from Creator which is retained inviolate. God never forfeits his character of Creator in order to be ubiquitously present (1 Kings 8:27; Ps. 139; Jer. 23:24; Acts 17:24). That Christian mysticism has often overlooked this gulf or tried to bridge it does not dispose of its cardinal importance for Christian doctrine. The limits as thus defined allow real omnipresence without identifying God with things. Within them Christianity holds that there are different degrees or modes of presence: "I am with you always" (Matt. 28:20); "where two or three are gathered in my name" (Matt. 18:20); "wherever I cause my name to be honored" (Exod. 20:24); "my Name shall be there" (1 Kings 8:29). In Roman Catholic theology transubstantiation, the doctrine of the "real presence" of Christ in the Mass, is based on the words "This is my body" (Luke 22:19). This diversity of presence is construed in personal terms: God is not by very nature inevitably one with or tied to the world. He is above and beyond creation. But by his sovereign will, he is everywhere, and by word and promise he covenants to be specially here and there, without prejudice to his ubiquity elsewhere.

J. K. S. REID

**Opus Dei** (Prelature of the Holy Cross and Opus Dei). Roman Catholic organization founded on

October 2, 1928, by the Spanish priest Josemaría Escrivá de Balaguer (1902–1975). Its aim is to spread, in all spheres of society, a deep awareness of the universal call to holiness and apostolate, in the fulfillment—with freedom and responsibility—of one's professional work. Spread to the five continents, it reported in 1986 more than 1000 priests incardinated in the prelature and 72,000 laypeople (men and women, single and married). The prelate is Alvaro del Portillo.

**Orangeism.** Predominantly Irish Protestant political and fraternal society named for the Dutch Royal House of Orange. It commemorates the "Glorious Revolution" of 1688 and 1689, when William III, prince of Orange, and his wife Mary became joint British sovereigns. English Orangeism as a religious and political movement commenced in Exeter Cathedral when William was invited to replace his father-in-law, James II, because it was suspected he was reestablishing the power of the Roman Catholic Church. A dean of Exeter wrote "The Qualifications of an Orangeman," and the liturgy which is still used. Landing at Torbay, Devon, in November 1688, William's ascendency was a bloodless revolution which secured the progress of the Reformation and modern democracy. James resisted in Ireland and generally appointed Roman Catholics to suppress Protestantism. Londonderry suffered seige and William was victor of the decisive Battle of the Boyne in July 1690. Land wars in which Orange troops fought in Ireland led to the reorganizing of Orange lodges after the Battle of the Diamond, Armagh, September 1795. In the late 1900s the organization of mainline Protestants had 1500 primary lodges, which were united through district and county lodges with the Grand Orange Lodge of Ireland.

Similar lodges exist in various Commonwealth countries, as well as Ghana, Togo, and the USA. They have a simple ritual, teach the evangelical faith, and encourage social and philanthropic practices. Where necessary, members may engage in political lobbying, but only in Northern Ireland is there a link with a political party. There is a democratic structure and officers led by a master are elected annually, by the several lodges. A world consultative council meets triennially but each national grand lodge is autonomous. Women's and young people's lodges are part of the Orange organization.

W. MARTIN SMYTH

**Orchard, William Edwin** (1877–1955). Roman Catholic. Born in Rugby, he studied at Westminster College, Cambridge, and London University. He was ordained to the ministry of the Congregational Church in 1904 and became minister of the King's Weigh House Church, London, in 1914. During his ministry he introduced many Catholic ritual forms into the worship of the church and was finally received into the Roman Catholic communion in 1932. He was ordained priest (sub condition) in 1935 and then preached and lectured in many areas. His books of prayers have been widely used. He wrote *Evolution of OT Religion* (1908), *The Temple, A Book of Prayers* (1913), *The Outlook for Religion* (1917), *The Devotional Companion* (1921), *Foundations of Faith* (4 vols., 1924–27), *Prayer* (1930), *The Inevitable Cross* (1933), *The Way of Simplicity* (1934), *The Cult of Our Lady* (1937), and *The Necessity for the Church* (1940).

F. W. DILLISTONE

**Orders, Major.** In the Roman Catholic Church, the three higher degrees of the priestly hierarchy, the subdeaconate, deaconate, and priesthood. The "sacrament of order" confers major orders. Episcopacy is not usually regarded as a distinct order, but rather as the fullness of the priesthood. Subdeacons take a vow of celibacy and of daily reciting the breviary. According to canon law, no one can be admitted to the major orders before age 22 for subdeacons, 23 for deacons, and 25 for priests. Three years of theological studies in an approved seminary are required from candidates to the subdeaconate; candidates to the deaconate may be ordained after the beginning of the fourth year; and candidates to the priesthood after the first semester of the fourth year of studies.

*See also* BREVIARY.

GEORGES A. BARROIS

**Orders, Ministerial.** The commission, responsibilities, privileges, and prerogatives conferred at ordination on the minister. The term was normally used in Episcopal settings, but the concept pertained throughout the Christian world. In the 20th century it became a subject attended by complex and contentious discussion. Almost every affirmation made about who could be ordained to the teaching or pastoral ministry and how that ministry functioned during the 1900s was denied or refuted by others on biblical, historical, or ecclesiastical grounds.

In the NT Jesus assembled 12 in an inner circle of followers (Matt. 10:1–5) and also appointed others to preach and minister (Luke 10:1). Dominical leadership was peculiarly invested in Peter (Matt. 16:18) and exercised by him without opposition even before Pentecost (Acts 1:15; 2:14). From the earliest days of the church the 12 (and soon others) assumed wider responsibilities in directing the community (Acts 2 and thereafter). This organization surrounding the apostles had roots in the OT patriarchs and current synagogue practice. Remarkably, however, the patriarchal leadership of the apostles drops from the view of the NT after Acts relates how Matthias replaced Judas (Acts 2:25–26). Petrine leadership continued, associated immediately with the authority vested in James (at Jerusalem) and later in Paul. This is why Roman Catholic papal pronouncements describe their authority as within the "Church of Peter and Paul."

If both historical precedent and situational realities shaped the ministerial organization of the primitive church, a crucial question was what aspects of that example were normative for the 20th-century church. In Vatican Council II and its document *Luman Gentium* the formation of the Apostolic College attempted to recover some of the lost importance of the patriarchal government example of "the Twelve." Vatican II also attempted to clarify the ministerial offices of bishop, priest, and deacon. In Roman church government this three-office structure was regarded as irreversibly mandated by Scripture. Many Protestant communions denied the biblical sanction for episcopal government, arguing that it mandated the structure and form used in their ministerial pattern. Congregational forms placed the ministers of the church in the NT role of elder/bishops and sometimes evangelists. Their two-office view also established an ordained commissioning of deacons in directing and administering many activities. Sometimes in practice much of the directing work is done by nonministerial professional and lay workers. Presbyterian government rejected episcopacy but had its own three-office ministry structure of deacons (acts of mercy), ruling elders (spiritual and governmental control), and teaching elder/bishop/pastors (spiritual teaching and leadership). In episcopal government control was exercised by ranks of ordained leaders elevated by further commissions. The congregational structure centers most authority for ordering of ministry at the congregational or local church level. Presbyterian government looked to graded church courts of elected, trained, and ordained ruling and teaching elders, who might or might not have parity with one another.

Whatever the design of ministerial orders, there was normally an appeal to a biblical mandate and the true leadership of the church by God in providence and the Holy Spirit. When due weight was given to the contingencies which infect human affairs, the statement that one order alone was legitimate for ordering the church was very bold. Unfortunately it contributed to the ongoing division of the people of God.

J. K. S. REID

**Orders, Minor.** In the Roman Catholic Church, the orders or degrees of *ostiarius* (doorkeeper), *lector* (reader), exorcist, and acolyte. They prepare clerics to the reception of the major, or sacred, orders. The names of the minor orders refer to charges and offices in usage in medieval churches. The tonsure, the act of setting apart the

individual and enrollment in the diocese, is a prerequisite to the reception of the minor orders. The determination of intervals of time between the tonsure and the single minor orders is left by canon law to the discretion of the ordaining bishop. He may not, however, confer them on the same day, and an interval of at least one year must be observed between the ordination to the order of acolyte and the access to the major orders. Abbots are permitted by canon law to confer the tonsure and minor orders upon their own subjects.

*See also* ORDERS, MAJOR.

GEORGES A. BARROIS

**Ordination.** From the Lat. *ordinare* (to organize or set in order), in ecclesiastical usage the act of separating and commissioning one for a role of special ministerial or priestly service, either for a specified mission or for life. It normally involves recognition of skills and worthiness God has invested in the individual, a period of preparation, and the consecration of that individual through the conferring of ordination status. The act of ordination traditionally centers in the laying on of hands by a bishop in episcopal church government, by those already ordained to the ruling or teaching eldership in the presbyterial form, and by ordained pastors, elders, and/or deacons in the congregational form. The act of ordination is meant to be a human affirmation of God's setting apart of the person and not so much that special spiritual authority is bestowed by virtue of the act itself. Operative divine grace does attach to the act of laying on of hands by the bishop in episcopal churches who follow a theology of apostolic succession. The theory is that special virtue granted to Peter was directly communicated by him to others in the laying on of hands. They in turn passed it on in unbroken succession to the modern church.

Biblical warrant for the investiture to ministerial office is drawn from the choosing by God of Aaron, his sons, and the tribe of Levi (Exod. 4:14–15; 28:41; 29:9; Deut. 33:8–11; Judges 17:13). Num. 8:10 records the laying on of hands. The OT observes the public recognition of the divine choice of prophets and kings as well. Jesus called out 12 (Mark 3:13–14; John 15:16), and Paul insisted that he had been set apart from birth (Gal. 1:1, 15). Matthias was selected with prayer and divine lot, Paul and Barnabas were especially commissioned at Antioch (Acts 13:1–4), and Timothy was instructed to use care in setting apart others (1 Tim. 5:22). The NT assumes that officers are set aside to govern, and must qualify for their work (for example, 1 Tim. 3:1–3; 5:17–20; 2 Tim. 2:1–2; Titus 1:5–9).

Throughout church history the status accompanying the ordained offices, and often the associated wealth and royal patronage, has led to a wide variety of problems and abuses. In the 1900s ordination tended to be a battleground for deeper theological divisions within communions. Since status and the opportunity to teach and interpret Scripture were exercised primarily by ordained individuals, modernists and conservatives both sought to exclude one another from ordination. The right to examine the theological positions and moral fitness of potential ministers was an especially bitter issue. Women fought for the right to be ordained to these status positions within the church, and an issue of the later century was specifically whether homosexuals could properly be ordained. Such issues helped splinter several mainline denominations, and even more conservative churches were touched by ordination-related controversies.

Ordination theologically refers to God's sovereign decrees and predestinating power over creation. This subject is related to God's omnipotence and omniscience.

**Organ.** *Since 1900.* The organ has undergone immense changes in mechanics and function. The development of electric and electropneumatic action, replacing cumbersome levers, made possible a lighter resistance in the key and the use of a single set of pipes at various pitches and in various divisions, manual and pedal. The standardization of console measurements at the recommendation of the American Guild of Organists, about 1920, encouraged organists to develop skills which could be easily transferred from one instrument to another.

The employment of the organ for nonecclesiastical purposes influenced church organ design. The instrument which was developed between 1910 and 1930 to accompany motion pictures was characterized by highly sensational effects, some of which found their way into church organs. This period witnessed the vogue of harp, chime, and vox humana stops in church organs. Before the radio became an important disseminator of fine music, the church or concert hall organ was in many communities the only medium available for the performance of symphonic and operatic literature. As a result, many stops were invented to imitate orchestral instruments and effects, some of which are still important components of church organs used to accompany large choral works originally written for chorus and orchestra. Film and electronic media rendered some of these inventions obsolete. Organ design then tended toward a more austere distinctively organlike tone. While the movement to imitate the organ of Bach's day or before is subject to the danger of extreme faddism, many of the instruments constructed at mid-century seemed to agree well with a contemporary theology of intellectualism and impersonality. An increasing problem was the cost of

building pipe organs. Early electric organs were invented which, amplifying feeble sounds by electronic means, imitate more or less successfully the tones of a pipe organ. The advantage of low cost did not in all cases compensate for the variations in console measurements, nor for the occasionally unattractive tone of these electric organs.

PAUL ALLWARDT

*Since 1955.* Breakthroughs in electronics and computerization caused major changes in the keyboard music industry and its religious applications. For churches which could afford organs, however, the technological advances actually enhanced the 20th-century revival of the pipe organ. New instruments were also introduced which were little more than cousins to anything previously in existence.

As console organs became smaller and computerized circuitry replaced vacuum tubes, even small congregations with limited financial resources were able to add organ music to worship. Sound technology, synthetic sound boards, and fabrics allowed some organs to come closer to a rich tone than had previously been possible. Nothing approaching the resonance and tonal colors of the pipe organ was possible through electronic amplification, however. As popular music groups experimented with new sounds and styles during the 1960s, small, portable electronic keyboards and synthesizers were developed which tried to innovate rather than emulate existing organ sounds. As music for these organs became more sophisticated and the keyboard's abilities more variable, musicianship began to replace sheer volume, and some contemporary Christian musicians began to take advantage of the new medium. From the concert stage these instruments found their way into evangelistic crusades, rallies, and eventually churches. Pentecostal and charismatic churches in particular used the new music styles and instrumentation.

Computers and electronics also affected more traditional organ music, however. Cabinet organs with small, attached pipes had been experimented with during the 1700s. In the mid-1900s better understanding of the nature of acoustics and new materials and engineering to focus sound allowed creation of portable pipe chests, usually hooked up electrically to consoles, which allowed churches to experience a basic pipe organ quality at a fraction of the cost, installation time, and space. Electronic innovations to organ design also allowed pipe organs of all sizes to be somewhat less sensitive to temperature and climate. Replacing fabric coverings of enclosed pipe chests of all sizes with fiberglass fabric allowed greater sound penetration. Computer-assisted acoustical design also allowed architects and organ builders to work together to match an organ to its auditorium.

While many of the great organs of Europe were damaged or destroyed in 20th-century wars, new restoration techniques brought some classics back to life. High-fidelity recordings of these instruments and extensive travel by Westerners assured that, whatever new styles and instruments might bring to church music, the pipe organ and its grand choral accompaniment would remain the epitome of awe-inspiring worship.

**Organ Transplants.** The antecedents of modern organ transplantation are older than usually imagined. At about the beginning of the 6th century B.C., Hindu surgeons attempted to reconstruct noses with transplanted flaps of skins. The 16th-century Italian surgeon Gasparo Tagliacozzi, using techniques similar to those of the Hindus, reconstructed noses with a flap of skin from the inner, upper arm of the patient; the arm was put in a cast and held to the face for two or three weeks; the skin flap was then cut away from the arm.

From the 18th century forward, the rapid progress of medicine—including the development of aseptic surgery, anesthesia, and blood transfusion (itself a kind of transplant)—gave surgeons the necessary elements for effective transplantation. In 1954, Boston doctors successfully transplanted a kidney from one twin brother to another. In 1967, the first human-to-human heart transplant was performed. More difficult organs, such as the liver, were soon transplanted with increasing promise. In the 1980s the kidney was the most common organ to be transplanted. Lungs and the pancreas were transplanted, as well as the liver and a host of other tissues, such as skin, the cornea, fascia, nerves, blood, and bone marrow.

With some exceptions, ethicists within Judaism, Islam, and Christianity accepted organ transplantation when performed with the proper consent. For Christians, four theological concerns were central to the position favoring transplantation: the unity of body and soul, the cultural mandate, the biblical bias for life, and the example of Jesus' bodily sacrifice.

*The Unity of Body and Soul.* The Christian understanding of a person as an ensouled body or an embodied soul means that changes in one's body are important to personal identity. Yet Christians have long interchanged bodily parts and used artificial parts without supposing a fundamental shift in identity. Eyeglasses, dentures, prostheses, and the donation or reception of blood are examples.

Persons change internally and externally throughout a life time. Internally they meet new friends, visit new countries, suffer tragedies, read different books and face other influences which can profoundly change them. Externally or bodily

they grow fingernails, hair, and cellular structure. Within soul and body, then, there is both change and consistency. Organ transplants are congruent with such an understanding of personhood. A bodily part may be changed, but the person retains identity.

*The Cultural Mandate.* Many theologians have understood the cultural mandate of Gen. 1:28 to mean that humanity should explore, cultivate, and develop the resources of the earth. The mandate logically includes human existence as one aspect of creation. As Anthony Hoekema writes, "Man is called by God to develop all the potentialities found in nature and in humankind as a whole. He must seek to develop not only agriculture, horticulture, and animal husbandry, but also science, technology, and art." According to such an interpretation, organ transplantation is a legitimate extension of humanity's mandate, the exercise of God-given creativity in the cultivation of natural potential.

*The Biblical Bias for Life.* Christianity has promoted medicine because of the religion's strong stand to protect life against disease and war as a corollary of the commandment not to murder (Exod. 20:13). Paul regarded death as the "last enemy" (1 Cor. 15:26). Although life is not the ultimate good—nor in itself "sacred"—the Bible is emphatically on the side of life. The Israelites are called to "choose life" (Deut. 30:19), and Jesus is said to come so that persons may have eternal life (John 3:16). Of course, what is in view in such passages is spiritual life and Jesus alone gained the final, conclusive victory over death, but medical triumphs over diseases and premature deterioration of organs imitate this great victory in a significant provisional sense.

*The Example of Jesus' Bodily Sacrifice.* Jesus saved those who would follow him from sin and death by offering up his body. Celebrating the Eucharist, Christians remember that they live because their Lord gave his body and his blood. The cross is the symbol of self-giving, and when Christians follow Christ they are called to make his cross their own. There are few more dramatic ways they can give than to share their bodies and their blood. There remain three major concerns surrounding organ transplantation: the determination of brain death, organ procurement, and organ allocation.

Until the 1960s, cessation of brain function inevitably followed from cessation of the cardiopulmonary function (or vice-versa). People did not live on in ambiguous states, for example where the heart beat after brain function had ceased. Respirators and other technological innovations made such states possible. The determination of death was no longer so simple a matter as placing a mirror under a person's nostrils. Machines could maintain blood and oxygen circulation even when the body could never again circulate blood and breathe on its own. The notion of "brain death" was therefore introduced.

The fear remained that an organ donor might be pronounced brain dead prematurely, for the sake of an organ recipient. Much of this fear stemmed from a confusion of brain death with what was technically called a "persistent vegetative state." In a persistent vegetative state only part of the brain is destroyed. The brain stem, the primitive part of the brain that enables reflexive actions such as breathing and digesting food, is usually intact. The injured person languished in a coma.

Organ donors have suffered incapacitation of their entire brains. The Catholic ethicist John Dedek explains that no one may be declared dead who has the potential for spontaneous respiration. "But one who has no hope of ever recovering the power of spontaneous respiration because of irreversible destruction of the brain is no longer a living being, even though his heart and lung functions are being mechanically maintained."

In the 1980s enough deaths (about 20,000 each year) occurred in the USA under conditions that would permit transplantation to supply more organs than needed. Yet in 1982, for example, only 3681 postmortem kidneys were transplanted in the country. The lack created debates over more "effective" but less ethical sorts of organ procurement. The prevailing policy, favored by the majority of Christian ethicists, was "express consent." No organs might be removed for transplantation unless the donor (or the donor's family) had expressly donated them. Some ethicists and physicians, bemoaning the shortage of organs available under this procedure, argued for a policy of "presumed consent." Under such a policy, organs could be taken for transplantation automatically, unless the deceased or family expressly forbade it. This policy was in effect by the late 1900s in some countries. Those opposed to presumed consent protested that it was statist coercion, making organ donation more a matter of "societal taking" than "personal giving."

Christian ethicists were more unanimous in opposing the commercialization of organ donation as a way to loosen the procurement bind. They vigorously fought proposals to sell organs and to deduct costs from hospital bills in return for organs.

Another concern was how to determine who received scarce organs. Medically, a complicated set of criteria evolved, factoring in the potential recipient's age, emotional stability, physical condition, nearness to death, and tissue-type. Ethicists argued against making estimated social worth or financial ability to pay determining factors. As the system stood at the end of the 1980s in the USA, relatively wealthy people were more likely to receive transplants. Programs were sought to make transplants more affordable, and technological advances lowered costs.

*See also* Bioethics.

*Bibliography.* P. Ramsey, *The Patient as Person* (1970); H. Smith, *Ethics and the New Medicine* (1970); J. F. Dedek, *Contemporary Medical Ethics* (1975); R. M. Veatch, *Case Studies in Medical Ethics* (1977); A. Hoekema, *Created in God's Image* (1986).

Robert G. Clouse and Rodney Clapp

**Original Righteousness.** Doctrine of the state of humanity in relation to God before Adam's fall into a state of sin and misery. In the 20th century widespread acceptance of evolution by theologians compromised the doctrine of original righteousness along with its cognate doctrine, original sin. In liberal theology the tendency was to conceive primitive man as either subethical or as morally innocent prior to the first conscious sin. The belief was that no man was ever like John Calvin's picture of unfallen Adam "when he had affections regulated by reason, and all his senses governed in proper order, and when, in the excellency of his nature, he truly resembled the excellence of his Creator" (*Institutes* 1.15.3).

The dialectical, or neo-orthodox, school, also accepting the general evolutionary hypothesis, nevertheless felt it necessary to cling to a strong doctrine of original sin, and therefore retained a concept of original righteousness similar to that first systematized by Augustine (354–430) and stressed by the Reformers. With the liberals, however, these theologians deny that it ever belonged to any historic being. Instead, the fall is Christian saga or legend. Each person is born with a corruption which presupposes sin. It was often implied by neo-orthodoxy, although rarely asserted, that original righteousness characterized a premundane or "superhistorical" existence of humanity.

Roman Catholic theology retained a slightly different conception of original righteousness. The Roman Catholic view is that humanity was created in a morally neutral state. God endowed human beings with special righteousness as a *superadditum donum*. It was this gift which Adam lost in the fall.

John N. Thomas

**Original Sin.** In its simplest terms the doctrine of original sin means that, as a result of the fall, every man is born corrupt, and it is usually held that he is also guilty. Out of his perverted *state* proceed his evil *acts*.

In Rom. 5:12–21 Paul asserts that "through one man sin entered into the world, and death through sin; and so death passed unto all men, for that all sinned." While a connection between the sin of Adam and of mankind generally is plainly asserted, scholars cannot agree whether Paul means that all men sinned *in* Adam or sinned personally, as Adam sinned. It is held also that the doctrine of original sin is contained or implied in Gen. 3 and in such OT passages as Ps. 51 and Isa. 59.

Patristic thinking received its most important formulation in Augustine (354–430) who taught that the race was *in* Adam, although it was sometimes said to exist in him seminally and sometimes in a realistic sense so as to share not only his nature but also his personality. As a result of this connection, men are born not only corrupt and guilty but also devoid of the freedom of choice which was Adam's before the fall.

In the Middle Ages Aquinas, whose teaching became in essence the official doctrine of the Roman Church, while holding with Augustine that original sin meant the loss of original righteousness, insisted that the latter was a super-added grace and not a part of man's created nature. Bereft of it, man is left in a state of conflict but retains in slightly impaired form his freedom of choice.

Luther and Calvin returned to the essentials of Augustinian anthropology and this has continued in conservative Protestantism.

In liberal Protestantism the general acceptance of the hypothesis of evolution led to development of the thesis that humans have no original corruption and guilt, but only morally neutral tendencies brought to human nature from its animal ancestry. These urge their own unrestricted expression and give rise to temptation when confronted by moral or spiritual law.

Dialectical or neo-orthodox theology sought to combine the acceptance of evolution with an Augustinian conception of original sin. This resulted in an admitted paradox: there was no historic Adam with whom our inborn sinfulness is connected; and yet it is due to some voluntary act prior to our birth. This left the explanation of original sin a complete mystery, but preserved the fact and faced the prevailing views of science.

**Bibliography.** F. R. Tennant, *The Sources of the Doctrines of the Fall and Original Sin* (1903); N. P. Williams, *The Ideas of the Fall and of Original Sin: Historical and Critical Study* (1927); J. G. Machen, *The Christian View of Man* (1937); E. Brunner, *Man in Revolt* (1939); R. Niebuhr, *The Nature and Destiny of Man*, vol. 1 (1941); J. M. Boyce, *God the Redeemer* (1978).

JOHN N. THOMAS

**Orphaned Missions.** A term used by Protestants from the early part of World War II to designate mission fields cut off from their supporting societies. In fact, the interchurch aid denoted by this term began with World War I. In 1914 German missionaries were expelled from their fields. J. H. Oldham of London rallied support from mission societies in Britain, Sweden, France, and the USA. Between 1917 and 1926 American help totaled $1.7 million. Largely through Oldham's work, the Versailles Treaty included a clause exempting German mission properties from confiscation.

World War II created a new orphaned mission problem. This time fields of societies in Germany, Denmark, Finland, France, Holland, and Norway were cut off from home support. The International Missionary Council (IMC) and the Lutheran World Federation (LWF) cooperated in recruiting gifts from churches in Britain, Australia, Sweden, Switzerland, South Africa, Canada, and the USA. From late 1939 through 1947 these gifts totaled nearly $6.4 million. All help was administered with an active regard for the trusteeship owed to native churches and to the European societies. In the absence of an early peace treaty, property settlements were negotiated with individual governments. In general, governments showed respect for mission properties.

Postwar Europe's economy required a continuation of interchurch mission aid. From 1948 to 1950 IMC invested $607,144, and the National Lutheran Council, American Committee of LWF, $2.2 million.

FREDRIK A. SCHIOTZ

**Orr, James** (1844–1913). Scottish theologian and apologist. Born in Glasgow, he studied at United Presbyterian Divinity Hall, Edinburgh, and Glasgow University. He was minister of East Bank United Presbyterian Church, Hawick (1874–91); he taught church history at United Presbyterian Divinity Hall (1891–1900), and then systematic theology and apologetics at United Free Church College, Glasgow (1900–1913). He campaigned for modified subscription to the Westminster Confession, edited several church magazines, and was a leading advocate of the United Free Church Union of 1900. While retreating from strict Calvinism, he defended evangelical orthodoxy with wide-ranging scholarship. He vigorously opposed Ritschlianism, the documentary hypotheses of the Pentateuch, aspects of Darwinian evolution, and all naturalistic Christologies. He was influential in Britain and North America, and contributed to *The Fundamentals*. His main works are *The Christian View* (1893), *The Ritschlian Theology* (1897), *The Progress of Dogma* (1901), *God's Image in Man* (1905), *The Problem of the OT* (1906), *The Virgin Birth* (1907), and *Revelation and Inspiration* (1910). He was also general editor for the *International Standard Bible Encyclopaedia* (1915).

GLEN G. SCORGIE

**Orthodox Churches.** See EASTERN ORTHODOX CHURCHES.

**Orthodox Presbyterian Church (OPC).** Protestant Calvinist denomination formed in the 1930s in a split within the northern branch of American Presbyterianism. Although signs of an incipient theological liberalism had been visible in the Presbyterian Church in the USA since

619

before the turn of the 20th century, the appearance of the *Auburn Affirmation* in January 1924, eventually signed by about 1300 PCUSA ministers, brought the controversy into the open. This document was regarded by conservatives as an attack on the vital doctrines of historic Christianity and the testimony of that church, and it set the stage for formation of the OPC.

The division occurred after a series of events convinced conservative leaders of the PCUSA that the tide had definitely turned in favor of theological liberalism. The conservative element, led by J. Gresham Machen, Clarence Edward Cartney, Carl McIntire and others, was unable to stem the tide. The reorganization of the governing board of Princeton Theological Seminary in 1929 led to the formation of Westminster Theological Seminary that year, for this change of administration gave the controlling power to the liberal element.

The study by the Laymen's Commission on World Missions, *Re-thinking Missions* (1932), represented a liberal approach which denigrated evangelism as a missionary enterprise and spurred the conservatives to form the Independent Board for Presbyterian Foreign Missions in 1933. This revolt against the denominational authority to conduct world missions resulted in disciplinary action by the General Assembly of the Presbyterian Church, USA, against Machen and others. The climax of this struggle was reached when Machen was placed on trial by New Brunswick Presbytery, found guilty of violating his ordination vows, and suspended from the ministry.

This decision led to the founding of the Presbyterian Church of America in 1936 by those who had been disciplined or were facing action. This new church adopted the Westminster Standards without amendment which had weakened their fidelity to the Scriptures. As a result of legal action by the PCUSA the name was ordered changed, and the denomination became the Orthodox Presbyterian Church. It suffered a further division in 1937 following Machen's sudden death under the leadership of Carl McIntire, primarily because of its alleged neglect of premillennialism as a mandated position in eschatology.

Although the OPC did not grow very much over the first four decades of its history, in the 1980s it became much more aggressive in its missionary outreach both in the USA and abroad and its membership approached 20,000. It continued to stress the doctrinal positions of the Westminster Confession of Faith and its Larger and Shorter Catechism.

C. GREGG SINGER

**Osservatore Romano.** Informational newspaper founded in Rome in 1861 and subsequently used by Pope Leo XIII for current publication of acts from the Holy See. It became the official journal of the Vatican. In the late 1900s it contained, in addition to communications from the papal government, reports on political and religious world problems. It was issued daily, except on Sundays.

GEORGES A. BARROIS

**Ottley, Robert Lawrence** (1856–1933). Anglican theologian. Born in Richmond, Yorkshire, he was educated at Oxford where he remained all his life except for a short time when he held the incumbency of Winterbourne Bassett (1897–1903). He was variously fellow, tutor, theological college vice-principal and principal, dean of Magdalen College, canon of Christ Church, and—from 1903 until his death—professor of pastoral theology. To the controversial *Lux Mundi* symposium volume (1889) he contributed the essay on Christian ethics. His other works include *Lancelot Andrewes* (1894), *The Doctrine of the Incarnation* (1896), *Aspects of the OT* (1897), *The Hebrew Prophets* (1898), *Short History of the Hebrews* (1902), *The Religion of Israel* (1905), *Christian Ideas and Ideals* (1909), *The Rule of Life and Love* (1913), *Christian Morals* (1915), and *Studies in the Confessions of St. Augustine* (1919).

**Otto, Rudolph** (1869–1937). Religious scholar. He taught theology at Göttingen (1898–1914), Breslau (1914–17), and Marburg (1917–37). He was a careful student of religions and of the mystical aspects of religion. His *Idea of the Holy* (1923; rev. ed., 1929) sets out his thesis that religion is basically the apprehension of the numinous which manifests itself to men who can know it only by religious insight. He also sought something of authority for the Christian faith because of its basis on biblical truth. His later books include *Naturalism and Religion* (1907), *Religious Essays, A Supplement to the Idea of the Holy* (1931), *Mysticism, East and West* (1932), *The Kingdom of God and the Son of Man: A Study in the History of Religion* (1937), and *Suende und Urschuld und andere Aufsaetze zur Theologie* (1932).

*Bibliography.* Theodor Siegfried, *Grundfragen der Theologie bei Rudolph Otto* (1931); J. M. Moore, *Theories of Religious Experience, with Special Reference to James, Otto and Bergson* (1938).

RAYMOND W. ALBRIGHT

**Outler, Albert C.** (1908– ). Methodist theologian. Born in Thomasville, Ga., he studied at Wofford College, Emory, and Yale universities (Ph.D., 1938). He pastored churches in Baxley, Gordon, and Macon, Ga., and then held professorships at Duke (1938–45), Yale (1945–51), and the Perkins School of Theology at Southern Methodist University (1951–74). His primary specialty is historical theology, but he is also interested in the contributions of the Anglican Wesleyan tradition to the rehabilitation of modern thought; he is regarded as one of the foremost 20th-century interpreters of John Wesley. An active churchman, he served on numerous commissions of the United Methodist Church and was its delegated observer at the Second Vatican Council. Among Outler's most important works are *Psychotherapy and the Christian Message* (1954), *The Christian Tradition and the Unity We Seek* (1957), *John Wesley* (1964), *Who Trusts in God?* (1968), *Evangelism in the Wesleyan Spirit* (1971), *Theology in the Wesleyan Spirit* (1975), *John and Charles Wesley* (1981), and *The Works of John Wesley: Sermons* (1985).

RICHARD V. PIERARD

**Ou-Yang, Ching-Wu** (1871–1943). Chinese Buddhist scholar. He organized the Chinese Buddhist Association (1912) to fight proposed state religion. He criticized the inability of Buddhist clergy to uphold their religion, and exemplified the shift of leadership to laypeople. The Chinese renaissance (1917) created an intellectual need which considered the Pure Land pietism of Yin Kuang too conservative. Ou-Yang, originally Hwayen, revived Wei Shih idealism, opposing Tai Hsu's monism. He founded the Institute of Inner Studies in Nanking (1922), which became the center of the idealistic movement, raising the intellectual level of Chinese Buddhism.

*See also* BUDDHISM.

EARL H. CRESSY

**Oxford Conference on Church, Community and State (1937).** A delegated gathering of world Christian groups which continued the work begun at the Universal Christian Conference on Life and Work held in Stockholm in 1925. Some 425 conference members were present from 40 countries. The Roman Catholic Church declined to participate; the German Evangelical Church, because of its situation under Nazi control, withdrew its initial acceptance. The theme of the conference was "the relation of the Church to the all-embracing claims of a communal life," in an age when the perennial problem of the relationship between church and state had reached a crisis. With the Faith and Order Conference (Edinburgh, 1937) the Oxford conference laid down guidelines for the future World Council of Churches. Many ecumenical leaders took an active part in the four-day proceedings, among them John Baillie, Reinhold Niebuhr, J. H. Oldham, Emil Brunner, T. S. Eliot, Hendrik Kraemer, V. S. Azariah, John A. Mackay, Henry P. Van Dusen, Cosmo Lang, and W. A. Visser't Hooft (who became the first general secretary of WCC). The conference report was published as *The Churches Survey Their Task* (1937), introduced by J. H. Oldham.

J. D. DOUGLAS

**Oxford Group**. *See* BUCHMAN, FRANK NATHAN DANIEL.

**Oxford Movement.** *See* ANGLO-CATHOLICISM.

# Pp

**Pacifism.** In Christian ethics a doctrinal and practical dedication to peace. Biblical pacifists support their position on scriptural grounds, while secular pacifists rely on moral and philosophical arguments. Because of the difficulty in interpreting biblical statements about war, the example of the early church has been extremely important in modern discussions on the subject among Christians. Most early church leaders advocated nonviolence, even in the face of bitter persecution. This changed, however, with the official toleration of Christianity in the Edict of Milan (313) and the partnership between church and state born in the reign of Constantine (312–37). From the early 4th century and through the medieval period, Christians followed the "just war" approach popularized by Augustine (354–430). Augustine's conception actually gave pacifistic motivation to taking up arms, since the goal of a just war was to institute justice and restore peace.

During the Reformation era Anabaptists returned to the strict pacifism of the early church, refusing to participate in the violent, coercive activities of the states. Their approach was passed on to such groups as the Mennonites. The Quakers of 17th-century England adopted a nonviolent lifestyle that they have maintained for over three centuries. At the end of the 20th century the leading contemporary institution through which they maintained their peace interest was the American Friends Service Committee. After World War II they joined in peace activities with individuals from other Protestant and Roman Catholic churches.

World wars and the technological developments culminating in the thermonuclear bomb led to increasing recognition of the pacifist position around the world. Pacifist groups were especially active and powerful between the wars (1919–39), as pacifism became linked with isolationism in the USA. Despite the unpopularity of their position during World War II, conscientious objectors were recognized by law in the USA and in England. Instead of facing imprisonment as was common during World War I, pacifists were allowed to do alternative service. Many pacifists worked in national parks, schools, and hospitals. However, many objected on principle even to conscription for nonviolent service and refused to participate.

The popularity of pacifism as a religious ideal or a life philosophy declined during World War II and the cold war, but in the USA the Vietnam conflict led to a resurgence. Churches that advocated the new pacifism were heavily influenced by those who advocated a total repudiation of war. A primary argument was that Augustine's just war had been rendered absurd by the potential for nuclear annihilation. Pacifism, therefore, appeared to be the most realistic theological position available to Christians. Ironically, at the same time pacifism was resurfacing in the church, a new theology justifying armed conflict also arose. This "theology of revolution" espoused by many liberation theologians supported guerrilla warfare and terrorism as a means to remedy political and social injustices. Borrowing from Marxist social analysis, these individuals believed revolution and war to be synonymous terms and that conflict to establish a classless society was the way to universal peace.

In response to liberation theology those who supported Western capitalism advocated limited wars, fought with conventional weapons, to counter terrorist activities. Some went so far as to accept limited use of nuclear weapons. These disagreements demonstrated that there was no consensus that pacifism was an inherent part of the Christian message. Even those who believed in nonviolence could not agree about how far the teaching should be extended. Should a person reject the use of violence in any situation, or is it enough to refuse to engage in the coercive activities of the state? Further debate among pacifists revolved around the question: What should be the attitude of a pacifist who is conscripted into the armed forces? Some were willing to engage in noncombatant duty for the military. Others would accept work of national importance under civilian direction. For still others, no form of service for the government would be ethically acceptable. Those with the last position preferred to accept any legal penalties in order to keep a peace witness.

*See also* PEACE MOVEMENTS.

*Bibliography.* M. E. Curti, *Peace or War: The American Struggle* (1936); G. F. Nuttall, *Christian Pacifism in History* (1958); R. H. Bainton, *Christian Attitudes Toward War and Peace: A Historical Survey and Critical Re-Evaluation* (1960); P. Ramsey, *War and Christian Conscience* (1961); R. G. Clouse, *War, Four Christian Views* (1981).

ROBERT G. CLOUSE

**Packer, James Innell** (1926– ). Anglican theologian. Born in Gloucestershire, England, he was educated at Oxford University (D. Phil., 1954), and after ordination in the Church of England he was senior tutor at Tyndale Hall, Bristol (1955–61), librarian (1961/62) and warden (1962–69) at Latimer House, Oxford, principal of Tyndale Hall, Bristol (1969–71), and associate principal, Trinity College, Bristol (1972–79). He then went to Canada where he was professor of historical and systematic theology, Regent College, Vancouver (1979– ). One of the foremost scholars in the evangelical field, he has written prolifically. Among his books are *"Fundamentalism" and the Word of God* (1958), *Evangelism and the Sovereignty of God* (1961), *Knowing God* (1973), *I Want to Be a Christian* (1977), *Beyond the Battle for the Bible* (1980), *Freedom and Authority* (1982), *Keep in Step with the Spirit* (1984), *Meeting God* (1986), *God in Our Midst* (1987), and *Hot Tub Religion* (1987).

**Paisley, Ian Richard Kyle** (1926– ). Irish preacher and politician. Born the son of a Baptist minister, he was educated at Reformed Presbyterian Theological Hall, Belfast. Ordained in 1946, he was appointed minister of Ravenhill Road Evangelical Hall. He founded the Free Presbyterian Church of Ulster in 1951, of which he has since been moderator of synod. He was active in politics as well as in church affairs. He was elected member of the Northern Ireland Stormont Parliament in 1969 (which later was suspended), the Westminster Parliament in 1974 as a Protestant Unionist, and the European Parliament. He founded and was a leader of the Democratic Unionist party. A colorful orator and preacher and powerful advocate of the Protestant cause in Northern Ireland, he was described as the "most able Irish politician in decades." In church matters he was a vigorous controversialist, fundamentalist, and antiecumenist in his policies, with a large popular following. His Free Presbyterian Church had approximately 50 congregations in the mid-1980s.

S. W. MURRAY

**Pakistan.** Populous southern Asian country with an area of 796,095 sq. km. (307,374 sq. mi.). In 1987, the population was estimated to be nearly 106.2 million. Formerly part of Great Britain's Indian Empire, its history was linked with that of India until it became a separate dominion in 1947. In 1956 a republic was proclaimed, consisting of West and East Pakistan, with more than 1000 miles of India dividing the two parts. East Pakistan announced its secession in 1971, and the "Democratic Government of Bangladesh" was proclaimed the following year. West Pakistan became simply Pakistan, and left the Commonwealth in protest against Great Britain's recognition of the new state.

Islam was the state religion of Pakistan from 1956. The country later provided the base for both the World Muslim Congress and the World Federation of Islamic Missions. Until the late 1980s the government was associated with the assiduous application of Islamic law, notably in the punishment meted out to offenders—sometimes so harsh that it provoked international protest. Even then, however, the acids of modernity were eating into traditionalist structures, and a growing secularism received new impetus with the change of government in 1988, when the advent of a woman prime minister raised new questions. Islam had previously known division, particularly in the expulsion of the Ahmadis in 1974, an allegedly heretical sect whose activities became known among Muslims in some British cities.

Only about 3.5 million inhabitants were non-Islamic in the mid-1980s. Of these, close to one-third were Hindus. The territory originally had a much higher Hindu population, but some 5.5 million left when India was partitioned in 1947. The majority of the remaining non-Muslims were Christians. It was estimated by at least one authority that the Christian population might double by the year 2000.

J. D. DOUGLAS

**Palau, Luis** (1934– ). Argentinian evangelist. Born in Buenos Aires, he became a Christian when a child, and at age 18 began preaching on weekends. By 1957 he helped to organize a tent evangelism and radio ministry. After further training in Bible studies at Portland, Oreg., he was an evangelist to Spanish-speaking people, later forming his own international team. Through evangelistic campaigns, Bible conferences, films, television, radio, and literature, the outreach has now extended to many millions of people all over the world. His published works include *The Schemer and the Dreamer* (1976), *The Moment to Shout* (1977), *Heart after God* (1978), *Scottish Fires of Revival* (with D. L. Jones) (1980), *Walk on Water, Pete* (1981), and the autobiographical *Luis Palau: Calling the Nations to Christ* (with D. L. Jones) (1983).

J. D. DOUGLAS

**Palestine Exploration Fund (PEF).** Organization formed on June 22, 1865, to procure and publish information about the geography, history, people, and climate of the Holy Land. The full title of the society is the Society for the Accurate and Systematic Investigation of the Archeology, the Topography, the Geology and Physical Geography, the Manners and Customs of the Holy Land for Biblical Illustration. PEF was a reinstitution of the Palestine Association, which had been formed in 1804. An executive committee comprising specialists in architecture, numismatics, epigraphy, archeology, philology, art, natural science, history, and even military tactics directed the society's work. Its most substantial support came through donations.

Some of the earliest and most important work done in the Holy Land was conducted by this society. The first expedition sent to Palestine (1865) was directed by Sir Charles Wilson and concentrated on Jerusalem's topography. Later expeditions in the 1870s under Sir Charles Warren, Captain Stewart, Captain Conder, and Captain Kitchener resulted in the publication of the *Survey of Western Palestine* (6 vols.). PEF sent Sir Flinders Petrie in 1890, and later F. J. Bliss and A. C. Dickie to excavate Tell Hesi in southern Palestine. This excavation inaugurated the scientific method of stratigraphical dating currently used in Middle Eastern archeology. PEF publishes the *Palestine Exploration Quarterly*.

JOHN MCRAY

**Palmer, Albert Wentworth** (1879–1954). Congregationalist pastor. He studied at the University of California and Yale Divinity School. He served pastorates at Plymouth Church, Oakland, Calif. (1907–17); Central Union Church, Honolulu, Hawaii (1917–24); and Oak Park, Ill. (1924–30). He was president of the Chicago Theological Seminary (1930–46), moderator of the Congregational Christian Churches of USA (1946–48), and lecturer in religion at University of Southern California (1949–51). He was a liberal in theology. His books include *The Drift toward Religion* (1914), *The Human Side of Hawaii* (1924), *The New Christian Epic* (1929), *Paths to the Presence of God* (1931), *Orientals in American Life* (1934), *The Minister's Job* (1937), *The Art of Conducting Public Worship* (1939), *Come, Let Us Worship* (1941), *Aids to Worship* (1944), *The Light of Faith* (1945), and *How Religion Helps* (1949).

**Panama.** Republic occupying the narrowest part of Central America with an area of 77,082 sq. km. (29,762 sq. mi.) and a population of 2.3 million (1988).

In the late 1980s about 85 percent of the population was Roman Catholic. Until independence in 1903, the Catholic Church in Panama was closely linked to the Colombian Church. Church-state relations were historically cordial and no serious restrictions have been placed on church activities. The 1946 constitution recognized Catholicism as the predominant religion and provided for religious instruction in the public schools. The Catholic educational system consisted of the Catholic University and more than 40 schools run by various religious orders. Seventy-five percent of the priests in Panama were foreigners.

During the late 1960s and early 1970s the archbishop of Panama, Marcos McGrath, supported the efforts of progressive clergy to organize agricultural cooperatives and Christian-based communities. Nevertheless, in 1971, this did not discourage the military from murdering a Colombian priest working in the rain forests of Veraguas. His attempts to organize a cooperative movement amongst the peasantry enraged local landlords and politicians, who in turn enlisted the support of the National Guard. The incident resulted in a souring of church-state relations, and for several months after the murder the archbishop refused to attend any government functions. Two-and-one-half years later, a Protestant missionary was killed in the same area.

Protestants account for 12 percent of the total population, and their numbers have been growing significantly in recent years. The largest Protestant church is the Foursquare Gospel, a pentecostal church which arrived in 1928. Traditional denominations were strongest among the English-speaking Creole population and in the Canal Zone.

In the 1980s both the rural sections of Panama and the government became more hostile to Christian activity. Drugs passing through the country from Colombia or grown in Panama comprised a major export. In 1983 General Manuel Antonio Noriega, a practitioner of Voodoo religious beliefs, was brought to power by the National Guard. Christians were among dissidents kidnapped and killed before a U.S. military invasion (1989) forced Noriega to flee. In the wake of such turmoil both Protestants and Roman Catholics were cooperating more closely as a Christian community.

PHILIP J. WILLIAMS

**Panikkar, Raimundo** (1918– ). Theologian and philosopher of intrareligious dialog. Born in Barcelona, Spain, to a Hindu father and a Spanish Catholic mother, Panikkar studied and lectured in Europe, India, and the Americas, thinking and writing in four or more languages a constant stream of articles and books on the dialog that had been part of his own family's life.

Professor of comparative philosophy and history of religions at the University of California, Santa Barbara, since 1971, Panikkar first came to the notice of the English-speaking world with *The Unknown Christ of Hinduism* (1964) and its claim that the good Hindu is saved by Christ through the sacraments of Hinduism. This seemed to follow the fulfillment theology of John N. Farqhar's *Crown of Hinduism* (1913) and fit in with Karl Rahner's concept of "anonymous Christian"; but in a second (1981) much revised and enlarged edition of *The Unknown Christ*, Panikkar acknowledged that his position had become much more radical and that he stood at the confluence of four rivers: the Hindu, Christian, Buddhist, and secular traditions. This movement of thought can be seen in intervening publications such as *The Trinity and the Religious Experience of Man* (1973), *The Intrareligious Dialogue* (1978), and *Myth, Faith, and Hermeneutics: Cross-Cultural Studies* (1979). Panikkar has also published *The Vedic Experience* (1977), an annotated anthology of the Vedas for modern man.

PHILIP HILLYER

**Pannenberg, Wolfhart** (1928– ). German theologian. Born in Stettin (now Szczecin), Poland, he studied at the universities of Berlin, Göttingen, and Basel, lectured at Heidelberg (1955–58), then was successively professor of systematic theology at Wuppertal (1958–61), Mainz (1961–68), and Munich (1968– ). Originally a student of philosophy, he came to Christian faith through rational reflection concerning the meaning of human existence and history. In *Revelation as History* (1960) he voiced a strong protest against irrationalism in theology. This book provides the key to much of his later development, for example, the "from-below" approach to Christology (*Jesus—God and Man*), the apologetic approach to Christian doctrine (*The Apostles' Creed*), the concern to lead theology out of its isolation to meet the substantial challenge of the sciences (*Theology and the Philosophy of Science*), and the eschatological orientation which earned him the description, "a mysterious figure in the background" of "The Theology of Hope" (*Theology and the Kingdom of God*). Contending that he is a Christian because he is a modern and rational man, he has set himself the courageous and controversial task of demonstrating the reasonableness of Christian faith in the modern world.

CHARLES M. CAMERON

**Papal Blessing.** The benediction given by the pope or his delegates. It usually confers upon those who receive it the privilege of a plenary indulgence. In specific circumstances, it is extended to the faithful the world over, *Urbi et Orbi*, namely, "to the City (Rome) and to the Universe." A papal blessing, to be administered by delegated power, may be obtained by private persons on special occasions. Canon law empowers any priest assisting a dying person to impart the papal blessing.

GEORGES A. BARROIS

**Papua New Guinea.** Independent country occupying islands north of Australia in the Pacific Ocean with an area of 462,840 sq. km. (178,704 sq. mi.) and a population of 3.9 million (1987). Papua New Guinea is a member of both the United Nations and the British Commonwealth of Nations. Prior to 1973, New Guinea was under UN trusteeship, with Australia as the responsible nation. Australia's involvement in Papua began in 1886, and in New Guinea after World War I.

Eighty percent of the population lived in rural areas where tribal loyalties remained strong, and warfare with substantial ritual magic occasionally flared up. Along with a national parliamentary government, 20 provincial assemblies were established after 1976, in an endeavor to deal effectively with regional problems. Individual religious rights were guaranteed by law, with the stipulation that religion did not infringe on other humanitarian principles.

The indigenous culture contained numerous religious beliefs and practices. Many were based on magic, the appeasing of spirits, and the observance of taboos. Ancestor spirits were extremely important, and local deities could be heroes of nonhuman origin or animal-like in form. All serious events were seen as having some religious connotation, and religion was but one aspect of the accepted overall cosmic order.

Whatever the inroads made by Christianity, many of the old beliefs remained into the 1990s. This was hardly surprising given the relatively late arrival of the first missionaries. Contact with material-rich Europeans and Americans, particularly during World War II, led to an upsurge of "cargo cults," with their eschatological expectations of bounty for all. Such cults appeared in many variations; one in 1964 sought to break away from Australia and the installation of the president of the USA as leader.

Notwithstanding the deep roots and continued influence of traditional beliefs, more than 90 percent of the population claims to belong to the Christian faith. Of these some 31 percent are Catholics, 28 percent are Lutherans, 14.5 percent belong to the United Church of Papua New Guinea and the Solomon Islands, 5 percent are Anglicans, and 3.5 percent are Seventh-day Adventists. Other smaller groups, including Baptists, Nazarenes, and pentecostals, make up the remainder.

Missionary work was pioneered by Catholics on Woodlark Island in 1847, but disease and native antagonism forced the abandonment of the venture in 1857. Better fortune attended the efforts of the predominantly Congregationalist London Missionary Society (LMS), which made use of Melanesian and Polynesian converts in the work which began in 1871. More than 120 LMS missionaries were killed in the first 40 years, but they persisted, with Port Moresby as the focus of their endeavors. Prominent early leaders were William Lawes (1839–1907) and James Chalmers (1841–1901). Equally precarious at first was the Methodist mission near Rabaul, which began in 1875. Again Polynesian converts, led by George Brown (1835–1917), were used, and there was never a shortage of volunteers despite the insecurity. Methodist work spread to Manus Island and Bougainville from these beginnings. In 1882 Catholic missionaries returned, using a base of New Britain, prior to beginnings also in Papua in 1885, under Louis-Andre Navarre (1836–1932).

German annexation of north-eastern New Guinea, New Britain, and New Ireland in 1884 opened the way for Lutheran missionaries in that region in 1886. The first of these was Johannes Flierl (1858–1947), who labored there until 1930. Australian and American Lutherans provided support for this work, which had its origin in several German mission societies. By 1890, with Australian Anglicans wishing to participate in missions in Papua, it was clear that some demarcation of areas was needed. A conference that year led to agreements among LMS, Anglicans, and Methodists. Methodists began work in 1891 from a base on Dobu Island, off the southeast tip of Papua. Anglicans began work at Dogura in the same year, also making use of Pacific Island converts under the leadership of men such as Copland King (d. 1918). Seventh-day Adventist missions began inland from Port Moresby in 1908 and spread to Bougainville in 1924. Again use was made of native converts as evangelists. Smaller mission groups, under the overall aegis of the Evangelical Alliance, began work after World War II.

By independence there were more mission hospitals than government, and by far most students attended church-related schools. In addition the mission-founded churches had a considerable stake in the national economy through plantations, industries, and services established to support evangelistic ventures. Clearly missionaries were owed much by modern Papua New Guinea, whatever stresses were placed on the culture by their presence and efforts.

While the comity of missions continued to a considerable degree in rural areas of the late 1980s, the mobility of the population, higher education, and the effect of national recruitment for the police, armed services, and the bureaucracy have meant that there is denominational pluralism in urban centers. The contemporary ecumenical spirit led to improved relations among most Christians and to the appearance in 1968 of the United Church of Papua New Guinea and the Solomon Islands (based in churches begun by Methodists and Congregationalists). Most or all leadership in major denominations was indigenous by late century, and churches were maturing and playing a constructive role in the young nation.

**Bibliography.** P. Biskup, et al., *A Short History of New Guinea* (1970); P. Ryan, ed. *Encyclopedia of Papua-New Guinea*, 3 vols. (1972); T. Ahrens and J. Knight, eds., *Christ in Melanesia: Exploring Theological Issues* (1977); N. C. Habel, ed., *Powers, Plumes and Piglets: Phenomena of Melanesian Religion* (1979); J. Garrett, *To Live among the Stars: Christian Origins in Oceania* (1982); J. Hinnells, ed., *A Handbook of Living Religions* (1985).

IAN GILLMAN

**Papyri, Biblical and Early Christian.** Texts on papyrus and other materials, in particular parchment, ostraca, and wooden tablets, especially those texts found mainly in the sands of Egypt, as distinct from "manuscripts" preserved through the medieval library tradition. The extensive discovery and publication of papyri since the late century have had a growing significance for the study and interpretation of early Christianity and its literature. New evidence for the biblical text emerged in unexpected quantity, and documents illuminated the philological and historical backgrounds of the Bible reflecting everyday life and language of that era. Tens of thousands of papyri were known by the late 1900s, and some 40,000 had been published.

Study of Hebrew (and Greek) was revolutionized by the discovery in 1947 and after of the Dead Sea Scrolls, more than 500 Hebrew, Aramaic, and Greek texts from various locations in the vicinity of Qumran, including OT texts of the 1st centuries B.C. and A.D. An early Hebrew papyrus in Cambridge (the Nash Papyrus, dated as early as the 2d cent. B.C.) contains the Ten Commandments. Some fragments of pre-Masoretic Text have appeared on Babylonian incantation bowls and elsewhere.

Greek papyri from Egypt particularly contributed to textual knowledge (including non-LXX and pre-Hexaplaric material). Christian scribes favored the codex form for biblical texts, and used conventional abbreviations of certain words which had particular theological importance. These *nomina sacra* include an abbreviation for the word for Lord (Gk. *kyrios*), where Jewish scribes had been accustomed to write the Tetragrammaton (YHWH in Hebrew characters). Words for God, Jesus, Christ, Son, and Spirit, as well as more ordinary words for father, mother, and man, were abbreviated whether the meaning was "sacred" or "profane." While the mounting number of published texts continued to add to the paleographical data, dates based on handwriting remained approximate and were regarded with caution.

A. Rahlfs's *Verzeichnis der griechischen Hand-schriften des Alten Testaments* (1914) listed 50 different papyri ranging in date from the 2d or 3d to the 7th centuries A.D. His numbering system was continued and most references, prefixed by MS, follow it. The system of van Haelst's *Catalogue*, which registers more than 300 OT papyri and altogether more than 1000 literary papyri, also became widely used. Most documents were very fragmentary, only half a dozen containing an extensive amount of text. Among these were a fairly complete 4th-century roll preserving Pss. 30–55 (MS 2013), edited by C. F. G. Heinrici in 1903, and a valuable codex of Genesis (the "Berlin Genesis," containing Gen. 1–35) from the 3d or 4th century A.D. (MS 911).

After 1914 many new documents came to light, some surpassing previously known papyri in significance. By late century all biblical books were represented. A codex of the Minor Prophets (MS "X"), purchased in Cairo in 1916 by Charles Freer, was published by H. A. Sanders and Carl Schmidt in 1927, together with the Berlin Genesis, which had appeared at Achmim in 1906. The Freer collection in Washington also included substantial codex survivals of Deuteronomy and Joshua (MS "W") and the Psalms (MS 1219), acquired by Freer at Gizeh in 1906.

The famous Beatty papyri in Dublin, edited in the main by F. G. Kenyon in the 1930s, were purchased by A. Chester Beatty in Egypt in 1931. The Beatty papyri include seven manuscripts of the OT, three of the NT, and one of portions of 1 Enoch (hitherto unknown in Greek ), a Christian homily (Melito, *On the Pasch*), and an "Apocryphon of Ezekiel." The Beatty papyrus of Ezekiel, Daniel, and Esther (MS 967) was supplemented by leaves from the same codex in Princeton, Cologne, Madrid, and Barcelona. Codices acquired by M. Bodmer of Geneva in 1955/56 includes, as well as Coptic OT texts, the earliest substantial codex of the Psalms in Greek (P. Bodmer XXIV), and Pss. 33 and 34 (P. Bodmer IX) as part of a codex of miscellaneous texts. A papyrus from Antinoopolis, now in Oxford (P. Ant. I 8 + III 210), provides an important witness for the Book of Proverbs, with Hebraizing features. Some texts in the versions of Aquila or Symmachus have appeared; remains of a parchment roll in Vienna (G 39777) have parts of Pss. 68 and 80 in the version of Symmachus or a related version. Some unusual formats and combinations occur, such as the remains of a papyrus roll with Exodus on the recto (front side) and the Revelation on the verso (reverse side) (*London, B.M. Pap. 2053*), and a fragment of a papyrus roll with Pss. 11–14 on the recto and part of Isocrates' *Ad demonicum* on the verso (*B.M. Pap. 230*).

Of interest because of their early date from the 2d and 1st centuries B.C. were papyri in roll form. One of these was in Manchester and others were in Cairo. The former, with portions of Deuteronomy (MS 957), was published by C. H. Roberts in 1936. The latter, originally thought to be from a single roll but later proven to be from three (available in a photographic edition by Z. Aly, 1980), included substantial portions of Deuteronomy (MS 848) and also small portions of Deuteronomy (MS 847) and Genesis (MS 942).

Coptic biblical texts began to appear in the 3d century and provide new textual information. Early examples were a bilingual codex in Hamburg (*Pap. bil. 1*) with Ecclesiastes in both Greek and Coptic as well as the Song of Songs and Lamentations in Coptic and an apocryphal work (the Acts of Paul) in Greek ; the Savery Codex (formerly *Mississippi Crosby Codex I*) containing Jonah and an excerpt from 2 Maccabees, 1 Peter, and Melito's *On the Pasch*; and a codex in London with Deuteronomy, Jonah, and Acts (edited by E. A. W. Budge in 1912). A resurgence in Coptic studies in the later 1900s followed the discovery in 1945 near Nag Hammadi in Upper Egypt of 13 codices containing gnostic material (over 40 works in Coptic, and some Greek fragments in the bindings). A concerted effort was underway in the 1980s to catalog all Coptic literary texts (*Corpus dei Manoscritti Copti Letterari*). The rescuing of Nubian monuments threatened by dam construction along the Nile River led to discovery of OT and theological texts in Old Nubian.

The most extensive NT documents are the Chester Beatty papyri ($\mathfrak{P}^{45}$: Gospels and Acts; $\mathfrak{P}^{46}$: Pauline Epistles; $\mathfrak{P}^{47}$: Revelation) and Bodmer papyri ($\mathfrak{P}^{66}$: John; $\mathfrak{P}^{74}$: Acts; $\mathfrak{P}^{75}$: Luke and John). An excellent facsimile and text edition of the Chester Beatty papyri was published by Frederic Kenyon. The Bodmer papyri, appearing from 1956, also were reproduced in excellent facsimiles. By the 1980s there were more than 200 known NT papyri. More than 90 documents in a "P list" (restricted to texts on papyrus specifically) ranged in date from the 2d to 8th centuries. While mostly fragments, they added considerably to textual knowledge. The Gospels, in particular those of Matthew and John, were best represented. An edition of NT papyri, with an interlinear text of the 26th Nestle-Aland ed. of the Greek NT was in progress in the 1980s (*Das Neue Testament auf Papyrus*).

The versions available by the 1990s included several texts in Coptic—Matthew in the Scheide collection (edited by H. M. Schenke, 1981), Acts in the Glazier collection of the J. Pierpont Morgan Library, New York (G 67), and Acts and 1 Peter in the London and Savery miscellaneous codices. The Scheide text of Matthew has at the close the *Greater Doxology* (*Gloria in excelsis*) in Greek and Coptic. Texts in Old Nubian were appearing or being revised. A parchment fragment with portions of Luke 23–24 in Latin and

Gothic was found at Antinoopolis (Vetus Latina 36).

Some amazing discoveries of early Christian literature were also made. A number of papyri of parts of *The Shepherd* by Hermas were found; especially noteworthy is the 3d-century Ann Arbor codex containing one-fourth of the Greek text (P. Mich. 129). Several papyri contained *On the Pasch* by Melito of Sardis, and fragments of some other works tentatively attributed to him. In 1941 were found at Toura, a village near Cairo, works of Didymus the Blind. These were collected at Cairo.

Very fragmentary material, including a wide range of apocryphal and patristic works, came to light. In 1935 Bell and Skeat published one of the earliest Christian papyri, 2d-century fragments of an "unknown gospel" having many parallels with the canonical Gospels, especially John. Some papyri published as "sayings" (*logia*) of Jesus were identified as from the Gospel of Thomas, a work found in Coptic among the Nag Hammadi codices. Other identified apocrypha include the Protevangelium of James, the Acts of John, the Acts of Paul (for which the Hamburg papyrus referred to above is one of the principal witnesses), the Abgar-Jesus letters, and the Apocalypse of Peter. Pseudepigraphical works include the Apocalypse of Elias (a fragment in Florence being the only Greek witness), the 11th Ode of Solomon, 4 Esdras (otherwise extant only in Latin), and 1 Enoch (preserved complete only in Ethiopic). Gnostic works in Greek include the Gospel of Mary and the Sophia of Jesus Christ. Patristic authors represented include Ignatius, Aristides, Irenaeus, Hippolytus, Origen, Eusebius, Basil of Caesarea, Cyril of Alexandria, and Gregory of Nazianzus. There is a fragment of the Epistle of Barnabas, and from Dura on the Euphrates a fragment of the *Diatessaron* of Tatian. Among the hagiographa are two papyri of the *Acts of Phileas*. There are unidentified literary tests, liturgical pieces, prayers, hymns, creeds, amulets, and the like, a large number of which are Coptic. Many contain biblical quotations and allusions, as do many private letters. Official documents referring to Christians begin to appear from around the middle of the 3d century. By the 1980s more than 40 certificates of sacrifice (*libelli*) had been found from the Decian persecution (not specifically referring to Christians). Texts relating to the persecution of Christians in the late 3d and early 4th centuries give way to documents from the early 4th century onward which attest to the increasing Christianization of Egyptian society.

*See also* ARCHEOLOGY, BIBLICAL; DEAD SEA SCROLLS.

**Bibliography.** K. Aland, *Kurzgefasste Liste der griechischen Handschriften des Neuen Testaments* (1963); S. Jellicoe, *The Septuagint and Modern Study* (1968); B. M. Metzger, *The Text of the NT: Its Transmission, Corruption, and Restoration* (2d ed. 1968); M. Naldini, *Il Cristianesimo in Egitto. Lettere private nei papiri dei secoli III–V* (1968); K. Treu, *Archiv Für Papyrusforschung* 19 (1969); Enchoria (from 1971); F. G. Kenyon, *The Text of the Greek Bible* (3d rev. ed., 1975); K. Aland, ed., *Repertorium der griechischen christlichen Papyri*, vol. 1, *Biblische Papyri. Altes Testament, Neues Testament, Varia, Apokryphen* (1976); J. van Haelst, *Catalogue des papyrus littéraires juifs et chrétiens* (1976); B. M. Metzger, *The Early Versions of the NT: Their Origin, Transmission, and Limitations* (1977); C. H. Roberts, *Manuscript, Society and Belief in Early Christian Egypt* (1979); E. G. Turner, *Greek Papyri: An Introduction* (rev. ed., 1980); B. M. Metzger, *Manuscripts of the Greek Bible: An Introduction to Greek Palaeography* (1981); T. Orlandi, *Coptic Bibliography* (from 1982); W. Grunewald and K. Junack, *Das Neue Testament auf Papyrus*, vol. 1, *Die Katholischen Briefe* (1986); K. and B. Aland, *The Text of the NT* (1987); Discoveries in the Judaean Desert (from 1955).

STUART PICKERING

## Parables of Jesus Christ. *Parables and Gospel.*

The most important 20th-century advance made in the study of the parables is the growing realization that they must not be interpreted by themselves but rather as part of the gospel. However, according to their different views of the nature of the gospel, the scholars who adopt the above principle are far from agreement in their interpretations. Some arrange the parables according to the chronology of the Gospels and notice in them a progression from the elements of faith to its deepest mysteries. The form-critics (such as Rudolf Bultmann) and scholars indebted to them (A. T. Cadoux, B. T. D. Smith, Charles W. F. Smith, and W. H. Robinson) found in the parables both specimens of the method of Jesus' public teaching and of the problems confronting the primitive church. To others the parables are primarily a crystallized expression of the message Jesus brought (G. A. Buttrick, James Stirling, Emil Brunner, C. H. Dodd, and Henry T. Sell). Weinel and Koch find them invaluable as a mirror of the inner life of Jesus. Few are those who, like Brémond, see clearly that in the parables is a reflection of the messianic self-consciousness of Jesus and that in not a few of them he is speaking of his redemptive work.

*Purpose.* Much light has been thrown upon the parables by a careful study of their Hebrew-Jewish antecedents. Hence it appears that some of them, just like the parables of the rabbis, are "example stories," that is, they serve to illustrate certain difficult truths (such as The Good Samaritan, The Pharisee and the Publican, The Friend at Midnight, and The Hungry Children). But, as Albertz, Robinson, Cadoux, and others have pointed out, the parabolic form is also meant to hide something from the audience, just like the Hebrew *māshāl*. In some parables this is for polemical reasons. The story will carry the unsuspecting listeners away with it only to turn eventually against them (such as The Wicked Husbandmen). In the reference to Isa. 6:9–10 in Mark 4:11–12, the deceptiveness and ambiguity of the parabolic language, although not intended to exclude people from the saving truth, are shown, nevertheless, to bar them from any self-chosen way to the coming kingdom. Those only who follow Jesus will have in him the clue to the true application.

**Parable and Allegory.** So understood, the parables of Jesus (not the example stories) contain an allegorical element. Like the Jewish and the OT parables, those of Jesus are not specimens of a "natural theology" intended to teach people to find God in this world. Rather they are means of intimating a truth known to the narrator alone. Just as the rabbis, Jesus did not hesitate to introduce "unnatural" features whenever his message demanded such an emphasis (e.g., the hundredfold yield). Recognizing the presence of allegorical features is not tantamount to justifying allegorical interpretation which takes up each feature of the story without regard for the rest. A correct interpretation of the parables must find the point of comparison in the story as a whole, for each parable is designed to make only one point. Details of the story must be interpreted, however, in the light of the contribution they make to the plot of the story.

**Eschatology.** Seen in the context of the life-work and teaching of Jesus, the parables necessarily imply eschatological references. C. H. Dodd and his followers, while taking these eschatological references seriously, interpret them as "realized eschatology." Their view is based upon a most questionable textual and literary criticism. It would seem more appropriate to let the texts speak for themselves. Many of the parables are ways by which Jesus hinted at the revolutionary changes his coming would bring about in the history of Israel and mankind.

**Genuineness.** Following the general trend of NT criticism, most or all of the parables are often considered to be the work of the primitive church. Yet 20th-century scholarship has pointed out the typically Aramaic form of these narratives and their Palestinian background, which would make it impossible to ascribe them to any but the earliest period of the primitive church. There is nothing comparable in the whole post-Gospel literature. These considerations make it advisable, if not imperative, to regard Jesus as the author of all of them. Form criticism has stimulated a search for the "setting" of the parables for purposes of better understanding. But since many of them have been preserved without indication of their occasion, and the historical material in the Gospels is far from giving us a detailed and chronologically reliable picture of the frame of the life of Jesus, the settings suggested are in most instances purely gratuitous. This kind of research has shown, however, the importance of interpreting the parables against the background of the claims and hopes, prejudices and false beliefs of Jesus' contemporaries.

*See also* JESUS AS A TEACHER.

**Bibliography.** H. B. Swete, *The Parables of the Kingdom* (1920); A. Feldman, *The Parables and Similes of the Rabbis* (1924); G. A. Buttrick, *The Parables of Jesus* (1928); A. T. Cadoux, *The Parables of Jesus* (1931); C. H. Dodd, *The Parables of the Kingdom* (1935); W. O. E. Oesterley, *The Gospel Parables in the Light of Their Jewish Background* (1936); O. C. Quick, *The Realism of Christ's Parables* (1937); A. E. Barnett, *Understanding the Parables of Our Lord* (1940); O. A. Piper, *Evangelical Quarterly* 14 (1942): 42–53; J. Jeremias, *The Parables of Jesus* (ET, 1955); R. S. Wallace, *Many Things in Parables: Expository Studies* (1955); A. M. Hunter, *The Parables of Jesus* (1971); J. D. Crossan, *In Parables: The Challenge of the Historical Jesus* (1973); N. Perrin, *Jesus and the Language of the Kingdom* (1976); K. E. Bailey, *Poet and Peasant: A Literary Cultural Approach to the Parables in Luke* (1976); *Through Peasant Eyes: More Lucan Parables* (1980).

OTTO A. PIPER

**Paraguay.** Small South American republic with an area of 406,752 sq. km. (157,048 sq. mi.). By 1990 the population—95 percent Mestizo—of this land-locked South American republic was estimated to exceed 4.2 million. The Paraguay River naturally divides the fertile eastern region where most lived from the dry savannah of the western Chaco Boreal where cotton and cattle were the main commodities.

Through the 1900s Paraguay did not live up to its potential. When the Jesuits arrived in 1609 they devised a reduction system for evangelizing the Guaranis (settled farmers speaking a common language) while teaching them property use and regulating community life. Before their expulsion from Latin America in 1768 the Jesuits established 50 flourishing communes of as many as 4000 Guarani. Although a theological debate raged in Spain over whether "Indians" had souls, it was the colonial merchant class who felt threatened by an educated and organized tribal populace and machinated to destroy the communes and banish the Jesuits. Most of the Jesuit missionaries died in military clashes, on prison ships, or in Iberian dungeons. One vestige of this political experiment to empower a native tribe lingered in the universal use of the Guarani language—the only indigenous tongue in Latin America granted official and recognized status and used by 90 percent of the people.

Independence from Spanish colonial rule was achieved in 1811 but, as in the rest of the continent, this meant trading one overlord for another. In modern times, as a result of the fascist rule of General Alfredo Stroessner from 1954 one million Paraguayans emigrated with no plans to return. Haven was sought in Paraguay by fleeing Nazis, and later by Anastasio Somoza, Nicaragua's defeated dictator, whose life as a hotelier was cut short by assassination in 1980.

The impoverished industrial base was offset by goods from around the world brought up the Paraguay River to the port at Ascunción for resale to Brazilians and Argentines who flocked to towns along their common borders to buy "tax-free" merchandise.

Roman Catholics, 91.9 percent of the populace in the 1980s, were distributed among 282 parishes in one archdiocese and eight dioceses ministered by an archbishop, 15 bishops, 536 priests, 997 nuns, 103 brothers, one pontifical university, and 249 seminarians (1983). The 107,000 Protestants account for 2.5 percent of the population and were divided among 46 denominations (1987).

FAITH ANNETTE SAND

**Parapsychology.** Study of paranormal psychological phenomena (e.g., telepathy, clairvoyance, psychokinesis). Early psychical research by Sir Oliver Lodge (1885) suggested that the best way of confirming extrasensory perception (ESP) was by means of quantitative experiments such as card guessing, since the number of hits to be expected by chance could be determined statistically. Unfortunately such experiments, whatever their value as evidence, were extremely boring to carry out and comparatively tiresome even to read about. Early in the 20th century in Great Britain, Lodge and Gilbert Murray conducted experiments involving the reproduction of drawings and the guessing of subjects about who other than the percipient had written and spoken. These experiments seemed strongly to suggest the occurrence of telepathy (direct contact between mind and mind) or clairvoyance (knowledge of events where the normal conditions of knowledge do not obtain). In 1921 a group of psychologists in Holland carried out tests involving the correlation of letters with numbers by a young dentist, where meticulous precautions were taken to avoid the providing of sensory clues; in 187 tests the dentist succeeded 60 times, although by chance the number should have been about 3.9. In a series of experiments in 1928, it was found that the proportion of hits tended to decline as time went on; this curious phenomenon has been noted in subsequent card-guessing experiments. After tests conducted by the universities of London and Columbia and by the Society for Psychical Research all showed negative results, a new era in the subject was inaugurated in 1934 with the publication of *Extra-Sensory Perception* by J. B. Rhine, a psychologist working at Duke University in North Carolina. Rhine used a special pack of 25 cards with five patterns only, which had the dual advantage of making chance easier to assess and facing the percipient with a much simpler task. In preliminary mass experiments with university students the results were well above statistical chance, and some percipients stood notably above the rest. With one percipient, the odds against chance were of the order of $10^{20}$ to 1. It has been hazarded that these successes may have been due partly to Rhine's enthusiastic personality, and contrariwise that the falling-off effect, which occasionally descends to levels significantly *below* chance, were due to increasing boredom. In response to criticism of Rhine's work subsequent experiments were tightened, and participants were meticulously watched for any evidence of conscious or unconscious fraud. Rhine's mathematics were corroborated by the American Institute of Mathematical Statistics. In Great Britain S. B. Soal, after initial work with a medium, carried out apparently unsuccessful investigations with cards from 1934 to 1939. Following suggestions by Whately Carrington, who had noted similar effects in the guessing of drawings, Soal found that two of his subjects achieved high scores on either the card immediately *after* or the cards immediately *before* and *after* the target card. Work in parapsychology was also done in the USSR. L. L. Vasiliev discovered evidence that some subjects can be successfully "willed" by others to go to sleep, when these subjects have no normal means of knowing that this is being done to them at the time. Distance and the interposition of screens appeared to make no appreciable difference, and this discovery was judged to have some strategic importance.

*Bibliography.* R. Heywood, *The Sixth Sense* (1966); S. Ostrander and L. Schroeder, *Psychic Discoveries behind the Iron Curtain* (1971).

HUGO A. MEYNELL

**Pascendi Dominici Gregis.** Encyclical of Pope Pius X condemning modernism, issued on September 8, 1907, shortly after the decree *Lamentabili sane exitu.* The encyclical used officially the term "modernism" for the first time in Roman Catholic debate. Although modernists never intended to build a complete system of doctrine, the pope denounces agnosticism and immanentism as the two basic errors of their philosophy, leading to subjectivism and dogmatic relativism in theology and to an evolutionistic interpretation of history and Scripture, excluding supernatural elements. The pope endeavored to refute the agnosticism of the modernists by reference to the teaching of Vatican Council I on the knowledge of God and the objective value of the motives of credibility. He denounced the doctrine of vital immanence as implying pantheism. The immediate cause of modernism was, according to the pope, a perversion of the mind, with roots in curiosity and pride, rejecting scholastic philosophy, patristic tradition, and the official doctrine of the church. Bishops and other ordinaries were ordered to control the teaching of instructors in Catholic universities and seminaries, as well as the publication of books and periodicals and public addresses by Catholic priests.

*Bibliography.* American Catholic Quarterly Review 32 (1907): 705–30.

GEORGES A. BARROIS

**Passion.** In the English Bible the term used in Acts 1:3 of Jesus' last days on earth, particularly of Gethsemane and Calvary. The synoptic Gospels show a remarkable similarity of wording in telling how Jesus told his disciples about the sequence of events: "The Son of man must suffer many things, and be rejected by the elders and the chief priests and the scribes, and be killed" (Matt. 16:21; Mark 8:31; Luke 9:22). This suffering of many things, this passion, as all three writers add, led to resurrection and to entry into glory (Luke 24:26). Jesus' suffering was a necessary part of the Father's great plan (Luke 24:46; Acts 17:3) and was the fulfillment of prophecy. It also symbolized the obedience and the humility of the Son of God in coming to save a fallen world.

**Passion Sunday.** The fifth Sunday in Lent. In Roman Catholic churches, crosses are covered with a violet veil until the solemn unveiling of the altar cross on Good Friday. This observance commemorates the period during which Christ no longer walked openly among the people, but hid himself (John 11:54).

GEORGES A. BARROIS

**Pastoral Theology.** The theology of the practice of ministry. As contrasted with systematic theology, pastoral theology is concerned less with the structure of dogmatics and more with the application of theology to the experience of persons. In a sense, while systematic theology can be thought of as deductive in that it reasons downward from doctrinal beliefs about God to human experience, pastoral theology is inductive in that it reasons upward from human experiences to their theological implications. Although such a distinction is not entirely appropriate, it is true that pastoral theology can be thought of as practical, as opposed to theoretical.

Pastoral theology is concerned with two aspects of pastoral or pragmatic ministry: the theological meaning of life-events and the appropriate method by which Christian pastors should function in the practice of ministry. Although much of ministry throughout the ages has been concerned with the proclamative or prophetic function, pastoral care of persons has been a part of the Judeo-Christian tradition since the time of Cain and Abel. Care giving is a distinctive characteristic of NT faith where the writer of Galatians encourages Christians to "bear one another's burdens and thus fulfill the law of Christ" (Gal. 6:2). The meaning and method of such care giving provide the core of pastoral theology. Traditionally this has meant a combining of the prophetic and the priestly roles of ministry. As priests ministers have attempted to salve or heal the wounds and vicissitudes of life through prayer, sacraments, and presence. As prophets ministers have attempted to inspire and encourage persons to interpret these experiences religiously and to live in godly ways.

There are four classical traditions in pastoral theology: Roman Catholic, Lutheran, Anglican, and Reformed. The Catholic tradition began as early as the 2d century A.D. It perceived the problem of life as sin and recommended penance followed by acts of satisfaction as the solution. Yearly confession was mandated by the 13th century, and a whole system for cataloging sins and prescribed penalties leading to absolution was established by the 16th century. "Casuistry" was the term applied to this system for the care of souls. The goal of Catholic pastoral theology was to save souls and prepare them for heaven.

Although the Reformers rejected much of the mechanics of this model, they, too, designed methods for attending to the problem of sin. Luther became more concerned with the overall condition of faithlessness than with the enumeration of sins. Pride, self-righteousness, lack of trust, and anxiety were his concerns. The Lutheran approach induced feelings of despair and repentance. This was followed by encouragements to have faith.

Pastoral theology in Anglicanism was less interested in sinful feelings (as in Lutheranism) or specific sins (as in Catholicism). Anglicans emphasized the possibility of Christian growth based on the prevenient grace of God in salvation. Sin was conceived to be disorder—inward, interpersonal, and social. The pastoral task was to restore order and to guide parishioners in more holy living. There was little emphasis on private or public confession, and more emphasis on the pastor's role in the social order. Presence was emphasized over method.

The Reformed tradition perceived disobedience or idolatry as the core meaning of sin. Recommendations to pastors from this point of view included means for analyzing feelings and discerning hidden motives. This approach resembled Lutheranism more than Anglicanism. Stressing predestination, Reformed Christians desired concrete assurance that they were foreordained to salvation. Much of this form of pastoral theology was concerned with procedures to help people determine the true state of their souls and to achieve evidence of their security.

These four traditions continue to inform pastoral theology. The implicit pastoral theology of the social gospel movement, liberal Christianity, and avant-garde Catholicism follow the Anglican concern for "presence." Fundamentalist and charismatic/pentecostal pastoral theologies owe their essence to the Reformed and Anglican emphases on growth and assurance. Sacramental Catholicism also owes a debt to this tradition.

By far the dominant approach in contemporary pastoral theology was inspired by the Lutheran emphasis on reflective self-examination of experience. This has been the essence of the pastoral counseling movement. Procedures for understanding and accepting human frailty have been thoroughly developed alongside efforts to understand and communicate that experience in theological terms. At times these efforts have led to an overemphasis on contemporary psychotherapeutic methods for self-understanding without appropriate theological underpinnings.

Correctives to this overemphasis on client-centered therapy and psychoanalysis have become focal in contemporary pastoral theology. Paul Tillich (1952) and Daniel Day Williams (1961) represent the viewpoint that beneath all human experience are attempts to handle basic anxiety which can only be assuaged by faith. Thus it is the task of the pastor to communicate both understanding of the human situation as well as the answers of faith. This is "correlational" pastoral theology.

Another corrective to this secular psychotherapy overemphasis has been attempts by such persons as Seward Hiltner (1958) and Thomas Oden (1983) to reclaim the uniqueness of the pastoral role. Hiltner's emphasis on "shepherding" as the role which provides the umbrella for whatever the pastor does—be it preaching, visiting, administering, or counseling—is an example. This distinguishes the pastor from a counselor and captures the broad meaning of the priestly role. Oden combines the importance of Scripture and church tradition with reason and experience to determine the substance and technique for pastoral theology. Thus, the balance between meaning and method is preserved.

*Bibliography.* J. T. McNeil, *A History of the Cure of Souls* (1951); S. Hiltner, *Preface to Pastoral Theology* (1958); D. D. Williams, *The Minister and the Care of Souls* (1961); W. B. Oglesby, Jr., ed., *The New Shape of Pastoral Theology: Essays in Honor of Seward Hiltner* (1969); J. D. Whitehead and E. E. Whitehead, *Method in Ministry: Theological Reflection and Christian Ministry* (1980); E. B. Holifield, *A History of Pastoral Care in America* (1983); T. C. Oden, *Pastoral Theology: Essentials of Ministry* (1983).

H. Newton Malony

**Paton, William** (1886–1943). Missionary organizer, ecumenist, and writer. Born in England of Scottish parents, he was educated at Oxford and studied for the ministry at the Presbyterian Church of England's Westminster College, Cambridge. He was a member of the Student Christian Movement staff (1911–21), but his pacifist views and membership in the newly founded Fellowship of Reconciliation caused problems during World War I. In 1917 he was ordained ("to avoid conscription," says his biographer) and sent to India, where he was an evangelist and a YMCA-related worker among British troops; here "political realism" began to modify his pacifist stance. He was secretary of the National Christian Council of India, Burma, and Ceylon (1922–27),

then returned to Britain as joint secretary of the International Missionary Council and editor of the *International Review of Missions,* continuing both until his death. He was responsible for the organization of two major ecumenical gatherings: at Jerusalem (1928) and at Tambaram (1938). He edited the eight official volumes from the first, and seven from the second. Paton was a tireless champion of missions orphaned by war, an undertaking fraught with pitfalls and beset by misunderstandings. Writer of numerous articles and pamphlets, he also published a number of books, among them *Jesus Christ and the World's Religions* (1916; rev. 1927), *A Faith for the World* (1928), *World Community* (1938), *The Message of the World-Wide Church* (1939), *The Church and the New Order* (1941), and *The Ecumenical Church and World Order* (1942).

J. D. Douglas

**Patristics, 20th-Century Trends in.** Patristic study has traditionally involved the collection and correlation into critical editions of the writings of the church fathers. This type of work began with the Benedictines of St. Maury's in the 17th century. Nineteenth-century scholars responded to an even greater academic need for better critical and historical studies by producing invaluable collections that remained basic to much later study. These include J. P. Migne, *Patrologias curus completus,* Latin and Greek series; Adolf von Harnack, *Geschichte der altchristlichen Literatur bis auf Eusebius;* Johann von Otto, *Corpus apologetorum christianorum saeculi secundi;* Johann A. Möhler, *Patrologie oder christliche Literärgeschichte* (PL); Joseph B. Lightfoot, *The Apostolic Fathers;* Franz X. Funk, *Patres Apostolici;* the *Corpus scriptorum ecclesiasticorum latinorum* (the Vienne corpus of Latin fathers, since 1866), and *Die griechischen christlichen Schriftsteller der ersten drei Jahrhunderte* (the Berlin corpus of Greek fathers, since 1897).

Twentieth-century scholars were faced with the task of revising and reediting these collections. New evidence spread light on disputed authorship and the authenticity of texts. However, two World Wars disrupted all academic endeavors and the loss of books, existing research, and manuscripts in Europe, where much of this type of research was being done, was great. Also, many of these changes affected the Migne series, and the very size of the task was discouraging. Yet, a project was undertaken by Adalbert Hamman in 1956 to supplement the PL (Latin Fathers) series. Hamman corrected attributions of authorship, regrouped certain works, furnished the latest critical works of disputed writings, and added forgotten and newly discovered works. The fifth and final volume of *Patrologia Latina: Supplementum* appeared in 1971 with 17 fascicles. Patrology manuals were among the first materials to be revised or newly written in the 1950s: B. Altaner, *Patrologie: Leben, schriften und Lehre der Kirchenväter* (2d ed. 1950); J. Quasten, *Patrologie*, 3 vols. (1953); F. L. Cross, *The Early Christian Fathers* (1960); H. von Campenhausen, *Die griechischen Kirchenväter* (1956); and *Lateinische Kirchenväter* (1959). In 1951 the first International Patristic Conference met at Oxford, marking a renewed interest in patristic studies. The conference, which has been convened every four years, began publishing its proceedings after the 1955 conference; the *Studia Patristica* appears in the *Texte und Unterlichen Literatur* series.

The turn of the century also saw attention to Eastern church writings. The *Corpus scriptorum christianorum orientalism* was established as a critical edition series in 1903. The CSCO series comprises four series: Syriac, Coptic, Arabic, and Ethiopic. As of 1984 there were 465 fascicles in the collection. A number of translations and studies of oriental texts were being prepared in the 1980s. This was related to the increased awareness of NT scholars of versions of the early church Greek Bible. The Greek church fathers enjoyed the fullest attention of 20th-century patristic scholars. Study of the Greek fathers was seen to be essential to adequately understanding church history and the development of early church doctrine. However, their contribution has been overshadowed by a Western academic and theological romance with Rome and the Latin church. Although Migne did produce a large collection of Greek writings, and the Berlin corpus continued to update and publish new critical editions of individual works, no new series was begun until 1977. This was 24 years after its Latin counterpart was first published.

The *Corpus Christorum, Series graeca* was a welcome addition for many scholars and students of the ancient Greek church. This new attention is the result of research into the Greek Bible by NT scholars. Church historians regarded the early Christian dialog with the Greco-Roman world instead of as a separate entity from it. The major discovery of the 20th century that encouraged this thinking was the uncovering of the gnostic library at Nag Hammadi. These new texts gave the other side of the "orthodoxy" versus "heresy" debate of the early church. The Nag Hammadi texts shed new light on the philosophy and theology that early church fathers were protesting against, and filled in some of the dark corners of 2d-century Christianity. Church historians, with the aid of sociologists, anthropologists, and philologists, shifted their focus to the vast array of events and arguments of history rather than the ecclesia itself. The result has been the founding of a number of valuable research projects and study centers. The most important of these is the Le centre d'analyse et de documentation patristique de l'université des sciences humines de Strasbourg (est. 1967). The center organized a card index of all biblical citations and allusions in both Greek and Latin patristic literature. The project has already published two volumes of the *Biblica Patristica* (1975, 1982). Two related projects in France were the *L'inventoire générale des citations patristiques de la bible grecque* and the *Novi testamenti graeci editio maior critica*. Researchers from both of these projects collaborated in order to speed the work. The goal of the joint project was to cite all patristic passages that stemmed directly from biblical passages. The provisional lists were completed in 1973 and amounted to 432 authors and anonymous works; in 1975 the citations reached 300,000.

While the task regarding the Greek works was completed by 1980, studies of the Latin and oriental texts continued. Interest in the Greek church continued to grow. The American Institute for Patristic and Byzantine Studies was established in 1981 to increase knowledge of Byzantine authors. The Patriarchal Institute for Patristic Studies was founded at the Vlatadon Monastery in Thessalonica, Greece, to enhance theological research in patristic literature, and to take scholarly advantage of the rich ecclesiastical history of Mount Athos. The institute concentrated on the anthropology of the Cappadocian fathers, Christian hymnography, Eastern and Western church relations, 14th-century Thessalonican authors, and the theological literature after the fall of Constantinople. The institute has produced the journal *Kleronomia*, the monograph series *Analecta Vlatadon*, and a three-volume study, *Byzantine Hymnography*, edited by K. Mitsakis. The Mount Athos projects include the reproduction of manuscripts onto microfilm, the photographing of examples of Byzantine art on illuminated slides, the photographing of buildings, frescoes, icons, liturgical instruments, and documents, and the cataloging of all manuscripts at Athos. A 12-volume collection of Greek hymnography, *Analecta Hymnica Graeca*, was compiled and published from 1966 to 1980.

Nag Hammadi gnostic texts, written in Coptic, also gave birth to a new specialized field of research. The collection was published by E. J. Brill in three parts; the first was an eight-volume photographic facsimile series; the second was an English translation undertaken by the Institute of Antiquity and Christianity at Claremont Graduate School, California; and the third was a monograph series, the *Nag Hammadi Library* (1971). E. A. W. Budge edited the *Coptic Texts* in five volumes (repr., 1977). The most popular English edition appears to be by James E. Robinson, ed., *The Nag Hammadi Library in English* (1977).

Despite interest in the Greek and oriental materials, a strong need was felt for a more complete and updated critical Latin series. Such a series was undertaken by the *Corpus Christorum,*

*Series Latina,* inaugurated in 1953 with two volumes of Tertullian. The series was originally intended to be 175 volumes, but additional and longer studies, designated by a volume plus lettering system, have expanded it to more than 200 volumes. Latin church interest has centered around Augustine. Publications and institutes include: the Institut Patristico 'Augustinianum' (Rome); L'institut des études augustiniennes's Revue des études augustiniennes, Series recherches augustiniennes, Oeuveres de saint Augustin; the Augustinian Institute's *Augustinian Studies* (1970); the *St. Augustine Lecture Series; Augustiniana* (from 1951); *Augustinianum* (from 1961); and the Augustininus-Institut der Deutschen Augustiner's *Augustinus-Begriffslexikon.*

Because patristic study is international in scope a number of critical editions with translations have been published. The most notable of these critical translations is the French series *Sources chrétiennes* begun by Henri de Lubac and Jean Daniélou in 1941; in 1986 the series had 245 volumes. German studies include the *Studia patristica et liturgica* (1967); the *Beiheft zu den Studia patristica et liturgica* (1980); and the *Veröffentlichungen des Grabmann-institutes* (a medieval text study). Translations into Italian, Spanish, and Polish have been enhanced by specific projects from those countries. In 1972 the *Italian Patristic Publications and Projects* was established to concentrate on the Italian contribution. The *Quanderni di Vetera Christianorum* was one such project that emerged. This was a study in patristic rhetoric, exegesis, and biblical pattern. The Italian publication team for the *Corona patrum salesiana* announced in 1972 that they would update the series with critical texts and change the series name to *Corona Patrum.* A Spanish translation series, the *Scrinium patristicum lateranense,* appeared from 1964. *Avgvstnvs* (since 1956) was a Madrid theological journal dedicated to the study of St. Augustine and the Augustinian religious order. The *Bibliographie Patristique Polonaise* recorded all Polish research connected with Christian antiquity through the 8th century. The *Traditio Christiano* was introduced as a new collection of patristic texts simultaneously translated into French, German, and Italian; each volume was devoted to a specific theme of Christian faith.

The first English translations were British. These translations consisted of selections from the early church fathers and appeared in two major series: the *Ante-Nicene Fathers* (edited by A. Roberts and J. Donaldson, 1886–97) and *Nicene and Post-Nicene Fathers* (NPNF, edited by P. Schaff, 1886–1900). NPNF concentrates mainly on Augustine and Chrysostom. The earlier English translations in the *Library of the Fathers* (1838–88) was a 45-volume set edited by Pusey, Keble, and Newman. Unfortunately this edition was marred by the Anglo-Catholic tensions of Victorian England. The first American translations did not appear until after World War II; they included the *Ancient Christian Writers* series, first edited by J. Quasten and Plumbe in 1946. The series continued yearly to publish translations of major works. The *Fathers of the Church* appeared in 1947 and had published 75 volumes by 1984. The *Patristic Monograph Series* was first published by the Philadelphia Patristic Foundation in 1975. Students were given the opportunity to publish their dissertations by the Catholic University of America; *Patristic Studies* was comprised of doctoral dissertations that included text translations and commentary. *Studies in Christian Antiquity* (edited by Quasten) included dissertations which interpret single patristic texts. The *North American Patristic Society* was founded in 1970, and included scholars, students, and interested persons from the USA and Canada. The *Canadian Society of Patristic Studies/Association canadienne des études patristiques* was founded in 1975. Both societies were established to increase awareness of patristic studies and to encourage research in the field.

More specific European-orientated projects include those at the *Patristische Kommission der westdeutschen Akademien* which operated out of Göttingen, Heidelberg, Mainz, and Munich. Each center had a particular project but the general aim was to study Slavic ecclesiastical literature. The project concentrated on the Athanasian and pseudo-Athanasian writings, especially the Arian discourses, the Palestinian Psalm catenae, Didymus, the Syriac Pseudo-Dionysius, John Damascene's *Expositio fidei,* the corpus of Christian papyri, the *Bibliographia patristica,* and the works of Gregory of Nyssa. The *Corpus Troporum* project, an ancient Christian music project sponsored by the Swedish Council for Research in the Faculty of Arts, collected a variety of tropes from the first two centuries A.D. Studies in Christian Greek and Latin philology also increased in importance. A special philology section was established in the classics department at the Catholic University of Nijmegen, Holland. The university has published a number of studies, most of them dissertations, under three special categories; *Latinitas Christianorum primaeva* first appeared in 1932; *Graecitas Christianorum primaeva* issued its first publications in 1962; and *Graecitas et latinitas christianorum primaeva: Supplementa* (from 1964) published shorter studies that exceeded journal length.

One important addition to church history, NT, and patristic studies was in women's studies. From the late 1960s North American researchers became interested in women's history. No single study on women and the church fathers existed by the 1980s, but an awareness of women's history encouraged the translation of texts concerned with women's lives. Some of the better works include E. Clark, *Jerome, Chrysostom and Friends: Essays and Translations* (1979), S. Reiger Shore, translator, *John Chrysostom: On Virginity and Against Remarriage,* (1983), J. LaPorte, *Women in the Early Church* (1982), K. E. Borrenson, *Subordination and Equivalence: The Nature and Role of Women in Augustine and Thomas Aquinas* (1981), F. Dupriez, *La condition féminine et les peres de l'église latine* (1982), R. Gryson, *Le ministère des femmes dans l'église ancienne* (1976), R. Rader, *Male/Female Friendship in Early Christian Communities* (1983), G. Tavard, *Woman in Christian Tradition* (1974), and P. Wilson-Kastner, *A Lost Tradition: Woman Writers of the Early Church* (1981). A number of church history journals took particular interest in this area. *Signs* (University of Chicago) devoted issues to women and religion, and material appeared in the *Journal of the American Academy of Religion, Christian Century, Theological Studies,* and the *Journal of Feminist Studies in Religion.* The *Frau und Christentum* (1984–87) project at the *Institut für ökumenische Forschung* at the University of Tübingen had two focal points: "Women's Sexuality in Early Christianity" and "Women and Christianity in 20th-Century Germany." Doctoral dissertations were written on 19th- and 20th-century church history, and the Hebrew Bible from the perspective of feminist theology. The Institute for Antiquity and Christianity began a project entitled *Women in Papyrus Sources: Documentary Papyri Relating to Women from the Hellenistic, Roman, and Byzantine Periods* (1984) to shed light on patristic texts dealing with virginity and on patristic attitudes toward women.

In more general terms, scholars and students were provided with valuable research tools in the 20th century. Bibliographies, dictionaries, lexicons, indices, and concordances were completed and many older works revised and updated. G. Kittle's *Wörterbach zum Neuen Testament* remained invaluable. To this may be added Walter Bauer's *Griechisch-Deutsches Wörterbuch zum Neuen Testaments und der übrigen urchristlichen Literatur* (5th ed., 1958); the English translation was published by W. F. Arndt and F. Wilbur Gingrich in 1957. Since then an index to the work has been published: *An Index to the Bauer, Arndt and Gingrich Greek Lexicon* (1958, 2d. ed., 1981). The long-awaited *Greek Patristic Lexicon* was completed by G. W. H. Lampe (1961–68).

A number of other works exist, many designed for research of particular church fathers, works, or themes: T. Van Bavel, *Répertoire bibliographique de saint Augustin, 1950–1960* (1963), É. Lamirande, *Une siècle et demi d'études sur l'ecclésiologie de saint Augustin* (1962), *Fichier Augustinien: Maiters et Auteurs,* 4 vols. (1972), D. Lenfant, *Concordantiae Augustinianae* (1963), T. Miethe, *Augustinian Bibliography, 1970–1980, Catologus Verborum of the Corpus Christianorum: Thesaurus linguae Augustinianae, John, Psalms, De Trinitae, De civitate Dei, Confessionium* (1976), R. Gryson, *Littérature Arienne latin,* 3 vols. (1980), Berkowitz, *Index Arnobianus* (1967), *Index verborum et locvtionvm quae in sancti Cypriani;* E. J. Goodspeed, *Index Apologeticus* (1912, 1960), H. Kraft, *Clavis patrum apostolicorum* (1963), G. Claesson, *Index Tertullianus,* 3 vols. (1974/75), H. Quellet, *Concordance verbale du De corona de Tertullian* (1975), G. Müller, *Lexicon Athanasianum* (1952), M. Aubineau, *Index verborum Homiliorum Festalium* (1983), A. M. Malingrey, *Indices Chrysostomici* (1978), R. A. Krupp, *Saint John Chrysostom: A Scriptural Index* (1984), and W. Jaeger and H. Langerbeck, *Opera Gregorii Nysseni* (1952).

Technology has advanced such academics. The *Avgvstinvs-Lexikon* in Würzburg, Germany, produced a computer-processed Augustine concordance. A printed edition of the Augustinus-Lexicon was also in production. The *Banque d'information bibliographique en patristique,* at Laval University, Quebec, was being programmed in the 1980s. When completed the project would have on file texts and studies in patristic literature and various related disciplines. The use of word processors increased scholastic production and one company led in developing print wheels in Greek and Greek/Latin fonts. Typing elements in Greek and Armenian for at least one typewriter existed.

Patristic studies grew rapidly in a very short time. NT scholarship, the Nag Hammadi Library, women's studies, philology, anthropology, and sociology redirected the focus of patristics to place Christianity within a larger framework of culture, language, philosophy, and ancient religion. It was anticipated that patristic studies would continue to use a historical method stressing sociohistorical issues, and that patristic studies in theology would continue to stress themes centered on the Christian faith, and shift toward spotlighting the larger schema of Greco-Roman philosophical/religious thought. The vast amounts of biblical citations, lexicons, dictionaries, and concordances clarified and defined the subdisciplines of the field, making patristic study essential for understanding Christian antiquity.

Leslie J. MacDonald

**Patron Saints.** In Roman Catholic usage, saints designated by ecclesiastical authority as the heavenly protectors of a person, church, country, trade, or fraternity. Individuals receive the names of their patron saints at baptism or confirmation. Churches or parishes solemnize the feast of the patron saint with set liturgical rules. Local traditions and events, either historical or legendary, in the life of the saints determine countries' and guilds' choice of patrons. Thus St. Andrew is the patron of Scotland; St. Patrick, of Ireland; St. Rose of Lima, of the Americas; St. Christopher, of travelers; and St. Luke, of physicians. Popular superstitions have often credited the saints with healing powers for specific maladies; thus St. Hubert is invoked against rabies, St. Apollonia, against toothache, and St. Vitus, against epilepsy.

GEORGES A. BARROIS

**Pauck, Wilhelm** (1901–1981). American church historian. Born in Lassphe, Germany, he studied at the universities of Göttingen and Berlin. He came to Chicago Theological Seminary as an exchange student in 1925, and was appointed professor of church history there in 1926. In 1939 he was appointed professor of historical theology at the University of Chicago, and to the chair of history in 1945. From 1953 to 1967 he was professor at Union Theological Seminary, New York. He served terms as president of the American Society of Church History (1936), the American Theological Society (1946, 1963), and the American Society for Reformation Research, and was coeditor of *Church History* (1950–53). Among his publications are *Das Reich Gottes auf Erden* (1928); *Karl Barth, Prophet of a New Christianity?* (1932); with Richard Niebuhr and Francis Miller, *The Church Against the World* (1934); *The Heritage of the Reformation* (1950); with his wife Marion Pauck, volume 1 of *Paul Tillich: His Life and Thought* (1976); and works on Luther, Melanchthon, Bucer, Harnack, and Troeltsch. A collection of essays in his honor, edited by Jaroslav Pelikan, was published in 1968.

E. J. FURCHA

**Paul, The Apostle.** The late 1900s witnessed a remarkable interest in Paul. The dating of his letters was applied to their exegesis, and new attempts were made to resolve difficulties over chronology. The apostle's relation to Judaism was rigorously reexamined, often with revolutionary results. What precisely Paul the Christian believed about the Mosaic law was debated along with contextual and sociological questions.

*Chronology.* Traditionally, the Book of Acts has been used alongside Paul's epistles as a source for understanding Paul's early life, conversion, and missionary work, largely because Acts provides a consecutive narrative. However, there are problems in reconciling the accounts in Acts with those in the epistles. Gal. 1:11–24 suggests that immediately prior to his conversion and for three years afterwards Paul lived not in Jerusalem, as Acts seems to indicate (7:58–8:1, 3; 9:1–2, 26; 22:3), but probably in Damascus. Similarly, while Paul's letters mention two visits to Jerusalem (Gal. 1:18; 2:1) and that he hoped to make a third (Rom. 15:25; 1 Cor. 16:4), Acts makes apparent reference to five visits (9:26–28; 11:27–30; 15:1–4; 18:22; 21:17–19). Attempts to reconcile these differences have proved difficult, so many scholars assumed their inconsistency and used Acts and the epistles separately. Paul's own writings were taken as the primary source, while Acts was used where it offered no difficulties. The basis for new chronologies were writings that were almost universally accepted as Pauline: Galatians, 1 Thessalonians, 1–2 Corinthians, Romans, and Philippians.

This approach owed its origin to the American scholar, John Knox. He held that Paul made two missionary journeys. The first, which took place between the first and second visits to Jerusalem mentioned in Gal. 1:18 and 2:1, is alluded to in the reference to Syria and Cilicia in Gal. 1:21. Knox argued that Paul's work was not confined to Syria and Cilicia but included Macedonia, Greece, and Asia and kept him occupied until he returned to Jerusalem 14 years later (2:1). On this visit to Jerusalem Paul was urged to "remember the poor" (2:10) and he immediately left on his second missionary tour, proceeding through Asia Minor, Macedonia, and Greece for the purpose of organizing the collection of money. The money was collected and taken to Jerusalem three years after the request (Rom. 15:25; 1 Cor. 16:4). During this period Paul wrote Galatians, 1–2 Corinthians, and Romans. According to Knox, then, Paul was converted in A.D. 37 and visited Jerusalem in 40, 51, and 54. This reconstruction obviates the difficulty involved in harmonizing Acts and the epistles. It also accounts for what Paul did during the so-called hidden years between his first and second visits to Jerusalem. But it does not explain why Barnabas deserted Paul at Antioch (Gal. 2:13) after an 11-year partnership. Moreover, it reads a lot into the request of Gal. 2:10.

R. Jewett, following Knox, worked out a system in which he claimed to be able to identify not only the year but the month of various events. The crucifixion took place on April 3, 33; Paul's conversion on October 3 or 8, 34; the first Jerusalem visit in August–October 37; the second in August–October 51; and the third in June 57. This reconstruction depends in particular on Paul's escape from Aretas (Acts 9:19–25; 2 Cor. 11:32). Aretas cannot have been in charge of Damascus before the reign of Caligula, and therefore A.D. 37 is the earliest possible date for Paul's first visit to Jerusalem. This chronology is an improvement on that of Knox, but it has problems. Paul's conversion is at the more likely date of A.D. 34 and Galatians is dated before Romans. To date Philippians prior to 1–2 Corinthians and Colossians prior to Romans, however, is difficult to defend. Jewett's dating of Paul's first visit to Jerusalem depends on the assumption, based on Acts, that it immediately followed Paul's clandestine escape from Damascus. This is possible, but if the Acts chronology is abandoned there is no reason for thinking that the visit did not happen later in Paul's life; he himself mentions it at the very end of his list of hardships.

G. Lüdemann proposed a scheme similar to Knox's. He took issue with the dependence of chronologies on the Gallio reference in Acts 18:12. The inscription found at Delphi dates Gallio's tenure in office to A.D. 51 and 52. By making this their fixed point in Pauline chronology, by working forward and backward from this date, and by adding chronological data from Acts, scholars reach the improbable conclusion that the time lag between Paul's conversion and his first letter was about 19 years, about four times as great as the interval between the first and last of Paul's extant letters. Lüdemann argues that Luke tends to tell his readers everything about Paul's associations with a particular place when he mentions his first visit, even though Paul visited the place more than once. Thus he holds that Paul's accusation before Gallio belongs not to Paul's first visit to Corinth (c. A.D. 41) but to his last (A.D. 51 or 52).

Lüdemann dates Paul's conversion as A.D. 30 and his first visit to Jerusalem as 33. The following year Paul undertook his founding mission in Syria, Cilicia, and south Galatia with Barnabas, under the auspices of Antioch. This was followed by his independent mission in Europe from A.D. 41. Paul paid his second visit to Jerusalem in A.D. 47. Then followed a single major tour (A.D. 47–52) to collect money for the poor at Jerusalem, which ended with the delivery of the money and Paul's third and final visit to Jerusalem (spring, A.D. 52). The result is a chronology which, like that of Knox and Jewett, illumines the early period of Paul's career. First Thessalonians is dated about A.D. 41 and 1 Corinthians about 49.

Lüdemann added credence to the practice of using references to the collection as an aid for working out a chronology, but his reconstruction compresses Paul's four main epistles (Galatians, 1–2 Corinthians, Romans) into a brief period and sets the bulk of Paul's work before the Jerusalem Council. It makes the improbable suggestion that the conflict with Peter in Antioch (Gal. 2:11–13) occurred before the Jerusalem conference (Gal. 2:1–10) and was in fact the cause of the conference. Its suggestion that Paul's appearance before Gallio was not on his first but his last visit to Corinth goes against the plain sense of the context.

The new chronology proposed by Knox and his followers has the advantage of showing what occupied Paul during the otherwise empty-looking 14 years of Gal. 2:1. Paul's missionary activities are spread more evenly over his years as a missionary. It depends upon whether the collection was the purpose of the second journey or incidental to it and whether Gal. 2:10 refers to the collection at all. The reference to helping the poor in Gal. 2:10 does not in itself date Galatians in close proximity to the letters which actually mention Paul's collection. If Galatians is earlier than the Corinthian and Roman correspondence, then the case for taking the chronology of Acts more seriously was not closed.

The dating of Paul's writings bears on their interpretation. Differences in stress among epistles on a particular subject have sometimes been explained on the grounds that Paul's thought developed over the years. Development can, of course, be due to a variety of factors. If a lengthy period between the epistles in question can be provided for, however, this approach is obviously useful. However, given the uncertainty over chronology it was difficult to identify the overall time-span of the epistles or the time between particular epistles. The new chronology tends to bunch major epistles within a comparatively brief period, with Galatians placed fairly close to Romans. First Thessalonians is generally accepted as early and Colossians and Ephesians treated as "deutero-Pauline." If Galatians can be shown to be earlier than 1–2 Corinthians and Romans then it serves, along with 1 Thessalonians, as an important bench mark. This would mean that the close similarity between Galatians and Romans in their teaching on justification by faith can be taken as proof not that Galatians comes from the same period as Romans but that justification by faith was the central feature of Paul's theology throughout his ministry.

***Conversion and Call.*** Traditionally, the Western Church has interpreted Paul's conversion to mean deliverance from bondage to the Jewish law. Evidence for this is found in Rom. 7:7–25. The frustration and defeat described in these verses are taken together with statements in Galatians about Christ's setting free those "under the law" (3:13, 23–26; 4:3–5) as a transcript of Paul's own personal experience as a Jew before his conversion to Christianity. Support for this is often found in Acts 26:14 ("it is hard for you to kick against the goads"), which is interpreted to mean the stabs of truth or pangs of conscience (possibly over the death of Stephen) which Paul had done his best to ignore.

This view was believed in 1900s reinterpretation to owe more to the introspective conscience of Western Christendom than to Paul himself. Gal. 1:14 and Phil. 3:4–6 are cited as evidence that Paul as a Jew lived a secure and fulfilled life. He had no problems, no pangs of conscience, no shortcomings. When he says that he forgets what is behind and strains forward to what lies ahead (Phil. 3:13) what he refers to are his accomplishments, not his shortcomings. Noting the worth of his Jewish background, he says it is nothing when compared to "the surpassing greatness of knowing Christ Jesus my Lord" (3:8). Scholars like K. Stendahl and E. P. Sanders find no evidence that Paul was psychologically prepared for his conversion by the frustration and futility he experienced as a Jew under the Law. On the contrary, his own account of his conversion states that it was due to a revelation of Jesus Christ, graciously imparted to him by God (Gal. 1:11–17). That is to say, it was an objective experience, not owing to his state of mind. Similarly, it is argued that in 2 Cor. 3:7–17 the contrast Paul draws between the old covenant and the new is not one of crushing legalism and freedom in Christ, but is between that which had "splendor" and that which had "greater splendor." The fact that the Law does not give life does not mean that it is evil. On the contrary, it is "holy, righteous and good" (Rom. 7:12).

That Paul viewed Judaism positively is not to be doubted (Phil. 3:4–6), but clearly this is not the whole story. Paul has some very negative things to say about the Law. He calls the first covenant "the ministry that brought death" (2 Cor. 3:7). Paul could scarcely have written Rom. 1:18–2:29 had he not been convinced that the Jews were very well aware of sin. To suggest that Romans 7 contains no hint of Paul's own experience reduces this great passage to a purely theoretical treatise. If Paul's conversion had no experiential antecedents in his previous life, how is one to explain why and how Christ supersedes the Law? Or how are we to explain why Paul the Jew persecuted Christians and after his conversion was himself persecuted by Jews and Judaizers unless there was understood to be a radical difference between Christianity and Judaism?

Intimately connected to Paul's conversion was his call (as in Gal. 1:15–17, and Acts 9:15) to evangelize the Gentiles (Rom. 1:5, 13; 11:13; 15:16, 18; 1 Thess. 2:16). But even though his apostolate dates from the moment of his conversion it is not justifiable to speak, as Stendahl and others do, of Paul's Damascus road experience as a call rather than a conversion, on the grounds that Christianity at the time was still a reform movement within Judaism. Already at Antioch there was a congregation in which Gentile converts were living without reference to the Law (Gal. 2:11–13). Paul the Pharisee would hardly have persecuted Christians had he viewed them simply as reformed Jews.

***Paul and the Jewish Law.*** Paul's statements on the Law have always caused difficulty. On the one hand, he appears to devalue the Law (2 Cor. 3:7; Gal. 3:19) and on the other hand to extol it (Rom. 7:12). Between these appraisals are texts whose meaning is so unclear that they can be used to support either a positive or negative view of the Law (Rom. 10:4; Gal. 3:24). A common explanation was that Paul rejected not the Law but its misuse, so basically his view was positive. This view was supported by Sanders and others influenced by him, who argued that if there were Jews of Paul's time who tried to justify themselves by good works this did not itself define Judaism as a legalistic system. Judaism was based on the covenant, that is, grace. Similarly, J. D. G. Dunn

maintained that what Paul attacked was not the Law but the "works of the law": circumcision, food laws, and Sabbath observance. This was a useful distinction but it left unanswered Paul's clear statement of the need to be redeemed from the Law (Gal. 4:4; 5:1) and his description of the Law as "the ministry that brought death" (2 Cor. 3:7). Another explanation reconciled conflicting statements by seeing development in Paul's teaching. Following U. Wilckens, J. W. Drane, and others, Hans Hübner suggested that Paul met with such a violent reaction to his letter to the Galatians, both from Galatia and from the Jerusalem church, that he modified his teaching. The result of his rethinking was Romans. This view allowed allegedly conflicting statements on the Law to stand unreconciled.

That statements on the Law could not be resolved was accepted by H. Räisänen. He held that, contrary to the common view, there was a development or change of view between Galatians and Romans and that Paul did not have a coherent view of the Law. The result was that he could be negative or positive as suited his purpose. The consequences of this view are obvious—Paul was impaled upon an impossible dilemma: as a Jew he believed that the Law was divinely given, but as a Christian that it had been abolished by Christ.

Sanders maintained that Paul's understanding of the Law resulted, not from any personal experience of the futility of life under the Law, but from the fact that Gentiles were saved by Christ apart from the Law. Whereas Christ was indispensable to the salvation of the Gentiles the Law was not. When Sanders comes, however, to explain Paul's own position in regard to the Law he runs into difficulty, for he has already established that 1st-century Judaism was uniformly a religion of the covenant of grace. By not allowing that the Judaizers are evidence that some Jews understood obedience to the Law as a way to righteousness Sanders makes Paul's more radical statements about the Law at best unintelligible and at worst a misrepresentation of Judaism.

The attempt to approach the subject from the point of view of its social situation opened a new era in Pauline studies. M. Barth, G. Theissen, W. A. Meeks, and F. Watson argued that Paul's teaching spoke directly to his work in forming Law-free Gentile congregations and the issues this raised. Watson said that Paul went first to evangelize the Jews, and when this failed (Rom. 9:11) he turned to the Gentiles. In order to facilitate the entry of Gentiles into the church and insure the success of his Gentile mission, the requirements of the Jewish Law were not imposed on the Gentiles. The Gentile mission proved highly successful but soon ran into problems with the more conservative Jewish Christians. What Paul says about the Law is his subsequent attempt to legitimize the separate Gentile churches. The faith-works antithesis in his epistles is not to be interpreted as a theological contrast between salvation as the gift of God and salvation as earned by good works. It was rather more a sociological contrast between two different ways of life—"faith," the way followed by Paul's Gentile churches, and "works" followed by the Jewish churches, which continued their Jewish way of life. These were diametrically opposed, not because one represents grace and the other human performance—for Judaism acknowledged that supremacy of grace in election and the covenant—but because the Law was not practiced in Paul's churches.

This interpretation resolved the different views of the Law. In Galatians Paul is fighting to break the hold the Judaizers have over his converts and is obliged to devalue the Law (3:10, 19; 4:3, 9). In Romans he is asking Jewish Christians in Rome to recognize the validity of the separate Gentile churches in the city and knows that he stands a better chance of success if he acknowledges the essential goodness of the Law (7:12–13).

The sociological approach has opened up valuable insights. Unfortunately Watson begins by affirming that his approach does not exclude the possibility of a theological interpretation by Paul, but in the end comes close to turning Paul's theology into a rationalization of a practical problem. Paul makes it abundantly clear that his gospel was a response to a revelation from God (1 Cor. 9:1; 15:8; Gal. 1:12, 16; Eph. 3:3). However, what Watson writes about the respective contexts of Galatians and Romans did add weight to the view that the different statements on the Law in Galatians and Romans needed to be interpreted in the light of the contexts to which Paul was writing.

It was clear that at least some difficulties in Paul's statements on the Law might be resolved by treating his teaching indiscriminately, using his writings without taking context into account. It misrepresented Paul, however, to say that in Galatians he takes a wholly negative view of the Law while in Romans he takes a wholly positive view. A plausible case can be made for taking Gal. 3:21–26 to mean that the Law played a beneficient role in preparing the way for Christ. Likewise in Romans 7 statements about the goodness of the Law are matched by others which show that the Law allowed itself to be disastrously weakened by sin.

While Paul's theology undoubtedly represents reflection on what had actually happened in his missionary work, clearly he attached considerable importance to its revelation. What precisely this revelation was we are not told, but presumably it led to the discovery that Christ crucified was God's Messiah and that his death was necessary for salvation. Since crucifixion meant condemnation by the Law it followed that Christ's death on the cross exposed the inadequacy of the Law. If the death of Christ was necessary for salvation it must mean that salvation could come in no other way, and consequently Christ died for Jew and Gentile alike. Since the Gentiles were included salvation was not through the Law, for Gentiles were not under the Law.

***Righteousness and Justification.*** The meaning of the righteousness of God and the justification of the sinner by faith in Paul's teaching was debated at length. Protestant scholars, following Martin Luther, generally emphasized that the meaning of the Greek verb translated as "justify" or "make righteous" means "to pronounce righteous." The term thus has a forensic or juridical sense, signifying God's acquittal of the sinner. Catholic scholars, and notably the Council of Trent, tended to follow the Latin *iustificare* (the traditional translation of the Greek ) "to make righteous." Accordingly, the Catholic understanding of justification included aspects of salvation which the Reformers saw as belonging to sanctification rather than justification.

Much of the modern debate was influenced by R. Bultmann. He emphasized that righteousness refers not to the ethical quality of a person, but to a relationship. God reaches out to the ungodly and puts them in a right relationship with himself. Righteousness is thus not something which a person has on his own; it is given, as a judge declares a guilty person in a court of law to be innocent or righteous. This fundamental forensic sense which the verb has in Paul's writing came out of his Jewish tradition. In Judaism God's justifying action, which Israel sorely needed, also came to be thought of as eschatological. Paul shows that what was an eschatological hope for the Jews is now realized and experienced by Christians. In and through the life, death, and resurrection of Jesus Christ, God declares sinners to be forgiven and acquitted.

New ground was broken by E. Käsemann. He argued that the righteousness of God refers not to a status given by God or a status before God but to God's "salvation-creating power." The concept is essentially dynamic. The action or power of God is indeed expressed in the gift of righteousness to humanity, but the gift must never be thought of in isolation from the giver. Moreover, the righteousness of God, expressed in Jesus Christ, is cosmic inasmuch as Jesus is Lord of all. The strongly theocentric and cosmic character of Käsemann's interpretation influenced subsequent scholarship.

P. Stuhlmacher stressed the soteriological thrust of the righteousness of God in relation to the faithfulness of God as Creator toward his creation. God's saving word in Jesus Christ moves through the world, creating faith and thereby brings a new creation into being (2 Cor. 5:17; Gal. 6:15). Similarly, K. Kertelge emphasized the dynamic character of the concept but argued that, inasmuch as humanity is the object of God's action, a divine-human relationship is implied. He acknowledged the forensic character of righteousness; the divine acquittal recreates the sinner. It is in this sense that the justified person is a new creation in Christ. Kertelge also acknowledged the eschatological sense which the concept acquired in Judaism and the way in which this was transformed by Paul into terms of realized eschatology and made applicable to all races.

Another new era in interpreting Paul was again engineered by Sanders, who approached the subject from the point of view of God's covenant with Israel. Righteousness in the Israelite and Jewish tradition has to do with maintenance of one's place in the covenant. One belongs to the people of God by election or grace; one keeps one's place in the covenant by obedience (righteousness), observing the Law, and repenting of sins. In Paul, however, "to be made righteous" ("to be justified") refers to getting into—not to staying in—the people of God, which is made possible through the grace of God in Jesus Christ.

Most 20th-century scholars agreed that the primary sense of justification is dynamic, but that the meaning includes both the saving action of God and the new state or status of those who are put right with God. God's action in acquitting and forgiving those who are alienated and lost and without any entitlement whatever on their part does not leave unchanged those who repent but results in their becoming new beings (1 Cor. 6:11; 2 Cor. 5:17). The loving action of God in acquitting the guilty is made possible through the death of his own Son. At the same time the term refers not just to acquittal of past transgressions but also to the final acquittal (Gal. 5:5). The theological, as distinct from the christological and anthropological, meaning of justification and righteousness is crucial, and 1 Cor. 1:30 and 6:11 use righteousness as a synonym for salvation to teach the link between the justification or setting right of the individual and that of creation itself (Rom. 8:17–39; 2 Cor. 5:17; Gal. 6:15).

The debate about the meaning of God's justification inevitably raised afresh the question whether this is the heart of Paul's theology. Käsemann, G. Bornhamm, J. C. Beker, and others were sure that it is, while Sanders and H. Ridderbos followed A. Schweitzer in making participation in Christ or dying and rising with Christ the dominant concept. They argued that discussion of righteousness occurs only in Paul's polemical writings, and maintained that, while righteousness by faith can be derived from and understood on the basis of such other aspects of Paul's theology as life in Christ and in the Spirit, this is not true vice versa. In fact, the attempt to make any one aspect of Paul's thought central harms the whole. The juridical aspect of justification, while

expressing an essential aspect of salvation according to Paul, is not the exclusive concept in the light of which all the other aspects of Paul's teaching must be interpreted. Righteousness by faith is central in contexts where polemic demands it, but it remains one way among several used by Paul to describe salvation.

*Apocalyptic.* The place of apocalyptic in the thought of Paul also consumed considerable interest. M. Hengel showed the extent to which Jewish apocalyptic influenced Palestinian and diaspora Judaism, with the result that the long-standing distinction scholars made between Pharisaic Judaism and apocalyptic Judaism was rejected and Paul was regarded as a good example of how Pharisaic interest in the Law could coexist quite happily with apocalyptic hope.

Scholars frequently acknowledged the extent to which apocalyptic thought dominated the Thessalonian correspondence, but argued that it was less prominent in Paul's later writings, particularly Colossians. By contrast, C. L. Mearns proposed the novel view that Paul moved away from an early radical realized eschatology to a future advent hope. Beker argued that Paul's thought was consistently apocalyptic and controlled by the hope of the future cosmic triumph of God. In support of his interpretation Beker drew attention, not only to 1–2 Thessalonians, but also to 1 Corinthians 15, 2 Corinthians 5, and Rom. 8:17–30. He maintained that unless justice is done to the apostle's vision of the apocalyptic victory of God it is all too easy for his theology to be reduced to Christology or, worse, to anthropology. Beker's interpretation was a helpful corrective to those who failed to see the extent of the apocalyptic features in the theology of Paul, but many scholars believed that, by making the triumph of God wholly apocalyptic, he has overstated his case.

Apocalyptic is present not only in Paul's early but also in his later writings (Rom. 13:11; Phil. 3:20; 4:5), so that Paul did not lessen his future hope, unless Colossians is regarded as Pauline, and some are not willing to do that. Too much should not be made of the fact that the apocalyptic theme is all but absent from Galatians. The degree to which Paul modified or transformed Jewish apocalyptic thought is debated by scholars, but what is beyond doubt is that Paul broke down the fundamental chasm between the present and future ages or aeons by his teaching that in the death and resurrection and the gift of the Holy Spirit the new age has dawned. Paul's epistles share with apocalyptic a strong awareness of the pervasiveness of sin and evil, but he asserts the answer in the action of God in Jesus Christ. Since the righteousness of God is manifested in Jesus Christ the long-standing problem of theodicy in apocalyptic falls away. God's people still suffer, but their sufferings are transformed so that they play a part in God's redemptive plan (Rom. 8:16; cf. 2 Cor. 12.7; Phil. 3:10). Their sufferings are a sign of their solidarity with a world that longs to be set free from its "bondage to decay" (Rom. 8:21).

R. J. McKELVEY

***As A Preacher.*** In his own eyes the apostle stood out first as a preacher. The Book of Acts reports three sermons: at Antioch (Acts 17), Lystra (Acts 14), and Athens (Acts 17). The statement about the response to this sermon (7:34) seems not to justify the widespread opinion that Paul's preaching failed in Athens, compared with Corinth. Why compare a single sermon with a ministry of 18 months? The sermon at Athens contains a skillful "psychological approach." In addressing hearers not familiar with the OT, Paul began with something else. In speaking to Hebrews, or proselytes, he started with their Bible, his main source of preaching truths. Acts also records three defenses: before the Jews (chap. 22), the Romans (chap. 24), and a cross-section of his world (chap. 26). While not sermons, these addresses show his powers of intellect, riches of feeling, gifts of imagination, ability to adapt himself, lofty idealism, and strong practicality.

The epistles also reveal much about his preaching, especially to believers. 2 Cor. 1–5 contains his philosophy of preaching, showing that Paul believed in the primacy of preaching, as the main duty of the minister. He uniformly preached doctrine but never apart from ethics. As for influence, his preaching has largely dominated Protestant Christianity.

ANDREW W. BLACKWOOD

**Bibliography.** A. Schweitzer, *The Mysticism of Paul the Apostle* (ET, 1931); J. Lowe, *JTS* 62 (1941): 129–42; R. Bultmann, *Theology of the NT* (ET, 1951–55); C. H. Dodd, *NT Studies* (1954); C. E. B. Cranfield, *SJT* 17 (1964): J. Knox, *Chapters in a Life of Paul* (1964); W. D. Davies, *Paul and Rabbinic Judaism* (1965), 43–68; P. Stuhlmacher, *Gerechtigkeit Gottes bei Paulus* (1966); K. Kertelge, *"Rechtfertgung" bei Paulus* (1967); R. C. Tannehill, *Dying and Rising with Christ* (1967); E. Käsemann, *NT Questions of Today* (1969), 168–82; V. P. Furnish, *JAAR* 38 (1970): 289–303; G. Bornkamm, *Paul, Paulus* (1971); M. Hengel, *Judaism and Hellenism* (ET, 1974); J. W. Dranc, *Paul: Libertine or Legalist?* (1975); H. Ridderbos, *Paul: An Outline of His Theology* (1975); E. P. Sanders, *Paul and Palestinian Judaism* (1977); R. Jewett, *Dating Paul's Life* (1979); J. C. Beker, *Paul the Apostle* (1980); S. Kim, *The Origin of Paul's Gospel* (1981); C. L. Mearns, *NTS* 27 (1981): 137–57; *Paul and Paulinism: Essays in Honour of C. K. Barrett* (1982); R. Scroggs, *Interpretation* 36 (1982): 74–77; G. Theissen, *The Social Setting of Pauline Christianity* (1982); J. D. G. Dunn, *BJRL* 65 (1983): 85–122; H. Räisänen, *Paul and the Law* (1983); H. Hübner, *Law in Paul's Thought* (1984); L. E. Keck, *Interpretation* 38 (1984): 229–41; G. Lüdemann, *Paul, Apostle to the Gentiles: Studies in Chronology* (1984); J. Badenas, *Christ the End of the Law* (1985); J. D. G. Dunn, *NTS* 31 (1985): 523–42; J. M. G. Barclay, *Themelios* 12 (1986): 5–15; F. F. Bruce, *BJRL* 68 (1986): 273–95; N. Hyldahl, *Die paulinische Chronologie (Acta Theologica Danica XIX)* (1986); D. J. Lull, *JBL* 105 (1986): 481–98; F. Watson, *Paul, Judaism and the Gentiles* (1986); D. Moo, *SJT* 40 (1987): 287–307; H. Moore, *IBS* 9 (1987): 35–46.

**Paul VI** (1897–1978). Pope from 1963. Born Giovanni Battista Montini near Brescia, Italy, and son of a Catholic newspaper editor, he was educated at the Gregorian University and the University of Rome. He was ordained in 1920, and served in the Vatican diplomatic service until 1944. He then became archbishop of Milan, a cardinal in 1958, and five years later was elected pope in succession to John XXIII. Under his pontificate the second, third, and fourth sessions of Vatican II were held, the index of proscribed books was abolished, and the rule against eating meat on Fridays rescinded. In celebrating the Mass, Latin was replaced by other languages, and a wider variety of liturgical expression was permitted. In 1967 a new Synod of Bishops had its first meeting; it advised the pope then and subsequently on matters concerning canon law, human rights, celibacy, and justice and peace. Paul VI appointed cardinals from third world countries, pronounced against proposals for women priests, reorganized Vatican administration, and made 75 the normal retirement age for bishops. Like John XXIII, however, he was conservative in matters of faith and morals. He resisted the temper of the times in such encyclicals as *Sacerdotalis caelibates* (1967), which upheld priestly celibacy, and *Humanae vitae* (1968), which underlined the ban on birth control. He was the first pope since 1809 to travel outside Italy, and the first to travel by plane. Among his destinations were India, Israel, the USA, Colombia, Uganda, and the Far East. In his travels he persistently appealed for world peace and social justice. Never physically robust and confronted by many controversial issues, he battled on until a few weeks short of his 81st birthday.

**Bibliography.** James Walsh, ed., *The Mind of Paul* (1964); W. J. Wilson, *Paul, the Missionary Pope* (1968); J. F. Andrews, ed., *Paul VI: Critical Appraisals* (1970); *The Teachings of Pope Paul VI*, 11 vols. (1968–79).

J. D. DOUGLAS

**Paulist Fathers.** Roman Catholic organization founded by Fr. Isaac T. Hecker, in 1858, in New York City. Pius IX, in approving the society, suggested that its purpose should be the conversion of non-Catholics in America, and the Paulists worked almost totally in the USA among non-Catholics. Besides mission, youth, and parish work, the Paulists operated through information centers, broadcast and print media, hospitals, and convert instruction. Seventeen religious houses throughout the nation served the nearly 200 Paulists as bases of operations for their missionary endeavors. Paulists were encouraged to develop their own initiative while striving for personal sanctity. Seminary training was aimed at developing the most progressive methods of convert training in the new priest.

THOMAS J. McCARTHY

**Pawley, Bernard Clinton** (1911–1981). Anglican archdeacon and ecumenist. Educated at Oxford and at Wells Theological College, he served curacies in Stoke on Trent and Leeds before becoming an army chaplain in 1940. He was then rector of Elland (1945–55), diocesan secretary (1955–59) and canon-residentiary (1959–70) of Ely, canon-residentiary of St. Paul's Cathedral, London (1970–72), and archdeacon of Canterbury and canon-residentiary of Canterbury Cathedral (1972–81). A strong supporter of ecumenical relations, he wrote *Looking at the Vatican Council* (1962), *Anglican-Roman Relations* (1964), and *Rome and Canterbury Through Four Centuries* (1975).

**Pax Romana.** Confederation of various national Catholic university federations throughout the world. Founded in 1921 in Fribourg, Switzerland, there were 70 affiliated federations in the 1980s. From 1947 Pax Romana was composed of two autonomous sections, the International Movement of Catholic Students and the International Catholic Movement for Intellectual and Cultural Affairs. The organization sought to provide trained Christian leaders committed to the promotion of human dignity, the creation of social and economic structures for world justice, and better expression of Roman Catholic faith. It collected and disseminated news about universities, and fostered critical reflection on the nature and purpose of university education. It saw itself as a movement of laypeople who intellectually served the mission of the church in the world. It sponsored local, regional, and national meetings and seminars, and every three years held a major international congress. Its international coordinating office was in Paris, France.

MICHAEL SHARKEY

**Payne, Ernest Alexander** (1902–1980). British Baptist pastor, administrator, and ecumenical leader. Educated at Kings College, London, Regent's Parks Baptist College, Mansfield College, Oxford, and Marburg, he served on the staff of the Baptist Missionary Society, taught at Regent's Park College from 1940, and was secretary of the Baptist Union of Great Britain and Ireland from 1951 to 1967. He was president of the Baptist Union in 1977, and as such he proved an able administrator and a strong upholder of Baptist principles. He was largely responsible for renewed contact with the Baptists of Eastern Europe in the 1950s. While he was deeply involved in the Free Church Federal Council and the Baptist World Alliance his major contribution was to the ecumenical movement through the British Council of Churches and the World Council. He served on the central committee of the latter and was a vice-president (1954–1975). He was an able chairman with a clear mind and a gift for reconciliation. His contribution was recognized by the state when he was appointed a Companion of Honour in 1968. He was the author of many books, including *The Free Church Tradition* and *The Fellowship of Believers*. In addition he wrote over 70 articles for the *Baptist Quarterly*, mainly on Baptist history.

JAMES TAYLOR

**Payne, J. Barton** (1922–1979). American biblical scholar. Educated at the University of California (Berkeley), San Francisco Theological Seminary, and Princeton Theological Seminary (Ph.D.), he was professor of OT successively at Bob Jones University, Wheaton Graduate School of Theology, Trinity Evangelical Divinity School, and Covenant Theological Seminary.

Barton served as an ordained minister in the United Presbyterian, Evangelical Free, and Reformed Presbyterian churches. He worked in several archeological expeditions in Palestine and directed the Wheaton Graduate Summer School there. His prophecy conferences stressed the respective values of different interpretations and the practical impact prophecy should have. He was a man of great energy, delight in life, personal devotion, and love for family and missions. He died in a mountain climbing accident in Japan following a sabbatical spent lecturing throughout Asia and teaching Bible with his wife, Dorothy, in India. His approximately 200 publications include extensive translation work for the New International Version, the New American Standard Bible, and the Berkeley Version. He is well known for *The Theology of the Older Testament*, *The Encyclopedia of Biblical Prophecy*, "I–II Chronicles" in *The Expositor's Bible Commentary*, *An Outline of Hebrew History*, *Hebrew Vocabularies*, *Biblical Prophecy for Today*, and *Revelation in Sequence*. He also edited *New Perspectives on the OT*.

P. B. PAYNE

**Peace.** Completeness, soundness, or wholeness. The offer of peace is a major attraction of the Christian gospel in a frenetic world. *Shalōm* ("peace") is one of the OT's richest words. It occurs throughout the OT, but is most fully represented in the Book of Isaiah. The basic sense of freedom from war occurs in Isa. 32:18 and 39:8. God establishes a covenant of peace with his people (54:10) but decrees that the wicked know no peace (48:22; 57:21; Jer. 6:14). *Shalōm* implies well-being, wholeness, soundness, and so is translated in the Revised Standard Version as "welfare" (38:17), "prosperity" (66:12), and "whole (ness)" (53:5). It is linked with righteousness (32:16–18; 60:17) and joy (55:12). Inner well-being, even perfect peace (26:3; 57:19: lit., "peace, peace"), comes through trust in God. The meaning of the word made it suitable as a greeting (Gen. 43:23; Judg. 6:23; 1 Sam. 25:6).

The Gk. *eirēnē*, is the NT equivalent of *shalōm*, and carries its connotations. It is used as a greeting (e.g., in John 20:19, 21, 26, and at the head of most NT letters), but is not a mere convention (see, for instance, the exposition of it in 1 Cor. 1:3, 10–17). Christ, as the Prince of Peace (Isa. 9:6–7), came to effect peace with God (Luke 2:14; Acts 10:36) through his reconciling death (Rom. 1:1–11; Col. 1:20–22). He brought Jew and Gentile together in the very act of bringing them to God (Eph. 2:14–15). Christ's peace is wholeness (1 Thess. 5:23), and it blesses the inner life of the believer (Rom. 8:6; Col. 3:15). The peace of God is Christ's gift (John 14:27; 16:33; cf. Phil. 4:7) through the Spirit (Gal. 5:22), for he is the God of peace (Col. 14:33; 1 Thess. 5:23; Heb. 13:20). Christians should exhibit such peace in their dealings with each other (Mark 9:50; Rom. 12:18; 1 Cor. 7:15).

GEOFFREY W. GROGAN

**Peace Mission Movement.** *See* FATHER DIVINE'S PEACE MISSION.

**Peace Movements.** *Introduction.* From the beginning of the church, those who believed the use of force to be inconsistent with Christian ethics have practiced organized opposition to war, violence, and even self-defense. While the NT records with favor statements about soldiers, leaders often took a harsh view. Hippolytus, for example, in Church Order (c. 218) said regarding examination of converts that new Christians in the military were forbidden to kill, even under orders, and a Christian who wanted to join the army was put out of the church "for he has despised God." From their birth in the 12th century the Waldensians condemned war, although self-defense was allowed. Anabaptist groups such as the Mennonites created "peace churches" during the Reformation, and the Quakers brought pacifism to Pennsylvania in 1682.

Christian pacifistic movements have always stirred controversy. Romans saw Christian pacifism as proof of a traitorous bent. The Pennsylvania Quaker government nearly faced armed insurrection by angry Scottish colonists for failing to protect them from Indian attack. Unsympathetic fellow believers condemn pacifists for building theologies and interpreting Scripture to serve their agenda. Faced with such opposition, pacifist groups often looked outside the orthodox mainstream for support, thereby increasing their alienation from the orthodox.

*Pacifism's Golden Age.* With the increasing threat of world annihilation, 20th-century peace movements achieved unparalleled success in organizing and swaying public opinion and faced unparalleled opposition within churches. Already

at the turn of the century, the philosophy of Christian pacifism was aligned with liberal optimism that hoped for the evolutionary advance of humanity. In 1910 Andrew Carnegie established a bond fund of $10 million, with which he proposed to "hasten the abolition of International War." In the wake of World War I, pacifism swept the Protestant church in the USA and Europe. There were also strong Roman Catholic and Jewish organizations. The 1930s brought the apex of this grand crusade. Sixty-three nations signed the Kellog–Briand Pact of 1928, which attempted to outlaw war. In a clash between Chinese and Japanese in 1931 Christian war resisters physically interposed themselves between the armies. In 1938 Adolf Hitler capitalized on fervent English pacifism in the Munich agreement with Prime Minister Neville Chamberlain.

The focus of American pacifism in the 1930s—as later—was on college campuses, but religious and political forces were at work. By 1935 12 million Americans were in one or more of 37 organizations affiliated with the National Peace Conference. Leaders included the Socialist party and the American Communist party, although communist members drifted in and out of peace movements with changes in European politics. More conservative groups included the Carnegie Endowment for International Peace, the World Peace Foundation, the Woodrow Wilson Foundation, and the Church Peace Union. The National Council for the Prevention of War included the peace churches, the YWCA, and a collection of religious and labor groups. The Women's International League for Peace and Freedom (founded in 1915) gave an aggressive feminist perspective and was one of the abler lobbying groups. A key influence was the Fellowship of Reconciliation, which was born in England in 1914 as an organization of Christian churches. The makeup of American leadership, including Harry Emerson Fosdick and A. J. Muste, a former union organizer and disciple of Trotsky anarchism, attracted a variety of extremists. The War Resister's League was founded in 1923 to aid conscientious objectors (COs) who had faced imprisonment during World War I. This group advocated active resistance and was comprised mainly of radical socialists and anarchists which most Christian-related movements avoided.

The theologian of the cause was Reinhold Niebuhr, who tirelessly studied, wrote, and spoke. Niebuhr sought a peace theology on which the church at large could agree, one consistent with neo-orthodox theological understandings. His continual reevaluation, however, was a problem. First, he concluded that violence by the working class might sometimes be justifiable in the quest for a new social order. In 1934 he resigned from the Fellowship of Reconciliation he had chaired in 1932. Then Niebuhr so identified with German

Christians facing persecution and was so horrified by the events in Europe and the East that he shifted to a firm "just war" theological position and in the early 1940s spoke out militantly against pacifism and neutrality in the church through his journal, *Christianity and Crisis*.

The Munich Pact divided peace organizations, and World War II nearly destroyed them. Pacifists, however, were the first to speak out against nazism and to publicize anti-Jewish laws in Germany. They campaigned to ease immigration laws to admit European Jews to the USA. In general, groups opposed U.S. involvement in the war but forsook absolute pacifism. American communists so vacillated with the fortunes of the USSR that they lost credibility in the movement. They also were condemned for leading a series of labor strikes against manufacturers of war material in 1939 and 1940. The peace movement as a whole was blamed for American and British unpreparedness. Among Christians the Quakers, Mennonites, and Brethren most consistently opposed World War II. Of 10,000 who declared CO status during the war, two-thirds belonged to historic "peace churches."

**The Nuclear Rebirth.** If World War II nearly ended pacifism, Hiroshima and Nagasaki energized these organizations. Postwar resistance was not so identified with Christian principles as during the 1930s. The political left still dominated its philosophy. In 1945 the Committee for Non-Violent Revolution organized, and after the draft was reinstituted in 1947 the first draft card burning protest occurred. The new peace movement was first an antinuclear movement. The fearful potential for destruction awed the world, and highly respected personalities and scientists—particularly scientists who had worked in the Manhattan Project to develop the atomic bomb—sought to ban its further development.

The first international peace offensive, the Stockholm Appeal for World Peace, collected 500 million signatures in 1950. It was supported by a manifesto signed by Manhattan Project scientists. In 1955 the Vienna Appeal collected 650 million signatures, and a statement by 52 Nobel laureates called on all nations "to renounce force as a final resort of policy" or cease to exist. Albert Einstein and Bertrand Russell jointly issued a plea in 1955 for a world test ban, and Einstein made a 1957 world broadcast. Adlai Stevenson, the 1956 U.S. presidential candidate, promised to end nuclear testing. Journalist Norman Cousins, musician Oscar Hammerstein II, and union leader Walter Reuther organized the National Committee for a Sane Nuclear Policy (SANE). More radical was the Committee for Non-Violent Action, whose members risked death by entering nuclear test zones. Such organizations were widely portrayed as communist-front movements in the national

fear of communist aggression after the Korean War.

***Pacifism in the Late 1900s.*** On a world scale the tone for the late 20th century was set by creation of Britain's largest established peace movement, the Campaign for Nuclear Disarmament (CND), in 1958. In the USA a complex of ideologies intermingled, usually in sympathy with left-wing political agendas and certainly supported in some sense by Russian and Cuban agitation. But no one group or nation could control this diverse new uprising of idealists. During the Vietnam War a record 172,000 men claimed CO status, and 100,000 went to Canada, Sweden, France, and other countries. Pope John XXIII took a major stand with pacifism as a Christian philosophy in the encyclical *Pacem in terris* (1969). In 1972 the first serious candidate for the U.S. presidency to take a pacifist position, George McGovern, was nominated by a major political party.

Radicalism increased with the 1959 founding of the Student Peace Union (SPU), a pacifist-socialist coalition. Fueled by racial fighting in the South, the liberal coalition of peace and civil rights struggles included Christian groups already involved in the plight of the blacks. While peaceful protest had long been a pacifist theme, the nonviolent philosophies of Leo Tolstoy and Mohandas Gandhi gave to 1960s pacifists an intellectual affinity with Eastern religion closer than they had ever had with Christianity. Humanist ideals were tempered by an oppressive pessimism and meaninglessness from Friedrich Nietzsche which pervaded what was called the "hippie," "flower child," or simply the "lost" generation of young people. Three protesters burned themselves to death in 1965, and Students for a Democratic Society (SDS) organized rallies, "teach-ins," marches, draft card burnings, and more violent activities.

The Cuban missile crisis heightened fear that nuclear war was inevitable, but the first U.S.–USSR test ban treaty, signed in 1963, dampened international movements. Most were kept alive only by open support by national communist parties. CND returned to life over the issue of medium-range nuclear missiles in Western Europe. A 1980 rally drew 70,000 to Trafalgar Square in London. In 1981 as many as 150,000 attended a Hyde Park demonstration, while 350,000 marched in other European cities. In June 1982 a World Peace Day in New York City drew 500,000 demonstrators. By the late 1980s peace groups included Poets Against the Bomb, Teachers for Peace, Scientists Against Nuclear Arms, Journalists Against Nuclear Extermination, and the Medical Campaign Against Nuclear Weapons.

The modern nuclear movement was more aligned with environmentalist groups than with any other segment of society. There were fewer ties with civil rights groups after the 1970s. Main-line Christian denominations in the USA nearly all contributed money and energy to the antinuclear campaign, and the interfaith Religious Task Force of Mobilization for Survival was a leading force. The strategy of antinuclear activism was to lobby internationally for "nuclear-free zones" where neither nuclear power nor weapons could be introduced. By 1990 a world consensus against nuclear armaments seemed stronger than any pacifist movement had enjoyed in world history. This was, however, despite the cheerleading from many Christians, totally a secular pacifism.

See also PACIFISM.

**Bibliography.** R. L. Moellering, *Modern War and the Christian* (1969); L. S. Wittner, *Rebels Against War: The American Peace Movement, 1941–1960* (1969); C. DeBenedetti, *The Peace Reform in American History* (1980); J. J. Davis, *Evangelical Ethics: Issues Facing the Church Today* (1985); M. Meltzer, *Ain't Gonna Study War No More: The Story of America's Peace Seekers* (1985); G. C. Bennett, *The New Abolitionists: The Story of Nuclear Free Zones* (1987).

## Peake, Arthur Samuel (1865–1929). English Methodist scholar. Born in Leek, Staffordshire, he studied at Oxford and in 1890 was elected to a theological fellowship which he held seven years at Merton College. Although he had planned to seek orders in the Church of England, he answered a challenge from his own church and became the head of the Theological Institute at Manchester which, under his leadership, became the Hartley Primitive Methodist College. He also helped to inaugurate the theological faculty at the University of Manchester in which he became professor of biblical criticism and exegesis (1904–29). The ministry of the church greatly increased in his 29 years of service. His publications include *The Bible: Its Origin, Its Significance, and Its Abiding Worth* (1913), *The Problem of Suffering in the OT* (1904), and his widely studied *Commentary on the Bible* (1919), which he planned and edited. He also edited the *Holborn Review* (1919–29).

RAYMOND W. ALBRIGHT

## Peale, Norman Vincent (1898– ). American minister. Born in Bowersville, Ohio, he was educated at Ohio Wesleyan University and Boston University, and ordained in the Methodist Episcopal Church in 1922. He served congregations in Rhode Island and New York (1922–32), and then transferred to the Reformed Church in America as pastor of the Marble Collegiate Church in New York City, a position he held from 1932. He soon was known as a powerful speaker who delivered vivid, practical, and inspiring sermons. With *The Power of Positive Thinking* (1952), a national bestseller, Peale's reputation as a preacher of Christian optimism and self-confidence was assured. Author of some 20 books with variations on these themes and other topics, he also spread his views

via *Guideposts*, an inspirational magazine, and on syndicated radio and televison programs. Peale's awards include more than 15 honorary doctorates, the Freedom Foundation Award (5 times), the Clergyman of the Year Award (1964), and the Presidential Medal of Freedom (1984). He served on numerous boards, on presidential commissions, as president of the Reformed Church in America, and with many civic and social organizations.

JAMES A. DE JONG

## Pedersen, Johannes Peder Ejler (1883– ). Danish Semitics and Islamics scholar. Born in Illebolle, Denmark, he studied theology and Semitic philology at the University of Copenhagen (Dr. Phil., 1912), and Semitics and Islamics in Marburg, Leipzig, Berlin, Leiden, Paris, and Budapest. He taught Semitic philology in Copenhagen (1916–51). Many of his published writings are in Danish only; others include *Der Eid bei den Semiten und im Islam* (1914), *Israel* (4 vols., 1926, 1959), *Inscriptiones Semiticae* (1928), *Scepticisme Israelite* (1931), and *Al-Sulami, Tabaqat Al-Sufiyah I* (Arabic text, sayings of mystics) (1938). Shortly after his retirement, his services to Copenhagen University and his contributions to learning in general were recognized in a festschrift, *Studia orientalia* (1953).

## Peloubet, Francis Nathan (1831–1920). Congregationalist pastor. Born in New York City, he was educated at Williams College and Bangor Theological Seminary. He then held Massachusetts pastorates at Gloucester (1857–59), Oakham (1860–65), Attleboro (1866–71), and Natick (1872–84), retiring from the active ministry in 1884. From 1874 he was engaged as an editor of Sunday school literature. In theology he was a liberal conservative. He was the author of *Select Notes on the International Sunday School Lessons* (46 vols., 1875–1920), partly written in collaboration with his wife and with Amos Russell Wells; Sunday school quarterlies in three grades (1880ff.); *Suggestive Illustrations on the NT* (3 vols., comprising John, Acts, and Matthew; 1898/99); *Loom of Life* (1900); *The Teacher's Commentary* (2 vols., comprising Matthew and Acts; 1901); *The Front Line of the Sunday School Movement* (1904); *The Book of Job, the Problem of the Ages* (1906); and *Gates to the Prayer Country* (1907). He also edited a revision of W. Smith's abridged *Bible Dictionary* (1884) and *Select Songs for the Sunday School* (2 vols., 1884–93).

## Pentecostal Churches. A term descriptive of churches which emerged from the Holiness movement in the USA at the turn of the 20th century. Characteristically these churches embraced the view that a "baptism in the Holy Spirit" apart from that of regeneration was an experience of

empowerment for ministry, available to all believers. This spiritual baptism was accompanied by the ability to speak in tongues. A wide range of pentecostal organizations were alternatively called the "Apostolic Faith movement," "Latter Rain movement," "Full-Gospel movement" and (sometimes pejoratively) the "Tongues movement." The designation as "pentecostal" was based on their appeal to the experience of the 120 on the day of Pentecost (Acts 1:8; 2:4) as normative for the modern church.

Although this teaching arose among Charles Fox Parham and his students in Kansas and Texas (1901), it gained its primary impetus through the ministry of William Joseph Seymour, the black pastor of the Apostolic Faith Mission in Los Angeles, Calif. (1906). Reports of events at the mission in the city's newspapers attracted seekers and scoffers alike to the racially integrated, although predominantly black congregation at a time when most American religion was deeply segregated. *The Apostolic Faith*, a paper published by the mission from September 1906 to May 1908, spread news that the apostolic faith was being "restored" throughout the world. News of similar, almost simultaneous, "outpourings" elsewhere—from India and China, to Scandinavia—was published, along with short devotional homilies. The result was rapid growth, and some Holiness papers (such as *Word and Work*) and denominations (including the Church of God in Christ) took a pentecostal position almost overnight.

Pentecostals generally hold a high view of Scripture, and the need for personal salvation available only through faith in Jesus Christ. They typically understand themselves to receive the Holy Spirit at conversion (as described in Rom. 8:9) but anticipate a later "baptism in the Spirit" to receive additional power for ministry through the exercise of various spiritual gifts, including those listed in 1 Cor. 12:8–10. They tend to emphasize holiness in living and the imminent return of Christ. Their conviction that they are a "last-days" people motivates them strongly toward evangelism and world mission. Their vigorous mission emphasis has made the pentecostals among the fastest-growing churches worldwide, and at times has left them open to charges of proselytism. By 1984 they comprised the largest family of Protestant churches, in excess of 51 million persons. Pentecostal churches particularly were the largest Protestant presence in many traditionally Roman Catholic countries.

Traditionally most successful among the less educated, the lower classes, and among those of non-European cultural heritage, pentecostals since World War II have increasingly attracted middle- and upper-class adherents. Since 1970, pentecostal groups have founded the Charles H. Mason Theological Seminary (Atlanta, Ga.), the Assemblies of God Theological Seminary (Springfield, Mo.), and the Church of God School of Theology (Cleveland, Tenn.). They also produced an academic Society for Pentecostal Studies, which publishes a scholarly journal, *Pneuma*. This is paralleled in Europe by the European Pentecostal Theological Association. In the USA pentecostals led the way in mass media evangelism, through such well-known preachers as Oral Roberts, Jim Bakker (PTL), and Jimmy Swaggart, augmented by "charismatic" Pat Robertson (700 Club). Highly visible media personalities proved a mixed blessing in the 1980s. Robertson distinguished himself in a credible bid for the U.S. presidency (1988); Roberts and Swaggart were involved in scandal; and Bakker was sentenced to prison.

The earliest pentecostals were Holiness-pentecostals, who continued to hold to a Wesleyan view of sanctification as a postconversion crisis experience which "removed" their sin nature. It was anticipated that this would be followed by their "baptism in the Spirit." Among those denominations which continued to maintain this position were the Church of God (Cleveland) and the Church of God of Prophecy (Cleveland). Both came out of an organization founded by Tennessee revivalist Ambrose Jessup Tomlinson. Others with a perfectionist theology include the Pentecostal Holiness Church (Oklahoma City, Okla.) given its focus by Joseph Hillery King; The Apostolic Faith (Portland, Oreg.) founded by Florence Louise Crawford, and the Church of God in Christ (Memphis, Tenn.), led for 69 years by Charles Harrison Mason.

William H. Durham, originally pastor of the North Avenue Mission in Chicago, rejected the Wesleyan view of sanctification, and caused the first major doctrinal split within pentecostalism. Arguing that Jesus had finished the work of salvation, including sanctification, on the cross, his "finished-work" theory was taught from about 1910 onward. He died in 1912 at age 39, but his theological legacy led to establishment of a series of denominations which viewed sanctification as positional and progressive. Among these were the International Church of the Foursquare Gospel (Los Angeles, Calif.), founded by the flamboyant evangelist, Aimee Semple McPherson; the Open Bible Standard Churches (Des Moines, Iowa); and the largest pentecostal body, the Assemblies of God (Springfield, Mo.).

At a camp meeting near Pasadena, Calif., in 1913, Canadian evangelist Robert E. McAlister commented that in Acts Christians were baptized in the name of Jesus (Acts 2:38) rather than according to a Trinitarian formula (Matt. 28:19). Coupled with a revelation claimed by John G. Scheppe that there was power in "the name of Jesus," this led ultimately (1916) to a second doctrinal division, and the establishment of a third strand of pentecostalism. Known commonly as "Jesus Name," "Apostolic," "Oneness," or "Jesus Only" pentecostals, this group practiced baptism according to Acts 2:38, understood the name of God to be "Jesus," and proclaimed a modalistic understanding of the Godhead. The most radical of the pentecostal movements, it identifies the initial reception of the Spirit in a believer's life as "baptism in the Spirit," and anticipates the ability to speak in tongues as evidence of true salvation as well as empowerment for ministry. Denominations representing this strand of pentecostalism include the United Pentecostal Church (St. Louis, Mo.), the Pentecostal Assemblies of the World (Indianapolis, Ind., originally led by the gifted black preacher, Garfield Thomas Haywood), the Bible Way Churches (Washington, D.C.), and various other "apostolic" churches.

Pentecostals perceive themselves as a grassroots ecumenical movement. Understanding *koinōnia* fellowship, to be a work of the Spirit, they view human-organized ecumenical efforts with incredulity. Many pentecostals have cooperated in various healing crusades (such as F. F. Bosworth, William Branham, and Oral Roberts), the founding of the Pentecostal World Conference, the Pentecostal Fellowship of North America, the Full Gospel Business Men's International, and Women's Aglow Fellowship. The acceptance of pentecostals by U.S. evangelicals led to their participation in the National Association of Evangelicals (NAF), the Lausanne Committee for World Evangelization. No classical pentecostal church by the 1980s had joined the National Council of Churches but a few third world groups were affiliated with the World Council of Churches.

Due largely to the witness of David J. Du Plessis, pentecostal teaching found fertile ground within mainline churches, resulting in the neopentecostal or charismatic renewal movement. It emerged first in Protestant circles (1960), then in the Roman Catholic Church (1967). While many within this movement have had a renewed experience in their lives, few explained it in pentecostal terms. Yet it spread rapidly, bringing new vitality to the life, worship, and ministry of Christians around the world.

*See also* CHARISMATIC MOVEMENT; HOLINESS CHURCHES.

**Bibliography.** N. Bloch-Hoell, *The Pentecostal Movement* (1964); J. T. Nichol, *Pentecostalism* (1966); D. L. Gelpi, *Pentecostalism: A Theological Viewpoint* (1971); E. D. O'Connor, *The Pentecostal Movement in the Catholic Church* (1971); V. Synan, *The Holiness-Pentecostal Movement in the United States* (1971); S. Durasoff, *Bright Wind of the Spirit: Pentecostalism Today* (1972); W. J. Hollenweger, *The Pentecostals: The Charismatic Movement in the Churches* (1972); K. McDonnell, *Charismatic Renewal* (1976); R. M. Anderson, *Vision of the Disinherited: The Making of American Pentecostalism* (1979); K. McDonnell, ed., *Presence, Power, Praise: Documents on the Charismatic Renewal* (1980); F. T. Corum, *Like As of Fire* (1981); M. M. Poloma, *The Charismatic Movement: Is There a New Pentecost?* (1982); R. Quebedeaux, *The New Charismatics: How a Christian Renewal Movement Became a Part of the American Religious Mainstream* (1983); V. Synan, *In the Latter Days: The Outpouring of the Holy Spirit in the Twentieth Century* (1984); W. C. Fletcher, *Soviet Charismatics: The Pentecostals in the USSR* (1985); P. Hocken, *Streams of Renewal* (1986).

CECIL M. ROBECK, JR.

**Perry, Ralph Barton** (1876–1957). University professor. Born in Pultney, Vt., he studied at Princeton and Harvard (Ph.D., 1899). He taught philosophy at Williams (1899/1900), Smith (1900–1902), and Harvard (1902–46; emeritus, 1946– ). Among his books, those of greatest religious importance were *The Approach to Philosophy* (1905), *Present Philosophical Tendencies* (1912), *The New Realism* (1912), *The Present Conflict of Ideals* (1918), *Philosophy of the Recent Past* (1926), *General Theory of Vale* (1926), *A Defense of Philosophy* (1931), *The Thought and Character of William James* (1935), *The Meaning of the Humanities* (1938), *Puritanism and Democracy* (1944), and *Hope for Immortality* (1945).

RAYMOND W. ALBRIGHT

**Peru.** South American country facing the Pacific Ocean with an area of nearly 1.3 million sq. km. (496,225 sq. mi.) and a population of 19.8 million (1985).

An overwhelming majority of the population (about 96 percent) is nominally Roman Catholic. The Peruvian church did not suffer anticlerical measures comparable to those in Mexico or Central America. From 1859, the government budget included appropriations for the salaries of bishops and archbishops. Throughout most of Peru's history church-state relations were cordial and the formal separation of church and state did not occur until 1979. Since the late 1950s, however, the church has gradually distanced itself from the government and dominant economic groups. As early as 1958 church leaders criticized socioeconomic inequalities and called for meaningful reforms. The church's adoption of a more progressive stance on social issues was given significant impetus by the 1968 Medellín Conference and by the influx of foreign missionaries during the 1960s and 1970s. This change also coincided with the military dictatorship of Juan Velasco Alvarado (1968–75), which was responsible for implementing a number of social and economic reforms. During the conservative austerity measures of the military regime from 1975 to 1980, the church spoke out against government economic policies and human rights abuses. Progressive clergy and laypeople built a network of Christian base communities during the 1970s, designed to promote a grassroots church. Liberation theology was especially influential within progressive sectors and its leading exponent, Gustavo Gutiérrez, is a Peruvian-born priest. In the

1980s the church's increasingly progressive posture, combined with the government's shift to the right, led some of the bishops to moderate their positions. Nevertheless, because the progressive current is so well rooted within the church, the hierarchy remained vocal on human rights issues. In 1984 there were slightly over 2000 priests, 60 percent of them foreign-born.

The first Protestants arrived in 1849 and until the 1950s worked primarily among immigrant communities. Traditional denominations, which had been dominant, were replaced in the later 1900s by pentecostal and fundamentalist churches. By 1984 the total membership of these churches approached 700,000.

PHILIP J. WILLIAMS

**Peter, The Apostle.** Little is known for certain of Peter's career after he disappears from the record of Acts. Of his traditional association with Rome only his martyrdom is beyond reasonable doubt. He seems to have pursued his "mission to the circumcised" (Gal. 2:8) throughout the eastern Mediterranean world. From references in 1 Cor. 1:12, 3:22, and 9:5 it appears that he visited Corinth some time after Paul's evangelization of that city and that he had a following in the church there. After the lapse of Claudius's expulsion edict (Acts 18:2) he may have visited Rome (A.D. 55); if he returned there around 63 he was there when the Neronian persecution broke out two years later.

Excavations beneath St. Peter's between 1940 and 1950 revealed a 2d-century monument to Peter's (his "trophy") on the Vatican hill. Such a monument was mentioned by Gaius of Rome (see Euseb. *HE* 2.25.7). The suggestion that some bones found in the vicinity were actually Peter's cannot be substantiated.

*1 Peter.* E. J. Goodspeed held that 1 Peter was sent by the Roman church to Asia Minor in response to Heb. 5:12, to counteract the anti-imperial tendency of the Book of Revelation. R. Perdelwitz's view that 1 Pet. 1:3–4:11 is a baptismal discourse inserted in a letter was adopted by H. Windisch and F. W. Beare in their commentaries, as well as by B. H. Streeter in *The Primitive Church* (1929). W. Bornemann found in 1 Pet. 1:3–5:11 a baptismal sermon of Silvanus in Asia Minor around 90. F. L. Cross regarded 1:3–4:11 as a liturgical service (including baptism) for the eve of passover. This view, with similar ones, was subjected to a critical examination by C. F. D. Moule.

The Petrine authorship, with a life-setting in Rome on the eve of the Neronian persecution, was maintained by E. G. Selwyn and also, with a little hesitation, by J. N. D. Kelly. Probably a majority of students regarded the letter as post-Pauline, and therefore non-Petrine. F. W. Beare thought the proceedings against Christians in

Bithynia and Pontus under Pliny the younger (A.D. 112) to be a probable setting.

*2 Peter.* Opinion generally hardened against 2 Peter's authenticity, although Peter's authorship had vigorous defenders, such as E. M. B. Green. J. A. T. Robinson, dated 2 Peter before 1 Peter, holding that the earlier letter implied in 2 Pet. 3:1 was Jude, not 1 Peter.

F. F. BRUCE

*As a Preacher.* In the Gospels Peter appears as a young man of promise, in the Acts as a preacher with power, especially for evangelism. In sermons reported in the Acts Peter quoted much Scripture from memory. The pattern was that after a brief introduction, he first presented the facts from Scripture; second, how the facts pointed to Christ; third, the appeal growing out of this interpretation. He gained a hearing by appealing to the intellect, then spoke to the emotion and the will. He preached positively more than negatively. He did not shrink from addressing hearers directly. At Pentecost, largely by preaching, he opened the doors of the church to Jewish proselytes, and at Caesarea to men of Roman birth. In the NT he stands out as a prominent preacher.

*Bibliography.* *Personal Studies.* F. J. Foakes-Jackson, *Peter, Prince of Apostles* (1927); O. Cullmann, *Peter: Disciple-Apostle-Martyr* (2d ed., 1962); R. E. Brown, K. P. Donfried, and J. Reumann, eds., *Peter in the NT* (1973); C. P. Thiede, *Simon Peter: From Galilee to Rome* (1986).

*Peter and Rome.* G. Edmundson, *The Church in Rome in the First Century* (1913); H. Lietzmann, *Petrus und Paulus in Rome* (1927); M. Besson, *Saint Pierre et les Origines de la primauté romaine* (1928); K. Heussi, *War Petrus in Rom?* (1936), and *Die romische Petrustradition in kritischer Sicht* (1955); K. Aland, *NTS* 2 (1955–56): 267–75; J. M. C. Toynbee and J. B. Ward-Perkins, *The Shrine of St. Peter and the Vatican Excavations* (1957); E. Kirschbaum, *The Tombs of St. Peter and St. Paul* (ET, 1959); M. Guarducci, *The Tomb of St. Peter* (ET, 1960); T. W. Manson, *Studies in the Gospels and Epistles* (1962).

*Commentaries and Epistles.* R. Perdelwitz, *Die Mysterienreligionen und das Problem des I Petrusbriefes* (1911); W. Bornemann, *ZNW* 19 (1918): 143–65; E. J. Goodspeed, *New Chapters in NT Study* (1937).

*Commentaries on Petrine Epistles.* H. Windisch (1930), F. W. Beare (2d ed., 1958); C. E. B. Cranfield (1960); B. Reicke (1964), and J. N. D. Kelly (1969). *Commentaries on 1 Peter.* F. Hauck (1949); A. M. Stibbs and A. F. Walls (1959); E. Best (1971); J. H. Elliott, *A Home for the Homeless* (1981). *Commentaries on 2 Peter.* E. M. B. Green (1968); R. J. Bauckham (1983).

*Special Topics.* "Babylon" in 1 Pet. 5:13. E. T. Merrill, *Essays in Early Christian History* (1924); G. T. Manley, *EvQ* 16 (1944): 138–46. *Regarding 1 Peter.* P. Carrington, *The Primitive Christian Catechism: A Study in the Epistles* (1940); B. Reicke, *Disobedient Spirits and Christian Baptism* (1946); E. G. Selwyn, *SNTS Bulletin* 1 (1950): 39–50; F. L. Cross, *1 Peter: A Paschal Liturgy* (1954); J. H. Elliott, *A Home for the Homeless* (1981); C. F. D. Moule, *Essays in NT Interpretation* (1982): 133–45. *Regarding 2 Peter.* E. M. B. Green, *2 Peter Reconsidered* (1961); E. Käsemann, *Essays on NT Themes* (ET, 1964): 169–95; J. A. T. Robinson, *Redating the NT* (1976); T. Fornberg, *An Early Church in a Pluralistic Society* (1977).

ANDREW W. BLACKWOOD

## Petrie, William Matthew Flinders (1853–1942).

Lay archeologist. Born in Charlton, England, ill health prevented him from receiving a formal education, but he became interested in archeology as a boy and went on to become the greatest archeological genius of modern times. In 1880 he went to Egypt, where he undertook a long series of excavations on behalf of the Egypt Exploration Society and the British School of Archaeology in Egypt, which he headed. In 1926 excavating conditions in Egypt became too onerous, so he moved into Palestine, where he had inaugurated modern archeology in 1890. For the remainder of his life, until his death in Jerusalem, he worked and wrote in Palestine. Petrie was the author of close to 100 books, nearly all excavation reports. During the last 20 years of his life his pioneering methods were rapidly antiquated, and his efforts to reconstruct the history of Israel lost their validity.

*Bibliography.* W. M. F. Petrie, *Seventy Years in Archaeology* (1931).

WILLIAM F. ALBRIGHT

## Petry, Ray C. (1903– ).

Methodist layman. Born near Eaton, Ohio, he held degrees from Manchester College and the University of Chicago (Ph.D., 1932). From 1929 to 1937 he taught history at Manchester College and religion at McPherson College. From 1937 he held the chair of church history in the Divinity and Graduate School of Duke University. His books include *Francis of Assisi* (1941), *No Uncertain Sound* (1948), and *Preaching in the Great Tradition* (1950). He assisted in editing *The Chinese Christian Classics* and edited volume 10, *The Late Medieval Mystics*, in *The Library of Christian Classics*.

## Pfeiffer, Robert H. (1892–1958).

OT scholar and Assyriologist. Born in Bologna, Italy, he studied at the universities of Geneva, Berlin, and Tübingen, and became pastor of the Methodist Church in Sanborn, N.Y. (1916–19). He then studied at Harvard University (Ph.D., 1922), and remained there as instructor, assistant professor, and lecturer (1922–53), curator of the Semitic Museum (1931–58), and professor of Semitic language and literature (1953–58). He taught in the same field at Boston University (1924–30; 1947–58). He directed the archeological excavations at Nuzi (Kirkuk, Iraq) in 1928/29. He contributed articles to many reference works, including *The Interpreter's Bible, The New Schaff-Herzog Encyclopedia of Religious Knowledge,* and *The Encyclopedia Americana.* He wrote *State Letters of Assyria* (1935), *The Archives of Shilwateshub* (1942), *Introduction to the OT* (1941, 1948), *History of NT Times* (1949), and *Il Giudaismo* (1951), and edited the *Journal of Biblical Literature* (1943–47).

## Phenomenology of Religion.

Study of the development of a human consciousness or self-awareness of God-concepts within evolution-based philosophy; comparative study of religious phenomena. Phenomenology of religion can refer to at least two areas of intellectual enquiry. It can refer to the philosophical movement rooted in the thought of Edmund Husserl (1859–1938). This tradition included Martin Heidegger, Jean Paul Sartre, Maurice Merleau-Ponty, and Paul Ricoeur. Accordingly phenomenology of religion would be that part of phenomenological philosophy devoted to the study of religion. The second meaning of the term refers to a school of thinkers who have applied descriptive methods to the study of the history and comparison of religions. Prominent were Mircea Eliade, Rudolph Otto, Gerardus van der Leeuw, and Joachim Wach. Tending to be religious sociologists or anthropologists rather than philosophers, their primary concern was to examine the data of primitive religions with an eye to the more symbolic and ritualistic forms of religious expression rather than the theological, doctrinal, or philosophical aspects.

In neither sense is phenomenology of religion to be equated with the philosophy of religion, which seeks some explanation and justification of particular theological statements or beliefs. Phenomenology attempts to describe rather than to explain or justify. Further, phenomenology attempts to examine actual practices whereas the philosophy of religion tends to deal with ideal archetypes—not with how people do believe but with how people ought to believe.

Phenomenology understood as a philosophical method is interested in the "raw data" of a person's experience, often described as "essences." The method is purported to be primarily descriptive in its intent and, when applied to religion, is often seen as a neutral means of understanding and describing religious experience. However, in the late 19th and early 20th centuries the phenomenological students formed the conviction that all religions were basically similar and that any apparent differences were due to cultural manifestations and influences. The attempt to locate essences turned into the attempt to reduce each religion to lowest common denominators which no religion would ever endorse. The study advanced from that low, but at the end of the 20th century it was not completely freed from this mistake of the early phenomenologists.

Central issues in contemporary sociological study of religion surrounded the description of religions and questions about the nature of that description. Many attempts were made to delineate the forms of a particular religion, attempting to identify types of symbols, rituals, or practices. The issue about the nature of description centered on the relationship between the observer and the practitioner. For example, could one accurately describe Christianity without being a Christian? Was something lost when there was a "critical distance" between the phenomenologist and the actual believer or community of believers? Some phenomenologists of religion, such as Brede Kristensen, argued that it is necessary to look at religious phenomena from the standpoint of a believer. Empathy with the particular religion under scrutiny is the foremost requirement. Others argued that such neutral empathy is both impossible in practice and unnecessary in principle. In the end a dilemma arose which haunted the phenomenology of religion through the century. If empathy is not required then inevitably the observer's own presuppositions affect the results. If empathy is required the problem becomes how honest empathy is truly possible. The overarching problem is the attempt to study religion from a strictly neutral descriptive point of view. What tended to happen was that religion, of whatever variety, was cast in the mold of 20th-century Western enlightened secular man. It was a noble aim to study the world's religions honestly and sensitively. It could not be done from a neutral standpoint, however, and until this fact was honestly confronted, the phenomenology of religion would not become very fruitful.

See also PHILOSOPHY OF RELIGION.

**Bibliography.** M. Eliade, *The Sacred and the Profane* (1961); J. D. Bettis, ed., *The Phenomenology of Religion* (1969); N. Smart, *The Phenomenon of Religion* (1973); E. J. Sharpe, *Comparative Religion* (1975).

RICHARD LINTS

**Philippians, Epistle to the.** See PAUL, THE APOSTLE.

**Philippine Independent Church.** See SOUTHEAST ASIA.

**Philippines.** See SOUTHEAST ASIA.

**Philipson, David** (1862–1949). Rabbi. Born in Wabash, Ind., he was educated at the University of Cincinnati and Hebrew Union College. He was rabbi at Har Sinai Congregation, Baltimore, Md. (1884–88), and at B'ne Israel Congregation, Cincinnati, Ohio (1888–1938; emeritus, 1938–49). He also served as a member of the faculty of Hebrew Union College (homiletics, 1891–1905; history of reform Judaism, 1905–47). He was the president of the Central Conference of American Rabbis (1907–9), on the board of editors of the new Bible translation, consulting editor of the *Jewish Encyclopedia*, chairman of the board of editors of Union of American Hebrew Congregations and Hebrew Union College Annual, vice-president of the American Jewish Historical Society, and a member of the synagogue council of America. He wrote *Old European Jewries* (1894),

*The Oldest Jewish Congregation in the West* (1894; rev. ed., 1924), *A Holiday Sheaf* (1898), *The Jew in English Fiction* (1899, 1902, 1911, 1919), *The Reform Movement in Judaism* (1907; rev. ed., 1931), *Max Lilienthal—American Rabbi* (1915), *Centenary Papers and Others* (1919), *History of Hebrew Union College* (1925), and *My Life as an American Jew* (1941). He edited *The Selected Writings of Isaac M. Wise* (1900), *Reminiscences by Isaac M. Wise* (1901), and *Letters of Rebecca Gratz* (1929).

RAYMOND W. ALBRIGHT

**Phillips, John Bertram** (1906–1982). Anglican clergyman and scholar. Born in Barnes, Middlesex, he held various short-term appointments in the London area, then was successively vicar in Lee (1940–44) and Redhill (1945–55), prebendary of Chichester Cathedral (1957–60), and canon of Salisbury Cathedral (1964–69). A prolific writer who believed in making righteousness readable, he produced several books that reached the religious best-seller category. Among his publications are *Letters to Young Churches* (1947), *Your God Is Too Small* and *Making Men Whole* (1952), *Plain Christianity* (1954), *The Young Church in Action* (1955), *NT Christianity* (1956), *St. Luke's Life of Christ* (1956), *The Book of Revelation* (1957), *The NT in Modern English* (1958), *A Man Called Jesus* (1959), *God Our Contemporary* (1960), *Good News* (1963), *Four Prophets* (1963), *Ring of Truth* (1967), and *Peter's Portrait of Jesus* (1976).

J. D. DOUGLAS

**Phillips, Walter Alison** (1864–1950). Church of England historian. Born in Lewisham, London, he studied at Merchant Taylor's School, London, and Merton College, Oxford. In 1905 he became chief assistant editor of the *Encyclopaedia Britannica* (11th ed.). In 1912 he joined the staff of the *Times*. He was Lecky professor of modern history at Trinity College, Dublin (1914–39). His chief works are *Modern Europe* (1899), *The Confederation of Europe* (1913), and *The Revolution in Ireland* (1923). He edited *History of the Church of Ireland*.

**Philosophical Theology.** See THEOLOGY, 20TH-CENTURY TRENDS IN.

**Philosophy of Religion.** The branch of philosophy that studies philosophical questions that arise out of reflection about religious claims, beliefs, and practices. Such questions would include: What is the nature of religion and of God? What does it mean to say that God is omnipotent or omniscient? What is prayer? How should "miracle" be defined? Are miracles possible? What is revelation? What is faith and how is it related to reason? What reasons or arguments, if any, support belief in the existence of God or survival after death? What is the nature of religious experience and what criteria, if any, serve to distinguish genuine religious experiences from the spurious? What is the relation between religion and science? How have modern developments in science made religious belief less plausible, and the two fields incompatible? What is the relation between religion and ethics? Is religious belief a necessary condition for living a consistently moral life? What is the nature and function of religious language, and how does it differ from other uses of language?

In the mid-1900s the philosophy of religion was regarded in many academic circles as dead, shown to be irrelevant by the attacks of a system known as logical positivism. During the 1940s and 1950s, the philosophical agenda was set largely by thinkers hostile to theism; Catholic and Protestant philosophers sympathetic to a traditional or orthodox brand of Christian theism were on the defensive.

The philosophical climate, changed, however, and most philosophers finally recognized that it was logical positivism that was dead. Its false claims were unmasked in a flood of books and articles after World War II. By the later 1900s agenda was set, for the most part, by respected philosophers sympathetic to theism. The list of just the American philosophers recognized as pace-setters in the field included Alvin Plantinga, George Mavrodes, William Alston, Robert M. Adams, Marilyn McCord Adams, Keith Yandell, and Nicholas Wolterstorff, and other members of the Society of Christian Philosophers. The society's journal, *Faith and Philosophy*, was a platform for discussions in the philosophy of religion. The list of influential philosophers of religion in Great Britain included Richard Swinburne, Paul Heim, and Peter Geach, among others.

A widely discussed topic of the late 20th century was the rationality of belief in God. A group of philosophers led by Plantinga challenged the previously dominant assumption that a major test for the rationality of any belief was the ability of its proponents to prove that belief. In the case of God's existence, belief in God was alleged to be rational only if one could provide rational supporting proofs or reasons. If such proofs or arguments could not be provided, the belief was judged substandard. Plantinga and others replied that belief in God is properly basic—by which they meant that a person is perfectly justified in accepting that belief, even if unable to produce supporting arguments. The case for this position was laid out in *Faith and Rationality*, edited by Plantinga and Wolterstorff.

For Plantinga, belief in God is in the same epistemological boat as belief in other minds or that the world continues to exist when no one is perceiving it. Even though it is not possible to prove that other minds exist, it is rational to believe that

they do. Likewise, even if it were not possible to prove that God exists, it is rational to believe it. Plantinga, however, also believed that proofs are available should believers decide that they would like some; but the arguments are not necessary to make the Christian's belief rational.

Whether Plantinga (and others) were correct in their claim that the theistic arguments are not necessary, discussion of these arguments continued to retain its place at or near the center of the philosophy of religion. Advances in the logic of necessity and refinements of the techniques of analytic philosophy made interaction on the theistic arguments much more technical; but according to those at home with them, these techniques also made the debates more productive. Unfortunately, the highly technical nature of the ideas tended to make the whole matter much less accessible to nonphilosophers. Ironically, the more plausible theistic arguments became to professional philosophers, the less intelligible they become to the masses.

Plantinga also gave the ontological argument for God's existence a novel twist in *God, Freedom, and Evil*, in which he based a version of the argument on the semantics of possible worlds. Some philosophers, such as the Roman Catholic Frederick Copleston, continued to insist that a properly formulated version of the cosmological argument still merited respect. The teleological argument was refined, revised, and brought up to date, taking into account such modern challenges as Darwinism, by thinkers such as F. R. Tennant. Richard Swinburne (*The Existence of God*, 1979) offered interesting and challenging appraisal of the theistic arguments.

A perennial problem for philosophers of religion has been the problem of evil. Critics of theism often alleged that the existence of evil is logically incompatible with the existence of a good and omnipotent God. This kind of logical attack against theism (logical in the sense that it maintains that a logical contradiction exists at the heart of theism) has received its most influential reply from Plantinga in such books as *God and Other Minds* (1967), *God, Freedom, and Evil* (1974) and *The Nature of Necessity* (1975). Thanks largely to such work, former advocates of the logical or deductive problem of evil were forced to abandon this line of attack. In its place, these antitheists advanced various versions of an inductive form of the problem of evil in which the existence of evil is said to make belief in God improbable or less plausible. An excellent survey of replies to this argument can be found in Michael Peterson's *Evil and the Christian God*.

From the 1970s many philosophers of religion turned their attention to the concept of God, in particular to the attributes of God. Examples of the issues encountered were: What does it mean to say that God is omnipotent, omniscient, or immutable? Can an omnipotent being do absolutely anything or are there logical constraints upon God's power? Can an omniscient being know the future free actions of human beings and, if so, how can those creatures really be free, given the fact that God knows what they will do? What is God's relation to time? Is God timeless in the sense that he is totally outside of time? Most of these issues are discussed in Ronald Nash's *Concept of God.*

Confusion resulting from incorrect thinking about the nature of God and God's relation to the world created new interest in the system known as panentheism or process theology. According to this approach, God and the world are mutually eternal and mutually interdependent. Process theology sees God, not as a complete or an unsurpassably perfect being, but as one whose present "perfection" is constantly being surpassed. God, like the world, is subject to process, change, and development. For philosophically alert individuals, the 20th-century arena of the philosophy of religion was full of interesting and exciting debates. While systematic theology was characterized by a lack of innovation, some of the most creative thinking about theoretical issues in religion was being done by professional philosophers. Thanks to the work of a growing number of such individuals, the philosophy of religion was restored to a place of importance and honor in the field of philosophy.

*See also* PHENOMENOLOGY OF RELIGION.

**Bibliography.** *Surveys.* B. Brody, ed., *Readings in the Philosophy of Religion* (1974); W. Rowe, *Philosophy of Religion: An Introduction* (1978); J. Hick, *Philosophy of Religion* (3d ed., 1983); W. Abraham, *An Introduction to the Philosophy of Religion* (1985); R. H. Nash, *Faith and Reason: Searching for a Rational Faith* (1988).

*Studies of Philosophical Problems.* C. S. Lewis, *Miracles* (1960) and *The Problem of Pain* (1962); G. Mavrodes, ed., *The Rationality of Belief in God* (1970); A. Plantinga, *God, Freedom and Evil* (1974); M. Peterson, *Evil and the Christian God* (1982); R. H. Nash, *The Concept of God* (1983); A. Plantinga and N. Walterstorff, eds., *Faith and Rationality* (1983); R. H. Nash, *Process Theology* (1987).

RONALD H. NASH

**Pickens, Claude Leon, Jr.** (1900– ). Episcopalian Islamics scholar. Born in Alexandria, Va., he studied at the University of Michigan, the Theological Seminary in Virginia, and Columbia University. He served in the Diocese of Hankow (O.-Hsiang) (1926–50); he was canon of St. Paul's Cathedral, Hankow; F.R.G.S., secretary of Society of Friends of the Moslems in China; and associate editor of *Muslim World*, contributing articles pertaining to Chinese Islam. He made surveys of Muslims in northeast Tibet, inner Mongolia, and northwest China (1933, 1936), accompanied by S. M. Zwemer and missionaries to China. He compiled the *Annotated Bibliography of Literature on Islam in China.*

**Pieper, Francis (Franz August Otto)** (1852–1931). Lutheran theologian, editor, and church leader. Born in Pomerania, he studied there at the gymnasium of Colberg, at Northwestern University, Watertown, Wis., and at Concordia Theological Seminary, St. Louis, Mo. He was Lutheran pastor at Manitowoc, Wis. (1875–78), professor of theology at Concordia Seminary (1878–87), president there from 1887, and president of the Lutheran Synod of Missouri, Ohio, and other states from 1899. In these positions and as editor of *Lehre und Wehre,* he played an important part in shaping the theological orientation of a large section of the American Lutheran clergy. He wrote *Das Grundbekenntnis der evangelischlutherischen Kirche* (1880), *Lehre von der Rechtfertigung* (1889), *Gesetz und Evangelium* (1892), *Distinctive Doctrines of the Lutheran Church* (1892), *Unsere Stellung in Lehre und Praxis* (1896), *Lehrstellung der Missouri-Synode* (1897), *Christ's Work* (1898), *Das Wesen des Christentums* (1903), *Zur Einigung* (1913), *Conversion and Election* (1913), *Christliche Dogmatik* (1917, 1920, 1924), *Die rechte Weltanschauung* (1923), *Das Fundament des christlichen Glaubens* (1925), and *A Brief Statement of the Missouri Synod's Doctrinal Position* (1931).

**Pietilä, Antti Jaakko** (1878–1932). Evangelical Lutheran scholar. Born in Oulu, Finland, he studied at the University of Helsinki and taught dogmatics and ethics there (1919–32). He belonged to the so-called School of Erlangen (J. C. K. von Hofmann), but his theological thinking was on native base and he held the viewpoints of the revival movements. He wrote *The Christian Safety of Salvation* (1905), *Drei Versuchungsgeschichten: Zarathustra, Buddha, Christus* (1910), *Die Entwicklung des Offenbarungsbegriffs seit Schleiermacher* (1918), *The Ethics of Christ and the Present Time* (1918), *The Ethics of Society* (1925), and *Christian Dogmatics,* (3 vols., 1930–32).

LENNART PINOMAA

**Pijper, Frederik** (1859–1926). Reformed pastor and professor. Born in Hoogwoud, the Netherlands, he studied theology at the University of Utrecht, receiving his doctorate in 1883. After serving as pastor at Eenigenburg, Veendam, and Berkhout, he became professor of church history at the University of Leiden (1897). He wrote *Geschiedenis der boete en biecht in de Christelijke Kerk* (1891), *Bibliotheca Reformatoria Neerlandica* (10 vols., 1903–14), *Middeleeuwsch Christendom* (1917), *Beknopt handboek tot de geschiedenis des Christendoms* (1924). He was a leading editor of the *Nederlandsch archief voor kerkgeschiedenis.*

ALBERT HYMA

**Pike, James Albert.** (1913–1969). Anglican bishop. Born in Oklahoma City, he graduated from the Jesuit College of Santa Clara, became an agnostic, and entered law school at Yale University where he earned the J. D. in 1938. He then worked for the Securities and Exchange Commission and taught at the Catholic University of America and Georgetown University. During World War II he was part of Advanced Naval Intelligence. After the war and the break-up of his first marriage, he began the study of theology which led to his ordination as an Episcopal priest in 1946. He then held a series of important positions within the Episcopal Church, ranging from dean of the Cathedral of St. John the Divine to bishop of the Episcopal bishopric of California (1958–1966). His numerous publications, covering many of the social, political, and theological issues of the day, brought him fame and controversy. He was accused of heresy for denying the virgin birth, the trinity, the incarnation, and the second coming, and was finally censured by his fellow bishops in 1966. He then developed an interest in the occult. During a trip to the Holy Land in 1969, he apparently became lost and fell to his death in the desert.

ROBERT V. SCHNUCKER

**Piper, Otto A.** (1891–1981). Presbyterian scholar. Born in Lichte, Germany, he studied theology and philosophy at Jena, Marburg, Paris, and Göttingen. After military service in World War I, he taught systematic theology at Göttingen (1920–30) and Münster (1930–33), where he succeeded Karl Barth. Forced by the Nazis to leave Germany, he taught philosophy of religion at Swansea, Wales (1934–36), and Bangor, North Wales (1936/37), before settling at Princeton Theological Seminary in 1937, where he taught until his death. He devoted himself to European relief work following World War II and received the officer's Cross of the Order of Merit from the president of BundesRepublik Deutschland. Among his many significant works are *Weltliches Christentum* (1924), *Theologie and Reine Lehre*, (1926), *Die Grundlagen der evangelischen Ethik* (2 vols., 1928/29), *Recent Developments in German Protestantism* (1934), *God in History* (1939), *The Christian Interpretation of Sex* (1941), and *The Biblical View of Sex and Marriage* (1959). A festschrift in his honor appeared in 1962 entitled *Current Issues in NT Interpretation*, edited by W. Klassen and G. F. Snyder.

WALTER A. ELWELL

**Pittenger, William Norman** (1905– ). Anglican theologian. Born in Bogota, N.J., he was educated at Princeton University and General Theological Seminary, N.Y. He joined the faculty of General Theological Seminary in 1935 as a tutor and retired in the mid-1960s as professor of apologetics. After his "retirement," he taught at Kings College, Cambridge University, but has since retired from this position also. A prolific author, he is particularly noted for his works on the Eucharist and Christology and for his commitment to process theology. Pittenger's process thought, however, has some unusual sources including the writings of William Porcher and DuBose, which Pittenger collected in the book, *Unity in the Faith* (1957). This process orientation results in a strong emphasis on the development of Christian doctrine through the centuries and on the need to reformulate these doctrines in each new age. His view of God is pantheistic. Pittenger stresses that the Christian God who is known to us in Jesus Christ is related to all of creation. He also wrote *The Word Incarnate: A Study of the Doctrine of the Person of Christ* (1959).

STEPHEN T. FRANKLIN

**Pius XI** (1857–1939). Pope from 1922 to 1939. Born Ambrogio Dominiano Achille Ratti in Desio, province of Milan, he studied theology at Saint Charles Seminary, Milan, and was sent to the Lombard College in Rome for graduate training. He was ordained a priest in 1879, and obtained doctorates in theology, canon law, and philosophy (1882). After a few months of parish ministry, he served for five years on the faculty of Saint Charles Seminary, after which he was appointed doctor (i.e., research staff member) of the Ambrosian Library, Milan (1888). At this time of his life, he sought a diversion from the sedentary life of a scholar in mountain climbing. In 1907 he succeeded Ceriani as head of the Ambrosian, and in 1911, he was appointed vice-prefect of the Vatican Library in Rome under Ehrle, S. J. When Ehrle resigned after the outbreak of World War I, Ratti became prefect of the Vatican Library. Ratti was sent as apostolic visitor to Poland and the Baltic provinces (1918) in order to study and promote the reorganization of church life in those territories, which had been deeply affected by the impact of war and the shifting of political allegiance. In 1919 he was appointed papal nuncio to the Polish government, and consecrated archbishop (titular) of Lepanto. He was called back to Italy to succeed the late Ferrari on the archiepiscopal see of Milan (1921) and was created cardinal the same year. Upon his election as pope (1922), he took the name of Pius XI. Pius XI confirmed Gasparri in his charge as secretary of state and, with the assistance of this prelate, negotiated the so-called Lateran treaty (1929), between the Holy See and the Italian (fascist) government. The pope was recognized officially as the temporal sovereign of the City of the Vatican and its dependences, and the authority of the Italian government over Rome and sundry parts of the former Pontifical States, was acknowledged by the papal government. The Lateran treaty was supplemented by a concordat, with a view to insure the cooperation of the papal and the royal government in matters of common concern. These agreements consummated the ruin of the *Partito Popolare Italiano*, a democratic Christian movement which had become internally divided and which the Vatican was not eager to uphold. The pope's effort at improving the relations between the Holy See and secular powers was repeatedly thwarted by the emergence of totalitarian ideologies. In France, he condemned the ultranationalist (and monarchist) movement of the *Action Franÿaise*, which had the following of a considerable number of Catholics who had felt encouraged by the condemnation of the democratic *Sillon* under Pius X. The situation was more delicate in Italy and in Germany, where the fascist and Nazi governments were threatening the liberty of the church. Pius XI solemnly rebuked Mussolini's measures against Catholic Action in the encyclical *Non abbiamo bisogno* (1931). Atheistic communism was similarly branded in the encyclical *Divini redemptoris* (1937). Pius XI gave special attention to ecclesiastical problems arising in the following fields:

(1) Promotion of Missions: The pope's policy aimed at centralizing the control of foreign missions in Rome, reorganizing missionary districts, and hastening the formation of indigenous clergy and the consecration of indigenous bishops.

(2) Social Problems: An attempt was made at formulating anew the social doctrine of the Roman Church in the encyclical *Quadragesimo anno* (1931). The doctrine of the church on the nature and social function of the Christian family was stated in the encyclical *Casti connubii* (1930). The development of Catholic Action, that is, of lay movements, cooperating with the clergy under the authority of the hierarchy, was actively promoted.

(3) Union of Churches: The principles and conditions of a Roman ecumenism were expounded in the encyclical *Mortalium animos* (1928). Another encyclical, *Rerum orientalium* (1928), marks the effort made to foster the growth of Uniate Churches in harmony with their traditions, while preliminary studies for the codification of Eastern canon law were ordered by the pope in order to achieve a greater integration of all ecclesiastical bodies within the Roman obedience.

(4) Ecclesiastical Studies: The encyclical *Studiorum ducem* (1923) reaffirmed the belief that Thomism constitutes the outstanding means of expression for Catholic doctrine, and the apostolic constitution *Deus scientiarum Dominus* (1931) was issued in view of a thorough reorganization of ecclesiastical studies within the Roman Church. There was no radical softening of the attitude of the papacy toward modernists, especially in the field of biblical research.

**Bibliography.** M. Bierbaum, *Das Papsttum, Leben und Werk Pius XI* (1937); R. Fontenelle, *Pie XI* (1939); L. Browne-Olf, *Pius XI, Apostle of Peace* (1938); G. Galbiati, *Papa Pio XI* (1939); F. C. Roux, *Huit ans au Vatican, 1932–1940* (1947); M. Maccarone, Il nazional-socialismo e la S. R. Sede (1947); *Enciclopedia Cattolica* (vol. 9, 1952). The official documents of Pius XI are found in the *Acta Apostolicae Sedis;* cf. M. Claudia Carlen, *A Guide to the Encyclicals of the Roman Pontiffs from Leo XIII to the Present Day 1878–1937* (1939).

GEORGES A. BARROIS

**Pius XII** (1876–1958). Pope from 1939. Born Eugenio Pacelli in Rome in a family actively devoted to the service of the papacy for several generations, he studied theology at the Gregorian University and at the Pontifical Athenaeum of the Roman Seminary, obtaining the degrees of doctor of theology and *doctor utriusque juris*. Ordained a priest in 1899, he was assigned in 1901 to the section of Extraordinary Ecclesiastical Affairs, of which he became prosecretary (1912) and secretary (1915). In 1917, Pacelli was sent as papal nuncio to Munich with the title archbishop of Sardes, and he conveyed the pope's plan for peace to the imperial government of Germany. After World War I, he became accredited to the German Republic and transferred his residence to Berlin. He was instrumental in preparing the concordats and solemn agreements between the Holy See and the German states under the pontificate of Pius XI. Pacelli was recalled to Rome and created cardinal in 1929; he became secretary of state to Pius XI in 1930, after whose death he was elected pope (1939), in an unprecedented short conclave. He took the name of Pius XII, and appointed Maglione his secretary of state. After the death of this prelate in 1944, Pius XII took on himself the direction of the Vatican diplomacy, with the help of Tardini in the section of Extraordinary Ecclesiastical Affairs and Montini in the section of Ordinary Ecclesiastical Affairs.

The rapid deterioration of international politics in 1939 and the outbreak of World War II confronted Pius XII with problems similar to those with which Benedict XV had wrestled during the totality of his reign. The Vatican's intense diplomatic activity during the summer months of 1939 proved futile for the preservation of the peace, and the only course which remained open was for the pope to maintain close contacts with the secular powers, in order to humanize the war and bring about peace negotiations. For these reasons the appointment of Myron Taylor as personal envoy of President Roosevelt in 1940 was most welcome at the Vatican. The pope also communicated with Washington through his Apostolic Delegate and through Spellman, archbishop of New York (cardinal since 1945). On October 20, 1939, the pope protested against the violation of the natural rights of individuals and states in the encyclical *Summi Pontificatus*. In an address to the members of the Pontifical Court, on Christmas Eve 1939, he enumerated five essential conditions for a just and honorable peace: (1) adequate reparations whenever a nation's right to independence was violated; (2) progressive disarmament by mutual agreement of the nations concerned; (3) creation or development of international institutions for the prevention or arbitration of differences; (4) revision of treaties or conventions which would have become obsolete; (5) Christian justice and charity as the essential foundations of real peace. The pope disapproved of the formula "unconditional surrender" coined by the Allies; he feared that the unlimited pursuit of their war aims might create in Central Europe a vacuum favorable to the development of communism.

During the war years and after the cessation of hostilities, the Vatican contributed to the relief of civilian populations, especially in Rome and Italy, and set up an office for gathering information on displaced persons, prisoners of war, and civilian internees.

Atheistic and materialistic communism was denounced and unambiguously condemned. A decree of the Holy Office (1949) threatened with automatic excommunication Roman Catholics taking or retaining membership in communist organizations. While rejecting the principle of the separation of church and state, the diplomacy of the Vatican made allowance provisionally for the de facto regime prevailing in most of the democratic nations. It upheld the privileged situation of the Roman Church in Italy and Spain, and expressed no dissatisfaction with the laws of these countries restricting the liberty of other churches or the civil status of individuals not sharing in the Roman Catholic faith. Pius XII strove to maintain the independence of the Roman Church and of the Uniate Churches in the countries behind the Iron Curtain. He raised a strong protest against the arrest of Mindszenty, primate of Hungary, and fought the attempts of the governments of Czechoslovakia and Hungary at creating or favoring National Catholic churches not organically related to the Holy See. In Yugoslavia, he protested against the condemnation of Stepinac, archbishop of Zagreb who had been charged with supporting reactionary elements hostile to the Tito regime in predominantly Roman Catholic Croatia.

In his government of the Roman Church, Pius XII endeavored to stress its universal, supranational character. The promotion of new cardinals in the Consistories of 1946 and 1953 reversed the former majority in the Sacred College, which then (1953) counted only 26 Italian members. There remained, however, an overwhelming proportion of Italian prelates in the central administration of the church. Pius XII defined the dogma of the assumption in 1950. He upheld the principles of his predecessors with regard to biblical studies in the encyclical *Divino afflante Spiritu* (1943), and took position against philosophical existentialism in the encyclical *Humani generis* (1950).

*Bibliography.Wartime Correspondence between Pius XII and President Roosevelt* (1947); J. O. Smit, *Pope Pius XII* (1949); M. Claudia Carlen, *Guide to the Documents of Pius XII, 1939—49* (1951); O. Halecki and J. F. Murray, *Eugene Pacelli, Pope of Peace* (1954); N. Padellaro, *Portrait of Pius XII* (ET, 1956); K. Burton, *Witness of the Light: The Life of Pope Pius XII* (1958); R. Hochhuth, *The Representative* (ET, 1963); S. Friedlander, *Pius XII and the Third Reich* (ET, 1966); C. Falconi, *The Silence of Pius XII* (1970).

GEORGES A. BARROIS

**Plymouth Brethren.** A body of Christians tracing their origin to the evangelical revival in Britain early in the 19th century. Commonly known as Plymouth Brethren because of their first substantial congregation in that English city in 1831, they dislike any label other than Christian. Their basic distinctive is their strong determination to take Scripture, rather than doctrinal formularies or ecclesiastical traditions, as normative. They subscribe to doctrines commonly held by evangelicals with the exception of a related group, commonly known as "Exclusive" Brethren, who have developed eccentric doctrines. Their early leaders espoused the premillennial view of the second advent of Christ, and some developed novel views of a "secret rapture" of true believers prior to Christ's return in glory. They stressed the unity of all believers in the body of Christ and their duty to propagate the NT gospel and live devoted lives.

Formative leaders include John Nelson Darby (1800–1882), graduate of Trinity College, Dublin and Irish curate; Benjamin Wills Newton (1807–99), fellow of Exeter College, Oxford; George Müller (1805–98), a German who settled in Bristol where he founded a famous orphanage; Henry Craik (1805–66), a Scotsman trained for ministry in the Church of Scotland; and Anthony Norris Groves (1795–1853), who became a missionary in Baghdad and India. Initial growth took place in the west of England—London and other large towns and parts to the north of England. Substantial growth, particularly in Ireland and Scotland, followed evangelical revival movements in the later 19th century.

Personal differences between Darby and Newton—both strongminded men—together with disagreements on prophetic matters and ministry in the church, led to a rift in 1845 which was widened in 1849. The year 1849 marks the final separation of Darby and his followers from other Brethren. The former, often described as Exclusives, accepted Darby's teaching that the church was "in ruins" in its outward structure, that NT teaching about church order no longer applied, and that the duty of Christians was to obey Christ's command to break bread weekly in remembrance of him to claim his promised presence. Darby propagated his views in Switzerland,

France, other European countries, and later in North America, the Caribbean, and New Zealand. He wrote voluminously and translated the Bible into French and German as well as English. After his death in 1882 his followers divided into numerous mutually exclusive groups, and the movement became discredited by excesses during the 1950s and 1960s.

Open or Christian Brethren, as they were variously called, who did not follow Darby's line, looked to men such as Müller and Groves as exemplars. They had few commanding figures or outstanding propagators of their viewpoint. Leading characteristics were: tenacious adherence to Scripture (often interpreted dispensationally); diligent evangelistic preaching at home and abroad; the multiplication of autonomous churches practicing believer's baptism; and weekly celebration of the Lord's supper in open, nonliturgical worship. There was also strong emphasis on Bible teaching, prayer, and sometimes various forms of social service. Leadership structures varied, involving either a board of male members, known as leading brethren, or boards of elders and deacons usually chosen by the church. In the late 1900s an increasing number used full-time paid workers in ministry positions. Open Brethren usually did not insist on uniformity in secondary matters of doctrine and polity, and they tended to cooperate with other evangelicals and to contribute to interdenominational societies and activities. Open Brethren largely avoided divisions, apart from one caused by a "Needed Truth" movement in 1887.

Because of emigration and missionary activities, Brethren communities were spread through the English-speaking world and in many other countries. They were particularly prevalent in Argentina, New Zealand, Singapore, and parts of central Africa, where F. S. Arnot was an outstanding pioneer. Missionary agencies included Müller's Scripture Knowledge Institution (founded in 1834) and *Echoes of Service* (founded in 1872), a missionary magazine. Similar service agencies existed in Australia, Canada, France, Germany, New Zealand, Switzerland, and the USA, with a total of 1200 missionaries worldwide.

In the late 1900s there was a marked tendency among Open Brethren to take their place among other Protestant denominations, although many resisted ecumenism. There was still no denominational structure or point of reference, aside from the Christian Brethren Research Fellowship, founded in 1963 in Britain. Estimates of numerical strength varied wildly. There were perhaps, 50,000 Open Brethren in Britain and 10,000 to 20,000 Exclusives, and 500,000 Brethren worldwide.

*Bibliography.* W. R. Neatby, *A History of the Plymouth Brethren* (1902); H. H. Rowdon, *The Origins of the Brethren* (1967); F. R. Coad, *A History of the Brethren Movement* (1968); J. N. Darby, *Collected Writings* (34 vols., repr. ed., 1971); W. T. Stunt, et al., *Turning the World Upside Down* (1972); F. A. Tatford, *That the World May Know*, 10 vols. (1982–86).

HAROLD H. ROWDON

**Pocket Testament League.** League whose aim is to encourage everyone to carry, read, and use the Bible. In 1893 Helen Cadbury, a child in Birmingham, England, formed a Bible club with her friends. After her 1908 marriage to American evangelist Charles Alexander, the couple launched the Pocket Testament League as a worldwide movement. It has extended its work to 33 countries, and 3 to 4 million copies of the Gospel of John were distributed annually in the 1980s. The league's methods included personal evangelism using the Bible, simple Bible studies for all age groups, training seminars and conferences, and school visits and local outreach.

**Poland.** Northeast European country with an area of 312,683 sq. km. (120,728 sq. mi.) and a population of 38 million (1988). Even before the communist state was dismantled in 1989 and 1990, Poland was the only country in Eastern Europe where the church was stronger than the state and enjoyed greater authority and legitimacy. A distinctive combination of religious faith and patriotism in the national mind took root in the 19th century. During this time of partitions, the Catholic Church preserved Poland's national identity. Since the shift of the borders at the end of World War II Poland has been a nearly homogeneously Catholic country with over 90 percent of the population pledging allegiance to the Catholic Church. Over 95 percent of Polish children are baptized into the Catholic Church. In 1985, 86 bishops and three cardinals formed a plenary conference of the Polish episcopate which regularly issued communiques and pastoral letters on the country's current problems, both religious and sociopolitical. These documents are read in all churches.

Apart from the Roman Catholic Church there are over 30 churches and denominations which are recognized by the Polish authorities. Non-Catholic Christian churches represent less than 3 percent of the population; among them the largest is the Polish Autocephalous Orthodox Church with over 800,000 members. Protestants constitute a tiny minority of about 100,000. The Lutherans, approximately 80,000 in number, are the largest group. As the majority of Lutherans are of German origin, their number has been constantly declining due to emigration to West Germany, especially since the Polish-German Peace treaty in 1970. The Polish Ecumenical Council (PEC), created in 1945, coordinates the activities of the country's non-Roman Catholic Christians. This organization is linked to the World Council of Churches. The only significant Christian minority which, for political reasons, has been denied official recognition is the Eastern-rite Catholic Church. This denomination embraces 250,000 to 500,000 Ukrainians living in Poland. Since 1956 the authorities have granted de facto recognition to an arrangement developed during the previous decades, whereby 50 Eastern-rite Catholic priests work as assistants to the Roman Catholic parish priests in areas largely populated by Ukrainians.

Non-Christian groups include a few thousand Muslims and several thousand non-Christian gypsies. Out of the 3.25 million Jews in Poland in 1938, 2.9 million died in the Holocaust. After 1945 a large proportion of survivors have emigrated to Israel as a direct consequence of the anti-Semitic policy of the Polish communist authorities. In 1980 only 5000 Jews remained in Poland.

The Marxist-Leninist Polish United Workers' party came to power in 1947, and eradication of religion became one of the state's main aims. Since 1950 the Office for Religious Affairs controlled the activities of the churches, and one member of the Communist party's central committee supervised church affairs. There was also a special church department within the Ministry of the Interior. Throughout the postwar period the state authorities attempted to limit religious activity within church buildings, and no religious associations were allowed, with the exception from 1956 of the few Catholic Intellectuals' Clubs (KIKs). Christian culture was barred from the state-controlled mass media and Christian elements were removed from the history textbooks. From 1960 religious instruction was forbidden in schools. The churches had no legal status.

Before 1956 the state tried to destroy all religious denominations indiscriminately. From 1956, however, non-Catholic Christian churches enjoyed increased toleration as a result of the authorities' goal of offsetting the power of the Roman Catholic Church. Even the Jehovah's Witnesses, persecuted elsewhere in Eastern Europe, began to receive official concessions in the late 1970s. Only at times of political crisis (in 1956, 1968, 1970, 1976, and 1980) was there short-lived rapprochement between the state and the Catholic Church in which antireligious policies were temporarily eased in return for the church's help in stabilizing the country politically.

The state was unable to destroy the Catholic Church, but made great efforts to limit its influence; yet ironically the government relied on the church to preserve internal order. From the 1970s the Catholic Church experienced a revival, boosted by the election of Polish Cardinal Karol Wojtyla as John Paul II. In 1985 every third Catholic priest ordained in Europe was a Pole, contributing to the total of 22,381 Polish priests, both diocesan and monastic. In addition, 95 per-

cent of Polish workers recently declared themselves as believers in an official census, and the proportion of secondary school children professing a religious outlook rose from 62 percent in 1977 to 75 percent in 1983.

In the events of 1989 the state's control proved to have been largely ineffective. One of the first events of the reform was passage of three new laws by the parliament guaranteeing freedom of conscience, the right of public profession of faith, church access to media, and full legal status for the Roman Catholic Church. Catholic influence through the Solidarity was strong in the new government structure which was emerging in late 1990.

See Norman Davies, *God's Playground: A History of Poland* (2 vols., 1981).

PHILIP WALTERS

**Poling, Daniel Alfred** (1884–1968). Reformed Church of America pastor. Born in Portland, Oreg., he studied at Dallas (Oregon) College, Lafayette Seminary, and Ohio State University. He was pastor of the Marble Collegiate Dutch Reformed Church, New York (1922–30); of Baptist Temple, Philadelphia (1936–48); and thereafter chaplain, Chapel of Four Chaplains, Philadelphia, and president of the World's Christian Endeavor Union. Among his many publications are *Mothers of Men* (1914), *Learn to Live* (1923), *An Adventure in Evangelism* (1925), *Radio Talks to Young People* (1926), *Between Two Worlds* (1930), *Youth Marches* (1937), *A Preacher Looks at War* (1943), *Prayers for the Armed Forces* (1950), *Mine Eyes Have Seen* (1959), *Jesus Says to You* (1961), and *He Came from Galilee* (1965). He was widely known as a syndicated columnist. He edited *The Christian Endeavor World* and *The Christian Herald*.

J. D. DOUGLAS

**Polity, Ecclesiastical.** In the course of Christian history three main types of church government have emerged—the congregational or independent, the presbyterian, and the episcopal. The congregational emphasizes the autonomy of the local congregation. The presbyterian stresses the parity of elders or presbyters, lay and clerical, and their responsibilities of government in a graded hierarchy of church courts—local church session, presbytery, synod, and general assembly. The episcopal is based on the bishop as its key ruling figure.

Throughout the 20th century the question of church polity has continued to be actively discussed for several reasons: (1) Historical research has proceeded apace into the organization and government of the early church. (2) Even before 1900 the various old-line denominations had begun to build up world organizations in an interchurch movement, including the Lambeth

Conference, the Alliance of Churches Holding the Presbyterian System, the Methodist Ecumenical Conference, and the International Congregational Council. This movement grew with such groups as the Baptist World Alliance and Lutheran World Federation and, among other things, it brought the question of church polity to the fore. (3) This question emerged in connection with the world ecumenical movement, in which the churches sought to articulate their fundamental unity in Jesus Christ as their common Lord.

The chief matters which most scholars are agreed may be summed up thus: Although Jesus Christ founded the church as his body, he did not prescribe for it a fixed pattern of organization. In the NT churches no one form of government universally prevailed. The Anglican scholar, B. H. Streeter, stated that "no one form of church order is primitive, possessing the sanction of apostolic precedent." In later NT times the usual form of church government was by a group of responsible officials known as "presbyters." The term "bishop," when used in the NT, refers to these presbyters, denoting the character of their office, which was to supervise the local Christian community. By the end of the 2d century the monarchical episcopate had become the standard pattern of church organization. Hans Lietzmann suggested that in difficult times "the concentration of power in the hands of a single person offered the surest guarantee of good leadership." But as to how this development took place, Anglican L. E. Elliott-Binns observed that "the process by which the bishop came to be distinguished from his fellow presbyters, and at last to occupy a position of authority over them and the Church, can no longer be traced."

The Faith and Order branch of what became the World Council of Churches concerned itself with the theological and doctrinal factors underlying the present "unhappy divisions" among the churches of Christendom. At its conference at Lausanne, Switzerland, in 1927, Faith and Order set forth the following "principle of comprehension": "In view of (1) the place which the episcopate, the council of presbyters, and the congregation of the faithful, respectively, had in the constitution of the Early Church; and (2) the fact that Episcopal, Presbyteral, and Congregational systems of government are each today, and have been for centuries, in Christendom; and (3) the fact that Episcopal, Presbyteral, and Congregational systems are each believed by many to be essential to the good order of the Church, we therefore recognize that these several elements must all, under conditions which require further study, have an appropriate place in the order of life of a re-united Church and that each separate communion, recalling the abundant blessing of God vouchsafed to its ministry in the past, should gladly bring to the common life of the united Church its own spiritual treasures."

This "principle of comprehension" was embodied in the Church of South India as organic merger which took place in 1947 and which embraced former Congregationalists, Presbyterians, and Episcopalians. In the constitution of this church it was stated that "the Church of South India recognizes that Episcopal, Presbyteral, and Congregational elements must all have their place in its order of life." In conformity with this idea, the basic unit became the local congregation of the faithful. Congregations within a given geographical area were organized into a diocese. Each diocese, although headed by a bishop, was administered by a diocesan council which included, besides the bishop and his assistant, all pastoral ministers, and at least an equal number of laymen. The highest court in the Church of South India was the synod, consisting of all the bishops and at least two ministerial presbyters and four laymen from each diocese. The moderator and deputy of this synod were chosen from the ranks of the bishops.

The South Indian Church, from its official inauguration in 1947, continued to grow through merger and extensive communion with other bodies and set the pattern, at least in regard to church polity, for non-Roman organic union.

**Bibliography.** P. C. Simpson, *Church Principles* (1923); H. N. Bate, ed., *Faith and Order, Lausanne 1927* (1927); B. H. Streeter, *The Primitive Church* (1929); J. L. Schaver, *The Polity of the Churches* (1947); L. E. Elliott-Binns, *The Beginnings of Western Christendom* (1948); H. Lietzmann, *The Founding of the Church Universal* (1950).

NORMAN V. HOPE

## Poole-Connor, Edward Joshua (1872–1962).

English evangelical leader, pastor, and author. He had little formal theological training but served effectively in a number of churches, including two periods in Talbot Tabernacle, London. Always kindly and courteous, he was nevertheless not afraid of controversy and was outspoken in his views. He believed that the decline of the church was due to the advances of modernism and higher criticism. He opposed any form of compromise with those who denied the basic doctrines of the faith, particularly the verbal inspiration of Scripture. He lost sympathy with denominationalism. He realized the value of bringing together the many churches and pastors lacking denominational affiliation and support. In 1922 he founded the Fellowship of Undenominational and Unattached Churches and Missions, which later became the Fellowship of Independent Evangelical Churches. He was a strong advocate of an evangelical unity in which essential truth was firmly held but freedom observed on "nonessentials." In his many writings he fearlessly opposed compromise and error, and criticized, for example, the New English Bible, the World

Council of Churches, and Billy Graham's cooperation with those who did not hold his view of Scripture. He served as editor of the *Bible League Quarterly,* a journal which warned against compromise and provided scholarly answers to the higher critics. He helped revive All Nations' College after World War II, and was briefly its principal. In 1952 he was one of the founders of the British Evangelical Council. He was involved in the North Africa Mission and with the founding of the Evangelical Library.

JAMES TAYLOR

**Porteus, Norman Walker** (1898– ). Scottish OT scholar. Born in Haddington, he studied at the universities of Edinburgh, Oxford, Berlin, Tübingen, and Münster, and after ordination he was minister of Crossgates (1929–31). He was professor of Hebrew and Oriental languages at St. Andrews University (1931–34), and professor of OT language, literature, and theology at Edinburgh University (1934–37), transferring to the chair of Hebrew and Semitic languages there in 1937, a post he held until retirement in 1968. He was also principal of New College, Edinburgh (1964–68). He was the author of *Das Buch Daniel* (ET, 1965), *Living the Mystery* (1967), and *OT and History* (1972). Apart from articles in theological dictionaries and journals, he contributed to *Barth Festschrift* (1936), *Record and Revelation* (1938), *The OT and Modern Study* (1951), *Peake's Commentary on the Bible* (1962), *Hinton Davies Festschrift* (1970), and *Eichrodt Festschrift* and *Von Rad Festschrift* (1971).

**Portugal.** Republic of Southwestern Europe, covering an area of 89,348 sq. km. (34,497 sq. mi.). Of its 10.25 million population (1986), about 93 percent are Roman Catholics. There are about 75,000 Protestants.

In 1908 King Carlos was assassinated; his son, Manuel II, was deposed two years later. Stability only returned to the country in 1933 when a new constitution was adopted. At that time Antonio de Oliveira Salazar emerged as a virtual dictator, remaining in control until a coup d'état on April 25, 1974. A leftist government then came to power, producing greater religious freedom for non-Catholics. It also aligned Portugal with the more liberal movements of modern Europe. The Roman Catholic Church moderated the revolutionary leanings of the new government by prohibiting the faithful to vote for communist candidates; the result was a moderate socialism.

In modern times faithful worship among Portugal's Catholics has declined. In the 1980s no more than 5 percent were in worship weekly. In Lisbon about 24 percent attended once a week. Of those who ignored the church, 18 percent said they attended Mass from time to time, 23 percent said they attended only rarely, and 29 percent said they never attend. Still, the shrine of the virgin at Fatima continued to be a popular symbol of faith, drawing more than 400,000 pilgrims a year. In 1951 Pius XII closed the Holy Year at Fatima, and more than one million attended.

Portugal at late century was a study in contrast. The south was largely irreligious. In addition to low worship attendance, there was only one priest for every 4500 residents. In the center and north of the country, Catholicism thrived, with one priest for every 600 Catholics. In some villages weekly Mass attendance was virtually total.

Because of the dominance of the Roman Catholic Church, Protestantism could claim only 1000 adherents in 1900. By 1970 that number had increased to 56,700 (0.7 percent). One year after the coup there were 64,000 (0.7 percent), and in 1988 that number had increased to about 75,000. This represented a slight decline in the size of the Roman Catholic Church, and most defectors had become irreligious or atheists. The officially irreligious grew in number from 173,000 (2 percent) in 1970 to 296,000 (3.3 percent) in 1985. Atheists increased in number from 30,000 in 1970 to 120,000 (1.3 percent) in 1985.

The largest Protestant church in Portugal was the Assemblies of God, with 250 congregations, 7500 members, and as many as 24,000 adherents. The American Conservative Baptist missionaries had started 51 churches with 3150 members and about 5100 adherents. The Christian (Plymouth) Brethren had 120 assemblies with 4000 members and 8000 adherents. Protestant missionaries established several training centers for Portuguese young people. The Assemblies of God maintained a Bible training center with 51 students. Greater Europe Mission had 24 resident and 80 correspondence students. Other training institutes were operated by Baptists and Presbyterians.

Jehovah's Witnesses entered Portugal in 1925. In 1985 they had 113 worship centers with 9088 members and 19,500 adherents. They experienced their major growth after the departure of Salazar in 1974. Although there were only about 800 identifiable Jews, there were 100,000 Marranos (crypto-Jews) whose ancestors adopted Catholicism to avoid persecution after 1497.

Because of Portugal's former possession of Mozambique, and because of immigration from Pakistan, Guinea-Bissau, Timor, Macao, and North Africa, there was a small Muslim minority, which in the mid-1980s had remained constant at 800 for 20 years.

WAYNE DETZLER

**Postmillennialism.** *See* MILLENNIUM.

**Poteat, Edwin McNeill** (1892–1955). Baptist pastor. Born in New Haven, Conn., he studied at Furman University and Southern Baptist Theological Seminary, Louisville, Ky. He was a missionary in China (1917–29); associate professor of philosophy and ethics, University of Shanghai (1927–29); pastor of Pullen Memorial Baptist Church, Raleigh, N.C. (1929–37, 1948– ); pastor of Euclid Ave. Baptist Church, Cleveland, Ohio (1937–44); and president of Colgate-Rochester Divinity School, Rochester, N.Y. (1944–48). He wrote *Coming to Terms with the Universe* (1931), *Jesus and the Liberal Mind* (1933), *Reverend John Doe, D.D.* (1934), *Thunder over Sinai* (1935), *The Social Manifesto of Jesus* (1936), *These Shared His Passion* (1938), *These Shared His Cross* (1939), *These Shared His Power* (1940), *Centurion* (1941), *Four Freedoms and God* (1942), *Over the Sea the Sky* (1943), *Last Reprieve?* (1945), *Parables of Crisis* (1950), and *God Makes the Difference* (1951). He was the expositor of Pss. 42–89 in *The Interpreter's Bible*.

## Potter, Philip A.

**Potter, Philip A.** (1921– ). Ecumenical leader. Born in Roseau, Dominica, West Indies, of a Roman Catholic father and a Protestant mother, he studied law and theology in Kingston, Jamaica. From 1947 onwards he attended numerous ecumenical gatherings. He served as a pastor of the Methodist church in Haiti (1950–54), was the executive secretary of the World Council of Churches (WCC) youth department (1954–60), chairman of the World Student Christian Federation (1960–68), director of the Division of World Mission and Evangelism of the WCC (1967–72), and general secretary of the WCC (1972–84). Potter gave strong theological, ethical, and spiritual guidance to the work of the World Council, especially in his insistence on the fundamental unity of witness and service, which the gospel commands and makes possible, and the correlation of faith and action. Among his numerous works is *Life in All Its Fulness* (1981).

A. J. VAN DER BENT

## Power, Christianity and the Problem of.

The word *power* comes from the Middle English *poer* or *pouer*, and ultimately from the Latin *posse, potesse*, meaning "to be able." It means, most broadly, an "ability to effect a result" or "to act." It implies a concentration of some kind of force which can be made to do work. Regarding natural laws the "problem" of power is the problem of making such mechanical arrangements that the force or energy employed may accomplish a desired physical result. The release of energy from the atom must be under conditions which control the result. But when the problem under consideration regards human relations the power is that used to influence—and in the last analysis to coerce—others. Under what conditions, if ever, is the use of power to influence and coerce ever morally and spiritually justifiable?

Interpersonal power has been sought and gloried in throughout the ages; the problem of its technical use, with and without consideration of the moral and spiritual problems involved, has been long and earnestly studied. The Caesars and Napoleons are the great practical students of the subject. The most controversial and misunderstood theoretical study to appear was by Italian philosopher Niccolò Machiavelli, *The Prince* (1513). More helpful works on the philosophy of politics have been works such as Plato's *Republic* and *Laws*, Aristotle's *Ethics* and *Politics*, Thomas Hobbes' *Leviathan* (1651), Jean-Jacques Rousseau's *Social Contract* (1762), Jeremy Bentham's *Principles of Morals and Legislation*, John S. Mill's *Essay on Liberty* (1859) and his *Considerations on Representative Government*. The problem of power is usually studied from the point of view that power can be effectively, technically, and morally employed, and it is or may be good; but it conversely needs to be closely guided and controlled against misuse.

The rise of totalitarianism, of scandals in governments, and of new psychological techniques to influence thinking have all worked to instill in the mind of modern man a growing sensitivity to the moral and spiritual aspects of the problem of power. In some cases the mood has been toward a sweeping condemnation of the use of power as such. This is probably due, primarily, to the humanism which regards the individual as the possessor of unalienable rights—a conception which sharpens disdain for inevitable invasions of such alleged rights by the social use of power. It is due also to the greater concentrations of such power in modern history, and therefore to the greater potential for evil results. Human societies have become more tightly organized, in ever larger units, with ever more terrible forms of power available in a "shrinking world." Hobbes and Rousseau, although they assumed or asserted that the use of power could be justified under certain conditions, recognized that justification is always necessary. In their wake arose thinkers who acknowledged a certain temporary or permanent necessity for the employment of power, but they still regarded it as bad in itself—an unfortunate necessity or necessary evil.

The latter conception passed through certain stages. At first, the individual was regarded as the ultimate repository of all rights. The surrender or invasion of those rights was necessarily an evil. The necessities of social organization, however, did justify the invasion of some individual liberty because it served the interests of the individual. Power, therefore, must be permitted under the most stringent safeguards and to the least degree possible. Mill may be regarded as the classic exponent of this view. It was still a basic assumption in 20th-century American discussion. It was often a basis, expressed or unacknowledged, of the criticisms of "creeping socialism" and "the welfare state."

The same evaluation of the use of social power has been carried over, but along with a repudiation of individualism, into Marxist communism. Here the state is simply equated with coercive power, at present possessed by the exploiting class and employed in their interests. Power must be seized and used, with violence, by the proletariat in revolution and during an intermediate socialist period. But when the classless society has been consolidated, the employment of coercive power in human relations will no longer be necessary, and the state will wither away. In reply, it was pointed out that that has not been the experience in communist countries; that Joseph Stalin in the 1950s and several Eastern bloc governments in the 1980s finally repudiated the theory. Such a repudiation is inevitable, since men are more radically evil than this theory assumes. The employment of power to coerce, whether it is morally right or not, will always be necessary.

Others, horrified by the ruthlessness of modern life, have accepted, often without qualification, Lord Acton's dictum, "Power always corrupts; and absolute power corrupts absolutely." Usually the latter part of the dictum has been emphasized to condemn all forms of alleged or real totalitarianism or the employment of armed force. The first part of the dictum, if taken with complete seriousness and acted upon consistently, would lead to anarchism. Although the use of power has often been associated with the corruption both of those who used it and of those upon whom it has been brought to bear, it is not clear that "power always corrupts." For example, the authority of a parent is a social use of power, but, if wisely used, it seems to have a beneficial effect on both parent and child. As shown in homes and schools where power is not exercised, it can be dangerous, as it certainly is misleading, thus to locate the responsibility for corruption. Power is simply capacity—for a good result, an evil result, or, more normally, for a mixed result. The Christian understanding is that power corrupts because innate corruption in human hearts corrupts the use of power. The problem is not primarily one of power but of human character.

The solution to be worked toward, but not too sanguinely expected, is that human character be improved, and the agency to be relied upon to do that is not diminution or abolition of the use of power but a way to transform people and make the use of power less necessary and also less alluring. If it may be granted that this transforming power is to be found in Jesus Christ, the hope of an ultimate solution, and of proximate approaches to a solution, may be found in the triumph of Christianity. The history and present condition of Christianity, "spotty" though the record is, show that such an expectation is not without justification. Although Christian leaders and organizations have abused power, sought alliances with centers of power which were not enlightened by love and justice, failed to make a fully constructive use of power, still its record is much better than that of any other. The church has possessed within itself an ability to regenerate both itself and human society in general.

Behind all this, however, lies a deeper problem. It is the problem of the moral and spiritual justifiability of using power to influence the thought and actions of any other individual or group. Granted that forceful persuasion is inevitable and inescapable, is it not still an affront to the dignity of people and to God, even if that suasion is in the cause of justice or evangelism? Does not power belong only to God? The Christian answer has been that power does belong ultimately to God alone. But, in making us members one of another in the unity of his human family, he has associated us with himself in the employment of certain essential kinds of power. Use of such authority is commanded, so it is morally and religiously justified. So long as it is employed in obedience to and dependence upon God, and consequently in harmony with the welfare of ourselves and all humanity, the power of the Christian is a gift to enable service.

***Bibliography.*** B. Russell, *Power* (1938); J. MacLaurin, *The United Nations and Power Politics* (1951); Lord Radcliffe, *The Problem of Power* (1952); R. Niebuhr, *Christianity and Power Politics* (repr. ed., 1969); J. G. Davies, *Christians, Politics, and Violent Revolution* (1976); E. R. Norman, *Christianity and the World Order* (1979).

ANDREW K. RULE

## Practical Theology, 20th-Century Developments in.

At the dawn of the 20th century practical theology was still feeling the 19th-century influence of Friedrich Schleiermacher's account of the nature and relationships of the subject. His *Brief Outline of the Study of Theology* (1811, rev. ed., 1830) depicted practical theology as "the crown" and completion of theological study. The purpose and goal of theology was to equip leaders of the church for their task. Theology as a whole was seen as a vocational subject like law or medicine, rather than as a general enquiry into truth like mathematics or metaphysics, which are not linked to a specific community or occupation. Practical theology, he affirmed, is an ecclesial and scholarly subject closely related to the more theoretical parts of theological study. It cannot be separated from the church; indeed Schleiermacher tied it so closely to the tasks of the clergy that it became not so much a theory of the practice of the church as the study of the techniques of ministry. But he also insisted that it was a scholarly or scientific study; its ecclesial interest must be linked to a scientific spirit. Practical theology is concerned to understand and interpret the tasks of the church, and of the ordained ministry in particular. It can do this only by close interaction with historical, systematic, and biblical theologies.

Schleiermacher's vision tended, as time passed, to become circumscribed so that practical theology was usually confined entirely to matters of clerical technique, as the traditional subdivisions might suggest—liturgics, homiletics, pastoral care (or "poimenics"), and catechetics. This narrowing of interest neglected important areas of theological concern, but it was probably necessary if theology was to take seriously its role in the formation of clergy, its responsibility to the church, and its relevance to the whole person. More serious was the tendency for practical theology to lose its concern for scholarly rigor and to become little more than tips on how to perform as a minister. These fruits of experience were rarely subjected to rigorous critical examination. This type of study was sometimes rudely, but not quite inaccurately, referred to as "practically theology" by irreverent students. It sought to induct students into a recognized, secure, and unchallenged pattern of ministry.

This understanding of practical theology gives the pivotal role to the professional formation of clergy, analogous to the other forms of professional education. But the professional model of ministry is ambivalent. It suggests that the ordained ministry should have standards of accountability and skills which are fully professional, and that practical theology has a special concern for critical and responsible formation. But, on the other hand, if the Christian ministry comes to regard itself as a *profession*, a question is raised about the status of the rest of the church: Are the other members of the royal priesthood of the whole people of God to be considered as "clients" or "patients"—as recipients of ministry rather than participants in ministry?

Within the general parameters of Schleiermacher's approach there have been three particularly important developments this century—the suggestion that practical theology is essentially about how to communicate the gospel; the identification of practical theology with pastoral care; and the suggestion that practical theology is the study of the whole life of the church.

For Karl Barth the central question for practical theology was how the Word of God may be served by human words. Practical theology, like all theology, is centrally concerned with proclamation—through the sermon, through teaching, through the witness of Christian lives, and through pastoral care. This last is defined by Barth's friend and colleague, Thurneysen, as the "specific communication to the individual of the message proclaimed in general in the sermon to the congregation." Practical theology is seen as an ecclesial discipline, devoted to serving the church,

and above all the church's preaching. And although the content of proclamation is given by exegesis and dogmatics, its form and presentation is shaped by practical theology which, although a theological discipline in its own right, is also required to borrow insights and seek help from secular disciplines as appropriate. Practical theology is thus a subordinate study, which has to do with the application of the truths with which dogmatics and exegesis directly engage.

Seward Hiltner and a large and influential school of mainly American theologians tended to see practical theology as centered not on preaching but on the pastoral activity of the church. Hiltner believed that an examination of the life of the church from what he calls "the shepherding perspective" will produce theological wisdom. The analytical tools are for the most part not theological but borrowed from modern psychology and psychiatry. A therapeutic model for pastoral care, and indeed for the function of the church, tends to be dominant. In more recent times strenuous and effective efforts have been made to recover a theological grounding for pastoral care without abandoning the productive relationship with psychiatry and psychology, particularly in the work of theologians such as Tom Oden and Alastair Campbell.

The third line of development was associated with Karl Rahner, who saw practical theology as "an original science" charged with the responsibility for "a theological analysis of the particular present situation. The church was to carry out the special self-realization appropriate to it at any given moment." Rahner was concerned with asserting that practical theology is not "a mere hotchpotch of practical consequences" of the other disciplines but a theological discipline in its own right. For Rahner, practical theology was not as confined to the ecclesiastical realm or to the functions of the pastor, as it was for Barth, Thurneysen, or Hiltner. Instead it asked what God is doing in the church and in the world, and how believers and those Rahner called "anonymous Christians" should respond. To fulfill its task it needs to give close attention to the findings of the human sciences and the other theological disciplines, but it is not subordinate or derivative.

There were significant efforts to break away from the confines suggested by Schleiermacher, asserting that practical theology must engage with the life of the world, as well as in the activity of the church and the work of ministry. Its concern was with practice as such, as well as with Christian practice, the practice of the church, and the practice of ministry. This broader understanding of the responsibilities of the subject more closely associated ministry with Christian ethics so that a normative approach to practice became an indispensable component of any serious practical theology. Reinhold Niebuhr represented this kind of practical theologian as one who sought to discern how the light of Christian faith could illumine in practical ways a whole generation about what was happening in their day. This was more than "applied theology" in the sense of taking conclusions ready-made from systematic theology or from the Bible and applying them to reality; such theology interacted between his experience of the challenges of his day and the Christian tradition, a dialectic of theory and practice. Today's political theologians and especially the liberation theologians of Latin America often affirm that they are practical theologians, and that theology arises out of engagement in the life of the world and world-transforming praxis.

This raises what is now the central issue in practical theology—the relationship of theory and practice. Much stimulus for this discussion has been derived from Marxism. Karl Marx wrote in the *Theses on Feuerbach* (1845): "The question of whether objective truth can be attributed to human thinking is not a question of theory, but a practical question. In practice man must prove the truth, that is the reality and power, the this-sidedness of his thinking. . . . The philosophers have only interpreted the world, in various ways; the point, however, is to change it." Theologians who are sympathetic with such a view point out that from the beginning Christianity has been a way rather than a metaphysic, that the disciples are repeatedly enjoined in the Gospels to be "doers" rather than mere "hearers," and that Christianity is more than theory or speculation. The truth is something to be done, and to be loved, not something to be examined in a detached fashion. Christianity is about conversion, about transformation rather than explanation. Theology is concerned with the doing of the truth rather than with the contemplation of the truth. Thus some theologians spoke of the priority of praxis (J.B. Metz) or claimed that "the new criterion of theology and of faith is to be found in practice" (J. Moltmann). This led to an oversimplified view that theory emerges spontaneously out of immersion in activity, and some of the liberation theologians were accused of reducing the Christian message to a political program. But it remains true that theology does have to do with changing the world, with conversion, with the mission of the church, and with the attempt to understand reality within the horizon of the coming kingdom.

In the late 1900s there was a recovery of awareness that all theology must be practical, and attention was given to the relationship of theory and practice. The discipline of practical theology engaged in a vigorous self-examination which placed traditional responsibilities in a far broader context, reassessed its nature and methods as a practical science and clarified its relationships to the other theological disciplines and to the social sciences. Practical theology was never as lively and interesting as during the later 20th century.

**Bibliography.** W. Pannenberg, *Theology and the Philosophy of Science* (ET, 1976); R. Gill, *Prophecy and Praxis* (1981); D. P. McCann, *Christian Realism and Liberation Theology: Practical Theologies in Conflict* (1981); D. S. Browning, *Practical Theology: The Emerging Field in Theology, Church and World* (1983); A. V. Campbell, *Moderated Love* (1983); T. C. Oden, *Pastoral Theology: Essentials of Ministry* (1983); A. V. Campbell, *Rediscovering Pastoral Care* (rev. ed., 1986); J. W. de Gruchy, *Theology and Ministry in Context and Crisis* (1987); D. B. Forrester, *A Practical Theology for Today* (1988).

DUNCAN B. FORRESTER

**Pratt, James Bissett** (1875–1944). Unitarian teacher and scholar. Born in Elmira, N.Y., he was educated at Williams College, Harvard (Ph.D., 1905), Columbia Law School, and the University of Berlin. After teaching Latin in Berkeley School, New York (1900), and at Elmira Free Academy (1900–1902), he came to teach philosophy at Williams (1905–44). He studied native religions in India (1913/14); Buddhism in Siam, China, and Japan (1923/24); and spent a year studying the religions in Indo-China, India, and Java (1931/32). He wrote *Psychology of Religious Belief* (1907), *What Is Pragmatism?* (1909), *India and Its Faiths* (1915), *Democracy and Peace* (1916), *The Religious Consciousness* (1920), *Matter and Spirit* (1922), *The Pilgrimage of Buddhism* (1928), *Adventures in Philosophy* (1931), *Personal Realism* (1937), *Naturalism* (1939), and *Can We Keep the Faith?* (1941). He also coauthored *Essays in Critical Realism* (1920).

RAYMOND W. ALBRIGHT

**Prayer, Book of Common.** See COMMON PRAYER, BOOK OF.

**Predestination.** See CALVINISM; COMMON GRACE.

**Preexistence.** The idea that before their birth on this planet, human beings have existed in other forms; also the doctrine that the Son existed in the Trinity before the incarnation. One form of this belief is metempsychosis or the repeated reappearance on earth of the same soul in various bodies, human or animal, as in the Hindu religion. This has never been entertained by Christian theology. Some individual theologians, however, have supported the idea that all human souls have existed in a premundane state. This is usually held in combination with a doctrine of a pretemporal fall. The advocacy of this idea by Origen and Erigena has been counted against them as heresy. The hypothesis has no basis in Scripture; it is unnecessary (contrary to Origen's opinion) for the explanation of original guilt, and has no confirmation from human consciousness. The idea of preexistence, in a universal sense, thrives only in the atmosphere of theosophy.

The preexistence of Christ is a part of orthodox Christology. Some Anabaptist and Lutheran theology envisages Christ's human nature as preexistent. Roman and Reformed theology finds in the NT and in logic only the preexistence of the divine Logos. It is not Christ's "reasonable soul," his human self, or human nature, which is said to have existed "before the world was." Whatever the origin of the human soul the arguments against preexistence would hold in the case of Jesus as much as in other cases; his human soul must, if truly human, have originated as other souls do. Therefore, the doctrine of Christ's preexistence is not a parallel to doctrines of the origins of souls, but a unique doctrine stemming from his unique deity. It is supported in Scripture principally by NT representations, though auxiliary support has been claimed from such OT references as Isa. 9:6 ("Everlasting Father.") There is little evidence from the Synoptics, although Jesus' reference to Psalm 110 in Matt. 22:41–45 might indicate his own preexistence. Even if it could be demonstrated, however, that the historical Jesus made no reference to and was not conscious of his preexistence, this would not constitute disproof, as we are by no means certain of the interior state of an incarnate Mind. In Paul there is clear teaching of Christ's preexistence, on an ascending scale. Christ is first the "man from heaven" (1 Cor. 15:47; see also 2 Cor. 8:9). In Phil. 2:5–11 Paul goes further: Christ exists *en morphē theou*, "in the form of God." This is a step toward Paul's highest conception, already in part on the Johannine level, in Col. 1:15–17. Here the preexistence is not simple existence, but is creative in the highest sense. The final step is taken in the Gospel of John, especially in the first chapter, where the preexistence, again creative, is associated explicitly with deity. Consciousness of preexistence is in John ascribed unequivocally to Christ (3:13; 6:33–51; 8:58). The latter with its resemblance to Exod. 3:14, looks like a hint of eternal preexistence. The prayer of John 17 is unintelligible apart from the presupposition of preexistence. Whether such passages are taken as verbatim reporting or as dramatic interpretation depends on one's view of the Fourth Gospel. The writer's intention is at all events quite clear. The Apocalypse, regardless of the question of its authorship, suggests a preexistence in 1:17, 22:13, and the idea is clearly in Hebrews. Since NT thought is oriented toward the future, it does not emphasize Christ's preexistence; but this belief in any case would be a necessary corollary of belief in Christ's deity. One could accept, as Arius did, preexistence in some sense without accepting full deity; but deity cannot be predicated in the "consubstantial" sense without at the same time predicating preexistence.

KENNETH J. FOREMAN

**Prefect, Apostolic.** *See* CONGREGATIONS, ROMAN.

**Preiss, Théodore Martin** (1910–1950). French Reformed. Born in Mullhouse, France, he studied at Strasbourg Theological Faculty and at the Sorbonne, Paris. He then was director of studies at the Strasbourg Protestant Seminary for five years. At the Amsterdam Youth Conference (1938), he was named part-time traveling secretary of the World Student Christian Federation. His work was interrupted by the World War II (1939), during which he was prisoner about two months. Released as an Alsatian, he was appointed minister by the Alsace Reformed Church at Guebwiller. Two years later, in 1942, he escaped from Alsace (then occupied by the Germans) to take up the NT chair in Montpellier Theological Faculty. He took an active part in French resistance with his colleagues and students and suffered illness as a result. His main work was a thesis on "the Son of Man," which he was unable to complete because of his illness. Notes from lectures Preiss gave on that subject have been published in the Review of the Montpellier Theological Faculty, *Etudes Théologiques et Religieuses*, 26/3 (1951) under the title "Le Fils de l'Homme, fragments d' un cours de Christologie du Nouveau Testament." He wrote *Le Temoignage Interieur du Saint Esprit* (1946), and most of his articles published in various reviews have been collected in *La Vie en Christ* (1952).

**Bibliography.** A. Bielschowsky, in *Verbum Caro*, 17 (1951). Articles on Th. Preiss: O. Cullmann, in *Verbum Caro*, 16 (1950); R. Mackie, in *Student World*, 4 (1950); P. Bonnard, in *Revue de Théologie et de Philosophie* (1950); R. Mehl, Pref. to *La Vie en Christ* (1952).

RAYMOND W. ALBRIGHT

**Prelate.** Title of certain ecclesiastical dignitaries. The Code of Canon Law, while recognizing the honorific title of prelate given by the Holy See to some clerics without jurisdiction (as, for instance, several officers or dignitaries of the pontifical court), states that the name of prelate applies primarily to secular and regular clerics having either local or personal external powers of jurisdiction. Some prelates, instituted by the pope in the same manner as residential bishops and having ordinary jurisdiction over a territory not connected with a bishopric, are known as prelates (or abbots) *nullius*, that is, *nullius dioceseos*.

GEORGES A. BARROIS

**Premillennialism.** *See* MILLENNIUM.

**Presbyter, Presbyterate.** *In the Ancient Church.* The word *presbyteros* occurs sparsely in nonbiblical, pre-Christian literature. The problem in pinpointing the origin of the presbyterial office in the early church still attracts attention. Otto Scheel (*Die Kirche im Urchristentum*, 1912) contended that the Christian church was not modeled after the Jewish synagogue with its elders, nor after other possible parallels in its pagan environment, but was a unique creation of Christianity. However, the facts that many of the early churches were founded by people who were Jews, were started in the synagogue, and had a Jewish membership still favor immediate Jewish influence. Christian August Bugge (*Das Problem der ältesten Kirchenverfassung,* 1924) regarded the organization of the early church as based on Jewish prophetic and pagan mystery principles. The presbyter represented a certain gradation of the spiritual order.

The development of the office seems to have lacked uniformity. Presbyters were at least found in churches founded by Paul and likely in other churches (see James 5:14; 1 Pet. 5:1). It is not absolutely clear in these two instances whether presbyters were in office by virtue of election or seniority. Bishop and presbyter were interchangeable terms.

These offices of bishop and presbyter existed separately in the church later, and it might be due to continued fluctuation of the terms that the *Didache* (c. A.D. 100–130) does not mention presbyters at all, but only bishops (*episkopoi*—note the plural) and deacons (*diakonoi*) as office-bearers who were to be elected by the people (15.1).

Early in the subapostolic periods 1 Clement (c. A.D. 96) appears to distinguish between the bishop (singular) and the presbyters (plural) (45. 1, 5; cf. 54. 2; 57. 1). Ignatius (d. 135) writes of a threefold office, bishop, presbyter, and deacon, and it appears to be a legitimate inference that the presbyters comprised the presbytery (*presbyterion*) which was headed by the bishop (*Letter to the Ephesians* 4). Ignatius admonished obedience to the bishop as to Jesus Christ (*Trallians* 2), who presides "after the likeness of God," and to the presbyters who "[hold office] after the likeness of the council of the apostles" (*Magnesians* 6). The Eucharist, baptism, and love feasts were under the jurisdiction of the bishop or of one appointed by him (*Smyrnaeans* 8).

The close relationship between bishop and presbyter comes out further in the use of the same prayer of ordination for the two except for the exchange of the words "presbyter" and "presbyterate" for "bishop" and "episkonate," respectively, and for the omission of enthronization in the case of presbyters (*Canones Hippolyti* 4. 30–32; see also Hieronymous, *Epistola,* 146, *Ad evangelum* 1). The Nicene Creed mentions both bishops and presbyters in the administering of the Eucharist to deacons (Canon 18). The Synod of Laodicea (c. A.D. 343–381?) decreed that both bishops and presbyters should instruct and baptize converts from the heresy of the Phrygians (Canon 8).

Eventually the office of the presbyter was taken up in the priesthood of the Roman Catholic Church and emerged again during the Reformation as an office which could be held by laymen.

***In Presbyterianiam.*** The presbyterian form of church government is based on the principle of representative government and of one spiritual order which is vested in the presbyters. A series of ascending judicatories—session, presbytery, synod, and general assembly—exercise government (the general assembly does not occur in all cases of presbyterian government). Each judicatory has original power in its own sphere.

Presbyters are usually elected by the communicant members of a congregation, subject to the approval of a higher judicatory, the presbytery.

DANIEL J. THERON

***In Modern Times.*** Even before the end of the 19th century it had become clear that the Puritan-Presbyterian claim that the presbyterian form of church government alone has NT sanction was simplistic and misleading. Subsequent research has proved that presbyterian church government, as set up in Reformed churches during the 16th century, was no exact replica of NT models, and was designed according to local needs and circumstances.

Since the Genevan church was only citywide in extent, it had no graded hierarchy of courts characteristic of modern Presbyterianism. This development took place in France (1559). Although John Knox, leader of the Scottish Reformation from 1560, was a disciple of John Calvin, he did not establish a purely presbyterian organization. His church had superintendents who, without sacerdotal pretensions, discharged functions of former bishops. Only with the Second Book of Discipline, adopted in 1581 under Andrew Melville's leadership, did the Scottish Church become strictly presbyterian in government, and the system of church courts was derived mainly from France.

The justification for presbyterian polity rests on the grounds that it is faithful to the spirit of the NT church, in which authority was democratically delegated from below, and it has proved reasonably effective in enabling the church to fulfill its divinely given functions. Efforts to strengthen the government of some presbyterian bodies by centralized officials and boards with quasi-episcopal authority has occurred in some denominations.

*See also* PRESBYTERIANS.

***Bibliography.*** A. J. Maclean, *The Ancient Church Orders* (1910); C. H. Turner, *Studies in Early Church History,* 2 vols. (1912); E. Sehling, *Geschichte der protestantischen Kirchenverfassung* (2d ed., 1914); J. N. Ogilvie, *The Presbyterian Churches of Christendom,* (1925); J. L. Ainslie, *The Doctrines of Ministerial Order in the Reformed Churches of the 16th and 17th Centuries* (1940); R. S. Louden, *The True Face of the Kirk* (1963).

NORMAN V. HOPE

## Presbyterian Church in America (PCA). A

conservative denomination founded in 1973 as a

continuation of the Old School wing of the Presbyterian Church in the United States (Southern). This element, admittedly small, was an effective minority and became increasingly concerned with liberal theological tendencies in the church. The drift toward religious liberalism became a strong current in the late 1930s when the general assembly failed to find modernist church historian Ernest Trice Thompson of Union Theological Seminary in Richmond, Va., guilty of heresy. The prevailing mood of national unity during the crisis of U.S. involvement in World War II brought about a surface truce between conservatives and the growing liberal elements.

Soon after the appointment of Thompson to the faculty of Union Seminary, the Fellowship of Saint James was formed there. Allegedly a discussion group for the school's graduates, the organization secretly planned and carried out a strategy of agitation for union with the Presbyterian Church in the USA (Northern), which was much more liberal than the PCUS. Those seeking reunion began a systematic program after 1945 to bring the polity and theology of the Southern church into a close harmony with those of the Northern PCUSA.

The general assembly of the PCUS in 1953 sent to the presbyteries a "plan of union" with the Northern church. The conservative element was able to defeat this plan because the denomination's governing rules required a favorable vote on such a motion by three-fourths of the presbyteries. The union movement was relatively localized, so not enough presbyteries supported the plan to bring about their desired union.

The defeat of this plan was the last major victory that the conservative element achieved, and it spurred the liberal group to adopt new tactics to strengthen their efforts.

The conservatives' stand was that the Southern church must not be swallowed by a larger denomination that no longer stood for historic Presbyterianism in either doctrine or polity. Through the 1960s, as they realized that Union was inevitable, the Old School wing decided to form a new "Continuing Presbyterian Church," maintaining the historic testimony of the PCUS and faithful to the Westminster Standards. They also sought to hold the Old School positions proclaimed by James Henley Thornwell, Robert L. Dabney, Benjamin M. Palmer, and other 19th-century Southern theologians. The *Southern Presbyterian Journal*, founded in 1942 by L. Nelson Bell, John R. Richardson, Henry Dendy, and others to advance the conservative cause, was the key motivating force for withdrawing from the PCUS. As the lines of conflict became more openly drawn, three major conservative organizations were formed: The Presbyterian Evangelistic Fellowship in 1958; Concerned Presbyterians in 1965, aimed at the laity; and Presbyterian Churchmen United, to broaden ministerial support, in 1968.

After a series of meetings beginning in 1970, the first general assembly of the Continuing Presbyterian Church movement met in late 1973 in Birmingham, Ala., to organize the new denomination. First known as the National Presbyterian Church, its name was changed in 1974 to the Presbyterian Church in America (PCA). At its inception the PCA included 225 churches and approximately 40,000 members. By 1986 the membership was more than 151,000 members. Heavily involved in world missions and evangelism, the PCA's rapid growth also stemmed from a continuing exodus of churches from the PCUS, especially during the final period of merger with the PCUSA (1983). In 1982 the PCA also received a smaller Northern Presbyterian denomination, the Reformed Presbyterian Church, Evangelical Synod. Unity discussion with the Orthodox Presbyterian Church continued through the 1980s.

Denominational offices were located at Atlanta, Ga. Covenant College, Lookout Mountain, Tenn., and Covenant Seminary, St. Louis. Mo., became denominational institutions with the merger of the Reformed Presbyterian Church. Greenville (S.C.) Seminary and John Knox Seminary, Ft. Lauderdale, Fla., were affiliated with the PCA through its presbyteries. The PCA joined the National Association of Evangelicals (NAE) in 1986.

*Bibliography.* F. Smith, *The History of the Presbyterian Church in America* (1985).

C. GREGG SINGER

## Presbyterian Church in the United States (PCUS).

Popularly known as the Southern Presbyterian Church. It was organized in Augusta, Ga., in 1861 as a result of the passage of the Gardner Spring Resolution by the Old School general assembly of the Presbyterian Church in the USA that year. It has been widely supposed, and even dogmatically asserted, that slavery was at the root of the movement to leave the Northern Wing of the Old School. This is not the case. The Gardner Spring Resolution was at the heart of the problem since it placed the Old School church on record as supporting the federal government in the Civil War.

While many Northern and Southern Presbyterians desired to hold their church intact despite the hostilities, the Southern leaders in the Old School general assembly felt that the Northern radicals' position was a violation of their doctrine of the purity of the church. The church must remain free from any involvement, as the church, in political and economic matters of the state and concentrate upon the preaching of the gospel, emphasizing this task as the proclamation of the whole counsel of God to a lost and needy world.

The presbyteries and leaders who seceded from the Old School general assembly met at the First Presbyterian Church in Augusta, constituting the Presbyterian Church in the Confederate States of America. After the war it assumed the name of the Presbyterian Church in the United States, remaining independent of the merger of the Old and New School churches of the North in 1869. The PCUS remained true to the Westminster Confession of Faith and adopted the views of its leaders (Robert Dabney, James Henley Thornwell, and Benjamin M. Palmer) in regard not only to the purity of the church but also to the equality of the teaching and ruling elders to govern the church at all levels. They also carried on the Old School emphasis that activities must be carried on by committees responsible to the general assembly, not by semi-independent and self-perpetuating boards. The PCUS thus remained Old School in theology and "Thornwellian" in polity. It also was devoted to the missionary task of the church, and soon after its founding it sent out missionaries to various parts of the world—Brazil, China, and the Congo. More than the Presbyterian groups of the North it became noted for its missionary zeal.

Theologically it remained orthodox until well into the 20th century. Some suggest that its doctrinal decline became noticeable with the appointment of modernist church historian Ernest Trice Thompson to the faculty of the Union Theological Seminary in Richmond, Va. The founding of a study and strategy group of Union graduates in about 1940 furthered the spread of theological liberalism among young ministers who entered the ministry of the church. A movement also began for union with the Presbyterian Church in the USA (Northern). It was not, however, until the end of World War II that this movement gained ground within the church, particularly in the border states and synods which supported Union Seminary in Richmond.

The first proposal which passed in the general assembly of 1953 was defeated in the presbyteries. The ensuing battle for control by the two parties continued, creating a chasm which finally erupted with the withdrawal of many of the conservatives in 1973. This resulted in the founding of the Presbyterian Church in America (PCA). Some conservative pastors and congregations opted to carry on the battle within the church, but reunification of the PCUS and the PCUSA into a reorganized PCUSA was accomplished in 1983.

**Bibliography.** E. T. Thompson, *Presbyterians in the South*, 3 vols. (1963–73).

C. Gregg Singer

# Presbyterian Church in the USA (PCUSA).

North America's largest ecclesiastical body holding to a presbyterian form of church government.

A mainline Protestant denomination, the PCUSA at the end of the 1980s was a church with great ethnic, political, and religious diversity. Through the century it led in national and world ecumenical endeavors, establishing dialog with other Christian and non-Christian bodies. Human rights, feminism, and other social concerns dominated the work of the church.

What were four denominations in 1900 joined over the 20th century to create the church as it existed in 1990. The dominant of these four, the Northern church, also called the PCUSA, in 1930 became the first of the dominant American religious bodies to ordain women as ruling elders, admitting them to church leadership at all levels. In 1956 women were ordained as ministers, and the church promoted feminist concerns throughout the 1970s and 1980s. By 1988 well over one-half of the total membership was made up of women. In the 1960s the PCUSA's Commission on Religion and Race was a leader in the American civil rights struggle, and from 1967 was greatly influenced by the black theology movement founded by James Cone of Union Theological Seminary. Mainline Presbyterians were instrumental in founding the Federal Council of Churches in 1908, the World Council of Churches in 1948, and the National Council of Churches in 1950.

With this political, social, and theological activism, which has been a thread through PCUSA life since the first general assembly in 1789, have come repercussions. In 1988 there were 2.9 million members in the PCUSA. This was up from 2.6 million in 1977, but reflected a substantial net loss considering the 1983 merger of the Northern and Southern mainline churches, which added nearly 878,000. The 1988 number of synods (16), presbyteries (177), and churches (11,573) was also in decline. At its 1990 general assembly, renewal, evangelism, and reorganization vied with abortion and homosexuality as concerns.

Historically the PCUSA is Augustinian and Calvinist in theology. Its sole credal statement before the 20th century was the Westminster Confession of Faith and Larger and Shorter Catechisms. This statement of belief, however, was found to be too strong a stand on the sovereignty of God, human depravity, and inerrancy of the Bible for the mood of the 20th-century church. In 1903 its doctrinal statements were rewritten in some details to pave the way for the Cumberland Presbyterian Church to join in 1906. Cumberland Presbyterians had broken from the PCUSA in 1809 in the wake of Second Great Awakening revivalism because they believed in human free will and rejected depravity. Many Cumberland Presbyterians found the PCUSA still incompatible in 1906, and the Cumberland church split as a result of the merger.

Two other important mergers were to follow. In 1958 the PCUSA changed its name to the United Presbyterian Church, USA, when it joined forces with the far smaller United Presbyterian Church in North America (UPCNA). Through the 1940s the PCUSA and the Fellowship of Saint James movement within the Southern Presbyterian Church in the USA worked toward a three-way union with the UPCNA. A master plan for union was developed in 1954, but voted down by Southern conservatives. Only the UPCNA accepted at the time. The reunion of Northern and Southern churches, healing the 1861 Civil War division, was finally accomplished in a lengthy process that lasted from 1968 to 1983. Some Southern presbyteries were merged on a trial basis from 1968. When most conservatives withdrew from the PCUS in 1973 the final roadblock to reunification was removed.

Meanwhile, both mainline Presbyterian churches had made a final break with the Westminster Confession of Faith. An updated *Confession of '67* was framed and adopted in an effort to make the faith of the church more acceptable to other groups in the world ecumenical movement and to more accurately reflect current teachings and concerns. The brief statement stresses God's love and reconciliation and faith in Jesus Christ in generally neo-orthodox terms. The 1903 version of the Westminster Confession was retained by the church as a more-or-less historical document in its book of Confessions.

These and other factors contributed to a tumultuous century for the PCUSA. Ever since it was transplanted to America from its north European and Scotch-Irish homelands, Presbyterian Calvinists have tended toward two disparate mindsets. One wing of the American church has sought to be uncompromisingly biblical in its approach to life and the church, carefully stressing the glory and awe of God, as expressed in the original Westminster Confession. This conservatism has often been evangelistic in its own right but conservatives also tended to be unbending and quietistic. The second mindset, which became dominant after 1801 when the Plan of Union brought Congregationalists in the PCUSA, has strived toward openness to other views. It has been more outward reaching and activistic in applying faith to current issues.

In the 1700s this diversity led to dissension over subscription to the confessional standards and finally a split over revivalism in 1741. In the 1800s European theologies and liberalism aggravated long tensions and caused the New School-Old School schism of the 1830s, contributed to the North-South split in 1861, and led to controversy and heresy trials in the 1880s and 1890s.

The more activistic and more liberal wing came to the fore at about the turn of the 20th century and dominated the PCUSA thereafter. In 1914 ecumenist and liberal J. Ross Stevenson was named president of Princeton Seminary, the bastion of Presbyterian orthodoxy. Conservatives, who came to be called fundamentalists, began a bitter battle which came to a head in 1924 when the activistic group, known as the modernists, published their Auburn Affirmation. From 1926 they completely controlled both the general assembly and Princeton Seminary.

Conservatives responded by founding Westminster Seminary in Philadelphia and the Independent Board of Foreign Missions, cutting themselves off from the mission agency structure of their denomination. An independent board, they said, was needed to disavow denominational missionaries who had abandoned both evangelism and the Bible for neo-orthodox theology and a syncretistic worldview. Leaders of this rebellion were immediately tried for heresy, and the general assembly upheld their convictions in 1936. A large body of conservatives left the church, founding what was to become the Bible Presbyterian Church and the Orthodox Presbyterian Church. The Southern churches, which had remained more theologically conservative, did not experience the same crisis point until the 1960s and 1970s.

After what came to be known as the fundamentalist-modernist controversy, the PCUSA was freed to move in its own directions, and its activistic, ecumenical, and conciliatory approach to faith and life characterized the PCUSA from that time.

# Presbyterians. *Introduction.*

The Greek term *presbyterion*, translated "bishop" or "elder," provides the basis for the word "presbyterian." One of three systems of church government—with congregational and episcopacy—a Presbyterian church usually adheres to Reformed (sometimes called Calvinist or Augustinian) doctrine. In presbyterian government, ruling and teaching elders chosen by the local congregation have spiritual responsibility over the people. Elders also represent the congregation in higher church bodies—presbytery, synod, and general assembly. Presbyterianism has roots in the work of John Calvin. From Geneva, Switzerland, it spread into Hungary, Czechoslovakia, Poland, France, the Low Countries, England, and Scotland. Although the first synod was convened by the Huguenots in Paris in 1559, Presbyterian church order took firmest root under the leadership of John Knox in Scotland. In 1560 he brought about the first general assembly, at which the Scots adopted a confession of faith and a book of discipline. In the next century Scottish and English Presbyterians played a key role with congregational and Anglican Puritans at the Westminster Assembly (1643–49) in writing the Westminster Confession of Faith, Larger and Shorter Catechisms, form of government, and directory for worship. Although these five statements were not embraced by the Church of England, they were adopted by the Church of Scotland, and eventually became the standards of faith for modern presbyterian movements, particularly in the USA.

During the final decades of the 20th century, half-millennial celebrations marked the birth of the principal "reformers." For the Reformed tradition, with its bent toward presbyterian polity, the roots run deeper and earlier than the principal reformers Calvin (1509–64) and Knox (c. 1513–72) to include the spirit of defiance in the martyrdom of John Hus (1369–1415) and a recognition of the necessity of vernacular Scripture instilled by John Wycliffe (1320–84). In the most generic sense "Reformed" means the Protestant doctrinal tradition which originated in continental Europe during the Reformation, and "presbyterian" refers to the philosophy of church government the Reformed tradition tended to adopt in English-speaking countries. In 1970 the presbyterian movement could be subdivided into 354 distinct denominations—286 of white European origin and 68 of nonwhite indigenous origin. It included 83,296 churches with 19.8 million adult members in 129 countries. The total Reformed religious community grew from 34.2 million in 1970 to 40.2 million in 1980 and 43.4 million in 1985.

***20th-Century Trends.*** North American presbyterianism in the 20th century was characterized by large churches which joined in the overall "mainline decline" and smaller, splinter groups that experienced growth, although much of this growth was the reshuffling of Presbyterians from one group to another. A partial exception to this trend was the Presbyterian Church in America (PCA), which was influenced by a Southern revival movement in the 1950s, and which had a distinct passion for evangelistic growth after its formation in the 1970s. Still, the primary reason why the PCA grew so quickly was that it continually absorbed whole congregations from the Presbyterian Church in the United States (PCUS) and eventually a whole denomination. In general the U.S. Presbyterian churches grew from 300,000 before the American Civil War (1860) to 3.25 million (1960), not an impressive advance given the growth in American population during that period. By 1990 the "unchurched" Americans alone had reached 44 percent of the total population.

Within world Christendom the most significant development for Presbyterian groups was in Korean churches, which experienced the greatest growth rate. Four denominations began Korean missions between 1884 and 1898. Presbyterianism remains the principal tradition within noncommunist South Korea, although it has also undergone splintering and mergering and has faced serious challenges growing out of pluralism and the Korean War (1950–53).

The initial few thousand Presbyterians in Korea topped 2 million in 1970, 3 million in 1975, and 4.5 million in 1985, not including 21 indigenous offshoots of Presbyterian origin that exceeded 2.5 million in 1970, 4 million in 1975, and 5 million in 1985. Of South Korea's total population of 37.5 million, 11.5 million are professing Christians and 9.5 million of them are Presbyterians.

Worldwide the Presbyterians increased from 1970 to 1985 by nearly 5 million from 32.4 to 39.3 million. This was exceeded within Protestant churches only by United Churches (65 million members in 1985), and Lutherans (43.5 million in 1985). Protestant communions in general claimed 277 million members in 1985.

***International Presbyterianism.*** Confusing, often horrendous, events of the 20th century moved world Presbyterians closer to one another and toward ecumenism in general. That search for unity began in 1875 with the founding of the Alliance of the Reformed Churches Throughout the World Holding the Presbyterian System. The World Presbyterian Alliance met 11 times before World War I, and five more times between the European wars. At the 18th meeting in Princeton, N.J., in 1954 it reorganized with 66 constituent bodies and 40 million adherents in 45 countries, not all of whom were originally defined either as Presbyterian or Reformed. By 1968 there were 110 Alliance member communions, 46 of which were called "younger churches" which had developed mostly from missions into autonomous, indigenous organizations; 24 alone were African.

The diversity of this "world conciliarism" movement was such that at the Nairobi meeting (1970) the World Presbyterian Alliance and the International Congregational Council were dissolved and reorganized as the World Alliance of Reformed Churches (WARC), with 125 Presbyterian and Congregational bodies. By 1982 there were 157 constituent bodies at the the Second General Council meeting in Ottawa. Within the greater Reformed (Presbyterian) tradition there were 39.7 million affiliated with member churches; an additional 4.6 million were affiliated with both WARC and the Reformed Evangelical Synod (RES), 4.4 million to WARC and the World Methodist Council (WMC), and 197,000 to WARC and the International Federation of Free Evangelical Churches (IFFEC), a total of 48.9 million. Reformed Christians also played key roles in the world ecumenical movement and the founding of the World Council of Churches in 1948.

***National Presbyterian Churches.*** The map of Presbyterianism is best illustrated by the history of divisions and reunions within the Church of Scotland. This tendency to splinter and merge was transplanted to regions where Scottish missionaries worked. In Scotland itself the major divisions included: Cameronian covenanters versus Episcopalians (1690), the first "secession" (1733), burghers versus antiburghers (1747), Auld Licht versus New Licht (1799 and 1806), and the second "secession" (1761). To further complicate matters, reunions gathered several New Licht groups into the United Secession (1820) and United Presbyterian (1847) churches. The established Church of Scotland itself split off the Free Church of Scotland in 1843. The Free Church merged with the United Presbyterians and then returned to its parent body in 1929. With other groups splitting off with each merger, little of each original segment survived in Scotland or elsewhere.

Major national church unions outside Scotland included four bodies uniting to form the Reformed Church of France in 1938. The Church of Christ in Japan was organized on the eve of war in 1941. Two Reformed churches of Neuchâtel, Switzerland, reunited in 1943, and the Church of Central Rhodesia was formed in 1945. The Dutch Reformed Church united two bodies in 1946. The United Church of Christ in the Philippines came into existence in 1948, as did the Evangelical Church in Germany, which is more of a federation.

One important development occurred when the Church of South India was formed in 1947, involving Presbyterians, Dutch Reformed, and Congregationalists, with Methodists and the Anglican Church of India, Burma, and Ceylon. In 1970 the Church of North India united Presbyterians and Congregationalists (who had joined in 1924) with Anglicans, Baptists, Brethren, Disciples of Christ, and Methodists. A similar union of Anglicans, Presbyterians, and Methodists was accomplished in Nigeria (1965). In 1966 Presbyterians and Congregationalists formed the United Church of Jamaica-Grand Cayman; and the free and national churches in Switzerland, divided since the 19th century, reunited in the Evangelical Reformed Church of Canton Vaud.

The first union across confessional boundaries in England was the 1972 merger of the United Reformed Church, the Presbyterian Church of England, and the Congregational Church in England and Wales. Congregationalists had already incorporated the Presbyterian Church in Wales. In 1981 the British Disciples of Christ entered this union. In 1977 a Council for World Mission (CWM) succeeded the London Missionary Society (1795), the Commonwealth Missionary Society (1836), and the Overseas Mission of the Presbyterian Church of England (1847).

In 1972 the United Congregational Church of Southern Africa was formed from United Congregational churches and the Association of Disciples of Christ. The Tsonga Presbyterian Church was added in 1978. Australian Presbyterians,

Congregationalists, and Methodists united in 1974, forming the Uniting Church of Australia (1977); 30 percent of the Presbyterians remained outside this union, however. In 1978 the United Protestant Church of Belgium, the Reformed Church of Belgium, and the Belgium District of the Reformed Churches in the Netherlands united.

***North American Presbyterianism.*** Presbyterianism reached the New World through the French Huguenots and the Dutch, German, English, and Scottish settlers. The largest single group of American Presbyterians prior to 1800 were the Scotch-Irish. By 1706 Francis Makemie had organized the first presbytery, and the first synod met in 1716. In 1789 the first American general assembly met in Philadelphia at the same time as the ratification of the Constitution of the United States. The new church was named the Presbyterian Church in the United States of America (PCUSA). Between 1800 and 1840 its membership grew from 20,000 to 220,000, and in 1812 Princeton Seminary was established to furnish a better-educated ministry.

Revivalism and evangelism, interchurch relations with less doctrinally oriented congregational churches, theological issues, and slavery soon divided the American Presbyterian movement. The Second Awakening's fervor and antitheological bias resulted in the establishment of the Cumberland Presbyterian Church in 1810. The "Plan of Union" between Presbyterians and Congregationalists to govern cooperative frontier church planting resulted in deep disagreements over church government and theology. Social issues aggravated existing tensions, which in 1837 split the denomination between conservatives (the Old School) and liberals and social activists (the New School). The New School was mostly a congregationally minded Northern church and the Old School branch a broader movement with much of its strength in the South. Thus the hostilities of the American Civil War contributed to a further split in the Old School church into Northern and Southern denominations. In 1869 the Northern New and Old School Presbyterians reunited in a compromise regional church, retaining the PCUSA name. The Presbyterian Church in the United States (Southern) remained separate until 1983.

Darwinism and liberal theologies divided the PCUSA from the moment of reunion. A statement of reconciliation between liberals and conservatives did not end the factionalism, and in 1903 the Northern church adopted a revised Westminster Confession that took away many distinctives of Reformed theology to allow non-Reformed Presbyterians to join the church. By 1906 most Cumberland Presbyterians united, and in 1920 the Welsh Calvinist Methodist Church joined the union.

Other presbyterian bodies also developed in North America. Scottish and Scotch-Irish immigrants from the "seceder movement" who had created several small churches in 1782 merged them into the United Presbyterian Church of North America. Although theologically conservative, the United Presbyterians were social activists, especially in the antislavery movement and in the temperance cause. Members of the Dutch Reformed Church also arrived in the USA and Canada in large numbers in the 1840s and 1850s. This church did not involve itself in the affairs of other Presbyterian bodies and was far more numerous on the western frontier of both countries. Some Scottish churches, such as the Reformed Presbyterian Church, also avoided entanglement with the mainline churches.

Among mainline churches the hope of reunification resurfaced after World War II. Conservatives had already largely abandoned the Northern church in a mid-1930s split, and the Southern church was moving toward neo-orthodox theology. The Northern church division was led in 1936 by J. Gresham Machen (1881–1937), forming the Orthodox Presbyterian Church. Machen's sudden death aggravated disagreements within this conservative movement, and the Bible Presbyterian Church split away. The Bible Presbyterian Church itself split in the 1950s, the dominant group eventually becoming the Reformed Presbyterian Church, Evangelical Synod.

In 1957 the United Presbyterians were merged into the Northern church, and the new denomination sought to redefine itself theologically in the Confession of 1967. Historic Christian confessions were retained in the Book of Confessions as historical tradition. In 1969 the move toward final reunification of the PCUS and PCUSA began with the formation of experimental joint presbyteries. This forced a final confrontation with conservatives in the Southern church, who left to form the Presbyterian Church in America in 1973. A decade later the union of the PCUS and PCUSA was accomplished, creating a 4-million-member denomination.

Also in 1957 the General Council of the Congregational Christian Churches and the Evangelical and Reformed Church united into the United Church of Christ. Both groups represented previous consolidations. After these mergers the principal nonmerged churches included the Christian Reformed Church and the Reformed Church in America, both with a strong Dutch heritage.

The Consultation on Church Union (COCU) resulted from an initiative of the 1961 UPCUSA General Assembly. Episcopalians, Methodists, and the United Church of Christ were invited to explore organic union; the Evangelical United Brethren and the Disciples of Christ joined the movement in 1963. A draft plan of union in 1970 gave way to a flexible movement of cooperation by 1974 among a variety of presbyterian and congregational bodies.

Conservative churches also moved toward cooperation in the late 1900s. An active federation, the North American Presbyterian and Reformed Council (NAPRC), represented several denominations. In 1982 the PCA received the Reformed Presbyterian Church, Evangelical Synod—itself a conservative union of small churches in the 1960s—and reunion with the Orthodox Presbyterian Church was considered.

American Presbyterian memberships (1988) included: Associate Presbyterian Church of North America, 36,543; Associate Reformed Presbyterian Church, 36,543; Bible Presbyterian Church, 8,000; Cumberland Presbyterian Church, 98,037; Evangelical Presbyterian Church, 30,000; Korean Presbyterian Church in America, 24,000; Orthodox Presbyterian Church, 14,300; Presbyterian Church in America, 188,083; Reformed Presbyterian Church of North America (Covenanters), 5,111; and Second Cumberland Presbyterian Church, 15,000.

In Canada a series of unions reduced eight Presbyterian bodies to four before 1875, when these four united to form the Presbyterian Church in Canada. In 1925 a majority merged with the Methodist and Congregational churches to form the United Church of Canada, to which was added the Evangelical United Brethren in 1968. The United Church had grown to 2.28 million members by 1985, though the church was in decline from 1970. Those who declined to enter the 1925 union continued as the Presbyterian Church in Canada. Formal conversations with Anglicans by this denomination occurred until 1945 and from 1961. Its membership was 213,483 in 1988 and also was declining in numbers.

**Bibliography**. B. Quinn, et al., eds., *Churches and Church Membership in the United States* (1974, 1982); J. G. Melton with J. V. Geisendorfer, *A Dictionary of Religious Bodies in the United States Compiled from the Files of the Institute for the Study of American Religion* (1977); J. M. Gorton, *The Encyclopedia of American Religions* (1978); D. B. Barrett, *World Christian Encyclopedia: A Comparative Study of Churches and Religions in the Modern World, A.D. 1900–2000* (1982). See also the minutes of various general assemblies and the annuals, R. McHenry et al., *Britannica Book of the Year*, and C. H. Jacquet, Jr., ed., *Yearbook of American and Canadian Churches*.

ROBERT V. SCHNUCKER AND CLYDE CURRY SMITH

**Press, Religion and the Secular.** The existence throughout the world of thousands of religious newspapers and magazines attests to the inability or unwillingness of the secular press to print enough religious news and views. This situation differs in various countries. In those nations or regions where religion is important to the culture the secular press usually gives more attention to religion than in lands where religion is a minor concern.

Even in countries where religion has an important place, the privately owned secular press is limited in the quantity of material it can publish. The amount of church news, a lack of knowledge among media professionals, the controversial nature of many religious issues, and secularization, which breeds a lack of interest among some readers, all mean that publishers cannot be expected to make their papers or magazines voices of religion.

Conflict has long existed between the professional journalist and the professional religionist. The journalist, seeking to attract all readers, secular and religious alike, generally resists the pressures from the religionist for more space and attention to the causes which lack a wide appeal. The religionist, on the other hand, sees the press chiefly as a tool. Only when he realizes that the secular press in free-enterprise systems must be a profit-making enterprise and must sell a great proportion of its space to advertisers, does the religionist understand that the press cannot serve the church freely.

Misunderstandings and bitterness were reduced in those religious bodies which organized news bureaus or helped train their clergy and other church workers. Guidance in the proper preparation of materials for the press, instruction in the differences between news and paid advertising, and other directions for cooperation with journalists helped alleviate some of what was accurately or not called media bias.

The place of religion in the secular press occasionally is studied by researchers in journalism, sociology, and religion. In the USA over the 1900s the trends were as follows: (1) Religion played a minor part in metropolitan secular newspapers and secular national magazines but a somewhat larger part in country weeklies and none in secular specialized periodicals. Many metropolitan newspapers came to hire a religion reporter, but the demand for space far exceeded the supply. In radio and television there was almost no time available, except at a high cost. In the late 1900s public access cable stations did allow some opportunity for media exposure in city markets, at a cost. (2) The secular press was more likely to cover *church*, rather than *religious*, information, the distinction being that religious information has to do with a philosophy of life whereas church information has to do with the activities of organized groups, such as local churches or denominations. (3) Despite appearances, no particular denominational groups regularly obtained more or less space than others, although in communities where a given creed was unusually strong there might be preferential treatment.

As a result of difficulties in getting their news across to the public some large denominations developed state-of-the-art publishing houses and magazines. In communist and controlled press countries, such as the USSR from the 1960s and Poland in the early 1980s, a thriving underground press developed. Direct mail operations helped some urban churches target and distribute printed and photocopied newsletters. As computer-based word processing systems replaced older duplicating machines, this could be done with a great deal of sophistication. Church news and issues-related magazines were also within reach of more groups with photo-offset printing, "desk-top" publishing, and other advances. As secular news became more of a problem the church was forced to take more innovative directions.

**Bibliography.** J. L. Fortson, *How to Make Friends for Your Church* (1943); M. Muggeridge, *Christ and the Media* (1977); V. S. Owens, *The Total Image: Selling Jesus in the Modern Age* (1980); Daughters of St. Paul, *Media Impact and You* (1981).

ROLAND E. WOLSELEY

**Pringle-Pattison, Andrew Seth** (1856–1931). Scottish philosopher. He was educated at the University of Edinburgh and in Germany, and held the chair of logic and philosophy at University College, Cardiff (1883–87); logic, rhetoric, and metaphysics at the University of St. Andrews (1887–91); and logic and metaphysics at the University of Edinburgh (1891–1919). Opposed to mechanistic evolutionary naturalism, he sought constantly to preserve the judgment of values and to avoid the loss of the individual self in any absolute. Among his publications are *The Idea of God in the Light of Recent Philosophy* (1917), *The Idea of Immortality* (1922), and *Studies in the Philosophy of Religion* (1930).

**Prior, Prioress.** In several religious orders, especially the mendicant orders, with the exception of the Franciscans, the title given to the elected superior of a local convent formally erected. The designated official is next in rank to the abbot, and historically was responsible for the work of deans and monks or nuns.

**Procurator.** In monasteries and other religious communities, the official in charge of the temporal goods of the house. He is also called syndic or cellarer. The term is used in the Church of Scotland for the legal officer who advises the courts of the church in judicial matters.

**Profanity.** That which profanes (a verb) or is profane (an adjective); from the Latin *pro*, meaning "before" or "in front of," and *fanus*, "a temple." Thus the profane is that which does not belong to the sacred. Profane may simply refer to the common or secular, but in modern usage the term more commonly means the unhallowed and the polluted. In this sense "to profane" is to pollute, and profanity is that which pollutes. From this merely ethical meaning, the religious significance is never far distant. To profane is to treat the sacred as if it were not sacred whether through oversight, indifference, ignorance, or deliberately. It may involve an act or attitude directed against sacred ritual, or it may have a more moral and spiritual dimension. The object ultimately affronted may be personal, as in the Scriptures, or impersonal or semipersonal, as in the taboos of the Polynesians. The act of profaning expresses an attitude of careless indifference, disregard, or active contempt.

In Heb. 12:16 Esau is said in literal translation to have been "a profane person" because he sold his birthright for food. The NIV uses the word "godless" to describe Esau's disregard for the holy. The birthright was God-given, and his light sacrifice of it was an affront to the Giver. In Lev. 18–22, there are six references to profaning "the name" of God. It might be done by worshiping Molech (18:21; 20:3), or by swearing falsely (19:12). It might be done by the priests in treating disrespectfully the people's offerings (22:2). In Mal. 1:12 an attitude of regarding the temple sacrifices as a "burden," and the offering of animals which are torn and lame and sick, are characterized as profaning the name of God. In Lev. 21:4 priests were forbidden to profane themselves by touching the dead. In Neh. 13:18, working upon the sacred Sabbath is said to desecrate or profane it; and in Acts 24:6 Paul is charged with profaning the temple by bringing into it one thought to be uncircumcised. In Ezek. 44:23, one of the duties of the priests in the restored temple is to "teach my people the difference between the holy and the common [profane], and show them how to distinguish between the unclean and the clean." In all these cases, the profaning is represented as something evil, a calamity or a misdeed; but Jesus, in defending his disciples for plucking and eating corn on the Sabbath, asked, "Haven't you read in the law, how that on the Sabbath days the priests in the temple desecrate the day and yet are innocent?" (Matt. 12:5).

It is against this background that the modern characterization of certain forms of speech as profanity is to be understood. Such speech is polluting because it involves an indifference to or a defiance of that which should be treated as sacred. The sacredness may be naturalistically considered, such as the purity of a human person or the value of certain ideals or relationships. But in the fullest use of the term profanity expresses carelessness or enmity toward God.

ANDREW K. RULE

**Proofs of God's Existence.** Rational or philosophical demonstrations or logical arguments offered to support theistic faith. Whether faith depends on understanding, or as was more widely held among 20th-century Christians, faith issues in understanding, understanding is essential to faith. The proofs of God's existence are an effort to explain and to defend faith through

understanding. Christianity is a religion of revelation with both supernatural and natural aspects. The theistic proofs seek to discover how far the basic fact of the supernatural revelation may be supported by sound reason based on an appeal to the facts of natural revelation. Within the discipline known as apologetics, proof strives to bring these two aspects of revelation into a systematic harmony. The widespread conviction, therefore, that theistic argument is irrelevant to real religion would appear to be more pious than intelligent.

Two of the three "metaphysical" proofs—the cosmological and the teleological—were already elaborated in pre-Christian times. The roots of the third—the ontological—may be found in Plato, although he never developed it into a theistic argument. Augustine (A.D. 354–430) and Erigena (810–80) were aware of the ontological argument, but Anselm of Canterbury (1033–1109) is usually designated its "father." Since his time, philosophers have accepted or rejected it, but all have had to take account of it. Prior to the time of David Hume (1711–76) and Immanuel Kant (1724–1804), each of the three arguments, if accepted as valid, was regarded as an independent proof, sufficient without aid from any other to compel the assent of the intellect. But the critical treatment to which these men subjected theistic argument convinced subsequent thinkers that: (1) they are arguments, but not demonstrative proofs; (2) they do not stand alone but mutually support one another; and (3) taken together, they still constitute an argument and not a demonstration which may not be logically disputed. Kant's negative attitude toward the possibility of metaphysical theistic argument has appealed to many, as has his preference for a moral argument. It was commonly asserted by the liberal theologians of the 19th century that only moral argument is valid or religiously relevant. Georg Hegel (1770–1831), however, presented an ontological argument; Rudolf Lotze (1817–81) worked out an argument which began with cosmological reasoning, and moved through teleological to ontological stages. Robert Flint and J. Orr presented the three along with others. The concentration of 19th-century liberals on moral argument was charged to "cosmic blindness" by conservative and neo-orthodox apologists of the 20th century. A strong tendency to advocate a teleological philosophy and argument and arguments based on epistemology, religions, history, and psychology received increasing attention during the 1900s.

The cosmological argument, on which Thomas Aquinas depended heavily, moves from the observation that something now exists to the conclusion that something must exist necessarily. The objection that a "necessity" is not the same as a god is not serious so long as this argument is simply one strand in a wider argument. But if the premise is accepted that behind every effect lies a cause, the fact of the universe's existence is a ground for postulating that there was a first cause—an "unmoved mover." Hume and Sir Arthur Eddington denied the objective validity of the causal concept, and Kant refused to affirm it. If its objective validity is restricted to the relating of particulars within the world of sensory experience, then its use in the cosmological argument must be pronounced invalid. If the causal relation is admitted to involve time sequence, the cosmological argument becomes caught in an "infinite temporal regress," against modern conceptions that matter in motion is eternal. If the cause is identified with the logical "ground" the argument ends in a pantheistic conclusion.

The teleological argument rests on the analogy that the organization of the objective world is like that of a work of human contrivance. Since there is design there must be a personal, creative designer. The objections—that only an architect, not a creator, is indicated; he cannot be said to be infinite since the world is finite; and an analogical argument such as this cannot amount to a proof—are not serious. Since it is usually allowed that the only alternatives for world order are chance and design, the important question is how valid and strong the analogy to human inventions works to favor design. Hume decided the differences are too great. If the objective world can be adequately explained without the use of teleological categories, then the analogy is false; if teleological categories are required, then a valid analogy exists. Science in the late 1900s gave added validity to this argument. The breaking of the genetic structure vastly increased understanding of the complexity of biological processes. Darwinian natural evolution remained unsubstantiated after a century and was deemed inadequate by many scientists to explain the advance planning through which nature adapts to environment. R. E. D. Clark developed a popular but often disputed argument that the continual tendency is for natural processes to run down according to the second law of thermodynamics, while chance assumes the opposite.

The moral, esthetic, epistemological, historical, and religious argument are commonly presented in isolation from other reasoning, but they are concrete forms of teleological reasoning and serve to personalize the theism to which teleological reasoning leads.

The moral argument maintains that the existence of God is somehow implied in moral experience. Its validity depends on whether this claim can be substantiated and moral experience shown to be universally valid. Kant's claim that the existence of God is a postulate of the moral reason, William Paley's contention that moral commands require divine sanction, and the argument based on a hedonistic calculus, did not carry conviction

in the 20th century. The tendency was to base an argument instead on the unconditional nature of moral imperatives. W. R. Sorley, Hastings Rashdall, and Elton Trueblood used this argument extensively, stressing a universal moral consciousness which would be meaningless without an ultimate legislator. C. S. Lewis argued that the moral instinct bolsters the higher but weaker impulse and is independent of society's need for order. Bertrand Russell, however, used similar reasoning to argue that if there is an ultimate god such a being is either weak or arbitrary and evil.

The epistemological argument seeks to show that, in the process whereby truth is attained, there is something which points directly to the existence of a God of truth or to belief in a power that makes truth true and relevant.

The religious argument, also called experientialism, has been most fervently denied by modern sociologists and anthropologists but is still used to defend historically the belief that a universal religious consciousness has existed, indicating an object. Friedrich Schleiermacher and Rudolf Otto took the argument deeper to assert that religion, with its belief in God, is inseparable either from the essential constitution of human nature or from its inevitable development. On the other hand, Henri Bergson and many contemporaries found in the direct experience, not of mankind in general, but of religious mystics the highest justification for belief in the existence of God. Opponents have claimed that such assertions belong within psychology rather than philosophy and offer no justification for belief other than the desire to believe.

Historical arguments may rest on a philosophy of divinely directed history or on the historical reality of some particular God-sponsored institution. History may be regarded as the creative work, not of individuals, but of a super-individual Power or Spirit, which is identified with God. The contention of Walter R. Matthews that evolution requires the effective control of every stage by a process which strives toward a specific end can be conceived only in terms of a Mind transcendent to the process is another argument based on natural history. Alan Richardson, on the other hand, pointing to the fact of the historical existence of the church, urges that a sufficient cause for this phenomenon must be acknowledged and maintains that this can only be the truth of the basic convictions on which the church is founded, and thus gets a theistic argument.

The ontological argument, which had something of a resurgence in process theology through Charles Hartshorne, is that for every thought there is an object to which it refers. Total illusion is impossible. The idealistic contention is that value is the best clue to reality. To those who accept Platonic idealistic epistemology its force is overwhelming; to those who do not, this argument seems completely empty.

**Bibliography.** I. Kant, *Critique of Pure Reason* (ET, 1934); G. H. Clark, *A Christian View of Men and Things* (1952); D. Hume, *Dialogues Concerning Natural Theology* (1963); J. H. Gerstner, *Reasons for Faith* (repr. ed., 1967); C. Hartshorne, *A Natural Theology for Our Time* (1967); C. Van Til, *A Christian Theory of Knowledge* (1969); H. S. Kushner, *When Bad Things Happen to Good People* (1981); N. Geisler and W. Corduan, *Philosophy of Religion* (2d ed., 1988).

ANDREW K. RULE

## Protestant Episcopalians.

Usually a designation for members of the Protestant Episcopal Church in the United States of America but applicable to the Reformed Episcopal Church and various Methodist bodies. Historically only Americans call themselves Protestant Episcopalians, highlighting a dual emphasis on identifying with the Reformation and with episcopal polity.

By the late 20th century the term was fading from use. A revised preamble to the constitution of the Protestant Episcopal Church, USA, authorized dropping the word "Protestant" for most purposes since the denomination had long been known as the Episcopal church. Further, Episcopalians had undergone a liturgical renewal movement that stressed their Roman Catholic roots and moved the altar and liturgy to a central place in worship. Active negotiations with Roman Catholics were moving toward healing the 16th-century schism caused by Henry VIII.

The Protestant Episcopal Church in the USA is predominantly modernist, but it encompasses a conservative evangelical wing. Diversity has characterized the group from its beginnings in the American Revolution when Loyalist clergy and laity fled the rebellion, and remaining members of the Church of England sought to form an episcopal church on American soil. Connecticut Episcopalians dispatched Samuel Seabury to Scotland for ordination as an American bishop in 1784 after England rebuffed their request. Led by William White, the irenic rector of Christ Church, Philadelphia, the first national convention was convened in 1785. In 1787 Parliament finally authorized ordination of two bishops and in 1789 the official break with the Church of England was finalized. Under White and likeminded churchmen, the American denomination merged Swedish and German Lutherans, Northern High-Church episcopalians who followed Roman Catholic practices, and Low-Church Southern evangelicals.

This broad base proved durable. The American church survived disestablishment of pro-Anglican governments in Virginia, Maryland, South Carolina, and New York, withdrawal of Loyalists, and loss of mission support from England's Society for the Propagation of the Gospel in Foreign Parts. Ties remained between American and Anglican episcopalians, and Queen Victoria was a particular patron of American church projects. Southern dioceses split away to form the Protestant Episcopal Church in the Confederate States of America, but the national body reunited in 1865.

Growing theological liberalism followed the Civil War, and the Protestant Episcopalians suffered their only major split in 1873 when a large group of conservatives formed the Reformed Episcopal Church.

In the late 20th century the Protestant Episcopal Church had declined in membership. There were 93 dioceses, including 3 million members and 12,000 clergy in the 1970s. The mainline body was active in NCC and WCC. It used an American version of the Book of Common Prayer, last revised in 1928, and technically subscribed to the Apostle's and Nicene creeds. Women were ordained to all offices.

A vestry made up of the rector (priest) and laity governs the local church, and deacons are ordained, usually as a step toward priesthood. Dioceses are headed by bishops, and every three years a general convention is convened, comprised of the House of Bishops and a House of Deputies made up of priests and laity. An executive council administers between conventions.

## Protestantism. *Definition of Term.*

A collective name for all denominations, sects, groups, and religious associations which developed out of the Reformation, as well as cultural phenomena pertaining to them. Originally it was a technical term in the field of church history, but in the 20th century it became more a cultural concept, especially after a number of orthodox Protestant denominations identified themselves as evangelical rather than Protestant, since their leaders wish to emphasize the preaching of the pure gospel in preference to the negative idea of a protest against Rome. On the other hand, modern historical research has devoted itself to an increasing extent to the influence exerted by the Reformation upon modern civilization and institutions. In this field of intellectual activity the name "Protestantism" is indispensable. Historically it was derived rather accidentally from the "Protest" of the Lutheran representatives assembled at the so-called Second Reichstag (Diet) of Speier on April 19, 1529. The delegates from a number of Lutheran states objected to the attempt made at the meeting by the Catholic members in the Holy Roman Empire to prohibit all innovation in the field of religion. Evangelical leaders thus became known as "Protestants." The subsequent extension of the term is justified in that the only thing that all the multifarious institutions and cultural manifestations known as Protestant have in common is the opposition to the Roman Catholic Church and Catholic thought as expressed in literature, art, science, and culture in general, an opposition in the name of individual responsibility before God.

***Old and New Protestantism.*** A dichotomy between the period before 1700, now called Old Protestantism, and the New Protestantism since that era was a major hypothesis of 20th-century historical research. The unyielding stability of ecclesiastical traditions, founded in the authority of official creeds of the Reformation times, covered subtle differences in intent and culture. There was often a misunderstanding of the Reformation as great as that of the "Enlightenment" historians of the 18th century and the liberal historiography of the 19th century. It appeared as if the leaders in the Reformation wanted above all things to break apart the shackles forged by church and dogma, to make theological thought more subjective, and to free the world from the religious ties of tradition. Even Roman Catholics emphasized the idea that Protestantism was a revolution. They accused the orthodox Protestants of the 16th century of having been responsible for the apostasy of the modern world. They concluded that this apostasy resulted from the schism in the church and the destruction of the medieval civilization in the West. When seen in this light, the Reformation was closely connected with the Renaissance, running parallel with it; these two phenomena were considered merely the early stepping stones from medieval bondage to modern liberty of spirit and the secularization of modern culture.

Ernst Troeltsch (from 1906) first theorized that Martin Luther's Reformation was much closer to the Middle Ages than to the spirit of the period since 1700, and that the real transition from the Middle Ages to the "modern world" came in the 18th century and was at first attacked most bitterly from all directions. The historians concerned with secular affairs were even more vehement in their adverse criticism than were the theologians. This thesis was later strongly reinforced by the observation that the decisive changes in the social sciences and institutions which brought about the end of the medieval world did not occur either until the 18th century. In the age of rationalism cultural and religious changes were produced which showed a much greater chasm between the 18th century and the age of the Reformation than that between the Reformation and the Middle Ages. The New Protestantism flourished in an entirely different intellectual climate from that of the earlier type. The remarkable changes since 1700 are so pervasive that no amount of "Luther renaissance" attempted by modern theologians and no planned "restorations" of the confessional churches could lead the 20th century back to the days of Luther. Protestantism of the late 1900s did show signs of fidelity to the creeds of the 16th century, but a fundamental return to the actual spirit of the Reformers was out of the question. Old Protestantism and the New Protestantism were much farther apart than are the modern Roman Catholic Church from its predecessor in the Middle Ages. The great difference arose in the secular alterations affecting mental and spiritual attitudes and habits. These changes were not the result of the Reformation but of entirely different phenomena.

***Old Protestantism and the Middle Ages.*** The more deeply research delved into the Reformers, the more certain it appeared that for them the Reformation was not a revolution, but a return to and an absolute restoration of primitive Christianity. They sought to continue, improve, and heal the medieval church. The so-called Luther renaissance in Germany, begun with the great Luther studies of Karl Holl in about 1910, annihilated the idea that the first Reformers made common cause with that secularization of the European mind and spirit born in the Italian Renaissance and continued through the so-called Enlightenment to the 20th century. Renaissance and Reformation were related in a very superficial sense, particularly in the reform program of the Erasmian circle aiming at what has been somewhat erroneously called Christian humanism. The latter was in fact a sort of compromise, a middle way. In essence Renaissance and Reformation were widely apart from each other, and in their cultural effects hostile to each other. The Old Protestantism, far from wanting to promote the secularization of human institutions and thought, placed itself in the position of a road block as the forces of paganism advanced toward apostasy. For a short time it actually assisted in the process of new devotion, even among the Roman Catholic adversaries. Without the Reformation the restoration of Catholic piety in the age of the Jesuit baroque would not have been entirely possible.

What separated Luther from the Middle Ages was his new dogma, which flowed from a new, quite direct experience of the reality of God. His was a radical approach to the sacramental system. He wished to break away from all mediation between God and man in the process of salvation. In his opinion all came from God, nothing from man. Thus he sought to undermine the old sacramental system of the Middle Ages. But many who later studied this remarkable development of Luther's theology, including even Holl, came to an erroneous conclusion. They were correct that Luther did develop a startling exegesis which exerted profound influence in all directions. It led to the destruction of the priestly office as conceived by medieval theologians, and it also sought to teach a new sense of the duties of the Christian. However, Luther was not so far removed from medieval theology and ethics as is often widely claimed.

Undoubtedly he departed from medieval traditions the furthest in the field of dogma, especially in the dogma of salvation. Modern studies dealing with Luther's earliest writings confirmed afresh this statement. Nevertheless, even his conception of "justification" is based less exactly on Paul than Luther himself imagined, and more on the Augustinian and strictly medieval concept. This is what Troeltsch also saw regarding absolution and divine grace. The early Reformers were mistaken in their belief that they had brought about the restoration of NT Christianity in its original form. As evangelical theologians emancipated themselves from Luther's interpretation of the Scriptures, they sought to use the profound literature of the Reformers, but stumbled upon repercussions of scholastic traditions in these writings, even in the doctrine of the sacramental system.

In the realm of politics and economics medieval traditions influenced the Old Protestantism more than in the field of doctrine. It is erroneous to allege that Luther's concept of the two kingdoms (the kingdom of God and the kingdom of the world—a true Augustinian idea) meant the emancipation of the civil government from the duties of Christian ethics and as a result the founding of the totalitarian state in the modern world. What he did help destroy was the temporal power of the hierarchy, and with that naturally also the whole grand system of a Christian civilization built up as a unit, which, however, had long been in the process of disruption, particularly in the states of the Italian Renaissance. What he put in its place was the same "Christian authority" well known to the late Middle Ages, with far-reaching social activities performed by the clergy, together with the customary labors tending toward salvation from sin and damnation, physical well-being, and Christian education for its subjects. It was freed from the right of supervision and from the close contact with the papacy, the "spiritual government," but by no means from the command of Christian ethics, which was urged upon it with the increased earnestness of those who preached repentance. State churches placed the civil ruler as *summus episcopus* for each state. These were not free associations of newly awakened members, but rather true medieval churches of the population at large, although without the priestly hierarchy. For that reason they were unable to organize themselves without the aid of the civil government. That which thus was instituted in Germany was a new type of confessional state, unique in its nature all over Europe, whose civil rulers for several generations sought to make Christian education one of their main objectives and were narrowly confined in their efforts to usurp temporal power.

In the framework of medieval civilization the leadership of religious principles guided all forms of life and society, and the age of the Reformation with its new religious ardor and hard confessional struggles did not weaken these principles but rather strengthened them. This was also true of Zurich, the scene of Ulrich Zwingli's activities, and especially of Geneva, the city of John Calvin. The research of Walter Köhler on the marriage laws of Zurich and the consistory of Geneva delineated the heavy hand of religious ordinances set forth by the Protestant clergy. These went far beyond the medieval traditions. Finally, the most radical reformers of the Old Protestantism, the Anabaptists and the neomystics (spiritualists), whom Luther fought as fanatics, aimed at a spiritualizing of life, even a complete abandonment of all ties with the world by the Christian community. They actually went so far as to refuse military service and taking up the duties of magistrates. They neither owned nor administered private property nor charged interest on loans. What this all amounted to was the refusal to utilize all the facilities of ordinary and customary practices which render life profitable in a material sense. The love ethics of the Sermon on the Mount of Jesus, applied to a new order of society, was transferred from the monastery to the laity as a whole. Anabaptists accused the official people's churches of the Reformation of being associations of the baptized, not of the truly converted and regenerated. They further charged that these churches let themselves be forced to make compromises with the world, with the result that they were unable and unworthy to conduct a truly spiritual life. The "Inner Word," as it was first most impressively formulated by Thomas Münzer, has sometimes been seen as a forerunner of modern spiritual movements. It actually was a reverberation of medieval mysticism. The English Baptists of the 17th century manifested a novel type of personal devotion, nearer to the individualism of the 20th century.

***Protestantism and the Modern World.*** It must be granted at the outset that the distance which separates the Protestantism of recent times from the religious movements of the 16th century is enormous. Nevertheless this supposition does not imply that the Reformation must be looked upon merely as a late form of medieval religion. The overwhelming power of the thrust led to the religious and social development of modern society. This thrust, far beyond the intention of the Reformers, helped to destroy the medieval system of thought and life which, without the outer aid of the papacy, could no longer be maintained. The temporal power of the papacy had been greatly diminished since the Great Schism of 1378 and the reforming councils of the 15th century. But the revolt of so large a portion of the West against Rome changed to a marked extent the relation between church and state. There was no longer Western ecclesiastical authority recognized everywhere as a matter of course, and never since that time has it been possible to restore such an *ordo mundi,* as conceived in a medieval sense. The authority of the Bible, which in the Old Protestantism was to take the place of the ecclesiastical power as the seat of recognized knowledge, was subject to a manifold theological interpretation; as a result it was not a real substitute. The faith of the Protestants was based upon revealed truths which the Reformers as well as earlier church leaders did not doubt in the least. This is one reason they were not at all tolerant in the modern sense of the word, for they did not tolerate any public preaching of whatever doctrine might happen to please the speaker at the moment. But faith was to be a personal matter and placed each Christian in direct touch with God. Vast strides in the development of Western civilization were accomplished in the deepening of Christian piety, the religious appeal to each individual, the freeing of Christian ethics from false legalities and from the confessional to a pure ethics of sentiment and conviction, the extension of religious duties to society as a whole, and the elimination of monastic and priestly asceticism from the catalog of virtues. Such changes were not merely on the upper levels. For one thing, the moral, religious, and secular education of the masses was undertaken with great zeal by the Reformers and their churches, a zeal which found very little counterpart in the states of the Italian Renaissance. It unquestionably impelled the Catholic authorities to devote new energies to this tremendous task. The secularization of church property as a result of the Reformation also carried in its train many upheavals. Notably in England it caused an economic and social revolution. One of the most complicated and also the most important tasks for historians is to trace the influence of the Reformation upon the general culture of modern countries in the West.

The effect of Lutheranism on secular culture was confined more than was Calvinism to the sphere of spiritual life. In politics the Lutheran churches and forms of civil government were able to develop freely only in the north, particularly in Sweden. In the small states of the Holy Roman Empire they were too closely dependent upon the civil rulers to play a part of their own. It used to be fashionable to argue that they educated the German people to become humble and dutiful subjects of the rulers, but this sort of thing was common in all German lands, and even more so in the Reformed Calvinistic states, while the Catholic areas went further than the Protestant states. In those regions where the Catholic or Counter-Reformation was most successful the local nobility and political estates were suppressed. At all times German Lutheranism, in contrast with Calvinism and Zwinglianism, has exhibited a nonpolitical trend. On the other hand,

in higher cultural activity Lutheranism developed very fruitful activity, notably in music, literature, and philosophy. Lutheran influences upon German idealism were pronounced and highly beneficial. But Lutheranism became fully qualified for this task only after it had experienced strong inner changes, especially since the orthodox types of Old Lutheranism were superseded by the movement known as pietism. The latter powerfully affected the lay elements of the German population and replaced to a large extent the stubborn dogmatism of the orthodox Lutheran sermons with a new piety, much more strongly imbued with throbbing religious fervor. August H. Francke's pietism and his famous slogan of "Pray and work!" found numerous followers at the court of the soldier king Frederick William at Potsdam, where a new bureaucracy was formed by Prussian government officials and army officers. It seems that Francke's pietism played a remarkable part in forming Prussian spiritual traditions.

The Calvinistic share in the development of modern political and social institutions and thought seems at first glance enormous and many-sided when the whole compass of modern civilization is examined. Calvin's concept of the *politia Christiana,* built in the confines of a Swiss canton which was strongly municipal in character, instead of a German monarchical state, views the citizens as members of a political association, not as subjects. It was much easier to form democratic forms of government in Geneva than in Saxony or Brandenburg. Not without reason is Calvinism looked upon as the breeding ground of liberal and democratic thought, as distinguished from the monarchical and authoritarian attitude of Lutheranism. Nevertheless, one must be very careful not to derive political differences from differences in theology. The political theories of Luther and Calvin are not nearly so widely apart as has often been imagined. The power of the sword was wielded as much in Calvinistic as in Lutheran countries. The Genevan Reformer was neither a revolutionary nor a democratic champion. On the contrary, he favored conservative and aristocratic ideals. But political circumstances forced the Reformed areas to struggle against Catholic authorities with limited assistance from the aristocratic estates. The Lutherans relied heavily upon princes in their fight against Rome. Out of the Calvinistic revolutions the political maxims of liberty for all citizens arose first in France and the Netherlands, later in England, and also to some extent in North America. At the beginning the old theme of three estates representing the masses of the people (as in the pamphlets issued shortly after the massacre of St. Bartholomew's Night in 1572) was the leading slogan. There was opposition to a strong monarchy. Afterward the Puritans and Independents in

England fomented a great revolution and introduced republican principles under the leadership of Oliver Cromwell. In social reform the so-called Levelers became the precursors of democratic legislators during the 19th century. Liberty and equality were ideas to conjure with, as the "Beggars of Holland" arose against mighty Spain and the Puritans dared to defy the Stuart dynasty. Without the religious zeal of the Calvinists it would not have been possible to found the liberal governments of England and Holland, which became the center of the later attempts made to establish parliamentary government in nearly all European countries. Their enthusiasm was a fruit of real Calvinistic thought. They fought as if directly elected by God for this purpose. The theology of the Swiss reformers evinced a harder core than that of Luther. It also aroused great practical energies.

***Origin and General Character of the New Protestantism.*** It is impossible to make a detailed comparison between the effects of early Protestant theology and various secular factors which facilitated the rise of modern society and institutions. The same may be said about the social evolution thesis of Max Weber and others concerning the rise of modern capitalism. The influence of the Protestant ethic upon capitalistic society was so subtle that no amount of research will ever determine exactly how Protestantism vied with secular forces to bring about free enterprise as contrasted with communism. The worldly love of material possessions and religious fervor which seeks to foster a feeling of security and divine favor are in practice difficult to distinguish. At any rate it is certain that the treatises of Protestant writers during the 17th century which set forth capitalistic tendencies—particularly those by Puritans and Baptists—do not belong to the Old but to New Protestantism.

Distinguishing New Protestantism from Old means recognizing the introduction of foreign elements into the religious spirit of the Reformation. A radical subjectivity of piety, activated largely by such sects as Anabaptists and spiritualists, in the 16th century refused to submit to ecclesiastical authority and teaching. It is still impossible to determine exactly how the religious subjectivity originated. In part it may have been an exaggerated form of Lutheran biblicism and the principle of free and individual interpretation of the Scriptures and ecclesiastical tradition. In part it likely grew out of medieval sects, such as the Joachimistic apocalyptists, with their mystical and pietistic ideas and habits. The early Baptists in Switzerland, Germany, the Dutch Republic, and England and other elements supported the religious zeal of the Puritans, some of the Presbyterians, and the Congregationalists in their struggle against episcopacy, and the Anglican doctrines and church government. As Indepen-

dents they assisted Oliver Cromwell in obtaining victory for his party. Numerous ramifications of these early Protestant denominations in England and the Netherlands have attracted the attention of historians, but two types of influence on the New Protestantism will illustrate the process.

First, the originally pure theological concept of the "inner light" of God's revelation in the heart of the individual became ever more mixed with the "natural light" of reason, and often designated as common sense. The religious subjectivity which turned against ecclesiastical authorities gradually became a political subjectivity which fought for free conventicles and independent congregations, as well as for political democracy, meaning popular sovereignty. In this manner the political rationalism of the 18th century was developed. Men like John Locke derived much of their political thought from Puritans and Independents. Locke spent four years in the Dutch Republic, just before the Glorious Revolution of 1688. He took with him to England important theories about religious and political liberty, which thus far had not been widely accepted by the English leaders. The notion that political and religious democracy developed first in England and spread from there into various continental countries is contradicted by thousands of pamphlets published in the Dutch Republic during the 17th century. Nowhere else did so much literature appear that led to the so-called Enlightenment.

Second, it must not be lightly assumed that religious and intellectual toleration in the modern sense of the word developed entirely out of the thought and practices of the Anabaptists and the Baptists. The Independents fought primarily for their own liberty, and they often became (especially in North America) as intolerant as the Calvinistic pastors had been before them. As soon as the persecuted churches had the good fortune to achieve local power above other denominations they forgot about their previous experiences as humble martyrs for their faith. The appearance of a Roger Williams, the Baptist founder of Rhode Island, was by no means a normal phenomenon. The idea of toleration was readily derived from the theory of a general priesthood of all believers, a theory that appealed far more to the Anabaptists than to the state churches of the large denominations. But most Independents were at first so afraid of what they called worldly society that they could not contribute much to the shaping of lasting institutions and ideas. They certainly were in no position to fashion the far-famed thesis of "the general rights of man." This is particularly true of the German spiritualist Sebastian Franck, a compiler whose alleged modernity and intellectual importance have often been overemphasized. In the struggle of the English Independents in the 17th century the idea of a separation of church and state won wide acceptance. Modern toleration in general owes more to secular than to religious factors. The first important case of this development may be seen in the political adherents of Chancellor L'Hôpital, who during the Huguenot wars spoke for the national government in his appeal for reconciliation between the two great religious parties. Similar ideas are to be found among the Dutch patricians of the 17th century, who, largely because of their economic interests, opposed the Calvinistic zealots who could not tolerate the existence of non-Calvinistic congregations in New Amsterdam. These patricians were equally critical of the leaders in the Catholic Reformation, particularly those Spanish agents of autocracy who tried in vain to block the rising tide of liberty in the Dutch Republic. The influence of the Dutch universities in this respect was very important.

It is not difficult to understand that the religious neutrals were chiefly responsible for the rise of modern toleration. Moreover, the need to preserve the modern state caused a speedy end to the religious wars. But the politicians received support from a theological movement that found its origin more in the spirit of the Renaissance than in that of the Reformation. Its roots went down to the Neo-Platonism of Florence, back in particular to Marcilio Ficino; and they were nourished especially by the anti-Trinitarianism of the Socinians. Also in the Dutch Republic there was a new spirit of liberalism among the Arminians, while in England scholars and church leaders drew heavily upon the thought of Jacobus Arminius. These liberals sowed the seeds of rational criticism as they fled from one country to another. Some went a long way toward the ultimate goal of skepticism and worldliness; others, including Hugo Grotius, were content to accept a compromise with the deeply religious thinkers. The dogma of the Trinity and that of the incarnation of the Logos were deemed incompatible with human reason. The attempt by Erasmus to concentrate on an ethical rather than a theological core of Christianity—the love ethics of Jesus—to simplify the creeds in general was seized upon by numerous theologians and preachers. They were precursors of the rationalists, but their liberal theology made only a slight contribution to the general process of secularization of European thought. This secularization began at the end of the Middle Ages and expanded in all directions. About the middle of the 17th century this process produced the first great philosophical systems of modern times, and it played havoc with orthodox theology in many flourishing universities. This made much more rapid progress among the Protestants than among the Roman Catholics since Protestantism did not have such a close corporation as the theological faculties in the Catholic universities. There was no papal authority, nor such a rigid and supposedly infallible creed as that fashioned by the Council of Trent. Division among the leading Protestants greatly facilitated the onward march of skepticism and infidelity. It would be a gross falsification of the facts to assume that the Reformation was largely responsible for these phenomena in the New Protestantism. The real origin of this secularization was not the Reformation, which increased religious fervor, but a weakening, in humanism, of the old concept that man was sinful and born in corruption, a vacillating creature, dependent upon God for his own good. The Renaissance had taught the doctrine of human self-confidence. In its attempt to restore classical civilization it introduced a new feeling of respect for human reason. This renewal of self-confidence made scientific progress possible on a large scale. It was seen correctly that man could learn much from the study of nature, as distinguished from the realm of religion and theology.

The Protestant world had to come to terms with this secular movement. It could adapt itself to secular ideas, adopting them until it was literally overwhelmed and diluted by them. It could deliberately stiffen its attitude, restoring the Old Protestant heritage to its full validity, or withdrawing into the ivory tower of pious sentiments and world rejection. It could also enter the arena, whereby great risks are run and great victories won. The various Protestant strategies cover most of the intellectual movements of the last 250 years. The road of Protestantism is more insecure than that of the Catholic Church, but it has tended to be more productive as regards general culture. At times it seemed as though the original driving power of the Protestant faith was flagging and with it Protestant influence on general culture. Produced shortly before World War I, Troeltsch's presentation of events reads almost like an epilogue. In the great cultural crises of the 20th century, however, the forces of the faith broke out anew with astounding vitality. When faith in secular culture had suffered immense disillusionment and was utterly shaken in its complacency, the inner vitality of Protestantism stood with its attacking forces.

**Bibliography.** K. Holl, *Gesammelte Aufsätze zur Kirchengeschichte*, 3 vols. (3d ed., 1923); K. Barth, *Die protestantische Theologie im 19. Jahrhundert* (1947); J. H. Nichols, *Primer for Protestants* (1947); O. Brunner, *Adliges Landleben und europäischer Geist* (1949); H. T. Kerr, Jr., *Positive Protestantism* (1950); E. Hirsch, *Geschichte der neueren protestantischen Theologie im Zusammenhang mit den allgemeinen Bewegungen des europäischen Denkens*, 2 vols. (1949, 1951); K. S. Latourette, *A History of Christianity* (1953); L. Bouyer, *The Spirit and Forms of Protestantism* (ET, 1956); J. B. Cobb, Jr., *Varieties of Protestantism* (1960); G. W. Forell, *The Protestant Faith* (1960); K. Heim, *The Nature of Protestantism* (ET, 1963); W. Pauck, *The Heritage of the Reformation* (rev. ed., 1968); D. C. Steinmetz, *Reformers in the Wings* (1971); M. E. Marty, *Protestantism* (1972).

GERHARD RITTER

***Protocols of the Elders of Zion.*** A highly influential document that propagates the myth of a Jewish conspiracy to enslave the world, an idea which originated during the French Revolution and found increasing acceptance in the late 19th century, especially in Russia. The work was first published in a Russian newspaper in 1903 and soon after in books by Sergei Nilus (1905) and G. V. Butmi (1906). Translations of it reached the West in 1919. Major German, English, and French editions of the document appeared in 1920, and Henry Ford popularized it in the USA.

The "protocols" consist of 24 fragmentary lectures that comprise approximately 90 pages. The main themes include a critique of liberalism, an analysis of the methods used by Jews to achieve world domination, and a description of this new world-state. However, commentators give confusing accounts concerning the lectures' time and location. In 1921 the *Times* of London revealed that the works were lifted from a tract satirizing the regime of Napoleon III that was published in 1864 by French lawyer Maurice Joly. Further research suggested that the document was fabricated in Paris around 1897 or 1898 by the Russian secret police for use by the reactionary right to check liberalizing tendencies.

The *Protocols* soon became part of the stock-in-trade of Jew-haters everywhere, notably in Nazi Germany. Such American Christian anti-Semites as Charles E. Coughlin and Gerald B. Winrod made extensive use of it. The spurious nature of the *Protocols* was exposed in a celebrated trial in Berne in 1934 and 1935. In these proceedings the Swiss Jewish community brought suit on the basis of a law that banned the publication or distribution of offensive writings. The court ruled that the work was indecent, plagiarized from Joly, and was "ridiculous nonsense." Two defendants were fined, but the sentence was quashed on appeal in 1937 because the literature was not salacious per se. Even though the *Protocols* have been completely discredited, the tract is still distributed by extremist book sellers.

*See also* ANTI-SEMITISM.

**Bibliography.** J. S. Curtiss, *An Appraisal of the Protocols of Zion* (1942); N. Cohn, *Warrant for Genocide* (1966).

RICHARD V. PIERARD

**Province.** (1) In the Roman Church, the ecclesiastical territory placed under the jurisdiction of an archbishop or metropolitan, namely his own diocese and the suffragan dioceses. According to canon law, the metropolitan and the bishops of his province must convene every 20 years in a provincial or metropolitan council.

(2) A territorial circumscription of some religious orders, chiefly the mendicant orders and regular clerics, under the ordinary jurisdiction of a superior, prior, or minister provincial.

*See also* BISHOP, SUFFRAGAN.

GEORGES A. BARROIS

**Psalmody.** A term sometimes applied to the use in worship of hymns and—more precisely—psalms. Most scholars agree that the psalms originally were connected with Hebrew worship, and that they still lend themselves admirably to liturgy. In modern times they have suffered from wooden versifications and unworthy tunes. Hymns that paraphrase psalms include Martin Luther's "Ein' feste Burg ist unser Gott," and Isaac Watts's "O God, Our Help in Ages Past." The singing of psalms in worship is more common in Scotland than in the USA. The exclusive use—an inheritance from followers of Calvin—has almost disappeared, except among a few very small bodies. The Associate Reformed Presbyterian (ARP) Church was one of the last denominations to sanction use of hymns, and the ARP and some other Reformed churches retain the psalter in addition to the hymnal. The use of psalms in worship is a form of objective worship which avoids the "I and me songs," with their subjectivity and sentimentalism.

ANDREW W. BLACKWOOD

**Pseudepigrapha, OT.** Jewish or Jewish-Christian writings produced between c. 220 B.C. and A.D. 200, aside from rabbinic works, or the writings of Philo or Josephus. Questions remain about what to include within the collection. R. H. Charles (1913) included 17; H. F. D. Sparks (1984) 25, and the definitive edition of J. H. Charlesworth (1983–85) included 52, plus a supplement of 13 fragments.

Many of these writings were pseudonymous R. H. Charles argued that the supremacy of the Mosaic law and scribal traditions in this period made revival of OT prophecy impossible; second, the canon was formed, so nothing could be added. Thus these books were written to sustain the Jewish people in their faith under persecution, and give hope for the future. According to Charlesworth, the fluid state of the OT collection permitted some Jews and Christians to consider these books seriously, even on the level of Scripture in some instances.

Rather than classifying these works by Palestinian or Alexandrian origin, Charlesworth classified them by genre:

***Apocalyptic Literature and Related Works*** (19 works). Ethiopic, Slavonic and Hebrew Apocalypses of Enoch; Sibylline Oracles; Treatise of Shem; Apocryphon of Ezekiel; Apocalypse of Zephaniah; 4 Ezra; Greek Apocalypse of Ezra; Vision of Ezra; Questions of Ezra; Revelation of Ezra; Apocalypse of Sedrach; 2 Baruch; 3 Baruch; Apocalypse of Abraham; Apocalypse of Adam; Apocalypse of Elijah; and Apocalypse of Daniel.

***Testaments*** (often with apocalyptic sections; eight works). Testaments of the Twelve Patriarchs; Testament of Job; testaments of Abraham, Isaac, and Jacob, respectively; Testament of Moses; Testament of Solomon; and Testament of Adam.

***Expansions of the "Old Testament" and Legends*** (13 works). Letter of Aristeas; Jubilees; Martyrdom and Ascension of Isaiah; Joseph and Asenath; Life of Adam and Eve; Pseudo-Philo; The Lives of the Prophets; Ladder of Jacob; 4 Baruch; Jannes and Jambres; History of the Rechabites; Eldad and Modad; and History of Joseph.

***Wisdom and Philosophical Literature*** (five works). Ahiqar; 3 and 4 Maccabees; Pseudo-Phocylides; and Sentences of the Syriac Menander.

***Prayers, Psalms, and Odes*** (seven works). More Psalms of David; Prayer of Manasseh; Psalms of Solomon; Hellenistic Synagogal Prayers; Prayer of Joseph; Prayer of Jacob; and Odes of Solomon.

A series of 13 fragments of lost Judeo-Hellenistic works are also categorized as poetry, oracle, drama, philosophy, chronography, history, or romance.

The criteria for pseudepigraphic documents are that the work should be partially, and preferably totally, Jewish or Jewish-Christian, dating from the period 200 B.C. to A.D. 200. It should claim to be inspired, be related in form or content to the OT, and ideally be attributed to an OT figure, often claiming to be the speaker or author. These works are of interest to both Jewish and Christian readers, for they contain rich theological insights into such concepts as sin and evil, the nature of God, and the resurrection and entrance into paradise.

*See also* APOCRYPHA, OT.

**Bibliography.** R. H. Charles, *The Apocrypha and Pseudepigrapha of the OT in English*, 2 vols. (1913), and *Religious Development between the Old and New Testaments* (1914); O. Eissfeldt, *The OT: An Introduction* (1965); M. Hengel, *Judaism and Hellenism*, vol. 1 (1974); J. H. Charlesworth, *The Pseudepigrapha and Modern Research* (1976); M. Stone, *Scriptures, Sects and Visions: A Profile of Judaism from Ezra to the Jewish Revolt* (1980); G. W. Nickelsburg, *Jewish Literature between the Bible and the Mishnah* (1981); J. H. Charlesworth, *The OT Pseudepigrapha*, 2 vols. (1983–85); H. F. D. Sparks, *The Apocryphal OT* (1984); J. H. Charlesworth, *The OT Pseudepigrapha and the NT* (1985).

WALTER MCGREGOR DUNNETT

**Psychiana.** Organization founded in 1929 by Frank B. Robinson, a pharmacist, in Moscow, Idaho. It is rather unique in that it was from its beginning primarily a "mail order" faith, its membership recruited almost entirely through advertising. Robinson was the son of an English Baptist minister, but at age 14 was sent to Canada. He studied for the Baptist ministry, but a variety of circumstances led him to change his plans and eventually to sever his connections entirely with the church. He fell under the influence of New Thought and on one occasion had a remarkable conversion experience. An ardent evangelist for his newfound faith, he decided to prepare a series of lessons and circulate them by means of advertising. Borrowing money, he printed the first lessons and spent the entire remaining sum on one ad in the magazine, *Psychology*. That advertisement, "I Talked with God," afterward appeared in a variety of American periodicals. In less than 15 years one million people had bought his lessons or books, and he had built up a substantial organization in Moscow.

He was ordained by one of the bishops of the Old Catholic Church and incorporated the movement, with himself as "archbishop of Moscow." A small board of directors, consisting of himself and four other ordained clergymen, became the ruling body. Tentative efforts were made to form local societies, but membership remained primarily an individual matter, the students having direct relationship only to the central office.

Robinson's was the typical New Thought emphasis on health, prosperity, and happiness. He stressed the theme of the availability of God's power to every man. There is nothing needed by a person, he declared, which the power of God cannot bring if one will but meet the conditions. These conditions were explained in the lessons and numerous books issued from Moscow. Robinson's death in 1948 left the movement under the direction of his son, Alfred W. Robinson. The organization published *The Psychiana Bulletin* and *The Way*.

**Bibliography.** F. B. Robinson, *The Strange Autobiography of Frank B. Robinson* (1941); *Your God Power* (1943); M. Bach, *They Have Found a Faith* (1946); C. S. Braden, *These Also Relieve* (1949).

CHARLES S. BRADEN

**Psychiatry.** A branch of medicine which studies and treats mental and emotional disorders. A psychiatrist is a physician who has specialized training in the diagnosis, treatment, and prevention of such disorders.

***History.*** Attempts to understand and treat mental and emotional disorders reach back as far as recorded history. Primitive people generally attributed disordered behavior to forces acting outside the body. Such forces were deemed to be supernatural and included evil spirits, witches, gods, and magicians. Since disordered behavior and feelings were judged to be the punishment of the gods for some offense committed by the individual, others in the society were usually reluctant to intervene lest they too should incur the wrath of the gods. When they did intervene, treatment usually took the form of exorcisms, incantations, and charms. Less humane treatment involved chipping a hole in the individual's head to allow the evil spirit to depart from the body. Horrible-tasting or -smelling concoctions and the use of starvation or floggings were other strategies designed to make the body of the possessed person an undesirable place of habitation for the evil spirits.

Modern psychiatry is primarily derived from the approach of the Greek priests of the period 800 to 700 B.C., who began to supplement incantations and exorcisms with recommendations of kindness and suggestions for the use of physical and recreational activities. The writings of Hippocrates (460–375 B.C.) were crucial in moving psychiatry toward a more scientific basis. His classification of mental disorders into mania, melancholia, and phrenitis (brain fever) and his description of these disorders in terms of the assumed underlying physiological causes were an important step in this direction.

Contemporary Western psychiatry represents a convergence of two traditions, the biomedical and the psychological. The biomedical tradition is rooted in the work of German psychiatrist Emil Kraepelin (1856–1926). Kraepelin argued that mental disorders are biomedical disorders, that is, diseases. His system of classification became the basis of most modern psychiatric classification systems. The psychological tradition in psychiatry was founded in the work of the French physicians Franz Anton Mesmer (1734–1815), Jean-Martin Charcot (1825–93), Pierre Janet (1859–1947), and most importantly, the Viennese psychiatrist Sigmund Freud (1856–1939). These theorists assumed that while some mental disorders may at times have a biomedical basis, the primary cause of most emotional and psychological problems was psychological. More specifically, they assumed that the most important dynamics of the disorder were unconscious conflicts. Developed by Freud, psychoanalysis continued to be a dominant force in 20th-century psychiatry.

The biomedical and psychological traditions in psychiatry each had periods of dominance in their rivalry for control of the discipline. By late century Western psychiatry appeared to be returning to its medical roots, with an increasing number of psychiatrists holding primarily to biomedical hypotheses about the origin of mental disorders and responding to these assumptions with pharmacological treatment.

***Training and Certification.*** Psychiatric training begins with a minimum of three years of premedical college, followed by four years of medical school study and a four-year residency in psychiatry. Certification by the American Board of Psychiatry and Neurology, required for teaching appointments in medical schools and desirable for clinical positions, is possible after two additional years of experience and the passing of a comprehensive oral and written examination. Approximately 45 percent of U.S. psychiatrists were certified in the late 1980s.

In addition to general (adult) certification, specialized certification is available in child, administrative, and forensic psychiatry. Other areas of specialization include biological psychiatry, psychoanalysis, geriatric psychiatry, and preventive psychiatry.

***Relationship to Other Health Professions and Christianity.*** The major difference between clinical psychologists and psychiatrists is that clinical psychologists are not medical doctors. Rather, they hold a Ph.D. with specialized training which overlaps considerably with that of psychiatrists but also complements psychiatric training in several areas. Clinical psychologists are usually better trained in the use of psychological tests and in the conduct of research. They are not qualified to prescribe drugs and are usually not as well trained in the diagnosis of mental disorders. However, they are often better trained in psychotherapy. As psychiatry returned to its biological roots, more of the psychotherapy was left to psychologists, social workers, and other nonmedical psychotherapists.

Psychiatry's relationship to religion has often been one of conflict. Freud viewed religion as, at best, a symptom of neuroses and, at worst, a cause of such disorders. Such generalizations were personal opinions. Applying Freud's own methods to himself, it appears that his views of religion were biased by his own religious and spiritual conflicts. This is not to suggest that the psychoanalytic view of religion makes no contribution to the Christian. Psychoanalysis promoted an understanding of the relationship between religious commitments and the rest of personality, particularly the way in which these commitments can aid the integration of personality or damage it as a sham center. However, Freud's personal views of religion also contributed greatly to the hostility of the relationship between psychiatry and Christianity.

Psychoanalysis is not inherently anti-Christian, nor is the more biomedical approach to psychiatry. While the latter grew out of a reductionistic view of persons as biological machines, it is also entirely consistent with a view of persons as embodied spirits. Psychiatrists have greatly assisted persons, both Christian and non-Christian, who suffer from serious mental disorders. While the Christian faces many challenges in relating to the discipline of psychiatry, it is an important sphere of kingdom service for those who seek to bring all things under Christ's subjection.

*See also* PSYCHOTHERAPY.

**Bibliography.** A. M. Freedman, H. I. Kaplan, and B. J. Sadock, eds., *Comprehensive Textbook of Psychiatry* (1975); L. C. Kolb and H. K. Brodie, *Modern Clinical Psychiatry* (1982); E. R. Wallace, *Pastoral Psychology* 31 (1983): 215–43.

DAVID G. BENNER

**Psychical Research.** Investigation of alleged phenomena ("hauntings," telepathy, clairvoyance, and similar extrasensory reports) which appear to resist explanation by science as usually understood. It should not be confused with spiritism or spiritualism, which is a set of beliefs and practices, although it has been largely concerned with investigation of phenomena claimed by spiritualists. "Psychic phenomena" have occurred or are assumed to have occurred throughout history; while Saul outlawed mediumship, he consulted a medium just before his death (1 Sam. 28:7–25). After the beginnings of the scientific movement in the 17th century, educated people tended more and more to disbelieve the occurrence of such phenomena, although there were always notable dissenting figures (e.g., Emanuel Swedenborg, who based his whole account of heaven and hell on supposed encounters with departed spirits, and whose feats of paranormal cognition impressed the philosopher Immanuel Kant). A new era in the subject evolved from 1886 with the founding of the Society for Psychical Research by a number of intellectuals at the University of Cambridge, England. Notable among these founders were Henry Sidgwick, the moral philosopher, and Frederic Myers, the classical scholar. Life after death is maintained by many psychical researchers to be unproven, since communication through mediums of what is apparently known only to dead "communicators" can always be attributed to telepathy or clairvoyance by the medium. A methodological breakthrough in the subject was made by Robert Crookall, who pointed out that the difficulty would disappear if one tested accounts of the immediate afterlife by "communicators" for their coherence one with another. This suggestion had been made by the philosopher Henri Bergson and the physicist Oliver Lodge, but Crookall was the first to carry it out. Crookall concluded his research with the provocative judgment that belief in life after death is about as securely founded as belief in evolution. Recent improvements in medicine, resulting in revival of the clinically dead, have produced a rash of accounts of interest to those concerned with evidence for life after death (discussed by E. Kübler-Ross, R. Moody, and others). Research continued but was hampered by shortage of funds and the hostility of many in the academic community, especially natural scientists. Fraud by some mediums has tended to throw pall of doubt over phenomena which can not be so easily discarded.

*Bibliography.* F. W. H. Myers, *Human Personality and Its Survival of Bodily Death* (1907); R. Heywood, *The Sixth Sense* (1966); I. Currie, *You Cannot Die* (1978).

HUGO A. MEYNELL

## Psychology, Counseling.

A specialty within psychology developed after World War II within the early 20th-century movements of vocational guidance, mental hygiene, and mental measurement. Counseling psychology emphasizes positive aspects of growth and adjustment with a develop-

mental orientation. It is the specialty of psychology which focuses on helping people to resolve crises, cope with personal or social problems, increase problem-solving ability, make decisions, improve psychological well-being, and develop plans for the future. Counseling psychologists regard those who come to them for help as "clients" who possess potential resources and personal strengths necessary to aid themselves in resolving dilemmas.

Individuals and groups of all ages use the services as a means of coping with problems of education, career, marriage, family, health, sex, aging, and disabling conditions of a social or physical nature. Usually, clients of counseling psychologists are people who function reasonably well in society but who experience interpersonal or environmental conflicts. The concerns of clients may stem from social, vocational, educational, developmental, health-related, or emotional sources. Counseling psychologists usually deal with anxiety or frustration instead of severe disability or disintegration; they focus on normal development as opposed to personality restructuring or rebuilding. They also work with preventive programs, helping people to improve coping skills and adaptability to life situations.

Clients' needs are usually assessed through tests, interviews, written inventories, and observations. In general, such assessments do not diagnose psychopathology. They instead point to strengths and personal methods of coping. Unlike some other psychological specialties, those providing counseling psychological services are designed to appraise growth potential and deal with everyday crises in development, helping to improve basic interpersonal, social, psychological, and life skills. Counseling procedures may include interviews, observation, and assessing educational skills, aptitudes, interests, emotions, attitudes, personality characteristics, and other abilities. One-on-one and group discussions, teaching communication skills and demonstrating problem-solving or decision-making techniques and career planning, are tools used in this practice.

Career counseling, interest measurement, personal counseling, and psychological education are examples of services offered. Direct therapy, called "interventions," involves psychological and educational theories rather than psychiatry. These interventions are used to prevent problems, deal with problems in the individual's life, or help the person return to mental well-being after a psychological trauma.

The services of counseling psychologists are used by individuals, couples, families, and groups. These services are offered in educational, rehabilitative, and health organizations, as well as in other public and private agencies. Historically, most counseling psychologists have worked in colleges and universities; however, these psychologists today may work, as well, in hospitals, clinics, businesses, government agencies, mental health centers, or private practice.

Training of counseling psychologists is similar to that received by clinical psychology professionals, but there have been differences between counseling and clinical psychologists in where they work, the focus of their work, and the clients with whom they work. Clinical psychologists are likely to work in medical settings. Counseling psychologists, on the other hand, have been more likely to receive training and experience and to work in counseling centers and educational institutions. In the late 1900s more of them also received special training needed for working in medical settings. Regardless of setting, counseling psychologists focus less on diagnosis than do clinical psychologists and more on educational techniques to enhance the lives of normal individuals. The counseling psychologist works primarily with adults and adolescents; few work only with children. Clinical psychologists, however, are much more likely to work exclusively or secondarily with children.

To understand a client's situation, counseling psychologists strive for an objective measure of aptitude, learning ability, personality, and interests. A clinical psychologist would tend to use projective techniques and tests, or neuropsychological tests. Clinical psychologists usually address a client's behavioral deficits or level of effective functioning. Counseling psychologists look for ways to help an individual deal with a specific problem and focus on particular goals within a limited time frame. Clinical interventions may be similar, but, since they are used more often with moderately to severely disturbed individuals, they are often more long-term, extensive, and pervasive in the individual's life. In either field scientific research is used to assess how effectively different techniques accomplished goals.

Counseling psychologists have a Ph.D. degree. Doctoral programs exist in regionally accredited university graduate schools in such departments as psychology, counseling, educational psychology, or education. The American Psychological Association accredits such doctoral programs on the basis of number and quality of faculty, organization of courses and other instruction, and the quality of library, computer, and other facilities. Ph.D. programs in counseling psychology require four to five years of graduate study in such areas as human development, learning, and several types of psychology. These programs require practical training experiences. Such training in counseling centers, clinics, hospitals, or other related agencies helps to insure that counseling psychologists will be able to handle many types of client concern. Counseling psychologists follow the training and ethical standards of the American Psychological Association.

In the USA in the late 1900s services of a counseling psychologist could be found primarily through university counseling centers, community mental and health centers, and hospitals. Some large churches staffed programs, and a growing industrial field provided services at the workplace. Counseling psychologists' services, such as stress management, parenting classes, or weight control, were frequently sponsored by community agencies.

*See also* COUNSELING, PASTORAL.

**Bibliography.** M. E. Hahn, *American Psychologist* 10 (1955): 282; American Psychological Association, *Ethical Principles in the Conduct of Research with Human Participants* (1973), and *Ethical Standards of Psychologists* (rev. ed., 1977); B. Fretz, *The Counseling Psychologist* 10 (1982): 15–19; American Psychological Association Education and Training Committee, *Counseling Psychology* (1983/84).

ELIZABETH A. SCHILSON

## Psychology of Religion.

Historically, attempts to explain what were taken to be uniquely "religious" experiences, such as conversion or mysticism, employing the concepts of psychological theory. Later psychology of religion included investigations of mundane psychological processes, such as cognition, perception, and emotion as they function in one's consideration of what is ultimately real. Psychology of religion may be identified as an organized movement chiefly in the history of American psychology.

*The Golden Age* (1900–1920). Most of the figures who established psychology as an independent discipline in the USA at the beginning of the 20th century belonged to the functionalist movement. Although they employed diverse methods to investigate a range of problems, all sought to explain psychological processes as developments in the evolutionary struggle for survival. The majority rejected orthodox Christian beliefs but advocated a religion of high moral consciousness largely compatible with the dominant liberal Protestantism of the day.

G. Stanley Hall, who may have played the greatest role in establishing the early academic departments and psychological journals, received early training as a Protestant minister. He later endeavored to reinterpret the "truth of Jesus Christ" in the language of functionalist psychology. This concern encouraged a generation of psychologists to identify the value which religious practices held for human survival and to raise human moral consciousness. Among the significant works in this early period were: E. D. Starbuck, *The Psychology of Religion* (1899), Edward Schribner Ames, *The Psychology of Religious Experience* (1910), James Leuba, *Psychological Study of Religion* (1912), and, most influential, W. James, *The Varieties of Religious Experience* (1902).

*Displacement from the Mainstream of Psychology* (1920–60). By the mid-1920s academic psychology's interest in the psychology of religion had become dormant. The functionalist movement lost its dominant position to the more blatantly reductionist tenets of John Watson's behaviorism. Behaviorists accepted only concepts that could be translated into measurable experimental operations, that is, stimuli in the environment and the muscular responses they produce. Religion, like any other human experience, was considered reducible to simple stimulus-response sequences. Its explanation required no special branch of psychology. The few remaining psychologists of religion did not respond to this challenge by developing convincing alternative paradigms for theory and research. What little empirical work remained in the field was judged irrelevant to the major interests of the discipline.

At the same time, organized religion grew wary of the concerns that psychology of religion had embraced. The destruction resulting from World War I gave little support to the moral optimism of previous decades. When neo-orthodox theology was introduced in America it tempered liberal enthusiasm for changing human psychological functions with a renewed emphasis on the action of a transcendent God. Combined with the fundamentalists' hostility toward Darwinian thinking, these changes in Protestant Christianity broke apart the supportive constituency that had surrounded psychology of religion.

During the next 30 years, psychology of religion was largely neglected within academic psychology. Nevertheless, several new sources of ideas emerged which had a lasting influence.

First, the major personality theorists associated with clinical practice frequently applied their ideas to analyses of religion. In *Future of an Illusion* (1927) Sigmund Freud argued that the Judeo-Christian belief in God the Father is a form of cultural neurosis which may be traced to the helplessness of early childhood. Carl Jung proposed that religious symbols express a deeper realization of self, including unconscious as well as conscious aspects of man's identity. Gordon Willard Allport, the only American among these predominantly European theorists, extended his criteria for identifying mature and immature personalities to a parallel distinction between intrinsic and extrinsic styles of faith.

Second, an increasing number of ministers and counselors were convinced that they needed to better understand the religious experience of clients who suffered mental and physical illnesses. This empathetic concern led these counselors to establish systematic training in pastoral counseling and standards of professional competence in their field. Anton Boisen, a leader in the movement, suggested that clients may confront intense personal conflicts in both psychopathol-

ogy and religion, but only religious experiences carry the unique potential for conflict resolution. His writings helped the pastoral counseling movement to construct interview techniques and case history methods for studying religious experience in clinical settings. Following this lead, theological seminaries and mental hospitals became the chief institutional centers for psychology of religion through the 1950s.

*Late 1900s Developments and Links to Mainstream Psychology* (1960– ). From the early 1960s, a number of important developments indicated increasing interest in psychology of religion. New journals were devoted exclusively to social scientific research in religion, among them the *Journal for the Scientific Study of Religion, Journal of Religion and Health, Review of Religious Research*, and the *Journal for Psychology and Theology*. Empirical studies dealing with psychology of religion also appeared in the journals of the American Psychological Association with surprising frequency. Indeed, in the mid-1970s this professional body organized its Division 36: "Psychologists Interested in Religious Issues."

These institutional developments reflected increases in both the quantity and quality of theory and research in this field. Certain studies continued to investigate the traditional categories of dramatic religious experiences, employing methods superior to those used in previous research. However, much research focused instead on mundane psychological processes involved in a person's wrestling with religious questions. By drawing upon established theoretical traditions in other areas of psychology, this research moved psychology of religion closer to the mainstream of the discipline.

For example, numerous studies applied variants of Jean Piaget's understanding of cognitive development to children's comprehension of religious and moral concepts. Goldman (1964) describes three stages in a child's consciousness of religious history: a preoperational stage during which reality and fantasy are not distinguished, a concrete operational stage in which distinguishing real events from fantasy is of central importance, and a final formal operational stage in which an adolescent can gain a fuller appreciation of the context of meaning surrounding any record of real events and can understand the significance of myth and symbol across historical periods. Similar stages were identified in the development of children's moral reasoning, religious group identity, and conceptions of God. These analyses indicated how religious concepts of the Scriptures should be communicated to children at each stage.

Allport's distinction between intrinsic and extrinsic religion produced a tradition of research on different styles of personal faith. Hunt and King (1971) describe a pattern of intrinsic-committed faith which employs abstract principles and multiple categories in reasoning and tolerates alternative interpretations of experience. They contrast this with an extrinsic-consensual faith in which persons prefer to reason through their faith with concrete religious material, use a few simple categories for evaluation, and are intolerant of other viewpoints. The researchers say the latter pattern has a high correlation to negative interpretations of one's own death and expressions of racial prejudice, among a large number of other variables they investigated.

Since persons often rely on religion to help them explain the unexplainable, theories which deal with our commonsense accounts of life events should find a place in the psychology of religion. Social psychology has made a major contribution in this regard through the body of concepts contained in attribution theory. These ideas have influenced research on a variety of religious themes, from how persons assign responsibility for tragic life consequences to when one is likely to experience intense religious emotions.

In the case of emotions, attribution theory predicts that religious emotion will be produced by both physiological arousal of the autonomic nervous system and the availability of an explanation which attributes the arousal to a religious source, for example, an encounter with the Holy Spirit. Studies demonstrated the powerful effects achieved by adroit manipulation of both factors in worship rituals.

The brief review of contemporary theory and research presented above represents the efforts of psychologists to incorporate accepted research methods with religious topics. Essentially, these methods were developed within a hypothetico-deductive model of scientific explanation which assumed that behavior is universally determined. Others in the field found good reason to challenge this model and its underlying assumption.

An important critical viewpoint observed that the empirical research was influenced by the prior beliefs, values, and faith commitments of the psychologists themselves. Voiced by those in the Christian tradition, such as M. S. Van Leeuwen, these arguments pointed out a need for alternative approaches to explanation compatible with the belief that persons are responsible, self-determining agents before God. From this perspective a new agenda might regard the explanation of how all psychological processes function if, in fact, humans are inherently religious in their relationship with God.

*Bibliography.* P. W. Pruyser, *A Dynamic Psychology of Religion* (1968); J. E. Dittes, *Handbook of Social Psychology* (2d ed., 1969); J. M. Yinger, *The Scientific Study of Religion* (1970); M. Argyle and B. Beit-Hallahmi, *The Social Psychology of Religion* (1975); C. D. Batson and W. L. Ventis, *The Religious Experience: A Social-Psychological Perspective* (1982); B. Spilka, R. Hood, and R. Gorsuch, *The Psychology of Religion: An Empir-*

*ical Approach* (1985); M. S. Van Leeuwen, *The Person in Psychology: A Contemporary Christian Appraisal* (1985).

GLENN D. WEAVER

**Psychotherapy.** More than 250 distinguishable 20th-century theories, encompassing a wide variety of theoretical approaches and techniques. One of the major problems of the field was self-definition. There was much disagreement about what psychotherapy was, how it was to be carried out, and by whom it was to be conducted. Perhaps the best-known definition of psychotherapy was that of Jerome Frank, who described it as a work conducted by a trained, socially sanctioned healer whose healing powers are accepted by the sufferer; it involves a sufferer who is seeking relief through the medium of the healer, and it consists of contacts between the healer and sufferer through which the healer tries to produce certain changes in the sufferer's emotional state, attitudes, or behavior.

The American Psychological Association for legislative purposes defined psychotherapy as "the use of learning, conditioning methods, and emotional reactions, in a professional relationship, to assist a person or persons to modify feelings, attitudes, and behavior which are intellectually, socially, or emotionally maladaptive or ineffectual." It has also been stated that "individual verbal psychotherapy is a procedure wherein two persons engage in a prolonged series of emotion-arousing interactions, mediated primarily by verbal exchanges, the purposes of which is to produce changes in the behaviors of one of the pair." Others suggest that psychotherapy is defined by who does it.

In real life many people engage in activities which could be described as psychotherapy. Professional practitioners include physicians, psychologists, social workers, psychiatric nurses, pastoral counselors, and a wide variety of paraprofessionals. Although the number and variety of psychotherapeutic approaches and techniques proliferated from the 1960s, almost all of them fall within three broad categories.

*Psychoanalytic.* These flow from the psychoanalytic theory of Sigmund Freud, which is the cornerstone or foundation of all modern psychotherapy. Virtually all forms of psychotherapy derived from or were developed in reaction to psychoanalysis. Its basic premise is that of uncovering, understanding, and resolving unconscious motivation and conflict as well as the forces that guide the individual. The goal of psychotherapy is first to uncover the unconscious process and then to reconstruct one's personality on the basis of this knowledge. This is a long-term process which usually requires several hundred hours of intensive psychotherapy stretched out over years.

*Behavioral.* The behavioral approaches originated in reaction to the perception that psychoanalysis lacked scientific precision. The three major thrusts of behavioral therapy include: *classical* or *respondent* conditioning (Ivan Pavlov and Watson), *operant* conditioning (B. F. Skinner), and *cognitive behavior therapy* (Wolpe, Beck, Ellis, and Meichenbaum). In the strict behavioral sense the primary focus in psychotherapy is on modifying behavior through a systematic process of looking at and altering the antecedents and consequences of behavior. The emphasis is primarily on behavior and action allowing for the role of thought and the importance of the individual's internal dialog in the behavior change process. Patient and therapist work collaboratively to discover "cognitive distortion" or thinking errors that lead to negative feelings and dysfunctional behavior. The goal of psychotherapy is not to "cure" patients but to develop effective coping strategies that help him to deal with everyday life. Psychotherapy using this approach tends to be relatively brief, often as few as five to 10 sessions.

***Existential-Humanistic.*** The roots of existential-humanistic psychotherapy rest deeply in philosophy and particularly in the writings of Jean-Paul Sartre, Martin Heidegger, and Paul Tillich. This is a meaningful alternative to the psychoanalytic theories which focus on the unconscious process and to behavioral views based on observable actions. Here the central theme is that of empowering people to determine their own destiny and meaning in life. The emphasis is clearly on "being" in the present rather than on environmentally based determinants or the past. The major contributors to this school are Fritz Perls, Viktor Frankl, and Carl Rogers. Rogers' "client-centered" therapy had the greatest impact. Rogers' approach emphasizes the conditions necessary for psychological growth, such as unconditional positive regard, empathetic understanding, and genuineness. The main thrust is that psychological growth occurs when these three conditions are met in any interaction between two people.

No one school predominated, and a number of forms of psychotherapy came into use. Some of these were directed toward a wide range of problems, while others were highly specific and targeted toward more specific disorders. Late-1900s trends suggested a movement toward more eclectic approaches, briefer periods of therapy, and higher accountability and efficacy of treatment.

*Bibliography.* A. J. Enelow, *Elements of Psychotherapy* (1977); C. H. Patterson, *Theories of Counseling and Psychotherapy* (3d ed., 1980); W. G. Herron and S. Rouslin, *Issues in Psychotherapy* (1982); B. E. Gilliland, et al., *Theories and Strategies in Counseling and Psychotherapy* (1984); S. L. Garfield and A. E. Bergin, *Handbook of Psychotherapy and Behavior Change* (1986); D. G. Benner, ed., *Christian Counseling and Psychotherapy* (1987); A. E. Ivey, M. B. Ivey, and L. Simek-Downing, *Counseling and Psychotherapy: Integrating Skills, Theory, and Practice* (1987).

H. L. LABRENTZ

**Puerto Rico.** *See* WEST INDIES.

**Pullan, Leighton** (1865–1941). Anglican. He studied at Oxford and was ordained a deacon in 1891, and a priest in 1892. He was theological lecturer at St. Joseph College (1889–1930; fellow, 1892–1930), and lecturer in church history at Oxford (1927–30). His books include *Lectures on Religion* (1896), *History of Early Christianity* (1898), *History of the Book of Common Prayer* (1900), *The Books of the NT* (1901), *The Christian Tradition* (1902), *The Church of the Fathers* (1905), *The Atonement* (1906), *The Gospels* (1912), *Religion since the Reformation* (1923), *The Significance of Nicea* (1925), *Mrs. Eddy's Christian Science* (1928), and *From Justinian to Luther* (1930).

RAYMOND W. ALBRIGHT

**Pulpit.** From the Lat. *pulpitum*, "raised platform." In ecclesiastical use, a stand on which the speaker delivers a sermon in Christianity and Islam. Technically the pulpit differs from the lectern, and sanctuaries with a divided chancel traditionally place a lectern to the right of worshipers and the pulpit to the left. In modern practice the distinction has become less important in Protestant churches.

Throughout church history the pulpit as a furnishing carried symbolic overtones related to a theology of worship. Ezra once spoke from a wooden pulpit, podium, or platform (Neh. 4:8), the only specific reference in Scripture to such a stand. The assumption is made that when Moses and the prophets addressed the people, they used natural or constructed platforms, both to be seen and heard and to demonstrate the high and separate holiness of God's message they were empowered to proclaim. Figuratively the idea is conveyed by Moses as he stands on a hilltop, raising the "staff of God" over the warriors as they fought the Amalekites at Rephidim (Exod. 17:9). Nothing like the pulpit was established in the cultic practices of Israel, however, either in the temple or the synagogue. When Jesus, for example, spoke in Nazareth, he stood at his seat, was given the scroll, read from it, and sat to teach (Luke 4:16, 20).

In the early church a reading desk or place of preaching did develop. This arrangement changed with the rise of the Roman See and the sacramental system during the 4th and 5th centuries. The churches at Rome used stonework, architectural plans, and existing structures from pagan temples and other public buildings. These large, cavernous basilicas were copied throughout Europe. Conforming practice to architecture, the public stood in the open nave of what became the medieval cathedrals, looking on into the sanctuary where the Mass was sacrificed and the worship led. The focal point was the altar. As the medieval church invariably faced east toward

Jerusalem, the lectern was on the right (south) and the pulpit was on the left (north). The dual form of pulpit and lectern became known as the *ambos*, the Latin word for "both." In the exuberant art of the Gothic era in the 11th to 14th centuries all elements of worship architecture, including the pulpit, became richly carved and ornamented.

Reformation practice disdained ornamentation, claiming that it lead to idolatry. Thus the altar was removed or denigrated to a lesser place of status. The pulpit was elevated in importance. Depending on the constraints of architecture and congregation's financial resources, the pulpit retained much of its elaborate art and might be physically installed at the center or suspended above the level of the worshipers. It also was eventually redesigned to include a sounding board so the sermon could be heard more clearly. Lutheran and Anglican churches, which gave greater stress to sacramental aspects of worship as well as proclamation, tended to keep the divided chancel and centralized altar, but an attempt was still made to visually set the preacher in greater prominence.

Open air preaching and nonliturgical churches organized out of the First and Second awakenings in Britain and America contributed to a degrading of symbolism which continued into the 20th century. Particularly in Protestant North America, decor became more a matter of taste than of theology. Crosses and other visual symbols of faith often became the focal point of design. In baptistic churches a baptistry was a central element of many worship centers. Few Christians in the 1900s pondered the significance of the position of their pulpit. Theological presuppositions, however, remained in traditional worship settings, consciously or unconsciously denoting the relative importance given to various elements of public worship practice.

**Qatar.** *See* GULF STATES.

**Quadragesimo Anno.** Encyclical of Pope Pius XI published May 15, 1931, the 40th anniversary of *Rerum novarum.* The contents of the earlier encyclical are reasserted and extended. Private property, fair wages, and the interdependence of capital and labor are defended. Socialism and communism are condemned. It is recommended that the social order, distorted by individualism, be reconstructed by restoring medieval guilds (*ordines*) which embrace both employers and workers in each trade or profession.

**Bibliography.** Latin text in *Acta Apostolicae Sedis*, 22:177–228; English in J. Husslein, *Social Wellsprings* (1942), 2:178–234.

THEODORE TAPPERT

**Quakers.** *See* FRIENDS, SOCIETY OF.

**Quayle, William Alfred** (1860–1925). Methodist bishop. Born in Parkville, Mo., he studied at Baker University. Ordained to the Methodist ministry in 1886, he taught ancient languages at Baker (1886–88), taught Greek (1888–91), and was president of Baker (1890–94). He served pastorates in Kansas City, Mo. (1894–97), Indianapolis (1897–1900), Kansas City (1900–1904), and St. James' Church, Chicago (1904–8). He was elected to the episcopate in 1908. Among his books are *The Poet's Poet and Other Essays* (1897), *The Blessed Life* (1900), *Books and Life* (1901), *The Song of Songs* (1910), *The Pastor-Preacher* (1911), *The Climb to God* (1913), *Poems* (1914), *Recovered Yesterdays in Literature* (1916), *The Dynamite of God* (1918), *The Throne of Grace* (1919), *Books as a Delight* (1920), *The Uncommon Common Place* (1921), *With Earth and Sky* (1922), and *The Healing Shadow* (1923).

RAYMOND W. ALBRIGHT

**Qur'an.** *See* KORAN.

# Rr

**Race Relations.** The study of race and race relations is fraught with controversy, and ideological and psychological considerations make an objective discussion of the topic almost impossible. The very definition of race itself is hotly debated. Physical anthropologists, usually reflecting Darwinian evolutionary agenda, have tried to reduce *Homo sapiens* to racial subspecies, but their taxonomies range from three to 20 categories. Many use the term casually to refer to a human group sharing certain cultural characteristics like religion or language, although this is better designated as ethnicity. Race can best be defined as referring to a group that is socially determined on the basis of physical criteria.

Racism (or racialism) is the belief that organic, genetically transmitted differences (whether real or imagined) within human groups are associated with the presence or absence of certain socially relevant qualities or abilities. This belief results in invidious distinctions between groups; it is not objectively discerned physical differences as such that create races, but the recognition that they are socially different. Only when the group differences in physical appearance overlap with dissimilarities in status and culture are the variations interpreted racially. This most likely occurs when groups come into contact through migration. Migration may come in the form of military conquest and the establishment of political and economic dominance over an indigenous people or gradual frontier expansion which pushes back and subdues an aboriginal population. It also may be caused by involuntary migration due to slavery or indentured servitude, or voluntary movement into a country by alien groups seeking economic opportunity or political freedom. In any event, the one group is assumed to have hereditary superiority and the other inferiority.

Although humans have always made distinctions on the basis of physical features, these tended to be based on xenophobic and social class differences. Only in modern times has there been a real awareness of racial differentiations.

The turning point in Western racial attitudes came with the onset of the transatlantic slave trade and the rationalizations for African inferiority that were developed to justify slavery. This was accentuated by European imperialism and the subjugation of large parts of Africa and Asia.

Carolus Linnaeus, a Swedish botanist, in 1758 made the first crude attempt to classify people by race, and in the following century physical anthropologists and social Darwinists endeavored to put racism on a scientific basis. It was popularized in such important works as Arthur de Gobineau's *Essay on the Inequality of the Human Races* (1853–55) and Houston Stewart Chamberlain's *Foundations of the Nineteenth Century* (1911), and the writings of the Americans Lathrop Stoddard and Madison Grant. Racism was preached by anti-Semites who propagated the myth of a superior "Aryan" race, and this found its ultimate expression in Adolf Hitler, national socialism, and the Holocaust. In Nazi Germany "racial science" (*Rassenkunde*) was elevated to the status of an academic discipline. Racial theories were also used to justify the manner in which *Herrenvolk* democracies in North America and South Africa subjugated subordinate groups through legalized segregation and apartheid and the aboriginal populations in Australia and New Zealand were reduced to inferior status. Asians have also experienced discrimination in the USA through immigration restrictions, the internment of citizens of Japanese ancestry during World War II, and pressures on the new immigrants from Indochina and Korea.

Although racial issues were muted in Muslim countries because of the universal claims inherent in Islam, and a few relatively successful multiracial societies came into being in places like Hawaii and Brazil, nevertheless by the late 20th century racial discrimination was a global problem. Relations in Africa between such peoples as the Hutu and Tutsi in Burundi and the Fulani and Hausa in northern Nigeria took on a racial cast. In India, members of lighter-skinned caste groupings predominated over darker ones, and the Harijans (Untouchables) were subjected to severe disadvantages. The Tamils in Sri Lanka and Malaysia, Moros in the Philippines, mountain People in Taiwan, Burakamin and Koreans in Japan, and Chinese in Malaysia and Indonesia have also experienced discrimination. The same is true with East and West Indians in Great Britain, Turks in West Germany and Bulgaria, West Indians and Indonesians in the Netherlands, Africans and Asians from the former colonies in France, Greeks and Armenians in Turkey, and the Roma and Sinti (Gypsies) throughout Europe. In some Latin American countries, "Indians" are victims of brutal treatment at the hands of mestizo or white military dictators.

During the evolution of Western racism, the Christian churches remained largely indifferent to the plight of minorities. For example, anti-Semitic parties in Germany received support from Lutheran preachers, British churches backed imperialistic expansion under the Union Jack, blacks were systematically excluded from white congregations in the USA, and Dutch Reformed churches were the spiritual bastions of apartheid in South Africa. The chink in the armor of Western Christian racism was, however, their missionary outreach. This put parishioners in contact with other cultures and peoples, and the converts were seen as brothers and sisters in Christ.

The turning point in Christian engagement with the race question came in 1924 with the publication of three books—*The Clash of Colour* by missionary publicist Basil J. Mathews, *Of One Blood* by Presbyterian mission executive Robert E. Speer, and *Christianity and the Race Problem* by J. H. Oldham, secretary of the International Missionary Council. They identified the race issue as a primary test for Christianity in the 20th century and clarified that the question facing Christians was not personal relations between blacks and whites but the institutional racism in economic and political structures. From this point on, leading "mainline" church figures worked for more harmonious race relations, and Christian leaders from Asia and Africa were involved in ecumenical gatherings. After World War II evangelical figures such as Billy Graham began preaching against racism and held meetings throughout the world except South Africa, where he refused to come until finally he was allowed to address integrated audiences.

The black church played the key role in enabling American blacks to maintain a sense of identity and self-worth even as they suffered under the burdens of discrimination: accordingly the freedom movement was born and nourished in the bosom of the black church, and many of its leaders, most notably Martin Luther King, Jr., were clergymen. In turn, they were backed by white denominational leaders and a handful of evangelicals. Many American churches then sought to assist other peoples of color, such as Vietnamese and Latin American refugees. In the 1970s and 1980s both Protestant and Roman Catholic figures in Britain worked to ameliorate racial discrimination against blacks, while their counterparts in Germany pursued similar objectives on behalf of Turks and Gypsies. The Catholic Church selected its prelates without regard to race, and the various popes in the last half of the century publicly condemned racism. The Christian Conference of Asia promoted consultations and consciousness-raising programs for Asian minorities who were victims of racial discrimination in their own lands. The World Council of Churches funded an aggressive but controversial program to combat racism that worked to liberate white-ruled territories in the southern part of Africa. Church bodies outside South Africa took a strong stand, while leaders of the South African Church of all theological views, such as Desmond Tutu and Beyers Naude and the authors of the Kairos Document (1985), spoke out against apartheid. Many congregations integrated themselves in spite of official displeasure.

Churches in Western countries produced religious education literature and encouraged pastors to preach that racism is sin, but the flow of peoples from third world countries into Europe and North America presented an ongoing problem, with both economic and racial dimensions. Further, the desire of racial and ethnic minorities to maintain a separate existence so they could build up their own community institutions seemed to make the prospect of an integrated Christian church less certain. Still, the continuing struggle against imperialism and economic underdevelopment and evangelical efforts to reach every part of the world with the gospel give hope that Christians can achieve the goal of harmonious race relations on a global basis.

*Bibliography.* K. Haselden, *The Racial Problem in Christian Perspective* (1959); P. L. van den Berghe, *Race and Racism: A Comparative Perspective* (1967); M. Benton, *Race Relations* (1968); P. Mason, *Patterns of Dominance* (1970); *Race Relations* (1970); J. Verkuyl, *Break Down the Walls: A Christian Cry for Racial Justice* (1973); A. Montagu, *Man's Most Dangerous Myth: The Fallacy of Race* (1974); L. Kuyper, *Race, Class, and Power* (1979); R. T. Kendall, *Christians and Race* (1982).

RICHARD V. PIERARD

**Rad, Gerhard von** (1901–1971). German OT scholar. Born in Nuremburg, he studied at the universities of Erlangen and Tübingen, and was vicar in parishes of the Evangelical Lutheran Church of Bavaria (1925–28). He was assistant and docent at Erlangen and Leipzig (1929–34), and he was professor ordinarius for OT at Jena (1934–45), Göttingen (1945–49), and Heidelberg (1949– ). He wrote *Das Gottesvolk im Deuteronomium* (1929), *Das chronistische Geschichtsbild* (1930), *Die Priester-*

*schrift im Hexateuch* (1934), *Das formgeschichtliche Problem des Hexateuch* (1938), *Deuteronomiumstudien* (1947), and *Der heilige Krieg im alten Israel* (1951). A festschrift was published in his honor on his 70th birthday: *Probleme Biblischer Theologie* (ed. H. W. Wolff, 1971).

**Radhakrishnan, Sarvepalli** (1888–1975). Indian philosopher, teacher, statesman, and writer. Radhakrishnan had a distinguished academic career in Indian universities and at Oxford, where he was professor of Eastern religions and ethics (1936–52). He was Indian ambassador to the USSR (1949–52), vice-president of India (1952–62), and president of India (1962–67). Radhakrishnan's writings aimed to defend Hindu philosophy. His position was neo-Vedantist and he attempted to synthesize Vedanta with Western liberal rationalism. He had a distinctive emphasis on ethics—possibly because of Christian influence during his studies at Madras Christian College. He used Christian terminology (e.g., "the Evil One," denied by nondualism), but only metaphorically. He held that mystical experiences are essentially one. Therefore, he regarded religious dogmas and scriptures as distortions of reality through human intermediaries and as inhibitions to genuine inquiry and spiritual growth. He hoped religions would grow toward the truth by accepting experience as primary; experience was his authority, with human reason as the final arbiter. Thus Radhakrishnan's greatest weakness was his failure to account for divine revelation as the source of religious truth; his greatest achievement was creative reinterpretation of aspects of Indian philosophy, making them comprehensible and acceptable to the West. He wrote *The Hindu View of Life* (1927), *An Idealistic View of Life* (1932), and *Eastern Religions and Western Thought* (1939).

*Bibliography.* P. Nagaraja Rao, et al., *Radhakrishnan Reader* (1969).

ANTHONY P. STONE

**Ragaz, Leonhard** (1862–1945). Swiss Reformed pastor and Christian social action pioneer. Born in Canton-Graubuenden, Switzerland, he was educated at the universities of Basel, Jena, and Berlin, and ordained as a Reformed minister in 1890. After short periods as rural minister and teacher, he became senior pastor in Chur in 1895 and was increasingly involved in educational programs for workers. In 1902 he accepted a call to the cathedral in Basel, where his profound social concern involved him in controversy. At the same time he continued his scholarly pursuits and in 1908 was appointed professor of systematic and practical theology at Zurich University. When World War I began, he denounced violence as a solution, attributing it to the kingdom of evil; he was later to also denounce fascism, nazism, and communism. On a visit to America he found a kindred spirit in Walter Rauschenbusch and found the status of black people "utterly offensive." He became disillusioned with the institutional church and criticized clericalism ("an alliance between power and religion") as downgrading God. In 1921 Ragaz gave up his chair, renouncing a secure income to represent Christ in poverty. He settled in a working-class area of Zurich and established an educational center. He championed the League of Nations, supported disarmament, and warned that failure to deal adequately with material needs had helped drive the workers into the arms of materialistic philosophy. Social change and religious reform were, in his view, interdependent. During World War II the government of neutral Switzerland banned his monthly journal *Neue Wege*, but he continued to distribute it secretly. His publications include *Dein Reich komme* (2 vols., 1908), *Die neue Schweiz* (1971), *Weltreich, Religion und Gottesherrschaft* (2 vols., 1922), *Der Kampf um das Reich Gottes in Blumhardt, Vater und Sohn—und weiter!* (1925), *Das Reich und die Nachfolge* (1938), *Die Geschichte der Sache Christi* (1945), *Die Bibel—eine Deutung* (7 vols., 1947–50), *Mein Weg: Eine Autobiographie* (2 vols., 1952), Ch. Ragaz and M. Mattmüller, *Leonhard Ragaz in seinen Briefen* (2 vols., 1966–83).

J. D. DOUGLAS

**Rahner, Karl** (1904–1984). German Roman Catholic theologian. Born in Freiburg, he entered the Jesuit Order in 1922 and was ordained in 1932. He taught at Innsbruck, but the Nazis abolished the faculty in 1939. During World War II he ministered in Vienna and elsewhere. He was then professor of philosophy at Munich and later professor of theology at Münster, retiring in 1971. A warm supporter of Christian unity, his was a voice often heard during and after Vatican II, much to the dismay of more conservative forces. For a time he was under a publications ban. Some, nevertheless, have called him the most important theologian since Aquinas, with an influence that extended beyond his own church. He held that faith had become largely removed from everyday living, and he was concerned that the church adapt itself to the spiritual needs of the age. He wrote more than 30 books, among which in English translation are *The Eternal Yes* (1958), *Encounters with Silence* (1960), *Theology for Renewal* (1963), *On Heresy* (1964), *Nature and Grace* (1964), *Studies in Modern Theology* (1965), *Christian in the Marketplace* (1967), *Spiritual Exercises* (1967), *On Prayer* (1968), *Concerning Vatican II* (1969), *The Shape of the Church to Come* (1973), *Allow Yourself to Be Forgiven* (1975), *Foundations of Christian Faith* (1978), and *Professions: A Look Back at Eighty Years* (1985). For many his name is best known for *The Encyclope-*

*dia of Theology* (1975). It was said that his writing was so abtruse that his theologian brother Hugo remarked, "When I am an old man and have the time I want to translate Karl's writings—into German."

J. D. DOUGLAS

**Rall, Harris Franklin** (1870–1964). Methodist pastor and professor. Born in Council Bluffs, Iowa, he studied at the universities of Iowa, Yale, Berlin, and Wittenberg-Halle (Ph.D., 1899). He was pastor of Trinity Methodist Church, New Haven (1900–1904) and of First Church, Baltimore (1904–10); president at Iliff School of Theology, Denver (1910–15); and professor of theology, Garrett Biblical Institute, Evanston, Ill. (1915–45). His writings include *NT History* (1914), *A Working Faith* (1914), *A Life of Jesus* (1917), *The Teachings of Jesus* (1918), *Modern Premillennialism* (1920), *The Coming Kingdom* (1924), *The Meaning of God* (1925), with S. S. Cohon, *Christianity and Judaism Compare Notes* (1927), *A Faith for Today* (1936), *Christianity: An Inquiry into Its Nature and Truth* (1940 [received the Fiftieth Anniversary Bross Prize Award of $15,000]), *According to Paul* (1944), and *The Christian Faith and Way* (1947). He edited *A Guide for Bible Readers* (8 vols., 1945–47).

**Ramabai, Sarasvati** (1858–1922). Indian educator. Born in the forests of southern India, she was the daughter of a learned Brahmin who educated her in Indian lore. Her father lost his property and became blind; he, his wife, and their eldest daughter all died of starvation. Ramabai became a lecturer on the importance of female education, and was received with honor in the highest circles. When her lawyer husband died soon after their marriage, she established in Poona the Areja Mahita Somaj, a society of like-minded women concerned about the education of their sex and about child-marriage. In 1883 she went to England, was converted from Hinduism to Christianity, and for three years taught Sanskrit at Cheltenham Ladies' College. In 1886 she visited the USA and raised much money by lecturing and through the associations formed by her friends, so that on her return to India in 1889 she was able to realize her ambition of opening an unsectarian school for high-caste Hindu girls, especially child-widows, in Bombay. In 1896, during a severe famine in the central provinces, she established at Kedgoan an orphanage for over 300 women and children, called Mukti Sadan. This "House of Salvation" was a rescue hospital and training institution for sick, helpless, and broken women. In recognition of her superb service she received the Kaisar-i-Hind gold medal in 1919. She also supervised a new Marathi translation of the Bible, Sanskrit free from the taint of Hinduism. She wrote *The High-Caste Hindu Woman* (1887) and *Testimony* (1917).

**Ramsay, William Mitchell** (1851–1939). Scottish classicist and archeologist. Born in Glasgow, he was educated at the universities of Aberdeen, Oxford, and Göttingen. He became a fellow of Exeter College, Oxford, in 1882; a fellow of Lincoln College in 1885, and professor of classical art (1885–86); and professor of humanity at Aberdeen University (1886–1911). He was knighted by King Edward VII in 1906. He early acquired an interest in the antiquities and geography of Asia Minor, and for more than 30 years spent substantial periods there. His findings and reflections were incorporated in numerous volumes, among which are *The Historical Geography of Asia Minor* (1890), *The Church in the Roman Empire* (1893), *St. Paul the Traveller and the Roman Citizen* (1895), *Historical Commentary on Galatians* (1899), *The Letters to the Seven Churches of Asia* (1905), *The Cities of St. Paul* (1907), *The First Christian Century* (1911), *The Teaching of Paul in Terms of the Present Day* (1913), *The Bearing of Recent Research on the Trustworthiness of the NT* (1914), and *Asianic Elements in Greek Civilization* (1927).

J. D. DOUGLAS

**Ramsey, Arthur Michael** (1904–1988). Archbishop of Canterbury and theologian. Educated at Magdalene College, Cambridge, he was ordained in 1928. He became professor of divinity at Durham University (1940) and professor of divinity at Cambridge (1950). Two years later he was consecrated bishop to the see of Durham, from where he moved in 1956 to become archbishop of York. In 1961 he became archbishop of Canterbury, retiring in 1974. During his time there he saw the Church of England take synodical government into its system (1970). As a theologian he combined a catholic churchmanship with Barthian insights on the basis of his commitment to biblical theology.

As an ecumenist he worked hard to bring about the union of the English Methodist Church and the Church of England. In 1967 he made a famous "Common Declaration" with Pope Paul VI which led to the setting up of the Anglican–Roman Catholic International Commission to examine doctrines at issue between the two churches, but he was very disappointed by the rejection of his proposals in 1969 and 1972.

His varied concerns and interests are evident in his works: *The Gospel and the Catholic Church* (1936), *The Resurrection of Christ* (1945), *The Glory of God and the Transfiguration of Christ* (1949), *From Gore to Temple* (1960), *Relations with Rome* (1964), *Sacred and Secular* (1965), and *God, Christ and the World* (1969).

PETER TOON

**Ramsey, Ian Thomas** (1915–1972). Anglican bishop and theologian. Born in Bolton, England, he studied at Cambridge University. In 1951 he became professor of the Christian religion at Oxford University and a fellow of Oriel College. Although he participated in ecclesiastical matters and was canon theologian at Leicester Cathedral, his intellectual work was primarily on the frontier between Christian theology and contemporary philosophy; he tried to illuminate both directions simultaneously. In 1966 he was appointed bishop of Durham, where he brought the same broadness of mind and wide sympathy to his pastoral work as he had done to his academic. Further, he was very active on a variety of church committees and the affairs of the House of Lords. He wrote several books, including *Freedom and Immortality* (1960), *Religious Language* (1963), *Models and Mystery* and *Religion and Science: Conflict and Synthesis* (1964), *Christian Discourse: Some Logical Explorations* (1965), *Our Understanding of Prayer* (1971), and *Christian Empiricism* (1974).

PETER TOON

**Ransom.** See REDEEMER.

**Ras Shamra** ("Fennel Head"; more correctly, Ras esh-Shamra). Tell (city mound) on the Syrian coast, about seven miles north of Latakia, which was an important Canaanite cultural center during the Amarna Age. Discovered accidentally in 1928 by a Syrian plowman, the site was excavated by French archeologist C. F. A. Schaeffer (1929–73, with a nine-year break because of World War II), and the work is still continuing. There are five distinct strata of occupation; the bottom stratum dates from the 5th and possibly the 6th millennium B.C. The top two strata, covering the period 2100–1200 B.C., have yielded findings of immense value for biblical studies. During these last two periods of occupation the name of the city was Ugarit. A low mound on the shore of nearby Minet el-Beida ("Whitehaven") marks the site of its port town.

The objects brought to light by the less extensive exploration of the second stratum of Ugarit include iconic representations of deities, one of them with an Egyptian inscription. These finds suffice to establish that Baal-zephon was already the principal deity worshiped at this site—under that very Semitic name—in the first half of the 2d millennium B.C., and that consequently its dominant population must already have been Semitic at that time. In the top stratum there have been exposed, among other things, a temple of Dagon and a temple of Baal (or Baal-zephon), and between the two a building in which were stored a large number of tablets, some inscribed with Babylonian cuneiform writing but most with a hitherto unknown script which has come to be known as Ugaritic. The building in question is usually referred to as the library. Most of the texts in the new alphabet are in Ugaritic; a few are in Hurrian (Horite). The presence of Hurrians at Ugarit is confirmed by the occurrence of Hurrian proper names in the various non-Hurrian texts.

Most of the texts found in the library are poetic in form and religious in content. Two votive inscriptions were found in one of the temples. Tablets containing letters, lists, and other nonliterary documents were found in another building. Most of the tablets date from around 1375 B.C.

*Origin of the Ugaritic Alphabet.* Two of the tablets (one of them defective) contain nothing but a list of the 30 signs of the new alphabet; 22 have equivalents in the common North Semitic (Hebrew) aleph-beth and occupy the same position as in the latter with the other eight being inserted at various points. This doubtless indicates that the cuneiform alphabet was merely an adaptation of the ordinary linear one, which must therefore have been perfected by 1400 B.C. at the latest.

*Analysis of the Three Great Epics.* The most important of the poetic texts are the epics of Baal, Aqhat, and Keret. Unfortunately all three are fragmentary.

The epic of Baal is completely mythological. Its purpose is to glorify Baal, also called Hadd (which probably means "thunder" or "thunderer"; cf. Hadad in biblical proper names such as Benhadad) and often referred to as the rider of the clouds (Ps. 68:5 [MT 4]) and the prince, lord of the earth. It is he who, by his quickening rain, ensures the earth's fertility. The epic tells how, with the help of his sister the warrior goddess Anath and the craftsman god Kothar wa-Khasis (Skillful and Clever), he vanquished first a series of marine beings and then Mut or Mot, who seems to be an objectification of the principle of sterility. All this was no doubt suggested by observation, on the one hand, of the furious beating of the sea against the land in an apparent attempt to engulf it during the stormy Syrian winter, and, on the other, of the apparent danger of dessication and famine during the hot, rainless summer.

The epic of Aqhat is only half mythological. Its hero is a human being, the only son of the pious judge or king, Daniel. Aqhat hunts with a composite bow, a gift of the craftsman god. Anath asks him to surrender this bow to her in exchange for riches or immortality. The youth refuses so Anath commissions an assassin to slay him—apparently after filching his bow. Somehow the corpse is consumed by a female vulture without being revived. Daniel splits the vulture open and buries his son's remains; his daughter Paghat takes revenge for her brother's death. Here the text breaks off. That Aqhat is a youth and a hunter and refuses the request of a goddess is reminiscent of the story of Adonis. However, there is no

695

hint in this poem of a desire on the part of the goddess for the youth himself. His death is followed by blight and drought; but in the present text that seems to be a consequence of the crime as such, not of any Tammuz-like quality in Aqhat. Nevertheless, the epic may be a variation on the Adonis–Tammuz theme, and the missing conclusion may have told of some arrangements which Daniel obtained from the gods for his son to return to the land of the living for six months of the year.

The epic of Keret is, finally, a legend pure and simple. King Keret, who reigns at Khubur, has lost his wife and children or—according to another interpretation—seven successive wives. He grieves because of the probable extinction of his line, but is instructed in a dream by El (or the Kindly One, El Benign), the head of the Ugaritic pantheon, to mobilize all the manpower of his realm, march upon Udum, and lay siege to it until its king, Pabel, tries to buy him off. He is then to reply that the only tribute he will accept is Pabel's lovely daughter Hurriya. Keret thus wins Hurriya and she bears him sons and daughters. It seems, however, that he owes this felicity, at least in part, to El's consort, the mother goddess Asherah, who has been moved to bestow it upon him by certain vows—which Keret fails to keep. He is consequently smitten with a terminal illness. His younger son Elhau and his daughter Tithmanet display true grief. Finally El takes pity on Keret and dispatches a certain female being, Sha'tequat, to heal him. It is while he is recuperating that, for the first time in this episode, his eldest son Yassib appears on the scene. He has the impudence to suggest that since his father is neglecting the duties of kingship he should step down and make room for his son. Keret curses him roundly. The tablet(s) containing the rest of the story is (are) missing. Keret is represented as a demigod, a descendant of El, but he was doubtless a historical character. One of the purposes of the poem may have been to explain why he was succeeded on the throne by his younger son Elhau rather than his firstborn (cf. 1 Kings 1–2).

*OT Affinities.* The Ras Shamra texts teach us a good deal about Canaanite religion and folklore, and at the same time beguile by their affinity with biblical poetry. At every turn one finds meters, varieties of parallelism, pairs of parallel synonyms, phrases, and stock similes also found in biblical poetry. Thus, when we read (III. AB. A. 8–10): "Lo, thine enemies, O Baal / Lo, thine enemy wilt thou smite / Lo, thou wilt cut off thine adversary / Thou wilt win thine everlasting kingdom / Thy dominion of generation and generation," we promptly compare the tricolon with Ps. 92:10(9) and the dicolon with Pss. 145:13 and 146:10. We even find in the Baal epic a reference to the smiting of Leviathan, who is furnished with the same epithets as in Isa. 27:1, and to

whom are attributed a multiplicity of heads (seven) as in Ps. 74:13. By "thine enemy" or "thine adversary," the lines quoted above mean a being to whom one refers in parallelism as sea/river. This sea is also alluded to as an ancient foe of Yahweh in one of the Bible verses cited for Leviathan (Ps. 74:13) and with the parallelism sea/river(s) in Hab. 3:8. On the whole, the texts have shed a great deal of light on the wider cultural milieu of biblical literature—its ideas, tastes, and lexicography. In some cases it has even suggested near-certain emendations of the biblical text. At the same time, Ugaritic poetry is vastly inferior to biblical poetry, even as the crude Ugaritian god-concept is vastly inferior to the biblical one. In particular, it should be noted that in Hebrew poetry Leviathan and Sea are not gods but rebellious creatures of Yahweh (in Ps. 104:26, Leviathan is even said to have been created by Yahweh "to play with"!), and in Ps. 92:10 they have even been replaced by "the doers of iniquity."

Whether the people of Ugarit were Canaanites has been argued back and forth. In any case, the principal aid in the interpretation of the Ugarit texts has been the Hebrew Bible; and it is obvious from the known Phoenician (i.e., Canaanite) inscriptions and from Canaanisms in the Tell el-Amarna letters and elsewhere that Phoenician literature would have been even more helpful, were it extant. On practical grounds, therefore, the provisional classification of Ugaritic as ancient North Phoenician is the best one.

The affinities of biblical with Ugaritic literature are no doubt due in part to Canaanite influence upon Israel after the Israelite settlement in Canaan (cf. the construction and furnishing of Solomon's temple by Phoenicians). But this can hardly be the whole explanation. Israel, which came into being as such at or not long before the moment when it adopted Mosaic monotheism, contained according to its own traditions Mesopotamian, Egyptian, and Canaanite elements, and had spent the preceding century or centuries on the margin of Canaanite civilization. At any rate, it was not a cultural tabula rasa. And while the Mosaic revolution was a much more profound change than the American Revolution, in neither case did the new nation disdain to retain, nor could it help retaining, from the culture from which it branched off, whatever elements were compatible with, or capable of being adapted to, the principles of the revolution.

*Bibliography.* C. F. A. Schaeffer, *Mission de Ras Shamra* (1929–78); W. F. Albright, *Catholic Biblical Quarterly* (Jan. 1945): 5–31; H. L. Ginsberg, *Biblical Achaeologist* 8/2 (May 1945): 4158; *Encyclopedia of Literature* (1946), 117–120; idem, *Ancient Near Eastern Texts Relating to the OT* (1950), 128–55; C. H. Gordon, *Ugaritic Handbook* (1947); idem, *Ugaritic Literature* (1949); T. H. Gaster, *Thespis: Ritual, Myth, and Drama* (1950), 113–313; U. Cassuto, *Entsiqlopediyah* (1950), 1: cols. 79–89, 795; G. R.

Driver, *Canaanite Myths and Legends* (1956); J. Gray, *The Legacy of Canaan* (1965).

H. Louis Ginsberg

**Rastafarians.** A messianic, millennial West Indian cult, centered mainly in Jamaica. The roots of the movement lie in the teachings of Marcus Garvey (1887–1940). His message of black nationalism, propagated in the 1920s in the USA became the basis for numerous subsequent black nationalist movements. Garvey is considered a major prophet by the Rastafarians—"John the Baptist." After Prince Ras (*Lord*) Tafari was crowned as Emperor Haile Selassie in 1930, Leonard P. Howell and other Jamaicans began preaching that the emperor was the living God as revealed in Rev. 19:16 and prepared their followers to migrate to Ethiopia. The strong attachment to "ganja" (marijuana) as a sacrament and the traditional plaited hair-style, the "dreadlock," became common under Howell, who dominated the movement for almost three decades. Confrontation between the authorities and the cult was common.

The cult loosely organized and diversified through the 20th century. Present membership in the 1980s was estimated at 70,000 to 100,000 although some sources placed the membership at more than 200,000. The six basic beliefs of the movement are: (1) Haile Selassie I is the living God; (2) the black man is the reincarnation of the ancient Israelites who, because of the white man, are in exile in Jamaica; (3) the white man is inferior to the black man; (4) the Jamaican situation is a hopeless hell; (5) Ethiopia is heaven; and (6) the black man will rule the world of the future. These are not creeds but commonly accepted tenets; many variations can be found. Most reject marriage by civil authority as part of a white man's culture. The widespread use of marijuana as a sacramental element has brought the group into continuing conflict with the authorities.

**Bibliography.** J. Owens, *Dread: The Rastafarians in Jamaica* (1976); L. E. Barrett, *The Rastafarians: Sounds of Cultural Dissonance* (1977).

Melvin E. Dieter

**Ratcliff, Edward Craddock** (1896–1967). Anglican theologian. After graduating from Cambridge, he was ordained in 1922. He was vice-principal of Westcott House, Cambridge (1924–29); fellow and praelector in church history, Queen's College, Oxford (1930–43); professor of liturgical theology at the University of London (1945–47); and professor of divinity at Cambridge (1947–58). His publications include *The English Coronation Service* (1936), *The Booke of Common Prayer of the Churche of England* (1949), *The Coronation Service of Queen Elizabeth II* (1953), and *From Uniformity to Unity* (1962). He contributed to *Biblical and Patristic Studies in Memory of R. P. Casey* (1963).

**Rauschenbusch, Walter** (1861–1918). Proponent of social Christianity. Born in Rochester, N.Y., he was influenced by the thought of Albrecht Ritschl and the revivalist spirit of Lyman Beecher, Charles G. Finney, and Dwight L. Moody. Rauschenbusch developed his own theological position of Christian socialism, in turn leaving his mark on generations of North American pastors, ethicists, and Christian laypersons. While he retained liberal tendencies, he was not uncritical of professional evangelism. After three years at the gymnasium in Gütersloh and studies in arts and theology at Rochester, he was ordained to become minister of the Second German Baptist Church, New York City in 1886. He was appointed professor of NT interpretation in the German department of Rochester Theological Seminary in 1897 and to the chair of church history in the theology department in 1903. He established, in 1887, a loose affiliation with fellow Baptist ministers Leighton Williams and Nathaniel Schmidt, known as "the little Society of Jesus." It gave impetus in 1890 to the formation of the Brotherhood of the Kingdom which had its own "rule" of eight points and strove to bring a renewed awareness of the work of the Spirit of God to Baptist ecclesiastical circles. The Evangelical Alliance of Josiah Strong ("Save America for the world's sake") had some influence on his activities in these years. A short-lived monthly people's paper, *For the Right* (Oct. 1889– March 1891), reflects his interest in social Christianity during his years in the pastorate. His fight for temperance as one of the ways to effect basic social change is noteworthy. Of his four books in German and seven in English, the most significant are *Christianity and the Social Order* (1907), *Prayers of the Social Awakening* (1910), *Christianizing the Social Order* (1912), *The Social Principles of Jesus* (1916), and *A Theology for the Social Gospel* (1918).

E. J. Furcha

**Raven, Charles Earle** (1885–1964). Anglican theologian. After graduating from Cambridge he was ordained in 1909 and was fellow, dean, and lecturer in theology at Emmanuel College, Cambridge (1909–20); rector of Bletchingley (1920–24); canon of Liverpool (1924–32); university professor of divinity (1932–50) and master of Christ's College (1939–50) at Cambridge; and warden of Madingley Hall, Cambridge (1950–54). He was much in demand as a lecturer, a strong advocate of pacifism, and made distinguished contributions to both theological and scientific studies. His publications include *Apollinarianism* (1923), *The Creator Spirit* (1927), *Jesus and the Gospel of Love* (1931), *War and the Christian* (1938), *Science, Religion, and the Future* (1943), *Good News of God* (1944), *Science, Medicine, and Morals*

697

(1959), and *Teilhard de Chardin: Scientist and Seer* (1962).

**Read, David Haxton Carswell** (1910– ). Presbyterian pastor. Born in Cupar, Fife, Scotland, he studied at the universities of Edinburgh, Paris, Montpelier, Strasbourg, and Marburg, and in Palestine. He was ordained in the Church of Scotland in 1936 and ministered in Edinburgh. From 1940 to 1945 he was a prisoner of war in Germany. He was chaplain to Edinburgh University (1949–55) and a chaplain to Queen Elizabeth (1952–55), then in 1956 he became pastor of Madison Avenue Presbyterian Church, New York City. A regular preacher on the National Radio Pulpit and the Protestant Hour, he was named by *Time* magazine in 1979 as one of the seven great preachers in America. His numerous books include *The Spirit of Life* (1939), *Prisoners' Quest* (1944), *The Communication of the Gospel* (1952), *I Am Persuaded* (1962), *Whose God Is Dead?* (1966), *Christian Ethics* (1968), *Unfinished Easter* (1978), and *The Faith Is Still There* (1980).

JAMES McCLANAHAN

**Redeemer.** One who buys back or liberates by paying a ransom price. In the OT the term is generally used of an individual who buys back either property which has been sold or a family member who has been enslaved (Lev. 25:25–34, 47–55). The latter meaning of the term is also used in reference to God, especially in the Book of Isaiah (see Job 19:25; Pss. 19:14; 78:35; Prov. 23:11; Isa. 41:14; 43:14; 54:5; 60:16; Jer. 50:34). A kinsman-redeemer was occasionally an avenger of blood.

The exodus occupies a central place in the OT. The meaning of God as Redeemer, therefore, is largely derived from this event. God delivered his people from bondage in Egypt with his mighty acts of judgment and his outstretched arm (Exod. 6:6; Deut. 15:15). The OT does not state that God paid some sort of price for this deliverance (Isa. 52:3); the stress is placed instead on God's mighty strength and power in freeing his people.

The term "redeemer" is never used in reference to Christ in the NT, although "redemption" is (see 1 Cor. 1:30). Nonetheless, the portrayal of Christ as Redeemer is very evident both in the Gospels and in Paul's writings.

Mark 10:45 is the most significant NT passage concerning Christ's role and mission as Redeemer. Jesus, as Servant, gave his life to pay the price to release us from bondage to sin and death (cf. Isa. 52:13–53:12). Paul develops this thought more fully in his writings. Christ has redeemed us from the curse of the Law (Gal. 3:13; 4:5). Paul associates redemption with justification (Rom. 3:24). Because Christ paid the ransom for us through his death, we are released from guilt and judgment. The blood of Christ is the ransom price for the forgiveness of sins (Eph. 1:7).

In the early church one theory of the atonement held that sinners were captives of Satan. Christ's death was the ransom price paid to Satan by God to free sinners. Although Christ's death is expiatory, it was not paid as a price to anyone. Moreover, the Bible does not portray God carrying on some sort of business deal with Satan. The work of Christ as Redeemer is ultimately a mystery.

*See also* SALVATION.

**Bibliography.** W. A. Elwell, ed., *Evangelical Dictionary of Theology* (1984); P. J. Achtemeier, ed., *Harper's Bible Dictionary* (1985); G. W. Bromiley, ed., *ISBE*, vol. 4 (1988); W. A. Elwell, ed., *Baker Encyclopedia of the Bible*, vol. 2 (1988).

**Reed, Luther Dotterer** (1873–1972). Lutheran leader in the Liturgical movement. Born in North Wales, Pa., he studied at Franklin and Marshall College; Lutheran Theological Seminary, Philadelphia, Pa; and the University of Leipzig. From 1895 to 1904 he was pastor of Lutheran congregations in Pittsburgh and Jeannette, Pa. At Lutheran Theological Seminary, Mt. Airy, Philadelphia, he held positions as director of the Krauth Memorial Library (1906), professor of liturgics and church art (1911), president (1939–45), and president emeritus (1945– ). Involved in the Liturgical movement in the Protestant Church for more than half a century, he was president of the Lutheran Liturgical Association (1898–1906) and edited its *Memoirs;* chairman of the joint committee which prepared the text and music of the *Common Service Book* (1917); and chairman of the joint commissions which prepared a new Service Book and Hymnal for the Lutheran Churches in the USA and Canada. In collaboration with Harry G. Archer he published *Psalter and Canticles Pointed for Chanting* (1897), *Choral Service Book* (1901), *Music of the Responses* (1903), and *Season Vespers* (1905). He wrote *The Lutheran Liturgy* (1947) and edited *History of the First English Evan. Lutheran Church in Pittsburgh* (1919) and *The Philadelphia Seminary Biographical Record* (1923).

**Rees, Paul Stromberg** (1900– ). American pastor and educator. Born in Providence, R.I., he graduated from the University of Southern California after having been ordained to the ministry in the Evangelical Covenant Church. He ministered in California and Michigan before transferring to First Covenant Church, Minneapolis (1938–58). He was vice-president of World Vision (1958–75) and edited its magazine (1964–72). His many publications include *If God Be for Us* (1940), *The Face of Our Lord* (1951), *Christian! Commit Yourself* (1957), *Proclaiming the NT*

(1964), *Men of Action in the Book of Acts* (1966), and *Don't Sleep Through the Revolution* (1969).

EARLE E. CAIRNS

**Reeves, Richard Ambrose** (1899–1980). Anglican bishop. Born in Norwich, England, he was educated at Cambridge, the College of the Resurrection at Mirfield, and General Theological Seminary, New York. Ordained in 1926, he served parishes in England and Scotland before consecration as bishop of Johannesburg in 1949. His opposition to apartheid was so strenuous that the South African government deported him; this led to his resignation from his diocese in 1961. In England he was general secretary of the Student Christian Movement (1962–66), but returned then to parish work in Sussex, where he also served as assistant bishop in the diocese of Chichester. Among his writings are *Shooting at Sharpeville: The Agony of South Africa* (1960), *South Africa—Yesterday and Tomorrow* (1962), *Let the Facts Speak* (1962), and *Calvary Now* (1965).

**Reformation Studies in the 20th Century.** During the 19th century some of the great editions of the Reformers' works were produced or begun. *Corpus Reformatorum*, embracing Philipp Melanchthon (1834–60), John Calvin (1863–1900) and Ulrich Zwingli (1905– ); *Weimarer Ausgabe* of Martin Luther (1883– ); and the Parker Society's collection of the English Reformers (1841–55). But few secondary studies produced before 1900 remained standard scholarly tools after 1950 (an exception being the biography by J. Köstlin, *Life of Luther,* 2 vols. [1875], esp. 5th rev. ed., G. Kawerau, ed. [1903]). There were enormous advances in every area of Reformation study in the 20th century, which were chronicled in the field's leading journal, *Archiv für Reformationsgeschichte* (1903– ). This article will concentrate on the period after World War II, with special reference to works in English. Even so it is necessarily selective.

*The Reformation in Medieval Perspective.* A volume by this name edited by S. E. Ozment (1971) suggested the new tendency to emphasize the continuities between late medieval religion and its 16th-century renewal. Greater attention was paid to the prevalence of cries for "reform in head and members" from such leading churchmen as Jean Gerson (1361–1429) in the pre-Reformation centuries (see, e.g., F. Oakley, *The Western Church in the Later Middle Ages* [1979], and Ozment, *The Age of Reform: 1250–1550* [1980]). The conciliarist reform program was not totally suppressed in the 15th century but haunted the popes in the 16th. The conciliar movement's remaining influence is one reason the Council of Trent failed to pronounce on the nature of the church (see H. Jedin, *A History of the Council of Trent,* 2 vols. [ET, 1957–61]).

Those reformers traditionally presented as forerunners of Protestantism were studied in the context of their time (see G. Leff, *Heresy in the Later Middle Ages: The Relation of Heterodoxy to Dissent,* 2 vols. [1967]). John Hus was viewed increasingly within indigenous Czech reform, less obviously heterodox than John Wycliffe (see H. Kaminsky, *A History of the Hussite Revolution* [1967]). By the late 1900s Wycliffe and Hus were less commonly interpreted as clearcut advocates of *"sola Scriptura,"* and Wycliffe was even presented as spokesman for an abortive reform initiative sponsored by the king and court which aimed at an "autonomous national church" in England. Antecedents of some features of the Radical Reformation were identified in late medieval piety, especially mysticism, but debate continued about others, such as sacramentarian views of the Lord's supper.

In theology continuity also received greater stress, with increasing attention to Augustinianism, with its effect on Luther, and nominalism which no longer was regarded as incompatible with mysticism (H. Oberman, *The Harvest of Medieval Theology: Gabriel Biel and Late Medieval Nominalism* [2d ed., 1967]). Oberman was the preeminent, if controversial, scholar in this field. Among his important works are *Forerunners of the Reformation: The Shape of Late Medieval Thought* (rev. ed., 1981) and *The Dawn of the Reformation* (1986). With C. Trinkaus he edited *The Pursuit of Holiness in Late Medieval and Renaissance Religion* (1971), and he was one editor of the *Studies in Medieval and Reformation Thought* series (1966– ).

Various qualifications (such as rising expectations among churchmen and stereotyped propaganda from the Reformed apologists) redrew the traditional picture of late medieval Catholicism as universally corrupt and oppressive (see G. Strauss, *Manifestations of Discontent in Germany on the Eve of the Reformation* [1971]). But scholars still divided over the question posed by Luther's personal history of the adequacy of the forms of pre-Reformation religion to satisfy profound religious needs. Did the penitential system aggravate rather than relieve, and was Catholicism burdensome and exacting? T. N. Tentler in *Sin and Confession on the Eve of the Reformation* (1977) disputed the common verdict; Ozment's *Reformation in the Cities: The Appeal of Protestantism to Sixteenth-Century Germany and Switzerland* (1975) found it confirmed. John Bossy, *Christianity in the West 1400–1700* (1985), concerned himself with the persistence of "traditional Christianity" under Reformation stress.

*The Humanists.* Pride of place belonged to Desiderius Erasmus. Following the magnificent edition of his letters by P. S. Allen and H. M. Allen, *Opus epistolarum Des. Erasmi Roterdami* (12 vols., 1906–58), work began on a complete new edition (1969– ) and a complete English translation (1974– ) of his works. Biographies abounded, including Roland H. Bainton, *Erasmus of Christendom* (1969), and J. D. Tracy, *Erasmus: The Growth of a Mind* (1972). It became more common to consider his "theology," as in J. B. Payne, *Erasmus: His Theology of the Sacraments* (1970), and the serious religious and theological concerns of the humanists in general (see L. W. Spitz, *The Religious Renaissance of the German Humanists* [1964], and C. Trinkaus, *"In Our Image and Likeness": Humanity and Divinity in Italian Humanist Thought*, 2 vols. [1970]). This reassessment extended to estimates of Melanchthon and the high proportion of northern humanists who became Protestants.

There was growing acceptance of P. O. Kristeller's argument in *Renaissance Thought* (1961) that humanism denoted, not a philosophical position or set of beliefs, but a network of intellectual interests preoccupied with language and the "liberal arts" of grammar, rhetoric, and logic. Its significance for the Reformation lay, above all, in the application of new methods of study to the Scriptures, and was reflected in the high premium placed on "educated godliness" (*pietas litterata*) in the pedagogy of Protestant communities.

**Luther.** Although Reformation scholars increasingly recognized the work of other Reformers, the Luther industry showed no signs of relenting. An excellent introduction was B. Lohse, *Martin Luther* (1986). Among biographies, Bainton's *Here I Stand* (1950) enjoyed continuing appeal. The preoccupation with the early Luther dominated, especially in M. Brecht, *Martin Luther: His Road to Reformation, 1483–1521* (1985), but the imbalance was being redressed, as in H. Bornkamm, *Luther in Mid-Career, 1521–1530* (1983), M. U. Edwards, *Luther's Last Battles: Politics and Polemics, 1521–46* (1983), and H. Junghans, ed., *Leben und Werk Martin Luthers von 1526 bis 1546* (2 vols., 1983). The freshest 1980s presentation was Oberman's *Luther: Mensch zwischen Gott und Teufel* (1982), which depicted him, as he saw himself, caught up in an apocalyptic conflict between God and Satan. Pamphlets and cartoons hailed Luther as prophet of the end, but an even more alien Luther emerges in Oberman's *Roots of Antisemitism* (1983).

Catholic interest in Luther blossomed. Pioneer of a more sympathetic approach was J. Lortz, *Reformation in Germany* (2 vols., 1968). *Luther: A Life* (1982), by J. M. Todd, was at times uncritically favorable. Peter Manns, Otto Pesch, and Jared Wicks interpreted Luther from their standpoint as Catholics. Not only do ecumenically minded Protestants commend him as a theologian for Catholics, but representative Lutherans and Catholics discuss *Luther's Ecumenical Significance* (Manns and H. Meyer, eds., 1983). The

timing of Luther's break with Rome is a major question for this dialog.

Finishing touches were being put on the Weimar edition of Luther's works in the late 1980s. English students used the 55-volume "American edition" of *Luther's Works*, which was edited by J. Pelikan and H. T. Lehmann from 1958 to 1986. J. Benzing, *Lutherbibliographie* (1966), listed all publications of Luther's writings in his lifetime. No English counterpart existed to K. Aland, *Hilfsbuch zum Lutherstudium* (3d ed., 1970).

Scholars still struggled to identify the date of Luther's breakthrough to a new understanding of "the righteousness of God" (the title of a distinguished study by E. G. Rupp, 1953). There was a growing consensus that the "breakthrough" may have evolved in stages between 1512 and 1520. One issue was the contributions of a distinctive school of Augustinian theology, through which Johannes von Staupitz inspired Luther (see D. C. Steinmetz, *Luther and Staupitz: An Essay in the Intellectual Origins of the Protestant Reformation* [1980]; Oberman, *Masters of the Reformation* [1981]; and other studies). Whether the Ninety-Five Theses were actually posted in 1517 fomented a vigorous controversy around the 1967 anniversary.

Among studies of Luther's teaching, *Luther's Theology of the Cross* by W. von Loewenich (1929; ET, 1976) had wide influence, as did P. Althaus, *The Theology of Martin Luther* (1966); W. D. J. Cargill-Thompson, *The Political Thought of Martin Luther* (1984); I. D. K. Siggins, *Martin Luther's Doctrine of Christ* (1970); and M. Lienhard, *Luther: Witness to Jesus Christ* (1982).

**Other Reformers.** An adequate English biography of Melanchthon was still needed, but there were W. Maurer, *Der junge Melanchthon zwischen Humanismus und Reformation* (2 vols., 1967–69), and R. Stupperich, *Melanchthon* (ET, 1965). Late 1900s studies, including P. Fraenkel's *Testimonia Patrum: The Function of the Patristic Argument in the Theology of Melanchthon* (1960), in general vindicated his right to a place alongside Luther. *Supplementa Melanchthoniana* (1910–68) provided works lacking from *Corpus Reformatorum*. A selected *Studienausgabe* was also in progress (1951– ), and his correspondence was being critically edited by H. Scheible *Briefwechsel* (1977– ).

Martin Bucer gained increasing appreciation on his own terms, and not only as a teacher of Calvin. An edition of his works was making headway (*Deutsche Schriften*, 1960– , and *Opera Latina*, 1955– ). Hastings Eells' pioneer biography *Martin Bucer* (1931) needed replacement, and a comprehensive account of his theology was called for, in addition to W. P. Stephens, *The Holy Spirit in the Theology of Martin Bucer* (1970). But his standing as a distinctive Reformer with a strong grasp of church, community, social ethics, and pastoral ministry was granted (see G. Hamman, *Entre la secte et la cit. Le projet d' Eglise du Reformateur Martin Bucer* [1984]).

Zwingli was handsomely treated, with a major biography in George R. Potter, *Zwingli* (1976), and substantial interpretations of his theology, such as G. W. Locher, *Zwingli's Thought: New Perspectives* (1981), and W. P. Stephens, *The Theology of Huldrych Zwingli* (1985). R. C. Walton, *Zwingli's Theocracy* (1967), contributed to the debate whether there was a "fall" in the Zurich Reformation. Johann H. Bullinger lacked a worthy biography, but a critical edition of his works was begun in 1972. The anniversary collection, U. Gabler and E. Herkenrath, eds., *Heinrich Bullinger, 1504–1575* (2 vols., 1975), surveyed the field, with welcome monographs from J. W. Baker, *Heinrich Bullinger and the Covenant: The Other Reformed Tradition* (1980), and others.

A range of other Reformers was introduced in Steinmetz, *Reformers in the Wings* (1971), while a comprehensive biographical dictionary was available in Stupperich, *Reformatorenlexikon* (1984). *Guillaume Farel, 1489–1565* presented that reformer in 1930. Works by P. McNair (*Peter Martyr in Italy* [1967]) and M. W. Anderson (1975) deal with phases of Peter Martyr Vermigli's career, J. M. Kittelson has produced a fine life of Wolfgang Capito (1975), P. E. Hughes a useful one of Lefèvre d' Étaples (1985), and Rupp's *Patterns of Reformation* (1969) includes an account of Johannes Oecolampadius (1482–1531).

*The Reformation Movement.* Of general histories in English, H. J. Grimm, *The Reformation Era* (2d ed., 1973), Ozments, *The Age of Reform,* E. G. Léonard, *A History of Protestantism* (2 vols., 1965–67), and L. W. Spitz, *The Protestant Reformation, 1517–1559* (1985) were among the best. A. G. Dickens gave a sharp overview in *Reformation and Society in Sixteenth-Century Europe* (1966), and W. R. Estep an even-handed account in *Renaissance and Reformation* (1986). Grimm, Léonard, and Spitz contain particularly full bibliographical guidance.

*Pamphlets and Popular Religion.* The interest aroused by G. Strauss's book, *Luther's House of Learning: Indoctrination of the Young in the German Reformation* (1978), is symptomatic of an enlarged concern with the reception of the Protestant gospel. From visitation records Strauss discovered massive ignorance and a lack of discipline among rural folk, but his exposure of the "failure" of the Reformation has not gone uncontested. Its "success" was more obvious in the towns.

An important area was the study of pamphlets (see H. J. Köhler, ed., *Flugschriften als Massenmedium der Reformationszeit* [1981]) and other popular written and pictorial forms. R. W. Scribner's *For the Sake of Simple Folk: Popular Propaganda for the German Reformation* (1981) is a splendid example of research using cartoons and other media. Pamphlets were widely catalogued and reproduced on microfiche.

Popular religion (broadly, religion as practiced and experienced rather than as defined and prescribed) became fashionable, partly through the acclaim accorded to Emmanuel Le Roy Ladurie and Carlo Ginzburg. Other influential works included Keith Thomas, *Religion and the Decline of Magic* (1971), and Jean Delumeau, *Catholicism between Luther and Voltaire* (1977). Among numerous focal points on this ill-defined front might be mentioned: rituals and their significance in social and emotional life; the fluid boundaries between religion and superstition or paganism; religious subcultures; localized religion at all levels of society; the religion of the lower classes; and witchcraft and the occult.

*Urban Reformation.* The trailblazing study of reformation in urban areas was B. Moeller's *Imperial Cities and the Reformation* (1972), which argued that the evangelical message, as articulated by urban Reformers like Zwingli and Bucer, not only answered to the late medieval civic consciousness of being a holy community but was institutionalized by means appropriate to urban life, such as public disputations. In *The German Nation and Martin Luther* (1974) Dickens uttered the dictum, "the Reformation was an urban event." Studies of city reformations proliferated, such as M. U. Chrisman, *Strasbourg and the Reform* (1967), Strauss on Nuremburg in L. P. Buck and J. W. Zophy, eds., *The Social History of the Reformation* (1972), Strauss in *Nuremburg in the Sixteenth Century* (2d ed., 1976), and H. C. Rublack on Constance (1971). Important collections of papers have been edited by W. J. Mommsen, et al., *Stadtbürgertum und Adel in der Reformation* (1979), and Moeller, *Stadt und Kirche im 16. Jahrhundert,* (1978). T. A. Brady contributed a massive analysis, *Ruling Class, Regime and Reformation at Strasbourg, 1520–1555* (1978), with a weighty introduction on the historiographical issues involved, and also *Turning Swiss: Cities and Empire, 1450–1550* (1985). According to K. von Greyerz, *The Late City Reformation in Germany: The Case of Colmar, 1522–1628* (1980), later reformations followed a different pattern. Magisterial initiative was a major factor. H. Schilling (e.g., in the Mommsen and Moeller collections) and others looking specifically at the North German cities. A research institute in Tübingen took special interest in urban reform studies.

Regarding the cities, themes attracting major interest included poor relief and social welfare, with a trend to question the claim that Protestantism was the decisive catalyst for change, educational reform and innovation, and the impact of the printing revolution. The last required approaches from many angles, such as levels of literacy, Latin and the vernacular, output and distribution, and the transformation in styles of learning and thinking. Studies included L. Febvre and H. J. Martin, *The Coming of the Book* (1976), and E. Eisenstein, *The Printing Press as an Agent of Change* (2 vols., 1979).

*Revolution and the Peasants' War.* The massive influence of social history brought to sharp focus the theme of revolution—whether in a more constitutional form in Geneva, as in R. M. Kingdon, ed., *Transition and Revolutions: Problems and Issues of European Renaissance and Reformation History* (1974), the apocalyptic millenarianism of Anabaptist Münster in 1534 and 1535, or the socioeconomic Peasants' War. About the Anabaptist and peasant revolts German Marxist historians were voluble. Scribner and G. Benecke compiled *The German Peasants' War, 1525: New Viewpoints* (1979). Whether the failure of the uprising turned the Reformation from a popular movement into a magistrates' or princes' Reformation is still debated. A forceful interpretation by P. Blickle, *The Revolution of 1525: The German Peasants' War from a New Perspective* (1981), views the Lutheran gospel as a major factor unifying the disparate grievances and protests of *the common man* (an increasingly frequent term in this context—see Brady's *Turning Swiss* for a discussion of the Reformation of the common man). Nevertheless, the precise relation between the evangelical message and the peasants' demands (as distinct from their articulate spokesmen's) remained a matter under study (see Oberman, *The Dawn of the Reformation*).

**The Reformation's Radicals.** Until the 20th century Anabaptism languished under the dismissive denigration inspired by the magisterial Reformers themselves (see L. Verduin, *The Reformers and Their Stepchildren* [1964]). Anabaptist rehabilitation was spearheaded by Mennonite scholars, many in the USA, through the *Mennonite Quarterly Review* (1927– ), *The Mennonite Encyclopedia* (4 vols., H. S. Bender, et al., eds., 1955–59), and the writings of Bender (esp. *Conrad Grabel, 1498–1526* [1950]), J. C. Wenger, John Horsch, Robert Friedmann, J. H. Yoder, and others. This phase of study was marked by G. F. Hershberger, ed., *The Recovery of the Anabaptist Vision* (1957), and the resulting works were covered in H. Hillerbrand, *A Bibliography of Anabaptism, 1520–1630* (1962).

These endeavors emphasized the biblicist restitutionism of the evangelical Anabaptists, particularly the Swiss Brethren, who, as a kind of "free church," maintained the original thrust of the Zürich Reformation, refusing Zwingli's compromises with the state. This mainstream, orthodox Anabaptism distanced itself from the revolutionary and eccentric fringes—Thomas Müntzer's violent apocalypticism, the Münsterites' rebellious "kingdom of the saints," the anti-Trinitarians,

spiritualist free-thinkers, and other groups. Non-Mennonite scholars contributed, such as F. H. Littell (*The Anabaptist View of the Church* [1952; rev. ed., *The Origins of Sectarian Protestantism* (1964)]) and Bainton. Bainton especially admired the Anabaptists as pioneers of pacifism, toleration, and liberty.

Few Reformation books had an impact as massive as G. H. Williams, *The Radical Reformation* (1962). In part a vast compilation of Mennonite scholarship, it also set the Anabaptists alongside two other main categories of radicals—the spiritualists and the rationalists (with many subdivisions) and traced the connections among them. Although it implied too sharp a dichotomy between the radical and magisterial reformations, Williams' work foreshadowed fresh departures in the study of the Reformation's "left wing," which qualified or overturned some central theses of the Bender school. Other books followed the influence of pre-Reformation mysticism on Müntzer and South German Anabaptism (H. J. Goertz, W. O. Packull), noted the relation between *Mysticism and Dissent* (Ozment, 1973) or monasticism (see K. R. Davis, *Anabaptism and Asceticism: A Study in Intellectual Origins* [1974]). Others studied Andreas von Carlstadt's role as a pioneer of some radical teachings; the social composition of Anabaptism—especially C. P. Clasen, *Anabaptism: A Social History, 1525–1618* (1972), which probably exaggerates its numerical insignificance; the links between Anabaptists and the Peasants' revolt (J. M. Stayer, *Anabaptists and the Sword* [1972]); and the identification of different groupings with separate origins, such as Goertz, *Die Täufer. Geschichte und Deutung* (1980). These works distinguished three independent traditions: Swiss Brethren; South German-Austrian, and North German-Dutch. Their description of the mass-movement aspirations of some early leaders conflicts with Troeltsch's typology of Anabaptism as a "sect" of separated believers. The histories also explored its historical and social dimensions—asking whether Anabaptism was a network of withdrawn cells, or a prominent current in a broad stream of radicalism.

Basic research continued with accounts of Carlstadt and Müntzer in Rupp's *Patterns of Reformation*, K. Deppermann's life of Melchior Hoffman, (1987), and editions and translations of primary sources. *Quellen zur Geschichte der Wiedertäufer* (1930–38) and *Täufer* (1951– ) are the main series of documentary material, while *Classics of the Radical Reformation* (1973– ) presents Anabaptist writings. Spiritualists and other groups also were studied. One example was R. E. McLaughlin's life of Kasper von Ossig Schwenckfeld (1986).

**England and Scotland.** The stubborn representation of the English Reformation as an act (or succession of acts) of state was undermined by Dickens, *The English Reformation* (1964), which noted the climate for religious change, the role of laity, and local variations in reform structure. All of these nuances eventually created a more complex picture with fewer dominant motifs. C. Cross, *Church and People 1450–1660: The Triumph of the Laity in the English Church* (1976) stands in the Dickensian lineage. Local and regional studies abounded, such as Dickens on the diocese of York, Cross on towns such as Hull and Leeds, C. Haigh on Lancashire, and P. Clark on Kent. The Lollards were studied by Dickens, M. Aston, A. Hudson, and others, for its input into both mainstream and sectarian Protestantism. The lines of continental influence were carefully distinguished, as in D. Baker, ed., *Reform and Reformation: England and the Continent, c.1500–c.1750* (1979). The institutional framework of reform within clergy, finance and church courts, attracted interest, as in R. O'Day and F. Heal, eds., *Continuity and Change: Personnel and Administration in the Church of England, 1500–1642* (1976) and *Church and Society in England, Henry VIII to James I* (1977). Among period studies especially notable were D. M. Loades' *Reign of Mary Tudor* (1979), and P. Collinson's *Religion of Protestants: The Church in English Society, 1559–1625* (1982), together with his fine biography of Edmund Grindal, *Archbishop Grindal, 1519–1583: The Struggle for a Reformed Church* (1979). The writings of J. J. Scarisbrick are also insightful. *Reformation and the English People* (1984) challenged Dickens' conclusions. In the realm of thought *The Apocalyptic Tradition in Reformation Britain, 1530–1695*, by K. R. Firth (1979), was one of several books on this subject.

Gordon Donaldson's important but controversial reading of *The Scottish Reformation* (1960) was chiefly concerned with ecclesiastical structures and minimized the continuity between the early Knoxian and episcopal phases and the later Presbyterian Melvillian era. Among those who contested this interpretation was J. Kirk, for example, in his edition of *The Second Book of Discipline* (1980; see J. K. Cameron's edition of the *First Book* [1972]). I. B. Cowan highlighted *Regional Aspects of the Scottish Reformation* (1978) and focused more closely on "Church and Society in 16th-century Scotland" in *The Scottish Reformation* (1982). In *Court, Kirk, and Community: Scotland, 1470–1625* (1981) J. Wormald recognized both religious and political motivations. Intellectual and cultural currents were at the fore in *Essays on the Scottish Reformation 1513–1625*, edited by D. McRoberts, (1964). M. Lynch produced a solid local analysis, no doubt the harbinger of many others, in *Edinburgh and the Reformation*, (1981).

On Knox himself the best studies since *John Knox* by Eustace Percy (1937) came from outside Scotland—P. Janton's French biography (1967) and Janton's study of Knox's ecclesiology (1972); R. L. Greaves, *Theology and Revolution in the Scottish Reformation: Studies in the Thought of John Knox* (1980); and R. G. Kyle, *The Mind of John Knox* (1984). Knox's *History of the Reformation in Scotland* was finely edited by W. C. Dickinson (2 vols., 1949).

***Catholic Reform.*** The terms "Reform Restoration," and "Renewal" are now commonly used as alternatives to the traditional "Counter-Reformation," but the debate encapsuled in the two types of designations continued. Jedin's history of the Council of Trent and its antecedents and his *Reformation and Counter Reformation* (1980) were among substantial works. The question of continuity between late medieval and post-Reformation Catholicism underlay many discussions. Delumeau's stimulating *Catholicism between Luther and Voltaire*, reflecting the approach of French scholarship, magnified the achievements of Roman Catholic reform at the expense of pre-Reformation religion, while in A. D. Wright, *The Counter-Reformation: Catholic Europe and the non-Christian World* (1982), Catholic reform, like Protestant, is said to be hostile to medieval superstition. Valuable general accounts were given by M. R. O'Connell, *The Counter Reformation, 1558–1610* (1974), Dickens, *The Counter Reformation* (1969), and H. O. Evenett (1968), who, like Delumeau, rejected the traditional view of the Tridentine era as one of decline, setting the issue into national context.

In an ecumenical age interest is drawn to reforming churchmen such as Gasparo Contarini (1484–1542) (P. C. Matheson, *Cardinal Contarini at Regensburg* [1972]), Johann Gropper (1503–59), Jacopo Sadoleto (R. M. Douglas, *Jacopo Sadoleto, 1477–1547* [1972]), and Reginald Pole (1500–1558) (W. Schenk, *Reginald Pole, Cardinal of England* [1950]; D. Fenlon, *Heresy and Obedience in Tridentine Italy* [1972]; E. G. Gleason, *Reform Thought in Sixteenth Century Italy* [1981]). Catholic theologians were surveyed by E. Iserloh, ed., *Katholische Theologen der Reformationszeit* (1984– ), their works catalogued by T. Klaiber, ed., *Katholische Kontroverstheologen und Reformer des 16. Jahrhunderts: Ein Werkverzeichnis* (1978) and edited in *Corpus Catholicorum* (1919– ). Sources for Germany are appearing in *Acta Reformationis Catholicae* (1959– ).

In *Christianity in the West, 1400–1700* (1985) and other studies Boss has pursued an interest in parochial Catholic piety, while an account of urban Catholic Reform was given by R. P. Hsia, *Society and Religion in Münster* (1984). Catholic missions received their due by Delumeau (see also, G. Schurhammer's 4-vol. life of Francis Xavier [1973–81]).

***Women and the Reformation.*** This relative newcomer to Reformation studies reflected the general interest in historical studies on the role of women. Bainton assembled three volumes on *Women of the Reformation—in Germany and Italy* (1971), *in France and England* (1973) and *from Spain to Scandinavia* (1977). More synthetic accounts were restricted to essays in wider surveys. Among these were R. R. Ruether, ed., *Religion and Sexism: Images of Women in the Jewish and Christian Traditions* (1974), and R. L. Greaves, ed., *Triumph over Silence: Women in Protestant History* (1985). The consensus of such works is that the Reformers straddled tradition and innovation in their attitudes toward the role of women. Liberating them from the monastic devaluation of sex and marriage, they decreed for them a new domestic inferiority. The idea is reflected in Ozment's title, *When Fathers Ruled: Family Life in Reformation Europe* (1983). J. L. Irwin's collection of sources on *Womanhood in Radical Protestantism, 1525–1675* (1979) did not reveal a markedly freer status for women than in mainstream Protestantism. In Italy and France, noblewomen enjoyed opportunities for achievement in humanist salons and courts and hence in promoting religious reform, and in Germany Reformers' wives, such as Katherine Zell at Strasbourg, were occasionally prominent, especially in charitable works. Another Katherine, Frau Luther, does not lack for biographers, but the Reformation's impact on the experience of marriage, as distinct from the Reformers' teaching about it, is one of many topics awaiting further research.

**Bibliography.** B. J. Kidd, *Documents Illustrative of the Continental Reformation* (1911); H. J. Hillerbrand, *The Reformation in Its Own Words* (1964); *Library of Christian Classics* (1953–70); R. H. Bainton and E. W. Gritsch, *Bibliography of the Continental Reformation: Materials Available in English* (1972); S. Ozment, ed., *Reformation Europe: A Guide to Research* (1982); A. G. Dickens and J. Tonkin, *A Historiography of the Reformation* (1985); R. W. Scribner, *The German Reformation* (1986). See also annual reviews in *Bibliographie Internationale de l'Humanisme et de la Renaissance*, *Archiv für Reformationsgeschichte* and *Sixteenth Century Journal.*

DAVID F. WRIGHT

**Reformed Church, Christian.** *See* CHRISTIAN REFORMED CHURCH IN AMERICA.

**Reformed Church in Northwest Germany, Evangelical.** Church created by royal decree on April 12, 1882, when the king of Prussia ordered the 124 "reformed" congregations scattered throughout the area then known as the Province of Hannover to become incorporated as an independent territorial church. Member congregations are located in East Frisia and the districts of Bentheim, Göttingen, Osnabrück, the Lower Weser, Lower Saxony, and Stuttgart.

Although the Reformed tradition in northwest Germany is rooted in the thought of Zwingli, Calvin, Beza, and Bullinger, its direct spiritual father is John à Lasco. He was called as pastor of Emden and superintendent in 1542. From this "mother church" the Reformed tradition in the remainder of northwest Germany was largely nurtured. The Peace of Westphalia (1648) helped give the Reformed tradition in Germany external shape. The Heidelberg Confession as well as the Confession of the Synod of Dort have significantly influenced its spiritual direction. In some areas, other confessional statements and church orders played influential roles.

Reformed congregations and the dominant Lutheran churches coexisted until 1882, both working through a common consistorium. As a result, the Evangelical-Reformed Church of N.W. Germany has retained a structure which combines presbyterial and consistorial elements.

A few of the congregations maintained their traditions in a largely Roman Catholic environment (District of Lingen). In other areas, Huguenot refugees established congregations which have retained their unique characteristics to this day (Altona, Celle, Hannover, and Lübeck). Congregations are closely linked through a *Kirchenvertrag* (church covenant).

E. J. FURCHA

**Reformed Church in the United States.** American church founded in the early 18th century by German, Swiss, Dutch, and Huguenot pioneers in Pennsylvania and neighboring colonies. The first congregation was organized by Johann Philip Boehm in eastern Pennsylvania in 1725; the church received its official name in 1869, when the term "German" was dropped. It was one of the first denominations to join the Federal Council of the Churches of Christ, organized in 1908. It merged into the Evangelical and Reformed Church in 1934 and in 1957 merged with the Congregational and Christian churches to form the United Church of Christ. However, the Eureka Classis in South Dakota refused to become part of the united church, and continued as the Reformed Church in the United States. It recognizes the Heidelberg Catechism as its standard of doctrine. In 1980, there were 26 organized congregations with 4008 members and 27 active ministers.

**Bibliography.** F. S. Mead, *Handbook of Denominations in the United States* (1980).

**Reformed Episcopalians.** A denomination formed in an 1873 schism from the Protestant Episcopal Church over ritualism within the Episcopal churches. The Reformed Episcopal Church (REC) achieved the height of its numerical growth in the USA in 1915, when it had 11,606 communicant members on the rolls of its three synods (Chicago, New York-Philadelphia, and Canada) and two missionary jurisdictions (Special South and Pacific Coast). An English branch, the Reformed Episcopal Church—U.K., also existed side-by-side with a small sister-church of REC, the Free Church of England (FCE).

During the 20th century, as the immediate causes for REC's organization faded into the past, those numbers began to slip (9660 in 1930; 7652 in 1960), and the number of synodical and missionary jurisdictions was reduced to three synods (Chicago, New York-Philadelphia, and Charleston-Atlanta-Charlotte) and new missionary jurisdiction. In 1927, the Reformed Episcopal Church—U.K. merged with the Free Church of England. The Canadian synod, lacking its own bishop, gradually declined until in 1930 it petitioned the General Council of REC to be transferred to the jurisdiction of the Free Church of England. But FCE was no more successful than REC in providing episcopal oversight, and in 1945 the Canadian synod was returned to REC jurisdiction. By 1960, the Canadian Reformed Episcopal Church had virtually disappeared.

On the other hand, a number of institutions within REC grew and flourished. REC's theological seminary in Philadelphia, opened in 1887, grew from a student body of 13 in 1890 to more than 100 in 1976. Reformed Episcopal foreign missions grew from a single station in India to include missionary work in France, Germany, Uganda, and Kenya. The Missionary Jurisdiction of the South (USA), organized in 1875 to serve black freedmen, was granted full synodical status in 1975, along with its own theological educational facility.

Reformed Episcopal interest in ecumenical relations, which was one of the major motives in the founding of REC, declined during much of the 20th century. In 1912 efforts by the Church of Jesus (Puerto Rico) to achieve organic union with REC were rebuffed, despite Bishop R. L. Rudolph's decision to consecrate a bishop for them. In 1918 REC called for a national conference on "Organic Union of the Churches," but the response of only six denominations to the call chilled further moves in that direction. Although REC had a founding role in the organizing of another ecumenical organization, the Federal Council of Churches, REC found itself increasingly at odds with the council's theological positions and withdrew from the council in 1945 after a tumultuous debate.

In 1939 the Protestant Episcopal Church (PEC) opened talks with representatives of REC, looking toward reunion of the churches. A committee of the PEC House of Bishops in 1941 petitioned the Lambeth Conference to extend provincial recognition to REC. But the 1948 Lambeth Conference failed to respond favorably, and nothing further came of the talks. Not until 1987, when REC voted to affiliate with the National Association of Evangelicals, did REC initiate any new ecumenical approaches. Then in the same year, the New York-Philadelphia Synod gave a cordial response to ecumenical overtures from the Episcopal Church's diocese of Pennsylvania, and in 1988, the Episcopal General Convention authorized extending the talks to the national level.

The general theological climate of REC has remained conservative and evangelical. But as the founding generation of old Episcopalians died off by the 1920s, REC acquired a distinctively dispensational and fundamentalist tenor. In the 1950s, however, the influence of Robert K. Rudolph and F. C. Kuehner turned REC back toward the Calvinist theology which had always been latent in the old Episcopal evangelicals. In the 1980s there was a renewed interest in REC's Anglican and Episcopal roots. A major revision of REC's Book of Common Prayer was undertaken between 1912 and 1930, the last such significant revision before 1990.

ALLEN C. GUELZO

## Reformed League (Reformierter Bund).

A voluntary organization that was formed in 1884 to foster closer cooperation among the scattered Reformed churches in Germany. It did not concern itself with internal matters of its member bodies but rather represented their interests alongside the numerically much larger Lutheran and united communions there. It supported the establishment of study centers at the universities, a theological school at Wuppertal, and the publication of books and magazines from a Reformed perspective. Its chief administrative organs are an executive board (*Moderamen*) and a biennial general assembly. During the Nazi era "church struggle" it identified and worked with the Confessing Church. After Word War II, congregations and individual persons were allowed to be members as well and its purpose was declared to be that of maintaining the Reformed confession and order of worship. Under pressure from the communist authorities in East Germany, a separate league was formed there but the two were reunited after 1990. In the 1980s the League adopted a strong position against apartheid in South Africa and actively worked for its ending. More controversial was the statement, "The Church's Responsibility for Peace in Light of Its Confessing Commitment to Jesus Christ." Issued by the executive in 1982 and approved by the general assembly in 1984, it labeled the nuclear arms race as blasphemy against God and in opposition to the basic principles of the Christian faith and declared that a *status confessionis* in the matter existed. It is a constituent body of the World Alliance of Reformed Churches.

RICHARD V. PIERARD

## Reid, John Kelman Sutherland (1910– ).

Scottish theologian. Born in Leith, he was educated at the universities of Edinburgh, Heidelberg, Marburg, and Strasburg. He was professor of philosophy at the University of Calcutta, India (1935–37), then returned to serve the Church of Scotland. He was minister of Craigmillar Park, Edinburgh (1939–52), interrupted by four years as a military chaplain during World War II; professor of theology at Leeds University (1952–61); and professor at Aberdeen University, first of Christian dogmatics (1961–70) and then of systematic theology (1970–76). Among his publications are *The Church's Standing Orders* (1943), *Human Destiny* (1954), *The Authority of Holy Scripture* (1957), *Our Life in Christ* (1963), and *Christian Apologetics* (1969). He translated works of Calvin and Cullmann, and was joint editor of the *Scottish Journal of Theology* from its first publication in 1947.

**Religion, Psychology of.** A form of human behavior or motivation that, in whatever expression, can be classified by psychologists, sociologists, or anthropologists as different from or similar to other forms of human expressions. When people kneel in prayer, sing hymns, recite creeds, study Scripture, confess sin, minister to the needy, preach a sermon, memorize a text, prepare a church budget, or lay on hands, they involve the classical psychological functions of volition, affection, and cognition. Thus, religion has a facet uniquely amenable to analysis by the human sciences, which provide a perspective not available to the theologian. The human facet of religion is studied by psychologists, sociologists, psychiatrists, and philosophers, as well as by scholars in religious studies.

*Dimensions of Religion.* Religion, as human behavior, is multidimensional. Charles Glock, in a monograph on religious commitment (1962), offered the first complex theoretical model to categorize religious behavior. It included five dimensions—the *ideological*, the *ritualistic*, the *experiential*, the *intellectual*, and the *consequential*. The ideological dimension pertained to religious beliefs, the ritualistic to practices, the experiential to feelings, the intellectual to knowledge, and the consequential to effects. As M. J. Meadow and Richard Kahoe state in *Psychology of Religion*, these dimensions allow objective comparison of religion with other human processes: "For any venture in which people engage, we can ask what they think about it, how they go about doing it, what kinds of feelings and experiences are associated with it, how much they know about what they are doing, and what consequences it has for the rest of their lives."

Researchers are not unanimous in the division of these dimensions, nor do they agree about what unique aspects of religion truly separate it from other sorts of behavior. Some psychologists see religious behavior strictly as instances of general human behavior; participants in Fundamentalists Anonymous, which deals with perceived personal problems relating to religion, pattern their group dynamics after Alcoholics Anonymous. Other researchers regard religious behaviors as uniquely prominent; relationships among a complex of behaviors with a religious motivation may shed light on general human behaviors. For example, the mass suicide at Jonestown, Guyana, in 1979 powerfully illustrated the influence of a charismatic leader, raising perplexing questions for psychologists interested in the phenomena of persuasion. Still other researchers emphasize the unique interaction among religious and nonreligious behaviors. Religion produces an attitude which pervades all areas of thought. For Christians, the problem of suffering affects not only their worldview but also their relationship to God and their understanding of the gospel.

Finally, some researchers emphasize basically unique variables in religion: As a religious person the human searches for something beyond the self, whether the search reaches outward to a god or inward to an indwelling spirit.

*Historical Developments since 1950.* Within the 20th century developments that marked the 1950s were pivotal in the relationship between the social sciences and religion. With the publication of Gordon Allport's *Individual and His Religion* (1950), the psychology of religion regained respectability in American academia and professional psychology, from which it had been banished for at least two decades. Allport's influence was reinforced by Robert Brodie MacLeod's *Religious Perspectives of College Teaching in Experimental Psychology* (1951). The application of psychology to Christian education was institutionalized in the *Lumen Vitae Studies in Religious Psychology*, which primarily featured the contributions of European scholars. The brief appearance of the *Journal of Psychotherapy as a Religious Process* (1954–56) attempted (albeit unsuccessfully) to organize the community of psychological scholars interested in the religious dimensions of psychotherapy.

The Religious Research Fellowship, now the Religious Research Association (RRA), was launched in 1951 to promote institutional and church-based religious research, thus subjecting the institutional church to the rigorous scrutiny of experimental social science. In 1959 the group founded the *Review of Religious Research*. The (National) Academy of Religion and Mental Health (ARMH) emerged in 1954 to publicize and analyze the results of behavioral research, to promote both spiritual and mental well-being. With the founding of the Christian Association for Psychological Studies (CAPS) in 1952 the Christian psychology movement organized with similar goals to those of the American Catholic Psychological Association (ACPA), founded in 1947.

During the 1960s many of these initial efforts matured into definitive movements with their own journals and professional credentials. The *Journal for the Scientific Study of Religion* was founded in 1961 to publish research of the scholars who had met since 1949 as the Committee (now the Society) for the Scientific Study of Religion (SSSR). These scholars sought to "(1) bring together social scientists and religious persons; (2) pursue joint research; (3) stimulate students and scholars to work on religion as a research topic; and (4) create an audience who would read religious research." ACPA published the *Catholic Psychological Record* (1963–68), and the Franciscans founded *Insight: Quarterly Review of Religion and Mental Health*, which focused on the "crossroads of psychology, phenomenology, psychiatry and theology." Similar goals were expressed by the publishers of *Inward Light: Journal of the Friends Conference on Religion and Psychology*, founded in 1937, which endeavored to "be an organ of expression and intercommunication among those concerned with cultivating the inner life and relating it to the problems of our time." ARMH launched the *Journal of Religion and Health*, a quarterly which sought to combine spiritual, physical, and emotional aspects of human well-being.

The increasing emphasis on scholarly, rather than apologetic, studies resulted in the transformation of the *Journal of Bible and Religion* (founded in 1933) to the *Journal of the American Academy of Religion* in 1967. The Faculty Christian Fellowship contributed its *Faith Learning Studies: A Series Examining the Academic Disciplines*, and included as its third volume *Psychology* by Joseph Havens (1964). In 1964 a revolutionary development took place at Fuller Theological Seminary when the Graduate School of Psychology matriculated the first students to earn the doctorate in clinical psychology with a cocurriculum in theology and a series of "integration seminars" cotaught by a theologian and a psychologist. At the end of the decade, the monumental and influential *Handbook of Social Psychology* (1969) featured a lengthy chapter on the psychology of religion by James E. Dittes of Yale University, cementing the foundation laid by Allport nearly two decades earlier.

During the 1970s and 1980s one witness to the large community of Christian psychologists was publication of the massive *Baker Encyclopedia of Psychology* (1985). Christian psychologists could disseminate their ideas in the *Journal of Psychology and Theology* (published by the Rosemead Graduate School of Psychology) or the *Journal of Psychology and Christianity* (published by CAPS). Jewish scholars had the *Journal of Psychology and Judaism*. In 1976, Psychologists Interested in Religious Issues (previously ACPA) was approved as a division of the American Psychological Association (APA), thus legitimating the psychology of religion and its disciplinary kin. The voluminous literature in this area is documented in two major bibliographies by Donald Capps, Lewis Rambo, and Paul Ransohoff (1976) and later by Hendrika Vande Kemp (1984), and its history was eloquently summarized by David Wulff (1985), whose review provides an international perspective. A landmark publication was Richard Gorsuch's chapter on the "Psychology of Religion" in the 1988 *Annual Review of Psychology*.

The 1970s witnessed great interest in religious experience and mysticism, giving birth to transpersonal psychology and "new religions." The "Jesus People" transfused traditional religious groups with new forms of ritual and liturgy. The "Flower People" and drug researchers spawned an interest in altered states of consciousness, multiple realities, and state-specific sciences (Charles Tart), the varieties of unconscious experience (Stanislav Grof), and the legitimacy of drug-induced mystical states (Walter H. Clark). The novels of Carlos Castaneda (e.g., *Separate Reality* [1972], *Journey to Ixtlan* [1973], and *The Teachings of Don Juan* [1973]) inspired the religious quests of millions. But the 1970s ended with the Jonestown massacre, inspiring research into darker, unique aspects of "the new religions" led by sociologists of religion such as James Richardson.

***Significant Areas of Research and Interest.*** Research in American psychology of religion from 1950 was also profoundly affected by the murder of millions in the Holocaust and the racial prejudice that became overt during and after World War II. Research was spurred by publication of *The Authoritarian Personality* (1950), which found that churchgoers tended to be more prejudiced than the nonreligious. Significant publications on this topic included Nathan Ackerman and Marie Jahoda, *Anti-Semitism and Emotional Disorder* (1950); Erich Neuman, *Depth Psychology and a New Ethic*, with editions in 1949, and 1969; Allport, *The Nature of Prejudice* (1954); and Milton Rokeach, *The Open and Closed Mind* (1960). There followed an attempt to clarify Allport's distinction between extrinsic and intrinsic religious orientation. Rokeach's research on dogmatism was both fruitful and controversial. Many evangelical Christians criticized his distinction between the content and process of religious thought. Related research has applied Julian Rotter's "locus of control" to religious behavior.

Research on religious development was motivated in the 1980s by the growing interest in spiritual development and charismatic religious groups, as well as the earlier tradition of religious education. Followers of Jean Piaget and other cognitive developmentalists (or "genetic epistemologists") were concerned with religious knowledge, stressing that cognitive structures limit the child's grasp of religious concepts, and thus affect teaching of doctrine and creeds. Such thinkers as Richard Perry emphasized the continuation of intellectual and ethical development into the college years, demonstrating the movement from dualistic to multiplistic and relativistic thinking which must ultimately culminate in commitment. In this time of development ethical thinking is affected and the individual is more vulnerable to charismatic leaders and persuasion. Research on moral development indicates that the person grows through being challenged by new problems that cannot be resolved at a previous level of development; thus persons do not progress beyond the complexity of the problems posed by their culture. Thus, spiritual directors must pose intellectual and ethical challenges and encourage movement away from familiar settings for growth to occur. This research lends little support for such educational programs as "values clarification"; it also leaves unanswered questions about the ultimate source of values and criteria for their evaluation.

Psychoanalysts and clinical psychologists often imply that an interest in religion is symptomatic of mental illness. Perhaps the best illustration of the close connection between psychosis and religious ideation published during this time was Rokeach, *The Three Christs of Ypsilanti: A Narrative Study of Three Lost Men* (1964). From the opposite perspective, Anton Boisen, the founder of Clinical Pastoral Education, continued to advance his belief that religious growth may be the outcome of psychosis in *Out of the Depths: An Autobiographical Study of Mental Disorder* (1960). Highly influential was O. H. Mowrer's *Crisis in Psychiatry and Religion* (1961), which emphasized that "disingenuous amorality may be the cause of personality disorder and deviation." Mowrer stressed the importance of confession and the small group model of the early church, and inspired the founding of integrity therapy.

Bernard Spilka, Ralph Hood, and Gorsuch reviewed the variety of possible relationships between religion and mental health. Religion may foster the expression of psychopathology by condoning peculiar behavior; glossolalia, conversion, mystical experiences, and scrupulosity may be (but are not necessarily) connected with mental disorder. Religion may also act as a social control; the environment of the institutional church, doctrines and creeds, and religious leaders all serve to channel, direct, and limit behavior. Religion may also serve as a haven for the deviant; in communal living, one's life may be directed and controlled, sparing difficult decision making, there is less fear of rejection and isolation, and the security of divine protection. For some, such as Boisen, religious expression serves a therapeutic function. Conversion, prayer, and other experiences lead to *metanoia*, a transformation of the person. But religion can also foster escape from reality and reinforce other ego defenses that block growth and perpetuate destructive patterns.

Meadow and Kahoe's text attempts to put several of these variables into perspective. They relate the research on belief to religious faith, on guilt and shame to conscience, on volition to hope, and on altruism to religious love. This approach illustrates at least a rudimentary level of integration often missing, since early psychologists of religion tended to use religious categories to organize their textbooks. It is still common to find chapters or sections on religious experience, mysticism, conversion, prayer, ecstatic experiences, and worship. An exception to this, organized entirely by the categories of ego psychology, is Paul Pruyser, *A Dynamic Psychology of Religion* (1968). Pruyser also contributed a study of doubt, *Between Belief and Unbelief* (1972), applying object-relations theory to understand the affective component of belief. This work is related to other developmental research using projection theories, which assume that one's concept of God will reflect early experiences with significant others. The best theoretical examples of this are the works of Anna-Maria Rizzuto and John McDargh.

***The Status of Religion.*** In 1944, the Edward W. Hazen Foundation and the American Council on Education cosponsored a study of religion in college textbooks. The rationale of the study was that religion is part of culture, and a large part of the population believes the heritage should be transmitted. This fact is frequently obscured, denied, or distorted by modern modes of thinking, and these trends discourage the development of religion. Faculties and teachers might play a far more constructive, beneficial role to society through a more enlightened study and appraisal of religion as a phase of culture.

Allport was commissioned to conduct the study of psychology textbooks. He concluded that roughly one-third of the 50 texts reviewed gave religion "the silent treatment." Only one was viewed as openly hostile, but the typical treatment failed to put religion in perspective for the student seeking a philosophy of life, or it ultimately regarded religious persons with condescension, as somehow "managed" by religion. Only three texts applied semisystematic treatment to religion, despite the fact that religious behavior is found in every known culture.

Four decades later the situation remained much the same. Although the psychology of religion has gained academic respect, the typical undergraduate will fail to encounter religious behavior in a psychology course, or will find it treated as a relic or a symptom. The challenge remains to steer the narrow channel between psychologism and dogmatism in the religious life.

***Bibliography.*** G. W. Allport, *College Reading and Religion* (1948); E. Neuman, *Depth Psychology and a New Ethic* (1949;

rev. ed., 1969); N. W. Ackerman and M. Jahoda, *Anti-Semitism and Emotional Disorder: A Psychoanalytic Interpretation* (1950); T. W. Adorno, et al., *The Authoritarian Personality* (1950); G. W. Allport, *The Individual and His Religion* (1950); *The Nature of Prejudice* (1954); M. Rokeach, *The Open and Closed Mind* (1960); C. Y. Glock, *Religious Education, Research Supplement* (1962); P. W. Pruyser, *A Dynamic Psychology of Religion* (1968); J. E. Dittes, *Handbook of Social Psychology*, vol. 5 (2d ed., 1969); P. W. Pruyser, *Between Belief and Unbelief* (1974); D. Capps, L. Rambo, and P. Ransohoff, *Psychology of Religion: A Guide to Information Sources* (1975); M. H. Spero, *Judaism and Psychology: Halakhic Perspectives* (1980); J. F. Byrnes, *The Psychology of Religion* (1984); R. J. Lovinger, *Working with Religious Issues in Therapy* (1984); M. J. Meadow and R. D. Kahoe, *Psychology of Religion: Religion in Individual Lives* (1984); H. Vande Kemp, *Psychology and Theology in Western Thought, 1672–1965: A Historical and Annotated Bibliography* (1984); D. Benner, ed., *Baker Encyclopedia of Psychology* (1985); B. Spilka, R. W. Hood, Jr., and R. L. Gorsuch, *The Psychology of Religion: An Empirical Approach* (1985); E. M. Stern, ed., *Psychotherapy and the Religiously Committed Patient* (1985); D. M. Wulff, *Approaches to the Study of Religion*, vol. 2, *The Social Sciences* (1985); R. L. Gorsuch, *Annual Review of Psychology* (1988).

HENDRIKA VANDE KEMP

**Religion, Philosophy of.** *See* PHILOSOPHY OF RELIGION.

**Religion and Life Movement.** English lay organization initiated in 1940 by the Commission of the Churches and sponsored since 1942 by the British Council of Churches. Between 1940 and 1946 nearly 150 "Religion and Life Weeks" were organized in communities of all types and sizes, with Anglican and Free Church and occasionally Roman Catholic cooperation. The aim was to bring home to the people the bearing of religion on family life, education, industry, and international affairs, and to prepare them to face post-war problems. Besides public meetings there were special gatherings for ministers, women, and youth. The "weeks" quickened the sense of reponsibility in the churches, revealed the possibilities of cooperative action, and led in many places to the setting up of local councils of churches modeled on, and generally associated with, the British Council of Churches.

PHILIP WATSON

**Religion and Literature.** *See* LITERATURE, RELIGION AND.

**Religious Education.** *See* EDUCATION, CHRISTIAN.

**Religious Science and Philosophy.** *See* NEW THOUGHT.

**Remission of Sins.** English translation in various passages of the KJV, of Gk. *aphesis,* meaning a "sending away" or "dismissal." Its meaning is further explicated by the fact that it is translated as "forgiveness" in the KJV of Acts 5:31; 13:38; 26:18; Eph. 1:7; Col. 1:14; and invariably "forgiveness" in the RSV which does not use the word

"remission." In the Ephesians-Colossians passage, it is parallel with *apolutrōsis* ("redemption" or "deliverance") and in Heb. 10:18 with the phrase "no longer remember." The remitter or forgiver of sins is always God, except in John 20:23 where it is the Spirit-filled believer. Remission is connected with repentance as its condition (Mark 1:4; Luke 24:47; Acts 2:38), and with baptism (Luke 3:3; 24:47; Acts 2:38). It is proclaimed for Israel (Luke 1:77; Acts 5:31; 13:38) and for all believers (Acts 10:43; as well as by implication—Eph. 1:7; Col. 1:14; Heb. 9:22; 10:18). It is associated with Christ or his name (Acts 2:38; 26:18); it is said to be "in him" (Eph. 1:7; Col. 1:14). In Matt. 26:18 and Heb. 9:22 it is connected with the death of Christ, specifically with his shed blood. Roman Catholics interpret John 20:23 to mean that priests, through apostolic succession, have divine authority to forgive sins. Protestants, on the contrary, interpreting this passage in the light of the NT as a whole, explain it as referring to the spiritual sensitivity of the Spirit-filled Christian community, which will have inspired insight to discern between sins unrepented of (and therefore unforgiven) and sins which are truly repented of. The Roman Catholic applies this to the priest's absolution in the confessional, while the Protestant applies it to confession of acknowledged transgression of God's Law.

KENNETH J. FOREMAN

**Reordination.** A second or repeated ordination. During the Middle Ages, priests ordained in schismatic or heretical bodies and admitted to Catholic priesthood after their conversion were normally reordained, along with priests whose Catholic ordination was irregular. Priests ordained not in conformity with the canons were deemed to lack the supernatural powers necessary for the administration of the sacraments. Today, the Roman Church repeats schismatic or Catholic ordinations only if their validity or completeness is doubted.

GEORGES A. BARROIS

**Rerum Orientalium.** Encyclical issued by Pope Pius XI on September 8, 1928, promoting the study of the history, doctrine, and liturgy of the Eastern Church. The pope recalls in chronological order the endeavors of the Holy See to bring the dissident Christians of the East back to the Roman communion. He applies the general principles of Roman ecumenism, formulated in the encyclical *Mortalium animos* to the particular problem of bringing about a reunion with the Eastern Church. In view of this task, he recommends that Roman Catholic priests apply themselves to special studies in the Oriental Institute founded in Rome by Pope Benedict XV.

*Bibliography.* Original text in *Acta Apostolicae Sedis* (1928), 20:277–88; ET in *Catholic Mind,* 26:421–31.

GEORGES A. BARROIS

**Restoration of All.** The Scriptures teach that creation, as it came from God's hand, was good (Gen. 1:31); that the fall of man was the cause of cosmic corruption (Gen. 3:17–19; Rom. 8:20); that events in the natural order will accompany the redemption of man (Acts 2:19–20); and that, in the final consummation, sin and all of its effects will be overcome. Creation itself will be delivered at last from the bondage of corruption (Rom. 8:21; see also Isa. 65:17; 1 Cor. 15:28; Eph. 1:20–22; Phil. 2:9–11; Col. 1:17, 20; 2 Pet. 3:12, 13; Rev. 21:5).

The doctrine of a final restoration of all is not without problems, however. That events in human history, like sin and redemption, could have effects in inanimate nature can only seem superstitious and bizarre. The law of entropy, apparently universal in the natural order, is interpreted to mean that creation is inexorably headed toward, not any kind of restoration, but complete exhaustion. Bertrand Russell's "a Freeman's Worship" is perhaps only the best known of a large number of such interpretations. There are those who predict that atomic fission will lead, not only to the destruction of the human race, but also to the very annihilation of this planet.

The reply that such conclusions, based on naturalistic considerations, do not touch the basis of the doctrine of the final restoration may be true enough; but the latter doctrine is also not lacking in difficulties. For if the scriptural record of supernatural revelation teaches such a doctrine, it also seems to teach that not all personal beings will be finally restored (Matt. 25:41; Rev. 20:10). It has been argued, of course, by universalists that these and similar passages do not mean what they have been commonly interpreted to mean. They contend that the adjective *aiōnios* means, not "eternal," but "age-long"; that we are now in one of the "ages" into which the Scriptures divide history; that the punishment of the unrepentant will last through this age only; and that then all will be restored. If this interpretation of Scripture can be maintained, then there will be no difficulty in accepting a doctrine of universal restoration on the basis of the supernatural revelation. But although etymologically the adjective *aiōnios* does mean "age-long," its use in the NT to express the eternity of God himself (Heb. 9:14) and of the life which believers receive from him (Matt. 25:46; John 3:15) shows that it had now come to mean "eternal." Furthermore, the unendingness of the fate of the wicked is clearly expressed in passages where this adjective is not employed (Matt. 7:12; Mark 9:44, 45; Jude :7; cf. Rev. 20:10, 14).

The Scriptures therefore seem to teach both a final restoration of all and the exclusion of some personal beings from that restoration. This dilemma can be resolved by understanding the "all" collectively, not distributively, so that the totality, the system of things, is to be restored but not every particular being that has ever existed within it.

ANDREW K. RULE

**Resurrection of Christ.** *NT Claims and Modern Assessments.* For preaching that Jesus had been raised from the dead, Paul was jeered (Acts 17:32). Yet the resurrection of Jesus Christ remained at the center of the apostolic proclamation. Paul even told the Corinthians that "if Christ has not been raised, your faith is futile" (1 Cor. 15:17; see also Rom. 8:11). He sees Jesus' resurrection as a non-negotiable component of Christian belief. In contrast, one of the 20th century's most influential NT scholars denies that the tomb was empty because "a corpse cannot become alive again" (Rudolf Bultmann, *Der Spiegel*), and the eminent British churchman G. W. H. Lampe regards "the story of the empty tomb as myth rather than literal history" (Lampe and D. M. Mackinnon, *The Resurrection*). In modern times, as in ancient, the resurrection of Jesus is a focal point of controversy.

It cannot be denied that Jesus' followers, who the evidence suggests were not easily convinced of his resurrection, fervently believed and proclaimed that Jesus appeared to and taught them following his public execution (attested outside the NT by Josephus and Tacitus). It is widely conceded that the existence of this remarkable conviction can be traced to within five years of the date of the crucifixion. The NT records some 11 different appearances, not including Paul's personal experience, of the risen Jesus. He reportedly appeared to the Eleven on at least four occasions (Luke 24:36–49; John 20:19–29; Matt. 28:16–20; Acts 1:3–8); to women at the tomb (Matt. 28:9–10); to Mary Magdalene (John 20:11–18); to Peter (Luke 24:34; 1 Cor. 15:5); to disciples on the Emmaus road (Luke 24:13–31); to James (1 Cor. 15:7); to seven disciples fishing (John 21:1–23); and finally to a crowd of some 500 (1 Cor. 15:6).

When these accounts are combined with Paul's personal experience (Gal. 1:12; cf. Acts 9:1–8; 22:6–11; 26:12–18), a double validation of Christ's resurrection emerges from the sources (see W. L. Craig, *Historical Argument for the Resurrection of Jesus*). Both the Gospels and Paul set forth historical proof (see Acts 1:3), the Gospels by relating appearances to the Eleven and others associated with them, Paul by stressing that many of the these witnesses, himself included, were available to testify to the veracity of the reports. Contemporary gospel criticism in some quarters has tended to deny that Jesus' resurrection could have happened. This tendency has been in evidence since the Enlightenment. Some critics continue to adopt a rigid reliance on historical science to rule out Jesus' resurrection on a priori grounds. Others point out, however, that nothing in the NT portrayal is intrinsically impossible either scientifically or historically (Grant Osborne, *Resurrection Narratives*). Wolfhart Pannenberg concurs that the resurrection "need not appear meaningless from the presuppositions of modern thought" (*Jesus, God and Man*).

Views which discount Christ's resurrection must come up with satisfactory alternative explanations for the claims of the sources. William Wrede asserted that Paul's vision of the risen Jesus on the Damascus road was quite real, to Paul at least, but was ultimately a function of epileptic fits to which he was prone (*Paul*). F. C. Baur, following D. F. Strauss, portrayed the gospel accounts of the resurrection as visions, by which he appears to mean hallucinations (*Vorlesungen über neutestamentliche Theologie*). Still older theories suggested that Jesus did not really die on the cross but only swooned, reviving in the cool tomb and escaping into subsequent anonymity, or that the women visited the wrong tomb, or that Jesus' disciples stole the body. Such explanations raised more questions than they answered and were widely abandoned, even by those who doubted Jesus' resurrection (see J. P. Moreland, *Scaling the Secular City*).

It is sometimes assumed that ancient legends and myths uncovered through the comparative study of religions suffice to explain the NT accounts. The early church's proclamation, it is said, reflects the concurrence of previously circulated religious belief or superstition and the fertile precritical imaginations of Jesus' followers, who seized on "resurrection" to preserve the hope their beloved but deceased mentor had kindled in them. Yet such scholars as Helmer Ringgren, J. N. D. Anderson, Bruce Metzger, and Pannenberg point out that great care must be exercised in drawing parallels between the NT accounts and ostensibly similar ones in other religious or philosophical traditions. On close scrutiny the alleged parallels become doubtful. One is left with a conceptual background that is confined primarily to (1) the OT as understood in rabbinic and apocalyptic Judaism, and (2) Jesus' teaching about himself, as noted in Hans Bayer, *Jesus' Predictions*. Such a background is not comprehensive enough an explanation of the NT accounts apart from the event itself, though it does give pointers as to how the resurrection was understood and applied generally by some at the time.

Where Jesus' resurrection is taken seriously 20th-century critics attempted to discount the corporeality of Jesus' resurrection form. Hans Küng denied a bodily resurrection in physiological terms, although he was willing to accept a Jesus whose resurrected body was understood not so much physiologically as personally (*Eternal Life?*). Leonhard Goppelt adopted a similar view in his *Theology of the NT*, as did Pannenberg, who claimed that gospel accounts are interlaced with legend, particularly in maintaining that Christ made corporeal appearances (*Jesus, God and Man*).

On the other hand, Osborne maintained that the evidence strongly suggests a physical resurrection (*Resurrection Narratives*), and Pinchas Lapide, who noted that "some modern Christian theologians are ashamed of the material facticity of the resurrection," averred that the four gospels "complete with each other in illustrating the tangible, substantial dimension" of Jesus' resurrection (*Resurrection of Jesus*). Robert Gundry argued convincingly that an understanding of *sōma* which radically separates the physical body from the personality goes beyond the semantic possibility of the word's NT usage ("Sōma" *in Biblical Theology*). Paul knows nothing of a totally dematerialized, resurrected Jesus. One treads precarious ground, then, in arguing for the theological significance of the resurrection appearances while denying that they were physical. Oscar Cullmann observed that ancient Greek conceptions of the immortality of the soul are often imposed on the NT reports in violation of their own stated claims (*Immortality of the Soul*). Picking up on this has given scholars their only evidence to advocate, in essence, a spiritual but not a physical resurrection. Nevertheless Scripture is clearly not on their side.

In sum, while the tendency to deny Jesus' resurrection outright declined in the later 1900s it was often reinterpreted to remove its supernaturalism in violation of the full claims of the sources. The veracity of the resurrection narratives is eminently plausible in the present century no less than in the first, when Jesus' bodily resurrection was scoffed at by Jew and Gentile alike, as in Acts 23:8.

Yet plausibility does not automatically translate into theological serviceability. The NT is not only concerned to assert the reality of Jesus' rise and attendant exaltation; it moves from that point forward to confessions of theological significance.

***Theological Significance.*** The NT writers, convinced of the literal truth of the resurrection, predicated several theological corollaries on this claim. In Acts, Jesus' resurrection has a pronounced apologetic function. It validates OT prophecy (2:31) by demonstrating that he is the Messiah (3:15–16; Rom. 1:4). The resurrection proves central to apostolic preaching, even when stringent critical methods are applied to the sources, as C. H. Dodd noted (*Apostolic Preaching*). At no known stratum of gospel tradition is belief in Jesus' resurrection absent. The modern attempt to call the resurrection "not a historical but nevertheless a real event" (*Eternal Life?*) is seriously out of sympathy with the realism of the early Christians, who from earliest times endured hardship rather than deny the actuality of what they had witnessed and its implications (e.g., Acts 5:30–42; 13:26–52; 17:1–9; 23:6–10; 2 Tim. 2:8–13).

Jesus' resurrection is the basis for Paul's preaching of the cross. His death provides a perfect sacrifice for sins, and his resurrection establishes that God has accepted the payment which the Son has tendered for debt incurred by sinners (Rom. 4:21–25; Heb. 1:3). Death and estrangement from God have been replaced by life in the resurrected Christ and reconciliation to God (Rom. 5:10; 1 Cor. 15:55–57). Because Jesus has been raised, persons can experience spiritual rebirth and live in unshakable hope (1 Pet. 1:3; Eph. 1:18–20).

The resurrection of Jesus, exalted and interceding for his people at God's right hand, is the cornerstone of Christian living. In the wake of his atoning crucifixion, Jesus' real and continuing life is the means by which the Christian triumphs over sin (Rom. 6:4–10). Frail and failure-prone humans are infused with transforming potential by "the Spirit of him who raised Jesus from the dead" (Rom. 8:11). Christ's salvation avails for all who look to God for the deliverance effected by his resurrection; believers discover that they were raised proleptically with him and can now be mastered by the redeeming and liberating virtues imparted by the living God rather than the foibles and vices symptomatic of Christless children of Adam (Col. 3:1–4).

Modern theology is perhaps emerging from an era in which Christ's resurrection received inadequate attention or, too often, suffered misguided analysis. Peter Carnley observes that the affirmation that Christ was the raised, exalted Lord of the Christian community indisputably charged the church with a powerful assessment of Jesus' function and identity (*Structure of Resurrection Belief*). Jesus himself apparently intended that his resurrection would comprise the heart of the Christian message. His first followers could not conceive what "resurrection" of "the Son of Man" might entail (Mark 9:9–10, 31, 33–34; see Bayer, *Jesus' Predictions*). Thomas roundly doubted all hearsay evidence until his own eyes scotched his cynicism (John 20:24–29). Yet, if the cross would draw men to Jesus (John 3:14; 12:32; 13:31), the resurrection bound Jesus' followers to the life of devotion and service to which he summoned them (cf. Matt. 28:16–20). The final writing of the NT conveys greetings "from Jesus Christ . . . the firstborn from the dead" (Rev. 1:5). On the basis of Christ's triumph over sin and death by a bodily resurrection to newness of life, each Christian is promised, and is witness to, an analogous experience.

**Bibliography.** F. C. Baur, *Vorlesungen über neutestamentliche Theologie;* C. H. Dodd, *The Apostolic Preaching and Its Developments* (1937); O. Cullman, *Immortality of the Soul or Resurrection of the Dead?* (1958); W. Wrede, *Paul* (repr. 1962); G. W. H. Lampe and D. M. Mackinnon, *The Resurrection: A Dialogue* (1966); R. Bultmann, *"Der Spiegel" in the NT* (1970); R. E. Brown, *The Virginal Conception and Bodily Resurrection of Jesus* (1973); G. E. Ladd, *I Believe in the Resurrection of Jesus* (1975); R. H. Gundry, "Sōma" *in Biblical Theology, with Emphasis on Pauline Theology* (1976); W. Pannenburg, *Jesus, God and Man* (2d ed., 1977); U. Wilckens, *Resurrection* (1978); L. Goppelt, *Theology of the NT,* vol. 1 (1981); P. Lapide, *The Resurrection of Jesus* (1983); H. Küng, *Eternal Life?* (1984); G. Osborne, *The Resurrection Narratives* (1984); P. Perkins, *Resurrection: NT Witnesses and Contemporary Reflection* (1984); J. Wenham, *Easter Enigma: Are the Resurrection Accounts in Conflict?* (1984); H. Bayer, *Jesus' Predictions of Vindication and Resurrection* (1985); W. L. Craig, *The Historical Argument for the Resurrection of Jesus during the Deist Controversy* (1985); P. Carnley, *The Structure of Resurrection Belief* (1987); G. R. Habermas and A. G. N. Flew, *Did Jesus Rise from the Dead?* (1987); J. P. Moreland, *Scaling the Secular City* (1987).

ROBERT W. YARBROUGH

**Retreat.** Period during which a group of believers withdraws to a secluded place for a time of prayer, meditation, study, and instruction. Retreats have been especially popular in the Catholic Church. Priests and religious usually make an annual retreat. Among Protestants retreats assume many forms. For example, a group of ministers or laypeople may go to a secluded rural cottage for a weekend. They meet for devotions and meditate privately. In arranging for a retreat leaders should keep the numbers small, the program simple, and emphasize spirituality rather than philosophic thought.

ANDREW W. BLACKWOOD

**Revelation.** Revelation is the act of God in which he discloses or communicates truth to human beings. There is a great chasm between God and man. God is pure spirit; in man, spirit is united with body. We cannot go beyond the veil of flesh to establish relations with a spiritual Being. In revelation God himself takes the initiative in bridging the barrier between Creator and creature, between pure Spirit and embodied spirit. He makes himself known through his word and his works.

The act of revelation takes place in the arena of history. The gospel is the good news of the mighty acts of God in history. God called Abraham to leave his country and home to go to the promised land. God revealed himself to Moses as the God of Abraham, Isaac, and Jacob. His claim to Israel's loyalty was based on the fact that he brought the people out of the land of Egypt. He revealed his power and purpose in the crucial events of Israel's history; he also sent the prophets, the qualified interpreters of these events, to be the bearers of his word. In the fullness of time, he sent his Son who manifested God in the context of human life. Christ endured the torment of death and rose from the grave. God sent his Spirit at Pentecost.

Revelation is the event in which God communicates his truth to man; inspiration, as the term is used in theology, is the process by which this divine message is committed to writing. Scholars differ in their theories as to the nature and the extent of inspiration; but, at the heart of the Christian faith, there is the conviction that God through Scripture reveals to man that knowledge which is necessary to salvation.

Scripture becomes the word of God to us as the Holy Spirit bears witness in our heart that this is indeed the word of God. The Westminster Confession of Faith concludes its statement on the authority of Scripture (1.4) by saying that "our full persuasion and assurance of the infallible truth and divine authority thereof, is from the inward work of the Holy Spirit, bearing witness by and with the word in our hearts."

Through revelation man apprehends truth which cannot be reached by reason alone. The great truths of Scripture cannot be reduced to some rational system which man can work out for himself without the aid of revelation. Schleiermacher sought to cut the tie between Christian thought and a revelation grounded in history. He built on the feeling of dependence, rather than on pure reason. He sought, in his *Christian Faith*, to produce a system of thought which was not dependent on objective revelation. The theology of crisis rejected such an idea. Nevertheless, the truth of revelation is not irrational. Paul tells Felix about the Christian proclamation that begins with the witness to the resurrection; but he insists that he is not crazy and that he speaks the words of truth (Acts 24).

The NT church was a reality long before the NT in its present form was written; prophets and apostles were living bearers of the word of the Lord. As the church moved farther away from the event of revelation it became necessary to establish a standard by which the preaching of the church could be judged. The church needed to distinguish between authoritative and nonauthoritative writings. The rise of heresy forced the formation of a canon. The written word became the standard of preaching, and in time also the source of preaching. Apart from it, we have little knowledge of the events through which God revealed himself. The unique significance of the Bible is that it is to this book that we must go for our knowledge of the revelation of himself which God has given in the prophets and in his Son.

Our interest in the method of revelation should not supplant our concern with the content of the message which God has communicated to man. This body of truth is known as the deposit of faith. Yet we must be careful not to state revealed truth in terms of a series of propositions which can be laid hold of apart from faith. There must be a note of personal encounter in all of our dealings with revelation. The Bible reveals its message to those who seek to know and follow the truth. The proclamation of the gospel will always be a stumbling block to those who refuse to receive it. Obedience is the road to spiritual knowledge. But

the proclamation of the gospel does become the wisdom of God and the power of God to those who respond to it. Through revelation, the Christian enters into an assured knowledge of the character of God; he comes to know the will of God for him in the decisions of his earthly life; and he lays hold on the hope of the salvation which God has prepared for those who love him.

**Bibliography.** E. F. Scott, *The NT Idea of Revelation* (1935); E. Brunner, *Revelation and Response* (ET, 1947); F. C. Grant, *Introduction to NT Thought* (1950); B. B. Warfield, *The Inspiration and Authority of the Bible* (1951); G. C. Berkouwer, *General Revelation* (1955); H. W. Robinson, *Inspiration and Revelation in the OT* (4th ed., 1956); J. Baillie, *The Idea of Revelation in Recent Thought* (1956); C. F. H. Henry, ed., *Revelation and the Bible: Contemporary Evangelical Thought* (1959); B. Ramm, *Special Revelation and the Word of God* (1961); H. D. McDonald, *Ideas of Revelation* (1962); G. Moran, *Theology of Revelation* (1966); K. Rahner, *Hearers of the Word* (1969); L. Morris, *I Believe in Revelation* (1976).

HOLMES ROLSTON

## Revelation, Book of. *Introduction.*

The last book of the Bible, commonly called Revelation, is usually set within the class of literature termed *apocalyptic* (Gk. *apokalupsis*, "an uncovering"). This type of literature flourished in the last two centuries B.C. and the first century A.D. (with occasional examples outside that period). Such books present problems because they abound in strange symbolism which was evidently designed to make what was said intelligible to the initiated but meaningless to those outside. Apocalyptic books were underground writings, produced by the oppressed. They proceed from a deep conviction that evil is strong, that the righteous are powerless to overcome it, but that in the end God will intervene and overthrow all the might of evil. The apocalyptists were thus both pessimistic and optimistic: pessimistic about the possibility of the defeat of the evil they saw, but optimistic because they were sure that in the end God would prevail.

Apocalypses often claim to have been written by some great one of the past such as Enoch or Abraham, and they may present past history as a prophecy in the mouth of the supposed author. In some respects Revelation is not a typical apocalypse. It names its author as John, not some great one of the past, and there is no attempt to rewrite history. Rather John stands in the present, and boldly contemplates the evil he sees, confident that in due course God will completely overthrow it all. Repeatedly he calls his book a prophecy (as in 1:3, and 22:7). He sees his present world not simply as a place dominated by evil but as the stage on which God has worked out his purpose of redemption.

*Author and Date.* Traditionally the John who claims to have written this book (1:1–4) has been understood as the apostle John. Most modern scholars hold that another John is meant, but we should bear in mind that we have knowledge of very few people named John at this time; only later did that name become common among Christians. The Greek is very curious and not at all like the Greek of John's Gospel and epistles. As, however, we know very little about the role of an amanuensis in the 1st century this proves nothing about authorship. If different amanuenses were used, or if John wrote one book himself, community of authorship could be defended. There are some striking resemblances among all the Johannine writings, but all that is certain about the author is that he was called John and that the traditional ascription to John the apostle has been neither proved nor disproved.

It is clear that the book was written in a time of persecution and a time when worship of the emperor was widespread. Tradition puts the writing of the book during the reign of the emperor Domitian, in the last decade of the 1st century. The only alternative to attract any great support suggests the reign of Nero. This is possible, but the churches in chaps. 2 and 3 seem to have been developing for some time. Ephesus had left its first love (2:4); Laodicea had acquired wealth (3:17), although the city was destroyed by an earthquake in A.D. 60/61 and must have had time for recovery. The reign of Domitian seems the probable date.

*Interpretation.* There are four main ways in which the book has been understood. (1) The "preterist" view sees the book as the 1st-century circumstances in which the writer found himself. For all subsequent Christians it has only historical interest. (2) The "futurist" view takes the opposite extreme. It sees the book, after the first three chapters, as concerned with what will happen at the end of the world. For all Christians except those in the last generation the book is merely a forecast. (3) The "historicist" view is that all of human history is surveyed in one great sweep. Within this view each interpreter has seemed to find the symbols pointing irresistibly to his own time and place, although nobody has given a convincing reason why the book should be almost exclusively concerned with the history of Western Europe. (4) The "idealist" view sees the book as concerned with great ideas and principles, not with actual happenings. It is thus relevant at all times, but the absence of any secure historical reference is a disadvantage.

None of these views is completely satisfactory, and the actual situation may include elements from more than one of them. The book was written to a little church, which had accepted the faith that Jesus was the Son of God and that he had died to put away the sins of those who believe in him. In due course he would come back again and establish that kingdom in which righteousness reigns and justice is done. But Jesus did not come back and believers suffered as much as ever. Was it all a delusion? No, says John, with the utmost firmness. The power of evil

is real, but that is no more than a temporary aberration. To see things from the perspective of heaven is to see that it is the power of God that matters. John's symbols and visions take his readers behind the scenes and make them face ultimate reality. His book is both a call to faith and a theology of power.

*Bibliography.* R. H. Charles, *A Critical and Exegetical Commentary on the Revelation of St. John,* 2 vols. (1920); H. H. Rowley, *The Relevance of Apocalyptic: A Study of Jewish and Christian Apocalypses from Daniel to Revelation* (3d ed., 1963); G. B. Caird, *A Commentary on the Revelation of St. John the Divine* (1966); I. T. Beckwith, *The Apocalypse of John* (repr. 1967); G. E. Ladd, *A Commentary on the Revelation of John* (1972); G. R. Beasley-Murray, *The Book of Revelation* (1974); P. D. Hanson, *The Dawn of Apocalyptic* (1975); W. Schmithals, *The Apocalyptic Movement: Introduction and Interpretation* (ET, 1975); J. M. Ford, *Revelation* (1975); R. H. Mounce, *The Book of Revelation* (1977); J. P. Sweet, *Revelation* (1979).

LEON MORRIS

## Reverend, The.

From the Lat. *reverendus,* gerund of *revereri,* "to pay respect," it is the most common title of a minister. In the Church of England a bishop is "right reverend" and an archbishop, "most reverend." As an adjective, "reverend" never permits a plural. To write "Rev. Jones" is incorrect. The term requires an additional title before the family name. Correct forms include: "The Rev. John H. Jones," "The Rev. Mr. Jones," or "The Rev. Dr. Jones." Like Spurgeon, ministers often prefer to be addressed as "Mister," or "Pastor." Friends and others eschew such titles. Titles such as reverend have no scriptural basis.

ANDREW W. BLACKWOOD

## Revival of Religion.

Spontaneous spiritual awakening or renewal within an individual or group. In 20th-century usage evangelistic preaching rallies, called "revivals," became part of the Protestant culture in some Western denominations. Historically the term has described various phenomena, but in the most effectual revivals regeneration of non-Christians was seen as secondary to heightened commitment and piety within Christian individuals and the organized Christian church. Renewal, not rebirth is the dominant picture, as God lifts his people dramatically and supernaturally to higher levels of living and mission.

*Scriptural Concept.* In biblical usage a spiritual revival or renewal, although calling for a response from individuals, is clearly recognized to be a work of God (Ps. 85:6; Hab. 3:2). Revivals were reported in the times of the Judges, Samuel, Elijah, Josiah, Hezekiah, and the return of the exiles from Babylon. Ezekiel's vision of the resurrection of dry bones (Ezek. 37:1–14) predicts revival for the nation of Israel. Isaiah looked for the renewal of individual righteousness to be "like streams of water in the desert" in the coming reign of Messiah (Isa. 32:2).

The revival spoken of by Joel, that God would pour out his Spirit on all flesh (2:28–29), was applied by Luke to the awakening of the church at Pentecost (Acts 2:17–21). Pentecost has been used as the biblical prototype of revivals in the church.

*Pre-1900s Revivalism.* Some of the most dramatic examples of revival within church history occurred during the 1500s in the Reformation, the 1600s in the nonconformist church of northern Europe and Britain, the 1700s in pietistic movements in Europe and the great awakenings of 1730s and 1790s in America and Great Britain, and the 1800s in great movements of the American Civil War period and the Western missionary movement. The 20th century has arguably seen less revivalism than the 19th century, and much of the 20th-century impetus resulted from 1800s work. Undeniably, however, in Wales, Africa, China, and South Korea amazing awakenings took place. Revitalizations in the West tended to be within individual congregations and small spiritual movements, although the post-Vatican Council II Roman Catholic Church enjoyed new spiritual vitality in some circles and Protestantism was infected with an unusual dose of revitalization in the Jesus movement and the related charismatic influences of the late 1960s and early 1970s.

The modern popular conception of revivalism was framed in the Second Great Awakening camp meetings in the American South (early 1800s) and particularly in the "new means" evangelism of Charles Finney. Finney and other evangelists active through the mid-1800s used psychological techniques—such as the protracted meeting and the anxious bench—and high-pressure confrontation to influence hearers to turn to Christ or reform as Christians. The human response was all important, and revivals were reduced to an almost scientific formula of means guaranteed to elicit a subjective response.

A participant in the First Great Awakening in America, Jonathan Edwards, recognized revival as first a work of God and only secondarily a work of the preacher or a response of the hearer. Some notably successful evangelists of the 1700s and 1800s, included Charles Wesley (1707–88), George Whitefield (1714–70), Asahel Nettleton (1783–1844), Ashbel Green (1762–1848), and Charles Spurgeon (1834–92). As a result at least two types of revival movement were active as the church entered the 20th century. Both used means, but the revivalist who believed these awakenings were strictly a work of God's Spirit regarded those means an ardent prayer, confession of sins, and biblical preaching. Those who regarded the revival as a human manifestation stressed emotionalism and motivation.

*20th-Century Revivals.* One of the most influential revivals of church history began in the bleak mining communities of Wales and in Welsh universities in 1904 and 1905. In its height for about one and one-half years, the revival began in Presbyterian and Methodist churches in the area around Cardiff. In that short period it produced 100,000 converts and spread through Welsh Christian communities around the world to the general society. In Cardiff the reforming influence was immediate. Police, for example, estimated that drunkenness decreased 60 percent and the jail population 40 percent. A decade later the moral influence among the entire Welsh nation was still felt.

The single most dynamic individual of the revival was Evan Roberts, a mystical, pietistic preacher influenced by the Keswick Conventions. As news and the effects of the movement spread ministers from around the Western world and some mission leaders traveled to Wales, and later to Ireland and Scotland, to observe the work of Roberts and his fellow evangelists. A large Welsh community in Pennsylvania was infected with the spirit of the revival, as were Welsh groups located in Scandinavia, and Argentina.

Welsh ministers converted or challenged to enter the ministry took the spiritual influence throughout Great Britain, and so many entered missionary service that Welsh evangelism-minded missionaries are regarded as the main reasons for the explosive growth of the African churches. Their influence on American church movements, particularly American pentecostalism, was pervasive and impossible to fully assess. The Welsh revivals, according even to some secular historians, helped prepare Great Britain for the trauma of World War I. Partly because of the awakening in Great Britain a world hunger for revivalism was born.

The work in North America was most extensive in the Methodist Church. It tended to be pietistic, nonconfessional, and greatly interested in social reform issues. W. E. Biederwolf, a revivalist, was named to head a department of evangelism in the new Federal Council of Churches. J. Wilbur Chapman and Billy Sunday introduced mass evangelism meetings. By 1911 there were 600 professional evangelists in the USA. By then the movement had lost its church base and had become commercialized and divisive. The strong liberalism of the early 1900s affected the work with the influence of the social gospel.

From Argentina revival was introduced to large sections of South America. Brazil began a seven-year revival movement in 1905, mainly centering in Baptist missions and pentecostals. In Chile a widespread effort centered in Baptist and Methodist missions.

Most important to the church history of the 20th century, however, was the African revival, which actually began in British Ceylon and India. When the Orange Free State and the South

African Republic rebelled the English army set up internment camps for political leaders and prisoners of war in Ceylon and India. Afrikaner prisoner chaplains led a prayer-based movement within the camps which spread through the Dutch Reformed Church in mass revivals after the war. Other origins of this revival are traced to a series of evangelistic meetings in Capetown with English evangelist Gipsy Smith. An evangelistic Missions of Peace evangelistic organization began in 1904 after early reports of the Welsh revival. With the infusion of English evangelistic spirit from these revivals the spiritual awakening of old mission churches and evangelistic growth spread through the southern half of Africa by 1920. The dominant evangelist of the movement was Rees Howell. The African revival stressed the unity of the body of Christ, evangelism, Scripture, and confession of sin. It involved social activism.

The revivals which may have the greatest impact on the 21st century occurred in the East, however. The first, about which much still was unknown in the 1980s, occurred on the Chinese mainland, beginning in the mid-1950s. At the proclamation of the People's Republic of China in 1949 all remaining missionaries were deported, leaving an indigenous church of less than one million people. So tight was the national controls over Chinese life that little information was available regarding the welfare of the Christians until the thaw in East-West relations in 1979. In that time the Christian population grew more than 50 times its mission size, to around 50 million people.

Communist policy in the 1950s sought to nationalize the church and allow it to die by attrition. The Three-Self Patriotic Movement was instituted as the only recognized church organization. Instead of joining, however, many Chinese Christians began an underground house church movement, studying hand-copied Scripture portions and training evangelistic teams to go into the unreached areas of the country. Most of these evangelists were quickly arrested and often executed but the secret churches grew at a phenomenal rate. Intense persecution during the Cultural Revolution (1965–69), nonexistent organization, and the lack of Bibles available caused serious problems with theology which extended into the late century, but the small cells of believers developed an informal structure centering on prayer, reading such materials as were available, and disciplined spiritual and moral life. It was estimated that potentially China might become a predominantly Christian nation in the early 2100s.

In the USA one of the more unusual awakenings in history occurred outside church organizations as well. Growing out of the drug culture and the youth rebellion of the 1960s, an intense charismatic revival stirred college campuses beginning in 1967. Some American parachurch organizations, such as Campus Crusade for Christ and InterVarsity Christian Fellowship, were able to identify the phenomenon and harness some of its enthusiasm; cultic groups also arose from the lack of spiritual direction and the distrust of organized churches which characterized what became known as the "Jesus Movement" or the "Jesus Revolution." As persons converted within the movement did enter churches they contributed to the charismatic influences on the 1970s American Christian culture.

Roy Fisher of Southwestern Baptist Theology Seminary, an early student of the Jesus Movement, identified 15 characteristics of this movement, which he said coincided remarkably with the experience of 1st-century Christianity. The Jesus people, he observed, (1) emphasized love; (2) emphasized the person of Jesus; (3) were usually Bible-based in doctrine; (4) looked for miraculous happenings; (5) demanded individual purity; (6) were enthusiastic; (7) practiced bold witnessing; (8) had a theology of hope and (9) joy; (10) were tolerant of failings of new converts; (11) were suspected by the establishment; (12) were strongly eschatological in outlook; (13) were dogmatic in belief; (14) had radically changed lives; and (15) were divided over the issue of "tongues." The appeal of the movement was to an unchurched drug culture and counter-culture who were living in a spiritual vacuum.

In many other countries revivals occurred, and evangelism increased despite prevailing secularization of "Western" countries. Interest in classic revival and revivalism was shown in great international conferences in Amerstam and Seoul in the 1980s and in regional prayer gatherings in numerous other places.

*Bibliography.* B. A. Weisberger, *They Gathered at the River: The Story of the Great Revivalists and Their Impact upon Religion in America* (1958); W. G. McLoughlin, *Modern Revivalism* (1959); W. S. Cannon, *The Jesus Revolution: New Inspiration for Evangelicals* (1971); J. B. Boles, *The Great Revival, 1787–1805* (1972); W. McLoughlin, *Revivals, Awakenings, and Reform: An Essay on Religious and Social Change in America, 1607–1977* (1978); R. Lovelace, *Dynamics of Spiritual Life* (1979); E. E. Cairns, *An Endless Line of Splendor* (1986); and several historical works by J. E. Orr.

**Revolution and Christianity.** *Political Revolution.* The medieval concept of government subjected to the universal ethics of natural law was seriously weakened during the 16th century so that the problem of the relationship of Christians to political and social revolutionary movements was raised afresh. At the outset Catholics and Protestants alike tended to emphasize the divine right of kings and to deny the right of resistance by subjects. Luther, fearing a social revolt which would jeopardize religious reform, warned that the powers that be are ordained of God and that the first duty of Christian subjects is obedience. The Christian who is wronged or persecuted is not to actively resist, but to suffer, to plead, and to pray. The Lutheran tradition has generally continued to follow a conservative path, strengthening monarchical power and resisting revolutionary currents. Anglicanism, especially in its first century, emphasized obedience and nonresistance to kings.

Calvin also advocated loyalty and submission to civil authority. He persistently urged obedience both to Christian and non-Christian rulers; he shrank from every suggestion of revolution. Nevertheless he had no liking for monarchy, for he preferred "aristocracy tempered by democracy," and he distinguished between law-abiding and tyrannical rulers. He maintained that duly elected magistrates had the right and obligation to resist an evil ruler on behalf of oppressed constituents. Although most cautiously stated, this opened the way for democratic and revolutionary thinking in the Reformed tradition. Stimulated by the conditions under which they lived, Calvinists slowly worked out the elements of constitutionalism, ideas of natural rights, and the principles of resistance to tyranny by responsible authority. In 17th-century England this Calvinist tradition combined with that of Anabaptist and Independent sects to produce a new movement that was both religious and political. In the Puritan Revolution this movement had its opportunity and the foundation of Anglo-American liberal democracy was laid; revolution was undergirded by Christian forces. The movement suffered temporary eclipse in the Restoration of 1660 but won limited victories after the Glorious Revolution of 1689 and has been a factor in English life ever since.

In the American colonies these currents, stemming in large measure from Puritan sources, had considerable opportunity. Leading American denominations, especially Congregational, Presbyterian, and Baptist, staunchly supported the Revolution. Revolutionary leaders also were influenced by the Enlightenment, and a few held rationalistic, deistic, or unitarian ideas. Anglicans were sharply divided by the Revolution; some favored the mother country while others, often influenced by the rationalist currents which had swept southern Episcopalianism, played major roles in the Revolution. American Catholics in general supported the Revolution, seeking larger liberties for themselves. Although Roman Catholicism has often shown an affinity for monarchical government and only became hostile to the authoritarian ideal in the Latin American context of the late 1900s, there are strands of antiabsolutist thought in Catholic political theory. Jesuits such as Juan de Mariana, Luis de Molina, Robert Bellarmine, and Francisco Suárez developed theories of responsible government and the restraint of kings. Catholicism generally adjusted to various patterns of government.

The American Revolution was guided by a concept of higher law, while in the French Revolution the law was defined by the general will as expressed in a legislative majority, giving a unitary, intolerant, egalitarian character to French democracy. The Catholic Church consistently opposed the Revolution. Pope Pius VI sought to call the nation back to the Christian doctrine of obedience to kings. The church was separated from the state during the Revolution and was divided into three segments, each with a different attitude toward the Revolution. Napoleon healed the schisms and reestablished Catholicism, but the antipathy of church to revolution continued throughout the 19th century, with some notable exceptions, as in Belgium and Ireland. Protestants in England and America at first welcomed the French Revolution as the end of the old regime, but there was reaction against its excesses, and a conservative stamp marked 19th-century Protestantism. In the face of 20th-century totalitarianism there has been general Christian acceptance of the right of revolution, evident notably in Lutheran circles.

***Social Revolution.*** By the mid-1800s the effects of the Industrial Revolution were shattering traditional ways and stimulating social revolution. Socialism was steadily resisted by Catholicism, but adjustment to social crisis was prepared for by the encyclical *Rerum novarum* of Leo XIII (1891), which approved trade unionism as a means to social justice. Although the gulf between Protestantism and socialism remained wide, there were points of contact. Groups of Christian socialists exhorted the churches to be aware of the cry for social justice, and on Protestant soil socialism tended to be less atheistic and violent, more humane and parliamentary. Antireligious communism was steadily opposed by most Christians. Catholicism regarded it with extreme hostility. Some liberal Protestants, remembering the social injustices under the czars, at first viewed the revolution hopefully, but as the record of purges, prison camps, church closings, and threats to democratic nations became clear, the Protestant churches became increasingly antagonistic. Christianity's positive approach to the social revolution has been through Christian social movements which have influenced both Catholicism and Protestantism and enabled them to deal with social and industrial changes with some creativity.

ROBERT T. HANDY

***20th-Century Developments.*** The 1900s tested Reformation theologies of the Christian's responsibility to the state. Atheist totalitarian revolutions brought many antireligious policies to the surface. Some revolutionary movements sought to use Christian activities for political purposes. In some Oriental, Middle East, and African countries Christianity was outlawed as a revolutionary movement inimical to the values of society, and in some traditionally Christian countries there were social upheavals within church and state. In general Christian reaction to national revolution continued trends from 19th-century philosophy and theology.

The world church in general was politically conservative through the first half of the century. One major exception was Northern Ireland's centuries-old conflict with the English, a division which cut along Protestant-Catholic lines. Since Irish society revolved around the church, leaders on both sides cultivated political alliances within their respective Christian communities. In the turbulent 1920s and 1930s Spanish Roman Catholics felt compelled to side with revolutionary forces because of the anti-Catholic policies of the socialist Second Republic government. Catholics were identified with a conservative movement which General Francisco Franco needed for his army-led revolution in 1936. The Spanish Christians thus found themselves de facto allies with Nazi Germany and fascist Italy in the Spanish Civil War.

In Europe, however, both Protestants and Catholics found themselves in opposition to national socialism. Government leaders sought to pacify Christians through strict controls over ministers and their activities. A large number of believers, symbolized by the Confessing Church movement in Germany, openly or secretly joined antigovernment bodies. The "underground," particularly in the Low Countries, was largely comprised of Christians. Some Christians joined resistance armies; the dominant ethic of the Christian underground, however, was to avoid violence while doing all that was humanly possible to ameliorate injustice.

Different kinds of revolutionary fervor were waiting to be unleashed in the West, however. The first of these to surface came in the American civil rights movement which largely arose within the black churches. This was a social revolutionary struggle with pacifistic methods which borrowed from nonviolent Hindu philosophy. Reaction by local government was occasionally violent and was supportive by white Christians. The race crisis, centered in urban and southern areas, was an issue which reached across all of American society and pitted black against white and black Christian against white Christian.

In the USA a peaceful revolution in attitudes eventually began, but in South Africa much deeper political and historical factors caused the sides to entrench. Christian revolutionists—predominantly blacks, mixed-race "coloreds," and Asians—allied with socialist and communist movements against a system of white Afrikaner supremacy and segregation known as apartheid. From the institution of apartheid in 1949 racial tensions in both society and church slowly heightened into a bitter civil conflict which infected the region four decades later. Related to civil rights was the antiwar and antinuclear movements, in which Christians were involved in the USA and Europe. Such movements were primarily influenced by modernist Protestant and Roman Catholic theologies, although many conservative Christians became involved in the civil rights struggles in the USA and South Africa, and some were sympathetic toward pacifist aims. On one set of issues the revolutionists were primarily evangelical conservative Protestants and Roman Catholics—abortion, withholding food and water from some infants and elderly persons, and euthanasia. In the USA and Canada successful legal maneuvers to legalize and even promote the right of women to end their pregnancies stimulated intense reactions among those who viewed all persons as created by God in his image. Largely nonviolent, the "right-to-life" movement was mostly nonviolent but was decidedly revolutionary in its attitude toward the society's legal system.

One of the most deliberately reasoned theological approaches to the problem of Christianity and revolutionary struggle was that of Jürgen Moltmann, especially as applied by Gustavo Gutiérrez and José Míguez-Bonino. Their liberation theology was designed to frame a response to injustices within Latin American society. The theology was used, with some adjustments, in other third world contexts of the late 1900s and the American civil rights movement in the 1970s.

Basically liberation theology taught that "authentic" Christian practice (called praxis) focuses Christ's love by liberating the oppressed. Strongly anticipating Christ's kingdom, the church strives to create that kingdom by destroying the sin of disruption and oppression. While liberation theology was born within Roman Catholicism it had an enormous impact on the thinking of mainline churches from the late 1960s through the 1980s. By 1990 its black theology counterpart, designed by James Cone in the USA, was waning, and the active participation of some priests and nuns in left-wing South American coups dampened public support when the new governments themselves became oppressive. The movement was, however, the one uniquely 20th-century approach to revolution from a Christian tradition.

*Bibliography.* W. Rauschenbusch, *Christianity and the Social Crisis* (1907); C. Dawson, *Religion and the Modern State* (1936); J. T. McNeill, *Christian Hope for World Society* (1937); J. H. Nichols, *Democracy and the Churches* (1951); G. Gutiérrez, *A Theology of Liberation* (ET, 1973); A. F. Holmes, ed., *War and Christian Ethics* (1975); J. Míguez-Bonino, *Doing Theology in a Revolutionary Situation* (1975); S. N. Gundry and A. F. Johnson, eds., *Tensions in Contemporary Theology* (2d ed., 1976).

**Reward.** The completion of a deed; a consequence of action. Sometimes reward is referred to as wages. In God's covenant with Israel he promised good things for obedience, disaster and death for violation. The history of the judges and kings was written in terms of reward for faithfulness and punishment for sin and idolatry. Earthly victory and national welfare depended on obedience (as in Josh. 1:7–9; Judg. 2).

In the psalms and wisdom literature reward and punishment were applied to individual life. Ps. 1 points the contrast between the wise pious man and the ungodly fool, but the counterpoint is in Ps. 103:10: "He does not treat us as our sins deserve." Echoing Ps. 73, Proverbs and Ecclesiastes sound a pessimistic note in observing that the righteous suffer and the wicked prosper, or that a common fate awaits all. Job struggles with his friends because he sees no strict pattern of reward for righteousness and punishment for evil. Jesus speaks primarily of earthly rewards as flowing from God's grace (Matt. 6:25–34; 7:11). Jesus advises seeking reward in the spiritual relation with God (Matt. 6:4, 6, 18), or in the age to come (Matt. 6:20; Mark 10:21). He also calls for service without thought of reward (e.g., Luke 9:57–62; 14:25–33). The reward motive is played down also in Matt. 20:1–16, Mark 8:35, and Luke 17:7–10. Putting the kingdom first was the true priority (Matt. 6:33). Paul's great theme is that God in Christ freely justifies the believer and that he thereupon enters into the privileges of the new life in Christ where he enjoys the gifts of the Spirit in reward and victory. The Christian shares in Christ's reward but is also individually accountable (Rom. 2:6–11; 14:10; cf. 1 Cor. 3: 10–17). Like Jesus, Paul seldom refers to reward in this life beyond what flows from obedience (Eph. 6:2) or God's gracious provision (Phil. 4:17–19). Usually he projects the rewards into the future life, when the great reward will be the possession of eternal life (Gal. 6:8).

**Rhodesia.** *See* SOUTH AFRICA, REPUBLIC OF; SOUTHERN AFRICA.

**Rice, John R.** (1895–1980). Fundamentalist evangelist and author. Born in Cooke County, Tex., Rice was educated at Decatur Baptist College, Baylor University, and Southwestern Baptist Theological Seminary. He taught and coached athletics at Wayland Baptist College (1921/22), served churches in Texas, and then entered full-time evangelism in 1940. Perhaps the most prominent mid-century fundamentalist, Rice authored well over 100 books and pamphlets. He founded (1934) and edited the weekly *Sword of the Lord,* founded (1959) and organized the "Voice of Revival" radio program, and conducted the popular "Sword Conferences" on revival and soul winning.

NORRIS A. MAGNUSON

**Richards, George Warren** (1869–1955). Evangelical and Reformed pastor and educator. Born in Farmington, Pa., he studied at Muhlenberg College, Franklin and Marshall College (D.D., 1902), Theological Seminary of the Reformed Church in the United States, and at the universities of Berlin and Erlangen. He pastored the Salem Reformed Church, Allentown, Pa. (1890–99). He was professor of church history in the Theological Seminary of the Reformed Church in the United States (1899–1939; president, 1920–39). He was visiting professor at the Biblical Seminary of New York (1932–38), and visiting professor of historical theology at Temple University (1935–51). He was the editor of the *Reformed Church Review* (1904–11); president of the Alliance of Reformed Churches Holding the Presbyterian System (1929–33); and president of the Evangelical and Reformed Church (1934–38; emeritus, 1940– ). Among his publications are *The Heidelberg Catechism—Historical and Doctrinal Studies* (1913), *Christian Ways of Salvation* (1923), *Beyond Fundamentalism and Modernism* (1934), and *Creative Controversies in Christianity* (1938). With C. N. Heller, he published translations of Zwingli's *True and False Religion* and *Reply to Emser.* He also did translations of two volumes of sermons by Barth and Thurneysen under the English titles *Come Holy Spirit* (1933) and *God's Search for Man* (1935).

RAYMOND W. ALBRIGHT

**Richardson, Alan** (1905–1975). Anglican scholar and dean of York. Born in Wigan, Lancashire, he was educated at the universities of Liverpool and Oxford, and at Ridley Hall, Cambridge. After brief periods as Student Christian Movement (SCM) secretary, curate, and theological college chaplain, he was vicar of Cambo (1934–38); SCM study secretary (1938–43); canon of Durham Cathedral (1943–53); professor of Christian theology, University of Nottingham (1953–64); and dean of York (1964–75). He wrote *Creeds in the Making* (1935), *Miracle Stories of the Gospels* (1941), *Preface to Bible Study* (1943), *Christian Apologetics* (1948), *Science, History and Faith* (1950), *Biblical Doctrine of Work* (1952), *Genesis I–X* (1953), *Introduction to the Theology of the NT* (1958), *Sacred and Profane* (1964), *Religion in Contemporary Debate* (1966), and *The Political Christ* (1973). In addition, he edited *Theological Word Book of the Bible* (1950), and *A Dictionary of Christian Theology* (1969).

**Richardson, Cyril Charles** (1909–1976). Anglican church historian. Born in London, he studied at the University of Saskatchewan; Emmanuel College, Saskatoon; Union Theological Seminary, New York; and the University of Göttingen. Professor of church history at Union Theological Seminary from 1949, he contributed extensively to symposia and periodicals. Richardson wrote *The Christianity of Ignatius of Antioch* (1935), *The Church Through the Centuries* (1938), *The Sacrament of Reunion* (1940), *The Eucharist in Zwingli and Cranmer* (1949), *Early Christian Fathers* (1953), and *The Doctrine of the Trinity* (1958). He edited *The Pocket Bible* (1951).

**Riley, William Bell** (1861–1947). Fundamentalist leader, Baptist minister, and educator. A graduate of Hanover College (Indiana) and Southern Baptist Theological Seminary, he served churches in Kentucky, Indiana, and Illinois, before becoming pastor of the First Baptist Church of Minneapolis (1897–1942). He founded the Northwestern Bible School (1902), Seminary (1935), and College (1944). Among the most prominent fundamentalist leaders, he was president of the World's Christian Fundamentals Association for a decade after its founding in 1919, and leader of the fundamentalist forces among Northern Baptists. He lectured and wrote extensively in opposition to evolution and communism. He authored nearly 20 books in addition to the 40-volume *Bible of the Expositor and the Evangelist.*

NORRIS A. MAGNUSON

**Ritschl, Otto Karl Albrecht** (1860–1944). German Protestant theologian. Son of Albrecht Ritschl, he was born in Bonn, educated at the universities of Göttingen, Bonn, and Giessen, and in 1885 became privatdocent for church history at the University of Halle. In 1889 he became associate professor at Kiel, returning in 1894 to Bonn where he became full professor of systematic theology from 1897. It had been said that, building on his father's foundations, he helped to develop the disciplined study of the history of dogma. He wrote *De epistulis Cyprianicis* (1885), *Cyprian von Karthago und die Verfassung der Kirche* (1885), *Schleiermacher's Stellung zum Christentum in seinen Reden über die Religion* (1888), *Das christliche Lebensideal in Luthers Auffassung* (1889), *Albrecht Ritschls Leben* (2 vols., 1892–96), *über Welturteile* (1895), *Nietzsches Welt- und Lebensanschauung in ihrer Entstehung und Entwicklung* (1897), *Die Causalbetrachtung in der Geisteswissenschaft* (1901), *Wissenschaftliche Ethik und moralische Gesetzebung* (1903), *Die freie Wissenschaft und der Idealismus auf den deutschen Universitäten* (1905), *System und systematische Methode in der Geschichtedes wissenschaftlichen Sprachgebrauchs und der philosophischen Methodologie* (1906), and *Dogmengeschichte des Protestantismus* (4 vols., 1908–27).

**Ritter, Gerhard** (1888–1967). Evangelical educator. Born in Sooden an der Werra, Hesse, he studied at the universities of Munich, Leipzig, Berlin, and Heidelberg (Dr. Phil., 1911). He taught at secondary schools in Kassel, Magdeburg (1912–14), and was a soldier in World War I (1915–18). He became research assistant and lecturer in Heidelberg (1919–21), and later was professor of modern history in Hamburg (1924/25) and then in Freiburg (Baden) (1925– ). He was imprisoned by the Gestapo (1944), tried at the Volksgerichtshof, Berlin, but was set free in 1945 by the approaching Russian army. His writings include *Studien zur Spätscholastik* (3 vols., 1921–27), *Luther, Gestalt und Tat* (5th ed., 1949), *Die Heidelberger Universität*, Bd. I: *Das Mittelalter 1386–1509* (1936), *Die Neugestaltung Europas im Zeitalter der Reformation und der Glaubenskämpfe* (1942, 2d ed., 1950), *Die Weltwirkung der Reformation* (1940), *Die Dämonie der Macht* (1940, 6th ed., 1948), *Vom sittlichen Problem der Macht* (1948), *Friedrich d. Grosse* (1936, 2d ed., 1942), *Stein. Eine politische Biographie* (2 vols., 1931), and *Europa und die deutsche Frage* (1948).

**River Brethren.** Small groups of evangelical Christians who emerged from a nucleus of about 30 Anabaptist families who fled severe persecution in Basel, Switzerland in 1750 for England. Finally settling in Lancaster County, Pa., in early 1752, in about 1770 these and other German-speaking people of Lutheran, Mennonite, and Baptist churches formed brotherhoods in response to a revival movement in the area. They reacted to formalism in their respective churches, but did not agree among themselves on the mode of baptism and the interpretation of Scripture. Those who practiced threefold immersion came to be known by 1778 as River Brethren, probably because their settlements were along the Susquehanna River, Pa. Jacob Engel, one of the original Basel families, became their first minister. Splinter groups emerged over disagreements regarding specific applications of Scripture to practices in worship and conduct. One such group evolved in 1828 under John Wenger, another in 1860 under John Swank. Some formed a union in 1883 with the Evangelical United Mennonites, known as the Mennonite Brethren in Christ or simply, "Brethren in Christ." Later this group became the United Missionary Church. Other splinter groups in the mid-19th century were the "Yorkers" (Old Order Brethren) and the "Brinsers," later referred to as United Zion's Children. The modern organizational structure emerged around 1820. During the Civil War the group had to gain official recognition in order to maintain its pacifist practices. Incorporation took place in 1904.

Brethren in Christ combine Anabaptist and pietist tenets. They are essentially congregational, although there are district and state councils and a general conference. They recognize three orders of ministry: bishop, minister, and deacon. Bishops are in charge of the worship and administration of the denomination, ministers perform teaching duties, and deacons take responsibility for the physical well-being of the denomination.

Active missionary outreach, pursuit of nonresistance, and educational work through two colleges and two academies and participation in the Mennonite Central Committee characterized the denomination in the 1900s. Most congregations were found in Pennsylvania and Canada, with a publishing house in Nappanee, Ind. The denomination listed 16,382 members in 1986 in 173 congregations. It published the *Evangelical Visitor.* Care must be taken not to confuse the several Brethren groups which, despite their many common theological tenets, differ in their respective development and growth. These include the United Brethren, the Brethren in Christ Fellowship, and the Church of the United Brethren in Christ.

*See also* UNITED BRETHREN IN CHRIST.

**Bibliography.** A. W. Climenhaga, *History of the Brethren in Christ Church* (1942); J. A. Huffman, *History of the Mennonite Brethren in Christ Church* (1986).

E. J. FURCHA

**Roberts, David Everett** (1911–1955). Presbyterian educator. Born in Omaha, Nebr., he studied at Occidental College, Union Theological Seminary, Edinburgh University (Ph.D., 1936), Oxford, Marburg, and Göttingen. He was on the faculty of Union Theological Seminary from 1936, dean of students (1939–45), and Marcellus Hartley professor of the philosophy of religion (1950). He was a member of the staff of the study department of the World Council of Churches (1949). His chief activities, besides teaching, were college student work and training in pastoral counseling. He wrote *Psychotherapy and a Christian View of Man* (1950), and he and H. P. Van Dusen edited *Liberal Theology* (1942).

**Roberts, Edward Howell** (1895–1954). Pastor and educator. Born in Middle Granville, N.Y., he studied at Ripon College, Wis.; University of Wisconsin; Princeton Theological Seminary; University of Southern California; and University of California. He was assistant pastor of First Presbyterian Church in New Rochelle, N.Y. (1923), and did educational work in Los Angeles (1926–30). He held positions at Princeton Theological Seminary as instructor in systematic theology (1930–37); registrar (1932–37); dean of students (1937–45); associate professor of homiletics (1937–53); dean (1945–54); and professor of homiletics (1953/54). He was executive secretary of the American Association of Theological Schools (1938–42) and president (1952–54).

**Roberts, Granville Oral** (1918– ). American evangelist and administrator. Born near Ada, Okla., he studied at Oklahoma Baptist University and Phillips University. He considered himself basically an evangelist, having been ordained in the Pentecostal Holiness Church at the age of 18. He served various pastorates for short periods (1941–47), then began what developed into a worldwide outreach of crusades, broadcasting, and literature. He was the founder of the Oral Roberts Evangelistic Association, and among the many institutions and projects that emerged from his work is Oral Roberts University (1963). In 1968 he became a Methodist minister. Among his published writings are *If You Need Healing, Do These Things* (1947), *God Is a Good God* (1960), *If I Were You* (1967), *Miracle of Seed-Faith* (1970), his autobiography, *The Call* (1971), *The Miracle Book* (1972), *A Daily Guide to Miracles* (1976), and *Don't Give Up* (1980).

**Roberts, Thomas D'Esterre** (1893–1976). Roman Catholic archbishop. Born in Le Havre, France, he entered the Jesuit Order in 1909 and was ordained in 1925. He served as a schoolmaster and was rector of St. Francis Xavier's College, Liverpool, when he was appointed archbishop of Bombay, India in 1937. There he had a remarkable ministry among the poor, the lowly, and the lost. In 1950 he resigned and returned to England, but not before making successful overtures to the pope to appoint an Indian to replace him. His deeply held convictions that found him at odds with the hierarchy, notably on birth control and on the evil waste of war (see his chapter in *Objections to Roman Catholicism*, ed. Michael de la Bedoyere, 1964, pp. 165–84) made him the center of controversy in his latter years. He was the author of *Black Popes* (1954).

J. D. DOUGLAS

**Robertson, Archibald Thomas** (1863–1934). American NT scholar. Born near Chatham, Va., he was educated at Wake Forest College and then at Southern Baptist Theological Seminary, where he taught until his death. He was instructor in NT interpretation (1888–92), professor of biblical introduction (1892–95), and professor of NT interpretation (1895–1934). His numerous books include *Syllabus of NT Greek Syntax* (1900), *Bibliography of NT Greek* (1903), *Teaching of Jesus Concerning God the Father* (1904), *Key-Words in the Teaching of Jesus* (1906), *Epochs in the Life of Paul* (1909), *Commentary on Matthew* (1910), *John the Loyal* (1911), *Studies in the Epistle of James* (1915), *The Divinity of Christ in the Gospel of John* (1916), *Making Good in the Ministry* (1918), *Studies in Mark's Gospel* (1919), *Harmony of the Gospels* (1922), *The Minister and His Greek NT* (1923), *An Introduction to the Textual Criticism of the NT* (1925), *Paul and the Intellectuals* (1928), *Word Pictures in the NT* (6 vols., 1930–33), *A New Short Grammar of the Greek Testament* (1931), and *Passing on the Torch and Other Ser-*

*mons* (1934). He was editor and contributing editor to many biblical series, including the Hastings' Dictionaries and "The 1911 Bible," and was also a member of the revision committee for the American Standard Bible.

RAYMOND W. ALBRIGHT

**Robinson, Henry Wheeler** (1872–1945). Baptist minister, professor, and lecturer. Born in Northampton, he was educated at Regent's Park College, London; Edinburgh University; Mansfield College, Oxford; Marburg University; and Strasburg University. He served as minister of Pitlochry Baptist Church (1900–1903) and Coventry (1903–6). He was professor of philosophy of religion in Rawdon College, Leeds (1906–20), and principal of Regent's Park College (1920–42). During his time as principal, the college moved from London to Oxford. Speaker's Lecturer in biblical studies at the University of Oxford, Robinson became an acknowledged leader in OT studies in Great Britain. He wrote *The Christian Doctrine of Man* (1911), *The Religious Ideas of the OT* (1913), *The Cross of Job* (1916), *The Life and Faith of the Baptists* (1927), *The Christian Experience of the Holy Spirit* (1928), *The History of Israel* (1938), *Suffering, Human and Divine* (1939), *Redemption and Revelation* (1942), and *Inspiration and Revelation*. He also edited *Record and Revelation* (1938).

F. W. DILLISTONE

**Robinson, John Arthur Thomas** (1919–1983). Anglican theologian and bishop. Born in Canterbury, he was educated at Cambridge where his Ph.D. thesis in 1946 was said by his examiner to have been "the best ever to have come my way." Accepted by William Temple for ordination, he was a curate in Bristol (1945–48); chaplain of Wells Theological College (1948–51); and fellow and dean of Clare College, Cambridge (1951–59). In 1959 he was consecrated suffragan bishop of Woolwich and, according to his biographer, "was soon recognized as the leading radical of the Church of England." His views were reflected in *Honest to God* (1963) which sold over a million copies and caused an outcry in more conservative circles. In 1969 he returned to Cambridge as fellow, dean of chapel, and lecturer in theology at Trinity College, but failed to win further academic or ecclesiastical promotion. He was much in demand as a lecturer worldwide, and participated in the translation of the New English Bible. Among his numerous other published works are *Jesus and His Coming* (1957), *The New Reformation?* (1965), *In the End God* (1968), *Christian Freedom in a Permissive Society* (1970), *The Human Face of God* (1973), *Redating the NT* (1976), *Truth Is Two-Eyed* (1979), *The Roots of a Radical* (1980), *The Priority of John* (1985), and *Where Three Ways Meet* (1987).

J. D. DOUGLAS

**Robinson, Lucien Moore** (1858–1932). Episcopalian. Born in Hartford, Maine, he was educated at Harvard and Haverford. After serving as assistant rector at the Church of the Epiphany, Philadelphia (1888–92), he taught liturgics and ecclesiastical polity at the Philadelphia Divinity School (1891–1928). He was the custodian of the standard *Book of Common Prayer*, wrote *Introduction to the Prayer Book* (1911), and edited Murray's *Manual of Mythology* (1895).

RAYMOND W. ALBRIGHT

**Robinson, Theodore Henry** (1881–1964). English OT scholar. Born in Edenbridge, Kent, he studied at the universities of Cambridge, London, and Göttingen. He held positions as professor of Hebrew and Syriac in Bengal (1908–15), and lecturer (1915–27) and professor (1927–44) of Semitic languages at University College, Cardiff. His famous partnership with Oesterley produced *Hebrew Religion* (1930), *History of Israel* (1932), and *Introduction to the Books of the OT* (1934). His works also include *Prophecy and the Prophets* (1923), *Poets and Poetry in the OT* (1947), and *A Short Comparative History of Religions* (1951).

**Robson, James** (1890–1981). Scottish minister and Arabic scholar. Born in Port Glasgow, he studied at Glasgow University and taught Hebrew there, but left to serve with the YMCA in Mesopotamia and India during World War I (1916–18). He was lecturer at Forman Christian College, Lahore, India (1918–19); missionary at Sheikh Othman, Aden (1919–26); minister at Shandon, Scotland (1926–28); lecturer in Arabic at Glasgow University (1928–49); and professor of Arabic, Manchester University (1949–58). Among his writings are *Ion Keith-Falconer of Arabia* (1924), *Christ in Islam* (1929), *Tracts on Listening to Music* (1938), *Ancient Arabian Musical Instruments* (1938), and *An Introduction to the Science of Tradition* (1953). He was sectional editor on Islam in *A Dictionary of Comparative Religion* (1970).

**Rockwell, William Walker** (1874–1958). Congregationalist. Born in Pittsfield, Mass., he studied at Harvard, Andover, Göttingen (Ph.D., 1914), and Marburg (Th.D., 1930). He was instructor at Andover (1904–5) before going to Union Theological Seminary, N.Y., were he was professor of church history (1905–25), librarian (1925–42), and later achieved emeritus status (1942– ). He was secretary and editor (1912–17) and president (1926) of the American Society of Church History. His publications include *Die Doppelehe des Landgrafen Philipp von Hessen* (1904), *Liber Miraculorum Sancti Cornelii Ninivensis* (1914, indexed ed., 1925), and *Rival Presuppositions in the Writing of Church History* (1934).

# Roman Catholic Church since 1950.

The profound changes in the Roman Catholic Church since 1950, arguably more far-reaching than any in the previous three or four centuries, led inevitably to altered relations with the world outside the church. It seems best therefore to first address changes within the church and then external relations.

A momentous development came with the encyclical *Divino afflante Spiritu* published by Pius XII in 1943. The attitude prevalent since the condemnation of modernism by Pius X in the papal decree *Lamentabili sane exitu* (1907) and the encyclical *Pascendi dominici gregis* (1907) had been that the Scriptures and theology ought to be approached in scholastic terms. The 1943 encyclical, however, opened the Scriptures to investigation using modern methods that integrated Scripture and tradition more closely. The results were dramatic. Theologians studied the Bible with concern for the context of their writing and the intention of the author as well as its literal content. They investigated dogmas in terms of their development within the faith experience of the church that defined them. The philosophical categories of Aristotle and Thomas Aquinas that were popular before 1950 gave way to historical and literary categories. Systematic theologians such as Karl Rahner were inspired to use Thomism in new ways, regarding developments in philosophy and especially in epistemology. Historical studies, which had been going on since the beginning of the century, caused an interaction among sacramental theology, ecclesiology, and dogma, integrating theological thought and pastoral ministry in an extraordinarily effective way. These new principles came into play when Pius XII defined the dogma of the assumption in 1950. He based the decision on constant Catholic piety through the ages and the dignity of Mary contained in Scripture.

The new stress on pastoral theology brought about changes in the sacraments that affected all Catholics. Parents received instruction to prepare them for infant baptism and their role in the Christian development of the child. Penance, now known as the sacrament of reconciliation, emphasized counseling the penitent, with face-to-face confession an option. The sacrament of the sick, formerly extreme unction, was administered more frequently, in keeping with historical study of the practice of the early church, and a revived permanent diaconate provided more ministers under holy orders. Dioceses required more thorough preparation for marriage and confirmation than before as a defense against divorce and loss of faith. Perhaps the most obvious of all liturgical changes concerned the Eucharist. The Benedictines and Josef Jungmann, a Jesuit, led a movement first to follow the Mass using missals, then to revise the lectionary, use the vernacular,

and have the priest face the people to make the altar a eucharistic banquet table. Changes in church architecture using modern materials and forms followed, and the altar was more centrally located. After Vatican Council II the homily regained an important part in the service of the Word. In the process, however, the stately Latin language and the beautiful Gregorian chant suffered a decline, offset somewhat by new hymns with origins in national musical traditions.

Moral theology did not seem to benefit directly from the changes. With the rise of concern for correcting injustice and with the decline of eschatology, a certain confusion entered church discipline, particularly in the areas of situational and sexual ethics. Pope Paul VI refused to be swayed by the majority of a commission he had established, and his encyclical, *Humanae vitae* (1968), repeated earlier condemnations of artificial birth control and abortion. Reaffirmation by John Paul II was followed in 1987 by a papal admonition against *in vitro* fertilization, surrogate motherhood, and other forms of medical and technological interference in human reproduction. Opinion polls in developed countries indicated widespread opposition among Catholics to papal teaching, but the popes remained firm. On the other hand, a rise in concern for social justice on a worldwide scale led to revised conceptions of evangelization and unprecedented social involvement by Catholics. This was especially true in Latin America, where social activists developed a theology of liberation. In addition, the openness to differences among cultures fostered a movement for inculturation and a reliance on native clergy to lead the church.

Accompanying developments in moral theology and missiology was a demographic shift in church membership away from Europe and North America southward to Latin America and the third world. A decline in churchgoing in Western Europe was offset by rapid population growth in the traditionally Catholic countries of Latin America and conversions in Africa and Asia. While the percentage of Christians of all sorts in the developed countries fell from 77 percent in 1900 to 72 percent in 1965 to a projected 65 percent by the year 2000, the percentage in Latin America and the third world grew from 6 percent in 1900 to 15 percent in 1965 to a projected 23 percent of the total population by 2000. The Vatican recognized this shift by including more representatives of the third world in the curia and by enlarging the number of cardinals. It was dramatized by the election of a Pole, Karol Wojtyla, as pope John Paul II after the one-month reign of the Italian John Paul I.

A less felicitous demographic development affected the clerical and religious states of life. After rising sharply in the 1950s, the number of candidates for the priesthood dropped in the

1960s, and departures among priests, nuns, and brothers took on alarming proportions. Many of those who left were young, which raised the average age of the remaining members. Religious orders of women in the West were especially hard hit, although the Jesuits, the largest order of men in the church, dropped from 36,000 in 1965 to 29,000 in 1974 and 25,000 in 1986. Nevertheless, Mother Teresa of Calcutta founded a new congregation that flourished. Shortages of priests increased debate about the rule of celibacy, the ordination of women, and the role of the laity in ministry. Popes reaffirmed the traditional stance on celibacy and women's ordination, but laypeople were increasingly involved in eucharistic ministry, liturgy, ministry to the sick, catechetics, and financial administration.

Developments in individual and communal spirituality influenced the demand for new kinds of leadership. A retreat movement for adults grew in the 1950s and 1960s; a charismatic movement followed. A number of religious congregations revised their rules after Vatican II to adapt the spirit of their founders to modern conditions. Religious habits were often put aside for lay dress. As teaching orders involved in Catholic education in the West declined they were replaced by lay teachers. Significant too, was the emergence of secular institutes such as Opus Dei, whose members took vows but did not live in community. Another effect of Vatican II on the communal life of the church came with the revision of the Code of Canon Law which was promulgated in 1983.

As the relatively high degree of centralization under Pius XII gave way to episcopal collegiality and respect for diverse cultural backgrounds after Vatican II, the homogeneity of the Roman Catholic Church came to be based less in outward conformity. A remarkable diversity began to appear among different groups, sometimes excessively liberal, as in Holland during the experimentation after Vatican II, and sometimes strictly conservative, as among churches in communist countries. The difficulty of reconciling these divergent trends made the task of governing the church unusually difficult. The Vatican censured theologians such as Hans Küng in Europe, Charles Curran in North America, and Leonardo Boff in Brazil, and intervened in the governance of the Jesuits, all of which made headlines in the secular news media. The Catholic press and communications media, which had lost influence and consisted mostly of occasional periodicals, were not equal to explaining Catholic positions cogently to answer hostile secular media or the controlled press of Eastern countries. Energetic visits around the world by John Paul II, his uncompromising quest for unity and orthodoxy, and the well-publicized good will shown to him in most places did much to offset internal and external criticism.

The role of the church in education also changed significantly from 1950. For a variety of reasons, notably a different attitude toward religious freedom and the impossibility of providing materially for all Catholic children, church leaders no longer pressed Catholic parents to send their children to Catholic schools. Instead they emphasized that Christians should act as a leaven in the fact-oriented disciplines of public education. Church-related schools also began to accept increasing numbers of non-Catholic students.

Ferment in the Roman Catholic Church necessarily colored attitudes toward other religious and political bodies. One important development was the rise of ecumenism. Substantial agreement on approaches to Scripture among Catholic, Anglican, and mainline Protestant theologians, as well as a recognition that fault lay on all sides in the historic divisions, paved the way for statements which highlighted common ground on doctrinal matters such as the Eucharist, marriage, holy orders, and the primacy of the Roman See. A Secretariat for Promoting Christian Unity under Cardinal Augustin Bea, set up by John XXIII in 1960, was followed by Roman Catholic participation at the plenary meeting of the World Council of Churches (WCC) in 1961 and Catholic membership on the Commission for Faith and Order of the WCC by the mid-1970s. Nonetheless, Paul VI in 1969 rejected full membership by the Roman Catholic Church. The Anglican decision to ordain women and the rise of biblical fundamentalism with its aggressive proselytizing among Catholics detracted from the ecumenical spirit of the previous three decades.

Ultimately, incompatible attitudes toward authority in the church, including the knotty question of papal infallibility, dampened ecumenical efforts in the 1980s. A church commission on dialog with atheists and unbelievers met with little success. Despite renewed interest among Westerners toward the Eastern churches and ecumenical initiatives pursued by John XXIII, Paul VI, and Patriarch Athenagoras, as well as membership of Orthodox churches in WCC, the fragmentation among Orthodox churches, their difficulties with communist regimes, and their historic isolation dashed hopes for unity between East and West. Relations between Catholics and Muslims became worse, if anything, during this time, nor did the Vatican extend diplomatic recognition to the state of Israel.

Regarding church-state relations in the West, the close association of the Catholic Church with political parties characteristic of the previous century began to loosen after World War II. Catholic Action continued to provide focal points for social engagement seeking not to be excessively involved in politics. Formerly Catholic political parties in Western Europe broadened to include all Christians and became a Christian Democratic political movement that stood for Christian values and moderate capitalism. Catholics such as Konrad Adenauer (West Germany), Alcide De Gasperi (Italy), and Charles de Gaulle (France) brought a Christian focus to politics as they maintained the understanding built in the Nazi concentration camps among Catholics, socialists, and secular humanists. Religious pluralism was acknowledged at Vatican II by an important statement on the inviolability of conscience, religious liberty, and the saving action of God among people of good will. These developments had been anticipated by the work of John Courtney Murray, who reexamined the problem of relations between church and state in the light of the broader question of the church in society.

The diplomatic practice of arranging concordats between the Vatican and governments on questions of mutual interest like education, religious institutes, marriage, and church property continued after World War II. It was, however, qualified by more regional agreements between bishops and states and by ad hoc protocols with governments hesitant to conclude biding agreements or hostile to church ideology. Direct involvement by the Vatican with secular governments was also modified by an increasing willingness of national bishops conferences to address political concerns directly. The American bishops issued pastoral letters on nuclear weapons and on the economy, and the bishops of the Philippines, led by Cardinal Jaime Sin, played an important part in ending the Marcos dictatorship there.

Relations with communist countries were characterized by a period of extreme alienation in the 1950s following the imprisonment of Cardinals Stefan Wyszynski in Poland, Jozsef Mindszenty in Hungary, and Aloysius Stepinac in Yugoslavia, along with large numbers of clergy and religious. The death of Joseph Stalin and movements to shake off Soviet hegemony led to slight improvements, and the eastern policy of the Vatican under Paul VI, implemented by Archbishop Agostino Casaroli, eased relations with communist states. The Soviet invasion of Czechoslovakia in 1968 and the association of the church with the outlawed Solidarity labor union in Poland once again chilled relations. They were not helped by an assassination attempt on John Paul II by a Turk with connections to Bulgaria. A small schismatic church barely survived intense persecution in China.

The contemporary Roman Catholic Church has demonstrated vigor that was hard to predict before 1950, courageously reforming its interior life with faith in the guidance of the Holy Spirit, and with equal courage providing the world with ongoing witness to the presence of Jesus Christ.

**Bibliography.** T. T. Love, *John Courtney Murray: Contemporary Church-State Theory* (1965); L. Gilkey, *Catholicism Confronts Modernity: A Protestant View* (1975); W. Buhlmann, *The Coming of the Third Church: An Analysis of the Present and Future of the Church* (1977); J. Hitchcock, *Catholicism and Modernity* (1979); W. McSweeney, *Roman Catholicism: The Search for Relevance* (1980); H. Jedin, ed., *The Church in the Modern Age* (1981); P. Nichols, *The Pope's Divisions: The Roman Catholic Church Today* (1981); M. Bavarel, *New Communities, New Ministries* (1983); L. Urban, *Look What They've Done to My Church* (1985).

MICHAEL ZEPS

**Romania.** A former socialist republic, overthrown in what came to be called the "velvet revolution" in December 1989 and reorganized as a democratic republic. Romania's area is 237,500 sq. km. (91,700 sq. mi.) and its population about 23 million (1985). The population includes a number of ethnic and religious minorities, including at least 15 denominations. The Orthodox Church was dominant, although it was a Reformed pastor, Laszlo Toke, whose stand against government control of his denomination and mistreatment of ethnic Hungarians, led to demonstrations that resulted in the toppling of the Ceausescu regime. A key point in the December revolution occurred when a Baptist, Petru Dugulescu, led 100,000 Romanians and Hungarians in the Lord's Prayer in Timisoara's largest square. The following day a similar number returned to hear Dugulescu preach.

The socialist constitution guaranteed "freedom to practice a religious confession." The Romanian Communist party, however, was firmly committed to the cultivation of a dialectical and materialist worldview. Through the late 1980s it was often made clear in the media that this program entailed opposition to religion. A department of cults (i.e., religious affairs), was charged with overseeing—and, in practice, restricting—the activities of religious groups. Most restriction was achieved subtly by administrative means, rather than by force of law. The authorities' aim generally was to obtain religious leaders' acquiescence in, or even support for, their restrictive measures. In this way open conflict between official church leaderships and the state could be avoided; but individual clergy and laity, and sometimes local church communities, did come into conflict with state and party authorities from time to time.

The Romanian Orthodox Church, which claimed about 75 percent of the population, has been closely identified with the Romanian state and its temporal rulers from the time it was granted autocephaly in 1885. After the Russian army drove out occupying Nazis in August 1944 the USSR held Romania until its communist government was firmly in control. Following a difficult period of transition in the late 1940s, there emerged an Orthodox Church which was no less loyal to its new communist government—at the official level at least—than it had been to the right-wing regime in power a few years earlier. The patriarch who led the church for almost three decades from his appointment in 1948, Justinian Marina, a member of the Communist party, argued in his theological writings for a "servant church," loyally playing its part in the new social order. The church officially recognized the patriarch of Moscow rather than the ecumenical patriarchate of Constantinople. This loyalty did not protect the church, which has a rich monastic tradition, from the draconian controls imposed on the monasteries in the 1950s. Land and money were confiscated; Christian schools were nationalized. The Orthodox Church did nevertheless enjoy a privileged position in many respects, compared with the other denominations in Romania.

In 1948, when Romania unilaterally abrogated its concordat with the Vatican and subsequently expelled the papal nuncio, Catholics formed the next largest religious group in the country, but this group included the 1.5 million Eastern-rite Catholics (Uniates) who were in 1948 forcibly merged with the Orthodox Church. The Uniates continued in existence unofficially. Unlike the Eastern-rite Catholics, who are Romanians, the Latin-rite Catholic Church was made up largely of members of the country's Hungarian and German communities. The Reformed and Lutheran churches similarly were closely identified with the ethnic minority groups.

So-called "Neo-Protestants"—principally Baptists, pentecostals, and Brethren—had among them about 500,000 adherents, less than 3 percent of the population. They enjoyed marked growth in the 1980s, however, and include some of the country's largest and most active churches. Partly for this reason, members of these churches engaged, disproportionately often, in disputes with authority, on several occasions involving entire local churches. Issues of contention included the provision of church buildings and the appointment of clergy.

Among many events of 1989 and 1990 which had an impact on religious practice was the forced retirement of Orthodox patriarch Teoctist and other church leaders accused of collaboration with the authorities. An evangelical reform movement within the Orthodox Church, the Lord's Army, was legalized, and mass evangelism events were televised beginning in January. A Romanian Evangelical Alliance, made up of a variety of evangelical groups, including the Lord's Army, was organized.

**Bibliography.** T. Beesou, *Discretion and Valor* (rev. ed., 1982).
PHILIP WALTERS

**Romans, Epistle to the.** *See* PAUL, THE APOSTLE.

**Romero y Galdames, Oscar Arnulfo** (1917–1980). Salvadoran archbishop and martyr. Born in Ciudad Barrios, El Salvador, he was ordained in 1942 and proved himself a conscientious and somewhat conservative priest. He served the national bishops' conference and then that of the Central American bishops as general secretary. In 1970 he was consecrated as auxiliary bishop to the archbishop of San Salvador. He was transferred in 1974 to the diocese of Santiago de Maria. To the dismay of progressives he was appointed archbishop in 1977. His own views meanwhile had been changing because of acts of political violence and the repression of the poor. His public utterances and actions became more outspoken when a few days after his inauguration police opened fire on a demonstration, killing many people. It was the beginning of a brutal persecution that took the lives of thousands, including priests and nuns, and ended with the murder of the archbishop himself as he preached in his own cathedral. He had been nominated the previous year for the Nobel Peace Prize by a large number of American and British parliamentarians. Some of the archbishop's "Thoughts" were compiled and translated by James Brockman in *The Church Is All of You* (1984).

J. D. DOUGLAS

**Rookmaaker, Hendrik Roelof ("Hans")** (1922–1977). Dutch scholar. Born in the Hague, he was educated at the Municipal University of Amsterdam and received his doctorate there in 1959. He was lecturer in the history of art at Leiden University (1958–65), and professor of the same subject in the Free University of Amsterdam (1965–77). From 1973 he also taught in the Kortenhoeve Community, an extension of Francis Schaeffer's Swiss L'Abri Community. In his late teens Rookmaaker was a prisoner of war and barely escaped execution. During his three-month imprisonment he had nothing to do but read Scripture—and that was the turning-point of his life. Toward the end of World War II, during a second term of imprisonment, he discovered Herman Dooyeweerd's *New Critique of Theoretical Thought* and applied the Christian vision articulated there to art history, asking how an artist's work reflects his beliefs. Rookmaaker traced the history of philosophy through the work of artists in his best-known work, *Modern Art and the Death of a Culture* (1970). Emphasizing that what a man believes makes him live in a certain way, he held that Christians today must understand the spirit of the age. His approach involved learning from the past without being bound by it. He has had a significant influence on the art world. More generally, he has helped many people understand the attitudes, problems, and concerns of the times in which they live.

CHARLES M. CAMERON

**Rosen, Moishe.** *See* JEWS FOR JESUS

**Rosicrucians.** An occult sect dating back by some very obscure and dubious claims to the early 15th century and Christian Rosencreuz (Rosycross). The *Fama Faternitas of the Meritorious Order of the Rosy Cross* (1614), *The Confession of the Rosicrucian Fraternity* (1615), and *The Chymical Wedding of Christian Rosencreuz* (1616) purportedly were written by Rosencreuz in 1459 to describe mystical secrets he learned in the East; they constitute the foundational documents of the movement. Most scholars accept the claim of Johann Valentine Andrae (1586–1684) that he wrote the writings and the history which they purported to provide as a hoax. Nevertheless, some were attracted to this new philosophical combination of alchemy, science, and the occult; a loosely organized fraternal movement continued to propagate the stories, gradually dying out by the end of the 17th century.

The current version of Rosicrucianism was organized in England by Robert Wentworth Little in 1866. A later revision of his work, *The General Statutes of the Order of Knights of the Red Cross of Rome and Constantine,* identifies the order with Freemasonry. Its religious conception is akin to theosophy and gnosticism, borrowing from reincarnation theories and the Bible. Rosicrucian colleges, as the local units are designated, eventually sprang up throughout the 19th-century British Empire, in the USA, and across continental Europe. The most widely known branch of the contemporary movement is AMORC (The Ancient Mystical Order Rosae Crucis) established in 1915. H. Spencer Lewis led this revival of the movement, adhering to his theory that its existence was cyclical—flourishing for 108 years and remaining quiescent for an equal period. AMORC maintains its headquarters and a center for research and teaching at San Jose, Calif. Another branch of the movement, the Rosicrucian Fraternity, grew up around the leadership of R. Swinburne Clymer, who wrote *The Rosicrucians: Their Teachings . . .* in 1902. Its headquarters are at Quakertown, Pa. A third contemporary group, Societas Rosicruciana in America, has headquarters in New York City.

*Bibliography.* H. S. Lewis, *Rosicrucian Questions and Answers with Complete History of the Rosicrucian Order* (repr. 1959); A. E. Waite, *The Brotherhood of the Rosy Cross* (repr. 1961); R. S. Clymer, *The Rosy Cross, Its Teachings* (repr. 1965); C. Rosencreuz, *Chymische Hochzeit* (repr. 1973).

MELVIN E. DIETER

**Rossis, Zikos** (1838–1933). Greek Orthodox educator. Born in Derbizani, Greece, he studied at the Rizarion Seminary in Athens, and at the universities of Athens and Leipzig (Ph.D., 1866). He lectured in homiletics and fundamental theology at Athens University (1867– ) and taught at the same time at Rizarion Seminary as professor of dogmatics and moral theology (1881–1911). He participated in the Boon Union Conferences (with Old Catholics and Anglicans) in 1874 and 1875. In his numerous articles on reunion he endorsed a very conservative point of view. His main work is his *System of Dogmatics of the Eastern Orthodox Church* (1903, in Greek) of which only volume 1 was published.

GEORGES FLOROVSKY

**Rowe, Henry Kalloch** (1869–1941). American church historian. Born in Dorchester, Mass., he was educated at Brown University, Harvard, and Boston University (Ph.D., 1905). He was a teacher in academies and private schools (1893–1903) and instructor in history at Boston University (1903–6); he thereafter taught church history at what became Andover-Newton Theological Institution (1906–39). Among his writings are *Landmarks in Christian History* (1912), *Society, Its Origin and Development* (1916), *History of Religion in the United States* (1924), *Modern Pathfinders of Christianity* (1928), *History of the Christian People* (1931), and *History of Andover Theological Seminary* (1933).

**Rowley, Harold Henry** (1890–1969). English OT scholar. Born in Leicester, he studied at the universities of Bristol and Oxford, Bristol Baptist College, and Mansfield College in Oxford. He became a missionary to China (1922), where he served as associate professor of OT at Shantung Christian University (1924–29). On returning to Britain he held posts as lecturer in Semitic languages at the University College of South Wales, Cardiff (1930), professor of Semitic languages at the University College of North Wales, Bangor (1935), and professor of Hebrew at the Victoria University of Manchester (1945–59). His publications include *The Aramaic of the OT* (1929), *Darius the Mede and the Four World Empires in the Book of Daniel* (1935), *Israel's Mission to the World* (1939), *The Relevance of the Bible* (1942), *The Relevance of Apocalyptic* (1944), *The Missionary Message of the OT* (1945), *The Rediscovery of the OT* (1946), *The Growth of the OT* (1950), *The Biblical Doctrine of Election* (1950), *From Joseph to Joshua* (1950), *Submission in Suffering and Other Essays on Eastern Thought* (1951), *The Servant of the Lord and Other Essays on the OT* (1951), *The Zadokite Fragments and the Dead Sea Scrolls* (1952), The *Unity of the Bible* (1953), *The Faith of Israel* (1956), *Men of God* (1963), *From Moses to Qumran* (1963), *Worship in Ancient Israel* (1967), and *Job,* a New Century Bible Commentary (1970). He edited *Studies in OT Prophecy* (1950), *The OT and Modern Study* (1951), *A Companion to the Bible* (2d ed., 1963), and was coeditor of *Peake's Commentary on the Bible* (2d ed.,

727

1962) and *Hastings' Dictionary of the Bible* (2d ed., 1963).

F. F. BRUCE

**Royce, Josiah** (1855–1916). American philosopher. Born in Grass Valley, Calif., he graduated from the University of California, and was instructor in English literature and logic there (1878–82). He then joined the faculty at Harvard and from 1892 was professor of the history of philosophy. It was said that religious problems drove him to philosophy. In his concept of God he progressed from universal thought to universal experience to universal selfhood, but failed to reach personality. From his emphasis in ethical teaching he became known as a "philosopher of loyalty." He was a Neo-Hegelian idealist. He authored *Religious Aspect of Philosophy* (1885), *Spirit of Modern Philosophy* (1892), *Studies of Good and Evil* (1898), *Conception of Immortality* (1900), *The World and the Individual* (1900–1901), *Philosophy of Loyalty* (1908), and *Race Questions, Provincialism, and Other American Questions* (1908).

**Rozanov, Basil** (1856–1919). Eastern Orthodox. Born in Vetluga, Russia, he studied at the graduate school of history at the University of Moscow, and for a time was teacher of history and geography in the high school there. Later he entered civil service at St. Petersburg. At the same time he became a standing contributor to the conservative newspaper, *Novoje Vriemja*, "The New Time," edited by Souvorin. The first important book of Rozanov was a kind of philosophical commentary on the Legend of the Great Inquisitor of Dostojevsky (1890). Later on Rozanov concentrated on the problems of sex and *eros*, and shifted far from Christianity. He attacked Christianity violently, especially in two of his books: *The Dark Face*, a metaphysics of Christianity (1911), and *Moonlight Man* (1913). In place of Christianity he proposed his own "natural" (in fact, phallic) religion, based on his interpretation of the OT, the sexual piety of medieval Judaism, and the ancient religions of Egypt. Somehow he wanted to preserve the externals of traditional Christianity, which impressed him esthetically. His last work, *The Apocalypsis of the Russian Revolution*, also in an anti-Christian vein, was published posthumously.

*Bibliography.* D. S. Mirsky, *A History of Russian Literature,* ed. and abridged by Francis J. Whitfield (1949).

GEORGES FLOROVSKY

**Rumania.** *See* ROMANIA.

**Runcie, Robert Alexander Kennedy** (1921– ). Archbishop of Canterbury. After World War II service as a combatant officer and winning the Military Cross, he graduated from both Oxford and Cambridge and was ordained in 1950. He was a curate in Gosforth (1950–52); chaplain (1953–54) and vice-principal (1954–56) of Westcott House, Cambridge; fellow and dean of Trinity Hall, Cambridge (1956–60); principal of Cuddesdon College, Oxford (1960–69); and bishop of St. Albans (1970–80). Appointed to Anglicanism's top post in 1980, he was drawn involuntarily into controversies of the time. While he was criticized variously for fence-sitting, theological liberalism, and ecclesiastical partisanship, often on flimsy evidence, he did not shrink from speaking out forcefully or from taking unpopular stances where he considered it necessary to do so. He was deeply concerned with social and humanitarian causes at home and abroad, and after the Falklands War conducted an official service devoid of the triumphalist notes many expected. Church unity has been one of his major preoccupations, reflected in his longtime relations with Eastern Orthodoxy, and in his welcome of Pope John Paul II to Canterbury in 1982—the first pontiff to visit Protestant Britain. Runcie has published few major works; he wrote *Windows onto God* and *Seasons of the Spirit*, both of which appeared in 1983, and edited *Cathedral and City: St. Albans Ancient and Modern* (1978).

J. D. DOUGLAS

**Russia.** *See* UNION OF SOVIET SOCIALIST REPUBLICS.

**Russian Orthodox Church.** *See* EASTERN ORTHODOX CHURCHES.

**Rwanda, Republic of.** An east-central African republic with an area of 26,338 sq. km. (10,169 sq. mi.) and a population of 6 million (1985). During the 20th century, the religious history of Rwanda presented a complex interaction among traditional and modern forces. While 73 percent were identified as Christian in the 1980s, about half of the people believed in, and practiced, traditional African religion. Some one-half of the population were Roman Catholic, while the remainder observed any of a number of religions, including Islam (420,000), Hinduism (1300), Protestantism (525,000), and Bahái (7,500). Approximately one percent of the non-Rwandan African population professes to be Muslim. Freedom to practice any religion is guaranteed by the country's constitution.

*Non-Christian Religions*. Traditional animistic beliefs promote the notion that "good and evil spirits" battle for control of the human soul; they proclaim that all humans and animals possess the same principal life force, *Imana*, which is manifested in a physical existence. In animals this invisible soul disappears when the creature dies, but in humans it is transformed into a *bazimu*, the spirit of the dead. Eventually the personal identity of the dead is absorbed into an identity force in the spiritual world. Rwandans have great pride in this religion, which promotes integrity, understanding oneself, and the exercise of personal judgment as essential characteristics of a well-developed individual. Rwandan religious leaders and theologians attempted to correlate these beliefs with Christian doctrines. The resulting syncretism claimed that the only way to obtain happiness is to work toward the improvement of one's destiny, and not try to escape it.

*Christianity*. Of those who were professing Christians, most were converts from some form of traditional African beliefs. The Christian churches actively sought converts, and a growing number of influential Christians were in government, economic, and mercantile affairs. Since such elements of Christianity as the existence of a nonmaterial soul, a supreme being, and the life of the spirit after death are similar to traditional beliefs, churches have been successful in attracting and converting from traditional religion.

The religious institutions in Rwanda have, since colonial days, provided for the education of their members and of citizens generally. The Roman Catholic and Protestant churches operate most of the elementary schools, technical colleges, and a university established in 1963. Rwanda has been able to improve the quality of higher education. Citizens used to have to travel to Zaire for study.

*Indigenous Churches*. Rwanda's indigenous Christian churches are almost nonexistent. The first congregation was established in 1970 by the Kimbanguist from Zaire and, in 1975, a second congregation of the Church of Jesus Christ on Earth by the prophet Kimbangu was added.

The continued involvement of religious institutions will drastically affect the future of Rwanda's Protestant, Catholic, and indigenous churches, and will strengthen the hand of well-trained bishops, priests, pastors, and lay leaders whose commitment to Rwanda and to religious ideals and humanities will be the foundations of the new Republic of Rwanda.

*Bibliography*. P. Falk, *The Growth of the Church in Africa* (1978); R. F. Manyeto, *The ABC of Modern Africa* (1979); R. F. Nyrop, *Rwanda: A Country Study* (1985); P. E. Dostert, *Africa, 1986* (21st rev. ed., 1986).

PATRICE MUYUMBA

# Ss

**Sabatier, Louis Auguste** (1839–1901). French liberal Protestant theologian. Born in Vallon, he studied at the Protestant theological faculty at Montauban and at the universities of Tübingen and Heidelberg. After a four-year pastorate, he became professor of Reformed dogmatics in Strasbourg, but was expelled for his French sympathies in 1872. In 1877 he established a Protestant Theological Faculty in Paris, and became its dean. In 1866 he joined the new religious science department of the École des Hautes Études at the Sorbonne. For Sabatier the feeling of dependence and of prayer was the original element in religion; concepts, dogmas, ecclesiastical forms, and practices were merely derivative. Sabatier maintained that the study of the derivation of these elements was a task which had to be performed by psychologists and historians. His best-known books are *The Apostle Paul* (3d ed., 1896), *Outlines of a Philosophy of Religion* (1897), and *Religions of Authority and the Religion of the Spirit* (1904).

ANDREW K. RULE

**Sacraments.** Outward and visible signs of an inward and spiritual grace. They are recognized by virtually all Christian denominations as means of grace, although the place of the sacraments has always loomed large in ecumenical discussions.

The NT does not speak of sacraments as such, although the Greek word later used for this concept, *mysterion*, does occasionally occur in reference to the gospel or the content of the Christian faith. The word was first used in its modern sense by the 4th-century catechist, Cyril of Jerusalem. The Latin word *sacramentum*, which means "oath," has an older history, being used of sacramental signs by Tertullian about A.D. 200, and becoming standard thereafter. In medieval theology the two concepts were fused, and the signs were regarded as proofs of the presence of God's grace at work.

The Protestant Reformers rejected the tendency to confuse the sign with the reality and developed a sacramental theology based on the covenant principle. As signs of the covenant, the sacraments bore witness to God's grace but did not necessarily confer it. The Reformers also limited the number of sacraments to two on the grounds that only baptism and the Eucharist were clearly instituted by Jesus. These two were the sacraments of the gospel, each bearing witness to the atoning work of Christ on the cross, albeit in different aspects.

Today Roman and Anglican Catholics, as well as Eastern Orthodox, regard the sacraments as effective channels of God's grace and give them a central place in the worship of the church. Rome has gone further and defines the operation of the sacraments by the term *ex opere operato*, which means that valid administration alone guarantees the effective presence and working of God's grace. Rome has also developed a doctrine of the real presence of Christ in the eucharistic elements, which allows them to be worshiped after they have been consecrated, although it may be true that this practice is less common today than it once was.

Luther developed a sacramental teaching similar to the Catholic one, but regarded Christ's presence as purely spiritual. For this reason, he rejected the medieval doctrine of transubstantiation and substituted what has come to be called "consubstantiation." Christ is said to be present alongside the consecrated elements, not actually in them; only a right reception by faith can guarantee their efficacy.

Zwingli developed a more radical sacramental theology, claiming that the signs were of merely symbolic value and thus made no difference to anyone's faith. This view is not generally espoused by mainline churches today, although it is held in practice by many evangelicals. Quakers and the Salvation Army do not normally make use of the sacraments.

Calvin's view, enshrined in the Thirty-Nine Articles of religion and the Westminster Confession of Faith, is the most widely accepted in traditional English-speaking Protestantism. It lies somewhere between that of Luther and Zwingli. Calvin rejected both Luther's doctrine of consubstantiation and Zwingli's theology, instead developing the view that the sacraments are sure witnesses of God's grace, guarding against false teaching, and also effectual signs, confirming and strengthening the faith already in us. The sacraments are an assurance to believers, as well as an evangelistic tool. Baptism presses the claims of the gospel, while communion challenges Christians to consider the quality of their faith and their relationship with Christ. It was for this reason that Calvin encouraged serious preparation before receiving communion.

There has been considerable controversy in the past about the number of sacraments. The Eastern Orthodox Church does not recognize any fixed number, but in practice gives special prominence to the Eucharist and, of course, also practices baptism. Other sacramental acts are accepted as such, but are not accorded specific recognition.

The Roman Catholic Church accepts seven sacraments, a number which first appeared in the 12th century and was formally acknowledged at the Council of Florence in 1439. The traditional sacraments are divided into two groups: baptism, confirmation, the Eucharist, penance, and extreme unction on the one hand, and holy orders and matrimony on the other. The first group could be administered to any Christian, while the second group was mutually exclusive (one was either in orders or at liberty to marry, but not both). In practice, of course, this division is indefensible, and is not universally practiced even in the Roman Church, which admits married priests in the Eastern rite and recently in the Western rite as well (in the case of converts from among the already married Protestant clergy).

Protestants generally accept only two sacraments, baptism and the Eucharist, although some denominations grant that the five others accepted by Rome may have a sacramental character. Matrimony is almost universally accepted as a valid ordinance among Protestants, and most denominations have an ordained ministry. Confirmation, in one form or another, is also widespread. On the other hand, penance and extreme unction are rare and often objected to, although the latter has recently become more common as an act of healing.

Protestants generally maintain that the validity and efficacy of the sacraments depend on right reception by faith. This has led to controversy over baptism, since some Protestants believe that it is only after a personal profession of faith that right reception of the sacrament can be guaranteed, whereas others believe that the sacrament may be administered to infants as part of God's covenant promises. Infant communion, however, remains unusual (apart from the practice of the Eastern Orthodox Church), because it is generally argued that the logic of the sacrament itself demands the ability to discern the body and blood of Christ, which would automatically exclude young children.

In recent years, the different Christian churches have moved closer to a genuine recognition of each other's baptism, although the position of the Orthodox Churches is unclear and some Protestant converts to Rome have been rebaptized. Baptists and others who reject infant baptism are increasingly willing to accept a profession of faith from a person who was baptized in infancy instead of insisting on rebaptism. However, this is not the position taken by the majority of sectarian groups, which practice rebaptism on a wide scale.

Intercommunion is somewhat less common on the whole, but it too is gaining wider acceptance as the barriers between denominations break down. The other sacraments, or sacramentals, are less significant, and are almost always recognized, although the Roman Catholic and Eastern Orthodox Churches officially expect their members to be married within their own church and may not recognize a non-Catholic or non-Orthodox marriage as valid.

**Bibliography.** J. Martos, *Doors to the Sacred* (1981).

GERALD BRAY

**Sacred College.** See CARDINALS, COLLEGE OF.

**Sacrilege.** Is classified by Roman Catholic moral theology among sins against the virtue of religion and defined as the irreverent treatment of persons, places, and things dedicated to God or consecrated to sacred purposes. Thus sacrilege may be personal, as when violence is done to priests or clerics; local, when sinful acts are committed in a church; real, as abuse of the sacraments, and theft or misuse of sacred objects.

GEORGES A. BARROIS

**Salesians.** Members of the Society of St. Francis of Sales, one of the largest Roman Catholic religious congregations. The society was founded by St. Giovanni Bosco (1815–1888) in Turin, Italy. Its primary purpose is Christian education, particularly of lower-class youth. It also has a number of printing and publishing houses (Don Bosco is the patron saint of Catholic publishers). In 1987 there were Salesians in 99 nations.

**Salvation.** Deliverance from sin. The word points to what God has provided/done, continues to provide/do, and will provide/do for unworthy, sinful human beings.

In the OT, salvation has this threefold reference. It gains explicit meaning in God's relationship with the descendants of Abraham whom he calls to be his elect people, to have communion with himself, and to bear his message to the world. The Lord saves this people from oppressors and enemies (e.g., in the exodus); he delivers them from plagues and famine; he helps individual Israelites with their problems and troubles (as the Psalter well attests). In the Prophets salvation is that which God has in store for the future—the glorious age of the Messiah, a regenerated cosmos, perfect fellowship between God and his people, and a kingdom of peace, righteousness, and love. The Israelites, therefore, as God's family, looked back to great acts of salvation, experienced present deliverance, and looked forward to the final great act of salvation inaugurating the perfect age of the kingdom of God. Salvation was all that which God did for his elect people to draw them into a right and permanent relationship with himself. And because they were a people in a given time and place, this salvation included all kinds of physical, temporal benefits which were signs of his love and care for his people.

In the ministry of Jesus we see again that salvation is used of God to make people whole. Jesus cures physical and mental diseases and restores people to a right relationship with God. His healings, miracles, exorcisms, and works of mercy are all signs of the wholeness which lies within the provision of salvation by God. However, we see in the teaching and acts of Jesus that salvation also involves the removal of the barrier of sin, which lies between human beings and their Creator. Jesus saw himself as the ransom and sacrifice by which this barrier could and would be everlastingly removed and thus the new and living way opened to God for repentant human beings. He went to the cross as the Suffering Servant, the Lamb of God, and the obedient Son, in order to make salvation (in its fullest and everlasting sense) a permanent possibility and gift from God to mankind. What the OT sacrifices had imperfectly achieved, he, as the pure Lamb of God, perfectly accomplished. He was gloriously vindicated in his resurrection from the dead and exaltation into heaven. No wonder his disciples preached that God's salvation now comes to mankind in no other name than in the name of Jesus.

In the Book of Acts and the Epistles, the physical healings and benefits that fellowship with God include are not emphasized as much as the right relationship with God the Father through Jesus in the power of the Holy Spirit. Salvation is based on what Jesus has done and now is—he is the Lord and Christ seated at the Father's right hand in heaven. Salvation is entry into a living relationship and fellowship with God through the Holy Spirit in the name of Jesus in anticipation of a richer, fuller experience of God in the life of the age to come—the age of the kingdom after the resurrection of the dead and the judgment of the

nations. So the gospel is both the gospel of the kingdom of God and the gospel of salvation in the name of Jesus, the Christ and Lord; this gospel is to be proclaimed throughout the world and converts are to gather in churches to worship God together and in their fellowship begin to experience the joys of the future kingdom of God.

We may say, then, that salvation can involve (especially in OT terms of the temporal blessings experienced by the covenant people of God) freedom and deliverance from injustice, oppression, poverty, and disease in the present world and age. Further, since the future age of the kingdom will be wholly free of evil and sin, it may also be claimed that God wills at all times and in all places the removal of all sinfulness and evil. This is the general usage which is found in much contemporary theology (see, e.g., the reports of the assemblies of the World Council of Churches since the 1970s) and explains the involvement of churches in pronouncements and activities to promote "justice and peace" in this world. A major question arises, however, as to whether in this emphasis the churches are losing the right and full orientation of the concept of salvation as presented in the Bible.

Within traditional theology over the centuries, salvation has been presented as primarily (but not exclusively) eschatological—that which God will wholly and finally provide through Christ for his redeemed people in the new cosmos of the kingdom of God of the age to come. He will provide this because Jesus Christ died as a sacrifice for us, to remove the power and effects of sin and to allow God to remake the universe and to restore believing sinners into holy communion with himself forever. In the present age, sinners, in union with the exalted Jesus through the Holy Spirit, experience both in their hearts and in fellowship with other Christians foretastes of the glorious life of the future kingdom. Thus their lives are characterized by faith, hope, and love. Sometimes as signs of the wholeness that is to come, God gives physical (miraculous) healing to members of the church, the body of Christ. So salvation is said to be a past event (achieved for mankind in the death and resurrection of Jesus); a future event (in the perfect kingdom of heaven); and a present experience of union with Christ in faith and love.

The nature of salvation may be set out in greater detail in the following statements:

*Salvation is what the world needs.* For traditional, orthodox Christianity this statement means that both people and the cosmos itself need to be regenerated and renewed in order to become what God wills that they should be. The problem is sin—rebellion and disobedience against God—which is the root of all evil and injustice, war and wickedness. Thus the message of the forgiveness of sin and reconciliation with

God through Christ is of utmost importance. The promise of the future kingdom of God is to be declared as part of the whole counsel of God.

For some, racism, sexism, injustice, hunger, war, and deprivation constitute the "sin" from which people need to be saved: thus salvation includes both words and action aimed at improving the lot of the "poor" by changing the structures and contexts which cause their "poverty" and bondage. Liberation theology is an intellectual presentation of human liberation from the various ills and evil structures of society in the name of Jesus Christ. It is often informed by a Marxist view of history.

*Salvation is what God has provided, is providing, and will provide.* Orthodox theology usually traces the origins of salvation to the inner decisions of God as Trinity and then follows its historical realization in the election of Israel, culminating in the death and resurrection of Jesus, the Messiah. Its fulfillment is to be in the age to come, when peace and righteousness, joy and justice will be supremely present. This approach assumes that God is both transcendent (outside his creation) and immanent (acting within his creation), and that, as such, he brings into the creation a new order and power which will eventually constitute the center of the new creation of the age to come. This new order and power is Jesus, the Second Adam (the new Man) and the Holy Spirit, who acts in Jesus' name in the present age.

Those who explain salvation in primarily this-worldly terms of the liberation of human beings from evil structures and systems tend to see God, the Savior, as definitely immanent but hardly (if at all) transcendent and supernatural. The hope is that this world will itself become the kingdom of God through the removal of evil and sin (thus the need for social, political, and environmental activity to work with God to bring about this end).

*Salvation has its historical focus in the death of Jesus on the cross and its everlasting agent and center in Jesus himself as the risen, exalted Messiah and Lord.* Throughout the centuries, efforts have been made by theologians to explain how the death of Jesus on the cross at Calvary is an act of God which effectively deals with the power and effects of human sin. Thus there are various theories of the atonement which portray it as God's victory over Satan, sin, and death; as a penal and substitutionary sacrifice constituting a propitiation of the wrath of God against sin; and as the bringing of incorruption and immortality into the reach of mankind. No single theory can contain the whole truth for what God achieved in the death of Jesus for our sins is more than words can tell. God vindicated Jesus from death and exalted him to his right hand in heaven. Therefore God, the Savior, offers salvation now in the name of Jesus, who was once dead but is now risen. Through the preaching, teaching, and sacraments of the church, God's salvation in Jesus is offered and conveyed to all who believe; and this salvation has as its central reality a spiritual union with Jesus through the Holy Spirit in faith. Further, the future life of the kingdom of God will be centered also upon Jesus, the Lamb of God, who will be both its Light and Temple.

*Salvation will be completed and fully experienced and enjoyed only in the life of the kingdom of God of the age to come.* Only after the parousia of Jesus as the Son of Man, the resurrection of the dead, the judgment of the nations, and the inauguration of the everlasting kingdom of heaven will the elect people of God (true believers) know full salvation. Although the power and love of the kingdom are experienced now by the individual believer and within the corporate fellowship of the household of faith, that power and love are only the foretaste and firstfruit of the fullness of the glory that shall be revealed. Only when the children of God are clothed in their resurrection bodies and living in the new heaven and earth and seeing the glory of God in the face of Jesus Christ will they truly be fully and finally saved from all sin, evil, corruption, and mortality. At the end of his *City of God*, Augustine described this final state in these words: "There we shall rest and we shall see; we shall see and we shall love; we shall love and we shall praise. Behold, what shall be in the end shall never end."

*Salvation is both individual and corporate.* The whole point of the proclamation of the gospel and the call to people to repent and believe is that individuals should personally respond and enter (through regeneration and conversion) into a right relationship with God the Father through Jesus Christ the Lord. But although salvation is a personal reality it is not individualistic. It is being saved into God's family, to become a brother/sister of Jesus, himself the elder brother. In fact, the church as the body of Christ, temple of the Holy Spirit, and household of faith is intended by God to be the visible expression of what his salvation is all about—a reconciled, loving, believing, trusting, faithful, worshiping, caring, obedient people. What the future kingdom will be like is to be indicated by the life and witness, worship and service of the church in this age.

*Salvation is to be offered to all people through the proclamation of the gospel, but it will not be accepted by all; therefore all people will not be saved.* Although the Bible suggests that the kingdom of heaven will be inhabited by countless thousands of redeemed people, enjoying the fullness of God's salvation, it nowhere promises that all people will be saved. In fact, there is a definite warning, often repeated, of the possibility of hell for those who refuse God's gracious offer of salvation.

Where salvation is presented by churches primarily in this-worldly terms of liberation from evil it is usually accompanied by the belief that whatever new order God will bring in the future, it will be for all people. Universalism (the doctrine that all will eventually be saved) has been a very common teaching within the churches of Europe and America in the 20th century, even where the older idea of salvation as deliverance from the effects and power of sin has continued to be held as the basic or primary meaning of salvation. One important reason for this has been because God has been described solely as the God of love while other aspects of his holy being and character (e.g., his purity, righteousness, and glory) have been neglected. The only universalism which the Bible knows is that of people of all ages, races, and languages being everlastingly united to the Lord Jesus in heaven in praise of God the Father, in the power of the Holy Spirit.

*Salvation as God's present activity and provision (in Christ through the Holy Spirit) places an obligation upon his church to promote righteousness and justice in the present sinful world and evil age, in anticipation of the perfection and fullness of the glorious age of salvation which is yet to dawn.* This world and age are the sphere of present salvation and the whole creation groans in expectation for the liberation of the children of God from all sin and evil. Thus, recognizing moves for justice and peace in this world as possible signs of God's care and love for the human race, the church is to encourage and support all that which truly ennobles and dignifies human beings as creatures of God made in his image and likeness. The signs are not, however, God's salvation as such. They are indicators which ought to turn people to God in Christ's name, looking for his full and final salvation from "outside" time and history.

**Bibliography.** G. Aulen, *Christus Victor* (1931); J. J. King, *The Necessity of the Church for Salvation* (1960); E. M. B. Green, *The Meaning of Salvation* (1965); M. M. Thomas, *Salvation and Humanization* (1971); D. Bloesch, *Jesus as Victor! Karl Barth's Doctrine of Salvation* (1976); D. Wells, *The Search for Salvation* (1978); L. Morris, *The Atonement* (1983).

PETER TOON

**Salvation Army.** An international, nonsectarian evangelistic and social service organization, rooted in the Methodist evangelism and "Holiness" preaching of William and Catherine Booth. The Salvation Army began to take its well-known form after 1865 when the Booths began their ministry in the slums of East London. The work of the Christian Revival Association (soon to become The Christian Mission) expanded rapidly, with 13 "preaching stations" and an average of nearly 150 weekly services by the time of the first formal report in 1868. Six years later that average had increased nearly tenfold, resulting in more than 3000 conversions during the previous year. By the turn of the century the Army was reporting as many as one-third of a million converts annually, with as many as 50,000 of them in the USA. Evangelism continues to be a central concern; during its centennial year, for example, the Army reported about 100,000 converts.

In 1878 The Christian Mission assumed the name "The Salvation Army." During the next several years the first edition of the Army's Orders and Regulations was published, the *War Cry* was begun, and, in 1880, the first contingent of Salvationists was sent to the USA, beginning an international expansion that within a brief period of time was to carry the Army into France, India, Sweden, Canada, Switzerland, and other countries. Growth was rapid, as the Army expanded from fewer than 100 British Isles corps in 1878 to a worldwide total of 3500 by 1898 and 7000 six years later. In 1981 the Army had 24,700 officers in 15,200 corps and some 3000 social welfare agencies in an increasing number of countries (89 in early 1986).

From the beginning of their work in East London the Booths sought to meet material as well as spiritual needs. The Army's presence in the slums brought them into contact with pressing human need that in its turn prompted them to respond with concern and practical assistance. In addition, their growing knowledge of slum conditions resulted in an increasing identification with the poor and a developing critique of what seemed to them to be an unjust social order. The Christian Mission's outreach in 1868 included temperance meetings, soup kitchens, and employment assistance. That kind of social outreach expanded during the 1870s and 1880s, but it was the publication of William Booth's *In Darkest England and the Way Out* (1890) that served as the major impetus for the Army's social program, publicizing social ills, offering a large-scale remedy, and reflecting on and deepening its identification with the poor.

Despite extensive opposition during its early years, the Salvation Army gradually became a popular organization with widespread support. Among the reasons for its increasing popularity were the quality and extent of its service to Allied soldiers during World War I, which brought Salvationists forcibly to the attention of the general population.

The social program has continued in the late 20th century. Homes and centers for alcoholics, food distribution centers, homes for women, men's industrial homes, occupational centers, prison-gate homes, residential centers for the elderly, children's homes, day care centers, camps, clubs and play centers, homes and institutes for the handicapped, counseling services, family welfare, employment assistance, missing person searches, hospitals, dispensaries, and schools constitute only a part of the Salvation Army's ongoing social ministry.

Standing in the Wesleyan tradition, the Salvation Army has had from the beginning a strong Holiness emphasis, which for them undergirded the extent and effectiveness of their social efforts. That heritage has also placed them firmly in the tradition of evangelical Protestant theology. The Army continues to be marked by conservative theology, evangelism, and practical service.

*See also* HOLINESS CHURCHES.

**Bibliography.** H. Redwood, *God in the Slums* (1931); John Ervine, *God's Soldier*, 2 vols. (1934); R. Sandall, *The History of the Salvation Army*, 3 vols. (1947–55); H. Wisbey, Jr., *Soldiers Without Swords: A History of the Salvation Army in the United States* (1955); S. Chesham, *Born to Battle: The Salvation Army in America* (1965); R. Collier, *The General Next to God: The Story of William Booth and the Salvation Army* (1965); N. Magnuson, *Salvation in the Slums; Evangelical Social Work, 1865–1920* (1977).

NORRIS A. MAGNUSON

**Sanctification.** *See* SALVATION.

**Sanday, William** (1843–1920). Church of England scholar. Born in Holme Pierrepont, Nottinghamshire, he was educated at Balliol College, Oxford, and Corpus Christi College, Oxford, and was ordered deacon in 1867 and ordained priest two years later. He was fellow of Trinity College, Oxford (1866–73); in charge of Navestock, Romford (1869–71); lecturer of St. Nicholas, Abingdon (1871/72); vicar of Great Waltham, Chelmsford (1872/73); rector of Barton-on-the-Heath, Warwickshire (1873–76); principal of Hatfield Hall, Durham (1876–83); Dean Ireland's professor of the exegesis of Scripture at the University of Oxford and tutorial fellow of Exeter College, Oxford (1883–95); and after 1895 Lady Margaret professor of divinity and canon of Christ Church, Oxford. He was also examining chaplain to the bishop of Durham (1879–81); select preacher at Cambridge in 1880, 1892, and 1903; Whitehall preacher in 1889/90; and Bampton lecturer in 1893. He was honorary fellow of Exeter College from 1898; chaplain in ordinary to the king; and a fellow of the British Academy from 1903. Besides his contributions to Hastings' *Dictionary of the Bible*, he wrote or edited *The Study of the NT* (1883), *What the First Christians Thought about Christ* (1886), *Free Thinking: A Brief Review of Mrs. Besant on the Evidences of Christianity* (1886), *The Fullness of Revelation in the NT* (1894), *The Synoptic Gospels* (1900), *A New Marcion: Being a Criticism of Mr. F. C. Conybeare's "Myth, Magic, and Morals"* (1909), *Personality in Christ and Ourselves* (1911), *Studies in the Synoptic Problem* (1911), *The Primitive Church and Reunion* (1913), *Bishop Gore's Challenge to Criticism* (1914), *The Life-Work of Samuel Rolles Driver* (1914), *The Deeper Causes of the War* (1914), *The Meaning of the War for Germany and Great Britain: An Attempt at Synthesis* (1915), *Form and Content in the Christian Tradition*

(1916), *In View of the End: A Retrospect and a Prospect* (1916), *When Should the War End?* (1917), *Divine Overruling* (1920), *The NT Background* (1920), and *The Position of Liberal Theology* (1920). He also contributed to volume 7 of *Old-Latin Biblical Texts,* entitled *Novum Testamentum sancti Irenaei* (1923).

RAYMOND W. ALBRIGHT

**Sangster, William Edwyn Robert** (1900–1960). English Methodist minister. Born in London, he was educated at Richmond College and at London University. He was ordained in the Methodist Church in 1926. He ministered in various English and Welsh circuits before beginning a 16-year term at Westminster Central Hall that saw great crowds gathering to hear him preach. President of the Methodist Conference in 1950, he later became secretary of his denomination's home missions department. His numerous publications include *Why Jesus Never Wrote a Book* (1932), *God Does Guide Us* (1934), *He Is Able* (1936), *Methodism Can Be Born Again* (1938), *These Things Abide* (1939), *Ten Statesmen and Jesus Christ* (1941), *The Path to Perfection* (Ph.D. diss., 1943); *The Craft of Sermon Illustration* (1946), *Let Me Commend* (1949), *The Pure in Heart* (1954), *The Secret of Radiant Life* (1957), *Power in Preaching* (1958), and *Give God a Chance* (1959).

**Saudi Arabia.** Independent kingdom in southwestern Asia with a total area of 2,150,000 sq. km. (830,000 sq. mi.) and a total population of 10.1 million (1983 est.). Present-day Saudi Arabia is the result of the expansionism in the 1920s of Najdi (central Arabian) ruler Abd al-Aziz (Ibn Saud), the scion of a dynasty that had embraced the militant, ultraorthodox Unitarian movement (better known as Wahhabism by nonadherents) nearly two centuries earlier. Wahhabism is a Sunni Islamic movement distinguished by its adoption of the strict Hanbali school of jurisprudence. It banned such practices as wearing silk clothing and shaving beards. Sufi worship at saints' tombs came in for special hostility since the practice could easily degenerate into saint worship. The early Wahhabis suspected the authenticity of other forms of Islam and were in turn widely regarded in the Islamic world as heretics. The gap between them and other Sunni Muslims, however, has subsequently eroded.

Abd al-Aziz started to curb his movement's zeal almost as soon as he completed his conquests. He suppressed the fanatical Ikhwan (Brothers) military force when it rebelled against him, and he used cunning arguments to counter conservative religious objections to such innovations as the telephone. In more recent years, the royal family has come to be seen by some Muslims as corrupt and secretly addicted to forbidden practices. Such was the thrust of the abortive revolt in 1979 by rigid Wahhabis in the Great Mosque of Mecca that shocked the regime and alerted it to the need to reassert its own faithfulness to Islam.

Saudi Arabia remains a theocratic state. The shari'a (Islamic law) is strictly enforced and, in the absence of the kinds of modern law codes adopted in other Muslim countries, is the basis of the kingdom's legal system. All royal enactments require certification by the ulama that they are consistent with the shari'a. The ulama occupy important positions, particularly in education and the judiciary, although the creation of new courts to enforce nonshari'a rules have eaten into their monopoly on the judicial function. Religious policemen (*mutawwin*) see that people pray at the prescribed times and generally seek out the lax.

Not all the population is Wahhabi or Hanbali. Outside Najd, other Sunni schools of jurisprudence have survived—Shafi'is is in the Hijaz (the West) and Malikis in the Gulf region. Perhaps 5 percent—but concentrated in the oil-producing eastern province and disproportionately represented among the workers in the oil fields—is Shi'ite (Twelvers). The latter have always been victims of discrimination by the Saudis. Shi'ite dislike of the monarchy has been given new inspiration by the Iranian revolution. Riots and demonstrations by Shi'ites during 1979/80 (not to be confused with the Sunni revolt in Mecca) frightened the regime.

While all Saudis are Muslims, the expatriate workforce includes many Christians. In keeping with surviving ultraorthodox demands (and contrary to usual Islamic doctrines of religious toleration), Saudi Arabia is unique in the Islamic world in banning the open practice of other religions. No churches are permitted. But in keeping with the more pragmatic attitude of the 20th-century Saudi monarchy, non-Muslim worship is unhindered if conducted discreetly.

**Bibliography.** J. P. Piscatori, ed., *Islam and Development: Religion and Sociopolitical Change* (1980); F. A. Sankari, *Islamic Resurgence in the Arab World* (1982); G. E. Perry, *The Middle East: Fourteen Islamic Centuries* (1983); J. P. Piscatori, ed., *Islam in the Political Process* (1983); A. Al-Yassini, *Religion and State in the Kingdom of Saudi Arabia* (1985); R. H. Dekmejian, *Islam in Revolution: Fundamentalism in the Arab World* (1985).

ELEANOR H. PERRY

**Sayers, Dorothy Leigh** (1893–1957). Anglican writer and scholar. Born in Oxford, she graduated from Oxford University in 1915 with a degree in medieval literature. In 1923 she published her first novel, *Whose Body?* a detective story featuring her enduring literary creation, Lord Peter Wimsey. This was followed by a steady stream of popular detective fiction, finishing with *Busman's Holiday* (1937). Religion later engaged her literary powers, as in *The Man Born to Be King* (1942), an acclaimed series of radio plays on the life of Christ. Her most impressive religious book was *The Mind of the Maker* (1941), which explored literary creativity as an analog of the Trinity; others were *Begin Here* (1941) and *Creed or Chaos?* (1947). She translated Dante's *Inferno* (1949) and *Purgatorio* (1955), but died before completing the *Paradiso*. A collection of essays, *Introductory Papers on Dante*, was published in 1954. Sayers was associated with the circle whose members included C. S. Lewis, Charles Williams, and J. R. R. Tolkien.

NICK NEEDHAM

**Scepticism.** Philosophical perspective that true, reliable knowledge is unattainable in certain areas of investigation (science, morality, metaphysics, theology). Scepticism has played a curious but significant role in Christian theology. This is true of both Catholic and Protestant thought. William of Ockham (d. 1349) denied universality to existences apart from discourse. He then went on to affirm the impossibility of a philosophical demonstration of God's existence and the soul's immortality, making faith the sole ground of religious belief. In this sense Martin Luther was an Ockhamist. When Immanuel Kant concluded in his *Critique of Pure Reason* (1781) the impropriety of applying a priori categories (inner and outer) to the regulative ideas of self, God, and the world, he was only saying that any metaphysics is not demonstrable in the realm of pure reason. He affirmed that such religious ideas as God, human freedom (basic to morals), and immortality rest upon a sheer though necessary postulate of the practical reason. It was Henry Mansel (1820–1871) who saw in Kantian scepticism the opportunity to decry reason and assert the need of revelation to provide the lack. Many Protestant theologians continue to reassert the negative and sceptical character of human reason in matters relating to theology, affirming, therefore, the need of supernatural revelation. To counteract this questionable virtue of dichotomizing reason and faith many discriminating theologians have seen the need to reconsider Kant's philosophy which led to rational scepticism so as to make philosophy and theology once more brothers in religious inquiry and faith.

Scepticism often rests upon the questionable assumption that a finite mind cannot know the infinite, the partial the absolute. Finite knowledge may not lead to knowledge of the infinite, but such impossibility does not necessarily support complete scepticism. One may not know for certain but this fact does not necessarily preclude knowledge (*argumentum ad ignorantiam*). Most discriminating religious thinkers today affirm that reason itself is an adventure of faith and that reason and faith are not antithetical. Scepticism, it need hardly be pointed out, frequently disguises stubbornness of spirit and betrays a dogmatism as real as the dogmatism it condemns.

VERGILIUS FERM

## Schaeffer, Francis August (1912–1984).
American scholar and pastor. Born in Germantown, Pa., he became a Christian at the age of 18 after reading the Bible, beginning with Genesis, for about six months. He attended Hampden-Sydney College, Westminster Theological Seminary, and Faith Theological Seminary. He helped to found Faith Seminary after a split with Westminster in 1937. After ordination as the first pastor in the Bible Presbyterian denomination, he served in three different denominations over a period of 10 years. During part of this time he served as moderator of the Great Lakes Presbytery of the Bible Presbyterian Church.

He traveled throughout Europe for three months in 1947 to evaluate the state of the church in Europe as a representative of the Independent Board for Presbyterian Foreign Missions and as the American Secretary for the Foreign Relations Department of the American Council of Christian Churches. Upon returning to the USA he was asked to move to Europe to begin the work necessary for the formation of the International Council of Christian Churches. Thus in 1948 the Schaeffers moved to Lausanne, Switzerland, as missionaries.

During the early 1950s Schaeffer went through a spiritual crisis. He recognized that something was wrong with both his own life and the separated movement in general. He carefully reconsidered his Christian commitment and his priorities. He concluded that there was a great deal of imbalance in both his life and the movement. He thus emerged from this struggle with a new certainty about his faith, a new emphasis on the blood of Christ and the work of the Holy Spirit, and a new direction in his life which would unfold over the coming years. During 1953/54 he traveled across the country speaking 346 times during 515 days about the deeper spiritual life. These talks which grew out of his spiritual crisis later became the basis for his book *True Spirituality* and the spiritual basis of L'Abri Fellowship, founded in 1955.

One of the major themes of this new direction was the lordship of Christ in all areas of life. Schaeffer's work is concerned with the history of Western civilization, abortion, medical ethics, the environment, and politics.

He continued speaking and writing right up until the time of his death. As a pastor he had a personal impact on the lives of many people; as a theologian he led the fight against liberalism and its impact on the church; and on social issues he challenged millions of evangelicals to bring their faith to life. Schaeffer was truly a sensitive man of God who sought to bring the gospel to 20th-century people, showing what it means to believe it, to think it through, and to live it out.

His books include *Escape from Reason* (1968), *How Should We Then Live?* (1976), *Whatever Happened to the Human Race?* (1979), *Pollution and the Death of Man* (1970), and *A Christian Manifesto* (1980).

JAMES INGRAM

## Schaff, David Schley (1852–1929).
American church historian. Born in Mercersburg, Pa., he graduated from Yale and Union Theological seminaries. He was minister of the Presbyterian church at Hastings, Nebr. (1877–81), associate editor of the *Schaff-Herzog Encyclopaedia* (1881–83), minister of the First Presbyterian Church, Kansas City, Mo. (1883–89), professor of church history at Lane Theological Seminary, Cincinnati (1897–1903), professor of ecclesiastical history and history of doctrine at Western Theological Seminary (1903–25), and lecturer on American church history at Union Theological Seminary, N.Y. (1925–29). He continued the *History of the Christian Church* begun by his father, Philip Schaff, writing volume 5 (2 pts., 1907–10). Among his other publications are *The Life of Philip Schaff* (1897), *John Huss . . . after Five Hundred Years* (1951), and *The Reformation and Its Influence* (1917).

RAYMOND W. ALBRIGHT

## Scheel, (Jürgen) Otto (Einar Immanuel)
(1876–1954). German church historian. Born in Tondern, Sleswick-Holstein, he was educated at the universities of Halle and Kiel, and was privat-docent for systematic theology at the latter institution from 1900 to 1905, when he was made titular professor. He taught church history at Tübingen (1906–24) and was professor of German history at Kiel (1924–33). In theology he belonged to the modern historical and critical school. His works include *Die Anschauung Augustin's von Christi Person and Werke* (1901), *Luthers Stellung zur heiligen Schrift* (1902), *Wie erhalten wir das Erbe der Reformation in den geistigen Kämpfen der Gegenwart?* (Leipzig, 1904), *Die dogmatische Behandlung der Tauflehre in der modernen positiven Theologie* (1906), *Individualismus und Gemeinschaftsleben in der Auseinandersetzung Luthers mit Karlstadt, 1524–25* (1907), and *Die moderne Religionspsychologie* (1908). He was a coeditor of the first edition of *Die Religion in Geschichte und Gegenwart*. He was especially interested in studies in the early church which led to *Die Kirche im Urchristentum* (1912); and he devoted much of his later years to Luther studies, the results of which appeared in *Martin Luther* (2 vols., 1915–17; 3d ed., 1921–30).

RAYMOND W. ALBRIGHT

**Schermerhorn, William David** (1871–1942). Methodist scholar. Born in Lincoln, Kans., he was educated at Kansas Wesleyan University, Garrett Biblical Institute, and the University of Chicago. Ordained to the Methodist ministry in 1899, he was pastor in Lincoln, Kans. (1899–1901), Chicago (1901–4), and Wilson, Kans. (1904–5). After serving as a missionary in India (1905–10) he became professor of English Bible at Kansas Wesleyan (1911/12); taught NT interpretation at Garrett (1912–17); was president of Dakota Wesleyan, S.D. (1917–22); and was professor of church history and missions at Garrett (1922–39). He also taught missions at Northwestern University (1922–27) and spent September 1931, to March 1932, in the Orient on a study trip for the American Society of Church History. He wrote *Beginnings of the Christian Church* (1929) and *The Christian Mission in the Modern World* (1933).

RAYMOND W. ALBRIGHT

**Schillibeeckx, Edward Cornelius Florentius Alfons** (1914– ). Dominican scholar. Born in Antwerp, Belgium, he taught dogmatic theology at Louvain (1943–45, 1947–58). He was appointed professor of dogmatics and the history of theology at the University of Nijmegen in 1958. In 1965 he helped to found the international theological journal *Concilium*. His *Jesus* received acclaim in the wider theological world but disapproval from the Vatican (he was summoned to Rome in Dec. 1979). His controversial *Ministry* (1981) caused even greater concern. He was the first theologian to receive the Erasmus Prize (1982) in recognition of his important contribution to European culture. He retired that same year. He has received the highest civil honor in the Netherlands—Commander of the Order of Orange-Nassau. He has been described as "one of the very greatest theologians" (J. Bowden). His major works are *Jesus: An Experiment in Christology* (1974) and *Christ: The Christian Experience in the Modern World* (1977).

CHARLES M. CAMERON

**Schmauk, Theodore Emanuel** (1920– ). Lutheran editor and scholar. Born in Lancaster, Pa., he studied at the University of Pennsylvania. He was ordained to the Lutheran ministry in 1883. His career was devoted to general denominational work. He served as editor-in-chief of the *Lutheran Church Review* (1895–1920), editor of the Lutheran Sunday School Lessons and General Council Graded Series (1896–1911), literary editor of *The Lutheran* (1889–1920), and lecturer in Christian faith, apologetics, and ethics at the Lutheran Theological Seminary, Mt. Airy, Philadelphia (1911–20). Among his works are *Bible History* (1899), *The Early Churches of the Lebanon Valley* (1902), *History of the Lutheran Churches in Pennsylvania from the Original Sources* (1903), *The Confessions and Confessional Principle of the Lutheran Church* (1909), and *Christianity and Christian Union* (1913). He edited an annotated edition of Benjamin Rush's *Account of German Inhabitants of Pennsylvania* (1910).

RAYMOND W. ALBRIGHT

**Schutz, Roger.** *See* TAIZÉ.

**Schwarze, William Nathaniel** (1875–1948). Moravian scholar. Born in Chaska, Minn., he was educated at Moravian College, Bethlehem, Pa. (Ph.D., 1910), and at the Moravian Theological Seminary. Ordained to the ministry of the Moravian Church in 1896, he served as pastor of Bruederfeld and Bruederheim, Alberta, Canada (1896–1900). After directing the Buxton Grove Theological Seminary for native ministers in St. John's Antigua, B.W.I. (1900–1903), he became professor of philosophy and church history at Moravian College (1903–43) and president of Moravian College and Theological Seminary (1928–43; emeritus, 1943–48). He was also the archivist of the Northern Province of North America (1905–48) and president of the Moravian Historical Society, an incumbency during which the modern quarters of the society in Bethlehem were constructed. He wrote *History of Moravian College and Theological Seminary* (1910) and *John Huss, the Martyr of Bohemia* (1915). He translated David Zeisberger's, *History of the North American Indians* (1910).

RAYMOND W. ALBRIGHT

**Schweitzer, Albert** (1875–1965). Protestant theologian, organist, and missionary surgeon. Born in Kayserburg, Upper Alsace, he studied at the University of Strasbourg (Ph.D., 1899). He also studied in Paris and Berlin. He was made a privatdocent in theology at Strasbourg in 1902 while curate at the church of St. Nicolaus. In 1903 while studying in Paris with C. M. Widor he was made organist of the J. S. Bach Society, a position which he held until 1911. He and Widor edited a definitive edition of Bach's works for the organ. In 1906 he wrote (in French) a biography and commentary on J. S. Bach. A German edition appeared in 1908 and an English translation in 1911. In 1906 he published *Von Reimarus zu Wrede*, later translated as *The Quest of the Historical Jesus*, which interprets Jesus' teaching in the light of the eschatological beliefs of his time. Schweitzer caught the imagination of the religious world when he left his pastorate and professorship in Europe in 1913 to build a hospital in Lambarene, French Equatorial Africa, and became its missionary surgeon. Most of his time thereafter was spent in Africa, interrupted by several lecture trips to Europe and one to America in 1949 in connection with the Goethe Festival. His works include *Paul and His Interpreters* (1912),

*On the Edge of the Primeval Forest* (1922), *Christianity and the Religions of the World* (1923), *The Decay and Restoration of Civilization* (1923), *Out of My Life and Thought* (1933), and *Indian Thought and Its Development* (1936).

**Bibliography.** A. A. Roback, ed., *Albert Schweitzer Jubilee Book.*

JULIUS SEELYE BIXLER

**Schwenkfelders of America.** Exponents of the theological tenets of Caspar Schwenckfeld von Ossig (1489–1561), a member of the lesser nobility of Silesia. They came to Pennsylvania between 1731 and 1737 because of severe persecution during the so-called Counter-Reformation. The bulk of these Silesian immigrants settled within a 50-mile radius of Philadelphia. Their arrival in America is observed annually in Memorial Day [Gedächtnistag] services on September 24. While the last identifiable exponent of Schwenckfeld's teaching on the European Continent died in 1826, the group continued to thrive in North America.

For more than a generation after their arrival in North America, Schwenkfelders maintained loose associations, reading their revered teacher's books and being served by appointed elders who helped in instructing the young and led in the study of the Scriptures and in corporate worship. Incorporation and adoption of a constitution came in 1782, probably because of pressure from the Moravian missioner August Gottlieb Spangenberg, who wanted them to join the Herrnhut Brethren. A statement of 17 points of agreement, signed by 41 "house fathers," constitutes the act of agreement. After several revisions it came to be known as the "Formula for the government and discipline of the Schwenkfelder Society." (The society later became a "church.") The first meetinghouse of the society was built in 1790 at Hosensack, Pa., to be followed by a second in 1791 and a third at Towamencin in 1793. Others were to be built and rebuilt in the course of the 19th and 20th centuries. There are five duly incorporated congregations (Palm, Central, Philadelphia, Norriston, Lansdale) with a current total membership of about 3000 (the largest in their history). The group maintains a first-rate research library on Schwenkfeldiana and related matters in Pennsburg, Pa. It has supported through a board of publications the printing of the 19-volume *Corpus Schwenckfeldianorum* and other books about their founder and the history and teaching of the Schwenkfelder Church.

The group has maintained the Perkiomen School for Boys since 1892 and publishes the periodical *The Schwenkfeldian.* Headquarters are in Pennsburg. The church's polity is congregationalist. Its general conference meets semiannually. In 1985 15 clergy served the denomination.

Schwenkfelders are christological, practice the sacraments of baptism and the Eucharist, and defend the sole authority of the Scriptures. In keeping with the teaching of their founder, they believe the Bible to be "dead letter" unless it is illumined by the indwelling Word. In older practices, marriage was encouraged between members of their community; the consent of a spiritual superior was required, although "mixed" marriages were not unknown. A "Charity Fund" assures that no Schwenkfelder is left destitute.

**Bibliography.** H. W. Kriebel, *The Schwenckfelders in America* (1904); C. D. Hartranft, et al., eds., *Corpus Schwenckfeldianorum* (1907–61); P. L. Maier, *Caspar Schwenckfeld on the Person and Work of Christ* (1959); E. J. Furcha, *Schwenckfeld's Concept of the New Man* (1970); S. G. Schultz, *Caspar Schwenckfeld von Ossig, 1489–1561* (1977); W. K. Meschter, *Twentieth Century Schwenkfelders* (1984); R. Emmet McLaughlin, *Caspar Schwenckfeld. Reluctant Rebel. His Life to 1540* (1985).

E. J. FURCHA

**Science and Religion** (1950–86). The issues which have concerned scientists and theologians in the latter part of the 20th century have included both those which were prominent during the previous century, such as the broad aspects of the relationship between the sciences and theology, and new issues, such as the development of a theological discussion of ecological issues. These new developments have been brought about by advances in science and technology, so that topics such as genetic engineering, which were formerly considered only in principle, now become practical possibilities. This does not necessarily alter the questions at issue, but makes the assertion that science, as opposed to technology, is "value-free," difficult to sustain in practice. Indeed, one question which now concerns many scientists is simply that of the legitimate limitation, because of its ethical implications, of research which is technically possible. It is now realized, also, that the selection of topics for research is determined not only by overt personal interests but by the values held by the community in general. The current debate over *in vitro* fertilization of human ova is a case in point.

Even where there is a reluctance to acknowledge the traditional values of Christian theology, or where they have been rejected, there has in some cases developed a concern expressed in terms of other religious value-systems (e.g., Zen Buddhism). This seems to recognize an interdependence of mankind and the material environment which makes harmony desirable and disharmony destructive. There have indeed been attempts to attribute the destructiveness of much modern Western technology to a literal understanding of the biblical injunction to mankind to "fill the earth and subdue it. Rule over the fish of the sea and the birds of the air and over every living creature that moves on the ground" (Gen. 1:28). A balanced study of OT teaching, taken as a whole, leads to a different conclusion. Most Christian theologians, indeed, see the ecological problem as an aspect of the self-centeredness of mankind.

Several series of Gifford Lectures (e.g., those by Raven [1951/52], von Weiszäcker [1959/60], Hardy [1963–65], Jaki [1975/76], Eccles [1977/78], and Moltmann [1984/85]) have dealt specifically with aspects of science and religion, and Polanyi's series on personal knowledge (1951/52) also raised important questions about reductionism which are relevant to a proper understanding of the world. Further, two series of Bampton Lectures, those by Mascall (1956) and Peacocke (1978), have been very influential. Other symposia, such as *The Sciences and Theology in the Twentieth Century*, edited by Peacocke, illustrate the breadth of contemporary interest in the topic.

The first half of the present century saw advances in both the physical and the biological sciences which have had implications for theology. Einstein's theory of relativity, wave mechanics and quantum mechanics, and the more recent developments in thermodynamics have influenced the development of cosmological theory. In the biological sciences, the development of molecular biology, with its insights into molecular mechanisms underlying biological processes, has made it possible to discuss genetic change in specific molecular terms instead of speculating about it with hypothetical models. The assertion by Jacques Monod that life can now be understood in terms of "chance and necessity," that is, in terms of statistical factors determining change, followed by exact copying according to chemical laws, is striking in its simplicity, even if it does not necessarily lead to his conclusion that there is no longer any place for God in the universe. It invokes the old "God of the gaps" and does not recognize the Christian insight that the whole universe is contingent upon God's will for its existence.

If the tendency of the 18th century was to consider God as transcendent, creating the universe and perhaps giving the solar system its initial angular momentum, the emphasis of the 20th century may be on seeing God as immanent in the world he has created. The interest in A. N. Whitehead's "process theology" has perhaps led in that direction. The suggestion that, contrary to most previous Christian thought, God is not immune from change, but that the evolution of living systems affects him so that "God perfects the world, and the world perfects God" (Birch and Cobb) indicates this direction of thought. The French Jesuit paleontologist, Teilhard de Chardin, had suggested something similar in his concept of the evolution of the universe to the "omega point," when the perfect man would be manifested as a result of the evolutionary process. This type of thinking may lead to a form of pantheism.

Numerous authors have written books which seek to set out a basis for relating scientific and biblical thought. As is evident, the approach taken will depend upon the author's views of science and the Bible. Following in the 19th-century tradition of authors such as Hugh Miller and J. W. Dawson, Bernard Ramm's *Christian View of Science and Scripture* attempted to combine contemporary scientific theories with a belief in the divine inspiration of Scripture. Ramm makes a distinction between "progressive creationism" and "theistic evolutionism" and aligns himself with the former. Other writers would prefer to see God's activity in the evolutionary process. Indeed, it can reasonably be held that everything that has happened since the creation of the universe was implicit in the properties of the initial atoms of the primeval creation, formed as they were when conditions were right. It is to be remembered that any theory of the origin of the universe, or of life, can be justified only ex post facto; the opportunities for repetition of the event, by the very nature of things, can hardly be expected to occur. Mascall and Peacocke, in their Bampton Lectures, attempt boldly to confront biblical theology with the necessity to take account of contemporary scientific understanding of nature. As philosophical realists, they believe that scientific endeavor is not merely an intellectual game, but is gradually approaching a view of the world at all levels to which the word "reality" may not unreasonably be applied. They draw attention to the limitations of the "models" which scientists use as bases for their thought.

A question on which there has been much discussion, and some disagreement, is the use of metaphor in Scripture. That it is used seems obvious, but whether the description of creation in the first chapters of the Book of Genesis, for example, is metaphorical, continues to be a subject for debate. It is widely held that these chapters are not to be taken in what may be called a "naive literalist" manner. On the other hand, some have held that the events described are to be considered to have occurred just as we read them in translation, giving the words their "natural" meaning. This is held to mean that the earth was created in six periods of 24 hours, and that the history of the earth is to be compressed within about 6000 years. Adherents of this view (see, e.g., the writings of Henry M. Morris and his school) set out to discredit conventional methods for the determination of the age of the earth from radiometric and other physical methods. Those who practice these methods accept that there are in them experimental uncertainties, but they do not believe that the uncertainties are great enough to render the methods useless. Further, they point out that there is a fair degree of concordance obtained from different independent techniques.

To say that the existence of the world is "contingent" means that it is not "necessary." Among theologians who have discussed the relation between scientific and theological understanding of the natural world, T. F. Torrance has done much to reemphasize the notions of contingence and contingent order in the context of modern thought. He makes the point that these notions, essential for natural science, derive from outside it, namely, from Christian theology—a point which has sometimes been overlooked in the heat of the debate. Indeed, a case for the dependence of the rise of modern science upon the supportive environment of 17th-century Christian Europe has been well argued by Hooykaas and others.

In pre-Darwinian discussions of apologetics, the argument from design for the creation of the world by God took a prominent place. Indeed, one of the greatest triumphs of the theory of evolution, in the view of many of its supporters, was that it turned the idea of design in the universe on its head and allowed the development of an alternative: we are here because we have been the best survivors. Some Christians have felt that this was not an adequate explanation, that the conditions necessary for life as we know it are so finely adjusted as to make it highly unlikely that they have come about "by chance." In recent years, a somewhat similar idea has arisen in quite a different way. Observing that the fundamental constants of nature, the electromagnetic and gravitational fine-structure constants, have values which lead to the structures we observe in the cosmos, some cosmologists have asked why these constants have the values they do. To them it seems that we are here to observe the structure of the universe because of a contingent fact. This is a crude statement of what has been called "anthropic cosmological principle," which, as it has been said, attempts to answer the question "Why is the universe as we observe it?" by asserting that "if it were otherwise there would not be anyone to ask the question" (S. Hawking).

**Bibliography.** B. Ramm, *The Christian View of Science and Scripture* (1954); I. G. Barbour, *Issues in Science and Religion* (1966); R. H. Bube, *The Human Quest* (1971); A. R. Peacocke, *Science and the Christian Experiment* (1971); R. Hooykaas, *Religion and the Rise of Modern Science* (1972); M. Jeeves, ed., *Behavioural Sciences: A Christian Perspective* (1984); C. F. H. Henry, ed., *Horizons of Science* (1978); D. M. Mackay, *Science, Chance and Providence* (1978); D. Burke, ed., *Creation and Evolution* (1985); C. A. Russell, *Crosscurrents: Interactions between Science and Faith* (1985); J. Polkinghorne, *One World* (1986).

J. ALAN FRIEND

**Scientology.** Eclectic movement combining elements of psychiatry, science fiction, and religion, and claiming some 2 million adherents worldwide. Membership is gained through a lengthy series of residential courses. These courses involve the study of an esoteric psychotherapy and training which, it is claimed, substantially increases intellectual and mental abilities and removes mental aberrations caused by negative experiences earlier in life or inherited via a reincarnated spirit.

The organization was founded by an American science fiction writer, L. Ron Hubbard (1911–1986), whose book *Dianetics: The Modern Science of Mental Health* was widely read in the USA in the early 1950s. Facing strong criticism of Hubbard's teachings and bankruptcy, the organization moved to Great Britain in 1954, where its world headquarters have remained. Hubbard led the movement until 1966, and continued to be involved in teaching until his death.

Although scientologists refer to themselves as a church, their beliefs are basically humanistic, with no place for a personal, supernatural God. The highest aim of man is to realize his full human potential; this is achieved through participation in the church's courses and through self-effort. The history of the church of scientology has been a stormy one, marked in particular by attacks on and from governments and the media. Some governments, including that of Great Britain, have placed restrictions on scientologists' activities.

PETER HICKS

**Scofield, Cyrus Ingerson** (1843–1921). Congregationalist scholar. Born in Lenawee County, Mich., and reared in Tennessee, he was educated privately and served in the Army of Northern Virginia under General Lee, receiving the Confederate Cross of Honor. Admitted to the Kansas bar he was elected to the Kansas House of Representatives from Atchison and Nemaha counties. President Grant appointed him U.S. attorney for Kansas. Converted to Christianity in 1879, he was ordained to the Congregational ministry in 1882 and served as pastor of First Church, Dallas, Tex. (1882–95, 1902–7), and Moody Church, Northfield, Mass. (1895–1902). His later years were devoted to Scofield Correspondence Bible School and to lecturing in Europe and America. His most famous work was *The Scofield Reference Bible*, the editing of which he completed in 1909. He also wrote *Rightly Dividing the Word of Truth* (1885), *Addresses on Prophecy* (1900), *The Doctrine of the Holy Spirit* (1906), *Lectures on Galatians* (1907), and *Bible of 1911* (1911).

**Bibliography.** A. S. Gaebelein, *The History of the Scofield Reference Bible* (1943).

RAYMOND W. ALBRIGHT

**Scopes Trial.** Trial in Dayton, Tenn., in 1925, of 24-year-old John Thomas Scopes for teaching evolution in the county high school which brought to a dramatic head a series of attacks by fundamentalists upon modern science. They challenged the right of tax-supported schools to teach any theory of the origin of man which denied the biblical account of divine creation. Tennessee was the first state to acquiesce to their pressure when a bill (1925) made it a legal offense to teach biological evolution in universities, normal schools, and other public schools of the state.

Scopes challenged what he regarded as an affront to academic freedom. He was defended by Chicago criminal lawyer Clarence Darrow at the expense of the American Civil Liberties Union. The prosecution was led by Christian statesman William Jennings Bryan, whose efforts had been largely responsible for the enactment of antievolution laws in several Southern states. The issue was not to determine whether Scopes had violated the law—that was freely admitted—but whether evolution was to be taught in tax-supported institutions. The trial became a duel of wits between Bryan, the spokesman for fundamentalism, and Darrow, the defender of academic freedom whose agnosticism blurred the principle which he supported.

Scopes was convicted and fined $100. The decision was later reversed by the supreme court of Tennessee on the technical grounds that the fine was too large, although the statute itself was upheld. The real issue of science versus fundamentalism remained unsettled.

**Bibliography.** L. H. Allen, ed., *Bryan and Darrow at Dayton* (1925); H. Steele Commager, *The American Mind* (1950); P. Hibben, *The Peerless Leader* (1929); M. Shipley, *War on Modern Science* (1927).

ROBERT G. TORBET

## Scotland.

Country occupying the northern third of the British mainland with an area more than half that of England and Wales (78,772 sq. km. [30,414 sq. mi.]) and a total population of 5.1 million (1981). Scotland has an ecclesiastical scene very different from that in England with whom it has shared a sovereign since 1603 and a parliament since 1707.

The 1900 merger of the Free Church and the United Presbyterian Church to form the United Free Church was quickly followed by a movement for union with the parent Church of Scotland. There were several reasons for this: (1) The appointment of parish ministers by patrons instead of through election by congregations had been abolished in 1874, thus removing one great barrier. (2) The 1900 union was such a success as to encourage further experimentation. (3) The practical sympathy shown by Church of Scotland representatives toward the United Free Church regarding legal difficulties had created a friendly atmosphere for negotiations. (4) The growth of Roman Catholicism in Scotland constituted a challenge which indicated union as the path of wisdom. (5) Secularism was affecting Scotland, creating the problem of the so-called churchless million who had no vital connection with organized religion in any form. This showed the need for closing ranks.

Negotiations lasted from 1908 to 1929. Two basic issues had to be faced. The Church of Scotland stood for the national recognition of religion. The United Free Church maintained the spiritual freedom of the church from any kind of secular control. Through parliamentary legislation a compromise was effected which precluded state interference in "matters of doctrine, worship, government, and discipline," and the union took place in 1929, giving the expanded Church of Scotland a membership of over 1.25 million. The secularism that has affected the whole of Western Christendom is reflected in a steady drop in Church of Scotland membership to 870,527 in 1985.

Roman Catholics form the next largest religious body in Scotland. Since achieving legal toleration under the Catholic Emancipation Act of 1829, the number of Catholics has grown consistently in the country. This increase has come about chiefly through large-scale immigration from the Republic of Ireland and the tradition of large Catholic families. The Catholic Church in Scotland is organized in two provinces—St. Andrews-Edinburgh and Glasgow—and claims a baptized total of about 800,000, concentrated overwhelmingly in the Lowlands. The fact that these individuals were originally non-Scottish in culture as well as non-Protestant in religion has created some tension.

The influence of minority Presbyterians who failed to enter the successive church unions is now not great. The Reformed Presbyterians who stand squarely on the Covenants of 1638 and 1643, now number no more than about 250. The Original Seceders rejoined the Church of Scotland in 1956. The remnant of the Free Church which declined union in 1900 have about 17,000 members and adherents. A breakaway group from the latter, the Free Presbyterian Church, numbers about 5000. The United Free Church has about 9000 members.

Said to represent the unbroken episcopal tradition of the Scottish Reformation, the Episcopal Church in Scotland resembles the Church of England in doctrine, worship, and government. It has seven bishops and some 35,000 communicant members.

Congregationalists number about 18,500 members and adherents, Baptists about 14,500, Christian Brethren about 16,000, and Methodists about 9000. The Salvation Army probably number about 6000. Among the sects there are an estimated 7000 Jehovah's Witnesses, 12,000 Mormons, and 7000 scientologists. There are also about 28,000 Muslims, 10,000 Hindus, and 10,000 Sikhs.

Union negotiations among Christian churches are at a virtual standstill. Most of them, however, cooperate in the work of such interdenominational bodies as the Scottish Churches Council. At conferences Roman Catholics are increasingly found as active observers.

J. D. DOUGLAS

## Scott, Robert Balgarnie Young (1899–1987).

Canadian OT scholar and clergyman. Born in Toronto, he studied at the University of Toronto (Ph.D., 1928), Union College, Toronto, and New College, University of Edinburgh, and was ordained in the United Church of Canada in 1926. He was professor of OT at Union College, Vancouver (1928–31), Union Theological College, Montreal (1931–55), and McGill University faculty of divinity (1948–55; dean, 1948/49), and professor of religion, Princeton University (1955–68). He was one of the founders of the Canadian Society of Biblical Studies (1933), and was later its president (1972). He was also president of the Society of Biblical Literature (1960), and the recipient of five honorary degrees for his biblical scholarship. He wrote *The Relevance of the Prophets* (1944, rev. 1968), *Treasures from Judean Caves* (1955), *Isaiah 1–39*, Interpreter's Bible (1956), *The Psalms as Christian Praise* (1958), *Proverbs and Ecclesiastes*, Anchor Bible (1965), *The Way of Wisdom in the OT* (1971), and the lyrics to 10 widely published hymns. He coedited and contributed to *Towards the Christian Revolution* (1936).

GLEN G. SCORGIE

## Scroggie, William Graham (1877–1958).

British Bible teacher, pastor, and author. Born in Great Malvern, his early background was Christian Brethren, although he eventually trained for the Baptist ministry at Spurgeon's College, London. He was forced to leave his first two pastorates in London and Yorkshire because of his opposition to theological liberalism in one and worldliness in the other. Two years of intense, private study of Scripture preceded his 10-year pastorate at Sunderland and 17 years at Charlotte Chapel, Edinburgh (which city's university gave him an honorary D.D.). His final pastorate of seven years at the Metropolitan Tabernacle, London, was preceded by two years traveling and preaching in New Zealand, Australia, the USA, and Canada. Although he retired due to ill health in 1944, he gave in 1954 his 12th series of Bible readings at the Keswick Convention. His gift of Bible teaching and survey is reflected in his numerous publications, most notably *The Land and Life of Rest* (1950), *The Unfolding Drama of Redemption: The Bible as a Whole* (2 vols., 1957), and four volumes on the psalms.

JAMES TAYLOR

## Secrecy of the Confessional. *See* CONFESSIONAL, SECRECY OF THE.

## Sects and Cults.

Religious groups defined by believers in terms of deviation from theological orthodoxy. Thus Roman Catholics may call Lutherans a sect while Anglicans often describe Mormonism as a cult. In both Judaism and Islam similar theological definitions exist as they do with slightly different emphases in other world religions.

In the theological sense sects tend to be groups which have broken from a dominant tradition but which retain some aspects of that tradition. Cults on the other hand tend to be groups which the orthodox consider totally wrong and therefore outside the tradition and beyond the pale of salvation.

Theological definitions are helpful for believers but they do not enable scholars to compare traditions or to comment on the social dynamics of religious groups. Therefore toward the end of the 19th century and in the early years of this century various sociologists led by Max Weber (1864–1920) and Ernst Troeltsch (1865–1923) began using what they called "ideal types" to identify similar forms of religious movements in terms of their social expression.

An ideal type is not a real thing but rather an approximation which concentrates on the salient features of particular, observable social groups. As used by Weber an ideal type denotes social arrangements peopled by rational beings and is used to describe theoretical models of institutions, social relations, and political systems which are "ideal" in the sense of being constructed entirely according to the theoretical laws that explain them.

When they came to study religious movements Weber and Troeltsch proposed a threefold typology which made use of the terms "church," "sect," and "mysticism," "spiritual idealism" or "cult." Later, in the 1920s H. Richard Niebuhr suggested that "denomination" should be added to complete this typology and make sense of the American situation. Therefore to understand the sociological use of "sect" one must begin by understanding what sociologists mean by "church."

In sociology the term "church" is used to refer to a religious organization which is universalist in scope. The model of the ideal-type church is rooted in the medieval Roman Catholic notion of the church theoretically embracing every member of society. Thus, anyone living in Europe during the Middle Ages was considered to be a Christian, and baptism was usually administered automatically to children just as all members of society participated in the Mass unless excommunicated by the church. In such a situation it was assumed that Europeans were Christians and therefore members of the Church of Christ which was unquestionably the Roman Catholic Church. As a result church membership was virtually compulsory and a requirement for citizenship.

The Reformers questioned the automatic assumption that all church members were Christians. No longer did attendance at Mass and participation in the sacraments guarantee that a person was a Christian. Martin Luther (1483–1546) and the other Reformers emphasized the necessity for each individual to exercise a personal faith. As a result individual choice and personal commitment became the hallmark of the Christian. Sociologically this insistence on personal decision and choice signifies a sectarian movement or sect which forms in essence a voluntary society. No longer is it assumed that everyone in a particular society is a Christian or that membership in the church is compulsory for all members of society. Rather, Christians are people who elect to join a particular group because they believe that its teachings contain the truth and that it promotes "true religion."

The third typology introduced at this stage was that of "mystical religion" which is sometimes referred to by Weber and Troeltsch as "mysticism," "spiritual religion," or the "cult." Here cult was taken to signify a small, inner-directed, highly mystical group of intellectuals. Thus the Quakers became the prime example of spiritual religion and therefore the cult. Troeltsch describes such groups as being based on personal, inward experience, and held together by purely interpersonal ties and lacking a permanent form. He argues that they often lead to an exaggerated, highly emotional form of piety and although highly creative are inherently unstable.

The word "cult" has also been used by evangelical Christians to signify theologically unorthodox groups. This usage seems to have begun with books like H. van Baalen's *Chaos of the Cults* (1934) and has been popularized through works like Walter Martin's best seller *The Kingdom of the Cults* (1965). Here cults are identified as spiritually dangerous because they lead people away from the truth of Christianity.

During the 1970s, the word "cult" was picked up by journalists to describe new religious movements which were appealing to young people in Western society, such as the Unification Church, Hare Krishna, and transcendental meditation. The journalistic use of "cult" soon took on a highly derogatory meaning and came to signify a group which was considered "dangerous" because it was supposed to "brainwash" its members and present some undefined threat to social order. The Jonestown tragedy in 1979 added a bizarre and sensational element to journalistic writing about cults.

The emergence of a highly committed, high-profile, anticult movement in the late 1970s soon meant that the word began to lose all objective meaning. Therefore, most social scientists today prefer to talk about "new religious movements" rather than cults.

In surveying the church-sect typology of Weber and Troeltsch H. Richard Niebuhr pointed out that it did not take into account the predominantly American phenomenon of religious groups which behave like ideal-type churches but because they minister only to certain members of a given society are technically classified as sects.

Typical of this type of religious group are Methodists and Baptists. In theory both are conversionist groups which exist in terms of a voluntary principle. But, in practice, in many areas to be born a Methodist or Baptist means that a person will be considered a Christian. Therefore, while their explicit theology might demand personal commitment and cause sociologists to classify them as sectarian groups, their practice or implicit theology accepts anyone who is either born into their community or who simply attends one of their churches in a given area.

To describe this type of group Niebuhr proposed the use of the term "denomination." In his typology a denomination is a sectarian movement which has developed characteristics more properly belonging to a church. Another way of saying this is to describe a denomination as a sect on the way to becoming a church. Yet, the nature of modern society is such that the denomination can never fully attain the role of a church because it can never dominate a given geographical area and make membership of the religious community it represents a prerequisite for citizenship.

Today in most Western countries the established churches, such as the Anglicans in England, display characteristics which make them look more like denominations than the typology of the church proposed by Weber. Perhaps only in Southern Ireland and similar Roman Catholic countries does one still find institutions approaching the ideal-type church. However, in using church-sect typologies it must be remembered that they were never intended to exactly duplicate the real world and that they can be applied with modification to non-Christian societies for the purpose of comparison and social analysis.

*Bibliography.* H. Richard Niebuhr, *The Social Sources of Denominationalism* (1929); E. Troeltsch, *The Social Teachings of the Christian Churches* (1931); M. Weber, *The Sociology of Religion* (repr., 1964); R. Robertson, *The Sociological Interpretation of Religion* (1972); R. Stark and W. S. Bainbridge, *The Future of Religion: Secularization, Revival and Cult Formation* (1985); I. Hexham and K. Poewe, *Understanding Cults and New Religions* (1986).

IRVING HEXHAM

**Secularism.** Originally the self-chosen designation of a society of agnostics who regarded belief in anything transcendent as an impediment to progress, the word has assumed a variety of usages based on its etymology (the recognition of only one *saeculum*).

Secularism may be used to describe the thought of outspokenly atheistic and agnostic leaders, such as Comte, Marx, John Dewey, Bertrand Russell, Freud, and Sartre, with their complete emancipation from the supernatural and all transcendent absolutes. The extremes of optimism (the world is subject to rational control by scientific method or predetermined to issue in utopia) and of pessimism (life is meaningless) are represented.

The most prevalent usage of the term is its reference to "practical atheism" and "this-worldliness" reflected in all areas of thought and life. God is not so much denied as ignored. This age is for all practical purposes the only one. Man's autonomy is assumed; he makes his own rules on the basis of more or less enlightened self-interest. While some are still riding high with the intoxication of power, the mood of most has turned to despair, apparent especially in literature and art and the disintegration of the forms of community. It is not always clear whether it is the specifically Christian or any transcendent being whatsoever which is being repudiated. Sometimes the word becomes synonymous with "materialism" as a catchall for all that is a denial of the "spiritual" and traditional values.

More rarely the term refers to recognition of only one *saeculum*—not taking seriously the "new age" in Christ which runs concurrently with the old aeon until its promised triumph in the resurrection.

*Bibliography.* J. Richard Spann, ed., *The Christian Faith and Secularism* (1948); C. T. Craig, ed., *The Challenge of our Culture* (1946); T. O. Wedel, *The Christianity of Main Street* (1950).

MARTIN J. HEINECKEN

**Sell, Edward** (1839–1932). Anglican missionary and Islamics scholar. Born in Wantage, England, he finished his education at the Church Missionary College, was ordained in 1862, and began missionary service in India that was to last 67 years. He was principal of a high school for Muslims in Madras (1865–81), then became CMS secretary for the dioceses of Madras and Travancore, and acted also on behalf of the SPCK. He became a leading authority on Islam. His many publications include *The Faith of Islam* (1880), *The Historical Development of the Qur'an* (1897), *Essays on Islam* (1901), *Islam: Its Rise and Progress* (1907), *The Religious Orders of Islam* (1908), *The Khulafa'r-Rashidun* (1909), *The Cult of Ali* (1909), *The Battles of Badr and Uhud* (1909), *Al-Qur'an* (1909), *Sufism* (1910), *The Druses* (1910), *Ghazwas and Siriyas* (1911), 10 books on OT literature and *The Messianic Hope* (1929), and various articles in the *Encyclopaedia of Religion and Ethics*.

**Selwyn, Edward Gordon** (1885–1959). Anglican scholar. Born in Liverpool, he was educated at Cambridge and ordained in 1909. He was fellow and lecturer at Corpus Christi College, Cambridge (1909–13), warden of Radley College (1913–18), rector of Redhill, Havant (1919–30), editor of *Theology* (1920–33), and dean of Winchester from 1931. He wrote *The Approach to Christianity* (1925), *The Epistle of Christian Courage* (1939), and *The First Epistle of St. Peter* (1946). He edited *Essays Catholic and Critical* (1926) and *A Short History of Christian Thought* (1937).

**Senegal.** *See* WEST AFRICA.

**Septuagint.** Greek translation of the Hebrew OT. The exact origin of this version is obscure and shrouded in legend. The term originally referred to the Greek Pentateuch, which was translated during the reign of Ptolemy II Philadelphus (285–246 B.C.) in Alexandria, Egypt. The name "Septuagint" comes from the Greek word for "seventy" (hence LXX). The number 70 may be an approximation for 72, referring to the 72 Jewish translators allegedly brought to Egypt by Ptolemy II Philadelphus. The number may, on the other hand, have been traditional (cf. the number of elders in Moses' day [Exod. 24:1, 9]; the membership of the Sanhedrin; the generally accepted reading of Luke 10:1, 17). The *Letter of Aristeas* suggests that in its final form the Greek Pentateuch was the product of editorial harmonization. Probably by 150 B.C. most of the OT existed in Greek. Eventually the term "Septuagint" was applied to the entire Greek OT previous to revision or retranslation. Hence it would be more accurate to speak of the Old Greek version, but the term LXX is well established in this restricted sense. Naturally the style varies in different books, and the verison is of unequal merit.

Considerable research has been done on the LXX in the 20th century. P. E. Kahle (*The Cairo Geniza* [1947]) maintained that there were earlier translations of the Pentateuch, of which a revision was made in the time of Ptolemy; this then became the standard Greek Torah. For the other books of the OT he postulated additional independent Greek renderings. When the church needed a canonical text of the entire OT, it simply took one form of the various texts and adapted it for Christian readers. Kahle did not believe that there was one original Old Greek version, and consequently the manuscripts of the LXX would not go back to a single archetype. In contrast, P. de Lagarde saw the problems involved and the correct methodology for recovering the text of the original LXX. He was followed by A. Rahlfs (*Septuaginta Studien*, 3. Heft, [1911]; *Septuaginta, Genesis* [1926]). Rahlfs was also the editor of a complete text (*Septuaginta id est V. T. Graece iuxta LXX Interpretes* [Stuttgart, 1935]). A thoroughgoing attempt at establishing the text of one LXX book on Lagardian principles was made by M. L.

Margolis (*The Book of Joshua in Greek* [1931], pts. 1–4). He maintained that the text "as it appears at the top of the page is the nearest approach to the Greek original as it left the hands of the translator(s)." The methods initiated by Lagarde were successfully applied by J. A. Montgomery in two commentaries in the International Critical Commentary series: *Daniel* (1927) and *Kings* (1951). For an appreciation of Lagardian principles and extensive bibliography on LXX work in general, see H. M. Orlinsky, *JAOS* 61 (1941): 81–91; idem, *Biblical Archaeologist* 9 (1946); idem, "Current Progress in Septuagint Research," in H. R. Willoughby, ed., *The Study of the Bible Today and Tomorrow* (1947); and idem, "Margolis' Work in the Septuagint," in *Max Leopold Margolis, Scholar and Teacher* (1952). In this volume J. Reider also presents a complete bibliography of the writings of that LXX scholar. In defense of Lagarde's principles and the work of Rahlfs, see P. Katz, *TZ* 5 (1949): 1–24; and "Recovery of Original LXX—A Study in the History of Transmission and Text. Criticism," in *Actes du Premier Congrès de la Féd. Int. des Assoc. Études d'Classiques* (1951), 165–82.

It is now recognized that Hebrew texts in Greek transcription were used by Jews; an example of such a text is the second column of the Hexapla. F. Wutz advanced the theory that the LXX was rendered from a Hebrew text written in Greek characters (*Die Transkriptionen von der Septuaginta bis zu Hieronymus* [1925–33]). A great deal of research was expended to prove this hypothesis, but it has not been accepted by scholars.

From Egypt the LXX spread to all parts of the Hellenistic-Jewish world, and over time different text traditions developed in centers like Alexandria, Caesarea, and Antioch. The possibility of prerecensional revisions on the basis of local Hebrew texts must in this connection receive serious consideration. The LXX became the OT of the Christians, who used it in their controversies with the Jews, even though it differed from the Hebrew text then in vogue. Accordingly the need arose for another translation or rendering of the OT. Theodotion did not produce a new version, but apparently worked on a tradition current in Asia Minor, which is referred to by biblical scholars as Ur-Theodotion or pre-Theodotion. In connection with the three main recensions of the Greek Bible some attention must be given to the background of Lucian's text. The appearance of Lucianic readings preceding Lucian (martyred A.D. 311/12) along with their occurrence in Old Latin texts has raised complicated problems which are still unresolved, and accordingly an Ur-Lucian or a pre-Lucianic version native to Antioch and Syria has been postulated.

The LXX represents a pre-Masoretic Hebrew text and accordingly is important for textual and exegetical studies. The methods of translation, however, must be noted. Extreme literalism and freedom of rendering are frequently found in the same verse or adjacent verses. Also certain definite exegetical principles were employed by the translators. For theological reasons some expressions concerning God, which were regarded as crude or offensive, were attenuated, and anthropomorphisms were frequently removed. In many cases this was achieved by the translator's manipulation of Hebrew roots. Yet the translators did not intentionally set out to rewrite the original, and these exegetical principles were not consistently followed (see C. T. Fritsch, *The Anti-Anthropomorphisms of the Greek Pentateuch* [1943]; H. S. Gehman, *JBL* 68 [1949]: 231–40; idem, *JAOS* 70 [1950]: 292–96; D. H. Gard, *The Exegetical Method of the Greek Translator of the Book of Job*, J. B. L. Monograph series, vol. 8 [1952]; J. W. Wevers, *CBQ* 14 [1952]: 40–56; ibid. 15 [1953]: 30–45). The LXX accordingly cannot be used in a merely mechanical manner to emend the Masoretic Text.

Linguistic studies of LXX Greek which deserve mention include H. St. J. Thackeray, *A Grammar of the OT in Greek According to the Septuagint* (1909); H. S. Gehman, *VT* 1 (1951): 81–90; and idem, ibid. 3 (1953): 141–48. In connection with the Greek OT should also be noted J. Reider, *Prolegomena to a Greek-Hebrew and Hebrew-Greek Index to Aquila* (1916); J. H. Moulton, *Grammar of NT Greek*, vol. 1 (3d ed., 1908); idem, with W. F. Howard, ibid., vol. 2 (1929). This grammar has many references to the LXX and an appendix on Semiticisms in the NT.

An indispensable handbook to LXX studies is H. B. Swete, *An Introduction to the OT in Greek*, revised by R. R. Ottley (1914). For manuscripts and versions, see F. G. Kenyon, *The Text of the Greek Bible* (1937); and idem, *Our Bible and the Ancient Manuscripts* (4th ed., 1939). A general work on the LXX is R. R. Ottley, *A Handbook to the Septuagint* (1920). According to H. M. Orlinsky, the Tetrapla was not a separate edition of Origen's critical work with the omission of the two Hebrew columns of the Hexapla, but the term was loosely used for the Hexapla when the four Greek columns (Tetrapla) were stressed rather than all six (Hexapla).

Among Greek papyri of the OT should be noted 2d-century B.C. fragments of Deuteronomy (23: 24[26]–24:3; 25:1–3; 26:12; 17–19; 28:31–33). It is important that this text agrees with A and Theodotion rather than with B; for these texts, see C. H. Roberts, *Two Biblical Papyri in the John Rylands Library Manchester* (1936). The Chester Beatty Papyri, dating variously from the first half of the 2d, 3d, and 4th centuries A.D., contain portions of Genesis, Numbers, Deuteronomy, Isaiah, Jeremiah, Ezekiel, Daniel, Esther, and Ecclesiasticus (see F. G. Kenyon, *The Chester Beatty Biblical Papyri;* fasc. 4 [1934]; 5 [1935]; 6 [1937]; 7 [1937]). The John H. Scheide Biblical Papyri of

42 pages, which contain, with some losses, Ezekiel 19:12–39:29, are dated to the early 3d century and come from the same codex as the Chester Beatty Papyrus of this book (Kenyon IX; Rahlfs and Ziegler no. 967). They have been published in photographic reproduction and transcription with critical apparatus, introductory chapters, and notes under the editorship of A. C. Johnson, H. S. Gehman, and E. H. Kase (1938); see also H. S. Gehman, *JAOS* 58 (1938): 92–102; idem, *JBL* 57 (1938): 281–87; and J. Ziegler, *ZAW* 61 (1945–48): 76–94.

In addition to the editions of the LXX of Swete and Rahlfs there is the large Cambridge edition of *The OT in Greek* begun under the editorship of A. E. Brooke and N. McLean. Another important edition of the LXX with an extensive critical apparatus is the *Septuaginta, Vetus Testamentum Graecum (Auctoritate Societatis Litterarum Gottingensis editum)*.

*Bibliography.* J. Barr, *Comparative Philology and the Text of the OT* (1968); S. Jellicoe, *Septuagint and Modern Study* (1968); J. Ziegler, *Sylloge, Gesammelte Aufsätze zur Septuaginta* (1971); X. Jacques, *List of Septuagint Words Sharing Common Elements* (1972); R. A. Kraft, ed., *Septuagint Lexicography* (1972); S. P. Brock, C. T. Fritsch, and S. Jellicoe, *Classified Bibliography of the Septuagint* (1973); S. Jellicoe, ed., *Studies in the Septuagint: Origins, Recensions, and Interpretations* (1974); F. M. Cross and S. Talmon, eds., *Qumran and the History of the Biblical Text* (1975); F. G. Kenyon, *Text of the Greek Bible* (3d rev. ed., 1975); D. Barthélemy, *Études d'histoire du texte l'AT* (1978); E. Würthwein, *Text of the OT* (4th ed., 1979).

HENRY S. GEHMAN

## Serbian Orthodox Church in America (SOCA).

Church formed by immigrants from the area now called Yugoslavia in California in 1894. It was first called St. Sava's, in honor of the first archbishop of the Serbian Orthodox Church (13th cent.).

By 1921, there were 24 congregations in the USA, and the patriarch in Belgrade agreed to recognize them as the diocese of North America. In 1926, Mardarije was appointed as bishop. His successor, Dionisije, was appointed in 1940.

In the early 1960s, citing the large territory of his diocese, Dionisije requested that it be elevated to a metropolitinate and that two assistant bishops be approved. The patriarchate responded by deposing Dionisije, accusing him of financial and sexual misconduct, and replacing the single diocese with three: Middle Eastern-Canadian, Middle Western, and Western. Three priests of American churches were appointed as bishops. The Middle Western diocese includes the headquarters of SOCA at St. Sava's Monastery in Libertyville, Ill., where the episcopal council and national assembly meet to govern the church. In 1983, a separate Canadian diocese was created.

Dionisije resisted the charges, claiming that the true causes were his outspoken anticommunism and the patriarch's intention, at the behest of Tito's government, to make the American churches dependent upon Belgrade. A large minority of church members sided with Dionisije, at least for a time, leading to numerous schisms in local congregations, occasionally accompanied by violent demonstrations, and to law suits which were finally settled in 1976 by decision of the U.S. Supreme Court favoring the patriarchal party.

In 1986 SOCA had 77 parishes with about 100,000 members. It is a self-governing church which acknowledges the authority of the Holy Synod and patriarch of the Serbian Orthodox Church in Yugoslavia.

*Bibliography.* Dionisije, *Patriarch Gherman's Violations of the Holy Canons, Rules and Regulations of the Serbian Orthodox Church* (1965); D. Vrga, *Changes and Socio-Religious Conflict in an Ethnic Minority Group, the Serbian Orthodox Church in America* (1975).

PAUL D. STEEVES

**Sermon.** A popular oral address proclaiming religious truth contained in Scripture. A function of the OT prophets which developed into an integral part of synagogue worship, it was the primary activity of the apostles (Acts 20:27; 1 Cor. 1:17–18). Paul presents preaching as a responsibility of Timothy as a pastor (2 Tim. 4:2). The biblical purpose of preaching is to offer salvation through the interpretation of the Holy Spirit in the hearts of hearers and to equip and strengthen the church.

The practice of biblical preaching was reborn with the renewal of the place of Scripture in the Reformation. The nonconformist church in England and Puritan believers in North America contributed a foundation of powerful, Bible-centered proclamation for the 20th century. Much of the power of the 19th-century pulpit was centered in the revival movement, and even secular newspapers printed the texts of such dynamic preachers as Charles Spurgeon. In the 20th century, as church attendance declined and alternative media made the average church-goer more discriminating, new, more lively communication styles and practices were developed and taught in theological schools.

The basic varieties of the sermon of the late 1900s church were: (1) The homily, a brief series of observations and exhortations drawn from a short passage of Scripture, primarily used on occasions when a longer message would be inappropriate. (2) The topical sermon, which compiles all or most of what Scripture teaches on a given subject. It draws from all parts of the Bible to develop the topic and so can be a powerful communicative tool. (3) The textual-topical sermon also draws from throughout the Word, yet is anchored to one text. Such a method is often used for series of sermons on the Ten Commandments or the "fruit of the Spirit" (Gal. 5:22–23). (4) The textual sermon draws its main points from the development of an idea in a small passage of Scripture. The text dictates the organization of the message, and each point is developed with microscopic examination. (5) The expository sermon draws all main and subpoints from the flow of the text, and it is considered the most biblical and systematic way to teach. A single subject is covered throughout the sermon, but it must be the subject that was in view when the biblical author penned his words.

Preaching methods of the 20th century differed in various cultural and theological contexts, and they involved all the dramatic techniques of secular discourse and theater. The important considerations were that the sermon maintain interest, and was persuasive and informative in religious content. Most important in distinguishing sermons from other forms of communication was that the sermon be based on Scripture.

## Sermon on the Mount. *Structure.* The Sermon on the Mount (Matt. 5–7) is the first of five or six compilations of Jesus' sayings which the Evangelist inserts into his narrative. The sermon appears in the Gospel just after the beginning of Jesus' ministry and the call of his first disciples. Its apparent purpose is to set forth Jesus' new interpretation of the Law as a guide for those who aspire to the kingdom of heaven. The sermon begins with nine Beatitudes (5:3–12). Then follow sayings on the responsibilities of the disciples and the relation between the old and new Law (5:13–20); six contrasts between the old and new applications of the Law (5:21–48); three contrasts between the old religious practice and the new (6:1–18); and a group of sayings on various aspects of the religious life, leading up to the golden rule (6:19–7:12). The sermon concludes with warnings (7:13–27), the last of which is the parable of the two houses.

*Sources.* Some relationship exists between this and the much shorter "Sermon on the Plain" (Luke 6:20–49), which begins and concludes in similar fashion. It is often suggested that Matthew and Luke drew on the so-called Q source. If Luke's sermon is substantially that of Q, Matthew may have woven this in with a second discourse from a special source M (perhaps represented by Matt. 5:4–5, 7–10, 21–28, 33–37; 6:1–7, 16–18), together with other Q materials which Luke places in various parts of his Gospel. On the other hand, Luke, who shows little interest in controversies about the Jewish law, may have abbreviated a Q sermon which originally was longer. In this case, some of Matthew's special material may have been part of Q. Earlier collections seem, in any event, to lie behind the Sermon on the Mount, and it is usually thought unlikely that Jesus would have given all this teaching on a single occasion.

*Teaching.* The Sermon on the Mount is in harmony with Jesus' other teaching. It is eschatological, that is, it presupposes the coming judgment and the kingdom of God. Albert Schweitzer and others have regarded all of Jesus' ethical teaching as an interim-ethic—such extreme demands would not have been made if the end of the age were not in view—but it is more commonly held that both Jesus' eschatology and his ethics are determined by his profound faith in God's sovereignty and omnipotence, and that his view of the will of God would have been the same whether the kingdom should come early or late. Many of the sermon's moral teachings have no necessary relationship to eschatological belief.

Maxims in the sermon (and elsewhere in the Gospels) are similar in form to the wisdom literature of the OT (see, e.g., 5:25–26, 29–30; most of the passage on anxious care [6:25–34]; and the golden rule [7:12]). Jesus' wisdom sayings often reveal a more intense concentration on the will and activity of God, as contrasted with the wisdom books, whose advice is often worldly and prudential. Jesus apparently uses what are otherwise secular proverbs to impart a religious message, but he, undoubtedly, treasures and respects the traditional wisdom of his people. The Sermon on the Mount, in fact, presents him in the roles of prophet, lawgiver, and sage.

The sayings in the sermon exhibit more than one attitude toward the Jewish law. The antitheses of chapter 5 are a prophetic and radical criticism of the Jewish law as it was commonly understood. Not only murder and adultery, but the impulses behind them, must be rooted out. Divorce, retaliation, and oath taking, which were presupposed by the Law, are excluded. The demand for love of enemies is grounded in the example of God, and the follower of Jesus must, like Job, be "perfect." Although this prepares the way for Paul and Marcion, it is assumed to be the true understanding of the OT Law itself, which is not destroyed but completed (5:17). On the other hand, Matt. 5:18–19 expresses the authority of the Law more strongly than any other part of the Gospels, and even draws the rabbinic distinction between lesser and greater commandments. The temple and Jewish forms of piety are taken for granted as a normal part of life, even though Jesus deals critically with certain observances (5:23–24; 6:1–8, 16–18). This twofold attitude is found elsewhere in the Gospels. For example, Matt. 23:16–22 holds all oaths equally binding, while Mark 7:9–13 protests against inforcing an oath which conflicts with the duty to father or mother and Mark 7:15 sweeps away the distinction between clean and unclean foods.

The sermon contains little christological material, such as is found in Matt. 11:25–30, except for the suggestion that Jesus' disciples call him "Lord" (7:21–22), the phrases "for my sake" (5:11) and "I am come" (5:17), and the formula "You have heard that it was said to the ancients . . . but I say unto you" (5:21–22, etc.), which suggest unique authority. The legal sayings are maxims, unlike the specific rulings on Sabbath observance and other issues, which elsewhere in the Gospels are often in connection with short anecdotes. No parables are included, and there is little emphasis on repentance or on seeking and saving that which is lost. On the other hand, the Beatitudes are a unique feature of the sermon. These promise to those who are poor in spirit (the religious "poor" of the psalms who live by trust and prayer), who mourn, who hunger and thirst for righteousness, and who exhibit the qualities of meekness, mercy, and peacemaking, that they will inherit the kingdom of heaven and become God's sons. Thus, although performance is demanded, the way of life rests on a relationship with God in faith, prayer, and presumably repentance.

***The Meaning of the Sermon and Its Practicability.*** Since the sermon as it stands is probably a compilation, its theological purpose is not necessarily identical with that of the separate sayings contained in it. It is an entire new Torah or teaching tradition, made up not only of legal sayings but of general directions for the religious life. Its sources may have taken form before the Christian movement was clearly differentiated from the synagogue. Although it contains promises and intimations of divine help, it is largely in the form of demands for right action and implies that the way of life is through obedience to these commandments. The Evangelist who gave the sermon its present form probably expected it to be observed literally. A satisfactory interpretation must deal with the sayings themselves in the light of all of Jesus' teachings. Modern theologians, as they attempt this task, have raised two separate but interrelated questions: (1) the purpose of Jesus in pronouncing the more radical sayings; and (2) the extent to which the teaching of the sermon can be observed and applied by present-day Christians.

In answer to the first question, it is sometimes argued that Jesus' purpose was to put an end to the legal way of life altogether by showing that the will of God is too far-reaching to be comprehended in any law code, for God demands unbounded love for himself and for one's neighbor. Others hold that Jesus expanded the Law's meaning in a prophetic direction but had no hostility to the legal principle of obedience, and expected that his disciples in their everyday affairs could and would observe his most extreme demands.

The problem of the practicability of the commandments arises because Christians do not as a matter of fact find themselves living in strict accord with the sermon; they are keenly conscious of their participation in society and their responsibility for it. Thus some hold that the more extreme commands can be kept only by the "perfect." Others regard all the commandments as equally binding on everyone, so that a Christian dare not participate in resistance to an enemy even if by nonparticipation he must defy the society in which he lives. Another group of interpreters holds that the sermon pictures an ethical ideal toward which one can only strive, or by which one's character may be transformed. Still others believe that the purpose of the sermon is to drive men to repentance and despair of their own efforts; thus it presupposes a message of grace and forgiveness which is completed only by Paul's doctrine of atonement through the cross. A few exegetes take even the command against worry (6:25–34) as a law which convicts man of lack of trust in God. On the other hand, others argue that the several parts of the sermon require different approaches and that not all the sayings can be applied according to a single set of principles.

***Bibliography.*** C. Gore, *The Sermon on the Mount* (1900); B. W. Bacon, *The Sermon on the Mount* (1902); P. Fiebig, *Jesu Bergpredigt* (1924); H. J. Vogels, *Synoptische Studien zur Bergpredigt* (1924); A. D. Lindsay, *The Moral Teaching of Jesus* (1937); M. Dibelius, *The Sermon on the Mount* (1940); H. Windisch, *The Meaning of the Sermon on the Mount* (1951); R. Bultmann, *Theology of the NT* (1951); A. M. Perry, *JBL*, 54 (1935): 103–16; A. N. Wilder, *The Interpreter's Bible* (1951) 7: 155–64.

SHERMAN E. JOHNSON

# Sertillanges, Antonin Gilbert (1863–1948).

Born in Clermont-Ferrand, France, he entered the Dominican Order in 1883. He was professor of philosophy at the *Institut Catholique*, Paris (1900–1922), and was elected a member of the *Académie des Sciences Morales et Politiques* (1918). His major works are *Saint Thomas d'Aquin* (Les Grands Philosophes) (1910), *La philosophie morale de Saint Thomas d'Aquin* (1916), *Catéchisme des incroyants* (1930), and *Le Christianisme et les philosophies* (1939–41).

GEORGES A. BARROIS

# Seventh-day Adventists. The largest American Adventist group. Seventh-day Adventists trace their beginnings to the prophecies and visions of Ellen G. White (1827–1915). After the "Great Disappointment," in which Christ's second coming failed to materialize in 1843/44, followers of Adventist teaching divided into several factions. The majority abandoned their earlier belief that a significant event occurred in 1844, and asserted that the 2300-year prophecy of Dan. 8 would occur some time in the future. Others spiritualized the predictions of events in 1844. Adventists led by White concluded that an event had occurred in 1844—a change in Christ's ministry *in heaven,* in which he had moved from the heavenly Holy to the Most Holy Place. The group also focused upon the Ten Commandments. White had a vision of the tablets of stone upon which the commandments were inscribed. She saw a halo around the fourth, on keeping the seventh

day holy (hence the group's name). Followers of White worshiped on Saturday and emphasized other OT teachings as well. Seventh-day Adventists hold the writings of White in the highest esteem, "as inspired counsels from the Lord." Doctrinally Seventh-day Adventists resemble the Baptist and Disciples of Christ churches at many points. One distinctive belief is that humans are by nature mortal, but may receive immortality through acceptance of God's grace in Christ. They practice baptism by immersion and footwashing, and abstain from alcohol and tobacco. They maintain several publishing houses and mission works outside the USA.

*Bibliography.* B. Herndon, *The Seventh Day: The Story of the Seventh-day Adventists* (1960); D. F. Neufeld, ed., *The Seventh Day Adventist Encyclopedia* (1976); A. W. Spalding, *Origin and History of Seventh-day Adventists*, 4 vols. (1976).

R. MILTON WINTER

**Sex, Ethics of.** The sexual revolution, which had its beginnings in the USA after World War I as condoms and diaphrams became accessible and reliable, reached its climax in the early 1980s. After World War II, the development of alternative methods of contraception (creams, jellies, pills, sponges, IUDs) coincided with and complemented a worldwide concern for population control, and, in the USA, the formal appearance of the Women's Liberation movement. By the 1970s the population rate in the USA and much of Western Europe approached the zero goal and many people on both sides of the Atlantic took a more relaxed attitude toward pre- and extramarital sex since sex could now be "safe." Data in the USA soon revealed that most teenagers had experienced sexual intercourse before the end of high school, and teenage pregnancy became a growing problem. Many adults accepted the idea that any form of sexual behavior between consenting adults was permissible. This in turn permitted public acknowledgment of the Gay Rights movement, with homosexuals and lesbians unabashedly asserting their lifestyle.

These changing attitudes toward sexual relations were paralleled by a movement which argued that it is a woman's right to terminate her pregnancy. The U.S. Supreme Court ruled that such was the case for the first trimester of pregnancy. In the second trimester, it was to be the decision of the woman in consultation with her physician. Although polls have consistently shown that about 80 percent of the population supports this ruling, it has come under severe attack by the Roman Catholic Church and other groups as being a violation of God's law and intentions.

While the vast majority of the population continued to endorse marriage as the ethical state for sex and for raising a family, the divorce rate climbed to about 40 percent of all who married.

The single parent came to the public's attention. It seemed that the traditional mores for sex, contraception, abortion, marriage, and parenting were in eclipse. However, the recognition of the seriousness of Herpes and the discovery of AIDS (Acquired Immune Deficiency Syndrome) brought home some of the unfortunate consequences of the sexual revolution. AIDS, a fatal disease, has caused many to reevaluate their ethical concepts, particularly since the disease seems to be spreading into the heterosexual population. There is now an urgency in the call for a return to the traditional religious values and ethics which once governed sex and marriage.

*Bibliography.* J. T. Noonan, Jr., *Contraception, A History of Its Treatment by the Catholic Theologians and Canonists* (1965); M. S. Calderone and E. W. Johnson, *The Family Book about Sexuality* (1981); E. Fuchs, *Sexual Desire and Love: Origins and History of the Christian Ethic of Sexuality and Marriage* (1983); G. A. Larue, *Sex and the Bible* (1983); M. F. Schwar, et al., *Sex and Gender* (1983); M. R. Cosby, *Sex in the Bible, An Introduction to What Scripture Teaches Us about Sexuality* (1984); L. S. Cahill, *Between the Sexes, Foundations for a Christian Ethics of Sex* (1985); P. Gardella, *Innocent Ecstasy, How Christianity Gave America an Ethic of Sexual Pleasure* (1985).

ROBERT V. SCHNUCKER

**Seychelles.** Independent republic in the Indian Ocean northeast of Madagascar, made up of 115 islands with a total land area of about 376 sq. km. (145 sq. mi.) and with a population of 66,700 (1985 est.). A former British colony, the islands became independent in 1976, but remained within the British Commonwealth. The overwhelming majority of Seychellois profess at least nominal Christianity: 85 percent are Roman Catholics, 10 percent Protestants. Before 1980 there was much superstition and dependence on the outward rites of baptism and confirmation; since then there has been a marked religious revival which, among other things, is confronting the serious problem of immorality and occult practices. An indigenous pentecostal house group, which began in 1982, has grown to over 1000 members. Anglicans have established a theological training course. Membership in the Seventh-day Adventist Church has tripled and they cooperate in evangelism with other denominations. A one-party socialist government allows the Sunday morning services from the Roman Catholic and Anglican cathedrals to be broadcast live on alternate Sundays, and has been helpful to FEBA's radio ministry. The Seychelles Creole NT (Creole is the language of 96 percent of the population) has now been translated by the Bible Society of Mauritius.

JOHN L. FEAR

**Shamanism.** Broadly defined, the ritual practices of certain religious leaders who enter ecstatic trances in order to secure healing and spiritual well-being for themselves and their communities. Shamanism may be most clearly identified in loosely organized religious systems in which the shamans act as gifted individuals who can control their own possession by the spirits rather than as cultic functionaries who have been trained to fill ceremonial roles. I. M. Lewis (1986) has summarized the controversy among cultural anthropologists regarding the precision with which the term should be applied.

In his landmark study, M. Eliade (1972) singles out the practitioner's ecstatic journey beyond the self "to heaven, to the lower world, or to the depths of the ocean" as characteristic of pure shamanism. A celestial journey is a feature of the practice in Siberian and Central Asian tribes from whose language the word "shaman" comes. In North American Eskimo tribes shamans enter trances in order to journey to the bottom of the sea, the home of Sedna, goddess of the animals. By communicating these experiences to the tribe, the shaman reestablishes communal harmony with the spirits and defends the tribe against famine and disease.

While anthropologists have described the structure of shamanistic ritual (Levi-Strauss) or its functions in a given cultural milieu (Radcliffe-Brown), psychologists have attempted to identify the mechanisms which produce the trance. J. Jaynes' hypothesis (1976) regarding mental processes in the early bicameral mind suggests that the spirits' voices are mediated by a primitive interaction between the right and left hemispheres of the brain. Lilly (1977) relates hallucinogenic visions to spontaneous retinal firings caused by sensory deprivation. Research in the field of psychoneuroimmunology has led some to propose that ecstatic experiences may have healing benefits because they moderate the effects of psychological stress on the body.

*Bibliography.* A. R. Radcliffe-Brown, *Structure and Function in Primitive Society* (1952); C. Levi-Strauss, *Structural Anthropology* (1963); M. Eliade, *Shamanism: Archaic Techniques of Ecstasy* (1972); J. Jaynes, *The Origin of Consciousness in the Breakdown of the Bicameral Mind* (1976); J. C. Lilly, *The Deep Self* (1977); M. Harner *The Way of the Shaman* (1980); S. Karkar, *Shamans, Mystics and Doctors* (1982).

GLENN D. WEAVER

## Shantymen's Christian Association (SCA).
Canadian frontier mission agency. Founded in 1907 by William Henderson, a Presbyterian, SCA seeks to evangelize workers in remote mining projects, lumber camps, and Indian communities. (Lumber workers in isolated northern regions used to live in shanties—hence the name.) Missionaries serve in nine of the nation's ten provinces. Oil and gas exploration projects across Canada's vast northern regions provide new challenges to the mobile force. The itinerant missionaries, traveling by terrain vehicle, motorcycle, boat, plane, or on foot, are, for many in those areas, their only contact with the church. They engage in personal evangelism and conduct meetings in homes, schools, mess halls, and bunkhouses. The *Shantyman,* SCA's monthly publication, is its evangelistic organ. The agency's headquarters is in Mississauga, Ontario.

LESLIE K. TARR

## Shaver, Erwin Leander (1840–1970). Leader
in religious education. Born in Eau Claire, Wis., he studied at Lawrence College, Garrett Biblical Institute, and Teachers College, Columbia University. He was ordained into the Methodist ministry in 1917 and transferred to the Congregational Church in 1923. He taught religious education at a Methodist school, Hendrix College, Arkansas, from 1920 to 1922, when he was fired for defending the teaching of evolution. He was then employed as secretary by the Congregational Division of Christian Education. In 1942 he joined the staff of the International Council of Religious Education, where he was executive director of Weekday Religious Education. When ICRE became a part of the National Council of Churches in 1950, his program was included in its division of education and ministry. He retired in 1957. He was a leading figure in released time religious education, a phenomenon which peaked in the late 1940s with 2.2. million elementary-age children in all 48 states enrolled in instructional programs, 42 percent of which actually took place in school classrooms. Shaver's *Weekday Church School* (1956) is the most complete record of the history, philosophy, and influence of the released time education movement in the American public schools. He also authored numerous books on curriculum and teaching methodology for Sunday schools and weekday classes.

RICHARD V. PIERARD

## Sheen, Fulton John (1895–1979). Roman
Catholic bishop, preacher, television evangelist, educator, and author. Born in El Paso, Ill., he was educated at St. Viator's College and St. Paul's Seminary, and was ordained in 1919. His academic performance opened the door to the Catholic University of America and the University of Louvain in Belgium, where he earned his doctorate in 1923. After obtaining an *agrégé en philosophie* with highest honors in 1925, he taught theology at St. Edmund's College in Ware, England. There followed a brief stint as a parish priest; he was then transferred to the Catholic University as teacher of philosophy. He rose quickly to full professor, and as a priest to papal chamberlain, domestic prelate, bishop, and archbishop. A superb evangelist, he wrote more than 50 popular books, and in 1930 began the television program, "The Catholic Hour." This led to live broadcasts of services, and in 1951, his "Life Is Worth Living" series. He reached millions in his ministry as the most prominent spokesman of the Catholic Church in America.

JACK MITCHELL

## Shellabear, William Girdlestone (1862–1947).

Missionary. Born in Wells, Norfolk, England, he studied at Haileybury, Woolwich, and Chatham. He then became a captain engineer for the Singapore Harbour Mining Defences. In 1890 he joined the Malay Mission of the Methodist Episcopal Church of the USA. He developed the mission press and wrote and published much Malayan Christian literature. He revised the Malay Bible for the B. & F. Bible Society, and was president of the Straits Branch of the Royal Asiatic Society. He taught languages and Islamics at Drew Theological Seminary in Madison, N.J. (1920–25), and at the Kennedy School of Missions, Hartford (1925–34). He wrote *Practical Malay Grammar* (1890), *Malay-English Vocabulary* (1902), and many articles on Islamic subjects in *The Moslem World*. After retirement he prepared much Christian literature in Malay verse.

**Bibliography.** R. L. Archer, *The Moslem World* (July 1947).

EDWIN E. CALVERLEY

## Shepherd, Massey Hamilton, Jr. (1913– ).

Episcopalian clergyman and liturgics scholar. Born in Wilmington, N.C., he studied at the universities of South Carolina and Chicago (Ph.D., 1937). He taught at the divinity school of the University of Chicago (1937–40) and was professor of church history at the Episcopal Theological School, Cambridge, Mass. (1940–54), before appointment in 1954 as professor of liturgics and church history at Church Divinity School of the Pacific, Berkeley, Calif. His chief interests were in the promotion of the liturgical movement, and his writings are largely concerned with that field. They include *The Living Liturgy* (1946), *At All Times and in All Places* (1947), *The Oxford American Prayer Book Commentary* (1950), *The Worship of the Church* (1952), *The Reform of Liturgical Worship* (1961), and *Liturgy and Education* (1965).

## Sheppard, David Stuart (1929– ).

Anglican bishop. After graduation from Cambridge, he served a curacy at St. Mary's, Islington, London, then moved to the East End of the capital to become warden of the Mayflower Family Centre, Canning Town (1957–69). He succeeded J. A. T. Robinson as bishop of Woolwich (1969–75) before becoming bishop of Liverpool. A mutual concern for the plight of the inner city led to a unique and ongoing cooperation with the Roman Catholic archbishop, Derek Worlock. Sheppard's social concern and winsome personality, coupled with his reputation as a former English cricket captain, have gained him a wide hearing among the unchurched and the resentment of the national government whose policies he has criticized. His published works include *Parson's Pitch*

(1964), *Built as a City* (1974), *Bias to the Poor* (1983), and *The Other Britain* (1984).

J. D. DOUGLAS

## Sheppard, Hugh Richard Lawrie (1880–1937).

Anglican dean, preacher, and pacifist. Born in Windsor, where his father was a minor canon highly regarded by Queen Victoria, he was educated at Cambridge and Cuddesdon College. After brief periods in chaplaincy and pastoral work, chiefly at Oxford House, he began a memorable incumbency at St. Martin-in-the-Fields, London (1914–27). Through his preaching and a profound social concern expressed in practical ways, he brought new life to a moribund West End church. He wrote for the popular press, made a significant contribution in the early days of religious broadcasting, and became known also as a tireless espouser of the pacifist cause. Illness forced his resignation in 1927; the same reason made him relinquish the deanery of Canterbury in 1931 after a two-year tenure. As canon and precentor of St. Paul's Cathedral, London, he maintained strong, independent views as he struggled against sickness and harrowing domestic difficulties. The unique appeal he had made to ordinary people was underlined when 100,000 people came to pay their respects as his body lay in state. His publications include *Two Days Before* (1924), *The Human Parson* (1924), and *The Impatience of a Parson* (1927).

J. D. DOUGLAS

## Sherrill, Henry Knox (1890–1980).

American Episcopal bishop and ecumenist. Born in Brooklyn, N.Y., he graduated from Yale University, was ordained to the Protestant Episcopal ministry, and appointed to a parish in Boston. After service as an army chaplain in World War I, he was rector of churches in Brookline (1919–23) and Boston (1923–30), and bishop of the diocese of Massachusetts (1930–47). In 1947 he was chosen as presiding bishop of the Episcopal Church where he remained until his retirement in 1958. He was the first president of the National Council of Churches of Christ in the United States (1950–52), and was a president of the World Council of Churches (1954–61). He authored *William Lawrence: Later Years of a Happy Life* (1943), *The Church's Ministry in Our Time* (1949), and *Among Friends* (1962).

RICHARD V. PIERARD

## Sherrill, Lewis Joseph (1892–1957).

American scholar. Educated at Austin College, Louisville Presbyterian Theological Seminary, Northwestern University, Yale University (Ph.D., 1929), and Harvard University, he was Presbyterian pastor at Covington, Tenn. (1921–25), professor of religious education at Louisville Presbyterian Theological Seminary (1925–50; dean,

1930–50), and professor of practical theology at Union Theological Seminary (1950–57). He was executive secretary (1935–38) and president (1938–40) of the American Association of Theological Schools, and the author of numerous books, including *The Gift of Power* (1955).

## Shields, Thomas Todhunter (1873–1955).

Canadian pastor and fundamentalist leader. Born in Bristol, England, he immigrated with his family to Canada in 1888. He ministered to several Baptist congregations before becoming pastor in 1910 of Jarvis Street Baptist Church, Toronto, the largest church of the denomination in Canada, a post he held until his death. A leading North American fundamentalist, he founded the weekly *Gospel Witness* in 1922. He was founder and first president of the Baptist Bible Union, a coalition of Canadian and American fundamentalists. His protest against liberal teaching in the denomination's McMaster University led to his expulsion in 1927 from the Baptist Convention of Ontario and Quebec. He led that year in the formation of the Union of Regular Baptist Churches of Ontario and Quebec and of Toronto Baptist Seminary. He cooperated with American fundamentalist Carl McIntire in forming the International Council of Christian Churches in 1948, in reaction to the World Council of Churches founded in the same year. Shields was recognized as an able preacher; his sermons were widely distributed through the *Gospel Witness* and books which he authored.

LESLIE K. TARR

## Shi'ism.

Main minority branch of Islam. Shi'ites are united in the belief that 'Ali ibn Abi Talib, the fourth Caliph, was the first Imam or true successor to Muhammad. Shi'ites comprise about 15 percent of all Muslims in the world, from small minorities in East Africa, India, Pakistan, and much of the Arab world, to half the population of Iraq, and 95 percent or more of the populations of Yemen and Iran.

Shi'ism arose as a result of the dispute over the succession to Muhammad in 632. The majority chose Abu Bakr as the first Caliph. He and his two successors, Umar and Uthman, had been "companions" of Muhammad. But the "Party of 'Ali" (*shi'at 'Ali*) believed that Muhammad himself had appointed 'Ali, his cousin and the husband of his daughter Fatimah, to be his successor. They held that the successor ought to be a member of Muhammad's "family," not merely a companion. Thus when Uthman was murdered in 656 and 'Ali was elected as fourth Caliph, his followers regarded him as the first Imam. 'Ali's leadership was challenged by Mu'awiya, governor of Syria, who had himself proclaimed Caliph. After 'Ali's murder in A.D. 661, he was succeeded by his two sons Hassan and Hussein. The martyrdom of Imam Hussein at Karbala in southern Iraq on the

10th of Muharram 680 is perhaps the most important event in Shi'ite history. Celebrated annually as the holiday of "Ashura," this event is deeply emotional.

Shi'ism is divided into two major and several minor branches. The main branch is so-called Twelver Shi'ism (*Ithna 'Ashariyah*), which holds that the Twelfth Imam, Muhammad al-Mahdi, went into occultation about 874; he is hence known as the Hidden Imam. Although he has representatives on earth, the Twelvers await his return to restore peace, justice, and perfection. This expectation has shaped the psychology of Twelver Shi'ism in a fundamental way. Twelver Shi'ism has been the official religion of Iran since Shah Ismail proclaimed it in 1502; it is also prevalent in Iraq. "Twelvers" are also found in Afghanistan, India, Pakistan, Lebanon, and parts of East Africa. (The discussion of general Shi'ite beliefs below will focus primarily on Twelver ideas.)

"Sevener," or Ismaili Shi'ism, regards the seventh Imam, Muhammad ibn Isma'il (d. A.D. 799), as hidden but living on earth and therefore present to men. It does not, of course, look for the return of the Mahdi as does the Twelver belief. Historically Ismailis have been revolutionaries and challenge the existing powers. The "Assassins," a group of Ismailis located in the Elburz Mountains and in mountain fortresses in Syria, gained their name from one activity characteristic of them; other Ismailis were also politically active in the early years of Islam. The Fatimid Dynasty of Egypt (909–1171) was led by members of this sect. Recently the Ismailis have become politically more quietist; most of them are now followers of the Aga Khan and have developed a prosperous business community with an elaborate program of education, welfare, and self-help. They are especially prevalent in India, Pakistan, and East Africa, with smaller communities in Iran, Syria, and Egypt.

A third branch of Shi'ism is the Zaydi form, dominant in Yemen, which recognizes the fifth Imam, Muhammad al-Baqir (d. A.D. 733), as the last. It rejects any form of Hidden Imamism and holds that even a member of the "family" can be accepted as Imam only after claiming the title publicly and backing up this claim by force.

In theology and religious practice the Shi'ites share much with the majority Sunni. Their daily prayers and activities differ very little from those of the Sunni. They agree on the major principles of *Tawhid* (the unity of God), prophecy (the extraordinary role of Muhammad and the other prophets who preceded him), and eschatology. The main points of difference from the Sunni involve the concepts of the Imamate and justice (*'adl*).

The Imamate is the central idea of Shi'ite Islam. The Imams are the true successors to the

Prophet, equal to him in every way except the giving of the Koran and the Law (*Shar'iah*). They are the witnesses of God on earth and possess perfect knowledge of the Koran and of God. They are, in short, the perfect representatives of the Prophet. The basis for this view of the Imam lies in the Shi'ite distinction between reality and its human expression. For them any worldly manifestation, no matter how excellent, is only a partial reflection of the ultimate truth. Even the Koran itself has an outer literal and an inner spiritual meaning. Shi'ites share the literal meaning (*zahir*) with the Sunni, but they believe the inner allegorical meaning (*batin*) is revealed through the Imams. The law (*Shar'iah*) is external, but the truth (*haqiq*) is internal.

The Imamate represents the inner or "spiritual" aspect of Islam, in contrast to the exterior or "legal" aspect represented by the Sunni Caliphate. 'Ali and his successors are regarded as divinely led leaders of the faithful whose authority derives from their God-given insight into the esoteric side of Islam. If the exoteric is the Koran, the Traditions (*Hadith*), and the Law, the esoteric is their spirit.

Whereas the Sunnis, the "People of tradition (*sunnah*) and the consensus of the community ('*ijma*)," had "closed the canon" in the 3d century, leaving all future interpretation to the community of Islam (the *umma*), the Shi'ites had in the Imam a provision for ongoing reinterpretation with the full spiritual authority of the Prophet. Even in his absence, the Shi'ites retained the right of *ijtihad* (independent judgment) and vested this right in *mojtaheds*, who were representatives of the Imam. This gave the Shi'ite community a divinely guided leader to follow. It also gave them an argument against the "majoritarianism" of the Sunni community. The Shi'ites (who were usually in the minority) implicitly rejected the assumption that the majority was necessarily right. They were willing to challenge *ijma*, which was the foundation of Sunni law and belief. This gave them spiritual strength in challenging superior force.

It should be pointed out that the Shi'ite view of a "spiritual" inner character of religion has affinities with Sufi mysticism. Sufism has flourished in both Sunni and Shi'ite branches of Islam, but it can be argued that it has a greater affinity with Shi'ism.

The Shi'ite view of justice ('*adl*) makes them potentially revolutionary, in contradistinction to the Sunnis. For the Shi'ites, justice is an essential feature of both God's character and human society. Justice is not merely what God happens to declare, but rather is an inherent characteristic of God, who by his very nature must do justice. In other words, justice is of the very essence of the universe and not merely a divine fiat. In relation to the world, justice is a condition of the legitimacy of any regime. But in actual fact all earthly regimes fall short of the perfection required by God and represented by the Imam. This demand for perfect justice has had two opposite results. One is quietism, in which Shi'ites have turned away from political and social issues to scientific, philosophical, and theological activity—on the assumption that nothing significant can be done until the return of the Mahdi, who will restore all things. The other result is revolutionary challenge. The early Isma'ilis illustrate this position, as do contemporary Iranian and other revolutionists. When the sense of injustice is aroused and connected with possible action, the Shi'ite doctrine of '*adl* becomes an instrument for radical change. This occurred in Iran in 1979 when followers of Ayatollah Rouholla Khomeini overthrew the Shah and established their own Islamic Republic.

An important aspect of Shi'ite religious life is the emotionalism associated with the veneration of 'Ali and his sons (especially Hussein). Martyrs occupy a special place in Shi'ite theology and practice, as evidenced by the nature of the ceremonies at Ashura. During these processions the story of Karbala is chanted by the men as they march, rhythmically beating themselves with ceremonial chains. Passion plays depict the tragedy of Hussein's death and evoke great feeling and weeping. This emotionalism has also penetrated into the poetry and culture of Shi'ite societies.

As with justice, so emotionalism has had two different political and social outcomes. One form of emotionalism has virtually glorified the minority character of Shi'ism and the "oppressed" state of its people; under certain conditions this has led to an emotional embrace of "oppressedness" rather than action to eliminate it. But under other circumstances it has produced intense commitment to action regardless of the cost. The Khomeini revolution brought out crowds of people who defied the overwhelming power of the Shah and, with hardly a weapon, overthrew his regime. Martyrdom was welcomed by many in the Iran-Iraq War following 1980.

In addition to the universal Islamic obligation to make a pilgrimage to Mecca (*Hajj*), the Shi'ites make pilgrimages to the tombs of the Imams (*imam-zadehs*). Such locations include Najaf, 'Ali's burial place; Karbala, where Hussein and his family are interred; Masshad, the location of the tomb of 'Ali Rida, the 8th Imam; and Samarra, where the 10th and 11th Imams are buried and where the 12th Imam went into occultation.

**Bibliography.** D. M. Donaldson, *The Shi'ite Religion* (1933); J. N. Hollister, *The Shi'a of India* (1953); B. Lewis, *The Assassins* (1968); S. N. Makarem, *The Doctrine of the Ismailis* (1972); S. H. Nasr, *Ideals and Realities of Islam* (1975); A. Tabataba'i, *Shiite Islam* (1975); A. A. Sachedina, *Islamic Messianism* (1981); H. Enayat, *Modern Islamic Political Thought* (1982); S. A. Arjomand, *The Shadow of God and the Hidden Imam* (1984).

M. Howard Mattsson-Boze

**Shinto.** The native religion of Japan. The term "Shinto" means "the way of the gods." The Shinto gods possess sacred power. Sometimes there are distinct gods with distinct identities; sometimes there is only a nebulous sense of numinous power. The gods, when differentiated, take many forms: clan ancestors; the souls of powerful leaders; living people who for some reason inspire awe; people who express the national identity of the Japanese; influences associated with historical events; and local forces of nature as found, for example, in an unusual rock or beautiful waterfall. None of the Shinto deities may be described as an eternal and sovereign king, creator of heaven and earth. Shinto deities may be awesome, but they are usually more modest, best described as uncanny or eerie. Some deities manifest themselves as warm and reassuring and as maintaining proper harmony, while other deities can bring harm and discord.

The Kojiki and the Nihongi are the earliest collections of the legends of Shinto, dating from the early 8th century A.D. The legends themselves, however, are often much older. They concern various acts of creation (including the creation of Japan), ritual pollution and purification, disruptive and cooperative behavior, and events and persons connected with the emperor's family. According to these legends, Jimmu, a descendant of the sun-goddess Amaterasu, established the Japanese imperial dynasty.

The many shrines which dot the Japanese countryside are the most visible expression of Shinto. These shrines are often located in places of great beauty; but even where that is not possible (in, e.g., a back street of Tokyo), the buildings themselves often elicit a sense of calmness and harmony.

Every shrine, no matter how small, represents a sacred space which can give power to as well as purify those who enter it. One major function of the priests is to perform purification ceremonies. Shinto shrines and priests also provide opportunities to dedicate crops, rice wine, and other items to the gods. Many shrines also sponsor festivals (called *matsuri*). These festivals are not only times of fun, gossip, and business—very much like an American county fair—but also reaffirm the solidarity of the local community, such as a farming village or perhaps a small neighborhood in a city. Such festivals foster harmony of neighbor with neighbor as well as harmony between the community and the local deities.

A few Shinto shrines possess national significance. The ancient shrine at Ise is the abode of Amaterasu, who is both the sun-goddess and the divine ancestress of the line of Japanese emperors. In Tokyo the Meiji shrine is dedicated to the Emperor Meiji, who reigned during the Meiji Restoration in the 1860s. The Meiji Restoration consisted of the "return" of the Japanese govern-ment to the emperor and Japan's reopening to the outside world, particularly the Western world. Also in Tokyo is the important Yasukuni Shrine which enshrines those who have died on behalf of the emperor since the Meiji Restoration. Yasukuni Shrine was established in the late 19th century, and Meiji Shrine in the early 20th. In contrast, the Izumo Shrine on the Japan Sea marks one of the most ancient of Shinto's sacred locations, its origins predating the introduction of writing. Izumo is the home of Susanoo, whom the ancient legends picture as quarreling with Amaterasu, the patron deity of the imperial line. Izumo also hosts a fall festival in which all the gods of Japan are said to gather together to consult on the future of the country. Kyoto is the site of the Fushimi Inari Shrine, established by a nobleman in 711. Worship focuses on the fox, with many symbols of agricultural abundance and fertility, both male and female. It is still the scene of many shamanistic folk practices.

Ever since the arrival of Buddhism in the mid-6th century, Shinto has had to share the religious affections of the Japanese. Some Buddhists have seen the Shinto gods as guardians of the Buddha. More common was the theory of dual manifestation in which the Shinto gods were conceived as the local manifestations of Buddhist figures. During times of nationalistic revival, the Japanese sometimes reversed this, claiming that the Buddhist figures were in fact manifestations of the Shinto deities. In 1872, a law was passed requiring the elimination of all Buddhist influences from Shinto shrines. It was an ancient practice for small Buddhist figures to be placed within Shinto precincts, a practice which has since been resumed.

Because of its ancient connections with pre-Buddhist Japan, Shinto has been a carrier of Japanese nationalism. Motoori Norinaga (1730–1801) and Hirata Atsutane (1776–1843) developed a tradition of National Learning (Kokugaku), which uses the collections of Shinto legends as its primary texts. This heritage fed into the militarism of the 1920s and 1930s, when participation in highly nationalistic Shinto rituals was required of all residents of the Japanese Empire, including the colonies of Taiwan and Korea. The defeat of the imperial forces in World War II was a catastrophe for Shinto. The Shinto ceremonies in the neighborhoods retained their meaning, but the national rituals lost their significance when the postwar secular constitution mandated the elimination of Shinto's status as the state cult.

The miraculous revival of the postwar Japanese economy and Japan's development into a financial superpower have gone hand-in-hand with a revival of Shinto. There is growing agitation for greater legal recognition of the role of the emperor in connection with Shinto. Recently the prime ministers have made visits to Yasukuni Shrine in their official role. The postwar controversy over the role of Shinto on the national scale must be contrasted with its ongoing role in village and neighborhood life, where its ceremonies have little to do directly with matters of state and everything to do with the continuity of the rhythms of Japanese culture from time immemorial.

**Bibliography.** S. Matsumoto, *Studies in Shinto Thought* (1964); J. M. Kitagawa, *Religion in Japanese History* (1966); *Japanse Religion: A Survey by the Agency for Cultural Affairs* (1982).

STEPHEN T. FRANKLIN

## Shoemaker, Samuel Moor (1893–1963).

American preacher and writer. Deeply influenced by John R. Mott, Robert Speer, and others at D. L. Moody's Northfield Conferences in 1911 and 1912, and educated at Princeton University and General and Union Theological seminaries in New York City, he experienced, while with the YMCA in China (1917–19), a conversion that was "the great turning point" of his life. Ordained in 1921, he became rector of Calvary Episcopal Church in New York City four years later. He exercised leadership in Frank Buchman's Oxford Group until breaking with Buchman in 1941. Shoemaker's involvement in social ministries, including assisting in the formulation of the "Twelve Steps" of Alcoholics Anonymous, expanded with the "Pittsburgh Experiment" following his move to that city in 1952 as rector of Calvary Episcopal Church. His work in both parishes was also marked by personal evangelism, small groups, and a ministry of radio preaching, speaking on college and seminary campuses, and writing. He wrote nearly 30 books, among the most widely read of which were *A Young Man's View of the Ministry* (1923) and *With the Holy Spirit and with Fire* (1960).

NORRIS A. MAGNUSON

## Sick, Ministering to the. One of the most delicate and important pastoral responsibilities. It calls for sensitivity, spiritual poise, common sense, discretion, and devotion to Christ and the patient. It affords pastors an opportunity to demonstrate their faith. The first principle pastors must bear in mind is that of the physician: "Do no harm."

A second principle that pastors must remember is that they symbolize the presence of God in Christ. Many sick persons feel that unless pastors visit, God has forgotten; unless they have cleared their consciences with pastors, so that they understand, God does not understand. When illness comes, especially if unusual or prolonged, the feeling of isolation increases. The greatest mistake pastors can make is not to call, or to seem not to care.

The following rules are important: (1) Find out when it is convenient to call. Ask a member of the family or a friend. (2) Upon entering the sickroom, adjust your mood to that of the patient. (3) Speak in a natural voice, suitable to the sickroom—loud enough to be heard, but not so loud that you can be heard in the next room. You have come to call upon a sick person, not to attract attention to yourself. (4) Shake hands only if the sick person puts out a hand. Shake with a firm but not a hard grasp. Remember the weakened condition of the patient. (5) If there is another visitor or member of the family present, express your interest in the patient, but do not stay, unless the patient insists or unless the other visitor offers to leave. More than two people is a crowd. (6) Sit down only if you are asked to do so. Be careful not to sit so that the patient faces the light or has to strain to see you. (7) Inquire how things are going, but do not ask the diagnosis. The patient may tell you. (8) Give the patient a chance to talk. (9) If the conversation lags or if the patient becomes restless, prepare to leave. (10) When you are ready to leave, stand up, express your best wishes, go to the door, and leave. Do not linger.

**Bibliography.** R. C. Cabot and R. L. Dicks, *The Art of Ministering to the Sick* (1936); R. L. Dicks, *Comfort Ye My People* (1946); idem, *Thy Health Shall Spring Forth* (1945); C. Scherzer, *Springs of Living Water* (1950); idem, *The Church and Healing* (1950); H. F. Dunbar, *Mind and Body* (1947); and the journals *The Pastor,* and *Religion and Health*.

RUSSELL L. DICKS

## Sierra Leone. *See* WEST AFRICA.

## Sigtuna. Center of Christian missions in Sweden. In 1915 M. Björkquist, later bishop of Stockholm, established Sigtuna Foundation (*Sigtunastifeltsen*) to provide a center for and to cultivate Lutheran faith and culture. In 1917 a people's high school was established in which, besides regular school subjects, the theory of life and the forming of character are taught. In 1926 the Sigtuna Humanistic Public School, a boarding school with a college as well as a school for the lower grades, was founded. The foundation also arranges courses on religious, cultural, and social problems of current interest. Through conferences and open discussions the foundation offers opportunities for contact between different social groups. A guest house provides opportunities for study and meditation.

In 1984 the institute was relocated in Uppsala. Although *Sigtunastiftelsen* has become a large institution, many maintain that its original aims are the same.

CARL-GUSTAF ANDRÉN AND ANTONIO BARBOSA DA SILVA

## Sikhism. Religion founded by Guru Nanak at the end of the 15th century A.D. in the area of Pakistan and northwest India. The word "Sikh" in

its Pali and Sanskrit roots means "disciple." Today there are over 10 million Sikhs. Some 80 percent live in the Punjab State of India, while the others are scattered throughout the rest of India, South Asia, Great Britain, the USA, and Canada. They are an industrious and prosperous people. Their religion combines elements of Hinduism, Islam, and mysticism.

Sikhism is founded on the teachings of its 10 Gurus (spiritual teachers) who lived from A.D. 1469 to 1708. The founder, Guru Nanak (1469–1539), drew his insights from two main sources: the Hindu Bhakti movement and sufism, or Islamic mysticism. Their salient features—the importance of meditation on God and the repetition of his names, the concept of a personal God, and eagerness to have union with him—became the starting points of Guru Nanak's teachings.

Nanak had an orthodox Hindu upbringing in a *Kshatriya* family near Lahore. Once he had a vision of God, who commissioned him to go out into the world to preach. In association with a Muslim musician, Mardana, he produced many hymns through which he popularized the new faith, and undertook four extensive teaching tours.

Nine other Gurus followed him, each appointing a successor. It is held that they passed their inspiration, light, and authority successively to each other, like one candle lit from another. Arjun Mal (1563–1606) made an initial collection of the canonical scriptures and also organized Sikhism. He built the Hari Mandir, the Golden Temple, at Amritsar, which has been the center of the religious and political activities of the Sikhs.

Gobind Singh (1666–1708), the last of the line of the ten Gurus, gave Sikhism its present form. Sikhism, a passive faith during the entire 16th century, gradually took on a political and military character because of Muslim persecution, including the assassination of two Gurus. Gobind started a new fraternity, called *Khalsa* (the pure), initially of five men who were baptized and given the common surname *Singh* (lion). Women received the corresponding name *Kaur* (lioness). Both names are commonly used today. Gobind declared the guruship as ceased but passed its essential character and function to both the canonical scripture which he completed and to the Sikh community as a whole.

After a series of defeats and the death of many at the hands of the Mughal rulers, the Sikhs gradually rose in political power under the leadership of Ranjit Singh. He united all the Sikhs, established an empire, and was crowned as Maharaja of Punjab in 1801. After his death, the British took advantage of the internal power struggle of the Sikhs and defeated them, annexing their empire in 1849.

Initially, the Sikhs were loyal to the British and were given certain special privileges. But later on, unrest developed and they joined India's freedom movement under Gandhi. In 1947 at the partition of India and Pakistan, because of a bitter Sikh-Muslim riot, over 2 million Sikhs were forced to flee to India.

Sikhism teaches monotheism and prohibits the worship of idols or pictures, although it is held that God is everywhere in creation. God is One, he is the Truth, and he is the Creator. He is the true Teacher and, therefore, often addressed as *Wah Guru* (Hail Teacher). He is known as God of love through meditation.

*Adi Granth*, the only canonical scripture, is the ultimate spiritual authority. Its main content is some 6000 hymns composed by the first five Gurus. Other scriptures of less importance are the *Dasam Granth* (the 10th volume), the life stories of Nanak, the traditions of *Khalsa*, and a collection of folklore.

The Hindu theory of *samsara* (the cycle of birth, death, and rebirth) is basic to Sikhism's understanding of man, sin, and salvation. Until one achieves *sahaj* (love-union) with God, one goes through the transmigration of the soul. The true spiritual pilgrimage is an inward one and not to holy places.

The Guru concept is at the heart of Sikhism. God himself is the true Guru, and his message to humanity first came primarily through 10 select Gurus. The *Adi Granth* is itself "the Living Guru," and so also the Sikh community as a whole. Each person is expected to have a Guru for spiritual guidance.

Sikhism made major departures from Hinduism in rejecting the worship of idols, ritual purifications by water, elaborate rituals, and hereditary priesthood. The important religious duties of each Sikh are the recitation of the names of God, meditation on him, and the singing of hymns and faithful study of the sacred book. Central to everything one does is the *Adi Granth*. People bow down before it in worship, babies are named by its use, newly married couples walk around it four times, there are long hours and days of reading from it on special occasions, and it is the central object in the temples. Regular worship is held in the temple or *Guradwara* (the door of the Guru).

The *Khalsa* Sikhs are distinguished by five symbols, the Punjab names of which all begin with the letter "k": *kesh*, or uncut hair; *kangha*, or comb to keep hair clean; *kara*, or metal bangle; *kaccha*, or knee-length underwear; and *kirpan*, or dagger. It is the ambition of each youth to be initiated into membership in the community by *pahul* (the ceremony of baptism) and become a *Khalsa*.

The Sikh community is a religious and ethnic entity. The Sikhs have a deep sense of community solidarity, and they help each other in their progress. Although three broad ethnic divisions—the untouchables, the higher castes, and the agricultural groups—are recognized within the community, there is no rigid caste system. Equality of all including women and the dignity of labor are affirmed.

Since the turn of this century, many Sikhs have migrated to Great Britain and North America, where they are quite visible. They make every effort to help the new generation of Sikhs remain faithful to the fundamentals of the faith.

In the present-day affairs of the Sikhs, the Akali party has great authority. Religion and politics are not separated. A small group of extremists, through their terrorist activities, have been pressing their long-standing demand for an independent Sikh state, *Khalistan*. In India, although the Sikh community is a small minority of less than 2 percent, it has produced some of the nation's best farmers, athletes, poets, military personnel, industrialists, and political leaders (including one of its recent presidents).

*Bibliography.* M. A. Macauliff, *The Sikh Religion: Its Gurus, Sacred Writings and Authors* (1909); K. Singh, *A History of the Sikhs,* 2 vols. (1963, 1979); W. H. McLeod, *Guru Nanak and the Sikh Religion* (1968); G. Singh, *The Religion of the Sikhs* (1971); P. S. Sambhi and W. O. Cole, *The Sikhs: Their Religious Beliefs and Practices* (1978).

Saphir Athyal

**Silence in Worship.** The most thorough experience of the use of silence in worship has been that of the Religious Society of Friends. The Quaker experience began in the middle of the 17th century, not by a preconceived plan but spontaneously. Groups of Seekers were thrilled by the conviction that Christ had come to lead and teach his people. The living Christ, they felt convinced, could be known directly and immediately. Consequently, the early Friends gathered to hear Christ's direct teaching to their own hearts. How could they listen unless they first became still? Accordingly, in the powerful Quaker gatherings of that day, men and women began by gathering in silence, but they always were free to break it by the spoken word, provided they felt that Christ had led them to speak. Most Christian groups today have not adopted the Quaker way of worship.

D. Elton Trueblood

**Silver, Abba Hillel** (1893–1963). Rabbi. Born in Lithuania, he studied at the University of Cincinnati and at Hebrew Union College, and was successively rabbi in Wheeling, W.Va. (1915–17), and, from 1917, at The Temple, Cleveland. He wrote *Messianic Speculations in Israel* (1927), *Democratic Impulse in Jewish History* (1928), *Religion in a Changing World* (1930), *World Crisis and Jewish Survival* (1941), *Vision and Victory* (1949), *Where Judaism Differed* (1956), and *Moses and the Original Torah* (1961).

**Simpson, Albert Benjamin** (1844–1919). Founder of the Christian and Missionary Alliance. Born in Cavendish, Prince Edward Island, Canada, Simpson graduated in 1865 from Knox College (Presbyterian) in Toronto. Following a Canadian pastorate, he went in 1874 to Louisville, Ky., to become minister of the influential Chestnut Street Presbyterian Church (renamed Broadway Tabernacle). His emphasis was on evangelism. He became minister in 1880 of Thirteenth Street Presbyterian Church in New York but resigned the following year to found the independent Gospel Tabernacle, which conducted inner city ministry and evangelism. Simpson was an exponent of the "fourfold gospel," which proclaimed Christ as "Savior, Sanctifier, Healer, and Coming King." His evangelical theology was coupled with an emphasis on sanctification, premillennial eschatology, divine healing, and missions. He organized the Christian Alliance (1887) and the International Missionary Alliance (1889), which merged in 1897 to become the Christian and Missionary Alliance. Editor of the *Alliance Weekly* from its inception in 1887, he also authored about 70 books and many hymns.

Leslie K. Tarr

**Simpson, James Young** (1873–1934). Presbyterian. Born in Edinburgh, he was educated at Edinburgh University, Christ's College, Cambridge, and New College, Edinburgh. He traveled widely and lectured in the USA. He was professor of natural science, New College, Edinburgh. He was president of the Latvian-Lithuanian Frontier Court of Arbitration (1921). He wrote *The Spiritual Interpretation of Nature* (1912), *Landmarks in the Struggle between Science and Religion* (1925), and *Nature, Cosmic, Human and Divine* (1929).

F. W. Dillistone

**Simpson, William John Sparrow** (1858–1952). Anglican. He was educated at Trinity College, Cambridge. Ordained in 1882, he was vicar of St. Mark's, Regent's Park (1888–1904), and chaplain of St. Mary's Hospital, Ilford (1904–52). He wrote *The Church and the Bible* (1897), *The Catholic Conception of the Church* (1914), *Reconciliation and Atonement* (1916), *Reconciliation between God and Man* (1917), *The Prayer of Consecration* (1917), *French Catholics in the Nineteenth Century* (1918), *Broad Church Theology* (1919), *Archbishop Bramhall* (1930), *St. Augustine: On the Spirit and the Letter* (1930), *The Letters of St. Augustine* (1930), *St. Augustine's Conversion* (1930), *South Indian Schemes* (1930), *The History of the Anglo-Catholic Revival from 1845* (1932), *Dispensations* (1936), and *The Ministry and the Eucharist* (1942).

Raymond W. Albright

**Singapore.** Independent Southeast Asian island republic 42 km. (26 mi.) long and 23 km. (14 mi.) wide. Its total area is 626 sq. km. (242 sq. mi.). Singapore is a pluralistic society whose people are largely descendants of immigrants from the Malay Peninsula, China, the Indian subcontinent, and Sri Lanka. In 1988, it had a population of 2.6 million, which was made up of 76.0 percent Chinese, 15.1 percent Malays, 6.5 percent Indians (including Pakistanis, Bangladeshis, and Sri Lankans), and 2.4 percent "others." In the 1980 census, information concerning religion was asked of persons aged 10 years and older. Respondent replies revealed that 10.3 percent were Christians (Roman Catholics, 4.6 percent; non-Catholics, 5.7 percent), 26.7 percent Buddhists, 29.3 percent Taoists (a loose term which includes those who believed in the teachings of Confucius, practiced ancestor worship, or worshiped the various Chinese deities), 16.3 percent Muslims, 3.6 percent Hindus, 0.6 percent other religions, and 13.2 percent no religion. The replies also showed that most of the religions were ethnocentric: 99.2 percent of Buddhists and Taoists stated that they were Chinese, 99.4 percent of Malays were Muslims, and 99.7 percent of Hindus were Indians. Only Christians seemed to be more cosmopolitan with 79.1 percent being Chinese, 7.8 percent Indians, 0.4 percent Malays, and 12.7 percent other ethnic groups (primarily Caucasians and Eurasians).

Although freedom of worship is guaranteed by the constitution, the Muslim community is the only faith to have a special body (Muslim Religious Council of Singapore) empowered by an act of parliament to carry out wide-ranging functions, such as advising the government on matters relating to the faith, promoting the welfare of Muslims, building and administering mosques, and handling of pilgrimage affairs. Hindus and Sikhs also have statutory boards which advise the government and administer religious buildings and endowment funds, but their roles are more limited. The constitution also provides for a Presidential Council for Minority Rights which examines bills passed by parliament to insure that they will not be disadvantageous to persons of any one ethnic or religious group. Equal recognition is given to the four major religions (Chinese, Islam, Christian, and Hindu) in that six out of the 10 annual public holidays are associated with these faiths. The Inter-Religious Organization, a private body set up in 1949, seeks to promote goodwill among leaders and followers of various religions.

In January 1984, religious knowledge was introduced as a compulsory subject for secondary school students. It was a two-year course and students could opt for any one of the following: Bible Knowledge, Islamic Studies, Buddhist Studies, Confucian Ethics, Hindu Studies, or Sikh Studies. However, in recent years there has been increased religious fervor and assertiveness among religious groups. Competition for followers and converts has become more intense. Concern has also been expressed over the possibility of religious groups venturing into politics, or political parties using religious sentiments to garner popular support. Therefore, the government is introducing legislation which will enable it to take preemptive action against religious and racial strife. The Ministry of Education has also reversed its earlier policy of making Religious Knowledge a compulsory subject for students in upper secondary schools.

BOBBY E. K. SNG

**Sizoo, Joseph Richard** (1885–1966). American pastor. Born in the Netherlands, he came to the USA in 1891, was educated at Hope College, Mich., and New Brunswick Theological Seminary. He returned to Amsterdam for ordination in the Dutch Reformed Church in 1910. He then became a missionary in South India (1910/11), minister of First Church, Walden, N.Y. (1911–17), of Second Church, Somerville, N.J. (1917–24), of New York Avenue Presbyterian Church, Washington, D.C. (1924–36), and of St. Nicholas Collegiate Church, N.Y. (1936–47). He then became president of New Brunswick Theological Seminary (1947–52). After official retirement he was professor of religion and director of chapel at George Washington University. His works include *Abraham Lincoln—A Heritage and a Hope* (1924), *William Jennings Bryan* (1925), *I Believe in the Bible* (1958), and *Still We Can Hope* (1966).

**Skoss, Solomon Leon** (1884–1953). Jewish scholar. Born in Perm, Russia, he studied Hebrew and rabbinic literature in Hebrew academies (Yeshiboth) in the USSR, the universities of Denver and Pennsylvania, Dropsie College (Ph.D., 1926), and Université Egyptiènne and School of Oriental Studies, Cairo, Egypt. He was a fellow at Dropsie College (1922–25) and taught Arabic there. He specialized in Judeo-Arabic literature, biblical Hebrew philology, and biblical exegesis of the 10th and 11th centuries A.D. His works include *The Arabic Commentary of 'Alī ben Suleimān on Genesis* (1928), *A Chapter on Permutation in Hebrew from David al-Fāsī's Dictionary "Jāmi' al-Alfāz"* (1932), *The Hebrew-Arabic Dictionary of the Bible Kitāb Jāmi' al-Alfāz of David ben Abraham al-Fāsī* (vol. 1, 1936; vol. 2, 1945), and *Saadia Gaon's Grammatical Work "Kutub al-Lughah": A Study of Inflection in Hebrew* (1942), and *A Study of Hebrew Vowels* (1951).

**Slack, Kenneth** (1917–1987). English minister, ecumenist, and writer. After graduating from Liverpool University, he studied theology at Westminster College, Cambridge, and in 1941 was ordained in the Presbyterian Church of England.

After ministering briefly in Shrewsbury, he was a Royal Air Force chaplain (1942–46) and for his work was appointed a Member of the Order of the British Empire (M.B.E.). He was minister of St. James', Edgware (1946–55), general secretary of the British Council of Churches (1955–65), minister of St. Andrew's, Cheam (1965–67), minister of the City Temple (1967–75), director of Christian Aid (1975–82), and minister of Kensington United Reformed Church (1982–87). He was moderator of the Free Church Federal Council (1983/84) and a well known religious journalist and broadcaster. His publications include *The Christian Conflict* (1960), *The British Churches Today* (1961), *Despatch from New Delhi* (1962), *Is Sacrifice Outmoded?* (1966), *Uppsala Report* (1968), *Martin Luther King* (1970), *George Bell* (1971), *Nairobi Narrative* (1976), and *Seven Deadly Sins* (1985).

## Slavery (20th Century).

**Slavery (20th Century).** While no account of slavery in the 20th century would be complete without a major section on the Nazi concentration camps of 1939–44 and the Soviet labor camps of 1917–56 and after, such examples of systematic, state-run oppression by no means exhaust or even represent the extent and nature of modern slavery.

Although over 300 agreements to eliminate slavery in different parts of the world were signed in the 19th century, the practice has persisted in various forms right up to the present day. This has happened despite the provisions of such measures as the League of Nations International Slavery Convention (1926), the International Labour Organization (ILO) Forced Labour Convention (1930), article 4 of the Universal Declaration of Human Rights (1948), and the United Nations Supplementary Convention on the Abolition of Slavery, the Slave Trade, and Institutions and Practices Similar to Slavery (1956). The latter convention extended the basic concept of slavery to include debt-bondage, serfdom, and the exploitation of women and children. Other contemporary manifestations of slavery noted in a UN report in 1984 included apartheid (described as a "collective slavery-like practice"), colonialism, forced labor, illicit traffic in migrant workers, and prostitution.

International supervision of the observance of these conventions has always been sporadic; only in 1974 did the UN Sub-Commission on Prevention of Discrimination and Protection of Minorities set up a permanent Working Group on Slavery, which meets annually. Owing to the subject's sensitivity the chief sources of information for the working group have been independent, nongovernment organizations like the International Council of Women, the International Commission of Jurists, the Minority Rights Group, the International Abolitionist Federation, and the world's oldest human rights group, the Anti-Slavery Society.

The Anti-Slavery Society for the Protection of Human Rights, which sprang from the reforming zeal of Sir Thomas Fowell Buxton and other colleagues of William Wilberforce, has united since 1909 the interests of the British and Foreign Anti-Slavery Society, founded in 1839, and the Aborigines Protection Society, founded in 1837. It reported in 1971 that slavery had a major role in 17 African, 15 Asian, and 6 Latin American countries, but it has not been slow to follow up less systematic or more isolated violations of ILO and UN conventions in Europe and North America, mostly concerned with the exploitation of child labor, particularly in the case of the children of migrants or minority groups.

Perhaps the most widespread slaverylike practice of today is child labor—the employment of children under the age of 12 or 15 or the minimum school-leaving age, especially on tasks whose nature or setting renders them suitable for adults only. Such exploitation is tolerated to some degree in more than 40 countries, including Spain, Italy, Morocco, South Africa, and Thailand. It is reported to be very extensive in Colombia, Bangladesh, and Pakistan, and its practice has been legalized in India despite the constitution and international conventions. Debt-bondage or bonded labor among adults is also more prevalent on the Indian subcontinent than elsewhere, although it is not insignificant in southern Italy, Sicily, Peru, and Ecuador.

While the Anti-Slavery Society is concerned with all forms of slavery defined in the relevant ILO and UN conventions (and also, with its Aborigines Protection Society "hat" on, champions persecuted tribal minorities in Brazil, Bangladesh, the Philippines, and elsewhere), other nongovernment organizations like Amnesty International and the World Council of Churches (WCC) focus on particular issues. Amnesty International takes up the cases of individual prisoners of conscience, including those sentenced to forced labor on account of their political or religious views. The WCC Migration Secretariat and Programme to Combat Racism alert the churches to the situation of migrant labor in all parts of the world and to human rights violations in South Africa, placing particular emphasis on conditions facing women during and after the UN Decade for Women (1976–85).

**Bibliography.** United Nations, *Report on Slavery* (1966); J. Ennew, *Debt-Bondage: A Survey* (1981); United Nations, *Exploitation of Child Labour* (1982); *Slavery* (1984); *The United Nations and Human Rights* (1984); World Council of Churches, *Women under Racism* (1984); *Migrant Women Claim Their Rights: Nairobi and After* (1986); C. Humana, *The Economist World Human Rights Guide* (1986); André Jacques, *The Stranger Within Your Gates* (1986); R. Sawyer, *Slavery in the Twentieth Century* (1986).

PHILIP HILLYER

**Slessor, Mary Mitchell** (1848–1915). Scottish missionary. Born into a poverty-stricken family in Aberdeen (her father was an alcoholic), she received only a modest education and worked in a textile mill in Dundee to help support her family. A deeply devout girl, she devoted all of her free time to religious activities and urban mission work. Her dream of foreign service was fulfilled in 1876 when the United Presbyterian Church of Scotland sent her to its mission at Calabar in eastern Nigeria. Slessor proved to be a pioneer missionary almost without peer, as she quickly mastered the local language and worked as a teacher, preacher of the gospel, and minister to the ill. She strove to eliminate the inhuman practices engendered by traditional religious beliefs, such as the murder of twins, trial by ordeal, and human sacrifice to atone for accidents which befell the communities. Local chiefs utilized her services as an arbiter in disputes; and to combat poverty she encouraged local residents to establish more extensive trading connections between the interior and coastal area. The British colonial authorities appointed her a vice-consul in 1892; she was the first woman to hold that rank in the empire. She organized an African court and coordinated the tribal customs with the new British laws. Deeply concerned with winning the people to Christ, she saw all her efforts as directed toward that end, and her tough constitution, cool nerve, and utter disregard of personal comfort enabled her to be a powerful influence in the advance of Christianity in Nigeria. She gave her life unreservedly to the people, even to the point of adopting their dress and lifestyle and taking in African children as her own.

RICHARD V. PIERARD

**Smith, C. Henry** (1875–1948). Mennonite historian. Born in Metamora, Ill., he studied at the universities of Illinois and Chicago (Ph.D., 1907). He taught at Elkhart Institute, Ind. (1898–1900), was dean at Goshen College, Ind. (1908–13), and taught at Bluffton College, Ohio (1913–48). He was the pioneer Mennonite historian and coeditor of the *Mennonite Encyclopedia*. Most outstanding among his writings are *The Mennonites of America* (1909), *The Mennonites* (1920), *The Coming of the Russian Mennonites* (1927), *The Mennonite Immigration to Pennsylvania in the Eighteenth Century* (1929), and *The Story of the Mennonites* (3d ed., 1950).

*Bibliography.* Mennonite Life 5/2 (Apr. 1950): 3–10; Mennonite Quarterly Review 22/1 (Jan. 1949): 5–21.

CORNELIUS KRAHN

**Smith, George Adam** (1856–1942). Scottish biblical scholar. Born in Calcutta, India, he was educated at the universities of Edinburgh, Tübingen, and Leipzig, traveled extensively in Egypt and Syria, and in 1880 became assistant minister at the West Free Church, Brechin, and tutor in Hebrew in the Free Church College, Aberdeen. He was then minister of Queen's Cross Free Church, Aberdeen (1882–92), professor of OT language, literature, and theology at the United Free Church College, Glasgow (1892–1909), and principal of Aberdeen University (1909–35). He strove to obtain better industrial conditions for workers, became a royal chaplain and was knighted by King George V, continued to travel widely around biblical sites, and was greatly in demand as lecturer in the USA and England. His works include *The Book of Isaiah* (2 vols., 1888, 1890), *The Preaching of the OT to the Age* (1893), *Historical Geography of the Holy Land* (1894), *Book of the Twelve Prophets* (2 vols., 1896, 1897), *Life of Henry Drummond* (1898), *Modern Criticism and the Preaching of the OT* (1901), *Forgiveness of Sins, and Other Sermons* (1904), *Jerusalem: The Topography, Economics and History from the Earliest Times to A.D. 70* (2 vols., 1908), *The Early Poetry of Israel* (1913), and *Jeremiah* (1923). He wrote *The Kirk in Scotland* (1930) with John Buchan.

J. D. DOUGLAS

**Smith, Gerald Birney** (1868–1929). Baptist scholar. Born in Middlefield, Mass., he graduated from Brown, Columbia, and Union Theological seminaries. He did further graduate work at Berlin, Marburg, and Paris. He was Latin tutor at Oberlin Academy (1891/92), taught mathematics and modern languages at Worcester Academy (1892–95), and taught theology at the University of Chicago (1900–1929). He was the managing editor of the *American Journal of Theology* (1909–20) and editor of the *Journal of Religion* (1921–27). He wrote *Practical Theology* (1903), *Social Idealism and Changing Theology* (1913), *Principles of Christian Living* (1924), and *Current Christian Thinking* (1927). With E. D. Burton and J. M. P. Smith he wrote *Biblical Conception of Atonement* (1909). He edited and contributed to *A Guide to the Study of the Christian Religion* (1916). With Shailer Mathews, he edited *A Dictionary of Religion and Ethics* (1921).

RAYMOND W. ALBRIGHT

**Smith, Rodney ("Gipsy")** (1860–1947). English evangelist. Born of Gipsy parents at Epping Forest near London, he was converted at a Primitive Methodist meeting in Cambridge when he was 16, and subsequently became an officer in the newly formed Salvation Army. In 1882 he began what was to become a worldwide ministry. A popular evangelist, as well as writer, singer, and evangelical ecumenist, Smith had a noteworthy influence on the shape of early 20th-century evangelism through his work with the National Council of Evangelical Free Churches. He was a pioneer in the use of radio in the service of the gospel in Great Britain, the USA, and Australia, was a popular advocate of large-scale evangelism to students, and anticipated some of today's most pressing issues, including alcohol abuse, the need for Christian perspectives on ecology, and the protection of ethnic minorities. In his labors following World War I—during which he served with the YMCA in France—Smith was associated with the cause of Methodism in Britain, working with its home missions department. Proud of his Romany origins, he was well able to converse in the ancient language, learned from his father, Cornelius, who also was an evangelist. Gipsy Smith died on board the liner *Queen Mary* on its first postwar Southampton–New York crossing. His published works include *Gipsy Smith, His Life and Work* (1901), *A Mission of Peace* (1904), *Evangelical Talks* (1922), and *The Beauty of Jesus* (1932).

DAVID LAZELL

**Smith, Henry Preserved** (1847–1927). American biblical scholar. Born in Troy, Ohio, he was educated at Marietta College, Amherst College, Lane Theological Seminary, and the universities of Berlin and Leipzig. He served Lane Theological Seminary as instructor in church history (1874/75) and Hebrew (1875/76), and as professor of Hebrew and OT exegesis (1877–93). He was then professor of biblical literature at Amherst College (1898–1906), and professor of Hebrew language and literature at Meadville Theological School, Pa. (1907–13). Finally he was librarian and professor of Hebrew at Union Theological Seminary, N.Y. (1913–25). In theology he affirmed his "belief in religion as the life of God in the human soul, and in the Christian religion as the fullest measure of that life, mediated through Jesus Christ." He had been ordained as a Presbyterian minister in 1875, but was suspended for alleged heretical teaching by the Presbytery of Cincinnati in 1893. Six years later he was received into the Congregational ministry. His published works include *Inspiration and Inerrancy* (1893), *The Bible and Islam* (1896), *Critical Commentary on the Books of Samuel* (1899), *OT History* (1904), *The Religion of Israel* (1914), *Essays in Biblical Interpretation* (1921), and the autobiographical *Heretic's Defense* (1926).

**Smith, Herbert Augustine** (1874–1952). Congregationalist musician. Born in Naperville, Ill., he studied at Northwestern (now North Central) College, the American Conservatory of Music, and the Oberlin Conservatory of Music. He taught hymnology and church music at the Chicago Theological Seminary (1901–16) and Boston University (1917–44); he was director of fine arts in religion (1921–33), director of the department of sacred music, College of Music (1934–44), and director of music, Chautauqua, N.Y. (1921–28). He wrote *Worship in the Church*

*School through Music, Pageantry and Pictures* (1928), *Lyric Religion* (1931), and *Organization and Administration of Choirs* (1933). He composed the following pageants: *The Immortality of Love and Service* (1919), *The City Beautiful* (1919), *The Commonwealth of God* (1920), *The Stars and Stripes* (1920), and *The Light of the World* (1922). He compiled and edited *The Hymnal for American Youth* (1919), *The Century Hymnal* (1921), *The Army and Navy Hymnal* (1922), *Hymns for the Living Age* (1923), *The American Student Hymnal* (1928), *The New Hymnal for American Youth* (1930), *Praise and Service* (1932), and *The New Church Hymnal* (1937).

RAYMOND W. ALBRIGHT

**Smith, John Coventry** (1903–1984). Pastor, ecumenist, and administrator. Born in Stamford, Ont., he was educated at Muskingum College, Ohio, and at Pittsburgh-Xenia Seminary (now Pittsburgh Theological Seminary). He ministered briefly in Four Mile United Presbyterian Church in rural Pennsylvania (1928/29) before appointment as a missionary to Japan. During World War II he was imprisoned by the Japanese for six months, but was then allowed to return to the USA, where he served churches in the Pittsburgh area and worked on behalf of Japanese-Americans. In 1948 he joined the executive staff of the Board of Foreign Missions of the Presbyterian Church USA, in which before his retirement in 1970 he held many key positions. He traveled widely at home and abroad on denominational and ecumenical business, and served a seven-year term as president of the World Council of Churches. He was moderator of the general assembly of the United Presbyterian Church (1968/69). His autobiography is *From Colonialism to World Community, the Church's Pilgrimage.*

**Smith, John Merlin Powis** (1866–1932). Baptist scholar. Born in London, he was educated at Des Moines College and the University of Chicago (Ph.D., 1899). He served as literary secretary to President William R. Harper (1899–1906), and taught Semitic language and literature at Chicago (1899–1932). He was associate editor of *Biblical World* (1906–20), the *American Journal of Theology* (1907–20), the *Journal of Religion* (1920–32), and the *American Journal of Semitic Languages and Literatures* (1907–15; editor, 1915–32). He wrote commentaries on Micah, Zephaniah, Nahum, and Malachi (*International Critical Series*) (1911/12), commentaries on Amos, Hosea, and Micah (*Bible for Home and School*) (1914), *The Prophet and His Problems* (1914), *Harper-Smith's Hebrew Method and Manual* (1921), *Harper-Smith's Elements of Hebrew* (1921), *The Religion of the Psalms* (1922), *The Moral Life of the Hebrews* (1923), *The Prophets and Their Times* (1925), and *The Psalms* (1926). With E. D. Burton and G. B. Smith, he wrote *Biblical Ideas of Atonement* (1909). With A. R. Gordon, T. J. Meek, and L. Waterman, he wrote *A Guide to the Study of the Christian Religion* (1916). With E. J. Goodspeed, he wrote *The Bible—An American Translation* (1931). He contributed to Hastings' *Dictionary of the Bible* (1909), the *Dictionary of Religion and Ethics* (1921), the *Standard Bible Dictionary* (1925), and the *Encyclopaedia Britannica* (1929). He was a member of the commission appointed by the International Council of Religious Education to revise the American Standard Version of the Bible (1930).

RAYMOND W. ALBRIGHT

**Smith, Oswald Jeffrey** (1889–1986). Canadian pastor, evangelist, missionary leader, author, and hymnist. Born in Erneston, Ont., Smith graduated from Toronto Bible College and McCormick Theological Seminary in Chicago. In 1928 he founded the People's Church, an independent congregation in Toronto that majored in evangelism and world missions. He was its senior pastor until 1959 when he was succeeded by his son Paul. Smith popularized the "faith promise" concept of missionary giving, and, in his lifetime, the congregation contributed millions of dollars to overseas missions. A tireless advocate of world evangelization, he addressed missionary conventions around the world and advised churches on promotion of missions. He conducted evangelistic missions on every continent. He was the author of 35 books, which were translated into 128 languages and had a distribution of more than 6 million. He also wrote about 100 hymns.

LESLIE K. TARR

**Smith, Preserved** (1880–1941). Born in Cincinnati, Ohio, he studied at Amherst College, Columbia University (Ph.D., 1907), the University of Berlin, and the University of Sorbonne. He taught at Williams College (1904–6), Amherst (1907–14), Harvard (1919/20), and was professor of history at Cornell (1922–41). He was a productive scholar, contributing to the *Encyclopaedia Britannica* and the *New International Encyclopaedia*, and writing many reviews in English, French, and German journals. His publications include *Life and Letters of Martin Luther* (1911), *Luther's Correspondence* (1913, 1917), *The Age of the Reformation* (1920), *Erasmus* (1923), and *A History of Modern Culture* (2 vols., 1930–34).

ERNEST G. SCHWIEBERT

**Smith, Ronald Gregor** (1913–1968). Scottish theologian. Born in Edinburgh and educated at the universities of Edinburgh, Munich, Marburg, and Copenhagen, he was ordained in the Church of Scotland in 1939. He ministered in Selkirk (1939–44) and was a military chaplain (1944–46). In 1947 he joined the staff of SCM Press. In 1956

he was appointed professor of divinity at Glasgow University, a post he held until his death. Among his publications are *Still Point* (1943), *Between Man and Man* (1947), *The New Man* (1956), *J. G. Hamaan* (1960), *A Theological Perspective of the Secular, Christian Scholar* (1960), *The Nature of Faith* (1961), *The Last Years* (1965), and *Secular Christianity* (1965).

**Smith, Wilbur Moorehead** (1894–1976). Bible expositor, author, and bibliophile. Born in Chicago, he studied at Moody Bible Institute (1913/14) and the College of Wooster (1914–17). He was ordained to the Presbyterian ministry in 1922 and served four pastorates (1918–37). He taught at Moody Bible Institute (1938–47), became professor of English Bible at Fuller Theological Seminary, Pasadena, Calif. (1947–63), then professor of English Bible at Trinity Evangelical Divinity School, Deerfield, Ill. (1963–67; emeritus, 1967–78). A great book collector, he offered students and pastors guidance in profitable reading through such widely circulated annotated reading lists as *Some Much Needed Books in Biblical and Theological Literature* (1934), *Profitable Bible Study* (1939), and *55 Best Books on Prophecy* (1940). His other works include *The Supernaturalness of Christ* (2d ed., 1974), *Therefore Stand* (1945), *Great Sermons on the Death of Christ* (1964), and *The Biblical Doctrine of Heaven* (1968). He exercised a broad influence on Christian education by editing an annual volume of *Peloubet's Select Notes on the International Sunday School Lessons* (1935–70).

GLEN G. SCORGIE

**Smyth, Samuel Phillips Newman** (1843–1925). Congregational pastor and writer. Born in Brunswick, Maine, he was educated at Bowdoin College and Andover Theological Seminary. After a short ministry at Providence, R.I., he was pastor of the First Congregational Church, Bangor, Maine (1870–75), the First Presbyterian Church, Quincy, Ill. (1876–82), and the First Congregational Church, New Haven, Conn. (1882–1908). He was a fellow of Yale University (1899–1921), and was active in movements for unity and cooperation among the churches. Among his many published works are *The Religious Feeling: A Study for Faith* (1877), *The Orthodox Theology of To-day* (1881), *Christian Facts and Forces* (1887), *Personal Creeds* (1890), *Christian Ethics* (1892), *The Place of Death in Evolution* (1897), *Through Science to Faith* (1902), *Passing Protestantism and Coming Catholicism* (1908), *Modern Belief in Immortality* (1910), *Constructive Natural Theology* (1913), *A Story of Church Unity* (1923), and *Recollections and Reflections* (1926).

**Snaith, Norman Henry** (1898–1982). English OT scholar. Educated at Oxford, he was ordained

763

a Methodist minister in 1921, and engaged in pastoral work. He taught Hebrew and OT at Wesley College, Leeds (1936–67), where he was also principal from 1961. He was lecturer in biblical studies at Oxford (1961–65). He was president of the Society for OT Study (1957) and of the Methodist Conference (1958/59). His publications include *Studies in the Psalter* (1934), *Have Faith in God* (1935), *The Distinctive Ideas of the OT* (1944), *The Jews from Cyrus to Herod* (1949), *New Men in Christ Jesus* (1952), *Mercy and Sacrifice* (1953), *Commentary on Amos, Hosea and Micah* (1956), *Leviticus and Numbers* (1966), *The Book of Job* (1968), and *The God That Never Was* (1971).

**Social Gospel.** The full impact of the Industrial Revolution with its large-scale production, concentration of economic power, urbanization, and inequalities in the distribution of wealth and income created serious problems for Christians in the 19th century. The individualistic and conservative social philosophies that had been generally accepted by Christians seemed inadequate to aggressive groups which pressed for a social interpretation of the Christian faith. Their new versions of Christianity were based on the message of the prophets and the teachings of Jesus, supported by the traditional sense of responsibility of the church for society and informed by the new social sciences. It was the confident hope of Christian leaders that the application of Christian principles to the ordering of society would lead to the rectification of serious social evils and pave the way for the establishment of the kingdom of God on earth. The Social Gospel movement was made up of a number of strands, differentiated by various theological, denominational, social, and political emphases.

In Europe the Christian social movement was manifest in various ways under the leadership of such men as H. F. R. Lamennais and C. H. Saint-Simon in France; Giuseppe Mazzini in Italy; Hermann Kutter and Leonhard Ragaz in Switzerland; and J. H. Wichern, Friedrich Naumann, and Adolf von Harnack in Germany. In England social concern was evident in the Christian Socialist movement of 1848–54 under the leadership of Maurice and Kingsley, and was continued in the work of such men as Ruskin, Headlam, Holland, and Gore. A network of organizations, publications, and conferences vigorously implemented these movements. In Roman Catholicism the social concern was prominent in such undertakings as the papal encyclical *Rerum novarum* and the work of the archbishop of Mainz, W. E. von Ketteler.

In America the social interpretation of Christianity, despite the work of early prophets such as Theodore Parker, did not gain a significant following until the last quarter of the 19th century,

when violent labor strife and deteriorating urban living conditions troubled certain Christian leaders and made them receptive to influences stemming from European Christian social movements, certain radical social trends, and the discipline of sociology. These leaders enunciated new patterns of thought and programs of action; their Social Gospel movement had its own conservative and right wings, but its main body was reformist and progressive in nature. It was found chiefly in Congregational, Presbyterian, Episcopal, Baptist, and Methodist churches, and was geographically strongest in the Northeast and Midwest.

Basic emphases included criticism of competition and its rationalization in classical economics, concern for fair play and simple justice for the worker, protest against the ethics of avaricious business leaders, and attack on the social evils of burgeoning urban centers. The movement was conditioned by both the evangelical tradition in American theology, which combined an emphasis on salvation with the desire to ameliorate the evils of society, and by the liberal tradition, which sought to interpret the Christian faith in terms of the intellectual currents of the late 19th century in which scientific and historical thinking played a significant role. Advocates tended to be idealistic, optimistic, and somewhat utopian in their expectation that the kingdom of God would come on earth in the not-too-distant future and to a great extent through men's efforts. They were inclined to understand Jesus' kingdom teachings in the light of their own evolutionary thinking. They focused their attention on urban problems and slighted the rural areas. The movement was led largely by the clergy, and was never more than a minority movement in American Protestantism—although an important and creative minority at its peak of influence in the early years of the 20th century. Prominent leaders included Washington Gladden, a Congregationalist who is often named the father of the Social Gospel; Graham Taylor, a seminary teacher prominent in the Settlement House movement; George D. Herron, a fiery and leftward-moving social prophet of the 1890s; William D. P. Bliss, an indefatigable writer and organizer; and Walter Rauschenbusch, a Baptist professor who is generally considered to be the foremost exponent of the movement. Various societies, such as the Church Association for the Advancement of the Interests of Labor (CAIL) and the Brotherhood of the Kingdom, contributed to the spread of the movement, as did a number of journals, such as the *Kingdom* and the *Christian Socialist*. An extensive literature was created as many volumes on the social teachings of Jesus and on social problems from the Christian viewpoint appeared. Novels, of which Charles M. Sheldon's *In His Steps* is a conspicuous example, popularized the movement. Seminary curricula were revised to accommodate the social emphasis. The Federal Council of the Churches of Christ, founded in 1908 at the height of Social Gospel movement, contributed to its increase. The organization of social action agencies in leading denominations was another result of the Social Gospel movement.

After World War I the optimism of the earlier period began to fade, first in Europe and then in America. Hope in the coming of the kingdom of God on earth as a result of human activity lessened; the idealistic basis of the movement was challenged by reality; the liberal theological orientation of the Social Gospel movement was subject to sharp criticism by neo-orthodoxy; the strategy of the movement was attacked as naive and unrealistic. By the time of World War II the movement as a creative force was greatly limited, although it left a permanent mark on the churches.

**Bibliography.** C. H. Hopkins, *The Rise of the Social Gospel in American Protestantism, 1865–1915* (1940); C. E. Hudson and M. B. Reckitt, *The Church and the World* (vols. 2–3, 1940); H. F. May, *Protestant Churches and Industrial America* (1949).

ROBERT T. HANDY

**Socialism, Christian.** *See* CHRISTIAN SOCIALISM.

**Sociology of Religion.** Perspective for viewing religious reality which blends theory and empirical data to analyze religion, a phenomenon whose empirical reality is often far from clear. Sociology's approach to religion differs from that of most other academic disciplines in its insistence on empirical evidence to support its theories, evidence that comes through patterned presentations of seemingly unpatterned data. That which distinguishes the sociology of religion from the other social sciences which also empirically study religious phenomena is its emphasis on the social—an emphasis that recognizes an interplay among individuals, groups, and large-scale organizations.

There are two major perspectives within sociology: the "social organizational" and the "social psychological." The social organizational focuses on the study of institutions, while the social psychological emphasizes the interface between individuals and the larger social order. The former is generally regarded as an objective study of objective "social facts," the latter as an objective study of subjective perceptions. There is an interface between the two approaches, but before considering this intimate connection, it is necessary to discuss each as it has been applied to the study of religion in society.

***Religion as a Social Institution.*** Society may be viewed as a totality comprised of interlocking institutions, including the family, economy, polity, and religion. Among the many institutions which make up modern society, religion is one of the oldest. Given its undisputed importance in the history of humankind, the religious institution was central in the theorizing of the founding fathers of sociology.

Auguste Comte, putative founder of the discipline, observed with mixed emotion a breakdown of Catholicism in 19th-century France. While recognizing the historical role the church played in maintaining order in medieval Europe, Comte welcomed the arrival of the scientific age which was at odds with traditional religion. This new age needed a new religion, and Comte believed that sociology could serve as a scientific religious surrogate. Emile Durkheim, the master who gave sociology its distinctive thrust, accepted the functional importance of religion as an integrative force but departed from Comte's "religion of sociology." His model for the "sociology of religion" is an approach that is still accepted today. Durkheim's definition of religion as a "unified system of beliefs and practices relative to sacred things, that is to say, things set apart or forbidden—beliefs and practices which unite into a single moral community called a Church all those that adhere to them" is a benchmark for the institutional approach. It marks as religious those things that are considered sacred, with an emphasis on beliefs and practices that are collective or the property of the group (rather than the individual). Durkheim's definition and his classic *Elementary Forms of Religious Life* provided the base for a structural-functional approach to the study of religious phenomena—an approach that studies the structure of religious institutions and the purpose or function served by its beliefs and practices for the social order. Much contemporary empirical research seeks to identify the beliefs and practices and to determine the functions served by facets of organized religion.

One of the organizational issues that has received much attention from sociology is the attempt to distinguish among churches, denominations, sects, and cults. Unlike European countries, the USA has never known a "church" in the Durkheimian sense of the term. As a harbor for those seeking religious freedom, America is an example of religious pluralism in which no single religious belief has united the country. This stands in contrast to the religious beliefs and practices which Durkheim believed unified clans and tribes as well as the medieval Catholicism which for centuries served as the religion of the West. The USA provides an example of a religious mosaic made up of denominations, sects, and cults. Denominations represent the well-established religions which have made their peace with "the world," including Episcopalianism, Methodism, Lutheranism, Judaism, and Catholicism. Sects are religious protest groups which have splintered off established denominations and which in turn may become denominations themselves. An example may be provided by the so-called Holiness and pentecostal sects, which include groups such as the Nazarenes, Wesleyan Methodists, Christian Missionary Alliance, Salvation Army, and the Assemblies of God. The Holiness movement, and later the pentecostal movement which sprung from it, originated in conflicts over the accommodative spirit of a post-Civil War Methodism (which itself originated as a sect of Anglicanism). One of these groups, the Assemblies of God, is now the 12th largest Protestant denomination in the USA with over 2 million members (over 16 million worldwide). It has long abandoned most of its sectlike qualities, including a separation from the larger culture and a withdrawal from "worldly" values and institutions. While sects represent a break from an established denomination or sect, sociologically speaking cults are cultural imports or new religions that are dramatically different from the dominant religious worldview. The International Society for Krishna Consciousness (ISCON) or the Holy Spirit Society for the Unification of Worldwide Christianity (the Unification Church or "Moonies"), one with its roots in Hinduism and the other a syncretic expression of Christianity and oriental philosophies, provide illustrations of cults which have entered the religious mosaic of the West. Such descriptive attempts identify different forms of religious organization as frequently intraorganizational; that is, they focus on providing a sociological description of a single religious institution.

Those taking an institutional approach may seek to determine the impact of religion on other institutions and/or on the larger society. These scholars may utilize the integration model of structural functionalism, or they may employ the conflict model of Marxism. For Karl Marx, religion was a product of the economic substructure and a means through which the economic order, complete with its injustices, was legitimized. Whether employing the model of a well-oiled machine where all the parts or institutions of society work together or one of society being an institutional battleground, those sociologists using an interinstitutional approach focus on the relationship between religion and other parts of the social order.

***Religion as Interpretation.*** Comte, Durkheim, and Marx, although producing very different theories in the sociology of religion, do share a materialistic bent in emphasizing what Durkheim called "social facts." Another of the founding fathers, Max Weber, provided a somewhat different thrust to the sociological enterprise in insisting that sociology be an "interpretative" science. Weber's social-psychological analysis is on a macro or institutional level and provides a bridge between the dominant functionalist approach to religion and the less prominent social-psychological perspective. His classic *Protestant Ethic and the Spirit of Capitalism* provides a model for an objective study of subjective perceptions. In his attempt to refute and modify Marx's claim that religion was a by-product of the economic system, Weber brilliantly argued that the values of Protestantism served as an important factor in the rise of capitalism. He showed how theological conceptions become part of deeper felt orientations of human beings which in turn must be recognized and interpreted in sociological analysis.

Interpretative sociology places its emphasis on the meanings that persons attach to their beliefs and actions. Rather than responding directly to social stimuli (whether historical, culturally normative, or demographic), human beings, say interpretive sociologists, act on the basis of the meanings they attach to such "objective" facts and situations. The quest for a better understanding of the meanings persons attach to religious phenomena has facilitated the development of a social-psychological approach which weds psychological to sociological theory. William James and Georg Simmel are classic theorists who have inspired contemporary social psychologists of religion who are working on a micro level of analysis which focuses on interpretative efforts between and among individuals. A topic of particular recent interest to social psychologists of religion has been that of conversion to new religious movements, including rich descriptive studies of members of various groups ranging from Catholic charismatics to members of ISCON.

***Toward a Dialectical Sociology.*** Contemporary social theorist Peter Berger has done more than any sociologist to theoretically integrate the social organization and social-psychological approach in the study of religion. Berger asserts that there are three options for maintaining religious reality amid the onslaught of modern secularism. The reductive option—which reduces religious beliefs to rational thought—may be a favorite of liberal theologians, but in the long run robs religion of its function of providing meaning for life. The deductive option of simply reiterating a faith perspective, an approach of fundamentalism, is also doomed to failure in the modern world which seeks meaning but which is skeptical of traditional religious formulations. Berger believes that it is through the inductive option, or religious experience, that religion may be revitalized in modern secular society.

Such experiences, however, occur within a larger social context, with the objective social world serving as either a supporting plausibility system or a constraining system. Subjective perceptions do deviate from this institutionally normative world and collective experiences can result in a new externalized reality. The dialectical tension between the objective (the normative and institutional) and the subjective (the perceived world of meanings and experiences) makes the social world an ever-changing dynamic.

Within Berger's model the two sociological approaches complement each other. There is room for the social-psychological perspective of followers of James and Simmel who emphasize religious experience as well as for Weberian analysis which recognizes the importance of charisma for vital religious movements. At the same time such interpretive components as religious experience and charisma give rise to stable institutional matrixes which are the focus of organizational analysis inspired by Comte, Marx, and Durkheim.

**Bibliography.** W. James, *The Varieties of Religious Experience* (1902); E. Durkheim, *The Elementary Forms of Religious Life* (1915); M. Weber, *The Sociology of Religion* (1922); K. Marx and F. Engels, *On Religion* (1957); M. Weber, *The Protestant Ethic and the Spirit of Capitalism* (1958); K. Marx, *The Economic and Philosophic Manuscripts of 1844* (1964); P. Berger, *The Sacred Canopy* (1967); P. Berger, *The Heretical Imperative* (1979); T. F. and J. O'Dea, *The Sociology of Religion* (1983); M. Poloma, *The Assemblies of God at the Crossroads: Charisma and Institutional Dilemmas* (1989).

MARGARET M. POLOMA

## Sockman, Ralph Washington (1889–1970).

American Methodist minister. Born in Mount Vernon, Ohio, he was educated at Ohio Wesleyan University, Union Theological Seminary, and Columbia University (Ph.D., 1917). He was intercollegiate secretary of the YMCA (1911–13), and associate minister (1915–17) and minister (1917–61) of Madison Avenue Methodist Episcopal Church. During that time he served terms as president of the Board of World Peace of the Methodist Church, president of the Church Peace Union, director of the Hall of Fame for Famous Americans, and associate professor at Union Theological Seminary. His numerous works include *Suburbs of Christianity* (1924), *Morals of Tomorrow* (1931), *Paradoxes of Jesus* (1936), *The Highway of God* (1942), *The Lord's Prayer* (1947), *How to Believe* (1953), *The Whole Armor of God* (1955), and *The Meaning of Suffering* (1961).

J. D. DOUGLAS

## Söderblom, Nathan (1866–1931).

Lutheran ecumenist. Born in Trono, Sweden, he studied at the universities of Uppsala and Paris (D.Theol., 1901). He was pastor of the Swedish parish in Paris (1894–1901), professor of comparative religion in the Theological Faculty at Uppsala University (1901–14), professor at the University of Leipzig (1912–14), and archbishop of Uppsala (1914–31). A noted scholar in the field of comparative religion, he outgrew the rationalism of the liberal epoch while preserving the positive values of sound critical scholarship. Under his primacy a revival of church life took place in Sweden. His enthusiasm for Christian unity, kindled in his youth, made him one of the outstanding leaders of the ecumenical movement. He was the chief organizer of the first Conference on Life and Work in Stockholm (1925). In 1930 he received the Nobel Peace Prize. His writings include *Christian Fellowship* (1923), *The Living God* (1933), and *The Nature of Revelation* (1933).

**Bibliography.** N. Söderblom, *In Memoriam* (1931); H. G. G. Herklots, *Nathan Söderblom, Apostle of Christian Unity* (1948); J. G. H. Hoffmann, *Nathan Söderblom, Prophéte de l'oecumenisme* (1948).

YNGVE BRILIOTH

## Solomon Islands. See SOUTH PACIFIC, ISLANDS OF THE.

## Solzhenitsyn, Alexander (1918– ).

Soviet dissident writer. Born in Rostov-on-Don, he was educated at Rostov and Moscow universities. In 1941 he joined the army. The close of the war, however, saw Solzhenitsyn commencing a harrowing 11-year period of imprisonment for having criticized Stalin in a letter. Finally released in 1956, he took up a teaching post in a secondary school.

Solzhenitsyn's sensation-making *One Day in the Life of Ivan Denisovich*, a description of life in a Stalinist prison camp, appeared in 1962 in the Soviet journal *New World*. But he soon experienced difficulty in publishing further in the USSR. Two memorable novels, *Cancer Ward* and *The First Circle*, were published in the West in 1968. Both depict the individual's struggle to achieve personal integrity in the face of agonizing oppression, whether from cancer or a totalitarian state. Soviet authorities scented ideological heresy, and Solzhenitsyn was expelled from the Writers' Union. In 1970 he was awarded (in his absence) the Nobel Prize for literature. In 1973 the first two parts of his projected seven-part history of the Soviet labor camp system, entitled *The Gulag Archipelago*, were published in Paris. He was consequently arrested for treason in 1974 and deported from the USSR. He currently lives in Vermont.

A traditional orthodox faith underlies Solzhenitsyn's writings. He sees art as a means of helping man to discover truth, which he ultimately defines in spiritual terms. His Christian values are clearly expressed in his 1972 letter to the patriarch of Moscow.

NICK NEEDHAM

## Somalia.

Independent republic in northeastern Africa which covers between 565,000 and 668,000 sq. km. (218,000 and 258,000 sq. mi.) and has a population of about 5.3 million (1983 est.). Formed from territories governed respectively by Great Britain and Italy, Somalia became independent in 1960, and has been controlled by a revolutionary council since 1969. Islam is the official religion, claiming all but about 12,000 of the total population. Roman Catholic missionaries have been in the region since the 1880s, but native converts to Christianity have never exceeded a few hundred. In 1972 all church property was nationalized by law, although some churches and schools are still controlled by the ecclesiastical authorities. The Roman Catholic presence has decreased as priests and nuns leave the country. Protestant work, established two decades after that of the Catholics and operated largely by Mennonite and Sudan Interior Mission personnel under restrictions, was terminated in 1976 with the expulsion of Protestant missionaries.

J. D. DOUGLAS

## Son of God. *See* CHRISTOLOGY.

## Son of Man.

In the OT this phrase is used in the sense of: (1) a man, or of man as such (cf. the synonymous parallelism in Num. 23:19; Job 25:6; Pss. 8:4; 80:17; Isa. 51:12; Jer. 49:33); (2) a semitechnical epithet (God addresses the prophet Ezekiel as such); (3) Israel, or, more probably, Israel's king (see Ps. 80:17, where the Targum renders "son of man" as "king Messiah"); and (4) once in Dan. 7:13 in the Aramaic phrase *kebar enosh* (like a son of man). Here the one "like a son of man" is a being standing over against the animal representatives of the worldly kingdoms; in the interpretation given within the chapter he either personifies or represents the "saints of the Most High."

In the NT the phrase is rendered *ho huios tou anthrōpou*, except in John 5:27 and Rev. 1:13 (*huios anthrōpou*). The first reference probably and the second indubitably refer to Dan. 7:13. Except for Acts 7:53 and Rev. 1:13, the phrase occurs only in the Gospels and is always used by Jesus, except in John 12:34 where the Jews quote him. A number of problems are associated with the use of the phrase.

What lies behind its use in Dan. 7:13? Various scholars have suggested influences from Babylonian, Canaanite, and Egyptian sources, from Persian Zoroastrianism, and from gnostic speculation. Is the Son of Man the mythological primal man, the Ugaritic Baal taking over the rule of the senior god El, or is he the king in the alleged New Year Enthronement Festival? Thus far the study of the origins of this phrase have not produced any generally accepted conclusions.

There can be little doubt that the apocalyptic use of the phrase took its rise from Dan. 7. The Similitudes of Enoch (1 Enoch 32–71) have been variously dated between the 1st century B.C. and the 3d century A.D., but even accurate dating does not definitively settle the period of origin of oral traditions lying behind it. Most scholars regard the Gospels and the Similitudes as quite independent of each other, but both owing their use of the phrase to Dan. 7. In the Similitudes the Son of Man is an important figure, almost certainly personal. He precedes the creation; is hidden in the heavens; is manifested from time to time in various righteous historical figures (notably Enoch); and will eventually be revealed to judge the wicked. The Apocalypse of Ezra is certainly not earlier than A.D. 70. Its vision of a manlike figure from the sea seems to be based on Dan. 7 (and possibly the Similitudes of Enoch). It could hardly have influenced the NT writers.

In John 12:34 the crowd believes Jesus is using "Son of Man" as a synonym for "messiah." Does this mean the two were normally identified in contemporary Judaism? In fact, evidence for this is lacking. It is, however, interesting to note that the strongly anti-Christian Rabbi Akiba identified one of the thrones of Dan. 7:9 as the messiah's.

Sayings of Jesus such as Mark 9:12 indicate that Jesus believed the Scriptures to teach that the Son of Man would suffer. Is there an element of suffering in Dan. 7 itself? Dan. 7:21 states that the little horn will wage war against the saints and will prevail over them (cf. also v. 25). This appears, however, to be before the saints receive the kingdom and it is only in connection with that reception that the Son of Man is mentioned (Dan. 7:13–14).

There are many references to righteous suffering in the psalms. Psalms 22 and 69 in particular are often quoted or alluded to in the passion narratives. None of the occurrences of the term in the psalms, however, are in a context of innocent suffering. The Qumran sectaries were interested in the suffering element in the Isaianic servant songs, relating these sufferings to their own experience of persecution, but there is no link, in their writings, between these passages and the Son of Man. The Targum of Jonathan links the servant and the messiah but identifies neither with the Son of Man. First Enoch 37–71 contains some phrases applied to the Son of Man, which are also found in the servant songs. Although this phenomenon is interesting, it denotes nothing more than common characteristics shared by the two figures.

The many occurrences of the term in the Gospels may be classified as follows: (1) references to Jesus' present ministry (Matt. 8:20; 11:18, 19; 16:13; Mark 2:10, 27, 28; Luke 12:10); (2) references to Jesus' sufferings (Matt. 26:2; Mark 8:31; 9:12, 31; 10:33, 45; Luke 17:25; 22:22, 48); and (3) references to Jesus' exaltation (Matt. 10:23, 32, 33; Mark 8:38; Luke 12:8, 9; 18:8; 21:36; 22:69). The Johannine tradition contains fewer references but each class is represented.

What are we to make of these sayings? Some take the radical view that the sayings were invented by the early church. Bultmann thought that the exaltation group of sayings may have been authentic words of Jesus. The evidence that the term came from Jesus himself, however, is strong.

What did the term mean for Jesus? Some, taking their cue from somewhat oblique references like Mark 2:28 and Matt. 16:13, assert that Jesus was speaking about some heavenly figure other than himself. This would then make John the Baptist the forerunner of a forerunner! Such references, along with others, are better understood, as most scholars maintain, as uses of the phrase as a simple substitute for "I."

Jesus taught that the sufferings of the Son of Man were both necessary and biblical. A passage like Mark 9:27–31 certainly suggests that in his mind "Son of Man" was a kind of middle term between "Christ" and "Suffering Servant." The linking of these OT figures was a distinctive feature of Jesus' understanding of himself and his place in the plan of God. The exaltation passages indicate his conviction that he would ultimately triumph and judge and reign. "Son of Man" therefore becomes a major programmatic term for Jesus, linking his lowly life and sufferings with his exaltation and glory. The Johannine sayings even relate it to his preexistence, so that the entire course of his experience—from preexistence through suffering to glory—is bound up with his claim to be the Son of Man.

*Bibliography.* R. Otto, *The Kingdom of God and the Son of Man* (1953); O. Cullmann, *The Christology of the NT* (1963); A. J. B. Higgins, *Jesus and the Son of Man* (1964); R. H. Fuller, *The Foundations of NT Christology* (1965); H. E. Tödt, *The Son of Man in the Synoptic Tradition* (1965); C. K. Barrett, *Jesus and the Gospel Tradition* (1967); M. D. Hooker, *The Son of Man in Mark* (1967); M. Black, *BJRL* 45 (1962/63): 305–18; J. Jeremias, *NT Theology* (1971); I. H. Marshall and O. Michel, *NIDNTT* (1978): 607–68; F. F. Bruce, *Christ the Lord: Studies in Christology presented to Donald Guthrie* (1982), 50–70.

GEOFFREY W. GROGAN

## Soper, Edmund Davison (1876–1961).

Methodist scholar. Born in Tokyo, he was educated at Dickinson College and Drew Theological Seminary. He was professor of history of religion and missions at Ohio Wesleyan University, Drew Theological Seminary, Northwestern University, Duke University, and Garrett Biblical Institute; president of Ohio Wesleyan University; and visiting professor in theological colleges in India, Singapore, and Manila. His best-known books are *The Religions of Mankind* and *The Philosophy of the Christian World Mission.*

## Sorcery and Soothsaying.

The use of magic to gain knowledge of the supernatural. The soothsayer predicts the future, while the necromancer communicates with the spirits of the dead. Sorcery in the narrow sense is magic used with evil intent; it is intended to cause damage or death or to win the unlawful or forbidden. Amulets or rosaries, for example, may be worn to thwart harmful influences. While the basis of sorcery and soothsaying is primitive animism, the untutored masses of religious devotees throughout the world have retained these primitive and false theories and practices, as in the case, for instance, of the "evil eye."

*Bibliography.* A. LeRoy, *The Religion of the Primitives* (1922); R. S. Rattray, *Religion and Art in Ashanti* (1927).

JOHN CLARK ARCHER

## Sorley, William Ritchie (1855–1935).

Born in Selkirk, he was educated at Edinburgh University, Tübingen, Berlin, and Cambridge. He was a fellow of Trinity College, Cambridge (1883), professor of philosophy at Cardiff (1888–94), professor of moral philosophy at Aberdeen (1894–1900), and professor of moral philosophy at Cambridge (1900–1933). He wrote *The Ethics of Naturalism* (1885), *Moral Values and the Idea of God* (1914/15), and many articles supporting his theistic philosophy.

F. W. DILLISTONE

## Soteriology. See REDEEMER; SALVATION.

## Souter, Alexander (1873–1949).

Scottish NT and patristics scholar. Educated at Aberdeen and Cambridge universities, he was professor of NT Greek and exegesis at Mansfield College, Oxford (1903–11), and professor of humanity at Aberdeen University until his retirement in 1937. Souter's speciality was the Latin of the early Christian centuries; his major patristic writings were in this field, including *A Study of Ambrosiaster* (1905), *Pelagius' Expositions of Thirteen Epistles of St. Paul* (3 vols., 1922–31), and *The Earliest Latin Commentaries on the Epistles of St. Paul* (1927). After retirement he was editor-in-chief of the projected *Oxford Latin Dictionary;* his *Glossary of Later Latin,* A.D. 150–600, published posthumously in 1949, was originally planned as an appendix to the dictionary. However, Souter was better known to the Christian reading public for his series of aids for the study of the Greek NT: the *Oxford Greek Testament* (1910), a critical apparatus for the text of the Revised Version; *The Text and Canon of the NT* (1913); and *A Pocket Lexicon to the Greek NT* (1916).

NICK NEEDHAM

## South Africa, Republic of.

Country in southern Africa with an area of 1,223,404 sq. km. (472,359 sq. mi.) and a population of 31.9 million (1983). The Republic of South Africa has been one of the most active and successful Christian mission fields in Africa. Scottish, English, Dutch, German, Scandinavian, Swiss, French, and American missionaries arrived in the 19th century. As a result of their work, over 79 percent of the total population professes Christianity.

Four major ethnic groups—African (over 73 percent of the total population), European (15 percent), coloured (8.8 percent), and Asian (3.1 percent)—make up the estimated nearly 32 million people of the Republic. Only the Asians, chiefly from the Indian subcontinent, are not overwhelmingly Christian. Some 77 percent of the Africans (the chief subgroups include the Zulus, Xhosas, Tswanas, Pedis, Sothos, Tsongas, Swazis, and Vendas) claim Christianity, 93 percent of the whites (approximately three-fifths are Afrikaners, two-fifths English-speaking), and 90 percent of the coloureds whose ethnic background is a mixture of African, European, and Malay. The various Protestant groups comprise about 39 percent of the total population with the Dutch Reformed churches dominating followed by Methodists, Lutherans, Presbyterians, Congregationalists, and the Apostolic Faith Mission. Roman Catholics account for slightly less than 9 percent of the total population, and Anglicans (Church of the Province of South Africa) approximately 8 percent. There are also small conservative Evangelical churches. Unique among Africans are strong independent Christian churches, perhaps claiming 20 percent of the total South African population.

Other religious groups include tribal religionists (their percentage has dropped from over 50 percent in 1911 to the current 16 percent; the majority of the Venda, Shangaan, and Pedi people continue to be followers), Hindus (2 percent of the total population confined almost entirely to the Asian community), Muslims (1.3 percent Urdu- and Gujarati-speaking peoples of Indian descent, and an Afrikaans-speaking Muslim community known as Cape Malays officially classified as coloured), and Jews (0.6 percent white middle-class communities in the larger cities such as Cape Town and Johannesburg).

Although Catholicism came with Portuguese explorers in 1501, the first permanent Christian congregation was established by the Dutch in Cape Town in 1652. The Dutch Reformed Church (Nederduitse Gereformeerde Kerk, NGK) has continued to be the dominant faith of the Afrikaaners in South Africa. In the early years, it tended to be involved exclusively with the white settlers, ignoring other communities until the beginning of the 19th century. In 1824 NGK gained autonomy from the mother church in the Netherlands at a time when the latter was shedding some of its strict Calvinist theology under the impact of the Enlightenment. The South African church kept its staunch Calvinism, buttressed by Scottish Presbyterianism and the evangelical enthusiasm of Andrew Murray, Jr. In 1857 NGK decreed that blacks and whites had to attend separate services. Between 1853 and 1866, five schisms took place within NGK in the Transvaal and the Orange Free State. Two of these groups—the Nederduits Hervormde Kerk and the Gereformeerde Kerk—continue to the present day. The larger NGK and the two smaller churches have the allegiance of some 42 percent of the white population of South Africa, including

virtually all the political leaders of the present ruling National party responsible for institutionalizing the apartheid policy. They have insisted that apartheid is the will of God and have sometimes been referred to as the "National party at prayer." NGK has been instrumental in creating three successful "daughter" or "mission" churches, including the Black Nederduitse Gereformeerde Kerk in Afrika with 900,000 members and the Coloured Nederduitse Gereformeerde Sending Kerk (NGSK) with 500,000 members.

Moravians first established a mission work among the Khoisan (Hottentot) peoples in 1737. Shortly after 1795, when Great Britain first gained control of the Cape, English and Scottish missionaries arrived. The London Missionary Society's best-known early missionaries included Johannes van der Kemp, Robert Moffat, David Livingstone, and John Philip, the latter being particularly outspoken against the slavery practiced by the Dutch Boers. Today this society is merged with other missions and churches in the United Congregational Church of Southern Africa. In 1806 Methodists built a small chapel in Cape Town and ten years later the first Methodist missionaries arrived. The Methodist Church of Southern Africa has the largest African membership of all the mainline churches and has been in the forefront in the opposition to apartheid.

One of the more notable contributions of the Scottish Presbyterians was the founding in 1841 of the Lovedale school which became a major African educational center. Lutheranism arrived in South Africa under the work of German, Swedish, Norwegian, and North American mission groups. The Apostolic Faith Mission, a pentecostal body founded in 1908, consists of substantial blacks, whites, and coloureds and is the only denomination outside the Dutch Reformed Church to have a significant number of Afrikaans-speaking members.

Roman Catholicism developed more slowly as freedom of worship was not officially granted until 1870. The Catholic Church has expanded rapidly, particularly since the 1950s. Anglican missions reached South Africa in 1821 and its first bishop was appointed in 1847.

Black South African Christians have had to face three ecclesiastical alternatives—to become members of white-controlled mission churches, to join multiracial denominations dominated by white leadership, or to organize their own independent groups. Two independent churches emerged as early as the 1890s—"Ethiopian" churches, which emphasize African independence but are patterned after the established bodies from which they seceded; and "Zionist" churches, which attempt to blend the Christian faith and African traditions (including prophecy, dreams, healing, and ecstatic expressions). Many of the latter groups are also known for their messianic leaders. These churches have grown rapidly, one reason being that they have enabled many urban blacks, whose tribal connections have been weakened, to cope with the alien world of the townships. Of the 3000 independent churches, the largest groups include the Zion Christian Church and the Nazarite Baptist Church. Black American churches have played a significant role in the founding of several groups.

The Reformed, Lutherans, and Presbyterians have developed separate churches for whites and blacks in contrast to the Anglicans, Congregationalists, Methodists, and Roman Catholics, who adhere to a policy of one church (although residential segregation frequently limits integration at the parish level). The latter groups have been in the forefront in the struggle against apartheid with notable African leaders including Nobel Peace Prize winners Chief Albert Luthuli and Anglican Archbishop Desmond Tutu being counted among their membership. Since 1966, there has been a growing black theology movement defined as the theology of the oppressed. An outstanding individual in the movement is Lutheran Bishop Manas Buthelezi, a leader in the South African Council of Churches.

Changes have also been occurring in the Reformed tradition. In 1982, Reverend Allan Boesak of the coloured NGSK was elected president of the World Alliance of Reformed Churches. In 1961 the white NGK withdrew from the World Council of Churches following the Cottesloe Consultation convened in response to the 1960 Sharpeville massacre. The Christian Institute of South Africa was founded in 1963 by C. F. Beyers Naudé whose initial aim was to work within NGK to bring about change. Ostracized by NGK, the Christian Institute turned its attention to the so-called mission and English-speaking churches, and then to support black movements before it was banned by the white minority government in 1977. Stirrings of dissent against the apartheid system in NGK continue to be heard, including a 1982 statement by 123 ministers calling on the church to play "a much greater role of reconciliation," and an October 1986 synod decision declaring its doors open to all races.

In late 1990 political and religious developments in South Africa remained uncertain. The apartheid system was increasingly attacked, and NGK was moving from its position of support for the government policy. The situation was complicated by escalated violence between political and tribal factions in the black townships.

*Bibliography.* J. Du Plessis, *A History of Christian Missions in South Africa* (1911); A. Moorrees, *Die Nederduitse Gereformeerde Kerk in Suid-Afrika, 1652–1873* (1937); B. G. M. Sundkler, *Bantu Prophets in South Africa* (1948); B. Kruger, *The Pear Tree Blossoms: The History of the Moravian Church in South Africa, 1737–1869* (1966); P. Hinchliff, *The Church in South Africa* (1968); idem, *The Anglican Church in South Africa* (1969); D. R. Briggs and J. Wing, *The Harvest and the Hope* (1970); J. M. Sales, *The Planting of the Churches in South Africa* (1971); B. Moore, ed., *The Challenge of Black Theology in South Africa* (1973); B. A. Pauw, *Christianity and Xhosa Tradition: Belief and Ritual among Xhosa-speaking Christians* (1975); M. West, *Bishops and Prophets in a Black City: African Independent Churches in Soweto and Johannesburg* (1975); B. G. M. Sundkler, *Zulu Zion and Some Swasi Zionists* (1976); J. W. de Gruchy, *The Church Struggle in South Africa* (1979); E. Regehr, *Perceptions of Apartheid: The Churches and Political Change in South Africa* (1979); M. Hope and J. Young, *The South African Churches in a Revolutionary Situation* (1981); P. Walshe, *Church versus State in South Africa: A Case of the Christian Institute* (1983); A. A. Boesak, *Black and Reformed Apartheid, Liberation and the Calvinist Tradition* (1984); R. J. Neuhaus, *Dispensations: The Future of South Africa as South Africans See It* (1986).

ALAN H. WINQUIST

**Southeast Asia.** A densely populated region that comprises the peninsula directly south of China and thousands of islands south and east of the peninsula. The land is heavily forested and has rich soil and an abundance of natural resources. Most of the people continue to live in small farming villages where they work the land with crude agricultural implements.

Most of Southeast Asia was governed by European colonial regimes until after World War II, when revolutionary forces in a number of countries began winning independence. Since then the spread of communism has been a significant factor, and by the middle of the 1970s, the whole of Vietnam, Cambodia, and Laos were under the control of communist forces. At that time Christian missionaries were expelled, and today their numbers are severely limited in the region.

The dominant religion on the peninsula is Buddhism. Virtually every village has a pagoda or some other Buddhist shrine, and Buddhist monks are numerous, except in regions where communist domination has repressed religious freedom. Islam is expanding rapidly in the region, and has become the chief religion in Malaysia. Only in the Philippines is Christianity the major religion.

The *Philippines*, with more than 50 million inhabitants, is the most populous of the Southeast Asian nations. Christianity began to flourish, especially after the era of Spanish rule, and today some 94 percent of Filipinos profess to be Christian, 85 percent of whom are Roman Catholic. Six percent of the Christians are adherents of indigenous groups, and fewer than 4 percent are Protestants. The largest non-Christian religion is Islam (Sunnis of the Shafiite rite), which was introduced in the country by Malaysians in the 1830s.

The Catholic faith was brought to the Philippines in 1521, when a priest arrived with Magellan's expedition. In the decades that followed, Augustinians and Dominicans began missionary endeavors, and in the 17th and 18th centuries the country became a base of operations for Catholic missionary ventures to Japan, China, and Cambodia. Despite the size and importance of the Catholic Church, it long remained under the control of outsiders. It was not until 1905 that the first bishop was consecrated, and not until 1960 that the Philippines had its own cardinal. Because of its size, the Catholic Church has considerable influence in Filipino politics—a factor that was particularly evident after the 1986 elections when Ferdinand Marcos was ousted and Corazon Aquino assumed the presidency. Her closest advisors were Jaime Cardinal Sin, archbishop of Manila, and Fathers Joaquin Bernas and Catalino Arevalo, both prominent Jesuits.

Partly because of a severe shortage of priests, Filipino Catholicism is not as doctrinally pure as it is in the West. It contains many elements of folk religion, and it has been the source of many independent indigenous churches. The largest of these churches is the Philippine Independent Church, which was officially organized in 1902 by Father Gregorio Aglipay and nationalist leader Isabelo de Los Reyes. The movement initially attracted large numbers of people and there was a mass exodus from the Catholic Church. Membership declined, however, after the supreme court ruled in 1906 that all properties belonged to the Catholic Church. The movement has since become affiliated with the Anglican Church. Another large indigenous church is the Church of Christ, which is very authoritarian and insists that there is no salvation outside its membership.

Protestant missionaries began work in the Philippines after the country was annexed by the USA in 1898. The Presbyterians were the first to come, followed by the Methodists, Baptists, Disciples of Christ, Christian and Missionary Alliance, and the Seventh-day Adventists. Pentecostal bodies entered later but have been among the fastest-growing of the Protestant groups. Today there are more than 350 Christian organizations in the country, most of which are based in the USA. The Philippine church has its own mission program, and in recent years has been sending a considerable number of missionaries abroad.

In *Vietnam*, the second most populous country in Southeast Asia, approximately 55 percent of the people are Buddhists. Mahayana Buddhism was introduced in the 2d century, and it was the dominant strain until 1930 when all Buddhists were joined together in the United Buddhist Church. Many of the Buddhists, however, combine their beliefs with folk religions, which include Confucian and Taoist beliefs as well as magic and astrology. Outside Buddhism proper, there are a number of newer syncretistic Buddhist sects. The largest is the Cao Daist Missionary Church, a mixture of Buddhism, Confucianism, and Catholicism. It was founded in 1919 and its membership has grown to nearly 3 million.

Fewer than 8 percent of the population professes to be Christian, over half of whom are Roman Catholic. The first missionary effort was conducted by Franciscans, who arrived in 1580 from the Philippines. They were joined in the decades that followed by Jesuits and Dominicans. The largest Protestant missionary effort has been that of the Christian and Missionary Alliance, which began its work in 1911. Robert A. Jaffray, who had served for 15 years in China, initiated the work out of concern for the more than 20 million people who had no Protestant witness. Out of that mission work and the work of other evangelical missions was developed the Evangelical Church. Later indigenous evangelical churches were started independently of the mission churches, and in the 1960s they united to form the Church of Christ.

During the Vietnam War, the missions endured many setbacks and tragedies. Missionaries were captured and killed by the Viet Cong, and Vietnamese Christians were brutally persecuted. Missionaries, many of whom had a long untainted record of selfless humanitarian service, had hoped they could remain in the country to care for the people, but they were treated as enemies. The huge leprosarium and mission hospital at Banmethuot founded by the Alliance was attacked, and Dr. Ardel Vietti, Archie Mitchell, the hospital director, and Dan Gerber, a Mennonite staff worker, were taken captive, never to be heard from again. During the Tet offensive in January 1968, five more missionaries lost their lives. Later two other missionaries, Betty Olsen and Hank Blood, died after an agonizing captivity by the Viet Cong. It was in the tribal areas where the Alliance work had seen the most success, and it was here that the native people suffered the most. Nearly 300 believers were studying at the Nhatrang Bible Institute, and many of them and their families were brutalized by the enemy soldiers.

*Laos*, a country of fewer than 4 million people, is the only land-locked nation in Southeast Asia. The people are more isolated than in other areas of the peninsula, and traditional tribal religions still flourish. Buddhism is the dominant religion, but approximately one-third of the population remain traditionalists, despite missionary efforts by Buddhists.

Christians comprise less than 2 percent of the population, and only a small minority of these are Protestants. The first Catholic missionaries arrived in 1630 and began working among the Thai Lao peoples of the plains. In 1950, Catholic missionaries began working among the mountain tribal people, where significant gains have been made. The first Protestant missionaries were Swiss Brethren who arrived in 1902. They were later joined by Alliance missionaries whose work gave birth to the Gospel Church, the largest Protestant body in the country. The most successful evangelistic outreach has been among the Montagnard tribal peoples.

*Kampuchea* (Cambodia) has seen bitter political turmoil since the 1970s. Millions of people were either killed or brutally displaced from their homes during the terrifying years of the communist Khmer Rouge regime led by Pol Pot. Religious activities were forbidden, Christian leaders were killed, mosques were demolished, and Buddhist temples were looted. Images of Buddha were used for kindling or hurled into the rivers. Because of their vast numbers, Buddhist monks suffered the most. An estimated 50,000 were murdered during the three years of the Pol Pot regime.

Theravada (or Hinayana) Buddhism is predominant, a religion that is quickly recognized by its ornate pagodas and saffron-robed monks begging in the streets. Tribal religion is practiced by the Montagnard tribes, and Muslims comprise over 2 percent of the population. There are approximately 50,000 professing Christians (less than one percent of the population), and only about 10,000 of these are Protestants. The Christian and Missionary Alliance began work in 1922 and has been the most active mission in the area since. There was a significant period of growth in the early 1970s, but in 1975 all missionaries were evacuated.

*Thailand* (Siam), with some 45 million Buddhists, has the largest Buddhist population of any Southeast Asian country. It is a land with more than 24,000 temples and 200,000 monks and is a center of Theravada Buddhism. A recent reform program encourages monks to be involved in social outreach and educates them for university teaching. Islam is the second largest religion with some 2 million adherents. Christianity claims only a half-million, and most of them are viewed as immigrants or foreigners. Most of the Catholics are either Vietnamese or Chinese, and most of the Protestants are either Chinese or Montagnard tribespeople.

Protestant missionary work has a long history, beginning in 1828 with missionaries from the Netherlands and England. Within a decade they were joined by missionaries from the American Board, the American Baptists, and Presbyterians. Other missions joined the effort in the 20th century, and in 1934 the Presbyterians, Baptists, Disciples of Christ, and Lutherans combined their efforts to form the Church of Christ in Thailand, which is the largest Protestant church in the country. Greatest growth in recent years has been enjoyed by the United Pentecostals, who began their work after World War II.

*Malaysia* is the only significant stronghold of Islam in Southeast Asia. It is comprised of three regions: Peninsular Malaysia, adjacent to and south of Thailand; and Sarawak and Sabah, both located on the north side of the island of Borneo. Islam is the state religion, with some 7 million adherents (approximately 50 percent of the population). Muslim traders arrived in Peninsular Malaysia in the 13th century and within two centuries it became the major faith of the region. The largest ethnic group (second only in size to Malay) is Chinese, and the second largest religion, adhered to by approximately 25 percent of the population, is Chinese folk religion. Buddhism ranks third in size.

The fast-growing major religion in Malaysia is Christianity. In 1900 professing Christians comprised less than 2 percent of the population. By 1970 they had surpassed 5 percent, and by the year 2000 it is estimated they will approach 7.5 percent. This growth represents both Catholic and Protestant segments of the church. Catholic missionary work began in the 16th century. The Portuguese arrived first and were later joined by the famous Jesuit missionary Francis Xavier.

The first Protestants in Malaysia were Dutch immigrants, who arrived in the 1640s. The first Protestant missionary was sponsored by the London Missionary Society in 1814. In the decades that followed, Anglicans and other denominations and mission societies arrived, but the work continued at a slow pace until after World War II and after China was closed to missionaries. Many missionaries reestablished their work in Southeast Asia. The Methodists have the largest Protestant work in the country, and sponsor large educational, medical, and agricultural programs. There are many independent churches, the largest of which is the True Jesus Church, which was brought to the region by Chinese immigrants.

*Brunei* is a small region on the island of Borneo that is bounded on three sides by Malaysia. It is a sultanate under British protection with a population of less than 300,000. The state religion is Islam, and the sultan is the head of state, but there is a sizable population of Muslims, and Christians make up 8 percent of the population. Of the latter, Catholics and Anglicans are most numerous. Methodist and Seventh-day Adventists are also active in Brunei.

*Bibliography.* E. F. Irwin, *With Christ in Indo-China* (1937); W. T. Thomas and R. B. Manikam, *The Church in Southeast Asia* (1956); H. E. Dowdy, *The Bamboo Cross* (1964); A. L. Tuggy, *The Philippine Church: Growth in a Changing Society* (1971); D. Cho, ed., *New Forces in Missions* (1976); H. R. Cowles, *Operation Heartbeat* (1976); D. Barrett, *World Christian Encyclopedia* (1982).

RUTH A. TUCKER

**Southern Africa.** Today Southern Africa is best known for apartheid and the racial policies of the Afrikaner Nationalist government which are in turn related to Calvinism and the Dutch Reformed Church. A century ago Southern Africa was the springboard for the evangelization of Africa and a source of hope on a "dark" continent. Yet whatever the differences between the past and present many observers in both periods would agree that the future of South Africa is in embryo the future of the world. If Christianity succeeds here then its future is assured. Should the gospel be rejected then Christians face decline and a very uncertain future.

Surveying the history of religion in Southern Africa one must begin with indigenous religious systems. Too often African religions are dismissed by theologians as "animism" or assimilated in an essentially Christian frame of reference. However, the various indigenous religions of Southern Africa are as distinct as the religions of India. True, just as Buddhism and various Hindu systems share the common metaphysics of yoga, rebirth, karma, and samsara, so too African religions share a concern with witchcraft and ancestors. But here, as in India, the similarity between different religious beliefs ends. To group all African religions under a common head is a gross misrepresentation that reflects a racist bias.

The available evidence, which of necessity is based on the reports of missionaries and traders, seems to indicate that prior to white contact there was considerable interaction between African societies and Arab, Cape "coloured," and other "foreign" groups. Therefore, long before the arrival of white missionaries and traders influential Africans had some knowledge of both Christianity and Islam.

African traditional beliefs as they existed before the arrival of Europeans are, however, very difficult to reconstruct. At best it seems that some African groups, nations, clans, or families were essentially "secular" in their understanding of the world. As a result, certain missionaries described them as being "without God." Other Africans, however, were decidedly religious. Some believed in a whole hierarchy of gods or spiritual beings while others had a strong belief in one supreme being. For certain groups "god" was highly personal while others viewed god in essentially impersonal terms. Each group had its own beliefs; generalization simply distorts the situation.

With the beginning of Dutch settlement in 1652, Calvinism through the medium of the Dutch Reformed Church was introduced to the Cape. Strong evidence exists, however, to show that the original settlers were not particularly religious and shared many aspects of European folk religion and superstition. As the settlement expanded the influence of religion declined until the beginning of the 19th century when apart from the immediate area around Cape Town there seems to be little evidence of a viable Christianity in South Africa.

Moravian missionaries arrived in 1792 followed by the London Missionary Society in 1799 and later on other groups like the Methodists, Lutherans, and Anglicans. Initially the missionaries were sent to the so-called coloured people. Only later did they expand their activities beyond the Cape frontier to Natal and the hinterland. Still later South Africa was to become the base for evangelism throughout Africa south of the Sahara.

Four events mark the development of Southern African Christianity in the 19th century. The first is the decision by the Dutch Reformed Church to adopt a homogeneous church principle and allow "people of colour" to meet separately from the "white" congregation. The second is the outbreak of evangelistic revivals under the leadership of Andrew Murray (1828–1917) which began in 1860. The third is the dispute between Bishop Colenso and the missionary Henry Callaway over the nature and significance of polygamy in 1861. Finally, in 1892 the first recorded "Ethiopian" African Independent Church was founded on the Witwatersrand.

The first event has often been blamed for the creation of apartheid but this is far too simplistic a notion and is not backed by solid historical evidence. The motive for this decision was evangelistic not racist; nevertheless the unexpected and unintended effect may have been to isolate white Christians from other racial groups.

The second event had far-reaching effects in Europe and North America because it popularized the piety of Andrew Murray and through his writings gave an impetus to ideas about "faith healing" and similar charismatic gifts. In many ways these revivals can be said to have led directly to the development of pentecostalism and eventually to the modern charismatic movement.

The third event is far more complex an issue and concerns the relationship between Christianity and culture. On the surface Bishop Colenso took the more humane view by defending certain aspects of polygamy and under specific conditions allowing some polygamists to become full members of the church. Henry Callaway rejected Colenso's argument and presented his own case based on personal observation of polygamous families. He argued that polygamy enslaved women and was a social evil. Today most people would instinctively agree with Colenso and see Callaway as ethnocentric. But, in fact, both Colenso and Callaway were steeped in Zulu culture and by the standards of their time were very enlightened. The debate they engaged in serves as a warning about judging the past too harshly and assuming that all valid cultural knowledge originated in the 20th century.

Finally, the development of a strong African Independent Church movement free from missionary control saw the emergence of African forms of Christianity which, while criticized by many whites, undoubtedly express the aspirations of many common people. Although they originally lacked theological sophistication there can be no doubt that the vigor of the independent churches had a profound effect upon Africans in established mission churches and through them on Christianity generally.

It is a mistake to think of South African Christianity as isolated from the rest of the world throughout the 19th century. Bishop Colenso made a significant contribution to religion in *The Pentateuch and Book of Joshua Critically Examined* (1862). Rather than being an isolated individual on the frontier of a great empire, Colenso emerges as a leader of the intellectual thought of his time. Similarly Andrew Murray's writings on prayer, Christian living, obedience, and piety profoundly influenced British and American evangelicalism, giving direction to both the emerging fundamentalist movement and pentecostalism.

From 1899 to 1902 South African society was torn apart by the Second Anglo-Boer War. In the aftermath of war and the recognition that over one-third of all Boer/Afrikaner women and children had died in British concentration camps a vigorous Nationalist movement developed which sought to preserve Afrikaner culture from destruction by both British and African cultures. Supported by a religious revival legitimized by the invention of a Calvinist historiography, Afrikaner Nationalism developed its characteristic doctrine of apartheid. At the same time a civil religion developed which gave sacred sanction to Afrikaner actions and political activities.

But if the use of Christian symbols created apartheid those same symbols led a small but significant number of Afrikaners to place faith and loyalty to God over commitment to their volk. As a result the Christian Institute led by Geyser and Naudé was created to oppose apartheid on biblical and Reformed grounds. The institute's journal (*Pro Veritate*) quickly became the leading voice of opposition in South Africa. Similarly, the South African Calvinist Society, which propagates its views through its journal *Woord en Daad*, developed a critical stance toward the abuses of Nationalist policy and the use of religion to legitimate political actions.

Other Christian opposition groups developed primarily out of Anglican and Roman Catholic communities. More recently the evangelical organization Africa Enterprise has taken the lead in organizing conservative Christian opposition to the racial policies of the South African government. In particular the work of the National Initiative for Reconciliation, founded at a conference organized by Africa Enterprise in 1985, deserves mention.

Within the black community African "independent" churches began to develop toward the end of the 19th century. Originally they broke away from their parent bodies largely because of the racism of white missionaries, but increasingly their prime motivation became the development of an authentic African Christianity. From them

various pentecostal beliefs and practices found their way back into white congregations and eventually, largely as a result of the work of David du Plessis, into world pentecostalism and the charismatic movement. Finally, in the early 1970s a vigorous black theology movement developed which gave rise to a renewed investigation of African traditions and indigenous theologies.

Christian missions have had a strong impact on all the independent countries of Southern Africa. Malawi is an example of a successful state where Presbyterianism holds sway. In other countries, such as Zimbabwe, newer political ideologies coexist alongside strong religious movements some of which are Christian, other of which are revivals of older traditional religions. For example, Shona diviners or spirit mediums played an important role in the Rhodesian-Zimbabwian civil war which led to the independence of Zimbabwe.

In many of these countries dissident religious groups like Jehovah's Witnesses experience periodic persecution although the most severe repression occurred in Zambia where Alice Lenshina's Lumpa movement was ruthlessly suppressed by the slaughter of thousands of its members by the Zambian army in 1964. The situation in Namibia, formerly German South West Africa, is different again. Here the Lutheran Church has taken a strong stand in support of the South African People's Organisation (SWAPO) which is fighting against South African rule. But while the Lutherans draw support from the northern Ovambo, the traditional rulers of much of the country, the Herero, are less likely to support SWAPO.

Among the Herero, in their own Lutheran-based independent church movement, the Oruuano Church, various prophetic leaders and faith-healing missions are at least as important as explicitly political groups. Yet this statement in itself is misleading because in Africa religious movements tend to be political even when they are ostensibly religious. The division between religion and politics in the North American or European sense is simply not made.

Clearly Christianity in Southern Africa has made a profound impact upon both white and black cultures. But it has also affected the rest of the world and continues to be a source of both inspiration and dismay to all Christians.

**Bibliography.** B. G. Sundkler, *Bantu Prophets in South Africa* (1961); J. McCracken, *Politics and Christianity in Malawi, 1875–1940* (1977); I. Hexham, *The Irony of Apartheid: The Struggle for National Independence of Afrikaner Calvinism Against British Imperialism* (1981); W. M. J. van Binsberger, *Religious Change in Zambia: Exploratory Studies* (1981); K. Poewe, *The Namibian Herero: A History of Their Social Disintegration and Survival* (1985); W. de Gruchy, *The Church Struggle in South Africa* (1986); B. Tlhagale and I. Mosala, *The Unquestionable Right to Be Free: Black Theology from South Africa* (1986).

IRVING HEXHAM

# Southern Baptist Convention (SBC).

Largest member body in the Baptist World Alliance, numbering more than 14 million baptized believers in some 37,000 churches in all 50 states of the USA. SBC was formed on May 8, 1845, in Augusta, Ga. Baptists in the South separated from the Triennial Convention over issues arising out of the abolition movement. Other factors such as the freedom to carry on missionary activities without regard to the slavery issue and differences over the nature of denominational structure also contributed to the separation.

Theologically, Southern Baptists are evangelicals who give a high priority to the Bible in determining their faith and order. They baptize only believers by immersion and hold that neither baptism nor the Lord's supper convey sacramental grace. Missions constitutes their primary reason for being and has made SBC one of the most aggressive missionary bodies in Christendom. As far as soteriology is concerned Southern Baptists can be classified generally as modified Calvinists. They are heirs of the Free Church tradition which includes both Calvinist and Arminian strains. The churches are congregational in polity and nonliturgical in order. Preaching constitutes the central act of worship. Strong congregational ecclesiology coupled with a sense of destiny have helped to determine the convention's relationship with other Christian communions.

SBC has steadfastly refused to join the National and World Councils of Churches. However, it cooperates with agencies of the National Council of Churches on projects of mutual interest. Although not a part of institutional ecumenism, SBC took the lead in the formation of the Baptist World Alliance in London (1905) and continues to participate in this organization which embraces the majority of Baptists in the world today.

The organization of SBC seems deceptively simple, but in reality is very complex. In Southern Baptist polity, the autonomy of the local church is jealously guarded and yet the principle of cooperation commands the loyalty of the most Southern Baptists. Local congregations are related to SBC in the same way they are related to the state conventions and local associations. The relationship is both voluntary and financial. The churches are organized into associations, state conventions, and SBC to carry on denominational programs and ministries which would be otherwise impossible. Therefore, the work of the convention, which meets annually, is promoted through four boards, seven commissions, and six seminaries.

Of these agencies the foreign and home mission boards sponsor 7556 missionaries. Missionary work in the USA is provided in 87 different languages under the direction of "home missionaries." The foreign mission board supports 3816 missionaries who serve in 110 countries. The Sunday school board is responsible for publishing enterprises, the operation of book stores, and two summer retreat centers. The annuity board provides retirement and insurance programs for local church and denominational employees. The commissions are charged with the operation of various facets of the convention's institutional ministries. In 1985, a total of 12,697 students were enrolled in the six seminaries. Colleges and universities are operated by state conventions. In 1985 these institutions numbered 53 with a total enrollment of 105,000 students.

The complex organization of SBC, which meets only once a year, involves a maze of interrelationships between churches which send "messengers" to the convention and "trustees" nominated by the state conventions and elected by SBC to direct the work of the boards, commissions, and seminaries. The convention's budget and day-by-day operation is coordinated by an executive committee. Financial support of the convention's work is provided by the "cooperative program" which divides the total receipts from the churches according to an agreed-upon formula. There is no creed which binds Southern Baptists together but there is a confession of faith first adopted in 1925 and revised in 1963 which contains a summary of doctrines held in common. The preface indicates that the confession is not intended to take the place of the Bible or of Christ who is declared sole Lord of the conscience. Apparently a spirit of mutual trust and cooperation within biblical parameters makes for a viable denomination.

**Bibliography.** W. W. Barnes, *The Southern Baptist Convention* (1954); *Encyclopedia of Southern Baptists*, 4 vols. (1958–82); *Southern Baptist Convention Annual* (1963); R. A. Baker, *The Southern Baptist Convention and Its People, 1607–1972* (1974); *Southern Baptist Convention Annual* (1986).

W. R. ESTEP

# Southern Christian Leadership Conference (SCLC).

Organization established by Martin Luther King, Jr., in 1957 in Atlanta, Ga., to bring about the equality of blacks in all aspects of American life. The movement espoused nonviolent social change; conducted leadership training programs for blacks; engaged in vigorous voter registration to insure the enfranchisement of blacks for city, state, and national elections; and organized the powerful civil rights march on Washington, D.C., in 1963. SCLC was instrumental in creating the environment which brought about the 1964 Civil Rights Act and the Voting Rights Act of 1965. After the 1968 assassination of King in Memphis, Tenn., Ralph David Abernathy assumed leadership. The organization no longer conducted national campaigns for equality, and the staff was cut from 150 to 61 in 1970. In 1972 the organization suffered a split with Jesse Jackson, who led a group interested in economic equality goals. The Jackson group moved to Chicago and took the name PUSH (People United to Save Humanity). SCLC continues today but in greatly reduced form.

ROBERT V. SCHNUCKER

**South India, Church of (CSI).** First union of episcopal and nonepiscopal churches, inaugurated on September 27, 1947, at St. George's Cathedral, Madras. At its inauguration CSI had 1.1 million members, made up of 500,000 former Anglicans of the Church of India, Burma, and Ceylon, 290,000 members of the South India United Church (a 1908 union of Presbyterians and Congregationalists and one area of the Reformed and Lutheran Basel Mission), and 220,000 Methodists.

This pioneering union had its roots in the Tranquebar Conference of 1919 which proposed union between Anglicans and the South India United Church on the basis of Scripture, the creeds, and the "historic episcopate, locally adapted," the latter being accepted as a fact which did not involve any theory of its origins or doctrinal significance. The developing scheme, which soon added the sacraments of baptism and the Lord's supper to its basis to equate it with the Lambeth Quadrilateral (1888), received equivocal reactions from successive Lambeth conferences. Full communion between Anglican churches and the Church of South India has been delayed so that CSI no longer has any nonepiscopally ordained presbyters (a problem avoided by the unification rite adopted by the Church of North India in 1970).

Some 40,000 Anglicans in the Nandyal district of South India refused to join CSI in 1947, but later became members of a Church of North India diocese which was subsequently transferred to CSI. Reunion talks with other churches in South India were initiated in 1948. The North Tamil Church Council of the South Indian United Church joined CSI in 1950. Other talks continued through the 1900s. CSI-Lutheran conversations produced agreed statements (1959) and a draft scheme (1969) for the formation of the Church of Christ in South India with five Lutheran bodies, now part of the United Evangelical Lutheran Churches in India, a 1975 federation with a total membership of 1.5 million. CSI has also been involved in conversations with the Mar Thoma Church (with which it has been in communion since 1958) and the Church of North India, joining with them in a joint council which came out of a 1975 recommendation to act together in mission and work toward the inauguration of a single "Bharat Christian Church."

CSI is governed by a synod with a moderator elected from the diocesan bishops. Each diocese has a diocesan council and each congregation a pastorate committee. Forms of worship devised for use in the church are collected in *The Book of Common Worship* (1963) and its *Supplement* (1967). CSI's present membership stands at about 1.6 million.

*Bibliography.* J. E. L. Newbigin, *The Reunion of the Church* (1948); B. Sundkler, *Church of South India* (1954); T. S. Garrett, *Worship in the Church of South India* (1965).

PHILIP HILLYER

**South Pacific, Islands of the.** Area covering most of the region known as Polynesia and some of Melanesia and consisting of a multitude of islands, independent nations, and a few remaining colonial dependencies, with an overall population of just under 1.5 million. Its distance from east to west is comparable to that between London and Honolulu, or between New York and Bombay; its overall area is at least four times that of Europe or the USA, but the actual total land area falls between that of Austria and Hungary.

The South Pacific came to the attention of Europe with the voyages of James Cook (1769–79). This coincided with the emergence of missionary societies after the evangelical awakening in England and the USA. The London Missionary Society (LMS) was founded in 1795, and pioneered missionary work in this vast area. In 1796 the first missionaries were sent out: 4 clergymen, 25 tradesmen, 4 wives, and 3 children. From a staging post in Sydney they began work in Tahiti, Tonga, and the Marquesas. The early years were marked by failure rather than success, and by 1800 only seven missionaries were left in the whole area.

However, by 1820 the tide had turned in Tahiti, and considerable progress was evident by the late 1830s, when French presence and interests gave support to Catholic missions. In due time LMS handed over its responsibilities in Tahiti to the French Protestant Missionary Society, but, well before doing so, one of its agents had developed a missionary strategy of great significance. John Williams (1796–1839) arrived in Tahiti in 1817, and was apparently the first to recognize the possibility of spreading Christianity throughout Oceania by means of native evangelists. By 1834 he is reported to have sent such evangelists to every island of importance within 3200 km. (2000 mi.) of Tahiti.

The cost in human lives was high, partly because of intertribal warfare in the area and partly because of the hatred engendered by some European traders and slavers. Many native evangelists were killed, as were pioneer missionaries like John Williams and the anglican bishop John Patterson. But equally remarkable is the devotion of native evangelists and the constant supply of volunteers for such a hazardous ministry. It says much both about the people themselves and the way in which they were introduced to and embraced Christianity.

As well as engendering hatred of Europeans among not a few Pacific islanders, the same Europeans introduced their own national rivalries into the area. France was not content to see the area become an English enclave, and the Americans and Germans also defended their interests. This led to curious political situations in Samoa and the New Hebrides, the latter being jointly "ruled" by Great Britain and France from 1906 until independence in 1980. But it also led to competition between Christian denominations, particularly between Catholics and Protestants, the former backed by France and the latter generally finding reluctant support from Great Britain.

Fearful of imperialism at first, missionaries in the end appealed for intervention by a great power to solve the chaos (e.g., Fiji became a British colony in 1874). Not dissimilar patterns were to be found elsewhere. On the other hand, Tonga remains to this day an independent kingdom, but has what closely approximates an established Methodist Church.

While some islanders, not least from the Solomons and Fiji, were enticed by "blackbirders" aboard ships and "persuaded" to become indentured laborers on sugar plantations in Australia, others resisted attempts to persuade them to labor on foreign-sponsored plantations in Fiji. This led British and Australian entrepreneurs to rely on indentured laborers from India. So Hinduism and Islam were brought into Fiji, and today the descendants of those who came from India outnumber the native Fijians. In New Caledonia French and Asian emigres and descendants of the convicts once sent there have a similar relationship to the native kanaks, who seek the sort of independence enjoyed by their cousins in the Solomons and Vanuatu.

Despite such dissuasives, the vast majority of the inhabitants of Oceania are Christians of one persuasion or another. The spectrum ranges from Congregationalists, Catholics, Presbyterians, Methodists, and Anglicans to various pentecostal groups, Seventh-day Adventists, Latter-day Saints, and Jehovah's Witnesses. Various "cargo cults" are to be found as is the continuing influence of traditional religions, which still claim the allegiance of up to 10 percent of the population. Also present are Baha'is, Hindus, and Muslims, with smaller numbers of Buddhists and Taoists.

Autonomous island churches mirror autonomous island nations, with combined resources linked in such bodies as the Pacific Conference of Churches and the Pacific Theological College, both dating from 1966. Of the former Roman Catholics have been full members since 1976. Indeed, the post-Vatican II scene has placed considerable challenges before Roman Catholics, particularly in their relationships with other Christians. The impact of tourism, economic and social development, the mobility of peoples, the legacies of colonialism and its economic imperialism, unease about French nuclear testing and colonial dependencies, and other great power tensions pose continuing challenges to all. However, Christianity's roots are deep, and tested and proved in strength.

*Bibliography.* N. Gunson, *Messengers of Grace: Evangelical Missionaries in the South Seas, 1797–1860* (1978); J. Garrett, *To Live among the Stars* (1982); *The Far East and Australasia, 1986* (1985); J. Hinnells, ed., *A Handbook of Living Religions* (1985).

IAN GILLMAN

**Soviet Union.** *See* UNION OF SOVIET SOCIALIST REPUBLICS.

**Space Exploration.** Investigation of the extent of the universe beyond the limits of the earth's atmosphere by means of spacecraft. Astronomy explores the same space, but obtains its data by analysis of electromagnetic signals (light and radio waves) that are received on the surface of the earth from space itself. Until the development of rockets (1946), all that scientists had deduced about space resulted from observations through the distorting atmosphere of the earth.

Space exploration is carried out with space probes—spacecraft which are launched at an orbital velocity higher than earth's and thereby escape the earth's gravitational pull or attraction. They then orbit the earth or continue on to other planets in the solar system.

The mechanical principles of space flight and, thus, space exploration were first articulated in Isaac Newton's *Mathematical Principles of Natural Philosophy* (1687). However, the capability to actually send a spacecraft into space had to wait until the development of rockets with engines powerful enough to provide sufficient thrust to propel the rocket or spacecraft into orbit beyond the earth's atmosphere. This was first achieved by the Germans in their development of V-1 and V-2 rockets at the end of World War II.

Konstantin Tsiolkovsky is known as the "father of space research." In his papers on the subject of rocket travel, the first of which appeared in 1902 (although actually written about 1895), he laid down the scientific principles of astronautics.

In 1926, Robert H. Goddard fired the first liquid-propellant rocket from Auburn, Mass. He undertook fundamental research in rocketry, but his results were not publicized.

The launching of Sputnik I by the USSR on October 4, 1957, opened the space age and paved the way for manned flight. Sputnik carried a radio transmitter, signals from which were picked up all over the world.

In January 1959, the Soviet Luna 1 bypassed the moon at 4000 miles; in September of the same year Luna 2 crash-landed there; and in October 1959, Luna 3 circled the moon and sent back the first photographs of the far side.

The first manned space flight was achieved on April 12, 1961, by Yuri Gagarin, who completed a full circuit of the earth in Vostok 1. He reached an altitude of 203 miles and the journey took 1 hour, 40 minutes.

On May 5, 1961, Alan Shepard became the first American in space. He achieved a suborbital flight lasting 15 minutes. On February 11, 1962, John Glenn completed a full orbit of the earth.

Successful space-docking operations were carried out in December 1965, by Gemini 6 (Thomas P. Stafford and Walter M. Schira, Jr.) and Gemini 7 (James A. Lovell, Jr., and Frank Borman). This was an essential preliminary to the success of the Apollo program, which was to land astronauts on the surface of the moon.

During 1967, the U.S. program of lunar mapping with Orbiter vehicles was continued. By the end of the year, the entire surface of the moon had been charted satisfactorily, enabling the choice of possible landing sites.

The final triumph of the Apollo program came on July 20, 1969, when Neil Armstrong and Edwin Aldrin, Jr., in Eagle, the lunar module of Apollo 11, made a successful landing on the Mare Tranquillitatis and walked on the moon.

In May 1971, America launched its first probe designed to go into closed orbit around Mars. Mariner 9 reached its target in November 1971, and operated until October 1972, sending over 7000 high-quality pictures of the Martian surface.

The first Jupiter probe, Pioneer 10, was launched on March 2, 1972; it bypassed Jupiter in December 1973, at a distance of 82,000 miles, sending back pictures and valuable information about the Jovian magnetosphere. It is now on its way out of the solar system.

Skylab, the first U.S. space-station, was launched in 1973. It suffered damage during the ascent, and was repaired in orbit by the first crew. A second crew went up to Skylab in July 1973.

Mariner 10, launched in November 1973, was the first two-planet probe. In February 1974, it bypassed Venus, sending pictures, and in March 1974, it sent the first close-range pictures of Mercury. After two more active passes the craft lost contact.

In October 1975, the USSR landed a probe on Venus and obtained a picture from the surface. Venera 9 operated for 53 minutes after landing before being put out of action by adverse conditions. Venera 10 was equally successful a month later.

Launched in August 1975, Viking 1, from the USA, landed successfully in the Chryse region of Mars in July 1976, at once sending data and pictures. Its "twin," Viking 2, landed in the Utopia region in September 1976.

On August 20, 1977, Voyager 2 was launched on its journey to Jupiter and Saturn. It was followed on September 5, 1977, by Voyager 1, which, traveling in a more economical orbit, bypassed Jupiter (Mar. 5, 1979) and Saturn (Nov. 12, 1980) before Voyager 2. Two additional moons of Jupiter and three of Saturn were discovered. A complex system of rings, including two which appeared to be braided, were also discovered around Saturn. Voyager 2 flew by Jupiter in February 1981, and Saturn in August of the same year, providing greater detail about the two planets. Voyager 2 was then programmed to bypass Uranus, which it did on January 24, 1986. Ten new moons were discovered and delicate rings around the planet were studied. A strong methane atmosphere provided a perpetual haze over the planet. Voyager 2 was then programed to fly by Neptune in 1989.

In December 1978, Pioneer Venus 1 and 2, from the USA, and Venera 11 and 12, from the USSR, reported important new information about the high temperature and high concentration of argon-36 in the atmosphere of Venus.

In 1980, Soviet cosmonauts Valery V. Ryumin and Leonid I. Popov spent a record-breaking 185 days aboard the Salyut 6 space-station, returning to earth in Soyuz 37 on October 11.

On April 12, 1982, the space shuttle Columbia was launched from the Kennedy Space Center in Florida and landed at Edwards Air Force Base in California on April 14. This was the first launched vehicle to be returned intact for use in a later launch. Shuttle flights were repeated with success through 1985. In addition to the shuttle Columbia, shuttles Challenger, Discovery, and Atlantis were launched.

On March 2, 1983, the USSR launched Cosmos 1443 and carried out an unmanned docking with the Salyut 7 space-station, making steady progress in the ultimate establishment of a multi-manned space-station. Called a "space tug" by the Soviets, Cosmos 1443 provided electrical power as well as living and work space for its crew.

On January 25, 1983, the Infrared Astronomical Satellite was launched and detected swarms of large particles around the star Vega. Some astronomers suggested that these were planets—the first to be detected outside the solar system.

During 1984 and 1985, both the USA and the USSR used their spacecraft to carry out many scientific experiments—the USA using space shuttles and the USSR using the Salyut space-station.

On January 28, 1986, the space shuttle Challenger disintegrated 73 seconds after takeoff, killing the seven crew members: mission commander Francis "Dick" Scobee, pilot Michael Smith, mission specialists Ellison Onizuka, Judith Resnik, and Ronald McNair, teacher-in-space Sharon Christa McAuliffe, and Hughes Aircraft engineer Gregory Jarvis. This accident halted the U.S. manned space program until the entire program could be reevaluated for safety.

Five probes were launched in 1984/85 to investigate Halley's Comet as it made its appearance in 1986: Giotto, launched by the European Space Agency; Vegas 1 and 2, launched by the USSR; and Suisei and Sakigake, launched by Japan. These probes showed the comet to be a black lump spewing out jets of water vapor and dust.

On February 19, 1986, the USSR launched its newest space-station, Mir (Peace). It was a marked improvement on the Salyut series, providing support for 12 crew members and docking facilities for four additional laboratory modules.

The future of space exploration seemed assured. The USSR seemed headed toward permanent habitation of their Mir space-station and the USA seemed to be working toward a resumption of the space shuttle program early in 1988. Once the shuttle program was again in place, the USA planned to launch the Magellan Venus Radar Mapper mission early in April 1989; the Galileo Jupiter Orbiter and Atmospheric Probe spacecraft in October 1989; and, finally, the Mars Orbiter in September 1992.

Other nations besides the USSR and the USA have launched satellites: Japan, France, Great Britain, Italy, West Germany, the Netherlands, Spain, India, Canada, China, Indonesia, Nato, the European Space Agency, Czechoslovakia, the Arab League, Brazil, and Mexico.

OLLIN J. DRENNAN

**Spain.** Large country occupying some 85 percent of the Iberian peninsula, covering 504,750 sq. km. (194,885 sq. mi.). The country has a population of 37 million (1985), of whom Roman Catholics number 35,895,900 and Protestants 33,500. The history of Christianity in Spain can be traced back to the early Christian era. Some scholars maintain that Paul traveled to Spain, although Rom. 15:24 does not specifically support this conjecture. Others have identified James as a founder of the church in Spain. These apostolic roots are highly debatable. By the time of Tertullian, nonetheless, a flourishing Spanish church is supposed to have existed. In A.D. 300 the Council of Elvira was held, which speaks of the status of Spanish dioceses by that date. At the third Council of Toledo (589) the Arian church accepted Catholicism. In the 8th century Muslim Moors threatened the Spanish church. By 732 they reached Tours, where Charles Martel halted their advance.

From about 1000 until the 1490s Christians in Spain were persecuted by the Moors. However, Spain was reconquered for Catholicism by 1492, when Granada was taken. The reestablishment of Catholicism was completed when Aragon and Castile were united in 1494. In 1479 Ferdinand and Isabella introduced the Inquisition. Jews and Muslims were systematically sought out and tried. More than 350,000 Jews (Marranos) were accused of heresy, and 12,000 were burned at the stake. Incipient Reformation sympathizers were treated with similar brutality. The Reformation was largely eradicated from Spain. The Counter-Reformation was born on Spanish soil. Among its forerunners were St. Teresa, St. John of the Cross, and Ignatius Loyola. Loyola's Jesuits became the shock troops of the war against the Reformation, especially in France and England.

During the 18th and 19th centuries Catholicism experienced a decline in Spain. The church became increasingly corrupt, as it succumbed to materialism and immorality. In 1767 Charles III expelled the Jesuits from the country. The French occupation of Spain in 1808 introduced anticlericalism and this further depleted the spiritual resources of Spanish Catholicism. Regionalism also tore apart the fabric of the national church, until the 1936–39 civil war restored nationalism to the Spanish people. From 1939 until 1975 Franco forged an iron image of Spanish Catholicism. National order and religious rigidity were of the same piece. A new Concordat was completed under the pontificate of Pius XII in 1953, which designated the Catholic Church as "the only religion of the Spanish nation." However, under pressure from other European nations and at the urging of the USA, a religious liberty law passed the Cortes in 1967.

New liberties followed the death of Franco in November 1975. The Holy See relinquished some degree of control over the internal government of the Spanish nation. By 1978 Protestants gained new freedom to bury their dead, perform marriages, and receive converted Catholics into their churches. The Act of 1978 states: "The public authorities will keep in mind the religious beliefs of the Spanish society and will maintain cooperation with the Catholic Church and the other confessions." As a result of these new liberties, the face of Spanish Catholicism has changed. In January 1966 the Steinmetz Institute surveyed urban women, and it was discovered that 78 percent practiced their religion at least weekly; 6 percent practiced every two weeks; and 3 percent practiced seldom or never. Nine years later a survey revealed that only 14 percent of people under 30 practiced their faith more than once a week, as did 19 percent of the over 30-year-olds. When asked whether they practiced their faith weekly, 36 percent of the under-30-year-olds and 38 percent of the over-30-year-olds said they went to Mass at least weekly.

As the Catholic Church has loosened its grip on Spanish society, Protestantism has grown. In 1900 there were very few Protestants. By 1975 there were 31,500 (0.1 percent) Protestants and that number grew to 33,500 (0.1 percent) by 1985. Most of the Protestant movements entered Spain as missionary movements, mostly from England and the USA. The Christian (Plymouth)

Brethren entered Spain in 1868. One year later the American Baptists started their work. They were followed by the Swedish Baptists in 1881 and the Southern Baptists in 1921. The largest Protestant groups in Spain are predictably the pentecostals. The Philadelphia Churches claim 13,500 adherents. There are 6000 in fellowship with Brethren Assemblies and 15,000 adherents. (The informal nature of the Assemblies helped them to thrive in the years prior to Franco's death.) Southern Baptists claim approximately 7500 members.

Other religious movements have burgeoned since 1975. For instance, in 1950 there were 93 Jehovah's Witnesses in Spain. By 1970 that number had grown to 10,086. Now there are approximately 39,500. Mormon missionaries also reached Spain in significant numbers. Now they claim approximately 7200 members.

Not only have Protestant churches grown in Spain since the death of Franco; disaffection with Catholicism has spread. In 1900 only 2000 people called themselves irreligious in Spain; by 1985 the number of irreligious had grown to 705,000 (2 percent). In 1900 there were no registered atheists in Spain; by 1985 there were 176,000.

Despite the long history of Muslim presence in Spain, their number is no longer significant. There are presently only 5200 Muslims in Spain, most of them in Madrid. In 1900 there were no officially registered Jews in Spain. Now there are approximately 8900. There are, however, 200,000 Marranos (Crypto-Jews), who were forcibly converted to Catholicism. They are identified as Catholics, although they secretly observe Jewish rites. There were 195 members of Bahai in 1961. By 1985 their number had grown to 4500, and they maintain about a dozen spiritual assemblies.

Since 1975 Protestantism has emerged from a ghetto complex in Spain. However, there has not been spectacular growth among the Protestants. Furthermore, there is still a good deal of division among them. Predictably they have few indigenous leaders. To remedy this lack Greater Europe Mission, Operation Mobilization, and TEAM have launched extension courses to provide biblical education.

Among the larger North American and British missions now working in Spain are the Southern Baptist Convention, OMS, Worldwide Evangelistic Crusade, TEAM, Assemblies of God, Greater Europe Mission, CAM International, and European Christian Mission. There are also about 30 missionaries from Latin America in Spain.

*Bibliography.* Anuario Evangelico Espanol (1983); D. G. Vought, *Protestants in Modern Spain: A Struggle for Religious Pluralism* (1973); D. B. Barrett, ed., *World Christian Encyclopedia* (1982).

WAYNE DETZLER

**Speiser, Ephraim Avigdor** (1902–1965). Jewish scholar. Born in Skalat, Poland, he came to the USA in 1920 and studied at the University of Pennsylvania and at Dropsie College (Ph.D., 1924). He was visiting professor at the Hebrew University of Jerusalem (1927), annual professor at the American School of Oriental Research in Baghdad (1927/28), professor of Semitics at the University of Pennsylvania (1931–54), where he was also professor of Hebrew and Semitic language and literature (1954–64), and university professor of oriental studies (1965). He directed excavations in Mesopotamia in 1927, 1930–32, and 1936/37. In Bible studies he contributed evidence for the view that the essential authenticity of the historical background of the OT has been abundantly confirmed by archeological records. He is the author of *Mesopotamian Origins* (1930), *Excavations at Tepe Gawra* (1936), *Introduction to Hurrian* (1941), *The United States and the Near East* (1947; rev. ed., 1951), and *Genesis* (1964).

**Spellman, Francis Joseph** (1889–1967). American cardinal. Born in Whitman, Mass., he studied at Fordham College, N.Y., and the North American College, Rome. Ordained to the priesthood in 1916, he engaged in pastoral work and held various administrative positions in the archdiocese of Boston. In 1925 he was called to Rome to serve on the staff of the Secretariat of State, under the government of Pius XI. He was nominated auxiliary bishop of Boston (1932), and became archbishop of New York (1939), in which capacity he played an influential part in the development of relations between Pope Pius XII and the president of the USA. He was created cardinal in 1946. He was the author of several devotional books and works of religious fiction, among them *What America Means to Me and Other Poems and Prayers* (1953).

**Sperry, Willard L. (Aroyd)** (1882–1954). Congregationalist theologian. Born in Peabody, Mass., he studied at Olivet (Mich.) College, Queen's College, Oxford, and Yale. He was assistant minister and then pastor of the First Church, Fall River, Mass. (1908–13), and pastor of the Central Congregational Church, Boston (1914–22). He was lecturer, then professor of practical theology at Andover Theological Seminary (1917–25). After 1908 he was affiliated with Harvard Divinity School. When the two institutions merged in 1922, Sperry became dean. After the judicial dissolution of the union (1926) Sperry in due course came to serve in a threefold capacity (1929–53): as continuing dean of the Harvard Divinity School, as professor of Christian morals, and as chaplain to the university (chairman of the board of preachers). The most important of his writings are *The Disciplines of Liberty* (1921), *Reality in Worship* (1925), *The Paradox of Religion* (1927),

*The Divine Reticence* (1927), *Yes, But—The Bank-ruptcy of Apologetics* (1931), *What You Owe Your Child* (1935), *Wordsworth's Anti-Climax* (1935), *We Prophesy in Part* (1938), *Strangers and Pilgrims: Studies in the Classics of Christian Devotion* (1939), *What We Mean by Religion* (1941), *Religion in America* (1945), *Jesus Then and Now* (1949), and *The Ethical Basis of Medical Practice* (1951). He drafted the Faith and Order Commission's report, *The Non-Theological Factors in the Making and Unmaking of Church Union* (1937), and participated in the revision of the OT for the Revised Standard Version.

*Bibliography.* Harvard Divinity School *Bulletin* (1953); W. L. Sperry, *Summer Yesterdays in Maine* (1941); idem, *Thirteen Americans* (1953).

GEORGE H. WILLIAMS

**Spinka, Matthew** (1890–1972). Church historian. Born in Stitary, Czechoslovakia, he came to the USA in 1905. He earned a Ph.D. at the University of Chicago and a Th.D. from the Faculty of Protestant Theology, Prague. He taught church history at Central Theological Seminary, Dayton, Ohio (1920–26), served as librarian and associate professor of church history at Chicago Theological Seminary and the Divinity School of the University of Chicago (1926–43), and was professor of church history at Hartford Theological Seminary (1943–55). Among his publications are *The Church and the Russian Revolution* (1927), *A History of Christianity in the Balkans* (1933), *Christianity Confronts Communism* (1936), *John Hus and the Czech Reform* (1941), *John Amos Comenius* (1943), *Nicolas Berdyaev* (1950), *From Wyclif to Erasmus* (1953), *The Church in Soviet Russia* (1956), *John Hus at the Council of Constance* (1965), *John Hus: A Biography* (1968), and *Letters of John Hus* (1972). He edited *Church History* (1932–49) and *A History of Illinois Congregational and Christian Churches*.

J. D. DOUGLAS

**Spiritualism, Spiritism.** Communication with spirits is a feature of religious life that is virtually as old as humanity itself. "Spiritism" is the general term given to the phenomenon; "spiritualism" is a more specific designation referring to the particular expression of spiritism which emerged in the latter half of the 19th century and survives today in organized form.

The origin of spiritualism can be traced to events that occurred in upstate New York in 1848. Margaret and Katie Fox, two teenage girls, heard mysterious rappings that they later attributed to a murdered peddler, allegedly buried beneath their Hydesville home. The much publicized rappings launched spiritualism as a popular movement which eventually spread to England and Europe. At its height the spiritualist craze claimed over 10 million believers with some distinguished adherents, including Sherlock Holmes' creator Sir Arthur Conan Doyle, physicist Sir Oliver Lodge, and eminent biologist Alfred R. Wallace.

The central and distinguishing figure of spiritualism was the "medium," who served as the contact between the seen and unseen worlds. It was through mediums, usually while in trance, that the spirits directly spoke, wrote, or drew. It was also in the presence of mediums that spiritistic phenomena, like the Hydesville rappings, occurred. As the movement grew the repertoire became more elaborate and more exotic: tables were tilted and turned, musical instruments were played, objects were leviated, messages were spoken or written—all seemingly effected by invisible presences which on occasion materialized, in whole or in part, to be visibly seen or captured on film.

Popular fascination with spiritism prompted the formation of organizations to investigate spiritistic phenomena scientifically. In 1882 England's Society of Psychical Research was founded and in 1884 the American Society for Psychical Research was established, with William James among its first members. The contemporary discipline of parapsychology is a direct descendant of these organizations.

Skeptics justifiably dismissed the movement as fraudulent. Mediums were routinely exposed; few survived critical scrutiny, Douglas D. Home (1833–1886) being a notable exception. What was not dismissed as fraud was often explained away as collective hallucination, self-delusion, or dementia. A third less skeptical explanation considered the phenomena real but attributed them to latent powers of the mind, not to spirits.

Spiritualism's indebtedness to the Austrian physician Franz Mesmer (1734–1815) can be seen in its use of trance and in the "magnetic" theory often cited to explain how spiritistic phenomena were produced. Mesmer was the grandfather of hypnotism. He used trance-induction techniques in his practice and suggested that healing could be effected in trance states because of a current of energy, which he called "animal magnetism," that passed from healer to patient. Although Mesmer's primary intent was curing illness, those he put into trance, or "mesmeric sleep," occasionally spoke and exhibited clairvoyant gifts, and spiritistic phenomena sometimes occurred.

Spiritualism's central belief is implicit in the spirit contact foundational to it: the dead continue to exist and communication with them is possible. That belief found its place in the broader framework of an emanationist cosmology supplied by spiritualist theoreticians like Andrew Jackson Davis, who were in turn heavily influenced by the Neo-Platonist mystic and seer Emmanuel Swedenborg (1688–1772).

Like emanationist cosmologies in general, the spiritualist's variation blurs the distinction between the creature and Creator, reducing God to Infinite Intelligence and affirming that humanity and all of nature are extensions or expressions of it. The spiritualists, like Swedenborg before them, believed in a progressive spiritual evolution which continued beyond the grave, the deceased passing through various stages eventually to become pure spirit once again. The spiritualists thus rejected the biblical doctrine of resurrection and with it the redemptive significance of the death and resurrection of Jesus Christ. A final judgment was also ruled out, the eternal possibility of reform in this life and the hereafter becoming an explicit tenet of faith for the National Spiritualist Association of Churches. Reincarnation found a place in the spiritism of Allan Kardec in France but was generally shunned.

Since the spiritualist excitement of the 19th century, popular enthusiasm for contacting spirits has risen and fallen in waves. It has erupted in times of acute social crisis, emerging with renewed vigor on the heels of both World Wars. In the wake of the occult revival and widespread interest in Eastern mysticism during the countercultural era of the 1960s, spiritism has once more seen new life. Ram Dass and other countercultural heroes led the way in the 1970s. By the mid-1980s spiritism had again become a cultural fad, largely due to the efforts of Shirley MacLaine who gave it mass-media exposure. But this latest wave is only marginally related to 19th-century spiritualism. Spiritistic phenomena are all but absent; the doctrine of reincarnation is the rule rather than exception; and Eastern monism provides the framework for spiritistic discourse and the theories enthusiasts use to explain it.

**Bibliography.** E. W. Capron, *Modern Spiritualism, Its Facts and Fanticisms, Its Consistencies and Contradictions* (1855); F. Podmore, *Modern Spiritualism: A History and a Criticism,* 2 vols. (1902); A. C. Doyle, *The History of Spiritualism,* 2 vols. (1926); L. Spence, *An Encyclopaedia of Occultism* (1960); J. Webb, *The Occult Underground* (1974); *The Occult Establishment* (1976); R. L. Moore, *In Search of White Crows: Spiritualism, Parapsychology, and American Culture* (1977); R. M. and C. R. Goldfarb, *Spiritualism and Nineteenth-Century Letters* (1978); R. Brandon, *The Spiritualists: The Passion for the Occult in the Nineteenth and Twentieth Centuries* (1983); J. Oppenheim, *The Other World: Spiritualism and Psychical Research in England, 1850–1914* (1985); L. Barrow, *Independent Spirits: Spiritualism and English Plebeians* (1986).

ROBERT BURROWS

**Spirituals, Negro.** *See* GOSPEL SONGS.

*Spiritus Paraclitus.* Encyclical of Pope Benedict XV issued on September 15, 1920, on the occasion of the 15th centenary of the death of St. Jerome. After a brief survey of the life and works of Jerome, the pope restates the Roman Catholic position with regard to Scripture. The Bible, composed by men who were inspired by the Holy Spirit, has God himself as its principal Author, the individual authors of single canonical books being his instruments. Their activity, however, ought not to be described as automatic writing. In consequence, the Bible is said to be absolutely free from error as was already declared in the encyclical *Providentissimus Deus* of Leo XIII. Apparent anomalies extant in Scripture may not be explained by distinguishing primary and secondary elements, of which the latter would not be guaranteed; nor by opposing absolute to relative teaching; nor by the hypothesis of implicit quotations, on which the sacred author would not pass judgment; nor by assuming the existence in the Bible of pseudohistorical narratives or literary patterns which would seem to give fiction an appearance of reality. These and similar principles of criticism are condemned as being incompatible with the traditional exegesis of the Roman Church.

GEORGES A. BARROIS

**Sri Lanka.** Island country in the Indian Ocean with an area of 64,652 sq. km. (24,962 sq. mi.) and a population of 16.2 million (1985). In Sri Lanka 69.3 percent of the population are Buddhists of the Theravada School. Nearly all of them belong to the Sinhala race. Buddhism was introduced in the 3d century B.C. by Mahinda, son of the Indian king Asoka. Popular religion includes non-Buddhist practices like using exorcists (*kattadiyas*) to cast off spells, worship at shrines of Hindu deities, and the use of horoscopes.

Buddhism suffered a serious setback under colonial rule. A revival was spearheaded by American theosophist Henry Olcott in the late 1800s. He founded top-rank Buddhist educational institutions. Itinerant preacher Anagarika Dharmapala (1864–1933) helped raise the religious and national consciousness of the people. He founded the Mahabodhi Society devoted to restoring neglected Buddhist holy places in India.

Recently missionaries have gone to many parts of the world. The Buddhist clergy (*sangha*) play a prominent role in the politics of Sri Lanka which they regard as the *Dhammadipa* (the island serves as guardian of Buddhist teaching). The idea that Sri Lanka is a Buddhist nation has been promoted, but although the constitution gives Buddhism a prominent place, it also guarantees freedom of religion.

Tamils constitute 15.5 percent of the population; 85 percent of them are Hindus. Most Sri Lankan Hindus are adherents of the Saiva Siddhanta School which developed in Tamil Nadu, South India, during medieval times. This and the common Tamil language have inspired close contacts with Tamil Nadu, evidenced by Tamil Nadu's support of the Tamil campaign for greater autonomy.

Hinduism, like Buddhism, experienced a revival during British rule under Arumuka Navalar (1822–1879). Following a visit to Sri Lanka by Swami Vivekananda in 1893 a branch of the Ramakrishna mission was formed giving impetus to the revival, especially under Swami Vipulananda. Hinduism has no organization comparable to the Buddhist *sangha* and thus no establishment which could command the allegiance of all the Hindus in Sri Lanka. Indian guru Satya Sai Bāba has a growing number of devotees from different races and religions.

The Muslims are a small (7.6 percent) but influential community. Most are Moors, descended from 12th- and 13th-century Arab traders. They speak a dialect of Tamil. The Malays are Javanese who came as soldiers with the Dutch, although some may have come earlier. The Bohras are a small merchant community from Gujarat, India, who belong to the Ismaili sect. Evidences of the worldwide Muslim revival are seen in the rebuilding of mosques and a fervent devotion to religion and community by most Muslims.

Nestorians from Persia visited Sri Lanka in the 6th century, but Christianity took root only during colonial rule. The Portuguese (1505–1658) encouraged, and sometimes enforced, Roman Catholicism. The Dutch (1640–1796) encouraged the Dutch Reformed Church. The Anglicans, Methodists, Congregationalists, Baptists, and the Salvation Army came during the time of British rule (1796–1948). Since independence the older churches have faced embarrassment over their colonialist ties.

Christians, who include Sinhalese, Tamils, and Burghers (Portuguese and Dutch extraction), are down to 7.5 percent of the population (from 9.1 percent in 1946). Ninety percent are Roman Catholic. Theologians like Aloysius Pieris, Michael Rodrigo, Tissa Balasuriya, D. T. Niles, Lynn de Silva, Wesley Ariyarajah, and Lakshman Wickremasinghe have focused on pluralism, interreligious dialog, and the sociopolitical implications of Christianity. Newer charismatic churches and evangelical organizations are active in evangelism and growing in numbers. Some older churches voted in the 1970s to form a united church, but dissenters stalled the move through court action.

*Bibliography.* J. R. Carter, ed., *Religiousness in Sri Lanka* (1979); K. M. de Silva, *A History of Sri Lanka* (1981).

AJITH FERNANDO

**Stählin, Ernst** (1889–1980). Swiss church historian. Born in Basel, he studied at the universities of Basel, Göttingen, Berlin, and Magdeburg, taught at the University of Basel in 1916, and succeeded in 1927 his own teacher, Paul Wernle, in the chair of modern church history which he held until his own retirement in 1961. He served as rector of the university for three terms. His research and publications focused on three main areas: (1) the life and work of the Basel Reformer Oecolampadius; (2) Swiss Protestantism; and (3) the "kingdom of God" theological tenet in the history of Christianity. A festschrift, *Gottesreich und Menschenreich*, was presented to him on his 80th birthday in 1969.

From 1929 to 1936 he was editor-in-chief of the *Kirchenblatt für die reformierte Schweiz.* Noteworthy publications include a two-volume selection of the work of Johan Caspar Lavater (1943), a seven-volume selection of texts on kingdom of God proclamations throughout Christian history, *Die Verkündigung des Reiches Gottes in der Kirche Jesu Christi* (1951–65), and *Briefe und Akten zum Leben Oekolampads* (2 vols., 1927–34). A detailed list of his work is given in *Gottesreich und Menschenreich*, supplemented in a memorial tribute in *Zwingliana* 15 (1980/81): 299–302.

E. J. FURCHA

**Stählin, Wilhelm** (1883–1975). German Lutheran theologian. Born in Gunzenhausen, he studied at Erlangen, Rostock, and Berlin (Dr. Phil.). After pastorates in Egloffstein, Upper Franconia (1910–17), and the St. Lorenz Church, Nuremberg (1917–26), he joined the University of Muenster, Westphalia, as professor of practical theology (1926–57). From 1944 to 1952 he functioned as bishop of the Evangelical-Lutheran Church, Oldenburg.

By his involvement in the Christian youth movement and as a director of the youth associations (1922–32) he contributed significantly to renewal of church life by relating youth organizations to church structures. He cofounded the so-called Berneuchen movement (1931) and played a leading role in the formation of the male fraternal organization of the evangelical St. Michael Brotherhood. He cofounded in 1946 the Evangelical-Catholic ecumenical working group, helping the German Protestant churches gain renewed appreciation for the catholicity of the Christian tradition in liturgy, diaconal service, prayer, sacramental life, and proclamation of the gospel.

Among his works are *Fieber und Heil in der Jugendbewegung* (1921), *Jesus und die Jugend* (1922), *Das Berneuchener Buch* (1926), *Was ist lutherisch?* (1952), and *Die Feier des Neuen Bundes* (1963).

E. J. FURCHA

**Stalker, James** (1848–1927). Scottish scholar and minister. Born in Crieff, Perthshire, he was educated at the universities of Edinburgh, Berlin, and Halle, and ministered in Kirkcaldy and Glasgow before appointment in 1902 as professor of church history in the United Free Church College, Aberdeen, a post he held until 1926. Much in demand as a lecturer at home and abroad, he was known as a theologian who rested his faith "on the threefold foundation of Scripture, tradition, and personal experience, with emphasis on the third." His publications include *The Life of Jesus Christ* (1879), *The Life of St. Paul* (1884), *Imago Christi* (1889), *The Preacher and His Models* (1891), *The Seven Deadly Sins* (1901), *The Seven Cardinal Virtues* (1902), *John Knox, His Ideas and Ideals* (1904), *The Atonement* (1908), and *The Ethic of Jesus According to the Synoptic Gospels* (1909).

J. D. DOUGLAS

**Stamm, John Samuel** (1878–1956). Evangelical United Brethren theologian. Born near Alida, Kans., he studied at North Western College, Naperville, Ill., Evangelical Theological Seminary, Naperville, Ill., and the University of Chicago. He served pastorates at Macon, Mo. (1899–1901), Glasgow, Mo. (1901–3), Manhattan, Ill. (1903–7), Downers Grove, Ill. (1907–12), and Oak Park, Ill. (1912–19). He was professor of systematic theology at Evangelical Theological Seminary, Naperville, Ill. (1919–25), and bishop of the Evangelical and Evangelical United Brethren Church (1926–50). He also served as president of the Evangelical School of Theology, Reading, Pa. (1935–41), and president of the Federal Council of the Churches of Christ in America (1948–50). He is the author of *Evangelism and Christian Experience*.

**Stapleton, Ammon** (1850–1916). United Evangelical (now Evangelical United Brethren) scholar. Born in Earl, Pa., he served in the Union Army under General Sheridan, and then studied at Central Pennsylvania (now Albright) College. Ordained to the Evangelical ministry in 1875, he served 20 years as a pastor, then as presiding elder (1895–1907), and later as pastor of St. Paul's Church, York, Pa., and St. Paul's Church, Williamsport, Pa. He was influential in the formation of the Historical Society of the United Evangelical Church, forerunner of the Historical Society of the Evangelical United Brethren Church. He wrote *Natural History of the Bible* (1885), *Compendium of Church History* (1896), *Evangelical Annals,* containing also *A History of the United Evangelical Church* (1900), *Memorials of the Huguenots in America* (1901), *Flashlights on Evangelical History* (1908), *Old Time Evangelical Evangelism, being the Life and Times of Albright* (1911), and *The Henkel Memorial* (1912). He contributed the nucleus of the Historical Society of the Evangelical United Brethren Church's collection of Evangelicana.

RAYMOND W. ALBRIGHT

**Stapleton, Ruth Carter** (1929–1983). Evangelist, spiritual therapist, and author. Born in Archery, Ga., she attended Georgia State College for Women (1946–48), Methodist College, and the University of North Carolina. During the 1950s she suffered severe mental depression, following which, she began to promote holistic health through "inner healing." As a combination of self-help and theology, her teaching advocated spiritual, emotional, and physical healing through prayer, psychology, meditation, exercise, and diet. She led workshops and retreats throughout the world and operated Behold Inc. as well as a 35-acre retreat center called "Holovita" ("whole life"). Her ministry reached Protestants, Catholics, and people such as her elder brother, former president Jimmy Carter. Her best-selling books include *The Gift of Inner Healing* (1976), *Experiencing Inner Healing* (1977), and *Brother Billy* (1978).

JACK MITCHELL

**Starbuck, Edwin Diller** (1866–1947). Writer on psychology of religion. Born in Bridgeport, Ill., he was educated at Indiana University, Harvard University, and Clark University (Ph.D., 1897). He was professor of mathematics at Vincennes University, Ind. (1891–93), assistant professor of education at Leland Stanford Jr. University, Calif. (1897–1903), professor of education at Earlham College, Ind. (1904–6), professor of philosophy at the State University of Iowa (1906–30), professor of philosophy and director of character research at the University of Southern California (1930–39), and professor of psychology there (1939–45). His theological position can be described as that of monistic idealism. His interest in theology is evident in his contributions to the psychology of religion, among which were *Psychology of Religion* (1899), *Biblical World* (Jan. 1907/8), and *Homiletic Review* (1907–9). He wrote widely on character education.

HARRY G. GOODYKOONTZ

**Steere, Douglas Van** (1901– ). Quaker scholar. Born in Harbor Beach, Mich., he was educated at Michigan State College, Oxford University, and Harvard (Ph.D., 1931). He was assistant (1928–31), associate (1931–41), and professor (1941–64) of philosophy at Haverford College, and was a writer and lecturer on religious subjects, especially the nurture of the inward life. He was active in the work of Quaker Service, especially in missions to Poland, Germany, and Scandinavia after World War II. In religious philosophy he was a critical realist with strong mystical leanings. Among his many books are *Prayer and Worship* (1938), *On Beginnings from Within* (1943), *Doors into Life* (1948), *On Listening to One Another* (1955), *Work and Contemplation* (1957), *Dimensions of Prayer* (1963), *Spiritual Counsel and Letters of Baron von Hügel* (coauthor, 1963), *Mutual Irradiation* (1970), and *On Speaking out of the Silence* (1972).

**Stewardship.** Recognition of God's ownership of all material resources and of life itself, including one's thoughts, time, talents, energy, influence, and possessions. The term is much broader than the tithe, but may include it. Stewardship is not merely a scheme to raise money for the church, but a means of entering actively into partnership with God. It may be compared to the battery of an automobile, which is meant not to store up power for itself but to give its energy for the benefit of other parts of the car. Stewardship in the loftiest sense is the noblest expression of the Christian ideal, and provides the motive power for mighty achievements. It does so by leading the way to discipline, sacrifice, and service, through which one finds the victorious life. According to Paul, we must remember "the words the Lord Jesus himself said: 'It is more blessed to give than to receive'" (Acts 20:35). Such stewardship involves not only the use of time, talents, and money, but also the trusteeship of all that has come from God. As Christians we are stewards of the gospel, which the Lord has committed to us for the work of evangelism and missions. According to Peter we should be good stewards of God's grace (1 Pet. 4:10). Christ used parables to show the virtues of good stewards, who may be administrators, supervisors, managers of estates, or trusted servants. Paul placed more stress on the spiritual implications: "So then, men ought to regard us as servants of Christ and as those entrusted with the secret things of God. Now it is required that those who have been given a trust must prove faithful" (1 Cor. 4:1–2). Stewardship calls for faith in God and the realization that life and possessions are gifts from him, to be used for the benefit of others, with a thoroughgoing dedication of one's total resources and powers in the unselfish service to fellow men—all in the spirit of the cross (Mark 10:45).

ROBERT CASHMAN

**Stewart, James Stuart** (1896– ). Scottish preacher and writer. Educated at the universities of St. Andrews, Edinburgh, and Bonn, he was minister of St. Andrew's, Auchterarder (1924–28), Beechgrove, Aberdeen (1928–35), and North Morningside, Edinburgh (1935–46) before appointment as professor of NT language, literature, and theology at New College, Edinburgh (1947–66). He lectured widely in the USA, and was moderator of the general assembly of the Church of Scotland in 1963. Among his publications are *The Life and Teaching of Jesus Christ* (1932), *A Man in Christ* (1935), *The Strong Name* (1941), *Heralds of God* (1945), *A Faith to Proclaim* (1953), *Thine Is the Kingdom* (1956), *The Wind of the Spirit* (1968), *River of Life* (1972), and *King for Ever* (1975).

**Stoltz, Karl Ruf** (1884–1943). Congregationalist scholar. Born in Traverse City, Mich., he studied at Baldwin-Wallace, Garrett Biblical Institute, Northwestern University, and the University of Iowa (Ph.D., 1911). He was professor of religious education at Wellesley College (1912–24), professor of biblical literature and religious education at the YMCA College, Chicago (1924–27), and professor of English Bible and dean of the School of Religious Education, Hartford Seminary Foundation (1927–43). He wrote *Psychology of Prayer* (1923), *Evolution and Genesis* (1927), *Pastoral Psychology* (1932), *Psychology of Religious Living* (1937), *Tricks Our Minds Play on Us* (1939), and *Making the Most of the Rest of Life* (1941). He was coauthor of *Jesus and a Boy's Philosophy of Life* (1926), *Studies in Religious Education* (1931), and *Religion and the Church Tomorrow* (1936).

RAYMOND W. ALBRIGHT

**Stonehouse, Ned Bernard** (1902–1962). NT scholar. Born in Grand Rapids, Mich., he was educated at Calvin College, Princeton Theological Seminary, and the Free University of Amsterdam (Th.D., 1929). He was instructor in NT at Westminster Theological Seminary (1929/30), and was appointed assistant professor in 1930 and professor in 1937. He was ordained to the ministry of the Presbyterian Church in 1932, and transferred to the Orthodox Presbyterian Church in 1936. Among his published works are *The Witness of Matthew and Mark to Christ* (1944), *The Witness of Luke to Christ* (1951), *J. Gresham Machen: A Biographical Memoir* (1954), and *Paul before the Areopagus and Other NT Studies* (1957). He edited *The New International Commentary on the NT* (9 vols., 1951– ).

JACK MITCHELL

**Stott, John Robert Walmsley** (1921– ). Anglican preacher and scholar. Born in London, he graduated from Cambridge. He was ordained in the Church of England, and was curate (1945–50) and then rector (1950–75) of All Souls', Langham Place, London. He became a leader in the movement to bring evangelical Christianity back into the mainstream of his church's life and thinking. Apart from a remarkable ministry in his influential London parish, he had a wider appeal at home and abroad in the conduct of university missions and other student occasions. He was appointed a chaplain to the queen in 1959. Even after his resignation in 1975 he maintained links with All Souls' as rector emeritus, and it was from there that he founded the Institute for Contemporary Christianity, of which he was director (1982–86) and then president. His numerous publications include *Men with a Message* (1954), *Basic Christianity* (1958), *Fundamentalism and Evangelism* (1959), *The Epistles of John* (1964), *Our Guilty Silence* (1967), *The Message of Gala-*

tians (1968), *Christ the Controversialist* (1970), *Understanding the Bible* (1972), *Christian Mission in the Modern World* (1975), *The Lausanne Covenant* (1975), *God's New Society* (1979), *I Believe in Preaching* (1982), *Issues Facing Christians Today* (1984), and *The Cross of Christ* (1986).

J. D. DOUGLAS

**Streeter, Burnet Hillman** (1874–1937). Anglican scholar. Born in Croydon, he was educated at Queen's College, Oxford, and ordained in 1899. He became fellow and dean of Pembroke College, Oxford (1899–1905); fellow of Queen's (1905–33); provost of Queen's College, Oxford (1933–37); professor of exegesis, Oxford University (1932/33); and a fellow of the British Academy. He had close associations with both the Student Christian Movement and the movement founded by Frank Buchman. Streeter's main interest was the philosophy of religion, on which he wrote *Reality: A New Correlation of Science and Religion* (1926), *The Buddha and the Christ* (1932), and *The Spirit* (1919). But his most important work was in the field of NT studies. He wrote an essay in the *Oxford Studies in the Synoptic Problem* (1911) and *The Four Gospels: A Study of Origins* (1924). He edited *Foundations* (1912), *Concerning Prayer* (1916), and *Adventure* (1927).

F. W. DILLISTONE

**Strenopoulos, Germanos** (1872–1951). Greek Orthodox ecumenist. Born in Dellionae, Eastern Thrace, he studied at the Theological College of Halki and at the universities of Halle, Leipzig, Strasbourg, and Lausanne (Ph.D., 1903). He served as professor and principal of the Halki College, and was consecrated bishop in 1912, with the title of metropolitan of Seleucia. In 1922 he was appointed exarch of the ecumenical patriarch in Western and Central Europe, with the title of metropolitan of Thyateira, and settled in London. He was very active in the negotiations between Greek and Anglican churches and in the ecumenical movement from its very beginning. He was one of the joint presidents of the World Council of Churches from its inauguration in 1948. His main writings are *Hippolyts philosophische Anschauungen* (1903), *Kyrilos Loukais* (1951), and numerous articles on various subjects in Greek, English, German, and Swiss periodicals.

GEORGES FLOROVSKY

**Stritch, Samuel Alphonsus** (1887–1958). Cardinal. Born in Nashville, Tenn., he studied at Saint Gregory's Seminary, Cincinnati, Ohio, and the North American College, Rome. Ordained to the priesthood in 1909, he engaged in pastoral and administrative work in the diocese of Nashville, of which he became chancellor (1917). He was consecrated bishop of Toledo, Ohio

(1921), became archbishop of Milwaukee, Wis. (1930), and was transferred to the archdiocese of Chicago (1940). He was created cardinal on February 18, 1946, under the pontificate of Pius XII. He played an outstanding part in the organization of the National Catholic Welfare Conference, an agency created to coordinate the educational, social, and civic endeavors of Roman Catholics in the USA.

GEORGES A. BARROIS

**Strong, Philip Nigel Warrington** (1899–1983). Anglican archbishop and missionary. Born in Sutton-on-the Hill, Derbyshire, he graduated from Selwyn College, Cambridge, trained at Bishops' College, Cheshunt, and was ordained in 1922. After 14 years of pastoral ministry in inner city parishes in the north of England, he was consecrated bishop of New Guinea in 1936. He arrived in New Guinea in 1937 to catch the growing support for this Anglo-Catholic mission after the Depression. This growth, however, was destroyed by the Japanese invasion during which both white missionaries and native clergy lost their lives. The recovery after World War II was delayed by a further disaster when in 1951 the eruption of Mt. Lamington wiped out a mission station and caused further loss of life. Although Strong was described as a "colorful eccentric" bachelor and as "authoritarian," he continued the work toward indigenization and saw the consecration of the first native cleric as assistant bishop in 1960. After 26 years in New Guinea, he became archbishop of Brisbane in 1962 and was elected primate of Australia in 1966. He retired in 1970. His diaries of his missionary years were published in 1981.

NOEL S. POLLARD

**Student Organizations, Religious (North American).** Student religious organizations have been indigenous to American campus life for over two centuries. Much of the history of the churches in America and of the religious life of colleges can be written around the creative religious and social pioneering of these organizations. Earliest records of voluntary student religious societies in North America date back to the 1690s at Harvard. Cotton Mather (1663–1728) was a key figure in encouraging Christian piety among the students, and early societies in New England colleges came to be called Mather Societies. By 1800 evangelistic revivals (the Second Great Awakening) had reached college campuses to turn the tide of post-Revolutionary secularism.

In 1802, under the strong preaching of Timothy Dwight (1752–1817), one-third of the students at Yale were converted. At Williams College in 1806 a group of undergraduates under the leadership of Samuel J. Mills (1783–1818) took refuge from a storm during their regularly scheduled prayer meeting, the now famous "Haystack Prayer Meeting." This group of student volunteers began the first student foreign missionary society in North America and later influenced the formation of the first church-sponsored sending agency, the Board of Commissioners for Foreign Missions. As early as 1856, 58 students at the University of Michigan and Virginia formed chapters of the YMCA, an organization begun in London in 1844 by George Williams because of his concern for the spiritual welfare of young men. Spontaneous student leadership spread the YMCA movement across U.S. campuses. In 1877 Luther Wishard (1854–1925) was appointed the first American YMCA secretary, followed by John R. Mott in 1888. Wishard had been active in the student Y at Hanover College and Princeton. He hoped to unite the work in all the colleges, the ultimate goal being the conversion of students and their subsequent commitment to active Christian service. Strong emphasis was laid on personal prayer life, Bible study, evangelism, and social outreach, with an increasing concern for world missions.

Dwight Moody used his conference grounds at Northfield, Mass., to hold summer student conferences. There, in July 1888, a student executive was formed with representatives from several cooperating movements. John R. Mott was chosen to represent the YMCA, Nettie Dunn the YWCA, and Robert Wilder the Inter-Seminary Movement. Mott was unanimously chosen as chairman and Wilder was named traveling secretary. In December 1888 the movement was officially organized as the Student Volunteer Movement for Foreign Missions (SVM). In the space of a generation, 175,000 students signed the SVM pledge and 21,000 went overseas from North American colleges. The motto of SVM was: The Evangelization of the World in This Generation.

In 1895 the World's Student Christian Federation (WSCF), an international federation of national student movements similar to SVM, was formed with John R. Mott as general secretary. For the next 25 years, the story of SVM is one of constant growth and outreach. Nothing since has touched the religious life of the total student body with the impact of SVM, some colleges having 50 percent of the student body as members.

From the high point of 1920, SVM experienced a rapid decline and, for a number of reasons, by 1940 it had almost ceased to be an important influence in student religious life. Chief among the reasons was the acceptance of higher critical thought. This undercut biblical authority and emphasized social concerns which blotted out the need for Christian conversion. In 1959 SVM merged with the United Student Christian Council (ecumenical federation of Protestant agencies and denominational student ministries) and the Inter-Seminary Movement to form the National Student Christian Federation (NSCF). In 1966

this group allied with the Roman Catholic National Newman Student Federation and other groups to form the University Christian Movement (UCM). Ten years later UCM voted itself out of existence.

In the early 20th century the steady growth of the college population, particularly in state universities, made it increasingly difficult for the Christian associations alone to serve the varied needs of the campus. As churches realized that many of their students were attending state colleges, denominational groups began to establish student centers next to secular campuses. The Methodist Church began the first such center in 1913 at the University of Illinois, followed shortly by other members of the National Council of Churches. Most denominational student ministries soon followed the trend toward an increasingly liberal theology, with growing ecumenical emphasis. At most church-related and public colleges the campus religious atmosphere moved toward accepting higher critical theology as the norm.

The period prior to 1900 was predominantly the Protestant era of higher education. Religious societies were voluntary associations of, by, and for Protestant students who bound themselves together by personal, moral, and religious earnestness and sought to translate personal faith into the larger life of the campus and the world. Not until 1895 did the Newman Club begin as the campus movement for Roman Catholic students on non-Catholic campuses. The first full-time rabbi for Jewish student work was appointed at the University of Illinois in 1923.

The church-aligned student ministries included: Wesley Foundation (Methodist), Westminster Foundation (Presbyterian), Canterbury House (Episcopalian), Roger Williams Foundation (American Baptist), Baptist Student Movement (Southern Baptist), Lutheran Campus Ministry (American Lutheran Church), Lutheran Chapel (Lutheran Church—Missouri Synod), Newman Club (Roman Catholic), and B'nai B'rith Hillel Foundation (Jewish). Typically, an ordained minister was designated as a student worker in the denominational budget and was often given a building adjacent to the campus and a great deal of freedom—a pattern that continues to some extent today. In this same time period other Christian denominations opted against getting involved on secular campuses, feeling that the strong liberal views presented matched a liberal theology of which they disapproved. Their separation from the mainstream of higher education thus left the large state universities without the benefit of their point of view.

The Inter-Seminary Movement (a fellowship of seminary students and faculties) within the student Y had been one of its successful programs, but conflict between liberal and evangelical theology came to a head when a delegation of students from Princeton Seminary at the 1924 conference found themselves in disagreement with doctrinal statements on almost every point. In 1925 representatives from six conservative Christian theological institutions formed the League of Evangelical Students (LES), presenting a reasoned position for the Bible as God's Word, Jesus Christ as truly God as well as man, and other basic tenets of Christianity delineated in a series of papers published from 1910 to 1915 as *The Fundamentals*. LES groups spread to various campuses, dominated by seminarians who did careful apologetic work and gave conservative students a "reasonable" faith for an environment hostile to biblical Christianity in a way never before true in university life. Their defensive stance was highly intellectual and often beyond younger students' comprehension. By its very nature, the group neglected outreach.

An evangelical student movement, Inter-Varsity Fellowship, crossed the Atlantic from England to Canada in 1928 as Inter-Varsity Christian Fellowship of Canada. Ten years later it came to the USA as Inter-Varsity Christian Fellowship of USA, incorporated in 1940. Convinced that IVCF would pursue truth as well as evangelism, the League agreed that its chapters should be absorbed by IVCF student groups. During World War II and immediately after, student-led IVCF groups spread to most major campuses in the USA with a threefold purpose: evangelism, discipleship, and missions. In 1946 IVCF held its first student missions conference in Toronto. In 1948 the conference was moved to the University of Illinois in Urbana, where it continues to be held triennially with as many as 17,000 students attending. This conference has been a major influence in the world mission of the U.S. church since the demise of SVM.

With the rapid growth of enrollment in colleges and universities following World War II, other parachurch groups similar to IVCF commenced student work, so that by 1960 numerous groups, such as Campus Crusade for Christ, Navigators, International Students, Inc., and other local groups were ministering to students. By 1970 many evangelical and independent churches located near campuses had started their own student programs.

Student unrest and disillusionment during the late 1960s and 1970s challenged every religious student group on campus. Some groups essentially disappeared; others became more evangelical. Many became involved in civil rights and political rallies. The drug culture brought in Eastern religious thought and a sense of "lostness" that led other groups to become more evangelistic. Students were questioning and confused, looking for answers and new meaning to life. Rock music became a dominant cultural influ-

ence. Students tended to desert a group with no clear message, and when social issues changed, some groups lost their reason for being.

A resultant explosion occurred in student ministries in the 1970s and 1980s, so today some campuses list as many as 50 or 60 different groups. Plurality in religious thought on American campuses, caused in part by the influx of a wider spectrum of students, some from other countries, means that the religious affairs office on many campuses now lists Muslim, Buddhist, Hare Krishna, Scientology, Theosophical, and Baha'i, along with the traditional Judeo-Christian groups. The campus mirrors the world around it as it never has before. The elitism of higher education, the narrow age span, and the predominance of affluent white males is a thing of the past. Religious student organizations reflect this shift.

The philosophy for student ministry is as varied as the number of groups. Most ministries have nonstudent leaders who provide program ideas and seek to interest students. Many groups exist to maintain basic beliefs and commitment; others promote strong social concerns; some are evangelistic, seeking to win new converts. Some emphasize personal piety; others are issue-oriented and impersonal. Some are closely associated with a denomination or local church; others are interdenominational. Many are church-centered rather than campus-centered. Most are missions to students; a few are student-led missions.

*Bibliography.* C. P. Shedd, *The Church Follows Its Students* (1938); E. A. Walter, ed., *Religion and the State University* (1958), D. Howard, *Student Power in World Evangelism* (1970); J. D. Douglas, ed., *The New International Dictionary of the Christian Church* (1974).

KEITH AND GLADYS HUNT

## Student Organizations, Religious (Worldwide).

Informal student groups for Bible study, prayer, and missionary endeavor have surfaced wherever student life has had a sufficiently coherent social nature and there have been active Christians present. Many early groups left no records. They often met secretly for fear of disapproval by the authorities who wanted all religious activities under their control. In 1768, for instance, eight students were expelled from Oxford for meeting privately for Bible study and prayer. In such an atmosphere no one advertised their activities. Apart from groups such as the White Horse Inn in the early 16th century, the group led by Henry Scougal (1650–1708) in Aberdeen is probably the earliest on record. He was the son of a bishop and so perhaps the group was deemed acceptable.

By the mid-19th century it was common for British and North American students, especially medical students, to form such groups. Often they had among their other aims prayer for foreign missionary work. Guy's Hospital, London, formed such a group in 1845 and the Cambridge Prayer Union was formed in 1848 primarily for those preparing for the ministry. The Cambridge Missionary Union was established in 1858. The two Cambridge groups later formed the Cambridge Inter-Collegiate Christian Union (CICCU) in 1877 with a strong evangelistic emphasis. In the same year a group was formed in Japan at the Sapporo Agricultural College, probably the earliest student group outside Europe and North America. Their aim was "mutual assistance and encouragement" so that they could "confess Christ according to His command and . . . perform with true fidelity every Christian duty." This was not untypical of many of the early groups. Evangelism was a natural result in most cases.

Organized Christian "movements," however, did not emerge until the late 19th century by which time it was not regarded as so improper for students to organize their own activities. In Great Britain CICCU took an interest in helping likeminded students. Beginning in Oxford and the London medical schools they began to stimulate groups in other universities and joined forces with some already in existence in Scotland. A national movement emerged and became the very influential Student Christian Movement (SCM). By 1895 conferences were being held in Great Britain, including some for the encouragement of missionary interest. A large percentage of missionaries going abroad for the Church of England and interdenominational societies, such as the China Inland Mission, were recent university graduates. The SCM staff then became interested in attracting and influencing speakers and students of nonevangelical traditions. At the same time liberal tendencies in theology had penetrated theological colleges and faculties, and a more ecumenical spirit began to prevail.

The British SCM was already linked with other European movements. At a conference in Sweden in 1895 the World Student Christian Federation (WSCF) was formed with six national movements represented. Until 1900 these developments were almost without exception what would now be called "evangelical," stressing the authority and reliability of Scripture and the substitutionary death of Christ. By 1905 there was tension between the strongly evangelical tradition represented principally by CICCU and the rest of the British SCM. In 1910 this led to CICCU disaffiliating from the rest. It went its way as an independent group so that an SCM was started in Cambridge alongside it. This seems to have been the only place where such an explicit division took place so early.

World War I suspended almost all activity, but as soon as ex-servicemen returned to the universities in 1919 the same fundamental theological divisions became evident and in an even sharper form. CICCU and SCM leaders in Cambridge met to discuss possible union. It became clear, however, that their theological differences were deep, and they went their separate ways. New but usually tiny evangelical Christian Unions began to appear in other British universities as SCM adopted a liberal and ecumenical—even eclectic—theology. The first British national conference of evangelical groups, the Inter-Varsity Conference, took place in London in 1919 and the Inter-Varsity Fellowship (now UCCF, Universities and Colleges Christian Fellowship) was formally established in 1928.

Meanwhile, somewhat parallel developments had been taking place in Scandinavia under the leadership of Hallesby and others. Similar new evangelical movements emerged in other countries in Europe and in 1928 the British Inter-Varsity Fellowship sent one of its members (Howard Guiness) on a tour through Canada, Australia, New Zealand, and India. In many of these places he found small groups of evangelical students meeting separately from SCM. He did much to encourage them to come out into the open and be bold and confident in preaching the gospel. International conferences of evangelical students were held annually in Europe starting in Norway in 1934 (the Norwegian Evangelical Movement was the first separate evangelical movement founded in 1924). In 1937 the conference was in Hungary. In 1939 it was in Cambridge and attracted about 800 students from all over Europe and other countries.

In 1945, when World War II was over, much of Europe was in confusion, but student work of an evangelical nature began to blossom. It was decided that the mere holding of conferences was not enough, but some kind of international organization ought to be set up. In 1946 the International Fellowship of Evangelical Students (IFES) constitution was drawn up and was accepted in 1947 by 10 national movements, including mainland China where the work flourished under good national leadership. The principle of indigenous leadership has always been strong in IFES and even where the work has been pioneered by foreigners, a staff of nationals has been appointed very quickly.

In the postwar years new universities were being established all over the world. In Africa, India, and the Far East groups of evangelical students joined IFES. IFES also sent its staff and encouraged member movements to send their graduates to teach in new universities and secondary schools. There was rapid growth of such work in Africa, the West Indies, Singapore, Taiwan, and Hong Kong. In Japan, India, the Philippines, and South America the work grew more slowly but surely. When IFES celebrated its 40th year, there was work associated with it going on in 130 countries.

Meanwhile WSCF and its former leaders helped set up the World Council of Churches, but had themselves become an entirely ecumenical body with, in most countries, a loss of clearly defined membership. Leadership at the student level was not always definitely Christian. It went into a rapid decline in most countries and has never recovered. Campus Crusade for Christ, Navigators, and some denominational agencies have also developed a student ministry in certain countries, but have not developed national movements and usually have fewer nationals in leadership positions.

*Bibliography.* T. Tatlow, *The Story of the Student Christian Movement of Great Britain and Ireland* (1933); R. P. Wilder, *The Student Volunteer Movement* (1938); R. Rouse, *The World Student Christian Federation* (1948); O. R. Barclay, *Whatever Happened to the Jesus Lane Lot?* (1977); D. Johnson, *Contending for the Faith* (1979); P. Lowman, *The Day of His Power* (1983).

OLIVER R. BARCLAY

**Stump, Joseph** (1866–1935). Lutheran theologian. Born in Marietta, Pa., he studied at Capital University, Columbus, and the Lutheran Theological Seminary, Mt. Airy, Philadelphia. Ordained to the Lutheran ministry in 1887, he served Lutheran parishes at Great Bend, Pa. (1887–89), Ephrata, Pa. (1889–92), and Grace Church, Phillipsburg, N.J. (1892–1915). He became professor of systematic theology at the Chicago Lutheran Theological Seminary, Maywood, Ill. (1915–20); dean and professor of systematic theology at the Chicago Lutheran Seminary (1920/21); and president and professor of systematic theology at Northwestern Lutheran Theological Seminary (1921–35). He wrote *Life of Philip Melanchthon* (1897), *Bible Story* (1898), *Bible Teachings* (1902), *An Explanation of Luther's Small Catechism* (1907), *Russellism, A Counterfeit Christianity* (1922), *The Christian Life, A Handbook of Christian Ethics* (1930), and *The Christian Faith, A System of Christian Dogmatics* (1932). He coauthored *An Explanation of the Common Service* (1908). He translated and edited Stark's *Daily Handbook* (1904).

RAYMOND W. ALBRIGHT

**Subdeacon.** *See* ORDERS, MAJOR.

**Substance Abuse.** Pathological use of a substance which lasts over a month and which results in impairment of functioning. The abuse of substances is an acutely contemporary problem which is increasingly demanding the attention and concern of societies around the world. Historical precedents can be seen in some societies such as the coca-smoking Indians of Colombia or the peyote-using Indians of the American Southwest. And while some writers in the "noble savage" tradition attempt to portray such historical use as innocent and harmless, most commen-

tators view substance abuse, both then and now, as harmful and ultimately destructive.

Substance abuse generally has become a problem in areas of the world where easily abused substances are in ready supply (as in the opium areas of Southeast Asia) or in affluent cultures where potential users have the resources to pay for imported substances. Hence, current drug-related problems are transnational in scope and involve almost all areas of the globe. The abuse of substances is generally banned by the laws of most countries in the world, but government enforcement of these laws is often frustrating and difficult. The lucrative potential of the illegal drug trade has attracted highly sophisticated criminal and black market activities.

Social commentators on contemporary culture have made many attempts to explain how substance abuse has come to have such a destructive presence in modern society. Is this trend simply the result of greater availability made possible by modern technology? Is the greater abuse of substances due to the increased pressures and stress of life in industrialized society? Has the rising affluence of many countries in the world satisfied the more basic needs of shelter, food, and safety so that modern urban dwellers now feel more keenly the existential angst of human life? Or does rising drug use reflect the moral vacuum of many secularized societies of the West which no longer offer hope to troubled persons? The answers to these questions most likely involve a complex combination of all of these suggestions.

Substances subject to abuse can range from products or medications legitimately purchased over the counter, to medications prescribed by a physician but misused by the patient, to substances which are generally illegal to purchase or use. Each of these three categories contains substances which occur naturally as well as those which are synthetically manufactured. Substances are either ingested, inhaled, or injected. Physiological response to the abused substance varies according to uniqueness of each agent and according to its effect on the central nervous system (stimulating it or depressing it). Some common phenomena among the many varied response patterns include euphoria, disorientation, poor coordination, and impaired sensory awareness.

The most insidious quality of substance abuse is that substance dependence can form with at least five classes of drugs: alcohol, barbiturates, opioids, amphetamines, and cannabis. Although addictions to these five types of substance will vary somewhat in features and characteristics, all are marked by symptoms of toleration and withdrawal. Toleration is present when increasing amounts of the drug are required to achieve the same desired effect. In the case of alcohol, there are marked variations in individual response so that the tolerance curve for each person will be idiosyncratic. Withdrawal occurs when a substance-specific syndrome follows reduced intake or cessation of intake. These withdrawal syndromes vary from mild to severe and require medical intervention.

Substance dependence may be psychological as well as physiological. Along with either type of dependence can occur a slow deterioration of functioning and quality of life. As more of the substance is required, more of one's energy, time, and motivation are devoted to maintenance of the habit. Financial, medical, and criminal complications frequently occur in the later stages of drug abuse.

Extensive research and experience have repeatedly documented two ingredients which are involved in successful treatment strategies: a multidisciplinary approach and group experience. The former becomes necessary because of the complex interconnectedness of psychological, physiological, and spiritual factors in substance abuse. Medical personnel can assist in monitoring the health of the recovering addict; mental health personnel can help identify the emotional needs involved in the abusive use of drugs; and spiritual counselors can help build a framework of life which will exclude future drug use. Admittedly, the spiritual dimension is the most frequently ignored in most drug rehabilitation facilities. The group dimension of effective treatment was first demonstrated by Alcoholics Anonymous. Currently almost all treatment regimens include some ongoing group involvement, especially in the final stages of recovery. The fact that peer support and accountability appear necessary for recovery may well be related to the dependency needs which may have fostered the drug involvement initially.

In the past the most common approach to the abuse of substances was a moral one; alcoholics were remanded for their ongoing bad, poor, and sinful involvements. Christians found support for this approach in scriptural discussions of drunkenness. The Bible frequently condemns drunkenness and holds people responsible and accountable for this behavior. Modern research has added much to our knowledge regarding the physiological effects of alcohol and the presence of a predictable syndrome which occurs with alcohol abuse. Thus many researchers prefer to describe alcoholism in terms of a disease. Does this medical emphasis contradict the Bible? This medical model can become offensive to biblical sensibilities only if it becomes exclusive. It is mandatory that substance abuse be viewed in the moral context in which it occurs. Individuals are not only responsible for behavior leading to substance abuse, but they are responsible for its ongoing presence and for taking steps to disengage from its snare.

**Bibliography.** APA, *Diagnostic and Statistical Manual* (3d ed., 1980); S. Cohen, *The Substance Abuse Problems* (1981); G. Bennett, et al., eds., *Substance Abuse: Pharmacologic, Developmental, and Clinical Perspectives* (1983); W. Lenters, *The Freedom We Crave: Addiction, the Human Condition* (1985).

JAMES R. BECK

**Sudan.** Independent country in east-central Africa, occupying 2,506,000 sq. km. (967,500 sq. mi.) with a population of 21.7 million (1985). The religious history of this African republic is largely the story of dynamic forms of Christianity clashing with equally potent varieties of Islam. This religious rivalry was centuries in the making. Christianity had the first thrust in ancient Nubia in the 4th century but was not established until the 6th century when monophysite missionaries converted the king of Nobatae, one of the ancient city-states of Nubia. Orthodox Christianity became dominant in A.D. 1000 and continued to grow until Muslim occupation in the 14th century. By 1504 Christian Nubia had collapsed with only vestigial elements surviving into the 19th century. Catholic missionaries began replanting Christianity in Sudan in 1842. Franciscans and Verona Fathers shouldered the work of evangelism and church planting throughout the 19th century. The Mahdist rebellion in 1881 obliterated much of their work but rebuilding of both structures and people began afresh in 1898. The very next year witnessed the beginning of the Anglican Church of Sudan.

Muslim hegemony over Sudan commenced in the 14th century when Muslim rule in central Nubia was established. Recent archeological evidence suggests that early Muslim regimes tolerated Christianity. By the 16th century a more ruthless Islam triumphed in Sudan, extending its influence throughout the country. This expansion had abated by the 19th century when a renewed Western Christianity sought to challenge Sudanese Islam's religious monopoly.

Mission activity in the south increased in the first half of the 20th century. The Catholic Church opened a number of new dioceses from 1900 to 1960. The Church Missionary Society furthered the growth of Anglicanism but still, like the Catholic Church, confined its efforts largely to the south. Presbyterian missionaries arrived in 1900 and worked among the Shilluk and Nuer tribes in the south. The Sudan United Mission began mission work in 1907 and helped to create the Sudanese Church of Christ represented in the mid-1970s by about 100 congregations and 53,000 affiliated individuals. The Africa Inland Mission and Sudan Interior Mission began work in Sudan in 1936 and 1937, respectively. By mid-century Jehovah's Witnesses and Seventh-day Adventists had established churches.

Christian mission activity was disrupted by the coming of Sudanese independence in 1956. A year later all 295 mission schools in the south were nationalized. In 1960 Qur'an schools (*khalwas*) began appearing all over the south, marking the commencement of forced islamization of the southern tribes of Sudan. The Missionary Societies Act of 1962 made preaching, teaching, and baptizing children under 18 illegal. Civil war between north and south erupted in 1963. In 1964 all missionaries were expelled, charged by the Khartoum government with fomenting secession of the south from the north. In 1972 Christian leaders representing the All Africa Conference of Churches helped to bring about the peace accord between Khartoum and the South Sudan Liberation Movement. Khartoum's failure to honor provisions for religious liberty in the south and the attempt to declare the primacy of Islamic law (*Sharia*) contributed to the outbreak of new hostilities between north and south in the early 1980s.

Today the religious profile of Sudan is still dominated by Islam and Christianity. Sunni and Sufi Islamic orders command the allegiance of 74 percent of the 21 million Sudanese. The high percentage of professing Muslims, mostly Sunnis, hides a deeply fragmented Islamic community. Sudanese Islam is dominated by numerous *tariqas* (brotherhoods). Two of these brotherhoods, the 3-million-member Ansar brotherhood and the one-million-member Khatmiya, supported rival political parties which were severely repressed in 1970 when the junta of 1969 led to the establishment of a socialist regime in 1970 and a one-party state in 1971.

Catholics represent over 5 percent of the population (approximately one million adherents). The Anglican Church is the largest Protestant group in the country (300,000). Orthodox Church strength is estimated at about 100,000. Faith mission churches remain small. The Africa Inland Church has about 1000 affiliated members while the Evangelical Church of Eastern Sudan (SIM) numbers about 1500.

Traditional religion claims 19 percent of the population. Most traditionalists belong to a constellation of tribes in the south that have been resistant to both Christianity and Islam. Anuak, Didinga, Dinka, Nuer, Shilluk, and Uduk tribes are numbered among those that have spurned missionary advances from both East and West.

Although Islam and Christianity have coexisted in Sudan for nearly a millennium, achieving dominance over traditional religion, the soul of Sudan remains troubled. Religion in modern Sudan continues to be a turbulent force.

**Bibliography.** D. Barrett, ed., *African Initiatives in Religion* (1971); A. Hastings, *History of African Christianity: 1950–1975* (1979); G. Vantini, *Christianity in the Sudan* (1981); D. Barrett, ed., *World Christian Encyclopedia* (1982); P. Bowers, *East Africa Journal of Evangelical Theology* 4/11 (1985).

MARK R. SHAW

**Sufism.** Mystical Islamic movement. The English word is derived from the Arabic *suf,* meaning "wool," after the early mystics adopted a coarse woolen garment to protest the luxury of the Umayyad court of the 7th and 8th centuries A.D. Sufism is the term used both for the devotion of the individual Muslim and for the confraternities, or Sufi "orders," that developed in the medieval period and that continue to the present day.

Although certain Western scholars have suggested that Sufism was entirely derived from Christianity, it is more appropriate to see it as the natural flowering of a spiritual movement within Islam. This is not to deny contacts between Christianity and Sufism, but rather to suggest that Sufism drew upon the language of the Koran and the example of Muhammad in its development. In its later stages it also drew upon several other cultures, and today the term covers movements which are rigidly orthodox as well as those which are more loosely associated with Islamic orthodoxy and can be more accurately described as syncretistic. A few writers go so far as to see Sufism as the esoteric core of all religions, thereby denying its specifically Islamic character.

Among the most prominent figures in early Sufism was Hasan al-Basri. Born in 642, he was appointed as a judge in the religious courts but resigned in protest against the harsh policies of the governor of Iraq. He believed that inner reflection was of the greatest importance and urged his friends to withdraw and read the Koran so that they might examine their actions according to its teaching. He was constantly upset about the insincerity of his own intentions. While he might not be counted a true mystic he nevertheless spoke of God's love for his servants and of their love for him.

The term "love" is used more than 30 times in the Koran to speak of this relationship and was to become one of the dominant themes in later Sufism. It is taken up in an austere form by Rabi'a, a female mystic who died in 801. There are, in fact, two women by this name, and their teachings are to be distinguished. Rabi'a of Basra came from humble origins and lived a life of extreme simplicity. She would spend whole nights in prayer and then take a short nap, waking up to repent of the time she had spent asleep. Although she had received many marriage proposals, she always refused. She is best known for her emphasis on the purity that man should seek in his love for God. She speaks of the love born of selfishness and the love worthy of God: "My God, if I have adored Thee in fear of Hell, burn me in its fire, and if in desire for Paradise, forbid it to me. But if I have not worshiped Thee except for Thine own self, then do not forbid me to see Thy face."

In the next phase in the development of Sufism there are marked tendencies toward ecstatic utterances. Abu Yazid of Bistam and Al-Hallaj of Baghdad are contrasting figures. The former lived in a small village where his excesses could be overlooked, but the latter deliberately thrust himself into the public spotlight in the capital city. Both were so caught up in the mystery of God that they could not restrain themselves. Abu Yazid spent the first half of his life in minute observance of pious duties but thereafter abandoned them. He felt that he was so close to God that anyone who saw him saw God: "I am Thou, Thou art me, and I am Thou." Some scholars have seen in this the influence of the Advaitan form of the Hindu Vedanta but both Abu Yazid and Al-Hallaj are always careful to preserve ultimately the creature-Creator distinction, however far their ecstasy may carry them. Al-Hallaj, as is well known, was executed because of his utterances. The first 40 years of his life were devoted to study, during which he spent a year in Mecca, living on bread and water and engaged in meditation. He then became a missionary, traveling in what is now Pakistan, China, and Turkey. He returned to Baghdad to speak of the God who had made him drunk with His love. He was imprisoned on suspicion of being associated with the antigovernment forces of the extreme Shi'a. It is an oversimplification to speak of his being executed for saying that he was the Truth (i.e., God). Al-Hallaj sought his own death in order to be united with God but he was also a victim of the politicians, an emphasis that is brought out in modern plays about him.

With the death of Al-Hallaj in 922 the Sufi movement was subject to persecution and suspicion. There were other martyrs and many small groups of Sufis were forced to meet in secret. In the 11th century there were several notable attempts to explain and justify the beliefs and practices of the Sufis to a wider public. By far the most significant was that of Al-Ghazalai (d. A.D. 1111). Born in Persia, he was attracted to the court in Baghdad and given patronage by Nizam al-Mulk, the vizier. He had studied the religious sciences and at an early age directed the foremost academy in Baghdad. However, he suffered a crisis of faith at the age of 37 and thereafter withdrew from public life. It has been argued that after the assassination of his patron by the extreme Shi'a he feared for his own life. It is much more likely that he realized that he had been seeking the world's recognition rather than spiritual progress. In his autobiography and elsewhere he stresses the importance of the inner personal experience of God; illumination is the highest type.

Not all the later Sufis would show such moderation. The Persian poets wrote "wine poetry" in which intoxication is a symbol for religious experience. Rumi, in his monumental "Mathnavi," developed other types of symbolism ("We are the

flute; The music is Thine"). Ibn 'Arabi, writing in Arabic, spoke of the courtship of a maiden, alluding to divine Wisdom. From the 12th century on Sufism became increasingly pantheistic, being influenced by Neo-Platonism.

From consideration of representative individuals we turn to the Sufi orders. The Sufis naturally gathered together to receive guidance from a master and for discussion. What distinguishes the orders is the provision for a rule of life and for discipline under a *shaykh* (master). By the 11th century the earliest of the orders was in existence and convents had been established. One rule of life from this period comprises ten injunctions, from personal cleanliness to frequent prayer and hospitality to the poor. The orders were named after the founding fathers, four of whom have primacy of honor. From these original orders a great variety of others developed, often adaptations to local conditions. Each order could trace its origins to one of the great teachers of the past as validation of its authority. Each emphasized a unique aspect of spirituality. Like Roman Catholic third orders, some exercised severe discipline, while others were much more open. In each case initiates gathered together for regular corporate devotions, notably recitations. Unlike Roman Catholicism, however, celibacy was never part of the vows. Convents for women were founded as early as the 12th century.

The Sufi orders soon became vehicles for the spread of Islam by peaceful means. Furthermore, they served as a countermeasure to the Shi'a who were threatening the Sunni rulers, especially in the fringe areas of central Asia and north Africa. The noted traveler of the 14th century, Ibn Battuta, wrote in some detail of his welcome in many Sufi convents, not only in Persia, Anatolia, and the Caucusus, but further afield on the Indian continent. It is clear that these centers were also important for the expansion of trade. At a slightly later stage convents were frequently built around the tomb of a holy man, whose influence continued after his death. A further development was the establishment of a hierarchical structure within the orders, with authority vested in the *shaykh*, to whom an oath of allegiance was taken. Under him were the masters, the initiates, and the novices. Manuals were written for the guidance of the novices. A typical manual had four parts, the first dealing with the beliefs proper to a Sufi, the second with the stages in spiritual growth, the third with rules of conduct, and the fourth with dispensations.

By the beginning of the 19th century the Sufi orders were a dominant influence in the more traditional societies, so much so that membership in an order was virtually synonymous with being a Muslim. From that time on it was recognized that not only the orders but also the main structures of Islam needed reform. The orders were attacked for their superstition and in Arabia the Wahhabis abolished them completely. At the same time, however, a small number of new orders were formed, each seeking a reformed ethos. In the 20th century the orders have suffered considerably from the increasing secularization of the Islamic world, mass movements in politics, and tighter government control. The most conspicuous example of the latter was in Turkey in 1925, when Ataturk dissolved all the orders because of their opposition to his reforms.

Recent studies have illuminated the present-day position of the orders. For the lowest classes in the cities and for the rural workers they retain their attraction, providing social status and also a means of coping with the harsh realities of life. The orders have suffered a drastic loss of influence as other social and political groups have taken over their role in the cities and as state education has undermined their influence over the young. Nevertheless, for those who are unaffected by these changes they provide a haven of traditional values, together with the support that a highly regulated society can give in personal crises or in moving from a village to a town. They may even help in providing accommodation or jobs. For the more highly educated middle classes the orders provide a brotherhood which sustains them in their professional work. For both the lower classes and the elite the assemblies involve the recitation of Koranic texts, chiefly the divine Names. Depending on the order, these group recitations may lead to ecstatic outbursts. Outward expression is much more restrained in elite groups, conforming to the teaching of the *shaykh*. Assemblies may meet twice a week, strengthening local fellowship. In addition, members visit other centers of their order. The orders teach professional members the religious value of work properly carried out. They are encouraged to spend time in meditation at regular intervals in the cells of their local center. They receive guidance from the local head of their order.

In conclusion, it is clear that some orders are adapting to changing conditions, while others have lost a substantial number of members to the new political movements. Notable orders include the Shadhiliyya, the Badawiyya, the Qadariyya, the Naqshbandiyya, the Tijaniyya of North Africa, and the Sanusiyya of Libya.

*Bibliography.* A. J. Arberry, *Sufism: An Account of the Mystics of Islam* (1950); J. S. Trimingham, *The Sufi Orders in Islam* (1971); M. Gilsenan, *Saint and Sufi in Modern Egypt* (1973); A. Schimmel, *Mystical Dimensions of Islam* (1976).

DAVID BREWSTER

**Suicide.** The act of intentionally killing oneself. The act of suicide may convey a message; it is a means by which one attempts to influence, persuade, manipulate, stimulate, or change feelings and/or behaviors in someone else. In fact, eight out of every 10 persons who kill themselves have given definite warnings of their suicidal intentions. Moreover, statistics show that people who have had a suicide in their families are more likely to commit suicide than those who do not. It seems, then, that suicide is a communicative gesture, intended to have some effect on survivors.

Myths about suicide include the following: (1) suicidal people are fully intent on dying; (2) people who talk about suicide never do it; (3) suicide happens without warning; (4) only crazy people commit suicide; (5) oppressive weather increases the suicide rate; (6) most suicides happen at night; (7) improvement following a suicidal crisis means the risk is over.

Although these are common myths about suicide, the facts tell a different story. For example, studies reveal that suicidal persons give many clues or warnings about their intentions. It is thought that most suicidal people are ambivalent about living or dying and gamble with death. Studies also reveal that most suicides occur on Mondays, in the springtime, and in the daytime. Most suicides occur within about three months following the beginning of improvement when the individual has the energy to put intentions into effect. Studies of hundreds of suicide notes indicate that suicidal persons are not necessarily mentally ill.

There are approximately 25,000 suicides per year in the USA; only one-ninth of suicide attempts actually result in death. High-risk individuals have the following characteristics: 45 years of age or older, solitary lifestyle, poor health, white, male, unemployed, retired, recently separated, divorced, widowed, and those who have made previous attempts. Also at risk are persons with severe depression, alcohol dependency, schizophrenia, personality disorder, or recently experienced major life stress.

Females make suicide attempts approximately three times as often as males, but males have a higher number of successful attempts. The dramatic difference in actual suicides for males is due to the lethality of method chosen. Females tend to choose methods with a lower probability of success and longer possible rescue time, such as gas, drug overdose, or cutting nonvital organs. Males choose more lethal methods with little or no rescue time, such as firearms, explosives, jumping from heights, or cutting vital organs.

Some danger signs of suicide potential include giving away prized possessions, depression, long grief reaction following a loss, sleep disturbance, loss of appetite or excessive eating, sustained deviation from normal behavior patterns, mentioning or being obsessed with death, accident proneness or death wishes, sudden unexplained elevation in mood, and previous attempts. Any of these can signal suicidal intentions.

Suicide has no single cause across the human race and it can have multiple causes within an individual. Suicidal persons are a heterogeneous group who may share only their self-destructive behavior. Therefore, suicide is not a distinct clinical entity.

**Bibliography.** R. W. Maris, *Pathways to Suicide: A Survey of Self-Destructive Behaviors* (1981); E. Robins, *The Final Months* (1981); K. Hawton and J. Catalan, *Attempted Suicide: A Practical Guide to Its Nature and Management* (1982); J. P. Soubrier and J. Vedrinne, eds., *Depression and Suicide* (1983).

ELIZABETH A. SCHILSON

**Sundar Singh, Sadhu** (1889–1929). Indian evangelist. Born in Rampur, Patiala State, India, he was a son of a Sikh landowner who was converted by a vision of Jesus Christ, was baptized at Simla on September 3, 1905, adopted a saffron-robed sadhu's life in North India, and chose Tibet for his field of Christian witness. From 1918 to 1922 he conducted a preaching tour of Asia, Europe, America, and Australia. In April 1929, he started alone for Tibet and since he never returned he presumably died there. He was a Christ-like "solitary," acclaimed for intuitive spiritual insight and loving service. He wrote *The Search after Reality* (1925) and *With and Without Christ* (1929).

**Bibliography.** B. H. Streeter and A. J. Appasamy, *The Sadhu* (1921); A. Parker, *Sadhu Sundar Singh: Called of God* (1920); M. Kent, *Hibbert Journal* (Oct. 1933); C. F. Andrews, *Christian Century* (Nov. 11, 1931).

WILSON M. HUME

**Sunday, William Ashley (Billy)** (1862–1935). American revivalist. Born in Iowa and converted through Chicago's Pacific Garden Mission in 1886, he was ordained in 1903. After retiring from a career as a major league baseball player in 1891, he was assistant secretary of the Chicago YMCA (1891–93), and then assistant to the prominent evangelist J. Wilbur Chapman for the next two and one-half years. Beginning his work as an independent evangelist in 1896 in Garner, Iowa, he moved gradually into larger cities across the nation, reaching the zenith of his career in New York in 1917 with an estimated 100,000 converts. He is said to have preached to as many as 100 million persons during his lifetime, with approximately one million converts. Distinguished by elaborate and effective organization and flamboyant preaching, Sunday's citywide meetings were generally held, after 1900, in wooden tabernacles designed and erected specifically for the crusades. Fundamentalist in theology, his dynamically preached emphases included patriotism, prohibition, and opposition to evolution. Sunday's popularity declined after 1902, and he concluded his career as he had begun it, preaching in small Midwestern cities and towns.

NORRIS A. MAGNUSON

**Sunday Observance.** The holy day for early Christians was Sunday, the first day of the week (called the Lord's Day in commemoration of the resurrection). Christian Sunday observance was not based on the Jewish Sabbath, the seventh day of the week, inasmuch as the Jewish legal system was no longer considered binding. However, the Lord's Day did come to assume certain features of the Jewish Sabbath, which in some respects provided a type for Christian Sunday observance. As Christianity became a legal and then a state religion, civil and ecclesiastical laws enforced strict Sunday observance; for example, a decree of Constantine in 321 made Sunday a day of rest from general labor.

In medieval times Sabbatarianism, the identification of the Lord's Day with the Jewish Sabbath and the application of the fourth (or third) commandment to its observance, was widespread and led to strict laws. In the late Middle Ages, the multiplication of holy days and the general decline of religion tended to obscure the distinctiveness of Sunday. The Reformers, reacting against medieval practices, rejected the Sabbatarian emphasis. The "Continental Sabbath" with its lack of restrictions and holiday atmosphere has since characterized Sunday observance in Europe.

English Puritanism revived the Sabbatarian idea, reacting against late medieval laxness and insisting that the Mosaic code did apply. This idea of Sunday as the Christian Sabbath and a day of worship set apart by legal restrictions was evident in the 1640–60 period, when manual labor and games were prohibited. The Puritan heritage in Great Britain (particularly Scotland) and America led to the Protestant acceptance of the idea, giving a distinctive and strict character to the Anglo-American Sunday quite different from that on the Continent.

In the 19th century the Sunday "blue laws" were modified as the Puritan tradition declined, a trend hastened by industrialization, technological improvement, and the desire to have Sunday as an unrestricted day of recreation. In America, immigration from the Continent further hastened the trend, vigorously but unsuccessfully opposed by certain Protestant organizations. Arguments for stricter observance of Sunday are now often based on the desire to have it as a day of rest and recreation, a "civil Sabbath."

**Bibliography.** R. Floody, *Scientific Basis of Sabbath and Sunday* (1906); P. Cotton, *From Sabbath to Sunday* (1933).

ROBERT T. HANDY

**Sunday School Movement.** Movement arising historically in connection with the philanthropic movements in 18th-century England which helped provide schools for the less privileged before tax-supported education was born. The "father" of the Sunday school was Robert

Raikes. He became a newspaper editor at age 22, taking over the *Gloucester Journal* from his father in 1757. The publisher went one afternoon to the slum district in search of a gardener. There he was jostled by a gang of ragged boys. He determined to do something about the condition of the children. Raikes took the problem to the Reverend Thomas Stock, the rector of the district, who collected names of 90 children, and together the two men undertook a strenuous visitation campaign. Far from being received with open arms, they were cursed and rejected by many people. Eventually they held a class in the kitchen of a Christian woman, Mrs. Meredith, who at first did the teaching.

While many of his biographers make the claim that Raikes marched unwilling pupils to the class with their feet hobbled like animals, one of those pupils later clarified the origin of the allegation. It was the parents of some of the wild urchins who afflicted their children and forced them to go to school, where they learned reading, writing, arithmetic, and the Word of God. It is clear that the first Sunday schools were serious educational ventures. Secular and religious teaching was administered with painful discipline; yet there was a deeply conscious religious atmosphere. Raikes wrote four of the early textbooks used in Sunday school.

Next Raikes began a Sunday school in his parish near his home. Several other schools sprang up around Gloucester. Not until three years later did Raikes use his newspaper as a platform to report and publicize Sunday school. Raikes maintained that starting with children, the lives of the slum-dwellers could be improved. His enthusiastic report caught the eyes of Christian leaders working in other vice-ridden areas; they responded to the plea of Raikes and started Sunday schools throughout England. John Wesley urged, "There must be a Sunday school wherever there is a Methodist Society."

Four years later, in 1784 John Wesley entered Leeds, England, and noted there were 26 schools with over 2000 students taught by 45 teachers. Wesley described the Sunday schools as "nurseries for Christians." He records in his journal under the date April 19, 1788, "We went on to Bolton, where I preached in the evening in one of the most elegant houses in the kingdom, and to one of the liveliest congregations. And this I must avow, there is not such a set of singers in any of the Methodist congregations in the three kingdoms. There cannot be; for we have near a hundred such trebles, boys and girls, selected out of our Sunday Schools, and accurately taught, as are not found together in any chapel, cathedral, or music room within the four seas. Besides, the spirit with which they all sing, and the beauty of many of them, so suits the melody, that I defy any

to exceed it; except the singing of angels in our Father's house."

At first Sunday school began at ten o'clock in the morning. At noon, the students had a break, then returned for another lesson. Then it was time for a whole group to be taken to church. This was as disagreeable to the parishioners as to the pupils, who were forced to attend church and were then herded back to Sunday school. At first only boys were enrolled, but almost immediately both boys and girls were accepted. Raikes insisted that students come to school with "clean hands, clean faces and their hair combed." A ragged child would not be turned away, but habits of cleanliness were not costly and could be acquired by all.

Early discipline problems were many and severe among the lawless students. They were of such proportion that the first teacher, Mrs. Meredith, resigned from her post shortly after the movement began, and the class was moved to the kitchen of Mrs. Chritchley. Originally, teachers were paid for their services and the use of their kitchen. However, in a letter to Mrs. Harris, Raikes suggested that instructors, as well as monitors, should be volunteers. Early classes used the Lancasterian system of instruction, a system of using advanced pupils to hear the lessons of the younger children.

In 1785 the Society for the Support and Encouragement of Sunday Schools Throughout the British Dominions (understandably shortened to "The Sunday School Society") was founded and became responsible for the rapid expansion of the movement. It financed and founded the new Sunday schools.

When Raikes died in 1811 there were 250,000 enrolled in Sunday school. By the time a statue was erected in his memory in 1831, Sunday schools in Great Britain were ministering weekly to 1.3 million children, approximately 25 percent of the population.

***The American Sunday School Movement.*** The people of Savannah, Ga., have historically claimed that the first Sunday school was started approximately 50 years before Raikes in their city when John Wesley taught the children on Sunday afternoon. Technically this effort is not considered a Sunday school because Wesley's efforts involved the children of Christians and catechism instruction, and the aim was edification of the pupil.

The first documented American Sunday school was held in 1785 at Oak Grove, Va., by William Elliott; both whites and blacks were instructed but at separate hours.

The Methodists were among the first to start Sunday schools, hence one of the reasons for their phenomenal growth as a denomination in the USA. Francis Asbury established a Sunday school in the home of Thomas Crenshaw of

Hanover County, Va., in 1786. In rapid-fire succession Sunday schools grew up in South Carolina, Maryland, Rhode Island, New York, and Pennsylvania. Within 11 years after Raikes began the first Sunday school in England, a new Sunday School Society was constituted in Philadelphia on January 11, 1791. Within three months they raised $3968 for the establishment of Sunday schools. After this, Sunday school societies sprang up in other cities.

The Sunday school movement mushroomed over the USA, tied more heavily to evangelism, whereas the movement in England was tied more to general education. In the early 1800s denominations began organizing their own Sunday schools as they saw their children going to Sunday schools operated by interdenominational agencies.

From the early days, Sunday schools conducted contests and offered incentives to stimulate attendance and study. Raikes gave away books, shoes, and pants for faithful attendance. Once he offered a $20 gold piece to any boy who could memorize the Book of Proverbs.

Toward the end of the 1700s, the Christ Congregational Church in New York gave a silver medal to the student bringing the most visitors during the year.

Lowell Mason (the song writer), superintendent of the Savannah (Ga.) Sabbath School, wrote out this regulation in 1818: "Tickets are given for good behavior in school and in church, for diligently attending to lessons and memorizing Scripture. Extra tickets shall be given for extra lessons, discretionally by the teacher." When the idea of prizes for bringing a visitor was criticized, Mason answered, "Anyone who procures a new scholar shall receive a monthly ticket." A ticket was worth 1/16 of a dollar and could be exchanged for books.

Beginning in 1830 the Mississippi Valley Enterprise captured the imagination of Sunday school enthusiasts on the eastern seaboard. The area west of the Alleghenies to the Rocky Mountains had a population of 4 million people within 1.3 million sq. mi. An area almost void of religious influence, the American Sunday School Union spearheaded a massive evangelistic thrust, passing in May a resolution to start a Sunday school in every town in the Mississippi Valley, wanting this accomplished in two years. Two thousand people unanimously voted and contributed over $17,000 to the project. Large gatherings in Boston, Mass., Washington, D.C., and Charleston, S.C., kicked off the project, including senators, members of Congress, and notables such as Daniel Webster and Francis Scott Key. Over 80 missionaries were employed and sent out. Their strategy was to organize people into a Sunday school and provide a library. Clarence Benson, a historian of the movement, estimated that over one million volumes were thus placed in circulation, giving further momentum to the growth of literacy in the USA.

One of the most renowned of those missionaries was Stephen Paxson, himself reached for Christ through the American Sunday School Union. "Stuttering Stephen" had overcome the double handicap of a limp and stammering to become a successful businessman and hatter. His daughter Mary brought him to Sunday school where he was converted.

Paxson caught the vision of the great task of the American Sunday School Union. He set out on his horse, "Robert Raikes," to establish Sunday schools in Indiana and Illinois. The horse according to tradition reflected his master's zeal, habitually stopping to wait for Paxson to minister to any child they passed. Paxson registered the names of 83,000 children reached for God and within a span of 25 years established 1314 Sunday schools.

Within 50 years, observers note that 80 percent of all the churches in the Mississippi Valley came out of Sunday schools. In one year alone, 17,000 persons made professions of faith. From 1824 to 1874, there were 61,299 Sunday schools organized, with 407,244 teachers and 2,650,784 pupils.

This era is called "the Babel period" because there were no Sunday school curriculum materials. The Sunday school libraries contained children's fiction books. Classes were "taught" by children reading out loud while teachers "heard the lesson." During the 1830s question and answer books were printed by Sunday School Societies.

Sunday school took a decided upturn immediately after the Civil War. *The Sunday School Teacher* was published in 1866, suggesting a curriculum which comprehensively and consistently explained and applied the Scripture. Out of this grew the *International Uniform Lesson* which was originally followed by most denominations. The *Sunday School Times*, first published in 1866, became the vehicle to spread Sunday school lessons throughout America. At one time, this weekly newspaper had the largest circulation of any newspaper or magazine in the USA.

State and county Sunday school conventions became the driving force after the Civil War, although they had been officially organized earlier. The first International Sunday School Convention was held in Baltimore in 1875. These conventions were unlike modern-day Sunday school conventions. Today, individuals from publishing houses and colleges instruct the laypeople "how to do it" in small workshops. The original conventions were massive rallies where laypeople motivated other laypeople to the work of Sunday school. Small committees worked on resolutions, strategy, and plans. They were in fact great Sunday school revival meetings. In most conventions a large parade was organized, attempting to make a great impact on the cities.

In 1884, the conventions reported 8.7 million Sunday school students in the USA. Because of their accomplishments many thought the millennium could be ushered in. Instead of looking to spiritual horizons, the Sunday school movement began turning academic. In 1903, the Religious Education Association was formed out of the conventions. The Sunday School Convention had its name changed to the International Sunday School Council of Religious Education, and in 1924, the name became the International Council of Religious Education.

In the early 1900s, theological liberalism crept into theological seminaries and sifted down into the churches. Theological liberalism minimized the imperative to teach the Bible and the zeal for evangelistic outreach. Sunday school, which had been one of the most important agencies for the expansion of work of God in the USA in the preceding century, began to decline after 1916.

During these years, most mainline denominations developed their own Sunday school literature. Most conservatives think Sunday schools lost their excitement because of a growing rational approach to the Scriptures. In reaction to liberalism, Moody Bible Institute was founded in the late 1800s. In the following years, numerous other Bible institutes were raised up by God to meet the need of growing biblical illiteracy.

God raised up interdenominational publishing houses such as Scripture Press (Wheaton, Ill.); Gospel Light Press (Glendale, Calif.); Union Gospel Press (Cleveland, Ohio); and David C. Cook Publishing Company (Elgin, Ill.). These were innovative in their dedication to biblical content, evangelistic fervor, and doctrinal orthodoxy. These laid the foundation for a Sunday school revival after the Second World War.

During the 1950s, a new spirit spread across Sunday school. Attendance took a new upturn in most denominations. Since America has experienced somewhat of a spiritual revival after every major war, the mainline denominations were growing along with the new smaller evangelical denominations and independent churches. But some suggested the growth among liberal-oriented denominations was a sociological phenomenon. A new interdenominationalism grew up around organizations such as Youth for Christ, World Vision, and other organizations committed to conservative Christianity. Large Sunday school conventions were reintroduced by the National Sunday School Association. Over 50,000 people attended the Michigan Sunday School Convention in Cobo Hall, Detroit, Mich., in 1963. The Sunday school contests of *Christian Life* magazine captured the attention of the

church world between 1948–57 and gave impetus to Sunday school growth.

The postwar Sunday school explosion reached a high around 1965. About this time mainline denominations began registering deficits in attendance and offerings. The Gallup Poll reflected a deterioration of public confidence in the church. Articles began to appear in the popular media questioning the effectiveness of Sunday school. *Life* magazine asked, "What is the most wasted hour of the week?" The *New York Times* accused Sunday school of being irrelevant and inefficient.

However, the evangelical denominations continued to grow. In 1968, NSSA published a press release claiming a 3.5 percent growth of its Sunday school's attendance.

*Christian Life* magazine introduced the listing of the 100 largest Sunday schools in 1968, which rocked the complacency of the Sunday school world. Its message got through to the religious community that Sunday schools true to the Word of God were still growing in number and vitality. During the early 1970s, there came a mild Sunday school upsurge among segments of the evangelical world. The causes of growth were Sunday school busing, continued interest in evangelism, saturation advertisement, and a commitment to biblical education.

The decade of the 1970s has been characterized as the age of the big Sunday schools. When *Christian Life* magazine began its listing, only 20 Sunday schools in America averaged over 2000 in attendance. Within the next seven years, over 60 Sunday schools reached that level. But these are only 100 out of 350,000 Sunday schools in America. Some considered this a "drop in the bucket," asking, "Why be concerned about the large ones?" But these successful Sunday schools prove that it was still possible to grow, effectively teach the Word of God, produce godly living, and saturate communities with the gospel.

During the 1980s the Sunday schools again faced other challenges as statistics revealed the continual slide in mainline denominations and a gradual plateauing in most evangelical groups. The decline in live births after the baby boom dropoff in 1965 produced fewer children for Sunday school enrollment. Growing secularism made biblical education less valued and growing commitment to pleasure on Sunday squeezed others out of Sunday school attendance. The traditional methods of door-to-door evangelism, busing, and contests no longer were as effective as previously. Fewer visitors came to Sunday school, but attendance at the worship grew in evangelical churches.

The rise of charismatic churches with their emphasis on excitement, raised hands, and praise music has tended to extend worship to two hours, canceling adult Sunday school. Also, a growing number of "baby boomer" churches with emphasis on drama and contemporary music aimed at the unchurched (called "seeker services") has caused them also to cancel adult Sunday school. They have joined the growing number of mainline churches. They have conducted Sunday school for children during the worship service, leaving adults out of the Sunday school loop. While some of these groups are providing home cells for Bible study and pastoral care, the growth of biblical illiteracy could be linked to the decline in Sunday school.

Sunday school is a school now usually connected with a church for religious instruction. While commonly thought of as instruction for the young, many modern Sunday schools offer religious education for all ages. The church has always instructed its young and new converts. But the school begun by Raikes had four new characteristics not previously brought together in one agency. First, Raikes attempted to teach all children, not just those within the church. Second, the curriculum was Bible-oriented, not just the catechism or church doctrine. Third, the purpose was to change the lifestyle of the pupils or bring them to faith in Christ. Fourth, the teachers were laypeople, not clergy. Even though the first Sunday schools were organized separately from churches and denominations, they were brought into the church and have been described for over 100 years as "the reaching, teaching, winning and maturing arm of the church."

ELMER L. TOWNS

**Surinam.** Independent country on the northeastern coast of South America occupying 163,265 sq. km. (63,037 sq. km.). Since 1975 this former Dutch colony has had political independence which has been marked by instability. The current military government, established by a coup in 1980, presides over a bankrupt economy deprived of promised aid from the Netherlands due to its repressive policies, and is threatened by guerrilla activity in the eastern countryside.

Of the total population of 400,000, one-half is currently living in the Netherlands, having emigrated in the mid-1970s due to fear of the Dutch withdrawal. The ethnic diversity is great with the majority composed of East Indians (155,000), followed by Creole (142,000), Indonesians (67,000), blacks (44,500), and Amerindians (13,000).

The government does not interfere in religious activity. Protestants, with 22 denominations, form the largest Christian group. Of these the Moravian Brethren have a membership of 56,000, followed by the Dutch Reformed Church (6200), the Lutheran Church (4000), the Evangelical Church (World Team; 3100), and Seventh-day Adventists (1900). The pentecostal churches are growing and currently have 2000 adherents (1987). There are two Baptist and four Wesleyan Methodist congregations. The Roman Catholic Church numbers

85,000. The Jewish community, having emigrated from Brazil in 1663, has two synagogues in Paramaribo, the capital, and has been reduced to 150 due to unsettled conditions. Hindus (East Indians) total 100,000 and Muslims 80,000. Bush Negroes, emancipated slaves of West Africa who reverted to jungle living and their former animistic religion, number over 10,000. The Amerindians in significant numbers have accepted evangelical Christianity.

There are 140 evangelical missionaries in Surinam, representing 21 agencies. There are four Bible institutes. The Bible Society and the Summer Institute of Linguistics are involved in seven translation projects.

LEONARD MEZNAR

**Surrogacy.** Practice whereby one woman carries a child for another with the intention to hand over the child after birth. Hagar served as a surrogate for Sarah and bore Ishmael as Abraham's son. Hindu mythology has an account of surrogacy in the birth story of Krishna.

Modern contract surrogacy emerged with the development of artificial insemination and *in vitro* fertilization techniques in the 1970s. Hundreds of children have been born by surrogate means since then. In some instances single persons have commissioned surrogate births using anonymous donors of sperm or ovum.

Surrogacy takes a number of forms. A woman may provide an egg which is fertilized *in vitro* (outside the body) by her husband's sperm and then transferred to a surrogate womb for gestation. Or a surrogate's egg may be fertilized by the husband's sperm. Or there may be an anonymous donor of either sperm or egg which is inserted into a surrogate womb.

Objections to surrogacy are both moral and legal. The Roman Catholic Church condemns surrogacy (and artificial insemination) as a violation of the biological and spiritual unity of the marriage relationship. Others express concern about the exploitation of mother and child, since the mother-child bond rooted in pregnancy and delivery is negated by the surrogacy contract. Moreover, lineage is confounded at the same time as "mother," "father," and "child" are confused.

Legal problems arise with the enforcement of a contract between a requesting party and a surrogate. It is difficult to compel strict performance of contracted personal service (surrogate behavior during gestation cannot be controlled; and the surrogate may choose to keep the child).

Debate centers on three questions. First, because a child will inevitably discover its origins, might the psychological consequences to both mother and child render surrogacy morally wrong? Second, might the legal ambiguity of any surrogate contract allow either party to violate the agreement by aborting the fetus, claiming ownership of the child, or rejecting a defective child? And third, does payment of a fee for surrogate services imply that a child is being bought and that women are subject to exploitation for surrogate service?

A British government commission in 1984 published a condemnation of surrogacy as part of its report on the social and ethical implications of technologies which treat infertility ("The Warnock Report on Human Fertilisation and Embryology"). The report, with two members dissenting, recommended that informal surrogacy agreements be made unenforceable, and advocated criminal penalties for agencies making commercial arrangements for surrogate childbirth. Legislation regulating and/or prohibiting surrogate contracts has been proposed and debated in both Great Britain and the USA. Moral debate is not expected to end legislation.

*Bibliography.* A. C. Varga, *The Main Issues in Bioethics* (1980); N. P. Keane, *The Surrogate Mother* (1981); T. A. Shannon, ed., *Bioethics* (1981); S. Gorovitz, et al., eds., *Moral Problems in Medicine* (1983); M. D. Bayles, *Reproductive Ethics* (1984); M. Warnock, *A Question of Life. The Warnock Report on Human Fertilisation and Embryology* (1984).

D. L. JOHNSON

**Svenska Kyrkans Diakonistyrelse (Svenska Kyrkans Centralråd** since 1966). Organization established in 1910 to work in collaboration with clergy and laypersons and in harmony with diocesan boards to promote a richer development of the congregational life and the charities of the Church of Sweden. The archbishop was chairman and six other members of the board were appointed by the assembly.

The board, through special committees and secretaries, carried on SKD's activities for the promotion of better church attendance, publications, Sunday schools, youth activities, scouting, social welfare, films, and radio. It aimed to be a central organ, occupying an official ecclesiastical position, to aid and stimulate voluntary church work. It supplied books, papers, and religious films, and arranged lectures, courses, and meetings, partly for evangelization.

The SKD *Bokförlag*, or publishing house, was started in 1910. Only literature approved by SKD was published.

On the initiative of SKD the Laymen's School of the Swedish Church was founded in 1922, and in 1923 was located in Sigtuna. Its function was to train laypersons for congregational activities. The school had courses for Sunday school teachers and junior leaders, preparatory courses for applicants for admission to training schools, courses in Christian culture, and courses for social workers.

From 1966 SKD became what is now called *Svenska kyrkans centralråd för evangelisation och församlingsarbete.* (In everyday speech: *Svenska kyrkans centralråd:* The Swedish Church's central

board.) The central board carries on its various activities through a director and a secretary. It is constituted by, inter alia, nine committees (*nämnder*) which are coordinated under the church assembly and its board. Its activities are financed by several foundations which are closely connected with the church. By and large, the central board works to attain the original goals or ideals of SKD.

CARL-GUSTAF ANDRÉN AND ANTONIO BARBOSA DA SILVA

**Sweden.** Northern European constitutional monarchy occupying 450,089 sq. km. (173,780 sq. mi.) with a population of 8.3 million (1988). At the beginning of the 20th century the leadership of H. Hjärne (professor of history), J. A. Eklund (later bishop of Karlstad), and Nathan Söderblom (later archbishop) helped to bring about a change for the better in the Church of Sweden. The Young Church Movement (Ungkyrkorörelsen) arose in Uppsala in 1908, inspired by Eklund and theologically influenced by E. M. Billing, later bishop of Västerås. It was closely connected with the Student Christian Movement, which had earlier gained admission into Uppsala (1901) and Lund (1902). The leader was Manfred Björkquist, later bishop of Stockholm. *Svenska Kyrkans Diakonistyrelse* (SKD—known later as Svenska Kyrkans CENTRALRÅD) was founded at the same time as the Young Church Movement, which was supported by SKD. Sigtunastiftelsen also emanates from the Young Church Movement.

On the initiative of Söderblom the Church of Sweden was brought into the ecumenical movement. Efforts to achieve a peaceful end to World War I and ecumenical meetings held in Stockholm in 1925 were fruits of his leadership. Archbishop Y. Brilioth, chairman of the Faith and Order Commission of the World Council of Churches, continued this work. Bishop A. Nygren was elected president of the Lutheran World Federation in 1947. Ecumenism remained very topical within the Church of Sweden. For example, the Life and Peace Christian World Conference was held in Uppsala under the presidency of Archbishop Olof Sundby. The Swedish Ecumenical Council established the Life and Peace Institute in 1985 in Uppsala. The Church of Sweden is also engaged in dialog with non-Christian religions.

The revival movements begun in the 19th century still have considerable influence and constitute the main body of the *Kyrkliga förbundet för evangelisk-luthersk tro* (the Church Alliance for the Evangelical and Lutheran Faith), which stresses faithfulness to the Bible and the Lutheran Confessions.

Representatives of liberal theology/liberalism, inspired by Adolf von Harnack, founded the Religious Reform Federation (Religiösa reformförbundet) in 1929 under the guidance of E. Linderholm. In 1934 the Oxford Group gained a following, especially among students and clergy. The liturgical movement is more recent and is interested chiefly in the revival of Christian life centering in prayer and holy communion.

Since 1948 the most important issue the Church of Sweden faces is the question concerning the right of women to become priests. Today (1986) most of the Swedish bishops (13 in number) ordain women.

Closely connected with this question is the conservative movement's effort to bring about a spiritual revival in the Swedish Church. This movement has founded a synod for the reformation and renewal of the church as an evangelical Lutheran Church. The synod struggles intensively to separate the church from the state. Bishop Gärtner is one of the most important leaders of the synod. This is perhaps one of the reasons why the synod is against the consecration of women as priests.

Ninety-six percent of the population are officially members of the Swedish Church. A law concerning religious liberty (1951) made it possible to leave the established church without joining another religious denomination recognized by the state. However, it is possible to be member of both a Free church and the state church. In 1981 there were 92,900 Roman Catholics, 20,000 Jews, 6900 Methodists, 35,600 members of the Salvation Army, 21,300 Baptists, 97,200 pentecostals, 6000 members of Helgelseförbundet (sanctification union), 13,200 members of *Svenska Alliansmissionen* (Swedish Alliance Mission), 80,800 members of Svenska Missionsförbundet (the Swedish Church of Mission), 19,500 members of Örebromissionen (the Swedish *national* Baptists), 63,000 members of the Orthodox Church, 37,000 Muslims, 16,800 members of Jehovah's Witnesses, and 6200 members of the Mormon Church. In addition, there are small numbers in Sri Chinmoy Center, Divine Light Mission, International Society for Krishna, Consciousness (Hare Krishnarörelsen), the Unification Church, Sidda Yoga Dham, Maranatah, and Livets Ord (Theology of Prosperity/Success) Uppsala. In 1918 a committee for collaboration with the free churches was instituted.

The church assembly was reorganized in 1948 and 1982. It presently consists of 251 members, "instead of the previous 96 reformed Church Assemblies, which are democratically elected without discrimination between clergy and laity but the clergy exert a de facto influence in the discussion of doctrinal issues" (*Kyrkohistorisk* , pp. 56f.). Every year since 1919 the bishops have had an unofficial meeting. The general meeting *(Allmänna Kyrkliga Mötet)* is held every year, and there the clergy and laypeople discuss ecclesiastical questions.

At the jubilee of the Reformation (1917) a new translation of the Bible was approved. A new hymnal was approved in 1937 and a revised liturgy in 1942. In 1933 the Board of the Church of Sweden Missions to Seamen was founded. This mission is carried out through affiliated churches in foreign ports. In 1981 a new translation of the NT was approved. The translation of the OT is continuing. A new hymnal was approved in 1986 by the general assembly. The Church of Sweden has mission fields in Africa, Asia, and South America. It is worth noting that the highest authority of the Church of Sweden in matter of legislation has been the parliament (*Riksdagen*), not the king, since 1982. The archbishop of Sweden is bishop of his diocese (Uppsala) and presiding bishop of the Church of Sweden.

At the turn of the century the Church of Sweden experienced a theological revival in Uppsala through Erik Stave, professor of OT, and Nathan Söderblom, professor of comparative religion, and in Lund through Pehr Eklund, dean of Lund. Einar Billing had great influence on systematic theology. Regarding the NT, A. Fridrichsen of Uppsala, who introduced a new approach to the NT (known as the realistic interpretation) as a reaction against liberal theologians' use of the historical critical method—an approach which a priori excludes the transempirical dimension of the gospel—continued this development. H. Odeberg made studies in rabbinical literature. The historian H. Holmquist (d. 1945) inaugurated the extensive work, *Svenska Kyrkans Historia*, with H. Pleijel, of Lund. The latter was editor of the *Samlingar och studier till Svenska Kyrkans historia*. Since 1900 important studies in church history have been published in *Kyrkohistorisk Årsskrift*, edited by Harry Lenhammar of Uppsala. Thorough research work in Luther was begun. In addition to E. M. Billing, especially G. Aulén and A. Nygren have made important contributions. Some of the best-known contemporary theologians are G. Wingren, B. Hägglund, H. Lyttkens, and P. E. Persson (Lund); H. Riesenfeld, A. Gyllenkrok, B. Sundkler, A. Jeffner, R. Holte, and H. Hof (Uppsala).

**Bibliography.** *Svenska Kyrkans* (yearly since 1921); G. K. A. Bell, ed., *The Stockholm Conference 1925* (1926); G. Aulén, *Theologische Blaetter* (1928); E. Rodhe, *Svenska Kyrkam omkring sekelskiftet* (1930); F. Siegmund-Schultz, ed., *Ekklesia* (1935); N. F. S. Ferré, *Swedish Contributions to Modern Theology* (1939); Y. Brilioth, *Kyrkokunskap* (1946); H. M. Waddams, *The Swedish Church* (1946); H. Pleijel, *Kyrkohistoriska arkivet i Lund* (1950); H. Lenhammar, *Allmänna Kyrkliga Mötet 1908–1973, Målsättning och funktion;* Acta Universitatis Upsaliensis, *Uppsala University 500 Years* (1976); *Studia Historico-Ecclesiastica Upsaliensia* (1977); G. Bexell, *Teologisk etik i Sverige sedan 1920-talet* (1981); G. Gustafsson, *Religion i Sverige* (1981); Swedish Society of Church History, *Synoden och svenska kyrkan* (1983); *Partierna staten och kyrkan* (1985); A. B. da Silva, *Themelios* 11/3 (1986).

CARL-GUSTAF ANDRÉN AND ANTONIO BARBOSA DA SILVA

**Swedenborgians.** *See* NEW JERUSALEM, CHURCH OF THE.

**Swedish Theology.** *See* LUNDENSIAN THEOLOGY.

**Sweet, William Warren** (1881–1958). American historian. Born in Baldwin, Kans., he was educated at Ohio Wesleyan University, Drew Theological Seminary, Crozer Theological Seminary, and the University of Pennsylvania (Ph.D., 1912). He served two Methodist churches in the Philadelphia area (1909–11) before teaching history at Ohio Wesleyan University (1911–13) and DePaul University (1913–27). He was professor of history of American Christianity, University of Chicago (1927–46). After official retirement he taught church history at Garrett Biblical Institute (1946–48), and from 1948 was professor of history and chairman of faculty, Perkins School of Theology. His writings include *The Story of Religion in America* (1930), *Methodism in American History* (1933), *Religion on the American Frontier* (4 vols., 1931–46), *Religion in Colonial America* (1942), *Revivalism in America* (1944), *The American Churches* (1947), and *Religion in the Development of American Culture, 1740–1865* (1952).

**Swenson, David Ferdinand** (1876–1940). Congregationalist philosopher. Born in Sweden, he came to America in 1882. He graduated from the University of Minnesota and spent the remainder of his life teaching philosophy at that university. Deeply religious and interested in logical and epistemological problems, he believed that objectivity is attained only by turning inward. An early discoverer of Kierkegaard, he became an eminent interpreter and translator of the Danish philosopher. He wrote *Something about Kierkegaard* (1941), *Faith of a Scholar* (posthumously published, 1948), and an introduction to Eduard Geismar's *Lectures on the Religious Thought of Soren Kierkegaard*. He translated the following works of Kierkegaard: *Concluding Unscientific Postscript* (1941), *Philosophical Fragments* (1937, with introduction), *Thoughts on Crucial Situations* (1941), and four volumes of *Edifying Discourses* (1943–45), the latter completed after his death by his widow, Lillian M. Swenson.

JOHANNES KNUDSEN

**Swete, Henry Barclay** (1835–1917). Church of England theologian. Born in Bristol, he was educated at Gonville and Caius College, Cambridge, and was ordered deacon in 1858 and ordained priest in the following year. He was curate of Blagdon, Somerset (1858–65), All Saints', Cambridge (1866–68), and Tor Mohun, Devonshire (1869–72), and rector of Ashdon, Essex (1877–90). He was fellow of his college (1858–77), tutor (1872–75), divinity lecturer at Cambridge

(1875–77), professor of pastoral theology at King's College, London (1882–90), and served as Regius Professor of Divinity at Cambridge until 1915; he became honorary chaplain to the king in 1911. He contributed articles to Smith and Wace's *Dictionary of Christian Biography* and Hastings' *Dictionary of the Bible*. Other works he wrote or edited include *The Psalms of Solomon with the Greek Fragments of the Book of Enoch* (1899), *Essays on Some Theological Questions of the Day* (1905), *The Holy Spirit in the Ancient Church* (1912), *The Last Discourse and Prayer of Our Lord: A Study of St. John XIV–XVII* (1913), *The Holy Catholic Church: The Communion of Saints* (1915), *The Forgiveness of Sins: A Study in the Apostles' Creed* (1916), *The Life of the World to Come* (1917), *Essays on the Early History of the Church and the Ministry* (1918), *A Remembrance* (1918), and *The Parables of the Kingdom* (1920).

RAYMOND W. ALBRIGHT

**Switzerland.** Small central European country covering 41,288 sq. km. (15,941 sq. mi.). With a population of 6.7 million (1985), the republic has 3,555,500 Roman Catholics and 2,890,800 Protestants.

Switzerland was evangelized early in the Christian era. The Abbey of St. Maurice was erected in A.D. 300, and the Abbey of Romainmotiers dates back to 400. Missionaries associated with Columba founded the Abbey of St. Gall in 613.

During the Reformation, Swiss Reformers presented a credible alternative to Lutheranism. In 1519 Zwingli began to preach Reformation doctrines, and soon the churches in Baden, St. Gall, Bern, Basel, and Schaffhausen followed his teachings. Zwingli was slain in the confessional wars in 1531. Meanwhile Calvin established his version of the Reformation in Geneva. There he formulated a cohesive doctrinal structure which today is the basis of Presbyterianism, the Reformed Church, and other Protestant groups. Not only did Calvin create a doctrinal system, but he also applied Christian truth to the structure of society.

Until this century Catholicism was the minority religion in Switzerland. In 1900 there were 1,346,000 Catholics and 1,916,000 Protestants. However, immigration has changed that balance. Now there is a considerable Catholic majority in the country.

There are major theological faculties at the universities of Berne, Basel, Geneva, Neuchâtel, and Lausanne. This has made the Swiss a force in the field of theology. Among the best-known Swiss theologians are Barth, Brunner, and evangelical Rene Pâche.

Switzerland is the home of many international organizations, among which are the Red Cross and the World Council of Churches (WCC). With its headquarters in Geneva, WCC has conducted many consultations in Switzerland. Evangelist

Billy Graham has also conducted missions in Switzerland in 1955, 1960, 1970, and 1974. His 1974 crusade was held in conjunction with the international Congress on World Evangelization at Lausanne.

In addition to the major churches of Switzerland, there are many smaller groups. The Christian Brethren have 45 assemblies and 2500 members with an adherent circle of 5000; Baptists have 14 churches with 1422 members and 3000 adherents; the Evangelical Free Churches have 113 churches and 2750 members with a circle of 5000 adherents; the Methodists have 330 and 18,350 members; the Salvation Army claims 15,000 members and 30,000 adherents. The number of officially irreligious in Switzerland have grown from 5700 (1900) to 69,200 (1975) and 91,200 (1985). The number of atheists has increased from 1000 (1900) to 33,700 (1985).

When Tibet was overrun by communist forces, some 500 refugees fled to Switzerland and there are now 2000 Buddhists. Other religious movements have headquarters in Switzerland, such as Ramakrishna Mission, the Divine Light Mission, ISKCON (Hare Krishna), and the Theosophical Society.

There are several evangelical theological training institutions in Switzerland. The Freie Evangelische Akademie in Basel is a graduate-level faculty. Bible institute training is offered at St. Chrischona, Aarau, Beatenberg, Walzenhausen, and Bienenberg. In francophone Switzerland there are training centers at Emmaus, LeRoc, and Centre Biblique International.

*Bibliography.* Handbuch der Reformierten schweiz (1962); H. Mol, ed., *Western Religion* (1972); D. B. Barrett, ed., *World Christian Encyclopedia* (1982).

WAYNE DETZLER

**Sword of the Spirit, The.** A movement and society organized in August 1941 by Arthur Cardinal Hinsley, archbishop of Westminster, England, for bringing the principles of the Christian faith and natural law to bear in support of national unity during World War II and of social reconstruction thereafter. The hope that Catholics and Protestants might join on an equal footing in such a movement was disappointed, but the Sword was able to work on the basis of parallel activity in a common cause. Since its founder's death (in 1943) and the end of hostilities, it has continued as the organ of English Roman Catholic concern for questions of social order.

*Bibliography.* The Sword, monthly bulletin; J. C. Heenan, *Cardinal Hinsley* (1944).

EDWARD R. HARDY

**Sykes, Norman** (1897–1961). Anglican church historian. Born in Yorkshire, he was educated at the universities of Leeds and Oxford, and was ordained in 1923. He was lecturer in history,

King's College, London (1924–31), professor of history at the University of London (1933–44), and professor of ecclesiastical history at the University of Cambridge (1944–58). His published works include *Edmund Gibson* (1926), *Church and State in England since the Reformation* (1929), *The Crisis of the Reformation* (1938), *The English Religious Tradition* (1953), *Old Priest and New Presbyter* (1956), *William Wake, Archbishop of Canterbury, 1657–1737* (1957), *From Sheldon to Secker* (1959), and *Man as Churchman* (1960).

J. D. DOUGLAS

**Symbolism, Church.** Attitudes toward the use of symbols in worship differ widely, but the trend is toward increased use. Liturgical bodies still give them a large place in architecture and forms of worship. Groups formerly opposed to such signs of inward grace now introduce the cross, lighted candles, vestments, and liturgical colors. The result occasionally seems grotesque, as when a red light keeps burning over an altar, which ought to mean "the reservation of the Sacrament." Such "improvements" by unskilled hands seem ludicrous, but various writers, such as V. O. Vogt in the USA and Robert Will on the Continent, have shown how to combine use of symbols with worship free from fixed forms. The situation calls for study of worship historically, and for keeping the balance between religion and art. When art becomes an end in itself it ceases to serve as a handmaid of religion. When religion ignores art childlike folk feel starved in their quest for "the beauty of holiness." Since the days of the apostles, followers of Christ seldom have found the right balance. The next generation may discover the golden mean.

*See also* ART AND THE CHURCH.

ANDREW W. BLACKWOOD

**Synoptic Problem.** *See* GOSPEL AND GOSPELS.

**Syria.** Independent country in Southwest Asia covering 185,180 sq. km. (71,498 sq. mi.). Muslims (mostly Sunnis) command 89.6 percent of Syria's population (10,267,000). During A.D. 660–750 Damascus ruled the Umayyad Empire. Later Syria was ruled by Egyptian Mamelkes, Asian Mongols, and Ottoman Turks (until 1918). Most Muslims identify with Sunnis; however, a branch of the Shias (Shi'ites), the Alawites, make up 11 percent of the population. They acknowledge a trinity: Muhammad, Salman, and Ali. Their secret tenets include seven reincarnations. They have no mosques, exclude women from formal rites, and drink wine during religious ceremonies.

The Druze sect (also in Lebanon and Palestine) was founded by Arasi (11th cent.) who identified Egyptian caliph Al-Hakim as the incarnation of Allah. The sect combines Jewish, Christian, and

Muslim beliefs. The 200,000 adherents are centered mostly in Djebel Druze, and represent only 0.2 percent of the Syrian population. Yazidi religion is a complex syncretism of Islam, Judaism, Manichaeism, Zoroastrianism, and Nestorianism, although Islamic thought prevails. Most of the 12,000 followers are located near Aleppo in the north. Many Jews have emigrated to Israel since World War II, although a tiny Arabic-speaking Sefardi community remains.

Christianity in Syria antedates Paul's conversion. Antioch later became an important Christian center in the Roman Empire. Controversies over the nature of Christ in succeeding centuries resulted in the Nestorian and Jacobite sects; Catholic Uniate churches came into being in the 11th century with the Maronites accepting Roman authority in 1516. Eastern rite churches subsequently resulted in the formation of additional Uniate churches, including Chaldean, Armenian, Greek Melkite, and Syrian Catholic bodies. The Greek Orthodox Church continues to be the largest denomination in Syria. Although persecuted Armenians have come to Syria from Turkey and Iraq, recently many Christians are emigrating out of Syria.

Protestant missions began in Syria in the 19th century. Protestants, however, are suspect to both Muslim and Eastern rite Christians, as well as to the Alawite government. Many contemporary Christians have had technical or university training; the army and the government also boast significant numbers of Christians. Christians are integrating themselves more into the mainstream of Syrian life; this means that they are also becoming increasingly secularized. However, this development may lead to a wider and more influential role by Christians. On the other hand, evidence suggests that it may cause an intensification of fundamentalist Islamic movements. All in all, Christians comprise 8.9 percent of the Syrian population, while nonreligious groups total about 1.2 percent (which may possibly double before the end of the century). The percentage of Christians will possibly decline to only 7.0 percent of the total population by the year 2000.

Against developments that seem to favor religion, there are evidences of suppression of any group or movement that attempts to challenge the government. A new constitution in 1973 saw Islam as the religion of the head of the state only, and no longer the state's faith. Riots followed in overt opposition. Christians have advocated a constitution which would recognize Islam for the majority of all Syrians but not as the official faith of the state. In 1982, the banned Muslim Brotherhood sought to overthrow the government in Hamah. President Assad (an Alawite) quelled the rebellion by military force with massive destruction in the city and the death of an estimated 3000 to 10,000 people. There is considerable apprehension among the small number of evangelical Christians who fear persecution may occur particularly if the government becomes unstable.

**Bibliography.** R. M. Haddad, *Syrian Christians in Muslim Society* (1970); F. Ajami, *The Arab Predicament: Arab Political Thought since 1967* (1981); J. F. Devlin, *Syria: Modern State in an Ancient Land* (1983); G. J. Jennings, *Welcome into the Middle East!* (1986).

GEORGE J. JENNINGS

# Tt

**Taft, Charles Phelps** (1897–1983). Lawyer and ecumenical leader. Born into a distinguished family in Cincinnati, Ohio, he graduated from Yale University, then practiced law in Cincinnati. He served on the city council at various times between 1938 and 1977 and was mayor from 1955 to 1957. He was senior warden of Christ Episcopal Church, Cincinnati, and a lay deputy at several triennial conventions of the Protestant Episcopal Church. He was president of the Federal Council of Churches (1947/48), an Episcopal delegate to the founding assembly of the World Council of Churches (WCC) (1948), and during the 1950s served as a member of the central committee of WCC, general board of the National Council of Churches (NCC), and chair of the department of the church and economic life in NCC. He was author of four books including *Why I Am for the Church* (1947).

RICHARD V. PIERARD

**Tagore, Rabindrānāth** (1861–1941). Brahmo-Samājist and Hindu. Born in Calcutta, he was a nationalist Indian poet, novelist, musician, painter, and social reformer. A universal humanitarian with strong mystical tinge, he was essentially an ethicist and conciliator. In 1901 he established the famous Shāntīniketan School at Bolpur, Bengal, which later developed into the international University of Vishwabhāratī. He was awarded the Nobel Prize for literature in 1913. He was a leader of the early 20th-century Bengali literary renaissance; he wrote 100,000 lines of poetry and composed over 3000 songs. Among his best-known English writings are *Gītanjalī* (1912), *Sādhanā* (1913), *Gorā* (1924), *The Religion of Man* (1931), *Collected Poems & Plays* (1941), and *The Gardener* (1943).

*Bibliography.* E. J. Thompson, *Rabindrānāth Tagore, Poet and Dramatist* (1926); S. Rādhākrishnan, *The Philosophy of Rabindrānāth Tagore* (1918).

WILSON M. HUME

**Tai Hsu** (1885–1947). Chinese Buddhist abbot. He was the leader of Buddhist reform in China to regenerate clergy, rededicate property to benefit the people, and reconstruct doctrine in agreement with science. He founded *Hai Chao Yin*, a monthly which still continues (1920); Wuchang Buddhist Institute (1922); and the Institute of Chinese and Tibetan Studies near Chungking, implementing the trend toward Tibetan mysticism (1933). Tai Hsu promoted social service and education. He made international contacts, largely intellectual, and promoted monism, encouraging Wei Shih idealism harmonized with Hwayen and Tientai. His lectures and essays were published under the title *Fa-hsiang Wei-shih Hsueh* (*Dharma-character Idealistic Philosophy*) (1938).

EARL H. CRESSY

**Taiwan.** Large Pacific island off the Chinese mainland with a population of 19,511,000 (1985 est.). Roman Catholicism was introduced to Taiwan in the early 17th century by Spanish missionaries from the Philippines, but the missions were abandoned late in that century and Catholic priests did not return to the island until the 1890s. Protestant Christianity on the island was introduced by the English Presbyterian Mission, whose personnel visited Taiwan in 1859 and established their first permanent station in 1865. Both the Roman Catholics and the Presbyterians found converts slow in coming and both groups suffered periods of persecution. Since the English Presbyterians sought to convert the Taiwanese (along with the Hakka and aborigines who also lived on the island) they later came to be linked with the Taiwanese politically when the island was occupied first by the Japanese in 1895 and then by the Chinese Nationalist government in 1945. Presbyterian services are usually conducted in Taiwanese.

Hospitals and educational institutions were established early and others refugeed from the mainland in 1949, including several universities. Several Christian seminaries currently train clergy and church workers. Christian publications have always been an integral part of the work of the church. At present there are approximately 80 presses and printing houses in Taiwan, of which 40 are Roman Catholic; 25 are Protestant, ecumenical, or interdenominational; and the others are Lutheran, Presbyterian, or Baptist. Most presses are quite small, employing fewer than 20 people, but several employ more than 50 people and one more than 200. Some of these publishing houses came from the mainland in 1949, but the majority of them date from the 1960s. Most presses are located in Taipei and are run by Chinese, although there are exceptions. In addition to printed works they produce movies, video cassettes, and television and radio programs for audiences in Taiwan and China.

Presently, the Roman Catholics and some 80 Protestant groups are active on Taiwan; these include both foreign mission agencies and indigenous associations. In 1980 the Christian population of the island was 1,288,140 of whom 470,000 were Roman Catholics. This is somewhat less than one percent of the population. The Christian groups which are currently the most rapidly growing are the charismatic, evangelical ones whose converts usually come from the Presbyterian or other Protestant churches.

KATHLEEN L. LODWICK

**Taizé.** The place near Cluny in southeastern France where Roger Schutz (1915– ) and six of his friends began a Protestant monastic order on Easter Sunday 1947. The order is the result of Schutz's study of early Christian monasticism as part of his doctorate at the University of Lausanne in the early 1940s. During the Vichy regime, Schutz provided shelter to Jews and others at Taizé. In 1942 he was forced to leave his château and went to Geneva where he made contact with Max Thurian and others interested in a Protestant monastic movement. By 1944 he had returned to Taizé and by 1947, seven took the vows of celibacy, obedience, and common property. The Rule of Taizé was completed by 1952. There were 70 members in the community by 1968. The members usually dress as laypeople except during worship when a white robe with a cowl is worn. Offices are said three times a day. There is a novitiate of two to three years. Upon being admitted to the order, one may stay at Taizé or go into other parts of the world to work at one's profession and promote Christian unity.

ROBERT V. SCHNUCKER

**Talmud.** Hebrew word meaning "teaching." The term has a range of meaning. In its narrowest sense it refers to the Babylonian Talmud; in its broader sense the term includes the extensive literature of Jewish religious lore, especially that produced between the 1st and 5th centuries A.D.

Both the Babylonian and Palestinian talmuds are arranged as commentaries on the *Mishna* oral traditions, and the word *Talmud* is sometimes taken to include the *Mishna* as well (the Babylonian Aramaic synonym *Gemara* is sometimes used to refer to the *Talmud* exclusive of the *Mishna*). The *Mishna* is the most authoritative compilation of the Jewish rabbinic-Pharisaic oral law, achieving its final form under the redaction of Rabbi Judah the Prince, in Hebrew, at the beginning of the 3d century A.D. It collects the teachings of the *Tanna'im,* teachers who lived primarily from the middle of the 1st century, and is devoted principally to legal topics. As distinct from other rabbinic works of that period, the *Mishna* is arranged topically, not as a commentary on a biblical book (*Midrash*), and it is devoted principally to legal subjects, which are called *Halakah* ("the way in which one walks"). It is divided into six orders or general legal areas: (1) *Zera'im* ("Seeds") on agricultural regulations; (2) *Mo'ed* ("Feasts") on Sabbath regulations and festivals; (3) *Nashim* ("Women") on family law; (4) *Nezikin* ("Damages") on civil and criminal law; (5) *Kodashim* ("Consecrated Things") on sacrifices and the temple cult; and (6) *Tohoroth* ("Purifications") on ritual purity. The orders are divided into 60 tractates on specific topics, and these in turn into numbered chapters and individual laws. The classification is not strictly followed; for example, the tractate dealing with blessings and the daily liturgy is in the order *Zera'im,* on vows in *Nashim,* and the moral maxims of the "Ethics of the Fathers" (*Abot*) in *Nezikin.*

With its publication (orally, in accordance with the doctrine of oral law) the *Mishna* gained universal acceptance among the Jews of Israel and Babylonia and became the center of the theological teaching in both areas. The scholars of the later period were known as *Amora'im,* and operated in the academies of Tiberias, Sephoris, and Caesarea, in Israel, and in Sura, Nahardea, Pumbedita, and Mahoza in Babylonia. According to an authoritative medieval tradition, the Babylonian Talmud was completed in 499, while the Palestinian Talmud was probably redacted about a century earlier. Both contain tractates that appear to have emanated from different editions, notably the tractate *Nezikim* in the Palestinian Talmud, which Saul Lieberman has traced to mid-4th-century Caesarea. Current scholarship emphasizes that the editorial process of the Babylonian Talmud probably extended many years after 499, and was achieved largely by *Sabora'im,* the successors of the *Amora'im.* The two talmuds are similar in developing some aspects of the earlier Tanna'itic period as well as introducing new approaches. Those earlier collections, including the *Mishna,* consist largely of disputes among rabbis. The equivalent units in the talmudic period are known as *memras,* formal, Hebrew dicta (while the commentary on these passages is generally in *Amoraic*, a language not normally used in earlier texts). Whereas the *Mishna* generally limits itself to setting out opposing positions, the talmuds contain sophisticated proof, refutation, and discussion of various opinions. These are presented as face-to-face confrontations between rabbis, or as hypothetical discussions. Proof-texts are cited for and against the various interpretations from biblical verses, from the *Mishna* or external Tanna'itic teachings (*baraita*), from the dicta of authoritative *Amora'im*, or from logical reasoning. Underlying all the discussion is an assumption of the perfection of the *Mishna*, nearly equal to the sanctity of the Bible itself. The talmuds take for granted that every word of the *Mishna* was carefully chosen and that the authors were aware of all their implications. This type of dialectical reasoning is applied to explaining disputes in the *Mishna* or other Tanna'itic sources, or those between *Amora'im;* as well as to resolve contradictions between or within sources. The talmuds explain the *Mishna* in several ways: by determining correct readings, defining difficult words, providing the sources and reasons for the various opinions, declaring which opinions are normative, extending the legal principles to new applications, and the like. Thus, a discrepancy in the *Mishna* might variously be explained by either applying the two statements to different situations, by claiming that they represent the views of two different teachers, or by emending one of the sources.

The organization of the talmuds is not systematic, and it is likely to connect topics by the flimsiest threads. It does, however, observe certain esthetic standards, such as the arrangement of material in numerically symmetrical patterns (especially in multiples of seven). Neither the Palestinian nor the Babylonian Talmud, as they have survived, covers the whole of the *Mishna*. Neither expounds more than one tractate of the order *Tohorot* (Niddah, dealing with rules of menstrual impurity) since the rules of ritual purity were no longer practicable after the destruction of the second temple. The Babylonian Talmud does not comment on most of *Zera'im*, which is not in force outside Israel, but contains tractates from *Kodashim*. The Palestinian Talmud, on the other hand, has a full talmud on the former order, but not on the latter. Neither comments upon the nonlegal *Abot*. Both talmuds devote considerable space to *aggadah*, nonlegal matters. In the Babylonian Talmud, this amounts to about a third, in the Palestinian about a sixth of the total (the Palestinian schools produced many separate collections of this material). Talmudic *aggadah* discusses a wide variety of subjects, ranging from biblical exegesis and homiletics to theology and folklore.

The texts of the talmuds have been preserved in various degrees of accuracy. The situation of the Palestinian Talmud is particularly unfortunate since it was eclipsed early in the Middle Ages by its Babylonian cousin. The only complete text is the Leiden MS, on which was based the *editio princeps* (Venice 1523), although important partial and fragmentary texts have been discovered, especially from the Cairo Genizah. The printed editions of the Babylonian Talmud also go back to the first full printing of Venice (1521–23), which was preceded by publication of individual tractates in Italy, Spain and Portugal. Most surviving MSS date from late medieval Europe, although here too the hundreds of oriental fragments unearthed in the Cairo Genizah have revolutionized modern understanding of the talmudic text.

The Babylonian Talmud was recognized by all rabbinic Jews as a central source of law. Various genres of literature were devoted to its explication: commentaries were composed both to facilitate its understanding and to continue the dialectical process as a way of extracting new possibilities of meaning. Codes were designed to turn the rambling theoretical discussions into actual lawbooks. In the *Responsa* literature, the foremost rabbis used the Talmud to answer practical questions addressed to them. Hermeneutical manuals and introductions were also composed.

*Bibliography.* G. F. Moore, *Judaism in the First Centuries of the Christian Era: The Age of the Tannaim* (1927–30); H. L. Strack, *Introduction to the Talmud and Midrash* (1931); J. Kaplan, *The Redaction of the Babylonian Talmud* (1933); I. Epstein, ed., *The Babylonian Talmud* (ET, 1948–52); R. N. N. Rabbinowicz, *Diqduqé Soferim* (2d ed., 1960); S. Lieberman, *Hellenism in Jewish Palestine* (2d ed., 1962); E. E. Urbach, *The Sages: Their Concepts and Beliefs* (1975); A. Steinsalz, *The Essential Talmud* (ET, 1976).

ELIEZER SEGAL

## Tambaram Conference

**Tambaram Conference** (1938). The second world meeting of the International Missionary Council (IMC), convened at Madras Christian College, Tambaram, South India, December 12–29, 1938. It was deliberately staged in the East for the "upbuilding of the younger Churches." By 1938 the IMC included 14 member missions from "sending" countries and 12 councils of churches or missions in "receiving" countries, so at Tambaram the younger churches had, for the first time, as many delegates as the older churches. Half of the 471 delegates from 69 countries were under 35.

The Tambaram theme was evangelism. Many preparatory studies were circulated, including *Evangelism for the World Today* (1938), edited by J. R. Mott, but the most controversial and most discussed was the study commissioned from the Dutch missionary theologian C. F. Kraemer on *The Christian Mission in a Non-Christian World* (1938). In contrast to the fulfillment theology of J. N. Farquhar's *Crown of Hinduism* (1913) which was so influential at the 1928 IMC meeting in

Jerusalem, and in opposition to the liberal approach of W. E. Hocking's *Re-Thinking Missions* (1932), Kraemer proposed a radical discontinuity between the gospel and all other religions. His position was questioned by the Madras "Rethinking Group" and by A. G. Hogg, who argued that Christianity's uniqueness lay not in its creation by the occurrence of revelation but in the uniqueness of that revelation.

Further discussion of this issue and of other conference findings on church and society and the relationship between older and younger churches was cut short by the outbreak of World War II or preempted by subsequent moves toward the end of colonialism. However, Tambaram's identification of the need for a properly trained indigenous ministry eventually bore fruit in the creation of the Theological Education Fund.

*See also* INTERNATIONAL MISSIONARY COUNCIL.

**Bibliography.** International Missionary Council, *The World Mission of the Church* (1939), and *The Tambaram Series*, 7 vols. (1939); C. F. Hallencreutz, *Kraemer Towards Tambaram* (1966); D. J. Hesselgrave and E. Rommen, *Contextualization: Meanings, Methods, and Models* (1989).

PHILIP HILLYER

**Tanzania.** *See* EAST AFRICA.

**Taoism.** Both a philosophy and a religious tradition of China, literally "the teaching of the way." Taoism is in reality a series of religious movements worshiping the Tao and its manifestations of magic, alchemy, and meditative practices which were believed to lead to immortality. Taoist movements were founded in China in the 2d century A.D. by Ling Chang Tao-ling and are typically communal, invoking sacred powers to recreate a cosmic harmony for the sake of blessings to individuals and society. These movements are esoteric in nature and their full traditions can only be transmitted to the initiated. Characteristically they are messianic and eschatological, envisioning the immanent end of all things and the creation of a new righteous, harmonious order ruled by the Tao.

The millenarianism of Taoist movements is often highly political, seeking military dominance to attain messianic goals. Ethically they teach restraint and humility. Transgressors are believed to face divine punishment and therefore confession is essential to obtain forgiveness. Taoist scriptures are often concerned with ritual as much as practice and doctrine. Revelation is not limited to one period or person but frequently occurs, creating rival movements, each with its own sacred writings.

Cosmologically Taoists believe that the Tao is the origin of all things and in its original state is permanent and unchanging. Yet this essence gives birth to a "breath" which brings into being primordial chaos. This in turn produces movement through the active principle of *yang* and the stillness of *yin*. The interaction of *yin* and *yang* causes the phenomenological world to function through the five fundamental agents of wood, fire, earth, metal, and water, producing the ever-changing universe.

In the universe the harmony of the Tao has been disturbed and within the human body are forces which tempt humans away from harmony. The cosmos is thus populated by an array of hierarchical forces. Below the Tao (a personal god sometimes called the Jade Emperor) are heaven, earth, and water, the "three officials," and below them is a vast bureaucracy of gods inhabiting the nine heavens. Below these are demons, humans, animals, and ghosts. To keep harmony in the cosmos the divine emanations of the Tao order society by establishing human rulers, the governance extending from emperors through their ministers and armies to the common people.

The Taoist priesthood exists to teach the arts that lead to personal immortality and to combat evil forces on earth by supporting the divinely approved government. The goal of Taoism is immortality. The immortals are believed to be birdlike creatures who live on divine food on the top of high mountains. Historically various Chinese emperors mounted expeditions to explore mountains and discover the home of the immortals as well as their sacred island Péng-lai. Another popular belief within Taoism is that the immortals often appeared in disguise among humans to transmit wisdom and magical powers to worthy individuals.

Taoists conceive of a union between the spiritual and the physical. Immortality is the conserving and harmonious transformation of the mind and body through the individual's energies. As a result hygienic and dietary disciplines play an important role in Taoist ritual and practice. Breathing techniques were also developed, as well as various sexual practices intended to preserve the essence of life by avoiding ejaculation or the female orgasm. Good deeds, humility, impartiality, and control over the passions were also considered prerequisites to restoring personal harmony.

Various Taoist movements developed throughout Chinese history, and Taoism has often locked in bitter struggle with its chief rival, Buddhism. In the late 1900s Taoist practices survived outside of China, although little was known about the state of Taoism in China itself. Taoist influences could be seen in new religious movements like the Unification Church and certain "New Age" spiritual and ecological groups in North America.

**Bibliography.** H. Welch, *Taoism: The Parting of the Way* (1966); M. Saso and D. W. Chappell, eds., *Buddhist and Taoist Studies* (1977).

IRVING HEXHAM

**Tappert, Theodore Erhardt** (1904–1973). Reformation scholar, educator, and author. Born in Meriden, Conn., he was educated at Wagner College, Lutheran Theological Seminary in Philadelphia, Columbia University, and the University of Pennsylvania. He taught at the Lutheran Theological Seminary for 42 years until his death. A prolific author and editor, his works include *Road to Reformation* (1946), *Luther's Letters of Spiritual Counsel* (1955), and *The Mature Luther* (1959). He was editor of *Selected Writings of Martin Luther* (4 vols., 1967). He also translated and edited works of Hermann Sasse, Henry Melchoir Muhlenberg, Heinrich Boehmer, P. J. Spener, and Luther.

JACK MITCHELL

**Tareev, Michael** (1866–1934). Eastern Orthodox theologian. He studied at the Moscow Theological Academy, in which he was later professor of moral theology. He was an enemy of intellectualism in theology and wanted instead to reinterpret Christianity in terms of spirituality. The central idea in his system was that of *kenosis*. Christianity as an "inner" religion had, in his opinion, nothing to do with the secular life. In his last years he was working on a history of Russian theology (the manuscript seems to have been lost). His main work is *Foundations of Christianity* (in Russian, 5 vols., 1908–11).

*Bibliography.* N. Gorodetzky, *The Humiliated Christ in Modern Russian Thought* (1938).

GEORGES FLOROVSKY

**Tawney, Richard Henry** (1880–1962). Anglican professor. Born in Calcutta, he studied at Rugby and Oxford, and was professor of economic history at the University of London (1931–49). He is most widely known for his book, *Religion and the Rise of Capitalism* (1926), which is a revision and an elaboration of Max Weber's thesis in *The Protestant Ethic and the Spirit of Capitalism* (1904). He also wrote *The Agrarian Problem in the Sixteenth Century* (1912), *The Acquisitive Society* (1920), and *Equality* (1931).

WINTHROP S. HUDSON

**Taylor, John Vernon** (1914– ). Anglican missionary, writer, and bishop. Educated at Cambridge, he pursued theological studies at Oxford, and after ordination served parishes in London and Lancashire before going to Uganda as warden of Bishop Tucker College, Mukono (1945–54). He was then successively research worker on the International Missionary Council (1955–59), Africa Secretary of the Church Missionary Society (1959–63), general secretary of that society (1963–74), and bishop of Winchester (1975–85). He was also a lucid and thought-provoking writer. His publications include *Man in the Midst* (1955), *Christianity and Politics in Africa* (1957), *The*

*Growth of the Church in Buganda* (1958), *Christians of the Copperbelt* (1961), *The Primal Vision* (1963), *The Go-Between God* (1972), *Enough Is Enough* (1975), *Weep Not for Me* (1986), and *A Matter of Life and Death* (1986).

J. D. DOUGLAS

**Tchernowitz, Chaim** (1870–1949). Jewish scholar. Born in Sebej, White Russia, he was ordained rabbi in 1896 and in the following year became rabbi in Odessa where he founded a rabbinical Yeshiva. There he introduced the study of secular subjects in Hebrew and coordinated modern science with Talmudic knowledge; his innovation led him to adopt the pseudonym Rav Tzair (the young rabbi). He studied further at the University of Wurzburg (Ph.D., 1914) and in 1923 he came to the USA as professor in Talmud at the Jewish Institute of Religion, New York City. He is most widely known for his studies in Talmudic and rabbinic literature and for his essays. In New York, he founded and edited the Hebrew monthly, *Bitzaron*. Among his writings the best known are *Letholedoth Hashulhan Aruch* (1897/98), *Shiurim Bethalmud* (1913), *Kitzur Hatalmud* (1919–23), *Toledoth Hahalachab* (4 vols., 1934–50), *Massecheth Zichronoth* (1945), *Toledoth Haposekim* (3 vols., 1946), and *Hevlei Genlah* (1949).

*Bibliography.* F. Lachower, *Toledoth Harsafruth Haivrith Hahavashah*, book 3; M. Waxman, *A History of Jewish Literature*, vol. 4; *Bitzaron* (Rav Tzair Jubilee Issue) (Apr. 1948).

LOUIS FINKELSTEIN

***Te Deum.*** Title of the so-called Ambrosian hymn taken from the opening words (*Te Deum laudamus*). This hymn has been regarded from early times as a classic expression of the Christian faith on a par with the liturgical confessions. Legend holds that at the time of Augustine's baptism (387), Ambrose intoned the hymn and sang it alternately with Augustine. However, it was probably composed by Niketas, bishop of Remesiana (Bela Palanka in Yugoslavia), who died between 335 and 414. Niketas may have been, if not the first author of the *Te Deum*, as Dom Morin asserted, at least responsible for its definitive arrangement.

*Bibliography.* P. Cagin, *L'euchologie latine, I: Te Deum ou Illatio* (1905); W. A. Patin, *Niceta von Remesiana* (1909); A. E. Burn, *The Hymn Te Deum and Its Author* (1925).

GEORGES A. BARROIS

**Teilhard de Chardin, Pierre** (1881–1955). Jesuit paleontologist and philosopher. Educated in France and England, he was ordained priest in 1911, and in 1920 became professor of geology at the Institut Catholic, Paris. He went on paleontological expeditions to China in 1923 and in 1926, having been deprived of his Paris teaching post because of the theological implications of his lectures on evolution. Returning to France after

810

World War II, Teilhard was forbidden to either speak or publish articles on theological or philosophical topics, and was prevented from accepting a professorship at the College de France. He moved to the USA in 1951 to work at the Werner-Gren Foundation and died in New York. Teilhard wrote nearly 400 papers, but, because his Roman Catholic superiors withheld permission, his theological and philosophical works were published only after his death, beginning with *The Phenomenon of Man* (1959). This appeared in English with a foreword by Julian Huxley commending many of Teilhard's ideas, except the central theme of "Christogenesis" or fulfillment of all things in and through the Omega point, the universal cosmic Christ. Teilhard's vocabulary and style were unique; he introduced concepts such as "cosmogenesis," "planetization," and "noosphere" in writings that bounced between science, theology, and mysticism. Despite justified scientific and theological criticisms of his evolutionary optimism, Teilhard's main achievement was his unification of science and theology. Teilhard's other works available in English include *Le Milieu Divin* (1960), *The Future of Man* (1964), *Hymn of the Universe* (1965), *Towards the Future* (1975), and *The Heart of the Matter* (1978).

***Bibliography.*** C. Cuénot, *Teilhard de Chardin: A Biographical Study* (1965); M. and E. Lukas, *Teilhard—A Biography* (1977); M. Le Morvan, ed., *The Human Search* (1979); A. Hanson, ed., *Teilhard Reassessed* (1970).

PHILIP HILLYER

**Temperance Movement.** Organized effort to discourage the sale and consumption of intoxicating beverages, motivated by a desire to reform society. The movement was the result of a conjunction of various technological, social, and theological developments. Although Jews and Christians warned against drunkenness (as in Proverbs; Eph. 5:18, etc.), alcoholic drinks traditionally have been considered part of God's good creation. Wine, with bread, is a central Jewish social and religious symbol; the Christian Eucharist uses it to symbolize—and in Roman theology to present again—the incarnation, asserting that what God had created and humans had corrupted through sin, represents or is even a vehicle for redeeming grace. Pious Christians have gone to lengths to avoid even the appearance of drunkenness by diluting wine with water (a common practice among the more circumspect circles of the ancient world); monks continued this practice long after undiluted table wine became common in Christian Europe. In the late Middle Ages, Heinrich of Langenstein (d. 1397), a leading theologian at Paris and Vienna, may be taken as typical of the Catholic attitude: he encouraged Viennese, whose income from wine trade was considerable, to restrict the growing of wine grapes, since wine's higher alcoholic content led to more drunkenness than did beer brewed from grain. Thus temperance or moderation in the use of alcohol has often been characteristic of Christian teaching.

The modern temperance movement's advocacy of complete abstinence from alcoholic beverages arose in the 19th century. In the 17th and 18th centuries distilled liquor—initially made by distilling fruits (brandy, *Branntwein*) and later from various grains (whiskey, vodka, gin) or sugar cane by-products (rum)—became readily available at cheap prices. Distilled spirits were used for medicinal purposes as early as A.D. 1100 in Europe. They became widespread only from the 17th century as merchants, especially the Dutch, found spirits easier to store and transport and more profitable to sell than wine or beer. By the early 18th century cheap gin was causing great social dislocation in London and elsewhere.

The temperance movement in a strict sense began in North America. Although a full range of alcohol from beer to rum was consumed in the colonies, especially at social celebrations, traditional social norms kept drunkenness in check. Consumption continued to grow after the American Revolution, reaching 7.1 gallons of absolute alcohol annually for each adult over 15 years of age by 1810. Perhaps half of that amount was taken in the form of distilled spirits. The problem became acute on the frontier, in part because social norms were particularly weak there and partly because grain made into whiskey was far more easily transported than grain itself and became a medium of exchange. Between 1790 and 1830, when drinking in the USA was at its highest level, the country was going through its unruly adolescence in which democratic liberty and rugged individualism were often uncritically exalted. The temperance movement represented, to a large degree, an effort by moral and religious elites to temper unchecked individualism and to establish a new set of social norms. It was part of a much larger effort to "reform" America; antiprofanity, antislavery, antiwar efforts prison reform, women's rights, Sunday "blue laws," and many other causes were enthusiastically supported by clergy and lay reformers.

In 1784 the Philadelphia physician Benjamin Rush warned about the dangers to physical and moral health posed by distilled liquor. In Germany, Christoph Wilhelm Hufeland, court physician in Berlin, made similar claims; in Britain Thomas Trotter's Edinburgh Latin dissertation (1788) was published as *An Essay, Medical, Philosophical, and Chemical, on Drunkenness* (1804). Stimulated by Rush, Presbyterians throughout New England and the Middle Atlantic states passed resolutions against intemperance (1811/12). Quakers and Methodists had denounced the use of distilled spirits as early as the 1780s. What later became the American Temperance Society was organized nationwide in 1826. With the organization came a shift from advocating moderate use of alcohol and the denunciation of hard liquor to the advocacy of total abstinence from all nonmedicinal alcohol. The American Temperance Society endorsed total abstinence in 1836. Lyman Beecher's *Six Sermons on Intemperance*, delivered in 1825 and published in 1826, greatly encouraged the change. Average annual absolute alcohol consumption dropped from seven gallons to three gallons per person between 1830 and 1840.

Leaders in the movement succeeded in convincing legislators in many states to pass prohibition laws, beginning with the famous Maine Law in 1851; distilled liquor already had been banned in Maine in 1846. Most of these laws, however, had been repealed or enforcement had lapsed by the late 1850s. The nation's attention was diverted to the question of the abolition of slavery.

After the Civil War, a new temperance movement began in 1873 and 1874 when women in Hillsboro, Ohio, began holding prayer vigils and boycotts in front of drug stores and taverns, primarily in opposition to illegal and unlicensed liquor sales. This women's crusade developed into the Women's Christian Temperance Union, which enjoyed mass support. Once more the temperance movement was part of a larger cluster of reform efforts, among them women's rights, "home protection" (women's suffrage), antiprostitution, and education. As America became industrialized, urban poverty and social ills encouraged alcoholism. The fact that most residents of the cities were non-Protestants who defended moderate social drinking based on the traditional social norms limiting drunkenness, made the evils of urban alcoholism seem worse to the largely Protestant leadership of the temperance movement. As Roman Catholic leaders, who had always preached against drunkenness, perceived that traditional social limits on drinking were dissolving in the new urban settings, some of them also began to encourage abstinence. A few had done so already in the 1830s. Business leaders and industrialists, such as Andrew Carnegie and, later, Henry Ford, encouraged the temperance movement as a way to make the labor force more productive.

Politicians, caught between immigrant constituencies and "progressive" urban reformers, wavered. Several independent prohibition parties emerged. Organization of the Anti-Saloon League (1895) marked the final stage: the emergence of a bipartisan, politically activist movement dedicated to a legislative prohibition of the manufacture and sale of beverage alcohol. Intense lobbying and electoral politics on the local, state, and national level led to the 18th Amendment to the Constitution and its enabling legislation, the Volstead Act, in 1918 (effective, Jan. 1, 1920).

In the 1970s historians began to take a much more positive view of the temperance movement and the Prohibition era. Statistical studies show that consumption of alcohol did drop during Prohibition, from 2.6 gallons per capita annually to about one gallon in 1934, immediately after repeal. Deaths from alcohol-related diseases declined. Looking back, scholars view temperance advocates no longer as fundamentalist fanatics seeking authoritarian control of a society in the midst of change; rather, they are understood, both before the Civil War and after, as progressive reformers seeking to establish new social norms. The linkage between the movement for women's suffrage and temperance has been studied.

After the repeal of national prohibition laws, Alcoholics Anonymous continued the total abstinence approach, with a quasi-religious faith in the "twelve steps" to recovery from alcoholism. Scientific research on alcoholism developed significantly. Consumption of alcohol slowly increased to the levels of the early 1900s (2.82 gallons per person in the late 1970s).

The temperance movement developed in other industrialized Protestant countries. In Northern Germany, as an example, high grain production in Prussia east of the Elbe River stimulated distilling in the early 19th century. Schnapps, especially after it began to be distilled from potatoes, became a cheap drink for the laboring masses. German middle-class liberals joined with pietist Protestants to encourage abstinence from distilled liquors, especially after Robert Baird, a representative of the American Temperance Society, published *Histoire des sociétés de tempérance des Unis d'Amerique* (1836; German trans., 1837). Johann Gerhard Oncken, leader of the Baptist movement in Germany, had founded a temperance society at Hamburg as early as 1830. Unlike the American movement, the German temperance advocates encouraged the moderate use of beer and wine as alternatives to distilled spirits. The defeat of the liberal constitutional movement in 1848 set back the temperance movement in a manner similar to the Civil War in the USA. In the 1870s a rebirth took place, leading to the founding of the *Deutscher Verein* in 1878. *Deutscher Verein* worked with government administrators to control alcoholism through the licensing of taverns, taxation, and discretionary treatment of drunkards. Annual absolute alcohol consumption dropped from 10.2 liters a person in 1873 to 9.1 liters in 1900 and 6.9 liters in 1913.

In addition to these social factors, subtle theological changes were also at work. It is likely that the Protestant rejection of a sacramental theology in which created things are real vehicles for God's grace encouraged the modern "scientific" distinction between physical and spiritual reality. No longer capable both of being used salvifically, the "fruit of the earth and product of human hands," became at first a "neutral" natural product, which ironically was respiritualized as "demon rum."

**Bibliography.** T. L. Smith, *Revivalism and Social Reform in Mid-Nineteenth Century America* (1957); M. Keller, ed., *International Bibliography of Studies on Alcohol, 1901–1950*, 2 vols. (1966); B. Harrison, *Drink and the Victorians: The Temperance Question in England, 1815–1872* (1971); N. Clark, *Deliver Us from Evil: An Interpretation of American Prohibition* (1976); J. S. Blocker, Jr., *Give to the Winds Thy Fears: Woman's Temperance Crusade, 1873–1874* (1979); W. J. Rorabaugh, *The Alcoholic Republic: An American Tradition* (1979); A. E. Dingle, *The Campaign for Prohibition in Victorian England: The United Kingdom Alliance, 1872–1895* (1980); M. E. Lender and J. K. Martin, *Drinking in America: A History* (1982); M. E. Lender, ed., *Dictionary of American Temperance Biography: From Temperance Reform to Alcohol Research, the 1600s to the 1980s* (1984); J. S. Roberts, *Drink, Temperance, and the Working Class in Nineteenth Century Germany* (1984); K. A. Kerr, *Organized for Prohibition: A New History of the Anti-Saloon League* (1985); R. Bordin, *Frances Willard: A Biography* (1986).

DENNIS D. MARTIN

**Temple, William** (1881–1942). Anglican. Born in Exeter, Devonshire, he was educated at Rugby School and Balliol College, Oxford, and was president of Oxford Union (1904). During his time as a fellow and lecturer in philosophy, Queen's College, Oxford (1904–10), he was ordained deacon in the Church of England (1908). He became headmaster of Repton School (1910–14); rector of St. James, Picadilly, London (1914–18); canon of Westminster (1919–21); bishop of Manchester (1921–29); archbishop of York (1929–42); and archbishop of Canterbury (1942–44). In his ministry he took a leading part in social movements, becoming president of the Worker's Educational Association; in missionary affairs, being one of the delegates at the Jerusalem Conference (1928); in ecumenical relationships, presiding over the Edinburgh Conference (1937); and in forward movements in his own church. He gave the Gifford Lectures in Scotland and lectured in the USA. He wrote many books and articles, including *The Faith and Modern Thought; Church and Nation* (1915), *Mens Creatrix* (1917), *Christus Veritas* (1924), *Essays on Christian Politics* (1927), *Nature, Man and God* (1934), *Readings in St. John's Gospel* (1939), and *Christianity and Social Order* (1942). He contributed to the book *Foundations* and edited *The Pilgrim* (1920–27). He was chairman of the commission which produced the report entitled *Doctrine in the Church of England*.

F. W. DILLISTONE

**Templeton Prize.** Annual award recognizing those who through original and pioneering ways have advanced understanding of the knowledge and love of God. It was established in 1972 by Sir John Templeton. Nominations were sought from leaders of all the world's major religions, but the Templeton Foundation also considered others whose names were submitted. A board of judges and advisors participated in the decision. By 1987 the prize was worth $330,000 and its recipient was Stanley L. Jaki, a Hungarian-born Benedictine monk, a world authority on physics described as "one of the greatest of all modern champions of a positive relation of theology to rigorous science." In 1988 the prize went to the Burmese-born Muslim leader Inamullah Khano. Other winners have included Mother Teresa of Calcutta, Brother Roger of the Taizé monastic community, evangelist Billy Graham, and Russian author Aleksandr Solzhenitsyn.

J. D. DOUGLAS

**Tennant, Frederick Robert** (1886–1957). Anglican. Born in Burslem, Staffs, he was educated at Caius College, Cambridge, and ordained in 1891. He became chaplain of Caius College (1897–99); rector of Hockwold (1903–13); lecturer in theology and fellow of Trinity College, Cambridge (1913– ); and a fellow of the British Academy (1935). He wrote *The Origin and Propagation of Sin* (1902), *The Sources of the Doctrine of the Fall and Original Sin* (1903), *The Concept of Sin* (1912), *Philosophical Theology* (vol. 1, 1928; vol. 2, 1930), and *The Nature of Belief* (1943).

F. W. DILLISTONE

**Tenney, Merrill Chapin** (1904–1985). NT scholar and educator. Born in Chelsea, Mass., he was educated at Nyack Missionary Training Institute, Gordon College, Boston University, and Harvard University (Ph.D., 1944). His area of specialization was biblical and patristic Greek. After teaching at Gordon College for many years, he joined the Wheaton College faculty in 1944 as professor of Bible and theology. He was the dean of the graduate school from 1947 to 1971, and then continued teaching until his retirement in 1977. Tenney was not known as an innovator but rather as one who reverenced the Scriptures and made the complexities of NT scholarship understandable to the students of his day. He was revered as a teacher but reached a far wider audience through his published works, which include *Resurrection Realities* (1945), *John: The Gospel of Belief* (1948), *Galatians: The Charter of Christian Liberty* (1951), *The Genius of the Gospels* (1956), *Interpreting Revelation* (1957), *NT Survey* (1961), and *NT Times* (1965). His best-known edited work is the *Zondervan Pictorial Encyclopedia of the Bible* (4 vols., 1975).

WALTER A. ELWELL

**Teresa, Mother** (1910– ). Founder of the Missionaries of Charity. Born Agnes Gonxha Bojaxhiv in Skopje, Albania, she joined the Irish Loreto Sisters in order to become a missionary in India. Arriving in Calcutta in 1929, she took life vows in 1937 and joined Entally Loreto school as a geography teacher, but felt called in 1946 to work in the slums. Her new vocation was recognized by

Rome in 1948 and the Missionaries of Charity was accepted as a diocesan religious congregation in 1950, its members taking a fourth vow "to give wholehearted and free service to the poorest of the poor."

Mother Teresa acknowledges that their children's home, home for dying destitutes, and relief programs are not the whole answer to Calcutta's problems, but she sees the work done there and elsewhere as a necessary drop in the ocean performed in the spirit of Matt. 25. Mother Teresa took Indian citizenship in 1949 and has been honored with the various Indian awards, as well as internationally with the first Templeton Prize for Progress in Religion (1973), the Nobel Peace Prize (1979), and many honorary degrees. Prizes and donations further the work of the Missionaries of Charity, which has expanded worldwide since gaining papal recognition in 1965. Mother Teresa founded the parallel Missionary Brothers of Charity in 1963 and received permission in 1966 for Brother Andrew (Ian Travers-Ball, an Australian Jesuit who came to India in 1954) to become their head, or "General Servant." Since 1975 the Brothers have also made foundations outside India. By 1986 there were over 2400 Sisters and more than 370 Brothers in India and across the world from Venezuela to Taiwan.

PHILIP HILLYER

**Terrorism.** The use or threat of violence to create fear and destabilize society. Terrorist organizations or individuals seek to further some cause, not by directly attacking state military and political forces but by spreading panic and fear in society through indiscriminate attacks on people and property. Terrorism is not a political ideology but a strategy—a way of seeking change in the institutions and practices of a state.

Students of terrorism generally emphasize four distinctive features of this phenomenon. First, it involves violence against people. Since the aim is to create fear, every member of society becomes a potential target. Children, diplomats, political leaders, businesspeople, and military personnel are particularly attractive victims. Whereas war destruction is aimed chiefly at soldiers and military installations, the terrorist makes no distinction between combatants and noncombatants. The most effective terrorism avoids obvious targets identified with the regime, party, or policy being fought. Destruction and death must come by chance.

Second, terrorism seeks to achieve its aims through psychological rather than physical means. The goal of terrorism is to break the bond of community solidarity, to call into public question the established rules and institutions by which community stability and order are maintained. It does so by carrying out dramatic acts, demonstrating the vulnerability of the state and the inability of government to protect people from lawlessness. Lacking the ability to defeat police and military forces, terrorists avoid direct engagement with them altogether. Since the government has a monopoly of power within a state, terrorists use violence to psychologically equalize their position, drawing power by creating an invincible public perception. Brian Jenkins, a student of terrorism, explains that, "You don't do terrorism to kill people. You do it to create an echo that makes you larger than life. No echo, no success." This is why the number of deaths or even the number of hijackings and bombings is not an adequate measure of the impact of terrorism on society. The chief test is the degree to which terrorism has destabilized society and harmed the fabric of community solidarity.

Third, terrorism is usually a deliberate, methodical, and organized campaign to implement defined political objectives. While terrorists employ seemingly random violence, their aims and strategy are carefully planned to maximize the impact of their limited resources and personnel. Whether the actions are carried out by individuals, small groups, or large organizations, publicity is their agent. Terrorists seek to carry out acts of violence which will receive prominent television, radio, and press coverage. This is why common terrorist tactics include bombings in highly populated areas, hijackings, and kidnapping—each of which has proven an effective psychological weapon in modern democratic societies.

The importance of the media is demonstrated by the widespread coverage of European and Middle East terrorism in 1985 and 1986, with the result that American travel to Western Europe declined precipitously, especially during the summer of 1986. The importance of publicity was particularly demonstrated by the use of terrorism by the Palestinian Liberation Organization (PLO). The PLO policy of random civilian violence brought much publicity and gave universal recognition to the cause of Palestinian statehood.

Discipline and organization are vital to terrorist organizations. In order to accomplish their objectives groups rely on secrecy, discipline, and effective organization. The organized character of modern terrorism was illustrated by the Irish Republican Army (IRA) in planting 49 bombs in 22 Northern Ireland towns in one night. Simultaneous bombings at airline ticket counters at Rome and Vienna airports, and multiple bombings in Paris during 1986 were also the results of careful coordination.

Fourth, terrorism is violence perpetrated by nongovernment agents, although governments may give important support. There can be no doubt that governments have carried out untold evil against their own citizens. Joseph Stalin's genocidal campaigns against the peasant landowners (kulaks) in the 1920s and the forced enslavement of millions of workers in Siberia are examples, as are Pol Pot's massacre and forced starvation of some 2 million Cambodians and the Argentine military government's campaign in the 1970s against opponents, resulting in the disappearance of 10,000 children and adults. Some define such indiscriminate violence as state terrorism, but it is important to distinguish between authorized, indiscriminate government violence and the unauthorized, indiscriminate violence of nongovernment groups. The identification of terrorism with nongovernment actors does not mean that states have not supported terrorism. The increasing impact of terrorism in the later 1900s derived partly from government sponsorship of international terrorist organizations. The governments of Libya, Iran, and Syria, for example, were alleged to be major supporters of Palestinian terrorism. The USSR directly or indirectly trained and equipped terrorists. But, while states sponsored transnational terrorism, most terrorism was undertaken by organizations and agents not under the control of any state. Their independence was usually a carefully guarded asset.

Guerrilla warfare, a form of unconventional warfare carried out largely in rural areas, also differs from terrorism. Like terrorism, guerrilla warfare seeks to undermine an existing regime and guerrilla fighters occasionally use terrorism as a tool. Random, indiscriminate killing simply to achieve fear is not their major strategy. Their chief aim is to topple a regime through a war of attrition which engages military forces sporadically only when advantageous to the irregulars and which seeks to undermine the political and economic order through random killings and destructions. A goal of guerrilla warfare is to gain rural support, strangling urban areas and forcing the capitulation of ruling elites. In Nicaragua, for example, groups such as the Sandinistas in the 1970s and the contras in the 1980s were guerrillas, not terrorists.

Throughout history, groups have conspired to challenge the power of rulers by carrying out assassinations, sudden raids, and other acts of terror. But modern terrorism is a more pervasive and international phenomenon. Historically, terrorism was chiefly a problem within state boundaries. As the world became more interdependent economically and politically after World War II, and mass media made publicity easier to achieve, the nature of terrorism became increasingly transnational. Major financial and military support was readily available from foreign sources, especially revolutionary governments. The effects of terrorism similarly changed. Whereas the effects of past terrorist activities were generally confined to individual states, terrorism through the last half of the 20th century was a global cancer, affecting many countries simultaneously.

Much of the international terrorism in this period was rooted in two contemporary political movements—communist totalitarianism and Islamic radicalism. While the political aims of these movements differed, they shared an abhorrence of democratic values and an acceptance of violence as a weapon for political change. Individuals attracted to both movements shared a deep, zealous commitment to their revolutionary political and religious ideologies and were capable of self-sacrifice for a cause they considered larger than themselves. Radical Shi'ite Muslims in Iran and Lebanon, for example, eagerly sacrificed their lives in service of the holy cause of Islam.

Modern international terrorism was pioneered in the 1960s by the PLO, which introduced airline hijacking as an international weapon, and European radical groups, which dramatized the vulnerability of modern society through bold kidnappings, assassinations, and bombings. Terrorists had greater international impact during the 1980s than during any previous period in history. During the early 1980s some 350 to 450 terrorist acts were committed each year, resulting in the deaths of hundreds of people annually. Particularly in the summer of 1985 and through 1986, terrorists succeeded in carrying out a number of bold and dramatic acts of violence. Some of the most important of these included the June 1985 hijacking of a Trans-World Airlines (TWA) airplane in the Middle East, the midair explosion of an Air India jet, the seizure in October of the Italian cruise ship *Achille Lauro*, the November hijacking of an Egyptian airliner and the subsequent bloody rescue attempt in Malta, the December massacres at El Al Airlines ticket counters at the Rome and Vienna airports, the April 1986 explosion on a TWA airliner on its way from Rome to Athens, and the April explosion at a West Berlin discotheque. Since many of these acts were carried out against travelers, foreign travel to Western Europe and the Middle East declined precipitously during 1986.

Motivation of modern terrorists by clearly defined political objectives contrasts with late 19th-century terrorism in Europe, and especially in Russia, which was guided chiefly by the ideology of anarchism. Major goals of terrorist organizations in the late 1900s were varied. Some groups, such as the Kurds in Iran, the Basques in Spain, and the Croatians in Yugoslavia, seek to establish a new national state. Such an organization as the PLO has a complex political agenda involving creation of one state and destruction of another. Groups such as the Armed Forces for National Liberation of Puerto Rico, the IRA, and the PLO seek to liberate a territory from control of others. Organizations may seek to subvert existing political regimes (such as the Tupamaros of Uruguay and the Montoneros of Argentina attempted to do in the 1960s and 1970s). Some groups, such as the Red Brigade of Italy, the Weatherman Underground in the USA, and the Baader Meinhof group from West Germany, because of a profound alienation from existing society, seek the radical transformation of the contemporary sociopolitical order.

Given the superior military power and technical skill of the state, terrorists have seldom succeeded in their political objectives. Authoritarian and totalitarian regimes will be largely immune to the threat of terrorism, but if democracies adopt a siege mentality and seek to contain terrorists solely by restricting social freedom, terrorists will have succeeded in undermining the central tenet of an open, pluralistic society. The challenge facing Western democracies in the midst of international terrorism was to devise a low-level, long-term strategy involving intelligence and counter-terrorism to identify and destroy the breeding and training grounds which stimulated the intense hatred and encouraged the belief that such tragic methods could succeed.

MARK R. AMSTUTZ

**Tertiaries.** Members of monastic third orders after the first order of monks and the second order of nuns. These laypeople take simple vows, remain outside a monastery or convent, and follow to some degree a portion of a monastic rule. The juridical status of the various third orders in the Roman Catholic Church is now determined by canons 702–707 of the Code of Canon Law. The formation of new third orders in addition to those already authorized is forbidden, and while religious superiors may receive individuals into their third order, the erection of new sodalities of tertiaries requires the approval of the local ordinary. Various congregations of Dominican, Franciscan, and Carmelite sisters, who engage in some active ministry like teaching, nursing, or missionary work, are sometimes called regular third orders. These activists contrast to the contemplative branch of the same religious family, or second order.

GEORGES A. BARROIS

**Thailand.** *See* SOUTHEAST ASIA.

**Theodicy.** From the title of a work of Gottfried Leibniz (1646–1716), *Théodicée* (from Gk. *theos*, meaning "God," and *dike*, meaning "justice"). Theodicy is thus a philosophical attempt to vindicate the justice and goodness of God, especially in view of the fact of evil, which is normally felt or judged to constitute a challenge to such attributes of God. It is sometimes insisted that God would have prevented evil if he could, and is in the course of a long struggle to eliminate it, but that his power is limited (William James, H. G. Wells). A variant of this is the doctrine of E. S. Brightman (*The Problem of God* and *The Philosophy of*

*Religion*) and his followers that evil is the result of a "given" within the nature of God himself which he has not yet been able to overcome. Still another form is the contention that God created a kingdom of moral persons with free will. Personality involves freedom and since moral personality can be achieved only through the struggle against evil, God must permit evil.

Other forms of theodicy seek their end by working on the concept of evil itself. There is the doctrine of Augustine and others that evil is negative and so was not created by God. The British Neo-Hegelians have taught that this world is a "vale of soul making," that soul making requires struggle against evil, and that evil is therefore a good, a positive element in making this the best of all possible worlds. A corollary is that evil is to be compared with the dark and ugly shading in a perfect picture, which nevertheless is an indispensable contribution to the perfection of the whole.

A philosopher such as Cyril Joad, on the contrary (see his *God and Evil*), after years of feeling driven by the fact of evil to adopt an agnostic position, was finally forced by a deeper and more intimate reconsideration of the same facts to a belief in God. It is doubtful that, in his later view, the evil in the world would call for a theodicy; it rather constitutes one. The atheist position, especially popular in the 1960s and 1970s, was that theism's answers to evil were hopelessly irrational and that humanistic determinism offered the only coherent consideration of the human predicament. The human constructs of the various major theodicies, however, are all logically consistent if their basic premises regarding God, evil, and human freedom are accepted. Theodicies are merely apologetic extensions of various theological systems and do not stand apart from their inherent worldview and doctrine of God.

ANDREW K. RULE

**Theological Education, Recent Trends in (U.K.).** In the late 20th century theological education in the United Kingdom was offered by a wide variety of institutions and agencies. A comprehensive range of university courses included liturgy and pastoralia. Comparative religion was a popular subject, and subsidiary courses permitted students to relate theology to such subjects as sociology and politics. Students proceeded not only to ordination but a variety of professions. Part-time educational programs and facilitated contextual training for ordinands were available.

Like other departments in faculties of arts, theology and religious studies had a low priority as government policy emphasized scientific and technological subjects. Senior staff were not always replaced on retirement, and syllabuses had to be revised to cope with the loss of staff. This worried theological colleges which used universities for part of their ordination training and all who valued the pursuit of theology in the environment provided by the universities.

Theological colleges in such places as London, Oxford, Cambridge, Bristol, Birmingham, Manchester, Durham, and Edinburgh made extensive use of the universities. Other colleges introduced their own degree programs, validated by the Council for National Academic Awards, while others administered nondegree programs. Theological education by extension courses were provided by the Open University; St. John's College, Nottingham; Calvin Theological College; Westminster College, Oxford; and St. Colm's College, Edinburgh. Wolsey Hall, Oxford, administered a correspondence B.D. degree program at the University of London, and correspondence courses leading to other qualifications were available at such institutions as the London Bible College and the Bible Training Institute of Glasgow.

A relative newcomer to the field of theological education and training for ministry, training courses prepared as many priests and ministers as did all other theological colleges. These seminaries "without walls" served people in secular occupations through residential weekends, weeknight seminars, weekend placements, and summer schools over a three- or four-year period leading to qualifications for stipendiary as well as nonstipendiary and lay ministries. Some of these courses built on the student's secular work experience for theological reflection and encouraged students to view their workplace as their sphere of ministry and mission after completion of their training. Students normally studied 10 hours or spent as much as one-half of this time on church or community work, integrating theory and practice. Courses might link with universities and lead to university qualifications.

Academic studies increasingly meshed with practical and professional training ordination, and ecclesiastical and secular placements exposed students to contemporary issues facing Christian ministry and mission. The addition of new courses and the consequent overloading of the syllabuses, pressure by special interest groups, the challenge of theological diversity in a pluralistic church, and different perceptions of the church's role in society all raised fundamental questions about the needs of church ministry and how to meet such needs. Piecemeal programs needed more clearly defined rationale, but widely differing perceptions made agreement on objectives and methods difficult. How best to use increasingly limited university facilities became a matter of debate, some colleges extensively supplementing university studies with practical courses and others dissatisfied with the content and style of academic theology to such an extent that they attempted themselves to provide all needed studies and training. Influenced by the

third world, various schemes widened the context of study to include not only local churches but also local communities. Scripture and Christian tradition were combined with social and political issues to set the agenda for ministerial training.

Theological colleges traditionally used the linear model, which concentrated on teaching the *text*, for example, the Bible or one of the major academic disciplines of theology. Educators assumed the truths or principles learned could and would be subsequently applied in the *context* in which the student subsequently ministered. This model in varying degrees gave way to an integrated model in which theory was applied to practice and experience, followed by reflection. The method used student placements, ranging from two-week pastoral observation to assignments which might run throughout the whole of the academic session. By the 1980s internship training in local churches was required of all students training at colleges for the ministry of the United Reformed Churches in the final or fourth year of training.

The need to relate theology to the wider concerns of life led to new and innovative forms of training. The Urban Theology Unit in Sheffield provided a range of courses specifically designed to relate theological education to community concerns. Academic work linked with social analysis, church and community work in various community settings, and courses led to either a diploma in theology and mission or community studies or a doctorate in ministry. The doctoral program included work with the New York Theological Seminary.

At Manchester the Baptist, Congregational, and United Reformed Church colleges offered a fully integrated four-year course with three components: college-university, church, and community. Training in each continued throughout the four years, replacing the one-year internship program and exposing students to the challenge presented by the community as well as the church. The time devoted to each area varied from year to year. In the first year, students spent more time on theological study and community analysis and reflection than on pastoral involvement. The second and third years increased pastoral work, while academic work decreased and community and church work increased in the final years. The church placements were in the same area as the community placement and students reflected on their experience in the community not only with the college staff but also with members of the local church. Skills and communication, education, and motivation were highly regarded, and each local congregation chose a pastoral support group of laypersons to assist the college staff in the training of the student. Training for ministry became a partnership between the local church and the college, with the laity playing an essential role. The concept is that what the student learns about the implications of theology for life is essentially what each church member needs to know and vice versa. The course's strong mission orientation encouraged students to view the deprived areas of the cities as their possible sphere of ministry.

A number of colleges less successfully integrated forms of theological education and training for ministry because of their geographical isolation from areas of great human need so some purchased property in urban priority areas as extension centers of the college. Thus St. John's Anglican College, Durham, maintained an Urban Studies Unit in Gateshead. A staff member and students lived in the area and attempted to relate their study and training to the needs of the local community during the students' final year of training.

Theological education was also undertaken by ecclesiastical and paraecclesiastical agencies. Both denominational and ecumenical centers provided postordination training for the clergy, including the Westminster Pastoral Foundation in London, St. George's House in Windsor, and the Northern Institute of Upholland; others such as the Manchester Christian Institute and the North of England Institute for Christian Education trained both clergy and laity. The William Temple Foundation in Manchester and the Northern Churches Training Group explored church and society relationships. Initiatives in education and training appeared likely to result from two seminal studies produced by the Church of England, the *Tiller* report and *Faith in the City*.

In the meantime ecumenical cooperation in theological education and ministerial training grew. The Cambridge Federation for Theological Colleges, like the Oxford Certificate in Theology, standardized training. Anglican and Free Church staff and students shared a common site in Birmingham (the Queen's College) and Manchester (the Northern Federation for Training in Ministry). Some of the training courses were ecumenical.

Among issues needing attention from educators remained aims and objectives of theological study within the differences of opinion over the church's role in society and the differing perceptions of faith and commitment within a pluralistic church. In ecumenical institutions planning a common core curriculum required a good deal of imagination and patience. Further, staff needed to be trained themselves in the skills of theological reflection. Help on social analysis was available from professionals in social and community work, and collaborative theological education enriched both fields, but those responsible for training for Christian ministry needed to be competent not only in academic theology but in the art of reflecting theologically on contemporary

culture in the light of the gospel. Contextual training assisted both staff and students in discerning what makes the gospel good news in today's world, but its value depended both upon the degree to which staff and students became involved in the local community and upon the rigor of their study of the gospel and the Christian tradition.

Spiritual formation was included in all the courses leading to ordination, but personal spirituality continued to give problems. College communities were often fragmented, with some students living on campus and others in the community and pursuing a variety of courses, so that attendance at corporate acts of worship was affected. Questions by students concerning the nature and understanding of prayer in relation to Christian action also influenced the situation.

Training for lay members of the church featured prominently in theological education. As noted above, some plans trained laypeople and ordinands together, while others used laypeople to train ordinands. Much remained to be done to help laypeople become more effective both as church workers and in their own secular occupations.

**Bibliography.** J. J. Vincent, ed., *Alternative Theological Education* (1979); *The Cherwell Report: The Commission for Priestly Formation, Roman Catholic Episcopal Conference of England and Wales* (1979); J. Stein, ed., *Ministries for the 1980s* (1979); *Ministerial Formation: Report on the Consultation on Ministerial Formation* (1979); J. Tiller, *A Strategy for the Church's Ministry* (1983); P. H. Vaughan, ed., *Training for Diversity of Ministry* (1983); Archbishop of Canterbury's Commission on Urban Priority Areas, *Faith in the City: A Call for Action by Church and Nation* (1985).

R. J. McKelvey

## Theological Education in the USA, Trends in.

In the 20th century the procedures for training ministers underwent sweeping changes. Germany no longer dominated the field, although significant work still took place in universities there, and American doctoral students were attracted to these, as well as to university-related theological faculties in Switzerland, Scotland, England, and the Netherlands. However, the majority of ministers were schooled at seminaries in the USA and Canada, and the North American model of professional training was widely followed in Latin America, Africa, and Asia.

Although many clergy valued the academic training they received in seminary, educators tended to regard the traditional German model of the theological sciences with its fourfold divisions of Bible, systematic theology (dogmatics), church history (historical theology), and practical theology (catechetics, homiletics, and liturgics) as inadequate. New areas of study contributed to the transformation of the minister from being a comprehensive interpreter and shepherd of the faith to a position as manager of a local institution. Accordingly, theological education increasingly took on the character of a melange of introductions to a wide variety of disciplines, and in the opinion of some critics the academic studies had little relevance to the clergyperson's successful functioning in the real world of institutional ministry. Moreover, the diversity of undergraduate education received by seminary students (with no one accepted preseminary program even in the liberal arts like those for law or medicine) built no common fund of knowledge for their studies. This further hindered them from receiving a unified, consistent theological training.

Debate raged among educators from the 1960s about the very nature of the enterprise and the need for "reform." Much of the argumentation centered around "praxis," an emphasis which flowed particularly from black, feminist, and liberation theologies. More concerns were expressed about culture, spirituality, oppression/liberation, and experiential faith. The need was seen for seminaries to engage in case studies and field education. Doctrinal orthodoxy, theological reflection, and scholarly inquiry were deemphasized by liberal mainline and some conservative institutions.

Theological education for the laity received more attention. The discipling of believers, mediating the Christian tradition to them, and equipping them for service may well be the most important task facing the church in the 21st century. To insure Christianity's forward movement, training for the laity is as important as that for the clergy, but theological study narrowed to the education of clergy and theology converted into a science accessible mostly to scholars. "Christian" or "religious" education failed to provide ordered learning for the believer regarding the texts, history, beliefs, and practices of the faith. This problem was made worse by the professionalization of theology (as restricted to the seminary), an overemphasis on homiletics (simple exposition of the authoritative text as settled truth and its passive acceptance as application to life), and a generalizing of education. Teaching in the Christian community lacked order as a systematized, sequential process of the layperson's life as a believer.

Because of the open-endedness and laissez-faire nature of North American Christianity, the quality of theological instruction was very uncertain. The Association of Theological Schools in the United States and Canada (ATS), founded in 1918, tried to deal with the problem by formally accrediting graduate education and upholding high standards. In 1968 it even proposed a model curriculum for theological education, with entry and exit requirements and an emphasis on shared responsibility of faculty members for the spiritual formation of ministerial students and of departments for socially responsible theology and ministry. This was never fully accepted. In the 1980s

ATS included 204 member institutions and trained about 75 to 80 percent of all graduate-level theological students in North America. To broaden their educational outreach, over one-third of these shared library and faculty resources and course cross-listing with other colleges, universities, and seminaries.

Nevertheless, many people received only a modicum of theological education for the pastorate, either in Bible institutes and colleges and university religious studies programs or through correspondence courses and on-the-job service. There is no way of determining how many ministers were trained in this fashion, but the numbers were substantial in fundamentalist, pentecostal, and nondenominational bodies and in black and ethnic churches where pastors were called by local congregations with little or no attention paid to ordination standards.

In academics increasing emphasis was placed upon theological study as professional or "vocational" education. Hence, there was more concern with "practical" subjects, skills, and techniques, and less with the "life of the mind." Still, great uncertainty existed within theological institutions as to whether practical experience should be given in the school or gained through internships or at the place of first employment. To resolve this difficulty, seminaries incorporated more course work from the social and behavioral sciences into the professional curriculum and stressed continuing education once the person was on the job. The general theory was that the complex nature of the minister's work—involving the functions of teacher, physician, social worker, lawyer, and manager—necessitated at least a superficial instruction in these and other areas. Further complicating the picture was the trend for graduates to enter a wide variety of specialized ministries, such as institutional and industrial chaplaincies, Christian education, campus ministry, itinerant evangelism, mass communications, overseas development, or national church boards and agencies.

Enrollments in seminaries increased after World War II due to the resurgence of evangelicalism and the transformation of conservative Bible institutes into regular colleges which fed students into graduate-level theological schools. However, enrollments in Roman Catholic and major Protestant denominational seminaries stagnated or declined in the 1960s, and several were closed or merged with other schools, while evangelical seminaries and Southern Baptist institutions flourished. By the late 1980s five Southern Baptist institutions ranked among the top 10 in enrollment, headed by the 4000-student Southwestern Baptist Theological Seminary in Fort Worth, Tex. Four evangelical seminaries (led by Fuller in Pasadena, Calif.) made this select group. The only mainline school among these 10 leaders was the Presbyterian Church (USA) Princeton Theological Seminary in New Jersey. However, demographic patterns contributed to a leveling of enrollments in evangelical seminaries, and Southern Baptist enrollment slipped with internal denominational strife in the 1980s.

The most important demographic development from the 1970s was the influx of women and older students. These nontraditional students included people making a midlife career change and ministers wishing to improve their skills. Conservative denominations continued to discourage women from entering the ministry, but the percent of women in seminary student bodies rose from 10 percent in 1972 to 27 percent in 1987; in mainline Protestant schools their share of student bodies was considerably higher. Between 1976 and 1987 the amount of women in preordination degree programs doubled, while in absolute numbers male enrollments declined slightly. In 1987 the number of women completing degree work and qualifying as candidates for ordination ranged from 29.8 percent in the American Baptist Churches to 47.6 percent in the United Church of Christ and 52.8 percent in the United Church of Canada. These data encompass the 201 schools that reported to ATS in 1988.

Theological seminaries have sought to redress the imbalance of racial and ethnic minorities in their student populations, but success has been limited. Between 1972 and 1987 the black enrollment increased from 2.6 percent to 6 percent of the student total. Much of this was in traditionally black institutions, and it included an increase in the proportion of women among black seminarians from 8.7 percent to 29.4 percent. The ratio of women to men among black theological students is now higher than the ratio among whites. In 1987 Hispanics comprised only 2.5 percent and native Americans 0.24 percent of seminary student bodies. Pacific and Asian-Americans made up 3 percent, proportionally a better representation at graduate levels than for other minorities.

A major development was the almost universal substitution of the M.Div. (Master of Divinity) for the B.D. (Bachelor of Divinity) as the professional theological degree. Students complained that people in other fields received masters or even doctoral degrees in their graduate studies, and thus they were disadvantaged. The new programs normally did not require any more time to complete than the traditional three-year ones, and alumni who held B.D. degrees could trade them in for the more prestigious M.Div. At the postgraduate level, most institutions replaced the traditional Th.D. and S.T.D. degrees with the Ph.D. A significant curricular innovation was the D.Min. (Doctor of Ministry) degree designed for full-time professionals currently in ministry who wished to improve their competence. It involved an addi-

tional year or two of work beyond the M.Div., and work often was done on a part-time basis. Among other things, it required the completion of a study project which tended to be more practically oriented than the academic dissertation customary in a Ph.D. program.

**Bibliography.** W. A. Brown, et al., *The Education of American Ministers* (1934); H. R. Niebuhr, D. D. Williams, and J. M. Gustafson, *The Advancement of Theological Education* (1957); *Theological Education* 5 (Spring 1969); E. Farley, *Theologia: The Fragmentation and Unity of Theological Education* (1983); C. M. Wood, *Vision and Discernment: An Orientation in Theological Study* (1985); Association of Theological Schools in the United States and Canada, *Fact Book on Theological Education* (1987/88); E. Farley, *The Fragility of Knowledge: Theological Education in the Church and the University* (1988); D. T. Hessel, ed., *Theological Education for Social Ministry* (1988); J. C. Hough, Jr., and B. G. Wheeler, *Beyond Clericalism: The Congregation as a Focus for Theological Education* (1988); K. Schuth, *Reason for the Hope: The Future of Roman Catholic Theologates* (1989).

RICHARD V. PIERARD

## Theological Schools in the United States and Canada, Association of (ATS).

Founded in 1918, the recognized accrediting agency for graduate professional theological education. More than 200 seminaries were members in the 1980s. The association promoted the improvement of theological education through research and publication of its findings along with the use of advisory and counseling teams for its constituent members. ATS also conducted seminars and other meetings for seminary faculty and administrators. It engaged in long-range planning to effectively use the resources available for theological education. ATS was a member in the Council on Postsecondary Accreditation and worked cooperatively with regional accrediting associations, other professional associations, state departments of education, the National Catholic Education Association, and professional organizations such as the American Academy of Religion, the American Theological Library Association, and the Academy of Parish Clergy.

ROBERT V. SCHNUCKER

## Theology, 20th-Century Trends in. *From 1900.*

In Western Christendom at the beginning of the 20th century three divergent theological positions occupied the field: Post-Tridentine Roman theology represented Roman orthodoxy; Protestantism was sharply divided between Protestant scholasticism, represented by such leaders as B. B. Warfield, A. Kuyper, and A. H. Strong, and liberalism, represented by, among others, William Adams Brown and A. C. McGiffert. Liberalism stemmed from Friedrich Schleiermacher but was tending more and more toward outright humanism. The Roman and Protestant conservatives were supernaturalistic and had much in common except for divergent views on soteriology and ecclesiology. In reaction to liberalism they tended to ignore or oppose modern culture. Modernism or liberalism loosely denoted views all the way from slight modifications of orthodoxy to systems or ideas indistinguishable from nontheistic humanism. In general, Roman orthodoxy rested on the authority of the church; Protestant scholasticism on the authority of the Bible, interpreted by the classical creeds (Westminster, Augsburg, or Dort); liberalism attempted to dispense with the idea of authority in favor of a freer, more inductive and empirical basis of belief. In the USA, where liberalism especially flourished, it was characterized by a strongly naturalistic bias, a "low" Christology, the interpretation of the Bible as a record of human experience and opinion, and the rejection of miracles. It voiced an optimistic humanism, speaking of man's "fall upward," of sin as maladjustment, of salvation as a working out of higher possibilities along evolutionary lines, of eschatology (if any) in Platonic rather than biblical terms, and of the kingdom of God as an indefinitely improvable system of human society. There were many variations and shadings of belief.

Neo-Thomism in the Roman Church continued into the 20th century. Papal influence on dogma was also strong, dogma being now finally defined by the pope alone. In orthodox Protestant circles the impacts of historical, biblical, and other sciences made themselves felt; and World War I shocked the optimism of liberals. From about 1914 to the mid-century, certain trends in Protestant thought can be followed.

***The Theology of Crisis.*** This, like Neo-Thomism, is a professed return to earlier theologies. The publication in 1919 of a commentary on Romans by Karl Barth marks the beginning of this important movement. Often called neo-orthodoxy, this school goes back philosophically to Kierkegaard and Kant, and theologically to the early Reformers, especially Martin Luther. As it first appeared, it was a violent protest against the humanism, "historicism," and "psychologism" within German theology. Under the leadership of Barth and Emil Brunner (*The Divine Human Encounter* [ET, 1943]; *Man in Revolt* [ET, 1947]; *The Divine Imperative* [ET, 1957]; *Revelation and Reason* [1946]) neo-orthodoxy penetrated all Protestant thinking, even if only to stimulate violent reaction. It was characterized by: (1) a deliberate attempt to eliminate from Christian theology all nonbiblical elements; (2) an appeal to the teachings of the Reformers themselves; (3) a fresh insistence on the classical creeds; (4) thoroughgoing insistence on the transcendence of God as opposed to all immanentism; (5) a stress on the radical nature of sin; (6) an interpretation of revelation as being primarily the self-disclosure of a person rather than the unveiling of propositions; and (7) a strong emphasis on the importance and necessity of personal decision and commitment; hence the name sometimes given, "existential"

theology, as concerned with the desperate need of the essential self.

***Qualified Liberalism.*** On the liberal side, there emerged a point of view which may be described as evangelical liberalism, not neo-orthodoxy but affected by it. The positions of Edwin Lewis (*A Christian Manifesto* [1934]; *The Faith We Declare* [1939]) or Walter Marshall Horton (*Our Christian Faith* [1947]; *Realistic Theology* [1934]) or H. H. Farmer (*God and Men* [1947]) are representative. While affirming the rights of historical criticism, such thinkers accepted the Bible as the supreme authority for faith, emphasized the reality and seriousness of sin, and (without too much attention to traditional formulas) strived to maintain a balance of transcendence and immanence. They emphasized the necessity of redemption from sin and Christ as the power of God unto salvation. There lingered an "unreconstructed" liberalism which carried on the humanist tradition. At the extreme of this spectrum was the view represented by Henry Nelson Wieman in *The Growth of Religion* (1938), *The Source of Human Good* (1946), and an essay in *Religious Liberals Reply* (1947), whose interpretation of Christianity used much of the traditional terminology without the traditional meaning.

***Biblical Theology.*** Most Protestants took more seriously than in the 19th century the Bible's authority. Biblical studies shifted from purely linguistic, literary, and historical-critical problems to theology, although in the main there was no attempt to discard critical views. In the latter years of the half-century especially, there has been a strong revival of biblical theology. Important scholars in this field included R. Bultmann, O. Cullmann, O. Proksch, Walther Eichrodt, C. H. Dodd, T. W. and William Manson, Sir Edwin Hoskyns, and A. G. Hebert, along with revived interest in Peter Taylor Forsyth. At the beginning of this period NT theology was dominant; in the latter part of it, interest in OT thought was renewed. Satisfactory synthesis of the scientific and theological approaches remained a problem.

***Philosophical Theology.*** Able exponents, such as F. R. Tennant, A. E. Taylor, William Temple, N. P. Williams, Reinhold Niebuhr, and D. C. Macintosh, were less disposed by the fifth decade of the century to construct purely rationalistic schemes or to attempt to expunge all mysteries from Christian faith. Nevertheless, however close to orthodoxy philosophical theology came, there remained a real difference between theologians who thought of paradox as the inevitable mark of God upon history, and those who deplored paradox as a theologian's word for intellectual failure.

***Other Voices.*** The Swedish scholars were somewhat in a class by themselves, although close to the neo-orthodox. Notably, Anders Nygren in *Agape and Eros* (1939), rejecting the classic concept of charity, reinterpreted the doctrine of love; and Bishop Gustaf Aulen's *Christus Victor* (1931) rehabilitated and reespoused the "ransom" theory of the atonement. Aulen's *Faith of the Christian Church* (ET, 1960) is a more systematic presentation of a theology which has issued out of the modern "Lutherforschung." Nels F. S. Ferre (*The Christian Understanding of God* [1951]) reinterpreted theology by combining evangelical insight with the metaphysic of Alfred North Whitehead. Paul Tillich's *Systematic Theology* (3 vols., 1951–63), stressed revelation and the Logos as center of the new life, yet was classed by some as neognostic.

Generally in theology from 1900 to 1950 there was a more christocentric approach and at the same time a greater stress on transcendence stopping short of sheer predestinarian omnipotence. Greater stress was given to the human element in revelation and to the focus of revelation in Christ; in Christology there was a more serious recognition of Christ's true humanity; in soteriology a return to the idea of atonement by vicarious sacrifice, yet with less emphasis on, or denial of, a penal element. In anthropology greater recognition was made of man's creatureliness, his finite, sinful nature; in ecclesiology a recovery of the meaning and authority of the church; in eschatology a revival of biblical categories and a reinterpretation of apocalyptic as a valid philosophy of history and destiny.

KENNETH J. FOREMAN

*From 1950.* Theological literature from 1950 on increasingly reflected evangelical, neoliberal, and humanist criticism of neo-orthodoxy. Ecumenical church union retained a vulnerable doctrine of religious authority; defection from objective biblical inspiration nurtured a proliferation of rival views. James D. Smart depicted *The Divided Mind of Modern Theology* (1967) through the lengthened impact of Barth and Bultmann, but the post-Bultmannian revolt paced by Ernst Käsemann (*The Testament of Jesus* [1968]) called for more continuity with the Jesus of history.

Neoliberalism sought to buttress confidence in reason and order by recycling process theology (Schubert M. Ogden, *The Reality of God and Other Essays* [1966]) which some promoted as a Christian conceptuality (John Cobb, Jr., *A Christian Natural Theology, Based on the Thought of Alfred North Whitehead* [1965]). The theory views the universe as necessary to God. Its appeal lay in reviving philosophical reasoning and nonmiraculous theism. It shaped no adequate doctrine of Jesus Christ. French Jesuit Pierre Teilhard de Chardin (1881–1955) sought to unite the cosmic and redemptive spheres in a comprehensive evolution toward "point Omega," unveiling Christ as central (*The Divine Milieu: An Essay on the Interior Life* [1960]) but minimizing Jesus of Nazareth.

Liberal theology was oriented mainly to social activism. The theology of revolution provided a supposed biblical sanction for Marxist theory by appealing to the Hebrew exodus and to apocalyptic judgment. Both revolution and liberation theologies did not exclude violence as an instrument for social change, and they lacked a means of producing the wealth that they proposed to redistribute. Contemporary social theologies differed from those of the early 1950s in their evident suspicion of Western democracy and free enterprise and their distrust of orderly change. Unlike humanism, which is consciously atheistic, such works as Gustavo Gutiérrez, *A Theology of Liberation* (1973) invoked a supposedly biblical rationale for socialist solutions. Whereas modernism's corollary at the beginning of the century was optimistic idealism, neoliberalism increasingly involved both God and man in the suffering of the world.

Professing to speak as evangelicals was a spectrum somewhat to the left of traditional orthodoxy, most notably Barth (1886–1968), who followed his multivolume *Church Dogmatics* (1936–62) with *Evangelical Theology: An Introduction* (ET, 1963). Barth rejected both general and scriptural propositional revelation to promote internal personal confrontation; he subordinated all divine perfections to freedom and love and was open to universal salvation. Barthian emphasis on divine self-communication influenced the dogmatic theology of numerous contemporaries. Otto Weber (1902–66) sought in *Foundations on Dogmatics* (1981, 1983) to overcome the antithesis between theology of the incarnation and theology of the cross. In *The Evangelical Faith* (ET, 1976–79), Helmut Thielicke (1908–86) correlated modernist, evangelical, and neo-orthodox elements to herald the divine kerygma revealed in Christ through the Holy Spirit. Rejecting the rationalism of the liberal Cartesian approach of Schleiermacher, Bultmann, and Tillich and the non-Cartesian objective historical approach, he founded his views on God's demand for a decision. Answering this call shapes a new self-understanding by incorporating sinners into the salvation event. Broadly following the Apostles' Creed, his trinitarian exposition depicts the Father as the source of revelation and the Son as the form of revelation, and develops his Christology in terms of Christ's three offices rather than his two natures.

More evangelically orthodox was G. C. Berkouwer (1903– ) and his massive *Studies in Dogmatics* (1949– ). In contrast to Cornelius Van Til (1895–1987) who viewed Barth's flawed epistemology as vitiating all his work (see Van Til, *The New Modernism: An Appraisal of the Theology of Barth and Brunner* [1947], and *Christianity and Barthianism* [1962]), Berkouwer focused on the centrality of Barth's "triumphant grace." As developed, he protested, the concept shapes an exaggerated Christomonism and unjustifiably implies universalism (*The Triumph of Grace in the Theology of Karl Barth* [ET, 1956]). Berkouwer ruled out natural theology but, contrary to Barth, insisted that God does speak through general revelation. Critics later disputed Berkouwer's concessions to Barth's view of Scripture and an emphasis that the truth of theology is known only to personal faith. Still more Barthian, and moving to Barth's left, is *Christian Faith* (1979) by Hendrikus Berkhof (1914– ) of Leiden.

Thomas F. Torrance (1913– ) extended Barth's influence. Strengthening the cognitive aspect of revelation in *Theology in Reconstruction* (1965) he nonetheless halted short of propositional divine disclosure. Torrance's creative work was on theology-and-science frontiers. In *Space, Time and Incarnation* (1969) and *Divine and Contingent Order* (1981) he maintained that contemporary science illumines and reinforces theology's content and procedures. In the name of science he shied away from all purely objective knowledge, contending that Christian theology functions analogically to scientific knowledge and that, moreover, Christian theology has its own logic (*God and Rationality* [1971]). In America Barth's limitations on scriptural revelation influenced both Donald G. Bloesch (1928– ) (*Essentials of Evangelical Theology* [2 vols., 1978]) and Bernard L. Ramm (1916– ). In *After Fundamentalism: The Future of Evangelical Theology* (1982) Ramm champions Barth's epistemology. Dale Moody's *Word of Truth: A Summary of Christian Doctrine Based on Biblical Revelation* (1981) reflects Brunner's influence more than Barth's. Gabriel Fackre's *Christian Story* (rev. ed., 1984) sets traditional evangelical dogmatics in the context of narrative theology; while open to universal salvation, he bases redemption solely on Christ's atonement.

Barth's epistemology was vigorously contested by Gordon H. Clark (*Karl Barth's Theological Method* [1963]) no less than by Van Til. A gifted evangelical philosopher, Clark (1902–85) wrote numerous influential works, including *A Christian View of Men and Things* (1952). Also criticizing Barth's views as compromising Reformed theology, Fred H. Klooster in *The Significance of Barth's Theology* (1961) extended earlier strictures by Louis Berkhof (1873–1957) in *Systematic Theology* (1938). The most extensive evangelical contribution was the six-volume *God, Revelation and Authority* (1976–82) by Carl F. H. Henry (1913– ) which, in deliberate contrast to Barth's priority for internal volition, wrestled with introductory metaphysical concerns and stressed that God makes intelligible divine disclosure in objective scriptural form. Millard J. Erickson's three-volume *Christian Theology* (1983–85) also vigorously advances evangelical orthodoxy against contemporary alternatives.

Formation in 1950 of the Evangelical Theological Society (ETS) marked the emergence of a growing cadre of scholars who championed scriptural orthodoxy. The resurgence of evangelical orthodoxy was perhaps the late 20th century's most striking feature. Among intellectual developments were formation of Fuller Theological Seminary, Gordon-Conwell Theological Seminary, and Trinity Evangelical Divinity School, and establishment in 1956 of *Christianity Today* as a journal rivaling the prestigious liberal *Christian Century*. An international scholarship supportive of evangelical theism was growing. Experiential and charismatic excesses moderated this momentum, however, and evangelical forces divided internally over the issue of biblical inerrancy.

In England C. S. Lewis (1898–1963) contributed to renewed interest in biblical theism through his brilliant literary exposure of the inconsistencies and weaknesses of contemporary alternatives (such as *The Screwtape Letters* [1942] and *Surprised by Joy* [1955]). Little emerged in Britain in systematic theology except, perhaps, Leonard Hodgson (1889–1969), *For Faith and Freedom* (1956–57). Instead, NT studies and philosophical concerns were the cognitive battleground. Mediating scholars held the line against radical scriptural criticism. Dodd (1884–1973) reinforced the validity of the NT record of Jesus despite critical biblical views. Yet Dodd stressed "realized eschatology" at the expense of a future eschatological climax, and shunned retributory and propitiatory aspects of divine atonement. Evangelical spokesmen, notably F. F. Bruce (1910–1990) (*Are the NT Documents Reliable?* [1954]) who wrote numerous commentaries, R. V. G. Tasker (1895– ) (*The Biblical Doctrine of the Wrath of God* [1951]) and the Australian scholar Leon Morris (1914– ) (*The Apostolic Preaching of the Cross* [1955]) took firmer ground. At Cambridge Charles F. D. Moule (1908– ) championed a high primitive Christology in *The Origin of Christology* (1977) against those who consider the deity of Christ a postapostolic perspective. Noteworthy was Donald Guthrie's *NT Theology* (1981) in England, and George E. Ladd's *Theology of the NT* (1974) in America.

Scholastic theology was given a new contemporary turn by A. M. Farrer (1904–68) and then by E. L. Mascall (1905– ) (*The Openness of Being: Natural Theology Today* [1971]). Sustained by contributions of gifted philosophers (Jacques Maritain, 1882–1973; Etienne Gilson, 1884–1978; and Frederick Coplestone, 1907– ), its theological pacemakers have been Karl Rahner (1904–84) and Bernard Lonergan (1904–84). Extensive Catholic-Protestant dialog followed the new ecumenical thrust attending the election of Pope John XXIII (1958–63) who set aggiornamento in motion. Both Rahner (*Theological Investigations* [translated serially since 1961]) and Lonergan

(*Insight and Method in Theology* [1958, 1972]) affirm a natural theology of sorts, and both insist on special revelation, although in the name of personal confrontation they share with neo-orthodoxy the rejection of scriptural verbal revelation. Critics note the anthropocentric focus of Rahner's doctrine of revelation which accommodates his view of an "anonymous Christ" in nonbiblical religions. Both Rahner and Hans Küng (1928– ) spoke of all church formulations as time-bound, but Küng ventured to put the dogma of papal infallibility in that context (*Infallible? An Inquiry* [ET, 1971]; *On Being a Christian* [1976]).

Defection from christological orthodoxy was demonstrated by leading British churchmen in *The Myth of God Incarnate* (1977), whose editor, John Hick, affirmed in *God and the Universe of Faiths: Essays in the Philosophy of Religion* (1973) that all religions are in soteric contact with the same Ultimate and that Christian discovery of salvation in Christ does not preclude salvation through rival faiths. Anglican bishop J. A. T. Robinson (1919–83), whose *Honest to God* (1963) was among earlier books by liberal churchmen attesting a radical departure from orthodox theism, was influenced by Tillich.

Paul Tillich (1886–1965) radically restated his Lutheran tradition by promoting existential analysis and theological solution in the context of a broadly panentheistic—if not atheistic—view of the ultimacy of an impersonal Ground of all being. Tillich's *Systematic Theology* (3 vols., 1950–63) attracted fewer secularists to Christian beliefs than it enlisted intellectuals in forsaking supernatural theism. Death-of-God theology was indebted to his emphasis that predications about God lack objective validity; Tillich conceded that his ultimate Ground was likewise no more than a faith-construct.

John Macquarrie (1919– ) opted for theism not in its evangelical, orthodox form. "Dialectical theism" is what he called his panentheism in *In Search of Humanity* (1982) and *In Search of Deity* (1984). His philosophical anthropology reflected a distaste for a fixed view of man. He considered man the panentheistic microcosm of a dynamic universe and moved from self-transcendence through estrangement to the transcendent. This approach offered a natural theology independent of Christian revelation which separated his view from that of Jürgen Moltmann. Wolfhart Pannenberg (*Jesus—God and Man* [ET, 1968]) and Moltmann (*Theology of Hope: On the Ground and the Implications of a Christian Eschatology* [1965]) promoted a one-layer theory of reality keyed to the future of God. Moltmann (1926– ) and Pannenberg (1928– ) are most significant as a corrective to Oscar Cullmann's *Salvation in History* (ET, 1967), which commendably placed divine revelation on a historical time-line but detached biblical

salvation history from divine control of history generally.

Efforts to overcome the disintegrating consequences of radical biblical criticism are made by narrative expositors such as Hans W. Frei (1922– ) (*The Eclipse of Biblical Narrative: A Study in Eighteenth and Nineteenth Century Hermeneutics* [1974]) and by canonical expositors such as Brevard S. Childs (1923– ) (*Introduction to the OT as Scripture* [1979]). Speaking of the authority of the text these views intend something quite different from what is meant by evangelical orthodoxy, and their exposition of revelation and of history is often ambiguous. What is of special value in Childs' emphasis is that the reliability and meaning of the canon is not to be discovered by going behind the text to earlier and often highly problematical sources.

Berkouwer rightly comments that in theology "there is more doubt and uncertainty now than there was at the beginning" of the century (*A Half Century of Theology*). To almost every question that the world asks, professedly Christian theologians give conflicting answers. If theology a generation ago already reflected influential personalities more than closely knit systems, today even influential individuals are declining in number. No towering thinker currently dominates the theological scene. A bewildering pluralism—secular humanism, process theology, theology of hope, theology of revolution, liberation theology, narrative theology, canonical theology—competes with evangelical orthodoxy for attention. Contemporary theology exhibits what Lonnie D. Kliever calls "runaway pluralism." Neo-orthodox encounter involving nonpropositional transcendent revelation is giving way again to an experience-centered anthropological theology. The term *evangelical* has itself become somewhat obscure through widening misappropriation of the designation encouraged through evangelical defection from full biblical authority.

**Bibliography.** *From 1900.* W. M. Horton, *Contemporary English Theology* (1936); H. R. Mackintosh, *Types of Modern Theology* (1937); W. M. Horton, *Contemporary Continental Theology* (1938); C. F. H. Henry, *Fifty Years of Protestant Theology* (1950); A. Nash, *Protestant Thought in the Twentieth Century: Whence and Whither?* (1951).

*From 1950. Surveys.* P. E. Hughes, *Creative Minds in Contemporary Theology* (2d ed., 1969); H. Zahrnt, *The Question of God: Protestant Theology in the 20th Century* (ET, 1969); H. Cunliffe-Jones, *Christian Theology since 1600* (1970); J. Macquarrie, *Twentieth-Century Religious Thought: The Frontiers of Philosophy and Theology, 1900–1970* (1971); A. I. C. Heron, *A Century of Protestant Theology* (1980); L. D. Kliever, *The Shattered Spectrum: A Survey of Contemporary Theology* (1981); M. E. Marty and D. G. Peerman, *A Handbook of Christian Theologians* (rev. ed., 1984).

CARL F. H. HENRY

**Theology of Crisis.** See CRISIS, THEOLOGY OF.

**Theosophy.** A modern gnostic philosophy or religion, from Gk. *theos* (God) and *sophia* (wisdom). From the mid-19th century, particularly in England and the USA, theosophy-type groups were popular among those seeking a more mystical philosophy or a religion built around naturalistic evolutionary concepts. While theosophical systems have varied they revolve around an eternal "first cause," an infinite reality within which all things exist. Creation manifests this source or *Logos* in a "trinity" of matter, spirit, and consciousness. Within consciousness are units of consciousness—individuals—each of which is a divine son or *monad*. There is an evolution of consciousness which parallels the evolution of form in the universe; so monads progress through reincarnation, which is in general governed by the laws of Hindu karma. It is the destiny of human spirit to infinitely progress in the perfection of the divine nature within.

The most successful Western organization teaching principles of theosophy was the Theosophical Society, founded in 1875 by the Russian mystic Helena Petrovna Blavatsky, Henry Steel Olcott, who became the society's founding president, and William Q. Judge. An experienced medium and occultist, Madame Blavatsky completed her first major book, *Isis Unveiled*, in 1877. Two years later she and Olcott journeyed to India, a transforming spiritual experience for both. Theosophy played a role in establishing the East, especially India and Tibet, as a source of occultic wisdom for the West and the focus of many a seeker's pilgrimage. It was instrumental in the popularizing of such concepts as karma and reincarnation. Blavatsky was deeply involved in various forms of spiritism and claimed to receive occultic initiations from the "masters of ancient wisdom" for whom she was said to be a messenger. The syncretistic teaching of theosophy claims to encompass the truths that form the basis of all true religions. In that sense it claims to be a universal world religion.

After Blavatsky's death in 1891 the movement experienced internal dissension and eventually split into the Theosophical Society in America, with headquarters in Wheaton, Ill., and the Theosophical Society, led from Altadena, Calif. In 1912 the Krotona Institute of Theosophy, located in Ojai, Calif., was founded by A. P. Warrington.

**Bibliography.** R. S. Ellwood, *Alternative Altars* (1979); J. G. Melton, *Encyclopedic Handbook of Cults in America* (1986).

RONALD ENROTH

**Therapy.** *See* COUNSELING, PASTORAL; PSYCHOTHERAPY.

**Thessalonians, Epistles to the.** *See* PAUL, THE APOSTLE.

**Thielicke, Helmut** (1908–1985). German Protestant theologian. Born into a pastor's family in Wuppertal-Barmen, he studied at various uni-

versities and received doctorates in theology and philosophy. He then taught at Erlangen and Heidelberg, but had to take a pastorate when he was dismissed in 1940. The following year the Nazi regime banned him from traveling and speaking because he criticized official racial doctrine. After the war he became famous as a preacher and reached large audiences through his sermons, pamphlets, and radio and television talks. In 1945 he assumed a professorship at Tübingen and then moved to Hamburg in 1954, serving a term as rector at both universities. In his many writings Thielicke stressed the proclamation of the Word of God as the church's primary task and the necessity of applying the Scriptures to ethical dilemmas. God's answer to human alienation as seen in the dichotomy that had developed between the sacred and secular realms of life was to enable restoration by bringing humankind to new life in Christ; thus individual renewal was the key to genuine social reconstruction. Thielicke was the most articulate exponent of conservative evangelical theology in postwar Germany, and because over 20 of his books were translated into English, his prestige and influence spread elsewhere. Among his works are *The Waiting Father* (1959), *How the World Began* (1961), *Nihilism, Its Origin and Nature* (1962), *Life Can Begin Again* (1963), *Between Heaven and Earth* (1965), *I Believe, the Christian Creed* (1968), *How Modern Should Theology Be?* (1970), and *Faith the Great Adventure* (1985). By far the most important are his three-volume works, *Theological Ethics* (1966–75) and *The Evangelical Faith* (1974–82).

RICHARD V. PIERARD

**Third Order.** *See* TERTIARIES.

**Thomas, George F.** (1899–1977). Philosopher of religion. Born in Ladonia, Tex., he studied at Southern Methodist, Oxford, and Harvard (Ph.D., 1919) universities. He held teaching posts in philosophy and religion at Southern Methodist (1923–25), Swarthmore (1927–31), Dartmouth (1931–37), North Carolina (1937–40), and Princeton (1940–68). He was a member of the advisory committee of the World Council of Churches and the Joint Committee on Approaches to Unity of the Protestant Episcopal Church. A prolific writer, his works include *Spirit and Its Freedom* (1938), *Poetry, Religion and the Spiritual Life* (1951), *Christian Ethics and Moral Philosophy* (1955), *Religious Philosophies of the West* (1965), and *Philosophy and Religious Belief* (1969). He also edited *The Vitality of the Christian Tradition* (1944).

RICHARD V. PIERARD

**Thomas, M. M.** (1916– ). Indian lay theologian, social analyst, and ecumenical leader. Thomas's road to a democratic "redefinition of Marxism,

Gandhism and Liberalism within the framework of the theology and realistic anthropology of Christian Neo-orthodoxy" is charted in *The Ideological Quest within My Christian Commitment: 1939–1954* (1983), a collection of papers arising from his work with the Kerala Youth Christian Council of Action, as youth secretary of the Mar Thoma Church, and as a staff member of the World's Student Christian Federation. He believed that Christianity must be relevant to the modern world and keep in dialog with contemporary religions; this belief found sustained expression in his association with P. D. Devanandan in the activities of the Christian Institute for the Study of Religion and Society, Bangalore. He was the institute's second director (1963–76) and was involved in the production of its influential journal, *Religion and Society*. Thomas's thought reached a wider audience through his participation in the World Council of Churches (as a chairman of the central committee) and the East Asian Christian Conference, and through many publications. His basic position, outlined in *The Christian Response to the Asian Revolution* (1966) and *Some Theological Dialogues* (1977), is applied to the Indian situation in *Salvation and Humanisation* (1971), *The Acknowledged Christ of the Indian Renaissance* (2d ed., 1976), and its sequel, *The Secular Ideologies of India and the Secular Meaning of Christ* (1976), and culminates in *Risking Christ for Christ's Sake: Towards an Ecumenical Theology of Pluralism* (1987).

PHILIP HILLYER

**Thomas, Norman Mattoon** (1884–1968). Presbyterian socialist. Born in Marion, Ohio, he was educated at Princeton University and Union Theological Seminary. He was ordained in 1911 and was associate minister in the Brick Presbyterian Church, New York (1910/11), and pastor of the East Harlem Church and chairman of the American Parish (1911–18). He was the founder and editor of *World Tomorrow* (1918–21); secretary of the Fellowship of Reconciliation; director of the League for Industrial Democracy (1922); socialist candidate for governor of New York (1924); twice candidate for mayor of New York City; and candidate for president of the United States. He demitted the ministry in 1931. He wrote *The Conscientious Objector in America* (1923), *Is Conscience a Crime?* (revision of preceding, 1927), *America's Way Out—A Program for Democracy* (1930), *As I See It* (1932), with Paul Blanshard, *What's the Matter with New York?* (1932), *Human Exploitation* (1934), *War—No Profit, No Glory, No Need* (1935), *Socialism on the Defensive* (1938), *We Have a Future* (1941), *What Is Our Destiny?* (1944), *Appeal to the Nations* (1947), and *A Socialist's Faith* (1951).

RAYMOND W. ALBRIGHT

**Thompson, Ernest Trice** (1894–1985). American Presbyterian scholar. Born in Texarkana, Tex., he studied at Hampden-Sydney College, Columbia University, and Union Theological Seminary, Virginia. Shortly after ordination he was appointed to teach church history and church polity at Union Seminary (1922–64), and thereafter was a visiting professor at Austin Presbyterian Theological Seminary (1965–70). He was contributing editor to the *Presbyterian Standard* (1924–31); associate editor (1931–37) and editor (1937–43) of *Presbyterian of the South;* and editor (1943–46) and then coeditor of the *Presbyterian Outlook*. He was the first president of the Virginia Council of Churches and an active proponent of the reunion between Southern and Northern branches of American Presbyterianism. He was moderator of the general assembly of the Presbyterian Church, USA, in 1959. His published works include *Presbyterian Missions in the Southern States* (1934), *Changing Emphases in American Preaching* (1943), *The Sermon on the Mount and Its Meaning for Today* (1946), *The Changing South* (1950), *The Gospel According to Mark and Its Meaning for Today* (1954), *The Spirituality of the Church* (1961), *Presbyterians in the South* (3 vols., 1963–73), and *Plenty and Want* (1972).

WILLIAM H. BERGER

**Thomson, George Thomas** (1887–1958). Presbyterian. Born in Edinburgh, he was educated at Edinburgh University, Christ Church in Oxford, and Berlin. He held pastorates at Tain (1920–24) and St. Boswell's (1924–28), and was professor of systematic theology at Aberdeen University (1928–36) and professor of Christian dogmatics at Edinburgh University (1936–52). He was a leading interpreter of the theology of Karl Barth in Britain. He translated Barth's *Doctrine of the Word of God* and *Dogmatics in Outline* and Heppe's *Reformierte Dogmatik*.

F. W. DILLISTONE

**Tikhon (Bellavin)** (1865–1925). Eastern Orthodox. Born in Toropetz, Russia, he studied at Pskov Theological Seminary and St. Petersburg Theological Academy. He was ordained priest (1891) and consecrated bishop of Ljublin (1898). In 1899 he was appointed bishop of Alaska and Aleout Islands; in 1905 he was raised to the rank of archbishop. He was fully aware of the special situation of the Orthodox Church in America and recommended its reorganization into an "Exarchate" under the authority of the church in Russia, but with a wide autonomy of various national groups: Syrian, Serbian, Greek. Each of them had to have its own bishop and administration, under the presidency of the archbishop. The plan was not realized, but a Syrian bishop was appointed as a suffragan to the archbishop. He was much concerned with the use of the English language for worship and preaching, and it was upon his initiative that Isabel Hapgood undertook her translation of the *Service Book* of the Orthodox Church (1906). In 1903 he started a theological school at Minneapolis, which was transformed into a seminary in 1905 in order to train local candidates for the ministry in America (after Tikhon's time it was transferred to Tenafly, N.J., and then closed after the Russian Revolution). He also founded a monastery at South Canaan, Pa. (St. Tikhon's monastery). He was interested in friendly relations with the Anglican Church, but these relations became rather tense after Tikhon reordained an Anglican priest and used him for ministry in the Orthodox Church. A formal protest was made by the presiding bishop of the Protestant Episcopal Church to the Russian Synod. In 1907 he was transferred to the chair of Jaroslavl, and then to Vilna. In 1917 he was elected metropolitan of Moscow and in the same year, after the plenary council of the Russian Church had reshaped the organization of the Russian church and restored the office of patriarch, he was elected patriarch of Moscow and all Russia. He had enormous moral authority. In the beginning he took a strong stand against the communist regime, but later on, for the benefit of the church, had to come to certain practical terms with the authorities. He was arrested in 1922, but was released after some months. The "Council" of 1923, convened by the modernist group of the clergy and at that time supported by the Bolsheviks, deposed the patriarch and pretended to assume the supreme authority in the church. This action was never recognized by the majority and finally the "Living Church" disintegrated (now it has been disavowed by the government itself). The name of the patriarch soon became a symbol of piety and order in Russia.

*See also* EASTERN ORTHODOX CHURCHES; RUSSIAN ORTHODOX CHURCH.

**Bibliography**. Memorandum of Tikhon on the reorganization of the church in America, in English supplement to the *Russian Orthodox American Messenger* (Mar., 1906); W. C. Emhardt, *Religion in Soviet Russia, Anarchy* (1929); important documents in translation; N. S. Timasheff, *Religion in Soviet Russia* (1942); P. B. Anderson, *People, Church and State in Modern Russia* (1944).

GEORGES FLOROVSKY

**Tillich, Paul** (1886–1965). German-American theologian. Born in rural Prussia, he studied at various universities, and received a Ph.D. at Breslau for a dissertation on Schelling. He was ordained to the Protestant ministry in 1912, and during World War I served as an army chaplain. He began teaching at Marburg in 1924, moved to Dresden in 1925, and to Frankfurt in 1929. Forced by the Nazis to leave Germany, he was appointed professor of philosophical theology at Union Theological Seminary, New York, in 1933. He spent the remainder of his life in the USA, teaching at Columbia, Harvard, and Chicago universities. He was influenced by Platonism, medieval mysticism, German idealism, and, above all, existentialism. He insisted that philosophy and theology should play complementary roles, with the former posing questions and the latter answering them. He stressed the wholeness of God, and that no single system of thought could ever encompass the totality of God, thus concluding that theology could never be final. God is the ground of all being, and what we have found (or rejected) is only a reduced image of him. For Tillich, God is "ultimate concern" and the term contains a double meaning of both the attitude and the reality to which it is directed. He also showed how theology uses the language of symbols and that these participate in the process of creation and destruction, integration and fragmentation. Symbols have creative power which flows from the human unconscious, and they point beyond themselves to God who is the ground of being. How they participate in this reality, however, is not clear. Among his major works are *Interpretation of History* (1936), *The Protestant Era* (1936), *The Courage to Be* (1952), *Theology of Culture* (1959), *Morality and Beyond* (1963), and above all *Systematic Theology* (3 vols., 1951–63).

RICHARD V. PIERARD

**Time.** Augustine confessed that he knew what time was until someone asked him what it was; then he did not know. The long history of discussion reveals that men in general might well make that confession their own. Attitudes toward the reality of time vary widely. There is a long tradition which regards the temporal as the hallmark of unreality. For Plato, time is merely the moving image of eternity. For rationalists of the Enlightenment, reality is to be found only in timelessly valid truths. For F. H. Bradley "there is no history or progress in the Absolute." This evaluation of the temporal has played a large part in religious thinking. This point of view finds reality only in the eternal, conceived as the timeless. It is possible, however, to agree that reality is to be found only in the eternal and still to attribute reality to time by conceiving of eternity as infinite time transcended. In flat contradiction to the view of the rationalists is Henri Louis Bergson's emphatic assertion that time is "the very stuff of reality," and 20th-century thought was more sympathetic with the evaluation of Bergson than with that of the rationalists. For, as Benito Mussolini once remarked, "history has our age by the throat." There are, however, other views. Immanuel Kant, for example, held that time, being a "form of sensibility" is universally characteristic of the "phenomenal world," but he refused to attribute it to the "noumenal world." Karl Heim suggested that our world is under the form of time because of the fall.

All efforts to deal with time conceptually run into difficulties. The physicists have had to grapple with the problem because motion is a function of time. Theirs is the "objective" or "absolute" time—"clock time," characterized by infinite divisibility into identical and mutually exclusive units, which can be counted and dealt with mathematically. But that this obviously useful device cannot be pressed too far was already made dramatically clear by the paradoxes of Zeno (335–263 B.C.). It incurs the difficulties: (1) since the spatial points in mathematics are dimensionless, points of time analogous to them would also be dimensionless, and even an infinite number of dimensionless points would not constitute a duration; (2) the moving time of experience now becomes a static line along which something else moves and, in its movement, involves dynamic time; so that now we have two times instead of one; and (3) as Kant pointed out, whatever moves time must have had a beginning and cannot have had a beginning. Further, this method of dealing with time contains no provision for representing its unidirectional character and it cancels out the characteristic of experienced time according to which one and the same block of it may be immensely long to one observer and almost unnoticeably fleeting to another. Some of the phenomena of subatomic physics have led physicist James Hopwood Jeans to suggest that the intraatomic world may not be in such time at all. Many of the phenomena of astronomical physics lead the scientists to associate the one dimension of time with the three dimensions of space to form a four-dimensional, space-time continuum; and the possibility of continuums of more than four dimensions has been envisaged.

Humans also must deal with "psychological time"—the experience of duration which is revealed to "intuition" or introspection—the time which Bergson regarded as "the very stuff of reality." Even if it should prove to be transparent, the problem of its relation to objective time still remains. This time also is divisible, if only into a past and a future separated or connected by the "specious present." Thus the problem of continuity and divisibility emerges again, although not, at first sight, in such an acute form. It does become mystifying, however, when the character of the specious present is considered. For, as William James expressed it, the specious present is a "saddle-back," not a "knife-edge." It contains something of the "no longer" and something of the "not yet" in an experience which, nevertheless, is a unitary present. It is an actual piece of duration. Further, as measured in terms of objective time, its length is variable, depending perhaps on innate characteristics of the person involved, on his freshness or tiredness at the time, on his inter-

est or lack of interest in what is transpiring, and so forth. Variableness of length, as measured by objective time, is indeed characteristic of psychological time—any block of objective time may be but a fleeting moment or an interminable period of psychological time. Thus psychological time refuses to fit into the tidy patterns of objective time; and yet the two must somehow be related. Psychological time must be real because humans are aware of it as a purely inner experience to consciousness; but is it the only real time, the objective time being merely an "artificial" schematization for some limited purpose? Or is objective time the only real time, psychological time being the result of some subjective warping? Are both real time; and, if so, how are they related? Or is time as such unreal?

*Bibliography.* I. Kant, *Critique of Pure Reason* (ET, 1896); F. H. Bradley, *Appearance and Reality: A Metaphysical Essay* (1902); H. Bergson, *Time and Free Will: An Essay on the Immediate Data of Consciousness* (1913); K. Heim, *The New Divine Order* (1930); O. Cullman, *Christ and Time* (ET, 1950); J. Barr, *Biblical Words for Time* (1962).

ANDREW K. RULE

**Timothy, Epistles to.** *See* PAUL, THE APOSTLE.

**Tisserant, Eugène** (1884–1972). Cardinal. Born in Nancy, France, he was ordained to the priesthood (1907) and called to Rome to serve on the staff of the Vatican Library (1908). He became proprefect of this institution under Mercati (1930). His scholarly interests extended to the entire field of the languages and literatures of the ancient Near East, with particular emphasis on the history of the Eastern Churches. He is noted for his editions of early Christian manuscripts and his critical studies. He was created cardinal in 1936, under the pontificate of Pius XI, and was subsequently consecrated archbishop (titular) of Iconium (1937). In 1946, he received the cardinal's title of Porto and Santa Rufina, a suburbicarian diocese. He was appointed secretary of the Congregation for the Eastern Church (1936), of which he had been a consultor for ten years. Two years later, he was made president of the Pontifical Biblical Commission, of which he had been a consultor since 1914 and a voting member since his elevation to the cardinalate. He was also a member of the commission for the codification of the canon law of the Eastern Church; of the Tribunal of the *Signatura;* and of the Congregations of the Consistory, of the Sacraments, of the Propaganda, of Rites, and of Seminaries and Universities. In addition, he was dean of the Sacred College.

GEORGES A. BARROIS

**Tithe.** The gift or payment of a tenth of one's income to the church, or other religious and charitable agencies. The custom is of ancient origin (Gen. 14:20; 28:22). Tithes were paid to God as tokens of homage and gratitude. The NT does not show that Jesus or his disciples stressed tithing. The church owes much of her conception of Christian stewardship to Paul. A number of denominations consider tithing basic. Many other church members find it a vital stage in the development of Christian stewardship—not as a binding obligation, but as a minimum working standard.

ROBERT CASHMAN

**Tittle, Ernest Fremont** (1885–1949). Methodist. Born in Springfield, Ohio, he graduated from Ohio Wesleyan University and Drew Theological Seminary. He was minister of Ohio Methodist churches at Christiansburg (1908–10), Dayton (1910–13), Delaware (1913–16), Columbus (1916–18), and Evanston, Ill. (1918–49). He served in France with the YMCA in World War I, and after his return took a pacifist position which he held uncompromisingly to the end of his life. He wrote *What Must the Church Do to Be Saved?* (1921), *The Religion of the Spirit* (1928), *The Foolishness of Preaching* (1930), *We Need Religion* (1931), *Jesus after Nineteen Centuries* (1932), *A World That Cannot Be Shaken* (1933), *A Way to Life* (1935), *Christians in an Unchristian Society* (1939), *The Lord's Prayer* (1942), and three volumes published posthumously: *A Mighty Fortress*, *The Gospel According to Luke*, and *A Book of Pastoral Prayers*.

PAUL HUTCHINSON

**Titus, Epistle to.** See PAUL, THE APOSTLE.

**Togo.** See WEST AFRICA.

**Tolkien, John Ronald Reuel** (1892–1973). English writer. After graduating from Oxford he served in the army (1915–18) before beginning his academic career as reader (1920–24) and professor (1924/25) of English at Leeds University. He returned to Oxford as professor of Anglo-Saxon (1925–45). Among his publications are *A Middle English Vocabulary* (1922), *Chaucer as a Philologist* (1934), *The Hobbit* (1937), *On Fairy-Stories* (1938), *The Homecoming of Beorhtnoth* (1953), the phenomenally successful trilogy *The Lord of the Rings* (1954/55), *The Road Goes Ever On* (1968), and *The Silmarillion* (1968).

J. D. DOUGLAS

**Tonga.** See SOUTH PACIFIC, ISLANDS OF THE.

**Tongues.** See GLOSSOLALIA.

**Torah.** Hebrew word for "teaching," "guidance," or "instruction." While the Bible applies this word to such matters as wisdom, moral teachings common in Proverbs, or prophecy, it refers particularly to the five first books of the Hebrew Bible, "the books of Moses" (Gk. *Pentateuch*). The Pentateuch itself speaks in certain legal passages of "the *Torah* of" (as in Exod. 13:9; Lev. 6:9, 14, 25, and throughout the Levitical law), and occasionally refers to the whole of God's teachings through Moses as such (as in Exod. 24:12; Deut. 1:5; 4:44; 33:4). The term is particularly common in Deuteronomy, where it frequently refers to the text of the Deuteronomic covenant (Deut. 31:9, 24, 26). Although modern critical scholarship sees the Pentateuch as a composite work redacted from documents, Jewish tradition regards all the Torah, with the possible exception of the closing section describing Moses' death (Deut. 34), as a unified work divinely revealed by God to Moses at Mount Sinai. At its core stands the legislation, which a Talmudic tradition classifies as 613 commandments—248 positive and 365 negative. Much Jewish scholarship was directed to the classification, explication, and elaboration of these commandments.

In later Jewish writings the term took on additional meanings. The standard rendering in the LXX as *nomos*, "law," reflects a belief that the main purpose of the Torah was to be sought in its legal code, a belief reflected in the fact that the Tanna'im scribes generally restricted their exegesis to the legal passages of the Pentateuch. On the other hand, a widespread approach (as early as in Ben Sira 1:1ff.) identifies the pre-existent Wisdom described in Prov. 8:22–36 with the Torah. This lends to it the metaphysical status of an entity whose existence preceded creation and by means of which God fashioned the universe. A similar image is found in the writings of Philo of Alexandria. This theme was generally rejected by medieval Jewish rationalists, or they interpreted it symbolically to mean that the world exists for the sake of the Torah. The Jewish Kabbalistic mystics (c. A.D. 1100–1700) identified the Torah with one or another of 10 emanations (*sepirot*) from God. Modern Jewish thinkers, since Benedict Spinoza (1632–77) and Moses Mendelssohn (1729–86), have studied the relationship between the theological (universal) and the legislative (distinctly Jewish) elements of the Torah. Rabbinic dicta in the Mishna emphasize that the existence of the world depends on the Torah (as in Abot 1:2). The validity of the Torah was generally held to be eternal, and would continue in the messianic era. In some instances in rabbinic literature, as well as in Paul and John (Rom. 3:19, and, quoting Jesus, John 10:34), "Torah" refers to the whole of the Hebrew Bible, although Jewish scholars have generally upheld a distinction between the Torah (Pentateuch) and "Words of Tradition" (the rest of the Bible), which was regarded as less sacred. The prophetic writings were seen as essential elements of the covenant with Israel which consisted mostly of adherence to the law of the Torah. Through keeping the Torah Israel was to become "a kingdom of priests and a holy people" (Exod. 19:6). Accordingly, the totality of the law is considered binding on Israel alone; the rest of mankind was given the "seven Noahide commandments," basic moral rules. The rabbis made various attempts to epitomize the Torah or to isolate "fundamental" teachings. This issue arose in the teaching of Jesus (Matt. 7:12; 22:40; Mark 12:29–31). Rabbinic sources developed the doctrine of the "two Torahs": in addition to the written Torah, there exists an oral Torah—consisting of ancestral traditions, interpretations, and legislation—which enjoys equal authority with the written Torah, and (according to some formulations) was also revealed to Moses. Although frequently expressed in polemical contexts as a way of asserting Israel's special attachment to the "secret" oral tradition, the insistence on not writing down the oral Torah (a prohibition which was literally enforced through the Talmudic era) was also intended to preserve its flexibility and humaneness. This reverence for extrabiblical traditions as being from God was the main dividing line between the Pharisees and other second-temple sects and was presented in the Mishna (Sanhedrin 10:1) as a virtual dogma. Rabbinic law distinguishes between Torah and rabbinic law, the latter being of lesser authority.

Jewish tradition emphasizes the importance of studying Torah as a distinct obligation, whether for its own sake or with a view to practical application. Accordingly, public reading from it, and other forms of study, constitute a central component of the liturgy.

**Bibliography.** S. Schechter, *Some Aspects of Rabbinic Theology* (1909); C. H. Dodd, *The Bible and the Greeks* (1935); Y. Kaufmann, *The Religion of Israel: From Its Beginnings to the Babylonian Exile* (1960); W. Harvey, in G. Wigoder, ed., *Jewish Values* (1974); E. Urbach, *The Sages, Their Concepts and Beliefs* (1975).

ELIEZER SEGAL

**Torrance, Thomas Forsyth** (1913– ). Scottish theologian. Born of missionary parents in Chengtu, Szechuan, China, he was educated at the universities of Edinburgh, Basel (D.Theol., 1946), and Oxford, and pursued research in Jerusalem, Athens, Berlin, and Marburg. He was professor of systematic theology at Auburn Theological Seminary, N.Y. (1938/39), but then returned to Scotland, and after ordination was minister at Alyth (1940–47) and at Beechgrove, Aberdeen (1947–50). He then occupied the chairs of church history (1950–52) and Christian dogmatics (1952–79) at New College, Edinburgh. He helped to found the prestigious *Scottish Journal of Theology*, was moderator of the Church of Scotland general assembly (1976/77), lectured widely throughout the world, is a member of many learned societies, and was for a term president of the Academie Internationale des Sciences Religieuses. In 1978 he was awarded the Templeton Prize, given to "those who through original

and pioneering ways advanced the knowledge and love of God." Apart from his monumental work as joint editor of Karl Barth's *Church Dogmatics*, he has written numerous books, including *Calvin's Doctrine of Man* (1948), *Royal Priesthood* (1955), *When Christ Comes and Comes Again* (1957), *Theology in Reconstruction* (1965), *Theological Science* (1969), *Spirit, Truth and Incarnation* (1969), *God and Rationality* (1971), *Theology in Reconciliation* (1975), *Space, Time and Resurrection* (1976), *The Ground and Grammar of Theology* (1980), *The Christian Frame of Mind* (1985), and *Reality and Scientific Theology* (1985).

J. D. DOUGLAS

**Torrey, Charles Cutler** (1863–1956). Congregationalist. Born in East Hardwick, Vt., he studied at Bowdoin College, Andover Theological Seminary, and the University of Strasbourg. He was instructor and professor at Andover Seminary (1892–1900) and professor of Semitic languages at Yale University (1900–1932; professor emeritus, 1932– ). He established the American School of Oriental Research at Jerusalem (1900–1901). He has written *The Translations Made from the Original Aramaic Gospels* (1912), *The Composition and Date of Acts* (1916), *The Second Isaiah* (1928), *Pseudo-Ezekiel and the Original Prophecy* (1930), *The Jewish Foundation of Islam* (1933), *The Four Gospels* (1933, 2d ed., 1947), *The Apocryphal Literature* (1945), *Our Translated Gospels* (1936), *Documents of the Primitive Church* (1941), and *The Lives of the Prophets* (1946).

**Torrey, Reuben Archer** (1856–1928). American pastor and evangelist. Born in Hoboken, N.J., he graduated in arts and theology at Yale, and also studied at the universities of Leipzig and Erlangen. He was pastor of the Congregational Church, Garretsville, Ohio (1878–82), and the Open Door Church, Minneapolis (1883–86), superintendent of Chicago Evangelization Society and Moody Bible Institute (1889–1908), and pastor of the Chicago Avenue Church, Chicago (1894–1905). From 1901 he engaged in evangelistic work worldwide, after which he was dean of the Bible Institute of Los Angeles (1912–24) and pastor of the Church of the Open Door, Los Angeles (1915–24). His last years were spent as special lecturer at Moody Bible Institute, Chicago. Among his many books were *How I Bring Men to Christ* (1893), *Baptism with the Holy Spirit* (1895), *What the Bible Teaches* (1908), *How to Promote and Conduct a Successful Revival* (1901), *Talks to Men* (1904), *The Person and Work of the Holy Spirit* (1910), *The Voice of God in the Present Hour* (1917), *The Fundamental Doctrines of the Christian Faith* (1919), *How to Be Saved and How to Be Lost* (1923), *The Power of Prayer and the Prayer of*

*Power* (1924), and *Lectures on the First Epistle of John* (1929).

**Totalitarianism.** A theory of centralized, "total" government and politics that emerged in the 20th century. Although widely used by theorists and popular commentators alike, the term so eludes definition that many believe it to be virtually unusable as an analytical concept. The Italian fascists, who coined it in the late 1920s, founded a regime that fell far short of being totalitarian, and the German National Socialists (Nazis) did not really succeed in their intention to create a total state. The Soviet Communists have never accepted it as a valid description of their system. Some historians have applied the concept of totalitarianism to a variety of earlier regimes, such as those of ancient Egypt, Sparta, the ideal state of Plato's "Republic," Ch'in or Han dynasties of ancient China, imperial Rome, Maurya India, the Inca empire, John Calvin's Geneva, and the Zulu under Chief Shaka, and to compare it with other forms of authoritarian rule, also vaguely defined, like absolutism, autocracy, despotism, caesarism, dictatorship, and even "post-totalitarian" systems. Its attractiveness as a polemical device was excellently illustrated through the distinction made by one American government official in the 1980s: "authoritarian" regimes were those who were aligned with the USA; "totalitarian" ones were Marxist-Leninist or other dictatorships of which the USA disapproved. Benjamin Barber has aptly suggested that in light of the many discrepancies in usage and ambiguities in definition surrounding the term, "totalitarianism is to modern political science what reason was to Luther: a conceptual harlot of uncertain parentage, belonging to no one but at the service of all."

Although totalitarianism was used pejoratively against the Axis in World War II, Western scholars paid little attention to the concept until the early 1950s, and it is absent from most reference works published before then. The ensuing popularization was based on two premises. One was that the similarities in character between the communist regime in the Soviet Union and the regimes of fascist Italy and Nazi Germany were greater than the differences between them. The other was that the Soviet system drew its inspiration from sources that were antithetical to the democratic way of life. In the cold war era an outpouring of serious literature on the topic occurred—spearheaded by Hannah Arendt's *Origins of Totalitarianism* and Carl Friedrich and Zbigniew Brzezinski's, *Totalitarian Dictatorship and Autocracy*—but this interest rapidly declined after the 1960s as scholars examined the very real differences that existed within the fascist and communist systems. The quest for a "generic fascism" proved elusive, while the changing character of the communist order—as reflected through

de-Stalinization, the Sino-Soviet rivalry, Eurocommunism, polycentrism in the Soviet bloc, and in the 1980s the more open "glasnost" policy—destroyed theories of a monolithic Marxist-Leninist system.

The value of the totalitarian hypothesis is that it calls attention to real, qualitative differences between previous dictatorships and those which emerged after World War I. The distinctive elements in the new tyrannies were: (1) statism in which boundaries between the state and social groupings, even the individual personality, were dissolved under state control; (2) an officially espoused ideology of some kind; (3) the mobilization of all citizens under a mythical position within the ideology; (4) the unrestrained use of violence, terror, and propaganda to keep the populace in line; (5) elimination of all rival associations which might threaten the dictatorship of the "party"; and (6) centralized control of economic power. This contemporary quest for "total" control's uniqueness was that it occurred within the context of mass democracy and modern technology.

Herbert Spiro wrote that the most distinctive element shared by systems labeled as totalitarian was their ruthless pursuit of a single, positively formulated goal; other possible goals were disregarded or subordinated to the all-important one. This might be imperial power, racial hegemony, the dictatorship of the proletariat, or the rapid industrialization of a backward economy. The resources of the system were harnessed to accomplish the goal, no distractions from this single-minded purpose were permitted, nor would opposition to or disagreement with the process take place. The elites at the top determined the procedures for attaining the goal. The problem confronting the leaders was, however, that if it were achieved, then the raison d'être for the system would be removed. Hence, the movements depended not only on heroic leadership and universal terror but also on permanent crisis and revolution, conditions impossible to sustain indefinitely. Even such governments which survived the wars instigated policies which were not flexible enough to grapple with problems of the real world.

Looking at the matter somewhat differently, novelist and social critic George Orwell contended that the attack upon the concept of objective truth lay at the core of the concept of totalitarianism. A system seeking total power would attempt to control the past as well as the future, that is, to maintain mastery over memory, consciousness, and the inner self. It would try to create a "new" individual whose consciousness was shaped by the party or leader and who did not have any personal existence independent of the collectivity. Psychiatry and other devices of mind control have been used to govern the inner life of human beings as well as their overt actions in some statist societies. The objective, Orwell said, would be to arbitrarily define "truth" by appropriating such words as democracy, peace, and liberation, obscuring the violence central to the system. The "lie" not only concealed violence from the individual but also legitimated it. Historically fascist totalitarian regimes constructed an ideological facade which required "improvement on the truth" because of the vast discrepancy existing between the ideological claim and the actual nature of its rule.

At bottom totalitarianism refers to a religious system. The political system rests on a totalist myth that makes a moral and cultural appeal and replaces the traditional source of order and values, which is essentially religious faith. The total state and its leader(s) become the new god that determines values and demands the ultimate allegiance of the citizenry. Movements that might be construed as totalitarian reflect the moral crisis of civilization. Autocracies of the West during the 1900s have resulted from the decline of Christian culture with its emphasis on moral judgment and self-sacrifice for a cause which transcends human government. Christian culture also works against totalist government by affirming the value of the individual, who has the capacity for self-responsibility.

Considerable scholarship has been devoted to uncovering the origins of states whose governing style uses totalitarian aims and methods. Explanations for their rise are set into four general categories: One category of theories traces it to the complexities of modern societies and economies, or even to the link between modern society and socialism's response to its problems through economic centralization and bureaucratization. A second category connects the emergence of mass political movements and the great military and economic disasters of the 20th century. Especially after World War I the calamities of depression and inflation undermined commitments to traditional values, atomized the masses, and made them susceptible to manipulation by political extremists. A third type of explanation is that the deterministic political implications of the philosophies of Jean-Jacques Rousseau, Karl Marx, and Friedrich Nietzsche laid the theoretical groundwork for totalitarianism. A fourth traces its origins to anti-Semitism and racial imperialism. Those who value this interpretation underscore the utter unpredictability of the Nazi and Soviet systems, and suggest that dictators who follow totalitarian-type policies are motivated by a desire to eliminate the ability to distinguish fact from fiction and to persuade people of the insignificance of human beings.

So many exceptions can be found that no one explanation is satisfactory. In fact, the usefulness of the term for propaganda purposes clearly exceeds its value as a tool for political analysis. By the 1980s it had degenerated into a contentless, emotive slogan appropriated by polemicists or a synonym for authoritarian. True totalistic style was most clearly approximated, not at the level of the state, but in much smaller groups, such as communitarian societies and religious cults.

*See also* CHURCH AND STATE; COMMUNISM, MARXIST.

***Bibliography.*** C. J. Friedrich, ed., *Totalitarianism* (1954); J. L. Talmon, *The Origins of Totalitarianism* (2d ed., 1960); C. J. Friedrich and Z. K. Brzezinski, *Totalitarian Dictatorship and Autocracy* (2d ed., 1965); B. Moore, Jr., *Social Origins of Dictatorship and Democracy* (1966); H. Buchheim, *Totalitarian Rule: Its Nature and Characteristics* (ET, 1968); *International Encyclopedia of the Social Sciences* (1968); C. J. Friedrich, M. Curtis, and B. B. Barber, *Totalitarianism in Perspective: Three Views* (1969); K. D. Bracher, *The German Dictatorship: The Origins, Structure and Effect of National Socialism* (1970); H. Arendt, *The Origins of Totalitarianism* (rev. ed., 1973); J. L. Radel, *Roots of Totalitarianism: The Ideological Sources of Fascism, National Socialism, Communism* (1974); A. J. Gregor, *Italian Fascism and Developmental Dictatorship* (1977); E. A. Menze, *Totalitarianism Reconsidered* (1981); P. Hollander, *Many Faces of Socialism: Essays in Comparative Sociology and Politics* (1983); I. Howe, ed., *1984 Revisited* (1983); S. F. Cohen, *Rethinking the Soviet Experience: Politics and History since 1917* (1985).

RICHARD V. PIERARD

**Tournier, Paul** (1898–1986). Physician, editor, and author. Born in Geneva, Switzerland, he received his M.D. degree from the University of Geneva in 1923, and later served as a physician in the Swiss Army (1939–45). An early believer of what was later termed psychosomatic illness, he was committed to the theory that the origins of illness were not simply physical, but also emotional and spiritual. An early work, *La Médecine de la personne* (1940), which was translated as *The Healing of Persons* (1965), articulated his position and was initially criticized but later accepted. He authored numerous works that have been translated into 13 languages. His best-known English translations are *The Meaning of Persons* (1957), *Guilt and Grace: A Psychological Study* (1962), *To Understand Each Other* (1967), *The Person Reborn* (1966), and *Learning to Grow Old* (1972).

JACK MITCHELL

**Toy, Crawford Howell** (1836–1919). Orientalist and theist. Born in Norfolk, Va., he was educated at the University of Virginia. Later he taught (1856–59) and studied at the Southern Baptist Theological Seminary, Greenville, S.C. After brief spells as a Greek teacher, Confederate soldier, and graduate student, he was professor of Hebrew at the Southern Baptist Theological Seminary (1869–79) and professor of Hebrew and Oriental languages at Harvard University (1880–1909). He wrote *History of the Religion of Israel* (1882), *Quotations in the NT* (1884), *Judaism and Christianity* (1890), *Commentary on Proverbs*

(1899), and *Introduction to the History of Religions* (1913). He was editor of the *Jewish Encyclopedia* and also prepared the Hebrew text and English translation of Ezekiel for the *Polychrome Bible* (1899).

**Toynbee, Arnold Joseph** (1889–1975). British historian. Born in London, he was educated at Oxford where he became a fellow and tutor of Balliol College (1912–15), followed by government service in World War I. He was then professor of Byzantine and modern Greek language and history at the University of London (1919–24) and director of studies at the Royal Institute of International Affairs and research professor of international history at the London School of Economics (1925–55). A profound and wide-ranging scholar, he published works on ancient history as well as studies of modern problems in international affairs. His greatest work was *A Study of History* (12 vols., 1934–61) in which he discussed the rise and decline of 21 civilizations, including the Western, whose downfall he regarded as almost inevitable. Among his other books were *Civilization on Trial* (1948), *The World and the West* (1953), *An Historian's Approach to Religion* (1956), *East to West: A Journey Round the World* (1958), and a history of China and Japan entitled *Half the World* (1973).

J. D. DOUGLAS

**Transgression.** English word derived from Lat. *transgressio*, "a going across." This word often denotes a violation of a command or law. The word "trespass" has essentially the same meaning, and is derived from the Old French *trespasser*, "to go across." Transgression is most frequently represented in the OT by the verb *pāshă'* and the noun *pěshă'*, both of which define transgression as rebellion. They describe sin as personal and voluntary and imply a superior or an authority against whom revolt is carried out (Hos. 7:13). The two words together occur over 130 times in the OT. Much can be learned about transgression and its forgiveness by a study of Pss. 32 and 51.

For a detailed study of transgression and rebellion the following Hebrew words and their cognates must also be considered: *bāghǎdh*, "deal treacherously" (Ps. 59:5); *mā'ăl*, "act unfaithfully" (1 Chron. 5:25); *'āvăr*, "pass over" (Josh. 7:11); *mārǎdh*, "rebel" (Dan. 9:9); *mārāh*, "be contentious" (Jer. 4:17); and *sārăr*, "turn aside" (Isa. 1:23). *'Āvăr* is particularly associated with transgressing the covenant and the Law.

In the NT transgression is denoted chiefly by a family of three words: *parabainō*, "to go past" (Matt. 15:3); *parabasis*, "a going over" (Heb. 2:2), and *parabatēs*, "transgressor" (Gal. 2:18). Transgression is going contrary to the Law (Rom. 2:27;

4:15; Gal. 3:19; James 2:9, 11). *Parerchomai*, "to go past," is used with the meaning of "transgress" in Luke 15:29. Closely associated with the idea of transgression are *anomos*, "lawless" (Luke 22:37); *anomia*, "lawlessness" (1 John 3:4); and *paraptōma*, "a falling aside, trespass" (Matt. 6:14).

ARNOLD B. RHODES

**Transplants, Organ.** *See* ORGAN TRANSPLANTS.

**Trichotomy.** Term from Gk. *tricha*, "triply," and *tomos* "a cut," suggesting that human personality consists of three mutually exclusive and collectively exhaustive principles: body, mind or soul, and spirit. In the christological controversies, Apollinarius sought to provide for the full deity and sinlessness of Christ on the basis of a trichotomist view. He maintained that sin in man resides in the spirit, and that in Christ the human spirit was not present, its place being taken by the divine Logos. This form of Christology was condemned by the church without, however, distinguishing between trichotomy and dichotomy.

ANDREW K. RULE

**Trinidad and Tobago.** *See* WEST INDIES.

**Troeltsch, Ernst Peter Wilhelm** (1865–1923). German theologian. Born in Haunstetten, near Augsburg, he was educated at the universities of Erlangen, Berlin, and Göttingen. He was associate professor at Bonn (1892–1904), professor of systematic theology at Heidelberg (1904–8), and professor of theology at Berlin (1908–1923). He became the leading theologian of the religiohistorical school. He sensed the interrelatedness of religion and social culture. Although he was conscious that the former is much more than the fruit of the latter, he was constantly at a loss to say just where his suggested "syntheses of culture" were final and where they were steps to further synthesis. In all this he posited human freedom rather than a mere discovery of an ever-emerging and determined cultural pattern in the world. His philosophy of history may be called nonsceptical relativism. His most fruitful productions came in the last decade of his life: *Absolutheit des Christentums* (2d ed., 1912), *Christian Thought* (1923), and *The Social Teachings of the Christian Churches* (2 vols., 1931, 1951). Among his earlier publications were *Vernunft und Offenbarung bei Johann Gerhard und Melanchthon* (1891), *Richard Rothe* (1899), *Politische Ethik und Christentum* (1904), *Das Historische in Kants Religionsphilosophie* (1904), *Psychologie und Erkenntnistheorie in der Religionswissenschaft* (1905), *Die Bedeutung des Protestantismus für die Enstehung der modernen Welt* (1906), and *Die Trennung von Staat und Kirche* (1907).

**Trueblood, David Elton** (1900– ). Evangelical Quaker philosopher-theologian. Educated at Brown, Harvard, and Johns Hopkins (Ph.D., 1934) universities, he was converted to evangelical theology through the influence of C. S. Lewis. He taught at Guilford College (1927–30), and Haverford College (1933–36), Stanford University (1936–45), where he was also university chaplain, and Earlham College (1945–70). From 1930 to 1933 he was executive secretary of the Baltimore Yearly Meeting of Friends. Author of more than 30 books, he has preached and lectured widely, edited *The Friend* for more than a decade, and during 1954 and 1955, served as chief of religious policy for the United States Information Agency. Founder in 1946 of what soon became the Yokefellows (committed to common spiritual and vocational disciplines), Trueblood was a major force in the church renewal movement that developed after mid-century. Several of his books, including *The Company of the Committed* (1961) and *The Incendiary Fellowship* (1967), reflect his interest in that movement. Others, including *The Trustworthiness of Religious Experience* (1939), *The Predicament of Modern Man* (1944), *Alternative to Futility* (1948), and *The Life We Prize* (1951), reflect his large apology for the Judeo-Christian spiritual tradition.

NORRIS A. MAGNUSON

**Tunisia.** *See* NORTH AFRICA.

**Turin, Shroud of.** Also called "the holy shroud," a linen cloth alleged to be the winding sheet in which Jesus was laid in the tomb. Long an object of veneration, especially among Roman Catholics but also among many Protestants, tests in 1988 showed the cloth and its sepia-toned image of a nude male with hands over his loins to be an elaborate 14th-century hoax.

The 14-foot-3-inch-by-3-foot-7-inch cloth shows a frontal image on one side and a rear image on the other, with apparent blood stains indicating wounds suffered in a crucifixion. The image is shadowy, losing distinctness at close range. World interest attached to the relic after 1898 when it was exhibited and an official photograph was taken. Further photographs and studies were made at subsequent exhibitions as interest developed.

The shroud first appeared in 1357 at the dedication for the chapel of Lirey, France, established by Geoffrey de Charny. Within a few years questions were raised about its authenticity, but in 1453 it was given to the duke of Savoy and moved to the Cathedral of Turin where it was encased in a silver box. In 1532 during a fire at the cathedral, prompt action saved the shroud, but some molten silver burned through the cloth. Water stains also resulted from the fire, and other patterned holes indicate that, while folded, a hot poker-like instrument was thrust through it. Poor Clare nuns patched some holes and put on a backing to strengthen the cloth.

Modern interest was heightened by the fact that the image of a man with long hair, mustache, and beard, is negative. This led even some scientists to theorize that a burst of energy accompanying the resurrection might explain the image. Others observed that Luke 24:12 carefully described Jesus' grave cloths as strips of linen. In 1978 a team of 24 scientists and technicians from around the world were allowed to conduct nondestructive tests over five days. While the majority report was inconclusive, a minority report by Walter C. McCrone related that the image itself was most likely painted on, using a thin water-color substance commonly used in 14th-century art.

More conclusive tests were allowed after an updated carbon-14 ($C^{14}$) test was developed which allowed definitive tests for age with destruction of a much smaller sample than had previously been possible. The Vatican, which took ownership of the cloth in 1983, allowed the test in the summer of 1988, and the results were released that October. The cloth was shown to have been woven in the 14th century.

**Turkey.** Middle Eastern republic which comprises territory in Europe and Asia Minor, covering a total area of 779,452 sq. km. (300,948 sq. mi.) and with a population of 52.8 million (1987 est.)

During much of the 19th century the Ottoman Empire was considered "the sick man" of Europe. The final death blow came when political leaders led the country into World War I on the side of the Central Powers, confident that Germany would win and counting on popular support because of a longstanding fear of Russia. Defeat in that war resulted in the disintegration of the old Ottoman Empire, occupation by Allied forces of strategic parts of Turkey, and the presence of Greek troops in Smyrna (Izmir), which rekindled national feeling among the Muslim-Turkish population. In 1923 an international treaty recognized for the first time a completely independent Turkey controlling all territories where Turkish populations predominated.

The war had also caused the almost entire liquidation of the large Armenian population on suspicion of disloyalty to the empire. During the subsequent struggle for independence the Greek community was greatly diminished. However, over 100,000 Greeks lived in Istanbul and nearby islands until 1955, when Turkish mobs destroyed Greek churches and property in retaliation for Greek persecution of the Turkish minority in Cyprus. Approximately 2000 Greeks remain in the Istanbul area today.

In 1924, under Kemal Ataturk, Turkey adopted a new constitution and ceased to be a Muslim state. The old religious law yielded to modern codes of criminal, civil, and commercial law. The lunar law of Islam was cast aside in favor of the Western calendar, and a modified Latin alphabet replaced Arabic letters. Western ideas increasingly influenced education, industry, literature, art, and to some extent politics.

During this period of rapid social revolution, religious developments were of special significance. For two decades the secularized state canceled all religious instruction in Turkish schools. Mission schools and hospitals were permitted, but functioned under the same restrictions imposed on Turkish institutions. Tension slackened between Muslim and Christian, perhaps because of growing irreligion and materialism. Gradually during the last half of the 20th century a new trend evolved. "Christian propaganda" was totally curtailed, while Islamic teaching was freely propagated. In fact, a court order put a temporary ban on sales of the Bible.

In 1980 religious affiliation figures showed that 99.2 percent were Sunni Muslims; 0.5 percent were Christians (mostly Greek Orthodox); and that the Jewish population had dwindled to about 7000.

**Tyrrell, George Henry** (1861–1909). Roman Catholic writer. Born in Dublin, Ireland, he left Anglicanism for Roman Catholicism in 1879, and in 1880 became a Jesuit. He studied philosophy at Stonyhurst and theology at St. Beuno's, Wales, and soon became known as one of the ablest Roman Catholic writers in England. From an ultramontane and scholastic position he gradually advanced to an attitude of distinct modernism. Although admonished for his views on hell in 1900 he did not come into serious conflict with his communion until 1906 when in his *Much-Abused Letter* he denied that Roman Catholic theology is perfect and inerrant, and held that the visible church is but a mutable organism subject to development and modification. This incurred the extreme displeasure of the ecclesiastical authorities, and on his refusal to retract the above teachings, he was expelled from the Jesuit order. He was also forbidden to officiate in the archdiocese of Westminster, and he declined the proffered right to exercise priestly functions in the archdiocese of Mecheln on condition that he submit any future writings to the censor. When, in 1907, he sharply criticized the encyclical *Pascendi* he incurred the minor excommunication. Theologically he described himself as a "liberal Roman Catholic." His works, some of which have gone through repeated editions and have been translated into German and French, include *Hard Sayings* (1898), *External Religion* (1899), *Faith of the Millions* (2 vols., 1901), *Lex Orandi* (1903), *Lex Credendi* (1906), *Oil and Wine* (1907), *Through Scylla and Charybdis* (1907), *Medievalism* (1908), and *Christianity at the Cross Roads* (1909).

# Uu

**Uganda.** *See* EAST AFRICA.

**Ukrainian Orthodox Church in America.**
Five distinct churches, totaling about 250,000,
who represent Ukrainian Christians in North
America: (1) The Ukrainian Orthodox Church of
the USA (UOCUSA); (2) The Ukrainian Greek
Orthodox Church (UGOC); (3) The Ukrainian
Orthodox Church in America (UOCA); (4) The
Holy Ukrainian Autocephalous Orthodox Church
(HUAOC); and (5) The Sobornopravna Ukrainian
Autocephalous Orthodox Church (SUAOC). These
churches came into existence because the overthrow of Russian tsarism (1917) offered Ukrainians the opportunity for political and religious
independence from the Russians. Their history
has been one of alternating disputes and cooperation.

Two lines of development nurtured the
Ukrainian churches in Canada and the USA.
Ukrainian immigrants, who included communicants of Catholic or Russian Orthodox churches,
organized their own bodies: the UGOC in Canada
in 1918 and the UOCUSA in 1920. At the same
time, in the newly created republic of Ukraine,
nationalistic church leaders formed the Ukrainian
Autocephalous Orthodox Church (UAOC), breaking away from the Russian Orthodox Church.
These two lines merged when the UAOC sent
Bishop Ivan Teodorovych to America as head of
both North American groups. Teodorovych led
the UOCUSA until 1971, when he was succeeded
by Metropolitan Mstyslav Skrypnyk. Teodorovych
resigned from the UGOC in 1946 and was
replaced by Skrypnyk. In the UGOC Skrypnyk
was succeeded in 1951 by Metropolitan Ilarion
Ohienko.

From the time of his appointment there was
doubt about the canonical validity of Teodorovych's consecration. His superiors in Ukraine
had been ordained as bishops by a presbytery of
priests and laymen, not by other bishops as
required by Orthodox law. Because of controversy
over Teodorovych's credentials, in 1926 some

Ukrainian congregations in America formed the
UOCA. In 1932, the patriarch of Constantinople
consecrated Joseph Zuk as the first bishop for
this church.

The major Orthodox churches relate with one
another through the Standing Conference of
Canonical Orthodox Bishops in America, created
in 1960. The UOCUSA and UGOC, with more
than 200,000 members between them, do not participate in this consultation with non-Ukrainian
Orthodox, but the UOCA, with 40,000 members,
does. This means that the much smaller
Ukrainian body is the one that is accorded legitimacy by other Orthodox communions.

Emigrants from Ukraine after World War II
created the two small autocephalous churches,
HUAOC and SUAOC, concluding that the larger
groups had compromised themselves by subordination to non-Ukrainian church authority; these
two groups claimed to be the true successors of
the UAOC of their homeland.

*Bibliography.* Ukraine: A Concise Encyclopedia, vol. 2 (1971);
A. Serafim, *The Quest for Orthodox Church Unity in America*
(1973); D. J. Dunn, *Religions and Modernization in the Soviet
Union* (1977); P. Yuzyk, *The Ukrainian Greek Orthodox Church
of Canada* (1981).

PAUL D. STEEVES

**Unamuno y Jugo, Miguel de** (1864–1937).
One of the greatest figures in the intellectual life
of Spain, and one of the outstanding men of letters of the 20th century. Born in Bilbao in 1864,
he became professor of Greek at the University of
Salamanca while still in his 20s. A voluminous
writer, his work includes poetry, drama, fiction,
essays on all sorts of topics, as well as studies in
philosophy and religion. The work for which he is
best known in the English-speaking world is *The
Tragic Sense of Life* (1912). In 1914, because of his
anticlerical attitudes, Unamuno was deposed
from the rectorship of the University of Salamanca. In 1927 he was exiled from Spain to the
island of Fuerte Ventura. Escaping to France, he
took up residence in the border town of Hendaye.
With the advent of the Spanish Republic in 1931,

Unamuno again became rector of the University of Salamanca.

Unamuno arrogantly claimed to understand the Spanish soul better than did Spain's greatest writer, Cervantes, the creator of *Don Quixote,* maintaining that he, himself, was Quixote come to life again. Steeped in the mystic lore and classical literature of his country, he became their best interpreter. An incessant traveler throughout the Iberian Peninsula, he wrote descriptions of beauty and spirit. Unamuno had a poignant sense of the tragic element in life at a time when Europe and the West were complacently unaware of impending doom before the outbreak of World War I.

Unamuno was deeply influenced by Søren Kierkegaard long before the latter became known outside Scandinavia. A highly individualistic writer, he was, nevertheless, widely conversant with world literature. He learned 16 languages in order to be able to read the original works of authors who interested him.

Unamuno's other leading works include *The Agony of Christianity* (1928).

JOHN A. MACKAY

## Underhill, Evelyn (Mrs. Stuart Moore)

(1875–1941). Writer on spiritual religion, religious poet, and spiritual counselor. Her widely read *Mysticism* (1911) began in a frame of interpretation deeply influenced by the vitalism of Henri Bergson but under the influence of Friedrich von Hügel and late in her life, of Jacques Maritain, later editions moved steadily in the direction of realism. Her own interpretation of spiritual religion shows a growing maturity and original power as it advances from *The Life of the Spirit and the Life of To-day* (1922) to *The Golden Sequence* (1933) and *Mixed Pasture* (1933). As a religious poet her little volumes *Immanence* and *Theophanies* contain some poems that rank with the best of writings of the 17th-century English mystical poets. Her *Concerning the Inner Life* (1956), her retreat addresses, such as *The Fruits of the Spirit* (1962), and her posthumously published *Letters* establish firmly her reputation as a spiritual counselor. An Anglican with Catholic sympathies, her *Worship* (1936) shows a grasp of the significance of liturgical worship but she could not understand the theology within free Protestant worship.

DOUGLAS V. STEERE

## Unger, Merrill F.

(1909–1980). Bible scholar, pastor, and author. Born in Baltimore, he was educated at Johns Hopkins University (Ph.D., 1947), Southern Baptist Theological Seminary, Nyack Missionary College, and Dallas Theological Seminary (Th.D., 1945). From 1934 to 1940, he was pastor of West Ferry Church in Buffalo, N.Y. He also pastored Winnetka Church, Dallas, Tex.

(1943/44), and Bible Presbyterian Church, Baltimore (1945–47). His teaching career began at Gordon College, Boston, where he was assistant professor of Greek (1947/48). He then taught at Dallas Theological Seminary as professor and chairman of the OT department until he was made professor emeritus in 1967. Among his most significant works are *Introductory Guide to the OT* (1951), *Archeology and the OT* (1954), *Unger's Bible Dictionary* (3d ed., 1960), and *Unger's Bible Handbook* (1966).

JACK MITCHELL

**Uniate Churches.** More properly called "Eastern Catholic" because they comprise people whose ethnic and religious identity distinguish them from the Latin Church. Sometimes called "Greek Catholics," the churches serve Armenians, Arabs, Slavs, Romanians, Egyptians, and Indians, as well as Greeks. They recognize the authority of the bishop of Rome. Before 1962, their most obvious distinctive was their use in worship of traditional languages instead of Latin.

The Uniate churches emerged during attempts to overcome the rupture between Constantinople and Rome (1054). The search for unity actually produced further schisms. Within national churches some believers allied with Rome while others, usually the majority, refused to do so. Those who opted for Rome became the Uniates. Ukrainian rite Catholics, for example, whose 4 million members constitute more than half of the world's Uniates, began as the church of the Russians in the 10th century. It was headed by the metropolitan of Kiev, appointed by the patriarch of Constantinople. In the schism of the 11th century, the Russians sided with the Orthodox. When the Council of Florence (1439) effected a short-lived reunion of Catholic and Orthodox churches, the Russians separated from Constantinople. When Poland was annexed by Russia in the 16th century many Russian Orthodox found themselves under Catholic rule. After decades of conflict Polish Metropolitan Ragoza of Kiev consented to submit to Rome. The Union of Brest (1596) brought churches under Kiev's administration into a Catholic Church which retained the Slavonic liturgy. That church subsequently became known as the Ukrainian (or Ruthenian) Catholic Church. Not all of the Orthodox in Polish Ukraine submitted to Rome. An opposing faction arose immediately and appointed an Orthodox metropolitan of Kiev, producing two denominations of Ukrainians, Catholics and Orthodox, using similar liturgies. The Catholic party was labeled "uniate" by their opponents in the Ukrainian Orthodox group and originally referred specifically to those who adhered to the Union of Brest. It was a term of reproach but came to be used to designate other national churches which affiliated with Rome on the

Russo-Ukrainian pattern. Because of its pejorative connotation, Eastern Catholics reject "Uniate."

Officially, Eastern Catholics are divided into five major "rites," four of which are further subdivided into national churches: (1) the Byzantine rite includes Ukrainians, Russians, Greeks, Bulgarians, Italo-Greeks, Melkites of Syria, and a few others; (2) the rite of Antioch includes Syrians, Maronites, and Malankarese; (3) the Alexandrian rite includes Coptic and Ethiopian Catholics; (4) the Chaldean rite includes Chaldeans and Malabarese; and (5) the Armenian rite. "Rite" refers to the entire system of church discipline, covering more than simply the patterns of worship. It includes, for example, rules about marriage, clergy, and institutions. In the 20th century, a complex process has been underway to create a single code of canon law to govern all Eastern Catholics.

Uniate Christians have suffered as minorities in their native territories. Before the 20th century, their difficulties usually came from their privileged Orthodox counterparts. In the 20th century, countries with Uniate churches have experienced the rise to power of militant Islam or atheistic communist parties. In areas that came under communist rule, the Uniate Church was formally liquidated and its parishes incorporated into the Orthodox Church. Thousands of Catholics resisted assimilation and created a vigorous underground which is commonly called the "catacomb church" of the Soviet Union.

*Bibliography.* I. Vlasovs'kyi, *Outline History of the Ukrainian Orthodox Church* (1956); D. Attwater, *The Christian Churches of the East* (1961); J. D. Faris, *Studia Canonica* 17 (1983); B. R. Bociurkiw, *Ukrainian Churches under Soviet Rule* (1984); I. Hvat, *The Catacomb Ukrainian Catholic Church and Pope John Paul II* (1984). See also the periodical *Diakonia*.

PAUL D. STEEVES

**Unification Church.** A Korean sect started by the Rev. Sun Myung Moon. Born of Presbyterian parents in Korea in 1920, Moon claimed that Jesus spoke to him on a Korean hillside in 1936 and commissioned him to finish the work of salvation which Jesus had failed to complete. In 1954 he organized his followers into the Holy Spirit Association for the Unification of World Christianity. The book *Divine Principle* (1957) set out the essential beliefs of the church. The group moved its main evangelistic efforts to the USA in 1972. Moon's involvement in politics, together with the aggressive witnessing and fund-raising methods of his converts aroused widespread political and religious antagonism. Membership in the USA is about 30,000 and less than one million worldwide.

Moon acknowledges that his theology does not conform with the basic beliefs of traditional orthodox Christianity. He teaches that God's initial plan for the earth failed because Satan seduced Eve, who, in turn, seduced Adam and polluted the human family. Christ, a perfect man (not divine), then came to marry a perfect Eve, have children, and reestablish a pure family. He failed in his mission, however, because John the Baptist doubted him. This, in turn, caused the Jewish leaders to reject him. Consequently, Christ's death on the cross achieved only spiritual salvation for humankind. The Lord of the Second Advent (some followers believe he is Moon) finally will come to establish the perfect family. Thereby the cycle of restoration will begin which will bring all people into harmony with one another and with God in one great family of love.

MELVIN E. DIETER

**Union Church.** A church used jointly by congregations of different confessions. Since the 16th century Protestants and Catholics in some parts of western Germany conducted public worship at different hours in the same building, called *simultaneum* or *Simultankirche*. In the Palatinate, especially, union cemeteries existed alongside union churches. Similar arrangements were introduced into America by German colonists, and union churches, often with union cemeteries and schools, were established in Pennsylvania and other states during the 18th and 19th centuries. Most were erected for Lutheran and Reformed congregations, each confession preserving its identity despite the use of common property. In a few cases Moravians, Mennonites, and others participated. The motive was predominantly economic. Most unions separated but there were still union churches in Pennsylvania in the second half of the 20th century.

The term is sometimes loosely applied to nondenominational community churches, as well as to territorial churches in Germany in which Lutherans and Reformed have a common ecclesiastical administration.

THEODORE TAPPERT

**Union of Soviet Socialist Republics (USSR).** The world's first socialist state and the largest nation geographically, occupying 15 percent of the earth's land surface. In 1990 ethnic unrest and political and economic instability associated with the perestroika reforms brought the USSR to the brink of dissolution. Even in the USSR's flagship region, Moscow, there was serious political debate for withdrawal from the national government. Political independence seemed likely in some districts and the move from a controlled, socialistic economic system to a free market economy inevitable. It was founded in the October Revolution of 1917 in the overthrow of the tzarist Russian Empire and named the Russian Soviet Federative Socialist Republic (RSFSR). It was reorganized in 1922 as the USSR from the former regions of Russia, the Ukraine,

Byelorussia, and the Caucuses. Also called the Soviet Union, "Russia" as a generic term for the vast area was popularly used, although it went out of existence as a political name with the demise of the RSFSR. Divided into 15 union republics in the late 1900s, the USSR encompassed, including the White Sea and the Sea of Azov, 22.4 million sq. km. (8.65 million sq. mi.), and its population in 1988 was 286.7 million. Officially an atheistic state, its principal religion remained Orthodox. The Communist party of the Soviet Union (CPSU) has always intended that religion should eventually die out or be eradicated, but its actual policy toward religion has varied with current political realities since 1917. After the October Revolution the fledgling Bolshevik regime was too preoccupied with government problems to regard religion. By the 1920s larger churches were targets of antireligious activists, and from 1927 through the 1930s persecution of religion proceeded on a massive scale: millions perished, and institutional church life was almost totally destroyed. After the Nazi invasion of the USSR in 1941, this policy changed, partly due to the patriotic stance of the Russian Orthodox Church, which rallied the faithful to the defense of the nation. Moreover, in areas occupied by the Nazis' long-closed churches and monasteries reopened, and the populace flocked to them. It was clear that faith remained alive despite repression. At the end of the war new territories incorporated into the western part of the USSR contained flourishing church communities. Joseph Stalin now wanted to keep the churches "above ground," where their activities could be monitored, rather than driving them "underground."

This pattern of limited officially recognized church activity under close state control continued, with the exception of the antireligious campaign conducted on Nikita Krushchev's personal initiative from 1959 to 1964. This campaign, unexpected and ferocious, involved the arrest of priests, pastors, and believers and the closure of two-thirds of all legally functioning Orthodox churches. It demonstrated to believers how precarious their situation was. The accommodation initiated by Stalin involved no change in Soviet law and would continue only as long as it suited the authorities.

In the mid-1980s the Russian Orthodox Church was by far the largest communion, numbering about 50 million and distributed throughout the USSR, with its heartland in Ukraine, Russia, Moldavia, and Byelorussia. There were about 5.5 million Roman Catholics, mostly in Lithuania and other western areas, and possibly around 1.5 million Eastern rite Catholics (Uniates), mostly in western Ukraine. The Uniates were the largest religious group in the USSR which was completely illegal. Their church was forcibly incorporated into the Russian Orthodox Church after

World War II. Baptists were the largest evangelical group, numbering well over 3 million, followed by pentecostals with about 500,000. Both groups were found throughout the USSR, although they were strongest in the Ukraine. Other smaller groups included Lutherans, Mennonites, Methodists, Seventh-day Adventists, Jehovah's Witnesses, True Orthodox, Old Believers, and other sects of Orthodox origin. The Georgian Orthodox Church in Georgia and the Armenian Apostolic Church in Armenia continued to command the allegiance of the bulk of their countrymen.

The Constitution of 1977 guaranteed "the right to profess any religion or not to profess any religion, to perform religious rites or to conduct atheist propaganda" (art. 52). A basic inequality was inherently maintained because "propaganda" permitted a far wider range of activities than "rites." Believers' legal activities defined in the Law on Religious Associations, adopted in 1929 and revised in 1975, made clear that the only legal activity was worship. Worship could take place only within a building registered for that purpose by the state. In practice, the state limited the number of places of worship for all religious groups to an extremely inadequate level, undermining their one legal right by bureaucratic means. The law recognized as legal only local religious communities, each of which had to consist of at least 20 adult members. Some denominations, mostly the Orthodox, the Baptists, and the Muslims, have maintained centralized administrations, without basis in law, at the discretion of the secular authorities. Some denominations, such as the Roman Catholics and Jews, are permitted no centralized organizations. In a similar way, some denominations had facilities for training clergy or for publishing a limited amount of literature, journals and Scripture, but others did not, and no facilities permitted were adequate for the needs of the denominations.

The responsibility for seeing that legislation on religion was obeyed, and for registering places of worship, rested with the Council for Religious Affairs (CRA), under the Council of Ministers of the USSR. Under a central administration in Moscow, departments monitored the various religious groups and placed commissioners at the republican and regional level. The local commissioners observe the religious communities very closely, especially the priests, pastors, and bishops, and, in some documented cases, have interfered in church life. The close surveillance of church life in the USSR was demonstrated graphically in a secret report of the CRA to the CPSU which reached the West in 1979. It described the systematic monitoring of the activities of Russian Orthodox clergy and its strategy to limit both the effectiveness of their witness and the range of activities open to believers. Active priests and bishops who tried to build church life by zealous preaching or by encouraging young men to train for the priesthood were singled out for questioning and "educative" measures.

State control of the churches into the 1980s was most clearly seen in church involvement in the "peace" campaign. Soviet churchmen were not permitted to offer any independent, Christian input into the debate, but only to support Soviet government initiatives. Groups who permitted a centralized administration were used most prominently—the Orthodox, Baptists, and Muslims. In return for their willingness to endorse Soviet foreign policy aims they were reportedly given permission to train more theological students, to produce more religious literature, and other concessions. The government policy has made life harder for the religious citizens in other ways. Atheists tended to be given the responsible jobs with prospects of promotion. In the education system scientific atheism was the only acceptable worldview, and examinations in it were compulsory.

Dissent in the churches against both state repression and subservience by church leaders heightened in the 1960s, mostly as a response to the Khrushchev campaign. It blossomed in the 1970s, during the brief period of detente, as did human rights activity generally, and attracted publicity in the West. Until some loosening under perestroika reforms in the late 1980s dissent of all kinds was repressed, and a new campaign was undertaken against religious activists. The number of known religious prisoners increased to around the 400 mark by the mid-1980s. Sentences were longer than previously, and from 1982 resentencing of prisoners by the camp authorities began.

The Soviet authorities usually sentenced the most troublesome religious dissenters under articles of the Criminal Code dealing not with infringements of the laws on religion but with economic, political, and other crimes. The leaders of the registered churches routinely disowned the dissenters in their ranks as malcontents and criminals unrepresentative of the mass of the believers. There was, however, a wealth of unofficially produced documentation (*samizdat*) which has reached the West demonstrating that criminal charges against religious dissenters were spurious and that in the vast majority of cases the dissenters were arrested because they attempted to expand the range of action open to believers who wished to witness to their faith.

The most effective and persistent religious dissent in the USSR was by Roman Catholic believers in Lithuania, where the vast majority of the population was Catholic, and priests and laypersons united in articulating their opposition to Moscow's religious policies. The *samizdat Chronicle of the Lithuanian Catholic Church*, document-

ing cases of the infringements of believers' rights, was the most important religious *samizdat* journal still appearing regularly in the USSR through the 1980s. In 1979 almost 150,000 people demonstrated their strength by signing a petition to the authorities asking for the reopening of a Catholic church in Klaipeda.

Despite pressures placed on them, nearly all churches in the USSR grew in the postwar period. From the 1960s many young and educated people began to accept religious faith, a phenomenon which refuted the predictions of Marxist-Leninist theory. The possibility of a "renaissance" or "revival" movement, particularly in the Russian Orthodox Church, was discussed.

The Jewish community in the USSR numbered as many as 3 million in the 1980s, although not all were religious. From the 1960s, however, there was a revival of religious Judaism among Soviet Jewry. For many this expressed itself in a desire to emigrate to Israel. Some 250,000 Jews did succeed in emigrating during the 1970s, but, despite a vigorous emigration campaign, many more who applied to do so were forced to remain in the USSR. Those who remained suffered from a severe shortage of synagogues and rabbis. Soviet authorities condemned the teaching of Hebrew, and some teachers were sentenced to labor camps.

Islam also remained strong in the USSR: with from 45 to 50 million Muslims the USSR was the world's fifth largest Islamic country. They were found chiefly in Soviet Central Asia and the Caucasus, governed by four officially recognized "Spiritual Directorates." A strong unofficial movement in the form of the mystical Sufi brotherhoods evaded state control. There were registered mosques, mullahs, and medressehs (theological colleges), and the Koran was published, but none of these met the needs. The Sufi brotherhoods served as an outlet for religious expression. Islam resisted atheist propaganda, and the Muslim way of life survived more or less intact, despite frequent criticisms in the Soviet press of such practices as the payment of bride-money (*kalym*). The Muslim population presented a demographic problem for Moscow since their birth rate exceeded that of the Russians and a volatile political dilemma with the rise of Islamic fundamentalism in Iran and Afghanistan on the USSR's southern borders. As in the Russian Orthodox Church, Muslims increasingly turned to the values of their culture and history, and they have traditionally held strong national self-identification.

By the later 1900s there were no more than 500,000 Buddhists in Buryatia in the Soviet Far East. They had three registered temples (datsans) and appeared reasonably free to follow their way of life. Some interest in Buddhism was shown by urban intellectuals, and an unknown number converted.

The sweeping societal changes of 1989 and 1990 brought more freedom to religious groups than at any previous time during Marxist control. In early December 1989 Mikhail Gorbachev became the first Soviet leader to confer openly with a pope. That Christmas American television preacher Robert Schuller spoke to an estimated 200 million on Soviet television. Religious literature and Bibles moved into the country with official cooperation. This situation created problems. After decades of underground, largely informal existence, many Protestant, Catholic, and Orthodox groups lacked structure and leadership to openly shepherd an estimated 50 million believers. Also, the political climate of the Soviet Union remained so uncertain that some feared a coup might yet undo the reform movement.

**Bibliography.** L. Kochan, *The Jews in Soviet Russia since 1917* (rev. ed., 1978); M. Bourdeaux, *Land of Crosses: The Struggle for Religious Freedom in Lithuania, 1939–1978* (1979); T. E. Sawyer, *The Jewish Minority in the Soviet Union* (1979); W. Sawatsky, *Soviet Evangelicals since World War II* (1981); S. Akiner, *Islamic Peoples of the Soviet Union* (1983); T. Beeson, *Discretion and Valour: Religious Conditions in Russia and Eastern Europe* (rev. ed., 1983); *Religious Minorities in the Soviet Union* (rev. ed., 1984); D. Pospielovsky, *The Russian Church under the Soviet Regime, 1971–1982*, 2 vols. (1984); A. Bennigsen and S. E. Wimbush, *Mystics and Commissars: Sufism in the Soviet Union* (1985); J. Ellis, *The Russian Orthodox Church: A Contemporary History* (1986).

PHILIP WALTERS

**Unitarians.** A monotheistic religion born within Christianity which recognizes the existence of a transcendent God, but denies the deity of Jesus Christ and the Holy Spirit. The term "unitarian" refers to belief in God as one Person in a unified Godhead rather than as three Persons or a Trinity in the Godhead. The Unitarian conception of Christ's atonement is that it was not a literal vicarious substitute to pay for human sins but rather was a moral act by a man chosen by God that was designed to bring a unity between God and man.

Arius (d. 336), a priest in Alexandria, Egypt, may have been the first to popularize the antitrinitarian views that came to characterize later Unitarians. His teaching that Christ was a created being rather than coequal and coeternal with God the Father led to the Arian controversy whose doctrines the Council of Nicea condemned in A.D. 325. Arianism nearly extinguished Western orthodoxy when it was championed by rulers in the 330s and 340s.

Faustus Paulus Socinus, 16th-century Italian antitrinitarian theologian, is often regarded as the first "modern" Unitarian. He was forced to flee Italy frequently because of charges of heresy lodged against him as a result of the expression of his position. After 1579 he spent much of his time working among the infant Unitarian societies then forming in Poland, although he encountered considerable opposition there also. Because of his influence in the development of the doctrine, Unitarians in Europe are often referred to as Socinians.

Michael Servetus was another prominent Unitarian proponent of the 16th century. Although he did not form a national Unitarian body as did Socinus, he spread antitrinitarian ideas throughout the Continent. A renowned Spanish medical doctor, Servetus gained prominence as a Unitarian thinker in a 1531 article he published which questioned the Trinity and denied original sin. Denounced throughout Europe for his views, Servetus fled from one city to another supporting himself through the practice of medicine. While living in Vienna in 1553 he published *Christianismi restitutio*, a complete denial of all Christian orthodoxy. Condemned to death by the Roman Catholic authorities, he was burned as a heretic in Geneva later that year.

Despite their continental roots, Unitarians have been most numerous in England and especially the USA. Former Anglican priest Theophilus Lindsey organized the first distinctly Unitarian congregation in England in 1774, which met at Essex Chapel, London. English Unitarians started to receive greater acceptance in the latter 1800s and particularly began to grow in the 20th century.

In the USA Unitarians became most numerous. Beginning in 1785 the congregation meeting at King's Chapel, Boston, was considered the first Unitarian body. English minister and chemist Joseph Priestley was the most prominent Unitarian of that period, arriving in 1794 from England where his support of the French Revolution had stirred hatred. A follower of Lindsey, he continued to pursue his two-faceted career of medical research and the preaching of Unitarian doctrines until his death in 1804.

American Unitarians of the early 19th century included such prominent figures of the time as William Ellery Channing and Ralph Waldo Emerson. Unitarians then stressed a more intuitive piety as a result of the Romantic movement of the period. By the late 19th century, however, Unitarians were coming increasingly under the influence of German biblical criticism and adopted a distinctly antisupernaturalist posture. Twentieth-century Unitarians have continued to embrace this trend. They support an ongoing search for truth in which they explore a variety of writings and traditions. They emphasize the freedom of the individual from the restraints of creeds and dogmas, including the literal teachings of the Bible, view Jesus Christ only as a great prophet, and consider the Bible to be merely a significant collection of religious writings. Since 1961, most Unitarians have been affiliated with the combined Unitarian Universalist Association.

**Bibliography.** W. E. Channing, *The Works of William E. Channing, D. D.* (1877); E. B. Gordon, *The Leaven of the Sad-*

ducees (1926); E. M. Wilbur, *A History of Unitarianism,* 2 vols. (1945–62); D. B. Parke, *The Epic of Unitarianism: Original Writings from the History of Liberal Religion* (1957); C. L. Scott, *The Universalist Church of America: A Short History* (1957); E. Albee, *A History of English Unitarianism* (1962); H. H. Cheetham, *Unitarianism and Universalism: An Illustrated History* (1962); E. M. Wilbur, *Our Unitarian Heritage* (1963); G. W. Cooke, *Unitarianism in America* (1972); D. H. Meyer, *Winterthur Portfolio* (1973); R. B. Tapp, *Religion among the Unitarian Universalists: Converts in the Stepfathers' House* (1973); D. W. Howe, *The Unitarian Conscience: Harvard Moral Philosophy, 1805–1861* (1975); C. Cashdollar, *Church History* (1976); G. Williams, *American Universalism* (1976); D. C. Strange, *Harvard Library Bulletin* (1977); P. B. Wintersteen, *Christology in American Unitarianism* (1977).

JACK W. TRAYLOR

## United Arab Emirates. *See* GULF STATES.

## United Brethren in Christ.
Two churches bear this name in slightly different forms and at different times. The Church of the United Brethren in Christ (Old Constitution) has continued under the name since 1889. While they share with other Brethren groups a trinitarian doctrine of God and hold baptism and the Lord's supper to be ordinances of the church, they enforce strict discipline among members regarding the use of alcohol, membership in secret societies, and rejection of any form of "carnal" aggression. A college and seminary are maintained in Huntington, Ind., and several schools in mission areas. Membership in 1980 was about 28,000 in some 280 congregations.

The Evangelical United Brethren, who originated with Philip William Otterbein and Martin Boehm in the late 18th century, merged in 1946 with the Evangelical Church to become the Evangelical United Brethren Church (EUB). In turn, this body merged into the United Methodist Church in the USA (1968), while the North West Canada Conference later joined with the United Church of Canada.

E. J. FURCHA

## United Church of Canada.
Canada's largest Protestant denomination. It was founded in 1925 through union of the Presbyterian Church in Canada, the Methodist Church (Canada, Newfoundland, and Bermuda), the Congregational Churches of Canada, and a number of local union churches in western Canada. Some Congregational churches and about one-third of the Presbyterians voted against union (the latter constituted the continuing Presbyterian Church in Canada). Declaring itself to be "not merely a united but a uniting Church," the denomination engaged in ongoing merger discussions with other churches. In 1968, it absorbed the (eastern) Canada Conference of the Evangelical United Brethren Church. The Western Canada Conference of that church voted against union and formed the Evangelical Church in Canada. Union discussions began in 1944 with the Anglican

Church, the nation's second largest Protestant denomination, and were widened in 1969 to include the Christian Church (Disciples of Christ). The Anglicans withdrew from the discussions in 1975, and the Christian Church suspended discussions in 1985.

The United Church's commitment to ecumenism was reflected in its ongoing involvement in the Canadian Council of Churches and the World Council of Churches. It maintains relations with the World Methodist Conference and the World Alliance of Reformed Churches. The church's doctrinal stance, as set forth in the basis of Union, was orthodox, and candidates for ordination were required to express "essential agreement" with that doctrinal declaration. Subsequent supplementary and explanatory statements offered contemporary expressions and elaborations of its theological position. In practice, the United Church was regarded by its leadership and outside observers as theologically liberal. Within the denomination the United Church Renewal Fellowship sought to rally evangelicals within the church and to counter liberal tendencies. Tensions in the 1980s developed over perceived leftist sociopolitical pronouncements and over the proposal to ordain self-professed homosexuals.

In the late 1900s there were 12 regional conferences, including 92 presbyteries and about 2400 congregations. Although Canada is officially bilingual, the denomination had few French-speaking churches. The biennial general council is the church's highest court. The majority of delegates to that body were designated by the regional conferences. The general council formulated church policy and elected the denomination's moderator for a two-year term. Congregations chose their own ministers, although the presbytery ratified the appointment and inducted the minister. From 1936, the church permitted ordination of women and by the late 1980s there were more than 400 female ministers. The church, in 1980, elected a woman minister, Lois Wilson, to be moderator. Administration was centralized in Toronto where the *United Church Observer* was also published. Theological education was offered at six institutions across Canada.

From 1950, the denomination was involved in making political, economic, and social pronouncements and in lobbying government. It actively supported interchurch coalitions and task forces on such issues as native rights, disarmament, and other social justice concerns. Those pronouncements and involvements have produced some tensions between church activists, on the one hand, and evangelical church members and establishment persons on the other. In common with other Canadian mainline denominations, the United Church declined in membership over the late 20th century, but it remained the largest Protestant denomination in seven of Canada's 10 provinces.

LESLIE K. TARR

**United Church of Christ (UCC).** A product of the modern ecumenical movement and the only major American denomination which traces its ancestry back to each major family of the Protestant Reformation—Anglican, Reformed, Lutheran, and Anabaptist. In the emblem of UCC an adaptation of the words of John 17:11, "That they may all be one," indicates the emphasis the denomination placed from its beginning in 1957 on being both a united and a uniting church.

The union of 1957 brought together the Evangelical and Reformed Church and the General Council of the Congregational Christian Churches, both of which had long American and European roots and were themselves the products of earlier unions.

In 1959 a statement of faith was approved by the second general synod of the new church, and a new constitution was adopted in 1961. More than 100,000 members dissented from the union and formed a Wisconsin-based National Association and an Illinois-based Conservative Congregational Christian Conference. By 1986 UCC included 6408 congregations, and nearly 1.7 million members in 49 states. Membership was heaviest in the East and North. The membership was predominantly white and middle class. While 223 churches had more than 1000 members, 51 percent of the congregations had fewer than 200.

Theologically liberal in its doctrinal orientation, this mainline ecclesiastical organization includes a wide variety of views on polity and theology. Its inclusivity was intentional, an experiment in church union designed to create a melting pot American communion as a model for the church as a whole.

*Bibliography.* D. Horton, *The United Church of Christ: Its Origins, Organization, and Role in the World Today* (1962); L. H. Gunnemann, *The Shaping of the United Church of Christ* (1977); B. B. Zikmund, *Hidden Histories in the United Church of Christ* (1984); L. H. Zuck, *Socially Responsible Believers* (1968).

LOWELL H. ZUCK

**United Free Church of Scotland.** A body formed through a union in 1900 of the majority of the Free Church of Scotland and the United Presbyterian Church. Previous efforts at union had broken down in 1873 due to the strength of opposition in the Free Church. Several factors brought the two groups together: a disestablishment campaign in national politics; adoption by both of doctrinal declaratory acts concerning adherence to the Westminster Confession of Faith; the shared spiritual awakening under Dwight L. Moody and Ira Sankey; and the introduction of instrumental music and hymns in public worship. In 1898 both churches accepted a formula mandatory for ministers and office bearers to sign, pledging their adherence to the fundamental doctrines of the faith and to the principles of Presbyterian church government. The Declaratory Acts of 1879 and 1892 found full expression in the formula. In 1929 the United Free Church merged into the Church of Scotland. A minority refused to enter the union, and they organized the United Free Church of Scotland. In 1985 it had 84 congregations and a membership of 10,118 served by 35 ministers. It was engaged in overseas work in Africa, East Asia, and Australia.

ALISTAIR J. DRUMMOND

**United Methodist Church.** A mainline denomination produced by the mergers of two prominent denominations in the 20th century brought about the United Methodist Church. In 1939 the Methodist Episcopal Church, the Methodist Episcopal Church South, and the Methodist Protestant Church united to create the Methodist Church. The second merger united this body in 1968 with the Church of the Evangelical United Brethren. The new denomination of nearly 11 million members formed under the United Methodist Church name.

American Methodist roots go back to the work of John Wesley in Georgia in the 1760s, shaped and modified over subsequent centuries by such typically American-grown features as revival camp meetings, saddlebag preachers, and an adaptable connectional system. Although major schisms occurred in American Methodist history, the various groups retained evangelical piety, a similar polity, and a basic Arminianism. The first major split took place in 1790. In the early 19th century the African Methodist Episcopal Church and the African Methodist Episcopal Zion Church evolved as separate bodies. The Methodist Episcopal Church, South, came into existence in 1844 over the question of slavery.

The "Evangelical United Brethren Church" was formed in 1946 through a merger of the "United Brethren in Christ" and the "Evangelical Church." Both groups had their roots in the Anabaptist/pietist traditions of Americans of German origin.

Philip William Otterbein (1726–1813), a Reformed pastor, served German-speaking settlers in Pennsylvania in the early 1750s. After a conversion experience he became associated with the Mennonite preacher Martin Boehme (1725–1813). By 1800 both men were recognized as superintendents (later, bishops) of the "German Evangelical Reformed Church." Since 1837, English is the dominant language in corporate worship, although German continued to be used until about 1930. The *Discipline* adopted by this rapidly growing denomination was similar to that of the Methodists.

Jacob Albright (1759–1808), a Lutheran lay preacher in the pietist tradition, attracted followers in Pennsylvania. They were originally known as "Albright's people" but adopted the name "Evangelical Association" in 1816. A division in 1891 was followed by a reunion in 1922. It resulted in the "Evangelical Church," founded in Detroit. Dissenters at the time formed the "Evangelical Congregational Church."

The Methodist as well as the Evangelical Brethren stream brought into the United Methodist Church a strong focus on the centrality of the Scriptures, a social consciousness, an open attitude to tradition, and the willingness to change in nonessentials. Representing almost one-half of world Methodism, the denomination claimed some 10 million members and 1.5 million "preparatory members" in the USA and some 350,000 members in Asia, Africa, and Europe (1985). There were five regional "jurisdictions," each of which was led by bishops and had responsibility for the annual conference within each jurisdiction. The general conference met every four years. The denomination maintained a publishing house and several educational institutions. Life and work of the United Methodist Church was coordinated by a number of general boards and commissions.

**Bibliography.** S. E. Ahlstrom, *A Religious History of the American People* (1972); F. A. Norwood, *The Story of American Methodism* (1974).

E. J. FURCHA

# United Presbyterian Church in the USA.
*See* PRESBYTERIANS.

# United Reformed Church, United Kingdom (URC).
A body formed in 1972 from the Presbyterian Church of England and the Congregational Church in England and Wales. The Reformed Association of Churches of Christ joined in 1981. The URC, a church in the Reformed tradition, was a member of the British Council of Churches, World Alliance of Reformed Churches, and the World Council of Churches. It has 1800 local church fellowships served by 750 stipendiary ministers and 150 auxiliary ministers. In the 1980s it had about 135,000 members. Each region of the country had a provincial synod with a full-time moderator who exercises pastoral care for the ministers in that area. The general assembly meets once a year, and a moderator is elected each year as the national representative of the church. The URC shares in world mission through the Council for World Mission.

# United States of America (USA).
A federal republic of 50 states, consisting of about 9.4 million sq. km. (3.6 million sq. mi.) and 244 million population (1988). The population is mostly comprised of immigrants and their descendants from the 17th century on, primarily European Protestants and Roman Catholics. Racial and ethnic groups from outside Europe contributed considerable religious and social diversity to the USA in the 20th century. In 1980 the population included 11.7 percent black, mostly descended from slaves, 6.4 percent Hispanic, 1.5 percent Asian or Pacific Islander, and .6 percent native American Indian, Eskimo, and Aleut. The course of Christianity in America over most of the 20th century involved adaptation to a pluralizing society without and a splintering church within. These tendencies did not become openly evident, however, until after World War I. As the 20th century dawned, Christianity in the USA reached its zenith of influence and prestige. Ecclesiastical leadership and the larger national ethos were conditioned by a historic Protestant majority. Drawing on the older Anglo-Saxon religious heritage and extended by the evangelical revivals of the 19th century, majority Protestantism was closely identified with the development of the nation. Also present was a growing Roman Catholic minority whose influence on American religious life increased with each decade.

Statistics on church membership and attendance lacked consistency, but a surge in church membership during the 1890s was evident. By the new century about half the U.S. population of 76 million formally belonged to a Christian parish; approximately one-third of church members were Roman Catholic. More significant than membership numbers was the impact that hundreds of thousands of congregations, deeply entrenched in the social structure, exercised on the values and cultural core of the nation.

The prevailing outlook of most American Christians was progressive, optimistic, and confident. Reflective of Western Christendom as a whole, church supporters believed that the spread of foreign missions and the advances of civilization abroad under Western leadership would prepare for the coming kingdom of God. Only a coterie of premillennialists, Seventh-day Adventists, and other millennially oriented groups questioned the theological optimism of the era.

***Denominational Variety.*** In no other society were Christians so separated into competing groups, a condition that partially explains the dynamism of the American churches. Resulting from mobility and freedom of choice, American believers belonged to almost 300 denominations, which were divided by ecclesiastical and doctrinal tradition, sectionalism, ethnic or social ties, or styles of religious experience. Overlapping layers of immigrants since colonial days had contributed to this mixture. Strong-minded religious leaders frequently formed new, independent church bodies, or even launched fresh movements that promoted some theological distinctive.

Standing in the forefront, and somewhat resembling an establishment, were the historic denominations, often termed *mainline*. All of these derived from theological and ecclesiastical movements of the Reformation and were carried to America before 1776. The most prominent were the Baptists, Methodists, Presbyterians, Lutherans, Congregationalists, and Episcopalians. Except for the latter two, these vast communions were segmented into regional or ethnic units. In keeping with the racial segregation of the times there were black counterparts to most church bodies. In fact, the black churches provided the one self-defining institution open to black control. As such, these congregations became a focal point for cultural identity and mobilization.

Adding to the variety were a host of smaller denominations that continued to hold services in the foreign language of their immigrant constituencies, or who had split off from the mainline for any of a variety of reasons. In addition, the turn of the century witnessed the emergence of Holiness groups that stressed Wesleyan sanctification or the glossolalia of pentecostalism. Representative among the former is the Church of the Nazarene (1895), and the latter, the Assemblies of God (1914). The historic "peace" churches—the Friends, Mennonites, and Old Order Amish—constituted another tradition which heavily influenced religious life in Pennsylvania, the Ohio River Valley, and the prairies of the West. In the industrial cities Eastern Orthodox parishes multiplied as immigrants came from the Balkans and Russia.

Supporting these churchly structures was a galaxy of denominational colleges, theological seminaries, publishing houses, conference grounds, mission societies, charity centers, and youth organizations, the YMCA being the best known. Many of the above were chartered as parachurch, nonprofit corporations and effectively mobilized lay volunteerism.

### The Quest for Unity amidst Theological Debate.
Protestant leaders in America and other lands recognized that the world missionary movement demanded interdenominational teamwork. Impetus for cooperation came from the leadership of John R. Mott of the Student Volunteer Movement (SVM), founded in 1886 with the aid of Evangelist Dwight L. Moody. Under the motto, "The Evangelization of the World in This Generation," SVM before 1930 dispatched more than 20,000 missionaries overseas, thousands of whom were women. Increasing international contacts led to the Edinburgh World Missionary Conference in 1910. Most historians date the beginning of the ecumenical Christian unity movement from that gathering. Two years earlier the Federal Council of Churches was founded to foster unity among American denominations. The rise of local, state, national, and international councils signaled Protestant efforts to deal with a divided Christianity.

Concurrently, forces of theological cleavage erupted in American Christianity, the most basic theoretical controversy since the Reformation. The parties deemed "liberal" or "modernist" tried to combine Christian theology with the emerging social and natural sciences. This entailed displacing traditional views of biblical authority and the gospel stress on individual salvation, while embracing Darwinian evolution, higher criticism of the Bible and confidence in human rationality. Jesus was not the divine Savior of lost sinners but the great moral teacher pointing the way to social justice. In oversimplified terms this view became designated the *social gospel*. Claiming to combine Christianity with modern thought, the liberals emphasized reason and intuition as the basis for religious authority. Among the most prominent spokesmen were Washington Gladden, Walter Rauschenbusch, and Harry Emerson Fosdick.

The conservatives mounted a countermovement to defend orthodoxy. The authority and infallibility of the Bible, the virgin birth and physical resurrection, the substitutionary atonement, and the second coming were touchstone issues. Princeton's B. B. Warfield and J. Gresham Machen became well-known apologists. *The Fundamentals*, a 12-volume series by numerous authors initiated in 1910, argued the orthodox case in millions of freely distributed booklets. Many northern conservatives were influenced by the publication of the Scofield Reference Bible in 1909, which stressed a dispensational, premillennial eschatology. Most of the newly founded Bible institutes subscribed to this view, which rejected a gradually unfolding kingdom of God in human affairs. Final confrontation between liberal and conservative forces, however, did not occur in the denominations until after World War I.

### The Churches in War, Peace, and Depression.
The churches heartily joined all Americans in the 1917 crusade "to make the world safe for democracy." Despite a burgeoning peace movement before 1914, both Protestants and Roman Catholics embraced the military effort of World War I with abandon. Only the historic peace churches, along with the Jehovah's Witnesses, questioned American entry. A prevailing mood of "civil religion" seemed to dissolve distinctions between the Christian religion and the nation. Wartime consensus helped enact Prohibition, long a Protestant goal, when the 18th Amendment took effect in 1920.

Immediately after the armistice, unity-minded Protestants launched the Interchurch World Movement of North America to promote faith, democracy, and peace. The effort proved short-lived. Instead, in the 1920s America's churches faced accelerating secularization, an outburst of nativist intolerance, and internecine theological conflict in the denominations. As a result the Protestant Puritan heritage that had helped define the American ethos since colonial times lost its hold on public life. The forces challenging Christianity were formidable. Among these were skepticism, overconfidence in science, evolutionary optimism, consumerism, and media-influenced lifestyles. Except in remote areas, neighborhood parishes no longer played the formative role in community and family life.

The conservative Protestants, who opposed these trends and criticized the liberal theologians who accommodated to them, became known as fundamentalists. While most denominations sustained fundamentalist-modernist confrontations during the 1920s, the only ones to suffer permanent schisms were the Northern Baptist Convention and the Presbyterian Church in the USA. In contrast, the Southern denominations generally remained theologically conservative although their liberal movements were organizing. In that region fundamentalists attempted to outlaw evolutionary teaching in the public schools. The sensationalized 1925 Scopes Trial in Tennessee dramatized the issue. Unable to achieve orthodox uniformity in the mainline denominations, or forestall the secular drift of the larger society, many fundamentalists edged to the fringe as the culture dramatically shifted. Eventually they formed a subculture and institutional base of their own, the dominant form of which developed into the evangelical movement in the 1940s. More conservative groups tended toward small denominations and independent assemblies which perpetuated a separatistic, Bible-based Christianity.

The churches endured the Great Depression of the 1930s with difficulty. Budgets were trimmed, missionaries recalled, and charity funds exhausted. Membership gains were modest, the most observable occurring in smaller evangelistic and Holiness circles. Mainline Protestantism was unprepared theologically and economically for reverses in American society and a collapse of confidence in inevitable human progress.

Sparked by the diverse theologies of Europeans Karl Barth, Emil Brunner, and Paul Tillich, based in the existential philosophy of Søren Kierkegaard, a gradual rethinking began in American theology. This trend, usually labeled neo-orthodoxy, emphasized human sinfulness, divine transcendence, and God's redemptive work in Christ. Although subject to the conclusions of higher criticism, the Bible served in a mystical sense as the bearer of divine revelation. Americans Reinhold and H. Richard Niebuhr furthered the revision of theological liberalism by insisting on the tragic and amoral nature of society and the self-centeredness of individuals. In both Catholic and Protestant circles the nature of the church and Christology became topics of vital concern.

***World War II and Postwar Revival.*** The repudiation of war as an instrument of national policy attracted many clergy in the 1920s and 1930s.

Nazism in Europe and Japanese aggression in Asia, however, made absolute pacifism difficult. When the USA entered World War II the churches met the challenge, but none glorified the conflict or made it a holy cause, although much that was holy was understood to be at stake. More than 8000 chaplains of all faiths served in the military. With suffering so extensive and the struggle so fierce, a new tide of religious sentiment arose in foxholes, battleship chapels, military hospitals, and home congregations.

The surge of religious activity, unknown since 1920, continued after the war for at least a decade and a half. This occurred in contrast to the continued decline of churchly influence in Europe. Membership in all religious groups grew twice as fast as the population. New buildings were constructed, especially in expanding suburbs. Religious books, including the new Revised Standard Version of the Bible (1950), topped best-seller lists. The phrase "under God" was inserted in the "Pledge of Allegiance," and "In God We Trust" became the official national motto. Using the latest communication techniques, mass evangelism was revitalized. As the "cold war" with the Soviets intensified, millions sought religious counsel on television and in books from Roman Catholic Fulton J. Sheen, Rabbi Joshua Liebman, and evangelist Billy Graham. Polls indicated that half the population attended a weekly religious service in 1955, and by 1960 70 percent belonged to a religious body. Some social scientists questioned the depth of discipleship generated, but it was evident that America was the most outwardly religious of any industrialized country.

Roman Catholicism comprised the largest single Christian constituency in the country. Until World War II the Roman Church was absorbed with serving the needs of ethnic immigrant parishioners, who divided into vast communities of Italians, Polish, Hungarians, Bohemians, Portuguese, Mexicans, Puerto Ricans, and others. By the 20th century the older German and Irish groups, with Irish dominating the clergy, had been Americanized. At mid-century further Americanization struggles within and anti-Catholic prejudice outside the Roman Church subsided. Practice and thought were strengthened by a fresh emphasis on scriptural study by the laity and liturgical renewal, which eventually included the vernacular Mass. The election of reforming pope John Paul XXIII in 1958 and Catholic John F. Kennedy to the presidency in 1960 signaled a coming of age of Catholicism in America.

The world flowering of ecumenism became the primary accomplishment of postwar mainline Protestantism; 147 church bodies from 44 countries joined together at Amsterdam in 1948 to form the World Council of Churches, "a fellowship of churches which accept our Lord Jesus Christ as God and Savior." At Cleveland, Ohio, in

1950 the National Council of Churches of Christ in the USA was launched, which brought together various strains of mainline Christianity and superseded the Federal Council of 1908. Denominational mergers also characterized the drive for unity. In 1957 the United Church of Christ enveloped four traditions (Congregational, Christian, Lutheran, and Reformed). The next year the United Presbyterians merged with the Presbyterian Church in the USA. By 1960 96 percent of all Lutherans belonged to either the American Lutheran Church, the Lutheran Church in America, or the Lutheran Church–Missouri Synod. The Methodists, North and South, and the smaller Protestant Methodist Church had unified in 1939, and subsequently joined with the Evangelical United Brethren in 1968. Standing outside the ecumenical movement, numerous smaller, conservative denominations formed the National Association of Evangelicals in 1943. The Southern Baptist Convention, operating independently, continued as the largest single Protestant denomination. By 1980 Southern Baptist membership would approach 14 million.

Foreign missions greatly expanded in the postwar world, largely due to the increased awareness of servicemen returning from overseas. Postwar prosperity supplied the necessary funds. As Western colonialism retreated, the transcultural nature of the gospel was stressed. Added to traditional medical and educational missions were innovations such as broadcasting. During the 1960s about 25,000 North Americans comprised the majority of Protestant mission workers worldwide. In contrast Roman Catholic missionaries (60,000 in the 1970s) outnumbered all others, the Maryknoll Fathers of the Foreign Missionary Society of America being the best known from the USA.

*Pluralism and Protest.* During the 1960s the religious resurgence and societal consensus of the previous decade gave way to domestic ferment unknown since the Civil War. Secularization was enhanced by court decisions outlawing voluntary prayers in the schools and official observances that suggested "excessive governmental entanglement with religion." A new era of realism in the media signaled the erosion of traditional restraints and the decline of biblical morality as the basis for public law. Disenchanted youths, protesting the Vietnam War and the inherited social order, developed a counterculture that challenged all authority. Racial injustices, coupled with political assassinations and urban riots, telegraphed widening societal rifts. Clearly the institutional church could no longer claim to represent America's cultural center. For many the country, along with Western civilization itself, had entered a "Post-Christian" era. Christianity would have to compete in the public arena with alterna-

tive value systems, lifestyles, and even Eastern religions.

The churches reflected no unified reaction to the tides of change. A new radical theology sought to make the ancient faith relevant to moderns by eschewing traditional doctrinal distinctions and "other-worldliness," which were termed "God-talk." Human relationships, situational ethics, and the divine in the secular became bywords, along with the controversial "death of God" concept. Gabriel Vahanian, Thomas J. J. Altizer, and Harvey Cox were representative radical authors.

Both Protestant and Catholic leaders struggled to communicate Christianity to a society increasingly subjective, relativistic, and privatistic about religious matters. Experimentation and informality infused fresh worship styles, and the rules for numerous Protestant clergy moved toward counseling or social activism. A unique youth movement, the Jesus People, exhibited a fluid, often communal approach to fellowship. The Vatican Council II (1962–65) introduced change at the Catholic parish level, including more lay participation and interfaith contact as well as termination of meatless Fridays. Although debated in lay circles, authoritative teachings on abortion, divorce, contraception, celibacy, and papal infallibility were not amended.

The black churches and mainline Protestantism supplied much of the moral force working to end racial segregation in the South. A Baptist minister, Martin Luther King, Jr., and his Southern Christian Leadership Conference provided primary leadership in mobilizing for the national civil rights legislation passed in 1964. As black populations burgeoned in Northern cities the historic black denominations, such as the African Methodist Episcopal Church (1816) and the National Baptist Convention, USA (1886), competed with a growing pentecostal movement. Some black writers, typified by James H. Cone, developed a black liberation theology. Nevertheless the black churches continued as centers of community structure and the National Baptist Convention (5.5 million) remained the nation's fourth largest denomination.

*Conservative Resurgence.* By the 1970s a surge in conservative and evangelical Protestantism took America by surprise. The 1976 election of Southern Baptist Jimmy Carter to the presidency highlighted the term "born again." In a poll that year 48 percent of Protestants and 18 percent of Catholics claimed such a religious experience. *Newsweek* dubbed 1976 "The Year of the Evangelical." Mass evangelism, especially Billy Graham, and television ministries expanded the gospel outreach. No one theological or ecclesiastical tradition encompasses the evangelical religious style. Minimally it represented an outlook committed to a literal, authoritative Bible, personal conversion to Christ, and an obligation to share the gospel and pursue good works. The spread of charismatic practice in America and overseas in many denominations also aided the evangelical renaissance. The Assemblies of God, numbering more than 3 million, constituted one of America's largest and fastest growing evangelical denominations. The National Association of Evangelicals served as a cooperative framework for millions of parishioners scattered across 90 denominations and religious groups. Other conservative church bodies, such as Eastern Orthodox Churches, and the Lutheran Church–Missouri Synod, registered growth. The election of Pope John Paul II in 1978 reaffirmed theological conservatism in Roman Catholicism.

The more liberal and pluralistic mainline denominations underwent membership decline amidst internal debates. Ordination of women, homosexual issues, and political goals were the most controversial. In response traditionalists founded two new bodies, the Anglican Orthodox Church and the Presbyterian Church in America. Mergers marked a continuing quest for unity and larger membership bases. In 1983 Northern and Southern Presbyterians, separated since the Civil War, created the Presbyterian Church, USA, which became the fifth largest denomination in the country. Lutheran consultations considered unification of all Lutherans except the Missouri Synod.

Internationally the World Council of Churches has assembled every seven years. A growing third world membership has directed that body toward reformist political and economic positions. Conservative evangelicals proclaimed both evangelism and the alleviation of exploitation as essential ministries at Lausanne in 1974. Church leaders in North America generally became increasingly aware that the majority of Christians worldwide no longer resided in the West, a demographic development with implications for the future of Christianity in America in particular.

**Bibliography.** G. Hammar, *Christian Realism in American Theology: A Study of Reinhold Niebuhr, W. M. Horton, and H. P. Van Dusen* (1940); H. S. Smith, ed., *American Christianity: An Historical Interpretation with Representative Documents*, 2 vols. (1960–63); R. T. Handy, ed., *The Social Gospel in America, 1870–1920* (1966); E. Wakin and J. F. Scheuer, *The De-Romanization of the American Catholic Church* (1966); H. W. Schneider, *Religion in 20th Century America* (rev. ed., 1967); P. A. Carter, *The Decline and Revival of the Social Gospel: Social and Political Liberalism in American Protestant Churches, 1920–1940* (rev. ed., 1971); J. H. Kane, *A Global View of Christian Missions: From Pentecost to the Present* (1971); S. E. Ahlstrom, *Religious History of the American People* (1972); R. T. Handy, *History of the Churches in the United States and Canada* (1976); M. E. Marty, *A Nation of Behavers in the United States* (1976); D. M. Kelley, *Why Conservative Churches Are Growing: A Study in the Sociology of Religion* (1977); J. W. Carroll, D. W. Johnson, and M. E. Marty, *Religion in America: 1950 to the Present* (1979); G. M. Marsden, *Fundamentalism and American Culture: The Shaping of Twentieth-Century Evangelicalism, 1870–1925* (1980); F. S. Mead, *Handbook of Denominations in the United States* (7th ed., 1980); P. W. Williams, *Popular Religion in America: Symbolic Change and the Modernization Process in Historical Perspective* (1980); D. B. Barrett, ed., *World Christian Encyclopedia: A Comparative Study of Churches and Religions in the Modern World, A.D. 1900–2000* (1982); J. J. Hennesey, *American Catholics: A History of the Roman Catholic Community in the United States* (1982); M. A. Noll, ed., *Handbook to Christianity in America* (1983).

THOMAS A. ASKEW

**United Zion's Children.** *See* RIVER BRETHREN.

## Unity of the Church (Moravian Brethren).

Otherwise known as *Unitas Fratrum*, Unity of the Brethren or Moravian Church. This body traces its origins as a distinct branch of the Christian church to Bohemia (Czechoslovakia) in 1457. It developed out of the national revival of religion in Czechoslovakia, of which John Hus (1373–1415) was a prominent figure. Despite periodic persecution, membership in the *Unitas Fratrum* grew rapidly in the years which preceded the Reformation. By 1517 there were at least 200,000 Brethren and over 400 parishes. The Brethren continued in a "living fellowship in Christ" until the outbreak of the Thirty Years' War (1618–48); in 1627 all Protestant churches in Bohemia and Moravia, including those of the Brethren, were proscribed. During the years which followed, John Amos Comenius (1592–1670), an outstanding Moravian, was its bishop.

In the 1720s a few families from Moravia, Bohemia, Silesia, and Poland, who had kept the traditions of the *Unitas Fratrum*, emigrated to Saxony where Nicolaus Ludwig von Zinzendorf (1700–1760) was offering them religious freedom. They built a village which they named Herrnhut. Under Zinzendorf, who quickly became their spiritual as well as their temporal leader, the *Unitas Fratrum* became a renewed church. Within the next decade the church established relations with evangelical Christians in Western Europe, Great Britain, and America.

In 1732 the Brethren began their foreign missions. A century later, there were 209 Moravian missionaries at 41 missions in the West Indies, South, Central, and North America, Greenland, and Africa. Foreign missions occupied the largest part of the Brethren's work during the 19th century. In continental Europe diaspora work (spiritual renewal among European Protestants) was next in importance to foreign missions. During this century unity synods met approximately decennially; that of 1848 allowed the church in Britain and North America to become autonomous.

By 1914 there were 156 mission stations, 367 European and American missionaries, 111 native missionaries, and 2059 native helpers in North, Central, and South America; the West Indies; South and East Africa; Tibet, and Australia. They reported having reached—through church, school, or preaching place—more than 100,000 people in the year 1913. Since then Moravian congregations in former mission fields have been encouraged to become completely self supporting. In 1984 there were 17 provinces. The *Unitas Fratrum* suffered during both World Wars, particularly after the division of Germany following World War II, which put Herrnhut, and other Moravian centers in East Germany.

The *Unitas Fratrum* is basically Presbyterian in polity. It has retained from its earliest days the threefold order of ministry: bishop, presbyter, and deacon. Each province is governed by an elected synod, and the entire *Unitas Fratrum* is represented at a unity synod which meets every seven years. Among the traditions handed down to Moravians by Zinzendorf is the personal devotional book *Daily Texts* (*Losungen*), published annually and now available in 34 languages. It is widely read by Moravians and non-Moravians and has a circulation of 1.25 million copies.

The total membership of the *Unitas Fratrum* (1984) is 444,437, of which 261,489 are communicants. The British province has a membership of 3754, the Continental, 19,274, the two American provinces a total of 55,932, with the greatest membership of all provinces being that of Tanzania (Western), with 51,748. The *Unitas Fratrum* is a charter member of the World Council of Churches.

*Bibliography.* B. E. Michel, *The Moravian Church, Its History, Faith and Ministry* (1978); *Moravian Daily Texts*, with statistical supplement (pub. annually); *Church Order of the Unitas Fratrum (Moravian Church) with appendix: 1981* (1981); J. T. Hamilton and K. G. Hamilton, *History of the Moravian Church, the Renewed Unitas Fratrum, 1722–1957* (2d ed., 1983).

DAVINA DAVIS

## Unity School of Christianity.

Perhaps the largest mail-order religious organization in the world. The movement was founded in 1889 in Kansas City, Mo., by Charles and Myrtle Fillmore. Claiming experiences of healing from various physical ailments, including tuberculosis, Myrtle Fillmore converted to Christian Science in 1887. Soon afterwards her husband Charles also claimed a dramatic healing, and together they began a new movement that today involves millions of people around the world.

The Fillmores did not intend to found a church or denomination. They envisioned an organization, supplementary to existing churches, which would offer counseling, prayer, and healing through publications, classes, and the mass media. Today, however, Unity does operate local autonomous churches or centers, staffed by licensed, ordained ministers, many of whom are women. The administrative center for the movement is Unity Village, a corporate municipality located outside Kansas City, Mo. The organization operates an extensive telephone counseling ministry, provides retreats and classes for laypersons, and administers a two-year training program at the Unity Ministerial School. Three monthly publications receive wide circulation: *Unity Magazine, Daily Word,* and *Wee Wisdom,* America's oldest continuing magazine for children.

The Fillmores were heavily influenced by the New Thought movement. Charles, who was familiar with the spiritualists and the theosophists, incorporated a modified version of reincarnation into his teaching. Unity's purpose is to equip people to cope with life's problems through prayer, right thinking, and the realization that God is within everyone. Unity's God is not the God of traditional Christian theology but rather an impersonal, universal principle. Prayer is employed as affirmation, not entreaty. According to Unity, everyone can realize and express divine potential, an idea common to Eastern and New Age sects. Unity teaching exhibits fundamental differences with orthodox Christianity in their views of the Trinity, the atonement of Jesus Christ, the resurrection, and the Bible.

*Bibliography.* W. R. Martin, *The Kingdom of the Cults* (1977); G. W. Braswell, Jr., *Understanding Sectarian Groups in America* (1986).

RONALD ENROTH

## Universalism.

A theology which holds that in the fullness of time all souls will be released from the penalties of sin and be restored to God. Technically known as *apokatastasis pantōs* ("restoration of all"), universalism denies the doctrines of eternal punishment and the salvation only of an elect. While based on biblical passages such as Acts 3:21, Rom. 5:18–19, 1 Cor. 15:22, and Eph. 1:9–10, the first clearly universalist writings date from the Greek church fathers, most notably Clement of Alexandria (c. A.D. 150–c. 215), his student Origen (c. 185–c. 254), and Gregory of Nyssa (330–c. 395). Augustine of Hippo (354–430) strongly opposed universal salvation and the theology of Origen was eventually declared heretical at the Fifth Ecumenical Council in 534.

In Western Europe universalism almost completely disappeared during the Middle Ages and was rejected, too, by the magisterial Protestant Reformers who held a strongly predestinarian view of salvation. Within the Radical Reformation, however, a few spiritualist and Anabaptist writers, notably Hans Denck (c. 1495–1527), revived the idea. It later came to fuller expression in radical German pietism, particularly through the influence of the mystical theosophist Jacob Boehme (1575–1624). Pietist universalism was brought to America by George De Benneville (1703–1793) and through such sectarian groups as the Dunkers (today, Church of the Brethren).

The formation of a church in which universal salvation was an explicit and central article of faith took place in America during the late 18th century. John Murray (1741–1815), an earlier exponent of the Whitefield-Wesleyan revival, arrived in New England in 1770 and organized the first Universalist congregation at Gloucester, Mass., in 1779. Universalist ideas were also developing about the same time around certain liberal Congregational clergy, of whom Charles Chauncy (1705–1787) is representative. Some Baptists also adopted universal salvation as they moved from their English Calvinist roots. Elhanan Winchester (1751–1797), for example, organized a Universalist congregation in Philadelphia in 1781. Winchester developed a compelling biblical argument for restorationism in his *Universal Restoration, Exhibited in Four Dialogues* (1788, 1792).

From this theologically diverse and noncoherent movement, a Universalist denomination began to take shape. A loosely agreed upon statement of faith, the Winchester Confession, was also adopted in 1803. Doctrinal statements were also formulated in 1899 and 1935. It was Hosea Ballou (1771–1852), however, who proved to be the dominant spokesman for the movement in the early 19th century. His classic *Treatise on the Atonement* (1805) posits a moral (rather than substitutionary) view of Christ's redeeming sacrifice. He taught that death brings the unregenerate soul to repentance, thus denying any hell punishment. An influential pastor and editor, Ballou moved the Universalist church closer to Unitarianism.

Twentieth-century Universalism, now clearly a liberal faith, was shaped largely by Clarence Skinner (1881–1949). He articulated a wider vision of universalist thought which sought to explore the commonality of all faiths. Ties were sought with the major world non-Christian and native American religions. Modern Universalists have emphasized such beliefs as the reasonableness of moral action, the tolerance of diversity, and the brotherhood of all humanity. The long felt cooperation between Universalists and Unitarians led to a formal merger of the two churches in 1961 into the Unitarian-Universalist Association.

Universalism as a belief in the final salvation of all persons continued to have an appeal through the 20th century. Neo-orthodox theology as shaped by the Swiss theologian Karl Barth (1886–1968) gave it a new respect. While Barth did not directly teach *apokatastasis*, certain passages of the massive *Church Dogmatics* (1936–39) stress the irresistible universal triumph of God's grace. A few Protestants also defended the idea of a "Hades Gospel," which gives a second chance to confess Christ for those who have not yet heard it. Mormon theology offers a similar "second chance."

*Bibliography.* T. Whittmore, *The Modern History of Universalism* (1860); H. Ballou, *The Ancient History of Universalism: From the Time of the Apostles to Its Condemnation in the Fifth General Council, A.D. 553* (2d rev. ed., 1872); R. Eddy, *Universalism in America: A History,* 2 vols. (1884–86); H. H. Allen and R. Eddy, *History of the Unitarians and Universalists in the United*

States (1894); C. R. Skinner, *The Social Implications of Universalism* (1915); C. R. Skinner and A. S. Cole, *Hell's Ramparts Fell: The Life of John Murray* (1941); C. R. Skinner, *A Religion for Greatness* (1945); A. D. Bell, *The Life and Times of George De Benneville, 1703–1793* (1953); G. C. Berkouwer, *The Triumph of Grace in the Theology of Karl Barth* (1956); C. L. Scott, *The Universalist Church in America: A Short History* (1957); R. A. Byerly, "A Biblical Critique of Universalism in Contemporary Theology" (unpub. thesis, Temple University, 1959); E. Cassara, *Hosea Ballou: The Challenge to Orthodoxy* (1961); A. Harnack, *History of Dogma* (ET, 3d ed., 1961); R. E. Miller, *The Larger Hope: The First Century of the Universalist Church in America* (1961); C. Irwin, "Pietist Origins of American Universalism" (unpub. thesis, Tufts University, 1966); E. Cassara, *Universalism in America: A Documentary History* (1971); G. H. Williams, *American Universalism: A Bicentennial Historical Essay* (1971).

DAVID B. ELLER

**Unrai, Wogihara** (d. 1937). Buddhist priest and scholar. Born in Kitatanabemachi, Wakayama Prefecture, Japan, he studied at the Buddhist College attached to the Jodo Sect, and the University of Strassburg (Ph.D., 1905). He was professor of Sanskrit and Pāli at the Taisho College (1905–37), and became lecturer at Tokyo Imperial University (1912–19). He wrote many articles on the theology and history of Buddhism and especially on Buddhist Sanskrit. His studies and critical publications include *Mahāvyutpatti* (2d ed., 1927), *Bodhisattvabhūmi* (1930–36), *Haribhadra's Abhisamayālaṁkārālokā Prajñāpāramitavyākhyā* (1932–35), and *Saddharmapuṇḍarīka-sūtra* (1934–35). His Sanskrit-Japanese dictionary with reference to Chinese translation of Buddhist scripture was partly issued after his death.

S. MATSUNAMI

**Upper Volta.** *See* WEST AFRICA.

**Uppsala Assembly, World Council of Churches.** The fourth WCC world assembly, convened in Uppsala, Switzerland, July 4–19, 1968. Its theme of "Behold, I Make All Things New" was carried forward in six sections: the Holy Spirit and the catholicity of the church; renewal in missions; world economic and social development; toward justice and peace in international affairs; worship; and toward new styles of living.

Despite its interest in catholicity, the assembly marked an end of an era of ecumenical movement and the beginning of a new orientation toward social and political activism. Papers spoke of the church's boldness "in speaking of itself as the sign of the coming unity of mankind" and noted that secular efforts at conciliation and unification often seemed more effective than those of the church. Therefore, the call was made to seek "a new openness" to the world situation. Economic inequalities dominated debate. The assembly recommended that churches set aside one percent of their total income for development aid and that they encourage their governments to follow suit from their GNP. The percentage was to be increased in subsequent years.

The ongoing divisions of the church in philosophy and theology were recognized, and little could be accomplished to alleviate them. Roman Catholic observers were involved and Jesuit Robert Tucci told the assembly that Roman Catholic membership might be in the offing. Yet discussions revealed that the Protestant view of the church as a spiritual entity and the Roman Catholic conception of the church as an ecclesiastical government could not be resolved. Unity of people, and not of the church, was stressed. Divisiveness was interjected into the meeting by a militant youth faction, whose delegates were highly critical of the ecumenical establishment. This group staged demonstrations, demanding more recognition in the assembly.

Little that was new in theology came out of discussions and papers. Christians were called to "venture out towards unknown horizons" in distinguishing the ethics of the gospel from their cultural contexts. Contextualization discussions revolved around birth control and sexual ethics, family patterns, and changes in societal roles, but delegates reached no consensus. A wide number of innovative liturgies were presented, and it was asserted that the only true worship speaks to social injustices and divisions among humanity.

Actions taken radically affected the organization and focus of WCC work. Several subunits were added: the Programme to Combat Racism (PCR), the Commission on the Churches' Participation in Development (CCPD), the Christian Medical Commission (CMC), the Dialogue with People of Living Faiths and Ideologies (DFI), and education. Besides considering the question of Roman Catholic participation, deeper relations with national and regional councils was a priority.

Presidents elected to lead the WCC for terms in succeeding years were Patriarch German, Hans Lilje, Daniel T. Niles, Kiyoko Takeda Cho, Ernest A. Payne, John Coventry Smith, and Alphaeus H. Zulu. Indian theologian M. M. Thomas was named moderator of the central committee.

*See also* WORLD COUNCIL OF CHURCHES (WCC).

A. J. VAN DER BENT

**Uruguay.** South America's smallest nation geographically, which alternated between military dictatorship and republic in the latter 1900s. Officially called the Eastern Republic of Uruguay (República Orientale del Uruguay), the population of about 3.1 million (1990) was known as "Orientales" and was 10 percent mestizo, 89 percent Iberian descent, and a small number of

Europeans, mulattos, and blacks. The country is largely Atlantic coastal plain, and 12 percent of its 176,215 sq. km. (68,037 sq. mi.) is arable. Well-watered rolling, grassy plains and hills have sustained a thriving cattle and sheep industry. Almost half of the nation's people live in the capital, Montevideo, a port on the Rio de la Plata, which stretches 170 miles by 140 miles and drains almost one-third of South America's watershed. Uruguay was once considered the continent's most democratic country (women's suffrage was instituted in 1932) and one of its most prosperous economies, with an advanced social welfare program.

The urbane and sophisticated populace—with a literacy rate of 96 percent—were among the first to decry the influx of capital from the industrial nations which began to divert the wealth of the country north, lowering the standard of living. In the ensuing struggle between the Tupamaros (leftist guerrillas drawn from the upper classes) and the corrupted military and government officials, a repressive dictatorship was established and political prisoners were tortured and killed.

Civilian government was restored in 1985, ending 12 years of crushing rule, but the effects of the huge international debt remain and the country faces the crisis common to the region—runaway inflation, underemployment, and an economy dependent on exports. During the repressive military era 400,000 Uruguayans emigrated with no plan of returning.

Historically nonreligious, Uruguayans have been the least Catholic of all South America. Fully 37 percent were self-proclaimed atheists (1987) although the Roman Catholics claimed 66 percent of the people. These statistics likely counted many of the same people, since not all baptized remained in the faith. The country was divided into one archdiocese and nine dioceses with 222 parishes served by one archbishop, 11 bishops, 552 priests, 1641 nuns, and 148 brothers (1983). Reflecting the country's ills Jesuit Juan Luis Segundo in 1959 published *Función de la Iglesia en la Realidad Rioplatense*, which opened a new era of contemporary Latin American theology in what subsequently was termed liberation theology.

The 59,600 evangelicals comprise only 1.9 percent of the populace, making it the smallest percentage in Latin America, yet strong Protestant voices have emerged from this tiny number, including Emilio Castro, once general secretary of the World Council of Churches (WCC). Missionary agencies from 15 countries support 115 missionaries, and there are 36 Protestant denominations.

FAITH ANNETTE SAND

# Vv

**Valentine, Milton** (1825–1906). Lutheran. Born near Uniontown, Md., he studied at Pennsylvania (now Gettysburg) College, Gettysburg, Pa. Ordained a Lutheran minister in October 1852, he served pastorates at Winchester, Va. (1852/53), Greensburg, Pa. (1853/54), and after serving as principal of the Emaus Institute, Middletown, Pa. (1854–59), returned to the pastorate, St. Matthew's Church, Reading, Pa. He became professor of ecclesiastical history in the Lutheran Theological Seminary, Gettysburg (1866–68); president of Pennsylvania College, Gettysburg, (1868–84); and professor of systematic theology and chairman of the faculty, Lutheran Theological Seminary, Gettysburg (1884–1903; emeritus, 1903–6). He served several terms as joint editor of the *Lutheran Quarterly* (1871–76; 1880–85; and again after 1898). He wrote *Natural Theology or Rational Theism* (1885), *Theoretical Ethics* (1897), *Christian Truth and Life* (1898), and *Christian Theology* (1906).

Raymond W. Albright

**Vancouver Assembly, World Council of Churches.** The sixth assembly, convened in 1983, the most representative world gathering in the history of the ecumenical movement. Its theme, "Jesus Christ—the Life of the World," involved work on witnessing in a divided world; taking steps toward unity; moving toward participation; healing and sharing life in community; confronting threats to peace and survival; struggling for justice and human dignity; learning in community; and communicating credibly. Renewal was stressed in the areas of interfaith unity, mission, evangelism, justice, and peace. A feature of the meeting was a large tent in which thousands worshiped each day with the delegates.

The WCC assembly continued to be dominated by a social and political emphasis, revolving around the "realized eschatology" of liberation theology. There were signs of growth in maturity in ecumenical fellowship as delegates dealt realistically with the sharp divisions and tragic conflicts among one another and in the world. Messages stressed the unity of world society, even though it be torn by tension and conflict, and sought to link peace and justice as an operating principle of WCC-affiliated churches. The assembly suggested that member churches continue to jointly discuss their mutual commitment to bringing the reality of justice, peace, and integrity to all creation.

Beyond approaching ecumenicity from a more eschatological perspective, the assembly again attempted to open the door to other forms of unity with a document on "Baptist, Eucharist and Ministry." Churches were asked to comment on the document and its inherent understandings by 1986. Contextualization in world evangelism continued to be given attention; discussion of Christian witness centered in the contexts of culture, worship, the situation of the poor, the life of children, and the pluralistic world, with its religions. Future steps for collaboration between WCC and the Roman Catholic Church were outlined.

Priority areas for WCC activities for the following seven years included growth toward unity, justice and peace, a vital and coherent theology, new self-understandings by churches, and confessing, learning community. Presidents elected to terms to carry out these mandates were R. Nita Barrow, Marga Búhring, Paulos Mar Gregorios, Johannes W. Hempel, W. F. Khotso Makhulu, and Lois M. Wilson. Heinz-Joachim Held was named to moderate the central committee.

*See also* World Council of Churches (WCC).

A. J. Van Der Bent

**Van Dusen, Henry Pitney** (1897–1975). American ecumenical leader, educator, and author. Born in Philadelphia, Pa., he studied at Princeton University; New College, Edinburgh; Union Theological Seminary; and Edinburgh University (Ph.D., 1932). A theological liberal and advocate of justice and human rights, in 1924 he was ordained a Presbyterian Church in the USA minister despite conservative objection. In 1924 he began his long career at Union Theological

Seminary as an instructor. He held chairs of theology (1936–63), and was president of the seminary (1945–63). Following his educational career, he traveled widely promoting world Christianity, and was a leader of the World Council of Churches (WCC). Among his numerous books were *In Quest of Life's Meaning* (1926), *The Plain Man Seeks for God* (1933), *For the Healing of the Nations* (1940), *East Indies Discoveries* (1944), and *God in Education* (1951).

JACK MITCHELL

**Van Dyke, Henry Jackson** (1852–1933). Presbyterian. Born in Germantown, Pa., he studied at Princeton College, Princeton Theological Seminary, and the University of Berlin. He was pastor at United Congregational Church, Newport, R.I. (1879–82), and the Brick Presbyterian Church, New York City (1883–1900). He became professor of English literature at Princeton (1900–1923), U.S. government minister to the Netherlands and Luxemburg (1913–17), American lecturer at the University of Paris (1908/9), and moderator of the general assembly of the Presbyterian Church, USA (1902/3). He was a prolific writer. His later books include *The Spirit of America* (1910), *Fighting for Peace* (1917), *The Valley of Vision* (1919), *Golden Stars* (1919), *Camp Fires and Guide Posts* (1921), *Companionable Books* (1922), *Six Days of the Week* (1924), *Half-Told Tales* (1925), *The Golden Key* (1926), *Chosen Poems* (1927), *Even unto Bethlehem* (1928), *The Man Behind the Book* (1929), and *Gratitude* (1930).

RAYMOND W. ALBRIGHT

**Van Til, Cornelius** (1895–1987). Christian Reformed theologian. Born in Grootegast, Groningen, the Netherlands, Van Til was raised in the piety and orthodoxy arising from the 1834 secession movement from the Dutch Reformed Church. In 1905 he emigrated with his family to Highland, Ind., and eventually attended Calvin College, Princeton Seminary, and Princeton University (Ph.D., 1927). He served as pastor in Spring Lake (Mich.) Christian Reformed Church (1927/28) and then became instructor in apologetics at Princeton Seminary (1928/29). In the wake of the Auburn Affirmation (1924) modernists were on the ascendancy and took control of the Princeton Seminary board of trustees. In 1929 Van Til resigned, along with Oswald T. Allis, J. Gresham Machen, and Robert Dick Wilson, and organized Westminster Seminary, where Van Til was professor of apologetics (1929–76).

He developed a distinctive approach to theology and apologetics called presuppositionalism, which rejected classic theology's assumption that the question of God must be settled by an appeal to facts and laws. The non-Christian will be unable to see the God behind the facts, Van Til said, until that person has the concept of God as

a category of thought. The apologetic task, therefore, is to expose the error of the unbelieving mind by showing that life and reality make sense only on the basis of Christian presuppositions. The work of the Christian is to seek God's presuppositions, found in Scripture, and so imperfectly to think God's thoughts after him.

These insights were disseminated in more than 250 articles and in some 30 books, including *The New Modernism: An Appraisal of the Theology of Barth and Brunner* (1946), *Christianity and Idealism* (1955), *The Defence of the Faith* (1955), *Christianity and Barthianism* (1962), *A Christian Theory of Knowledge* (1969), and *The New Hermeneutic* (1974).

JAMES A. DE JONG

**Vanuatu.** *See* SOUTH PACIFIC, ISLANDS OF THE.

**Varnava (Rossitch)** (1880–1937). Serbian Orthodox. Born in Plevlye, Old Serbia, he studied at the Theological Seminary of Prizren, Serbia, and the Theological Academy of St. Petersburg. He served as a chaplain to the Serbian Legation at Constantinople (1905–10), was consecrated bishop (1910), and was elected patriarch of Serbia (1930). He was very active in the organization of the Serbian national patriarchate, restored after World War I, and achieved its stabilization. He died in the middle of an acute conflict in the realm caused by the concordat of Jugoslavia with the Vatican to which he was strongly opposed.

GEORGES FLOROVSKY

**Vatican Council II** (1962–1965). The 21st ecumenical council of the Roman Catholic Church and a major turning point in Catholic life. Papal announcement on January 25, 1959, that a council would be convened evoked astonishment in church and world. In office only 90 days, Pope John XXIII suddenly and unexpectedly, at the "motion of the Holy Spirit," announced his intention to convene an ecumenical council. Leo XII, Pius XI, and Pius XII had evidently entertained the idea, but nothing had come of it.

Vatican Council I (1869/70) had left the church in ambivalence. Its major accomplishment had been to equip the papal office with unprecedented and final authority. Many thought that in the so-called new church there would be no place for a general council. The dogma of immaculate conception required no more than papal letters intimating a decision already taken. A second question remained untouched: What was now the role of bishops? Vatican Council I had been deferred. In 1959 it was at first uncertain whether John's council would be Vatican I continued or a quite new agenda.

What John had in mind was to call a diocesan synod to update the 1917 Canon Law, and to summon an ecumenical council. His encyclical,

*Ad Petri Cathedram* (July 3, 1959) foresaw a council "to advance the development of the Christian faith" and "the adaptation of ecclesiastical discipline to contemporary conditions"; and the hope was expressed that "those who are separated from the Apostolic See will see in it a warm invitation to seek and find unity."

Churches other than Rome would be involved. More than 100 non-Catholics observed at one time or another. A message on November 14, 1960, told the preparatory committees that the proclamation of new dogmas would not be a principal end. "On every hand, the battlelines are drawn against what is good and true . . . there are temptations and the lure of material advantage." In the face of this, the pope wished to "effect a renewal of Faith's strength." The language was to be Latin, the official language of the church and the only tongue which all the participants shared.

***Chronology.*** The council opened on October 11, 1962, with 2540 voting delegates present. As directed by *motu proprio*, various commissions drew up schemata (draft documents). A new pope opened session two, Paul VI having succeeded John XXIII in June 1963. On December 7, 1965, the pope and Patriarch Athenagoras I, in Rome and Istanbul, expressed mutual regret for mistakes in the past and hope for future reconciliation. On December 9 session four ended, and with it the council.

***Emphases.*** (1) *Aggiornamento* (a refurbishing) of the church was to be achieved by a continuous return to the sources of Christian life in revelation and tradition and adjustment to the "changed conditions of the times." (2) For the first time in the history of councils, the Roman Church in an opening message addressed, not merely its members, but "all Men and Nations." A new universal orientation for the church was being signaled. (3) The new orientation was demonstrated in new social ministries and awareness, such as showing concern for the poor, and condemning discrimination. The council expressed a greater optimism concerning salvation, that "whoever fears God and does what is right is acceptable to God." This constituted a significant shift of emphasis to the subjective in Roman Catholic soteriology. It also fostered new religious freedom, abrogating, after one of the council's most heated debates, the long-accepted maxim that "error has no rights." (4) Inferred in this was a renovated understanding of the church. The laity's important role was emphasized by, among others, delegate Karol Wojtyla, the future John Paul II. The ecclesiastical importance of the church organization in holding Peter's "keys" as the "body of Christ" was not rejected, but it was supplemented by a concept of the church as the "people of God."

***Documents.*** The new ideas were proclaimed in four major documents: *Lumen gentium* (the church), *Dei verbum* (revelation), *Sacrosanctum concilium* (liturgy), and *Gaudium et spes* (the church in the modern world). One decree *Unitatis redintegratio* (Ecumenism) was also issued.

An initial draft of *Dei verbum* proposed two sources of revelation, Scripture and church tradition. This reaffirmed the interpretation of the Council of Trent and was least acceptable to other churches. A large majority of Vatican II delegates voted against the draft in secret ballots, and dramatic papal action withdrew it. Rewritten, it was passed with virtual unanimity three weeks before the council closed. Both sources were, in the end, retained, but the place of tradition was somewhat redefined. Tradition was expounded, not as independent of Scripture, but as its "agent"; "it takes the Word of God and explains it." The magisterium serves the Word of God. On the debit side, the council's exegetical methods were less than satisfactory. Karl Rahner complained that Scripture was to be quoted as "dicta probantia, to give substance to what is known on other grounds." On the other hand, the document encouraged exegetical study of the Bible in collaboration with "separated brethren" (Protestants) and promoted private reading.

Four major points are made in *Lumen gentium*. (1) The hierarchical structure of the church, placed first in the first draft, was in a second preceded by "the people of God" and followed by "the laity." This drastically supplanted Pius XII's *Mystici corporis Christi* understanding of the church as the continuing incarnation of Christ. The new emphasis conceived of the church as a pilgrim people pressing forward, closer to the understanding of Augustine. Encounter with this active people means contact with a God whose active grace lives within it, and this constitutes the mystery of the church. This appreciation of the oneness of the church was a major development. In baptism priesthood and laity enjoy a basic oneness before the "sacrament of orders" superimposes distinction. The yawning fissures between bishop and priest and priest and layperson were mended. The same message is conveyed in articles on the bishops' pastoral office, priestly formation, and the apostolate of the laity. Alongside this functional diversity there remained an inflexible pattern: "The Father sends Christ, Christ sends the Apostles, the Apostles make their successors the bishops sharers in this mission," and bishops hand down ministry "in lesser degree" to priests. This latter statement seemed to many to subvert the attempt to recover integrated unity.

In his address inaugurating session three Paul VI designated collegiality "the weightiest subject to be discussed" by the synod. Collegiality set the government of the Roman Church on a broader basis, reversing the process toward centralization of authority that originated in the Gregorian Reform of the 11th and 12th centuries. The pope's primacy over both pastors and laity was untouched, and many Roman Catholic leaders and theologians have deplored that development of this key concept seems to have been aborted. Karl Rahner, for example, regrets that episcopal synods have only a consultational, and not a deliberative vote.

*Unitatis redintegratio* heralds a changed attitude toward other churches. "Separated Christians" were designated individuals to whom the name *Christian* could not be denied. By the time pope and observers met at the end of the council, the bodies to which they belonged were recognized as Christian ecclesial entities. *Mystici corporis Christi*, understanding the church as structured society complete with hierarchy, implied a disjunction: either a person was part of this body or was utterly apart from Christ's body. But the fact that Jesus Christ called, gathered, and promised to be with a people opened the door to recognizing other churches as realizations of the church of Christ. They are defective, but only structurally. Identification of the church of Christ with the Church of Rome was effectively repudiated. The church was now said to *subsist* in the Roman Church. The new thought on baptism fortifies this conclusion. As priests and faithful are equally "disciples of the Lord," so "separated Christians" are truly baptized, and the church is "linked" in many ways with them. This new attitude was dramatically exemplified when Rome and Constantinople mutually expunged sentences of anathema and expressed hope for reconciliation. Nothing quite so dramatic was apparent in the policies of Rome toward the churches of the West. That there was no relaxation of canon law regarding "mixed marriages" caused disappointment. On the other hand, proliferating joint commissions set up with the World Council of Churches (WCC) and the Christian world communions testified to Rome's commitment to ecumenism under John Paul II.

The opening "Message to Humanity" with its unprecedented address to "all men and nations" set a scenario in which something about "The Church in the Modern World" was inevitable. This look to the world was expressed by a document regarding non-Christian religions, with its celebrated statement concerning the Jews: "What happened to Christ in his Passion cannot be attributed to all Jews without distinction then alive, nor to Jews of today"; and also to declarations concerning religious freedom. The church has the duty to scrutinize "the signs of the times and of interpreting them in the light of the Gospel." Some delegates thought this too pragmatic an approach. The message set the stage for several subsequent actions by Vatican II. The council refused to condemn atheism and communism. Embargo was placed on discussion of birth control, which eventually received papal clarification in *Humanae vitae* in 1968. Marriage "is not instituted solely for procreation." First in importance were "mutual help and service." The principle of military deterrence by national preparedness was approved as "the most effective way by which peace of a sort can be maintained."

*Sacrosanctum concilium* was the first document to be completed and was of major importance to the liturgical life of the church. At this point Catholic laity shared actively in the work initiated by John XXIII. Heated controversy divided those crusading for retaining tradition from others tolerant of innovation. The issue was of supreme importance since Roman theology regards the Mass as "performing the 'work of salvation' through sacrifice and sacrament." The council's intention was to stimulate more intelligent participation by worshipers. Hence elements of liturgy which served no sacramental purpose were discarded. The council deliberately adopted change. Participation was promoted by translation of Latin forms into the language of the people. Scripture was also elevated.

***Extraordinary General Assembly of the Synod of Bishops.*** At this conference, November 24 to December 8, 1985, the council "really let the ecumenical genie out of the bottle, and opened Pandora's box of trouble and hope," according to G. B. Caird. The assembly was convened to "celebrate" the work of Vatican II, and to take stock of the situation 20 years after its close. No synod can cancel or repudiate a council, but it can do a lot of different things with what a council said. It was by no means clear what the synod would do with Vatican II. Two documents prefaced the meeting: the unofficial Ratzinger Report, which was widely but wrongly interpreted as hostile to further or continued change, and the official 9000-word document prepared by Cardinal Daneels entitled "Relator." The subsequent *Synod Report* showed the church unequivocally set to move forward and committed to "deeply understanding Vatican II and bringing it into the practice of the Church." "The church becomes more credible if it speaks less about itself and more and more about Christ crucified," for "all the importance of the Church is derived from its connection with Christ." Koinonia was set as the criterion for "the correct relation between unity and uniformity in the Church." Sharing at all levels was recommended, as was collaboration between laypeople and clergy. This new interest in the laity characterized the consultative document on *Vocation and Mission of the Laity in the Church and in the World*. The report "Ecclesiology of Communion" expressed ongoing interest in ecumenism. The church "desires that the incomplete communion with non-Catholic Churches may reach full communion."

**The Future.** The radical Catholic Rahner, writing of the enduring significance of Vatican Council II, observed that it was the Roman Church's first reflections on the justification of having pluralism within the church: "The importance of bishops in dogmatic developments, and the autonomy of dioceses, are becoming clear. The *de facto* abolition of Latin as the language of worship, the growing importance of national conferences, the autonomy of many Churches which has developed through external political circumstances—these and many other symptoms show that the age in which uniformity prevailing within the Latin Church was taken for granted is over."

*Bibliography.* H. Daniel-Rops, *The Second Vatican Council* (ET, 1962); G. C. Berkouwer, *The Second Vatican Council and the New Catholicism* (1965); H. Küng, *The Living Church* (1965) and *The Changing Church* (1965); Y. M. J. Congar, et al., *L'Eglise de Vatican II*, 3 vols. (1965–66), *Acta Ap Sedis*, vols. 56–58 (1964–66); W. M. Abbott, ed., *The Documents of Vatican II* (1966); B. C. Butler, *The Theology of Vatican II* (1967); G. B. Caird, *Our Dialogue with Rome* (1967); B. C. Pawley, ed., *The Second Vatican Council: Studies by Eight Anglican Observers* (1967); H. Vorgrimler, ed., *Commentary on the Documents of Vatican II*, 5 vols. (1967–69); L. J. Suenens, *Coresponsibility in the Church* (1968); K. Rahner, *Theological Investigations*, vol. 6 (ET, 1969) and vol. 14 (1976); K. Wojtyla, *Sources of Renewal: The Implementation of the Second Vatican Council* (ET, 1980); *The Ratzinger Report* (1985); *Synod Report, Extraordinary Synod of Bishops, 1985* (1986).

J. K. S. Reid

**Vedder, Henry Clay** (1853–1935). Church historian and editor. Born in De Ruyter, N.Y., he was educated at the University of Rochester and Rochester Theological Seminary. He served on the editorial staff of *The Examiner* (1876–92), was editor of the *Baptist Quarterly Review* (1885–92), and editor-in-chief of *The Examiner* (1892–94). In 1894 he became professor of church history in Crozer Theological Seminary, Chester, Pa., until retirement in 1926. From 1929 until his death he was on the editorial staff of the Chester *Times*. Among his many publications are *Baptists and Liberty of Conscience* (1885), *A Short History of the Baptists* (1891), *The Dawn of Christianity* (1894), *The Baptists* (1903), *Balthasar Hübmaier, the Leader of the Anabaptists* (1905), *Church History Handbooks* (4 vols., 1909/10), *Socialism and the Ethics of Jesus* (1912), *The Reformation in Germany* (1913), *The Gospel of Jesus and the Problems of Democracy* (1914), *The Johannine Writings and the Johannine Problem* (1917), *The Fundamentals of Christianity* (1921), and *Short History of Baptist Missions* (1927).

**Venezuela.** A republic on the Caribbean coast of South America. Once impoverished, vast oil deposits made Venezuela, an OPEC founder, one of South America's most prosperous nations. Yet its population, estimated at 19.7 million (1990) and living on 912,050 sq. km. (352,143 sq. mi.) of land, did not benefit equally from this valuable resource in the late 1900s. As in all of Latin America, the prosperous upper and middle classes, which tended to be from the 20 percent of Iberian-descent, lived far removed from the tribulations of the laborers, comprised mainly of the 69 percent mestizos and 9 percent blacks. Although its per capita income was the highest in Latin America, over 9 million workers earned less than $1480 annually (1987), and the oil crisis of the 1980s caused the unemployment rate to soar to 16 percent in 1985 with underemployment aggravating the economy even more. While 85 percent of the people were urban dwellers, the 2 percent indigenous lived mainly outside the market economy.

To escape the oppressive heat of tropical lowlands of the Orinoco River Delta or the humid and malaria-ridden Maracaibo Basin, most of the population clustered in the Venezuelan Highlands where the capital, Caracas, rests at 3164 feet. Angel Falls, the world's highest, is in the south in the tropical Guiana Highlands whose jungles steadily were being cleared to create huge cattle ranches. Eight years of compulsory school was attended by 82 percent of the school-aged children and 8 percent of the people were literate (1985).

The country's 91 percent devout Roman Catholic population was divided into 1002 parishes in six archdioceses and 18 dioceses served by two cardinals, four archbishops, 33 bishops, 1975 priests, 3862 nuns, 234 brothers, 496 seminarians, and one pontifical university (1983).

The small (2.1 percent) Protestant population of 530,700 is served by 474 foreign missionaries, many working with the tribal people. There were 26 denominations present (1985). Both Catholics and Protestants concentrated on maintaining teachers in the educational system.

Faith Annette Sand

**Versions of the Bible.** *See* Bible Translations (Modern).

**Vidler, Alec Roper** (1899– ). Ecclesiastical historian and Anglican theologian. After studies at Cambridge, he was ordained (1922) and served in industrial Newcastle and Birmingham. An Anglo-Catholic, he came into conflict at Birmingham with his liberal bishop, E. W. Barnes, who discouraged the Anglo-Catholic practice of reserving the sacraments. He joined the Oratory of the Good Shepherd and between 1931 and 1938 was part of the Oratory House at Cambridge, developing his gifts as a pastor, preacher, and writer with *The Modernist Movement in the Roman Church* (1934), *The Gospel of God and the Authority of the Church* (with W. L. Knox, 1937), and *God's Demand and Man's Response* (1938). He was warden of St. Deniol's Library, Harwarden (1939–48), taking over the editorship of *Theology* (1939–65). While at St. Deniol's he wrote *God's Judgment on Europe* (1940), *Secular Despair and Christian Faith* (1941), *Christ's Strange Work* (1944), *The Orb and the Cross* (1945), and *Good News for Mankind* (1947). He was influenced by Reinhold Niebuhr and Karl Barth and challenged traditional post-Enlightenment liberalism and demanded a return to the gospel, emphasizing the reality of sin and the necessity of justification by faith. He remained a popular preacher, especially in university missions. In the postwar period, partly under the influence of his study of F. D. Maurice (*The Theology of F. D. Maurice* [1948]), he came to put less emphasis on sin and a "gospel of despair."

He became a canon of St. George's Chapel, Windsor (1948–56), writing *Christian Belief* (1950), *Prophecy and Papacy* (1954), and *Christian Belief and This World* (1956). The works reflected his concern with the central meaning of the Christian gospel and its relationship to the world and his continued interest in Roman Catholic liberalism. As dean of King's College, Cambridge (1956–67) he became the center of a group of younger theologians who, dissatisfied with prevailing orthodoxy and anxious to explore foundations, published a controversial book of essays edited by Vidler, *Soundings* (1962). Vidler himself wrote historical studies: *The Church in an Age of Revolution: 1789 to the Present Day* (1961), *A Century of Social Catholicism* (1964), *Twentieth Century Defenders of the Faith* (1965), *F. D. Maurice and Company* (1966), and *A Variety of Catholic Modernists* (1970). In retirement he became involved in local politics and was mayor of his native Rye, Sussex (1972–74). He and lifelong friend Malcolm Muggeridge collaborated in producing a television series on Paul in 1970, which also resulted in the book, *Paul, Envoy Extraordinary* (1972).

C. PETER WILLIAMS

**Vietnam.** *See* SOUTHEAST ASIA.

**Vig, Peder Sorensen** (1854–1929). Lutheran. Born in Egtved, Denmark, he studied at the University of Copenhagen; was ordained at Neenah, Wis. (1885); and served pastorates in Shelby County, Iowa (1885–87). He was professor at the seminary of the Danish Lutheran Church at Luck, Wis. (1887–92), at Elk Horn, Iowa (1894–96), and at Trinity Seminary, Blair, Nebr., the seminary of the United Danish Lutheran Church in America (1896 intermittently to 1928); and president of Trinity (1909–26). He was knighted by the king of Denmark. In theology he was conservative. He was a noted teacher and historian with many minor publications. His major publications are

his contributions to *Danske i Amerika* (1908) and *Danske i Kamp* (1917).

**Bibliography.** T. P. Beck, *The Professor, P. S. Vig* (1946).

JOHANNES KNUDSEN

**Vigilanti Cura.** Encyclical of June 29, 1936, in which Pius XI discusses motion pictures, especially with the American bishops who had previously established the Legion of Decency. The importance of motion pictures for recreation and propaganda is recognized, but the encyclical deplores that many films are morally and religiously harmful, recommends extension of the Legion's pledge to boycott such films, and proposes national offices—under Catholic Action—to review all productions.

**Bibliography.** Latin text, *Acta Apostolicae Sedis*, vol. 28; ET, J. Husslein, *Social Wellsprings*, vol. 2 (1942).

THEODORE TAPPERT

**Visser 'T Hooft, Willem Adolf** (1900–1985). Dutch ecumenist. Born in Haarlem, he was educated at the University of Leiden, and thereafter was on the staff of the YMCA before becoming general secretary of the World Student Christian Federation. In 1938 he began his notable work as general secretary of what developed into the World Council of Churches (WCC). A versatile linguist, he edited *The Student World* (1928–38) and *Ecumenical Review* (1948–66). Among his many publications were *The Background of the Social Gospel in America* (1928), *Anglo-Catholicism and Orthodoxy* (1933), "*None Other Gods*" (1937), *Wretchedness and Greatness of the Church* (1944), *The Struggle of the Dutch Church* (1946), *Le Conseil oecuménique des Eglises* (1946), *The Kingship of Christ: An Interpretation of Recent European Theology* (1947), *The Ecumenical Movement and the Racial Problem* (1954), *No Other Name: The Choice between Syncretism and Christian Universalism* (1963), *Memoirs* (1973), *Has the Ecumenical Movement a Future?* (1974), *The Fatherhood of God in an Age of Emancipation* (1982), and *The Genesis and Formation of the World Council of Churches* (1982). He coauthored, with A. Bea, *Peace among Christians* (ET, 1967).

J. D. DOUGLAS

**Vogel, Heinrich** (1902– ). Lutheran theologian. Born in Pröttlin, he studied at Berlin and Jena, then was for many years pastor in Dobbrikow, Mark Brandenburg. In the church struggle of the Nazi era he was a member of the Confessional Synod and a leader of the illegal Berlin church seminary (Kirchliche Hochschule) of the Confessional Church. For his activities he was repeatedly imprisoned. From 1946 he served as professor of systematic theology both at Humboldt University in East Berlin, from which he retired in 1967, and at the Kirchliche Hochschule in

West Berlin until his retirement in 1969. Vogel tried to bridge the gap between East and West and was recipient of high honors from both sides. He was awarded the *Vaterländische Verdienstorden* of the GDR (1960) and received the *Grosse Verdienstkreuz zum Bundesverdienstkreuz* of the FRG. He also was given the Wladimir Order of the Russian Orthodox Patriarchate Moscow in 1958. Vogel is best known for his christological treatises. He appealed to a wider public through his sermons, hymns, and poems. A festschrift in his honor appeared in 1962. His collected works (12 vols.) were published in the late 1980s by Radius-Verlag in Stuttgart.

ERIC GELDBACH

**Volunteers of America.** Urban evangelical welfare organization founded in 1896 in New York City by Ballington and Maud Booth. It was run on more democratic lines than the Salvation Army but retained uniforms and ranks. It aids about 2 million persons each year at about 600 centers in more than 100 cities in the USA. Units hold church services, Bible studies, and Sunday schools, and give personal counseling. There are camps, homes for the aged, maternity homes, day nurseries and salvage centers, and services in prisons form an important part of the work. After Ballington Booth's death in 1940 the movement was led by Maud Booth to 1948 and from 1948 by son Charles B. Booth. There were about 33,000 adherents in the 1980s.

*See also* SALVATION ARMY.

EARLE E. CAIRNS

**Voskamp, Carl J.** (1859–1937). Lutheran missionary. Born in Antwerp, Belgium, he was sent in 1884 to Canton province, China, by the Berlin Missionary Society and was shifted to Shantung province in 1898 to open new missionary work. He remained in Shantung (after 1925 under American auspices) until his death. The veteran missionary was the author and translator of numerous books, tracts, and hymns in Chinese.

THEODORE TAPPERT

**Vosté, Jacques Marie** (1883–1949). Roman Catholic. Born in Bruges, Belgium, he entered the Dominican Order in 1900. He studied at the Dominican College and the University of Louvain; and the École Biblique of Jerusalem. He taught NT exegesis at the Collegium Angelicum, Rome (1911); and was appointed consultor (1929) and secretary (1939) of the Pontifical Biblical Commission. In addition to numerous studies and monographs, which embody the substance of his courses, he edited texts and manuscripts from Syriac authors, such as the Commentary of Theodore of Mopsuestia on the Fourth Gospel, and the works of Mar Ishodad of Merw.

GEORGES A. BARROIS

**Wace, Henry** (1836–1924). Anglican scholar. Born in London, he was educated at Oxford, and after ordination served two curacies in London. He was then lecturer of Grosvenor Chapel (1870–72); chaplain (1872–80) and preacher (1880–96) of Lincoln's Inn, London; rector of St. Michael's, Cornhill (1896–1903); and dean of Canterbury (1903–24). He also served as professor of ecclesiastical history (1875–83) and principal (1883–96) of King's College, London. He edited or collaborated with others in several works and was the author of *Christianity and Morality* (1876), *The Foundations of Faith* (1880), *The Gospel and Its Witnesses* (1883), *Some Central Points of Our Lord's Ministry* (1890), *The Sacrifice of Christ* (1898), *Confession and Absolution* (1902), *The Bible and Modern Investigation* (1903), *Principles of the Reformation* (1910), *Prophecy, Jewish and Christian* (1911), *The War and the Gospel* (1917), *The Story of the Passion* (1922), and *The Story of the Resurrection* (1923).

**Wach, Joachim** (1898–1955). Episcopalian. Born in Chemnitz, Germany, he studied at Munich, Freiburg, Berlin, Leipzig (Ph.D., 1922), and Heidelberg (Th.D., 1928). He was privatdocent and professor of the history of religions at the University of Leipzig (1924–35). He came to the USA in September 1935, taught at Brown University (1935–46), and was professor of the history of religions on the Federated Theological Faculty of the University of Chicago from 1946. He wrote *Religionswissenschaft* (1924), *Das Verstehen, Geschichte der Hermeneutik im 19. Jahrhundert* (1926–33), *Meister und Jünger* (1925), *Sociology of Religion* (1944), and *Types of Religious Experience, Christian and Non-Christian* (1951).

**Waldensian Church (Waldenses).** A pre-Reformation church renewal movement which survived intense persecutions and existed through the 20th century as a small European Protestant denomination. In 1979 the Italian Methodist church joined the tiny remaining Waldensian church, increasing its membership to about 25,000, with a community of about twice that size. While most remaining churches are in Italy, there are congregations in Argentina, Uruguay, and the USA; the two of Valdese, N.C., were founded by Waldensian immigrants in 1893. Despite their small number the Waldenses maintain a publishing house, social agencies, hospitals, and African missions. The church is governed through an annual synod, headed by an elected moderator and an executive board. In the 20th century the group has been greatly affected by liberal and radical theologies and political movements.

The beginnings of the Waldensian church movement remained a matter of study and disagreement in the late 20th century, mainly because the perennial efforts to exterminate the believers also destroyed the documents of their history. The Waldenses themselves identify their beginnings in the major Christian renewal that penetrated Western Europe's church and society in the 12th century. The renewal emphasized the sufferings and death of Jesus Christ, the Bible, personal devotion, and preaching, all within the traditional sacramental system. In order to reform the church, stress was placed on the divinely given prerogatives of hierarchy and priesthood. Among those stirred was a prosperous layman named Peter Valdes or Waldo at Lyons, France. Waldo undertook a disciplined lifestyle with a medieval ascetic emphasis on poverty. Rather than turning toward the monastic cloister, he began to share the life that he had found in Christ. This preaching soon caused trouble with the church, for as a layman he was taking upon himself a task restricted to the clergy. Waldo and those who were associating themselves with him were excommunicated in 1184.

Waldo and his colleagues, called the Poor Men of Lyons, fanned out through southern France and northern Italy and into parts of Germany, Switzerland, Austria, and Bohemia. To facilitate their underground evangelism the vernacular was used in Bible reading and worship. Practices and beliefs seen as contrary to Scripture in the sacrament of penance were jettisoned, such as purgatory, prayers for the dead, veneration of images, and indulgences. The doctrine of transubstantiation was denied. Waldensians developed an alternative church with an itinerant preaching leadership committed to poverty and celibacy, a millenarian and prophetic bent, and with a vision for restoring the apostolic church. Most were exterminated during the 13th century by the crusade and inquisition. In remote areas of the Cottian Alps, however, a small remnant kept a low profile, and occasionally conformed to the Catholic Church when harassment became unbearable. This was particularly true in the southwestern Alps, on the Piedmont or Italian side as well as the French, and in Calabria near Naples.

Contact with Protestantism was first effected by William Farel in 1526, and by 1560 Waldensians had fully embraced the Calvinistic Reformation. Parishes were erected, clergy from the Academy at Geneva were settled, and a confession of faith was produced. The French and Calabrian churches were swept away by the Counter-Reformation, but those in Piedmont survived. To their natural tenacity and shrewdness was added the Calvinistic conviction that they were a New Israel who occupied a special place in the divine plan and were under the unremitting care of a sovereign providence. The diplomacy of certain Protestant nations was also a key factor in their survival.

Toward the end of the 17th century the life of the Waldenses hung by a thread, and for a few years all were driven into exile in Switzerland and Germany. But Piedmont transferred its political alliances and they were welcomed back to a life of limited toleration. The spirit of the Enlightenment gradually overcame the Waldensians of the 18th century and they became mostly concerned with preserving the status quo.

In the 1820s the Second Evangelical Awakening touched the Waldenses. Theological students trained at Lausanne returned with a dynamic faith, while Felix Neff, "the apostle of the French Alps," breathed new life into Waldensianism on occasional visits. Evangelical Anglicans gave strong financial support and also political aid where possible. The revitalized church engaged in evangelism and church planting outside their traditional area, established scores of schools, and developed a theological institution, a publishing house, and various social agencies. There was also a social vision which led to cooperation with liberal forces for the achievement of religious liberty and the unification of Italy. During the middle of the 19th century migration began to South America, with about 20 Waldensian congrega-

tions ultimately being planted in western Uruguay and adjacent parts of Argentina.

*Bibliography.* M. Lambert, *Medieval Heresy: Popular Movements from Bogomil to Hus* (1976); G. Tourn, *The Waldensians: The First 800 Years (1174–1974)* (1980); E. Cameron, *The Reformation of the Heretics: The Waldenses of the Alps 1480–1580* (1984).

IAN S. RENNIE

**Wales.** A principality of the United Kingdom, located to the west of England on the island of Great Britain and comprising 20,760 sq. km. (8,017 sq. mi.). Its population of nearly 3 million in the late 1980s retain distinctive cultural and linguistic traditions. In religious identification Presbyterians compose 32 percent of the people, Anglicans 28.5 percent, Roman Catholics 18.5 percent, and others 21 percent.

Nothing is known of the introduction of Christianity to Wales, but it apparently was well established during the Roman occupation (from A.D. 78). Welsh bishops attended the Synod of Arles (314). Christianity enjoyed a renaissance during the 6th century. Welsh Christianity continued as a distinctive movement despite the pleas of Augustine of Canterbury (603). In fact, the Welsh church was isolated until 750, when it accepted belatedly the Roman method of calculating Easter. At the time of the Norman Conquest (1066), the Welsh Church was still a national church. It did not submit formally to Canterbury until the middle of the 12th century. The Celtic church surrendered its forms only reluctantly, however. After 1323 the pope intervened in the election of Welsh bishops.

The Protestant Reformation took on Welsh forms when the literature was translated into Welsh. In 1567 the Book of Common Prayer and the NT appeared in Welsh. In 1588 William Morgan's Welsh Bible appeared. Puritanism gained ground in Welsh Protestantism. In 1735 the Evangelical Revival broke out under the leadership of Howel Harris, and he was soon joined by William Williams and Daniel Rowland. Subsequent revivals occurred in 1859 to 1860 and 1904 and 1905. Although more than 90 percent claimed to be Christians in Wales in the 1980s, religious practice was negligible. Fewer than 14 percent worshiped regularly. Many Welsh people considered themselves to be religious, but their practice did not agree with their profession.

Several sociological phenomena contributed to the erosion of popular religion in Wales. Many moved from the valleys into the cities, and this urbanization cut their connection to the church. High unemployment further diminished religious commitment in the middle and working classes. The passing of the revival generation robbed families of religious influence.

Although church attendance in Wales still surpassed that of England (9 percent), it represented a secularization which made many churches redundant. The trend of religion in Wales was downward through the latter half of the 20th century.

WAYNE DETZLER

**Walker, Alan Edgar** (1911– ). Australian Methodist minister and social activist. Born in Sydney, he graduated from the city's university and was ordained in the Methodist Church (now part of the Uniting Church of Australia) (1935). He served first in a ministry to young people, and then was superintendent of a circuit in the coal mining town of Cessnock, New South Wales, where he first expressed Christian social views. The pattern of his vigorous ministry appeared while he was superintendent of the Waverley Methodist Mission (1944–54), and afterwards in the influential Sydney Central Methodist Mission, which he built around a cinema in which he ran a popular "Pleasant Sunday Afternoon" program (1958–78). He participated in activities of the World Council of Churches, the United Nations, the World Methodist Council, and other bodies. He created the Life Line Centre in 1963, and began a telephone counseling ministry that spread rapidly throughout the world. He retired in 1978, but became the World Methodist Council's director of evangelism, was made Knight of the British Empire in 1981, and continued to write and travel. Among his publications are *The Whole Gospel for the Whole World* (1957), *A New Mind for a New Age* (1959), *How Jesus Helped People* (1964), *God the Disturber* (1973), *The New Evangelism* (1975), *Life Begins at Christ* (1979), *Standing Up to Preach* (1983), and *Life in the Holy Spirit* (1986).

NOEL S. POLLARD

**Walker, Williston** (1860–1922). American church historian. Born in Portland, Maine, he was educated at Amherst college, Hartford Theological Seminary, and the University of Leipzig (Ph.D., 1888). He was an associate in history at Bryn Mawr College (1888/89), professor of Germanic and Western church history at Hartford Theological Seminary (1889–1901), and professor of ecclesiastical history at Yale Divinity School (1901–22). Among his published works are *The Increase of Royal Power under Philip Augustus* (1888), *The Creeds and Platforms of Congregationalism* (1893), *A History of the Congregational Church in the United States* (1894), *The Reformation* (1900), *Ten New England Leaders* (1901), *John Calvin: The Organiser of Reformed Protestantism (1509–1564)*, and *Great Men of the Christian Church* (1908). The book for which he is best known, however, and which is still widely used in church history classes, is *A History of the Christian Church* (1918; many times reprinted).

**Wand, John William Charles** (1885–1977). Anglican bishop and church historian. Born in Grantham, Lincolnshire, he was educated at Oxford, and after ordination served curacies in Benwell (1908–11) and Lancaster (1911–14). He was vicar-choral of Sarum (1914–19); vicar of St. Mark, Sarum (1919–25); and Royal Air Force chaplain (1922–25). He went to Oxford as dean of Oriel College (1925–34) and university lecturer (1931–34) before going to Australia as archbishop of Brisbane (1934–43). Returning to England, he was bishop of Bath and Wells (1943–45) and bishop of London (1945–55). He was knighted by Queen Elizabeth II in 1955 and became a member of her Privy Council. Among his many books are *The Golden String* (1926), *The Development of Sacramentalism* (1928), *History of the Modern Church* (1930), *The Old Faith and the New Age* (1933), *I and II Peter and Jude* (1934), *History of the Early Church* (1935), *First Century Christianity* (1937), *NT Letters* (1944), *God and Goodness* (1947), *The Latin Doctors* (1948), *The Authority of the Scriptures* (1949), *The Greek Doctors* (1950), *The Four Councils* (1950), *What the Church of England Stands For* (1951), *The Life of Jesus Christ* (1955), *The Church Today* (1960), *Atonement* (1962), *Changeful Page* (1965), *Transfiguration* (1967), *Reflections on the Gospel* (1969), *Christianity: A Historical Religion?* (1972), and *Letters on Preaching* (1974).

J. D. DOUGLAS

**Wang, Hao-Jan (Wang K'uan)** (1848–1919). Muslim. Born in Peking, while on a visit to Mecca, Cairo, and Constantinople (1906), Caliph Hamid gave him 1000 books. Two Turkish scholars returned to China with him, and he established schools in Peking and organized the Arabic Normal School, where Arabic, Chinese, and science were taught. He was head of Arabic literature section of the Bureau of Mongolian and Tibetan Affairs. He founded the Muslim Forward Movement (1911).

CLAUDE L. PICKENS, JR.

**Ward, Harry F.** (1873–1967). Born in Chiswick, England, he studied at the University of Southern California, Northwestern, and Harvard; was head resident, Northwestern University Settlement (1898/99); minister of churches in Chicago (1900–1912); professor of social service, Boston University, School of Theology (1913–18); and professor of Christian ethics, Union Theological Seminary (1918–41). He was secretary of the Methodist Federation for Social Service (1912–45), chairman of the American Civil Liberties Union (1920–40), and chairman of the American League for Peace and Democracy (1934–40). Among his books are *The New Social Order* (1919), *Our Economic Morality* (1929), *Which*

861

*Way Religion?* (1931), *In Place of Profit* (1933), and *Democracy and Social Change* (1941).

**Ward, James** (1843–1925). Psychologist and philosopher. Born in Hull, England, he graduated from Spring Hill College near Birmingham and intended to enter the Congregationalist ministry. A scholarship at Berlin and Göttingen changed his theological views. For a year he preached at Emmanuel Chapel in Cambridge but gave it up and discarded church membership and credal commitment. In Trinity College, Cambridge, he became a fellow in the moral sciences. In 1897 he was made professor of mental philosophy and logic. He was Gifford lecturer at Aberdeen (1895–98) and at St. Andrews (1907–10). In 1904 he lectured at Berkeley, Calif., and visited various American universities, as well as the St. Louis Exposition where he gave a lecture. His early work was mainly in psychology, but after 1894 he turned to philosophical writing. Avoiding agnosticism and materialism, he said God's existence is unprovable but without faith in it we cannot make sense of our total experience. Besides articles, he published *The Realm of Ends* (1911), *Heredity and Memory* (1913), *Psychological Principles* (1918), *A Study of Kant* (1922), and *Naturalism and Agnosticism* (repr. ed., 1971).

JOSEPH FLETCHER

**Warfield, Benjamin Breckinridge** (1851–1921). American Reformed theologian. Born in Lexington, Ky., he was educated at the College of New Jersey, Princeton Theological Seminary, and the University of Leipzig. He was professor of NT language and literature at Western Theological Seminary, Allegheny, Pa. (1878–87), and professor of didactic and polemical theology at Princeton Theological Seminary (1887–1921). One of the nation's most prominent conservative theologians within the "Old Princeton" theology, he was the editor of *The Presbyterian and Reformed Review* (1890–1903) and of Augustine's *Anti-Pelagian Writings* (1887), and the author of 20 books and numerous pamphlets and articles on biblical and theological topics. Among his most important works are *Introduction to the Textual Criticism of the NT* (1886), *The Acts and Pastoral Epistles* (1902), *The Lord of Glory* (1907), *The Savior of the World* (1914), *The Plan of Salvation* (1915), and *Counterfeit Miracles* (1918). The 10-volume posthumous compilation of his sermons, pamphlets, and articles includes *Revelation and Inspiration* (1927), *Biblical Doctrines* (1929), *Christianity and Criticism* (1929), *Studies in Tertullian and Augustine* (1930), *Calvin and Calvinism* (1931), *Perfectionism* (1931), *Studies in Theology* (1932), and *Critical Reviews* (1932). He was deeply committed to the principles of Calvinism as expressed in the Westminster Confession of Faith and in his time was the foremost exponent of the plenary inspiration and inerrancy of Scripture.

RICHARD V. PIERARD

**Warneck, Gustav** (1834–1910). Founder of the science of missiology. Son of an artisan in Naumburg, Germany, he studied for the ministry, pastored a church, served six years on the home staff of the Barmen (Rhine) Mission (1871–77), and then devoted his life to academic endeavors. In 1874 he founded the important scholarly journal of German Protestant missions, the *Allgemeine Missionszeitschrift*, and in 1879 initiated the practice of holding regular missions conferences in the German churches. In a paper in 1888 he proposed the holding of regular international missionary conferences supported by a continuation committee to coordinate Protestant work overseas, a vision that came to fruition after his death in the Edinburgh Conference (1910) and the formation of the International Missionary Council (1921). His comprehensive historical study, *Outline of a History of Protestant Missions from the Reformation to the Present Time* (1902), and a three-volume synthesis of mission theory, *Evangelische Missionslehre* (1892–1903), placed missiology on a solid scientific footing and paved the way for its subsequent development as a significant scholarly discipline in theological education.

RICHARD V. PIERARD

**Warnshuis, Abbe Livingston** (1877–1958). Reformed Church in America mission leader. Born in Clymer, N.Y., he studied at Hope College and New Brunswick Theological Seminary. He was a missionary to China (1900–1915), and participated in conferences resulting in the organization of the United Church in China. In 1915 he became national evangelistic secretary of the China Continuation Committee, predecessor of the National Christian Council. In 1920 he moved to London to serve as secretary, associated with Joseph H. Oldham of the International Missionary Council (IMC); he opened the New York office of IMC in 1925 and served conjointly as a secretary of the Foreign Missions Conference of North America (1925–42). He served as foreign counselor of the Church Committee on Overseas Relief and Reconstruction (1943–45). He wrote *Language Lessons in Amoy Vernacular* (1911). He edited *Talmage's Dictionary of Amoy Vernacular* (rev. ed.), *Directory of Foreign Missions* (1933), and *The Christian Message for the World Today* (repr. ed., 1971). He was coeditor of *The Jerusalem Meeting, I.M.C.* (1928), and *The Madras Series, I.M.C.* (1938).

**Washington, Booker Taliaferro** (1856–1915). American educator. Born in Franklin County, Va., he was educated at Hampton Institute and at Wayland Seminary, Washington, D.C.

He taught at Hampton Institute (1880/81), and thereafter was principal of the Tuskegee Normal and Industrial Institute, Alabama. He was a leader in educating and improving the lot of black Americans. Among his published works were *Future of the American Negro* (1899), *Sowing and Reaping* (1900), *Up from Slavery* (1901), *Character Building* (1902), *Story of My Life and Work* (1903), *Working with the Hands* (1904), *Tuskegee and Its People* (1905), *Life of Frederick Douglass* (1907), *The Negro in Business* (1907), and *The Story of the Negro* (1909). He collaborated with W. E. B. Du Bois in *The Negro in the South* (1907).

**Waterhouse, Eric Stickland** (1879–1964). English Methodist minister and scholar. After graduating from London University, he was a Wesleyan minister in various circuits in southeast England before appointment as lecturer in philosophy (1920–40) and principal (1940–51) of Richmond College, Surrey. Meanwhile he served as professor of religion in London University (1931–51). Among his publications were *What Is Salvation?* (1932), *The Philosophical Approach to Religion* (1933), *The Dawn of Religion* (1936), and *Psychology and Pastoral Work* (1939). He wrote articles for Hastings' *Encyclopaedia of Religion and Ethics* (13 vols., 1920–30).

**Waterman, Leroy** (1875–1972). Baptist Orientalist. Born in Pierpont, Ohio, he studied at Hillsdale (Mich.) College and Divinity School and at the universities of Oxford, Berlin, and Chicago (Ph.D., 1912). He was professor of Hebrew language and literature, Hillsdale College (1902–10); professor of OT and history of religions, Meadville Theological School (1913–15); and professor of Semitics, University of Michigan (1915–45). He was annual professor of the American Schools of Oriental Research, Baghdad (1927/28); and director of the University of Michigan Archeological Expeditions to Iraq and Palestine (1928–32). His books include *Some Koujunjik Letters and Related Texts* (1912), *Business Documents of the Hammurabi Period* (1916), *The Royal Correspondence of the Assyrian Empire* (1930–36), *First Preliminary Report of Excavations in Iraq* (1931), *Second Preliminary Report* (1933), *Preliminary Report of Excavations at Sepphoris, Palestine* (1937), *Religion Faces the World Crisis* (1943), and *The Song of Songs as a Dramatic Poem* (1948). He was a translator for *The Bible—An American Translation* (1935) and a member of the translation committee of the RSV (1937–52). He edited volume 14 of R. F. Harper, *Assyrian and Babylonian Letters* (1914).

**Watt, Hugh** (1879–1968). Scottish church historian. Born in Kilmaurs, Ayrshire, he was educated at the universities of Glasgow, Marburg, Berlin, and Halle and was minister in Waterbeck

(1907–12) and Bearsden North (1912–19) before becoming professor of church history at New College, Edinburgh (1919–50; principal and dean, 1946–50). He was moderator of the Church of Scotland general assembly in 1950. He was the author of *Representative Churchmen of Twenty Centuries* (1926), *Thomas Chalmers and the Disruption* (1943), *The Published Writings of Thomas Chalmers* (1943), *New College, Edinburgh—A Centenary History* (1946), *Recalling the Scottish Covenants* (1946), and *John Knox in Controversy* (1950).

**Weatherhead, Leslie Dixon** (1893–1976). Methodist pastor and writer. Born in London and educated at London University, Richmond Theological College, and Manchester University, he served as a combatant officer and chaplain in World War I. He was minister of the English Methodist Church in Madras, India (1919–22), and then returned to minister in Manchester (1922–25), Leeds (1925–36), and the City Temple, London (1936–60). He was president of the Methodist Conference (1955/56) and of the Institute of Religion and Medicine (1966/67). For many years he specialized in psychological studies and lectured and wrote on the relationship between psychology and religion. He was a certified teacher, lecturer, and examiner in psychology. His many publications include *Discipleship* (1934), *How Can I Find God?* (1934), *Why Do Men Suffer?* (1936), *The Mastery of Sex Through Psychology and Religion* (1939), *The Will of God* (1944), *A Plain Man Looks at the Cross* (1945), *Psychology, Religion and Healing* (1951), *Life Begins at Death* (1969), and *The Busy Man's OT* (1971).

TIM LENTON

**Webster, Douglas** (1920–1986). Anglican missiologist. After graduating from Oxford, he served curacies in Lancashire and London before becoming lecturer in the London College of Divinity (1947–52). He joined the Church Missionary Society, first as education secretary (1953–61), then as theologian-missioner (1961–65). He was later professor of missions at the Selly Oak Colleges, Birmingham (1966–69) and canon-residentiary of St. Paul's Cathedral (1969–84). Among his publications were *What Is Evangelism?* (1959), *Local Church and World Mission* (1962), *In Debt to Christ: A Study in the Meaning of the Cross* (1964), *Pentecostalism and Speaking with Tongues* (1964), *Unchanging Mission* (1965), *Yes to Mission* (1966), *Not Ashamed* (1970), and *Good News from John* (1974).

J. D. DOUGLAS

**Weil, Simone** (1909–1943). French social activist and mystic. From a middle-class French-Jewish background, she gave up a career in classics and philosophy to identify with the oppressed. Despite ill health she worked in factories and alongside farm laborers. She joined the anti-Franco brigade in the Spanish Civil War; identifying herself with the Jewish victims of nazism, she died in England of self-imposed starvation. Her short life was dominated by searches for social justice and truth. The first led her to a practical form of socialism. The second led from agnosticism, through a number of mystical experiences (from 1938), to being acclaimed by some a "Catholic saint outside the Church." She was never baptized. Her writings, many of which were in the form of letters, essays, and poems, include *Waiting for God* (ET, 1951), and *The Notebooks of Simone Weil* (ET, 1956).

PETER HICKS

**Weissenberg, Joseph** (1885–1936). German religious figure regarded as a reincarnation of Christ by adherents who formed what they called the Evangelical Johannean Church According to the Revelation of St. John. After leaving his wife he called his mistress the virgin Mary and had several children by her.

**Welch, Adam Cleghorn** (1864–1943). Presbyterian OT scholar. Born in Jamaica, he studied at Edinburgh, Erlangen, and Halle. Ordained in 1887, he served as minister in Waterbeck, Helensburgh, and Glasgow (1887–1913), and as professor of OT, New College, Edinburgh (1913–34). His works include *The Code of Deuteronomy* (1924), *The Psalter in Life, Worship, and History* (1926), *Jeremiah: His Time and His Work* (1928), *Deuteronomy: The Framework to the Code* (1932), and *The Work of the Chronicler: Its Purpose and Its Date* (1939).

ELMER E. FLACK

**Wellhausen, Julius** (1844–1918). German Protestant pioneer of higher criticism techniques. Born in Hameln, he studied at Göttingen (Ph.D., 1870). He was privatdocent in the theological faculty at Göttingen, then professor of OT at Griefswald (1872–82). After long controversy regarding his liberal view of the inspiration of Scripture, he resigned and became professor of Semitics at Halle (1882–85), Marburg (1885–92), and Göttingen (from 1892). He is best known for his theory that the Pentateuch was postexilic and he presented the most accepted explanation for the theory that the five books were a composite redacted by a later author who worked primarily with a late "P" document. He also was a leading scholar of his day in Islamic studies. His most important study was *Geschichte Israels* (1878), translated in 1883 as the *History of Israel*. Among his other extensive writings were *Der Text der Bücher Samuels untersucht* (1871), *Composition des Hexateuchs* (3d ed., 1899), *Prolegomena zur Geschichte Israels* (6th ed., 1905), *Das Evangelium Marci übersetzt* (2d ed., 1909), *Israelitische und jüdische Geschichte* (7th ed., 1914), and *Kritische Analyse der Apostelgeschichte* (1914). With others he wrote *Die Christliche Religion, mit Einschluss der israelitische-jüdischen Religion* (1906).

**Wells, Amos Russell** (1862–1933). Congregationalist-Presbyterian editor. Born in Glen Falls, N.Y., he studied at Antioch College and taught Greek there (1883–92). He was editor of *The Christian Endeavor World* (1891–33). Until his death he also edited Peloubet's *Notes on the International Sunday School Lessons* (1901–33). Theologically he was a conservative Calvinist. A prolific writer, among his later books are *Everyday Poems* (1910), *Sunday School Essentials* (1911), *Expert Endeavor* (1911), *The Ideal Adult Bible Class* (1912), *Ten Don'ts for Teachers* (1913), *The Arithmetic of Friendship* (1913), *A Treasure of Hymns* (1914), *A Successful Sunday School Superintendent* (1915), *Union Work* (1916), *Cyclopedia of Twentieth Century Illustrations* (1918), *Collected Poems* (1921), *Romance of Right Living* (1923), *Progressive Endeavor* (1925), *The Glorious Names of Jesus* (1926), *Know Your Bible?* (1927), *The Daily Digest* (1927), *Think on These Things* (1928), *Walk in His Ways* (1930), *The Devotional Year Book* (1931), and *Bible Sayings* (1931).

RAYMOND W. ALBRIGHT

**Wenger, John Christian** (1910– ). Mennonite church historian. Born in Honey Brook, Pa., he studied at Goshen College and at the universities of Michigan, Basel, and Zurich (Th.D., 1939). He was professor at Goshen College (1938–70). He was ordained as deacon and preacher in the Mennonite Church and appointed a bishop in 1941. He also was on the Mennonite Publishing Board (1946–71), member of the presidium, Mennonite World Conference (1963–72), assistant editor, *Mennonite Quarterly Review*, and assistant editor, *Mennonite Encyclopedia* (1946–59). He edited the *Complete Writings of Menno Simons* (1956) and published several works on Mennonite history and theology. Among these are *Glimpses of Mennonite History and Doctrine* (1940), *The Doctrines of the Mennonites* (1950), *The Mennonite Church in America* (1966), and *Faithfully George R.: The Life and Thought of George R. Brunk I (1871–1938)* (1978).

E. J. FURCHA

**Wentz, Abdel Ross** (1883–1976). Church historian. Born in York County, Pa., he studied at Gettysburg College, Gettysburg Seminary, and the universities of Leipzig, Tübingen, Berlin, and George Washington (Ph.D., 1914). He was professor of history at Gettysburg College (1909–16); and professor of church history at Gettysburg Seminary (from 1916; president, 1940–51). He was a member of the American Bible Revision Committee and president of the Foreign Missions Board of the United Lutheran Church. He wrote *The Beginnings of the German Element in York County, Pennsylvania* (1916), *History of the Lutheran Synod of Maryland* (1920), *When Two Worlds Met: The Diet of Worms, 1521* (1921), *The Lutheran Church in American History* (2d ed., 1933), *History of the Gettysburg Theological Seminary . . . 1826–1926* (1926), *Fliedner the Faithful* (1936), and *A New Strategy for Theological Education* (1937). He was coauthor of *The Lutheran Churches of the World* (1929).

J. D. DOUGLAS

**Wesleyan Church.** Branch of the Methodist church begun in the Wesleyan Holiness revival of the 19th century. The late 20th-century denomination was formed in 1968 through the merger of the Pilgrim Holiness Church and the Wesleyan Methodist Church of America. Orange Scott and other Methodist abolitionists organized the Wesleyan Methodist connection in 1843 in protest against the Methodist Episcopal Church's failure to advocate an immediate end to slavery. Strong commitment to the Wesleyan doctrine of Christian perfection involved the new denomination in the Holiness revival which began in the American churches at that time. The Pilgrim Holiness Church, begun in 1897, was a product of the same movement, as small Holiness evangelistic associations, camp meeting fellowships, and local and overseas mission agencies born in the revival coalesced into more formal denominational structures.

Wesleyan membership worldwide was about 200,000 in the 1980s, with about 150,000 of these in the USA. Other centers were in Sierra Leone, South Africa, Zambia, the Caribbean, Mexico, and the Philippines. The American church maintained four liberal-arts colleges, two Bible colleges, and a seminary foundation for graduate theological training in the USA.

The denomination was Wesleyan in doctrine, affirming the basic creeds of the Christian church, with particular concern for the Wesleyan doctrine of entire sanctification as a second work of grace in the believer's heart subsequent to regeneration. The denomination held membership in the Christian Holiness Association and the National Association of Evangelicals.

*See also* HOLINESS CHURCHES.

MELVIN E. DIETER

**West Africa.** A diverse and varied region, with about one-half of the total population of sub-Saharan Africa and the continent's most populous nation, Nigeria. Of its approximately 176 million people about 73 million are Muslims and 66 million Christians (1986). The remainder are classified as traditional religionists. It is estimated that West Africa is composed of about 600 ethnolinguistic groups, each with a distinctive culture and language.

Geographically the region's four topographical zones include an Atlantic coastal area along the western rim, the forest zone of tropical rain forest, the savanna of grassfields which extends from the forest to the fourth zone, the Saharan desert. Within the region are the countries of Benin (formerly Dahomey), Burkina Faso (formerly Upper Volta), Cameroon, Chad, Gambia, Ghana, Guinea, Guinea-Bissau, Ivory Coast, Liberia, Mali, Mauritania, Niger, Nigeria, Senegal, Sierra Leone, Togo, and Western Sahara.

Until the late 19th century West Africa was dominated by indigenous societies and states (like the Yoruba and Hausa) and inland empires (like Ghana, Mali, and Songhai). European influence was limited to coastal bases used for trade in slaves, palm oil, gold, ivory, and other local products. These coastal bases originated with 15th-century European expansionism in which the Portuguese were followed by the Dutch, French, British, and Germans. These nations established their own bases or conquered rival ports. The arrival of Europeans brought Christianity to West Africa, although Christianity had been present in North Africa from the 1st century A.D. This initial presence of Christianity was dominated by Roman Catholic missionaries. Little happened in church growth in West Africa in general for the next 350 years. By the mid-19th century there were only about 10,000 Christians in West Africa, most of whom were receptives from the slave trade or settlers in the bases.

This inactivity came to an end in the latter 19th century as European powers claimed the interior of Africa, using the coastal bases as starting points. Protestant churches and agencies also entered the missionary movement in full force. The modern period of missions in West Africa was dominated primarily by Protestants, but both branches of Christianity took missions seriously in the early 20th century. The carving of Africa into colonies, known as the partition of Africa, brought vast sections of Africa under European control for the first time and set the future course for Africa. By the beginning of the 20th century areas colonized included the future nations of Benin, Burkina Faso, Chad, Guinea, Ivory Coast, Mali, Mauritania, Niger, and Senegal by France; Guinea-Bissau by Portugal; Western Sahara by Spain; Gambia, Ghana, Nigeria, and Sierra Leone by Great Britain, and Togo and Cameroon by Germany. After World War I German colonies were divided and administered by France and Britain until their independence. Liberia, as a nation for repatriated slaves, was independent from 1847.

This partitioning process was generally peaceable, with Britain and France claiming the largest territory. Each moved to the interior from their coastal bases along navigable rivers. The French moved eastward up the Senegal River and then over and down the Niger River. At the same time they moved south into the Saharan desert from Algeria and north from Gabon. As they moved into the interior the French encountered increasing resistance from Muslim groups and states. The British moved inward from the coast along the Gambia River and up the Niger River, as well as from their coastal bases in Sierra Leone and Gold Coast. Germany claimed Togo and Cameroon from coastal bases. These colonial claims (except Germany's) lasted until after World War II.

As the 20th century began, European colonial powers wanted to pacify and develop their colonies. First, the desire was to economically develop the colonies by introducing cash crops into the subsistence economies predominant in Africa. The French encouraged groundnuts, cotton, palm oil, and cocoa in various places, while the British in some of their colonies promoted rubber, cocoa, and timber and the Germans started various plantation products. In order to provide markets for these goods, the colonial powers built roads and railroads from the coast to interior sources of these products and developed a taxation system to go along with them. European impact varied widely from colony to colony and even within colonies, with greater involvement usually related to more significant economic or political interests in a region. West Africa, because of its generally hostile environment, did not have any large European settler colonies. Therefore most colonies were controlled by a relatively small band of colonial officials and military.

As European colonialism increased, so also did missionary involvement, which moved into the interior as well. At the beginning of the 20th century mission emphasis was on training an African clerical class and providing Africans with a knowledge of the Bible. In addition there was a commitment to a "civilizing" role which included the promotion of Western culture, with new agricultural techniques, hygiene, literacy, Western humanitarian values, and the replacement of slavery with legitimate trade. Missionary expansion at the time of colonial imperialism helped Africans to identify missions with political domination; however, missions often defended Africans against colonial interests and abuses and therefore were not always appreciated by colonial officers or traders.

In the early 20th century European colonial powers attempted to define their colonial policies. The French developed associations in which French and colonists would cooperate and develop together with a centralized government ruled by a governor-general in Dakar under the French government. Lieutenant-governors were directly responsible for the various territories. This close relationship was facilitated by the fact that France's West African colonies were contiguous to one another The desire was to gradually raise the cultural and responsibility level for Africans and their societies.

The British followed a policy of indirect rule. They actively sought to cooperate with African traditional systems and rulers, who were employed as liaisons for British policy, programs, and taxation. By ruling through local chiefs and elders, they minimized administrative costs and gradually introduced modern ideas of government and society. This approach was conducive to Britain's more scattered colonies along the West African coast where each one was ruled separately.

As missionary work grew during the early 20th century, the stress was placed on establishing churches and then organizing schools and medical dispensaries around the churches. These schools provided a trained elite for church, education, or government work and thereby a means of social mobility. After World War I, when there was a dearth of missionaries, many African churches, while still under the control of the European church leadership, developed their own leaders. There also was an emphasis on converting Africans to Christianity before the rising tide of Islam reached them. In this endeavor to build a national leadership and to evangelize, the importance of the mission school and trained catechist was vital and resulted both in trained church leaders and also an elite who would soon lead the nationalist and independence movements.

West Africa was a leader in African nationalist movements and Pan-Africanism, which encouraged all blacks to organize to resist European colonial supremacy. This came to a head after World War II. Before the war, colonial governments, while generally keeping a loose hold on their colonies, considered colonialism to be a long-term commitment. However, the disruption of World War II and the disaster that resulted preoccupied Europeans and African nationalists saw their opportunity to pursue the freedom for which the war was fought. While this political movement was occurring, there was a growth after World War II of the number of missionaries in West Africa and the church began a major postwar boom.

Some people gained from colonialism and others suffered. Those who gained included indigenous rulers, traders, educated coastal people, and Muslim collaborators with French association or British indirect rule. Africans harmed by colonialism were those who resisted European rule or who were conscripted as laborers to work on roads, railroads, mines, and plantations. Their resentment fueled the nationalist movements. As the momentum for self-government and independence grew, the European governments, with the exception of Portugal in Guinea-Bissau, lost much of their desire to retain their colonies. Reforms were granted to gradually give African colonies autonomy. Kwame Nkrumah led his country to independence from Britain in 1957 and set the precedent for other British colonies, many of whom received self-government in the early 1960s. Guinea gained independence from France in 1958, leading to the independence of the other French West African states in 1960. Portuguese colonies achieved their independence later. Amilcar Cabral led the anti-Portuguese movement in Africa and helped Guinea-Bissau achieve sovereignty in 1974.

The church was not immune to these momentous changes. Many nationalist leaders were educated in mission schools and identified with European political values learned there, but the reaction of mission-based churches was mixed to liberation movements. Some supported the movements, others saw them as threatening the stability of society and ushering in the unknown, and others decided to adjust to whatever circumstances resulted. Mission churches cautiously waited to see what a postcolonial government would decide about the role of the church in society.

One significant factor in West African church history is that of the independent churches which separated themselves from the mission churches. These churches were often regional and developed their own doctrines, interpretation of the Bible, worship, ecclesiastical structure, and responses to political and religious issues. Frequently these divided into two large groupings. One, known as Ethiopian-style, became characterized by breaking with an established church or mission and closely retaining its style, only under African leadership. The other variety was the Zionist-style, often a charismatic and prophetic group centered around a leader who shaped the doctrine and procedures of the group without reference to traditional churches. These churches were usually local, but an estimated 5000 of them covered Africa near the end of the 20th century. These independent churches were often considered the precursors to African nationalism because they were reactions against European dominance and developed indigenous African leadership.

The role of the church in West Africa from the 1950s has modified to adjust to the new circumstances. Since independence, African governments have shared third world concerns for creating political stability and consensus and for stimulating economic development for their nations. This has meant confronting such issues as one-party states, military coups, regional differences, and debt payments. In these situations the church has encouraged public morals and ethics. But it also has changed in other ways. Since independence the churches—mission and independent—have accommodated to changing political, economic, and social situations. By the late 1900s the churches were administered by Africans with the mission agencies in a subsidiary role. The African church was also leading in the analysis of the relationship of Christianity to traditional African religions and to the distinctives of Christian theology for the African scene. The emphasis was on an African perspective of doctrine, worship, and symbols, making Christianity meaningful in the African context. This search, stimulated by an African awareness of their shared experience, led to greater cooperation among African churches of all nations and sects through conferences and consultations. They gravitated toward two groups; one identified with the World Council of Churches and the other with the World Evangelical Fellowship. Nevertheless cooperation on a regional and continental basis has become a major feature of postcolonial Africa. Greater cooperation among Christians has also led to an increasing dialog and understanding between Christians and Muslims, particularly in those states and regions where both religions are in close proximity. There has tended to be generally a much larger growth rate than in the West in the number of Christians throughout West Africa and all of Africa.

The West African church made a significant transition in a very brief time of 150 years. It made the transition from small communities identified with various European coastal enclaves, to expanding colonial missions, and finally to independent church bodies with their own agendas.

Civil war in Liberia created an uncertain political climate in the region in the late 1980s, and one missionary was murdered by rebel forces in 1990. Most mission organizations withdrew their foreign nationals from the country in mid-1990. In late 1990 other countries also faced instability and uncertain futures.

**Bibliography.** K. S. Latourette, *Christianity in a Revolutionary Age*, vol. 5 (1962); S. C. Neill, *A History of Christian Missions* (1964); R. Oliver and A. Atmore, *Africa since 1800* (1972); A. Hastings, *A History of African Christianity, 1950–1975* (1979); O. U. Kalu, ed., *A History of Christianity in West Africa* (1980); L. Sanneh, *West African Christianity: The Religious Impact* (1983); P. B. Clarke, *West Africa and Christianity* (1986).

CHARLES W. WEBER

**Western Samoa.** *See* SOUTH PACIFIC, ISLANDS OF THE.

**West Indies.** Islands of the Caribbean Basin, consisting of the Greater Antilles (Cuba, Hispaniola, Jamaica, and Puerto Rico), the Lesser Antilles (including the Leeward, Windward, and

Virgin Islands), and the Bahamas. Because these islands represent one of the most strategic regions of the world, competition among European colonial powers led to extensive contraband trade and frequent exchange of ownership of individual islands before the 19th century. The original Arawak and Carib populations disappeared. The demand for plantation labor resulted in forced migration of Africans as slaves and enticements to Asians and others to emigrate later. As a consequence, many languages and ethnic groups, including a small Jewish minority, were represented. Most people spoke creole variations of European mother tongues. The independent island nations were among the most densely populated in the world. The largest single religious affiliation was Roman Catholicism, a fact emphasized by several papal visits to the area in the late 1900s. African animism persisted in folk religions, characterized by divination, spell casting, curing, and spirit possession phenomena. The abolition of slavery began in the region in Haiti in 1793. Emancipation from Britain came in 1838, and slavery ended altogether in 1886.

***Spanish-Speaking Areas.*** *Puerto Rico.* This is the easternmost and smallest of the Greater Antilles. Discovered by Columbus in 1493, it was a Spanish colony until the USA acquired it in 1898. Although Congress granted Puerto Ricans USA citizenship in 1917, they did not gain internal political autonomy until 1952.

The Spanish created the first Roman Catholic diocese in 1511, but the strength of the church remained precarious. The USA instituted a policy of separation of church and state. Occasionally controversies erupted when bishops opposed government policies regarding contraception and secular education, notably in 1937 and 1960. In the late 1900s most priests were either from Spain or the USA, but all bishops were Puerto Rican. Approximately 90 percent of the population was at least nominally Catholic in the 1980s.

The Spanish introduced religious toleration in 1868. Shortly thereafter, Puerto Rican converts formed the first Presbyterian congregation. In 1873, Anglicans organized and constructed the first Protestant church building. During the U.S. military occupation, major Protestant denominations sent missionaries to the island.

Ecumenical cooperation has characterized Protestant work in Puerto Rico. Noncompeting denominations agreed in 1899 to concentrate in distinct territories. Various churches formed the Evangelical Union in 1905 (which became the Evangelical Council). In 1919 the union founded an interdenominational seminary. In 1931, three Protestant churches merged into the United Evangelical Church. Among missionary-fostered denominations, the Methodists are known for their educational ministries and Adventists for contributions to public health. The self-support-

ing Pentecostal Church of God is the largest non-Catholic body. It was introduced by Puerto Rican emigrés returning from Hawaii and emphasizes lay witnessing.

*Dominican Republic.* This occupies the eastern two-thirds of Hispaniola. Two-thirds of the adult Afro-Spanish people remained illiterate in the late 1900s. The first New World bishopric was established in Santo Domingo in 1511, but the position was frequently vacant. The University of San Tomás dates from 1538. The Jesuits entered the area in 1650. Roman Catholicism was the state religion from 1844. In 1880 and 1912 archbishops were chosen as presidents. Church and state relations are governed by a 1954 concordat. The hierarchy supported the dictatorship of Rafael Trujillo until 1959 but opposed his anticlerical successor, Juan Bosch.

The Dominican Republic was the last Latin American country to receive sustained Protestant missionary activity, and Protestants comprised the smallest proportion of the total population of any Latin American country. Nevertheless, their contribution was felt through International Hospital and the Librería Dominicana Publishing House.

*Cuba.* The largest of the Greater Antilles, half of the island is flat and fertile. Dominican missionaries came to Cuba in 1512, and even in the middle of the 20th century most priests were Spanish. Bishop Juan José Di'az de Espada succeeded in expanding education and the number of parishes early in the 19th century. Following abortive independence efforts, some Cuban exiles in the late 1860s embraced Protestantism and became pastors upon their return to the island. Early in the 20th century, Methodists founded several schools, notably in small towns. In 1947, Presbyterians, Methodists, and Episcopalians founded Union Theological Seminary in Matanzas. Following U.S. occupation in 1898, church and state were separated along North American lines. The revolution which Fidel Castro led in 1959 produced a confrontation with the Catholic hierarchy; all schools were nationalized and foreign priests were expelled in 1961. By the 1980s, the vast majority of Cubans had discontinued regular church attendance. The one-party state monopolized all Cuban media, including extensive film production and book publishing. Nevertheless, the example of socialist Cuba inspired liberation theology elsewhere.

***French-Speaking Areas.*** *Guadeloupe.* This area is the northernmost of the Windward Island group and consists of two large islands, Grand-Terre and Basse-Terre, and smaller islands, Marie Galantee and La Desirade, as well as the northern half of St. Maarten. This area of 1780 sq. km. (687 sq. mi.) contained 332,000 people (1985). Education was free and compulsory between 6 and 16 years of age. In 1981 there were 284 primary schools and 59 secondary schools. The Universitaire Antilles-Guyane and a teacher training school were located here. The majority of the population professed the Roman Catholic faith. This French colony also gained departmental status with France in 1946 and had regional status with Martinique and French Guiana.

*Martinique.* This French island in the Windward Islands has 1100 sq. km. (425 sq. mi.) and approximately 330,000 inhabitants (1984). A colony in 1635, it gained departmental status with France in 1946. In 1980, there were 229 primary schools and 3042 secondary schools. The majority of the populace was Roman Catholic.

*Haiti.* This nation of 6 million occupies the western third of Hispaniola. In the late 20th century Haiti was the poorest nation in the Western Hemisphere; most adults were illiterate. In 1697, Spain recognized the French presence in the colony of Saint-Domingue. In the following century, it became a sugar exporter, one of the richest colonies in the world. The prosperity depended upon labor of slaves who made up the vast majority of the population by the time of the French Revolution. Under the leadership of Toussaint L'Ouverture, the French colony experienced the only successful slave revolt in world history, and Haiti became the first independent nation of Latin America in 1804. After 1704, French Jesuits were especially active in both religious and scientific work. Independence disrupted Catholic ecclesiastical authority until the Vatican signed a concordat in 1860. In 1984, there were one archbishop, 6 bishops, and 420 priests, mostly French-born whites. The government subsidized both Roman Catholic and Protestant educational institutions. Most Haitian Protestant pastors were native. English missionaries introduced Methodism in 1807. In the 1960s, about 5 percent of all of Latin America's Protestants were Haitian.

*Dutch-Speaking Areas. Netherlands Antilles.* The Dutch founded colonies in the Caribbean in the 1630s. In the late 20th century, the Dutch area consisted of two island groups. Aruba, Curaçao and Bonaire in the Leeward Islands, covering 925 sq. km. (357 sq. mi.) and containing 216,453 inhabitants in 1981, represented the first island group. St. Eustatius, Saba, and the Dutch portion of St. Maarten in the Windward Islands, with 67 sq. km. (26 sq. mi.) and 15,479 residents (1981), was the second island group. Dutch was spoken in Aruba, Curaçao, and Bonaire, while English was predominant in the islands in the Windward group. In 1979, there were 215 nursery and primary schools, 68 secondary and vocational schools, two teacher training colleges, and one university. The Roman Catholic Church, with approximately 80 percent of the population, was the majority religion. The Anglican, Methodist, Dutch Reformed, and smaller Protestant denom-

inations numbered approximately 17,500 adherents.

*English-Speaking Area. Jamaica.* With 10,991 sq. km. (4244 sq. mi.), Jamaica is the third largest island in the Greater Antilles. Discovered by Columbus in 1494 but neglected by the Spanish, the island was seized by the British in 1655. Jamaica developed a slave-based sugar prosperity which declined in the mid-19th century, after emancipation and the adoption of free trade. A crown colony after 1866, it became an independent member of the British Commonwealth in 1962. Its 2.5 million people (1988) were governed by a two-party, parliamentary system of government. In the 1830s, half of the slaves in the British Empire worked in Jamaica. In the late 20th century over three-fourths of its predominantly rural people were descendants of slaves. Kingston, the capital, remained the only significant city. Earlier in the century, bananas, citrus, cocoa, and coffee diversified the previous sugar monoculture. In the 1950s, bauxite exports and tourism became important. At least 80 percent of the adults were literate. Higher education institutions included teachers' colleges; the College of Arts, Sciences, and Technology, and a branch of the University of the West Indies. Most Jamaicans were nominally Protestant, half of these Anglican. The first Anglican diocese was created in 1824. Quakers first expressed interest in missionary efforts among the slaves in 1671. Other Protestant missionaries came to Jamaica in the 18th century: Moravians (1754); Baptists (1783); and Methodists (1789). The First Baptist missionary was a freedman from the USA. Jamaican Baptists sent their first missionary to Africa in 1884. Afrosyncretic movements like the Rastafarians gained support from time to time. Ecumenism dated from the 1939 creation of the Jamaican Council of Churches.

*Antigua and Barbuda.* Located on the southern end of the Leeward Islands, these were discovered by Columbus in 1493, but they were not permanently settled until 1632. They remained a British colony from 1667 through 1958, a member of the Federation of the West Indies from 1958 through 1962, and a member of the free association in the Windward and Leeward Islands until achieving full independence within the British Commonwealth in November 1981. Antigua and Barbuda have 281 sq. km. (108 sq. mi.) and 161 sq. km. (62 sq. mi.), respectively, with a total population of 81,500 (1986). The majority were Anglican and Roman Catholic. The Anglican Church included the Diocese of Antigua in St. John's, which ministered to 60,000 members in 12 Caribbean islands. Other denominations included the Antigua Baptist Association, the Evangelical Lutheran Church, the Seventh-day Adventists—known for their public health efforts—the Moravians, Nazarenes, and Wesleyan

Holiness. The American Bible Society and the Divine Word Missions were active.

*The Bahamas.* This area of 29 inhabited and more than 2000 uninhabited islands and cays was a British crown colony from 1717 to 1964 and became an independent nation within the Commonwealth in 1973. The Bahamas cover 13,935 sq. km. (5382 sq. mi.) and contain 226,000 people (1984). Education was free and compulsory between 5 and 14 years. There were 78 primary schools, 7 junior high schools, 21 junior-senior high schools, 9 senior high schools, and 4 special schools. The College of the Bahamas provided higher education. The largest religious denominations in 1980 included 50,000 Baptists, 40,000 Roman Catholics, 38,400 Anglicans, 12,000 Methodists, and 10,000 Seventh-day Adventists. The Baptist World Relief and the Catholic Relief Services provided support to the community. Evangelistic organizations included the Gospel Missionary Union and the Southern Baptist Convention.

*Barbados.* The most easterly of the Caribbean islands comprised 430 sq. km. (166 sq. mi.) and 257,000 people (1988). An independent nation within the British Commonwealth, it had an elected assembly in 1652. In 1984, there were 114 primary schools, 21 secondary schools, a technical school, a teacher training school, a community college, a branch of the University of the West Indies, 15 government-supported independent schools, and a theological school. There were more than 90 religious denominations and sects. In 1970, there were 150,000 Anglicans, as well as Methodist, Moravian, and pentecostal groups, plus approximately 23,000 Roman Catholics and small groups of Hindus, Muslims, and Jews. The United Church Board for World Ministries was an active ecumenical organization. The Salvation Army, the Seventh-day Adventist World Development and Relief Agency, and Church World Service provided social services. The Caribbean Council of Churches published a monthly newsletter in Bridgetown.

*Dominica.* This island of 750 sq. km. (289 sq. mi.) in the Windward group had 82,503 people (1984). First settled by the French, Dominica became a British colony in 1759. After 1978 it became an independent republic within the British Commonwealth. In 1982, there were 58 primary and 8 secondary schools, a teacher training college, and a branch of the University of the West Indies. Roman Catholics comprised 80 percent of the religious population (1983), approximately 65,000 members. Other Christian churches included Methodist, pentecostal, Baptist, Church of Christ, Seventh-day Adventist, and Anglican denominations, as well as the Jehovah's Witnesses. A Gospel Broadcasting Corporation produced over 100 hours of religious programs each week. Missionary work was provided by the

Berean Mission, Inc., the Catholic Medical Mission Board, and St. Patrick's Missionary Society. Church World Service, Catholic Relief Services and the United Methodist Committee on Relief provided social services.

*Grenada.* This southernmost Windward Island was a British colony after 1783 and an independent nation within the British Commonwealth from 1974. In 1979 a revolution overthrew the parliamentary government and installed a socialist government and social reforms. Unrest and assassinations followed and in 1983 an invasion force of Caribbean and U.S. troops occupied the island, restoring the parliament. There were 113,000 people on 344 sq. km. (133 sq. mi.) (1982). Education was free and compulsory between six and 14 years. There were 68 primary schools and 20 secondary schools (1981), technical centers in each parish, a technical and vocational institute, a teacher's training college, and a branch of the University of the West Indies. Religious denominations included the Anglican communion, the Roman Catholic Church, Presbyterian, Methodist, Plymouth Brethren, Baptist, and Seventh-day Adventists. Missionary work was provided by the Berean Mission, Inc., and St. Patrick's Missionary Society. Church World Service and the United Methodist Committee on Relief provided social services.

*Saint Christopher (St. Kitts) and Nevis.* In the Leeward Islands, St. Kitts covers 176 sq. km. (68 sq. mi.) and Nevis 93 sq. km. (36 sq. mi.). They share 44,404 inhabitants (1980). Jointly settled by the British and French in the 1620s, these islands became an independent nation within the British Commonwealth in September 1983. There were 28 primary schools and 6 secondary schools (1982). The majority of the population were Anglican, while other denominations included the Methodist, Moravian, Seventh-day Adventist, Baptist, Church of God, Apostolic Faith, and Plymouth Brethren churches. Radio Paradise was a popular religious radio station. The American Bible Society was active.

*Saint Lucia.* This island has 616 sq. km. (238 sq. mi.) and 134,000 inhabitants (1984). It became an independent nation within the British Commonwealth in 1977, having been a British colony since 1814. Education was compulsory between 5 and 15 years of age. The Roman Catholic Church encompassed 85 percent of the population, with the remainder divided among the Anglican, Methodist, Baptist, Seventh-day Adventist, pentecostal, and Bethel Tabernacle churches. The *Catholic Chronicle* and the *Crusader* were religious publications. Catholic Relief Services of the United States Catholic Conference provided social services.

*Saint Vincent and the Grenadines.* These islands, in the Windwards, include 389 sq. km. (150 sq. mi.) and approximately 138,000 inhabitants

(1984). A British colony from 1763 through 1958 and a member of the Federation of the West Indies until 1962, these islands achieved full independence within the British Commonwealth in 1979. There were 30 preprimary schools, 62 primary schools, and 19 secondary schools (1982). Thirteen secondary schools were operated by religious organizations with government assistance. A teacher training college and a technical college operated. The Anglican Church was the largest denomination—the bishop of the Windward Islands and the archbishop of the West Indies had headquarters here. Other key denominations included the Methodists, Seventh-day Adventists, Baptists, and the Roman Catholic Church. The Catholic Medical Mission Board, the Salvation Army, and the United Methodist Committee on Relief provided necessary social services.

*Trinidad and Tobago.* These two islands north of the Venezuelan coast anchor the Caribbean island chain. Trinidad and Tobago had 1.7 million inhabitants (1984), and cover 5128 sq. km. (1980 sq. mi.). Trinidad and Tobago was an independent republic within the British Commonwealth from 1976, having been combined as a crown colony in 1888. Primary and secondary education was free and attendance officially compulsory between 6 and 12 years. The junior secondary school system for ages 12 to 14 was introduced in 1972 as a joint state and religious system. The nation was served by the Trinidad branch of the University of the West Indies, and three teacher training colleges, three government technical institutes and training centers, the Polytechnic Institute, and the East Caribbean Farm Institute. In 1980, 60 percent of the population was Christian (34 percent Roman Catholic; 15 percent Anglican), 25 percent Hindu, and 6 percent Muslim. Non-Creoles were mostly non-Christian. Lower-class Creoles of African descent professed membership in either formal religions or in the Shouter or Shango sects. The Christian Council of Trinidad and Tobago, created in 1967 to promote Christian unity, included the Roman Catholic, Anglican, Presbyterian, Methodist, and Moravian churches, the Lutheran Mission, and Salvation Army. The Ethiopian Orthodox Church and the Baptist Union were observers. The *Catholic News* was a periodical founded in 1892. Social services were provided by the Seventh-day Adventist World Development and Relief Agency, the Baptist World Relief, the Catholic Medical Mission Board, Catholic Relief Services, and Church World Service. Missionary and evangelistic activities were provided by the Moravian Church, the Southern Baptist Convention, and the Anglican communion.

*Anguilla.* This island and a smaller one are the most northerly of the Leeward group. Anguilla, a British dependency, cover 249 sq. km. (96 sq. mi.) and have 7019 inhabitants (1984). There were five preprimary centers, six state primary schools, and one state secondary school in the education system (1983). Religious denominations included the Anglicans, Methodists, Seventh-day Adventists, Baptists, Church of God, and the Roman Catholic Church, as well as Apostolic Faith and the Jehovah's Witnesses. The Caribbean Beacon Radio, a privately owned station, broadcast 20 hours of religious and commercial programs daily.

*Montserrat.* This island of 102 sq. km. (39.5 sq. mi.) is in the Leeward Island group and contains 11,793 persons (1984). It was a British possession since 1637. Education was compulsory until 14 years of age and provided free in state-supported schools. There were nine primary schools, two junior secondary schools, one private secondary school, and one technical college (1985). Principal church affiliations were the Anglican, Baptist, Methodist, pentecostal, Seventh-day Adventist, and Roman Catholic.

*The British Virgin Islands.* This area of 153 sq. km. (59 sq. mi.) consists of 40 mountainous islands (15 inhabited) in the northern Leeward Islands near the United States Virgin Islands. A British colony from the 1660s, after 1966 they were a semiautonomous dependency with 11,558 inhabitants (1983). There were 8 preprimary schools, 18 primary schools, and one secondary school (1984). The Methodist Church and the Church of God were predominant religious denominations. Others included the Anglicans, Seventh-day Adventists, Baptists, and the Roman Catholic Church.

*United States Virgin Islands.* A Danish colony from 1672 until 1917, the islands became a U.S. territory, consisting of St. Croix, St. Thomas, and St. John Islands, along with 50 smaller ones. Part of the Leeward group they had 102,410 inhabitants on 355 sq. km. (137 sq. mi.) in 1984. Religious denominations included the Roman Catholic Church with about 25,000 adherents (1984), Anglican, Lutheran, Methodist, Moravian, and Seventh-day Adventist churches.

*Bibliography.* H. J. Wiarda, *JChSt* 7 (Spring 1965); J. Gonzalez, *The Development of Christianity in the Latin Caribbean* (1969); I. S. Emmanuel and S. A. Emmanuel, *History of the Jews of the Netherlands Antilles* (1970); G. E. Simpson, *Religious Cults of the Caribbean: Jamaica, Trinidad, and Haiti* (1970); A. Hageman and P. E. Wheaton, eds., *Religion in Cuba Today* (1971); J. H. Parry and P. M. Sherlock, *A Short History of the West Indies* (3d ed., 1972); G. E. Simpson, *Caribbean Studies* 12 (July 1972); I. Hamid, ed., *Out of the Depth: Papers Presented at Four Missiology Conferences Held in Antigua, Guayana, Jamaica, and Trinidad, 1975* (1977); N. Erskine, *Decolonizing Theology: A Caribbean Perspective* (1981); S. D. Grazier, *JRTheol* 39 (Fall/Winter 1982–83); C. Wright, *Religion* 14 (Oct. 1984).

ROBERT H. CLAXTON AND JOHN A. JACKSON, JR.

**Weston, Frank** (1871–1924). Anglican missionary bishop and Anglo-Catholic. After graduating from Oxford, he was ordained and served curacies in London before joining the Universities' Mission to Central Africa in 1898. He was principal of Zanzibar's St. Andrew's Training College (1901–8) and bishop for the country (1908–24). A strong and persuasive High Church leader, he was president of the second Anglo-Catholic congress in London in 1923. He understood the African mind, and wrote against the system of forced labor in East Africa in *Serfs of Great Britain* (1920). Although he was a warm advocate of church reunion, he is remembered most for his opposition to a particular scheme for bringing together Christian missionary work in Kenya, a controversy which spread throughout the English-speaking world. His antimodernist views were reflected in his best-known book *The One Christ* (1907).

J. D. DOUGLAS

**Whale, John Seldon** (1896–1985). English Congregational scholar. Born in Mevagissey, Cornwall, he studied at Oxford and Cambridge, and after ordination was minister of Bowdon Downs Congregational Church, Manchester (1925–29). He was then professor of ecclesiastical history, Mansfield College, Oxford (1929–33); president of Cheshunt College, Cambridge (1933–43); headmaster of Mill Hill School (1943–51); and visiting professor of systematic theology, Drew University (1951–53). Among his publications were *The Christian Answer to the Problem of Evil* (1936), *The Right to Believe* (1938), *Christian Doctrine* (1941), *The Protestant Tradition: An Essay in Interpretation* (1955), *Victor and Victim: The Christian Doctrine of Redemption* (1960), and *Christian Reunion: Historic Divisions Reconsidered* (1971).

J. D. DOUGLAS

**White, Ellen Gould** (1827–1915). Seventh-day Adventist Church leader. Born in Gorham, Maine, into a Methodist family expelled in 1843 for embracing premillennial views, she became an Adventist under the influence of William Miller. Shortly afterwards the first of many "revelations" revealed to her the triumph of the Adventists over persecution. With the official establishment of the Seventh-day Adventist Church in 1863 in Battle Creek, Mich., White became its leader and her words were accepted as the "spirit of prophecy." Her *Steps to Christ* (1892) has gone through numerous editions in more than 100 languages, selling more than 20 million copies. Among her other publications is *Testimonies for the Church* (9 vols., 1855–1909). During the latter part of her life she established Seventh-day Adventism in Europe (1885–87) and Australia (1891–1900).

J. D. DOUGLAS

**White, Wilbert Webster** (1863–1944). American biblical scholar. Born in Ashland, Ohio, he studied at the University of Wooster, Xenia Theological Seminary, and Yale University (Ph.D.,

1891). He was Presbyterian pastor at Peotone, Ill. (1885/86); professor of Hebrew and OT literature at Xenia Theological Seminary (1890–95); taught at the Moody Bible Institute, Chicago (1895–97); engaged in Bible work in India and England (1897–1900); and was founder and president of the Bible Teachers' Training School, New York (1900–1940), which he soon transformed into the Biblical Seminary, New York. This school became the embodiment of his ideal that theological education should be centered in (and in large part consist of) biblical studies. He also conducted summer conferences for theological teachers and other religious leaders at the seminary's summer headquarters at Silver Bay, N.Y. His published works include *Inductive Studies in the Twelve Minor Prophets* (1894), *Thirty Studies in Jeremiah* (1895), *Thirty Studies in the Gospel by John* (1896), *Thirty Studies in the Revelation of Jesus Christ to John* (1898), *Studies in OT Characters* (1900), *Thirty Studies in the Gospel by Matthew* (1903), *The Resurrection of the Body "According to the Scriptures"* (1923), and *How to Study* (1930).

**Whitehead, Alfred North** (1861–1947). English philosopher and contributor to process theology. Born in Ramsgate, Kent, he studied at Trinity College, Cambridge. He was lecturer in mathematics at Trinity (1885–1910) and at University College, London (1911–14); professor, Imperial College of Science and Technology (1914–24); and professor of philosophy, Harvard University (1924–36). His earlier writings dealt with mathematics, logic, and the philosophy of science. From 1925, he constructed a subtle metaphysical system. Integral to this system is a conception of God as the source of "unactualized possibilities" (God's "primordial nature") and the conserver of actualized values (God's "consequent nature"). In the creative process there is interaction between the world of finite things ("actual occasions"), which are transient, and God, who is both primordial and everlasting. His writings include *Science and the Modern World* (1925), *Religion in the Making* (1926), *Process and Reality* (1929), *Adventures of Ideas* (1933), and *Modes of Thought* (1938).

**Bibliography.** P. A. Schilpp, ed., *The Philosophy of Alfred North Whitehead* (1941); R. B. Mellert, *What Is Process Theology?* (1975); C. Hartshorne, *Whitehead's View of Reality* (1981); D. W. Diehl, "Process Theology" in *Evangelical Dictionary of Theology*, ed. W. A. Elwell (1984).

WILLIAM A. CHRISTIAN, JR.

**Whitney, James Pounder** (1857–1929). Anglican historian. Born in Marsden, York, he was educated at King's College, Cambridge. Ordained in 1883, he served in parishes until 1900, then became principal of Bishop's College, Lennoxville, Canada (1900–1905); professor of ecclesiastical history at King's College, London (1905–18); and Dixie Professor at Cambridge (1919–39). He wrote *The History of the Reformation* (1940) and contributed to the *Cambridge Modern History*. He was joint editor of the *Cambridge Mediaeval History* (1907–22).

F. W. DILLISTONE

**Whitsunday.** The English name for Pentecost. Whitsunday is so called from the white robes worn by catechumens whose baptism, instead of taking place at Easter, was postponed until the vigil of Pentecost. Whitsuntide is the period extending from Saturday before Pentecost to Trinity Sunday.

**Whyte, Alexander** (1836–1921). Scottish Presbyterian preacher. Born in Kirriemuir, he was educated at Aberdeen University and at New College, Edinburgh. After ordination he was associate minister at Free St. John's, Glasgow (1866–70), and then colleague and successor at Free St. George's, Edinburgh (1870–1916), where crowds gathered to hear his dramatic and compelling preaching. During his later ministry there he served as principal and taught NT literature at New College (1909–18). A conservative, he still established and maintained friendly contact with scholars of very different churchmanship, including Cardinal Newman. His published works include *Commentary on the Shorter Catechism* (1892), *Appreciation of Jacob Behmen* (1895), *Lancelot Andrewes and His Private Devotions* (1895), *The Four Temperaments* (1895), *Santa Teresa* (1897), *Bible Characters* (6 vols., 1896–1902), *Bunyan Characters* (4 vols., 1893–1908), *The Apostle Paul* (1903), *Fraser of Brea* (1911), and *Thomas Shepard, Pilgrim Father and Founder of Harvard* (1909).

J. D. DOUGLAS

**Wiesel, Elie** (1928– ). Jewish scholar, writer, and spokesperson for survivors of the Nazi holocaust. Born in Sighet, Romania (Transylvania), in 1944 he was deported to the death camps at Auschwitz and Buchenwald. He studied at the Sorbonne, worked for Israeli, French, and American newspapers, and from 1972 to 1976 he was distinguished professor of Judaic studies, City College, New York. He then became professor in the humanities, university professor, and professor of religion at Boston University.

With *La Nuit* (1958; ET, *Night*, 1960), recollections of Auschwitz, Wiesel became a brilliant and relentless voice on behalf of Jewry against racism and oppression. In 25 major novels, Hasidic tales, Jewish legends, and plays, he has bid people of faith to journey from despair to affirmation, although he wrote that for him God had "died" in the Holocaust.

He has been awarded numerous honorary doctorates and has received major literary awards and citations for his powerful writing. His books,

written primarily in French, have been translated into many languages. He was made Commandeur de la Legion d'Honneur. In 1984 he was awarded the Congressional Gold Medal by the U.S. Senate and House of Representatives. In 1986 Wiesel was named recipient of the Nobel Peace Prize for his "commitment which originated in the sufferings of the Jewish people and has been widened to embrace all oppressed peoples and races."

He was chairman of the U.S. Holocaust Memorial Council and the U.S. President's Commission on the Holocaust.

Among his works are *The Town beyond a Wall* (1964), *A Beggar in Jerusalem* (1970), *Souls on Fire: Portraits and Legends of Hasidic Masters* (1972), *The Trial of God*, a play (1979), *The Testament* (1980), and *Signes d'Exode* (1985).

E. J. FURCHA

**Wilder, Amos Niveu** (1895– ). NT scholar, educator, and writer. Born in Madison, Wis., during World War I he served in the American Ambulance Field Service in France (1916/17) and was awarded France's Croix de Guerre medal. He studied at Yale University (Ph.D., 1933), Mansfield College, Oxford, and Harvard University, and after ordination (1926) served as pastor of the Congregational church in North Conway, N.H. (1925–28). He was associate professor of ethics and Christian evidences at Hamilton College (1930–33); professor of NT interpretation, Andover Newton Theological School (1933–43); professor of NT, Chicago Theological Seminary (1943–54); and professor of NT (1954–56) and of Divinity (1956–63) at Harvard. Wilder's academic pursuits also covered both biblical and modern literature. His literary works include poetry, theology, ethics, and literary criticism. Among his books are *Battle-Retrospect and Other Poems* (1923), *Eschatology and Ethics in the Teaching of Jesus* (1939), *Theology and Modern Literature* (1958), *Kerygma, Eschatology and Social Ethics* (1966), and *Theopoetic: Theology and the Religious Imagination* (1976).

JACK MITCHELL

**Wilkinson, John Thomas** (1894–1980). English Methodist scholar. After graduating from Manchester University, he trained for the Primitive Methodist ministry at Hartley Victoria College. After ordination he served in various English circuits (1917–46), was tutor in church history at Hartley Victoria College (1941–53) and principal (1953–59), and lecturer in history of church doctrine at Manchester University (1953–59). He was the author of *Richard Baxter and Margaret Charlton* (1927), *Principles of Biblical Interpretation* (1960), *No Apology* (1962), and *Interpretation and Community* (1963).

**Williams, George Huntston** (1914– ). Congregationalist and Unitarian minister. Born in Huntsburg, Ohio, he graduated from St. Lawrence University and Meadville Theological School, Chicago. He was ordained in the Christian Union Church, Rockford, Ill. (1940/41), from which he was called to Starr King School and Pacific School of Religion, Berkeley, Calif. (1941–47). He studied at the University of California and Union Theological Seminary (Th.D., 1946).

From 1947 he taught church history at Harvard Divinity School, becoming Hollis professor of divinity, Harvard University. Interested in the bearing of theology upon issues of church and state, Williams devoted his lifetime to studying the relationship of religious values and social life in such areas as the conservation of nature, racial justice, civil liberties, bioethics, and ecumenical concerns. He helped found Americans United for Life, and he participated in the World Congress of Jewish Studies (1961); was observer at Vatican Council II (1962–65); was guest of the patriarch of Moscow, 50th anniversary, restoration of the patriarchate (1968); and was Guggenheim Fellow, Marie-Curie Sklodowska University and Catholic University in Lublin (1972/73).

His works include *The Norman Anonymous of ca. 1100* (1951), *Frederic Henry Hedge* (1951), *Anselm and Atonement* (1959), *Wilderness and Paradise in Christian Thought* (1962), *The Radical Reformation* (1962), *The Polish Brethren 1601–1685* (1980), and *The Mind of John Paul II* (1981). Williams has edited many studies, such as *The Harvard Divinity School* (1954), *Anabaptist and Spiritual Writers* (1957), the papers of Harry A. Wolfson (1974/75), *Thomas Hooker: Writings in England and Holland* (1975), *Historia Reformationis Polonicae* (1988), and *Divinings: Pointers from the Harvard Heritage 1636–1986* (1988).

**Bibliography.** F. F. Church and T. George, eds., *Continuity and Discontinuity in Church History* (1979), and the symposium, "An Historian for all Seasons," in *AmJThPh* (May 1986).

RODNEY L. PETERSEN

**Williams, Norman Powell** (1883–1943). Anglican. He studied at Oxford. He was ordained deacon in 1908 and priest in 1909, having been a fellow of Magdalen College (1906–9). He served as librarian of Exeter College, Oxford (1910–16); assistant master at Eton College (1916/17); chaplain, fellow, and theological lecturer at Exeter College, Oxford (1909–27); and Lady Margaret Professor of Divinity and canon of Christ Church, Oxford, from 1927. He was the author of *The Ideas of the Fall and of Original Sin: A Historical and Critical Study* (1927) and *The Grace of God* (1930). He contributed to *Oxford Studies in the Synoptic Problem* (1911), *Encyclopaedia of Religion and Ethics* (1910–34), *Essays, Catholic and Critical* (1926), and *A New Commentary on Holy Scripture* (1928). With W. Sanday he wrote *Form and Content in the Christian Tradition* (1916) and with C. Harris edited *Northern Catholicism* (1933).

RAYMOND W. ALBRIGHT

**Willoughby, Harold Rideout** (1890–1962). Methodist. Born in North Haverhill, N.H., he studied at Wesleyan University, Garrett Biblical Institute, the University of Chicago (Ph.D., 1924), and the University of Berlin. He taught NT at the University of Chicago (1924–43), and was professor of Christian origins there from 1943. In NT studies he applied social-historical methods to the problems of Christian origins and investigated iconography of the Greek NT. He wrote *Pagan Regeneration* (1929), *Codex 2400 and Its Miniatures* (1933), *The Coverdale Psalter and the Quatrocentenary of the Printed English Bible* (1935), *The First Authorized Bible and the Cranmer Preface* (1942), *Soldiers' Bibles Through Three Centuries* (1944), and *The Study of the Bible Today and Tomorrow* (1947). He was coauthor of *A Short Introduction to the Gospels* (1926) with E. D. Burton, and with E. J. Goodspeed and D. W. Riddle, *The Rockefeller-McCormick NT* (1932); and he edited with E. C. Colwell, *The Four Gospels of Karahissar* (1936), with J. T. McNeill and M. Spinka, *Environmental Factors in Christian History* (1939), and with E. C. Colwell, *The Elizabeth Day McCormick Apocalypse* (2 vols., 1940).

**Wilson, J. Christy** (1881–1973). American missionary and Near Eastern scholar. Born in Columbus, Nebr., he was educated at Kansas University and at Princeton University and Princeton Theological Seminary. In 1919 he went as an evangelistic missionary to Tabriz, northwestern Iran, under the Presbyterian Board of Foreign Missions. During 20 years there he was chairman of the Near East Relief Committee for Iran and of the Near East Christian Council. Soon after the start of World War II he returned to the USA and was associate professor of ecumenics at Princeton Seminary (1940–62). He wrote several books in Persian, including one on the art, archeology, and architecture of Iran at the request of the Imperial Ministry of Education. Among his works in English were *The Christian Message to Islam* (1950), *Apostle to Islam: The Biography of Samuel M. Zwemer* (1952), and *Ministers in Training* (1957). He wrote a missionary column for the *Presbyterian Magazine*, and contributed articles on Near Eastern subjects for the *New Collier's Encyclopedia*.

J. CHRISTY WILSON, JR.

**Wilson, Robert Dick** (1856–1930). Presbyterian scholar and cofounder of Westminster Seminary. He studied at the College of New Jersey (Ph.D., 1886), Western Theological Seminary, and the University of Berlin (1881–83). He taught OT at Western Seminary (instructor, 1880/81, 1883–85; professor, 1885–1900) and was at Princeton Theological Seminary (1900–1929) during the modernist controversy. Among those who resigned when conservatives lost Princeton, he died soon after the start of Westminster Theological Seminary (1929/30). His writings include *Elements of Syriac Grammar* (1890), *Manual of Syriac* (1890), *Hebrew Syntax* (1902), *Hebrew Grammar for Beginners* (1907), *Hebrew Prose Composition* (1907), *Hebrew Illustrations* (1908), *Studies in the Book of Daniel* (repr. ed., 1972), *Is the Higher Criticism Scholarly?* (1922), and *Scientific OT Criticism* (1923).

L. A. LOETSCHER

**Wilson, Robert McLachlan** (1916– ). Scottish NT scholar. Born in Gourock, he graduated from Edinburgh University in Arts and Divinity, and later earned a Ph.D. at Cambridge. After ordination in the Church of Scotland, he was minister in Strathaven (1946–54) before going to St. Andrews to lecture in NT language and literature (1954–69), in which department he was appointed to a personal chair in 1969. He succeeded Matthew Black as professor of biblical criticism in 1978 and retired in 1983. Recognized as an international authority on gnosticism, he was elected a fellow of the British Academy in 1977. He was also editor of *NT Studies* (1977–83), but found time to continue preaching and to participate in church affairs. He edited and translated extensively in his specialized field. His own publications include *The Gnostic Problem* (1958), *Studies in the Gospel of Thomas* (1960), *The Gospel of Philip* (1962), and *Gnosis and the NT* (1968).

J. D. DOUGLAS

**Wise, Stephen Samuel** (1874–1949). Jewish writer and leader. Born in Budapest, he studied at the City College of New York and Columbia University (Ph.D., 1901). He was rabbi at Madison Avenue Synagogue, New York (1893–1900), and Beth Israel, Portland, Oreg. (1900–1906). In 1907 he founded and became rabbi of the Free Synagogue of New York where he remained until his death. He was interested in the Zionist movement and founded the first section of the Federation of American Zionists. Between 1936 and 1938, he was president of the American Jewish Congress, the World Jewish Congress, and the Zionist Organization of America. He also founded the eastern council of liberal rabbis; was founder and first president of the Jewish Institute of Religion; and served on religious, social, and government committees. Among his books is *The Ethics of Solomon Ibn Gabirol* (1901), and he coauthored with Jacob de Haas, *The Great Betrayal* (1930). He

also edited *Opinion,* a magazine about Jewish life and thought.

RAYMOND W. ALBRIGHT

**Wiseman, Donald John** (1918– ). English Assyriologist. After studies at London University he served in the Royal Air Force (1939–45), and was subsequently a chief intelligence officer, rising to the rank of group-captain (colonel). He resumed studies at Oxford and in 1948 was appointed assistant keeper in the British Museum's Western Asiatic antiquities department. He was professor of Assyriology at London University (1961–82), joint director of the British School of Archaeology in Iraq (1961–65), president of the Society for OT Studies (1980), and a fellow of the British Academy. A member of the Plymouth Brethren and a warm supporter of evangelical causes, he was chairman of Tyndale House for Biblical Research, Cambridge (1957–86). His publications include *The Alalakh Tablets* (1953), *Chronicles of Chaldaean Kings* (1956), *Illustrations from Biblical Archaeology* (1958), *Peoples of OT Times* (1973), *Essays on the Patriarchal Narratives* (1980), and *Nebuchadrezzar and Babylon* (1985). He was editor of the journal *Iraq* (1953–78) and joint editor of *Reallexikon der Assyrologie* (from 1959). He coedited with E. Yamauchi, *Archaeology and the Bible: An Introductory Study* (1979).

J. D. DOUGLAS

**Women, Ordination of.** A debate which became a conservative-modernist issue in a variety of 20th-century communions and related to the rise of the women's suffrage and feminism movements. Ordination (from Lat. *ordinare,* "to put in order or appoint") is a process in which churches confer on members the right to minister in specific ways. The right extends to the full support of people working outside the church (e.g., missionaries among unevangelized people). Ordination does not imply the right to a salary, but it does reserve for the ordained prerogatives and responsibilities denied to other "lay" members. For this reason ordination is seen to confer a valued status, and debates over the ordination of women took place within a social climate sensitive to personal value and liberty. "Ordination" within these debates involved the historic orders of bishop, presbyter (or priest), and deacon in episcopal church governments and equivalent posts in other churches. Since church leaders are by tradition ordained ministers, leadership in local or regional churches is perceived to be a function of ordained status.

*Development of the Question.* Jesus chose 12 men as apostles, to preach, heal, and have authority over demons (Matt. 10:1–4; Mark 3:13–19). Women accompanied them on preaching tours and "were helping to support them out of their own means" (Luke 8:1–3). In churches where Paul worked, presbyter-bishops or elders took care of congregations and deacons worked alongside (Acts 14:23; 20:28; Phil. 1:1). Phoebe was a servant or deacon to Paul and the church at Cenchreae and, according to one interpretation, Junia or Julia was an "apostle" (Rom. 16:1, 7). Euodia and Syntyche worked with Paul "in the cause of the gospel" (Phil. 4:2). Presbyter-bishops and deacons are to be "husbands of one wife" (1 Tim. 3:2, 12; Titus 1:6). Although described in the masculine gender, this grammatical convention does not necessarily exclude women from either office. One interpretation of "women" in 1 Tim. 3:11 is that it refers to "female deacons." "Widows" (1 Tim. 5:3–16) could also have indicated a position of authority originally, since in the 3d-century Syrian statement on church order, *Didascalia Apostolorum*, widows were excluded from giving instruction or administering sacraments. The *Apostolic Constitutions* (c. 381) agrees with the *Didascalia* that deaconesses could be ordained but says widows could not; a less influential, possibly private, document, *Testamentum Domini*, describes "lady presbyters" among the leading widows. By A.D. 343 women were not allowed to be presbyters (Council of Laodicea). Ordination of deaconesses continued, but *Apostolic Constitutions* argues that they should refrain from preaching and baptizing; prayer becomes their primary liturgical function. The Synod of Orleans (533) opposed their ordination in Gaul, but deaconesses were found elsewhere in the 11th century.

By the time of the Reformation "ordination" of women was a closed issue. Martin Luther argued that the place of women was the home; John Calvin would not let women usurp the prerogative of presbyters to baptize. But in 1836 Theodor Fliedner established a Protestant community of unmarried Lutheran women as an order of Protestant deaconesses at Kaiserwerth in Germany. The bishop of London ordained a deaconess in 1862. In the USA Lutherans in 1884, Anglicans in 1885, and Methodists in 1888 began ordaining deaconesses. The movement grew gradually and the 20th century extended the process. In the USA there were 100 women Congregational ministers by 1927; the Methodist Episcopal Church in 1924 authorized women lay preachers; and in 1956 the Presbyterian Church in the USA voted to ordain women and the mainline American Methodist Church gave full conference privileges to ordained women. In 1970 the Lutheran Church in America and in 1976 American Anglicans voted to ordain women, years after the Anglican bishop of Hong Kong had ordained the Reverend Li Tim Oi to the priesthood with the permission of his local synod. By 1975, of the 295 members of the World Council of Churches, 104 ordained women, 57 did not, and the rest did not

clarify their position. The ordaining churches were mainly denominations of East and West Europe and North America, with some in Asia, the Pacific, Caribbean, Latin America, and Africa. In some countries, such as Indonesia, churches did not follow the example of their own Western groups.

The general synod of the Church of England in 1975 voted that no fundamental theological objections remained to ordaining women. Roman Catholic leaders, including John Paul II, stood adamantly against movements to ordain women priests, although some observers anticipate women priests by the end of the century. In 1987 the Church of England, following the lead of the Anglicans in Wales, East Africa, and elsewhere, began the process of ordaining women deacons. The Orthodox Church shares the Roman Catholic stance, as do many indigenous churches around the third world.

**Debate.** Ecclesiastical tradition and social mores, as well as scriptural reasons, have stood between women and ordained office. Some traditionalists regard the male priest as an icon of the male Christ, the male OT priest, or the male Jesus as the model for the representative at the sacrament. Others note the choice of male apostles by a Jesus who affirmed women, and some ecumenists would prefer not to make the relatively minor issue of ordaining women yet another barrier between themselves and the Roman Catholic or Orthodox churches. Advocates of ordaining women tend to interpret the humanity of the exalted Jesus as inclusively male and female and reckon that social convention made it inappropriate for him to appoint female apostles. Further, they regard unity with churches who do ordain women as important as union with those which do not.

Another set of arguments belongs to social anthropology, some arguing that male domination is "natural" and therefore right, others that it is a social myth and wrong in the present climate. Ordination is a gateway to church leadership, and leadership has been exercised by women in church work in the 19th and 20th centuries despite the bar to ordination. Further, leadership by women outside the church, whether as monarch or business manager, has long been practiced and is a growing phenomenon; to refuse formal recognition of church leadership in such circumstances is seen by proponents as an inappropriate violation of an egalitarian standard of human justice.

Protestants, Catholics, and Orthodox on both sides are willing to allow scriptural authority in the debate, though they disagree greatly on its force. Most salient texts are drawn from Genesis 1–3 and the Pauline epistles. Advocates of women's ordination regard the fall as the source of inequality and male domination. Paul, they argue, affirmed universal equality in Christ in Gal. 3:28, but moderated this standard in the light of conventional rabbinic exegesis and particular needs of local churches to whom he wrote. Christians must discriminate between the universally valid Gal. 3:28 and the culture-appropriate 1 Cor. 11:3–16 and 1 Tim. 2:14

Opponents question the criteria offered for distinguishing between temporary and universal scriptural injunctions. Those who believe the Bible stands against ordaining women fall into two camps. Dispensationalists believe that male headship is rooted in the created order (Gen. 2) or the curse placed upon woman in Gen. 3:16 and followed by Paul in 1 Cor. 14:34. Within covenant theology, on the other hand, conservatives root their view in the nature of the Adamic and succeeding covenants. Subordination of women is not in itself inequality, but a difference in roles among equals. The curse of Gen. 3:16 has introduced conflict in that women and men both seek to dominate one another. Man's role is to carry the responsibility of the covenants as self-sacrificing head and covenantal representative of God within family and church. The covenantal approach stresses not equality but mutual subjection to one another, the authority of God and to separate identities given to men and women (Eph. 5:21–33). Those who desire women to have ordained status in the church see in male-only headship the curse, and Paul's commentary on it governed by 1st-century realities which have been carried forward as 20th-century myth.

*See also* DEACONESS; ORDINATION.

**Bibliography.** Archbishop of Canterbury's Committee, *The Ministry of Women* (1919); S. Goldberg, *The Inevitability of Patriarchy* (1977); G. W. Knight, III, *The NT Teaching on the Role of Men and Women* (1977); P. Moore, ed., *Man, Woman, Priesthood* (1978); G. Wenham, *Churchman* 92 (1978); R. Ruether and E. McLaughlin, *Women of Spirit: Female Leadership in the Jewish and Christian Traditions* (1979); C. F. Parvey, ed., *Ordination of Women in Ecumenical Perspective* (1980); I. Raming in *Concilium: Women in a Men's Church* (1980); E. S. Fiorenza, *In Memory of Her* (1983); T. Hopko, ed., *Women and the Priesthood* (1983); M. Furlong, ed., *Feminine in the Church* (1984); G. W. Knight, III, *NTS* 30 (1984); C. Crastin, *Biblical Headship and the Ordination of Women* (1986).

GERVAIS ANGEL

### Wood, Maurice Arthur Ponsonby (1916– ).

Anglican bishop. After graduating from Cambridge he was ordained and served a curacy at St. Paul's, Portman Square, London. He then became a naval chaplain (1943–47), served with the commandos, and won the distinguished service cross for bravery. Returning to the parish ministry, he was rector of St. Ebbe's, Oxford (1947–52); vicar of Islington (1952–61); principal of Oak Hill College, London (1961–71); and bishop of Norwich (1971–85). A leading supporter of evangelical causes, including Billy Graham crusades, he was the author of *Like a Mighty Army* (1956), *Comfort in Sorrow* (1957), *Your Suffering* (1959), *Christian

*Stability* (1966), *To Everyman's Door* (1968), *Into the Way of Peace* (1982), and *This Is Our Faith* (1985).

J. D. DOUGLAS

### Woolley, Paul (1902–1985).

American church historian. Graduate of Princeton University in arts and theology, he was one of the original faculty members of Westminster Theological Seminary in 1929, where he served as its registrar and church history teacher; he continued there until retirement. He was active in the formation of the Orthodox Presbyterian Church in 1936, managing editor of the *Westminster Theological Journal*, and one of the earliest contributors to *Christianity Today* magazine. A meticulous and single-minded lecturer, administrator, and counselor to generations of students at Westminster, he did not take time from these tasks to publish the lectures that reflected his comprehensive grasp of church history. In 1982 he was honored by fellow historians with the festschrift, *John Calvin: His Influence in the Western World*, ed. W. S. Reid.

J. D. DOUGLAS

### World Alliance of Reformed Churches (WARC).

Founded in 1875, the oldest international organization of Protestants with a confessional basis. In full title it is the "Alliance of the Reformed Churches Throughout the World Holding the Presbyterian System." The alliance is federative and advisory, existing to promote the common interests of its members in the context of the ecumenical movement. "In forming this Alliance," said the preamble to the original constitution, "the Presbyterian Churches do not mean to change their fraternal relations with other Churches, but will be ready, as heretofore, to join with them in Christian fellowship, and in advancing the cause of the Redeemer, on the general principle maintained and taught in the Reformed Confessions that the Church of God on earth, though composed of many members, is one body in the communion of the Holy Ghost, of which body Christ is the Supreme Head, and the Scriptures alone are the infallible law." What had been called the World Presbyterian Alliance in 1970 merged with the International Congregational Council to form the "World Alliance of Reformed Churches (Presbyterian and Congregational)." In 1987 the total membership was 164, of which 49 were in Asia, 39 in Africa, 37 in Europe, 21 in Latin and Central America, 11 in North America, and 7 in Australasia. Altogether WARC had representation in 82 countries. Its general council met at regular intervals.

### World Council of Churches (WCC).

International organization of world ecumenical outreach and interfaith cooperation. Officially formed in 1948, WCC has roots that reach back to the ecumenical movement of the early 1900s and to the intense conviction among many Christians of that time that divisions among churches had hampered the witness of the Christian faith throughout its history. WCC is the organized expression of three streams of ecumenical life. Two of these—the Faith and Order movement born at the Edinburgh World Missions Conference (1910) and the Life and Work Committee formed by the World Alliance for Promoting International Friendship in 1919—merged at the constituting assembly of WCC at Amsterdam (1948). The third stream, the missionary movement, organized in the International Missionary Council (IMC), was integrated into WCC at the assembly in New Delhi (1961). A provisional committee of the World Council of Churches in Process of Formation, meeting at Utrecht in 1938, laid the first solid foundation on which the permanent structure of the council was built over the next two decades.

***Basis and Authority.*** The basis of WCC, as expanded at New Delhi, is that WCC "is a fellowship of churches which confess the Lord Jesus Christ as God and Saviour according to the Scriptures and therefore seek to fulfill together their common calling to the glory of the one God, Father, Son and Holy Spirit." Membership is open to any church which can accept this basis, which is not a full confession of faith but rather a definition to clarify the limits of its membership. The council does not judge the sincerity with which member churches accept the basis. Some conservative churches have declined to join because the basis is not biblical enough and is too inclusive; some liberal churches will not accept so restrictive a trinitarian formula. WCC nevertheless represents most major Reformation and Orthodox churches—310 in total—representing 400 million. It includes, besides the historic churches founded in past centuries, several late 20th-century Pentecostal bodies and independent churches in Africa and Asia. Most successful church union negotiations have united member denominations. The seriousness with which such a vast number of churches have taken their membership in the world body has varied.

***Organization.*** The principal authority of WCC is that of assemblies composed of official representatives appointed by member churches. Governance between assembly meetings is maintained by an elected central committee with a maximum of 145 members. It normally meets annually and may act for the assembly. The central committee elects an executive committee of 16 members which normally meets twice a year. WCC may have a maximum of seven presidents who comprise the presidium. The moderator and vice-moderators of the central committee, together with the general secretary, are the recognized officers of WCC. W. A. Visser 't Hooft was the first general secretary, from 1948 to 1966. He was succeeded by Eugene C. Blake (1967–71), Philip A. Potter (1972–84), and Emilio Castro (from 1985).

From 1954 WCC was organized in three divisions: studies, ecumenical action, and interchurch aid, refugee and world service. A fourth division, world mission and evangelism, was added in 1961. A new three-unit structure was introduced in 1971 as an organization of priorities and projects. Program unit 1, *Faith and Witness,* comprises faith and order, world missions and evangelism, church and society, and "Dialogue with People of Living Faiths." Program unit 2, *Justice and Service,* comprises work regarding development, racism, interchurch aid, refugee services, international affairs, and medicine. Program unit 3, *Education and Renewal,* comprises education, women, renewal and congregational life, youth, biblical studies, and theological education. The work of each of the three program units is supervised, reviewed, and coordinated by a unit committee.

The staff of the general secretary coordinates the work of the three program units, monitors relations with churches and other ecumenical organizations, and interprets the work of the council. The general secretary heads the staff with the help of three deputies, each of whom moderates one of the program units. Related to the general secretariat is the communication department which informs the churches and the wider public about the work of WCC. English, French, German, and Spanish are the four operational languages of the council; at larger conferences Russian is added.

A substantial amount of money is channeled through WCC for ecumenically supported programs and relief and development projects. In 1983, the total was more than $44 million. The expenses for WCC's own programs and operations in that year were about $13 million. A resource sharing office seeks to find more meaningful ways for churches, both rich and poor, to share money and human and spiritual resources. The council's extensive archives and collection of books and papers relating to the ecumenical movement are available in the WCC library.

***Ecumenical Institute.*** Located at the Château de Bossey, Céligny, near Geneva, the Ecumenical Institute was founded in 1946 to train ecumenical leaders and to promote ecumenical theology within intercultural and interconfessional contexts. Seminars and conferences are organized, and the graduate school of ecumenical studies is open to pastors and laypeople of different confessions from all over the world.

***Assemblies.*** An assembly takes place every seven or eight years. Besides setting policy and allowing occasion for worldwide interchurch celebration, each assembly reflects some aspect of Christianity in contemporary history.

At *Amsterdam 1948*, 146 churches, mainly from Europe and North America, embarked on a new epoch in church history. The motto was: "We intend to stay together." There was a shared enthusiasm and a profound conviction that the Protestant churches, with a few exceptions, were marching on the road to visible and organic unity within the next few decades.

*Evanston 1954* reflected current tensions of the cold war. It also promoted the role of laypeople in the churches. Delegates resolved to dedicate themselves to God anew, "that He may enable us to grow together."

*New Delhi 1961* was marked by two major events. The 20th-century missionary movement became fully integrated into the council. After long deliberations the Orthodox churches in the socialist countries joined WCC. With this added mission dimension and representation, WCC embarked on its effort to link the concerns of unity, mission, and service as essential aspects of the church.

*Uppsala 1968* faced the growing gap between rich and poor nations, the disastrous effects of white racism, the ambiguity of new scientific discoveries, the tensions between generations, and the student revolts. Youth participants in great numbers were vocal and critical of what went on.

*Nairobi 1975* showed that the ecumenical movement had reached a higher level of maturity. There was a heated discussion on the violation of human rights in the Soviet Union.

*Vancouver 1983* was the most representative gathering ever held in the history of the ecumenical movement. The large worship tent became a symbol of the pilgrim church in the world and drew large crowds. The assembly tried to deal realistically with sharp divisions and conflicts in the world without allowing them to destroy the ecumenical fellowship.

**Bibliography.** H. E. Fey, ed., *The Ecumenical Advance: A History of the Ecumenical Movement*, vol. 2 (1970); W. A. Visser 't Hooft, *Memoirs* (1973); E. Lange, *And Yet It Moves: Dream and Reality of the Ecumenical Movement* (1979); P. A. Potter, *Life in All Its Fulness* (1981); A. J. van der Bent, *What in the World Is the World Council of Churches?* (1983); A. J. van der Bent, *Handbook of Member Churches, World Council of Churches* (1985). See also *Official Reports* of WCC assemblies and the periodicals *International Review of Mission* (from 1912), *Ecumenical Review* (from 1948), and *One World* (from 1974).

A. J. VAN DER BENT

## World Home Bible League (WHBL). Non-
denominational Scripture placement agency. Founded originally in 1938 as American Home Bible League by a Reformed Church in America layman, William Chapman, the organization assisted congregations and groups of American churches in community Scripture-placement projects. That focus broadened, and WHBL became involved with national churches abroad in placing Bibles, New Testaments, and Scripture portions in the languages of the country. Its Latin

American programs, for instance, included nationwide initiatives designed and authorized by national and regional government to place contemporary language New Testaments in the hands of all public school students and in military installations and prisons. Study aids and correspondence courses were available. *Brazil/New Life '90* project, for example, aimed to provide Scriptures for 25 million students by 1990. Similar programs were undertaken in Bolivia, Ecuador, Peru, and El Salvador. Other extensive endeavors are underway in Southeast Asia, Africa, the Middle East, and elsewhere. In the late 1980s WHBL merged with Bibles for India, a similar agency.

LESLIE K. TARR

**World Methodist Council.** *See* METHODIST COUNCIL, WORLD.

**World Presbyterian Alliance.** *See* WORLD ALLIANCE OF REFORMED CHURCHES.

**World Student Christian Federation.** *See* STUDENT ORGANIZATIONS, RELIGIOUS (WORLDWIDE).

**World Vision International.** One of the largest Christian humanitarian organizations. Founded in 1950 as an American agency by Bob Pierce to help Korean War orphans, by the late 1980s World Vision had international headquarters near Los Angeles, Calif., and regional centers in Canada, Great Britain, Finland, the Netherlands, Australia, Switzerland, West Germany, Africa, Hong Kong, Singapore, New Zealand, and Australia.

The organization followed six objectives: (1) Although initially an orphan sponsorship program, the organization changed its strategy to minister to nearly 400,000 children and their families (late 1980s) through developing community and family resources in 80 nations. (2) Emergency aid was provided to victims of natural disaster, famine, and war in more than 100 disaster projects. (3) More than 700 rural community development projects for health, nutrition, water, agriculture, and literacy aimed at giving self-reliance and hope. (4) World Vision's Missions Advanced Research and Communications Center (MARC) gathered and interpreted current information to aid mission agencies and national churches plan effective evangelism strategies. (5) Pastor and community leader training projects were sponsored to equip national churches and communities with program management skills. (6) Through its support and field offices one goal was to challenge people to see beyond their own needs to ministry opportunities around them.

In the late 1980s World Vision was carrying out these objectives in more than 3400 projects with an annual budget of well over $100 million (U.S.).

Most of its staff of about 3000 were nationals working in their own countries. Not a missionary sending agency, it worked primarily through local churches and partner agencies.

**Worship, Public.** Dialog between a group of believers and God, in which the group (congregation) expresses adoration, reverence, and praise toward God. The 20th century has observed a renewal in corporate worship after a period of decline. The theology of worship has explored new forms that speak to national and cultural contexts while retaining the function of personal and communal praise.

Every act of communication with God is a worship experience, but Judeo-Christian worship has historically stressed active, communal themes. From the birth of national Israel in the wilderness, individual sacrifice was replaced by a regulated cultic system. God was transcendent and utterly holy, and recognition of the distance between God and sinful worshipers was appreciated. God also was immanent, however, inviting individual and communal contact. Both the tabernacle and temple symbolized his beckoning to approach in reverent devotion. The sacrificial system involved outward acts, but the OT prophets continually called for inward, personal reality.

Outward acts and inward devotion melded in liturgy. For example, dedicated craftsmen created objects to be used in praise and obeisance. Inspired creativity was expressed in a liturgy of the Word—the psalms. A liturgy of active worship included Sabbath-keeping, festivals, and sacrifices, including the regulated tithe. The "service" of community study, preaching, prayer, and song characterized the synagogue.

The Christian church adopted and adapted various aspects of Jewish worship. Sacraments replaced sacrifices as signs and seals of God's immanent presence in grace. The Lord's Day became the Sabbath festival. Liturgy extended beyond the psalms to new songs extolling Christ and the Holy Spirit. Creeds were recited in unison; a ministry of the Word unveiled OT Scripture, apostolic writings, and gospel text. The prophetic message became central. Prayer remained integral, for the God worshiped was eminently approachable in Christ.

The Reformation reaffirmed NT worship principles and their inherent concept of God, condemning both the focus on a barely-approachable, all-transcendent God in the Mass, and the priesthood. The Reformed principle for public worship was that it must be carefully aligned with God's Word. Only practices directly sanctioned in the Bible were allowed. Two styles of public worship quickly developed, however. A formal, liturgical model centered in the Word and objective praise to God. The other, disdaining the coldness of objective worship, introduced a pietistic, subjective variety. Its regulative principle was that whatever Scripture did not forbid might be practiced. Subjective public worship enraptured worshipers in the immanent Jesus. More flexible and emotional, it stressed personal response and decision.

The great 19th-century revivals, the development of gospel music, and the success of Arminian and pentecostal theologies instituted subjective worship as a dominant force among 20th-century conservative, evangelical Christians. Inward renewal in public worship became outward repentance and ecstasy. This worship of God as immanent was far from post-Kantian liberal theology, which rejected revelation and made God utterly transcendent. As modern theologians found the Bible and God meaningless, church members found public and private worship irrelevant. Liturgical Protestants who retained the Reformed principle of worship were regarded by all other groups as out of touch with reality, especially in music, since some groups refused to use instruments or sang only psalms. Increasingly, Roman Catholics faced a similar dilemma.

As a result, the 20th century became a watershed for myriad theologies of worship, mirroring the confusion of theology in general. Where influenced by neo-orthodox thought, Western churches were pulled from the lethargic indifference of liberal worship to an interpersonal, subjective view that God encountered worshipers in celebration. In Barthian theological understanding this was more a celebration than a vertical interaction. Subjectively God might be immanent, but objectively he is totally separate. After reaching an apex in the USA in the 1950s, attendance in the mainline churches waned, signaling that the theme of festive interaction was inadequate. Christians attempting to hold liberal theologies continued to decline in most of Europe and North America until worship centers were virtually empty.

The growth of pentecostalism through the 20th century as a world movement assured that personal, subjective worship experience thrived. Many Reformed, conservative churches rethought and reformulated long-cherished liturgical practices. Their openness stemmed partly from a generation that held looser conceptions of the purpose of worship and partly from continual interaction with evangelicals from other traditions.

The most radical changes in worship were in Roman Catholicism after Vatican Council II. Theology did not change so much as there was a new hunger among pastors and laity for personal involvement in every part of worship. Homilies gained importance, the vernacular was used, Bible reading and study were encouraged, the liturgy of the Mass was brought closer to the people, and more interaction during worship brought worshipers closer to one another.

In general the 20th century was a time of learning to cope with changes that had already begun in ecclesiastical worship. Psychology added the understanding that worship is a "drama" and a "dialog." Christians participated in an ancient practice of dramatizing devotion. The dialog was among all worshipers of all religions. Worship was considered perfectly proper among Christians, Jews, Muslims, and even Hindus in some interfaith gatherings.

In more orthodox circles, those persons who planned worship services came to appreciate the psychological and spiritual drama involved in music, liturgy, processionals and recessionals, credal confessions, sacramental celebrations, and even in the offering. In such acts Christians communally share and portray their devotion to God and one another, and present a witness before the world. The idea that drama is a dimension of worship caused new understandings about how banners, paintings, and other decorations influence what takes place in the sanctuary. Music may be artistically professional, dramatic, and emotive, and yet still be suitable for praise.

As dialog, worship plans were more carefully constructed so that Christians might realize their direct communion with God. God's greeting, followed by choral and congregational anthems of praise, the reading of Scripture, a time of public confession of sin, credal recitations, a congregational prayer, offering, and the public proclamation of a message based in Scripture were all popular elements of modern worship that could be arranged so that the people spoke to themselves, to one another, and to God, and God spoke back, through Scripture, sacrament, and sermon.

The process of building modern Christian theologies of worship was far from complete as the century neared its end, but the concept of public worship in all the hues of modern Christian theology was a dynamic barometer of the general impact that theology was making on the believer. At the same time, the essence of worship remained God's revelation of himself to his children and their response of faith.

*Bibliography*. R. G. Turnbull, ed., *Baker's Dictionary of Practical Theology* (1967); R. G. Rayburn, *O Come, Let Us Worship: Corporate Worship in the Evangelical Church* (1980); L. Ryken, ed., *The Christian Imagination: Essays on Literature and the Arts* (1981).

## Worship in Non-Christian Religions. *Introduction.*

Appreciation for and study of world religions began in the late 1800s, but it still was in relative infancy in 1955 when Earl W. Count wrote the following article. When the mission movement began in the early 1800s the scriptures and practices of other faiths were regarded as curiosities in travel accounts. Beliefs and worship among those regarded as "the pitiable heathen" were denigrated as superstition.

That changed radically after Max Müller began introducing to the West a series of 50 translated world scriptures, *Sacred Books of the East* (1875), and in 1890 Sir J. G. Frazer stunned the Christian community with his theories in *The Golden Bough*. Frazer borrowed methods and concepts from Darwinian anthropologists for his model of progressive or evolutionary religious concepts. He saw humanity in the process of moving from animism through stages of polytheism toward mature monotheism. In Frazer and his colleagues the field of religious anthropology was born, and Christian ideas about their system being qualitatively unique and unchallengeable were undercut. Throughout the first half of the 20th century mission conferences and such leaders as Pearl Buck and William Hocking demanded that missions accept other forms of response to God. The massive transcultural migrations following World War II and development of world media inherently took some of the mystery out of non-Christian beliefs and showed their often sublime conceptions of the divine.

*The Phenomenon of Religion.* Several theories in modern times have been given as to what motivates religious expression. Immanuel Kant said that humans are religious because they are reasoning beings. The essence of religion is rooted in an awareness of moral responsibility, which must have an origin beyond the human experience. Sigmund Freud countered that religion is pathological, a projection of a father-image which the individual uses to avoid developing a mature, self-expressive ego. The Christian response, hinted at by Paul in Acts 17 and first developed by Augustine, is that religion is the human response to divine revelation. That response (worship) includes a variety of acts and attitudes. It involves some form of faith, surrender, and prayer. It implies a feeling of guilt and a need for salvation. Hendrik Kraemer divided all religious expression into two groups, conceding that the separation lines between those groups can be hazy. The first, "prophetic religions of revelation," includes Judaism, Christianity, and Islam. The second, "naturalist religions of transempirical realization," includes all forms of pantheism, Buddhism, and other mystical religions. Kraemer goes on to say that in the final analysis there is no "natural" religion, but there does seem to be a universal religious consciousness.

*Worship and Worldview.* For worship, as for religion, there can be no universal touchstone by which its presence in culture can be declared. It is always complex, and testifies to long development. Whatever its form it is a kinetic oractive expression of a culture's worldview. This makes its exploration difficult: people worship, and philosophers among them endeavor to rationalize it. But the philosophers also testify in terms of their own experience; ethnologists know that under the modal type of worship lies great variety of types of worship within the culture, even when people perform the external forms in common. A native may furnish a sincere explanation of the acts, but the investigator will have gained no more than an artificial generalization of the religious practices of a people. Left out will be intangibles that cannot be weighed objectively.

With this in mind some generalizations may still be helpful: (1) All worship attempts to secure a rapport between worshiper and superhuman powers that are in some degree personalized. (2) It always harnesses the emotions and esthetic perception. The former is a psychological and physiological matter, the latter a cultural factor. (3) Worship may be an individual, solitary performance, or it may be corporate. In any case, it involves ritual—be it as elaborate as a Polynesian or a Pueblo Indian public ceremony, or as reduced as the Quaker meeting.

*The Character of the Worshiped.* Attitude and expectations of the worshiper govern the deity or entity worshiped. The worshiped may be dead ancestors, natural phenomena associated with natural objects, or some defined or remote supreme being. There is no perfect correlation between the level of material achievement in a culture and their conceptual sophistication of deity. A supreme being is encountered, among the Algonquian Indians, East Africans, apparently some Australians, and others; yet the figure of this being may remain quite vague and is not actively worshiped. From the standpoint of worship, the sorts of gods are less important than what they are expected to do, how personal they seem, and how people adjust to them.

Volga Finns annually welcome their ancestors back to the village, entertain them at a sacrificial feast, and bespeak their continued benevolence; among the Cheremiss, a special hut is dedicated to the worship. The ancestors have become gods, yet they remain members of the family and so maintain interest in its welfare. Clearly, a natural power or a supreme being is not a member of the family or clan, yet his continued benevolence may be petitioned. Zuni Pueblo worship ancestors as part of a far more complex pattern which includes other spirits as well; any demarcation, moreover, between what some would call magic on the one hand and religion on the other is blurred. Nature is harmonious; men and gods fit; they possess roles. For that balance to continue, certain functions, including ceremonial, must be performed. If the ritual is maintained with perfect exactitude, the gods must do their share, for that is the nature of things. Precisely how and why this rite of deference and petition effects action from the gods is not determined. The Pueblo worldview does not pit humanity against a hostile, reluctant, or indifferent nature and arbitrary or whimsical supernaturals; hence the approach to the gods is not one of winning them over to "our" side or seeking reconciliation with them. And unlike the Volga Finns, where each family worships its own ancestors, the Zuni worship the ancestors of the people as a whole.

Corporate worship is hardly separable from drama. It may enlist recitation, music, dance, or material emblems, and is a way to interpret the worldview.

*The Emotional Side of Worship.* Varying degrees of fear and whatever else may enter into deference. The fear may actually mount to terror; it may remain as diffuse as anxiety. On the other hand, ancestors or other deities may be bargained with and chided if they fail to supply the benefits expected (Bantu Thonga and other African). Perhaps this behavior passes beyond the frame of worship; for it lacks deference and petition on the part of one who recognizes his inferiority. Yet what remains in common with deferential petition is a belief in the personality of the deity, his ability to do the superhuman, and his amenability to petition or persuasion.

That emotions must be disciplined in worship is widely recognized, but unbridled release of emotions also characterizes some forms of worship. For days prior to a Pueblo ceremonial, the priest must refrain from anger and all evil thoughts; else the elaborate ritual will "misfire." It is not the absence of emotion but the presence of the right kind and absence of the wrong kind, which is demanded.

Commonly, Christian worship includes petition for forgiveness of a transgression of divine will, with remission of a penalty; gratitude for past favor, and petition for continued favor. By contrast, the Hindu would pray for strength to stand up under the unremissible consequences of his transgression. The Buddhist would seek by meditation—what he considers to be the annihilation of emotion—to merge back into an ineffable infinity which is not personal and is not "deity." The Pueblo's thanks to the gods is a form of courtesy that reveals far less of a gap between the stations of man and god than in Christianity; it seeks no mystical union and does not develop adoration. The Navajo has no sense of the guilt or moral debit. Instead, religious exercise seeks to return the individual to the path of life from which somehow he has become deflected. All these marshal the same human urges and seek spiritual adjustment, hence they must be forms of worship; yet their patterns all differ as their conceptualizations of existence differ.

*Individual and Corporate Worship.* Within any culture all religious expression obviously must derive from the same worldview and the attitude of the society as to what an individual is. Among the Pueblos, individual self-assertion is less prized than is merging as a societal team. Corporate worship is the highest endeavor of which the entire society is capable. By contrast, among the Plains tribes self-assertion, the performance of highly individualistic and conspicuous deeds is the social ideal. The youth on the threshold of manhood enters upon a solitary quest for power that involves self-mortification and a plea to the spirits that some one of them will adopt him as a protégé. He prays, offers tobacco, fasts, weeps, and keeps vigil, until a spirit visits him in his trance and becomes his tutelary. The relationship is supposed to last for life. Plains tribal ceremonies include worship; but not as a focality of society.

The trance seeking of the Plains tribes suggests a form of mysticism. Yet the diametrically different worldview does not relate directly with the Christian or Hindu forms. Christianity, Judaism, and Islam have a Mesopotamian spiritual ancestry. In these great religions, humans stand out from the rest of creation, and above both them and creation is a deity with whom the individual seeks union through reconciliation. In the natural world, humanity is not at home. People fight it, and attempt to subdue it to their will (under divine sanction). Viewed anthropologically, this is a very exceptional attitude which leads to a distinct worship. The native American, while recognizing a human distinction, downplays its uniqueness among countless creatures; there may be bodily metamorphoses between animals and people which make human distinctiveness even less distinct. Acts of worship are directed toward maintaining harmony with the totality of nature. When some cultures kill an animal for food, they explain to the animal spirit represented by his victim the necessity for what has been done. Killing an animal is an unfortunate necessity; it must not jeopardize the human's place in a nature where the material and the spiritual do not have separate existences.

EARL W. COUNT

***Since 1955.*** By 1955, as noted above, the pitfalls of religious and cultural anthropology were becoming better understood, and the progressive theories of evolutionary anthropology were reconsidered as presuppositions. As techniques for research in various cultures were refined and more work was done by native scholars, archeology also pushed back the horizon of knowledge for some world religions. It was clear that much remained to be done.

Within the Christian church there were movements in two opposing directions in reaction to world religions and worship. In ecumenistic circles great strides were taken toward dialogs to understand and break down barriers separating world faiths. In Roman Catholic thought this move was signaled by Vatican Council II, especially its study document *Lumen gentium*, which expressed great appreciation for non-Christian faiths, even religions far removed from Christianity. God's light of revelation, the document related, is available in some degree to all persons. Men and women who follow such light as they have may find acceptance with God. More radical moves in this direction came within the World Council of Churches, particularly in its program of "Dialogue Between Men of Living Faiths." At Ajaltoun, Lebanon, in 1970, for example, one consultation assembled Christians, Buddhists, Hindus, and Muslims for conversation, joint prayer, and exploration of joint worship. Through its Theological Education Fund, WCC studied how to "contextualize" Christianity to be acceptable to divergent religions.

The evangelical community was exploring its own forms of contextualization. The focus of mission strategies was to carefully consider other religions and societies, not so Christianity could be syncretistically meshed with them, but in order that the Western baggage within Christian culture could be dropped and the essential faith applied in understandable forms. J. H. Bavinck in his system of "elenctics" applied this task with militant evangelistic force. He said Christians must understand other religions as perfectly as possible, so that their differences might be seen and proclaimed. The non-Christian, through the Holy Spirit, would see the failure of the former worldview and worship and be brought to repent of its "shame."

***Bibliography.*** E. B. Tylor, *Primitive Culture* (1871); J. G. Frazer, *The Golden Bough* (1890); J. Spieth, *Die Religion der Eweer* (1912); R. H. Lowie, *Anthropology Papers* 25 (1922); R. F. Benedict, *Memoir* 29 (1923); W. Schmidt, *Der Ursprung der Gottesidee* (1926–47); U. Holmberg, *Mythology of All Races* 4 (1927); R. L. Bunzel, *Annual Report* (1929/30); H. Kraemer, *The Christian Message in a Non-Christian World* (1938); R. H. Lowie, *Primitive Religion* (1948); J. H. Bavinck, *An Introduction to the Science of Missions* (ET, 1960); *The Church Between Temple and Mosque: A Study of the Relationship Between the Christian Faith and Other Religions* (repr. ed., 1981); S. Neill, *Christian Faith and Other Faiths* (1984); J. Finegan, *Myth and Mystery* (1989); D. J. Hesselgrave and E. Rommen, *Contextualization* (1989).

**Wrede, William** (1859–1906). Lutheran higher critical scholar. Born in Bücken, Hanover, he studied at Leipzig and Göttingen (1877–81). He was privatdocent, Göttingen (1891–93); professor extraordinary, Breslau (1893–95); and professor of NT, Breslau (1895–1906). Protagonist of a consistently historical method in the study of the NT, he contended that biblical theology should be superseded by the history of primitive Christian religion and thought, that the Gospels represent the theology of the primitive church rather than the history of Jesus, and that Paul was the real founder of Christianity. He wrote *Über Aufgabe und Methode der sogennante neutestamentlichen Theologie* (1897), *Das Messiasgeheimnis in den Evangelien* (1901), *TU*, 24 (1903), *Paulus* (2d ed.,

Wright, George Ernest

1907), and *Das literarische Rätsel des Hebräer-briefes* (1906).

OTTO A. PIPER

**Wright, George Ernest** (1909–1974). OT scholar, archeologist, author, and educator. Born in Zanesville, Ohio, he was educated at Wooster College, McCormick Theological Seminary, and Johns Hopkins University (Ph.D., 1937). He was ordained in the Presbyterian Church in the USA (1934). After a fellowship at McCormick Theological Seminary (1934–36), he was field secretary for the American Schools of Oriental Research (1938), assistant and associate professor at McCormick (1939–45), professor of OT history and theology (1945–58), and Parkman professor of divinity at Harvard (1958–74). In addition, he served as the archeological director of expeditions in Palestine, Gezer, and Cyprus (1956–74). A curator, author, and editor of numerous books and articles, his most significant works include *God Who Acts: Biblical Theology as Recital* (1958), and *The OT and Theology* (1969). With F. V. Filson he compiled *The Westminster Historical Atlas to the Bible* (rev. ed., 1956).

JACK MITCHELL

**Wühr, Wilhelm** (1905–1950). Roman Catholic. Born in Nuremberg, Bavaria, he studied at the University of Munich. He collaborated with others in completing Ludwig F. Pastor's *The History of the Popes* (1891–1961) to 1932. Nazi persecution kept him from finishing his degree at the University of Wurzburg where the necessary thesis had been accepted in 1935. He taught at Bayreuth (1937–40), but was suspended from office by Nazi persecution against the leaders of the Catholic youth movement (1940–45). After military service he served as professor of history at the Hochschule, Freising, near Munich (1947–50). He was a pioneer of Catholic youth activity in German settlements in Rumania (1930–38). He organized meetings of European Christian historians (1946–50). The publication of some of his works was forbidden, and one work was partly destroyed by bombs. He wrote *Studien zu Gregor VI.: Kirchenreform und Weltpolitik* (1930), *Die Emigranten der Franzoes. Revolution in baier.u. frank. Kreis* (1938), and *Das abendländische Bildungswesen im Mittelalter* (1950).

**Wundt, Wilhelm** (1832–1920). German philosopher. Born in Neckerau, he studied at the universities of Tübingen, Heidelberg, and Berlin; became privatdocent at Heidelberg in physiology (1857) and extraordinary professor (1864); was elected to the legislative chamber of Baden (1866); became extraordinary professor at Zurich (1874), and professor of philosophy at Leipzig (1875) where he was rector (1889/90). In psychol-

ogy his contributions were notable. His latter years were spent teaching philosophy at Leipzig, where he began the institute for experimental psychology. He also worked in physiological psychology and social psychology, testing the interrelations of art, language, religion, and morality. Works relating his work to religion and ethical philosophy include *Über die Aufgabe der Philosophie in der Gegenwart* (1874), *Der Spiritismus. Eine sogenannte wissenschaftliche Frage* (1879), *Logik* (2 vols., 1880–83), *Ethics* (3 vols., ET, 1897–1901), *Outlines of Psychology* (ET, 1902), *Völkerpsychologie* (10 vols., 1900–1920), *System der Philosophie* (2 vols., 1919), and *The Elements of Folkpsychology* (ET, 1916).

**Bibliography.** K. Thieme, *Zu Wundts Religionspsychologie* (1910); W. Nef, *Die Philosophie Wilhelm Wundts* (1923); P. S. Hess, *Das religiöse Bedürfnis eine kritische Studie anhand der Religionstheorie Wilhelm Wundts* (1935).

RAYMOND W. ALBRIGHT

**Wurm, Theophil** (1868–1953). Lutheran bishop. Born in Basel, Switzerland, he studied at theological seminaries in Maulbronn and Blaubeuren and at the universities of Tübingen and Berlin. He served churches in Stuttgart (1891–1913), Ravensburg (1913–20), and Reutlingen (1920–27); was prelate at Heilbronn (1927–29); and was church president (1929–53). He was a leader of the Confessional Church. Because of his opposition to the "German Christians" and to the national leadership in 1934 he was deposed by an illegally called synod and interned in his home by the police. After several weeks he was restored to office by Adolf Hitler. In 1945 he was elected the first president of the council of the Evangelical Church in Germany at its session in Treysa. He wrote *Jubiläumsschrift für die Evangelische Gesellschaft* (1905), *Ratgeber für Armenfreunde* (1909), *Evangelischer Glaube* (1930), *Lebensrätsel und Gottesglaube* (1932), *Die Botschaft der Kirche* (1935), and *Fünfzig Jahre im Dienst der Kirche* (1950).

RAYMOND W. ALBRIGHT

**Wysznski, Stefan** (1901–1981). Roman Catholic cardinal. Born in Zuzela, Poland, he was educated at the seminary in Wloclawek, ordained in 1924, and worked in an industrial parish in Wloclawek. In 1929 he earned a doctorate in sociology and church law at the Catholic University of Lublin, spent a year in Rome, and returned to become professor of sociology and canon law at the Higher Seminary, Wloclawek. During World War II he supported resistance against the German occupation. In 1946 he was made bishop of Lublin and rector of the city's Catholic University. In 1949 he became archbishop of Gniezno and Warsaw, and primate of Poland; in 1952 he was made cardinal. In 1953, after he had protested against state interference in church affairs, he was arrested and confined to monasteries for three years. After his release he negotiated a compromise with a less rigid administration, but church-state relations remained uneasy, especially when the government refused in 1966 to allow him to go on a visit to Rome, and would not permit foreign bishops to enter Poland for special celebrations at Czestochowa, a controversy that forced Paul VI to cancel a proposed visit to Poland. A staunch supporter of the working class and of human rights, Wysznski opposed the replacement of Latin in the Mass, and was conservative also in such matters as abortion, birth control, and clerical celibacy.

J. D. Douglas

# Yy

**Yahuda, Abraham Shalom Ezekiel** (1877–1951). Jewish Pentateuch scholar. A descendant of a Shephardic family that traced its origin to the scholars of Babylon, he was born in Jerusalem and educated at the universities of Heidelberg and Strasbourg. He taught biblical studies and Semitic languages at Berlin (1905–14); Hebrew language and literature at Madrid (1915–22); lectured at Oxford, Cambridge, Jerusalem, Cairo, and Yale; and at his death was research professor at the New School for Social Research in New York. In addition to books in Arabic and Hebrew, he published *The Language of the Pentateuch in Its Relation to Egyptian* (1933), and *Accuracy of the Bible* (1935).

Raymond W. Albright

**Yahweh.** A recreation of the Tetragrammaton Hebrew letters *YHWH*, a holy name for God which was never pronounced aloud in the reading of *Torah* from the late Second Temple period. Its pronunciation was lost by medieval Judaism. Through modern linguistics the pronunciation *Yahweh* was no longer based primarily on traditions preserved in late patristic sources. Both the vocalization *yahwê* and *yahû* (a shortened form used chiefly in personal names) were confirmed by a variety of ancient Near Eastern inscriptional materials from the 1st and 2d millennia B.C. These new sources of evidence included (1) transliterations of Hebrew personal names in Assyrian and Babylonian cuneiform documents from the 9th to the 5th centuries B.C.; (2) alphabetic inscriptions in Hebrew, Canaanite, and related tongues; and (3) transcriptions of West Semitic names and other linguistic materials from the 2d millennium B.C.

It became clear that no satisfactory attempt to recover the etymology and original meaning of "Yahweh" could ignore the laws governing the grammatical, especially the phonetic, evolution of Northwest Semitic. Attempts to derive the name from an original *ya, yah, yaw,* or *yahû* (popular among scholars after the discovery of the independent form *YHW* in the Egyptian papyri of the 5th-century B.C. from the Elephantine archives) were not helpful.

The derivation which now appears to fit best into the typical patterns of formation of divine names in the ancient Near East, and at the same time conform to the linguistic laws of old (prebiblical) Hebrew, is that first suggested by Jean Le Clerc early in the 18th century and developed in modern form by Paul Haupt and W. F. Albright. This view holds that *yahwê* was originally a finite *hiphil* verb derived from a causative stem of the Northwest Semitic root *hwy*, "to come into being" or "to exist." The divine name would thus go back to a verbal form meaning "he causes to come into existence," or in effect, "he creates." This etymology has had striking confirmation in the appearance of the form in question (not the divine name) in Amorite personal names from the early 2d millennium, and in a place-name in southeastern Palestine mentioned in an Egyptian document of the 13th century B.C. The causative stem *yahwê*, meaning "he creates," was current in the linguistic milieu of early Hebrew.

The name Yahweh appears to have been originally the first or key word of an ancient liturgical formula which proclaimed the creative activity of the deity. Such abbreviation of sentence names has abundant parallels among the names and appellations of ancient Semitic gods. It is likely that the obscure sentence of Exod. 3:14, and the expression *Yahweh Ṣĕbā'ôt* (originally, "he creates the [heavenly] armies") reflect formulae at least of the type from which the name *Yahweh* was derived.

Among etymologies proposed, S. Mowinckel and J. Montgomery contend that the name is a compound, *yahū* or *yahūwa*, "O He!" R. A. Bowman suggests that *Yahweh* means "Speaker" on the basis of Canaanite *hwt*, "a command."

No non-Israelite divine name "Yahweh" was yet identified for certain in ancient Near Eastern sources. A number of enigmatic readings (e.g., Ugaritic *yw*) have been equated with the Israelite divine name. Pre-Israelite origins remained shrouded in mystery.

The English transliteration *Jehovah* was dropped by most biblical translators of the 20th century. Masoretic scribes in medieval copies had developed the practice of pointing the vowels *yehōwāh* instead of *yahōwāh* to avoid breaking the taboo of using the holy name for God. This practice was misunderstood by English Bible translators.

**Bibliography**. *To 1950*. W. F. Albright, *From the Stone Age to Christianity* (2d ed., 1946); B. D. Eerdmans, G. J. Thierry, and B. Alfrink, *Oudtestamentische Studien* 5 (1948): 1–62; J. Obermann, *JBL* 68 (1949): 301–23; B. Alfrink, *Theologische Zeitschrift* 5 (1949).

*Since 1950*. R. L. Harris, G. L. Archer, Jr., and B. K. Waltke, eds., *Theological Wordbook of the OT*, vol. 2 (1980); W. A. Elwell, ed., *Evangelical Dictionary of Theology* (1984); G. J. Botterweck and H. Ringgren, *Theological Dictionary of the OT*, vol. 5 (1988).

FRANK MOORE CROSS, JR.

**Yang, Wen-Hui** (1837–1911). Buddhist layman chiefly responsible for revival of Buddhist literature in China. In 1880 the Japanese scholar Bunyiu Nanjio gave him Buddhist texts lost in China, especially the *Ch'eng Wei-shih Lun Shu-chi*, a mountain peak of Buddhist rationalism but too abstract for the Chinese mind. These Yang published in China (1901). He initiated large-scale Buddhist publication; established circulation centers in Peking, Tientsin, Shanghai, and Yangchow; and distributed about one million tracts. He was the teacher of Ou-yang Ching-wu.

EARL H. CRESSY

**Yemen.** The southwest corner of Arabia. The word *Yemen* has two possible origins. One is geographical. Arab traders sailing north in the Red Sea found Yemen to "the right hand" while pilgrims in Mecca praying toward Islam's center, the Kaaba, knew it to be "on the right." Another is historical. For Romans the region was *Arabia Felix* ("Fortunate Arabia"), reputedly a place of "prosperity" (*ymn*). Home of the Minaean, Sabean, and Himyaritic cultures in antiquity, Yemen embraced Islam before Muhammad's death in 632. Long a stopping point for merchants traveling between Europe and Asia and under Turkish rule, the Yemen area evolved into two nations by the 20th century.

*The People's Democratic Republic of Yemen* (formerly Southern Yemen). By 1839 the British East India Company established coaling stations in what was then the State of Aden. The opening of the Suez Canal in 1869 made Aden a crucial link in the "Imperial Life Line" from England to India. Independence came in 1967 when Britain recognized the Federation of South Arabia (a union of the Aden Protectorate and 16 small tribal states that had been joined as the Protectorate of South Arabia). Political instability and pro-Marxist regimes followed. Bounded by Saudi

Arabia and the Yemen Arab Republic to the north, Oman to the east, and with a 700-mile coast on the Indian Ocean to the south, the P.D.R. of Yemen has 287,683 sq. km. (111,075 sq. mi.) and a population of 2.5 million (1987 est.). Yemen has struggled with limited agricultural and mineral resources, the vagaries of international trade, and a limited income from fishing and oil refining. The population is predominately Sunni Muslim, with small Jewish, Hindu, and Christian communities. The Sunnis are of the Shafi'i School of Law (founded by ash-Shafi'i, a Muslim jurist, 767–820), said to be a *via media* between the conservatism of the Malikite and the liberalism of the Hanafite and Hanbalite schools. Shi'i Muslims are primarily guest workers from Northern Yemen. While British law was introduced in colonial times, Muslim (Shar'iah) Law was retained by the Arab majority, especially for matters of family and personal relationship. Tribal and traditional law are followed in the interior. Descendants of the Prophet Muhammad (sayyids) are elders (shaykhs) and continue to be important. Threats to the stability of Yemeni Islam are economic unrest, the role of migratory labor, the impact of the Iran-Iraq War of the 1980s, and the growth of both Marxism and Shi'ite fundamentalism.

*The Yemen Arab Republic* (or Northern Yemen). A center of culture and commerce in classical times North Yemen converted to Islam in 628 and came under the control of the powerful Rassite Dynasty in the 10th century. Shi'ites of the Zaydi School (along with the Ismaili and Jafari traditions one of the major interpretations of Shiism, or the belief that Muhammad willed Ali to be his successor), the Rassites gave Yemen a faith different from its Sunni neighbors. Ruled by the Turks from 1538 until 1918, Yemen's status as a sovereign nation was confirmed in 1934 in treaties with Saudi Arabia and Britain. With 195,000 sq. km. (75,290 sq. mi.), the Yemen Arab Republic is bounded by Saudi Arabia to the east and the People's Democratic Republic of Yemen to the south, with which it has boundary disputes, religious differences, and an ambivalent attitude concerning union. It faces the Red Sea on the west. Yemen's population is 6.9 million (1987). While the Kingdom of Yemen joined the Arab League in 1945 and in 1958 became part of the United Arab Republic with Egypt and Syria, turmoil began in 1962 with a military coup by officers with sympathies for President Gamal Abdel Nasser. They proclaimed a republic but civil war followed. Egypt and the USSR favored the coup, Saudi Arabia and Jordan supported the monarchy. Only in 1969 were the monarchists defeated. The Egyptians had withdrawn in 1967, but Soviet influence increased. In 1964 Shar'iah courts were established; officials were charged to uphold the Koran, the teachings of the Prophet, and Islam, and 1000 Koranic schools upheld Islamic values. A rich traditional Islam (known for its vital oral literature) through the 1980s competed with Marxism and alien ideas introduced by the 20 percent of the Yemenis who worked abroad.

*Bibliography.* H. Scott, *In the High Yemen* (1942); A. Faroughy, *Introducing Yemen* (1943); E. W. Bethmann, *Yemen on the Threshold* (1960); W. H. Ingrams, *The Yemen* (1963); M. W. Wenner, *Modern Yemen, 1918–1966* (1967); R. W. Stookey, *Yemen*.

C. GEORGE FRY

**Yin Kuang** (1861–1940). Chinese Buddhist abbot of the Pure Land (Paradise) sect. He made Pao-kuo Monastery in Soochow the center of a revival of popular Pure Land pietism through preaching holiness, faith in realizing one's Buddha nature, and combatting evil. He promoted lay organizations to satisfy spiritual longings by scripture study, meditation, and experiencing reality in the realm of the infinite Buddha.

EARL H. CRESSY

**Yorker Brethren.** *See* RIVER BRETHREN.

**Young, Edward Joseph** (1907–1968). OT scholar. Born in San Francisco, he studied at Stanford University, San Francisco Theological Seminary, Westminster Theological Seminary, the University of Leipzig, and Dropsie College, Philadelphia (Ph.D., 1943). He was ordained to the ministry of the Presbyterian Church in the USA in 1935, then transferred to the Orthodox Presbyterian Church in 1936 and was moderator of the latter's general assembly in 1956. He was a convinced Calvinist. He taught OT at Westminster (1936–68), chaired its faculty (1966–68), and edited its *Westminster Theological Journal*. Proficient in many languages and widely traveled, he took special interest in the prophetic writings. He is best known for his commentary on *The Book of Isaiah* (3 vols., 1965–72) in which he argued for unity of authorship. He was a vigorous champion of biblical inerrancy in such works as *Thy Word Is Truth: Some Thoughts on the Biblical Doctrine of Inspiration* (1957). Other works include *The Prophecy of Daniel* (1949), *My Servants the Prophets* (1952), *An Introduction to the OT* (rev. ed., 1960), language primers, and devotional writings. He was general editor of the *New International Commentary on the OT*.

GLEN G. SCORGIE

**Young Men's Christian Association (YMCA).** An international, interdenominational volunteer movement, originally organized to minister to young workingmen in the cities and to promote evangelism, Bible study, and prayer. Founded in London in 1844 through the efforts of a young Congregationalist draper named George Williams (1821–1905) and a circle of business associates from evangelical churches, the YMCA quickly spread to Canada (Montreal, 1851) and the USA (Boston, 1851). In 1855, the movement held its first world conference in Paris, when the World Alliance of Young Men's Christian Associations was formed. By that time, there were 379 associations in seven countries with a total membership of 30,360.

Inspired by reading Charles G. Finney's *Lectures on Revivals* (1835), Williams followed Finney's emphasis on blending personal evangelism and social work. The YMCA soon became known as the mission of the evangelistic churches to young men. Supported by the philanthropy of wealthy church members and adapting to the needs of young people moving to the cities, the YMCA enjoyed its greatest period of vitality from about 1870 to 1918, thanks to such leaders as Williams; Anthony Cooper, seventh earl of Shaftesbury (1801–85); Dwight L. Moody (1832–99), who was president of the Chicago YMCA from 1866 to 1872; and John R. Mott (1865–1955), who was general secretary from 1915 to 1928.

Emphasizing Christianity in practical work, the YMCA of this period stressed religious, educational, social, and physical growth. It was a pioneer in fostering athletic recreation and defending the value of "play," and its activities were designed to develop high standards of Christian character and citizenship. In World War I (1914–18) and World War II (1939–45), the "Y" was active in attending to the social and spiritual needs of military personnel and prisoners of war, and in World War II was one of the six founding members of the United Service Organization (USO). Through the 20th century the organization established broad, ecumenical ties and the World Alliance of YMCAs became heavily involved in work with refugee and rehabilitation services, and human rights and peace organizations.

Local YMCAs of the late 1900s operated a variety of hostels, clubs, cafeterias, gymnasia, vocational training centers, and other facilities. Each was an autonomous corporation, voluntarily affiliated with national councils and the World Alliance, which has headquarters in Geneva, Switzerland. YMCAs, especially in America, became interconfessional and less evangelical in orientation. The general emphasis became to give a healthy outlook on life through greater development of body, mind, and spirit. The World Alliance of YMCAs has a more Christian base, with full members (those committed to the Christian way of life) and associate members (those who are permitted to use facilities but not to participate in policy and management) in 90 countries. By far the largest number, some 11 million, are in the American YMCA.

*Bibliography.* C. H. Hopkins, *A History of the YMCA in North America* (1951); C. P. Shedd, ed., *History of the World Alliance of Young Men's Christian Associations* (1955); C. Binfield, *George Williams and the YMCA* (1973); C. H. Hopkins, *John R. Mott, 1865–1955: A Biography* (1979).

ROBERT D. LINDER

## Young Women's Christian Association (YWCA).

The oldest international women's organization, with its origins in England in 1851. It now spans more than 80 countries. The program of work in each member association is designed to respond to local needs, but worldwide there is uniform commitment to ideals of love and service. To remain an active world movement, a world council was held every fourth year and voted to designate issues of international importance. These issues became a focus for each association. Some 1980s issues included peace, health, energy and environment, refugees and migrants, and human rights.

A new development of the internationalism of the YWCA in the late 1900s was the program of "Co-operation for Development," in which developing and developed countries contributed both human and financial resources to projects managed by and for women. The World YWCA Office was in Geneva, Switzerland.

J. D. DOUGLAS

## Youth for Christ (YFC).

An international evangelical youth organization encouraging evangelism and Bible study. Youth for Christ had no single founder, and it arose in several northern cities almost simultaneously. Probably the first youth rally director in America was Lloyd Bryant, who organized weekly rallies for youth in New York City during the early 1930s. For seven years Bryant ministered to teenagers in Manhattan at the Christian and Missionary Alliance Tabernacle. He was soon followed by Jack Wyrtzen, Percy Crawford, Oscar Gillan, Roger Malsbary, and others.

Wyrtzen, a converted insurance salesman and dance band trombonist, proved to be the most enduring. He launched a radio broadcast called "Word of Life Hour" and linked it with rallies at Bryant's Alliance Tabernacle. The first rally was on October 25, 1941. Later rallies drew 20,000 to Madison Square Garden. By 1943 Saturday night rallies proliferated in American cities. Torrey Johnson, pastor of the Midwest Bible Church, organized the first rallies in Chicago in 1944 and led in organizing the national movement.

Coordination of the ministries came in 1945 when local leaders met at Winona Lake, Ind., and established Youth for Christ, International. Johnson was elected president. That year Billy Graham served as a traveling evangelist for the organization. Graham's evangelistic team was formed two years later, mostly from experienced Youth for Christ rally workers. During World War II and immediately following, Youth for Christ took special interest in servicemen. This link with American military men and women gave Youth for Christ a global vision. Scores of teams went to countries abroad where servicemen had been stationed.

In 1948 Bob Cook succeeded Johnson as president of the organization. Under Cook's leadership Youth for Christ in the 1950s turned to high school Bible clubs (Campus Life) as a more effective way to reach high schoolers. A Youth Guidance Program summer camping ministry was devised to help delinquent young people. By 1986 YFC counted 1065 Campus Life clubs in the USA and ministries in 56 foreign countries.

The larger significance of Youth for Christ lies in the number of evangelical ministries spawned by the movement. The Billy Graham Evangelistic Association is the largest and best known, but World Vision, International Students, Greater Europe Mission, Trans-World Radio, and Overseas Crusades also trace their roots to the early years of Youth for Christ.

*Bibliography.* M. Larson, *Twentieth Century Crusade* (1953); J. Hefley, *God Goes to High School* (1970); B. L. Shelley, *Fides* 18 (1986).

BRUCE L. SHELLEY

## Yugoslavia.

A Socialist Republic of southeastern Europe on the Balkan Peninsula. Yugoslavia in the 1980s had 255,804 sq. km. (98,766 sq. mi.) and 23 million people (1984). The three main religious denominations in Yugoslavia were the Orthodox Church (8 million members), the Roman Catholic Church (7 million members), and the Muslims (about 2 million). The country has a history of religious and national conflict, due to the close identification of nationality with religion. The traditional enmity between Catholics of the northern Croatia and the Orthodox in the more eastern Serbia came to a head in World War II, when the Croats formed an independent republic under German patronage. Their attempts to "convert" the Serbs to Catholicism by force involving large-scale massacres, have retarded ecumenical relations between the Catholic and Orthodox churches ever since. After the 1945 victory of Josip Broz Tito's largely Serbian communist partisans, many Catholic clergy were imprisoned or executed. Even Archbishop Stepinac, who had publicly protested against the massacres of Serbs and Jews, was imprisoned and died in exile. Only from 1968, when Catholic and Orthodox leaders first met and prayed together, were attempts made to foster ecumenism. In the 1980s the Catholics had about 2800 parishes and 4000 priests, many of them monks; they still were mostly Croats and Slovenes. The Orthodox Church had 2400 parishes but only 1400 priests. The great majority were Serbs, but there was a Macedonian Orthodox Church (one million members), as well as 30 Romanian parishes. The Serbian Orthodox Church was long headed by Patriarch German, who was elected in 1958.

The Muslims, who were converted under the long rule of the Ottoman Turks, were based in Kosovo, Bosnia-Herzegovina, and Macedonia. They had 2100 mosques and 1600 imams; their most active center was Sarajevo.

A number of small Protestant groups, with about 357,000 members altogether, were mainly in the northern territories and mostly national minorities. The Evangelical Lutheran Church (80,000 members) largely consisted of Slovak and Hungarians, as well as some Slovenes; it had 64 churches and 44 priests. The Calvinist Reformed Church had 59 churches and 43 ministers; its members were mostly Hungarians, with some Czechs and Germans. Almost 4000 Baptists included a variety of nationalities and had 54 churches and 15 prayer houses over the country. They had 20 pastors and were known for organizing youth activities, such as summer camps and coffee houses. The Seventh-day Adventist community was large enough to maintain 300 churches and 120 ministers. The Methodist Church had 4500 members, mostly German, with 40 churches but only 13 ministers. There were also small communities of pentecostals (72 churches), United Brethren (24 churches), and Jehovah's Witnesses (104 churches). Thirteen Old Catholic parishes existed, as well as an unknown number of Uniates (Eastern-rite Catholics), who were illegal. About 6000 Jews survived World War II, but by the 1980s there were 36 Jewish religious communities without any professional rabbis.

Church-state relations were better than in most East European countries. Although church property was nationalized and nonreligious "social activities" such as church sports clubs discouraged, relative toleration of religion existed from the mid-1950s. In 1970 the state restored full diplomatic relations with the Vatican (broken off in 1945). Catholic priests' associations, founded after the war, were largely distrusted as the state has tried to use them to divide the church. However, religious instruction of children was permitted and almost all religious communities had training facilities for clergy. Theological students could not be exempted from military service, as were other students. There was a vigorous, although censored, religious press and every denomination had at least one journal; the Catholics produced 67 publications, the Orthodox 10. However, the churches had no access to radio or television. The Bible is freely available and is sold in bookshops.

The reform movement within Yugoslavia in 1989 and 1990 was shadowed by ethnic unrest, particularly among Muslims, and the dramatic advances seen in other Eastern European countries were not so visible, partly because Yugoslavia was already one of the more independent states within the Soviet sphere. Among Christians the most dramatic undertaking was in a translation project to provide Bibles in the various dialects. As restrictions on religious literature loosened, mission groups struggled to meet the demand for Bibles in any Slavic language.

*Bibliography.* S. Alexander, *Church and State in Yugoslavia since 1945* (1979); T. Beeson, *Discretion and Valour* (rev. ed., 1982).

PHILIP WALTERS

Zz

**Zabriskie, Alexander Clinton** (1898–1956). Episcopalian clergyman and educator. Born in New York, he was educated at Groton, Princeton, Cambridge University, and the (Virginia) Protestant Episcopal Theological Seminary, Alexandria, Va. He taught in the seminary from 1925 and was dean of faculty (1940–50). His writings deal chiefly with Anglicanism and evangelicalism, and the mission and unity of the church. They include *Personal Evangelism* (1932), *Unity among Ourselves* (1940), *Charles Simeon: Anglican Evangelical* (1940), *Arthur Selden Lloyd: Missionary Statesman and Pastor* (1942), *Anglican Evangelicalism* (1943), *The Genius of Anglicanism* (1943/44), and *Bishop Brent, Crusader for Christian Unity* (1948). He also edited *Anglican Evangelicalism* (1943).

**Zahn, Theodor** (1838–1933). German NT scholar. Born in Mörs, he was educated at the universities of Basel, Erlangen, and Berlin. He was a teacher at the gymnasium in Neustrelitz (1861–65); became a lecturer at the University of Göttingen (1865), privatdocent (1868), associate professor (1871); and professor at Kiel (1877), at Erlangen (1878), and at Leipzig (1888). He taught pedagogics and NT exegesis at Erlangen (1892–1909). Generally a conservative scholar, he was very widely read in many fields and from them all drew support for his exegetical studies. He also did basic work in the critical study of NT canon, history, and authorship. His *Forschungen zur Geschichte des Neutestamentlichen Kanons und der altkirchlichen Literatur* (11 vols., 1881–1916) was completed after his retirement. Among other works of his extensive writings were *Missionsmethoden im Zeitalter der Apostel* (1886), *Geschichte des neutestamentlichen Kanons* (2 vols., 1889–92), *Einige Bemerkungen zu Adolf Harnacks Prüfung der Geschichte des neutestamentlichen Kanons* (1889), *Das Evangelium des Petrus* (1893), and *Introduction to the NT* (3 vols., ET, 1909). He edited, in collaboration with O. von Gebhardt and A. Harnack, the *Patrum apostolicorum opera* (3 vols., 5th ed., 1905), to which he contributed the volume on *Ignatii et Polycarpi epistulae, martyria, fragmenta* (1876), and *Kommentar zum Neuen Testament* (1903– ), for which he prepared the volumes on Matthew (1903), Galatians (1905), and John (1907). He also edited the *Acts of John* (1880).

RAYMOND W. ALBRIGHT

**Zaire.** The Republic of Zaire, formerly the Democratic Republic of the Congo, and earlier the Republic of the Congo. Now a country of 2.3 million sq. km. (905,568 sq. mi.) and 33 million people (1988) it was the largest African territory colonized between 1908 and 1960 by Belgium. During this era, the territory was part of what came to be known as the Belgian Congo and Ruanda-Rundi.

From 1885 to 1908, the region was organized into Congo Free State and was given to King Leopold II of Belgium. His ownership of this huge territory was characterized by extreme cruelty and exploitation. In 1960, the Belgian Congo became an independent republic, and in 1971, the Democratic Republic of Congo became the Republic of Zaire. In 1990 Zaire was the largest republic in the heart of Africa.

Most of the population lived in rural areas and sustained themselves by farming. Growing, crowded urban areas from 1960 developed alarmingly high unemployment. Zaire's diverse population contained numerous ethnic groups and languages.

***Roman Catholicism.*** As early as the 1400s contacts were made by Roman Catholic missionaries. Between 1482 and the late 1700s the coastal kingdom of the Congo established diplomatic relations with the Vatican. The kingdom adopted Roman Catholicism as its religion and several dozens, if not hundreds, of Bakongo men were inducted into the priesthood, despite the fact that from 1501 to 1863 millions of natives were captured and sold into slavery in North and South America.

The most significant Roman Catholic leaders between 1885 and 1960 were predominantly Belgians. There was a closely shared view of the colonial mission between the church and the colonial administration. The missionaries regarded themselves as having the responsibility to inculcate the capacity for hard work, decency, and reliability. Such an affinity between church and colonial authorities gave Catholic missions an almost total monopoly over the colonial educational system and a comparatively free hand to establish churches, schools, clinics, hospitals, and other institutions. Their success is shown by the large number of baptisms, strong notions of the family as the cornerstone of the church, and the high number and quality of clerical and lay leaders they generated. Cardinal Joseph Malula and many of his bishops and priests are credited not only with successful evangelization but also with efforts to "Africanize" or make the faith, beliefs, and practices more relevant. Some persons and groups also held church membership and African religious perceptions simultaneously.

The Zairian Catholic Church has distinguished itself through mission work in Burundi, Rwanda, Congo, Gabon, and the Central African Republic. Zairian Christianity near the end of the century was faced with the task of synthesizing important values and doctrines and assessing them in both the Judeo-Christian and African contexts, as well as the uniquely Zairian-Christian cultural history.

The Roman Catholics' historical claim to education, medicine, and other social institutions placed them in a position of national leadership. This, in part, was why the Roman Catholic Church emerged as a contending force for spiritual and political leadership. By 1975 and 1978 the Conference of Catholic Bishops of Zaire realized their responsibility and right to act both as pastors and citizens, speaking out against harsh political regimes on behalf of the people of Zaire. This was perhaps a noble and honorable mission, but it was also a complex one.

*Protestantism.* Since 1960 Protestants have also been engaged in the Africanization of church leadership and control. After 1954 efforts were made to liberalize both educational and urbanization policies to meet the demands for increased and skilled workers.

The first Protestant mission to Zaire was established among Bakongo people in the lower Zaire in 1878. Work expanded rapidly after 1900, and through the colonial period the missions spread. Missionaries wished to avoid conflicts so various provinces and regions were assigned to specific denominations. Missions were separated by long distances so a representative council of missionaries was organized to allow cooperation and contact. Pierre Shaumba (1959–65) and Jean Bokalaele (from 1965) were successive executive secretaries of the council. While this council wanted cooperation and to minimize competition among the different churches, from 1965 it developed into the Church of Christ in Zaire, comprising 53 different Protestant communities (churches and missionaries) by the 1970s. Rules of this federated denomination allowed members to transfer membership to another community, and under Shaumba and Bokeleale it developed a unified executive church government. Overall, however, the Church of Christ in Zaire has remained weak and silent in the face of growing authoritarian and dictatorial policies by the Joseph Mobutu regime. After his successful coup in 1965, Mobutu began to dismantle the socioeconomic, political, and moral fiber of the society. Protestant silence has weakened the church among the people.

*Independent Churches.* Outside of the main Protestant and Catholic churches are a number of Independent bodies, such as The Church of Jesus Christ on Earth, led by Simon Kimbangu. Kimbanguism developed in the 1930s and flourished into the 1980s, with its own missionary services in surrounding countries. By 1990 it was expected to soon reach into Angola and Southern Africa. With the volatile political situation and such movements, religion's future dimensions and meanings were full of potential and uncertainty.

*Bibliography.* J. Crawford, *Protestant Missions in Congo* (1973); P. Falk, *The Growth of the Church in Africa* (1979); R. F. Manyeto, *The ABC of Modern Africa* (1979); M. Roth, *Zaire: A Country Study* (3d ed., 1979); C. Young and T. Turner, *The Rise and Decline of the Zairism State* (1979); M. O. Crowder, *The Cambridge Encyclopedia of Africa* (1981); A. Rake, *New African Yearbook* (1985).

PATRICE MUYUMBA

**Zambia.** See SOUTHERN AFRICA.

**Zanzibar.** See EAST AFRICA.

**Zeitlin, Solomon** (1893–1976). Historian and rabbinic scholar, specializing in the Second Jewish Commonwealth. Born in Vitebsk, Russia, he was professor of rabbinic literature at Dropsie College, Philadelphia (from 1925), coeditor of the *Jewish Quarterly Review* (from 1940), and editor of *Jewish Apocryphal Literature.* He wrote *Megillat Taanit as a Source for Jewish Chronology and History in the Hellenistic and Roman Periods* (1922), *Josephus on Jesus* (1931), *The Canonisation of the Hebrew Scriptures* (1933), *The History of the Second Jewish Commonwealth Prolegomena* (1933), *The Book of Jubilees, Its Character and Its Significance* (1939), *Maimonides, A Biography* (1939), *Who Crucified Jesus?* (rev. ed., 1947), *The Sadducees and the Pharisees: Religious and Secular Leadership* (1943), *Judaism as a Religion* (1944), and *The First Book of Maccabees* (1950).

**Zenos, Andreas Constantinides** (1855–1942). Presbyterian. Born in Constantinople, he was educated at Robert College, Constantinople, was pastor of the Presbyterian church at Brandt, Pa. (1881–83), and in 1883 was appointed professor of Greek at Lake Forest University, where he remained five years. He was professor of NT exegesis at Hartford Theological Seminary (1888–91), church history at McCormick Theological Seminary, Chicago (1891–94), and historical theology at Presbyterian Theological Seminary, Chicago (1894–1932; dean, 1920–32). He wrote *Elements of Higher Criticism* (1895), *Compendium of Church History* (1896), *The Teaching of Jesus Concerning Christian Conduct* (1905), *The Son of Man* (1914), *The Plastic Age of the Gospel: A Manual of NT Theology* (1927), and *Presbyterianism in America: Past, Present and Prospective* (1937). He translated the "Ecclesiastical History" of Socrates for the *Nicene and Post-Nicene Fathers* (1890), and edited, with M. W. Jacobus and E. E. Nourse, *A New Standard Bible Dictionary* (3d ed., 1936).

RAYMOND W. ALBRIGHT

**Zimbabwe.** *See* SOUTHERN AFRICA.

**Zionism.** The philosophy of the Jewish people's restoration to "Zion," which early in Jewish history was identified with Jerusalem. After the Roman expulsion of the Jews from Jerusalem in A.D. 135 , this Zion idea was never divorced from Jewish thinking, and Jewish prayers (both individual and corporate) reiterated the desire to return to their homeland. Religious Jews dreamed of an end period of ultimate release from dispersion among the nations and a return to the land of promise, *Eretz Yisrael* ("land of Israel"). A handful of Jews had always remained in Palestine (a name the Romans had given the land to sever its connection with Judaism), and their numbers were augmented by refugees of the medieval expulsions from Europe, culminating in the Spanish Inquisition in the latter 1400s.

The actual term "Zionism" was not used until the 1890s. The advent of the 19th century found Palestine under the control of the Ottoman Empire, the group of Turks that at one time subdued the entire Middle East and was knocking on the door of Europe. Centuries of corrupt administration had taken their toll, and Ottoman Palestine was in a state of decline in the 1800s. By the 20th century, only 10 percent of the land was cultivated, and absentee landlords purchased hundreds of thousands of acres from the financially strapped Ottomans. By the end of World War I, 144 wealthy landowners owned approximately 750,000 acres in *Eretz Yisrael*.

In the latter decades of the 19th century, the rise of Hebrew literature, Jewish nationalism, and a fresh outbreak of anti-Semitism stimulated groups such as *Hoveve Zion* ("Lovers of Zion") to raise money to send Jewish settlers to Palestine. Pogroms in Czarist Russia from 1881 into the first decade of the 20th century engendered thousands of panic-stricken Jewish refugees who believed that *Eretz Yisrael* was their safest place of refuge. Agricultural settlements were also sponsored by benefactors such as Baron Edmond de Rothschild. By the outbreak of World War I in 1914, Jews had purchased more than 100,000 acres from large landowners and had reclaimed fertile cultivated areas from marsh areas and deserts. Jewish urban areas also expanded, and in 1909 a group of Jaffa Jews founded Tel Aviv, destined to become modern Israel's largest city.

Pre-modern Zionism emphasized a religious motive and quiet territorial settlement. With the publication of the small booklet entitled *Der Judenstaat (The Jewish State: An Attempt at a Modern Solution to the Jewish Question)* by Theodor Herzl in 1896, however, political Zionism was born and with it the modern conception of Zionism. A new era in Jewish history unfolded when Herzl, an Austrian journalist, changed from an advocate of Jewish assimilation to a belief that anti-Semitism was inevitable as long as the majority of Jewish people lived outside of their homeland. Herzl had wrestled with the rising anti-Semitism in Austria, France, and Germany.

For him, the climax of Jew-hatred was reached during the trial and subsequent public degradation of Captain Alfred Dreyfus with treason during 1894 and 1895. The French government charged Dreyfus with treason, but Herzl knew that his real crime was being a Jew. As a Paris correspondent for the *Neue Freie Presse (New Free Press)*, Herzl felt the bitterness of the French people against the Jewish people and knew that this one Jew was being tried and condemned for all Jew-hatred. The nation had judged the Jewish people unworthy of life as equals, in spite of the declarations of freedom and liberty in 1789. Two years after Herzl's death, a French Court of Appeals would pronounce that the evidence against Dreyfus was completely unsubstantiated.

In *Der Judenstaat* and subsequent articles and speeches, Herzl expounded political, economic, and technical efforts that he believed were necessary to create a functioning Jewish state. The First Zionist Congress met in 1897 and over 200 delegates from all over the world adopted the Basel Program. This program stressed that Zionism sought to create a legal home in Palestine for the Jewish people and would promote settlement, create worldwide organizations to bind Jews together, strengthen Jewish national consciousness, and obtain consent of the governments of the world.

Herzl's thinking was purely secular; in fact, he was an agnostic. The majority of his followers, however, were Orthodox southeastern Europeans, and while Herzl opposed turning Zionism into a cultural, religious, or piecemeal settlement society, he did make concessions to these advocates. This fragile alliance indicates the many facets of

Zionism during the 20th century. To Herzl, the main goal of Zionism was to obtain a political charter granting Jews sovereign rights in their homeland. Shortly after his death in 1904, approximately 70,000 Jewish people had settled in Palestine. A majority (at least 60 percent) lived in the cities. Zionism would be transformed into a mass movement and political power during World War I. The British issued the Balfour Declaration in 1917 which bestowed favor upon the establishment in Palestine of a Jewish national home.

Zionism was a minority movement and encountered opposition within the Jewish community. American Reform Judaism, for example, claimed that Palestine was no longer a Jewish land and that the USA was "Zion." To these non-Zionist Jews, Zionism was damaging to the fabric of Judaism and only served to stir up the Russians. Furthermore, they believed that Jews were not suited for the rigors of Palestine, where disease was rampant. In spite of the efforts of the few Zionist Reform Jews, such as Rabbi Stephen S. Wise, it was only the horror of the murder of 100,000 Jews by Russian army units from 1919 to 1921 and, ultimately, the horror of the Nazi Holocaust during World War II in which 6 million Jews were exterminated, that drew Zionists and non-Zionists together in support of Palestine as a Jewish commonwealth—a haven for the persecuted and homeless. In November 1947, a partition plan creating a Jewish state was endorsed by both the USA and the Soviet Union. It was passed by the General Assembly of the United Nations. The State of Israel was formally recognized on May 14, 1948, when British rule ended. Only a few radical non-Zionist Jews, in such organizations as the American Council for Judaism, continued their efforts to disembody the new Jewish state, cultivating support among academics, Christians, and government officials.

As with the pre-Holocaust Jewish community, Christians have battled over the Zionist movement for most of the 20th century. A strong contingent within the Christian community had an important part in supporting the Jewish people's restoration to "Zion." Within the millenarian tradition the conviction that the Jews would return to the Holy Land became an important dogma. As premillennialism gained ground during the 19th century, forming the core of the early fundamentalist-evangelical movement, adherents not only believed that the Jewish people would return, but also vocally supported the right of the Jews to be restored to their former homeland.

Even before Theodor Herzl's *Der Judenstaat*, fundamentalist-evangelical William E. Blackstone advocated the reestablishment of a Jewish state and circulated a petition urging the USA to return the land of Palestine to the Jewish people. The Blackstone Petition of 1891 was signed by 413 renowned Christian and Jewish leaders, including Melville W. Fuller, Chief Justice of the United States Supreme Court; Thomas B. Reed, Speaker of the House of Representatives; William McKinley, Congressman of Ohio and later President of the United States; and industrialists and banker, Cyrus H. McCormick, John D. Rockefeller, and J. P. Morgan. Through the State Department, the petition was distributed to the principal nations of the world. During World War I, Blackstone urged a new petition on President Woodrow Wilson, and in 1918 he was invited to address a Zionist mass meeting in Los Angeles.

Other Christians, such as Herzl's close friend William H. Hechler, worked diligently to promote political Zionism as the ultimate solution to the Jewish question. Hechler tried to encourage heads of state (including the Turkish sultan who controlled Palestine) to support Herzl's proposals, and he accompanied Herzl to Palestine in 1898 to meet with the Kaiser. The active support of such Christian Zionists in many countries influenced political action, and even the Balfour Declaration of 1917 was the product of religious as well as political activity. Individual Christian Zionists came from a broad spectrum of theological traditions.

Even liberal Protestantism, which has historically opposed Zionism, contributed clergymen through organizations such as the Christian Council on Palestine during World War II. As executive secretary of this council, a young liberal Christian Zionist minister from Pittsburgh, Carl Hermann Voss, ably assembled a broad spectrum of theological and academic members. The famed theologians Reinhold Niebuhr and Paul Tillich were part of the executive council of the Christian Council on Palestine as was renowned archeologist William Foxwell Albright. Even the evangelical editor of the *Christian Herald*, Daniel Poling, was an active participant on the council. Answering unequivocally a reader's question in October 1947, Poling declared to the nearly 400,000 *Christian Herald* readers: "I am a Christian Zionist who believes that Palestine should become, as promised, the Jewish state." Welcoming the new State of Israel, he never wavered from that position.

Such unequivocal Christian Zionism has not gone without attack. Christian missionary organizations in Arab lands have challenged its hindrance to evangelism and vehemently opposed it. It has been criticized by theologians as an erroneous political philosophy based on a spurious interpretation of the Bible which dictates that modern Palestine is the Jew's own special piece of real estate. These critics argue that Christian Zionism totally ignores the rights of Palestinian Arab people and that the Jews forfeited their title to the promised land through unfaithfulness long ago.

Today, the vast majority of Jewry worldwide, however, from Orthodox to Reform, now support the State of Israel. Although they do not always agree with the Jewish state, they understand its importance and significance to the preservation of the Jewish people. As the young state has strengthened, the definition of Zionism and what its current goals and purpose should be have been heatedly debated within the World Zionist Organization itself. Since 1968 the emphasis of *aliyah* (personal migration to Israel) has been seen by many as an ultimate, yet controversial, goal.

**Bibliography.** I. Cohen, *Theodor Herzl: Founder of Political Zionism* (1959); A. Hertzberg, *The Zionist Idea: A Historical Analysis and Reader* (1959); T. Herzl, *Diary*, ed. R. Patai and trans. H. Zohn, 5 vols. (1960); W. Laqueur, *A History of Zionism* (1972); H. Fishman, *American Protestantism and a Jewish State* (1973); N. W. Cohen, *American Jews and the Zionist Idea* (1975); D. A. Rausch, *Zionism Within Early American Fundamentalism* (1979).

DAVID A. RAUSCH

**Zöllner, Wilhelm** (1860–1937). Lutheran. He studied at Erlangen and Leipzig; was minister (1886–97); president of the deaconess institution at Kaiserswerth (1897–1905); superintendent-general of the church-province Westphalia (1905–31); and activated home mission and church press work. He was president of the Reichs-Kirchen-Ausschuss (1935–37) and, after attempting unsuccessfully to settle the struggle between government and church, he resigned. He wrote *Gnade und Wahrheit* (1903), *Wege und Ziele* (1917), *Frauennot und Frauenhilfe* (1918), *Die sozialen Aufgaben der Kirche* (1924), and *Im Dienst der Kirche* (1931).

ROBERT STUPPERICH

**Zoroastrianism.** Also called Mazdaism, the ancient religion of Persia whose traditional founder was the prophet Zoroaster, a Greek form of the Iranian Zarathustra. Around the 6th century B.C., when according to tradition he was 30 years old, Zoroaster had a religious experience in which he encountered God, whom he called *Ahura-Mazda*, the "Wise Lord." Following this and other revelations Zoroaster preached a new ethical religion which eventually became the state religion of Persia. In the 7th century A.D. the followers of Zoroaster were conquered by Muslim invaders and converted to Islam. A remnant survived in Iran while others fled to India. In the 1980s there were about 100,000 Zoroastrians, known as Parsis, the majority of whom are in India.

Zoroaster appears to have taught faith in God and the existence of an evil spirit named *Angra Mainyu*. This division between good and evil forces has often led to Zoroastrianism being characterized as a dualistic religion and it is arguable that indeed in A.D. 250 it took on a dualistic theology. A dualistic form of Zoroastrianism infected 4th-century Christianity in Manichaeism. However, the Parsis are clearly monotheistic and believe in the ultimate triumph of good over evil. Judgment occurs after death and the good go to paradise while the evil are punished.

Great emphasis is placed on ethical teachings and personal honesty in a world where harmony is to be desired and justice promoted. The world is viewed as a good place which is to be enjoyed; consequently asceticism has found little support within the Zoroastrian tradition.

Worship is performed on behalf of individuals by priests in fire temples where a perpetual flame is kept alive. Only males may become priests within a hereditary priesthood where priests may marry and raise families. Other rituals involve sacred clothing to be worn by both men and women and elaborate marriage and funeral ceremonies. There are no weekly observances or congregational worship but rather a recurring pattern of devotion on an annual basis.

*See also* MANICHEISM.

**Bibliography.** R. C. Zaehner, *The Dawn and Twilight of Zoroastrianism* (1961); M. N. Dhalla, *History of Zoroastrianism* (rev. ed., 1977).

IRVING HEXHAM

**Zwemer, Samuel Marinus** (1867–1952). Dutch Reformed. Born in Ottawa County, Mich., he attended Hope College and New Brunswick Seminary and went as a missionary to Bahrain and other Muslim countries (1891–1905). With James Cantine he founded the Arabian Mission of the Dutch Reformed Church. Zwemer was prominent in organizing conferences on Muslim work, as well as in representing the Muslim world at conferences in Europe and America. Later, from headquarters in Cairo, he became an itinerant missionary to Muslims on a world scale. He visited many missions, making notable contributions in South Africa and the Netherlands Indies, where he preached in Dutch, English, and Arabic. He also visited India and China several times. In the USA from 1905 to 1910 and on other visits he was an early leader of the Student Volunteer Movement and influenced many young people to enter missionary service.

He was the author of about 50 volumes in English and a number in Arabic. Translations of his books appeared in many languages. He was also founder and for 36 years the editor of the *Moslem World*. For nearly a decade after returning from the mission field Zwemer was professor of missions and the history of religion at Princeton Theological Seminary. After retirement he continued to speak widely throughout America and abroad.

**Bibliography.** J. Christy Wilson, *Apostle to Islam: A Biography of Samuel M. Zwemer* (1952).

J. CHRISTY WILSON, SR.

**Zwischen den Zeiten.** An influential neo-orthodox theological journal. The German theologian Friedrich Gogarten coined the phrase, which means "betwixt and between" in an article of 1920 in *Die christliche Welt*, in which he critiqued what he called the "Kulturprotestantismus" of modern theology. When Karl Barth and his friend Eduard Thurneysen two years later founded a periodical in conjunction with Gogarten and Georg Merz (as editor) they chose this phrase as its title to reflect the flux in which they found much of theological thought. Theology, they said, was betwixt the foundational assertions of biblical theology and between the possibility of a "new theology." Against much of theological liberalism, inherited from the 19th century, they sought to highlight the dialectical tension in contemporary statements about God and expressions of faith, acceptable to Christians in the modern scientific world. The periodical was begun in 1922, although its first issue did not appear until the spring of 1923. Through 1933 the periodical contained seminal articles by such prominent theologians as Karl and Heinrich Barth, Emil Brunner, Friedrich Gogarten, Gerhard von Rad, Ernst Wolf, W. Trillhaas, Emanuel Hirsch, Ernst Fuchs, Eduard Thurneysen, and Georg Merz. In addition, many issues carried remarks on current events and book reviews, along with articles by lesser-known theologians, scientists, and laypersons.

Barth and Thurneysen wrote some of their most provocative challenges to the then dominant expressions of Christian thought on Christian ethics, the task of proclamation, the church, confessionalism and political engagement, the German political situation, and other subjects.

In 1933 Gogarten parted company with some positions held by Barth and Thurneysen, and the journal was discontinued. Its last issue appeared in October. Although intended as a way-station of theological probing, the periodical proved to be a major contribution to 20th-century neo-orthodoxy and provided needed space in which to place pertinent issues before the church.

E. J. FURCHA